GUINNESS WORLD RECORDS™

BRITISH HIT SINGLES

15TH EDITION

www.britishhitsingles.com

ACKNOWLEDGEMENTS

EDITOR - **DAVID ROBERTS**

CHIEF CONSULTANT / CONTRIBUTOR - **DAVE McALEER**

ASSISTANT EDITOR - **JAMES BRADLEY**

DESK EDITOR - **MARY NOVAKOVICH**

ART EDITOR - **MARIA CENTORINO**

PROOFREADER - **ANDY GREGORY**

YEAR REVIEW WRITERS - **BRUNO MACDONALD AND KATE FREEMAN**

HEAD OF PICTURES / MEDIA DESK - **BETTY HALVAGI**

PRODUCTION DIRECTOR - **PATRICIA LANGTON**

PR - **THE OUTSIDE ORGANISATION AND CHRIS BURTON**

VICE PRESIDENT, PUBLISHING - **INGRID SELBERG**

WITH THANKS TO:

The Official UK Charts Company, Ian Castello-Cortes, Vicki Miles, Neil Hayes, Brian Southall, Ric Blaxill, Michael Heatley, Alan Smith, Jack Cocker, David D'Arcy, Claire Curtice, Claire Power, Jamie Thackwell, Roger Wemyss-Brooks, Janet Jones, Joyce Lee, John Einarson, Martin Downham, Chris Butters, Russtti Gaynor, Graham Betts, Richard M White, Phil Sutcliffe, Paul Du Noyer, Sylvie Simmons, Vincent Howcutt, Harriet Howe, Steve Earnshaw, Steve Hampson, Robin Clarke, Kate Stuart-Cox, Derek Christie, Andy Brobbin, Kevin Ennis, Allan Hollings, Lloyd Eckert, Neil Thompson, Ross Carter, Vez Ninja, Malcolm Smith, James Rigg, Gary James, Herman Verkade, Julian Barker, Ian Dewhirst, Mike Loveday and Chris Barnett

First edition 1977, Second edition 1979, Third edition 1981, Fourth edition 1983, Fifth edition 1985, Sixth edition 1987, Seventh edition 1989, Eighth edition 1991, Ninth edition 1993, Tenth edition 1995, Eleventh edition 1997, Twelfth edition 1999, Thirteenth edition 2000, Fourteenth edition 2001

Reprint 10 9 8 7 6 5 4 3 2 1 0

Published in Great Britain by
Guinness World Records Ltd,
338 Euston Road, London NW1 3BD

Printed and bound in Great Britain
by Bath Press

A catalogue record for this book is available from the British Library

ISBN 085112-187-X

Bibliography

Neil Young – Don't Be Denied: The Canadian Years by John Einarson
Meat Loaf – To Hell and Back by Meat Loaf and David Dalton
Beck! On a Backwards River: The Story of Beck by Rob Jovanovic
Marc Almond – Tainted Love The Autobiography
45 – Bill Drummond
Bryan Adams – Sandy Robertson

Feedback from our readers on points of accuracy or general enquiries are always welcomed.
So write to us at: **The Editor, Guinness World Records, British Hit Singles, 338 Euston Road London NW1 3BD,**
or email: **editor@15th.britishhitsingles.com VISIT OUR WEBSITE www.britishhitsingles.com**

CONTENTS

GUINNESS WORLD RECORDS™

BRITISH HIT SINGLES

15TH EDITION

THE TRACKS OF YOUR YEARS

THE OFFICIAL UK SINGLES CHART 50TH ANNIVERSARY

The UK singles chart celebrates its 50th birthday in 2002. In honour of this milestone, and to acknowledge the chart's importance as an essential thread running through popular music, our Book of British Hit Singles, which itself marks 25 years of chart action, celebrates with a very special gold edition

- **1952** Al Martino's 'Here in My Heart' tops the first chart
- **1958** Cliff Richard begins his run of hits over six decades
- **1961** Elvis scores four No.1s
- **1962** Elvis scores four No.1s again
- **1963** The Beatles begin a run of 11 consecutive chart-toppers
- **1966** Four Tops score the first No.1 on Motown's UK label
- **1968** Louis Armstrong becomes the oldest chart-topper
- **1969** 'Je T'aime ... Moi Non Plus' banned by the BBC
- **1972** The Osmond family begins three years of chart domination
- **1975** 'Bohemian Rhapsody' begins a nine-week stay at the top

▶ The very first chart-topper, Al Martino, NME journalist Derek Johnson and Dame Vera Lynn, who scored a hat-trick of hits in the first chart, all contribute their memories of 1950s UK pop. Additionally, in a veritable orgy of nostalgia, we have the personal memories of a different music celebrity for each one of the 50 years of the chart's life. The special features celebrating the half-century are the icing on the birthday cake. The bread-and-butter listings of all 25,000 singles and the 8,000 acts that created them are here in all their glory, together with the annual facts, stats and trivia that are the very gospels according to "the bible of pop".

And what of the future of the charts and the continued relevance of the British hit single? Well, against all the odds the importance of that single song remains the same. Still the million-selling singles keep coming; still the teen market dictates the shape and form of the Top 75; still those kids become adults and in years to come turn to our book to get a nostalgic buzz as they remember the tracks of their years.

David Roberts - Editor
British Hit Singles

◀ ▶ 50 years of pop separate the chart superstars of 1952-2002. Al Martino, the first chart-topper **left** and **right** 21st-century man, Robbie Williams

- **1977** 'Mull of Kintyre' becomes the UK's first two million-seller
- **1980** John Lennon has first of three consecutive posthumous No.1s
- **1982** Nicole has the 500th No.1 with 'A Little Peace'
- **1984** 'Do They Know It's Christmas?' bags more than 3.5 million sales
- **1986** Jackie Wilson hits the top posthumously 29 years after his chart debut
- **1989** Producers Stock Aitken and Waterman have seven No.1s
- **1991** '(Everything I Do) I Do It For You' sets a record 16 weeks at the top
- **1994** Whigfield is the first debut act to enter the chart at No.1
- **1995** Media interest is high as Blur and Oasis battle for the top spot
- **1997** World and UK sales records are broken by 'Candle in the Wind 1997'
- **2001** Hear'Say are the fastest selling debut act ever
- **2002** The UK chart celebrates its 50th birthday

THE VERY FIRST TOP 12

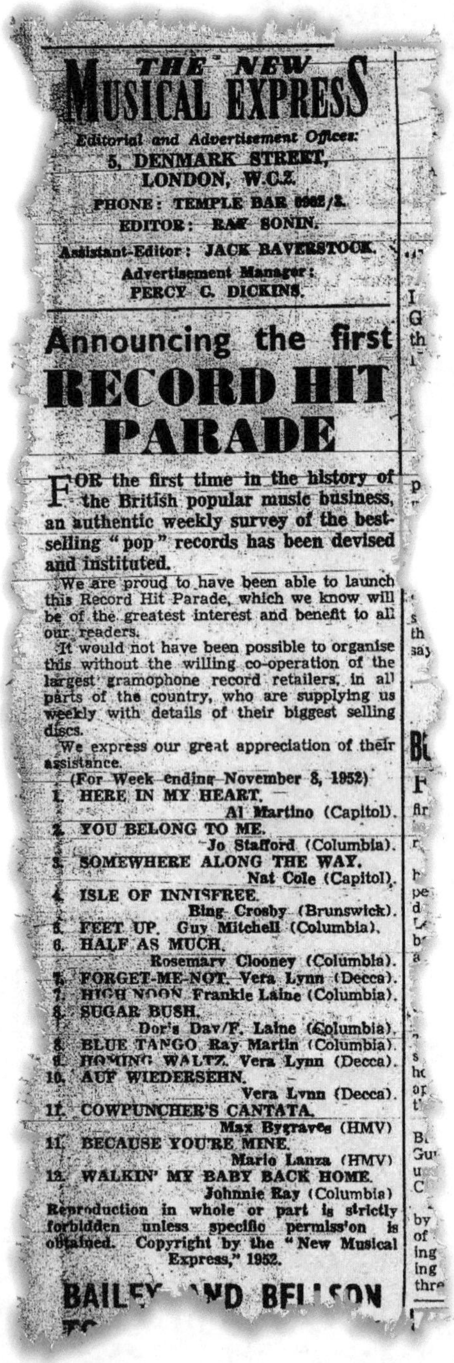
THE NEW MUSICAL EXPRESS
Editorial and Advertisement Offices:
5, DENMARK STREET,
LONDON, W.C.2.
PHONE: TEMPLE BAR 0902/3.
EDITOR: RAY SONIN.
Assistant-Editor: JACK BAVERSTOCK.
Advertisement Manager:
PERCY C. DICKINS.

Announcing the first
RECORD HIT PARADE

FOR the first time in the history of the British popular music business, an authentic weekly survey of the best-selling "pop" records has been devised and instituted.

We are proud to have been able to launch this Record Hit Parade, which we know will be of the greatest interest and benefit to all our readers.

It would not have been possible to organise this without the willing co-operation of the largest gramophone record retailers, in all parts of the country, who are supplying us weekly with details of their biggest selling discs.

We express our great appreciation of their assistance.

(For Week ending November 8, 1952)

1. HERE IN MY HEART. Al Martino (Capitol).
2. YOU BELONG TO ME. Jo Stafford (Columbia).
3. SOMEWHERE ALONG THE WAY. Nat Cole (Capitol).
4. ISLE OF INNISFREE. Bing Crosby (Brunswick).
5. FEET UP. Guy Mitchell (Columbia).
6. HALF AS MUCH. Rosemary Clooney (Columbia).
7. FORGET-ME-NOT. Vera Lynn (Decca).
7. HIGH NOON. Frankie Laine (Columbia).
8. SUGAR BUSH. Doris Day/F. Laine (Columbia).
8. BLUE TANGO. Ray Martin (Columbia).
9. HOMING WALTZ. Vera Lynn (Decca).
10. AUF WIEDERSEHN. Vera Lynn (Decca).
11. COWPUNCHER'S CANTATA. Max Bygraves (HMV)
11. BECAUSE YOU'RE MINE. Mario Lanza (HMV)
12. WALKIN' MY BABY BACK HOME. Johnnie Ray (Columbia)

Reproduction in whole or part is strictly forbidden unless specific permission is obtained. Copyright by the "New Musical Express," 1952.

The first Record Hit Parade was published on 14 November 1952 and featured 15 records because some had equal sales figures. Here is the lowdown on each hit using the title spellings as used in that week 50 years ago

1. HERE IN MY HEART
Al Martino

The big ballad singer's debut disc rocketed to the top on both sides of the Atlantic. In the US, where it appeared on the indie label BBS (owned by Dave Miller, who also launched the careers of The Four Aces and Bill Haley), it reportedly sold 100,000 in its first seven days. Philadelphian Martino (born Alfred Cini) was a boyhood friend of fellow chart entrant Mario Lanza, who dropped his own plans to record this song when Martino told him that he had his heart set on recording it. The record had already been the No.1 seller in the UK for several weeks before it started its nine-week run at the top of the NME chart.

2. YOU BELONG TO ME
Jo Stafford

This California-born song stylist initially came to the public's attention 11 years previously in 1941 as a member of Tommy Dorsey's renowned vocal team The Pied Pipers. Her version of the much recorded country composition sold more than two million copies. It not only topped the chart in her homeland but also became the first No.1 in the UK by a female performer. The track was produced and arranged by her husband Paul Weston.

3. SOMEWHERE ALONG THE WAY
Nat "King" Cole

The velvet-voiced Alabama-born singer/pianist first recorded in 1936 and had been a top-billing act since 1944, when he fronted the "coolest" combo in jazz music. This track was his follow-up to the memorable 'Unforgettable', and he was backed on it by the Nelson Riddle Orchestra. The B-side was his version of the No.12 hit 'Walkin' My Baby Back Home'. Amazingly, King's last Top 40 entry came 42 years later.

4. ISLE OF INNISFREE
Bing Crosby

Only Elvis Presley can match the 300 million singles sold by the singer born Harry Lillis Crosby. Composed by British songwriter Richard Farrelly, this ode to an island in Ireland gave Bing his highest placed UK hit, even though it was not among the 299 US Top 20 entries he amassed since going solo in 1931.

5. FEET UP
Guy Mitchell

Born Al Cernick in Detroit, Mitchell was one of the most popular US performers in Britain throughout the 1950s. This song about his baby (the sort that needs its nappy changed) was penned, as were most of his hits, by the decade's most successful songsmith, Bob 'How Much Is that Doggie in the Window' Merrill.

6. HALF AS MUCH
Rosemary Clooney
Mitch Miller was the first producer to spot the pop potential of covering Hank Williams's country hits – Tony Bennett's interpretation of Hank's 'Cold, Cold Heart' having topped the US chart in 1951. He was proved correct again when his production of this Hank C&W smash was an international bestseller. Clooney, who first found fame with Tony Pastor's Band in the late 1940s, was still picking up Grammy nominations in 2001.

7. FORGET-ME-NOT
Vera Lynn
The legendary vocalist sang with the Joe Loss Band in 1935 and later that year made her recording debut with the Charlie Kunz Band. The "Forces' Sweetheart" was the only act to have three singles on the chart. Johnny Johnston, whose group supplied backing vocals, composed this song or her.

7. HIGH NOON
Frankie Laine
The Academy Award-winning song, taken from the Gary Cooper movie of the same name, is probably best remembered for its opening line "Do not forsake me oh my darling". 'High Noon' was a bestseller for the legendary Laine and Western movie star Tex Ritter. It was one of very few records of the time on which the singer did a vocal overdub.

8. SUGAR BUSH
Doris Day and Frankie Laine
A sing-along song which was based on a folk tune that composer Joseph Marais had learned as a child in South Africa. The teaming of top solo artists for duets was not unusual at the time, and among singer/actress Day's other musical partners were Frank Sinatra and Johnnie Ray.

8. BLUE TANGO
Ray Martin
Leroy Anderson's composition 'Blue Tango' was the No.2 sheet music hit of the year, and Vienna-born, British-based orchestra leader and Columbia Records A&R man Martin had the top-selling version. The only instrumental single on the chart was also one of the first batch of 45rpm singles released in the UK.

9. HOMING WALTZ
Vera Lynn
Hit-makers Alma Cogan, Dickie Valentine, Billy Cotton and Teddy Johnson were among the other artists who recorded this Johnny Johnston song. According to the record's label, Vera was accompanied by "Soldiers, Sailors and Airmen of HM Forces", although she was actually joined by the Johnny Johnston Singers again.

10. AUF WIEDERSEHN
Vera Lynn
The biggest-selling British record of the year was also the first UK single ever to top the US Best Sellers (it spent nine weeks at the summit) and the only one to achieve that feat in the 1950s. The song sounded as if it had been written in the war years, but was actually penned in Germany in 1949. It goes without saying that the Johnny Johnston Singers can be heard on the catchy chorus.

11. COWPUNCHER'S CANTATA
Max Bygraves
The only single by a British male vocalist featured on this chart was a parody of several recent Western story songs. It includes Bygraves's humorous interpretations of Frankie Laine's bestsellers 'Mule Train' and 'Cry of the Wild Goose'. It might be hard to imagine but, at the time, the youthful London-born Bygraves was a cutting-edge comedian.

11. BECAUSE YOU'RE MINE
Mario Lanza
Born Alfredo Cocozza in Philadelphia, light operatic tenor/actor Lanza was as popular in the 1950s as Pavarotti is today. His highest placed UK hit was the title song of Mario's fourth film, in which he played an opera singer who became a GI. Lanza's untimely death at the age of 38 in Rome in 1959 is still shrouded in mystery.

12. WALKIN' MY BABY BACK HOME
Johnnie Ray
The hearing aid-wearing "Prince of Wails" sobbed himself into the hearts of thousands of teenage girls in 1952. He was mobbed wherever he performed and no doubt cried all the way to the bank. He ended a fantastic year by making this 1931 song popular again. Interestingly, when US DJs first heard Ray they presumed him to be a black female artist and his first hit, 'Cry', went on to top the R&B chart!

HOW THE CHART BEGAN

Former NME journalist Derek Johnson recalls the early days

Derek Johnson (centre) and wife Sheila chat with Maurice Kinn at the NME's 10th anniversary party

At the tail-end of 1951, promoter and agent Maurice Kinn embarked on a precarious career change. Fulfilling an ambition to run a music paper, he bought the ailing *Musical Express & Accordion Weekly* for £1,000 and relaunched it in March 1952 as the *New Musical Express*. He had already made up his mind to start the UK's first pop record chart. America had a chart, so why not here? The British sheet music sales chart had been of little interest to the general public at this time.

Maurice and advertising director Percy Dickins spent months preparing the ground, talking to people in the record industry and contacting record stores to seek their co-operation. By November 1952, the first "Record Hit Parade" was ready to go, supported by adverts in the national press, which immediately boosted *NME*'s circulation.

> **"It was all hands to the pump in the NME office with virtually everyone given their own list of shops to contact every Monday morning"**

The first chart was based on lists supplied by 53 record stores, mainly in London and the Home Counties, but also included cities such as Birmingham, Glasgow, Manchester and Belfast. It was all hands to the pump in the *NME* office with virtually everyone – including journalists, secretaries, advertising staff and Maurice himself – given their own list of shops to contact every Monday morning. The week's results were then collated by *NME*'s staff accountant Ted Hull, creating a final chart.

At this time, *NME* was a compact unit of just 24 members of staff. The offices were situated in London's Denmark Street, known as Tin Pan Alley and home to numerous music publishers, musicians and singers who popped in and out of their offices on the street.

The chart in the first week consisted of just a Top 12, due mainly to the fact that there were relatively few weekly releases. The chief factor contributing to this shortage was a distinct lack of the raw material used to manufacture the discs. This was a resin called shellac, in short supply at the end of the Second World War when important imports such as consumer goods and foodstuffs were considered a priority. I recall visiting the old Decca factory in New Malden in1954 and seeing vast mountains of waste shellac dust. Because of the shortage, this dust had to be recycled to meet the demands of new record releases.

It soon became clear that the singles chart was a big success. Record companies began quoting chart placings in their adverts and

NME's circulation jumped by 50 per cent. BBC radio remained aloof, and even in the mid-60s when I was presenting a daily review show, I was surprised to find that every word had to be scripted. Although the BBC had a monopoly at the time of the chart launch, by contrast Radio Luxembourg was in its heyday. Millions tuned in every night to hear the latest sounds presented by unscripted free-chatting DJs. During my time as programme administrator of Radio Luxembourg, based in London, I learned of the *NME*'s new enterprise and passed the chart listings to DJs in the Duchy who began a regular chart run-down every night. This, more than anything else, gave the chart widespread acceptance and credence.

In 1956, having previously worked as a promoter, manager and freelancer for the *NME*, I began full-time employment as their news editor and stayed with the *NME* for 30 years. By 1956 the chart had gradually grown to a Top 30. By now, supplies of shellac had become more readily available and the number of weekly releases grew accordingly. At the same time America was introducing a new means of processing records using a substance called vinyl.

The expansion of the chart meant a doubling of the number of stores contacted; even with the help of extra part-time *NME* staff to collect the data, the job became too much and the compilation was handed over to a firm of accountants.

Maurice Kinn died in 2000, having seen his foresight expand beyond his wildest dreams. Had he not conceived the idea of a pop record chart, there is no doubt someone else would have had the inspiration sooner or later, but Maurice was the innovator. As for me, being involved in the fledgling years of the Record Hit Parade was exciting. My three meetings with Elvis created great memories and co-hosting the *NME* poll concerts was special. But perhaps my most significant experience occurred on the day I first joined the *NME* full-time. I was immediately attracted to the receptionist / telephonist, a lovely, funny, friendly young blonde. She was just my style – so I married her. Sheila and I had 34 wonderful years together before she succumbed to cancer in 1995. It's gratifying to know that Sheila was also involved in the chart's development – because she, too, had her list of record stores to contact every Monday morning.

“Record companies began quoting chart placings in their adverts and NME's circulation jumped by 50 per cent”

The 1956 NME staff party line-up. Centre (standing) Derek Johnson and front row (left to right), editor Andy Gray, Berenice Kinn, Maurice Kinn, advertising director Percy Dickins (father of music industry kingpins Rob and Barry), Sheila Sweetman and circulation manager Tommy Rowe

AL MARTINO: THE FIRST No.1 ACT

The 1950s Al Martino

Fifty years on from the first UK singles chart, Al Martino is alive and well and still performing. British Hit Singles went to Beverly Hills to catch up with the man who took 'Here in My Heart' to the top of the very first singles chart

TAKE US BACK TO THE EARLY 1950s. WHERE DID 'HERE IN MY HEART' COME FROM AND HOW DID IT GET RECORDED?

Bill Borelli, who wrote the song, had seen me in the Arthur Godfrey talent scout show and he thought I'd do his song justice. He came to New York to look for me and came into a restaurant and sat opposite me. We got into a conversation because he said he was from Philadelphia and I was from Philadelphia. He still didn't know I was the man he was searching for. He told me he was looking for a singer by the name of Al Martino. For a second, I thought he was putting me on or kidding me. I introduced myself and his head nearly dropped in the soup. After he got over the shock, he told me about his song, came up to my apartment and played it to me. It didn't take me very long to realise that this was a great song.

First of all I had to tell him that I wasn't recording for any company, and he said we're going to record it ourselves on our own label. Mr Borelli had only enough money to book eight musicians but I took the initiative and got Monty Kelly [the song's arranger] to hire a 52-piece orchestra. When he realised we had gone way overboard on

Madonna's got one, Kylie's got one and now Al Martino has a Guinness World Records British Hit Singles No.1 award to mark the very first chart-topper 50 years ago

"He put the record on and the switchboard lit up like a Christmas tree"

this he had to go back and look for investors – Borelli, Busillo and Smith, who ended up as the investors and gave their names to the label, BBS.

HOW DID 'HERE IN MY HEART' GET DISTRIBUTED, SOLD AND PROMOTED?

I had taken the record to Capitol Records in Los Angeles. I drove my car out there but they turned it down. I then had no alternative but to turn it over to an independent company who would distribute it for me, but I had to give up my royalties to do that. Dave Miller, who owned the independent label, had a network of disc jockeys who could promote the record, and the first play was in May 1952 by Barry Kaye in Philadelphia on WCAU. He put the record on and the switchboard lit up like a Christmas tree. That's when I knew we had something. In the US chart it jumped very quickly to No.1.

HOW DID YOU FIRST DISCOVER THAT YOUR RECORD HAD MADE NO.1 IN THE FIRST NEW MUSICAL EXPRESS UK CHART?

I had a manager who told me I was No.1 in England and that the Palladium wanted to book me. The *New Musical Express* was owned by Maurice Kinn and he had just started this magazine. I didn't get to work the Palladium until 1953 and I got to England during the coronation of Queen Elizabeth. The Queen had a birthday party for Winston Churchill at the Dorchester and they invited me to sit at the table with Winston and his two daughters. I had wonderful conversations with Mr Churchill. Quite a guy, and a wonderful sense of humour. Everyone had an escort. But I didn't have one and Mr Churchill didn't have one. So when everyone got up to dance, the only people left at the table were Mr Churchill and I. He whispered over to me, "Mr Martino, I hope you're not going to ask me to dance!"

'HERE IN MY HEART' DID EVENTUALLY END UP ON THE CAPITOL LABEL. HOW DID THAT HAPPEN?

Originally Capitol took me but not the record. The condition was that if ▶

they signed me they would have to help to promote the record.

DO YOU STILL PERFORM 'HERE IN MY HEART'?

I don't believe I can leave the stage without singing it. I've done it every single night I'm performing for the past 50 years. There is no way you can exclude it.

IS IT YOUR MOST SUCCESSFUL SONG?

'Spanish Eyes' was many years later. At that time you had a bigger market. You've got all of Europe, America, Canada, Australia. The distribution was much larger and therefore you're gonna sell more records. I assume 'Spanish Eyes' in Britain was a pretty big hit too? I think some disc jockey had discovered it.

HOW ABOUT RE-RELEASING 'HERE IN MY HEART' TO CELEBRATE THE 50TH ANNIVERSARY OF OUR UK CHART?

It's not an impossibility. Capitol Records EMI has the second version of it. It would be a splendid idea and I'm looking at it from a producer's point of view, not an artist's point of view. I have gotten so many people call me in the past 10 years to have it released and I've turned them all down. It just cannot buck up against what's happening today. Other artists would have been anxious to put it out, but that would have been a mistake. But now, 50 years later, you've got a hook, a reason to do it and that's the difference.

DO YOU STILL FOLLOW WHAT'S HAPPENING IN THE CHARTS TODAY?

I used to follow the British charts quite a lot, but lately I haven't because of all the rock. I don't expect to see a great ballad in the Top 10. I had my nose in the music business totally back in the 50s, 60s, even the 70s. But all of that has diminished. I couldn't keep up. Many records I couldn't relate to. Like rap. How could I possibly relate to that? It took me a long time to accept rock. Let's talk about The Beatles. The Beatles' moms and dads were coming in to see me in Liverpool. Here I am, No.1 artist at Capitol Records, and Sir Joseph Lockwood [of EMI who would later sign The Beatles] comes along and purchases Capitol and it becomes a British-orientated label.

Some of the songs of today are great, but the performances are only to deliver the song. You don't have to have a great voice but you have a great song – that's fantastic. Now you have any kind of a voice that can sell it. Can you imagine Elton John singing 'Here in My Heart'? It's impossible, but I can't take anything away from him because he's a great writer. It was Bobby Darin, it was Paul Anka, who started the singer-songwriter era. They both made demonstration records of their own songs and would go to a record company to try to sell those songs. The record company would say, we don't have anybody to sing that stuff so why don't you put it out? Atlantic was, I think, the first to do that with Bobby's 'Splish Splash'. There's a fine example of how good the song is. Let's reverse it now and say Paul McCartney calls me and says, "Al, I've got a great song called 'Yesterday' – would you record it?" Of course I would have recorded it. It was a great song.

> **"Can you imagine Elton John singing 'Here in My Heart'? It's impossible, but I can't take anything away from him because he's a great writer"**

BEFORE WE FINISH, WE MUST ASK YOU ABOUT YOUR ROLE IN PERHAPS THE GREATEST MOVIE OF ALL TIME

It was a stroke of luck that a book was written called *The Godfather*. I read the book with the Johnny Fontaine role in there. This role was huge, with Johnny Fontaine in nearly every chapter. So, after I was cast in the role of Johnny Fontaine by producer Al Ruddy, a man by the name of Frank Sinatra went on the warpath and tried to get Paramount to exclude that part because he thought it was too much like his life. I convinced Mario Puzo, the author, not to pay any attention to Frank's tantrums but the part did get reduced at Frank's insistence. There was even a time when Frank tried to convince Coppola [the director] he could play the Don's part. See how important the Johnny Fontaine role was? The Fontaine role was why you had those lines like "I'll make him an offer he can't refuse". And what about the horse's head? Without Johnny Fontaine, there would have been no horse's head.

WHAT ARE YOUR FUTURE PLANS?

I work quite often. I just came off a three-month tour and I'm ready to go out again next week! I haven't toured Great Britain in 10 years. I haven't had any offers. I would love to play over there again. If we do get a tour there we will credit it to The Book of British Hit Singles.

CHART MILESTONES

The official UK charts used to compile The Book of British Hit Singles have altered in size and format on a number of occasions. Here are the major changes since the chart began in 1952. The day of the week when the chart has been released to the public has varied. It should be noted that the chart entry dates used in this book are usually later (now almost a week later) than that announcement

14 NOVEMBER 1952
First chart was a Top 12 (but actually included 15 records) compiled for the New Musical Express. Date of chart was a Friday. For a full description of how this first chart began, see pages 6 - 9

1 OCTOBER 1954
Chart became a Top 20 and then a Top 25 for one week only on 30 December 1955

13 APRIL 1956
Top 30 established

4 MARCH 1960
Last NME Top 30 used by this book

10 MARCH 1960
Week ending 5 March data inaugurated the first Record Retailer chart used in this book. Date of chart changed to a Thursday

3 JANUARY 1963
Now a Top 50 independently audited for Record Retailer

5 JULY 1967
Date of chart changed to a Wednesday

12 FEBRUARY 1969
Top 50 now compiled for Record Retailer and the BBC by British Market Research Bureau

9 AUGUST 1969
Date of chart changed to a Saturday

6 FEBRUARY 1971
Postal strike responsible for limiting the chart to a Top 40 for seven weeks. Top 50 resumed on 27 March 1971

6 JANUARY 1973
Top 30 only, for one week

22 DECEMBER 1973
Top 30 only, for one week

JULY 1977
First edition of The Guinness Book of British Hit Singles published

6 MAY 1978
Top 75 began

8 JANUARY 1983
Chart compilation taken over by Gallup

DECEMBER 1992
The chart produced in association with the BPI and Bard became the copyright of Chart Information Network Co Ltd, or CIN for short. Gallup's compilation was based on a minimum of 500 record outlets including vinyl, cassette and CD singles

12 FEBRUARY 1994
Chart compilation taken over by Millward Brown and the sample of record outlets increased to more than 1,000

JULY 2001
Chart Information Network Co Ltd changed its name to the Official UK Charts company

29 DECEMBER 2001
Last Top 75 chart of the year incorporated into this current edition of British Hit Singles

IT'S WORTH REMEMBERING...

▶ A final note about which charts have been used in compiling this book. Establishing an "official chart", with a variety to choose from in the early days, was not an easy task for the compilers of this book when it was first published in 1977.

In the 1960s, the charts compiled by NME and Melody Maker were more widely quoted and equally accurate compared with those of Record Retailer. However, since Record Retailer was the music industry trade chart and the only Top 50 that was published throughout the 1960s, this book's original authors decided it was the best chart for their purposes.

THE VINYL REVIVAL

When all around us are strapping on their MP3 watches and burning CDs, what's with this article on vinyl in the 21st century? Industry hacks spent the early 90s pronouncing vinyl dead, but read on, because those black vinyl discs are back in the racks

Left: John Cusack in 'High Fidelity' sorting through his Bob Dylan bootlegs

▶ Vinyl was undoubtedly the most important music format of the 20th century. Its predecessor shellac was heavy, fragile and expensive to manufacture. When vinyl hit the record stores in the early 50s, its advantages were obvious and its unwieldy forerunner was soon replaced. But if you'd ventured into a record shop in the mid-1990s, actual records were the last thing you were likely to find.

Much like the battle between Betamax and VHS, the format wars in the audio arena have been bitterly contested, with far more factions in the fray. Eight-track cartridges, DATs, and digital compact cassettes are just a few of the victims in the race to establish a new standard medium for pre-recorded music. But by far the biggest upheaval in the home audio stakes came when CDs took the crown from vinyl.

So why did vinyl nearly die? The massive drop in vinyl sales over the past 20 years was partly down to a coffer-swelling opportunity for the major record companies. With Sony, for example, producing expensive new CD players, and Sony Music producing the CDs to play in them, it was in their interests to build demand for the software, and thereby fuel demand for the hardware. They did this by promoting CDs on the basis of their audio superiority and wild claims that they were indestructible. Yeah, right. Did they tell us how easy they were to scratch, and that CDs are just as prone to jumping and skipping as vinyl? Having blinded us with science, the majors proceeded to repackage and resell our record collections back to us at immense profits, convincing us that CDs had rendered vinyl redundant, and consigned our 33s and 45s to the dustbin of history.

Riding the tide of the vinyl revolution, a group of companies is filling the gap left by the majors, and dealing vinyl to those disenchanted with the digital alternatives. The world's largest is Simply Vinyl, founded by Mike Loveday in 1997 to reissue classic rock records on lovingly packaged 180g virgin vinyl. Simply Vinyl and other companies reproduce the original records as faithfully as possible for the diehard vinylist, and they count Paul Weller and Mark Lamarr among their customers.

Mike Loveday explains: "In the early days the major labels were relentlessly reissuing everything on CD without due care and attention to sound. You had a lot of people who wanted to replace their vinyl collection with CDs so it would 'last for ever', only to find that when they played them, The Rolling Stones didn't sound like The Rolling Stones and The Who didn't sound like The Who." A&R for Simply Vinyl, Ian Dewhirst, continues: "Most of our buyers swear by vinyl. They believe that the analogue listening experience is much more fulfilling than the digital one." We could fill a book with the arguments for and against the sound quality of vinyl in comparison with CDs, but in layman's terms the digitising process loses small sections of the analogue signal which gives vinyl sound the warmth and fullness its fans crave.

A key driver of vinyl sales in recent years has been DJ culture. With kids now more likely to be spending their pocket money on turntables than on guitars, budding DJs have led to booming sales of 12" singles. The 12" hit the shops in the late 1970s after disco DJs popularised the format which allowed them to play longer versions of the cuts by legends such as Nile Rodgers and Giorgio Moroder, and needed six or seven minutes to develop rather than the paltry three or four you could squeeze on a 7". The first 12" to hit the charts was The Undisputed Truth's 'U + Me = Love' in 1977, and the biggest 12" to date has been New Order's classic 'Blue Monday' which shifted more than 600,000 copies in the UK and three million worldwide.

Twenty years later, with Ibiza now a summer institution, 12" vinyl imports often entered the singles chart under their own steam, and club DJs forced the majors to give these anthems a full release. One infamous example was 'Music Sounds Better with You' by Stardust, a one-off side project by Daft Punk's Thomas Bangalter on his own indie label Roule. When it reached No.55 thanks to word of mouth and club ubiquity, Virgin picked up the track and rush-released it. The track reached No.2 and spent half a year on the chart.

The frequent reports of the death of vinyl have therefore been massively exaggerated, with vinyl pressing plants across the UK unable to meet with the increased demand over the past few years. Any music freak who's been to the movies over the past year or two must have noticed the resurgence of vinyl on celluloid. In Cameron Crowe's *Almost Famous* there was many a lingering shot of William digging through his sister's record collection as though he'd found lost treasure, and Quentin Tarantino's movie *Jackie Brown* set the mood by sticking a classic Delfonics track on the turntable. But more than any other movie, the big-screen version of Nick Hornby's *High Fidelity* left vinyl junkies in danger of an overdose. The true star of the movie was undoubtedly John Cusack's impressively large and well-ordered record collection.

High Fidelity managed to make sense of the vinyl junkie's addiction. Vinyl has many advantages over the CD for the music obsessives. For a start, seeing one of Warhol's classic sleeves reduced to CD size, or a classic Led Zep gatefold shrunk into a digi-pak, makes record cover art redundant. CDs may well be more easily transportable but they crack and shatter with age, whereas a cared-for record sleeve takes on a tactile patina like an old leather sofa. According to Chris Barnett from Simply Vinyl: "I think that there's something immense and wonderful about a 12" record and appreciating the artwork in its full size and glory and all the detail you can see there. It's a piece of art. A CD is just a little plastic box that has no real value as such. The artwork's all compressed – you have to squint to look at it. It's just a consumer good. The two things are realms apart. Flicking through racks of records is fantastic. It's such a buzz trying to find what you're after, but where's the fun of doing that with CDs?"

As for how the UK compares with rest of the world, 63 per cent of British households still own a turntable, and although vinyl albums in the UK represent just 2 per cent of music sales, that represents a massive 23.7 per cent of the world market. All of this goes to show that vinyl is alive and well in the UK, and suggests it'll be the obsessive music lover's format of choice for years to come. If you want to start record collecting, HMV and Virgin megastores now stock most new releases on vinyl. For second-hand records, specialist genres and rarer items, check Yellow Pages for your local vinyl record shop. The majority are staffed by friendly, knowledgable vinyl hounds who'll guide you through the racks. It's hard to imagine having friends around in 20 years' time for a nostalgic search through old MP3 files. So go on, go up to the loft and dig out that old turntable and that battered box of dusty 45s – just don't forget to save your CDs for beermats.

"I think there's something immense and wonderful about a 12" record... it's a piece of art"

READERS' TOP 100

▶ We asked you, the readers of British Hit Singles, to vote for your favourite singles and you didn't let us down. The response from perhaps the best qualified judges of 50 years of hits resulted in more than 31,000 votes for singles, with 'Bohemian Rhapsody' coming in at No.1. Here is what Queen's Brian May had to say about the clear winner of our poll.

Queen's 'Bohemian Rhapsody': clear winner in our poll

"The life expectancy of '**Bohemian Rhapsody**' seems to increase with age. The history of the track since 1975 has been even more surprising. Even though – incredibly – a quarter of a century has passed, wherever polls are conducted, all around the globe, 'Bo Rhap' (as it became affectionately known) still always crops up at or near the top of the list. In this latest poll, the song was so far ahead of any rival that even months before the deadline its position was unimpeachable. It has become a classic phenomenon, and one which no one will ever allow us to forget! Thank you, people, for the memory."

BRITISH HIT SINGLES READERS' TOP 100 SINGLES: 1952 - 2002

1. BOHEMIAN RHAPSODY Queen
2. IMAGINE John Lennon
3. HEY JUDE Beatles
4. DANCING QUEEN Abba
5. LIKE A PRAYER Madonna
6. ANGELS Robbie Williams
7. PENNY LANE / STRAWBERRY FIELDS FOREVER Beatles
8. WANNABE Spice Girls
9. YESTERDAY Beatles
10. LET IT BE Beatles
11. SMELLS LIKE TEEN SPIRIT Nirvana
12. DON'T LOOK BACK IN ANGER Oasis
13. NOTHING COMPARES 2 U Sinead O'Connor
14. SUSPICIOUS MINDS Elvis Presley
15. BILLIE JEAN Michael Jackson
16. LOSING MY RELIGION R.E.M.
17. HOTEL CALIFORNIA Eagles
18. (EVERYTHING I DO) I DO IT FOR YOU Bryan Adams
19. A WHITER SHADE OF PALE Procol Harum
20. WITH OR WITHOUT YOU U2
21. CANDLE IN THE WIND 1997 / SOMETHING ABOUT THE WAY YOU LOOK TONIGHT Elton John
22. I WILL ALWAYS LOVE YOU Whitney Houston
23. BABY ONE MORE TIME Britney Spears
24. VOGUE Madonna
25. HEARTBEAT / TRAGEDY Steps
26. THRILLER Michael Jackson
27. NEVER EVER All Saints
28. MY HEART WILL GO ON Celine Dion
29. I TURN TO YOU Melanie C
30. WONDERWALL Oasis
31. AMERICAN PIE Don McLean
32. EVERYBODY HURTS R.E.M.
33. CARELESS WHISPER George Michael
34. BAKER STREET Gerry Rafferty
35. BRIDGE OVER TROUBLED WATER Simon and Garfunkel
36. I'LL BE MISSING YOU Puff Daddy and Faith Evans featuring 112
37. I CAN'T GET NO (SATISFACTION) Rolling Stones
38. BITTER SWEET SYMPHONY Verve
39. I HEARD IT THROUGH THE GRAPEVINE Marvin Gaye
40. WUTHERING HEIGHTS Kate Bush
41. BETTER THE DEVIL YOU KNOW Kylie Minogue
42. VIENNA Ultravox
43. SHE LOVES YOU Beatles
44. MUSIC Madonna
45. EVERY BREATH YOU TAKE Police
46. LAYLA Derek and the Dominoes
47. THE WINNER TAKES IT ALL Abba
48. HEARTBREAK HOTEL Elvis Presley
49. MY SWEET LORD George Harrison
50. I'M NOT IN LOVE 10cc
51. GOOD VIBRATIONS Beach Boys
52. UNCHAINED MELODY Righteous Brothers
53. BACK FOR GOOD Take That
54. STAN Eminem
55. WITHOUT YOU Nilsson
56. GOD ONLY KNOWS Beach Boys
57. DON'T YOU WANT ME Human League
58. I DON'T WANT TO MISS A THING Aerosmith
59. BAT OUT OF HELL Meat Loaf
60. HELP! Beatles
61. HEROES David Bowie
62. PURPLE RAIN Prince
63. CAN'T GET YOU OUT OF MY HEAD Kylie Minogue
64. LIKE A ROLLING STONE Bob Dylan
65. GOD SAVE THE QUEEN Sex Pistols
66. CHINA IN YOUR HAND T'Pau
67. HERO Mariah Carey
68. WHOLE AGAIN Atomic Kitten
69. LOVE IS ALL AROUND Wet Wet Wet
70. SPACE ODDITY David Bowie
71. MAKE ME SMILE (COME UP AND SEE ME) Steve Harley and Cockney Rebel
72. KNOWING ME KNOWING YOU Abba
73. THE DRUGS DON'T WORK Verve
74. TEENAGE KICKS Undertones
75. SUMMER OF '69 Bryan Adams
76. CARS Gary Numan
77. MR BLUE SKY Electric Light Orchestra
78. 2 BECOME 1 Spice Girls
79. ROCK DJ Robbie Williams
80. PURE SHORES All Saints
81. SULTANS OF SWING Dire Straits
82. HOLLER Spice Girls
83. INTO THE GROOVE Madonna
84. BELIEVE Cher
85. INDEPENDENT WOMEN PART 1 Destiny's Child
86. TAINTED LOVE Soft Cell
87. I WILL SURVIVE Gloria Gaynor
88. MY GENERATION Who
89. DAY TRIPPER / WE CAN WORK IT OUT Beatles
90. COMMON PEOPLE Pulp
91. WATERLOO SUNSET Kinks
92. YOU'VE LOST THAT LOVIN' FEELIN' Righteous Brothers
93. VOODOO CHILE Jimi Hendrix
94. JAILHOUSE ROCK Elvis Presley
95. SWEET CHILD O' MINE Guns N' Roses
96. ANARCHY IN THE UK Sex Pistols
97. ETERNAL FLAME Bangles
98. WITHOUT YOU Mariah Carey
99. ALL ALONG THE WATCHTOWER Jimi Hendrix
100. HOW DO I LIVE LeAnn Rimes

THE 916 NUMBER ONE HITS

▶ All the UK chart-toppers are listed here in chronological order, with date, blobs (••••) indicating the weeks at the top, song, act name, writers, producers and sales awards. For those people anxious to pinpoint the No.1 on a particular day visit our website: www.britishhitsingles.com but note that on these pages, every chart reflects the top sellers in the seven-day period ending the Saturday before the chart date. The all-important Christmas No.1 is the last hit listed in each year, except in 1993 when Mr Blobby returned to No.1 in the nick of time at the expense of Take That.

Please note that the equivalent US positions are taken from the Billboard "Best Sellers" chart up to 4 Aug 1958 when the Hot 100 was launched and this chart has been used since then. The US peak positions for some 2001 singles may be improved by 2002 chart action.

KEY TO SYMBOLS

SILVER, GOLD AND PLATINUM CERTIFICATION
Singles from 1973-1988 required sales of 250,000 to go silver, 500,000 to go gold and one million to go platinum. From 1 Jan 1989 to now: 200,000 (silver), 400,000 (gold) and 600,000 (platinum)

PLATINUM - ✪
GOLD - ●
SILVER - ⊙
ONE-HIT WONDER - ❶
STRAIGHT IN AT UK NO.1 - ◆
WEEKS AT NO.1 - •••••••

1953: Mantovani, whose biggest hit 'Song From The Moulin Rouge' was his only chart-topper, although he did help out David Whitfield on his 1954 No.1 'Cara Maria'

1952

1. 14 Nov ••••••••• HERE IN MY HEART Al Martino Writers: Pat Genero, Lou Levinson and Bill Borrelli. Producer: Voyle Gilmore. **US peak: 1.** ◆

1953

2. 16 Jan • YOU BELONG TO ME Jo Stafford Writers: Pee Wee King, Redd Stewart and Chilton Price. Producer: Paul Weston. **US peak: 1.**

3. 23 Jan • COMES A-LONG A-LOVE Kay Starr Writer: Al Sherman. Producer: Mitch Miller. **US peak: 22.**

4. 30 Jan • OUTSIDE OF HEAVEN Eddie Fisher Writers: Sammy Gallop and Chester Conn. Producer: Hugo Winterhalter. **US peak: 10.**

5. 6 Feb ••••• DON'T LET THE STARS GET IN YOUR EYES Perry Como Writer: Slim Willet, Cactus Pryor and Barbara Trammel. Producer: Eli Obertsein. **US peak: 1.**

6. 13 Mar •••• SHE WEARS RED FEATHERS Guy Mitchell Writer: Bob Merrill. Producer: Mitch Miller.

7. 10 Apr • BROKEN WINGS Stargazers Writers: John Jerome and Bernard Gunn. Producer: Dick Rowe.

8. 17 Apr • (HOW MUCH IS) THAT DOGGIE IN THE WINDOW Lita Roza Writer: Bob Merrill. Producer: Dick Rowe.

9. 24 Apr ••••••••• 3 Jul •••••• 21 Aug ••• I BELIEVE Frankie Laine Writers: Erwin Drake, Irvin Graham, Jimmy Shirl and Al Stillman. Producer: Mitch Miller. **US peak: 2.**

10. 26 Jun • I'M WALKING BEHIND YOU Eddie Fisher featuring Sally Sweetland Writer: Billy Reid. Producer: Hugo Winterhalter. **US peak: 1.**

11. 14 Aug • SONG FROM 'THE MOULIN ROUGE' Mantovani and his Orchestra Writer: Georges Auric. Producer: Frank Lee. **US peak: 13.**

12. 11 Sep •••••• LOOK AT THAT GIRL Guy Mitchell Writer: Bob Merrill. Producer: Mitch Miller.

13. 23 Oct •• HEY JOE! Frankie Laine Writer: Boudleaux Bryant. Producer: Mitch Miller. **US peak: 11.**

1956: Doris Day tops the charts with a song from Hitchcock's movie 'The Man Who Knew Too Much'

14. 6 Nov • 11 Dec (equal top) • ANSWER ME David Whitfield Writers: Gerhard Winkler and Fred Rauch; English lyrics by Carl Sigman. Producer: Bunny Lewis.

15. 13 Nov •••••••• 11 Dec (equal top) ANSWER ME Frankie Laine Writers: Gerhard Winkler and Fred Rauch; English lyrics by Carl Sigman. Producer: Mitch Miller.

1954

16. 8 Jan ••••••••• OH, MEIN PAPA Eddie Calvert Writers: Paul Burkhard; English lyrics by John Turner and Geoffrey Parsons. Producer: Norrie Paramor. **US peak: 9**.

17. 12 Mar ••••• 23 Apr • I SEE THE MOON Stargazers Writer: Meredith Wilson. Producer: Dick Rowe.

18. 16 Apr • 7 May •••••••• SECRET LOVE Doris Day Writers: Paul Francis Webster and Sammy Fain. Producer: Ray Heindorf. **US peak: 1**.

19. 30 Apr • SUCH A NIGHT Johnnie Ray Writer: Lincoln Chase. Producer: Mitch Miller.

20. 2 Jul •••••••••• CARA MIA David Whitfield with Chorus and Mantovani and his Orchestra Writers: Lee Lange and Tulio Trapani (aka producer Bunny Lewis and arranger Mantovani). Producer: Bunny Lewis. **US peak: 10**.

21. 10 Sep • LITTLE THINGS MEAN A LOT Kitty Kallen Writers: Carl Stultz and Edith Lindermann. Producer: Milt Gabler **US peak: 1**. ❶

22. 17 Sep ••• THREE COINS IN THE FOUNTAIN Frank Sinatra Writers: Sammy Cahn and Jule Styne. Producer: Voyle Gilmore. **US peak: 7**.

23. 8 Oct •••• 19 Nov • HOLD MY HAND Don Cornell Writers: Jack Lawrence and Richard Myers. Producer: Bob Thiele. **US peak: 5**.

24. 5 Nov •• MY SON, MY SON Vera Lynn Writers: Bob Howard, Melville Farley and Eddie Calvert. Producer: Frank Lee.

25. 26 Nov • THIS OLE HOUSE Rosemary Clooney Writer: Stuart Hamblen. Producer: Mitch Miller. **US peak: 1**.

26. 3 Dec ••••• LET'S HAVE ANOTHER PARTY Winifred Atwell Writers: Nat D Ayer, Clifford Grey, James W Tate, Ray Henderson, Mort Dixon, Albert Fitz, William Penn, Gus Cahn, Walter Donaldson, Leslie Stuart, Harry Armstrong, Ted Snyder, Leo Wood, Harry Wood. Producer: Johnny Franz.

1955

27. 7 Jan • 21 Jan •• THE FINGER OF SUSPICION Dickie Valentine Writers: Al Lewis and Paul Mann. Producer: Dick Rowe.

28. 14 Jan • 4 Feb •• MAMBO ITALIANO Rosemary Clooney Writer: Bob Merrill. Producer: Mitch Miller. **US peak: 10**.

29. 18 Feb ••• SOFTLY, SOFTLY Ruby Murray Writers: Mark Paul and Pierre Dudan; English lyrics by Paddy Roberts. Producer: Norrie Paramor.

30. 11 Mar ••••••• GIVE ME YOUR WORD Tennessee Ernie Ford Writers: George Wyle and Irving Taylor. Producer: Lee Gillette.

31. 29 Apr •• CHERRY PINK AND APPLE BLOSSOM WHITE Perez Prado Writer: Louis Guilielmi Louiguy. Producer: Herman Diaz. **US peak: 1**.

32. 13 May •• STRANGER IN PARADISE Tony Bennett Writers: Robert Wright and George Forrest. Producer: Mitch Miller. **US peak: 2**.

33. 27 May •••• CHERRY PINK AND APPLE BLOSSOM WHITE Eddie Calvert Writer: Louis Guilielmi Louiguy. Producer: Norrie Paramor.

34. 24 Jun ••• UNCHAINED MELODY Jimmy Young Writers: Alex North and Hy Zaret. Producer: Dick Rowe.

35. 15 Jul •• DREAMBOAT Alma Cogan Writer: Al Hoffman. Producer: Walter Ridley.

36. 29 Jul ••••••••••• ROSE MARIE Slim Whitman Writers: Rudolf Friml, Otto Harbach and Oscar Hammerstein II. Producer: Lew Chudd.

37. 14 Oct •••• THE MAN FROM LARAMIE Jimmy Young Writers: Lester Lee and Ned Washington. Producer: Dick Rowe.

38. 11 Nov •• HERNANDO'S HIDEAWAY Johnston Brothers Writers: Richard Adler and Jerry Ross. Producer: Hugh Mendl.

39. 25 Nov ••• 6 Jan 1956 •• ROCK AROUND THE CLOCK Bill Haley and his Comets Writers: Jimmy de Knight (James Myers) and Max C Freedman. Producer: Milt Gabler. **US peak: 1**.

40. 16 Dec ••• CHRISTMAS ALPHABET Dickie Valentine Writers: Buddy Kaye and Jules Loman. Producer: Dick Rowe.

1956

41. 20 Jan •••• SIXTEEN TONS Tennessee Ernie Ford Writer: Merle Travis. Producer: Lee Gillette. **US peak: 1**.

42. 17 Feb •••• MEMORIES ARE MADE OF THIS Dean Martin Writers: Terry Gilkyson, Richard Dehr and Frank Miller. Producer: Lee Gillette. **US peak: 1**.

43. 16 Mar •• 6 Apr • IT'S ALMOST TOMORROW Dreamweavers Writers: Wade Buff and Eugene Adkinson. Producers: Wade Buff, Eugene Adkinson and Milt Gabler. **US peak: 8**. ❶

44. 30 Mar • ROCK AND ROLL WALTZ Kay Starr Writers: Dick Ware and Shorty Allen. Producer: Joe Carlton. **US peak: 1**.

45. 13 Apr ••• THE POOR PEOPLE OF PARIS Winifred Atwell Writers: Marguerite Monnot and René Rouzaud. Producer: Hugh Mendl.

46. 4 May •••••• NO OTHER LOVE Ronnie Hilton Writers: Richard Rodgers and Oscar Hammerstein II. Producer: Walter Ridley.

47. 15 Jun ••••• I'LL BE HOME Pat Boone Writers: Ferdinand Washington and Stan Lewis. Producer: Randy Wood. **US peak: 6**.

48. 20 Jul ••• WHY DO FOOLS FALL IN LOVE? Teenagers featuring Frankie Lymon Writers: Frankie Lymon, Jimmy Merchant and Herman Santiago. Producer: Richard Barrett **US peak: 6**.

49. 10 Aug ••••••WHATEVER WILL BE, WILL BE (QUE SERA, SERA) Doris Day Writers: Ray Evans and Jay Livingston. Producer: Mitch Miller. **US peak: 3**.

50. 21 Sep •••• LAY DOWN YOUR ARMS Anne Shelton Writers: Leon Land and Ake Gerhard. Producer: Johnny Franz. **US peak: 59**.

51. 19 Oct •••• A WOMAN IN LOVE Frankie Laine Writer: Frank Loesser. Producer: Mitch Miller. **US peak: 19**.

1957: Harry Belafonte, who had the Christmas No.1 with 'Mary's Boy Child'

52. 16 Nov ••••••• JUST WALKIN' IN THE RAIN Johnnie Ray Writers: Johnny Bragg and Robert S Riley. Producer: Mitch Miller. **US peak: 3**.

1957

53. 4 Jan • 18 Jan • 1 Feb (equal top) • SINGING THE BLUES Guy Mitchell Writer: Melvin Endsley. Producer: Mitch Miller. **US peak: 1**.

54. 11 Jan • SINGING THE BLUES Tommy Steele and the Steelmen Writer: Melvin Endsley. Producer: Hugh Mendl.

55. 25 Jan • 1 Feb (equal top) • 8 Feb •• THE GARDEN OF EDEN Frankie Vaughan Writer: Denise Norwood. Producer: Johnny Franz.

56. 22 Feb ••••••• YOUNG LOVE Tab Hunter Writers: Carole Joyner and Ric Cartey. Producer: Billy Vaughn. **US peak: 1**.

57. 12 Apr ••••• CUMBERLAND GAP Lonnie Donegan Writer: Traditional, arranged by Lonnie Donegan. Producer: Alan Freeman.

58. 17 May • ROCK-A-BILLY Guy Mitchell Writers: Woody Harris and Eddie V Deane. Producer: Mitch Miller. **US peak: 10**.

59. 24 May •• BUTTERFLY Andy Williams Writer: Anthony September (aka Kal Mann and Bernie Lowe). Producer: Archie Bleyer. **US peak: 4**.

60. 7 Jun ••• YES TONIGHT, JOSEPHINE Johnnie Ray Writers: Winfield Scott and Dorothy Goodman. Producer: Mitch Miller.

61. 28 Jun •• GAMBLIN' MAN / PUTTIN' ON THE STYLE Lonnie Donegan Writers: Woody Guthrie and Lonnie Donegan / traditional arranged by Norman Cazden. Producer: Alan Freeman and Michael Barclay (recorded live at the London Palladium).

62. 12 Jul ••••••• ALL SHOOK UP Elvis Presley Writers: Otis Blackwell and Elvis Presley. Producer: Steve Sholes. **US peak: 1**.

63. 30 Aug ••••••••• DIANA Paul Anka Writer: Paul Anka. Producer: Don Costa. **US peak: 1**.

64. 1 Nov ••• THAT'LL BE THE DAY Crickets Writers: Buddy Holly, Jerry Allison and Norman Petty. Producer: Norman Petty. **US peak: 1**.

65. 22 Nov ••••••• MARY'S BOY CHILD Harry Belafonte Writer: Jester Hairston. Producer: Rene Farnon. **US peak: 12**.

1958

66. 10 Jan •• GREAT BALLS OF FIRE Jerry Lee Lewis Writers: Otis Blackwell and Jack Hammer. Producer: Sam Phillips. **US peak: 2**.

67. 24 Jan ••• JAILHOUSE ROCK Elvis Presley Writers: Jerry Leiber and Mike Stoller. Producer: Steve Sholes. **US peak: 1**. ◆

68. 14 Feb •• THE STORY OF MY LIFE Michael Holliday Writers: Burt Bacharach and Hal David. Producer: Norrie Paramor.

69. 28 Feb •••••••• MAGIC MOMENTS Perry Como Writers: Burt Bacharach and Hal David. Producer: Joe Reisman. **US peak: 3**.

70. 25 Apr ••• WHOLE LOTTA WOMAN Marvin Rainwater Writer: Marvin Rainwater. Producer: Jim Vinneau. **US peak: 60**.

71. 16 May •••••• WHO'S SORRY NOW? Connie Francis Writers: Ted Snyder, Bert Kalmar and Herman Ruby. Producer: Harry Myerson. **US peak: 5**.

72. 27 Jun • 4 Jul (equal top) • ON THE STREET WHERE YOU LIVE Vic Damone Writers: Alan Jay Lerner and Frederick Loewe. Producer: Mitch Miller. **US peak: 8**.

73. 4 Jul (equal top) • 11 Jul •••••• ALL I HAVE TO DO IS DREAM / CLAUDETTE Everly Brothers Writers: Felice and Boudleaux Bryant / Roy Orbison. Producer: Archie Bleyer. **US peaks: 1 / 30**

74. 22 Aug ••••• WHEN Kalin Twins Writers: Jack Reardon and Paul Evans. Producer: Jack Pleis. **US peak: 5**. ❶

75. 26 Sep •••••• CAROLINA MOON / STUPID CUPID Connie Francis Writers: Benny Davis and Joe Burke / Neil Sedaka and Howard Greenfield. Producers: Connie Francis and Leroy Holmes. **US peaks: 14 / 8**

76. 7 Nov ••• IT'S ALL IN THE GAME Tommy Edwards Writers: Charles Gates Dawes and Carl Sigman. Producer: Harry Myerson. **US peak: 1**.

77. 28 Nov ••• HOOTS MON Lord Rockingham's XI Writer: Harry Robinson. Producers: Hugh Mendl and Jack Good.

78. 19 Dec ••••• IT'S ONLY MAKE BELIEVE Conway Twitty Writers: Conway Twitty and Jack Nance. Producer: Jim Vinneau. **US peak: 1**.

1959

79. 23 Jan • THE DAY THE RAINS CAME Jane Morgan Writers: Gilbert Becaud; English lyrics by Carl Sigman. Producer: Vic Schoen. **US peak: 21**.

80. 30 Jan ••• ONE NIGHT / I GOT STUNG Elvis Presley Writers: Dave Bartholomew and Pearl King / Aaron Schroeder and David Hill. Producers: Steve Sholes and Chet Atkins. **US peaks: 4 / 8**

81. 20 Feb •••• AS I LOVE YOU Shirley Bassey Writers: Jay Livingston and Ray Evans. Producer: Johnny Franz.

1960: Ricky Valance had his chart-topper banned by the BBC for the record's reference to death

82. 20 Mar • SMOKE GETS IN YOUR EYES Platters Writers: Jerome Kern and Otto Harbach. Producer: Buck Ram. **US peak: 1**.

83. 27 Mar •••• SIDE SADDLE Russ Conway Writer: Trevor Stanford. Producer: Norman Newell.

84. 24 Apr ••• IT DOESN'T MATTER ANYMORE Buddy Holly Writer: Paul Anka. Producer: Dick Jacobs. **US peak: 13**.

85. 15 May ••••• A FOOL SUCH AS I / I NEED YOUR LOVE TONIGHT Elvis Presley Writers: William Trader / Sid Wayne and Bix Reichner. Producers: Steve Sholes and Chet Atkins. **US peaks: 2 / 4**

86. 19 Jun •• ROULETTE Russ Conway Writer: Trevor Stanford. Producer: Norman Newell.

87. 3 Jul •••• DREAM LOVER Bobby Darin Writer: Bobby Darin. Producer: Ahmet Ertegun. **US peak: 2**.

88. 31 Jul •••••• LIVING DOLL Cliff Richard and the Drifters Writer: Lionel Bart. Producer: Norrie Paramor. **US peak: 30**.

89. 11 Sep •••• ONLY SIXTEEN Craig Douglas Writer: Barbara Campbell (aka Lou Adler, Herb Alpert and Sam Cooke). Producer: Bunny Lewis.

90. 9 Oct • HERE COMES SUMMER Jerry Keller Writer: Jerry Keller. Producer: Richard Wolf. **US peak: 14**. ❶

91. 16 Oct •• MACK THE KNIFE Bobby Darin Writers: Bertolt Brecht and Kurt Weill; English lyrics by Marc Blitzstein. Producer: Ahmet Ertegun. **US peak: 1**.

92. 30 Oct ••••• TRAVELLIN' LIGHT Cliff Richard and the Shadows Writers: Sid Tepper and Roy C Bennett. Producer: Norrie Paramor.

93. 4 Dec ••• (one week equal) WHAT DO YOU WANT Adam Faith Writer: Les Vandyke. Producer: John Burgess; arranged by John Barry.

94. 18 Dec •••••• (one week equal) WHAT DO YOU WANT TO MAKE THOSE EYES AT ME FOR Emile Ford and the Checkmates Writers: Joseph McCarthy, Howard Johnson and Jimmy Monaco. Producer: Michael Barclay.

1960

95. 29 Jan • STARRY EYED Michael Holliday Writers: Earl Shuman and Mort Garson. Producer: Norrie Paramor.

96. 5 Feb •••• WHY Anthony Newley Writers: Bob Marcucci and Peter de Angelis. Producer: Ray Horricks.

97. 10 Mar • POOR ME Adam Faith Writer: Les Vandyke. Producer: John Burgess.

98. 17 Mar •• RUNNING BEAR Johnny Preston Writer: J P Richardson. Producer: J P Richardson. **US peak: 1**.

99. 31 Mar •••• MY OLD MAN'S A DUSTMAN Lonnie Donegan Writers: Traditional; new lyrics by Lonnie Donegan, Peter Buchanan and Beverley Thorn. Producer: Michael Barclay and Alan Freeman (recorded live at the Gaumon, Doncaster).

100. 28 Apr • DO YOU MIND Anthony Newley Writer: Lionel Bart. Producer: Ray Horricks. **US peak: 91**.

101. 5 May ••••••• CATHY'S CLOWN Everly Brothers Writers: Don and Phil Everly. Producer: Wesley Rose. **US peak: 1**.

102. 23 Jun •• THREE STEPS TO HEAVEN Eddie Cochran Writers: Eddie and Bob Cochran. Producers: Jerry Capeheart and Eddie Cochran.

103. 7 Jul ••• GOOD TIMIN' Jimmy Jones Writers: Fred Tobias and Clint Ballard Jr. Producer: Otis Blackwell. **US peak: 3**.

104. 28 Jul • 11 Aug •• PLEASE DON'T TEASE Cliff Richard and the Shadows Writers: Pete Chester and Bruce Welch. Producer: Norrie Paramor.

105. 4 Aug • SHAKIN' ALL OVER Johnny Kidd and the Pirates Writers: Frederick Heath and Gus Robinson. Producer: Walter Ridley.

106. 25 Aug ••••• APACHE Shadows Writer: Jerry Lordan. Producer: Norrie Paramor.

107. 29 Sep ••• TELL LAURA I LOVE HER Ricky Valance Writers: Jeff Barry and Ben Raleigh. Producer: Norrie Paramor. ❶

108. 20 Oct •• ONLY THE LONELY Roy Orbison Writer: Roy Orbison and Joe Melson. Producer: Fred Foster. **US peak: 2**.

109. 3 Nov •••••••• IT'S NOW OR NEVER Elvis Presley Writers: Eduardo di Capua, Aaron Shroeder and Wally Gold. Producers: Steve Sholes and Chet Atkins. **US peak: 1**. ◆

110. 29 Dec •• I LOVE YOU Cliff Richard and the Shadows Writer: Bruce Welch. Producer: Norrie Paramor.

1961

111. 12 Jan •• POETRY IN MOTION Johnny Tillotson Writers: Paul Kauffman and Mike Anthony. Producer: Archie Bleyer. **US peak: 2**.

112. 26 Jan •••• ARE YOU LONESOME TONIGHT? Elvis Presley Writers: Ray Turk and Lou Handman. Producers: Steve Sholes and Chet Atkins. **US peak: 1**.

113. 23 Feb • SAILOR Petula Clark Writers: Fini Busch and Werner Scharfenburger. Producer: Alan Freeman.

114. 2 Mar ••• WALK RIGHT BACK / EBONY EYES Everly Brothers Writers: Sonny Curtis / John D Loudermilk. Producer: Wesley Rose. **US peaks: 7 / 8**

115. 23 Mar •••••• WOODEN HEART Elvis Presley Writers: Bert Kaempfert, Kay Twomey, Fred Wise and Ben Weisman. Producer: Steve Sholes.

116. 4 May •• BLUE MOON Marcels Writers: Richard Rodgers and Lorenz Hart. Producer: Stu Phillips. **US peak: 1**.

117. 18 May • ON THE REBOUND Floyd Cramer Writer: Floyd Cramer. Producer: Chet Atkins. **US peak: 4**.

118. 25 May • YOU'RE DRIVING ME CRAZY Temperance Seven Writer: Walter Donaldson. Producer: George Martin.

119. 1 Jun •••• SURRENDER Elvis Presley Writers: Ernesto and B G De Curtis; English lyrics by Doc Pomus and Mort Shuman. Producer: Steve Sholes. **US peak: 1**.

120. 29 Jun ••• RUNAWAY Del Shannon Writers: Del Shannon and Max Crook. Producers: Harry Balk and Irving Micahnik. **US peak: 1**.

121. 20 Jul •• TEMPTATION Everly Brothers Writers: Nacio Herb Brown and Arthur Freed. Producer: Wesley Rose. **US peak: 27**.

122. 3 Aug • WELL I ASK YOU Eden Kane Writer: Les Vandyke. Producer: Bunny Lewis.

123. 10 Aug ••• YOU DON'T KNOW Helen Shapiro Writers: John Schroeder and Mike Hawker. Producer: Norrie Paramor.

124. 31 Aug ••• 28 Sep • JOHNNY REMEMBER ME John Leyton Writer: Geoff Goddard. Producer: Joe Meek.

125. 21 Sep • REACH FOR THE STARS / CLIMB EV'RY MOUNTAIN Shirley Bassey Writers: Udo Jurgens; English lyrics by David West / Richard Rodgers and Oscar Hammerstein II. Producer: Norman Newell.

126. 5 Oct • KON-TIKI Shadows Writer: Michael Carr. Producer: Norrie Paramor.

127. 12 Oct • MICHAEL Highwaymen Writer: Traditional, arranged by Dave Fisher. Producer: Dave Fisher. **US peak: 1**.

128. 19 Oct ••• WALKIN' BACK TO HAPPINESS Helen Shapiro Writers: John Schroeder and Mike Hawker. Producer: Norrie Paramor. **US peak: 100**.

129. 9 Nov •••• LITTLE SISTER / HIS LATEST FLAME Elvis Presley Writers: Doc Pomus and Mort Shuman. Producers: Steve Sholes and Chet Atkins. **US peaks: 5 / 4**.

130. 7 Dec ••• TOWER OF STRENGTH Frankie Vaughan Writers: Burt Bacharach and Bob Hilliard. Producer: Johnny Franz.

131. 28 Dec •• MOON RIVER Danny Williams Writers: Henry Mancini and Johnny Mercer. Producer: Norman Newell.

1962

132. 11 Jan •••••• THE YOUNG ONES Cliff Richard and the Shadows Writers: Sid Tepper and Roy C Bennett. Producer: Norrie Paramor. ◆

133. 22 Feb •••• ROCK-A-HULA BABY / CAN'T HELP FALLING IN LOVE Elvis Presley Writers: Fred Wise, Ben Weisman and Dolores Fuller / George David Weiss, Hugo Peretti and Luigi Creatore. Producer: Steve Sholes. **US peaks: 23 / 2**.

134. 22 Mar •••••••• WONDERFUL LAND Shadows Writer: Jerry Lordan. Producer: Norrie Paramor.

135. 17 May • NUT ROCKER B Bumble and the Stingers Writer: Pyotr Ilyich Tchaikovsky. Producer: Kim Fowley. **US peak: 23**. ❶

136. 24 May ••••• GOOD LUCK CHARM Elvis Presley Writers: Aaron Schroeder and Wally Gold. Producers: Chet Atkins and Steve Sholes. **US peak: 1**.

1961: Petula Clark, whose first No.1 followed post-war radio success in 'Meet the Huggetts'

137. 28 Jun •• COME OUTSIDE Mike Sarne with Wendy Richard Writer: Charles Blackwell. Producer: Charles Blackwell.

138. 12 Jul •• I CAN'T STOP LOVING YOU Ray Charles Writer: Don Gibson. Producer: Sid Feller. **US peak: 1**.

139. 26 Jul ••••••• I REMEMBER YOU Frank Ifield Writers: Johnny Mercer and Victor Scherzinger. Producer: Norrie Paramor. **US peak: 5**.

140. 13 Sep ••• SHE'S NOT YOU Elvis Presley Writers: Doc Pomus, Jerry Leiber and Mike Stoller. Producers: Chet Atkins and Steve Sholes. **US peak: 5**.

141. 4 Oct ••••• TELSTAR Tornados Writer: Joe Meek. Producer: Joe Meek. **US peak: 1**.

142. 8 Nov ••••• LOVESICK BLUES Frank Ifield Writers: Irving Mills and Cliff Friend. Producer: Norrie Paramor. **US peak: 44**.

143. 13 Dec ••• RETURN TO SENDER Elvis Presley Writers: Otis Blackwell and Winfield Scott. Producers: Chet Atkins and Steve Sholes. **US peak: 2**.

1963

144. 3 Jan ••• THE NEXT TIME / BACHELOR BOY Cliff Richard and the Shadows Writers: Buddy Kaye and Philip Springer / Bruce Welch and Cliff Richard. Producer: Norrie Paramor. **US peak: 0 / 99**.

145. 24 Jan • DANCE ON Shadows Writers: Valerie and Elaine Murtagh and Ray Adams. Producer: Norrie Paramor.

146. 31 Jan ••• DIAMONDS Jet Harris and Tony Meehan Writer: Jerry Lordan. Producer: Dick Rowe.

147. 21 Feb ••• THE WAYWARD WIND Frank Ifield Writers: Stan Labowsky and Herb Newman. Producer: Norrie Paramor.

148. 14 Mar •• 4 Apr • SUMMER HOLIDAY Cliff Richard and the Shadows Writers: Bruce Welch and Brian Bennett. Producer: Norrie Paramor.

149. 29 Mar • FOOT TAPPER Shadows Writers: Hank B Marvin and Bruce Welch. Producer: Norrie Paramor.

150. 11 Apr ••• HOW DO YOU DO IT? Gerry and the Pacemakers Writer: Mitch Murray. Producer: George Martin. **US peak: 9**.

151. 2 May ••••••• FROM ME TO YOU Beatles Writers: John Lennon and Paul McCartney. Producer: George Martin. **US peak: 41**.

152. 20 Jun •••• I LIKE IT Gerry and the Pacemakers Writer: Mitch Murray. Producer: George Martin. **US peak:17**.

153. 18 Jul •• CONFESSIN' (THAT I LOVE YOU) Frank Ifield Writers: Al J Neiburg, Doc Daugherty and Ellis Reynolds. Producer: Norrie Paramor. **US peak: 58**.

154. 1 Aug • (YOU'RE THE) DEVIL IN DISGUISE Elvis Presley Writers: Bill Giant, Bernie Baum and Florence Kaye. Producers: Chet Atkins and Steve Sholes. **US peak: 3**.

155. 8 Aug •• SWEETS FOR MY SWEET Searchers Writers: Doc Pomus and Mort Shuman. Producer: Tony Hatch.

156. 22 Aug ••• BAD TO ME Billy J Kramer and the Dakotas Writers: John Lennon and Paul McCartney. Producer: George Martin. **US peak: 9**.

1962: Ray Charles had one of the three transatlantic chart-toppers this year

157. 12 Sep •••• 28 Nov •• SHE LOVES YOU Beatles Writers: John Lennon and Paul McCartney. Producer: George Martin. **US peak: 1**.

158. 10 Oct ••• DO YOU LOVE ME Brian Poole and the Tremeloes Writer: Berry Gordy Jr. Producer: Mike Smith.

159. 31 Oct •••• YOU'LL NEVER WALK ALONE Gerry and the Pacemakers Writers: Richard Rodgers and Oscar Hammerstein II. Producer: George Martin. **US peak: 48**.

160. 12 Dec ••••• I WANT TO HOLD YOUR HAND Beatles Writers: John Lennon and Paul McCartney. Producer: George Martin. **US peak: 1**.

1964

161. 16 Jan •• GLAD ALL OVER Dave Clark Five Writers: Dave Clark and Mike Smith. Producer: Dave Clarke. **US peak: 6**.

162. 30 Jan ••• NEEDLES AND PINS Searchers Writers: Sonny Bono and Jack Nitzsche. Producer: Tony Hatch. **US peak: 13**.

163. 20 Feb • DIANE Bachelors Writers: Erno Rapee and Lew Pollack. Producer: Michael Barclay. **US peak: 10**.

164. 27 Feb ••• ANYONE WHO HAD A HEART Cilla Black Writers: Burt Bacharach and Hal David. Producer: George Martin.

165. 19 Mar •• LITTLE CHILDREN Billy J Kramer and the Dakotas Writers: Mort Shuman and John Leslie McFarland. Producer: George Martin. **US peak: 7**.

166. 2 Apr ••• CAN'T BUY ME LOVE Beatles Writers: John Lennon and Paul McCartney. Producer: George Martin. **US peak: 1**

167. 23 Apr •• A WORLD WITHOUT LOVE Peter and Gordon Writers: John Lennon and Paul McCartney. Producer: Norman Newell. **US peak: 1**.

168. 7 May •• DON'T THROW YOUR LOVE AWAY Searchers Writers: Jimmy Wisner and Billy Jackson. Producer: Tony Hatch. **US peak: 16**.

169. 21 May • JULIET Four Pennies Writers: Mike Wilsh, Fritz Fryer and Lionel Morton. Producer: Johnny Franz.

170. 28 May •••• YOU'RE MY WORLD Cilla Black Writers: Umberto Bindi, Gino Paoli and Carl Sigman. Producer: George Martin. **US peak: 26**.

171. 25 Jun •• IT'S OVER Roy Orbison Writers: Roy Orbison and Bill Dees. Producer: Wesley Rose. **US peak: 9**.

172. 9 Jul • THE HOUSE OF THE RISING SUN Animals Writers: Traditional, arranged by Alan Price. Producer: Mickie Most. **US peak: 1**.

173. 16 Jul • IT'S ALL OVER NOW Rolling Stones Writers: Bobby and Shirley Womack. Producer: Andrew Loog Oldham. **US peak: 26**.

174. 23 Jul ••• A HARD DAY'S NIGHT Beatles Writers: John Lennon and Paul McCartney. Producer: George Martin. **US peak: 1**.

175. 13 Aug •• DO WAH DIDDY DIDDY Manfred Mann Writers: Jeff Barry and Ellie Greenwich. Producer: John Burgess. **US peak: 1**.

176. 2 7Aug •• HAVE I THE RIGHT? Honeycombs Writers: Ken Howard and Alan Blaikley. Producer: Joe Meek. **US peak: 5**.

177. 10 Sep •• YOU REALLY GOT ME Kinks Writers: Ray Davies. Producer: Shel Talmy. **US peak: 7**.

178. 24 Sep •• I'M INTO SOMETHING GOOD Herman's Hermits Writers: Carole King and Gerry Goffin. Producer: Mickie Most. **US peak: 13**.

179. 8 Oct •• 12 Nov • OH, PRETTY WOMAN Roy Orbison Writers: Roy Orbison and Bill Dees. Producer: Wesley Rose. **US peak: 1**.

180. 22 Oct ••• (THERE'S) ALWAYS SOMETHING THERE TO REMIND ME Sandie Shaw Writers: Burt Bacharach and Hal David. Producer: Tony Hatch. **US peak: 52**.

181. 19 Nov •• BABY LOVE Supremes Writers: Brian Holland, Lamont Dozier and Eddie Holland. Producers: Brian Holland, Lamont Dozier and Eddie Holland. **US peak: 1**.

182. 3 Dec • LITTLE RED ROOSTER Rolling Stones Writer: Willie Dixon. Producer: Andrew Loog Oldham.

183. 10 Dec ••••• I FEEL FINE Beatles Writers: John Lennon and Paul McCartney. Producer: George Martin. **US peak: 1**.

1964: The Honeycombs, featuring drummer Ann Lantree who turned 21 during the group's chart-topping spell

1965

184. 14 Jan •• YEH, YEH Georgie Fame Writers: Rogers Grant, Pat Patrick and Jon Hendricks. Producer: Tony Palmer. **US peak: 21**.

185. 28 Jan • GO NOW! Moody Blues Writers: Larry Banks and Milton Bennett. Producer: Denny Cordell. **US peak: 10**.

186. 4 Feb •• YOU'VE LOST THAT LOVIN' FEELIN' Righteous Brothers Writers: Phil Spector, Barry Mann and Cynthia Weil. Producer: Phil Spector. **US peak: 1**.

187. 18 Feb • TIRED OF WAITING FOR YOU Kinks Writers: Ray Davies. Producer: Shel Talmy. **US peak: 6**.

188. 25 Feb •• I'LL NEVER FIND ANOTHER YOU Seekers Writers: Tom Springfield. Producer: Tom Springfield. **US peak: 4**.

189. 11 Mar • IT'S NOT UNUSUAL Tom Jones Writers: Les Reed and Gordon Mills. Producer: Peter Sullivan. **US peak: 10**.

190. 18 Mar ••• THE LAST TIME Rolling Stones Writers: Mick Jagger and Keith Richard. Producer: Andrew Loog Oldham. **US peak: 9**.

191. 8 Apr • CONCRETE AND CLAY Unit 4 Plus 2 Writers: Brian Parker and Tommy Moeller. Producer: John L Barker. **US peak: 28**.

192. 15 Apr • THE MINUTE YOU'RE GONE Cliff Richard Writers: Jimmy Gately. Producer: Norrie Paramor.

193. 22 Apr ••• TICKET TO RIDE Beatles Writers: John Lennon and Paul McCartney. Producer: George Martin. **US peak: 1**.

194. 13 May • KING OF THE ROAD Roger Miller Writer: Roger Miller. Producer: Jerry Kennedy. **US peak: 4**.

195. 20 May • WHERE ARE YOU NOW (MY LOVE) Jackie Trent Writers: Jackie Trent and Tony Hatch. Producer: Tony Hatch.

196. 27 May ••• LONG LIVE LOVE Sandie Shaw Writer: Chris Andrews. Producer: Chris Andrews.

197. 17 Jun • 1 Jul • CRYING IN THE CHAPEL Elvis Presley Writer: Artie Glenn. Producer: Steve Sholes. **US peak: 3**.

198. 24 Jun • 8 Jul •• I'M ALIVE Hollies Writer: Clint Ballard Jr. Producer: Ron Richards.

199. 22 Jul •• MR TAMBOURINE MAN Byrds Writer: Bob Dylan. Producer: Terry Melcher. **US peak: 1**.

200. 5 Aug ••• HELP! Beatles Writers: John Lennon and Paul McCartney. Producer: George Martin. **US peak: 1**.

201. 26 Aug •• I GOT YOU BABE Sonny and Cher Writer: Sonny Bono. Producer: Sonny Bono. **US peak: 1**.

202. 9 Sep •• (I CAN'T GET NO) SATISFACTION Rolling Stones Writers: Mick Jagger and Keith Richard. Producer: Andrew Loog Oldham. **US peak: 1**.

203. 23 Sep • MAKE IT EASY ON YOURSELF Walker Brothers Writers: Burt Bacharach and Hal David. Producer: Johnny Franz. **US peak: 16**.

204. 30 Sep ••••• TEARS Ken Dodd Writers: Billy Uhr and Frank Capano. Producer: Norman Newell.

205. 4 Nov ••• GET OFF OF MY CLOUD Rolling Stones Writers: Mick Jagger and Keith Richard. Producer: Andrew Loog Oldham. **US peak: 1**.

206. 25 Nov ••• THE CARNIVAL IS OVER Seekers Writer: Tom Springfield. Producer: Tom Springfield.

207. 16 Dec ••••• DAY TRIPPER / WE CAN WORK IT OUT Beatles Writers: John Lennon and Paul McCartney. Producer: George Martin. **US peaks: 5 / 1**.

1966

208. 20 Jan • KEEP ON RUNNIN' Spencer Davis Group Writer: Jackie Edwards. Producer: Chris Blackwell. **US peak: 76**.

209. 27 Jan ••• MICHELLE Overlanders Writers: John Lennon and Paul McCartney. Producer: Tony Hatch. ❶

210. 17 Feb •••• THESE BOOTS ARE MADE FOR WALKIN' Nancy Sinatra Writer: Lee Hazlewood. Producer: Lee Hazlewood. **US peak: 1**.

211. 17 Mar •••• THE SUN AIN'T GONNA SHINE ANYMORE Walker Brothers Writers: Bob Crewe and Bob Gaudio. Producer: Johnny Franz. **US peak: 13**.

212. 14 Apr •• SOMEBODY HELP ME Spencer Davis Group Writer: Jackie Edwards. Producer: Chris Blackwell. **US peak: 47**.

213. 28 Apr • YOU DON'T HAVE TO SAY YOU LOVE ME Dusty Springfield Writers: Pino Donaggio, Vito Pallavicini, Vicki Wickham and Simon Napier-Bell. Producer: Johnny Franz. **US peak: 4**.

214. 5 May ••• PRETTY FLAMINGO Manfred Mann Writer: Mark Barkan. Producer: John Burgess. **US peak: 29**.

215. 26 May • PAINT IT BLACK Rolling Stones Writers: Mick Jagger and Keith Richard. Producer: Andrew Loog Oldham. **US peak: 1**.

216. 2 Jun ••• STRANGERS IN THE NIGHT Frank Sinatra Writers: Bert Kaempfert, Charlie Singleton and Eddie Snyder. Producer: Jimmy Bowen. **US peak: 1**.

217. 23 Jun •• PAPERBACK WRITER Beatles Writers: John Lennon and Paul McCartney. Producer: George Martin. **US peak: 1**.

218. 7 Jul •• SUNNY AFTERNOON Kinks Writer: Ray Davies. Producer: Shel Talmy. **US peak: 14**.

219. 21 Jul • GET AWAY Georgie Fame Writer: Clive Powell. Producer: Tony Palmer. **US peak: 70**.

220. 28 Jul • OUT OF TIME Chris Farlowe and the Thunderbirds Writers: Mick Jagger and Keith Richard. Producer: Mick Jagger.

221. 4 Aug •• WITH A GIRL LIKE YOU Troggs Writer: Reg Presley. Producer: Larry Page. **US peak: 29**.

222. 18 Aug •••• YELLOW SUBMARINE / ELEANOR RIGBY Beatles Writers: John Lennon and Paul McCartney. Producer: George Martin. **US peaks: 2 / 11**.

1965: The Walker Brothers were NOT brothers and none of them was born with the name Walker

223. 15 Sep • ALL OR NOTHING Small Faces Writers: Steve Marriott and Ronnie Lane. Producers: Steve Marriott and Ronnie Lane.

224. 22 Sep ••••• DISTANT DRUMS Jim Reeves Writer: Cindy Walker. Producer: Chet Atkins. **US peak: 45**.

225. 27 Oct ••• REACH OUT I'LL BE THERE Four Tops Writers: Brian Holland, Lamont Dozier and Eddie Holland. Producers: Brian Holland and Lamont Dozier. **US peak: 1**.

226. 17 Nov •• GOOD VIBRATIONS Beach Boys Writers: Brian Wilson and Mike Love. Producer: Brian Wilson. **US peak: 1**.

227. I Dec ••••••• GREEN GREEN GRASS OF HOME Tom Jones Writer: Claude "Curly" Putnam Jr. Producer: Peter Sullivan. **US peak: 11**.

1967

228. 19 Jan •••• I'M A BELIEVER Monkees Writer: Neil Diamond. Producer: Jeff Barry. **US peak: 1**

229. 16 Feb •• THIS IS MY SONG Petula Clark Writer: Charlie Chaplin. Producer: Ernie Freeman. **US peak: 3**.

230. 2 Mar •••••• RELEASE ME (AND LET ME LOVE AGAIN) Engelbert Humperdinck Writers: Eddie Miller, Robert Yount, Dub Williams and Robert Harris. Producer: Charles Blackwell. **US peak: 4**.

231. 13 Apr •• SOMETHIN' STUPID Nancy and Frank Sinatra Writer: C Carson Parks. Producers: Jimmy Bowen and Lee Hazelwood. **US peak: 1**.

232. 27 Apr ••• PUPPET ON A STRING Sandie Shaw Writers: Bill Martin and Phil Coulter. Producer: Ken Woodman.

233. 18 May ••• SILENCE IS GOLDEN Tremeloes Writers: Bob Gaudio and Bob Crewe. Producer: Mike Smith. **US peak: 11**.

234. 8 Jun •••••• A WHITER SHADE OF PALE Procol Harum Writers: Keith Reid and Gary Brooker. Producer: Denny Cordell. **US peak: 5**.

235. 19 Jul ••• ALL YOU NEED IS LOVE Beatles Writers: John Lennon and Paul McCartney. Producer: George Martin. **US peak: 1**

236 9 Aug •••• SAN FRANCISCO (BE SURE TO WEAR SOME FLOWERS IN YOUR HAIR) Scott McKenzie Writer: John Phillips. Producers: Lou Adler and John Phillips. **US peak: 4**.

237. 6 Sep ••••• THE LAST WALTZ Engelbert Humperdinck Writers: Les Reed and Barry Mason. Producer: Peter Sullivan. **US peak: 25**.

238. 11 Oct •••• MASSACHUSETTS Bee Gees Writers: Barry, Robin and Maurice Gibb. Producers: Robert Stigwood and the Bee Gees. **US peak: 11**.

239. 8 Nov •• BABY, NOW THAT I FOUND YOU Foundations Writers: Tony Macaulay and John McLeod. Producer: Tony Macaulay. **US peak: 11**.

240. 22 Nov •• LET THE HEARTACHES BEGIN Long John Baldry Writers: Tony Macaulay and John McLeod. Producer: Tony Macaulay. **US peak: 88**.

241. 6 Dec ••••••• HELLO, GOODBYE Beatles Writers: John Lennon and Paul McCartney. Producer: George Martin. **US peak: 1**.

1968

242. 24 Jan • THE BALLAD OF BONNIE AND CLYDE Georgie Fame Writers: Mitch Murray and Peter Callender. Producer: Mike Smith. **US peak: 7**.

243. 31 Jan •• EVERLASTING LOVE Love Affair Writers: Buzz Cason and Mac Gayden. Producer: Mike Smith.

244. 14 Feb •• MIGHTY QUINN Manfred Mann Writer: Bob Dylan. Producer: Mike Hurst. **US peak: 10**.

245. 28 Feb ••• CINDERELLA ROCKAFELLA Esther and Abi Ofarim Writer: Mason Williams. Producers: Abi Ofarim and Chaim Semel. **US peak: 68**.

246. 20 Mar • THE LEGEND OF XANADU Dave Dee, Dozy, Beaky, Mick and Tich Writers: Ken Howard and Alan Blaikley. Producer: Steve Rowland.

247. 27 Mar •• LADY MADONNA Beatles Writers: John Lennon and Paul McCartney. Producer: George Martin. **US peak: 4**.

248. 10 Apr •• CONGRATULATIONS Cliff Richard Writers: Bill Martin and Phil Coulter. Producer: Norrie Paramor. **US peak: 99**.

1966: Chris Farlowe tops the chart with a song penned by Jagger and Richards

249. 24 Apr •••• WHAT A WONDERFUL WORLD / CABARET Louis Armstrong Writers: George David Weiss and George Douglas / John Kander and Fred Ebb. Producer: Bob Thiele. **US peak: 32**.

250. 22 May •••• YOUNG GIRL Gary Puckett and the Union Gap Writer: Jerry Fuller. Producer: Jerry Fuller. **US peak: 2**

251. 19 Jun •• JUMPIN' JACK FLASH Rolling Stones Writers: Mick Jagger and Keith Richards. Producer: Jimmy Miller. **US peak: 3**.

252. 3 Jul ••• BABY COME BACK Equals Writer: Eddy Grant. Producer: Ed Kassner. **US peak: 32**.

253. 24 Jul • I PRETEND Des O'Connor Writers: Les Reed and Barry Mason. Producer: Norman Newell.

254. 31 Jul •• 21 Aug • MONY MONY Tommy James and the Shondells Writers: Bobby Bloom, Richie Cordell, Bo Gentry and Tommy James. Producers: Bo Gentry and Richie Cordell. **US peak: 3**.

255. 14 Aug • FIRE Crazy World of Arthur Brown Writers: Vincent Crane, Arthur Brown, Peter Ker and Michael Finesilver. Producer: Kit Lambert. **US peak: 2.** ❶

256. 28 Aug • DO IT AGAIN Beach Boys Writers: Brian Wilson and Mike Love. Producer: Brian Wilson. **US peak: 20**.

257. 4 Sep • I'VE GOTTA GET A MESSAGE TO YOU Bee Gees Writers: Barry, Robin and Maurice Gibb. Producers: Robert Stigwood and the Bee Gees. **US peak: 8**.

258. 11 Sep •• HEY JUDE Beatles Writers: John Lennon and Paul McCartney. Producer: George Martin. **US peak: 1**.

259. 25 Sep •••••• THOSE WERE THE DAYS Mary Hopkin Writers: Gene Raskin and Alexander Vertinski. Producer: Paul McCartney. **US peak: 2**.

260. 6 Nov • WITH A LITTLE HELP FROM MY FRIENDS Joe Cocker Writers: John Lennon and Paul McCartney. Producer: Denny Cordell. **US peak: 68**.

1969: Bobbie Gentry, who droppd her real name on seeing the movie 'Ruby Gentry'

261. 13 Nov •••• THE GOOD, THE BAD AND THE UGLY Hugo Montenegro and his Orchestra Writer: Ennio Morricone. Producer: Hugo Montenegro. **US peak: 2**.

262. 11 Dec ••• 8 Jan • LILY THE PINK Scaffold Writers: John Gorman, Mike McGear and Roger McGough. Producer: Norrie Paramor.

1969

263. 1 Jan • 15 Jan •• OB-LA-DI, OB-LA-DA Marmalade Writers: John Lennon and Paul McCartney. Producer: Mike Smith.

264. 29 Jan • ALBATROSS Fleetwood Mac Writer: Peter Green. Producer: Mike Vernon.

265. 5 Feb • BLACKBERRY WAY Move Writer: Roy Wood. Producer: Jimmy Miller.

266. 12 Feb •• (IF PARADISE IS) HALF AS NICE Amen Corner Writers: Lucio Battisti and Jack Fishman. Producer: Shel Talmy.

267. 26 Feb •••• WHERE DO YOU GO TO MY LOVELY Peter Sarstedt Writer: Peter Sarstedt. Producer: Shel Talmy. **US peak: 70**.

268. 26 Mar ••• I HEARD IT THROUGH THE GRAPEVINE Marvin Gaye Writers: Norman Whitfield and Barrett Strong. Producer: Norman Whitfield. **US peak: 1**.

269.16 Apr • ISRAELITES Desmond Dekker and the Aces Writers: Desmond Dekker and Leslie Kong. Producer: Leslie Kong. **US peak: 9** .

270. 23 Apr •••••• GET BACK Beatles with Billy Preston Writers: John Lennon and Paul McCartney. Producer: George Martin. **US peak: 1.** ◆

271. 4 Jun • DIZZY Tommy Roe Writers: Tommy Roe and Freddy Weller. Producer: Steve Barri. **US peak: 1**.

272. 11 Jun ••• BALLAD OF JOHN AND YOKO Beatles Writers: John Lennon and Paul McCartney. Producers: George Martin and The Beatles. **US peak: 8**.

273. 2 Jul ••• SOMETHING IN THE AIR Thunderclap Newman Writer: Speedy Keen. Producer: Pete Townshend. **US peak: 37**.

274. 23 Jul ••••• HONKY TONK WOMEN Rolling Stones Writers: Mick Jagger and Keith Richard. Producer: Jimmy Miller. **US peak: 1**.

275. 30 Aug ••• IN THE YEAR 2525 (EXORDIUM & TERMINUS) Zager and Evans Writer: Rick Evans. Producers: Denny Zager and Rick Evans. **US peak: 1.** ❶

276. 20 Sep ••• BAD MOON RISING Creedence Clearwater Revival Writer: John Fogerty. Producer: John Fogerty. **US peak: 2**

277. 11 Oct • JE T'AIME ... MOI NON PLUS Jane Birkin and Serge Gainsbourg Writer: Serge Gainsbourg. Producer: Jack Baverstock. **US peak: 58.** ❶

278 . 18 Oct • I'LL NEVER FALL IN LOVE AGAIN Bobbie Gentry Writers: Burt Bacharach and Hal David. Producer: Kelso Herston.

279. 25 Oct •••••••• SUGAR SUGAR Archies Writers: Jeff Barry and Andy Kim. Producer: Jeff Barry. **US peak: 1.** ❶

280. 20 Dec •••••• TWO LITTLE BOYS Rolf Harris Writers: Theodore Morse and Edward Madden. Producer: Martin Clarke.

1970

281. 31 Jan ••••• LOVE GROWS (WHERE MY ROSEMARY GOES) Edison Lighthouse Writers: Barry Mason and Tony Macaulay. Producer: Tony Macaulay. **US peak: 5**.

282. 7 Mar ••• WAND'RIN' STAR Lee Marvin Writers: Alan Jay Lerner and Frederick Loewe. Producer: Tom Mack. ❶

283. 28 Mar ••• BRIDGE OVER TROUBLED WATER Simon and Garfunkel Writer: Paul Simon. Producers: Paul Simon, Art Garfunkel and Roy Halee. **US peak: 1**

284. 18 Apr •• ALL KINDS OF EVERYTHING Dana Writers: Denny Lindsay and Jackie Smith. Producer: Ray Horricks.

285. 2 May •• SPIRIT IN THE SKY Norman Greenbaum Writer: Norman Greenbaum. Producer: Eric Jacobson. **US peak: 3.** ❶

286. 16 May ••• BACK HOME England World Cup Squad Writers: Bill Martin and Phil Coulter. Producers: Bill Martin and Phil Coutler.

287. 6 Jun • YELLOW RIVER Christie Writer: Jeff Christie. Producer: Mike Smith. **US peak: 23**.

288. 13 Jun ••••••• IN THE SUMMERTIME Mungo Jerry Writer: Ray Dorset. Producer: Barry Murray. **US peak: 3**.

289. 1 Aug •••••• THE WONDER OF YOU Elvis Presley Writer: Baker Knight. Producers: Elvis Presley and Felton Jarvis. **US peak: 9**.

290. 12 Sep • THE TEARS OF A CLOWN Smokey Robinson and the Miracles Writer: Henry Cosby, William Robinson and Stevie Wonder. Producers: Henry Cosby and William Robinson. **US peak: 1**.

291. 19 Sep •••••• BAND OF GOLD Freda Payne Writers: Ron Dunbar and Edith Wayne. Producers: Brian Holland, Lamont Dozier and Eddie Holland. **US peak: 3**.

292. 31 Oct ••• WOODSTOCK Matthews Southern Comfort Writer: Joni Mitchell. Producer: Ian Matthews. **US peak: 23**. ❶

293. 21 Nov • VOODOO CHILE Jimi Hendrix Experience Writer: Jimi Hendrix. Producer: Jimi Hendrix.

294. 28 Nov •••••• I HEAR YOU KNOCKING Dave Edmunds Writers: Dave Bartholomew and Pearl King. Producer: Dave Edmunds. **US peak: 4**.

1971

295. 9 Jan ••• GRANDAD Clive Dunn Writers: Herbie Flowers and Kenny Pickett. Producer: John Cameron and Clive Dunn. ❶

296. 30 Jan ••••• MY SWEET LORD George Harrison Writer: George Harrison. Producers: Phil Spector and George Harrison. **US peak: 1**.

297. 6 Mar •• BABY JUMP Mungo Jerry Writer: Ray Dorset. Producer: Barry Murray.

298. 20 Mar •••••• HOT LOVE T. Rex Writer: Marc Bolan. Producer: Tony Visconti. **US peak: 72**.

299. 1 May •• DOUBLE BARREL Dave and Ansil Collins Writer: Winston Riley. Producer: Winston Riley. **US peak: 22**.

300. 15 May ••••• KNOCK THREE TIMES Dawn Writers: Irwin Levine and L Russell Brown. Producers: Dave Appell and The Tokens. **US peak: 1**.

301. 19 Jun ••••• CHIRPY CHIRPY CHEEP CHEEP Middle of the Road Writer: Lally Scott. Producers: Giacomo Tosti and Ignacio Greco.

302. 24 Jul •••• GET IT ON T. Rex Writer: Marc Bolan. Producer: Tony Visconti. **US peak: 10**.

303. 21 Aug •••• I'M STILL WAITING Diana Ross Writer: Deke Richards. Producers: Deke Richards and Hal Davis. **US peak: 63**.

304. 18 Sep ••• HEY GIRL DON'T BOTHER ME Tams Writer: Ray Whitley. Producer: Rick Hall. **US peak: 41**.

305. 9 Oct ••••• MAGGIE MAY Rod Stewart Writers: Rod Stewart and Martin Quittenton. Producer: Rod Stewart. **US peak: 1**.

306. 13 Nov •••• COZ I LUV YOU Slade Writers: Noddy Holder and Jim Lea. Producer: Chas Chandler.

307. 11 Dec •••• ERNIE (THE FASTEST MILK MAN IN THE WEST) Benny Hill Writer: Benny Hill. Producer: Walter Ridley.

1972

308. 8 Jan •••• I'D LIKE TO TEACH THE WORLD TO SING New Seekers Writers: Roger Cook, Roger Greenaway, William Backer and Billy Davis. Producer: David Mackay. **US peak: 7**.

309. 5 Feb •• TELEGRAM SAM T. Rex Writer: Marc Bolan. Producer: Tony Visconti. **US peak: 67**.

310. 19 Feb ••• SON OF MY FATHER Chicory Tip Writers: Giorgio Moroder, Peter Belotte and Michael Holm. Producer: Roger Easterby and Des Champ. **US peak: 91**.

311. 11 Mar ••••• WITHOUT YOU Nilsson Writers: Peter Ham and Tom Evans. Producer: Richard Perry. **US peak: 1**.

312. 15 Apr ••••• AMAZING GRACE Pipes and Drums and Military Band of the Royal Scots Dragoon Guards Writers: Traditional. Producer: Peter Kerr. **US peak: 11**.

313. 20 May •••• METAL GURU T. Rex Writer: Marc Bolan. Producer: Tony Visconti.

314. 17 Jun •• VINCENT Don McLean Writer: Don McLean. Producer: Ed Freeman. **US peak: 12**.

315. 1 Jul • TAKE ME BAK 'OME Slade Writers: Noddy Holder and Jim Lea. Producer: Chas Chandler. **US peak: 97**.

316. 8 Jul ••••• PUPPY LOVE Donny Osmond Writer: Paul Anka. Producers: Mike Curb and Ray Ruff. **US peak: 3**.

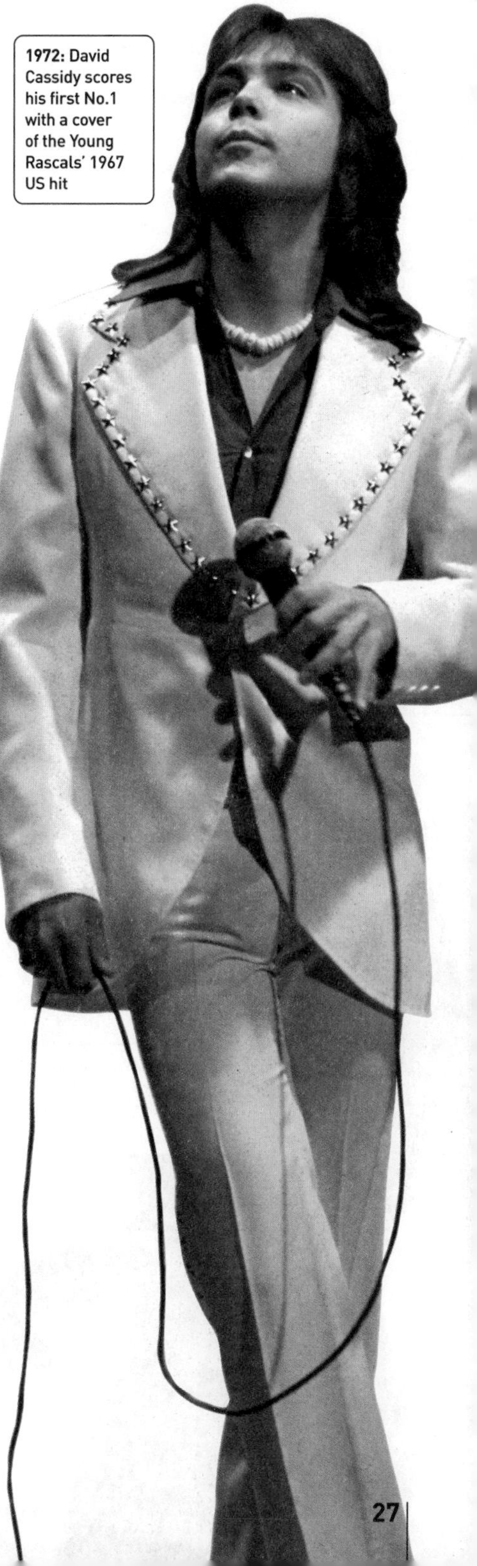

1972: David Cassidy scores his first No.1 with a cover of the Young Rascals' 1967 US hit

317. 12 Aug ••• SCHOOL'S OUT Alice Cooper Writers: Alice Cooper and Michael Bruce. Producer: Bob Ezrin. **US peak: 7**.

318. 2 Sep • YOU WEAR IT WELL Rod Stewart Writers: Rod Stewart and Martin Quittenton. Producer: Rod Stewart. **US peak: 13**.

319. 9 Sep ••• MAMA WEER ALL CRAZEE NOW Slade Writers: Noddy Holder, Jim Lea. Producer: Chas Chandler. **US peak: 76**.

320. 30 Sep •• HOW CAN I BE SURE David Cassidy Writers: Felix Cavaliere and Eddie Brigati. Producer: Wes Farrow. **US peak: 25**.

321. 14 Oct •••• MOULDY OLD DOUGH Lieutenant Pigeon Writers: Nigel Fletcher and Robert Woodward. Producer: Stavely Makepiece.

1974: Alvin Stardust (born Bernard Jewry) spent seven days at the top

322. 11 Nov •• CLAIR Gilbert O'Sullivan Writer: Gilbert O'Sullivan. Producer: Gordon Mills. **US peak: 2**.

323. 25 Nov •••• MY DING-A-LING Chuck Berry Writer: Chuck Berry. Producer: Esmond Edwards. **US peak: 1**.

324. 23 Dec ••••• LONG HAIRED LOVER FROM LIVERPOOL Little Jimmy Osmond Writer: Christopher Kingsley. Producers: Mike Curb and Perry Botkin Jr. **US peak: 38**.

1973

325. 27 Jan ••••• BLOCKBUSTER Sweet Writers: Nicky Chinn and Mike Chapman. Producer: Phil Wainman. **US peak: 73**.

326. 3 Mar •••• CUM ON FEEL THE NOIZE Slade Writers: Noddy Holder and Jim Lea. Producer: Chas Chandler. **US peak: 98**. ◆

327. 31 Mar • THE TWELFTH OF NEVER Donny Osmond Writers: Jay Livingston and Paul Francis Webster. Producers: Mike Curb and Don Costa. **US peak: 8**.

328. 7 Apr •• GET DOWN Gilbert O'Sullivan Writer: Gilbert O'Sullivan. Producer: Gordon Mills. **US peak: 7**.

329. 21 Apr •••• TIE A YELLOW RIBBON ROUND THE OLD OAK TREE Dawn Writers: Irwin Levine and L Russell Brown. Producers: Hank Medress and David Appell. **US peak: 1**.

330. 19 May •••• SEE MY BABY JIVE Wizzard Writer: Roy Wood. Producer: Roy Wood. ●

331. 16 Jun • CAN THE CAN Suzi Quatro Writers: Nicky Chinn and Mike Chapman. Producers: Nicky Chinn and Mike Chapman. **US peak: 56**. ⊙

332. 23 Jun • RUBBER BULLETS 10cc Writers: Kevin Godley, Lol Creme and Graham Gouldman. Producers: 10cc. **US peak: 73**.

333. 30 Jun ••• SKWEEZE ME PLEEZE ME Slade Writers: Noddy Holder and Jim Lea. Producer: Chas Chandler. ◆⊙

334. 21 Jul • WELCOME HOME Peters and Lee Writers: Jean-Alphonse Dupré, Stanislas Beldone; English lyrics by Bryan Blackburn. Producer: Johnny Franz.

335. 28 Jul •••• I'M THE LEADER OF THE GANG (I AM) Gary Glitter Writers: Gary Glitter and Mike Leander. Producer: Mike Leander. ●

336. 25 Aug •••• YOUNG LOVE Donny Osmond Writers: Carole Joyner and Ric Cartey. Producer: Mike Curb and Don Costa. **US peak: 25**. ⊙

337. 22 Sep • ANGEL FINGERS Wizzard Writer: Roy Wood. Producer: Roy Wood. ⊙

338. 29 Sep •••• EYE LEVEL Simon Park Orchestra Writers: Simon Park and Jack Trombey. Producer: Simon Park. ❶✪

339. 27 Oct ••• DAYDREAMER / THE PUPPY SONG David Cassidy Writers: Terry Dempsey / Harry Nilsson. Producer: Rick Jarrard.

340. 17 Nov •••• I LOVE YOU LOVE ME LOVE Gary Glitter Writers: Gary Glitter and Mike Leander. Producer: Mike Leander. ✪

341. 15 Dec ••••• MERRY XMAS EVERYBODY Slade Writers: Noddy Holder and Jim Lea. Producer: Chas Chandler. ◆✪

1974

342. 19 Jan • YOU WON'T FIND ANOTHER FOOL LIKE ME New Seekers Writers: Tony Macaulay and Geoff Stephens. Producer: Tommy Oliver. ●

343. 26 Jan •••• TIGER FEET Mud Writers: Nicky Chinn and Mike Chapman. Producers: Nicky Chinn and Mike Chapman. ●

344. 23 Feb •• DEVIL GATE DRIVE Suzi Quatro Writers: Nicky Chinn and Mike Chapman. Producers: Nicky Chinn and Mike Chapman. ●

345. 9 Mar • JEALOUS MIND Alvin Stardust Writer: Peter Shelley. Producer: Peter Shelley.

346. 16 Mar ••• BILLY, DON'T BE A HERO Paper Lace Writers: Mitch Murray and Peter Callander. Producers: Mitch Murray and Peter Callander. **US peak: 96**. ●

347. 6 Apr •••• SEASONS IN THE SUN Terry Jacks Writers: Jacques Brel; English lyrics by Rod McKuen. Producer: Terry Jacks. **US peak: 1**. ⊙

348. 4 May •• WATERLOO Abba Writers: Björn Ulvaeus, Benny Andersson and Stig Anderson. Producers: Björn Ulvaeus and Benny Andersson. **US peak: 6**. ⊙

1975: Texan Johnny Nash, whose reggae-flavoured chart-topper was one of 11 UK hits

349. 18 May •••• SUGAR BABY LOVE Rubettes Writers: Wayne Bickerton and Tony Waddington. Producer: Wayne Bickerton. **US peak: 37.** ●

350. 15 Jun • THE STREAK Ray Stevens Writer: Ray Stevens. Producer: Ray Stevens. **US peak:1.** ⊙

351. 22 Jun • ALWAYS YOURS Gary Glitter Writers: Mike Leander and Gary Glitter. Producer: Mike Leander. ⊙

352. 29 Jun •••• SHE Charles Aznavour Writers: Charles Aznavour and Herbert Kretzmer. Producer: Eddie Barclay. ⊙

353. 27 Jul ••• ROCK YOUR BABY George McCrae Writers: Harry W Casey and Richard Finch. Producers: Harry W Casey and Richard Finch. **US peak: 1.** ●

354. 17 Aug •• WHEN WILL I SEE YOU AGAIN Three Degrees Writers: Kenny Gamble and Leon Huff. Producers: Kenny Gamble and Leon Huff. **US peak: 2.** ●

355. 31 Aug ••• LOVE ME FOR A REASON Osmonds Writer: Johnny Bristol. Producer: Mike Curb. **US peak: 10.** ●

356. 21 Sep ••• KUNG FU FIGHTING Carl Douglas Writer: Karl Douglas. Producer: Biddu. **US peak: 1.** ●

357. 12 Oct • ANNIE'S SONG John Denver Writer: John Denver. Producer: Milt Okun. **US peak: 1.** ⊙

358. 19 Oct • SAD SWEET DREAMER Sweet Sensation Writer: D E S Parton. Producer: D E S Parton and Tony Hatch. **US peak: 14.** ⊙

359. 26 Oct ••• EVERYTHING I OWN Ken Boothe Writer: David Gates. Producer: Lloyd Chalmers. ⊙

360. 16 Nov ••• GONNA MAKE YOU A STAR David Essex Writer: David Essex. Producer: Jeff Wayne. ●

361. 7 Dec •• YOU'RE THE FIRST, THE LAST, MY EVERYTHING Barry White Writers: Barry White, Tony Sepe and Peter Radcliffe. Producer: Barry White. **US peak: 2.**

362. 21 Dec •••• LONELY THIS CHRISTMAS Mud Writers: Nicky Chinn and Mike Chapman. Producer: Nicky Chinn and Mike Chapman. ●

1975

363. 18 Jan • DOWN DOWN Status Quo Writers: Francis Rossi and Robert Young. Producers: Status Quo.

364. 25 Jan • MS GRACE Tymes Writers: John Hall and Johanna Hall. Producer: Billy Jackson. **US peak: 91.** ⊙

365. 1 Feb ••• JANUARY Pilot Writer: David Paton. Producer: Alan Parsons. **US peak: 87.** ⊙

366. 22 Feb •• MAKE ME SMILE (COME UP AND SEE ME) Steve Harley and Cockney Rebel Writer: Steve Harley. Producer: Steve Harley and Alan Parsons. **US peak: 96.** ⊙

367. 8 Mar •• IF Telly Savalas Writer: David Gates. Producer: Snuff Garrett. ⊙

368. 22 Mar •••••• BYE BYE BABY Bay City Rollers Writers: Bob Gaudio and Bob Crewe. Producer: Phil Wainman.

369. 3 May •• OH BOY Mud Writers: Sonny West, Norman Petty and Bill Tilghman. Producers: Nicky Chinn and Mike Chapman. ⊙

370. 17 May ••• STAND BY YOUR MAN Tammy Wynette Writers: Billy Sherrill and Tammy Wynette. Producer: Billy Sherrill. **US peak: 19.** ●

371. 7 Jun ••• WHISPERING GRASS Windsor Davies and Don Estelle Writers: Fred and Doris Fisher. Producer: Walter Ridley. ●

372. 28 Jun •• I'M NOT IN LOVE 10cc Writers: Graham Gouldman and Eric Stewart. Producer: 10cc. **US peak: 2.**

373. 12 Jul • TEARS ON MY PILLOW Johnny Nash Writer: Ernie Smith. Producer: Johnny Nash. ⊙

374. 19 Jul ••• GIVE A LITTLE LOVE Bay City Rollers Writers: Johnny Goodison and Phil Wainman. Producer: Phil Wainman.

375. 09 Aug • BARBADOS Typically Tropical Writers: Jeffrey Calvert and Max West. Producers: Jeffrey Calvert and Max West. ➊⊙

376. 16 Aug ••• CAN'T GIVE YOU ANYTHING (BUT MY LOVE) Stylistics Writers: Hugo Peretti, Luigi Creatore and George David Weiss. Producers: Hugo Peretti and Luigi Creatore. **US peak: 51.** ●

377. 6 Sep •••• SAILING Rod Stewart Writer: Gavin Sutherland. Producer: Tom Dowd. **US peak: 58.** ⊙

378. 4 Oct ••• HOLD ME CLOSE David Essex Writer: David Essex. Producer: Jeff Wayne. ●

379. 25 Oct •• I ONLY HAVE EYES FOR YOU Art Garfunkel Writers: Harry Warren and Al Dubin. Producer: Richard Perry. **US peak: 18.** ✪

380. 8 Nov •• SPACE ODDITY David Bowie Writer: David Bowie. Producer: Gus Dudgeon. **US peak: 15.**

381. 22 Nov • D.I.V.O.R.C.E. Billy Connolly Writers: Billy Connolly, Claude Putnam Jr and Bobby Braddock. Producer: Phil Coulter. ⊙

382. 29 Nov ••••••••• BOHEMIAN RHAPSODY Queen Writer: Freddie Mercury. Producers: Roy Thomas Baker and Queen. **US peak: 9.** ✪✪

1976

383. 31 Jan •• MAMMA MIA Abba Writers: Stig Anderson, Björn Ulvaeus and Benny Andersson. Producers: Björn Ulvaeus and Benny Andersson. **US peak: 32.** ⊙

384. 14 Feb • FOREVER AND EVER Slik Writers: Bill Martin and Phil Coulter. Producers: Bill Martin and Phil Coulter. ●

385. 21 Feb •• DECEMBER '63 (OH WHAT A NIGHT) Four Seasons Writers: Bob Gaudio and Judy Parker. Producer: Bob Gaudio. **US peak: 1.** ●

386. 6 Mar ••• I LOVE TO LOVE (BUT MY BABY LOVES TO DANCE) Tina Charles Writers: Jack Robinson and James Bolden. Producer: Biddu. ●

387. 27 Mar •••••• SAVE YOUR KISSES FOR ME Brotherhood of Man Writers: Tony Hiller, Martin Lee and Lee Sheridan. Producer: Tony Hiller. **US peak: 27.** ●

388. 8 May •••• FERNANDO Abba Writers: Stig Anderson, Björn Ulvaeus and Benny Andersson. Producers: Björn Ulvaeus and Benny Andersson. **US peak: 13.** ●

389. 5 Jun • NO CHARGE J J Barrie Writer: Harlan Howard. Producer: Bill Amesbury. ➊⊙

390. 12 Jun •• COMBINE HARVESTER (BRAND NEW KEY) Wurzels Writer: Melanie Safka. Producer: Bob Barrett. ⊙

391. 26 Jun ••• YOU TO ME ARE EVERYTHING Real Thing Writers: Ken Gold and Micky Denne. Producer: Ken Gold. **US peak: 64.** ⊙

392. 17 Jul • THE ROUSSOS PHENOMENON EP Demis Roussos Writers: 'Forever and Ever', 'So Dreamy', 'My Friend the Wind' Stylianos Vlaviano and Robert Costandinos; 'Sing an Ode to Love' Stylianos Vlaviano, Charalampe Chalkitis and Robert Costandinos. Producer: Demis Roussos. ⊙

393. 24 Jul •••••• DON'T GO BREAKING MY HEART Elton John and Kiki Dee Writers: Ann Orson and Carte Blanche (aka Elton John and Bernie Taupin). Producer: Gus Dudgeon. **US peak: 1.**

394. 4 Sep •••••• DANCING QUEEN Abba Writers: Stig Anderson, Benny Andersson and Björn Ulvaeus. Producers: Benny Andersson and Björn Ulvaeus. **US peak: 1.** ⊙

395. 16 Oct •••• MISSISSIPPI Pussycat Writer: Werner Theunissen. Producer: Eddy Hilberts. ●

396. 13 Nov ••• IF YOU LEAVE ME NOW Chicago Writer: Peter Cetera. Producer: James Guerico. **US peak: 1.** ●

397. 4 Dec ••• UNDER THE MOON OF LOVE Showaddywaddy Writers: Tommy Boyce and Curtis Lee. Producer: Mike Hurst. ●

398. 25 Dec ••• WHEN A CHILD IS BORN (SOLEADO) Johnny Mathis Writers: Fred Jay and Di Damicco Ciro. Producer: Jack Gold. ●

1977

399. 15 Jan •••• DON'T GIVE UP ON US David Soul Writer: Tony Macaulay. Producer: Tony Macaulay. **US peak: 1.** ✪

1977: Baccara, the first female duo to hit the top spot

400. 12 Feb • DON'T CRY FOR ME ARGENTINA Julie Covington Writers: Tim Rice and Andrew Lloyd Webber. Producer: Tim Rice and Andrew Lloyd Webber. ●

401. 19 Feb ••• WHEN I NEED YOU Leo Sayer Writers: Albert Hammond and Carole Bayer Sager. Producer: Richard Perry. **US peak: 1.** ●

402. 12 Mar ••• CHANSON D'AMOUR Manhattan Transfer Writer: Wayne Shanklin. Producer: Richard Perry. ●

403. 2 Apr ••••• KNOWING ME KNOWING YOU Abba Writers: Stig Anderson, Benny Andersson and Björn Ulvaeus. Producers: Benny Andersson and Björn Ulvaeus. **US peak: 14.**

404. 7 May •• FREE Deniece Williams Writers: Deniece Williams, Hank Redd, Nathan Watts and Susaye Green. Producers: Maurice White and Charles Stepney. **US peak: 25.** ⊙

405. 21 May •••• I DON'T WANT TO TALK ABOUT IT / FIRST CUT IS THE DEEPEST Rod Stewart Writers: Danny Whitten / Cat Stevens. Producer: Tom Dowd. **US peaks: 46 / 21.** ⊙

406. 18 Jun • LUCILLE Kenny Rogers Writers: Roger Bowling and Hal Bynum. Producer: Larry Butler. **US peak: 5.** ⊙

407. 25 Jun • SHOW YOU THE WAY TO GO Jacksons Writers: Kenny Gamble and Leon Huff. Producers: Kenny Gamble and Leon Huff. **US peak: 28.** ⊙

408. 2 Jul ••• SO YOU WIN AGAIN Hot Chocolate Writer: Russ Ballard. Producer: Mickie Most. **US peak: 31.** ⊙

409. 23 Jul •••• I FEEL LOVE Donna Summer Writers: Giorgio Moroder, Pete Bellotte and Donna Summer. Producer: Giorgio Moroder and Pete Bellotte. **US peak: 6.** ●

410. 20 Aug • ANGELO Brotherhood of Man Writers: Tony Hiller, Martin Lee and Lee Sheridan. Producer: Tony Hiller. ✪

411. 27 Aug • FLOAT ON Floaters Writers: Arnold Ingram, James Mitchell Jr and Marvin Willis. Producer: Woody Wilson. **US peak: 2.** ➊⊙

412. 3 Sep ••••• WAY DOWN Elvis Presley Writer: Layng Martine Jr. Producer: Elvis Presley and Felton Jarvis. **US peak: 18.** ●

413. 8 Oct ••• SILVER LADY David Soul Writers: Tony Macaulay and Geoff Stephens. Producer: Tony Macaulay. **US peak: 52**. ●

414. 29 Oct • YES SIR I CAN BOOGIE Baccara Writers: Frank Dostal and Rolf Soja. Producer: Rolf Soja. ⊙

415. 5 Nov •••• THE NAME OF THE GAME Abba Writers: Stig Anderson, Benny Andersson and Björn Ulvaeus. Producers: Benny Andersson and Björn Ulvaeus. **US peak: 12**. ●

416. 3 Dec ••••••••• MULL OF KINTYRE / GIRLS' SCHOOL Wings Writers: Paul McCartney and Denny Laine. Producer: Paul McCartney. **US peak: 0 / 32**. ✪✪

1978

417. 4 Feb • UPTOWN TOP RANKING Althia and Donna Writers: Althia Forest, Donna Reid and Errol Thompson. Producer: Joe Gibson. ❶⊙

418. 11 Feb • FIGARO Brotherhood of Man Writers: Tony Hiller, Martin Lee and Lee Sheridan. Producer: Tony Hiller.

419. 18 Feb ••• TAKE A CHANCE ON ME Abba Writers: Benny Andersson and Björn Ulvaeus. Producers: Benny Andersson and Björn Ulvaeus. **US peak: 3**. ●

420. 11 Mar •••• WUTHERING HEIGHTS Kate Bush Writer: Kate Bush. Producer: Andrew Powell. ●

421. 8 Apr ••• MATCHSTALK MEN AND MATCHSTALK CATS AND DOGS Brian and Michael Writer: Michael Coleman. Producer: Kevin Parrott. ❶●

422. 29 Apr •• NIGHT FEVER Bee Gees Writers: Barry, Robin and Maurice Gibb. Producers: Barry, Robin and Maurice Gibb, Karl Richardson and Albhy Galuten. **US peak: 1**.

423. 13 May ••••• RIVERS OF BABYLON / BROWN GIRL IN THE RING Boney M Writers: Traditional, arranged by Frank Farian and Hans-Georg Mayer. Producer: Frank Farian. **US peak: 30**. ⊙

424. 17 Jun ••••••••• YOU'RE THE ONE THAT I WANT John Travolta and Olivia Newton-John Writer: John Farrar. Producer: John Farrar. **US peak: 1**.

1979: Gloria Gaynor's No.1 was a disco favourite and is now perhaps the most popular karaoke choice of all time

425. 19 Aug ••••• THREE TIMES A LADY Commodores Writer: Lionel Richie Jr. Producer: James Carmichael and the Commodores. **US peak: 1**. ●

426. 23 Sep • DREADLOCK HOLIDAY 10cc Writers: Eric Stewart and Graham Gouldman. Producers: Eric Stewart and Graham Gouldman. **US peak: 44**. ●

427. 30 Sep ••••••• SUMMER NIGHTS John Travolta and Olivia Newton-John Writers: Warren Casey and Jim Jacobs. Producer: Louis St Louis. **US peak: 5**. ✪

428. 18 Nov •• RAT TRAP Boomtown Rats Writer: Bob Geldof. Producer: Mutt Lange.

429. 2 Dec • DA YA THINK I'M SEXY Rod Stewart Writers: Rod Stewart and Carmen Appice. Producer: Tom Dowd. **US peak: 1**. ●

430. 9 Dec •••• MARY'S BOY CHILD – OH MY LORD Boney M Writers: Jester Harrison, Frank Farian and Fred Jay. Producer: Frank Farian. **US peak: 85**. ⊙

1979

431. 6 Jan ••• YMCA Village People Writers: Jacques Morali, Henri Belolo and Victor Willis. Producer:Jacques Morali. **US peak: 2**. ✪

432. 27 Jan • HIT ME WITH YOUR RHYTHM STICK Ian Dury and the Blockheads Writers: Ian Dury and Chas Jankel. Producer: Chas Jankel. ●

433. 3 Feb •••• HEART OF GLASS Blondie Writers: Chris Stein and Deborah Harry. Producer: Mike Chapman. **US peak: 1**. ●

434. 3 Mar •• TRAGEDY Bee Gees Writers: Barry, Maurice and Robin Gibb. Producer: Bee Gees, Karl Richardson and Albhy Galuten. **US peak: 1**.

435. 17 Mar •••• I WILL SURVIVE Gloria Gaynor Writers: Dino Fekaris and Freddie Perren. Producers: Dino Fekaris and Freddie Perren. **US peak: 1**.

436. 14 Apr •••••• BRIGHT EYES Art Garfunkel Writer: Mike Batt. Producer: Mike Batt. ⊙

437. 26 May ••• SUNDAY GIRL Blondie Writer: Chris Stein. Producer: Mike Chapman. ⊙

438. 16 Jun •• RING MY BELL Anita Ward Writer: Frederick Knight. Producer: Frederick Knight. **US peak: 1**. ❶●

439. 30 Jun •••• ARE 'FRIENDS' ELECTRIC? Tubeway Army Writer: Gary Numan. Producer: Gary Numan. ●

440. 28 Jul •••• I DON'T LIKE MONDAYS Boomtown Rats Writer: Bob Geldof. Producer: Phil Wainman. **US peak: 73**. ⊙

441. 25 Aug •••• WE DON'T TALK ANYMORE Cliff Richard Writer: Alan Tarney. Producer: Bruce Welch. **US peak: 7**. ●

442. 22 Sep • CARS Gary Numan Writer: Gary Numan. Producer: Gary Numan. **US peak: 9**. ●

443. 29 Sep ••• MESSAGE IN A BOTTLE Police Writer: Sting. Producer: The Police and Nigel Gray. **US peak: 74**. ●

444. 20 Oct • VIDEO KILLED THE RADIO STAR Buggles Writers: Bruce Woolley, Trevor Horn and Geoff Downes. Producers: Trevor Horn and Geoff Downes. **US peak: 40**.

445. 27 Oct ••• ONE DAY AT A TIME Lena Martell Writer: Kris Kristofferson. Producer: George Elrick. ❶ ●

446. 17 Nov ••• WHEN YOU'RE IN LOVE WITH A BEAUTIFUL WOMAN Dr Hook Writer: Even Stevens. Producer: Ron Haffkine. **US peak: 6**. ●

447. 8 Dec • WALKING ON THE MOON Police Writer: Sting. Producer: The Police and Nigel Gray. ●

1979: Dr Hook were the subject of premature excitement on 10 Nov when Radio 1 DJ Paul Burnett announced that the band were No.1. A computer error had given him the wrong information and Dr Hook had to wait a further week before toppling Lena Martell

448. 15 Dec ••••• ANOTHER BRICK IN THE WALL (PT.2) Pink Floyd Writer: Roger Waters. Producers: Roger Waters, Bob Ezrin and Dave Gilmour. **US peak: 1.** ✪

1980

449. 19 Jan •• BRASS IN POCKET Pretenders Writers: Chrissie Hynde and James Honeyman-Scott. Producer: Chris Thomas. **US peak: 14.** ●

450. 2 Feb •• THE SPECIAL AKA LIVE EP Writers: Jerry Dammers, Lloyd Chalmers, Dimitri Tiomkin, Paul Francis Webster; Sydney Roy Crooks, Jackie Robinson, George Agard; Harry Johnson; Morty Naismith and Roy Ellis. Producers: Jerry Dammers and Dave Jordan. ⊙

451. 16 Feb •• COWARD OF THE COUNTY Kenny Rogers Writers: Roger Bowling and B E Wheeler. Producer: Larry Butler. **US peak: 3.**●

452. 1 Mar •• ATOMIC Blondie Writers: Chris Stein and Debbie Harry. Producer: Mike Chapman. **US peak: 39**.

453. 15 Mar • TOGETHER WE ARE BEAUTIFUL Fern Kinney Writer: Ken Leray. Producers: Caron Whitsett, Wolf Stephenson and Tommy Couch. ●

454. 22 Mar ••• GOING UNDERGROUND / DREAMS OF CHILDREN Jam Writer: Paul Weller. Producer: Vic Coppersmith-Heaven. ◆●

455. 12 Apr •• WORKING MY WAY BACK TO YOU – FORGIVE ME GIRL Detroit Spinners Writers: Sandy Linzer, Denny Randell and Michael Zager. Producer: Michael Zager. **US peak: 2.** ⊙

456. 26 Apr • CALL ME Blondie Writers: Giorgio Moroder and Debbie Harry. Producer: Giorgio Moroder. **US peak: 1**.

457. 3 May •• GENO Dexy's Midnight Runners Writers: Kevin Rowland and Al Archer. Producer: Pete Wingfield.

458. 17 May •• WHAT'S ANOTHER YEAR Johnny Logan Writer: Shay Healy. Producers: Bill Whelan and Dave Pennefather. ⊙

459. 31 May ••• THEME FROM M*A*S*H (SUICIDE IS PAINLESS) Mash Writers: Mike Altman and Johnny Mandel. Producer: Thomas Z Shephard. ❶⊙

460. 21 Jun ••• CRYING Don McLean Writers: Roy Orbison and Joe Melson. Producer: Larry Butler. **US peak: 5.** ⊙

461. 12 Jul •• XANADU Olivia Newton-John and Electric Light Orchestra Writer: Jeff Lynne. Producer: Jeff Lynne. **US peak: 8.** ⊙

462. 26 Jul •• USE IT UP AND WEAR IT OUT Odyssey Writers: Sandy Linzer and L Russell Brown. Producer: Sandy Linzer. ⊙

463. 9 Aug •• THE WINNER TAKES IT ALL Abba Writers: Benny Andersson and Björn Ulvaeus. Producers: Benny Andersson and Björn Ulvaeus. **US peak: 8.** ●

464. 23 Aug •• ASHES TO ASHES David Bowie Writer: David Bowie. Producers: David Bowie and Tony Visconti.

465. 6 Sep • START Jam Writer: Paul Weller. Producer: Vic Coppersmith-Heaven. ⊙

466. 13 Sep •• FEELS LIKE I'M IN LOVE Kelly Marie Writer: Ray Dorset. Producer: Pete Yellowstone. ●

467. 27 Sep •••• DON'T STAND SO CLOSE TO ME Police Writer: Sting. Producers: The Police and Nigel Gray. **US peak: 10.** ◆●

468. 25 Oct ••• WOMAN IN LOVE Barbra Streisand Writers: Barry and Robin Gibb. Producer: Barry Gibb, Karl Richardson and Albhy Galuten. **US peak: 1**.

469. 15 Nov •• THE TIDE IS HIGH Blondie Writer: John Holt. Producer: Mike Chapman. **US peak: 1.** ●

470. 29 Nov ••• SUPER TROUPER Abba Writer: Benny Andersson and Björn Ulvaeus. Producers: Benny Andersson and Björn Ulvaeus. **US peak: 45.** ●

471. 20 Dec • (JUST LIKE) STARTING OVER John Lennon Writer: John Lennon. Producers: John Lennon, Yoko Ono and Jack Douglas. **US peak: 1.** ●

472. 27 Dec •• THERE'S NO ONE QUITE LIKE GRANDMA St Winifred's School Choir Writer: Gordon Lorenz. Producer: Peter Tattersall. ❶●

1981

473. 10 Jan •••• IMAGINE John Lennon Writer: John Lennon. Producers: John Lennon, Yoko Ono and Phil Spector. **US peak: 3**.

474. 7 Feb •• WOMAN John Lennon Writer: John Lennon. Producers: John Lennon, Yoko Ono and Jack Douglas. **US peak: 2.** ⊙

475. 21 Feb ••• SHADDAP YOU FACE Joe Dolce Music Theatre Writer: Joe Dolce. Producers: Joe Dolce and Ian McKenzie. **US peak: 53.** ➊●

476. 14 Mar •• JEALOUS GUY Roxy Music Writer: John Lennon. Producer: Bryan Ferry and Rhett Davies. ●

477. 28 Mar ••• THIS OLE HOUSE Shakin' Stevens Writer: Stuart Hamblen. Producer: Stuart Coleman. ●

478. 18 Apr ••• MAKING YOUR MIND UP Bucks Fizz Writers: Andy Hill and John Danter. Producer: Andy Hill.

479. 9 May ••••• STAND AND DELIVER Adam and the Ants Writers: Adam Ant and Marco Pirroni. Producer: Chris Hughes. ◆

480. 13 Jun •• BEING WITH YOU Smokey Robinson Writer: William "Smokey" Robinson. Producer: George Tobin and Mike Piccirillo. **US peak: 2.** ●

481. 27 Jun •• ONE DAY IN YOUR LIFE Michael Jackson Writers: Sam Brown III and Renee Armand. Producer: Sam Brown III. **US peak: 55.** ●

482. 11 Jul ••• GHOST TOWN Specials Writer: Jerry Dammers. Producer: John Collins. ●

483. 1 Aug •••• GREEN DOOR Shakin' Stevens Writers: Bob Davie and Marvin Moore. Producer: Stuart Coleman. ●

484. 29 Aug • JAPANESE BOY Aneka Writer: Bobby Heatlie. Producer: Neil Ross. ⊙

485. 5 Sep •• TAINTED LOVE Soft Cell Writer: Ed Cobb. Producer: Mike Thorne. **US peak: 8.** ●

486. 19 Sep •••• PRINCE CHARMING Adam and the Ants Writers: Marco Pirroni and Adam Ant. Producers: Chris Hughes, Marco Pirroni and the Ants. ●

487. 17 Oct •••• IT'S MY PARTY Dave Stewart with Barbara Gaskin Writers: Herb Weiner, Wally Gold and John Gluck Jr. Producer: Dave Stewart. **US peak: 72.** ●

488. 14 Nov • EVERY LITTLE THING SHE DOES IS MAGIC Police Writer: Sting. Producers: Hugh Padgham and The Police. **US peak: 3.** ⊙

489. 21 Nov •• UNDER PRESSURE Queen and David Bowie Writers: Queen and David Bowie. Producers: Queen and David Bowie. **US peak: 29.** ⊙

490. 5 Dec • BEGIN THE BEGUINE (VOLVER A EMPEZAR) Julio Iglesias Writer: Cole Porter; Spanish lyrics by Julio Iglesias. Producer: Ramon Arousa. ⊙

491. 12 Dec ••••• DON'T YOU WANT ME Human League Writers: Jo Callis, Phil Oakey and Philip Adrian Wright. Producers: Martin Rushent and Human League. **US peak: 1.**

1982

492. 16 Jan •• LAND OF MAKE BELIEVE Bucks Fizz Writers: Andy Hill and Peter Sinfield. Producer: Andy Hill. ●

493. 30 Jan • OH JULIE Shakin' Stevens Writer: Shakin' Stevens. Producer: Stuart Coleman. ●

494. 6 Feb • THE MODEL / COMPUTER LOVE Kraftwerk Writers: Ralf Hutter, Karl Bartos and Emil Schulz. Producer: Ralf Hutter and Florian Schneider.

495. 13 Feb ••• A TOWN CALLED MALICE / PRECIOUS Jam Writer: Paul Weller. Producers: Pete Wilson and The Jam. ◆●

496. 6 Mar ••• THE LION SLEEPS TONIGHT Tight Fit Writers: Hugo Peretti, Luigi Creatore, George David Weiss, Solomon Linda, Paul Campbell. Producer: Tim Friese-Greene. ●

497. 27 Mar ••• SEVEN TEARS Goombay Dance Band Writers: Wolff-Ekkehardt, Stein and Wolfgang Jass. Producer: Jochen Petersen. ●

498. 17 Apr • MY CAMERA NEVER LIES Bucks Fizz Writers: Andy Hill and Nicola Martin. Producer: Andy Hill. ⊙

499. 24 Apr ••• EBONY AND IVORY Paul McCartney with Stevie Wonder Writer: Paul McCartney. Producer: George Martin. **US peak: 1.**●

500. 15 May •• A LITTLE PEACE Nicole Writers: Ralph Siegel and Bernd Meinunger. Producers: Clive Langer and Alan Winstanley. ⊙

501. 29 May •• HOUSE OF FUN Madness Writers: Mike Barson and Lee Thompson. Producer: Clive Langer and Alan Winstanley. ⊙

502. 12 Jun •• GOODY TWO SHOES Adam Ant Writers: Adam Ant and Marco Pirroni. Producers: Adam Ant, Marco Pirroni and Chris Hughes. **US peak: 12.**

503. 26 Jun • I'VE NEVER BEEN TO ME Charlene Writers: Ron Miller and Ken Hirsch. Producers: Ron Miller, Berry Gordy and Don Costa. **US peak: 3.** ➊⊙

504. 3 Jul •• HAPPY TALK Captain Sensible Writers: Richard Rodgers and Oscar Hammerstein II. Producer: Tony Mansfield.

505. 17 Jul ••• FAME Irene Cara Writers: Michael Gore and Dean Pitchford. Producer: Michael Gore. **US peak: 4.** ●

506. 7 Aug •••• COME ON EILEEN Dexy's Midnight Runners and the Emerald Express Writers: Kevin Rowland, Jimmy Patterson and Kevin Adams. Producers: Clive Langer and Alan Winstanley. **US peak: 1.**

507. 4 Sep •••• EYE OF THE TIGER Survivor Writers: Frankie Sullivan and Jim Peterik. Producers: Frankie Sullivan and Jim Peterik. **US peak: 1** ●

508. 2 Oct ••• PASS THE DUTCHIE Musical Youth Writers: Jackie Mittoo, Fitzroy Simpson and Lloyd Ferguson. Producer: Peter Collins. **US peak: 10.** ●

1980: A hat-trick of chart-toppers for Debbie Harry, lead singer with Blondie, within 12 months

509. 23 Oct ••• DO YOU REALLY WANT TO HURT ME Culture Club Writers: Culture Club. Producer: Steve Levine. **US peak: 2.** ●

510. 13 Nov ••• I DON'T WANNA DANCE Eddy Grant Writer: Eddy Grant. Producer: Eddy Grant. **US peak: 53.** ●

511. 4 Dec •• BEAT SURRENDER Jam Writer: Paul Weller. Producer: Peter Wilson. ◆ ⊙

512. 18 Dec •••• SAVE YOUR LOVE Renée and Renato Writers: John and Sue Edward. Producer: John Edward. ●

1983

513. 15 Jan •• YOU CAN'T HURRY LOVE Phil Collins Writers: Brian Holland, Lamont Dozier, Eddie Holland. Producers: Phil Collins and Hugh Padgham. **US peak: 10.** ●

514. 29 Jan ••• DOWN UNDER Men At Work Writers: Colin Hay and Ron Strykert. Producer: Peter Mclan. **US peak: 1.** ●

515. 19 Feb •• TOO SHY Kajagoogoo Writers: Kajagoogoo, lyrics by Limahl and Nick Beggs. Producers: Nick Rhodes and Colin Thurston. **US peak: 5.** ●

516. 5 Mar • BILLIE JEAN Michael Jackson Writer: Michael Jackson. Producer: Quincy Jones. **US peak: 1.** ●

517. 12 Mar •• TOTAL ECLIPSE OF THE HEART Bonnie Tyler Writer: Jim Steinman. Producer: Jim Steinman. **US peak: 1.**

518. 26 Mar •• IS THERE SOMETHING I SHOULD KNOW Duran Duran Writers: Duran Duran. Producers: Duran Duran and Ian Little. **US peak: 4.** ◆

519. 9 Apr ••• LET'S DANCE David Bowie Writer: David Bowie. Producers: David Bowie and Nile Rodgers. **US peak: 1.** ●

520. 30 Apr •••• TRUE Spandau Ballet Writer: Gary Kemp. Producers: Tony Swain, Steve Jolley and Spandau Ballet. **US peak: 4.** ●

521. 28 May • CANDY GIRL New Edition Writers: Maurice Starr and Michael Jonzun. Producers: Maurice Starr and Michael Jonzun. **US peak: 46.** ⊙

522. 4 Jun •••• EVERY BREATH YOU TAKE Police Writer: Sting. Producers: Hugh Padgham and The Police. **US peak: 1.** ⊙

523. 2 Jul ••• BABY JANE Rod Stewart Writers: Rod Stewart and Jay Davis. Producers: Rod Stewart and Tom Dowd, co-produced by Jim Cregan and George Tutko. **US peak: 14.** ⊙

524. 23 Jul ••• WHEREVER I LAY MY HAT (THAT'S MY HOME) Paul Young Writers: Marvin Gaye, Norman Whitfield and Barrett Strong. Producer: Laurie Latham. **US peak: 70.** ●

525. 13 Aug ••• GIVE IT UP KC and the Sunshine Band Writers: Harry Casey and Debra Carter. Producers: Harry Casey and Richard Finch. **US peak: 18.** ●

526. 3 Sep ••• RED RED WINE UB40 Writer: Neil Diamond. Producers: UB40 and Ray "Pablo" Falconer. **US peak: 1.** ●

527. 24 Sep •••••• KARMA CHAMELEON Culture Club Writers: Culture Club. Producer: Steve Levine. **US peak: 1.** ✪

528. 5 Nov ••••• UPTOWN GIRL Billy Joel Writer: Billy Joel. Producer: Phil Ramone. **US peak: 3.**

529. 10 Dec ••••• ONLY YOU Flying Pickets Writer: Vince Clarke. Producers: Flying Pickets and John Sherry. ●

1983: Two weeks at the top for Bonnie Tyler, the girl with a powerful rasping delivery from the South Wales village of Skewen

1984

530. 14 Jan •• PIPES OF PEACE Paul McCartney Writer: Paul McCartney. Producer: George Martin. ⊙

531. 28 Jan ••••• RELAX Frankie Goes To Hollywood Writers: Peter Gill, Holly Johnson and Mark O'Toole. Producer: Trevor Horn. **US peak: 10.** ✪

532. 3 Mar ••• 99 RED BALLOONS Nena Writers: Joern-Uwe Fahrenkrog-Peterson and Carlo Karges; Producers: Reinhold Heil and Manne Präker. **US peak: 2.** ●

533. 24 Mar •••••• HELLO Lionel Richie Writer: Lionel Richie. Producers: Lionel Richie and James Anthony Carmichael. **US peak: 1.** ●

534. 5 May •••• THE REFLEX Duran Duran Writers: Duran Duran. Producers: Alex Sadkin, Ian Little and Duran Duran; remixed by Nile Rodgers. **US peak: 1.**

535 2 Jun •• WAKE ME UP BEFORE YOU GO-GO Wham! Writer: George Michael. Producer: George Michael. **US peak: 1.** ●

536. 16 Jun ••••••••• TWO TRIBES Frankie Goes To Hollywood Writers: Peter Gill, Holly Johnson and Mark O'Toole. Producer: Trevor Horn. **US peak: 43.** ◆✪

537. 18 Aug ••• CARELESS WHISPER George Michael Writers: George Michael and Andrew Ridgeley. Producer: George Michael. **US peak: 1.** ✪

538. 8 Sep •••••• I JUST CALLED TO SAY I LOVE YOU Stevie Wonder Writer: Stevie Wonder. Producer: Stevie Wonder. **US peak: 1.** ✪

539. 20 Oct ••• FREEDOM Wham! Writer: George Michael. Producer: George Michael. **US peak: 3.** ●

540. 10 Nov ••• I FEEL FOR YOU Chaka Khan Writer: Prince. Producer: Arif Mardin. **US peak: 3.**

541. 1 Dec • I SHOULD HAVE KNOWN BETTER Jim Diamond Writers: Jim Diamond and Graham Lyle. Producer: Kip Williams.

542. 8 Dec • THE POWER OF LOVE Frankie Goes To Hollywood Writers: Peter Gill, Holly Johnson, Brian Nash and Mark O'Toole. Producer: Trevor Horn. ●

1984: Nena was both the group's name and vocalist Gabriele Kerner's stage name

543. 15 Dec ••••• DO THEY KNOW IT'S CHRISTMAS Band Aid Writers: Bob Geldof and Midge Ure. Producer: Midge Ure. **US peak: 13.** ◆✪✪✪

1985

544. 19 Jan ••• I WANT TO KNOW WHAT LOVE IS Foreigner Writer: Mick Jones. Producers: Alex Sadkin and Mick Jones. **US peak: 1.** ●

545. 9 Feb •••• I KNOW HIM SO WELL Elaine Paige and Barbara Dickson Writers: Tim Rice, Björn Ulvaeus and Benny Andersson. Producers: Tim Rice, Björn Ulvaeus and Benny Andersson. ●

546. 9 Mar •• YOU SPIN ME RIGHT ROUND (LIKE A RECORD) Dead or Alive Writers: Dead or Alive. Producer: Mike Stock, Matt Aitken and Pete Waterman. **US peak: 11.** ●

547. 23 Mar •••• EASY LOVER Philip Bailey (duet with Phil Collins) Writers: Philip Bailey, Phil Collins and Nathan East. Producer: Phil Collins. **US peak: 2.**●

548. 20 Apr •• WE ARE THE WORLD USA for Africa Writers: Michael Jackson and Lionel Richie. Producer: Quincy Jones. **US peak: 1.** ⊙

549. 4 May • MOVE CLOSER Phyllis Nelson Writer: Phyllis Nelson. Producer: Yves Dessca. ❶●

550. 11 May ••••• 19 Paul Hardcastle Writers: Paul Hardcastle, William Coutourie, Jonas McCord and Mike Oldfield. Producer: Paul Hardcastle. **US peak: 15.** ●

551. 15 Jun •• YOU'LL NEVER WALK ALONE The Crowd Writers: Richard Rodgers and Oscar Hammerstein II. Producers: Graham Gouldman and Ray Levy. ●

552. 29 Jun •••• FRANKIE Sister Sledge Writer: Joy Denny. Producer: Nile Rodgers. **US peak: 75.** ●

553. 27 Jul • THERE MUST BE AN ANGEL (PLAYING WITH MY HEART) Eurythmics Writers: Dave Stewart and Annie Lennox. Producer: David A Stewart. **US peak: 22.**

554. 3 Aug •••• INTO THE GROOVE Madonna Writers: Madonna and Steve Bray. Producers: Madonna and Steve Bray. ●

555. 31 Aug • I GOT YOU BABE UB40, guest vocals by Chrissie Hynde Writer: Sonny Bono. Producers: UB40 and Ray "Pablo" Falconer. **US peak: 28.** ●

556. 7 Sep •••• DANCING IN THE STREET David Bowie and Mick Jagger Writers: Ivy Hunter, William Stevenson and Marvin Gaye. Producers: Clive Langer and Alan Winstanley. **US peak: 7.** ◆●

557. 5 Oct • IF I WAS Midge Ure Writers: Midge Ure and Danny Mitchell. Producer: Midge Ure. ⊙

558. 12 Oct ••••• THE POWER OF LOVE Jennifer Rush Writers: Candy de Rouge, Gunther Mende, Jennifer Rush and Mary Susan Applegate. Producers: Candy de Rouge and Gunther Mende. **US peak: 67. US peak: 57.** ✪

559. 16 Nov •• A GOOD HEART Feargal Sharkey Writer: Maria McKee. Producer: David A Stewart. **US peak: 67.** ●

560. 30 Nov •• I'M YOUR MAN Wham! Writer: George Michael. Producer: George Michael. **US peak: 3.** ●

561. 14 Dec •• SAVING ALL MY LOVE FOR YOU Whitney Houston Writers: Michael Masser and Gerry Goffin. Producer: Michael Masser. **US peak: 1.** ●

562. 28 Dec •• MERRY CHRISTMAS EVERYONE Shakin' Stevens Writer: Bob Heatlie. Producer: Dave Edmunds. ●

1986

563. 11 Jan •• WEST END GIRLS Pet Shop Boys Writers: Neil Tennant and Chris Lowe. Producer: Stephen Hague. **US peak: 1.** ●

564. 25 Jan •• THE SUN ALWAYS SHINES ON TV A-Ha Writer: Paul Waaktaar. Producer: Alan Tarney. **US peak: 20.**

565. 8 Feb •••• WHEN THE GOING GETS TOUGH, THE TOUGH GET GOING Billy Ocean Writers: Wayne Braithwaite, Barry J Eastmond, R J "Mutt" Lange and Billy Ocean. Producer: R J "Mutt" Lange. **US peak: 2.** ⊙

566. 8 Mar ••• CHAIN REACTION Diana Ross Writers: Barry, Robin and Maurice Gibb. Producers: Barry Gibb, Karl Richardson and Albhy Galuten. **US peak: 66.** ●

567. 29 Mar ••• LIVING DOLL Cliff Richard and the Young Ones, featuring Hank B Marvin Writer: Lionel Bart. Producer: Stuart Coleman. ●

568. 19 Apr ••• A DIFFERENT CORNER George Michael Writer: George Michael. Producer: George Michael. **US peak: 7.** ●

569. 10 May • ROCK ME AMADEUS Falco Writers: Rob Bolland, Ferdi Bolland and Falco. Producers: Rob Bolland and Ferdi Bolland. **US peak: 1.** ●

570. 17 May ••• THE CHICKEN SONG Spitting Image Writers: Philip Pope, Robert Grant and Doug Naylor. Producer: Philip Pope. ⊙

571. 7 Jun ••• SPIRIT IN THE SKY Doctor and the Medics Writer: Norman Greenbaum. Producer: Craig Leon. **US peak: 69.** ⊙

572. 28 Jun •• THE EDGE OF HEAVEN Wham! Writer: George Michael. Producer: George Michael. **US peak: 10.** ⊙

573. 12 Jul ••• PAPA DON'T PREACH Madonna Writers: Brian Elliott; additional lyrics by Madonna. Producers: Madonna and Stephen Bray. **US peak: 1.** ●

574. 2 Aug ••• THE LADY IN RED Chris de Burgh Writer: Chris de Burgh. Producer: Paul Hardiman. **US peak: 3.** ●

575. 23 Aug ••• I WANT TO WAKE UP WITH YOU Boris Gardiner Writer: Ben Peters. Producer: Willie Lindo. ●

576. 13 Sep •••• DON'T LEAVE ME THIS WAY Communards with Sarah Jane Morris Writers: Kenny Gamble, Leon Huff and Cary Gilbert. Producer: Mike Thorne. **US peak: 40.** ●

577. 11 Oct • TRUE BLUE Madonna Writers: Madonna and Stephen Bray. Producers: Madonna and Stephen Bray. **US peak: 3.** ⊙

578. 18 Oct ••• EVERY LOSER WINS Nick Berry Writers: Simon May, Stewart James and Bradley James. Producers: Simon May, Stewart James and Bradley James.

579. 8 Nov •••• TAKE MY BREATH AWAY Berlin Writers: Giorgio Moroder and Tom Whitlock. Producer: Giorgio Moroder. **US peak: 1.** ●

580. 6 Dec •• THE FINAL COUNTDOWN Europe Writer: Joey Tempest. Producer: Kevin Elson. **US peak: 8.** ●

581. 20 Dec • CARAVAN OF LOVE Housemartins Writers: Ernie Isley, Chris Jasper and Marvin Isley. Producer: John Williams. ●

582. 27 Dec •••• REET PETITE Jackie Wilson Writers: Berry Gordy and Tyran Carlo. Producer: Carl Davis. **US peak: 62.**

1987

583. 24 Jan •• JACK YOUR BODY Steve "Silk" Hurley Writer: Steve "Silk" Hurley. Producer: Steve "Silk" Hurley. ●

584. 7 Feb •• I KNEW YOU WERE WAITING (FOR ME) George Michael and Aretha Franklin Writers: Simon Climie and Denis Morgan. Producer: Narada Michael Walden. **US peak: 1.** ●

585. 21 Feb ••• STAND BY ME Ben E King Writers: Jerry Leiber, Mike Stoller and Ben E King. Producers: Jerry Leiber and Mike Stoller. **US peak: 9.**

586. 14 Mar •• EVERYTHING I OWN Boy George Writer: David Gates. Producer: Steve Levine. ⊙

587. 28 Mar • RESPECTABLE Mel and Kim Writer: Mike Stock, Matt Aitken and Pete Waterman. Producers: Mike Stock, Matt Aitken and Pete Waterman. ●

1987: Mel and Kim's appearance on Ferry Aid's 'Let It Be' knocked their own single off the top

588. 4 Apr ••• LET IT BE Ferry Aid Writers: John Lennon and Paul McCartney. Producers: Mike Stock, Matt Aitken and Pete Waterman. ◆●

589. 25 Apr •• LA ISLA BONITA Madonna Writers: Madonna and Patrick Leonard. Producers: Madonna and Patrick Leonard. **US peak: 4.** ⊙

590. 9 May •••• NOTHING'S GONNA STOP US NOW Starship Writers: Diane Warren and Albert Hammond. Producer: Narada Michael Walden. **US peak: 1.** ●

591. 6 Jun •• I WANNA DANCE WITH SOMEBODY (WHO LOVES ME) Whitney Houston Writers: George Merrill and Shannon Rubicam. Producer: Narada Michael Walden. **US peak: 1.** ●

592. 20 Jun •• STAR TREKKIN' The Firm Writers: Grahame Lister and John O'Connor. Producers: Grahame Lister and John O'Connor. ⊙

593. 4 Jul ••• IT'S A SIN Pet Shop Boys Writers: Neil Tennant and Chris Lowe. Producers: Julian Mendelsohn and Stephen Hague. **US peak: 9.** ⊙

594. 25 Jul • WHO'S THAT GIRL Madonna Writers: Madonna and Patrick Leonard. Producers: Madonna and Patrick Leonard. **US peak: 1.** ⊙

595. 1 Aug •• LA BAMBA Los Lobos Writer: Traditional, arranged by Ritchie Valens. Producer: Mitchell Froom. **US peak: 1.**

596. 15 Aug •• I JUST CAN'T STOP LOVING YOU Michael Jackson Writer: Michael Jackson. Producers: Quincy Jones and Michael Jackson. **US peak: 1.**

597. 29 Aug •••••• NEVER GONNA GIVE YOU UP Rick Astley Writers: Mike Stock, Matt Aitken and Pete Waterman. Producers: Mike Stock, Matt Aitken and Pete Waterman. **US peak: 1.** ●

598. 3 Oct •• PUMP UP THE VOLUME / ANITINA (THE FIRST TIME I SEE SHE DANCE) M/A/R/R/S Writers: Steven and Martin Young, A R Kane, C J Mackintosh, John Fryer and Dave Darrell / A R Kane and Colourbox. Producer: Martin Young. **US peak: 13.** ❶ ⊙

599. 17 Oct •••• YOU WIN AGAIN Bee Gees Writers: Barry, Robin and Maurice Gibb. Producers: Arif Mardin with Barry, Robin and Maurice Gibb; co-produced by Brian Trench. **US peak: 75**.

600. 14 Nov ••••• CHINA IN YOUR HAND T'Pau Writers: Carol Decker and Ron Rogers. Producer: Roy Thomas Baker. ●

601. 19 Dec •••• ALWAYS ON MY MIND Pet Shop Boys Writers: Mark James, Johnny Christopher and Wayne Thompson. Producers: Julian Mendelsohn and Pet Shop Boys. **US peak: 4**. ●

1988

602. 16 Jan •• HEAVEN IS A PLACE ON EARTH Belinda Carlisle Writers: Rick Nowels and Ellen Shipley. Producer: Rick Nowels. **US peak: 1**. ●

603. 30 Jan ••• I THINK WE'RE ALONE NOW Tiffany Writer: Ritchie Cordell. Producer: George E Tobin. **US peak: 1**. ●

604. 20 Feb ••••• I SHOULD BE SO LUCKY Kylie Minogue Writers: Mike Stock, Matt Aitken and Pete Waterman. Producers: Mike Stock, Matt Aitken and Pete Waterman. **US peak: 28**. ●

605. 26 Mar •• DON'T TURN AROUND Aswad Writers: Diane Warren and Albert Hammond. Producer: Chris Porter.

606. 9 Apr ••• HEART Pet Shop Boys Writers: Neil Tennant and Chris Lowe. Producers: Andy Richards and Pet Shop Boys. ⊙

607. 30 Apr •• THEME FROM S EXPRESS S Express Writers: Mark Moore and Pascal Gabriel. Producers: Mark Moore and Pascal Gabriel. **US peak: 91**. ⊙

608. 14 May • PERFECT Fairground Attraction Writer: Mark E Nevin. Producers: Fairground Attraction and Kevin Moloney. **US peak: 80**. ⊙

609. 21 May •••• WITH A LITTLE HELP FROM MY FRIENDS / SHE'S LEAVING HOME Wet Wet Wet / Billy Bragg with Cara Tivey Writers: John Lennon and Paul McCartney. Producers: 'With A Little Help From My Friends' Wet Wet Wet / 'She's Leaving Home' John Porter and Kenny Jones. ⊙

610. 18 Jun • DOCTORIN' THE TARDIS Timelords Writers: Mike Chapman, Nicky Chinn, Roy Grainer, Gary Glitter, Mike Leander, Timelords. Producers: Timelords. **US peak: 66**.

611. 25 Jun •• I OWE YOU NOTHING Bros Writers: The Brothers (Nicky Graham and Tom Watkins). Producer: Nicky Graham.

612. 9 Jul •••• NOTHING'S GONNA CHANGE MY LOVE FOR YOU Glenn Medeiros Writers: Michael Masser and Gerry Goffin. Producer: Jay Stone. **US peak: 12**. ●

613. 6 Aug ••••• THE ONLY WAY IS UP Yazz and the Plastic Population Writers: George Jackson, Johnny Henderson. Producers: Coldcut (Matt Black and Jonathan Moore). **US peak: 96**. ●

614. 10 Sep •• A GROOVY KIND OF LOVE Phil Collins Writers: Toni Wine and Carole Bayer Sager. Producers: Phil Collins and Anne Dudley. **US peak: 1**. ⊙

615. 24 Sep •• HE AIN'T HEAVY HE'S MY BROTHER Hollies Writers: Bob Russell and Bobby Scott. Producer: Ron Richards. **US peak: 7**.

616. 8 Oct • DESIRE U2 Writers: U2, lyrics by Bono. Producer: Jimmy Iovine. **US peak: 3**. ⊙

617. 15 Oct •• ONE MOMENT IN TIME Whitney Houston Writers: Albert Hammond and John Bettis. Producer: Narada Michael Walden. **US peak: 5**. ⊙

618. 29 Oct ••• ORINOCO FLOW (SAIL AWAY) Enya Writers: Enya Brennan and Roma Ryan. Producer: Nicky Ryan. **US peak: 24**. ⊙

619. 19 Nov ••• THE FIRST TIME Robin Beck Writers: Gavin Spencer, Tom Anthony and Terry Boyle. Producers: Gavin Spencer and Tom Anthony. ❶⊙

620. 10 Dec •••• MISTLETOE AND WINE Cliff Richard Writers: Leslie Stewart, Jeremy Paul and Keith Strachan. Producer: Cliff Richard. ●

1989

621. 7 Jan ••• ESPECIALLY FOR YOU Kylie Minogue and Jason Donovan Writers: Mike Stock, Matt Aitken, Pete Waterman. Producers: Mike Stock, Matt Aitken and Pete Waterman. ●

622. 28 Jan •••• SOMETHING'S GOTTEN HOLD OF MY HEART Marc Almond with special guest Gene Pitney Writers: Roger Cook and Roger Greenaway. Producer: Bob Kraushaar. ●

1988: Tiffany's first UK live appearance was at Newcastle's Eldon Square Shopping Centre

623. 25 Feb •• BELFAST CHILD Simple Minds Writers: Traditional; lyrics by Simple Minds. Producers: Trevor Horn and Steve Lipson. ⊙

624. 11 Mar •• TOO MANY BROKEN HEARTS Jason Donovan Writers: Mike Stock, Matt Aitken and Pete Waterman. Producers: Mike Stock, Matt Aitken and Pete Waterman. ●

625. 25 Mar ••• LIKE A PRAYER Madonna Writers: Madonna and Patrick Leonard. Producers: Madonna and Patrick Leonard. **US peak: 1**. ●

626. 15 Apr •••• ETERNAL FLAME Bangles Writers: Susanna Hoffs, Billy Steinberg, Tom Kelly. Producer: Davitt Sigerson. **US peak: 1**. ⊙

627. 13 May • HAND ON YOUR HEART Kylie Minogue Writers: Mike Stock, Matt Aitken, and Pete Waterman. Producers: Mike Stock, Matt Aitken and Pete Waterman. ●

628. 20 May ••• FERRY 'CROSS THE MERSEY Christians, Holly Johnson, Paul McCartney, Gerry Marsden and Stock Aitken Waterman Writer: Gerry Marsden. Producers: Mike Stock, Matt Aitken and Pete Waterman. ◆

629. 10 Jun •• SEALED WITH A KISS Jason Donovan Writers: Gary Geld, Peter Udell. Producers: Mike Stock, Matt Aitken and Pete Waterman. ◆

630. 24 Jun •••• BACK TO LIFE (HOWEVER DO YOU WANT ME) Soul II Soul featuring Caron Wheeler Writers: Beresford Romeo, Caron Wheeler, Simon Law and Nellee Hooper. Producers: Jazzie B (Beresford Romeo) and Nellee Hooper. **US peak: 4.** ⊙

631. 22 Jul •• YOU'LL NEVER STOP ME LOVING YOU Sonia Writers: Mike Stock, Matt Aitken and Pete Waterman. Producers: Mike Stock, Matt Aitken and Pete Waterman.

632. 5 Aug ••••• SWING THE MOOD Jive Bunny and the Mastermixers Medley produced by: Andy Pickles and Les Hemstock. ✪ **US peak: 11**

633. 9 Sep •••••• RIDE ON TIME Black Box Writers: Dan Hartman, Daniele Davoli, Marco Limoni and Valerio Semplici. Producer: Groove Groove Melody. **US peak: 33.**

634. 21 Oct ••• THAT'S WHAT I LIKE Jive Bunny and the Mastermixers Medley produced by: Andy Pickles, Les Hemstock and Ian Morgan. **US peak: 69.** ●

635. 11 Nov •• ALL AROUND THE WORLD Lisa Stansfield Writers: Lisa Stansfield, Ian Devaney and Andy Morris. Producers: Ian Devaney and Andy Morris. **US peak: 3.** ●

636. 25 Nov ••• YOU GOT IT (THE RIGHT STUFF) New Kids on the Block Writer: Maurice Starr. Producers: Maurice Starr and Michael Jonzun. **US peak: 3.** ●

637. 16 Dec • LET'S PARTY Jive Bunny and the Mastermixers Medley produced by: Andy Pickles and Ian Morgan. ◆●

638. 23 Dec ••• DO THEY KNOW IT'S CHRISTMAS? Band Aid II Writers: Bob Geldof and Midge Ure. Producers: Mike Stock, Matt Aitken and Pete Waterman. ◆✪

1990

639. 13 Jan •• HANGIN' TOUGH New Kids on the Block Writer: Maurice Starr. Producer: Maurice Starr. **US peak: 1.**

640. 27 Jan • TEARS ON MY PILLOW Kylie Minogue Writers: Sylvester Bradford and Al Lewis. Producers: Mike Stock, Matt Aitken and Pete Waterman. ⊙

641. 3 Feb •••• NOTHING COMPARES 2 U Sinead O'Connor Writer: Prince. Producer: Sinead O'Connor. **US peak: 1.** ✪

642. 3 Mar •••• DUB BE GOOD TO ME Beats International featuring Lindy Layton Writers: Norman Cook, Jimmy Jam and Terry Lewis. Producer: Norman Cook. **US peak: 76.** ●

643. 31 Mar •• THE POWER Snap! Writers: Benito Benites, John "Virgo" Garrett III. Producers: Snap!. **US peak: 2.** ⊙

644. 14 Apr •••• VOGUE Madonna Writers: Madonna and Shep Pettibone. Producers: Madonna and Shep Pettibone. **US peak: 1.** ●

645. 12 May •••• KILLER Adamski Writers: Adam Tinley and Sealhenry Samuel. Producer: Adamski.

646. 9 Jun •• WORLD IN MOTION Englandneworder Writers: New Order and Keith Allen. Producer: Stephen Hague. ●

647. 23 Jun ••••• SACRIFICE / HEALING HANDS Elton John Writers: Elton John and Bernie Taupin. Producer: Chris Thomas. **US peak: 18 / 13.** ✪

648. 28 Jul •••• TURTLE POWER Partners In Kryme Writers: James P Alpern and Richard A Usher Jr. Producers: Partners In Kryme. **US peaks: 13.** ❶⊙

649. 25 Aug ••• ITSY BITSY TEENY WEENY YELLOW POLKA DOT BIKINI Bombalurina Writers: Lee Pockriss and Paul Vance. Producer: Nigel Wright. ⊙

650. 15 Sep •• THE JOKER Steve Miller Band Writer: Steve Miller. Producer: Steve Miller. **US peak: 1.** ⊙

651. 29 Sep •••• SHOW ME HEAVEN Maria McKee Writers: Joshua Rifkin, Eric Rackin and Maria McKee. Producer: Paul Staveley O'Duffy.

652. 27 Oct • A LITTLE TIME Beautiful South Writers: Paul Heaton and Dave Rotheray. Producer: Mike Hedges.

653. 3 Nov •••• UNCHAINED MELODY Righteous Brothers Writers: Hy Zaret and Alex North. Producer: Phil Spector. **US peak: 4.**

654. 1 Dec •••• ICE ICE BABY Vanilla Ice Writers: Vanilla Ice, Earthquake, David Bowie and Queen. Producer: Vanilla Ice. **US peak: 1.** ✪

655. 29 Dec • SAVIOUR'S DAY Cliff Richard Writer: Chris Eaton. Producers: Cliff Richard and Paul Moessl. ⊙

1989: Buy the Jive Bunny single or the rabbit gets it!

1991

656 5 Jan •• BRING YOUR DAUGHTER... TO THE SLAUGHTER Iron Maiden Writer: Bruce Dickinson. Producer: Martin Binch. ◆

657 19 Jan • SADNESS PART ONE Enigma Writers: Michael Cretu, Franz Gregorian and David Fairstein. Producer: Michael Cretu. **US peak: 5.** ⊙

658 26 Jan • INNUENDO Queen Writers: Queen. Producers: Queen and David Richards. ◆⊙

659 2 Feb •• 3AM ETERNAL KLF featuring Children of the Revolution Writers: Jim Cauty, Bill Drummond and Ricardo Lyte. Producers: KLF. **US peak: 5.** ⊙

660 16 Feb ••• DO THE BARTMAN Simpsons Writer: Bryan Loren. Producer: Bryan Loren. ●

661 9 Mar •• SHOULD I STAY OR SHOULD I GO Clash Writers: The Clash. Producer: Mick Jones. **US peak: 45.**

662 23 Mar • THE STONK Hale and Pace and the Stonkers Writers: Joe Griffiths, Gareth Hale and Norman Pace. Producer: Brian May. ❶

663 30 Mar ••••• THE ONE AND ONLY Chesney Hawkes Writer: Nik Kershaw. Producers: Alan Shacklock and Nik Kershaw. **US peak: 10.** ●

664 4 May ••••• THE SHOOP SHOOP SONG (IT'S IN HIS KISS) Cher Writer: Rudy Clark. Producer: Peter Asher. **US peak: 33.** ●

665 8 Jun ••• I WANNA SEX YOU UP Color Me Badd Writer: Dr Freeze. Producer: Dr Freeze. **US peak: 2.** ⊙

666 29 Jun •• ANY DREAM WILL DO Jason Donovan Writers: Tim Rice and Andrew Lloyd Webber. Producer: Nigel Wright. ●

667 13 Jul •••••••••••••••• (EVERYTHING I DO) I DO IT FOR YOU Bryan Adams Writers: Bryan Adams, Michael Kamen and Robert John "Mutt" Lange. Producer: Robert John "Mutt" Lange. **US peak: 1.** ✪

668 2 Nov • THE FLY U2 Writers: U2. Producer: Daniel Lanois. **US peak: 58.** ◆⊙

669 9 Nov •• DIZZY Vic Reeves and The Wonder Stuff Writers: Tommy Roe and Freddy Weller. Producer: Mick Glossop. ⊙

1991: Color Me Badd were four school friends from Oklahoma City who saw their UK No.1 'I Wanna Sex You Up' stall at No.2 in the States despite double-platinum sales – the only single to achieve that feat in 1991

670. 23 Nov •• BLACK OR WHITE Michael Jackson Writer: Michael Jackson. Producers: Michael Jackson and Bill Bottrell. **US peak: 1.** ◆⊙

671. 7 Dec •• DON'T LET THE SUN GO DOWN ON ME George Michael and Elton John Writers: Elton John and Bernie Taupin. Producer: George Michael. **US peak: 1.** ◆⊙

672. 21 Dec ••••• BOHEMIAN RHAPSODY / THESE ARE THE DAYS OF OUR LIVES Queen Writers: Freddie Mercury / Queen. Producers: 'Bohemian Rhapsody' Roy Thomas Baker and Queen; 'These Are the Days of Our Lives' Queen and David Richards. **US peak: 2.** ◆✪

1992

673. 25 Jan •••• GOODNIGHT GIRL Wet Wet Wet Writers: Graeme Clark, Tommy Cunningham, Neil Mitchell, Marti Pellow. Producers: Wet Wet Wet.

674. 22 Feb •••••••• STAY Shakespear's Sister Writers: Siobhan Fahey, Marcella Detroit and Guiot (Dave Stewart). Producers: Chris Thomas, Alan Moulder and Shakespear's Sister. **US peak: 4.** ●

675. 18 Apr ••• DEEPLY DIPPY Right Said Fred Writers: Richard Fairbrass, Fred Fairbrass and Rob Manzoli. Producer: Tommy D. ⊙

676. 9 May ••••• PLEASE DON'T GO / GAME BOY KWS Writers: Harry W Casey, Richard Finch / Chris King, Winston Williams. Producers: Chris King and Winston Williams. **US peak: 6.** ●

677 13 Jun ••••• ABBA-ESQUE (EP) Erasure Writers: 'Lay All Your Love on Me', 'Take a Chance on Me', 'Voulez-Vous' Benny Andersson, Björn Ulvaeus; 'S.O.S.' Benny Andersson, Björn Ulvaeus and Stig Anderson. Producer: Dave Bascombe. ◆●

678. 18 Jul ••• AIN'T NO DOUBT Jimmy Nail Writers: Guy Pratt, Danny Schogger, Jimmy Nail and Charlie Dore. Producers: Guy Pratt, Danny Schogger and Jimmy Nail. ●

679. 8 Aug •••••• RHYTHM IS A DANCER Snap! Writers: Benito Benitez, John "Virgo" Garrett III, Thea Austin and Durron Butler. Producers: Snap!. **US peak: 5.** ●

680. 19 Sep •••• EBENEEZER GOODE Shamen Writers: Colin Angus and Richard West (Mr C). Producers: Shamen. ⊙

681. 17 Oct •• SLEEPING SATELLITE Tasmin Archer Writers: Tasmin Archer, John Beck and John Hughes. Producer: Paul "Wix" Wickens. **US peak: 32** ⊙

682. 31 Oct ••• THE END OF THE ROAD Boyz II Men Writers: L A Reid, Babyface and Daryl Simmons. Producers: L A Reid and Babyface. **US peak: 1.**

683. 21 Nov •• WOULD I LIE TO YOU Charles and Eddie Writers: Mick Leeson and Peter Vale. Producer: Josh Deutsch. **US peak: 13.** ✪

684. 5 Dec •••••••••• I WILL ALWAYS LOVE YOU Whitney Houston Writer: Dolly Parton. Producer: David Foster. **US peak: 1** ✪✪

1992: Tasmin Archer's debut single 'Sleeping Satellite' would be her only Top 10 hit

1993

685. 13 Feb ••••• NO LIMIT 2 Unlimited Writers: Anita Dels, Ray Slijngaard, Phil Wilde and Jean Paul de Coster. Producers: Phil White and Jean Paul de Coster.

686. 20 Mar •• OH CAROLINA Shaggy Writer: John Folkes. Producer: Sting International. **US peak: 59.** ●

687. 3 Apr •••• YOUNG AT HEART Bluebells Writers: Bobby Hodgens and Siobhan Fahey. Producers: Colin Fairley and Robert Andrews.

688. 1 May ••• FIVE LIVE (EP) George Michael and Queen with Lisa Stansfield Writers: 'Somebody to Love' Freddie Mercury; 'Killer Papa Was a Rolling Stone' Seal, Adam Tinley, Norman Whitfield and Barrett Strong; 'These Are the Days of Our Lives' Queen; 'Calling You' Bob Telson. Producers: 'Somebody to Love' and 'These Are the Days of Our Lives' George Michael, Queen and David Richards; 'Killer Papa Was a Rolling Stone' and 'Calling You' George Michael and Chris Porter. ◆●

689. 22 May ••• ALL THAT SHE WANTS Ace of Base Writers: Joker and Buddha. Producers: Denniz Pop, Jonas "Joker" Berggren and Ulf "Buddha" Ekberg. **US peak: 2.** ✪

690. 12 Jun •• (I CAN'T HELP) FALLING IN LOVE WITH YOU UB40 Writers: Hugo Peretti, Luigi Creatore and George David Weiss. Producers: UB40. **US peak: 1.** ✪

691. 26 Jun ••• DREAMS Gabrielle Writers: Gabrielle and Tim Laws. Producers: Richie Fermie. **US peak: 26.** ●

692. 17 Jul •••• PRAY Take That Writer: Gary Barlow. Producers: Steve Jervier, Paul Jervier and Jonathan Wales. ◆ ●

693. 14 Aug •• LIVING ON MY OWN Freddie Mercury Writer: Freddie Mercury. Producers: Mack and Freddie Mercury; rearranged, produced and recorded by NMB (Serge Ramaekers, Colin Peter and Carl Ward). ●

694. 28 Aug •••• MR VAIN Culture Beat Writers: Steven Lewis, Noise Katzmann and Jay Supreme. Producers: Torsten Fenslau. **US peak: 17.** ●

695. 25 Sep •• BOOM! SHAKE THE ROOM Jazzy Jeff and the Fresh Prince Writers: Will Smith, Lee Haggard, Walter Williams, Ken Mayberry, Leroy Bonner, Clarence Satchell, Marshall Jones, Jimmy "Diamond" Williams, Merv Pierce, Billy Beck and Ralph Middlebrook. Producer: Mr Lee. **US peak: 13.** ⊙

696. 9 Oct •• RELIGHT MY FIRE Take That featuring Lulu Writer: Dan Hartman. Producers: Joey Negro and Andrew Livingstone. ◆⊙

697. 23 Oct ••••••• I'D DO ANYTHING FOR LOVE (BUT I WON'T DO THAT) Meat Loaf Writer: Jim Steinman. Producer: Jim Steinman. **US peak: 1.** ✪

698. 11 Dec • 25 Dec •• MR BLOBBY Mr Blobby Writers: Paul Shaw and David Rogers. Producers: Paul Shaw and David Rodgers. ✪

699. 18 Dec • BABE Take That Writer: Gary Barlow. Producers: Steve Jervier, Paul Jervier and Jonathan Wales. ◆✪

1994

700. 8 Jan •• TWIST AND SHOUT Chaka Demus and Pliers with Jack Radics and Taxi Gang Writers: Bert Berns and Phil Medley. Producers: Sly Dunbar, Robbie Shakespeare and Lloyd "Gitsy" Willis. ●

701. 22 Jan •••• THINGS CAN ONLY GET BETTER D:Ream Writers: Peter Cunnah and Jamie Petrie. Producers: D:Ream with Tom Frederikse.

702. 19 Feb •••• WITHOUT YOU Mariah Carey Writers: Pete Ham and Tom Evans. Producers: Walter Afanasieff and Mariah Carey. **US peak: 3.** ◆●

703. 19 Mar ••• DOOP Doop Writers: Frederick Ridderhof. Producer: Peter Garnefski. ❶●

704. 9 Apr •• EVERYTHING CHANGES Take That Writers: Gary Barlow, Mike Ward, Eliot Kennedy and Cary Baylis. Producers: Mike Ward and Eliot Kennedy. ◆⊙

705. 23 Apr •• THE MOST BEAUTIFUL GIRL IN THE WORLD Symbol (Prince) Writer: Symbol. Producers: Symbol and Ricky P. **US peak: 3.**

706. 7 May • THE REAL THING Tony Di Bart Writers: Lucinda Drayton, Tony Di Bart and Andy Blissett. Producers: Rhyme Time Productions; remixed by the Joy Brothers. ⊙

707. 14 May • INSIDE Stiltskin Writer: Peter Lawlor. Producer: Peter Lawlor. ⊙

708. 21 May •• COME ON YOU REDS Manchester United Football Squad Writers: Francis Rossi, Andy Brown and John Edwards. Producers: Status Quo. ⊙

709. 4 Jun ••••••••••••••• LOVE IS ALL AROUND Wet Wet Wet Writer: Reg Presley. Producers: Wet Wet Wet and Graeme Duffin. **US peak: 45.** ✪✪

710. 17 Sep •••• SATURDAY NIGHT Whigfield Writers: Larry Pignagnoli and Davide Riva. Producer: Larry Pignagnoli. ◆✪

711. 15 Oct •• SURE Take That Writers: Gary Barlow, Robbie Williams and Mark Owen. Producers: Brothers In Rhythm. ◆⊙

712. 29 Oct •••• BABY COME BACK Pato Banton Writer: Eddy Grant. Producers: Susan Stoker and Michael Railton. ✪

713. 26 Nov •• LET ME BE YOUR FANTASY Baby D Writer: Floyd Dyce. Producer: Floyd Dice. ⊙

714. 10 Dec ••••• STAY ANOTHER DAY East 17 Writers: Tony Mortimer, Rob Kean and Dominic Hawken. Producers: Phil Harding, Ian Curnow and Rob Kean. ✪

1995

715. 14 Jan ••• COTTON EYE JOE Rednex Writers: Jan Ericsson, Oban and Pat Reiniz. Producer: Pat Reiniz. **US peak: 25.** ✪

716. 4 Feb ••••••• THINK TWICE Celine Dion Writers: Andy Hill and Pete Sinfield. Producer: Chris Neil. **US peak: 95.** ✪

717. 25 Mar • LOVE CAN BUILD A BRIDGE Cher, Chrissie Hynde and Neneh Cherry with Eric Clapton Writers: Naomi Judd, John Jarvis and Paul Overstreet. Producer: Peter Asher. ⊙

718. 1 Apr • DON'T STOP (WIGGLE WIGGLE) Outhere Brothers Writers: Hula Mahone, Craig Simpkins, Keith Mayberry and Aladino. Producers: Outhere Brothers. ●

719. 8 Apr •••• BACK FOR GOOD Take That Writer: Gary Barlow. Producers: Chris Porter and Gary Barlow. **US peak: 7.** ◆

720. 6 May • SOME MIGHT SAY Oasis Writer: Noel Gallagher. Producers: Owen Morris and Noel Gallagher. ◆●

721. 13 May • DREAMER Livin' Joy Writers: Paolo Visnadi and Janice Robinson. Producers: Livin' Joy. **US peak: 72.** ◆

722. 20 May ••••••• UNCHAINED MELODY / WHITE CLIFFS OF DOVER Robson Green and Jerome Flynn Writers: Alex North and Hy Zaret / Walter Kent and Janice Robinson. Producers: Mike Stock and Matt Aitken. ◆✪✪✪

723. 8 Jul •••• BOOM BOOM BOOM Outhere Brothers Writers: Hula Mahone and Keith Mayberry. Producers: Outhere Brothers. **US peak: 65.** ●

724. 5 Aug ••• NEVER FORGET Take That Writer: Gary Barlow. Producers: Jim Steinman, Brothers In Rhythm and Dave James. ◆●

725. 26 Aug •• COUNTRY HOUSE Blur Writers: Damon Albarn / Blur. Producer: Stephen Street. ◆

726. 9 Sep •• YOU ARE NOT ALONE Michael Jackson Writer: R Kelly. Producer: R Kelly. **US peak: 1.** ●

727. 23 Sep • BOOMBASTIC Shaggy Writer: Orville Burrell, Robert Livingstone and King Floyd. Producers: Robert Livingston and Shaun Pizzonia. **US peak: 3.** ◆●

728. 30 Sep •••• FAIRGROUND Simply Red Writer: Mick Hucknall. Producers: Mick Hucknall and Stewart Levine. ◆✪

729. 28 Oct •• GANGSTA'S PARADISE Coolio featuring LV Writers: Artis Ivey Jr, Stevie Wonder, Larry Sanders and Doug Rasheed. Producer: Doug Rasheed. **US peak: 1.** ◆✪

730. 11 Nov •••• I BELIEVE / UP ON THE ROOF Robson Green and Jerome Flynn Writers: Ervin Drake, Irvin Graham, Jimmy Shirl and Al Stillman / Gerry Coffin and Carole King. Producers: Mike Stock and Matt Aitken. ◆✪

731. 9 Dec •••••• EARTH SONG Michael Jackson Writer: Michael Jackson. Producers: Michael Jackson and David Foster. ◆✪

1996

732. 20 Jan • JESUS TO A CHILD George Michael Writer: George Michael. Producer: George Michael. **US peak: 7.** ◆⊙

733. 27 Jan ••••• SPACEMAN Babylon Zoo Writer: Jas Mann. Producers: Jas Mann and Steve Power. ◆

734. 2 Mar • DON'T LOOK BACK IN ANGER Oasis Writer: Noel Gallagher. Producers: Owen Morris and Noel Gallagher. **US peak: 55.** ◆✪

735. 9 Mar ••• HOW DEEP IS YOUR LOVE Take That Writers: Robin, Barry and Maurice Gibb. Producers: Chris Porter and Take That. ◆✪

736. 30 Mar ••• FIRESTARTER Prodigy Writers: Liam Howlett, Keith Flint, Trevor Horn and Art of Noise. Producer: Liam Howlett . **US peak: 30.** ◆●

737. 20 Apr •• RETURN OF THE MACK Mark Morrison Writer: Mark Morrison. Producers: Phill Chill and Mark Morrison. **US peak: 2.** ✪

738. 4 May ••• FASTLOVE George Michael Writers: George Michael, Patrice Rushen and Fred Washington. Producers: George Michael and Jon Douglas. **US peak: 8.** ◆

739. 25 May • OOH AAH...JUST A LITTLE BIT Gina G Writers: Simon Tauber, Steve Rodway. Producer: Steve Rodway. **US peak: 12.** ✪

740. 1 Jun • 6 Jul • THREE LIONS (THE OFFICIAL SONG OF THE ENGLAND FOOTBALL TEAM) Baddiel and Skinner and Lightning Seeds Writers: Ian Broudie, Frank Skinner and David Baddiel. Producers: Dave Bascombe, Ian Broudie and Simon Rogers. ◆✪

741. 8 Jun •••• 13 Jul • KILLING ME SOFTLY Fugees Writers: Norman Gimbel, Charles Fox. Producers: Wyclef Jean, Lauryn Hill, Jerry Duplessis and Prakazrel Michel. ◆✪✪

742. 20 Jul • FOREVER LOVE Gary Barlow Writer: Gary Barlow. Producers: Chris Porter and Take That. ◆●

743. 27 Jul ••••••• WANNABE Spice Girls Writers: Richard Stannard, Matthew Rowe and Spice Girls. Producers: Richard Stannard and Matt Rowe. **US peak: 1.** ✪

744. 14 Sep • FLAVA Peter Andre Writer: Peter Andre, Andy Whitmore, Wayne Hector and Cee. Producer: Andy Whitmore. ◆⊙

745. 21 Sep •• READY OR NOT Fugees Writers: Wyclef Jean, Pras Michel, Lauryn Hill, William Hart and Thomas Bell. Producers: Fugees and Jerry Duplessis. ●

1996: Gina G's 'Ooh Aah ... Just a Little Bit' spent 25 weeks on the singles chart

746. 5 Oct • BREAKFAST AT TIFFANY'S Deep Blue Something Writer: Todd David Pipes. Producer: Dave Castell. **US peak: 5**

747. 12 Oct • SETTING SUN Chemical Brothers Writers: Ed Simons, Tom Rowlands and Noel Gallagher. Producers: Chemical Brothers. ◆⊙

748. 19 Oct • WORDS Boyzone Writers: Robin, Barry and Maurice Gibb. Producers: Phil Harding and Ian Curnow. ◆✪

749. 26 Oct •• SAY YOU'LL BE THERE Spice Girls Writers: Spice Girls and Eliot Kennedy. Producers: Andy Watkins and Paul Wilson. **US peak: 3.** ◆✪

750. 9 Nov •• WHAT BECOMES OF THE BROKEN HEARTED / SATURDAY NIGHT AT THE MOVIES / YOU'LL NEVER WALK ALONE Robson Green and Jerome Flynn Writers: James Dean, Paul Riser and William Weatherspoon / Barry Mann and Cynthia Weil / Richard Rodgers and Oscar Hammerstein II. Producers: Mike Stock and Matt Aitken. ◆●

751. 23 Nov •• BREATHE Prodigy Writers: Liam Howlett, Keith Flint and Maxim. Producer: Liam Howlett. ◆✪

752. 7 Dec • I FEEL YOU Peter Andre Writers: Peter Andre, Glen Goldsmith, Terry Jones and Oliver Jacobs. Producers: Cutfather and Joe. ◆⊙

753. 14 Dec • A DIFFERENT BEAT Boyzone Writers: Ronan Keating, Stephen Gately, Shane Lynch, Keith Duffy, Ray Hedges and Martin Brannigan Producer: Ray Hedges ◆●

754. 21 Dec • KNOCKIN' ON HEAVEN'S DOOR / THROW THESE GUNS AWAY Dunblane Writers: Bob Dylan / Edward Christopher and Thomas Millar. Producer: Peter Cobbin. ❶◆●

755. 28 Dec ••• 2 BECOME 1 Spice Girls Writers: Spice Girls, Richard Stannard and Matt Rowe. Producers: Richard Stannard and Matt Rowe **US peak: 4.** ◆✪

1997

756. 18 Jan • PROFESSIONAL WIDOW (IT'S GOT TO BE BIG) Tori Amos Writer: Tori Amos. Producer: Tori Amos.

757. 25 Jan • YOUR WOMAN White Town Writer: Jyoti Mishra. Producer: Jyoti Mishra. **US peak: 23.** ◆⊙

1997: LL Cool J means Ladies Love Cool James

758. 1 Feb • BEETLEBUM Blur Writers: Damon Albarn, Graham Coxon, Alex James and Dave Rowntree. Producer: Stephen Street. ◆

759. 8 Feb • AIN'T NOBODY LL Cool J Writers: David Wolinski. Producer: Rashaad Smith. **US peak: 46.** ◆

760. 15 Feb • DISCOTHEQUE U2 Writers: Bono, The Edge, Adam Clayton, Larry Mullen and Simon Pyke. Producer: Mark Ellis (aka Flood). **US peak: 10.** ◆⊙

761. 22 Feb ••• DON'T SPEAK No Doubt Writers: Gwen Stefani and Eric Stefani. Producer: Matthew Wilder. ◆●

762. 15 Mar ••• MAMA / WHO DO YOU THINK YOU ARE Spice Girls Writers: Spice Girls, Richard Stannard, Matt Rowe / Spice Girls, Andy Watson and Paul Wilson. Producers: Richard Stannard, Matt Rowe / Andy Watkins and Paul Wilson. ◆✪

763. 5 Apr • BLOCK ROCKIN' BEATS Chemical Brothers Writers: Tom Rowlands, Ed Simons and Jesse Weaver. Producers: Chemical Brothers. ◆

764. 12 Apr ••• I BELIEVE I CAN FLY R Kelly Writer: R Kelly. Producer: R Kelly. **US peak: 2.** ✪

765. 3 May • BLOOD ON THE DANCE FLOOR Michael Jackson Writers: Michael Jackson and Teddy Riley. Producers: Michael Jackson and Teddy Riley. **US peak: 42.** ◆

766. 10 May • LOVE WON'T WAIT Gary Barlow Writers: Madonna and Shep Pettibone. Producer: Stephen Lipson. ◆⊙

767. 17 May •• YOU'RE NOT ALONE Olive Writers: Tim Kellett and Robin Taylor-Firth. Producers: Robin Taylor-Firth and Tim Kellett. **US peak: 56.** ◆

768. 31 May • I WANNA BE THE ONLY ONE Eternal featuring BeBe Winans Writers: BeBe Winans and James Lawrence. Producers: Dennis Charles and Ronnie Wilson. ◆●

769. 07 Jun ••• MMMBOP Hanson Writers: Isaac, Taylor and Zach Hanson. Producers: Dust Brothers and Stephen Lironi. **US peak: 1.** ◆✪

770. 28 Jun ••• 26 Jul ••• I'LL BE MISSING YOU Puff Daddy and Faith Evans (featuring 112) Writer: Sting. Producers: Sean Combs and Stevie J. **US peak: 1.** ◆

771. 19 Jul • D'YOU KNOW WHAT I MEAN? Oasis Writer: Noel Gallagher. Producers: Owen Morris and Noel Gallagher. ◆✪

772. 16 Aug •••• MEN IN BLACK Will Smith Writers: Will Smith, Patrice Rushen, Terry McFadden and Fred Washington. Producers: Poke and Tone. ◆✪

773. 13 Sep • THE DRUGS DON'T WORK Verve Writer: Richard Ashcroft. Producers: Martin "Youth" Glover and The Verve. ◆⊙

774. 20 Sep ••••• CANDLE IN THE WIND 1997 / SOMETHING ABOUT THE WAY YOU LOOK TONIGHT Elton John Writers: Elton John and Bernie Taupin. Producer: George Martin / Chris Thomas. **US peak: 1.** ◆✪✪✪✪✪✪✪✪

775. 25 Oct • SPICE UP YOUR LIFE Spice Girls Writers: Spice Girls, Richard Stannard and Matt Rowe. Producers: Richard Stannard and Matt Rowe. **US peak: 18.** ◆✪

776. 1 Nov •••• BARBIE GIRL Aqua Writers: Soren Rasted, Claus Noreen, Rene Dif and Lene Nykstrom. Producers: Johnny Jam, Delgado, Soren Rasted and Claus Noreen. **US peak: 7.**

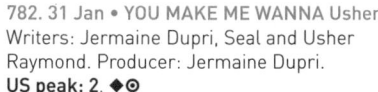

777. 29 Nov •• 10 Jan 1998 • PERFECT DAY Various Writer: Lou Reed. Producers: Mark Sayer-Wade,Tolga Kashif (The Music Sculptors) and Simon Hanhart. ◆✪✪

778. 13 Dec •• TELETUBBIES SAY EH-OH! Teletubbies Writers: Andrew McCrorie-Shand and Andrew Davenport. Producers: Andrew McCrorie-Shand and Steve James. ◆✪✪

779. 27 Dec •• TOO MUCH Spice Girls Writers: Spice Girls, Andy Watkins and Paul Wilson. Producers: Andy Watkins and Paul Wilson. **US peak: 9.** ◆✪

1998

780. 17 Jan • NEVER EVER All Saints Writers: Rickidy Raw and Shaznay Lewis. Producers: Cameron McVey and Magnus Fiennes. **US peak: 4.** ⊙

781. 24 Jan • ALL AROUND THE WORLD Oasis Writer: Noel Gallagher. Producers: Owen Morris and Noel Gallagher. ◆

782. 31 Jan • YOU MAKE ME WANNA Usher Writers: Jermaine Dupri, Seal and Usher Raymond. Producer: Jermaine Dupri. **US peak: 2.** ◆⊙

783. 7 Feb •• DOCTOR JONES Aqua Writers: Soren Rasted, Claus Noreen, Rene Dif and Lene Nykstrom. Producers: Johnny Jam, Delgado, Soren Rasted and Claus Noreen. ◆✪✪

784. 21 Feb • 14 Mar • MY HEART WILL GO ON Celine Dion Writers: James Horner and Will Jennings. Producers: Walter Afanasieff and James Horner. **US peak: 1.** ◆

785. 28 Feb • BRIMFUL OF ASHA Cornershop Writer: Tjinder Singh. Producer: Tjinder Singh; re-mixed by Norman Cook. ◆●

786. 7 Mar • FROZEN Madonna Writers: Madonna and Patrick Leonard. Producers: Madonna, William Orbit and Patrick Leonard. **US peak: 2.** ◆●

1998: **Aqua originally went under the name Joyspeed**

787. 21 Mar •••••• IT'S LIKE THAT Run-DMC vs Jason Nevins Writers: Joseph Simmons, Darryl McDaniels and Lawrence Smith. Producers: Joseph Simmons and Larry Smith, additional production and re-mix by Jason Nevins. ◆✪

788. 2 May • ALL THAT I NEED Boyzone Writers: Carl Sturken and Evan Rogers. Producers: Carl Sturken and Evan Rogers. ◆

789. 9 May • 23 May • UNDER THE BRIDGE / LADY MARMALADE All Saints Writers: Anthony Kiedis, Michael Balzary, John Frusciante and Chad Smith / Bob Crewe and Kenny Nolan. Producers: Nellee Hooper and Karl Gordon / Jonny Douglas and John Benson. ◆

790. 16 May • TURN BACK TIME Aqua Writers: Soren Rasted; Claus Noreen, Rene Dif and Lene Nykstrom. Producers: Johnny Jam, Delgado, Soren Rasted and Claus Noreen. ◆

791. 30 May • FEEL IT Tamperer featuring Maya Writers: Michael Jackson and Jackie Jackson. Producers: Alex Farolfi and Mario Fargetta. ⊙

792. 6 Jun •• C'EST LA VIE B*Witched Writers: B*Witched, Ray Hedges, Tracey Ackerman and Martin Brannigan. Producer: Ray Hedges. **US peak: 9.** ◆⊙

793. 20 Jun ••• 3 LIONS '98 Baddiel and Skinner and Lightning Seeds Writers: Ian Broudie, David Baddiel and Frank Skinner. Producer: Ian Broudie. ◆✪

794. 11 Jul • BECAUSE WE WANT TO Billie Writers: Dion Rambo, Jacques Richmond, Wendy Page and Jim Marr. Producers: Jim Marr and Wendy Page. ◆⊙

795. 18 Jul • FREAK ME Another Level Writers: Roy Murray and Keith Sweat. Producer: Fitzgerald Scott. ◆

796. 25 Jul • DEEPER UNDERGROUND Jamiroquai Writers: Jason Kay and Toby Smith. Producer: Jay Kay. ◆

797. 1 Aug •• VIVA FOREVER Spice Girls Writers: Spice Girls, Richard Stannard and Matt Rowe. Producers: Richard Stannard and Matt Rowe. ◆✪

798. 15 Aug ••• NO MATTER WHAT Boyzone Writers: Andrew Lloyd Webber and Jim Steinman. Producers: Jim Steinman, Andrew Lloyd Webber and Nigel Wright. ◆●

799. 5 Sep • IF YOU TOLERATE THIS YOUR CHILDREN WILL BE NEXT Manic Street Preachers Writers: James Dean Bradfield, Sean Moore and Nick Jones. Producer: Dave Eringa. ◆⊙

800. 12 Sep • BOOTIE CALL All Saints Writers: Shaznay Lewis and Karl Gordon. Producer: Karl Gordon. ◆●

801. 19 Sep • MILLENNIUM Robbie Williams Writers: Robbie Williams, Guy Chambers, John Barry and Leslie Bricusse. Producers: Guy Chambers and Steve Power. ◆●

802. 26 Sep • I WANT YOU BACK Melanie B featuring Missy 'Misdemeanor' Elliott Writers: Missy Elliott, Gerard Thomas and Donald Holmes. Producers: Missy Elliott, Gerald Thomas and Gerald Holmes. ◆⊙

803. 3 Oct 98 •• ROLLERCOASTER B*Witched Writers: B*Witched, Ray Hedges, Tracey Ackerman, Martin Brannigan. Producer: Ray Hedges. ◆✪

804. 17 Oct • GIRLFRIEND Billie Writers: Dion Rambo and Jacques Richmond. Producers: Jim Marr and Wendy Page. ◆⊙

805. 24 Oct • GYM AND TONIC Spacedust Writers: Spacedust. Producers: Duncan Glasson and Paul Glancy. ◆⊙

806. 31 Oct ••••••• BELIEVE Cher Writers: Brian Higgins, Paul Barry, Steve Torch, Matt Gray, Stuart McLennen and Timothy Powell. Producers: Mark Taylor and Brian Rawling. **US peak: 1**. ◆✪✪

807. 19 Dec • TO YOU I BELONG B*Witched Writers: B*Witched, Ray Hedges, Tracey Ackerman, Martin Brannigan. Producer: Ray Hedges. ◆

808. 26 Dec • GOODBYE Spice Girls Writers: Spice Girls, Richard Stannard and Matt Rowe. Producers: Richard Stannard and Matt Rowe. **US peak: 11**. ◆✪

1999

809. 2 Jan • CHOCOLATE SALTY BALLS (PS I LOVE YOU) Chef Writer: Trey Parker. Producer: Rick Rubin. ✪

810. 9 Jan • HEARTBEAT / TRAGEDY Steps Writers: Jackie James / Barry, Maurice and Robin Gibb. Producers: Dan Frampton and Pete Waterman / Mark Topham, Karl Twigg and Paul Waterman. ✪

811. 16 Jan • PRAISE YOU Fatboy Slim Writers: Norman Cook and Camille Yarborough. Producer: Fatboy Slim. **US peak: 36**. ◆⊙

812. 23 Jan • A LITTLE BIT MORE 911 Writer: Bobby Gosh. Producers: Trevor Steel and John Holliday. ◆⊙

813. 30 Jan • PRETTY FLY (FOR A WHITE GUY) Offspring Writers: Dexter Holland, Robert John "Mutt" Lange, Joe Elliott and Steve Clark. Producer: Dave Jerdan. **US peak: 53**. ◆

814. 6 Feb • YOU DON'T KNOW ME Armand Van Helden featuring Duane Harden Writers: Armand Van Helden and Duane Harden. Producer: Armand Van Helden. ◆⊙

815. 13 Feb • MARIA Blondie Writer: Jimmy Destri. Producer: Craig Leon. **US peak: 82**. ◆

816. 20 Feb • FLY AWAY Lenny Kravitz Writer: Lenny Kravitz. Producer: Lenny Kravitz. **US peak: 12**. ◆⊙

817. 27 Feb •• BABY ONE MORE TIME Britney Spears Writer: Max Martin. Producers: Max Martin and Rami Yacoub. **US peak: 1**. ◆⊙

818. 13 Mar •• WHEN THE GOING GETS TOUGH Boyzone Writers: Wayne Braithwaite, Barry Eastmond, Mutt Lange and Billy Ocean. Producer: Steve Mac. ◆✪

819. 27 Mar • BLAME IT ON THE WEATHERMAN B*Witched Writers: Ray Hedges, Tracey Ackerman, Martin Brannigan and Andy Caine. Producer: Ray Hedges. ◆

820. 3 Apr •• FLAT BEAT Mr Oizo Writer: Quentin Dupieux. Producer: Quentin Dupieux. ◆✪

821. 17 Apr •• PERFECT MOMENT Martine McCutcheon Writers: Wendy Page and Jim Marr. Producer: Tony Moran. ◆●

822. 1 May •• SWEAR IT AGAIN Westlife Writers: Steve Mac and Wayne Hector. Producer: Steve Mac. **US peak: 20**. ◆●

823. 15 May • I WANT IT THAT WAY Backstreet Boys Writers: Max Martin and Andreas Carlsson. Producers: Max Martin and Kristian Lundin. **US peak: 6**. ◆⊙

1999: Ricky Martin had a trans atlantic chart-topper that shook everybody's bon bons and stayed on the chart for 17 weeks

824. 22 May • YOU NEEDED ME Boyzone Writer: Randy Goodrum. Producer: Steve Mac. ◆●

825. 29 May •• SWEET LIKE CHOCOLATE Shanks & Bigfoot Writers: Stephen Meade and Daniel Langsman. Producers: Shanks & Bigfoot. ◆✪

826. 12 Jun • EVERYBODY'S FREE (TO WEAR SUNSCREEN) Baz Luhrmann Writers: Tim Cox, Nigel Swanston and Mary Schmich. Producer: Nellee Hooper. ◆●

827. 19 Jun • BRING IT ALL BACK S Club 7 Writers: Elliot Kennedy, Mike Percy, Tim Lever and S Club 7. Producers: Eliot Kennedy, Mike Percy and Tim Lever. ◆✪

828. 26 Jun • BOOM, BOOM, BOOM, BOOM!! Vengaboys Writers: Dennis Van Den Driessen and Wessel Van Diepen. Producers: Danski and DJ Delmundo. **US peak: 84.** ●

829. 03 Jul •• (9PM) TILL I COME ATB Writers: Andre Tanneberger, Arcos Ferrerons, Gilabert Posadas and Garrido Rivera. Producer: Andre Tanneberger. ◆✪

830. 17 Jul ••• LIVIN' LA VIDA LOCA Ricky Martin Writers: Robi Rosa and Desmond Child. Producers: Desmond Child and Robi Rosa. **US peak: 1.** ◆✪

831. 07 Aug •• WHEN YOU SAY NOTHING AT ALL Ronan Keating Writers: Paul Overstreet and Don Schlitz. Producer: Stephen Lipson. ◆●

832. 21 Aug • IF I LET YOU GO Westlife Writers: Jorgen Elofsson, Per Magnusson and David Kreuger. Producers: Per Magnusson and David Kreuger. ◆⊙

833. 28 Aug • MI CHICO LATINO Geri Halliwell Writers: Geri Halliwell, Paul Wilson and Andy Watkins. Producers: Paul Wilson and Andy Watkins. ◆⊙

834. 04 Sep •• MAMBO NO.5 (A LITTLE BIT OF...) Lou Bega Writers: Perez Prado, David LuBega and Christian Pletschacher. Producers: Frank Leo, Lou Bega, Donald Fact and Zippy Davids. **US peak: 3.** ◆

835. 18 Sep • WE'RE GOING TO IBIZA! Vengaboys Writers: Jeff Calvert and Geraint Hughes. Producers: Danski and DJ Delmundo. ◆●

836. 25 Sep ••• BLUE (DA BA DEE) Eiffel 65 Writers: Massimo Gabutti, Maurizio Lobina and Gianfranco Randone. Producers: Massimo Etabucci and Luciano Zucchet. **US peak: 6.** ◆

837. 16 Oct •• GENIE IN A BOTTLE Christina Aguilera Writers: Steve Kipner, David Frank and Pam Sheyne. Producers: Steve Kipner and David Frank. **US peak: 1.** ◆

838. 30 Oct • FLYING WITHOUT WINGS Westlife Writers: Steve Mac and Wayne Hector. Producer: Steve Mac. ◆

839. 06 Nov • KEEP ON MOVIN' Five Writers: Richard Stannard, Julian Gallagher, Jay Brown, Abs Breen and Sean Conlon. Producers: Richard Stannard and Julian Gallagher. ◆⊙

840. 13 Nov • LIFT ME UP Geri Halliwell Writers: Geri Halliwell, Tracey Ackerman, Andy Watkins and Paul Wilson. Producers: Paul Wilson and Andy Watkins. ◆ ⊙

841. 20 Nov • SHE'S THE ONE / IT'S ONLY US Robbie Williams Writers: Karl Wallinger / Guy Chambers and Steve Power. Producers: Guy Chambers and Steve Power. ◆●

842. 27 Nov • KING OF THE CASTLE Wamdue Project Writer: Chris Brann. Producer: Chris Brann. ◆●

843. 04 Dec ••• THE MILLENNIUM PRAYER Cliff Richard Writers: Traditional, arranged by Paul Field and Stephen Deal. Producer: Nigel Wright. ✪✪

844. 25 Dec •••• I HAVE A DREAM / SEASONS IN THE SUN Westlife Writers: Benny Andersson and Björn Ulvaeus / Jacques Brel and Rod McKuen. Producers: Dan Frampton and Pete Waterman / Mark Topham, Karl Twigg. ◆✪

2000

845. 22 Jan • THE MASSES AGAINST THE CLASSES Manic Street Preachers Writers: James Dean Bradfield, Sean Moore and Nick Jones. Producer: Dave Eringa. ◆

846. 29 Jan • BORN TO MAKE YOU HAPPY Britney Spears Writers: Kristian Lundin and Andreas Carlsson. Producer: Kristian Lundin. ◆

847. 05 Feb •• RISE Gabrielle Writers: Bob Dylan, Louise Bobb, Ferdy Under-Hamilton and Ollie Dagois. Producer: Johnny Dollar. ◆●

848. 19 Feb • GO LET IT OUT Oasis Writer: Noel Gallagher. Producers: Noel Gallagher and Mark Stent. ◆⊙

849. 26 Feb •• PURE SHORES All Saints Writers: Shaznay Lewis and William Orbit. Producer: William Orbit. ◆✪

850. 11 Mar • AMERICAN PIE Madonna Writers: Don McLean. Producers: William Orbit and Madonna **US peak: 29.** ◆●

851. 18 Mar • DON'T GIVE UP Chicane featuring Bryan Adams Writers: Nick Bracegirdle, Bryan Adams and Ray Hedges. Producers: Chicane and Ray Hedges. ◆⊙

852. 25 Mar • BAG IT UP Geri Halliwell Writers: Geri Halliwell, Paul Wilson and Andy Watkins. Producers: Paul Wilson and Andy Watkins. ◆⊙

853. 1 Apr • NEVER BE THE SAME AGAIN Melanie C / Lisa 'Left Eye' Lopes Writers: Melanie Chisholm, Rhett Lawrence, Lisa Lopes and Paul Cruz. Producer: Rhett Lawrence. ◆●

854. 8 Apr • FOOL AGAIN Westlife Writers: Jorgen Elofsson, Per Magnusson and David Kreuger. Producers: Per Magnusson and David Kreuger. ◆

855. 15 Apr • FILL ME IN Craig David Writers: Craig David and Mark Hill. Producer: Mark Hill. **US peak: 15** ◆●

856. 22 Apr •• TOCA'S MIRACLE Fragma, vocals by Coco Writers: Ramon Zenker, Dirk Duderstadt, Marco Duderstadt, Victor Imbres and Rob Davis. Producer: Ramon Zenker. **US peak: 99.** ◆●

857. 6 May • BOUND 4 DA RELOAD (CASUALTY) Oxide & Neutrino Writers: Alex Rivers, Kenneth Freeman and Mark Oseitutu. Producers: Alex Rivers (DJ Oxide) and Mark Oseitutu (MC Neutrino). ◆⊙

858. 13 May • OOPS! ... I DID IT AGAIN Britney Spears Writers: Max Martin and Rami Yacoub. Producers: Max Martin and Rami Yacoub. **US peak: 9.** ◆⊙

859. 20 May • DON'T CALL ME BABY Madison Avenue Writers: Cheyne Coates, Andy Van Dorsselaer, Duane Morrison and Guiseppe Chierchia. Producers: Andy van Dorsselaer and Cheyne Coates. **US peak: 88.** ◆

860. 27 May • DAY & NIGHT Billie Piper Writers: Eliot Kennedy, Tim Lever, Billie Piper and Mark Cawley. Producers: Eliot Kennedy, Tim Lever and Mike Percy. ◆⊙

861. 3 Jun ••• IT FEELS SO GOOD Sonique Writers: Sonia Clarke, Simon Belofsky, Graeme Pleeth and Linus Burdick. Producers: Sonia Clarke, Simon Belofsky and Graeme Pleeth. **US peak: 8.** ◆

862. 24 Jun • YOU SEE THE TROUBLE WITH ME Black Legend Writers: Barry White and Ray Parker Jr. Producers: Jackie Reverse and Enrico Ferrari. ◆⊙

863. 1 Jul • SPINNING AROUND Kylie Minogue Writers: Ira Shickman, Dinky Bingham, Kara DioGuardi and Paula Abdul. Producer: Mike Spencer. ◆⊙

864. 8 Jul • THE REAL SLIM SHADY Eminem Writers: Marshall Mathers, Andre Young and Melvin Bradfield. Producers: Dr Dre and Mel Bradford **US peak: 4.** ◆⊙

2000: LeAnn Rimes recorded her first album 'After All' aged 11

865. 15 Jul • BREATHLESS Corrs Writers: Robert John "Mutt" Lange and Corrs. Producers: Robert John "Mutt" Lange. **US peak: 34.** ◆⊙

866. 22 Jul • LIFE IS A ROLLERCOASTER Ronan Keating Writers: Rick Nowels and Gregg Alexander. Producers: Rick Nowels and Gregg Alexander. ◆●

867. 29 Jul • WE WILL ROCK YOU Five and Queen Writers: Brian May, Abs Breen and Jay Brown. Producers: Richard Stannard, Brian May and Julian Gallagher. ◆

868. 5 Aug • 7 DAYS Craig David Writers: Craig David, Mark Hill and Darren Hill. Producer: Mark Hill. **US peak: 33.** ◆

869. 12 Aug • ROCK DJ Robbie Williams Writers: Robbie Williams, Guy Chambers, Kelvin Andrews, Nelson Pigford and Ekundayo Paris. Producers: Guy Chambers and Steve Power. ◆✪

870. 19 Aug • I TURN TO YOU Melanie C Writers: Melanie Chisholm, Rick Nowels and Billy Steinberg. Producer: Rick Nowels. ◆⊙

871. 26 Aug • GROOVEJET (IF THIS AIN'T LOVE) Spiller, lead vocals by Sophie Ellis-Bextor Writers: Cristiano Spiller, Sophie Ellis-Bextor, Robert Davis, Vince Montana Jr and Ron Walker. Producer: Cristiano Spiller and Boris Dlugosch. ❶◆●

872. 2 Sep • MUSIC Madonna Writers: Madonna Ciccone and Mirwais Ahmadzai. Producers: Madonna and Mirwais Ahmadzai. **US peak: 1.** ◆●

873. 9 Sep • TAKE ON ME A1 Writers: Pal Waaktaar, Mags Furuholmen and Morten Harket. Producers: Graham Stack and Mark Taylor. ◆

874. 16 Sep •• LADY (HEAR ME TONIGHT) Modjo Writers: Yann Destagnol, Romain Tranchart, Nile Rodgers and Bernard Edwards. Producers: Yann Destagnol and Romain Tranchart. **US peak: 81.** ◆●

875. 30 Sep •• AGAINST ALL ODDS Mariah Carey and Westlife Writer: Phil Collins. Producers: Mariah Carey and Steve Mac. ◆⊙

876. 14 Oct • BLACK COFFEE All Saints Writers: Tom Nichols, Alexander Soos and Kirsty Elizabeth Roper. Producer: William Orbit. ◆●

877. 21 Oct • BEAUTIFUL DAY U2 Writers: Adam Clayton, David Evans, Paul Hewson and Larry Mullen. Producers: Daniel Lanois and Brian Eno. **US peak: 21.** ◆⊙

878. 28 Oct • STOMP Steps Writers: Mark Topham, Karl Twigg and Rita Campbell. Producers: Mark Topham, Karl Twigg and Paul Waterman. ◆

879. 4 Nov • HOLLER / LET LOVE LEAD THE WAY Spice Girls Writers: Rodney Jerkins, LeShawn Daniels, Fred Jerkins III and Spice Girls / Same writers plus Harvey Mason Jr. Producers: Rodney Jerkins / Rodney Jerkins and Harvey Mason Jr. ◆⊙

880. 11 Nov • MY LOVE Westlife Writers: Pelle Nylen, Per Magnusson, David Kreuger and Jorgan Elofsson. Producers: Per Magnusson and David Kreuger. ◆

881. 18 Nov • SAME OLD BRAND NEW YOU A1 Writers: Eric Foster White, Ben Adams, Mark Read and Christian Ingebrigtsen. Producer: Eric Foster White. ◆

882. 25 Nov • CAN'T FIGHT THE MOONLIGHT LeAnn Rimes Writer: Diane Warren. Producer: Trevor Horn. **US peak: 71.** ◆●

883. 2 Dec • INDEPENDENT WOMEN PART 1 Destiny's Child Writers: Samuel Barnes, Jean Oliver, Cory Rooney and Beyoncé Knowles. Producers: Olivier Jean (Poke) and Sam Barnes (Tone), Cory Rooney and Beyoncé Knowles. **US peak: 1.** ◆●

884. 9 Dec • NEVER HAD A DREAM COME TRUE S CLUB 7 Writers: Cathy Dennis and Simon Ellis. Producers: Cathy Dennis, Oskar Paul and Stephen Lipson. **US peak: 10.** ◆●

885. 16 Dec • STAN Eminem Writers: Marshall Mathers, Dido Armstrong and Paul Herman. Producer: Mark James. **US peak: 51.** ◆✪

886. 23 Dec ••• CAN WE FIX IT Bob the Builder Writer: Paul K. Joyce. Producer: Grant Mitchell. ❶✪

2001

887. 13 Jan • TOUCH ME Rui Da Silva featuring Cassandra. Writers: Rui Da Silva and Cassandra Fox. Producer: Rui Da Silva. ◆❶⊙

888. 20 Jan • LOVE DON'T COST A THING Jennifer Lopez Writers: Damon Sharpe, Greg Lawson, Georgetta Franklin, Jeremy Monroe

and Amii Harris. Producer: Ric Wake. **US peak: 3.** ◆⊙

889. 27 Jan •• ROLLIN' Limp Bizkit Writers: Wes Borland, Sam Rivers, John Otto and Fred Durst. Producer: Terry Date. **US peak: 65.** ◆⊙

890. 10 Feb •••• WHOLE AGAIN Atomic Kitten Writers: Stuart Kershaw, Andy McCluskey, Bill Padley and Jim Godfrey. Producers: Engine. ◆✪

891. 10 Mar • IT WASN'T ME Shaggy featuring Ricardo "Rikrok" Ducent Writers: Orville Burrell, Ricardo Ducent, Shaun Pizzonia and Brian Thompson. Producer: Shaun Pizzonia. **US peak: 1.** ◆✪

892. 17 Mar • UPTOWN GIRL Westlife Writer: Billy Joel. Producer: Steve Mac. ◆✪

893. 24 Mar ••• PURE AND SIMPLE Hear'Say Writers: Pete Kirtley, Tim Hawes and Alison Clarkson. Producers: Pete Kirtley and Tim Hawes (Jiant). ◆✪

894. 14 Apr •• WHAT TOOK YOU SO LONG Emma Bunton Writers: Martin Harrington, Richard Stannard, Julian Gallagher, Emma Bunton, John Themis and David Morgan. Producers: Richard Stannard and Julian Gallagher. ◆⊙

895. 28 Apr • SURVIVOR Destiny's Child Writers: Beyoncé Knowles, Anthony Dent, Matthew Knowles. Producers: Anthony Dent and Beyoncé Knowles. **US peak: 2.** ◆⊙

896. 5 May • 26 May • DON'T STOP MOVIN' S Club 7 Writers: Simon Ellis, Shephard Solomon and S Club 7. Producer: Simon Ellis. ◆✪

897. 12 May •• IT'S RAINING MEN Geri Halliwell Writers: Paul Jabara and Paul Shaffer. Producer: Stephen Lipson. ◆●

898. 2 Jun • DO YOU REALLY LIKE IT DJ Pied Piper and the Masters of Ceremonies Writers: Eugene and Ronald Mwohia, Steve Wickham, Paul Newman and Ashley Livingstone. Producers: Eugene and Ronald Mwohia. ◆●❶

899. 9 Jun ••• ANGEL Shaggy featuring Rayvon Writers: Orville Burrell, Ahmet Ertegun, Eddie Curtis, Chip Taylor, Ricardo Ducent, Nigel Staff, Shaun Pizzonia, Dave Kelly and Steve Miller. Producer: Shaun Pizzonia. **US peak: 1.** ◆✪

2001: Blue secured two No.1 hits and were nominated for two 2002 Brit Awards

900. 30 Jun • LADY MARMALADE Christina Aguilera, Lil' Kim, Mya and Pink Writers: Bob Crewe and Kenny Nolan. Producers: Ron Fair, Missy Elliott and Dana Stinson. **US peak: 1.** ◆●

901. 7 Jul • WAY TO YOUR LOVE Hear'Say Writers: Mikkel S Eriksen, Hallgeir Rustan and Tor Erik Hermansen. Producers: Mikkel S Eriksen, Hallgeir Rustan and Tor Erik Hermansen (Stargate). ◆

902. 14 Jul • ANOTHER CHANCE Roger Sanchez Writers: Roger Sanchez and Steve Lukather. Producer: Roger Sanchez. ◆⊙

903. 21 Jul •• ETERNITY / ROAD TO MANDALAY Robbie Williams Writers: Robbie Williams and Guy Chambers. Producers: Guy Chambers and Steve Power. ◆

904. 4 Aug •• ETERNAL FLAME Atomic Kitten Writers: Susanna Hoffs, Billy Steinberg and Tom Kelly. Producer: Andy Wright. ◆●

905. 18 Aug • 21 SECONDS So Solid Crew Writers: Dwayne Vincent, Ashley Walters, Jermaine Williams, Shane Neil, Lisa Maffia, Michael Harvey, Marvin Dawkins, Jason Moore, Darren Weir, Jason Phillips and Mahtari Aminu. Producer: Synth. ◆⊙

906. 25 Aug •• LET'S DANCE Five Writers: Martin Harrington, Ash Howes, Julian Gallagher, Richard Stannard, Richard Breen, Sean Conlon and Jason Brown. Producers: Richard Stannard and Julian Gallagher. ◆

907. 8 Sep • TOO CLOSE Blue Writers: Keir Gist, Darren Lighty, Robert Huggar, Raphael Brown, Robert Ford, Denzil Miller, James Moore, Kurt Walker and Lawrence Smith. Producer: Ray Ruffin. ◆⊙

908. 15 Sep • MAMBO NO.5 Bob the Builder Writers: Perez Prado, Lou Bega, Christian Pletschacher. Lyric adapted by Grant Mitchell and Graham Dickson. Producer: Grant Mitchell. ◆●

909. 22 Sep • HEY BABY (UHH, AHH) DJ Otzi Writers: Bruce Channel and Margaret Cobb. Producers: Klaus Biedermann, Claus Marcus and Christian Seitz. ◆✪

910. 29 Sep •••• CAN'T GET YOU OUT OF MY HEAD Kylie Minogue Writers: Cathy Dennis and Rob Davis. Producers: Cathy Dennis and Rob Davis. ◆✪

911. 27 Oct ••• BECAUSE I GOT HIGH Afroman Writer: Joseph Foreman. Producers: Joseph Foreman and Headfridge. **US peak: 13.** ◆❶●

912. 17 Nov • QUEEN OF MY HEART Westlife Writers: Steve McCutcheon, Wayne Hector, Steve Robson and John McLaughlin. Producer: Steve Mac. ◆⊙

913. 24 Nov • IF YOU COME BACK Blue Writers: Ray Ruffin, Nicole Formescu, Ian Hope and Lee Brennan. Producer: Ray Ruffin. ◆⊙

914. 1 Dec • HAVE YOU EVER S Club 7 Writers: Cathy Dennis, Andrew Frampton and Christopher Braide. Producer: Stephen Lipson. ◆

915. 8 Dec •• GOTTA GET THRU THIS Daniel Bedingfield Writer: Daniel Bedingfield. Producer: Daniel Bedingfield. ❶●◆

916. 22 Dec •• SOMETHIN' STUPID Robbie Williams and Nicole Kidman Writer: Carson C Parks. Producers: Guy Chambers and Steve Power. ◆⊙

STATISTICS 2001

British Hit Singles chart consultant Dave McAleer selects the points worth noting in a year in which the world's fastest changing chart finally slowed down a little. There were a dozen fewer chart-toppers than in 2000 and the average entry stayed longer

▶ The year may well be remembered as the year of *Popstars*, as around the world local winners of that very successful TV show helped to lift sales of both singles and albums. *Popstars* helped to create artists whose initial sales (in their country of origin) often surpassed those of any previous chart debutantes.

The UK was the only major territory to increase total record sales at a time when CDR copying and MP3 downloading affected world markets. Although, UK singles sales fell by 8 per cent overall, sales of four specific chart-toppers went through the roof. After a year in which only one single passed the 750,000 sales mark, it's good to see that a smash can still sell more than a million, with releases by both Shaggy and Hear'Say joining the seven-figure set and Kylie and Atomic Kitten also very close to the million mark. The Kittens and Destiny's Child showed there was still plenty of life left in the girl group format, while Westlife, Blue and Five proved that British-based boy bands were still tops. In the mixed group category S Club 7 and Steps continued to rack up Top 5 hits, and only time will tell whether Hear'Say will renew their season ticket to the top rungs of the chart.

Hitherto unknown dance acts still debuted at No.1 and, following an all-time low year, American rock bands made a strong comeback – grabbing four of the Top 5 slots one week. European acts lost some ground, while hip hop and rap had its best year yet, often monopolising the Top 20. Chart-toppers Afroman and the year's best-selling act Shaggy helped to brighten up the best sellers.

Solo acts were a little thin on the ground in 2001 – a state of affairs likely to change in 2002 thanks to *Pop Idol*. The year's leading ladies included a quartet of ex-Spice Girls and Australia's favourite female, Kylie Minogue, who proved that pop princesses, like boomerangs, can come back. The singing and swinging Robbie Williams remained the millennium's No.1 male in a year in which the two all-time leading acts, Elvis Presley and Cliff Richard, both added to their total chart weeks.

The success of British acts around the world improved in 2001, with better showings for UK-produced singles and albums in most territories, and hits from both rock stalwarts and more recent favourites such as Atomic Kitten, Craig David, Dido, Gorillaz, Radiohead, S Club 7 and Travis.

It's an eye opener to compare the world's two most important charts. In the US, 87 singles entered the Top 20 in 2001 compared with 342 in Britain, and of those UK entries 148 spent one week in the Top 20 compared with just two in the US. The average US hit spent 10 weeks in the Top 20 compared with less than three in the UK. When talking about the US singles chart it should be noted that total sales dropped by an amazing 41 per cent in 2001, making an overall drop of 72 per cent in the past 36 months. In the country where airplay alone can take a record to the top, sales reached an all-time low when a single topped the best sellers with sales below 20,000.

The UK Top 75 may be volatile, but with our weekly singles sales being the envy of every other country it is almost certainly the healthiest and most active chart in the world.

Shaggy - Most weeks on chart and biggest-selling artist in 2001

New singles released in 2001: 7,242
(6,414 in 2000)

Biggest-selling single in 2001:
'It Wasn't Me' Shaggy 1,150,000
(Can We Fix It by Bob the Builder with 853,151 in 2000)

Total No.1 hits in 2001: 31
(43 in 2000)

Most weeks on chart by any single in 2001:
'Pure and Simple' Hear'Say - 25 weeks
('Amazed' by Lonestar with 22 weeks in 2000)

New chart entries in 2001: 851
(846 in 2000)

Most weeks at No.1 in 2001:
4 'Whole Again' Atomic Kitten and 'Can't Get You Out of My Head' Kylie Minogue
(Westlife 3 and Sonique 3 in 2000)

Singles sales in 2001: 51.2 million
(55.7 million in 2000)

Biggest-selling act in 2001:
Shaggy - 1,910,000
(Westlife with 1,244,000 singles in 2000)

Most weeks on chart by any act in 2001: Shaggy 54 (Craig David with 58 in 2000)

Average first-week sales of a new No.1 in 2001: **141,500**
(119,753 in 2000)

▶ 2001 BEST SELLERS

Figures supplied by the The Official UK Charts Company

1.	**IT WASN'T ME** Shaggy featuring Ricardo "Rikrok" Ducent	1,150,000
2.	**PURE AND SIMPLE** Hear'Say	1,100,000
3.	**CAN'T GET YOU OUT OF MY HEAD** Kylie Minogue	990,000
4.	**WHOLE AGAIN** Atomic Kitten	940,000
5.	**HEY BABY (UHH, AHH)** DJ Otzi	750,000
6.	**UPTOWN GIRL** Westlife	745,000
7.	**DON'T STOP MOVIN'** S Club 7	700,000
8.	**ANGEL** Shaggy featuring Rayvon	590,000
9.	**TEENAGE DIRTBAG** Wheatus	550,000
10.	**BECAUSE I GOT HIGH** Afroman	490,000

▶ 2001 CHART STAYERS

By weeks on chart and peak positions. 75 points for a week at No.1, 74 for a week at No.2 and so on, down to one point for one week at the bottom chart position of No.75

1.	**WHOLE AGAIN** Atomic Kitten	1,315
2.	**TEENAGE DIRTBAG** Wheatus	1,189
3.	**HEY BABY (UHH, AHH)** DJ Otzi	1,131
4.	**IT WASN'T ME** Shaggy featuring Ricardo "Rikrok" Ducent	1,088
5.	**PURE AND SIMPLE** Hear'Say	1,058
6.	**DON'T STOP MOVIN'** S Club 7	1,045
7.	**CLINT EASTWOOD** Gorillaz	944
8.	**CAN'T GET YOU OUT OF MY HEAD** Kylie Minogue	935
9.	**ANGEL** Shaggy featuring Rayvon	874
10.	**CASTLES IN THE SKY** Ian Van Dahl	850

POP REVIEW OF THE YEAR

JANUARY

At the top of the chart, Rui Da Silva and Cassandra inject Ibizan warmth into winter with 'Touch Me'. Jennifer Lopez eyebrow-raisingly claims her 'Love Don't Cost a Thing', and Limp Bizkit become rock's rockingest with 'Rollin' (Air Raid Vehicle)'... Bizkit-esque boyband Linkin Park crash the UK chart with the limpet-like 'Hybrid Theory' album and Marilyn Manson plays dead live while his engagement to actress Rose McGowan unravels after two years. "There is great love, but our lifestyle difference is, unfortunately, even greater," declares Ms McGowan... Metallica are hobbled by the exit of bassist Jason Newsted after 14 years as "Jason New-Boy" but Def Leppard squeeze money from Madonna whose MadGuy Films finances a TV movie about the Sheffield superstars... Guns N' Roses and Oasis play the Rock in Rio festival at which Britney is captured swearing backstage... Fisticuffing Five lads Ritchie and J are remanded on bail after a Dublin pub punch-up in 2000... Madge steps out with new hubby Guy Ritchie at the LA premiere of *Snatch*, but otherwise pursues her new Anglocentric angle: reportedly having elocution lessons and being pestered by Lourdes to take tea with the Queen... Ash declare their desire to "wipe Westlife off the planet". Tim and Rick tell Radio 1: "They just stand around on cliffs looking like gimps"... When not standing around on cliffs looking like a gimp, Westlife's Bryan is propping up pillows for pregnant girlfriend Kerry, whose place in Atomic Kitten is taken by Jenny of Precious... A *Heat* magazine poll rates Robbie and Kylie the sexiest man and woman on the planet... Destiny's Child, Stevie Wonder, Mary J Blige and Whitney Houston help Wyclef Jean to raise money for the underprivileged at a New York gig. Of another star on the bill, Clef enthuses: "I love Charlotte Church – she's hot!"... Mary J Blige pops up again as part of Aerosmith's all-star rendition of 'Walk This Way' during the Superbowl, although Steven Tyler's eyes are on Britney Spears who, he enthuses to *Q*, was "wearing an Aerosmith T-shirt cut down to her yahoos! I tell you, these are the moments I live for"... While Britney scores Stateside with 'Stronger' and kickstarts a global ad campaign for Skechers trainers, her 'Baby One More Time' is revived to astonishing effect by Darius Danesh, most celebrated entrant in TV's wannabe showcase *Popstars*... In a troubled month for So Solid Crew, most of them are kept out of an over-subscribed party to launch the Dreem Teem's 'In Session' album, as are Usher and The Architechs... Posh and Becks are reportedly interested in buying an island, while 20-year-old Mark Oliver is found guilty of receiving items stolen from Posh's suitcase last year... Making a star of Kate Hudson (Mrs Chris Robinson of the Black Crowes), giving employment to Peter Frampton and reviving Elton John's 'Tiny Dancer', Cameron Crowe's movie *Almost Famous* opens over here... Steps announce plans to conquer the US... While the Beatles stay atop the album chart with '1', George Harrison predicts: "The planet is doomed"... soulster James Carr, best known for 'The Dark End of the Street', dies of cancer on the 7th... Jessica Michalik, 15, dies after a heart attack during Limp Bizkit's set in Sydney. "The loss of her life," state the band, "will impact ours forever."

January: Westlife remain unflustered by Ash's bashing on Radio 1

FEBRUARY

Risen from the ashes, Atomic Kitten go numero uno for four weeks with the slow-burning 'Whole Again'. Among the losers are Wheatus, whose 'Teenage Dirtbag' nonetheless becomes one of the year's top sellers and gives Iron Maiden another glimpse of fame via the song's name-checks. Other runners-up are U2 with 'Stuck in a Moment You Can't Get Out Of'... Bono and the boys reapply for the job of "the best band in the world" at a one-off gig at London's Astoria – and are rewarded for their "godlike genius" at the NME Carling awards, which also rates them best rock act. Coldplay win best new act, single ('Yellow') and Radio 1 session. The Evening Session wins Best Radio Show, Radiohead are Best Band and Eminem Best Hip Hop/Rap Act... Simulated shenanigans of the Ecstasy and chainsaw variety cause controversy as Eminem's tour hits Britain, while his gran pleads for peace on Radio 4: "I want to stop this war between us." Faring better is Elton John, who duets with Mr Mathers on 'Stan' at the Grammys. "I'd heard of Elton John," says Shady, "but I didn't know he was gay." An unruffled Elt responds, "I don't know what planet he must live on." At the ceremony, U2 bag three awards for 'Beautiful Day'... Two of the year's hypes hit the headlines: The Strokes make their UK live debut and *Popstars* picks the five finalists who become Hear'Say... Four months after its release, Dido's 'No Angel' tops the album chart on its way to becoming a multiplatinum monster. The late Eva Cassidy's three-year-old 'Songbird' heads the same way after her version of 'Over the Rainbow' is played on *TOTP2*. "I was sat there, tears rolling down," Ozzy Osbourne tells *Q*, "and ended up buying four copies of the CD." Toploader's 'Dancin' in the Moonlight' staggers into the Top 10 after 13 weeks on the chart and Outkast release their tribute to Erykah Badu's mom, 'Ms Jackson'... Madonna moots a duet with Pavarotti but nixes a rumoured hook-up with Britney, then beats the latter to Best International Female at the Brits. Westlife win Best British Pop Act, with *EastEnders*' Phil Mitchell embellishing their performance of 'Uptown Girl'. Robbie runs away with Best British Male, Best Video and Best British Single for 'Rock DJ' but is obliged to quash reports of romance with Geri: "I think the world of her but that's it, thanks very much." Ms Halliwell helpfully presents one of the Robster's trophies with: "According to the press he's been giving me one, so let me return the favour and give him one!" In an evening short on outrage, Noel Gallagher declares: "Over the years, these awards have been accused of not having a sense of humour. But when A1 win the Best Newcomer, you know someone has got to be taking the piss." Craig David returns home empty-handed, buoyed only by U2 – who win the Outstanding Contribution to British Music – dedicating 'One' to him... The Vengaboys are ordered to slice a shot of Westlife from their latest video... Starsailor enjoy the first of several successes with the Top 20 'Fever'... Britney's mum thinks the video for 'Don't Let Me Be the Last To Know', featuring frisky frolics with a male model, is too much, and tells her to ▶

> **"I was sat there, tears rolling down, and ended up buying four copies of the CD"**
> Ozzy Osbourne on Eva Cassidy's 'Over the Rainbow'

February: Two out of three kittens turn out for the presentation of their British Hit Singles No.1 awards for 'Whole Again'. Jen and Lil faced the cameras at HMV Oxford Street, London. Tash: we've still got your award, so give us a call!

tone it down. Meanwhile, her boyfriend **Justin Timberlake** and his **'N Sync** compadres team up with Bart's boy band **Party Posse** in **The Simpsons**... In an expensive month for **Pearl Jam** diehards, the Seattle survivors issue a bootlegger-battling 25 live albums... **Jennifer Lopez** is the first woman to top the US album and film charts at the same time, with 'J.Lo' and *The Wedding Planner* respectively... Guitarist **John Fahey** dies on the 22nd and the Glastonbury festival is cancelled after overcrowding last year.

WE'RE No1

Popstars ecstatic as they break Britney's record for first single

By POLLY GRAHAM

POPSTARS band Hear'Say last night spoke of their delight as their first single shot to Number One.

selling debut track ever. It smashed the record held by Britney Spears, whose first single Baby One More Time

Suzanne Shaw said: "I'm gobsmacked." Singer Noel Sullivan added: "It's absolutely amazing."

Colleague Myleene Klass said it was "living proof dreams can come true".

MARCH

Atop the chart, raunch replaces romance as **Atomic Kitten** give way to **Shaggy** and **Rikrok**'s anthemic 'It Wasn't Me'... **Westlife**'s Comic Relief cover of **Billy Joel**'s 'Uptown Girl' follows and wins the Westies their biggest first-week sales of 292,000... But that figure's eclipsed by **Hear'Say**, whose 549,823 in a week make 'Pure and Simple' the most successful debut single in chart history and the third fastest-selling behind 'Do They Know It's Christmas?' and 'Candle in the Wind'. 'Pure and Simple' marks a return to the top for one of its co-writers: cartoon coquette Alison "**Betty Boo**" Clarkson... Joining the Kittens, the Shagster and the Popstars among 2001's mega-sellers is the non-No.1 **'Clint Eastwood'** by **Damon Albarn**'s cartoon hip-hoppers **Gorillaz**. Anxious **Blur** fans are informed by bassist **Alex James**: "When Damon finishes with the Banana Splits, we'll do another Blur record"... **S Club 7** manager **Simon Fuller** plots Popstars II: *Pop Idol*... In a troubled month for rapular romance, **Kim Mathers** files for divorce from on-off-on hubby **Eminem** and, despite being found not guilty on a weapons charge, **Puff Daddy**'s dumped by **J.Lo**. Charitably, Puffy gives the gift of laughter by changing his name: "I'm rockin' with **P Diddy** now." Equally mirthfully, **Eminem**, **Snoop Dogg**, **Missy Elliott** and other rap acts promise not to use bad language or be offensive at the Black College Reunion festival in Florida... In a troubled month for indie types, **Manic Street Preachers** release two singles simultaneously and play live for Castro in Cuba but earn as many headlines as sales for their 'Know Your Enemy' album. **Neil Codling** leaves **Suede** and **At The Drive-In** announce an indefinite hiatus... Driving proves problematic for **Westlife** – whose Nicky emerges unscathed from a car crash in London – and **Madonna**, whose hubby-helmed 'What It Feels Like for a Girl' video features scenes of vehicular naughtiness... **The Avalanches** are the first recipients of an official blessing for a Madge sample when her highness approves their hijacking of 'Holiday' for 'Stay Another Season'... In a troubled month for pop, S Clubbers Bradley, Jon and Paul are arrested for possession of cannabis in London ("We have," they confess, "been very stupid") and **Westlife**'s Kian is beaten up in Dublin... 80,000 tickets for **U2**'s gig at Dublin's Slane Castle sell out in 45 minutes and their Elevation tour kicks off in Miami in front of fans including **Lenny Kravitz**, **Howie B** and **Pearl Jam**. Absent owing to glandular fever is support act **PJ Harvey**... **J.Lo** teams

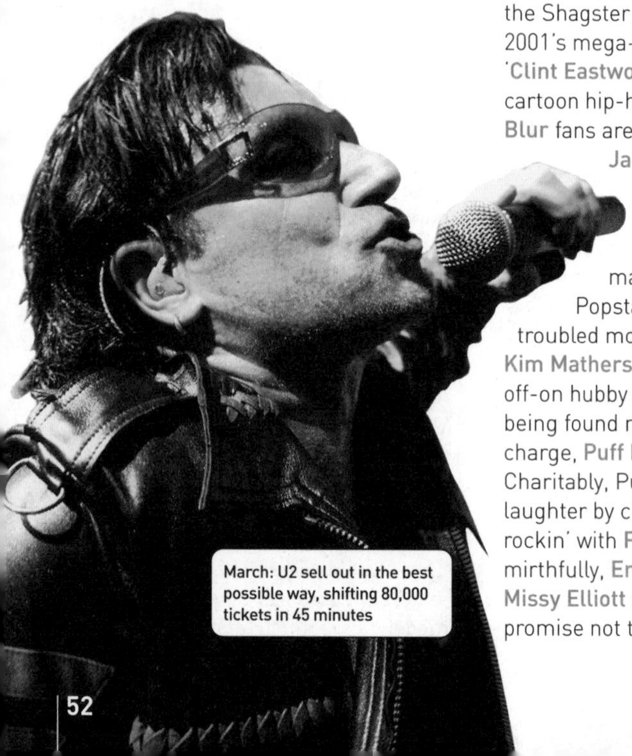

March: U2 sell out in the best possible way, shifting 80,000 tickets in 45 minutes

up with Andy Hilfiger, younger brother of Tommy, to launch a clothing line... Steps announce they have "absolutely no plans to split"... *NME* readers rate Robbie "villain of the year". Hero? L Gallagher, who may or may not be chortling when Williams is pushed offstage in Germany... Shania Twain is reported to be pregnant... "Childhood has become the great casualty of modern-day living," mourns Michael Jackson in an address to the Oxford Union... Sporting complementary robotic styling, Daft Punk and Aerosmith drop new albums, the former to more acclaim than the latter despite the Smiffs' hit 'Jaded'. Tyler and co are also inducted into the Rock and Roll Hall of Fame, as are Queen... Nelly Furtado gives the world 'Whoa, Nelly!' on the back of her hit 'I'm Like a Bird'... The grumpy 'Mr Writer' is another humongous hit for Stereophonics, who sell tickets by the truckload for summer stadium gigs... Britney stars in a Pepsi ad and starts filming a movie. Meanwhile, Justin Timberlake books slots in Brit's LA studio, fuelling rumours she wants him to go solo... In a tough month for the girls of Spice, Victoria endures a grilling from Ali G for the BBC's Comic Relief charity show and Geri's London flat is burgled by crims who graffiti the walls and steal £80,000 worth of property ...The Village People's biker Glenn Hughes succumbs to lung cancer on the 4th and heart failure claims The Mamas and the Papas' main man John Phillips on the 18th.

"When Damon finishes with the Banana Splits, we'll do another Blur record"
Alex James

APRIL

It's Girl Power at No.1, but not as we know it: baby Bunton slinks in with 'What Took You So Long', then Destiny's Child steamroller 'Survivor' to the top... Further down the chart but destined to linger longer in the ear is Missy Elliott's 'Get Ur Freak On', soon a must-have mobile ringtone... The Grand Dame of Girl Power – who's belatedly answering to the name Mrs Ritchie – ties with The Beatles for the most number of US gold singles by anyone who isn't Elvis. Even more spectacularly, 80,000 tickets sold in four hours and more than a thousand people camping outside London venue Earls Court testify to the box-office bonanza that is the Drowned World Tour... In a wimpy month for rock 'n' roll raucousness, R.E.M.'s Peter Buck is arrested after an alleged yoghurty incident on a flight to London, and Eminem – erroneously rumoured to be dating Beyoncé of Destiny's Child – is given two years' probation for possessing an illegal weapon... If they need help with legal fees, the door to knock on is the one marked Mariah, since she's just signed a multi-million-dollar deal with Virgin... Travis cover Queen's 'Killer Queen' and Robbie Williams is involved in what royal bassist John Deacon reportedly describes as "a really bad" cover of 'We Are the Champions'. Meanwhile, Rob's underwear goes under the hammer for charity. "Little Robbie did well in those pants," he promises... Westlife announce plans to work with Bryan Adams, while wedding bells start to ring for 'lifer Nicky and the daughter of the Irish prime minister... Ash keep Janet Jackson at bay as 'Free All Angels' edges ahead of 'All for You' in album sales. Comrades-in-crunch Feeder and Stereophonics make it three out of five for rock-rocking rock at the top of the chart, with Fear Factory's 'Digimortal' bringing up the rear... Mel B plays a Nelson Mandela tribute at London's Trafalgar Square, although more are there to see headliners R.E.M. Mel remains, however, a firm favourite ▶

April: Destiny's Child shower their fans in kisses

▶ with SisQo. "She ain't married no more, right?" he quizzes *Q*. "I would love to put The Dragon on her"... Sting is sued for breaking up a man's marriage – or so the story has it when he guests on *Ally McBeal*. Equally glamorously, Lee Steps appears in *Crossroads* as himself... Depeche Mode return with 'Dream On' and Guns N' Roses announce gigs for June – later postponed, then cancelled due to guitarist Buckethead feeling a bit poorly... Gabba gabba gone: lymphatic cancer claims Joey Ramone on the 15th... Charles and Eddie's Charles Pettigrew dies on the 6th.

▶ MAY

Spring has sprung and S Club 7 bloom at number one with 'Don't Stop Movin''. Then Geri's cover of the Weather Girls' 'It's Raining Men' flips its aerobicised arse to pole position – only for S Club to bounce back to the top... Craig David bags a hat-trick of Ivor Novello songwriting awards. All Saints also earn one for 'Pure Shores' although the band has ceased to exist... In a troubled month for So Solid Crew, associate Neutrino (as in Oxide and) is shot in the leg outside a London club... Papa Roach ride the crest of the metal revival, scoring another hit off the 'Infest' album with 'Between Angels and Insects' and dragging soon-to-be stars Alien Ant Farm over for a UK tour... Commercially moribund but still able to drop jaws at a thousand paces, Mötley Crüe confess all in their autobiography *The Dirt*... Dane Bowers pitches his songwriting weight aboard the Westlife wagon in a bid to break them Stateside. "Bryan can't dance," he allows, "but the rest are OK"... While the Aussie Family Association tries to prevent "equal opportunity offender" Slim Shady from touring Down Under, the Vatican asks Britney, Justin Timberlake and Faith Hill to read prayers on a CD accompanying the Pope's new books... Robbie tells a German news agency the Royal Family are robots... There's another bouncing Bono boy as the U2 singer becomes a father for the fourth time. He also finds time to speechify at Harvard University, pondering "Is wasting inspiration a crime?"... Travis make their live comeback after seven months, including a cover of Mott the Hoople's 'All the Young Dudes'... Oasis (remember them?) tour the States with the Black Crowes but without drummer Alan White, whose "hyper mobile thumb" obliges brother Steve to step up to the stool... Ricky Martin, Shaggy, Backstreet Boys and Christina Aguilera get gongs at the World Music Awards in Monte Carlo... Billie Piper marries Chris Evans in Las Vegas, while the *EastEnders* press office confirms actor Jack Ryder has found lurve with Kym Hear'Say... R.E.M. return with 'Imitation of Life' from the number one album 'Reveal'. The latter's release coincides with Michael Stipe's stop-it-the-suspense-is-killing-us confession that he's gay... The Stereo MCs stagger

May: S Club 7's 'Don't Stop Movin'' hits the top spot and will go on to bag the Record of the Year award in December

May: Mariah Carey puts on a brave face

previous two back into the chart... Björk premieres her 'Vespertine' album in New York... Anastacia guests on *Ally McBeal*... "I'm honestly really, really delirious and stressed out and overworked and doing too much," announces Mariah Carey from the middle of a promotional whirlwind. "This is a freaking complete clown fest..." ... No more Mr Nice Guy: crooner Perry Como passes away on the 12th and songwriter James Myers rocks around the clock no longer as of the 9th.

JUNE

Vying with 'It Wasn't Me' as the catchphrase of 2001, 'Do You Really Like It' pushes DJ Pied Piper and the Masters of Ceremony's "lovin' it, lovin' it, lovin' it" into the national consciousness. Shaggy and Rayvon hit back with 'Angel', whose parent album 'Hotshot' is number one too. (The latter also becomes the year's No.2 bestseller Stateside.) Then it's wave your knickers to their feet with 'Deep Down and Dirty' while Eddy Grant enjoys a renaissance with the remixed 'Electric Avenue', as does Paul McCartney with the transatlantic smash album 'Wingspan'... DMX's first lady of rap, Eve, makes good on her US success with the UK hit 'Who's That Girl' and the album 'Scorpion', the latter also the source of the Dr Dre-produced Gwen Stefani duet 'Let Me Blow Ya Mind'... Towering above everyone, Destiny's Child go platinum with the 'Survivor' album, bringing their in the air time as Christina Aguilera, Lil' Kim, Mya, Pink and Missy Elliott return 'Lady Marmalade' to No.1 a mere three years since it was there voulez-vousing with All Saints. As debate rages over Christina's latest image, Boy George tells *Q*: "She looks like the kind of girl I would have hung out with at school"... Missy plays what Teletext describes as "the most bonkers show ever in London" at the Brixton Academy, Hear'Say tour the UK and Barcelona gets the first glimpse of Madonna's cowpunk kung-fu live extravaganza... Another 80,000 tickets find good homes as U2's second Slane Castle gig sells out in 90 minutes... While his DJ, Uncle Kracker, enjoys solo success with 'Follow Me' (a UK hit in October), Kid Rock finds lurve with Pamela Anderson, who's number 16 in this year's *FHM* poll of the 100 Sexiest Women in the World. The top three is a pop takeover for Britney, Rachel of S Club and, reigning supreme for a second year, J.Lo. Also in are Louise (14), Beyoncé (15), Shania Twain (21), Geri (28), Stepsters Lisa, Claire and Faye (29, 49, 56), Toni Braxton (31), Dannii Minogue (32), Kylie (44), Christina Aguilera (45), Billie (48), S Clubber Hannah (63), Emma Bunton (71), Andrea Corr (75), Aqua's Lene (90), Vanessa-Mae (91) and Mariah (99)... Britney's charms don't work on dance producer BT, who insists she acquire a cooler music collection before he'll work with her... Radiohead score their second number one album within 12 months with 'Amnesiac', The Strokes go Top 20 with 'Hard to Explain' and Basement Jaxx give a home to label-less singer Kele Le Roc with the rollicking 'Romeo'... Travis tour the US with Dido and recreate their flan-flinging video for 'Sing' on *Top of the Pops*. 'The Invisible Band' returns them to the top of the album chart, ahead of D12 and Muse, before they embark on a tour of the Far East with Coldplay... Neil Young headlines a rain-soaked Fleadh festival in London's Finsbury Park, churning up the mud for a Destiny's Child gig one week later, while Limp Bizkit and a reformed Roxy Music play UK arenas... Elton John auctions 20 of his classic cars at Christie's... Jon Bon Jovi addresses the Oxford Union, advising his audience to "stay humble"... In an embarrassing month for rap, Mandy Moore announces: "Eminem has

"I'm honestly really, really delirious and stressed out and overworked and doing too much" Mariah Carey

always been sweet to me"... **Prince** becomes a Jehovah's Witness... Three legends are lost: boom-booming bluesman **John Lee Hooker** on the 21st and, on the 30th, country guru **Chet Atkins** and jazz saxophonist **Joe Henderson**.

JULY

Hear'Say leap Stepsishly to the top of the chart with 'The Way to Your Love', although more enduringly romantic is its successor: **Roger Sanchez**'s blend of heartbreaking house and a **Toto** sample in 'Another Chance'. **Robbie** rounds off the month with 'Eternity'/'Road to Mandalay' and thousands turn out for his stadium gigs. "I ask **Elvis** to look over me when I'm on stage," says Rob. "I've got a tattoo of a prayer: '**Elvis**, grant me sincerity'"... Backstreet Boy **AJ** and **Metallica**'s **James Hetfield** head for rehab while, reportedly rambling about rainbows, damaged diva Mariah ends up in hospital. This somewhat scuppers the UK chart showing of her Cameo-sampling 'Loverboy', although it winds up among the biggest US successes of the year... Swapping pharmacy for topography, **D12** reinvent 'Purple Pills' as 'Purple Hills', coming undone only when one of the CDs is disqualified from the chart for including a free sticker. It's a huge hit anyway and the Emster has further cause for celebration when he's granted a visa to perform in Australia, as long as he avoids "inciting discord"... Despite being beneath the US legal drinking age, **Britney** admits to the occasional bevvy: "I like to celebrate if something comes up... One drink here, one drink there... I never overdo anything, honestly!"... **Train** drive their US smash 'Drops of Jupiter (Tell Me)' into the UK chart... **Radiohead** play a homecoming gig at Oxford's South Park – and lend their voices to the US series of the same name, in which they help **Cartman** to get revenge... The stars are out for **Madonna** live in London, including Matt from **Muse**, **Sugababes**, **Robbie**, **P Diddy**, **Kylie**, **Dido**, **Paul Oakenfold**, **William Orbit** and **Ewan McGregor**... **The Edge** teams up with **Angelina Jolie** in U2's *Tomb Raider*-flogging video for 'Elevation' while **Belinda Carlisle** – not exactly the **Lara Croft** of AOR but you know what we mean – strips for *Playboy* to prove women don't "have to be 20 years old or a size zero to be sexually viable". Also pushing the erotic envelope is UK movie *Intimacy*, the rock 'n' roll element of which is supporting actress **Marianne Faithfull**... 2001's shiniest star of soul, 20-year-old **Alicia Keys**, tops the US album chart with 'Songs in A Minor' while fellow pin-up **Usher**'s '8701' wins the UK pole position on the back of smash singles 'Pop Ya Collar' and 'U Remind Me'... **Westlife** deny plans to split amid reports of a solo deal for Shane... **Sinead O'Connor** is wed in a secret ceremony and will later be spied singing on **Massive Attack**'s work in progress... A baby boy is born to **Liam Gallagher** and **Nicole Appleton**. **Scott Five** also becomes a dad... With '19/2000' flying high in the chart, **Gorillaz** decline a Mercury Music Prize nomination for their debut album. "Sounds a bit heavy, man!" declares bassist Murdoc. "Like carrying a dead albatross round your neck for eternity... Why don't you nominate some other Muppet?" The award organisers concede defeat next month, despite the Parlophone label maintaining their mickey-taking monkeys are still in the running... Beckingham Palace goes online, with **Posh** giving visitors to her website a tour of a cartoon house based on her own home. Vic's old pal **Mel B** and record label Virgin part company after her 'Hot' album's frosty reception. Politician-in-the-making Mel says she left to spend more time with daughter Phoenix and find a more attentive new label... Meanwhile, **Mel C** admits she hasn't felt comfortable in the group for the past two years and doesn't "intend to do any more work with the **Spice Girls**". Days later, Sporty claims the Spices are still together... Having earlier revealed she finds a man's sexual apparatus frightening,

"I ask Elvis to look over me when I'm on stage. I've got a tattoo of a prayer: 'Elvis, grant me sincerity'" Robbie Williams

July: Madonna wows an all-star audience in London including Robbie and Kylie

Geri goes girl-on-girl mad for her Party in the Park performance of 'Scream If You Wanna Go Faster'... "You can take away the parade but you can't take away the love!" declares Pete Tong as Radio 1's Love Weekend – replacing the axed Love Parade – kicks off in Newcastle... Ol' Dirty Bastard is imprisoned despite fears for his safety inside. The Wu-Tang Clan declare that, in the event of mishap, "ODB has informed his wife to sue New York City and the government for Bill Cosby billions"... Cancer claims 'Everybody's Talkin'' composer Fred Neil on the 7th and folkstress Mimi Fariña on the 18th... Also lost are R&B singer Ernie K-Doe (5th), Lynyrd Skynyrd bassist Leon Wilkeson (27th), John Peel's right-hand man John Walters (31st) and Napster – the "temporarily" shut down music server remains dormant for the rest of the year.

August: So Solid Crew take over the top spot from Atomic Kitten with their bass heavy garage anthem '21 Seconds'

AUGUST

Giving generously to the Bangles' pensions, Atomic Kitten return 'Eternal Flame' to number one and Five score their final chart-topper with the irresistible 'Let's Dance'. Of is-he-or-isn't-he-in bandmate Sean, J admits: "We no longer have a clue. He's always had a bit of a hard time doing what we do"... Sophie Ellis-Bextor's 'Take Me Home' is runner-up to Five after a media-concocted attempt to replicate Groovejet's battle with Posh last year. "It's not a brilliant time for music," says Soph. "I think that sometimes we have a tendency to get used... If we start at a low standard, everybody gets used to it and forgets that they might deserve something better"... In between the Atomic and Five number ones, So Solid Crew prove you can be tighter than a tight thing even when you outnumber the Wu-Tang with '21 Seconds', while Asher D maintains their rock 'n' roll credentials with a gun-related arrest... Also hitting big (and topping the US chart) is 'Bootylicious', with which Destiny's Child flaunt their "jelly" to a grateful nation... Weezer bassist Mikey Welsh reportedly disappears, turning up in a psychiatric hospital... The Prodigy's disappearing act ends when they hit European festival stages... Doubtless prompting much checking of locked doors chez Dre, the doctor's Death Row nemesis Suge Knight is released from jail... Dre's deputy Eminem duets with Marilyn Manson at the Reading festival and wins the approval of Travis. "The moral majority get upset but it's pantomime," they tell Radio 1. "It's like getting upset at Widow Twanky." Flames lick the stage courtesy of firestarters Green Day and Queens of the Stone Age – the latter doubtless hoping to warm the cockles of bassist Nick Oliveri who performs naked. More fetchingly, PJ Harvey models a microscopic black ensemble... Two of Madonna's bras fetch £15,000 each in an online auction... Amid a media maelstrom including a full-page rave from *The Sun*'s Dominic Mohan, White Stripes make their UK live debut. Siblings Jack and Meg White excite attention with the mischievous suggestion that they're actually a divorced couple... U2 launch their UK tour in Manchester watched by Noel Gallagher. The shows – some supported by Nelly Furtado – go on even when Bono's father loses his fight with cancer. "He's left the planet," says the singer,"Just like Elvis"... An optimistic ad agency is reported to want Robbie to be the new Milk Tray man... Usher's own mobile interrupts his performance of 'U Remind Me' on a US TV show... Metal money is spent ▶

▶ on Slipknot's 'Iowa' and Staind's 'Break the Cycle', both of which smash to the top of the chart. (Radio 2 nonetheless pledges always to feature the number one in its relaunched album chart show.) System of a Down Sum 41 Slayer and Alien Ant Farm reinforce the rock takeover. At metal magazine *Kerrang*'s awards, Muse win Best British Act, to the pleasure of leader Matt: "What we're doing is being seen as hard rock. When we first came out, everyone thought it was like whingeing indie crap"... At the more mature end of the rock spectrum, New Order return to the Top 10 after six years with 'Crystal', The Cult get gigular and Mercury Rev release the stunning 'All Is Dream' album... Also keeping cash registers ringing are David Gray's 'White Ladder', which tops the album chart after 66 weeks, Atomic Kitten's 'Right Now', repackaged to capitalise on their revival, and 'The Very Best of Prince', which returns the dumper-consigned maestro to the spotlight for the first time since 1999... Meanwhile, in a year of disappointing placings for such legends as Paul McCartney and Rod Stewart, 60-year-old Bob Dylan bucks the trend with his top five album 'Love and Theft'... The Charlatans update their sound from *Exile*-era Stones to, erm, *Emotional Rescue*-era Stones with a quality single, 'Love Is the Key'... Björk is awarded France's National Order of Merit... Emma Bunton announces a wish to write songs for new artists while Victoria causes ripples with a fake lip-ring... Veteran harmonicist Larry Adler falls victim to pneumonia on the 6th and Shoop Shooping soul singer Betty Everett dies on the 19th, but most mourned internationally is young R&B sensation turned movie star Aaliyah, killed in a plane crash in the Bahamas on the 25th.

▶ SEPTEMBER

Scoring one of the most jaw-droppingly rude hits since Simply Red's 'The Right Thing', the appropriately named Blue top the chart with 'Too Close'. Then it's a quick race through humour – Bob the Builder's 'Mambo No.5' – and horror – DJ Otzi's 'Hey Baby' – to the all-conquering Kylie's 'Can't Get You Out of My Head'. Despite divine omnipresence in the media, Victoria enters at number six with 'Not Such an Innocent Girl'. "Kylie's been around a lot longer than I have," Vic concedes. "Now it's just about me letting people know what I'm capable of on my own. I'm not expecting that overnight"... *Popstars* also-rans Liberty hit with 'Thinking It Over', produced by Mark from Artful Dodger. He also helps Melanie Blatt to find her feet after All Saints, with 'Twenty Four Seven'... The omens look ominous for Michael Jackson, whose comeback gigs in New York are blighted by Whitney flouncing off the bill and Marlon Brando mumbling about machetes. He's also upstaged by Alien Ant Farm's storming hit metal mangling of 'Smooth Criminal'... The Strokes saucily sleeved 'Is This It' makes number two in the album chart... In the bookshops *Somebody Someday* outsells *Learning to Fly* three to one. Robbie announces he has no plans to ponder Posh's bio: "I don't have any interest in reading any book right now. I only colour them in and look at the pictures." Fellow academic Britney announces she spends her time "freakin' organising my rubber bands. I love it. It makes me happy". She'll need plenty after a burglary at her home in Florida. And to the consternation of fans Down Under, she reportedly wails: "Where the hell is that place? Who'd travel 16 hours to go there?" Brit also antagonises animal lovers with her racy performance at the MTV

September: Gorillaz go platinum Stateside

> **" We had a wicked time, but it's come to an end "** Five

Video Awards, cavorting with a snake... Six-gong big winner at the awards is the Christopher Walken-starring 'Weapon of Choice' by Fatboy Slim. Michael Jackson presents his self-titled Vanguard award to U2. Robbie's 'Rock DJ' wins best special effects and Mick Jagger – producer of this month's plucky Brit movie *Enigma* – hands over Best Video From a Film to Christina Aguilera for 'Lady Marmalade'. Marmalade alma mater *Moulin Rouge* opens in the UK, allowing audiences to see Kylie as the absinthe fairy and hear Jim Broadbent lick new life into 'Like a Virgin'... The Chemical Brothers release a long-awaited new single but are eclipsed by French fromage 'Starlight' by Supermen Lovers... Also scoring direct hits are Mary J Blige with the Dr Dre-produced 'Family Affair' and the Dre-sampling 'What Would You Do' by City High... Hip hop of another hue tops the US chart courtesy of J.Lo's 'I'm Real'. La Lopez celebrates by marrying Cris Judd in LA where, no way ominously for the groom, J.Lo's manager is the best man... Mariah Carey's movie *Glitter* falls just short of the US Top 10 while Gorillaz are the first British act of 2001 to have a platinum album in the States... In a very odd month for So Solid Crew, crew member Harvey adds a rap to Mel C's cover of 'Bohemian Rhapsody', also featuring opera singer Russell Watson... Catatonia split up, as do Five. "We had a wicked time," say J and co, "but it's come to an end"... D12 and Hear'Say play shows as announced but the rest of the pop world is rocked by September 11th terrorist atrocities in New York, whose victims include Backstreet Boys stage technician Danny Lee on Flight 11... On the worst night to win anything, PJ Harvey is awarded the Mercury Music Prize for 'Songs From the City, Songs From the Sea'... Ten days later, the US telethon. *A Tribute to Heroes* opens with Bruce Springsteen's new 'My City of Ruins' and closes with Willie Nelson leading a version of 'America the Beautiful'. Along the way, Neil Young covers 'Imagine', Limp Bizkit's Fred and Wes play Pink Floyd's 'Wish You Were Here' and Mariah sings 'Hero'.

▶ OCTOBER

After keeping even Michael Jackson's 'You Rock My World' at bay, Kylie is bumped by Afroman's giggly stoner rap 'Because I Got High', but reigns supreme in the album chart with 'Fever' and gets her own *An Audience With...* on ITV, during which she reinterprets her Jason Donovan duet 'Especially For You' with Kermit... In a troubled month for So Solid Crew, Mis-Teeq become Britain's biggest garage act with their 'Lickin' on Both Sides' album – although both bands do well at the Mobos, where Usher waltzes off with Best R&B Act and Best Album... In a mournful month for metal, masked axeman Wes Borland walks out on Limp Bizkit and Terrorvision conclude their farewell tour at home in Bradford... Savage Garden and Elastica split up, as do – officially, at last – Mr and Mrs Shady... Well-heeled Robbie fans pack London's Albert Hall for the live launch of his 'Swing When You're Winning' album. Also on board are Rupert Everett, Jane Horrocks and Jonathan Wilkes... A Performing Rights Society survey proves Robbie's 'Rock DJ' the most played song in British bars, pubs and restaurants... Rob's old mates Oasis blink back into the spotlight for a 10th anniversary tour of Britain, while fellow Britpop survivors Pulp flutter chart-wards with 'Sunrise'/'The Trees'... Untroubled by sales but the subject of much acclaim, Ryan Adams releases his 'Gold' album. "The only thing missing," enthuses *Uncut* magazine, "is a big bloody sign saying Genius At Work." Accompanying single 'New York, New York' boasts a video filmed in the city just before the Twin Towers massacre... Paul McCartney headlines the Concert for New York City at Madison Square Garden with Bowie, Mick 'n' Keef, Eric Clapton and Elton John, although most plaudits go to the unstoppable Who. In Washington, Michael Jackson's United We Stand gig boasts P Diddy, James Brown and Destiny's Child... Geri and Steps entertain RAF troops in Oman but the former faces accusations that she was paid to do so. "If it's true Geri Halliwell charged a fee," Vera Lynn tells *The Observer*, "then it's a very poor show." Steps chip in with: "We owed them a bit more than acting like stupid, over-demanding pop stars. ▶

▶ Geri Halliwell was well out of order"… As the world reels from another threat, metal veterans Anthrax rue that "suddenly our name is not so cool"… The world's most successful DJ, Paul Oakenfold, is signed to Madge's Maverick label… Britney glistens in the raunchy vid for new Neptunes-helmed Prince pastiche 'I'm a Slave 4 U'. Her mum can't be happy… Westlife deny plans to split and announce a new album and tour instead. "You might see some dance routines," Shane tells Radio 1. "I don't know if you'll see *good* dance routines"… Former Five bruiser J admits hitting a man who claimed Westlife were better in the Dublin pub palaver. He apologises and is ordered to pay more than £4,000 to charity… Snoop Dogg is busted for possession of marijuana and Jamiroquai's Jay Kay denies attacking a photographer and destroying camera equipment outside a London club in April. Insufficient evidence causes criminal charges to be dropped in November… S Clubbers Paul and Hannah confess to romance off-screen as well as on their TV show… In a temporary burst of doing what he does best, Elton John releases the 'Songs From the West Coast' album, before his role in a Royal Mail ad campaign proves Postman Pat has no rivals… Madonna, Eminem, Destiny's Child and Geri are immortalised as puppets for BBC Scotland's *Top of the Poppets*. A far from miffed Eminem asks if he can buy his… Boz Scaggs guests on *Ally McBeal*… Brian Harvey returns to the charts with his Wyclef collaboration 'Loving You (Ole Ole Ole)'… Androgyny rules – courtesy not so much of Garbage's comeback single as glamour queens The Ones, in town to promote dance anthem 'Flawless'. Group member Nashom dishes the dirt on his co-star from the film in which the song originated: "I don't want to say Robert De Niro was too big for his britches but…"… At *Q* magazine's 12th annual awards, there are bits of metal for Starsailor, Ash, Gorillaz, U2, Travis, Elvis Costello, the Manics, John Lydon, Radiohead and their producer Nigel Godrich, and Brian Eno. Sending jaws plunging to the floor, Kate Bush accepts the Classic Songwriter award with an orgasmic thank you… Warp records co-founder Rob Mitchell is killed by cancer on the 8th while Woodstock organiser John Roberts goes to the great gig in the sky on the 27th.

October: Squadron leader Geri Halliwell entertains the troops in Oman

▶ NOVEMBER

The number one spot is the site of short-lived skirmishes, as Westlife's 'Queen of My Heart' is toppled by Blue's 'If You Come Back' and S Club's 'Have You Ever'… Alicia Keys goes top three with 'Fallin''… In a troubled month for just about everyone, pop guru Jonathan King is jailed, So Solid Crew's Skat D is fined for breaking a girl's jaw, mucho-hyped hard rocker Andrew WK is concussed by a stage invader at his UK live debut and 300 people complain about strong language on the BBC's broadcast of Robbie's Albert Hall gig… More feathers are ruffled by host Ali G at the MTV Europe Awards, although Atomic Kitten claim not to mind being dubbed "slappers". The host town Frankfurt gives its streets temporary new names like Robbie Williams Avenue… Erroneous reports have Westlife ejected from a Manchester bar for singing and Madonna hospitalised by a bucking bronco onstage. In reality, Madge's only bruising results from her 'GHV2' album being kept at number two by Westlife's 'World of Our Own'… Meanwhile, Aphex Twin reveals La Ciccone declined an invitation to grunt like a pig on his latest album… Similarly strange but true, Muse revive Nina Simone's 'Feeling Good' for an audience-perplexing *Top of the Pops* performance… R.E.M. make a guest appearance in Homer's garage in *The Simpsons*… Last seen on New Order's summer tour, Billy Corgan debuts his new band Zwan in California…

> **"I'll miss him dearly and I'll always love him – he's my baby brother…"** Paul McCartney

> "Let's hope he's jamming with John"
>
> Keith Richards

Radiohead's live album 'I Might Be Wrong' is joined on the shelves by a best-of from proto-Radioheaders **Pink Floyd**. Meanwhile, **Bob the Builder** beats the Floyd to number one on the Australian album chart... Roundly ridiculed for not selling as well as **Robbie**'s 'Swing When You're Winning' (a feat replicated by virtually everyone else in Britain), **Mick Jagger** nonetheless wins respectable reviews, for his 'Goddess in the Doorway' album. Meanwhile, preparations are under way for the **Stones**' 40th anniversary... *South Park* and **Slim Shady** provide a cartoon cocktail in **Eminem**'s new video *The Slim Shady Show*. Mr Mathers is also spied kissing **Kim Basinger** on the set of an autobiographical movie in which Basinger plays his mother... Em's pal Elton adds another notch to *Ally McBeal*'s guest count, **Britney** joins **Beyoncé** in the role call for the new *Austin Powers* flick and anyone who waits to the very end of the *Jay and Silent Bob Strike Back* movie can see **Alanis Morissette** reprising her role as God... **Natalie Imbruglia** returns with the Morissettesque 'That Day' while a Vodafone ad rockets a re-released 'Bohemian Like You' by the **Dandy Warhols** into the hit parade... Basking in post-Kylie cool, **Dannii Minogue** storms back to chart life with 'Who Do You Love Now (Stringer)'... Twelve months after the flop 'Forever' album, **Emma** maintains the **Spice Girls** are still going strong, despite the closing of their fan club in June and rumours of a rift between **Mel B** and **Posh**. "There's always shit flying around me," muses Mel. "It used to bother me. Now I just duck"... The all-star Artists Against Aids project puts **Marvin Gaye**'s 'What's Going On' in the UK top 10 for the first time... "I'll miss him dearly and I'll always love him – he's my baby brother," says **Paul McCartney** when **George Harrison** is killed by cancer in LA on the 29th. "Let's hope he's jamming with John," says **Keith Richards**... Also lost are counterculture hero **Ken Kesey** (10th) and **Can** guitarist **Michael Karoli** (16th). ▶

DECEMBER

Gotta get Garage says Britain as it sends the unknown Daniel Bedingfield's 'Gotta Get Thru This' to number one for a fortnight. Thereafter, it's Robbie all the way as his 'Somethin' Stupid' duet with Nicole Kidman reigns through Christmas, despite selling fewer than half as many as Bob the Builder's festive chart-topper last year... A toothache-plagued Robbie cringes at the London premiere of his *Nobody Someday* rockumentary: "I was really ashamed and embarrassed because it was full of self-pity"... Critical reaction isn't much better for John Carpenter's movie *Ghosts of Mars*, starring Ice Cube – who makes a bid for the Christmas dollar with a greatest hits set... Mark Wahlberg stars in *Rock Star*, loosely based on the true tale of Judas Priest's singer Ripper Owens... A survey of 18-24-year-olds ranks 'Mary's Boy Child' by Boney M as the best Christmas hit, with Whitney's 'I Will Always Love You' the worst... Nicky Westlife and Faye Steps win Best Haircuts at the *Smash Hits* awards, while Most Fanciable gongs go to Ben A1 and Rachel S Club... S Club win Record of the Year for 'Don't Stop Movin'' while, in another triumph for the cleaning up of cannabis's image, Andrea Corr backs the drug's decriminalisation in Ireland... The Corrs grace the Royal Variety Performance, although *EastEnders* star Barbara Windsor is more entranced by J.Lo: "Jennifer said, 'Will you hold my hand?' So I just went like that and grabbed her bum." Her Maj, meanwhile, cops a royal eyeful of Kym Hear'Say thanks to a barely there outfit... Fellow under-dressed popstress PJ Harvey tops *Q*'s 100 Women Who Rock Your World poll... In a troubled month for So Solid Crew, their UK tour is cancelled amid security fears... In need of better security is Brian Harvey, bashed with a machete outside a Nottingham club... In a disastrous month for the Jacksons, Michael's R Kelly-composed 'Cry' is his lowest-charting single for eight years while Janet's Carly Simon hook-up 'Son of a Gun' is the least successful release from 'All For You'... While the world wakes up to the wonder of The Hives, their label Poptones runs into problems... J.Lo, Ja Rule and Kid Rock provide a tonic for troops at an MTV-organised gig in Germany... An astonishingly alive Shane McGowan leads the Pogues on a triumphant tour. Kirsty MacColl is mentioned each night prior to 'A Fairytale of New York', the most modern single to make it on to a Performing Rights Society list of the most-performed Christmas songs... Hear'Say see their 'Everybody' album go in at number 24. "Any other time of the year we might be number one," says Suzanne. Meanwhile, having declared half of Hear'Say unfit to be stars, *Pop Idol* judge Simon Cowell sets his sights on Geri: "She hasn't cut the mustard, simple as that." Harsh, but Geri's newie 'Calling' is falling down the chart after becoming her second single in a row not to top it... Big Country's Stuart Adamson is found dead in Hawaii on the 16th and soul pioneer Rufus Thomas dies on the 15th, as does Seventies singer Clifford T Ward on the 18th... In a sad day for Saturday mornings, Ant and Dec bow out of *SM:TV* and *CD:UK*. Their star-studded finales include Mariah as a maid of honour in spoof sitcom *Chums*... It's also black armbands for Steps fans on Boxing Day when our heroes call it a day, despite achievements including toppling Michael Jackson from the top of the album chart and introducing a *Carry On* element to Diana Ross's 'Chain Reaction'. "We have always said that when the time came we would leave as good friends and go out while we're on top," say the band. Appropriately, they've just made it into the *British Hit Singles* Top 100 most successful British chart acts.

December: A Boxing Day split for Steps leaves us with fond memories and these Corinthian Pop Star figurines to remember them by

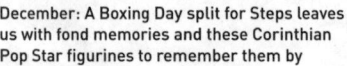

> **"We have always said that when the time came we would leave as good friends and go out while we're on top"** Steps

LISTS, STATS AND FACTS

THE TOP 10 BEST-SELLING SINGLES

The UK chart's all-time biggest sellers include four value-for-money double A sides and, astonishingly, two places inside the Top 10 for singles by Boney M.

1. **CANDLE IN THE WIND 1997 / SOMETHING ABOUT THE WAY YOU LOOK TONIGHT**
   Elton John 4,860,000
2. **DO THEY KNOW IT'S CHRISTMAS**
   Band Aid 3,550,000
3. **BOHEMIAN RHAPSODY**
   Queen 2,130,000
4. **MULL OF KINTYRE / GIRLS' SCHOOL**
   Wings 2,050,000
5. **RIVERS OF BABYLON / BROWN GIRL IN THE RING**
   Boney M 1,995,000
6. **YOUR'E THE ONE THAT I WANT**
   John Travolta and Olivia Newton-John 1,980,000
7. **RELAX**
   Frankie Goes To Hollywood 1,910,000
8. **SHE LOVES YOU**
   The Beatles 1,890,000
9. **UNCHAINED MELODY / (THERE'LL BE BLUEBIRDS OVER) THE WHITE CLIFFS OF DOVER**
   Robson Green and Jerome Flynn 1,840,000
10. **MARY'S BOY CHILD - OH MY LORD**
    Boney M 1,790,000

Producer Frank Farian's disco chartbusters Boney M, whose 'Rivers of Babylon' spent 40 weeks on the UK singles chart in the late 70s sales boom

TOP PRODUCERS

No.1s / Producer		Weeks at No.1
27	GEORGE MARTIN	98
27	NORRIE PARAMOR	96
17	MITCH MILLER	73
15	STEVE SHOLES	62
15	PETE WATERMAN	38
13	MATT AITKEN =	33
13	MIKE STOCK =	33
11	CHET ATKINS	42
10	BENNY ANDERSSON =	35
10	BJÖRN ULVAEUS =	35
10	JOHNNY FRANZ	28
9	MIKE CHAPMAN	24
8	DICK ROWE	24
8	GEORGE MICHAEL	20
7	MADONNA	18
7	NORMAN NEWELL	17
7	TONY HATCH	15
6	CHAS CHANDLER	20
6	TONY MACAULAY	19
6	MIKE SMITH	13
6	ANDREW LOOG OLDHAM	11
5	NICKY CHINN	13
5	TONY VISCONTI =	18
5	MIKE CURB =	18
5	PHIL SPECTOR	17
5	WALLY RIDLEY	16

No.1: George Martin

▶ The performers get their *Top of the Pops* performance, the writers their Ivor Novellos, but what of the producers? These unsung heroes of pop get little in the way of recognition. How many average Joes know their Norrie Paramors from their Dick Rowes? That may be changing in the hip hop and R&B arenas, with producers such as Timbaland stepping out of the shadows to cut solo tracks and put the MCs and soul divas in the shade, but it'll be a few years before they overtake the Chas Chandlers and Tony Viscontis of this world.

Notably absent from our league are several legends who have shaped pop in ways far greater than their singles chart record would suggest. Brian Wilson, Nile Rodgers and Kraftwerk's backroom dummies have influenced the way pop sounds today, but no one has left his mark more than George Martin, without whom The Beatles could never have progressed from 'Please Please Me' to 'I Am the Walrus' in just a few short years.

POSTHUMOUS CHART TOPPERS

▶ When a star is cut down in his or her prime, it always leads to a reappraisal of their work. It's a natural time to reflect on an artist's impact on music and their place in your record collection, with certain songs being given a new poignancy after the death of the performer. In fact, for Eddie Cochran, Jackie Wilson, Buddy Holly, Jim Reeves, Jimi Hendrix, John Lennon, Freddie Mercury and Aaliyah, the hits listed below represent their only solo No.1s. George Harrison's 'My Sweet Lord' is the only previous No.1 to return to the top after a star's death.

1959 **BUDDY HOLLY**
It Doesn't Matter Anymore

1960 **EDDIE COCHRAN**
Three Steps to Heaven

1966 **JIM REEVES**
Distant Drums

1970 **JIMI HENDRIX**
Voodoo Chile

1977 **ELVIS PRESLEY**
Way Down

1980 **JOHN LENNON**
Just Like Starting Over

1980 **JOHN LENNON**
Imagine

1981 **JOHN LENNON**
Woman

1986 **JACKIE WILSON**
Reet Petite (The Sweetest Girl in Town)

1993 **FREDDIE MERCURY**
Living on My Own (Remix)

2002 **AALIYAH**
More than a Woman

2002 **GEORGE HARRRISON**
My Sweet Lord

THE POP PREMIER LEAGUE

▶ Although there seems to be a move to grander classical music to greet the arrival of clubs as they take the field, many still employ feisty chart hits to set up both the fans and the team for the following 90 minutes of joy or misery.

Blood-stirringly good examples include Dave Clark Five's stomper 'Glad All Over' at Selhurst Park where Crystal Palace strut their stuff, Jeff Beck's 'Hi Ho Silver Lining' at Wolves' Molineux and Sham 69's 'If the Kids Are United' at Scunthorpe United's Glanford Park.

A copy of Manchester United's best performing single, the chart-topping 'Come On You Reds' from 1994

As for football clubs releasing records, perhaps this musical genre has run its course. The warped logic that dictated "we're in a cup final, so we must release a single" seems to have waned. So here is, maybe, the last role of dishonour.

Pos / Team		Hits per Team	Peak Pos	Wks on chart
1.	MANCHESTER UNITED	10	1	69
2.	LIVERPOOL	5	3	21
3.	TOTTENHAM HOTSPUR	5	5	33
4.	CHELSEA	5	5	23
5.	ARSENAL	4	9	16
6.	LEEDS UNITED	2	10	13
7.	EVERTON	2	14	8
8.	NEWCASTLE*	2	26	3
9.	SUNDERLAND**	2	41	6
10.	NOTTINGHAM FOREST	1	24	6
11.	WEST HAM UNITED	1	31	2
12.	STOKE CITY***	1	34	2
13.	MIDDLESBROUGH	1	44	1
14.	FULHAM****	1	46	1
15.	CRYSTAL PALACE	1	50	2
16.	RANGERS	1	54	2
17.	COVENTRY CITY	1	61	2
18.	BRIGHTON AND HOVE ALBION	1	65	2

** Newcastle listed in British Hit Singles Artist A-Z as both Black & White Army and Toon Travellers*
*** Sunderland listed in British Hit Singles Artist A-Z as Simply Red and White and A Love Supreme*
**** Stoke City listed in British Hit Singles Artist A-Z as The Potters*
***** Fulham listed in British Hit Singles Artist A-Z as Tony Rees and the Cottagers*

THE TOP 10 ONE-HIT WONDERS

▶ Ultimate one-hit wonders are acts who have just one entry in the UK singles chart but, spectacularly, their one and only visit to the Top 75 bags a No.1. Nothing before and nothing after. Here is the flash-in-the-pan Top 10 ranked by weeks at No.1.

1. **THE ARCHIES** - Sugar Sugar - **1969 (26 wks on chart / 8 at No.1)**
2. **THE KALIN TWINS** - When - **1958 (18 wks on chart / 5 at No.1)**
3. **THE SIMON PARK ORCHESTRA** - Eye Level - **1973 (24 wks on chart / 4 at No.1)**
4. **PARTNERS IN KRYME** - Turtle Power - **1990 (10 wks on chart / 4 at No.1)**
5. **CLIVE DUNN** - Grandad - **1971 (27 wks on chart / 3 at No.1)**
6. **LEE MARVIN** - Wand'rin' Star - **1970 (23 wks on chart / 3 at No.1)**
7. **BRIAN AND MICHAEL** - Matchstalk Men and Matchstalk Cats and Dogs - **1978 (19 wks on chart / 3 at No.1)**

10. = **DREAMWEAVERS** - It's Almost Tomorrow - **1956 (18 wks on chart / 3 at No.1)**
10. = **LENA MARTELL** - One Day at a Time - **1979 (18 wks on chart / 3 at No.1)**
10. = **MATTHEWS SOUTHERN COMFORT** - Woodstock - **1970 (18 wks on chart / 3 at No.1)**

WEDDING TOP 20

▶ Listed below are the Top 20 of songs extolling the virtues of marriage as an institution, with no 'D.I.V.O.R.C.E.' to be seen. An honourable mention should go to The Wedding Present, who once had a hit with 'Nobody's Twisting Your Arm'

1. **THE WEDDING** - Julie Rogers ....(3) (23)
2. **SHE WEARS MY RING** Solomon King ....(3) (18)
3. **LOVE AND MARRIAGE** Frank Sinatra ....(3) (8)
4. **(I'M ALWAYS HEARING) WEDDING BELLS** Eddie Fisher ....(5) (11)
5. **WHITE WEDDING** - Billy Idol ....(6) (15)
6. **BAND OF GOLD** - Don Cherry ....(6) (11)
6. **SHOTGUN WEDDING** - Roy C ....(6) (11)
8. **WEDDING BELLS** Godley and Creme ....(7) (11)
9. **LET'S JUMP THE BROOMSTICK** Brenda Lee ....(12) (5)
10. **PEGGY SUE GOT MARRIED** Buddy Holly ....(13) (10)
11. **MARRY ME** - Mike Preston ....(14) (10)
12. **THIS GOLDEN RING** Fortunes ....(15) (9)
13. **LOVE IS A GOLDEN RING** Frankie Laine ....(19) (5)
14. **KISS THE BRIDE** - Elton John ....(20) (7)
15. **WEDDING RING** Russ Hamilton ....(20) (6)
16. **LET'S GET MARRIED** Proclaimers ....(21) (4)
17. **CHAPEL OF LOVE** Dixie Cups ....(22) (8)
18. **I'M GONNA GET MARRIED** Lloyd Price ....(23) (5)
20. **THIRD FINGER LEFT HAND** Pearls ....(31) (6)
20. **HAWAIIAN WEDDING SONG** Julie Rogers ....(31) (6)

Calculated by (peak position) and (weeks on chart)

Julie Rogers is top of the Wedding Top 20 and appropriately wears a very large ring on the third finger of her left hand

TOP 10 MOVIE THEMES

1. **ROCK AROUND THE CLOCK**
   Bill Haley and His Comets .... **5 weeks at No.1 (57)**
2. **THE GOOD THE BAD AND THE UGLY**
   Hugo Montenegro and His Orchestra .... **4 weeks at No.1 (24)**
3. **MEN IN BLACK**
   Will Smith .... **4 weeks at No.1 (16)**
4. **YELLOW SUBMARINE**
   The Beatles .... **4 weeks at No.1 (14)**
5. **THE MAN FROM LARAMIE**
   Jimmy Young .... **4 weeks at No.1 (12)**
6. **JAILHOUSE ROCK**
   Elvis Presley .... **3 weeks at No.1 (25)**
7. **THREE COINS IN THE FOUNTAIN**
   Frank Sinatra .... **3 weeks at No.1 (19)**

9.= **SUMMER HOLIDAY**
   Cliff Richard and The Shadows .... **3 weeks at No.1 (18)**

9.= **WOODSTOCK**
   Matthews Southern Comfort.................... **3 weeks at No.1 (18)**

10. **HELP!**
   The Beatles .... **3 weeks at No.1 (17)**

▶ To qualify, the theme must also be the title of the movie so no place here for the likes of these chart-toppers: 'Wand'rin Star', '(Everything I Do) I Do It For You', 'Love Is All Around' and 'I Will Always Love You'. These, then, are the cinematic cream of the crop.

Figures in brackets indicate total weeks single spent on chart. All the artists credited with the above singles sang the music in the actual movie except in the case of 'The Man From Laramie' and 'Woodstock' where Crosby, Stills, Nash and Young rocked out on the Joni Mitchell composition.

Bill Haley and His Comets, whose 'Rock Around the Clock' thrilled cinema audiences and stormed the charts back in the mid-50s

NAMES AIN'T NOTHING BUT A NUMBER

▶ One Love, It Takes Two, Three Lions... Numbers have always played a part in pop. So, donning the anoraks, we've come up with two top 10-type Top 10s, made up of the biggest song featuring each number from one to 10 in the title, and same again for band names.

The following were discounted from the song title Top 10: Part 1, 2 etc, 4 meaning for, and EP titles such as Five Live were also discounted in an effort to include songs where the number formed a proper part of the title. Also, songs or bands with more than one number in the title ('2 Become 1', 911) were discounted as well.

Song		Band
ONE DAY IN YOUR LIFE Lena Martell	1	**A1**
TWO LITTLE BOYS Rolf Harris	2	**U2**
KNOCK THREE TIMES Dawn	3	**Three Degrees**
IT'S FOUR IN THE MORNING Faron Young	4	**Four Tops**
MAMBO NO.5 (A LITTLE BIT OF...) Lou Bega	5	**Dave Clark Five**
THE SIX TEENS Sweet	6	**Double Six**
7 DAYS Craig David	7	**S Club 7**
ACTIV 8 (COME WITH ME) Altern 8	8	**Altern 8**
(9PM) TILL I COME ATB	9	**Nine Inch Nails**
PERFECT 10 Beautiful South	10	**10 CC**

TOP 10 ACTS WITHOUT A NUMBER ONE HIT

Billy Fury: His best chart performing release was 'Jealousy', which stalled at No.2. 'Kon-Tiki' by The Shadows was the record that prevented Billy (real name Ronald Wycherly) from hitting the top; a feat he never achieved despite 281 weeks of chart action

▶ The following acts all have the unhappy distinction of having spent an age on the chart without ever taking up residence at the top spot. Nat "King" Cole could, perhaps, have felt the most aggrieved. Three times during his 248 weeks on chart he made No.2, but never the top spot. Acts which have never had a No.1, listed in order of weeks spent on chart, followed by their best performing single based on chart weeks:

1. **BILLY FURY**
   (281 weeks)
   Jealousy .... **peak pos 2**
2. **JANET JACKSON**
   (274 weeks)
   The Best Things in Life Are Free................ **peak pos 2**
3. **NAT "KING" COLE**
   (248 weeks)
   When I Fall In Love...... **peak pos 2**
4. **WHO**
   (247 weeks)
   My Generation and I'm a Boy...................... **peak pos 2**
5. **DEPECHE MODE**
   (240 weeks)
   People Are People....... **peak pos 4**
6. **TINA TURNER**
   (224 weeks)
   What's Love Got to Do with It .... **peak pos 3**
7. **BRENDA LEE**
   (210 weeks)
   Speak to Me Pretty......... **peak pos 3**
8. **BON JOVI**
   (208 weeks)
   Always .... **peak pos 2**
9. **KOOL AND THE GANG**
   (207 weeks)
   Joanna / Tonight........... **peak pos 2**
10. **TEMPTATIONS**
    (203 weeks)
    My Girl .... **peak pos 2**

TOP 100 POP ACTS

▶ This annual check on the fortunes of the 100 best chart performers is compiled according to the number of weeks they have spent on the UK singles chart since the first hit parade in 1952.

Any tied position is decided according to the weeks they have spent at No.1, No.2 and so on. Listed below is this year's placing in bold (with last year's for comparison), the act name, the number of weeks they have spent on chart, No.1 hits tally and the total number of hits achieved.

LY	TY	Artist	Wks on Chart	No.1s	Total Hits
1	**1**	Elvis Presley	1,173	17	132
2	**2**	Cliff Richard	1,145	14	125
3	**3**	Shadows	770	12	63
4	**4**	Elton John	576	4	76
▲ 6	**5**	Madonna	568	10	55
▼ 5	**6**	Diana Ross	560	2	77
7	**7**	Michael Jackson	493	7	53
8	**8**	Rod Stewart	477	6	62
9	**9**	Beatles	456	17	32
10	**10**	David Bowie	447	5	66
11	**11**	Frank Sinatra	440	3	38
12	**12**	Queen	419	6	51
13	**13**	Stevie Wonder	415	2	54
14	**14**	Status Quo	413	1	56
15	**15**	Paul McCartney	410	4	52
16	**16**	Tom Jones	390	2	41
17	**17**	Rolling Stones	366	8	48
18	**18**	Bee Gees	354	5	38
19	**19**	Roy Orbison	345	3	34
20	**20**	Everly Brothers	344	4	30
21	**21**	UB40	330	3	48
22	**22**	Shirley Bassey	326	2	31
23	**23**	Perry Como	322	2	26
24	**24**	Jim Reeves	322	1	26
25	**25**	Lonnie Donegan	321	3	30
26	**26**	Hollies	318	2	32
27	**27**	Four Tops	318	1	33
▲ 29	**28**	Whitney Houston	312	4	32
▼ 28	**29**	Oasis	309	5	17
30	**30**	Pat Boone	308	1	27
31	**31**	Supremes	306	1	31
32	**32**	Prince	305	1	51
33	**33**	Donna Summer	299	1	42
34	**34**	Hot Chocolate	283	1	35
35	**35**	Frankie Laine	281	4	27
36	**36**	Beach Boys	281	2	32
37	**37**	Billy Fury	281	-	29
38	**38**	Slade	279	6	36
39	**39**	Shakin' Stevens	277	4	37
▲ 46	**40**	Kylie Minogue	275	6	33
41	**41**	Janet Jackson	274	-	38
▼ 40	**42**	Madness	268	1	32
▼ 41	**43**	ELO	255	1	29
▲ 65	**44**	U2	254	4	34
▼ 43	**45**	Abba	252	9	26
▲ 49	**46**	Mariah Carey	252	2	28
▼ 43	**47**	Adam Faith	251	2	24
▼ 45	**48**	George Michael	249	7	27
49	**49**	Nat "King" Cole	248	-	33
▼ 47	**50**	Petula Clark	247	2	28
▼ 48	**51**	Who	247	-	31
▼ 50	**52**	Connie Francis	244	2	24
▲ 63	**53**	Depeche Mode	240	-	38
▼ 52	**54**	Engelbert Humperdinck	239	2	16
▼ 53	**55**	T. Rex	236	4	30
▼ 54	**56**	Bryan Adams	235	2	33
▼ 55	**57**	Jacksons	235	1	27
▼ 56	**58**	Olivia Newton-John	234	3	26
▼ 57	**59**	Andy Williams	234	1	22
▼ 58	**60**	Ken Dodd	233	1	19
▼ 59	**61**	Frankie Vaughan	232	2	31
▼ 60	**62**	Celine Dion	230	2	23
▼ 62	**63**	Phil Collins	228	3	31
▼ 61	**64**	Pet Shop Boys	227	4	34
▲ 69	**65**	Cher	226	3	31
▼ 64	**66**	Tina Turner	224	-	36
▼ 66	**67**	Fleetwood Mac	223	1	27
▼ 67	**68**	Duran Duran	222	2	30
▼ 68	**69**	Tremeloes	222	2	21
70	**70**	Manfred Mann	217	3	22
71	**71**	Kinks	215	3	24
72	**72**	Bon Jovi	215	-	28
▼ 72	**73**	Simply Red	214	1	31
▼ 73	**74**	Boyzone	213	6	16
-	**75**	Robbie Williams	213	5	16
▼ 74	**76**	Gene Pitney	212	1	22
▼ 75	**77**	Dusty Springfield	211	1	26
▼ 76	**78**	Herman's Hermits	211	1	20
▼ 77	**79**	Brenda Lee	210	-	22
▼ 78	**80**	Wet Wet Wet	209	3	26
▼ 79	**81**	Showaddywaddy	209	1	23
▼ 80	**82**	Eurythmics	208	1	28
▼ 81	**83**	Kool and the Gang	207	-	23
▼ 83	**84**	Jam	205	4	21
▼ 84	**85**	Erasure	203	1	28
▼ 85	**86**	Temptations	203	-	28
▲ 89	**87**	Marvin Gaye	202	1	25
▼ 86	**88**	Bananarama	202	-	27
▼ 87	**89**	Duane Eddy and the Rebels	201	-	23
▼ 88	**90**	OMD	201	-	30
▼ 90	**91**	David Essex	199	2	25
▼ 91	**92**	Bill Haley and His Comets	199	1	16
▼ 92	**93**	John Lennon	197	3	20
-	**94**	Steps	196	2	15
▼ 93	**95**	Cilla Black	194	2	21
▼ 94	**96**	Kim Wilde	194	-	30
▼ 95	**97**	Stranglers	194	-	34
▼ 96	**98**	David Whitfield	190	2	19
▼ 97	**99**	Buddy Holly	190	1	23
▼ 98	**100**	Neil Sedaka	190	-	19

Kylie Minogue: biggest gaining female artist in the British Hit Singles Top 100 Pop Acts

LIVERPOOL: CAPITAL CITY OF POP

liverpool
welcomes you
The UK's
Capital of Pop

▲ **Above:** Council leader Mike Storey was delighted with the World Capital City of Pop honour – but joked that the city council would now have to change its gateway signs billing Liverpool as the UK capital of pop. "We keep on getting bigger and better. Now, there's just the universe to take on!"

▼ **Below:** The world's press assembled to capture the presentation of the British Hit Singles No.1 award in front of Liverpool landmark the Yellow Submarine with local Beatles cover band The Blue Meanies in attendance.

With a population of 461,481 and 54 No.1 hit singles from its inhabitants, Liverpool is the capital city of pop

▶ From a list of more than 900 No.1 hits since the singles chart began in 1952, Liverpool's 54 chart-toppers (including 17 by The Beatles) begin with Lita Roza in 1953 and end with Atomic Kitten in 2001. To celebrate these poptastic statistics, the city of Liverpool erected a Wall of Fame in Mathew Street, opposite the world-famous Cavern Club, where gold discs for each one of the Liverpool No.1 chart-toppers are displayed.

In recognition of Liverpool's pop status, British Hit Singles editor David Roberts presented the city representatives – the Lord Mayor, councillor Gerry Scott, Sir Bob Scott and council leader Mike Storey – with the award for being the UK's No.1 pop city in relation to the size of the population. As it turned out, no one could find a city anywhere in the world to beat Liverpool, so a World Record certificate was the icing on the cake and a place in the Guinness World Records Book 2002 was secured.

Here's how Liverpool ranks against the UK pop competition for No.1 singles:

1. LIVERPOOL
Population 461,481 – 54 No.1s
A No.1 for every 8,545 Scousers

2. CARDIFF
Population 350,000 – 8 No.1s
A No.1 for every 43,750 Cardiff citizens

3. LONDON
Population 7,825,000 – 107 No.1s
A No.1 for every 73,131 Londoners

4. MANCHESTER
Population 2,281,000 – 23 No.1s
A No.1 for every 99,173 Mancunians

5. GLASGOW
Population 1,648,000 – 16 No.1s
A No.1 for every 103,000 Glaswegians

Outside the UK, let's also hear it for Dublin. A recent surge in No.1s has given them a total of 21 from a population of one million, which translates into a chart-topper for every 47,619 Dubliners.

Note that acts qualify only if all or most members of a group are born in or form a band in the city. Newcastle's surprising non-appearance in our chart, with just two No.1 acts (Jimmy Nail and The Animals), was not helped by a no-show by The Police (not all Geordies) and Sting's unexpected lack of solo No.1s.

A-Z BY ARTIST

▶ Here starts the listing of every band, solo singer, duo, trio and orchestra that has achieved the distinction of at least one week at No.75 in the UK singles chart

Kylie Minogue (left), queen of hit singles in 2001, and Dido (right), the biggest selling UK albums artist in the past 12 months

HOW TO USE THIS SECTION

This fictitious act entry illustrates how to use the symbols and information contained in this section of the book

WE FEAR CHANGE 466 Top 500 *UK male rock band, originally from Hertfordshire, formed in 1994 out of the ashes of indie band The Rumble Brothers, which imploded in 1993 after a tempestuous three years. Boasting Martin "Barney" Barranes of Red 57 on guitar, original Rumble Brothers Eric Watson (b) and Martin Downham (v/g), the friction continues with Gary Smith (v), Steve Hughes (g) and Tony Sweet (d). (130 WEEKS).*

			pos	wks
15 Oct 94		**LOVE LET ME DOWN** *Guinness World Records 008*	22	13
14 Jan 95	●	**ALBURY DAYS** *Guinness World Records 009* ◆	9	19
22 Apr 95	★	**LAST NIGHT (WE CAN FLY)** *Guinness World Records 010*	1	22
30 Sep 95	●	**BORN AGAIN** *Guinness World Records 011* ▲	4	9
6 Oct 95		— **ALBURY DAYS (re-entry)** *Guinness World Records 009*	49	4
3 Feb 96		**I WISH I WAS A ROBOT** *Guinness World Records 012* [1]	2	36
24 Aug 96	●	**(LIVING IN A) HICK TOWN** *Guinness World Records 013*	3	8
3 Feb 96	★	**THE SORROW ROOM (LIVE EP)** *Guinness World Records 014* ■	1	9
22 Mar 97		**THE GAME OF LIFE** *Guinness World Records 015*	32	4
12 Sep 98		**SEAHORSES** *Guinness World Records 016* [2]	19	4
22 Dec 01		**ALBURY DAYS (re-mix)** *Guinness World Records 017*	72	2+

[1] We Fear Change featuring The Gary & Mary Smith All-Stars
[2] We Fear Change featuring Rick Rumble's Rhythm & Booze Orchestra

Tracks on The Sorrow Room (Live EP): Sorrow Room / Last Night (We Can Fly) / I Nearly Came Back for You / Sally Seven Days

See also MARV DOWLING, RED 57

Key to the annotations:

- Act name
- Total weeks on chart
- UK Top 10 hit
- UK No.1 hit
- All re-entries indented
- Date of chart entry, traditionally week ending date (currently Saturday)
- Refers to a footnote indicating a change to the name of the act for a particular single or a collaboration with another artist
- Cross-reference linking act to associated act or acts
- Indicates an act within the list of Top 500 acts of all time, calculated by weeks on chart. See also page 69
- Peak position / weeks on chart
- UK million seller
- US No.1
- UK entry at No.1
- Still on chart in Jan 2002
- Label / catalogue numbers generally taken from the seven-inch vinyl single before Jan 1993 and CD single after this time
- EP track titles

MINI-BIOGRAPHY ABBREVIATIONS

b. – born, d. – died, b – bass guitar, d – drums, fl – flute, g – guitar, k – keyboard, prc – percussion, prog – programming, s – saxophone, syn – synthesizer, t – trumpet, v – vocals

In this edition, for the first time, the act biographies include the real names (if different surnames) of all solo artists and duos scoring a Top 20 hit and the lead vocalists on all chart-toppers

A

A *UK, male vocal / instrumental group (6 WEEKS)* pos/wks

7 Feb 98		**FOGHORN** *Tycoon TYCD 5*	63	1
11 Apr 98		**NUMBER ONE** *Tycoon TYCD 6*	47	1
27 Jun 98		**SING-A-LONG** *Tycoon TYCD 7*	57	1
24 Oct 98		**SUMMER ON THE UNDERGROUND** *Tycoon TYCD 8*	72	1
5 Jun 99		**OLD FOLKS** *Tycoon TYCD 9*	54	1
21 Aug 99		**I LOVE LAKE TAHOE** *Tycoon TYCD 10*	59	1

A CAMP *Sweden / US, female / male vocal / instrumental group led by Nina Persson (1 WEEK)* pos/wks

1 Sep 01		**I CAN BUY YOU** *Stockholm 0152162*	46	1

A1 (469 Top 500) *Top UK boy band who have written and played on their recordings: Mark Read, Paul Marazzi, Ben Adams and Norwegian Christian Ingebrigtsen. Quartet, who scored two No.1s in a nine-week period, were winners of 2001 Brits Newcomer award (74 WEEKS)* pos/wks

3 Jul 99	●	**BE THE FIRST TO BELIEVE** *Columbia 6674222*	6	9
11 Sep 99	●	**SUMMERTIME OF OUR LIVES** *Columbia 6678322*	5	6
13 Nov 99		**SUMMERTIME OF OUR LIVES (re-entry)** *Columbia 6678322*	62	2
20 Nov 99	●	**EVERYTIME / READY OR NOT** *Columbia 6681872*	3	11
4 Mar 00	●	**LIKE A ROSE** *Columbia 6689032*	6	12
9 Sep 00	★	**TAKE ON ME** *Columbia 6695902* ■	1	10
18 Nov 00	★	**SAME OLD BRAND NEW YOU** *Columbia 6705202* ■	1	10
2 Dec 00		**TAKE ON ME (re-entry)** *Columbia 6695902*	69	1
3 Mar 01	●	**NO MORE** *Columbia 6708742*	6	8
12 May 01		**NO MORE (re-entry)** *Columbia 6708742*	64	5

A PERFECT CIRCLE *US, male vocal / instrumental group (2 WEEKS)* pos/wks

18 Nov 00		**THE HOLLOW** *Virgin VUSCD 181*	72	1
13 Jan 01		**3 LIBRAS** *Virgin VUSCD 184*	49	1

A+ *US, male rapper – Andre Levins (9 WEEKS)* pos/wks

13 Feb 99	●	**ENJOY YOURSELF** *Universal UND 56230*	5	9

A.R.E. WEAPONS *US, male vocal / insrumental group (1 WEEK)* pos/wks

4 Aug 01		**STREET GANG** *Rough Trade RTRADESCD 022*	72	1

A*TEENS *Sweden, male / female vocal group (19 WEEKS)* pos/wks

4 Sep 99		**MAMMA MIA** *Stockholm 5613432*	12	5
11 Dec 99		**SUPER TROUPER** *Stockholm 5615002*	21	5
26 May 01	●	**UPSIDE DOWN** *Stockholm 1588492*	10	7
27 Oct 01		**HALFWAY AROUND THE WORLD** *Stockholm 0153612*	30	2

A vs B *UK, male production duo (1 WEEK)* pos/wks

9 May 98		**RIPPED IN 2 MINUTES** *Positiva CDTIV 89*	49	1

AALIYAH *US, female vocalist – Aaliyah Haughton (50 WEEKS)* pos/wks

2 Jul 94		**BACK AND FORTH** *Jive JIVECD 357*	16	5
15 Oct 94		**(AT YOUR BEST) YOU ARE LOVE** *Jive JIVECD 359*	27	2
11 Mar 95		**AGE AIN'T NOTHING BUT A NUMBER** *Jive JIVECD 369*	32	2
13 May 95		**DOWN WITH THE CLIQUE** *Jive JIVECD 377*	33	2
9 Sep 95		**THE THING I LIKE** *Jive JIVECD 382*	33	2
3 Feb 96		**I NEED YOU TONIGHT** *Big Beat A 8130CD* [1]	66	1
24 Aug 96		**IF YOUR GIRL ONLY KNEW** *Atlantic A 5669CD*	21	2
23 Nov 96		**GOT TO GIVE IT UP** *Atlantic A 5632CD*	37	2
24 May 97		**IF YOUR GIRL ONLY KNEW / ONE IN A MILLION (re-issue)** *Atlantic A 5610CD*	15	3
30 Aug 97		**4 PAGE LETTER** *Atlantic AT 0010CD1*	24	2
22 Nov 97		**THE ONE I GAVE MY HEART TO / HOT LIKE FIRE** *Atlantic AT 0017CD*	30	2
18 Apr 98		**JOURNEY TO THE PAST** *Atlantic AT 0026CD*	22	3
12 Sep 98		**ARE YOU THAT SOMEBODY?** *Atlantic AT 0047CD*	11	4
22 Jul 00	●	**TRY AGAIN** *Virgin VUSCD 167* ▲	5	11
21 Oct 00		**TRY AGAIN (re-entry)** *Virgin VUSCD 167*	75	1
21 Jul 01		**WE NEED A RESOLUTION** *Blackground VUSCD 206* [2]	20	4
1 Sep 01		**WE NEED A RESOLUTION (re-entry)** *Blackground VUSCD 206* [2]	65	2

[1] Junior M.A.F.I.A. featuring Aaliyah [2] Aaliyah featuring Timbaland

ABBA (45 Top 500) *The most successful Swedish recording act in the UK: Björn Ulvaeus (g/v), Benny Andersson (k/v), Agnetha Faltskog (v), and Norwegian Anni-Frid (Frida) Lyngstad (v). 'Waterloo' was the first Scandinavian No.1 in the UK and the biggest ever Eurovision Song Contest-winning hit in the US (252 WEEKS)* pos/wks

20 Apr 74	★	**WATERLOO** *Epic EPC 2240*	1	9
13 Jul 74		**RING RING** *Epic EPC 2452*	32	5
12 Jul 75		**I DO I DO I DO I DO I DO** *Epic EPC 3229*	38	6
20 Sep 75	●	**S.O.S.** *Epic EPC 3576*	6	10
13 Dec 75	★	**MAMMA MIA** *Epic EPC 3790*	1	14
27 Mar 76	★	**FERNANDO** *Epic EPC 4036*	1	15
21 Aug 76	★	**DANCING QUEEN** *Epic EPC 4499* ▲	1	15
20 Nov 76	●	**MONEY MONEY MONEY** *Epic EPC 4713*	3	12
26 Feb 77	★	**KNOWING ME KNOWING YOU** *Epic EPC 4955*	1	13
22 Oct 77	★	**THE NAME OF THE GAME** *Epic EPC 5750*	1	12
4 Feb 78	★	**TAKE A CHANCE ON ME** *Epic EPC 5950*	1	10
16 Sep 78	●	**SUMMER NIGHT CITY** *Epic EPC 6595*	5	9
3 Feb 79	●	**CHIQUITITA** *Epic EPC 7030*	2	9
5 May 79	●	**DOES YOUR MOTHER KNOW** *Epic EPC 7316*	4	9
14 Jul 79	●	**ANGELEYES / VOULEZ-VOUS** *Epic EPC 7499*	3	11
20 Oct 79	●	**GIMME GIMME GIMME (A MAN AFTER MIDNIGHT)** *Epic EPC 7914*	3	12
15 Dec 79	●	**I HAVE A DREAM** *Epic EPC 8088*	2	10
2 Aug 80	★	**THE WINNER TAKES IT ALL** *Epic EPC 8835*	1	10
15 Nov 80	★	**SUPER TROUPER** *Epic EPC 9089*	1	12
18 Jul 81	●	**LAY ALL YOUR LOVE ON ME** *Epic EPC A13 1456*	7	7
12 Dec 81	●	**ONE OF US** *Epic EPC A 1740*	3	10
20 Feb 82		**HEAD OVER HEELS** *Epic EPC A 2037*	25	7
23 Oct 82		**THE DAY BEFORE YOU CAME** *Epic EPC A 2847*	32	6
11 Dec 82		**UNDER ATTACK** *Epic EPC A 2971*	26	8
12 Nov 83		**THANK YOU FOR THE MUSIC** *CBS A 3894*	33	6
5 Sep 92		**DANCING QUEEN (re-issue)** *Polydor PO 231*	16	5

'Lay All Your Love on Me' was available only on 12" vinyl in the UK

ABBACADABRA *UK, male / female vocal / instrumental group (1 WEEK)* pos/wks

5 Sep 92		**DANCING QUEEN** *PWL International PWL 246*	57	1

Russ ABBOT *UK, male vocalist Russell Roberts (22 WEEKS)* pos/wks

6 Feb 82		**A DAY IN THE LIFE OF VINCE PRINCE** *EMI 5249*	61	1
20 Feb 82		**A DAY IN THE LIFE OF VINCE PRINCE (re-entry)** *EMI 5249*	75	1
29 Dec 84	●	**ATMOSPHERE** *Spirit FIRE 4*	7	13
13 Jul 85		**ALL NIGHT HOLIDAY** *Spirit FIRE 6*	20	7

Gregory ABBOTT *US, male vocalist (13 WEEKS)* pos/wks

22 Nov 86	●	**SHAKE YOU DOWN** *CBS A 7326* ▲	6	13

ABC (336 Top 500) *Glossy but witty pop group formed 1980, in Sheffield, South Yorkshire, UK. Led by stylish vocalist Martin Fry b. 9 Mar 1959. First UK group of the 1980s to prise four Top 20 hits off debut album (1982's 'The Lexicon of Love') and were equally successful Stateside (93 WEEKS)* pos/wks

31 Oct 81		**TEARS ARE NOT ENOUGH** *Neutron NT 101*	19	8
20 Feb 82	●	**POISON ARROW** *Neutron NT 102*	6	11
15 May 82	●	**THE LOOK OF LOVE** *Neutron NT 103*	4	11
4 Sep 82	●	**ALL OF MY HEART** *Neutron NT 104*	5	8
15 Jan 83		**THE LOOK OF LOVE (re-entry)** *Neutron NT 103*	71	1
5 Nov 83		**THAT WAS THEN THIS IS NOW** *Neutron NT 105*	18	4
21 Jan 84		**S.O.S.** *Neutron NT 106*	39	5
10 Nov 84		**HOW TO BE A MILLIONAIRE** *Neutron NT 107*	49	4
6 Apr 85		**BE NEAR ME** *Neutron NT 108*	26	4
15 Jun 85		**VANITY KILLS** *Neutron NT 109*	70	1

16 Jan 86		**OCEAN BLUE** *Neutron NT 110*	51	3
6 Jun 87		**WHEN SMOKEY SINGS** *Neutron NT 111*	11	10
5 Sep 87		**THE NIGHT YOU MURDERED LOVE** *Neutron NT 112*	31	8
28 Nov 87		**KING WITHOUT A CROWN** *Neutron NT 113*	44	3
27 May 89		**ONE BETTER WORLD** *Neutron NT 114*	32	4
23 Sep 89		**THE REAL THING** *Neutron NT 115*	68	1
14 Apr 90		**THE LOOK OF LOVE (re-mix)** *Neutron NT 116*	68	1
27 Jul 91		**LOVE CONQUERS ALL** *Parlophone R 6292*	47	2
11 Jan 92		**SAY IT** *Parlophone R 6298*	42	3
22 Mar 97		**STRANGER THINGS** *Blatant / Deconstruction 453632*	57	1

The act was a UK, male vocal / instrumental group for first six hits, and a UK / US, male / female vocal / instrumental group for the next four; male duo 87-92 and Martin Fry alone for 'Stranger Things'

Paula ABDUL *US, female vocalist (67 WEEKS)* pos/wks

4 Mar 89	●	**STRAIGHT UP** *Siren SRN 111* ▲	3	13
3 Jun 89		**FOREVER YOUR GIRL** *Siren SRN 112* ▲	24	6
19 Aug 89		**KNOCKED OUT** *Siren SRN 92*	45	3
2 Dec 89		**(IT'S JUST) THE WAY THAT YOU LOVE ME** *Siren SRN 101*	74	1
7 Apr 90	●	**OPPOSITES ATTRACT** *Siren SRN 124* [1] ▲	2	13
21 Jul 90		**KNOCKED OUT (re-mix)** *Virgin America VUS 23*	21	5
29 Sep 90		**COLD HEARTED** *Virgin America VUS 27* ▲	46	3
22 Jun 91	●	**RUSH RUSH** *Virgin America VUS 38* ▲	6	11
31 Aug 91		**THE PROMISE OF A NEW DAY** *Virgin America VUS 44* ▲	52	2
18 Jan 92		**VIBEOLOGY** *Virgin America VUS 53*	19	6
8 Aug 92		**WILL YOU MARRY ME** *Virgin America VUS 58*	73	1
17 Jun 95		**MY LOVE IS FOR REAL** *Virgin America VUSCD 91* [2]	28	3

[1] Paula Abdul with the Wild Pair [2] Paula Abdul featuring Ofra Haza

ABI *UK, male vocalist (2 WEEKS)* pos/wks

13 Jun 98		**COUNTING THE DAYS** *Kuku CDKUKU 1*	44	2

ABIGAIL *UK, female vocalist (4 WEEKS)* pos/wks

16 Jul 94		**SMELLS LIKE TEEN SPIRIT** *Klone CDKLONE 25*	29	4

ABNEA – *See Johan GIELEN*

Colonel ABRAMS *US, male vocalist (35 WEEKS)* pos/wks

17 Aug 85	●	**TRAPPED** *MCA MCA 997*	3	23
7 Dec 85		**THE TRUTH** *MCA MCA 1022*	53	3
8 Feb 86		**I'M NOT GONNA LET YOU** *MCA MCA 1031*	24	7
15 Aug 87		**HOW SOON WE FORGET** *MCA MCA 1179*	75	2

ABSOLUTE *US, male production / instrumental duo (3 WEEKS)* pos/wks

18 Jan 97		**I BELIEVE** *AM:PM 5820752* [1]	38	2
14 Mar 98		**CATCH ME** *AM:PM 5825032*	69	1

[1] Absolute featuring Suzanne Palmer

ABSOLUTELY FABULOUS – *See PET SHOP BOYS*

AC/DC (215 Top 500) *Internationally acclaimed Australia-based quintet: Angus Young (g), Malcolm Young (g), Bon Scott (v) (d. 1980), Cliff Williams (b), Phillip Rudd (d). Brian Johnson (ex-Geordie) replaced Scott in 1980. No act has had more hits (28) without a Top 10 than AC/DC (126 WEEKS)* pos/wks

10 Jun 78		**ROCK 'N' ROLL DAMNATION** *Atlantic K 11142*	24	9
1 Sep 79		**HIGHWAY TO HELL** *Atlantic K 11321*	56	4
2 Feb 80		**TOUCH TOO MUCH** *Atlantic K 11435*	29	9
28 Jun 80		**DIRTY DEEDS DONE DIRT CHEAP** *Atlantic HM 2*	47	3
28 Jun 80		**HIGH VOLTAGE (LIVE VERSION)** *Atlantic HM 1*	48	3
28 Jun 80		**IT'S A LONG WAY TO THE TOP (IF YOU WANNA ROCK 'N' ROLL)** *Atlantic HM 3*	55	3
28 Jun 80		**WHOLE LOTTA ROSIE** *Atlantic HM 4*	36	8
13 Sep 80		**YOU SHOOK ME ALL NIGHT LONG** *Atlantic K 11600*	38	6
29 Nov 80		**ROCK 'N' ROLL AIN'T NOISE POLLUTION** *Atlantic K 11630*	15	8
6 Feb 82		**LET'S GET IT UP** *Atlantic K 11706*	13	6
3 Jul 82		**FOR THOSE ABOUT TO ROCK (WE SALUTE YOU)** *Atlantic K 11721*	15	6
29 Oct 83		**GUNS FOR HIRE** *Atlantic A 9774*	37	4
4 Aug 84		**NERVOUS SHAKEDOWN** *Atlantic A 9651*	35	5
6 Jul 85		**DANGER** *Atlantic A 9532*	48	4
18 Jan 86		**SHAKE YOUR FOUNDATIONS** *Atlantic A 9474*	24	5
24 May 86		**WHO MADE WHO** *Atlantic A 9425*	16	5
30 Aug 86		**YOU SHOOK ME ALL NIGHT LONG (re-issue)** *Atlantic A 9377*	46	4
16 Jan 88		**HEATSEEKER** *Atlantic A 9136*	12	6
2 Apr 88		**THAT'S THE WAY I WANNA ROCK 'N' ROLL** *Atlantic A 9098*	22	5
22 Sep 90		**THUNDERSTRUCK** *Atco B 8907*	13	5
24 Nov 90		**MONEYTALKS** *Atco B 8886*	36	3
27 Apr 91		**ARE YOU READY** *Atco B 8830*	34	3
17 Oct 92		**HIGHWAY TO HELL (LIVE)** *Atco B 8479*	14	4
6 Mar 93		**DIRTY DEEDS DONE DIRT CHEAP (LIVE)** *Atco B 6073CD*	68	1
10 Jul 93		**BIG GUN** *Atco B 8396CD*	23	3
30 Sep 95		**HARD AS A ROCK** *Atlantic A 4368CD*	33	2
11 May 96		**HAIL CAESAR** *East West 7559660512*	56	1
15 Apr 00		**STIFF UPPER LIP** *EMI CDSTIFF 100*	65	1

ACE *UK, male vocal / instrumental group (10 WEEKS)* pos/wks

9 Nov 74		**HOW LONG** *Anchor ANC 1002*	20	10

Richard ACE *Jamaica, male vocalist (2 WEEKS)* pos/wks

2 Dec 78		**STAYIN' ALIVE** *Blue Inc. INC 2*	66	2

ACE OF BASE (305 Top 500) *Swedish pop-reggae outfit comprising three Berggren family members, Linn (v), Jenny (v), Jonas "Joker" (k) and Ulf "Buddha" Ekberg (k), all from Gothenburg. Only Swedish act to top the US album chart with 'The Sign' (titled 'Happy Nation' outside US) in 1994 (100 WEEKS)* pos/wks

8 May 93	★	**ALL THAT SHE WANTS** *London 8612702*	1	16
28 Aug 93		**WHEEL OF FORTUNE** *London 8615452*	20	6
13 Nov 93		**HAPPY NATION** *London 8619272*	42	3
26 Feb 94	●	**THE SIGN** *London ACECD 1* ▲	2	16
11 Jun 94	●	**DON'T TURN AROUND** *London ACECD 2*	5	11
15 Oct 94		**HAPPY NATION (re-issue)** *London 8610972*	40	3
14 Jan 95		**LIVING IN DANGER** *London ACECD 3*	18	4
11 Nov 95		**LUCKY LOVE** *London ACECD 4*	20	5
27 Jan 96		**BEAUTIFUL LIFE** *London ACECD 5*	15	6
25 Jul 98	●	**LIFE IS A FLOWER** *London ACECD 7*	5	11
10 Oct 98	●	**CRUEL SUMMER** *London ACECD 8*	8	5
19 Dec 98		**ALWAYS HAVE, ALWAYS WILL** *London ACECD 9*	12	10
17 Apr 99		**EVERYTIME IT RAINS** *London ACECD 10*	22	4

ACEN *UK, male producer (4 WEEKS)* pos/wks

8 Aug 92		**TRIP II THE MOON** *Production House PNT 042*	38	3
10 Oct 92		**TRIP II THE MOON (re-mix)** *Production House PNT 042RX*	71	1

ACES – *See Desmond DEKKER and the ACES*

Tracy ACKERMAN – *See Q*

ACT *UK / Germany, male / female vocal / instrumental group (2 WEEKS)* pos/wks

23 May 87		**SNOBBERY AND DECAY** *ZTT ZTAS 28*	60	2

ACT ONE *US, male / female vocal / instrumental group (6 WEEKS)* pos/wks

18 May 74		**TOM THE PEEPER** *Mercury 6008 005*	40	6

ACZESS *UK, male producer (1 WEEK)* pos/wks

27 Oct 01		**DO WHAT WE WOULD** *INCredible 6719782*	65	1

ADAM and the ANTS (200 Top 500) *Warpaint-wearing, colourfully costumed 'Antmusic' innovators: included Stuart (Adam Ant) Goddard (v) and Marco Pirroni (g). The London-based act was 1981's top chart act with nine hits. Also in that year, they amassed 91 chart weeks – a total not bettered until 1996 (130 WEEKS)* pos/wks

2 Aug 80		**KINGS OF THE WILD FRONTIER** *CBS 8877*	48	5
11 Oct 80	●	**DOG EAT DOG** *CBS 9039*	4	16
6 Dec 80	●	**ANTMUSIC** *CBS 9352*	2	18
27 Dec 80	●	**YOUNG PARISIANS** *Decca F13803*	9	13
24 Jan 81		**CARTROUBLE** *Do It DUN 10*	33	9
24 Jan 81		**ZEROX** *Do It DUN 8*	45	9
21 Feb 81	●	**KINGS OF THE WILD FRONTIER (re-entry)** *CBS 8877*	2	13

UK No.1 ★ UK Top 10 ● Still on chart + UK million seller ◆ UK entry at No.1 ■ US No.1 ▲

1952

IN THE YEAR IN WHICH ANNE FRANK'S DIARY OF HER EXPERIENCES IN THE SECOND WORLD WAR WAS PUBLISHED, 'SINGIN' IN THE RAIN' BROKE NEW HOLLYWOOD RECORDS, AND DWIGHT "IKE" EISENHOWER WAS ELECTED PRESIDENT OF THE US, **DAME VERA LYNN**, WHO HAD THREE HITS IN THE VERY FIRST CHART, RECALLS A FORTUITOUS VISIT TO A SWISS BIERKELLER...

"I'm surprised, looking back, that 'Auf Wiedersehen' was so high up in the chart. As I've travelled around, it's not the sort of song people ask for. At the time, I was in a show in London, 'London Laughs' at the Adelphi with Tony Hancock and Jimmy Edwards, and it had been running for about 18 months. I was getting a bit fatigued, so my husband and I went to Switzerland for 10 days' rest. I used to hear this tune on the radio, and at the beer parlour where we went one evening everyone would get up and and sing it and swing their beer tankards. So, I thought, this is a great song and when we got back I tried to find it. Some months later I found it and I rang Decca to say I want to record this tune, and I said it hasn't got any English lyrics to it yet. That was organised and I went in the studio and it became a terrific hit. It's such a simple song that I was a bit surprised it made No.1 in the States."

SINGLE OF THE YEAR
'Here in My Heart' Al Martino

9 May 81 ★ **STAND AND DELIVER** *CBS A 1065* ■ 1 15
12 Sep 81 ★ **PRINCE CHARMING** *CBS A 1408* 1 12
12 Dec 81 ● **ANT RAP** *CBS A 1738* 3 10
27 Feb 82 **DEUTSCHER GIRLS** *Ego 5* 13 6
13 Mar 82 **THE ANTMUSIC EP (THE B-SIDES)** *Do It DUN 20* 46 4

Tracks on The Antmusic EP (The B-sides): Friends / Kick / Physical

See also Adam ANT

A.D.A.M. featuring AMY
France, male / female vocal / instrumental duo (11 WEEKS) pos/wks

1 Jul 95 **ZOMBIE** *Eternal YZ 951CD* 16 11

Arthur ADAMS *US, male vocalist (5 WEEKS)* pos/wks

24 Oct 81 **YOU GOT THE FLOOR** *RCA 146* 38 5

Bryan ADAMS (56 Top 500) *Globally successful rock singer / songwriter / guitarist, b. 5 Nov 1959, Kingston, Ontario. He has had more UK hits than any other Canadian artist and was the biggest-selling singles artist in the UK in 1991 (235 WEEKS)* pos/wks

12 Jan 85 **RUN TO YOU** *A&M AM 224* 11 12
16 Mar 85 **SOMEBODY** *A&M AM 236* 35 7
25 May 85 **HEAVEN** *A&M AM 256* ▲ 38 5
10 Aug 85 **SUMMER OF '69** *A&M AM 267* 42 7
2 Nov 85 **IT'S ONLY LOVE** *A&M 285* [1] 29 6
21 Dec 85 **CHRISTMAS TIME** *A & M AM 297* 55 2
22 Feb 86 **THIS TIME** *A & M AM 295* 41 7
12 Jul 86 **STRAIGHT FROM THE HEART** *A & M AM 322* 51 3
28 Mar 87 **HEAT OF THE NIGHT** *A & M ADAM 2* 50 2
20 Jun 87 **HEARTS ON FIRE** *A & M ADAM 3* 57 3
17 Oct 87 **VICTIM OF LOVE** *A & M AM 407* 68 2
29 Jun 91 ★ **(EVERYTHING I DO) I DO IT FOR YOU** *A & M AM 789* ◆ ▲ 1 24
14 Sep 91 **CAN'T STOP THIS THING WE STARTED** *A & M AM 612* 12 6
23 Nov 91 **THERE WILL NEVER BE ANOTHER TONIGHT** *A & M AM 838* 32 3
28 Dec 91 **(EVERYTHING I DO) I DO IT FOR YOU (re-entry)** *A & M AM 789* 73 1
22 Feb 92 ● **THOUGHT I'D DIED AND GONE TO HEAVEN** *A & M AM 848* 8 7
18 Jul 92 **ALL I WANT IS YOU** *A & M AM 879* 22 5
26 Sep 92 **DO I HAVE TO SAY THE WORDS** *A & M AM 0068* 30 3
30 Oct 93 ● **PLEASE FORGIVE ME** *A & M 5804232* 2 16
15 Jan 94 ● **ALL FOR LOVE** *A & M 5804772* [2] ▲ 2 13
22 Apr 95 ● **HAVE YOU EVER REALLY LOVED A WOMAN** *A & M 5810282* ▲ 4 9
11 Nov 95 **ROCK STEADY** *Capitol CDCL 763* [3] 50 2
1 Jun 96 ● **THE ONLY THING THAT LOOKS GOOD ON ME IS YOU** *A & M 5813692* 6 7
24 Aug 96 ● **LET'S MAKE A NIGHT TO REMEMBER** *A & M 5815672* 10 8
23 Nov 96 **STAR** *A & M 5820252* 13 4
8 Feb 97 ● **I FINALLY FOUND SOMEONE** *A & M 5820832* [4] 10 7
19 Apr 97 **18 TIL I DIE** *A & M 5821852* 22 3
20 Dec 97 **BACK TO YOU** *A & M 5824752* 18 7
21 Mar 98 **I'M READY** *A & M 5825352* 20 4
10 Oct 98 **ON A DAY LIKE TODAY** *Mercury MERCD 516* 13 5
12 Dec 98 ● **WHEN YOU'RE GONE** *A & M 5828212* [5] 3 19
15 May 99 ● **CLOUD NUMBER 9** *A&M / Mercury 5828492* 6 9
18 Dec 99 **THE BEST OF ME** *Mercury / A & M 4971952* 47 1
22 Jan 00 **THE BEST OF ME (re-entry)** *Mercury / A & M 4971952* 55 2
18 Mar 00 ★ **DON'T GIVE UP** *Xtravaganza XTRAV 9CDS* [6] ■ 1 14

[1] Bryan Adams and Tina Turner [2] Bryan Adams, Rod Stewart and Sting [3] Bonnie Raitt and Bryan Adams [4] Barbra Streisand and Bryan Adams [5] Bryan Adams featuring Melanie C [6] Chicane featuring Bryan Adams

Gayle ADAMS *US, female vocalist (1 WEEK)* pos/wks

26 Jul 80 **STRETCHIN' OUT** *Epic EPC 8791* 64 1

Marie ADAMS – *See Johnny OTIS SHOW*

Oleta ADAMS *US, female vocalist (36 WEEKS)* pos/wks

24 Mar 90 **RHYTHM OF LIFE** *Fontana OLETA 1* 52 2
3 Nov 90 **RHYTHM OF LIFE (re-entry)** *Fontana OLETA 1* 56 3
12 Jan 91 ● **GET HERE** *Fontana OLETA 3* 4 12
13 Apr 91 **YOU'VE GOT TO GIVE ME ROOM / RHYTHM OF LIFE (re-issue)** *Fontana OLETA 4* 49 3
29 Jun 91 **CIRCLE OF ONE** *Fontana OLETA 5* 73 1
28 Sep 91 **DON'T LET THE SUN GO DOWN ON ME** *Fontana TRIBO 1* 33 5
25 Apr 92 **WOMAN IN CHAINS (re-issue)** *Fontana IDEA 16* [1] 57 1
10 Jul 93 **I JUST HAD TO HEAR YOUR VOICE** *Fontana OLECD 6* 42 3
7 Oct 95 **NEVER KNEW LOVE** *Fontana OLECD 9* 22 3
16 Dec 95 **RHYTHM OF LIFE (re-mix)** *Fontana OLECD 10* 38 2
10 Feb 96 **WE WILL MEET AGAIN** *Mercury OLECD 11* 51 1

[1] Tears For Fears featuring Oleta Adams

The original release of 'Woman in Chains' credited Tears For Fears only

Ryan ADAMS *US, male vocalist (1 WEEK)* pos/wks

8 Dec 01 **NEW YORK NEW YORK** *Lost Highway 1722232* 53 1

Cliff ADAMS ORCHESTRA *UK, orchestra (2 WEEKS)* pos/wks

28 Apr 60 **THE LONELY MAN THEME** *Pye International 7N 25056* 39 2

ADAMSKI
UK, male instrumentalist / producer – Adam Tinley (39 WEEKS) pos/wks

20 Jan 90 **N-R-G** *MCA MCA 1386* 12 6
7 Apr 90 ★ **KILLER** *MCA MCA 1400* 1 18
8 Sep 90 ● **THE SPACE JUNGLE** *MCA MCA 1435* 7 8
17 Nov 90 **FLASHBACK JACK** *MCA MCA 1459* 46 2
9 Nov 91 **NEVER GOIN' DOWN / BORN TO BE ALIVE** *MCA MCS 1578* [1] 51 2
4 Apr 92 **GET YOUR BODY** *MCA MCS 1613* [2] 68 1
4 Jul 92 **BACK TO FRONT** *MCA MCS 1644* 63 1
11 Jul 98 **ONE OF THE PEOPLE** *ZTT ZTT 101CD* [3] 56 1

[1] Adamski featuring Jimi Polo / Adamski featuring Soho [2] Adamski featuring Nina Hagen [3] Adamski's Thing

Featured vocalist on 'Killer' was Seal

ADDAMS and GEE *UK, male instrumental duo (1 WEEK)* pos/wks

20 Apr 91 **CHUNG KUO (REVISITED)** *Debut DEBT 3108* 72 1

ADDIS BLACK WIDOW *US, male rap duo (2 WEEKS)* pos/wks

3 Feb 96 **INNOCENT** *Mercury Black Vinyl MBVCD 1* 42 2

ADDRISI BROTHERS *US, male vocal duo (3 WEEKS)* pos/wks

6 Oct 79 **GHOST DANCER** *Scotti Brothers K 11361* 57 3

ADEVA *US, female vocalist – Patricia Daniels (66 WEEKS)* pos/wks

14 Jan 89 **RESPECT** *Cooltempo COOL 179* 17 9
25 Mar 89 **MUSICAL FREEDOM (MOVING ON UP)** *Cooltempo COOL 182* [1] 22 8
12 Aug 89 **WARNING** *Cooltempo COOL 185* 17 8
21 Oct 89 **I THANK YOU** *Cooltempo COOL 192* 17 7
16 Dec 89 **BEAUTIFUL LOVE** *Cooltempo COOL 195* 57 5
28 Apr 90 **TREAT ME RIGHT** *Cooltempo COOL 200* 62 2
6 Apr 91 **RING MY BELL** *Cooltempo COOL 224* [2] 20 5
19 Oct 91 **IT SHOULD'VE BEEN ME** *Cooltempo COOL 236* 48 3
29 Feb 92 **DON'T LET IT SHOW ON YOUR FACE** *Cooltempo COOL 248* 34 4
6 Jun 92 **UNTIL YOU COME BACK TO ME** *Cooltempo COOL 254* 45 3
17 Oct 92 **I'M THE ONE FOR YOU** *Cooltempo COOL 264* 51 2
11 Dec 93 **RESPECT (re-mix)** *Network NWKCD 79* 65 1
27 May 95 **TOO MANY FISH** *Virgin America VUSCD 89* [3] 34 2
18 Nov 95 **WHADDA U WANT (FROM ME)** *Virgin America VUSCD 98* [3] 36 2
6 Apr 96 **DO WATCHA DO** *Avex UK AVEXCD 24* [4] 54 1
4 May 96 **I THANK YOU (re-mix)** *Cooltempo CDCOOLS 318* 37 2
12 Apr 97 **DO WATCHA DO (re-mix)** *Distinctive DISNCD 28* [4] 60 1
26 Jul 97 **WHERE IS THE LOVE? / THE WAY THAT YOU FEEL** *Distinctive DISNCD 31* 54 1

[1] Paul Simpson featuring Adeva [2] Monie Love vs Adeva [3] Frankie Knuckles featuring Adeva [4] Hyper Go Go and Adeva

ADICTS *UK, male vocal / instrumental group (1 WEEK)* pos/wks

14 May 83 **BAD BOY** *Razor RZS 104* 75 1

ADIEMUS *UK, male instrumental duo (2 WEEKS)* pos/wks

14 Oct 95	**ADIEMUS** *Venture VEND 4*	**48**	2

Larry ADLER – *See Kate BUSH*

ADONIS featuring 2 PUERTO RICANS, A BLACK MAN AND A DOMINICAN *US, male vocal / instrumental group (4 WEEKS)* pos/wks

13 Jun 87	**DO IT PROPERLY ('NO WAY BACK') / NO WAY BACK** *London LON 136*	**47**	4

ADRENALIN M.O.D.
UK, male instrumental / production group (5 WEEKS) pos/wks

8 Oct 88	**O-O-O** *MCA RAGAT 2*	**49**	5

ADULT NET
UK / US, male / female vocal / instrumental group (2 WEEKS) pos/wks

10 Jun 89	**WHERE WERE YOU** *Fontana BRX 2*	**66**	2

ADVENTURES *UK, male vocal / instrumental group (24 WEEKS)* pos/wks

15 Sep 84	**ANOTHER SILENT DAY** *Chrysalis CHS 2000*	**71**	2
1 Dec 84	**SEND MY HEART** *Chrysalis CHS 2001*	**62**	4
13 Jul 85	**FEEL THE RAINDROPS** *Chrysalis AD 1*	**58**	3
9 Apr 88	**BROKEN LAND** *Elektra EKR 69*	**20**	10
2 Jul 88	**DROWNING IN THE SEA OF LOVE** *Elektra EKR 76*	**44**	4
13 Jun 92	**RAINING ALL OVER THE WORLD** *Polydor PO 211*	**68**	1

ADVENTURES OF STEVIE V
UK, male / female vocal / production group (22 WEEKS) pos/wks

21 Apr 90 ●	**DIRTY CASH** *Mercury MER 311*	**2**	13
29 Sep 90	**BODY LANGUAGE** *Mercury MER 331*	**29**	5
2 Mar 91	**JEALOUSY** *Mercury MER 337*	**58**	3
27 Sep 97	**DIRTY CASH (re-mix)** *Avex Trax AVEXCDX 57*	**69**	1

ADVERTS *UK, male / female vocal / instrumental group (11 WEEKS)* pos/wks

27 Aug 77	**GARY GILMORE'S EYES** *Anchor ANC 1043*	**18**	7
4 Feb 78	**NO TIME TO BE 21** *Bright BR 1*	**34**	4

AEROSMITH (341 Top 500) *Godfathers of contemporary heavy rock scene, formed 1970 New Hampshire, US. Multi-platinum album act's UK success came only after front men Steven Tyler (v) and Joe Perry (g) teamed with rappers Run-DMC on 'Walk This Way' (1986). Group's first US No.1 single (1998) came 25 years after chart debut (92 WEEKS)* pos/wks

17 Oct 87	**DUDE (LOOKS LIKE A LADY)** *Geffen GEF 29*	**45**	5
16 Apr 88	**ANGEL** *Geffen GEF 34*	**69**	2
9 Sep 89	**LOVE IN AN ELEVATOR** *Geffen GEF 63*	**13**	8
24 Feb 90	**DUDE (LOOKS LIKE A LADY) (re-issue)** *Geffen GEF 72*	**20**	5
14 Apr 90	**RAG DOLL** *Geffen GEF 76*	**42**	4
1 Sep 90	**THE OTHER SIDE** *Geffen GEF 79*	**46**	2
10 Apr 93	**LIVIN' ON THE EDGE** *Geffen GFSTD 35*	**19**	4
3 Jul 93	**EAT THE RICH** *Geffen GFSTD 46*	**34**	3
30 Oct 93	**CRYIN'** *Geffen GFSTD 56*	**17**	6
18 Dec 93	**AMAZING** *Geffen GFSTD 63*	**57**	3
2 Jul 94	**SHUT UP AND DANCE** *Geffen GFSTD 75*	**24**	4
20 Aug 94	**SWEET EMOTION** *Columbia 6604492*	**74**	1
5 Nov 94	**CRAZY / BLIND MAN** *Geffen GFSTD 80*	**23**	4
8 Mar 97	**FALLING IN LOVE (IS HARD ON THE KNEES)** *Columbia 6640752*	**22**	4
21 Jun 97	**HOLE IN MY SOUL** *Columbia 66645012*	**29**	2
27 Dec 97	**PINK** *Columbia 6648722*	**38**	2
12 Sep 98 ●	**I DON'T WANT TO MISS A THING** *Columbia 6664082* ▲	**4**	20
26 Jun 99	**PINK (re-issue)** *Columbia 6675342*	**13**	6
17 Mar 01	**JADED** *Columbia 6709312*	**13**	7

AFRICAN BUSINESS *Italy, male vocal / instrumental group (1 WEEK)* pos/wks

17 Nov 90	**IN ZAIRE** *Urban URB 64*	**73**	1

AFRO CELT SOUND SYSTEM *UK / Ireland / France / Guinea, male vocal / instrumental group (1 WEEK)* pos/wks

29 Apr 00	**RELEASE** *Realworld RWSCD 10*	**71**	1

AFRO MEDUSA
UK, male production duo and Spain, female vocalist (2 WEEKS) pos/wks

28 Oct 00	**PASILDA** *Rulin RULIN 6CDS*	**31**	2

AFROMAN *US, male vocalist – Joseph Foreman (13 WEEKS)* pos/wks

6 Oct 01	**BECAUSE I GOT HIGH (import)** *Universal 0152822*	**45**	3
27 Oct 01 ★	**BECAUSE I GOT HIGH** *Universal MCSTD 40266* ■	**1**	10+

AFTER 7 *US, male vocal group (3 WEEKS)* pos/wks

3 Nov 90	**CAN'T STOP** *Virgin America VUS 31*	**54**	3

AFTER THE FIRE *UK, male vocal / instrumental group (12 WEEKS)* pos/wks

9 Jun 79	**ONE RULE FOR YOU** *CBS 7025*	**40**	6
8 Sep 79	**LASER LOVE** *CBS 7769*	**62**	2
9 Apr 83	**DER KOMMISSAR** *CBS A 2399*	**47**	4

AFTERNOON BOYS – *See Steve WRIGHT*

AFTERSHOCK *US, male vocal / instrumental duo – Frost Rivera and Guy Routte (8 WEEKS)* pos/wks

21 Aug 93	**SLAVE TO THE VIBE** *Virgin America VUSCD 75*	**11**	8

AFX *UK, male instrumentalist / producer – Richard James (1 WEEK)* pos/wks

11 Aug 01	**2 REMIXES BY AFX** *MEN 1 MEN 1CD*	**69**	1

See also POLYGON WINDOW; APHEX TWIN

AGE OF CHANCE
UK, male / female vocal / instrumental group (13 WEEKS) pos/wks

17 Jan 87	**KISS** *Fon AGE 5*	**50**	6
30 May 87	**WHO'S AFRAID OF THE BIG BAD NOISE!** *Fon VS 962*	**65**	2
20 Jan 90	**HIGHER THAN HEAVEN** *Virgin VS 1228*	**53**	5

AGE OF LOVE *Italy, male instrumental / production trio (6 WEEKS)* pos/wks

5 Jul 97	**THE AGE OF LOVE – THE REMIXES** *React CDREACT 100*	**17**	4
19 Sep 98	**AGE OF LOVE** *React CDREACT 135*	**38**	2

AGENT 00 *UK, male production duo (1 WEEK)* pos/wks

7 Mar 98	**THE MAGNIFICENT** *Inferno CDFERN 002*	**65**	1

AGENT PROVOCATEUR
UK, male / female vocal / production group (1 WEEK) pos/wks

22 Mar 97	**AGENT DAN** *Epic AGENT 3CD*	**49**	1

AGENT SUMO *UK, male production duo (2 WEEKS)* pos/wks

9 Jun 01	**24 HOURS** *Virgin VSCDT 1806*	**44**	2

AGNELLI & NELSON
Ireland, male DJ duo – Chris Agnelli and Robbie Nelson (13 WEEKS) pos/wks

15 Aug 98	**EL NINO** *Xtravaganza 0091575 EXT*	**21**	4
11 Sep 99	**EVERYDAY** *Xtravaganza XTRAV 2CDS*	**17**	4
17 Jun 00	**EMBRACE** *Xtravaganza XTRAV 11CDS*	**35**	2
9 Sep 00	**HUDSON STREET** *Xtravaganza XTRAV 13CDS*	**29**	2
7 Apr 01	**VEGAS** *Xtravaganza XTRAV 23CDS*	**48**	1

Christina AGUILERA (421 Top 500) *Internationally successful photogenic pop vocalist, b. 18 Dec 1980, New York. Four US chart-toppers and the winner of 1999 Best New Artist Grammy and World Music Awards in 2000 and 2001 (79 WEEKS)* pos/wks

11 Sep 99	**GENIE IN A BOTTLE (import)** *RCA 701062*	**50**	5
16 Oct 99 ★	**GENIE IN A BOTTLE** *RCA 74321705482* ■ ▲	**1**	19

26 Feb 00 ● WHAT A GIRL WANTS *RCA 74321737522* ▲ 3 13
22 Jul 00 I TURN TO YOU *RCA 74321765472* 19 6
11 Nov 00 ● COME ON OVER BABY (ALL I WANT IS YOU) *RCA 74321799912* ▲ 8 7
6 Jan 01 COME ON OVER BABY (ALL I WANT IS YOU) (re-entry) *RCA 74321799912* 65 1
10 Mar 01 ● NOBODY WANTS TO BE LONELY *Columbia 6709462* [1] 4 12
30 Jun 01 ★ LADY MARMALADE *Interscope / Polydor 4975612* [2] ■ ▲ 1 16

[1] Ricky Martin and Christina Aguilera [2] Christina Aguilera, Lil' Kim, Mya & Pink

A-HA (193 Top 500) *Norway's biggest-selling act: Morten Harket (v), Pal Waaktaar (g), Magna Furuholmen (k). This globally popular teen-targeted trio was noted for its innovative videos and stage shows (133 WEEKS)* pos/wks

28 Sep 85 ● TAKE ON ME *Warner Bros. W 9006* ▲ 2 19
28 Dec 85 ★ THE SUN ALWAYS SHINES ON TV *Warner Bros. W 8846* 1 12
5 Apr 86 ● TRAIN OF THOUGHT *Warner Bros. W 8736* 8 8
14 Jun 86 ● HUNTING HIGH AND LOW *Warner Bros. W 6663* 5 10
4 Oct 86 ● I'VE BEEN LOSING YOU *Warner Bros. W 8594* 8 7
6 Dec 86 ● CRY WOLF *Warner Bros. W 8500* 5 9
28 Feb 87 MANHATTAN SKYLINE *Warner Bros. W 8405* 13 6
4 Jul 87 ● THE LIVING DAYLIGHTS *Warner Bros. W 8305* 5 9
26 Mar 88 ● STAY ON THESE ROADS *Warner Bros. W 7936* 5 6
18 Jun 88 THE BLOOD THAT MOVES THE BODY *Warner Bros. W 7840* 25 4
27 Aug 88 TOUCHY! *Warner Bros. W 7749* 11 7
3 Dec 88 YOU ARE THE ONE *Warner Bros. W 7636* 13 10
13 Oct 90 CRYING IN THE RAIN *Warner Bros. W 9547* 13 7
15 Dec 90 I CALL YOUR NAME *Warner Bros. W 9462* 44 5
26 Oct 91 MOVE TO MEMPHIS *Warner Bros. W 0070* 47 2
5 Jun 93 DARK IS THE NIGHT *Warner Bros. W 0175CD* 19 4
18 Sep 93 ANGEL *Warner Bros. W 0195CD* 41 3
26 Mar 94 SHAPES THAT GO TOGETHER *Warner Bros. W 0236CD* 27 3
3 Jun 00 SUMMER MOVED ON *WEA WEA 275CD* 33 2

AHMAD *US, male rapper (2 WEEKS)* pos/wks

9 Jul 94 BACK IN THE DAY *Giant 74321212042* 64 2

AIDA *Holland, male production duo (1 WEEK)* pos/wks

19 Feb 00 FAR AND AWAY *48K / Perfecto SPECT 03CDS* 58 1

AIR *France, male instrumental / production duo Benoît Dunkel and Nicolas Godin (14 WEEKS)* pos/wks

21 Feb 98 SEXY BOY *Virgin VSCDT 1672* 13 4
16 May 98 KELLY WATCH THE STARS *Virgin VSCDT 1690* 18 3
21 Nov 98 ALL I NEED *Virgin VSCDT 1702* 29 3
26 Feb 00 PLAYGROUND LOVE *Virgin VSCDT 1764* [1] 25 2
2 Jun 01 RADIO #1 *Virgin VSCDT 1803* 31 2

[1] Sung by Gordon Tracks

AIR SUPPLY *UK / Australia, male vocal / instrumental group (Russell Hitchcock and Graham Russell) (17 WEEKS)* pos/wks

27 Sep 80 ALL OUT OF LOVE *Arista ARIST 362* 11 11
2 Oct 82 EVEN THE NIGHTS ARE BETTER *Arista ARIST 474* 44 4
20 Nov 93 GOODBYE *Giant 74321153462* 66 2

AIRHEAD *UK, male vocal / instrumental group (10 WEEKS)* pos/wks

5 Oct 91 FUNNY HOW *Korova KOW 47* 57 3
21 Dec 91 COUNTING SHEEP *Korova KOW 48* 35 5
7 Mar 92 RIGHT NOW *Korova KOW 49* 50 2

AIRHEADZ *UK, male DJ / production duo (2 WEEKS)* pos/wks

28 Apr 01 STANLEY (HERE I AM) *AM:PM CDAMPM 145* 36 2

AIRSCAPE *Belgium / Holland, male instrumental / production group leader Johann Gielen (5 WEEKS)* pos/wks

9 Aug 97 PACIFIC MELODY *Xtravaganza 0091165* 27 2
29 Aug 98 AMAZON CHANT *Xtravaganza 0091605 EXT* 46 1
4 Dec 99 L'ESPERANZA *Xtravaganza EXTRAV 7CD* 33 2

See also BLUE BAMBOO; CUBIC 22; TRANSFORMER 2

Laurel AITKEN and the UNITONE *Jamaica / Cuba, male vocal / instrumental group (3 WEEKS)* pos/wks

17 May 80 RUDI GOT MARRIED *I-Spy SEE 6* 60 3

AKA *UK, male vocal group (2 WEEKS)* pos/wks

12 Oct 96 WARNING *RCA 74321360662* 43 2

AKABU featuring Linda CLIFFORD *UK, male producer (Dave Lee) and US, female vocalist (1 WEEK)* pos/wks

15 Sep 01 RIDE THE STORM *NRK Sound Division NRKCD 053* 69 1

See also Joey NEGRO; Li KWAN; RAVEN MAIZE; JAKATTA; HED BOYS

Jewel AKENS *US, male vocalist (8 WEEKS)* pos/wks

25 Mar 65 THE BIRDS AND THE BEES *London HLN 9954* 29 8

AKIN *UK, female vocal duo (1 WEEK)* pos/wks

14 Jun 97 STAY RIGHT HERE *WEA WEA 117CD* 60 1

ALABAMA 3 *UK, male vocal / instrumental group (3 WEEKS)* pos/wks

22 Nov 97 SPEED AT THE SOUND OF LONELINESS *Elemental ELM 42CDS 1721* 72 1
11 Apr 98 AIN'T GOIN' TO GOA *Elemental ELM 45CDS1* 40 2

ALANA – *See MK*

ALARM *UK, male vocal / instrumental group (64 WEEKS)* pos/wks

24 Sep 83 68 GUNS *IRS PFP 1023* 17 7
21 Jan 84 WHERE WERE YOU HIDING WHEN THE STORM BROKE *IRS IRS 101* 22 6
31 Mar 84 THE DECEIVER *IRS IRS 103* 51 4
3 Nov 84 THE CHANT HAS JUST BEGUN *IRS IRS 104* 48 4
2 Mar 85 ABSOLUTE REALITY *IRS ALARM 1* 35 6
28 Sep 85 STRENGTH *IRS IRM 104* 40 4
18 Jan 86 SPIRIT OF '76 *IRS IRM 109* 22 5
26 Apr 86 KNIFE EDGE *IRS IRM 112* 43 3
17 Oct 87 RAIN IN THE SUMMERTIME *IRS IRM 144* 18 5
12 Dec 87 RESCUE ME *IRS IRM 150* 48 2
20 Feb 88 PRESENCE OF LOVE *IRS IRM 155* 44 3
16 Sep 89 SOLD ME DOWN THE RIVER *IRS EIRS 123* 43 3
4 Nov 89 A NEW SOUTH WALES / THE ROCK *IRS EIRS 129* 31 5
3 Feb 90 LOVE DON'T COME EASY *IRS EIRS 134* 48 3
27 Oct 90 UNSAFE BUILDING 1990 *IRS ALARM 2* 54 2
13 Apr 91 RAW *IRS ALARM 3* 51 2

'A New South Wales' features Morriston Orpheus Male Voice Choir. 'Sold Me Down The River' was joined by 'Yn Gymreag' for the first week on chart

Morris ALBERT *Brazil, male vocalist – Morris Kaisermann (10 WEEKS)* pos/wks

27 Sep 75 ● FEELINGS *Decca F 13591* 4 10

ALBERTA *Sierra Leone, female vocalist (3 WEEKS)* pos/wks

26 Dec 98 YOYO BOY *RCA 74321640602* 48 3

ALBERTO Y LOS TRIOS PARANOIAS *UK, male vocal / instrumental group (5 WEEKS)* pos/wks

23 Sep 78 HEADS DOWN NO NONSENSE MINDLESS BOOGIE *Logo GO 323* 47 5

Al ALBERTS – *See FOUR ACES*

ALBION *Holland, male producer – Ferry Corsten (1 WEEK)* pos/wks

3 Jun 00 AIR 2000 *Platipus PLATCD 73* 59 1

See also SYSTEM F; VERACOCHA; MOONMAN; GOURYELLA; Ferry CORSTEN

ALCATRAZ *US, male instrumental / production duo – Jean-Philippe Aviance and Victor Imbres (4 WEEKS)* pos/wks

17 Feb 96 GIV ME LUV *AM:PM 5814332* 12 4

1953

IN THE YEAR IN WHICH QUEEN ELIZABETH II WAS CROWNED IN WESTMINSTER ABBEY, THE STARGAZERS BECAME THE FIRST BRITISH ACT TO TOP THE UK CHART, STALIN DIED IN MOSCOW AND HILLARY AND TENZING CONQUERED EVEREST, **JOHN ALLISON** OF THE ALLISONS GETS ALL INSPIRED BY SOME HARMONY SINGING...

"Life was very simple in 1953. My family had no television and my dad controlled the wireless. At weekends the house was often filled with the music from BBC Children's Favourites with Uncle Mac, Forces and then 'Family Favourites', 'The Billy Cotton Band Show', musical spots on 'Take It From Here' and 'Educating Archie' and then, during the week, 'Workers Playtime'. I was 13 and a choirboy at Saint Dionis, Parsons Green. I loved close harmony singing and my personal interest was certainly kindled by people like Dickie Valentine, David Whitfield, Frankie Laine, Guy Mitchell and particularly the **Beverley Sisters** who charted for the first time that year with 'I Saw Mommy Kissing Santa Claus'. They all seemed to be associated with big dance bands or orchestras and I didn't have the faintest idea how that came about. Unknown to me, the rock 'n' roll beat was about to happen and the emergence of the guitar as an easily acquired common instrument to ease the passage of so many in the world of entertainment. I had certainly decided that popular music would be a nice, satisfying way to earn a living. It would be four years until the craze for skiffle and the discovery that simple do-it-yourself guitar music would open up the way for so many of us. The rest, as the cliché goes, is music history."

SINGLE OF THE YEAR
'I Believe' Frankie Laine

ALCAZAR *Sweden, male / female vocal trio (4 WEEKS)* pos/wks

8 Dec 01 **CRYING AT THE DISCOTHEQUE** *Arista 743893432*.....13 4+

ALDA *Iceland, female vocalist – Alda Olafsdottir (14 WEEKS)* pos/wks

29 Aug 98 ● **REAL GOOD TIME** *Wildstar CDWILD 7*.....7 7
26 Dec 98 **GIRLS NIGHT OUT** *Wildstar CDWILD 10*.....20 7

Cali ALEMAN – *See Tito PUENTE Jr and the LATIN RHYTHM featuring Tito PUENTE, INDIA and Cali ALEMAN*

ALENA *Jamaica, female vocalist (5 WEEKS)* pos/wks

13 Nov 99 **TURN IT AROUND** *Wonderboy WBOYD 16*.....14 5

ALESSI *US, male vocal duo – Billy and Bobby Alessi (11 WEEKS)* pos/wks

11 Jun 77 ● **OH LORI** *A & M AMS 7289*.....8 11

ALEX PARTY *Italy / UK, male / female vocal / instrumental group. Leader Paolo Visnadi (28 WEEKS)* pos/wks

18 Dec 93 **SATURDAY NIGHT PARTY** *Cleveland City Imports CCICD 17000*.....49 6
28 May 94 **SATURDAY NIGHT PARTY (READ MY LIPS) (re-entry)** *Cleveland City Imports CCICD 17000*.....29 4
18 Feb 95 ● **DON'T GIVE ME YOUR LIFE** *Systematic SYSCD 7*.....2 13
18 Nov 95 **WRAP ME UP** *Systematic SYSCD 22*.....17 3
19 Oct 96 **READ MY LIPS (re-mix)** *Systematic SYSCD 30*.....28 2

'Read My Lips' in 1996 is a remix of the first hit with added vocals

See also LIVIN' JOY

ALEXIA *Italian, female vocalist – Alessia Aquilani (15 WEEKS)* pos/wks

21 Mar 98 ● **UH LA LA LA** *Dance Pool ALEX 1CD*.....10 9
13 Jun 98 **GIMME LOVE** *Dance Pool ALEX 2CDZ*.....17 4
10 Oct 98 **THE MUSIC I LIKE** *Dance Pool ALEX 3CD*.....31 2

ALFI and HARRY *US, male vocalist / instrumentalist – David Seville under two false names (5 WEEKS)* pos/wks

23 Mar 56 **THE TROUBLE WITH HARRY** *London HLU 8242*.....15 5

See also David SEVILLE; CHIPMUNKS

ALFIE *UK, male vocal / instrumental group (1 WEEK)* pos/wks

8 Sep 01 **YOU MAKE NO BONES** *Twisted Nerve TN 033CD*.....61 1

John ALFORD *UK, male vocalist (12 WEEKS)* pos/wks

17 Feb 96 **SMOKE GETS IN YOUR EYES** *Love This LUVTHISCD 7*.....13 5
25 May 96 ● **BLUE MOON / ONLY YOU** *Love This LUVTHISCD 9*.....9 4
23 Nov 96 **IF / KEEP ON RUNNING** *Love This LUVTHISCD 15*.....24 3

ALI *UK, male vocalist (2 WEEKS)* pos/wks

23 May 98 **LOVE LETTERS** *Wild Card 5698092*.....63 1
24 Oct 98 **FEELIN' YOU** *Wild Card 5676992*.....63 1

Tatyana ALI *US, female vocalist (18 WEEKS)* pos/wks

14 Nov 98 ● **DAYDREAMIN'** *Epic 6665462*.....6 5
13 Feb 99 ● **BOY YOU KNOCK ME OUT** *MJJ / Epic 6669372* [1].....3 8
15 May 99 **BOY YOU KNOCK ME OUT (re-entry)** *MJJ / Epic 6669372* [1].....69 1
19 Jun 99 **EVERYTIME** *Epic / MJJ 674742*.....20 4

[1] Tatyana Ali featuring Will Smith

ALI and FRAZIER *UK, female vocal duo (4 WEEKS)* pos/wks

7 Aug 93 **UPTOWN TOP RANKING** *Arista 74321158842*.....33 4

ALIBI *UK, male vocal duo (2 WEEKS)* pos/wks

15 Feb 97 **I'M NOT TO BLAME** *Urgent 74321434762*.....51 1
7 Feb 98 **HOW MUCH I FEEL** *Urgent 74321548472*.....58 1

ALICE BAND *UK / Ireland / US, female vocal / instrumental group (1 WEEK)* pos/wks

23 Jun 01 **ONE DAY AT A TIME** *Instant Karma KARMA 5CD*.....52 1

ALICE DEEJAY *Holland, male / female production / vocal group (50 WEEKS)* pos/wks

31 Jul 99 ● **BETTER OFF ALONE** *Positiva CDTIV 113* [1].....2 16
4 Dec 99 ● **BACK IN MY LIFE** *Positiva CDTIV 121*.....4 15
15 Jul 00 ● **WILL I EVER** *Positiva CDTIV 134*.....7 10
21 Oct 00 **THE LONELY ONE** *Positiva CDTIV 145*.....16 5
10 Feb 01 **CELEBRATE OUR LOVE** *Positiva CDTIV 149*.....17 4

[1] DJ Jurgen presents Alice Deejay

ALICE IN CHAINS *US, male vocal / instrumental group (14 WEEKS)* pos/wks

23 Jan 93 **WOULD** *Columbia 6588882*.....19 3
20 Mar 93 **THEM BONES** *Columbia 6590902*.....26 3
5 Jun 93 **ANGRY CHAIR** *Columbia 6593652*.....33 2
23 Oct 93 **DOWN IN A HOLE** *Columbia 6597512*.....36 2
11 Nov 95 **GRIND** *Columbia 6626232*.....23 2
10 Feb 96 **HEAVEN BESIDE YOU** *Columbia 6628935*.....35 2

ALIEN ANT FARM *US, male vocal / instrumental group (16 WEEKS)* pos/wks

30 Jun 01 **MOVIES** *Dreamworks / Polydor 4508992*.....53 1
8 Sep 01 **SMOOTH CRIMINAL (import)** *Dreamworks / Polydor 4508852*.....74 2
29 Sep 01 ● **SMOOTH CRIMINAL** *Dreamworks / Polydor DRMDM 50887*.....3 12
29 Dec 01 **SMOOTH CRIMINAL (re-entry)** *Dreamworks / Polydor DRMDM 50887*.....73 1+

ALIEN VOICES featuring THREE DEGREES *UK, male producer – Andros Georgiou (2 WEEKS)* pos/wks

26 Dec 98 **LAST CHRISTMAS** *Wildstar CDWILD 15* [1].....54 2

See also Andy G's STARSKY & HUTCH ALL STARS; BOOGIE BOX HIGH

ALISHA *US, female vocalist (2 WEEKS)* pos/wks

25 Jan 86 **BABY TALK** *Total Control TOCO 6*.....67 2

ALISHA'S ATTIC *UK, female vocal duo – Shellie and Karen Poole (47 WEEKS)* pos/wks

3 Aug 96 **I AM I FEEL** *Mercury AATCD 1*.....14 10
2 Nov 96 **ALISHA RULES THE WORLD** *Mercury AATCD 2*.....12 6
15 Mar 97 **INDESTRUCTIBLE** *Mercury AATCD 3*.....12 6
12 Jul 97 **AIR WE BREATHE** *Mercury AATCD 4*.....12 6
19 Sep 98 **THE INCIDENTALS** *Mercury AATCD 5*.....13 7
9 Jan 99 **WISH I WERE YOU** *Mercury AATCD 6*.....29 5
17 Apr 99 **BARBARELLA** *Mercury AATCD 7*.....34 2
24 Mar 01 **PUSH IT ALL ASIDE** *Mercury AATDD8*.....24 4
28 Jul 01 **PRETENDER GOT MY HEART** *Mercury AATCD 9*.....43 1

ALL ABOUT EVE *UK, female / male vocal / instrumental group (47 WEEKS)* pos/wks

31 Oct 87 **IN THE CLOUDS** *Mercury EVEN 5*.....47 5
23 Jan 88 **WILD HEARTED WOMAN** *Mercury EVEN 6*.....33 4
9 Apr 88 **EVERY ANGEL** *Mercury EVEN 7*.....30 5
30 Jul 88 ● **MARTHA'S HARBOUR** *Mercury EVEN 8*.....10 8
12 Nov 88 **WHAT KIND OF FOOL** *Mercury EVEN 9*.....29 4
30 Sep 89 **ROAD TO YOUR SOUL** *Mercury EVEN 10*.....37 4
16 Dec 89 **DECEMBER** *Mercury EVEN 11*.....34 5
28 Apr 90 **SCARLET** *Mercury EVEN 12*.....34 2
15 Jun 91 **FAREWELL MR SORROW** *Mercury EVEN 14*.....36 2
10 Aug 91 **STRANGE WAY** *Vertigo EVEN 15*.....50 3
19 Oct 91 **THE DREAMER** *Vertigo EVEN 16*.....41 2
10 Oct 92 **PHASED (EP)** *MCA MCS 1688*.....38 2
28 Nov 92 **SOME FINER DAY** *MCA MCS 1706*.....57 1

Tracks on Phased (EP): Phased / Mine / Infra Red / Ascent-Descent

ALL BLUE *UK, male vocal duo (1 WEEK)* pos/wks

21 Aug 99 **PRISONER** *WEA WEA 213CD1*.....73 1

ALL-4-ONE *US, male vocal group (23 WEEKS)* pos/wks

			pos	wks
2 Apr 94		SO MUCH IN LOVE *Atlantic A 7261CD*	60	1
18 Jun 94	●	I SWEAR *Atlantic A 7255CD* ▲	2	18
19 Nov 94		SO MUCH IN LOVE (re-mix) *Atlantic A 7216CD*	49	2
15 Jul 95		I CAN LOVE YOU LIKE THAT *Atlantic A 8193CD*	33	2

ALL SAINTS (267 Top 500)

From All Saints Road, London, a cooler, R&B-motivated vocal girl group in the wake of The Spice Girls. Melanie Blatt, London, Shaznay Lewis, London, Nicole Appleton, Canada, Natalie Appleton, Canada. Crowned Best Breakthrough Artists in the 1998 MTV Europe Music Awards. Group split in 2001 (109 WEEKS) pos/wks

			pos	wks
6 Sep 97	●	I KNOW WHERE IT'S AT *London LONCD 398*	4	8
22 Nov 97	★	NEVER EVER *London LONCD 407* ◆	1	24
9 May 98	★	UNDER THE BRIDGE / LADY MARMALADE *London LONCD 408* ■	1	14
12 Sep 98	★	BOOTIE CALL *London LONCD 415* ■	1	11
5 Dec 98	●	WAR OF NERVES *London LONCD 421*	7	11
26 Feb 00	★	PURE SHORES *London LONCD 444* ■	1	16
14 Oct 00	★	BLACK COFFEE *London LONCD 454* ■	1	16
27 Jan 01	●	ALL HOOKED UP *London LONCD 456*	7	6
24 Feb 01		BLACK COFFEE (re-entry) *London LONCD 454*	71	1
10 Mar 01		BLACK COFFEE (2nd re-entry) *London LONCD 454*	69	1
17 Mar 01		ALL HOOKED UP (re-entry) *London LONCD 456*	59	1

THE ALL SEEING I *UK, male vocal / instrumental group (17 WEEKS)* pos/wks

			pos	wks
28 Mar 98		BEAT GOES ON *ffrr FCD 334*	11	7
23 Jan 99	●	WALK LIKE A PANTHER '98 *ffrr FCD 351* [1]	10	7
18 Sep 99		1ST MAN IN SPACE *ffrr FCD 370* [2]	28	3

[1] The All Seeing I featuring Tony Christie [2] The All Seeing I featuring Phil Oakey

ALL STAR CHOIR – *See Donna SUMMER*

ALL-STARS – *See Louis ARMSTRONG*

ALL-STARS – *See Junior WALKER and the ALL-STARS*

ALL SYSTEMS GO *UK, male vocal / instrumental group (2 WEEKS)* pos/wks

			pos	wks
18 Jun 88		POP MUZIK *Unique NIQ 03*	63	2

Richard ALLAN *UK, male vocalist (1 WEEK)* pos/wks

			pos	wks
24 Mar 60		AS TIME GOES BY *Parlophone R 4634*	43	1

Steve ALLAN *UK, male vocalist (2 WEEKS)* pos/wks

			pos	wks
27 Jan 79		TOGETHER WE ARE BEAUTIFUL *Creole CR 164*	67	1
10 Feb 79		TOGETHER WE ARE BEAUTIFUL (re-entry) *Creole CR 164*	70	1

Donna ALLEN *US, female vocalist (27 WEEKS)* pos/wks

			pos	wks
18 Apr 87	●	SERIOUS *Portrait 650744 7*	8	12
3 Jun 89	●	JOY AND PAIN *BCM BCM 257*	10	10
21 Jan 95		REAL *Epic 6610992*	34	2
11 Oct 97		SATURDAY *AM:PM 5823752* [1]	29	3

[1] East 57th Street featuring Donna Allen

Keith ALLEN – *See BLACK GRAPE; Joe STRUMMER; FAT LES*

ALLISONS *UK, male vocal / instrumental duo – John Allison (Brian Alford) and Bob Allison (Colin Day) (27 WEEKS)* pos/wks

			pos	wks
23 Feb 61	●	ARE YOU SURE *Fontana H 294*	2	16
18 May 61		WORDS *Fontana H 304*	34	5
15 Feb 62		LESSONS IN LOVE *Fontana H 362*	30	6

ALLNIGHT BAND *UK, male instrumental group (3 WEEKS)* pos/wks

			pos	wks
3 Feb 79		THE JOKER (THE WIGAN JOKER) *Casino Classics CC 6*	50	3

ALLSTARS *UK, male / female vocal group (11 WEEKS)* pos/wks

			pos	wks
23 Jun 01		BEST FRIENDS *Islands CID 775*	20	5
1 Sep 01		BEST FRIENDS (re-entry) *Islands CID 775*	66	2
22 Sep 01		THINGS THAT GO BUMP IN THE NIGHT / IS THERE SOMETHING I SHOULD KNOW *Island CID 783*	12	4

ALLURE *US, female vocal group (8 WEEKS)* pos/wks

			pos	wks
14 Jun 97		HEAD OVER HEELS *Epic 6645942* [1]	18	3
10 Jan 98		ALL CRIED OUT *Epic 6652715* [2]	12	5

[1] Allure featuring NAS [2] Allure featuring 112

ALMIGHTY *UK, male vocal / instrumental group (22 WEEKS)* pos/wks

			pos	wks
30 Jun 90		WILD AND WONDERFUL *Polydor PO 75*	50	2
2 Mar 91		FREE 'N' EASY *Polydor PO 127*	35	2
11 May 91		DEVIL'S TOY *Polydor PO 144*	36	2
29 Jun 91		LITTLE LOST SOMETIMES *Polydor PO 151*	42	2
3 Apr 93		ADDICTION *Polydor PZCD 261*	38	2
29 May 93		OUT OF SEASON *Polydor PZCD 266*	41	2
30 Oct 93		OVER THE EDGE *Polydor PZCD 298*	38	2
24 Sep 94		WRENCH *Chrysalis CDCHS 5014*	26	2
14 Jan 95		JONESTOWN MIND *Chrysalis CDCHS 5017*	26	3
16 Mar 96		ALL SUSSED OUT *Chrysalis CDCHS 5030*	28	2
25 May 96		DO YOU UNDERSTAND *Raw Power RAWX 1022*	38	1

Marc ALMOND (254 Top 500)

Distinctive vocalist who first found fame fronting chart regulars Soft Cell, b. 9 Jul 1957, Southport, UK. His only No.1 also gave co-vocalist Gene Pitney his first British chart-topper and sold more than one million copies in Europe alone (112 WEEKS) pos/wks

			pos	wks
2 Jun 83		BLACK HEART *Some Bizarre BZS 19* [1]	49	3
2 Jun 84		THE BOY WHO CAME BACK *Some Bizarre BZS 23*	52	5
1 Sep 84		YOU HAVE *Some Bizarre BZS 24*	57	3
20 Apr 85	●	I FEEL LOVE (MEDLEY) *Forbidden Fruit BITE 4* [2]	3	12
24 Aug 85		STORIES OF JOHNNY *Some Bizarre BONK 1*	23	5
26 Oct 85		LOVE LETTER *Some Bizarre BONK 2*	68	3
4 Jan 86		THE HOUSE IS HAUNTED (BY THE ECHO OF YOUR LAST GOODBYE) *Some Bizarre GLOW 1*	55	3
7 Jun 86		A WOMAN'S STORY *Some Bizarre GLOW 2* [3]	41	5
18 Oct 86		RUBY RED *Some Bizarre GLOW 3*	47	3
14 Feb 87		MELANCHOLY ROSE *Some Bizarre GLOW 4*	71	1
3 Sep 88		TEARS RUN RINGS *Parlophone R 6186*	26	7
5 Nov 88		BITTER SWEET *Some Bizarre R 6194*	40	3
14 Jan 89	★	SOMETHING'S GOTTEN HOLD OF MY HEART *Parlophone R 6201* [4]	1	12
8 Apr 89		ONLY THE MOMENT *Parlophone R 6210*	45	2
3 Mar 90		A LOVER SPURNED *Some Bizarre R 6229*	29	4
19 May 90		THE DESPERATE HOURS *Some Bizarre R 6252*	45	2
23 Mar 91		SAY HELLO WAVE GOODBYE '91 (re-recording) *Mercury SOFT 1* [5]	38	3
18 May 91	●	TAINTED LOVE (re-issue) *Mercury SOFT 2* [5]	5	8
28 Sep 91		JACKY *Some Bizarre YZ 610*	17	6
11 Jan 92		MY HAND OVER MY HEART *Some Bizarre YZ 633*	33	5
25 Apr 92	●	THE DAYS OF PEARLY SPENCER *Some Bizarre YZ 638*	4	7
27 Mar 93		WHAT MAKES A MAN A MAN (LIVE) *Some Bizarre YZ 720CD*	60	2
13 May 95		ADORED AND EXPLORED *Some Bizarre MERCD 431*	25	3
29 Jul 95		THE IDOL *Some Bizarre MERCD 437*	44	2
30 Dec 95		CHILD STAR *Some Bizarre MERCD 450*	41	1
28 Dec 96		YESTERDAY HAS GONE *EMI Premier CDPRESX 13* [6]	58	1
11 Jan 97		YESTERDAY HAS GONE (re-entry) *EMI Premier CDPRESX 13* [6]	69	1

[1] Marc and the Mambas [2] Bronski Beat and Marc Almond [3] Marc Almond and the Willing Sinners [4] Marc Almond featuring special guest star Gene Pitney [5] Soft Cell / Marc Almond [6] PJ Proby and Marc Almond featuring the My Life Story Orchestra

I Feel Love medley comprises: I Feel Love / Love to Love You Baby / Johnny Remember Me. Original versions of 'Say Hello Wave Goodbye' (1982) and 'Tainted Love' (1981) credited to Soft Cell alone

ALOOF *UK, male vocal / instrumental group (6 WEEKS)* pos/wks

			pos	wks
19 Sep 92		ON A MISSION *Cowboy RODEO 5*	64	1
18 May 96		WISH YOU WERE HERE ... *East West EW 038CD*	61	1
30 Nov 96		ONE NIGHT STAND *East West EW 067CD*	30	2
1 Mar 97		WISH YOU WERE HERE ... (re-mix) *East West EW 083CD1*	43	1
29 Aug 98		WHAT I MISS THE MOST *East West EW 179CD1*	70	1

Herb ALPERT (279 Top 500) *Leader of the US's biggest-selling instrumental act, The Tijuana Brass, b. 31 Mar 1935, Los Angeles. The multi-talented trumpet-toting star's band had four albums simultaneously in the US Top 10 in the mid-1960s. He sold his A&M label for $300 million in 1989 and his publishing company for $350 million in 2000 (106 WEEKS)* pos/wks

		pos	wks
3 Jan 63	THE LONELY BULL (EL SOLO TORRO) *Stateside SS 138* [1]	22	9
9 Dec 65 ●	SPANISH FLEA *Pye International 7N 25335* [2]	3	20
24 Mar 66	TIJUANA TAXI *Pye International 7N 25352* [2]	37	4
27 Apr 67	CASINO ROYALE *A & M AMS 700* [2]	27	14
3 Jul 68 ●	THIS GUY'S IN LOVE WITH YOU *A & M AMS 727* ▲	3	16
26 Mar 69	THIS GUY'S IN LOVE WITH YOU (re-entry) *A & M AMS 727*	47	1
9 Apr 69	THIS GUY'S IN LOVE WITH YOU (2nd re-entry) *A & M AMS 727*	49	1
7 May 69	THIS GUY'S IN LOVE WITH YOU (3rd re-entry) *A & M AMS 727*	50	1
18 Jun 69	WITHOUT HER *A & M AMS 755* [2]	36	5
12 Dec 70	JERUSALEM *A & M AMS 810* [2]	47	1
2 Jan 71	JERUSALEM (re-entry) *A & M AMS 810* [2]	42	2
13 Oct 79	RISE *A & M AMS 7465* ▲	13	13
19 Jan 80	ROTATION *A & M AMS 7500*	46	3
21 Mar 87	KEEP YOUR EYE ON ME *Breakout USA 602*	19	9
6 Jun 87	DIAMONDS *Breakout USA 605*	27	7

[1] Tijuana Brass [2] Herb Alpert and the Tijuana Brass

Alpert provides vocals on 'This Guy's in Love With You' and 'Without Her'. Janet Jackson provides uncredited vocals on 'Diamonds'

ALPHA-BETA – *See Izhar COHEN and the ALPHA-BETA*

ALPHAVILLE *Germany, male vocal / instrumental group (13 WEEKS)* pos/wks

		pos	wks
18 Aug 84 ●	BIG IN JAPAN *WEA Int. X9505*	8	13

ALSOU *Russia, female vocalist (3 WEEKS)* pos/wks

		pos	wks
12 May 01	BEFORE YOU LOVE ME *Mercury 1589142*	27	3

Gerald ALSTON *US, male vocalist (1 WEEK)* pos/wks

		pos	wks
15 Apr 89	ACTIVATED *RCA ZB 42681*	73	1

ALTERED IMAGES
UK, male / female vocal / instrumental group (60 WEEKS) pos/wks

		pos	wks
28 Mar 81	DEAD POP STARS *Epic EPC A 1023*	67	2
26 Sep 81 ●	HAPPY BIRTHDAY *Epic EPC A 1522*	2	17
12 Dec 81 ●	I COULD BE HAPPY *Epic EPC A 1834*	7	12
27 Mar 82	SEE THOSE EYES *Epic EPC A 2198*	11	7
22 May 82	PINKY BLUE *Epic EPC A 2426*	35	6
19 Mar 83 ●	DON'T TALK TO ME ABOUT LOVE *Epic EPC A 3083*	7	7
28 May 83	BRING ME CLOSER *Epic EPC A 3398*	29	6
16 Jul 83	LOVE TO STAY *Epic EPC A 3582*	46	3

ALTERN 8 *UK, male instrumental / production duo – Mark Archer and Chris Peat (34 WEEKS)* pos/wks

		pos	wks
13 Jul 91	INFILTRATE 202 *Network NWK 24*	28	7
16 Nov 91 ●	ACTIV 8 (COME WITH ME) *Network NWK 34*	3	9
8 Feb 92	FREQUENCY *Network NWKT 37*	41	1
11 Apr 92 ●	EVAPOR 8 *Network NWK 38*	6	6
4 Jul 92	HYPNOTIC ST-8 *Network NWK 49*	16	4
10 Oct 92	SHAME *Network NWKTEN 56* [1]	74	1
12 Dec 92	BRUTAL-8-E *Network NWK 59*	43	5
3 Jul 93	EVERYBODY *Network NWKCD 73*	58	1

[1] Altern 8 vs Evelyn King

ALTHIA and DONNA *Jamaica, female vocal duo – Althia Forest and Donna Reid (11 WEEKS)* pos/wks

		pos	wks
24 Dec 77 ★	UPTOWN TOP RANKING *Lightning LIG 506*	1	11

ALVIN and the CHIPMUNKS – *See CHIPMUNKS*

ALY-US *US, male vocal / instrumental group (2 WEEKS)* pos/wks

		pos	wks
21 Nov 92	FOLLOW ME *Cooltempo COOL 266*	43	2

Shola AMA *UK, female vocalist – Mathurin Campbell (50 WEEKS)* pos/wks

		pos	wks
19 Apr 97 ●	YOU MIGHT NEED SOMEBODY *WEA WEA 097CD1*	4	14
30 Aug 97 ●	YOU'RE THE ONE I LOVE *WEA WEA 121CD1*	3	8
29 Nov 97	WHO'S LOVING MY BABY *WEA WEA 145CD1*	13	7
21 Feb 98	MUCH LOVE *WEA WEA 154CD1*	17	3
11 Apr 98	SOMEDAY I'LL FIND YOU / I'VE BEEN TO A MARVELLOUS PARTY *EMI CDTCB 001* [1]	28	3
17 Apr 99 ●	TABOO *WEA WEA 203CD* [2]	10	8
6 Nov 99	STILL BELIEVE *WEA WEA 239CD1*	26	3
29 Apr 00	IMAGINE *WEA WEA 252 CD*	24	4

[1] Shola Ama and Craig Armstrong / Divine Comedy [2] Glamma Kid featuring Shola Ama

Eddie AMADOR *US, male DJ / producer (5 WEEKS)* pos/wks

		pos	wks
24 Oct 98	HOUSE MUSIC *Pukka CDPUKKA 18*	37	2
22 Jan 00	RISE *Defected DEFECT 9CDS*	19	3

AMAR *UK, female vocalist / instrumentalist – Amar Nagi (1 WEEK)* pos/wks

		pos	wks
9 Sep 00	SOMETIMES IT SNOWS IN APRIL *Blanco Y Negro NEG 129CD*	48	1

AMAZULU *UK, female / male vocal / instrumental group (57 WEEKS)* pos/wks

		pos	wks
6 Jul 85	EXCITABLE *Island IS 201*	12	13
23 Nov 85	DON'T YOU JUST KNOW IT *Island IS 233*	15	11
15 Mar 86	THE THINGS THE LONELY DO *Island IS 267*	43	6
31 May 86 ●	TOO GOOD TO BE FORGOTTEN *Island IS 284*	5	13
13 Sep 86	MONTEGO BAY *Island IS 293*	16	9
10 Oct 87	MONY MONY *EMI EM 32*	38	5

AMBASSADOR *Holland, male DJ / production group (1 WEEK)* pos/wks

		pos	wks
12 Feb 00	ONE OF THESE DAYS *Platipus PLATCD 69*	67	1

AMBASSADORS OF FUNK featuring MC MARIO
UK, male DJ and rapper – Simon Harris and Einstein (8 WEEKS) pos/wks

		pos	wks
31 Oct 92 ●	SUPERMARIOLAND *Living Beat SMASH 23*	8	8

See also Simon HARRIS

AMBER *Holland, female vocalist – Marie Cremers (2 WEEKS)* pos/wks

		pos	wks
24 Jun 00	SEXUAL *Substance SUBS 2CDS*	34	2

AMEN *US, male vocal / instrumental group (1 WEEK)* pos/wks

		pos	wks
17 Feb 01	TOO HARD TO BE FREE *Virgin VUSCD 191*	72	1
21 Jul 01	THE WAITING 18 *Virgin VUSCD 207*	61	1

AMEN CORNER *UK, male vocal / instrumental group lead vocal – Andy Fairweather-Low (67 WEEKS)* pos/wks

		pos	wks
26 Jul 67	GIN HOUSE BLUES *Deram DM 136*	12	10
11 Oct 67	THE WORLD OF BROKEN HEARTS *Deram DM 151*	24	6
17 Jan 68 ●	BEND ME, SHAPE ME *Deram DM 172*	3	12
31 Jul 68 ●	HIGH IN THE SKY *Deram DM 197*	6	13
29 Jan 69 ★	(IF PARADISE IS) HALF AS NICE *Immediate IM 073*	1	11
25 Jun 69 ●	HELLO SUZIE *Immediate IM 081*	4	10
14 Feb 76	(IF PARADISE IS) HALF AS NICE (re-issue) *Immediate IMS 103*	34	5

See also FAIR WEATHER; Andy FAIRWEATHER-LOW

AMEN UK *UK, male / female vocal / production group (6 WEEKS)* pos/wks

		pos	wks
8 Feb 97	PASSION *Feverpitch CDFVR 1015*	15	4
28 Jun 97	PEOPLE OF LOVE *Feverpitch CDFVR 18*	36	2

AMERICA *US, male vocal / instrumental group (20 WEEKS)* pos/wks

		pos	wks
18 Dec 71	HORSE WITH NO NAME *Warner Bros. K 16128*	49	2
8 Jan 72 ●	HORSE WITH NO NAME (re-entry) *Warner Bros. K 16128* ▲	3	11
25 Nov 72	VENTURA HIGHWAY *Warner Bros. K 16219*	43	4
6 Nov 82	YOU CAN DO MAGIC *Capitol CL 264*	59	3

AMERICAN BREED *US, male vocal / instrumental group (6 WEEKS)* pos/wks

		pos	wks
7 Feb 68	BEND ME SHAPE ME *Stateside SS 2078*	24	6

UK No.1 ★ UK Top 10 ● Still on chart + UK million seller ◆ UK entry at No.1 ■ US No.1 ▲

AMERICAN HI-FI *US, male vocal / instrumental group (3 WEEKS)* pos/wks

8 Sep 01 **FLAVOR OF THE WEAK** *Mercury 5886722* **31** 3

AMERICAN MUSIC CLUB
US, male vocal / instrumental group (4 WEEKS) pos/wks

24 Apr 93 **JOHNNY MATHIS' FEET** *Virgin VSCDG 1445* **58** 2
10 Sep 94 **WISH THE WORLD AWAY** *Virgin VSCDX 1512* **46** 2

AMES BROTHERS *US, male vocal group (6 WEEKS)* pos/wks

4 Feb 55 ● **THE NAUGHTY LADY OF SHADY LANE** *HMV B 10800* **6** 6

'With Hugo Winterhalter and his Orchestra'

AMIL – *See JAY-Z*

AMIRA *US, female vocalist – Amira McNiel (7 WEEKS)* pos/wks

13 Dec 97 **MY DESIRE** *VC VCRD 27* **51** 1
8 Aug 98 **MY DESIRE (re-mix)** *VC Recordings VCRD 36* **46** 2
10 Feb 01 **MY DESIRE (2nd re-mix)** *VC Recordings VCRD 71* **20** 4

AMNESIA – *See Frank'o MOIRAGHI featuring AMNESIA*

Cherie AMORE *France, female vocalist (2 WEEKS)* pos/wks

15 Apr 00 **I DON'T WANT NOBODY (TELLIN' ME WHAT TO DO)** *Eternal / WEA WEA 262CD* **33** 2

Vanessa AMOROSI *Australia, female vocalist (10 WEEKS)* pos/wks

23 Sep 00 ● **ABSOLUTELY EVERYBODY** *Mercury 1582972* **7** 10

AMOS *UK, male vocalist / rapper / producer (12 WEEKS)* pos/wks

3 Sep 94 **ONLY SAW TODAY – INSTANT KARMA** *Positiva CDTIV 16* **48** 2
25 Mar 95 **LET LOVE SHINE** *Positiva CDTIV 24* **31** 2
7 Oct 95 **CHURCH OF FREEDOM** *Positiva CDTIV 38* **54** 1
12 Oct 96 **STAMP!** *Positiva CDTIV 65* **11** 5
31 May 97 **ARGENTINA** *Positiva CDTIV 74* **30** 2

Tori AMOS *US, female vocalist / instrumentalist – piano (64 WEEKS)* pos/wks

23 Nov 91 **SILENT ALL THESE YEARS** *East West YZ 618* **51** 3
1 Feb 92 **CHINA** *East West YZ 7531* **51** 2
21 Mar 92 **WINTER** *East West A 7504* **25** 4
20 Jun 92 **CRUCIFY** *East West A 7479* **15** 6
22 Aug 92 **SILENT ALL THESE YEARS (re-issue)** *East West A 7433* **26** 4
22 Jan 94 ● **CORNFLAKE GIRL** *East West A 7281CD* **4** 6
19 Mar 94 ● **PRETTY GOOD YEAR** *East West A 7263CD* **7** 4
28 May 94 **PAST THE MISSION** *East West YZ 7257CD* **31** 3
15 Oct 94 **GOD** *East West A 7251CD* **44** 2
13 Jan 96 **CAUGHT A LITE SNEEZE** *East West A 5524CD1* **20** 3
23 Mar 96 **TALULA** *East West A 8512CD1* **22** 2
3 Aug 96 **HEY JUPITER / PROFESSIONAL WIDOW** *East West A 5494CD* **20** 9
9 Nov 96 **BLUE SKIES** *Perfecto PERF 130CD1* [1] **26** 2
11 Jan 97 ★ **PROFESSIONAL WIDOW (IT'S GOT TO BE BIG) (re-mix)** *East West A 5450CD* **1** 10
2 May 98 **SPARK** *Atlantic AT 0031CD* **16** 3
13 Nov 99 **GLORY OF THE 80'S** *Atlantic AT 0077CD1* **46** 1

[1] BT featuring Tori Amos

AMOURE *UK, male production duo – Rod Edwards and Nick Magnus (2 WEEKS)* pos/wks

27 May 00 **IS THAT YOUR FINAL ANSWER? (WHO WANTS TO BE A MILLIONAIRE – THE SINGLE)** *Celador MILLION 2* **33** 2

AMPS *US, male / female vocal / instrumental group (1 WEEK)* pos/wks

21 Oct 95 **TIPP CITY** *4AD BAD 5015CD* **61** 1

AMY – *See A.D.A.M. featuring AMY*

ANASTACIA *US, female vocalist – Anastacia Newkirk (38 WEEKS)* pos/wks

30 Sep 00 ● **I'M OUTTA LOVE** *Epic 6695782* **6** 17
3 Feb 01 **NOT THAT KIND** *Epic 6707632* **11** 7
31 Mar 01 **NOT THAT KIND (re-entry)** *Epic 6707632* **62** 1
2 Jun 01 **COWBOYS & KISSES** *Epic 6712622* **28** 5
25 Aug 01 **MADE FOR LOVIN' YOU** *Epic 6717172* **27** 3
1 Dec 01 **PAID MY DUES** *Epic 6721252* **14** 5

AND WHY NOT? *UK, male vocal / instrumental group (18 WEEKS)* pos/wks

14 Oct 89 **RESTLESS DAYS (SHE CRIES OUT LOUD)** *Island IS 426* **38** 7
13 Jan 90 **THE FACE** *Island IS 444* **13** 8
21 Apr 90 **SOMETHING YOU GOT** *Island IS 452* **39** 3

... AND YOU WILL KNOW US BY THE TRAIL OF DEAD
US, male vocal / instrumental group (1 WEEK) pos/wks

11 Nov 00 **MISTAKES AND REGRETS** *Domino RUG 114CD* **69** 1

Angry ANDERSON *Australia, male vocalist (13 WEEKS)* pos/wks

19 Nov 88 ● **SUDDENLY** *Food For Thought YUM 113* **3** 13

Carl ANDERSON *US, male vocalist (4 WEEKS)* pos/wks

8 Jun 85 **BUTTERCUP** *Streetwave KHAN 45* **49** 4

Carleen ANDERSON *US, female vocalist (17 WEEKS)* pos/wks

12 Feb 94 **NERVOUS BREAKDOWN** *Circa YRCDG 112* **27** 4
28 May 94 **MAMA SAID** *Circa YRCD 114* **26** 4
13 Aug 94 **TRUE SPIRIT** *Circa YRCD 118* **24** 3
14 Jan 95 **LET IT LAST** *Circa YRCD 119* **16** 3
7 Feb 98 **MAYBE I'M AMAZED** *Circa YRCD 128* **24** 2
25 Apr 98 **WOMAN IN ME** *Circa YRCD 129* **74** 1

See also BRAND NEW HEAVIES

Gillian ANDERSON – *See HAL featuring Gillian ANDERSON*

Lynn ANDERSON *US, female vocalist (20 WEEKS)* pos/wks

20 Feb 71 ● **ROSE GARDEN** *CBS 5360* **3** 20

Moira ANDERSON *UK, female vocalist (2 WEEKS)* pos/wks

27 Dec 69 **THE HOLY CITY** *Decca F 12989* **43** 2

Sunshine ANDERSON *US, female vocalist (8 WEEKS)* pos/wks

2 Jun 01 ● **HEARD IT ALL BEFORE** *Atlantic AT 0100CD* **9** 7
22 Sep 01 **LUNCH OR DINNER** *Atlantic AT 0109CD* **57** 1

Laurie ANDERSON
US, female vocalist / multi-instrumentalist (6 WEEKS) pos/wks

17 Oct 81 ● **O SUPERMAN** *Warner Bros. K 17870* **2** 6

Leroy ANDERSON and his "POPS" CONCERT ORCHESTRA
US, orchestra (4 WEEKS) pos/wks

28 Jun 57 **FORGOTTEN DREAMS** *Brunswick 05485* **28** 1
12 Jul 57 **FORGOTTEN DREAMS (re-entry)** *Brunswick 05485* **30** 1
6 Sep 57 **FORGOTTEN DREAMS (2nd re-entry)** *Brunswick 05485* **24** 2

John ANDERSON BIG BAND *UK, big band (5 WEEKS)* pos/wks

21 Dec 85 **GLENN MILLER MEDLEY** *Modern GLEN 1* **63** 2
11 Jan 86 **GLENN MILLER MEDLEY (re-entry)** *Modern GLEN 1* **61** 3

Glenn Miller Medley comprises the following tracks: In the Mood / American Patrol / Little Brown Jug / Pennsylvania 65000

ANDERSON BRUFORD WAKEMAN HOWE
UK, male vocal / instrumental group (2 WEEKS) pos/wks

24 Jun 89 **BROTHER OF MINE** *Arista 112379* **63** 2

See also YES

Peter ANDRE (391 Top 500)

Australian-raised teen-dream vocalist with six-pack stomach, b. 27 Feb 1973, Middlesex, UK. Chart-topping debut album 'Natural' included platinum single 'Mysterious Girl' and two UK No.1s. However, his ventures into more mature R&B-flava'd tracks proved less accessible to his previously large fan base (83 WEEKS) pos/wks

10 Jun 95		**TURN IT UP** *Mushroom D 1000*	64 1
16 Sep 95		**MYSTERIOUS GIRL** *Mushroom D 11921*	53 2
16 Mar 96		**ONLY ONE** *Mushroom D 1307*	16 3
13 Apr 96		**ONLY ONE (re-entry)** *Mushroom D 1307*	69 1
1 Jun 96	●	**MYSTERIOUS GIRL (re-issue)** *Mushroom D 2000* [1]	2 18
14 Sep 96	★	**FLAVA** *Mushroom D 2003* ■	1 9
7 Dec 96	★	**I FEEL YOU** *Mushroom D 1521* ■	1 9
1 Mar 97		**I FEEL YOU (re-entry)** *Mushroom D 1521*	65 1
8 Mar 97	●	**NATURAL** *Mushroom DX 1577*	6 8
15 Mar 97		**I FEEL YOU (2nd re-entry)** *Mushroom D 1521*	74 1
10 May 97		**NATURAL (re-entry)** *Mushroom DX 1577*	58 1
24 May 97		**NATURAL (2nd re-entry)** *Mushroom DX 1577*	68 2
9 Aug 97	●	**ALL ABOUT US** *Mushroom MUSH 5CD*	3 8
1 Nov 97		**ALL ABOUT US (re-entry)** *Mushroom MUSH 5CD*	75 1
8 Nov 97	●	**LONELY** *Mushroom MUSH 16CD*	6 5
3 Jan 98		**LONELY (re-entry)** *Mushroom MUSH 16CD*	68 4
24 Jan 98		**ALL NIGHT ALL RIGHT** *Mushroom MUSH 21CD* [2]	16 4
25 Jul 98	●	**KISS THE GIRL** *Mushroom MUSH 34CDSX*	9 5

[1] Peter Andre featuring Bubbler Ranx [2] Peter Andre featuring Warren G

ANDREW WK

US, male vocalist / producer – Andrew Wilkes-Krier (4 WEEKS) pos/wks

10 Nov 01		**PARTY HARD** *Mercury 5888132*	19 4

Chris ANDREWS *UK, male vocalist (36 WEEKS)* pos/wks

7 Oct 65	●	**YESTERDAY MAN** *Decca F 12236*	3 15
2 Dec 65		**TO WHOM IT CONCERNS** *Decca F 22285*	13 10
14 Apr 66		**SOMETHING ON MY MIND** *Decca F 22365*	45 1
28 Apr 66		**SOMETHING ON MY MIND (re-entry)** *Decca F 22365*	41 2
2 Jun 66		**WHAT'CHA GONNA DO NOW** *Decca F 22404*	40 4
25 Aug 66		**STOP THAT GIRL** *Decca F 22472*	36 4

Eamonn ANDREWS *Ireland, male vocalist (3 WEEKS)* pos/wks

20 Jan 56		**THE SHIFTING WHISPERING SANDS (PARTS 1 & 2)** *Parlophone R 4106*	18 3

'With Ron Goodwin and his Orchestra and Chorus'

ANEKA *UK, female vocalist – Mary Sandeman (16 WEEKS)* pos/wks

8 Aug 81	★	**JAPANESE BOY** *Hansa HANSA 5*	1 12
7 Nov 81		**LITTLE LADY** *Hansa HANSA 8*	50 4

Dave ANGEL *UK, male DJ / producer (1 WEEK)* pos/wks

2 Aug 97		**TOKYO STEALTH FIGHTER** *Fourth & Broadway BRCD 355*	58 1

Simone ANGEL *Holland, female vocalist (1 WEEK)* pos/wks

13 Nov 93		**LET THIS FEELING** *A & M 5803652*	60 1

ANGELETTES *UK, female vocal group (5 WEEKS)* pos/wks

13 May 72		**DON'T LET HIM TOUCH YOU** *Decca F 13284*	35 5

ANGELHEART *UK, female producer (2 WEEKS)* pos/wks

6 Apr 96		**COME BACK TO ME** *Hi-Life 5776312* [1]	68 1
22 Mar 97		**I'M STILL WAITING** *Hi-Life 5735452* [2]	74 1

[1] Angelheart featuring Rochelle Harris [2] Angelheart featuring Aletia Bourne

ANGELIC *UK, male / female production / vocal duo – Amanda O'Riordan and Darren Tate (16 WEEKS)* pos/wks

17 Jun 00		**IT'S MY TURN** *Serious MCSTD 40235*	11 10
24 Feb 01		**CAN'T KEEP ME SILENT** *Serious SERR 023CD*	12 4
10 Nov 01		**STAY WITH ME** *Serious SERR 35CD*	36 2

See also CITIZEN CANED

ANGELIC UPSTARTS

UK, male vocal / instrumental group (30 WEEKS) pos/wks

21 Apr 79		**I'M AN UPSTART** *Warner Bros. K 17354*	31 8
11 Aug 79		**TEENAGE WARNING** *Warner Bros. K 17426*	29 6
3 Nov 79		**NEVER 'AD NOTHIN'** *Warner Bros. K 17476*	52 4
9 Feb 80		**OUT OF CONTROL** *Warner Bros. K 17558*	58 3
22 Mar 80		**WE GOTTA GET OUT OF THIS PLACE** *Warner Bros. K 17576*	65 2
2 Aug 80		**LAST NIGHT ANOTHER SOLDIER** *Zonophone Z 7*	51 4
7 Feb 81		**KIDS ON THE STREET** *Zonophone Z 16*	57 3

Bobby ANGELO and the TUXEDOS

UK, male vocal / instrumental group (6 WEEKS) pos/wks

10 Aug 61		**BABY SITTIN'** *HMV POP 892*	30 6

ANGELS *US, female vocal group (1 WEEK)* pos/wks

3 Oct 63		**MY BOYFRIEND'S BACK** *Mercury AMT 1211* ▲	50 1

ANGELS OF LIGHT – *See PSYCHIC TV*

ANGELWITCH *UK, male vocal / instrumental group (1 WEEK)* pos/wks

7 Jun 80		**SWEET DANGER** *EMI 5064*	75 1

ANIMAL *US, male puppet vocal and instrumental – drums (3 WEEKS)* pos/wks

23 Jul 94		**WIPE OUT** *BMG Kidz 74321219532*	38 3

ANIMAL NIGHTLIFE

UK, male / female vocal / instrumental group (22 WEEKS) pos/wks

13 Aug 83		**NATIVE BOY (UPTOWN)** *Innervision A3584*	60 3
18 Aug 84		**MR SOLITAIRE** *Island IS 193*	25 12
6 Jul 85		**LOVE IS JUST THE GREAT PRETENDER** *Island IS 200*	28 6
5 Oct 85		**PREACHER, PREACHER** *Island IS 245*	67 1

ANIMALHOUSE *UK, male vocal / instrumental group (1 WEEK)* pos/wks

15 Jul 00		**READY TO RECEIVE** *Boilerhouse / Arista 74321771072*	61 1

ANIMALS (154 Top 500)

Ground-breaking Newcastle band: Eric Burdon (v), Alan Price (k), Brian "Chas" Chandler (b) (d. 1996), Hilton Valentine (g), John Steel (d). They were the first hit act produced by Mickie Most and, after The Tornados and The Beatles, the third UK group to top the US singles chart (147 WEEKS) pos/wks

16 Apr 64		**BABY LET ME TAKE YOU HOME** *Columbia DB 7247*	21 8
25 Jun 64	★	**THE HOUSE OF THE RISING SUN** *Columbia DB 7301* ▲	1 12
17 Sep 64	●	**I'M CRYING** *Columbia DB 7354*	8 10
4 Feb 65	●	**DON'T LET ME BE MISUNDERSTOOD** *Columbia DB 7445*	3 9
8 Apr 65	●	**BRING IT ON HOME TO ME** *Columbia DB 7539*	7 11
15 Jul 65	●	**WE'VE GOTTA GET OUT OF THIS PLACE** *Columbia DB 7639*	2 12
28 Oct 65	●	**IT'S MY LIFE** *Columbia DB 7741*	7 11
17 Feb 66		**INSIDE – LOOKING OUT** *Decca F 12332*	12 8
2 Jun 66	●	**DON'T BRING ME DOWN** *Decca F 12407*	6 8
27 Oct 66		**HELP ME GIRL** *Decca F 12502* [1]	14 10
15 Jun 67		**WHEN I WAS YOUNG** *MGM 1340* [2]	45 3
6 Sep 67		**GOOD TIMES** *MGM 1344* [2]	20 11
18 Oct 67	●	**SAN FRANCISCAN NIGHTS** *MGM 1359* [2]	7 10
14 Feb 68		**SKY PILOT** *MGM 1373* [2]	40 3
15 Jan 69		**RING OF FIRE** *MGM 1461* [2]	35 5
7 Oct 72		**THE HOUSE OF THE RISING SUN (re-issue)** *RAK RR 1*	25 6
18 Sep 82		**THE HOUSE OF THE RISING SUN (re-entry of re-issue)** *RAK RR 1*	11 10

[1] Eric Burdon and session musicians billed as The Animals [2] Eric Burdon and The Animals

ANIMOTION

US / UK, male / female vocal / instrumental group (12 WEEKS) pos/wks

11 May 85	●	**OBSESSION** *Mercury PH 34*	5 12

Paul ANKA (188 Top 500) *Celebrated Canadian singer / songwriter, b. 30 Jul 1941, Ottawa. He topped the UK and US charts aged 16 and was the youngest transatlantic chart regular of the 1950s. He also penned big hits for Buddy Holly, Tom Jones, Donny Osmond and 'My Way' for Frank Sinatra (134 WEEKS)*

			pos	wks
9 Aug 57	★	**DIANA** *Columbia DB 3980* ◆ ▲	1	25
8 Nov 57	●	**I LOVE YOU, BABY** *Columbia DB 4022*	3	15
8 Nov 57		**TELL ME THAT YOU LOVE ME** *Columbia DB 4022*	25	2
31 Jan 58	●	**YOU ARE MY DESTINY** *Columbia DB 4063*	6	13
30 May 58		**CRAZY LOVE** *Columbia DB 4110*	26	1
26 Sep 58		**MIDNIGHT** *Columbia DB 4172*	26	1
30 Jan 59	●	**(ALL OF A SUDDEN) MY HEART SINGS** *Columbia DB 4241*	10	13
10 Jul 59	●	**LONELY BOY** *Columbia DB 4324* ▲	3	17
30 Oct 59	●	**PUT YOUR HEAD ON MY SHOULDER** *Columbia DB 4355*	7	12
26 Feb 60		**IT'S TIME TO CRY** *Columbia DB 4390*	28	1
31 Mar 60		**PUPPY LOVE** *Columbia DB 4434*	33	4
14 Apr 60		**IT'S TIME TO CRY (re-entry)** *Columbia DB 4390*	47	1
5 May 60		**PUPPY LOVE (re-entry)** *Columbia DB 4434*	37	3
15 Sep 60		**HELLO YOUNG LOVERS** *Columbia DB 4504*	44	1
15 Mar 62		**LOVE ME WARM AND TENDER** *RCA 1276*	19	11
26 Jul 62		**A STEEL GUITAR AND A GLASS OF WINE** *RCA 1292*	41	4
28 Sep 74	●	**(YOU'RE) HAVING MY BABY** *United Artists UP 35713* [1] ▲	6	10

[1] Paul Anka featuring Odia Coates

ANOTHER LEVEL (405 Top 500) *Soulful, teen-targeted UK pop vocal group; Dane Bowers, Wayne Williams, Mark Baron, Bobak Kianoush. Credible quartet, who have had hits with top US rap stars TQ, Jay-Z and Ghostface Killah, were nominated for a Brit award in 1999 but split in 2000 (81 WEEKS)*

			pos	wks
28 Feb 98	●	**BE ALONE NO MORE** *Northwestside 74321551982*	6	9
18 Jul 98	★	**FREAK ME** *Northwestside 74321582362* ■	1	12
7 Nov 98	●	**GUESS I WAS A FOOL** *Northwestside 74321621202*	5	13
23 Jan 99	●	**I WANT YOU FOR MYSELF** *Northwestside 7432164632* [1]	2	8
10 Apr 99		**BE ALONE NO MORE** *Northwestside 74321658472* [2]	11	9
12 Jun 99	●	**FROM THE HEART** *Northwestside 74321673012*	6	10
28 Aug 99		**FROM THE HEART (re-entry)** *Northwestside 74321673012*	74	1
4 Sep 99	●	**SUMMERTIME** *Northwestside 74321694672* [3]	7	7
13 Nov 99	●	**BOMB DIGGY** *Northwestside 74321712212*	6	12

[1] Another Level / Ghostface Killah [2] Another Level featuring Jay-Z [3] Another Level featuring TQ

ANOUCHKA – *See Terry HALL*

Adam ANT *Innovative and flamboyant pop idol, b. Stuart Goddard, 3 Nov 1954, London. He left Adam and The Ants at their peak and immediately topped the UK chart and scored his first ever US hit. Later made his mark as an actor (69 WEEKS)*

			pos	wks
22 May 82	★	**GOODY TWO SHOES** *CBS A 2367*	1	11
18 Sep 82	●	**FRIEND OR FOE** *CBS A 2736*	9	8
27 Nov 82		**DESPERATE BUT NOT SERIOUS** *CBS A 2892*	33	7
29 Oct 83	●	**PUSS 'N BOOTS** *CBS A 3614*	5	11
10 Dec 83		**STRIP** *CBS A 3589*	41	6
22 Sep 84		**APOLLO 9** *CBS A 4719*	13	8
13 Jul 85		**VIVE LE ROCK** *CBS A 6367*	50	4
17 Feb 90		**ROOM AT THE TOP** *MCA MCA 1387*	13	7
28 Apr 90		**CAN'T SET RULES ABOUT LOVE** *MCA MCA 1404*	47	2
11 Feb 95		**WONDERFUL** *EMI CDEMS 366*	32	3
3 Jun 95		**GOTTA BE A SIN** *EMI CDEMS 379*	48	2

See also ADAM and the ANTS

ANT & DEC (414 Top 500) *Newcastle-born child actors and Geordie jokers Anthony McPartlin and Declan Donnelly (aka PJ & Duncan) initially recorded under their character aliases from the children's TV series Byker Grove. They scored impressive 12 Top 20 entries within three years. These one-time pop idols are now popular TV presenters (81 WEEKS)*

			pos	wks
18 Dec 93		**TONIGHT I'M FREE** *Telstar CDSTAS 2706*	62	3
23 Apr 94		**WHY ME** *Telstar CDSTAS 2719*	27	4
23 Jul 94	●	**LET'S GET READY TO RHUMBLE** *XSrhythm CDANT 1*	9	11
8 Oct 94		**IF I GIVE YOU MY NUMBER** *XSrhythm CDANT 2*	15	7
3 Dec 94		**ETERNAL LOVE** *XSrhythm CDANT 3*	12	9
25 Feb 95		**OUR RADIO ROCKS** *XSrhythm CDANT 4*	15	5
29 Jul 95		**STUCK ON U** *XSrhythm CDANT 5*	12	5
14 Oct 95		**U KRAZY KATZ** *XSrhythm CDANT 6*	15	4
2 Dec 95		**PERFECT** *Telstar CDANT 7*	16	7
20 Mar 96		**STEPPING STONE** *Telstar CDANT 8*	11	5
24 Aug 96	●	**BETTER WATCH OUT** *Telstar CDANT 9*	10	4
23 Nov 96		**WHEN I FALL IN LOVE** *Telstar CDANT 10*	12	8
15 Mar 97	●	**SHOUT** *Telstar CDDEC 11*	10	5
10 May 97		**FALLING** *Telstar CDDEC 12*	14	4

All hits up to and including 20 Mar 96 credited to PJ & Duncan

ANTARCTICA *Australia, male producer – Steve Gibbs (2 WEEKS)*

			pos	wks
29 Jan 00		**RETURN TO REALITY** *React CDREACT 173*	53	1
8 Jul 00		**ADRIFT (CAST YOUR MIND)** *React CDREACT 172*	72	1

Mark ANTHONI – *See FIRE ISLAND*

Billie ANTHONY *UK, female vocalist – Philomena Brown (16 WEEKS)*

			pos	wks
15 Oct 54	●	**THIS OLE HOUSE** *Columbia DB 3519*	4	16

This release was 'With Eric Jupp and his Orchestra'

Marc ANTHONY *US, male vocalist (3 WEEKS)*

			pos	wks
13 Nov 99		**I NEED TO KNOW** *Columbia 6683612*	28	3

See also Louie VEGA and Marc ANTHONY

Miki ANTHONY *UK, male vocalist (7 WEEKS)*

			pos	wks
3 Feb 73		**IF IT WASN'T FOR THE REASON THAT I LOVE YOU** *Bell 1275*	27	7

Richard ANTHONY
France, male vocalist (Richard Anthony Bush) (15 WEEKS)

			pos	wks
12 Dec 63		**WALKING ALONE** *Columbia DB 7133*	37	5
2 Apr 64		**IF I LOVED YOU** *Columbia DB 7235*	48	1
23 Apr 64		**IF I LOVED YOU (re-entry)** *Columbia DB 7235*	18	9

Ray ANTHONY and His ORCHESTRA *US, orchestra (2 WEEKS)*

			pos	wks
4 Dec 53	●	**DRAGNET** *Capitol CL 13983*	7	1
8 Jan 54		**DRAGNET (re-entry)** *Capitol CL 13983*	11	1

ANTHRAX *US, male vocal / instrumental group (37 WEEKS)*

			pos	wks
28 Feb 87		**I AM THE LAW** *Island IS LAW 1*	32	5
27 Jun 87		**INDIANS** *Island IS 325*	44	4
5 Dec 87		**I'M THE MAN** *Island IS 338*	20	6
10 Sep 88		**MAKE ME LAUGH** *Island IS 379*	26	3
18 Mar 89		**ANTI-SOCIAL** *Island IS 409*	44	3
1 Sep 90		**IN MY WORLD** *Island IS 470*	29	2
5 Jan 91		**GOT THE TIME** *Island IS 476*	16	4
6 Jul 91		**BRING THE NOISE** *Island IS 490* [1]	14	5
8 May 93		**ONLY** *Elektra EKR 166CD*	36	3
11 Sep 93		**BLACK LODGE** *Elektra EKR 171CD*	53	2

[1] Anthrax featuring Chuck D

ANTI-NOWHERE LEAGUE
UK, male vocal / instrumental group (10 WEEKS)

			pos	wks
23 Jan 82		**STREETS OF LONDON** *WXYZ ABCD 1*	48	5
20 Mar 82		**I HATE . . . PEOPLE** *WXYZ ABCD 2*	46	3
3 Jul 82		**WOMAN** *WXYZ ABCD 4*	72	2

ANTI-PASTI – *See EXPLOITED*

ANTICAPPELLA
Italy / UK, male / female vocal / instrumental group (12 WEEKS)

			pos	wks
16 Nov 91		**231** *PWL Continental PWL 205*	24	4
18 Apr 92		**EVERY DAY** *PWL Continental PWL 220*	45	2
25 Jun 94		**MOVE YOUR BODY** *Media MCSTD 1980* [1]	21	3
1 Apr 95		**EXPRESS YOUR FREEDOM** *Media MCSTD 2048*	31	2
25 May 96		**231 / MOVE YOUR BODY (re-mix)** *Media MCSTD 40037*	54	1

[1] Anticappella featuring MC Fixx It

ANTONIA – *See BOMB THE BASS*

ANTS – *See ADAM and the ANTS*

ANUNA – *See Bill WHELAN featuring ANUNA and the RTE CONCERT ORCHESTRA*

APACHE INDIAN *UK, male vocalist – Steven Kapur (33 WEEKS)* pos/wks

28 Nov 92		**FE' REAL** *Ten TEN 416* [1]	33	3
2 Jan 93		**ARRANGED MARRIAGE** *Island CID 544*	16	6
27 Mar 93		**CHOK THERE** *Island CID 555*	30	4
14 Aug 93	●	**NUFF VIBES (EP)** *Island CID 560*	5	10
22 Oct 93		**MOVIN' ON** *Island CID 580*	48	2
7 May 94		**WRECKX SHOP** *MCA MCSTD 1969* [2]	26	2
11 Feb 95		**MAKE WAY FOR THE INDIAN** *Island CID 586* [3]	29	2
22 Apr 95		**RAGGAMUFFIN GIRL** *Island CID 606* [4]	31	2
29 Mar 97		**LOVIN' (LET ME LOVE YOU)** *Coalition COLA 002CD*	53	1
18 Oct 97		**REAL PEOPLE** *Coalition COLA 019CD*	66	1

[1] Maxi Priest featuring Apache Indian [2] Wreckx-N-Effect featuring Apache Indian [3] Apache Indian and Tim Dog [4] Apache Indian with Frankie Paul

The listed flip side of 'Fe' Real' was 'Just Wanna Know' by Maxi Priest. Tracks on Nuff Vibes (EP): Boom Shack a Lak / Fun / Caste System / Warning

APHEX TWIN
UK, male instrumentalist / producer – Richard James (12 WEEKS) pos/wks

9 May 92		**DIGERIDOO** *R&S RSUK 12*	55	2
27 Nov 93		**ON** *Warp WAP 39CD*	32	3
8 Apr 95		**VENTOLIN** *Warp WAP 60CD*	49	1
26 Oct 96		**GIRL / BOY (EP)** *Warp WAP 78CD*	64	1
18 Oct 97		**COME TO DADDY** *Warp WAP 94CD*	36	2
3 Apr 99		**WINDOWLICKER** *Warp WAP 105CD*	16	3

Tracks on Girl / Boy (EP): Girl / Boy Song / Milkman / Inkey $ / Beatles Under My Carpet. The EP was incorrectly listed in the chart and, because of its length, should have been considered an album

See also POLYGON WINDOW; AFX

APHRODITE'S CHILD
Greece, male vocal / instrumental group (7 WEEKS) pos/wks

6 Nov 68		**RAIN AND TEARS** *Mercury MF 1039*	29	7

APOLLO presents HOUSE OF VIRGINISM *Sweden, male instrumentalist and Sweden, male vocal / instrumental group (1 WEEK)* pos/wks

17 Feb 96		**EXCLUSIVE** *Logic 74321324102*	67	1

APOLLO FOUR FORTY
UK, male instrumental / production group (52 WEEKS) pos/wks

22 Jan 94		**ASTRAL AMERICA** *Stealth Sonic SSXCD 2* [1]	36	2
5 Nov 94		**LIQUID COOL** *Stealth Sonic SSXCD 3* [1]	35	2
25 Mar 95		**(DON'T FEAR) THE REAPER** *Stealth Sonic SSXCD 4* [1]	35	2
27 Jul 96		**KRUPA** *Stealth Sonic SSXCD 5*	23	4
28 Sep 96		**KRUPA (re-entry)** *Stealth Sonic SSXCD 5*	24	4
15 Feb 97	●	**AIN'T TALKIN' 'BOUT DUB** *Stealth Sonic SSXCDX 6*	7	7
5 Jul 97		**RAW POWER** *Stealth Sonic SSXCD 7*	32	3
11 Jul 98		**RENDEZ-VOUS '98** *Epic 6661102* [2]	12	6
8 Aug 98	●	**LOST IN SPACE** *Stealth Sonic SSX 9CD*	4	9
28 Aug 99	●	**STOP THE ROCK** *Epic SSX 10CD*	10	6
27 Nov 99		**HEART GO BOOM** *Epic SSX 11CD*	57	1
9 Dec 00		**CHARLIE'S ANGELS 2000** *Epic SSX 13CD*	29	6

[1] Apollo 440 [2] Jean-Michel Jarre and Apollo 440

Fiona APPLE *US, female vocalist (2 WEEKS)* pos/wks

26 Feb 00		**FAST AS YOU CAN** *Columbia 6689962*	33	2

Kim APPLEBY *UK, female vocalist (31 WEEKS)* pos/wks

3 Nov 90	●	**DON'T WORRY** *Parlophone R 6272*	2	10
9 Feb 91	●	**G.L.A.D.** *Parlophone R 6281*	10	6
29 Jun 91		**MAMA** *Parlophone R 6291*	19	8
19 Oct 91		**IF YOU CARED** *Parlophone R 6297*	44	3
31 Jul 93		**LIGHT OF THE WORLD** *Parlophone CDR 6352*	41	2
13 Nov 93		**BREAKAWAY** *Parlophone CDR 6362*	56	1
12 Nov 94		**FREE SPIRIT** *Parlophone CDR 6397*	51	1

See also MEL and KIM

APPLEJACKS
UK, male / female vocal / instrumental group (29 WEEKS) pos/wks

5 Mar 64	●	**TELL ME WHEN** *Decca F 11833*	7	13
11 Jun 64		**LIKE DREAMERS DO** *Decca F 11916*	20	11
15 Oct 64		**THREE LITTLE WORDS (I LOVE YOU)** *Decca F 11981*	23	5

APPLES *UK, male vocal / instrumental group (1 WEEK)* pos/wks

23 Mar 91		**EYE WONDER** *Epic 6566717*	75	1

Charlie APPLEWHITE *US, male vocalist (1 WEEK)* pos/wks

23 Sep 55		**BLUE STAR** *Brunswick 05416*	20	1

This release was 'With Victor Young and His Orchestra and Chorus'

Helen APRIL – *See John DUMMER and Helen APRIL*

APRIL WINE *Canada, male vocal / instrumental group (9 WEEKS)* pos/wks

15 Mar 80		**I LIKE TO ROCK** *Capitol CL 16121*	41	5
11 Apr 81		**JUST BETWEEN YOU AND ME** *Capitol CL 16184*	52	4

AQUA (380 Top 500) *Scandinavian Europop: Claus Noreen, Denmark, Soren Rasted, Denmark, fronted by the flame-haired Lene Nystrom, Norway, and the bald-headed Rene Dif, Denmark. 'Barbie Girl' was a global smash and their debut album 'Aquarium' sold more than 14 million worldwide. Ceased to be in 2001 having racked up total album / single sales of more than 28 million (85 WEEKS)* pos/wks

25 Oct 97	★	**BARBIE GIRL** *Universal UMD 80413* ◆	1	24
7 Feb 98	★	**DOCTOR JONES** *Universal UMD 80457* ■	1	14
25 Apr 98		**BARBIE GIRL (re-entry)** *Universal UMD 80413*	66	2
16 May 98	★	**TURN BACK TIME** *Universal UMD 80490* ■	1	10
1 Aug 98	●	**MY OH MY** *Universal UMD 85058*	6	9
17 Oct 98		**MY OH MY (re-entry)** *Universal UMD 85058*	66	2
26 Dec 98		**GOOD MORNING SUNSHINE** *Universal UMD 85086*	18	7
26 Feb 00	●	**CARTOON HEROES** *Universal MCSTD 40226*	7	9
13 May 00		**CARTOON HEROES (re-entry)** *Universal MCSTD 40226*	73	2
10 Jun 00		**AROUND THE WORLD** *Universal MCSTD 40234*	26	6

AQUA MARINA – *See FAB*

AQUARIAN DREAM
US, male / female vocal / instrumental group (1 WEEK) pos/wks

24 Feb 79		**YOU'RE A STAR** *Elektra LV 7*	67	1

ARAB STRAP *UK, male vocal / instrumental duo (4 WEEKS)* pos/wks

13 Sep 97		**THE GIRLS OF SUMMER (EP)** *Chemikal Underground CHEM 017CD*	74	1
4 Apr 98		**HERE WE GO / TRIPPY** *Chemikal Underground CHEM 20CD*	48	1
10 Oct 98		**(AFTERNOON) SOAPS** *Chemikal Underground CHEM 27CD*	74	1
10 Feb 01		**LOVE DETECTIVE** *Chemikal Underground CHEM 049CD*	66	1

Tracks on The Girls of Summer (EP): Hey! Fever / Girls of Summer / The Beautiful Barmaids of Dundee / One Day After School

ARCADIA *UK, male vocal / instrumental group (13 WEEKS)* pos/wks

26 Oct 85	●	**ELECTION DAY** *Odeon NSR 1*	7	7
25 Jan 86		**THE PROMISE** *Odeon NSR 2*	37	4
26 Jul 86		**THE FLAME** *Odeon NSR 3*	58	2

Arcadia was Duran Duran sideline band featuring Simon Le Bon, Nick Rhodes and Roger Taylor

See also DURAN DURAN

Tasmin ARCHER *UK, female vocalist (37 WEEKS)* pos/wks

12 Sep 92	★	**SLEEPING SATELLITE** *EMI EM 233*	1	15
2 Jan 93		**SLEEPING SATELLITE (re-entry)** *EMI EM 233*	67	2

THE OFFICIAL UK SINGLES CHART 50TH ANNIVERSARY

1954

IN THE YEAR IN WHICH ROGER BANNISTER BROKE THE FOUR-MINUTE MILE, BILL HALEY AND HIS COMETS SCORED THE FIRST ROCK 'N' ROLL HIT WITH 'SHAKE RATTLE AND ROLL' AND DISCOTHEQUE ENTERED THE DICTIONARY, **SHAKIN' STEVENS**, WHO WAS JUST SIX AT THE TIME, GIVES US THE BENEFIT OF HIS RESEARCH INTO THE ORIGIN OF HIS BIGGEST HIT ...

“As the story goes, the inspiration for 'This Ole House' came to Stuart Hamblen during a hunting trip in the Sierra Mountains. Caught in a blizzard, he sheltered in an old shack where he found the body of an old prospector. In 1954 he released his recording of the song and in the same year **Rosemary Clooney** and Billie Anthony also released their covers of this country song. There's no trace of Stuart Hamblen having charted in the UK, but Billie Anthony reached No.4, while Rosemary went to No.1 in the same month. Twenty-seven years later I recorded this song with a different arrangement, which became my first UK No.1 and the title of an album – both of which became international hits. Since 1954 this classic song has been covered by scores of artists, ranging through to Caravan, Bobby Bare, The Shadows, Billie Jo Spears, Bill Black's Combo, Jimmy Dean, Boxcar Willie and NRBQ, a US band whose version first brought the song to my attention.”

SINGLE OF THE YEAR
'Cara Mia' David Whitfield

		pos	wks
20 Feb 93	**IN YOUR CARE** *EMI CDEMS 260*	16	6
29 May 93	**LORDS OF THE NEW CHURCH** *EMI CDEM 266*	26	4
21 Aug 93	**ARIENNE** *EMI CDEM 275*	30	4
8 Jan 94	**SHIPBUILDING** *EMI CDEM 302*	40	4
23 Mar 96	**ONE MORE GOOD NIGHT WITH THE BOYS** *EMI CDEM 401*	45	2

ARCHIES *US, male / female cartoon vocal group – lead vocal Ron Dante (26 WEEKS)* pos/wks

		pos	wks
11 Oct 69 ★	**SUGAR, SUGAR** *RCA 1872* ▲	1	26

See also CUFFLINKS

ARCHITECHS
UK, male production duo and female vocalist (19 WEEKS) pos/wks

		pos	wks
7 Oct 00 ●	**BODY GROOVE** *Go. Beat / Polydor GOBCD33* [1]	3	14
7 Apr 01	**SHOW ME THE MONEY** *Go. Beat GOBCD 38*	20	4
18 Aug 01	**SHOW ME THE MONEY (re-entry)** *Go. Beat GOBCD 38*	65	1

[1] Architechs featuring Nana

Jann ARDEN *Canada, female vocalist (2 WEEKS)* pos/wks

		pos	wks
13 Jul 96	**INSENSITIVE** *A & M 5812652*	40	2

Tina ARENA *Australia, female vocalist (32 WEEKS)* pos/wks

		pos	wks
15 Apr 95 ●	**CHAINS** *Columbia 6611255*	6	11
12 Aug 95	**HEAVEN HELP MY HEART** *Columbia 6620975*	25	5
2 Dec 95	**SHOW ME HEAVEN** *Columbia 6626975*	29	3
3 Aug 96	**SORRENTO MOON (I REMEMBER)** *Columbia 6635435*	22	4
27 Jun 98	**WHISTLE DOWN THE WIND** *Really Useful 5672192*	24	5
24 Oct 98	**IF I WAS A RIVER** *Columbia 6665605*	43	2
13 Mar 99	**BURN** *Columbia 6667442*	47	1
20 May 00	**LIVE FOR THE ONE I LOVE** *Columbia 6691332*	63	1

ARGENT *UK, male vocal / instrumental group (27 WEEKS)* pos/wks

		pos	wks
4 Mar 72 ●	**HOLD YOUR HEAD UP** *Epic EPC 7786*	5	12
10 Jun 72	**TRAGEDY** *Epic EPC 85115*	34	7
24 Mar 73	**GOD GAVE ROCK AND ROLL TO YOU** *Epic EPC 1243*	18	8

See also SAN JOSE *featuring* Rodriguez ARGENTINA; SILSOE

India.ARIE *US, female vocalist (5 WEEKS)* pos/wks

		pos	wks
30 Jun 01	**VIDEO** *Motown TMGCD 1505*	32	3
20 Oct 01	**BROWN SKIN** *Motown TMGCD 1507*	29	2

ARIEL *Argentina, male DJ / producer – Ariel Belloso (6 WEEKS)* pos/wks

		pos	wks
27 Mar 93	**LET IT SLIDE** *Deconstruction 74321134512*	57	2
21 Jun 97	**DEEP (I'M FALLING DEEPER)** *Wonderboy WBOYD 005*	47	1
17 Jun 00	**A9** *Essential Recordings ESCD 15*	28	3

ARIZONA featuring ZEITIA *UK, male production / instrumental duo and female vocalist (1 WEEK)* pos/wks

		pos	wks
12 Mar 94	**I SPECIALIZE IN LOVE** *Union City UCRCD 27*	74	1

Ship's Company and Royal Marine Band of HMS ARK ROYAL
UK, male choir and marine band (6 WEEKS) pos/wks

		pos	wks
23 Dec 78	**THE LAST FAREWELL** *BBC RESL 61*	46	6

ARKARNA
UK, male vocal / instrumental / production group (3 WEEKS) pos/wks

		pos	wks
25 Jan 97	**HOUSE ON FIRE** *WEA WEA 088CD1*	33	2
2 Aug 97	**SO LITTLE TIME** *WEA WEA 108CD1*	46	1

Joan ARMATRADING *UK, female vocalist (53 WEEKS)* pos/wks

		pos	wks
16 Oct 76 ●	**LOVE AND AFFECTION** *A & M AMS 7249*	10	9
23 Feb 80	**ROSIE** *A & M AMS 7506*	49	5
14 Jun 80	**ME MYSELF I** *A & M AMS 7527*	21	11
6 Sep 80	**ALL THE WAY FROM AMERICA** *A & M AMS 7552*	54	3
12 Sep 81	**I'M LUCKY** *A & M AMS 8163*	46	5
16 Jan 82	**NO LOVE** *A & M AMS 8179*	50	5
19 Feb 83	**DROP THE PILOT** *A & M AMS 8306*	11	10
16 Mar 85	**TEMPTATION** *A & M AM 238*	65	2
26 May 90	**MORE THAN ONE KIND OF LOVE** *A & M AM 561*	75	1
23 May 92	**WRAPPED AROUND HER** *A & M AM 877*	56	2

ARMIN *Holland, male DJ producer – Armin Van Buuren (4 WEEKS)* pos/wks

		pos	wks
14 Feb 98	**BLUE FEAR** *Xtravaganza 0091485 EXT*	45	1
12 Feb 00	**COMMUNICATION** *AM:PM CDAMPM 129*	18	3

ARMOURY SHOW *UK, male vocal / instrumental group (6 WEEKS)* pos/wks

		pos	wks
25 Aug 84	**CASTLES IN SPAIN** *Parlophone R 6079*	69	2
26 Jan 85	**WE CAN BE BRAVE AGAIN** *Parlophone R 6087*	66	1
17 Jan 87	**LOVE IN ANGER** *Parlophone R 6149*	63	3

Craig ARMSTRONG – *See* Shola AMA

Louis ARMSTRONG (333 Top 500) *Best known jazz artist of the 20th century, b. 4 Aug 1901, New Orleans, US, (not 4 Jul 1900 according to previous claims by the man himself) d. Jul 1971. This ground-breaking, trumpet-playing gravel-voiced vocalist, known as "Satchmo", is the oldest performer to top either the UK or US charts (93 WEEKS)* pos/wks

		pos	wks
19 Dec 52 ●	**TAKES TWO TO TANGO** *Brunswick 04995*	6	10
13 Apr 56 ●	**A THEME FROM THE THREEPENNY OPERA (MACK THE KNIFE)** *Philips PB 574* [1]	8	11
15 Jun 56	**TAKE IT SATCH (EP)** *Philips BBE 12035* [1]	29	1
13 Jul 56	**THE FAITHFUL HUSSAR** *Philips PB 604* [1]	27	2
6 Nov 59	**MACK THE KNIFE (A THEME FROM THE THREEPENNY OPERA)** *Philips PB 967* [1]	24	1
4 Jun 64 ●	**HELLO, DOLLY!** *London HLR 9878* [2] ▲	4	14
7 Feb 68 ★	**WHAT A WONDERFUL WORLD / CABARET** *HMV POP 1615* [3] / [1]	1	29
26 Jun 68	**THE SUNSHINE OF LOVE** *Stateside SS 2116*	41	7
16 Apr 88	**WHAT A WONDERFUL WORLD (re-issue)** *A & M AM 435* [3]	53	5
19 Nov 94 ●	**WE HAVE ALL THE TIME IN THE WORLD** *EMI CDEM 357*	3	11
18 Mar 95	**WE HAVE ALL THE TIME IN THE WORLD (re-entry)** *EMI CDEM 357*	66	2

[1] Louis Armstrong and his All-Stars [2] Louis Armstrong and the All Stars [3] Louis Armstrong Orchestra & Chorus

Take It Satch (EP) tracks: Tiger Rag / Mack the Knife / The Faithful Hussar / Back O'Town Blues. 'Mack the Knife' is a re-issue of 'Theme From The Threepenny Opera' under a different title. 'Cabaret' was not listed with 'What a Wonderful World' until 14 Feb 1968

ARMY OF LOVERS
Sweden / France, male / female vocal / group (12 WEEKS) pos/wks

		pos	wks
17 Aug 91	**CRUCIFIED** *Ton Son Ton WOK 2007*	47	5
28 Dec 91	**OBSESSION** *Ton Son Ton WOK 2009*	67	1
15 Feb 92	**CRUCIFIED (re-issue)** *Ton Son Ton WOK 2017*	31	5
18 Apr 92	**RIDE THE BULLET** *Ton Son Ton WOK 2018*	67	1

ARNEE and the TERMINATERS
UK, male vocal / instrumental group (7 WEEKS) pos/wks

		pos	wks
24 Aug 91 ●	**I'LL BE BACK** *Epic 6574177*	5	7

ARNIE'S LOVE
US, male / female vocal / instrumental group (3 WEEKS) pos/wks

		pos	wks
26 Nov 83	**I'M OUT OF YOUR LIFE** *Streetwave WAVE 9*	67	3

David ARNOLD – *See* Nina PERSSON *and* David ARNOLD; BJÖRK; David McALMONT; PROPELLERHEADS

Eddy ARNOLD *US, male vocalist (21 WEEKS)* pos/wks

		pos	wks
17 Feb 66 ●	**MAKE THE WORLD GO AWAY** *RCA 1496*	8	17
26 May 66	**I WANT TO GO WITH YOU** *RCA 1519*	49	1
9 Jun 66	**I WANT TO GO WITH YOU (re-entry)** *RCA 1519*	46	2
28 Jul 66	**IF YOU WERE MINE MARY** *RCA 1529*	49	1

UK No.1 ★ UK Top 10 ● Still on chart + UK million seller ◆ UK entry at No.1 ■ US No.1 ▲

PP ARNOLD *US, female vocalist (37 WEEKS)*

Date		Title / Label	pos	wks
4 May 67		THE FIRST CUT IS THE DEEPEST *Immediate IM 047*	18	10
2 Aug 67		THE TIME HAS COME *Immediate IM 055*	47	2
24 Jan 68		(IF YOU THINK YOU'RE) GROOVY *Immediate IM 061*	41	4
10 Jul 68		ANGEL OF THE MORNING *Immediate IM 067*	29	11
24 Sep 88		BURN IT UP *Rhythm King LEFT 27* [1]	14	10

[1] Beatmasters with PP Arnold

ARPEGGIO *US, male / female vocal group (3 WEEKS)*

Date		Title / Label	pos	wks
31 Mar 79		LOVE AND DESIRE (PART 1) *Polydor POSP 40*	63	3

ARRESTED DEVELOPMENT *US, male / female vocal / instrumental / rap group (39 WEEKS)*

Date		Title / Label	pos	wks
16 May 92		TENNESSEE *Cooltempo COOL 253*	46	4
11 Jul 92		TENNESSEE (re-entry) *Cooltempo COOL 253*	54	3
24 Oct 92	●	PEOPLE EVERYDAY *Cooltempo COOL 265*	2	14
9 Jan 93	●	MR WENDAL / REVOLUTION *Cooltempo CDCOOL 268*	4	9
3 Apr 93		TENNESSEE (re-issue) *Cooltempo CDCOOL 270*	18	6
28 May 94		EASE MY MIND *Cooltempo CDCOOL 293*	33	3

Steve ARRINGTON *US, male vocalist (19 WEEKS)*

Date		Title / Label	pos	wks
27 Apr 85	●	FEEL SO REAL *Atlantic A 9576*	5	10
6 Jul 85		DANCIN' IN THE KEY OF LIFE *Atlantic A 9534*	21	8
7 Sep 85		DANCIN' IN THE KEY OF LIFE (re-entry) *Atlantic A 9534*	75	1

ARRIVAL *UK, male / female vocal / instrumental group (20 WEEKS)*

Date		Title / Label	pos	wks
10 Jan 70	●	FRIENDS *Decca F 12986*	8	9
6 Jun 70		I WILL SURVIVE *Decca F 13026*	16	11

ARROLA – See *RUFF DRIVERZ*

ARROW *Montserrat, male vocalist (15 WEEKS)*

Date		Title / Label	pos	wks
28 Jul 84		HOT HOT HOT *Cooltempo ARROW 1*	59	5
13 Jul 85		LONG TIME *London LON 70*	30	7
3 Sep 94		HOT HOT HOT (re-mix) *The Hit Label HLC 7*	38	3

ARROWS *US / UK, male vocal / instrumental group (16 WEEKS)*

Date		Title / Label	pos	wks
25 May 74	●	A TOUCH TOO MUCH *RAK 171*	8	9
1 Feb 75		MY LAST NIGHT WITH YOU *RAK 189*	25	7

ARSENAL FC *UK, male football team vocal group (16 WEEKS)*

Date		Title / Label	pos	wks
8 May 71		GOOD OLD ARSENAL *Pye 7N 45067* [1]	16	7
15 May 93		SHOUTING FOR THE GUNNERS *London LONCD 342* [2]	34	3
23 May 98	●	HOT STUFF *Grapevine AFCCD 1*	9	5
3 Jun 00		ARSENAL NUMBER ONE / OUR GOAL *Grapevine CDGPS280*	46	1

[1] Arsenal FC First Team Squad [2] Arsenal FA Cup Squad featuring Tippa Irie and Peter Hunnigale

ART COMPANY *Holland, male vocal / instrumental group (11 WEEKS)*

Date		Title / Label	pos	wks
26 May 84		SUSANNA *Epic A 4174*	12	11

ART OF NOISE *UK, male / female instrumental / production group (65 WEEKS)*

Date		Title / Label	pos	wks
24 Nov 84	●	CLOSE (TO THE EDIT) *ZTT ZTPS 01*	8	19
13 Apr 85		MOMENTS IN LOVE / BEAT BOX *ZTT ZTPS 02*	51	4
9 Nov 85		LEGS *China WOK 5*	69	1
22 Mar 86	●	PETER GUNN *China WOK 6* [1]	8	9
21 Jun 86		PARANOIMIA *China WOK 9* [2]	12	9
18 Jul 87		DRAGNET *China WOK 14*	60	4
29 Oct 88	●	KISS *China CHINA 11* [3]	5	7
12 Aug 89		YEBO *China CHINA 18* [4]	63	3
16 Jun 90		ART OF LOVE *China CHINA 23*	67	1
11 Jan 92		INSTRUMENTS OF DARKNESS (ALL OF US ARE ONE PEOPLE) *China WOK 2012*	45	5
29 Feb 92		SHADES OF PARANOIMIA *China WOK 2014*	53	2
26 Jun 99		METAFORCE *ZTT ZTT 129CD*	53	1

[1] Art of Noise featuring Duane Eddy [2] Art of Noise featuring Max Headroom [3] Art of Noise featuring Tom Jones [4] Art of Noise featuring Mahlathini and the Mahotella Queens

ART OF TRANCE *UK, male instrumentalist / producer (3 WEEKS)*

Date		Title / Label	pos	wks
31 Oct 98		MADAGASCAR *Platipus PLAT 43CD*	69	1
7 Aug 99		MADAGASCAR (re-mix) *Platipus PLAT 58CD*	48	2

ARTEMESIA *Holland, male producer – Patrick Prinz (4 WEEKS)*

Date		Title / Label	pos	wks
15 Apr 95		BITS + PIECES *Hooj Choons HOOJ 31CD*	46	2
23 Sep 95		BITS + PIECES (re-entry) *Hooj Choons HOOJ 31CD*	75	1
12 Aug 00		BITS AND PIECES (re-mix) *Tidy Trax TIDT 141CD*	51	1

See also ETHICS; MOVIN' MELODIES; SUBLIMINAL CUTS

ARTFUL DODGER *UK, male production / instrumental duo – Mark Hill and Peter Devereux (69 WEEKS)*

Date		Title / Label	pos	wks
11 Dec 99	●	RE-REWIND THE CROWD SAY BO SELECTA *Public Demand / Relentless RELENT 1CDS* [1]	2	17
4 Mar 00	●	MOVIN TOO FAST *Locked On XL LOX 117CD* [2]	2	11
10 Jun 00		MOVIN TOO FAST (re-entry) *Locked On XL LOX 117CD* [2]	64	1
15 Jul 00	●	WOMAN TROUBLE *Public Demand / ffrr FCD 380* [3]	6	10
25 Nov 00	●	PLEASE DON'T TURN ME ON *Public Demand / ffrr FCD 388* [4]	4	10
17 Mar 01		THINK ABOUT ME *ffrr FCD 394* [5]	11	8
15 Sep 01	●	TWENTYFOURSEVEN *ffrr / Public Demand FCD 400* [6]	6	9
15 Dec 01		IT AIN'T ENOUGH *ffrr / Public Demand FCD 401* [7]	20	3+

[1] Artful Dodger featuring Craig David [2] Artful Dodger and Romina Johnson [3] Artful Dodger and Robbie Craig featuring Craig David [4] Artful Dodger featuring Lifford [5] Artful Dodger featuring Michelle Escoffery [6] Artful Dodger featuring Melanie Blatt [7] Dreem Teem vs Artful Dodger featuring MZ May and MC Alistair

Neil ARTHUR *UK, male vocalist (2 WEEKS)*

Date		Title / Label	pos	wks
5 Feb 94		I LOVE I HATE *Chrysalis CDCHSS 5005*	50	2

ARTIST – See *PRINCE*

ARTISTS AGAINST AIDS WORLDWIDE *US / Ireland, all-star male / female vocal ensemble (7 WEEKS)*

Date		Title / Label	pos	wks
17 Nov 01	●	WHAT'S GOING ON *Columbia 6721172*	6	7+

ARTISTS UNITED AGAINST APARTHEID *International, male / female vocal / instrumental charity assembly (8 WEEKS)*

Date		Title / Label	pos	wks
23 Nov 85		SUN CITY *Manhattan MT 7*	21	8

ASAP *UK, male vocal / instrumental group (4 WEEKS)*

Date		Title / Label	pos	wks
14 Oct 89		SILVER AND GOLD *EMI EM 107*	60	2
3 Feb 90		DOWN THE WIRE *EMI EM 131*	67	2

ASCENSION *UK, male / female vocal / DJ / production group (3 WEEKS)*

Date		Title / Label	pos	wks
5 Jul 97		SOMEONE *Perfecto PERF 141CD*	55	1
15 Jul 00		SOMEONE (re-mix) *Code Blue BLU 011CD1*	43	2

ASH *Ireland, male / female, vocal / instrumental group (53 WEEKS)*

Date		Title / Label	pos	wks
1 Apr 95		KUNG FU *Infectious INFECT 21CD*	57	1
12 Aug 95		GIRL FROM MARS *Infectious INFECT 24CD*	11	5
21 Oct 95		ANGEL INTERCEPTOR *Infectious INFECT 27CD*	14	4
27 Apr 96	●	GOLDFINGER *Infectious INFECT 39CD*	5	5
6 Jul 96	●	OH YEAH *Infectious INFECT 41CD*	6	7
28 Sep 96		OH YEAH (re-entry) *Infectious INFECT 41CD*	69	1
25 Oct 97	●	A LIFE LESS ORDINARY *Infectious INFECT 50CD*	10	5
3 Oct 98		JESUS SAYS *Infectious INFECT 59CD*	15	4
5 Dec 98		WILD SURF *Infectious INFECT 61CDS*	31	2
10 Feb 01	●	SHINING LIGHT *Infectious INFECT 98CD*	8	4
14 Apr 01		BURN BABY BURN *Infectious INFECT 99CDS*	13	6

21 Jul 01		**SOMETIMES** *Infectious INFECT 101CDS*	21	6
13 Oct 01		**CANDY** *Infectious INFECT 106CDS*	20	3

Act were male only trio before 1997 hit

ASH – *See QUENTIN and ASH*

ASHA *Italy, female vocalist (2 WEEKS)*

			pos	wks
8 Jul 95		**JJ TRIBUTE** *Ffrreedom TABCD 228*	38	2

ASHAYE *UK, male vocalist (3 WEEKS)*

			pos	wks
15 Oct 83		**MICHAEL JACKSON MEDLEY** *Record Shack SOHO 10*	45	3

Tracks on medley: Don't Stop Til You Get Enough / Wanna Be Startin' Something / Shake Your Body Down to the Ground / Blame It on the Boogie

Richard ASHCROFT *UK, male vocalist (18 WEEKS)*

			pos	wks
15 Apr 00	●	**A SONG FOR THE LOVERS** *Hut / Virgin HUTCD 128*	3	10
24 Jun 00		**MONEY TO BURN** *Hut / Virgin HUTCD 136*	17	4
1 Jul 00		**A SONG FOR THE LOVERS (re-entry)** *Hut / Virgin HUTCD 128*	61	1
23 Sep 00		**C'MON PEOPLE (WE'RE MAKING IT NOW)** *Hut / Virgin HUTCD 138*	21	3

See also VERVE

John ASHER *UK, male vocalist (6 WEEKS)*

			pos	wks
15 Nov 75		**LET'S TWIST AGAIN** *Creole CR 112*	14	6

ASHFORD and SIMPSON *US, male / female vocal duo – Nickolas Ashford and Valerie Simpson (22 WEEKS)*

			pos	wks
18 Nov 78		**IT SEEMS TO HANG ON** *Warner Bros. K 17237*	48	4
5 Jan 85	●	**SOLID** *Capitol CL 345*	3	15
20 Apr 85		**BABIES** *Capitol CL 355*	56	3

ASHTON, GARDNER AND DYKE *UK, male vocal / instrumental group (14 WEEKS)*

			pos	wks
16 Jan 71	●	**THE RESURRECTION SHUFFLE** *Capitol CL 15665*	3	14

ASIA *UK, male vocal / instrumental group (13 WEEKS)*

			pos	wks
3 Jul 82		**HEAT OF THE MOMENT** *Geffen GEF A2494*	46	5
18 Sep 82		**ONLY TIME WILL TELL** *Geffen GEF A2228*	54	3
13 Aug 83		**DON'T CRY** *Geffen A 3580*	33	5

ASIA BLUE *UK, female vocal group (2 WEEKS)*

			pos	wks
27 Jun 92		**ESCAPING** *Atomic WNR 882*	50	2

ASIAN DUB FOUNDATION *UK, male vocal / instrumental group (7 WEEKS)*

			pos	wks
21 Feb 98		**FREE SATPAL RAM** *ffrr FCD 326*	56	1
2 May 98		**BUZZIN'** *ffrr FCD 335*	31	2
4 Jul 98		**BLACK WHITE** *ffrr FCD 337*	52	1
18 Mar 00		**REAL GREAT BRITAIN** *ffrr FCD 376*	41	2
3 Jun 00		**NEW WAY, NEW LIFE** *ffrr FCD 378*	49	1

ASSEMBLY *UK, male vocal / instrumental group (10 WEEKS)*

			pos	wks
12 Nov 83	●	**NEVER NEVER** *Mute TINY 1*	4	10

See also ERASURE

ASSOCIATES *UK, male vocal / instrumental group (47 WEEKS)*

			pos	wks
20 Feb 82	●	**PARTY FEARS TWO** *Associates ASC 1*	9	10
8 May 82		**CLUB COUNTRY** *Associates ASC 2*	13	10
7 Aug 82		**LOVE HANGOVER / 18 CARAT LOVE AFFAIR** *Associates ASC 3*	21	8
16 Jun 84		**THOSE FIRST IMPRESSIONS** *WEA YZ 6*	43	6
1 Sep 84		**WAITING FOR THE LOVEBOAT** *WEA YZ 16*	53	4
19 Jan 85		**BREAKFAST** *WEA YZ 28*	49	6
17 Sep 88		**HEART OF GLASS** *WEA YZ 310*	56	3

'18 Carat Love Affair' listed until 28 Aug only. Act was duo on 1982 hits

ASSOCIATION *US, male vocal / instrumental group (8 WEEKS)*

			pos	wks
22 May 68		**TIME FOR LIVIN'** *Warner Bros. WB 7195*	23	8

Rick ASTLEY (342 Top 500) *Soulful-voiced pop vocalist, b. 6 Feb 1966, Warrington, UK. Brit award-winning, US chart-topping debut hit was 1987's best-selling UK single. No British solo male can match his seven consecutive (mostly Stock, Aitken Waterman produced) Top 10 hits in the 1980s (91 WEEKS)*

			pos	wks
8 Aug 87	★	**NEVER GONNA GIVE YOU UP** *RCA PB 41447* ▲	1	18
31 Oct 87	●	**WHENEVER YOU NEED SOMEBODY** *RCA PB 41567*	3	12
12 Dec 87	●	**WHEN I FALL IN LOVE / MY ARMS KEEP MISSING YOU** *RCA PB 41683*	2	10
27 Feb 88	●	**TOGETHER FOREVER** *RCA PB 41817* ▲	2	9
24 Sep 88	●	**SHE WANTS TO DANCE WITH ME** *RCA PB 42189*	6	10
26 Nov 88	●	**TAKE ME TO YOUR HEART** *RCA PB 42573*	8	10
11 Feb 89	●	**HOLD ME IN YOUR ARMS** *RCA PB 42615*	10	8
26 Jan 91	●	**CRY FOR HELP** *RCA PB 44247*	7	7
30 Mar 91		**MOVE RIGHT OUT** *RCA PB 44407*	58	2
29 Jun 91		**NEVER KNEW LOVE** *RCA PB 44737*	70	1
4 Sep 93		**THE ONES YOU LOVE** *RCA 74321160142*	48	2
13 Nov 93		**HOPELESSLY** *RCA 74321175642*	33	2

Before 9 Jan 1988, 'When I Fall in Love' was listed by itself. After that date 'My Arms Keep Missing You' was the side listed

ASTRO TRAX *UK, male / female vocal / production trio (1 WEEK)*

			pos	wks
24 Oct 98		**THE ENERGY (FEEL THE VIBE)** *Satellite 74321622052*	74	1

ASWAD (416 Top 500) *Seminal reggae outfit formed 1975 London, UK. Featured former child actor Brinsley Forde (v), b. 1952, Guyana. They signed to Island in 1976, topped the chart with an old Tina Turner B-side and followed it into the Top 20 with a Bucks Fizz B-side (80 WEEKS)*

			pos	wks
3 Mar 84		**CHASING FOR THE BREEZE** *Island IS 160*	51	3
6 Oct 84		**54-46 (WAS MY NUMBER)** *Island IS 170*	70	3
27 Feb 88	★	**DON'T TURN AROUND** *Mango IS 341*	1	12
21 May 88		**GIVE A LITTLE LOVE** *Mango IS 358*	11	8
24 Sep 88		**SET THEM FREE** *Mango IS 383*	70	2
1 Apr 89		**BEAUTY'S ONLY SKIN DEEP** *Mango MNG 105*	31	6
22 Jul 89		**ON AND ON** *Mango MNG 708*	25	8
18 Aug 90		**NEXT TO YOU** *Mango MNG 753*	24	6
17 Nov 90		**SMILE** *Mango MNG 767* [1]	53	2
30 Mar 91		**TOO WICKED (EP)** *Mango MNG 771*	61	2
31 Jul 93		**HOW LONG** *Polydor PZCD 252* [2]	31	5
9 Oct 93		**DANCEHALL MOOD** *Bubblin' CDBUBB 1*	48	2
18 Jun 94	●	**SHINE** *Bubblin' CDBUBB 3*	5	14
17 Sep 94		**WARRIORS** *Bubblin' CDBUBB 4*	33	3
18 Feb 95		**YOU'RE NO GOOD** *Bubblin' CDBUBB 5*	35	3
5 Aug 95		**IF I WAS** *Bubblin' CDBUBB 6*	58	1

[1] Aswad featuring Sweetie Irie [2] Yazz and Aswad

Tracks on Too Wicked (EP): Best of My Love / Warrior Re-Charge / Fire / I Shot the Sheriff

AT THE DRIVE-IN *US, male vocal / instrumental group (3 WEEKS)*

			pos	wks
19 Aug 00		**ONE ARMED SCISSOR** *Grand Royal GR 091CD*	64	1
16 Dec 00		**ROLODEX PROPAGANDA** *Grand Royal / Virgin VUSCD 189*	54	1
24 Mar 01		**INVALID LITTER DEPT** *Grand Royal / Virgin VUSCD 193*	50	1

Gali ATARI – *See MILK AND HONEY featuring Gali ATARI*

ATB *Germany, male producer – Andre Tanneberger (52 WEEKS)*

			pos	wks
13 Mar 99		**(9PM) TILL I COME** *Ministry of Sound DATA 1*	68	1
22 May 99		**(9PM) TILL I COME (German import)** *Club Tools CLU 66066*	72	3
19 Jun 99		**(9PM) TILL I COME (Australian import)** *Dancenet DNET 131*	63	1
19 Jun 99		**(9PM) TILL I COME (German import) (re-entry)** *Club Tools CLU 66066*	47	2
3 Jul 99	★	**(9PM) TILL I COME** *Sound of Ministry MOSCDS 132* ■	1	15
9 Oct 99		**DON'T STOP (import)** *Club Tools CLU 66406*	61	2
23 Oct 99	●	**DON'T STOP** *Sound of Ministry MOSCDS 134*	3	9
1 Jan 00		**DON'T STOP (re-entry)** *Sound of Ministry MOSCDS 134*	48	4
25 Mar 00	●	**KILLER** *Sound of Ministry MOSCDS 138*	4	8

		pos	wks
17 Jun 00	**KILLER (re-entry)** *Sound of Ministry MOSCDS 138*	74	1
27 Jan 01	**THE FIELDS OF LOVE** *Club Tools / Edel 0124095 CLU* [1]	16	4
30 Jun 01	**LET U GO** *Kontour 0117335 KTR*	34	2

[1] ATB featuring York

A.T.F.C. presents ONEPHATDEEVA

UK, male producer – Aydin Hasirci (8 WEEKS) pos/wks

		pos	wks
30 Oct 99	**IN AND OUT OF MY LIFE** *Defected DEFECT 8CDS*	11	5
16 Sep 00	**BAD HABIT** *Defected DFECT 19CDS* [1]	17	3

[1] A.T.F.C. presents Onephatdeeva featuring Lisa Millett

ATGOC *Italy, male instrumentalist / producer (2 WEEKS)* pos/wks

		pos	wks
21 Nov 98	**REPEATED LOVE** *Wonderboy WBOYD 012*	38	2

Chet ATKINS *US, male instrumentalist – guitar (2 WEEKS)* pos/wks

		pos	wks
17 Mar 60	**TEENSVILLE** *RCA 1174*	46	1
5 May 60	**TEENSVILLE (re-entry)** *RCA 1174*	49	1

ATLANTA RHYTHM SECTION

US, male vocal / instrumental group (4 WEEKS) pos/wks

		pos	wks
27 Oct 79	**SPOOKY** *Polydor POSP 74*	48	4

ATLANTIC OCEAN *Holland, male instrumental duo – Rene Van Der Weyde and Lex Van Coeverden (14 WEEKS)* pos/wks

		pos	wks
19 Feb 94	**WATERFALL** *Eastern Bloc BLOCCD 001*	22	6
2 Jul 94	**BODY IN MOTION** *Eastern Bloc BLOCCD 009*	15	4
26 Nov 94	**MUSIC IS A PASSION** *Eastern Bloc BLOCCDX 017*	59	1
30 Nov 96	**WATERFALL (re-mix)** *Eastern Bloc BLOC 104CD*	21	3

ATLANTIC STARR

US, male / female vocal / instrumental group (48 WEEKS) pos/wks

		pos	wks
9 Sep 78	**GIMME YOUR LOVIN'** *A & M AMS 7380*	66	3
29 Jun 85	**SILVER SHADOW** *A & M AM 260*	41	6
7 Sep 85	**ONE LOVE** *A & M AM 273*	58	4
15 Mar 86 ●	**SECRET LOVERS** *A & M AM 307*	10	12
24 May 86	**IF YOUR HEART ISN'T IN IT** *A & M AM 319*	48	4
13 Jun 87 ●	**ALWAYS** *Warner Bros. W 8455* ▲	3	14
12 Sep 87	**ONE LOVER AT A TIME** *Warner Bros. W 8327*	57	3
27 Aug 94	**EVERYBODY'S GOT SUMMER** *Arista 74321228072*	36	2

ATLANTIS vs AVATAR *UK, male production group featuring female vocalist – Miriam Stockley (2 WEEKS)* pos/wks

		pos	wks
28 Oct 00	**FIJI** *Inferno CDFERN 34*	52	2

Natacha ATLAS – *See Jean-Michel JARRE*

ATMOSFEAR *UK, male instrumental trio (7 WEEKS)* pos/wks

		pos	wks
17 Nov 79	**DANCING IN OUTER SPACE** *MCA 543*	46	7

ATOMIC KITTEN *UK, female vocal trio (63 WEEKS)* pos/wks

		pos	wks
11 Dec 99 ●	**RIGHT NOW** *Innocent SINCD 15*	10	9
8 Apr 00 ●	**SEE YA** *Innocent SINCD 17*	6	6
1 Jul 00	**SEE YA (re-entry)** *Innocent SINCD 17*	74	1
15 Jul 00 ●	**I WANT YOUR LOVE** *Innocent SINCD 18*	10	5
21 Oct 00	**FOLLOW ME** *Innocent SINCD 22*	20	5
10 Feb 01 ★	**WHOLE AGAIN** *Innocent SINCD24* ◆ ■	1	22
21 Jul 01	**WHOLE AGAIN (re-entry)** *Innocent SINCD24*	73	1
4 Aug 01 ★	**ETERNAL FLAME** *Innocent SINCD 27* ■	1	14

ATOMIC ROOSTER *UK, male vocal / instrumental group (25 WEEKS)* pos/wks

		pos	wks
6 Feb 71	**TOMORROW NIGHT** *B & C CB 131*	11	12
10 Jul 71 ●	**THE DEVIL'S ANSWER** *B & C CB 157*	4	13

ATTRACTIONS – *See Elvis COSTELLO*

Winifred ATWELL (234 Top 500) *The 'Queen of the Ivories' (and Elton John's early idol) b. 27 Apr 1914, Trinidad, d. 28 Feb 1983. Britain's all-time top female instrumentalist earned a couple of gold discs for her popular party medleys and hosted a very successful TV series in 1957 (117 WEEKS)* pos/wks

		pos	wks
12 Dec 52	**BRITANNIA RAG** *Decca F 10015*	11	1
9 Jan 53 ●	**BRITANNIA RAG (re-entry)** *Decca F 10015*	5	5
15 May 53	**CORONATION RAG** *Decca F 10110*	12	1
29 May 53 ●	**CORONATION RAG (re-entry)** *Decca F 10110*	5	5
25 Sep 53	**FLIRTATION WALTZ** *Decca F 10161*	12	1
9 Oct 53 ●	**FLIRTATION WALTZ (re-entry)** *Decca F 10161*	10	1
6 Nov 53	**FLIRTATION WALTZ (2nd re-entry)** *Decca F 10161*	12	1
4 Dec 53 ●	**LET'S HAVE A PARTY** *Philips PB 213*	2	9
23 Jul 54 ●	**RACHMANINOFF'S 18TH VARIATION ON A THEME BY PAGANINI (THE STORY OF THREE LOVES)** *Philips PB 234*	9	7
1 Oct 54	**RACHMANINOFF'S 18TH VARIATION ON A THEME BY PAGANINI (THE STORY OF THREE LOVES) (re-entry)** *Philips PB 234*	19	2
26 Nov 54	**LET'S HAVE A PARTY (re-entry)** *Philips PB 213*	14	6
26 Nov 54 ★	**LET'S HAVE ANOTHER PARTY** *Philips PB 268*	1	8
4 Nov 55 ●	**LET'S HAVE A DING DONG** *Decca F 10634*	3	10
16 Mar 56 ★	**THE POOR PEOPLE OF PARIS** *Decca F 10681*	1	16
18 May 56	**PORT-AU-PRINCE** *Decca F 10727* [1]	18	6
20 Jul 56	**LEFT BANK (C'EST A HAMBOURG)** *Decca F 10762*	14	7
26 Oct 56 ●	**MAKE IT A PARTY** *Decca F 10796*	7	12
22 Feb 57	**LET'S ROCK 'N' ROLL** *Decca F 10852*	28	2
15 Mar 57	**LET'S ROCK 'N' ROLL (re-entry)** *Decca F 10852*	24	2
6 Dec 57 ●	**LET'S HAVE A BALL** *Decca F 10956*	4	6
7 Aug 59	**THE SUMMER OF THE SEVENTEENTH DOLL** *Decca F 11143*	24	2
27 Nov 59 ●	**PIANO PARTY** *Decca F 11183*	10	7

[1] Winifred Atwell and Frank Chacksfield

Various hits listed above were medleys as follows: Let's Have a Party: If You Knew Suzie / The More We Are Together / That's My Weakness Now / Knees Up Mother Brown / Daisy Bell / Boomps A Daisy / She Was One Of The Early Birds / Three O'Clock In The Morning. Let's Have Another Party: Somebody Stole My Gal / I Wonder Where My Baby Is Tonight / When The Red Red Robin / Bye Bye Blackbird / Sheik Of Araby / Another Little Drink / Lilly Of Laguna / Honeysuckle and The Bee / Broken Doll / Nellie Dean. Let's Have a Ding Dong: Ain't She Sweet / Oh Johnny Oh Johnny Oh / Oh You Beautiful Doll / Yes We Have No Bananas / Happy Days Are Here Again / I'm Forever Blowing Bubbles / I'll Be Your Sweetheart / If These Lips Could Only Speak / Who's Taking You Home Tonight. Make It a Party: Who Were You With Last Night / Hello Hello Who's Your Lady Friend / Yes Sir That's My Baby / Don't Dilly Dally On the Way / Beer Barrel Polka / After the Ball / Peggy O'Neil / Meet Me Tonight in Dreamland / I Belong To Glasgow / Down at the Old Bull and Bush. Let's Rock 'n' Roll: Singin' The Blues / Green Door / See You Later Alligator / Shake Rattle and Roll / Rock Around the Clock / Razzle Dazzle. Let's Have a Ball: Music Music Music / This Ole House / Heartbreaker / Woody Woodpecker / Last Train to San Fernando / Bring a Little Water Sylvie / Puttin' On The Style / Don't You Rock Me Daddy-O. Piano Party: Baby Face / Comin' Thru' The Rye / Annie Laurie / Little Brown Jug / Let Him Go Let Him Tarry / Put Your Arms Around Me Honey / I'll Be With You in Apple Blossom Time / Shine On Harvest Moon / Blue Skies / I'll Never Say 'Never Again' Again / I'll See You In My Dreams

AUDIOWEB *UK, male vocal / instrumental group (12 WEEKS)* pos/wks

		pos	wks
14 Oct 95	**SLEEPER** *Mother MUMCD 69*	74	1
9 Mar 96	**YEAH** *Mother MUMCD 72*	73	1
15 Jun 96	**INTO MY WORLD** *Mother MUMCD 76*	42	1
19 Oct 96	**SLEEPER (re-mix)** *Mother MUMCD 78*	50	2
15 Feb 97	**BANKROBBER** *Mother MUMCD 85*	19	2
24 May 97	**FAKER** *Mother MUMCD 91*	70	1
25 Apr 98	**POLICEMAN SKANK … (THE STORY OF MY LIFE)** *Mother MUMCD 100*	21	2
4 Jul 98	**PERSONAL FEELING** *Mother MUMCD 104*	65	1
20 Feb 99	**TEST THE THEORY** *Mother MUMCD 110*	56	1

Brian AUGER – *See Julie DRISCOLL, Brian AUGER and the TRINITY*

AURA – *See POPPERS presents AURA*

AURORA *UK, male production duo – aka Dive (12 WEEKS)* pos/wks

		pos	wks
5 Jun 99	**HEAR YOU CALLING** *Additive 12AD 040*	71	1

		pos	wks
5 Feb 00	**HEAR YOU CALLING (re-issue)** *Positiva CDTIV 124*	17	4
23 Sep 00 ●	**ORDINARY WORLD** *Positiva CDTIV 139* [1]	5	7

[1] Aurora featuring Naimee Coleman

See also DIVE

AURRA *US, male / female vocal / instrumental group (18 WEEKS)*

		pos	wks
4 May 85	**LIKE I LIKE IT** *10 TEN 45*	51	5
19 Apr 86	**YOU AND ME TONIGHT** *10 TEN 71*	12	8
21 Jun 86	**LIKE I LIKE IT (re-issue)** *10 TEN 126*	43	5

Adam AUSTIN *UK, male vocalist (1 WEEK)*

		pos	wks
13 Feb 99	**CENTERFOLD** *Media PSRCA 0107*	41	1

David AUSTIN *UK, male vocalist (3 WEEKS)*

		pos	wks
21 Jul 84	**TURN TO GOLD** *Parlophone R 6068*	68	3

Patti AUSTIN *US, female vocalist (11 WEEKS)*

		pos	wks
12 Feb 83	**BABY COME TO ME** *Qwest K 15005* [1] ▲	11	10
5 Sep 92	**I'LL KEEP YOUR DREAMS ALIVE** *Ammi AMMI 101* [2]	68	1

[1] Patti Austin and James Ingram [2] George Benson and Patti Austin

AUTECHRE *UK, male instrumental duo (1 WEEK)*

		pos	wks
7 May 94	**BASSCAD** *Warp WAP 44CD*	56	1

AUTEURS *UK, male / female vocal / instrumental group (9 WEEKS)*

		pos	wks
27 Nov 93	**LENNY VALENTINO** *Hut HUTCD 36*	41	2
23 Apr 94	**CHINESE BAKERY** *Hut HUTDX 41*	42	2
6 Jan 96	**BACK WITH THE KILLER AGAIN** *Hut HUTCD 65*	45	3
24 Feb 96	**LIGHT AIRCRAFT ON FIRE** *Hut HUTCD 66*	58	1
3 Jul 99	**THE RUBETTES** *Hut HUTCD 113*	66	1

AUTUMN *UK, male vocal / instrumental group (6 WEEKS)*

		pos	wks
16 Oct 71	**MY LITTLE GIRL** *Pye 7N 45090*	37	6

Peter AUTY and the SINFONIA OF LONDON conducted by Howard BLAKE *UK, male vocalist with UK orchestra (9 WEEKS)*

		pos	wks
14 Dec 85	**WALKING IN THE AIR** *Stiff LAD 1*	42	5
19 Dec 87	**WALKING IN THE AIR (re-issue)** *CBS GA 3950*	37	4

See also DIGITAL DREAM BABY

AVALANCHES *Australia, male production group (12 WEEKS)*

		pos	wks
7 Apr 01	**SINCE I LEFT YOU** *XL Recordings XLS 128CD*	16	7
21 Jul 01	**FRONTIER PSYCHIATRIST** *XL Recordings XLS 134CD*	18	5

Frankie AVALON *US, male vocalist – Francis Avallone (15 WEEKS)*

		pos	wks
10 Oct 58	**GINGERBREAD** *HMV POP 517*	30	1
24 Apr 59	**VENUS** *HMV POP 603* ▲	16	6
22 Jan 60	**WHY** *HMV POP 688* ▲	20	4
28 Apr 60	**DON'T THROW AWAY ALL THOSE TEARDROPS** *HMV POP 727*	37	4

AVALON BOYS – *See LAUREL and HARDY with the AVALON BOYS featuring Chill WILLS*

AVERAGE WHITE BAND
UK, male vocal / instrumental vocal group (47 WEEKS)

		pos	wks
22 Feb 75 ●	**PICK UP THE PIECES** *Atlantic K 10489* ▲	6	9
26 Apr 75	**CUT THE CAKE** *Atlantic K 10605*	31	4
9 Oct 76	**QUEEN OF MY SOUL** *Atlantic K 10825*	23	7
28 Apr 79	**WALK ON BY** *RCA XC 1087*	46	5
25 Aug 79	**WHEN WILL YOU BE MINE** *RCA XB 1096*	49	5
26 Apr 80	**LET'S GO ROUND AGAIN PT.1** *RCA AWB 1*	12	11
26 Jul 80	**FOR YOU FOR LOVE** *RCA AWB 2*	46	4
26 Mar 94	**LET'S GO ROUND AGAIN (re-mix)** *The Hit Label HLC 5*	56	2

Kevin AVIANCE *US, male vocalist (1 WEEK)*

		pos	wks
13 Jun 98	**DIN DA DA** *Distinctive DISNCD 42*	65	1

AVONS *UK, male / female vocal trio (22 WEEKS)*

		pos	wks
13 Nov 59 ●	**SEVEN LITTLE GIRLS SITTING IN THE BACK SEAT** *Columbia DB 4363*	3	13
7 Jul 60	**WE'RE ONLY YOUNG ONCE** *Columbia DB 4461*	49	1
21 Jul 60	**WE'RE ONLY YOUNG ONCE (re-entry)** *Columbia DB 4461*	45	1
27 Oct 60	**FOUR LITTLE HEELS** *Columbia DB 4522*	45	2
1 Dec 60	**FOUR LITTLE HEELS (re-entry)** *Columbia DB 4522*	49	1
26 Jan 61	**RUBBER BALL** *Columbia DB 4569*	30	4

AWESOME *UK, male vocal group (2 WEEKS)*

		pos	wks
8 Nov 97	**RUMOURS** *Universal MCSTD 40145*	58	1
21 Mar 98	**CRAZY** *Universal MCSTD 40195*	63	1

AWESOME 3 *UK, male / female vocal / instrumental group (8 WEEKS)*

		pos	wks
8 Sep 90	**HARD UP** *A & M AM 591*	55	3
3 Oct 92	**DON'T GO** *Citybeat CBE 1271*	75	1
4 Jun 94	**DON'T GO (re-mix)** *Citybeat CBX 771CD*	45	2
26 Oct 96	**DON'T GO (2nd) (re-mix)** *XL XLS 78CD* [1]	27	2

[1] Awesome 3 featuring Julie McDermott

Hoyt AXTON *US, male vocalist (4 WEEKS)*

		pos	wks
7 Jun 80	**DELLA AND THE DEALER** *Young Blood YB 82*	48	4

AXUS *UK, male / female vocal / production duo (1 WEEK)*

		pos	wks
26 Sep 98	**ABACUS (WHEN I FALL IN LOVE)** *INCcredible INCRL 8CD*	62	1

Roy AYERS *US, male vocalist / instrumentalist – vibraphone (13 WEEKS)*

		pos	wks
21 Oct 78	**GET ON UP, GET ON DOWN** *Polydor AYERS 7*	41	4
13 Jan 79	**HEAT OF THE BEAT** *Polydor POSP 16* [1]	43	5
2 Feb 80	**DON'T STOP THE FEELING** *Polydor STEP 6*	56	3
16 May 98	**EXPANSIONS** *Soma Recordings SOMA 65CDS* [2]	68	1

[1] Roy Ayers and Wayne Henderson [2] Scott Grooves featuring Roy Ayers

AYLA *Germany, male producer – Ingo Kunzi (3 WEEKS)*

		pos	wks
4 Sep 99	**AYLA** *Positiva CDTIV 117*	22	3

AZ *US, male rapper – Anthony Cruz (1 WEEK)*

		pos	wks
30 Mar 96	**SUGARHILL** *Cooltempo CDCOOL 315*	67	1

AZ YET *US, male vocal group (10 WEEKS)*

		pos	wks
1 Mar 97	**LAST NIGHT** *LaFace 74321423202*	21	3
21 Jun 97 ●	**HARD TO SAY I'M SORRY** *LaFace 74321481482* [1]	7	7

[1] Az Yet featuring Peter Cetera

Charles AZNAVOUR
France, male vocalist – Shanaur Aznavourian (29 WEEKS)

		pos	wks
22 Sep 73	**THE OLD FASHIONED WAY** *Barclay BAR 20*	50	1
20 Oct 73	**THE OLD FASHIONED WAY (re-entry)** *Barclay BAR 20*	38	12
22 Jun 74 ★	**SHE** *Barclay BAR 26*	1	14
27 Jul 74	**THE OLD FASHIONED WAY (2nd re-entry)** *Barclay BAR 20*	47	2

AZTEC CAMERA (475 Top 500) *Sensitive, tuneful pop band formed 1980, and centred around teenage singer / songwriter Roddy Frame, b. 29 Jan 1964, East Kilbride, Scotland. Album 'Love' was among nominations for Best British Album at 1989 Brit awards (74 WEEKS)*

		pos	wks
19 Feb 83	**OBLIVIOUS** *Rough Trade RT 122*	47	6
4 Jun 83	**WALK OUT TO WINTER** *Rough Trade RT 132*	64	4
5 Nov 83	**OBLIVIOUS (re-issue)** *WEA AZTEC 1*	18	11
1 Sep 84	**ALL I NEED IS EVERYTHING / JUMP** *WEA AC 1*	34	6
13 Feb 88	**HOW MEN ARE** *WEA YZ 168*	25	9
23 Apr 88 ●	**SOMEWHERE IN MY HEART** *WEA YZ 181*	3	14
6 Aug 88	**WORKING IN A GOLDMINE** *WEA YZ 199*	31	5
8 Oct 88	**DEEP AND WIDE AND TALL** *WEA YZ 154*	55	3
7 Jul 90	**THE CRYING SCENE** *WEA YZ 492*	70	3
6 Oct 90	**GOOD MORNING BRITAIN** *WEA YZ 521* [1]	19	8

18 Jul 92		**SPANISH HORSES** *WEA YZ 688*	52	3
1 May 93		**DREAM SWEET DREAMS** *WEA YZ 740CD1*	67	2

[1] Aztec Camera and Mick Jones

'Jump' listed only from 22 Sep 1984 to end of chart run

AZTEC MYSTIC – *See DJ ROLANDO AKA AZTEC MYSTIC*

AZURE *Italy / US, male / female vocal / DJ duo (1 WEEK)*

			pos	wks
25 Apr 98		**MAMA USED TO SAY** *Inferno CDFERN 005*	56	1

AZYMUTH *Brazil, male instrumental group (8 WEEKS)*

			pos	wks
12 Jan 80		**JAZZ CARNIVAL** *Milestone MRC 101*	19	8

Bob AZZAM and His ORCHESTRA and CHORUS *Egypt, bandleader and his orchestra (14 WEEKS)*

			pos	wks
26 May 60		**MUSTAPHA** *Decca F 21235*	23	14

B

Derek B *UK, male rapper (Derek Boland) (15 WEEKS)*

			pos	wks
27 Feb 88		**GOODGROOVE** *Music of Life 7NOTE 12*	16	6
7 May 88		**BAD YOUNG BROTHER** *Tuff Audio DRKB 1*	16	6
2 Jul 88		**WE'VE GOT THE JUICE** *Tuff Audio DRKB 2*	56	3

Howie B *UK male instrumentalist / producer (4 WEEKS)*

			pos	wks
19 Jul 97		**ANGELS GO BALD: TOO** *Polydor 5711672*	36	2
18 Oct 97		**SWITCH** *Polydor 5717112*	62	1
11 Apr 98		**TAKE YOUR PARTNER BY THE HAND** *Polydor 5693272* [1]	74	1

[1] Howie B featuring Robbie Robertson

JAZZIE B – *See Maxi PRIEST; SOUL II SOUL*

Jon B *US, male vocalist (5 WEEKS)*

			pos	wks
17 Oct 98		**THEY DON'T KNOW** *Epic 6663975*	32	2
26 May 01		**DON'T TALK** *Epic 6712792*	29	3

Lisa B *US, female vocalist (9 WEEKS)*

			pos	wks
12 Jun 93		**GLAM** *ffrr FCD 210*	49	2
25 Sep 93		**FASCINATED** *ffrr FCD 218*	35	3
8 Jan 94		**YOU AND ME** *ffrr FCD 226*	39	4

Lorna B *UK, female vocalist (6 WEEKS)*

			pos	wks
28 Jan 95		**DO YOU WANNA PARTY** *Steppin' Out SPONCD 2* [1]	36	3
1 Apr 95		**SWEET DREAMS** *Steppin' Out SPONCD 3* [1]	37	2
15 Mar 97		**FEELS SO GOOD** *Avex UK AVEXCD 53*	69	1

[1] DJ Scott featuring Lorna B

Melanie B *UK, female vocalist – Melanie Brown (36 WEEKS)*

			pos	wks
26 Sep 98	★	**I WANT YOU BACK** *Virgin VSCDT 1716* [1] ■	1	9
10 Jul 99		**WORD UP** *Virgin VSCDT 1735* [2]	14	7
25 Sep 99		**WORD UP (re-entry)** *Virgin VSCDT 1735* [2]	71	1
7 Oct 00	●	**TELL ME** *Virgin VSCDT 1777*	4	7
3 Mar 01	●	**FEELS SO GOOD** *Virgin VSCDT 1787*	5	8
16 Jun 01		**LULLABY** *Virgin VSCDT 1798*	13	4

[1] Melanie B featuring Missy 'Misdemeanor' Elliott [2] Melanie G

See also SPICE GIRLS

Sandy B *US, female vocalist (8 WEEKS)*

			pos	wks
20 Feb 93		**FEEL LIKE SINGIN'** *Nervous SANCD 1*	60	1
18 May 96		**MAKE THE WORLD GO ROUND** *Champion CHAMPCD 322*	73	1
24 May 97		**MAKE THE WORLD GO ROUND (re-mix)** *Champion CHAMPCD 327*	35	2
8 Nov 97		**AIN'T NO NEED TO HIDE** *Champion CHAMPCD 331*	60	1
28 Feb 98		**MAKE THE WORLD GO ROUND (2nd re-mix)** *Champion CHAMPCD 333*	20	3

Stevie B *US, male vocalist Steven Hill (9 WEEKS)*

			pos	wks
23 Feb 91	●	**BECAUSE I LOVE YOU (THE POSTMAN SONG)** *Polydor PO 126* ▲	6	9

Tairrie B *US, female rapper (2 WEEKS)*

			pos	wks
1 Dec 90		**MURDER SHE WROTE** *MCA MCA 1455*	71	2

Mark B & BLADE *UK, Male rap / production duo (4 WEEKS)*

			pos	wks
10 Feb 01		**THE UNKNOWN** *Wordplay WORDCDS 011*	49	1
26 May 01		**YA DON'T SEE THE SIGNS** *Worldplay WORDCDSE 019*	23	3

Eric B and RAKIM *US, male DJ / rap duo (Eric Barrier and William Griffin Jr) (26 WEEKS)*

			pos	wks
7 Nov 87		**PAID IN FULL** *Fourth & Broadway BRW 78*	15	6
20 Feb 88		**MOVE THE CROWD** *Fourth & Broadway BRW 88*	53	2
12 Mar 88		**I KNOW YOU GOT SOUL** *Cooltempo COOL 146*	13	6
2 Jul 88		**FOLLOW THE LEADER** *MCA MCA 1256*	21	5
19 Nov 88		**THE MICROPHONE FIEND** *MCA MCA 1300*	74	1
12 Aug 89		**FRIENDS** *MCA MCA 1352* [1]	21	6

[1] Jody Watley with Eric B and Rakim

B B and Q BAND *US, male vocal / instrumental group (15 WEEKS)*

			pos	wks
18 Jul 81		**ON THE BEAT** *Capitol CL 202*	41	5
6 Jul 85		**GENIE** *Cooltempo COOL 110* [1]	40	4
20 Sep 86		**(I'M A) DREAMER** *Cooltempo COOL 132*	35	5
17 Oct 87		**RICOCHET** *Cooltempo COOL 154*	71	1

[1] Brooklyn Bronx and Queens

B BUMBLE and the STINGERS *US, male instrumental group (26 WEEKS)*

			pos	wks
19 Apr 62	★	**NUT ROCKER** *Top Rank JAR 611*	1	15
3 Jun 72		**NUT ROCKER (re-issue)** *Stateside SS 2203*	19	11

B-CREW *US, female vocal group (1 WEEK)*

			pos	wks
20 Sep 97		**PARTAY FEELING** *Positiva CDTIV 78*	45	1

B15 PROJECT featuring Crissy D and Lady G *UK / Jamaica, male production duo and female vocalists (10 WEEKS)*

			pos	wks
17 Jun 00	●	**GIRLS LIKE US** *Ministry of Sound RELENT 3CDS*	7	8
19 Aug 00		**GIRLS LIKE US (re-entry)** *Ministry of Sound RELENT 3CDS*	55	2

B-52's *US, male / female vocal / instrumental group (61 WEEKS)*

			pos	wks
11 Aug 79		**ROCK LOBSTER** *Island WIP 6506*	37	5
9 Aug 80		**GIVE ME BACK MY MAN** *Island WIP 6579*	61	3
7 May 83		**(SONG FOR A) FUTURE GENERATION** *Island IS 107*	63	2
10 May 86		**ROCK LOBSTER / PLANET CLAIRE (re-issue)** *Island BFT 1*	12	7
3 Mar 90	●	**LOVE SHACK** *Reprise W 9917*	2	13
19 May 90		**ROAM** *Reprise W 9827*	17	7
18 Aug 90		**CHANNEL Z** *Reprise W 9737*	61	2
20 Jun 92		**GOOD STUFF** *Reprise W 0109*	21	6
12 Sep 92		**TELL IT LIKE IT T-I-IS** *Reprise W 0130*	61	3
9 Jul 94	●	**(MEET) THE FLINTSTONES** *MCA MCSTD 1986* [1]	3	12
30 Jan 99		**LOVE SHACK 99** *Reprise W 0461CD*	66	1

[1] BC-52's

'Planet Claire' listed only from 17 May 1986

B-MOVIE *UK, male vocal / instrumental group (7 WEEKS)* pos/wks

18 Apr 81 **REMEMBRANCE DAY** *Deram DM 437* 61 3
27 Mar 82 **NOWHERE GIRL** *Some Bizarr/DDe BZZ 8* 67 4

B REAL / BUSTA RHYMES / COOLIO / LL COOL J / METHOD MAN
US, male rappers (6 WEEKS) pos/wks

5 Apr 97 ● **HIT 'EM HIGH (MONSTARS' ANTHEM)** *Atlantic A 5449CD* 8 6

B-TRIBE *Spain, male / female vocal / instrumental group (4 WEEKS)* pos/wks

25 Sep 93 **¡FIESTA FATAL!** *East West YZ 770CD* 64 4

B*WITCHED (379 Top 500) *Ireland's most successful female group, Edele and Keavy Lynch, Sinead O'Carroll and Lindsay Armaou. Youngest girl group to top the chart, they sold more than one million copies of their debut album in the US and were the first act to enter at No.1 with their first four singles (85 WEEKS)* pos/wks

6 Jun 98 ★ **C'EST LA VIE** *Glow Worm / Epic 6660532* ■ 1 19
3 Oct 98 ★ **ROLLERCOASTER** *Glow Worm / Epic 6664752* ■ 1 15
19 Dec 98 ★ **TO YOU I BELONG** *Glow Worm / Epic 6667712* ■ 1 12
27 Mar 99 ★ **BLAME IT ON THE WEATHERMAN** *Glow Worm / Epic 6670335* ■ ..1 9
27 Mar 99 **TO YOU I BELONG (re-entry)** *Glow Worm / Epic 6667712* 64 2
16 Oct 99 ● **JESSE HOLD ON** *Glow Worm / Epic 6679612* 4 10
18 Dec 99 **I SHALL BE THERE** *Glow Worm / Epic 683332* [1] 13 9
8 Jan 00 **JESSE HOLD ON (re-entry)** *Glow Worm / Epic 6679612* 60 2
8 Apr 00 **JUMP DOWN** *Glow Worm / Epic 6691282* 16 5
27 May 00 **JUMP DOWN (re-entry)** *Glow Worm / Epic 6691282* 62 2

[1] B*witched featuring Ladysmith Black Mambazo

BABE INSTINCT *UK, female vocal group (2 WEEKS)* pos/wks

16 Jan 99 **DISCO BABES FROM OUTER SPACE** *Positiva CDTIV 103* 21 2

Alice BABS *Sweden, female vocalist (1 WEEK)* pos/wks

15 Aug 63 **AFTER YOU'VE GONE** *Fontana TF 409* 43 1

BABY BUMPS *UK, male / female vocal / instrumental duo – Sean Casey and Lisa Millett (6 WEEKS)* pos/wks

8 Aug 98 **BURNING** *Delirious DELICD 10* 17 4
26 Feb 00 **I GOT THIS FEELING** *Sound of Ministry MOSCDS 137* 22 2

BABY D *UK, male / female vocal / instrumental group (45 WEEKS)* pos/wks

18 Dec 93 **DESTINY** *Production House PNC 057* 69 1
23 Jul 94 **CASANOVA** *Production House PNC 065* 67 1
19 Nov 94 ★ **LET ME BE YOUR FANTASY** *Systematic SYSCD 4* 1 14
3 Jun 95 ● **(EVERYBODY'S GOT TO LEARN SOMETIME) I NEED YOUR LOVING** *Systematic SYSCD 11* 3 12
13 Jan 96 ● **SO PURE** *Systematic SYSCD 21* 3 7
6 Apr 96 **TAKE ME TO HEAVEN** *Systematic SYSCD 26* 15 5
2 Sep 00 **LET ME BE YOUR FANTASY (re-mix)** *Systematic SYSCD 35* 16 5

BABY DC featuring IMAJIN
US, male rapper Derrick Coleman Jr and vocal group (1 WEEK) pos/wks

24 Apr 99 **BOUNCE, ROCK, SKATE, ROLL** *Jive 0522142* 45 1

BABY FORD *UK, male instrumentalist keyboards (16 WEEKS)* pos/wks

10 Sep 88 **OOCHY KOOCHY (F.U. BABY YEAH YEAH)** *Rhythm King 7BFORD 1* 58 6
24 Dec 88 **CHIKKI CHIKKI AHH AHH** *Rhythm King 7BFORD 2* 75 1
7 Jan 89 **CHIKKI CHIKKI AHH AHH (re-entry)** *Rhythm King 7BFORD 2* 54 3
17 Jun 89 **CHILDREN OF THE REVOLUTION** *Rhythm King 7BFORD 4* 53 4
17 Feb 90 **BEACH BUMP** *Rhythm King 7BFORD 6* 68 2

BABY JUNE *UK, male vocalist – Tim Hegarty (1 WEEK)* pos/wks

15 Aug 92 **HEY! WHAT'S YOUR NAME** *Arista 115271* 75 1

BABY O *US, male / female vocal / instrumental group (5 WEEKS)* pos/wks

26 Jul 80 **IN THE FOREST** *Calibre CAB 505* 46 5

BABY ROOTS *UK, male vocalist (1 WEEK)* pos/wks

1 Aug 92 **ROCK ME BABY** *ZYX ZYX 68027* 71 1

BABYBIRD *UK, male vocalist / instrumentalist (35 WEEKS)* pos/wks

10 Aug 96 **GOODNIGHT** *Echo ECSCD 24* 28 2
12 Oct 96 ● **YOU'RE GORGEOUS** *Echo ECSD 26* 3 16
1 Feb 97 **CANDY GIRL** *Echo ECSCD 31* 14 3
17 May 97 **CORNERSHOP** *Echo ECSCD 33* 37 2
9 May 98 **BAD OLD MAN** *Echo ECSCD 60* 31 2
22 Aug 98 **IF YOU'LL BE MINE** *Echo ECSCX 65* 28 4
27 Feb 99 **BACK TOGETHER** *Echo ECSCD 73* 22 3
25 Mar 00 **THE F-WORD** *Echo ECSCD 92* 35 2
3 Jun 00 **OUT OF SIGHT** *Echo ECSCD 97* 58 1

BABYFACE *US, male vocalist – Kenneth Edmonds (23 WEEKS)* pos/wks

9 Jul 94 **ROCK BOTTOM** *Epic 6601832* 50 4
1 Oct 94 **WHEN CAN I SEE YOU** *Epic 6606592* 35 3
9 Nov 96 **THIS IS FOR THE LOVER IN YOU** *Epic 6639352* 12 5
8 Mar 97 **EVERYTIME I CLOSE MY EYES** *Epic 6642492* 13 4
19 Jul 97 ● **HOW COME, HOW LONG** *Epic 6646202* [1] 10 5
25 Oct 97 **SUNSHINE** *Northwestside 74321528702* [2] 25 2

[1] Babyface featuring Stevie Wonder [2] Jay-Z featuring Babyface and Foxy Brown

BABYLON ZOO
UK, male vocalist / multi-instrumentalist – Jas Mann (20 WEEKS) pos/wks

27 Jan 96 ★ **SPACEMAN** *EMI CDEM 416* ◆ ■ 1 14
27 Apr 96 **ANIMAL ARMY** *EMI CDEM 425* 17 3
5 Oct 96 **THE BOY WITH THE X-RAY EYES** *EMI CDEMS 440* 32 2
6 Feb 99 **ALL THE MONEY'S GONE** *EMI CDEM 519* 46 1

BABYS *US / UK, male vocal / instrumental group (3 WEEKS)* pos/wks

21 Jan 78 **ISN'T IT TIME** *Chrysalis CHS 2173* 45 3

BACCARA *Spain, female vocal duo – Maria Mendiola and Mayte Mateos (25 WEEKS)* pos/wks

17 Sep 77 ★ **YES SIR I CAN BOOGIE** *RCA PB 5526* 1 16
14 Jan 78 ● **SORRY I'M A LADY** *RCA PB 5555* 8 9

Burt BACHARACH *US, orchestra and chorus (12 WEEKS)* pos/wks

20 May 65 ● **TRAINS AND BOATS AND PLANES** *London HL 9968* 4 11
1 May 99 **TOLEDO** *Mercury 8709652* [1] 72 1

[1] Elvis Costello / Burt Bacharach

BACHELORS (101 Top 500) *Irish vocal / instrumental trio, who were one of the few popular non-rock groups of the 1960s: brothers Declan and Con Cluskey and John Stokes. This Dublin act had hits on both sides of the Atlantic with revivals of popular pre-rock ballads (187 WEEKS)* pos/wks

24 Jan 63 ● **CHARMAINE** *Decca F 11559* 6 19
4 Jul 63 **FARAWAY PLACES** *Decca F 11666* 36 3
29 Aug 63 **WHISPERING** *Decca F 11712* 18 10
23 Jan 64 ★ **DIANE** *Decca F 11799* 1 19
19 Mar 64 ● **I BELIEVE** *Decca F 11857* 2 17
4 Jun 64 ● **RAMONA** *Decca F 11910* 4 13
13 Aug 64 ● **I WOULDN'T TRADE YOU FOR THE WORLD** *Decca F 11949* 4 16
3 Dec 64 ● **NO ARMS CAN EVER HOLD YOU** *Decca F 12034* 7 12
1 Apr 65 **TRUE LOVE FOR EVER MORE** *Decca F 12108* 34 6
20 May 65 ● **MARIE** *Decca F 12156* 9 12
28 Oct 65 **IN THE CHAPEL IN THE MOONLIGHT** *Decca F 12256* 27 10
6 Jan 66 **HELLO, DOLLY!** *Decca F 12309* 38 4
17 Mar 66 ● **THE SOUND OF SILENCE** *Decca F 12351* 3 13
7 Jul 66 **CAN I TRUST YOU** *Decca F 12417* 26 7
1 Dec 66 **WALK WITH FAITH IN YOUR HEART** *Decca F 22523* 21 9
6 Apr 67 **OH HOW I MISS YOU** *Decca F 22592* 30 8
5 Jul 67 **MARTA** *Decca F 22634* 20 9

Randy BACHMAN – *See BUS STOP; BACHMAN-TURNER OVERDRIVE*

UK No.1 ★ UK Top 10 ● Still on chart + UK million seller ◆ UK entry at No.1 ■ US No.1 ▲

Tal BACHMAN *Canada, male vocalist / guitarist (2 WEEKS)* pos/wks

30 Oct 99 **SHE'S SO HIGH** *Columbia 6679932* 30 2

BACHMAN-TURNER OVERDRIVE

Canada, male vocal / instrumental group (18 WEEKS) pos/wks

16 Nov 74 ● **YOU AIN'T SEEN NOTHING YET** *Mercury 6167 025* ▲ 2 12
1 Feb 75 **ROLL ON DOWN THE HIGHWAY** *Mercury 6167 071* 22 6

See also Randy BACHMAN

BACK TO THE PLANET

UK, male / female vocal / instrumental group (2 WEEKS) pos/wks

10 Apr 93 **TEENAGE TURTLES** *Parallel LLLCD 3* 52 1
4 Sep 93 **DAYDREAM** *Parallel LLLCD 8* 52 1

BACKBEAT BAND *US, male vocal / instrumental group (5 WEEKS)* pos/wks

26 Mar 94 **MONEY** *Virgin VSCDX 1489* 48 3
23 Apr 94 **MONEY (re-entry)** *Virgin VSCDX 1489* 73 1
14 May 94 **PLEASE MR POSTMAN** *Virgin VSCDX 1502* 69 1

BACKBEAT DISCIPLES – *See Arthur BAKER*

BACKROOM BOYS – *See Frank IFIELD*

BACKSTREET BOYS (138 Top 500) *American boy band vocal quintet (Brian Littrell, Nick Carter, AJ McLean, Howie Dorough, Kevin Richardson) created teen hysteria in Europe before becoming 1999's top-selling act in their homeland. Their 14 consecutive UK Top 10 entries is a record for a US group (154 WEEKS)* pos/wks

28 Oct 95 **WE'VE GOT IT GOIN' ON** *Jive JIVECD 386* 54 1
16 Dec 95 **I'LL NEVER BREAK YOUR HEART** *Jive JIVECD 389* 42 3
1 Jun 96 **GET DOWN (YOU'RE THE ONE FOR ME)** *Jive JIVECD 394* 14 8
24 Aug 96 ● **WE'VE GOT IT GOIN' ON (re-issue)** *Jive JIVECD 400* 3 7
16 Nov 96 ● **I'LL NEVER BREAK YOUR HEART (re-issue)** *Jive JIVERCD 406* 8 8
18 Jan 97 ● **QUIT PLAYING GAMES (WITH MY HEART)** *Jive JIVECD 409* 2 10
29 Mar 97 ● **ANYWHERE FOR YOU** *Jive JIVECD 416* 4 6
31 May 97 **ANYWHERE FOR YOU (re-entry)** *Jive JIVECD 416* 72 1
14 Jun 97 **ANYWHERE FOR YOU (2nd re-entry)** *Jive JIVECD 416* 70 1
2 Aug 97 ● **EVERYBODY (BACKSTREET'S BACK)** *Jive JIVECD 426* 3 11
11 Oct 97 ● **AS LONG AS YOU LOVE ME** *Jive JIVECD 434* 3 19
14 Feb 98 ● **ALL I HAVE TO GIVE** *Jive JIVECD 445* 2 12
15 May 99 ★ **I WANT IT THAT WAY** *Jive 0523392* ■ 1 14
30 Oct 99 ● **LARGER THAN LIFE** *Jive 0550562* 5 14
26 Feb 00 **SHOW ME THE MEANING OF BEING LONELY (import)** *Jive IMPORT 9250082* 66 1
4 Mar 00 ● **SHOW ME THE MEANING OF BEING LONELY** *Jive 9250082* 3 9
3 Jun 00 **SHOW ME THE MEANING OF BEING LONELY (re-entry)** *Jive 9250082* 51 2
24 Jun 00 ● **THE ONE** *Jive 9250662* 8 7
9 Sep 00 **THE ONE (re-entry)** *Jive 9250662* 75 1
18 Nov 00 ● **SHAPE OF MY HEART** *Jive 9251442* 4 9
24 Feb 01 ● **THE CALL** *Jive 9251702* 8 5
7 Jul 01 **MORE THAN THAT** *Jive 9252342* 12 5

BACKYARD DOG *UK, male vocal / production group (6 WEEKS)* pos/wks

7 Jul 01 **BADDEST RUFFEST** *East West EW 233CD* 15 5
25 Aug 01 **BADDEST RUFFEST (re-entry)** *East West EW 233CD* 69 1

BAD ANGEL – *See BOOTH and the BAD ANGEL*

BAD BOYS INC *UK, male vocal group (31 WEEKS)* pos/wks

14 Aug 93 **DON'T TALK ABOUT LOVE** *A & M 5803412* 19 5
2 Oct 93 **WHENEVER YOU NEED SOMEONE** *A & M 5804032* 26 3
11 Dec 93 **WALKING ON AIR** *A & M 5804692* 24 6
21 May 94 ● **MORE TO THIS WORLD** *A & M 5806072* 8 7
23 Jul 94 **TAKE ME AWAY (I'LL FOLLOW YOU)** *A & M 5806912* 15 6
17 Sep 94 **LOVE HERE I COME** *A & M 5807752* 26 4

BAD COMPANY *UK, male vocal / instrumental group (23 WEEKS)* pos/wks

1 Jun 74 **CAN'T GET ENOUGH** *Island WIP 6191* 15 8
22 Mar 75 **GOOD LOVIN' GONE BAD** *Island WIP 6223* 31 6
30 Aug 75 **FEEL LIKE MAKIN' LOVE** *Island WIP 6242* 20 9

BAD ENGLISH *UK / US, male vocal / instrumental group (3 WEEKS)* pos/wks

25 Nov 89 **WHEN I SEE YOU SMILE** *Epic 655347 1* ▲ 61 3

BAD HABIT BOYS *Germany, male production duo (1 WEEK)* pos/wks

1 Jul 00 **WEEKEND** *Inferno CDFERN 28* 41 1

BAD MANNERS (263 Top 500) *Good-time ska band fronted by shaven-headed Buster Bloodvessel (b. Douglas Trendle, 6 Sep 1958, London). Spent more weeks on UK chart in 1980 (45) than anyone bar Madness. Even after the hits, they remained a popular live attraction (111 WEEKS)* pos/wks

1 Mar 80 **NE-NE NA-NA NA-NA NU-NU** *Magnet MAG 164* 28 14
14 Jun 80 **LIP UP FATTY** *Magnet MAG 175* 15 14
27 Sep 80 ● **SPECIAL BREW** *Magnet MAG 180* 3 13
6 Dec 80 **LORRAINE** *Magnet MAG 181* 21 12
28 Mar 81 **JUST A FEELING** *Magnet MAG 187* 13 9
27 Jun 81 ● **CAN CAN** *Magnet MAG 190* 3 13
26 Sep 81 ● **WALKING IN THE SUNSHINE** *Magnet MAG 197* 10 9
21 Nov 81 **BUONA SERA** *Magnet MAG 211* 34 9
1 May 82 **GOT NO BRAINS** *Magnet MAG 216* 44 5
31 Jul 82 ● **MY GIRL LOLLIPOP (MY BOY LOLLIPOP)** *Magnet MAG 232* 9 7
30 Oct 82 **SAMSON AND DELILAH** *Magnet MAG 236* 58 3
14 May 83 **THAT'LL DO NICELY** *Magnet MAG 243* 49 3

BAD MEETS EVIL featuring EMINEM and ROYCE DA 5'9"

US, male producer and male rappers (1 WEEK) pos/wks

1 Sep 01 **SCARY MOVIES** *Mole UK MOLEUK 045* 63 1

See also EMINEM

BAD NEWS *UK, male vocal group (5 WEEKS)* pos/wks

12 Sep 87 **BOHEMIAN RHAPSODY** *EMI EM 24* 44 5

BAD RELIGION *US, male vocal / instrumental group (2 WEEKS)* pos/wks

11 Feb 95 **21ST CENTURY (DIGITAL BOY)** *Columbia 6611435* 41 2

BAD SEEDS – *See Nick CAVE and the BAD SEEDS*

BAD YARD CLUB – *See David MORALES*

Angelo BADALAMENTI – *See ORBITAL*

Wally BADAROU *France, male instrumentalist keyboards (6 WEEKS)* pos/wks

19 Oct 85 **CHIEF INSPECTOR** *Fourth & Broadway BRW 37* 46 6

BADDIEL and SKINNER and the LIGHTNING SEEDS *UK, male vocal group David Baddiel, Frank Skinner (Christopher Collins) and The Lightning Seeds (28 WEEKS)* pos/wks

1 Jun 96 ★ **THREE LIONS (THE OFFICIAL SONG OF THE ENGLAND FOOTBALL TEAM)** *Epic 6632732* ■ 1 15
20 Jun 98 ★ **3 LIONS '98** *Epic 6660982* ■ 1 13

BADFINGER *UK, male vocal / instrumental group (34 WEEKS)* pos/wks

10 Jan 70 ● **COME AND GET IT** *Apple 20* 4 11
9 Jan 71 ● **NO MATTER WHAT** *Apple 31* 5 12
29 Jan 72 ● **DAY AFTER DAY** *Apple 40* 10 11

BADLY DRAWN BOY *UK, male vocalist / producer / instrumentalist – Damon Gough (9 WEEKS)* pos/wks

4 Sep 99 **ONCE AROUND THE BLOCK** *Twisted Nerve / XL Recordings TNXL 003CD* 46 2
17 Jun 00 **ANOTHER PEARL** *Twisted Nerve / XL Recordings TNXL 004CD* 41 1
16 Sep 00 **DISILLUSION** *Twisted Nerve / XL Recordings TNXL 005CD* 26 2

25 Nov 00	**ONCE AROUND THE BLOCK (re-issue)** *Twisted Nerve / XL Recordings TNXL 009CD*	27	2
19 May 01	**PISSING IN THE WIND** *Twisted Nerve / XL Recordings TNXL 010CD*	22	2

BADMAN *UK, male producer – Julian Brettle (3 WEEKS)* pos/wks

2 Feb 91	**MAGIC STYLE** *Citybeat CBE 759*	61	3

Erykah BADU *US, female vocalist – Erica Wright (17 WEEKS)* pos/wks

19 Apr 97	**ON & ON** *Universal UND 561117*	12	4
14 Jun 97	**NEXT LIFETIME** *Universal UND 56132*	30	3
29 Nov 97	**APPLE TREE** *Universal UND 56150*	47	1
11 Jul 98	**ONE** *Elektra E 3833CD1* [1]	23	3
6 Mar 99	**YOU GOT ME** *MCA MCSTD 48110* [2]	31	2
15 Sep 01	**SWEET BABY** *Epic 6718822* [3]	23	4

[1] Busta Rhymes featuring Erykah Badu [2] Roots featuring Erykah Badu [3] Macy Gray featuring Erykah Badu

Joan BAEZ *US, female vocalist (47 WEEKS)* pos/wks

6 May 65	**WE SHALL OVERCOME** *Fontana TF 564*	26	10
8 Jul 65 ●	**THERE BUT FOR FORTUNE** *Fontana TF 587*	8	12
2 Sep 65	**IT'S ALL OVER NOW, BABY BLUE** *Fontana TF 604*	22	8
23 Dec 65	**FAREWELL ANGELINA** *Fontana TF 639*	35	3
20 Jan 66	**FAREWELL ANGELINA (re-entry)** *Fontana TF 639*	49	1
28 Jul 66	**PACK UP YOUR SORROWS** *Fontana TF 727*	50	1
9 Oct 71 ●	**THE NIGHT THEY DROVE OLD DIXIE DOWN** *Vanguard VS 35138*	6	12

BAHA MEN *Bahamas, male vocal group (28 WEEKS)* pos/wks

14 Oct 00 ●	**WHO LET THE DOGS OUT** *Edel 0115425 ERE*	2	23
3 Feb 01	**YOU ALL DAT** *Edel 0124855 ERE*	14	5

'You All Dat' features vocal by Imani Coppola

Carol BAILEY *UK, female vocalist (2 WEEKS)* pos/wks

25 Feb 95	**FEEL IT** *Multiply CDMULTY 3*	41	2

Philip BAILEY *US, male vocalist (20 WEEKS)* pos/wks

9 Mar 85 ★	**EASY LOVER** *CBS A 4915* [1]	1	12
18 May 85	**WALKING ON THE CHINESE WALL** *CBS A 6202*	34	8

[1] Philip Bailey (duet with Phil Collins)

See also EARTH WIND AND FIRE

Merril BAINBRIDGE *Australia, female vocalist (1 WEEK)* pos/wks

7 Dec 96	**MOUTH** *Gotham 74321431012*	51	1

Adrian BAKER *UK, male vocalist (8 WEEKS)* pos/wks

19 Jul 75 ●	**SHERRY** *Magnet MAG 34*	10	8

See also GIDEA PARK

Anita BAKER *US, female vocalist (22 WEEKS)* pos/wks

15 Nov 86	**SWEET LOVE** *Elektra EKR 44*	13	10
31 Jan 87	**CAUGHT UP IN THE RAPTURE** *Elektra EKR 49*	51	5
8 Oct 88	**GIVING YOU THE BEST THAT I GOT** *Elektra EKR 79*	55	3
30 Jun 90	**TALK TO ME** *Elektra EKR 111*	68	2
17 Sep 94	**BODY & SOUL** *Elektra EKR 190CD*	48	2

Arthur BAKER *US, male producer / multi-instrumentalist (7 WEEKS)* pos/wks

20 May 89	**IT'S YOUR TIME** *Breakout USA 654* [1]	64	2
21 Oct 89	**THE MESSAGE IS LOVE** *Breakout USA 668* [2]	38	5

[1] Arthur Baker featuring Shirley Lewis [2] Arthur Baker and the Backbeat Disciples featuring Al Green

See also Wally JUMP Jr and the CRIMINAL ELEMENT

Hylda BAKER and Arthur MULLARD
UK, female / male comedy duo (6 WEEKS) pos/wks

9 Sep 78	**YOU'RE THE ONE THAT I WANT** *Pye 7N 46121*	22	6

George BAKER SELECTION
Holland, male / female vocal / instrumental group (10 WEEKS) pos/wks

6 Sep 75 ●	**PALOMA BLANCA** *Warner Bros. K 16541*	10	10

BALAAM AND THE ANGEL
UK, male vocal / instrumental group (2 WEEKS) pos/wks

29 Mar 86	**SHE KNOWS** *Virgin VS 842*	70	2

Long John BALDRY *UK, male vocalist (36 WEEKS)* pos/wks

8 Nov 67 ★	**LET THE HEARTACHES BEGIN** *Pye 7N 17385*	1	13
28 Aug 68	**WHEN THE SUN COMES SHINING THRU** *Pye 7N 17593*	29	7
23 Oct 68	**MEXICO** *Pye 7N 17563*	15	8
29 Jan 69	**IT'S TOO LATE NOW** *Pye 7N 17664*	21	8

BALEARIC BILL *UK / Belgium, DJ / production trio (2 WEEKS)* pos/wks

2 Oct 99	**DESTINATION SUNSHINE** *Xtravaganza XTRAV 3CDS*	36	2

Edward BALL *UK, male vocalist (2 WEEKS)* pos/wks

20 Jul 96	**THE MILL HILL SELF HATE CLUB** *Creation CRESCD 233*	57	1
22 Feb 97	**LOVE IS BLUE** *Creation CRESCD 244*	59	1

Michael BALL *UK, male vocalist (39 WEEKS)* pos/wks

28 Jan 89 ●	**LOVE CHANGES EVERYTHING** *Really Useful RUR 3*	2	14
28 Oct 89	**THE FIRST MAN YOU REMEMBER** *Really Useful RUR 6* [1]	68	2
10 Aug 91	**IT'S STILL YOU** *Polydor PO 160*	58	2
25 Apr 92	**ONE STEP OUT OF TIME** *Polydor PO 206*	20	7
12 Dec 92	**IF I CAN DREAM (EP)** *Polydor PO 248*	51	1
26 Dec 92	**IF I CAN DREAM (EP) (re-entry)** *Polydor PO 248*	68	1
11 Sep 93	**SUNSET BOULEVARD** *Polydor PZCD 293*	72	1
30 Jul 94	**FROM HERE TO ETERNITY** *Columbia 6606905*	36	3
17 Sep 94	**THE LOVERS WE WERE** *Columbia 6607972*	63	2
9 Dec 95	**THE ROSE** *Columbia 6614535*	42	4
17 Feb 96	**(SOMETHING INSIDE) SO STRONG** *Columbia 6629005*	40	2

[1] Michael Ball and Diana Morrison

Tracks on If I Can Dream (EP): If I Can Dream / You Don't Have to Say You Love Me / Always on My Mind / Tell Me There's a Heaven

Kenny BALL and his JAZZMEN (184 Top 500)
Top UK trad jazz band leader, b. 22 May 1930, Essex. His Dixieland band was at the forefront of the early 1960s jazz revival. Their biggest hit, 'Midnight in Moscow', reached runner-up spot on both sides of the Atlantic (136 WEEKS) pos/wks

23 Feb 61	**SAMANTHA** *Pye Jazz Today 7NJ 2040*	13	15
11 May 61	**I STILL LOVE YOU ALL** *Pye Jazz 7NJ 2042*	24	6
31 Aug 61	**SOMEDAY (YOU'LL BE SORRY)** *Pye Jazz 7NJ 2047*	28	6
9 Nov 61 ●	**MIDNIGHT IN MOSCOW** *Pye Jazz 7NJ 2049*	2	21
15 Feb 62 ●	**MARCH OF THE SIAMESE CHILDREN** *Pye Jazz 7NJ 2051*	4	13
17 May 62 ●	**THE GREEN LEAVES OF SUMMER** *Pye Jazz 7NJ 2054*	7	14
23 Aug 62	**SO DO I** *Pye Jazz 7NJ 2056*	14	8
18 Oct 62	**THE PAY-OFF (AMOI DE PAYER)** *Pye Jazz 7NJ 2061*	23	6
17 Jan 63 ●	**SUKIYAKI** *Pye Jazz 7NJ 2062*	10	13
25 Apr 63	**CASABLANCA** *Pye Jazz 7NJ 2064*	21	11
13 Jun 63	**RONDO** *Pye Jazz 7NJ 2065*	24	8
22 Aug 63	**ACAPULCO 1922** *Pye Jazz 7NJ 2067*	27	6
11 Jun 64	**HELLO, DOLLY!** *Pye Jazz 7NJ 2071*	30	7
19 Jul 67	**WHEN I'M SIXTY FOUR** *Pye 7N 17348*	43	2

BALTIMORA *Ireland, male vocalist – Jimmy McShane (12 WEEKS)* pos/wks

10 Aug 85 ●	**TARZAN BOY** *Columbia DB 9102*	3	12

Charli BALTIMORE *US, female rapper (4 WEEKS)* pos/wks

1 Aug 98	**MONEY** *Epic 6662272*	12	4

BAM BAM *US, male vocalist / instrumentalist (2 WEEKS)* pos/wks

19 Mar 88	**GIVE IT TO ME** *Serious 70US 10*	65	2

Afrika BAMBAATAA

US, male DJ / producer / rapper – Kevin Donovan (33 WEEKS) pos/wks

28 Aug 82	**PLANET ROCK** *21 POSP 497* [1]	53	3
10 Mar 84	**RENEGADES OF FUNK** *Tommy Boy AFR 1* [1]	30	4
1 Sep 84	**UNITY (PART 1 – THE THIRD COMING)** *Tommy Boy AFR 2* [2]	49	5
27 Feb 88	**RECKLESS** *EMI EM 41* [3]	17	8
12 Oct 91	**JUST GET UP AND DANCE** *EMI USA MT 100*	45	3
17 Oct 98	**GOT TO GET UP** *Multiply CDMULTY 42*	22	4
18 Sep 99 ●	**AFRIKA SHOX** *Hard Hands HAND 057CD1* [4]	7	5
25 Aug 01	**PLANET ROCK** *Tommy Boy TBCD 2266* [5]	47	1

[1] Afrika Bambaataa and the Soul Sonic Force [2] Afrika Bambaataa and James Brown [3] Afrika Bambaataa and Family featuring UB40 [4] Leftfield / Bambaataa [5] Paul Oakenfold presents Afrika Bambaataa and Soulsonic Force

BAMBOO *UK, male producer – Andrew Livingstone (12 WEEKS)* pos/wks

17 Jan 98 ●	**BAMBOOGIE** *VC Recordings VCRD 29*	2	10
4 Jul 98	**THE STRUTT** *VC Recordings VCRD 35*	36	2

BANANARAMA (88 Top 500)

Britain's most charted female group: Sarah Dallin, Keren Woodward, Siobhan Fahey. The London-based trio were also best sellers in the US, where 'Venus' topped the chart. Fahey, who married Eurythmic Dave Stewart, left in 1988 to form Shakespear's Sister and was replaced by Jacqui O'Sullivan (202 WEEKS) pos/wks

13 Feb 82 ●	**IT AIN'T WHAT YOU DO IT'S THE WAY THAT YOU DO IT** *Chrysalis CHS 2570* [1]	4	10
10 Apr 82 ●	**REALLY SAYING SOMETHING** *Deram NANA 1* [2]	5	10
3 Jul 82 ●	**SHY BOY** *London NANA 2*	4	11
4 Dec 82	**CHEERS THEN** *London NANA 3*	45	7
26 Feb 83 ●	**NA NA HEY HEY KISS HIM GOODBYE** *London NANA 4*	5	10
9 Jul 83 ●	**CRUEL SUMMER** *London NANA 5*	8	10
3 Mar 84 ●	**ROBERT DE NIRO'S WAITING** *London NANA 6*	3	11
26 May 84	**ROUGH JUSTICE** *London NANA 7*	23	7
24 Nov 84	**HOTLINE TO HEAVEN** *London NANA 8*	58	2
24 Aug 85	**DO NOT DISTURB** *London NANA 9*	31	6
31 May 86 ●	**VENUS** *London NANA 10* ▲	8	13
16 Aug 86	**MORE THAN PHYSICAL** *London NANA 11*	41	5
14 Feb 87	**TRICK OF THE NIGHT** *London NANA 12*	32	5
11 Jul 87	**I HEARD A RUMOUR** *London NANA 13*	14	9
10 Oct 87 ●	**LOVE IN THE FIRST DEGREE** *London NANA 14*	3	12
9 Jan 88	**I CAN'T HELP IT** *London NANA 15*	20	6
9 Apr 88 ●	**I WANT YOU BACK** *London NANA 16*	5	10
24 Sep 88	**LOVE, TRUTH AND HONESTY** *London NANA 17*	23	8
19 Nov 88	**NATHAN JONES** *London NANA 18*	15	9
25 Feb 89 ●	**HELP** *London LON 222* [3]	3	9
10 Jun 89	**CRUEL SUMMER (re-mix)** *London NANA 19*	19	6
28 Jul 90	**ONLY YOUR LOVE** *London NANA 21*	27	4
5 Jan 91	**PREACHER MAN** *London NANA 23*	20	6
20 Apr 91	**LONG TRAIN RUNNING** *London NANA 24*	30	5
29 Aug 92	**MOVIN' ON** *London NANA 25*	24	5
28 Nov 92	**LAST THING ON MY MIND** *London NANA 26*	71	2
20 Mar 93	**MORE MORE MORE** *London NACPD 27*	24	4

[1] Fun Boy Three and Bananarama [2] Bananarama with Fun Boy Three [3] Bananarama / La Na Nee Nee Noo Noo

The listed flip side of 'Love in the First Degree' was 'Mr Sleaze' by Stock Aitken Waterman. Act was a duo for last three hits

BAND *Canada / US, male vocal / instrumental group (18 WEEKS)* pos/wks

18 Sep 68	**THE WEIGHT** *Capitol CL 15559*	21	9
4 Apr 70	**RAG MAMA RAG** *Capitol CL 15629*	16	9

BAND AID *International, male / female vocal / instrumental charity assembly (26 WEEKS)* pos/wks

15 Dec 84 ★	**DO THEY KNOW IT'S CHRISTMAS?** *Mercury FEED 1* ◆ ■	1	13
7 Dec 85 ●	**DO THEY KNOW IT'S CHRISTMAS? (re-entry)** *Mercury FEED 1*	3	7
23 Dec 89 ★	**DO THEY KNOW IT'S CHRISTMAS?** *PWL/Polydor FEED 2* [1] ■	1	6

[1] Band Aid II

BAND AID: Adam Clayton, Bono (U2); Bob Geldof, Johnny Fingers, Simon Crowe, Peter Briquette (Boomtown Rats); David Bowie; Paul McCartney; Holly Johnson (Frankie Goes To Hollywood); Midge Ure, Chris Cross (Ultravox); Simon Le Bon, Nick Rhodes, Andy Taylor, John Taylor, Roger Taylor (Duran Duran); Paul Young; Tony Hadley, Martin Kemp, John Keeble, Gary Kemp, Steve Norman (Spandau Ballet); Martyn Ware, Glenn Gregory (Heaven 17); Francis Rossi, Rick Parfitt (Status Quo); Sting; Boy George, Jon Moss (Culture Club); Marilyn; Keren Woodward, Sarah Dallin, Siobhan Fahey (Bananarama); Jody Watley (Shalamar); Paul Weller; Robert "Kool" Bell, James Taylor, Dennis Thomas (Kool and the Gang); George Michael. BAND AID II: Bananarama, Big Fun, Bros, Cathy Dennis, D Mob, Jason Donovan, Kevin Godley, Glen Goldsmith, Kylie Minogue, The Pasadenas, Chris Rea, Cliff Richard, Jimmy Somerville, Sonia, Lisa Stansfield, Technotronic, Wet Wet Wet

BAND AKA *US, male vocal / instrumental group (12 WEEKS)* pos/wks

15 May 82	**GRACE** *Epic EPC A 2376*	41	5
5 Mar 83	**JOY** *Epic EPC A 3145*	24	7

BAND OF GOLD

Holland, male / female vocal / instrumental group (11 WEEKS) pos/wks

14 Jul 84	**LOVE SONGS ARE BACK AGAIN (MEDLEY)** *RCA 428*	24	11

BAND OF THIEVES – *See Luke GOSS and the BAND OF THIEVES*

BANDA SONARA *UK, male producer – Gerald Elms (2 WEEKS)* pos/wks

6 Oct 01	**GUITARRA G** *Defected DFECT 36CDS*	50	2

BANDERAS *UK, female vocal / instrumental duo – Sally Herbert and Caroline Buckley (16 WEEKS)* pos/wks

23 Feb 91	**THIS IS YOUR LIFE** *London LON 290*	16	10
15 Jun 91	**SHE SELLS** *London LON 298*	41	6

BANDWAGON – *See Johnny JOHNSON and the BANDWAGON*

Honey BANE *UK, female vocalist (8 WEEKS)* pos/wks

24 Jan 81	**TURN ME ON TURN ME OFF** *Zonophone Z 15*	37	5
18 Apr 81	**BABY LOVE** *Zonophone Z 19*	58	3

BANG *UK, male vocal duo (2 WEEKS)* pos/wks

6 May 89	**YOU'RE THE ONE** *RCA PB 42715*	74	2

BANGLES (326 Top 500)

Melodic pop-rock quartet formed 1981, Los Angeles, California, US. Comprised Susanna Hoffs (v), sisters Vicki (g) and Debbi Peterson (d) and Michael Steele (b). Split 1989, having become the most successful all-female band in chart history, then reformed for a tour in 2000. 'Eternal Flame' returned to top in 2001 by Atomic Kitten (94 WEEKS) pos/wks

15 Feb 86 ●	**MANIC MONDAY** *CBS A 6796*	2	12
26 Apr 86	**IF SHE KNEW WHAT SHE WANTS** *CBS A 7062*	31	7
5 Jul 86	**GOING DOWN TO LIVERPOOL** *CBS A 7255*	56	3
13 Sep 86 ●	**WALK LIKE AN EGYPTIAN** *CBS 650071 7* ▲	3	19
10 Jan 87	**WALKING DOWN YOUR STREET** *CBS BANGS 1*	16	6
18 Apr 87	**FOLLOWING** *CBS BANGS 2*	55	3
6 Feb 88	**HAZY SHADE OF WINTER** *Def Jam BANGS 3*	11	10
5 Nov 88	**IN YOUR ROOM** *CBS BANGS 4*	35	6
18 Feb 89 ★	**ETERNAL FLAME** *CBS BANGS 5* ▲	1	18
10 Jun 89	**BE WITH YOU** *CBS BANGS 6*	23	8
14 Oct 89	**I'LL SET YOU FREE** *CBS BANGS 7*	74	1
9 Jun 90	**WALK LIKE AN EGYPTIAN (re-issue)** *CBS BANGS 8*	73	1

Tony BANKS – *See FISH*

BANNED *UK, male vocal / instrumental group (6 WEEKS)* pos/wks

17 Dec 77	**LITTLE GIRL** *Harvest HAR 5145*	36	6

BANSHEES – *See SIOUXSIE and the BANSHEES*

Buju BANTON *Jamaica, male vocalist (1 WEEK)* pos/wks

7 Aug 93	**MAKE MY DAY** *Mercury BUJCD 2*	72	1

Pato BANTON *UK, male vocalist – Patrick Murray (37 WEEKS)* pos/wks

1 Oct 94 ★	**BABY COME BACK** *Virgin VSCDT 1522*	1	18

11 Feb 95	THIS COWBOY SONG *A & M 5809652* [1]	15	6
8 Apr 95	BUBBLING HOT *Virgin VSCDT 1530* [2]	15	7
20 Jan 96	SPIRITS IN THE MATERIAL WORLD *MCA MCSTD 2113* [3]	36	2
27 Jul 96	GROOVIN' *IRS CDEIRS 195* [4]	14	4

[1] Sting featuring Pato Banton [2] Pato Banton with Ranking Roger [3] Pato Banton with Sting [4] Pato Banton and the Reggae Revolution

The sleeve of 'Baby Come Back' credits Ali and Robin Campbell

BAR CODES featuring Alison BROWN
UK, male / female vocal group (1 WEEK) pos/wks

17 Dec 94	SUPERMARKET SWEEP *Blanca Casa BC 101CD*	72	1

BAR-KAYS *US, male vocal / instrumental group (15 WEEKS)* pos/wks

23 Aug 67	SOUL FINGER *Stax 601 014*	33	7
22 Jan 77	SHAKE YOUR RUMP TO THE FUNK *Mercury 6167 417*	41	4
12 Jan 85	SEXOMATIC *Club JAB 10*	51	4

Chris BARBER'S JAZZ BAND
UK, male jazz band, – Chris Barber trombone (30 WEEKS) pos/wks

13 Feb 59 ●	PETITE FLEUR *Pye Nixa NJ 2026*	3	22
31 Jul 59	PETITE FLEUR (re-entry) *Pye Nixa NJ 2026*	22	2
9 Oct 59	LONESOME (SI TU VOIS MA MERE) *Columbia DB 4333* [1]	27	2
4 Jan 62	REVIVAL *Columbia SCD 2166*	50	2
1 Feb 62	REVIVAL (re-entry) *Columbia SCD 2166*	43	2

[1] Chris Barber featuring Monty Sunshine

BARBRA and NEIL – *See Barbra STREISAND; Neil DIAMOND*

BARCLAY JAMES HARVEST
UK, male vocal / instrumental group (9 WEEKS) pos/wks

2 Apr 77	LIVE (EP) *Polydor 2229 198*	49	1
16 Apr 77	LIVE (EP) (re-entry) *Polydor 2229 198*	49	1
26 Jan 80	LOVE ON THE LINE *Polydor POSP 97*	63	2
22 Nov 80	LIFE IS FOR LIVING *Polydor POSP 195*	61	3
21 May 83	JUST A DAY AWAY *Polydor POSP 585*	68	2

Tracks on Live (EP): Rock 'n' Roll Star / Medicine Man (Parts 1 & 2)

BARDO *UK, male / female vocal duo – Sally Ann Triplett and Stephen Fischer (8 WEEKS)* pos/wks

10 Apr 82 ●	ONE STEP FURTHER *Epic EPC A2265*	2	8

BARDOT *Australia, female vocal group (1 WEEK)* pos/wks

14 Apr 01	POISON *East West EW 229CD*	45	1

BAREFOOT MAN *Germany, male vocalist (7 WEEKS)* pos/wks

5 Dec 98	BIG PANTY WOMAN *Plaza PZACD 082*	21	7

BARENAKED LADIES
Canada, male vocal / instrumental group (12 WEEKS) pos/wks

20 Feb 99 ●	ONE WEEK *Reprise W 468CD* ▲	5	8
15 May 99	IT'S ALL BEEN DONE *Reprise W 476CD*	28	2
24 Jul 99	CALL AND ANSWER *Reprise W498CD1*	52	1
11 Dec 99	BRIAN WILSON *Reprise W 511CD1*	73	1

BARKIN BROTHERS featuring Johnnie FIORI
UK, male production group and US female vocalist (2 WEEKS) pos/wks

15 Apr 00	GONNA CATCH YOU *Brothers Organisation BRUVCD 15*	51	2

Gary BARLOW *UK, male vocalist (47 WEEKS)* pos/wks

20 Jul 96 ★	FOREVER LOVE *RCA 74321397922* ■	1	16
10 May 97 ★	LOVE WON'T WAIT *RCA 74321470842* ■	1	7
26 Jul 97	LOVE WON'T WAIT (re-entry) *RCA 74321470842*	64	1
26 Jul 97	SO HELP ME GIRL *RCA 74321501202*	11	7
9 Aug 97	LOVE WON'T WAIT (2nd re-entry) *RCA 74321470842*	67	1
20 Sep 97	SO HELP ME GIRL (re-entry) *RCA 74321501202*	64	4
15 Nov 97 ●	OPEN ROAD *RCA 74321518292*	7	5
17 Jul 99	STRONGER *RCA 74321682002*	16	4
9 Oct 99	FOR ALL THAT YOU WANT *RCA 74321701012*	24	2

See also TAKE THAT

Gary BARNACLE – *See BIG FUN; SONIA*

BARNBRACK *UK, male vocal / instrumental group (7 WEEKS)* pos/wks

16 Mar 85	BELFAST *Homespun HS 092*	45	7

Jimmy BARNES – *See INXS*

Richard BARNES *UK, male vocalist (10 WEEKS)* pos/wks

23 May 70	TAKE TO THE MOUNTAINS *Philips BF 1840*	35	6
24 Oct 70	GO NORTH *Philips 6006 039*	49	1
7 Nov 70	GO NORTH (re-entry) *Philips 6006 039*	38	3

BARRACUDAS *UK / US, male vocal / instrumental group (6 WEEKS)* pos/wks

16 Aug 80	SUMMER FUN *Zonophone Z 5*	37	6

Wild Willy BARRETT – *See John OTWAY and Wild Willy BARRETT*

Amanda BARRIE and Johnny BRIGGS
UK, female / male vocal duo (3 WEEKS) pos/wks

16 Dec 95	SOMETHING STUPID *EMI Premier CDEMS 411*	35	3

The listed flip side of 'Something Stupid' was 'Always Look on the Bright Side of Life' by the Coronation Street Cast

JJ BARRIE *Canada, male vocalist – Barrie Authors (11 WEEKS)* pos/wks

24 Apr 76 ★	NO CHARGE *Power Exchange PX 209*	1	11

Featured vocalist is Vicki Brown

Ken BARRIE *UK, male vocalist (15 WEEKS)* pos/wks

10 Jul 82	POSTMAN PAT *Post Music PP 001*	44	8
25 Dec 82	POSTMAN PAT (re-entry) *Post Music PP 001*	54	3
24 Dec 83	POSTMAN PAT (2nd re-entry) *Post Music PP 001*	59	4

BARRON KNIGHTS (328 Top 500) *Britain's princes of pop parody, formed Leighton Buzzard, UK, fronted by Duke D'Mond (b. Richard Palmer). Group's humorous hit medleys proved popular in the 1960s and 1970s and helped to stop pop music taking itself too seriously (94 WEEKS)* pos/wks

9 Jul 64 ●	CALL UP THE GROUPS *Columbia DB 7317* [1]	3	13
22 Oct 64	COME TO THE DANCE *Columbia DB 7375* [1]	42	2
25 Mar 65 ●	POP GO THE WORKERS *Columbia DB 7525* [1]	5	13
16 Dec 65 ●	MERRY GENTLE POPS *Columbia DB 7780* [1]	9	7
1 Dec 66	UNDER NEW MANAGEMENT *Columbia DB 8071* [1]	15	9
23 Oct 68	AN OLYMPIC RECORD *Columbia DB 8485*	35	4
29 Oct 77 ●	LIVE IN TROUBLE *Epic EPC 5752*	7	10
2 Dec 78 ●	A TASTE OF AGGRO *Epic EPC 6829*	3	10
8 Dec 79	FOOD FOR THOUGHT *Epic EPC 8011*	46	6
4 Oct 80	THE SIT SONG *Epic EPC 8994*	44	4
6 Dec 80	NEVER MIND THE PRESENTS *Epic EPC 9070*	17	8
5 Dec 81	BLACKBOARD JUMBLE *CBS A 1795*	52	5
19 Mar 83	BUFFALO BILL'S LAST SCRATCH *Epic EPC A 3208*	49	3

[1] The Barron Knights with Duke D'Mond

Joe BARRY *US, male vocalist (1 WEEK)* pos/wks

24 Aug 61	I'M A FOOL TO CARE *Mercury AMT 1149*	49	1

Len BARRY *US, male vocalist – Leonard Borisoff (24 WEEKS)* pos/wks

4 Nov 65 ●	1-2-3 *Brunswick 05942*	3	14
13 Jan 66 ●	LIKE A BABY *Brunswick 05949*	10	10

THE OFFICIAL UK SINGLES CHART 50TH ANNIVERSARY

1955

FROM THE YEAR WHEN MARILYN MONROE HIT THE SILVER SCREEN IN 'THE SEVEN YEAR ITCH', JAMES DEAN INVENTED THE TEENAGER IN 'REBEL WITHOUT A CAUSE', AND RUBY MURRAY BECAME THE FIRST ACT TO HAVE FIVE SINGLES SIMULTANEOUSLY IN THE TOP 20, **TOM JONES** RECALLS SOME PERSONAL MEMORIES ...

"There was a guy on BBC radio called Jack Jackson who used to do a show called 'Off the Record', and he would play what was going on in America. I loved it: Jerry Lee Lewis, Elvis of course, and **Bill Haley**'s 'Rock Around The Clock'. Before that, before rock 'n' roll, I used to like Tennessee Ernie Ford, who made a bunch of boogie records – 'Catfish Boogie', 'Blackberry Boogie' – before he did 'Sixteen Tons'. All of it was really just black music – and that's how I learned to sing, like a black American."

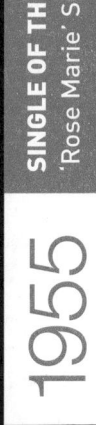

SINGLE OF THE YEAR
'Rose Marie' Slim Whitman

John BARRY ORCHESTRA (435 Top 500) *Early UK rock 'n' roll bandleader, who arranged Adam Faith's hits and found global fame writing film scores (including many for James Bond), b. Jonathan Barry Prendergast, 3 Nov 1933, York, UK. This Oscar and Grammy winner received an OBE in 1999 (78 WEEKS)*

Date		Title / Label	pos	wks
4 Mar 60	●	**HIT AND MISS** *Columbia DB 4414* [1]	10	12
28 Apr 60		**BEAT FOR BEATNIKS** *Columbia DB 4446*	40	2
9 Jun 60		**HIT AND MISS (re-entry)** *Columbia DB 4414* [1]	45	1
14 Jul 60		**NEVER LET GO** *Columbia DB 4480*	49	1
18 Aug 60		**BLUEBERRY HILL** *Columbia DB 4480*	34	3
8 Sep 60		**WALK DON'T RUN** *Columbia DB 4505* [2]	49	1
22 Sep 60		**WALK DON'T RUN (re-entry)** *Columbia DB 4505* [2]	11	13
8 Dec 60		**BLACK STOCKINGS** *Columbia DB 4554* [2]	27	9
2 Mar 61		**THE MAGNIFICENT SEVEN** *Columbia DB 4598* [2]	48	1
16 Mar 61		**THE MAGNIFICENT SEVEN (re-entry)** *Columbia DB 4598* [2]	45	2
6 Apr 61		**THE MAGNIFICENT SEVEN (2nd re-entry)** *Columbia DB 4598* [2]	50	1
8 Jun 61		**THE MAGNIFICENT SEVEN (3rd re-entry)** *Columbia DB 4598* [2]	47	1
26 Apr 62		**CUTTY SARK** *Columbia DB 4806* [2]	35	2
1 Nov 62		**THE JAMES BOND THEME** *Columbia DB 4898*	13	11
21 Nov 63		**FROM RUSSIA WITH LOVE** *Ember S 181*	44	1
19 Dec 63		**FROM RUSSIA WITH LOVE (re-entry)** *Ember S 181*	39	2
11 Dec 71		**THEME FROM 'THE PERSUADERS'** *CBS 7469* [3]	13	15

[1] John Barry Seven + Four [2] John Barry Seven [3] John Barry

Michael BARRYMORE *UK, male vocalist (4 WEEKS)*

Date		Title / Label	pos	wks
16 Dec 95		**TOO MUCH FOR ONE HEART** *EMI CDEM 412*	25	4

Lionel BART *UK, male vocalist (3 WEEKS)*

Date		Title / Label	pos	wks
25 Nov 89		**HAPPY ENDINGS (GIVE YOURSELF A PINCH)** *EMI EM 121*	68	1
23 Dec 89		**HAPPY ENDINGS (GIVE YOURSELF A PINCH) (re-entry)** *EMI EM 121*	71	2

Bart & Homer – *See SIMPSONS*

BARTHEZZ *Holland, male producer – Bart Claessen (4 WEEKS)*

Date		Title / Label	pos	wks
22 Sep 01		**ON THE MOVE** *Positiva CDTIV 158*	18	4

BAS NOIR *US, female vocal duo (1 WEEK)*

Date		Title / Label	pos	wks
11 Feb 89		**MY LOVE IS MAGIC** *10 TEN 257*	73	1

Rob BASE and DJ E-Z ROCK
US, male rap / DJ duo – Robert Ginyard and Rodney Bryce (19 WEEKS)

Date		Title / Label	pos	wks
16 Apr 88		**IT TAKES TWO** *Citybeat CBE 724*	24	6
14 Jan 89		**GET ON THE DANCE FLOOR** *Supreme SUPE 139*	14	7
4 Mar 89		**IT TAKES TWO (re-entry)** *Citybeat CBE 724*	49	3
22 Apr 89		**JOY AND PAIN** *Supreme SUPE 143*	47	3

BASEMENT BOYS present ULTRA NATE
US, male production group and US female vocalst (1 WEEK)

Date		Title / Label	pos	wks
23 Feb 91		**IS IT LOVE?** *Eternal YZ 509*	71	1

BASEMENT JAXX *UK, male DJ / producer duo – Simon Ratcliffe and Felix Buxton (48 WEEKS)*

Date		Title / Label	pos	wks
31 May 97		**FLY LIFE** *Multiply CDMULTY 21*	19	3
1 May 99	●	**RED ALERT** *XL Recordings XLS 100CD*	5	10
14 Aug 99	●	**RENDEZ-VU** *XL Recordings XLS 110CD*	4	8
6 Nov 99		**JUMP 'N SHOUT** *XL Recordings XLS 116CD*	12	5
15 Apr 00		**BINGO BANGO** *XL Recordings XLS 120CD*	13	4
16 Jun 01	●	**ROMEO** *XL Recordings XLS 132CD*	6	10
6 Oct 01		**JUS 1 KISS** *XL Recordings XLS 136CD*	23	3
3 Nov 01		**JUS 1 KISS (re-entry)** *XL Recordings XLS 136CD*	66	1
8 Dec 01	●	**WHERE'S YOUR HEAD AT?** *XL Recordings XLS 140CD*	9	4

BASIA *Poland, female vocalist (9 WEEKS)*

Date		Title / Label	pos	wks
23 Jan 88		**PROMISES** *Epic BASH 4*	48	4
28 May 88		**TIME AND TIDE** *Epic BASH 5*	61	3
14 Jan 95		**DRUNK ON LOVE** *Epic 6611582*	41	2

Count BASIE – *See Frank SINATRA*

Toni BASIL *US, female vocalist – Antonia Basilotta (16 WEEKS)*

Date		Title / Label	pos	wks
6 Feb 82	●	**MICKEY** *Radialchoice TIC 4* ▲	2	12
1 May 82		**NOBODY** *Radialchoice TIC 2*	52	4

Olav BASOSKI *Holland, male producer (1 WEEK)*

Date		Title / Label	pos	wks
26 Aug 00		**OPIUM SCUMBAGZ** *Defected DFECT 20CDS*	56	1

Alfie BASS – *See Michael MEDWIN, Bernard BRESSLAW, Alfie BASS and Leslie FYSON*

Fontella BASS *US, female vocalist (15 WEEKS)*

Date		Title / Label	pos	wks
2 Dec 65		**RESCUE ME** *Chess CRS 8023*	11	10
20 Jan 66		**RECOVERY** *Chess CRS 8027*	32	5

Norman BASS *Germany, male producer (4 WEEKS)*

Date		Title / Label	pos	wks
21 Apr 01		**HOW U LIKE BASS** *Substance SUBS 10CDS*	17	4

BASS BOYZ *UK, male producer – James Sammon (1 WEEK)*

Date		Title / Label	pos	wks
28 Sep 96		**GUNZ AND PIANOZ** *Polydor 5753432*	74	1

See also PIANOMAN

BASS BUMPERS
Germany / UK, male / female vocal / instrumental group (4 WEEKS)

Date		Title / Label	pos	wks
25 Sep 93		**RUNNIN'** *Vertigo VERCD 78*	68	1
5 Feb 94		**THE MUSIC'S GOT ME** *Vertigo VERCD 84*	25	3

BASS JUMPERS
Holland, male producer and female vocalist (1 WEEK)

Date		Title / Label	pos	wks
13 Feb 99		**MAKE UP YOUR MIND** *Pepper 0530112*	44	1

BASS-O-MATIC *UK, male multi-instrumentalist / producer – William Orbit (19 WEEKS)*

Date		Title / Label	pos	wks
12 May 90		**IN THE REALM OF THE SENSES** *Virgin VS 1265*	66	3
1 Sep 90	●	**FASCINATING RHYTHM** *Virgin VS 1274*	9	11
22 Dec 90		**EASE ON BY** *Virgin VS 1295*	61	4
3 Aug 91		**FUNKY LOVE VIBRATIONS** *Virgin VS 1355*	71	1

See also William ORBIT

Shirley BASSEY (22 Top 500) *Internationally acclaimed vocalist and cabaret entertainer, b. 8 Jan 1937, Cardiff, Wales. With 30 hit singles (spanning a record 42-year period for a female) and 34 hit albums, she is Britain's most successful female chart artist. Honoured with a damehood in 2000 (326 WEEKS)*

Date		Title / Label	pos	wks
15 Feb 57	●	**THE BANANA BOAT SONG** *Philips PB 668*	8	10
23 Aug 57		**FIRE DOWN BELOW** *Philips PB 723*	30	1
6 Sep 57		**YOU, YOU ROMEO** *Philips PB 723*	29	2
19 Dec 58		**AS I LOVE YOU** *Philips PB 845*	27	2
26 Dec 58	●	**KISS ME, HONEY HONEY, KISS ME** *Philips PB 860*	3	17
9 Jan 59	★	**AS I LOVE YOU (re-entry)** *Philips PB 845*	1	17
31 Mar 60		**WITH THESE HANDS** *Columbia DB 4421*	38	2
21 Apr 60		**WITH THESE HANDS (re-entry)** *Columbia DB 4421*	43	2
12 May 60		**WITH THESE HANDS (2nd re-entry)** *Columbia DB 4421*	41	2
4 Aug 60	●	**AS LONG AS HE NEEDS ME** *Columbia DB 4490*	2	30
11 May 61	●	**YOU'LL NEVER KNOW** *Columbia DB 4643*	6	17
27 Jul 61	★	**REACH FOR THE STARS / CLIMB EV'RY MOUNTAIN** *Columbia DB 4685*	1	16
23 Nov 61	●	**I'LL GET BY (AS LONG AS I HAVE YOU)** *Columbia DB 4737*	10	8
23 Nov 61		**REACH FOR THE STARS / CLIMB EV'RY MOUNTAIN (re-entry)** *Columbia DB 4685*	40	2
15 Feb 62		**TONIGHT** *Columbia DB 4777*	21	8
26 Apr 62		**AVE MARIA** *Columbia DB 4816*	31	4
31 May 62		**FAR AWAY** *Columbia DB 4836*	24	13
30 Aug 62	●	**WHAT NOW MY LOVE?** *Columbia DB 4882*	5	17

Date	Title / Label	pos	wks
28 Feb 63	WHAT KIND OF FOOL AM I? *Columbia DB 4974*	47	2
26 Sep 63	● I (WHO HAVE NOTHING) *Columbia DB 7113*	6	20
23 Jan 64	MY SPECIAL DREAM *Columbia DB 7185*	32	7
9 Apr 64	GONE *Columbia DB 7248*	36	5
15 Oct 64	GOLDFINGER *Columbia DB 7360*	21	9
20 May 65	NO REGRETS *Columbia DB 7535*	39	4
11 Oct 67	BIG SPENDER *United Artists UP 1192*	21	15
20 Jun 70	● SOMETHING *United Artists UP 35125*	4	21
2 Jan 71	THE FOOL ON THE HILL *United Artists UP 35156*	48	1
23 Jan 71	SOMETHING (re-entry) *United Artists UP 35125*	50	1
27 Mar 71	(WHERE DO I BEGIN) LOVE STORY *United Artists UP 35194*	34	9
7 Aug 71	FOR ALL WE KNOW *United Artists UP 35267*	46	1
21 Aug 71	● FOR ALL WE KNOW (re-entry) *United Artists UP 35267*	6	23
15 Jan 72	DIAMONDS ARE FOREVER *United Artists UP 35293*	38	6
3 Mar 73	● NEVER NEVER NEVER *United Artists UP 35490*	8	18
14 Jul 73	NEVER NEVER NEVER (re-entry) *United Artists UP 35490*	48	1
22 Aug 87	THE RHYTHM DIVINE *Mercury MER 253* [1]	54	2
16 Nov 96	'DISCO' LA PASSIONE *East West EW 072CD* [2]	41	1
20 Dec 97	HISTORY REPEATING *Wall of Sound WALLD 036* [3]	19	7
23 Oct 99	WORLD IN UNION *Universal TV 4669402* [4]	35	3

[1] Yello featuring Shirley Bassey [2] Chris Rea and Shirley Bassey [3] Propellerheads featuring Miss Shirley Bassey [4] Shirley Bassey / Bryn Terfel

BASSHEADS
UK, male / female vocal / instrumental group (19 WEEKS) pos/wks

Date	Title / Label	pos	wks
16 Nov 91	● IS THERE ANYBODY OUT THERE? *Deconstruction R 6303*	5	8
30 May 92	BACK TO THE OLD SCHOOL *Deconstruction R 6310*	12	4
28 Nov 92	WHO CAN MAKE ME FEEL GOOD *Deconstruction R 6326*	38	2
28 Aug 93	START A BRAND NEW LIFE (SAVE ME) *Deconstruction CDR 6353*	49	2
15 Jul 95	IS THERE ANYBODY OUT THERE? (re-mix) *Deconstruction 74321293882*	24	3

BASSTOY *US, male / female vocal / instrumental duo (1 WEEK)* pos/wks

Date	Title / Label	pos	wks
27 May 00	RUNNIN *Neo NEOCD 029*	62	1

BATES *Germany, male vocal / instrumental group (1 WEEK)* pos/wks

Date	Title / Label	pos	wks
3 Feb 96	BILLIE JEAN *Virgin International DINSD 151*	67	1

Mike BATT with the NEW EDITION
UK, male vocalist with male / female vocal group (8 WEEKS) pos/wks

Date	Title / Label	pos	wks
16 Aug 75	● SUMMERTIME CITY *Epic EPC 3460*	4	8

See also WOMBLES

BAUHAUS *UK, male vocal / instrumental group (35 WEEKS)* pos/wks

Date	Title / Label	pos	wks
18 Apr 81	KICK IN THE EYE *Beggars Banquet BEG 54*	59	3
4 Jul 81	THE PASSION OF LOVERS *Beggars Banquet BEG 59*	56	2
6 Mar 82	KICK IN THE EYE (EP) *Beggars Banquet BEG 74*	45	4
19 Jun 82	SPIRIT *Beggars Banquet BEG 79*	42	5
9 Oct 82	ZIGGY STARDUST *Beggars Banquet BEG 83*	15	7
22 Jan 83	LAGARTIJA NICK *Beggars Banquet BEG 88*	44	4
9 Apr 83	SHE'S IN PARTIES *Beggars Banquet BEG 91*	26	6
29 Oct 83	THE SINGLES 1981-'83 *Beggars Banquet BEG 100E*	52	4

Tracks on Kick in the Eye (EP): Kick in the Eye (Searching for Satori) / Harry / Earwax. The Singles 1981-83 was an EP: The Passion of Lovers / Kick In The Eye / Spirit / Ziggy Stardust) / Lagartija Nick / She's In Parties

Les BAXTER his Chorus and Orchestra
US, orchestra and chorus (9 WEEKS) pos/wks

Date	Title / Label	pos	wks
13 May 55	● UNCHAINED MELODY *Capitol CL 14257*	10	9

BAY CITY ROLLERS (238 Top 500)
Tartan teen sensations from Edinburgh: Leslie McKeown (v), Eric Faulkner (g), Stuart Wood (g), Alan Longmuir (b), Derek Longmuir (d). They were the first of many acts heralded as 'Biggest Group Since The Beatles' and one of the most screamed-at teeny-bopper acts of the 70s (116 WEEKS) pos/wks

Date	Title / Label	pos	wks
18 Sep 71	● KEEP ON DANCING *Bell 1164*	9	13
9 Feb 74	● REMEMBER (SHA-LA-LA) *Bell 1338*	6	12
27 Apr 74	● SHANG-A-LANG *Bell 1355*	2	10
27 Jul 74	● SUMMERLOVE SENSATION *Bell 1369*	3	10
12 Oct 74	● ALL OF ME LOVES ALL OF YOU *Bell 1382*	4	10
8 Mar 75	★ BYE BYE BABY *Bell 1409*	1	16
12 Jul 75	★ GIVE A LITTLE LOVE *Bell 1425*	1	9
22 Nov 75	● MONEY HONEY *Bell 1461*	3	9
10 Apr 76	● LOVE ME LIKE I LOVE YOU *Bell 1477*	4	9
11 Sep 76	● I ONLY WANNA BE WITH YOU *Bell 1493*	4	9
7 May 77	IT'S A GAME *Arista 108*	16	6
30 Jul 77	YOU MADE ME BELIEVE IN MAGIC *Arista 127*	34	3

BAZ *UK, female vocalist (2 WEEKS)* pos/wks

Date	Title / Label	pos	wks
15 Dec 01	BELIEVERS *One Little Indian 313 TP7CD1*	36	2

BBC CONCERT ORCHESTRA, BBC SYMPHONY CHORUS cond. Stephen JACKSON *UK, orchestra, chorus and conductor (3 WEEKS)* pos/wks

Date	Title / Label	pos	wks
22 Jun 96	ODE TO JOY (FROM BEETHOVEN'S SYMPHONY NO.9) *Virgin VSCDT 1591*	36	3

BBE *France / Italy, male instrumental group (20 WEEKS)* pos/wks

Date	Title / Label	pos	wks
28 Sep 96	● SEVEN DAYS AND ONE WEEK *Positiva CDTIV 67*	3	9
29 Mar 97	● FLASH *Positiva CDTIV 73*	5	5
14 Feb 98	DESIRE *Positiva CDTIV 87*	19	3
30 May 98	DEEPER LOVE (SYMPHONIC PARADISE) *Positiva CDTIV 93*	19	3

BBG *UK, male vocal / instrumental group (10 WEEKS)* pos/wks

Date	Title / Label	pos	wks
28 Apr 90	SNAPPINESS *Urban URB 54* [1]	28	5
11 Aug 90	SOME KIND OF HEAVEN *Urban URB 59*	65	2
23 Mar 96	LET THE MUSIC PLAY *MCA MCSTD 40029* [2]	46	1
18 May 96	SNAPPINESS (re-mix) *Hi-Life 5762972*	50	1
5 Jul 97	JUST BE TONIGHT *Hi-Life 5738972* [2]	45	1

[1] BBG featuring Dina Taylor [2] BBG featuring Erin

BBM *UK, male vocal / instrumental group (2 WEEKS)* pos/wks

Date	Title / Label	pos	wks
6 Aug 94	WHERE IN THE WORLD *Virgin VSCD 1495*	57	2

BBMAK *UK, male vocal group (16 WEEKS)* pos/wks

Date	Title / Label	pos	wks
28 Aug 99	BACK HERE *Telstar CDSTAS 3053*	37	2
24 Feb 01	● BACK HERE (re-issue) *Telstar CDSTAS 3166*	5	10
26 May 01	● STILL ON YOUR SIDE *Telstar CDSTAS 3185*	8	4

BC-52's – *See B-52's*

BE BOP DELUXE *UK, male vocal / instrumental group (13 WEEKS)* pos/wks

Date	Title / Label	pos	wks
21 Feb 76	SHIPS IN THE NIGHT *Harvest HAR 5104*	23	8
13 Nov 76	HOT VALVES (EP) *Harvest HAR 5117*	36	5

Tracks on Hot Valves (EP): Maid in Heaven / Blazing Apostles / Jet Silver and the Dolls of Venus / Bring Back the Spark

See also Bill NELSON

BEACH BOYS (36 Top 500)
California family band famous for their harmonies. The most successful and consistently popular US group of the rock era: Brian Wilson (b/k/v), Mike Love (v), Carl Wilson (g/v) (d. 1998), Al Jardine (g/v), Dennis Wilson (d/v) (d. 1983) (281 WEEKS) pos/wks

Date	Title / Label	pos	wks
1 Aug 63	SURFIN' U.S.A. *Capitol CL 15305*	34	7
9 Jul 64	● I GET AROUND *Capitol CL 15350* ▲	7	13
29 Oct 64	WHEN I GROW UP (TO BE A MAN) *Capitol CL 15361*	44	2
19 Nov 64	WHEN I GROW UP (TO BE A MAN) (re-entry) *Capitol CL 15361*	27	5
21 Jan 65	DANCE, DANCE, DANCE *Capitol CL 15370*	24	6
3 Jun 65	HELP ME, RHONDA *Capitol CL 15392* ▲	27	10
2 Sep 65	CALIFORNIA GIRLS *Capitol CL 15409*	26	8
17 Feb 66	● BARBARA ANN *Capitol CL 15432*	3	10
21 Apr 66	● SLOOP JOHN B *Capitol CL 15441*	2	15
28 Jul 66	● GOD ONLY KNOWS *Capitol CL 15459*	2	14
3 Nov 66	★ GOOD VIBRATIONS *Capitol CL 15475* ▲	1	13
4 May 67	● THEN I KISSED HER *Capitol CL 15502*	4	11
23 Aug 67	● HEROES AND VILLAINS *Capitol CL 15510*	8	9
22 Nov 67	WILD HONEY *Capitol CL 15521*	29	6

17 Jan 68 DARLIN' *Capitol CL 15527* 11 14
8 May 68 FRIENDS *Capitol CL 15545* 25 7
24 Jul 68 ★ DO IT AGAIN *Capitol CL 15554* 1 14
25 Dec 68 BLUEBIRDS OVER THE MOUNTAIN *Capitol CL 15572* 33 5
26 Feb 69 ● I CAN HEAR MUSIC *Capitol CL 15584* 10 13
11 Jun 69 ● BREAK AWAY *Capitol CL 15598* 6 11
16 May 70 ● COTTONFIELDS *Capitol CL 15640* 5 17
3 Mar 73 CALIFORNIA SAGA – CALIFORNIA *Reprise K 14232* 37 5
3 Jul 76 GOOD VIBRATIONS (re-issue) *Capitol CL 15875* 18 7
10 Jul 76 ROCK AND ROLL MUSIC *Reprise K 14440* 36 4
31 Mar 79 HERE COMES THE NIGHT *Caribou CRB 7204* 37 8
16 Jun 79 ● LADY LYNDA *Caribou CRB 7427* 6 11
29 Sep 79 SUMAHAMA *Caribou CRB 7846* 45 4
29 Aug 81 BEACH BOYS MEDLEY *Capitol CL 213* 47 4
22 Aug 87 ● WIPEOUT *Urban URB 5* [1] 2 12
19 Nov 88 KOKOMO *Elektra EKR 85* ▲ 25 9
2 Jun 90 WOULDN'T IT BE NICE *Capitol CL 579* 58 1
29 Jun 91 DO IT AGAIN (re-issue) *Capitol EMCT 1* 61 2
2 Mar 96 FUN FUN FUN *PolyGram TV 5762972* [2] 24 4

[1] Fat Boys and the Beach Boys [2] Status Quo with the Beach Boys

Walter BEASLEY *US, male vocalist (3 WEEKS)* pos/wks

23 Jan 88 I'M SO HAPPY *Urban URB 14* 70 3

BEASTIE BOYS *US, male rap group (59 WEEKS)* pos/wks

28 Feb 87 (YOU GOTTA) FIGHT FOR YOUR RIGHT (TO PARTY) *Def Jam 650418 7* 11 11
30 May 87 NO SLEEP TILL BROOKLYN *Def Jam BEAST 1* 14 7
18 Jul 87 ● SHE'S ON IT *Def Jam BEAST 2* 10 8
3 Oct 87 GIRLS / SHE'S CRAFTY *Def Jam BEAST 3* 34 4
11 Apr 92 PASS THE MIC *Capitol 12CL 653* 47 2
4 Jul 92 FROZEN METAL HEAD (EP) *Capitol 12CL 665* 55 1
9 Jul 94 GET IT TOGETHER / SABOTAGE *Capitol CDCL 716* 19 4
26 Nov 94 SURE SHOT *Capitol CDCL 726* 27 3
4 Jul 98 ● INTERGALACTIC *Grand Royal CDCL 803* 5 7
7 Nov 98 BODY MOVIN' *Grand Royal CDCL 809* 15 4
16 Jan 99 BODY MOVIN' (re-entry) *Grand Royal CDCL 809* 69 1
29 May 99 REMOTE CONTROL / 3 MCS & 1 DJ *Grand Royal CDCL 812* 21 3
18 Dec 99 ALIVE *Grand Royal CDCL 818* 28 4

Tracks on Frozen Metal Head (EP): Jimmy James / Jimmy James (Original) / Drinkin' Wine / The Blue Nun

BEAT (340 Top 500) *Birmingham, UK-based band who married ska and new wave influences, formed 1978; Dave Wakeling (v/g), Ranking Roger (v), Andy Cox (g) and David Steele (b). After 1983 break-up, former two launched General Public and latter pair formed Fine Young Cannibals (92 WEEKS)* pos/wks

8 Dec 79 ● TEARS OF A CLOWN / RANKING FULL STOP *2 Tone CHSTT 6* 6 11
23 Feb 80 ● HANDS OFF – SHE'S MINE *Go Feet FEET 1* 9 9
3 May 80 ● MIRROR IN THE BATHROOM *Go Feet FEET 2* 4 9
16 Aug 80 BEST FRIEND / STAND DOWN MARGARET (DUB) *Go Feet FEET 3* 22 9
13 Dec 80 ● TOO NICE TO TALK TO *Go Feet FEET 4* 7 11
18 Apr 81 DROWNING / ALL OUT TO GET YOU *Go Feet FEET 6* 22 8
20 Jun 81 DOORS OF YOUR HEART *Go Feet FEET 9* 33 6
5 Dec 81 HIT IT *Go Feet FEET 11* 70 2
17 Apr 82 SAVE IT FOR LATER *Go Feet FEET 333* 47 4
18 Sep 82 JEANETTE *Go Feet FEET 15* 45 3
4 Dec 82 I CONFESS *Go Feet FEET 16* 54 3
30 Apr 83 ● CAN'T GET USED TO LOSING YOU *Go Feet FEET 17* 3 11
2 Jul 83 ACKEE 1-2-3 *Go Feet FEET 18* 54 4
27 Jan 96 MIRROR IN THE BATHROOM (re-mix) *Go Feet 74321232062* 44 2

BEAT RENEGADES

UK, male production duo – Ian Bland and Paul Fitzpatrick (1 WEEK) pos/wks

19 May 01 AUTOMATIK *Slinky Music SLINKY 014CD* 73 1

See also RED; DREAM FREQUENCY

BEAT SYSTEM *UK, male vocal / instrumental group (3 WEEKS)* pos/wks

3 Mar 90 WALK ON THE WILD SIDE *Fourth & Broadway BRW 163* 63 2
18 Sep 93 TO A BRIGHTER DAY (O' HAPPY DAY) *ffrr FCD 217* 70 1

BEATCHUGGERS featuring Eric CLAPTON *Denmark, male producer Michael Linde and UK, male singer / instrumentalist (2 WEEKS)* pos/wks

18 Nov 00 FOREVER MAN (HOW MANY TIMES) *ffrr FCD 386* 26 2

BEATLES (9 Top 500) *World's most successful group. John Lennon (v/g) b. 9 Oct 1940, Liverpool, d. 8 Dec 1980, New York, Paul McCartney (v/b) b. 18 Jun 1942, Liverpool, George Harrison (v/g) b. 24 Feb 1943, Liverpool, d. 29 Nov 2001, Ringo Starr (Richard Starkey) (v/d) b. 7 Jul 1940, Liverpool.. Achievements include: most No.1 singles and albums in the UK and US. Within three months of their US chart debut in 1964, they held all the Top 5 single chart places, had a record 14 simultaneous entries on Billboard Top 100 and had the two top-selling albums. During those 12 weeks they earned six gold singles and sold four million albums. Their album 'Sgt. Pepper's Lonely Hearts Club Band' is the biggest seller ever in the UK, and the group is the No.1 all-time US best-selling album act. They split in 1970 but in 1996, Anthology' sold 10 million worldwide in only four weeks. 2000's '1' collection is the world's fastest selling album ever with 23.5 million in its first month (and 10 million more since) and was the top-selling album of 2000 in the UK. The Beatles, who were awarded MBEs in 1965, have sold an estimated one billion records (456 WEEKS)* pos/wks

11 Oct 62 LOVE ME DO *Parlophone R 4949* ▲ 17 18
17 Jan 63 ● PLEASE PLEASE ME *Parlophone R 4983* 2 18
18 Apr 63 ★ FROM ME TO YOU *Parlophone R 5015* 1 21
6 Jun 63 MY BONNIE *Polydor NH 66833* [1] 48 1
29 Aug 63 ★ SHE LOVES YOU *Parlophone R 5055* ◆ ▲ 1 31
5 Dec 63 ★ I WANT TO HOLD YOUR HAND *Parlophone R 5084* ◆ ▲ 1 21
26 Mar 64 ★ CAN'T BUY ME LOVE *Parlophone R 5114* ◆ ▲ 1 14
9 Apr 64 SHE LOVES YOU (re-entry) *Parlophone R 5055* 42 2
14 May 64 I WANT TO HOLD YOUR HAND (re-entry) *Parlophone R 5084* 48 1
11 Jun 64 AIN'T SHE SWEET *Polydor 52 317* 29 6
9 Jul 64 CAN'T BUY ME LOVE (re-entry) *Parlophone R 5114* 47 1
16 Jul 64 ★ A HARD DAY'S NIGHT *Parlophone R 5160* ▲ 1 13
3 Dec 64 ★ I FEEL FINE *Parlophone R 5200* ◆ ▲ 1 13
15 Apr 65 ★ TICKET TO RIDE *Parlophone R 5265* ▲ 1 12
29 Jul 65 ★ HELP! *Parlophone R 5305* ▲ 1 14
9 Dec 65 ★ DAY TRIPPER / WE CAN WORK IT OUT *Parlophone R 5389* ◆ ▲ 1 12
16 Jun 66 ★ PAPERBACK WRITER *Parlophone R 5452* ▲ 1 11
11 Aug 66 ★ YELLOW SUBMARINE / ELEANOR RIGBY *Parlophone R 5493* 1 13
23 Feb 67 ● PENNY LANE / STRAWBERRY FIELDS FOREVER *Parlophone R 5570* ▲ 2 11
12 Jul 67 ★ ALL YOU NEED IS LOVE *Parlophone R 5620* ▲ 1 13
29 Nov 67 ★ HELLO, GOODBYE *Parlophone R 5655* ▲ 1 12
13 Dec 67 ● MAGICAL MYSTERY TOUR (DOUBLE EP) *Parlophone SMMT/MMT 1* 2 12
20 Mar 68 ★ LADY MADONNA *Parlophone R 5675* 1 8
4 Sep 68 ★ HEY JUDE *Apple R 5722* ▲ 1 16
23 Apr 69 ★ GET BACK *Apple R 5777* [2] ■ ▲ 1 17
4 Jun 69 ★ THE BALLAD OF JOHN AND YOKO *Apple R 5786* 1 14
8 Nov 69 ● SOMETHING / COME TOGETHER *Apple R 5814* ▲ 4 12
14 Mar 70 ● LET IT BE *Apple R 5833* ▲ 2 9
24 Oct 70 LET IT BE (re-entry) *Apple R 5833* 43 1
13 Mar 76 ● YESTERDAY *Apple R 6013* ▲ 8 7
27 Mar 76 HEY JUDE (re-entry) *Apple R 5722* 12 7
27 Mar 76 PAPERBACK WRITER (re-entry) *Parlophone R 5452* 23 5
3 Apr 76 GET BACK (re-entry) *Apple R 5777* [2] 28 5
3 Apr 76 STRAWBERRY FIELDS FOREVER (re-entry) *Parlophone R 5570* 32 3
10 Apr 76 HELP! (re-entry) *Parlophone R 5305* 37 3
10 Jul 76 BACK IN THE USSR *Parlophone R 6016* 19 6
7 Oct 78 SGT. PEPPER'S LONELY HEARTS CLUB BAND – WITH A LITTLE HELP FROM MY FRIENDS *Parlophone R 6022* 63 3
5 Jun 82 ● BEATLES MOVIE MEDLEY *Parlophone R 6055* 10 9
16 Oct 82 ● LOVE ME DO (re-entry) *Parlophone R 4949* 4 7
22 Jan 83 PLEASE PLEASE ME (re-entry) *Parlophone R 4983* 29 4
23 Apr 83 FROM ME TO YOU (re-entry) *Parlophone R 5015* 40 4
3 Sep 83 SHE LOVES YOU (2nd re-entry) *Parlophone R 5055* 45 3
26 Nov 83 I WANT TO HOLD YOUR HAND (2nd re-entry) *Parlophone R 5084* 62 2
31 Mar 84 CAN'T BUY ME LOVE (2nd re-entry) *Parlophone R 5114* 53 2
21 Jul 84 A HARD DAY'S NIGHT (re-entry) *Parlophone R 5160* 52 2
8 Dec 84 I FEEL FINE (re-entry) *Parlophone R 5200* 65 1
20 Apr 85 TICKET TO RIDE (re-entry) *Parlophone R 5265* 70 2
30 Aug 86 YELLOW SUBMARINE / ELEANOR RIGBY (re-entry) *Parlophone R 5493* 63 1

28 Feb 87		PENNY LANE (re-entry) / STRAWBERRY FIELDS FOREVER (2nd re-entry) *Parlophone R 5570*	65	2
18 Jul 87		ALL YOU NEED IS LOVE (re-entry) *Parlophone R 5620*	47	3
5 Dec 87		HELLO GOODBYE (re-entry) *Parlophone R 5655*	63	1
26 Mar 88		LADY MADONNA (re-entry) *Parlophone R 5675*	67	1
10 Sep 88		HEY JUDE (2nd re-entry) *Apple R 5722*	52	2
22 Apr 89		GET BACK (2nd re-entry) *Apple R 5777* [2]	74	1
17 Oct 92		LOVE ME DO (2nd re-entry) *Parlophone R 4949*	53	1
1 Apr 95	●	BABY IT'S YOU *Apple CDR 6406*	7	6
8 Jul 95		BABY IT'S YOU (re-entry) *Apple CDR 6406*	71	1
16 Dec 95	●	FREE AS A BIRD *Apple CDR 6422*	2	8
16 Mar 96	●	REAL LOVE *Apple CDR 6425*	4	7

[1] Tony Sheridan and the Beatles [2] Beatles with Billy Preston

Tracks on Magical Mystery Tour (EP): Magical Mystery Tour / Your Mother Should Know / I Am the Walrus / Fool on the Hill / Flying / Blue Jay Way

See also Paul McCARTNEY; Ringo STARR; John LENNON; George HARRISON

BEATMASTERS *UK, male / female production group (47 WEEKS)* pos/wks

			pos	wks
9 Jan 88	●	ROK DA HOUSE *Rhythm King LEFT 11* [1]	5	11
24 Sep 88		BURN IT UP *Rhythm King LEFT 27* [2]	14	10
22 Apr 89	●	WHO'S IN THE HOUSE *Rhythm King LEFT 31* [3]	8	9
12 Aug 89	●	HEY DJ – I CAN'T DANCE (TO THAT MUSIC YOU'RE PLAYING) / SKA TRAIN *Rhythm King LEFT 34* [4]	7	11
2 Dec 89		WARM LOVE *Rhythm King LEFT 37* [5]	51	2
21 Sep 91		BOULEVARD OF BROKEN DREAMS *Rhythm King 6573617*	62	1
16 May 92		DUNNO WHAT IT IS (ABOUT YOU) *Rhythm King 6580017* [6]	43	3

[1] Beatmasters featuring the Cookie Crew [2] Beatmasters with PP Arnold [3] The Beatmasters with Merlin [4] Beatmasters featuring Betty Boo [5] Beatmasters featuring Claudia Fontaine [6] Beatmasters featuring Elaine Vassell

BEATNUTS *US, male rap duo (1 WEEK)* pos/wks

			pos	wks
14 Jul 01		NO ESCAPIN' THIS *Epic 6713412*	47	1

BEATRICE – *See Mike KOGLIN*

BEATS INTERNATIONAL *UK, male / female vocal / instrumental group leader – Norman Cook (30 WEEKS)* pos/wks

			pos	wks
10 Feb 90	★	DUB BE GOOD TO ME *Go.Beat GOD 39* [1]	1	13
12 May 90	●	WON'T TALK ABOUT IT *Go.Beat GOD 43*	9	7
15 Sep 90		BURUNDI BLUES *Go.Beat GOD 45*	51	3
2 Mar 91		ECHO CHAMBER *Go.Beat GOD 51*	60	2
21 Sep 91		THE SUN DOESN'T SHINE *Go.Beat GOD 59*	66	2
23 Nov 91		IN THE GHETTO *Go.Beat GOD 64*	44	3

[1] Beats International featuring Lindy Layton

See also FREAKPOWER; PIZZAMAN; Norman COOK; FATBOY SLIM; MIGHTY DUB KATZ; HOUSEMARTINS

BEAUTIFUL PEOPLE
UK, male instrumental / production group (1 WEEK) pos/wks

			pos	wks
28 May 94		IF 60S WERE 90S *Essential ESSX 2037*	74	1

BEAUTIFUL SOUTH (145 Top 500) *Ex-Housemartins Paul Heaton (v/g) and Dave Hemingway (v) (from the beautiful north of England) formed the band that featured Briana Corrigan (v) (replaced by Jacqui Abbot 1994-2000). Heaton and Dave Rotheray (g) write the witty and ironic songs (151 WEEKS)* pos/wks

			pos	wks
3 Jun 89	●	SONG FOR WHOEVER *Go! Discs GOD 32*	2	11
23 Sep 89	●	YOU KEEP IT ALL IN *Go! Discs GOD 35*	8	8
2 Dec 89		I'LL SAIL THIS SHIP ALONE *Go! Discs GOD 38*	31	8
6 Oct 90	★	A LITTLE TIME *Go! Discs GOD 47*	1	14
8 Dec 90		MY BOOK *Go! Discs GOD 48*	43	6
16 Mar 91		LET LOVE SPEAK UP ITSELF *Go! Discs GOD 53*	51	2
11 Jan 92		OLD RED EYES IS BACK *Go! Discs GOD 66*	22	6
14 Mar 92		WE ARE EACH OTHER *Go! Discs GOD 71*	30	3
13 Jun 92		BELL BOTTOMED TEAR *Go! Discs GOD 78*	16	5
26 Sep 92		36D *Go! Discs GOD 88*	46	2
12 Mar 94		GOOD AS GOLD *Go! Discs GODCD 110*	23	5
4 Jun 94		EVERYBODY'S TALKIN' *Go! Discs GODCD 113*	12	8
3 Sep 94		PRETTIEST EYES *Go! Discs GODCD 119*		
12 Nov 94		ONE LAST LOVE SONG *Go! Discs GODCD 122*	14	5
18 Nov 95		PRETENDERS TO THE THRONE *Go! Discs GODCD 134*	18	4
12 Oct 96	●	ROTTERDAM *Go! Discs GODCD 155*	5	9
14 Dec 96	●	DON'T MARRY HER *Go! Discs GODCD 158*	8	10
29 Mar 97		BLACKBIRD ON THE WIRE *Go! Discs 5821252*	23	5
5 Jul 97		LIARS' BAR *Go! Discs 5822492*	43	1
3 Oct 98	●	PERFECT 10 *Go! Discs 5664832*	2	14
19 Dec 98		DUMB *Go! Discs 5667532*	16	7
13 Mar 99		DUMB (re-entry) *Go! Discs 5667532*	72	1
20 Mar 99		HOW LONG'S A TEAR TAKE TO DRY? *Go! Discs 8708212*	12	6
10 Jul 99		THE TABLE *Go! Discs 5621652*	47	2
7 Oct 00		CLOSER THAN MOST *Go! Discs / Mercury 5629672*	22	4
23 Dec 00		THE RIVER / JUST CHECKIN' *Go! Discs / Mercury 5727552*	59	1
17 Nov 01		THE ROOT OF ALL EVIL *Go! Discs / Mercury 5888702*	50	1

BEAVIS and BUTT-HEAD – *See CHER*

Gilbert BECAUD *France, male vocalist (12 WEEKS)* pos/wks

			pos	wks
29 Mar 75	●	A LITTLE LOVE AND UNDERSTANDING *Decca F 13537*	10	12

BECK *US, male vocalist – David Campbell (27 WEEKS)* pos/wks

			pos	wks
5 Mar 94		LOSER *Geffen GFSTD 67*	15	6
29 Jun 96		WHERE IT'S AT *Geffen GFSTD 22156*	35	2
16 Nov 96		DEVIL'S HAIRCUT *Geffen GFSTD 22183*	22	2
8 Mar 97		THE NEW POLLUTION *Geffen GFSTD 22205*	14	5
24 May 97		SISSYNECK *Geffen GFSTD 22253*	30	2
8 Nov 97		DEADWEIGHT *Geffen GFSTD 22293*	23	3
19 Dec 98		TROPICALIA *Geffen GFSTD 22365*	39	2
20 Nov 99		SEXX LAWS *Geffen 4971812*	27	3
8 Apr 00		MIXED BIZNESS *Geffen 4973002*	34	2

Jeff BECK *UK, male vocalist / instrumentalist – guitar (57 WEEKS)* pos/wks

			pos	wks
23 Mar 67		HI-HO SILVER LINING *Columbia DB 8151*	14	14
2 Aug 67		TALLYMAN *Columbia DB 8227*	30	3
28 Feb 68		LOVE IS BLUE (L'ARMOUR EST BLEU) *Columbia DB 8359*	23	7
9 Jul 69		GOO GOO BARABAJAGAL (LOVE IS HOT) *Pye 7N 17778* [1]	12	9
4 Nov 72		HI-HO SILVER LINING (re-issue) *RAK RR 3*	17	11
5 May 73		I'VE BEEN DRINKING *RAK RR 4* [2]	27	6
9 Oct 82		HI-HO SILVER LINING (re-entry of re-issue) *RAK RR 3*	62	4
7 Mar 92		PEOPLE GET READY *Epic 6577567* [2]	49	3

[1] Donovan with the Jeff Beck Group [2] Jeff Beck and Rod Stewart

Robin BECK *US, female vocalist (13 WEEKS)* pos/wks

			pos	wks
22 Oct 88	★	THE FIRST TIME *Mercury MER 270*	1	13

Peter BECKETT – *See Barry GRAY ORCHESTRA*

Victoria BECKHAM *UK, female vocalist (28 WEEKS)* pos/wks

			pos	wks
26 Aug 00	●	OUT OF YOUR MIND *Nulife 74321753342* [1]	2	16
6 Jan 01		OUT OF YOUR MIND (re-entry) *Nulife 74321753342* [1]	58	4
29 Sep 01	●	NOT SUCH AN INNOCENT GIRL *Virgin VSCDT 1816*	6	5
24 Nov 01		NOT SUCH AN INNOCENT GIRL (re-entry) *Virgin VSCDT 1816*	46	3

[1] True Steppers and Dane Bowers featuring Victoria Beckham *See also SPICE GIRLS*

BEDAZZLED *UK, male instrumental group (1 WEEK)* pos/wks

			pos	wks
4 Jul 92		SUMMER SONG *Columbia 6581627*	73	1

Daniel BEDINGFIELD
New Zealand, male vocalsit / producer (4 WEEKS) pos/wks

			pos	wks
8 Dec 01	★	GOTTA GET THRU THIS *Relentless RELENT 27CD* ■	1	4+

BEDLAM *UK, male DJ / production duo (1 WEEK)* pos/wks

			pos	wks
6 Feb 99		DA-FORCE *Playola 0091695 PLA*	68	1

BEDLAM AGO GO *UK, male vocal / instrumental group (1 WEEK)* pos/wks

			pos	wks
4 Apr 98		SEASON NO.5 *Sony S2 BDLM 2CD*	57	1

…ocal / instrumental group (9 WEEKS) pos/wks

	…AT YOU DREAM OF *Stress CDSTR 23* [1]	25 3
	SET IN STONE / FORBIDDEN ZONE *Stress CDSTR 80*	71 1
6 Nov 99	**HEAVEN SCENT** *Bedrock BEDRCDS 001*	35 3
8 Jul 00	**VOICES** *Bedrock BEDRCDS 005*	44 2

[1] Bedrock featuring KYO

BEDROCKS *UK, male vocal / instrumental group (7 WEEKS)* pos/wks

18 Dec 68	**OB-LA-DI, OB-LA-DA** *Columbia DB 8516*	20 7

Celi BEE and the BUZZY BUNCH
US, male / female vocal / instrumental group (1 WEEK) pos/wks

17 Jun 78	**HOLD YOUR HORSES BABE** *TK TKR 6032*	72 1

BEE GEES (18 Top 500)
All-time top family recording act, who are members of the exclusive 100 million-plus sales club, are Isle of Man, UK, born and Australian raised Barry, Robin and Maurice Gibb. As composers, they have wrote hits for many top acts and had 10 UK No. 1s. In 1978 they penned four consecutive US chart-toppers (three of which they also produced). Their 'Saturday Night Fever' album is the world's biggest selling soundtrack and they were first group to have UK Top 20s in five decades. Distinctive trio have won countless trophies including the World Music Legend Award (1997) and Brits Outstanding Contribution to British Music (1997) (354 WEEKS) pos/wks

27 Apr 67	**NEW YORK MINING DISASTER 1941** *Polydor 56 161*	12 10
12 Jul 67	**TO LOVE SOMEBODY** *Polydor 56 178*	50 1
26 Jul 67	**TO LOVE SOMEBODY (re-entry)** *Polydor 56 178*	41 4
20 Sep 67 ★	**(THE NIGHT THE LIGHTS WENT OUT IN) MASSACHUSETTS** *Polydor 56 192*	1 17
22 Nov 67 ●	**WORLD** *Polydor 56 220*	9 16
31 Jan 68 ●	**WORDS** *Polydor 56 229*	8 10
27 Mar 68	**JUMBO / THE SINGER SANG HIS SONG** *Polydor 56 242*	25 7
7 Aug 68 ★	**I'VE GOTTA GET A MESSAGE TO YOU** *Polydor 56 273*	1 15
19 Feb 69 ●	**FIRST OF MAY** *Polydor 56 304*	6 11
4 Jun 69	**TOMORROW, TOMORROW** *Polydor 56 331*	23 8
16 Aug 69 ●	**DON'T FORGET TO REMEMBER** *Polydor 56 343*	2 15
28 Mar 70	**I.O.I.O.** *Polydor 56 377*	49 1
5 Dec 70	**LONELY DAYS** *Polydor 2001 104*	33 9
29 Jan 72	**MY WORLD** *Polydor 2058 185*	16 9
22 Jul 72 ●	**RUN TO ME** *Polydor 2058 255*	9 10
28 Jun 75 ●	**JIVE TALKIN'** *RSO 2090 160* ▲	5 11
31 Jul 76 ●	**YOU SHOULD BE DANCING** *RSO 2090 195* ▲	5 10
13 Nov 76	**LOVE SO RIGHT** *RSO 2090 207*	41 4
29 Oct 77 ●	**HOW DEEP IS YOUR LOVE** *RSO 2090 259* ▲	3 15
4 Feb 78 ●	**STAYIN' ALIVE** *RSO 2090 267* ▲	4 12
15 Apr 78 ★	**NIGHT FEVER** *RSO 002* ▲	1 20
13 May 78	**STAYIN' ALIVE (re-entry)** *RSO 2090 267*	63 6
25 Nov 78 ●	**TOO MUCH HEAVEN** *RSO 25* ▲	3 13
17 Feb 79 ★	**TRAGEDY** *RSO 27* ▲	1 10
14 Apr 79	**LOVE YOU INSIDE OUT** *RSO 31* ▲	13 9
5 Jan 80	**SPIRITS (HAVING FLOWN)** *RSO 52*	16 7
17 Sep 83	**SOMEONE BELONGING TO SOMEONE** *RSO 96*	49 4
26 Sep 87 ★	**YOU WIN AGAIN** *Warner Bros. W 8351*	1 15
12 Dec 87	**E.S.P.** *Warner Bros. W 8139*	51 5
15 Apr 89	**ORDINARY LIVES** *Warner Bros. W 7523*	54 3
24 Jun 89	**ONE** *Warner Bros. W 2916*	71 1
2 Mar 91 ●	**SECRET LOVE** *Warner Bros. W 0014*	5 11
21 Aug 93	**PAYING THE PRICE OF LOVE** *Polydor PZCD 284*	23 5
27 Nov 93 ●	**FOR WHOM THE BELL TOLLS** *Polydor PZCD 299*	4 14
16 Apr 94	**HOW TO FALL IN LOVE PART 1** *Polydor PZDD 311*	30 4
1 Mar 97 ●	**ALONE** *Polydor 5735272*	5 9
21 Jun 97	**I COULD NOT LOVE YOU MORE** *Polydor 5712232*	14 3
8 Nov 97	**STILL WATERS (RUN DEEP)** *Polydor 5718892*	18 3
18 Jul 98 ●	**IMMORTALITY** *Epic 6661682* [1]	5 12
7 Apr 01	**THIS IS WHERE I CAME IN** *Polydor 5879772*	18 5

[1] Celine Dion with Bee Gees

See also Robin GIBB; Barry GIBB

BEENIE MAN
Jamaica, male vocalist / toaster / rapper Moses David (21 WEEKS) pos/wks

20 Sep 97	**DANCEHALL QUEEN** *Island Jamaica IJCD 2018*	70 1
7 Mar 98 ●	**WHO AM I** *Greensleeves GRECD 588*	10 5
8 Aug 98	**FOUNDATION** *Shocking Vibes SVJCDS1*	69 1
4 Mar 00 ●	**MONEY** *Parlophone Rhythm Series CDRHYTHM 27* [1]	5 9
24 Mar 01	**GIRLS DEM SUGAR** *Virgin VUSCD 173* [2]	13 5

[1] Jamelia featuring Beenie Man [2] Beenie Man featuring Mya

BEF featuring Lalah HATHAWAY
US, male production group and US, female vocalist (5 WEEKS) pos/wks

27 Jul 91	**FAMILY AFFAIR** *Ten TEN 369*	37 5

Lou BEGA *Germany, male vocalist – David Lubega (21 WEEKS)* pos/wks

7 Aug 99	**MAMBO NO.5 (A LITTLE BIT OF...) (import)** *Ariola 74321658012*	31 4
4 Sep 99 ★	**MAMBO NO.5 (A LITTLE BIT OF ...)** *RCA 74321696722* ■	1 15
18 Dec 99	**I GOT A GIRL** *RCA 74321720642*	55 2

BEGGAR and CO *UK, male vocal / instrumental group (15 WEEKS)* pos/wks

7 Feb 81	**(SOMEBODY) HELP ME OUT** *Ensign ENY 201*	15 10
12 Sep 81	**MULE (CHANT NO. 2)** *RCA 130*	37 5

BEGINNING OF THE END
US, male vocal / instrumental group (6 WEEKS) pos/wks

23 Feb 74	**FUNKY NASSAU** *Atlantic K 10021*	31 6

BEIJING SPRING *UK, female vocal duo (5 WEEKS)* pos/wks

23 Jan 93	**I WANNA BE IN LOVE AGAIN** *MCA MCSTD 1709*	43 3
8 May 93	**SUMMERLANDS** *MCA MCSTD 1761*	53 2

BEL AMOUR *France, male / female production / vocal trio (3 WEEKS)* pos/wks

12 May 01	**BEL AMOUR** *Credence CDCRED 010*	23 3

BEL CANTO *UK, male vocal / instrumental group (1 WEEK)* pos/wks

14 Oct 95	**WE'VE GOT TO WORK IT OUT** *Good Groove CDGG 2*	65 1

Harry BELAFONTE (366 Top 500)
Singer / actor, civil rights campaigner and driving force behind USA for Africa b. 1 Mar 1927, New York, US. Started transatlantic calypso craze in 1957 when his LP, 'Calypso', topped the US chart for 31 weeks. Became Unicef goodwill ambassador in 1987 (87 WEEKS) pos/wks

1 Mar 57 ●	**BANANA BOAT SONG (DAY-O)** *HMV POP 308* [1]	2 18
14 Jun 57 ●	**ISLAND IN THE SUN** *RCA 1007*	3 25
6 Sep 57	**SCARLET RIBBONS** *HMV POP 360* [2]	18 6
1 Nov 57 ★	**MARY'S BOY CHILD** *RCA 1022*	1 12
22 Aug 58	**LITTLE BERNADETTE** *RCA 1072* [3]	16 7
28 Nov 58 ●	**MARY'S BOY CHILD (re-entry)** *RCA 1022* ◆	10 6
12 Dec 58	**THE SON OF MARY** *RCA 1084*	18 4
11 Dec 59	**MARY'S BOY CHILD (2nd re-entry)** *RCA 1022*	30 1
21 Sep 61	**THERE'S A HOLE IN MY BUCKET** *RCA 1247* [4]	32 2
12 Oct 61	**THERE'S A HOLE IN MY BUCKET (re-entry)** *RCA 1247* [4]	34 6

[1] Harry Belafonte with Tony Scott's Orchestra and Chorus and Millard Thomas, Guitar
[2] Harry Belafonte and Millard Thomas [3] Belafonte [4] Harry Belafonte and Odetta

Maggie BELL *UK, female vocalist (12 WEEKS)* pos/wks

15 Apr 78	**HAZELL** *Swansong SSK 19412*	37 3
13 May 78	**HAZELL (re-entry)** *Swansong SSK 19412*	74 1
17 Oct 81	**HOLD ME** *Swansong BAM 1* [1]	11 8

[1] B A Robertson and Maggie Bell

William BELL *US, male vocalist – William Yarborough (22 WEEKS)* pos/wks

29 May 68	**A TRIBUTE TO A KING** *Stax 601 038*	31 7
20 Nov 68 ●	**PRIVATE NUMBER** *Stax 101* [1]	8 14
26 Apr 86	**HEADLINE NEWS** *Absolute LUTE 1*	70 1

[1] Judy Clay and William Bell

BELL and JAMES *US, male vocal duo (3 WEEKS)* pos/wks

31 Mar 79	LIVIN' IT UP (FRIDAY NIGHT) *A & M AMS 7424*	68	1
14 Apr 79	LIVIN' IT UP (FRIDAY NIGHT) (re-entry) *A & M AMS 7424*	59	2

BELL & SPURLING
UK, male vocal duo – Martin Bellamy and John Spurling (6 WEEKS) pos/wks

13 Oct 01 ●	SVEN SVEN SVEN *Eternal WEA 336CD*	7	6

Archie BELL and the DRELLS
US, male vocal / instrumental group (33 WEEKS) pos/wks

7 Oct 72	HERE I GO AGAIN *Atlantic K 10210*	11	10
27 Jan 73	THERE'S GONNA BE A SHOWDOWN *Atlantic K 10263*	36	5
8 May 76	SOUL CITY WALK *Philadelphia International PIR 4250*	13	10
11 Jun 77	EVERYBODY HAVE A GOOD TIME *Philadelphia International PIR 5179*	43	4
28 Jun 86	DON'T LET LOVE GET YOU DOWN *Portrait A 7254*	49	4

BELL BIV DEVOE *US, male vocal group (29 WEEKS)* pos/wks

30 Jun 90	POISON *MCA MCA 1414*	19	11
22 Sep 90	DO ME *MCA MCA 1440*	56	3
15 Aug 92 ●	THE BEST THINGS IN LIFE ARE FREE *Perspective PERSS 7400* [1]	2	13
9 Oct 93	SOMETHING IN YOUR EYES *MCA MCSTD 1934*	60	2

[1] Luther Vandross and Janet Jackson with special guests BBD and Ralph Tresvant

BELL BOOK & CANDLE
Germany, male / female vocal / instrumental group (1 WEEK) pos/wks

17 Oct 98	RESCUE ME *Logic 74321616882*	63	1

Freddie BELL and the BELLBOYS
US, male vocal / instrumental group (10 WEEKS) pos/wks

28 Sep 56 ●	GIDDY-UP-A DING DONG *Mercury MT 122*	4	10

BELLAMY BROTHERS
US, male vocal duo – Howard and David Bellamy (29 WEEKS) pos/wks

17 Apr 76 ●	LET YOUR LOVE FLOW *Warner Bros. K 16690* ▲	7	12
21 Aug 76	SATIN SHEETS *Warner Bros. K 16775*	43	3
11 Aug 79 ●	IF I SAID YOU HAVE A BEAUTIFUL BODY WOULD YOU HOLD IT AGAINST ME *Warner Bros. K 17405*	3	14

BELLBOYS – *See Freddie BELL and the BELLBOYS*

BELLATRIX
Iceland, male / female vocal / instrumental group (1 WEEK) pos/wks

16 Sep 00	JEDI WANNABE *Fierce Panda NING 101CD*	65	1

BELLE and the DEVOTIONS *UK, female vocal group (8 WEEKS)* pos/wks

21 Apr 84	LOVE GAMES *CBS A 4332*	11	8

Regina BELLE *US, female vocalist (13 WEEKS)* pos/wks

21 Oct 89	GOOD LOVIN' *CBS 655230*	73	1
11 Dec 93	A WHOLE NEW WORLD (ALADDIN'S THEME) *Columbia 6599002* [1] ▲	12	12

[1] Regina Belle and Peabo Bryson

BELLE & SEBASTIAN
UK, male / female vocal / instrumental group (12 WEEKS) pos/wks

24 May 97	DOG ON WHEELS *Jeepster JPRCDS 001*	59	1
9 Aug 97	LAZY LINE PAINTER JANE *Jeepster JPRCDS 002*	41	2
25 Oct 97	3... 6... 9 SECONDS OF LIGHT (EP) *Jeepster JPRCDS 003*	32	2
3 Jun 00	LEGAL MAN *Jeepster JPRCD 018*	15	3
30 Jun 01	JONATHAN DAVID *Jeepster JPRCDS 022*	31	2
8 Dec 01	I'M WAKING UP TO US *Jeepster JPRCDS 023*	39	2

Tracks on 3... 6... 9 Seconds Of Light (EP): A Century of Fakers / Le Pastie de la Bourgeoisie / Beautiful / Put The Book Back On The Shelf

BELLE STARS *UK, female vocal / instrumental group (42 WEEKS)* pos/wks

5 Jun 82	IKO IKO *Stiff BUY 150*	35	6
17 Jul 82	THE CLAPPING SONG *Stiff BUY 155*	11	9
16 Oct 82	MOCKINGBIRD *Stiff BUY 159*	51	3
15 Jan 83 ●	SIGN OF THE TIMES *Stiff BUY 167*	3	11
16 Apr 83	SWEET MEMORY *Stiff BUY 174*	22	9
13 Aug 83	INDIAN SUMMER *Stiff BUY 185*	52	3
14 Jul 84	80s ROMANCE *Stiff BUY 200*	71	1

BELLEFIRE *Ireland, female vocal group (4 WEEKS)* pos/wks

14 Jul 01	PERFECT BLISS *Virgin VSCDT 1807*	18	4

BELLINI *Germany, male vocal / production group (7 WEEKS)* pos/wks

27 Sep 97 ●	SAMBA DE JANEIRO *Virgin DINSD 165*	8	7

Louis BELLSON – *See Duke ELLINGTON*

BELLY *US, male / female vocal / instrumental group (9 WEEKS)* pos/wks

23 Jan 93	FEED THE TREE *4AD BAD 3001CD*	32	3
10 Apr 93	GEPETTO *4AD BAD 2018CD*	49	2
4 Feb 95	NOW THEY'LL SLEEP *4AD BAD 5003CD*	28	2
22 Jul 95	SEAL MY FATE *4AD BAD 5007CD*	35	2

BELMONTS – *See DION*

BELOUIS SOME *UK, male vocalist – Neville Keighley (26 WEEKS)* pos/wks

27 Apr 85	IMAGINATION *Parlophone R 6097*	50	7
18 Jan 86	IMAGINATION (re-issue) *Parlophone R 1986*	17	10
12 Apr 86	SOME PEOPLE *Parlophone R 6130*	33	7
16 May 87	LET IT BE WITH YOU *Parlophone R 6154*	53	2

BELOVED *UK, male / female vocal / instrumental duo (47 WEEKS)* pos/wks

21 Oct 89	THE SUN RISING *WEA YZ 414*	26	7
27 Jan 90	HELLO *WEA YZ 426*	19	7
24 Mar 90	YOUR LOVE TAKES ME HIGHER *East West YZ 463*	39	3
9 Jun 90	TIME AFTER TIME *East West YZ 482*	46	4
10 Nov 90	IT'S ALRIGHT NOW *East West YZ 541*	48	3
23 Jan 93 ●	SWEET HARMONY *East West YZ 709CD*	8	10
10 Apr 93	YOU'VE GOT ME THINKING *East West YZ 738CD*	23	4
14 Aug 93	OUTERSPACE GIRL *East West YZ 726CD*	38	2
30 Mar 96	SATELLITE *East West EW 034CD*	19	3
10 Aug 96	EASE THE PRESSURE *East West EW 058CD*	43	2
30 Aug 97	THE SUN RISING (re-issue) *East West EW 122CD1*	31	2

Act was male only before 1993

BELTRAM *US, male producer – Joey Beltram (4 WEEKS)* pos/wks

28 Sep 91	ENERGY FLASH (EP) *RandS RSUK 3*	52	2
7 Dec 91	THE OMEN *RandS RSUK 7* [1]	53	2

[1] Program 2 Beltram

Tracks on Energy Flash (EP): Energy Flash / Psycho Bass / My Sound / Sub-Base Experience

Pat BENATAR *US, female vocalist – Patricia Andrzejewski (53 WEEKS)* pos/wks

21 Jan 84	LOVE IS A BATTLEFIELD *Chrysalis CHS 2747*	49	5
12 Jan 85	WE BELONG *Chrysalis CHS 2821*	22	9
23 Mar 85	LOVE IS A BATTLEFIELD (re-issue) *Chrysalis PAT 1*	17	10
15 Jun 85	SHADOWS OF THE NIGHT *Chrysalis PAT 2*	50	4
19 Oct 85	INVINCIBLE (THEME FROM 'THE LEGEND OF BILLIE JEAN') *Chrysalis PAT 3*	53	3
15 Feb 86	SEX AS A WEAPON *Chrysalis PAT 4*	67	3
2 Jul 88	ALL FIRED UP *Chrysalis PAT 5*	19	10
1 Oct 88	DON'T WALK AWAY *Chrysalis PAT 6*	42	5
14 Jan 89	ONE LOVE *Chrysalis PAT 7*	59	3
30 Oct 93	SOMEBODY'S BABY *Chrysalis CDCHS 5001*	48	1

David BENDETH
Canada, male vocalist and multi-instrumentalist (5 WEEKS) pos/wks

8 Sep 79	FEEL THE REAL *Sidewalk SID 113*	44	5

BENELUX and Nancy DEE
Belgium / Holland / Luxembourg, female vocal group (4 WEEKS) pos/wks

25 Aug 79 **SWITCH** *Scope SC 4* 52 4

Eric BENET *US, male vocalist (5 WEEKS)* pos/wks

22 Mar 97 **SPIRITUAL THANG** *Warner Bros. W 0390CD* 62 1
1 May 99 **GEORGY PORGY** *Warner Bros. W478CD2* [1] 28 3
5 Feb 00 **WHY YOU FOLLOW ME** *Warner Bros. W491CD* 48 1

[1] Eric Benet featuring Faith Evans

Nigel BENN – *See PACK featuring Nigel BENN*

Simone BENN – *See VOLATILE AGENTS featuring Simone BENN*

BENNET *UK, male vocal / instrumental group (3 WEEKS)* pos/wks

22 Feb 97 **MUM'S GONE TO ICELAND** *Roadrunner RR 22853* 34 2
3 May 97 **SOMEONE ALWAYS GETS THERE FIRST** *Roadrunner RR 22983* 69 1

Chris BENNETT – *See MUNICH MACHINE*

Tony BENNETT *US, male vocalist – Anthony Benedetto (61 WEEKS)* pos/wks

15 Apr 55 ★ **STRANGER IN PARADISE** *Philips PB 420* 1 16
16 Sep 55 **CLOSE YOUR EYES** *Philips PB 445* 18 1
13 Apr 56 **COME NEXT SPRING** *Philips PB 537* 29 1
5 Jan 61 **TILL** *Philips PB 1079* 35 2
18 Jul 63 **THE GOOD LIFE** *CBS AAG 153* 27 13
6 May 65 **IF I RULED THE WORLD** *CBS 201735* 40 5
27 May 65 **(I LEFT MY HEART) IN SAN FRANCISCO** *CBS 201730* 46 2
30 Sep 65 **(I LEFT MY HEART) IN SAN FRANCISCO (re-entry)** *CBS 201730* 40 5
9 Dec 65 **(I LEFT MY HEART) IN SAN FRANCISCO (2nd re-entry)** *CBS 201730* 25 7
23 Dec 65 **THE VERY THOUGHT OF YOU** *CBS 202021* 21 9

Boyd BENNETT and his ROCKETS
US, male vocalist and male vocal / instrumental group (2 WEEKS) pos/wks

23 Dec 55 **SEVENTEEN** *Parlophone R 4063* 16 2

Cliff BENNETT and the REBEL ROUSERS
UK, male vocal / instrumental group (23 WEEKS) pos/wks

1 Oct 64 ● **ONE WAY LOVE** *Parlophone R 5173* 9 9
4 Feb 65 **I'LL TAKE YOU HOME** *Parlophone R 5229* 42 3
11 Aug 66 ● **GOT TO GET YOU INTO MY LIFE** *Parlophone R 5489* 6 11

Peter E BENNETT with the CO-OPERATION CHOIR
UK, male vocalist and choir (1 WEEK) pos/wks

7 Nov 70 **THE SEAGULL'S NAME WAS NELSON** *RCA 1991* 45 1

Gary BENSON *UK, male vocalist (Harry Hyams) (8 WEEKS)* pos/wks

9 Aug 75 **DON'T THROW IT ALL AWAY** *State STAT 10* 20 8

George BENSON (170 Top 500) *Grammy-winning guitarist / vocalist, b. 22 Mar 1943, Pennsylvania, US. This one-time child prodigy topped the US chart in 1976 with the triple-platinum album 'Breezin'. He was also a major live attraction in Britain during the 1980s (143 WEEKS)* pos/wks

25 Oct 75 **SUPERSHIP** *CTI CTSP 002* [1] 30 6
4 Jun 77 **NATURE BOY** *Warner Bros. K 16921* 26 6
24 Sep 77 **THE GREATEST LOVE OF ALL** *Arista 133* 27 7
31 Mar 79 **LOVE BALLAD** *Warner Bros. K 17333* 29 9
26 Jul 80 ● **GIVE ME THE NIGHT** *Warner Bros. K 17673* 7 10
4 Oct 80 ● **LOVE X LOVE** *Warner Bros. K 17699* 10 8
7 Feb 81 **WHAT'S ON YOUR MIND** *Warner Bros. K 17748* 45 5
19 Sep 81 **LOVE ALL THE HURT AWAY** *Arista ARIST 428* [2] 49 3
14 Nov 81 **TURN YOUR LOVE AROUND** *Warner Bros. K 17877* 29 11
23 Jan 82 **NEVER GIVE UP ON A GOOD THING** *Warner Bros. K 17902* 14 10
21 May 83 **LADY LOVE ME (ONE MORE TIME)** *Warner Bros. W 9614* 11 10
16 Jul 83 **FEEL LIKE MAKIN' LOVE** *Warner Bros. W 9551* 28 7
24 Sep 83 ● **IN YOUR EYES** *Warner Bros. W 9487* 7 10
17 Dec 83 **INSIDE LOVE (SO PERSONAL)** *WEA Int. W 9427* 57 5
19 Jan 85 **20 / 20** *Warner Bros. W 9120* 29 9
20 Apr 85 **BEYOND THE SEA (LA MER)** *Warner Bros. W 9014* 60 3
16 Aug 86 **KISSES IN THE MOONLIGHT** *Warner Bros. W 8640* 60 4
29 Nov 86 **SHIVER** *Warner Bros. W 8523* 19 9
14 Feb 87 **TEASER** *Warner Bros. W 8437* 45 4
27 Aug 88 **LET'S DO IT AGAIN** *Warner Bros. W 7780* 56 3
5 Sep 92 **I'LL KEEP YOUR DREAMS ALIVE** *Ammi AMMI 101* [3] 68 1
11 Jul 98 **SEVEN DAYS** *MCA MCSTD 48083* [4] 22 3

[1] George "Bad" Benson [2] Aretha Franklin and George Benson [3] George Benson and Patti Austin [4] Mary J Blige featuring George Benson

BENTLEY RHYTHM ACE *UK, male instrumental duo – Mike Stokes and Richard March (7 WEEKS)* pos/wks

6 Sep 97 **BENTLEY'S GONNA SORT YOU OUT!** *Parlophone CDRS 6476* 17 4
27 May 00 **THEME FROM GUTBUSTER** *Parlophone CDRS 6537* 29 2
2 Sep 00 **HOW'D I DO DAT** *Parlophone CDRS 6543* 57 1

Brook BENTON *US, male vocalist (18 WEEKS)* pos/wks

10 Jul 59 **ENDLESSLY** *Mercury AMT 1043* 28 2
6 Oct 60 **KIDDIO** *Mercury AMT 1109* 42 3
3 Nov 60 **KIDDIO (re-entry)** *Mercury AMT 1109* 41 3
16 Feb 61 **FOOLS RUSH IN** *Mercury AMT 1121* 50 1
13 Jul 61 **THE BOLL WEEVIL SONG** *Mercury AMT 1148* 30 9

BENZ *UK, male rap / vocal group (9 WEEKS)* pos/wks

16 Dec 95 **BOOM ROCK SOUL** *Hacktown 74321329652* 62 2
16 Mar 96 **URBAN CITY GIRL** *Hacktown 74321348732* 31 3
25 May 96 **MISS PARKER** *Hacktown 74321377292* 35 2
29 Mar 97 **IF I REMEMBER** *Hendricks CDBENZ 1* 59 1
9 Aug 97 **ON A SUN-DAY** *Hendricks CDBENZ 2* 73 1

Ingrid BERGMAN – *See Dooley WILSON*

BERLIN *US, male / female vocal / instrumental group – lead vocal Terri Nunn (39 WEEKS)* pos/wks

25 Oct 86 ★ **TAKE MY BREATH AWAY (LOVE THEME FROM 'TOP GUN')** *CBS A 7320* ▲ 1 15
17 Jan 87 **YOU DON'T KNOW** *Mercury MER 237* 39 6
14 Mar 87 **LIKE FLAMES** *Mercury MER 240* 47 3
20 Feb 88 **TAKE MY BREATH AWAY (LOVE THEME FROM 'TOP GUN') (re-entry)** *CBS A 7320* 52 3
13 Oct 90 ● **TAKE MY BREATH AWAY (re-issue)** *CBS 656361 7* 3 12

Elmer BERNSTEIN *US, orchestra (11 WEEKS)* pos/wks

18 Dec 59 ● **STACCATO'S THEME** *Capitol CL 15101* 4 10
10 Mar 60 **STACCATO'S THEME (re-entry)** *Capitol CL 15101* 40 1

Leonard BERNSTEIN, ORCHESTRA and CHORUS
US, male conductor, orchestra and chorus (4 WEEKS) pos/wks

2 Jul 94 **AMERICA – WORLD CUP THEME 1994** *Deutsche Grammophon USACD 1* 44 4

BERRI *UK, female vocalist – Beverley Sleight (22 WEEKS)* pos/wks

26 Nov 94 **THE SUNSHINE AFTER THE RAIN** *Ffrreedom TABCD 223* [1] 26 6
2 Sep 95 ● **THE SUNSHINE AFTER THE RAIN (re-mix)** *Ffrreedom TABCD 232* 4 11
2 Dec 95 **SHINE LIKE A STAR** *Ffrreedom TABCD 239* 20 5

[1] New Atlantic / U4EA featuring Berri

LaKiesha BERRI *US, female vocalist (1 WEEK)* pos/wks

5 Jul 97 **LIKE THIS AND LIKE THAT** *Adept ADPTCD 7* 54 1

Chuck BERRY (345 Top 500) *First guitar-playing rock star, b. 18 Oct 1926, Missouri, US. Often called rock 'n' roll's premier poet and most influential instrumentalist. "Duck walking" legend was among the first acts inducted into the Rock and Roll Hall of Fame (91 WEEKS)* pos/wks

21 Jun 57 **SCHOOL DAY (RING! RING! GOES THE BELL)** *Columbia DB 3951* 24 2

UK No.1 ★ UK Top 10 ● Still on chart + UK million seller ◆ UK entry at No.1 ■ US No.1 ▲

THE OFFICIAL UK SINGLES CHART 50TH ANNIVERSARY

1956

FROM THE YEAR OF THE FIRST EUROVISION SONG CONTEST, WHEN HUNGARY REBELLED AGAINST THE SOVIETS AND CALLED FOR DEMOCRACY, AND BOTH SKIFFLE AND ELVIS PRESLEY EXPLODED ON TO THE SCENE, **CLIFF RICHARD** THINKS BACK TO ONE INFLUENTIAL DAY IN PARTICULAR ...

“Had there been no Elvis there would have been no Cliff Richard. 'Heartbreak Hotel' was the first one. I was a teenager when I heard it with my friends in my home town – there was a car that had stopped, the driver had left the engine running with the radio on and we heard 'Since my baby left me...'. Wow! Before the end of the song the car drove off, so we didn't know who it was. We all listened for days, maybe weeks, to all the different radio stations and finally they played it and said 'It's by a man named **Elvis Presley**'. So it was straight down to the record shop. When I was young I dreamed that I would wake up and I was Elvis, it was that bad.”

SINGLE OF THE YEAR
'Just Walking in the Rain' Johnnie Ray

12 Jul 57		SCHOOL DAY (RING! RING! GOES THE BELL) (re-entry) *Columbia DB 3951*	24	2
25 Apr 58		SWEET LITTLE SIXTEEN *London HLM 8585*	16	5
11 Jul 63		GO GO GO *Pye International 7N 25209*	38	6
10 Oct 63	●	LET IT ROCK / MEMPHIS TENNESSEE *Pye International 7N 25218*	6	13
19 Dec 63		RUN RUDOLPH RUN *Pye International 7N 25228*	36	6
13 Feb 64		NADINE (IS IT YOU) *Pye International 7N 25236*	27	6
2 Apr 64		NADINE (IS IT YOU) (re-entry) *Pye International 7N 25236*	43	1
7 May 64	●	NO PARTICULAR PLACE TO GO *Pye International 7N 25242*	3	12
20 Aug 64		YOU NEVER CAN TELL *Pye International 7N 25257*	23	8
14 Jan 65		THE PROMISED LAND *Pye International 7N 25285*	26	6
28 Oct 72	★	MY DING-A-LING *Chess 6145 019* ▲	1	17
3 Feb 73		REELIN' AND ROCKIN' *Chess 6145 020*	18	7

Dave BERRY (451 Top 500) *Unique charismatic performer b. Dave Grundy, 6 Feb 1941, Sheffield, UK. Major European star, whose 'This Strange Effect' is among Holland's biggest sellers. Stage act influenced Alvin Stardust, and several punk bands acknowledge him as an inspiration (77 WEEKS)*

			pos	wks
19 Sep 63		MEMPHIS TENNESSEE *Decca F 11734* [1]	19	13
9 Jan 64		MY BABY LEFT ME *Decca F 11803* [1]	41	1
23 Jan 64		MY BABY LEFT ME (re-entry) *Decca F 11803* [1]	37	8
30 Apr 64		BABY IT'S YOU *Decca F 11876*	24	6
6 Aug 64	●	THE CRYING GAME *Decca F 11937*	5	12
26 Nov 64		ONE HEART BETWEEN TWO *Decca F 12020*	41	2
31 Dec 64		ONE HEART BETWEEN TWO (re-entry) *Decca F 12020*	45	1
25 Mar 65	●	LITTLE THINGS *Decca F 12103*	5	12
22 Jul 65		THIS STRANGE EFFECT *Decca F 12188*	37	6
30 Jun 66	●	MAMA *Decca F 12435*	5	16

[1] Dave Berry and the Cruisers

Mike BERRY *UK, male vocalist (51 WEEKS)*

			pos	wks
12 Oct 61		TRIBUTE TO BUDDY HOLLY *HMV POP 912* [1]	24	6
3 Jan 63	●	DON'T YOU THINK IT'S TIME *HMV POP 1105* [1]	6	12
11 Apr 63		MY LITTLE BABY *HMV POP 1142* [1]	34	7
2 Aug 80	●	THE SUNSHINE OF YOUR SMILE *Polydor 2059 261*	9	12
29 Nov 80		IF I COULD ONLY MAKE YOU CARE *Polydor POSP 202*	37	9
5 Sep 81		MEMORIES *Polydor POSP 287*	55	5

[1] Mike Berry and the Outlaws

Nick BERRY *UK, male vocalist (24 WEEKS)*

			pos	wks
4 Oct 86	★	EVERY LOSER WINS *BBC RESL 204*	1	11
27 Dec 86		EVERY LOSER WINS (re-entry) *BBC RESL 204*	72	2
13 Jun 92	●	HEARTBEAT *Columbia 6581517*	2	8
31 Oct 92		LONG LIVE LOVE *Columbia 6587597*	47	3

Adele BERTEI – See *JELLYBEAN*

BEST COMPANY *UK, male vocal duo (1 WEEK)*

			pos	wks
27 Mar 93		DON'T YOU FORGET ABOUT ME *ZYX ZYX 69468*	65	1

BEST SHOT *UK, male rap group (2 WEEKS)*

			pos	wks
5 Feb 94		UNITED COLOURS *East West YZ 795CD*	64	2

BETA BAND *UK, male vocal / instrumental group (3 WEEKS)*

			pos	wks
14 Jul 01		BROKE / WON *Regal Recordings REG 60CD*	30	2
27 Oct 01		HUMAN BEING *Regal Recordings REG 65CD*	57	1

Martin BETTINGHAUS – See *Timo MAAS*

BEVERLEY SISTERS *UK, female vocal trio (34 WEEKS)*

			pos	wks
27 Nov 53		I SAW MOMMY KISSING SANTA CLAUS *Philips PB 188*	11	1
11 Dec 53	●	I SAW MOMMY KISSING SANTA CLAUS (re-entry) *Philips PB 188*	6	4
13 Apr 56		WILLIE CAN *Decca F 10705*	23	4
1 Feb 57		I DREAMED *Decca F 10832*	24	2
13 Feb 59	●	LITTLE DRUMMER BOY *Decca F 11107*	6	13
20 Nov 59		LITTLE DONKEY *Decca F 11172*	14	7

23 Jun 60		GREEN FIELDS *Columbia DB 4444*	48	1
7 Jul 60		GREEN FIELDS (re-entry) *Columbia DB 4444*	29	2

Frankie BEVERLY – See *MAZE featuring Frankie BEVERLY*

BEYOND *UK, male vocal / instrumental group (1 WEEK)*

			pos	wks
21 Sep 91		RAGING 'EP' *Harvest HARS 530*	68	1

Tracks on Raging (EP): Great Indifference / Nail / Eve of My Release

BG THE PRINCE OF RAP *Germany, male rapper (2 WEEKS)*

			pos	wks
18 Jan 92		TAKE CONTROL OF THE PARTY *Columbia 6576330*	71	2

BIBLE *UK, male vocal / instrumental group (8 WEEKS)*

			pos	wks
20 May 89		GRACELAND *Chrysalis BIB 4*	51	4
26 Aug 89		HONEY BE GOOD *Ensign BIB 5*	54	4

BIBLE OF DREAMS – See *Johnny PANIC and the BIBLE OF DREAMS*

BIDDU *UK, orchestra – leader: Biddu Appaiah (13 WEEKS)*

			pos	wks
2 Aug 75		SUMMER OF '42 *Epic EPC 3318*	14	8
17 Apr 76		RAIN FOREST *Epic EPC 4084*	39	4
11 Feb 78		JOURNEY TO THE MOON *Epic EPC 5910*	41	1

BIG APPLE BAND – See *Walter MURPHY and the BIG APPLE BAND*

BIG AUDIO DYNAMITE
UK / US, male vocal / instrumental group (27 WEEKS)

			pos	wks
22 Mar 86		E=MC2 *CBS A 6963*	11	9
7 Jun 86		MEDICINE SHOW *CBS A 7181*	29	5
18 Oct 86		C'MON EVERY BEATBOX *CBS 650147*	51	3
21 Feb 87		V THIRTEEN *CBS BAAD 2*	49	5
28 May 88		JUST PLAY MUSIC *CBS BAAD 4*	51	3
12 Nov 94		LOOKING FOR A SONG *Columbia 6610182* [1]	68	2

[1] Big Audio

BIG BAD HORNS – See *LITTLE ANGELS*

BIG BAM BOO *UK / Canada, male vocal / instrumental duo (2 WEEKS)*

			pos	wks
28 Jan 89		SHOOTING FROM MY HEART *MCA MCA 1281*	61	2

BIG BASS vs Michelle NARINE
Canada, male production group and female vocalist (1 WEEK)

			pos	wks
2 Sep 00		WHAT YOU DO *Stonebridge / Edel 0110965ERE*	67	1

BIG BEN *UK, clock (2 WEEKS)*

			pos	wks
1 Jan 00		MILLENNIUM CHIMES *London BIGONE 2000*	53	2

BIG BEN BANJO BAND *UK, instrumental group (6 WEEKS)*

			pos	wks
10 Dec 54	●	LET'S GET TOGETHER NO.1 *Columbia DB 3549*	6	4
9 Dec 55		LET'S GET TOGETHER AGAIN NO.1 *Columbia DB 3676*	19	1
30 Dec 55		LET'S GET TOGETHER AGAIN NO.1 (re-entry) *Columbia DB 3676*	18	1

These hits were both medleys as follows: Let's Get Together No.1: I'm Just Wild About Harry / April Showers / Rock-a-Bye Your Baby / Swanee / Darktown Strutters Ball / For Me and My Gal / Oh You Beautiful Doll / Yes Sir That's My Baby / Let's Get Together

BIG BOPPER *US, male vocalist – JP Richardson (8 WEEKS)*

			pos	wks
26 Dec 58		CHANTILLY LACE *Mercury AMT 1002*	30	1
9 Jan 59		CHANTILLY LACE (re-entry) *Mercury AMT 1002*	12	7

BIG BOSS STYLUS presents RED VENOM
UK, male production duo and male rapper – Mike Neilson (1 WEEK)

			pos	wks
31 Jul 99		LET'S GET IT ON *All Around the World CDGLOBE 195*	72	1

BIG C – See *Alex WHITCOMBE and BIG C*

UK No.1 ★ UK Top 10 ● Still on chart + UK million seller ◆ UK entry at No.1 ■ US No.1 ▲

BIG COUNTRY (298 Top 500) *Distinctively Scottish-sounding rock quartet from Dunfermline, Scotland: Stuart Adamson b. 11 Apr 1958, d. 16 Dec 2001, (v/g, ex-Skids), Bruce Watson (g), Tony Butler (b), Mark Brzezicki (d). These frequent early-1980s chart visitors achieved five Top 10 albums including the 1984 No.1 'Steeltown' and were well known for Watson's bagpipe-like guitar sound (103 WEEKS)* pos/wks

26 Feb 83 ●	**FIELDS OF FIRE (400 MILES)** *Mercury COUNT 2*	10	12
28 May 83	**IN A BIG COUNTRY** *Mercury COUNT 3*	17	7
3 Sep 83 ●	**CHANCE** *Mercury COUNT 4*	9	9
21 Jan 84 ●	**WONDERLAND** *Mercury COUNT 5*	8	8
29 Sep 84	**EAST OF EDEN** *Mercury MER 175*	17	6
1 Dec 84	**WHERE THE ROSE IS SOWN** *Mercury MER 185*	29	7
19 Jan 85	**JUST A SHADOW** *Mercury BCO 8*	26	4
12 Apr 86 ●	**LOOK AWAY** *Mercury BIGC 1*	7	8
21 Jun 86	**THE TEACHER** *Mercury BIGC 2*	28	4
20 Sep 86	**ONE GREAT THING** *Mercury BIGC 3*	19	6
29 Nov 86	**HOLD THE HEART** *Mercury BIGC 4*	55	2
20 Aug 88	**KING OF EMOTION** *Mercury BIGC 5*	16	5
1 Oct 88	**KING OF EMOTION (re-entry)** *Mercury BIGC 5*	74	1
5 Nov 88	**BROKEN HEART (THIRTEEN VALLEYS)** *Mercury BIGC 6*	47	4
4 Feb 89	**PEACE IN OUR TIME** *Mercury BIGC 7*	39	3
12 May 90	**SAVE ME** *Mercury BIGC 8*	41	3
21 Jul 90	**HEART OF THE WORLD** *Mercury BIGC 9*	50	2
31 Aug 91	**REPUBLICAN PARTY REPTILE (EP)** *Vertigo BIC 1*	37	2
19 Oct 91	**BEAUTIFUL PEOPLE** *Vertigo BIC 2*	72	1
13 Mar 93	**ALONE** *Compulsion CDPULSS 4*	24	3
1 May 93	**SHIPS (WHERE WERE YOU)** *Compulsion CDPULSS 6*	29	3
10 Jun 95	**I'M NOT ASHAMED** *Transatlantic TRAX 1009*	69	1
9 Sep 95	**YOU DREAMER** *Transatlantic TRAD 1012*	68	1
21 Aug 99	**FRAGILE THING** *Track TRACK 0004A* [1]	69	1

[1] Big Country featuring Eddi Reader

Tracks on Republican Party Reptile (EP): Republican Party Reptile / Comes a Time / You Me and the Truth

BIG DADDY *US, male vocal group (8 WEEKS)* pos/wks

9 Mar 85	**DANCING IN THE DARK** *Making Waves SURF 1033*	21	8

BIG DADDY KANE *US, male rapper (6 WEEKS)* pos/wks

13 May 89	**RAP SUMMARY / WRATH OF KANE** *Cold Chillin' W 2973*	52	2
26 Aug 89	**SMOOTH OPERATOR** *Cold Chillin' W 2804*	65	1
13 Jan 90	**AIN'T NO STOPPIN' US NOW** *Cold Chillin' W 2635*	44	3

BIG DISH *UK, male vocal / instrumental group (5 WEEKS)* pos/wks

12 Jan 91	**MISS AMERICA** *East West YZ 529*	37	5

BIG FAMILY – *See JT and the BIG FAMILY*

BIG FUN *UK, male vocal group (33 WEEKS)* pos/wks

12 Aug 89 ●	**BLAME IT ON THE BOOGIE** *Jive JIVE 217*	4	11
25 Nov 89 ●	**CAN'T SHAKE THE FEELING** *Jive JIVE 234*	8	9
17 Mar 90	**HANDFUL OF PROMISES** *Jive JIVE 243*	21	6
23 Jun 90	**YOU'VE GOT A FRIEND** *Jive CHILD 90* [1]	14	6
4 Aug 90	**HEY THERE LONELY GIRL** *Jive JIVE 251*	62	1

[1] Big Fun and Sonia featuring Gary Barnacle

BIG MOUNTAIN
US, male / female vocal / instrumental group (15 WEEKS) pos/wks

4 Jun 94 ●	**BABY I LOVE YOUR WAY** *RCA 74321198062*	2	14
24 Sep 94	**SWEET SENSUAL LOVE** *Giant 74321234642*	51	1

BIG PUN – *See Jennifer LOPEZ*

BIG ROLL BAND – *See Zoot MONEY and the BIG ROLL BAND*

BIG RON
UK, male producer – Aaron Gilbert (aka Jules Verne) (1 WEEK) pos/wks

11 Mar 00	**LET THE FREAK** *48k SPECT 06CDS*	57	1

BIG ROOM GIRL featuring Darryl PANDY *UK, male production / instrumental duo and US, male vocalist (2 WEEKS)* pos/wks

20 Feb 99	**RAISE YOUR HANDS** *VC Recordings VCRD 44* [1]	40	2

[1] BIG ROOM GIRL featuring Darryl PANDY

See also RHYTHM MASTERS

BIG SOUND – *See Simon DUPREE and the BIG SOUND*

BIG SOUND AUTHORITY
UK, male / female vocal / instrumental group (12 WEEKS) pos/wks

19 Jan 85	**THIS HOUSE (IS WHERE YOUR LOVE STANDS)** *Source BSA 1*	21	9
8 Jun 85	**A BAD TOWN** *Source BSA 2*	54	3

BIG SUPREME *UK, male vocal group (5 WEEKS)* pos/wks

20 Sep 86	**DON'T WALK** *Polydor POSP 809*	58	3
14 Mar 87	**PLEASE YOURSELF** *Polydor POSP 840*	64	2

BIG THREE *UK, vocal / instrumental group (17 WEEKS)* pos/wks

11 Apr 63	**SOME OTHER GUY** *Decca F 11614*	37	7
11 Jul 63	**BY THE WAY** *Decca F 11689*	22	10

BIG TIME CHARLIE *UK, male DJ / production duo (4 WEEKS)* pos/wks

23 Oct 99	**ON THE RUN** *Inferno CDFERN 18*	22	2
18 Mar 00	**MR DEVIL** *Inferno CDFERN 24* [1]	39	2

[1] Big Time Charlie featuring Soozy Q

Barry BIGGS *Jamaica, male vocalist (46 WEEKS)* pos/wks

28 Aug 76	**WORK ALL DAY** *Dynamic DYN 101*	38	5
4 Dec 76 ●	**SIDESHOW** *Dynamic DYN 118*	3	16
23 Apr 77	**YOU'RE MY LIFE** *Dynamic DYN 127*	36	4
9 Jul 77	**THREE RING CIRCUS** *Dynamic DYN 128*	22	8
15 Dec 79	**WHAT'S YOUR SIGN GIRL** *Dynamic DYN 150*	55	7
20 Jun 81	**WIDE AWAKE IN A DREAM** *Dynamic DYN 10*	44	6

Ronald BIGGS – *See SEX PISTOLS*

Ivor BIGGUN *UK, male vocalist (15 WEEKS)* pos/wks

2 Sep 78	**WINKER'S SONG (MISPRINT)** *Beggars Banquet BOP 1* [1]	22	12
12 Sep 81	**BRAS ON 45 (FAMILY VERSION)** *Dead Badger BOP 6* [2]	50	3

[1] Ivor Biggun and the Red Nosed Burglars [2] Ivor Biggun and the D Cups

BILBO *UK, male vocal / instrumental group (7 WEEKS)* pos/wks

26 Aug 78	**SHE'S GONNA WIN** *Lightning LIG 548*	42	7

Mr Acker BILK and his PARAMOUNT JAZZ BAND (117 Top 500)
First UK act to top US chart in 1960s, b. 28 Jan 1929, Somerset, UK. Band leader / clarinettist / vocalist was at forefront of UK trad-jazz revival. 'Stranger on the Shore' spent more than one year on chart and was voted No.1 Instrumental of 1962 in the US. Made an MBE in the 2001 honours list (171 WEEKS) pos/wks

22 Jan 60 ●	**SUMMER SET** *Columbia DB 4382*	5	19
9 Jun 60	**GOODNIGHT SWEET PRINCE** *Melodisc MEL 1547*	50	1
18 Aug 60	**WHITE CLIFFS OF DOVER** *Columbia DB 4492*	30	9
8 Dec 60 ●	**BUONA SERA** *Columbia DB 4544*	7	18
13 Jul 61 ●	**THAT'S MY HOME** *Columbia DB 4673*	7	17
2 Nov 61	**STARS AND STRIPES FOREVER / CREOLE JAZZ** *Columbia SCD 2155*	22	10
30 Nov 61 ●	**STRANGER ON THE SHORE** *Columbia DB 4750* [1] ◆ ▲	2	55
15 Mar 62	**FRANKIE AND JOHNNY** *Columbia DB 4795*	42	2
26 Jul 62	**GOTTA SEE BABY TONIGHT** *Columbia SCD 2176*	24	9
27 Sep 62	**LONELY** *Columbia DB 4897* [1]	14	11
24 Jan 63	**A TASTE OF HONEY** *Columbia DB 4949* [1]	16	9
21 Aug 76 ●	**ARIA** *Pye 7N 45607* [2]	5	11

[1] Mr Acker Bilk with the Leon Young String Chorale [2] Acker Bilk, his Clarinet and Strings

BILL *UK, male vocalist (1 WEEK)*

Date	Title / Label	pos	wks
23 Oct 93	**CAR BOOT SALE** *Mercury MINCD 1*	73	1

BILLIE – *Billie PIPER*

BILLIE – *See H2O*

BIMBO JET
France, male / female vocal / instrumental group (10 WEEKS)

Date	Title / Label	pos	wks
26 Jul 75	**EL BIMBO** *EMI 2317*	12	10

BINARY FINARY
UK, male production duo – Matt Lewis and Ricky Grant (9 WEEKS)

Date	Title / Label	pos	wks
10 Oct 98	**1998** *Positiva CDTIV 98*	24	3
28 Aug 99	**1999** *Positiva CDTIV 118*	11	6

Umberto BINDI *Italy, male vocalist (1 WEEK)*

Date	Title / Label	pos	wks
10 Nov 60	**IL NOSTRO CONCERTO** *Oriole CB 1577*	47	1

BINI and MARTINI *Italy, male production duo (2 WEEKS)*

Date	Title / Label	pos	wks
4 Mar 00	**HAPPINESS (MY VISION IS CLEAR)** *Azuli AZNYCDX 113*	53	1
10 Mar 01	**BURNING UP** *Azuli AZNY 137*	65	1

See also ECLIPSE; GOODFELLAS featuring Lisa MILLETT; HOUSE OF GLASS

BIOHAZARD *US, male vocal / instrumental group (4 WEEKS)*

Date	Title / Label	pos	wks
9 Jul 94	**TALES FROM THE HARD SIDE** *Warner Bros. W 0254CD*	47	2
20 Aug 94	**HOW IT IS** *Warner Bros. W 0259CD*	62	2

La BIONDA *Italy, male / female vocal group (4 WEEKS)*

Date	Title / Label	pos	wks
7 Oct 78	**ONE FOR YOU ONE FOR ME** *Philips 6198 227*	54	4

BIOSPHERE *Norway, male instrumentalist – Ger Jenssen, keyboards (2 WEEKS)*

Date	Title / Label	pos	wks
29 Apr 95	**NOVELTY WAVES** *Apollo APOLLO 20CDX*	51	2

BIRDLAND *UK, male vocal / instrumental group (7 WEEKS)*

Date	Title / Label	pos	wks
1 Apr 89	**HOLLOW HEART** *Lazy LAZY 13*	70	1
8 Jul 89	**PARADISE** *Lazy LAZY 14*	70	1
3 Feb 90	**SLEEP WITH ME** *Lazy LAZY 17*	32	3
22 Sep 90	**ROCK 'N' ROLL NIGGER** *Lazy LAZY 20*	47	1
2 Feb 91	**EVERYBODY NEEDS SOMEBODY** *Lazy LAZY 24*	44	1

BIRDS *UK, male vocal / instrumental group (1 WEEK)*

Date	Title / Label	pos	wks
27 May 65	**LEAVING HERE** *Decca F 12140*	45	1

Jane BIRKIN and Serge GAINSBOURG
UK / France, female / male vocal duo (34 WEEKS)

Date	Title / Label	pos	wks
30 Jul 69 ●	**JE T'AIME . . . MOI NON PLUS** *Fontana TF 1042*	2	11
4 Oct 69 ★	**JE T'AIME . . . MOI NON PLUS (re-issue)** *Major Minor MM 645*	1	14
7 Dec 74	**JE T'AIME . . . MOI NON PLUS (2nd re-issue)** *Antic K 11511*	31	9

BIS *UK, male / female vocal / instrumental group (9 WEEKS)*

Date	Title / Label	pos	wks
30 Mar 96	**THE SECRET VAMPIRE SOUNDTRACK (EP)** *Chemikal Underground CHEM 003CD*	25	2
22 Jun 96	**BIS VS THE DIY CORPS (EP)** *Teen-C SKETCH 001CD*	45	1
9 Nov 96	**ATOM POWERED ACTION (EP)** *Wiiija WIJ 55CD*	54	1
15 Mar 97	**SWEET SHOP AVENGERZ** *Wiiija WIJ 67CD*	46	1
10 May 97	**EVERYBODY THINKS THAT THEY'RE GOING TO GET THEIRS** *Wiiija WIJ 69CD*	64	1
14 Nov 98	**EURODISCO** *Wiiija WIJ 86CD*	37	2
27 Feb 99	**ACTION AND DRAMA** *Wiiija WIJ 95CD*	50	1

Tracks on The Secret Vampire Soundtrack (EP): Kandy Pop / Secret Vampires / Teen-C Power / Diska. Tracks on Bis vs The DIY Corps (EP): This Is Fake DIY / Burn the Suit / Dance to the Disco Beat. Tracks on Atom Powered Action (EP): Starbright Boy / Wee Love / Team Theme / Cliquesuck

BISCUIT BOY *UK, male vocal / instrumental trio (1 WEEK)*

Date	Title / Label	pos	wks
15 Sep 01	**MITCH** *Mercury 5887582*	75	1

Elvin BISHOP *US, male instrumentalist – guitar (4 WEEKS)*

Date	Title / Label	pos	wks
15 May 76	**FOOLED AROUND AND FELL IN LOVE** *Capricorn 2089 024*	34	4

Hit has vocal (uncredited) by Mickey Thomas

BITI – *See DEGREES OF MOTION featuring BITI*

BIZARRE INC
UK, male / female vocal / instrumental group (49 WEEKS)

Date	Title / Label	pos	wks
16 Mar 91	**PLAYING WITH KNIVES** *Vinyl Solution STORM 25R*	43	5
14 Sep 91	**SUCH A FEELING** *Vinyl Solution STORM 32S*	13	9
23 Nov 91 ●	**PLAYING WITH KNIVES (re-issue)** *Vinyl Solution STORM 38S*	4	8
3 Oct 92 ●	**I'M GONNA GET YOU** *Vinyl Solution STORM 46S* [1]	3	12
2 Jan 93	**I'M GONNA GET YOU (re-entry)** *Vinyl Solution STORM 46S* [1]	72	1
27 Feb 93	**TOOK MY LOVE** *Vinyl Solution STORM 60CD* [1]	19	5
23 Mar 96	**KEEP THE MUSIC STRONG** *Some Bizarre MERCD 451*	33	2
6 Jul 96	**SURPRISE** *Some Bizarre MERCD 462*	21	3
14 Sep 96	**GET UP SUNSHINE STREET** *Some Bizarre MERCD 471*	45	2
13 Mar 99	**PLAYING WITH KNIVES (re-mix)** *Vinyl Solution VC01CD1*	30	2

[1] Bizarre Inc featuring Angie Brown

BIZZ NIZZ
US / Belgium, male / female vocal / instrumental group (11 WEEKS)

Date	Title / Label	pos	wks
31 Mar 90 ●	**DON'T MISS THE PARTYLINE** *Cooltempo COOL 203*	7	11

BIZZI *UK, male vocalist (1 WEEK)*

Date	Title / Label	pos	wks
6 Dec 97	**BIZZI'S PARTY** *Parlophone Rhythm CDRHYTHM 7*	62	1

BJÖRK (483 Top 500) *Captivating, eccentric, uncompromising, female singer / songwriter, b. Björk Gudmundsdottir, 21 Nov 1965, Reykjavik, Iceland. Formerly a member of The Sugarcubes, artist she was a double Brits winner in 1994 (Best International Female and Best International Newcomer) (73 WEEKS)*

Date	Title / Label	pos	wks
27 Apr 91	**OOOPS** *ZTT ZANG 19* [1]	42	3
19 Jun 93	**HUMAN BEHAVIOUR** *One Little Indian 112 TP7CD*	36	2
4 Sep 93	**VENUS AS A BOY** *One Little Indian 122 TP7CD*	29	4
23 Oct 93	**PLAY DEAD** *Island CID 573* [2]	12	6
4 Dec 93	**BIG TIME SENSUALITY** *One Little Indian 132 TP7CD*	17	8
19 Mar 94	**VIOLENTLY HAPPY** *One Little Indian 142 TP7CD*	13	4
6 May 95 ●	**ARMY OF ME** *One Little Indian 162 TP7CD*	10	5
26 Aug 95	**ISOBEL** *One Little Indian 172 TP7CD*	23	3
25 Nov 95 ●	**IT'S OH SO QUIET** *One Little Indian 182 TP7CD*	4	15
24 Feb 96 ●	**HYPERBALLAD** *One Little Indian 192 TP7CD*	8	4
9 Nov 96	**POSSIBLY MAYBE** *One Little Indian 193 TP7CD*	13	3
1 Mar 97	**I MISS YOU** *One Little Indian 194 TP7CDL*	36	2
20 Dec 97	**BACHELORETTE** *One Little Indian 212 TP7CD*	21	5
17 Oct 98	**HUNTER** *One Little Indian 222 TP7CD*	44	1
12 Dec 98	**ALARM CALL** *One Little Indian 232 TP7CDL*	33	2
19 Jun 99	**ALL IS FULL OF LOVE** *One Little Indian 242 TP7CD*	24	2
18 Aug 01	**HIDDEN PLACE** *One Little Indian 332 TP7CD*	21	2
17 Nov 01	**PAGAN POETRY** *One Little Indian 352 TP7CD*	38	2

[1] 808 State featuring Björk [2] Björk and David Arnold

BJÖRN AGAIN
Australia, male / female vocal / instrumental group (8 WEEKS)

Date	Title / Label	pos	wks
24 Oct 92	**ERASURE-ISH (A LITTLE RESPECT / STOP!)** *M & G MAGS 32*	25	3
12 Dec 92	**SANTA CLAUS IS COMING TO TOWN** *M & G MAGS 35*	55	4
27 Nov 93	**FLASHDANCE ... WHAT A FEELING** *M &G MAGCD 50*	65	1

BK *UK, male producer – Ben Keen (3 WEEKS)*

Date	Title / Label	pos	wks
25 Nov 00	**HOOVERS AND HORNS** *Nukleuz NUKC 0185* [1]	57	2
8 Dec 01	**FLASH** *Nukleuz NUKP 0361* [2]	67	1

[1] Fergie and BK [2] BK and Nick Sentience

See CORTINA

BLACK *UK, male vocalist – Colin Vearncombe (35 WEEKS)* pos/wks

			pos	wks
27 Sep 86		WONDERFUL LIFE *Ugly Man JACK 71*	72	1
27 Jun 87	●	SWEETEST SMILE *A &M AM 394*	8	10
22 Aug 87	●	WONDERFUL LIFE *A & M AM 402*	8	9
16 Jan 88		PARADISE *A & M AM 422*	38	3
24 Sep 88		THE BIG ONE *A & M AM 468*	54	4
21 Jan 89		NOW YOU'RE GONE *A & M AM 491*	66	2
4 May 91		FEEL LIKE CHANGE *A & M AM 780*	56	2
15 Jun 91		HERE IT COMES AGAIN *A & M AM 753*	70	1
5 Mar 94		WONDERFUL LIFE (re-issue) *PolyGram TV 5805552*	42	3

'Wonderful Life' on A & M is a re-recording. It was re-issued on PolyGram TV in 1994

Cilla BLACK (95 Top 500) *Undoubtedly one of Britain's favourite female vocalists / entertainers of the past 50 years, b. Priscilla White, 27 May 1943, Liverpool. After handing in her Top 20 season ticket, she has become an award-winning and extremely popular TV presenter (194 WEEKS)* pos/wks

			pos	wks
17 Oct 63		LOVE OF THE LOVED *Parlophone R 5065*	35	6
6 Feb 64	★	ANYONE WHO HAD A HEART *Parlophone R 5101*	1	17
7 May 64	★	YOU'RE MY WORLD *Parlophone R 5133*	1	17
6 Aug 64	●	IT'S FOR YOU *Parlophone R 5162*	7	10
14 Jan 65	●	YOU'VE LOST THAT LOVIN' FEELIN' *Parlophone R 5225*	2	9
22 Apr 65		I'VE BEEN WRONG BEFORE *Parlophone R 5269*	17	8
13 Jan 66	●	LOVE'S JUST A BROKEN HEART *Parlophone R 5395*	5	11
31 Mar 66	●	ALFIE *Parlophone R 5427*	9	12
9 Jun 66	●	DON'T ANSWER ME *Parlophone R 5463*	6	10
20 Oct 66		A FOOL AM I (DIMMELO PARLAMI) *Parlophone R 5515*	13	9
8 Jun 67		WHAT GOOD AM I? *Parlophone R 5608*	24	7
29 Nov 67		I ONLY LIVE TO LOVE YOU *Parlophone R 5652*	26	11
13 Mar 68	●	STEP INSIDE LOVE *Parlophone R 5674*	8	9
12 Jun 68		WHERE IS TOMORROW *Parlophone R 5706*	39	3
12 Feb 69	●	SURROUND YOURSELF WITH SORROW *Parlophone R 5759*	3	12
9 Jul 69	●	CONVERSATIONS *Parlophone R 5785*	7	12
13 Dec 69		IF I THOUGHT YOU'D EVER CHANGE YOUR MIND *Parlophone R 5820*	20	9
20 Nov 71	●	SOMETHING TELLS ME (SOMETHING IS GONNA HAPPEN TONIGHT) *Parlophone R 5924*	3	14
2 Feb 74		BABY WE CAN'T GO WRONG *EMI 2107*	36	6
18 Sep 93		THROUGH THE YEARS *Columbia 6596982*	54	1
30 Oct 93		HEART AND SOUL *Columbia 6598562* [1]	75	1

[1] Cilla Black with Dusty Springfield

Frank BLACK *US, male vocalist (4 WEEKS)* pos/wks

			pos	wks
21 May 94		HEADACHE *4AD BAD 4007CD*	53	1
20 Jan 96		MEN IN BLACK *Dragnet 6627862*	37	2
27 Jul 96		I DON'T WANT TO HURT YOU (EVERY SINGLE TIME) *Dragnet 6634635*	63	1

Jeanne BLACK *US, female vocalist (4 WEEKS)* pos/wks

			pos	wks
23 Jun 60		HE'LL HAVE TO STAY *Capitol CL 15131*	41	4

BLACK and WHITE ARMY
UK, 250 Newcastle United football fan vocalists (2 WEEKS) pos/wks

			pos	wks
23 May 98		BLACK & WHITE ARMY *Toon TOON 1CD*	26	2

BLACK BOX (472 Top 500) *Although little known in their homeland, house instrumental / production trio (Mirko Limoni, Valerio Semplici, Daniele Davoli) had UK's best-selling single of 1989, using a Loleatta Holloway vocal sample mimed by French model Katrin Quinol. First Italian act to achieve three Top 10 entries (74 WEEKS)* pos/wks

			pos	wks
12 Aug 89	★	RIDE ON TIME *Deconstruction PB 43055*	1	22
17 Feb 90	●	I DON'T KNOW ANYBODY ELSE *Deconstruction PB 43479*	4	8
2 Jun 90		EVERYBODY EVERYBODY *Deconstruction PB 43715*	16	5
3 Nov 90	●	FANTASY *Deconstruction PB 43895*	5	11
15 Dec 90		THE TOTAL MIX *Deconstruction PB 44235*	12	8
6 Apr 91		STRIKE IT UP *Deconstruction PB 44459*	16	8
14 Dec 91		OPEN YOUR EYES *Deconstruction PB 45053*	48	4
14 Aug 93		ROCKIN' TO THE MUSIC *Deconstruction 74321158122*	39	2
24 Jun 95		NOT ANYONE *Mercury MERCD 434*	31	2
20 Apr 96		I GOT THE VIBRATION / A POSITIVE VIBRATION *Manifesto MERCD 459* [1]	21	3
22 Feb 97		NATIVE NEW YORKER *Manifesto FESCD 18* [1]	46	1

[1] Blackbox

BLACK BOX RECORDER
UK, male / female vocal / instrumental group (4 WEEKS) pos/wks

			pos	wks
22 Apr 00		THE FACTS OF LIFE *Nude NUD 48CD1*	20	3
15 Jul 00		THE ART OF DRIVING *Nude NUD 51CD1*	53	1

BLACK CONNECTION
Italy, male / female vocal / production group (3 WEEKS) pos/wks

			pos	wks
14 Mar 98		GIVE ME RHYTHM *Xtravaganza/Edel 0091465 EXT*	32	2
24 Oct 98		I'M GONNA GET YA BABY *Xtravaganza 0091615 EXT*	62	1

BLACK CROWES *US, male vocal / instrumental group (28 WEEKS)* pos/wks

			pos	wks
1 Sep 90		HARD TO HANDLE *Def American DEFA 6*	45	5
12 Jan 91		TWICE AS HARD *Def American DEFA 7*	47	3
22 Jun 91		JEALOUS AGAIN / SHE TALKS TO ANGELS *Def American DEFA 8*	70	1
24 Aug 91		HARD TO HANDLE (re-issue) *Def American DEFA 10*	39	4
26 Oct 91		SEEING THINGS *Def American DEFA 13*	72	1
2 May 92		REMEDY *Def American DEFA 16*	24	3
26 Sep 92		STING ME *Def American DEFA 21*	42	2
28 Nov 92		HOTEL ILLNESS *Def American DEFA 23*	47	3
11 Feb 95		HIGH HEAD BLUES / A CONSPIRACY *American 74321258492*	25	2
22 Jul 95		WISER TIME *American 74321298272*	34	2
27 Jul 96		ONE MIRROR TOO MANY *American 74321398572*	51	1
7 Nov 98		KICKING MY HEART AROUND *American Recordings 6666665*	55	1

BLACK DIAMOND *US, male vocalist (1 WEEK)* pos/wks

			pos	wks
17 Sep 94		LET ME BE *Systematic SYSCD 1*	56	1

BLACK DOG featuring Ofra HAZA *UK, male instrumentalist / producer – Ken Downie and Israel, female vocalist (1 WEEK)* pos/wks

			pos	wks
3 Apr 99		BABYLON *Warner Esp. WESP 006 CD1*	65	1

BLACK DUCK *UK, male rapper (5 WEEKS)* pos/wks

			pos	wks
17 Dec 94		WHIGGLE IN LINE *Flying South CDDUCK 1*	33	5

BLACK EYED PEAS *US, male rap trio (4 WEEKS)* pos/wks

			pos	wks
10 Oct 98		JOINTS & JAMS *Interscope IND 95604*	53	1
12May 01		REQUEST + LINE *Interscope 4970532* [1]	31	3

[1] featuring Macy GRAY

BLACK GORILLA
UK, male / female vocal / instrumental group (6 WEEKS) pos/wks

			pos	wks
27 Aug 77		GIMME DAT BANANA *Response SR 502*	29	6

BLACK GRAPE *UK, male vocal / instrumental group (25 WEEKS)* pos/wks

			pos	wks
10 Jun 95	●	REVEREND BLACK GRAPE *Radioactive RAXTD 16*	9	5
5 Aug 95	●	IN THE NAME OF THE FATHER *Radioactive RAXTD 19*	8	4
2 Dec 95		KELLY'S HEROES *Radioactive RAXTD 22*	17	5
25 May 96	●	FAT NECK *Radioactive RAXTD 24*	10	3
29 Jun 96	●	ENGLAND'S IRIE *Radioactive RAXTD 25* [1]	6	4
1 Nov 97		GET HIGHER *Radioactive RAXTD 32*	24	3
7 Mar 98		MARBLES *Radioactive RAXTD 33*	46	1

[1] Black Grape featuring Joe Strummer and Keith Allen

BLACK LACE (393 Top 500) *Group formed for 1979 Eurovision Song Contest re-emerged in 1983 as a duo, Colin Routh and Alan Barton (d. 23 Mar 1995). Maligned much 'Superman' and 'Agadoo' have remained popular party favourites (83 WEEKS)* pos/wks

			pos	wks
31 Mar 79		MARY ANN *EMI 2919*	42	4
24 Sep 83	●	SUPERMAN (GIOCA JOUER) *Flair FLA 105*	9	18
30 Jun 84	●	AGADOO *Flair FLA 107*	2	30

Date		Title / Label	Pos	Wks
24 Nov 84	●	**DO THE CONGA** *Flair FLA 108*	10	9
1 Jun 85		**EL VINO COLLAPSO** *Flair LACE 1*	42	5
7 Sep 85		**I SPEAKA DA LINGO** *Flair LACE 2*	49	4
7 Dec 85		**HOKEY COKEY** *Flair LACE 3*	31	6
20 Sep 86		**WIG WAM BAM** *Flair LACE 5*	63	3
26 Aug 89		**I AM THE MUSIC MAN** *Flair LACE 10*	52	3
22 Aug 98		**AGADOO (re-recording)** *NOW CDWAG 260*	64	1

BLACK LEGEND *Italy, male production duo (22 WEEKS)* pos/wks

Date		Title / Label	Pos	Wks
20 May 00		**YOU SEE THE TROUBLE WITH ME (import)** *Rise RISECD 072*	52	5
24 Jun 00	★	**YOU SEE THE TROUBLE WITH ME** *Eternal WEA 282CD* ■	1	15
4 Aug 01		**SOMEBODY** *WEA WEA 328CD* [1]	37	2

[1] Shortie vs Black Legend

No.1 version features a 'karaoke' re-recording of the original Barry White vocal by UK vocalist Spoonface

BLACK MACHINE *France / Nigeria, male vocal / instrumental duo – Herry Iyere Innocent and Alasson Wat (5 WEEKS)* pos/wks

Date		Title / Label	Pos	Wks
9 Apr 94		**HOW GEE** *London LONCD 348*	17	5

BLACK MAGIC *US, male producer – Lil' Louis (2 WEEKS)* pos/wks

Date		Title / Label	Pos	Wks
1 Jun 96		**FREEDOM (MAKE IT FUNKY)** *Positiva CDTIV 51*	41	2

See also LIL' LOUIS

BLACK RIOT *US, male producer (3 WEEKS)* pos/wks

Date		Title / Label	Pos	Wks
3 Dec 88		**WARLOCK / A DAY IN THE LIFE** *Champion CHAMP 75*	68	3

'A Day in the Life' listed only from 17 Dec 1988

BLACK ROB *US, male rapper – Robert Ross (8 WEEKS)* pos/wks

Date		Title / Label	Pos	Wks
12 Aug 00		**WHOA** *Puff Daddy / Arista 74321782732*	44	2
6 Oct 01		**BAD BOY FOR LIFE** *Bad Boy / Arista 74321889982* [1]	13	6

[1] P.Diddy featuring Black Rob and Mark Curry

BLACK SABBATH *UK, vocal / instrumental group (70 WEEKS)* pos/wks

Date		Title / Label	Pos	Wks
29 Aug 70	●	**PARANOID** *Vertigo 6059 010*	4	18
3 Jun 78		**NEVER SAY DIE** *Vertigo SAB 001*	21	8
14 Oct 78		**HARD ROAD** *Vertigo SAB 002*	33	4
5 Jul 80		**NEON KNIGHTS** *Vertigo SAB 3*	22	9
16 Aug 80		**PARANOID (re-issue)** *Nems BSS 101*	14	12
6 Dec 80		**DIE YOUNG** *Vertigo SAB 4*	41	7
7 Nov 81		**MOB RULES** *Vertigo SAB 5*	46	4
13 Feb 82		**TURN UP THE NIGHT** *Vertigo SAB 6*	37	5
15 Apr 89		**HEADLESS CROSS** *IRS EIRS 107*	62	1
13 Jun 92		**TV CRIMES** *IRS EIRSP 178*	33	2

Group UK only for first three hits and re-issue of 'Paranoid'

BLACK SHEEP *US, male rap duo (1 WEEK)* pos/wks

Date		Title / Label	Pos	Wks
19 Nov 94		**WITHOUT A DOUBT** *Mercury MERCD 417*	60	1

BLACK SLATE *UK / Jamaica, male vocal / instrumental group (15 WEEKS)* pos/wks

Date		Title / Label	Pos	Wks
20 Sep 80	●	**AMIGO** *Ensign ENY 42*	9	9
6 Dec 80		**BOOM BOOM** *Ensign ENY 47*	51	6

BLACK UHURU *Jamaica, male vocal / instrumental group (9 WEEKS)* pos/wks

Date		Title / Label	Pos	Wks
8 Sep 84		**WHAT IS LIFE?** *Island IS 150*	56	6
31 May 86		**THE GREAT TRAIN ROBBERY** *Real Authentic Sound RAS 7018*	62	3

Band of the BLACK WATCH *UK, military band (22 WEEKS)* pos/wks

Date		Title / Label	Pos	Wks
30 Aug 75	●	**SCOTCH ON THE ROCKS** *Spark SRL 1128*	8	14
13 Dec 75		**DANCE OF THE CUCKOOS (THE 'LAUREL AND HARDY' THEME)** *Spark SRL 1135*	37	8

Tony BLACKBURN *UK, male vocalist (7 WEEKS)* pos/wks

Date		Title / Label	Pos	Wks
24 Jan 68		**SO MUCH LOVE** *MGM 1375*	31	4
26 Mar 69		**IT'S ONLY LOVE** *MGM 1467*	42	3

BLACKBYRDS *US, male vocal / instrumental group (6 WEEKS)* pos/wks

Date		Title / Label	Pos	Wks
31 May 75		**WALKING IN RHYTHM** *Fantasy FTC 114*	23	6

BLACKFOOT *US, male vocal / instrumental group (5 WEEKS)* pos/wks

Date		Title / Label	Pos	Wks
6 Mar 82		**DRY COUNTY** *Atco K 11686*	43	4
18 Jun 83		**SEND ME AN ANGEL** *Atco B 9880*	66	1

J BLACKFOOT *US, male vocalist (4 WEEKS)* pos/wks

Date		Title / Label	Pos	Wks
17 Mar 84		**TAXI** *Allegiance ALES 2*	48	4

BLACKFOOT SUE *UK, male vocal / instrumental group (15 WEEKS)* pos/wks

Date		Title / Label	Pos	Wks
12 Aug 72	●	**STANDING IN THE ROAD** *Jam 13*	4	10
16 Dec 72		**SING DON'T SPEAK** *Jam 29*	36	5

BLACKGIRL *US, female vocal group (3 WEEKS)* pos/wks

Date		Title / Label	Pos	Wks
16 Jul 94		**90s GIRL** *RCA 74321217882*	23	3

BLACKHEARTS – *See Joan JETT and the BLACKHEARTS*

Honor BLACKMAN – *See Patrick MacNEE and Honor BLACKMAN*

BLACKNUSS *Sweden, male / female vocal / instrumental group (1 WEEK)* pos/wks

Date		Title / Label	Pos	Wks
28 Jun 97		**DINAH** *Arista 74321479762*	56	1

BLACKOUT *UK, male production / instrumental duo – Marc Dillon and Pat Dickins (1 WEEK)* pos/wks

Date		Title / Label	Pos	Wks
27 Mar 99		**GOTTA HAVE HOPE** *Multiply CDMULTY 47*	46	1

BLACKOUT *UK, male / female vocal / rap group (8 WEEKS)* pos/wks

Date		Title / Label	Pos	Wks
31 Mar 01		**MR DJ** *Independiente ISOM 48MS*	19	7
6 Oct 01		**GET UP** *Independiente ISOM 52MS*	67	1

Bill BLACK'S COMBO *US, male instrumentalist – bass (8 WEEKS)* pos/wks

Date		Title / Label	Pos	Wks
8 Sep 60		**WHITE SILVER SANDS** *London HLU 9090*	50	1
3 Nov 60		**DON'T BE CRUEL** *London HLU 9212*	32	7

BLACKSTREET *US, male vocal group (70 WEEKS)* pos/wks

Date		Title / Label	Pos	Wks
19 Jun 93		**BABY BE MINE** *MCA MCSTD 1772* [1]	37	3
13 Aug 94		**BOOTI CALL** *Interscope A 8250CD*	56	1
11 Feb 95		**U BLOW MY MIND** *Interscope A 8222CD*	39	2
27 May 95		**JOY** *Interscope A 8195CD*	56	2
19 Oct 96	●	**NO DIGGITY** *Interscope IND 95003* [2] ▲	9	7
8 Mar 97		**GET ME HOME** *Def Jam DEFCD 32* [3]	11	5
26 Apr 97	●	**DON'T LEAVE ME** *Interscope IND 95534*	6	10
27 Sep 97	●	**FIX** *Interscope IND 97521*	7	5
13 Dec 97		**(MONEY CAN'T) BUY ME LOVE** *Interscope IND 95563*	18	6
4 Apr 98	●	**I GET LONELY** *Virgin VSCDT 1683* [4]	5	7
27 Jun 98		**THE CITY IS MINE** *Northwestside 74321588012* [5]	38	2
12 Dec 98	●	**TAKE ME THERE** *Interscope IND 95620* [6]	7	9
17 Apr 99		**GIRLFRIEND / BOYFRIEND** *Interscope IND 95640* [7]	11	7
10 Jul 99		**GET READY** *Puff Daddy / Arista 74321682602* [8]	32	4

[1] BLACKstreet featuring Teddy Riley [2] BLACKstreet featuring Dr Dre [3] Foxy Brown featuring BLACKstreet [4] Janet featuring BLACKstreet [5] Jay-Z featuring BLACKstreet [6] BLACKstreet and Mya featuring Mase and Blinky Blink [7] BLACKstreet with Janet [8] Mase featuring BLACKstreet

BLACKWELLS *US, male vocal group (2 WEEKS)* pos/wks

Date		Title / Label	Pos	Wks
18 May 61		**LOVE OR MONEY** *London HLW 9334*	46	2

Richard BLACKWOOD *UK, male rapper (16 WEEKS)* pos/wks

Date		Title / Label	Pos	Wks
17 Jun 00	●	**MAMA – WHO DA MAN?** *East West MICKY 01CD1*	3	7
16 Sep 00	●	**1.2.3.4. GET WITH THE WICKED** *East West MICKY 05CD1*	10	6
25 Nov 00		**SOMEONE THERE FOR ME** *Hopefield / East West MICKY 06CD*	23	3

BLADE – *See Mark B & BLADE*

BLAGGERS I.T.A. *UK, male vocal / instrumental group (7 WEEKS)* pos/wks

12 Jun 93	**STRESSS** *Parlophone CDITA 1*	56	2
9 Oct 93	**OXYGEN** *Parlophone CDITA 2*	51	2
8 Jan 94	**ABANDON SHIP** *Parlophone CDITA 3*	48	3

BLAHZAY BLAHZAY *US, male rap duo (1 WEEK)* pos/wks

2 Mar 96	**DANGER** *Mercury Black Vinyl MBVCD 2*	56	1

Vivian BLAINE *US, female vocalist – Vivienne Stapleton (1 WEEK)* pos/wks

10 Jul 53	**BUSHEL AND A PECK** *Brunswick 05100*	12	1

BLAIR – *See Terry HALL*

BLAIR *UK, male vocalist (5 WEEKS)* pos/wks

2 Sep 95	**HAVE FUN GO MAD** *Mercury MERCD 443*	37	3
6 Jan 96	**LIFE** *Mercury MERCD 447*	44	2

Peter BLAKE *UK, male vocalist (4 WEEKS)* pos/wks

8 Oct 77	**LIPSMACKIN' ROCK 'N' ROLLIN'** *Pepper UP 36295*	40	4

BLAME *UK, male instrumental / production duo (2 WEEKS)* pos/wks

11 Apr 92	**MUSIC TAKES YOU** *Moving Shadow SHADOW 11*	48	2

BLAMELESS *UK, male vocal / instrumental group (5 WEEKS)* pos/wks

4 Nov 95	**TOWN CLOWNS** *China WOKCD 2046*	56	1
23 Mar 96	**BREATHE (A LITTLE DEEPER)** *China WOKCD 2070*	27	3
1 Jun 96	**SIGNS...** *China WOKCD 2077*	49	1

BLANCMANGE *Electronic pop duo with penchant for Eastern rhythms, formed 1981 Blackburn, Lancashire, UK, split 1987. Comprised Neil Arthur (v/g), Stephen Luscombe (k). 'The Day Before You Came' was the first Abba hit to reach a higher position as a cover (71 WEEKS)* pos/wks

17 Apr 82	**GOD'S KITCHEN / I'VE SEEN THE WORD** *London BLANC 1*	65	2
31 Jul 82	**FEEL ME** *London BLANC 2*	46	5
30 Oct 82 ●	**LIVING ON THE CEILING** *London BLANC 3*	7	14
19 Feb 83	**WAVES** *London BLANC 4*	19	9
7 May 83 ●	**BLIND VISION** *London BLANC 5*	10	8
26 Nov 83	**THAT'S LOVE, THAT IT IS** *London BLANC 6*	33	8
14 Apr 84 ●	**DON'T TELL ME** *London BLANC 7*	8	10
21 Jul 84	**THE DAY BEFORE YOU CAME** *London BLANC 8*	22	8
7 Sep 85	**WHAT'S YOUR PROBLEM** *London BLANC 9*	40	5
10 May 86	**I CAN SEE IT** *London BLANC 11*	71	2

Billy BLAND *US, male vocalist (10 WEEKS)* pos/wks

19 May 60	**LET THE LITTLE GIRL DANCE** *London HL 9096*	15	10

BLANK & JONES *Germany, production duo (7 WEEKS)* pos/wks

26 Jun 99	**CREAM** *Devia DVNT 31CDS*	24	3
27 May 00	**AFTER LOVE** *Nebula NEBCDS 3*	57	1
30 Sep 00	**THE NIGHTFLY** *Nebula NEBCD 010*	55	1
3 Mar 01	**BEYOND TIME** *Gang Go / Edel 01245115 GAG*	53	2

BLAQUE IVORY *US, female vocal group (3 WEEKS)* pos/wks

3 Jul 99	**808** *Columbia 6674962*	31	3

BLAST featuring VDC
Italy, male / female vocal / instrumental group (5 WEEKS) pos/wks

18 Jun 94	**CRAYZY MAN** *UMM MCSTD 1982*	22	3
12 Nov 94	**PRINCES OF THE NIGHT** *UMM MCSTD 2011*	40	2

Melanie BLATT – *See ALL SAINTS; ARTFUL DODGER*

BLAZE featuring Palmer BROWN
US, male production duo and US, male vocalist (2 WEEKS) pos/wks

10 Mar 01	**MY BEAT** *Black & Blue / Kickin' NEOCD 053*	53	2

BLEACHIN' *UK, male vocal / instrumental group (4 WEEKS)* pos/wks

22 Jul 00	**PEAKIN'** *Boiler House / Arista 74321774812*	32	3
2 Sep 00	**PEAKIN' (re-entry)** *Boiler House / Arista 74321774812*	70	1

BLESSID UNION OF SOULS
US, male vocal / instrumental group (6 WEEKS) pos/wks

27 May 95	**I BELIEVE** *EMI CDEM 374*	29	5
23 Mar 96	**LET ME BE THE ONE** *EMI CDEM 387*	74	1

BLESSING *UK, male vocal / instrumental group (13 WEEKS)* pos/wks

11 May 91	**HIGHWAY 5** *MCA MCS 1509*	42	6
18 Jan 92	**HIGHWAY 5 (re-mix)** *MCA MCS 1603*	30	6
19 Feb 94	**SOUL LOVE** *MCA MCSTD 1940*	73	1

Mary J BLIGE (285 Top 500) *Original queen of hip hop and soul, b. 11 Jan 1971, Atlanta, Georgia, US. Transatlantic chart regular since platinum-selling debut album 'What's The 411?' (1992). Recorded with numerous top acts including Elton John, Puff Daddy, Eric Clapton, Lauryn Hill, Bono, R Kelly, Wyclef Jean and Aretha Franklin (105 WEEKS)* pos/wks

28 Nov 92	**REAL LOVE** *Uptown MCS 1721*	68	2
27 Feb 93	**REMINISCE** *Uptown MCSTD 1731*	31	4
12 Jun 93	**YOU REMIND ME** *Uptown MCSTD 1770*	48	3
28 Aug 93	**REAL LOVE (re-mix)** *Uptown MCSTD 1922*	26	4
4 Dec 93	**YOU DON'T HAVE TO WORRY** *Uptown MCSTD 1948*	36	2
14 May 94	**MY LOVE** *Uptown MCSTD 1972*	29	3
10 Dec 94	**BE HAPPY** *Uptown MCSTD 2033*	30	4
15 Apr 95	**I'M GOIN' DOWN** *Uptown MCSTD 2053*	12	4
29 Jul 95 ●	**I'LL BE THERE FOR YOU – YOU'RE ALL I NEED TO GET BY** *Def Jam DEFDX 11* [1]	10	5
30 Sep 95	**MARY JANE (ALL NIGHT LONG)** *Uptown MCSTD 2088*	17	4
16 Dec 95	**(YOU MAKE ME FEEL LIKE A) NATURAL WOMAN** *Uptown MCSTD 2108*	23	3
30 Mar 96	**NOT GON' CRY** *Arista 74321358252*	39	2
1 Mar 97	**CAN'T KNOCK THE HUSTLE** *Northwestside 74321447192* [2]	30	2
17 May 97	**LOVE IS ALL WE NEED** *Uptown MCSTD 48053*	15	4
16 Aug 97 ●	**EVERYTHING** *MCA MCSTD 48059*	6	9
29 Nov 97	**MISSING YOU** *MCA MCSTD 48071*	19	3
3 Jan 98	**MISSING YOU (re-entry)** *MCA MCSTD 48071*	72	1
31 Jan 98	**MISSING YOU (2nd re-entry)** *MCA MCSTD 48071*	74	1
11 Jul 98	**SEVEN DAYS** *MCA MCSTD 48083* [3]	22	3
13 Mar 99 ●	**AS** *Epic 6670122* [4]	4	10
21 Aug 99	**ALL THAT I CAN SAY** *MCA MCSTD 40215*	29	3
11 Dec 99	**DEEP INSIDE** *MCA MCSTD 40224*	42	2
29 Apr 00	**GIVE ME YOU** *MCA MCSTD 40230*	19	4
16 Dec 00 ●	**911** *Columbia 6706122* [5]	9	10
6 Oct 01 ●	**FAMILY AFFAIR** *MCA MCSTD 40267* ▲	8	13

[1] Method Man featuring Mary J Blige [2] Jay-Z featuring Mary J Blige [3] Mary J Blige featuring George Benson [4] George Michael and Mary J Blige [5] Wyclef Jean featuring Mary J Blige

BLIND MELON *US, male vocal / instrumental group (13 WEEKS)* pos/wks

12 Jun 93	**TONES OF HOME** *Capitol CDCL 687*	62	2
11 Dec 93	**NO RAIN** *Capitol CDCL 699*	17	6
9 Jul 94	**CHANGE** *Capitol CDCL 717*	35	3
5 Aug 95	**GALAXIE** *Capitol CDCLS 755*	37	2

BLINK *Ireland, male vocal / instrumental group (1 WEEK)* pos/wks

16 Jul 94	**HAPPY DAY** *Lime CDR 6385*	57	1

BLINK 182 *US, male vocal / instrumental group (29 WEEKS)* pos/wks

2 Oct 99	**WHAT'S MY AGE AGAIN?** *MCA MCSTD 40219*	38	2
25 Mar 00 ●	**ALL THE SMALL THINGS** *MCA MCSTD 40223*	2	10
8 Jul 00	**WHAT'S MY AGE AGAIN? (re-issue)** *MCA MCSZD 40219*	17	6
14 Jul 01	**THE ROCK SHOW** *MCA MCSTD 40259*	14	7
6 Oct 01	**FIRST DATE** *MCA MCSTD 40264*	31	3
3 Nov 01	**FIRST DATE (re-entry)** *MCA MCSTD 40264*	74	1

BLINKY BLINK – *See BLACKSTREET*

BLOCKHEADS – *See Ian DURY and the BLOCKHEADS*

BLOCKSTER *UK / Italy, male production group (11 WEEKS)* pos/wks

			pos	wks
16 Jan 99	●	**YOU SHOULD BE ...** *Sound of Ministry MOSCDS 128*	3	9
24 Jul 99		**GROOVELINE** *Sound of Ministry MOSCDS 131*	18	2

Kristine BLOND *Denmark, female vocalist (5 WEEKS)* pos/wks

			pos	wks
11 Apr 98		**LOVE SHY** *Reverb BNOISE 1CD*	22	3
11 Nov 00		**LOVE SHY (re-mix)** *Relentless RELENT 4CDS*	28	2

BLONDIE (121 Top 500) *Influential New York-based quintet, fronted by ex-Bunny Girl Deborah Harry (v) (b. 1 Jul 1945, Miami) and fiancé Chris Stein (g). Few acts were more popular internationally 1978-1981, and no other US act in the 1980s matched their three No.1s (169 WEEKS)* pos/wks

			pos	wks
18 Feb 78	●	**DENIS** *Chrysalis CHS 2204*	2	14
6 May 78	●	**(I'M ALWAYS TOUCHED BY YOUR) PRESENCE DEAR** *Chrysalis CHS 2217*	10	9
26 Aug 78		**PICTURE THIS** *Chrysalis CHS 2242*	12	11
11 Nov 78	●	**HANGING ON THE TELEPHONE** *Chrysalis CHS 2266*	5	12
27 Jan 79	★	**HEART OF GLASS** *Chrysalis CHS 2275* ◆ ▲	1	12
19 May 79	★	**SUNDAY GIRL** *Chrysalis CHS 2320*	1	13
29 Sep 79	●	**DREAMING** *Chrysalis CHS 2350*	2	8
24 Nov 79		**UNION CITY BLUE** *Chrysalis CHS 2400*	13	10
23 Feb 80	★	**ATOMIC** *Chrysalis CHS 2410*	1	9
12 Apr 80	★	**CALL ME** *Chrysalis CHS 2414* ▲	1	9
8 Nov 80	★	**THE TIDE IS HIGH** *Chrysalis CHS 2465* ▲	1	12
24 Jan 81	●	**RAPTURE** *Chrysalis CHS 2485* ▲	5	8
8 May 82		**ISLAND OF LOST SOULS** *Chrysalis CHS 2608*	11	9
24 Jul 82		**WAR CHILD** *Chrysalis CHS 2624*	39	4
3 Dec 88		**DENIS (re-mix)** *Chrysalis CHS 3328*	50	3
11 Feb 89		**CALL ME (re-mix)** *Chrysalis CHS 3342*	61	2
10 Sep 94		**ATOMIC (re-mix)** *Chrysalis CDCHS 5013*	19	4
8 Jul 95		**HEART OF GLASS (re-mix)** *Chrysalis CSCHS 5023*	15	3
28 Oct 95		**UNION CITY BLUE (re-mix)** *Chrysalis CDCHS 5027*	31	2
13 Feb 99	★	**MARIA** *Beyond 74321645632* ■	1	12
12 Jun 99		**NOTHING IS REAL BUT THE GIRL** *Beyond 74321669472*	26	3

See also Deborah HARRY

BLOOD SWEAT AND TEARS
US / Canada, male vocal / instrumental group (6 WEEKS) pos/wks

			pos	wks
30 Apr 69		**YOU'VE MADE ME SO VERY HAPPY** *CBS 4116*	35	6

BLOODHOUND GANG
US, male vocal / instrumental group (21 WEEKS) pos/wks

			pos	wks
23 Aug 97		**WHY'S EVERYBODY ALWAYS PICKIN' ON ME?** *Geffen GFSTD 22252*	56	1
15 Apr 00	●	**THE BAD TOUCH** *Geffen 4972672*	4	14
2 Sep 00		**THE BALLAD OF CHASEY LAIN** *Geffen 4973812*	15	6

Male / female act for 1997 debut hit

BLOODSTONE *US, male vocal / instrumental group (4 WEEKS)* pos/wks

			pos	wks
18 Aug 73		**NATURAL HIGH** *Decca F 13382*	40	4

Bobby BLOOM *US, male vocalist (24 WEEKS)* pos/wks

			pos	wks
29 Aug 70	●	**MONTEGO BAY** *Polydor 2058 051*	3	14
12 Dec 70		**MONTEGO BAY (re-entry)** *Polydor 2058 051*	42	3
9 Jan 71		**HEAVY MAKES YOU HAPPY** *Polydor 2001 122*	31	5
9 Jan 71		**MONTEGO BAY (2nd re-entry)** *Polydor 2058 051*	47	2

BLOOMSBURY SET *UK, male vocal / instrumental group (3 WEEKS)* pos/wks

			pos	wks
25 Jun 83		**HANGING AROUND WITH THE BIG BOYS** *Stiletto STL 13*	56	3

Tanya BLOUNT *US, female vocalist (1 WEEK)* pos/wks

			pos	wks
11 Jun 94		**I'M GONNA MAKE YOU MINE** *Polydor PZCD 315*	69	1

Kurtis BLOW *US, male rapper (23 WEEKS)* pos/wks

			pos	wks
15 Dec 79		**CHRISTMAS RAPPIN'** *Mercury BLOW 7*	30	6
11 Oct 80		**THE BREAKS** *Mercury BLOW 8*	47	4
16 Mar 85		**PARTY TIME (THE GO-GO EDIT)** *Club JAB 12*	67	1
15 Jun 85		**SAVE YOUR LOVE (FOR NUMBER 1)** *Club JAB 14* [1]	66	2
18 Jan 86		**IF I RULED THE WORLD** *Club JAB 26*	24	8
8 Nov 86		**I'M CHILLIN'** *Club JAB 42*	64	2

[1] René and Angela featuring Kurtis Blow

BLOW MONKEYS *UK, male vocal / instrumental group (46 WEEKS)* pos/wks

			pos	wks
1 Mar 86		**DIGGING YOUR SCENE** *RCA PB 40599*	12	10
17 May 86		**WICKED WAYS** *RCA MONK 2*	60	2
31 Jan 87	●	**IT DOESN'T HAVE TO BE THIS WAY** *RCA MONK 4*	5	8
28 Mar 87		**OUT WITH HER** *RCA MONK 5*	30	6
30 May 87		**(CELEBRATE) THE DAY AFTER YOU** *RCA MONK 6* [1]	52	2
15 Aug 87		**SOME KIND OF WONDERFUL** *RCA MONK 7*	67	1
6 Aug 88		**THIS IS YOUR LIFE** *RCA PB 42149*	70	2
8 Apr 89		**THIS IS YOUR LIFE (re-mix)** *RCA PB 42695*	32	5
15 Jul 89		**CHOICE?** *RCA PB 42885* [2]	22	6
14 Oct 89		**SLAVES NO MORE** *RCA PB 43201* [2]	73	2
26 May 90		**SPRINGTIME FOR THE WORLD** *RCA PB 43623*	69	2

[1] Blow Monkeys with Curtis Mayfield [2] Blow Monkeys featuring Sylvia Tella

BLU PETER *UK, male DJ / producer (1 WEEK)* pos/wks

			pos	wks
21 Mar 98		**TELL ME WHAT YOU WANT / JAMES HAS KITTENS** *React CDREACT 285*	70	1

BLUE *UK, male vocal / instrumental group (8 WEEKS)* pos/wks

			pos	wks
30 Apr 77		**GONNA CAPTURE YOUR HEART** *Rocket ROKN 522*	18	8

BLUE *UK, male vocal group (31 WEEKS)* pos/wks

			pos	wks
2 Jun 01	●	**ALL RISE** *Innocent SINCD 28*	4	13
8 Sep 01	★	**TOO CLOSE** *Innocent SINCD 30* ■	1	13
24 Nov 01	★	**IF YOU COME BACK** *Innocent SINCD 32* ■	1	6+

Babbity BLUE *UK, female vocalist (2 WEEKS)* pos/wks

			pos	wks
11 Feb 65		**DON'T MAKE ME (FALL IN LOVE WITH YOU)** *Decca F 12053*	48	2

Barry BLUE *UK, male vocalist – Barry Green (48 WEEKS)* pos/wks

			pos	wks
28 Jul 73	●	**(DANCING) ON A SATURDAY NIGHT** *Bell 1295*	2	15
3 Nov 73	●	**DO YOU WANNA DANCE** *Bell 1336*	7	12
2 Mar 74		**SCHOOL LOVE** *Bell 1345*	11	9
3 Aug 74		**MISS HIT AND RUN** *Bell 1364*	26	7
26 Oct 74		**HOT SHOT** *Bell 1379*	23	5

See also CRY SISCO!

BLUE ADONIS featuring LIL' MISS MAX
Belgium, male production duo, female vocalist (3 WEEKS) pos/wks

			pos	wks
17 Oct 98		**DISCO COP** *Serious SERR 002CD*	27	3

BLUE AEROPLANES
UK, male / female vocal / instrumental group (3 WEEKS) pos/wks

			pos	wks
17 Feb 90		**JACKET HANGS** *Ensign ENY 628*	72	1
26 May 90		**. . . AND STONES** *Ensign ENY 632*	63	2

BLUE AMAZON *UK, male production duo / female vocalist (2 WEEKS)* pos/wks

			pos	wks
17 May 97		**AND THEN THE RAIN FALLS** *Sony S2 BAS 301 CD*	53	1
1 Jul 00		**BREATHE** *Subversive SUB 61D*	73	1

BLUE BAMBOO *Belgium, male producer – Johan Gielen (4 WEEKS)* pos/wks

			pos	wks
3 Dec 94		**ABC AND D . . .** *Escapade CDJAPE 6*	23	4

See also AIRSCAPE; CUBIC 22; TRANSFORMER 2

BLUE BOY *UK, male producer – Alexis Blackmore (16 WEEKS)* pos/wks

			pos	wks
1 Feb 97	●	**REMEMBER ME** *Pharm CDPHARM 1*	8	13
23 Aug 97		**SANDMAN** *Sidewalk CDSWALK 001*	25	3

UK No.1 ★ UK Top 10 ● Still on chart + UK million seller ◆ UK entry at No.1 ■ US No.1 ▲

BLUE FEATHER *Holland, male vocal / instrumental group (4 WEEKS)* pos/wks

			pos	wks
3 Jul 82		LET'S FUNK TONIGHT *Mercury MER 109*	50	4

BLUE FLAMES – *See Georgie FAME*

BLUE GRASS BOYS – *See Johnny DUNCAN and the BLUE GRASS BOYS*

BLUE HAZE *UK, male vocal / instrumental group (6 WEEKS)* pos/wks

			pos	wks
18 Mar 72		SMOKE GETS IN YOUR EYES *A & M AMS 891*	32	6

BLUE JEANS – *See Bob B SOXX and the BLUE JEANS*

BLUE MELONS *UK, male / female vocal / instrumental group (1 WEEK)* pos/wks

			pos	wks
8 Jun 96		DO WAH DIDDY DIDDY *Fundamental FUNDCD 1*	70	1

BLUE MERCEDES *UK, male vocal / instrumental duo (18 WEEKS)* pos/wks

			pos	wks
10 Oct 87		I WANT TO BE YOUR PROPERTY *MCA BONA 1*	23	11
13 Feb 88		SEE WANT MUST HAVE *MCA BONA 2*	57	2
23 Jul 88		LOVE IS THE GUN *MCA BONA 3*	46	5

BLUE MINK (394 Top 500) *UK-based session musician supergroup with writers Roger Cook and Roger Greenaway providing the classic pop songs for group members Roger Cook (v), Madeline Bell b. 23 Jul 1942, Newark, New Jersey, US (v), Roger Coulam (k), Herbie Flowers (b), Barry Morgan (d). Greenaway received OBE in 2001 (83 WEEKS)* pos/wks

			pos	wks
15 Nov 69	●	MELTING POT *Philips BF 1818*	3	15
28 Mar 70	●	GOOD MORNING FREEDOM *Philips BF 1838*	10	10
19 Sep 70		OUR WORLD *Philips 6006 042*	17	9
29 May 71	●	BANNER MAN *Regal Zonophone RZ 3034*	3	14
11 Nov 72		STAY WITH ME *Regal Zonophone RZ 3064*	11	13
17 Feb 73		STAY WITH ME (re-entry) *Regal Zonophone RZ 3064*	43	2
3 Mar 73		BY THE DEVIL (I WAS TEMPTED) *EMI 2007*	26	9
23 Jun 73	●	RANDY *EMI 2028*	9	11

BLUE NILE *UK, male vocal / instrumental group (4 WEEKS)* pos/wks

			pos	wks
30 Sep 89		THE DOWNTOWN LIGHTS *Linn LKS 3*	67	1
29 Sep 90		HEADLIGHTS ON THE PARADE *Linn LKS 4*	72	1
19 Jan 91		SATURDAY NIGHT *Linn LKS 5*	50	2

BLUE OYSTER CULT *US, male vocal / instrumental group (14 WEEKS)* pos/wks

			pos	wks
20 May 78		(DON'T FEAR) THE REAPER *CBS 6333*	16	14

BLUE PEARL
UK / US, male / female vocal / instrumental group (29 WEEKS) pos/wks

			pos	wks
7 Jul 90	●	NAKED IN THE RAIN *Big Life BLR 23*	4	13
3 Nov 90		LITTLE BROTHER *Big Life BLR 32*	31	5
11 Jan 92		(CAN YOU) FEEL THE PASSION *Big Life BLR 67*	14	6
25 Jul 92		MOTHER DAWN *Big Life BLR 73*	50	2
27 Nov 93		FIRE OF LOVE *Logic 74321170292* [1]	71	1
4 Jul 98		NAKED IN THE RAIN '98 (re-recording) *Malarky MLKD 7*	22	2

[1] Jungle High with Blue Pearl

BLUE RONDO A LA TURK
UK, male vocal / instrumental group (9 WEEKS) pos/wks

			pos	wks
14 Nov 81		ME AND MR SANCHEZ *Virgin VS 463*	40	4
13 Mar 82		KLACTOVEESEDSTEIN *Diable Noir VS 476*	50	5

BLUE ZOO *UK, male vocal / instrumental group (17 WEEKS)* pos/wks

			pos	wks
12 Jun 82		I'M YOUR MAN *Magnet MAG 224*	55	3
16 Oct 82		CRY BOY CRY *Magnet MAG 234*	13	10
28 May 83		I JUST CAN'T (FORGIVE AND FORGET) *Magnet MAG 241*	60	4

BLUEBELLS *UK, male vocal / instrumental group (49 WEEKS)* pos/wks

			pos	wks
12 Mar 83		CATH / WILL SHE ALWAYS BE WAITING *London LON 20*	62	2
9 Jul 83		SUGAR BRIDGE (IT WILL STAND) *London LON 27*	72	1
24 Mar 84		I'M FALLING *London LON 45*	11	12
23 Jun 84	●	YOUNG AT HEART *London LON 49*	8	12
1 Sep 84		CATH (re-issue) *London LON 54*	38	7
9 Feb 85		ALL I AM (IS LOVING YOU) *London LON 58*	58	3
27 Mar 93	★	YOUNG AT HEART (re-issue) *London LONCD 338*	1	12

BLUENOTES – *See Harold MELVIN and the BLUENOTES*

BLUES BAND *UK, male vocal / instrumental group (2 WEEKS)* pos/wks

			pos	wks
12 Jul 80		BLUES BAND (EP) *Arista BOOT 2*	68	2

Tracks on Blues Band (EP): Maggie's Farm / Ain't it Tuff / Diddy Wah Diddy / Back Door Man

BLUES BROTHERS
US, male vocal duo – John Belushi and Dan Ackroyd (8 WEEKS) pos/wks

			pos	wks
7 Apr 90		EVERYBODY NEEDS SOMEBODY TO LOVE *East West A7591*	12	8

For the first two weeks, the flip side of 'Everybody Needs Somebody to Love' – 'Think' by Aretha Franklin – was listed

BLUETONES *UK, male vocal / instrumental group (41 WEEKS)* pos/wks

			pos	wks
17 Jun 95		ARE YOU BLUE OR ARE YOU BLIND *Superior Quality BLUE 001CD*	31	2
14 Oct 95		BLUETONIC *Superior Quality BLUE 002CD*	19	3
3 Feb 96	●	SLIGHT RETURN *Superior Quality BLUE 003CD*	2	8
11 May 96	●	CUT SOME RUG / CASTLE ROCK *Superior Quality BLUE 005CD*	7	5
20 Jul 96		CUT SOME RUG / CASTLE ROCK (re-entry) *Superior Quality BLUE 005CD*	73	1
28 Sep 96	●	MARBLEHEAD JOHNSON *Superior Quality BLUE 006CD*	7	6
21 Feb 98	●	SOLOMON BITES THE WORM *Superior Quality BLUED 007*	10	3
9 May 98		IF ... *Superior Quality BLUED 009*	13	5
8 Aug 98		SLEAZY BED TRACK *Superior Quality BLUED 010*	35	2
4 Mar 00		KEEP THE HOME FIRES BURNING *Superior Quality BLUED 012*	13	3
20 May 00		AUTOPHILIA *Superior Quality BLUED 013*	18	3

Colin BLUNSTONE *UK, male vocalist (29 WEEKS)* pos/wks

			pos	wks
12 Feb 72		SAY YOU DON'T MIND *Epic EPC 7765*	15	9
11 Nov 72		I DON'T BELIEVE IN MIRACLES *Epic EPC 8434*	31	6
17 Feb 73		HOW COULD WE DARE TO BE WRONG *Epic EPC 1197*	45	2
14 Mar 81		WHAT BECOMES OF THE BROKEN HEARTED *Stiff BROKEN 1* [1]	13	10
29 May 82		TRACKS OF MY TEARS *PRT 7P 236*	60	2

[1] Dave Stewart. Guest vocals: Colin Blunstone

See also ARGENT; Neil MacARTHUR; ZOMBIES

BLUR (195 Top 500) *Prime movers of Britpop: Damon Albarn (v/k), Graham Coxon (g), Alex James (b), Dave Rowntree (d). They won a record four Brit awards in 1995, and their first No.1 caused a media storm when it outpaced 'Roll With It' by Britpop rivals Oasis (132 WEEKS)* pos/wks

			pos	wks
27 Oct 90		SHE'S SO HIGH / I KNOW *Food FOOD 26*	48	3
27 Apr 91	●	THERE'S NO OTHER WAY *Food FOOD 29*	8	8
10 Aug 91		BANG *Food FOOD 31*	24	4
11 Apr 92		POPSCENE *Food FOOD 37*	32	2
1 May 93		FOR TOMORROW *Food CDFOODS 40*	28	4
10 Jul 93		CHEMICAL WORLD *Food CDFOODS 45*	28	4
16 Oct 93		SUNDAY SUNDAY *Food CDFOOD 46*	26	3
19 Mar 94	●	GIRLS AND BOYS *Food CDFOODS 47*	5	7
11 Jun 94		TO THE END *Food CDFOODS 50*	16	5
3 Sep 94	●	PARKLIFE *Food CDFOOD 53*	10	7
19 Nov 94		END OF A CENTURY *Food CDFOOD 56*	19	3
26 Aug 95	★	COUNTRY HOUSE *Food CDFOODS 63* ■	1	11
9 Sep 95		COUNTRY HOUSE *Food FOODS 63*	57	1
25 Nov 95	●	THE UNIVERSAL *Food CDFOODS 69*	5	9
24 Feb 96	●	STEREOTYPES *Food CDFOOD 73*	7	5
11 May 96	●	CHARMLESS MAN *Food CDFOOD 77*	5	6
1 Feb 97	★	BEETLEBUM *Food CDFOODS 89* ■	1	5
19 Apr 97	●	SONG 2 *Food CDFOODS 93*	2	5
26 Apr 97		BEETLEBUM (re-entry) *Food CDFOODS 89*	59	2
28 Jun 97	●	ON YOUR OWN *Food CDFOOD 98*	5	5
27 Sep 97		MOR *Food CDFOOD 107*	15	3
6 Mar 99	●	TENDER *Food CDFOODS 117*	2	10
10 Jul 99		COFFEE + TV *Food CDFOODS 122*	11	7

		pos	wks
27 Nov 99	NO DISTANCE LEFT TO RUN *Food CDFOOD 123*	14	3
22 Jan 00	NO DISTANCE LEFT TO RUN (re-entry) *Food CDFOOD 123*	65	1
28 Oct 00 ●	MUSIC IS MY RADAR *Food / Parlophone CDFOODS 135*	10	7
13 Jan 01	MUSIC IS MY RADAR (re-entry) *Food / Parlophone CDFOODS 135*	66	2

Chart rules allow for a maximum of three formats; the 7-inch of 'Country House', already available on two CDs and cassette, was therefore listed separately

BM DUBS present MR RUMBLE featuring BRASS TOOTH and KEE *UK, male production group (2 WEEKS)*

		pos	wks
17 Mar 01	WHOOMP THERE IT IS *Incentive CENT 16CDS*	32	2

BMR featuring FELICIA *Germany, male producers – Michi Lange featuring female vocalist (2 WEEKS)*

		pos	wks
1 May 99	CHECK IT OUT (EVERYBODY) *AM:PM CDAMPM 120*	29	2

BMU *US / UK, male vocal group (2 WEEKS)*

		pos	wks
18 Feb 95	U WILL KNOW *Mercury MERCD 420*	23	2

BOB and EARL
US, male vocal duo – Bobby Relf and Earl Nelson (13 WEEKS)

		pos	wks
12 Mar 69 ●	HARLEM SHUFFLE *Island WIP 6053*	7	13

BOB and MARCIA *Jamaica, male / female vocal duo – Bob Andy and Marcia Griffiths (25 WEEKS)*

		pos	wks
14 Mar 70 ●	YOUNG GIFTED AND BLACK *Harry J HJ 6605*	5	12
5 Jun 71	PIED PIPER *Trojan TR 7818*	11	13

BOB THE BUILDER *UK, male silicone puppet building contractor – Neil Morrissey (38 WEEKS)*

		pos	wks
16 Dec 00 ★	CAN WE FIX IT *BBC Music WMSS 60372*	1	18
28 Apr 01	CAN WE FIX IT (re-entry) *BBC Music WMSS 60372*	59	2
2 Jun 01	CAN WE FIX IT (2nd re-entry) *BBC Music WMSS 60372*	54	2
15 Sep 01 ★	MAMBO NO.5 *BBC Music WMSS 60442* ■	1	16+

BOBBYSOCKS *Norway / Sweden, female vocal duo (4 WEEKS)*

		pos	wks
25 May 85	LET IT SWING *RCA PB 40127*	44	4

Su Su BOBIEN – *See MASS SYNDICATE featuring Su Su BOBIEN*

Andrea BOCELLI *Italy, male vocalist (24 WEEKS)*

		pos	wks
24 May 97 ●	TIME TO SAY GOODBYE (CON TE PARTIRO) *Coalition COLA 003CD* [1]	2	14
25 Sep 99	CANTO DELLA TERRA *Polydor / Sugar 5613192*	25	4
18 Dec 99	AVE MARIA *Philips 4644852*	65	1
1 Jul 00	CANTO DELLA TERRA (re-entry) *Polydor / Sugar 5613192*	24	5

[1] Sarah Brightman and Andrea Bocelli

Karen BODDINGTON and Mark WILLIAMS
Australia, female / male vocal duo (1 WEEK)

		pos	wks
2 Sep 89	HOME AND AWAY *First Night SCORE 19*	73	1

BODY COUNT *US, male rap / instrumental group (4 WEEKS)*

		pos	wks
8 Oct 94	BORN DEAD *Rhyme Syndicate SYNDG 4*	28	2
17 Dec 94	NECESSARY EVIL *Virgin VSCDX 1529*	45	2

See also ICE-T

BODYSNATCHERS
UK, female vocal / instrumental group (12 WEEKS)

		pos	wks
15 Mar 80	LET'S DO ROCK STEADY *2 Tone CHSTT 9*	22	9
19 Jul 80	EASY LIFE *2 Tone CHSTT 12*	50	3

Humphrey BOGART – *See Dooley WILSON*

Hamilton BOHANNON
US, male vocalist / instrumentalist – drums (38 WEEKS)

		pos	wks
15 Feb 75	SOUTH AFRICAN MAN *Brunswick BR 16*	22	8
24 May 75 ●	DISCO STOMP *Brunswick BR 19*	6	12
5 Jul 75	FOOT STOMPIN' MUSIC *Brunswick BR 21*	23	6
6 Sep 75	HAPPY FEELING *Brunswick BR 24*	49	3
26 Aug 78	LET'S START THE DANCE *Mercury 6167 700*	56	4
13 Feb 82	LET'S START TO DANCE AGAIN *London HL 10582*	49	5

BOILING POINT *US, male vocal / instrumental group (6 WEEKS)*

		pos	wks
27 May 78	LET'S GET FUNKTIFIED *Bang BANG 1312*	41	6

Marc BOLAN – *See T. REX*

CJ BOLLAND *Belgium, male producer (10 WEEKS)*

		pos	wks
5 Oct 96	SUGAR IS SWEETER *Internal LIECD 35*	11	5
17 May 97	THE PROPHET *ffrr FCD 300*	19	3
3 Jul 99	IT AIN'T GONNA BE ME *Essential Recordings ESCD 5*	35	2

See also RAVESIGNAL III

Michael BOLTON (252 Top 500) *Soulful rock balladeer / songwriter who initially recorded under his real name, Michael Bolotin (b. 26 Feb 1953, Connecticut, US), and fronted recording groups The Nomads and Blackjack (113 WEEKS)*

		pos	wks
17 Feb 90 ●	HOW AM I SUPPOSED TO LIVE WITHOUT YOU *CBS 655397 7* ▲	3	10
28 Apr 90 ●	HOW CAN WE BE LOVERS *CBS 655918 7*	10	10
21 Jul 90	WHEN I'M BACK ON MY FEET AGAIN *CBS 656077 7*	44	5
20 Apr 91	LOVE IS A WONDERFUL THING *Columbia 6567717*	23	8
27 Jul 91	TIME LOVE AND TENDERNESS *Columbia 6569897*	28	7
9 Nov 91 ●	WHEN A MAN LOVES A WOMAN *Columbia 6574887* ▲	8	9
8 Feb 92	STEEL BARS *Columbia 6577257*	17	6
9 May 92	MISSING YOU NOW *Columbia 6579917* [1]	28	4
31 Oct 92	TO LOVE SOMEBODY *Columbia 6584557*	16	6
26 Dec 92	DRIFT AWAY *Columbia 6588657*	18	5
13 Mar 93	REACH OUT I'LL BE THERE *Columbia 6588972*	37	4
13 Nov 93	SAID I LOVED YOU BUT I LIED *Columbia 6598762*	15	8
26 Feb 94	SOUL OF MY SOUL *Columbia 6601772*	32	3
14 May 94	LEAN ON ME *Columbia 6604132*	14	7
9 Sep 95 ●	CAN I TOUCH YOU ... THERE *Columbia 6624385*	6	9
2 Dec 95	A LOVE SO BEAUTIFUL *Columbia 6627092*	27	5
16 Mar 96	SOUL PROVIDER *Columbia 6629812*	35	3
8 Nov 97	THE BEST OF LOVE / GO THE DISTANCE *Columbia 6652802*	14	4

[1] Michael Bolton featuring Kenny G

BOMB THE BASS *UK, male producer – Tim Simenon (50 WEEKS)*

		pos	wks
20 Feb 88 ●	BEAT DIS *Mister-ron DOOD 1*	2	9
27 Aug 88 ●	MEGABLAST / DON'T MAKE ME WAIT *Mister-ron DOOD 2* [1]	6	9
26 Nov 88 ●	SAY A LITTLE PRAYER *Rhythm King DOOD 3* [2]	10	10
27 Jul 91 ●	WINTER IN JULY *Rhythm King 6572757*	7	9
9 Nov 91	THE AIR YOU BREATHE *Rhythm King 6575387*	52	3
2 May 92	KEEP GIVING ME LOVE *Rhythm King 6579887*	62	2
1 Oct 94	BUG POWDER DUST *Stoned Heights BRCD 300* [3]	24	3
17 Dec 94	DARKHEART *Stoned Heights BRCD 305* [4]	35	3
1 Apr 95	1 TO 1 RELIGION *Stoned Heights BRCD 313* [5]	53	1
16 Sep 95	SANDCASTLES *Fourth & Broadway BRCD 324* [6]	54	1

[1] Bomb The Bass featuring Merlin and Antonia / Bomb The Bass featuring Lorraine and Lose [2] Bomb the Bass featuring Maureen [3] Bomb The Bass featuring Justin Warfield [4] Bomb The Bass featuring Spikey Tee [5] Bomb The Bass featuring Carlton [6] Bomb The Bass featuring Bernard Fowler

See also ANTONIA

BOMBALURINA *UK, male / female vocal group (20 WEEKS)*

		pos	wks
28 Jul 90 ★	ITSY BITSY TEENY WEENY YELLOW POLKA DOT BIKINI *Carpet CRPT 1*	1	13
24 Nov 90	SEVEN LITTLE GIRLS SITTING IN THE BACKSEAT *Carpet CRPT 2* [1]	18	7

[1] Bombalurina featuring Timmy Mallett

BOMBERS *Canada, male / female vocal / instrumental group (10 WEEKS)* pos/wks

Date		Title / Label	pos	wks
5 May 79		**(EVERYBODY) GET DANCIN'** *Flamingo FM 1*	37	7
18 Aug 79		**LET'S DANCE** *Flamingo FM 4*	58	3

BOMFUNK MC'S *Finland, male DJ / rap duo – Raymond Ebanks and DJ Gismo (21 WEEKS)* pos/wks

Date		Title / Label	pos	wks
5 Aug 00	●	**FREESTYLER** *Dancepool DPS 2CD*	2	12
2 Dec 00		**UP ROCKING BEATS** *INCredible 6706132*	11	9

BON *Germany, male vocal duo – Guy Gross and Claus Capek (5 WEEKS)* pos/wks

Date		Title / Label	pos	wks
3 Feb 01		**BOYS** *Epic 6707092*	15	5

BON JOVI (72 Top 500) *Globally popular New Jersey band: Jon Bon Jovi (v), Richie Sambora (g), David Bryan (k), Alec John Such (b), Tico Torres (d). The UK's biggest-selling album act of 1994. Estimated 75 million albums sold worldwide (215 WEEKS)* pos/wks

Date		Title / Label	pos	wks
31 Aug 85		**HARDEST PART IS THE NIGHT** *Vertigo VER 22*	68	1
9 Aug 86		**YOU GIVE LOVE A BAD NAME** *Vertigo VER 26* ▲	14	10
25 Oct 86	●	**LIVIN' ON A PRAYER** *Vertigo VER 28* ▲	4	15
11 Apr 87		**WANTED DEAD OR ALIVE** *Vertigo JOV 1*	13	7
15 Aug 87		**NEVER SAY GOODBYE** *Vertigo JOV 2*	21	5
24 Sep 88		**BAD MEDICINE** *Vertigo JOV 3* ▲	17	7
10 Dec 88		**BORN TO BE MY BABY** *Vertigo JOV 4*	22	7
29 Apr 89		**I'LL BE THERE FOR YOU** *Vertigo JOV 5* ▲	18	7
26 Aug 89		**LAY YOUR HANDS ON ME** *Vertigo JOV 6*	18	6
9 Dec 89		**LIVING IN SIN** *Vertigo JOV 7*	35	6
24 Oct 92	●	**KEEP THE FAITH** *Jambco JOV 8*	5	6
23 Jan 93		**BED OF ROSES** *Jambco JOVCD 9*	13	6
15 May 93	●	**IN THESE ARMS** *Jambco JOVCD 10*	9	7
7 Aug 93		**I'LL SLEEP WHEN I'M DEAD** *Jambco JOVCD 11*	17	5
2 Oct 93		**I BELIEVE** *Jambco JOVCD 12*	11	6
26 Mar 94	●	**DRY COUNTY** *Jambco JOVCD 13*	9	6
24 Sep 94	●	**ALWAYS** *Jambco JOVCD 14*	2	18
17 Dec 94	●	**PLEASE COME HOME FOR CHRISTMAS** *Jambco JOVCD 16*	7	6
25 Feb 95	●	**SOMEDAY I'LL BE SATURDAY NIGHT** *Jambco JOVDD 15*	7	7
4 Mar 95		**PLEASE COME HOME FOR CHRISTMAS (re-entry)** *Jambco JOVCD 16*	46	4
10 Jun 95	●	**THIS AIN'T A LOVE SONG** *Mercury JOVCD 17*	6	9
30 Sep 95	●	**SOMETHING FOR THE PAIN** *Mercury JOVCD 18*	8	7
25 Nov 95	●	**LIE TO ME** *Mercury JOVCD 19*	10	8
9 Mar 96	●	**THESE DAYS** *Mercury JOVCD 20*	7	6
6 Jul 96		**HEY GOD** *Mercury JOVCD 21*	13	5
10 Apr 99		**REAL LIFE** *Reprise W 479CD*	21	5
3 Jun 00	●	**IT'S MY LIFE** *Mercury 5627682*	3	13
9 Sep 00	●	**SAY IT ISN'T SO** *Mercury 5688972*	10	6
18 Nov 00		**SAY IT ISN'T SO (re-entry)** *Mercury 5688972*	73	1
9 Dec 00		**THANK YOU FOR LOVING ME** *Mercury 5727302*	12	6
19 May 01	●	**ONE WILD NIGHT** *Mercury 5729502*	10	7

See also Jon BON JOVI

Jon BON JOVI
US, male vocalist/instrumentalist – John Bongiovi Jr (34 WEEKS) pos/wks

Date		Title / Label	pos	wks
4 Aug 90		**BLAZE OF GLORY** *Vertigo JBJ 1* ▲	13	8
10 Nov 90		**MIRACLE** *Vertigo JBVJ 2*	29	5
14 Jun 97	●	**MIDNIGHT IN CHELSEA** *Mercury MERCD 488*	4	7
30 Aug 97	●	**QUEEN OF NEW ORLEANS** *Mercury MERCD 493*	10	4
15 Nov 97		**JANIE, DON'T TAKE YOUR LOVE TO TOWN** *Mercury 5749872*	13	3

See also BON JOVI

Ronnie BOND *UK, male vocalist (5 WEEKS)* pos/wks

Date		Title / Label	pos	wks
31 May 80		**IT'S WRITTEN ON YOUR BODY** *Mercury MER 13*	52	5

Gary 'U.S.' BONDS *US, male vocalist – Gary Anderson (39 WEEKS)* pos/wks

Date		Title / Label	pos	wks
19 Jan 61		**NEW ORLEANS** *Top Rank JAR 527* [1]	16	11
20 Jul 61	●	**QUARTER TO THREE** *Top Rank JAR 575* [1] ▲	7	13
30 May 81		**THIS LITTLE GIRL** *EMI America EA 122*	43	6
22 Aug 81		**JOLE BLON** *EMI America EA 127*	51	3
31 Oct 81		**IT'S ONLY LOVE** *EMI America EA 128*	43	3
17 Jul 82		**SOUL DEEP** *EMI America EA 140*	59	3

[1] U.S. Bonds

BONE *UK, male vocal / instrumental duo (1 WEEK)* pos/wks

Date		Title / Label	pos	wks
2 Apr 94		**WINGS OF LOVE** *Deconstruction 74321176282*	55	1

BONE THUGS-N-HARMONY *US, male rap group (22 WEEKS)* pos/wks

Date		Title / Label	pos	wks
4 Nov 95		**1ST OF THA MONTH** *Epic 6625172*	32	2
10 Aug 96	●	**THA CROSSROADS** *Epic 6635502* ▲	8	11
9 Nov 96		**1ST OF THA MONTH (re-issue)** *Epic 6638505*	15	4
15 Feb 97		**DAYS OF OUR LIVEZ** *East West A 3982CD*	37	2
26 Jul 97		**LOOK INTO MY EYES** *Epic 6647862*	16	3

Elbow BONES and the RACKETEERS
US, male group leader and female backing group (9 WEEKS) pos/wks

Date		Title / Label	pos	wks
14 Jan 84		**A NIGHT IN NEW YORK** *EMI America EA 165*	33	9

BONEY M (119 Top 500) *Internationally successful West Indian vocal group: Bobby Farrell, Marcia Barrett, Liz Mitchell, Maisie Williams. This German-based quartet was assembled by producer Frank Farian (later behind controversial duo Milli Vanilli) (170 WEEKS)* pos/wks

Date		Title / Label	pos	wks
18 Dec 76	●	**DADDY COOL** *Atlantic K 10827*	6	13
12 Mar 77	●	**SUNNY** *Atlantic K 10892*	3	10
25 Jun 77	●	**MA BAKER** *Atlantic K 10965*	2	13
29 Oct 77	●	**BELFAST** *Atlantic K 11020*	8	13
29 Apr 78	★	**RIVERS OF BABYLON / BROWN GIRL IN THE RING** *Atlantic/Hansa K 11120* ◆	1	40
7 Oct 78	●	**RASPUTIN** *Atlantic/Hansa K 11192*	2	10
2 Dec 78	★	**MARY'S BOY CHILD – OH MY LORD** *Atlantic/Hansa K 11221* ◆	1	8
3 Mar 79	●	**PAINTER MAN** *Atlantic/Hansa K 11255*	10	6
28 Apr 79	●	**HOORAY HOORAY IT'S A HOLI-HOLIDAY** *Atlantic/Hansa K 11279*	3	9
11 Aug 79		**GOTTA GO HOME / EL LUTE** *Atlantic/Hansa K 11351*	12	11
15 Dec 79		**I'M BORN AGAIN** *Atlantic/Hansa K 11410*	35	7
26 Apr 80		**MY FRIEND JACK** *Atlantic/Hansa K 11463*	57	5
14 Feb 81		**CHILDREN OF PARADISE** *Atlantic/Hansa K 11637*	66	2
21 Nov 81		**WE KILL THE WORLD (DON'T KILL THE WORLD)** *Atlantic/Hansa K 11689*	39	5
24 Dec 88		**MEGAMIX / MARY'S BOY CHILD (re-mix)** *Ariola 111947*	52	3
5 Dec 92	●	**BONEY M MEGAMIX** *Arista 74321125127*	7	9
17 Apr 93		**BROWN GIRL IN THE RING (re-mix)** *Arista 74321137052*	38	3
8 May 99		**MA BAKER – SOMEBODY SCREAMED** *Logic 74321653872* [1]	22	2
29 Dec 01		**DADDY COOL 2001(re-mix)** *BMG 74321913512*	47	1+

[1] Boney M vs Horny United

'Brown Girl in the Ring' listed with 'Rivers of Babylon' only from 5 Aug 1978, peaking at No.2. 'El Lute' listed with 'Gotta Go Home' only from 29 Sep 1979. The 1988 and 1992 megamixes are different

Graham BONNET *UK, male vocalist (15 WEEKS)* pos/wks

Date		Title / Label	pos	wks
21 Mar 81	●	**NIGHT GAMES** *Vertigo VER 1*	6	11
13 Jun 81		**LIAR** *Vertigo VER 2*	51	4

Graham BONNEY *UK, male vocalist – Graham Bradley) (8 WEEKS)* pos/wks

Date		Title / Label	pos	wks
24 Mar 66		**SUPERGIRL** *Columbia DB 7843*	19	8

BONO *Ireland, male vocalist (25 WEEKS)* pos/wks

Date		Title / Label	pos	wks
25 Jan 86		**IN A LIFETIME** *RCA PB 40535* [1]	20	5
10 Jun 89		**IN A LIFETIME (re-issue)** *RCA PB 42873* [1]	17	7
4 Dec 93	●	**I'VE GOT YOU UNDER MY SKIN** *Island CID 578* [2]	4	9
9 Apr 94		**IN THE NAME OF THE FATHER** *Island CID 593* [3]	46	2
23 Oct 99		**NEW DAY** *Columbia 6682122* [4]	23	2

[1] Clannad featuring Bono [2] Frank Sinatra with Bono [3] Bono and Gavin Friday [4] Wyclef Jean featuring Bono

I've Got You Under My Skin was the listed B-side of 'Stay (Faraway So Close)' by U2.

See also U2

BONZO DOG DOO-DAH BAND
UK, male vocal / instrumental group (14 WEEKS) pos/wks

Date		Title / Label	pos	wks
6 Nov 68	●	**I'M THE URBAN SPACEMAN** *Liberty LBF 15144*	5	14

Betty BOO *UK, female rapper – Alison Clarkson (55 WEEKS)* pos/wks

			pos	wks
12 Aug 89	●	**HEY DJ – I CAN'T DANCE (TO THAT MUSIC YOU'RE PLAYING) / SKA TRAIN** *Rhythm King LEFT 34* [1]	7	11
19 May 90	●	**DOIN' THE DO** *Rhythm King LEFT 39*	7	12
11 Aug 90	●	**WHERE ARE YOU BABY?** *Rhythm King LEFT 43*	3	10
1 Dec 90		**24 HOURS** *Rhythm King LEFT 45*	25	8
8 Aug 92		**LET ME TAKE YOU THERE** *WEA YZ 677*	12	8
3 Oct 92		**I'M ON MY WAY** *WEA YZ 693*	44	3
10 Apr 93		**HANGOVER** *WEA YZ 719CD*	50	3

[1] Beatmasters featuring Betty Boo

BOO RADLEYS *UK, male vocal / instrumental group (27 WEEKS)* pos/wks

			pos	wks
20 Jun 92		**DOES THIS HURT / BOO! FOREVER** *Creation CRE 128*	67	1
23 Oct 93		**WISH I WAS SKINNY** *Creation CRESCD 169*	75	1
12 Feb 94		**BARNEY (. . . & ME)** *Creation CRESCD 178*	48	2
11 Jun 94		**LAZARUS** *Creation CRESCD 187*	50	2
11 Mar 95	●	**WAKE UP BOO!** *Creation CRESCD 191*	9	8
13 May 95		**FIND THE ANSWER WITHIN** *Creation CRESCD 202*	37	3
29 Jul 95		**IT'S LULU** *Creation CRESCD 211*	25	2
7 Oct 95		**FROM THE BENCH AT BELVIDERE** *Creation CRESCD 214*	24	2
17 Aug 96		**WHAT'S IN THE BOX (SEE WATCHA GOT)** *Creation CRESCD 220*	25	2
19 Oct 96		**C'MON KIDS** *Creation CRESCD 236*	18	2
1 Feb 97		**RIDE THE TIGER** *Creation CRESCD 248X*	38	1
17 Oct 98		**FREE HUEY** *Creation CRESCD 299X*	54	1

BOO-YAA T.R.I.B.E. *US, male rap group (6 WEEKS)* pos/wks

			pos	wks
30 Jun 90		**PSYKO FUNK** *Fourth & Broadway BRW 179*	43	3
6 Nov 93		**ANOTHER BODY MURDERED** *Epic 6597942* [1]	26	3

[1] Faith No More and Boo-Yaa T.R.I.B.E.

BOOGIE BOX HIGH *UK, male vocal / instrumental group – leader Andros Georgiou (11 WEEKS)* pos/wks

			pos	wks
4 Jul 87	●	**JIVE TALKIN'** *Hardback 7BOSS 4*	7	11

See also ALIEN VOICES featuring the THREE DEGREES; Andy G's STARSKY & HUTCH ALL STARS

BOOGIE DOWN PRODUCTIONS
US, male rap / production duo (2 WEEKS) pos/wks

			pos	wks
4 Jun 88		**MY PHILOSOPHY / STOP THE VIOLENCE** *Jive JIVEX 170*	69	2

BOOKER T and the MG's *US, male instrumental group (43 WEEKS)* pos/wks

			pos	wks
11 Dec 68		**SOUL LIMBO** *Stax 102*	30	9
7 May 69	●	**TIME IS TIGHT** *Stax 119*	4	18
30 Aug 69		**SOUL CLAP '69** *Stax 127*	35	4
15 Dec 79	●	**GREEN ONIONS** *Atlantic K 10109*	7	12

BOOM – *See Boris DLUGOSCH*

BOOM! *UK, male / female vocal group (5 WEEKS)* pos/wks

			pos	wks
27 Jan 01		**FALLING** *London LONCD 458*	11	5

Taka BOOM – *See EYE TO EYE featuring Taka BOOM; Joey NEGRO*

BOOM BOOM ROOM *UK, male vocal / instrumental group (1 WEEK)* pos/wks

			pos	wks
8 Mar 86		**HERE COMES THE MAN** *Fun After All FUN 101*	74	1

BOOMTOWN RATS (219 Top 500) *New wave group named after a band in a Woody Guthrie novel. Fronted by charismatic Bob Geldof (b. 5 Oct 1954, Dublin), who was later knighted for organising Live Aid. The Mutt Lange produced 'Rat Trap' was the first new wave No.1 (123 WEEKS)* pos/wks

			pos	wks
27 Aug 77		**LOOKING AFTER NO.1** *Ensign ENY 4*	11	9
19 Nov 77		**MARY OF THE 4TH FORM** *Ensign ENY 9*	15	9
15 Apr 78		**SHE'S SO MODERN** *Ensign ENY 13*	12	11
17 Jun 78	●	**LIKE CLOCKWORK** *Ensign ENY 14*	6	13
14 Oct 78	★	**RAT TRAP** *Ensign ENY 16*	1	15
21 Jul 79	★	**I DON'T LIKE MONDAYS** *Ensign ENY 30*	1	12
17 Nov 79		**DIAMOND SMILES** *Ensign ENY 33*	13	10
26 Jan 80	●	**SOMEONE'S LOOKING AT YOU** *Ensign ENY 34*	4	9
22 Nov 80	●	**BANANA REPUBLIC** *Mercury BONGO 1*	3	11
31 Jan 81		**THE ELEPHANT'S GRAVEYARD (GUILTY)** *Mercury BONGO 2*	26	6
12 Dec 81		**NEVER IN A MILLION YEARS** *Mercury MER 87*	62	4
20 Mar 82		**HOUSE ON FIRE** *Mercury MER 91*	24	8
18 Feb 84		**TONIGHT** *Mercury MER 154*	73	1
19 May 84		**DRAG ME DOWN** *Mercury MER 163*	50	3
2 Jul 94		**I DON'T LIKE MONDAYS (re-issue)** *Vertigo VERCD 87*	38	2

See also Bob GELDOF

Clint BOON EXPERIENCE
UK, male / female vocal / instrumental group (3 WEEKS) pos/wks

			pos	wks
6 Nov 99		**WHITE NO SUGAR** *Artful CDARTFUL 32*	61	1
5 Feb 00		**BIGGEST HORIZON** *Artful CDARTFUL 33*	70	1
5 Aug 00		**DO WHAT YOU DO (EARWORM SONG)** *Artful CDARTFUL 34*	63	1

Daniel BOONE *UK, male vocalist – Peter Lee Stirling) (25 WEEKS)* pos/wks

			pos	wks
14 Aug 71		**DADDY DON'T YOU WALK SO FAST** *Penny Farthing PEN 764*	17	15
1 Apr 72		**BEAUTIFUL SUNDAY** *Penny Farthing PEN 781*	48	1
15 Apr 72		**BEAUTIFUL SUNDAY (re-entry)** *Penny Farthing PEN 781*	21	9

Debby BOONE *US, female vocalist (2 WEEKS)* pos/wks

			pos	wks
24 Dec 77		**YOU LIGHT UP MY LIFE** *Warner Bros. K 17043* ▲	48	2

Pat BOONE (30 Top 500) *Major rival to Elvis in late 1950s, b. 1 Jun 1934, Florida. This clean-cut vocalist was voted the World's Outstanding Male Singer in the UK in 1957. He was seldom absent from the UK or US charts during the early rock 'n' roll years (308 WEEKS)* pos/wks

			pos	wks
18 Nov 55	●	**AIN'T THAT A SHAME** *London HLD 8172*	7	9
27 Apr 56	★	**I'LL BE HOME** *London HLD 8253*	1	22
27 Jul 56		**LONG TALL SALLY** *London HLD 8291*	27	3
17 Aug 56		**I ALMOST LOST MY MIND** *London HLD 8303*	14	7
24 Aug 56		**LONG TALL SALLY (re-entry)** *London HLD 8291*	18	4
7 Dec 56	●	**FRIENDLY PERSUASION (THEE I LOVE)** *London HLD 8346*	3	21
11 Jan 57		**AIN'T THAT A SHAME (re-entry)** *London HLD 8172*	22	2
11 Jan 57		**I'LL BE HOME (re-entry)** *London HLD 8253*	19	2
1 Feb 57	●	**DON'T FORBID ME** *London HLD 8370*	2	16
26 Apr 57		**WHY BABY WHY** *London HLD 8404*	17	7
5 Jul 57	●	**LOVE LETTERS IN THE SAND** *London HLD 8445* ▲	2	21
27 Sep 57	●	**REMEMBER YOU'RE MINE / THERE'S A GOLDMINE IN THE SKY** *London HLD 8479*	5	18
6 Dec 57	●	**APRIL LOVE** *London HLD 8512* ▲	7	23
13 Dec 57		**WHITE CHRISTMAS** *London HLD 8520*	29	1
4 Apr 58	●	**A WONDERFUL TIME UP THERE** *London HLD 8574 (A)*	2	17
11 Apr 58	●	**IT'S TOO SOON TO KNOW** *London HLD 8574 (B)*	7	12
27 Jun 58	●	**SUGAR MOON** *London HLD 8640*	6	12
29 Aug 58		**IF DREAMS CAME TRUE** *London HLD 8675*	16	11
5 Dec 58		**GEE, BUT IT'S LONELY** *London HLD 8739*	30	1
16 Jan 59		**I'LL REMEMBER TONIGHT** *London HLD 8775*	28	1
6 Feb 59		**I'LL REMEMBER TONIGHT (re-entry)** *London HLD 8775*	21	1
20 Feb 59		**I'LL REMEMBER TONIGHT (2nd re-entry)** *London HLD 8775*	18	7
10 Apr 59		**WITH THE WIND AND THE RAIN IN YOUR HAIR** *London HLD 8824*	21	3
22 May 59		**FOR A PENNY** *London HLD 8855*	28	3
26 Jun 59		**FOR A PENNY (re-entry)** *London HLD 8855*	19	6
31 Jul 59		**'TWIXT TWELVE AND TWENTY** *London HLD 8910*	18	6
18 Sep 59		**'TWIXT TWELVE AND TWENTY (re-entry)** *London HLD 8910*	26	1
23 Jun 60		**WALKING THE FLOOR OVER YOU** *London HLD 9138*	40	2
14 Jul 60		**WALKING THE FLOOR OVER YOU (re-entry)** *London HLD 9138*	46	1
4 Aug 60		**WALKING THE FLOOR OVER YOU (2nd re-entry)** *London HLD 9138*	39	2
6 Jul 61		**MOODY RIVER** *London HLD 9350* ▲	18	10
7 Dec 61	●	**JOHNNY WILL** *London HLD 9461*	4	13
15 Feb 62		**I'LL SEE YOU IN MY DREAMS** *London HLD 9504*	27	9
24 May 62		**QUANDO, QUANDO, QUANDO** *London HLD 9543*	41	4
12 Jul 62	●	**SPEEDY GONZALES** *London HLD 9573*	2	19
15 Nov 62		**THE MAIN ATTRACTION** *London HLD 9620*	12	11

'There's a Goldmine in the Sky' was listed only for the week of 27 Sep 1957. It peaked at No.23. 'A Wonderful Time Up There' and 'It's Too Soon To Know' were both on the same single release

1957

FROM THE YEAR IN WHICH SPUTNIK BLASTED INTO SPACE GIVING RUSSIA THE LEAD IN THE SPACE RACE, THE EUROPEAN ECONOMIC COMMUNITY OR COMMON MARKET WAS FOUNDED, AND TOMMY STEELE BECAME THE FIRST BRITISH ROCK 'N' ROLLER TO TOP THE CHART, **ROGER DALTREY** REMEMBERS A LIFE-CHANGING EXPERIENCE...

"The first time I saw Elvis, I thought he was someone who'd landed from Mars. They showed a clip from the Ed Sullivan show – it was 'Hound Dog' – and I just thought, that's what I'm going to be. It motivated my whole life. I was at grammar school and I went in the next day and said to the teacher: 'Did you see that **Elvis Presley** on TV last night?' And he said: 'Yes! Disgusting, wasn't it?' I thought, that'll do me."

SINGLE OF THE YEAR
'Diana' Paul Anka

BOOT ROOM BOYZ – *See LIVERPOOL FC*

Duke BOOTEE – *See GRANDMASTER FLASH, Melle MEL and the FURIOUS FIVE*

BOOTH and the BAD ANGEL

UK / US, male vocal / instrumental duo (4 WEEKS) pos/wks

22 Jun 96		I BELIEVE *Fontana BBCD 1*	25	3
11 Jul 98		FALL IN LOVE WITH ME *Mercury MERCD 503*	57	1

Ken BOOTHE *Jamaica, male vocalist (22 WEEKS)* pos/wks

21 Sep 74	★	EVERYTHING I OWN *Trojan TR 7920*	1	12
14 Dec 74		CRYING OVER YOU *Trojan TR 7944*	11	10

BOOTHILL FOOT-TAPPERS

UK, male / female vocal / instrumental group (3 WEEKS) pos/wks

14 Jul 84		GET YOUR FEET OUT OF MY SHOES *Go! Discs TAP 1*	64	3

BOOTSY'S RUBBER BAND

US, male vocal / instrumental group (3 WEEKS) pos/wks

8 Jul 78		BOOTZILLA *Warner Bros. K 17196*	43	3

BOOTZILLA ORCHESTRA – *See Malcolm McLAREN*

BOSS *US, male producer - David Morales (1 WEEK)* pos/wks

27 Aug 94		CONGO *Cooltempo CDCOOL 296*	54	1

See also BAD YARD CLUB; David MORALES

BOSTON *US, male vocal / instrumental group (13 WEEKS)* pos/wks

29 Jan 77		MORE THAN A FEELING *Epic EPC 4658*	22	8
7 Oct 78		DON'T LOOK BACK *Epic EPC 6653*	43	5

Eve BOSWELL *Hungary, female vocalist – Eva Keleti (13 WEEKS)* pos/wks

30 Dec 55	●	PICKIN' A-CHICKEN *Parlophone R 4082* [1]	9	7
2 Mar 56		PICKIN' A-CHICKEN (re-entry) *Parlophone R 4082* [1]	16	3
6 Apr 56		PICKIN' A-CHICKEN (2nd re-entry) *Parlophone R 4082* [1]	20	3

[1] 'with Glen Somers and his Orchestra'

Judy BOUCHER *St Vincent, female vocalist (23 WEEKS)* pos/wks

4 Apr 87	●	CAN'T BE WITH YOU TONIGHT *Orbitone OR 721*	2	14
4 Jul 87		YOU CAUGHT MY EYE *Orbitone OR 722*	18	9

Peter BOUNCER – *See SHUT UP AND DANCE*

BOUNCING CZECKS *UK, male vocal / instrumental group (1 WEEK)* pos/wks

29 Dec 84		I'M A LITTLE CHRISTMAS CRACKER *RCA 463*	72	1

BOUNTY KILLER *Jamaica, male rapper – Rodney Price (1 WEEK)* pos/wks

27 Feb 99		IT'S A PARTY *Edel 0066135 BLA*	65	1

BOURGEOIS TAGG *US, male vocal / instrumental duo (6 WEEKS)* pos/wks

6 Feb 88		I DON'T MIND AT ALL *Island IS 353*	35	6

BOURGIE BOURGIE *UK, male vocal / instrumental group (4 WEEKS)* pos/wks

3 Mar 84		BREAKING POINT *MCA BOU 1*	48	4

Toby BOURKE with George MICHAEL *UK male vocalist (4 WEEKS)* pos/wks

7 Jun 97	●	WALTZ AWAY DREAMING *Aegean AECD 01*	10	4

Aletia BOURNE – *See ANGELHEART*

BOW WOW WOW

UK / Burma, female / male vocal / instrumental group (54 WEEKS) pos/wks

26 Jul 80		C30, C60, C90, GO *EMI 5088*	34	7
6 Dec 80		YOUR CASSETTE PET *EMI WOW 1*	58	6
28 Mar 81		W.O.R.K. (N.O. NAH NO NO MY DADDY DON'T) *EMI 5153*	62	3
15 Aug 81		PRINCE OF DARKNESS *RCA 100*	58	4
7 Nov 81		CHIHUAHUA *RCA 144*	51	4
30 Jan 82	●	GO WILD IN THE COUNTRY *RCA 175*	7	13
1 May 82		SEE JUNGLE (JUNGLE BOY) / TV SAVAGE *RCA 220*	45	3
5 Jun 82	●	I WANT CANDY *RCA 238*	9	8
31 Jul 82		LOUIS QUATORZE *RCA 263*	66	2
12 Mar 83		DO YOU WANNA HOLD ME? *RCA 314*	47	4

Your Cassette Pet listed as Louis Quatorze on 6 Dec 1980 only. Tracks on Your Cassette Pet (available only as a cassette) are: Louis Quatorze / Gold He Said / Umo-Sex-Al Apache / I Want My Baby On Mars / Sexy Eiffel Towers / Giant Sized Baby Thing / Fools Rush In / Radio G String. RCA 263 is disc version of track on EMI WOW 1 Cassette

BOWA featuring MALA

US, male / female vocal / instrumental duo (1 WEEK) pos/wks

7 Dec 91		DIFFERENT STORY *Dead Dead Good GOOD 8*	64	1

Dane BOWERS – *See TRUE STEPPERS; DANE; ANOTHER LEVEL*

David BOWIE (10) (Top 500)

Chameleon-like singer / songwriter / entertainer b. David Jones 8 Jan 1947, Brixton, London. Noted for his changes of character and fashion, he became Ziggy Stardust, Aladdin Sane and The Thin White Duke. His striking appearance was enhanced by an unfortunate school playground incident that changed the colour of one of his blue eyes to green when stabbed by a compass. Voted most influential artist in an NME poll in 2000. Among his many accolades and awards, for both recording and songwriting, is the 1996 Brit Award for Outstanding Contribution to British Music. (He is the only act to reject induction into the Rock and Roll Hall of Fame.) No UK act can better the 10 albums he charted with simultaneously in the Top 100 in 1983, and no British male can match his eight No.1 albums. This often sampled performer has starred in movies, acted on Broadway, painted and recorded music with many of the world's leading acts. In 1999 he released the first virtual album and became the first major act to make a full album available for download, releasing the first enhanced CD single (1995) and being the first singer / songwriter to go to the stock market selling interest in his back catalogue, raising $55 million in the process (447 WEEKS) pos/wks

6 Sep 69		SPACE ODDITY *Philips BF 1801*	48	1
20 Sep 69	●	SPACE ODDITY (re-entry) *Philips BF 1801*	5	13
24 Jun 72	●	STARMAN *RCA 2199*	10	11
16 Sep 72		JOHN I'M ONLY DANCING *RCA 2263*	12	10
9 Dec 72	●	THE JEAN GENIE *RCA 2302*	2	13
14 Apr 73	●	DRIVE-IN SATURDAY *RCA 2352*	3	10
30 Jun 73	●	LIFE ON MARS *RCA 2316*	3	13
15 Sep 73	●	THE LAUGHING GNOME *Deram DM 123*	6	12
20 Oct 73	●	SORROW *RCA 2424*	3	15
23 Feb 74	●	REBEL REBEL *RCA LPBO 5009*	5	7
20 Apr 74		ROCK 'N' ROLL SUICIDE *RCA LPBO 5021*	22	7
22 Jun 74		DIAMOND DOGS *RCA APBO 0293*	21	6
28 Sep 74	●	KNOCK ON WOOD *RCA 2466*	10	6
1 Mar 75		YOUNG AMERICANS *RCA 2523*	18	7
2 Aug 75		FAME *RCA 2579* ▲	17	8
11 Oct 75	★	SPACE ODDITY (re-issue) *RCA 2593*	1	10
29 Nov 75	●	GOLDEN YEARS *RCA 2640*	8	10
22 May 76		TVC 15 *RCA 2682*	33	4
19 Feb 77	●	SOUND AND VISION *RCA PB 0905*	3	11
15 Oct 77		HEROES *RCA PB 1121*	24	8
21 Jan 78		BEAUTY AND THE BEAST *RCA PB 1190*	39	3
2 Dec 78		BREAKING GLASS (EP) *RCA BOW 1*	54	7
5 May 79	●	BOYS KEEP SWINGING *RCA BOW 2*	7	10
21 Jul 79		DJ *RCA BOW 3*	29	5
15 Dec 79		JOHN I'M ONLY DANCING (AGAIN) (1975) / JOHN I'M ONLY DANCING (1972) *RCA BOW 4*	12	8
1 Mar 80		ALABAMA SONG *RCA BOW 5*	23	5
16 Aug 80	★	ASHES TO ASHES *RCA BOW 6*	1	10
1 Nov 80	●	FASHION *RCA BOW 7*	5	12
10 Jan 81		SCARY MONSTERS (AND SUPER CREEPS) *RCA BOW 8*	20	6
28 Mar 81		UP THE HILL BACKWARDS *RCA BOW 9*	32	6
14 Nov 81	★	UNDER PRESSURE *EMI 5250* [1]	1	11
28 Nov 81		WILD IS THE WIND *RCA BOW 10*	24	10
6 Mar 82		BAAL (EP) *RCA BOW 11*	29	5
10 Apr 82		CAT PEOPLE (PUTTING OUT FIRE) *MCA 770*	26	6
27 Nov 82	●	PEACE ON EARTH – LITTLE DRUMMER BOY *RCA BOW 12* [2]	3	8

UK No.1 ★ UK Top 10 ● Still on chart + UK million seller ◆ UK entry at No.1 ■ US No.1 ▲

26 Mar 83 ★ **LET'S DANCE** *EMI America EA 152* ▲ 1 14
11 Jun 83 ● **CHINA GIRL** *EMI America EA 157* 2 8
24 Sep 83 ● **MODERN LOVE** *EMI America EA 158* 2 8
5 Nov 83 **WHITE LIGHT, WHITE HEAT** *RCA 372* 46 3
22 Sep 84 ● **BLUE JEAN** *EMI America EA 181* 6 8
8 Dec 84 **TONIGHT** *EMI America EA 187* 53 4
9 Feb 85 **THIS IS NOT AMERICA (THE THEME FROM 'THE FALCON AND THE SNOWMAN')** *EMI America EA 190* [3] 14 7
8 Jun 85 **LOVING THE ALIEN** *EMI America EA 195* 19 6
27 Jul 85 **LOVING THE ALIEN (re-entry)** *EMI America EA 195* 67 1
7 Sep 85 ★ **DANCING IN THE STREET** *EMI America EA 204* [4] ■ 1 12
15 Mar 86 ● **ABSOLUTE BEGINNERS** *Virgin VS 838* 2 9
21 Jun 86 **UNDERGROUND** *EMI America EA 216* 21 6
8 Nov 86 **WHEN THE WIND BLOWS** *Virgin VS 906* 44 4
4 Apr 87 **DAY-IN DAY-OUT** *EMI America EA 230* 17 6
27 Jun 87 **TIME WILL CRAWL** *EMI America EA 237* 33 4
29 Aug 87 **NEVER LET ME DOWN** *EMI America EA 239* 34 6
7 Apr 90 **FAME (re-mix)** *EMI-USA FAME 90* 28 4
22 Aug 92 **REAL COOL WORLD** *Warner Bros. W 0127* 53 1
27 Mar 93 ● **JUMP THEY SAY** *Arista 74321139422* 9 6
12 Jun 93 **BLACK TIE WHITE NOISE** *Arista 74321148682* [5] 36 2
23 Oct 93 **MIRACLE GOODNIGHT** *Arista 74321162262* 40 2
4 Dec 93 **BUDDHA OF SUBURBIA** *Arista 74321177052* [6] 35 3
23 Sep 95 **THE HEART'S FILTHY LESSON** *RCA 74321307032* 35 2
2 Dec 95 **STRANGERS WHEN WE MEET / THE MAN WHO SOLD THE WORLD (LIVE)** *RCA 74321329402* 39 2
2 Mar 96 **HALLO SPACEBOY** *RCA 74321353842* 12 4
8 Feb 97 **LITTLE WONDER** *RCA 74321452072* 14 3
26 Apr 97 **DEAD MAN WALKING** *RCA 74321475852* 32 2
30 Aug 97 **SEVEN YEARS IN TIBET** *RCA 74321512542* 61 1
21 Feb 98 **I CAN'T READ** *Velvet ZYX 87578* 73 1
2 Oct 99 **THURSDAY'S CHILD** *Virgin VSCDT 1753* 16 3
18 Dec 99 **UNDER PRESSURE (re-mix)** *Parlophone CDQUEEN 28* [1] 14 7
5 Feb 00 **SURVIVE** *Virgin VSCDT 1767* 28 2
29 Jul 00 **SEVEN** *Virgin VSCDT 1776* 32 2

[1] Queen and David Bowie [2] David Bowie and Bing Crosby [3] David Bowie and the Pat Metheny Group [4] David Bowie and Mick Jagger [5] David Bowie featuring Al B Sure! [6] David Bowie featuring Lenny Kravitz

Tracks on Breaking Glass (EP): Breaking Glass / Art Decade / Ziggy Stardust. All three versions of 'John I'm Only Dancing' are different. Tracks on Baal (EP): Baal's Hymn / Remembering Marie A. / Ballad of the Adventurers / The Drowned Girl / Dirty Song

See also TIN MACHINE

George BOWYER *UK, male vocalist (2 WEEKS)* pos/wks

22 Aug 98 **GUARDIANS OF THE LAND** *Boys BYSCD 01* 33 2

BOX TOPS *US, male vocal / instrumental group (33 WEEKS)* pos/wks

13 Sep 67 ● **THE LETTER** *Stateside SS 2044* ▲ 5 12
20 Mar 68 **CRY LIKE A BABY** *Bell 1001* 15 12
23 Aug 69 **SOUL DEEP** *Bell 1068* 22 9

BOY GEORGE *UK, male vocalist – George O'Dowd (46 WEEKS)* pos/wks

7 Mar 87 ★ **EVERYTHING I OWN** *Virgin BOY 100* 1 9
6 Jun 87 **KEEP ME IN MIND** *Virgin BOY 101* 29 4
18 Jul 87 **SOLD** *Virgin BOY 102* 24 5
21 Nov 87 **TO BE REBORN** *Virgin BOY 103* 13 7
5 Mar 88 **LIVE MY LIFE** *Virgin BOY 105* 62 2
18 Jun 88 **NO CLAUSE 28** *Virgin BOY 106* 57 3
8 Oct 88 **DON'T CRY** *Virgin BOY 107* 60 2
4 Mar 89 **DON'T TAKE MY MIND ON A TRIP** *Virgin BOY 108* 68 2
19 Sep 92 **THE CRYING GAME** *Spaghetti CIAO 6* 22 4
12 Jun 93 **MORE THAN LIKELY** *Gee Street GESCD 49* [1] 40 3
1 Apr 95 **FUNTIME** *Virgin VSCDG 1538* 45 2
1 Jul 95 **IL ADORE** *Virgin VSCDX 1543* 50 2
21 Oct 95 **SAME THING IN REVERSE** *Virgin VSCDT 1561* 56 1

[1] PM Dawn featuring Boy George

See also CULTURE CLUB

BOY MEETS GIRL *US, male / female vocal duo – Shannon Rubicam and George Merrill (13 WEEKS)* pos/wks

3 Dec 88 ● **WAITING FOR A STAR TO FALL** *RCA PB 49519* 9 13

BOY WUNDA – *See PROGRESS presents the BOY WUNDA*

Jimmy BOYD *US, male vocalist (22 WEEKS)* pos/wks

8 May 53 ● **TELL ME A STORY** *Philips PB 126* [1] 5 15
11 Sep 53 **TELL ME A STORY (re-entry)** *Philips PB 126* [1] 12 1
27 Nov 53 ● **I SAW MOMMY KISSING SANTA CLAUS** *Columbia DB 3365* ▲ 3 6

[1] Jimmy Boyd – Frankie Laine

Jacqueline BOYER *France, female vocalist (2 WEEKS)* pos/wks

28 Apr 60 **TOM PILLIBI** *Columbia DB 4452* 33 2

BOYS *US, male vocal group (5 WEEKS)* pos/wks

12 Nov 88 **DIAL MY HEART** *Motown ZB 42245* 61 2
29 Sep 90 **CRAZY** *Motown ZB 44037* 57 3

BOYSTOWN GANG *US, male / female vocal group (20 WEEKS)* pos/wks

22 Aug 81 **AIN'T NO MOUNTAIN HIGH ENOUGH – REMEMBER ME (MEDLEY)** *WEA DICK 1* 46 6
31 Jul 82 ● **CAN'T TAKE MY EYES OFF YOU** *ERC 101* 4 11
9 Oct 82 **SIGNED SEALED DELIVERED (I'M YOURS)** *ERC 102* 50 3

BOYZ – *See HEAVY D and the BOYZ*

BOYZ II MEN (408 Top 500) *R&B vocal harmony quartet formed 1988 in Philadelphia (brothers Nathan and Wanya Morris, Shawn Stockman, Michael McCary) were Motown's biggest sellers in the 1990s. The Beatles are the only group to have spent longer at the top of the US chart (81 WEEKS)* pos/wks

5 Sep 92 ★ **END OF THE ROAD** *Motown TMG 1411* ▲ 1 21
19 Dec 92 **MOTOWNPHILLY** *Motown TMG 1402* 23 6
27 Feb 93 **IN THE STILL OF THE NITE (I'LL REMEMBER)** *Motown TMGCD 1415* 27 4
3 Sep 94 ● **I'LL MAKE LOVE TO YOU** *Motown TMGCD 1431* ▲ 5 12
26 Nov 94 **ON BENDED KNEE** *Motown TMGCD 1433* ▲ 20 3
24 Dec 94 **I'LL MAKE LOVE TO YOU (re-entry)** *Motown TMGCD 1431* 57 3
22 Apr 95 **THANK YOU** *Motown TMGCD 1438* 26 3
8 Jul 95 **WATER RUNS DRY** *Motown TMGCD 1443* 24 3
9 Dec 95 ● **ONE SWEET DAY** *Columbia 6626035* [1] ▲ 6 11
20 Jan 96 **HEY LOVER** *Def Jam DEFCD 14* [2] 17 4
20 Sep 97 ● **4 SEASONS OF LONELINESS** *Motown 8606992* ▲ 10 6
6 Dec 97 **A SONG FOR MAMA** *Motown 8607372* 34 2
25 Jul 98 **CAN'T LET HER GO** *Motown 8607952* 23 3

[1] Mariah Carey and Boyz II Men [2] LL Cool J featuring Boyz II Men

BOYZONE (74 Top 500) *Irish boy band vocal quintet who became international teen idols: Ronan Keating, Stephen Gately, Mikey Graham, Keith Duffy, Shane Lynch. They achieved the best ever start to a UK singles career with 16 consecutive Top 5 singles (213 WEEKS)* pos/wks

10 Dec 94 ● **LOVE ME FOR A REASON** *Polydor 8512802* 2 13
29 Apr 95 ● **KEY TO MY LIFE** *Polydor PZCD 342* 3 8
12 Aug 95 ● **SO GOOD** *Polydor 5797732* 3 6
25 Nov 95 ● **FATHER AND SON** *Polydor 5775762* 2 16
9 Mar 96 ● **COMING HOME NOW** *Polydor 5775702* 4 9
19 Oct 96 ★ **WORDS** *Polydor 5755372* ■ 1 14
14 Dec 96 ★ **A DIFFERENT BEAT** *Polydor 5732052* ■ 1 10
1 Mar 97 **A DIFFERENT BEAT (re-entry)** *Polydor 5732052* 74 1
15 Mar 97 **A DIFFERENT BEAT (2nd re-entry)** *Polydor 5732052* 62 4
22 Mar 97 ● **ISN'T IT A WONDER** *Polydor 5735472* 2 7
17 May 97 **ISN'T IT A WONDER (re-entry)** *Polydor 5735472* 44 7
2 Aug 97 ● **PICTURE OF YOU** *Polydor 5713112* 2 18
6 Dec 97 ● **BABY CAN I HOLD YOU / SHOOTING STAR** *Polydor 5691672* 2 14
2 May 98 ★ **ALL THAT I NEED** *Polydor 5698732* ■ 1 10
18 Jul 98 **ALL THAT I NEED (re-entry)** *Polydor 5698732* 49 4
15 Aug 98 ★ **NO MATTER WHAT** *Polydor 5675672* ◆ ■ 1 15
5 Dec 98 ● **I LOVE THE WAY YOU LOVE ME** *Polydor 5631992* 2 13

		pos	wks
13 Mar 99 ★	**WHEN THE GOING GETS TOUGH** *Polydor 5699132*■	1	14
22 May 99 ★	**YOU NEEDED ME** *Polydor 5639332*■	1	12
17 Jul 99	**WHEN THE GOING GETS TOUGH (re-entry)** *Polydor 5699132*	57	2
28 Aug 99	**YOU NEEDED ME (re-entry)** *Polydor 5639332*	60	3
4 Dec 99 ●	**EVERY DAY I LOVE YOU** *Polydor 5615802*	3	13

See also Ronan KEATING; Stephen GATELY; Mikey GRAHAM; KEITH 'N' SHANE

BRAD *US, male vocal / instrumental group (1 WEEK)*

		pos	wks
26 Jun 93	**20TH CENTURY** *Epic 6592482*	64	1

Scott BRADLEY *UK, male vocalist (1 WEEK)*

		pos	wks
15 Oct 94	**ZOOM** *Hidden Agenda HIDDCD 1*	61	1

Paul BRADY *UK, male vocalist (1 WEEK)*

		pos	wks
13 Jan 96	**THE WORLD IS WHAT YOU MAKE IT** *Mercury PBCD 5*	67	1

Billy BRAGG *UK, male vocalist (51 WEEKS)*

		pos	wks
16 Mar 85	**BETWEEN THE WARS (EP)** *Go! Discs AGOEP 1*	15	6
28 Dec 85	**DAYS LIKE THESE** *Go! Discs GOD 8*	43	5
28 Jun 86	**LEVI STUBBS' TEARS** *Go! Discs GOD 12*	29	6
15 Nov 86	**GREETINGS TO THE NEW BRUNETTE** *Go! Discs GOD 15* [1]	58	2
14 May 88 ★	**SHE'S LEAVING HOME** *Childline CHILD 1* [2]	1	11
10 Sep 88	**WAITING FOR THE GREAT LEAP FORWARDS** *Go! Discs GOD 23*	52	3
8 Jul 89	**WON'T TALK ABOUT IT** *Go.Beat GOD 33* [3]	29	6
6 Jul 91	**SEXUALITY** *Go! Discs GOD 56*	27	5
7 Sep 91	**YOU WOKE UP MY NEIGHBOURHOOD** *Go! Discs GOD 60*	54	2
29 Feb 92	**ACCIDENT WAITING TO HAPPEN (EP)** *Go! Discs GOD 67*	33	3
31 Aug 96	**UPFIELD** *Cooking Vinyl FRYCD 051*	46	1
17 May 97	**THE BOY DONE GOOD** *Cooking Vinyl FRYCD 064*	55	1

[1] Billy Bragg with Johnny Marr and Kirsty MacColl [2] Billy Bragg with Cara Tivey [3] Norman Cook featuring Billy Bragg

Tracks on Between the Wars (EP): Between the Wars / Which Side Are You On / World Turned Upside Down / It Says Here. Tracks on Accident Waiting to Happen (EP): Accident Waiting to Happen / Revolution / Sulk / The Warmest Room. 'She's Leaving Home' was listed with the flip side 'With a Little Help from My Friends' by Wet Wet Wet. 'Won't Talk About It' was listed with the flip side 'Blame It on the Bassline' by Norman Cook featuring MC Wildski

BRAIDS *US, female vocal duo (3 WEEKS)*

		pos	wks
2 Nov 96	**BOHEMIAN RHAPSODY** *Atlantic A 5640CD*	21	3

BRAIN BASHERS *UK, male / female DJ / production duo (1 WEEK)*

		pos	wks
1 Jul 00	**DO IT NOW** *Tidy Trax TIDY 137 CD*	64	1

BRAINBUG *Italy, male producer – Alberto Bertapelle (7 WEEKS)*

		pos	wks
3 May 97	**NIGHTMARE** *Positiva CDTIV 76*	11	5
22 Nov 97	**BENEDICTUS / NIGHTMARE** *Positiva CDTIV 86*	24	2

BRAINCHILD
Germany, male producer – Matthias Hoffmann (2 WEEKS)

		pos	wks
30 Oct 99	**SYMMETRY C** *Multiply CDMULTY 55*	31	2

Wilfrid BRAMBELL and Harry H CORBETT
UK, male vocal TV comedy duo (12 WEEKS)

		pos	wks
28 Nov 63	**STEPTOE AND SON AT BUCKINGHAM PALACE (PARTS 1 & 2)** *Pye 7N 15588*	25	12

Bekka BRAMLETT – *See Joe COCKER*

BRAN VAN 3000
Canada, male / female vocal / instrumental group (15 WEEKS)

		pos	wks
6 Jun 98	**DRINKING IN L.A.** *Capitol CDCL 802*	34	2
21 Aug 99 ●	**DRINKING IN L.A. (re-issue)** *Capitol CDCL 811*	3	11
16 Jun 01	**ASTOUNDED** *Virgin VUSCD 194* [1]	40	2

[1] Bran Van 3000 featuring Curtis Mayfield

BRAND NEW HEAVIES
UK / US, male / female vocal / instrumental group (68 WEEKS)

		pos	wks
5 Oct 91	**NEVER STOP** *ffrr F 165*	43	3
15 Feb 92	**DREAM COME TRUE** *ffrr F 180*	24	4
18 Apr 92	**ULTIMATE TRUNK FUNK (EP)** *ffrr F 185*	19	6
1 Aug 92	**DON'T LET IT GO TO YOUR HEAD** *ffrr BNH 1*	24	4
19 Dec 92	**STAY THIS WAY** *ffrr BNH 2*	40	5
26 Mar 94	**DREAM ON DREAMER** *ffrr BNHCD 3*	15	4
11 Jun 94	**BACK TO LOVE** *ffrr BNHCD 4*	23	4
13 Aug 94	**MIDNIGHT AT THE OASIS** *ffrr BNHCD 5*	13	6
5 Nov 94	**SPEND SOME TIME** *ffrr BNHCD 6*	26	4
11 Mar 95	**CLOSE TO YOU** *ffrr BNHCD 7*	38	3
12 Apr 97	**SOMETIMES** *ffrr BNHCD 8*	11	5
28 Jun 97	**YOU ARE THE UNIVERSE** *ffrr GNHCD 9*	21	4
18 Oct 97 ●	**YOU'VE GOT A FRIEND** *London BNHCD 10*	9	8
10 Jan 98	**SHELTER** *London BNHCD 11*	31	4
11 Sep 99	**SATURDAY NITE** *ffrr BNHCD12*	35	2
29 Jan 00	**APPARENTLY NOTHING** *ffrr BNHCD 13*	32	2

The first 10 hits are credited 'featuring N'Dea Davenport' on either the sleeve or the label. She was replaced by Siedah Garrett from 1979 to 1999 and Carleen Anderson from 1999. Tracks on Ultimate Trunk Funk (EP): Never Stop / Stay This Way / Mr Tanaka. BNH 2 is a re-mixed version of the track on the Ultimate Trunk Funk EP

Johnny BRANDON *UK, male vocalist (12 WEEKS)*

		pos	wks
11 Mar 55 ●	**TOMORROW** *Polygon P 1131* [1]	8	6
29 Apr 55	**TOMORROW (re-entry)** *Polygon P 1131* [1]	16	2
1 Jul 55	**DON'T WORRY** *Polygon P 1163*	18	4

[1] Johnny Brandon with the Phantoms and the Norman Warren Music

BRANDY *US, female vocalist – Brandy Norwood (62 WEEKS)*

		pos	wks
10 Dec 94	**I WANNA BE DOWN** *Atlantic A7217CD*	44	3
3 Jun 95	**I WANNA BE DOWN (re-mix)** *Atlantic A 7186CD*	36	3
3 Feb 96	**SITTIN' UP IN MY ROOM** *Arista 74321344012*	30	4
6 Jun 98 ●	**THE BOY IS MINE** *Atlantic AT 0036CD* [1] ▲	2	20
10 Oct 98 ●	**TOP OF THE WORLD** *Atlantic AT 0046CD* [2]	2	8
12 Dec 98	**HAVE YOU EVER?** *Atlantic AT 0058CD* ▲	13	8
9 Jan 99	**TOP OF THE WORLD (re-entry)** *Atlantic AT 0046CD* [2]	61	1
19 Jun 99	**ALMOST DOESN'T COUNT** *Atlantic AT0068CD1*	15	5
16 Jun 01 ●	**ANOTHER DAY IN PARADISE** *WEA WEA 327CD1* [3]	5	10

[1] Brandy and Monica [2] Brandy featuring Mase [3] Brandy and Ray J

Laura BRANIGAN *US, female vocalist (33 WEEKS)*

		pos	wks
18 Dec 82 ●	**GLORIA** *Atlantic K 11759*	6	13
7 Jul 84 ●	**SELF CONTROL** *Atlantic A 9676*	5	17
6 Oct 84	**THE LUCKY ONE** *Atlantic A 9636*	56	3

BRASS CONSTRUCTION
US, male vocal / instrumental group (35 WEEKS)

		pos	wks
3 Apr 76	**MOVIN'** *United Artists UP 36090*	23	6
5 Feb 77	**HA CHA CHA (FUNKTION)** *United Artists UP 36205*	37	5
26 Jan 80	**MUSIC MAKES YOU FEEL LIKE DANCING** *United Artists UP 615*	39	6
28 May 83	**WALKIN' THE LINE** *Capitol CL 292*	47	3
16 Jul 83	**WE CAN WORK IT OUT** *Capitol CL 299*	70	2
7 Jul 84	**PARTYLINE** *Capitol CL 335*	56	4
27 Oct 84	**INTERNATIONAL** *Capitol CL 341*	70	2
9 Nov 85	**GIVE AND TAKE** *Capitol CL 377*	62	3
28 May 88	**MOVIN' 1988 (re-mix)** *Syncopate SY 11*	24	4

BRASSTOOTH – *See BM DUBS*

BRAT *UK, male vocalist – Roger Kitter (8 WEEKS)*

		pos	wks
10 Jul 82	**CHALK DUST – THE UMPIRE STRIKES BACK** *Hansa SMASH 1*	19	8

BRAVADO *UK, male / female vocal / instrumental group (3 WEEKS)*

		pos	wks
18 Jun 94	**HARMONICA MAN** *Peach PEACHCD 5*	37	3

BRAVEHEARTS – *See QB FINEST*

BRAVO ALL STARS
UK / US, male / female vocal / instrumental group (2 WEEKS) pos/wks

29 Aug 98		**LET THE MUSIC HEAL YOUR SOUL** *Edel 0039335 ERE*	36	2

Artists featured: Backstreet Boys, Aaron Carter, Scooter, 'N Sync, Caught in the Act, The Boyz, Blumchen, Gil, Squeezer, Mr President, Touche, R'N'G and the Moffatts

Alan BRAXE and Fred FALKE
France, male production duo (3 WEEKS) pos/wks

25 Nov 00		**INTRO** *Vulture / Credence CDCRED 006*	35	3

Dhar BRAXTON *US, female vocalist (8 WEEKS)* pos/wks

31 May 86		**JUMP BACK (SET ME FREE)** *Fourth & Broadway BRW 47*	32	8

Toni BRAXTON (392 Top 500) *Sultry, sexy soul / R&B vocalist, b. 7 Oct 1968, Maryland, US, who won Best New Artist Grammy in 1993 and was one of America's top selling pop and R&B artists of the 1990s. Her biggest hits have been ballads from the pens of top writers Babyface, Diane Warren, R Kelly and Rodney Jerkins (83 WEEKS)* pos/wks

18 Sep 93		**ANOTHER SAD LOVE SONG** *LaFace 74321163502*	51	2
15 Jan 94	●	**BREATHE AGAIN** *LaFace 74321185442*	2	12
2 Apr 94		**ANOTHER SAD LOVE SONG (re-issue)** *LaFace 74321196682*	15	8
9 Jul 94		**YOU MEAN THE WORLD TO ME** *LaFace 74321214702*	30	5
3 Dec 94		**LOVE SHOULDA BROUGHT YOU HOME** *LaFace 74321249412*	33	3
13 Jul 96	●	**YOU'RE MAKIN' ME HIGH** *LaFace 74321395402* ▲	7	11
2 Nov 96	●	**UN-BREAK MY HEART** *LaFace 74321410632* ▲	2	19
24 May 97	●	**I DON'T WANT TO** *LaFace 74321468612*	9	8
8 Nov 97		**HOW COULD AN ANGEL BREAK MY HEART** *LaFace 74321531982* [1]	22	4
29 Apr 00	●	**HE WASN'T MAN ENOUGH** *LaFace 74321757852*	5	11

[1] Toni Braxton with Kenny G

BRAXTONS *US, female vocal group (7 WEEKS)* pos/wks

1 Feb 97		**SO MANY WAYS** *Atlantic A 5469CD*	32	2
29 Mar 97		**THE BOSS** *Atlantic A 5441CD*	31	3
19 Jul 97		**SLOW FLOW** *Atlantic AT 0001CD*	26	2

BREAD *US, male vocal / instrumental group (46 WEEKS)* pos/wks

1 Aug 70	●	**MAKE IT WITH YOU** *Elektra 2101 010* ▲	5	14
15 Jan 72		**BABY I'M A WANT YOU** *Elektra K 12033*	14	10
29 Apr 72		**EVERYTHING I OWN** *Elektra K 12041*	32	6
30 Sep 72		**THE GUITAR MAN** *Elektra K 12066*	16	9
25 Dec 76		**LOST WITHOUT YOUR LOVE** *Elektra K 12241*	27	7

BREAK MACHINE *US, male vocal group (32 WEEKS)* pos/wks

4 Feb 84	●	**STREET DANCE** *Record Shack SOHO 13*	3	14
12 May 84	●	**BREAKDANCE PARTY** *Record Shack SOHO 20*	9	8
14 Jul 84		**BREAKDANCE PARTY (re-entry)** *Record Shack SOHO 20*	65	2
11 Aug 84		**ARE YOU READY?** *Record Shack SOHO 24*	27	8

BREAKBEAT ERA *UK, male / female drum and bass trio (5 WEEKS)* pos/wks

18 Jul 98		**BREAKBEAT ERA** *XL Recordings XLS 95CD*	38	2
21 Aug 99		**ULTRA – OBSCENE** *XL Recordings XLS 107CD*	48	2
11 Mar 00		**BULLITPROOF** *XL Recordings XLS 115CD*	65	1

BREAKFAST CLUB *US, male vocal / instrumental group (3 WEEKS)* pos/wks

27 Jun 87		**RIGHT ON TRACK** *MCA MCA 1146*	54	3

BREATHE *UK, male vocal / instrumental group (27 WEEKS)* pos/wks

30 Jul 88	●	**HANDS TO HEAVEN** *Siren SRN 68*	4	12
22 Oct 88		**JONAH** *Siren SRN 95*	60	3
3 Dec 88		**HOW CAN I FALL?** *Siren SRN 102*	48	7
11 Mar 89		**DON'T TELL ME LIES** *Siren SRN 109*	45	5

Freddy BRECK *Germany, male vocalist (4 WEEKS)* pos/wks

13 Apr 74		**SO IN LOVE WITH YOU** *Decca F 13481*	44	4

BRECKER BROTHERS *US, male vocal / instrumental group (5 WEEKS)* pos/wks

4 Nov 78		**EAST RIVER** *Arista ARIST 211*	34	5

BREEDERS
US / UK, female / male vocal / instrumental group (6 WEEKS) pos/wks

18 Apr 92		**SAFARI (EP)** *4AD BAD 2003*	69	1
21 Aug 93		**CANNONBALL (EP)** *4AD BAD 3011CD*	40	3
6 Nov 93		**DIVINE HAMMER** *4AD BAD 3017CD*	59	1
23 Jul 94		**HEAD TO TOE (EP)** *4AD BADD 4012*	68	1

Tracks on Safari (EP): Do You Love Me Now / Don't Call Home / Safari / So Sad About Us. Tracks on Cannonball (EP): Cannonball / Cro-Aloha / Lord of the Thighs / 900. Tracks on Head to Toe (EP): Head to Toe / Shocker In Gloom Town / Freed Pig

See also THROWING MUSES; PIXIES

BREEKOUT KREW *US, male vocal duo (3 WEEKS)* pos/wks

24 Nov 84		**MATT'S MOOD** *London LON 59*	51	3

Ann BREEN *Ireland, female vocalist (2 WEEKS)* pos/wks

19 Mar 83		**PAL OF MY CRADLE DAYS** *Homespun HS 052*	69	1
7 Jan 84		**PAL OF MY CRADLE DAYS (re-entry)** *Homespun HS 052*	74	1

Jo BREEZER *UK, female vocalist (2 WEEKS)* pos/wks

13 Oct 01		**VENUS AND MARS** *Columbia 6717612*	27	2

BRENDON *UK, male vocalist – Brendon Dunning (9 WEEKS)* pos/wks

19 Mar 77		**GIMME SOME** *Magnet MAG 80*	14	9

Maire BRENNAN *Ireland, female vocalist (12 WEEKS)* pos/wks

16 May 92		**AGAINST THE WIND** *RCA PB 45399*	64	2
5 Jun 99	●	**SALTWATER** *Xtravaganza XTRAV 1CDS* [1]	6	10

[1] Chicane featuring Maire Brennan of Clannad

Rose BRENNAN *Ireland, female vocalist (9 WEEKS)* pos/wks

7 Dec 61		**TALL DARK STRANGER** *Philips PB 1193*	31	9

Walter BRENNAN *US, male vocalist (3 WEEKS)* pos/wks

28 Jun 62		**OLD RIVERS** *Liberty LIB 55436*	38	3

Tony BRENT *UK, male vocalist – Reginald Bretagne (52 WEEKS)* pos/wks

19 Dec 52	●	**WALKIN' TO MISSOURI** *Columbia DB 3147*	9	2
2 Jan 53	●	**MAKE IT SOON** *Columbia DB 3187*	9	4
9 Jan 53	●	**WALKIN' TO MISSOURI (re-entry)** *Columbia DB 3147*	7	5
23 Jan 53		**GOT YOU ON MY MIND** *Columbia DB 3226*	12	1
13 Mar 53	●	**MAKE IT SOON (re-entry)** *Columbia DB 3187*	9	3
30 Nov 56		**CINDY, OH CINDY** *Columbia DB 3844*	16	6
8 Feb 57		**CINDY, OH CINDY (re-entry)** *Columbia DB 3844*	30	1
28 Jun 57		**DARK MOON** *Columbia DB 3950*	17	14
28 Feb 58		**THE CLOUDS WILL SOON ROLL BY** *Columbia DB 4066*	24	3
9 May 58		**THE CLOUDS WILL SOON ROLL BY (re-entry)** *Columbia DB 4066*	20	2
5 Sep 58		**GIRL OF MY DREAMS** *Columbia DB 4177*	16	7
24 Jul 59		**WHY SHOULD I BE LONELY?** *Columbia DB 4304*	24	4

Bernard BRESSLAW *UK, male actor (11 WEEKS)* pos/wks

5 Sep 58	●	**MAD PASSIONATE LOVE** *HMV POP 522*	6	11

See also Michael MEDWIN, Bernard BRESSLAW, Alfie BASS and Leslie FYSON

Teresa BREWER *US, female vocalist – Theresa Breuer (53 WEEKS)* pos/wks

11 Feb 55	●	**LET ME GO LOVER** *Vogue/Coral Q 72043* [1]	9	10
13 Apr 56	●	**A TEAR FELL** *Vogue/Coral Q 72146*	2	15
13 Jul 56	●	**A SWEET OLD FASHIONED GIRL** *Vogue/Coral Q 72172*	3	15
10 May 57		**NORA MALONE** *Vogue/Coral Q 72224*	26	2
23 Jun 60		**HOW DO YOU KNOW IT'S LOVE** *Coral Q 72396*	21	11

[1] Teresa Brewer with The Lancers

BRIAN and MICHAEL
UK, male vocal duo – Brian Burke and Michael Coleman (19 WEEKS) pos/wks

		pos	wks
25 Feb 78 ★	**MATCHSTALK MEN AND MATCHSTALK CATS AND DOGS** *Pye 7N 46035*	1	19

BRICK *US, male vocal / instrumental group (4 WEEKS)* pos/wks

		pos	wks
5 Feb 77	**DAZZ** *Bang 004*	36	4

Edie BRICKELL and the NEW BOHEMIANS
US, female / male vocal / instrumental group (10 WEEKS) pos/wks

		pos	wks
4 Feb 89	**WHAT I AM** *Geffen GEF 49*	31	7
27 May 89	**CIRCLE** *Geffen GEF 51*	74	1
1 Oct 94	**GOOD TIMES** *Geffen GFSTD 78* [1]	40	2

[1] Edie Brickell

Alicia BRIDGES *US, female vocalist (11 WEEKS)* pos/wks

		pos	wks
11 Nov 78	**I LOVE THE NIGHT LIFE (DISCO ROUND)** *Polydor 2066 936*	32	10
8 Oct 94	**I LOVE THE NIGHT LIFE (DISCO ROUND) (re-mix)** *Mother MUMCD 57*	61	1

Johnny BRIGGS – *See Amanda BARRIE and Johnny BRIGGS*

BRIGHOUSE AND RASTRICK BRASS BAND
UK, male brass band (13 WEEKS) pos/wks

		pos	wks
12 Nov 77 ●	**THE FLORAL DANCE** *Transatlantic BIG 548*	2	13

Bette BRIGHT *UK, female vocalist (5 WEEKS)* pos/wks

		pos	wks
8 Mar 80	**HELLO I AM YOUR HEART** *Korova KOW 3*	50	5

Sarah BRIGHTMAN (312 Top 500) *Multi-faceted Hot Gossip dancer turned pop and classical star, b. 14 Aug 1960, Hertfordshire, UK. Singer / actress, and ex-wife of Andrew Lloyd Webber. 'Time To Say Goodbye' was the biggest selling single in Germany (2.5 million). At times she held three of the top four places on the US Classical Crossover chart (98 WEEKS)* pos/wks

		pos	wks
11 Nov 78 ●	**I LOST MY HEART TO A STARSHIP TROOPER** *Ariola/Hansa AHA 527* [1]	6	14
7 Apr 79	**THE ADVENTURES OF THE LOVE CRUSADER** *Ariola/Hansa AHA 538* [2]	53	5
30 Jul 83	**HIM** *Polydor POSP 625* [3]	55	4
23 Mar 85 ●	**PIE JESU** *HMV WEBBER 1* [4]	3	8
11 Jan 86 ●	**THE PHANTOM OF THE OPERA** *Polydor POSP 800* [5]	7	10
4 Oct 86 ●	**ALL I ASK OF YOU** *Polydor POSP 802* [6]	3	16
10 Jan 87 ●	**WISHING YOU WERE SOMEHOW HERE AGAIN** *Polydor POSP 803*	7	11
11 Jul 92	**AMIGOS PARA SIEMPRE (FRIENDS FOR LIFE)** *Really Useful RUR 10* [7]	11	11
24 May 97 ●	**TIME TO SAY GOODBYE (CON TE PARTIRO)** *Coalition COLA 003CD* [8]	2	14
23 Aug 97	**WHO WANTS TO LIVE FOREVER** *Coalition COLA 014CD*	45	1
6 Dec 97	**JUST SHOW ME HOW TO LOVE YOU** *Coalition COLA 035CD* [9]	54	2
14 Feb 98	**STARSHIP TROOPERS** *Coalition COLA 040CD*	58	1
13 Feb 99	**EDEN** *Coalition COLA 065CD*	68	1

[1] Sarah Brightman and Hot Gossip [2] Sarah Brightman and the Starship Troopers [3] Sarah Brightman and the London Philharmonic [4] Sarah Brightman and Paul Miles-Kingston [5] Sarah Brightman and Steve Harley [6] Cliff Richard and Sarah Brightman [7] José Carreras and Sarah Brightman [8] Sarah Brightman and Andrea Bocelli [9] Sarah Brightman and the LSO featuring José Cura

The listed flip side of 'Wishing You Were Somehow Here Again' was 'The Music of the Night' by Michael Crawford. COLA 040CD is a dance re-mix of AHA 527

BRIGHTON AND HOVE ALBION FC
UK, male football team vocalists (2 WEEKS) pos/wks

		pos	wks
28 May 83	**THE BOYS IN THE OLD BRIGHTON BLUE** *Energy NRG 2*	65	2

BRILLIANT *UK, male / female vocal / instrumental group (13 WEEKS)* pos/wks

		pos	wks
19 Oct 85	**IT'S A MAN'S MAN'S MAN'S WORLD** *Food FOOD 5*	58	5
22 Mar 86	**LOVE IS WAR** *Food FOOD 6*	64	4
2 Aug 86	**SOMEBODY** *Food FOOD 7*	67	4

Danielle BRISEBOIS *US, female vocalist (1 WEEK)* pos/wks

		pos	wks
9 Sep 95	**GIMME LITTLE SIGN** *Epic 6610782*	75	1

Johnny BRISTOL *US, male vocalist (16 WEEKS)* pos/wks

		pos	wks
24 Aug 74 ●	**HANG ON IN THERE BABY** *MGM 2006 443*	3	11
19 Jul 80	**MY GUY – MY GIRL (MEDLEY)** *Atlantic / Hansa K 11550* [1]	39	5

[1] Amii Stewart and Johnny Bristol

BRIT PACK *UK, Ireland, male vocal group (2 WEEKS)* pos/wks

		pos	wks
12 Feb 00	**SET ME FREE** *When! WENX 2000*	41	2

BRITS – *See VARIOUS ARTISTS (MONTAGES)*

BROCK LANDARS *UK, male vocal / production duo (2 WEEKS)* pos/wks

		pos	wks
11 Jul 98	**S.M.D.U.** *Parlophone CDBLUE 001*	49	2

BROKEN ENGLISH *UK, male vocal / instrumental group (13 WEEKS)* pos/wks

		pos	wks
30 May 87	**COMIN' ON STRONG** *EMI EM 5*	18	10
3 Oct 87	**LOVE ON THE SIDE** *EMI EM 55*	69	3

BRONSKI BEAT (430 Top 500) *Electronic dance trio formed 1984 London, UK: Steve Bronski (k), Larry Steinbachek (k) and the plaintive falsetto of Jimmy Somerville (v), who left in 1985 for The Communards (replaced by John Foster). First openly gay hit pop group, split in 1989 (78 WEEKS)* pos/wks

		pos	wks
2 Jun 84 ●	**SMALLTOWN BOY** *Forbidden Fruit BITE 1*	3	13
22 Sep 84 ●	**WHY?** *Forbidden Fruit BITE 2*	6	10
1 Dec 84	**IT AIN'T NECESSARILY SO** *Forbidden Fruit BITE 3*	16	11
20 Apr 85 ●	**I FEEL LOVE (MEDLEY)** *Forbidden Fruit BITE 4* [1]	3	12
30 Nov 85 ●	**HIT THAT PERFECT BEAT** *Forbidden Fruit BITE 6*	3	14
29 Mar 86	**COME ON, COME ON** *Forbidden Fruit BITE 7*	20	7
1 Jul 89	**CHA CHA HEELS** *Arista 112331* [2]	32	7
2 Feb 91	**SMALLTOWN BOY (re-mix)** *London LON 287* [3]	32	4

[1] Bronski Beat and Marc Almond [2] Eartha Kitt and Bronski Beat [3] Jimmy Somerville with Bronski Beat

Tracks on medley: I Feel Love / Love to Love You Baby / Johnny Remember Me

Jet BRONX and the FORBIDDEN *UK, male vocal / instrumental group – featuring TV presenter Loyd Grossman (1 WEEK)* pos/wks

		pos	wks
17 Dec 77	**AIN'T DOIN' NOTHIN'** *Lightning LIG 50*	49	1

BROOK BROTHERS
UK, male vocal duo – Geoff and Ricky Brook (35 WEEKS) pos/wks

		pos	wks
30 Mar 61 ●	**WARPAINT** *Pye 7N 15333*	5	14
24 Aug 61	**AIN'T GONNA WASH FOR A WEEK** *Pye 7N 15369*	13	10
25 Jan 62	**HE'S OLD ENOUGH TO KNOW BETTER** *Pye 7N 15409*	37	1
16 Aug 62	**WELCOME HOME BABY** *Pye 7N 15453*	33	6
21 Feb 63	**TROUBLE IS MY MIDDLE NAME** *Pye 7N 15498*	38	4

Bruno BROOKES – *See Liz KERSHAW and Bruno BROOKES*

BROOKLYN BOUNCE *Germany, male production duo, and male / female vocal group (1 WEEK)* pos/wks

		pos	wks
30 May 98	**THE MUSIC'S GOT ME** *Club Tools 0064795 CLU*	67	1

BROOKLYN, BRONX and QUEENS – *See B B and Q BAND*

Elkie BROOKS (348 Top 500) *Husky-voiced female vocalist, professional at age 15, b. Elaine Bookbinder, 25 Feb 1945, Salford, UK. Blues, jazz then rock phases (in Vinegar Joe with Robert Palmer) followed by a solo career which featured an impressive 20-year run of 15 hit albums from 1977 (91 WEEKS)* pos/wks

		pos	wks
2 Apr 77 ●	**PEARL'S A SINGER** *A & M AMS 7275*	8	9
20 Aug 77 ●	**SUNSHINE AFTER THE RAIN** *A & M AMS 7306*	10	9
25 Feb 78	**LILAC WINE** *A & M AMS 7333*	16	7

3 Jun 78 ONLY LOVE CAN BREAK YOUR HEART *A & M AMS 7353* 43 5
11 Nov 78 DON'T CRY OUT LOUD *A & M AMS 7395* 12 11
5 May 79 THE RUNAWAY *A & M AMS 7428* 50 5
16 Jan 82 FOOL IF YOU THINK IT'S OVER *A & M AMS 8187* 17 10
1 May 82 OUR LOVE *A & M AMS 8214* 43 5
17 Jul 82 NIGHTS IN WHITE SATIN *A & M AMS 8235* 33 5
22 Jan 83 GASOLINE ALLEY *A & M AMS 8305* 52 5
22 Nov 86 ● NO MORE THE FOOL *Legend LM 4* 5 16
4 Apr 87 BREAK THE CHAIN *Legend LM 8* 55 3
11 Jul 87 WE'VE GOT TONIGHT *Legend LM 9* 69 1

Garth BROOKS *US, male vocalist (15 WEEKS)* pos/wks

1 Feb 92 SHAMELESS *Capitol CL 646* 71 1
22 Jan 94 THE RED STROKES / AIN'T GOING DOWN *Liberty CDCLS 704* 13 5
16 Apr 94 STANDING OUTSIDE THE FIRE *Liberty CDCL 712* 28 4
18 Feb 95 THE DANCE / FRIENDS IN LOW PLACES *Capitol CDCL 735* 36 3
17 Feb 96 SHE'S EVERY WOMAN *Capitol CDCL 767* 55 1
13 Nov 99 LOST IN YOU *Capitol CDCL 814* 70 1

Mel BROOKS *US, male actor / rapper – Melvin Kaminsky (10 WEEKS)* pos/wks

18 Feb 84 TO BE OR NOT TO BE (THE HITLER RAP) *Island IS 158* 12 10

Meredith BROOKS *US, female vocal / instrumentalist (13 WEEKS)* pos/wks

2 Aug 97 ● BITCH *Capital CDCL 790* 6 10
6 Dec 97 I NEED *Capital CDCLS 794* 28 2
7 Mar 98 WHAT WOULD HAPPEN *Capital CDCL 798* 49 1

Norman BROOKS *Canada, male vocalist – Norman Arie (1 WEEK)* pos/wks

12 Nov 54 A SKY-BLUE SHIRT AND A RAINBOW TIE *London L 1228* 17 1

BROS (388 Top 500) *Top teen appeal act; twins Matt Goss (v) and Luke Goss (d), b. 29 Sep 1968, London, UK, and Craig Logan (b) – who left in 1989. Sold out tours, broke sales records, and won Brits Best Newcomer of 1988 award (84 WEEKS)* pos/wks

5 Dec 87 WHEN WILL I BE FAMOUS? *CBS ATOM 2* 62 2
9 Jan 88 ● WHEN WILL I BE FAMOUS? (re-entry) *CBS ATOM 2* 2 13
19 Mar 88 ● DROP THE BOY *CBS ATOM 3* 2 10
18 Jun 88 ★ I OWE YOU NOTHING *CBS ATOM 4* 1 11
17 Sep 88 ● I QUIT *CBS ATOM 5* 4 8
3 Dec 88 ● CAT AMONG THE PIGEONS / SILENT NIGHT *CBS ATOM 6* 2 8
29 Jul 89 ● TOO MUCH *CBS ATOM 7* 2 7
7 Oct 89 ● CHOCOLATE BOX *CBS ATOM 8* 9 6
16 Dec 89 ● SISTER *CBS ATOM 9* 10 6
10 Mar 90 MADLY IN LOVE *CBS ATOM 10* 14 4
13 Jul 91 ARE YOU MINE? *Columbia 6569707* 12 5
21 Sep 91 TRY *Columbia 6574047* 27 4

Act was duo for last six hits

BROTHER BEYOND *UK, male vocal / instrumental group (58 WEEKS)* pos/wks

4 Apr 87 HOW MANY TIMES *EMI EMI 5591* 62 3
8 Aug 87 CHAIN-GANG SMILE *Parlophone R 6160* 57 3
23 Jan 88 CAN YOU KEEP A SECRET? *Parlophone R 6174* 56 4
30 Jul 88 ● THE HARDER I TRY *Parlophone R 6184* 2 14
5 Nov 88 ● HE AIN'T NO COMPETITION *Parlophone R 6193* 6 10
21 Jan 89 BE MY TWIN *Parlophone R 6195* 14 6
1 Apr 89 CAN YOU KEEP A SECRET (re-mix) *Parlophone R 6197* 22 5
28 Oct 89 DRIVE ON *Parlophone R 6233* 39 4
9 Dec 89 WHEN WILL I SEE YOU AGAIN *Parlophone R 6239* 43 5
10 Apr 90 TRUST *Parlophone R 6245* 53 2
19 Jan 91 THE GIRL I USED TO KNOW *Parlophone R 6265* 48 2

BROTHER BROWN featuring FRANK'EE *Denmark, male DJ / production duo and female vocalist (5 WEEKS)* pos/wks

2 Oct 99 UNDER THE WATER *ffrr FCD 367* 18 4
24 Nov 01 STAR CATCHING GIRL *Rulin / MOS RULIN 21CDS* 51 1

BROTHER LOVE – *See PRATT and McCLAIN with BROTHERLOVE*

BROTHERHOOD *UK, male rap group (1 WEEK)* pos/wks

27 Jan 96 ONE SHOT / NOTHING IN PARTICULAR *Bite It BHOODD 3* 55 1

BROTHERHOOD OF MAN (315 Top 500) *Triple chart-topping UK vocal group formed by producer / composer Tony Hiller, which originally featured Tony Burrows (Edison Lighthouse, White Plains, etc). Their two-boy two-girl line-up in 1976 broke voting record for Eurovision Song Contest and had the contest's biggest selling UK hit (97 WEEKS)* pos/wks

14 Feb 70 ● UNITED WE STAND *Deram DM 284* 10 9
4 Jul 70 WHERE ARE YOU GOING TO MY LOVE *Deram DM 298* 22 10
13 Mar 76 ★ SAVE YOUR KISSES FOR ME *Pye 7N 45569* ◆ 1 16
19 Jun 76 MY SWEET ROSALIE *Pye 7N 45602* 30 7
26 Feb 77 ● OH BOY (THE MOOD I'M IN) *Pye 7N 45656* 8 12
9 Jul 77 ★ ANGELO *Pye 7N 45699* 1 12
14 Jan 78 ★ FIGARO *Pye 7N 46037* 1 11
27 May 78 BEAUTIFUL LOVER *Pye 7N 46071* 15 12
30 Sep 78 MIDDLE OF THE NIGHT *Pye 7N 46117* 41 6
3 Jul 82 LIGHTNING FLASH *EMI 5309* 67 2

BROTHERS *UK, male vocal group (9 WEEKS)* pos/wks

29 Jan 77 ● SING ME *Bus Stop Bus 1054* 8 9

BROTHERS FOUR *US, male vocal group (2 WEEKS)* pos/wks

23 Jun 60 GREENFIELDS *Philips PB 1009* 49 1
7 Jul 60 GREENFIELDS (re-entry) *Philips PB 1009* 40 1

BROTHERS GRIMM – *See JAZZ and the BROTHERS GRIMM*

BROTHERS IN RHYTHM *UK, male instrumental / production duo – Dave Seaman and Steve Anderson (12 WEEKS)* pos/wks

16 Mar 91 SUCH A GOOD FEELING *Fourth & Broadway BRW 228* 64 2
14 Sep 91 SUCH A GOOD FEELING (re-issue) *Fourth & Broadway BRW 228 210* 14 8
30 Apr 94 FOREVER AND A DAY *Stress CDSTR 36* [1] 51 2

[1] Brothers in Rhythm present Charvoni

BROTHERS JOHNSON *US, male vocal / instrumental duo – George and Louis Johnson (34 WEEKS)* pos/wks

9 Jul 77 STRAWBERRY LETTER 23 *A & M AMS 7297* 35 5
2 Sep 78 AIN'T WE FUNKIN' NOW *A & M AMS 7379* 43 6
4 Nov 78 RIDE-O-ROCKET *A & M AMS 7400* 50 4
23 Feb 80 ● STOMP *A & M AMS 7509* 6 12
31 May 80 LIGHT UP THE NIGHT *A & M AMS 7526* 47 4
25 Jul 81 THE REAL THING *A & M AMS 8149* 50 3

BROTHERS LIKE OUTLAW featuring Alison EVELYN *UK, male / female vocal group (1 WEEK)* pos/wks

23 Jan 93 GOOD VIBRATIONS *Gee Street GESCD 44* 74 1

Edgar BROUGHTON BAND *UK, male vocal / instrumental group (10 WEEKS)* pos/wks

18 Apr 70 OUT DEMONS OUT *Harvest HAR 5015* 39 5
23 Jan 71 APACHE DROPOUT *Harvest HAR 5032* 49 1
6 Feb 71 APACHE DROPOUT (re-entry) *Harvest HAR 5032* 35 2
13 Mar 71 APACHE DROPOUT (2nd re-entry) *Harvest HAR 5032* 35 1
27 Mar 71 APACHE DROPOUT (3rd re-entry) *Harvest HAR 5032* 33 1

Alison BROWN – *See BAR CODES featuring Alison BROWN*

Angie BROWN – *See BIZARRE INC; MOTIV 8*

Bobby BROWN (222 Top 500) *Swingbeat superstar, b. 5 Feb 1969, Massachusetts, who married Whitney Houston in 1992. He joined a re-formed New Edition in 1996, the vocal group in which he topped the chart with 'Candy Girl' aged 14 (123 WEEKS)* pos/wks

6 Aug 88 DON'T BE CRUEL *MCA MCA 1268* 42 7
17 Dec 88 ● MY PREROGATIVE *MCA MCA 1299* ▲ 6 17
25 Mar 89 DON'T BE CRUEL (re-issue) *MCA MCA 1310* 13 8

			pos	wks
20 May 89	●	EVERY LITTLE STEP *MCA MCA 1338*	6	9
15 Jul 89	●	ON OUR OWN (FROM GHOSTBUSTERS II) *MCA MCA 1350*	4	9
23 Sep 89		ROCK WIT'CHA *MCA MCA 1367*	33	6
25 Nov 89		RONI *MCA MCA 1384*	21	7
9 Jun 90		THE FREE STYLE MEGA-MIX *MCA MCA 1421*	14	7
30 Jun 90		SHE AIN'T WORTH IT *London LON 265* [1] ▲	12	9
22 Aug 92		HUMPIN' AROUND *MCA MCS 1680*	19	6
17 Oct 92		GOOD ENOUGH *MCA MCS 1704*	41	4
19 Jun 93		THAT'S THE WAY LOVE IS *MCA MCSTD 1783*	56	2
22 Jan 94		SOMETHING IN COMMON *MCA MCSTD 1957* [2]	16	5
25 Jun 94		TWO CAN PLAY THAT GAME *MCA MCSTD 1973*	38	3
1 Apr 95	●	TWO CAN PLAY THAT GAME (re-entry) *MCA MCSTD 1973*	3	12
8 Jul 95	●	HUMPIN' AROUND (re-mix) *MCA MCSTD 2073*	8	6
14 Oct 95		MY PREROGATIVE (re-mix) *MCA MCSTD 2094*	17	3
3 Feb 96		EVERY LITTLE STEP (re-mix) *MCA MCSTD 48004*	25	2
22 Nov 97		FEELIN' INSIDE *MCA MCSTD 48067*	40	1

[1] Glenn Medeiros featuring Bobby Brown [2] Bobby Brown and Whitney Houston

Carl BROWN – *See DOUBLE TROUBLE*

Crazy World of Arthur BROWN

UK, male vocal / instrumental group (14 WEEKS) pos/wks

			pos	wks
26 Jun 68	★	FIRE *Track 604 022*	1	14

Dennis BROWN *Jamaica, male vocalist (18 WEEKS)* pos/wks

			pos	wks
3 Mar 79		MONEY IN MY POCKET *Lightning LV 5*	14	9
3 Jul 82		LOVE HAS FOUND ITS WAY *A & M AMS 8226*	47	6
11 Sep 82		HALFWAY UP HALFWAY DOWN *A & M AMS 8250*	56	3

Diana BROWN and Barrie K SHARPE

UK, female / male vocal duo (11 WEEKS) pos/wks

			pos	wks
2 Jun 90		THE MASTERPLAN *ffrr F 133*	39	6
1 Sep 90		SUN WORSHIPPERS (POSITIVE THINKING) *ffrr F 144*	61	2
23 Mar 91		LOVE OR NOTHING *ffrr F 152*	71	1
27 Jun 92		EATING ME ALIVE *ffrr F 190*	53	2

Errol BROWN *UK, male vocalist (13 WEEKS)* pos/wks

			pos	wks
4 Jul 87		PERSONAL TOUCH *WEA YZ 130*	25	8
28 Nov 87		BODY ROCKIN' *WEA YZ 162*	51	2
14 Feb 98		IT STARTED WITH A KISS *EMI CDHOT 101* [1]	18	3

[1] Hot Chocolate featuring Errol Brown

See also HOT CHOCOLATE

Foxy BROWN *US, female rapper – Inga Marchand (25 WEEKS)* pos/wks

			pos	wks
21 Sep 96		TOUCH ME TEASE ME *Def Jam DEFCD 18* [1]	26	3
8 Mar 97		GET ME HOME *Def Jam DEFCD 32* [2]	11	5
10 May 97		AIN'T NO PLAYA *Northwestside 74321474842* [3]	31	2
21 Jun 97	●	I'LL BE *Def Jam 5710432* [4]	9	5
11 Oct 97		BIG BAD MAMMA *Def Jam 5749792* [5]	12	3
25 Oct 97		SUNSHINE *Northwestside 74321528702* [6]	25	2
13 Mar 99		HOT SPOT *Def Jam 8708352*	31	2
8 Sep 01		OH YEAH *Def Jam 5887312*	27	3

[1] Case featuring Foxy Brown [2] Foxy Brown featuring BLACKstreet [3] Jay-Z featuring Foxy Brown [4] Foxy Brown featuring Jay-Z [5] Foxy Brown featuring Dru Hill [6] Jay-Z featuring Babyface and Foxy Brown

Gloria D BROWN *US, female vocalist (3 WEEKS)* pos/wks

			pos	wks
8 Jun 85		THE MORE THEY KNOCK, THE MORE I LOVE YOU *10 TEN 52*	57	3

Horace BROWN *US, male vocalist (7 WEEKS)* pos/wks

			pos	wks
25 Feb 95		TASTE YOUR LOVE *Uptown MCSTD 2026*	58	1
18 May 96		ONE FOR THE MONEY *Motown 8605232*	12	4
12 Oct 96		THINGS WE DO FOR LOVE *Motown 8605712*	27	2

Ian BROWN *UK, male vocal / instrumentalist (30 WEEKS)* pos/wks

			pos	wks
24 Jan 98	●	MY STAR *Polydor 5719872*	5	4
4 Apr 98		CORPSES *Polydor 5696552*	14	4
20 Jun 98		CAN'T SEE ME *Polydor 5440452*	21	3
20 Feb 99	●	BE THERE *Mo Wax MW 108CD1* [1]	8	6
6 Nov 99		LOVE LIKE A FOUNTAIN *Polydor 5615162*	23	3
19 Feb 00	●	DOLPHINS WERE MONKEYS *Polydor 5616372*	5	4
17 Jun 00		GOLDEN GAZE *Polydor 5618442*	29	2
29 Sep 01		F.E.A.R. *Polydor 5872842*	13	4

[1] Unkle featuring Ian Brown

See also STONE ROSES

James BROWN (292 Top 500) *"Soul Brother No.1", b. 3 May 1928, South Carolina, US. The most charted R&B performer of all time has influenced numerous musical styles since the mid-1950s. Only Elvis Presley has enjoyed more US pop chart entries (104 WEEKS)* pos/wks

			pos	wks
23 Sep 65		PAPA'S GOT A BRAND NEW BAG *London HL 9990* [1]	25	7
24 Feb 66		I GOT YOU *Pye International 7N 25350* [1]	29	6
16 Jun 66		IT'S A MAN'S MAN'S MAN'S WORLD *Pye International 7N 25371* [1]	13	9
10 Oct 70		GET UP I FEEL LIKE BEING A SEX MACHINE *Polydor 2001 071*	32	7
27 Nov 71		HEY AMERICA *Mojo 2093 006*	47	3
18 Sep 76		GET UP OFFA THAT THING *Polydor 2066 687*	22	6
29 Jan 77		BODY HEAT *Polydor 2066 763*	36	4
10 Jan 81		RAPP PAYBACK (WHERE IZ MOSES?) *RCA 28*	39	5
2 Jul 83		BRING IT ON . . . BRING IT ON *Sonet SON 2258*	45	4
1 Sep 84		UNITY (PART 1 – THE THIRD COMING) *Tommy Boy AFR 2* [2]	49	5
27 Apr 85		FROGGY MIX *Boiling Point FROG 1*	50	3
1 Jun 85		GET UP I FEEL LIKE BEING A SEX MACHINE (re-issue) *Boiling Point POSP 751*	47	5
25 Jan 86	●	LIVING IN AMERICA *Scotti Brothers A 6701*	5	10
1 Mar 86		GET UP I FEEL LIKE BEING A SEX MACHINE (re-entry of re-issue) *Boiling Point POSP 751*	46	4
18 Oct 86		GRAVITY *Scotti Brothers 650059 7*	65	2
30 Jan 88		SHE'S THE ONE *Urban URB 13*	45	3
23 Apr 88		THE PAYBACK MIX *Urban URB 17*	12	6
4 Jun 88		I'M REAL *Scotti Brothers JSB 1* [3]	31	4
23 Jul 88		I GOT YOU (I FEEL GOOD) (re-issue) *A & M AM 444*	52	3
16 Nov 91		GET UP (I FEEL LIKE BEING A) SEX MACHINE (2nd re-issue) *Polydor PO 185*	69	2
24 Oct 92		I GOT YOU (I FEEL GOOD) (re-mix) *FBI FBI 9* [4]	72	1
17 Apr 93		CAN'T GET ANY HARDER *Polydor PZCD 262*	59	2
17 Apr 99		FUNK ON AH ROLL *Inferno / Eagle EAGXA 073*	40	2
22 Apr 00		FUNK ON AH ROLL (re-mix) *Eagle EAGXS 127*	63	1

[1] James Brown and the Famous Flames [2] Afrika Bambaataa and James Brown [3] James Brown featuring Full Force [4] James Brown vs Dakeyne

'Froggy Mix' is a medley of 12 James Brown songs. The listed flip side of 'I Got You (I Feel Good)' was 'Nowhere to Run' by Martha Reeves and the Vandellas

Jennifer BROWN *Sweden, female vocalist (1 WEEK)* pos/wks

			pos	wks
1 May 99		TUESDAY AFTERNOON *RCA 74321604092*	57	1

Joanne BROWN – *See Tony OSBORNE SOUND*

Jocelyn BROWN (432 Top 500) *Super session singer from North Carolina who relocated to New York, b. 25 Nov 1950. She has sung backing vocals for such acts as John Lennon, Bruce Springsteen, Luther Vandross, Diana Ross and Bob Dylan and has had UK hits with 10 separate recording acts (78 WEEKS)* pos/wks

			pos	wks
21 Apr 84		SOMEBODY ELSE'S GUY *Fourth & Broadway BRW 5*	13	9
22 Sep 84		I WISH YOU WOULD *Fourth & Broadway BRW 14*	51	3
15 Mar 86		LOVE'S GONNA GET YOU *Warner Bros. W 8889*	70	1
29 Jun 91	●	ALWAYS THERE *Talkin Loud TLK 10* [1]	6	9
14 Sep 91		SHE GOT SOUL *A & M AM 819* [2]	57	3
7 Dec 91	●	DON'T TALK JUST KISS *Tug SNOG 2* [3]	3	11
20 Mar 93		TAKE ME UP *A & M AMCD 210* [4]	61	1
11 Jun 94		NO MORE TEARS (ENOUGH IS ENOUGH) *Bell 74321209032* [5]	13	7
8 Oct 94		GIMME ALL YOUR LOVIN' *Bell 74321231322* [6]	22	3
13 Jul 96	●	KEEP ON JUMPIN' *Manifesto FESCD 11* [7]	8	6
10 May 97		IT'S ALRIGHT, I FEEL IT! *Talkin Loud TLCD 22* [8]	26	2
12 Jul 97	●	SOMETHING GOIN' ON *Manifesto FESCD 25* [7]	5	10
25 Oct 97		I AM THE BLACK GOLD OF THE SUN *Talkin Loud TLCD 26* [8]	31	2
22 Nov 97		HAPPINESS *Sony S3 KAMCD 2* [9]	45	1

1958

FROM THE YEAR IN WHICH BUSBY'S BABES DIED IN A TRAGIC AIR CRASH, BILL AND MARK RICHARDS INVENTED THE SKATEBOARD, AND 'JAILHOUSE ROCK' BY ELVIS PRESLEY BECAME THE FIRST SINGLE TO ENTER THE CHART AT NO.1, **DAVID CROSBY** REMEMBERS HOW HE GOT HOOKED ON HARMONY ...

"I started singing harmony when I was about six, seven years old with my family – we used to do corny stuff like sit around together with 'The Fireside Book of Folk Songs' and sing folk songs. And the first record I ever bought was a harmony record: **The Everly Brothers'** 'All I Have to Do Is Dream'. The way they just edged up into a tone together was scary. There's a certain point, if you do it really well, where the individuals submit their ego to something bigger – they link up and all of a sudden this bubble pops into existence where the whole is greater than the sum of the parts and it's about this thing you create together."

SINGLE OF THE YEAR 'Magic Moments' Perry Como
ALBUM OF THE YEAR 'South Pacific' Soundtrack

2 May 98		FUN *INCredible INCRL 2CD*	33	2
29 Aug 98		AIN'T NO MOUNTAIN HIGH ENOUGH *INCredible INCRL 7CD*	35	2
27 Mar 99		I BELIEVE *Playola 0091705 PLA*	62	1
3 Jul 99		IT'S ALL GOOD *INCredible INCRL 14CD*	54	1
11 Mar 00		BELIEVE *Defected DFECT 14CD3* [10]	45	2
27 Jan 01		BELIEVE (re-mix) *Defected DFECT 26CDS* [10]	42	2

[1] Incognito featuring Jocelyn Brown [2] Jamestown featuring Jocelyn Brown [3] Right Said Fred. Guest vocals: Jocelyn Brown [4] Sonic Surfers featuring Jocelyn Brown [5] Kym Mazelle and Jocelyn Brown [6] Jocelyn Brown and Kym Mazelle [7] Todd Terry featuring Martha Wash and Jocelyn Brown [8] Nuyorican Soul featuring Jocelyn Brown [9] Kamasutra featuring Jocelyn Brown [10] Ministers De La Funk featuring Jocelyn Brown

See also Todd TERRY PROJECT

Joe BROWN and the BRUVVERS

339 Top 500 *Chirpy Cockney singer / guitarist, b. 13 May 1941, Lincolnshire, UK. Brown was one of the original artists managed by early rock impresario Larry Parnes. Voted Top UK Vocal Personality in 1962 NME Poll (92 WEEKS)* pos/wks

			pos	wks
17 Mar 60		THE DARKTOWN STRUTTERS' BALL *Decca F 11207*	34	6
26 Jan 61		SHINE *Pye 7N 15322* [1]	33	6
11 Jan 62		WHAT A CRAZY WORLD WE'RE LIVING IN *Piccadilly 7N 35024*	37	2
17 May 62	●	A PICTURE OF YOU *Piccadilly 7N 35047*	2	19
13 Sep 62		YOUR TENDER LOOK *Piccadilly 7N 35058*	31	6
15 Nov 62	●	IT ONLY TOOK A MINUTE *Piccadilly 7N 35082*	6	13
7 Feb 63	●	THAT'S WHAT LOVE WILL DO *Piccadilly 7N 35106*	3	14
21 Feb 63		IT ONLY TOOK A MINUTE (re-entry) *Piccadilly 7N 35082*	50	1
27 Jun 63		NATURE'S TIME FOR LOVE *Piccadilly 7N 35129*	26	6
26 Sep 63		SALLY ANN *Piccadilly 7N 35138*	28	9
29 Jun 67		WITH A LITTLE HELP FROM MY FRIENDS *Pye 7N 17339* [1]	32	4
14 Apr 73		HEY MAMA *Ammo AMO 101* [1]	33	6

[1] Joe Brown

Karen BROWN – *See DJ's RULE*

Kathy BROWN *US, female vocalist (1 WEEK)*

			pos	wks
20 Sep 97		TURN ME OUT (TURN TO SUGAR) (RE-MIX) *ffrr FCD* [1]	63	1
10 Apr 99		JOY *Azuli AZNYCDX 094*	63	1
10 Apr 99		LOVE IS NOT A GAME *Defected DFECT 31CDS* [2]	63	1
10 Apr 99		OVER YOU *Defected DFECT 28CDS* [3]	63	1

[1] Praxis featuring Kathey Brown [2] J. Majik featuring Kathy Brown [3] Warren Clarke featuring Kathy Brown

See also PRAXIS; J. MAJIK featuring Kathy BROWN; Warren CLARKE featuring Kathy BROWN

Miquel BROWN *US, female vocalist (7 WEEKS)*

			pos	wks
18 Feb 84		HE'S A SAINT, HE'S A SINNER *Record Shack SOHO 15*	68	4
24 Aug 85		CLOSE TO PERFECTION *Record Shack SOHO 48*	63	3

Palmer BROWN – *See BLAZE featuring Palmer BROWN*

Peter BROWN *US, male vocalist (9 WEEKS)*

			pos	wks
11 Feb 78		DO YA WANNA GET FUNKY WITH ME *TK TKR 6009*	43	4
17 Jun 78		DANCE WITH ME *TK TKR 6027*	57	5

Polly BROWN *UK, female vocalist (5 WEEKS)*

			pos	wks
14 Sep 74		UP IN A PUFF OF SMOKE *GTO GT 2*	43	5

Roy 'Chubby' BROWN

UK, male comedian – Royston Vasey (22 WEEKS)

			pos	wks
13 May 95		LIVING NEXT DOOR TO ALICE (WHO THE F**K IS ALICE) *N.O.W. CDWAG 245* [1]	64	2
12 Aug 95	●	LIVING NEXT DOOR TO ALICE (WHO THE F**K IS ALICE) (re-entry) *N.O.W. CDWAG 245* [1]	3	17
21 Dec 96		ROCKIN' GOOD CHRISTMAS *PolyStar 5732612*	51	3

[1] Smokie featuring Roy 'Chubby' Brown

Sam BROWN *UK, female vocalist (35 WEEKS)*

			pos	wks
11 Jun 88		STOP *A & M AM 440*	52	3
4 Feb 89	●	STOP (re-entry) *A & M AM 440*	4	12
13 May 89		CAN I GET A WITNESS *A & M AM 509*	15	7
3 Mar 90		WITH A LITTLE LOVE *A & M AM 539*	44	4
5 May 90		KISSING GATE *A & M AM 549*	23	8
26 Aug 95		JUST GOOD FRIENDS *Dick Bros. DDICK 014CD1* [1]	63	1

[1] Fish featuring Sam Brown

Sharon BROWN *US, female vocalist (11 WEEKS)*

			pos	wks
17 Apr 82		I SPECIALIZE IN LOVE *Virgin VS 494*	38	9
26 Feb 94		I SPECIALIZE IN LOVE (re-mix) *Deep Distraxion OILYCD 025*	62	2

BROWN SAUCE *UK, male / female vocal group (12 WEEKS)*

			pos	wks
12 Dec 81		I WANNA BE A WINNER *BBC RESL 101*	15	12

BROWN SUGAR – *See SEX CLUB featuring BROWN SUGAR*

Duncan BROWNE *UK, male vocalist (8 WEEKS)*

			pos	wks
19 Aug 72		JOURNEY *RAK 135*	23	6
22 Dec 84		THEME FROM 'THE TRAVELLING MAN' *Towerbell TOW 64*	68	2

Jackson BROWNE *US, male vocalist (14 WEEKS)*

			pos	wks
1 Jul 78		STAY *Asylum K 13128*	12	11
18 Oct 86		IN THE SHAPE OF A HEART *Elektra EKR 42*	66	2
25 Jun 94		EVERYWHERE I GO *Elektra EKR 184CD1*	67	1

Ronnie BROWNE – *See SCOTTISH RUGBY TEAM with Ronnie BROWNE*

Tom BROWNE *US, male instrumentalist – trumpet (24 WEEKS)*

			pos	wks
19 Jul 80	●	FUNKIN' FOR JAMAICA (NY) *Arista ARIST 357*	10	11
25 Oct 80		THIGHS HIGH (GRIP YOUR HIPS AND MOVE) *Arista ARIST 367*	45	5
30 Jan 82		FUNGI MAMA (BEBOPAFUNKADISCOLYPSO) *Arista ARIST 450*	58	4
11 Jan 92		FUNKIN' FOR JAMAICA (re-mix) *Arista 114998*	45	4

BROWNS *US, male / female vocal group – Jim Ed, Maxine and Bonnie Brown (13 WEEKS)*

			pos	wks
18 Sep 59	●	THE THREE BELLS *RCA 1140* ▲	6	13

BROWNSTONE *US, female vocal group (24 WEEKS)*

			pos	wks
1 Apr 95	●	IF YOU LOVE ME *MJJ 6614135*	8	12
15 Jul 95		GRAPEVYNE *MJJ 6620942*	16	4
23 Sep 95		I CAN'T TELL YOU WHY *MJJ 6623775*	27	2
17 May 97		5 MILES TO EMPTY *Epic 6640962*	12	4
27 Sep 97		KISS AND TELL *Epic 6649852*	21	2

BROWNSVILLE STATION

US, male vocal / instrumental group (6 WEEKS)

			pos	wks
2 Mar 74		SMOKIN' IN THE BOYS' ROOM *Philips 6073 834*	27	6

Dave BRUBECK QUARTET *US, male instrumental group (30 WEEKS)*

			pos	wks
26 Oct 61	●	TAKE FIVE *Fontana H 339*	6	15
8 Feb 62		IT'S A RAGGY WALTZ *Fontana H 352*	36	3
17 May 62		UNSQUARE DANCE *CBS AAG 102*	14	12

Tommy BRUCE and the BRUISERS

UK, male vocal / instrumental group (21 WEEKS)

			pos	wks
26 May 60	●	AIN'T MISBEHAVIN' *Columbia DB 4453*	3	16
8 Sep 60		BROKEN DOLL *Columbia DB 4498*	36	4
22 Feb 62		BABETTE *Columbia DB 4776* [1]	50	1

[1] Tommy Bruce

Claudia BRUCKEN *Germany, female vocalist (2 WEEKS)*

			pos	wks
11 Aug 90		ABSOLUT(E) *Island IS 471*	71	1
16 Feb 91		KISS LIKE ETHER *Island IS 479*	63	1

BRUISERS *UK, male instrumental group (7 WEEKS)*

			pos	wks
8 Aug 63		BLUE GIRL *Parlophone R 5042*	31	6
26 Sep 63		BLUE GIRL (re-entry) *Parlophone R 5042*	47	1

Frank BRUNO *UK, male vocalist (4 WEEKS)* pos/wks

23 Dec 95	**EYE OF THE TIGER** *RCA 74321336282*	28	4

BRUNO and LIZ – *See Liz KERSHAW and Bruno BROOKES*

Tyrone BRUNSON *US, male instrumentalist – bass (5 WEEKS)* pos/wks

25 Dec 82	**THE SMURF** *Epic EPC A 3024*	52	5

BRUVVERS – *See Joe BROWN and the BRUVVERS*

Dora BRYAN *UK, female actress – Dora Broadbent (6 WEEKS)* pos/wks

5 Dec 63	**ALL I WANT FOR CHRISTMAS IS A BEATLE** *Fontana TF 427*	20	6

Kéllé BRYAN *UK, female vocalist (4 WEEKS)* pos/wks

2 Oct 99	**HIGHER THAN HEAVEN** *1st Avenue / Mercury MERCD 522*	14	4

See also ETERNAL

Anita BRYANT *US, female vocalist (6 WEEKS)* pos/wks

26 May 60	**PAPER ROSES** *London HLL 9144*	49	1
30 Jun 60	**PAPER ROSES (re-entry)** *London HLL 9144*	45	1
14 Jul 60	**PAPER ROSES (2nd re-entry)** *London HLL 9144*	24	2
6 Oct 60	**MY LITTLE CORNER OF THE WORLD** *London HLL 9171*	48	2

Peabo BRYSON *US, male vocalist (35 WEEKS)* pos/wks

20 Aug 83 ●	**TONIGHT I CELEBRATE MY LOVE** *Capitol CL 302* [1]	2	13
16 May 92 ●	**BEAUTY AND THE BEAST** *Epic 6576607* [2]	9	7
17 Jul 93	**BY THE TIME THIS NIGHT IS OVER** *Arista 74321157142* [3]	56	3
11 Dec 93	**A WHOLE NEW WORLD (ALADDIN'S THEME)** *Columbia 6599002* [4] ▲	12	12

[1] Peabo Bryson and Roberta Flack [2] Celine Dion and Peabo Bryson [3] Kenny G with Peabo Bryson [4] Regina Belle and Peabo Bryson

BT *US, male producer – Brian Transeau (26 WEEKS)* pos/wks

18 Mar 95	**EMBRACING THE SUNSHINE** *East West YZ 895CD*	34	2
16 Sep 95	**LOVING YOU MORE** *Perfecto PERF 110CD* [1]	28	2
10 Feb 96	**LOVING YOU MORE (re-mix)** *Perfecto PERF 117CD* [1]	14	3
9 Nov 96	**BLUE SKIES** *Perfecto PERF 130CD1* [2]	26	2
19 Jul 97	**FLAMING JUNE** *Perfecto PERF 145CD1*	19	4
29 Nov 97	**LOVE, PEACE & GREASE** *Perfecto PERF 153CD1*	41	1
10 Jan 98	**FLAMING JUNE (re-mix)** *Perfecto PERF 157CD1*	28	4
18 Apr 98	**REMEMBER** *Perfecto PERF 160CD1*	27	2
21 Nov 98	**GODSPEED** *Renaissance RENCD 002*	54	1
9 Oct 99	**MERCURY AND SOLACE** *Headspace HEDSCD 001*	38	2
24 Jun 00	**DREAMING** *Headspace HEDSCD 002* [3]	38	2
23 Jun 01	**NEVER GONNA COME BACK DOWN** *Ministry of Sound MOSBT CDS1*	51	1

[1] BT featuring Vincent Covello [2] BT featuring Tori Amos [3] BT featuring Kirsty Hawkshaw

BT EXPRESS *US, male instrumental / vocal group (11 WEEKS)* pos/wks

29 Mar 75	**EXPRESS** *Pye International 7N 25674*	34	6
26 Jul 80	**DOES IT FEEL GOOD / GIVE UP THE FUNK (LET'S DANCE)** *Calibre CAB 503*	52	4
23 Apr 94	**EXPRESS (re-mix)** *PWL International PWCD 285*	67	1

BUBBLEROCK – *See Jonathan KING*

Catherine BUCHANAN – *See JELLYBEAN*

Roy BUCHANAN *US, male instrumentalist – guitar (3 WEEKS)* pos/wks

31 Mar 73	**SWEET DREAMS** *Polydor 2066 307*	40	3

BUCKETHEADS *US, male producer – Kenny Gonzalez (16 WEEKS)* pos/wks

4 Mar 95 ●	**THE BOMB! (THESE SOUNDS FALL INTO MY MIND)** *Positiva CDTIV 33*	5	13
20 Jan 96	**GOT MYSELF TOGETHER** *Positiva CDTIV 48*	12	3

Lindsey BUCKINGHAM *US, male vocalist (7 WEEKS)* pos/wks

16 Jan 82	**TROUBLE** *Mercury MER 85*	31	7

See also FLEETWOOD MAC

Jeff BUCKLEY *US, male vocalist (3 WEEKS)* pos/wks

27 May 95	**LAST GOODBYE** *Columbia 6620422*	54	2
6 Jun 98	**EVERYBODY HERE WANTS YOU** *Columbia 6657912*	43	1

BUCKS FIZZ (147 Top 500) *Chart-topping mixed quartet: Cheryl Baker, Mike Nolan, Jay Aston (replaced by Shelley Preston in 1985) and Bobby G (Gubby). Formed for the 1981 Eurovision Song Contest, they were the last UK winners for 16 years (150 WEEKS)* pos/wks

28 Mar 81 ★	**MAKING YOUR MIND UP** *RCA 56*	1	12
6 Jun 81	**PIECE OF THE ACTION** *RCA 88*	12	9
15 Aug 81	**ONE OF THOSE NIGHTS** *RCA 114*	20	10
28 Nov 81 ★	**THE LAND OF MAKE BELIEVE** *RCA 163*	1	16
27 Mar 82 ★	**MY CAMERA NEVER LIES** *RCA 202*	1	8
19 Jun 82 ●	**NOW THOSE DAYS ARE GONE** *RCA 241*	8	9
27 Nov 82 ●	**IF YOU CAN'T STAND THE HEAT** *RCA 300*	10	11
12 Mar 83	**RUN FOR YOUR LIFE** *RCA FIZ 1*	14	7
18 Jun 83 ●	**WHEN WE WERE YOUNG** *RCA 342*	10	8
1 Oct 83	**LONDON TOWN** *RCA 363*	34	6
17 Dec 83	**RULES OF THE GAME** *RCA 380*	57	6
25 Aug 84	**TALKING IN YOUR SLEEP** *RCA FIZ 2*	15	9
27 Oct 84	**GOLDEN DAYS** *RCA FIZ 3*	42	4
29 Dec 84	**I HEAR TALK** *RCA FIZ 4*	34	8
22 Jun 85	**YOU AND YOUR HEART SO BLUE** *RCA PB 40233*	43	4
14 Sep 85	**MAGICAL** *RCA PB 40367*	57	3
7 Jun 86 ●	**NEW BEGINNING (MAMBA SEYRA)** *Polydor POSP 794*	8	10
30 Aug 86	**LOVE THE ONE YOU'RE WITH** *Polydor POSP 813*	47	3
15 Nov 86	**KEEP EACH OTHER WARM** *Polydor POSP 835*	45	4
5 Nov 88	**HEART OF STONE** *RCA PB 42035*	50	3

BUCKSHOT LEFONQUE
US, male vocal / instrumental group (1 WEEK) pos/wks

6 Dec 97	**ANOTHER DAY** *Columbia 6653762*	65	1

Roy BUDD *UK, male instrumentalist – piano (1 WEEK)* pos/wks

10 Jul 99	**GET CARTER** *Cinephile CINX 1003*	68	1

BUDGIE *UK, male vocal / instrumental group (2 WEEKS)* pos/wks

3 Oct 81	**KEEPING A RENDEZVOUS** *RCA BUDGIE 3*	71	2

BUFFALO G *Ireland, female vocal / rap duo – Olive Tucker and Naomi Lynch (4 WEEKS)* pos/wks

10 Jun 00	**WE'RE REALLY SAYING SOMETHING** *Epic 6694182*	17	3
8 Jul 00	**WE'RE REALLY SAYING SOMETHING (re-entry)** *Epic 6694182*	74	1

BUFFALO TOM *US, male vocal / instrumental group (5 WEEKS)* pos/wks

23 Oct 99 ●	**GOING UNDERGROUND : CARNATION** *Ignition IGNSCD 16*	6	5

B side by Liam Gallagher and Steve Cradock

BUG KANN and the PLASTIC JAM
UK, male / female vocal / instrumental group (2 WEEKS) pos/wks

31 Aug 91	**MADE IN TWO MINUTES** *Optimum Dance BKPJ 1S* [1]	70	1
26 Feb 94	**MADE IN 2 MINUTES (re-mix)** *PWL International PWCD 286*	64	1

[1] Bug Kann and Plastic Jam featuring Patti Low and Doogie

BUGGLES *UK, male vocal / instrumental duo – Trevor Horn and Geoff Downes (28 WEEKS)* pos/wks

22 Sep 79 ★	**VIDEO KILLED THE RADIO STAR** *Island WIP 6524*	1	11
26 Jan 80	**THE PLASTIC AGE** *Island WIP 6540*	16	8
5 Apr 80	**CLEAN CLEAN** *Island WIP 6584*	38	5
8 Nov 80	**ELSTREE** *Island WIP 6624*	55	4

James BULLER *UK, male vocalist (1 WEEK)* pos/wks

6 Mar 99	**CAN'T SMILE WITHOUT YOU** *BBC Music WMSS 60092*	51	1

Silvah BULLET – *See Jonny L*

BULLETPROOF *UK, male producer – Paul Chambers (1 WEEK)* pos/wks

10 Mar 01	**SAY YEAH / DANCE TO THE RHYTHM** *Tidy Trax TIDY 148CD*	62	1

BUMP *UK, male instrumental / production duo (5 WEEKS)* pos/wks

4 Jul 92	**I'M RUSHING** *Good Boy EDGE7 1*	40	4
11 Nov 95	**I'M RUSHING (re-mix)** *Deconstruction 74321320692*	45	1

BUMP & FLEX *UK, male / female vocal / production duo (1 WEEK)* pos/wks

23 May 98	**LONG TIME COMING** *Heat Recordings HEATCD 014*	73	1

BUNKER KRU – *See HARLEQUIN 4s / BUNKER KRU*

BUNNYMEN – *See ECHO and the BUNNYMEN*

Emma BUNTON *UK, female vocalist (35 WEEKS)* pos/wks

13 Nov 99 ●	**WHAT I AM** *VC Recordings VCRD 53* [1]	2	12
14 Apr 01 ★	**WHAT TOOK YOU SO LONG** *Virgin VSCDT 1796* ■	1	12
8 Sep 01 ●	**TAKE MY BREATH AWAY** *Virgin VSCDT 1814*	5	9
22 Dec 01	**WE'RE NOT GONNA SLEEP TONIGHT** *Virgin VSCDT 1821*	20	2+

[1] Tin Tin Out featuring Emma Bunton

See also SPICE GIRLS

Eric BURDON – *See ANIMALS*

Geoffrey BURGON *UK, orchestra (4 WEEKS)* pos/wks

26 Dec 81	**BRIDESHEAD THEME** *Chrysalis CHS 2562*	48	4

Keni BURKE *US, male vocalist (4 WEEKS)* pos/wks

27 Jun 81	**LET SOMEBODY LOVE YOU** *RCA 93*	59	3
18 Apr 92	**RISIN' TO THE TOP** *RCA PB 49103*	70	1

Hank C BURNETTE *Sweden, male multi-instrumentalist (8 WEEKS)* pos/wks

30 Oct 76	**SPINNING ROCK BOOGIE** *Sonet SON 2094*	21	8

Johnny BURNETTE *US, male vocalist (48 WEEKS)* pos/wks

29 Sep 60 ●	**DREAMIN'** *London HLG 9172*	5	16
12 Jan 61 ●	**YOU'RE SIXTEEN** *London HLG 9254*	3	12
13 Apr 61	**LITTLE BOY SAD** *London HLG 9315*	12	12
10 Aug 61	**GIRLS** *London HLG 9388*	37	5
17 May 62	**CLOWN SHOES** *Liberty LIB 55416*	35	3

Rocky BURNETTE *US, male vocalist (7 WEEKS)* pos/wks

17 Nov 79	**TIRED OF TOEIN' THE LINE** *EMI 2992*	58	7

Jerry BURNS *UK, female vocalist (1 WEEK)* pos/wks

25 Apr 92	**PALE RED** *Columbia 6579467*	64	1

Ray BURNS *UK, male vocalist (19 WEEKS)* pos/wks

11 Feb 55 ●	**MOBILE** *Columbia DB 3563* [1]	4	13
26 Aug 55	**THAT'S HOW A LOVE SONG WAS BORN** *Columbia DB 3640* [2]	14	6

[1] Ray Burns with Eric Jupp and His Orchestra [2] Ray Burns with the Coronets

BURRELLS – *See RESONANCE featuring The BURRELLS*

Malandra BURROWS *UK, female vocalist (10 WEEKS)* pos/wks

1 Dec 90	**JUST THIS SIDE OF LOVE** *Yorkshire Television DALE 1*	11	8
18 Oct 97	**CARNIVAL IN HEAVEN** *Warner.esp WESP 001CD*	49	1
29 Aug 98	**DON'T LEAVE ME** *Warner.esp WESP 004CD*	54	1

Jenny BURTON *US, female vocalist (2 WEEKS)* pos/wks

30 Mar 85	**BAD HABITS** *Atlantic A 9583*	68	2

BURUNDI STEIPHENSON BLACK *Burundi, drummers and chanters with orchestral additions by Mike Steiphenson of France (14 WEEKS)* pos/wks

13 Nov 71	**BURUNDI BLACK** *Barclay BAR 3*	31	14

BUS 75 – *See WHALE*

BUS STOP *UK, male production group (19 WEEKS)* pos/wks

23 May 98 ●	**KUNG FU FIGHTING** *All Around the World CDGLOBE 173* [1]	8	11
24 Oct 98	**YOU AIN'T SEEN NOTHIN' YET** *All Around the World CDGLOBE 187* [2]	22	4
10 Apr 99	**JUMP** *All Around the World CDGLOBE 186*	23	3
7 Sep 00	**GET IT ON** *All Around the World CDGLOBE225* [3]	59	1

[1] Bus Stop featuring Carl Douglas [2] Bus Stop featuring Randy Bachman [3] Bus Stop featuing T. Rex

Lou BUSCH and his Orchestra
US, orchestra and chorus – aka Joe 'Fingers' Carr (17 WEEKS) pos/wks

27 Jan 56 ●	**ZAMBESI** *Capitol CL 14504*	2	17

BUSH *UK, male vocal / instrumental group (13 WEEKS)* pos/wks

8 Jun 96	**MACHINEHEAD** *Interscope IND 95505*	48	2
1 Mar 97 ●	**SWALLOWED** *Interscope IND 95528*	7	5
7 Jun 97	**GREEDY FLY** *Interscope IND 95536*	22	2
1 Nov 97	**BONE DRIVEN** *Interscope IND 95553*	49	1
4 Dec 99	**THE CHEMICALS BETWEEN US** *Trauma / Polydor 4972222*	46	1
18 Mar 00	**WARM MACHINE** *Trauma / Polydor 4972752*	45	1
3 Jun 00	**LETTING THE CABLES SLEEP** *Trauma / Polydor 4973352*	51	1

Kate BUSH (123 Top 500) *Unmistakable singer / songwriter with operatic vocal ability, b. 30 Jul 1958, Kent. Discovered by Dave Gilmour of Pink Floyd. First British female to top the singles chart with a self-composed song and the first to have a UK No.1 album (168 WEEKS)* pos/wks

11 Feb 78 ★	**WUTHERING HEIGHTS** *EMI 2719*	1	12
13 May 78	**WUTHERING HEIGHTS (re-entry)** *EMI 2719*	75	1
10 Jun 78 ●	**MAN WITH THE CHILD IN HIS EYES** *EMI 2806*	6	11
11 Nov 78	**HAMMER HORROR** *EMI 2887*	44	6
17 Mar 79	**WOW** *EMI 2911*	14	10
15 Sep 79 ●	**ON STAGE (EP)** *EMI MIEP 2991*	10	9
26 Apr 80	**BREATHING** *EMI 5058*	16	7
5 Jul 80 ●	**BABOOSHKA** *EMI 5085*	5	10
4 Oct 80	**ARMY DREAMERS** *EMI 5106*	16	9
6 Dec 80	**DECEMBER WILL BE MAGIC AGAIN** *EMI 5121*	29	7
11 Jul 81	**SAT IN YOUR LAP** *EMI 5201*	11	7
7 Aug 82	**THE DREAMING** *EMI 5296*	48	3
17 Aug 85 ●	**RUNNING UP THAT HILL** *EMI KB 1*	3	11
26 Oct 85	**CLOUDBUSTING** *EMI KB 2*	20	6
1 Mar 86	**HOUNDS OF LOVE** *EMI KB 3*	18	5
10 May 86	**THE BIG SKY** *EMI KB 4*	37	3
1 Nov 86 ●	**DON'T GIVE UP** *Virgin PGS 2* [1]	9	11
8 Nov 86	**EXPERIMENT IV** *EMI KB 5*	23	4
30 Sep 89	**THE SENSUAL WORLD** *EMI EM 102*	12	5
2 Dec 89	**THIS WOMAN'S WORK** *EMI EM 119*	25	5
10 Mar 90	**LOVE AND ANGER** *EMI EM 134*	38	3
7 Dec 91	**ROCKET MAN (I THINK IT'S GOING TO BE A LONG LONG TIME)** *Mercury TRIBO 2*	12	8
18 Sep 93	**RUBBERBAND GIRL** *EMI CDEM 280*	12	5
27 Nov 93	**MOMENTS OF PLEASURE** *EMI CDEM 297*	26	3
16 Apr 94	**THE RED SHOES** *EMI CDEMS 316*	21	3
30 Jul 94	**THE MAN I LOVE** *Mercury MERCD 408* [2]	27	2
19 Nov 94	**AND SO IS LOVE** *EMI CDEMS 355*	26	2

[1] Peter Gabriel and Kate Bush [2] Kate Bush and Larry Adler

Tracks on On Stage (EP): Them Heavy People / Don't Push Your Foot on the Heartbrake / James and the Cold Gun / L'Amour Looks Something Like You

BUSTER *UK, male vocal / instrumental group (1 WEEK)* pos/wks

19 Jun 76	**SUNDAY** *RCA 2678*	49	1

Bernard BUTLER *UK, male vocal / instrumentalist (21 WEEKS)*

Date		Title / Label	pos	wks
27 May 95	●	YES *Hut HUTCD 53* [1]	8	8
4 Nov 95		YOU DO *Hut HUTDG 57* [1]	17	4
17 Jan 98		STAY *Creation CRESCD 281*	12	4
28 Mar 98		NOT ALONE *Creation CRESCD 289*	27	3
27 Jun 98		A CHANGE OF HEART *Creation CRESCD 297*	45	1
23 Oct 99		YOU MUST GO ON *Creation CRESCD 324*	44	1

[1] McAlmont and Butler

See also SUEDE

Jonathan BUTLER
South Africa, male vocalist / instrumentalist – guitar (18 WEEKS)

Date		Title / Label	pos	wks
25 Jan 86		IF YOU'RE READY (COME GO WITH ME) *Jive JIVE 109* [1]	30	7
8 Aug 87		LIES *Jive JIVE 141*	18	11

[1] Ruby Turner featuring Jonathan Butler

BUTTERSCOTCH *UK, male vocal group (11 WEEKS)*

Date		Title / Label	pos	wks
2 May 70		DON'T YOU KNOW *RCA 1937*	17	11

BUTTHOLE SURFERS *US, male vocal / instrumental group (1 WEEK)*

Date		Title / Label	pos	wks
5 Oct 96		PEPPER *Capitol CDCL 778*	59	1

BUZZCOCKS *UK, male vocal / instrumental group (53 WEEKS)*

Date		Title / Label	pos	wks
18 Feb 78		WHAT DO I GET *United Artists UP 36348*	37	3
13 May 78		I DON'T MIND *United Artists UP 36386*	55	2
15 Jul 78		LOVE YOU MORE *United Artists UP 36433*	34	6
23 Sep 78		EVER FALLEN IN LOVE (WITH SOMEONE YOU SHOULDN'T'VE) *United Artists UP 36455*	12	11
25 Nov 78		PROMISES *United Artists UP 36471*	20	10
10 Mar 79		EVERYBODY'S HAPPY NOWADAYS *United Artists UP 36499*	29	6
21 Jul 79		HARMONY IN MY HEAD *United Artists UP 36541*	32	6
25 Aug 79		SPIRAL SCRATCH (EP) *New Hormones ORG 1*	31	6
6 Sep 80		ARE EVERYTHING / WHY SHE'S A GIRL FROM THE CHAINSTORE *United Artists BP 365*	61	3

Tracks on Spiral Scratch (EP): Breakdown / Time's Up / Boredom / Friends of Mine. Sleeve of EP (not the label) credits Buzzcocks with Howard Devoto. 'Why She's a Girl from the Chainstore' listed from 13 Sep 1980

BUZZY BUNCH – *See Celi BEE and the BUZZY BUNCH*

BVSMP *US, male rap / vocal group (12 WEEKS)*

Date		Title / Label	pos	wks
23 Jul 88	●	I NEED YOU *Debut DEBT 3044*	3	12

BY ALL MEANS *US, male vocal group (2 WEEKS)*

Date		Title / Label	pos	wks
18 Jun 88		I SURRENDER TO YOUR LOVE *Fourth & Broadway BRW 102*	65	2

Max BYGRAVES (198 Top 500)

One of Britain's best-loved entertainers, b. 16 Oct 1922, London. The comedian / singer / songwriter was the only British male on the first UK singles chart. He had five Top 20 'sing-a-long' hit albums in just 15 months of the 1970s (131 WEEKS)

Date		Title / Label	pos	wks
14 Nov 52		COWPUNCHER'S CANTATA *HMV B 10250*	11	1
2 Jan 53	●	COWPUNCHER'S CANTATA (re-entry) *HMV B 10250*	8	1
23 Jan 53	●	COWPUNCHER'S CANTATA (2nd re-entry) *HMV B 10250*	6	5
6 Mar 53	●	COWPUNCHER'S CANTATA (3rd re-entry) *HMV B 10250*	10	1
14 May 54	●	(THE GANG THAT SANG) HEART OF MY HEART *HMV B 10654*	7	8
10 Sep 54	●	GILLY GILLY OSSENFEFFER KATZENELLEN BOGEN BY THE SEA *HMV B 10734*	7	7
5 Nov 54		GILLY GILLY OSSENFEFFER KATZENELLEN BOGEN BY THE SEA (re-entry) *HMV B 10734*	20	1
21 Jan 55		MISTER SANDMAN *HMV B 10801*	16	1
18 Nov 55	●	MEET ME ON THE CORNER *HMV POP 116*	2	11
17 Feb 56		THE BALLAD OF DAVY CROCKETT *HMV POP 153*	20	1
25 May 56		OUT OF TOWN *HMV POP 164*	18	7
5 Apr 57		HEART *Decca F 10862* [1]	14	8
2 May 58	●	YOU NEED HANDS / TULIPS FROM AMSTERDAM *Decca F 11004* [2]	3	25
22 Aug 58		LITTLE TRAIN / GOTTA HAVE RAIN *Decca F 11046*	28	2
2 Jan 59		(I LOVE TO PLAY) MY UKULELE *Decca F 11077*	19	4
18 Dec 59	●	JINGLE BELL ROCK *Decca F 11176*	7	4
10 Mar 60	●	FINGS AIN'T WOT THEY USED T'BE *Decca F 11214*	5	15
28 Jul 60		CONSIDER YOURSELF *Decca F 11251*	50	1
1 Jun 61		THE BELLS OF AVIGNON *Decca F 11350*	36	5
19 Feb 69		YOU'RE MY EVERYTHING *Pye 7N 17705*	50	1
5 Mar 69		YOU'RE MY EVERYTHING (re-entry) *Pye 7N 17705*	34	3
6 Oct 73		DECK OF CARDS *Pye 7N 45276*	13	15
9 Dec 89		WHITE CHRISTMAS *Parkfield PMS 5012*	71	4

[1] Max Bygraves With Malcolm Lockyer and his Orchestra [2] Max Bygraves with the Clark Bros and both sides with Eric Rodgers and his Orchestra

Cowpuncher's Cantata is a medley with the following songs: Cry of the Wild Goose / Riders in the Sky / Mule Train / Jezebel. 'Tulips from Amsterdam' was listed with 'You Need Hands' from 9 May 1958

BYKER GROOOVE! *UK, female vocal group (3 WEEKS)*

Date		Title / Label	pos	wks
24 Dec 94		LOVE YOUR SEXY . . . !! *Groove GROVD 01*	48	3

Charlie BYRD – *See Stan GETZ*

Debra BYRD – *See Barry MANILOW*

Donald BYRD *US, male instrumentalist – trumpet (6 WEEKS)*

Date		Title / Label	pos	wks
26 Sep 81		LOVING YOU / LOVE HAS COME AROUND *Elektra K 12559*	41	6

Gary BYRD and the GB EXPERIENCE *US, male rapper and male / female vocal / instrumental group (9 WEEKS)*

Date		Title / Label	pos	wks
23 Jul 83	●	THE CROWN *Motown TMGT 1312*	6	9

Features uncredited vocals by Stevie Wonder

BYRDS *US, male vocal / instrumental group (52 WEEKS)*

Date		Title / Label	pos	wks
17 Jun 65	★	MR TAMBOURINE MAN *CBS 201765* ▲	1	14
12 Aug 65	●	ALL I REALLY WANT TO DO *CBS 201796*	4	10
11 Nov 65		TURN! TURN! TURN! (TO EVERYTHING THERE IS A SEASON) *CBS 202008* ▲	26	8
5 May 66		EIGHT MILES HIGH *CBS 202067*	24	9
5 Jun 68		YOU AIN'T GOING NOWHERE *CBS 3411*	45	3
13 Feb 71		CHESTNUT MARE *CBS 5322*	19	8

Edward BYRNES and Connie STEVENS
US, male / female vocal duo (8 WEEKS)

Date		Title / Label	pos	wks
5 May 60		KOOKIE, KOOKIE (LEND ME YOUR COMB) *Warner Bros. WB 5*	27	8

See also Connie STEVENS

BYSTANDERS *UK, male vocal / instrumental group (1 WEEK)*

Date		Title / Label	pos	wks
9 Feb 67		98.6 *Piccadilly 7N 35363*	45	1

C

Andy C – *See SHIMON and Andy C*

Melanie C (468 Top 500)

Former Sporty Spice (b. Melanie Chisholm, 12 Jan 1974, Liverpool, UK) has appeared on 11 No.1 hits – a total never bettered by any female artist. Only woman to top the UK chart solo and as part of a duo, quartet and quintet (74 WEEKS)

Date		Title / Label	pos	wks
12 Dec 98	●	WHEN YOU'RE GONE *A & M 5828212* [1]	3	19
9 Oct 99	●	GOIN' DOWN *Virgin VSCDT 1744*	4	4
13 Nov 99		GOIN' DOWN (re-entry) *Virgin VSCDT 1744*	64	2
4 Dec 99	●	NORTHERN STAR *Virgin VSCDT 1748*	4	11
1 Apr 00	★	NEVER BE THE SAME AGAIN *Virgin VSCDT 1762* [2] ■	1	14

22 Jul 00 **NEVER BE THE SAME AGAIN (re-entry)** *Virgin VSCDT 1762* [2] 70 2
19 Aug 00 ★ **I TURN TO YOU** *Virgin VSCDT 1772* ■ 1 12
9 Dec 00 **IF THAT WERE ME** *Virgin VSCDT 1786* 18 8
3 Mar 01 **IF THAT WERE ME (re-entry)** *Virgin VSCDT 1786* 72 2

[1] Bryan Adams featuring Melanie C [2] Melanie C / Lisa 'Left Eye' Lopes

See also SPICE GIRLS

Roy C *US, male vocalist – Roy C Hammond (24 WEEKS)* pos/wks

21 Apr 66 ● **SHOTGUN WEDDING** *Island WI 273* 6 11
25 Nov 72 ● **SHOTGUN WEDDING (re-issue)** *UK 19* 8 13

C & C MUSIC FACTORY / CLIVILLES & COLE *US, male instrumental / production duo (Robert Clivilles and David Cole) featuring male / female vocalists / rappers (53 WEEKS)* pos/wks

15 Dec 90 ● **GONNA MAKE YOU SWEAT (EVERYBODY DANCE NOW)** *CBS 6564540* [1] ▲ 3 12
30 Mar 91 **HERE WE GO** *Columbia 6567557* [1] 20 7
6 Jul 91 ● **THINGS THAT MAKE YOU GO HMMM...** *Columbia 6566907* [1] 4 11
23 Nov 91 **JUST A TOUCH OF LOVE (EVERYDAY)** *Columbia 6575247* [2] 31 3
18 Jan 92 **PRIDE (IN THE NAME OF LOVE)** *Columbia 6577017* [3] 15 5
14 Mar 92 **A DEEPER LOVE** *Columbia 6578497* [3] 15 5
3 Oct 92 **KEEP IT COMIN' (DANCE TILL YOU CAN'T DANCE NO MORE)** *Columbia 6584307* [4] 34 3
27 Aug 94 **DO YOU WANNA GET FUNKY** *Columbia 6607622* [5] 27 3
18 Feb 95 **I FOUND LOVE / TAKE A TOKE** *Columbia 6612112* [6] 26 2
11 Nov 95 **I'LL ALWAYS BE AROUND** *MCA MCSTD 40001* [5] 42 2

[1] C & C Music Factory (featuring Freedom Williams) [2] C & C Music Factory featuring Zelma Davis [3] Clivilles and Cole [4] C & C Music Factory featuring Q Unique and Deborah Cooper [5] C & C Music Factory [6] C & C Music Factory / C & C Music Factory featuring Martha Wash

ÇA VA ÇA VA *UK, male vocal / instrumental group (8 WEEKS)* pos/wks

18 Sep 82 **WHERE'S ROMEO** *Regard RG 103* 49 5
19 Feb 83 **BROTHER BRIGHT** *Regard RG 105* 65 3

Montserrat CABALLE – *See Freddie MERCURY*

CABANA *Brazil, male / female vocal / instrumental duo (1 WEEK)* pos/wks

15 Jul 95 **BAILANDO CON LOBOS** *Hi-Life 5792512* 65 1

CABARET VOLTAIRE *UK, male vocal / instrumental group (8 WEEKS)* pos/wks

18 Jul 87 **DON'T ARGUE** *Parlophone R 6157* 69 2
4 Nov 89 **HYPNOTISED** *Parlophone R 6227* 66 2
12 May 90 **KEEP ON** *Parlophone R 6250* 55 2
18 Aug 90 **EASY LIFE** *Parlophone R 6261* 61 2

CABLE *UK, male vocal / instrumental group (2 WEEKS)* pos/wks

14 Jun 97 **FREEZE THE ATLANTIC** *Infectious INFECT 38CD* 44 2

Albert CABRERA – *See David MORALES*

CACIQUE *UK, male / female vocal / instrumental group (1 WEEK)* pos/wks

1 Jun 85 **DEVOTED TO YOU** *Diamond Duel DISC 1* 69 1

CACTUS WORLD NEWS *Ireland, male vocal / instrumental group (7 WEEKS)* pos/wks

8 Feb 86 **YEARS LATER** *MCA MCA 1024* 59 3
26 Apr 86 **WORLDS APART** *MCA MCA 1040* 58 3
20 Sep 86 **THE BRIDGE** *MCA MCA 1080* 74 1

CADETS with Eileen REID *Ireland, male / female vocal / instrumental group (1 WEEK)* pos/wks

3 Jun 65 **JEALOUS HEART** *Pye 7N 15852* 42 1

Susan CADOGAN *UK, female vocalist (19 WEEKS)* pos/wks

5 Apr 75 ● **HURT SO GOOD** *Magnet MAG 23* 4 12
19 Jul 75 **LOVE ME BABY** *Magnet MAG 36* 22 7

Athena CAGE – *See Keith SWEAT*

Al CAIOLA *US, orchestra, Al Caiola – guitar (6 WEEKS)* pos/wks

15 Jun 61 **THE MAGNIFICENT SEVEN** *HMV POP 889 / London HLT 9294* 34 6

CAKE *US, male vocal / instrumental group (7 WEEKS)* pos/wks

22 Mar 97 **THE DISTANCE** *Capricorn 5742212* 22 3
31 May 97 **I WILL SURVIVE** *Capricorn 5744712* 29 2
1 May 99 **NEVER THERE** *Capricorn 8708112* 66 1
3 Nov 01 **SHORT SKIRT LONG JACKET** *Columbia 6720402* 63 1

CALIBRE CUTS – *See VARIOUS ARTISTS (MONTAGES)*

CALIFORNIA SUNSHINE *Israel / Italy, male / female DJ / production group (1 WEEK)* pos/wks

16 Aug 97 **SUMMER '89** *Perfecto PERF 143CD* 56 1

CALL *US, male vocal / instrumental group (6 WEEKS)* pos/wks

30 Sep 89 **LET THE DAY BEGIN** *MCA MCA 1362* 42 6

Terry CALLIER *US, male vocalist (4 WEEKS)* pos/wks

13 Dec 97 **BEST BIT (EP)** *Heavenly HVN 72CD* [1] 36 3
23 May 98 **LOVE THEME FROM SPARTACUS** *Talkin' Loud TLCD 32* 57 1

[1] Beth Orton featuring Terry Callier

Tracks on Best Bit (EP): Skimming Stone / Dolphins / Lean On Me

Eddie CALVERT 415 Top 500 *The Man with the Golden Trumpet', b. 13 Mar 1922, Lancashire, UK, d. 7 Aug 1978, South Africa. 'Oh Mein Papa' spent nine weeks at the top – a record for an instrumental (80 WEEKS)* pos/wks

18 Dec 53 ★ **OH, MEIN PAPA** *Columbia DB 3337* 1 21
8 Apr 55 ★ **CHERRY PINK AND APPLE BLOSSOM WHITE** *Columbia DB 3581* 1 21
13 May 55 **STRANGER IN PARADISE** *Columbia DB 3594* 14 4
29 Jul 55 ● **JOHN AND JULIE** *Columbia DB 3624* 6 11
9 Mar 56 **ZAMBESI** *Columbia DB 3747* 18 1
23 Mar 56 **ZAMBESI (re-entry)** *Columbia DB 3747* 13 6
7 Feb 58 ● **MANDY (LA PANSE)** *Columbia DB 3956* 9 14
20 Jun 58 **LITTLE SERENADE** *Columbia DB 4105* 28 2

Donnie CALVIN – *See ROCKER'S REVENGE featuring Donnie CALVIN*

CAMEO *US, male vocal / instrumental group (71 WEEKS)* pos/wks

31 Mar 84 **SHE'S STRANGE** *Club JAB 2* 37 8
13 Jul 85 **ATTACK ME WITH YOUR LOVE** *Club JAB 16* 65 2
14 Sep 85 **SINGLE LIFE** *Club JAB 21* 15 10
7 Dec 85 **SHE'S STRANGE (re-issue)** *Club JAB 25* 22 8
22 Mar 86 **A GOODBYE** *Club JAB 28* 65 2
30 Aug 86 ● **WORD UP** *Club JAB 38* 3 13
29 Nov 86 **CANDY** *Club JAB 43* 27 9
25 Apr 87 **BACK AND FORTH** *Club JAB 49* 11 9
17 Oct 87 **SHE'S MINE** *Club JAB 57* 35 4
29 Oct 88 **YOU MAKE ME WORK** *Club JAB 70* 74 1
28 Jul 01 **LOVERBOY** *Virgin VUSCD 211* [1] 12 4
15 Sep 01 **LOVERBOY (re-entry)** *Virgin VUSCD 211* [1] 53 1

[1] Mariah featuring Cameo

Andy CAMERON *UK, male vocalist (8 WEEKS)* pos/wks

4 Mar 78 ● **ALLY'S TARTAN ARMY** *Klub 03* 6 8

CAM'RON featuring MASE *US, male rappers – Cameron Giles and Mason Betha (4 WEEKS)* pos/wks

19 Sep 98 **HORSE AND CARRIAGE** *Epic 6662612* 12 4

CAMILLA – *See MOJOLATORS featuring CAMILLA*

Tony CAMILLO'S BAZUKA
US, male instrumental / vocal group (5 WEEKS) pos/wks

31 May 75 **DYNOMITE (PART 1)** *A & M AMS 7168* 28 5

CAMISRA *UK, male DJ / producer – 'Tall Paul' Newman (12 WEEKS)* pos/wks

21 Feb 98 ● **LET ME SHOW YOU** *VC Recordings VCRD 31* 5 8
11 Jul 98 **FEEL THE BEAT** *VC Recordings VCRD 39* 32 2
22 May 99 **CLAP YOUR HANDS** *VC Recordings VCRD 49* 34 2

See also PARTIZAN; ESCRIMA; TALL PAUL; GRIFTERS

CAMOUFLAGE featuring MYSTI
UK, male / female vocal / instrumental group (3 WEEKS) pos/wks

24 Sep 77 **BEE STING** *State STAT 58* 48 3

CAMP LO *US, male rap duo (1 WEEK)* pos/wks

16 Aug 97 **LUCHINI AKA (THIS IS IT)** *ffrr FCD 305* 74 1

CAMPAG VELOCET
UK, male female vocal / instrumental group (1 WEEK) pos/wks

19 Feb 00 **VITO SATAN** *Pias Recordings PIASX 010CD* 75 1

Ali CAMPBELL *UK, male vocalist (18 WEEKS)* pos/wks

20 May 95 ● **THAT LOOK IN YOUR EYE** *Kuff KUFFDG 1* 5 10
26 Aug 95 **LET YOUR YEAH BE YEAH** *Kuff KUFFD 2* 25 4
9 Dec 95 **SOMETHIN' STUPID** *Kuff KUFFDG 5* [1] 30 4

[1] Ali and Kibibi Campbell

See also Pato BANTON; UB40

Danny CAMPBELL and SASHA
UK, male vocalist and male DJ / producer (1 WEEK) pos/wks

31 Jul 93 **TOGETHER** *ffrr FCD 212* 57 1

See also SASHA

Don CAMPBELL – *See GENERAL SAINT*

Ellie CAMPBELL *UK, female vocalist (5 WEEKS)* pos/wks

3 Apr 99 **SWEET LIES** *Jive / Eastern Bloc 0519222* 42 1
14 Aug 99 **SO MANY WAYS** *Jive / Eastern Bloc 0519362* 26 3
9 Jun 01 **DON'T WANT YOU BACK** *Jive 9201302* 50 1

Ethna CAMPBELL *UK, female vocalist (11 WEEKS)* pos/wks

27 Dec 75 **THE OLD RUGGED CROSS** *Philips 6006 475* 33 11

Ian CAMPBELL FOLK GROUP
UK, male vocal / instrumental group (5 WEEKS) pos/wks

11 Mar 65 **THE TIMES THEY ARE A-CHANGIN'** *Transatlantic SP 5* 42 2
1 Apr 65 **THE TIMES THEY ARE A-CHANGIN' (re-entry)** *Transatlantic SP 5* 47 1
15 Apr 65 **THE TIMES THEY ARE A-CHANGIN' (2nd re-entry)** *Transatlantic SP 5* 46 2

Glen CAMPBELL (314 Top 500) *Top session guitarist and singer who became one of the 1960s biggest selling country and easy listening artists, b. 22 Apr 1936, Arkansas, US. Other credits include part-time member of The Beach Boys and vocalist with The Crickets (98 WEEKS)* pos/wks

29 Jan 69 ● **WICHITA LINEMAN** *Ember EMBS 261* 7 13
7 May 69 **GALVESTON** *Ember EMBS 263* 14 10
6 Dec 69 ● **ALL I HAVE TO DO IS DREAM** *Capitol CL 15619* [1] 3 14
7 Feb 70 **TRY A LITTLE KINDNESS** *Capitol CL 15622* 45 2
9 May 70 ● **HONEY COME BACK** *Capitol CL 15638* 4 19
26 Sep 70 **EVERYTHING A MAN COULD EVER NEED** *Capitol CL 15653* 32 5
21 Nov 70 ● **IT'S ONLY MAKE BELIEVE** *Capitol CL 15663* 4 14
27 Mar 71 **DREAM BABY** *Capitol CL 15674* 39 3
4 Oct 75 ● **RHINESTONE COWBOY** *Capitol CL 15824* ▲ 4 12
26 Mar 77 **SOUTHERN NIGHTS** *Capitol CL 15907* ▲ 28 6

[1] Bobbie Gentry and Glen Campbell

Jo Ann CAMPBELL *US, female vocalist (3 WEEKS)* pos/wks

8 Jun 61 **MOTORCYCLE MICHAEL** *HMV POP 873* 41 3

Junior CAMPBELL *UK, male vocalist (18 WEEKS)* pos/wks

14 Oct 72 ● **HALLELUJAH FREEDOM** *Deram DM 364* 10 9
2 Jun 73 **SWEET ILLUSION** *Deram DM 387* 15 9

Kibibi CAMPBELL – *See Ali CAMPBELL*

Naomi CAMPBELL *UK, female vocalist (3 WEEKS)* pos/wks

24 Sep 94 **LOVE AND TEARS** *Epic 6608352* 40 3

Pat CAMPBELL *Ireland, male vocalist (5 WEEKS)* pos/wks

15 Nov 69 **THE DEAL** *Major Minor MM 648* 31 5

Stan CAMPBELL *UK, male vocalist (3 WEEKS)* pos/wks

6 Jun 87 **YEARS GO BY** *WEA YZ 127* 65 3

Tevin CAMPBELL *US, male vocalist (2 WEEKS)* pos/wks

18 Apr 92 **TELL ME WHAT YOU WANT ME TO DO** *Qwest W 0102* 63 2

CAN *Germany, male vocal / instrumental group (10 WEEKS)* pos/wks

28 Aug 76 **I WANT MORE** *Virgin VS 153* 26 10

CANDIDO *US, male multi-instrumentalist (3 WEEKS)* pos/wks

18 Jul 81 **JINGO** *Excalibur EXC 102* 55 3

CANDLEWICK GREEN
UK, male vocal / instrumental duo (8 WEEKS) pos/wks

23 Feb 74 **WHO DO YOU THINK YOU ARE** *Decca F 13480* 21 8

CANDY FLIP *UK, male vocal / instrumental duo – Rick Peel and Danny 'Dizzy' Deo (14 WEEKS)* pos/wks

17 Mar 90 ● **STRAWBERRY FIELDS FOREVER** *Debut DEBT 3092* 3 10
14 Jul 90 **THIS CAN BE REAL** *Debut DEBT 3099* 60 4

CANDY GIRLS *UK, male / female instrumental / production duo – Rachel Auburn and Paul Masterson (10 WEEKS)* pos/wks

30 Sep 95 **FEE FI FO FUM** *VC VCRD 1* [1] 23 4
24 Feb 96 **WHAM BAM** *VC VCRD 6* [1] 20 4
7 Dec 96 **I WANT CANDY** *Feverpitch CDFVR 1013* [2] 30 2

[1] Candy Girls featuring Sweet Pussy Pauline [2] Candy Girls featuring Valerie Malcolm

See also YOMANDA; SLEAZESISTERS; HI-GATE

CANDYLAND *UK, male vocal / instrumental group (1 WEEK)* pos/wks

9 Mar 91 **FOUNTAIN O' YOUTH** *Non Fiction YES 4* 72 1

CANDYSKINS *UK, male vocal / instrumental group (4 WEEKS)* pos/wks

19 Oct 96 **MRS HOOVER** *Ultimate TOPP 051CD* 65 1
8 Feb 97 **MONDAY MORNING** *Ultimate TOPP 055CD* 34 2
3 May 97 **HANG MYSELF ON YOU** *Ultimate TOPP 059CD* 65 1

CANIBUS *US, male rapper (3 WEEKS)* pos/wks

27 Jun 98 **SECOND ROUND KO** *Universal UND 56198* 35 2
10 Oct 98 **HOW COME** *Interscope IND 95598* [1] 52 1

[1] Youssou N'Dour and Canibus

CANNED HEAT *US, male vocal / instrumental group (41 WEEKS)* pos/wks

24 Jul 68 ● **ON THE ROAD AGAIN** *Liberty LBS 15090* 8 15
1 Jan 69 **GOING UP THE COUNTRY** *Liberty LBF 15169* 19 10
17 Jan 70 ● **LET'S WORK TOGETHER** *Liberty LBF 15302* 2 15
11 Jul 70 **SUGAR BEE** *Liberty LBF 15350* 49 1

Freddy CANNON *US, male vocalist – Freddy Picariello (53 WEEKS)* pos/wks

14 Aug 59	TALLAHASSEE LASSIE *Top Rank JAR 135*	17	8
1 Jan 60 ●	WAY DOWN YONDER IN NEW ORLEANS *Top Rank JAR 247*	3	17
4 Mar 60	CALIFORNIA HERE I COME *Top Rank JAR 309*	25	2
17 Mar 60	INDIANA *Top Rank JAR309*	42	1
24 Mar 60	CALIFORNIA HERE I COME (re-entry) *Top Rank JAR 309*	46	1
19 May 60	THE URGE *Top Rank JAR 369*	18	10
20 Apr 61	MUSKRAT RAMBLE *Top Rank JAR 548*	32	5
28 Jun 62	PALISADES PARK *Stateside SS 101*	20	9

BLU CANTRELL *US, female vocalist (6 WEEKS)* pos/wks

24 Nov 01	HIT 'EM UP STYLE (OOPS!) *Arista 74321891632*	12	6

Jim CAPALDI *UK, male vocalist (17 WEEKS)* pos/wks

27 Jul 74	IT'S ALL UP TO YOU *Island WIP 6198*	27	6
25 Oct 75 ●	LOVE HURTS *Island WIP 6246*	4	11

CAPERCAILLIE
UK, male / female vocal / instrumental group (3 WEEKS) pos/wks

23 May 92	A PRINCE AMONG ISLANDS (EP) *Survival ZB 45393*	39	2
17 Jun 95	DARK ALAN (AILEIN DUINN) *Survival SURCD 55*	65	1

Tracks on A Prince Among Islands (EP): Coisich a Ruin (Walk My Beloved) / Fagail Bhearnaraid (Leaving Bernaray) / The Lorn Theme / Gun Teann Mi Ris Na Ruinn Tha Seo (Remembrance)

CAPPADONNA – *See WU-TANG CLAN*

CAPPELLA *Italy, male / female production / vocal group (68 WEEKS)* pos/wks

9 Apr 88	PUSH THE BEAT / BAUHAUS *Fast Globe FGL 1*	60	2
6 May 89	HELYOM HALIB *Music Man MMPS 7004*	11	9
23 Sep 89	HOUSE ENERGY REVENGE *Music Man MMPS 7009*	73	1
27 Apr 91	EVERYBODY *ffrr F158*	66	1
18 Jan 92	TAKE ME AWAY *PWL Continental PWL 210* [1]	25	5
3 Apr 93 ●	U GOT 2 KNOW *Internal Dance IDC 1*	6	11
14 Aug 93	U GOT 2 KNOW (re-mix) *Internal Dance IDCR 2*	43	3
23 Oct 93 ●	U GOT 2 LET THE MUSIC *Internal Dance IDC 3*	2	12
19 Feb 94 ●	MOVE ON BABY *Internal Dance IDC 4*	7	7
18 Jun 94 ●	U & ME *Internal Dance IDCC 6*	10	7
15 Oct 94	MOVE IT UP / BIG BEAT *Internal Dance IDC 7*	16	6
16 Sep 95	TELL ME THE WAY *Systematic SYSCD 17*	17	3
6 Sep 97	BE MY BABY *Nukleuz PSNC 0072*	53	1

[1] Cappella featuring Loleatta Holloway

See also 49ers

CAPRICCIO *UK, production duo (2 WEEKS)* pos/wks

27 Mar 99	EVERYBODY GET UP *Defected DEFECT 2CDS*	44	2

CAPRICE *US, female vocalist (5 WEEKS)* pos/wks

4 Sep 99	OH YEAH *Virgin VSCDT 1745*	24	3
10 Mar 01	ONCE AROUND THE SUN *Virgin VSCDT 1750*	24	2

CAPRICORN *Belgium, male DJ (1 WEEK)* pos/wks

29 Nov 97	20 HZ (NEW FREQUENCIES) *R&S RS 97126CD*	73	1

Tony CAPSTICK and the CARLTON MAIN / FRICKLEY COLLIERY BAND *UK, male vocalist and male instrumental band (8 WEEKS)* pos/wks

21 Mar 81 ●	THE SHEFFIELD GRINDER / CAPSTICK COMES HOME *Dingles SID 27*	3	8

CAPTAIN BEAKY – *See Keith MICHELL*

CAPTAIN HOLLYWOOD PROJECT
US / Germany, male / female vocal / instrumental group (31 WEEKS) pos/wks

22 Sep 90 ●	I CAN'T STAND IT *BCM BCMR 395* [1]	7	10
24 Nov 90	ARE YOU DREAMING *BCM BCM 07504* [1]	17	10
27 Mar 93	ONLY WITH YOU *Pulse 8 CDLOSE 40*	67	1
6 Nov 93	MORE AND MORE *Pulse 8 CDLOSE 50*	23	5
5 Feb 94	IMPOSSIBLE *Pulse 8 CDLOSE 54*	29	3
11 Jun 94	ONLY WITH YOU (re-issue) *Pulse 8 CDLOSE 62*	61	1
1 Apr 95	FLYING HIGH *Pulse 8 CDLOSE 82*	58	1

[1] Twenty 4 Seven featuring Captain Hollywood

CAPTAIN SENSIBLE *UK, male vocalist – Ray Burns (31 WEEKS)* pos/wks

26 Jun 82 ★	HAPPY TALK *A & M CAP 1*	1	8
14 Aug 82	WOT *A & M CAP 2*	26	7
24 Mar 84 ●	GLAD IT'S ALL OVER / DAMNED ON 45 *A & M CAP 6*	6	10
28 Jul 84	THERE ARE MORE SNAKES THAN LADDERS *A & M CAP 7*	57	5
10 Dec 94	THE HOKEY COKEY *Have A Nice Day CDHOKEY 1*	71	1

CAPTAIN and TENNILLE *US, male instrumentalist / keyboards and female vocalist – Daryl Dragon and Toni Tennille (24 WEEKS)* pos/wks

2 Aug 75	LOVE WILL KEEP US TOGETHER *A & M AMS 7165* ▲	32	5
24 Jan 76	THE WAY I WANT TO TOUCH YOU *A & M AMS 7203*	28	6
4 Nov 78	YOU NEVER DONE IT LIKE THAT *A & M AMS 7384*	63	3
16 Feb 80 ●	DO THAT TO ME ONE MORE TIME *Casablanca CAN 175* ▲	7	10

Irene CARA *US, female vocalist (33 WEEKS)* pos/wks

3 Jul 82 ★	FAME *RSO 90*	1	16
4 Sep 82	OUT HERE ON MY OWN *RSO 66*	58	3
4 Jun 83 ●	FLASHDANCE . . . WHAT A FEELING *Casablanca CAN 1016* ▲	2	14

CARAMBA *Sweden, male vocalist / multi-instrumentalist dog impersonator – Michael Tretow (6 WEEKS)* pos/wks

12 Nov 83	FEDORA (I'LL BE YOUR DAWG) *Billco BILL 101*	56	6

CARAVELLES *UK, female vocal duo – Lois Wilkinson and Andrea Simpson (13 WEEKS)* pos/wks

8 Aug 63 ●	YOU DON'T HAVE TO BE A BABY TO CRY *Decca F 11697*	6	13

CARDIGANS
Sweden, male / female vocal / instrumental group (66 WEEKS) pos/wks

17 Jun 95	CARNIVAL *Trampolene PZCD 345*	72	1
30 Sep 95	SICK AND TIRED *Stockholm 5773112*	34	3
2 Dec 95	CARNIVAL (re-entry) *Trampolene PZCD 345*	35	2
17 Feb 96	RISE AND SHINE *Trampolene 5778252*	29	2
21 Sep 96	LOVEFOOL *Stockholm 5752952*	21	4
7 Dec 96	BEEN IT *Stockholm 5759672*	56	1
3 May 97 ●	LOVEFOOL (re-issue) *Stockholm 5710502*	2	13
6 Sep 97	YOUR NEW CUCKOO *Stockholm 5716632*	35	2
17 Oct 98	MY FAVOURITE GAME *Stockholm 5679912*	14	18
6 Mar 99 ●	ERASE / REWIND *Stockholm 5635332*	7	9
24 Jul 99	HANGING AROUND *Stockholm 5612682*	17	4
25 Sep 99 ●	BURNING DOWN THE HOUSE *Gut CDGUT 26* [1]	7	7

[1] Tom Jones and The Cardigans

See also A CAMP

CARE *UK, male vocal / instrumental duo (4 WEEKS)* pos/wks

12 Nov 83	FLAMING SWORD *Arista KBIRD 2*	48	4

Mariah CAREY (46 Top 500) *Record-shattering vocalist / songwriter, b. 27 Mar 1970, New York. Since her 1990 chart debut she has sold more than 120 million albums worldwide and has topped the US singles chart 15 times – only Elvis Presley has spent longer at the top. In 2001 signed record-breaking $20 million per album deal with Virgin (252 WEEKS)* pos/wks

4 Aug 90 ●	VISION OF LOVE *CBS 6559320* ▲	9	12
10 Nov 90	LOVE TAKES TIME *CBS 6563647* ▲	37	8
26 Jan 91	SOMEDAY *Columbia 6565837* ▲	38	5
1 Jun 91	THERE'S GOT TO BE A WAY *Columbia 6569317*	54	3
5 Oct 91	EMOTIONS *Columbia 6574037* ▲	17	9
11 Jan 92	CAN'T LET GO *Columbia 6576627*	20	7
18 Apr 92	MAKE IT HAPPEN *Columbia 6579417*	17	5
27 Jun 92 ●	I'LL BE THERE *Columbia 6581377* ▲	2	9
21 Aug 93 ●	DREAMLOVER *Columbia 6594445* ▲	9	10
6 Nov 93 ●	HERO *Columbia 6598122* ▲	7	15

1959

IN THE YEAR IN WHICH FIDEL CASTRO LED THE CUBAN REVOLUTION WITH CHE GUEVARA LEADING THE TROOPS, FRANK LLOYD WRIGHT'S GUGGENHEIM MUSEUM OPENED IN NEW YORK, WILLIAM BURROUGHS'S 'THE NAKED LUNCH' WAS PUBLISHED AND THE DEATH OF BUDDY HOLLY RESULTED IN THE FIRST POSTHUMOUS NO.1, **FRANÇOISE HARDY** FEELS CLIFF'S CROSS-CHANNEL INFLUENCE ...

“I was very influenced by **Cliff Richard**'s music, 'Living Doll' especially. That and Paul Anka's 'Lonely Boy' were the first records I ever bought at a store opposite the Galeries Lafayette in Paris. These were really the artists that made me want to write songs and sing myself.”

SINGLE OF THE YEAR 'Living Doll' Cliff Richard
ALBUM OF THE YEAR 'South Pacific' Soundtrack

1959

19 Feb 94	★	**WITHOUT YOU** *Columbia 6599192* ■	1	14
18 Jun 94	●	**ANYTIME YOU NEED A FRIEND** *Columbia 6603542*	8	10
17 Sep 94	●	**ENDLESS LOVE** *Epic 6608062* [1]	3	10
10 Dec 94	●	**ALL I WANT FOR CHRISTMAS IS YOU** *Columbia 6610702*	2	7
7 Jan 95		**ENDLESS LOVE (re-entry)** *Epic 6608062* [1]	70	2
4 Feb 95		**ENDLESS LOVE (2nd re-entry)** *Epic 6608062* [1]	55	4
11 Mar 95		**ALL I WANT FOR CHRISTMAS IS YOU (re-entry)** *Columbia 6610702*	59	1
23 Sep 95	●	**FANTASY** *Columbia 6624952* ▲	4	11
9 Dec 95	●	**ONE SWEET DAY** *Columbia 6626035* [2] ▲	6	11
17 Feb 96	●	**OPEN ARMS** *Columbia 6629772*	4	6
22 Jun 96	●	**ALWAYS BE MY BABY** *Columbia 6633345* ▲	3	10
6 Sep 97	●	**HONEY** *Columbia 6650192* ▲	3	8
13 Dec 97		**BUTTERFLY** *Columbia 6653365*	22	6
13 Jun 98	●	**MY ALL** *Columbia 6660592* ▲	4	8
19 Dec 98	●	**WHEN YOU BELIEVE** *Columbia 6667522* [3]	4	11
27 Mar 99		**WHEN YOU BELIEVE (re-entry)** *Columbia 6667522* [3]	68	2
10 Apr 99		**I STILL BELIEVE** *Columbia 6670732*	16	7
6 Nov 99	●	**HEARTBREAKER** *Columbia 6683012* [4] ▲	5	13
11 Mar 00	●	**THANK GOD I FOUND YOU** *Columbia 6690582* [5] ▲	10	9
20 May 00		**THANK GOD I FOUND YOU (re-entry)** *Columbia 6690582* [5]	71	1
30 Sep 00	★	**AGAINST ALL ODDS** *Columbia 6698872* [6] ■	1	11
13 Mar 01		**AGAINST ALL ODDS (re-entry)** *Columbia 6698872* [6]	68	1
28 Jul 01		**LOVERBOY** *Virgin VUSCD 211* [7]	12	4
15 Sep 01		**LOVERBOY (re-entry)** *Virgin VUSCD 211* [7]	53	1
29 Dec 01		**NEVER TOO FAR / DON'T STOP (FUNKIN' 4 JAMAICA)** *Virgin VUSCD 228* [8]	32	1+

[1] Luther Vandross and Mariah Carey [2] Mariah Carey and Boyz II Men [3] Mariah Carey and Whitney Houston [4] Mariah Carey featuring Jay-Z [5] Mariah Carey featuring Joe and 98 Degrees [6] Mariah Carey and Westlife [7] Mariah featuring Cameo [8] Mariah Carey / Mariah Carey featuring Mystikal

Although he is uncredited, 'I'll Be There' is a duet with Trey Lorenz

CARL – *See CLUBHOUSE*

Belinda CARLISLE

161 Top 500 *Lead vocalist of the first really successful all-girl rock group, The Go-Gos; b. 17 Aug 1958, Hollywood. She married the son of British-born film star James Mason in 1992 and her career fared even better in the UK than in her homeland (145 WEEKS)* pos/wks

12 Dec 87	★	**HEAVEN IS A PLACE ON EARTH** *Virgin VS 1036* ▲	1	14
27 Feb 88	●	**I GET WEAK** *Virgin VS 1046*	10	9
7 May 88	●	**CIRCLE IN THE SAND** *Virgin VS 1074*	4	11
6 Aug 88		**MAD ABOUT YOU** *IRS IRM 118*	67	3
10 Sep 88		**WORLD WITHOUT YOU** *Virgin VS 1114*	34	6
10 Dec 88		**LOVE NEVER DIES . . .** *Virgin VS 1150*	54	5
7 Oct 89	●	**LEAVE A LIGHT ON** *Virgin VS 1210*	4	10
9 Dec 89		**LA LUNA** *Virgin VS 1230*	38	6
24 Feb 90		**RUNAWAY HORSES** *Virgin VS 1244*	40	5
26 May 90		**VISION OF YOU** *Virgin VS 1264*	41	4
13 Oct 90	●	**(WE WANT) THE SAME THING** *Virgin VS 1219*	6	10
22 Dec 90		**SUMMER RAIN** *Virgin VS 1323*	23	10
20 Apr 91		**VISION OF YOU (re-entry)** *Virgin VS 1264*	71	1
28 Sep 91		**LIVE YOUR LIFE BE FREE** *Virgin VS 1370*	12	7
16 Nov 91		**DO YOU FEEL LIKE I FEEL** *Virgin VS 1383*	29	4
11 Jan 92		**HALF THE WORLD** *Virgin VS 1388*	35	4
29 Aug 92		**LITTLE BLACK BOOK** *Virgin VS 1428*	28	5
25 Sep 93		**BIG SCARY ANIMAL** *Virgin VSCDT 1472*	12	6
27 Nov 93		**LAY DOWN YOUR ARMS** *Virgin VSCDG 1476*	27	6
13 Jul 96	●	**IN TOO DEEP** *Chrysalis CDCHS 5033*	6	7
21 Sep 96	●	**ALWAYS BREAKING MY HEART** *Chrysalis CDCHS 5037*	8	6
30 Nov 96		**LOVE IN THE KEY OF C** *Chrysalis CDCHS 5044*	20	3
1 Mar 97		**CALIFORNIA** *Chrysalis CDCHSS 5047*	31	2
27 Nov 99		**ALL GOD'S CHILDREN** *Virgin VSCDT 1756*	66	1

Bob CARLISLE *US, male vocalist (2 WEEKS)* pos/wks

30 Aug 97		**BUTTERFLY KISSES** *Jive JIVECD 249*	56	2

Don CARLOS – *See SINGING DOGS*

Sara CARLSON – *See MANIC MCs featuring Sara CARLSON*

CARLTON *UK, male vocalist (3 WEEKS)* pos/wks

16 Feb 91		**LOVE AND PAIN** *Smith & Mighty SNM 4*	56	2
1 Apr 95		**1 TO 1 RELIGION** *Stoned Heights BRCD 313* [1]	53	1

[1] Bomb the Bass featuring Carlton

Carl CARLTON *US, male vocalist (8 WEEKS)* pos/wks

18 Jul 81		**SHE'S A BAD MAMA JAMA (SHE'S BUILT, SHE'S STACKED)** *20th Century TC 2488*	34	8

Larry CARLTON – *See Mike POST*

CARLTON MAIN / FRICKLEY COLLIERY BAND – *See Tony CAPSTICK and the CARLTON MAIN / FRICKLEY COLLIERY BAND*

CARMEL *UK, female / male vocal / instrumental group (19 WEEKS)* pos/wks

6 Aug 83		**BAD DAY** *London LON 29*	15	9
11 Feb 84		**MORE, MORE, MORE** *London LON 44*	23	7
14 Jun 86		**SALLY** *London LON 90*	60	3

Eric CARMEN *US, male vocalist (7 WEEKS)* pos/wks

10 Apr 76		**ALL BY MYSELF** *Arista 42*	12	7

Jean CARN – *See Bobby M featuring Jean CARN*

Kim CARNEGIE *UK, female vocalist (1 WEEK)* pos/wks

19 Jan 91		**JAZZ RAP** *Best ZB 44085*	73	1

Kim CARNES *US, female vocalist (15 WEEKS)* pos/wks

9 May 81	●	**BETTE DAVIS EYES** *EMI America EA 121* ▲	10	9
8 Aug 81		**DRAW OF THE CARDS** *EMI America EA 125*	49	4
9 Oct 82		**VOYEUR** *EMI America EA 143*	68	2

CARNIVAL featuring RIP vs RED RAT

UK, male production duo and Jamaica, male vocalist (1 WEEK) pos/wks

12 Sep 98		**ALL OF THE GIRLS (ALL AI-DI GIRL DEM)** *Pepper 0530072*	51	1

See also RIP PRODUCTIONS

Renato CAROSONE and his SEXTET

Italy, male vocalist and instrumental backing group (1 WEEK) pos/wks

4 Jul 58		**TORERO – CHA CHA CHA** *Parlophone R 4433*	25	1

Mary-Chapin CARPENTER *US, female vocalist (6 WEEKS)* pos/wks

20 Nov 93		**HE THINKS HE'LL KEEP HER** *Columbia 6598632*	71	1
7 Jan 95		**ONE COOL REMOVE** *Columbia 6611342* [1]	40	3
3 Jun 95		**SHUT UP AND KISS ME** *Columbia 6613675*	35	2

[1] Shawn Colvin with Mary-Chapin Carpenter

CARPENTERS

116 Top 500 *All-time biggest-selling brother / sister duo: Karen Carpenter (v/d) (d. 4 Feb 1983), Richard Carpenter (k/v). This Connecticut couple was among the world's most popular pop / MOR acts of the 1970s before Karen's tragic anorexia-associated death (173 WEEKS)* pos/wks

5 Sep 70	●	**(THEY LONG TO BE) CLOSE TO YOU** *A & M AMS 800* ▲	6	18
9 Jan 71		**WE'VE ONLY JUST BEGUN** *A & M AMS 813*	28	7
18 Sep 71		**SUPERSTAR / FOR ALL WE KNOW** *A & M AMS 864*	18	13
1 Jan 72		**MERRY CHRISTMAS DARLING** *A & M AME 601*	45	1
23 Sep 72	●	**I WON'T LAST A DAY WITHOUT YOU / GOODBYE TO LOVE** *A & M AMS 7023*	9	16
7 Jul 73	●	**YESTERDAY ONCE MORE** *A & M AMS 7073*	2	17
20 Oct 73	●	**TOP OF THE WORLD** *A & M AMS 7086* ▲	5	18
2 Mar 74		**JAMBALAYA (ON THE BAYOU) / MR GUDER** *A & M AMS 7098*	12	11
8 Jun 74		**I WON'T LAST A DAY WITHOUT YOU (re-issue)** *A & M AMS 7111*	32	5
18 Jan 75	●	**PLEASE MR POSTMAN** *A & M AMS 7141* ▲	2	12
19 Apr 75	●	**ONLY YESTERDAY** *A & M AMS 7159*	7	10
30 Aug 75		**SOLITAIRE** *A & M AMS 7187*	32	5
20 Dec 75		**SANTA CLAUS IS COMIN' TO TOWN** *A & M AMS 7144*	37	4

27 Mar 76		**THERE'S A KIND OF HUSH (ALL OVER THE WORLD)** *A & M AMS 7219*	22	6
3 Jul 76		**I NEED TO BE IN LOVE** *A & M AMS 7238*	36	5
8 Oct 77	●	**CALLING OCCUPANTS OF INTERPLANETARY CRAFT (THE RECOGNISED ANTHEM OF WORLD CONTACT DAY)** *A & M AMS 7318*	9	9
11 Feb 78		**SWEET SWEET SMILE** *A & M AMS 7327*	40	4
22 Oct 83		**MAKE BELIEVE IT'S YOUR FIRST TIME** *A & M AM 147*	60	3
8 Dec 90		**MERRY CHRISTMAS DARLING / (THEY LONG TO BE) CLOSE TO YOU (re-issue)** *A & M AM 716*	25	5
13 Feb 93		**RAINY DAYS AND MONDAYS** *A & M AMCD 0180*	63	2
24 Dec 94		**TRYIN' TO GET THE FEELING AGAIN** *A & M 5807612*	44	2

'I Won't Last a Day Without You' AMS 7023 listed by itself 23 Sep 1972 at No.49. 'Goodbye to Love', the other side, listed by itself from 30 Sep 1972, until the end of the record's chart run. 'Mr Guder' listed with 'Jambalaya' from 16 Mar 1974, until the end of the chart run

Dick CARR – *See Slim DUSTY*

Joe 'Fingers' CARR *US, male instrumentalist – piano, Lou Busch under a false name (5 WEEKS)* pos/wks

29 Jun 56		**PORTUGUESE WASHERWOMAN** *Capitol CL 14587*	20	5

See also Lou BUSCH and his Orchestra

Linda CARR *US, female vocalist (12 WEEKS)* pos/wks

12 Jul 75		**HIGHWIRE** *Chelsea 2005 025* [1]	15	8
5 Jun 76		**SOLD MY ROCK 'N' ROLL (GAVE IT FOR FUNKY SOUL)** *Spark SRL 1139* [2]	36	4

[1] Linda Carr and the Love Squad [2] Linda and the Funky Boys

Pearl CARR and Teddy JOHNSON *UK, female / male vocal duo (19 WEEKS)* pos/wks

20 Mar 59		**SING LITTLE BIRDIE** *Columbia DB 4275*	12	8
6 Apr 61		**HOW WONDERFUL TO KNOW** *Columbia DB 4603* [1]	23	11

[1] Teddy Johnson and Pearl Carr

Suzi CARR *US, female vocalist (1 WEEK)* pos/wks

8 Oct 94		**ALL OVER ME** *Cowboy RODEO 947CD*	45	1

Valerie CARR *US, female vocalist (2 WEEKS)* pos/wks

4 Jul 58		**WHEN THE BOYS TALK ABOUT THE GIRLS** *Columbia DB 4131*	29	1
18 Jul 58		**WHEN THE BOYS TALK ABOUT THE GIRLS (re-entry)** *Columbia DB 4131*	30	1

Vikki CARR *US, female vocalist – Florencia Bisenta De Casillas Martinez Cardona (26 WEEKS)* pos/wks

1 Jun 67	●	**IT MUST BE HIM (SEUL SUR SON ETOILE)** *Liberty LIB 55917*	2	20
30 Aug 67		**THERE I GO** *Liberty LBF 15022*	50	1
12 Mar 69		**WITH PEN IN HAND** *Liberty LBF 15166*	43	1
26 Mar 69		**WITH PEN IN HAND (re-entry)** *Liberty LBF 15166*	39	2
30 Apr 69		**WITH PEN IN HAND (2nd re-entry)** *Liberty LBF 15166*	40	2

Raffaella CARRA *Italy, female vocalist (12 WEEKS)* pos/wks

15 Apr 78	●	**DO IT DO IT AGAIN** *Epic EPC 6094*	9	12

Paul CARRACK *UK, male vocalist (18 WEEKS)* pos/wks

16 May 87		**WHEN YOU WALK IN THE ROOM** *Chrysalis CHS 3109*	48	5
18 Mar 89		**DON'T SHED A TEAR** *Chrysalis CHS 3164*	60	3
6 Jan 96		**EYES OF BLUE** *IRS CDEIRS 192*	40	4
6 Apr 96		**HOW LONG** *IRS CDEIRS 193*	32	5
24 Aug 96		**EYES OF BLUE (re-mix)** *IRS CDEIRS 194*	45	1

CARRAPICHO – *See CHILLI featuring CARRAPICHO*

José CARRERAS *Spain, male vocalist (19 WEEKS)* pos/wks

11 Jul 92		**AMIGOS PARA SIEMPRE (FRIENDS FOR LIFE)** *Really Useful RUR 10* [1]	11	11
30 Jul 94		**LIBIAMO / LA DONNA E MOBILE** *Teldec YZ 843CD* [2]	21	4
25 Jul 98		**YOU'LL NEVER WALK ALONE** *Decca 4607982* [3]	35	4

[1] José Carreras and Sarah Brightman [2] José Carreras featuring Placido Domingo and Luciano Pavarotti with Mehta [3] José Carreras, Placido Domingo and Luciano Pavarotti with Mehta

Tia CARRERE *US, female vocalist (6 WEEKS)* pos/wks

30 May 92		**BALLROOM BLITZ** *Reprise W 0105*	26	6

Jim CARREY *Canada, male vocalist (3 WEEKS)* pos/wks

21 Jan 95		**CUBAN PETE** *Columbia 6606625*	31	3

CARRIE *US / UK, male vocal / instrumental group (2 WEEKS)* pos/wks

14 Mar 98		**MOLLY** *Island CID 687*	56	1
9 May 98		**CALIFORNIA SCREAMIN'** *Island CID 694*	55	1

Dina CARROLL (309 Top 500) *Brit award-winning Best Female Vocalist of 1994 b. 21 Aug 1968, Newmarket, UK. Soul / dance vocalist's 'So Close' was the biggest-selling debut album by a British female artist in the 1990s, and she was the only UK woman to have two simultaneous Top 10 singles that decade (in 1993) (99 WEEKS)* pos/wks

2 Feb 91	●	**IT'S TOO LATE** *Mercury ITM 3* [1]	8	14
15 Jun 91		**NAKED LOVE (JUST SAY YOU WANT ME)** *Mercury ITM 4* [2]	39	3
11 Jul 92		**AIN'T NO MAN** *A & M AM 0001*	16	8
10 Oct 92		**SPECIAL KIND OF LOVE** *A & M AM 0088*	16	5
5 Dec 92		**SO CLOSE** *A & M AM 0101*	20	8
27 Feb 93		**THIS TIME** *A & M AMCD 0184*	23	6
15 May 93		**EXPRESS** *A & M 5802632*	12	6
16 Oct 93	●	**DON'T BE A STRANGER** *A & M 5803892*	3	13
11 Dec 93	●	**THE PERFECT YEAR** *A & M 5804812*	5	11
28 Sep 96	●	**ESCAPING** *Mercury / First Avenue DCCD 1*	3	8
21 Dec 96		**ONLY HUMAN** *Mercury / First Avenue DCCD 2*	33	4
24 Oct 98		**ONE, TWO, THREE** *Mercury / First Avenue MERCD 514*	16	4
24 Jul 99		**WITHOUT LOVE** *Manifesto / First Avenue FESCD 57*	13	7
16 Jun 01		**SOMEONE LIKE YOU** *Mercury / First Avenue 5689062*	38	2

[1] Quartz introducing Dina Carroll [2] Quartz and Dina Carroll

Ron CARROLL – *See SUPERFUNK; KLUSTER Featuring Ron CARROLL*

Ronnie CARROLL *Ireland, male vocalist – Ronald Cleghorn (50 WEEKS)* pos/wks

27 Jul 56		**WALK HAND IN HAND** *Philips PB 605*	13	8
29 Mar 57		**THE WISDOM OF A FOOL** *Philips PB 667*	20	2
31 Mar 60		**FOOTSTEPS** *Philips PB 1004*	36	3
22 Feb 62		**RING-A-DING GIRL** *Philips PB 1222*	46	3
2 Aug 62	●	**ROSES ARE RED (MY LOVE)** *Philips 326532 BF*	3	16
15 Nov 62		**IF ONLY TOMORROW** *Philips 326550 BF*	33	4
7 Mar 63	●	**SAY WONDERFUL THINGS** *Philips 326574 BF*	6	14

Jasper CARROTT *UK, male comedian / vocalist – Bob Davies (15 WEEKS)* pos/wks

16 Aug 75	●	**FUNKY MOPED / MAGIC ROUNDABOUT** *DJM DJS 388*	5	15

CARS *US, male vocal / instrumental group (51 WEEKS)* pos/wks

11 Nov 78	●	**MY BEST FRIEND'S GIRL** *Elektra K 12301*	3	10
17 Feb 79		**JUST WHAT I NEEDED** *Elektra K 12312*	17	10
28 Jul 79		**LET'S GO** *Elektra K 12371*	51	4
5 Jun 82		**SINCE YOU'RE GONE** *Elektra K 13177*	37	4
29 Sep 84	●	**DRIVE** *Elektra E 9706*	5	11
3 Aug 85	●	**DRIVE (re-entry)** *Elektra E 9706*	4	12

Aaron CARTER *US, male vocalist (29 WEEKS)* pos/wks

29 Nov 97	●	**CRUSH ON YOU** *Ultra Pop 0099605 ULT*	9	8
7 Feb 98	●	**CRAZY LITTLE PARTY GIRL** *Ultra Pop 0099645 ULT*	7	6
28 Mar 98		**I'M GONNA MISS YOU FOREVER** *Ultra Pop 0099725 ULT*	24	5
4 Jul 98		**SURFIN' USA** *Ultra Pop 0099805 ULT*	18	5
16 Sep 00		**I WANT CANDY** *Jive 9250892*	31	3
28 Oct 00		**AARON'S PARTY (COME GET IT)** *Jive 9251272*	51	2

Clarence CARTER *US, male vocalist (13 WEEKS)* pos/wks

10 Oct 70	●	**PATCHES** *Atlantic 2091 030*	2	13

CARTER – THE UNSTOPPABLE SEX MACHINE
UK, male vocal / instrumental duo – James 'Jim Bob' Morrison and Leslie 'Fruitbat' Carter (46 WEEKS) pos/wks

26 Jan 91		**BLOODSPORT FOR ALL** *Rough Trade R 20112687*	48	2
22 Jun 91		**SHERIFF FATMAN** *Big Cat USM 1*	23	7
26 Oct 91		**AFTER THE WATERSHED** *Big Cat USM 2*	11	5
11 Jan 92		**RUBBISH** *Big Cat USM 3*	14	5
25 Apr 92	●	**THE ONLY LIVING BOY IN NEW CROSS** *Big Cat USM 4*	7	5
4 Jul 92		**DO RE ME SO FAR SO GOOD** *Chrysalis USM 5*	22	3
28 Nov 92		**THE IMPOSSIBLE DREAM** *Chrysalis USM 6*	21	3
4 Sep 93		**LEAN ON ME I WON'T FALL OVER** *Chrysalis CDUSM 7*	16	3
16 Oct 93		**LENNY AND TERENCE** *Chrysalis CDUSM 8*	40	2
12 Mar 94		**GLAM ROCK COPS** *Chrysalis CDUSMS 10*	24	3
19 Nov 94		**LET'S GET TATTOOS** *Chrysalis CDUSMS 30*	30	3
4 Feb 95		**THE YOUNG OFFENDER'S MUM** *Chrysalis CDUSMS 12*	34	3
30 Sep 95		**BORN ON THE 5TH OF NOVEMBER** *Chrysalis CDUSM 13*	35	2

CARTER TWINS *Ireland, male vocal duo (1 WEEK)* pos/wks

8 Mar 97		**THE TWELFTH OF NEVER / TOO RIGHT TO BE** *RCA 74321453082*	61	1

Junior CARTIER *UK, male producer – Jon Carter (1 WEEK)* pos/wks

6 Nov 99		**WOMEN BEAT THEIR MEN** *Nucamp CAMPD 3X*	70	1

CARTOONS
Denmark, male / female vocal / instrumental group (30 WEEKS) pos/wks

3 Apr 99	●	**WITCH DOCTOR** *Flex / EMI CDTOONS 001*	2	13
19 Jun 99	●	**DOODAH!** *Flex / EMI CDTOON 002*	7	11
4 Sep 99		**AISY WAISY** *Flex/ EMI CDTOONS 003*	16	5
16 Oct 99		**DOODAH! (re-entry)** *Flex / EMI CDTOON 002*	73	1

Sam CARTWRIGHT – *See VOLCANO*

CARVELLS
UK, male vocalist / instrumentalist – Alan Carvell (4 WEEKS) pos/wks

26 Nov 77		**THE L.A. RUN** *Creole CR 143*	31	4

CASCADES *US, male vocal group (16 WEEKS)* pos/wks

28 Feb 63	●	**RHYTHM OF THE RAIN** *Warner Bros. WB 88*	5	16

CASE – *See Foxy BROWN and JA RULE*

Ed CASE *UK, male producer – Edward Makromallies (4 WEEKS)* pos/wks

21 Oct 00		**SOMETHING IN YOUR EYES** *Red Rose CDRROSE 003*	38	2
15 Sep 01		**WHO?** *Columbia 6718302* [1]	29	2

[1] Ed Case and Sweetie Irie

Natalie CASEY *UK, female vocalist (1 WEEK)* pos/wks

7 Jan 84		**CHICK CHICK CHICKEN** *Polydor CHICK 1*	72	1

Johnny CASH *US, male vocalist (59 WEEKS)* pos/wks

3 Jun 65		**IT AIN'T ME BABE** *CBS 201760*	28	8
6 Sep 69	●	**A BOY NAMED SUE** *CBS 4460*	4	19
23 May 70		**WHAT IS TRUTH** *CBS 4934*	21	11
15 Apr 72	●	**A THING CALLED LOVE** *CBS 7797* [1]	4	13
22 Jul 72		**A THING CALLED LOVE (re-entry)** *CBS 7797* [1]	48	1
3 Jul 76		**ONE PIECE AT A TIME** *CBS 4287* [2]	32	7

[1] Johnny Cash with the Evangel Temple Choir [2] Johnny Cash with the Tennessee Three

Pat CASH – *See John McENROE and Pat CASH with the FULL METAL RACKETS*

CA$HFLOW *US, male vocal / instrumental group (8 WEEKS)* pos/wks

24 May 86		**MINE ALL MINE / PARTY FREAK** *Club JAB 30*	15	8

CASHMERE *US, male vocal / instrumental group (11 WEEKS)* pos/wks

19 Jan 85		**CAN I** *Fourth & Broadway BRW 19*	29	8
23 Mar 85		**WE NEED LOVE** *Fourth & Broadway BRW 22*	52	3

CASINO *UK, male vocal / production group (2 WEEKS)* pos/wks

17 May 97		**SOUND OF EDEN** *Worx WORXCD 005*	52	1
10 Jul 99		**ONLY YOU** *Pow! CDPOW 006*	72	1

CASINOS *US, male vocal group (7 WEEKS)* pos/wks

23 Feb 67		**THEN YOU CAN TELL ME GOODBYE** *President PT 123*	28	7

CASSANDRA – *See Rui DA SILVA featuring CASSANDRA*

David CASSIDY (268 Top 500) *Top teen idol of 1970s, b. 12 Apr 1950, New York. This photogenic singer / actor first found fame via the TV series The Partridge Family. His UK chart career took off as his US sales slowed down. Returned to Top 5 album chart in 2001 (109 WEEKS)* pos/wks

8 Apr 72	●	**COULD IT BE FOREVER / CHERISH** *Bell 1224*	2	17
16 Sep 72	★	**HOW CAN I BE SURE** *Bell 1258*	1	11
25 Nov 72		**ROCK ME BABY** *Bell 1268*	11	9
24 Mar 73	●	**I'M A CLOWN / SOME KIND OF A SUMMER** *Bell MABEL 4*	3	12
13 Oct 73	★	**DAYDREAMER / THE PUPPY SONG** *Bell 1334*	1	15
11 May 74	●	**IF I DIDN'T CARE** *Bell 1350*	9	8
27 Jul 74		**PLEASE PLEASE ME** *Bell 1371*	16	6
5 Jul 75		**I WRITE THE SONGS / GET IT UP FOR LOVE** *RCA 2571*	11	8
25 Oct 75		**DARLIN'** *RCA 2622*	16	8
23 Feb 85	●	**THE LAST KISS** *Arista ARIST 589*	6	9
11 May 85		**ROMANCE (LET YOUR HEART GO)** *Arista ARIST 620*	54	6

See also PARTRIDGE FAMILY

Eva CASSIDY *US, female vocalist (9 WEEKS)* pos/wks

21 Apr 01		**OVER THE RAINBOW** *Blix Street / Hot HIT 16*	61	1
12 May 01		**OVER THE RAINBOW (re-entry)** *Blix Street / Hot HIT 16*	42	6
30 Jun 01		**OVER THE RAINBOW (2nd re-entry)** *Blix Street / Hot HIT 16*	74	1
25 Aug 01		**OVER THE RAINBOW (3rd re-entry)** *Blix Street / Hot HIT 16*	73	1

CASSIUS *France, DJ production duo – Philippe Zdar and Hubert Blanc-Francart (12 WEEKS)* pos/wks

23 Jan 99	●	**CASSIUS 1999** *Virgin DINSD 177*	7	7
15 May 99		**FEELING FOR YOU** *Virgin DINSD 181*	16	4
20 Nov 99		**LA MOUCHE** *Virgin DINSD 188*	53	1

CAST *UK, male vocal / instrumental group (55 WEEKS)* pos/wks

15 Jul 95		**FINETIME** *Polydor 5795072*	17	4
30 Sep 95		**ALRIGHT** *Polydor 5799272*	13	4
20 Jan 96	●	**SANDSTORM** *Polydor 5778732*	8	5
30 Mar 96	●	**WALKAWAY** *Polydor 5762852*	9	7
26 Oct 96	●	**FLYING** *Polydor 5754772*	4	5
5 Apr 97	●	**FREE ME** *Polydor 5736512*	7	6
21 Jun 97		**FREE ME (re-entry)** *Polydor 5736512*	64	1
28 Jun 97	●	**GUIDING STAR** *Polydor 5711732*	9	6
13 Sep 97	●	**LIVE THE DREAM** *Polydor 5716852*	7	5
15 Nov 97		**I'M SO LONELY** *Polydor 5690592*	14	3
8 May 99	●	**BEAT MAMA** *Polydor 5635932*	9	5
7 Aug 99		**MAGIC HOUR** *Polydor 5612272*	28	3
28 Jul 01		**DESERT DROUGHT** *Polydor 5871752*	45	1

CAST FROM CASUALTY *UK, male / female vocal group (6 WEEKS)* pos/wks

14 Mar 98	●	**EVERLASTING LOVE** *Warner.esp WESP 003CD*	5	6

CAST OF THE NEW ROCKY HORROR SHOW
UK, male / female vocal group (1 WEEK) pos/wks

12 Dec 98		**THE TIMEWARP** *Damn It Janet DAMJAN 1CD*	57	1

Roy CASTLE *UK, male vocalist (3 WEEKS)* pos/wks

22 Dec 60		**LITTLE WHITE BERRY** *Philips PB 1087*	40	3

CASUALS *UK, male vocal / instrumental group (26 WEEKS)* pos/wks

14 Aug 68 ●	**JESAMINE** *Decca F 22784*	2	18
4 Dec 68	**TOY** *Decca F 22852*	30	8

CAT *UK, male vocalist – Danny John-Jules (4 WEEKS)* pos/wks

23 Oct 93	**TONGUE TIED** *EMI CDEM 286*	17	4

CATATONIA *UK, male / female vocal / instrumental group (50 WEEKS)* pos/wks

3 Feb 96	**SWEET CATATONIA** *Blanco Y Negro NEG 85CD*	61	1
4 May 96	**LOST CAT** *Blanco Y Negro NEG 88CD1*	41	1
7 Sep 96	**YOU'VE GOT A LOT TO ANSWER FOR** *Blanco Y Negro NEG 93CD1*	35	2
30 Nov 96	**BLEED** *Blanco Y Negro NEG 97CD1*	46	1
18 Oct 97	**I AM THE MOB** *Blanco Y Negro NEG 107CD*	40	2
31 Jan 98 ●	**MULDER AND SCULLY** *Blanco Y Negro NEG 109CD*	3	10
2 May 98 ●	**ROAD RAGE** *Blanco Y Negro NEG 112CD*	5	8
1 Aug 98	**STRANGE GLUE** *Blanco Y Negro NEG 113CD*	11	6
7 Nov 98	**GAME ON** *WEA NEG 114CD*	33	2
10 Apr 99 ●	**DEAD FROM THE WAIST DOWN** *Blanco Y Negro NEG 115CD*	7	8
24 Jul 99	**LONDINIUM** *Blanco Y Negro NEG 117CD*	20	3
13 Nov 99	**KARAOKE QUEEN** *Blanco Y Negro NEG 119CD*	36	2
4 Aug 01	**STONE BY STONE** *Blanco Y Negro NEG 134CD*	19	3
8 Sep 01	**STONE BY STONE (re-entry)** *Blanco Y Negro NEG 134CD*	68	1

CATCH *UK, male vocal / instrumental group (1 WEEK)* pos/wks

17 Nov 90	**FREE (C'MON)** *ffrr F 147*	70	1

CATCH *UK, male vocal instrumental group (6 WEEKS)* pos/wks

11 Oct 97	**BINGO** *Virgin VSCDT 1656*	23	4
21 Feb 98	**DIVE IN** *Virgin VSCDT 1665*	44	2

CATHERINE WHEEL
UK, male vocal / instrumental group (12 WEEKS) pos/wks

23 Nov 91	**BLACK METALLIC (EP)** *Fontana CW 1*	68	1
8 Feb 92	**BALLOON** *Fontana CW 2*	59	1
18 Apr 92	**I WANT TO TOUCH YOU** *Fontana CW 3*	35	2
9 Jan 93	**30TH CENTURY MAN** *Fontana CWCD 4*	47	2
10 Jul 93	**CRANK** *Fontana CWCD 5*	66	1
16 Oct 93	**SHOW ME MARY** *Fontana CWCDA 6*	62	1
5 Aug 95	**WAYDOWN** *Fontana CWCD 7*	67	1
13 Dec 97	**DELICIOUS** *Chrysalis CDCHS 5071*	53	1
28 Feb 98	**MA SOLITUDA** *Chrysalis CDCHS 5077*	53	1
2 May 98	**BROKEN NOSE** *Chrysalis CDCHS 5086*	48	1

Tracks on Black Metallic (EP): Black Metallic / Crawling Over Me / Let Me Down Again / Saccharine

Lorraine CATO *UK, female vocalist (3 WEEKS)* pos/wks

6 Feb 93	**HOW CAN YOU TELL ME IT'S OVER** *Columbia 6587662*	46	2
3 Aug 96	**I WAS MADE TO LOVE YOU** *MCA MCSTD 40055*	41	1

CATS *UK, male instrumental group (2 WEEKS)* pos/wks

9 Apr 69	**SWAN LAKE** *BAF 1*	48	1
21 May 69	**SWAN LAKE (re-entry)** *BAF 1*	50	1

CATS UK *UK, female vocal group (8 WEEKS)* pos/wks

6 Oct 79	**LUTON AIRPORT** *WEA K 18075*	22	8

Nick CAVE and the BAD SEEDS
Australia / Germany, male vocal / instrumental group (12 WEEKS) pos/wks

11 Apr 92	**STRAIGHT TO YOU / JACK THE RIPPER** *Mute MUTE 140*	68	1
12 Dec 92	**WHAT A WONDERFUL WORLD** *Mute MUTE 151* [1]	72	1
9 Apr 94	**DO YOU LOVE ME** *Mute CDMUTE 160*	68	1
14 Oct 95	**WHERE THE WILD ROSES GROW** *Mute CDMUTE 185* [2]	11	4
9 Mar 96	**HENRY LEE** *Mute CDMUTE 189* [3]	36	1
22 Feb 97	**INTO MY ARMS** *Mute CDMUTE 192*	53	1
31 May 97	**(ARE YOU) THE ONE THAT I'VE BEEN…** *Mute CDMUTE 206*	67	1
31 Mar 01	**AS I SAT SADLY BY HER SIDE** *Mute CDMUTE 249*	42	1
2 Jun 01	**FIFTEEN FEET OF PURE WHITE SNOW** *Mute CDMUTE 262*	52	1

[1] Nick Cave and Shane McGowan [2] Nick Cave and Kylie Minogue [3] Nick Cave and the Bad Seeds and PJ Harvey

CAVEMAN *UK, male rap group (2 WEEKS)* pos/wks

9 Mar 91	**I'M READY** *Profile PROF 330*	65	2

CCS *UK, male vocal / instrumental group (55 WEEKS)* pos/wks

31 Oct 70	**WHOLE LOTTA LOVE** *RAK 104*	13	13
27 Feb 71 ●	**WALKIN'** *RAK 109*	7	16
4 Sep 71 ●	**TAP TURNS ON THE WATER** *RAK 119*	5	13
4 Mar 72	**BROTHER** *RAK 126*	25	8
4 Aug 73	**BAND PLAYED THE BOOGIE** *RAK 154*	36	5

CECIL *UK, male vocal / instrumental group (2 WEEKS)* pos/wks

25 Oct 97	**HOSTAGE IN A FROCK** *Parlophone CDRS 6471*	68	1
28 Mar 98	**THE MOST TIRING DAY** *Parlophone CDR 6490*	69	1

CELEDA *US, female vocalist (5 WEEKS)* pos/wks

5 Sep 98	**MUSIC IS THE ANSWER (DANCIN' AND PRANCIN)** *Twisted UK TWCD 10038* [1]	36	3
12 Jun 99	**BE YOURSELF** *Twisted UK TWCD 10049*	61	1
23 Oct 99	**MUSIC IS THE ANSWER (DANCIN' AND PRANCIN)** *Twisted UK TWCD 10052* [2]	50	1

[1] Danny Tenaglia and Celeda [2] Celeda with Danny Tenaglia

CELETIA *UK, female vocalist (3 WEEKS)* pos/wks

11 Apr 98	**REWIND** *Big Life BLRD 142*	29	2
8 Aug 98	**RUNAWAY SKIES** *Big Life BLRD 144*	66	1

CENTORY *US, male rapper (1 WEEK)* pos/wks

17 Dec 94	**POINT OF NO RETURN** *EMI CDEM 354*	67	1

CENTRAL LINE *UK, male vocal / instrumental group (30 WEEKS)* pos/wks

31 Jan 81	**(YOU KNOW) YOU CAN DO IT** *Mercury LINE 7*	67	3
15 Aug 81	**WALKING INTO SUNSHINE** *Mercury MER 78*	42	10
30 Jan 82	**DON'T TELL ME** *Mercury MER 90*	55	3
20 Nov 82	**YOU'VE SAID ENOUGH** *Mercury MER 117*	58	3
22 Jan 83	**NATURE BOY** *Mercury MER 131*	21	8
11 Jun 83	**SURPRISE SURPRISE** *Mercury MER 133*	48	3

CERRONE *France, male producer / multi-instrumentalist – Jean-Marc Cerrone (21 WEEKS)* pos/wks

5 Mar 77	**LOVE IN C MINOR** *Atlantic K 10895*	31	4
29 Jul 78 ●	**SUPERNATURE** *Atlantic K 11089*	8	12
13 Jan 79	**JE SUIS MUSIC** *CBS 6918*	39	4
10 Aug 96	**SUPERNATURE (re-mix)** *Encore CDCOR 013*	66	1

A CERTAIN RATIO *UK, male vocal / instrumental group (3 WEEKS)* pos/wks

16 Jun 90	**WON'T STOP LOVING YOU** *A & M ACR 540*	55	3

Peter CETERA *US, male vocalist (20 WEEKS)* pos/wks

2 Aug 86 ●	**GLORY OF LOVE** *Full Moon W 8662* ▲	3	13
21 Jun 97 ●	**HARD TO SAY I'M SORRY** *La Face 74321481482* [1]	7	7

[1] Az Yet featuring Peter Cetera

See also CHICAGO

Frank CHACKSFIELD and his ORCHESTRA
UK, orchestra (41 WEEKS) pos/wks

3 Apr 53 ●	**LITTLE RED MONKEY** *Parlophone R 3658* [1]	10	3
22 May 53 ●	**TERRY'S THEME FROM 'LIMELIGHT'** *Decca F 10106*	2	24
12 Feb 54 ●	**EBB TIDE** *Decca F 10122*	9	2
24 Feb 56	**IN OLD LISBON** *Decca F 10689*	15	4

18 May 56	**PORT-AU-PRINCE** *Decca F 10727* [2]	18	6
31 Aug 56	**DONKEY CART** *Decca F 10743*	26	2

[1] Frank Chacksfield's Tunesmiths, featuring Jack Jordan – clavioline [2] Winifred Atwell and Frank Chacksfield

CHAIRMEN OF THE BOARD (446 Top 500) *Superior 70s soul group fronted by distinctive singer / songwriter Norman (General) Johnson, b. 23 May 1944, Virginia, US. Detroit-based quartet, who recorded on Holland, Dozier and Holland's Invictus label, are regarded as legends by US "beach" (vintage soul) music fans (77 WEEKS)* pos/wks

22 Aug 70 ●	**GIVE ME JUST A LITTLE MORE TIME** *Invictus INV 501*	3	13
14 Nov 70 ●	**YOU'VE GOT ME DANGLING ON A STRING** *Invictus INV 504*	5	13
20 Feb 71	**EVERYTHING'S TUESDAY** *Invictus INV 507*	12	9
15 May 71	**PAY TO THE PIPER** *Invictus INV 511*	34	7
4 Sep 71	**CHAIRMAN OF THE BOARD** *Invictus INV 516*	48	2
15 Jul 72	**WORKING ON A BUILDING OF LOVE** *Invictus INV 519*	20	8
7 Oct 72	**ELMO JAMES** *Invictus INV 524*	21	7
16 Dec 72	**I'M ON MY WAY TO A BETTER PLACE** *Invictus INV 527*	38	1
6 Jan 73	**I'M ON MY WAY TO A BETTER PLACE (re-entry)** *Invictus INV 527*	30	5
23 Jun 73	**FINDERS KEEPERS** *Invictus INV 530*	21	9
13 Sep 86	**LOVERBOY** *EMI EMI 5585* [1]	56	3

[1] Chairmen of the Board featuring General Johnson

CHAKACHAS
Belgium, male / female vocal / instrumental group (8 WEEKS) pos/wks

11 Jan 62	**TWIST TWIST** *RCA 1264*	48	1
27 May 72	**JUNGLE FEVER** *Polydor 2121 064*	29	7

George CHAKIRIS *US, male vocalist (1 WEEK)* pos/wks

2 Jun 60	**HEART OF A TEENAGE GIRL** *Triumph RGM 1010*	49	1

CHAKKA BOOM BANG
Holland, male instrumental / production group (1 WEEK) pos/wks

20 Jan 96	**TOSSING AND TURNING** *Hooj Choons HOOJCD 39*	57	1

CHAKRA *UK, male / female vocal / instrumental group (5 WEEKS)* pos/wks

18 Jan 97	**I AM** *WEA WEA 091CD*	24	2
23 Aug 97	**HOME** *WEA WEA 116CD2*	46	1
23 Oct 99	**LOVE SHINES THROUGH** *WEA WEA 227CD*	67	1
26 Aug 00	**HOME (re-mix)** *WEA WEA 266CD*	47	1

Sue CHALONER *UK, female vocalist (1 WEEK)* pos/wks

22 May 93	**MOVE ON UP** *Pulse 8 CDLOSE 41*	64	1

Richard CHAMBERLAIN *US, male actor (36 WEEKS)* pos/wks

7 Jun 62	**THEME FROM 'DR KILDARE' (THREE STARS WILL SHINE TONIGHT)** *MGM 1160*	12	10
1 Nov 62	**LOVE ME TENDER** *MGM 1173*	15	11
21 Feb 63	**HI-LILI, HI-LO** *MGM 1189*	20	9
18 Jul 63	**TRUE LOVE** *MGM 1205*	30	6

Bryan CHAMBERS – *See CLEPTOMANIACS featuring Bryan CHAMBERS*

CHAMELEON *UK, male vocal / instrumental group (2 WEEKS)* pos/wks

18 May 96	**THE WAY IT IS** *Stress CDSTR 65*	34	2

CHAMELEONS – *See LORI and the CHAMELEONS*

CHAMPAIGN *US, male / female vocal / instrumental group (13 WEEKS)* pos/wks

9 May 81 ●	**HOW 'BOUT US** *CBS A 1046*	5	13

CHAMPIONSHIP LEGEND – *See RAZE*

CHAMPS *US, male instrumental group (10 WEEKS)* pos/wks

4 Apr 58 ●	**TEQUILA** *London HLU 8580* ▲	5	9
17 Mar 60	**TOO MUCH TEQUILA** *London HLH 9052*	49	1

CHAMPS BOYS *France, male instrumental group (6 WEEKS)* pos/wks

19 Jun 76	**TUBULAR BELLS** *Philips 6006 519*	41	6

CHANCE – *See SUNKIDS featuring CHANCE*

Gene CHANDLER *US, male vocalist – Eugene Dixon (29 WEEKS)* pos/wks

5 Jun 68	**NOTHING CAN STOP ME** *Soul City SC 102*	41	4
3 Feb 79	**GET DOWN** *20th Century BTC 1040*	11	11
1 Sep 79	**WHEN YOU'RE NUMBER 1** *20th Century TC 2411*	43	5
28 Jun 80	**DOES SHE HAVE A FRIEND** *20th Century TC 2451*	28	9

CHANELLE *US, female vocalist – Charlene Munford (9 WEEKS)* pos/wks

11 Mar 89	**ONE MAN** *Cooltempo COOL 183*	16	8
10 Dec 94	**ONE MAN (re-mix)** *Deep Distraxion OILYCD 031*	50	1

CHANGE *US, male / female vocal / instrumental group (43 WEEKS)* pos/wks

28 Jun 80	**A LOVER'S HOLIDAY / GLOW OF LOVE** *WEA K 79141*	14	8
6 Sep 80	**SEARCHING** *WEA K 79156*	11	10
2 Jun 84	**CHANGE OF HEART** *WEA YZ 7*	17	10
11 Aug 84	**YOU ARE MY MELODY** *WEA YZ 14*	48	4
16 Mar 85	**LET'S GO TOGETHER** *Cooltempo COOL 107*	37	7
25 May 85	**OH WHAT A FEELING** *Cooltempo COOL 109*	56	2
13 Jul 85	**MUTUAL ATTRACTION** *Cooltempo COOL 111*	60	2

See also Luther VANDROSS

CHANGING FACES *US, female vocal duo – Cassandra Lucas and Charisse Rose (12 WEEKS)* pos/wks

24 Sep 94	**STROKE YOU UP** *Big Beat A 8251CD*	43	3
26 Jul 97 ●	**G.H.E.T.T.O.U.T.** *Atlantic AT 0003CD*	10	5
1 Nov 97	**I GOT SOMEBODY ELSE** *Atlantic AT 0014CD*	42	1
4 Apr 98	**TIME AFTER TIME** *Atlantic AT 0027CD*	35	2
1 Aug 98	**SAME TEMPO** *A&M 5826952*	53	1

Bruce CHANNEL *US, male vocalist (28 WEEKS)* pos/wks

22 Mar 62 ●	**HEY! BABY** *Mercury AMT 1171* ▲	2	12
26 Jun 68	**KEEP ON** *Bell 1010*	12	16

CHANNEL X
Belgium, male / female vocal / instrumental group (1 WEEK) pos/wks

14 Dec 91	**GROOVE TO MOVE** *PWL Continental PWL 209*	67	1

CHANSON *US, male / female vocal group (7 WEEKS)* pos/wks

13 Jan 79	**DON'T HOLD BACK** *Ariola ARO 140*	33	7

CHANTAL – *See MOONMAN*

CHANTAYS *US, male instrumental group (14 WEEKS)* pos/wks

18 Apr 63	**PIPELINE** *London HLD 9696*	16	14

CHANTER SISTERS *UK, female vocal group (5 WEEKS)* pos/wks

17 Jul 76	**SIDE SHOW** *Polydor 2058 735*	43	5

CHAOS *UK, male vocal group (2 WEEKS)* pos/wks

3 Oct 92	**FAREWELL MY SUMMER LOVE** *Arista 74321116397*	55	2

Harry CHAPIN *US, male vocalist (5 WEEKS)* pos/wks

11 May 74	**W.O.L.D.** *Elektra K 12133*	34	5

Simone CHAPMAN – *See ILLEGAL MOTION featuring Simone CHAPMAN*

Tracy CHAPMAN *US, female vocalist (15 WEEKS)* pos/wks

11 Jun 88 ●	**FAST CAR** *Elektra EKR 73*	5	12
30 Sep 89	**CROSSROADS** *Elektra EKR 95*	61	3

CHAPTERHOUSE *UK, male vocal / instrumental group (3 WEEKS)* pos/wks

			pos	wks
30 Mar 91		**PEARL** *Dedicated STONE 003*	67	1
12 Oct 91		**MESMERISE** *Dedicated HOUSE 001*	60	2

CHAQUITO and HIS ORCHESTRA
UK, male arranger / conductor – Johnny Gregory (1 WEEK) pos/wks

			pos	wks
27 Oct 60		**NEVER ON SUNDAY** *Fontana H 265*	50	1

CHARLATANS 445 Top 500 *North country boys from Northwich who came to prominence as part of the "Madchester" scene. Tim Burgess (v) b. 30 May 1968, Manchester, UK, and Rob Collins (k) b. 23 Feb 1963, d. 23 Jul 1996. Act has seven Top 10 albums including three No.1s (77 WEEKS)* pos/wks

			pos	wks
2 Jun 90	●	**THE ONLY ONE I KNOW** *Situation Two SIT 70T*	9	9
22 Sep 90		**THEN** *Situation Two SIT 74T*	12	5
9 Mar 91		**OVER RISING** *Situation Two SIT 76*	15	5
17 Aug 91		**INDIAN ROPE** *Dead Dead Good GOOD 1T*	57	1
9 Nov 91		**ME. IN TIME** *Situation Two SIT 84*	28	3
7 Mar 92		**WEIRDO** *Situation Two SIT 88*	19	4
18 Jul 92		**TREMELO SONG (EP)** *Situation Two SIT 97T*	44	2
5 Feb 94		**CAN'T GET OUT OF BED** *Beggars Banquet BBQ 27CD*	24	3
19 Mar 94		**I NEVER WANT AN EASY LIFE IF ME AND HE WERE EVER TO GET THERE** *Beggars Banquet BBQ 31CD*	38	1
2 Jul 94		**JESUS HAIRDO** *Beggars Banquet BBQ 32CD1*	48	2
7 Jan 95		**CRASHIN' IN** *Beggars Banquet BBQ 44CD*	31	2
27 May 95		**JUST LOOKIN' / BULLET COMES** *Beggars Banquet BBQ 55CD*	32	3
26 Aug 95		**JUST WHEN YOU'RE THINKIN' THINGS OVER** *Beggars Banquet BBQ 60CD*	12	3
7 Sep 96	●	**ONE TO ANOTHER** *Beggars Banquet BBQ 301CD*	3	6
5 Apr 97	●	**NORTH COUNTRY BOY** *Beggars Banquet BBQ 309CD*	4	5
21 Jun 97	●	**HOW HIGH** *Beggars Banquet BBQ 312CD*	6	5
21 Jun 97		**NORTH COUNTRY BOY (re-entry)** *Beggars Banquet BBQ 309CD*	74	1
1 Nov 97		**TELLIN' STORIES** *Beggars Banquet BBQ 318CD*	16	3
16 Oct 99		**FOREVER** *Universal MCSTD 40220*	12	3
18 Dec 99		**MY BEAUTIFUL FRIEND** *Universal MCSTD 40225*	31	3
27 May 00		**IMPOSSIBLE** *Universal MCSTD 40231*	15	3
8 Sep 01		**LOVE IS THE KEY** *Universal MCSTD 40262*	16	3
1 Dec 01		**A MAN NEEDS TO BE TOLD** *Universal MCSTD 40271*	31	2

Tracks on Tremelo Song (EP): Tremelo Song / Happen to Die / Normality Swing

CHARLENE *US, female vocalist – Charlene Duncan (12 WEEKS)* pos/wks

			pos	wks
15 May 82	★	**I'VE NEVER BEEN TO ME** *Motown TMG 1260*	1	12

Don CHARLES *UK, male vocalist (5 WEEKS)* pos/wks

			pos	wks
22 Feb 62		**WALK WITH ME MY ANGEL** *Decca F 11424*	39	5

Ray CHARLES 202 Top 500 *Rock era's first "genius", b. Ray Charles Robinson, 23 Sep 1930, Georgia. This blind singer / songwriter / pianist and band leader had a US chart career spanning six decades. In 1994 he received a prestigious National Medal of Arts from US President Clinton (130 WEEKS)* pos/wks

			pos	wks
1 Dec 60		**GEORGIA ON MY MIND** *HMV POP 792* ▲	47	1
15 Dec 60		**GEORGIA ON MY MIND (re-entry)** *HMV POP 792*	24	7
19 Oct 61	●	**HIT THE ROAD JACK** *HMV POP 935* ▲	6	12
14 Jun 62	★	**I CAN'T STOP LOVING YOU** *HMV POP 1034* ▲	1	17
13 Sep 62	●	**YOU DON'T KNOW ME** *HMV POP 1064*	9	13
13 Dec 62		**YOUR CHEATING HEART** *HMV POP 1099*	13	8
28 Mar 63		**DON'T SET ME FREE** *HMV POP 1133*	37	3
16 May 63	●	**TAKE THESE CHAINS FROM MY HEART** *HMV POP 1161*	5	20
12 Sep 63		**NO ONE** *HMV POP 1202*	35	7
31 Oct 63		**BUSTED** *HMV POP 1221*	21	10
24 Sep 64		**NO ONE TO CRY TO** *HMV POP 1333*	38	3
21 Jan 65		**MAKIN' WHOOPEE** *HMV POP 1383*	42	4
10 Feb 66		**CRYIN' TIME** *HMV POP 1502*	50	1
21 Apr 66		**TOGETHER AGAIN** *HMV POP 1519*	48	1
5 Jul 67		**HERE WE GO AGAIN** *HMV POP 1595*	38	1
19 Jul 67		**HERE WE GO AGAIN (re-entry)** *HMV POP 1595*	45	2
20 Dec 67		**YESTERDAY** *Stateside SS 2071*	44	4
31 Jul 68		**ELEANOR RIGBY** *Stateside SS 2120*	36	9
13 Jan 90		**I'LL BE GOOD TO YOU** *Qwest W 2697* [1]	21	7

[1] Quincy Jones featuring Ray Charles and Chaka Khan

See also INXS

Suzette CHARLES *US, female vocalist (2 WEEKS)* pos/wks

			pos	wks
21 Aug 93		**FREE TO LOVE AGAIN** *RCA 74321158372*	58	2

Tina CHARLES *UK, female vocalist (Tina Hoskins) (63 WEEKS)* pos/wks

			pos	wks
7 Feb 76	★	**I LOVE TO LOVE (BUT MY BABY LOVES TO DANCE)** *CBS 3937*	1	12
1 May 76		**LOVE ME LIKE A LOVER** *CBS 4237*	31	7
21 Aug 76	●	**DANCE LITTLE LADY DANCE** *CBS 4480*	6	13
4 Dec 76	●	**DR LOVE** *CBS 4779*	4	10
14 May 77		**RENDEZVOUS** *CBS 5174*	27	6
29 Oct 77		**LOVE BUG – SWEETS FOR MY SWEET (MEDLEY)** *CBS 5680*	26	4
11 Mar 78		**I'LL GO WHERE YOUR MUSIC TAKES ME** *CBS 6062*	27	8
30 Aug 86		**I LOVE TO LOVE (re-mix)** *DMC DECK 1*	67	3

See also 5000 VOLTS

CHARLES and EDDIE *US, male vocal duo – Charles Pettigrew and Eddie Chacon (30 WEEKS)* pos/wks

			pos	wks
31 Oct 92	★	**WOULD I LIE TO YOU** *Capitol CL 673*	1	17
20 Feb 93		**N.Y.C. (CAN YOU BELIEVE THIS CITY)** *Capitol CDCL 681*	33	5
22 May 93		**HOUSE IS NOT A HOME** *Capitol CDCLS 688*	29	4
13 May 95		**24-7-365** *Capitol CDCLS 747*	38	4

Dick CHARLESWORTH and his CITY GENTS
UK, male jazz band group, Dick Charlesworth – clarinet (1 WEEK) pos/wks

			pos	wks
4 May 61		**BILLY BOY** *Top Rank JAR 558*	43	1

CHARLOTTE *UK, female vocalist (4 WEEKS)* pos/wks

			pos	wks
12 Mar 94		**QUEEN OF HEARTS** *Big Life BLRD 106*	54	1
2 May 98		**BE MINE** *Parlophone Rhythm CDRHYTHM 10*	59	1
29 May 99		**SKIN** *Parlophone Rhythm Series CDRHYTHM 20*	56	1
4 Sep 99		**SOMEDAY** *Parlophone Rhythm Series CDRHYTHM 23*	74	1

CHARME *US, male / female vocal group (2 WEEKS)* pos/wks

			pos	wks
17 Nov 84		**GEORGY PORGY** *RCA 464*	68	2

CHARO and the SALSOUL ORCHESTRA
US, female vocalist and orchestra (4 WEEKS) pos/wks

			pos	wks
29 Apr 78		**DANCE A LITTLE BIT CLOSER** *Salsoul SSOL 101*	44	4

CHARVONI – *See BROTHERS IN RHYTHM*

CHAS and DAVE *UK, male vocal / instrumental duo – Chas Hodges and Dave Peacock (66 WEEKS)* pos/wks

			pos	wks
11 Nov 78		**STRUMMIN'** *EMI 2874* [1]	52	3
26 May 79		**GERTCHA** *EMI 2947*	20	8
1 Sep 79		**THE SIDEBOARD SONG (GOT MY BEER IN THE SIDEBOARD HERE)** *EMI 2986*	55	3
29 Nov 80	●	**RABBIT** *Rockney 9*	8	11
12 Dec 81		**STARS OVER 45** *Rockney KOR 12*	21	8
13 Mar 82	●	**AIN'T NO PLEASING YOU** *Rockney KOR 14*	2	11
17 Jul 82		**MARGATE** *Rockney KOR 15*	46	4
19 Mar 83		**LONDON GIRLS** *Rockney KOR 17*	63	3
3 Dec 83		**MY MELANCHOLY BABY** *Rockney KOR 21*	51	6
3 May 86	●	**SNOOKER LOOPY** *Rockney POT 147* [2]	6	9

[1] Chas and Dave with Rockney [2] Matchroom Mob with Chas and Dave

See also TOTTENHAM HOTSPUR FA CUP FINAL SQUAD

Tara CHASE – *See Sonny JONES featuring Tara CHASE*

CHEAP TRICK *US, male vocal / instrumental group (14 WEEKS)* pos/wks

			pos	wks
5 May 79		**I WANT YOU TO WANT ME** *Epic EPC 7258*	29	9

2 Feb 80		**WAY OF THE WORLD** *Epic EPC 8114*	73	2
31 Jul 82		**IF YOU WANT MY LOVE** *Epic EPC A 2406*	57	3

Oliver CHEATHAM *US, male vocalist (5 WEEKS)* pos/wks

2 Jul 83		**GET DOWN SATURDAY NIGHT** *MCA 828*	38	5

CHECK 1-2 – *See Craig McLACHLAN*

Chubby CHECKER (256 Top 500) *The "King of the Twist", b. Ernest Evans, 3 Oct 1941, South Carolina, US. This rotund vocalist helped to make the Twist the most popular dance of the rock era. 'The Twist' was the only single to top the US chart on two separate occasions (112 WEEKS)* pos/wks

22 Sep 60		**THE TWIST** *Columbia DB 4503* ▲	49	1
6 Oct 60		**THE TWIST (re-entry)** *Columbia DB 4503*	44	1
30 Mar 61		**PONY TIME** *Columbia DB 4591* ▲	27	6
17 Aug 61		**LET'S TWIST AGAIN** *Columbia DB 4691*	37	3
28 Dec 61	●	**LET'S TWIST AGAIN (re-entry)** *Columbia DB 4691*	2	27
11 Jan 62		**THE TWIST (2nd re-entry)** *Columbia DB 4503* ▲	14	10
5 Apr 62		**SLOW TWISTIN'** *Columbia DB 4808*	23	8
19 Apr 62		**TEACH ME TO TWIST** *Columbia DB 4802* [1]	45	1
9 Aug 62		**DANCIN' PARTY** *Columbia DB 4876*	19	13
23 Aug 62		**LET'S TWIST AGAIN (2nd re-entry)** *Columbia DB 4691*	46	1
13 Sep 62		**LET'S TWIST AGAIN (3rd re-entry)** *Columbia DB 4691*	49	3
1 Nov 62		**LIMBO ROCK** *Cameo Parkway P 849*	32	10
20 Dec 62		**JINGLE BELL ROCK** *Cameo Parkway C 205* [1]	40	3
31 Oct 63		**WHAT DO YA SAY** *Cameo Parkway P 806*	37	4
29 Nov 75	●	**LET'S TWIST AGAIN / THE TWIST (re-issue)** *London HLU 10512*	5	10
18 Jun 88	●	**THE TWIST (YO, TWIST)** *Urban URB 20* [2]	2	11

[1] Chubby Checker and Bobby Rydell [2] Fat Boys and Chubby Checker

CHECKMATES – *See Emile FORD and the CHECKMATES*

CHECKMATES LTD *US, male vocal / instrumental group (8 WEEKS)* pos/wks

15 Nov 69		**PROUD MARY** *A & M AMS 769*	30	8

Judy CHEEKS *US, female vocalist (15 WEEKS)* pos/wks

13 Nov 93		**SO IN LOVE (THE REAL DEAL)** *Positiva CDTIV 6*	27	3
7 May 94		**REACH** *Positiva CDTIV 12*	17	4
4 Mar 95		**THIS TIME / RESPECT** *Positiva CDTIV 28*	23	2
17 Jun 95		**YOU'RE THE STORY OF MY LIFE / AS LONG AS YOU'RE GOOD TO ME** *Positiva CDTIV 34*	30	3
13 Jan 96		**REACH (re-mix)** *Positiva CDTIV 42*	22	3

CHEETAHS *UK, male vocal / instrumental group (6 WEEKS)* pos/wks

1 Oct 64		**MECCA** *Philips BF 1362*	36	3
21 Jan 65		**SOLDIER BOY** *Philips BF 1383*	39	3

CHEF *US, male cartoon vocalist – Isaac Hayes (13 WEEKS)* pos/wks

26 Dec 98	★	**CHOCOLATE SALTY BALLS (PS I LOVE YOU)** *Columbia 6667985*	1	13

CHELSEA FC *UK, male football team vocalists (22 WEEKS)* pos/wks

26 Feb 72	●	**BLUE IS THE COLOUR** *Penny Farthing PEN 782*	5	12
14 May 94		**NO ONE CAN STOP US NOW** *RCA 74321210452*	23	3
17 May 97		**BLUE DAY** *WEA WEA 112CD* [1]	22	5
27 May 00		**BLUE TOMORROW** *Telstar TV CFCCD 2000*	22	2

[1] Suggs & Co featuring Chelsea Team

See also STAMFORD BRIDGE

CHEMICAL BROTHERS *UK, male instrumental / production duo – Tom Rowlands and Ed Simons (53 WEEKS)* pos/wks

17 Jun 95		**LEAVE HOME** *Junior Boy's Own CHEMSD 1*	17	4
9 Sep 95		**LIFE IS SWEET** *Junior Boy's Own CHEMSD 2*	25	3
27 Jan 96		**LOOPS OF FURY (EP)** *Junior Boy's Own CHEMSD 3*	13	1
12 Oct 96	★	**SETTING SUN** *Junior Boy's Own CHEMSD 4* ■	1	7
5 Apr 97	★	**BLOCK ROCKIN' BEATS** *Virgin CHEMSD 5* ■	1	6
28 Jun 97		**BLOCK ROCKIN' BEATS (re-entry)** *Virgin CHEMSD 5*	69	1
20 Sep 97		**ELEKTROBANK** *Virgin CHEMSD 6*	17	4
12 Jun 99	●	**HEY BOY HEY GIRL** *Virgin CHEMSD 8*	3	10
14 Aug 99	●	**LET FOREVER BE** *Virgin CHEMSD 9*	9	7
23 Oct 99		**OUT OF CONTROL** *Virgin CHEMSD 10*	21	4
22 Sep 01	●	**IT BEGAN IN AFRIKA** *Virgin CHEMSD 12*	8	4
3 Nov 01		**IT BEGAN IN AFRIKA (re-entry)** *Virgin CHEMSD 12*	53	2

Tracks on Loops of Fury (EP): Loops of Fury / (The Best Part of) Breaking Up / Get Upon It Like This / Chemical Beats. Uncredited vocal on 'Setting Sun' and 'Let Forever Be' by Noel Gallagher and on 'Out of Control' by Bernard Sumner

CHEQUERS *UK, male vocal / instrumental group (10 WEEKS)* pos/wks

18 Oct 75		**ROCK ON BROTHER** *Creole CR 111*	21	5
28 Feb 76		**HEY MISS PAYNE** *Creole CR 116*	32	5

CHER (65 Top 500) *Perennially popular vocalist, b. Cherilyn LaPierre, 20 May 1946, California. She was half of the most successful husband / wife duo ever, Sonny and Cher, and had an equally stunning run of solo smashes. At the age of 52 she is the oldest female solo singer to top the chart (226 WEEKS)* pos/wks

19 Aug 65	●	**ALL I REALLY WANT TO DO** *Liberty LIB 66114*	9	10
31 Mar 66	●	**BANG BANG (MY BABY SHOT ME DOWN)** *Liberty LIB 66160*	3	12
4 Aug 66		**I FEEL SOMETHING IN THE AIR** *Liberty LIB 12034*	43	2
22 Sep 66		**SUNNY** *Liberty LIB 12083*	32	5
6 Nov 71	●	**GYPSIES TRAMPS AND THIEVES** *MCA MU 1142* ▲	4	13
16 Feb 74		**DARK LADY** *MCA 101* ▲	36	3
16 Mar 74		**DARK LADY (re-entry)** *MCA 101*	45	1
19 Dec 87	●	**I FOUND SOMEONE** *Geffen GEF 31*	5	10
2 Apr 88		**WE ALL SLEEP ALONE** *Geffen GEF 35*	47	5
2 Sep 89	●	**IF I COULD TURN BACK TIME** *Geffen GEF 59*	6	14
13 Jan 90		**JUST LIKE JESSE JAMES** *Geffen GEF 69*	11	11
7 Apr 90		**HEART OF STONE** *Geffen GEF 75*	43	5
11 Aug 90		**YOU WOULDN'T KNOW LOVE** *Geffen GEF 77*	55	3
13 Apr 91	★	**THE SHOOP SHOOP SONG (IT'S IN HIS KISS)** *Epic 6566737*	1	15
13 Jul 91	●	**LOVE AND UNDERSTANDING** *Geffen GFS 5*	10	8
12 Oct 91		**SAVE UP ALL YOUR TEARS** *Geffen GFS 11*	37	5
7 Dec 91		**LOVE HURTS** *Geffen GFS 16*	43	5
18 Apr 92		**COULD'VE BEEN YOU** *Geffen GFS 19*	31	4
14 Nov 92		**OH NO NOT MY BABY** *Geffen GFS 29*	33	4
16 Jan 93		**MANY RIVERS TO CROSS** *Geffen GFSTD 31*	37	3
6 Mar 93		**WHENEVER YOU'RE NEAR** *Geffen GFSTD 32*	72	1
15 Jan 94		**I GOT YOU BABE** *Geffen GFSTD 64* [1]	35	3
18 Mar 95	★	**LOVE CAN BUILD A BRIDGE** *London COCD 1* [2]	1	8
28 Oct 95	●	**WALKING IN MEMPHIS** *WEA WEA 021CD1*	11	7
20 Jan 96	●	**ONE BY ONE** *WEA WEA 032CD*	7	9
27 Apr 96		**NOT ENOUGH LOVE IN THE WORLD** *WEA WEA 052CD*	31	2
17 Aug 96		**THE SUN AIN'T GONNA SHINE ANYMORE** *WEA WEA 071CD*	26	3
31 Oct 98	★	**BELIEVE** *WEA WEA 175CD* ◆ ■ ▲	1	26
6 Mar 99	●	**STRONG ENOUGH** *WEA WEA 201CD1*	5	10
8 May 99		**BELIEVE (re-entry)** *WEA WEA 175CD*	59	2
19 Jun 99		**ALL OR NOTHING** *WEA WEA 212CD1*	12	7
6 Nov 99		**DOVE L'AMORE** *WEA WEA 230CD1*	21	3
17 Nov 01	●	**THE MUSIC'S NO GOOD WITHOUT YOU** *WEA WEA 337CD*	8	7+

[1] Cher with Beavis and Butt-Head [2] Cher, Chrissie Hynde and Neneh Cherry with Eric Clapton

See also SONNY and CHER; MEAT LOAF

CHERI *Canada, female vocal duo – Rosalind Hunt and Lyn Cullerier (9 WEEKS)* pos/wks

19 Jun 82		**MURPHY'S LAW** *Polydor POSP 459*	13	9

CHEROKEES *UK, male vocal / instrumental group (5 WEEKS)* pos/wks

3 Sep 64		**SEVEN DAFFODILS** *Columbia DB 7341*	33	5

CHERRELLE *US, female vocalist – Cheryl Norton (26 WEEKS)* pos/wks

28 Dec 85	●	**SATURDAY LOVE** *Tabu A 6829* [1]	6	11
1 Mar 86		**WILL YOU SATISFY?** *Tabu A 6927*	57	3
6 Feb 88		**NEVER KNEW LOVE LIKE THIS** *Tabu 6513827* [2]	26	7
6 May 89		**AFFAIR** *Tabu 654673 7*	67	2
24 Mar 90		**SATURDAY LOVE (re-mix)** *Tabu 6558007* [1]	55	2
2 Aug 97		**BABY COME TO ME** *One World OWECD 1* [2]	56	1

[1] Cherrelle with Alexander O'Neal [2] Alexander O'Neal featuring Cherrelle

Don CHERRY *US, male vocalist (11 WEEKS)*

		pos	wks
10 Feb 56 ●	BAND OF GOLD *Philips PB 549*	6	11

Eagle-Eye CHERRY *Sweden, male vocalist (28 WEEKS)*

		pos	wks
4 Jul 98 ●	SAVE TONIGHT *Polydor 5695952*	6	13
14 Nov 98 ●	FALLING IN LOVE AGAIN *Polydor 5630252*	8	8
20 Mar 99	PERMANENT TEARS *Polydor 5636752*	43	1
29 Apr 00	ARE YOU STILL HAVING FUN *Polydor 5618032*	21	4
11 Nov 00	LONG WAY AROUND *Polydor 5677812* [1]	48	2

[1] Eagle-Eye Cherry featuring Neneh Cherry

Neneh CHERRY (311 Top 500) *Sassy, strident rapper-singer, b.10 Mar 1964, Stockholm, Sweden, raised in New York and relocated to UK early 1980s. Stepdaughter of jazz trumpeter Don Cherry and sister of Eagle-Eye Cherry. Winner of 1990 Best New Female award in Rolling Stone and at the Brits (98 WEEKS)*

		pos	wks
10 Dec 88 ●	BUFFALO STANCE *Circa YR 21*	3	13
20 May 89 ●	MANCHILD *Circa YR 30*	5	10
12 Aug 89	KISSES ON THE WIND *Circa YR 33*	20	6
23 Dec 89	INNA CITY MAMMA *Circa YR 42*	31	7
29 Sep 90	I'VE GOT YOU UNDER MY SKIN *Circa YR 53*	25	5
3 Oct 92	MONEY LOVE *Circa YR 83*	23	4
16 Jan 93	BUDDY X *Circa YRCD 98*	35	3
25 Jun 94 ●	7 SECONDS *Columbia 6605082* [1]	3	21
24 Dec 94	7 SECONDS (re-entry) *Columbia 6605082* [1]	54	4
18 Mar 95 ★	LOVE CAN BUILD A BRIDGE *London COCD 1* [2]	1	8
3 Aug 96 ●	WOMAN *Hut HUTCD 70*	9	7
14 Dec 96	KOOTCHI *Hut HUTDG 75*	38	2
22 Feb 97	FEEL IT *Hut HUTCD 79*	68	1
6 Nov 99	BUDDY X 99 *4 Liberty LIBTCD 33* [3]	15	5
11 Nov 00	LONG WAY AROUND *Polydor 5677812* [4]	48	2

[1] Youssou N'Dour (featuring Neneh Cherry) [2] Cher, Chrissie Hynde and Neneh Cherry with Eric Clapton [3] Dreem Teem vs Neneh Cherry [4] Eagle-Eye Cherry featuring Neneh Cherry

CHI-LITES (358 Top 500) *Supreme soft-soul vocal quartet from Chicago, fronted by Eugene Record, b. 23 Dec 1940, Illinois, US, who originally formed group with Marshall Thompson as the Hi-Lites. Record also produced and wrote the vast majority of their many transatlantic hits (89 WEEKS)*

		pos	wks
28 Aug 71	(FOR GOD'S SAKE) GIVE MORE POWER TO THE PEOPLE *MCA MU 1138*	32	6
15 Jan 72 ●	HAVE YOU SEEN HER *MCA MU 1146*	3	12
27 May 72	OH GIRL *MCA MU 1156* ▲	14	9
23 Mar 74 ●	HOMELY GIRL *Brunswick BR 9*	5	13
20 Jul 74	I FOUND SUNSHINE *Brunswick BR 12*	35	5
2 Nov 74 ●	TOO GOOD TO BE FORGOTTEN *Brunswick BR 13*	10	11
21 Jun 75 ●	HAVE YOU SEEN HER / OH GIRL (re-issue) *Brunswick BR 20*	5	9
13 Sep 75 ●	IT'S TIME FOR LOVE *Brunswick BR 25*	5	10
31 Jul 76 ●	YOU DON'T HAVE TO GO *Brunswick BR 34*	3	11
13 Aug 83	CHANGING FOR YOU *R & B RBS 215*	61	3

CHIC (353 Top 500) *Acclaimed, ground-breaking funk-disco collective, formed 1976, New York City by Nile Rodgers (g), b. 19 Sep 1952 and Bernard Edwards (b), b. 31 Oct 1952; d. 18 Apr 1996, who became one of the top songwriter / production teams of the 80s. 'Good Times' was sampled on first rap hit, 'Rapper's Delight', by Sugarhill Gang (90 WEEKS)*

		pos	wks
26 Nov 77 ●	DANCE DANCE DANCE (YOWSAH YOWSAH YOWSAH) *Atlantic K 11038*	6	12
1 Apr 78 ●	EVERYBODY DANCE *Atlantic K 11097*	9	11
18 Nov 78 ●	LE FREAK *Atlantic K 11209* ▲	7	16
24 Feb 79 ●	I WANT YOUR LOVE *Atlantic LV 16*	4	11
30 Jun 79 ●	GOOD TIMES *Atlantic K 11310* ▲	5	11
13 Oct 79	MY FORBIDDEN LOVER *Atlantic K 11385*	15	8
8 Dec 79	MY FEET KEEP DANCING *Atlantic K 11415*	21	9
12 Mar 83	HANGIN' *Atlantic A 9898*	64	1
19 Sep 87	JACK LE FREAK *Atlantic A 9198*	19	6
14 Jul 90	MEGACHIC – CHIC MEDLEY *East West A 7949*	58	2
15 Feb 92	CHIC MYSTIQUE *Warner Bros. W 0083*	48	3

CHICAGO (407 Top 500) *Pioneering jazz-rock group included Peter Cetera (v / b) b. 13 Sep 1944. Group relocated from city of the same name to California, US, in 1967. Released longest numerical sequence of album titles (majority going platinum in the US) – the most recent being Chicago 26 (1999) (81 WEEKS)*

		pos	wks
10 Jan 70 ●	I'M A MAN *CBS 4715* [1]	8	11
18 Jul 70 ●	25 OR 6 TO 4 *CBS 5076*	7	13
9 Oct 76 ★	IF YOU LEAVE ME NOW *CBS 4603* ▲	1	16
5 Nov 77	BABY WHAT A BIG SURPRISE *CBS 5672*	41	3
21 Aug 82 ●	HARD TO SAY I'M SORRY *Full Moon K 79301* ▲	4	15
27 Oct 84 ●	HARD HABIT TO BREAK *Full Moon W 9214*	8	13
26 Jan 85	YOU'RE THE INSPIRATION *Warner Bros. W 9126*	14	10

[1] Chicago Transit Authority

CHICANE
UK, male producer / instrumentalist – Nick Bracegirdle (48 WEEKS)

		pos	wks
21 Dec 96	OFFSHORE *Xtravaganza 0091005*	14	7
14 Jun 97	SUNSTROKE *Xtravaganza 0091125*	21	3
13 Sep 97	OFFSHORE '97 (re-mix) *Xtravaganza 0091255 EXT* [1]	17	4
20 Dec 97	LOST YOU SOMEWHERE *Xtravaganza 0091415*	35	3
10 Oct 98	STRONG IN LOVE *Xtravaganza 0091675EXT* [2]	32	2
5 Jun 99 ●	SALTWATER *Xtravaganza XTRAV 1CDS* [3]	6	10
18 Mar 00 ★	DON'T GIVE UP *Xtravaganza XTRAV 9CDS* [4] ■	1	14
22 Jul 00	NO ORDINARY MORNING / HALCYON *Xtravaganza XTRAV 12CDS*	28	3
28 Oct 00	AUTUMN TACTICS *Xtravaganza XTRAV 17CDS*	44	2

[1] Chicane with Power Circle [2] Chicane featuring Mason [3] Chicane featuring Maire Brennan of Clannad [4] Chicane featuring Bryan Adams

Chicane are Disco Citizens under another name

CHICKEN SHACK
UK, male / female vocal / instrumental group (19 WEEKS)

		pos	wks
7 May 69	I'D RATHER GO BLIND *Blue Horizon 57-3153*	14	13
6 Sep 69	TEARS IN THE WIND *Blue Horizon 57-3160*	29	6

CHICKEN SHED THEATRE *UK, youth theatre company (6 WEEKS)*

		pos	wks
27 Dec 97	I AM IN LOVE WITH THE WORLD *Columbia 6654172*	15	6

CHICORY TIP *UK, male vocal / instrumental group (34 WEEKS)*

		pos	wks
29 Jan 72 ★	SON OF MY FATHER *CBS 7737*	1	13
20 May 72	WHAT'S YOUR NAME *CBS 8021*	13	8
31 Mar 73	GOOD GRIEF CHRISTINA *CBS 1258*	17	13

CHIEFTAINS *Ireland, male vocal / instrumental group (4 WEEKS)*

		pos	wks
18 Mar 95	HAVE I TOLD YOU LATELY THAT I LOVE YOU *RCA 74321271702* [1]	71	1
12 Jun 99	I KNOW MY LOVE *RCA Victor 74321670622* [2]	37	3

[1] Chieftains with Van Morrison [2] Chieftains featuring The Corrs

CHIFFONS *US, female vocal group (40 WEEKS)*

		pos	wks
11 Apr 63	HE'S SO FINE *Stateside SS 172* ▲	16	12
18 Jul 63	ONE FINE DAY *Stateside SS 202*	29	6
26 May 66	SWEET TALKIN' GUY *Stateside SS 512*	31	8
18 Mar 72 ●	SWEET TALKIN' GUY (re-issue) *London HL 10271*	4	14

CHILD *UK, male vocal / instrumental group (22 WEEKS)*

		pos	wks
29 Apr 78	WHEN YOU WALK IN THE ROOM *Ariola Hansa AHA 511*	38	5
22 Jul 78 ●	IT'S ONLY MAKE BELIEVE *Ariola Hansa AHA 522*	10	12
28 Apr 79	ONLY YOU (AND YOU ALONE) *Ariola Hansa AHA 536*	33	5

Jane CHILD *Canada, female vocalist (8 WEEKS)*

		pos	wks
12 May 90	DON'T WANNA FALL IN LOVE *Warner Bros. W 9817*	22	8

CHILDLINERS *UK / Australia, male / female vocal group (6 WEEKS)*

		pos	wks
16 Dec 95 ●	THE GIFT OF CHRISTMAS *London LONCD 376*	9	6

CHILDREN FOR RWANDA *UK, male / female choir (2 WEEKS)* pos/wks

10 Sep 94	**LOVE CAN BUILD A BRIDGE** *East West YZ 849CD*	57	2

CHILDREN OF THE NIGHT *UK, male vocalist / producer (2 WEEKS)* pos/wks

26 Nov 88	**IT'S A TRIP (TUNE IN, TURN ON, DROP OUT)** *Jive JIVE 189*	52	2

CHILDREN OF THE REVOLUTION – *See KLF*

Toni CHILDS *US, female vocalist (4 WEEKS)* pos/wks

25 Mar 89	**DON'T WALK AWAY** *A & M AM 462*	53	4

CHILI HI FLY *Australia, male DJ / production duo (2 WEEKS)* pos/wks

18 Mar 00	**IS IT LOVE?** *Ministry of Sound MOSCDS 141*	37	2

CHILL FAC-TORR *US, male vocal / instrumental group (8 WEEKS)* pos/wks

2 Apr 83	**TWIST (ROUND 'N' ROUND)** *Phillyworld PWS 109*	37	8

CHILLI featuring CARRAPICHO *US / Ghana / Brazil, male / female vocal / instrumental group (1 WEEK)* pos/wks

20 Sep 97	**TIC, TIC TAC** *Arista 74321511332*	59	1

CHIMES *UK, male / female vocal / instrumental group (28 WEEKS)* pos/wks

19 Aug 89	**1-2-3** *CBS 655166 7*	60	3
2 Dec 89	**HEAVEN** *CBS 655432 7*	66	2
6 Jan 90	**HEAVEN (re-entry)** *CBS 655432 7*	69	3
19 May 90 ●	**I STILL HAVEN'T FOUND WHAT I'M LOOKING FOR** *CBS CHIM 1*	6	9
28 Jul 90	**TRUE LOVE** *CBS CHIM 2*	48	3
29 Sep 90	**HEAVEN (re-issue)** *CBS CHIM 3*	24	6
1 Dec 90	**LOVE COMES TO MIND** *CBS CHIM 4*	49	2

CHIMIRA *South Africa, female vocalist (1 WEEK)* pos/wks

6 Dec 97	**SHOW ME HEAVEN** *Neoteric NRDCD 11*	70	1

CHINA BLACK *UK, male vocal / instrumental duo – Errol Reid and Simon Fung (35 WEEKS)* pos/wks

16 Jul 94 ●	**SEARCHING** *Wild Card CARDD 7*	4	16
29 Oct 94	**STARS** *Wild Card CARDD 9*	19	7
17 Dec 94	**SEARCHING (re-entry)** *Wild Card CARDD 7*	54	4
11 Feb 95	**ALMOST SEE YOU (SOMEWHERE)** *Wild Card CARDW 15*	31	2
3 Jun 95	**SWING LOW SWEET CHARIOT** *PolyGram TV SWLOW 2* [1]	15	6

[1] Ladysmith Black Mambazo featuring China Black

CHINA CRISIS *UK, male vocal / instrumental group (66 WEEKS)* pos/wks

7 Aug 82	**AFRICAN AND WHITE** *Inevitable INEV 011*	45	5
22 Jan 83	**CHRISTIAN** *Virgin VS 562*	12	9
21 May 83	**TRAGEDY AND MYSTERY** *Virgin VS 587*	46	6
15 Oct 83	**WORKING WITH FIRE AND STEEL** *Virgin VS 620*	48	5
14 Jan 84 ●	**WISHFUL THINKING** *Virgin VS 647*	9	8
10 Mar 84	**HANNA HANNA** *Virgin VS 665*	44	3
30 Mar 85	**BLACK MAN RAY** *Virgin VS 752*	14	9
1 Jun 85	**KING IN A CATHOLIC STYLE (WAKE UP)** *Virgin VS 765*	19	9
7 Sep 85	**YOU DID CUT ME** *Virgin VS 799*	54	3
8 Nov 86	**ARIZONA SKY** *Virgin VS 898*	47	4
24 Jan 87	**BEST KEPT SECRET** *Virgin VS 926*	36	5

CHINA DRUM *UK, male vocal / instrumental group (4 WEEKS)* pos/wks

2 Mar 96	**CAN'T STOP THESE THINGS** *Mantra MNT 8CD*	65	1
20 Apr 96	**LAST CHANCE** *Mantra MNT 10CD*	60	1
9 Aug 97	**FICTION OF LIFE** *Mantra MNT 21CD*	65	1
27 Sep 97	**SOMEWHERE ELSE** *Mantra MNT 022CD1*	74	1

Jonny CHINGAS *US, male instrumentalist (6 WEEKS)* pos/wks

19 Feb 83	**PHONE HOME** *CBS A 3121*	43	6

CHIPMUNKS *US, chipmunk vocal trio (12 WEEKS)* pos/wks

24 Jul 59	**RAGTIME COWBOY JOE** *London HLU 8916* [1]	11	8
19 Dec 92	**ACHY BREAKY HEART** *Epic 6588837* [2]	53	3
14 Dec 96	**MACARENA** *Sony Wonder 6639981* [3]	65	1

[1] David Seville and the Chipmunks [2] Alvin and the Chipmunks featuring Billy Ray Cyrus [3] Los Del Chipmunks

The Chipmunk characters were created by David Seville, who died in 1972. His son resurrected the act in 1980

See also David SEVILLE

CHIPPENDALES *UK / US, male vocal group (4 WEEKS)* pos/wks

31 Oct 92	**GIVE ME YOUR BODY** *XSrhythm XSR 3*	28	4

George CHISHOLM – *See JOHNSTON BROTHERS*

CHOCOLATE PUMA
Holland, male production duo – DJ Dobri and DJ Zki (9 WEEKS) pos/wks

24 Mar 01 ●	**I WANNA BE U** *Cream/Parlophone CREAM 13CD*	6	8
2 Jun 01	**I WANNA BE U (re-entry)** *Cream/Parlophone CREAM 13CD*	68	1

See also JARK PRONGO; TOMBA VIRA; GOODMEN

CHOO CHOO PROJECT
US, male / female production / instrumental vocal duo (3 WEEKS) pos/wks

15 Jan 00	**HAZIN' & PHAZIN'** *Defected DEFECT 10CDS*	21	3

See also Harry 'Choo-Choo' ROMERO

CHOPS-EMC + EXTENSIVE
UK, male instrumental group and rapper (1 WEEK) pos/wks

8 Aug 92	**ME' ISRAELITES** *Faze 2 FAZE 6*	60	1

CHORDETTES *US, female vocal group (25 WEEKS)* pos/wks

17 Dec 54	**MR SANDMAN** *Columbia DB 3553* ▲	11	8
31 Aug 56 ●	**BORN TO BE WITH YOU** *London HLA 8302*	8	9
18 Apr 58 ●	**LOLLIPOP** *London HLD 8584*	6	8

CHORDS *UK, male vocal / instrumental group (17 WEEKS)* pos/wks

6 Oct 79	**NOW IT'S GONE** *Polydor 2059 141*	63	2
2 Feb 80	**MAYBE TOMORROW** *Polydor POSP 101*	40	5
26 Apr 80	**SOMETHING'S MISSING** *Polydor POSP 146*	55	3
12 Jul 80	**THE BRITISH WAY OF LIFE** *Polydor 2059 258*	54	3
18 Oct 80	**IN MY STREET** *Polydor POSP 185*	50	4

CHRIS and JAMES *UK, male instrumental / production duo (3 WEEKS)* pos/wks

17 Sep 94	**CALM DOWN (BASS KEEPS PUMPIN')** *Stress 12STR 38*	74	1
4 Nov 95	**FOX FORCE FIVE** *Stress CDSTR 61*	71	1
7 Nov 98	**CLUB FOR LIFE '98** *Stress CDSTR 85*	66	1

Neil CHRISTIAN
UK, male vocalist – Christopher Tidmarsh (10 WEEKS) pos/wks

7 Apr 66	**THAT'S NICE** *Strike JH 301*	14	10

Roger CHRISTIAN *UK, male vocalist (3 WEEKS)* pos/wks

30 Sep 89	**TAKE IT FROM ME** *Island IS 427*	63	3

CHRISTIANS (389 Top 500) *Soul / gospel-influenced UK pop group; vocalist brothers Russell, Roger (who went solo in 1986) and Garry Christian plus Henry Priestman (k/v). In1974, the brothers appeared on TV talent show Opportunity Knocks. Their self-titled debut album went double platinum (84 WEEKS)* pos/wks

31 Jan 87	**FORGOTTEN TOWN** *Island IS 291*	22	11
13 Jun 87	**HOOVERVILLE (AND THEY PROMISED US THE WORLD)** *Island IS 326*	21	10
26 Sep 87	**WHEN THE FINGERS POINT** *Island IS 335*	34	7
5 Dec 87	**IDEAL WORLD** *Island IS 347*	14	13
23 Apr 88	**BORN AGAIN** *Island IS 365*	25	7
15 Oct 88 ●	**HARVEST FOR THE WORLD** *Island IS 395*	8	7
20 May 89 ★	**FERRY 'CROSS THE MERSEY** *PWL PWL 41* [1] ■	1	7

23 Dec 89		WORDS *Island IS 450*	18	8
7 Apr 90		I FOUND OUT *Island IS 453*	56	2
15 Sep 90		GREENBANK DRIVE *Island IS 466*	63	2
5 Sep 92		WHAT'S IN A WORD *Island IS 536*	33	5
14 Nov 92		FATHER *Island IS 543*	55	2
6 Mar 93		THE BOTTLE *Island CID 549*	39	3

[1] Christians, Holly Johnson, Paul McCartney, Gerry Marsden and Stock Aitken Waterman

CHRISTIE *UK, male vocal / instrumental group (37 WEEKS)* pos/wks

2 May 70	★	YELLOW RIVER *CBS 4911*	1	22
10 Oct 70		SAN BERNADINO *CBS 5169*	49	1
24 Oct 70	●	SAN BERNADINO (re-entry) *CBS 5169*	7	13
25 Mar 72		IRON HORSE *CBS 7747*	47	1

David CHRISTIE *France, male vocalist (12 WEEKS)* pos/wks

14 Aug 82	●	SADDLE UP *KR KR 9*	9	12

John CHRISTIE *Australia, male vocalist (6 WEEKS)* pos/wks

25 Dec 76		HERE'S TO LOVE (AULD LANG SYNE) *EMI 2554*	24	6

Lou CHRISTIE *US, male vocalist – Lugee Sacco (35 WEEKS)* pos/wks

24 Feb 66		LIGHTNIN' STRIKES *MGM 1297* ▲	11	8
28 Apr 66		RHAPSODY IN THE RAIN *MGM 1308*	37	2
13 Sep 69	●	I'M GONNA MAKE YOU MINE *Buddah 201 057*	2	17
27 Dec 69		SHE SOLD ME MAGIC *Buddah 201 073*	25	8

Tony CHRISTIE *UK, male vocalist – Tony Fitzgerald (54 WEEKS)* pos/wks

9 Jan 71		LAS VEGAS *MCA MK 5058*	21	9
8 May 71	●	I DID WHAT I DID FOR MARIA *MCA MK 5064*	2	17
20 Nov 71		IS THIS THE WAY TO AMARILLO *MCA MKS 5073*	18	13
10 Feb 73		AVENUES AND ALLEYWAYS *MCA MKS 5101*	37	4
17 Jan 76		DRIVE SAFELY DARLIN' *MCA 219*	35	4
23 Jan 99	●	WALK LIKE A PANTHER '98 *ffrr FCD 351* [1]	10	7

[1] The All Seeing I featuring Tony Christie

Shawn CHRISTOPHER *US, female vocalist (10 WEEKS)* pos/wks

4 May 91		ANOTHER SLEEPLESS NIGHT *Arista 114186*	50	4
21 Mar 92		DON'T LOSE THE MAGIC *Arista 115097*	30	5
2 Jul 94		MAKE MY LOVE *BTB BTBCD 502*	57	1

CHUCKS *UK, male / female vocal group (7 WEEKS)* pos/wks

24 Jan 63		LOO-BE-LOO *Decca F 11569*	22	7

CHUMBAWAMBA
UK, male / female vocal / instrumental group (31 WEEKS) pos/wks

18 Sep 93		ENOUGH IS ENOUGH *One Little Indian 79 TP7CD* [1]	56	2
4 Dec 93		TIMEBOMB *One Little Indian 89 TP7CD*	59	1
23 Aug 97	●	TUBTHUMPING *EMI CDEM 486*	2	20
31 Jan 98	●	AMNESIA *EMI CDEM 498*	10	5
13 Jun 98		TOP OF THE WORLD (OLE, OLE, OLE) *EMI CDEM 511*	21	3

[1] Chumbawamba and Credit to the Nation

Chubby CHUNKS *UK, male instrumentalist / producer (2 WEEKS)* pos/wks

4 Jun 94		TESTAMENT 4 *Cleveland City CLECD 13017* [1]	52	1
29 May 99		I'M TELLIN YOU (re-mix) *Cleveland City CLECD 13052* [2]	61	1

[1] Chubby Chunks Volume II [2] Chubby Chunks featuring Kim Ruffin

CHUPITO *Spain, male vocalist (2 WEEKS)* pos/wks

23 Sep 95		AMERICAN PIE *Eternal WEA 018CD*	54	2

Charlotte CHURCH *UK, female vocalist (4 WEEKS)* pos/wks

25 Dec 99		JUST WAVE HELLO *Sony Classical 6685312*	34	4

CHYNA – *See INCOGNITO*

CICA – *See PQM featuring CICA*

CICERO *UK, male vocalist – Dave Cicero (12 WEEKS)* pos/wks

18 Jan 92		LOVE IS EVERYWHERE *Spaghetti CIAO 3*	19	8
18 Apr 92		THAT LOVING FEELING *Spaghetti CIAO 4*	46	3
1 Aug 92		HEAVEN MUST HAVE SENT YOU BACK *Spaghetti CIAO 5*	70	1

CINDERELLA *US, male vocal / instrumental group (7 WEEKS)* pos/wks

6 Aug 88		GYPSY ROAD *Vertigo VER 40*	54	2
4 Mar 89		DON'T KNOW WHAT YOU GOT (TILL IT'S GONE) *Vertigo VER 43*	54	2
17 Nov 90		SHELTER ME *Vertigo VER 51*	55	2
27 Apr 91		HEARTBREAK STATION *Vertigo VER 53*	63	1

CINDY and the SAFFRONS *UK, female vocal group (3 WEEKS)* pos/wks

15 Jan 83		PAST, PRESENT AND FUTURE *Stiletto STL 9*	56	3

CINERAMA *UK, male / female vocal / instrumental duo (1 WEEK)* pos/wks

18 Jul 98		KERRY KERRY *Cooking Vinyl FRYCD 072*	71	1

Gigliola CINQUETTI *Italy, female vocalist (27 WEEKS)* pos/wks

23 Apr 64		NON HO L'ETA PER AMARTI *Decca F 21882*	17	17
4 May 74	●	GO (BEFORE YOU BREAK MY HEART) *CBS 2294*	8	10

CIRCA featuring DESTRY
UK, male production group and US, male vocalist (1 WEEK) pos/wks

27 Nov 99		SUN SHINING DOWN *Inferno CDFERN 22*	70	1

CIRCUIT *UK, male / female vocal / instrumental group (3 WEEKS)* pos/wks

20 Jul 91		SHELTER ME *Cooltempo COOL 237*	44	2
1 Apr 95		SHELTER ME (re-issue) *Pukka CDPUKA 2*	50	1

CIRCULATION *UK, male production duo (1 WEEK)* pos/wks

1 Sep 01		TURQUOISE *Hooj Choons HOOJ 109*	64	1

CIRRUS *UK, male vocal group (1 WEEK)* pos/wks

30 Sep 78		ROLLIN' ON *Jet 123*	62	1

CITIZEN CANED *UK, male producer – Darren Tate (2 WEEKS)* pos/wks

7 Apr 01		THE JOURNEY *Serious SERR 029CD*	41	2

See also ANGELIC

CITY BOY *UK, male vocal / instrumental group (20 WEEKS)* pos/wks

8 Jul 78	●	5-7-0-5 *Vertigo 6059 207*	8	12
28 Oct 78		WHAT A NIGHT *Vertigo 6059 211*	39	5
15 Sep 79		THE DAY THE EARTH CAUGHT FIRE *Vertigo 6059 238*	67	3

CITY GENTS – *See Dick CHARLESWORTH and his CITY GENTS*

CITY HIGH *US, male / female vocal / rap trio (13 WEEKS)* pos/wks

6 Oct 01	●	WHAT WOULD YOU DO? *Interscope / Polydor IND 97617*	3	13+

CITY SPUD – *See NELLY*

CJ & CO *US, male vocal / instrumental group (2 WEEKS)* pos/wks

30 Jul 77		DEVIL'S GUN *Atlantic K 10956*	43	2

Gary CLAIL ON-U SOUND SYSTEM
UK, male vocal / instrumental group (19 WEEKS) pos/wks

14 Jul 90		BEEF *RCA PB 43843* [1]	64	2
30 Mar 91	●	HUMAN NATURE *Perfecto PB 44401*	10	9
8 Jun 91		ESCAPE *Perfecto PB 44563*	44	3
14 Nov 92		WHO PAYS THE PIPER *Perfecto 74321117017*	31	3
22 May 93		THESE THINGS ARE WORTH FIGHTING FOR *Perfecto 74321147222*	45	2

[1] Gary Clail On-U Sound System featuring Bim Sherman

See also PRIMAL SCREAM

CLAIRE and FRIENDS
UK, female vocalist and young male / female friends (11 WEEKS) pos/wks

7 Jun 86		IT'S 'ORRIBLE BEING IN LOVE (WHEN YOU'RE 8 1/2) *BBC RESL 189*	13	11

CLANNAD *Ireland, male / female vocal group (29 WEEKS)* pos/wks

6 Nov 82	●	THEME FROM 'HARRY'S GAME' *RCA 292*	5	10
2 Jul 83		NEW GRANGE *RCA 340*	65	1
12 May 84		ROBIN (THE HOODED MAN) *RCA HOOD 1*	42	5
25 Jan 86		IN A LIFETIME *RCA PB 40535* [1]	20	5
10 Jun 89		IN A LIFETIME (re-issue) *RCA PB 42873* [1]	17	7
10 Aug 91		BOTH SIDES NOW *MCA MCS 1546* [2]	74	1

[1] Clannad featuring Bono [2] Clannad and Paul Young

Jimmy CLANTON *US, male vocalist (1 WEEK)* pos/wks

21 Jul 60		ANOTHER SLEEPLESS NIGHT *Top Rank JAR 382*	50	1

Eric CLAPTON (148 Top 500) *Rock guitar player, b. Eric Clapp, 30 Mar 1945, Surrey. Prior to long and lucrative solo career he recorded with hitmakers The Yardbirds, Cream, Blind Faith and Derek and the Dominoes. Multi-Grammy-winning singer-guitarist and mega-grossing live performer (150 WEEKS)* pos/wks

20 Dec 69		COMIN' HOME *Atlantic 584 308* [1]	16	9
12 Aug 72	●	LAYLA *Polydor 2058 130* [2]	7	11
27 Jul 74	●	I SHOT THE SHERIFF *RSO 2090 132* ▲	9	9
10 May 75		SWING LOW SWEET CHARIOT *RSO 2090 158*	19	9
16 Aug 75		KNOCKIN' ON HEAVEN'S DOOR *RSO 2090 166*	38	4
24 Dec 77		LAY DOWN SALLY *RSO 2090 264*	39	6
21 Oct 78		PROMISES *RSO 21*	37	7
6 Mar 82	●	LAYLA (re-issue) *RSO 87* [2]	4	10
5 Jun 82		I SHOT THE SHERIFF (re-issue) *RSO 88*	64	2
23 Apr 83		THE SHAPE YOU'RE IN *Duck W 9701*	75	1
16 Mar 85		FOREVER MAN *Warner Bros. W 9069*	51	4
4 Jan 86		EDGE OF DARKNESS *BBC RESL 178* [3]	65	3
17 Jan 87		BEHIND THE MASK *Duck W 8461*	15	11
20 Jun 87		TEARING US APART *Duck W 8299* [4]	56	3
27 Jan 90		BAD LOVE *Duck W 2644*	25	7
14 Apr 90		NO ALIBIS *Duck W 9981*	53	3
16 Nov 91		WONDERFUL TONIGHT (LIVE) *Duck W 0069*	30	7
8 Feb 92		TEARS IN HEAVEN *Reprise W 0081*	50	3
7 Mar 92	●	TEARS IN HEAVEN (re-entry) *Reprise W 0081*	5	9
1 Aug 92		RUNAWAY TRAIN *Rocket EJS 29* [5]	31	4
29 Aug 92		IT'S PROBABLY ME *A & M AM 883* [6]	30	5
3 Oct 92		LAYLA (ACOUSTIC) (re-recording) *Duck W 0134*	45	3
15 Oct 94		MOTHERLESS CHILD *Duck W 0271CD*	63	1
18 Mar 95	★	LOVE CAN BUILD A BRIDGE *London COCD 1* [7]	1	8
20 Jul 96		CHANGE THE WORLD *Reprise W 0358CD*	18	5
4 Apr 98		MY FATHER'S EYES *Duck W 0443CD*	33	2
4 Jul 98		CIRCUS *Duck W 0447CD*	39	2
18 Nov 00		FOREVER MAN (HOW MANY TIMES) *ffrr FCD 386* [8]	26	2

[1] Delaney and Bonnie and Friends featuring Eric Clapton [2] Derek and the Dominoes [3] Eric Clapton featuring Michael Kamen [4] Eric Clapton and Tina Turner [5] Elton John and Eric Clapton [6] Sting with Eric Clapton [7] Cher, Chrissie Hynde and Neneh Cherry with Eric Clapton [8] Beatchuggers featuring Eric Clapton

CLARISSA – *See DJ VISAGE featuring CLARISSA*

Dee CLARK *US, male vocalist (9 WEEKS)* pos/wks

2 Oct 59		JUST KEEP IT UP (AND SEE WHAT HAPPENS) *London HL 8915*	26	1
11 Oct 75		RIDE A WILD HORSE *Chelsea 2005 037*	16	8

Gary CLARK *UK, male vocalist (8 WEEKS)* pos/wks

30 Jan 93		WE SAIL ON THE STORMY WATERS *Circa YRCDX 93*	34	4
3 Apr 93		FREEFLOATING *Circa YRCDX 94*	50	3
19 Jun 93		MAKE A FAMILY *Circa YRCDX 105*	70	1

Loni CLARK *US, female vocalist (6 WEEKS)* pos/wks

5 Jun 93		RUSHING *A & M 5802862*	37	2
22 Jan 94		U *A & M 5804752*	28	3
17 Dec 94		LOVE'S GOT ME ON A TRIP SO HIGH *A & M 5808872*	59	1

Petula CLARK (50 Top 500) *Britain's most consistently successful female vocalist, b. 15 Nov 1932, Surrey. Before her 34-year chart span, she starred in movies and was voted Britain's Top TV Personality. First UK female to win a Grammy and be named Top Female Vocalist of the Year in the US in 1966 (247 WEEKS)* pos/wks

11 Jun 54		THE LITTLE SHOEMAKER *Polygon P 1117*	12	1
25 Jun 54	●	THE LITTLE SHOEMAKER (re-entry) *Polygon P 1117*	7	9
18 Feb 55		MAJORCA *Polygon P 1146*	12	4
25 Mar 55		MAJORCA (re-entry) *Polygon P 1146*	18	1
25 Nov 55	●	SUDDENLY THERE'S A VALLEY *Pye Nixa N 15013*	7	10
26 Jul 57	●	WITH ALL MY HEART *Pye Nixa N 15096*	4	18
15 Nov 57	●	ALONE *Pye Nixa N 15112*	8	12
28 Feb 58		BABY LOVER *Pye Nixa N 15126*	12	7
26 Jan 61	★	SAILOR *Pye 7N 15324*	1	15
13 Apr 61		SOMETHING MISSING *Pye 7N 15337*	44	1
13 Jul 61	●	ROMEO *Pye 7N 15361*	3	15
16 Nov 61	●	MY FRIEND THE SEA *Pye 7N 15389*	7	13
8 Feb 62		I'M COUNTING ON YOU *Pye 7N 15407*	41	2
28 Jun 62		YA YA TWIST *Pye 7N 15448*	14	11
20 Sep 62		YA YA TWIST (re-entry) *Pye 7N 15448*	45	2
2 May 63		CASANOVA / CHARIOT *Pye 7N 15522*	39	7
12 Nov 64	●	DOWNTOWN *Pye 7N 15722* ▲	2	15
11 Mar 65		I KNOW A PLACE *Pye 7N 15772*	17	8
12 Aug 65		YOU BETTER COME HOME *Pye 7N 15864*	44	3
14 Oct 65		ROUND EVERY CORNER *Pye 7N 15945*	43	3
4 Nov 65		YOU'RE THE ONE *Pye 7N 15991*	23	9
10 Feb 66	●	MY LOVE *Pye 7N 17038* ▲	4	9
21 Apr 66		A SIGN OF THE TIMES *Pye 7N 17071*	49	1
30 Jun 66	●	I COULDN'T LIVE WITHOUT YOUR LOVE *Pye 7N 17133*	6	11
2 Feb 67	★	THIS IS MY SONG *Pye 7N 17258*	1	14
25 May 67		DON'T SLEEP IN THE SUBWAY *Pye 7N 17325*	12	11
13 Dec 67		THE OTHER MAN'S GRASS (IS ALWAYS GREENER) *Pye 7N 17416*	20	9
6 Mar 68		KISS ME GOODBYE *Pye 7N 17466*	50	1
30 Jan 71		THE SONG OF MY LIFE *Pye 7N 45026*	41	1
13 Feb 71		THE SONG OF MY LIFE (re-entry) *Pye 7N 45026*	32	11
15 Jan 72		I DON'T KNOW HOW TO LOVE HIM *Pye 7N 45112*	47	1
29 Jan 72		I DON'T KNOW HOW TO LOVE HIM (re-entry) *Pye 7N 45112*	49	1
19 Nov 88	●	DOWNTOWN '88 (re-mix) *PRT PYS 19*	10	11

Roland CLARK – *See Armand VAN HELDEN*

Dave CLARK FIVE (115 Top 500) *Beat Boom superstars from Tottenham, London: Dave Clark (d), Mike Smith (v/k), Lenny Davidson (g), Denis Payton (s), Rick Huxley (g). In the first years of the "British Invasion", this foot-stomping quintet was second only to The Beatles in the US (174 WEEKS)* pos/wks

3 Oct 63		DO YOU LOVE ME *Columbia DB 7112*	30	6
21 Nov 63	★	GLAD ALL OVER *Columbia DB 7154*	1	19
20 Feb 64	●	BITS AND PIECES *Columbia DB 7210*	2	11
28 May 64	●	CAN'T YOU SEE THAT SHE'S MINE *Columbia DB 7291*	10	11
13 Aug 64		THINKING OF YOU BABY *Columbia DB 7335*	26	4
22 Oct 64		ANYWAY YOU WANT IT *Columbia DB 7377*	25	5
14 Jan 65		EVERYBODY KNOWS *Columbia DB 7453*	37	4
11 Mar 65		REELIN' AND ROCKIN' *Columbia DB 7503*	24	8
27 May 65		COME HOME *Columbia DB 7580*	16	8
15 Jul 65	●	CATCH US IF YOU CAN *Columbia DB 7625*	5	11
11 Nov 65		OVER AND OVER *Columbia DB 7744* ▲	45	4
19 May 66		LOOK BEFORE YOU LEAP *Columbia DB 7909*	50	1
16 Mar 67		YOU GOT WHAT IT TAKES *Columbia DB 8152*	28	8
1 Nov 67	●	EVERYBODY KNOWS *Columbia DB 8286*	2	14
28 Feb 68		NO ONE CAN BREAK A HEART LIKE YOU *Columbia DB 8342*	28	7
18 Sep 68	●	THE RED BALLOON *Columbia DB 8465*	7	11
27 Nov 68		LIVE IN THE SKY *Columbia DB 8505*	39	6
25 Oct 69		PUT A LITTLE LOVE IN YOUR HEART *Columbia DB 8624*	31	4
6 Dec 69	●	GOOD OLD ROCK 'N' ROLL *Columbia DB 8638*	7	12
7 Mar 70	●	EVERYBODY GET TOGETHER *Columbia DB 8660*	8	8
4 Jul 70		HERE COMES SUMMER *Columbia DB 8689*	44	3

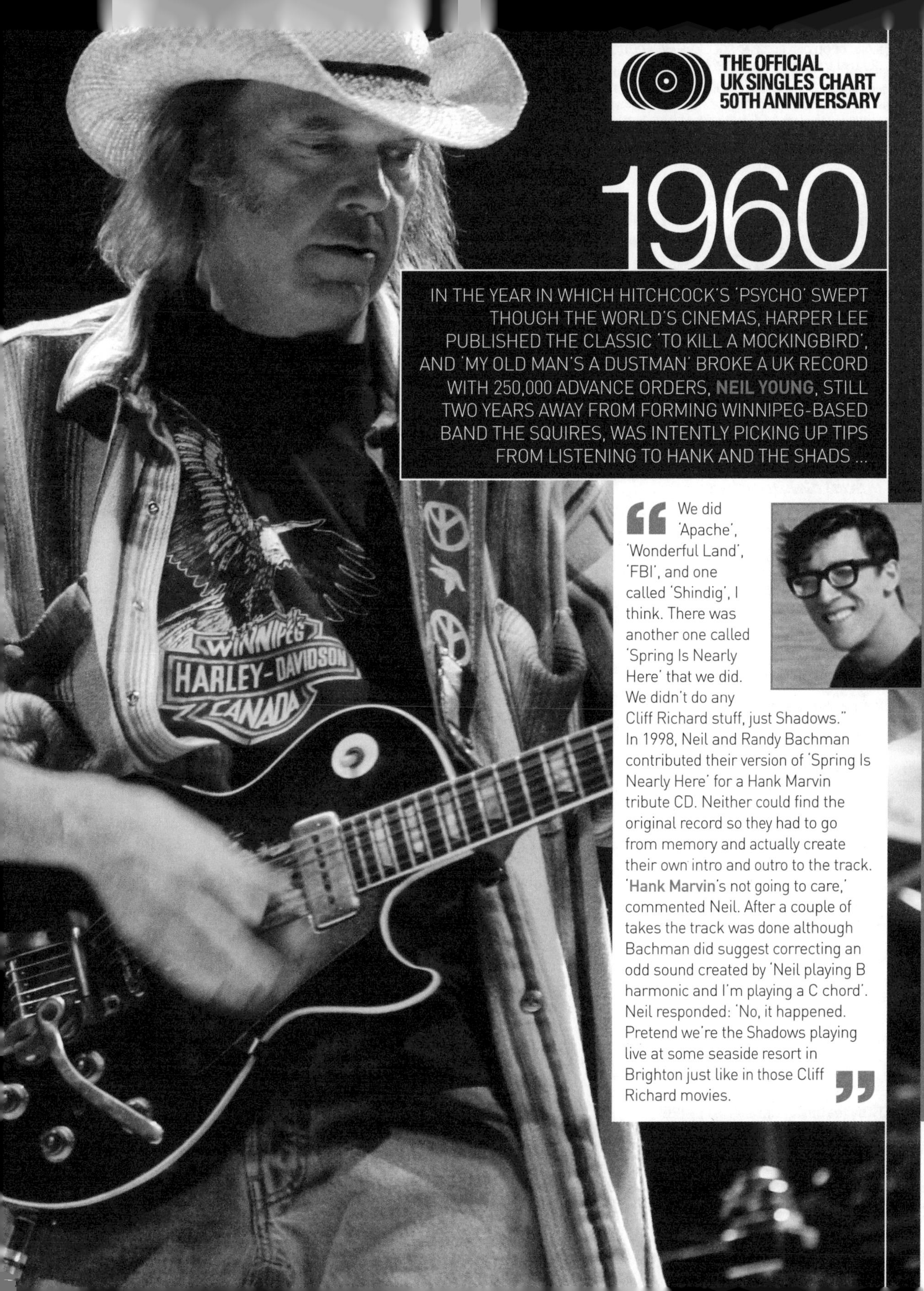

1960

IN THE YEAR IN WHICH HITCHCOCK'S 'PSYCHO' SWEPT THOUGH THE WORLD'S CINEMAS, HARPER LEE PUBLISHED THE CLASSIC 'TO KILL A MOCKINGBIRD', AND 'MY OLD MAN'S A DUSTMAN' BROKE A UK RECORD WITH 250,000 ADVANCE ORDERS, **NEIL YOUNG**, STILL TWO YEARS AWAY FROM FORMING WINNIPEG-BASED BAND THE SQUIRES, WAS INTENTLY PICKING UP TIPS FROM LISTENING TO HANK AND THE SHADS ...

"We did 'Apache', 'Wonderful Land', 'FBI', and one called 'Shindig', I think. There was another one called 'Spring Is Nearly Here' that we did. We didn't do any Cliff Richard stuff, just Shadows." In 1998, Neil and Randy Bachman contributed their version of 'Spring Is Nearly Here' for a Hank Marvin tribute CD. Neither could find the original record so they had to go from memory and actually create their own intro and outro to the track. '**Hank Marvin**'s not going to care,' commented Neil. After a couple of takes the track was done although Bachman did suggest correcting an odd sound created by 'Neil playing B harmonic and I'm playing a C chord'. Neil responded: 'No, it happened. Pretend we're the Shadows playing live at some seaside resort in Brighton just like in those Cliff Richard movies."

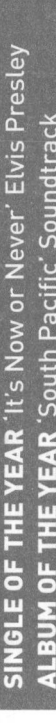

SINGLE OF THE YEAR 'It's Now or Never' Elvis Presley
ALBUM OF THE YEAR 'South Pacific' Soundtrack

7 Nov 70		**MORE GOOD OLD ROCK 'N' ROLL** *Columbia DB 8724*	**34**	6
1 May 93		**GLAD ALL OVER (re-issue)** *EMI CDEMCT 8*	**37**	3

'Everybody Knows' on DB 7453 and 'Everybody Knows' on DB 8286 are two different songs. The two Rock 'n' Roll titles are medleys as follows: Good Old Rock 'n' Roll / Sweet Little Sixteen / Long Tall Sally / Whole Lotta Shakin' Goin' On / Blue Suede Shoes / Lucille / Reelin' and Rockin' / Memphis Tennessee. More Good Old Rock 'n' Roll Music / Blueberry Hill / Good Golly Miss Molly / My Blue Heaven / Keep a Knockin' / Loving You / One Night / Lawdy Miss Clawdy

Dave CLARKE *UK, male producer (7 WEEKS)* pos/wks

30 Sep 95		**RED THREE: THUNDER / STORM** *Deconstruction 74321306992*	**45**	2
3 Feb 96		**SOUTHSIDE** *Bush 74321335382*	**34**	2
15 Jun 96		**NO ONE'S DRIVING** *Bush 74321380162*	**37**	2
8 Dec 01		**THE COMPASS** *Skint SKINT 73CD*	**46**	1

John Cooper CLARKE *UK, male vocalist (3 WEEKS)* pos/wks

10 Mar 79		**GIMMIX! PLAY LOUD** *Epic EPC 7009*	**39**	3

Rick CLARKE *UK, male vocalist (2 WEEKS)* pos/wks

30 Apr 88		**I'LL SEE YOU ALONG THE WAY** *WA WA 1*	**63**	2

Sharon D CLARKE – *See FPI PROJECT; SERIOUS ROPE*

Warren CLARKE featuring Kathy BROWN
UK, male producer and US, female vocalist (1 WEEK) pos/wks

2 Jun 01		**OVER YOU** *Defected DFECT 28CDS*	**42**	1

Julian CLARY – *See JOAN COLLINS FAN CLUB*

CLASH (186 Top 500) *Leading lights of the UK punk rock explosion: Joe Strummer (b. John Mellor) (v/g), Mick Jones (g/v), Paul Simonon (b), Topper Headon (d). Their third LP, 'London Calling' (first released 1979), was voted Best Album of the 1980s by Rolling Stone magazine (135 WEEKS)* pos/wks

2 Apr 77		**WHITE RIOT** *CBS 5058*	**38**	3
8 Oct 77		**COMPLETE CONTROL** *CBS 5664*	**28**	2
4 Mar 78		**CLASH CITY ROCKERS** *CBS 5834*	**35**	4
24 Jun 78		**(WHITE MAN) IN HAMMERSMITH PALAIS** *CBS 6383*	**32**	7
2 Dec 78		**TOMMY GUN** *CBS 6788*	**19**	10
3 Mar 79		**ENGLISH CIVIL WAR (JOHNNY COMES MARCHING HOME)** *CBS 7082*	**25**	6
19 May 79		**THE COST OF LIVING (EP)** *CBS 7324*	**22**	8
15 Dec 79		**LONDON CALLING** *CBS 8087*	**11**	10
9 Aug 80		**BANKROBBER** *CBS 8323*	**12**	10
6 Dec 80		**THE CALL UP** *CBS 9339*	**40**	6
24 Jan 81		**HITSVILLE UK** *CBS 9480*	**56**	4
25 Apr 81		**THE MAGNIFICENT SEVEN** *CBS 1133*	**34**	5
28 Nov 81		**THIS IS RADIO CLASH** *CBS A 1797*	**47**	6
1 May 82		**KNOW YOUR RIGHTS** *CBS A 2309*	**43**	3
26 Jun 82		**ROCK THE CASBAH** *CBS A 2429*	**30**	10
25 Sep 82		**SHOULD I STAY OR SHOULD I GO / STRAIGHT TO HELL** *CBS A 2646*	**17**	9
12 Oct 85		**THIS IS ENGLAND** *CBS A 6122*	**24**	5
12 Mar 88		**I FOUGHT THE LAW** *CBS CLASH 1*	**29**	5
7 May 88		**LONDON CALLING (re-issue)** *CBS CLASH 2*	**46**	3
21 Jul 90		**RETURN TO BRIXTON** *CBS 656072 7*	**57**	2
2 Mar 91	★	**SHOULD I STAY OR SHOULD I GO (re-issue)** *Columbia 6566677*	**1**	9
13 Apr 91		**ROCK THE CASBAH (re-issue)** *Columbia 6568147*	**15**	6
8 Jun 91		**LONDON CALLING (re-issue)** *Columbia 6569467*	**64**	2

Tracks on The Cost of Living (EP): I Fought the Law / Groovy Times / Gates of the West / Capital Radio. CBS CLASH 1 is a re-issue of a track from The Cost of Living (EP)

CLASS ACTION featuring Chris WILTSHIRE
US, female vocal group (3 WEEKS) pos/wks

7 May 83		**WEEKEND** *Jive JIVE 35*	**49**	3

CLASSICS IV *US, male vocal / instrumental group (1 WEEK)* pos/wks

28 Feb 68		**SPOOKY** *Liberty LBS 15051*	**46**	1

CLASSIX NOUVEAUX
UK, male vocal / instrumental group (34 WEEKS) pos/wks

28 Feb 81		**GUILTY** *Liberty BP 388*	**43**	7
16 May 81		**TOKYO** *Liberty BP 397*	**67**	3
8 Aug 81		**INSIDE OUTSIDE** *Liberty BP 403*	**45**	5
7 Nov 81		**NEVER AGAIN (THE DAYS TIME ERASED)** *Liberty BP 406*	**44**	4
13 Mar 82		**IS IT A DREAM** *Liberty BP 409*	**11**	9
29 May 82		**BECAUSE YOU'RE YOUNG** *Liberty BP 411*	**43**	4
30 Oct 82		**THE END ... OR THE BEGINNING** *Liberty BP 414*	**60**	2

CLAWFINGER
Norway / Sweden, male vocal / instrumental group (1 WEEK) pos/wks

19 Mar 94		**WARFAIR** *East West YZ 804CD1*	**54**	1

Judy CLAY – *See William BELL*

Merry CLAYTON *US, female vocalist (1 WEEK)* pos/wks

21 May 88		**YES** *RCA PB 49563*	**70**	1

Adam CLAYTON and Larry MULLEN
Ireland, male instrumental duo (12 WEEKS) pos/wks

15 Jun 96	●	**THEME FROM 'MISSION: IMPOSSIBLE'** *Mother MUMCD 75*	**7**	12

See also U2

CLAYTOWN TROUPE
UK, male vocal / instrumental group (3 WEEKS) pos/wks

16 Jun 90		**WAYS OF LOVE** *Island IS 464*	**57**	2
14 Mar 92		**WANTED IT ALL** *EMI USA MT 102*	**74**	1

Johnny CLEGG and SAVUKA
UK / South Africa, male vocal / instrumental group (1 WEEK) pos/wks

16 May 87		**SCATTERLINGS OF AFRICA** *EMI EMI 5605*	**75**	1

See also JULUKA

CLEOPATRA *UK, female vocal group – Cleopatra, Zainam and Yonah Higgins (31 WEEKS)* pos/wks

14 Feb 98	●	**CLEOPATRA'S THEME** *WEA WEA 133CD*	**3**	10
16 May 98	●	**LIFE AIN'T EASY** *WEA WEA 159CD1*	**4**	7
22 Aug 98	●	**I WANT YOU BACK** *WEA WEA 172CD1*	**4**	7
6 Mar 99		**A TOUCH OF LOVE** *WEA WEA 199CD1*	**24**	4
29 Jul 00		**COME AND GET ME** *WEA WEA 216CD1*	**29**	3

CLEPTOMANIACS featuring Bryan CHAMBERS
UK, male production group and UK, male vocalist (3 WEEKS) pos/wks

3 Feb 01		**ALL I DO** *Defected DFECT 27 CDS*	**23**	3

CLICK *US, male rap group (1 WEEK)* pos/wks

29 Jun 96		**SCANDALOUS** *Jive JIVECD 393*	**54**	1

Jimmy CLIFF *Jamaica, male vocalist – James Chambers (33 WEEKS)* pos/wks

25 Oct 69	●	**WONDERFUL WORLD, BEAUTIFUL PEOPLE** *Trojan TR 690*	**6**	13
14 Feb 70		**VIETNAM** *Trojan TR 7722*	**47**	1
28 Feb 70		**VIETNAM (re-entry)** *Trojan TR 7722*	**46**	2
8 Aug 70	●	**WILD WORLD** *Island WIP 6087*	**8**	12
19 Mar 94		**I CAN SEE CLEARLY NOW** *Columbia 6601982*	**23**	5

Buzz CLIFFORD *US, male vocalist (13 WEEKS)* pos/wks

2 Mar 61		**BABY SITTIN' BOOGIE** *Fontana H 297*	**17**	13

Linda CLIFFORD *US, female vocalist (13 WEEKS)* pos/wks

10 Jun 78		**IF MY FRIENDS COULD SEE ME NOW** *Curtom K 17163*	**50**	5
5 May 79		**BRIDGE OVER TROUBLED WATER** *RSO 30*	**28**	7
16 Sep 01		**RIDE THE STORM** *NRK Sound Division NRKCD 053* [1]	**69**	1

[1] Akabu featuring Linda Clifford

CLIMAX BLUES BAND *UK, male vocal / instrumental group (9 WEEKS)* pos/wks

9 Oct 76	●	COULDN'T GET IT RIGHT *BTM SBT 105*	10	9

Simon CLIMIE *UK, male vocalist (2 WEEKS)* pos/wks

19 Sep 92		SOUL INSPIRATION *Epic 6582837*	60	2

See also CLIMIE FISHER

CLIMIE FISHER *UK, male vocal / instrumental duo – Simon Climie and Rob Fisher (44 WEEKS)* pos/wks

5 Sep 87		LOVE CHANGES (EVERYTHING) *EMI EM 15*	67	2
12 Dec 87	●	RISE TO THE OCCASION *EMI EM 33*	10	11
12 Mar 88	●	LOVE CHANGES (EVERYTHING) (re-mix) *EMI EM 47*	2	12
21 May 88		THIS IS ME *EMI EM 58*	22	5
20 Aug 88		I WON'T BLEED FOR YOU *EMI EM 66*	35	4
24 Dec 88		LOVE LIKE A RIVER *EMI EM 81*	22	7
23 Sep 89		FACTS OF LOVE *EMI EM 103*	50	3

Patsy CLINE *US, female vocalist – Virginia Hensley (17 WEEKS)* pos/wks

26 Apr 62		SHE'S GOT YOU *Brunswick 05866*	43	1
29 Nov 62		HEARTACHES *Brunswick 05878*	31	5
8 Dec 90		CRAZY *MCA MCA 1465*	14	11

CLINIC *UK, male vocal / instrumental group (2 WEEKS)* pos/wks

22 Apr 00		THE RETURN OF EVIL BILL *Domino RUG 093CD*	70	1
4 Nov 00		THE SECOND LINE *Domino RUG 116CD*	56	1

George CLINTON *US, male vocalist (10 WEEKS)* pos/wks

4 Dec 82		LOOPZILLA *Capitol CL 271*	57	5
26 Apr 86		DO FRIES GO WITH THAT SHAKE *Capitol CL 402*	57	2
27 Aug 94		BOP GUN (ONE NATION) *Fourth & Broadway BRCD 308* [1]	22	3

[1] Ice Cube featuring George Clinton

CLIVILLES & COLE – *See C & C MUSIC FACTORY / CLIVILLES & COLE*

CLOCK *UK, male production / instrumental duo (70 WEEKS)* pos/wks

30 Oct 93		HOLDING ON *Media MRLCD 007*	66	1
21 May 94		THE RHYTHM *Media MCSTD 1971*	28	2
10 Sep 94		KEEP THE FIRES BURNING *Media MCSTD 1998*	36	3
4 Mar 95	●	AXEL F / KEEP PUSHIN' *Media MCSTD 2041*	7	9
1 Jul 95	●	WHOOMPH! (THERE IT IS) *Media MCSTD 2059*	4	9
26 Aug 95	●	EVERYBODY *Media MCSTD 2077*	6	5
18 Nov 95		IN THE HOUSE *Media MCSTD 40005*	23	3
24 Feb 96		HOLDING ON 4 U (re-mix) *Media MCSTD 40019*	27	2
7 Sep 96		OH WHAT A NIGHT *Power Station MCSTD 40057*	13	10
22 Mar 97	●	IT'S OVER *Media MCSTD 40100*	10	5
18 Oct 97		U SEXY THING *Media MCSTD 40138*	11	9
17 Jan 98		THAT'S THE WAY (I LIKE IT) *Media MCSTD 40148*	11	4
11 Jul 98		ROCK YOUR BODY *Media MCSTD 40160*	30	3
28 Nov 98		BLAME IT ON THE BOOGIE *Media MCSTD 40191*	16	4
31 Jul 99		SUNSHINE DAY *Media MCSTD 40208*	58	1

Rosemary CLOONEY (403 Top 500) *Top 50s female vocalist and 90s Grammy-nominated granny, b. 23, May 1928, Kentucky, US. Award-winning balladeer and jazz song stylist was at the forefront of first mambo craze in mid-1950s. Sampled on original Shaft 1999 recording '(Mucho Mambo) Sway' which has appeared on a number of compilation albums (81 WEEKS)* pos/wks

14 Nov 52	●	HALF AS MUCH *Columbia DB 3129*	3	9
5 Feb 54	●	MAN (UH-HUH) *Philips PB 220*	7	5
8 Oct 54	★	THIS OLE HOUSE *Philips PB 336* ▲	1	18
17 Dec 54	★	MAMBO ITALIANO *Philips PB 382* [1]	1	16
20 May 55	●	WHERE WILL THE DIMPLE BE? *Philips PB 428* [1]	6	13
30 Sep 55	●	HEY THERE *Philips PB 494* ▲	4	11
29 Mar 57		MANGOS *Philips PB 671*	25	2
26 Apr 57		MANGOS (re-entry) *Philips PB 671*	17	7

[1] Rosemary Clooney and the Mellomen

From 19 Feb 1954, other side of 'Man (Uh-Huh)', 'Woman (Uh-Huh)', by Jose Ferrer was also credited

CLOUD *UK, male instrumental group (1 WEEK)* pos/wks

31 Jan 81		ALL NIGHT LONG / TAKE IT TO THE TOP *UK Champagne FUNK 1*	72	1

CLOUDBURST – *See DISCO TEX presents CLOUDBURST*

CLOUT *South Africa, female vocal / instrumental group (15 WEEKS)* pos/wks

17 Jun 78	●	SUBSTITUTE *Carrere EMI 2788*	2	15

CLS *US, male vocal / production duo (1 WEEK)* pos/wks

30 May 98		CAN YOU FEEL IT *Satellite 74321580162*	46	1

CLUB NOUVEAU *US, male / female vocal / instrumental group (12 WEEKS)* pos/wks

21 Mar 87	●	LEAN ON ME *King Jay W 8430* ▲	3	12

CLUB 69 *Austria / US, male / female vocal / instrumental duo (6 WEEKS)* pos/wks

5 Dec 92		LET ME BE YOUR UNDERWEAR *ffrr F 204*	33	5
14 Nov 98		ALRIGHT *Twisted UK TWCD 10039* [1]	70	1

[1] Club 69 featuring Suzanne Palmer

CLUBHOUSE *Italy, male vocal / instrumental group (40 WEEKS)* pos/wks

23 Jul 83		DO IT AGAIN – BILLIE JEAN (MEDLEY) *Island IS 132*	11	6
3 Dec 83		SUPERSTITION – GOOD TIMES (MEDLEY) *Island IS 147*	59	3
1 Jul 89		I'M A MAN – YEKE YEKE (MEDLEY) *Music Man MMPS 7003*	69	3
20 Apr 91		DEEP IN MY HEART *ffrr F 157*	59	2
22 Jun 91		DEEP IN MY HEART (re-entry) *ffrr F 157*	55	2
4 Sep 93		LIGHT MY FIRE *PWL Continental PWCD 272* [1]	59	1
13 Nov 93		LIGHT MY FIRE (re-entry) *PWL Continental PWCD 272* [1]	45	5
25 Dec 93		LIGHT MY FIRE (2nd re-entry) *PWL Continental PWCD 272* [1]	53	6
30 Apr 94	●	LIGHT MY FIRE (re-mix) *PWL Continental PWCD 288* [1]	7	8
23 Jul 94		LIVING IN THE SUNSHINE *PWL Continental PWCD 309* [1]	21	3
11 Mar 95		NOWHERE LAND *PWL International PWCD 318* [1]	56	1

[1] Clubhouse featuring Carl

CLUBZONE *UK / Germany, male vocal / instrumental group (1 WEEK)* pos/wks

19 Nov 94		HANDS UP *Logic 74321236982*	50	1

CLUELESS *US, male / female vocal / production group (1 WEEK)* pos/wks

5 Apr 97		DON'T SPEAK *ZYX ZYX 660738*	61	1

Jeremy CLYDE – *See Chad STUART and Jeremy CLYDE*

CLYDE VALLEY STOMPERS *UK, male instrumental group (8 WEEKS)* pos/wks

9 Aug 62		PETER AND THE WOLF *Parlophone R 4928*	25	8

CO-CO *UK, male / female vocal / instrumental group (7 WEEKS)* pos/wks

22 Apr 78		BAD OLD DAYS *Ariola Hansa AHA 513*	13	7

CO-OPERATION CHOIR – *See Peter E BENNETT with the CO-OPERATION CHOIR*

COAST 2 COAST featuring DISCOVERY *Ireland, male production duo and female vocalist (1 WEEK)* pos/wks

16 Jun 01		HOME *Religion 0126955 RLG*	44	1

COAST TO COAST *UK, male vocal / instrumental group (22 WEEKS)* pos/wks

31 Jan 81	●	(DO) THE HUCKLEBUCK *Polydor POSP 214*	5	15
23 May 81		LET'S JUMP THE BROOMSTICK *Polydor POSP 249*	28	7

COASTERS *US, male vocal group (32 WEEKS)* pos/wks

27 Sep 57		SEARCHIN' *London HLE 8450*	30	1
15 Aug 58		YAKETY YAK *London HLE 8665*	12	8
27 Mar 59	●	CHARLIE BROWN *London HLE 8819*	6	12
30 Oct 59		POISON IVY *London HLE 8938*	15	7
9 Apr 94		SORRY BUT I'M GONNA HAVE TO PASS *Rhino A 4519CD*	41	4

Odia COATES – *See Paul ANKA*

Luis COBOS featuring Placido DOMINGO *Spain, male orchestra conductor and Spain, male vocalist (2 WEEKS)* pos/wks

16 Jun 90		NESSUN DORMA FROM 'TURANDOT' *Epic 656005 7*	59	2

Eddie COCHRAN (351 Top 500) *Legendary rock 'n' roll singer / songwriter and guitarist b. 3 Oct 1938, Oklahoma, US, d. 17 Apr 1960, Wiltshire, UK. Distinctive and influential 'teen rebel' rocker, whose songs have been recorded by such stars as Cliff Richard, Beach Boys, Sex Pistols and The Who (90 WEEKS)* pos/wks

7 Nov 58		SUMMERTIME BLUES *London HLU 8702*	18	6
13 Mar 59	●	C'MON EVERYBODY *London HLU 8792*	6	13
16 Oct 59		SOMETHIN' ELSE *London HLU 8944*	22	3
22 Jan 60		HALLELUJAH, I LOVE HER SO *London HLW 9022*	28	1
5 Feb 60		HALLELUJAH, I LOVE HER SO (re-entry) *London HLW 9022*	22	3
12 May 60	★	THREE STEPS TO HEAVEN *London HLG 9115*	1	15
6 Oct 60		SWEETIE PIE *London HLG 9196*	38	3
3 Nov 60		LONELY *London HLG 9196*	41	1
15 Jun 61		WEEKEND *London HLG 9362*	15	16
30 Nov 61		JEANNIE, JEANNIE, JEANNIE *London HLG 9460*	31	4
25 Apr 63		MY WAY *Liberty LIB 10088*	23	10
24 Apr 68		SUMMERTIME BLUES (re-issue) *Liberty LBF 15071*	34	8
13 Feb 88		C'MON EVERYBODY (re-issue) *Liberty EDDIE 501*	14	7

Tom COCHRANE *Canada, male vocalist (2 WEEKS)* pos/wks

27 Jun 92		LIFE IS A HIGHWAY *Capitol CL 660*	62	2

COCK ROBIN *US, male / female vocal / instrumental group (12 WEEKS)* pos/wks

31 May 86		THE PROMISE YOU MADE *CBS A 6764*	28	12

Joe COCKER (355 Top 500) *Throaty emotive pop / rock singer b. 20 May 1944, Sheffield, UK, whose first single was released in 1964. 'Up Where We Belong' won both Oscar and Grammy awards for the vocalist, who was still scoring Top 20 albums across Europe into the 21st century (89 WEEKS)* pos/wks

22 May 68		MARJORINE *Regal-Zonophone RZ 3006*	48	1
2 Oct 68	★	WITH A LITTLE HELP FROM MY FRIENDS *Regal-Zonophone RZ 3013*	1	13
27 Sep 69	●	DELTA LADY *Regal-Zonophone RZ 3024*	10	11
4 Jul 70		THE LETTER *Regal-Zonophone RZ 3027*	39	6
26 Sep 81		I'M SO GLAD I'M STANDING HERE TODAY *MCA 741* [1]	61	3
15 Jan 83	●	UP WHERE WE BELONG *Island WIP 6830* [2] ▲	7	13
14 Nov 87		UNCHAIN MY HEART *Capitol CL 465*	46	4
13 Jan 90		WHEN THE NIGHT COMES *Capitol CL 535*	65	2
7 Mar 92		(ALL I KNOW) FEELS LIKE FOREVER *Capitol CL 645*	25	5
9 May 92		NOW THAT THE MAGIC HAS GONE *Capitol CL 657*	28	6
4 Jul 92		UNCHAIN MY HEART (re-issue) *Capitol CL 664*	17	6
21 Nov 92		WHEN THE NIGHT COMES (re-issue) *Capitol CL 674*	61	3
13 Aug 94		THE SIMPLE THINGS *Capitol CDCLS 722*	17	5
22 Oct 94		TAKE ME HOME *Capitol CDCLS 729* [3]	41	3
17 Dec 94		LET THE HEALING BEGIN *Capitol CDCLS 727*	32	5
23 Sep 95		HAVE A LITTLE FAITH *Capitol CDCLS 744*	67	2
12 Oct 96		DON'T LET ME BE MISUNDERSTOOD *Parlophone CDCLS 779*	53	1

[1] Crusaders, featured vocalist Joe Cocker [2] Joe Cocker and Jennifer Warnes
[3] Joe Cocker featuring Bekka Bramlett

COCKEREL CHORUS *UK, male Tottenham Hotspur Football Club Supporters vocal group (12 WEEKS)* pos/wks

24 Feb 73		NICE ONE CYRIL *Youngblood YB 1017*	14	12

COCKNEY REBEL – *See Steve HARLEY and COCKNEY REBEL*

COCKNEY REJECTS *UK, male vocal / instrumental group (22 WEEKS)* pos/wks

1 Dec 79		I'M NOT A FOOL *EMI 5008*	65	2
16 Feb 80		BADMAN *EMI 5035*	65	3
26 Apr 80		THE GREATEST COCKNEY RIPOFF *Zonophone Z 2*	21	7
17 May 80		I'M FOREVER BLOWING BUBBLES *Zonophone Z 4*	35	5
12 Jul 80		WE CAN DO ANYTHING *Zonophone Z 6*	65	2
25 Oct 80		WE ARE THE FIRM *Zonophone Z 10*	54	3

COCO *UK, female vocalist (2 WEEKS)* pos/wks

8 Nov 97		I NEED A MIRACLE *Positiva CDTIV 81*	39	2

See FRAGMA

COCONUTS *US, female vocal group (3 WEEKS)* pos/wks

11 Jun 83		DID YOU HAVE TO LOVE ME LIKE YOU DID *EMI America EA 156*	60	3

See also Kid CREOLE and the COCONUTS

COCTEAU TWINS
UK, male / female vocal / instrumental group (25 WEEKS) pos/wks

28 Apr 84		PEARLY-DEWDROPS' DROPS *4AD 405*	29	5
30 Mar 85		AIKEA-GUINEA *4AD AD 501*	41	3
23 Nov 85		TINY DYNAMINE (EP) *4AD BAD 510*	52	2
7 Dec 85		ECHOES IN A SHALLOW BAY (EP) *4AD BAD 511*	65	1
25 Oct 86		LOVE'S EASY TEARS *4AD AD 610*	53	1
8 Sep 90		ICEBLINK LUCK *4AD AD 0011*	38	3
2 Oct 93		EVANGELINE *Fontana CTCD 1*	34	2
18 Dec 93		WINTER WONDERLAND / FROSTY THE SNOWMAN *Fontana COCCD 1*	58	1
26 Feb 94		BLUEBEARD *Fontana CTCD 2*	33	2
7 Oct 95		TWINLIGHTS (EP) *Fontana CTCD 3*	59	1
4 Nov 95		OTHERNESS (EP) *Fontana CTCD 4*	59	1
30 Mar 96		TISHBITE *Fontana CTCD 5*	34	2
20 Jul 96		VIOLAINE *Fontana CTCD 6*	56	1

Tracks on Tiny Dynamine (EP): Pink Orange Red / Ribbed and Veined / Plain Tiger / Sultitan Itan. Tracks on Echoes in a Shallow Bay (EP): Great Spangled Fritillary / Melonella / Pale Clouded White / Eggs and Their Shells. Tracks on Twinlights (EP): Golden-Vein / Half-Gifts / Pink Orange Red / Rilkean Heart. Tracks on Otherness (EP): Cherry Coloured Funk / Feet Like Fins / Seekers Who Are Lovers / Violaine

C.O.D *US, male vocal / instrumental group (2 WEEKS)* pos/wks

14 May 83		IN THE BOTTLE *Streetwave WAVE 2*	54	2

CODE RED *UK, male vocal group (7 WEEKS)* pos/wks

6 Jul 96		I GAVE YOU EVERYTHING *Polydor 5763992*	50	1
16 Nov 96		THIS IS OUR SONG *Polydor 5756332*	59	1
14 Jun 97		CAN WE TALK… *Polydor 5710992*	29	2
9 Aug 97		IS THERE SOMEONE OUT THERE? *Polydor 5714652*	34	2
4 Jul 98		WHAT WOULD YOU DO IF…? *Polydor 569932*	55	1

COFFEE *US, female vocal group (13 WEEKS)* pos/wks

27 Sep 80		CASANOVA *De-Lite MER 38*	13	10
6 Dec 80		SLIP AND DIP / I WANNA BE WITH YOU *De-Lite DE 1*	57	3

Alma COGAN (265 Top 500) *Very popular 1950s radio, TV and recording star, b. 19 May 1932, d. 26 Oct 1966. The singer, who was renowned for her glamour and was known as the "gal with the giggle in her voice", was the youngest English female to top the chart in the 1950s (110 WEEKS)* pos/wks

19 Mar 54	●	BELL BOTTOM BLUES *HMV B 10653*	4	9
27 Aug 54		LITTLE THINGS MEAN A LOT *HMV B 10717*	11	2
8 Oct 54		LITTLE THINGS MEAN A LOT (re-entry) *HMV B 10717*	19	1
22 Oct 54		LITTLE THINGS MEAN A LOT (2nd re-entry) *HMV B 10717*	18	2
3 Dec 54	●	I CAN'T TELL A WALTZ FROM A TANGO *HMV B 10786*	6	11
27 May 55	★	DREAMBOAT *HMV B 10872*	1	16
23 Sep 55		THE BANJO'S BACK IN TOWN *HMV B 10917 (A)*	17	1
14 Oct 55		GO ON BY *HMV B 10917 (B)*	16	4
16 Dec 55		TWENTY TINY FINGERS *HMV POP 129(A)*	17	1
23 Dec 55	●	NEVER DO A TANGO WITH AN ESKIMO *HMV POP 129(B)*	6	5
30 Mar 56		WILLIE CAN *HMV POP 187* [1]	13	8
13 Jul 56		THE BIRDS AND THE BEES *HMV POP 223*	25	4
10 Aug 56		WHY DO FOOLS FALL IN LOVE *HMV POP 223*	22	3
2 Nov 56		IN THE MIDDLE OF THE HOUSE *HMV POP 261*	26	1
23 Nov 56		IN THE MIDDLE OF THE HOUSE (re-entry) *HMV POP 261*	20	3
18 Jan 57		YOU, ME AND US *HMV POP 284*	18	6
29 Mar 57		WHATEVER LOLA WANTS (LOLA GETS) *HMV POP 317*	26	2
31 Jan 58		THE STORY OF MY LIFE *HMV POP 433*	25	2
14 Feb 58		SUGARTIME *HMV POP 450*	16	10
2 May 58		SUGARTIME (re-entry) *HMV POP 450*	30	1

23 Jan 59	**LAST NIGHT ON THE BACK PORCH** *HMV POP 573*	**27**	2
18 Dec 59	**WE GOT LOVE** *HMV POP 670*	**26**	4
12 May 60	**DREAM TALK** *HMV POP 728*	**48**	1
11 Aug 60	**TRAIN OF LOVE** *HMV POP 760*	**27**	5
20 Apr 61	**COWBOY JIMMY JOE** *Columbia DB 4607*	**37**	6

[1] Alma Cogan with Desmond Lane – Penny Whistle

Shaye COGAN *US, female vocalist (1 WEEK)* pos/wks

24 Mar 60	**MEAN TO ME** *MGM 1063*	**40**	1

Izhar COHEN and the ALPHA-BETA *Israel, male / female vocal group (7 WEEKS)* pos/wks

13 May 78	**A BA NI BI** *Polydor 2001 781*	**20**	7

Marc COHN *US, male vocalist (15 WEEKS)* pos/wks

25 May 91	**WALKING IN MEMPHIS** *Atlantic A 7747*	**66**	4
10 Aug 91	**SILVER THUNDERBIRD** *Atlantic A 7657*	**54**	3
12 Oct 91	**WALKING IN MEMPHIS (re-issue)** *Atlantic A 7585*	**22**	5
29 May 93	**WALK THROUGH THE WORLD** *Atlantic A 7340CD*	**37**	3

COLA BOY *UK, male / female vocal / instrumental duo – Andrew Midgely and Janey Lee Grace (7 WEEKS)* pos/wks

6 Jul 91 ●	**7 WAYS TO LOVE** *Arista 114526*	**8**	7

COLD JAM featuring GRACE *US, male / female vocal / instrumental group (2 WEEKS)* pos/wks

28 Jul 90	**LAST NIGHT A DJ SAVED MY LIFE** *Big Wave BWR 39*	**64**	2

COLDCUT *UK, male production duo – Matt Black and Jonathan Moore (39 WEEKS)* pos/wks

20 Feb 88 ●	**DOCTORIN' THE HOUSE** *Ahead of Our Time CCUT 27* [1]	**6**	9
10 Sep 88	**STOP THIS CRAZY THING** *Ahead of Our Time CCUT 4* [2]	**21**	7
25 Mar 89	**PEOPLE HOLD ON** *Ahead of Our Time CCUT 5* [3]	**11**	9
3 Jun 89	**MY TELEPHONE** *Ahead of Our Time CCUT 6*	**52**	2
16 Dec 89	**COLDCUT'S CHRISTMAS BREAK** *Ahead of Our Time CCUT 7*	**67**	3
26 May 90	**FIND A WAY** *Ahead of Our Time CCUT 8* [4]	**52**	2
4 Sep 93	**DREAMER** *Arista 74321156642*	**54**	2
22 Jan 94	**AUTUMN LEAVES** *Arista 74321171052*	**50**	2
16 Aug 97	**MORE BEATS & PIECES** *Ninja Tune ZENCDS 58*	**37**	2
16 Jun 01	**REVOLUTION** *Ninja Tune ZENCDS 88*	**67**	1

[1] Coldcut featuring Yazz and the Plastic Population [2] Coldcut featuring Junior Reid and the Ahead of Our Time Orchestra [3] Coldcut featuring Lisa Stansfield [4] Coldcut featuring Queen Latifah

COLDPLAY *UK, male vocal / instrumental group (23 WEEKS)* pos/wks

18 Mar 00	**SHIVER** *Parlophone CDR 6536*	**35**	3
8 Jul 00 ●	**YELLOW** *Parlophone CDR 6538*	**4**	11
4 Nov 00 ●	**TROUBLE** *Parlophone CDR 6549*	**10**	9

Andy COLE *UK, male vocalist / footballer (1 WEEK)* pos/wks

18 Sep 99	**OUTSTANDING** *WEA WEA 224CD*	**68**	1

Cozy COLE *US, male instrumentalist – drums (1 WEEK)* pos/wks

5 Dec 58	**TOPSY (PARTS 1 AND 2)** *London HL 8750*	**29**	1

George COLE – *See Dennis WATERMAN*

Lloyd COLE *UK, male vocalist (62 WEEKS)* pos/wks

26 May 84	**PERFECT SKIN** *Polydor COLE 1* [1]	**71**	1
9 Jun 84	**PERFECT SKIN (re-entry)** *Polydor COLE 1* [1]	**26**	8
25 Aug 84	**FOREST FIRE** *Polydor COLE 2* [1]	**41**	6
17 Nov 84	**RATTLESNAKES** *Poldor COLE 3* [1]	**65**	2
14 Sep 85	**BRAND NEW FRIEND** *Polydor COLE 4* [1]	**19**	8
9 Nov 85	**LOST WEEKEND** *Polydor COLE 5* [1]	**17**	7
18 Jan 86	**CUT ME DOWN** *Polydor COLE 6* [1]	**38**	4
3 Oct 87	**MY BAG** *Polydor COLE 7* [1]	**46**	4
9 Jan 88	**JENNIFER SHE SAID** *Polydor COLE 8* [1]	**31**	5
23 Apr 88	**FROM THE HIP (EP)** *Polydor COLE 9* [1]	**59**	2
3 Feb 90	**NO BLUE SKIES** *Polydor COLE 11*	**42**	4
7 Apr 90	**DON'T LOOK BACK** *Polydor COLE 12*	**59**	3
31 Aug 91	**SHE'S A GIRL AND I'M A MAN** *Polydor COLE 14*	**55**	2
25 Sep 93	**SO YOU'D LIKE TO SAVE THE WORLD** *Fontana VIBE D1*	**72**	2
16 Sep 95	**LIKE LOVERS DO** *Fontana LCDD 1*	**24**	3
2 Dec 95	**SENTIMENTAL FOOL** *Fontana LCDD 2*	**73**	1

[1] Lloyd Cole and the Commotions

Tracks on From the Hip (EP): From the Hip / Please / Lonely Mile / Love Your Wife

MJ COLE *UK, male producer – Matt Coleman (16 WEEKS)* pos/wks

23 May 98	**SINCERE** *AM:PM 5826912*	**38**	2
6 May 00 ●	**CRAZY LOVE** *Talkin Loud TLCD 59*	**10**	7
12 Aug 00	**SINCERE (re-mix)** *Talkin Loud TLCD 60*	**13**	5
2 Dec 00	**HOLD ON TO ME** *Talkin Loud TLCD 62* [1]	**35**	2

[1] MJ Cole featuring Elizabeth Troy

Nat "King" COLE (49) Top 500 *One of the 20th century's most distinctive song stylists, b. 17 Mar 1917, Alabama, d. 15 Feb 1965. His 41-year chart span is proof that the highly regarded vocalist's recordings are timeless (248 WEEKS)* pos/wks

14 Nov 52 ●	**SOMEWHERE ALONG THE WAY** *Capitol CL 13774*	**3**	7
19 Dec 52 ●	**BECAUSE YOU'RE MINE** *Capitol CL 13811*	**6**	2
2 Jan 53	**FAITH CAN MOVE MOUNTAINS** *Capitol CL 13811*	**11**	1
16 Jan 53	**FAITH CAN MOVE MOUNTAINS (re-entry)** *Capitol CL 13811*	**12**	2
23 Jan 53 ●	**BECAUSE YOU'RE MINE (re-entry)** *Capitol CL 13811*	**10**	1
6 Feb 53 ●	**FAITH CAN MOVE MOUNTAINS (2nd re-entry)** *Capitol CL 13811*	**10**	1
13 Feb 53	**BECAUSE YOU'RE MINE (2nd re-entry)** *Capitol CL 13811*	**11**	1
24 Apr 53 ●	**PRETEND** *Capitol CL 13878*	**2**	18
14 Aug 53 ●	**CAN'T I** *Capitol CL 13937*	**9**	3
18 Sep 53 ●	**CAN'T I (re-entry)** *Capitol CL 13937*	**6**	4
18 Sep 53 ●	**MOTHER NATURE AND FATHER TIME** *Capitol CL 13912*	**7**	7
30 Oct 53 ●	**CAN'T I (2nd re-entry)** *Capitol CL 13937*	**10**	1
16 Apr 54 ●	**TENDERLY** *Capitol CL 14061*	**10**	1
10 Sep 54 ●	**SMILE** *Capitol CL 14149*	**2**	14
8 Oct 54	**MAKE HER MINE** *Capitol CL 14149*	**11**	2
25 Feb 55 ●	**A BLOSSOM FELL** *Capitol CL 14235*	**3**	10
26 Aug 55	**MY ONE SIN** *Capitol CL 14327*	**18**	1
16 Sep 55	**MY ONE SIN (re-entry)** *Capitol CL 14327*	**17**	1
27 Jan 56 ●	**DREAMS CAN TELL A LIE** *Capitol CL 14513*	**10**	9
11 May 56 ●	**TOO YOUNG TO GO STEADY** *Capitol CL 14573*	**8**	14
14 Sep 56	**LOVE ME AS THOUGH THERE WERE NO TOMORROW** *Capitol CL 14621*	**24**	2
5 Oct 56	**LOVE ME AS THOUGH THERE WERE NO TOMORROW (re-entry)** *Capitol CL 14621*	**11**	13
19 Apr 57 ●	**WHEN I FALL IN LOVE** *Capitol CL 14709*	**2**	20
5 Jul 57	**WHEN ROCK AND ROLL CAME TO TRINIDAD** *Capitol CL 14733*	**28**	1
18 Oct 57	**MY PERSONAL POSSESSION** *Capitol CL 14765*	**21**	2
25 Oct 57	**STARDUST** *Capitol CL 14787*	**24**	2
29 May 59	**YOU MADE ME LOVE YOU** *Capitol CL 15017*	**22**	3
4 Sep 59	**MIDNIGHT FLYER** *Capitol CL 15056*	**27**	1
18 Sep 59	**MIDNIGHT FLYER (re-entry)** *Capitol CL 15056*	**23**	3
12 Feb 60	**TIME AND THE RIVER** *Capitol CL 15111*	**29**	1
26 Feb 60	**TIME AND THE RIVER (re-entry)** *Capitol CL 15111*	**23**	2
31 Mar 60	**TIME AND THE RIVER (2nd re-entry)** *Capitol CL 15111*	**47**	1
26 May 60 ●	**THAT'S YOU** *Capitol CL 15129*	**10**	8
10 Nov 60	**JUST AS MUCH AS EVER** *Capitol CL 15163*	**18**	10
2 Feb 61	**THE WORLD IN MY ARMS** *Capitol CL 15178*	**36**	10
16 Nov 61	**LET TRUE LOVE BEGIN** *Capitol CL 15224*	**29**	10
22 Mar 62	**BRAZILIAN LOVE SONG (ANDORPHINA PRETA)** *Capitol CL 15241*	**34**	4
31 May 62	**THE RIGHT THING TO SAY** *Capitol CL 15250*	**42**	4
19 Jul 62	**LET THERE BE LOVE** *Capitol CL 15257* [1]	**11**	14
27 Sep 62 ●	**RAMBLIN' ROSE** *Capitol CL 15270*	**5**	14
20 Dec 62	**DEAR LONELY HEARTS** *Capitol CL 15280*	**37**	3
12 Dec 87 ●	**WHEN I FALL IN LOVE (re-issue)** *Capitol CL 15975*	**4**	7
22 Jun 91	**UNFORGETTABLE** *Elektra EKR 128* [2]	**19**	8
14 Dec 91	**THE CHRISTMAS SONG** *Capitol CL 641*	**69**	2
19 Mar 94	**LET'S FACE THE MUSIC AND DANCE** *EMI CDEM 312*	**30**	3

[1] Nat 'King' Cole with George Shearing [2] Natalie Cole and Nat 'King' Cole

See also Natalie COLE

Natalie COLE (371 Top 500) *Daughter of legendary Nat 'King' Cole who has a 20-year Grammy-winning span of her own, b. 6 Feb 1950, Los Angeles, US. 'Unforgettable' in 1991 was an electronically recorded duet with her late father. Nat and Natalie are the only dad and daughter who both have No.1 US albums (87 WEEKS)* pos/wks

Date		Title / Label	Pos	Wks
11 Oct 75		THIS WILL BE *Capitol CL 15834*	32	5
8 Aug 87		JUMP START *Manhattan MT 22*	44	8
26 Mar 88	●	PINK CADILLAC *Manhattan MT 35*	5	12
25 Jun 88		EVERLASTING *Manhattan MT 46*	28	6
20 Aug 88		JUMP START (re-issue) *Manhattan MT 50*	36	5
26 Nov 88		I LIVE FOR YOUR LOVE *Manhattan MT 57*	23	14
15 Apr 89	●	MISS YOU LIKE CRAZY *EMI-USA MT 63*	2	15
22 Jul 89		REST OF THE NIGHT *EMI-USA MT 69*	56	2
16 Dec 89		STARTING OVER AGAIN *EMI-USA MT 77*	56	4
21 Apr 90		WILD WOMEN DO *EMI-USA MT 81*	16	7
22 Jun 91		UNFORGETTABLE *Elektra EKR 128* [1]	19	8
16 May 92		THE VERY THOUGHT OF YOU *Elektra EKR 147*	71	1

[1] Natalie Cole and Nat 'King' Cole

Paula COLE *US, female vocalist (9 WEEKS)* pos/wks

Date		Title / Label	Pos	Wks
28 Jun 97		WHERE HAVE ALL THE COWBOYS GONE? *Warner Bros. W 0406CD*	15	8
1 Aug 98		I DON'T WANT TO WAIT *Warner Bros. W 0422CD*	43	1

Naimee COLEMAN – *See AURORA*

COLETTE – *See SISTER BLISS*

John Ford COLEY – *See ENGLAND DAN and John Ford COLEY*

COLLAGE *US / Canada / Philippines, male vocal / instrumental group (5 WEEKS)* pos/wks

Date		Title / Label	Pos	Wks
21 Sep 85		ROMEO WHERE'S JULIET? *MCA MCA 1006*	46	5

COLLAPSED LUNG *UK, male vocal / instrumental group (8 WEEKS)* pos/wks

Date		Title / Label	Pos	Wks
22 Jun 96		LONDON TONIGHT / EAT MY GOAL *Deceptive BLUFF 029CD*	31	3
30 May 98		EAT MY GOAL (re-issue) *Deceptive BLUFF 060CD*	18	5

Dave and Ansil COLLINS *Jamaica, male vocal / instrumental duo – Dave Barker and Ansil Collins (27 WEEKS)* pos/wks

Date		Title / Label	Pos	Wks
27 Mar 71	★	DOUBLE BARREL *Technique TE 901*	1	15
26 Jun 71	●	MONKEY SPANNER *Technique TE 914* [1]	7	12

[1] Dave and Ansel Collins

Edwyn COLLINS *UK, male vocalist / instrumentalist (25 WEEKS)* pos/wks

Date		Title / Label	Pos	Wks
11 Aug 84		PALE BLUE EYES *Swamplands SWP1* [1]	72	2
12 Nov 94		EXPRESSLY (EP) *Setanta ZOP 001CD1*	42	3
17 Jun 95	●	A GIRL LIKE YOU (re-issue) *Setanta ZOP 003CD*	4	14
2 Mar 96		KEEP ON BURNING *Setanta ZOP 004CD1*	45	2
2 Aug 97		THE MAGIC PIPER (OF LOVE) *Setanta SETCDA 041*	32	3
18 Oct 97		ADIDAS WORLD *Setanta SETCDB 045*	71	1

[1] Paul QUINN and Edwyn COLLINS

The only track on all formats of Expressly (EP) was 'A Girl Like You'

See also ORANGE JUICE

Felicia COLLINS – *See LUKK featuring Felicia COLLINS*

Jeff COLLINS *UK, male vocalist (8 WEEKS)* pos/wks

Date		Title / Label	Pos	Wks
18 Nov 72		ONLY YOU *Polydor 2058 287*	40	8

Judy COLLINS (377 Top 500) *Distinctive folk / pop singer born 1 May 1939, Washington, US, and raised in Colorado. 'Both Sides Now' was the first Joni Mitchell composition to chart and 'Amazing Grace' spent longer on the chart than any other single by a female artist (86 WEEKS)* pos/wks

Date		Title / Label	Pos	Wks
17 Jan 70		BOTH SIDES NOW *Elektra EKSN 45043*	14	11
5 Dec 70	●	AMAZING GRACE *Elektra 2101 020*	5	32
24 Jul 71		AMAZING GRACE (re-entry) *Elektra 2101 020*	48	1
4 Sep 71		AMAZING GRACE (2nd re-entry) *Elektra 2101 020*	40	7
20 Nov 71		AMAZING GRACE (3rd re-entry) *Elektra 2101 020*	50	1
18 Dec 71		AMAZING GRACE (4th re-entry) *Elektra 2101 020*	48	2
22 Apr 72		AMAZING GRACE (5th re-entry) *Elektra 2101 020*	20	19
9 Sep 72		AMAZING GRACE (6th re-entry) *Elektra 2101 020*	46	2
23 Dec 72		AMAZING GRACE (7th re-entry) *Elektra 2101 020*	49	3
17 May 75	●	SEND IN THE CLOWNS *Elektra K 12177*	6	8

Michelle COLLINS *UK, female vocalist (3 WEEKS)* pos/wks

Date		Title / Label	Pos	Wks
27 Feb 99		SUNBURN *BBC Music WMSS 60082*	28	3

Phil COLLINS (63 Top 500) *Continually popular singer / songwriter (b. 31 Jan 1951, London) who simultaneously fronted Genesis (until 1996) and managed a successful solo career. Only members of The Beatles have appeared on more UK No.1 albums (228 WEEKS)* pos/wks

Date		Title / Label	Pos	Wks
17 Jan 81	●	IN THE AIR TONIGHT *Virgin VS102*	2	10
7 Mar 81		I MISSED AGAIN *Virgin VS 402*	14	8
30 May 81		IF LEAVING ME IS EASY *Virgin VS 423*	17	8
23 Oct 82		THRU' THESE WALLS *Virgin VS 524*	56	2
4 Dec 82	★	YOU CAN'T HURRY LOVE *Virgin VS 531*	1	16
19 Mar 83		DON'T LET HIM STEAL YOUR HEART AWAY *Virgin VS 572*	45	5
7 Apr 84	●	AGAINST ALL ODDS (TAKE A LOOK AT ME NOW) *Virgin VS 674* ▲	2	14
26 Jan 85		SUSSUDIO *Virgin VS 736* ▲	12	9
9 Mar 85	★	EASY LOVER *CBS A 4915* [1]	1	12
13 Apr 85	●	ONE MORE NIGHT *Virgin VS 755* ▲	4	9
27 Jul 85		TAKE ME HOME *Virgin VS 777*	19	9
23 Nov 85	●	SEPARATE LIVES *Virgin VS 818* [2] ▲	4	13
18 Jun 88	●	IN THE AIR TONIGHT (re-mix) *Virgin VS 102*	4	9
3 Sep 88	★	A GROOVY KIND OF LOVE *Virgin VS 1117* ▲	1	13
26 Nov 88	●	TWO HEARTS *Virgin VS 1141* ▲	6	11
4 Nov 89	●	ANOTHER DAY IN PARADISE *Virgin VS 1234* ▲	2	11
27 Jan 90	●	I WISH IT WOULD RAIN DOWN *Virgin VS 1240*	7	9
28 Apr 90		SOMETHING HAPPENED ON THE WAY TO HEAVEN *Virgin VS 1251*	15	7
28 Jul 90		THAT'S JUST THE WAY IT IS *Virgin VS 1277*	26	5
6 Oct 90		HANG IN LONG ENOUGH *Virgin VS 1300*	34	3
8 Dec 90		DO YOU REMEMBER (LIVE) *Virgin VS 1305*	57	5
15 May 93		HERO *Atlantic A 7360*	56	3
30 Oct 93	●	BOTH SIDES OF THE STORY *Virgin VSCDT 1500*	7	5
1 Jan 94		BOTH SIDES OF THE STORY (re-entry) *Virgin VSCDT 1500*	61	1
15 Jan 94		EVERYDAY *Virgin VSCDT 1505*	15	5
7 May 94		WE WAIT AND WE WONDER *Virgin VSCDT 1510*	45	2
5 Oct 96	●	DANCE INTO THE LIGHT *Face Value EW 066CD*	9	6
14 Dec 96		IT'S IN YOUR EYES *Face Value EW 076CD1*	30	4
12 Jul 97		WEAR MY HAT *Face Value EW 113CD*	43	2
7 Nov 98		TRUE COLORS *Virgin VSCDT 1715*	26	4
6 Nov 99		YOU'LL BE IN MY HEART *Edel / Walt Disney 0100735 DNY*	17	6
22 Sep 01		IN THE AIR TONITE *WEA WEA 331CD* [3]	26	2

[1] Philip Bailey (duet with Phil Collins) [2] Phil Collins and Marilyn Martin [3] Lil' Kim featuring Phil Collins

See also GENESIS

Rodger COLLINS *US, male vocalist (6 WEEKS)* pos/wks

Date		Title / Label	Pos	Wks
3 Apr 76		YOU SEXY SUGAR PLUM (BUT I LIKE IT) *Fantasy FTC 132*	22	6

Willie COLLINS *US, male vocalist (4 WEEKS)* pos/wks

Date		Title / Label	Pos	Wks
28 Jun 86		WHERE YOU GONNA BE TONIGHT? *Capitol CL 410*	46	4

Willie COLON *US, male vocalist (7 WEEKS)* pos/wks

Date		Title / Label	Pos	Wks
28 Jun 86		SET FIRE TO ME *A & M AM 330*	41	7

COLOR ME BADD *US, male vocal group (31 WEEKS)* pos/wks

Date		Title / Label	Pos	Wks
18 May 91	★	I WANNA SEX YOU UP *Giant W 0036*	1	14
3 Aug 91	●	ALL 4 LOVE *Giant W 0053* ▲	5	10
12 Oct 91		I ADORE MI AMOR *Giant W 0067* ▲	44	2
9 Nov 91		I ADORE MI AMOR (re-issue) *Giant W 0076*	59	2
22 Feb 92		HEARTBREAKER *Giant W 0078*	58	1

20 Nov 93		**TIME AND CHANCE** *Giant 74321168992*	62	1
16 Apr 94		**CHOOSE** *Giant 74321199432*	65	1

COLORADO *UK, female vocal group (3 WEEKS)* pos/wks

21 Oct 78		**CALIFORNIA DREAMIN'** *Pinnacle PIN 67*	45	3

COLOUR FIELD *UK, male vocal / instrumental group (18 WEEKS)* pos/wks

21 Jan 84		**THE COLOUR FIELD** *Chrysalis COLF 1*	43	4
28 Jul 84		**TAKE** *Chrysalis COLF 2*	70	1
26 Jan 85		**THINKING OF YOU** *Chrysalis COLF 3*	12	10
13 Apr 85		**CASTLES IN THE AIR** *Chrysalis COLF 4*	51	3

COLOUR GIRL *UK, female vocalist – Rebecca Skingley (5 WEEKS)* pos/wks

11 Mar 00		**CAN'T GET USED TO LOSING YOU** *4 Liberty LIBT CD037*	31	3
9 Sep 00		**JOYRIDER (YOU'RE PLAYING WITH FIRE)** *4 Liberty LIBT CD039*	51	1
3 Feb 01		**MAS QUE NADA** *4 Liberty LIBTCD 040* [1]	57	1

[1] Colour Girl featuring PSG

COLOURS featuring EMMANUEL & ESKA
UK, male instrumentalist / producer and female vocalist (1 WEEK) pos/wks

27 Feb 99		**WHAT U DO** *Inferno CDFERN 12*	51	1

See also Nitin SAWHNEY featuring ESKA; EN-CORE featuring Stephen EMMANUEL & ESKA

COLUMBO featuring OOE *UK, male production duo (1 WEEK)* pos/wks

15 May 99		**ROCKABILLY BOB** *V2 / Milkgems VVR 5006903*	59	1

Shawn COLVIN *US, female vocalist (12 WEEKS)* pos/wks

27 Nov 93		**I DON'T KNOW WHY** *Columbia 6598272*	62	1
12 Feb 94		**ROUND OF BLUES** *Columbia 6594282*	73	1
3 Sep 94		**EVERY LITTLE THING HE DOES IS MAGIC** *Columbia 6607742*	65	2
7 Jan 95		**ONE COOL REMOVE** *Columbia 6611342* [1]	40	3
12 Aug 95		**I DON'T KNOW WHY (re-issue)** *Columbia 6622725*	52	1
15 Mar 97		**GET OUT OF THIS HOUSE** *Columbia 6638522*	70	1
30 May 98		**SUNNY CAME HOME** *Columbia 6648022*	29	3

[1] Shawn Colvin with Mary-Chapin Carpenter

COMETS – *See Bill HALEY and his COMETS*

COMING OUT CREW *US, male / female vocal duo (1 WEEK)* pos/wks

18 Mar 95		**FREE, GAY AND HAPPY** *Out on Vinyl CDOOV 002*	50	1

COMMANDER TOM *Germany, male producer – Tom Weyer (1 WEEK)* pos/wks

23 Dec 00		**EYE BEE M** *Tripoli Trax TTRAX 069CD*	75	1

COMMENTATORS *UK, male impressionist – Rory Bremner (7 WEEKS)* pos/wks

22 Jun 85		**N-N-NINETEEN NOT OUT** *Oval 100*	13	7

COMMITMENTS
Ireland, male / female vocal / instrumental group (1 WEEK) pos/wks

30 Nov 91		**MUSTANG SALLY** *MCA MCS 1598*	63	1

COMMODORES (224 Top 500) *Top-notch US R&B combo: Lionel Richie (v/k), William King (t), Thomas McClary (g), Milan Williams (var), Ronald LaPread (b), Walter Orange (d). They were among the 1970s' biggest-selling groups, but lost ground when songwriter Richie went solo in 1982 (121 WEEKS)* pos/wks

24 Aug 74		**MACHINE GUN** *Tamla Motown TMG 902*	20	11
23 Nov 74		**THE ZOO (THE HUMAN ZOO)** *Tamla Motown TMG 924*	44	2
2 Jul 77	●	**EASY** *Motown TMG 1073*	9	10
8 Oct 77		**SWEET LOVE / BRICK HOUSE** *Motown TMG 1086*	32	6
11 Mar 78		**TOO HOT TO TROT / ZOOM** *Motown TMG 1096*	38	4
24 Jun 78		**FLYING HIGH** *Motown TMG 1111*	37	7
5 Aug 78	★	**THREE TIMES A LADY** *Motown TMG 1113* ▲	1	14
25 Nov 78		**JUST TO BE CLOSE TO YOU** *Motown TMG 1127*	62	4
25 Aug 79	●	**SAIL ON** *Motown TMG 1155*	8	10
3 Nov 79	●	**STILL** *Motown TMG 1166* ▲	4	11
19 Jan 80		**WONDERLAND** *Motown TMG 1172*	40	4
1 Aug 81		**LADY (YOU BRING ME UP)** *Motown TMG 1238*	56	5
21 Nov 81		**OH NO** *Motown TMG 1245*	44	3
26 Jan 85	●	**NIGHTSHIFT** *Motown TMG 1371*	3	14
11 May 85		**ANIMAL INSTINCT** *Motown ZB 40097*	74	1
25 Oct 86		**GOIN' TO THE BANK** *Polydor POSPA 826*	43	4
13 Aug 88		**EASY (re-issue)** *Motown ZB 41793*	15	11

Group was US / UK for 1985 and 1986 hits

COMMON *US, male rapper – Rasheed Lynn (3 WEEKS)* pos/wks

8 Nov 97		**REMINDING ME (OF SEF)** *Relativity 6560762* [1]	59	1
14 Oct 00		**THE LIGHT / THE 6TH SENSE** *MCA MCSTD 40237*	56	1
28 Apr 01		**GETO HEAVEN** *MCA MCSTD 40246* [2]	48	1

[1] Common featuring Chantay Savage [2] Common featuring Macy Gray

COMMOTIONS – *See Lloyd COLE*

COMMUNARDS (453 Top 500) *Controversial but melodic pop duo consisted of Bronski Beat's Jimmy Somerville (v) b. 22 Jun 1961, Glasgow, Scotland, and Richard Coles (k), b. 23 Jun 1962, Northampton, UK. Their No.1 cover marked the song's third Top 20 reading within a decade (76 WEEKS)* pos/wks

12 Oct 85		**YOU ARE MY WORLD** *London LON 77*	30	8
24 May 86		**DISENCHANTED** *London LON 89*	29	5
23 Aug 86	★	**DON'T LEAVE ME THIS WAY** *London LON 103* [1]	1	14
29 Nov 86	●	**SO COLD THE NIGHT** *London LON 110*	8	10
21 Feb 87		**YOU ARE MY WORLD (87) (re-mix)** *London LON 123*	21	6
12 Sep 87		**TOMORROW** *London LON 143*	23	7
7 Nov 87	●	**NEVER CAN SAY GOODBYE** *London LON 158*	4	11
20 Feb 88		**FOR A FRIEND** *London LON 166*	28	7
11 Jun 88		**THERE'S MORE TO LOVE** *London LON 173*	20	8

[1] Communards with Sarah Jane Morris

Perry COMO (23 Top 500) *One of the 20th century's most enduring entertainers, b. 18 May 1912, Pennsylvania, d. 12 May 2001. This easy-on-the-ear relaxed balladeer launched his career in 1933, collected 150 US chart entries, hosted an Emmy-winning TV series, and continued to score hits past the age of 60 (322 WEEKS)* pos/wks

16 Jan 53	★	**DON'T LET THE STARS GET IN YOUR EYES** *HMV B 10400* [1] ▲	1	15
4 Jun 54	●	**WANTED** *HMV B 10691* ▲	4	14
25 Jun 54	●	**IDLE GOSSIP** *HMV B 10667*	3	15
1 Oct 54		**WANTED (re-entry)** *HMV B 10691*	18	1
10 Dec 54		**PAPA LOVES MAMBO** *HMV B 10776*	16	1
30 Dec 55		**TINA MARIE** *HMV POP 103*	24	1
27 Apr 56		**JUKE BOX BABY** *HMV POP 191*	22	6
25 May 56	●	**HOT DIGGITY (DOG ZIGGITY BOOM)** *HMV POP 212*	4	13
21Sep 56	●	**MORE** *HMV POP 240*	10	11
28 Sep 56		**GLENDORA** *HMV POP 240*	18	6
14 Dec 56		**MORE (re-entry)** *HMV POP 240*	29	1
7 Feb 58	★	**MAGIC MOMENTS** *RCA 1036*	1	17
7 Mar 58	●	**CATCH A FALLING STAR** *RCA 1036*	9	10
9 May 58	●	**KEWPIE DOLL** *RCA 1055*	9	7
30 May 58		**I MAY NEVER PASS THIS WAY AGAIN** *RCA 1062*	15	8
5 Sep 58		**MOON TALK** *RCA 1071*	17	11
7 Nov 58	●	**LOVE MAKES THE WORLD GO 'ROUND** *RCA 1086*	6	14
21 Nov 58		**MANDOLINS IN THE MOONLIGHT** *RCA 1086*	13	12
27 Feb 59	●	**TOMBOY** *RCA 1111*	10	12
10 Jul 59		**I KNOW** *RCA 1126*	13	16
26 Feb 60	●	**DELAWARE** *RCA 1170*	3	13
10 May 62		**CATERINA** *RCA 1283*	37	4
14 Jun 62		**CATERINA (re-entry)** *RCA 1283*	45	2
30 Jan 71	●	**IT'S IMPOSSIBLE** *RCA 2043*	4	23
15 May 71		**I THINK OF YOU** *RCA 2075*	14	11
21 Apr 73	●	**AND I LOVE YOU SO** *RCA 2346*	3	31
25 Aug 73	●	**FOR THE GOOD TIMES** *RCA 2402*	7	27
8 Dec 73		**WALK RIGHT BACK** *RCA 2432*	33	10
12 Jan 74		**AND I LOVE YOU SO (re-entry)** *RCA 2346*	40	4
25 May 74		**I WANT TO GIVE** *RCA LPBO 7518*	31	6

[1] Perry Como with the Ramblers

Les COMPAGNONS DE LA CHANSON
France, male vocal group (3 WEEKS)

Date	Title	pos	wks
9 Oct 59	THE THREE BELLS (THE JIMMY BROWN SONG) *Columbia DB 4358*	27	1
23 Oct 59	THE THREE BELLS (THE JIMMY BROWN SONG) (re-entry) *Columbia DB 4358*	21	2

COMSAT ANGELS *UK, male vocal / instrumental group (2 WEEKS)*

Date	Title	pos	wks
21 Jan 84	INDEPENDENCE DAY *Jive JIVE 54*	75	1
4 Feb 84	INDEPENDENCE DAY (re-entry) *Jive JIVE 54*	71	1

CON FUNK SHUN *US, male vocal / instrumental group (2 WEEKS)*

Date	Title	pos	wks
19 Jul 86	BURNIN' LOVE *Club JAB 32*	68	2

CONCEPT *US, male vocalist / instrumentalist – keyboards (6 WEEKS)*

Date	Title	pos	wks
14 Dec 85	MR DJ *Fourth & Broadway BRW 40*	27	6

CONDUCTOR & THE COWBOY *UK, male production duo (2 WEEKS)*

Date	Title	pos	wks
20 May 00	FEELING THIS WAY *Serious SERR 016CD*	35	2

CONFEDERATES – *See Elvis COSTELLO*

CONGREGATION *UK, male / female choir (14 WEEKS)*

Date	Title	pos	wks
27 Nov 71	● SOFTLY WHISPERING I LOVE YOU *Columbia DB 8830*	4	14

CONGRESS *UK, male / female vocal / instrumental group (4 WEEKS)*

Date	Title	pos	wks
26 Oct 91	40 MILES *Inner Rhythm 7HEART 01*	26	4

Arthur CONLEY *US, male vocalist (15 WEEKS)*

Date	Title	pos	wks
27 Apr 67	● SWEET SOUL MUSIC *Atlantic 584 083*	7	14
10 Apr 68	FUNKY STREET *Atlantic 583 175*	46	1

CONNELLS *US, male vocal / instrumental group (11 WEEKS)*

Date	Title	pos	wks
12 Aug 95	74-75 *TVT LONCD 369*	14	8
16 Mar 96	74-75 (re-entry) *TVT LONCD 369*	21	3

Harry CONNICK Jr *US, male vocalist (11 WEEKS)*

Date	Title	pos	wks
25 May 91	RECIPE FOR LOVE / IT HAD TO BE YOU *Columbia 6568907*	32	6
3 Aug 91	WE ARE IN LOVE *Columbia 6572847*	62	2
23 Nov 91	BLUE LIGHT RED LIGHT (SOMEONE'S THERE) *Columbia 6575367*	54	3

Billy CONNOLLY
UK, male comedian / vocalist / instrumentalist (31 WEEKS)

Date	Title	pos	wks
1 Nov 75	★ D.I.V.O.R.C.E. *Polydor 2058 652*	1	10
17 Jul 76	NO CHANCE (NO CHARGE) *Polydor 2058 748*	24	5
25 Aug 79	IN THE BROWNIES *Polydor 2059 160*	38	7
9 Mar 85	SUPER GRAN *Stiff BUY 218*	32	9

Sarah CONNOR featuring TQ
Germany, female vocalist and US, male rapper (5 WEEKS)

Date	Title	pos	wks
13 Oct 01	LET'S GET BACK TO BED ...BOY *Epic 6718662*	16	5

CONQUERING LION *UK, male vocal group (1 WEEK)*

Date	Title	pos	wks
8 Oct 94	CODE RED *Mango CIDM 821*	53	1

Leena CONQUEST and HIP HOP FINGER
US, female vocalist (1 WEEK)

Date	Title	pos	wks
18 Jun 94	BOUNDARIES *BOUNDARIES*	67	1

Jess CONRAD *UK, male vocalist (13 WEEKS)*

Date	Title	pos	wks
30 Jun 60	CHERRY PIE *Decca F 1123*	39	1
26 Jan 61	MYSTERY GIRL *Decca F 11315*	44	1
9 Feb 61	MYSTERY GIRL (re-entry) *Decca F 11315*	18	9
11 Oct 62	PRETTY JENNY *Decca F 11511*	50	2

CONSORTIUM *UK, male vocal group (9 WEEKS)*

Date	Title	pos	wks
12 Feb 69	ALL THE LOVE IN THE WORLD *Pye 7N 17635*	22	9

Ann CONSUELO – *See SUBTERRANIA featuring Ann CONSUELO*

CONTOURS *US, male vocal group (6 WEEKS)*

Date	Title	pos	wks
24 Jan 70	JUST A LITTLE MISUNDERSTANDING *Tamla Motown TMG 723*	31	6

CONTRABAND *Germany / US, male / female vocal / instrumental group (2 WEEKS)*

Date	Title	pos	wks
20 Jul 91	ALL THE WAY FROM MEMPHIS *Impact American EM 195*	65	2

CONTROL *UK, male / female vocal / instrumental group (5 WEEKS)*

Date	Title	pos	wks
2 Nov 91	DANCE WITH ME (I'M YOUR ECSTASY) *All around the World GLOBE 105*	17	5

CONVERT *Belgium, male instrumental / production duo (7 WEEKS)*

Date	Title	pos	wks
11 Jan 92	NIGHTBIRD *A & M AM 845*	39	4
29 May 93	ROCKIN' TO THE RHYTHM *A & M 5802532*	42	2
31 Jan 98	NIGHTBIRD (re-issue) *Wonderboy WBOYD 008*	45	1

See also TRANSFORMER 2

CONWAY BROTHERS *US, male vocal group (10 WEEKS)*

Date	Title	pos	wks
22 Jun 85	TURN IT UP *10 TEN 57*	11	10

Russ CONWAY (111 Top 500) *Popular pianist and composer, b. Trevor Stanford, 2 Sep 1925, Bristol, d. 16 Nov 2000. Against the trends of the day this MOR piano player was the UK's top-selling artist in 1959 (178 WEEKS)*

Date	Title	pos	wks
29 Nov 57	PARTY POPS *Columbia DB 4031*	24	5
29 Aug 58	GOT A MATCH *Columbia DB 4166*	30	1
28 Nov 58	● MORE PARTY POPS *Columbia DB 4204*	10	7
23 Jan 59	THE WORLD OUTSIDE *Columbia DB 4234*	24	1
20 Feb 59	★ SIDE SADDLE *Columbia DB 4256*	1	30
6 Mar 59	THE WORLD OUTSIDE (re-entry) *Columbia DB 4234*	24	3
15 May 59	★ ROULETTE *Columbia DB 4298*	1	19
21 Aug 59	● CHINA TEA *Columbia DB 4337*	5	13
13 Nov 59	● SNOW COACH *Columbia DB 4368*	7	9
20 Nov 59	● MORE AND MORE PARTY POPS *Columbia DB 4373*	5	8
4 Mar 60	ROYAL EVENT *Columbia DB 4418*	15	7
21 Apr 60	FINGS AIN'T WOT THEY USED T'BE *Columbia DB 4422*	47	1
19 May 60	LUCKY FIVE *Columbia DB 4457*	14	9
29 Sep 60	PASSING BREEZE *Columbia DB 4508*	16	10
24 Nov 60	EVEN MORE PARTY POPS *Columbia DB 4535*	27	9
19 Jan 61	PEPE *Columbia DB 4564*	19	9
25 May 61	PABLO *Columbia DB 4649*	45	2
24 Aug 61	SAY IT WITH FLOWERS *Columbia DB 4665* [1]	23	10
30 Nov 61	● TOY BALLOONS *Columbia DB 4738*	7	11
22 Feb 62	LESSON ONE *Columbia DB 4784*	21	7
29 Nov 62	ALWAYS YOU AND ME *Columbia DB 4934*	33	4
3 Jan 63	ALWAYS YOU AND ME (re-entry) *Columbia DB 4934*	35	3

[1] Dorothy Squires and Russ Conway

'Always You and Me' featured Russ Conway talking as well as playing piano. Several of the discs were medleys as follows: Party Pops: When You're Smiling / I'm Looking over a Four-Leafed Clover / When You Wore a Tulip / Row Row Row / For Me and My Girl / Shine on Harvest Moon / By the Light of the Silvery Moon / Side By Side. More Party Pops: Music Music Music / If You Were the Only Girl in the World / Nobody's Sweetheart / Yes Sir That's My Baby / Some of these Days / Honeysuckle and the Bee / Hello Hello Who's Your Lady Friend / Shanty in Old Shanty Town. More and More Party Pops: Sheik of Araby / Who Were You With Last Night / Any Old Iron / Tiptoe Through the Tulips / If You Were the Only Girl in the World / When I Leave the World Behind. Even More Party Pops: Ain't She Sweet / I Can't Give You Anything But Love / Yes We Have No Bananas / I May Be Wrong / Happy Days and Lonely Nights / Glad Rag Doll

Martin COOK – *See Richard DENTON and Martin COOK*

Norman COOK *UK, male producer / multi-instrumentalist (10 WEEKS)*

Date	Title	pos	wks
8 Jul 89	WON'T TALK ABOUT IT / BLAME IT ON THE BASSLINE *Go.Beat GOD 33* [1]	29	6

1961

FROM THE YEAR IN WHICH YURI GAGARIN BECAME THE FIRST MAN TO VISIT SPACE, CND DEMONSTRATORS CLASHED WITH POLICE IN THE UK, DYLAN PLAYED HIS FIRST GIG IN GREENWICH VILLAGE AND ELVIS HAD A RECORD FOUR CHART TOPPERS, **GENE SIMMONS** REMEMBERS THAT MAGICAL MOMENT THAT IS BUYING YOUR FIRST RECORD ...

“The first record I bought was **Chubby Checker**, 'Let's Twist Again', at a small record store in Jackson's Heights in Queens. His real name was Ernest Evans, originally a chicken-plucker – when I fall in love with music I research it!”

SINGLE OF THE YEAR 'Wooden Heart' Elvis Presley
ALBUM OF THE YEAR 'GI Blues' Elvis Presley

			pos	wks
21 Oct 89		**FOR SPACIOUS LIES** *Go.Beat GOD 37* [2]	48	4

[1] Norman Cook featuring Billy Bragg / Norman Cook featuring MC Wildski [2] Norman Cook featuring Lester

See also FATBOY SLIM; FREAKPOWER; MIGHTY DUB KATZ; PIZZAMAN; BEATS INTERNATIONAL; HOUSEMARTINS

Peter COOK *UK, male comedian / vocalist (15 WEEKS)*

			pos	wks
17 Jun 65		**GOODBYE-EE** *Decca F 12158* [1]	18	10
15 Jul 65		**THE BALLAD OF SPOTTY MULDOON** *Decca F 12182*	34	5

[1] Peter Cook and Dudley Moore

Brandon COOKE featuring Roxanne SHANTE

UK, male producer and US, female rapper (3 WEEKS)

			pos	wks
29 Oct 88		**SHARP AS A KNIFE** *Club JAB 73*	45	3

See also Roxanne SHANTE

Sam COOKE (400 Top 500)

Gospel great turned soul superstar, b. 22 Jan 1931, Mississippi, US, d. 11 Dec 1964. Former leader of the Soul Stirrers and transatlantic hitmaker. Acclaimed singer / songwriter who influenced many R&B and pop vocalists including Otis Redding and Rod Stewart (82 WEEKS)

			pos	wks
17 Jan 58		**YOU SEND ME** *London HLU 8506* ▲	29	1
14 Aug 59		**ONLY SIXTEEN** *HMV POP 642*	23	4
7 Jul 60		**WONDERFUL WORLD** *HMV POP 754*	27	8
29 Sep 60	●	**CHAIN GANG** *RCA 1202*	9	11
27 Jul 61	●	**CUPID** *RCA 1242*	7	14
8 Mar 62	●	**TWISTIN' THE NIGHT AWAY** *RCA 1277*	6	14
16 May 63		**ANOTHER SATURDAY NIGHT** *RCA 1341*	23	12
5 Sep 63		**FRANKIE AND JOHNNY** *RCA 1361*	30	6
22 Mar 86	●	**WONDERFUL WORLD (re-issue)** *RCA PB 49871*	2	11
10 May 86		**ANOTHER SATURDAY NIGHT (re-issue)** *RCA PB 49849*	75	1

COOKIE CREW *UK, female rap duo (31 WEEKS)*

			pos	wks
9 Jan 88	●	**ROK DA HOUSE** *Rhythm King LEFT 11* [1]	5	11
7 Jan 89		**BORN THIS WAY (LET'S DANCE)** *ffrr FFR 19*	23	5
1 Apr 89		**GOT TO KEEP ON** *ffrr FFR 25*	17	9
15 Jul 89		**COME AND GET SOME** *ffrr F 110*	42	3
27 Jul 91		**SECRETS (OF SUCCESS)** *ffrr F159* [2]	53	3

[1] Beatmasters featuring the Cookie Crew [2] Cookie Crew featuring Danny D

COOKIES *US, female vocal group (1 WEEK)*

			pos	wks
10 Jan 63		**CHAINS** *London HLU 9634*	50	1

COOL DOWN ZONE

UK, male / female vocal / instrumental group (4 WEEKS)

			pos	wks
30 Jun 90		**HEAVEN KNOWS** *10 TEN 309*	52	4

COOL JACK *Italy, male instrumental / production duo (1 WEEK)*

			pos	wks
9 Nov 96		**JUS' COME** *AM:PM 5819892*	44	1

COOL, the FAB, and the GROOVY present Quincy JONES

UK, male production duo, US, male band and US, male producer / instrumentalist (1 WEEK)

			pos	wks
1 Aug 98		**SOUL BOSSA NOVA** *Manifesto FESCD 48*	47	1

Rita COOLIDGE *US, female vocalist (24 WEEKS)*

			pos	wks
25 Jun 77	●	**WE'RE ALL ALONE** *A & M AMS 7295*	6	13
15 Oct 77		**(YOUR LOVE HAS LIFTED ME) HIGHER AND HIGHER** *A & M AMS 7315*	49	1
29 Oct 77		**(YOUR LOVE HAS LIFTED ME) HIGHER AND HIGHER (re-entry)** *A & M AMS 7315*	48	1
4 Feb 78		**WORDS** *A & M AMS 7330*	25	8
25 Jun 83		**ALL TIME HIGH** *A & M AM 007*	75	1

COOLIO *US, male rapper – Artis Ivey Jr (62 WEEKS)*

			pos	wks
23 Jul 94		**FANTASTIC VOYAGE** *Tommy Boy TB 0617CD*	41	2
15 Oct 94		**I REMEMBER** *Tommy Boy TBXCD 635*	73	1
28 Oct 95	★	**GANGSTA'S PARADISE** *Tommy Boy MCSTD 2104* [1] ◆ ■ ▲	1	20
20 Jan 96	●	**TOO HOT** *Tommy Boy TBCD 718*	9	6
6 Apr 96		**1234 (SUMPIN' NEW)** *Tommy Boy TBCD 7721*	13	7
17 Aug 96		**IT'S ALL THE WAY LIVE (NOW)** *Tommy Boy TBCD 7731*	34	2
5 Apr 97	●	**HIT EM HIGH (THE MONSTARS' ANTHEM)** *Atlantic A 5449CD* [2]	8	6
7 Jun 97		**THE WINNER** *Atlantic A 5433CD*	53	1
19 Jul 97	●	**C U WHEN U GET THERE** *Tommy Boy TBCD 785* [3]	3	12
11 Oct 97		**OOH LA LA** *Tommy Boy TBCD 799*	14	5

[1] Coolio featuring LV [2] B Real / Busta Rhymes / Coolio / LL Cool J / Method Man [3] Coolio featuring 40 Thevz

COOLNOTES *UK, male / female vocal / instrumental group (28 WEEKS)*

			pos	wks
18 Aug 84		**YOU'RE NEVER TOO YOUNG** *Abstract Dance AD 1*	42	5
17 Nov 84		**I FORGOT** *Abstract Dance AD 2*	63	2
23 Mar 85		**SPEND THE NIGHT** *Abstract Dance AD 3*	11	9
13 Jul 85		**IN YOUR CAR** *Abstract Dance AD 4*	13	9
19 Oct 85		**HAVE A GOOD FOREVER** *Abstract Dance AD 5*	73	1
17 May 86		**INTO THE MOTION** *Abstract Dance AD 8*	66	2

COOLY'S HOT BOX – *See Roger SANCHEZ*

Alice COOPER (288 Top 500)

The alter ego of shock-rock vocalist Vincent Furnier, b. 4 Feb 1948, Detroit, US. Transatlantic chart-topper whose group was voted World's Top Band in 1972 in UK. Renowned for onstage shock-horror theatrics (104 WEEKS)

			pos	wks
15 Jul 72	★	**SCHOOL'S OUT** *Warner Bros. K 16188*	1	12
7 Oct 72	●	**ELECTED** *Warner Bros. K 16214*	4	10
10 Feb 73	●	**HELLO HURRAY** *Warner Bros. K 16248*	6	12
21 Apr 73	●	**NO MORE MR NICE GUY** *Warner Bros. K 16262*	10	10
19 Jan 74		**TEENAGE LAMENT 74** *Warner Bros. K 16345*	12	7
21 May 77		**(NO MORE) LOVE AT YOUR CONVENIENCE** *Warner Bros. K 16935*	44	2
23 Dec 78		**HOW YOU GONNA SEE ME NOW** *Warner Bros. K 17270*	61	6
6 Mar 82		**SEVEN AND SEVEN IS (live version)** *Warner Bros. K 17924*	62	3
8 May 82		**FOR BRITAIN ONLY / UNDER MY WHEELS** *Warner Bros. K 17940*	66	2
18 Oct 86		**HE'S BACK (THE MAN BEHIND THE MASK)** *MCA MCA 1090*	61	2
9 Apr 88		**FREEDOM** *MCA MCA 1241*	50	3
29 Jul 89	●	**POISON** *Epic 655061 7*	2	11
7 Oct 89		**BED OF NAILS** *Epic ALICE 3*	38	5
2 Dec 89		**HOUSE OF FIRE** *Epic ALICE 4*	65	2
22 Jun 91		**HEY STOOPID** *Epic 6569837*	21	6
5 Oct 91		**LOVE'S A LOADED GUN** *Epic 6574387*	38	3
6 Jun 92		**FEED MY FRANKENSTEIN** *Epic 6580927*	27	3
28 May 94		**LOST IN AMERICA** *Epic 6603472*	22	3
23 Jul 94		**IT'S ME** *Epic 6605632*	34	2

For the first five hits, 'Alice Cooper' was the name of the entire group, not just of the lead vocalist

Deborah COOPER – *See C & C MUSIC FACTORY / CLIVILLES & COLE*

Tommy COOPER *UK, male comedian / vocalist (3 WEEKS)*

			pos	wks
29 Jun 61		**DON'T JUMP OFF THE ROOF DAD** *Palette PG 9019*	40	2
20 Jul 61		**DON'T JUMP OFF THE ROOF DAD (re-entry)** *Palette PG 9019*	50	1

COOPER TEMPLE CLAUSE

UK, male vocal / instrumental group (1 WEEK)

			pos	wks
29 Sep 01		**LET'S KILL MUSIC** *Morning MORNING 9*	41	1

Julian COPE *UK, male vocalist (59 WEEKS)*

			pos	wks
19 Nov 83		**SUNSHINE PLAYROOM** *Mercury COPE 1*	64	1
31 Mar 84		**THE GREATNESS AND PERFECTION OF LOVE** *Mercury MER 155*	52	5
27 Sep 86		**WORLD SHUT YOUR MOUTH** *Island IS 290*	19	8
17 Jan 87		**TRAMPOLENE** *Island IS 305*	31	6
11 Apr 87		**EVE'S VOLCANO (COVERED IN SIN)** *Island IS 318*	41	5
24 Sep 88		**CHARLOTTE ANNE** *Island IS 380*	35	6
21 Jan 89		**5 O'CLOCK WORLD** *Island IS 399*	42	4
24 Jun 89		**CHINA DOLL** *Island IS 406*	53	2

Date	Title / Label	Pos	Wks
9 Feb 91	**BEAUTIFUL LOVE** *Island IS 483*	32	6
20 Apr 91	**EAST EASY RIDER** *Island IS 492*	51	3
3 Aug 91	**HEAD** *Island IS 497*	57	2
8 Aug 92	**WORLD SHUT YOUR MOUTH (re-issue)** *Island IS 534*	44	3
17 Oct 92	**FEAR LOVES THIS PLACE** *Island IS 545*	42	2
12 Aug 95	**TRY TRY TRY** *Echo ECSCD 11*	24	3
27 Jul 96	**I COME FROM ANOTHER PLANET BABY** *Echo ECSCD 22*	34	2
5 Oct 96	**PLANETARY SIT-IN (EVERY GIRL HAS YOUR NAME)** *Echo ECSCD 25*	34	1

See also TEARDROP EXPLODES

Imani COPPOLA *US, female vocalist / instrumentalist (3 WEEKS)* pos/wks

Date	Title / Label	Pos	Wks
28 Feb 98	**LEGEND OF A COWGIRL** *Columbia 6656015*	32	3

See also BAHA MEN

Harry H CORBETT – *See Wilfrid BRAMBELL and Harry H CORBETT*

Frank CORDELL and HIS ORCHESTRA *UK, orchestra (4 WEEKS)* pos/wks

Date	Title / Label	Pos	Wks
24 Aug 56	**SADIE'S SHAWL** *HMV POP 229*	29	2
16 Feb 61	**THE BLACK BEAR** *HMV POP 824*	44	2

Louise CORDET *UK, female vocalist – Louise Boisot (13 WEEKS)* pos/wks

Date	Title / Label	Pos	Wks
5 Jul 62	**I'M JUST A BABY** *Decca F 11476*	13	13

Chris CORNELL *US, male vocalist (1 WEEK)* pos/wks

Date	Title / Label	Pos	Wks
23 Oct 99	**CAN'T CHANGE ME** *A&M 4971732*	62	1

See also SOUNDGARDEN

Don CORNELL *US, male vocalist – Luigi Varlaro (23 WEEKS)* pos/wks

Date	Title / Label	Pos	Wks
3 Sep 54 ★	**HOLD MY HAND** *Vogue Q 2013*	1	21
22 Apr 55	**STRANGER IN PARADISE** *Vogue Q 72073*	19	2

Lynn CORNELL *UK, female vocalist (9 WEEKS)* pos/wks

Date	Title / Label	Pos	Wks
20 Oct 60	**NEVER ON SUNDAY** *Decca F 11277*	30	9

CORNERSHOP *UK, male vocal / instrumental duo (16 WEEKS)* pos/wks

Date	Title / Label	Pos	Wks
30 Aug 97	**BRIMFUL OF ASHA** *Wiiija WIJ 75CD*	60	1
28 Feb 98 ★	**BRIMFUL OF ASHA (re-mix)** *Wiiija WIJ 81CD* ■	1	12
16 May 98	**SLEEP ON THE LEFT SIDE** *Wiiija WIJ 80CD*	23	3

Charlotte CORNWELL – *See Julie COVINGTON, Rula LENSKA, Charlotte CORNWELL and Sue JONES-DAVIES*

Hugh CORNWELL

UK, male vocalist / instrumentalist – guitar (3 WEEKS) pos/wks

Date	Title / Label	Pos	Wks
24 Jan 87	**FACTS + FIGURES** *Virgin VS 922*	61	2
7 May 88	**ANOTHER KIND OF LOVE** *Virgin VS 945*	71	1

See also STRANGLERS

CO-RO featuring TARLISA

Germany, male / female vocal / production group (1 WEEK) pos/wks

Date	Title / Label	Pos	Wks
12 Dec 92	**BECAUSE THE NIGHT** *ZYX ZYX 68227*	61	1

CORONA *Brazil, male producer and female vocalist – Francesco Bontempi and Olga De Souza (44 WEEKS)* pos/wks

Date	Title / Label	Pos	Wks
10 Sep 94 ●	**THE RHYTHM OF THE NIGHT** *WEA YZ 837CD1*	2	14
31 Dec 94	**THE RHYTHM OF THE NIGHT (re-entry)** *WEA YZ 837CD1*	55	4
8 Apr 95 ●	**BABY BABY** *Eternal YZ 919CD*	5	8
22 Jul 95 ●	**TRY ME OUT** *Eternal YZ 955CD*	6	10
23 Dec 95	**I DON'T WANNA BE A STAR** *Eternal WEA 029CD*	22	6
22 Feb 97	**MEGAMIX** *Eternal WEA 092CD*	36	2

CORONATION STREET CAST featuring Bill WADDINGTON

UK, male / female vocal group (3 WEEKS) pos/wks

Date	Title / Label	Pos	Wks
16 Dec 95	**ALWAYS LOOK ON THE BRIGHT SIDE OF LIFE** *EMI Premier CDEMS 411*	35	3

The listed flip side of 'Always Look on the Bright Side of Life' was 'Something Stupid' by Amanda Barrie and Johnny Briggs

CORONETS *UK, male / female vocal group (7 WEEKS)* pos/wks

Date	Title / Label	Pos	Wks
26 Aug 55	**THAT'S HOW A LOVE SONG WAS BORN** *Columbia DB 3640* [1]	14	6
25 Nov 55	**TWENTY TINY FINGERS** *Columbia DB 3671*	20	1

[1] Ray Burns with the Coronets

Briana CORRIGAN *UK, female vocalist (2 WEEKS)* pos/wks

Date	Title / Label	Pos	Wks
11 May 96	**LOVE ME NOW** *East West EW 041CD1*	48	2

See also BEAUTIFUL SOUTH

CORRS (338 Top 500) *Internationally successful Irish sisters and brother group: Andrea, Caroline, Sharon and Jim Corr. Quartet, which has sold more than five million albums in the UK, was voted Best International Group at 1999 Brits. 'Talk On Corners' was the top UK album in 1998 (92 WEEKS)* pos/wks

Date	Title / Label	Pos	Wks
17 Feb 96	**RUNAWAY** *Atlantic A 5727CD*	49	2
7 Dec 96	**RUNAWAY (re-entry)** *Atlantic A 5727CD*	60	1
1 Feb 97	**LOVE TO LOVE YOU / RUNAWAY (re-issue)** *Atlantic A 5621CD*	62	1
25 Oct 97	**ONLY WHEN I SLEEP** *Atlantic AT 0015CD*	58	1
20 Dec 97	**I NEVER LOVED YOU ANYWAY** *Atlantic AT 0018CD*	43	2
28 Mar 98	**WHAT CAN I DO** *Atlantic AT 0029CD*	53	1
16 May 98 ●	**DREAMS** *Atlantic AT 0032CD*	6	10
29 Aug 98 ●	**WHAT CAN I DO (re-mix)** *Atlantic AT 0044CD*	3	11
28 Nov 98 ●	**SO YOUNG** *Atlantic AT 0057CD1*	6	13
27 Feb 99 ●	**RUNAWAY (re-mix)** *Atlantic AT 0062CD*	2	11
12 Jun 99	**I KNOW MY LOVE** *RCA Victor 74321670622* [1]	37	3
11 Dec 99	**RADIO** *Atlantic AT 0079CD*	18	9
15 Jul 00 ★	**BREATHLESS** *Atlantic AT 0084CD* ■	1	13
11 Nov 00	**IRRESISTIBLE** *Atlantic AT 0089CD*	20	5
13 Jan 01	**IRRESISTIBLE (re-entry)** *Atlantic AT 0089CD*	60	2
28 Apr 01	**GIVE ME A REASON** *Atlantic AT 0097CD*	27	2
10 Nov 01	**WOULD YOU BE HAPPIER?** *Atlantic AT 0115CD*	14	5

[1] Chieftains featuring The Corrs

Ferry CORSTEN – *See SYSTEM F; VERACOCHA; ALBION; GOURYELLA; MOONMAN*

CORTINA *UK, male producer – Ben Keen (2 WEEKS)* pos/wks

Date	Title / Label	Pos	Wks
24 Mar 01	**MUSIC IS MOVING** *Nukleuz NUKC 0159*	42	2

See also BK

Vladimir COSMA *Hungary, orchestra (1 WEEK)* pos/wks

Date	Title / Label	Pos	Wks
14 Jul 79	**DAVID'S SONG (MAIN THEME FROM 'KIDNAPPED')** *Decca FR 13841*	64	1

COSMIC BABY *Germany, male producer (1 WEEK)* pos/wks

Date	Title / Label	Pos	Wks
26 Feb 94	**LOOPS OF INFINITY** *Logic 74321191432*	70	1

COSMIC GATE *Germany, male production trio (7 WEEKS)* pos/wks

Date	Title / Label	Pos	Wks
4 Aug 01 ●	**FIRE WIRE** *Data DATA 24 CDS*	9	7

COSMIC ROUGH RIDERS

UK, male vocal / instrumental group (2 WEEKS) pos/wks

Date	Title / Label	Pos	Wks
4 Aug 01	**REVOLUTION (IN THE SUMMERTIME)** *Poptones MC 5047SCD*	35	1
29 Sep 01	**THE PAIN INSIDE** *Poptones MC 5052SCD*	36	1

COSMOS *UK, male production / instrumental duo (1 WEEK)* pos/wks

Date	Title / Label	Pos	Wks
18 Sep 99	**SUMMER IN SPACE** *Island Blue PFACD 3*	49	1

Don COSTA *US, orchestra (10 WEEKS)* pos/wks

		pos	wks
13 Oct 60	NEVER ON SUNDAY *London HLT 9195*	27	9
22 Dec 60	NEVER ON SUNDAY (re-entry) *London HLT 9195*	41	1

Nikka COSTA *US, female vocalist (1 WEEK)* pos/wks

		pos	wks
11 Aug 01	LIKE A FEATHER *Virgin VUSCD 199*	53	1

Elvis COSTELLO (110 Top 500) *Acclaimed singer / songwriter, b. Declan McManus, 25 Aug 1955, Liverpool. He emerged during punk explosion of 1976, but was soon accepted as a mainstream artist. Has clocked up 12 US Top 40 albums (179 WEEKS)* pos/wks

		pos	wks
5 Nov 77	WATCHING THE DETECTIVES *Stiff BUY 20*	15	11
11 Mar 78	(I DON'T WANT TO GO TO) CHELSEA *Radar ADA 3* [1]	16	10
13 May 78	PUMP IT UP *Radar ADA 10* [1]	24	10
28 Oct 78	RADIO RADIO *Radar ADA 24* [1]	29	7
10 Feb 79 ●	OLIVER'S ARMY *Radar ADA 31* [1]	2	12
12 May 79	ACCIDENTS WILL HAPPEN *Radar ADA 35* [1]	28	8
16 Feb 80 ●	I CAN'T STAND UP FOR FALLING DOWN *F. Beat XX 1*	4	8
12 Apr 80	HI FIDELITY *F. Beat XX 3*	30	5
7 Jun 80	NEW AMSTERDAM *F. Beat XX 5*	36	6
20 Dec 80	CLUBLAND *F. Beat XX 12* [1]	60	4
3 Oct 81 ●	A GOOD YEAR FOR THE ROSES *F. Beat XX 17*	6	11
12 Dec 81	SWEET DREAMS *F. Beat XX 19*	42	8
10 Apr 82	I'M YOUR TOY *F. Beat XX 21* [2]	51	3
19 Jun 82	YOU LITTLE FOOL *F. Beat XX 26*	52	3
31 Jul 82	MAN OUT OF TIME *F. Beat XX 28*	58	2
25 Sep 82	FROM HEAD TO TOE *F. Beat XX 30*	43	4
11 Dec 82	PARTY PARTY *A & M AMS 8267* [3]	48	6
11 Jun 83	PILLS AND SOAP *Imp IMP 001* [4]	16	4
9 Jul 83	EVERYDAY I WRITE THE BOOK *F. Beat XX 32*	28	8
17 Sep 83	LET THEM ALL TALK *F. Beat XX 33*	59	2
28 Apr 84	PEACE IN OUR TIME *Imposter TRUCE 1* [4]	48	3
16 Jun 84	I WANNA BE LOVED / TURNING THE TOWN RED *F. Beat XX 35*	25	6
25 Aug 84	THE ONLY FLAME IN TOWN *F. Beat XX 37*	71	2
4 May 85	GREEN SHIRT *F. Beat ZB 40085*	71	1
18 May 85	GREEN SHIRT (re-entry) *F. Beat ZB 40085*	68	1
1 Feb 86	DON'T LET ME BE MISUNDERSTOOD *F. Beat ZB 40555* [5]	33	4
30 Aug 86	TOKYO STORM WARNING *Imp IMP 007*	73	1
4 Mar 89	VERONICA *Warner Bros. W 7558*	31	6
20 May 89	BABY PLAYS AROUND (EP) *Warner Bros. W 2949*	65	1
4 May 91	THE OTHER SIDE OF SUMMER *Warner Bros. W 0025*	43	4
5 Mar 94	SULKY GIRL *Warner Bros. W 0234CD* [1]	22	3
30 Apr 94	13 STEPS LEAD DOWN *Warner Bros. W 0245CD* [1]	59	1
26 Nov 94	LONDON'S BRILLIANT PARADE *Warner Bros. W 0270CD1* [1]	48	2
11 May 96	IT'S TIME *Warner Bros. W 0348CD* [1]	58	1
1 May 99	TOLEDO *Mercury 8709652* [6]	72	1
31 Jul 99	SHE *Mercury MERCD 521*	19	8
9 Oct 99	SHE (re-entry) *Mercury MERCD 521*	57	2

[1] Elvis Costello and the Attractions [2] Elvis Costello and the Attractions with the Royal Philharmonic Orchestra [3] Elvis Costello and the Attractions with the Royal Horn Guards [4] Imposter [5] The Costello Show featuring the Confederates [6] Elvis Costello / Burt Bacharach

Tracks on Baby Plays Around (EP): Baby Plays Around / Poisoned Rose / Almost Blue / My Funny Valentine

COTTAGERS – *See Tony REES and the COTTAGERS*

Billy COTTON and his BAND *UK, male bandleader / vocalist, with band and chorus (25 WEEKS)* pos/wks

		pos	wks
1 May 53 ●	IN A GOLDEN COACH (THERE'S A HEART OF GOLD) *Decca F 10058* [1]	3	10
18 Dec 53	I SAW MOMMY KISSING SANTA CLAUS *Decca F 10206* [2]	11	3
30 Apr 54	FRIENDS AND NEIGHBOURS *Decca F 10299* [3]	12	1
14 May 54 ●	FRIENDS AND NEIGHBOURS (re-entry) *Decca F 10299* [3]	3	11

[1] Billy Cotton and his Band, vocals by Doreen Stephens [2] Billy Cotton and his Band, vocals by the Mill Girls and the Bandits [3] Billy Cotton and his Band, vocals by the Bandits

Mike COTTON'S JAZZMEN *UK, male instrumental band – Mike Cotton – trumpet (4 WEEKS)* pos/wks

		pos	wks
20 Jun 63	SWING THAT HAMMER *Columbia DB 7029*	36	4

John COUGAR – *See John Cougar MELLENCAMP*

COUGARS *UK, male instrumental group (8 WEEKS)* pos/wks

		pos	wks
28 Feb 63	SATURDAY NITE AT THE DUCK-POND *Parlophone R 4989*	33	8

COUNCIL COLLECTIVE *UK / US, male / female vocal / instrumental group (6 WEEKS)* pos/wks

		pos	wks
22 Dec 84	SOUL DEEP (PART 1) *Polydor MINE 1*	24	6

COUNT INDIGO *UK, male vocalist (1 WEEK)* pos/wks

		pos	wks
9 Mar 96	MY UNKNOWN LOVE *Cowboy RODEO 952CD*	59	1

COUNTING CROWS *US, male vocal / instrumental group (11 WEEKS)* pos/wks

		pos	wks
30 Apr 94	MR JONES *Geffen GFSTD 69*	28	2
9 Jul 94	ROUND HERE *Geffen GFSTD 74*	70	1
15 Oct 94	RAIN KING *Geffen GFSTD 82*	49	3
19 Oct 96	ANGELS OF THE SILENCES *Geffen GFSTD 22182*	41	1
14 Dec 96	A LONG DECEMBER *Geffen GFSTD 22190*	62	1
31 May 97	DAYLIGHT FADING *Geffen GFSTD 22247*	54	1
20 Dec 97	A LONG DECEMBER (re-entry) *Geffen GFSTD 22190*	68	1
30 Oct 99	HANGINAROUND *Geffen 4971842*	46	1

COUNTRYMEN *UK, male vocal group (2 WEEKS)* pos/wks

		pos	wks
3 May 62	I KNOW WHERE I'M GOING *Piccadilly 7N 35029*	45	2

COURSE *Holland, male / female vocal / DJ / production group (15 WEEKS)* pos/wks

		pos	wks
19 Apr 97 ●	READY OR NOT *The Brothers Organisation CDBRUV 2*	5	7
5 Jul 97 ●	AIN'T NOBODY *The Brothers Organisation CDBRUV 3*	8	6
20 Dec 97	BEST LOVE *The Brothers Organisation CDBRUV 6*	51	2

Tina COUSINS *UK, female vocalist (29 WEEKS)* pos/wks

		pos	wks
15 Aug 98 ●	MYSTERIOUS TIMES *Multiply CDMULTY 40* [1]	2	12
21 Nov 98	PRAY *Jive 0519162*	20	3
27 Mar 99	KILLIN' TIME *Jive / Eastern Bloc 0519232*	15	4
10 Jul 99	FOREVER *Jive 0519332*	45	2
9 Oct 99	ANGEL *Ebul / Jive 0519432*	46	1
22 Apr 00 ●	JUST AROUND THE HILL *Multiply CDMULTY 62* [1]	8	7

[1] Sash! featuring Tina Cousins

Don COVAY *US, male vocalist (6 WEEKS)* pos/wks

		pos	wks
7 Sep 74	IT'S BETTER TO HAVE (AND DON'T NEED) *Mercury 6052 634*	29	6

Vincent COVELLO – *See BT*

COVENTRY CITY CUP FINAL SQUAD *UK, male football team vocalists (2 WEEKS)* pos/wks

		pos	wks
23 May 87	GO FOR IT! *Sky Blue SKB 1*	61	2

COVER GIRLS *US, female vocal group (4 WEEKS)* pos/wks

		pos	wks
1 Aug 92	WISHING ON A STAR *Epic 6581437*	38	4

David COVERDALE and WHITESNAKE *UK, male vocalist and UK, male vocal / instrumental group (1 WEEK)* pos/wks

		pos	wks
7 Jun 97	TOO MANY TEARS *EMI CDEM 471* [1]	46	1

See also COVERDALE PAGE; WHITESNAKE; DEEP PURPLE

COVERDALE PAGE *UK, male vocal / instrumental duo (3 WEEKS)* pos/wks

		pos	wks
3 Jul 93	TAKE ME FOR A LITTLE WHILE *EMI CDEM 270*	29	2
23 Oct 93	TAKE A LOOK AT YOURSELF *EMI CDEM 279*	43	1

Julie COVINGTON *UK, female vocalist (29 WEEKS)* pos/wks

25 Dec 76 ★ **DON'T CRY FOR ME ARGENTINA** *MCA 260*..........1 15
3 Dec 77 **ONLY WOMEN BLEED** *Virgin VS 196*..........12 11
15 Jul 78 **DON'T CRY FOR ME ARGENTINA (re-entry)** *MCA 260*..........63 3

See also Julie COVINGTON, Rula LENSKA, Charlotte CORNWELL and Sue JONES-DAVIES

Julie COVINGTON, Rula LENSKA, Charlotte CORNWELL and Sue JONES-DAVIES *UK, female vocal group (6 WEEKS)* pos/wks

21 May 77 ● **OK?** *Polydor 2001 714*..........10 6

See also Julie COVINGTON

Warren COVINGTON – *See Tommy DORSEY ORCHESTRA starring Warren COVINGTON*

Patrick COWLEY – *See SYLVESTER*

Carl COX *UK, male producer (19 WEEKS)* pos/wks

28 Sep 91 **I WANT YOU (FOREVER)** *Perfecto PB 44885* [1]..........23 7
8 Aug 92 **DOES IT FEEL GOOD TO YOU** *Perfecto PB 74321102877* [1]..........35 3
6 Nov 93 **THE PLANET OF LOVE** *Perfecto 74321161772*..........44 2
9 Mar 96 **TWO PAINTINGS AND A DRUM (EP)** *Edel 0090715COX*..........24 2
8 Jun 96 **SENSUAL SOPHIS-TI-CAT / THE PLAYER** *Ultimatum 0090875COX*..........25 2
12 Dec 98 **THE LATIN THEME** *Edel 0091685 COX*..........52 1
22 May 99 **PHUTURE 2000** *Worldwide Ultimatum / Edel 0091715 COX*..........40 2

[1] DJ Carl Cox

Tracks on Two Paintings and a Drum (EP): Phoebus Apollo / Yum Yum / Siberian Snow Storm

Deborah COX *Canada, female vocalist (8 WEEKS)* pos/wks

11 Nov 95 **SENTIMENTAL** *Arista 74321324962*..........34 3
24 Feb 96 **WHO DO U LOVE** *Arista 74321337942*..........31 3
31 Jul 99 **IT'S OVER NOW** *Arista 74321686942*..........49 1
9 Oct 99 **NOBODY'S SUPPOSED TO BE HERE** *Arista 74321702102*..........55 1

Michael COX *UK, male vocalist (15 WEEKS)* pos/wks

9 Jun 60 ● **ANGELA JONES** *Triumph RGM 1011*..........7 13
20 Oct 60 **ALONG CAME CAROLINE** *HMV POP 789*..........41 2

Peter COX *UK, male vocalist (6 WEEKS)* pos/wks

2 Aug 97 **AIN'T GONNA CRY AGAIN** *Chrysalis CDCHS 5056*..........37 2
15 Nov 97 **IF YOU WALK AWAY** *Chrysalis CDCHSS 5069*..........24 2
20 Jun 98 **WHAT A FOOL BELIEVES** *Chrysalis CDCHS 5089*..........39 2

See also GO WEST

CRACKER *US, male vocal / instrumental group (9 WEEKS)* pos/wks

28 May 94 **LOW** *Virgin America VUSDG 80*..........43 4
23 Jul 94 **GET OFF THIS** *Virgin America VUSCD 83*..........41 3
3 Dec 94 **LOW (re-entry)** *Virgin America VUSDG 80*..........54 2

Sarah CRACKNELL *UK, female vocalist (1 WEEK)* pos/wks

14 Sep 96 **ANYMORE** *Gut CDGUT 3*..........39 1

See also SAINT ETIENNE

STEVE CRADOCK – *See OCEAN COLOUR SCENE; BUFFALO TOM*

CRAIG *UK, male vocalist – Craig Phillips (6 WEEKS)* pos/wks

23 Dec 00 **AT THIS TIME OF YEAR** *WEA WEA 321CD*..........14 5
10 Feb 01 **AT THIS TIME OF YEAR (re-entry)** *WEA WEA 321CD*..........56 1

Robbie CRAIG – *See ARTFUL DODGER*

Floyd CRAMER *US, male instrumentalist – piano (24 WEEKS)* pos/wks

13 Apr 61 ★ **ON THE REBOUND** *RCA 1231*..........1 14
20 Jul 61 **SAN ANTONIO ROSE** *RCA 1241*..........36 8
23 Aug 62 **HOT PEPPER** *RCA 1301*..........46 2

CRAMPS *US, male / female vocal / instrumental group (4 WEEKS)* pos/wks

9 Nov 85 **CAN YOUR PUSSY DO THE DOG?** *Big Beat NS 110*..........68 1
10 Feb 90 **BIKINI GIRLS WITH MACHINE GUNS** *Enigma ENV 17*..........35 3

CRANBERRIES *Ireland, male / female vocal / instrumental group (50 WEEKS)* pos/wks

27 Feb 93 **LINGER** *Island CID 556*..........74 1
12 Feb 94 **LINGER (re-issue)** *Island CID 559*..........14 11
7 May 94 **DREAMS** *Island CIDX 594*..........27 5
1 Oct 94 **ZOMBIE** *Island CID 600*..........14 6
3 Dec 94 **ODE TO MY FAMILY** *Island CIDX 601*..........26 6
11 Mar 95 **I CAN'T BE WITH YOU** *Island CID 605*..........23 5
12 Aug 95 **RIDICULOUS THOUGHTS** *Island CID 616*..........20 3
20 Apr 96 **SALVATION** *Island CID 633*..........13 5
13 Jul 96 **FREE TO DECIDE** *Island CID 637*..........33 3
17 Apr 99 **PROMISES** *Island US / Mercury 5725912*..........13 4
17 Jul 99 **ANIMAL INSTINCT** *Island US / Mercury 5621972*..........54 1

Les CRANE *US, male vocalist (14 WEEKS)* pos/wks

19 Feb 72 ● **DESIDERATA** *Warner Bros. K 16119*..........7 14

Whitfield CRANE – *See ICE-T; MOTORHEAD*

CRANES *UK, male / female vocal / instrumental group (2 WEEKS)* pos/wks

25 Sep 93 **JEWEL** *Dedicated CRANE 007CD*..........29 1
3 Sep 94 **SHINING ROAD** *Dedicated CRANE 008CD1*..........57 1

CRASH TEST DUMMIES *Canada, male / female vocal / instrumental group (20 WEEKS)* pos/wks

23 Apr 94 ● **MMM MMM MMM MMM** *RCA 74321201512*..........2 11
16 Jul 94 **AFTERNOONS & COFFEESPOONS** *RCA 74321219622*..........23 5
15 Apr 95 **THE BALLAD OF PETER PUMPKINHEAD** *RCA 74321276772* [1]..........30 4

[1] Crash Test Dummies featuring Ellen Reid

Beverley CRAVEN *UK, female vocalist (33 WEEKS)* pos/wks

20 Apr 91 ● **PROMISE ME** *Epic 6559437*..........3 13
20 Jul 91 **HOLDING ON** *Epic 6565507*..........32 7
5 Oct 91 **WOMAN TO WOMAN** *Epic 6574647*..........40 5
7 Dec 91 **MEMORIES** *Epic 6576617*..........68 2
25 Sep 93 **LOVE SCENES** *Epic 6595952*..........34 4
20 Nov 93 **MOLLIE'S SONG** *Epic 6598132*..........61 2

Billy CRAWFORD *US, male vocalist (2 WEEKS)* pos/wks

10 Oct 98 **URGENTLY IN LOVE** *V2 VVR 5003063*..........48 2

Jimmy CRAWFORD *UK, male vocalist – Ronald Lindsey (11 WEEKS)* pos/wks

8 Jun 61 **LOVE OR MONEY** *Columbia DB 4633*..........49 1
16 Nov 61 **I LOVE HOW YOU LOVE ME** *Columbia DB 4717*..........18 10

Michael CRAWFORD *UK, male vocalist – Michael Dumble-Smith (14 WEEKS)* pos/wks

10 Jan 87 ● **THE MUSIC OF THE NIGHT** *Polydor POSP 803*..........7 11
15 Jan 94 **THE MUSIC OF THE NIGHT** *Columbia 6597382* [1]..........54 3

[1] Barbra Streisand (duet with Michael Crawford)

The flip side of POSP 803 – 'Wishing You Were Somehow Here Again' by Sarah Brightman – was also listed

Randy CRAWFORD (463 Top 500) *Soulful jazz-slanted song stylist, b. 18 Feb 1952, Georgia, US. Has surprisingly proved more successful in Europe than her homeland, where she has yet to crack the pop Top 100. Winner of Brits Best Female Artist award in 1982 (75 WEEKS)* pos/wks

21 Jun 80 **LAST NIGHT AT DANCELAND** *Warner Bros. K 17631*..........61 2

Date		Title / Label	pos	wks
30 Aug 80	●	**ONE DAY I'LL FLY AWAY** *Warner Bros. K 17680*	2	11
30 May 81		**YOU MIGHT NEED SOMEBODY** *Warner Bros. K 17803*	11	13
8 Aug 81		**RAINY NIGHT IN GEORGIA** *Warner Bros. K 17840*	18	9
31 Oct 81		**SECRET COMBINATION** *Warner Bros. K 17872*	48	3
30 Jan 82		**IMAGINE** *Warner Bros. K 17906*	60	1
13 Feb 82		**IMAGINE (re-entry)** *Warner Bros. K 17906*	75	1
5 Jun 82		**ONE HELLO** *Warner Bros. K 17948*	48	4
19 Feb 83		**HE REMINDS ME** *Warner Bros. K 17970*	65	2
8 Oct 83		**NIGHT LINE** *Warner Bros. W 9530*	51	4
29 Nov 86	●	**ALMAZ** *Warner Bros. W 8583*	4	17
18 Jan 92		**DIAMANTE** *London LON 313* [1]	44	7
15 Nov 97		**GIVE ME THE NIGHT** *WEA WEA 142CD*	60	1

[1] Zucchero with Randy Crawford

See also CRUSADERS

Robert CRAY BAND *US, male vocal / instrumental group (5 WEEKS)* pos/wks

Date		Title / Label	pos	wks
20 Jun 87		**RIGHT NEXT DOOR (BECAUSE OF ME)** *Mercury CRAY 3*	50	4
20 Apr 96		**BABY LEE** *Silvertone ORECD 81* [1]	65	1

[1] John Lee Hooker with Robert Cray

CRAZY ELEPHANT *US, male vocal group (13 WEEKS)* pos/wks

Date		Title / Label	pos	wks
21 May 69		**GIMME GIMME GOOD LOVIN'** *Major Minor MM 609*	12	13

CRAZY TOWN *US, male vocal / rap / instrumental group (18 WEEKS)* pos/wks

Date		Title / Label	pos	wks
7 Apr 01	●	**BUTTERFLY** *Columbia 6710012* ▲	3	13
11 Aug 01		**REVOLVING DOOR** *Columbia 6714942*	23	5

CRAZYHEAD *UK, male vocal / instrumental group (4 WEEKS)* pos/wks

Date		Title / Label	pos	wks
16 Jul 88		**TIME HAS TAKEN ITS TOLL ON YOU** *Food FOOD 12*	65	2
25 Feb 89		**HAVE LOVE, WILL TRAVEL (EP)** *Food SGE 2025*	68	2

Tracks on Have Love, Will Travel (EP): Have Love Will Travel / Out on a Limb (Live) / Baby Turpentine (Live) / Snake Eyes (Live)

CREAM *UK, male vocal / instrumental group (59 WEEKS)* pos/wks

Date		Title / Label	pos	wks
20 Oct 66		**WRAPPING PAPER** *Reaction 591 007*	34	6
15 Dec 66		**I FEEL FREE** *Reaction 591 011*	11	12
8 Jun 67		**STRANGE BREW** *Reaction 591 015*	17	9
5 Jun 68		**ANYONE FOR TENNIS (THE SAVAGE SEVEN THEME)** *Polydor 56 258*	40	3
9 Oct 68		**SUNSHINE OF YOUR LOVE** *Polydor 56 286*	25	7
15 Jan 69		**WHITE ROOM** *Polydor 56 300*	28	8
9 Apr 69		**BADGE** *Polydor 56 315*	18	10
28 Oct 72		**BADGE (re-issue)** *Polydor 2058 285*	42	4

See also Eric CLAPTON

CREATION *UK, male vocal / instrumental group (3 WEEKS)* pos/wks

Date		Title / Label	pos	wks
7 Jul 66		**MAKING TIME** *Planet PLF 116*	49	1
3 Nov 66		**PAINTER MAN** *Planet PLF 119*	36	2

CREATURES

UK, male / female vocal / instrumental group (27 WEEKS) pos/wks

Date		Title / Label	pos	wks
3 Oct 81		**MAD EYED SCREAMER** *Polydor POSPD 354*	24	7
23 Apr 83		**MISS THE GIRL** *Wonderland SHE 1*	21	7
16 Jul 83		**RIGHT NOW** *Wonderland SHE 2*	14	10
14 Oct 89		**STANDING THERE** *Wonderland SHE 17*	53	2
27 Mar 99		**SAY** *Sioux SIOUX 6CD*	72	1

See also SIOUXSIE and the BANSHEES

CREDIT TO THE NATION *UK, male rap group (11 WEEKS)* pos/wks

Date		Title / Label	pos	wks
22 May 93		**CALL IT WHAT YOU WANT** *One Little Indian 94 TP7CD*	57	3
18 Sep 93		**ENOUGH IS ENOUGH** *One Little Indian 79 TP7CD* [1]	56	2
12 Mar 94		**TEENAGE SENSATION** *One Little Indian 124 TP7CD*	24	3
14 May 94		**SOWING THE SEEDS OF HATRED** *One Little Indian 134 TP7CD*	72	1
22 Jul 95		**LIAR LIAR** *One Little Indian 144 TP7CD*	60	1
12 Sep 98		**TACKY LOVE SONG** *Chrysalis CDCHS 5097*	60	1

[1] Chumbawamba and Credit to the Nation

CREED *US, male vocal / instrumental group (7 WEEKS)* pos/wks

Date		Title / Label	pos	wks
15 Jan 00		**HIGHER** *Epic 6683152*	47	1
20 Jan 01		**WITH ARMS WIDE OPEN** *Epic 6706952* ▲	13	5
29 Sep 01		**HIGHER (re-issue)** *Epic 6710642*	64	1

CREEDENCE CLEARWATER REVIVAL (327 Top 500) *Internationally successful combo who cleverly created original songs with 50s rock 'n' roll feel, fronted by John Fogerty b. 28 May 1945, California, US. Voted World's Top Group in UK Polls 1970/71 (beating The Beatles and The Rolling Stones) (94 WEEKS)* pos/wks

Date		Title / Label	pos	wks
28 May 69	●	**PROUD MARY** *Liberty LBF 15223*	8	13
16 Aug 69	★	**BAD MOON RISING** *Liberty LBF 15230*	1	15
15 Nov 69		**GREEN RIVER** *Liberty LBF 15250*	19	11
14 Feb 70		**DOWN ON THE CORNER** *Liberty LBF 15283*	31	6
4 Apr 70	●	**TRAVELLIN' BAND** *Liberty LBF 15310*	8	12
20 Jun 70	●	**UP AROUND THE BEND** *Liberty LBF 15354*	3	12
4 Jul 70		**TRAVELLIN' BAND (re-entry)** *Liberty LBF 15310*	46	1
5 Sep 70		**LONG AS I CAN SEE THE LIGHT** *Liberty LBF 15384*	20	9
20 Mar 71		**HAVE YOU EVER SEEN THE RAIN** *Liberty LBF 15440*	36	6
24 Jul 71		**SWEET HITCH-HIKER** *United Artists UP 35261*	36	8
2 May 92		**BAD MOON RISING (re-issue)** *Epic 6580047*	71	1

Kid CREOLE and the COCONUTS

US, male vocalist and female vocal group (58 WEEKS) pos/wks

Date		Title / Label	pos	wks
13 Jun 81		**ME NO POP I** *Ze WIP 6711* [1]	32	7
15 May 82	●	**I'M A WONDERFUL THING, BABY** *Ze WIP 6756*	4	11
24 Jul 82	●	**STOOL PIGEON** *Ze WIP 6793*	7	9
9 Oct 82	●	**ANNIE I'M NOT YOUR DADDY** *Ze WIP 6801*	2	8
11 Dec 82		**DEAR ADDY** *Ze WIP 6840*	29	7
10 Sep 83		**THERE'S SOMETHING WRONG IN PARADISE** *Island IS 130*	35	5
19 Nov 83		**THE LIFEBOAT PARTY** *Island IS 142*	49	4
14 Apr 90		**THE SEX OF IT** *CBS 655698 7*	29	5
10 Apr 93		**I'M A WONDERFUL THING BABY (re-mix)** *Island CID 551*	60	2

[1] Kid Creole and the Coconuts present Coati Mundi

See also COCONUTS

CRESCENDO *UK / US, male / female vocal / instrumental duo – Serena and Steve Hitchcock (5 WEEKS)* pos/wks

Date		Title / Label	pos	wks
23 Dec 95		**ARE YOU OUT THERE** *ffrr FCD 270*	20	5

CRESTERS – *See Mike SAGAR*

CREW CUTS *Canada, male vocal group (29 WEEKS)* pos/wks

Date		Title / Label	pos	wks
1 Oct 54		**SH-BOOM** *Mercury MB 3140* ▲	12	9
15 Apr 55	●	**EARTH ANGEL** *Mercury MB 3202*	4	20

Bernard CRIBBINS *UK, male actor (29 WEEKS)* pos/wks

Date		Title / Label	pos	wks
15 Feb 62	●	**HOLE IN THE GROUND** *Parlophone R 4869*	9	13
5 Jul 62	●	**RIGHT SAID FRED** *Parlophone R 4923*	10	10
13 Dec 62		**GOSSIP CALYPSO** *Parlophone R 4961*	25	6

CRICKETS (316 Top 500) *Band that originally featured Buddy Holly formed in Lubbock, Texas, US, best known members being Jerry Allison (d), Joe B Mauldin (b) and Sonny Curtis (g/v). Without Holly they recorded original versions of Top 10 hits 'I Fought The Law', 'Someone Someone', 'When You Ask About Love' and 'More Than I Can Say' (97 WEEKS)* pos/wks

Date		Title / Label	pos	wks
27 Sep 57	★	**THAT'LL BE THE DAY** *Vogue Coral Q 72279* ▲	1	14
27 Dec 57	●	**OH BOY** *Coral Q 72298*	3	15
10 Jan 58		**THAT'LL BE THE DAY (re-entry)** *Vogue Coral Q 72279*	29	1
14 Mar 58	●	**MAYBE BABY** *Coral Q 72307*	4	10
25 Jul 58		**THINK IT OVER** *Coral Q 72329*	11	7
24 Apr 59		**LOVE'S MADE A FOOL OF YOU** *Coral Q 72365*	26	1
8 May 59		**LOVE'S MADE A FOOL OF YOU (re-entry)** *Coral Q 72365*	30	1
15 Jan 60		**WHEN YOU ASK ABOUT LOVE** *Coral Q 72382*	27	1
12 May 60		**MORE THAN I CAN SAY** *Coral Q 72395*	42	1
26 May 60		**BABY MY HEART** *Coral Q 72395*	33	4
21 Jun 62	●	**DON'T EVER CHANGE** *Liberty LIB 55441*	5	13
24 Jan 63		**MY LITTLE GIRL** *Liberty LIB 10067*	17	9
6 Jun 63		**DON'T TRY TO CHANGE ME** *Liberty LIB 10092*	37	4

14 May 64	YOU'VE GOT LOVE *Coral Q 72472* [1]	40	6
2 Jul 64	(THEY CALL HER) LA BAMBA *Liberty LIB 55696*	21	10

[1] Buddy Holly and the Crickets

Although not credited on the records, Buddy Holly was featured on the first four hits

CRIMINAL ELEMENT ORCHESTRA – *See Wally JUMP Jr and the CRIMINAL ELEMENT*

CRISPY AND COMPANY
US, male vocal / instrumental group (11 WEEKS) pos/wks

16 Aug 75	BRAZIL *Creole CR 109*	26	5
27 Dec 75	GET IT TOGETHER *Creole CR 114*	21	6

CRITTERS *US, male vocal / instrumental group (5 WEEKS)* pos/wks

30 Jun 66	YOUNGER GIRL *London HL 10047*	38	5

Tony CROMBIE and his ROCKETS *UK, male vocal / instrumental group, Tony Crombie – drums (2 WEEKS)* pos/wks

19 Oct 56	TEACH YOU TO ROCK / SHORT'NIN' BREAD *Columbia DB 3822*	25	2

Bing CROSBY (319 Top 500) *The King of the Crooners. Bing released 2,500 tracks, 299 of which reached the US Top 20 (1931-1961) with estimated sales of more than 300,000,000, b. 3 May 1903, Washington, US, d.14 Oct 1977, Spain. 'White Christmas' (the most charted single in the US) is the No.2 all-time best-seller (97 WEEKS)* pos/wks

14 Nov 52 ●	THE ISLE OF INNISFREE *Brunswick 04900*	3	12
5 Dec 52 ●	ZING A LITTLE ZONG *Brunswick 04981* [1]	10	2
19 Dec 52 ●	SILENT NIGHT, HOLY NIGHT *Brunswick 03929*	8	2
19 Mar 54 ●	CHANGING PARTNERS *Brunswick 05244*	10	1
2 Apr 54 ●	CHANGING PARTNERS (re-entry) *Brunswick 05244*	9	1
23 Apr 54	CHANGING PARTNERS (2nd re-entry) *Brunswick 05244*	11	1
7 Jan 55	COUNT YOUR BLESSINGS INSTEAD OF SHEEP *Brunswick 05339*	18	1
21 Jan 55	COUNT YOUR BLESSINGS INSTEAD OF SHEEP (re-entry) *Brunswick 05339*	11	2
29 Apr 55	STRANGER IN PARADISE *Brunswick 05410*	17	2
27 Apr 56	IN A LITTLE SPANISH TOWN *Brunswick 05543*	22	3
23 Nov 56 ●	TRUE LOVE *Capitol CL 14645* [2]	4	27
24 May 57 ●	AROUND THE WORLD *Brunswick 05674*	5	15
9 Aug 75	THAT'S WHAT LIFE IS ALL ABOUT *United Artists UP 35852*	41	4
3 Dec 77 ●	WHITE CHRISTMAS *MCA 111* ◆ ▲	5	7
27 Nov 82 ●	PEACE ON EARTH – LITTLE DRUMMER BOY *RCA BOW 12* [3]	3	8
17 Dec 83	TRUE LOVE (re-issue) *Capitol CL 315* [2]	70	3
21 Dec 85	WHITE CHRISTMAS (re-issue) *MCA BING 1*	69	2
19 Dec 98	WHITE CHRISTMAS (2nd re-issue) *MCA MCSRD 48105*	29	4

[1] Bing Crosby and Jane Wyman [2] Bing Crosby and Grace Kelly [3] David Bowie and Bing Crosby

David CROSBY featuring Phil COLLINS
US / UK, male vocalist / instrumentalists (3 WEEKS) pos/wks

15 May 93	HERO *Atlantic A 7360*	56	3

See also CROSBY, STILLS, NASH and YOUNG; Phil COLLINS

CROSBY, STILLS, NASH and YOUNG
US / UK / Canada, male vocal / instrumental group (12 WEEKS) pos/wks

16 Aug 69	MARRAKESH EXPRESS *Atlantic 584 283* [1]	17	9
21 Jan 89	AMERICAN DREAM *Atlantic A 9003*	55	3

[1] Crosby, Stills and Nash

See also Stephen STILLS; Neil YOUNG; David CROSBY featuring Phil COLLINS

CROSS *UK / US, male vocal / instrumental group (1 WEEK)* pos/wks

17 Oct 87	COWBOYS AND INDIANS *Virgin VS 1007*	74	1

Christopher CROSS
US, male vocalist – Christopher Geppert (27 WEEKS) pos/wks

19 Apr 80	RIDE LIKE THE WIND *Warner Bros. K 17582*	69	1
14 Feb 81	SAILING *Warner Bros. K 17695* ▲	48	6
17 Oct 81	ARTHUR'S THEME (BEST THAT YOU CAN DO) *Warner Bros. K 17847* ▲	56	4
9 Jan 82 ●	ARTHUR'S THEME (BEST THAT YOU CAN DO) (re-entry) *Warner Bros. K 17847*	7	11
5 Feb 83	ALL RIGHT *Warner Bros. W 9843*	51	5

CROW *Germany, male production duo – David Rzenno and David Nothroff (1 WEEK)* pos/wks

19 May 01	WHAT YA LOOKIN' AT *Tidy Trax TIDY 153CD*	60	1

Sheryl CROW (449 Top 500) *Multi-Grammy-winning pop singer / songwriter born 11 Feb 1962, Missouri, US. The one-time backing singer for Michael Jackson and George Harrison became the first US female soloist to score six UK hits off debut LP (1993's Tuesday Night Music Club) (77 WEEKS)* pos/wks

18 Jun 94	LEAVING LAS VEGAS *A & M 5806472*	66	1
5 Nov 94 ●	ALL I WANNA DO *A & M 5808452*	4	13
11 Feb 95	STRONG ENOUGH *A & M 5809212*	33	4
27 May 95	CAN'T CRY ANYMORE *A & M 5810552*	33	3
29 Jul 95	RUN BABY RUN *A & M 5811492*	24	4
11 Nov 95	WHAT I CAN DO FOR YOU *A & M 5812292*	43	1
21 Sep 96 ●	IF IT MAKES YOU HAPPY *A & M 5819032*	9	6
30 Nov 96	EVERYDAY IS A WINDING ROAD *A & M 5820232*	12	6
29 Mar 97	HARD TO MAKE A STAND *A & M 5821492*	22	3
12 Jul 97 ●	A CHANGE WOULD DO YOU GOOD *A & M 5822092*	8	5
18 Oct 97	HOME *A & M 0440312*	25	2
13 Dec 97	TOMORROW NEVER DIES *A & M 5824572*	12	9
12 Sep 98 ●	MY FAVORITE MISTAKE *Polydor 5827632*	9	6
5 Dec 98	THERE GOES THE NEIGHBORHOOD *A&M 5828092*	19	7
6 Mar 99	ANYTHING BUT DOWN *A&M / Polydor 5828272*	19	4
11 Sep 99	SWEET CHILD O' MINE *Columbia 6678882*	30	3

CROWD *International, male / female vocal / instrumental charity assembly (11 WEEKS)* pos/wks

1 Jun 85 ★	YOU'LL NEVER WALK ALONE *Spartan BRAD 1*	1	11

CROWDED HOUSE *New Zealand / Australia, male vocal / instrumental group (64 WEEKS)* pos/wks

6 Jun 87	DON'T DREAM IT'S OVER *Capitol CL 438*	27	8
22 Jun 91	CHOCOLATE CAKE *Capitol CL 618*	69	2
2 Nov 91	FALL AT YOUR FEET *Capitol CL 626*	17	7
29 Feb 92 ●	WEATHER WITH YOU *Capitol CL 643*	7	9
20 Jun 92	FOUR SEASONS IN ONE DAY *Capitol CL 655*	26	5
26 Sep 92	IT'S ONLY NATURAL *Capitol CL 661*	24	4
2 Oct 93	DISTANT SUN *Capitol CDCLS 697*	19	6
20 Nov 93	NAILS IN MY FEET *Capitol CDCLS 701*	22	4
19 Feb 94	LOCKED OUT *Capitol CDCLS 707*	12	4
11 Jun 94	FINGERS OF LOVE *Capitol CDCLS 715*	25	3
24 Sep 94	PINEAPPLE HEAD *Capitol CDCLS 723*	27	3
22 Jun 96	INSTINCT *Capitol CDCLS 774*	12	4
17 Aug 96	NOT THE GIRL YOU THINK YOU ARE *Capitol CDCLS 776*	20	3
9 Nov 96	DON'T DREAM IT'S OVER (re-issue) *Capitol CDCL 780*	25	2

See also FINN; Neil FINN; Tim FINN

CROWN HEIGHTS AFFAIR
US, male vocal / instrumental group (34 WEEKS) pos/wks

19 Aug 78	GALAXY OF LOVE *Mercury 6168 801*	24	10
11 Nov 78	I'M GONNA LOVE YOU FOREVER *Mercury 6168 803*	47	4
14 Apr 79	DANCE LADY DANCE *Mercury 6168 804*	44	4
3 May 80 ●	YOU GAVE ME LOVE *De-Lite MER 9*	10	12
9 Aug 80	YOU'VE BEEN GONE *De-Lite MER 28*	44	4

Julee CRUISE *US, female vocalist (14 WEEKS)* pos/wks

10 Nov 90 ●	FALLING *Warner Bros. W 9544*	7	11
2 Mar 91	ROCKIN' BACK INSIDE MY HEART *Warner Bros. W 0004*	66	2
11 Sep 99	IF I SURVIVE *Distinctive DISNCD 55* [1]	52	1

[1] Hybrid featuring Julee Cruise

CRUISERS – *See Dave BERRY*

CRUSADERS *US, male vocal / instrumental group (16 WEEKS)* pos/wks

Date		Title	Pos	Wks
18 Aug 79	●	**STREET LIFE** *MCA 513*	5	11
26 Sep 81		**I'M SO GLAD I'M STANDING HERE TODAY** *MCA 741* [1]	61	3
7 Apr 84		**NIGHT LADIES** *MCA MCA 853*	55	2

[1] Crusaders, featured vocalist Joe Cocker

Vocalist on 'Street Life' was Randy Crawford, though uncredited

CRUSH *UK, female vocal duo (3 WEEKS)* pos/wks

Date		Title	Pos	Wks
24 Feb 96		**JELLYHEAD** *Telstar CDSTAS 2809*	50	2
3 Aug 96		**LUV'D UP** *Telstar CDSTAS 2833*	45	1

Bobby CRUSH *UK, male instrumentalist – piano (4 WEEKS)* pos/wks

Date		Title	Pos	Wks
4 Nov 72		**BORSALINO** *Philips 6006 248*	37	4

CRW *Italy, male producer – Mauro Picotto (6 WEEKS)* pos/wks

Date		Title	Pos	Wks
26 Feb 00		**I FEEL LOVE** *VC Recordings VCRD 63*	15	4
25 Nov 00		**LOVIN'** *VC Recordings VCRD 77*	49	2

See also Mauro PICOTTO

CRY BEFORE DAWN *Ireland, male vocal / instrumental group (2 WEEKS)* pos/wks

Date		Title	Pos	Wks
17 Jun 89		**WITNESS FOR THE WORLD** *Epic GONE 3*	67	2

CRY OF LOVE *US, male / female vocal / instrumental group (1 WEEK)* pos/wks

Date		Title	Pos	Wks
15 Jan 94		**BAD THING** *Columbia 6600462*	60	1

CRY SISCO! *UK, male producer – Barry Blue (9 WEEKS)* pos/wks

Date		Title	Pos	Wks
2 Sep 89		**AFRO DIZZI ACT** *Escape AWOL 1*	42	8
20 Jan 90		**AFRO DIZZI ACT (re-entry)** *Escape AWOL 1*	70	1

See also Barry BLUE

CRYIN' SHAMES *UK, male vocal / instrumental group (7 WEEKS)* pos/wks

Date		Title	Pos	Wks
31 Mar 66		**PLEASE STAY** *Decca F 12340*	26	7

CRYPT-KICKERS – *See Bobby 'Boris' PICKETT and the CRYPT-KICKERS*

CRYSTAL METHOD *US, male instrumental duo (4 WEEKS)* pos/wks

Date		Title	Pos	Wks
11 Oct 97		**(CAN YOU) TRIP LIKE I DO** *Epic 6650862* [1]	39	2
7 Mar 98		**KEEP HOPE ALIVE** *Sony S2 CM 3CD*	71	1
8 Aug 98		**COMIN' BACK** *Sony S2 CM 4CD*	73	1

[1] Filter and The Crystal Method

CRYSTAL PALACE WITH THE FAB FOUR *UK, male football team vocalists and UK male group (2 WEEKS)* pos/wks

Date		Title	Pos	Wks
12 May 90		**GLAD ALL OVER / WHERE EAGLES FLY** *Parkfield PMS 5019*	50	2

CRYSTALS *US, female vocal group (54 WEEKS)* pos/wks

Date		Title	Pos	Wks
22 Nov 62		**HE'S A REBEL** *London HLU 9611* ▲	19	13
20 Jun 63	●	**DA DOO RON RON** *London HLU 9732*	5	16
19 Sep 63	●	**THEN HE KISSED ME** *London HLU 9773*	2	14
5 Mar 64		**I WONDER** *London HLU 9852*	36	3
19 Oct 74		**DA DOO RON RON (re-issue)** *Warner Spector K 19010*	15	8

CSILLA *Hungary, female vocalist (1 WEEK)* pos/wks

Date		Title	Pos	Wks
13 Jul 96		**MAN IN THE MOON** *Worx WORXCD 001*	69	1

CUBAN BOYS *UK, male / female production group (9 WEEKS)* pos/wks

Date		Title	Pos	Wks
25 Dec 99	●	**COGNOSCENTI VS INTELLIGENTSIA** *EMI CDCUBAN 001*	4	7
19 Feb 00		**COGNOSCENTI VS INTELLIGENTSIA (re-entry)** *EMI CDCUBAN 001*	58	2

CUBIC 22 *Belgium, male instrumental / production duo – Peter Ramson and Danny Van Wauwe (7 WEEKS)* pos/wks

Date		Title	Pos	Wks
22 Jun 91		**NIGHT IN MOTION** *XL Recordings XLS 20*	15	7

See also AIRSCAPE; BLUE BAMBOO; TRANSFORMER 2

CUD *UK, male vocal / instrumental group (16 WEEKS)* pos/wks

Date		Title	Pos	Wks
19 Oct 91		**OH NO WON'T DO (EP)** *A & M AMB 829*	49	2
28 Mar 92		**THROUGH THE ROOF** *A & M AM 857*	44	2
30 May 92		**RICH AND STRANGE** *A & M AM 871*	24	3
15 Aug 92		**PURPLE LOVE BALLOON** *A & M AM 0024*	27	3
10 Oct 92		**ONCE AGAIN** *A & M AM 0081*	45	1
12 Feb 94		**NEUROTICA** *A & M 5805172*	37	2
2 Apr 94		**STICKS AND STONES** *A & M 5805472*	68	1
3 Sep 94		**ONE GIANT LOVE** *A & M 5807292*	52	2

Tracks on Oh No Won't Do (EP): Oh No Won't Do / Profession / Ariel / Price of Love

CUFFLINKS *US, male vocal group, leader – Ron Dante (30 WEEKS)* pos/wks

Date		Title	Pos	Wks
29 Nov 69	●	**TRACY** *MCA MU 1101*	4	16
14 Mar 70	●	**WHEN JULIE COMES AROUND** *MCA MU 1112*	10	14

See also ARCHIES

CULT (419 Top 500) *UK gothic rock stars who became US heavy rock heroes previously recorded as Southern Death Cult and Death Cult. West Yorkshire band's constant members Ian Astbury (v) and Billy Duffy (g). Group, who relocated to US in 1988, topped the UK album chart with hits collection in 1993 (80 WEEKS)* pos/wks

Date		Title	Pos	Wks
22 Dec 84		**RESURRECTION JOE** *Beggars Banquet BEG 122*	74	2
25 May 85		**SHE SELLS SANCTUARY** *Beggars Banquet BEG 135*	15	17
28 Sep 85		**SHE SELLS SANCTUARY (re-entry)** *Beggars Banquet BEG 135*	61	2
5 Oct 85		**RAIN** *Beggars Banquet BEG 147*	17	8
30 Nov 85		**REVOLUTION** *Beggars Banquet BEG 152*	30	7
28 Feb 87		**LOVE REMOVAL MACHINE** *Beggars Banquet BEG 182*	18	7
2 May 87		**LIL' DEVIL** *Beggars Banquet BEG 188*	11	7
22 Aug 87		**WILD FLOWER (DOUBLE SINGLE)** *Beggars Banquet BEG 195D*	24	2
29 Aug 87		**WILD FLOWER** *Beggars Banquet BEG 195*	30	4
1 Apr 89		**FIRE WOMAN** *Beggars Banquet BEG 228*	15	4
8 Jul 89		**EDIE (CIAO BABY)** *Beggars Banquet BEG 230*	32	5
18 Nov 89		**SUN KING / EDIE (CIAO BABY) (re-issue)** *Beggars Banquet BEG 235*	39	2
10 Mar 90		**SWEET SOUL SISTER** *Beggars Banquet BEG 241*	42	4
14 Sep 91		**WILD HEARTED SON** *Beggars Banquet BEG 255*	40	2
29 Feb 92		**HEART OF SOUL** *Beggars Banquet BEG 260*	51	1
30 Jan 93		**SHE SELLS SANCTUARY (re-mix)** *Beggars Banquet BEG 253CD*	15	4
8 Oct 94		**COMING DOWN** *Beggars Banquet BBQ 40CD*	50	1
7 Jan 95		**STAR** *Beggars Banquet BBQ 45CD*	65	1

Tracks on double single: Wild Flower / Love Trooper / Outlaw (live) / Horse Nation (live)

CULT JAM – *See LISA LISA*

Smiley CULTURE *UK, male vocalist – David Emanuel (13 WEEKS)* pos/wks

Date		Title	Pos	Wks
15 Dec 84		**POLICE OFFICER** *Fashion FAD 7012*	12	10
6 Apr 85		**COCKNEY TRANSLATION** *Fashion FAD 7028*	71	1
13 Sep 86		**SCHOOLTIME CHRONICLE** *Polydor POSP 815*	59	2

CULTURE BEAT *UK / US / Germany, male / female vocal / instrumental group (46 WEEKS)* pos/wks

Date		Title	Pos	Wks
3 Feb 90		**CHERRY LIPS (DER ERDBEERMUND)** *Epic 6556337*	55	3
7 Aug 93	★	**MR VAIN** *Epic 6594682*	1	15
6 Nov 93	●	**GOT TO GET IT** *Epic 6597212*	4	11
15 Jan 94	●	**ANYTHING** *Epic 6600252*	5	8
2 Apr 94		**WORLD IN YOUR HANDS** *Epic 6602292*	20	4
27 Jan 96		**INSIDE OUT** *Epic 6626562*	32	2
15 Jun 96		**CRYING IN THE RAIN** *Epic 6633582*	29	2
28 Sep 96		**TAKE ME AWAY** *Epic 6637552*	52	1

THE OFFICIAL UK SINGLES CHART 50TH ANNIVERSARY

1962

IN THE YEAR IN WHICH MARILYN MONROE WAS FOUND DEAD IN HER BED AFTER OVERDOSING ON SLEEPING PILLS, THE CUBAN MISSILE CRISIS WAS PEACEFULLY RESOLVED, ANDY WARHOL INVENTED POP ART AND DECCA RECORDS TURNED DOWN THE BEATLES AND SIGNED BRIAN POOLE AND THE TREMELOES INSTEAD, **MARIANNE FAITHFULL** TAKES HER MUM SHOPPING FOR HER FIRST SINGLE ...

“The first record I remember buying was 'Venus in Blue Jeans' – who was it by? **Mark Wynter**? I think I was in my early teens. I made my mother go with me to the record shop in Reading town centre and buy it for me.”

SINGLE OF THE YEAR 'Wonderful Land' Shadows
ALBUM OF THE YEAR 'Blue Hawaii' Elvis Presley

CULTURE CLUB (229 Top 500) *Internationally successful London-based quartet, whose flamboyant lead singer, Boy George (b. George O'Dowd, 14 Jun 1961, Kent), attracted considerable media attention. In 1984, they won both Brit (Best Group) and Grammy Awards (Best New Artist). Original members reunited for late 1990s tours (119 WEEKS)* pos/wks

18 Sep 82 ★	DO YOU REALLY WANT TO HURT ME *Virgin VS 518*	1	18
27 Nov 82 ●	TIME (CLOCK OF THE HEART) *Virgin VS 558*	3	12
9 Apr 83 ●	CHURCH OF THE POISON MIND *Virgin VS 571*	2	9
17 Sep 83 ★	KARMA CHAMELEON *Virgin VS 612* ◆ ▲	1	20
10 Dec 83 ●	VICTIMS *Virgin VS 641*	3	10
24 Mar 84 ●	IT'S A MIRACLE *Virgin VS 662*	4	9
6 Oct 84 ●	THE WAR SONG *Virgin VS 694*	2	8
1 Dec 84	THE MEDAL SONG *Virgin VS 730*	32	4
5 Jan 85	THE MEDAL SONG (re-entry) *Virgin VS 730*	74	1
15 Mar 86 ●	MOVE AWAY *Virgin VS 845*	7	7
31 May 86	GOD THANK YOU WOMAN *Virgin VS 861*	31	5
31 Oct 98 ●	I JUST WANNA BE LOVED *Virgin VSCDT 1710*	4	10
7 Aug 99	YOUR KISSES ARE CHARITY *Virgin VSCDT 1736*	25	4
27 Nov 99	COLD SHOULDER / STARMAN *Virgin VSCDT 1758*	43	2

See also BOY GEORGE

Larry CUNNINGHAM and the MIGHTY AVONS
Ireland, male vocal / instrumental group (11 WEEKS) pos/wks

10 Dec 64	TRIBUTE TO JIM REEVES *King KG 1016*	40	8
25 Feb 65	TRIBUTE TO JIM REEVES (re-entry) *King KG 1016*	46	3

CUPID'S INSPIRATION
UK, male vocal / instrumental group (19 WEEKS) pos/wks

19 Jun 68 ●	YESTERDAY HAS GONE *Nems 56 3500*	4	11
2 Oct 68	MY WORLD *Nems 56 3702*	33	8

CURE (162 Top 500) *Goth rock giants: Robert Smith (v/g), Lol Tolhurst (k), Simon Gallup (b), Porl Thompson (g), Boris Williams (d), who went from UK cult heroes to stadium-packing supergroup. Voted Best Group at 1991 Brit Awards (145 WEEKS)* pos/wks

12 Apr 80	A FOREST *Fiction FICS 10*	31	8
4 Apr 81	PRIMARY *Fiction FICS 12*	43	6
17 Oct 81	CHARLOTTE SOMETIMES *Fiction FICS 14*	44	4
24 Jul 82	HANGING GARDEN *Fiction FICS 15*	34	4
27 Nov 82	LET'S GO TO BED *Fiction FICS 17*	44	4
8 Jan 83	LET'S GO TO BED (re-entry) *Fiction FICS 17*	75	1
9 Jul 83	THE WALK *Fiction FICS 18*	12	8
29 Oct 83 ●	THE LOVE CATS *Fiction FICS 19*	7	11
7 Apr 84	THE CATERPILLAR *Fiction FICS 20*	14	7
27 Jul 85	IN BETWEEN DAYS *Fiction FICS 22*	15	10
21 Sep 85	CLOSE TO ME *Fiction FICS 23*	24	8
3 May 86	BOYS DON'T CRY *Fiction FICS 24*	22	6
18 Apr 87	WHY CAN'T I BE YOU? *Fiction FICS 25*	21	5
4 Jul 87	CATCH *Fiction FICS 26*	27	6
17 Oct 87	JUST LIKE HEAVEN *Fiction FICS 27*	29	5
20 Feb 88	HOT HOT HOT!!! *Fiction FICSX 28*	45	3
22 Apr 89 ●	LULLABY *Fiction FICS 29*	5	6
2 Sep 89	LOVESONG *Fiction FICS 30*	18	7
31 Mar 90	PICTURES OF YOU *Fiction FICS 34*	24	6
29 Sep 90	NEVER ENOUGH *Fiction FICS 35*	13	5
3 Nov 90	CLOSE TO ME (re-mix) *Fiction FICS 36*	13	5
28 Mar 92 ●	HIGH *Fiction FICS 39*	8	3
11 Apr 92	HIGH (re-mix) *Fiction FICSX 41*	44	1
23 May 92 ●	FRIDAY I'M IN LOVE *Fiction FICS 42*	6	7
17 Oct 92	A LETTER TO ELISE *Fiction FICS 46*	28	2
4 May 96	THE 13TH *Fiction 5764692*	15	2
29 Jun 96	MINT CAR *Fiction FISCD 52*	31	2
14 Dec 96	GONE *Fiction FICD 53*	60	1
29 Nov 97	WRONG NUMBER *Fiction FICD 54*	62	1
10 Nov 01	CUT HERE *Fiction 5873892*	54	1

See also GLOVE

CURIOSITY *UK, male vocal / instrumental group (58 WEEKS)* pos/wks

13 Dec 86 ●	DOWN TO EARTH *Mercury CAT 2* [1]	3	18
4 Apr 87	ORDINARY DAY *Mercury CAT 3* [1]	11	7
20 Jun 87 ●	MISFIT *Mercury CAT 4* [1]	7	9
19 Sep 87	FREE *Mercury CAT 5* [1]	56	2
16 Sep 89	NAME AND NUMBER *Mercury CAT 6*	14	9
25 Apr 92 ●	HANG ON IN THERE BABY *RCA PB 45377*	3	10
29 Aug 92	I NEED YOUR LOVIN' *RCA 74321111377*	47	2
30 Oct 93	GIMME THE SUNSHINE *RCA 74321168602*	73	1

[1] Curiosity Killed the Cat

CURLS – *See Paul EVANS*

José CURA – *See Sarah BRIGHTMAN*

Mark CURRY – *See PUFF DADDY*

Chantal CURTIS *France, female vocalist (3 WEEKS)* pos/wks

14 Jul 79	GET ANOTHER LOVE *Pye 7P 5003*	51	3

TC CURTIS *Jamaica, male vocalist / instrumentalist (4 WEEKS)* pos/wks

23 Feb 85	YOU SHOULD HAVE KNOWN BETTER *Hot Melt VS 754*	50	4

CURVE *UK, male / female vocal / instrumental duo (14 WEEKS)* pos/wks

16 Mar 91	THE BLINDFOLD (EP) *AnXious ANX 27*	68	1
25 May 91	COAST IS CLEAR *AnXious ANX 30*	34	3
9 Nov 91	CLIPPED *AnXious ANX 35*	36	2
7 Mar 92	FAIT ACCOMPLI *AnXious ANXT 36*	22	3
18 Jul 92	HORROR HEAD (EP) *AnXious ANXT 38*	31	2
4 Sep 93	BLACKERTHREETRACKER (EP) *AnXious ANXCD 42*	39	2
16 May 98	COMING UP ROSES *Universal UND 80489*	51	1

Tracks on The Blindfold (EP): Ten Little Girls / I Speak Your Every Word / Blindfold / No Escape from Heaven. Tracks on Horror Head (EP): Horror Head / Falling Free / Mission from God / Today Is Not the Day. Only track available on all formats of Blackerthreetracker (EP): Missing Link

CURVED AIR *UK, male / female vocal / instrumental group (12 WEEKS)* pos/wks

7 Aug 71 ●	BACK STREET LUV *Warner Bros. K 16092*	4	12

CUT 'N' MOVE
Denmark, male / female vocal / instrumental group (4 WEEKS) pos/wks

2 Oct 93	GIVE IT UP *EMI CDEM 273*	61	2
9 Sep 95	I'M ALIVE *EMI CDEM 375*	49	2

Frankie CUTLASS *US, male rapper (1 WEEK)* pos/wks

5 Apr 97	THE CYPHER: PART 3 *Epic 6641445*	59	1

Adge CUTLER – *See WURZELS*

CUTTING CREW
UK / Canada, male vocal / instrumental group (37 WEEKS) pos/wks

16 Aug 86 ●	(I JUST) DIED IN YOUR ARMS *Siren SIREN 21* ▲	4	12
25 Oct 86	I'VE BEEN IN LOVE BEFORE *Siren SIREN 29*	31	9
10 Jan 87	I'VE BEEN IN LOVE BEFORE (re-entry) *Siren SIREN 29*	70	1
7 Mar 87	ONE FOR THE MOCKINGBIRD *Siren SIREN 40*	52	5
21 Nov 87	I'VE BEEN IN LOVE BEFORE (re-mix) *Siren SRN 29*	24	8
22 Jul 89	(BETWEEN A) ROCK AND A HARD PLACE *Siren SRN 108*	66	2

CYBERSONIK *US, male instrumentalist / producers (1 WEEK)* pos/wks

10 Nov 90	TECHNARCHY *Champion CHAMP 264*	73	1

CYGNUS X *Germany, male producer – A C Bousten (5 WEEKS)* pos/wks

11 Mar 00	THE ORANGE THEME *Hooj Choons HOOJ 88CD*	43	2
18 Aug 01	SUPERSTRING *Xtravaganza XTRAV 28CDS*	33	3

Johnny CYMBAL *Canada, male vocalist (10 WEEKS)* pos/wks

14 Mar 63	MR BASS MAN *London HLR 9682*	24	10

CYPRESS HILL *US, male rap group (43 WEEKS)*

Date		Title	pos	wks
31 Jul 93		**INSANE IN THE BRAIN** *Ruff House 6595332*	32	4
2 Oct 93		**WHEN THE SH.. GOES DOWN** *Ruff House 6596702*	19	4
11 Dec 93		**I AIN'T GOIN' OUT LIKE THAT** *Ruff House 6596902*	15	7
26 Feb 94		**INSANE IN THE BRAIN (re-issue)** *Ruff House 6601762*	21	4
7 May 94		**LICK A SHOT** *Ruff House 6603192*	20	3
7 Oct 95		**THROW YOUR SET IN THE AIR** *Ruff House 6623542*	15	3
17 Feb 96		**ILLUSIONS** *Columbia 6629052*	23	2
10 Oct 98		**TEQUILA SUNRISE** *Columbia 6664935*	23	2
10 Apr 99		**DR GREENTHUMB** *Columbia 6671202*	34	2
26 Jun 99		**INSANE IN THE BRAIN** *INCredible INCRL 17CD* [1]	19	3
29 Apr 00		**(RAP) SUPERSTAR / (ROCK) SUPERSTAR** *Columbia 6692642*	13	5
16 Sep 00		**HIGHLIFE / CAN'T GET THE BEST OF ME** *Columbia 6697892*	35	2
8 Dec 01		**LOWRIDER / TROUBLE** *Columbia 6721662*	33	2

[1] Jason Nevins vs Cypress Hill

Billy Ray CYRUS *US, male vocalist (18 WEEKS)*

Date		Title	pos	wks
25 Jul 92	●	**ACHY BREAKY HEART** *Mercury MER 373*	3	10
10 Oct 92		**COULD'VE BEEN ME** *Mercury MER 378*	24	4
28 Nov 92		**THESE BOOTS ARE MADE FOR WALKIN'** *Mercury MER 384*	63	1
19 Dec 92		**ACHY BREAKY HEART** *Epic 6588837* [1]	53	3

[1] Alvin and the Chipmunks featuring Billy Ray Cyrus

CZR featuring DELANO
US, male production group and US, male vocalist (1 WEEK)

Date		Title	pos	wks
30 Sep 00		**I WANT YOU** *Credence CDCRED 002*	57	1

D

Asher D – *See OBI Project*

Crissy D – *See B15 Project featuring Crissy D & Lady G*

Chuck D *US, male rapper - Carlton Ridenhour (22 WEEKS)*

Date		Title	pos	wks
6 Jul 91		**BRING THE NOISE** *Island IS 490* [1]	14	5
26 Oct 96		**NO** *Mercury MERCD 476*	55	1
2 Dec 00	●	**OPERATION BLADE (BASS IN THE PLACE)** *Xtrahard / Xtravaganza X2H1 CDS* [2]	5	13
23 Jun 01		**ROCK DA FUNKY BEATS** *Xtrahard / Xtravaganza X2H3 CDS* [2]	19	3

[1] Anthrax featuring Chuck D [2] Public Domain featuring Chuck D

Danny D – *See COOKIE CREW*

Dimples D *US, female rapper – Crystal Smith (10 WEEKS)*

Date		Title	pos	wks
17 Nov 90		**SUCKER DJ** *FBI FBI 11*	17	10

Longsy D *UK, male instrumentalist / producer (7 WEEKS)*

Date		Title	pos	wks
4 Mar 89		**THIS IS SKA** *Big One VBIG 13*	56	7

Maxwell D *UK, male rapper – Maxwell Donaldson (2 WEEKS)*

Date		Title	pos	wks
15 Sep 01		**SERIOUS** *4 Liberty LIBTCD 046*	38	2

Nikki D *US, female rapper (6 WEEKS)*

Date		Title	pos	wks
6 May 89		**MY LOVE IS SO RAW** *Def Jam 6548987* [1]	34	5
30 Mar 91		**DADDY'S LITTLE GIRL** *Def Jam 6567347*	75	1

[1] Alyson Williams featuring Nikki D

Vicky D *US, female vocalist (6 WEEKS)*

Date		Title	pos	wks
13 Mar 82		**THIS BEAT IS MINE** *Virgin VS 486*	42	6

D BO GENERAL – *See URBAN SHAKEDOWN*

D.O.S.E. – *See Mark E SMITH*

D:REAM (473 Top 500) *Uplifting pop / dance act featuring Ulster–born Peter Cunnah (v) and Scotsman Al Mackenzie (k) who left 1993. 'Things Can Only Get Better' (first three-time Top 30 entrant in the 1990s) used as theme for Labour Party's 1997 general election campaign (74 WEEKS)*

Date		Title	pos	wks
4 Jul 92		**U R THE BEST THING** *FXU FXU 3*	72	1
30 Jan 93		**THINGS CAN ONLY GET BETTER** *Magnet MAG 1010CD*	24	5
24 Apr 93		**U R THE BEST THING (re-issue)** *Magnet MAG 1011CD*	19	8
31 Jul 93		**UNFORGIVEN** *Magnet MAG 1016CD*	29	3
2 Oct 93		**STAR / I LIKE IT** *Magnet MAG 1019CD*	26	4
8 Jan 94	★	**THINGS CAN ONLY GET BETTER (re-issue)** *Magnet MAG 1020CD*	1	16
26 Mar 94	●	**U R THE BEST THING (re-mix)** *Magnet MAG 1021CD*	4	10
18 Jun 94		**TAKE ME AWAY** *Magnet MAG 1025CD*	18	5
10 Sep 94		**BLAME IT ON ME** *Magnet MAG 1027CD*	25	5
8 Jul 95	●	**SHOOT ME WITH YOUR LOVE** *Magnet MAG 1034CD*	7	7
9 Sep 95		**PARTY UP THE WORLD** *Magnet MAG 1037CD*	20	6
11 Nov 95		**THE POWER (OF ALL THE LOVE IN THE WORLD)** *Magnet MAG 1039CD*	40	1
3 May 97		**THINGS CAN ONLY GET BETTER (2nd re-issue)** *Magnet MAG 1050CD*	19	3

D-SHAKE *Holland, male producer (Adrianus De Mooy) (8 WEEKS)*

Date		Title	pos	wks
2 Jun 90		**YAAAH / TECHNO TRANCE** *Cooltempo COOL 213*	20	6
2 Feb 91		**MY HEART THE BEAT** *Cooltempo COOL 228*	42	2

D-TEK *UK, male instrumental / production group (1 WEEK)*

Date		Title	pos	wks
6 Nov 93		**DROP THE ROCK (EP)** *Positiva 12TIV 5*	70	1

Tracks on Drop the Rock (EP): Drop the Rock / Chunkafunk / Drop the Rock (re-mix) / Don't Breathe

D TRAIN *US, male vocal / instrumental duo – James Williams and Hubert Eaves III (36 WEEKS)*

Date		Title	pos	wks
6 Feb 82		**YOU'RE THE ONE FOR ME** *Epic EPC A 2016*	30	8
8 May 82		**WALK ON BY** *Epic EPC A 2298*	44	6
7 May 83		**MUSIC PART 1** *Prelude A 3332*	23	7
16 Jul 83		**KEEP GIVING ME LOVE** *Prelude A 3497*	65	2
27 Jul 85		**YOU'RE THE ONE FOR ME (re-mix)** *Prelude ZB 40302*	15	11
12 Oct 85		**MUSIC (re-mix)** *Prelude ZB 40431*	62	2

D12 *US, male rap group (24 WEEKS)*

Date		Title	pos	wks
17 Mar 01	●	**SH!T ON YOU** *Interscope 4974962*	10	7
21 Jul 01	●	**PURPLE PILLS** *Shady / Interscope 4975692*	2	12
17 Nov 01		**FIGHT MUSIC** *Shady / Interscope 4976522*	11	5

Azzido DA BASS
Germany, male DJ / producer – Ingo Martens (12 WEEKS)

Date		Title	pos	wks
4 Mar 00		**DOOMS NIGHT** *Club Tools 0067285 CLU*	58	1
24 Jun 00		**DOOMS NIGHT (re-entry)** *Club Tools 0067285 CLU*	46	2
21 Oct 00	●	**DOOMS NIGHT (re-mix)** *Club Tools 0120285 CLU*	8	8
13 Jan 01		**DOOMS NIGHT (re-entry of re-mix)** *Club Tools 0120285 CLU*	70	1

DA BRAT *US, female rapper (1 WEEK)*

Date		Title	pos	wks
22 Oct 94		**FUNKDAFIED** *Columbia 6609212*	65	1

DA CLICK *UK, male rap group / female vocalist (8 WEEKS)*

Date		Title	pos	wks
16 Jan 99		**GOOD RHYMES** *ffrr FCD 353*	14	6
29 May 99		**WE ARE DA CLICK** *ffrr FCD 363*	38	2

DA FOOL *US, male DJ / producer – Mike Stewart (2 WEEKS)*

Date		Title	pos	wks
16 Jan 99		**NO GOOD** *ffrr FCD 352*	38	2

Ricardo DA FORCE *UK, male rapper – Ricardo Lyte (14 WEEKS)*

Date		Title	pos	wks
18 Mar 95		**PUMP UP THE VOLUME** *Stress CDSTR 49* [1]	51	2

16 Sep 95	●	STAYIN' ALIVE *All around the World CDGLOBE 131* [2]	2	11
31 Aug 96		WHY *ffrr FCD 280*	58	1

[1] Greed featuring Ricardo Da Force [2] N-Trance featuring Ricardo Da Force

DA HOOL *Germany, male instrumentalist / producer – Frank Tomiczek (13 WEEKS)*

			pos	wks
14 Feb 98		MEET HER AT THE LOVE PARADE *Manifesto FESCD 39*	15	4
22 Aug 98		BORA BORA *Manifesto FESCD 47*	35	3
28 Jul 01		MEET HER AT THE LOVE PARADE 2001 *Manifesto FESCD 85*	11	6

DA LENCH MOB *US, male rap group (2 WEEKS)*

			pos	wks
20 Mar 93		FREEDOM GOT AN A.K. *East West America A 8431CD*	51	2

DA MOB featuring JOCELYN BROWN *US, male / female vocal / instrumental group (3 WEEKS)*

			pos	wks
2 May 98		FUN *INCredible INCRL 2CD*	33	2
3 Jul 99		IT'S ALL GOOD *INCredible INCRL 14CD*	54	1

DA MUTTZ *UK, male production duo (aka Shaft) – Elliot Ireland and Alex Rizzo (10 WEEKS)*

			pos	wks
9 Dec 00		WASSUUP *Eternal WEA 319CD*	11	10

See also SHAFT

Rui DA SILVA featuring CASSANDRA *Portugal, male producer and UK female vocalist – Cassandra Fox (14 WEEKS)*

			pos	wks
13 Jan 01	★	TOUCH ME *Kismet / Arista 74321823992* ■	1	14

DA SLAMMIN' PHROGZ *France, male production duo (1 WEEK)*

			pos	wks
29 Apr 00		SOMETHING ABOUT THE MUSIC *WEA WEA 251CD*	53	1

DA TECHNO BOHEMIAN *Holland, male production trio (1 WEEK)*

			pos	wks
25 Jan 97		BANGIN' BASS *Hi-Life 5731772*	63	1

Paul DA VINCI *UK, male vocalist – Paul Prewer (8 WEEKS)*

			pos	wks
20 Jul 74		YOUR BABY AIN'T YOUR BABY ANYMORE *Penny Farthing PEN 843*	20	8

See also RUBETTES

Terry DACTYL and the DINOSAURS *UK, male vocal / instrumental group (16 WEEKS)*

			pos	wks
15 Jul 72	●	SEASIDE SHUFFLE *UK 5*	2	12
13 Jan 73		ON A SATURDAY NIGHT *UK 21*	45	4

Terry Dactyl is Jona Lewie

DADA *US, male vocal / instrumental group (1 WEEK)*

			pos	wks
4 Dec 93		DOG *IRS CDEIRSS 185*	71	1

DADDY FREDDY – See Simon HARRIS

DADDY'S FAVOURITE *UK, male DJ / producer (3 WEEKS)*

			pos	wks
21 Nov 98		I FEEL GOOD THINGS FOR YOU *Go.Beat GONCD 12*	44	2
9 Oct 99		I FEEL GOOD THINGS FOR YOU (re-issue) *Go.Beat GOBCD 22*	50	1

DAFFY DUCK featuring the GROOVE GANG *Germany, male instrumental / production group (3 WEEKS)*

			pos	wks
6 Jul 91		PARTY ZONE *East West YZ 592*	58	3

DAFT PUNK *France, male instrumental / production duo – Thomas Bangalter and Guy Manuel de Homem-Christo (35 WEEKS)*

			pos	wks
22 Feb 97	●	DA FUNK / MUSIQUE *Soma / Virgin VSCDT 1625*	7	5
26 Apr 97	●	AROUND THE WORLD *Virgin VSCDT 1633*	5	5
4 Oct 97		BURNIN' *Virgin VSCDT 1649*	30	2
28 Feb 98		REVOLUTION 909 *Virgin VSCDT 1682*	47	1
25 Nov 00	●	ONE MORE TIME *Virgin VSCDT 1791*	2	12
23 Jun 01		DIGITAL LOVE *Virgin VSCDT 1810*	14	7
17 Nov 01		HARDER BETTER FASTER STRONGER *Virgin VSCDT 1822*	25	3

Etienne DAHO – See SAINT ETIENNE

DAINTEES – See Martin STEPHENSON and the DAINTEES

DAISY CHAINSAW *UK, male / female vocal / instrumental group (6 WEEKS)*

			pos	wks
18 Jan 92		LOVE YOUR MONEY *Deva DEVA 001*	26	5
28 Mar 92		PINK FLOWER / ROOM ELEVEN *Deva 82 TP7*	65	1

DAJAE – See Junior SANCHEZ featuring DAJAE

DAKEYNE – See James BROWN; TINMAN

DAKOTAS *UK, male instrumental group (13 WEEKS)*

			pos	wks
11 Jul 63		THE CRUEL SEA *Parlophone R 5044*	18	13

See also Billy J KRAMER and the DAKOTAS

Jim DALE *UK, male vocalist – James Smith (22 WEEKS)*

			pos	wks
11 Oct 57	●	BE MY GIRL *Parlophone R 4343*	2	16
10 Jan 58		JUST BORN (TO BE YOUR BABY) *Parlophone R 4376*	27	1
17 Jan 58		CRAZY DREAM *Parlophone R 4376*	24	2
7 Mar 58		SUGARTIME *Parlophone R 4402*	25	3

DALE and GRACE *US, male / female vocal duo (2 WEEKS)*

			pos	wks
9 Jan 64		I'M LEAVING IT UP TO YOU *London HL 9807* ▲	42	2

DALE SISTERS *UK, female vocal trio – Julie, Hazel and Betty Dunderdale (7 WEEKS)*

			pos	wks
17 Mar 60		HEARTBEAT *HMV POP 710* [1]	33	1
23 Nov 61		MY SUNDAY BABY *Ember S 140*	36	6

[1] England Sisters

DALI'S CAR *UK, male vocal / instrumental duo (2 WEEKS)*

			pos	wks
3 Nov 84		THE JUDGEMENT IS THE MIRROR *Paradox DOX 1*	66	2

Roger DALTREY *UK, male vocalist (46 WEEKS)*

			pos	wks
14 Apr 73	●	GIVING IT ALL AWAY *Track 2094 110*	5	11
4 Aug 73		I'M FREE *Ode ODS 66302*	13	10
14 May 77		WRITTEN ON THE WIND *Polydor 2121 319*	46	2
2 Aug 80		FREE ME *Polydor 2001 980*	39	6
11 Oct 80		WITHOUT YOUR LOVE *Polydor POSP 181*	55	4
3 Mar 84		WALKING IN MY SLEEP *WEA U 9686*	56	3
5 Oct 85		AFTER THE FIRE *10 TEN 69*	50	5
8 Mar 86		UNDER A RAGING MOON *10 TEN 81*	43	5

See also WHO

DAMAGE *UK, male vocal group (59 WEEKS)*

			pos	wks
20 Jul 96		ANYTHING *Big Life BLRD 129*	68	1
12 Oct 96		LOVE II LOVE *Big Life BLRD 131*	12	6
14 Dec 96	●	FOREVER *Big Life BLRD 132*	6	9
22 Mar 97	●	LOVE GUARANTEED *Big Life BLRDA 133*	7	6
17 May 97	●	WONDERFUL TONIGHT *Big Life BLRDA 134*	3	8
14 Jun 97		LOVE GUARANTEED (re-entry) *Big Life BLRDA 133*	73	1
9 Aug 97		LOVE LADY *Big Life BLRDB 137*	33	2
1 Jul 00	●	GHETTO ROMANCE *Cooltempo CDCOOL 347*	7	7
28 Oct 00		RUMOURS *Cooltempo CDCOOLS 352*	22	4
31 Mar 01		STILL BE LOVIN' YOU *Cooltempo CDCOOLS 355*	11	6
19 May 01		STILL BE LOVIN' YOU (re-entry) *Cooltempo CDCOOLS 355*	74	1
14 Jun 01		SO WHAT IF I *Cooltempo CDCOOLS 357*	12	5
25 Aug 01		SO WHAT IF I (re-entry) *Cooltempo CDCOOLS 357*	70	1
15 Dec 01		AFTER THE LOVE HAS GONE *Cooltempo CDCOOL 360*	42	2

Carolina DAMAS – See SUENO LATINO

Bobby D'AMBROSIO *US, male DJ / producer (3 WEEKS)* pos/wks

2 Aug 97	**MOMENT OF MY LIFE** *Ministry of Sound MOSCDS 1* [1]	23	3

[1] Bobby D'Ambrosio featuring Michelle Weeks

DAMIAN *UK, male vocalist – Damian Davis (26 WEEKS)* pos/wks

26 Dec 87	**THE TIME WARP 2** *Jive JIVE 160*	51	6
27 Aug 88	**THE TIME WARP 2 (re-issue)** *Jive JIVE 182*	64	3
19 Aug 89 ●	**THE TIME WARP (re-mix)** *Jive JIVE 209*	7	13
16 Dec 89	**WIG WAM BAM** *Jive JIVE 236*	49	4

'The Time Warp' is a re-mix of 'The Time Warp 2'

DAMNED (447 Top 500) *Anarchic stalwarts of the UK punk rock scene: Dave Vanian (v), Brian James (g), Captain Sensible (b) and Rat Scabies (d). London-based band released the first UK punk single 'New Rose' (1976) and album 'Damned, Damned, Damned' (1977) (77 WEEKS)* pos/wks

5 May 79	**LOVE SONG** *Chiswick CHIS 112*	20	8
20 Oct 79	**SMASH IT UP** *Chiswick CHIS 116*	35	5
1 Dec 79	**I JUST CAN'T BE HAPPY TODAY** *Chiswick CHIS 120*	46	5
4 Oct 80	**HISTORY OF THE WORLD (PART 1)** *Chiswick CHIS 135*	51	4
28 Nov 81	**FRIDAY 13TH (EP)** *Stale One TRY 1*	50	4
10 Jul 82	**LOVELY MONEY** *Bronze BRO 149*	42	4
9 Jun 84	**THANKS FOR THE NIGHT** *Damned DAMNED 1*	43	4
30 Mar 85	**GRIMLY FIENDISH** *MCA GRIM 1*	21	7
22 Jun 85	**THE SHADOW OF LOVE (EDITION PREMIERE)** *MCA GRIM 2*	25	8
21 Sep 85	**IS IT A DREAM** *MCA GRIM 3*	34	4
8 Feb 86 ●	**ELOISE** *MCA GRIM 4*	3	9
19 Apr 86	**ELOISE (re-entry)** *MCA GRIM 4*	72	1
22 Nov 86	**ANYTHING** *MCA GRIM 5*	32	4
7 Feb 87	**GIGOLO** *MCA GRIM 6*	29	3
25 Apr 87	**ALONE AGAIN OR** *MCA GRIM 7*	27	6
28 Nov 87	**IN DULCE DECORUM** *MCA GRIM 8*	72	1

Tracks on Friday 13th (EP): Disco Man / Limit Club / Billy Bad Breaks / Citadel

Kenny DAMON *US, male vocalist (1 WEEK)* pos/wks

19 May 66	**WHILE I LIVE** *Mercury MF 907*	48	1

Vic DAMONE *US, male vocalist – Vito Farinola (22 WEEKS)* pos/wks

6 Dec 57	**AN AFFAIR TO REMEMBER (OUR LOVE AFFAIR)** *Philips PB 745*	29	1
31 Jan 58	**AN AFFAIR TO REMEMBER (OUR LOVE AFFAIR) (re-entry)** *Philips PB 745*	30	1
9 May 58 ★	**ON THE STREET WHERE YOU LIVE** *Philips PB 819*	1	17
1 Aug 58	**THE ONLY MAN ON THE ISLAND** *Philips PB 837*	24	3

DAN-I *UK, male vocalist (9 WEEKS)* pos/wks

10 Nov 79	**MONKEY CHOP** *Island WIP 6520*	30	9

Richie DAN *UK, male DJ / producer – Richard Gittens (3 WEEKS)* pos/wks

12 Aug 00	**CALL IT FATE** *Pure Silk CDPSR 1*	34	3

DANA (461 Top 500) *Petite teenager won Eurovision Song Contest for Ireland with her first hit in 1970. Born Rosemary Brown (later Scallon), 30 Aug 1951, London, UK. Winning debut hit sold more than two million and was also successful in Europe, Australia and South Africa. Ran for Irish presidency in 1997 (75 WEEKS)* pos/wks

4 Apr 70 ★	**ALL KINDS OF EVERYTHING** *Rex R 11054*	1	15
25 Jul 70	**ALL KINDS OF EVERYTHING (re-entry)** *Rex R 11054*	47	1
13 Feb 71	**WHO PUT THE LIGHTS OUT** *Rex R 11062*	14	11
25 Jan 75 ●	**PLEASE TELL HIM THAT I SAID HELLO** *GTO GT 6*	8	14
13 Dec 75 ●	**IT'S GONNA BE A COLD COLD CHRISTMAS** *GTO GT 45*	4	6
6 Mar 76	**NEVER GONNA FALL IN LOVE AGAIN** *GTO GT 55*	31	4
16 Oct 76	**FAIRYTALE** *GTO GT 66*	13	16
31 Mar 79	**SOMETHING'S COOKIN' IN THE KITCHEN** *GTO GT 243*	44	5
15 May 82	**I FEEL LOVE COMIN' ON** *Creole CR 32*	66	3

DANA INTERNATIONAL
Israel, female vocalist – Yaron Cohen (4 WEEKS) pos/wks

27 Jun 98	**DIVA** *Dance Pool DANA 1CD*	11	4

DANCE CONSPIRACY
UK, male instrumental / production duo (1 WEEK) pos/wks

3 Oct 92	**DUB WAR** *XL Recordings XLT 34*	72	1

DANCE FLOOR VIRUS
Italy, male vocal / instrumental group (2 WEEKS) pos/wks

21 Oct 95	**MESSAGE IN A BOTTLE** *Epic 6623742*	49	2

DANCE 2 TRANCE
Germany, male instrumental / production duo (8 WEEKS) pos/wks

24 Apr 93	**P.OWER OF A.MERICAN N.ATIVES** *Logic 74321139582*	25	4
24 Jul 93	**TAKE A FREE FALL** *Logic 74321153602*	36	3
4 Feb 95	**WARRIOR** *Logic 74321257722*	56	1

Evan DANDO – *See Kirsty MacCOLL; LEMONHEADS*

DANDY WARHOLS
US, male / female vocal / instrumental group (20 WEEKS) pos/wks

28 Feb 98	**EVERY DAY SHOULD BE A HOLIDAY** *Capitol CDCL 797*	29	2
2 May 98	**NOT IF YOU WERE THE LAST JUNKIE ON EARTH** *Capitol CDCL 800*	13	4
8 Aug 98	**BOYS BETTER** *Capitol CDCLS 805*	36	2
10 Jun 00	**GET OFF** *Capitol CDCLS 821*	38	2
9 Sep 00	**BOHEMIAN LIKE YOU** *Capitol CDCLS823*	42	1
7 Jul 01	**GODLESS** *Capitol CDCL 829*	66	1
10 Nov 01 ●	**BOHEMIAN LIKE YOU (re-issue)** *Parlophone / Capitol CDCLX 823*	5	8+

DANDYS *UK, male vocal / instrumental group (2 WEEKS)* pos/wks

14 Mar 98	**YOU MAKE ME WANT TO SCREAM** *Artificial ATFCD 3*	71	1
30 May 98	**ENGLISH COUNTRY GARDEN** *Artificial ATFCD 4*	57	1

DANE *UK, male vocalist – Dane Bowers (26 WEEKS)* pos/wks

26 Aug 01 ●	**OUT OF YOUR MIND** *Nulife 74321753342* [1]	2	16
3 Mar 01 ●	**SHUT UP AND FORGET ABOUT IT** *Arista 74321835342*	9	5
7 Jul 01 ●	**ANOTHER LOVER** *Arista 74321863412*	9	5

[1] TRUESTEPPERS and Dane Bowers featuring Victoria Beckham

D'ANGELO *US, male vocalist (11 WEEKS)* pos/wks

28 Oct 95	**BROWN SUGAR** *Cooltempo CDCOOL 307*	24	3
2 Mar 96	**COLD WORLD** *Geffen GFSTD 22114* [1]	40	2
2 Mar 96	**CRUISIN'** *Cooltempo CDCOOL 316*	31	2
15 Jun 96	**LADY** *Cooltempo CDCOOLS 323*	21	2
22 May 99	**BREAK UPS 2 MAKE UPS** *Def Jam 8709272* [2]	33	2

[1] Genius / GZA featuring D'Angelo [2] Method Man featuring D'Angelo

DANGER DANGER *US, male vocal / instrumental group (5 WEEKS)* pos/wks

8 Feb 92	**MONKEY BUSINESS** *Epic 6577517*	42	2
28 Mar 92	**I STILL THINK ABOUT YOU** *Epic 6578387*	46	2
13 Jun 92	**COMIN' HOME** *Epic 6581337*	75	1

Charlie DANIELS BAND
US, male vocal / instrumental group (10 WEEKS) pos/wks

22 Sep 79	**THE DEVIL WENT DOWN TO GEORGIA** *Epic EPC 7737*	14	10

Johnny DANKWORTH and his Orchestra *UK, male orchestral / group leader / instrumentalist - alto sax (33 WEEKS)* pos/wks

22 Jun 56 ●	**EXPERIMENTS WITH MICE** *Parlophone R 4185*	7	12
23 Feb 61 ●	**AFRICAN WALTZ** *Columbia DB 4590*	9	21

DANNII– *See Dannii MINOGUE*

DANNY and the JUNIORS *US, male vocal group (19 WEEKS)* pos/wks

17 Jan 58 ●	**AT THE HOP** *HMV POP 436* ▲	3	14
10 Jul 76	**AT THE HOP (re-issue)** *ABC 4123*	39	5

DANNY WILSON *UK, male vocal / instrumental group (28 WEEKS)* pos/wks

Date	Title / Label	pos	wks
22 Aug 87	**MARY'S PRAYER** *Virgin VS 934*	42	7
2 Apr 88 ●	**MARY'S PRAYER (re-entry)** *Virgin VS 934*	3	11
17 Jun 89	**THE SECOND SUMMER OF LOVE** *Virgin VS 1186*	23	9
16 Sep 89	**NEVER GONNA BE THE SAME** *Virgin VS 1203*	69	1

DANSE SOCIETY *UK, male vocal / instrumental group (5 WEEKS)* pos/wks

Date	Title / Label	pos	wks
27 Aug 83	**WAKE UP** *Society SOC 5*	61	3
5 Nov 83	**HEAVEN IS WAITING** *Society SOC 6*	60	2

Steven DANTE *UK, male vocalist – Steven Dennis (16 WEEKS)* pos/wks

Date	Title / Label	pos	wks
26 Sep 87	**THE REAL THING** *Chrysalis CHS 3167* [1]	13	10
9 Jul 88	**I'M TOO SCARED** *Cooltempo DANTE 1*	34	6

[1] Jellybean featuring Steven Dante

Dante THOMAS featuring PRAS
US, male vocalist & US, male rapper (3 WEEKS) pos/wks

Date	Title / Label	pos	wks
1 Sep 01	**MISS CALIFORNIA** *Elektra E7192CD* [1]	25	3

[1] Dante Thomas featuring Pras

Tonja DANTZLER *US, female vocalist (1 WEEK)* pos/wks

Date	Title / Label	pos	wks
17 Dec 94	**IN AND OUT OF MY LIFE** *ffrr FCD 246*	66	1

DANY – *See DOUBLE DEE featuring DANY*

DANZIG *US, male vocal / instrumental group (1 WEEK)* pos/wks

Date	Title / Label	pos	wks
14 May 94	**MOTHER** *American MOMDD 1*	62	1

DAPHNE *US, female vocalist (1 WEEK)* pos/wks

Date	Title / Label	pos	wks
9 Dec 95	**CHANGE** *Stress CDSTR 54*	71	1

DAPHNE & CELESTE *US, female vocal duo – Daphne DeConcetto and Celeste Cruz (28 WEEKS)* pos/wks

Date	Title / Label	pos	wks
5 Feb 00 ●	**OOH STICK YOU!** *Universal MCSTD 40209*	8	12
17 Jun 00	**UGLY** *Universal MCSTD 40232*	18	12
2 Sep 00	**SCHOOL'S OUT** *Universal MCSTD 40238*	12	4

Terence Trent D'ARBY (444 Top 500) *Unpredictable US pop / soul singer / songwriter, b. 15 Mar 1962, New York, US, whose success came after relocating to UK. Multi-million-selling, Grammy-winning debut album, 'Introducing the Hardline ...', was a worldwide hit. Winner of 1988 Brit award for Best International Newcomer (77 WEEKS)* pos/wks

Date	Title / Label	pos	wks
14 Mar 87 ●	**IF YOU LET ME STAY** *CBS TRENT 1*	7	13
20 Jun 87 ●	**WISHING WELL** *CBS TRENT 2* ▲	4	11
10 Oct 87	**DANCE LITTLE SISTER (PART ONE)** *CBS TRENT 3*	20	7
9 Jan 88 ●	**SIGN YOUR NAME** *CBS TRENT 4*	2	10
20 Jan 90	**TO KNOW SOMEONE DEEPLY IS TO KNOW SOMEONE SOFTLY** *CBS TRENT 6*	55	3
17 Apr 93	**DO YOU LOVE ME LIKE YOU SAY** *Columbia 6590732*	14	6
19 Jun 93	**DELICATE** *Columbia 6593312* [1]	14	6
28 Aug 93	**SHE KISSED ME** *Columbia 6595922*	16	7
20 Nov 93	**LET HER DOWN EASY** *Columbia 6598642*	18	7
8 Apr 95	**HOLDING ON TO YOU** *Columbia 6614235*	20	6
5 Aug 95	**VIBRATOR** *Columbia 6622585*	57	1

[1] Terence Trent D'Arby featuring Des'ree

Richard DARBYSHIRE *UK, male vocalist (7 WEEKS)* pos/wks

Date	Title / Label	pos	wks
20 Aug 88	**COMING BACK FOR MORE** *Chrysalis JEL 4* [1]	41	3
24 Jul 93	**THIS I SWEAR** *Dome CDDOME 1003*	50	3
12 Feb 94	**WHEN ONLY LOVE WILL DO** *Dome CDDOME 1008*	54	1

[1] Jellybean featuring Richard Darbyshire

DARE *UK, male vocal / instrumental group (7 WEEKS)* pos/wks

Date	Title / Label	pos	wks
29 Apr 89	**THE RAINDANCE** *A & M AM 483*	62	2
29 Jul 89	**ABANDON** *A & M AM 519*	71	2
10 Aug 91	**WE DON'T NEED A REASON** *A & M AM 755*	52	2
5 Oct 91	**REAL LOVE** *A & M AM 824*	67	1

Matt DAREY *UK, male producer / instrumentalist (9 WEEKS)* pos/wks

Date	Title / Label	pos	wks
9 Oct 99	**LIBERATION (TEMPTATION – FLY LIKE AN EAGLE)** *Incentive CENT 1CDS* [1]	19	3
22 Apr 00	**FROM RUSSIA WITH LOVE** *Liquid Asset ASSET CD003* [2]	40	2
15 Jul 00	**BEAUTIFUL** *Incentive CENT 7CDS* [3]	21	4

[1] Matt Darey presents Mash Up [2] Matt Darey Presents DSP [3] Matt Darey's Mash Up presents Marcella Woods

See also SUNBURST; MELT featuring LITTLE MS MARCIE; MDM

Bobby DARIN (131 Top 500) *Singer / songwriter / actor and multi-instrumentalist who had pop, rock, R&B, country and MOR hits, b. Walden Robert Cassotto, 14 May 1936, New York, d. 20 Dec 1973. This Grammy winner was posthumously inducted into the Rock and Roll Hall of Fame in 1990 (161 WEEKS)* pos/wks

Date	Title / Label	pos	wks
1 Aug 58	**SPLISH SPLASH** *London HLE 8666*	28	1
15 Aug 58	**SPLISH SPLASH (re-entry)** *London HLE 8666*	18	6
9 Jan 59	**QUEEN OF THE HOP** *London HLE 8737*	24	2
29 May 59 ★	**DREAM LOVER** *London HLE 8867*	1	19
25 Sep 59 ★	**MACK THE KNIFE** *London HLK 8939* ▲	1	16
22 Jan 60	**MACK THE KNIFE (re-entry)** *London HLK 8939*	30	1
29 Jan 60 ●	**LA MER (BEYOND THE SEA)** *London HLK 9034*	8	10
10 Mar 60	**MACK THE KNIFE (2nd re-entry)** *London HLK 8939*	50	1
31 Mar 60 ●	**CLEMENTINE** *London HLK 9086*	8	12
21 Apr 60	**LA MER (BEYOND THE SEA) (re-entry)** *London HLK 9034*	40	2
30 Jun 60	**BILL BAILEY** *London HLK 9142*	36	1
14 Jul 60	**BILL BAILEY (re-entry)** *London HLK 9142*	34	1
16 Mar 61 ●	**LAZY RIVER** *London HLK 9303*	2	13
6 Jul 61	**NATURE BOY** *London HLK 9375*	24	7
12 Oct 61 ●	**YOU MUST HAVE BEEN A BEAUTIFUL BABY** *London HLK 9429*	10	11
26 Oct 61	**THEME FROM 'COME SEPTEMBER'** *London HLK 9407* [1]	50	1
21 Dec 61 ●	**MULTIPLICATION** *London HLK 9474*	5	13
19 Jul 62 ●	**THINGS** *London HLK 9575*	2	17
4 Oct 62	**IF A MAN ANSWERS** *Capitol CL 15272*	24	6
29 Nov 62	**BABY FACE** *London HLK 9624*	40	4
25 Jul 63	**EIGHTEEN YELLOW ROSES** *Capitol CL 15306*	37	4
13 Oct 66 ●	**IF I WERE A CARPENTER** *Atlantic 584 051*	9	12
14 Apr 79	**DREAM LOVER / MACK THE KNIFE (re-issue)** *Lightning LIG 9017*	64	1

[1] Bobby Darin Orchestra

DARK STAR *UK, male vocal / instrumental group (6 WEEKS)* pos/wks

Date	Title / Label	pos	wks
26 Jun 99	**ABOUT 3AM** *Harvest CDEM 545*	50	1
15 Jan 00	**GRACEADELICA** *Harvest CDEMS 556*	25	3
13 May 00	**I AM THE SUN** *Harvest CDEMS 566*	31	2

DARKMAN *UK, male rapper (7 WEEKS)* pos/wks

Date	Title / Label	pos	wks
14 May 94	**YABBA DABBA DOO** *Wild Card CARDD 6*	49	2
20 Aug 94	**WHO'S THE DARKMAN** *Wild Card CARDD 8*	46	2
3 Dec 94	**YABBA DABBA DOO (re-issue)** *Wild Card CARDD 11*	37	2
21 Oct 95	**BRAND NEW DAY** *Wild Card 5771892*	74	1

DARLING BUDS
UK, male / female vocal / instrumental group (20 WEEKS) pos/wks

Date	Title / Label	pos	wks
8 Oct 88	**BURST** *Epic BLOND 1*	50	5
7 Jan 89	**HIT THE GROUND** *CBS BLOND 2*	27	5
25 Mar 89	**LET'S GO ROUND THERE** *CBS BLOND 3*	49	4
22 Jul 89	**YOU'VE GOT TO CHOOSE** *CBS BLOND 4*	45	3
2 Jun 90	**TINY MACHINE** *CBS BLOND 5*	60	2
12 Sep 92	**SURE THING** *Epic 6582157*	71	1

Guy DARRELL *UK, male vocalist (13 WEEKS)* pos/wks

Date	Title / Label	pos	wks
18 Aug 73	**I'VE BEEN HURT** *Santa Ponsa PNS 4*	12	13

James DARREN *US, male vocalist (25 WEEKS)* pos/wks

Date	Title / Label	pos	wks
11 Aug 60	**BECAUSE THEY'RE YOUNG** *Pye International 7N 25059*	29	7

UK No.1 ★ UK Top 10 ● Still on chart + UK million seller ◆ UK entry at No.1 ■ US No.1 ▲

14 Dec 61	**GOODBYE CRUEL WORLD** *Pye International 7N 25116*	28 9
29 Mar 62	**HER ROYAL MAJESTY** *Pye International 7N 25125*	36 3
21 Jun 62	**CONSCIENCE** *Pye International 7N 25138*	30 6

DARTS (236 Top 500) *Britain's best-known doo-wop vocal group; line-up included Den Hegarty, Griff Fender, Rita Ray and Bob Fish. The popular London-based eight-piece band had three successive No.2 hits with revivals of early US rock 'n' roll and R&B songs (117 WEEKS)* pos/wks

5 Nov 77 ●	**DADDY COOL / THE GIRL CAN'T HELP IT** *Magnet MAG 100*	6 13
28 Jan 78 ●	**COME BACK MY LOVE** *Magnet MAG 110*	2 12
6 May 78 ●	**BOY FROM NEW YORK CITY** *Magnet MAG 116*	2 13
5 Aug 78 ●	**IT'S RAINING** *Magnet MAG 126*	2 11
11 Nov 78	**DON'T LET IT FADE AWAY** *Magnet MAG 134*	18 11
10 Feb 79 ●	**GET IT** *Magnet MAG 140*	10 9
21 Jul 79 ●	**DUKE OF EARL** *Magnet MAG 147*	6 11
20 Oct 79	**CAN'T GET ENOUGH OF YOUR LOVE** *Magnet MAG 156*	43 6
1 Dec 79	**REET PETITE** *Magnet MAG 160*	51 7
31 May 80	**LET'S HANG ON** *Magnet MAG 174*	11 14
6 Sep 80	**PEACHES** *Magnet MAG 179*	66 3
29 Nov 80	**WHITE CHRISTMAS / SH-BOOM (LIFE COULD BE A DREAM)** *Magnet MAG 184*	48 7

DARUDE *Finland, male producer – Ville Virtanen (29 WEEKS)* pos/wks

24 Jun 00 ●	**SANDSTORM** *Neo NEOCD 033*	3 15
25 Nov 00 ●	**FEEL THE BEAT** *Neo NEOCD 045*	5 10
15 Sep 01	**OUT OF CONTROL (BACK FOR MORE)** *Neo NEOCD 067*	13 4

DAS EFX *US, male production / rap duo (5 WEEKS)* pos/wks

7 Aug 93	**CHECK YO SELF** *Fourth & Broadway BRCD 283* [1]	36 4
25 Apr 98	**RAP SCHOLAR** *East West E 3853CD* [2]	42 1

[1] Ice Cube featuring Das EFX [2] Das EFX featuring Redman

N'dea DAVENPORT *US, female vocalist (6 WEEKS)* pos/wks

11 Sep 93	**TRUST ME** *Cooltempo CDCOOL 278* [1]	34 2
20 Jun 98	**BRING IT ON** *Gee Street VVR5002033*	52 1
15 Dec 01	**YOU CAN'T CHANGE ME** *Defected DFECT 41CDS* [2]	25 3

[1] Guru featuring N'Dea Davenport [2] Roger Sanchez featuring Armand Van Helden and N'Dea Davenport

See also BRAND NEW HEAVIES; GURU

Anne-Marie DAVID *France, female vocalist (9 WEEKS)* pos/wks

28 Apr 73	**WONDERFUL DREAM** *Epic EPC 1446*	13 9

Craig DAVID (420 Top 500) *Critically lauded singer / songwriter, b. 5 May 1981, Southampton, UK. At 18 years, 11 months and 10 days he was the youngest British male to write and sing a No.1. Won numerous awards for his songs, records and videos. Debut album 'Born To Do It' went gold in 24 countries with UK sales exceeding 1.5 million (79 WEEKS)* pos/wks

11 Dec 99 ●	**RE-REWIND THE CROWD SAY BO SELECTA** *Public Demand / Relentless RELENT 1CDS* [1]	2 17
15 Apr 00 ★	**FILL ME IN** *Wildstar CDWILD 28* ■	1 14
15 Jul 00 ●	**WOMAN TROUBLE** *Public Demand / ffrr FCD 380* [2]	6 10
5 Aug 00 ★	**7 DAYS** *Wildstar CDWILD 30* ■	1 14
18 Nov 00	**7 DAYS (re-entry)** *Wildstar CDWILD 30*	74 1
2 Dec 00 ●	**WALKING AWAY** *Wildstar CDWILD 35*	3 13
31 Mar 01 ●	**RENDEZVOUS** *Wildstar CDWILD 36*	8 10

[1] Artful Dodger featuring Craig David [2] Artful Dodger and Robbie Craig featuring Craig David

FR DAVID *France, male vocalist – Robert Fitoussi (13 WEEKS)* pos/wks

2 Apr 83 ●	**WORDS** *Carrere CAR 248*	2 12
18 Jun 83	**MUSIC** *Carrere CAR 282*	71 1

DAVID and JONATHAN
UK, male vocal duo – Roger Greenaway & Roger Cook (22 WEEKS) pos/wks

13 Jan 66	**MICHELLE** *Columbia DB 7800*	11 6
7 Jul 66 ●	**LOVERS OF THE WORLD UNITE** *Columbia DB 7950*	7 16

See also BLUE MINK; PIPKINS

Jim DAVIDSON *UK, male vocalist (4 WEEKS)* pos/wks

27 Dec 80	**WHITE CHRISTMAS / TOO RISKY** *Scratch SCR 001*	52 4

Paul DAVIDSON *Jamaica, male vocalist (10 WEEKS)* pos/wks

27 Dec 75 ●	**MIDNIGHT RIDER** *Tropical ALO 56*	10 10

Dave DAVIES *UK, male vocalist (17 WEEKS)* pos/wks

19 Jul 67 ●	**DEATH OF A CLOWN** *Pye 7N 17356*	3 10
6 Dec 67	**SUSANNAH'S STILL ALIVE** *Pye 7N 17429*	20 7

See also KINKS

Windsor DAVIES and Don ESTELLE
UK, male comedy / vocal duo (16 WEEKS) pos/wks

17 May 75 ★	**WHISPERING GRASS** *EMI 2290*	1 12
25 Oct 75	**PAPER DOLL** *EMI 2361*	41 4

Billie DAVIS *UK, female vocalist – Carol Hedges (33 WEEKS)* pos/wks

30 Aug 62	**WILL I WHAT** *Parlophone R 4932* [1]	18 10
7 Feb 63 ●	**TELL HIM** *Decca F 11572*	10 12
30 May 63	**HE'S THE ONE** *Decca F 11658*	40 3
9 Oct 68	**I WANT YOU TO BE MY BABY** *Decca F 12823*	33 8

[1] Mike Sarne with Billie Davis

Billy DAVIS Jr – *See Marilyn McCOO and Billy DAVIS Jr*

Darlene DAVIS *US, female vocalist (5 WEEKS)* pos/wks

7 Feb 87	**I FOUND LOVE** *Serious 70US 1*	55 5

John DAVIS and the MONSTER ORCHESTRA
US, male vocal / instrumental group (2 WEEKS) pos/wks

10 Feb 79	**AIN'T THAT ENOUGH FOR YOU** *Miracle M 2*	70 2

Mac DAVIS *US, male vocalist (22 WEEKS)* pos/wks

4 Nov 72	**BABY DON'T GET HOOKED ON ME** *CBS 8250* ▲	29 6
15 Nov 80	**IT'S HARD TO BE HUMBLE** *Casablanca CAN 210*	27 16

Richie DAVIS – *See SHUT UP AND DANCE*

Roy DAVIS Jr featuring Peven EVERETT
US, male producer, male vocalist (4 WEEKS) pos/wks

1 Nov 97	**GABRIEL** *XL XLS 88CD*	22 4

Ruth DAVIS – *See Bo KIRKLAND and Ruth DAVIS*

Sammy DAVIS Jr *US, male vocalist (37 WEEKS)* pos/wks

29 Jul 55	**SOMETHING'S GOTTA GIVE** *Brunswick LAT 8296*	19 2
19 Aug 55	**SOMETHING'S GOTTA GIVE (re-entry)** *Brunswick LAT 8296*	11 5
9 Sep 55 ●	**LOVE ME OR LEAVE ME** *Brunswick 05428*	8 6
30 Sep 55	**THAT OLD BLACK MAGIC** *Brunswick 05450*	16 1
7 Oct 55	**HEY THERE** *Brunswick 05469*	19 1
4 Nov 55	**LOVE ME OR LEAVE ME (re-entry)** *Brunswick 05428*	18 2
20 Apr 56	**IN A PERSIAN MARKET** *Brunswick 05518*	28 1
28 Dec 56	**ALL OF YOU** *Brunswick 05629*	28 1
16 Jun 60	**HAPPY TO MAKE YOUR ACQUAINTANCE** *Brunswick 05830* [1]	46 1
22 Mar 62	**WHAT KIND OF FOOL AM I? / GONNA BUILD A MOUNTAIN** *Reprise R 20048*	26 8
13 Dec 62	**ME AND MY SHADOW** *Reprise R 20128* [2]	20 7
7 Feb 63	**ME AND MY SHADOW (re-entry)** *Reprise R 20128* [2]	47 2

[1] Sammy Davis Jr and Carmen McRae [2] Frank Sinatra and Sammy Davis Jr

Skeeter DAVIS *US, female vocalist – Mary Penick (13 WEEKS)* pos/wks

14 Mar 63	**END OF THE WORLD** *RCA 1328*	18 13

Spencer DAVIS GROUP (498 Top 500)

Big-selling Birmingham (UK) band: Spencer Davis (v/g), Peter York (d) and brothers Muff (b) and Steve Winwood (v/g/k). Both No.1s penned by reggae artist Jackie Edwards. Teenager Steve Winwood left 1967, and continued hit run with Blind Faith, Traffic and as a soloist (71 WEEKS)

			pos	wks
5 Nov 64		**I CAN'T STAND IT** *Fontana TF 499*	47	3
25 Feb 65		**EVERY LITTLE BIT HURTS** *Fontana TF 530*	43	2
18 Mar 65		**EVERY LITTLE BIT HURTS (re-entry)** *Fontana TF 530*	41	1
10 Jun 65		**STRONG LOVE** *Fontana TF 571*	50	1
24 Jun 65		**STRONG LOVE (re-entry)** *Fontana TF 571*	44	3
2 Dec 65	★	**KEEP ON RUNNING** *Fontana TF 632*	1	14
24 Mar 66	★	**SOMEBODY HELP ME** *Fontana TF 679*	1	10
1 Sep 66		**WHEN I COME HOME** *Fontana TF 739*	12	9
3 Nov 66	●	**GIMME SOME LOVING** *Fontana TF 762*	2	12
26 Jan 67	●	**I'M A MAN** *Fontana TF 785*	9	7
9 Aug 67		**TIME SELLER** *Fontana TF 854*	30	5
10 Jan 68		**MR SECOND CLASS** *United Artists UP 1203*	35	4

TJ DAVIS

UK, female vocalist (2 WEEKS)

			pos	wks
27 Jul 96		**BRILLIANT FEELING** *Arista 74321380902* [1]	72	1
29 Dec 01		**WONDERFUL LIFE** *Melting Pot MPRCD 20*	42	1+

[1] Full Monty Allstars featuring TJ Davis

Zelma DAVIS – *See C & C MUSIC FACTORY / CLIVILLES & COLE*

DAVIS PINCKNEY PROJECT – *See GO GO LORENZO and the DAVIS PINCKNEY PROJECT*

DAWN (270 Top 500)

Top-notch vocal trio fronted by one-time teenage hitmaker Tony Orlando (b. Michael Cassavitis, 3 Apr 1944, New York) and including Telma Hopkins and Joyce Vincent. Their 'Tie a Yellow Ribbon' was the top single of 1973 in both the UK and the US (109 WEEKS)

			pos	wks
16 Jan 71	●	**CANDIDA** *Bell 1118*	9	11
10 Apr 71	★	**KNOCK THREE TIMES** *Bell 1146* ▲	1	27
31 Jul 71	●	**WHAT ARE YOU DOING SUNDAY** *Bell 1169* [1]	3	12
10 Mar 73	★	**TIE A YELLOW RIBBON ROUND THE OLD OAK TREE** *Bell 1287* [1] ▲	1	39
4 Aug 73		**SAY, HAS ANYBODY SEEN MY SWEET GYPSY ROSE** *Bell 1322* [1]	12	15
5 Jan 74		**TIE A YELLOW RIBBON ROUND THE OLD OAK TREE (re-entry)** *Bell 1287* [1]	41	1
9 Mar 74		**WHO'S IN THE STRAWBERRY PATCH WITH SALLY** *Bell 1343* [2]	37	4

[1] Dawn featuring Tony Orlando [2] Tony Orlando and Dawn

Julie DAWN – *See Cyril STAPLETON and his Orchestra*

Liz DAWN – *See Joe LONGTHORNE*

DAWN OF THE REPLICANTS

UK, male vocal / instrumental group (2 WEEKS)

			pos	wks
7 Feb 98		**CANDLEFIRE** *East West EW 147CD1*	52	1
4 Apr 98		**HOGWASH FARM (THE DIESEL HANDS EP)** *East West EW 157CD*	65	1

Tracks on Hogwash Farm (The Diesel Hands EP): Hogwash Farm (re-built) / Night Train to Lichtenstein / The Duchess of Surin / Crow Valley

Dana DAWSON

US, female vocalist (14 WEEKS)

			pos	wks
15 Jul 95	●	**3 IS FAMILY** *EMI CDEM 378*	9	8
28 Oct 95		**GOT TO GIVE ME LOVE** *EMI CDEM 392*	27	2
4 May 96		**SHOW ME** *EMI CDEMS 423*	28	3
20 Jul 96		**HOW I WANNA BE LOVED** *EMI CDEMS 432*	42	1

Bobby DAY

US, male vocalist (2 WEEKS)

			pos	wks
7 Nov 58		**ROCKIN' ROBIN** *London HL 8726*	29	2

Darren DAY

UK, male vocalist (7 WEEKS)

			pos	wks
8 Oct 94		**YOUNG GIRL** *Bell 74321231082*	42	2
8 Jun 96		**SUMMER HOLIDAY MEDLEY** *RCA 74321384472*	17	4
9 May 98		**HOW CAN I BE SURE?** *Eastcoast DDCD 001*	71	1

Doris DAY (156 Top 500)

The Fifties' favourite singer / actress, b. Doris Kappelhoff, 3 Apr 1924, Cincinnati. The No.1 female movie star of that era, she also had numerous British hits (not to mention 25 US bestsellers) before the UK chart first started (146 WEEKS)

			pos	wks
14 Nov 52	●	**SUGARBUSH** *Columbia DB 3123* [1]	8	2
21 Nov 52	●	**MY LOVE AND DEVOTION** *Columbia DB 3157*	10	2
5 Dec 52	●	**SUGARBUSH (re-entry)** *Columbia DB 3123* [1]	8	6
3 Apr 53		**MA SAYS, PA SAYS** *Columbia DB3242* [2]	12	1
17 Apr 53		**FULL TIME JOB** *Columbia DB 3242* [2]	11	1
24 Jul 53	●	**LET'S WALK THAT-A-WAY** *Philips PB 157* [2]	4	14
2 Apr 54	★	**SECRET LOVE** *Philips PB 230* ▲	1	29
27 Aug 54	●	**THE BLACK HILLS OF DAKOTA** *Philips PB 287*	7	8
1 Oct 54	●	**IF I GIVE MY HEART TO YOU** *Philips PB 325* [3]	4	11
8 Apr 55	●	**READY, WILLING AND ABLE** *Philips PB 402*	7	9
9 Sep 55		**LOVE ME OR LEAVE ME** *Philips PB 479*	20	1
21 Oct 55		**I'LL NEVER STOP LOVING YOU** *Philips PB 497*	17	2
25 Nov 55		**I'LL NEVER STOP LOVING YOU (re-entry)** *Philips PB 497*	19	1
29 Jun 56	★	**WHATEVER WILL BE, WILL BE (QUE SERA, SERA)** *Philips PB 586*	1	22
13 Jun 58		**A VERY PRECIOUS LOVE** *Philips PB 799*	16	11
15 Aug 58		**EVERYBODY LOVES A LOVER** *Philips PB 843*	25	3
26 Sep 58		**EVERYBODY LOVES A LOVER (re-entry)** *Philips PB 843*	27	1
12 Mar 64	●	**MOVE OVER DARLING** *CBS AAG 183*	8	16
18 Apr 87		**MOVE OVER DARLING (re-issue)** *CBS LEGS 1*	45	6

[1] Doris Day and Frankie Laine [2] Doris Day and Johnnie Ray [3] Doris Day with The Mellomen

Inaya DAY

US, female vocalist (3 WEEKS)

			pos	wks
22 May 99		**JUST CAN'T GET ENOUGH** *AM:PM CDAMPM 121* [1]	39	2
7 Oct 00		**FEEL IT** *Positiva CDTIV 141*	51	1

[1] Harry 'Choo Choo' Romero presents Inaya Day

See also Boris DLUGOSCH

DAY ONE

UK, male vocal / instrumental duo (1 WEEK)

			pos	wks
13 Nov 99		**I'M DOIN' FINE** *Melankolic / Virgin SADD6*	68	1

Patti DAY

US, female vocalist (1 WEEK)

			pos	wks
9 Dec 89		**RIGHT BEFORE MY EYES** *Debut DEBT 3080*	69	1

DAYEENE

Sweden, female vocal duo (1 WEEK)

			pos	wks
17 Jul 99		**AND IT HURTS** *Pukka CDPUKKA 20*	63	1

Taylor DAYNE

US, female vocalist – Leslie Wundermann (54 WEEKS)

			pos	wks
23 Jan 88	●	**TELL IT TO MY HEART** *Arista 109616*	3	13
19 Mar 88	●	**PROVE YOUR LOVE** *Arista 109830*	8	10
11 Jun 88		**I'LL ALWAYS LOVE YOU** *Arista 111536*	41	7
18 Nov 89		**WITH EVERY BEAT OF MY HEART** *Arista 112760*	53	2
14 Apr 90		**I'LL BE YOUR SHELTER** *Arista 112996*	43	5
4 Aug 90		**LOVE WILL LEAD YOU BACK** *Arista 113277* ▲	69	1
3 Jul 93		**CAN'T GET ENOUGH OF YOUR LOVE** *Arista 74321147852*	14	8
16 Apr 94		**I'LL WAIT** *Arista 74321203472*	29	3
4 Feb 95		**ORIGINAL SIN (THEME FROM 'THE SHADOW')** *Arista 74321223462*	63	1
18 Nov 95		**SAY A PRAYER** *Arista 74321324292*	58	1
13 Jan 96		**TELL IT TO MY HEART (re-mix)** *Arista 74321335962*	23	3

DAYTON

US, male vocal group (1 WEEK)

			pos	wks
10 Dec 83		**THE SOUND OF MUSIC** *Capitol CL 318*	75	1

DAZZ BAND

US, male vocal / instrumental group (12 WEEKS)

			pos	wks
3 Nov 84		**LET IT ALL BLOW** *Motown TMG 1361*	12	12

DBM

Germany, male / female vocal / instrumental group (3 WEEKS)

			pos	wks
12 Nov 77		**DISCO BEATLEMANIA** *Atlantic K 11027*	45	3

UK No.1 ★ UK Top 10 ● Still on chart + UK million seller ◆ UK entry at No.1 ■ US No.1 ▲

D, B, M and T *UK, male vocal / instrumental group (8 WEEKS)*

		pos	wks
1 Aug 70	MR PRESIDENT *Fontana 6007 022*	33	8

See also Dave DEE, DOZY, BEAKY, MICK and TICH

Darryl D'BONNEAU – *See Barbara TUCKER; FONTANA*

D'BORA *US, female vocalist (4 WEEKS)*

		pos	wks
14 Sep 91	DREAM ABOUT YOU *Polydor PO 161*	75	1
1 Jul 95	GOING ROUND *Vibe MCSTD 2055*	40	2
30 Mar 96	GOOD LOVE REAL LOVE *Music Plant MCSTD 40023*	58	1

Nino DE ANGELO *Germany, male vocalist (5 WEEKS)*

		pos	wks
21 Jul 84	GUARDIAN ANGEL *Carrere CAR 335*	57	5

DE BOS *Holland, male DJ / producer (1 WEEK)*

		pos	wks
25 Oct 97	ON THE RUN *Jive JIVECD 433*	51	1

Chris DE BURGH *Son of a diplomat, Irish singer / songwriter b. Christopher John Davidson, 15 Oct 1948, Argentina. The first act to enter the Swiss album chart at No.1, he will, despite his international album sales success, be for ever remembered for the 1986 million-selling No.1 hit he wrote for and about his wife (71 WEEKS)*

		pos	wks
23 Oct 82	DON'T PAY THE FERRYMAN *A & M AMS 8256*	48	5
12 May 84	HIGH ON EMOTION *A & M AM 190*	44	5
12 Jul 86 ★	THE LADY IN RED *A & M AM 331*	1	14
20 Sep 86	FATAL HESITATION *A & M AM 346*	44	4
13 Dec 86	A SPACEMAN CAME TRAVELLING / THE BALLROOM OF ROMANCE *A & M AM 365*	40	5
21 Feb 87	THE LADY IN RED (re-entry) *A & M AM 331*	74	1
12 Dec 87	THE SIMPLE TRUTH (A CHILD IS BORN) *A & M AM 427*	69	2
2 Jan 88	THE SIMPLE TRUTH (A CHILD IS BORN) (re-entry) *A & M AM 427*	55	1
29 Oct 88 ●	MISSING YOU *A & M AM 474*	3	12
7 Jan 89	TENDER HANDS *A & M AM 486*	43	6
14 Oct 89	THIS WAITING HEART *A & M AM 528*	59	3
25 May 91	THE SIMPLE TRUTH (A CHILD IS BORN) (re-issue) *A & M RELF 1*	36	2
11 Apr 92	SEPARATE TABLES *A & M AM 863*	30	4
21 May 94	BLONDE HAIR BLUE JEANS *A & M 5805932*	51	1
9 Dec 95	THE SNOWS OF NEW YORK *A & M 5813132*	60	1
27 Sep 97	SO BEAUTIFUL *A & M 5823932*	29	4
18 Sep 99	WHEN I THINK OF YOU *A&M / Mercury 4971302*	59	1

DE CASTRO SISTERS with Skip Martin and His Orchestra
Cuba, female vocal group (1 WEEK)

		pos	wks
11 Feb 55	TEACH ME TONIGHT *London HL 8104*	20	1

DE-CODE featuring Beverli SKEETE
UK, male / female vocal / instrumental group (1 WEEK)

		pos	wks
18 May 96	WONDERWALL / SOME MIGHT SAY *Neoteric NRCD 2*	69	1

Etienne DE CRECY *France, male DJ / producer (3 WEEKS)*

		pos	wks
28 Mar 98	PRIX CHOC REMIXES *Different DIF 007CD*	60	1
20 Jan 01	AM I WRONG *XL Recordings XLS 127 CD*	44	2

DE FUNK featuring F45
Italy / UK, male production / vocal group (1 WEEK)

		pos	wks
25 Sep 99	PLEASURE LOVE *INCredible INCS 3CD*	49	1

Lennie DE ICE *UK, male producer (1 WEEK)*

		pos	wks
17 Apr 99	WE ARE I. E. *Distinctive DISNCD 50*	61	1

DE LA SOUL *US, male rap group (62 WEEKS)*

		pos	wks
8 Apr 89	ME MYSELF AND I *Big Life BLR 7*	22	8
8 Jul 89	SAY NO GO *Big Life BLR 10*	18	7
21 Oct 89	EYE KNOW *Big Life BLR 13*	14	7
23 Dec 89 ●	THE MAGIC NUMBER / BUDDY *Big Life BLR 14*	7	8
24 Mar 90	MAMA GAVE BIRTH TO THE SOUL CHILDREN *Gee Street GEE 26* [1]	14	7
27 Apr 91 ●	RING RING RING (HA HA HEY) *Big Life BLR 42*	10	7
3 Aug 91	A ROLLER SKATING JAM NAMED 'SATURDAYS' *Big Life BLR 55*	22	5
23 Nov 91	KEEPIN' THE FAITH *Big Life BLR 64*	50	2
18 Sep 93	BREAKADAWN *Big Life BLRD 103*	39	3
2 Apr 94	FALLIN' *Epic 6602622* [2]	59	1
29 Jun 96	STAKES IS HIGH *Tommy Boy TBCD 7730*	55	1
8 Mar 97	4 MORE *Tommy Boy TBCD 7779A* [3]	52	1
22 Jul 00	OOOH *Tommy Boy TBCD 2102* [4]	29	2
11 Nov 00	ALL GOOD *Tommy Boy TBCD 2154B* [5]	33	3

[1] Queen Latifah + De La Soul [2] Teenage Fanclub and De La Soul [3] De La Soul featuring Zhane [4] De La Soul featuring Redman [5] De La Soul featuring Chaka Khan

'Buddy' listed only until Jan 6 1990, peaking at No.8

See also JUNGLE BROTHERS

Donna DE LORY *US, female vocalist (1 WEEK)*

		pos	wks
24 Jul 93	JUST A DREAM *MCA MCSTD 1750*	71	1

Vincent DE MOOR *Holland, male producer (4 WEEKS)*

		pos	wks
16 Aug 97	FLOWTATION *XL Recordings XLS 89CD*	54	1
7 Apr 01	FLY AWAY *VC Recordings VCRD 87*	30	3

DE NADA *UK, male / female production / vocal group (4 WEEKS)*

		pos	wks
25 Aug 01	LOVE YOU ANYWAY *Wildstar CDWILD 37*	15	4

Lynsey DE PAUL
UK, female vocalist / songwriter – Lynsey Rubin (54 WEEKS)

		pos	wks
19 Aug 72 ●	SUGAR ME *MAM 81*	5	11
2 Dec 72	GETTING A DRAG *MAM 88*	18	8
27 Oct 73	WON'T SOMEBODY DANCE WITH ME *MAM 109*	14	7
8 Jun 74	OOH I DO *Warner Bros. K 16401*	25	6
2 Nov 74 ●	NO HONESTLY *Jet 747*	7	11
22 Mar 75	MY MAN AND ME *Jet 750*	40	4
26 Mar 77	ROCK BOTTOM *Polydor 2058 859* [1]	19	7

[1] Lynsey De Paul and Mike Moran

Tullio DE PISCOPO *Italy, male vocalist (4 WEEKS)*

		pos	wks
28 Feb 87	STOP BAJON . . . PRIMAVERA *Greyhound GREY 9*	58	4

Rebecca DE RUVO *Sweden, female vocalist (1 WEEK)*

		pos	wks
1 Oct 94	I CAUGHT YOU OUT *Arista 74321230782*	72	1

Teri DE SARIO *US, female vocalist (5 WEEKS)*

		pos	wks
2 Sep 78	AIN'T NOTHING GONNA KEEP ME FROM YOU *Casablanca CAN 128*	52	5

Stephanie DE SYKES
UK, female vocalist – Stephanie Ryton (17 WEEKS)

		pos	wks
20 Jul 74 ●	BORN WITH A SMILE ON MY FACE *Bradley's BRAD 7409* [1]	2	10
19 Apr 75	WE'LL FIND OUR DAY *Bradley's BRAD 7509*	17	7

[1] Stephanie De Sykes with Rain

William DE VAUGHN *US, male vocalist (10 WEEKS)*

		pos	wks
6 Jul 74	BE THANKFUL FOR WHAT YOU'VE GOT *Chelsea 2005 002*	31	5
20 Sep 80	BE THANKFUL FOR WHAT YOU'VE GOT (re-recording) *EMI 5101*	44	5

Tony DE VIT *UK, male DJ / producer (11 WEEKS)*

		pos	wks
4 Mar 95	BURNING UP *Icon ICONCD 001*	25	3
12 Aug 95	HOOKED *Labello Dance LAD 18CD* [1]	28	2
9 Sep 95	TO THE LIMIT *X:Plode BANG 1CD*	44	2

30 May 96	**I'LL BE THERE** *Labello Dance LAD 25CD1* [1]	37	2
28 Oct 00	**DAWN** *Tidy Trax TIDY 140CD*	56	2

[1] 99th Floor Elevators featuring Tony De Vit

DEACON BLUE (258 Top 500) *Scottish sextet with fervent following, led by singer / songwriter Ricky Ross (v) and featuring his wife Lorraine McIntosh (v). Named after the Steely Dan song, they achieved five Top 5 albums, including the million-selling 'When the World Knows Your Name' (112 WEEKS)* pos/wks

23 Jan 88	**DIGNITY** *CBS DEAC 4*	31	8
9 Apr 88	**WHEN WILL YOU MAKE MY TELEPHONE RING** *CBS DEAC 5*	34	7
16 Jul 88	**CHOCOLATE GIRL** *CBS DEAC 6*	43	7
15 Oct 88 ●	**REAL GONE KID** *CBS DEAC 7*	8	13
4 Mar 89	**WAGES DAY** *CBS DEAC 8*	18	6
20 May 89	**FERGUS SINGS THE BLUES** *CBS DEAC 9*	14	6
16 Sep 89	**LOVE AND REGRET** *CBS DEAC 10*	28	5
6 Jan 90	**QUEEN OF THE NEW YEAR** *CBS DEAC 11*	21	5
25 Aug 90 ●	**FOUR BACHARACH AND DAVID SONGS (EP)** *CBS DEAC 12*	2	9
25 May 91	**YOUR SWAYING ARMS** *Columbia 6568937*	23	4
27 Jul 91 ●	**TWIST AND SHOUT** *Columbia 6573027*	10	9
12 Oct 91	**CLOSING TIME** *Columbia 6575027*	42	3
14 Dec 91	**COVER FROM THE SKY** *Columbia 6576737*	31	4
28 Nov 92	**YOUR TOWN** *Columbia 6587867*	14	8
13 Feb 93	**WILL WE BE LOVERS** *Columbia 6589732*	31	4
24 Apr 93	**ONLY TENDER LOVE** *Columbia 6591842*	22	4
17 Jul 93	**HANG YOUR HEAD** *Columbia 6594602*	21	3
2 Apr 94	**I WAS RIGHT AND YOU WERE WRONG** *Columbia 6602222*	32	3
28 May 94	**DIGNITY** *Columbia 6604485*	20	3
28 Apr 01	**EVERYTIME YOU SLEEP** *Papillon BTFLY 0011*	64	1

Tracks on Four Bacharach and David Songs (EP): I'll Never Fall in Love Again / The Look of Love / Message to Michael / Are You There (With Another Girl). 'Dignity' in 1994 was the original recording of the song first issued in 1987 when it failed to chart

DEAD DRED *UK, male instrumental / production duo (2 WEEKS)* pos/wks

5 Nov 94	**DRED BASS** *Moving Shadow SHADOW 50CD*	60	2

DEAD END KIDS *UK, male vocal / instrumental group (10 WEEKS)* pos/wks

26 Mar 77 ●	**HAVE I THE RIGHT** *CBS 4972*	6	10

DEAD KENNEDYS *US, male vocal / instrumental group (9 WEEKS)* pos/wks

1 Nov 80	**KILL THE POOR** *Cherry Red CHERRY 16*	49	3
30 May 81	**TOO DRUNK TO FUCK** *Cherry Red CHERRY 24*	36	6

DEAD OR ALIVE *UK, male vocal / instrumental group (70 WEEKS)* pos/wks

24 Mar 84	**THAT'S THE WAY (I LIKE IT)** *Epic A 4271*	22	9
1 Dec 84 ★	**YOU SPIN ME ROUND (LIKE A RECORD)** *Epic A 4861*	1	23
20 Apr 85	**LOVER COME BACK TO ME** *Epic A 6086*	11	8
29 Jun 85	**IN TOO DEEP** *Epic A 6360*	14	8
21 Sep 85	**MY HEART GOES BANG (GET ME TO THE DOCTOR)** *Epic A 6571*	23	6
20 Sep 86	**BRAND NEW LOVER** *Epic A 650075 7*	31	4
10 Jan 87	**SOMETHING IN MY HOUSE** *Epic BURNS 1*	12	7
4 Apr 87	**HOOKED ON LOVE** *Epic BURNS 2*	69	2
3 Sep 88	**TURN ROUND AND COUNT 2 TEN** *Epic BURNS 4*	70	1
22 Jul 89	**COME HOME WITH ME BABY** *Epic BURNS 5*	62	2

DEAD PREZ *US, male rap duo (2 WEEKS)* pos/wks

13 Mar 00	**HIP HOP** *Epic 6689862*	41	2

DEADLY SINS *UK / Italy, male vocal / instrumental duo (2 WEEKS)* pos/wks

30 Apr 94	**WE ARE GOING ON DOWN** *Ffrreedom TABCD 220*	45	2

Hazell DEAN *Exuberant pop-dance singer, b. 27 Oct 1958, Essex, UK, who started recording in 1976. Became associated with frenetic Hi-NRG dance boom of the 1980s. Many of her hits were produced by Stock Aitken and Waterman including their first Top 10 entry, 'Whatever I Do' (71 WEEKS)* pos/wks

18 Feb 84	**EVERGREEN / JEALOUS LOVE** *Proto ENA 114*	63	3
21 Apr 84 ●	**SEARCHIN' (I GOTTA FIND A MAN)** *Proto ENA 109*	6	15
28 Jul 84 ●	**WHATEVER I DO (WHEREVER I GO)** *Proto ENA 119*	4	11
3 Nov 84	**BACK IN MY ARMS (ONCE AGAIN)** *Proto ENA 122*	41	4
2 Mar 85	**NO FOOL (FOR LOVE)** *Proto ENA 123*	41	5
12 Oct 85	**THEY SAY IT'S GONNA RAIN** *Parlophone R 6107*	58	4
2 Apr 88 ●	**WHO'S LEAVING WHO** *EMI EM 45*	4	11
25 Jun 88	**MAYBE (WE SHOULD CALL IT A DAY)** *EMI EM 62*	15	6
24 Sep 88	**TURN IT INTO LOVE** *EMI EM 71*	21	7
26 Aug 89	**LOVE PAINS** *Lisson DOLE 12*	48	4
23 Mar 91	**BETTER OFF WITHOUT YOU** *Lisson DOLE 19*	72	1

Jimmy DEAN *US, male vocalist – Seth Ward (17 WEEKS)* pos/wks

26 Oct 61 ●	**BIG BAD JOHN** *Philips PB 1187* ▲	2	13
8 Nov 62	**LITTLE BLACK BOOK** *CBS AAG 122*	33	4

Letitia DEAN and Paul MEDFORD
UK, female / male vocal duo (7 WEEKS) pos/wks

25 Oct 86	**SOMETHING OUTA NOTHING** *BBC RESL 203*	12	7

Sheryl DEANE – *See THRILLSEEKERS*

DEANNA – *See David MORALES*

DEAR JON *UK, female / male vocal / instrumental group (1 WEEK)* pos/wks

22 Apr 95	**ONE GIFT OF LOVE** *MDMC DEVCS 2*	68	1

DEATH IN VEGAS *UK, male instrumental / production duo – Richard Fearless and Tim Holmes (8 WEEKS)* pos/wks

2 Aug 97	**DIRT** *Concrete HARD 27CD*	61	1
1 Nov 97	**ROCCO** *Concrete HARD 29CD*	51	1
12 Feb 00 ●	**AISHA** *Concrete HARD 43CD*	9	4
6 May 00	**DIRGE** *Concrete HARD 44CD*	24	2

Uncredited vocal on 'Aisha' by Iggy Pop

DeBARGE *US, male / female vocal group (17 WEEKS)* pos/wks

6 Apr 85 ●	**RHYTHM OF THE NIGHT** *Gordy TMG 1376*	4	14
21 Sep 85	**YOU WEAR IT WELL** *Gordy ZB 40345* [1]	54	3

[1] El DeBarge with DeBarge

See also El DeBARGE; Chico DeBARGE

Chico DeBARGE *US, male vocalist (1 WEEK)* pos/wks

14 Mar 98	**IGGIN' ME** *Universal UND 56170*	50	1

See also DeBARGE

El DeBARGE *US, male vocalist (3 WEEKS)* pos/wks

28 Jun 86	**WHO'S JOHNNY ('SHORT CIRCUIT' THEME)** *Gordy ELD 1*	60	2
31 Mar 90	**SECRET GARDEN** *Qwest W 9992* [1]	67	1

[1] Quincy Jones featuring Al B Sure!, James Ingram, El DeBarge and Barry White

See also DeBARGE

Diana DECKER *US, female vocalist (10 WEEKS)* pos/wks

23 Oct 53 ●	**POPPA PICCOLINO** *Columbia DB 3325*	2	8
8 Jan 54 ●	**POPPA PICCOLINO (re-entry)** *Columbia DB 3325*	5	2

Dave DEE *UK, male vocalist (4 WEEKS)* pos/wks

14 Mar 70	**MY WOMAN'S MAN** *Fontana TF 1074*	42	4

See also Dave DEE, DOZY, BEAKY, MICK and TICH

Dave DEE, DOZY, BEAKY, MICK and TICH (172 Top 500) *Quirkily named UK quintet was very popular in late 1960s: Dave Dee (David Harman) (v), Dozy (Trevor Davies) (b), Beaky (John Dymond) (g), Mick (Michael Wilson) (d), Tich (Ian Amey) (g). Catchy productions and ultra-commercial songs (penned by managers Howard and Blaikley) ensured string of hits (141 WEEKS)* pos/wks

23 Dec 65	**YOU MAKE IT MOVE** *Fontana TF 630*	26	8
3 Mar 66 ●	**HOLD TIGHT!** *Fontana TF 671*	4	17
9 Jun 66 ●	**HIDEAWAY** *Fontana TF 711*	10	11
15 Sep 66 ●	**BEND IT!** *Fontana TF 746*	2	12

Date		Title / Label	pos	wks
8 Dec 66	●	**SAVE ME** *Fontana TF 775*	3	10
9 Mar 67		**TOUCH ME, TOUCH ME** *Fontana TF 798*	13	9
18 May 67	●	**OKAY!** *Fontana TF 830*	4	11
11 Oct 67	●	**ZABADAK!** *Fontana TF 873*	3	14
14 Feb 68	★	**THE LEGEND OF XANADU** *Fontana TF 903*	1	12
3 Jul 68	●	**LAST NIGHT IN SOHO** *Fontana TF 953*	8	11
2 Oct 68		**THE WRECK OF THE 'ANTOINETTE'** *Fontana TF 971*	14	9
5 Mar 69		**DON JUAN** *Fontana TF 1000*	23	9
14 May 69		**SNAKE IN THE GRASS** *Fontana TF 1020*	23	8

Jazzy DEE *US, male rapper / instrumentalist (5 WEEKS)* pos/wks

Date		Title / Label	pos	wks
5 Mar 83		**GET ON UP** *Laurie LRS 101*	53	5

Joey DEE and the STARLITERS

US, male vocal / instrumental group (8 WEEKS) pos/wks

Date		Title / Label	pos	wks
8 Feb 62		**PEPPERMINT TWIST** *Columbia DB 4758* ▲	33	8

Kiki DEE (423 Top 500) *First white UK artist to secure a recording deal with Tamla Motown, b. Pauline Matthews, 6 Mar 1947, Bradford, UK. Vocalist, much respected by her peers, who achieved an Olivier Award nomination in 1989 for her acting skills demonstrated in Willy Russell's West End stage hit 'Blood Brothers' (79 WEEKS)* pos/wks

Date		Title / Label	pos	wks
10 Nov 73		**AMOUREUSE** *Rocket PIG 4*	13	13
7 Sep 74		**I'VE GOT THE MUSIC IN ME** *Rocket PIG 12* [1]	19	8
12 Apr 75		**(YOU DONT KNOW) HOW GLAD I AM** *Rocket PIG 16* [1]	33	4
3 Jul 76	★	**DON'T GO BREAKING MY HEART** *Rocket ROKN 512* [2] ▲	1	14
11 Sep 76		**LOVING AND FREE / AMOUREUSE (re-issue)** *Rocket ROKN 515*	13	8
19 Feb 77		**FIRST THING IN THE MORNING** *Rocket ROKN 520*	32	5
11 Jun 77		**CHICAGO** *Rocket ROKN 526*	28	4
21 Feb 81		**STAR** *Ariola ARO 251*	13	10
23 May 81		**PERFECT TIMING** *Ariola ARO 257*	66	3
20 Nov 93	●	**TRUE LOVE** *Rocket EJSCX 32* [2]	2	10

[1] Kiki Dee Band [2] Elton John and Kiki Dee

On 18 Sep, 25 Sep and 2 Oct 1976, 'Loving and Free' was listed by itself. 'Chicago' was one side of a double-sided chart entry, the other being 'Bite Your Lip (Get Up and Dance)' by Elton John

Nancy DEE – *See BENELUX and Nancy DEE*

DEEE-LITE *US / Russia / Japan, male / female vocal / instrumental group (30 WEEKS)* pos/wks

Date		Title / Label	pos	wks
18 Aug 90	●	**GROOVE IS IN THE HEART / WHAT IS LOVE** *Elektra EKR 114*	2	13
24 Nov 90		**POWER OF LOVE / DEEE-LITE THEME** *Elektra EKR 117*	25	7
23 Feb 91		**HOW DO YOU SAY . . . LOVE / GROOVE IS IN THE HEART (re-mix)** *Elektra EKR 118*	52	2
27 Apr 91		**GOOD BEAT** *Elektra EKR 122*	53	3
13 Jun 92		**RUNAWAY** *Elektra EKR 148*	45	3
30 Jul 94		**PICNIC IN THE SUMMERTIME** *Elektra EKR 186CD1*	43	2

'What Is Love' listed only from 25 Aug 1990

DEEJAY PUNK-ROC *US, male DJ / producer (5 WEEKS)* pos/wks

Date		Title / Label	pos	wks
21 Mar 98		**DEAD HUSBAND** *Independiente ISOM 9MS*	71	1
9 May 98		**MY BEATBOX** *Independiente ISOM 12MS*	43	1
8 Aug 98		**FAR OUT** *Independiente ISOM 17MS*	43	2
20 Feb 99		**ROC-IN-IT** *Independiente ISOM 21MS* [1]	59	1

[1] Deejay Punk-Roc vs Onyx

DEEJAY SVEN – *See MC MIKER 'G' and Deejay SVEN*

Carol DEENE *UK, female vocalist (25 WEEKS)* pos/wks

Date		Title / Label	pos	wks
26 Oct 61		**SAD MOVIES (MAKE ME CRY)** *HMV POP 922*	44	3
25 Jan 62		**NORMAN** *HMV POP 973*	24	8
5 Jul 62		**JOHNNY GET ANGRY** *HMV POP 1027*	32	4
23 Aug 62		**SOME PEOPLE** *HMV POP 1058*	25	10

DEEP BLUE *UK, male producer – Sean O'Keefe (2 WEEKS)* pos/wks

Date		Title / Label	pos	wks
16 Apr 94		**HELICOPTER TUNE** *Moving Shadow SHADOW 41CD*	68	2

DEEP BLUE SOMETHING

US, male vocal / instrumental group (17 WEEKS) pos/wks

Date		Title / Label	pos	wks
6 Jul 96		**BREAKFAST AT TIFFANY'S** *Interscope IND 80032*	55	2
21 Sep 96	★	**BREAKFAST AT TIFFANY'S (re-entry)** *Interscope IND 80032*	1	12
7 Dec 96		**JOSEY** *Interscope IND 95518*	27	3

DEEP C *UK, male / female vocal / instrumental group (3 WEEKS)* pos/wks

Date		Title / Label	pos	wks
19 Jan 91		**AFRICAN REIGN** *M & G MAGS 4*	75	1
8 Jun 91		**CHILL TO THE PANIC** *M & G MAGS 10*	73	2

DEEP CREED '94 *US, male producer - Armand van Helden (1 WEEK)* pos/wks

Date		Title / Label	pos	wks
7 May 94		**CAN U FEEL IT** *Eastern Bloc BLOCCD 005*	59	1

DEEP DISH *Iran, male instrumental / production duo (4 WEEKS)* pos/wks

Date		Title / Label	pos	wks
26 Oct 96		**STAY GOLD** *Deconstruction 74321418222*	41	1
1 Nov 97		**STRANDED** *Deconstruction 74321512232*	60	1
3 Oct 98		**THE FUTURE OF THE FUTURE (STAY GOLD)** *Deconstruction 74321616252* [1]	31	2

[1] Deep Dish with Everything but the Girl

DEEP FEELING *UK, male vocal / instrumental group (5 WEEKS)* pos/wks

Date		Title / Label	pos	wks
25 Apr 70		**DO YOU LOVE ME** *Page One POF 165*	45	1
9 May 70		**DO YOU LOVE ME (re-entry)** *Page One POF 165*	34	4

DEEP FOREST *France, male instrumental duo - Eric Mouquet and Michael Sanchez (14 WEEKS)* pos/wks

Date		Title / Label	pos	wks
5 Feb 94	●	**SWEET LULLABY** *Columbia 6599242*	10	6
21 May 94		**DEEP FOREST** *Columbia 6604115*	20	4
23 Jul 94		**SAVANNA DANCE** *Columbia 6606355*	28	2
24 Jun 95		**MARTA'S SONG** *Columbia 6621402*	26	2

DEEP PURPLE (382 Top 500) *Long-running legendary heavy rock group. London band's ever-changing line-up ensured many spin-off groups, among them Rainbow (founded by ex-guitarist Ritchie Blackmore), Whitesnake (featuring ex-vocalist David Coverdale) and Gillan (started by ex-vocalist Ian Gillan) (85 WEEKS)* pos/wks

Date		Title / Label	pos	wks
15 Aug 70	●	**BLACK NIGHT** *Harvest HAR 5020*	2	21
27 Feb 71	●	**STRANGE KIND OF WOMAN** *Harvest HAR 5033*	8	12
13 Nov 71		**FIREBALL** *Harvest HAR 5045*	15	13
1 Apr 72		**NEVER BEFORE** *Purple PUR 102*	35	6
16 Apr 77		**SMOKE ON THE WATER** *Purple PUR 132*	21	7
15 Oct 77		**NEW LIVE AND RARE (EP)** *Purple PUR 135*	31	4
7 Oct 78		**NEW LIVE AND RARE II (EP)** *Purple PUR 137*	45	3
2 Aug 80		**BLACK NIGHT (re-issue)** *Harvest HAR 5210*	43	6
1 Nov 80		**NEW LIVE AND RARE III (EP)** *Harvest SHEP 101*	48	3
26 Jan 85		**PERFECT STRANGERS** *Polydor POSP 719*	48	3
15 Jun 85		**KNOCKING AT YOUR BACK DOOR / PERFECT STRANGERS** *Polydor POSP 749*	68	1
18 Jun 88		**HUSH** *Polydor PO 4*	62	2
20 Oct 90		**KING OF DREAMS** *RCA PB 49247*	70	1
2 Mar 91		**LOVE CONQUERS ALL** *RCA PB 49225*	57	2
24 Jun 95		**BLACK NIGHT (re-mix)** *EMI CDEM 382*	66	1

Tracks on New Live and Rare (EP): Black Night (Live) / Painted Horse / When a Blind Man Cries. New Live and Rare II (EP): Burn (Edited Version) / Coronarias Redig / Mistreated (Interpolating Rock Me Baby). New Live and Rare Volume 3 (EP): Smoke on the Water / Bird Has Flown / Grabsplatter

DEEP RIVER BOYS *US, male vocal group (1 WEEK)* pos/wks

Date		Title / Label	pos	wks
7 Dec 56		**THAT'S RIGHT** *HMV POP 263*	29	1

Scotti DEEP *US, male producer / instrumentalist (1 WEEK)* pos/wks

Date		Title / Label	pos	wks
15 Mar 97		**BROOKLYN BEATS** *Xtravaganza 0090095*	67	1

Rick DEES and his CAST OF IDIOTS *US, male vocalist with male / female vocal / instrumental group (9 WEEKS)* pos/wks

			pos	wks
18 Sep 76	●	**DISCO DUCK (PART ONE)** *RSO 2090 204* ▲	6	9

DEETAH *Chile, female vocalist (10 WEEKS)* pos/wks

			pos	wks
26 Sep 98		**RELAX** *ffrr FCDP 345*	11	8
1 May 99		**EL PARAISO RICO** *ffrr FCD 356*	39	2

DEF LEPPARD (257 Top 500) *Mainstream UK rock stalwarts who wooed US before their homeland: Joe Elliott (v), Phil Collen (g from 1983), Steve Clark (g) (d. 1991), Rick Savage (b), Rick Allen (d). In US achieved feat of two consecutive albums selling more than eight million (112 WEEKS)* pos/wks

			pos	wks
17 Nov 79		**WASTED** *Vertigo 6059 247*	61	3
23 Feb 80		**HELLO AMERICA** *Vertigo LEPP 1*	45	4
5 Feb 83		**PHOTOGRAPH** *Vertigo VER 5*	66	3
27 Aug 83		**ROCK OF AGES** *Vertigo VER 6*	41	4
1 Aug 87	●	**ANIMAL** *Bludgeon Riffola LEP 1*	6	9
19 Sep 87		**POUR SOME SUGAR ON ME** *Bludgeon Riffola LEP 2*	18	6
28 Nov 87		**HYSTERIA** *Bludgeon Riffola LEP 3*	26	5
9 Jan 88		**HYSTERIA (re-entry)** *Bludgeon Riffola LEP 3*	74	1
9 Apr 88		**ARMAGEDDON IT** *Bludgeon Riffola LEP 4*	20	5
16 Jul 88		**LOVE BITES** *Bludgeon Riffola LEP 5* ▲	11	8
11 Feb 89		**ROCKET** *Bludgeon Riffola LEP 6*	15	7
28 Mar 92	●	**LET'S GET ROCKED** *Bludgeon Riffola DEF 7*	2	7
27 Jun 92		**MAKE LOVE LIKE A MAN** *Bludgeon Riffola LEP 7*	12	5
12 Sep 92		**HAVE YOU EVER NEEDED SOMEONE SO BAD** *Bludgeon Riffola LEP 8*	16	5
30 Jan 93		**HEAVEN IS** *Bludgeon Riffola LEPCD 9*	13	5
1 May 93		**TONIGHT** *Bludgeon Riffola LEPCD 10*	34	3
18 Sep 93		**TWO STEPS BEHIND** *Bludgeon Riffola LEPCD 12*	32	4
15 Jan 94		**ACTION** *Bludgeon Riffola LEPCD 13*	14	5
14 Oct 95	●	**WHEN LOVE AND HATE COLLIDE** *Bludgeon Riffola LEPCD 14*	2	10
4 May 96		**SLANG** *Bludgeon Riffola LEPCD 15*	17	5
13 Jul 96		**WORK IT OUT** *Bludgeon Riffola LEPCD 16*	22	3
28 Sep 96		**ALL I WANT IS EVERYTHING** *Bludgeon Riffola LEPCD 17*	38	2
30 Nov 96		**BREATHE A SIGH** *Bludgeon Riffola LEPCD 18*	43	1
24 Jul 99		**PROMISES** *Bludgeon Riffola 5621362*	41	1
9 Oct 99		**GOODBYE** *Bludgeon Riffola 5622892*	54	1

DEFINITION OF SOUND
UK, male rap duo – Donald Weekes and Kevin Clark (25 WEEKS) pos/wks

			pos	wks
9 Mar 91		**WEAR YOUR LOVE LIKE HEAVEN** *Circa YR 61*	17	9
1 Jun 91		**NOW IS TOMORROW** *Circa YR 66*	46	4
8 Feb 92		**MOIRA JANE'S CAFE** *Circa YR 80*	34	4
19 Sep 92		**WHAT ARE YOU UNDER** *Circa YR 95*	68	1
14 Nov 92		**CAN I GET OVER** *Circa YR 97*	61	2
20 May 95		**BOOM BOOM** *Fontana DOSCD 1*	59	1
2 Dec 95		**PASS THE VIBES** *Fontana DOSCD 2*	23	3
24 Feb 96		**CHILD** *Fontana DOSCD 3*	48	1

DEFTONES *US, male vocal / instrumental group (4 WEEKS)* pos/wks

			pos	wks
21 Mar 98		**MY OWN SUMMER (SHOVE IT)** *Maverick W 0432CD*	29	2
11 Jul 98		**BE QUIET AND DRIVE (FAR AWAY)** *Maverick W 0445CD*	50	1
26 Aug 00		**CHANGE (IN THE HOUSE OF FLIES)** *Maverick W531CD*	53	1

DEGREES OF MOTION featuring BITI
US, female vocal group (21 WEEKS) pos/wks

			pos	wks
25 Apr 92		**DO YOU WANT IT RIGHT NOW** *ffrr F 184*	31	5
18 Jul 92		**SHINE ON** *ffrr F 192* [1]	43	3
7 Nov 92		**SOUL FREEDOM - FREE YOUR SOUL** *ffrr FX 201*	64	1
19 Mar 94	●	**SHINE ON (re-mix)** *ffrr FCD 229*	8	8
25 Jun 94		**DO YOU WANT IT RIGHT NOW (re-mix)** *ffrr FCD 236*	26	4

[1] Degrees of Motion featuring Biti with Kit West

DEJA *US, male / female vocal duo (1 WEEK)* pos/wks

			pos	wks
29 Aug 87		**SERIOUS** *10 TEN 132*	75	1

DEJA VU *UK, male vocal / instrumental duo (1 WEEK)* pos/wks

			pos	wks
5 Feb 94		**WHY WHY WHY** *Cowboy CDRODEO 941*	57	1

Desmond DEKKER and the ACES (500 Top 500) *First reggae act to top UK chart, leader b. Desmond Dacres, 16 Jul 1942, Kingston, Jamaica. Winner of Jamaican 'King of Bluebeat' award five times between 1963 and 1969. Despite obscure patois lyric, 'Israelites' reached Top 10 in UK (twice) and US (71 WEEKS)* pos/wks

			pos	wks
12 Jul 67		**007 (SHANTY TOWN)** *Pyramid PYR 6004*	14	11
19 Mar 69	★	**ISRAELITES** *Pyramid PYR 6058*	1	14
25 Jun 69	●	**IT MIEK** *Pyramid PYR 6068*	7	11
2 Jul 69		**ISRAELITES (re-entry)** *Pyramid PYR 6058*	45	1
10 Jan 70		**PICKNEY GAL** *Pyramid PYR 6078*	42	3
22 Aug 70	●	**YOU CAN GET IT IF YOU REALLY WANT** *Trojan TR 7777* [1]	2	15
10 May 75	●	**ISRAELITES (re-recording)** *Cactus CT 57* [1]	10	9
30 Aug 75		**SING A LITTLE SONG** *Cactus CT 73* [1]	16	7

[1] Desmond Dekker

DEL AMITRI *UK, male vocal / instrumental group (69 WEEKS)* pos/wks

			pos	wks
19 Aug 89		**KISS THIS THING GOODBYE** *A & M AM 515*	59	2
13 Jan 90		**NOTHING EVER HAPPENS** *A & M AM 536*	11	9
24 Mar 90		**KISS THIS THING GOODBYE (re-issue)** *A & M AM 551*	43	4
16 Jun 90		**MOVE AWAY JIMMY BLUE** *A & M AM 555*	36	6
3 Nov 90		**SPIT IN THE RAIN** *A & M AM 589*	21	6
9 May 92		**ALWAYS THE LAST TO KNOW** *A & M AM 870*	13	7
11 Jul 92		**BE MY DOWNFALL** *A & M AM 884*	30	4
12 Sep 92		**JUST LIKE A MAN** *A & M AM 0057*	25	4
23 Jan 93		**WHEN YOU WERE YOUNG** *A & M AMCD 0132*	20	3
18 Feb 95		**HERE AND NOW** *A & M 5809692*	21	4
29 Apr 95		**DRIVING WITH THE BRAKES ON** *A & M 5810072*	18	4
8 Jul 95		**ROLL TO ME** *A & M 5811312*	22	4
28 Oct 95		**TELL HER THIS** *A & M 5812172*	32	2
21 Jun 97		**NOT WHERE IT'S AT** *A & M 5822532*	21	3
6 Dec 97		**SOME OTHER SUCKER'S PARADE** *A&M 5824352*	46	1
13 Jun 98		**DON'T COME HOME TOO SOON** *A&M 5827052*	15	4
5 Sep 98		**CRY TO BE FOUND** *A&M MERCD 513*	40	2

DE'LACY *US, male / female vocal / instrumental group (16 WEEKS)* pos/wks

			pos	wks
2 Sep 95	●	**HIDEAWAY** *Slip 'N' Slide 74321310472*	9	10
31 Aug 96		**THAT LOOK** *Slip 'N' Slide 74321398322*	19	4
14 Feb 98		**HIDEAWAY 1998 (re-mix)** *Slip 'N'Slide 74321561052*	21	2

DELAGE *UK, female vocal group (2 WEEKS)* pos/wks

			pos	wks
15 Dec 90		**ROCK THE BOAT** *PWL / Polydor PO 113*	63	2

DELAKOTA *UK, male vocal / instrumental duo (3 WEEKS)* pos/wks

			pos	wks
18 Jul 98		**THE ROCK** *Go.Beat GOBCD 10*	60	1
19 Sep 98		**C'MON CINCINNATI** *Go.Beat GOBCD 11* [1]	55	1
13 Feb 99		**555** *Go.Beat GOBCD 14*	42	1

[1] Delakota featuring Rose Smith

DELANEY and BONNIE and FRIENDS *US, male / female vocal duo (Delaney and Bonnie Bramlett) and instrumental group (9 WEEKS)* pos/wks

			pos	wks
20 Dec 69		**COMIN' HOME** *Atlantic 584 308* [1]	16	9

[1] Delaney and Bonnie and Friends featuring Eric Clapton

See also Eric CLAPTON

DELANO – *See CZR featuring DELANO*

DELEGATION *UK, male vocal / instrumental group (7 WEEKS)* pos/wks

			pos	wks
23 Apr 77		**WHERE IS THE LOVE (WE USED TO KNOW)** *State STAT 40*	22	6
20 Aug 77		**YOU'VE BEEN DOING ME WRONG** *State STAT 55*	49	1

DELERIUM
Canada, male production duo – Rhys Fulber and Bill Leeb (23 WEEKS) pos/wks

			pos	wks
12 Jun 99		**SILENCE** *Nettwerk 398152*	73	1
5 Feb 00		**HEAVEN'S EARTH** *Nettwerk 331032*	44	1
14 Oct 00	●	**SILENCE (re-mix)** *Nettwerk 331072* [1]	3	16

1963

IN THE YEAR IN WHICH JFK WAS SHOT, THE PROFUMO AFFAIR CAUSED A MASSIVE SCANDAL IN LONDON, DR MARTIN LUTHER KING GAVE HIS LANDMARK 'I HAVE A DREAM' SPEECH IN FRONT OF ALMOST HALF A MILLION PEOPLE IN WASHINGTON DC, AND MERSEYBEAT ACTS RULED THE CHARTS, **OZZY OSBOURNE** RECALLS LIFE AS A BIRMINGHAM TEENAGE FAB FOUR FAN ...

“'She Loves You' was the very first record I ever bought – 13 years old, walking down the street in Aston with my money in my pocket – and as soon as I got it home I became a **Beatles** fanatic. Still am. It was a total obsession – if I saw their name in a magazine I'd cut it out and stick it on my wall. The first person I impersonated in front of the bedroom mirror was John Lennon. It was one of the saddest days in my life when he died.”

SINGLE OF THE YEAR 'From Me to You' Beatles
ALBUM OF THE YEAR 'Please Please Me' Beatles

7 Jul 01	**INNOCENTE (FALLING IN LOVE)** *Nettwerk 331172* [2]	**32**	3
24 Nov 01	**UNDERWATER** *Nettwerk 331422* [3]	**33**	2

[1] Delerium featuring Sarah McLachlan [2] Delerium featuring Leigh Nash [3] Delerium Featuring Rani. Sarah McLachlan's vocals (uncredited) also featured on the original hit version of 'Silence'

DELFONICS *US, male vocal group (23 WEEKS)* pos/wks

10 Apr 71	**DIDN'T I (BLOW YOUR MIND THIS TIME)** *Bell 1099*	**43**	1
24 Apr 71	**DIDN'T I (BLOW YOUR MIND THIS TIME) (re-entry)** *Bell 1099*	**22**	8
10 Jul 71	**LA-LA MEANS I LOVE YOU** *Bell 1165*	**19**	10
16 Oct 71	**READY OR NOT HERE I COME** *Bell 1175*	**41**	4

DELGADOS *UK, male / female vocal / instrumental group (2 WEEKS)* pos/wks

23 May 98	**PULL THE WIRES FROM THE WALL** *Chemikal CHEM 023CD*	**69**	1
3 Jun 00	**AMERICAN TRILOGY** *Chemikal Underground CHEM 039CD*	**61**	1

DELIRIOUS? *UK, male vocal / instrumental group (17 WEEKS)* pos/wks

1 Mar 97	**WHITE RIBBON DAY** *Furious? CDFURY 1*	**41**	2
17 May 97	**DEEPER** *Furious? CDFURY 2*	**20**	3
26 Jul 97	**PROMISE** *Furious? CDFURY 3*	**20**	2
15 Nov 97	**DEEPER (EP)** *Furious? CXFURY 4*	**36**	2
27 Mar 99	**SEE THE STAR** *Furious? CDFURY 5*	**16**	2
4 Mar 00	**IT'S OK** *Furious? CDFURY 6*	**18**	2
16 Jun 01	**WAITING FOR THE SUMMER** *Furious? CDFURY 7*	**26**	2
22 Dec 01	**I COULD SING OF YOUR LOVE FOREVER** *Furious? CDFURY 9*	**40**	2+

Tracks on Deeper (EP): Deeper / Summer of Love / Touch / Sanctify

'DELIVERANCE' SOUNDTRACK *US, male instrumental duo – Eric Weissberg on banjo and Steve Mandell on guitar (7 WEEKS)* pos/wks

31 Mar 73	**DUELLING BANJOS** *Warner Bros. K 16223*	**17**	7

DELLS *US, male vocal group (9 WEEKS)* pos/wks

16 Jul 69	**I CAN SING A RAINBOW - LOVE IS BLUE (MEDLEY)** *Chess CRS 8099*	**15**	9

DELORES – *See MONOBOY featuring DELORES*

DELRONS – *See REPARATA and the DELRONS*

DELTA – *See David MORALES; Crystal WATERS*

DELUXE *US, female vocalist (1 WEEK)* pos/wks

18 Mar 89	**JUST A LITTLE MORE** *Unyque UNQ 5*	**74**	1

DEM 2 *UK, male production duo (2 WEEKS)* pos/wks

24 Oct 98	**DESTINY** *Locked On LOX 101CD*	**58**	2

DEMETREUS – *See Christian FALK featuring DEMETREUS*

DEMOLITION MAN – *See PRIZNA featuring DEMOLITION MAN*

DEMON vs HEARTBREAKER *France, male production group (1 WEEK)* pos/wks

19 May 01	**YOU ARE MY HIGH** *Source SOURCDSE 1032*	**70**	1

D'EMPRESS – *See 187 LOCKDOWN*

Chaka DEMUS and PLIERS *Jamaica, male vocal duo (55 WEEKS)* pos/wks

12 Jun 93 ●	**TEASE ME** *Mango CIDM 806*	**3**	15
18 Sep 93 ●	**SHE DON'T LET NOBODY** *Mango CIDM 810*	**4**	10
18 Dec 93 ★	**TWIST AND SHOUT** *Mango CIDM 814* [1]	**1**	13
12 Mar 94	**MURDER SHE WROTE** *Mango CIDM 812*	**27**	4
18 Jun 94	**I WANNA BE YOUR MAN** *Mango CIDM 817*	**19**	6
27 Aug 94	**GAL WINE** *Mango CIDM 818*	**20**	4
1 Apr 95	**TWIST AND SHOUT (re-entry)** *Mango CIDM 814* [1]	**67**	1
31 Aug 96	**EVERY KINDA PEOPLE** *Island Jamaica IJCD 2005*	**47**	1
30 Aug 97	**EVERY LITTLE THING SHE DOES IS MAGIC** *Virgin VSCDT 1654*	**51**	1

[1] Chaka Demus and Pliers featuring Jack Radics and Taxi Gang

Terry DENE *UK, male vocalist – Terry Williams (20 WEEKS)* pos/wks

7 Jun 57	**A WHITE SPORT COAT** *Decca F 10895*	**18**	6
19 Jul 57	**START MOVIN'** *Decca F 10914*	**15**	8
26 Jul 57	**A WHITE SPORT COAT (re-entry)** *Decca F 10895*	**30**	1
16 May 58	**STAIRWAY OF LOVE** *Decca F 11016*	**16**	5

DENISE and JOHNNY *UK, male / female vocal duo – Denise Van Outen and Johnny Vaughan (12 WEEKS)* pos/wks

26 Dec 98 ●	**ESPECIALLY FOR YOU** *RCA 74321644722*	**3**	10
10 Apr 99	**ESPECIALLY FOR YOU (re-entry)** *RCA 74321644722*	**53**	2

Cathy DENNIS *UK, female vocalist (68 WEEKS)* pos/wks

21 Oct 89	**C'MON AND GET MY LOVE** *ffrr F 117* [1]	**15**	10
7 Apr 90	**THAT'S THE WAY OF THE WORLD** *ffrr F 132* [1]	**48**	3
4 May 91 ●	**TOUCH ME (ALL NIGHT LONG)** *Polydor CATH 3*	**5**	10
20 Jul 91	**JUST ANOTHER DREAM** *Polydor CATH 2*	**13**	7
5 Oct 91	**TOO MANY WALLS** *Polydor CATH 4*	**17**	7
7 Dec 91	**EVERYBODY MOVE** *Polydor CATH 5*	**25**	8
29 Aug 92	**YOU LIED TO ME** *Polydor CATH 6*	**34**	4
21 Nov 92	**IRRESISTIBLE** *Polydor CATH 7*	**24**	6
6 Feb 93	**FALLING** *Polydor CATHD 8*	**32**	2
12 Feb 94	**WHY** *ffrr FCD 227* [1]	**23**	3
10 Aug 96	**WEST END PAD** *Polydor 5752812*	**25**	2
1 Mar 97	**WATERLOO SUNSET** *Polydor 5759612*	**11**	5
21 Jun 97	**WHEN DREAMS TURN TO DUST** *Polydor 5711852*	**43**	1

[1] D Mob with Cathy Dennis

Dennis G – *See WIDEBOYS featuring Dennis G*

Jackie DENNIS *UK, male vocalist (10 WEEKS)* pos/wks

14 Mar 58 ●	**LA DEE DAH** *Decca F 10992*	**4**	9
27 Jun 58	**THE PURPLE PEOPLE EATER** *Decca F 11033*	**29**	1

Stefan DENNIS *Australia, male vocalist (8 WEEKS)* pos/wks

6 May 89	**DON'T IT MAKE YOU FEEL GOOD** *Sublime LIME 105*	**16**	7
7 Oct 89	**THIS LOVE AFFAIR** *Sublime LIME 113*	**67**	1

DENNISONS *UK, male vocal / instrumental group (13 WEEKS)* pos/wks

15 Aug 63	**BE MY GIRL** *Decca F 11691*	**46**	6
7 May 64	**WALKING THE DOG** *Decca F 11880*	**36**	7

Richard DENTON and Martin COOK *UK, male orchestra leaders - instrumental duo, guitar and keyboards (7 WEEKS)* pos/wks

15 Apr 78	**THEME FROM 'THE HONG KONG BEAT'** *BBC RESL 52*	**25**	7

John DENVER *US, male vocalist – Henry Deutschendorf (22 WEEKS)* pos/wks

17 Aug 74 ★	**ANNIE'S SONG** *RCA APBO 0295* ▲	**1**	13
12 Dec 81	**PERHAPS LOVE** *CBS A 1905* [1]	**46**	9

[1] Placido Domingo with John Denver

Karl DENVER 127 Top 500 *Versatile Scottish singer with multi-octave vocal range, b. Angus McKenzie, 16 Dec 1934, Glasgow (d. 21 Dec 1998). This unique artist, whose yodel-laced style added colour and contrast to the charts, reached the Top 20 with his first five singles (127 WEEKS)* pos/wks

22 Jun 61 ●	**MARCHETA** *Decca F 11360*	**8**	20
19 Oct 61 ●	**MEXICALI ROSE** *Decca F 11395*	**8**	11
25 Jan 62 ●	**WIMOWEH** *Decca F 11420*	**4**	17
22 Feb 62 ●	**NEVER GOODBYE** *Decca F 11431*	**9**	18
7 Jun 62	**A LITTLE LOVE, A LITTLE KISS** *Decca F 11470*	**19**	10
20 Sep 62	**BLUE WEEK-END** *Decca F 11505*	**33**	5
21 Mar 63	**CAN YOU FORGIVE ME** *Decca F 11608*	**32**	8
13 Jun 63	**INDIAN LOVE CALL** *Decca F 11674*	**32**	8
22 Aug 63	**STILL** *Decca F 11720*	**13**	15
5 Mar 64	**MY WORLD OF BLUE** *Decca F 11828*	**29**	6
4 Jun 64	**LOVE ME WITH ALL YOUR HEART** *Decca F 11905*	**37**	6
9 Jun 90	**LAZYITIS - ONE ARMED BOXER** *Factory FAC 2227* [1]	**46**	3

[1] Happy Mondays and Karl Denver

UK No.1 ★ UK Top 10 ● Still on chart + UK million seller ◆ UK entry at No.1 ■ US No.1 ▲

DENZIE – *See MONSTA BOY featuring DENZIE*

DEODATO *US, male multi-instrumentalist - Eumir Deodato (9 WEEKS)*

Date		Title / Label	pos	wks
5 May 73	●	ALSO SPRACH ZARATHUSTRA (2001) *Creed Taylor CTI 4000*	7	9

DEPARTMENT S

UK, male vocal / instrumental group (13 WEEKS)

Date		Title / Label	pos	wks
4 Apr 81		IS VIC THERE? *RCA1003*	22	10
11 Jul 81		GOING LEFT RIGHT *Stiff BUY 118*	55	3

DEPECHE MODE (53 Top 500)

Consistently successful synth-led Essex band: Dave Gahan (v), Martin Gore (syn), Andy Fletcher (b, syn), Vince Clarke (syn, replaced 1982 by Alan Wilder). One of the world's best-selling groups, who reached the UK Top 10 with their first 13 albums (240 WEEKS)

Date		Title / Label	pos	wks
4 Apr 81		DREAMING OF ME *Mute MUTE 013*	57	4
13 Jun 81		NEW LIFE *Mute MUTE 014*	11	15
19 Sep 81	●	JUST CAN'T GET ENOUGH *Mute MUTE 016*	8	10
13 Feb 82	●	SEE YOU *Mute MUTE 018*	6	10
8 May 82		THE MEANING OF LOVE *Mute MUTE 022*	12	8
28 Aug 82		LEAVE IN SILENCE *Mute BONG 1*	18	10
12 Feb 83		GET THE BALANCE RIGHT *Mute 7BONG 2*	13	8
23 Jul 83	●	EVERYTHING COUNTS *Mute 7BONG 3*	6	11
1 Oct 83		LOVE IN ITSELF *Mute 7BONG 4*	21	7
24 Mar 84	●	PEOPLE ARE PEOPLE *Mute 7BONG 5*	4	10
1 Sep 84	●	MASTER AND SERVANT *Mute 7BONG 6*	9	9
10 Nov 84		SOMEBODY / BLASPHEMOUS RUMOURS *Mute 7BONG 7*	16	6
11 May 85		SHAKE THE DISEASE *Mute BONG 8*	18	9
28 Sep 85		IT'S CALLED A HEART *Mute BONG 9*	18	4
22 Feb 86		STRIPPED *Mute BONG 10*	15	5
26 Apr 86		A QUESTION OF LUST *Mute BONG 11*	28	5
23 Aug 86		A QUESTION OF TIME *Mute BONG 12*	17	6
9 May 87		STRANGELOVE *Mute BONG 13*	16	5
5 Sep 87		NEVER LET ME DOWN AGAIN *Mute BONG 14*	22	4
9 Jan 88		BEHIND THE WHEEL *Mute BONG 15*	21	5
28 May 88		LITTLE 15 (import) *Mute LITTLE 15*	60	2
25 Feb 89		EVERYTHING COUNTS *Mute BONG 16*	22	7
9 Sep 89		PERSONAL JESUS *Mute BONG 17*	13	8
17 Feb 90	●	ENJOY THE SILENCE *Mute BONG 18*	6	9
19 May 90		POLICY OF TRUTH *Mute BONG 19*	16	6
29 Sep 90		WORLD IN MY EYES *Mute BONG 20*	17	6
27 Feb 93	●	I FEEL YOU *Mute CDBONG 21*	8	7
8 May 93		WALKING IN MY SHOES *Mute CDBONG 22*	14	4
25 Sep 93	●	CONDEMNATION *Mute CDBONG 23*	9	4
22 Jan 94	●	IN YOUR ROOM *Mute CDBONG 24*	8	4
15 Feb 97	●	BARREL OF A GUN *Mute CDBONG 25*	4	4
12 Apr 97	●	IT'S NO GOOD *Mute CDBONG 26*	5	5
28 Jun 97		HOME *Mute CDBONG 27*	23	4
1 Nov 97		USELESS *Mute CDBONG 28*	28	2
19 Sep 98		ONLY WHEN I LOSE MYSELF *Mute CDBONG 29*	17	3
5 May 01	●	DREAM ON *Mute CDBONG 30*	6	4
23 Jun 01		DREAM ON (re-entry) *Mute CDBONG 30*	75	1
11 Aug 01		I FEEL LOVED *Mute CDBONG 31*	12	6
17 Nov 01		FREELOVE *Mute CDBONG 32*	19	3

'BONG 16' is a live version of 'BONG 3'

DEPTH CHARGE *UK, male producer – Jonathan Kane (1 WEEK)*

Date		Title / Label	pos	wks
29 Jul 95		LEGEND OF THE GOLDEN SNAKE *DC DC 01CD*	75	1

DER DRITTE RAUM

Germany, male producer – Andreas Kruger (1 WEEK)

Date		Title / Label	pos	wks
4 Sep 99		HALLE BOPP *Additive 12AD 042*	75	1

DEREK and the DOMINOES – *See Eric CLAPTON*

Yves DERUYTER *Belgium, male DJ / producer (1 WEEK)*

Date		Title / Label	pos	wks
14 Apr 01		BACK TO EARTH *UK Bonzai UKBONZAICD01*	63	1

DESERT *UK, male production duo (1 WEEK)*

Date		Title / Label	pos	wks
20 Oct 01		LETTIN' YA MIND GO *Future Groove CDFGR 017*	74	1

DESIDERIO

UK / Holland, male production duo / female vocalist (1 WEEK)

Date		Title / Label	pos	wks
3 Jun 00		STARLIGHT *Code Blue BLU 010CD*	57	1

Kevin DESIMONE – *See Barry MANILOW*

DESIRELESS *France, female vocalist (19 WEEKS)*

Date		Title / Label	pos	wks
31 Oct 87		VOYAGE VOYAGE *CBS DESI 1*	53	6
14 May 88	●	VOYAGE VOYAGE (re-mix) *CBS DESI 2*	5	13

DESIYA featuring Melissa YIANNAKOU

UK, male / female vocal / instrumental duo (1 WEEK)

Date		Title / Label	pos	wks
1 Feb 92		COMIN' ON STRONG *Black Market 12MKT 2*	74	1

DESKEE *UK, male instrumentalist (3 WEEKS)*

Date		Title / Label	pos	wks
3 Feb 90		LET THERE BE HOUSE *Big One VBIG 19*	52	2
8 Sep 90		DANCE, DANCE *Big One VBIG 22*	74	1

DES'REE (493 Top 500)

Gospel / folk-tinged soul singer, b. Des'ree Weekes 30 Nov 1968, London, UK, who in 1999 picked up Brit award for Best Female and World Music Award for Top UK Act. 'You Gotta Be' was only single to reach the UK Top 20 three times in the 1990s and 'Life' was among Europe's biggest sellers in 1998 (72 WEEKS)

Date		Title / Label	pos	wks
31 Aug 91		FEEL SO HIGH *Dusted Sound 6573667*	51	5
11 Jan 92		FEEL SO HIGH (re-issue) *Dusted Sound 6576897*	13	7
21 Mar 92		MIND ADVENTURES *Dusted Sound 6578637*	43	3
27 Jun 92		WHY SHOULD I LOVE YOU *Dusted Sound 6580917*	44	3
19 Jun 93		DELICATE *Columbia 6593312* [1]	14	6
9 Apr 94		YOU GOTTA BE *Dusted Sound 6601342*	20	7
18 Jun 94		I AIN'T MOVIN' *Dusted Sound 6604672*	44	3
3 Sep 94		LITTLE CHILD *Dusted Sound 6604515*	69	1
11 Mar 95		YOU GOTTA BE (re-mix) *Dusted Sound 6613215*	14	8
20 Jun 98	●	LIFE *Sony S2 6659302*	8	15
7 Nov 98		WHAT'S YOUR SIGN? *Sony S2 6665162*	19	4
3 Apr 99	●	YOU GOTTA BE (2nd re-mix) *Dusted Sound / Sony S2 6668935*	10	8
16 Oct 99		AIN'T NO SUNSHINE *Universal Music TV 1564332* [2]	42	2

[1] Terence Trent D'Arby featuring Des'ree [2] Ladysmith Black Mambazo featuring Des'ree

DESTINY'S CHILD (299 Top 500)

Texas, US R&B quartet turned trio, fronted by Beyoncë Knowles, who also co-writes and co-produces these independent women responsible for three successive US No.1s. The only US girl group to top the UK chart twice (102 WEEKS)

Date		Title / Label	pos	wks
28 Mar 98	●	NO, NO, NO *Columbia 6656592* [1]	5	8
11 Jul 98		WITH ME *Columbia 6661472*	19	3
7 Nov 98		SHE'S GONE *Columbia 6664915* [2]	24	3
23 Jan 99		GET ON THE BUS *East West E 3780CD* [3]	15	5
24 Jul 99	●	BILLS, BILLS, BILLS *Columbia 6676902* ▲	6	9
30 Oct 99	●	BUG A BOO *Columbia 6681882*	9	7
8 Apr 00	●	SAY MY NAME *Columbia 6691882* ▲	3	11
29 Jul 00	●	JUMPIN' JUMPIN' *Columbia 6696292*	5	11
2 Dec 00	★	INDEPENDENT WOMEN PART 1 *Columbia 6705932* ■ ▲	1	15
28 Apr 01	★	SURVIVOR *Columbia 6711732* ■	1	13
4 Aug 01	●	BOOTYLICIOUS *Columbia 6717382* ▲	2	11
24 Nov 01	●	EMOTION *Columbia 6721112*	3	6+

[1] Destiny's Child featuring Wyclef Jean [2] Matthew Marsden featuring Destiny's Child [3] Destiny's Child featuring Timbaland

DESTRY – *See CIRCA featuring DESTRY; ZOO EXPERIENCE featuring DESTRY*

Marcella DETROIT *US, female vocalist - Marcella Levy (16 WEEKS)*

Date		Title / Label	pos	wks
12 Mar 94		I BELIEVE *London LONCD 347*	11	8
14 May 94		AIN'T NOTHING LIKE THE REAL THING *London LONCD 350* [1]	24	4
16 Jul 94		I'M NO ANGEL *London LOCDP 351*	33	4

[1] Marcella Detroit and Elton John

DETROIT EMERALDS *US, male vocal group (44 WEEKS)*

Date		Title / Label	pos	wks
10 Feb 73	●	FEEL THE NEED IN ME *Janus 6146 020*	4	15

5 May 73	**YOU WANT IT YOU GOT IT** *Westbound 6146 103*	12	9
11 Aug 73	**I THINK OF YOU** *Westbound 6146 104*	27	9
18 Jun 77	**FEEL THE NEED (re-recording)** *Atlantic K 10945*	12	11

DETROIT GRAND PU BAHS

US, male production / vocal group (3 WEEKS) pos/wks

8 Jul 00	**SANDWICHES** *Jive Electro 9230252*	29	3

DETROIT SPINNERS (335 Top 500)

Detroit-based R&B quintet known as The Spinners in US. Lead singers included G C Cameron, Phillippe Wynne (died on stage 1984) and John Edwards. Group, who unusually fared better after leaving Motown, have a 33-year US Top 40 span (93 WEEKS) pos/wks

14 Nov 70	**IT'S A SHAME** *Tamla Motown TMG 755* [1]	20	11
21 Apr 73	**COULD IT BE I'M FALLING IN LOVE** *Atlantic K 10283*	11	11
29 Sep 73 ●	**GHETTO CHILD** *Atlantic K 10359*	7	10
19 Oct 74	**THEN CAME YOU** *Atlantic K 10495* [2] ▲	29	6
11 Sep 76	**THE RUBBERBAND MAN** *Atlantic K 10807*	16	11
29 Jan 77	**WAKE UP SUSAN** *Atlantic K 10799*	29	6
7 May 77	**COULD IT BE I'M FALLING IN LOVE (EP)** *Atlantic K 10935*	32	3
23 Feb 80 ★	**WORKING MY WAY BACK TO YOU - FORGIVE ME GIRL - (MEDLEY)** *Atlantic K 11432*	1	14
10 May 80	**BODY LANGUAGE** *Atlantic K 11392*	40	7
28 Jun 80 ●	**CUPID - I'VE LOVED YOU FOR A LONG TIME (MEDLEY)** *Atlantic K 11498*	4	10
24 Jun 95	**I'LL BE AROUND** *Cooltempo CDCOOL 306* [3]	30	4

[1] Motown Spinners [2] Dionne Warwick and the Detroit Spinners [3] Rappin' 4-Tay featuring the Spinners

Tracks on Could It Be I'm Falling in Love (EP): Could It Be I'm Falling in Love / You're Throwing a Good Love Away / Games People Play / Lazy Susan

DETROIT WHEELS – *See Mitch RYDER and the DETROIT WHEELS*

DEUCE

UK, male / female vocal group (23 WEEKS) pos/wks

21 Jan 95	**CALL IT LOVE** *London LONCD 355*	11	10
22 Apr 95 ●	**I NEED YOU** *London LONCD 365*	10	5
19 Aug 95	**ON THE BIBLE** *London LONCD 368*	13	6
29 Jun 96	**NO SURRENDER** *Love This LUVTHISCD 10*	29	2

dEUS

Belgium, male vocal / instrumental group (7 WEEKS) pos/wks

11 Feb 95	**HOTEL LOUNGE (BE THE DEATH OF ME)** *Island CID 603*	55	1
13 Jul 96	**THEME FROM TURNPIKE (EP)** *Island CID 630*	68	1
19 Oct 96	**LITTLE ARITHMETICS** *Island CID 643*	44	2
15 Mar 97	**ROSES** *Island CID 645*	56	1
24 Apr 99	**INSTANT STREET** *Island CID 742*	49	1
3 Jul 99	**SISTER DEW** *Island CID 750*	62	1

Tracks on Theme from Turnpike (EP): Theme from Turnpike / Worried About Satan / Overflow / My Little Contessa

David DEVANT & HIS SPIRIT WIFE

UK, male vocal / instrumental group (2 WEEKS) pos/wks

5 Apr 97	**GINGER** *Rhythm King KIND 4CD*	54	1
21 Jun 97	**THIS IS FOR REAL** *Rhythm King KIND 5CD*	61	1

Sidney DEVINE

UK, male vocalist (1 WEEK) pos/wks

1 Apr 78	**SCOTLAND FOREVER** *Philips SCOT 1*	48	1

DEVO

US, male vocal / instrumental group (23 WEEKS) pos/wks

22 Apr 78	**(I CAN'T ME GET NO) SATISFACTION** *Stiff BOY 1*	41	8
13 May 78	**JOCKO HOMO** *Stiff DEV 1*	62	3
12 Aug 78	**BE STIFF** *Stiff BOY 2*	71	1
2 Sep 78	**COME BACK JONEE** *Virgin VS 223*	60	4
22 Nov 80	**WHIP IT** *Virgin VS 383*	51	7

DEVOTIONS – *See BELLE and the DEVOTIONS*

Howard DEVOTO – *See BUZZCOCKS; MAGAZINE*

DEXY'S MIDNIGHT RUNNERS (332 Top 500)

Maverick Birmingham UK-based post-punk group who split up in 1987. Led throughout radical personnel and stylistic changes by Kevin Rowland (v/g), b 17 Aug 1953. Transatlantic No.1, 'Come On Eileen', was the top selling UK single of 1982 (93 WEEKS) pos/wks

19 Jan 80	**DANCE STANCE** *Oddball Productions R 6028*	40	6
22 Mar 80 ★	**GENO** *Late Night Feelings R 6033*	1	14
12 Jul 80 ●	**THERE THERE MY DEAR** *Late Night Feelings R 6038*	7	9
21 Mar 81	**PLAN B** *Parlophone R 6046*	58	2
11 Jul 81	**SHOW ME** *Mercury DEXYS 6*	16	9
20 Mar 82	**THE CELTIC SOUL BROTHERS** *Mercury DEXYS 8* [1]	45	4
3 Jul 82 ★	**COME ON EILEEN** *Mercury DEXYS 9* [1] ◆ ▲	1	17
2 Oct 82 ●	**JACKIE WILSON SAID (I'M IN HEAVEN WHEN YOU SMILE)** *Mercury DEXYS 10* [2]	5	7
4 Dec 82	**LET'S GET THIS STRAIGHT (FROM THE START) / OLD** *Mercury DEXYS 11* [2]	17	9
2 Apr 83	**THE CELTIC SOUL BROTHERS** *Mercury DEXYS 12* [2]	20	6
22 Nov 86	**BECAUSE OF YOU** *Mercury BRUSH 1*	13	10

[1] Dexy's Midnight Runners with the Emerald Express [2] Kevin Rowland and Dexy's Midnight Runners

DEXYS 12 is a different version from DEXYS 8

Tony DI BART

UK, male vocalist (19 WEEKS) pos/wks

9 Apr 94 ★	**THE REAL THING** *Cleveland City Blues CCBCD 15001*	1	12
20 Aug 94	**DO IT** *Cleveland City Blues CCBCD 15003*	21	4
20 May 95	**WHY DID YA** *Cleveland City Blues CCBCD 15004*	46	1
2 Mar 96	**TURN YOUR LOVE AROUND** *Cleveland City Blues CCBCD 15006*	66	1
17 Oct 98	**THE REAL THING (re-mix)** *Cleveland City CLECD 13050*	51	1

Gregg DIAMOND BIONIC BOOGIE

US, male / female vocal group (3 WEEKS) pos/wks

20 Jan 79	**CREAM (ALWAYS RISES TO THE TOP)** *Polydor POSP 18*	61	3

Jim DIAMOND

UK, male vocalist (30 WEEKS) pos/wks

3 Nov 84 ★	**I SHOULD HAVE KNOWN BETTER** *A & M AM 220*	1	13
2 Feb 85	**I SLEEP ALONE AT NIGHT** *A & M AM 229*	72	1
18 May 85	**REMEMBER I LOVE YOU** *A & M AM 247*	42	5
22 Feb 86 ●	**HI HO SILVER** *A & M AM 296*	5	11

See also PhD

Neil DIAMOND (225 Top 500)

World-renowned singer / guitarist / songwriter, b. Noah Kaminsky, 24 Jan 1941, Brooklyn, US. First found international fame as writer of 'I'm a Believer' (Monkees), before going on to become one of the world's most popular live artists and biggest-selling album acts (with 36 US gold albums) (121 WEEKS) pos/wks

7 Nov 70 ●	**CRACKLIN' ROSIE** *Uni UN 529* ▲	3	17
20 Feb 71 ●	**SWEET CAROLINE** *Uni UN 531*	8	11
8 May 71 ●	**I AM . . . I SAID** *Uni UN 532*	4	12
13 May 72	**SONG SUNG BLUE** *Uni UN 538* ▲	14	13
14 Aug 76	**IF YOU KNOW WHAT I MEAN** *CBS 4398*	35	4
23 Oct 76	**BEAUTIFUL NOISE** *CBS 4601*	13	9
24 Dec 77	**DESIREE** *CBS 5869*	39	6
25 Nov 78 ●	**YOU DON'T BRING ME FLOWERS** *CBS 6803* [1] ▲	5	12
3 Mar 79	**FOREVER IN BLUE JEANS** *CBS 7047*	16	12
15 Nov 80	**LOVE ON THE ROCKS** *Capitol CL 16173*	17	12
14 Feb 81	**HELLO AGAIN** *Capitol CL 16176*	51	4
20 Nov 82	**HEARTLIGHT** *CBS A 2814*	47	7
21 Nov 92	**MORNING HAS BROKEN** *Columbia 6588267*	36	2

[1] Barbra and Neil

Barbra was Barbra Streisand

DIAMOND HEAD

UK, male vocal / instrumental group (2 WEEKS) pos/wks

11 Sep 82	**IN THE HEAT OF THE NIGHT** *MCA DHM 102*	67	2

DIAMONDS

Canada / US, male vocal group (17 WEEKS) pos/wks

31 May 57 ●	**LITTLE DARLIN'** *Mercury MT 148*	3	17

DIANA – *See Diana ROSS*

DICK and DEEDEE *US, male / female vocal duo (3 WEEKS)* pos/wks

26 Oct 61	**THE MOUNTAIN'S HIGH** *London HLG 9408*	37	3

Charles DICKENS *UK, male vocalist (8 WEEKS)* pos/wks

1 Jul 65	**THAT'S THE WAY LOVE GOES** *Pye 7N 15887*	37	8

Gwen DICKEY *US, female vocalist (13 WEEKS)* pos/wks

27 Jan 90	**CAR WASH** *Swanyard SYR 7*	72	2
2 Jul 94	**AIN'T NOBODY (LOVES ME BETTER)** *X-clusive XCLU 010CD* [1]	21	4
14 Feb 98	**WISHING ON A STAR** *Northwestside 74321554632* [2]	13	4
31 Oct 98	**CAR WASH (re-recording)** *MCA MCSTD 48096* [3]	18	3

[1] KWS and Gwen Dickey [2] Jay-Z featuring Gwen Dickey [3] Rose Royce featuring Gwen Dickey

See also ROSE ROYCE

Neville DICKIE *UK, male instrumentalist – piano (10 WEEKS)* pos/wks

25 Oct 69	**ROBIN'S RETURN** *Major Minor MM 644*	33	7
20 Dec 69	**ROBIN'S RETURN (re-entry)** *Major Minor MM 644*	43	3

DICKIES *US, male vocal / instrumental group (28 WEEKS)* pos/wks

16 Dec 78	**SILENT NIGHT** *A & M AMS 7403*	47	4
21 Apr 79 ●	**BANANA SPLITS (TRA LA LA SONG)** *A & M AMS 7431*	7	8
21 Jul 79	**PARANOID** *A & M AMS 7368*	45	6
15 Sep 79	**NIGHTS IN WHITE SATIN** *A & M AMS 7469*	39	5
16 Feb 80	**FAN MAIL** *A & M AMS 7504*	57	3
19 Jul 80	**GIGANTOR** *A & M AMS 7544*	72	2

Bruce DICKINSON *UK, male vocalist (23 WEEKS)* pos/wks

28 Apr 90	**TATTOOED MILLIONAIRE** *EMI EM 138*	18	5
23 Jun 90	**ALL THE YOUNG DUDES** *EMI EM 142*	23	5
25 Aug 90	**DIVE! DIVE! DIVE!** *EMI EM 151*	45	2
4 Apr 92 ●	**(I WANT TO BE) ELECTED** *London LON 319* [1]	9	5
28 May 94	**TEARS OF THE DRAGON** *EMI CDEM 322*	28	2
8 Oct 94	**SHOOT ALL THE CLOWNS** *EMI CDEMS 341*	37	2
13 Apr 96	**BACK FROM THE EDGE** *Raw Power RAWX 1012*	68	1
3 May 97	**ACCIDENT OF BIRTH** *Raw Power RAWX 1042*	54	1

[1] Mr Bean and Smear Campaign featuring Bruce Dickinson

See also IRON MAIDEN

Barbara DICKSON *UK, female vocalist (49 WEEKS)* pos/wks

17 Jan 76 ●	**ANSWER ME** *RSO 2090 174*	9	7
26 Feb 77	**ANOTHER SUITCASE IN ANOTHER HALL** *MCA 266*	18	7
19 Jan 80	**CARAVAN SONG** *Epic EPC 8103*	41	7
15 Mar 80	**JANUARY FEBRUARY** *Epic EPIC 8115*	11	10
14 Jun 80	**IN THE NIGHT** *Epic EPC 8593*	48	2
5 Jan 85 ★	**I KNOW HIM SO WELL** *RCA CHESS 3* [1]	1	16

[1] Elaine Paige and Barbara Dickson

DICTATORS *US, male vocal / instrumental group (2 WEEKS)* pos/wks

17 Sep 77	**SEARCH AND DESTROY** *Asylum K 13091*	49	1
1 Oct 77	**SEARCH AND DESTROY (re-entry)** *Asylum K 13091*	50	1

Bo DIDDLEY *US, male vocalist (10 WEEKS)* pos/wks

10 Oct 63	**PRETTY THING** *Pye International 7N 25217*	34	6
18 Mar 65	**HEY GOOD LOOKIN'** *Chess 8000*	39	4

DIDDY *UK, male producer (3 WEEKS)* pos/wks

19 Feb 94	**GIVE ME LOVE** *Positiva CDTIV 8*	52	1
12 Jul 97	**GIVE ME LOVE (re-mix)** *Feverpitch CDFVR 19*	23	2

P DIDDY – *See PUFF DADDY*

DIDO *UK, female vocalist – Florian Cloud de Bounevialle Armstrong (30 WEEKS)* pos/wks

24 Apr 01 ●	**HERE WITH ME** *Cheeky / Arista 74321832732*	4	12
2 Jun 01 ●	**THANK YOU** *Cheeky / Arista 74321853042*	3	10
22 Sep 01	**HUNTER** *Cheeky / Arista 74321885452*	17	8

DIESEL PARK WEST *UK, male vocal / instrumental group (15 WEEKS)* pos/wks

4 Feb 89	**ALL THE MYTHS ON SUNDAY** *Food FOOD 17*	66	2
1 Apr 89	**LIKE PRINCES DO** *Food FOOD 19*	58	3
5 Aug 89	**WHEN THE HOODOO COMES** *Food FOOD 20*	62	2
18 Jan 92	**FALL TO LOVE** *Food FOOD 35*	48	3
21 Mar 92	**BOY ON TOP OF THE NEWS** *Food FOOD 36*	58	2
5 Sep 92	**GOD ONLY KNOWS** *Food FOOD 39*	57	3

DIFFERENT GEAR vs POLICE *UK / Italy, male production group and UK / US, male vocal / instrumental trio (3 WEEKS)* pos/wks

5 Aug 00	**WHEN THE WORLD IS RUNNING DOWN** *Pagan PAGAN 039CDS*	28	3

DIFFORD and TILBROOK *UK, male vocal / instrumental duo (2 WEEKS)* pos/wks

30 Jun 84	**LOVE'S CRASHING WAVES** *A & M AM 193*	57	2

See also SQUEEZE

DIGABLE PLANETS *US, male / female vocal / instrumental group (2 WEEKS)* pos/wks

13 Feb 93	**REBIRTH OF SLICK (COOL LIKE DAT)** *Pendulum EKR 159CD*	67	2

DIGITAL DREAM BABY *UK, male producer – Steven Teear (4 WEEKS)* pos/wks

14 Dec 91	**WALKING IN THE AIR** *Columbia 6576067*	49	4

Hit is a dance re-mix of 'Walking in the Air' by vocalist Peter Auty

See also Peter AUTY and the SINFONIA OF LONDON conducted by Howard BLAKE

DIGITAL EXCITATION *Belgium, male producer – Frank de Wulf (2 WEEKS)* pos/wks

29 Feb 92	**PURE PLEASURE** *R&S RSUK 10*	37	2

DIGITAL ORGASM *Belgium, male / female vocal / instrumental group (14 WEEKS)* pos/wks

7 Dec 91	**RUNNING OUT OF TIME** *Dead Dead Good GOOD 009*	16	9
18 Apr 92	**STARTOUCHERS** *DDG International GOOD 13*	31	3
25 Jul 92	**MOOG ERUPTION** *DDG International GOOD 17*	62	2

DIGITAL UNDERGROUND *US, male rap group (4 WEEKS)* pos/wks

16 Mar 91	**SAME SONG** *Big Life BLR 40*	52	4

DILEMMA *Italy, male instrumental / production group (1 WEEK)* pos/wks

6 Apr 96	**IN SPIRIT** *ffrr FCD 274*	42	1

Ricky DILLARD – *See Farley 'Jackmaster' FUNK*

DIMESTARS *UK, male / female vocal / instrumental group (1 WEEK)* pos/wks

16 Jun 01	**MY SUPERSTAR** *Polydor 5870912*	72	1

D'INFLUENCE *UK, male / female vocal / instrumental group (10 WEEKS)* pos/wks

20 Jun 92	**GOOD LOVER** *East West A 8573* [1]	46	2
27 Mar 93	**GOOD LOVER (re-mix)** *East West America A 8439CD* [1]	61	1
24 Jun 95	**MIDNITE** *East West A 4418CD* [2]	58	1
16 Aug 97	**HYPNOTIZE** *Echo ECSCD 41*	33	2
11 Oct 97	**MAGIC** *Echo ECSCD 45*	45	1
5 Sep 98	**ROCK WITH YOU** *Echo ECSCD 56*	30	3

[1] D-Influence [2] D*Influence

Paolo DINI – See FPI PROJECT

Mark DINNING *US, male vocalist (4 WEEKS)*

			pos	wks
10 Mar 60		TEEN ANGEL *MGM 1053* ▲	37	3
7 Apr 60		TEEN ANGEL (re-entry) *MGM 1053*	42	1

DINOSAUR JR *US, male vocal / instrumental group (13 WEEKS)*

			pos	wks
2 Feb 91		THE WAGON *Blanco Y Negro NEG 48*	49	2
14 Nov 92		GET ME *Blanco Y Negro NEG 60*	44	1
30 Jan 93		START CHOPPIN' *Blanco Y Negro NEG 61CD*	20	3
12 Jun 93		OUT THERE *Blanco Y Negro NEG 63CD*	44	2
27 Aug 94		FEEL THE PAIN *Blanco Y Negro NEG 74CD*	25	3
11 Feb 95		I DON'T THINK SO *Blanco Y Negro NEG 77CD*	67	1
5 Apr 97		TAKE A RUN AT THE SUN *Blanco Y Negro NEG 103CD*	53	1

DINOSAURS – See Terry DACTYL and the DINOSAURS

DIO *UK / US, male vocal / instrumental group (22 WEEKS)*

			pos	wks
20 Aug 83		HOLY DIVER *Vertigo DIO 1*	72	2
29 Oct 83		RAINBOW IN THE DARK *Vertigo DIO 2*	46	3
11 Aug 84		WE ROCK *Vertigo DIO 3*	42	3
29 Sep 84		MYSTERY *Vertigo DIO 4*	34	4
10 Aug 85		ROCK 'N' ROLL CHILDREN *Vertigo DIO 5*	26	6
2 Nov 85		HUNGRY FOR HEAVEN *Vertigo DIO 6*	72	1
17 May 86		HUNGRY FOR HEAVEN (re-issue) *Vertigo DIO 7*	56	2
1 Aug 87		I COULD HAVE BEEN A DREAMER *Vertigo DIO 8*	69	1

DION *US, male vocalist – Dion DiMucci (35 WEEKS)*

			pos	wks
26 Jun 59		A TEENAGER IN LOVE *London HLU 8874* [1]	28	2
19 Jan 61		LONELY TEENAGER *Top Rank JAR 521*	47	1
2 Nov 61		RUNAROUND SUE *Top Rank JAR 586* ▲	11	9
15 Feb 62	●	THE WANDERER *HMV POP 971*	10	12
22 May 76		THE WANDERER (re-issue) *Philips 6146 700*	16	9
19 Aug 89		KING OF THE NEW YORK STREETS *Arista 112556*	74	2

[1] Dion and the Belmonts

Celine DION (62 Top 500) *French-Canadian vocalist who won the 1988 Eurovision Song Contest (for Switzerland), b. 30 Mar 1968, Quebec. She has sold a reported 130 million albums worldwide and is the only female with two UK million-selling singles as a solo artist (230 WEEKS)*

			pos	wks
16 May 92	●	BEAUTY AND THE BEAST *Epic 6576607* [1]	9	7
4 Jul 92		IF YOU ASKED ME TO *Epic 6581927*	60	2
14 Nov 92		LOVE CAN MOVE MOUNTAINS *Epic 6587787*	46	2
26 Dec 92		IF YOU ASKED ME TO (re-entry) *Epic 6581927*	57	3
3 Apr 93		WHERE DOES MY HEART BEAT NOW *Epic 6563265*	72	1
29 Jan 94	●	THE POWER OF LOVE *Epic 6597992* ▲	4	10
23 Apr 94		MISLED *Epic 6602922*	40	3
22 Oct 94	★	THINK TWICE *Epic 6606422* ◆	1	31
20 May 95	●	ONLY ONE ROAD *Epic 6613535*	8	8
9 Sep 95	●	TU M'AIMES ENCORE (TO LOVE ME AGAIN) *Epic 6624255*	7	9
2 Dec 95		MISLED (re-issue) *Epic 6626495*	15	6
2 Mar 96	●	FALLING INTO YOU *Epic 6629795*	10	10
1 Jun 96	●	BECAUSE YOU LOVED ME (THEME FROM 'UP CLOSE AND PERSONAL') *Epic 6632382* ▲	5	16
5 Oct 96	●	IT'S ALL COMING BACK TO ME NOW *Epic 6637112*	3	14
21 Dec 96	●	ALL BY MYSELF *Epic 6640622*	6	10
15 Mar 97		ALL BY MYSELF (re-entry) *Epic 6640622*	58	3
28 Jun 97		CALL THE MAN *Epic 6646922*	11	6
15 Nov 97	●	TELL HIM *Epic 6653052* [2]	3	15
20 Dec 97		THE REASON *Epic 6653812*	11	8
21 Feb 98	★	MY HEART WILL GO ON *Epic 6655472* ◆ ■ ▲	1	20
18 Jul 98	●	IMMORTALITY *Epic 6661682* [3]	5	12
28 Nov 98	●	I'M YOUR ANGEL *Epic 6666282* [4] ▲	3	13
10 Jul 99		TREAT HER LIKE A LADY *Epic 6675522*	29	3
11 Dec 99		THAT'S THE WAY IT IS *Epic 6684622*	12	11
8 Apr 00		THE FIRST TIME EVER I SAW YOUR FACE *Epic 6691942*	19	6
10 Jun 00		THE FIRST TIME EVER I SAW YOUR FACE (re-entry) *Epic 6691942*	74	1

[1] Celine Dion and Peabo Bryson [2] Barbra Streisand and Celine Dion [3] Celine Dion with Bee Gees [4] Celine Dion and R Kelly

KATHRYN DION – See 2 FUNKY 2 starring Kathryn DION

DIONNE *Canada, female vocalist (2 WEEKS)*

			pos	wks
23 Sep 89		COME GET MY LOVIN' *Citybeat CBC 745*	69	2

Wasis DIOP featuring Lena FIAGBE *Senegal, male producer and UK, female vocalist (2 WEEKS)*

			pos	wks
10 Feb 96		AFRICAN DREAM *Mercury MERCD 453*	44	2

DIRE STRAITS (232 Top 500) *Multi Brit- and Grammy- award-winning group led by vocalist / lead guitarist / songwriter Mark Knopfler, b. 12 Aug 1949, Glasgow. This London-based band, whose world tours attracted millions, is among the top five album-selling acts in the UK. Knopfler was honoured with an MBE in 2000 and, shortly afterwards, had a dinosaur named after him (119 WEEKS)*

			pos	wks
10 Mar 79	●	SULTANS OF SWING *Vertigo 6059 206*	8	11
28 Jul 79		LADY WRITER *Vertigo 6059 230*	51	6
17 Jan 81	●	ROMEO AND JULIET *Vertigo MOVIE 1*	8	11
4 Apr 81		SKATEAWAY *Vertigo MOVIE 2*	37	5
10 Oct 81		TUNNEL OF LOVE *Vertigo MUSIC 3*	54	3
4 Sep 82	●	PRIVATE INVESTIGATIONS *Vertigo DSTR 1*	2	8
22 Jan 83		TWISTING BY THE POOL *Vertigo DSTR 2*	14	7
18 Feb 84		LOVE OVER GOLD (LIVE) / SOLID ROCK (LIVE) *Vertigo DSTR 6*	50	3
20 Apr 85		SO FAR AWAY *Vertigo DSTR 9*	20	6
6 Jul 85	●	MONEY FOR NOTHING *Vertigo DSTR 10* ▲	4	16
26 Oct 85		BROTHERS IN ARMS *Vertigo DSTR 11*	16	13
11 Jan 86	●	WALK OF LIFE *Vertigo DSTR 12*	2	11
3 May 86		YOUR LATEST TRICK *Vertigo DSTR 13*	26	6
5 Nov 88		SULTANS OF SWING (re-issue) *Vertigo DSTR 15*	62	1
31 Aug 91		CALLING ELVIS *Vertigo DSTR 16*	21	4
2 Nov 91		HEAVY FUEL *Vertigo DSTR 17*	55	2
29 Feb 92		ON EVERY STREET *Vertigo DSTR 18*	42	2
27 Jun 92		THE BUG *Vertigo DSTR 19*	67	1
22 May 93		ENCORES (EP) *Vertigo DSCD 20*	31	3

Tracks on Encores (EP): Your Latest Trick / The Bug / Solid Rock / Local Hero (Wild Theme)

See also Mark KNOPFLER

DIRECKT *UK, male instrumental / production duo (2 WEEKS)*

			pos	wks
13 Aug 94		TWO FATT GUITARS (REVISITED) *UFG UFG 7CD*	36	2

DIRECT DRIVE *UK, male / female vocal / instrumental group (3 WEEKS)*

			pos	wks
26 Jan 85		ANYTHING? *Polydor POSP 728*	67	2
4 May 85		A.B.C. (FALLING IN LOVE'S NOT EASY) *Boiling Point POSP 742*	75	1

DIRTY ROTTEN SCOUNDRELS – See Lisa STANSFIELD

DIRTY VEGAS *UK, male production trio (4 WEEKS)*

			pos	wks
19 May 01		DAYS GO BY *Credence CDCRED 011*	27	4

DISCHARGE *UK, male vocal / instrumental group (3 WEEKS)*

			pos	wks
24 Oct 81		NEVER AGAIN *Clay CLAY 6*	64	3

DISCO ANTHEM *Holland, male producer – Lex van Coeverden (2 WEEKS)*

			pos	wks
18 Jun 94		SCREAM *Sweat MCSTD 1977*	47	2

DISCO CITIZENS *UK, male instrumental / production duo (5 WEEKS)*

			pos	wks
22 Jul 95		RIGHT HERE RIGHT NOW *Deconstruction 74321293872*	40	2
12 Apr 97		FOOTPRINT *Xtravaganza 0091115*	34	2
4 Jul 98		NAGASAKI BADGER *Xtravaganza 0091595 EXT*	56	1

See also CHICANE

DISCO EVANGELISTS *UK, male instrumental / production group (2 WEEKS)*

			pos	wks
8 May 93		DE NIRO *Positiva CDTIV 2*	59	2

DISCO TEX and the SEX-O-LETTES
US, male vocalist / female vocal group (22 WEEKS) pos/wks

23 Nov 74 ● **GET DANCING** *Chelsea 2005 013* 8 12
26 Apr 75 ● **I WANNA DANCE WIT CHOO** *Chelsea 2005 024* [1] 6 10

[1] Disco Tex and the Sex-O-Lettes featuring Sir Monti Rock III

DISCO TEX presents CLOUDBURST
UK, male / female production / vocal group (2 WEEKS) pos/wks

24 Mar 01 **I CAN CAST A SPELL** *Absolution CDABSOL 1* 35 2

See also FULL INTENTION; HUSTLERS CONVENTION featuring Dave LAUDAT and Ondrea DUVERNEY; SEX-O-SONIQUE

DISCOVERY – *See COAST 2 COAST featuring DISCOVERY*

DISPOSABLE HEROES OF HIPHOPRISY
US, male rap / instrumental duo (7 WEEKS) pos/wks

4 Apr 92 **TELEVISION THE DRUG OF THE NATION** *Fourth & Broadway BRW 241* 57 2
30 May 92 **LANGUAGE OF VIOLENCE** *Fourth & Broadway 12BRW 248* 68 1
19 Dec 92 **TELEVISION THE DRUG OF THE NATION (re-entry)** *Fourth & Broadway BRW 241* 44 4

Sacha DISTEL *France, male vocalist (27 WEEKS)* pos/wks

10 Jan 70 **RAINDROPS KEEP FALLING ON MY HEAD** *Warner Bros. WB 7345* 50 1
24 Jan 70 ● **RAINDROPS KEEP FALLING ON MY HEAD (re-entry)** *Warner Bros. WB 7345* 10 20
27 Jun 70 **RAINDROPS KEEP FALLING ON MY HEAD (2nd re-entry)** *Warner Bros. WB 7345* 43 4
1 Aug 70 **RAINDROPS KEEP FALLING ON MY HEAD (3rd re-entry)** *Warner Bros. WB 7345* 47 1
15 Aug 70 **RAINDROPS KEEP FALLING ON MY HEAD (4th re-entry)** *Warner Bros. WB 7345* 44 1

DISTURBED *US, male vocal / instrumental group (1 WEEK)* pos/wks

7 Apr 01 **VOICES** *Giant 74321848962* 52 1

DIVA *Norway, female vocal duo (2 WEEKS)* pos/wks

7 Oct 95 **THE SUN ALWAYS SHINES ON TV** *East West YZ 947CD* 53 1
20 Jul 96 **EVERYBODY (MOVE YOUR BODY)** *East West EW 035CD* 44 1

DIVA SURPRISE featuring Georgia JONES
US / Spain, male production duo and US, female vocalist (2 WEEKS) pos/wks

14 Nov 98 **ON THE TOP OF THE WORLD** *Positiva CDTIV 100* 29 2

DIVE *UK, male production duo - Sacha Collisson and Simon Greenaway (1 WEEK)* pos/wks

21 Feb 98 **BOOGIE** *WEA WEA 147CD1* 35 1

Hit featured vocalist Nasreen Shah

See also AURORA

DIVERSIONS
UK, male / female vocal / instrumental group (3 WEEKS) pos/wks

20 Sep 75 **FATTIE BUM BUM** *Gull GULS 18* 34 3

DIVINE *US, male vocalist – Harris Milstead (24 WEEKS)* pos/wks

15 Oct 83 **LOVE REACTION** *Design Communication DES 4* 65 2
14 Jul 84 **YOU THINK YOU'RE A MAN** *Proto ENA 118* 16 10
20 Oct 84 **I'M SO BEAUTIFUL** *Proto ENA 121* 52 2
27 Apr 85 **WALK LIKE A MAN** *Proto ENA 125* 23 7
20 Jul 85 **TWISTIN' THE NIGHT AWAY** *Proto ENA 127* 47 3

DIVINE *US, female vocal group (1 WEEK)* pos/wks

16 Oct 99 **LATELY** *Mushroom / Red Ant RA 002CDS* ▲ 52 1

DIVINE COMEDY
UK, male vocalist / instrumentalist – Neil Hannon (38 WEEKS) pos/wks

29 Jun 96 **SOMETHING FOR THE WEEKEND** *Setanta SETCD 26* 14 5
24 Aug 96 **BECOMING MORE LIKE ALFIE** *Setanta SETCD 27* 27 2
16 Nov 96 **THE FROG PRINCESS** *Setanta SETCD 32* 15 2
22 Mar 97 **EVERYBODY KNOWS (EXCEPT YOU)** *Setanta SETCDA 038* 14 4
11 Apr 98 **SOMEDAY I'LL FIND YOU / I'VE BEEN TO A MARVELLOUS PARTY** *EMI CDTCB 001* [1] 28 3
26 Sep 98 **GENERATION SEX** *Setanta SETCDA 050* 19 3
28 Nov 98 **THE CERTAINTY OF CHANCE** *Setanta SETCDA 067* 49 1
6 Feb 99 ● **NATIONAL EXPRESS** *Setanta SETCDA 069* 8 7
21 Aug 99 **THE POP SINGER'S FEAR OF THE POLLEN COUNT** *Setanta SETCDA 070* 17 4
13 Nov 99 **GIN SOAKED BOY** *Setanta SETCDA 071* 38 2
10 Mar 01 **LOVE WHAT YOU DO** *Parlophone CDRS 6554* 26 2
26 May 01 **BAD AMBASSADOR** *Parlaphone CRDS 6558* 34 2
10 Nov 01 **PERFECT LOVESONG** *Parlophone CDR 6561* 42 1

[1] Shola Ama and Craig Armstrong / Divine Comedy

DIVINYLS
Australia, male / female vocal / instrumental duo (12 WEEKS) pos/wks

18 May 91 ● **I TOUCH MYSELF** *Virgin America VUS 36* 10 12

DIXIE CHICKS *US, female vocal group (6 WEEKS)* pos/wks

3 Jul 99 **THERE'S YOUR TROUBLE** *Epic 6675162* 26 5
6 Nov 99 **READY TO RUN** *Epic 6682472* 53 1

DIXIE CUPS *US, female vocal group (16 WEEKS)* pos/wks

18 Jun 64 **CHAPEL OF LOVE** *Pye International 7N 25245* ▲ 22 8
13 May 65 **IKO IKO** *Red Bird RB 10024* 23 8

DIZZY HEIGHTS *UK, male rapper (4 WEEKS)* pos/wks

18 Dec 82 **CHRISTMAS RAPPING** *Polydor WRAP 1* 49 4

DJ ALIGATOR PROJECT
Denmark, male producer – Aliasghar Movasat (1 WEEK) pos/wks

7 Oct 00 **THE WHISTLE SONG** *EMI CDBLOW 001* 57 1

DJ ARABESQUE – *See Mario PIU*

DJ BADMARSH and SHRI featuring UK APACHE *India / Yemen, male instrumental / production duo and UK, male rapper (1 WEEK)* pos/wks

28 Jul 01 **SIGNS** *Outcaste OUT 38CD1* 63 1

DJ BOBO *Switzerland, male producer – René Baumann (4 WEEKS)* pos/wks

24 Sep 94 **EVERYBODY** *PWL Continental PWCD 312* 47 2
17 Jun 95 **LOVE IS ALL AROUND** *Avex UK AXEXCD 7* 49 2

DJ DADO *Italy, male producer – Roberto Gallo (9 WEEKS)* pos/wks

6 Apr 96 ● **X-FILES** *ZYX ZYX 8065R8* 8 6
14 Mar 98 **COMING BACK** *ffrr TABCD 247* 63 1
11 Jul 98 **GIVE ME LOVE** *VC Recordings VCRD 37* [1] 59 1
8 May 99 **READY OR NOT** *Chemistry CDKEM 006* [2] 51 1

[1] DJ Dado vs Michelle Weeks [2] DJ Dado and Simone Jay

DJ DAN presents NEEDLE DAMAGE
US, male DJ / production group (1 WEEK) pos/wks

5 May 01 **THAT ZIPPER TRACK** *Duty Free DF 026CD* 53 1

DJ DEE KLINE *UK, male DJ / producer – Nick Annand (6 WEEKS)* pos/wks

3 Jun 00 **I DON'T SMOKE** *East West EW 213CD* 11 6

DJ DISCIPLE *US, male DJ / producer (1 WEEK)* pos/wks

12 Nov 94 **ON THE DANCEFLOOR** *Mother MUMCD 55* 67 1

DJ DUKE *Denmark, male producer – Ken Larson (7 WEEKS)* pos/wks

			pos	wks
8 Jan 94		BLOW YOUR WHISTLE *ffrr FCD 228*	15	5
16 Jul 94		TURN IT UP (SAY YEAH) *ffrr FCD 235*	31	2

DJ E-Z ROCK – *See Rob BASE and DJ E-Z ROCK*

DJ EMPIRE presents Giorgio MORODER
Germany, male producer – Alexander Wilkie (1 WEEK) pos/wks

			pos	wks
12 Feb 00		THE CHASE (re-recording) *LOGIC 731482*	46	1

DJ ERIC *UK, male production trio (3 WEEKS)* pos/wks

			pos	wks
13 Feb 99		WE ARE LOVE *Distinctive DISNCD 49*	37	2
10 Jun 00		DESIRE *Distinctive DISNCD 56*	67	1

DJ 'FAST' EDDIE *US, male producer (15 WEEKS)* pos/wks

			pos	wks
11 Apr 87		CAN U DANCE *Champion CHAMP 41* [1]	71	2
14 Nov 87		CAN U DANCE (re-entry) *Champion CHAMP 41* [1]	67	2
21 Jan 89		HIP HOUSE / I CAN DANCE *DJ International DJIN 5*	47	4
11 Mar 89		YO YO GET FUNKY *DJ International DJIN 7*	54	3
28 Oct 89		GIT ON UP *DJ International 655366 7* [2]	49	4

[1] Kenny 'Jammin' Jason and 'Fast' Eddie Smith [2] DJ 'Fast' Eddie featuring Sundance

DJ FLAVOURS *UK, male producer – Neil Rumney (4 WEEKS)* pos/wks

			pos	wks
11 Oct 97		YOUR CARESS (ALL I NEED) *All Around the World CDGLOBE 160*	19	4

DJ GERT *Belgium, male DJ / producer – Gert Rossenbacker (1 WEEK)* pos/wks

			pos	wks
26 May 01		GIVE ME SOME MORE *Mostika 23200253*	50	1

DJ HYPE *UK, male producer (2 WEEKS)* pos/wks

			pos	wks
20 Mar 93		SHOT IN THE DARK *Suburban Base SUBBASE 20CD*	63	1
2 Jun 01		CASINO ROYALE / DEAD A'S *True Playaz TPRCD 004* [1]	58	1

[1] DJ Zinc / DJ Hype

DJ JAZZY JEFF & the FRESH PRINCE – *See JAZZY JEFF & the FRESH PRINCE*

DJ JEAN *Holland, DJ / producer – Jan Engelaar (11 WEEKS)* pos/wks

			pos	wks
11 Sep 99	●	THE LAUNCH *AM:PM CDAMPM 123*	2	11

DJ JURGEN presents Alice DEEJAY
Holland, male DJ / production group and female vocalist (16 WEEKS) pos/wks

			pos	wks
31 Jul 99	●	BETTER OFF ALONE *Positiva CDTIV 113*	2	16

See also ALICE DEEJAY

DJ KOOL *US, male rapper / DJ / producer – John Bowman (7 WEEKS)* pos/wks

			pos	wks
22 Feb 97	●	LET ME CLEAR MY THROAT *American 74321452092*	8	7

DJ KRUSH *Japan, male producer (2 WEEKS)* pos/wks

			pos	wks
16 Mar 96		MEISO *Mo Wax MW 042CD*	52	1
12 Oct 96		ONLY THE STRONG SURVIVE *Mo Wax MW 060CD*	71	1

DJ LUCK & MC NEAT *UK, male DJ / producers – Joel Samuels and Michael Rose (42 WEEKS)* pos/wks

			pos	wks
25 Dec 99	●	A LITTLE BIT OF LUCK *Red Rose CORROSLE 1*	9	15
27 May 00	●	MASTERBLASTER 2000 *Red Rose RROSE 002CD* [1]	5	8
7 Oct 00	●	AIN'T NO STOPPIN' US *Red Rose CDRROSE 004* [1]	8	6
17 Mar 01		PIANO LOCO *Island CID 773*	12	8
8 Sep 01		I'M ALL ABOUT YOU *Island CID 781* [2]	18	4
20 Oct 01		I'M ALL ABOUT YOU (re-entry) *Island CID 781* [2]	71	1

[1] DJ Luck & MC Neat featuring JJ [2] DJ Luck & MC Neat featuring Ari Gold

DJ MANTA *Holland, male / female DJ / production trio (1 WEEK)* pos/wks

			pos	wks
9 Oct 99		HOLDING ON *AM:PM CDAMPM 125*	47	1

DJ MIKO *Italy, male producer – Quartobaro Manier (10 WEEKS)* pos/wks

			pos	wks
13 Aug 94	●	WHAT'S UP *Systematic SYSCD 2*	6	10

DJ MILANO featuring SAMANTHA FOX
Italy, male DJ / producer and UK, female vocalist (2 WEEKS) pos/wks

			pos	wks
28 Mar 98		SANTA MARIA *All Around the World CDGLOBE 163*	31	2

See also Samantha FOX

DJ MISJAH and DJ TIM *Holland, male instrumental / production duo – Misjah Van Der Heiden and Tim Hoogestegger (4 WEEKS)* pos/wks

			pos	wks
23 Mar 96		ACCESS *Ffrreedom TABCD 240*	16	3
27 May 00		ACCESS (re-mix) *Tripoli Trax TTRAXCD 063*	45	1

DJ OTZI *Austria, male DJ / producer – Gerry Friedle (26 WEEKS)* pos/wks

			pos	wks
18 Aug 01		HEY BABY (import) *EMI 8892462*	41	5
22 Sep 01	★	HEY BABY (UHH, AHH) *EMI CDOTZI 001* ■	1	15+
1 Dec 01	●	DO WAH DIDDY *EMI CDOTZI 002*	9	5+
29 Dec 01		X-MAS TIME *EMI CDOTZI 003*	51	1+

DJ PIED PIPER and THE MASTERS OF CEREMONIES
UK, male rap / production group (14 WEEKS) pos/wks

			pos	wks
2 Jun 01	★	DO YOU REALLY LIKE IT *Relentless / MOS RELMOS 1CDS* ■	1	14

DJ POWER *Italy, male producer – Steve Gambaroli (2 WEEKS)* pos/wks

			pos	wks
7 Mar 92		EVERYBODY PUMP *Cooltempo COOL 252*	46	2

DJ PROFESSOR *Italy, male producer (6 WEEKS)* pos/wks

			pos	wks
10 Aug 91		WE GOTTA DO IT *Fourth & Broadway BRW 225* [1]	57	2
28 Mar 92		ROCK ME STEADY *PWL Continental PWL 219*	49	2
8 Oct 94		ROCKIN' ME *Citra CITRA 1CD* [2]	56	1
1 Mar 97		WALKIN' ON UP *Nukleuz MCSTD 40098* [3]	64	1

[1] DJ Professor featuring Francesco Zappala [2] Professor [3] DJ PROF-X-OR

DJ QUICKSILVER *Turkey / Belgium, male DJ / producer duo – Ohran Terzi with Tomasso De Donatis (29 WEEKS)* pos/wks

			pos	wks
5 Apr 97	●	BELLISSIMA *Positiva CDTIV 72*	4	17
6 Sep 97	●	FREE *Positiva CDTIVS 77*	7	7
21 Feb 98		PLANET LOVE *Positiva CDTIV 88*	12	5

DJ QUIK – *See TONY TONI TONÉ*

DJ RAP *UK, female vocalist / DJ / producer (5 WEEKS)* pos/wks

			pos	wks
4 Jul 98		BAD GIRL *Higher Ground HIGHS 8CD*	32	2
17 Oct 98		GOOD TO BE ALIVE *Higher Ground HIGHS 14CD*	36	2
3 Apr 99		EVERYDAY GIRL *Higher Ground HIGHS 19CD*	47	1

DJ ROLANDO AKA AZTEC MYSTIC
US, male DJ / producer – Rolando Rocha (2 WEEKS) pos/wks

			pos	wks
21 Oct 00		JAGUAR *430 West 430 WUKTCD1*	43	2

DJ SAKIN & FRIENDS
Germany, DJ / producer – Sakin Botzkurt (18 WEEKS) pos/wks

			pos	wks
20 Feb 99	●	PROTECT YOUR MIND (FOR THE LOVE OF A PRINCESS) *Positiva CDTIV 107*	4	10
8 May 99		PROTECT YOUR MIND (FOR THE LOVE OF A PRINCESS) (re-entry) *Positiva CDTIV 107*	71	1
5 Jun 99		NOMANSLAND (DAVID'S SONG) *Positiva CDTIV 112*	14	7

DJ SANDY VS HOUSETRAP
Germany, female DJ / producer and vocalist (2 WEEKS) pos/wks

			pos	wks
1 Jul 00		OVERDRIVE *Positiva CDTIV 133*	32	2

DJ SCOT PROJECT *Germany, male DJ / producer (2 WEEKS)* pos/wks

			pos	wks
27 Jul 96		U (I GOT THE FEELING) *Positiva CDTIV 55*	66	1
14 Feb 98		Y (HOW DEEP IS YOUR LOVE) *Perfecto PERF 158CD1*	57	1

THE OFFICIAL UK SINGLES CHART 50TH ANNIVERSARY

1964

IN THE YEAR IN WHICH NELSON MANDELA WAS IMPRISONED, MUHAMMAD ALI (THEN CASSIUS CLAY) BECAME WORLD HEAVYWEIGHT CHAMPION, JOHN COLTRANE RELEASED JAZZ MILESTONE 'A LOVE SUPREME' AND HAROLD WILSON'S LABOUR GOVERNMENT CAME TO POWER, **CILLA BLACK** TALKS ABOUT HER MOST SIGNIFICANT YEAR...

“It had to be 1964, really. That was the year that I had two successive number ones and then I was invited to appear in front of the Queen at the Royal Command Performance. My family all travelled down to London for the occasion. I think it was the first time they'd ever worn dinner suits before... They were that proud that they wore them all around London all day! I was just 21 and there I was singing 'You're My World' in front of the Queen... It doesn't get much better than that, surely? After the show, I was presented to the Queen...I had to wear gloves to shake her hand. Afterwards, I asked my dad what he thought about my performance. 'Oh, which one were you?' he replied. The whole family had been so transfixed by the presence of the Queen that they'd not taken their eyes off her and missed me altogether!”

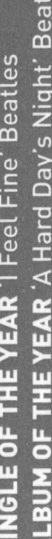

SINGLE OF THE YEAR 'I Feel Fine' Beatles
ALBUM OF THE YEAR 'A Hard Day's Night' Beatles

DJ SCOTT featuring Lorna B
UK, Scotland, male DJ and female vocalist (5 WEEKS) pos/wks

28 Jan 95	**DO YOU WANNA PARTY** *Steppin' Out SPONCD 2*	36	3
1 Apr 95	**SWEET DREAMS** *Steppin' Out SPONCD 3*	37	2

DJ Doc SCOTT *UK, male producer (2 WEEKS)* pos/wks

1 Feb 92	**NHS (EP)** *Absolute 2 ABS 001DJ*	64	2

Tracks on NHS (EP): Surgery / Night Nurse

DJ SEDUCTION *UK, male producer – John Kallum (8 WEEKS)* pos/wks

22 Feb 92	**HARDCORE HEAVEN / YOU AND ME** *Ffrreedom TAB 103*	26	5
11 Jul 92	**COME ON** *Ffrreedom TAB 111*	37	3

DJ SHADOW *US, male producer (7 WEEKS)* pos/wks

25 Mar 95	**WHAT DOES YOUR SOUL LOOK LIKE** *Mo Wax MW 027CD*	59	1
14 Sep 96	**MIDNIGHT IN A PERFECT WORLD** *Mo Wax MW 057CD*	54	1
9 Nov 96	**STEM** *Mo Wax MW 058CD*	74	1
11 Oct 97	**HIGH NOON** *Mo Wax MW 063CD*	22	2
20 Dec 97	**CAMEL BOBSLED RACE** *Mo Wax MW 084CD*	62	1
24 Jan 98	**WHAT DOES YOUR SOUL LOOK LIKE (PART 1)** *Mo Wax MW 087*	54	1

DJ SHORTY – *See Lenny FONTANA and DJ SHORTY*

DJ SUPREME *UK, male producer – Nick Destri (11 WEEKS)* pos/wks

5 Oct 96	**THA WILD STYLE** *Distinctive DISNCD 19*	39	2
3 May 97	**THA WILD STYLE (re-issue)** *Distinctive DISNCD 29*	24	2
6 Dec 97	**ENTER THE SCENE** *Distinctive DISNCD 40* [1]	49	1
21 Feb 98	**THA HORNS OF JERICHO** *All Around the World CDGLOBE 164*	29	2
16 Jan 99 ●	**UP TO THE WILDSTYLE** *All Around the World CDGLOBE 170* [2]	10	4

[1] DJ Supreme vs the Rhythm Masters [2] Porn Kings vs DJ Supreme

DJ TAUCHER
German, male DJ / producer – Ralf Armand Beck (1 WEEK) pos/wks

8 May 99	**CHILD OF THE UNIVERSE** *Additive 12AD 037*	74	1

DJ TIESTO *Holland, male producer – Tijs Verwest (54WEEKS)* pos/wks

12 May 01	**FLIGHT 643** *Nebula NEBCD 016*	56	1
29 Sep 01	**URBAN TRAIN** *VC Recordings / Nebula VCRD 95* [1]	22	3

[1] DJ Tiesto featuring Kirsty Hawshaw

See also GOURYELLA

DJ TIM – *See DJ MISJAH and DJ TIM*

DJ VISAGE featuring CLARISSA
Denmark / Germany, male DJ / producer / female vocalist (1 WEEK) pos/wks

10 Jun 00	**THE RETURN (TIME TO SAY GOODBYE)** *One Step Music OSMCDS 13*	58	1

DJ WHAT? – *See OBI PROJECT featuring HARRY, ASHER D & DJ WHAT?*

DJ ZINC *UK, male DJ / producer – Benjamin Pettit (4 WEEKS)* pos/wks

18 Nov 00	**138 TREK** *Phaze One PHAZE CDX03*	27	3
2 Jun 01	**CASINO ROYALE / DEAD A'S** *True Playaz TPRCD 004* [1]	58	1

[1] DJ Zinc / DJ Hype

DJAIMIN *Switzerland, male producer (2 WEEKS)* pos/wks

19 Sep 92	**GIVE YOU** *Cooltempo COOL 262*	45	2

DJH featuring STEFY
Italy, male instrumental / production group (14 WEEKS) pos/wks

16 Feb 91	**THINK ABOUT . . .** *RCA PB 44385*	22	6
13 Jul 91	**I LIKE IT** *RCA PB 44741*	16	7
19 Oct 91	**MOVE YOUR LOVE** *RCA PB 44965*	73	1

DJPC *Belgium, male producer (5 WEEKS)* pos/wks

26 Oct 91	**INSSOMNIAK** *Hype 7PUM 005*	62	4
29 Feb 92	**INSSOMNIAK (re-issue)** *Hype PUMR 005*	64	1

DJ's RULE *Canada, male instrumental / production duo (2 WEEKS)* pos/wks

2 Mar 96	**GET INTO THE MUSIC** *Distinctive DISNCD 9*	72	1
5 Apr 97	**GET INTO THE MUSIC (re-mix)** *Distinctive DISNCDD27* [1]	65	1

[1] DJ's Rule featuring Karen Brown

DJUM DJUM – *See LEFTFIELD*

Boris DLUGOSCH *Germany, male producer (8 WEEKS)* pos/wks

7 Dec 96	**KEEP PUSHIN'** *Manifesto FESCD 17* [1]	41	2
13 Sep 97	**HOLD YOUR HEAD UP HIGH** *Positiva CDTIV 79* [1]	23	2
16 Jun 01	**NEVER ENOUGH** *Positiva CDTIV 156* [2]	16	4

[1] Boris Dlugosch presents Booom! Vocals by Inaya Davis (aka Inaya Day) [2] Boris Dlugosch featuring Roisin Murphy

D'LUX *UK, male / female vocal / instrumental group (1 WEEK)* pos/wks

22 Jun 96	**LOVE RESURRECTION** *Logic 74321371012*	58	1

D'MENACE
UK, male production duo – Sandy Rivera and John Alvarez (3 WEEKS) pos/wks

8 Aug 98	**DEEP MENACE (SPANK)** *Inferno CDFERN 8*	20	3

D MOB *UK, male producer – Danny D (48 WEEKS)* pos/wks

15 Oct 88 ●	**WE CALL IT ACIEED** *ffrr FFR 13* [1]	3	12
3 Jun 89 ●	**IT IS TIME TO GET FUNKY** *ffrr F 107* [2]	9	10
21 Oct 89	**C'MON AND GET MY LOVE** *ffrr F 117* [3]	15	10
6 Jan 90 ●	**PUT YOUR HANDS TOGETHER** *ffrr F 124* [4]	7	8
7 Apr 90	**THAT'S THE WAY OF THE WORLD** *ffrr F 132* [3]	48	3
12 Feb 94	**WHY** *ffrr FCD 227* [3]	23	3
3 Sep 94	**ONE DAY** *ffrr FCDP 239*	41	2

[1] D Mob featuring Gary Haisman [2] D Mob featuring LRS [3] D Mob with Cathy Dennis [4] D Mob featuring Nuff Juice

DMX *US, male rapper – Earl Simmons (5 WEEKS)* pos/wks

15 May 99	**SLIPPIN'** *Def Jam 8707552*	30	2
15 Dec 01	**WHO WE BE** *Def Jam 5888512*	34	3

DNA *UK, male production duo – Neal Slateford and Nick Bett (29 WEEKS)* pos/wks

28 Jul 90 ●	**TOM'S DINER (re-mix)** *A & M AM 592* [1]	2	10
18 Aug 90	**LA SERENISSIMA** *Raw Bass RBASS 006*	34	8
3 Aug 91	**REBEL WOMAN** *DNA 7DNA 001* [2]	42	4
1 Feb 92	**CAN YOU HANDLE IT (re-recording)** *EMI EM 219* [3]	17	5
9 May 92	**BLUE LOVE (CALL MY NAME)** *EMI EM 226* [4]	66	2

[1] DNA featuring Suzanne Vega [2] DNA featuring Jazzi P [3] DNA featuring Sharon Redd [4] DNA featuring Joe Nye

D*NOTE *UK, male producer – Matt Winn (2 WEEKS)* pos/wks

12 Jul 97	**WAITING HOPEFULLY** *A & M 5822792*	46	1
15 Nov 97	**LOST AND FOUND** *VC VCRD 25*	59	1

Carl DOBKINS Jr *US, male vocalist (1 WEEK)* pos/wks

31 Mar 60	**LUCKY DEVIL** *Brunswick 05817*	44	1

Anita DOBSON *UK, female vocalist (13 WEEKS)* pos/wks

9 Aug 86 ●	**ANYONE CAN FALL IN LOVE** *BBC RESL 191* [1]	4	9
18 Jul 87	**TALKING OF LOVE** *Parlophone R 6159*	43	4

[1] Anita Dobson featuring the Simon May Orchestra

DR ALBAN *Nigeria, male vocalist – Alban Nwapa (28 WEEKS)* pos/wks

5 Sep 92 ●	**IT'S MY LIFE** *Logic 115330*	2	12
14 Nov 92	**ONE LOVE** *Logic 74321108727*	45	2

10 Apr 93		**SING HALLELUJAH!** *Logic 74321136202*	**16**	8
26 Mar 94		**LOOK WHO'S TALKING** *Logic 74321195342*	**55**	3
13 Aug 94		**AWAY FROM HOME** *Logic 74321222682*	**42**	2
29 Apr 95		**SWEET DREAMS** *Logic 74321251552* [1]	**59**	1

[1] Swing featuring Dr Alban

DOCTOR and the MEDICS *UK, male / female vocal / instrumental group – lead vocal Clive Jackson (25 WEEKS)*

			pos	wks
10 May 86	★	**SPIRIT IN THE SKY** *IRS IRM 113*	**1**	15
9 Aug 86		**BURN** *IRS IRM 119*	**29**	6
22 Nov 86		**WATERLOO** *IRS IRM 125* [1]	**45**	4

[1] Doctor and the Medics featuring Roy Wood

DR DRE *US, male rapper – Andre Young (66 WEEKS)*

			pos	wks
22 Jan 94		**NUTHIN' BUT A 'G' THANG / LET ME RIDE** *Death Row A 8328CD*	**31**	3
3 Sep 94		**DRE DAY** *Death Row A 8292CD*	**59**	2
15 Apr 95		**NATURAL BORN KILLAZ** *Death Row A 8197CD* [1]	**45**	2
10 Jun 95		**KEEP THEIR HEADS RINGIN'** *Priority PTYCD 103*	**25**	4
13 Apr 96	●	**CALIFORNIA LOVE** *Death Row DRWCD 3* [2]	**6**	8
19 Oct 96	●	**NO DIGGITY** *Interscope IND 95003* [3] ▲	**9**	7
11 Jul 98		**ZOOM** *Interscope IND 95594* [4]	**15**	3
14 Aug 99	●	**GUILTY CONSCIENCE** *Interscope IND 4971282* [5]	**5**	8
25 Mar 00	●	**STILL D.R.E.** *Interscope 4972742* [6]	**6**	10
10 Jun 00	●	**FORGOT ABOUT DRE** *Interscope 4973412* [7]	**7**	9
3 Feb 01	●	**THE NEXT EPISODE** *Interscope 4974762* [6]	**3**	10

[1] Dr Dre and Ice Cube [2] 2Pac featuring Dr Dre [3] BLACKstreet featuring Dr Dre [4] Dr Dre and LL Cool J [5] Eminem featuring Dr Dre [6] Dr Dre featuring Snoop Dogg [7] Dr Dre featuring Eminem

DR FEELGOOD *UK, male vocal / instrumental group (29 WEEKS)*

			pos	wks
11 Jun 77		**SNEAKIN' SUSPICION** *United Artists UP 36255*	**47**	3
24 Sep 77		**SHE'S A WIND UP** *United Artists UP 36304*	**34**	5
30 Sep 78		**DOWN AT THE DOCTOR'S** *United Artists UP 36444*	**48**	5
20 Jan 79	●	**MILK AND ALCOHOL** *United Artists UP 36468*	**9**	9
5 May 79		**AS LONG AS THE PRICE IS RIGHT** *United Artists YUP 36506*	**40**	6
8 Dec 79		**PUT HIM OUT OF YOUR MIND** *United Artists BP 306*	**73**	1

DR HOOK (287 Top 500) *Distinctive group fronted by vocalists Dennis Locorriere and Ray Sawyer; had eight years of regular UK / US hits. Early recordings often featured humorous anarchic Shel Silverstein songs, but this good-time New Jersey act had greater success with later gentler material (104 WEEKS)*

			pos	wks
24 Jun 72	●	**SYLVIA'S MOTHER** *CBS 7929* [1]	**2**	13
26 Jun 76	●	**A LITTLE BIT MORE** *Capitol CL 15871*	**2**	14
30 Oct 76	●	**IF NOT YOU** *Capitol CL 15885*	**5**	10
25 Mar 78		**MORE LIKE THE MOVIES** *Capitol CL 15967*	**14**	10
22 Sep 79	★	**WHEN YOU'RE IN LOVE WITH A BEAUTIFUL WOMAN** *Capitol CL 16039*	**1**	17
5 Jan 80	●	**BETTER LOVE NEXT TIME** *Capitol CL 16112*	**8**	8
29 Mar 80	●	**SEXY EYES** *Capitol CL 16127*	**4**	9
23 Aug 80		**YEARS FROM NOW** *Capitol CL 16154*	**47**	6
8 Nov 80		**SHARING THE NIGHT TOGETHER** *Capitol CL 16171*	**43**	4
22 Nov 80		**GIRLS CAN GET IT** *Mercury MER 51*	**40**	5
1 Feb 92		**WHEN YOU'RE IN LOVE WITH A BEAUTIFUL WOMAN (re-issue)** *Capitol EMCT 4*	**44**	4
6 Jun 92		**A LITTLE BIT MORE (re-issue)** *EMI EMCT 6*	**47**	4

[1] Dr Hook and the Medicine Show

DR MOUTHQUAKE – *See E-ZEE POSSEE*

DR OCTAGON *US, male producer – Keith Thornton (1 WEEK)*

			pos	wks
7 Sep 96		**BLUE FLOWERS** *Mo Wax MW 055CD*	**66**	1

DOCTOR SPIN *UK, male instrumental / production duo (8 WEEKS)*

			pos	wks
3 Oct 92	●	**TETRIS** *Carpet CRPT 4*	**6**	8

Ken DODD (60 Top 500) *Seasoned stand-up comedian-cum-balladeer, b. 8 Nov 1929, Liverpool. The tickling-stick-wielding troubadour was one of the most successful Merseyside acts in the mid-1960s, at times enjoying two Top 10 singles simultaneously (233 WEEKS)*

			pos	wks
7 Jul 60	●	**LOVE IS LIKE A VIOLIN** *Decca F 11248*	**8**	18
15 Jun 61		**ONCE IN EVERY LIFETIME** *Decca F 11355*	**28**	7
10 Aug 61		**ONCE IN EVERY LIFETIME (re-entry)** *Decca F 11355*	**47**	1
24 Aug 61		**ONCE IN EVERY LIFETIME (2nd re-entry)** *Decca F 11355*	**31**	10
1 Feb 62		**PIANISSIMO** *Decca F 11422*	**21**	15
29 Aug 63		**STILL** *Columbia DB 7094*	**35**	10
6 Feb 64		**EIGHT BY TEN** *Columbia DB 7191*	**22**	11
23 Jul 64		**HAPPINESS** *Columbia DB 7325*	**31**	13
26 Nov 64		**SO DEEP IS THE NIGHT** *Columbia DB 7398*	**31**	7
2 Sep 65	★	**TEARS** *Columbia DB 7659* ◆	**1**	24
18 Nov 65	●	**THE RIVER (LE COLLINE SONO IN FIORO)** *Columbia DB 7750*	**3**	14
12 May 66	●	**PROMISES** *Columbia DB 7914*	**6**	14
4 Aug 66		**MORE THAN LOVE** *Columbia DB 7976*	**14**	11
27 Oct 66		**IT'S LOVE** *Columbia DB 8031*	**36**	7
19 Jan 67		**LET ME CRY ON YOUR SHOULDER** *Columbia DB 8101*	**11**	10
30 Jul 69		**TEARS WON'T WASH AWAY THESE HEARTACHES** *Columbia DB 8600*	**22**	11
5 Dec 70		**BROKEN HEARTED** *Columbia DB 8725*	**15**	9
13 Feb 71		**BROKEN HEARTED (re-entry)** *Columbia DB 8725*	**38**	1
10 Jul 71		**WHEN LOVE COMES ROUND AGAIN (L'ARCA DI NOE)** *Columbia DB 8796*	**19**	16
18 Nov 72		**JUST OUT OF REACH (OF MY TWO EMPTY ARMS)** *Columbia DB 8947*	**29**	11
29 Nov 75		**(THINK OF ME) WHEREVER YOU ARE** *EMI 2342*	**21**	8
26 Dec 81		**HOLD MY HAND** *Images IMGS 0002*	**44**	5

Rory DODD – *See Jim STEINMAN*

DODGY *UK, male vocal / instrumental group (41 WEEKS)*

			pos	wks
8 May 93		**LOVEBIRDS** *A & M AMCD 0177*	**65**	2
3 Jul 93		**I NEED ANOTHER (EP)** *A & M 5803172*	**67**	2
6 Aug 94		**THE MELOD-EP** *Bostin 5806772*	**53**	1
1 Oct 94		**STAYING OUT FOR THE SUMMER** *Bostin 5807972*	**38**	2
7 Jan 95		**SO LET ME GO FAR** *Bostin 5809032*	**30**	3
11 Mar 95		**MAKING THE MOST OF** *Bostin 5809892* [1]	**22**	3
10 Jun 95		**STAYING OUT FOR THE SUMMER (re-mix)** *Bostin 5810952*	**19**	5
8 Jun 96		**IN A ROOM** *A & M 5816252*	**12**	6
10 Aug 96	●	**GOOD ENOUGH** *A & M 5818152*	**4**	8
16 Nov 96		**IF YOU'RE THINKING OF ME** *A & M 5819992*	**11**	4
15 Mar 97		**FOUND YOU** *A & M 5821332*	**19**	3
26 Sep 98		**EVERY SINGLE DAY** *A&M MERCD 512*	**32**	2

[1] Dodgy with the Kick Horns

Tracks on I Need Another (EP): I Need Another / If I Fall / Hendre DDU. Tracks on The Melod-EP: Melodies Haunt You / The Snake / Don't Go / Summer Fayre

Tim DOG *US, male rapper (3 WEEKS)*

			pos	wks
29 Oct 94		**BITCH WITH A PERM** *Dis-stress DISCD 1*	**49**	1
11 Feb 95		**MAKE WAY FOR THE INDIAN** *Island CID 586* [1]	**29**	2

[1] Apache Indian and Tim Dog

DOG EAT DOG *US, male vocal / instrumental group (7 WEEKS)*

			pos	wks
19 Aug 95		**NO FRONTS** *Roadrunner RR 23312*	**64**	1
3 Feb 96	●	**NO FRONTS (re-entry)** *Roadrunner RR 23312*	**9**	5
13 Jul 96		**ISMS** *Roadrunner RR 23083*	**43**	1

Nate DOGG *US, male rapper – Nathan Hale (14 WEEKS)*

			pos	wks
3 Feb 01		**OH NO** *Rawkus RWK 302* [1]	**24**	4
25 Aug 01		**WHERE I WANNA BE** *London LONCD 461* [2]	**14**	6
29 Sep 01		**AREA CODES** *Def Jam 5887722* [3]	**25**	3
13 Oct 01		**WHERE I WANNA BE (re-entry)** *London LONCD 461* [2]	**58**	1

[1] Mos Def and Nate Dogg featuring Pharoahe Monch [2] Shade Sheist featuring Nate Dogg and Kurupt [3] Ludacris featuring Nate Dogg

See also Warren G

DOGS D'AMOUR *UK, male vocal / instrumental group (15 WEEKS)* pos/wks

		pos	wks
4 Feb 89	HOW COME IT NEVER RAINS *China CHINA 13*	44	3
5 Aug 89	SATELLITE KID *China CHINA 17*	26	3
14 Oct 89	TRAIL OF TEARS *China CHINA 20*	47	3
23 Jun 90	VICTIMS OF SUCCESS *China CHINA 24*	36	3
15 Sep 90	EMPTY WORLD *China CHINA 27*	61	2
19 Jun 93	ALL OR NOTHING *China WOKCD 2033*	53	1

Ken DOH *UK, male producer – Michael Devlin (7 WEEKS)* pos/wks

		pos	wks
30 Mar 96 ●	NAGASAKI EP *ffrr FCD 272*	7	7

Track: Nagasaki (2 mixes) / I Need A Lover Tonight (2 mixes) / Kaki Traki

Joe DOLAN *Ireland, male vocalist (40 WEEKS)* pos/wks

		pos	wks
25 Jun 69 ●	MAKE ME AN ISLAND *Pye 7N 17738*	3	18
1 Nov 69	TERESA *Pye 7N 17833*	20	7
8 Nov 69	MAKE ME AN ISLAND (re-entry) *Pye 7N 17738*	48	1
28 Feb 70	YOU'RE SUCH A GOOD LOOKING WOMAN *Pye 7N 17891*	17	13
17 Sep 77	I NEED YOU *Pye 7N 45702*	43	1

Thomas DOLBY *UK, male vocalist / multi-instrumentalist – Thomas Robertson (51 WEEKS)* pos/wks

		pos	wks
3 Oct 81	EUROPA AND THE PIRATE TWINS *Parlophone R 6051*	48	3
14 Aug 82	WINDPOWER *Venice In Peril VIPS 103*	31	8
6 Nov 82	SHE BLINDED ME WITH SCIENCE *Venice In Peril VIPS 104*	49	4
16 Jul 83	SHE BLINDED ME WITH SCIENCE (re-issue) *Venice In Peril VIPS 105*	56	4
21 Jan 84	HYPERACTIVE *Parlophone Odeon R 6065*	17	9
31 Mar 84	I SCARE MYSELF *Parlophone Odeon R 6067*	46	5
16 Apr 88	AIRHEAD *Manhattan MT 38*	53	3
9 May 92	CLOSE BUT NO CIGAR *Virgin VS 1410*	22	5
11 Jul 92	I LOVE YOU GOODBYE *Virgin VS 1417*	36	4
26 Sep 92	SILK PYJAMAS *Virgin VS 1430*	62	2
22 Jan 94	HYPERACTIVE! (re-mix) *Parlophone CDEMCTS 10*	23	4

Joe DOLCE MUSIC THEATRE *US, male vocalist (10 WEEKS)* pos/wks

		pos	wks
7 Feb 81 ★	SHADDAP YOU FACE *Epic EPC 9518*	1	10

DOLL *UK, male / female vocal / instrumental group (8 WEEKS)* pos/wks

		pos	wks
13 Jan 79	DESIRE ME *Beggars Banquet BEG 11*	28	8

DOLLAR (207 Top 500) *Photogenic teen-targeted UK vocal duo, who were originally one-third of Guys and Dolls: David Van Day and Thereze Bazar. Their Top 10 hits came from writers as diverse as John Lennon, Paul McCartney, Trevor Horn, Erasure and themselves (128 WEEKS)* pos/wks

		pos	wks
11 Nov 78	SHOOTING STAR *Carrere 2871*	14	12
19 May 79	WHO WERE YOU WITH IN THE MOONLIGHT *Carrere CAR 110*	14	12
18 Aug 79 ●	LOVE'S GOTTA HOLD ON ME *Carrere CAR 122*	4	13
24 Nov 79 ●	I WANNA HOLD YOUR HAND *Carrere CAR 131*	9	14
25 Oct 80	TAKIN' A CHANCE ON YOU *WEA K 18353*	62	3
15 Aug 81	HAND HELD IN BLACK AND WHITE *WEA BUCK 1*	19	12
14 Nov 81 ●	MIRROR MIRROR (MON AMOUR) *WEA BUCK 2*	4	17
20 Mar 82	RING RING *Carrere CAR 225*	61	2
27 Mar 82 ●	GIVE ME BACK MY HEART *WEA BUCK 3*	4	9
19 Jun 82	VIDEOTHEQUE *WEA BUCK 4*	17	10
18 Sep 82	GIVE ME SOME KINDA MAGIC *WEA BUCK 5*	34	6
16 Aug 86	WE WALKED IN LOVE *Arista DIME 1*	61	4
26 Dec 87 ●	O L'AMOUR *London LON 146*	7	11
16 Jul 88	IT'S NATURE'S WAY (NO PROBLEM) *London LON 179*	58	3

Placido DOMINGO *Spain, male vocalist (28 WEEKS)* pos/wks

		pos	wks
12 Dec 81	PERHAPS LOVE *CBS A 1905* [1]	46	9
27 May 89	TILL I LOVED YOU *CBS 654843 7* [2]	24	9
16 Jun 90	NESSUN DORMA FROM 'TURANDOT' *Epic 656005 7* [3]	59	2
30 Jul 94	LIBIAMO / LA DONNA E MOBILE *Teldec YZ 843CD* [4]	21	4
25 Jul 98	YOU'LL NEVER WALK ALONE *Decca 4607982* [5]	35	4

[1] Placido Domingo with John Denver [2] Placido Domingo and Jennifer Rush [3] Luis Cobos featuring Placido Domingo [4] José Carreras featuring Placido Domingo and Luciano Pavarotti with Mehta [5] José Carreras, Placido Domingo and Luciano Pavarotti with Mehta

DOMINO *US, male rapper / vocalist (6 WEEKS)* pos/wks

		pos	wks
22 Jan 94	GETTO JAM *Chaos 6600402*	33	4
14 May 94	SWEET POTATOE PIE *Chaos 6603292*	42	2

Fats DOMINO (271 Top 500) *Pioneering rock 'n' roll singer / songwriter and pianist, b. 26 Feb 1928, New Orleans. Sold millions of rockin' records in pre-Haley / Presley years and is still among the biggest-selling artists and most successful composers of the rock era (109 WEEKS)* pos/wks

		pos	wks
27 Jul 56	I'M IN LOVE AGAIN *London HLU 8280*	28	1
17 Aug 56	I'M IN LOVE AGAIN (re-entry) *London HLU 8280*	12	13
30 Nov 56	BLUEBERRY HILL *London HLU 8330*	26	1
21 Dec 56 ●	BLUEBERRY HILL (re-entry) *London HLU 8330*	6	14
25 Jan 57	AIN'T THAT A SHAME *London HLU 8173*	23	2
1 Feb 57	HONEY CHILE *London HLU 8356*	29	1
29 Mar 57	BLUE MONDAY *London HLP 8377*	23	1
19 Apr 57	BLUE MONDAY (re-entry) *London HLP 8377*	30	1
19 Apr 57	I'M WALKIN' *London HLP 8407*	19	7
19 Jul 57	VALLEY OF TEARS *London HLP 8449*	25	1
28 Mar 58	THE BIG BEAT *London HLP 8575*	20	4
4 Jul 58	SICK AND TIRED *London HLP 8628*	26	1
22 May 59	MARGIE *London HLP 8865*	18	5
16 Oct 59	I WANT TO WALK YOU HOME *London HLP 8942*	14	5
18 Dec 59	BE MY GUEST *London HLP 9005*	11	8
19 Feb 60	BE MY GUEST (re-entry) *London HLP 9005*	19	3
17 Mar 60	COUNTRY BOY *London HLP 9073*	19	11
21 Jul 60	WALKING TO NEW ORLEANS *London HLP 9163*	19	10
10 Nov 60	THREE NIGHTS A WEEK *London HLP 9198*	45	2
5 Jan 61	MY GIRL JOSEPHINE *London HLP 9244*	32	4
27 Jul 61	IT KEEPS RAININ' *London HLP 9374*	49	1
30 Nov 61	WHAT A PARTY *London HLP 9456*	43	1
29 Mar 62	JAMBALAYA *London HLP 9520*	41	1
31 Oct 63	RED SAILS IN THE SUNSET *HMV POP 1219*	34	6
24 Apr 76	BLUEBERRY HILL (re-issue) *United Artists UP 35797*	41	5

DON PABLO'S ANIMALS *Italy, male production group (10 WEEKS)* pos/wks

		pos	wks
19 May 90 ●	VENUS *Rumour RUMA 18*	4	10

DON-E *UK, male vocalist – Donald McLean (8 WEEKS)* pos/wks

		pos	wks
9 May 92	LOVE MAKES THE WORLD GO ROUND *Fourth & Broadway BRW 242*	18	6
25 Jul 92	PEACE IN THE WORLD *Fourth & Broadway BRW 256*	41	1
28 Feb 98	DELICIOUS *Mushroom MUSH 20CD* [1]	52	1

[1] Deni Hines featuring Don-E

Lonnie DONEGAN (25 Top 500) *The 'King of Skiffle', b. 29 Apr 1931, Glasgow, Scotland. Britain's most successful and influential recording artist before The Beatles. Chalked up 28 successive Top 30 entries, and was the first UK male to score two US Top 10s. Album with Van Morrison and Chris Barber reached Top 20 in 2000 (321 WEEKS)* pos/wks

		pos	wks
6 Jan 56 ●	ROCK ISLAND LINE *Decca F 10647*	8	13
13 Apr 56	ROCK ISLAND LINE (re-entry) *Decca F 10647*	16	3
20 Apr 56	STEWBALL *Pye Nixa N 15036*	27	1
27 Apr 56 ●	LOST JOHN / STEWBALL (re-entry) *Pye Nixa N 15036*	2	17
11 May 56	ROCK ISLAND LINE (2nd re-entry) *Decca F 10647*	19	6
6 Jul 56	SKIFFLE SESSION (EP) *Pye Nixa NJE 1017*	20	2
7 Sep 56 ●	BRING A LITTLE WATER SYLVIE / DEAD OR ALIVE *Pye Nixa N 15071*	7	12
21 Dec 56	LONNIE DONEGAN SHOWCASE (LP) *Pye Nixa NPT 19012*	26	3
11 Jan 57	BRING A LITTLE WATER, SYLVIE / DEAD OR ALIVE (re-entry) *Pye Nixa N 15071*	30	1
18 Jan 57 ●	DON'T YOU ROCK ME DADDY-O *Pye Nixa N 15080*	4	17
5 Apr 57 ★	CUMBERLAND GAP *Pye Nixa N 15087*	1	12
7 Jun 57 ★	GAMBLIN' MAN / PUTTIN' ON THE STYLE *Pye Nixa N 15093*	1	19
11 Oct 57 ●	MY DIXIE DARLING *Pye Nixa N 15108*	10	15
20 Dec 57	JACK O' DIAMONDS *Pye Nixa 7N 15116*	14	7
11 Apr 58 ●	THE GRAND COOLIE DAM *Pye Nixa 7N 15129*	6	15
11 Jul 58	SALLY DON'T YOU GRIEVE / BETTY, BETTY, BETTY *Pye Nixa 7N 15148*	11	7
26 Sep 58	LONESOME TRAVELLER *Pye Nixa 7N 15158*	28	1
14 Nov 58	LONNIE'S SKIFFLE PARTY *Pye Nixa 7N 15165*	23	5

			pos	wks
21 Nov 58	●	**TOM DOOLEY** *Pye Nixa 7N 15172*	3	14
6 Feb 59	●	**DOES YOUR CHEWING GUM LOSE ITS FLAVOUR (ON THE BEDPOST OVERNIGHT** *Pye Nixa 7N 15181*	3	12
8 May 59		**FORT WORTH JAIL** *Pye Nixa 7N 15198*	14	5
26 Jun 59	●	**BATTLE OF NEW ORLEANS** *Pye 7N 15206*	2	16
11 Sep 59		**SAL'S GOT A SUGAR LIP** *Pye 7N 15223*	13	4
4 Dec 59		**SAN MIGUEL** *Pye 7N 15237*	19	4
24 Mar 60	★	**MY OLD MAN'S A DUSTMAN** *Pye 7N 15256*	1	13
26 May 60	●	**I WANNA GO HOME (THE WRECK OF THE 'JOHN B')** *Pye 7N 15267*	5	17
25 Aug 60	●	**LORELEI** *Pye 7N 15275*	10	8
24 Nov 60		**LIVELY** *Pye 7N 15312*	13	9
8 Dec 60		**VIRGIN MARY** *Pye 7N 15315*	27	5
11 May 61	●	**HAVE A DRINK ON ME** *Pye 7N 15354*	8	15
31 Aug 61	●	**MICHAEL, ROW THE BOAT / LUMBERED** *Pye 7N 15371*	6	11
18 Jan 62		**THE COMANCHEROS** *Pye 7N 15410*	14	10
5 Apr 62	●	**THE PARTY'S OVER** *Pye 7N 15424*	9	12
16 Aug 62		**PICK A BALE OF COTTON** *Pye 7N 15455*	11	10

'Stewball' had one week on the chart by itself on 20 Apr 1956. 'Lost John', the other side, replaced it on 27 Apr 1956, but 'Stewball' was given co-billing with 'Lost John' for the weeks of 11, 18 and 25 May 1956, peaking only at No.7. 'Dead or Alive' was not listed with 'Bring a Little Water Sylvie' for the week 7 Sep 1956. 'Putting on the Style' was not listed with 'Gamblin' Man' for the weeks of 7 and 14 Jun 1956. Tracks on Skiffle Session (EP): Railroad Bill / Stockalee / Ballad of Jesse James / Ol' Riley. Tracks on Lonnie Donegan Showcase (LP): Wabash Cannonball / How Long / How Long Blues / Nobody's Child / I Shall Not Be Moved / I'm Alabammy Bound / I'm a Rambling Man / Wreck of the Old '97 / Frankie and Johnny

Tanya DONELLY *US, female vocalist / instrumentalist (2 WEEKS)* pos/wks

			pos	wks
30 Aug 97		**PRETTY DEEP** *4AD BAD 7007CD*	55	1
6 Dec 97		**THE BRIGHT LIGHT** *4AD BAD 7012CD*	64	1

Ral DONNER *US, male vocalist (10 WEEKS)* pos/wks

			pos	wks
21 Sep 61		**YOU DON'T KNOW WHAT YOU'VE GOT (UNTIL YOU LOSE IT)** *Parlophone R 4820*	25	10

DONOVAN (306 Top 500) *Acclaimed Celtic singer / songwriter, b. Donovan Leitch, 10 May 1946, Glasgow. Initially dubbed British version of Bob Dylan, he enjoyed massive fame on both sides of the Atlantic in the 'flower power' years of the late 1960s (100 WEEKS)* pos/wks

			pos	wks
25 Mar 65	●	**CATCH THE WIND** *Pye 7N 15801*	4	13
3 Jun 65	●	**COLOURS** *Pye 7N 15866*	4	12
11 Nov 65		**TURQUOISE** *Pye 7N 15984*	30	6
8 Dec 66	●	**SUNSHINE SUPERMAN** *Pye 7N 17241* ▲	2	11
9 Feb 67	●	**MELLOW YELLOW** *Pye 7N 17267*	8	8
25 Oct 67	●	**THERE IS A MOUNTAIN** *Pye 7N 17403*	8	11
21 Feb 68	●	**JENNIFER JUNIPER** *Pye 7N 17457*	5	11
29 May 68	●	**HURDY GURDY MAN** *Pye 7N 17537*	4	10
4 Dec 68		**ATLANTIS** *Pye 7N 17660*	23	8
9 Jul 69		**GOO GOO BARABAJAGAL (LOVE IS HOT)** *Pye 7N 17778* [1]	12	9
1 Dec 90		**JENNIFER JUNIPER** *Fontana SYP 1* [2]	68	1

[1] Donovan with the Jeff Beck Group [2] Singing Corner meets Donovan

Jason DONOVAN (137 Top 500) *The top teen idol of the late 1980s, b. 1 Jun 1968, Melbourne. The Australian actor turned singer had an impressive array of UK hits after leaving TV soap 'Neighbours'. His debut LP, 'Ten Good Reasons', was the UK's top-selling album of 1989 (137 WEEKS)* pos/wks

			pos	wks
10 Sep 88	●	**NOTHING CAN DIVIDE US** *PWL PWL 17*	5	12
10 Dec 88	★	**ESPECIALLY FOR YOU** *PWL PWL 24* [1]	1	14
4 Mar 89	★	**TOO MANY BROKEN HEARTS** *PWL PWL 32*	1	13
10 Jun 89	★	**SEALED WITH A KISS** *PWL PWL 39* ■	1	10
9 Sep 89	●	**EVERY DAY (I LOVE YOU MORE)** *PWL PWL 43*	2	9
9 Dec 89	●	**WHEN YOU COME BACK TO ME** *PWL PWL 46*	2	11
7 Apr 90	●	**HANG ON TO YOUR LOVE** *PWL PWL 51*	8	7
30 Jun 90		**ANOTHER NIGHT** *PWL PWL 58*	18	5
1 Sep 90	●	**RHYTHM OF THE RAIN** *PWL PWL 60*	9	6
27 Oct 90		**I'M DOING FINE** *PWL PWL 69*	22	6
18 May 91		**RSVP** *PWL PWL 80*	17	5
22 Jun 91	★	**ANY DREAM WILL DO** *Really Useful RUR 7*	1	12
24 Aug 91	●	**HAPPY TOGETHER** *PWL PWL 203*	10	6
7 Dec 91		**JOSEPH MEGA REMIX** *Really Useful RUR 9* [2]	13	8
18 Jul 92		**MISSION OF LOVE** *Polydor PO 222*	26	4
28 Nov 92		**AS TIME GOES BY** *Polydor PO 245*	26	6
7 Aug 93		**ALL AROUND THE WORLD** *Polydor PZCD 278*	41	3

[1] Kylie Minogue and Jason Donovan [2] Jason Donovan and Original London Cast featuring Linzi Hately, David Easter and Johnny Amobi

DOOBIE BROTHERS *US, male vocal / instrumental group (45 WEEKS)* pos/wks

			pos	wks
9 Mar 74		**LISTEN TO THE MUSIC** *Warner Bros. K 16208*	29	7
7 Jun 75		**TAKE ME IN YOUR ARMS** *Warner Bros. K 16559*	29	5
17 Feb 79		**WHAT A FOOL BELIEVES** *Warner Bros. K 17314* ▲	31	10
5 May 79		**WHAT A FOOL BELIEVES (re-entry)** *Warner Bros. K 17314*	72	1
14 Jul 79		**MINUTE BY MINUTE** *Warner Bros. K 17411*	47	4
24 Jan 87		**WHAT A FOOL BELIEVES (re-issue)** *Warner Bros. W 8451* [1]	57	3
29 Jul 89		**THE DOCTOR** *Capitol CL 536*	73	2
27 Nov 93	●	**LONG TRAIN RUNNIN'** *Warner Bros. W 0217CD*	7	10
14 May 94		**LISTEN TO THE MUSIC (re-mix)** *Warner Bros. W 0228CD*	37	3

[1] Doobie Brothers featuring Michael McDonald

DOOGIE – *See BUG KANN and the PLASTIC JAM*

DOOLALLY *UK, male production duo – Stephen Meade and Daniel Langsmen (16 WEEKS)* pos/wks

			pos	wks
14 Nov 98		**STRAIGHT FROM THE HEART** *Locked On LOX 104CD*	20	6
2 Jan 99		**STRAIGHT FROM THE HEART (re-entry)** *Locked On LOX 104CD*	63	4
7 Aug 99	●	**STRAIGHT FROM THE HEART (re-issue)** *Chocolate Boy / Locked On LOX 112CD*	9	6

See also SHANKS & BIGFOOT

DOOLEYS (396 Top 500) *Largest UK family act to chart (seven members at times): Jim, John, Frank, Kathy, Helen, Anne Dooley plus Anne's husband Bob, and Alan Bogan. First mixed UK family group to notch up five Top 20 entries (83 WEEKS)* pos/wks

			pos	wks
13 Aug 77		**THINK I'M GONNA FALL IN LOVE WITH YOU** *GTO GT 95*	13	10
12 Nov 77	●	**LOVE OF MY LIFE** *GTO GT 110*	9	11
13 May 78		**DON'T TAKE IT LYIN' DOWN** *GTO GT 220*	60	3
2 Sep 78		**A ROSE HAS TO DIE** *GTO GT 229*	11	11
10 Feb 79		**HONEY I'M LOST** *GTO GT 242*	24	9
16 Jun 79	●	**WANTED** *GTO GT 249*	3	14
22 Sep 79	●	**THE CHOSEN FEW** *GTO GT 258*	7	11
8 Mar 80		**LOVE PATROL** *GTO GT 260*	29	7
6 Sep 80		**BODY LANGUAGE** *GTO GT 276*	46	4
10 Oct 81		**AND I WISH** *GTO GT 300*	52	3

Val DOONICAN (167 Top 500) *Popular balladeer and TV host, b. 3 Feb 1928, Waterford, Ireland. This relaxed crooner, who was known for his rocking chair and multi-coloured jumpers, had five successive Top 10 albums in the Swinging Sixties (143 WEEKS)* pos/wks

			pos	wks
15 Oct 64	●	**WALK TALL** *Decca F 11982*	3	21
21 Jan 65	●	**THE SPECIAL YEARS** *Decca F 12049*	7	12
8 Apr 65		**I'M GONNA GET THERE SOMEHOW** *Decca F 12118*	25	5
22 Apr 65		**THE SPECIAL YEARS (re-entry)** *Decca F 12049*	49	1
17 Mar 66	●	**ELUSIVE BUTTERFLY** *Decca F 12358*	5	12
3 Nov 66	●	**WHAT WOULD I BE** *Decca F 12505*	2	17
23 Feb 67		**MEMORIES ARE MADE OF THIS** *Decca F 12566*	11	12
25 May 67		**TWO STREETS** *Decca F 12608*	39	4
18 Oct 67	●	**IF THE WHOLE WORLD STOPPED LOVIN'** *Pye 7N 17396*	3	19
21 Feb 68		**YOU'RE THE ONLY ONE** *Pye 7N 17465*	37	4
12 Jun 68		**NOW** *Pye 7N 17534*	43	2
23 Oct 68		**IF I KNEW THEN WHAT I KNOW NOW** *Pye 7N 17616*	14	13
23 Apr 69		**RING OF BRIGHT WATER** *Pye 7N 17713*	48	1
4 Dec 71		**MORNING** *Philips 6006 177*	12	13
10 Mar 73		**HEAVEN IS MY WOMAN'S LOVE** *Philips 6028 031*	34	6
28 Apr 73		**HEAVEN IS MY WOMAN'S LOVE (re-entry)** *Philips 6028 031*	47	1

DOOP *Holland, male instrumental duo – Ferry Ridderhof and Peter Garnefski (12 WEEKS)* pos/wks

			pos	wks
12 Mar 94	★	**DOOP** *Citybeat CBE 774CD*	1	12

DOORS *US, male vocal / instrumental group (42 WEEKS)* pos/wks

16 Aug 67	**LIGHT MY FIRE** *Elektra EKSN 45014* ▲	49	1
28 Aug 68	**HELLO, I LOVE YOU** *Elektra EKSN 45037* ▲	15	12
16 Oct 71	**RIDERS ON THE STORM** *Elektra K 12021*	50	1
30 Oct 71	**RIDERS ON THE STORM (re-entry)** *Elektra K 12021*	22	10
20 Mar 76	**RIDERS ON THE STORM (re-issue)** *Elektra K 12203*	33	5
3 Feb 79	**HELLO I LOVE YOU (re-issue)** *Elektra K 12215*	71	2
27 Apr 91	**BREAK ON THROUGH** *Elektra EKR 121*	64	2
1 Jun 91 ●	**LIGHT MY FIRE (re-issue)** *Elektra EKR 125*	7	8
10 Aug 91	**RIDERS ON THE STORM (2nd re-issue)** *Elektra EKR 131*	68	1

D.O.P. *UK, male instrumental / production duo (2 WEEKS)* pos/wks

3 Feb 96	**STOP STARTING TO START STOPPING (EP)** *Hi-Life 5779472*	58	1
13 Jul 96	**GROOVY BEAT** *Hi-Life 5750652*	54	1

Tracks on Stop Starting to Stop Stopping (EP): Gusta / Dance to the House / Can You Feel It / How Do Y'All Feel

DOPE SMUGGLAZ *UK, male DJ / production trio (5 WEEKS)* pos/wks

5 Dec 98	**THE WORD** *Mushroom PERFCDS 1*	62	1
7 Aug 99	**DOUBLE DOUBLE DUTCH** *Perfecto PERF2CDS*	15	4

Charlie DORE *UK, female vocalist (2 WEEKS)* pos/wks

17 Nov 79	**PILOT OF THE AIRWAVES** *Island WIP 6526*	66	2

DOROTHY *UK, male instrumental duo (5 WEEKS)* pos/wks

9 Dec 95	**WHAT'S THAT TUNE (DOO DOO DOO DOO DOO-DOO-DOO-DOO-DOO-DOO)** *RCA 74321330912*	31	5

Lee DORSEY *US, male vocalist (36 WEEKS)* pos/wks

3 Feb 66	**GET OUT OF MY LIFE, WOMAN** *Stateside SS 485*	22	7
5 May 66	**CONFUSION** *Stateside SS 506*	38	6
11 Aug 66 ●	**WORKING IN THE COALMINE** *Stateside SS 528*	8	11
27 Oct 66 ●	**HOLY COW** *Stateside SS 552*	6	12

Marc DORSEY *US, male vocalist (1 WEEK)* pos/wks

19 Jun 99	**IF YOU REALLY WANNA KNOW** *Jive 0522592*	58	1

Tommy DORSEY ORCHESTRA starring Warren COVINGTON *US, orchestra – Warren Covington, male instrumentalist – trombone (19 WEEKS)* pos/wks

17 Oct 58 ●	**TEA FOR TWO CHA CHA** *Brunswick 05757*	3	19

DOUBLE *Switzerland, male vocal / instrumental duo – Kurt Maloo and Felix Haug (10 WEEKS)* pos/wks

25 Jan 86 ●	**THE CAPTAIN OF HER HEART** *Polydor POSP 779*	8	9
5 Dec 87	**DEVIL'S BALL** *Polydor POSP 888*	71	1

DOUBLE DEE featuring DANY *Italy, male vocal / instrumental duo (4 WEEKS)* pos/wks

1 Dec 90	**FOUND LOVE** *Epic 6563766*	63	2
25 Nov 95	**FOUND LOVE (re-mix)** *Sony S3 DANUCD 1*	33	2

DOUBLE 99 *UK, male instrumental / production duo – Tim Liken and Omar Adimora (9 WEEKS)* pos/wks

31 May 97	**RIPGROOVE** *Satellite 74321485132*	31	3
1 Nov 97	**RIPGROOVE (re-mix)** *Satellite 74321529322*	14	6

See also RIP PRODUCTIONS

007 – *See RED RAW featuring 007*

DOUBLE SIX *UK, male vocal / instrumental group (2 WEEKS)* pos/wks

19 Sep 98	**REAL GOOD** *Multiply CDMULTY 39*	66	1
12 Jun 99	**BREAKDOWN** *Multiply CDMULTY 50*	59	1

DOUBLE TROUBLE *UK, male instrumental / production duo – Leigh Guest and Michael Menson (35 WEEKS)* pos/wks

27 May 89	**JUST KEEP ROCKIN'** *Desire WANT 9* [1]	11	12
7 Oct 89 ●	**STREET TUFF** *Desire WANT 18* [2]	3	14
12 May 90	**TALK BACK** *Desire WANT 27* [3]	71	1
30 Jun 90	**LOVE DON'T LIVE HERE ANYMORE** *Desire WANT 32* [4]	21	6
15 Jun 91	**RUB-A-DUB** *Desire WANT 41*	66	2

[1] Double Trouble and the Rebel MC [2] Rebel MC and Double Trouble [3] With vocals by Janette Sewell [4] Double Trouble featuring Janette Sewell and Carl Brown

DOUBLE YOU? *Italy, male vocalist – Willie Morales (3 WEEKS)* pos/wks

2 May 92	**PLEASE DON'T GO** *ZYX ZYX 67487*	41	3

Rob DOUGAN *UK, male vocalist / instrumentalist / producer (1 WEEK)* pos/wks

4 Apr 98	**FURIOUS ANGELS** *Cheeky CHEKCD 025*	62	1

Carl DOUGLAS *Jamaica, male vocalist (39 WEEKS)* pos/wks

17 Aug 74 ★	**KUNG FU FIGHTING** *Pye 7N 45377* ▲	1	13
30 Nov 74	**DANCE THE KUNG FU** *Pye 7N 45418*	35	5
3 Dec 77	**RUN BACK** *Pye 7N 46018*	25	10
23 May 98 ●	**KUNG FU FIGHTING** *All Around the World CDGLOBE 173* [1]	8	11

[1] Bus Stop featuring Carl Douglas

Second listing for Kung Fu Fighting was not a re-mix of the original but Douglas's 1974 hit vocal sampled and used in a new recording by Bus Stop

Carol DOUGLAS *US, female vocalist (4 WEEKS)* pos/wks

22 Jul 78	**NIGHT FEVER** *Gull GULS 61*	66	4

Craig DOUGLAS (255 Top 500) *Clean-cut early Sixties teen idol, b. Terence Perkins, 12 Aug 1941, Isle of Wight. Voted Best New Singer of 1959; had eight cover versions among his nine Top 20 entries. He topped the bill on The Beatles' first major stage show (112 WEEKS)* pos/wks

12 Jun 59	**A TEENAGER IN LOVE** *Top Rank JAR 133*	13	11
7 Aug 59 ★	**ONLY SIXTEEN** *Top Rank JAR 159*	1	15
22 Jan 60 ●	**PRETTY BLUE EYES** *Top Rank JAR 268*	4	14
28 Apr 60 ●	**THE HEART OF A TEENAGE GIRL** *Top Rank JAR 340*	10	9
11 Aug 60	**OH! WHAT A DAY** *Top Rank JAR 406*	43	1
20 Apr 61 ●	**A HUNDRED POUNDS OF CLAY** *Top Rank JAR 556*	9	9
29 Jun 61 ●	**TIME** *Top Rank JAR 569*	9	14
22 Mar 62 ●	**WHEN MY LITTLE GIRL IS SMILING** *Top Rank JAR 610*	9	13
28 Jun 62 ●	**OUR FAVOURITE MELODIES** *Columbia DB 4854*	9	10
18 Oct 62	**OH, LONESOME ME** *Decca F 11523*	15	12
28 Feb 63	**TOWN CRIER** *Decca F 11575*	36	4

DOVE *Ireland, male / female vocal group (2 WEEKS)* pos/wks

11 Sep 99	**DON'T DREAM** *ZTT 135CD*	37	2

DOVES *UK, male vocal / instrumental group (7 WEEKS)* pos/wks

14 Aug 99	**HERE IT COMES** *Casino CHIP 003CD*	73	1
1 Apr 00	**THE CEDAR ROOM** *Heavenly HVN 95CD*	33	2
10 Jun 00	**CATCH THE SUN** *Heavenly HVN 96CD*	32	2
11 Nov 00	**THE MAN WHO TOLD EVERYTHING** *Heavenly HVN 98CD*	32	2

DOWLANDS *UK, male vocal duo (7 WEEKS)* pos/wks

9 Jan 64	**ALL MY LOVING** *Oriole CB 1897*	33	7

Robert DOWNEY Jr *US, male vocalist (1 WEEK)* pos/wks

30 Jan 93	**SMILE** *Epic 6589052*	68	1

Don DOWNING *US, male vocalist (10 WEEKS)* pos/wks

10 Nov 73	**LONELY DAYS, LONELY NIGHTS** *People PEO 102*	32	10

Will DOWNING *US, male vocalist (35 WEEKS)* pos/wks

2 Apr 88	**A LOVE SUPREME** *Fourth & Broadway BRW 90*	14	10
25 Jun 88	**IN MY DREAMS** *Fourth & Broadway BRW 104*	34	6

Date	Title / Label	pos	wks
1 Oct 88	**FREE** *Fourth & Broadway BRW 112*	58	5
21 Jan 89	**WHERE IS THE LOVE** *Fourth & Broadway BRW 122* [1]	19	7
28 Oct 89	**TEST OF TIME** *Fourth & Broadway BRW 146*	67	2
24 Feb 90	**COME TOGETHER AS ONE** *Fourth & Broadway BRW 159*	48	4
18 Sep 93	**THERE'S NO LIVING WITHOUT YOU** *Fourth & Broadway BRCD 278*	67	1

[1] Mica Paris and Will Downing

Jason DOWNS featuring MILK

US, male vocalist and US, male rapper (6 WEEKS)

Date	Title / Label	pos	wks
12 May 01	**WHITE BOY WITH A FEATHER** *Pepper 9230412*	19	5
14 Jul 01	**CATS IN THE CRADLE** *Pepper 9230442*	65	1

Lamont DOZIER – *See HOLLAND-DOZIER featuring Lamont DOZIER*

Charlie DRAKE

UK, male comedian / vocalist – Charles Sprigall (37 WEEKS)

Date	Title / Label	pos	wks
8 Aug 58 ●	**SPLISH SPLASH** *Parlophone R 4461*	7	11
24 Oct 58	**VOLARE** *Parlophone R 4478*	28	2
27 Oct 60	**MR CUSTER** *Parlophone R 4701*	12	12
5 Oct 61	**MY BOOMERANG WON'T COME BACK** *Parlophone R 4824*	14	11
1 Jan 72	**PUCKWUDGIE** *Columbia DB 8829*	47	1

DRAMATIS *UK, male vocal / instrumental group (8 WEEKS)*

Date	Title / Label	pos	wks
5 Dec 81	**LOVE NEEDS NO DISGUISE** *Beggars Banquet BEG 68* [1]	33	7
13 Nov 82	**I CAN SEE HER NOW** *Rocket XPRES 83*	57	1

[1] Gary Numan and Dramatis

Rusty DRAPER *US, male vocalist (4 WEEKS)*

Date	Title / Label	pos	wks
11 Aug 60	**MULE SKINNER BLUES** *Mercury AMT 1101*	39	4

DREAD ZEPPELIN *US, male vocal / instrumental group (3 WEEKS)*

Date	Title / Label	pos	wks
1 Dec 90	**YOUR TIME IS GONNA COME** *IRS DREAD 1*	59	1
13 Jul 91	**STAIRWAY TO HEAVEN** *IRS DREAD 2*	62	2

DREADZONE *UK, male instrumental group (15 WEEKS)*

Date	Title / Label	pos	wks
6 May 95	**ZION YOUTH** *Virgin VSCDG 1537*	49	2
29 Jul 95	**CAPTAIN DREAD** *Virgin VSCDG 1541*	49	2
23 Sep 95	**MAXIMUM (EP)** *Virgin VSCDT 1555*	56	2
6 Jan 96	**LITTLE BRITAIN** *Virgin VSCDG 1565*	20	6
30 Mar 96	**LIFE LOVE AND UNITY** *Virgin VSCDT 1583*	56	1
10 May 97	**EARTH ANGEL** *Virgin VSCDT 1593*	51	1
26 Jul 97	**MOVING ON** *Virgin VSCDT 1635*	58	1

Tracks on Maximum (EP): Maximum / Fight the Power 95 / One Way

DREAM *US, female vocal group (7 WEEKS)*

Date	Title / Label	pos	wks
17 Mar 01	**HE LOVES U NOT** *Puff Daddy / Arista 74321823542*	17	7

DREAM ACADEMY

UK, male / female vocal / instrumental group (10 WEEKS)

Date	Title / Label	pos	wks
30 Mar 85	**LIFE IN A NORTHERN TOWN** *Blanco Y Negro NEG 10*	15	8
14 Sep 85	**THE LOVE PARADE** *Blanco Y Negro NEG 16*	68	2

DREAM FREQUENCY *UK, male producer – Ian Bland (12 WEEKS)*

Date	Title / Label	pos	wks
12 Jan 91	**LOVE PEACE AND HARMONY** *Citybeat CBE 756*	71	2
25 Jan 92	**FEEL SO REAL** *Citybeat CBE 763* [1]	23	5
25 Apr 92	**TAKE ME** *Citybeat CBE 768*	39	3
21 May 94	**GOOD TIMES / THE DREAM** *Citybeat CBE 773CD*	67	1
10 Sep 94	**YOU MAKE ME FEEL MIGHTY REAL** *Citybeat CBE 775CD*	65	1

[1] Dream Frequency featuring Debbie Sharp

See also BEAT RENEGADES; RED

DREAM WARRIORS *Canada, male rap group (19 WEEKS)*

Date	Title / Label	pos	wks
14 Jul 90	**WASH YOUR FACE IN MY SINK** *Fourth & Broadway BRW 183*	16	8
24 Nov 90	**MY DEFINITION OF A BOOMBASTIC JAZZ STYLE** *Fourth & Broadway BRW 197*	13	8
2 Mar 91	**LUDI** *Fourth & Broadway BRW 206*	39	3

DREAMERS – *See FREDDIE and the DREAMERS*

DREAMHOUSE *UK, male vocal / instrumental group (2 WEEKS)*

Date	Title / Label	pos	wks
3 Jun 95	**STAY** *Chase CDPALACE 1*	62	2

DREAMWEAVERS *US, male / female vocal group (18 WEEKS)*

Date	Title / Label	pos	wks
10 Feb 56 ★	**IT'S ALMOST TOMORROW** *Brunswick 05515*	1	18

DREEM TEEM *UK, male DJ / production trio (12 WEEKS)*

Date	Title / Label	pos	wks
13 Dec 97	**THE THEME** *4 Liberty 74321542032*	34	4
6 Nov 99	**BUDDY X 99** *4 Liberty LIBTCD 33* [1]	15	5
15 Dec 01	**IT AIN'T ENOUGH** *ffrr / Public Demand FCD 401* [2]	20	3

[1] Dreem Teem vs Neneh Cherry [2] Dreem Teem vs Artful Dodger featuring MZ May and MC Alistair

DRELLS – *See Archie BELL and the DRELLS*

Eddie DRENNON and B.B.S. UNLIMITED

US, male vocal / instrumental group (6 WEEKS)

Date	Title / Label	pos	wks
28 Feb 76	**LET'S DO THE LATIN HUSTLE** *Pye International 7N 25702*	20	6

Alan DREW *UK, male vocalist (2 WEEKS)*

Date	Title / Label	pos	wks
26 Sep 63	**ALWAYS THE LONELY ONE** *Columbia DB 7090*	48	2

DRIFTERS (113 Top 500)

Ever changing, ever popular US group, founded in 1953 by Clyde McPhatter (d. 1972) and still active today, with erstwhile members including Ben E King, Johnny Moore (d. 1998) and Rudy Lewis (d. 1964). Inducted into Rock and Roll Hall of Fame in 1988 (176 WEEKS)

Date	Title / Label	pos	wks
8 Jan 60	**DANCE WITH ME** *London HLE 8988*	17	4
10 Mar 60	**DANCE WITH ME (re-entry)** *London HLE 8988*	35	1
3 Nov 60 ●	**SAVE THE LAST DANCE FOR ME** *London HLK 9201* ▲	2	18
16 Mar 61	**I COUNT THE TEARS** *London HLK 9287*	28	6
5 Apr 62	**WHEN MY LITTLE GIRL IS SMILING** *London HLK 9522*	31	3
10 Oct 63	**I'LL TAKE YOU HOME** *London HLK 9785*	37	5
24 Sep 64	**UNDER THE BOARDWALK** *Atlantic AT 4001*	45	4
8 Apr 65	**AT THE CLUB** *Atlantic AT 4019*	35	7
29 Apr 65	**COME ON OVER TO MY PLACE** *Atlantic AT 4023*	40	5
2 Feb 67	**BABY WHAT I MEAN** *Atlantic 584 065*	49	1
25 Mar 72	**AT THE CLUB** *Atlantic K 10148*	39	1
8 Apr 72 ●	**AT THE CLUB / SATURDAY NIGHT AT THE MOVIES (re-entry of re-issue)** *Atlantic K 10148*	3	19
26 Aug 72 ●	**COME ON OVER TO MY PLACE (re-issue)** *Atlantic K 10216*	9	11
4 Aug 73 ●	**LIKE SISTER AND BROTHER** *Bell 1313*	7	12
15 Jun 74 ●	**KISSIN' IN THE BACK ROW OF THE MOVIES** *Bell 1358*	2	13
12 Oct 74 ●	**DOWN ON THE BEACH TONIGHT** *Bell 1381*	7	9
8 Feb 75	**LOVE GAMES** *Bell 1396*	33	6
6 Sep 75 ●	**THERE GOES MY FIRST LOVE** *Bell 1433*	3	12
29 Nov 75 ●	**CAN I TAKE YOU HOME LITTLE GIRL** *Bell 1462*	10	10
13 Mar 76	**HELLO HAPPINESS** *Bell 1469*	12	8
11 Sep 76	**EVERY NITE'S A SATURDAY NIGHT WITH YOU** *Bell 1491*	29	7
18 Dec 76 ●	**YOU'RE MORE THAN A NUMBER IN MY LITTLE RED BOOK** *Arista 78*	5	12
14 Apr 79	**SAVE THE LAST DANCE FOR ME / WHEN MY LITTLE GIRL IS SMILING (re-issue)** *Lightning LIG 9014*	69	2

'Saturday Night at the Movies' received chart credit with 'At the Club' only after the re-issue's return to the chart on 8 Apr 1972

DRIFTERS – *See SHADOWS*

Julie DRISCOLL, Brian AUGER and the TRINITY

UK, female vocalist / male instrumental group (16 WEEKS)

Date	Title / Label	pos	wks
17 Apr 68 ●	**THIS WHEEL'S ON FIRE** *Marmalade 598 006*	5	16

DRIVER 67 *UK, male vocalist – Paul Phillips (12 WEEKS)* pos/wks

		pos	wks
23 Dec 78 ●	**CAR 67** *Logo GO 336*	7	12

DRIZABONE
UK / US, male / female vocal / instrumental group (18 WEEKS) pos/wks

		pos	wks
22 Jun 91	**REAL LOVE** *Fourth & Broadway BRW 223* [1]	16	8
26 Oct 91	**CATCH THE FIRE** *Fourth & Broadway BRW 232* [1]	54	2
23 Apr 94	**PRESSURE** *Fourth & Broadway BRCD 264*	33	2
15 Oct 94	**BRIGHTEST STAR** *Fourth & Broadway BRCD 293*	45	2
4 Mar 95	**REAL LOVE (re-recording)** *Fourth & Broadway BRCD 311*	24	4

[1] Driza Bone

Frank D'RONE *US, male vocalist (6 WEEKS)* pos/wks

		pos	wks
22 Dec 60	**STRAWBERRY BLONDE (THE BAND ROCKED ON)** *Mercury AMT 1123*	24	6

DRU HILL *US, male vocal group (42 WEEKS)* pos/wks

		pos	wks
15 Feb 97	**TELL ME** *Fourth & Broadway BRCD 342*	30	3
10 May 97	**IN MY BED** *Fourth & Broadway BRCD 353*	16	3
11 Oct 97	**BIG BAD MAMMA** *Def Jam 5749792* [1]	12	3
6 Dec 97	**5 STEPS** *Island Black Music CID 675*	22	3
24 Oct 98 ●	**HOW DEEP IS YOUR LOVE** *Island Black Music CID 725* [2]	9	7
16 Jan 99	**HOW DEEP IS YOUR LOVE (re-entry)** *Island Black Music CID 725* [2]	75	1
6 Feb 99 ●	**THESE ARE THE TIMES** *Island Black Music CID 733*	4	6
10 Jul 99 ●	**WILD WILD WEST** *Columbia 6675962* [3] ▲	2	16

[1] Foxy Brown featuring Dru Hill [2] Dru Hill featuring Redman [3] Will Smith featuring Dru Hill – additional vocals Kool Moe Dee

DRUGSTORE
UK / US / Brazil, male / female vocal / instrumental group (5 WEEKS) pos/wks

		pos	wks
10 Jun 95	**FADER** *Honey HONCD 7*	72	1
2 May 98	**EL PRESIDENT** *Roadrunner RR 22369* [1]	20	3
4 Jul 98	**SOBER** *Roadrunner RR22303*	68	1

[1] Additional vocals by Thom Yorke

DRUM CLUB *UK, male instrumental / production duo (1 WEEK)* pos/wks

		pos	wks
6 Nov 93	**SOUND SYSTEM** *Butterfly BFLD 10*	62	1

DRUM THEATRE *UK, male vocal / instrumental group (8 WEEKS)* pos/wks

		pos	wks
15 Feb 86	**LIVING IN THE PAST** *Epic A 6798*	67	2
17 Jan 87	**ELDORADO** *Epic EMU 1*	44	6

DRUPI *Italy, male vocalist – Giampiero Anelli (12 WEEKS)* pos/wks

		pos	wks
1 Dec 73	**VADO VIA** *A & M AMS 7083*	17	12

DSK
UK, male / female vocal / instrumental / production group (4 WEEKS) pos/wks

		pos	wks
31 Aug 91	**WHAT WOULD WE DO / READ MY LIPS** *Boy's Own BOI 6*	46	3
22 Nov 97	**WHAT WOULD WE DO (re-mix)** *Fresh FRSHD 63*	55	1

DSM *US, male rap group (4 WEEKS)* pos/wks

		pos	wks
7 Dec 85	**WARRIOR GROOVE** *10 DAZZ 45-7*	68	4

DSP – *See Matt DAREY*

DTI *US, male vocal / instrumental group (1 WEEK)* pos/wks

		pos	wks
16 Apr 88	**KEEP THIS FREQUENCY CLEAR** *Premiere UK ERE 501*	73	1

DTOX *UK, male / female vocal / instrumental group (1 WEEK)* pos/wks

		pos	wks
21 Nov 92	**SHATTERED GLASS** *Vitality VITal 1*	75	1

John DU CANN *UK, male vocalist (6 WEEKS)* pos/wks

		pos	wks
22 Sep 79	**DON'T BE A DUMMY** *Vertigo 6059 241*	33	6

John DU PREZ – *See MODERN ROMANCE*

DUB CONSPIRACY – *See TRU FAITH and DUB CONSPIRACY*

DUB PISTOLS
UK, male vocal / instrumental / production group (1 WEEK) pos/wks

		pos	wks
10 Oct 98	**CYCLONE** *CONCRETE HARD 36CD*	63	1

DUB WAR *UK, male vocal / instrumental group (5 WEEKS)* pos/wks

		pos	wks
3 Jun 95	**STRIKE IT** *Earache MOSH 138CD*	70	1
27 Jan 96	**ENEMY MAKER** *Earache MOSH 147CD*	41	2
24 Aug 96	**CRY DIGNITY** *Earache MOSH 163CDD*	59	1
29 Mar 97	**MILLION DOLLAR LOVE** *Earache MOSH 170CD1*	73	1

DUBLINERS *Ireland, male vocal / instrumental group (45 WEEKS)* pos/wks

		pos	wks
30 Mar 67 ●	**SEVEN DRUNKEN NIGHTS** *Major Minor MM 506*	7	17
30 Aug 67	**BLACK VELVET BAND** *Major Minor MM 530*	15	15
20 Dec 67	**MAIDS, WHEN YOU'RE YOUNG NEVER WED AN OLD MAN** *Major Minor MM 551*	43	3
28 Mar 87 ●	**THE IRISH ROVER** *Stiff BUY 258* [1]	8	8
16 Jun 90	**JACK'S HEROES / WHISKEY IN THE JAR** *Pogue Mahone YZ 500* [1]	63	2

[1] Pogues and the Dubliners

DUBSTAR *UK, male / female vocal / instrumental group (26 WEEKS)* pos/wks

		pos	wks
8 Jul 95	**STARS** *Food CDFOOD 61*	40	3
30 Sep 95	**ANYWHERE** *Food CDFOOD 67*	37	3
6 Jan 96	**NOT SO MANIC NOW** *Food CDFOOD 71*	18	5
30 Mar 96	**STARS (re-issue)** *Food CDFOODS 75*	15	6
3 Aug 96	**ELEVATOR SONG** *Food CDFOOD 80*	25	2
19 Jul 97	**NO MORE TALK** *Food CDFOOD 96*	20	3
20 Sep 97	**CATHEDRAL PARK** *Food CDFOOD 104*	41	1
7 Feb 98	**I WILL BE YOUR GIRLFRIEND** *Food CDFOODS 108*	28	2
27 May 00	**I (FRIDAY NIGHT)** *Food CDFOODS 128*	37	1

Ricardo 'Rikrok' DUCENT – *See SHAGGY*

Mary DUFF – *See Daniel O'DONNELL*

DUFFO *Australia, male vocalist (2 WEEKS)* pos/wks

		pos	wks
24 Mar 79	**GIVE ME BACK ME BRAIN** *Beggars Banquet BEG 15*	60	2

Stephen 'Tin Tin' DUFFY *UK, male vocalist (24 WEEKS)* pos/wks

		pos	wks
9 Jul 83	**HOLD IT** *Curve X 9763* [1]	55	4
2 Mar 85 ●	**KISS ME** *10 TIN 2*	4	11
18 May 85	**ICING ON THE CAKE** *10 TIN 3*	14	9

[1] Tin Tin

DUKE *UK, male vocalist (6 WEEKS)* pos/wks

		pos	wks
25 May 96	**SO IN LOVE WITH YOU** *Encore CDCOR 009*	66	1
26 Oct 96	**SO IN LOVE WITH YOU (re-issue)** *Pukka CDPUKKA 11*	22	4
11 Nov 00	**SO IN LOVE WITH YOU (re-mix)** *48k / Perfecto SPECT 08CDS*	65	1

George DUKE *US, male vocalist / instrumentalist (6 WEEKS)* pos/wks

		pos	wks
12 Jul 80	**BRAZILIAN LOVE AFFAIR** *Epic EPC 8751*	36	6

DUKE BAYSEE *UK, male vocalist (6 WEEKS)* pos/wks

		pos	wks
3 Sep 94	**SUGAR SUGAR** *Bell 74321228702*	30	4
21 Jan 95	**DO YOU LOVE ME** *Double Dekker CDDEK 1*	46	2

DUKES *UK, male vocal duo (13 WEEKS)* pos/wks

		pos	wks
17 Oct 81	**MYSTERY GIRL** *WEA K 18867*	47	7
1 May 82	**THANK YOU FOR THE PARTY** *WEA K 19136*	53	6

Candy DULFER
Holland, female instrumentalist – saxophone (14 WEEKS) pos/wks

		pos	wks
24 Feb 90 ●	**LILY WAS HERE** *RCA ZB 43045* [1]	6	12

1965

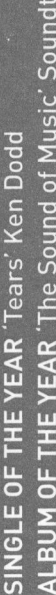

IN THE YEAR IN WHICH US FORCES BEGAN BOMBING MILITARY TARGETS IN VIETNAM, THE BEATLES WENT TO BUCKINGHAM PALACE TO MEET THE QUEEN AND RECEIVE THEIR MBEs, REPRESENTATIVES OF 110 NATIONS ATTENDED THE STATE FUNERAL OF SIR WINSTON CHURCHILL, AND AT TIMES UK ARTISTS HELD NINE OF THE US TOP 10 SLOTS, **JOHN MAYALL** DESCRIBES A CAREER-CHANGING ENCOUNTER IN A MOTORWAY SERVICE STATION ...

“The record that changed the course of my career was the **Yardbirds**' 'For Your Love' – or actually the B-side, 'Got to Hurry'. I heard it on a jukebox up on the motorway, the Blue Boar. Eric Clapton was leaving the group, and the timing was impeccable. He'd made such progress so quickly – I'd heard him about nine months before that and he hadn't seemed anything remarkable. By this time, he had something assured and special about him. I thought this is perfect I can't let this go by. So we signed him up for the Bluesbreakers.”

SINGLE OF THE YEAR 'Tears' Ken Dodd
ALBUM OF THE YEAR 'The Sound of Music' Soundtrack

			pos	wks
4 Aug 90		SAXUALITY *RCA PB 43769*	60	2

[1] David A Stewart featuring Candy Dulfer

DUM DUMS *UK, male vocal / instrumental group (15 WEEKS)* pos/wks

			pos	wks
11 Mar 00		EVERYTHING *Good Behavior CDGOOD 1*	21	5
8 Jul 00		CAN'T GET YOU OUT OF MY THOUGHTS *Good Behaviour GD GOOD 2*	18	5
23 Sep 00		YOU DO SOMETHING TO ME *Good Behaviour CD GOLD 3*	27	3
17 Feb 01		ARMY OF TWO *Good Behaviour CDGOOD 5*	27	2

Thuli DUMAKUDE *South Africa, male vocalist (1 WEEK)* pos/wks

			pos	wks
2 Jan 88		THE FUNERAL (SEPTEMBER 25, 1977) *MCA MCA 1228*	75	1

The listed flip side of 'The Funeral' was 'Cry Freedom' by George Fenton and Jonas Gwangwa

John DUMMER and Helen APRIL
UK, male / female vocal duo (3 WEEKS) pos/wks

			pos	wks
28 Aug 82		BLUE SKIES *Speed SPEED 8*	54	3

DUMONDE *Germany, male / female production / vocal group (3 WEEKS)* pos/wks

			pos	wks
27 Jan 01		TOMORROW *Variation VART 6*	60	1
19 May 01		NEVER LOOK BACK *Manifesto FESCD 83*	36	2

DUNBLANE *UK, male / female vocal / instrumental group (15 WEEKS)* pos/wks

			pos	wks
21 Dec 96	★	KNOCKIN' ON HEAVEN'S DOOR / THROW THESE GUNS AWAY *BMG 74321442182* ■	1	15

Johnny DUNCAN and the BLUE GRASS BOYS
US, male vocalist and UK, instrumental group (20 WEEKS) pos/wks

			pos	wks
26 Jul 57	●	LAST TRAIN TO SAN FERNANDO *Columbia DB 3959*	2	17
25 Oct 57		BLUE, BLUE HEARTACHES *Columbia DB 3996*	27	1
29 Nov 57		FOOTPRINTS IN THE SNOW *Columbia DB 4029*	27	1
3 Jan 58		FOOTPRINTS IN THE SNOW (re-entry) *Columbia DB 4029*	28	1

David DUNDAS *UK, male vocalist (14 WEEKS)* pos/wks

			pos	wks
24 Jul 76	●	JEANS ON *Air CHS 2094*	3	9
9 Apr 77		ANOTHER FUNNY HONEYMOON *Air CHS 2136*	29	5

Erroll DUNKLEY *Jamaica, male vocalist (14 WEEKS)* pos/wks

			pos	wks
22 Sep 79		OK FRED *Scope SC 6*	11	11
2 Feb 80		SIT DOWN AND CRY *Scope SC 11*	52	3

Clive DUNN *UK, male actor / vocalist (28 WEEKS)* pos/wks

			pos	wks
28 Nov 70	★	GRANDAD *Columbia DB 8726*	1	27
26 Jun 71		GRANDAD (re-entry) *Columbia DB 8726*	50	1

Simon DUPREE and the BIG SOUND
UK, male vocal / instrumental group (16 WEEKS) pos/wks

			pos	wks
22 Nov 67	●	KITES *Parlophone R 5646*	9	13
3 Apr 68		FOR WHOM THE BELL TOLLS *Parlophone R 5670*	43	3

DURAN DURAN (68 Top 500) *New Romantics turned teen idols: Simon Le Bon (v), Nick Rhodes (k), John Taylor (b), Andy Taylor (g), Roger Taylor (d). The Birmingham band's successive Top 10 hits included 'A View to a Kill' the best selling James Bond theme ever in the UK and the US. The three Taylors were unrelated (222 WEEKS)* pos/wks

			pos	wks
21 Feb 81		PLANET EARTH *EMI 5137*	12	11
9 May 81		CARELESS MEMORIES *EMI 5168*	37	7
25 Jul 81	●	GIRLS ON FILM *EMI 5206*	5	11
28 Nov 81		MY OWN WAY *EMI 5254*	14	11
15 May 82	●	HUNGRY LIKE THE WOLF *EMI 5295*	5	12
21 Aug 82	●	SAVE A PRAYER *EMI 5327*	2	9
13 Nov 82	●	RIO *EMI 5346*	9	11
26 Mar 83	★	IS THERE SOMETHING I SHOULD KNOW? *EMI 5371* ■	1	9
29 Oct 83	●	UNION OF THE SNAKE *EMI 5429*	3	7
24 Dec 83		UNION OF THE SNAKE (re-entry) *EMI 5429*	66	4
4 Feb 84	●	NEW MOON ON MONDAY *EMI DURAN 1*	9	7
28 Apr 84	★	THE REFLEX *EMI DURAN 2* ▲	1	14
3 Nov 84	●	WILD BOYS *Parlophone DURAN 3*	2	14
18 May 85	●	A VIEW TO A KILL *Parlophone DURAN 007* ▲	2	16
1 Nov 86	●	NOTORIOUS *EMI DDN 45*	7	6
3 Jan 87		NOTORIOUS (re-entry) *EMI DDN 45*	73	1
21 Feb 87		SKIN TRADE *EMI TRADE 1*	22	6
25 Apr 87		MEET EL PRESIDENTE *EMI TOUR 1*	24	5
1 Oct 88		I DON'T WANT YOUR LOVE *EMI YOUR 1*	14	5
7 Jan 89	●	ALL SHE WANTS IS *EMI DD 11*	9	5
22 Apr 89		DO YOU BELIEVE IN SHAME? *EMI DD 12*	30	4
16 Dec 89		BURNING THE GROUND *EMI DD 13*	31	5
4 Aug 90		VIOLENCE OF SUMMER (LOVE'S TAKING OVER) *Parlophone DD 14*	20	4
17 Nov 90		SERIOUS *Parlophone DD 15*	48	3
30 Jan 93	●	ORDINARY WORLD *Parlophone CDDDS 16*	6	9
10 Apr 93		COME UNDONE *Parlophone CDDDS 17*	13	8
4 Sep 93		TOO MUCH INFORMATION *Parlophone CDDDS 18*	35	3
25 Mar 95		PERFECT DAY *Parlophone CDDDS 20*	28	4
17 Jun 95		WHITE LINES (DON'T DO IT) *Parlophone CDDD 19* [1]	17	5
24 May 97		OUT OF MY MIND *Virgin VSCDT 1639*	21	2
30 Jan 99		ELECTRIC BARBARELLA *EMI CDELEC 2000*	23	3
10 Jun 00		SOMEONE ELSE NOT ME *Hollywood / Edel 0108845 HWR*	53	1

[1] Duran Duran featuring Melle Mel and Grandmaster Flash and the Furious Five

Group was UK / US from 'Burning the Ground'

See also POWER STATION; ARCADIA

Jimmy DURANTE *US, male vocalist (1 WEEK)* pos/wks

			pos	wks
14 Dec 96		MAKE SOMEONE HAPPY *Warner Bros. W 0385CD*	69	1

Judith DURHAM *Australia, female vocalist (5 WEEKS)* pos/wks

			pos	wks
15 Jun 67		THE OLIVE TREE *Columbia DB 8207*	33	5

See also SEEKERS

Ian DURY and the BLOCKHEADS
UK, male vocal / instrumental group (56 WEEKS) pos/wks

			pos	wks
29 Apr 78	●	WHAT A WASTE *Stiff BUY 27*	9	12
9 Dec 78	★	HIT ME WITH YOUR RHYTHM STICK *Stiff BUY 38* [1]	1	15
4 Aug 79	●	REASONS TO BE CHEERFUL (PT. 3) *Stiff BUY 50*	3	8
30 Aug 80		I WANT TO BE STRAIGHT *Stiff BUY 90*	22	7
15 Nov 80		SUEPERMAN'S BIG SISTER *Stiff BUY 100*	51	3
25 May 85		HIT ME WITH YOUR RHYTHM STICK (re-mix) *Stiff BUY 214*	55	4
26 Oct 85		PROFOUNDLY IN LOVE WITH PANDORA *EMI EMI 5534* [2]	45	5
27 Jul 91		HIT ME WITH YOUR RHYTHM STICK '91 *Flying FLYR 1*	73	1
11 Mar 00		DRIP FED FRED *Virgin VSCDT 1768* [3]	55	1

[1] Ian and the Blockheads [2] Ian Dury [3] Madness featuring Ian Dury

DUST BROTHERS *US, male production duo (1 WEEK)* pos/wks

			pos	wks
11 Dec 99		THIS IS YOUR LIFE *Restless 74321713962*	60	1

DUST JUNKYS *UK, male vocal / instrumental group (5 WEEKS)* pos/wks

			pos	wks
15 Nov 97		(NONSTOPOPERATION) *Polydor 5719732*	47	2
28 Feb 98		WHAT TIME IS IT? *Polydor 5694912*	39	2
16 May 98		NOTHIN' PERSONAL *Polydor 5699092*	62	1

DUSTED *UK, male production / instrumental duo (2 WEEKS)* pos/wks

			pos	wks
20 Jan 01		ALWAYS REMEMBER TO RESPECT AND HONOUR YOUR MOTHER *Go! Beat / Polydor GOBCD 36*	31	2

Slim DUSTY *Australia, male vocalist – David Kirkpatrick (15 WEEKS)* pos/wks

			pos	wks
30 Jan 59	●	A PUB WITH NO BEER *Columbia DB 4212* [1]	3	15

[1] Slim Dusty with Dick Carr and His Bushlanders

DUTCH FORCE *Holland, male producer - Benno De Goeij (2 WEEKS)* pos/wks

			pos	wks
6 May 00		DEADLINE *Inferno CDFERN 27*	35	2

UK No.1 ★ UK Top 10 ● Still on chart + UK million seller ◆ UK entry at No.1 ■ US No.1 ▲

Ondrea DUVERN – *See HUSTLERS CONVENTION featuring Dave LAUDAT and Ondrea DUVERNEY*

DWEEB *UK, male / female vocal / instrumental trio (2 WEEKS)*

Date	Title / Label	pos	wks
22 Feb 97	SCOOBY DOO *Blanco Y Negro NEG 100CD*	63	1
7 Jun 97	OH YEAH, BABY *Blanco Y Negro NEG 102CD1*	70	1

Sarah DWYER – *See LANGE featuring SARAH DWYER*

Bob DYLAN (182 Top 500)

The most influential folk / rock vocalist / guitarist ever, b. Robert Zimmerman, 24 May 1941, Minnesota, US. The legendary performer, who led the 1960s folk music movement, redefined the term and, indeed, image of the singer / songwriter. He was still adding to his impressive tally of Top 5 UK and US albums in 2001 (137 WEEKS)

Date	Title / Label	pos	wks
25 Mar 65 ●	TIMES THEY ARE A-CHANGIN' *CBS 201751*	9	11
29 Apr 65 ●	SUBTERRANEAN HOMESICK BLUES *CBS 201753*	9	9
17 Jun 65	MAGGIE'S FARM *CBS 201781*	22	8
19 Aug 65 ●	LIKE A ROLLING STONE *CBS 201811*	4	12
28 Oct 65 ●	POSITIVELY 4TH STREET *CBS 201824*	8	12
27 Jan 66	CAN YOU PLEASE CRAWL OUT YOUR WINDOW *CBS 201900*	17	5
14 Apr 66	ONE OF US MUST KNOW (SOONER OR LATER) *CBS 202053*	33	5
12 May 66 ●	RAINY DAY WOMEN NOS. 12 & 35 *CBS 202307*	7	8
21 Jul 66	I WANT YOU *CBS 202258*	16	9
14 May 69	I THREW IT ALL AWAY *CBS 4219*	30	6
13 Sep 69 ●	LAY LADY LAY *CBS 4434*	5	12
10 Jul 71	WATCHING THE RIVER FLOW *CBS 7329*	24	9
6 Oct 73	KNOCKIN' ON HEAVEN'S DOOR *CBS 1762*	14	9
7 Feb 76	HURRICANE *CBS 3878*	43	4
29 Jul 78	BABY STOP CRYING *CBS 6499*	13	11
28 Oct 78	IS YOUR LOVE IN VAIN *CBS 6718*	56	3
20 May 95	DIGNITY *Columbia 6620762*	33	2
11 Jul 98	LOVE SICK *Columbia 6659972*	64	1
14 Oct 00	THINGS HAVE CHANGED *Columbia 6693792*	58	1

DYNAMIX II featuring TOO TOUGH TEE

US, male vocal / instrumental group and rapper (4 WEEKS)

Date	Title / Label	pos	wks
8 Aug 87	JUST GIVE THE DJ A BREAK *Cooltempo COOL 151*	50	4

DYNASTY *US, male / female vocal / instrumental group (20 WEEKS)*

Date	Title / Label	pos	wks
13 Oct 79	I DON'T WANT TO BE A FREAK (BUT I CAN'T HELP MYSELF) *Solar FB 1694*	20	13
9 Aug 80	I'VE JUST BEGUN TO LOVE YOU *Solar SO 10*	51	4
21 May 83	DOES THAT RING A BELL *Solar E 9911*	53	3

Ronnie DYSON *US, male vocalist (6 WEEKS)*

Date	Title / Label	pos	wks
4 Dec 71	WHEN YOU GET RIGHT DOWN TO IT *CBS 7449*	34	6

E

Katherine E *US, female vocalist (7 WEEKS)*

Date	Title / Label	pos	wks
6 Apr 91	I'M ALRIGHT *Dead Dead Good GOOD 2*	41	5
18 Jan 92	THEN I FEEL GOOD *PWL Continental PWL 13*	56	2

Lizz E – *See FRESH 4 featuring Lizz E*

Sheila E *US, female vocalist / instrumentalist – percussion – Sheila Escovedo (9 WEEKS)*

Date	Title / Label	pos	wks
23 Feb 85	THE BELLE OF ST MARK *Warner Bros. W 9180*	18	9

E-LUSTRIOUS *UK, male instrumental / production duo (2 WEEKS)*

Date	Title / Label	pos	wks
15 Feb 92	DANCE NO MORE *MOS MOS 001T* [1]	58	1
2 Jul 94	IN YOUR DANCE *UFG UFG 6CD*	69	1

[1] E-Lustrious featuring Deborah French

E-MALE *UK, male vocal / instrumental group (1 WEEK)*

Date	Title / Label	pos	wks
31 Jan 98	WE ARE E-MALE *East West EW 137CD*	44	1

E-MOTION *UK, male vocal / instrumental duo – Alan Angus and Justin Oliver (7 WEEKS)*

Date	Title / Label	pos	wks
3 Feb 96	THE NAUGHTY NORTH AND THE SEXY SOUTH *Soundproof MCSTD 40017*	20	3
17 Aug 96	I STAND ALONE *Soundproof MCSTD 40061*	60	1
26 Oct 96	THE NAUGHTY NORTH AND THE SEXY SOUTH (re-mix) *Soundproof MCSTD 40076*	17	3

E-ROTIC

Germany / US, male / female vocal / instrumental group (2 WEEKS)

Date	Title / Label	pos	wks
3 Jun 95	MAX DON'T HAVE SEX WITH YOUR EX *Stip CDSTIP 2*	45	2

E-SMOOVE featuring Latanza WATERS

UK, male production team and US, female vocalist (1 WEEK)

Date	Title / Label	pos	wks
15 Aug 98	DEJA VU *AM:PM 5827671*	63	1

E-TYPE *Sweden, male vocalist (2 WEEKS)*

Date	Title / Label	pos	wks
23 Sep 95	THIS IS THE WAY *Ffrreedom TABCD 237*	53	1
24 Jun 00	CAMPIONE 2000 *Polydor 1580822*	58	1

E.U. – *See SALT-N-PEPA*

E-ZEE POSSEE

UK, male / female vocal / instrumental group (16 WEEKS)

Date	Title / Label	pos	wks
26 Aug 89	EVERYTHING STARTS WITH AN 'E' *More Protein PROT 1*	69	1
20 Jan 90	LOVE ON LOVE *More Protein PROT 3* [1]	59	3
17 Mar 90	EVERYTHING STARTS WITH AN 'E' (re-entry) *More Protein PROT 1*	15	8
30 Jun 90	THE SUN MACHINE *More Protein PROT 4*	62	3
21 Sep 91	BREATHING IS E-ZEE *More Protein PROT 12* [2]	72	1

[1] With Dr Mouthquake [2] E-Zee Possee featuring Tara Newley

E-TRAX *Germany, male production duo (1 WEEK)*

Date	Title / Label	pos	wks
9 Jun 01	LET'S ROCK *Tidy Trax TIDY 155CD*	60	1

E-Z ROLLERS

UK, male / female vocal / instrumental group (3 WEEKS)

Date	Title / Label	pos	wks
24 Apr 99	WALK THIS LAND *Moving Shadow 130CD1*	18	3

EAGLES *US, male vocal / instrumental group (51 WEEKS)*

Date	Title / Label	pos	wks
9 Aug 75	ONE OF THESE NIGHTS *Asylum AYM 543* ▲	23	7
1 Nov 75	LYIN' EYES *Asylum AYM 548*	23	7
6 Mar 76	TAKE IT TO THE LIMIT *Asylum K 13029*	12	7
15 Jan 77	NEW KID IN TOWN *Asylum K 13069* ▲	20	7
16 Apr 77 ●	HOTEL CALIFORNIA *Asylum K 13079* ▲	8	10
16 Dec 78	PLEASE COME HOME FOR CHRISTMAS *Asylum K 13145*	30	5
13 Oct 79	HEARTACHE TONIGHT *Asylum K 12394* ▲	40	5
1 Dec 79	THE LONG RUN *Elektra K 12404*	66	2
13 Jul 96	LOVE WILL KEEP US ALIVE *Geffen GFSTD 21980*	52	1

Robert EARL *UK, male vocalist – Brian Budge (27 WEEKS)*

Date	Title / Label	pos	wks
25 Apr 58	I MAY NEVER PASS THIS WAY AGAIN *Philips PB 805*	14	13
24 Oct 58	MORE THAN EVER (COME PRIMA) *Philips PB 867*	26	2
21 Nov 58	MORE THAN EVER (COME PRIMA) (re-entry) *Philips PB 867*	28	2
13 Feb 59	THE WONDERFUL SECRET OF LOVE *Philips PB 891*	17	10

Charles EARLAND *US, male instrumentalist – keyboards (5 WEEKS)*

Date	Title / Label	pos	wks
19 Aug 78	LET THE MUSIC PLAY *Mercury 6167 703*	46	5

Steve EARLE *US, male vocalist / instrumentalist – guitar (7 WEEKS)* pos/wks

			pos	wks
15 Oct 88		**COPPERHEAD ROAD** *MCA MCA 1280*	45	6
31 Dec 88		**JOHNNY COME LATELY** *MCA MCA 1301*	75	1

EARLY MUSIC CONSORT directed by David MUNROW
UK, male / female instrumental group (1 WEEK) pos/wks

			pos	wks
3 Apr 71		**HENRY VIII SUITE (EP)** *BBC RESL 1*	49	1

Tracks on Henry VIII Suite (EP): Fanfare, Passomezo du Roy, Gaillarde d'Escosse / Pavane, Mille Ducats / Larocque Gaillarde / Allemande / Wedding March, La Mourisque / If Love Now Reigned / Rone, Pourquoi

EARTH WIND AND FIRE (206 Top 500) *Colourful, mystical, Los Angeles-based group noted for flamboyant stage performances. Formed by Maurice White (d/v) and included Philip Bailey (v), Ronnie Laws (s/fl) and Verdine White (b). Few R&B acts outsold them in the late 1970s, when they achieved eight successive US Top 10 albums (128 WEEKS)* pos/wks

			pos	wks
12 Feb 77		**SATURDAY NITE** *CBS 4835*	17	9
11 Feb 78		**FANTASY** *CBS 6056*	14	10
13 May 78		**JUPITER** *CBS 6267*	41	5
29 Jul 78		**MAGIC MIND** *CBS 6490*	75	1
12 Aug 78		**MAGIC MIND (re-entry)** *CBS 6490*	54	4
7 Oct 78		**GOT TO GET YOU INTO MY LIFE** *CBS 6553*	33	7
9 Dec 78	●	**SEPTEMBER** *CBS 6922*	3	13
12 May 79	●	**BOOGIE WONDERLAND** *CBS 7292* [1]	4	13
28 Jul 79	●	**AFTER THE LOVE HAS GONE** *CBS 7721*	4	10
6 Oct 79		**STAR** *CBS 7902*	16	8
15 Dec 79		**CAN'T LET GO** *CBS 8077*	46	7
8 Mar 80		**IN THE STONE** *CBS 8252*	53	3
11 Oct 80		**LET ME TALK** *CBS 8982*	29	5
20 Dec 80		**BACK ON THE ROAD** *CBS 9377*	63	4
7 Nov 81	●	**LET'S GROOVE** *CBS A 1679*	3	13
6 Feb 82		**I'VE HAD ENOUGH** *CBS A 1959*	29	6
5 Feb 83		**FALL IN LOVE WITH ME** *CBS A 2927*	47	4
7 Nov 87		**SYSTEM OF SURVIVAL** *CBS EWF 1*	54	3
31 Jul 99		**SEPTEMBER 99 (re-mix)** *INCredible INCR 24CD*	25	3

[1] Earth Wind and Fire with the Emotions

EARTHLING *UK, male vocal / instrumental duo (2 WEEKS)* pos/wks

			pos	wks
14 Oct 95		**ECHO ON MY MIND PART II** *Cooltempo CDCOOL 312*	61	1
1 Jun 96		**BLOOD MUSIC (EP)** *Cooltempo CDCOOL 319*	69	1

Tracks on Blood Music (EP): First Transmission / Because the Night / Soup or No Soup / Infinite M

EAST 57th STREET featuring Donna ALLEN
UK, male production trio and US, female vocalist (3 WEEKS) pos/wks

			pos	wks
11 Oct 97		**SATURDAY** *AM:PM 5823752*	29	3

EAST OF EDEN *UK, male instrumental group (12 WEEKS)* pos/wks

			pos	wks
17 Apr 71	●	**JIG A JIG** *Deram DM 297*	7	12

EAST 17 (120 Top 500) *London-based singing, rapping and dancing lads with international teen appeal: Tony Mortimer (v/k), Brian Harvey (v), John Hendy (v), Terry Coldwell (v). Bad press and personal problems resulted in main songwriter Mortimer quitting, and a name change to E-17 for their short-lived 1998 comeback (170 WEEKS)* pos/wks

			pos	wks
29 Aug 92	●	**HOUSE OF LOVE** *London LON 325*	10	9
14 Nov 92		**GOLD** *London LON 331*	28	4
19 Dec 92		**GOLD (re-entry)** *London LON 331*	64	4
30 Jan 93	●	**DEEP** *London LOCDP 334*	5	10
10 Apr 93		**SLOW IT DOWN** *London LONCD 339*	13	7
26 Jun 93		**WEST END GIRLS** *London LONCD 344*	11	7
4 Dec 93	●	**IT'S ALRIGHT** *London LONCD 345*	3	14
14 May 94	●	**AROUND THE WORLD** *London LONCD 349*	3	13
1 Oct 94	●	**STEAM** *London LONCD 353*	7	8
3 Dec 94	★	**STAY ANOTHER DAY** *London LONCD 354*	1	15
25 Mar 95	●	**LET IT RAIN** *London LONCD 363*	10	7
6 May 95		**STAY ANOTHER DAY (re-entry)** *London LONCD 354*	64	1
17 Jun 95		**HOLD MY BODY TIGHT** *London LONCD 367*	12	7
4 Nov 95	●	**THUNDER** *London LONCD 373*	4	14
10 Feb 96	●	**DO U STILL** *London LONCD 379*	7	7
10 Aug 96		**SOMEONE TO LOVE** *London LONCD 385*	16	8
2 Nov 96	●	**IF YOU EVER** *London LONCD 388* [1]	2	15
18 Jan 97	●	**HEY CHILD** *London LONCD 390*	3	5
14 Nov 98	●	**EACH TIME** *Telstar CDSTAS 3017* [2]	2	10
13 Mar 99		**BETCHA CAN'T WAIT** *Telstar CDSTAS 3031* [2]	12	5

[1] East 17 featuring Gabrielle [2] E-17

EAST SIDE BEAT *Italy, male vocal / instrumental duo – Carl Fanini and Francesco Petrocchi (18 WEEKS)* pos/wks

			pos	wks
30 Nov 91	●	**RIDE LIKE THE WIND** *ffrr F 176*	3	11
19 Dec 92		**ALIVE AND KICKING** *ffrr F 206*	26	6
29 May 93		**YOU'RE MY EVERYTHING** *ffrr FCD 207*	65	1

Sheena EASTON (291 Top 500) *Scotland's most successful act Stateside, b. Sheena Orr, 27 Apr 1959, Glasgow. This vocalist was first seen in TV documentary 'The Big Time'. Reached the big time on both sides of the Atlantic and won the Grammy for Best New Artist of 1981 (104 WEEKS)* pos/wks

			pos	wks
5 Apr 80		**MODERN GIRL** *EMI 5042*	56	3
19 Jul 80	●	**9 TO 5** *EMI 5066* ▲	3	15
9 Aug 80	●	**MODERN GIRL (re-entry)** *EMI 5042*	8	12
25 Oct 80		**ONE MAN WOMAN** *EMI 5114*	14	6
14 Feb 81		**TAKE MY TIME** *EMI 5135*	44	5
2 May 81		**WHEN HE SHINES** *EMI 5166*	12	8
27 Jun 81	●	**FOR YOUR EYES ONLY** *EMI 5195*	8	13
12 Sep 81		**JUST ANOTHER BROKEN HEART** *EMI 5232*	33	8
5 Dec 81		**YOU COULD HAVE BEEN WITH ME** *EMI 5252*	54	3
31 Jul 82		**MACHINERY** *EMI 5326*	38	5
12 Feb 83		**WE'VE GOT TONIGHT** *Liberty UP 658* [1]	28	7
21 Jan 89		**THE LOVER IN ME** *MCA MCA 1289*	15	8
18 Mar 89		**DAYS LIKE THIS** *MCA MCA 1325*	43	3
15 Jul 89		**101** *MCA MCA 1348*	54	2
18 Nov 89		**THE ARMS OF ORION** *Warner Bros. W 2757* [2]	27	5
9 Dec 00		**GIVING UP GIVING IN** *Universal MCSTD 40244*	54	1

[1] Kenny Rogers and Sheena Easton [2] Prince with Sheena Easton

See also PRINCE

EASTSIDE CONNECTION *US, disco aggregation (3 WEEKS)* pos/wks

			pos	wks
8 Apr 78		**YOU'RE SO RIGHT FOR ME** *Creole CR 149*	44	3

Clint EASTWOOD *US, male actor (2 WEEKS)* pos/wks

			pos	wks
7 Feb 70		**I TALK TO THE TREES** *Paramount PARA 3004*	18	2

This is the flip of 'Wand'rin Star' by Lee Marvin and was listed with Marvin's A-side for two weeks only

Clint EASTWOOD and GENERAL SAINT
UK, male duo (8 WEEKS) pos/wks

			pos	wks
29 Sep 84		**LAST PLANE (ONE WAY TICKET)** *MCA MCA 910*	51	3
2 Apr 94		**OH CAROL!** *Copasetic COPCD 0009*	54	5

EASY RIDERS – *See Frankie LAINE*

EASYBEATS *Australia, male vocal / instrumental group (24 WEEKS)* pos/wks

			pos	wks
27 Oct 66	●	**FRIDAY ON MY MIND** *United Artists UP 1157*	6	15
10 Apr 68		**HELLO, HOW ARE YOU** *United Artists UP 2209*	20	9

EAT *UK / US, male / female vocal / instrumental group (1 WEEK)* pos/wks

			pos	wks
12 Jun 93		**BLEED ME WHITE** *Fiction FICCD 48*	73	1

EAT STATIC *UK, male production duo (3 WEEKS)* pos/wks

			pos	wks
22 Feb 97		**HYBRID** *Planet Dog BARK 024CD*	41	1
27 Sep 97		**INTERCEPTOR** *Planet Dog BARK 030CD*	44	1
27 Jun 98		**CONTACT...** *Planet Dog BARK 033CD*	67	1

Cleveland EATON *US, male instrumentalist – keyboards (6 WEEKS)* pos/wks

			pos	wks
23 Sep 78		**BAMA BOOGIE WOOGIE** *Gull GULS 63*	35	6

EAV *Austria, male vocal / instrumental group (4 WEEKS)* pos/wks

Date		Title / Label	pos	wks
27 Sep 86		**BA-BA-BANKROBBERY (ENGLISH VERSION)** *Columbia DB 9139*	63	4

EAZY-E *US, male rapper (3 WEEKS)* pos/wks

Date		Title / Label	pos	wks
6 Jan 96		**JUST TAH LET YOU KNOW** *Epic 6628162*	30	3

ECHO and the BUNNYMEN (378 Top 500) *Cult alternative rock group originally from Liverpool, UK, who named themselves after their drum machine. Ian McCulloch (v), b. 5 May 1959, frontman of this moody and atmospheric group, went solo 1988. Original line-up regrouped in 1997 (86 WEEKS)* pos/wks

Date		Title / Label	pos	wks
17 May 80		**RESCUE** *Korova KOW 1*	62	1
18 Apr 81		**SHINE SO HARD (EP)** *Korova ECHO 1*	37	4
18 Jul 81		**A PROMISE** *Korova KOW 15*	49	4
29 May 82		**THE BACK OF LOVE** *Korova KOW 24*	19	7
22 Jan 83	●	**THE CUTTER** *Korova KOW 26*	8	8
16 Jul 83		**NEVER STOP** *Korova KOW 28*	15	7
28 Jan 84	●	**THE KILLING MOON** *Korova KOW 32*	9	6
21 Apr 84		**SILVER** *Korova KOW 34*	30	5
14 Jul 84		**SEVEN SEAS** *Korova KOW 35*	16	7
19 Oct 85		**BRING ON THE DANCING HORSES** *Korova KOW 43*	21	7
13 Jun 87		**THE GAME** *WEA YZ 134*	28	4
1 Aug 87		**LIPS LIKE SUGAR** *WEA YZ 144*	36	4
20 Feb 88		**PEOPLE ARE STRANGE** *WEA YZ 175*	29	5
2 Mar 91		**PEOPLE ARE STRANGE (re-issue)** *East West YZ 567*	34	4
28 Jun 97	●	**NOTHING LASTS FOREVER** *London LOCDP 396*	8	6
13 Sep 97		**I WANT TO BE THERE WHEN YOU COME** *London LONCD 399*	30	2
8 Nov 97		**DON'T LET IT GET YOU DOWN** *London LOCDP 406*	50	1
27 Mar 99		**RUST** *London LONCD 424*	22	3
5 May 01		**IT'S ALRIGHT** *Cooking Vinyl FRY CD104*	41	1

Tracks on 'Shine So Hard' (EP): Crocodiles, All That Jazz, Zimbo, Over The Wall

ECHOBASS *UK, male producer – Simon Woodgate (1 WEEK)* pos/wks

Date		Title / Label	pos	wks
14 Jul 01		**YOU ARE THE WEAKEST LINK** *House of Bush CDANNE 001*	53	1

ECHOBEATZ *UK, male DJ / production duo – Dave De Braie and Paul Moody (5 WEEKS)* pos/wks

Date		Title / Label	pos	wks
25 Jul 98	●	**MAS QUE NADA** *Eternal WEA 176CD*	10	5

ECHOBELLY
UK / Sweden, male / female vocal / instrumental group (16 WEEKS) pos/wks

Date		Title / Label	pos	wks
2 Apr 94		**INSOMNIAC** *Fauve FAUV 1CD*	47	1
2 Jul 94		**I CAN'T IMAGINE THE WORLD WITHOUT ME** *Fauve FAUV 2CD*	39	2
5 Nov 94		**CLOSE...BUT** *Fauve FAUV 4CD*	59	1
2 Sep 95		**GREAT THINGS** *Fauve FAUV 5CD*	13	3
4 Nov 95		**KING OF THE KERB** *Fauve FAUV 7CD*	25	3
2 Mar 96		**DARK THERAPY** *Fauve FAUV 8CD*	20	3
23 Aug 97		**THE WORLD IS FLAT** *Epic 6648152*	31	2
8 Nov 97		**HERE COMES THE BIG RUSH** *Epic 6652452*	56	1

See also LITHIAM and Sonya MADAN

Billy ECKSTINE *US, male vocalist (48 WEEKS)* pos/wks

Date		Title / Label	pos	wks
12 Nov 54	●	**NO ONE BUT YOU** *MGM 763*	3	17
27 Sep 57		**PASSING STRANGERS** *Mercury MT 164* [1]	22	2
13 Feb 59	●	**GIGI** *Mercury AMT 1018*	8	14
12 Mar 69		**PASSING STRANGERS (re-issue)** *Mercury MF 1082* [1]	20	15

[1] Billy Eckstine and Sarah Vaughan

ECLIPSE
Italy, male producer / instrumentalist – Gianni Bini (4 WEEKS) pos/wks

Date		Title / Label	pos	wks
14 Aug 99		**MAKES ME LOVE YOU** *Azuli AZNYCDX 100*	25	4

See also BINI & MARTINI; GOODFELLAS featuring Lisa MILLETT; HOUSE OF GLASS

Silvio ECOMO *Holland, male producer (1 WEEK)* pos/wks

Date		Title / Label	pos	wks
15 Jul 00		**STANDING** *Hooj Choons HOOJ 098CD*	70	1

EDDIE and the HOT RODS
UK, male vocal / instrumental group (26 WEEKS) pos/wks

Date		Title / Label	pos	wks
11 Sep 76		**LIVE AT THE MARQUEE (EP)** *Island IEP 2*	43	5
13 Nov 76		**TEENAGE DEPRESSION** *Island WIP 6354*	35	4
23 Apr 77		**I MIGHT BE LYING** *Island WIP 6388*	44	3
13 Aug 77	●	**DO ANYTHING YOU WANNA DO** *Island WIP 6401* [1]	9	10
21 Jan 78		**QUIT THIS TOWN** *Island WIP 6411*	36	4

[1] Rods

Tracks on Live at the Marquee (EP): 96 Tears / Get out of Denver / Medley: Gloria / Satisfaction

EDDY *UK, female vocalist (2 WEEKS)* pos/wks

Date		Title / Label	pos	wks
9 Jul 94		**SOMEDAY** *Positiva CDTIV 14*	49	2

Duane EDDY and the REBELS (89 Top 500) *Twangy guitar legend, b. 26 Apr 1938, New York. Early rock's No.1 solo instrumentalist assembled a long string of UK and US hit singles and was one of the first rock acts to score on the album charts (201 WEEKS)* pos/wks

Date		Title / Label	pos	wks
5 Sep 58		**REBEL-ROUSER** *London HL 8669*	19	10
2 Jan 59		**CANNONBALL** *London HL 8764*	22	4
19 Jun 59	●	**PETER GUNN** *London HLW 8879* [1]	6	10
24 Jul 59		**YEP!** *London HLW B8879* [1]	17	5
4 Sep 59		**FORTY MILES OF BAD ROAD** *London HLW 8929*	11	9
11 Sep 59		**PETER GUNN (re-entry)** *London HLW 8879* [1]	27	1
18 Dec 59		**SOME KIND-A EARTHQUAKE** *London HLW 9007*	12	5
19 Feb 60		**BONNIE CAME BACK** *London HLW 9050*	12	10
28 Apr 60	●	**SHAZAM!** *London HLW 9104*	4	13
21 Jul 60	●	**BECAUSE THEY'RE YOUNG** *London HLW 9162*	2	18
10 Nov 60		**KOMMOTION** *London HLW 9225*	13	10
12 Jan 61	●	**PEPE** *London HLW 9257*	2	14
20 Apr 61	●	**THEME FROM DIXIE** *London HLW 9324*	7	10
22 Jun 61		**RING OF FIRE** *London HLW 9370*	17	10
14 Sep 61		**DRIVIN' HOME** *London HLW 9406*	30	4
5 Oct 61		**CARAVAN** *Parlophone R 4826* [1]	42	3
24 May 62		**DEEP IN THE HEART OF TEXAS** *RCA 1288* [1]	19	8
23 Aug 62	●	**BALLAD OF PALADIN** *RCA 1300* [1]	10	10
8 Nov 62	●	**(DANCE WITH THE) GUITAR MAN** *RCA 1316* [2]	4	16
14 Feb 63		**BOSS GUITAR** *RCA 1329* [2]	27	8
30 May 63		**LONELY BOY LONELY GUITAR** *RCA 1344* [2]	35	4
29 Aug 63		**YOUR BABY'S GONE SURFIN'** *RCA 1357* [2]	49	1
8 Mar 75	●	**PLAY ME LIKE YOU PLAY YOUR GUITAR** *GTO GT 11* [2]	9	9
22 Mar 86	●	**PETER GUNN** *China WOK 6* [3]	8	9

[1] Duane Eddy [2] Duane Eddy and the Rebelettes [3] Art of Noise featuring Duane Eddy

EDDY and the SOUL BAND
US, male / female vocal / instrumental group (7 WEEKS) pos/wks

Date		Title / Label	pos	wks
23 Feb 85		**THE THEME FROM 'SHAFT'** *Club JAB 11*	13	7

Randy EDELMAN
US, male vocalist / instrumentalist – piano (18 WEEKS) pos/wks

Date		Title / Label	pos	wks
6 Mar 76		**CONCRETE AND CLAY** *20th Century BTC 2261*	11	7
18 Sep 76		**UPTOWN UPTEMPO WOMAN** *20th Century BTC 2225*	25	7
15 Jan 77		**YOU** *20th Century BTC 2253*	49	2
17 Jul 82		**NOBODY MADE ME** *Rocket XPRES 81*	60	2

EDELWEISS
Austria, male / female vocal / instrumental group (10 WEEKS) pos/wks

Date		Title / Label	pos	wks
29 Apr 89	●	**BRING ME EDELWEISS** *WEA YZ 353*	5	10

EDEN *UK / Australia, male / female vocal / instrumental group (2 WEEKS)* pos/wks

Date		Title / Label	pos	wks
6 Mar 93		**DO U FEEL 4 ME** *Logic 74321135422*	51	2

Lyn EDEN – *See SMOKIN BEATS featuring Lyn EDEN*

EDISON LIGHTHOUSE *UK, male vocal / instrumental group lead vocal Tony Burrows (13 WEEKS)* pos/wks

Date		Title / Label	pos	wks
24 Jan 70	★	**LOVE GROWS (WHERE MY ROSEMARY GOES)** *Bell 1091*	1	12
30 Jan 71		**IT'S UP TO YOU PETULA** *Bell 1136*	49	1

Dave EDMUNDS (334 Top 500) *Former member of one-hit wonders Love Sculpture, b. 15 Apr 1944, Cardiff, Wales. Singer / guitarist and retro-sounding performer / producer's debut solo hit sold three million worldwide. He has produced many top acts including Dion, Everly Brothers, Del Shannon, Status Quo, Shakin' Stevens and Stray Cats (93 WEEKS)*

			pos	wks
21 Nov 70	★	**I HEAR YOU KNOCKING** *MAM 1* [1]	1	14
20 Jan 73	●	**BABY I LOVE YOU** *Rockfield ROC 1*	8	13
9 Jun 73	●	**BORN TO BE WITH YOU** *Rockfield ROC 2*	5	12
2 Jul 77		**I KNEW THE BRIDE** *Swansong SSK 19411*	26	8
30 Jun 79	●	**GIRLS TALK** *Swansong SSK 19418*	4	11
22 Sep 79		**QUEEN OF HEARTS** *Swansong SSK 19419*	11	9
24 Nov 79		**CRAWLING FROM THE WRECKAGE** *Swansong SSK 19420*	59	4
9 Feb 80		**SINGING THE BLUES** *Swansong SSK 19422*	28	8
28 Mar 81		**ALMOST SATURDAY NIGHT** *Swansong SSK 19424*	58	3
20 Jun 81		**THE RACE IS ON** *Swansong SSK 19425* [2]	34	6
26 Mar 83		**SLIPPING AWAY** *Arista ARIST 522*	60	4
7 Apr 90		**KING OF LOVE** *Capitol CL 568*	68	1

[1] Dave Edmunds' Rockpile [2] Dave Edmunds and the Stray Cats

Alton EDWARDS *Zimbabwe, male vocalist (9 WEEKS)*

			pos	wks
9 Jan 82		**I JUST WANNA (SPEND SOME TIME WITH YOU)** *Streetwave STRA 1897*	20	9

Dennis EDWARDS featuring Siedah GARRETT
US, male / female vocal duo (10 WEEKS)

			pos	wks
24 Mar 84		**DON'T LOOK ANY FURTHER** *Gordy TMG 1334*	45	5
20 Jun 87		**DON'T LOOK ANY FURTHER (re-issue)** *Gordy TMG 1334*	55	5

Rupie EDWARDS *Jamaica, male vocalist (16 WEEKS)*

			pos	wks
23 Nov 74	●	**IRE FEELINGS (SKANGA)** *Cactus CT 38*	9	10
8 Feb 75		**LEGO SKANGA** *Cactus CT 51*	32	6

Tommy EDWARDS *US, male vocalist (18 WEEKS)*

			pos	wks
3 Oct 58	★	**IT'S ALL IN THE GAME** *MGM 989* ▲	1	17
7 Aug 59		**MY MELANCHOLY BABY** *MGM 1020*	29	1

EELS *US, male vocal / instrumental group (23 WEEKS)*

			pos	wks
15 Feb 97	●	**NOVOCAINE FOR THE SOUL** *Dreamworks DRMCD 22174*	10	5
17 May 97	●	**SUSAN'S HOUSE** *Dreamworks DRMCD 22238*	9	5
13 Sep 97		**YOUR LUCKY DAY IN HELL** *Dreamworks DRMCD 22277*	35	2
26 Sep 98		**LAST STOP: THIS TOWN** *Dreamworks DRMCD 22346*	23	3
12 Dec 98		**CANCER FOR THE CURE** *Dreamworks DRMCD 22373*	60	1
26 Feb 00		**MR E'S BEAUTIFUL BLUES** *Dreamworks DRMCD 4509762*	11	4
24 Jun 00		**FLYSWATTER** *Dreamworks DRMCD 4509462*	55	1
22 Sep 01		**SOULJACKER PART 1** *Dreamworks DRMCD 4508922*	30	2

EFUA *UK, female vocalist (5 WEEKS)*

			pos	wks
3 Jul 93		**SOMEWHERE** *Virgin VSCDT 1463*	42	5

EGG *UK, male vocal / instrumental group (1 WEEK)*

			pos	wks
30 Jan 99		**GETTING AWAY WITH IT** *Indochina ID 079CD*	58	1

EGGS ON LEGS *UK, male vocalist (1 WEEK)*

			pos	wks
23 Sep 95		**COCK A DOODLE DO IT** *Avex UK AVEXCD 18*	42	1

EGYPTIAN EMPIRE *UK, male producer – Tim Taylor (2 WEEKS)*

			pos	wks
24 Oct 92		**THE HORN TRACK** *Ffrreedom TAB 115*	61	2

EIFFEL 65 *Italy, male vocal trio (36 WEEKS)*

			pos	wks
21 Aug 99		**BLUE (DA BA DEE) (import)** *Logic 74321688212*	39	5
25 Sep 99	★	**BLUE (DA BA DEE)** *Eternal WEA 226CD1* ■	1	21
19 Feb 00	●	**MOVE YOUR BODY** *Eternal WEA 255CD1*	3	10

808 STATE *UK, DJ / production / instrumental group (70 WEEKS)*

			pos	wks
18 Nov 89	●	**PACIFIC** *ZTT ZANG 1*	10	9
31 Mar 90		**THE EXTENDED PLEASURE OF DANCE (EP)** *ZTT ZANG 2T*	56	1
2 Jun 90	●	**THE ONLY RHYME THAT BITES** *ZTT ZANG 3* [1]	10	10
15 Sep 90		**TUNES SPLITS THE ATOM** *ZTT ZANG 6* [1]	18	7
10 Nov 90	●	**CUBIK / OLYMPIC** *ZTT ZANG 5*	10	10
16 Feb 91	●	**IN YER FACE** *ZTT ZANG 14*	9	6
27 Apr 91		**OOOPS** *ZTT ZANG 19* [2]	42	3
17 Aug 91		**LIFT / OPEN YOUR MIND** *ZTT ZANG 20*	38	4
29 Aug 92		**TIME BOMB / NIMBUS** *ZTT ZANG 33*	59	1
12 Dec 92		**ONE IN TEN (re-mix)** *ZTT ZANG 39* [3]	17	8
30 Jan 93		**PLAN 9** *ZTT ZANG 38CD*	50	2
26 Jun 93		**10 X 10** *ZTT ZANG 42CD*	67	1
13 Aug 94		**BOMBADIN** *ZTT ZANG 54CD*	67	1
29 Jun 96		**BOND** *ZTT ZANG 80CD*	57	1
8 Feb 97		**LOPEZ** *ZTT ZANG 87CD*	20	2
16 May 98		**PACIFIC / CUBIK (re-mixes)** *ZTT ZTT 98CD1*	21	3
6 Mar 99		**THE ONLY RHYME THAT BITES 99** *ZTT ZTT 125CD* [1]	53	1

[1] MC Tunes versus 808 State [2] 808 State featuring Björk [3] 808 State vs UB40

Tracks on The Extended Pleasure of Dance (EP): Cobra Bora / Ancodia / Cubik. 'Cubik' is a re-issue of one of the tracks from The Extended Pleasure of Dance (EP). 'Lopez' features the uncredited vocals of James Dean Bradfield, lead singer of the Manic Street Preachers

18 WHEELER *UK, male vocal / instrumental group (1 WEEK)*

			pos	wks
15 Mar 97		**STAY** *Creation CRESCD 249*	59	1

EIGHTH WONDER
UK, male / female vocal / instrumental group (25 WEEKS)

			pos	wks
2 Nov 85		**STAY WITH ME** *CBS A 6594*	65	2
20 Feb 88	●	**I'M NOT SCARED** *CBS SCARE 1*	7	13
25 Jun 88		**CROSS MY HEART** *CBS 651552 7*	13	8
1 Oct 88		**BABY BABY** *CBS BABE 1*	65	2

88.3 – *See Lisa MAY*

EINSTEIN *UK, male rapper (6 WEEKS)*

			pos	wks
18 Nov 89		**ANOTHER MONSTERJAM** *ffrr F 116* [1]	65	1
15 Dec 90		**TURN IT UP** *Swanyard SYD 9* [2]	42	4
24 Aug 96		**THE POWER 96** *Arista 74321398672* [3]	42	1

[1] Simon Harris featuring Einstein [2] Technotronic featuring Melissa and Einstein [3] Snap featuring Einstein

See also AMBASSADORS OF FUNK featuring MC MARIO

EL COCO *US, male vocal / instrumental group (4 WEEKS)*

			pos	wks
14 Jan 78		**COCOMOTION** *Pye International 7N 25761*	31	4

EL MARIACHI *US, male producer – Roger Sanchez (2 WEEKS)*

			pos	wks
9 Nov 96		**CUBA** *ffrr FCD 286*	38	2

See also FUNK JUNKEEZ; Roger SANCHEZ

ELASTICA *UK, female / male vocal / instrumental group (12 WEEKS)*

			pos	wks
12 Feb 94		**LINE UP** *Deceptive BLUFF 004CD*	20	3
22 Oct 94		**CONNECTION** *Deceptive BLUFF 010CD*	17	4
25 Feb 95		**WAKING UP** *Deceptive BLUFF 011CD*	13	4
24 Jun 00		**MAD DOG** *Deceptive BLUFF 077CD*	44	1

ELATE *UK, male / female vocal / instrumental trio (2 WEEKS)*

			pos	wks
26 Jul 97		**SOMEBODY LIKE YOU** *VC VCRD 22*	38	2

Donnie ELBERT *US, male vocalist (29 WEEKS)*

			pos	wks
8 Jan 72	●	**WHERE DID OUR LOVE GO?** *London HL 10352*	8	10
26 Feb 72		**I CAN'T HELP MYSELF** *Avco 6105 009*	11	10
29 Apr 72		**LITTLE PIECE OF LEATHER** *London HL 10370*	27	9

ELBOW *UK, male vocal / instrumental group (3 WEEKS)*

			pos	wks
5 May 01		**RED** *V2 VVR 5016153*	36	1
21 Jul 01		**POWDER BLUE** *V2 VVR 5016163*	41	1
20 Oct 01		**NEWBORN** *V2 VVR 5016173*	42	1

ELECTRA *UK, male vocal / instrumental group (7 WEEKS)* pos/wks

6 Aug 88	**JIBARO** *ffrr FFR 9*	54	3
30 Dec 89	**IT'S YOUR DESTINY / AUTUMN LOVE** *London F 121*	51	4

ELECTRAFIXION *UK, male vocal / instrumental group (6 WEEKS)* pos/wks

19 Nov 94	**ZEPHYR** *WEA YZ 865CD*	47	2
9 Sep 95	**LOWDOWN** *WEA YZ 977CD*	54	2
4 Nov 95	**NEVER** *Spacejunk WEA 022CD*	58	1
16 Mar 96	**SISTER PAIN** *Spacejunk WEA 037CD1*	27	1

ELECTRASY *UK, male vocal / instrumental group (7 WEEKS)* pos/wks

13 Jun 98	**LOST IN SPACE** *MCA MCSTD 40171*	60	1
5 Sep 98	**MORNING AFTERGLOW** *MCA MCSTD 40184*	19	4
28 Nov 98	**BEST FRIEND'S GIRL** *MCA MCSXD 40195*	41	2

ELECTRIBE 101
UK / Germany, male / female vocal / instrumental group (15 WEEKS) pos/wks

28 Oct 89	**TELL ME WHEN THE FEVER ENDED** *Mercury MER 310*	32	5
24 Feb 90	**TALKING WITH MYSELF** *Mercury MER 316*	23	5
22 Sep 90	**YOU'RE WALKING** *Mercury MER 328*	50	3
10 Oct 98	**TALKING WITH MYSELF '98 (re-mix)** *Manifesto FESDD 49*	39	2

ELECTRIC LIGHT ORCHESTRA (43 Top 500) *Ground-breaking and innovative UK group, fronted by multi-talented Jeff Lynne (v/g) from Birmingham and originally included Roy Wood (The Move). Their unique sound, which featured an orchestral string section, helped them to achieve numerous transatlantic hits (255 WEEKS)* pos/wks

29 Jul 72 ●	**10538 OVERTURE** *Harvest HAR 5053*	9	8
27 Jan 73 ●	**ROLL OVER BEETHOVEN** *Harvest HAR 5063*	6	10
6 Oct 73	**SHOWDOWN** *Harvest HAR 5077*	12	10
9 Mar 74	**MA-MA-MA-BELLE** *Warner Bros. K 16349*	22	8
10 Jan 76 ●	**EVIL WOMAN** *Jet 764*	10	8
3 Jul 76	**STRANGE MAGIC** *Jet 779*	38	3
13 Nov 76 ●	**LIVIN' THING** *Jet UP 36184*	4	12
19 Feb 77 ●	**ROCKARIA!** *Jet UP 36209*	9	9
21 May 77 ●	**TELEPHONE LINE** *Jet UP 36254*	8	10
29 Oct 77	**TURN TO STONE** *Jet UP 36313*	18	12
28 Jan 78 ●	**MR BLUE SKY** *Jet UP 36342*	6	11
10 Jun 78 ●	**WILD WEST HERO** *Jet JET 109*	6	14
7 Oct 78 ●	**SWEET TALKIN' WOMAN** *Jet 121*	6	9
9 Dec 78	**ELO (EP)** *Jet ELO 1*	34	8
19 May 79 ●	**SHINE A LITTLE LOVE** *Jet 144*	6	10
21 Jul 79 ●	**THE DIARY OF HORACE WIMP** *Jet 150*	8	9
1 Sep 79 ●	**DON'T BRING ME DOWN** *Jet 153*	3	9
17 Nov 79 ●	**CONFUSION / LAST TRAIN TO LONDON** *Jet 166*	8	10
24 May 80	**I'M ALIVE** *Jet 179*	20	9
21 Jun 80 ★	**XANADU** *Jet 185* [1]	1	11
2 Aug 80	**ALL OVER THE WORLD** *Jet 195*	11	8
22 Nov 80	**DON'T WALK AWAY** *Jet 7004*	21	10
1 Aug 81 ●	**HOLD ON TIGHT** *Jet 7011*	4	12
24 Oct 81	**TWILIGHT** *Jet 7015*	30	7
9 Jan 82	**TICKET TO THE MOON / HERE IS THE NEWS** *Jet 7018*	24	8
18 Jun 83	**ROCK 'N' ROLL IS KING** *Jet A 3500*	13	9
3 Sep 83	**SECRET MESSAGES** *Jet A 3720*	48	3
1 Mar 86	**CALLING AMERICA** *Epic A 6844*	28	7
11 May 91	**HONEST MEN** *Telstar ELO 100* [2]	60	1

[1] Olivia Newton-John and Electric Light Orchestra [2] Electric Light Orchestra Part 2

'Here Is the News' listed from 16 Jan 1982. Tracks on ELO (EP): Can't Get You Out of My Head / Strange Magic / Ma-Ma-Ma-Belle / Evil Woman

ELECTRIC PRUNES *US, male vocal / instrumental group (5 WEEKS)* pos/wks

9 Feb 67	**I HAD TOO MUCH TO DREAM (LAST NIGHT)** *Reprise RS 20532*	49	1
11 May 67	**GET ME TO THE WORLD ON TIME** *Reprise RS 20564*	42	4

ELECTRIC SOFT PARADE *UK, male vocal / instrumental group – led by Alex and Tom White (2 WEEKS)* pos/wks

4 Aug 01	**EMPTY AT THE END / SUMATRAN** *DB DB 006CD7* [1]	65	1
10 Nov 01	**THERE'S A SILENCE** *DB DB 007CD7*	52	1

[1] Soft Parade

ELECTRIQUE BOUTIQUE
UK / France, male production group (2 WEEKS) pos/wks

26 Aug 00	**REVELATION** *Data DATA 14CDS*	37	2

ELECTRONIC *UK, male vocal / instrumental group (36 WEEKS)* pos/wks

16 Dec 89	**GETTING AWAY WITH IT** *Factory FAC 2577*	12	9
27 Apr 91 ●	**GET THE MESSAGE** *Factory FAC 2877*	8	7
21 Sep 91	**FEEL EVERY BEAT** *Factory FAC 3287*	39	4
4 Jul 92 ●	**DISAPPOINTED** *Parlophone R 6311*	6	5
6 Jul 96	**FORBIDDEN CITY** *Parlophone CDR 6436*	14	4
28 Sep 96	**FOR YOU** *Parlophone CDR 6445*	16	2
15 Feb 97	**SECOND NATURE** *Parlophone CDR 6455*	35	2
24 Apr 99	**VIVID** *Parlopbone CDR 6514*	17	3

ELECTRONICAS *Holland, male instrumental group (8 WEEKS)* pos/wks

19 Sep 81	**ORIGINAL BIRD DANCE** *Polydor POSP 360*	22	8

ELECTROSET *UK, male instrumental / production group (4 WEEKS)* pos/wks

21 Nov 92	**HOW DOES IT FEEL** *ffrr F 203*	27	3
15 Jul 95	**SENSATION** *Ffrreedom TABCD 231*	69	1

ELEGANTS *US, male vocal group (2 WEEKS)* pos/wks

26 Sep 58	**LITTLE STAR** *HMV POP 520* ▲	25	2

ELEMENT FOUR
UK, male production duo – Paul Oakenfold and Andy Gray (11 WEEKS) pos/wks

9 Sep 00 ●	**BIG BROTHER UK TV THEME** *Channel 4 Music C4M 00072*	4	9
4 Aug 01	**BIG BROTHER UK TV THEME (re-entry)** *Channel 4 Music C4M 00072*	63	2

ELEVATION *UK, male instrumental / production duo (1 WEEK)* pos/wks

23 May 92	**CAN YOU FEEL IT** *Nova Mute 12NOMU 3*	62	1

ELEVATOR SUITE *UK, male production / instrumental trio (1 WEEK)* pos/wks

12 Aug 00	**BACK AROUND** *Infectious INFECT 85CDS*	71	1

ELEVATORMAN *UK, male instrumental / production group (4 WEEKS)* pos/wks

14 Jan 95	**FUNK AND DRIVE** *Wired WIRED 211*	37	3
1 Jul 95	**FIRED UP** *Wired WIRED 216*	44	1

ELGINS *US, male / female vocal group (20 WEEKS)* pos/wks

1 May 71 ●	**HEAVEN MUST HAVE SENT YOU** *Tamla Motown TMG 771*	3	13
9 Oct 71	**PUT YOURSELF IN MY PLACE** *Tamla Motown TMG 787*	28	7

ELIAS and his ZIG-ZAG JIVE FLUTES
South Africa, male instrumental group (14 WEEKS) pos/wks

25 Apr 58 ●	**TOM HARK** *Columbia DB 4109*	2	14

Yvonne ELLIMAN *US, female vocalist (44 WEEKS)* pos/wks

29 Jan 72	**I DON'T KNOW HOW TO LOVE HIM** *MCA MMKS 5077*	47	1
6 Nov 76 ●	**LOVE ME** *RSO 2090 205*	6	13
7 May 77	**HELLO STRANGER** *RSO 2090 236*	26	5
13 Aug 77	**I CAN'T GET YOU OUT OF MY MIND** *RSO 2090 251*	17	13
6 May 78 ●	**IF I CAN'T HAVE YOU** *RSO 2090 266* ▲	4	12

'I Don't Know How to Love Him' was one of four tracks on a maxi-single, two of which were credited during the disc's one week on the chart. The other track credited was 'Superstar' by Murray Head

Duke ELLINGTON *US, orchestra (4 WEEKS)* pos/wks

5 Mar 54 ●	**SKIN DEEP** *Philips PB 243* [1]	7	4

[1] Duke Ellington and his Orchestra with Louis Bellson (drums)

Lance ELLINGTON *UK, male vocalist (1 WEEK)* pos/wks

21 Aug 93	**LONELY (HAVE WE LOST OUR LOVE)** *RCA 74321158332*	57	1

Ray ELLINGTON *UK, male vocal / instrumental group (4 WEEKS)*

Date		Title / Label	pos	wks
15 Nov 62		THE MADISON *Ember S 102*	41	2
20 Dec 62		THE MADISON (re-entry) *Ember S 102*	36	2

Bern ELLIOTT and the FENMEN
UK, male vocal / instrumental group (22 WEEKS)

Date		Title / Label	pos	wks
21 Nov 63		MONEY *Decca F 11770*	14	13
19 Mar 64		NEW ORLEANS *Decca F 11852*	24	9

Joe ELLIOTT – *See Mick RONSON with Joe ELLIOTT*

Missy 'Misdemeanor' ELLIOTT
US, female rapper / producer (55 WEEKS)

Date		Title / Label	pos	wks
30 Aug 97		THE RAIN (SUPA DUPA FLY) *East West E 3919 CD*	16	3
29 Nov 97		SOCK IT 2 ME *East West E 3890CD*	33	2
25 Apr 98		BEEP ME 911 *East West E 3859CD*	14	3
22 Aug 98		HIT 'EM WIT DA HEE *East West E3824 CD1* [1]	25	3
22 Aug 98		MAKE IT HOT *East West E 3821 CD* [2]	22	4
26 Sep 98	★	I WANT YOU BACK *Virgin VSCDT 1716* [3] ■	1	9
21 Nov 98		5 MINUTES *Elektra E 3803CD* [4]	72	1
13 Mar 99		HERE WE COME *Virgin DINSD 179* [5]	43	1
25 Sep 99		ALL N MY GRILL *Elektra E 3742 CD* [6]	20	4
22 Jan 00		HOT BOYZ *Elektra E 7002CD* [7]	18	3
28 Apr 01	●	GET UR FREAK ON *East West / Elektra E 7206CD*	4	11
18 Aug 01	●	ONE MINUTE MAN *Elektra E 7245CD* [8]	10	8
13 Oct 01		SUPERFREAKON *East West / Elektra 7559672550*	72	1
22 Dec 01		SON OF A GUN (I BETCHA THINK THIS SONG IS ABOUT YOU) *Virgin VUSCD 232* [9]	13	2+

[1] Missy 'Misdemeanor' Elliott featuring Lil' Kim [2] Nicole featuring Missy 'Misdemeanor' Elliott and Mocha [3] Melanie B featuring Missy 'Misdemeanor' Elliott [4] Lil' Mo featuring Missy 'Misdemeanor' Elliott [5] Timbaland / Missy Elliott & Magoo [6] Missy 'Misdemeanor' Elliott featuring MC Solaar [7] Missy 'Misdemeanor' Elliott featuring Nas, Eve and Q Tip [8] Missy 'Misdemeanor' Elliott featuring Ludacris [9] Janet With Carly Simon featuring Missy Elliott

Greg ELLIS – *See Reva RICE and Greg ELLIS*

Joey B ELLIS *US, male rapper (10 WEEKS)*

Date		Title / Label	pos	wks
16 Feb 91		GO FOR IT (HEART AND FIRE) *Capitol CL 601* [1]	20	8
18 May 91		THOUGHT U WERE THE ONE FOR ME *Capitol CL 614*	58	2

[1] Rocky V featuring Joey B Ellis and Tynetta Hare

Shirley ELLIS *US, female vocalist (17 WEEKS)*

Date		Title / Label	pos	wks
6 May 65	●	THE CLAPPING SONG *London HLR 9961*	6	13
8 Jul 78		THE CLAPPING SONG (EP) *MCA MCEP 1*	59	4

Tracks on The Clapping Song (EP): The Clapping Song / Ever See a Diver Kiss His Wife While the Bubbles Bounce Above the Water / The Name Game / The Nitty Gritty. 'The Clapping Song' itself qualifies as a re-issue

ELLIS, BEGGS and HOWARD
UK, male vocal / instrumental group (8 WEEKS)

Date		Title / Label	pos	wks
2 Jul 88		BIG BUBBLES, NO TROUBLES *RCA PB 42089*	59	3
11 Mar 89		BIG BUBBLES, NO TROUBLES (re-entry) *RCA PB 42089*	41	5

Sophie ELLIS-BEXTOR *UK, female vocalist (15 WEEKS)*

Date		Title / Label	pos	wks
25 Aug 01	●	TAKE ME HOME (A GIRL LIKE ME) *Polydor 5872312*	2	12
15 Dec 01	●	MURDER ON THE DANCEFLOOR *Polydor 5704942*	2	3+

See also SPILLER

ELWOOD *US, male rapper / vocalist – Elwood Strickland (1 WEEK)*

Date		Title / Label	pos	wks
26 Aug 00		SUNDOWN *Palm Pictures PPCD 70342*	72	1

EMBRACE *UK, male vocal / instrumental group (38 WEEKS)*

Date		Title / Label	pos	wks
17 May 97		FIREWORKS (EP) *Hut HUTCD 84*	34	2
19 Jul 97		ONE BIG FAMILY (EP) *Hut HUTCD 86*	21	3
8 Nov 97	●	ALL YOU GOOD GOOD PEOPLE (EP) *Hut HUTCD 90*	8	4
6 Jun 98	●	COME BACK TO WHAT YOU KNOW *Hut HUTCD 93*	6	8
29 Aug 98	●	MY WEAKNESS IS NONE OF YOUR BUSINESS *Hut HUTCD 103*	9	4
13 Nov 99		HOOLIGAN *Hut HUTCD 123*	18	3
25 Mar 00		YOU'RE NOT ALONE *Hut / Virgin HUTCD 126*	14	3
10 Jun 00		SAVE ME *Hut / Virgin HUTCD 133*	29	2
15 Jul 00		SAVE ME (re-entry) *Hut / Virgin HUTCD 133*	67	1
19 Aug 00		I WOULDN'T WANNA HAPPEN TO YOU *Hut / Virgin HUTCD 137*	23	2
1 Sep 01		WONDER *Hut / Virgin HUTCD 142*	14	3
13 Oct 01		WONDER (re-entry) *Hut / Virgin HUTCD 142*	59	1
17 Nov 01		MAKE IT LAST *Hut / Virgin HUTCD 144*	35	2

Tracks on Fireworks (EP): The Last Gas / Now You're Nobody / Blind / Fireworks. Tracks on One Big Family (EP): One Big Family / Dry Kids / You've Only Got to Stop to Get Better / Butter Wouldn't Melt. Tracks on All You Good Good People (EP): All You Good Good People / You Don't Amount To Anything – This Time / The Way I Do / Free Ride

EMERSON – *See SASHA*

Keith EMERSON *UK, male instrumentalist – keyboards (5 WEEKS)*

Date		Title / Label	pos	wks
10 Apr 76		HONKY TONK TRAIN BLUES *Manticore K 13513*	21	5

See also EMERSON, LAKE and PALMER

EMERSON, LAKE and PALMER
UK, male instrumental group (13 WEEKS)

Date		Title / Label	pos	wks
4 Jun 77	●	FANFARE FOR THE COMMON MAN *Atlantic K 10946*	2	13

See also Keith EMERSON; Greg LAKE; ASIA

Dick EMERY *UK, male actor / vocalist (8 WEEKS)*

Date		Title / Label	pos	wks
26 Feb 69		IF YOU LOVE HER *Pye 7N 17644*	32	4
13 Jan 73		YOU ARE AWFUL (BUT I LIKE YOU) *Pye 7N 45202*	43	4

EMF *UK, male vocal / instrumental group (50 WEEKS)*

Date		Title / Label	pos	wks
3 Nov 90	●	UNBELIEVABLE *Parlophone R 6273* ▲	3	13
2 Feb 91	●	I BELIEVE *Parlophone R 6279*	6	7
27 Apr 91		CHILDREN *Parlophone R 6288*	19	5
31 Aug 91		LIES *Parlophone R 6295*	28	3
2 May 92		UNEXPLAINED (EP) *Parlophone SGE 2026*	18	4
19 Sep 92		THEY'RE HERE *Parlophone R 6321*	29	3
21 Nov 92		IT'S YOU *Parlophone R 6327*	23	3
25 Feb 95		PERFECT DAY *Parlophone CDRS 6401*	27	3
8 Jul 95	●	I'M A BELIEVER *Parlophone CDR 6412* [1]	3	8
28 Oct 95		AFRO KING *Parlophone CDRS 6416*	51	1

[1] EMF and Reeves and Mortimer

Tracks on Unexplained (EP): Getting Through / Far From Me / The Same / Search and Destroy

EMILIA *Sweden, female vocalist – Emilia Rydberg (14 WEEKS)*

Date		Title / Label	pos	wks
12 Dec 98	●	BIG BIG WORLD *Universal UMD 87190*	5	13
1 May 99		GOOD SIGN *Universal UMD 87206*	54	1

EMINEM (497 Top 500) *Controversy-courting, chainsaw-wielding, multi-award-winning rap superstar, whose name is Marshall Mathers (aka Slim Shady) b. 17 Oct 1974, Detroit. 'The Marshall Mathers LP' has sold more than 12 million (71 WEEKS)*

Date		Title / Label	pos	wks
10 Apr 99	●	MY NAME IS *Interscope IND 95638*	2	11
24 Jul 99		MY NAME IS (re-entry) *Interscope IND 95638*	68	1
14 Aug 99	●	GUILTY CONSCIENCE *Interscope IND 4971282* [1]	5	8
10 Jun 00	●	FORGOT ABOUT DRE *Interscope 4973412* [2]	7	9
8 Jul 00	★	THE REAL SLIM SHADY *Interscope 4973792* ■	1	15
14 Oct 00	●	THE WAY I AM *Interscope 4974252*	8	9
16 Dec 00	★	STAN *Interscope IND 97470* ■	1	16
21 Apr 01		STAN (re-entry) *Interscope IND 97470*	74	1
1 Sep 01		SCARY MOVIES *Mole UK MOLEUK 045* [3]	63	1

[1] Eminem featuring Dr Dre [2] Dr Dre featuring Eminem [3] Bad meets Evil featuring Eminem & Royce Da 5'9"

'Stan' features uncredited vocal by Dido

EMMA *UK, female vocalist (6 WEEKS)* pos/wks

28 Apr 90	**GIVE A LITTLE LOVE BACK TO THE WORLD** *Big Wave BWR 33*	33	6

EMMANUEL & ESKA – See *COLOURS featuring EMMANUEL & ESKA; EN-CORE featuring Stephen EMMANUEL & ESKA*

EMMIE *UK, female vocalist – Emma Norton-Smith (8 WEEKS)* pos/wks

23 Jan 99 ●	**MORE THAN THIS** *Indirect / Manifesto FESCD 52*	5	8

AN EMOTIONAL FISH
Ireland, male vocal / instrumental group (5 WEEKS) pos/wks

23 Jun 90	**CELEBRATE** *East West YZ 489*	46	5

EMOTIONS *US, female vocal group (28 WEEKS)* pos/wks

10 Sep 77 ●	**BEST OF MY LOVE** *CBS 5555* ▲	4	10
24 Dec 77	**I DON'T WANNA LOSE YOUR LOVE** *CBS 5819*	40	5
12 May 79 ●	**BOOGIE WONDERLAND** *CBS 7292* [1]	4	13

[1] Earth Wind and Fire with the Emotions

EMPIRION *UK, male instrumental / production group (2 WEEKS)* pos/wks

6 Jul 96	**NARCOTIC INFLUENCE** *XL XLS 72CD*	64	1
21 Jun 97	**BETA** *XL XLS 77CD*	75	1

EN VOGUE (397 Top 500) *Very Influential post-feminist R&B vocal quartet formed Oakland, California, US: Terry Ellis, Maxine Jones, Dawn Robinson (left 1995) and ex-beauty pageant winner Cindy Herron. Award-winning team blended hip hop and R&B and helped to launch the New Jill Swing movement (83 WEEKS)* pos/wks

5 May 90 ●	**HOLD ON** *East West America 7908*	5	11
21 Jul 90	**LIES** *East West America 7893*	44	4
4 Apr 92	**MY LOVIN'** *East West America A 8578*	69	3
9 May 92 ●	**MY LOVIN' (re-entry)** *East West America A 8578*	4	9
15 Aug 92	**GIVING HIM SOMETHING HE CAN FEEL** *East West America A 8524*	44	3
7 Nov 92	**FREE YOUR MIND / GIVING HIM SOMETHING HE CAN FEEL (re-issue)** *East West America A 8468*	16	8
16 Jan 93	**GIVE IT UP TURN IT LOOSE** *East West America A 8445CD*	22	4
10 Apr 93	**LOVE DON'T LOVE YOU** *East West America A 8424CD*	64	1
9 Oct 93	**RUNAWAY LOVE** *East West America A 8359CD*	36	3
19 Mar 94 ●	**WHATTA MAN** *ffrr FCD 222* [1]	7	10
11 Jan 97 ●	**DON'T LET GO (LOVE)** *East West A 3976CD*	5	16
14 Jun 97	**WHATEVER** *East West E 3642CD*	14	5
6 Sep 97	**TOO GONE, TOO LONG** *East West E 3908CD*	20	3
28 Nov 98	**HOLD ON (re-mix)** *East West E 3796 CD*	53	1
1 Jul 00	**RIDDLE** *Elektra E 7053CD*	33	2

[1] Salt-N-Pepa with En Vogue

EN-CORE featuring Stephen EMMANUEL & ESKA
UK, male producer / female vocalist (2 WEEKS) pos/wks

9 Sep 00	**COOCHY COO** *VC Recordings VCRD 72*	32	2

ENCORE *France, female vocalist – Sabine Ohmes (4 WEEKS)* pos/wks

14 Feb 98	**LE DISC JOCKEY** *Sum CDSUM 2*	12	4

ENERGISE *UK, male vocal / instrumental group (1 WEEK)* pos/wks

16 Feb 91	**REPORT TO THE DANCEFLOOR** *Network NWKT 16*	69	1

ENERGY 52
Germany, male DJ / producer – Paul Schmitz-Moormann (7 WEEKS) pos/wks

8 Mar 97	**CAFE DEL MAR** *Hooj Choons HOOJCD 51*	51	1
25 Jul 98	**CAFE DEL MAR '98 (re-mix)** *Hooj Choons HOOJ 64CD*	12	6

ENERGY ORCHARD *Ireland, male vocal / instrumental group (6 WEEKS)* pos/wks

27 Jan 90	**BELFAST** *MCA MCA 1392*	52	4
7 Apr 90	**SAILORTOWN** *MCA MCA 1402*	73	2

Harry ENFIELD *UK, male comedian / vocalist (7 WEEKS)* pos/wks

7 May 88 ●	**LOADSAMONEY (DOIN' UP THE HOUSE)** *Mercury DOSH 1*	4	7

ENGLAND DAN and John Ford COLEY
US, male vocal duo (12 WEEKS) pos/wks

25 Sep 76	**I'D REALLY LOVE TO SEE YOU TONIGHT** *Atlantic K 10810*	26	7
23 Jun 79	**LOVE IS THE ANSWER** *Big Tree K 11296*	45	5

ENGLAND RUGBY WORLD CUP SQUAD – See *UNION featuring the ENGLAND WORLD CUP SQUAD*

ENGLAND SISTERS – See *DALE SISTERS*

ENGLAND SUPPORTERS' BAND
UK, male instrumental group (4 WEEKS) pos/wks

27 Jun 98	**THE GREAT ESCAPE** *V2 VVR 5002163*	46	2
24 Jun 00	**THE GREAT ESCAPE 2000 (re-recording)** *V2 VVR 5014293*	26	2

ENGLAND UNITED
UK, male / female vocal / instrumental group (11 WEEKS) pos/wks

13 Jun 98 ●	**(HOW DOES IT FEEL TO BE) ON TOP OF THE WORLD** *London LONCD 414*	9	9
22 Aug 98	**(HOW DOES IT FEEL TO BE) ON TOP OF THE WORLD (re-entry)** *London LONCD 414*	61	2

ENGLAND WORLD CUP SQUAD
UK, male football team vocalists (46 WEEKS) pos/wks

18 Apr 70 ★	**BACK HOME** *Pye 7N 17920*	1	16
15 Aug 70	**BACK HOME (re-entry)** *Pye 7N 17920*	46	1
10 Apr 82 ●	**THIS TIME (WE'LL GET IT RIGHT) / ENGLAND WE'LL FLY THE FLAG** *England ER 1*	2	13
19 Apr 86	**WE'VE GOT THE WHOLE WORLD AT OUR FEET / WHEN WE ARE FAR FROM HOME** *Columbia DB 9128*	66	2
21 May 88	**ALL THE WAY** *MCA GOAL 1* [1]	64	2
2 Jun 90 ★	**WORLD IN MOTION . . .** *Factory / MCA FAC 2937* [2]	1	12

[1] England Football Team and the 'sound' of Stock, Aitken and Waterman
[2] Englandneworder

ENGLAND'S BARMY ARMY
UK, 5,000 male / female vocal cricket supporters (1 WEEK) pos/wks

12 Jun 99	**COME ON ENGLAND!** *Wildstar CDWILD 20*	45	1

Kim ENGLISH *US, female vocalist (7 WEEKS)* pos/wks

23 Jul 94	**NITE LIFE** *Hi-Life PZCD 323*	35	2
4 Mar 95	**TIME FOR LOVE** *Hi-Life HICD 8*	48	1
9 Sep 95	**I KNOW A PLACE** *Hi-Life 5798072*	52	1
30 Nov 96	**NITE LIFE (re-mix)** *Hi-Life 5755332*	35	2
26 Apr 97	**SUPERNATURAL** *Hi-Life 5736972*	50	1

Scott ENGLISH *US, male vocalist (10 WEEKS)* pos/wks

9 Oct 71	**BRANDY** *Horse HOSS 7*	12	10

ENIAC – See *Tom NOVY*

ENIGMA *UK, male / female vocal / instrumental group (15 WEEKS)* pos/wks

23 May 81	**AIN'T NO STOPPING** *Creole CR 9*	11	8
8 Aug 81	**I LOVE MUSIC** *Creole CR 14*	25	7

ENIGMA
Germany / Romania, male / female vocal / instrumental duo (45 WEEKS) pos/wks

15 Dec 90 ★	**SADNESS PART 1** *Virgin International DINS 101*	1	12
30 Mar 91	**MEA CULPA PART II** *Virgin International DINS 104*	55	3
10 Aug 91	**PRINCIPLES OF LUST** *Virgin International DINS 110*	59	2
11 Jan 92	**THE RIVERS OF BELIEF** *Virgin International DINS 112*	68	2
29 Jan 94 ●	**RETURN TO INNOCENCE** *Virgin International DINSD 123*	3	14
14 May 94	**THE EYES OF TRUTH** *Virgin International DINSD 126*	21	4
20 Aug 94	**AGE OF LONELINESS** *Virgin International DINSD 135*	21	5

25 Jan 97		**BEYOND THE INVISIBLE** *Virgin International DINSD 155*	**26**	2
19 Apr 97		**TNT FOR THE BRAIN** *Virgin International DINSD 161*	**60**	1

ENYA

Ireland, female vocalist / instrumentalist – Eithne Ni Bhraonain (63 WEEKS) pos/wks

15 Oct 88	★	**ORINOCO FLOW** *WEA YZ 312*	**1**	13
24 Dec 88		**EVENING FALLS . . .** *WEA YZ 356*	**20**	4
10 Jun 89		**STORMS IN AFRICA (PART II)** *WEA YZ 368*	**41**	4
19 Oct 91		**CARIBBEAN BLUE** *WEA YZ 604*	**13**	7
7 Dec 91		**HOW CAN I KEEP FROM SINGING?** *WEA YZ 365*	**32**	5
1 Aug 92	●	**BOOK OF DAYS** *WEA YZ 640*	**10**	6
14 Nov 92		**THE CELTS** *WEA YZ 705*	**29**	4
18 Nov 95	●	**ANYWHERE IS** *WEA WEA 023CD*	**7**	12
7 Dec 96		**ON MY WAY HOME** *WEA WEA 047CD*	**26**	2
13 Dec 97		**ONLY IF...** *WEA WEA 143CD*	**43**	2
25 Nov 00		**ONLY TIME** *WEA WEA 316CD*	**32**	3
31 Mar 01		**WILD CHILD** *WEA WEA 324CD*	**72**	1

EON *UK, male producer – Ian Bela (1 WEEK)* pos/wks

17 Aug 91		**FEAR: THE MINDKILLER** *Vinyl Solution STORM 33*	**63**	1

EPMD *US, male rap / DJ duo (1 WEEK)* pos/wks

15 Aug 98		**STRICTLY BUSINESS** *Parlophone CDR 6502*	**43**	1

See also MANTRONIK vs EPMD

EQUALS *UK, vocal / instrumental group (69 WEEKS)* pos/wks

21 Feb 68		**I GET SO EXCITED** *President PT 180*	**44**	4
1 May 68		**BABY COME BACK** *President PT 135*	**50**	1
15 May 68	★	**BABY COME BACK (re-entry)** *President PT 135*	**1**	17
21 Aug 68		**LAUREL AND HARDY** *President PT 200*	**35**	5
27 Nov 68		**SOFTLY SOFTLY** *President PT 222*	**48**	3
2 Apr 69		**MICHAEL AND THE SLIPPER TREE** *President PT 240*	**24**	7
30 Jul 69	●	**VIVA BOBBY JOE** *President PT 260*	**6**	14
27 Dec 69		**RUB A DUB DUB** *President PT 275*	**34**	7
19 Dec 70	●	**BLACK SKIN BLUE EYED BOYS** *President PT 325*	**9**	11

ERASURE (85 Top 500) *Award-winning UK duo formed by Vince Clarke (k) and Andy Bell (v). After hits with Depeche Mode, Yazoo and The Assembly, this act was Clarke's greatest success, scoring 15 Top 10 singles and having five albums enter at No.1 (203 WEEKS)* pos/wks

5 Oct 85		**WHO NEEDS LOVE LIKE THAT** *Mute MUTE 40*	**55**	2
25 Oct 86	●	**SOMETIMES** *Mute MUTE 51*	**2**	17
28 Feb 87		**IT DOESN'T HAVE TO BE** *Mute MUTE 56*	**12**	9
30 May 87	●	**VICTIM OF LOVE** *Mute MUTE 61*	**7**	9
3 Oct 87	●	**THE CIRCUS** *Mute MUTE 66*	**6**	10
5 Mar 88	●	**SHIP OF FOOLS** *Mute MUTE 74*	**6**	8
11 Jun 88		**CHAINS OF LOVE** *Mute MUTE 83*	**11**	7
1 Oct 88	●	**A LITTLE RESPECT** *Mute MUTE 85*	**4**	10
10 Dec 88	●	**CRACKERS INTERNATIONAL (EP)** *Mute MUTE 93*	**2**	13
30 Sep 89	●	**DRAMA!** *Mute MUTE 89*	**4**	8
9 Dec 89		**YOU SURROUND ME** *Mute MUTE 99*	**15**	9
10 Mar 90	●	**BLUE SAVANNAH** *Mute MUTE 109*	**3**	10
2 Jun 90		**STAR** *Mute MUTE 111*	**11**	7
29 Jun 91	●	**CHORUS** *Mute MUTE 125*	**3**	9
21 Sep 91	●	**LOVE TO HATE YOU** *Mute MUTE 131*	**4**	9
7 Dec 91		**AM I RIGHT? (EP)** *Mute MUTE 134*	**15**	6
11 Jan 92		**AM I RIGHT? (EP) (re-mix)** *Mute L12MUTE 134*	**22**	3
28 Mar 92	●	**BREATH OF LIFE** *Mute MUTE 142*	**8**	6
13 Jun 92	★	**ABBA-ESQUE (EP)** *Mute MUTE 144*■	**1**	12
7 Nov 92	●	**WHO NEEDS LOVE (LIKE THAT) (re-mix)** *Mute MUTE 150*	**10**	4
23 Apr 94	●	**ALWAYS** *Mute CDMUTE 152*	**4**	9
30 Jul 94	●	**RUN TO THE SUN** *Mute CDMUTE 153*	**6**	5
3 Dec 94		**I LOVE SATURDAY** *Mute CDMUTE 166*	**20**	6
23 Sep 95		**STAY WITH ME** *Mute CDMUTE 174*	**15**	4
9 Dec 95		**FINGERS AND THUMBS (COLD SUMMER'S DAY)** *Mute CDMUTE 178*	**20**	3
18 Jan 97		**IN MY ARMS** *Mute CDMUTE 190*	**13**	4
8 Mar 97		**DON'T SAY YOUR LOVE IS KILLING ME** *Mute CDMUTE 195*	**23**	2
21 Oct 00		**FREEDOM** *Mute CDMUTE 244*	**27**	2

Tracks on Crackers International (EP): Stop / The Hardest Part / Knocking on Your Door / She Won't Be Home. Tracks on Am I Right (EP): Am I Right / Carry On Clangers / Let It Flow / Waiting for Sex. Tracks on Am I Right (Re-mix EP): Am I Right / Chorus / Love to Hate You / Perfect Stranger. Tracks on Abba-esque (EP): Lay All Your Love on Me / SOS / Take a Chance on Me / Voulez-Vous. 'Take a Chance On Me' credits MC Kinky

See also KINKY

ERIC and the GOOD GOOD FEELING

UK, male / female vocal / instrumental group (1 WEEK) pos/wks

3 Jun 89		**GOOD GOOD FEELING** *Equinox EQN 1*	**73**	1

ERIK *UK, female vocalist (5 WEEKS)* pos/wks

10 Apr 93		**LOOKS LIKE I'M IN LOVE AGAIN** *PWL Sanctuary PWCD 252* [1]	**46**	2
29 Jan 94		**GOT TO BE REAL** *PWL International PWCD 278*	**42**	2
1 Oct 94		**WE GOT THE LOVE** *PWL International PWCD 305*	**55**	1

[1] Key West featuring Erik

ERIN – *See SHUT UP AND DANCE; BBG*

ERIRE – *See SCIENCE DEPARTMENT featuring DISCOVERY*

EROTIC DRUM BAND

Canada, male / female vocal / instrumental group (3 WEEKS) pos/wks

9 Jun 79		**LOVE DISCO STYLE** *Scope SC 1*	**47**	3

ERUPTION

Jamaica, male / female vocal / instrumental group (21 WEEKS) pos/wks

18 Feb 78	●	**I CAN'T STAND THE RAIN** *Atlantic K 11068* [1]	**5**	11
21 Apr 79	●	**ONE WAY TICKET** *Atlantic / Hansa K 11266*	**9**	10

[1] Eruption featuring Precious Wilson

Michelle ESCOFFERY – *See ARTFUL DODGER*

Shaun ESCOFFERY *UK, male vocalist (1 WEEK)* pos/wks

10 Mar 01		**SPACE RIDER** *Oyster Music OYSCD 4*	**52**	1

ESCORTS *UK, male vocal / instrumental group (2 WEEKS)* pos/wks

2 Jul 64		**THE ONE TO CRY** *Fontana TF 474*	**49**	2

ESCRIMA *UK, male producer – Paul Newman (4 WEEKS)* pos/wks

11 Feb 95		**TRAIN OF THOUGHT** *Ffrreedom TABCD 225*	**36**	2
7 Oct 95		**DEEPER** *Hooj Choons TABCD 236*	**27**	2

See also TALL PAUL; PARTIZAN; CAMISRA; GRIFTERS

ESKA – *See EN-CORE featuring Stephen EMMANUEL & ESKA; COLOURS featuring EMMANUEL & ESKA; Nitin SAWHNEY featuring ESKA*

ESKIMOS & EGYPT *UK, male vocal / instrumental group (4 WEEKS)* pos/wks

13 Feb 93		**FALL FROM GRACE** *One Little Indian EEF 96CD*	**51**	2
29 May 93		**UK-USA** *One Little Indian 99 TP7CD*	**52**	2

ESPIRITU *UK / France, male / female vocal / instrumental duo – Vanessa Quinones and Chris Chaplin (10 WEEKS)* pos/wks

6 Mar 93		**CONQUISTADOR** *Heavenly HVN 28CD*	**47**	2
7 Aug 93		**LOS AMERICANOS** *Heavenly HVN 33CD*	**45**	2
20 Aug 94		**BONITA MANANA** *Columbia 6606925*	**50**	1
25 Mar 95		**ALWAYS SOMETHING THERE TO REMIND ME** *WEA YZ 911CD* [1]	**14**	5

[1] Tin Tin Out featuring Espiritu

ESSENCE *UK, male production group and UK, female vocalist (2 WEEKS)* pos/wks

21 Mar 98		**THE PROMISE** *Innocent SINCD 1*	**27**	2

ESSEX *US, male / female vocal group (5 WEEKS)* pos/wks

			pos	wks
8 Aug 63		EASIER SAID THAN DONE *Columbia DB 7077* ▲	41	5

David ESSEX (91 Top 500) *Actor / teeny-bop star turned popular entertainer, b. David Cook, 23 Jul 1947, London. This singer / songwriter was voted No.1 British Male Vocalist (1974) and was a teen idol for more than a decade. Starred in the stage show 'Godspell' and graduated successfully to films (199 WEEKS)* pos/wks

			pos	wks
18 Aug 73	●	ROCK ON *CBS 1693*	3	11
10 Nov 73	●	LAMPLIGHT *CBS 1902*	7	15
11 May 74		AMERICA *CBS 2176*	32	5
12 Oct 74	★	GONNA MAKE YOU A STAR *CBS 2492*	1	17
14 Dec 74	●	STARDUST *CBS 2828*	7	10
5 Jul 75	●	ROLLING STONE *CBS 3425*	5	7
13 Sep 75	★	HOLD ME CLOSE *CBS 3572*	1	10
6 Dec 75		IF I COULD *CBS 3776*	13	8
20 Mar 76		CITY LIGHTS *CBS 4050*	24	4
16 Oct 76		COMING HOME *CBS 4486*	24	6
17 Sep 77		COOL OUT TONIGHT *CBS 5495*	23	6
11 Mar 78		STAY WITH ME BABY *CBS 6063*	45	5
19 Aug 78	●	OH WHAT A CIRCUS *Mercury 6007 185*	3	11
21 Oct 78		BRAVE NEW WORLD *CBS 6705*	55	3
3 Mar 79		IMPERIAL WIZARD *Mercury 6007 202*	32	8
5 Apr 80	●	SILVER DREAM MACHINE (PART 1) *Mercury BIKE 1*	4	11
14 Jun 80		HOT LOVE *Mercury HOT 11*	57	4
26 Jun 82		ME AND MY GIRL (NIGHT-CLUBBING) *Mercury MER 107*	13	10
11 Dec 82	●	A WINTER'S TALE *Mercury MER 127*	2	10
4 Jun 83		THE SMILE *Mercury ESSEX 1*	52	4
27 Aug 83	●	TAHITI (FROM 'MUTINY ON THE BOUNTY') *Mercury BOUNT 1*	8	11
26 Nov 83		YOU'RE IN MY HEART *Mercury ESSEX 2*	67	2
17 Dec 83		YOU'RE IN MY HEART (re-entry) *Mercury ESSEX 2*	59	4
23 Feb 85		FALLING ANGELS RIDING *Mercury ESSEX 5*	29	7
18 Apr 87		MYFANWY *Arista RIS 11*	41	7
26 Nov 94		TRUE LOVE WAYS *PolyGram TV TLWCD 2* [1]	38	3

[1] David Essex and Catherine Zeta Jones

Gloria ESTEFAN (108 Top 500) *Latin music's leading lady, b. Gloria Fajardo, 1 Dec 1957, Cuba. Successes in the dance and MOR fields have pushed her world sales to more than 35 million, with two of the vocalist's albums passing the one-million sales mark in the UK (182 WEEKS)* pos/wks

			pos	wks
16 Jul 88	●	ANYTHING FOR YOU *Epic 651673 7* [1] ▲	10	16
22 Oct 88	●	1-2-3 *Epic 652958 7* [1]	9	9
17 Dec 88		RHYTHM IS GONNA GET YOU *Epic 654514 7* [1]	16	9
31 Dec 88		1-2-3 (re-entry) *Epic 652958 7* [1]	72	1
11 Feb 89	●	CAN'T STAY AWAY FROM YOU *Epic 651444 7* [1]	7	12
15 Jul 89	●	DON'T WANNA LOSE YOU *Epic 655054 0* ▲	6	10
16 Sep 89		OYE MI CANTO (HEAR MY VOICE) *Epic 655287 7*	16	8
25 Nov 89		GET ON YOUR FEET *Epic 655450 7*	23	7
3 Mar 90		HERE WE ARE *Epic 6554737*	23	6
26 May 90		CUTS BOTH WAYS *Epic 655982 7*	49	5
26 Jan 91		COMING OUT OF THE DARK *Epic 6565747* ▲	25	5
6 Apr 91		SEAL OUR FATE *Epic 6567737*	24	7
8 Jun 91		REMEMBER ME WITH LOVE *Epic 6569687*	22	6
21 Sep 91		LIVE FOR LOVING YOU *Epic 6573827*	33	5
24 Oct 92		ALWAYS TOMORROW *Epic 6583977*	24	4
12 Dec 92	●	MIAMI HIT MIX / CHRISTMAS THROUGH YOUR EYES *Epic 6588377*	8	9
13 Feb 93		I SEE YOUR SMILE *Epic 6589612*	48	2
3 Apr 93		GO AWAY *Epic 6590952*	13	6
3 Jul 93		MI TIERRA *Epic 6593512*	36	3
14 Aug 93		IF WE WERE LOVERS / CON LOS ANOS QUE ME QUEDAN *Epic 6595702*	40	3
18 Dec 93		MONTUNO *Epic 6599972*	55	2
15 Oct 94		TURN THE BEAT AROUND *Epic 6606822*	21	6
3 Dec 94		HOLD ME THRILL ME KISS ME *Epic 6610802*	11	10
18 Feb 95		EVERLASTING LOVE *Epic 6611595*	19	5
18 Mar 95		HOLD ME THRILL ME KISS ME (re-entry) *Epic 6610802*	68	1
25 May 96		REACH *Epic 6632642*	15	6
3 Aug 96		REACH (re-entry) *Epic 6632642*	68	1
17 Aug 96		REACH (2nd re-entry) *Epic 6632642*	55	1
24 Aug 96		YOU'LL BE MINE (PARTY TIME) *Epic 6636505*	18	3
14 Dec 96		I'M NOT GIVING YOU UP *Epic 6640222*	28	3
6 Jun 98		HEAVEN'S WHAT I FEEL *Epic 6660042*	17	4
10 Oct 98		OYE *Epic 6664645*	33	2
16 Jan 99		DON'T LET THIS MOMENT END *Epic 6667472*	28	2
8 Jan 00		MUSIC OF MY HEART *Epic 6685272* [2]	34	3

[1] Gloria Estefan and Miami Sound Machine [2] 'N Sync / Gloria Estefan

'Christmas Through Your Eyes' was listed only from 19 Dec 1992

See also *MIAMI SOUND MACHINE*

Don ESTELLE – *See Windsor DAVIES and Don ESTELLE*

ESTHERO – *See Ian POOLEY*

Deon ESTUS *US, male vocalist / instrumentalist – bass (7 WEEKS)* pos/wks

			pos	wks
25 Jan 86		MY GUY – MY GIRL (MEDLEY) *Sedition EDIT 3310* [1]	63	3
29 Apr 89		HEAVEN HELP ME *Mika MIKA 2*	41	4

[1] Amii Stewart and Deon Estus

ETA *Denmark, male instrumental group (5 WEEKS)* pos/wks

			pos	wks
28 Jun 97		CASUAL SUB (BURNING SPEAR) *East West EW 110CD*	28	3
31 Jan 98		CASUAL SUB (BURNING SPEAR) (re-mix) *East West Dance EW 145CD*	28	2

ETERNAL (189 Top 500) *London-based vocal group with across-the-board appeal: sisters Easther and Vernett Bennett, Kéllé Bryan, Louise Nurding. First all-female act to shift more than one million copies of an album in the UK. Louise left for a successful solo career in 1995 followed by Kéllé four years later (134 WEEKS)* pos/wks

			pos	wks
2 Oct 93	●	STAY *EMI CDEM 283*	4	9
15 Jan 94	●	SAVE OUR LOVE *EMI CDEM 296*	8	7
30 Apr 94	●	JUST A STEP FROM HEAVEN *EMI CDEM 311*	8	10
20 Aug 94		SO GOOD *EMI CDEMS 339*	13	7
5 Nov 94	●	OH BABY I . . . *EMI CDEM 353*	4	13
24 Dec 94		CRAZY *EMI CDEMX 364*	15	7
21 Oct 95	●	POWER OF A WOMAN *EMI CDEM 396*	5	8
9 Dec 95	●	I AM BLESSED *EMI CDEMS 408*	7	12
9 Mar 96	●	GOOD THING *EMI CDEM 419*	8	6
17 Aug 96	●	SOMEDAY *EMI CDEMS 439*	4	9
7 Dec 96	●	SECRETS *EMI CDEM 459*	9	7
8 Mar 97	●	DON'T YOU LOVE ME *EMI CDEMS 465*	3	7
31 May 97	★	I WANNA BE THE ONLY ONE *EMI CDEM 472* [1] ■	1	15
11 Oct 97	●	ANGEL OF MINE *EMI CDEM 493*	4	13
30 Oct 99		WHAT 'CHA GONNA DO *EMI CDEM 552*	16	4

[1] Eternal featuring BeBe Winans

ETHER *UK, male vocal / instrumental group (1 WEEK)* pos/wks

			pos	wks
28 Mar 98		WATCHING YOU *Parlophone CDR 6491*	74	1

ETHICS *Holland, male producer – Patrick Prinz (5 WEEKS)* pos/wks

			pos	wks
25 Nov 95		TO THE BEAT OF THE DRUM (LA LUNA) *VC VCRD 5*	13	5

See also *ARTEMESIA; MOVIN' MELODIES; SUBLIMINAL CUTS*

ETHIOPIANS *Jamaica, male vocal / instrumental group (6 WEEKS)* pos/wks

			pos	wks
13 Sep 67		TRAIN TO SKAVILLE *Rio RIO 130*	40	6

Tony ETORIA *UK, male vocalist (8 WEEKS)* pos/wks

			pos	wks
4 Jun 77		I CAN PROVE IT *GTO GT 89*	21	8

EUROGROOVE *UK, male / female vocal group (7 WEEKS)* pos/wks

			pos	wks
20 May 95		MOVE YOUR BODY *Avex UK AVEXCD 4*	29	2
5 Aug 95		DIVE TO PARADISE *Avex UK AVEXCD 10*	31	2
21 Oct 95		IT'S ON YOU (SCAN ME) *Avex UK AVEXCD 17*	25	2
3 Feb 96		MOVE YOUR BODY (re-mix) *Avex UK AVEXCD 22*	44	1

EUROPE *Sweden, male vocal / instrumental group – lead vocal Joey Tempest (50 WEEKS)* pos/wks

1 Nov 86	★	THE FINAL COUNTDOWN *Epic A 7127*	1	15
31 Jan 87		ROCK THE NIGHT *Epic EUR 1*	12	9
18 Apr 87		CARRIE *Epic EUR 2*	22	8
20 Aug 88		SUPERSTITIOUS *Epic EUR 3*	34	5
1 Feb 92		I'LL CRY FOR YOU *Epic 6576977*	28	5
21 Mar 92		HALFWAY TO HEAVEN *Epic 6578517*	42	4
25 Dec 99		THE FINAL COUNTDOWN 2000 (re-recording) *Epic 6685042*	36	4

EURYTHMICS (82 Top 500) *Innovative and internationally popular duo formed by Brit award-winning Scottish vocalist Annie Lennox and multi-instrumentalist / songwriter / producer Dave Stewart, formerly known as The Tourists. The most charted male / female duo in the UK, whose greatest hits album sold more than two million copies in the UK and in Europe (208 WEEKS)* pos/wks

4 Jul 81		NEVER GONNA CRY AGAIN *RCA 68*	63	3
20 Nov 82		LOVE IS A STRANGER *RCA DA 1*	54	5
12 Feb 83	●	SWEET DREAMS (ARE MADE OF THIS) *RCA DA 2* ▲	2	14
9 Apr 83	●	LOVE IS A STRANGER (re-entry) *RCA DA 1*	6	8
9 Jul 83	●	WHO'S THAT GIRL? *RCA DA 3*	3	10
5 Nov 83	●	RIGHT BY YOUR SIDE *RCA DA 4*	10	11
21 Jan 84	●	HERE COMES THE RAIN AGAIN *RCA DA 5*	8	8
3 Nov 84	●	SEXCRIME (NINETEEN EIGHTY FOUR) *Virgin VS 728*	4	13
19 Jan 85		JULIA *Virgin VS 734*	44	4
20 Apr 85		WOULD I LIE TO YOU? *RCA PB 40101*	17	8
6 Jul 85	★	THERE MUST BE AN ANGEL (PLAYING WITH MY HEART) *RCA PB 40247*	1	13
2 Nov 85	●	SISTERS ARE DOIN' IT FOR THEMSELVES *RCA PB 40339* [1]	9	11
11 Jan 86		IT'S ALRIGHT (BABY'S COMING BACK) *RCA PB 40375*	12	8
14 Jun 86		WHEN TOMORROW COMES *RCA DA 7*	30	6
6 Sep 86	●	THORN IN MY SIDE *RCA DA 8*	5	11
29 Nov 86		THE MIRACLE OF LOVE *RCA DA 9*	23	9
28 Feb 87		MISSIONARY MAN *RCA DA 10*	31	4
24 Oct 87		BEETHOVEN (I LOVE TO LISTEN TO) *RCA DA 11*	25	5
26 Dec 87		SHAME *RCA DA 14*	41	6
9 Apr 88		I NEED A MAN *RCA DA 15*	26	5
11 Jun 88		YOU HAVE PLACED A CHILL IN MY HEART *RCA DA 16*	16	8
26 Aug 89		REVIVAL *RCA DA 17*	26	6
4 Nov 89		DON'T ASK ME WHY *RCA DA 19*	25	6
3 Feb 90		THE KING AND QUEEN OF AMERICA *RCA DA 20*	29	5
12 May 90		ANGEL *RCA DA 21*	23	6
9 Mar 91		LOVE IS A STRANGER (re-issue) *RCA PB 44265*	46	3
16 Nov 91		SWEET DREAMS (ARE MADE OF THIS) '91 *RCA PB 45031*	48	2
16 Oct 99		I SAVED THE WORLD TODAY *RCA 74321695632*	11	6
5 Feb 00		17 AGAIN *RCA 74321726262*	27	4

[1] Eurythmics and Aretha Franklin

See also Dave STEWART; Annie LENNOX

EUSEBE *UK, male / female vocal group (3 WEEKS)* pos/wks

26 Aug 95		SUMMERTIME HEALING *Mama's Yard CDMAMA 4*	32	3

EVANGEL TEMPLE CHOIR – *See Johnny CASH*

Faith EVANS *US, female vocalist (40 WEEKS)* pos/wks

14 Oct 95		YOU USED TO LOVE ME *Puff Daddy 74321299812*	42	2
23 Nov 96		STRESSED OUT *Jive JIVECD 404* [1]	33	2
28 Jun 97	★	I'LL BE MISSING YOU *Puff Daddy 74321499102* [2] ◆ ■ ▲	1	21
14 Nov 98		LOVE LIKE THIS *Puff Daddy 74321625592*	24	4
1 May 99		ALL NIGHT LONG *Puff Daddy / Arista 74321665692* [3]	23	3
1 May 99		GEORGY PORGY *Warner Bros. W478CD2* [4]	28	3
30 Dec 00		HEARTBREAK HOTEL *Arista 74321820572* [5]	26	5

[1] A Tribe Called Quest featuring Faith Evans and Raphael Saadiq [2] Puff Daddy and Faith Evans featuring 112 [3] Faith Evans featuring Puff Daddy [4] Eric Benet featuring Faith Evans [5] Whitney Houston featuring Faith Evans and Kelly Price

Maureen EVANS *UK, female vocalist (37 WEEKS)* pos/wks

22 Jan 60		THE BIG HURT *Oriole CB 1533*	26	2
17 Mar 60		LOVE KISSES AND HEARTACHES *Oriole CB 1540*	44	1
2 Jun 60		PAPER ROSES *Oriole CB 1550*	40	5
29 Nov 62	●	LIKE I DO *Oriole CB 1760*	3	18
27 Feb 64		I LOVE HOW YOU LOVE ME *Oriole CB 1906*	34	10
14 May 64		I LOVE HOW YOU LOVE ME (re-entry) *Oriole CB 1906*	50	1

Paul EVANS *US, male vocalist (14 WEEKS)* pos/wks

27 Nov 59		SEVEN LITTLE GIRLS SITTING IN THE BACK SEAT *London HLL 8968* [1]	25	1
31 Mar 60		MIDNITE SPECIAL *London HLL 9045*	41	1
16 Dec 78	●	HELLO THIS IS JOANIE (THE TELEPHONE ANSWERING MACHINE SONG) *Spring 2066 932*	6	12

[1] Paul Evans and the Curls

EVASIONS
UK, male / female vocal / rap / instrumental group (8 WEEKS) pos/wks

13 Jun 81		WIKKA WRAP *Groove GP 107*	20	8

EVE *US, female rapper – Eve Jeffers (20 WEEKS)* pos/wks

19 May 01	●	WHO'S THAT GIRL *Interscope 4975572*	6	8
25 Aug 01	●	LET ME BLOW YA MIND *Interscope / Polydor 4975932* [1]	4	12

[1] Eve featuring Gwen Stefani

See also Missy 'Misdemeanor' ELLIOTT

E.V.E. *UK / US, female vocal group (5 WEEKS)* pos/wks

1 Oct 94		GROOVE OF LOVE *Gasoline Alley MCSTD 2007*	30	3
28 Jan 95		GOOD LIFE *Gasoline Alley MCSTD 2038*	39	2

Alison EVELYN – *See BROTHERS LIKE OUTLAW featuring Alison EVELYN*

EVERCLEAR *US, male vocal / instrumental group (7 WEEKS)* pos/wks

1 Jun 96		HEARTSPARK DOLLARSIGN *Capitol CDCLS 773*	48	2
31 Aug 96		SANTA MONICA (WATCH THE WORLD DIE) *Capitol CDCL 775*	40	2
9 May 98		EVERYTHING TO EVERYONE *Capitol CDCL 799*	41	1
14 Oct 00		WONDERFUL *Capital CDCLS 824*	36	2

Betty EVERETT *US, female vocalist (14 WEEKS)* pos/wks

14 Jan 65		GETTING MIGHTY CROWDED *Fontana TF 520*	29	7
30 Oct 68		IT'S IN HIS KISS (THE SHOOP SHOOP SONG) *President PT 215*	34	7

Kenny EVERETT *UK, male vocalist (12 WEEKS)* pos/wks

12 Nov 77		CAPTAIN KREMMEN (RETRIBUTION) *DJM DJS 10810* [1]	32	4
26 Mar 83	●	SNOT RAP *RCA KEN 1*	9	8

[1] Kenny Everett and Mike Vickers

Peven EVERETT – *See Roy DAVIS Jr featuring Peven EVERETT*

EVERLAST *US, male vocalist – Erik Schrody (5 WEEKS)* pos/wks

27 Feb 99		WHAT IT'S LIKE *Tommy Boy TBCD 7470*	34	2
3 Jul 99		ENDS *Tommy Boy TBCD 346*	47	1
20 Jan 01		BLACK JESUS *Tommy Boy TBCD 2180*	37	2

See also HOUSE OF PAIN

Phil EVERLY *US, male vocalist (24 WEEKS)* pos/wks

6 Nov 82		LOUISE *Capitol CL 266*	47	6
19 Feb 83	●	SHE MEANS NOTHING TO ME *Capitol CL 276* [1]	9	9
10 Dec 94		ALL I HAVE TO DO IS DREAM *EMI CDEMS 359* [2]	14	6
25 Feb 95		ALL I HAVE TO DO IS DREAM (re-entry) *EMI CDEMS 359* [2]	58	3

[1] Phil Everly and Cliff Richard [2] Cliff Richard and Phil Everly

'All I Have to Do Is Dream' was listed with its flip side 'Miss You Nights' by Cliff Richard

See also EVERLY BROTHERS

1966

IN THE YEAR IN WHICH ENGLAND WON THE WORLD CUP, STAR TREK BOLDLY TOOK TO THE TV SCREENS, JOHN LENNON PROCLAIMED THE BEATLES MORE POPULAR THAN JESUS AND CHAIRMAN MAO'S SUPPORTERS UNLEASHED THEIR CULTURAL REVOLUTION, **DAVE DEE** OF DAVE DEE, DOZY, BEAKY, MICK AND TICH TALKS ABOUT A COUPLE OF THE FOUR TOP 10 HITS THE GROUP RACKED UP IN A YEAR IN WHICH THEY CLOCKED UP MORE WEEKS ON THE CHART THAN ANY OTHER ACT ...

"A lot of people don't remember 'You Make It Move' and our two prior singles, but 'Hold Tight' ... well, it is the group's anthem, really. I know we had bigger selling records later, but was the one that started it. When you go on stage, and I still perform with the band, 'Hold Tight' is the one the punters really remember, and the one they can sing. For the recording session we all stamped on the floorboards together in time with the drums, creating that huge, in-your-face drum sound. Tich's fuzz guitar work, though, plays an important part! This was, of course, the year that England won the World Cup and our happy-go-lucky song became sort of an anthem! 'Bend It' was very experimental. There weren't any other bands doing that sort of record. It was just us. It got people guessing as to what we would be doing for the next single! That created interest. This was the start of our musical world tour. Although we had a bouzouki player in, we ended up using a mandola, which is a bigger type of mandolin. It has eight strings but a deeper sound than a mandolin. We kept the bouzouki on, but it's buried in the track because the guy couldn't keep it in tune! Tich actually played the mandola!"

SINGLE OF THE YEAR 'Green Green Grass of Home' Tom Jones
ALBUM OF THE YEAR 'The Sound of Music' Soundtrack

EVERLY BROTHERS (20 Top 500) *Rock 'n' roll's foremost vocal duo: Don b. 1 Feb 1937 and Phil Everly b. 19 Jan 1939. The Kentucky-based brothers' distinctive harmony sound has influenced scores of latter groups including The Beatles. Duo, who were voted World's Top Group by NME readers in 1958, were supported by The Rolling Stones on 1963 UK tour. They achieved long string of transatlantic hits, many of which were self composed. They were the first duo / group inducted in Rock and Roll Hall of Fame, and were awarded a Lifetime Grammy in 1997. In 2001 they were elected into the Country Music Hall of Fame and their home state erected statues in their honour (344 WEEKS)* pos/wks

Date		Title / Label	pos	wks
12 Jul 57	●	BYE BYE LOVE *London HLA 8440*	6	16
8 Nov 57	●	WAKE UP LITTLE SUSIE *London HLA 8498* ▲	2	13
23 May 58	★	ALL I HAVE TO DO IS DREAM / CLAUDETTE *London HLA 8618* ▲	1	21
12 Sep 58	●	BIRD DOG *London HLA 8685* ▲	2	16
23 Jan 59	●	PROBLEMS *London HLA 8781*	6	12
22 May 59		TAKE A MESSAGE TO MARY *London HLA 8863*	29	1
29 May 59		POOR JENNY *London B-HLA 8863*	14	11
19 Jun 59		TAKE A MESSAGE TO MARY (re-entry) *London HLA 8863*	27	1
3 Jul 59		TAKE A MESSAGE TO MARY (2nd re-entry) *London HLA 8863*	20	8
11 Sep 59	●	('TIL) I KISSED YOU *London HLA 8934*	2	15
12 Feb 60		LET IT BE ME *London HLA 9039*	13	5
31 Mar 60		LET IT BE ME (re-entry) *London HLA 9039*	26	4
14 Apr 60	★	CATHY'S CLOWN *Warner Bros. WB 1* ▲	1	18
14 Jul 60	●	WHEN WILL I BE LOVED *London HLA 9157*	4	16
22 Sep 60	●	LUCILLE / SO SAD (TO WATCH GOOD LOVE GO BAD) *Warner Bros. WB 19*	4	15
15 Dec 60		LIKE STRANGERS *London HLA 9250*	11	10
9 Feb 61	★	WALK RIGHT BACK / EBONY EYES *Warner Bros. WB 33*	1	16
15 Jun 61	★	TEMPTATION *Warner Bros. WB 42*	1	15
5 Oct 61		MUSKRAT / DON'T BLAME ME *Warner Bros. WB 50*	20	6
18 Jan 62	●	CRYING IN THE RAIN *Warner Bros. WB 56*	6	15
17 May 62		HOW CAN I MEET HER *Warner Bros. WB 67*	12	10
25 Oct 62		NO ONE CAN MAKE MY SUNSHINE SMILE *Warner Bros. WB 79*	11	11
21 Mar 63		SO IT WILL ALWAYS BE *Warner Bros. WB 94*	23	11
13 Jun 63		IT'S BEEN NICE (GOODNIGHT) *Warner Bros. WB 99*	26	5
17 Oct 63		THE GIRL SANG THE BLUES *Warner Bros. WB 109*	25	9
16 Jul 64		THE FERRIS WHEEL *Warner Bros. WB 135*	22	10
3 Dec 64		GONE, GONE, GONE *Warner Bros. WB 146*	36	7
6 May 65		THAT'LL BE THE DAY *Warner Bros. WB 158*	30	4
20 May 65	●	THE PRICE OF LOVE *Warner Bros. WB 161*	2	14
26 Aug 65		I'LL NEVER GET OVER YOU *Warner Bros. WB 5639*	35	5
21 Oct 65		LOVE IS STRANGE *Warner Bros. WB 5649*	11	9
8 May 68		IT'S MY TIME *Warner Bros. WB 7192*	39	6
22 Sep 84		ON THE WINGS OF A NIGHTINGALE *Mercury MER 170*	41	9

'All I Have to Do Is Dream' was listed without Claudette for its first week on the chart but, from 30 May 1958, both sides were charted for 20 more weeks.

See also Phil EVERLY

EVERTON FOOTBALL CLUB
UK, male football team vocalists (8 WEEKS) pos/wks

Date		Title / Label	pos	wks
11 May 85		HERE WE GO *Columbia DB 9106* [1]	14	5
20 May 95		ALL TOGETHER NOW *MDMC DEVCS 3*	24	3

[1] Everton 1985

EVERYTHING BUT THE GIRL (322 Top 500) *Introspective pop duo formed 1982, Hull, UK: Tracey Thorn (v) b. 26 Sep 1962, Ben Watt (k) b. 6 Dec 1962. Gained greatest popularity after mid-90s conversion to low-key dance music. Remix of 'Missing' was the first single to spend an uninterrupted year on the US chart (96 WEEKS)* pos/wks

Date		Title / Label	pos	wks
12 May 84		EACH AND EVERY ONE *Blanco Y Negro NEG 1*	28	7
21 Jul 84		MINE *Blanco Y Negro NEG 3*	58	2
6 Oct 84		NATIVE LAND *Blanco Y Negro NEG 6*	73	2
2 Aug 86		COME ON HOME *Blanco Y Negro NEG 21*	44	7
11 Oct 86		DON'T LEAVE ME BEHIND *Blanco Y Negro NEG 23*	72	2
13 Feb 88		THESE EARLY DAYS *Blanco Y Negro NEG 30*	75	1
9 Jul 88	●	I DON'T WANT TO TALK ABOUT IT *Blanco Y Negro NEG 34*	3	9
27 Jan 90		DRIVING *Blanco Y Negro NEG 40*	54	2
22 Feb 92		COVERS (EP) *Blanco Y Negro NEG 54*	13	6
24 Apr 93		THE ONLY LIVING BOY IN NEW YORK (EP) *Blanco Y Negro NEG 62CD*	42	5
19 Jun 93		I DIDN'T KNOW I WAS LOOKING FOR LOVE (EP) *Blanco Y Negro NEG 64CD*	72	1
4 Jun 94		ROLLERCOASTER (EP) *Blanco Y Negro NEG 69CD*	65	1
20 Aug 94		MISSING *Blanco Y Negro NEG 71CD1*	69	1
28 Oct 95	●	MISSING (re-mix) *Blanco Y Negro NEG 84CD*	3	22
20 Apr 96	●	WALKING WOUNDED *Virgin VSCDT 1577*	6	6
29 Jun 96	●	WRONG *Virgin VSCDT 1589*	8	7
5 Oct 96		SINGLE *Virgin VSCDT 1600*	20	3
7 Dec 96		DRIVING (re-mix) *Blanco Y Negro NEG 99CD1*	36	2
1 Mar 97		BEFORE TODAY *Virgin VSCDT 1624*	25	2
3 Oct 98		THE FUTURE OF THE FUTURE (STAY GOLD) *Deconstruction 74321616252* [1]	31	2
25 Sep 99		FIVE FATHOMS *Virgin VSCDT 1742*	27	3
4 Mar 00		TEMPERAMENTAL *Virgin VSCDT 1761*	72	1
27 Jan 01		TRACEY IN MY ROOM *VC Recordings VCRD 78* [2]	34	2

[1] Deep Dish with Everything but the Girl [2] EBTG Vs Soul Vision

Tracks on Covers (EP): Love Is Strange / Tougher Than the Rest / Time After Time / Alison. Tracks on The Only Living Boy in New York (EP): The Only Living Boy in New York / Birds / Gabriel / Horses in the Room. Tracks on I Didn't Know I Was Looking For Love (EP): I Didn't Know I Was Looking For Love / My Head Is My Only House Unless It Rains / Political Science / A Piece of My Mind. Tracks on Rollercoaster (EP): Rollercoaster / Straight Back to You / Lights of Te Touan / I Didn't Know I Was Looking For Love (demo)

E'VOKE *UK, female vocal duo (6 WEEKS)* pos/wks

Date		Title / Label	pos	wks
25 Nov 95		RUNAWAY *Ffrreedom TABCD 238*	30	3
24 Aug 96		ARMS OF LOREN *Manifesto FESCD 10*	25	3

EVOLUTION *UK, male / female vocal / instrumental group (12 WEEKS)* pos/wks

Date		Title / Label	pos	wks
20 Mar 93		LOVE THING *Deconstruction 74321134272*	32	2
3 Jul 93		EVERYBODY DANCE *Deconstruction 74321152012*	19	5
8 Jan 94		EVOLUTIONDANCE PART ONE (EP) *Deconstruction 74321171912*	52	3
4 Nov 95		LOOK UP TO THE LIGHT *Deconstruction 74321318042*	55	1
19 Oct 96		YOUR LOVE IS CALLING *Deconstruction 74321422872*	60	1

Tracks on Evolutiondance Part One (EP): Escape 2 Alcatraz (remix) / Everybody / Don't Stop the Rain

EX PISTOLS *UK, male vocal / instrumental group (2 WEEKS)* pos/wks

Date		Title / Label	pos	wks
2 Feb 85		LAND OF HOPE AND GLORY *Virginia PISTOL 76*	69	2

EXCITERS *US, male / female vocal group (7 WEEKS)* pos/wks

Date		Title / Label	pos	wks
21 Feb 63		TELL HIM *United Artists UP 1011*	46	1
4 Oct 75		REACHING FOR THE BEST *20th Century BTC 1005*	31	6

EXETER BRAMDEAN BOYS' CHOIR *UK, male choir (3 WEEKS)* pos/wks

Date		Title / Label	pos	wks
18 Dec 93		REMEMBERING CHRISTMAS *Golden Sounds DSCC 1*	46	3

EXILE *US, male vocal / instrumental group (18 WEEKS)* pos/wks

Date		Title / Label	pos	wks
19 Aug 78	●	KISS YOU ALL OVER *RAK 279* ▲	6	12
12 May 79		HOW COULD THIS GO WRONG *RAK 293*	67	2
12 Sep 81		HEART AND SOUL *RAK 333*	54	4

EXOTERIX *UK, male producer – Duncan Millar (2 WEEKS)* pos/wks

Date		Title / Label	pos	wks
24 Apr 93		VOID *Positiva CDTIV 1*	58	1
5 Feb 94		SATISFY MY LOVE *Union UCRCD 26*	62	1

EXOTICA featuring Itsy FOSTER
UK / Italy, male / female vocal / instrumental group (1 WEEK) pos/wks

Date		Title / Label	pos	wks
16 Sep 95		THE SUMMER IS MAGIC *Polydor 5798392*	68	1

EXPLOITED *UK, male vocal / instrumental group (13 WEEKS)* pos/wks

Date		Title / Label	pos	wks
18 Apr 81		DOGS OF WAR *Secret SHH 110*	63	4
17 Oct 81		DEAD CITIES *Secret SHH 120*	31	5
5 Dec 81		DON'T LET 'EM GRIND YOU DOWN *Superville EXP 1003* [1]	70	1
8 May 82		ATTACK *Secret SHH 130*	50	3

[1] Exploited and Anti-Pasti

EXPOSÉ *US, female vocal group (1 WEEK)* pos/wks

28 Aug 93 **I'LL NEVER GET OVER YOU (GETTING OVER ME)** *Arista 74321158962* 75 1

EXPRESS OF SOUND
Italy, male instrumental / production group (1 WEEK) pos/wks

2 Nov 96 **REAL VIBRATION (WANT LOVE)** *Positiva CDTIV 66* 45 1

EXPRESSOS *UK, male / female vocal / instrumental group (5 WEEKS)* pos/wks

21 Jun 80 **HEY GIRL** *WEA K 18246* 60 3
14 Mar 81 **TANGO IN MONO** *WEA K 18431* 70 2

EXTENSIVE – *See CHOPS-EMC + EXTENSIVE*

EXTREME *US, male vocal / instrumental group (46 WEEKS)* pos/wks

8 Jun 91 **GET THE FUNK OUT** *A & M AM 737* 19 7
27 Jul 91 ● **MORE THAN WORDS** *A & M AM 792* ▲ 2 11
12 Oct 91 **DECADENCE DANCE** *A & M AM 773* 36 3
23 Nov 91 **HOLE HEARTED** *A & M AM 839* 12 7
2 May 92 **SONG FOR LOVE** *A & M AM 698* 12 6
5 Sep 92 **REST IN PEACE** *A & M AM 0055* 13 5
14 Nov 92 **STOP THE WORLD** *A & M AM 0096* 22 2
6 Feb 93 **TRAGIC COMIC** *A & M AMCD 0156* 15 4
11 Mar 95 **HIP TODAY** *A & M 5809932* 44 1

EYC *US, male vocal group (36 WEEKS)* pos/wks

11 Dec 93 **FEELIN' ALRIGHT** *MCA MCSTD 1952* 16 8
5 Mar 94 **THE WAY YOU WORK IT** *MCA MCSTD 1963* 14 7
14 May 94 **NUMBER ONE** *MCA MCSTD 1976* 27 5
30 Jul 94 **BLACK BOOK** *MCA MCSTD 1987* 13 6
10 Dec 94 **ONE MORE CHANCE** *MCA MCSTD 2025* 25 6
23 Sep 95 **OOH-AH-AA (I FEEL IT)** *Gasoline Alley MCSTD 2096* 33 2
2 Dec 95 **IN THE BEGINNING** *Gasoline Alley MCSTD 2107* 41 2

EYE TO EYE featuring Taka BOOM
UK, male producer and US, female vocalist (2 WEEKS) pos/wks

9 Jun 01 **JUST CAN'T GET ENOUGH (NO NO NO NO)** *Xtravaganza XTRAV 25CD* 36 2

EYES CREAM *Italy, male producer – Agostino Carollo (1 WEEK)* pos/wks

16 Oct 99 **FLY AWAY (BYE BYE)** *Accolade CDAC 001* 53 1

F

Adam F *UK, male producer – Adam Fenton (13 WEEKS)* pos/wks

27 Sep 97 **CIRCLES** *Positiva CDFJ 002* 20 3
7 Mar 98 **MUSIC IN MY MIND** *Positiva CDFJ 003* 27 3
15 Sep 01 **SMASH SUMTHIN'** *Def Jam 5886932* [1] 11 7
1 Dec 01 **STAND CLEAR** *Chrysalis CDEM 597* [2] 43 1

[1] Redman featuring Adam F [2] Adam F featuring M.O.P.

F45 – *See DE FUNK featuring F45*

F L B – *See FAT LARRY'S BAND*

F.L.O. – *See Rahni HARRIS and F.L.O.*

FAB *UK, male producers (11 WEEKS)* pos/wks

7 Jul 90 ● **THUNDERBIRDS ARE GO** *Brothers Organisation FAB 1* [1] 5 8
20 Oct 90 **THE PRISONER** *Brothers Organisation FAB 6* [2] 56 2
1 Dec 90 **THE STINGRAY MEGAMIX** *Brothers Organisation FAB 2* [3] 66 1

[1] FAB featuring MC Parker [2] FAB featuring MC Number 6 [3] FAB featuring Aqua Marina

FAB! *Ireland, female vocal group (1 WEEK)* pos/wks

1 Aug 98 **TURN AROUND** *Break Records BRCX 107* 59 1

Shelley FABARES *US, female vocalist (4 WEEKS)* pos/wks

26 Apr 62 **JOHNNY ANGEL** *Pye International 7N 25132* ▲ 41 4

FABIAN *US, male vocalist (1 WEEK)* pos/wks

10 Mar 60 **HOUND DOG MAN** *HMV POP 695* 46 1

Lara FABIAN *Belgium, female vocalist (1 WEEK)* pos/wks

28 Oct 00 **I WILL LOVE AGAIN** *Columbia 6694062* 63 1

FABULOUS BAKER BOYS *UK, male DJ / production trio (2 WEEKS)* pos/wks

15 Nov 97 **OH BOY** *Multiply CDMULTY 28* 34 2

FACE – *See David MORALES*

FACES *UK, male vocal / instrumental group (46 WEEKS)* pos/wks

18 Dec 71 ● **STAY WITH ME** *Warner Bros. K 16136* 6 14
17 Feb 73 ● **CINDY INCIDENTALLY** *Warner Bros. K 16247* 2 9
8 Dec 73 ● **POOL HALL RICHARD / I WISH IT WOULD RAIN** *Warner Bros. K 16341* 8 11
7 Dec 74 **YOU CAN MAKE ME DANCE SING OR ANYTHING (EVEN TAKE THE DOG FOR A WALK, MEND A FUSE, FOLD AWAY THE IRONING BOARD, OR ANY OTHER DOMESTIC SHORT COMINGS)** *Warner Bros. K 16494* [1] 12 9
4 Jun 77 **THE FACES (EP)** *Riva 8* 41 3

[1] Faces / Rod Stewart

Tracks on The Faces (EP): Memphis / You Can Make Me Dance Sing or Anything / Stay With Me / Cindy Incidentally

See also Rod STEWART

FACTORY OF UNLIMITED RHYTHM
Jamaica, male / female vocal / instrumental group (1 WEEK) pos/wks

1 Jun 96 **THE SWEETEST SURRENDER** *Kuff KUFFD 6* 59 1

Donald FAGEN *US, male vocalist (2 WEEKS)* pos/wks

3 Jul 93 **TOMORROW'S GIRLS** *Reprise W 0180CDX* 46 2

See also STEELY DAN

Joe FAGIN *UK, male vocalist (20 WEEKS)* pos/wks

7 Jan 84 ● **THAT'S LIVIN' ALRIGHT** *Towerbell TOW 46* 3 11
5 Apr 86 **BACK WITH THE BOYS AGAIN / GET IT RIGHT** *Towerbell TOW 84* 53 9

Yvonne FAIR *US, female vocalist (11 WEEKS)* pos/wks

24 Jan 76 ● **IT SHOULD HAVE BEEN ME** *Tamla Motown TMG 1013* 5 11

FAIR WEATHER *UK, male vocal / instrumental group (12 WEEKS)* pos/wks

18 Jul 70 ● **NATURAL SINNER** *RCA 1977* 6 12

Fair Weather is led by Andy Fairweather-Low

See also Andy FAIRWEATHER-LOW; AMEN CORNER

FAIRGROUND ATTRACTION *UK, female / male vocal / instrumental group – lead vocal Eddi Reader (27 WEEKS)* pos/wks

16 Apr 88 ★ **PERFECT** *RCA PB 41845* 1 13
30 Jul 88 ● **FIND MY LOVE** *RCA PB 42079* 7 10
19 Nov 88 **A SMILE IN A WHISPER** *RCA PB 42249* 75 1
28 Jan 89 **CLARE** *RCA PB 42607* 49 3

See also Eddi READER

FAIRPORT CONVENTION

UK, male / female vocal / instrumental group (9 WEEKS) pos/wks

			pos	wks
23 Jul 69		SI TU DOIS PARTIR *Island WIP 6064*	21	8
27 Sep 69		SI TU DOIS PARTIR (re-entry) *Island WIP 6064*	49	1

Andy FAIRWEATHER-LOW *UK, male vocalist (18 WEEKS)* pos/wks

			pos	wks
21 Sep 74	●	REGGAE TUNE *A & M AMS 7129*	10	8
6 Dec 75	●	WIDE EYED AND LEGLESS *A & M AMS 7202*	6	10

See also *AMEN CORNER; FAIR WEATHER*

Adam FAITH (47 Top 500) *Teen-idol vocalist turned top actor then financial wizard, b. Terence Nelhams, 23 Jun 1940, London. One of the most charted acts of the 1960s; became the first UK artist to lodge initial seven hits in the Top 5. Also one of the first UK acts to record original songs regularly (251 WEEKS)* pos/wks

			pos	wks
20 Nov 59	★	WHAT DO YOU WANT? *Parlophone R 4591*	1	19
22 Jan 60	★	POOR ME *Parlophone R 4623*	1	17
14 Apr 60	●	SOMEONE ELSE'S BABY *Parlophone R 4643*	2	13
30 Jun 60	●	WHEN JOHNNY COMES MARCHING HOME / MADE YOU *Parlophone R 4665*	5	13
15 Sep 60	●	HOW ABOUT THAT! *Parlophone R 4689*	4	14
17 Nov 60	●	LONELY PUP (IN A CHRISTMAS SHOP) *Parlophone R 4708*	4	11
9 Feb 61	●	WHO AM I! / THIS IS IT! *Parlophone R 4735*	5	14
27 Apr 61		EASY GOING ME *Parlophone R 4766*	12	10
20 Jul 61		DON'T YOU KNOW IT *Parlophone R 4807*	12	10
26 Oct 61	●	THE TIME HAS COME *Parlophone R 4837*	4	14
18 Jan 62		LONESOME *Parlophone R 4864*	12	9
3 May 62	●	AS YOU LIKE IT *Parlophone R 4896*	5	15
30 Aug 62	●	DON'T THAT BEAT ALL *Parlophone R 4930* [1]	8	11
13 Dec 62		BABY TAKE A BOW *Parlophone R 4964*	22	6
31 Jan 63		WHAT NOW *Parlophone R 4990* [1]	31	5
11 Jul 63		WALKIN' TALL *Parlophone R 5039*	23	6
19 Sep 63	●	THE FIRST TIME *Parlophone R 5061* [2]	5	13
12 Dec 63		WE ARE IN LOVE *Parlophone R 5091* [2]	11	12
12 Mar 64		IF HE TELLS YOU *Parlophone R 5109* [2]	25	9
28 May 64		I LOVE BEING IN LOVE WITH YOU *Parlophone R 5138* [2]	33	6
26 Nov 64		A MESSAGE TO MARTHA (KENTUCKY BLUEBIRD) *Parlophone R 5201*	12	11
11 Feb 65		STOP FEELING SORRY FOR YOURSELF *Parlophone R 5235*	23	6
17 Jun 65		SOMEONE'S TAKEN MARIA AWAY *Parlophone R 5289*	34	5
20 Oct 66		CHERYL'S GOIN' HOME *Parlophone R 5516*	46	2

[1] Adam Faith with Johnny Keating and his Orchestra [2] Adam Faith and the Roulettes

Horace FAITH *Jamaica, male vocalist – Horace Smith (10 WEEKS)* pos/wks

			pos	wks
12 Sep 70		BLACK PEARL *Trojan TR 7790*	13	10

Percy FAITH *Canada, orchestra (30 WEEKS)* pos/wks

			pos	wks
4 Mar 60	●	THE THEME FROM 'A SUMMER PLACE' *Philips PB 989* ▲	2	30

FAITH BROTHERS *UK, male vocal / instrumental group (6 WEEKS)* pos/wks

			pos	wks
13 Apr 85		THE COUNTRY OF THE BLIND *Siren SIREN 2*	63	3
6 Jul 85		A STRANGER ON HOME GROUND *Siren SIREN 4*	69	3

FAITH, HOPE AND CHARITY *US, male / female vocal group (4 WEEKS)* pos/wks

			pos	wks
31 Jan 76		JUST ONE LOOK *RCA 2632*	38	4

FAITH, HOPE AND CHARITY *UK, female vocal group (3 WEEKS)* pos/wks

			pos	wks
23 Jun 90		BATTLE OF THE SEXES *WEA YZ 480*	53	3

FAITH NO MORE *US, male vocal / instrumental group (65 WEEKS)* pos/wks

			pos	wks
6 Feb 88		WE CARE A LOT *Slash LASH 17*	53	3
10 Feb 90		EPIC *Slash LASH 21*	37	4
14 Apr 90		FROM OUT OF NOWHERE *Slash LASH 24*	23	6
14 Jul 90		FALLING TO PIECES *Slash LASH 25*	41	3
8 Sep 90		EPIC (re-issue) *Slash LASH 26*	25	5
6 Jun 92	●	MIDLIFE CRISIS *Slash LASH 37*	10	5
15 Aug 92		A SMALL VICTORY *Slash LASH 39*	29	5
12 Sep 92		A SMALL VICTORY (re-mix) *Slash LASHX 40*	55	1
21 Nov 92		EVERYTHING'S RUINED *Slash LASH 43*	28	3
16 Jan 93	●	I'M EASY / BE AGGRESSIVE *Slash LACDP 44*	3	7
13 Mar 93		I'M EASY / BE AGGRESSIVE (re-entry) *Slash LACDP 44*	75	1
6 Nov 93		ANOTHER BODY MURDERED *Epic 6597942* [1]	26	3
11 Mar 95		DIGGING THE GRAVE *Slash LASCD 51*	16	4
27 May 95		RICOCHET *Slash LASCD 53*	27	2
29 Jul 95		EVIDENCE *Slash LASCD 54*	32	3
31 May 97		ASHES TO ASHES *Slash LASCD 61*	15	3
16 Aug 97		LAST CUP OF SORROW *Slash LASCD 62*	51	1
13 Dec 97		THIS TOWN AIN'T BIG ENOUGH FOR BOTH OF US *Roadrunner RR 22513* [2]	40	2
17 Jan 98		ASHES TO ASHES (re-issue) *Slash LACDP 63*	29	3
7 Nov 98		I STARTED A JOKE *Slash LASCD 65*	49	1

[1] Faith No More and Boo-Yaa T.R.I.B.E. [2] Sparks vs Faith No More

Marianne FAITHFULL *UK, female vocalist (59 WEEKS)* pos/wks

			pos	wks
13 Aug 64	●	AS TEARS GO BY *Decca F 11923*	9	13
18 Feb 65	●	COME AND STAY WITH ME *Decca F 12075*	4	13
6 May 65	●	THIS LITTLE BIRD *Decca F 12162*	6	11
22 Jul 65	●	SUMMER NIGHTS *Decca F 12193*	10	10
4 Nov 65		YESTERDAY *Decca F 12268*	36	4
9 Mar 67		IS THIS WHAT I GET FOR LOVING YOU? *Decca F 22524*	43	2
24 Nov 79		THE BALLAD OF LUCY JORDAN *Island WIP 6491*	48	6

FAITHLESS *UK, male / female vocal / instrumental group (64 WEEKS)* pos/wks

			pos	wks
5 Aug 95		SALVA MEA (SAVE ME) *Cheeky CHEKCD 008*	30	2
9 Dec 95		INSOMNIA *Cheeky CHEKCD 010*	27	2
23 Mar 96		DON'T LEAVE *Cheeky CHEKCD 012*	34	2
26 Oct 96	●	INSOMNIA (re-issue) *Cheeky CHEKCD 017*	3	13
21 Dec 96	●	SALVA MEA (re-mix) *Cheeky CHEKCD 018*	9	7
26 Apr 97	●	REVERENCE *Cheeky CHEKCD 019*	10	3
15 Nov 97		DON'T LEAVE (re-mix) *Cheeky CHEKXCD 024*	21	2
5 Sep 98	●	GOD IS A DJ *Cheeky CHEKCD 028*	6	8
5 Dec 98		TAKE THE LONG WAY HOME *Cheeky CHEKCD 031*	15	6
1 May 99		BRING MY FAMILY BACK *Cheeky CHEKCD 035*	14	5
16 Jun 01	●	WE COME 1 *Cheeky 74321850842*	3	9
29 Sep 01		MUHAMMAD ALI *Cheeky 74321886442*	29	2
27 Oct 01		MUHAMMAD ALI (re-entry) *Cheeky 74321886442*	52	2
29 Dec 01		TARANTULA *Cheeky 7431903592*	29	1+

FALCO *Austria, male vocalist, – Johann Holzel (26 WEEKS)* pos/wks

			pos	wks
22 Mar 86	★	ROCK ME AMADEUS *A & M AM 278* ▲	1	15
31 May 86	●	VIENNA CALLING *A & M AM 318*	10	8
2 Aug 86		JEANNY *A & M AM 333*	68	1
27 Sep 86		THE SOUND OF MUSIK *WEA U 8591*	61	2

Christian FALK featuring DEMETREUS

Sweden, male producer and Sweden, male vocalist (3 WEEKS) pos/wks

			pos	wks
26 Aug 00		MAKE IT RIGHT *London LONCD 452*	22	3

Fred FALKE – See *Alan BRAXE and Fred FALKE*

FALL *UK, vocal / instrumental group – leader Mark E Smith (25 WEEKS)* pos/wks

			pos	wks
13 Sep 86		MR PHARMACIST *Beggars Banquet BEG 168*	75	1
20 Dec 86		HEY! LUCIANI *Beggars Banquet BEG 176*	59	1
9 May 87		THERE'S A GHOST IN MY HOUSE *Beggars Banquet BEG 187*	30	4
31 Oct 87		HIT THE NORTH *Beggars Banquet BEG 200*	57	5
30 Jan 88		VICTORIA *Beggars Banquet BEG 206*	35	3
26 Nov 88		BIG NEW PRINZ / JERUSALEM (DOUBLE SINGLE) *Beggars Banquet FALL 2/3*	59	2
27 Jan 90		TELEPHONE THING *Cog Sinister SIN 4*	58	1
8 Sep 90		WHITE LIGHTNING *Cog Sinister SIN 6*	56	2
14 Mar 92		FREE RANGE *Cog Sinister SINS 8*	40	1
17 Apr 93		WHY ARE PEOPLE GRUDGEFUL *Permanent CDSPERM 9*	43	1
25 Dec 93		BEHIND THE COUNTER *Permanent CDSPERM 13*	75	1
30 Apr 94		15 WAYS *Permanent CDSPERM 14*	65	1
17 Feb 96		THE CHISELERS *Jet JETSCD 500*	60	1

UK No.1 ★ UK Top 10 ● Still on chart + UK million seller ◆ UK entry at No.1 ■ US No.1 ▲

21 Feb 98		**MASQUERADE** *Artful CDARTFUL 1*	69	1

Tracks on 'Big New Prinz / Jerusalem' double single: Big New Prinz / Wrong Place Right Time Number Two / Jerusalem / Acid Priest 2088

See also Mark E SMITH

Harold FALTERMEYER
Germany, male instrumentalist – keyboards (23 WEEKS) pos/wks

			pos	wks
23 Mar 85		**AXEL F** *MCA MCA 949*	62	4
1 Jun 85	●	**AXEL F (re-entry)** *MCA MCA 949*	2	18
24 Aug 85		**FLETCH THEME** *MCA MCA 991*	74	1

Agnetha FALTSKOG *Sweden, female vocalist (12 WEEKS)* pos/wks

			pos	wks
28 May 83		**THE HEAT IS ON** *Epic A 3436*	35	6
13 Aug 83		**WRAP YOUR ARMS AROUND ME** *Epic A 3622*	44	5
22 Oct 83		**CAN'T SHAKE LOOSE** *Epic A 3812*	63	1

See also AB.BA

Georgie FAME (241 Top 500)
Critically acclaimed R&B / jazz vocalist / keyboard player, b. Clive Powell, 26 Jun 1943, Lancashire, UK. The one-time rock 'n' roll tour musician, who had a string of Sixties hits, is still a popular performer, often working with contemporaries such as Van Morrison and Bill Wyman (115 WEEKS) pos/wks

			pos	wks
17 Dec 64	★	**YEH, YEH** *Columbia DB 7428* [1]	1	12
4 Mar 65		**IN THE MEANTIME** *Columbia DB 7494* [1]	22	8
29 Jul 65		**LIKE WE USED TO BE** *Columbia DB 7633* [1]	33	7
28 Oct 65		**SOMETHING** *Columbia DB 7727* [1]	23	7
23 Jun 66	★	**GET AWAY** *Columbia DB 7946* [1]	1	11
22 Sep 66		**SUNNY** *Columbia DB 8015*	13	8
22 Dec 66		**SITTING IN THE PARK** *Columbia DB 8096* [1]	12	10
23 Mar 67		**BECAUSE I LOVE YOU** *CBS 202587*	15	8
13 Sep 67		**TRY MY WORLD** *CBS 2945*	37	5
13 Dec 67	★	**THE BALLAD OF BONNIE AND CLYDE** *CBS 3124*	1	13
9 Jul 69		**PEACEFUL** *CBS 4295*	16	9
13 Dec 69		**SEVENTH SON** *CBS 4659*	25	7
10 Apr 71		**ROSETTA** *CBS 7108* [2]	11	10

[1] Georgie Fame and the Blue Flames [2] Fame and Price Together

FAMILY *UK, male vocal / instrumental group (44 WEEKS)* pos/wks

			pos	wks
1 Nov 69		**NO MULE'S FOOL** *Reprise RS 27001*	29	7
22 Aug 70		**STRANGE BAND** *Reprise RS 27009*	11	12
17 Jul 71	●	**IN MY OWN TIME** *Reprise K 14090*	4	13
23 Sep 72		**BURLESQUE** *Reprise K 14196*	13	12

FAMILY CAT *UK, male vocal / instrumental group (4 WEEKS)* pos/wks

			pos	wks
28 Aug 93		**AIRPLANE GARDENS / ATMOSPHERIC ROAD** *Dedicated FCUK 003CD*	69	1
21 May 94		**WONDERFUL EXCUSE** *Dedicated 74321208432*	48	1
30 Jul 94		**GOLDENBOOK** *Dedicated 74321220072*	42	2

FAMILY COOKIN' – *See LIMMIE and the FAMILY COOKIN'*

FAMILY DOGG *UK, male / female vocal group (14 WEEKS)* pos/wks

			pos	wks
28 May 69	●	**A WAY OF LIFE** *Bell 1055*	6	14

FAMILY FOUNDATION
UK, male / female vocal / instrumental group (4 WEEKS) pos/wks

			pos	wks
13 Jun 92		**XPRESS YOURSELF** *380 PEW 1*	42	4

FAMILY STAND
US, male / female vocal / instrumental group (13 WEEKS) pos/wks

			pos	wks
31 Mar 90	●	**GHETTO HEAVEN** *East West A 7997*	10	11
17 Jan 98		**GHETTO HEAVEN (re-mix)** *Perfecto PERF 156CD1*	30	2

FAMILY STONE – *See SLY and the FAMILY STONE*

FAMOUS FLAMES – *See James BROWN*

FANTASTIC FOUR *US, male vocal group (4 WEEKS)* pos/wks

			pos	wks
24 Feb 79		**B.Y.O.F. (BRING YOUR OWN FUNK)** *Atlantic LV 14*	62	4

FANTASTICS *US, male vocal group (12 WEEKS)* pos/wks

			pos	wks
27 Mar 71	●	**SOMETHING OLD, SOMETHING NEW** *Bell 1141*	9	12

FANTASY UFO *UK, male instrumental group (6 WEEKS)* pos/wks

			pos	wks
29 Sep 90		**FANTASY** *XL XLT 15*	56	3
10 Aug 91		**MIND BODY SOUL** *Strictly Underground YZ 591* [1]	50	3

[1] Fantasy UFO featuring Jay Groove

FAR CORPORATION *UK / US / Germany / Switzerland, male vocal / instrumental group (11 WEEKS)* pos/wks

			pos	wks
26 Oct 85	●	**STAIRWAY TO HEAVEN** *Arista ARIST 639*	8	11

Don FARDON *UK, male vocalist – Donald Maughn (22 WEEKS)* pos/wks

			pos	wks
18 Apr 70		**BELFAST BOY** *Young Blood YB 1010*	32	5
10 Oct 70	●	**INDIAN RESERVATION** *Young Blood YB 1015*	3	17

FARGETTA *Italy / UK, male producer (3 WEEKS)* pos/wks

			pos	wks
23 Jan 93		**MUSIC** *Synthetic CDR 6334* [1]	34	2
10 Aug 96		**THE MUSIC IS MOVING** *Arista 74321381572*	74	1

[1] Fargetta and Anne-Marie Smith

Chris FARLOWE *UK, male vocalist – John Deighton (36 WEEKS)* pos/wks

			pos	wks
27 Jan 66		**THINK** *Immediate IM 023*	49	1
10 Feb 66		**THINK (re-entry)** *Immediate IM 023*	37	2
23 Jun 66	★	**OUT OF TIME** *Immediate IM 035*	1	13
27 Oct 66		**RIDE ON BABY** *Immediate IM 038*	31	7
16 Feb 67		**MY WAY OF GIVING IN** *Immediate IM 041*	48	1
29 Jun 67		**MOANIN'** *Immediate IM 056*	46	2
13 Dec 67		**HANDBAGS AND GLADRAGS** *Immediate IM 065*	33	6
27 Sep 75		**OUT OF TIME (re-issue)** *Immediate IMS 101*	44	4

FARM *UK, male vocal / instrumental group (54 WEEKS)* pos/wks

			pos	wks
5 May 90		**STEPPING STONE / FAMILY OF MAN** *Produce MILK 101*	58	4
1 Sep 90	●	**GROOVY TRAIN** *Produce MILK 102*	6	10
8 Dec 90	●	**ALL TOGETHER NOW** *Produce MILK 103*	4	12
13 Apr 91		**SINFUL! (SCARY JIGGIN' WITH DR LOVE)** *Siren SRN 138* [1]	28	5
4 May 91		**DON'T LET ME DOWN** *Produce MILK 104*	36	3
24 Aug 91		**MIND** *Produce MILK 105*	31	4
14 Dec 91		**LOVE SEE NO COLOUR** *Produce MILK 106*	58	4
4 Jul 92		**RISING SUN** *End Product 6581737*	48	3
17 Oct 92		**DON'T YOU WANT ME** *End Product 6584687*	18	5
2 Jan 93		**LOVE SEE NO COLOUR (re-mix)** *End Product 6588682*	35	4

[1] Pete Wylie with the Farm

FARMERS BOYS *UK, male vocal / instrumental group (17 WEEKS)* pos/wks

			pos	wks
9 Apr 83		**MUCK IT OUT** *EMI 5380*	48	6
30 Jul 83		**FOR YOU** *EMI 5401*	66	3
4 Aug 84		**IN THE COUNTRY** *EMI FAB 2*	44	5
3 Nov 84		**PHEW WOW** *EMI FAB 3*	59	3

John FARNHAM *Australia, male vocalist (17 WEEKS)* pos/wks

			pos	wks
25 Apr 87	●	**YOU'RE THE VOICE** *Wheatley PB 41093*	6	17

Joanne FARRELL *US, female vocalist (2 WEEKS)* pos/wks

			pos	wks
24 Jun 95		**ALL I WANNA DO** *Big Beat A 8194CD*	40	2

Joe FARRELL *US, male instrumentalist – saxophone (4 WEEKS)* pos/wks

			pos	wks
16 Dec 78		**NIGHT DANCING** *Warner Bros. LV 2*	57	4

Dionne FARRIS *US, female vocalist (6 WEEKS)* pos/wks

			pos	wks
18 Mar 95		**I KNOW** *Columbia 6613542*	47	2

27 May 95	I KNOW (re-entry) *Columbia 6613542*	41	3
7 Jun 97	HOPELESS *Columbia 6645165*	42	1

Gene FARROW and GF BAND

UK, male vocal / instrumental group (8 WEEKS) pos/wks

1 Apr 78	MOVE YOUR BODY *Magnet MAG 109*	33	5
13 May 78	MOVE YOUR BODY (re-entry) *Magnet MAG 109*	67	1
5 Aug 78	DON'T STOP NOW *Magnet MAG 125*	71	1
19 Aug 78	DON'T STOP NOW (re-entry) *Magnet MAG 125*	74	1

FASCINATIONS *US, female vocal group (6 WEEKS)* pos/wks

3 Jul 71	GIRLS ARE OUT TO GET YOU *Mojo 2092 004*	32	6

FASHION *UK, male vocal / instrumental group (12 WEEKS)* pos/wks

3 Apr 82	STREETPLAYER (MECHANIK) *Arista ARIST 456*	46	5
21 Aug 82	LOVE SHADOW *Arista ARIST 483*	51	5
18 Feb 84	EYE TALK *Epic 4106*	69	2

Susan FASSBENDER *UK, female vocalist (8 WEEKS)* pos/wks

17 Jan 81	TWILIGHT CAFE *CBS 9468*	21	8

FASTBALL *US, male vocal / instrumental trio (5 WEEKS)* pos/wks

3 Oct 98	THE WAY *Polydor 5699472*	21	5

FASTWAY *UK, male vocal / instrumental group (1 WEEK)* pos/wks

2 Apr 83	EASY LIVIN' *CBS A 3196*	74	1

FAT BOYS *US, male rap group (29 WEEKS)* pos/wks

4 May 85	JAIL HOUSE RAP *Sutra U 9123*	63	2
22 Aug 87 ●	WIPEOUT *Urban URB 5* [1]	2	12
18 Jun 88 ●	THE TWIST (YO, TWIST) *Urban URB 20* [2]	2	11
5 Nov 88	LOUIE LOUIE *Urban URB 26*	46	4

[1] Fat Boys and the Beach Boys [2] Fat Boys and Chubby Checker

FAT JOE – *See Jennifer LOPEZ*

FAT LADY SINGS *Ireland, male vocal / instrumental group (2 WEEKS)* pos/wks

17 Jul 93	DRUNKARD LOGIC *East West YZ 756CD*	56	2

FAT LARRY'S BAND *US, male vocal / instrumental group (26 WEEKS)* pos/wks

2 Jul 77	CENTER CITY *Atlantic K 10951*	31	5
10 Mar 79	BOOGIE TOWN *Fantasy FTC 168* [1]	46	4
18 Aug 79	LOOKING FOR LOVE TONIGHT *Fantasy FTC 179*	46	6
18 Sep 82 ●	ZOOM *Virgin VS 546*	2	11

[1] F.L.B.

FAT LES *UK, male / female vocal group (22 WEEKS)* pos/wks

20 Jun 98 ●	VINDALOO *Telstar CDSTAS 2982*	2	12
19 Dec 98	NAUGHTY CHRISTMAS (GOBLIN IN THE OFFICE) *Turtleneck NECKCD 001*	21	5
17 Jun 00 ●	JERUSALEM *Parlophone CDR 6540* [1]	10	3
5 Aug 00	JERUSALEM (re-entry) *Parlophone CDR 6540* [1]	55	2

[1] Fat Les 2000

FATBACK BAND *US, male vocal / instrumental group (67 WEEKS)* pos/wks

6 Sep 75	YUM YUM (GIMME SOME) *Polydor 2066 590*	40	6
6 Dec 75	(ARE YOU READY) DO THE BUS STOP *Polydor 2066 637*	18	10
21 Feb 76 ●	(DO THE) SPANISH HUSTLE *Polydor 2066 656*	10	7
29 May 76	PARTY TIME *Polydor 2066 682*	41	4
14 Aug 76	NIGHT FEVER *Spring 2066 706*	38	4
12 Mar 77	DOUBLE DUTCH *Spring 2066 777*	31	4
9 Aug 80	BACKSTROKIN' *Spring POSP 149* [1]	41	9
23 Jun 84	I FOUND LOVIN' *Master Mix CHE 8401*	49	4
4 May 85	GIRLS ON MY MIND *Atlantic/Cotillion FBACK 1* [1]	69	2
6 Sep 86	I FOUND LOVIN' (re-issue) *Important TAN 10*	55	5
5 Sep 87 ●	I FOUND LOVIN' (re-entry) *Master Mix CHE 8401*	7	12

[1] Fatback

FATBOY SLIM (485 Top 500) *Multi-aliased, superstar DJ / producer Norman Cook (b. Quentin Cook, 31 Jul 1963, Bromley, Kent, UK) finally achieved a solo No.1 in this guise, having already topped the chart with Housemartins and Beats International. Married TV / radio presenter Zoë Ball in 1999 (72 WEEKS)* pos/wks

3 May 97	GOING OUT OF MY HEAD *Skint SKINT 19CD*	57	1
1 Nov 97	EVERYBODY NEEDS A 303 *Skint SKINT 31CD*	34	2
20 Jun 98 ●	THE ROCKAFELLER SKANK *Skint SKINT 35CD*	6	10
17 Oct 98 ●	GANGSTER TRIPPIN' *Skint SKINT 39CD*	3	8
16 Jan 99 ★	PRAISE YOU *Skint SKINT 42CD* ■	1	12
1 May 99	BADDER BADDER SCHWING *Eye Q EYEUK 040CD* [1]	34	2
1 May 99 ●	RIGHT HERE RIGHT NOW *Skint SKINT 46CD*	2	10
28 Oct 00 ●	SUNSET (BIRD OF PREY) *Skint SKINT 58CD*	9	7
30 Dec 00	SUNSET (BIRD OF PREY) (re-entry) *Skint SKINT 58CD*	54	6
20 Jan 01	DEMONS *Skint SKINT 60CD* [2]	16	5
5 May 01 ●	STAR 69 *Skint SKINT 64CD*	10	7
15 Sep 01	YA MAMA / SONG FOR SHELTER *Skint SKINT 71CD*	30	2

[1] Freddy Fresh featuring Fatboy Slim [2] Fatboy Slim featuring Macy Gray

See also Norman COOK; BEATS INTERNATIONAL; MIGHTY DUB KATZ; HOUSEMARTINS; FREAKPOWER; PIZZAMAN; URBAN ALL STARS

FATHER ABRAHAM – *See SMURFS*

FATHER ABRAPHART and the SMURPS – *See Jonathan KING*

FATIMA MANSIONS

Ireland, male vocal / instrumental group (11 WEEKS) pos/wks

23 May 92	EVIL MAN *Radioactive SKX 56*	59	1
1 Aug 92	1000 % *Radioactive SKX 59*	61	3
19 Sep 92 ●	(EVERYTHING I DO) I DO IT FOR YOU *Columbia 6583827*	7	6
6 Aug 94	THE LOYALISER *Kitchenware SKCD 67*	58	1

'(Everything I Do) I Do It For You' was listed with 'Theme From M.A.S.H. (Suicide Is Painless)' by Manic Street Preachers

FBI – *See REDHEAD KINGPIN and the FBI*

FEAR FACTORY *US, male vocal / instrumental group (1 WEEK)* pos/wks

9 Oct 99	CARS *Roadrunner RR 21893*	57	1

Phil FEARON *UK, male vocalist (63 WEEKS)* pos/wks

23 Apr 83 ●	DANCING TIGHT *Ensign ENY 501* [1]	4	11
30 Jul 83	WAIT UNTIL TONIGHT (MY LOVE) *Ensign ENY 503* [1]	20	8
22 Oct 83	FANTASY REAL *Ensign ENY 507* [2]	41	6
10 Mar 84 ●	WHAT DO I DO *Ensign ENY 510* [2]	5	10
14 Jul 84 ●	EVERYBODY'S LAUGHING *Ensign ENY 514* [2]	10	10
15 Jun 85	YOU DON'T NEED A REASON *Ensign ENY 517* [2]	42	4
27 Jul 85	THIS KIND OF LOVE *Ensign ENY 521* [3]	70	3
2 Aug 86 ●	I CAN PROVE IT *Ensign PF 1*	8	9
15 Nov 86	AIN'T NOTHING BUT A HOUSEPARTY *Ensign PF 2*	60	2

[1] Galaxy featuring Phil Fearon [2] Phil Fearon and Galaxy [3] Phil Fearon and Galaxy featuring Dee Galdes

FEEDER *UK, male vocal / instrumental group (32 WEEKS)* pos/wks

8 Mar 97	TANGERINE *Echo ECSCD 32*	60	1
10 May 97	CEMENT *Echo ECSCX 36*	53	1
23 Aug 97	CRASH *Echo ECSCD 42*	48	1
18 Oct 97	HIGH *Echo ECSCD 44*	24	2
28 Feb 98	SUFFOCATE *Echo ECSCX 52*	37	1
3 Apr 99	DAY IN DAY OUT *Echo ECSCD 75*	31	2
12 Jun 99	INSOMNIA *Echo ECSCD 77*	22	3
21 Aug 99	YESTERDAY WENT TOO SOON *Echo ECSCD 79*	20	3
20 Nov 99	PAPERFACES *Echo ECSCD 85*	41	2
20 Jan 01 ●	BUCK ROGERS *Echo ECSCD 106*	5	6
14 Apr 01	SEVEN DAYS IN THE SUN *Echo ECSCD 107*	14	4

		pos	wks
19 May 01	**SEVEN DAYS IN THE SUN (re-entry)** *Echo ECSCD 107*	57	2
14 Jul 01	**TURN** *Echo ECSCD 116*	27	2
22 Dec 01	**JUST A DAY (EP)** *Echo ECSCD 121*	12	2+

Tracks on 'Just A Day' (EP): 'Just A Day', 'Can't Stop Losing You', 'Piece By Piece' (last track is video only)

Wilton FELDER *US, male instrumentalist – tenor sax (7 WEEKS)*

		pos	wks
1 Nov 80	**INHERIT THE WIND** *MCA 646*	39	5
16 Feb 85	**(NO MATTER HOW HIGH I GET) I'LL STILL BE LOOKIN' UP TO YOU** *MCA MCA 919* [1]	63	2

[1] Featuring Bobby Womack and introducing Alltrina Grayson

Bobby Womack uncredited vocalist on 'Inherit the Wind'

José FELICIANO
US, male vocalist / instrumentalist – guitar (23 WEEKS)

		pos	wks
18 Sep 68 ●	**LIGHT MY FIRE** *RCA 1715*	6	16
18 Oct 69	**AND THE SUN WILL SHINE** *RCA 1871*	25	7

FELIX *UK, male producer – Francis Wright (29 WEEKS)*

		pos	wks
8 Aug 92 ●	**DON'T YOU WANT ME** *Deconstruction 74321110507*	6	11
24 Oct 92	**IT WILL MAKE ME CRAZY** *Deconstruction 74321118137*	11	6
22 May 93	**STARS** *Deconstruction 74321147102*	29	3
12 Aug 95 ●	**DON'T YOU WANT ME (re-mix)** *Deconstruction 74321293972*	10	5
19 Oct 96	**DON'T YOU WANT ME (2nd) (re-mix)** *Deconstruction 74321418142*	17	4

Julie FELIX *US, female vocalist (19 WEEKS)*

		pos	wks
18 Apr 70	**IF I COULD (EL CONDOR PASA)** *RAK 101*	19	11
17 Oct 70	**HEAVEN IS HERE** *RAK 105*	22	8

FELIX DA HOUSECAT *US, male producer – Felix Stallings Jr (1 WEEK)*

		pos	wks
14 Jul 01	**SILVER SCREEN SHOWER SCENE** *City Rockers ROCKERS 1CD*	55	1

See also QWILO & FELIX DA HOUSECAT

FELLY – *See TECHNOTRONIC*

FE-M@IL *UK, female vocal group (2 WEEKS)*

		pos	wks
5 Aug 00	**FLEE FLY FLO** *Jive 9250592*	46	2

FEMME FATALE
US, male / female vocal / instrumental group (2 WEEKS)

		pos	wks
11 Feb 89	**FALLING IN AND OUT OF LOVE** *MCA MCA 1309*	69	2

FENDERMEN *US, male vocal / instrumental duo – guitars (9 WEEKS)*

		pos	wks
18 Aug 60	**MULE SKINNER BLUES** *Top Rank JAR 395*	50	1
1 Sep 60	**MULE SKINNER BLUES (re-entry)** *Top Rank JAR 395*	37	2
29 Sep 60	**MULE SKINNER BLUES (2nd re-entry)** *Top Rank JAR 395*	32	6

FENMEN – *See Bern ELLIOTT and the FENMEN*

Peter FENTON *UK, male vocalist (3 WEEKS)*

		pos	wks
10 Nov 66	**MARBLE BREAKS IRON BENDS** *Fontana TF 748*	46	3

George FENTON and Jonas GWANGWA
UK / South Africa, male instrumental / production duo (1 WEEK)

		pos	wks
2 Jan 88	**CRY FREEDOM** *MCA MCA 1228*	75	1

The listed flip side of 'Cry Freedom' was 'The Funeral' by Thuli Dumakude

Shane FENTON and the FENTONES
UK, male vocal / instrumental group (28 WEEKS)

		pos	wks
26 Oct 61	**I'M A MOODY GUY** *Parlophone R 4827*	22	8
1 Feb 62	**WALK AWAY** *Parlophone R 4866*	38	5
5 Apr 62	**IT'S ALL OVER NOW** *Parlophone R 4883*	29	7
12 Jul 62	**CINDY'S BIRTHDAY** *Parlophone R 4921*	19	8

See also FENTONES; Alvin STARDUST

FENTONES *UK, male instrumental group (4 WEEKS)*

		pos	wks
19 Apr 62	**THE MEXICAN** *Parlophone R 4899*	41	3
27 Sep 62	**THE BREEZE AND I** *Parlophone R 4937*	48	1

See also Shane FENTON and the FENTONES

FERGIE *Ireland, male DJ / producer – Robert Ferguson (3 WEEKS)*

		pos	wks
9 Sep 00	**DECEPTION** *Duty Free DF 020CD*	47	1
25 Nov 00	**HOOVERS & HORNS** *Nukleuz NUKC 0185* [1]	57	2

[1] Fergie & BK

Sheila FERGUSON *US, female vocalist (1 WEEK)*

		pos	wks
5 Feb 94	**WHEN WILL I SEE YOU AGAIN** *XSrhythm CDSTAS 2711*	60	1

See also THREE DEGREES

FERKO STRING BAND *US, male instrumental group (2 WEEKS)*

		pos	wks
12 Aug 55	**ALABAMA JUBILEE** *London HL 8140*	20	2

Luisa FERNANDEZ *Spain, female vocalist (8 WEEKS)*

		pos	wks
11 Nov 78	**LAY LOVE ON YOU** *Warner Bros. K 17061*	31	8

Pamela FERNANDEZ *US, female vocalist (3 WEEKS)*

		pos	wks
17 Sep 94	**KICKIN' IN THE BEAT** *Ore AG 5CD*	43	2
3 Jun 95	**LET'S START OVER / KICKIN' IN THE BEAT (re-mix)** *Ore AG 9CD*	59	1

FERRANTE and TEICHER *US, male instrumental duo, pianos – Arthur Ferrante and Louis Teicher (18 WEEKS)*

		pos	wks
18 Aug 60	**THEME FROM 'THE APARTMENT'** *London HLT 9164*	44	1
9 Mar 61 ●	**EXODUS (THEME FROM 'EXODUS')** *London HLT 9298 and HMV POP 881*	6	17

Exodus (Theme from 'Exodus') available first on London, then on HMV when the US label, United Artists, changed its UK outlet

Jose FERRER
US, male vocalist – Jose Vincente Ferrer y Centron (3 WEEKS)

		pos	wks
19 Feb 54 ●	**WOMAN (UH-HUH)** *Philips PB220*	7	3

'Woman (Uh-Huh)' coupled with 'Man (Uh-Huh)' by Rosemary Clooney

Tony FERRINO *UK, male vocalist – comedian Steve Coogan (2 WEEKS)*

		pos	wks
23 Nov 96	**HELP YOURSELF / BIGAMY AT CHRISTMAS** *RCA 74321430302*	42	2

Bryan FERRY (194 Top 500) *Stylish UK vocalist / songwriter, b. 26 Sep 1945, Tyne and Wear. Sophisticated singer who split his time between solo career and fronting the visually stimulating Roxy Music. Still having Top 20 albums in 2001 (133 WEEKS)*

		pos	wks
29 Sep 73 ●	**A HARD RAIN'S GONNA FALL** *Island WIP 6170*	10	9
25 May 74	**THE 'IN' CROWD** *Island WIP 6196*	13	6
31 Aug 74	**SMOKE GETS IN YOUR EYES** *Island WIP 6205*	17	8
5 Jul 75	**YOU GO TO MY HEAD** *Island WIP 6234*	33	3
12 Jun 76 ●	**LET'S STICK TOGETHER (LET'S WORK TOGETHER)** *Island WIP 6307*	4	10
7 Aug 76 ●	**EXTENDED PLAY (EP)** *Island IEP 1*	7	9
5 Feb 77 ●	**THIS IS TOMORROW** *Polydor 2001 704*	9	9
14 May 77	**TOKYO JOE** *Polydor 2001 711*	15	7
13 May 78	**WHAT GOES ON** *Polydor POSP 3*	67	2
5 Aug 78	**SIGN OF THE TIMES** *Polydor 2001 798*	37	8
11 May 85 ●	**SLAVE TO LOVE** *EG FERRY 1*	10	9
31 Aug 85	**DON'T STOP THE DANCE** *EG FERRY 2*	21	7
7 Dec 85	**WINDSWEPT** *EG FERRY 3*	46	3
29 Mar 86	**IS YOUR LOVE STRONG ENOUGH?** *EG FERRY 4*	22	7
10 Oct 87	**THE RIGHT STUFF** *Virgin VS 940*	37	6
13 Feb 88	**KISS AND TELL** *Virgin VS 1034*	41	5
29 Oct 88	**LET'S STICK TOGETHER (re-mix)** *EG EGO 44*	12	7
11 Feb 89	**THE PRICE OF LOVE (re-mix)** *EG EGO 46*	49	3
22 Apr 89	**HE'LL HAVE TO GO** *EG EGO 48*	63	1
6 Mar 93	**I PUT A SPELL ON YOU** *Virgin VSCDG 1400*	18	5

29 May 93 **WILL YOU LOVE ME TOMORROW** *Virgin VSCDG 1455* ... 23 5
4 Sep 93 **GIRL OF MY BEST FRIEND** *Virgin VSCDG 1488* ... 57 2
29 Oct 94 **YOUR PAINTED SMILE** *Virgin VSCDG 1508* ... 52 1
11 Feb 95 **MAMOUNA** *Virgin VSCDG 1528* ... 57 1

Tracks on Extended Play (EP): Price of Love / Shame Shame Shame / Heart on My Sleeve / It's Only Love

See also ROXY MUSIC

FERRY AID *International, male / female charity ensemble (7 WEEKS)* pos/wks

4 Apr 87 ★ **LET IT BE** *The Sun AID 1* ■ ... 1 7

FEVER featuring Tippa IRIE *UK, male production / instrumental group with male vocalist (1 WEEKS)* pos/wks

8 Jul 95 **STAYING ALIVE 95** *Telstar CDSTAS 2776* ... 48 1

Lena FIAGBE *UK, female vocalist (13 WEEKS)* pos/wks

24 Jul 93 **YOU COME FROM EARTH** *Mother MUMCD 42* [1] ... 69 1
23 Oct 93 **GOTTA GET IT RIGHT** *Mother MUMCD 44* ... 20 5
16 Apr 94 **WHAT'S IT LIKE TO BE BEAUTIFUL** *Mother MUMCD 49* ... 52 3
25 Jun 94 **VISIONS** *Mother MUMCD 53* ... 48 2
10 Feb 96 **AFRICAN DREAM** *Mercury MERCD 453* [2] ... 44 2

[1] Lena [2] Wasis Diop featuring Lena Fiagbe

Karel FIALKA *UK, male vocalist / multi-instrumentalist (12 WEEKS)* pos/wks

17 May 80 **THE EYES HAVE IT** *Blueprint BLU 2005* ... 52 4
5 Sep 87 ● **HEY MATTHEW** *IRS IRM 140* ... 9 8

FIAT LUX *UK, male vocal / instrumental group (4 WEEKS)* pos/wks

28 Jan 84 **SECRETS** *Polydor FIAT 2* ... 65 3
17 Mar 84 **BLUE EMOTION** *Polydor FIAT 3* ... 59 1

FICTION FACTORY *UK, male vocal / instrumental group (11 WEEKS)* pos/wks

14 Jan 84 ● **(FEELS LIKE) HEAVEN** *CBS A 3996* ... 6 9
17 Mar 84 **GHOST OF LOVE** *CBS A 3819* ... 64 2

FIDDLER'S DRAM *UK, male / female vocal / instrumental group (9 WEEKS)* pos/wks

15 Dec 79 ● **DAY TRIP TO BANGOR (DIDN'T WE HAVE A LOVELY TIME)** *Dingles SID 211* ... 3 9

FIDELFATTI featuring RONNETTE *Italy, male producer and female vocalist (1 WEEK)* pos/wks

27 Jan 90 **JUST WANNA TOUCH ME** *Urban URB 46* ... 65 1

Billy FIELD *Australia, male vocalist (3 WEEKS)* pos/wks

12 Jun 82 **YOU WEREN'T IN LOVE WITH ME** *CBS A 2344* ... 67 3

Ernie FIELD'S ORCHESTRA *US, orchestra (8 WEEKS)* pos/wks

25 Dec 59 **IN THE MOOD** *London HL 8985* ... 13 8

Gracie FIELDS *UK, female vocalist – Grace Stansfield (15 WEEKS)* pos/wks

31 May 57 ● **AROUND THE WORLD** *Columbia DB 3953* ... 8 8
2 Aug 57 **AROUND THE WORLD (re-entry)** *Columbia DB 3953* ... 24 1
6 Nov 59 **LITTLE DONKEY** *Columbia DB 4360* ... 30 1
20 Nov 59 **LITTLE DONKEY (re-entry)** *Columbia DB 4360* ... 20 5

Richard 'Dimples' FIELDS *US, male vocalist (4 WEEKS)* pos/wks

20 Feb 82 **I'VE GOT TO LEARN TO SAY NO** *Epic EPC A 1918* ... 56 4

FIELDS OF THE NEPHILIM *UK, male vocal / instrumental group (9 WEEKS)* pos/wks

24 Oct 87 **BLUE WATER** *Situation Two SIT 48* ... 75 1
4 Jun 88 **MOONCHILD** *Situation Two SIT 52* ... 28 3
27 May 89 **PSYCHONAUT** *Situation Two ST 57* ... 35 3
4 Aug 90 **FOR HER LIGHT** *Beggars Banquet BEG 244T* ... 54 1
24 Nov 90 **SUMERLAND (DREAMED)** *Beggars Banquet BEG 250* ... 37 1

FIERCE *UK, female vocal group (23 WEEKS)* pos/wks

9 Jan 99 **RIGHT HERE RIGHT NOW** *Wildstar CDWILD 13* ... 25 5
15 May 99 **DAYZ LIKE THAT** *Wildstar CDWILD 19* ... 11 5
14 Aug 99 **SO LONG** *Wildstar CDWILD 27* ... 15 5
12 Feb 00 ● **SWEET LOVE 2K** *Wildstar CDWILD 34* ... 3 8

5TH DIMENSION *US, male / female vocal group (21 WEEKS)* pos/wks

16 Apr 69 **AQUARIUS / LET THE SUNSHINE IN (MEDLEY)** *Liberty LBF 15193* ▲ ... 11 12
17 Jan 70 **WEDDING BELL BLUES** *Liberty LBF 15288* ▲ ... 16 9

5050 *UK, male production duo – Jason Powell and Andy Lysandrou (1 WEEK)* pos/wks

13 Oct 01 **WHO'S COMING ROUND** *Obsessive FIFTYCD 01* ... 54 1

50 GRIND featuring POKEMON ALLSTARS *UK, male vocal / instrumental group and Pokemon popsters (1 WEEK)* pos/wks

22 Dec 01 **GOTTA CATCH 'EM ALL** *Recognition CDREC 21* ... 57 1

52ND STREET *UK, male / female vocal / instrumental group (13 WEEKS)* pos/wks

2 Nov 85 **TELL ME (HOW IT FEELS)** *10 TEN 74* ... 54 5
11 Jan 86 **YOU'RE MY LAST CHANCE** *10 TEN 89* ... 49 4
8 Mar 86 **I CAN'T LET YOU GO** *10 TEN 114* ... 57 4

53RD & 3RD – *See Jonathan KING*

FILTER *US, male vocal / instrumental group (5 WEEKS)* pos/wks

11 Oct 97 **(CAN YOU) TRIP LIKE I DO** *Epic 6650862* [1] ... 39 2
18 Mar 00 **TAKE A PICTURE** *Reprise W 515CD* ... 25 3

[1] Filter and The Crystal Method

FINAL CUT – *See TRUE FAITH and Bridgette GRACE with FINAL CUT*

FINE YOUNG CANNIBALS (412 Top 500) *Politically aware pop / soul trio from Birmingham, UK: Roland Gift (v), ex-Beat members Andy Cox (g) and David Steele (b). Unmistakable vocalist Gift also acted in films, most notably 1989's Scandal. FYC, who were among 1989's biggest selling acts worldwide, won (and returned) two Brit awards in 1990 (81 WEEKS)* pos/wks

8 Jun 85 ● **JOHNNY COME HOME** *London LON 68* ... 8 13
9 Nov 85 **BLUE** *London LON 79* ... 41 6
11 Jan 86 ● **SUSPICIOUS MINDS** *London LON 82* ... 8 9
12 Apr 86 **FUNNY HOW LOVE IS** *London LON 88* ... 58 4
21 Mar 87 ● **EVER FALLEN IN LOVE** *London LON 121* ... 9 10
7 Jan 89 ● **SHE DRIVES ME CRAZY** *London LON 199* ▲ ... 5 11
15 Apr 89 ● **GOOD THING** *London LON 218* ▲ ... 7 8
19 Aug 89 **DON'T LOOK BACK** *London LON 220* ... 34 4
18 Nov 89 **I'M NOT THE MAN I USED TO BE** *London LON 244* ... 20 8
24 Feb 90 **I'M NOT SATISFIED** *London LON 252* ... 46 3
16 Nov 96 **THE FLAME** *ffrr LONCD 389* ... 17 3
11 Jan 97 **SHE DRIVES ME CRAZY (re-mix)** *ffrr LONCD 391* ... 36 2

See also TWO MEN, A DRUM MACHINE AND A TRUMPET

FINITRIBE *UK, male instrumental / production group (2 WEEKS)* pos/wks

11 Jul 92 **FOREVERGREEN** *One Little Indian 74 TP12F* ... 51 1
19 Nov 94 **BRAND NEW** *ffrr FCD 247* ... 69 1

FINK BROTHERS *UK, male vocal / instrumental duo (4 WEEKS)* pos/wks

9 Feb 85 **MUTANTS IN MEGA CITY ONE** *Zarjazz JAZZ 2* ... 50 4

FINN *New Zealand, male vocal / instrumental duo (5 WEEKS)* pos/wks

14 Oct 95 **SUFFER NEVER** *Parlophone CDRS 6417* ... 29 3
9 Dec 95 **ANGEL'S HEAP** *Parlophone CDRS 6421* ... 41 2

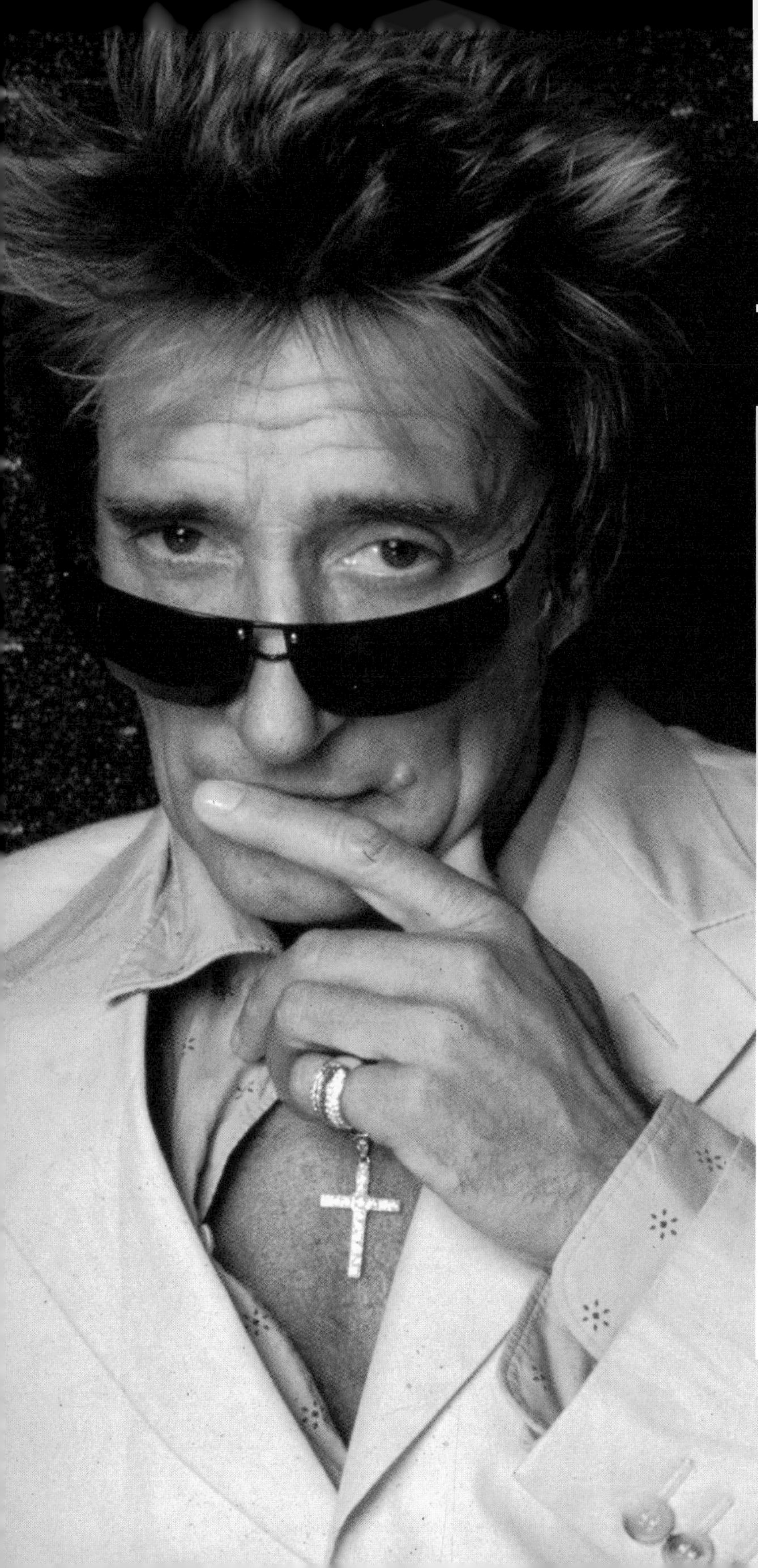

1967

IN THE YEAR IN WHICH WORLD-FAMOUS BOXING LEGEND MUHAMMAD ALI REFUSED THE VIETNAM DRAFT, CHE GUEVARA WAS SHOT DEAD, AND THE PSYCHEDELIC SOUNDS OF THE FLOWER CHILDREN WERE THE SOUNDTRACK TO THE SUMMER OF LOVE, **ROD STEWART** STARTS A LOVE AFFAIR WITH SOME SWEET SOUL MUSIC ...

"The one song that really made me fall in love with music in general and R&B in particular was **Arthur Conley**'s 'Sweet Soul Music'. That was a time when all the best music came out of America – songs like 'In the Midnight Hour' by Wilson Pickett, 'Just My Imagination' by The Temptations, 'It's All Over Now' by Bobby Womack. All these brilliant black singles. If someone put those all together on one CD, I'd buy it!"

SINGLE OF THE YEAR 'Hello, Goodbye' Beatles
ALBUM OF THE YEAR 'Sgt. Pepper's Lonely Hearts Club Band' Beatles

See also CROWDED HOUSE; Neil FINN; Tim FINN

Micky FINN – See URBAN SHAKEDOWN

Neil FINN *New Zealand, male vocalist / instrumentalist (6 WEEKS)*

		pos	wks
13 Jun 98	**SHE WILL HAVE HER WAY** *Parlophone CDR 6495*	**26**	2
17 Oct 98	**SINNER** *Parlophone CDR 6505*	**39**	1
7 Apr 01	**WHEREVER YOU ARE** *Parlophone CDRS 6557*	**32**	2
22 Sep 01	**HOLE IN THE ICE** *Parlophone CDRS 6563*	**43**	1

See also CROWDED HOUSE; FINN

Tim FINN *New Zealand, male vocalist (6 WEEKS)*

		pos	wks
26 Jun 93	**PERSUASION** *Capitol 6592482*	**43**	3
18 Sep 93	**HIT THE GROUND RUNNING** *Capitol CDCLS 694*	**50**	3

See also CROWDED HOUSE; FINN

Johnnie FIORI – See BARKIN BROTHERS featuring Johnnie FIORI

Elisa FIORILLO *US, female vocalist (14 WEEKS)*

		pos	wks
28 Nov 87 ●	**WHO FOUND WHO** *Chrysalis CHS JEL 1* [1]	**10**	10
13 Feb 88	**HOW CAN I FORGET YOU** *Chrysalis ELISA 1*	**50**	4

[1] Jellybean featuring Elisa Fiorillo

FIRE INC – See Jim STEINMAN

FIRE ISLAND *UK, male instrumental / production group (7 WEEKS)*

		pos	wks
8 Aug 92	**IN YOUR BONES / FIRE ISLAND** *Boy's Own BOIX 11*	**66**	1
12 Mar 94	**THERE BUT FOR THE GRACE OF GOD** *Junior Boy's Own JBO 18CD* [1]	**32**	3
4 Mar 95	**IF YOU SHOULD NEED A FRIEND** *Junior Boy's Own JBO 26CDS* [2]	**51**	1
11 Apr 98	**SHOUT TO THE TOP** *JBO JNR 5001573* [3]	**23**	2

[1] Fire Island featuring Love Nelson [2] Fire Island featuring Mark Anthoni [3] Fire Island featuring Loleatta Holloway

See also HELLER & FARLEY PROJECT; Pete HELLER; STYLUS TROUBLE

FIREBALLS *US, male vocal / instrumental group (17 WEEKS)*

		pos	wks
27 Jul 61	**QUITE A PARTY** *Pye International 7N 25092*	**29**	9
14 Nov 63	**SUGAR SHACK** *London HLD 9789* [1] ▲	**45**	4
19 Dec 63	**SUGAR SHACK (re-entry)** *London HLD 9789* [1]	**46**	4

[1] Jimmy Gilmer and the Fireballs

FIREHOUSE *US, male vocal / instrumental group (2 WEEKS)*

		pos	wks
13 Jul 91	**DON'T TREAT ME BAD** *Epic 6567807*	**71**	1
19 Dec 92	**WHEN I LOOK INTO YOUR EYES** *Epic 6588347*	**65**	1

FIRM *UK, male vocal / instrumental group (21 WEEKS)*

		pos	wks
17 Jul 82	**ARTHUR DALEY ('E'S ALRIGHT)** *Bark HID 1*	**14**	9
6 Jun 87 ★	**STAR TREKKIN'** *Bark TREK 1*	**1**	12

FIRM featuring Dawn ROBINSON
US, male rap group and US, female vocalist (3 WEEKS)

		pos	wks
29 Nov 97	**FIRM BIZ** *Columbia 6651612*	**18**	3

FIRST CHOICE *US, female vocal group (21 WEEKS)*

		pos	wks
19 May 73	**ARMED AND EXTREMELY DANGEROUS** *Bell 1297*	**16**	10
4 Aug 73 ●	**SMARTY PANTS** *Bell 1324*	**9**	11

FIRST CLASS *UK, male vocal group (10 WEEKS)*

		pos	wks
15 Jun 74	**BEACH BABY** *UK 66*	**13**	10

FIRST EDITION – See Kenny ROGERS

FIRST LIGHT *UK, male vocal / instrumental duo (5 WEEKS)*

		pos	wks
21 May 83	**EXPLAIN THE REASONS** *London LON 26*	**65**	3
28 Jan 84	**WISH YOU WERE HERE** *London LON 43*	**71**	2

FIRSTBORN *Ireland, male producer – Oisin Lunny (1 WEEK)*

		pos	wks
19 Jun 99	**THE MOOD CLUB** *Independiente ISOM 28MS*	**69**	1

FISCHER-Z *UK, male vocal / instrumental group (7 WEEKS)*

		pos	wks
26 May 79	**THE WORKER** *United Artists UP 36509*	**53**	5
3 May 80	**SO LONG** *United Artists BP 342*	**72**	2

FISH *UK, male vocalist (20 WEEKS)*

		pos	wks
18 Oct 86	**SHORT CUT TO SOMEWHERE** *Charisma CB 426* [1]	**75**	1
28 Oct 89	**STATE OF MIND** *EMI EM 109*	**32**	3
6 Jan 90	**BIG WEDGE** *EMI EM 125*	**25**	4
17 Mar 90	**A GENTLEMAN'S EXCUSE ME** *EMI EM 135*	**30**	3
28 Sep 91	**INTERNAL EXILE** *Polydor FISHY 1*	**37**	2
11 Jan 92	**CREDO** *Polydor FISHY 2*	**38**	2
4 Jul 92	**SOMETHING IN THE AIR** *Polydor FISHY 3*	**51**	2
16 Apr 94	**LADY LET IT LIE** *Dick Bros. DDICK 3CD1*	**46**	1
1 Oct 94	**FORTUNES OF WAR** *Dick Bros. DDICK 008CD1*	**67**	1
26 Aug 95	**JUST GOOD FRIENDS** *Dick Bros. DDICK 014CD1* [2]	**63**	1

[1] Fish and Tony Banks [2] Fish featuring Sam Brown

See also MARILLION

FISHBONE *US, male vocal / instrumental group (3 WEEKS)*

		pos	wks
1 Aug 92	**EVERYDAY SUNSHINE / FIGHT THE YOUTH** *Columbia 6581937*	**60**	2
28 Aug 93	**SWIM** *Columbia 6596252*	**54**	1

Cevin FISHER *US, male DJ / producer (9 WEEKS)*

		pos	wks
3 Oct 98	**THE FREAKS COME OUT** *Ministry of Sound MOSCDS 127* [1]	**34**	2
20 Feb 99	**(YOU GOT ME) BURNING UP** *Wonderboy WBOYD 013* [2]	**14**	4
7 Aug 99	**MUSIC SAVED MY LIFE** *Sm:)e Communications SM 90982*	**67**	1
20 Jan 01	**IT'S A GOOD LIFE** *Wonderboy WBOYD 022* [3]	**54**	1
24 Feb 01	**LOVE YOU SOME MORE** *Subversive SUB 68D* [4]	**60**	1

[1] Cevin Fisher's Big Break [2] Cevin Fisher / Loleatta Holloway [3] Cevin Fisher featuring Ramona Kelly [4] Cevin Fisher featuring Shelia Smith

Eddie FISHER (283 Top 500) *Leading 1950s heartthrob, b. 10 Aug 1929, Philadelphia. The US's most successful male singer between 1950 and 1954; accumulated many more UK hits in the pre-chart years. Married Elizabeth Taylor, Debbie Reynolds and Connie Stevens and is father of the actress Carrie Fisher (105 WEEKS)*

		pos	wks
2 Jan 53 ★	**OUTSIDE OF HEAVEN** *HMV B 10362*	**1**	16
23 Jan 53	**EVERYTHING I HAVE IS YOURS** *HMV B 10398*	**12**	1
6 Feb 53 ●	**EVERYTHING I HAVE IS YOURS (re-entry)** *HMV B 10398*	**8**	4
1 May 53 ●	**DOWNHEARTED** *HMV B 10450*	**3**	15
1 May 53	**OUTSIDE OF HEAVEN (re-entry)** *HMV B 10362*	**12**	1
22 May 53 ★	**I'M WALKING BEHIND YOU** *HMV B 10489* [1] ▲	**1**	18
6 Nov 53 ●	**WISH YOU WERE HERE** *HMV B 10564*	**8**	9
22 Jan 54 ●	**OH MY PAPA (O MEIN PAPA)** *HMV B 10614* ▲	**9**	1
5 Feb 54	**OH MY PAPA (O MEIN PAPA) (re-entry)** *HMV B 10614*	**11**	1
26 Feb 54 ●	**OH MY PAPA (O MEIN PAPA) (2nd re-entry)** *HMV B 10614*	**10**	1
12 Mar 54	**OH MY PAPA (O MEIN PAPA) (3rd re-entry)** *HMV B 10614*	**11**	1
29 Oct 54	**I NEED YOU NOW** *HMV B 10755* ▲	**16**	2
19 Nov 54	**I NEED YOU NOW (re-entry)** *HMV B 10755*	**13**	7
21 Jan 55	**I NEED YOU NOW (2nd re-entry)** *HMV B 10755*	**19**	1
18 Mar 55 ●	**(I'M ALWAYS HEARING) WEDDING BELLS** *HMV B 10839*	**5**	11
23 Nov 56 ●	**CINDY, OH CINDY** *HMV POP 273*	**5**	16

[1] Eddie Fisher with Sally Sweetland (soprano)

Mark FISHER featuring Dotty GREEN
UK, male instrumentalist – keyboards and female vocalist (2 WEEKS)

		pos	wks
29 Jun 85	**LOVE SITUATION** *Total Control TOCO 3*	**59**	2

Toni FISHER *US, female vocalist (1 WEEK)*

		pos	wks
12 Feb 60	**THE BIG HURT** *Top Rank JAR 261*	**30**	1

FITS OF GLOOM *UK / Italy, male vocal duo (4 WEEKS)* pos/wks

4 Jun 94	**HEAVEN** *Media MCSTD 1981*	**47**	2
5 Nov 94	**THE POWER OF LOVE** *Media MCSTD 2016* [1]	**49**	2

[1] Fits of Gloom featuring Lizzy Mack

Ella FITZGERALD *US, female vocalist (29 WEEKS)* pos/wks

23 May 58	**THE SWINGIN' SHEPHERD BLUES** *HMV POP 486*	**15**	5
16 Oct 59	**BUT NOT FOR ME** *HMV POP 657*	**25**	2
25 Dec 59	**BUT NOT FOR ME (re-entry)** *HMV POP 657*	**29**	1
21 Apr 60	**MACK THE KNIFE** *HMV POP 736*	**19**	9
6 Oct 60	**HOW HIGH THE MOON** *HMV POP 782*	**46**	1
22 Nov 62	**DESAFINADO** *Verve VS 502*	**38**	4
27 Dec 62	**DESAFINADO (re-entry)** *Verve VS 502*	**41**	2
30 Apr 64	**CAN'T BUY ME LOVE** *Verve VS 519*	**34**	5

Scott FITZGERALD *UK, male vocalist – William McPhail (12 WEEKS)* pos/wks

14 Jan 78 ●	**IF I HAD WORDS** *Pepper UP 36333* [1]	**3**	10
7 May 88	**GO** *PRT PYS 10*	**52**	2

[1] Scott Fitzgerald and Yvonne Keeley and the St Thomas More School Choir

FIVE (199 Top 500) *Superior all-boy vocal group: Abs Breen, Jay Brown, Sean Conlon, Rich Neville, Scott Robinson. Eponymous debut album sold more than four million worldwide. The only UK act to reach the Top 10 with every one of their first 11 releases split in 2001 (130 WEEKS)* pos/wks

13 Dec 97 ●	**SLAM DUNK (DA FUNK)** *RCA 74321537352*	**10**	9
14 Mar 98 ●	**WHEN THE LIGHTS GO OUT** *RCA 74321562312*	**4**	9
20 Jun 98 ●	**GOT THE FEELIN'** *RCA 74321584892*	**3**	13
12 Sep 98 ●	**EVERYBODY GET UP** *RCA 74321613752*	**2**	12
28 Nov 98 ●	**UNTIL THE TIME IS THROUGH** *RCA 74321632602*	**2**	12
31 Jul 99 ●	**IF YA GETTIN' DOWN** *RCA 74321689692*	**2**	12
6 Nov 99 ★	**KEEP ON MOVIN'** *RCA 74321709862* ■	**1**	17
18 Mar 00 ●	**DON'T WANNA LET YOU GO** *RCA 74321745292*	**9**	12
29 Jul 00 ★	**WE WILL ROCK YOU** *RCA 74321774022* [1] ■	**1**	12
4 Nov 00	**WE WILL ROCK YOU (re-entry)** *RCA 74321774022* [1]	**72**	1
25 Aug 01 ★	**LET'S DANCE** *RCA 74321875962* ■	**1**	12
3 Nov 01 ●	**CLOSER TO ME** *RCA 74321900742*	**4**	9+

[1] Five and Queen

FIVE SMITH BROTHERS *UK, male vocal group (1 WEEK)* pos/wks

22 Jul 55	**I'M IN FAVOUR OF FRIENDSHIP** *Decca F 10527*	**20**	1

FIVE STAR (173 Top 500) *Britain's best known black family act: Deniece, Doris, Stedman, Lorraine and Delroy Pearson. The Essex-based group became the youngest act to top the LP chart with the UK million-seller 'Silk and Steel'. In 1987 they were voted Top British Group in Smash Hits and at Brit Awards. Act relocated to US and had R&B success there in 2001 (140 WEEKS)* pos/wks

4 May 85	**ALL FALL DOWN** *Tent PB 40039*	**15**	12
20 Jul 85	**LET ME BE THE ONE** *Tent PB 40193*	**18**	9
14 Sep 85	**LOVE TAKE OVER** *Tent PB 40353*	**25**	9
16 Nov 85	**RSVP** *Tent PB 40445*	**45**	5
11 Jan 86 ●	**SYSTEM ADDICT** *Tent PB 40515*	**3**	11
12 Apr 86 ●	**CAN'T WAIT ANOTHER MINUTE** *Tent PB 40697*	**7**	10
26 Jul 86 ●	**FIND THE TIME** *Tent PB 40799*	**7**	10
13 Sep 86 ●	**RAIN OR SHINE** *Tent PB 40901*	**2**	11
22 Nov 86	**IF I SAY YES** *Tent PB 40981*	**15**	9
7 Feb 87 ●	**STAY OUT OF MY LIFE** *Tent PB 41131*	**9**	8
18 Apr 87 ●	**THE SLIGHTEST TOUCH** *Tent PB 41265*	**4**	9
22 Aug 87	**WHENEVER YOU'RE READY** *Tent PB 41477*	**11**	6
10 Oct 87	**STRONG AS STEEL** *Tent PB 41565*	**16**	7
5 Dec 87	**SOMEWHERE SOMEBODY** *Tent PB 41661*	**23**	6
4 Jun 88	**ANOTHER WEEKEND** *Tent PB 42081*	**18**	4
6 Aug 88	**ROCK MY WORLD** *Tent PB 42145*	**28**	4
17 Sep 88	**THERE'S A BRAND NEW WORLD** *Tent PB 42235*	**61**	2
19 Nov 88	**LET ME BE YOURS** *Tent PB 42343*	**51**	3
8 Apr 89	**WITH EVERY HEARTBEAT** *Tent PB 42693*	**49**	2
10 Mar 90	**TREAT ME LIKE A LADY** *Tent FIVE 1*	**54**	2
7 Jul 90	**HOT LOVE** *Tent FIVE 2*	**68**	1

FIVE THIRTY *UK, male vocal / instrumental group (4 WEEKS)* pos/wks

4 Aug 90	**ABSTAIN** *East West YZ 530*	**75**	1
25 May 91	**13TH DISCIPLE** *East West YZ 577*	**67**	1
3 Aug 91	**SUPERNOVA** *East West YZ 594*	**75**	1
2 Nov 91	**YOU (EP)** *East West YZ 624*	**72**	1

Tracks on You (EP): You / Cuddly Drug / Slow Train into the Ocean

5000 VOLTS *UK, male / female vocal / instrumental group (18 WEEKS)* pos/wks

6 Sep 75 ●	**I'M ON FIRE** *Philips 6006 464*	**4**	9
24 Jul 76 ●	**DR KISS KISS** *Philips 6006 533*	**8**	9

Vocals (uncredited) on 'I'm On Fire' by Tina Charles

FIXATE *UK, male vocal group (1 WEEK)* pos/wks

14 Jul 01	**24/7** *Epark EPKFIX CD1*	**42**	1

FIXX *UK, male vocal / instrumental group (8 WEEKS)* pos/wks

24 Apr 82	**STAND OR FALL** *MCA FIXX 2*	**54**	4
17 Jul 82	**RED SKIES** *MCA FIXX 3*	**57**	4

FKW *UK, male vocal / instrumental group (8 WEEKS)* pos/wks

2 Oct 93	**NEVER GONNA (GIVE YOU UP)** *PWL International PWCD 273*	**48**	2
11 Dec 93	**SEIZE THE DAY** *PWL International PWCD 279*	**45**	2
5 Mar 94	**JINGO** *PWL International PWCD 283*	**30**	3
4 Jun 94	**THIS IS THE WAY** *PWL International PWCD 307*	**63**	1

Roberta FLACK (425 Top 500) *Ground-breaking, song stylist / pianist, b. 10 Feb 1939, North Carolina, US. Recorded original hit 'Killing Me Softly with His Song' (written about Don McLean) and was the first black female soloist to top the US album chart, with 'First Take' in 1972 (79 WEEKS)* pos/wks

27 May 72	**THE FIRST TIME EVER I SAW YOUR FACE** *Atlantic K 10161* ▲	**14**	14
5 Aug 72	**WHERE IS THE LOVE** *Atlantic K 10202* [1]	**29**	7
17 Feb 73 ●	**KILLING ME SOFTLY WITH HIS SONG** *Atlantic K 10282* ▲	**6**	14
24 Aug 74	**FEEL LIKE MAKING LOVE** *Atlantic K 10467* ▲	**34**	7
6 May 78	**THE CLOSER I GET TO YOU** *Atlantic K 11099* [1]	**42**	4
17 May 80 ●	**BACK TOGETHER AGAIN** *Atlantic K 11481* [1]	**3**	11
30 Aug 80	**DON'T MAKE ME WAIT TOO LONG** *Atlantic K 11555*	**44**	7
20 Aug 83 ●	**TONIGHT I CELEBRATE MY LOVE** *Capitol CL 302* [2]	**2**	13
29 Jul 89	**UH-UH OOH OOH LOOK OUT (HERE IT COMES)** *Atlantic A 8941*	**72**	2

[1] Roberta Flack and Donny Hathaway [2] Peabo Bryson and Roberta Flack

FLAJ – *See GETO BOYS featuring FLAJ*

FLAMING LIPS *US, male vocal / instrumental group (4 WEEKS)* pos/wks

9 Mar 96	**THIS HERE GIRAFFE** *Warner Bros. W 0335CD*	**72**	1
26 Jun 99	**RACE FOR THE PRIZE** *Warner Bros. W 494CD1*	**39**	2
20 Nov 99	**WAITIN' FOR A SUPERMAN** *Warner Bros. W 505CD1*	**73**	1

FLAMINGOS *US, male vocal group (5 WEEKS)* pos/wks

4 Jun 69	**THE BOOGALOO PARTY** *Philips BF 1786*	**26**	5

With the Michael Sammes Singers

Michael THE FLANDERS *UK, male vocalist (3 WEEKS)* pos/wks

27 Feb 59	**THE LITTLE DRUMMER BOY** *Parlophone R 4528*	**20**	2
17 Apr 59	**THE LITTLE DRUMMER BOY (re-entry)** *Parlophone R 4528*	**24**	1

FLASH and the PAN

Australia, male vocal / instrumental group (15 WEEKS) pos/wks

23 Sep 78	**AND THE BAND PLAYED ON (DOWN AMONG THE DEAD MEN)** *Ensign ENY 15*	**54**	4
21 May 83 ●	**WAITING FOR A TRAIN** *Easybeat EASY 1*	**7**	11

Lester FLATT and Earl SCRUGGS

US, male instrumental duo – banjos (6 WEEKS) pos/wks

15 Nov 67	**FOGGY MOUNTAIN BREAKDOWN** *CBS 3038 and Mercury MF 1007*	**39**	6

The versions on the two labels were not the same cuts; CBS had a 1965 recording, Mercury a 1949 recording. The chart did not differentiate and listed both together

Fogwell FLAX and the ANKLEBITERS from FREEHOLD JUNIOR SCHOOL *UK, male vocalist and school choir (2 WEEKS)*

Date	Title / Label	pos	wks
26 Dec 81	ONE NINE FOR SANTA *EMI 5255*	68	2

FLEE-REKKERS *UK, male instrumental group (13 WEEKS)*

Date	Title / Label	pos	wks
19 May 60	GREEN JEANS *Triumph RGM 1008*	23	13

FLEETWOOD MAC (67 Top 500) *Record-breaking Anglo-American act. Members included: Mick Fleetwood (d), John McVie (b), Peter Green (g), Christine McVie (k/v), Lindsey Buckingham (g/v), Stevie Nicks (v). Grammy-winning album 'Rumours' sold more than 18 million copies in the US alone and has spent longer on the UK album chart than any other LP (223 WEEKS)*

Date	Title / Label	pos	wks
10 Apr 68	BLACK MAGIC WOMAN *Blue Horizon 57 3138*	37	7
17 Jul 68	NEED YOUR LOVE SO BAD *Blue Horizon 57 3139*	31	13
4 Dec 68 ★	ALBATROSS *Blue Horizon 57 3145*	1	20
16 Apr 69 ●	MAN OF THE WORLD *Immediate IM 080*	2	14
23 Jul 69	NEED YOUR LOVE SO BAD (re-issue) *Blue Horizon 57 3157*	32	6
13 Sep 69	NEED YOUR LOVE SO BAD (re-entry of re-issue) *Blue Horizon 57 3157*	42	3
4 Oct 69 ●	OH WELL *Reprise RS 27000*	2	16
23 May 70 ●	THE GREEN MANALISHI (WITH THE TWO-PRONG CROWN) *Reprise RS 27007*	10	12
12 May 73 ●	ALBATROSS (re-issue) *CBS 8306*	2	15
13 Nov 76	SAY YOU LOVE ME *Reprise K 14447*	40	4
19 Feb 77	GO YOUR OWN WAY *Warner Bros. K 16872*	38	4
30 Apr 77	DON'T STOP *Warner Bros. K 16930*	32	5
9 Jul 77	DREAMS *Warner Bros. K 16969* ▲	24	9
22 Oct 77	YOU MAKE LOVING FUN *Warner Bros. K 17013*	45	2
11 Mar 78	RHIANNON *Reprise K 14430*	46	3
6 Oct 79 ●	TUSK *Warner Bros. K 17468*	6	10
22 Dec 79	SARA *Warner Bros. K 17533*	37	8
25 Sep 82	GYPSY *Warner Bros. K 17997*	46	3
18 Dec 82 ●	OH DIANE *Warner Bros. FLEET 1*	9	15
4 Apr 87 ●	BIG LOVE *Warner Bros. W 8398*	9	12
11 Jul 87	SEVEN WONDERS *Warner Bros. W 8317*	56	4
26 Sep 87 ●	LITTLE LIES *Warner Bros. W 8291*	5	12
26 Dec 87	FAMILY MAN *Warner Bros. W 8114*	54	5
2 Apr 88 ●	EVERYWHERE *Warner Bros. W 8143*	4	10
18 Jun 88	ISN'T IT MIDNIGHT *Warner Bros. W 7860*	60	2
17 Dec 88	AS LONG AS YOU FOLLOW *Warner Bros. W 7644*	66	3
5 May 90	SAVE ME *Warner Bros. W 9866*	53	3
25 Aug 90	IN THE BACK OF MY MIND *Warner Bros. W 9739*	58	3

Group was UK and male only up to and including the re-issue of 'Albatross'

FLEETWOODS *US, male / female vocal group (8 WEEKS)*

Date	Title / Label	pos	wks
24 Apr 59 ●	COME SOFTLY TO ME *London HLU 8841* ▲	6	8

John '00' FLEMING *UK, male DJ / producer (2 WEEKS)*

Date	Title / Label	pos	wks
25 Dec 99	LOST IN EMOTION *React CDREACT 170*	74	1
12 Aug 00	FREE *React CDREACT 186*	61	1

La FLEUR *Holland, male / female vocal / instrumental group (4 WEEKS)*

Date	Title / Label	pos	wks
30 Jul 83	BOOGIE NIGHTS *Proto ENA 111*	51	4

FLICKMAN *Italy, male production duo – Andreas Mazzali and Giuliano Orlandi (6 WEEKS)*

Date	Title / Label	pos	wks
4 Mar 00	THE SOUND OF BAMBOO *Inferno CDFERN 25*	11	5
28 Apr 01	HEY! PARADISE *Inferno CDFERN 37*	69	1

KC FLIGHTT *US, male rapper (5 WEEKS)*

Date	Title / Label	pos	wks
1 Apr 89	PLANET E *RCA PT 49404*	48	4
12 May 01	VOICES *Hooj Choons HOOJ 106CD* [1]	59	1

[1] KC Flightt vs Funky Junction

Dread FLIMSTONE and the MODERN TONE AGE FAMILY *US, male vocal / instrumental group (1 WEEK)*

Date	Title / Label	pos	wks
30 Nov 91	FROM THE GHETTO *Urban URB 87*	66	1

Berni FLINT *UK, male vocalist (11 WEEKS)*

Date	Title / Label	pos	wks
19 Mar 77 ●	I DON'T WANT TO PUT A HOLD ON YOU *EMI 2599*	3	10
23 Jul 77	SOUTHERN COMFORT *EMI 2621*	48	1

FLINTLOCK *UK, male vocal / instrumental group (5 WEEKS)*

Date	Title / Label	pos	wks
29 May 76	DAWN *Pinnacle P 8419*	30	5

FLIP & FILL featuring Kelly LLORENNA *UK, male production duo and UK, female vocalist (3 WEEKS)*

Date	Title / Label	pos	wks
24 Mar 01	TRUE LOVE NEVER DIES *All Around the World CDGLOBE 240*	34	3

FLIPMODE SQUAD *US, male / female production / rap group (1 WEEK)*

Date	Title / Label	pos	wks
31 Oct 98	CHA CHA CHA *Elektra E 3810CD*	54	1

FLOATERS *US, male vocal group (11 WEEKS)*

Date	Title / Label	pos	wks
23 Jul 77 ★	FLOAT ON *ABC 4187*	1	11

A FLOCK OF SEAGULLS *UK, male vocal / instrumental group (46 WEEKS)*

Date	Title / Label	pos	wks
27 Mar 82	I RAN *Jive JIVE 14*	43	6
12 Jun 82	SPACE AGE LOVE SONG *Jive JIVE 17*	34	6
6 Nov 82 ●	WISHING (IF I HAD A PHOTOGRAPH OF YOU) *Jive JIVE 25*	10	12
23 Apr 83	NIGHTMARES *Jive JIVE 33*	53	3
25 Jun 83	TRANSFER AFFECTION *Jive JIVE 41*	38	5
14 Jul 84	THE MORE YOU LIVE, THE MORE YOU LOVE *Jive JIVE 62*	26	11
19 Oct 85	WHO'S THAT GIRL (SHE'S GOT IT) *Jive JIVE 106*	66	3

FLOORPLAY *UK, male instrumental / production duo (1 WEEK)*

Date	Title / Label	pos	wks
27 Jan 96	AUTOMATIC *Perfecto PERF 115CD*	50	1

FLOWERED UP *UK, male vocal / instrumental group (17 WEEKS)*

Date	Title / Label	pos	wks
28 Jul 90	IT'S ON *Heavenly HVN 3*	54	4
24 Nov 90	PHOBIA *Heavenly HVN 7*	75	1
11 May 91	TAKE IT *London FUP 1*	34	4
17 Aug 91	IT'S ON / EGG RUSH (re-recording) *London FUP 2*	38	3
2 May 92	WEEKENDER *Heavenly HVN 16*	20	5

FLOWERPOT MEN *UK, male vocal group (12 WEEKS)*

Date	Title / Label	pos	wks
23 Aug 67 ●	LET'S GO TO SAN FRANCISCO *Deram DM 142*	4	12

Mike FLOWERS POPS *UK, male / female vocal / instrumental group (14 WEEKS)*

Date	Title / Label	pos	wks
30 Dec 95 ●	WONDERWALL *London LONCD 378*	2	7
13 Apr 96	WONDERWALL (re-entry) *London LONCD 378*	52	2
8 Jun 96	LIGHT MY FIRE / PLEASE RELEASE ME *London LONCD 384*	39	2
28 Dec 96	DON'T CRY FOR ME ARGENTINA *Love This LUVTHIS 16*	30	3

Eddie FLOYD *US, male vocalist (29 WEEKS)*

Date	Title / Label	pos	wks
2 Feb 67	KNOCK ON WOOD *Atlantic 584 041*	50	1
2 Mar 67	KNOCK ON WOOD (re-entry) *Atlantic 584 041*	19	17
16 Mar 67	RAISE YOUR HAND *Stax 601 001*	42	3
9 Aug 67	THINGS GET BETTER *Stax 601 016*	31	8

FLUFFY *UK, female vocal / instrumental group (2 WEEKS)*

Date	Title / Label	pos	wks
17 Feb 96	HUSBAND *Parkway PARK 006CD*	58	1
5 Oct 96	NOTHING *Virgin VSCDT 1614*	52	1

FLUKE *UK, male instrumental / production group (20 WEEKS)*

Date	Title / Label	pos	wks
20 Mar 93	SLID *Circa YRCD 103*	59	1
19 Jun 93	ELECTRIC GUITAR *Circa YRCD 104*	58	2
11 Sep 93	GROOVY FEELING *Circa YRCD 106*	45	3
23 Apr 94	BUBBLE *Circa YRCD 110*	37	2
29 Jul 95	BULLET *Circa YRCD 121*	23	3
16 Dec 95	TOSH *Circa YRCD 122*	32	3
16 Nov 96	ATOM BOMB *Circa YRCD 125*	20	3

31 May 97		**ABSURD** *Virgin YRCD 126*	25	2
27 Sep 97		**SQUIRT** *Circa YRCD 127*	46	1

See also LUCKY MONKEYS

FLUSH – *See SLADE*

FLYING LIZARDS
UK, male / female vocal / instrumental group (16 WEEKS) pos/wks

4 Aug 79	●	**MONEY** *Virgin VS 276*	5	10
9 Feb 80		**TV** *Virgin VS 325*	43	6

FLYING PICKETS *UK, male vocal group (20 WEEKS)* pos/wks

26 Nov 83	★	**ONLY YOU** *10 TEN 14*	1	11
21 Apr 84	●	**WHEN YOU'RE YOUNG AND IN LOVE** *10 TEN 20*	7	8
8 Dec 84		**WHO'S THAT GIRL** *10 GIRL 1*	71	1

Jerome FLYNN – *See ROBSON and JEROME*

FM *UK, male vocal / instrumental group (11 WEEKS)* pos/wks

31 Jan 87		**FROZEN HEART** *Portrait DIDGE 1*	64	2
20 Jun 87		**LET LOVE BE THE LEADER** *Portrait MERV 1*	71	2
5 Aug 89		**BAD LUCK** *Epic 655031 7*	54	4
7 Oct 89		**SOMEDAY (YOU'LL COME RUNNING)** *CBS DINK 1*	64	2
10 Feb 90		**EVERYTIME I THINK OF YOU** *Epic DINK 2*	73	1

FOCUS *Holland, male instrumental group (21 WEEKS)* pos/wks

20 Jan 73		**HOCUS POCUS** *Polydor 2001 211*	20	10
27 Jan 73	●	**SYLVIA** *Polydor 2001 422*	4	11

FOG *US, male DJ / producer (4 WEEKS)* pos/wks

19 Feb 94		**BEEN A LONG TIME** *Columbia 6601212*	44	2
6 Jun 98		**BEEN A LONG TIME (re-mix)** *Pukka CDPUKKA 16*	27	2

Dan FOGELBERG *US, male vocalist (4 WEEKS)* pos/wks

15 Mar 80		**LONGER** *Epic EPC 8230*	59	4

Ben FOLDS *US, male singer / instrumentalist – piano (1 WEEK)* pos/wks

29 Sep 01		**ROCKIN' THE SUBURBS** *Epic 6718492*	53	1

See also Ben FOLDS FIVE

Ben FOLDS FIVE *US, male vocal / instrumental group (12 WEEKS)* pos/wks

14 Sep 96		**UNDERGROUND** *Caroline CDCAR 008*	37	2
1 Mar 97		**BATTLE OF WHO COULD CARE LESS** *Epic 6642302*	26	3
7 Jun 97		**KATE** *Epic 6645365*	39	2
18 Apr 98		**BRICK** *Epic 6656612*	26	3
24 Apr 99		**ARMY** *Epic 6672182*	28	2

FOLK IMPLOSION *US, male vocal / instrumental duo (1 WEEK)* pos/wks

15 Jun 96		**NATURAL ONE** *London LONCD 382*	45	1

Claudia FONTAINE – *See BEATMASTERS*

Wayne FONTANA (455 Top 500) *UK, male vocalist b. Glyn Ellis 28 Oct 1945, Manchester. All his hits were recorded on the Fontana label, resulting in the creation of the perfect pop quiz question (76 WEEKS)* pos/wks

11 Jul 63		**HELLO JOSEPHINE** *Fontana TF 404* [1]	46	2
28 May 64		**STOP LOOK AND LISTEN** *Fontana TF 451* [1]	37	4
8 Oct 64	●	**UM, UM, UM, UM, UM, UM** *Fontana TF 497* [1]	5	15
4 Feb 65	●	**GAME OF LOVE** *Fontana TF 535* [1] ▲	2	11
17 Jun 65		**JUST A LITTLE BIT TOO LATE** *Fontana TF 579* [1]	20	7
30 Sep 65		**SHE NEEDS LOVE** *Fontana TF 611* [1]	32	6
9 Dec 65		**IT WAS EASIER TO HURT HER** *Fontana TF 642*	36	6
21 Apr 66		**COME ON HOME** *Fontana TF 684*	16	12
25 Aug 66		**GOODBYE BLUEBIRD** *Fontana TF 737*	49	1
8 Dec 66		**PAMELA, PAMELA** *Fontana TF 770*	11	12

[1] Wayne Fontana and the Mindbenders

See also MINDBENDERS

FONTANA featuring Darryl D'BONNEAU
US, male producer and US, male vocalist (1 WEEK) pos/wks

24 Mar 01		**POW POW POW** *Strictly Rhythm SRUKCD 01*	62	1

Lenny FONTANA & DJ SHORTY *US, male production duo (2 WEEKS)* pos/wks

4 Mar 00		**CHOCOLATE SENSATION** *ffrr FCD 375*	39	2

FOO FIGHTERS *US, male vocal / instrumental group (32 WEEKS)* pos/wks

1 Jul 95	●	**THIS IS A CALL** *Roswell CDCL 753*	5	4
16 Sep 95		**I'LL STICK AROUND** *Roswell CDCL 757*	18	3
2 Dec 95		**FOR ALL THE COWS** *Roswell CDCL 762*	28	2
6 Apr 96		**BIG ME** *Roswell CDCL 768*	19	3
10 May 97		**MONKEY WRENCH** *Roswell CDCLS 788*	12	4
30 Aug 97		**EVERLONG** *Roswell CDCL 792*	18	3
31 Jan 98		**MY HERO** *Roswell CDCL 796*	21	2
29 Aug 98		**WALKING AFTER YOU; BEACON LIGHT** *Elektra E 4100CD* [1]	20	3
30 Oct 99		**LEARN TO FLY** *RCA 74321706622*	21	3
30 Sep 00		**BREAKOUT** *RCA 74321790102*	29	3
16 Dec 00		**NEXT YEAR** *RCA 74321809262*	42	2

[1] Foo Fighters: Ween

FOOL BOONA *UK, male DJ / producer – Colin Tevendale (1 WEEK)* pos/wks

10 Apr 99		**POPPED!!** *Virgin / VC Recordings / Uber Disko VCRD 46*	52	1

FOOL'S GARDEN *Germany, male vocal / instrumental group (4 WEEKS)* pos/wks

25 May 96		**LEMON TREE** *Encore CDCOR 014*	61	1
3 Aug 96		**LEMON TREE (re-issue)** *Encore CDCOR 018*	26	3

FOR REAL *US, female vocal group (2 WEEKS)* pos/wks

1 Jul 95		**YOU DON'T KNOW NOTHIN'** *A & M 5811232*	54	1
12 Jul 97		**LIKE I DO** *Rowdy 74321486582*	45	1

Bill FORBES *UK, male vocalist (1 WEEK)* pos/wks

15 Jan 60		**TOO YOUNG** *Columbia DB 4386*	29	1

David FORBES *UK, male producer (1 WEEK)* pos/wks

25 Aug 01		**QUESTIONS (MUST BE ASKED)** *Serious SERR 031CD*	57	1

FORBIDDEN – *See Jet BRONX and the FORBIDDEN*

FORCE & STYLES featuring Kelly LLORENNA
UK, male DJ duo (1 WEEK) pos/wks

25 Jul 98		**HEART OF GOLD** *Diverse VERSE 2CD*	55	1

FORCE M.D.'S *US, male vocal group (9 WEEKS)* pos/wks

12 Apr 86		**TENDER LOVE** *Tommy Boy IS 269*	23	9

Clinton FORD *UK, male vocalist (25 WEEKS)* pos/wks

23 Oct 59		**OLD SHEP** *Oriole CB 1500*	27	1
17 Aug 61		**TOO MANY BEAUTIFUL GIRLS** *Oriole CB 1623*	48	1
8 Mar 62		**FANLIGHT FANNY** *Oriole CB 1706*	22	10
5 Jan 67		**RUN TO THE DOOR** *Piccadilly 7N 35361*	25	13

Emile FORD and the CHECKMATES (368 Top 500) *First group to top the chart in the 1960s, fronted by vocalist b. Emile Sweatman 16 Oct 1937, Bahamas. UK-based multiracial act had five consecutive Top 20 entries – three with updates of oldies. NME readers voted them Best New Act 1960 (87 WEEKS)* pos/wks

30 Oct 59	★	**WHAT DO YOU WANT TO MAKE THOSE EYES AT ME FOR?** *Pye 7N 15225*	1	25
5 Feb 60	●	**ON A SLOW BOAT TO CHINA** *Pye 7N 15245*	3	14
26 May 60		**YOU'LL NEVER KNOW WHAT YOU'RE MISSING ('TIL YOU TRY)** *Pye 7N 15268*	12	9
1 Sep 60		**THEM THERE EYES** *Pye 7N 15282* [1]	18	16
8 Dec 60	●	**COUNTING TEARDROPS** *Pye 7N 15314*	4	12
2 Mar 61		**WHAT AM I GONNA DO** *Pye 7N 15331*	33	6

			pos	wks
18 May 61		HALF OF MY HEART *Piccadilly 7N 35003* [1]	50	1
22 Jun 61		HALF OF MY HEART (re-entry) *Piccadilly 7N 35003* [1]	42	3
8 Mar 62		I WONDER WHO'S KISSING HER NOW *Piccadilly 7N 35033* [1]	43	1

[1] Emile Ford

Lita FORD *UK, female vocalist (7 WEEKS)* pos/wks

			pos	wks
17 Dec 88		KISS ME DEADLY *RCA PB 49575*	75	1
20 May 89		CLOSE MY EYES FOREVER *Dreamland PB 49409* [1]	47	3
11 Jan 92		SHOT OF POISON *RCA PB 49145*	63	3

[1] Lita Ford duet with Ozzy Osbourne

Martyn FORD ORCHESTRA *UK, orchestra (3 WEEKS)* pos/wks

			pos	wks
14 May 77		LET YOUR BODY GO DOWNTOWN *Mountain TOP 26*	38	3

Mary FORD – *See Les PAUL and Mary FORD*

Penny FORD *US, female vocalist (7 WEEKS)* pos/wks

			pos	wks
4 May 85		DANGEROUS *Total Experience FB 49975* [1]	43	5
29 May 93		DAYDREAMING *Columbia 6590592*	43	2

[1] Pennye Ford

See also SNAP

Tennessee Ernie FORD *US, male vocalist (42 WEEKS)* pos/wks

			pos	wks
21 Jan 55	★	GIVE ME YOUR WORD *Capitol CL 14005*	1	24
6 Jan 56	★	SIXTEEN TONS *Capitol CL 14500* ▲	1	11
13 Jan 56	●	THE BALLAD OF DAVY CROCKETT *Capitol CL 14506*	3	7

Julia FORDHAM *UK, female vocalist (32 WEEKS)* pos/wks

			pos	wks
2 Jul 88		HAPPY EVER AFTER *Circa YR 15*	27	9
25 Feb 89		WHERE DOES THE TIME GO? *Circa YR 23*	41	5
31 Aug 91		I THOUGHT IT WAS YOU *Circa YR 69*	64	2
18 Jan 92		LOVE MOVES (IN MYSTERIOUS WAYS) *Circa YR 73*	19	9
30 May 92		I THOUGHT IT WAS YOU (re-mix) *Circa YR 90*	45	3
30 Apr 94		DIFFERENT TIME DIFFERENT PLACE *Circa YRCD 111*	41	3
23 Jul 94		I CAN'T HELP MYSELF *Circa YRCD 116*	62	1

FOREIGNER (427 Top 500) *Melodic Anglo-American rock group who amassed six US Top 10 albums. Featured Londoner Mick Jones (g) and New York native Lou Gramm (v). 'Waiting for a Girl Like You' stayed at No.2 in the US for a record-breaking 10 weeks (78 WEEKS)* pos/wks

			pos	wks
6 May 78		FEELS LIKE THE FIRST TIME *Atlantic K 11086*	39	6
15 Jul 78		COLD AS ICE *Atlantic K 10986*	24	10
28 Oct 78		HOT BLOODED *Atlantic K 11167*	42	3
24 Feb 79		BLUE MORNING BLUE DAY *Atlantic K 11236*	45	4
29 Aug 81		URGENT *Atlantic K 11665*	54	4
10 Oct 81		JUKE BOX HERO *Atlantic K 11678*	48	4
12 Dec 81	●	WAITING FOR A GIRL LIKE YOU *Atlantic K 11696*	8	13
8 May 82		URGENT (re-issue) *Atlantic K 11728*	45	5
8 Dec 84	★	I WANT TO KNOW WHAT LOVE IS *Atlantic A 9596* ▲	1	16
6 Apr 85		THAT WAS YESTERDAY *Atlantic A 9571*	28	6
22 Jun 85		COLD AS ICE (re-mix) *Atlantic A 9539*	64	2
19 Dec 87		SAY YOU WILL *Atlantic A 9169*	71	4
22 Oct 94		WHITE LIE *Arista 74321232862*	58	1

FORMATIONS *US, male vocal group (11 WEEKS)* pos/wks

			pos	wks
31 Jul 71		AT THE TOP OF THE STAIRS *Mojo 2027 001*	50	1
14 Aug 71		AT THE TOP OF THE STAIRS (re-entry) *Mojo 2027 001*	28	10

George FORMBY *UK, male vocalist / instrumentalist – ukulele (3 WEEKS)* pos/wks

			pos	wks
21 Jul 60		HAPPY GO LUCKY ME / BANJO BOY *Pye 7N 15269*	40	3

See also 2 IN A TENT

FORREST *US, male vocalist – Forrest M Thomas Jr (20 WEEKS)* pos/wks

			pos	wks
26 Feb 83	●	ROCK THE BOAT *CBS A 3163*	4	10
14 May 83		FEEL THE NEED IN ME *CBS A 3411*	17	8
17 Sep 83		ONE LOVER (DON'T STOP THE SHOW) *CBS A 3734*	67	2

Sharon FORRESTER *Jamaica, female vocalist (1 WEEK)* pos/wks

			pos	wks
11 Feb 95		LOVE INSIDE *ffrr FCD 253*	50	1

Lance FORTUNE *UK, male vocalist – Chris Morris (17 WEEKS)* pos/wks

			pos	wks
19 Feb 60	●	BE MINE *Pye 7N 15240*	4	12
5 May 60		THIS LOVE I HAVE FOR YOU *Pye 7N 15260*	26	5

FORTUNES *UK, male vocal / instrumental group (65 WEEKS)* pos/wks

			pos	wks
8 Jul 65	●	YOU'VE GOT YOUR TROUBLES *Decca F 12173*	2	14
7 Oct 65	●	HERE IT COMES AGAIN *Decca F 12243*	4	14
3 Feb 66		THIS GOLDEN RING *Decca F 12321*	15	9
11 Sep 71	●	FREEDOM COME, FREEDOM GO *Capitol CL 15693*	6	17
29 Jan 72	●	STORM IN A TEACUP *Capitol CL 15707*	7	11

45 KING (DJ MARK THE 45 KING)
US, male producer – Mark James (6 WEEKS) pos/wks

			pos	wks
28 Oct 89		THE KING IS HERE / THE 900 NUMBER *Dance Trax DRX 9*	60	5
11 Aug 90		THE KING IS HERE / THE 900 NUMBER (re-entry) *Dance Trax DRX 9*	73	1

49ers *Italy, male producer – Gianfranco Bortolotti (27 WEEKS)* pos/wks

			pos	wks
16 Dec 89	●	TOUCH ME *Fourth & Broadway BRW 157*	3	13
17 Mar 90		DON'T YOU LOVE ME *Fourth & Broadway BRW 167*	12	6
9 Jun 90		GIRL TO GIRL *Fourth & Broadway BRW 174*	31	3
6 Jun 92		GOT TO BE FREE *Fourth & Broadway BRW 255*	46	2
29 Aug 92		THE MESSAGE *Fourth & Broadway BRW 257*	68	1
18 Mar 95		ROCKIN' MY BODY *Media MCSTD 2021* [1]	31	2

[1] 49ers featuring Ann-Marie Smith

See also CAPPELLA

Itsy FOSTER – *See EXOTICA featuring Itsy FOSTER*

FOSTER and ALLEN
Ireland, male vocal duo – Mike Foster and Tony Allen (47 WEEKS) pos/wks

			pos	wks
27 Feb 82		A BUNCH OF THYME *Ritz RITZ 5*	18	11
30 Oct 82		OLD FLAMES *Ritz RITZ 028*	51	8
19 Feb 83		MAGGIE *Ritz RITZ 025*	27	9
29 Oct 83		I WILL LOVE YOU ALL MY LIFE *Ritz RITZ 056*	49	6
30 Jun 84		JUST FOR OLD TIME'S SAKE *Ritz RITZ 066*	47	6
29 Mar 86		AFTER ALL THESE YEARS *Ritz RITZ 106*	43	7

FOUNDATIONS *West Indies / UK / Sri Lanka, male vocal / instrumental group (57 WEEKS)* pos/wks

			pos	wks
27 Sep 67	★	BABY NOW THAT I'VE FOUND YOU *Pye 7N 17366*	1	16
24 Jan 68		BACK ON MY FEET AGAIN *Pye 7N 17417*	18	10
1 May 68		ANY OLD TIME (YOU'RE LONELY AND SAD) *Pye 7N 17503*	48	1
15 May 68		ANY OLD TIME (YOU'RE LONELY AND SAD) (re-entry) *Pye 7N 17503*	50	1
20 Nov 68	●	BUILD ME UP BUTTERCUP *Pye 7N 17636*	2	15
12 Mar 69	●	IN THE BAD BAD OLD DAYS (BEFORE YOU LOVED ME) *Pye 7N 17702*	8	10
13 Sep 69		BORN TO LIVE, BORN TO DIE *Pye 7N 17809*	46	3
12 Dec 98		BUILD ME UP BUTTERCUP (re-issue) *Castle NEEX 1001*	71	1

FOUNTAINS OF WAYNE
US, male vocal / instrumental group (7 WEEKS) pos/wks

			pos	wks
22 Mar 97		RADIATION VIBE *Atlantic 7567956262*	32	2
10 May 97		SINK TO THE BOTTOM *Atlantic A 5612CD*	42	1
26 Jul 97		SURVIVAL CAR *Atlantic AT 0004CD*	53	1
27 Dec 97		I WANT AN ALIEN FOR CHRISTMAS *Atlantic AT 0020CD*	36	2
20 Mar 99		DENISE *Atlantic AT 0053CD*	57	1

FOUR ACES *US, male vocal group (40 WEEKS)* pos/wks

			pos	wks
30 Jul 54	●	THREE COINS IN THE FOUNTAIN *Brunswick 05308* [1]	5	5
22 Oct 54		THREE COINS IN THE FOUNTAIN (re-entry) *Brunswick 05308* [1]	17	1
7 Jan 55	●	MISTER SANDMAN *Brunswick 05355* [1]	9	5

20 May 55	●	**STRANGER IN PARADISE** *Brunswick 05418*	6	6
18 Nov 55	●	**LOVE IS A MANY SPLENDORED THING** *Brunswick 05480* [1] ▲	2	13
19 Oct 56		**A WOMAN IN LOVE** *Brunswick 05589* [1]	19	3
4 Jan 57		**FRIENDLY PERSUASION (THEE I LOVE)** *Brunswick 05623* [1]	29	1
23 Jan 59		**THE WORLD OUTSIDE** *Brunswick 05773*	18	6

[1] Four Aces featuring Al Alberts

FOUR BUCKETEERS *UK, male / female vocal group (6 WEEKS)*

			pos	wks
3 May 80		**THE BUCKET OF WATER SONG** *CBS 8393*	26	6

FOUR ESQUIRES *US, male vocal group (2 WEEKS)*

			pos	wks
31 Jan 58		**LOVE ME FOREVER** *London HLO 8533*	23	2

4 HERO *UK, male instrumental group (6 WEEKS)*

			pos	wks
24 Nov 90		**MR KIRK'S NIGHTMARE** *Reinforced RIVET 1203*	73	2
9 May 92		**COOKIN' UP YAH BRAIN** *Reinforced RIVET 1216*	59	2
15 Aug 98		**STAR CHASERS** *Talkin' Loud TLCD 36*	41	1
3 Nov 01		**LES FLEUR** *Talkin' Loud TLCD 66*	53	1

'Mr Kirk's Nightmare' was titled 'Combat Dancing (EP)' in its first week on chart

400 BLOWS *UK, male vocal / instrumental duo (4 WEEKS)*

			pos	wks
29 Jun 85		**MOVIN'** *Illuminated ILL 61*	54	4

FOUR JAYS – *See Billy FURY*

FOUR KESTRELS – *See Billy FURY*

FOUR KNIGHTS *US, male vocal group (11 WEEKS)*

			pos	wks
4 Jun 54	●	**(OH BABY MINE) I GET SO LONELY** *Capitol CL 14076*	5	7
30 Jul 54	●	**(OH BABY MINE) I GET SO LONELY (re-entry)** *Capitol CL 14076*	10	4

FOUR LADS *Canada, male vocal group (23 WEEKS)*

			pos	wks
19 Dec 52	●	**FAITH CAN MOVE MOUNTAINS** *Columbia DB 3154* [1]	7	2
9 Jan 53	●	**FAITH CAN MOVE MOUNTAINS (re-entry)** *Columbia DB 3154* [1]	9	1
22 Oct 54	●	**RAIN, RAIN, RAIN** *Philips PB 311* [2]	8	16
28 Apr 60		**STANDING ON THE CORNER** *Philips PB 1000*	34	4

[1] Johnnie Ray and the Four Lads [2] Frankie Laine and the Four Lads

4 NON BLONDES
US, female / male vocal / instrumental group (19 WEEKS)

			pos	wks
19 Jun 93	●	**WHAT'S UP** *Interscope A 8412CD*	2	17
16 Oct 93		**SPACEMAN** *Interscope A 8349CD*	53	2

4 OF US *Ireland, male vocal / instrumental group (6 WEEKS)*

			pos	wks
27 Feb 93		**SHE HITS ME** *Columbia 6589192*	35	4
1 May 93		**I MISS YOU** *Columbia 6591722*	62	2

FOUR PENNIES *UK, male vocal / instrumental group – lead vocal Lionel Morton (56 WEEKS)*

			pos	wks
16 Jan 64		**DO YOU WANT ME TO** *Philips BF 1296*	47	1
6 Feb 64		**DO YOU WANT ME TO (re-entry)** *Philips BF 1296*	49	1
2 Apr 64	★	**JULIET** *Philips BF 1322*	1	15
16 Jul 64		**I FOUND OUT THE HARD WAY** *Philips BF 1349*	14	11
29 Oct 64		**BLACK GIRL** *Philips BF 1366*	20	12
7 Oct 65		**UNTIL IT'S TIME FOR YOU TO GO** *Philips BF 1435*	19	11
17 Feb 66		**TROUBLE IS MY MIDDLE NAME** *Philips BF 1469*	32	5

FOUR PREPS *US, male vocal group (23 WEEKS)*

			pos	wks
13 Jun 58	●	**BIG MAN** *Capitol CL 14873*	2	13
19 Sep 58		**BIG MAN (re-entry)** *Capitol CL 14873*	22	1
26 May 60		**GOT A GIRL** *Capitol CL 15128*	28	6
14 Jul 60		**GOT A GIRL (re-entry)** *Capitol CL 15128*	47	1
2 Nov 61		**MORE MONEY FOR YOU AND ME (MEDLEY)** *Capitol CL 15217*	39	2

Tracks on medley: Mr Blue / Alley Oop / Smoke Gets in Your Eyes / In This Whole Wide World / A Worried Man / Tom Dooley / A Teenager in Love – all songs feature new lyrics

FOUR SEASONS (146 Top 500) *No.1 US group of the early 1960s: Frankie Valli (v), Bob Gaudio (k/v), Nick Massi (b/v) (died 2000), Tommy DeVito (g/v). Falsetto-voiced Valli's quartet, the first group to score three US No.1s in succession, has a chart span there of almost 40 years (151 WEEKS)*

			pos	wks
4 Oct 62	●	**SHERRY** *Stateside SS 122* ▲	8	16
17 Jan 63		**BIG GIRLS DON'T CRY** *Stateside SS 145* ▲	13	10
28 Mar 63		**WALK LIKE A MAN** *Stateside SS 169* ▲	12	12
27 Jun 63		**AIN'T THAT A SHAME** *Stateside SS 194*	38	3
27 Aug 64	●	**RAG DOLL** *Philips BF 1347* [1] ▲	2	13
18 Nov 65	●	**LET'S HANG ON** *Philips BF 1439* [1]	4	16
31 Mar 66		**WORKING MY WAY BACK TO YOU** *Philips BF 1474* [2]	50	3
2 Jun 66		**OPUS 17 (DON'T YOU WORRY 'BOUT ME)** *Philips BF 1493* [2]	20	9
29 Sep 66		**I'VE GOT YOU UNDER MY SKIN** *Philips BF 1511* [2]	12	11
12 Jan 67		**TELL IT TO THE RAIN** *Philips BF 1538* [2]	37	5
19 Apr 75	●	**NIGHT** *Mowest MW 3024* [3]	7	9
20 Sep 75	●	**WHO LOVES YOU** *Warner Bros. K 16602*	6	9
31 Jan 76	★	**DECEMBER '63 (OH WHAT A NIGHT)** *Warner Bros. K 16688* ▲	1	10
24 Apr 76	●	**SILVER STAR** *Warner Bros. K 16742*	3	9
27 Nov 76		**WE CAN WORK IT OUT** *Warner Bros. K 16845*	34	4
18 Jun 77		**RHAPSODY** *Warner Bros. K 16932*	37	3
20 Aug 77		**DOWN THE HALL** *Warner Bros. K 16982*	34	5
29 Oct 88		**DECEMBER '63 (OH WHAT A NIGHT) (re-mix)** *BR 45277* [3]	49	4

[1] Four Seasons with the sound of Frankie Valli [2] Four Seasons with Frankie Valli [3] Frankie Valli and the Four Seasons

4 STRINGS *Holland, male / female production / vocal duo (3 WEEKS)*

			pos	wks
23 Dec 00		**DAY TIME** *AM:PM 139*	48	3

4 THE CAUSE *US, male / female vocal group (9 WEEKS)*

			pos	wks
10 Oct 98		**STAND BY ME** *RCA 74321622442*	12	9

FOUR TOPS (27 Top 500) *Unmistakable R&B vocal group from Detroit: Levi Stubbs, Renaldo Benson, Lawrence Payton (d. 1997), Abdul Fakir. The legendary Motown act performed together for a record 44 years (until Payton's death) and were inducted into the Rock and Roll Hall of Fame in 1990 (318 WEEKS)*

			pos	wks
1 Jul 65		**I CAN'T HELP MYSELF** *Tamla Motown TMG 515* ▲	23	9
2 Sep 65		**IT'S THE SAME OLD SONG** *Tamla Motown TMG 528*	34	8
21 Jul 66		**LOVING YOU IS SWEETER THAN EVER** *Tamla Motown TMG 568*	21	12
13 Oct 66	★	**REACH OUT I'LL BE THERE** *Tamla Motown TMG 579* ▲	1	16
12 Jan 67	●	**STANDING IN THE SHADOWS OF LOVE** *Tamla Motown TMG 589*	6	8
30 Mar 67	●	**BERNADETTE** *Tamla Motown TMG 601*	8	10
15 Jun 67		**SEVEN ROOMS OF GLOOM** *Tamla Motown TMG 612*	12	9
11 Oct 67		**YOU KEEP RUNNING AWAY** *Tamla Motown TMG 623*	26	7
13 Dec 67	●	**WALK AWAY RENEE** *Tamla Motown TMG 634*	3	11
13 Mar 68	●	**IF I WERE A CARPENTER** *Tamla Motown TMG 647*	7	11
21 Aug 68		**YESTERDAY'S DREAMS** *Tamla Motown TMG 665*	23	15
13 Nov 68		**I'M IN A DIFFERENT WORLD** *Tamla Motown TMG 675*	27	13
28 May 69		**WHAT IS A MAN** *Tamla Motown TMG 698*	16	11
27 Sep 69		**DO WHAT YOU GOTTA DO** *Tamla Motown TMG 710*	11	11
21 Mar 70	●	**I CAN'T HELP MYSELF (re-issue)** *Tamla Motown TMG 732*	10	11
30 May 70	●	**IT'S ALL IN THE GAME** *Tamla Motown TMG 736*	5	14
12 Sep 70		**IT'S ALL IN THE GAME (re-entry)** *Tamla Motown TMG 736*	48	2
3 Oct 70	●	**STILL WATER (LOVE)** *Tamla Motown TMG 752*	10	10
19 Dec 70		**STILL WATER (LOVE) (re-entry)** *Tamla Motown TMG 752*	44	2
1 May 71		**JUST SEVEN NUMBERS (CAN STRAIGHTEN OUT MY LIFE)** *Tamla Motown TMG 770*	36	5
26 Jun 71		**RIVER DEEP MOUNTAIN HIGH** *Tamla Motown TMG 777* [1]	11	10
25 Sep 71	●	**SIMPLE GAME** *Tamla Motown TMG 785*	3	11
20 Nov 71		**YOU GOTTA HAVE LOVE IN YOUR HEART** *Tamla Motown TMG 793* [1]	25	10
11 Mar 72		**BERNADETTE (re-issue)** *Tamla Motown TMG 803*	23	7
5 Aug 72		**WALK WITH ME TALK WITH ME DARLING** *Tamla Motown TMG 823*	32	6
18 Nov 72		**KEEPER OF THE CASTLE** *Probe PRO 575*	18	9
10 Nov 73		**SWEET UNDERSTANDING LOVE** *Probe PRO 604*	29	10
17 Oct 81	●	**WHEN SHE WAS MY GIRL** *Casablanca CAN 1005*	3	10
19 Dec 81		**DON'T WALK AWAY** *Casablanca CAN 1006*	16	11
6 Mar 82		**TONIGHT I'M GONNA LOVE YOU ALL OVER** *Casablanca CAN 1008*	43	4

26 Jun 82	**BACK TO SCHOOL AGAIN** *RSO 89*	62	2
23 Jul 88	**REACH OUT I'LL BE THERE (re-mix)** *Motown ZB 41943*	11	9
17 Sep 88	**INDESTRUCTIBLE** *Arista 111717* [2]	55	4
3 Dec 88 ●	**LOCO IN ACAPULCO** *Arista 111850*	7	13
25 Feb 89	**INDESTRUCTIBLE** *Arista 112074* [2]	30	7

[1] Supremes and the Four Tops [2] Four Tops featuring Smokey Robinson

The original US recording of 'Indestructible' was not issued until after the chart run of the UK- only mix

4MANDU *UK, male vocal group (6 WEEKS)* pos/wks

29 Jul 95	**THIS IS IT** *Final Vinyl 74321291222*	45	3
17 Feb 96	**DO IT FOR LOVE** *Arista 74321343902*	45	2
15 Jun 96	**BABY DON'T GO** *Arista 74321375914*	47	1

FOURMOST *UK, male vocal / instrumental group (64 WEEKS)* pos/wks

12 Sep 63 ●	**HELLO LITTLE GIRL** *Parlophone R 5056*	9	17
26 Dec 63	**I'M IN LOVE** *Parlophone R 5078*	17	12
23 Apr 64 ●	**A LITTLE LOVING** *Parlophone R 5128*	6	13
13 Aug 64	**HOW CAN I TELL HER** *Parlophone R 5157*	33	4
26 Nov 64	**BABY I NEED YOUR LOVIN'** *Parlophone R 5194*	24	12
9 Dec 65	**GIRLS, GIRLS, GIRLS** *Parlophone R 5379*	33	6

14-18 *UK, male vocalist – Peter Waterman (4 WEEKS)* pos/wks

1 Nov 75	**GOODBYE-EE** *Magnet MAG 48*	33	4

See also STOCK AITKEN WATERMAN

40 THEVZ – See COOLIO

Bernard FOWLER – See BOMB THE BASS

FOX *UK / US, male / female vocal / instrumental group (29 WEEKS)* pos/wks

15 Feb 75 ●	**ONLY YOU CAN** *GTO GT 8*	3	11
10 May 75	**IMAGINE ME IMAGINE YOU** *GTO GT 21*	15	8
10 Apr 76 ●	**S-S-S-SINGLE BED** *GTO GT 57*	4	10

Noosha FOX *UK, female vocalist (6 WEEKS)* pos/wks

12 Nov 77	**GEORGINA BAILEY** *GTO GT 106*	31	6

Samantha FOX (482 Top 500) *Former Sun 'Page 3 girl', b. 15 Apr 1966, London, UK, had big hits worldwide – including countries where she wasn't previously known for topless modelling. Only British female to register three Top 10 singles in the UK and US in 1980s (73 WEEKS)* pos/wks

22 Mar 86 ●	**TOUCH ME (I WANT YOUR BODY)** *Jive FOXY 1*	3	10
28 Jun 86 ●	**DO YA DO YA (WANNA PLEASE ME)** *Jive FOXY 2*	10	7
6 Sep 86	**HOLD ON TIGHT** *Jive FOXY 3*	26	5
13 Dec 86	**I'M ALL YOU NEED** *Jive FOXY 4*	41	6
30 May 87 ●	**NOTHING'S GONNA STOP ME NOW** *Jive FOXY 5*	8	9
25 Jul 87	**I SURRENDER (TO THE SPIRIT OF THE NIGHT)** *Jive FOXY 6*	25	7
17 Oct 87	**I PROMISE YOU (GET READY)** *Jive FOXY 7*	58	3
19 Dec 87	**TRUE DEVOTION** *Jive FOXY 8*	62	3
21 May 88	**NAUGHTY GIRLS (NEED LOVE TOO)** *Jive FOXY 9*	31	5
19 Nov 88	**LOVE HOUSE** *Jive FOXY 10*	32	6
28 Jan 89	**I ONLY WANNA BE WITH YOU** *Jive FOXY 11*	16	8
17 Jun 89	**I WANNA HAVE SOME FUN** *Jive FOXY 12*	63	2
28 Mar 98	**SANTA MARIA** *All Around the World CDGLOBE 163*	31	2

See also SOX

Bruce FOXTON *UK, male vocalist (9 WEEKS)* pos/wks

30 Jul 83	**FREAK** *Arista BFOX 1*	23	5
29 Oct 83	**THIS IS THE WAY** *Arista BFOX 2*	56	3
21 Apr 84	**IT MAKES ME WONDER** *Arista BFOX 3*	74	1

See also JAM

Inez FOXX *US, female vocalist (8 WEEKS)* pos/wks

23 Jul 64	**HURT BY LOVE** *Sue WI 323*	40	3
19 Feb 69	**MOCKINGBIRD** *United Artists UP 2269* [1]	36	2
19 Mar 69	**MOCKINGBIRD (re-entry)** *United Artists UP 2269* [1]	33	3

[1] Inez and Charlie Foxx

John FOXX *UK, male vocalist (31 WEEKS)* pos/wks

26 Jan 80	**UNDERPASS** *Virgin VS 318*	31	8
29 Mar 80	**NO ONE DRIVING (DOUBLE SINGLE)** *Virgin VS 338*	32	4
19 Jul 80	**BURNING CAR** *Virgin VS 360*	35	7
8 Nov 80	**MILES AWAY** *Virgin VS 382*	51	3
29 Aug 81	**EUROPE (AFTER THE RAIN)** *Virgin VS 393*	40	5
2 Jul 83	**ENDLESSLY** *Virgin VS 543*	66	3
17 Sep 83	**YOUR DRESS** *Virgin VS 615*	61	1

Tracks on double single: No One Driving / Glimmer / Mr No / This City

FPI PROJECT *Italy, male instrumental / production group (17 WEEKS)* pos/wks

9 Dec 89 ●	**GOING BACK TO MY ROOTS / RICH IN PARADISE** *Rumour RUMAT 9*	9	12
9 Mar 91	**EVERYBODY (ALL OVER THE WORLD)** *Rumour RUMA 29*	65	3
7 Aug 93	**COME ON (AND DO IT)** *Synthetic SYNTH 006CD*	59	1
13 Mar 99	**EVERYBODY (ALL OVER) (re-mix)** *99 North CDNTH 14*	67	1

'Going Back to My Roots' was a vocal track available in two formats and featured either Paolo Dini or Sharon Dee Clarke

FRAGGLES *UK / US, puppets from TV series (8 WEEKS)* pos/wks

18 Feb 84	**'FRAGGLE ROCK' THEME** *RCA 389*	33	8

FRAGMA *Germany / Spain, male / female production / vocal group (45 WEEKS)* pos/wks

25 Sep 99	**TOCA ME** *Positiva CDTIV 120*	11	6
22 Apr 00 ★	**TOCA'S MIRACLE (re-mix)** *Positiva CDTIV 128* [1] ■	1	15
12 Aug 00	**TOCA'S MIRACLE (re-entry of re-mix)** *Positiva CDTIV 128* [1]	52	2
13 Jan 01 ●	**EVERYTIME YOU NEED ME** *Positiva CDTIV 147* [2]	3	11
19 May 01 ●	**YOU ARE ALIVE** *Positiva CDTIVS 153*	4	9
8 Dec 01	**SAY THAT YOU'RE HERE** *Illustrious CDILLS 001*	25	2

[1] Vocals by Co Co [2] Fragma featuring Maria Rubia

Roddy FRAME *UK, male vocalist / instrumentalist (2 WEEKS)* pos/wks

19 Sep 98	**REASON FOR LIVING** *Independiente ISOM 18MS*	45	2

See also AZTEC CAMERA

Peter FRAMPTON *UK, male vocalist (24 WEEKS)* pos/wks

1 May 76 ●	**SHOW ME THE WAY** *A & M AMS 7218*	10	12
11 Sep 76	**BABY I LOVE YOUR WAY** *A & M AMS 7246*	43	5
6 Nov 76	**DO YOU FEEL LIKE WE DO** *A & M AMS 7260*	39	4
23 Jul 77	**I'M IN YOU** *A & M AMS 7298*	41	3

Connie FRANCIS (52 Top 500) *The original Italian-American queen of pop, b. Concetta Franconero, 12 Dec 1938, New Jersey. The most successful international female vocalist of the 1950s and 1960s and the first female solo artist to top the UK album chart (244 WEEKS)* pos/wks

4 Apr 58 ★	**WHO'S SORRY NOW** *MGM 975*	1	25
27 Jun 58	**I'M SORRY I MADE YOU CRY** *MGM 982*	11	10
22 Aug 58 ★	**CAROLINA MOON / STUPID CUPID** *MGM 985*	1	19
31 Oct 58	**I'LL GET BY** *MGM 993*	19	6
21 Nov 58	**FALLIN'** *MGM 993*	20	5
26 Dec 58	**YOU ALWAYS HURT THE ONE YOU LOVE** *MGM 998*	13	7
13 Feb 59 ●	**MY HAPPINESS** *MGM 1001*	4	14
29 May 59	**MY HAPPINESS (re-entry)** *MGM 1001*	30	1
3 Jul 59 ●	**LIPSTICK ON YOUR COLLAR** *MGM 1018*	3	16
11 Sep 59	**PLENTY GOOD LOVIN'** *MGM 1036*	18	6
4 Dec 59	**AMONG MY SOUVENIRS** *MGM 1046*	11	10
17 Mar 60	**VALENTINO** *MGM 1060*	27	8
19 May 60 ●	**MAMA / ROBOT MAN** *MGM 1076*	2	19
18 Aug 60 ●	**EVERYBODY'S SOMEBODY'S FOOL** *MGM 1086* ▲	5	13
3 Nov 60 ●	**MY HEART HAS A MIND OF ITS OWN** *MGM 1100* ▲	3	15
12 Jan 61	**MANY TEARS AGO** *MGM 1111*	12	9
16 Mar 61 ●	**WHERE THE BOYS ARE / BABY ROO** *MGM 1121*	5	14

1968

IN THE YEAR IN WHICH 10 MILLION FRENCH WORKERS AND STUDENTS WENT ON STRIKE, ENOCH POWELL MADE HIS INFAMOUS RIVERS OF BLOOD SPEECH, AND STANLEY KUBRICK PUSHED BACK THE LIMITATIONS OF CINEMA WITH '2001: A SPACE ODYSSEY', **BILL DRUMMOND** FROM KLF WAXES LYRICAL ABOUT FLEETWOOD MAC'S ONE AND ONLY CHART-TOPPER ...

"This is about being 15 in October 1968 and hearing 'Albatross' by **Fleetwood Mac**, for the first time late at night on Radio Luxembourg while lying in bed unable to get the idea of Linda Ballantyne's legs out of my mind. This is about the fact that an underground blues band went all the way to number one with the greatest instrumental single since 'Telstar', without having to sell out any of their purist principles by doing some cheesy, good-time, radio-friendly tune... Hang on a minute: it was not only the greatest instrumental since 'Telstar', it was the most moving, distinct, evocative, strange ... in fact, the greatest UK No.1 ever."

SINGLE OF THE YEAR 'Those Were the Days' Mary Hopkin
ALBUM OF THE YEAR 'John Wesley Harding' Bob Dylan

		pos	wks
15 Jun 61	BREAKIN' IN A BRAND NEW BROKEN HEART *MGM 1136*	12	11
14 Sep 61 ●	TOGETHER *MGM 1138*	6	11
14 Dec 61	BABY'S FIRST CHRISTMAS *MGM 1145*	30	4
26 Apr 62	DON'T BREAK THE HEART THAT LOVES YOU *MGM 1157* ▲	39	3
2 Aug 62 ●	VACATION *MGM 1165*	10	9
20 Dec 62	I'M GONNA BE WARM THIS WINTER *MGM 1185*	48	1
10 Jun 65	MY CHILD *MGM 1271*	26	6
20 Jan 66	JEALOUS HEART *MGM 1293*	44	2

Baby Roo listed with 'Where the Boys Are' for first eight weeks only

Jill FRANCIS *UK, female vocalist (1 WEEK)*

		pos	wks
3 Jul 93	MAKE LOVE TO ME *Glady Wax GW 003CD*	70	1

Claude FRANÇOIS *France, male vocalist (4 WEEKS)*

		pos	wks
10 Jan 76	TEARS ON THE TELEPHONE *Bradley's BRAD 7528*	35	4

Joe FRANK – *See HAMILTON, Joe FRANK and REYNOLDS*

FRANK AND WALTERS
Ireland, male vocal / instrumental group (13 WEEKS)

		pos	wks
21 Mar 92	HAPPY BUSMAN *Setanta HOO 2*	49	2
12 Sep 92	THIS IS NOT A SONG *Setanta HOO 3*	46	3
9 Jan 93	AFTER ALL *Setanta HOOCD 4*	11	5
17 Apr 93	FASHION CRISIS HITS NEW YORK *Setanta HOOCD 5*	42	3

FRANKE *UK, male vocalist – Franke Pharoah (3 WEEKS)*

		pos	wks
7 Nov 92	UNDERSTAND THIS GROOVE *China WOK 2028*	60	2
21 May 94	LOVE COME HOME *Triangle BLUESCD 001* [1]	73	1

[1] Our Tribe with Franke Pharoah and Kristine W

FRANK'EE – *See BROTHER BROWN featuring FRANK'EE*

FRANKIE GOES TO HOLLYWOOD (152 Top 500)
Fiercely marketed, controversial and regularly re-mixed Merseyside-based quintet fronted by Holly Johnson (b. 19 Feb 1960, Sudan). First act since Gerry and the Pacemakers to hit No.1 with initial three releases. During July 1984, 'Two Tribes' and 'Relax' held top two places in the chart (147 WEEKS)

		pos	wks
26 Nov 83 ★	RELAX *ZTT ZTAS 1* ◆	1	48
16 Jun 84 ★	TWO TRIBES *ZTT ZTAS 3* ◆ ■	1	20
10 Nov 84	TWO TRIBES (re-entry) *ZTT ZTAS 3*	73	1
1 Dec 84 ★	THE POWER OF LOVE *ZTT ZTAS 5*	1	11
16 Feb 85	RELAX (re-entry) *ZTT ZTAS 1*	58	4
23 Feb 85	THE POWER OF LOVE (re-entry) *ZTT ZTAS 5*	64	1
30 Mar 85 ●	WELCOME TO THE PLEASURE DOME *ZTT ZTAS 7*	2	11
6 Sep 86 ●	RAGE HARD *ZTT ZTAS 22*	4	7
22 Nov 86	WARRIORS (OF THE WASTELAND) *ZTT ZTAS 25*	19	8
7 Mar 87	WATCHING THE WILDLIFE *ZTT ZTAS 26*	28	6
2 Oct 93 ●	RELAX (re-issue) *ZTT FGTH 1CD*	5	7
20 Nov 93	WELCOME TO THE PLEASURE DOME (re-mix) *ZTT FGTH 2CD*	18	3
18 Dec 93 ●	THE POWER OF LOVE (re-issue) *ZTT FGTH 3CD*	10	7
26 Feb 94	TWO TRIBES (re-mix) *ZTT FGTH 4CD*	16	3
1 Jul 00 ●	THE POWER OF LOVE (re-mix) *ZTT ZTT 150CD*	6	6
9 Sep 00	TWO TRIBES (re-mix) *ZTT ZTT 154CD*	17	3
18 Nov 00	WELCOME TO THE PLEASURE DOME (re-mix) *ZTT 166CD*	45	1

Aretha FRANKLIN (107 Top 500)
The 'Queen of Soul Music', b. 25 Mar 1942, Tennessee, US. With six decades of recording behind her, this legendary gospel-influenced vocalist has won countless awards and amassed more pop and R&B hits than any other female in her homeland (182 WEEKS)

		pos	wks
8 Jun 67 ●	RESPECT *Atlantic 584 115* ▲	10	14
23 Aug 67	BABY I LOVE YOU *Atlantic 584 127*	39	4
20 Dec 67	CHAIN OF FOOLS / SATISFACTION *Atlantic 584 157*	43	2
10 Jan 68	SATISFACTION *Atlantic 584 157*	37	5
13 Mar 68	(SWEET SWEET BABY) SINCE YOU'VE BEEN GONE *Atlantic 584 172*	47	1
22 May 68	THINK *Atlantic 584 186*	26	9
7 Aug 68 ●	I SAY A LITTLE PRAYER *Atlantic 584 206*	4	14
22 Aug 70	DON'T PLAY THAT SONG *Atlantic 2091 027*	13	11
2 Oct 71	SPANISH HARLEM *Atlantic 2091 138*	14	9
8 Sep 73	ANGEL *Atlantic K 10346*	37	5
16 Feb 74	UNTIL YOU COME BACK TO ME (THAT'S WHAT I'M GONNA DO) *Atlantic K 10399*	26	8
6 Dec 80	WHAT A FOOL BELIEVES *Arista ARIST 377*	46	7
19 Sep 81	LOVE ALL THE HURT AWAY *Arista ARIST 428* [1]	49	3
4 Sep 82	JUMP TO IT *Arista ARIST 479*	42	5
23 Jul 83	GET IT RIGHT *Arista ARIST 537*	74	2
13 Jul 85	FREEWAY OF LOVE *Arista ARIST 624*	68	3
2 Nov 85 ●	SISTERS ARE DOIN' IT FOR THEMSELVES *RCA PB 40339* [2]	9	11
23 Nov 85	WHO'S ZOOMIN' WHO *Arista ARIST 633*	11	14
22 Feb 86	ANOTHER NIGHT *Arista ARIST 657*	54	6
10 May 86	FREEWAY OF LOVE (re-entry) *Arista ARIST 624*	51	3
25 Oct 86	JUMPIN' JACK FLASH *Arista ARIST 678*	58	3
31 Jan 87 ★	I KNEW YOU WERE WAITING (FOR ME) *Epic DUET 1* [3] ▲	1	9
14 Mar 87	JIMMY LEE *Arista RIS 6*	46	4
6 May 89	THROUGH THE STORM *Arista 112185* [4]	41	3
9 Sep 89	IT ISN'T, IT WASN'T, IT AIN'T NEVER GONNA BE *Arista 112545* [5]	29	5
7 Apr 90	THINK *East West A 7951*	31	2
27 Jul 91	EVERYDAY PEOPLE *Arista 114420*	69	1
12 Feb 94 ●	A DEEPER LOVE *Arista 74321187022*	5	7
25 Jun 94	WILLING TO FORGIVE *Arista 74321213342*	17	7
9 May 98	A ROSE IS STILL A ROSE *Arista 74321569742*	22	4
26 Sep 98	HERE WE GO AGAIN *Arista 74321612742*	68	1

[1] Aretha Franklin and George Benson [2] Eurythmics and Aretha Franklin [3] Aretha Franklin and George Michael [4] Aretha Franklin and Elton John [5] Aretha Franklin and Whitney Houston

'Think' on East West is a re-recording. It was the flip side of 'Everybody Needs Somebody to Love' by Blues Brothers and was listed for the first two weeks of that record's run

Erma FRANKLIN *US, female vocalist (10 WEEKS)*

		pos	wks
10 Oct 92 ●	(TAKE A LITTLE) PIECE OF MY HEART *Epic 6583847*	9	10

Rodney FRANKLIN *US, male instrumentalist – piano (9 WEEKS)*

		pos	wks
19 Apr 80 ●	THE GROOVE *CBS 8529*	7	9

Chevelle FRANKLYN / BEENIE MAN
Jamaica, female / male vocalists (1 WEEK)

		pos	wks
20 Sep 97	DANCEHALL QUEEN *Island Jamaica IJCD 2018*	70	1

FRANTIC FIVE – *See Don LANG*

FRANTIQUE *US, female vocal group (12 WEEKS)*

		pos	wks
11 Aug 79 ●	STRUT YOUR FUNKY STUFF *Philadelphia Int. PIR 7728*	10	12

Elizabeth FRASER – *See COCTEAU TWINS; MASSIVE ATTACK; Ian McCULLOCH; FUTURE SOUND OF LONDON*

Wendy FRASER – *See Patrick SWAYZE featuring Wendy FRASER*

FRASH *UK, male vocal / instrumental group (1 WEEK)*

		pos	wks
18 Feb 95	HERE I GO AGAIN *PWL International FLIPCD 1*	69	1

FRAZIER CHORUS
UK, male / female vocal / instrumental group (14 WEEKS)

		pos	wks
4 Feb 89	DREAM KITCHEN *Virgin VS 1145*	57	3
15 Apr 89	TYPICAL! *Virgin VS 1174*	53	2
15 Jul 89	SLOPPY HEART *Virgin VS 1192*	73	1
9 Jun 90	CLOUD 8 *Virgin VS 1252*	52	3
25 Aug 90	NOTHING *Virgin VS 1284*	51	3
16 Feb 91	WALKING ON AIR *Virgin VS 1330*	60	2

FREAKPOWER
UK / Canada, male vocal / instrumental group (20 WEEKS)

		pos	wks
16 Oct 93	TURN ON TUNE IN COP OUT *Fourth & Broadway BRCD 284*	29	5
26 Feb 94	RUSH *Fourth & Broadway BRCD 291*	62	2
18 Mar 95 ●	TURN ON TUNE IN COP OUT (re-issue) *Fourth & Broadway BRCD 317*	3	9

8 Jun 96	NEW DIRECTION *Fourth & Broadway BRCD 331*	60	1
9 May 98	NO WAY *Deconstruction 74321578572*	29	3

See also Norman COOK; BEATS INTERNATIONAL; PIZZAMAN; FATBOY SLIM; MIGHTY DUB KATZ; HOUSEMARTINS

FREAKY REALISTIC
UK / Japan, male / female vocal / instrumental group (3 WEEKS) pos/wks

3 Apr 93	KOOCHIE RYDER *Frealism FRECD 2*	52	2
3 Jul 93	LEONARD NIMOY *Frealism FRECD 3*	71	1

FREAKYMAN *Holland, male producer – Andre Van Den Bosch (1 WEEK)* pos/wks

27 Sep 97	DISCOBUG '97 *Xtravaganza 0091285 EXT*	68	1

Stan FREBERG *US, male vocalist (5 WEEKS)* pos/wks

19 Nov 54	SH-BOOM *Capitol CL 14187* [1]	15	2
27 Jul 56	ROCK ISLAND LINE / HEARTBREAK HOTEL *Capitol CL 14608* [2]	24	1
10 Aug 56	ROCK ISLAND LINE / HEARTBREAK HOTEL (re-entry) *Capitol CL 14608* [2]	29	1
12 May 60	THE OLD PAYOLA ROLL BLUES *Capitol CL 15122* [3]	40	1

[1] Stan Freberg with the Toads [2] Stan Freberg and his Sniffle Group [3] Stan Freberg with Jesse White

FRED & ROXY *UK, female vocal duo (2 WEEKS)* pos/wks

5 Feb 00	SOMETHING FOR THE WEEKEND *Echo ECSCD 81*	36	2

John FRED and the PLAYBOY BAND
US, male vocal / instrumental group (12 WEEKS) pos/wks

3 Jan 68 ●	JUDY IN DISGUISE (WITH GLASSES) *Pye International 7N 25442* ▲	3	12

FREDDIE and the DREAMERS (381 Top 500) *Fun beat group fronted and founded by the leaping, laughing Freddie Garrity, b. 14 Nov 1936, Manchester, UK. Immortalised in the 1965 film 'Every Day's a Holiday', which was re-titled 'Seaside Swingers' in the US where they topped the charts with 'I'm Telling You Now' (85 WEEKS)* pos/wks

9 May 63 ●	IF YOU GOTTA MAKE A FOOL OF SOMEBODY *Columbia DB 7032*	3	14
8 Aug 63 ●	I'M TELLING YOU NOW *Columbia DB 7086* ▲	2	11
7 Nov 63 ●	YOU WERE MADE FOR ME *Columbia DB 7147*	3	15
20 Feb 64	OVER YOU *Columbia DB 7214*	13	11
14 May 64	I LOVE YOU BABY *Columbia DB 7286*	16	8
16 Jul 64	JUST FOR YOU *Columbia DB 7322*	41	3
5 Nov 64 ●	I UNDERSTAND *Columbia DB 7381*	5	15
22 Apr 65	A LITTLE YOU *Columbia DB 7526*	26	5
4 Nov 65	THOU SHALT NOT STEAL *Columbia DB 7720*	44	3

FREDERICK – *See NINA and FREDERICK*

Dee FREDRIX *UK, female vocalist (5 WEEKS)* pos/wks

27 Feb 93	AND SO I WILL WAIT FOR YOU *East West YZ 725CD*	56	4
3 Jul 93	DIRTY MONEY *East West YZ 750CD*	74	1

FREE (464 Top 500) *Blues-orientated London rock quartet; Paul Rodgers (v), Paul Kossoff (g), Andy Fraser (b) and Simon Kirke (d); split 1973 when Rodgers and Kirke formed Bad Company (75 WEEKS)* pos/wks

6 Jun 70 ●	ALL RIGHT NOW *Island WIP 6082*	2	16
1 May 71 ●	MY BROTHER JAKE *Island WIP 6100*	4	11
27 May 72	LITTLE BIT OF LOVE *Island WIP 6129*	13	10
13 Jan 73 ●	WISHING WELL *Island WIP 6146*	7	10
21 Jul 73	ALL RIGHT NOW (re-entry) *Island WIP 6082*	15	9
18 Feb 78	FREE (EP) *Island IEP 6*	11	7
23 Oct 82	FREE (EP) (re-entry) *Island IEP 6*	57	3
9 Feb 91 ●	ALL RIGHT NOW (re-mix) *Island IS 486*	8	9

Tracks on Free (EP): All Right Now (long version) / My Brother Jake (re-issue) / Wishing Well (re-issue)

FREE – *See QUEEN; Wyclef JEAN; Pras MICHEL; QUEEN LATIFAH*

FREE SPIRIT *UK, male / female vocal duo (1 WEEK)* pos/wks

13 May 95	NO MORE RAINY DAYS *Columbia 6612822*	68	1

FREEEZ *UK, male vocal / instrumental group (48 WEEKS)* pos/wks

7 Jun 80	KEEP IN TOUCH *Calibre CAB 103*	49	3
7 Feb 81 ●	SOUTHERN FREEEZ *Beggars Banquet BEG 51* [1]	8	11
18 Apr 81	FLYING HIGH *Beggars Banquet BEG 55*	35	5
18 Jun 83 ●	I.O.U. *Beggars Banquet BEG 96*	2	15
1 Oct 83	POP GOES MY LOVE *Beggars Banquet BEG 98*	26	6
17 Jan 87	I.O.U. (re-mix) *Citybeat CBE 709* [2]	23	6
30 May 87	SOUTHERN FREEEZ (re-mix) *Total Control TOCO 14* [1]	63	2

[1] Freeez featuring Ingrid Mansfield Allman [2] Freeez featuring John Rocca

FREEFALL featuring Jan JOHNSTON *UK / Australia, male DJ / production duo and female vocalist (5 WEEKS)* pos/wks

28 Nov 98	SKYDIVE *Stress CDSTR 89*	75	1
22 Jul 00	SKYDIVE (re-mix) *Renaissance Recordings RENCDS 002*	43	2
8 Sep 01	SKYDIVE (I FEEL WONDERFUL) (2nd re-mix) *Incentive CENT 22CDS* [1]	35	2

FREEFALL featuring PSYCHOTROPIC
UK / US, male instrumental / production group (1 WEEK) pos/wks

27 Jul 91	FEEL SURREAL *ffrr FX 160*	63	1

FREEHOLD JUNIOR SCHOOL – *See Fogwell FLAX and the ANKLEBITERS from FREEHOLD JUNIOR SCHOOL*

Claire FREELAND *UK, female vocalist (1 WEEK)* pos/wks

21 Jul 01	FREE *Statuesque CDSTATU 1*	44	1

FREESTYLERS *UK, male instrumental / vocal group (5 WEEKS)* pos/wks

7 Feb 98	B-BOY STANCE *Freskanova FND 7* [1]	23	3
14 Nov 98	WARNING *Freskanova FND 14* [2]	68	1
24 Jul 99	HERE WE GO *Freskanova FND 19*	45	1

[1] Freestylers featuring Tenor Fly [2] Freestylers featuring Navigator

FREIHEIT *Germany, male vocal / instrumental group (9 WEEKS)* pos/wks

17 Dec 88	KEEPING THE DREAM ALIVE *CBS 652989 7*	14	9

Deborah FRENCH – *See E-LUSTRIOUS*

Nicki FRENCH *UK, female vocalist (18 WEEKS)* pos/wks

15 Oct 94	TOTAL ECLIPSE OF THE HEART *Bags of Fun BAGSCD 1*	54	1
14 Jan 95 ●	TOTAL ECLIPSE OF THE HEART (re-entry) *Bags of Fun BAGSCD 1*	5	12
22 Apr 95	FOR ALL WE KNOW *Bags of Fun BAGSCD 4*	42	2
15 Jul 95	DID YOU EVER REALLY LOVE ME *Love This LUVTHISCD 2*	55	1
27 May 00	DON'T PLAY THAT SONG AGAIN *RCA 74321764572*	34	2

FRENCH AFFAIR
France, male production duo / female vocalist (3 WEEKS) pos/wks

16 Sep 00	MY HEART GOES BOOM *Arista 74321780562*	44	3

Freddy FRESH *US, male producer – Frederick Schmid (3 WEEKS)* pos/wks

1 May 99	BADDER BADDER SCHWING *Eye Q EYEUK 040CD* [1]	34	2
31 Jul 99	WHAT IT IS *Eye Q EYEUK 043CD*	63	1

[1] Freddy Fresh featuring Fatboy Slim

Doug E FRESH and the GET FRESH CREW
US, male rap / DJ group (11 WEEKS) pos/wks

9 Nov 85 ●	THE SHOW *Cooltempo COOL 116*	7	11

FRESH 4 featuring Lizz E
UK, male DJ / production group and female vocalist (9 WEEKS) pos/wks

Date		Title / Label	Pos	Wks
7 Oct 89	●	**WISHING ON A STAR** *10 TEN 287*	10	9

FRESH PRINCE – See *JAZZY JEFF & the FRESH PRINCE*

FRESHIES *UK, male vocal / instrumental group (3 WEEKS)* pos/wks

Date		Title / Label	Pos	Wks
14 Feb 81		**I'M IN LOVE WITH THE GIRL ON A CERTAIN MANCHESTER MEGASTORE CHECKOUT DESK** *MCA 670*	54	3

Matt FRETTON *UK, male vocalist (5 WEEKS)* pos/wks

Date		Title / Label	Pos	Wks
11 Jun 83		**IT'S SO HIGH** *Chrysalis MATT 1*	50	5

FREUR *UK, male vocal / instrumental group (4 WEEKS)* pos/wks

Date		Title / Label	Pos	Wks
23 Apr 83		**DOOT DOOT** *CBS A 3141*	59	4

Glenn FREY *US, male vocalist (20 WEEKS)* pos/wks

Date		Title / Label	Pos	Wks
2 Mar 85		**THE HEAT IS ON** *MCA MCA 941*	12	12
22 Jun 85		**SMUGGLER'S BLUES** *BBC RESL 170*	22	8

See also EAGLES

FRIDA *Norway, female vocalist (12 WEEKS)* pos/wks

Date		Title / Label	Pos	Wks
21 Aug 82		**I KNOW THERE'S SOMETHING GOING ON** *Epic EPC A2603*	43	7
17 Dec 83		**TIME** *Epic A 3983* [1]	45	5

[1] Frida and B A Robertson

See also ABBA

Gavin FRIDAY – See *BONO*

Ralph FRIDGE *Germany, male producer – Ralf Fritsch (4 WEEKS)* pos/wks

Date		Title / Label	Pos	Wks
24 Apr 99		**PARADISE** *Additive 12AD 036*	68	1
8 Apr 00		**ANGEL** *Incentive CENT 6CDS*	20	3

Dean FRIEDMAN *US, male vocalist (22 WEEKS)* pos/wks

Date		Title / Label	Pos	Wks
3 Jun 78		**WOMAN OF MINE** *Lifesong LS 401*	52	5
23 Sep 78	●	**LUCKY STARS** *Lifesong LS 402*	3	10
18 Nov 78		**LYDIA** *Lifesong LS 403*	31	7

'Lucky Stars' features uncredited vocals by Denise Marsa

FRIENDS AGAIN *UK, male vocal / instrumental group (3 WEEKS)* pos/wks

Date		Title / Label	Pos	Wks
4 Aug 84		**THE FRIENDS AGAIN EP** *Mercury FA 1*	59	3

Tracks on The Friends Again EP: Lullaby On Board / Wand You Wave / Thank You for Being an Angel

FRIENDS OF MATTHEW
UK, male / female vocal / instrumental group (1 WEEK) pos/wks

Date		Title / Label	Pos	Wks
10 Jul 99		**OUT THERE** *Serious SERR 007CD*	61	1

FRIGID VINEGAR *UK, male rap / production duo (1 WEEK)* pos/wks

Date		Title / Label	Pos	Wks
21 Aug 99		**DOGMONAUT 2000 (IS THERE ANYONE OUT THERE?)** *Gut CDGUT 27*	53	1

FRIJID PINK *US, male vocal / instrumental group (16 WEEKS)* pos/wks

Date		Title / Label	Pos	Wks
28 Mar 70	●	**HOUSE OF THE RISING SUN** *Deram DM 288*	4	16

Robert FRIPP – See *David SYLVIAN*

Jane FROMAN *US, female vocalist (4 WEEKS)* pos/wks

Date		Title / Label	Pos	Wks
17 Jun 55		**I WONDER** *Capitol CL 14254*	14	4

FRONT 242 *Belgium / US, male vocal / instrumental group (1 WEEK)* pos/wks

Date		Title / Label	Pos	Wks
1 May 93		**RELIGION** *RRE RRE 106CD*	46	1

Christian FRY *UK, male vocalist (3 WEEKS)* pos/wks

Date		Title / Label	Pos	Wks
14 Nov 98		**YOU GOT ME** *Mushroom MUSH 33CDS*	45	2
3 Apr 99		**WON'T YOU SAY** *Mushroom MUSH 46CDS*	48	1

FUGAZI *US, male vocal / instrumental group (1 WEEK)* pos/wks

Date		Title / Label	Pos	Wks
20 Oct 01		**FURNITURE** *Dischord DIS 129CD*	61	1

FUGEES *US, male / female vocal / rap / production group (65 WEEKS)* pos/wks

Date		Title / Label	Pos	Wks
6 Apr 96		**FU-GEE-LA** *Columbia 6630662*	21	5
8 Jun 96	★	**KILLING ME SOFTLY** *Columbia 6633435* ◆ ■	1	20
14 Sep 96	★	**READY OR NOT** *Columbia 6637215*	1	12
30 Nov 96	●	**NO WOMAN, NO CRY** *Columbia 6639925*	2	9
15 Mar 97	●	**RUMBLE IN THE JUNGLE** *Mercury 5740692*	3	8
28 Jun 97		**WE TRYING TO STAY ALIVE** *Columbia 6646815* [1]	13	5
6 Sep 97		**THE SWEETEST THING** *Columbia 6649785* [2]	18	4
27 Sep 97		**GUANTANAMERA** *Columbia 6650852* [3]	25	2

[1] Wyclef Jean & The Refugee Allstars [2] Refugee Camp Allstars featuring Lauryn Hill [3] Wyclef Jean and The Refugee Allstars

See also Lauryn HILL; Wyclef JEAN; Pras MICHEL

FULL CIRCLE *US, male vocal group (5 WEEKS)* pos/wks

Date		Title / Label	Pos	Wks
7 Mar 87		**WORKIN' UP A SWEAT** *EMI America EA 229*	41	5

FULL FORCE *US, male vocal / instrumental group (37 WEEKS)* pos/wks

Date		Title / Label	Pos	Wks
4 May 85		**I WONDER IF I TAKE YOU HOME** *CBS A 6057* [1]	53	6
3 Aug 85		**I WONDER IF I TAKE YOU HOME (re-entry)** *CBS A 6057* [1]	12	11
21 Dec 85	●	**ALICE I WANT YOU JUST FOR ME** *CBS A 6640*	9	11
21 May 88		**NAUGHTY GIRLS (NEED LOVE TOO)** *Jive FOXY 9*	31	5
4 Jun 88		**I'M REAL** *Scotti Brothers JSB 1* [2]	31	4

[1] Lisa Lisa and Cult Jam with Full Force [2] James Brown featuring Full Force

FULL INTENTION
UK, male instrumental / production group (8 WEEKS) pos/wks

Date		Title / Label	Pos	Wks
6 Apr 96		**AMERICA (I LOVE AMERICA)** *Stress CDSTR 56*	32	2
10 Aug 96		**UPTOWN DOWNTOWN** *Stress CDSTR 67*	61	1
26 Jul 97		**SHAKE YOUR BODY (DOWN TO THE GROUND)** *Sugar Daddy CDSTR 82*	34	2
22 Nov 97		**AMERICA (I LOVE AMERICA) (re-mix)** *Sugar Daddy CDSTRX 56*	56	1
6 Jun 98		**YOU ARE SOMEBODY** *Sugar Daddy CDSD 001*	75	1
1 Sep 01		**I'LL BE WAITING** *Rulin RULIN 17CDS* [1]	44	1

[1] Full Intention presents Shena

See also SEX-O-SONIQUE; HUSTLERS CONVENTION featuring Dave LAUDAT and Ondrea DUVERNEY; DISCO TEX presents CLOUDBURST; SHENA

FULL METAL RACKETS – See *John McENROE and Pat CASH with the FULL METAL RACKETS*

FULL MONTY ALLSTARS featuring TJ DAVIS
UK, male vocal / instrumental group (1 WEEK) pos/wks

Date		Title / Label	Pos	Wks
27 Jul 96		**BRILLIANT FEELING** *Arista 74321380902*	72	1

Bobby FULLER FOUR
US, male vocal / instrumental group (4 WEEKS) pos/wks

Date		Title / Label	Pos	Wks
14 Apr 66		**I FOUGHT THE LAW** *London HL 10030*	33	4

FUN BOY THREE
UK vocal / instrumental trio – leader Terry Hall (70 WEEKS) pos/wks

Date		Title / Label	Pos	Wks
7 Nov 81		**THE LUNATICS (HAVE TAKEN OVER THE ASYLUM)** *Chrysalis CHS 2563*	20	12
13 Feb 82	●	**IT AIN'T WHAT YOU DO IT'S THE WAY THAT YOU DO IT** *Chrysalis CHS 2570* [1]	4	10
10 Apr 82	●	**REALLY SAYING SOMETHING** *Deram NANA 1* [2]	5	10
8 May 82		**THE TELEPHONE ALWAYS RINGS** *Chrysalis CHS 2609*	17	9
31 Jul 82		**SUMMERTIME** *Chrysalis CHS 2629*	18	8
15 Jan 83		**THE MORE I SEE (THE LESS I BELIEVE)** *Chrysalis CHS 2664*	68	1

5 Feb 83 ●	**TUNNEL OF LOVE** *Chrysalis CHS 2678*	10	10
30 Apr 83 ●	**OUR LIPS ARE SEALED** *Chrysalis FUNB 1*	7	10

[1] Fun Boy Three and Bananarama [2] Bananarama with Fun Boy Three

See also SPECIALS

FUN LOVIN' CRIMINALS

US, male vocal / rap / instrumental trio (31 WEEKS) pos/wks

8 Jun 96	**THE GRAVE AND THE CONSTANT** *Chrysalis CDCHS 5031*	72	1
17 Aug 96	**SCOOBY SNACKS** *Chrysalis CDCHS 5034*	22	3
16 Nov 96	**THE FUN LOVIN' CRIMINAL** *Chrysalis CDCHS 5040*	26	3
29 Mar 97	**KING OF NEW YORK** *Chrysalis CDCHS 5049*	28	3
5 Jul 97	**I'M NOT IN LOVE / SCOOBY SNACKS** *Chrysalis CDCHS 5060*	12	5
15 Aug 98	**LOVE UNLIMITED** *Chrysalis CDCHS 5096*	18	4
17 Oct 98	**BIG NIGHT OUT** *Chrysalis CDCHSS 5101*	29	2
8 May 99	**KOREAN BODEGA** *Chrysalis CDCHS 5108*	15	3
17 Feb 01 ●	**LOCO** *Chrysalis CDCHSS 5121*	5	6
1 Sep 01	**BUMP / RUN DADDY RUN** *Chrysalis CDCHSS 5128*	50	1

Farley 'Jackmaster' FUNK

US, male producer – Farley Williams (16 WEEKS) pos/wks

23 Aug 86 ●	**LOVE CAN'T TURN AROUND** *DJ International LON 105*	10	12
11 Feb 89	**AS ALWAYS** *Champion CHAMP 90* [1]	49	2
14 Dec 96	**LOVE CAN'T TURN AROUND** *4 Liberty LIBTCD 27* [2]	40	2

[1] Farley 'Jackmaster' Funk presents Ricky Dillard [2] Farley 'Jackmaster' Funk with Darryl Pandy.

'Love Can't Turn Around' in 1996 is a re-recording

FUNK D'VOID *Sweden, male producer – Lars Sandberg (1 WEEK)* pos/wks

20 Oct 01	**DIABLA** *Soma SOMA 112*	70	1

FUNK JUNKEEZ *US, male DJ / producer – Roger Sanchez (1 WEEK)* pos/wks

21 Feb 98	**GOT FUNK** *Evocative EVOKE 1CDS*	57	1

See also EL MARIACHI; Roger SANCHEZ

FUNK MASTERS

UK, male / female vocal / instrumental group (12 WEEKS) pos/wks

18 Jun 83 ●	**IT'S OVER** *Master Funk Records 7MP 004* [1]	8	12

[1] features Gonzales on Horns

FUNKADELIC *US, male vocal / instrumental group (13 WEEKS)* pos/wks

9 Dec 78 ●	**ONE NATION UNDER A GROOVE (PART 1)** *Warner Bros. K 17246*	9	12
21 Aug 99	**MOTHERSHIP RECONNECTION** *Virgin DINSD 185* [1]	55	1

[1] Scott Grooves featuring Parliament / Funkadelic

FUNKAPOLITAN *UK, male vocal / instrumental group (7 WEEKS)* pos/wks

22 Aug 81	**AS TIME GOES BY** *London LON 001*	41	7

FUNKDOOBIEST *US, male rap group (6 WEEKS)* pos/wks

11 Dec 93	**WOPBABALUBOP** *Immortal 6597112*	37	4
5 Mar 94	**BOW WOW WOW** *Immortal 6594052*	34	2

FUNKSTAR DE LUXE

Denmark, male producer / instrumentalist – Matt Ottesen (18 WEEKS) pos/wks

25 Sep 99 ●	**SUN IS SHINING** *Club Tools / Edel 0066895 CLU* [1]	3	10
22 Jan 00	**RAINBOW COUNTRY** *Club Tools 0067225CLU* [1]	11	6
13 May 00	**WALKIN IN THE NAME** *Club Tools 0067375 CLU* [2]	42	1
25 Nov 00	**PULL UP TO THE BUMPER** *Club Tools 0120375 CLU* [3]	60	1

[1] Bob Marley vs Funkstar De Luxe [2] Funkstar De Luxe vs Terry Maxx [3] Grace Jones vs Funkstar De Luxe

FUNKY BOYS – *See Linda CARR*

FUNKY BUNCH – *See MARKY MARK and the FUNKY BUNCH*

FUNKY CHOAD featuring Nick SKITZ *Australia / Italy, male production duo and Australia, male vocalist (1 WEEK)* pos/wks

29 Aug 98	**THE ULTIMATE** *ffrr FCD 341*	51	1

FUNKY GREEN DOGS

US, male / female vocal / production group (6 WEEKS) pos/wks

12 Apr 97	**FIRED UP!** *Twisted UK TWCD 10016*	17	3
28 Jun 97	**THE WAY** *Twisted UK TWCD 10026*	43	1
20 Jun 98	**UNTIL THE DAY** *Twisted UK TWCD 10034*	75	1
27 Feb 99	**BODY** *Twisted UK TWCD 110041*	46	1

FUNKY JUNCTION – *See KC FLIGHTT*

FUNKY POETS *US, male vocal group (1 WEEK)* pos/wks

7 May 94	**BORN IN THE GHETTO** *Epic 6603522*	72	1

FUNKY WORM *UK, male / female vocal / instrumental group (14 WEEKS)* pos/wks

30 Jul 88	**HUSTLE! (TO THE MUSIC . . .)** *Fon FON 15*	13	8
26 Nov 88	**THE SPELL!** *Fon FON 16*	61	3
20 May 89	**U + ME = LOVE** *Fon FON 19*	46	3

FUREYS *Ireland, male vocal group (14 WEEKS)* pos/wks

10 Oct 81	**WHEN YOU WERE SWEET SIXTEEN** *Ritz RITZ 003* [1]	14	11
3 Apr 82	**I WILL LOVE YOU (EV'RY TIME WHEN WE ARE GONE)** *Ritz RITZ 012*	54	3

[1] Fureys with Davey Arthur

FURIOUS FIVE – *See GRANDMASTER FLASH, Melle MEL and the FURIOUS FIVE*

FURNITURE *UK, male / female vocal / instrumental group (10 WEEKS)* pos/wks

14 Jun 86	**BRILLIANT MIND** *Stiff BUY 251*	21	10

Nelly FURTADO *Canada, female vocalist (26 WEEKS)* pos/wks

10 Mar 01 ●	**I'M LIKE A BIRD** *Dreamworks 4509192*	5	16
1 Sep 01 ●	**TURN OFF THE LIGHT** *Dreamworks DRMDM 50891*	4	10

Billy FURY (37 Top 500) *Early British rock 'n' roll star, b. Ronald Wycherley, 17 Apr 1941, Liverpool, d. 28 Jan 1983. Equalled Beatles' record of 24 hits in the 1960s, and spent 281 weeks on chart but without ever without reaching No.1 (281 WEEKS)* pos/wks

27 Feb 59	**MAYBE TOMORROW** *Decca F 11102*	22	3
27 Mar 59	**MAYBE TOMORROW (re-entry)** *Decca F 11102*	18	6
26 Jun 59	**MARGO** *Decca F 11128*	28	1
10 Mar 60 ●	**COLETTE** *Decca F 11200*	9	10
26 May 60	**THAT'S LOVE** *Decca F 11237* [1]	19	11
22 Sep 60	**WONDROUS PLACE** *Decca F 11267*	25	9
19 Jan 61	**A THOUSAND STARS** *Decca F 11311*	14	10
27 Apr 61	**DON'T WORRY** *Decca F 11334* [2]	40	2
11 May 61 ●	**HALFWAY TO PARADISE** *Decca F 11349*	3	23
7 Sep 61 ●	**JEALOUSY** *Decca F 11384*	2	12
14 Dec 61 ●	**I'D NEVER FIND ANOTHER YOU** *Decca F 11409*	5	15
15 Mar 62	**LETTER FULL OF TEARS** *Decca F 11437*	32	6
3 May 62 ●	**LAST NIGHT WAS MADE FOR LOVE** *Decca F 11458*	4	16
19 Jul 62 ●	**ONCE UPON A DREAM** *Decca F 11485*	7	13
25 Oct 62	**BECAUSE OF LOVE** *Decca F 11508*	18	14
14 Feb 63 ●	**LIKE I'VE NEVER BEEN GONE** *Decca F11582*	3	15
16 May 63 ●	**WHEN WILL YOU SAY I LOVE YOU** *Decca F 11655*	3	12
25 Jul 63 ●	**IN SUMMER** *Decca F 11701*	5	11
3 Oct 63	**SOMEBODY ELSE'S GIRL** *Decca F 11744*	18	7
2 Jan 64	**DO YOU REALLY LOVE ME TOO** *Decca F 11792*	13	10
30 Apr 64	**I WILL** *Decca F 11888*	14	12
23 Jul 64 ●	**IT'S ONLY MAKE BELIEVE** *Decca F 11939*	10	10
14 Jan 65	**I'M LOST WITHOUT YOU** *Decca F 12048*	16	10
22 Jul 65 ●	**IN THOUGHTS OF YOU** *Decca F 12178*	9	11
16 Sep 65	**RUN TO MY LOVIN' ARMS** *Decca F 12230*	25	7
10 Feb 66	**I'LL NEVER QUITE GET OVER YOU** *Decca F 12325*	35	5
4 Aug 66	**GIVE ME YOUR WORD** *Decca F 12459*	27	7
4 Sep 82	**LOVE OR MONEY** *Polydor POSP 488*	57	5

13 Nov 82	**DEVIL OR ANGEL** *Polydor POSP 528*	58	4
4 Jun 83	**FORGET HIM** *Polydor POSP 558*	59	4

[1] Billy Fury with the Four Jays [2] Billy Fury with the Four Kestrels

FUSED

Sweden, male instrumental / production duo / female vocalist (1 WEEK) pos/wks

20 Mar 99	**THIS PARTY SUCKS!** *Columbia 6669302*	64	1

FUTURE BREEZE *Germany, male production duo – Markus Boehme and Martin Hensing (2 WEEKS)* pos/wks

6 Sep 97	**WHY DON'T YOU DANCE WITH ME** *AM:PM 5823312*	50	1
20 Jan 01	**SMILE** *Nebula NEBCD 014*	67	1

FUTURE FORCE

UK / US, male / female vocal / instrumental duo (1 WEEK) pos/wks

17 Aug 96	**WHAT YOU WANT** *AM:PM 5816592*	47	1

FUTURE SOUND OF LONDON *UK, male instrumental / production duo – Brian Dougans and Gary Cobain (25 WEEKS)* pos/wks

23 May 92	**PAPUA NEW GUINEA** *Jumpin' & Pumpin' TOT 17*	22	6
6 Nov 93	**CASCADE** *Virgin VSCDT 1478*	27	3
30 Jul 94	**EXPANDER** *Jumpin' & Pumpin' CDSTOT 37*	72	1
13 Aug 94	**LIFEFORMS** *Virgin VSCDT 1484* [1]	14	3
27 May 95	**FAR-OUT SON OF LUNG AND THE RAMBLINGS OF A MADMAN** *Virgin VSCDT 1540*	22	3
26 Oct 96	**MY KINGDOM** *Virgin VSCDT 1605*	13	3
12 Apr 97	**WE HAVE EXPLOSIVE** *Virgin VSCDX 1616*	12	3
29 Sep 01	**PAPUA NEW GUINEA 2001 (re-mix)** *Jumpin' & Pumpin' CDSTOT 44*	28	3

[1] F.S.O.L. vocals by Elizabeth Fraser

See also HUMANOID

FUZZBOX – *See WE'VE GOT A FUZZBOX AND WE'RE GONNA USE IT*

Leslie FYSON – *See Michael MEDWIN, Bernard BRESSLAW, Alfie BASS and Leslie FYSON*

G

Bobby G *UK, male vocalist (12 WEEKS)* pos/wks

1 Dec 84	**BIG DEAL** *BBC RESL 151*	75	1
15 Dec 84	**BIG DEAL (re-entry)** *BBC RESL 151*	65	5
19 Oct 85	**BIG DEAL (2nd re-entry)** *BBC RESL 151*	46	6

See also BUCKS FIZZ

Dario G *UK, male DJ / production trio (39 WEEKS)* pos/wks

27 Sep 97 ●	**SUNCHYME** *Eternal WEA 130CD*	2	18
20 Jun 98 ●	**CARNAVAL DE PARIS** *Eternal WEA 162CD*	5	9
12 Sep 98	**SUNMACHINE** *Eternal WEA 173CD*	17	4
25 Mar 00	**VOICES** *Eternal WEA 256CD*	37	2
3 Feb 01 ●	**DREAM TO ME** *Manifesto FESCD 79*	9	6

Dennis G – *See WIDEBOYS featuring Dennis G*

Gina G *Australia, female vocalist – Gina Gardiner (51 WEEKS)* pos/wks

6 Apr 96 ★	**OOH AAH...JUST A LITTLE BIT** *Eternal WEA 041CD*	1	23
21 Sep 96	**OOH AAH...JUST A LITTLE BIT (re-entry)** *Eternal WEA 041CD*	62	1
5 Oct 96	**OOH AAH...JUST A LITTLE BIT (2nd re-entry)** *Eternal WEA 041CD*	64	1
9 Nov 96 ●	**I BELONG TO YOU** *Eternal WEA 081CD*	6	11
22 Mar 97 ●	**FRESH!** *Eternal WEA 095CD*	6	7
7 Jun 97	**TI AMO** *Eternal WEA 107CD1*	11	5
6 Sep 97	**GIMME SOME LOVE** *Eternal WEA 101CD1*	25	2
15 Nov 97	**EVERY TIME I FALL** *Eternal WEA 134CD*	52	1

Hurricane G – *See PUFF DADDY*

Kenny G *US, male instrumentalist – saxophone (26 WEEKS)* pos/wks

21 Apr 84	**HI! HOW YA DOIN'?** *Arista ARIST 561*	70	3
30 Aug 86	**WHAT DOES IT TAKE (TO WIN YOUR LOVE)** *Arista ARIST 672*	64	2
4 Jul 87	**SONGBIRD** *Arista RIS 18*	22	7
9 May 92	**MISSING YOU NOW** *Columbia 6579917* [1]	28	4
24 Apr 93	**FOREVER IN LOVE** *Arista 74321145552*	47	3
17 Jul 93	**BY THE TIME THIS NIGHT IS OVER** *Arista 74321157142* [2]	56	3
8 Nov 97	**HOW COULD AN ANGEL BREAK MY HEART** *LaFace 74321531982* [3]	22	4

[1] Michael Bolton featuring Kenny G [2] Kenny G with Peabo Bryson [3] Toni Braxton with Kenny G

Warren G *US, male rapper – Warren Griffin (59 WEEKS)* pos/wks

23 Jul 94 ●	**REGULATE** *Death Row A 8290CD* [1]	5	14
12 Nov 94	**THIS DJ** *RAL RALCD 1*	12	5
31 Dec 94	**THIS DJ (re-entry)** *RAL RALCD 1*	68	2
25 Mar 95	**DO YOU SEE** *RAL RALCD 3*	29	2
23 Nov 96 ●	**WHAT'S LOVE GOT TO DO WITH IT** *Interscope IND 97008* [2]	2	12
22 Feb 97 ●	**I SHOT THE SHERIFF** *Mercury DEFCD 31*	2	8
31 May 97	**SMOKIN' ME OUT** *Def Jam 5744432* [3]	14	5
10 Jan 98	**PRINCE IGOR** *Def Jam 5749652* [4]	15	7
24 Jan 98	**ALL NIGHT ALL RIGHT** *Mushroom MUSH 21CD* [5]	16	4

[1] Warren G and Nate Dogg [2] Warren G featuring Adina Howard [3] Warren G featuring Ron Isley [4] Warren G featuring Sissel [5] Peter Andre featuring Warren G

G NATION featuring ROSIE *UK, male production duo – Jake Moses and Mark Smith – and UK, female vocalist (1 WEEK)* pos/wks

9 Aug 97	**FEEL THE NEED** *Cooltempo CDCOOL 327*	58	1

Andy G's STARSKY & HUTCH ALL STARS

UK, male producer (1 WEEK) pos/wks

3 Oct 98	**STARSKY & HUTCH - THE THEME** *Virgin VSCDT 1708*	51	1

G-CLEFS *US, male vocal group (12 WEEKS)* pos/wks

30 Nov 61	**I UNDERSTAND** *London HLU 9433*	17	12

G.O.S.H. *UK, male / female charity ensemble (11 WEEKS)* pos/wks

28 Nov 87	**THE WISHING WELL** *MBS GOSH 1*	22	11

Eric GABLE *US, male vocalist (1 WEEK)* pos/wks

19 Mar 94	**PROCESS OF ELIMINATION** *Epic 6602282*	63	1

Peter GABRIEL (259 Top 500) *Award-winning singer / songwriter, b. 13 Feb 1950, Surrey, UK. Fronted Genesis until 1975, when replaced by Phil Collins. He broke through internationally with 'Sledgehammer', which also made him a video innovator. He is the driving force behind the Womad festival and is a tireless Amnesty International supporter (112 WEEKS)* pos/wks

9 Apr 77	**SOLSBURY HILL** *Charisma CB 301*	13	9
9 Feb 80 ●	**GAMES WITHOUT FRONTIERS** *Charisma CB 354*	4	11
10 May 80	**NO SELF CONTROL** *Charisma CB 360*	33	6
23 Aug 80	**BIKO** *Charisma CB 370*	38	3
25 Sep 82	**SHOCK THE MONKEY** *Charisma SHOCK 1*	58	5
9 Jul 83	**I DON'T REMEMBER** *Charisma GAB 1*	62	3
2 Jun 84	**WALK THROUGH THE FIRE** *Virgin VS 689*	69	3
26 Apr 86 ●	**SLEDGEHAMMER** *Virgin PGS 1* ▲	4	16
1 Nov 86 ●	**DON'T GIVE UP** *Virgin PGS 2* [1]	9	11
28 Mar 87	**BIG TIME** *Charisma PGS 3*	13	7
11 Jul 87	**RED RAIN** *Charisma PGS 4*	46	3
21 Nov 87	**BIKO (LIVE)** *Charisma PGS 6*	49	6
3 Jun 89	**SHAKIN' THE TREE** *Virgin VS 1167* [2]	61	3
22 Dec 90	**SOLSBURY HILL / SHAKING THE TREE (re-issue)** *Virgin VS 1322* [3]	57	4

			pos	wks
19 Sep 92		DIGGING IN THE DIRT *Realworld PGS 7*	24	4
16 Jan 93	●	STEAM *Realworld PGSDG 8*	10	7
3 Apr 93		BLOOD OF EDEN *Realworld PGSDG 9*	43	4
25 Sep 93		KISS THAT FROG *Realworld PGSDG 10*	46	3
25 Jun 94		LOVETOWN *Epic 6604802*	49	2
3 Sep 94		SW LIVE (EP) *Realworld PGSCD 11*	39	2

[1] Peter Gabriel and Kate Bush [2] Youssou N'Dour and Peter Gabriel [3] Peter Gabriel / Youssou N'Dour and Peter Gabriel

Tracks available on all formats of SW Live (EP): Red Rain / San Jacinto

GABRIELLE (163 Top 500) *Eyepatch-wearing soul / pop vocalist, born Louisa Gabrielle Bobb, 16 May 1970, London, UK. Broke record for highest chart debut when 'Dreams' entered at No.2. Voted Best British Newcomer at 1994 Brit Awards and Best British Female Vocalist in 1997 (144 WEEKS)* pos/wks

			pos	wks
19 Jun 93	★	DREAMS *Go.Beat GODCD 99*	1	15
2 Oct 93	●	GOING NOWHERE *Go.Beat GODCD 106*	9	7
11 Dec 93		I WISH *Go.Beat GODCD 108*	26	5
26 Feb 94		BECAUSE OF YOU *Go.Beat GODCD 109*	24	5
24 Feb 96	●	GIVE ME A LITTLE MORE TIME *Go.Beat GODCD 139*	5	18
22 Jun 96		FORGET ABOUT THE WORLD *Go.Beat GODCD 146*	23	5
5 Oct 96		IF YOU REALLY CARED *Go.Beat GODCD 153*	15	5
2 Nov 96	●	IF YOU EVER *London LONCD 388* [1]	2	15
1 Feb 97	●	WALK ON BY *Go.Beat GODCD 159*	7	8
9 Oct 99	●	SUNSHINE *Go.Beat GOBCD 23*	9	8
5 Feb 00	★	RISE *Go.Beat / Polydor GOBCD 25* ■	1	15
17 Jun 00	●	WHEN A WOMAN *Go.Beat / Polydor GOBCD 27*	6	8
4 Nov 00		SHOULD I STAY *Go.Beat / Polydor GOBCD 32*	13	7
21 Apr 01	●	OUT OF REACH *Go.Beat / Polydor GOLCD 39*	4	16
3 Nov 01	●	DON'T NEED THE SUN TO SHINE (TO MAKE ME SMILE) *Go.Beat / Polydor GOBCD 47*	9	7

[1] East 17 featuring Gabrielle

Yvonne GAGE *US, female vocalist (4 WEEKS)* pos/wks

			pos	wks
16 Jun 84		DOIN' IT IN A HAUNTED HOUSE *Epic A 4519*	45	4

Danni'elle GAHA *Australia, female vocalist (7 WEEKS)* pos/wks

			pos	wks
1 Aug 92		STUCK IN THE MIDDLE *Epic 6581247*	68	2
27 Feb 93		DO IT FOR LOVE *Epic 6584612*	52	2
12 Jun 93		SECRET LOVE *Epic 6592212*	41	3

Billy and Sarah GAINES *US, male / female vocal duo (1 WEEK)* pos/wks

			pos	wks
14 Jun 97		I FOUND SOMEONE *Expansion CDEXP 27*	48	1

Rosie GAINES *US, female vocalist (15 WEEKS)* pos/wks

			pos	wks
11 Nov 95		I WANT U *Motown 8604852*	70	1
31 May 97	●	CLOSER THAN CLOSE *Big Bang CDBBANG 1*	4	12
29 Nov 97		I SURRENDER *Big Bang CDBBANG 2*	39	2

Serge GAINSBOURG – *See Jane BIRKIN and Serge GAINSBOURG*

GALA *Italy, female vocalist – Gala Rizzatto (24 WEEKS)* pos/wks

			pos	wks
19 Jul 97	●	FREED FROM DESIRE *Big Life BLRD 135*	2	14
6 Dec 97		LET A BOY CRY *Big Life BLRD 140*	11	8
22 Aug 98		COME INTO MY LIFE *Big Life BLRD 147*	38	2

GALAXY – *See Phil FEARON*

Dee GALDES – *See Phil FEARON*

Eve GALLAGHER *UK, female vocalist (8 WEEKS)* pos/wks

			pos	wks
1 Dec 90		LOVE COME DOWN *More Protein PROT 6*	61	3
29 Dec 90		LOVE COME DOWN (re-entry) *More Protein PROT 6*	68	1
15 Apr 95		YOU CAN HAVE IT ALL *Cleveland City CLECD 13023*	43	2
28 Oct 95		LOVE COME DOWN (re-recording) *Cleveland City CLECD 13028*	57	1
6 Jul 96		HEARTBREAK *React CDREACT 78* [1]	44	1

[1] Mrs Wood featuring Eve Gallagher

Liam GALLAGHER – *See OASIS; BUFFALO TOM*

GALLAGHER and LYLE *UK, male vocal / instrumental duo – Benny Gallagher and Graham Lyle (27 WEEKS)* pos/wks

			pos	wks
28 Feb 76	●	I WANNA STAY WITH YOU *A & M AMS 7211*	6	9
22 May 76	●	HEART ON MY SLEEVE *A & M AMS 7227*	6	10
11 Sep 76		BREAKAWAY *A & M AMS 7245*	35	4
29 Jan 77		EVERY LITTLE TEARDROP *A & M AMS 7274*	32	4

Patsy GALLANT *Canada, female vocalist (9 WEEKS)* pos/wks

			pos	wks
10 Sep 77	●	FROM NEW YORK TO LA *EMI 2620*	6	9

Luke GALLIANA *UK, male vocalist (1 WEEK)* pos/wks

			pos	wks
12 May 01		TO DIE FOR *Jive 9201272*	42	1

GALLIANO *UK, male / female vocal / instrumental group (14 WEEKS)* pos/wks

			pos	wks
30 May 92		SKUNK FUNK *Talkin Loud TLK 23*	41	2
1 Aug 92		PRINCE OF PEACE *Talkin Loud TLK 24*	47	3
10 Oct 92		JUS' REACH (RECYCLED) *Talkin Loud TLK 29*	66	2
28 May 94		LONG TIME GONE *Talkin Loud TLKCD 48*	15	3
30 Jul 94		TWYFORD DOWN *Talkin Loud TLKCD 49*	37	2
27 Jul 96		EASE YOUR MIND *Talkin Loud TLCD 10*	45	2

James GALWAY *UK, male instrumentalist – flute (13 WEEKS)* pos/wks

			pos	wks
27 May 78	●	ANNIE'S SONG *RCA Red Seal RB 5085*	3	13

GAMBAFREAKS *Italy, male production duo (2 WEEKS)* pos/wks

			pos	wks
12 Sep 98		INSTANT REPLAY *Evocative EVOKE 7CDS* [1]	57	1
13 May 00		DOWN DOWN DOWN *Azuli AZNYCDX 116*	57	1

[1] Gambafreaks featuring Paco Rivaz

GANG OF FOUR *UK, male vocal / instrumental group (5 WEEKS)* pos/wks

			pos	wks
16 Jun 79		AT HOME HE'S A TOURIST *EMI 2956*	58	3
22 May 82		I LOVE A MAN IN UNIFORM *EMI 5299*	65	2

GANG STARR *US, male rap group (8 WEEKS)* pos/wks

			pos	wks
13 Oct 90		JAZZ THING *CBS 356377 7*	66	2
23 Feb 91		TAKE A REST *Cooltempo COOL 230*	63	1
25 May 91		LOVESICK *Cooltempo COOL 234*	50	3
13 Jun 92		2 DEEP *Cooltempo COOL 256*	67	2

GANT *UK, production duo – Julian Jonah and Danny Harrison (1 WEEK)* pos/wks

			pos	wks
27 Dec 97		SOUND BWOY BURIAL / ALL NIGHT LONG *Positiva CDTIV 85*	67	1

GAP BAND (402 Top 500) *Soul / funk / disco outfit from Tulsa, Oklahoma, US, featuring brothers Charlie, Ronnie and Robert Wilson. Named after Greenwood, Archer and Pine – three streets in their hometown. First British hit launched a 'rowing-boat' craze on UK dancefloors (82 WEEKS)* pos/wks

			pos	wks
12 Jul 80	●	OOPS UP SIDE YOUR HEAD *Mercury MER 22*	6	14
27 Sep 80		PARTY LIGHTS *Mercury MER 37*	30	8
27 Dec 80		BURN RUBBER ON ME (WHY YOU WANNA HURT ME) *Mercury MER 52*	22	11
11 Apr 81		HUMPIN' *Mercury MER 63*	36	6
27 Jun 81		YEARNING FOR YOUR LOVE *Mercury MER 73*	47	4
5 Jun 82		EARLY IN THE MORNING *Mercury MER 97*	55	3
19 Feb 83		OUTSTANDING *Total Experience TE 001*	68	2
31 Mar 84		SOMEDAY *Total Experience TE 5*	17	8
23 Jun 84		JAMMIN' IN AMERICA *Total Experience TE 6*	64	2
13 Dec 86	●	BIG FUN *Total Experience FB 49779*	4	12
14 Mar 87		HOW MUSIC CAME ABOUT (BOP B DA B DA DA) *Total Experience FB 49755*	61	2
11 Jul 87		OOPS UPSIDE YOUR HEAD (re-mix) *Club JAB 54*	20	8
18 Feb 89		I'M GONNA GIT YOU SUCKA *Arista 112016*	63	2

GARBAGE
US / UK, male / female vocal / instrumental group (59 WEEKS) pos/wks

			pos	wks
19 Aug 95		SUBHUMAN *Mushroom D 1138*	50	1
30 Sep 95		ONLY HAPPY WHEN IT RAINS *Mushroom D 1199*	29	3

2 Dec 95		QUEER *Mushroom D 1237*	13	4
23 Mar 96	●	STUPID GIRL *Mushroom D 1271*	4	7
23 Nov 96	●	MILK *Mushroom D 1494* [1]	10	7
18 Jan 97		MILK (re-entry) *Mushroom D 1494* [1]	74	1
9 May 98	●	PUSH IT *Mushroom MUSH 28CDS*	9	5
18 Jul 98	●	I THINK I'M PARANOID *Mushroom MUSH 35CDS*	9	5
17 Oct 98		SPECIAL *Mushroom MUSH 39CDS*	15	4
6 Feb 99	●	WHEN I GROW UP *Mushroom MUSH 43CDS*	9	7
5 Jun 99		YOU LOOK SO FINE *Mushroom MUSH 49CDS*	19	4
27 Nov 99		THE WORLD IS NOT ENOUGH *Radioactive RAXTD 40*	11	9
6 Oct 01		ANDROGYNY *Mushroom MUSH 94CDS*	24	2

[1] Garbage featuring Tricky

Adam GARCIA *Australia, male vocalist (5 WEEKS)* pos/wks

16 May 98		NIGHT FEVER *Polydor 5697972*	15	5

Scott GARCIA featuring MC STYLES
UK, male producer and UK, male rapper (3 WEEKS) pos/wks

1 Nov 97		A LONDON THING *Connected CDCONNECT 1*	29	3

Boris GARDINER
Jamaica, male vocalist / instrumentalist (38 WEEKS) pos/wks

17 Jan 70		ELIZABETHAN REGGAE *Duke DU 39*	48	1
31 Jan 70		ELIZABETHAN REGGAE (re-entry) *Duke DU 39*	14	13
26 Jul 86	★	I WANT TO WAKE UP WITH YOU *Revue REV 733*	1	15
4 Oct 86		YOU'RE EVERYTHING TO ME *Revue REV 735*	11	8
27 Dec 86		THE MEANING OF CHRISTMAS *Revue REV 740*	69	1

The first copies of 'Elizabethan Reggae', an instrumental, were printed with the label incorrectly crediting Byron Lee as the performer. The charts for the first entry, and the first four weeks of the re-entry, all reprinted this error. All charts and discs printed after 28 Feb 1970 gave Boris Gardiner the credit he deserved

Paul GARDINER *UK, male instrumentalist – bass (4 WEEKS)* pos/wks

25 Jul 81		STORMTROOPER IN DRAG *Beggars Banquet BEG 61*	49	4

Uncredited vocalist is Gary Numan

Art GARFUNKEL *US, male vocalist (37 WEEKS)* pos/wks

13 Sep 75	★	I ONLY HAVE EYES FOR YOU *CBS 3575*	1	11
3 Mar 79	★	BRIGHT EYES *CBS 6947*◆	1	19
7 Jul 79		SINCE I DON'T HAVE YOU *CBS 7371*	38	7

See also SIMON and GARFUNKEL

Judy GARLAND *US, female vocalist – Frances Gumm (2 WEEKS)* pos/wks

10 Jun 55		THE MAN THAT GOT AWAY *Philips PB 366*	18	2

Laurent GARNIER *France, male DJ / producer (4 WEEKS)* pos/wks

15 Feb 97		CRISPY BACON *F Communications F 055CD*	60	1
22 Apr 00		MAN WITH THE RED FACE *F Communications F 119CD*	65	1
11 Nov 00		GREED / THE MAN WITH THE RED FACE (re-issue) *F Communications F 127CDUK*	36	2

Lee GARRETT *US, male vocalist (7 WEEKS)* pos/wks

29 May 76		YOU'RE MY EVERYTHING *Chrysalis CHS 2087*	15	7

Leif GARRETT *US, male vocalist (14 WEEKS)* pos/wks

20 Jan 79	●	I WAS MADE FOR DANCIN' *Scotti Brothers K 11202*	4	10
21 Apr 79		FEEL THE NEED *Scotti Brothers K 11274*	38	4

Siedah GARRETT – *See BRAND NEW HEAVIES; Michael JACKSON; Dennis EDWARDS featuring Siedah GARRETT*

Lesley GARRETT and Amanda THOMPSON
UK, female vocal / instrumental duo (10 WEEKS) pos/wks

6 Nov 93		AVE MARIA *Internal Affairs KGBD 012*	16	10

David GARRICK *UK, male vocalist (16 WEEKS)* pos/wks

9 Jun 66		LADY JANE *Piccadilly 7N 35317*	28	7
22 Sep 66		DEAR MRS APPLEBEE *Piccadilly 7N 35335*	22	9

GARY'S GANG *US, male vocal / instrumental group (18 WEEKS)* pos/wks

24 Feb 79	●	KEEP ON DANCIN' *CBS 7109*	8	10
2 Jun 79		LET'S LOVEDANCE TONIGHT *CBS 7328*	49	4
6 Nov 82		KNOCK ME OUT *Arista ARIST 499*	45	4

Barbara GASKIN – *See Dave STEWART*

GAT DECOR *UK, male instrumental / production group (10 WEEKS)* pos/wks

16 May 92		PASSION *Effective EFFS 1*	29	4
9 Mar 96	●	PASSION (re-mix) *Way Of Life WAYDA 1*	6	6

Stephen GATELY *Ireland, male vocalist (19 WEEKS)* pos/wks

10 Jun 00	●	NEW BEGINNING / BRIGHT EYES *A&M / Polydor 5618192*	3	11
14 Oct 00		I BELIEVE *Polydor 5877472*	11	4
12 May 01		STAY *A&M / Mercury 5870672*	13	4

See also BOYZONE

David GATES *US, male vocalist (2 WEEKS)* pos/wks

22 Jul 78		TOOK THE LAST TRAIN *Elektra K 12307*	50	2

See also BREAD

GAY DAD *UK, male / female vocal / instrumental group (10 WEEKS)* pos/wks

30 Jan 99	●	TO EARTH WITH LOVE *London LONCD 413*	10	4
5 Jun 99		JOY! *London LONCD 428*	22	3
14 Aug 99		OH JIM *London LONCD 437*	47	1
31 Mar 01		NOW ALWAYS AND FOREVER *B Unique BUN 004CD*	41	1
22 Sep 01		TRANSMISSION *B Unique BUN 009CD*	58	1

GAY GORDON and the MINCE PIES
UK, male / female vocal / instrumental group (5 WEEKS) pos/wks

6 Dec 86		THE ESSENTIAL WALLY PARTY MEDLEY *Lifestyle XY 2*	60	5

Marvin GAYE (87 Top 500) *One of soul's most innovative and successful singer / songwriters, b. 2 Apr 1939, Washington DC, d. 1 Apr 1984. He went from doo-wop group member and session drummer to superstar. Posthumously awarded a Lifetime Achievement Grammy Award in 1996 (202 WEEKS)* pos/wks

30 Jul 64		ONCE UPON A TIME *Stateside SS 316* [1]	50	1
10 Dec 64		HOW SWEET IT IS *Stateside SS 360*	49	1
29 Sep 66		LITTLE DARLIN' (I NEED YOU) *Tamla Motown TMG 574*	50	1
26 Jan 67		IT TAKES TWO *Tamla Motown TMG 590* [2]	16	11
17 Jan 68		IF I COULD BUILD MY WHOLE WORLD AROUND YOU *Tamla Motown TMG 635* [3]	41	7
12 Jun 68		AIN'T NOTHIN' LIKE THE REAL THING *Tamla Motown TMG 655* [3]	34	7
2 Oct 68		YOU'RE ALL I NEED TO GET BY *Tamla Motown TMG 668* [3]	19	19
22 Jan 69		YOU AIN'T LIVIN' TILL YOU'RE LOVIN' *Tamla Motown TMG 681* [3]	21	8
12 Feb 69	★	I HEARD IT THROUGH THE GRAPEVINE *Tamla Motown TMG 686*▲	1	15
4 Jun 69		GOOD LOVIN' AIN'T EASY TO COME BY *Tamla Motown TMG 697* [3]	26	7
23 Jul 69	●	TOO BUSY THINKING 'BOUT MY BABY *Tamla Motown TMG 705*	5	16
30 Jul 69		GOOD LOVIN' AIN'T EASY TO COME BY (re-entry) *Tamla Motown TMG 697* [3]	48	1
15 Nov 69	●	ONION SONG *Tamla Motown TMG 715* [3]	9	12
9 May 70	●	ABRAHAM MARTIN AND JOHN *Tamla Motown TMG 734*	9	14
11 Dec 71		SAVE THE CHILDREN *Tamla Motown TMG 796*	41	6
22 Sep 73		LET'S GET IT ON *Tamla Motown TMG 868*▲	31	7
23 Mar 74	●	YOU ARE EVERYTHING *Tamla Motown TMG 890* [4]	5	12
20 Jul 74		STOP LOOK LISTEN (TO YOUR HEART) *Tamla Motown TMG 906* [4]	25	8
7 May 77	●	GOT TO GIVE IT UP (PT.1) *Motown TMG 1069*▲	7	10
24 Feb 79		POPS WE LOVE YOU *Motown TMG 1136* [5]	66	5
30 Oct 82	●	(SEXUAL) HEALING *CBS A 2855*	4	14

		pos	wks
8 Jan 83	**MY LOVE IS WAITING** *CBS A 3048*	34	5
18 May 85	**SANCTIFIED LADY** *CBS A 4894*	51	4
26 Apr 86 ●	**I HEARD IT THROUGH THE GRAPEVINE (re-issue)** *Tamla Motown ZB 40701*	8	8
14 May 94	**LUCKY LUCKY ME** *Motown TMGCD 1426*	67	1
6 Oct 01	**MUSIC** *Polydor 4976222* [6]	36	2

[1] Marvin Gaye and Mary Wells [2] Marvin Gaye and Kim Weston [3] Marvin Gaye and Tammi Terrell [4] Diana Ross and Marvin Gaye [5] Diana Ross, Marvin Gaye, Smokey Robinson and Stevie Wonder [6] Erick Sermon featuring Marvin Gaye

GAYE BYKERS ON ACID
UK, male vocal / instrumental group (2 WEEKS) pos/wks

		pos	wks
31 Oct 87	**GIT DOWN (SHAKE YOUR THANG)** *Purple Fluid VS 1008*	54	2

Crystal GAYLE *US, female vocalist – Brenda Gail Webb (28 WEEKS)* pos/wks

		pos	wks
12 Nov 77 ●	**DON'T IT MAKE MY BROWN EYES BLUE** *United Artists UP 36307*	5	14
26 Aug 78	**TALKING IN YOUR SLEEP** *United Artists UP 36422*	11	14

Michelle GAYLE *UK, female vocalist (52 WEEKS)* pos/wks

		pos	wks
7 Aug 93	**LOOKING UP** *RCA 74321154532*	11	6
24 Sep 94 ●	**SWEETNESS** *RCA 74321230192*	4	16
17 Dec 94	**I'LL FIND YOU** *RCA 74321247762*	26	7
27 May 95	**FREEDOM** *RCA 74321284692*	16	6
26 Aug 95	**HAPPY JUST TO BE WITH YOU** *RCA 74321302692*	11	7
8 Feb 97 ●	**DO YOU KNOW** *RCA 74321419282*	6	6
26 Apr 97	**SENSATIONAL** *RCA 74321419302*	14	4

Roy GAYLE – *See MIRAGE*

GAYLE & GILLIAN *Australia, female vocal duo (2 WEEKS)* pos/wks

		pos	wks
3 Jul 93	**MAD IF YA DON'T** *Mushroom CDMUSH 1*	75	1
19 Mar 94	**WANNA BE YOUR LOVER** *Mushroom D 11598*	62	1

Gloria GAYNOR (478 Top 500) *Legendary disco diva, b. 7 Sep 1949, New Jersey, US. Her transatlantic chart-topping feminist anthem and karaoke favourite proved it would survive by returning to the Top 5, in remixed form, 14 years after reaching No.1 (73 WEEKS)* pos/wks

		pos	wks
7 Dec 74 ●	**NEVER CAN SAY GOODBYE** *MGM 2006 463*	2	13
8 Mar 75	**REACH OUT I'LL BE THERE** *MGM 2006 499*	14	8
9 Aug 75	**ALL I NEED IS YOUR SWEET LOVIN'** *MGM 2006 531*	44	3
17 Jan 76	**HOW HIGH THE MOON** *MGM 2006 558*	33	4
3 Feb 79 ★	**I WILL SURVIVE** *Polydor 2095 017* ▲	1	15
6 Oct 79	**LET ME KNOW (I HAVE A RIGHT)** *Polydor STEP 5*	32	7
24 Dec 83	**I AM WHAT I AM (FROM 'LA CAGE AUX FOLLES')** *Chrysalis CHS 2765*	13	12
26 Jun 93 ●	**I WILL SURVIVE (re-mix)** *Polydor PZCD 270*	5	10
3 Jun 00	**LAST NIGHT** *Logic 74321738082*	67	1

GAZ *US, male vocal / instrumental group (4 WEEKS)* pos/wks

		pos	wks
24 Feb 79	**SING SING** *Salsoul SSOL 116*	60	4

GAZZA *UK, male vocalist - Paul Gascoigne (14 WEEKS)* pos/wks

		pos	wks
10 Nov 90 ●	**FOG ON THE TYNE (REVISITED)** *Best ZB 44083* [1]	2	9
22 Dec 90	**GEORDIE BOYS (GAZZA RAP)** *Best ZB 44229*	31	5

[1] Gazza and Lindisfarne

GBH *UK, male vocal / instrumental group (5 WEEKS)* pos/wks

		pos	wks
6 Feb 82	**NO SURVIVORS** *Clay CLAY 8*	63	2
20 Nov 82	**GIVE ME FIRE** *Clay CLAY 16*	69	3

Nigel GEE *UK, male producer (1 WEEK)* pos/wks

		pos	wks
27 Jan 01	**HOOTIN'** *Neo NEOCD 040*	57	1

J GEILS BAND *US, male vocal / instrumental group (20 WEEKS)* pos/wks

		pos	wks
9 Jun 79	**ONE LAST KISS** *EMI America AM 507*	74	1
13 Feb 82 ●	**CENTERFOLD** *EMI America EA 135* ▲	3	9
10 Apr 82	**FREEZE-FRAME** *EMI America EA 134*	27	7
26 Jun 82	**ANGEL IN BLUE** *EMI America EA 138*	55	3

Bob GELDOF *Ireland, male vocalist (15 WEEKS)* pos/wks

		pos	wks
1 Nov 86	**THIS IS THE WORLD CALLING** *Mercury BOB 101*	25	5
21 Feb 87	**LOVE LIKE A ROCKET** *Mercury BOB 102*	61	3
23 Jun 90	**THE GREAT SONG OF INDIFFERENCE** *Mercury BOB 104*	15	6
7 May 94	**CRAZY** *Vertigo VERCX 85*	65	1

See also BOOMTOWN RATS

GEM – *See OUR TRIBE / ONE TRIBE*

GEMINI *UK, male vocal duo (7 WEEKS)* pos/wks

		pos	wks
30 Sep 95	**EVEN THOUGH YOU BROKE MY HEART** *EMI CDEMS 391*	40	3
10 Feb 96	**STEAL YOUR LOVE AWAY** *EMI CDEMS 407*	37	2
29 Jun 96	**COULD IT BE FOREVER** *EMI CDEMS 426*	38	2

GEMS FOR JEM *UK, male instrumental / production duo (2 WEEKS)* pos/wks

		pos	wks
6 May 95	**LIFTING ME HIGHER** *Box 21 CDSBOKS 3*	28	2

GENE *UK, male vocal / instrumental group (22 WEEKS)* pos/wks

		pos	wks
13 Aug 94	**BE MY LIGHT BE MY GUIDE** *Costermonger COST 002CD*	54	1
12 Nov 94	**SLEEP WELL TONIGHT** *Costermonger COST 003CD*	36	2
4 Mar 95	**HAUNTED BY YOU** *Costermonger COST 004CD*	32	2
22 Jul 95	**OLYMPIAN** *Costermonger COST 005CD*	18	2
13 Jan 96	**FOR THE DEAD** *Costermonger COST 006CD*	14	3
2 Nov 96	**FIGHTING FIT** *Costermonger COST 009CD*	22	2
1 Feb 97	**WE COULD BE KINGS** *Polydor COSCD 10*	17	2
10 May 97	**WHERE ARE THEY NOW?** *Polydor COSCD 11*	22	2
9 Aug 97	**SPEAK TO ME SOMEONE** *Polydor COSCD 12*	30	2
27 Feb 99	**AS GOOD AS IT GETS** *Polydor COSCD 14*	23	2
24 Apr 99	**FILL HER UP** *Polydor COSCD 15*	36	2

GENE AND JIM ARE INTO SHAKES
UK, male vocal / instrumental duo (2 WEEKS) pos/wks

		pos	wks
19 Mar 88	**SHAKE! (HOW ABOUT A SAMPLING, GENE?)** *Rough Trade RT 216*	68	2

GENE LOVES JEZEBEL *UK, male vocal / instrumental group (7 WEEKS)* pos/wks

		pos	wks
29 Mar 86	**SWEETEST THING** *Beggars Banquet BEG 156*	75	1
14 Jun 86	**HEARTACHE** *Beggars Banquet BEG 161*	71	2
5 Sep 87	**THE MOTION OF LOVE** *Beggars Banquet BEG 192*	56	3
5 Dec 87	**GORGEOUS** *Beggars Banquet BEG 202*	68	1

GENERAL DEGREE – *See Richie STEPHENS*

GENERAL LEVY *UK, male vocalist (13 WEEKS)* pos/wks

		pos	wks
4 Sep 93	**MONKEY MAN** *ffrr FCD 214*	75	1
18 Jun 94	**INCREDIBLE** *Renk RENK 42 CD* [1]	39	3
10 Sep 94 ●	**INCREDIBLE (re-mix)** *Renk CD RENK 44* [1]	8	9

[1] M-Beat featuring General Levy

GENERAL PUBLIC *UK, male vocal / instrumental group (4 WEEKS)* pos/wks

		pos	wks
10 Mar 84	**GENERAL PUBLIC** *Virgin VS 659*	60	3
2 Jul 94	**I'LL TAKE YOU THERE** *Epic 6605532*	73	1

See also BEAT

GENERAL SAINT *UK, male vocalist (9 WEEKS)* pos/wks

		pos	wks
29 Sep 84	**LAST PLANE (ONE WAY TICKET)** *MCA MCA 910* [1]	51	3
2 Apr 94	**OH CAROL!** *Copasetic COPCD 0009* [1]	54	5
6 Aug 94	**SAVE THE LAST DANCE FOR ME** *Copasetic COPCD 12* [2]	75	1

[1] Clint Eastwood and General Saint [2] General Saint featuring Don Campbell

GENERATION X *UK, male vocal / instrumental group (31 WEEKS)* pos/wks

		pos	wks
17 Sep 77	**YOUR GENERATION** *Chrysalis CHS 2165*	36	4

		pos	wks
11 Mar 78	**READY STEADY GO** *Chrysalis CHS 2207*	47	3
20 Jan 79	**KING ROCKER** *Chrysalis CHS 2261*	11	9
7 Apr 79	**VALLEY OF THE DOLLS** *Chrysalis CHS 2310*	23	7
30 Jun 79	**FRIDAY'S ANGELS** *Chrysalis CHS 2330*	62	2
18 Oct 80	**DANCING WITH MYSELF** *Chrysalis CHS 2444* [1]	62	2
24 Jan 81	**DANCING WITH MYSELF (EP)** *Chrysalis CHS 2488* [1]	60	4

[1] Gen X

Tracks on Dancing With Myself (EP): Dancing With Myself / Untouchables / Rock On / King Rocker

See also Billy IDOL

GENERATOR *Holland, male producer – Robert Smit (1 WEEK)*

		pos	wks
23 Oct 99	**WHERE ARE YOU NOW?** *Tidy Trax TIDY 130CD*	60	1

GENESIS (104 Top 500) *Perennially popular UK group. Stalwart members are Tony Banks (k) and Mike Rutherford (g); others included Peter Gabriel (v), Phil Collins (v/d), Steve Hackett (g). These progressive 1970s rockers became a major act in the 1980s and had 10 consecutive Top 3 albums (187 WEEKS)*

		pos	wks
6 Apr 74	**I KNOW WHAT I LIKE (IN YOUR WARDROBE)** *Charisma CB 224*	21	7
26 Feb 77	**YOUR OWN SPECIAL WAY** *Charisma CB 300*	43	3
28 May 77	**SPOT THE PIGEON (EP)** *Charisma GEN 001*	14	7
11 Mar 78 ●	**FOLLOW YOU FOLLOW ME** *Charisma CB 309*	7	13
8 Jul 78	**MANY TOO MANY** *Charisma CB 315*	43	5
15 Mar 80 ●	**TURN IT ON AGAIN** *Charisma CB 356*	8	10
17 May 80	**DUCHESS** *Charisma CB 363*	46	5
13 Sep 80	**MISUNDERSTANDING** *Charisma CB 369*	42	5
22 Aug 81 ●	**ABACAB** *Charisma CB 388*	9	8
31 Oct 81	**KEEP IT DARK** *Charisma CB 391*	33	4
13 Mar 82	**MAN ON THE CORNER** *Charisma CB 393*	41	5
22 May 82 ●	**3 X 3 (EP)** *Charisma GEN 1*	10	8
3 Sep 83 ●	**MAMA** *Virgin / Charisma MAMA 1*	4	10
12 Nov 83	**THAT'S ALL** *Charisma / Virgin TATA 1*	16	11
11 Feb 84	**ILLEGAL ALIEN** *Charisma / Virgin AL1*	46	3
10 Mar 84	**ILLEGAL ALIEN (re-entry)** *Charisma / Virgin AL1*	70	1
31 May 86	**INVISIBLE TOUCH** *Virgin GENS 1* ▲	15	8
30 Aug 86	**IN TOO DEEP** *Virgin GENS 2*	19	9
22 Nov 86	**LAND OF CONFUSION** *Virgin GENS 3*	14	12
14 Mar 87	**TONIGHT TONIGHT TONIGHT** *Virgin GENS 4*	18	6
20 Jun 87	**THROWING IT ALL AWAY** *Virgin GENS 5*	22	8
2 Nov 91 ●	**NO SON OF MINE** *Virgin GENS 6*	6	6
4 Jan 92	**NO SON OF MINE (re-entry)** *Virgin GENS 6*	70	1
11 Jan 92 ●	**I CAN'T DANCE** *Virgin GENS 7*	7	9
18 Apr 92	**HOLD ON MY HEART** *Virgin GENS 8*	16	5
25 Jul 92	**JESUS HE KNOWS ME** *Virgin GENS 9*	20	7
21 Nov 92 ●	**INVISIBLE TOUCH (LIVE)** *Virgin GENS 10*	7	4
20 Feb 93	**TELL ME WHY** *Virgin GENDG 11*	40	3
27 Sep 97	**CONGO** *Virgin GENSD 12*	29	2
13 Dec 97	**SHIPWRECKED** *Virgin GENDX14*	54	1
7 Mar 98	**NOT ABOUT US** *Virgin GENSD 15*	66	1

Tracks on Spot the Pigeon (EP): Match of the Day / Pigeons / Inside and Out. Tracks on 3 x 3 (EP): Paperlate / You Might Recall / Me and Virgil

See also MIKE and the MECHANICS; Phil COLLINS; Steve HACKETT; FISH; Peter GABRIEL

Lee A GENESIS – *See Bob SINCLAR*

GENEVA *UK, male vocal / instrumental group (9 WEEKS)*

		pos	wks
26 Oct 96	**NO ONE SPEAKS** *Nude NUD 22CD*	32	2
8 Feb 97	**INTO THE BLUE** *Nude NUD 25CD*	26	2
31 May 97	**TRANQUILIZER** *Nude NUD 28 CD1*	24	2
16 Aug 97	**BEST REGRETS** *Nude NUD 31CD1*	38	1
27 Nov 99	**DOLLARS IN THE HEAVENS** *Nude NUD 46CD1*	59	1
11 Mar 00	**IF YOU HAVE TO GO** *Nude NUD 49CD1*	69	1

GENEVIEVE *France, female vocalist (1 WEEK)*

		pos	wks
5 May 66	**ONCE** *CBS 202061*	43	1

GENIUS CRU *UK, male production group (7 WEEKS)*

		pos	wks
3 Feb 01	**BOOM SELECTION** *Incentive CENT 17CDS*	12	5
27 Oct 01	**COURSE BRUV** *Incentive CENT 28CDS*	39	2

GENIUS / GZA featuring D'ANGELO *US, male rapper and US, male vocalist (2 WEEKS)*

		pos	wks
2 Mar 96	**COLD WORLD** *Geffen GFSTD 22114*	40	2

Bobbie GENTRY *US, female vocalist – Roberta Streeter (48 WEEKS)*

		pos	wks
13 Sep 67	**ODE TO BILLY JOE** *Capitol CL 15511* ▲	13	11
30 Aug 69 ★	**I'LL NEVER FALL IN LOVE AGAIN** *Capitol CL 15606*	1	19
6 Dec 69 ●	**ALL I HAVE TO DO IS DREAM** *Capitol CL 15619* [1]	3	14
21 Feb 70	**RAINDROPS KEEP FALLING ON MY HEAD** *Capitol CL 15626*	40	4

[1] Bobbie Gentry and Glen Campbell

GEORDIE *UK, male vocal / instrumental group (35 WEEKS)*

		pos	wks
2 Dec 72	**DON'T DO THAT** *Regal Zonophone RZ 3067*	32	7
17 Mar 73 ●	**ALL BECAUSE OF YOU** *EMI 2008*	6	13
16 Jun 73	**CAN YOU DO IT** *EMI 2031*	13	9
25 Aug 73	**ELECTRIC LADY** *EMI 2048*	32	6

Robin GEORGE *UK, male vocalist (2 WEEKS)*

		pos	wks
27 Apr 85	**HEARTLINE** *Bronze BRO 191*	68	2

Sophia GEORGE *Jamaica, female vocalist (11 WEEKS)*

		pos	wks
7 Dec 85 ●	**GIRLIE GIRLIE** *Winner WIN 01*	7	11

GEORGIA SATELLITES *US, male vocal / instrumental group (8 WEEKS)*

		pos	wks
7 Feb 87	**KEEP YOUR HANDS TO YOURSELF** *Elektra EKR 50*	69	1
16 May 87	**BATTLESHIP CHAINS** *Elektra EKR 58*	44	4
21 Jan 89	**HIPPY HIPPY SHAKE** *Elektra EKR 86*	63	3

GEORGIE PORGIE *US, male producer (3 WEEKS)*

		pos	wks
12 Aug 95	**EVERYBODY MUST PARTY** *Vibe MCSTD 2068*	61	1
4 May 96	**TAKE ME HIGHER** *Music Plant MCSTD 40031*	61	1
26 Aug 00	**LIFE GOES ON** *Neo NEOCD 039*	54	1

GEORGIO *US, male vocalist (3 WEEKS)*

		pos	wks
20 Feb 88	**LOVER'S LANE** *Motown ZB 41611*	54	3

Danyel GERARD *France, male vocalist (12 WEEKS)*

		pos	wks
18 Sep 71	**BUTTERFLY** *CBS 7454*	11	12

GERIDEAU *US, male vocalist (2 WEEKS)*

		pos	wks
27 Aug 94	**BRING IT ALL BACK 2 LUV** *Fruittree FTREE 10CD* [1]	65	1
4 Jul 98	**MASQUERADE** *Inferno CDFERN7*	63	1

[1] Project featuring Gerideau

GERRY and the PACEMAKERS (243 Top 500) *Record-breaking Merseybeat band: Gerry Marsden (v/g), Les Chadwick (b), Les McGuire (p), Freddie Marsden (d). Second Liverpool group to chart (after The Beatles), but first to reach No.1 and first act ever to top UK chart with their initial three singles (114 WEEKS)*

		pos	wks
14 Mar 63 ★	**HOW DO YOU DO IT?** *Columbia DB 4987*	1	18
30 May 63 ★	**I LIKE IT** *Columbia DB 7041*	1	15
10 Oct 63 ★	**YOU'LL NEVER WALK ALONE** *Columbia DB 7126*	1	19
16 Jan 64 ●	**I'M THE ONE** *Columbia DB 7189*	2	15
16 Apr 64 ●	**DON'T LET THE SUN CATCH YOU CRYING** *Columbia DB 7268*	6	11
3 Sep 64	**IT'S GONNA BE ALL RIGHT** *Columbia DB 7353*	24	7
17 Dec 64 ●	**FERRY 'CROSS THE MERSEY** *Columbia DB 7437*	8	13
25 Mar 65	**I'LL BE THERE** *Columbia DB 7504*	15	9
18 Nov 65	**WALK HAND IN HAND** *Columbia DB 7738*	29	7

GET FRESH CREW – *See Doug E FRESH and the GET FRESH CREW*

GET READY *UK, male vocal group (1 WEEK)*

			pos	wks
3 Jun 95		**WILD WILD WEST** *Mega GACXCD 2698*	65	1

GETO BOYS featuring FLAJ *US, male rap group (1 WEEK)*

			pos	wks
11 May 96		**THE WORLD IS A GHETTO** *Virgin America VUSCD 104*	49	1

Stan GETZ
US, male instrumentalist – tenor sax – Stanley Gayetzsky (29 WEEKS)

			pos	wks
8 Nov 62		**DESAFINADO** *HMV POP 1061* [1]	11	13
23 Jul 64		**THE GIRL FROM IPANEMA (GAROTA DE IPANEMA)** *Verve VS 520* [2]	29	10
25 Aug 84		**THE GIRL FROM IPANEMA (re-issue)** *Verve IPA 1* [3]	55	6

[1] Stan Getz and Charlie Byrd [2] Stan Getz and Joao Gilberto [3] Astrud Gilberto

The re-issue of 'The Girl From Ipanema' was credited only to Astrud Gilberto, the vocalist, even though it was exactly the same recording as the original hit

Amanda GHOST *UK, female vocalist (1 WEEK)*

			pos	wks
8 Apr 00		**IDOL** *Warner Brothers W 518CD*	63	1

GHOST DANCE *UK, male vocal / instrumental group (2 WEEKS)*

			pos	wks
17 Jun 89		**DOWN TO THE WIRE** *Chrysalis CHS 3376*	66	2

GHOSTFACE KILLAH *US, male rapper – Dennis Coles (13 WEEKS)*

			pos	wks
12 Jul 97		**ALL THAT I GOT IS YOU** *Epic 6646842*	11	4
23 Jan 99	●	**I WANT YOU FOR MYSELF** *Northwestside 74321643632* [1]	2	8
4 Nov 00		**MISS FAT BOOTY – PART II** *Rawkus RWK 282CD* [2]	64	1

[1] Another Level / Ghostface Killah [2] Mos Def featuring Ghostface Killah

Andy GIBB *UK, male vocalist (30 WEEKS)*

			pos	wks
25 Jun 77		**I JUST WANNA BE YOUR EVERYTHING** *RSO 2090 237* ▲	26	7
13 May 78		**SHADOW DANCING** *RSO 001* ▲	42	6
12 Aug 78	●	**AN EVERLASTING LOVE** *RSO 015*	10	10
27 Jan 79		**(OUR LOVE) DON'T THROW IT ALL AWAY** *RSO 26*	32	7

Barry GIBB – *See BEE GEES; Barbra STREISAND*

Robin GIBB *UK, male vocalist (21 WEEKS)*

			pos	wks
9 Jul 69	●	**SAVED BY THE BELL** *Polydor 56-337*	2	16
15 Nov 69		**SAVED BY THE BELL (re-entry)** *Polydor 56-337*	49	1
7 Feb 70		**AUGUST OCTOBER** *Polydor 56-371*	45	3
11 Feb 84		**ANOTHER LONELY NIGHT IN NEW YORK** *Polydor POSP 668*	71	1

See also BEE GEES

Steve GIBBONS BAND
UK, male vocal / instrumental group (14 WEEKS)

			pos	wks
6 Aug 77		**TULANE** *Polydor 2058 889*	12	10
13 May 78		**EDDY VORTEX** *Polydor 2059 017*	56	4

Georgia GIBBS *US, female vocalist – Freda Gibbons (2 WEEKS)*

			pos	wks
22 Apr 55		**TWEEDLE DEE** *Mercury MB 3196*	20	1
13 Jul 56		**KISS ME ANOTHER** *Mercury MT 110*	24	1

Debbie GIBSON *US, female vocalist / writer / producer (70 WEEKS)*

			pos	wks
26 Sep 87		**ONLY IN MY DREAMS** *Atlantic A 9322*	54	5
23 Jan 88	●	**SHAKE YOUR LOVE** *Atlantic A 9187*	7	8
19 Mar 88		**ONLY IN MY DREAMS (re-entry)** *Atlantic A 9322*	11	7
7 May 88		**OUT OF THE BLUE** *Atlantic A 9091*	19	7
9 Jul 88	●	**FOOLISH BEAT** *Atlantic A 9059* ▲	9	9
15 Oct 88		**STAYING TOGETHER** *Atlantic A 9020*	53	2
28 Jan 89		**LOST IN YOUR EYES** *Atlantic A 8970* ▲	34	7
29 Apr 89		**ELECTRIC YOUTH** *Atlantic A 8919*	14	8
19 Aug 89		**WE COULD BE TOGETHER** *Atlantic A 8896*	22	8
9 Mar 91		**ANYTHING IS POSSIBLE** *Atlantic A 7735*	51	2
3 Apr 93		**SHOCK YOUR MAMA** *Atlantic A 7386CD*	74	1
24 Jul 93		**YOU'RE THE ONE THAT I WANT** *Epic 6595222* [1]	13	6

[1] Craig McLachlan and Debbie Gibson

Don GIBSON *US, male vocalist (16 WEEKS)*

			pos	wks
31 Aug 61		**SEA OF HEARTBREAK** *RCA 1243*	14	13
1 Feb 62		**LONESOME NUMBER ONE** *RCA 1272*	47	3

Wayne GIBSON *UK, male vocalist (13 WEEKS)*

			pos	wks
3 Sep 64		**KELLY** *Pye 7N 15680*	48	2
23 Nov 74		**UNDER MY THUMB** *Pye Disco Demand DDS 2001*	17	11

GIBSON BROTHERS
Martinique, male vocal / instrumental group (54 WEEKS)

			pos	wks
10 Mar 79		**CUBA** *Island WIP 6483*	41	9
21 Jul 79	●	**OOH! WHAT A LIFE** *Island WIP 6503*	10	12
17 Nov 79	●	**QUE SERA MI VIDA (IF YOU SHOULD GO)** *Island WIP 6525*	5	11
23 Feb 80		**CUBA / BETTER DO IT SALSA (re-issue)** *Island WIP 6561*	12	9
12 Jul 80		**MARIANA** *Island WIP 6617*	11	10
9 Jul 83		**MY HEART'S BEATING WILD (TIC TAC TIC TAC)** *Stiff BUY 184*	56	3

GIDEA PARK
UK, male vocal / instrumentalist – Adrian Baker (19 WEEKS)

			pos	wks
4 Jul 81		**BEACH BOY GOLD** *Sonet SON 2162*	11	13
12 Sep 81		**SEASONS OF GOLD** *Polo POLO 14*	28	6

Johan GIELEN *Belgium, male producer (3 WEEKS)*

			pos	wks
18 Aug 01		**VELVET MOODS** *Data DATA 17T* [1]	74	1
22 Sep 01		**THE BEAUTY OF SILENCE** *Xtrahard / Xtravaganza X2H 5CDS* [2]	41	2

[1] Johan Gielen presents Abnea [2] Svenson and Gielen

See also BLUE BAMBOO; AIRSCAPE

GIFTED *UK, male instrumentalist (1 WEEK)*

			pos	wks
23 Aug 97		**DO I** *Perfecto PERF 140CD*	60	1

GIGOLO AUNTS *US, male vocal / instrumental group (4 WEEKS)*

			pos	wks
23 Apr 94		**MRS WASHINGTON** *Fire BLAZE 68CD*	74	1
13 May 95		**WHERE I FIND MY HEAVEN** *Fire BLAZE 87CD*	29	3

Astrud GILBERTO – *See Stan GETZ*

Joao GILBERTO – *See Stan GETZ*

Donna GILES *US, female vocalist (4 WEEKS)*

			pos	wks
13 Aug 94		**AND I'M TELLING YOU I'M NOT GOING** *Ore AG 4CD*	43	2
10 Feb 96		**AND I'M TELLING YOU I'M NOT GOING (re-issue)** *Ore AGR 4CD*	27	2

Johnny GILL *US, male vocalist (12 WEEKS)*

			pos	wks
23 Feb 91		**WRAP MY BODY TIGHT** *Motown ZB 44271*	57	2
28 Nov 92		**SLOW AND SEXY** *Epic 6587727* [1]	17	7
17 Jul 93		**THE FLOOR** *Motown TMGCD 1416*	53	1
29 Jan 94		**A CUTE SWEET LOVE ADDICTION** *Motown TMGCD 1420*	46	2

[1] Shabba Ranks featuring Johnny Gill

Vince GILL – *See Amy GRANT; Barbra STREISAND*

GILLAN *UK, male vocal / instrumental group (46 WEEKS)*

			pos	wks
14 Jun 80		**SLEEPIN' ON THE JOB** *Virgin VS 355*	55	3
4 Oct 80		**TROUBLE** *Virgin VS 377*	14	6
14 Feb 81		**MUTUALLY ASSURED DESTRUCTION** *Virgin VSK 103*	32	5
21 Mar 81		**NEW ORLEANS** *Virgin VS 406*	17	10
20 Jun 81		**NO LAUGHING IN HEAVEN** *Virgin VS 425*	31	6
10 Oct 81		**NIGHTMARE** *Virgin VS 441*	36	6
23 Jan 82		**RESTLESS** *Virgin VS 465*	25	7
4 Sep 82		**LIVING FOR THE CITY** *Virgin VS 519*	50	3

GILLETTE – *See 20 FINGERS*

Stuart GILLIES *UK, male vocalist (10 WEEKS)* pos/wks

31 Mar 73	**AMANDA** *Philips 6006 293*	13	10

Jimmy GILMER – *See FIREBALLS*

James GILREATH *US, male vocalist (10 WEEKS)* pos/wks

2 May 63	**LITTLE BAND OF GOLD** *Pye International 7N 25190*	29	10

Jim GILSTRAP *US, male vocalist (11 WEEKS)* pos/wks

15 Mar 75 ●	**SWING YOUR DADDY** *Chelsea 2005 021*	4	11

Gordon GILTRAP *UK, male instrumentalist – guitar (10 WEEKS)* pos/wks

14 Jan 78	**HEARTSONG** *Electric WOT 19*	21	7
28 Apr 79	**FEAR OF THE DARK** *Electric WOT 29* [1]	58	3

[1] Gordon Giltrap Band

GIN BLOSSOMS *US, male vocal / instrumental group (12 WEEKS)* pos/wks

5 Feb 94	**HEY JEALOUSY** *Fontana GINCD 3*	24	5
16 Apr 94	**FOUND OUT ABOUT YOU** *Fontana GINCD 4*	40	3
10 Feb 96	**TIL I HEAR IT FROM YOU** *A & M 5812272*	39	2
27 Apr 96	**FOLLOW YOU DOWN** *A & M 5815512*	30	2

GINGERBREADS – *See GOLDIE and the GINGERBREADS*

GINUWINE *US, male rapper – Elgin Lumpkin (22 WEEKS)* pos/wks

25 Jan 97	**PONY** *Epic 6641282*	16	6
24 May 97	**TELL ME DO U WANNA** *Epic 6645272*	16	3
6 Sep 97 ●	**WHEN DOVES CRY** *Epic 6649245*	10	5
14 Mar 98	**HOLLER** *Epic 6653372*	13	4
13 Mar 99 ●	**WHAT'S SO DIFFERENT?** *Epic 6670522*	10	4

GIPSY KINGS *France, male vocal / instrumental group (2 WEEKS)* pos/wks

3 Sep 94	**HITS MEDLEY** *Columbia 6606022*	53	2

Martine GIRAULT *UK, female vocalist (7 WEEKS)* pos/wks

29 Aug 92	**REVIVAL** *ffrr FX 195*	53	2
30 Jan 93	**REVIVAL (re-issue)** *ffrr FCD 205*	37	3
28 Oct 95	**BEEN THINKING ABOUT YOU** *RCA 74321316142*	63	1
1 Feb 97	**REVIVAL (re-mix)** *RCA 74321432162*	61	1

GIRESSE *UK, male DJ / production duo (1 WEEK)* pos/wks

14 Apr 01	**MON AMI** *Inferno CDFERN 36*	61	1

GIRL *UK, male vocal / instrumental group (3 WEEKS)* pos/wks

12 Apr 80	**HOLLYWOOD TEASE** *Jet 176*	50	3

GIRL NEXT DOOR – *See M&S presents GIRL NEXT DOOR*

GIRL THING *UK / Holland, female vocal group (13 WEEKS)* pos/wks

1 Jul 00 ●	**LAST ONE STANDING** *RCA 74321762412*	8	8
9 Sep 00	**LAST ONE STANDING (re-entry)** *RCA 74321762412*	65	2
18 Nov 00	**GIRLS ON TOP** *RCA 74321801162*	25	3

GIRLFRIEND *Australia, female vocal group (6 WEEKS)* pos/wks

30 Jan 93	**TAKE IT FROM ME** *Arista 74321114252*	47	4
15 May 93	**GIRL'S LIFE** *Arista 74321138452*	68	2

GIRLS @ PLAY *UK, female vocal group (7 WEEKS)* pos/wks

24 Feb 01	**AIRHEAD** *GSM GSMCDR 1*	18	5
13 Oct 01	**RESPECTABLE** *Redbus RBMCD101*	29	2

GIRLSCHOOL *UK, female vocal / instrumental group (25 WEEKS)* pos/wks

2 Aug 80	**RACE WITH THE DEVIL** *Bronze BRO 100*	49	6
21 Feb 81 ●	**ST VALENTINE'S DAY MASSACRE (EP)** *Bronze BRO 116* [1]	5	8
11 Apr 81	**HIT AND RUN** *Bronze BRO 118*	32	6
11 Jul 81	**C'MON LET'S GO** *Bronze BRO 126*	42	3
3 Apr 82	**WILDLIFE (EP)** *Bronze BRO 144*	58	2

[1] Motörhead and Girlschool (also known as Headgirl)

Tracks on St Valentine's Day Massacre (EP): Please Don't Touch / Emergency / Bomber. Tracks on Wildlife (EP): Don't Call It Love / Wildlife / Don't Stop

Junior GISCOMBE – *See JUNIOR*

GITTA *Denmark / Italy, male / female vocal / instrumental group (1 WEEK)* pos/wks

19 Aug 00	**NO MORE TURNING BACK** *Pepper 9230302*	54	1

GLADIATORS – *See NERO and the GLADIATORS*

GLADIATORS *UK, male / female vocal group (1 WEEK)* pos/wks

30 Nov 96	**THE BOYS ARE BACK IN TOWN** *RCA 74321417002*	70	1

GLAM *Italy, male instrumental / production group (2 WEEKS)* pos/wks

1 May 93	**HELL'S PARTY** *Six6 SIXCD 001*	42	2

GLAM METAL DETECTIVES *UK, male / female vocal group (2 WEEKS)* pos/wks

11 Mar 95	**EVERYBODY UP!** *ZTT ZANG 62CD*	29	2

GLAMMA KID *UK, male vocalist / rapper – Iyael Constable (25 WEEKS)* pos/wks

21 Nov 98	**FASHION '98** *WEA WEA 179CD*	49	1
17 Apr 99 ●	**TABOO** *WEA WEA 203CD* [1]	10	8
27 Nov 99 ●	**WHY** *WEA WEA 229 CD1*	10	10
2 Sep 00	**BILLS 2 PAY** *WEA WEA 268CD*	17	5
14 Oct 00	**BILLS 2 PAY (re-entry)** *WEA WEA 268CD*	69	1

[1] Glamma Kid featuring Shola Ama

GLASS TIGER *Canada, male vocal / instrumental group (18 WEEKS)* pos/wks

18 Oct 86	**DON'T FORGET ME (WHEN I'M GONE)** *Manhattan MT 13*	29	9
31 Jan 87	**SOMEDAY** *Manhattan MT 17*	66	2
26 Oct 91	**MY TOWN** *EMI EM 212*	33	7

'My Town' features the uncredited vocals of Rod Stewart

Mayson GLEN ORCHESTRA – *See Paul HENRY and the Mayson GLEN ORCHESTRA*

GLENN and CHRIS *UK, male footballers / vocal duo – Glenn Hoddle and Chris Waddle (8 WEEKS)* pos/wks

18 Apr 87	**DIAMOND LIGHTS** *Record Shack KICK 1*	12	8

Gary GLITTER (118 Top 500) *Glitter rock giant, b. Paul Gadd, 8 May 1940, Oxfordshire, UK. Started recording in 1960 (as Paul Raven), and was the first act to put his first 11 hits into the Top 10. This singer / songwriter remained a popular live performer until jailed in 1999 (170 WEEKS)* pos/wks

10 Jun 72 ●	**ROCK AND ROLL (PARTS 1 & 2)** *Bell 1216*	2	15
23 Sep 72 ●	**I DIDN'T KNOW I LOVED YOU (TILL I SAW YOU ROCK 'N' ROLL)** *Bell 1259*	4	11
20 Jan 73 ●	**DO YOU WANNA TOUCH ME? (OH YEAH)** *Bell 1280*	2	11
7 Apr 73 ●	**HELLO HELLO I'M BACK AGAIN** *Bell 1299*	2	14
21 Jul 73 ★	**I'M THE LEADER OF THE GANG (I AM)** *Bell 1321*	1	12
17 Nov 73 ★	**I LOVE YOU LOVE ME LOVE** *Bell 1337* ◆ ■	1	14
30 Mar 74 ●	**REMEMBER ME THIS WAY** *Bell 1349*	3	8
15 Jun 74 ★	**ALWAYS YOURS** *Bell 1359*	1	9
23 Nov 74 ●	**OH YES! YOU'RE BEAUTIFUL** *Bell 1391*	2	10
3 May 75 ●	**LOVE LIKE YOU AND ME** *Bell 1423*	10	6
21 Jun 75 ●	**DOING ALRIGHT WITH THE BOYS** *Bell 1429*	6	7
8 Nov 75	**PAPA OOM MOW MOW** *Bell 1451*	38	5
13 Mar 76	**YOU BELONG TO ME** *Bell 1473*	40	5
22 Jan 77	**IT TAKES ALL NIGHT LONG** *Arista 85*	25	6
16 Jul 77	**A LITTLE BOOGIE WOOGIE IN THE BACK OF MY MIND** *Arista 112*	31	5
20 Sep 80	**GARY GLITTER (EP)** *GTO GT 282*	57	3
10 Oct 81	**AND THEN SHE KISSED ME** *Bell BELL 1497*	39	5

UK No.1 ★ UK Top 10 ● Still on chart + UK million seller ◆ UK entry at No.1 ■ US No.1 ▲

THE OFFICIAL UK SINGLES CHART 50TH ANNIVERSARY

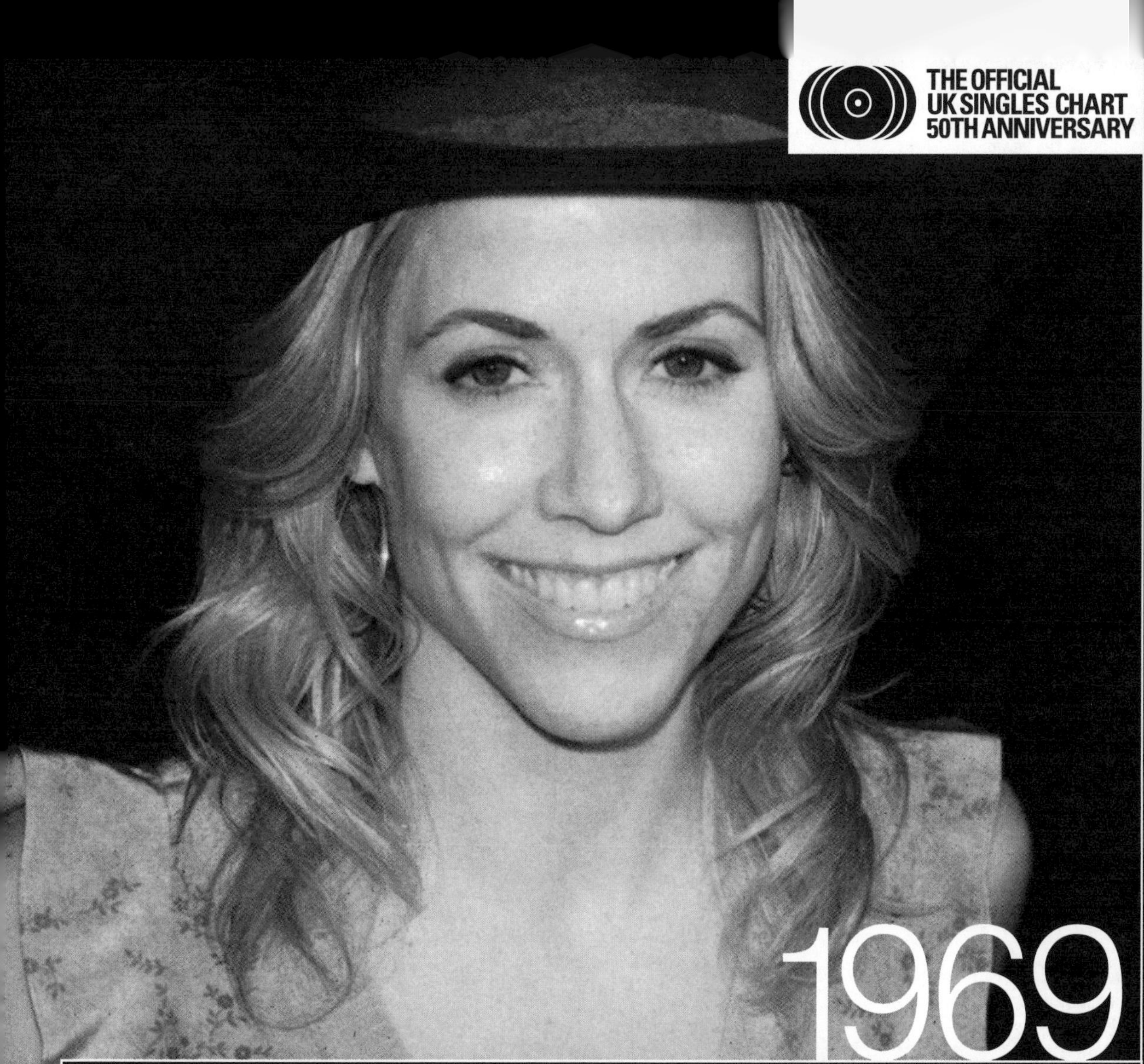

1969

IN THE YEAR THAT SAW THE LARGEST GLOBAL TELEVISION AUDIENCE EVER TUNING IN TO SEE NEIL ARMSTRONG BECOME THE FIRST MAN TO WALK ON THE MOON, HIPPIES PARTIED FOR PEACE AT WOODSTOCK AND THE WHO COMPLETED THE FIRST ROCK OPERA, 'TOMMY', **SHERYL CROW** GETS TRANSFORMED BY THE STONES ...

"I was 15 when I heard **The Rolling Stones**' album 'Let It Bleed' for the first time. It was the first record I'd heard that incorporated the country music I'd grown up listening to with rock 'n' roll. I went out and bought a guitar. I still play that record all the time – 'Honky Tonk Women'. Mick doing his kind of faux country twang transformed the way I perceived myself. I sang that song with the Stones a few years ago in a small club in Vegas. Someone sent me a picture of it and I still look at it and think, 'God, was I superimposed?'"

SINGLE OF THE YEAR 'Sugar Sugar' Archies
ALBUM OF THE YEAR 'Abbey Road' Beatles

5 Dec 81		**ALL THAT GLITTERS** *Bell BELL 1498*	48	5
23 Jun 84		**DANCE ME UP** *Arista ARIST 570*	25	5
1 Dec 84	●	**ANOTHER ROCK AND ROLL CHRISTMAS** *Arista ARIST 592*	7	7
10 Oct 92		**AND THE LEADER ROCKS ON** *EMI EM 252*	58	2
21 Nov 92		**THROUGH THE YEARS** *EMI EM 256*	49	3
16 Dec 95		**HELLO HELLO I'M BACK AGAIN (AGAIN!)** *Carlton Sounds 3036000192*	50	2

'Rock and Roll Part 1' not listed with 'Part 2' for weeks of 10 and 17 Jun 1972. Tracks on Gary Glitter (EP): I'm the Leader of the Gang (I Am) / Rock and Roll (Part 2) / Hello Hello I'm Back Again / Do You Wanna Touch Me? (Oh Yeah). All were re-issues. 'Hello Hello I'm Back Again (Again!)' in 1995 is a re-recording

GLITTER BAND *UK, male vocal / instrumental group (60 WEEKS)*

			pos	wks
23 Mar 74	●	**ANGEL FACE** *Bell 1348*	4	10
3 Aug 74	●	**JUST FOR YOU** *Bell 1368*	10	8
19 Oct 74	●	**LET'S GET TOGETHER AGAIN** *Bell 1383*	8	8
18 Jan 75	●	**GOODBYE MY LOVE** *Bell 1395*	2	9
12 Apr 75	●	**THE TEARS I CRIED** *Bell 1416*	8	8
9 Aug 75		**LOVE IN THE SUN** *Bell 1437*	15	8
28 Feb 76	●	**PEOPLE LIKE YOU AND PEOPLE LIKE ME** *Bell 1471*	5	9

See also Gary GLITTER

GLOBAL COMMUNICATION
UK, male instrumental / production duo (1 WEEK)

			pos	wks
11 Jan 97		**THE WAY / THE DEEP** *Dedicated GLOBA 002CD*	51	1

GLOVE *UK, male vocal / instrumental group (3 WEEKS)*

			pos	wks
20 Aug 83		**LIKE AN ANIMAL** *Wonderland SHE 3*	52	3

See also SIOUXSIE and the BANSHEES; CURE

GLOWORM *UK / US, male vocal / instrumental group (17 WEEKS)*

			pos	wks
6 Feb 93		**I LIFT MY CUP** *Pulse 8 CDLOSE 37*	20	4
14 May 94	●	**CARRY ME HOME** *Go.Beat GODCD 112*	9	11
6 Aug 94		**I LIFT MY CUP (re-issue)** *Pulse 8 CDLOSE 67*	46	2

GO GO LORENZO and the DAVIS PINCKNEY PROJECT
US, male vocal / instrumental group (8 WEEKS)

			pos	wks
6 Dec 86		**YOU CAN DANCE IF YOU WANT TO** *Boiling Point POSP 836*	46	8

GO-GO's *US, female vocal / instrumental group (10 WEEKS)*

			pos	wks
15 May 82		**OUR LIPS ARE SEALED** *IRS GDN 102*	47	6
26 Jan 91		**COOL JERK** *IRS AM 712*	60	1
18 Feb 95		**THE WHOLE WORLD LOST ITS HEAD** *IRS CDEIRS 190*	29	3

See also Belinda CARLISLE; Jane WIEDLIN

GO WEST (386 Top 500) *Songwriting duo specialising in radio-friendly white soul sounds; Peter Cox (v) and Richard Drummie (g/k/v). Best Newcomers at the 1986 Brit Awards had US Top 10 hit with 'King of Wishful Thinking', from the soundtrack of Pretty Woman (85 WEEKS)*

			pos	wks
23 Feb 85	●	**WE CLOSE OUR EYES** *Chrysalis CHS 2850*	5	14
11 May 85		**CALL ME** *Chrysalis GOW 1*	12	10
3 Aug 85		**GOODBYE GIRL** *Chrysalis GOW 2*	25	7
23 Nov 85		**DON'T LOOK DOWN – THE SEQUEL** *Chrysalis GOW 3*	13	10
29 Nov 86		**TRUE COLOURS** *Chrysalis GOW 4*	48	7
9 May 87		**I WANT TO HEAR IT FROM YOU** *Chrysalis GOW 5*	43	3
12 Sep 87		**THE KING IS DEAD** *Chrysalis GOW 6*	67	2
28 Jul 90		**THE KING OF WISHFUL THINKING** *Chrysalis GOW 8*	18	10
17 Oct 92		**FAITHFUL** *Chrysalis GOW 9*	13	6
16 Jan 93		**WHAT YOU WON'T DO FOR LOVE** *Chrysalis CDGOWS 10*	15	5
27 Mar 93		**STILL IN LOVE** *Chrysalis CDGOWS 11*	43	3
2 Oct 93		**TRACKS OF MY TEARS** *Chrysalis CDGOWS 12*	16	5
4 Dec 93		**WE CLOSE OUR EYES (re-mix)** *Chrysalis CDGOWS 13*	40	3

GOATS *US, male rap group (2 WEEKS)*

			pos	wks
29 May 93		**AAAH D YAAA / TYPICAL AMERICAN** *Ruff House 6593032*	53	2

'Typical American' listed only from 5 Jun 1993, peaking at No.65

GOD MACHINE *US, male vocal / instrumental group (2 WEEKS)*

			pos	wks
30 Jan 93		**HOME** *Fiction FICCD 47*	65	2

GODIEGO *Japan / US, male vocal / instrumental group (11 WEEKS)*

			pos	wks
15 Oct 77		**THE WATER MARGIN** *BBC RESL 50*	37	4
16 Feb 80		**GANDHARA** *BBC RESL 66*	56	7

'The Water Margin' is the English version of the song, which shared chart credit with the Japanese language version by Pete Mac Jr

GODLEY and CREME *UK, male vocal / instrumental duo – Kevin Godley and Lol Creme (36 WEEKS)*

			pos	wks
12 Sep 81	●	**UNDER YOUR THUMB** *Polydor POSP 322*	3	11
21 Nov 81	●	**WEDDING BELLS** *Polydor POSP 369*	7	11
30 Mar 85		**CRY** *Polydor POSP 732*	19	11
16 Aug 86		**CRY (re-entry)** *Polydor POSP 732*	66	3

See also 10 CC

GOD'S PROPERTY *US, male / female gospel choir (1 WEEK)*

			pos	wks
22 Nov 97		**STOMP** *B-rite Music IND 95559*	60	1

Andrew GOLD *US, male vocalist / instrumentalist – piano (36 WEEKS)*

			pos	wks
2 Apr 77		**LONELY BOY** *Asylum K 13076*	11	9
25 Mar 78	●	**NEVER LET HER SLIP AWAY** *Asylum K 13112*	5	13
24 Jun 78		**HOW CAN THIS BE LOVE** *Asylum K 13126*	19	10
14 Oct 78		**THANK YOU FOR BEING A FRIEND** *Asylum K 13135*	42	4

See also WAX

Ari GOLD – *See DJ LUCK and MC NEAT*

Brian and Tony GOLD – *See RED DRAGON with Brian and Tony GOLD*

GOLD BLADE *UK, male vocal / instrumental group (1 WEEK)*

			pos	wks
22 Mar 97		**STRICTLY HARDCORE** *Ultimate TOPP 056CD*	64	1

GOLDBUG *UK, male / female vocal / instrumental group (5 WEEKS)*

			pos	wks
27 Jan 96	●	**WHOLE LOTTA LOVE** *Acid Jazz JAZID 125CD*	3	5

GOLDEN EARRING *Holland, male vocal / instrumental group (16 WEEKS)*

			pos	wks
8 Dec 73	●	**RADAR LOVE** *Track 2094 116*	7	13
8 Oct 77		**RADAR LOVE** *Polydor 2121 335*	44	3

The 8 Oct 1977 version of Radar Love credits Golden Earring 'Live'

GOLDEN GIRLS *UK, male producer / instrumentalist (3 WEEKS)*

			pos	wks
3 Oct 98		**KINETIC** *Distinctive DISNCD 46*	38	2
4 Dec 99		**KINETIC '99 (re-mix)** *Distinctive DISNCD 59*	56	1

GOLDENSCAN *UK, male DJ / production duo (1 WEEK)*

			pos	wks
11 Nov 00		**SUNRISE** *VC Recordings VCRD 79*	52	1

GOLDFRAPP *UK, male / female vocal / instrumental group (2 WEEKS)*

			pos	wks
23 Jun 01		**UTOPIA** *Mute CDMUTE 264*	62	1
17 Nov 01		**PILOTS** *Mute CDMUTE 267*	68	1

GOLDIE *UK, male vocal / instrumental group (11 WEEKS)*

			pos	wks
27 May 78	●	**MAKING UP AGAIN** *Bronze BRO 50*	7	11

GOLDIE *UK, male producer – Clifford Price (16 WEEKS)*

			pos	wks
3 Dec 94		**INNER CITY LIFE** *ffrr FCD 251* [1]	49	2
9 Sep 95		**ANGEL** *ffrr FCD 266*	41	3
11 Nov 95		**INNER CITY LIFE (re-mix)** *ffrr FCD 267*	39	2
1 Nov 97		**DIGITAL** *ffrr FCD 316* [2]	13	3
24 Jan 98		**TEMPERTEMPER** *ffrr FCD 325* [2]	13	4
18 Apr 98		**BELIEVE** *ffrr FCD 332*	36	2

[1] Goldie presents Metalheadz [2] Goldie featuring KRS One

UK No.1 ★ UK Top 10 ● Still on chart + UK million seller ◆ UK entry at No.1 ■ US No.1 ▲

GOLDIE and the GINGERBREADS
US, female vocal / instrumental group (5 WEEKS) pos/wks

25 Feb 65 **CAN'T YOU HEAR MY HEART BEAT?** *Decca F 12070* 25 5

Bobby GOLDSBORO *US, male vocalist (47 WEEKS)* pos/wks

17 Apr 68 ● **HONEY** *United Artists UP2215* ▲ 2 15
4 Aug 73 ● **SUMMER (THE FIRST TIME)** *United Artists UP35558* 9 10
3 Aug 74 **HELLO SUMMERTIME** *United Artists UP35705* 14 10
29 Mar 75 ● **HONEY (re-issue)** *United Artists UP35633* 2 12

Glen GOLDSMITH *UK, male vocalist (24 WEEKS)* pos/wks

7 Nov 87 **I WON'T CRY** *Reproduction PB 41493* 34 7
12 Mar 88 **DREAMING** *Reproduction PB 41711* 12 11
11 Jun 88 **WHAT YOU SEE IS WHAT YOU GET** *Reproduction PB 42075* 33 5
3 Sep 88 **SAVE A LITTLE BIT** *Reproduction PB 42147* 73 1

GOMEZ *UK, male vocal / instrumental group (13 WEEKS)* pos/wks

11 Apr 98 **78 STONE WOBBLE** *Hut HUTCD 95* 44 1
13 Jun 98 **GET MYSELF ARRESTED** *Hut HUTCD 97* 45 1
12 Sep 98 **WHIPPIN' PICCADILLY** *Hut HUTCD 105* 35 3
10 Jul 99 **BRING IT ON** *Hut HUTCD 112* 21 3
11 Sep 99 **RHYTHM & BLUES ALIBI** *Hut HUTCD 114* 18 3
27 Nov 99 **WE HAVEN'T TURNED AROUND** *Hut HUTCD 117* 38 2

Leroy GOMEZ – *See SANTA ESMERALDA and Leroy GOMEZ*

GOMPIE *Holland, male vocal / instrumental group (12 WEEKS)* pos/wks

20 May 95 **ALICE (WHO THE X IS ALICE) (LIVING NEXT DOOR TO ALICE)** *Habana HABSCD 5* 34 5
2 Sep 95 **ALICE (WHO THE X IS ALICE) (LIVING NEXT DOOR TOALICE) (re-entry)** *Habana HABSCD 5* 17 7

GONZALES – *See FUNK MASTERS*

GONZALEZ *UK / US, male vocal / instrumental group (11 WEEKS)* pos/wks

31 Mar 79 **HAVEN'T STOPPED DANCING YET** *Sidewalk SID 102* 15 11

GOO GOO DOLLS *US, male vocal / instrumental trio (4 WEEKS)* pos/wks

1 Aug 98 **IRIS** *Reprise W 0449CD* 50 1
27 Mar 99 **SLIDE** *Edel / Hollywood / Third Rail 0102035 HWR* 43 1
17 Jul 99 **IRIS (re-issue)** *Hollywood 0102485 HWR* 26 2

GOOD GIRLS *US, female vocal group (1 WEEK)* pos/wks

24 Jul 93 **JUST CALL ME** *Motown TMGCD 1417* 75 1

GOODBYE MR MACKENZIE
UK, male / female vocal / instrumental group (13 WEEKS) pos/wks

20 Aug 88 **GOODBYE MR MACKENZIE** *Capitol CL 501* 62 2
11 Mar 89 **THE RATTLER** *Capitol CL 522* 37 6
29 Jul 89 **GOODWILL CITY / I'M SICK OF YOU** *Capitol CL 538* 49 2
21 Apr 90 **LOVE CHILD** *Parlophone R 6247* 52 2
23 Jun 90 **BLACKER THAN BLACK** *Parlophone R 6257* 61 1

GOODFELLAS featuring Lisa MILLETT
Italy, male production duo and UK, female vocalist (2 WEEKS) pos/wks

21 Jul 01 **SOUL HEAVEN** *Direction 6713852* 27 2

See also ECLIPSE; BINI & MARTINI; HOUSE OF GLASS

GOODFELLAZ *US, male vocal trio (2 WEEKS)* pos/wks

10 May 97 **SUGAR HONEY ICE TEA** *Wild Card 5736132* 25 2

GOODIES *UK, male comedy / vocal group (38 WEEKS)* pos/wks

7 Dec 74 ● **THE INBETWEENIES / FATHER CHRISTMAS DO NOT TOUCH ME** *Bradley's BRAD 7421* 7 9
15 Mar 75 ● **FUNKY GIBBON / SICK MAN BLUES** *Bradley's BRAD 7504* 4 10
21 Jun 75 **BLACK PUDDING BERTHA (THE QUEEN OF NORTHERN SOUL)** *Bradley's BRAD 7517* 19 7
27 Sep 75 **NAPPY LOVE / WILD THING** *Bradley's BRAD 7524* 21 6
13 Dec 75 **MAKE A DAFT NOISE FOR CHRISTMAS** *Bradley's BRAD 7533* 20 6

Cuba GOODING *US, male vocalist (2 WEEKS)* pos/wks

19 Nov 83 **HAPPINESS IS JUST AROUND THE BEND** *London LON 41* 72 2

GOODMEN *Holland, male instrumental / production duo – Rene Terhorst and Gaston Steenkist (19 WEEKS)* pos/wks

7 Aug 93 **GIVE IT UP** *Fresh Fruit TABCD 118* 23 5
9 Oct 93 ● **GIVE IT UP (re-entry)** *Fresh Fruit TABCD 118* 5 14

See also RIVA featuring Dannii MINOGUE; JARK PRONGO; TOMBA VIRA; CHOCOLATE PUMA

Ron GOODWIN and his Orchestra *UK, orchestra (24 WEEKS)* pos/wks

15 May 53 ● **TERRY'S THEME FROM 'LIMELIGHT'** *Parlophone R 3686* 3 23
28 Oct 55 **BLUE STAR (THE MEDIC THEME)** *Parlophone R 4074* 20 1

See also Eamonn ANDREWS

GOODY GOODY *US, female vocal duo (5 WEEKS)* pos/wks

2 Dec 78 **NUMBER ONE DEE JAY** *Atlantic LV 3* 55 5

GOOMBAY DANCE BAND *Germany / Montserrat, male / female vocal / instrumental group (16 WEEKS)* pos/wks

27 Feb 82 ★ **SEVEN TEARS** *Epic EPC A 1242* 1 12
15 May 82 **SUN OF JAMAICA** *Epic EPC A 2345* 50 4

GOONS *UK, male comedy / vocal group (30 WEEKS)* pos/wks

29 Jun 56 ● **I'M WALKING BACKWARDS FOR CHRISTMAS / BLUEBOTTLE BLUES** *Decca F 10756* 4 10
14 Sep 56 ● **BLOODNOK'S ROCK 'N' ROLL CALL / THE YING TONG SONG** *Decca E 10780* 3 10
21 Jul 73 ● **YING TONG SONG (re-issue)** *Decca F 13414* 9 10

'Bluebottle Blues' listed only from 13 Jul 1956. It peaked at No.5

Lonnie GORDON *US, female vocalist (23 WEEKS)* pos/wks

24 Jun 89 **(I'VE GOT YOUR) PLEASURE CONTROL** *ffrr F 106* [1] 60 3
27 Jan 90 ● **HAPPENIN' ALL OVER AGAIN** *Supreme SUPE 159* 4 10
11 Aug 90 **BEYOND YOUR WILDEST DREAMS** *Supreme SUPE 167* 48 2
17 Nov 90 **IF I HAVE TO STAND ALONE** *Supreme SUPE 181* 68 1
4 May 91 **GONNA CATCH YOU** *Supreme SUPE 185* 32 5
7 Oct 95 **LOVE EVICTION** *X:Plode BANG 2CD* 32 2

[1] Simon Harris featuring Lonnie Gordon

Lesley GORE *US, female vocalist (20 WEEKS)* pos/wks

20 Jun 63 ● **IT'S MY PARTY** *Mercury AMT 1205* ▲ 9 12
24 Sep 64 **MAYBE I KNOW** *Mercury MF 829* 20 8

GORILLAZ
UK / US, animated male vocal / production / instrumental group (35 WEEKS) pos/wks

17 Mar 01 ● **CLINT EASTWOOD** *Parlophone CDR 6552* 4 17
7 Jul 01 ● **19/2000** *Parlophone CDR 6559* 6 10
3 Nov 01 **ROCK THE HOUSE** *Parlophone CDRS 6565* 18 8

GORKY'S ZYGOTIC MYNCI
UK, male / female vocal / instrumental group (8 WEEKS) pos/wks

9 Nov 96 **PATIO SONG** *Fontana GZMCD 1* 41 1
29 Mar 97 **DIAMOND DEW** *Fontana GZMCD 2* 42 1
21 Jun 97 **YOUNG GIRLS & HAPPY ENDINGS / DARK NIGHT** *Fontana GZMCD 3* 49 1
6 Jun 98 **SWEET JOHNNY** *Fontana GZMCD 4* 60 1
29 Aug 98 **LET'S GET TOGETHER (IN OUR MINDS)** *Fontana GZMCD 5* 43 1
2 Oct 99 **SPANISH DANCE TROUPE** *Mantra / Beggars Banquet MNT 47CD* 47 1
4 Mar 00 **POODLE ROCKIN'** *Mantra / Beggars Banquet MNT 52CD* 52 1
15 Sep 01 **STOOD ON GOLD** *Mantra / Beggars Banquet MNT 64CD* 65 1

Eydie GORME *US, female vocalist (33 WEEKS)* pos/wks

24 Jan 58	LOVE ME FOREVER *HMV POP 432*	21	5
21 Jun 62 ●	YES MY DARLING DAUGHTER *CBS AAG 105*	10	9
31 Jan 63	BLAME IT ON THE BOSSA NOVA *CBS AAG 131*	32	6
22 Aug 63 ●	I WANT TO STAY HERE *CBS AAG 163* [1]	3	13

[1] Steve and Eydie

Luke GOSS and the BAND OF THIEVES
UK, male vocal / instrumental group (3 WEEKS) pos/wks

12 Jun 93	SWEETER THAN THE MIDNIGHT RAIN *Sabre CDSAB 1*	52	2
21 Aug 93	GIVE ME ONE MORE CHANCE *Sabre CDSAB 2*	68	1

See also BROS

Matt GOSS *UK, male vocalist (5 WEEKS)* pos/wks

26 Aug 95	THE KEY *Atlas 5811532*	40	2
27 Apr 96	IF YOU WERE HERE TONIGHT *Atlas 5762932*	23	3

See also BROS

Nigel GOULDING – *See Abigail MEAD and Nigel GOULDING*

Graham GOULDMAN *UK, male vocalist (4 WEEKS)* pos/wks

23 Jun 79	SUNBURN *Mercury SUNNY 1*	52	4

See also 10 CC; WAX

GOURYELLA *Holland, male production duo – Tijs Verwest and Ferry Corsten (11 WEEKS)* pos/wks

10 Jul 99	GOURYELLA *Code Blue BLU 001CD*	15	7
4 Dec 99	WALHALLA *Code Blue BLU 006CD*	27	2
23 Dec 00	TENSHI *Code Blue BLUE 017CD*	45	2

See also MOONMAN; Ferry CORSTEN; SYSTEM F; VERACOCHA

GQ *US, male vocal / instrumental group (6 WEEKS)* pos/wks

10 Mar 79	DISCO NIGHTS (ROCK FREAK) *Arista ARIST 245*	42	6

GRACE *UK, female vocalist – Dominique Atkins (24 WEEKS)* pos/wks

8 Apr 95 ●	NOT OVER YET *Perfecto PERF 104CD*	6	8
23 Sep 95	I WANT TO LIVE *Perfecto PERF 109CD*	30	2
24 Feb 96	SKIN ON SKIN *Perfecto PERF 116CD*	21	3
1 Jun 96	DOWN TO EARTH *Perfecto PERF 120CD*	20	2
28 Sep 96	IF I COULD FLY *Perfecto PERF 127CD*	29	2
3 May 97	HAND IN HAND *Perfecto PERF 129CD*	38	1
26 Jul 97	DOWN TO EARTH (re-mix) *Perfecto PERF 142CD1*	29	2
14 Aug 99	NOT OVER YET 99 *Code Blue BLU 004CD1* [1]	16	4

[1] Planet Perfecto featuring Grace

Bridgette GRACE – *See TRUE FAITH and Bridgette GRACE with FINAL CUT*

GRACE BROTHERS *UK, male instrumental duo (1 WEEK)* pos/wks

20 Apr 96	ARE YOU BEING SERVED *EMI Premier PRESCD 1*	51	1

Charlie GRACIE *US, male vocalist – Charlie Graci (41 WEEKS)* pos/wks

19 Apr 57	BUTTERFLY *Parlophone R 4290*	12	8
14 Jun 57 ●	FABULOUS *Parlophone R 4313*	8	16
23 Aug 57	I LOVE YOU SO MUCH IT HURTS / WANDERIN' EYES *London HLU 8467*	14	2
6 Sep 57 ●	WANDERIN' EYES *London HLU 8467*	6	12
6 Sep 57	I LOVE YOU SO MUCH IT HURTS *London HLU 8467*	20	2
10 Jan 58	COOL BABY *London HLU 8521*	26	1

'I Love You So Much It Hurts' and 'Wanderin' Eyes' were listed together for two weeks, then listed separately for a further two and 12 weeks respectively

Eve GRAHAM – *See NEW SEEKERS*

Jaki GRAHAM (465 Top 500) *Britain's foremost black female vocalist of the 1980s, b. 15 Sep 1956, Birmingham, UK, who was first introduced to the public via a duet with ex-Linx vocalist David Grant. The one-time UB40 backing vocalist helped to open doors for other UK female soul singers (75 WEEKS)* pos/wks

23 Mar 85 ●	COULD IT BE I'M FALLING IN LOVE *Chrysalis GRAN 6* [1]	5	11
29 Jun 85 ●	ROUND AND ROUND *EMI JAKI 4*	9	11
31 Aug 85	HEAVEN KNOWS *EMI JAKI 5*	59	3
16 Nov 85	MATED *EMI JAKI 6* [1]	20	10
3 May 86 ●	SET ME FREE *EMI JAKI 7*	7	12
9 Aug 86	BREAKING AWAY *EMI JAKI 8*	16	8
15 Nov 86	STEP RIGHT UP *EMI JAKI 9*	15	12
9 Jul 88	NO MORE TEARS *EMI JAKI 12*	60	2
24 Jun 89	FROM NOW ON *EMI JAKI 15*	73	2
16 Jul 94	AIN'T NOBODY *Pulse 8 CDLOSE 64*	44	2
4 Feb 95	YOU CAN COUNT ON ME *Avex UK AVEXCD 1*	62	1
8 Jul 95	ABSOLUTE E-SENSUAL *Avex UK AVEXCD 5*	69	1

[1] David Grant and Jaki Graham

Larry GRAHAM *US, male vocalist / instrumentalist – bass (4 WEEKS)* pos/wks

3 Jul 82	SOONER OR LATER *Warner Bros. K 17925*	54	4

Mikey GRAHAM *Ireland, male vocalist (6 WEEKS)* pos/wks

10 Jun 00	YOU'RE MY ANGEL *Public PR 001CDS*	13	5
14 Apr 01	YOU COULD BE MY EVERYTHING *Public PR 003CDS*	62	1

See also BOYZONE

Ron GRAINER ORCHESTRA *UK, orchestra (7 WEEKS)* pos/wks

9 Dec 78	A TOUCH OF VELVET A STING OF BRASS *Casino Classics CC 5*	60	7

GRAM'MA FUNK – *See GROOVE ARMADA; ILLICIT featuring GRAM'MA FUNK*

GRAND FUNK RAILROAD
US, male vocal / instrumental group (1 WEEK) pos/wks

6 Feb 71	INSIDE LOOKING OUT *Capitol CL 15668*	40	1

GRAND PLAZ *UK, male instrumental / production group (4 WEEKS)* pos/wks

8 Sep 90	WOW WOW – NA NA *Urban URB 60*	41	4

GRAND PRIX *UK, male vocal / instrumental group (1 WEEK)* pos/wks

27 Feb 82	KEEP ON BELIEVING *RCA 162*	75	1

GRAND PUBA *US, male rapper – Maxwell Dixon (6 WEEKS)* pos/wks

13 Jan 96	WHY YOU TREAT ME SO BAD *Virgin VSCDT 1566* [1]	11	5
30 Mar 96	WILL YOU BE MY BABY *GHQ 74321339092* [2]	53	1

[1] Shaggy featuring Grand Puba [2] Infiniti featuring Grand Puba

GRAND THEFT AUDIO *UK, male vocal / instrumental group (1 WEEK)* pos/wks

24 Mar 01	WE LUV U *Sci-Fi SCIFI 1CD*	70	1

GRANDAD ROBERTS AND HIS SON ELVIS
UK, male vocal duo (1 WEEK) pos/wks

20 Jun 98	MEAT PIE SAUSAGE ROLL *WEA WEA 160CD*	67	1

GRANDADDY *US, male vocal / instrumental group (3 WEEKS)* pos/wks

2 Sep 00	HEWLETT'S DAUGHTER *V2 VVR 5014333*	71	1
10 Feb 01	THE CRYSTAL LAKE *V2 VVR 5015153*	38	2

GRANDMASTER FLASH, Melle MEL and the FURIOUS FIVE
(375 Top 500) *Pioneering rap act who led the genre into more serious subjects. New York act fronted by Grandmaster Flash (Joseph Saddler) and Melle Mel (Melvin Glover). 'White Lines' took a record 25 weeks to make the Top 10 (87 WEEKS)* pos/wks

28 Aug 82 ●	THE MESSAGE *Sugarhill SHL 117* [1]	8	9
22 Jan 83	MESSAGE II (SURVIVAL) *Sugarhill SH 119* [2]	74	2
19 Nov 83	WHITE LINES (DON'T DON'T DO IT) *Sugarhill SH 130* [3]	60	3

11 Feb 84 ●	**WHITE LINES (DON'T DON'T DO IT) (re-entry)** *Sugarhill SH 130* [3]	7	38
30 Jun 84	**BEAT STREET BREAKDOWN** *Atlantic A 9659* [4]	42	7
22 Sep 84	**WE DON'T WORK FOR FREE** *Sugarhill SH 136* [4]	45	4
24 Nov 84	**WHITE LINES (DON'T DON'T DO IT) (2nd re-entry)** *Sugarhill SH 130* [3]	75	1
15 Dec 84 ●	**STEP OFF (PART 1)** *Sugarhill SH 139* [4]	8	12
5 Jan 85	**WHITE LINES (DON'T DON'T DO IT) (3rd re-entry)** *Sugarhill SH 130* [3]	73	1
16 Feb 85	**SIGN OF THE TIMES** *Elektra E 9677* [5]	72	1
16 Mar 85	**PUMP ME UP** *Sugarhill SH 141* [4]	45	6
8 Jan 94	**WHITE LINES (DON'T DO IT) (re-mix)** *WGAF WGAFCD 103* [3]	59	3

[1] Grandmaster Flash and the Furious Five [2] Melle Mel and Duke Bootee
[3] Grandmaster and Melle Mel [4] Grandmaster Melle Mel and the Furious Five
[5] Grandmaster Flash

See also DURAN DURAN

GRANDMIXER D.ST.
US, male DJ / producer – Derek Howells (3 WEEKS) pos/wks

24 Dec 83	**CRAZY CUTS** *Island IS 146*	73	2
14 Jan 84	**CRAZY CUTS (re-entry)** *Island IS 146*	71	1

GRANGE HILL CAST
UK, male / female vocal charity assembly (6 WEEKS) pos/wks

19 Apr 86 ●	**JUST SAY NO** *BBC RESL 183*	5	6

Gerri GRANGER *US, female vocalist (3 WEEKS)* pos/wks

30 Sep 78	**I GO TO PIECES (EVERYTIME)** *Casino Classics CC3*	50	3

Amy GRANT *US, female vocalist (39 WEEKS)* pos/wks

11 May 91 ●	**BABY BABY** *A & M AM 727* ▲	2	13
3 Aug 91	**EVERY HEARTBEAT** *A & M AM 783*	25	7
2 Nov 91	**THAT'S WHAT LOVE IS FOR** *A & M AM 666*	60	3
15 Feb 92	**GOOD FOR ME** *A & M AM 810*	60	1
13 Aug 94	**LUCKY ONE** *A & M 5807322*	60	1
22 Oct 94	**SAY YOU'LL BE MINE** *A & M 5808292*	41	2
24 Jun 95	**BIG YELLOW TAXI** *A & M 5809972*	20	10
14 Oct 95	**HOUSE OF LOVE** *A & M 5812332* [1]	46	2

[1] Amy Grant with Vince Gill

Andrea GRANT *UK, female vocalist (1 WEEK)* pos/wks

14 Nov 98	**REPUTATIONS (JUST BE GOOD TO ME)** *WEA WEA 192CD*	75	1

Boysie GRANT – *See Ezz RECO and the LAUNCHERS with Boysie GRANT*

David GRANT *UK, male vocalist (59 WEEKS)* pos/wks

30 Apr 83	**STOP AND GO** *Chrysalis GRAN 1*	19	9
16 Jul 83 ●	**WATCHING YOU WATCHING ME** *Chrysalis GRAN 2*	10	13
8 Oct 83	**LOVE WILL FIND A WAY** *Chrysalis GRAN 3*	24	6
26 Nov 83	**ROCK THE MIDNIGHT** *Chrysalis GRAN 4*	46	4
23 Mar 85 ●	**COULD IT BE I'M FALLING IN LOVE** *Chrysalis GRAN 6* [1]	5	11
16 Nov 85	**MATED** *EMI JAKI 6* [1]	20	10
1 Aug 87	**CHANGE** *Polydor POSP 871*	55	4
12 May 90	**KEEP IT TOGETHER** *Fourth & Broadway BRW 169*	56	2

[1] David Grant and Jaki Graham

Eddy GRANT (274 Top 500)
Former lead guitarist and songwriter for UK group The Equals, b. 5 Mar 1948, Plaisance, Guyana. Left group 1972, went into production and formed own label, Ice. Remix of transatlantic No.2 'Electric Avenue' returned him to the heights in 2001 (107 WEEKS) pos/wks

2 Jun 79	**LIVING ON THE FRONT LINE** *Ensign ENY 26*	11	11
15 Nov 80 ●	**DO YOU FEEL MY LOVE** *Ensign ENY 45*	8	11
4 Apr 81	**CAN'T GET ENOUGH OF YOU** *Ensign ENY 207*	13	10
25 Jul 81	**I LOVE YOU, YES I LOVE YOU** *Ensign ENY 216*	37	6
16 Oct 82 ★	**I DON'T WANNA DANCE** *Ice ICE 56*	1	15
15 Jan 83 ●	**ELECTRIC AVENUE** *Ice ICE 57*	2	9
19 Mar 83	**LIVING ON THE FRONT LINE / DO YOU FEEL MY LOVE (re-issue)** *Mercury MER 135*	47	4
23 Apr 83	**WAR PARTY** *Ice ICE 58*	42	4
29 Oct 83	**TILL I CAN'T TAKE LOVE NO MORE** *Ice ICE 60*	42	7
19 May 84	**ROMANCING THE STONE** *Ice ICE 61*	52	3
23 Jan 88 ●	**GIMME HOPE JO'ANNA** *Ice ICE 78701*	7	12
27 May 89	**WALKING ON SUNSHINE** *Blue Wave R 6217*	63	2
9 Jun 01 ●	**ELECTRIC AVENUE (re-mix)** *Ice / East West EW 232CD*	5	10
25 Aug 01	**ELECTRIC AVENUE (re-entry)** *Ice / East West EW 232CD*	71	2
24 Nov 01	**WALKING ON SUNSHINE (re-mix)** *Ice / East West EW 242CD*	57	1

Gogi GRANT *US, female vocalist – Audrey Arinsberg (11 WEEKS)* pos/wks

29 Jun 56 ●	**THE WAYWARD WIND** *London HLB 8282* ▲	9	11

Julie GRANT *UK, female vocalist (17 WEEKS)* pos/wks

3 Jan 63	**UP ON THE ROOF** *Pye 7N 15483*	33	3
28 Mar 63	**COUNT ON ME** *Pye 7N 15508*	24	9
24 Sep 64	**COME TO ME** *Pye 7N 15684*	31	5

Rudy GRANT *Guyana, male vocalist (3 WEEKS)* pos/wks

14 Feb 81	**LATELY** *Ensign ENY 202*	58	3

GRAPEFRUIT *UK, male vocal / instrumental group (19 WEEKS)* pos/wks

14 Feb 68	**DEAR DELILAH** *RCA 1656*	21	9
14 Aug 68	**C'MON MARIANNE** *RCA 1716*	31	10

GRASS-SHOW *Sweden, male vocal / instrumental group (2 WEEKS)* pos/wks

22 Mar 97	**1962** *Food CDFOOD 90*	53	1
23 Aug 97	**OUT OF THE VOID** *Food CDFOOD 103*	75	1

GRAVEDIGGAZ *US, male rap group (6 WEEKS)* pos/wks

11 Mar 95	**SIX FEET DEEP (EP)** *Gee Street GESCD 62*	64	1
5 Aug 95	**THE HELL (EP)** *Fourth & Broadway BRCD 326* [1]	12	3
24 Jan 98	**THE NIGHT THE EARTH CRIED** *Gee Street GEE 5001013*	44	1
25 Apr 98	**UNEXPLAINED** *Gee Street GEE 5001623*	48	1

[1] Tricky vs the Gravediggaz

Tracks on Six Feet Deep (EP): Bang Your Head / Mommy / Suicide. Tracks on The Hell 'EP': Hell Is Round the Corner / Hell Is Round the Corner (remix) / Psychosis / Tonite Is a Special Nite

David GRAY *UK, male vocalist (31 WEEKS)* pos/wks

4 Dec 99	**PLEASE FORGIVE ME** *IHT IHTCDS 003*	72	1
1 Jul 00 ●	**BABYLON** *IHT / East West EW 215CD1*	5	12
28 Oct 00	**PLEASE FORGIVE ME (re-issue)** *IHT / East West EW 219CD*	18	6
17 Mar 01	**THIS YEAR'S LOVE** *IHT / East West EW 228CD1*	20	5
28 Jul 01	**SAIL AWAY** *IHT / East West EW 234CD*	26	6
29 Dec 01	**SAY HELLO WAVE GOODBYE** *IHT / East West EW 244CD*	26	1

Dobie GRAY *US, male vocalist (11 WEEKS)* pos/wks

25 Feb 65	**THE "IN" CROWD** *London HL 9953*	25	7
27 Sep 75	**OUT ON THE FLOOR** *Black Magic BM 107*	42	4

Dorian GRAY *UK, male vocalist (7 WEEKS)* pos/wks

27 Mar 68	**I'VE GOT YOU ON MY MIND** *Parlophone R 5667*	36	7

Les GRAY *UK, male vocalist (5 WEEKS)* pos/wks

26 Feb 77	**A GROOVY KIND OF LOVE** *Warner Bros. K 16883*	32	5

See also MUD

Macy GRAY *US, female vocalist – Natalie McIntyre (49 WEEKS)* pos/wks

3 Jul 99	**DO SOMETHING** *Epic 6675932*	51	1
9 Oct 99 ●	**I TRY** *Epic 6681832*	6	22
25 Mar 00	**STILL** *Epic 6689822*	18	7
20 May 00	**STILL (re-entry)** *Epic 6689822*	65	2
5 Aug 00	**WHY DIDN'T YOU CALL ME** *Epic 6696682*	38	2
26 Aug 00	**WHY DIDN'T YOU CALL ME (re-entry)** *Epic 6696682*	74	1
20 Jan 01	**DEMONS** *Skint SKINT 60CD* [1]	16	5
28 Apr 01	**GETO HEAVEN** *MCA MCSTD 40246* [2]	48	1
12 May 01	**REQUEST + LINE** *Interscope 4970532* [3]	31	3

15 Sep 01		SWEET BABY *Epic 6718822* [4]	23	4
8 Dec 01		SEXUAL REVOLUTION *Epic 6721462*	45	1

[1] Fatboy Slim featuring Macy Gray [2] Common featuring Macy Gray [3] Black Eyed Peas featuring Macy Gray [4] Macy Gray featuring Erykah Badu

Barry GRAY ORCHESTRA *UK, orchestra (8 WEEKS)* pos/wks

11 Jul 81		THUNDERBIRDS *PRT 7P 216*	61	2
14 Jun 86		JOE 90 (THEME) / CAPTAIN SCARLET THEME *PRT 7PX 354* [1]	53	6

[1] Barry Gray Orchestra with Peter Beckett - keyboards

Alltrinna GRAYSON – *See Wilton FELDER*

GREAT WHITE *US, male vocal / instrumental group (5 WEEKS)* pos/wks

24 Feb 90		HOUSE OF BROKEN LOVE *Capitol CL 562*	44	2
16 Feb 91		CONGO SQUARE *Capitol CL 605*	62	1
7 Sep 91		CALL IT ROCK 'N' ROLL *Capitol CL 625*	67	2

Buddy GRECO *US, male vocalist (8 WEEKS)* pos/wks

7 Jul 60		THE LADY IS A TRAMP *Fontana H 255*	26	8

GREED featuring Ricardo DA FORCE
UK, male instrumental duo and UK, male rapper (2 WEEKS) pos/wks

18 Mar 95		PUMP UP THE VOLUME *Stress CDSTR 49*	51	2

GREEDIES *Ireland / UK / US, male vocal / instrumental group (5 WEEKS)* pos/wks

15 Dec 79		A MERRY JINGLE *Vertigo GREED 1*	28	5

Al GREEN *US, male vocalist (68 WEEKS)* pos/wks

9 Oct 71	●	TIRED OF BEING ALONE *London HL 10337*	4	13
8 Jan 72	●	LET'S STAY TOGETHER *London HL 10348* ▲	7	12
20 May 72		LOOK WHAT YOU DONE FOR ME *London HL 10369*	44	4
19 Aug 72		I'M STILL IN LOVE WITH YOU *London HL 10382*	35	5
16 Nov 74		SHA-LA-LA (MAKE ME HAPPY) *London HL 10470*	20	11
15 Mar 75		L.O.V.E. *London HL 10482*	24	8
3 Dec 88		PUT A LITTLE LOVE IN YOUR HEART *A & M AM 484* [1]	28	8
21 Oct 89		THE MESSAGE IS LOVE *Breakout USA 668* [2]	38	5
2 Oct 93		LOVE IS A BEAUTIFUL THING *Arista 74321162692*	56	2

[1] Annie Lennox and Al Green [2] Arthur Baker and the Backbeat Disciples featuring Al Green

Dotty GREEN – *See Mark FISHER featuring Dotty GREEN*

Jesse GREEN *Jamaica, male vocalist (26 WEEKS)* pos/wks

7 Aug 76		NICE AND SLOW *EMI 2492*	17	12
18 Dec 76		FLIP *EMI 2564*	26	8
11 Jun 77		COME WITH ME *EMI 2615*	29	6

Robson GREEN and Jerome FLYNN – *See ROBSON and JEROME*

GREEN DAY *US, male vocal / instrumental group (43 WEEKS)* pos/wks

20 Aug 94		BASKET CASE *Reprise W 0257CD*	55	2
29 Oct 94		WELCOME TO PARADISE *Reprise W 0269CDX*	20	3
28 Jan 95	●	BASKET CASE (re-issue) *Reprise W 0279CD*	7	6
18 Mar 95		LONGVIEW *Reprise W 0278CD*	30	3
20 May 95		WHEN I COME AROUND *Reprise W 0294CD*	27	3
7 Oct 95		GEEK STINK BREATH *Reprise W 0320CD*	16	3
6 Jan 96		STUCK WITH ME *Reprise W 0327CD*	24	3
6 Jul 96		BRAIN STEW / JADED *Reprise W 0339CD*	28	2
11 Oct 97		HITCHIN' A RIDE *Reprise W 0424CD*	25	2
31 Jan 98		TIME OF YOUR LIFE (GOOD RIDDANCE) *Reprise W 0430CD1*	11	5
9 May 98		REDUNDANT *Reprise W 0438CD1*	27	2
30 Sep 00		MINORITY *Reprise W 532CD*	18	3
23 Dec 00		WARNING *Reprise W 548CD1*	27	4
10 Nov 01		WAITING *Reprise W 570CD*	34	2

GREEN JELLY *US, male vocal / instrumental group (15 WEEKS)* pos/wks

5 Jun 93	●	THREE LITTLE PIGS *Zoo 74321151422*	5	8
14 Aug 93		ANARCHY IN THE UK *Zoo 74321159052*	27	3
25 Dec 93		I'M THE LEADER OF THE GANG *Arista 74321174892* [1]	25	4

[1] Hulk Hogan with Green Jelly

Norman GREENBAUM *US, male vocalist (20 WEEKS)* pos/wks

21 Mar 70	★	SPIRIT IN THE SKY *Reprise RS 20885*	1	20

Lorne GREENE *Canada, male actor / vocalist (8 WEEKS)* pos/wks

17 Dec 64		RINGO *RCA 1428* ▲	22	8

Lee GREENWOOD *US, male vocalist (6 WEEKS)* pos/wks

19 May 84		THE WIND BENEATH MY WINGS *MCA 877*	49	6

Iain GREGORY *UK, male vocalist (2 WEEKS)* pos/wks

4 Jan 62		CAN'T YOU HEAR THE BEAT OF A BROKEN HEART *Pye 7N 15397*	39	2

Johnny GREGORY – *See CHAQUITO; Russ HAMILTON*

Band of the GRENADIER GUARDS – *See ST JOHN'S COLLEGE SCHOOL CHOIR and the Band of the GRENADIER GUARDS*

GREYHOUND *Jamaica, male vocal / instrumental group (33 WEEKS)* pos/wks

26 Jun 71	●	BLACK AND WHITE *Trojan TR 7820*	6	13
8 Jan 72		MOON RIVER *Trojan TR 7848*	12	11
25 Mar 72		I AM WHAT I AM *Trojan TR 7853*	20	9

GRID *UK, male instrumental / production duo – Richard Norris and Dave Ball (47 WEEKS)* pos/wks

7 Jul 90		FLOATATION *East West YZ 475*	60	2
29 Sep 90		A BEAT CALLED LOVE *East West YZ 498*	64	4
25 Jul 92		FIGURE OF 8 *Virgin VSTG 1421*	50	3
3 Oct 92		HEARTBEAT *Virgin VST 1427*	72	2
13 Mar 93		CRYSTAL CLEAR *Virgin VSCDT 1442*	27	4
30 Oct 93		TEXAS COWBOYS *Deconstruction 74321167762*	21	3
4 Jun 94	●	SWAMP THING *Deconstruction 74321205842*	3	17
17 Sep 94		ROLLERCOASTER *Deconstruction 74321230772*	19	4
3 Dec 94		TEXAS COWBOYS (re-issue) *Deconstruction 74321244032*	17	6
23 Sep 95		DIABLO *Deconstruction 74321308402*	32	2

Zaine GRIFF *New Zealand, male vocalist (6 WEEKS)* pos/wks

16 Feb 80		TONIGHT *Automatic K 17547*	54	3
31 May 80		ASHES AND DIAMONDS *Automatic K 17610*	68	3

Billy GRIFFIN *US, male vocalist (12 WEEKS)* pos/wks

8 Jan 83		HOLD ME TIGHTER IN THE RAIN *CBS A 2935*	17	9
14 Jan 84		SERIOUS *CBS A 4053*	64	3

See also MIRACLES

Clive GRIFFIN *UK, male vocalist (5 WEEKS)* pos/wks

24 Jun 89		HEAD ABOVE WATER *Mercury STEP 4*	60	2
11 May 91		I'LL BE WAITING *Mercury STEP 6*	56	3

Roni GRIFFITH *US, female vocalist (4 WEEKS)* pos/wks

30 Jun 84		(THE BEST PART OF) BREAKING UP *Making Waves SURF 101*	63	4

GRIFTERS
UK, male production duo – Paul Newman and Brandon Block (1 WEEK) pos/wks

20 Feb 99		FLASH *Duty Free DF 004CD*	63	1

See also TALL PAUL; ESCRIMA; CAMISRA; PARTIZAN

GRIMETHORPE COLLIERY BAND – *See Peter SKELLERN*

Jay GROOVE – *See FANTASY UFO*

GROOVE ARMADA *UK, male production / instrumental duo – Andy Cato and Tom Findlay (22 WEEKS)*

		pos	wks
8 May 99	IF EVERYBODY LOOKED THE SAME *Pepper 0530292*	25	2
7 Aug 99	AT THE RIVER *Pepper 0530062*	19	5
27 Nov 99	I SEE YOU BABY *Pepper 9230002* [1]	17	4
15 Jan 00	I SEE YOU BABY (re-entry) *Pepper 9230002* [1]	70	2
25 Aug 01	SUPERSTYLIN' *Pepper 9230472*	12	6
13 Oct 01	SUPERSTYLIN' (re-entry) *Pepper 9230472*	67	1
17 Nov 01	MY FRIEND *Pepper 9230532*	36	2

[1] Groove Armada featuring Gram'ma Funk

GROOVE CONNEKTION 2 *UK, male producer / instrumentalist (1 WEEK)*

		pos	wks
11 Apr 98	CLUB LONELY *XL Recordings XLT 94CD*	54	1

GROOVE CORPORATION *UK / Italy, male / female vocal / instrumental group (1 WEEK)*

		pos	wks
16 Apr 94	RAIN *Six6 SIXCD 109*	71	1

GROOVE GANG – *See DAFFY DUCK featuring the GROOVE GANG*

GROOVE GENERATION featuring Leo SAYER *UK, male production group (3 WEEKS)*

		pos	wks
8 Aug 98	YOU MAKE ME FEEL LIKE DANCING *Brothers Org. CDBRUV 8*	32	3

GROOVE THEORY *UK, male vocal / instrumental duo (3 WEEKS)*

		pos	wks
18 Nov 95	TELL ME *Epic 6623882*	31	3

GROOVERIDER *UK, male DJ / producer (3 WEEKS)*

		pos	wks
26 Sep 98	RAINBOWS OF COLOUR *Higher Ground HIGHS 13CD*	40	2
19 Jun 99	WHERE'S JACK THE RIPPER *Higher Ground HIGHS 20CD*	61	1

Scott GROOVES *US, male DJ / producer (3 WEEKS)*

		pos	wks
16 May 98	EXPANSIONS *Soma Recordings SOMA 65CDS* [1]	68	1
28 Nov 98	MOTHERSHIP RECONNECTION *Soma Recordings SOMA 71CDS*	55	1
21 Aug 99	MOTHERSHIP RECONNECTION *Virgin DINSD 185* [2]	55	1

[1] Scott Grooves featuring Roy Ayers [2] Scott Grooves featuring Parliament / Funkadelic

Henry GROSS *US, male vocalist (4 WEEKS)*

		pos	wks
28 Aug 76	SHANNON *Life Song ELS 45002*	32	4

GROUND LEVEL *Australia, male instrumental / production group (2 WEEKS)*

		pos	wks
30 Jan 93	DREAMS OF HEAVEN *Faze 2 CDFAZE 14*	54	2

GROUP THERAPY *US, male rap group (1 WEEK)*

		pos	wks
30 Nov 96	EAST COAST / WEST COAST KILLAS *Interscope IND 95516*	51	1

Boring Bob GROVER – *See PIRANHAS*

GSP *UK, male instrumental / production duo (3 WEEKS)*

		pos	wks
3 Oct 92	THE BANANA SONG *Yoyo YOYO 1*	37	3

GTO *UK, male / female instrumental / production duo – Lee Newman and Michael Wells (7 WEEKS)*

		pos	wks
4 Aug 90	PURE *Cooltempo COOL 218*	57	3
7 Sep 91	LISTEN TO THE RHYTHM FLOW / BULLFROG *React REACT 7001*	72	2
2 May 92	ELEVATION *React REACT 4*	59	2

See also TECHNOHEAD; TRICKY DISCO

GUESS WHO *Canada, male vocal / instrumental group (14 WEEKS)*

		pos	wks
16 Feb 67	HIS GIRL *King KG 1044*	45	1
9 May 70	AMERICAN WOMAN *RCA 1943*	45	2
30 May 70	AMERICAN WOMAN (re-entry) *RCA 1943* ▲	19	11

GUN *UK, male vocal / instrumental trio (11 WEEKS)*

		pos	wks
20 Nov 68 ●	RACE WITH THE DEVIL *CBS 3734*	8	11

GUN *UK, male vocal / instrumental group (46 WEEKS)*

		pos	wks
1 Jul 89	BETTER DAYS *A & M AM 505*	33	9
16 Sep 89	MONEY (EVERYBODY LOVES HER) *A & M AM 520*	73	2
11 Nov 89	INSIDE OUT *A & M AM 531*	57	2
10 Feb 90	TAKING ON THE WORLD *A & M AM 541*	50	3
14 Jul 90	SHAME ON YOU *A & M AM 573*	33	4
14 Mar 92	STEAL YOUR FIRE *A & M AM 851*	24	4
2 May 92	HIGHER GROUND *A & M AM 869*	48	2
4 Jul 92	WELCOME TO THE REAL WORLD *A & M AM 885*	43	2
9 Jul 94 ●	WORD UP *A & M 5806672*	8	7
24 Sep 94	DON'T SAY IT'S OVER *A & M 5807572*	19	3
25 Feb 95	THE ONLY ONE *A & M 5809552*	29	3
15 Apr 95	SOMETHING WORTHWHILE *A & M 5810452*	39	2
26 Apr 97	CRAZY YOU *A & M 5821932* [1]	21	2
12 Jul 97	MY SWEET JANE *A & M 5822792* [1]	51	1

[1] G.U.N.

GUNS N' ROSES (275 Top 500) *Often controversial Los Angeles-based band. Best known line-up included W Axl Rose (b. William Bailey) (v), Slash (b. Saul Hudson) (g), Izzy Stradlin (b. Jeffrey Isbell) (g). The only act to hold the top two album spots in both the UK and the US on the week of releasing both records: Use Your Illusion 1 and 2 in 1991 (107 WEEKS)*

		pos	wks
3 Oct 87	WELCOME TO THE JUNGLE *Geffen GEF 30*	67	2
20 Aug 88	SWEET CHILD O' MINE *Geffen GEF 43* ▲	24	8
29 Oct 88	WELCOME TO THE JUNGLE / NIGHTRAIN (re-issue) *Geffen GEF 47*	24	5
18 Mar 89 ●	PARADISE CITY *Geffen GEF 50*	6	9
3 Jun 89 ●	SWEET CHILD O' MINE (re-issue) *Geffen GEF 55*	6	9
1 Jul 89 ●	PATIENCE *Geffen GEF 56*	10	7
2 Sep 89	NIGHTRAIN (re-issue) *Geffen GEF 60*	17	5
13 Jul 91 ●	YOU COULD BE MINE *Geffen GFS 6*	3	10
21 Sep 91 ●	DON'T CRY *Geffen GFS 9*	8	4
21 Dec 91 ●	LIVE AND LET DIE *Geffen GFS 17*	5	7
7 Mar 92 ●	NOVEMBER RAIN *Geffen GFS 18*	4	5
23 May 92 ●	KNOCKIN' ON HEAVEN'S DOOR *Geffen GFS 21*	2	9
21 Nov 92 ●	YESTERDAYS / NOVEMBER RAIN (re-issue) *Geffen GFS 27*	8	9
29 May 93	THE CIVIL WAR (EP) *Geffen GFSTD 43*	11	3
20 Nov 93 ●	AIN'T IT FUN *Geffen GFSTD 62*	9	3
4 Jun 94 ●	SINCE I DON'T HAVE YOU *Geffen GFSTD 70*	10	6
14 Jan 95 ●	SYMPATHY FOR THE DEVIL *Geffen GFSTD 86*	9	6

The re-issue of 'November Rain' was listed only from 28 Nov 1992. Tracks on The Civil War (EP): Civil War / Garden of Eden / Dead Horse / Interview

GURU *US, male rapper / producer – Keith Allam (12 WEEKS)*

		pos	wks
11 Sep 93	TRUST ME *Cooltempo CDCOOL 278* [1]	34	2
13 Nov 93	NO TIME TO PLAY *Cooltempo CDCOOL 282* [2]	25	3
19 Aug 95	WATCH WHAT YOU SAY *Cooltempo CDCOOL 308* [3]	28	3
18 Nov 95	FEEL THE MUSIC *Cooltempo CDCOOLS 313*	34	2
13 Jul 96	LIVIN' IN THIS WORLD / LIFESAVER *Cooltempo CDCOOL 320*	61	1
16 Dec 00	KEEP YOUR WORRIES *Virgin VUSCD 177* [4]	57	1

[1] Guru featuring N'Dea Davenport [2] Guru featuring Dee C Lee [3] Guru featuring Chaka Khan [4] Guru's Jazzmatazz featuring Angie Stone

GURU JOSH *UK, male producer – Paul Walden (14 WEEKS)*

		pos	wks
24 Feb 90 ●	INFINITY *Deconstruction PB 43475*	5	10
16 Jun 90	WHOSE LAW (IS IT ANYWAY)? *Deconstruction PB 43647*	26	4

Adrian GURVITZ *UK, male vocalist (16 WEEKS)*

		pos	wks
30 Jan 82 ●	CLASSIC *RAK 339*	8	13
12 Jun 82	YOUR DREAM *RAK 343*	61	3

GUS GUS *Iceland, male / female vocal / instrumental group (3 WEEKS)*

		pos	wks
21 Feb 98	POLYESTERDAY *4AD BAD 8002CD*	55	1
13 Mar 99	LADYSHAVE *4AD BAD 9001CD*	64	1
24 Apr 99	STARLOVERS *4AD BADD 9004CD*	62	1

GUSTO *US, male producer – Edward Green (8 WEEKS)* pos/wks

2 Mar 96 ●	DISCO'S REVENGE *Manifesto FESCD 6*	9	5
7 Sep 96	LET'S ALL CHANT *Manifesto FESCD 13*	21	3

Gwen GUTHRIE *US, female vocalist (25 WEEKS)* pos/wks

19 Jul 86 ●	AIN'T NOTHIN' GOIN' ON BUT THE RENT *Boiling Point POSP 807*	5	12
11 Oct 86	(THEY LONG TO BE) CLOSE TO YOU *Boiling Point POSP 822*	25	7
14 Feb 87	GOOD TO GO LOVER / OUTSIDE IN THE RAIN *Boiling Point POSP 841*	37	4
4 Sep 93	AIN'T NOTHIN' GOIN' ON BUT THE RENT (re-mix) *Polydor PZCD 276*	42	2

GUY *US, male vocal group (4 WEEKS)* pos/wks

4 May 91	HER *MCA MCS 1575*	58	4

GYPSYMEN *US, male producer – Todd Terry (2 WEEKS)* pos/wks

11 Aug 01	BABARRABATIRI *Sound Design SDES 09CDS*	32	2

H

HABIT *UK, male vocal / instrumental group (2 WEEKS)* pos/wks

30 Apr 88	LUCY *Virgin VS 1063*	56	2

Steve HACKETT
UK, male vocalist / instrumentalist – guitar (2 WEEKS) pos/wks

2 Apr 83	CELL 151 *Charisma CELL 1*	66	2

See also GENESIS

HADDAWAY
Trinidad and Tobago, male vocalist – Nester Haddaway (52 WEEKS) pos/wks

5 Jun 93 ●	WHAT IS LOVE *Logic 74321148502*	2	15
25 Sep 93 ●	LIFE *Logic 74321164212*	6	9
18 Dec 93 ●	I MISS YOU *Logic 74321181522*	9	14
2 Apr 94 ●	ROCK MY HEART *Logic 74321194122*	9	9
24 Jun 95	FLY AWAY *Logic 74321286942*	20	3
23 Sep 95	CATCH A FIRE *Logic 74321306652*	39	2

Tony HADLEY *UK, male vocalist (9 WEEKS)* pos/wks

7 Mar 92	LOST IN YOUR LOVE *EMI EM 222*	42	4
29 Aug 92	FOR YOUR BLUE EYES ONLY *EMI EM 234*	67	2
16 Jan 93	THE GAME OF LOVE *EMI CDEM 254*	72	1
10 May 97	DANCE WITH ME *VC VCRD 17* [1]	35	2

[1] Tin Tin Out featuring Tony Hadley

See also SPANDAU BALLET

Sammy HAGAR
US, male vocalist / instrumentalist – guitar (15 WEEKS) pos/wks

15 Dec 79	THIS PLANET'S ON FIRE / SPACE STATION NO. 5 *Capitol CL 16114*	52	5
16 Feb 80	I'VE DONE EVERYTHING FOR YOU *Capitol CL 16120*	36	5
24 May 80	HEARTBEAT / LOVE OR MONEY *Capitol RED 1*	67	2
16 Jan 82	PIECE OF MY HEART *Geffen GEFA 1884*	67	1
30 Jan 82	PIECE OF MY HEART (re-entry) *Geffen GEFA 1884*	67	2

See also VAN HALEN; MONTROSE

Paul HAIG *UK, male vocalist (3 WEEKS)* pos/wks

28 May 83	HEAVEN SENT *Island IS 111*	74	3

HAIRCUT 100 *UK, male vocal / instrumental group (47 WEEKS)* pos/wks

24 Oct 81 ●	FAVOURITE SHIRTS (BOY MEETS GIRL) *Arista CLIP 1*	4	14
30 Jan 82 ●	LOVE PLUS ONE *Arista CLIP 2*	3	12
10 Apr 82 ●	FANTASTIC DAY *Arista CLIP 3*	9	9
21 Aug 82 ●	NOBODY'S FOOL *Arista CLIP 4*	9	7
6 Aug 83	PRIME TIME *Polydor HC 1*	46	5

Curtis HAIRSTON *US, male vocalist (16 WEEKS)* pos/wks

15 Oct 83	I WANT YOU (ALL TONIGHT) *RCA 368*	44	5
27 Apr 85	I WANT YOUR LOVIN' (JUST A LITTLE BIT) *London LON 66*	13	7
6 Dec 86	CHILLIN' OUT *Atlantic A 9335*	57	4

Gary HAISMAN – *See D MOB*

HAL featuring Gillian ANDERSON
UK, male producers and US, female vocalist (3 WEEKS) pos/wks

24 May 97	EXTREMIS *Virgin VSCDT 1636*	23	3

HALE and PACE and the STONKERS *UK, male comedy duo – Gareth Hale and Norman Pace, and backing group (7 WEEKS)* pos/wks

9 Mar 91 ★	THE STONK *London LON 296*	1	7

Bill HALEY and his COMETS (92 Top 500) *Original 'King of Rock 'n' Roll', b. 6 Jul 1925, Detroit, d. 9 Feb 1981. The kiss-curl hairstyled frontman introduced rock to the world via a string of mid-1950s smashes, including 'Rock Around the Clock', the only record to return to the Top 20 on five occasions (199 WEEKS)* pos/wks

17 Dec 54 ●	SHAKE, RATTLE AND ROLL *Brunswick 05338*	4	14
7 Jan 55	ROCK AROUND THE CLOCK *Brunswick 05317*	17	2
15 Apr 55	MAMBO ROCK *Brunswick 05405*	14	2
14 Oct 55 ★	ROCK AROUND THE CLOCK (re-entry) *Brunswick 05317* ◆ ▲	1	17
30 Dec 55 ●	ROCK-A-BEATIN' BOOGIE *Brunswick 05509*	4	9
9 Mar 56 ●	SEE YOU LATER, ALLIGATOR *Brunswick 05530*	7	13
25 May 56 ●	THE SAINTS ROCK 'N ROLL *Brunswick 05565*	5	24
17 Aug 56 ●	ROCKIN' THROUGH THE RYE *Brunswick 05582*	3	18
14 Sep 56	RAZZLE DAZZLE *Brunswick 05453*	13	8
21 Sep 56 ●	ROCK AROUND THE CLOCK (2nd re-entry) *Brunswick 05317*	5	11
21 Sep 56	SEE YOU LATER, ALLIGATOR (re-entry) *Brunswick 05530*	12	8
9 Nov 56 ●	RIP IT UP *Brunswick 05615*	4	18
9 Nov 56	ROCK 'N ROLL STAGE SHOW (LP) *Brunswick LAT 8139*	30	1
23 Nov 56	RUDY'S ROCK *Brunswick 05616*	30	1
14 Dec 56	ROCK AROUND THE CLOCK (3rd re-entry) *Brunswick 05317*	24	2
14 Dec 56	RUDY'S ROCK (re-entry) *Brunswick 05616*	26	4
4 Jan 57	ROCK AROUND THE CLOCK (4th re-entry) *Brunswick 05317*	25	2
4 Jan 57	ROCKIN' THROUGH THE RYE (re-entry) *Brunswick 05582*	19	5
25 Jan 57	ROCK AROUND THE CLOCK (5th re-entry) *Brunswick 05317*	22	2
1 Feb 57	ROCK THE JOINT *London HLF 8371*	20	4
8 Feb 57 ●	DON'T KNOCK THE ROCK *Brunswick 05640*	7	8
3 Apr 68	ROCK AROUND THE CLOCK (re-issue) *MCA MU 1013*	20	11
16 Mar 74	ROCK AROUND THE CLOCK (2nd re-issue) *MCA 128*	12	10
25 Apr 81	HALEY'S GOLDEN MEDLEY *MCA 694*	50	5

Tracks on Rock 'n' Roll Stage Show (LP): Calling All Comets / Rockin' Through the Rye / A Rockin' Little Tune / Hide and Seek / Hey There Now / Goofin' Around / Hook Line and Sinker / Rudy's Rock / Choo Choo Ch'Boogie / Blue Comets Rock / Hot Dog Buddy Buddy / Tonight's the Night. Occasionally, some of the 'Rock Around the Clock' labels billed the song as '(We're Gonna) Rock Around the Clock'

Aaron HALL *US, male vocalist (3 WEEKS)* pos/wks

13 Jun 92	DON'T BE AFRAID *MCA MCS 1632*	56	2
23 Oct 93	GET A LITTLE FREAKY WITH ME *MCA MCSTD 1936*	66	1

Audrey HALL *Jamaica, female vocalist (20 WEEKS)* pos/wks

25 Jan 86	ONE DANCE WON'T DO *Germain DG7-1985*	20	11
5 Jul 86	SMILE *Germain DG 15*	14	9

Daryl HALL *US, male vocalist (26 WEEKS)* pos/wks

2 Aug 86	DREAMTIME *RCA HALL 1*	28	8
25 Sep 93	I'M IN A PHILLY MOOD *Epic 6595555*	59	2
8 Jan 94	STOP LOVING ME STOP LOVING YOU *Epic 6599982*	30	6

THE OFFICIAL UK SINGLES CHART 50TH ANNIVERSARY

1970

IN THE YEAR IN WHICH BOTH JIMI HENDRIX AND JANIS JOPLIN DIED, BRAZIL WON ITS THIRD WORLD CUP IN THE FIRST TELEVISED TOURNAMENT, THE APOLLO 13 ASTRONAUTS SURVIVED AN EXPLOSION IN THEIR SPACECRAFT AND GERMAINE GREER TOOK FEMINISM TO THE FRONT LINE IN 'THE FEMALE EUNUCH', TEENAGER **PADDY MCALOON** MAKES HIS OWN DISCS ...

"I think the first record I personally handed money over for was 'All Right Now' by Free at a shop called the Musicore in Durham, which no longer exists. You know in those days how they had those lone shops that just seemed to survive? There's a camera shop now. A very fine record. But one of the first records that was bought on my behalf was 'Ride a White Swan'. I was 13 when **Marc Bolan** was making records and that's who I wanted to be. I wanted to be Bolan so badly, like loads of kids did. I adored him. I wasn't then really writing songs although I was trying to because I didn't know how to do it, and what I would do was I would get a piece of paper and cut it into a disc that was shaped like a record and I'd write words on it and pretend that it was one."

SINGLE OF THE YEAR 'In The Summertime' Mungo Jerry
ALBUM OF THE YEAR 'Bridge Over Troubled Water' Simon and Garfunkel

26 Mar 94	I'M IN A PHILLY MOOD (re-entry) *Epic 6595555*	52	2
14 May 94	HELP ME FIND A WAY TO YOUR HEART *Epic 6604102*	70	1
2 Jul 94	GLORYLAND *Mercury MERCD 404* [1]	36	4
10 Jun 95	WHEREVER WOULD I BE *Columbia 6620592* [2]	44	3

[1] Daryl Hall and the Sounds of Blackness [2] Dusty Springfield and Daryl Hall

See also Daryl HALL and John OATES

Daryl HALL and John OATES (390 Top 500)

White, soul-influenced US duo: Daryl Hall (v), b. 11 Oct 1948, Philadelphia and John Oates (g) b. 7 Apr 1949, New York. Met at university in 1967, eventually becoming the most successful duo in US singles chart history, with 16 Top 10s and six No.1s (84 WEEKS)

		pos	wks
16 Oct 76	SHE'S GONE *Atlantic K 10828*	42	4
14 Jun 80	RUNNING FROM PARADISE *RCA RUN 1*	41	6
20 Sep 80	YOU'VE LOST THAT LOVIN' FEELIN' *RCA 1*	55	3
15 Nov 80	KISS ON MY LIST *RCA 15* ▲	33	8
23 Jan 82 ●	I CAN'T GO FOR THAT (NO CAN DO) *RCA 172* ▲	8	10
10 Apr 82	PRIVATE EYES *RCA 134* ▲	32	7
30 Oct 82 ●	MANEATER *RCA 290* ▲	6	11
22 Jan 83	ONE ON ONE *RCA 305*	63	3
30 Apr 83	FAMILY MAN *RCA 323*	15	7
12 Nov 83	SAY IT ISN'T SO *RCA 375*	69	3
10 Mar 84	ADULT EDUCATION *RCA 396*	63	2
20 Oct 84	OUT OF TOUCH *RCA 449* ▲	48	5
9 Feb 85	METHOD OF MODERN LOVE *RCA 472*	21	8
22 Jun 85	OUT OF TOUCH (re-mix) *RCA PB 49967*	62	3
21 Sep 85	A NIGHT AT THE APOLLO LIVE! *RCA PB 49935* [1]	58	2
29 Sep 90	SO CLOSE *Arista 113600* [2]	69	1
26 Jan 91	EVERYWHERE I LOOK *Arista 113980*	74	1

[1] Daryl Hall and John Oates featuring David Ruffin and Eddie Kendrick [2] Hall and Oates

'A Night at the Apollo Live!' is a medley of 'The Way You Do the Things You Do' and 'My Girl'

Lynden David HALL *UK, male vocal / instrumentalist (12 WEEKS)*

		pos	wks
25 Oct 97	SEXY CINDERELLA *Cooltempo CDCOOL 328*	45	2
14 Mar 98	DO I QUALIFY? *Cooltempo CDCOOLS 331*	26	2
4 Jul 98	CRESCENT MOON *Cooltempo CDCOOL 333*	45	1
31 Oct 98	SEXY CINDERELLA (re-issue) *Cooltempo CDCOOLS 340*	17	3
11 Mar 00	FORGIVE ME *Cooltempo CDCOOLS 346*	30	2
27 May 00	SLEEPING WITH VICTOR *Cooltempo CDCOOL 348*	49	1
23 Sep 00	LET'S DO IT AGAIN *Cooltempo CDCOOL 351*	69	1

Pam HALL *Jamaica, female vocalist (4 WEEKS)*

		pos	wks
16 Aug 86	DEAR BOOPSIE *Bluemountain BM 027*	54	4

Terry HALL *UK, male vocalist (6 WEEKS)*

		pos	wks
11 Nov 89	MISSING *Chrysalis CHS 3381*	75	1
27 Aug 94	FOREVER J *Anxious ANX 1024CDX*	67	1
12 Nov 94	SENSE *Anxious ANX 1027CD*	54	2
28 Oct 95	RAINBOWS (EP) *Anxious ANX 1033CD1*	62	1
14 Jun 97	BALLAD OF A LANDLORD *Southsea Bubble CDBUBBLE 1*	50	1

Tracks on Rainbows (EP): Chasing Rainbow / Mistakes / See No Evil / Ghost Train

The sleeve, not the label, of 'Missing' credits Terry, Blair and Anouchka

See also FUN BOY THREE; SPECIALS

Toni HALLIDAY – *See LEFTFIELD; Paul VAN DYK*

Geri HALLIWELL (364 Top 500)

Headline-grabbing former Ginger Spice (b. 6 Aug 1972, Watford, UK) sang on seven Spice Girls chart-toppers before achieving more solo No.1s than any other UK female. She is the only person to score as many as four consecutive No.1s both as a solo artist and as part of group (87 WEEKS)

		pos	wks
22 May 99 ●	LOOK AT ME *EMI CDEM 542*	2	12
28 Aug 99	LOOK AT ME (re-entry) *EMI CDEM 542*	60	2
28 Aug 99 ★	MI CHICO LATINO *EMI CDEM 548* ■	1	13
13 Nov 99 ★	LIFT ME UP *EMI CDEM 554* ■	1	15
4 Mar 00	LIFT ME UP (re-entry) *EMI CDEM 554*	62	2
25 Mar 00 ★	BAG IT UP *EMI CDEMS 560* ■	1	11
24 Jun 00	BAG IT UP (re-entry) *EMI CDEMS 560*	55	2
12 May 01 ★	IT'S RAINING MEN *EMI CDEMS 584* ■	1	15
11 Aug 01 ●	SCREAM IF YOU WANNA GO FASTER *EMI CDEMS 595*	8	9
27 Oct 01	SCREAM IF YOU WANNA GO FASTER (re-entry) *EMI CDEMS 595*	64	2
8 Dec 01 ●	CALLING *EMI CDEMS 606*	7	4

See also SPICE GIRLS

HALO JAMES *UK, male vocal / instrumental group (24 WEEKS)*

		pos	wks
7 Oct 89	WANTED *Epic HALO 1*	45	5
23 Dec 89 ●	COULD HAVE TOLD YOU SO *Epic HALO 2*	6	12
17 Mar 90	BABY *Epic HALO 3*	43	4
19 May 90	MAGIC HOUR *Epic HALO 4*	59	3

George HAMILTON IV *US, male vocalist (13 WEEKS)*

		pos	wks
7 Mar 58	WHY DON'T THEY UNDERSTAND *HMV POP 429*	22	9
18 Jul 58	I KNOW WHERE I'M GOIN' *HMV POP 505*	29	1
8 Aug 58	I KNOW WHERE I'M GOIN' (re-entry) *HMV POP 505*	23	3

Lynne HAMILTON *UK, female vocalist (11 WEEKS)*

		pos	wks
29 Apr 89 ●	ON THE INSIDE (THEME FROM 'PRISONER: CELL BLOCK H') *A1 A1 311*	3	11

Russ HAMILTON *UK, male vocalist – Ronald Hulme (26 WEEKS)*

		pos	wks
24 May 57 ●	WE WILL MAKE LOVE *Oriole CB 1359*	2	20
27 Sep 57	WEDDING RING *Oriole CB 1388* [1]	20	6

[1] Russ Hamilton with Johnny Gregory and his Orchestra with the Tonettes

HAMILTON, Joe FRANK and REYNOLDS

US, male vocal group (6 WEEKS)

		pos	wks
13 Sep 75	FALLIN' IN LOVE *Pye International 7N 25690* ▲	33	6

Marvin HAMLISCH *US, male instrumentalist – piano (13 WEEKS)*

		pos	wks
30 Mar 74	THE ENTERTAINER *MCA 121*	25	13

HAMMER *US, male rapper (68 WEEKS)*

		pos	wks
9 Jun 90 ●	U CAN'T TOUCH THIS *Capitol CL 578* [1]	3	16
6 Oct 90 ●	HAVE YOU SEEN HER *Capitol CL 590* [1]	8	7
8 Dec 90 ●	PRAY *Capitol CL 599* [1]	8	10
23 Feb 91	HERE COMES THE HAMMER *Capitol CL 610* [1]	15	5
1 Jun 91	YO!! SWEETNESS *Capitol CL 616* [1]	16	5
20 Jul 91	(HAMMER HAMMER) THEY PUT ME IN THE MIX *Capitol CL 607* [1]	20	4
26 Oct 91	2 LEGIT 2 QUIT *Capitol CL 636*	60	2
21 Dec 91 ●	ADDAMS GROOVE *Capitol CL 642*	4	9
21 Mar 92	DO NOT PASS ME BY *Capitol CL 650*	14	6
12 Mar 94	IT'S ALL GOOD *RCA 74321188612*	52	2
13 Aug 94	DON'T STOP *RCA 74321220012*	72	1
3 Jun 95	STRAIGHT TO MY FEET *Priority PTYCD 102* [2]	57	1

[1] MC Hammer [2] Hammer featuring Deion Saunders

Jan HAMMER

Czech Republic, male instrumentalist – keyboards (26 WEEKS)

		pos	wks
12 Oct 85 ●	MIAMI VICE THEME *MCA MCA 1000* ▲	5	8
19 Sep 87 ●	CROCKETT'S THEME *MCA MCA 1193*	2	12
1 Jun 91	CROCKETT'S THEME (re-issue) / CHANCER *MCA MCS 1541*	47	6

Albert HAMMOND *Gibraltar, male vocalist (11 WEEKS)*

		pos	wks
30 Jun 73	FREE ELECTRIC BAND *Mums 1494*	19	11

Beres HAMMOND – *See Maxi PRIEST*

Herbie HANCOCK

US, male vocalist / instrumentalist – keyboards (41 WEEKS)

		pos	wks
26 Aug 78	I THOUGHT IT WAS YOU *CBS 6530*	15	9
3 Feb 79	YOU BET YOUR LOVE *CBS 7010*	18	10
30 Jul 83 ●	ROCKIT *CBS A 3577*	8	12
8 Oct 83	AUTODRIVE *CBS A 3802*	33	4

21 Jan 84	**FUTURE SHOCK** *CBS A 4075*	54	3
4 Aug 84	**HARDROCK** *CBS A 4616*	65	3

HANDBAGGERS *UK, male / female vocal / instrumental group (1 WEEK)* pos/wks

15 Jun 96	**U FOUND OUT** *Tidy Trax TIDY 104CD*	55	1

HANDLEY FAMILY *UK, male / female vocal group (7 WEEKS)* pos/wks

7 Apr 73	**WAM BAM** *GL 100*	30	7

HANI *US, male DJ / producer (1 WEEK)* pos/wks

11 Mar 00	**BABY WANTS TO RIDE** *Neo NEO CD025*	70	1

Jayn HANNA *UK, female vocalist (2 WEEKS)* pos/wks

13 Apr 96	**LOVELIGHT (RIDE ON A LOVE TRAIN)** *VC VCRD 10*	42	1
1 Feb 97	**LOST WITHOUT YOU** *VC VCRD 16*	44	1

HANNAH – *See MAN WITH NO NAME*

HANNAH *UK, female vocalist – Hannah Waddingham (2 WEEKS)* pos/wks

21 Oct 00	**OUR KIND OF LOVE** *Telstar CDSTAS 3149*	41	2

HANNAH and her SISTERS – *See Hannah JONES*

HANOI ROCKS
Finland / UK, male vocal / instrumental group (2 WEEKS) pos/wks

7 Jul 84	**UP AROUND THE BEND** *CBS A 4513*	61	2

HANSON *US, male vocal / instrumental group (47 WEEKS)* pos/wks

7 Jun 97 ★	**MMMBOP** *Mercury 5745012* ■ ▲	1	13
13 Sep 97 ●	**WHERE'S THE LOVE** *Mercury 5749032*	4	9
22 Nov 97 ●	**I WILL COME TO YOU** *Mercury 5680672*	5	9
28 Mar 98	**WEIRD** *Mercury 5685412*	19	5
4 Jul 98	**THINKING OF YOU** *Mercury 5688132*	23	6
5 Sep 98	**THINKING OF YOU (re-entry)** *Mercury 5688132*	69	1
29 Apr 00	**IF ONLY** *Mercury 5627502*	15	4

HAPPENINGS *US, male vocal group (14 WEEKS)* pos/wks

18 May 67	**I GOT RHYTHM** *Stateside SS 2013*	28	9
16 Aug 67	**MY MAMMY** *Pye International 7N 25501 and BT Puppy BTS 45530*	34	5

Pye gave the US BT Puppy label its own identification halfway through the success of 'My Mammy'

HAPPY CLAPPERS
UK, male / female vocal / instrumental group (19 WEEKS) pos/wks

3 Jun 95	**I BELIEVE** *Shindig SHIN 4CD*	21	3
26 Aug 95	**HOLD ON** *Shindig SHIN 7CD*	27	2
18 Nov 95 ●	**I BELIEVE (re-issue)** *Shindig SHIN 9CD*	7	8
15 Jun 96	**CAN'T HELP IT** *Coliseum TOGA 004CD*	18	3
21 Dec 96	**NEVER AGAIN** *Coliseum TOGA 012CD*	49	1
22 Nov 97	**I BELIEVE 97** *Coalition COLA 027CD*	28	2

HAPPY MONDAYS *UK, male vocal / instrumental group (53 WEEKS)* pos/wks

30 Sep 89	**WFL** *Factory FAC 2327*	68	2
25 Nov 89	**MADCHESTER RAVE ON (EP)** *Factory FAC 2427*	19	14
7 Apr 90 ●	**STEP ON** *Factory FAC 2727*	5	11
9 Jun 90	**LAZYITIS - ONE ARMED BOXER** *Factory FAC 2227* [1]	46	3
20 Oct 90 ●	**KINKY AFRO** *Factory FAC 3027*	5	7
9 Mar 91	**LOOSE FIT** *Factory FAC 3127*	17	7
30 Nov 91	**JUDGE FUDGE** *Factory FAC 3327*	24	3
19 Sep 92	**STINKIN THINKIN** *Factory FAC 3627*	31	3
21 Nov 92	**SUNSHINE AND LOVE** *Factory FAC 3727*	62	1
22 May 99	**THE BOYS ARE BACK IN TOWN** *London LONCD 432*	24	2

[1] Happy Mondays and Karl Denver

Tracks on Madchester Rave On (EP): Hallelujah / Holy Ghost / Clap Your Hands / Rave On

See also BLACK GRAPE

Paul HARDCASTLE *UK, male producer (66 WEEKS)* pos/wks

7 Apr 84	**YOU'RE THE ONE FOR ME - DAYBREAK - AM** *Total Control TOCO 1*	41	4
28 Jul 84	**GUILTY** *Total Control TOCO 2*	55	3
22 Sep 84	**RAIN FOREST** *Bluebird BR 8*	41	5
17 Nov 84	**EAT YOUR HEART OUT** *Cooltempo COOL 102*	59	4
4 May 85 ★	**19** *Chrysalis CHS 2860*	1	16
15 Jun 85	**RAIN FOREST (re-issue)** *Bluebird / 10 BR 15*	53	4
9 Nov 85	**JUST FOR MONEY** *Chrysalis CASH 1*	19	5
1 Feb 86 ●	**DON'T WASTE MY TIME** *Chrysalis PAUL 1* [1]	8	11
21 Jun 86	**FOOLIN' YOURSELF** *Chrysalis PAUL 2*	51	3
11 Oct 86	**THE WIZARD** *Chrysalis PAUL 3*	15	6
9 Apr 88	**WALK IN THE NIGHT** *Chrysalis PAUL 4*	54	3
4 Jun 88	**40 YEARS** *Chrysalis PAUL 5*	53	2

[1] Paul Hardcastle featuring Carol Kenyon

'Just for Money' features the voices of Laurence Olivier, Bob Hoskins, Ed O'Ross and Alan Talbot, who are credited on the sleeve only

See also SILENT UNDERDOG

HARDCORE RHYTHM TEAM
UK, male vocal / production group (1 WEEK) pos/wks

14 Mar 92	**HARDCORE - THE FINAL CONFLICT** *Furious FRUT 001*	69	1

Duane HARDEN – *See Armand VAN HELDEN; POWERHOUSE*

HARDFLOOR *Germany, male instrumental / production group (6 WEEKS)* pos/wks

26 Dec 92	**HARDTRANCE ACPERIENCE** *Harthouse UK HARTUK 1*	56	4
10 Apr 93	**TRANCESCRIPT** *Harthouse UK HARTUK 5CD*	72	1
25 Oct 97	**ACPERIENCE (re-mix)** *Eye-q EYEUK 018CD1*	60	1

Tim HARDIN *US, male vocalist (1 WEEK)* pos/wks

5 Jan 67	**HANG ON TO A DREAM** *Verve VS 1504*	50	1

Carolyn HARDING – *See PROSPECT PARK / Carolyn HARDING*

Mike HARDING *UK, male comedian (8 WEEKS)* pos/wks

2 Aug 75	**ROCHDALE COWBOY** *Rubber ADUB 3*	22	8

Françoise HARDY *France, female vocalist (27 WEEKS)* pos/wks

25 Jun 64	**TOUS LES GARÇONS ET LES FILLES** *Pye 7N 15653*	36	7
31 Dec 64	**ET MÊME** *Pye 7N 15740*	31	5
25 Mar 65	**ALL OVER THE WORLD** *Pye 7N 15802*	16	15

Tynetta HARE – *See Joey B ELLIS*

NIKI HARIS – *See SNAP*

Morten HARKET *Norway, male vocalist (1 WEEK)* pos/wks

19 Aug 95	**A KIND OF CHRISTMAS CARD** *Warner Bros. W 0304CD*	53	1

See also A-HA

HARLEM COMMUNITY CHOIR – *See John LENNON*

HARLEQUIN 4s / BUNKER KRU *US, male / female vocal / instrumental group with UK, male production duo (4 WEEKS)* pos/wks

19 Mar 88	**SET IT OFF** *Champion CHAMP 64*	55	4

Steve HARLEY and COCKNEY REBEL *Distinctive singer / songwriter b. Steven Nice, 27. Feb 1951, London, UK, fronted band until he went solo in 1977. His self-penned No.1 'Make Me Smile' returned to the Top 40 in 1995 after being used in a Carlsberg TV commercial (69 WEEKS)* pos/wks

11 May 74 ●	**JUDY TEEN** *EMI 2128* [1]	5	11
10 Aug 74 ●	**MR SOFT** *EMI 2191* [1]	8	9
8 Feb 75 ★	**MAKE ME SMILE (COME UP AND SEE ME)** *EMI 2263*	1	9
7 Jun 75	**MR RAFFLES (MAN IT WAS MEAN)** *EMI 2299*	13	6
31 Jul 76 ●	**HERE COMES THE SUN** *EMI 2505* [2]	10	7
6 Nov 76	**LOVE'S A PRIMA DONNA** *EMI 2539* [2]	41	4

20 Oct 79 **FREEDOM'S PRISONER** *EMI 2994* [2] 58 3
13 Aug 83 **BALLERINA (PRIMA DONNA)** *Stiletto STL 14* [2] 51 5
11 Jan 86 ● **THE PHANTOM OF THE OPERA** *Polydor POSP 800* [3] 7 10
25 Apr 92 **MAKE ME SMILE (COME UP AND SEE ME) (re-issue)** *EMI EMCT 5* [2] 46 2
30 Dec 95 **MAKE ME SMILE (COME UP AND SEE ME) (2nd re-issue)** *EMI CDHARLEY 1* 33 3

[1] Cockney Rebel [2] Steve Harley [3] Sarah Brightman and Steve Harley

HARLEY QUINNE *UK, male vocal group (8 WEEKS)* pos/wks

14 Oct 72 **NEW ORLEANS** *Bell 1255* 19 8

HARMONIX *UK, male producer – Hamish Brown (2 WEEKS)* pos/wks

30 Mar 96 **LANDSLIDE** *Deconstruction 74321330762* 28 2

HARMONY GRASS *UK, male vocal / instrumental group (7 WEEKS)* pos/wks

29 Jan 69 **MOVE IN A LITTLE CLOSER BABY** *RCA 1772* 24 7

Ben HARPER *US, male vocalist / instrumentalist (1 WEEK)* pos/wks

4 Apr 98 **FADED** *Virgin VUSCD 134* 54 1

Charlie HARPER *UK, male vocalist (1 WEEK)* pos/wks

19 Jul 80 **BARMY LONDON ARMY** *Gem GEMS 35* 68 1

HARPERS BIZARRE *US, male vocal group (13 WEEKS)* pos/wks

30 Mar 67 **59TH STREET BRIDGE SONG (FEELIN' GROOVY)** *Warner Bros. WB 5890* 34 7
4 Oct 67 **ANYTHING GOES** *Warner Bros. WB 7063* 33 6

HARPO *Sweden, male vocalist (6 WEEKS)* pos/wks

17 Apr 76 **MOVIE STAR** *DJM DJS 400* 24 6

T HARRINGTON – *See Rahni HARRIS and F.L.O.*

Anita HARRIS *UK, female vocalist (50 WEEKS)* pos/wks

29 Jun 67 ● **JUST LOVING YOU** *CBS 2724* 6 30
11 Oct 67 **THE PLAYGROUND** *CBS 2991* 46 3
24 Jan 68 **ANNIVERSARY WALTZ** *CBS 3211* 21 9
14 Aug 68 **DREAM A LITTLE DREAM OF ME** *CBS 3637* 33 8

Emmylou HARRIS *US, female vocalist (6 WEEKS)* pos/wks

6 Mar 76 **HERE THERE AND EVERYWHERE** *Reprise K 14415* 30 6

Jet HARRIS *UK, male instrumentalist – bass (18 WEEKS)* pos/wks

24 May 62 **BESAME MUCHO** *Decca F 11466* 22 7
16 Aug 62 **MAIN TITLE THEME FROM 'THE MAN WITH THE GOLDEN ARM'** *Decca F 11488* 12 11

See also Jet HARRIS and Tony MEEHAN; SHADOWS

Jet HARRIS and Tony MEEHAN
UK, male instrumental duo – bass and drums (39 WEEKS) pos/wks

10 Jan 63 ★ **DIAMONDS** *Decca F 11563* 1 13
25 Apr 63 ● **SCARLETT O'HARA** *Decca F 11644* 2 13
5 Sep 63 ● **APPLEJACK** *Decca F 11710* 4 13

See also Jet HARRIS; Tony MEEHAN COMBO; SHADOWS

Keith HARRIS and ORVILLE
UK, male ventriloquist vocalist with duck (20 WEEKS) pos/wks

18 Dec 82 ● **ORVILLE'S SONG** *BBC RESL 124* 4 11
24 Dec 83 **COME TO MY PARTY** *BBC RESL 138* [1] 44 4
14 Dec 85 **WHITE CHRISTMAS** *Columbia DB 9121* 40 5

[1] Keith Harris and Orville with Dippy

Major HARRIS *US, male vocalist (9 WEEKS)* pos/wks

9 Aug 75 **LOVE WON'T LET ME WAIT** *Atlantic K 10585* 37 7
5 Nov 83 **ALL MY LIFE** *London LON 37* 61 2

Max HARRIS *UK, orchestra (10 WEEKS)* pos/wks

1 Dec 60 **GURNEY SLADE** *Fontana H 282* 11 10

Rahni HARRIS and F.L.O. *US, male instrumental group (7 WEEKS)* pos/wks

16 Dec 78 **SIX MILLION STEPS (WEST RUNS SOUTH)** *Mercury 6007 198* 43 7

Hit has credit 'vocals by T Harrington and O Rasbury'

Richard HARRIS *Ireland, male actor (18 WEEKS)* pos/wks

26 Jun 68 ● **MACARTHUR PARK** *RCA 1699* 4 12
8 Jul 72 **MACARTHUR PARK (re-issue)** *Probe GFF 101* 38 6

Rochelle HARRIS – *See ANGELHEART*

Rolf HARRIS (438 Top 500)
Lovable Australian musician, artist and presenter b. 30 Mar 1930, can lay claim to having some of the unlikeliest hits in the history of the UK charts. His only No.1 was a song written in 1903 by Theodore F Morse and Edward Madden and was the final chart-topper of the 60s (77 WEEKS) pos/wks

21 Jul 60 ● **TIE ME KANGAROO DOWN SPORT** *Columbia DB 4483* [1] 9 13
25 Oct 62 ● **SUN ARISE** *Columbia DB 4888* 3 16
28 Feb 63 **JOHNNY DAY** *Columbia DB 4979* 44 2
16 Apr 69 **BLUER THAN BLUE** *Columbia DB 8553* 30 8
22 Nov 69 ★ **TWO LITTLE BOYS** *Columbia DB 8630* 1 24
20 Jun 70 **TWO LITTLE BOYS (re-entry)** *Columbia DB 8630* 50 1
13 Feb 93 ● **STAIRWAY TO HEAVEN** *Vertigo VERCD 73* 7 6
1 Jun 96 **BOHEMIAN RHAPSODY** *Living Beat LBECD 41* 50 1
25 Oct 97 **SUN ARISE (re-recording)** *EMI CDROO 001* 26 3
14 Oct 00 **FINE DAY** *Tommy Boy TBCD 2155* 24 3

[1] Rolf Harris with his wobble board and The Rhythm Spinners

Ronnie HARRIS *UK, male vocalist (3 WEEKS)* pos/wks

24 Sep 54 **THE STORY OF TINA** *Columbia DB 3499* 12 3

Sam HARRIS *US, male vocalist (2 WEEKS)* pos/wks

9 Feb 85 **HEARTS ON FIRE / OVER THE RAINBOW** *Motown TMG 1370* 67 2

Simon HARRIS *UK, male / DJ producer (17 WEEKS)* pos/wks

19 Mar 88 **BASS (HOW LOW CAN YOU GO)** *ffrr FFR 4* 12 6
29 Oct 88 **HERE COMES THAT SOUND** *ffrr FFR 12* 38 4
24 Jun 89 **(I'VE GOT YOUR) PLEASURE CONTROL** *ffrr F 106* [1] 60 3
18 Nov 89 **ANOTHER MONSTERJAM** *ffrr F 116* [2] 65 1
10 Mar 90 **RAGGA HOUSE (ALL NIGHT LONG)** *Living Beat 7SMASH 9* [3] 56 3

[1] Simon Harris featuring Lonnie Gordon [2] Simon Harris featuring Einstein [3] Simon Harris featuring Daddy Freddy

See also AMBASSADORS OF FUNK featuring MC MARIO

George HARRISON (398 Top 500)
Former Beatles guitarist, much inspired by Eastern musicians, born 25 Feb 1943, Liverpool UK, died 29 Nov 2001. First ex-Beatle to score a solo UK No.1 single, and only act in history to make UK and US Top 5 with back-to back triple albums (82 WEEKS) pos/wks

23 Jan 71 ★ **MY SWEET LORD** *Apple R 5884* ▲ 1 17
14 Aug 71 ● **BANGLA DESH** *Apple R 5912* 10 9
2 Jun 73 ● **GIVE ME LOVE (GIVE ME PEACE ON EARTH)** *Apple R 5988* ▲ 8 10
21 Dec 74 **DING DONG** *Apple R 6002* 38 5
11 Oct 75 **YOU** *Apple R 6007* 38 5
10 Mar 79 **BLOW AWAY** *Dark Horse K 17327* 51 5
23 May 81 **ALL THOSE YEARS AGO** *Dark Horse K 17807* 13 7
24 Oct 87 ● **GOT MY MIND SET ON YOU** *Dark Horse W 8178* ▲ 2 14
6 Feb 88 **WHEN WE WAS FAB** *Dark Horse W 8131* 25 7
25 Jun 88 **THIS IS LOVE** *Dark Horse W 7913* 55 3

Noel HARRISON *UK, male vocalist (14 WEEKS)* pos/wks

26 Feb 69 ●	**THE WINDMILLS OF YOUR MIND** *Reprise RS 20758*	8	14

HARRY – *See OBI PROJECT featuring HARRY, ASHER D & DJ WHAT?*

Deborah HARRY *US, female vocalist (52 WEEKS)* pos/wks

1 Aug 81	**BACKFIRED** *Chrysalis CHS 2526* [1]	32	6
15 Nov 86 ●	**FRENCH KISSIN' IN THE USA** *Chrysalis CHS 3066* [1]	8	10
28 Feb 87	**FREE TO FALL** *Chrysalis CHS 3093* [1]	46	4
9 May 87	**IN LOVE WITH LOVE** *Chrysalis CHS 3128* [1]	45	5
7 Oct 89	**I WANT THAT MAN** *Chrysalis CHS 3369*	13	10
2 Dec 89	**BRITE SIDE** *Chrysalis CHS 3452*	59	4
31 Mar 90	**SWEET AND LOW** *Chrysalis CHS 3491*	57	3
5 Jan 91	**WELL DID YOU EVAH!** *Chrysalis CHS 3646* [2]	42	4
3 Jul 93	**I CAN SEE CLEARLY NOW** *Chrysalis CDCHSS 4900*	23	4
18 Sep 93	**STRIKE ME PINK** *Chrysalis CDCHSS 5000*	46	2

[1] Debbie Harry [2] Deborah Harry and Iggy Pop

See also BLONDIE

HARRY J ALL STARS *Jamaica, male instrumental group (25 WEEKS)* pos/wks

25 Oct 69 ●	**LIQUIDATOR** *Trojan TR 675*	9	20
29 Mar 80	**LIQUIDATOR (re-issue)** *Trojan TRO 9063*	42	5

Re-issue of 'Liquidator' coupled with re-issue of 'Long Shot Kick De Bucket' by The Pioneers

Richard HARTLEY / Michael REED ORCHESTRA
UK, male instrumentalist – synthesizer, orchestra (10 WEEKS) pos/wks

25 Feb 84 ●	**THE MUSIC OF TORVILL AND DEAN (EP)** *Safari SKATE 1*	9	10

Tracks on EP: Bolero / Capriccio Espagnole Opus 34 (Nos. 4 and 5) by Richard Hartley; Barnum on Ice / Discoskate by the Michael Reed Orchestra

Dan HARTMAN *US, male vocalist (34 WEEKS)* pos/wks

21 Oct 78 ●	**INSTANT REPLAY** *Blue Sky SKY 6706*	8	15
13 Jan 79	**THIS IS IT** *Blue Sky SKY 6999*	17	8
18 May 85	**SECOND NATURE** *MCA MCA 957*	66	2
24 Aug 85	**I CAN DREAM ABOUT YOU** *MCA MCA 988*	12	8
1 Apr 95	**KEEP THE FIRE BURNIN'** *Columbia 6611552* [1]	49	1

[1] Dan Hartman starring Loleatta Holloway

Alex HARVEY BAND – *See SENSATIONAL Alex HARVEY BAND*

Brian HARVEY *UK, male vocalist (5 WEEKS)* pos/wks

28 Apr 01	**STRAIGHT UP NO BENDS** *Edel 0126605 ERE*	26	2
27 Oct 01	**LOVING YOU (OLE OLE OLE)** *Blacklist 0132325 ERE* [1]	20	3

[1] Brian Harvey and the Refugee Crew

See also TRUE STEPPERS; EAST 17

Lee HARVEY – *See N*E*R*D featuring Lee HARVEY & VITA*

PJ HARVEY *UK, female vocalist – Polly Jean Harvey (22 WEEKS)* pos/wks

29 Feb 92	**SHEELA-NA-GIG** *Too Pure PURE 008*	69	1
1 May 93	**50 FT QUEENIE** *Island CID 538*	27	2
17 Jul 93	**MAN-SIZE** *Island CID 569*	42	2
18 Feb 95	**DOWN BY THE WATER** *Island CID 607*	38	2
22 Jul 95	**C'MON BILLY** *Island CID 614*	29	2
28 Oct 95	**SEND HIS LOVE TO ME** *Island CID 610*	34	2
9 Mar 96	**HENRY LEE** *Mute CDMUTE 189* [1]	36	1
23 Nov 96	**THAT WAS MY VEIL** *Island CID 648*	75	1
26 Sep 98	**A PERFECT DAY ELISE** *Island CID 718*	25	2
23 Jan 99	**THE WIND** *Island CID 730*	29	2
25 Nov 00	**GOOD FORTUNE** *Island CID 769*	41	2
10 Mar 01	**A PLACE CALLED HOME** *Island CID 771*	43	2
20 Oct 01	**THIS IS LOVE** *Island CID 785*	41	1

[1] Nick Cave and the Bad Seeds and PJ Harvey

For the first three hits PJ Harvey was the name of the entire group, not just the lead singer

Steve HARVEY *UK, male vocalist (6 WEEKS)* pos/wks

28 May 83	**SOMETHING SPECIAL** *London LON 25*	46	4
29 Oct 83	**TONIGHT** *London LON 36*	63	2

HARVEY DANGER *US, male vocal / instrumental group (1 WEEK)* pos/wks

1 Aug 98	**FLAGPOLE SITTA** *Slash LASCD 64*	57	1

Gordon HASKELL *UK, male vocalist (1 WEEK)* pos/wks

29 Dec 01 ●	**HOW WONDERFUL YOU ARE** *Flying Sparks TDBCDS 04*	2	1+

David HASSELHOFF *US, male vocalist (2 WEEKS)* pos/wks

13 Nov 93	**IF I COULD ONLY SAY GOODBYE** *Arista 74321172262*	35	2

Tony HATCH *UK, orchestra (1 WEEK)* pos/wks

4 Oct 62	**OUT OF THIS WORLD** *Pye 7N 15460*	50	1

Juliana HATFIELD *US, female vocalist / instrumetalist (2 WEEKS)* pos/wks

11 Sep 93	**MY SISTER** *Mammoth YZ 767CD* [1]	71	1
18 Mar 95	**UNIVERSAL HEART-BEAT** *East West YZ 916CD*	65	1

[1] Juliana Hatfield Three

Donny HATHAWAY – *See Roberta FLACK*

Lalah HATHAWAY *US, female vocalist (10 WEEKS)* pos/wks

1 Sep 90	**HEAVEN KNOWS** *Virgin America VUS 28*	66	2
2 Feb 91	**BABY DON'T CRY** *Virgin America VUS 35*	54	3
27 Jul 91	**FAMILY AFFAIR** *Ten TEN 369*	37	5

HATIRAS featuring SLARTA JOHN *Canada, male producer – George Hatiras and UK, male rapper – Mark James (5 WEEKS)* pos/wks

27 Jan 01	**SPACED INVADER** *Defected DFECT 25CDS*	14	5

HAVANA *UK, male instrumental / production group (1 WEEK)* pos/wks

6 Mar 93	**ETHNIC PRAYER** *Limbo LIMBO 007CD*	71	1

HAVEN *UK, male vocal / instrumental group (1 WEEK)* pos/wks

22 Sep 01	**LET IT LIVE** *Radiate RDT 3*	72	1

Nic HAVERSON *UK, male vocalist (3 WEEKS)* pos/wks

30 Jan 93	**HEAD OVER HEELS** *Telstar CDHOH 1*	48	3

Chesney HAWKES *UK, male vocalist (25 WEEKS)* pos/wks

23 Feb 91 ★	**THE ONE AND ONLY** *Chrysalis CHS 3627*	1	16
22 Jun 91	**I'M A MAN NOT A BOY** *Chrysalis CHS 3708*	27	5
28 Sep 91	**SECRETS OF THE HEART** *Chrysalis CHS 3681*	57	3
29 May 93	**WHAT'S WRONG WITH THIS PICTURE** *Chrysalis CDCHS 3969*	63	1

Screamin' Jay HAWKINS *US, male vocalist (3 WEEKS)* pos/wks

3 Apr 93	**HEART ATTACK AND VINE** *Columbia 6591092*	42	3

Sophie B HAWKINS *US, female vocalist (37 WEEKS)* pos/wks

4 Jul 92	**DAMN I WISH I WAS YOUR LOVER** *Columbia 6581077*	14	9
12 Sep 92	**CALIFORNIA HERE I COME** *Columbia 6583177*	53	3
6 Feb 93	**I WANT YOU** *Columbia 6587772*	49	2
13 Aug 94	**RIGHT BESIDE YOU** *Columbia 6606915*	13	12
26 Nov 94	**DON'T DON'T TELL ME NO** *Columbia 6610152*	36	5
11 Mar 95	**AS I LAY ME DOWN** *Columbia 6612125*	24	6

Edwin HAWKINS SINGERS
US, male / female vocal group (13 WEEKS) pos/wks

21 May 69 ●	**OH HAPPY DAY** *Buddah 201 048*	2	12
23 Aug 69	**OH HAPPY DAY (re-entry)** *Buddah 201 048*	43	1

Kirsty HAWKSHAW – *See DJ TIESTO; BT*

HAWKWIND *UK, male vocal / instrumental group with female dancer (28 WEEKS)* pos/wks

Date		Title / Label	pos	wks
1 Jul 72	●	**SILVER MACHINE** *United Artists UP 35381*	3	15
11 Aug 73		**URBAN GUERRILLA** *United Artists UP 35566*	39	3
21 Oct 78		**SILVER MACHINE (re-entry)** *United Artists UP 35381*	34	5
19 Jul 80		**SHOT DOWN IN THE NIGHT** *Bronze BRO 98*	59	3
15 Jan 83		**SILVER MACHINE (2nd re-entry)** *United Artists UP 35381*	67	2

Bill HAYES *US, male vocalist (9 WEEKS)* pos/wks

Date		Title / Label	pos	wks
6 Jan 56	●	**THE BALLAD OF DAVY CROCKETT** *London HLA 8220* [1] ▲	2	9

[1] with Archie Bleyer's Orchestra

Isaac HAYES *US, male vocalist / multi-instrumentalist (35 WEEKS)* pos/wks

Date		Title / Label	pos	wks
4 Dec 71	●	**THEME FROM 'SHAFT'** *Stax 2025 069* ▲	4	12
3 Apr 76	●	**DISCO CONNECTION** *ABC 4100* [1]	10	9
26 Dec 98	★	**CHOCOLATE SALTY BALLS (PS I LOVE YOU)** *Columbia 6667985* [2]	1	13
30 Sep 00		**THEME FROM SHAFT (re-recording)** *LaFace / Arista 74321792582*	53	1

[1] Isaac Hayes Movement [2] Chef

HAYSI FANTAYZEE *UK, male / female vocal duo – Jeremy Healy and Kate Garner (25 WEEKS)* pos/wks

Date		Title / Label	pos	wks
24 Jul 82		**JOHN WAYNE IS BIG LEGGY** *Regard RG 100*	11	10
13 Nov 82		**HOLY JOE** *Regard RG 104*	51	3
22 Jan 83		**SHINY SHINY** *Regard RG 106*	16	10
25 Jun 83		**SISTER FRICTION** *Regard RG 108*	62	2

Justin HAYWARD *UK, male vocalist (20 WEEKS)* pos/wks

Date		Title / Label	pos	wks
25 Oct 75	●	**BLUE GUITAR** *Threshold TH 21* [1]	8	7
8 Jul 78	●	**FOREVER AUTUMN** *CBS 6368*	5	13

[1] Justin Hayward and John Lodge

See also MOODY BLUES

Leon HAYWOOD *US, male vocalist (11 WEEKS)* pos/wks

Date		Title / Label	pos	wks
15 Mar 80		**DON'T PUSH IT, DON'T FORCE IT** *20th Century Fox TC 2443*	12	11

HAYWOODE *UK, female vocalist – Sharon Haywoode (31 WEEKS)* pos/wks

Date		Title / Label	pos	wks
17 Sep 83		**A TIME LIKE THIS** *CBS A 3651*	48	7
29 Sep 84		**I CAN'T LET YOU GO** *CBS A 4664*	63	4
13 Apr 85		**ROSES** *CBS A 6069*	65	3
5 Oct 85		**GETTING CLOSER** *CBS A 6582*	67	2
21 Jun 86		**ROSES (re-issue)** *CBS A 7224*	11	11
13 Sep 86		**I CAN'T LET YOU GO (re-issue)** *CBS 650076 7*	50	4

Ofra HAZA *Israel, female vocalist (12 WEEKS)* pos/wks

Date		Title / Label	pos	wks
30 Apr 88		**IM NIN'ALU** *WEA YZ 190*	15	8
17 Jun 95		**MY LOVE IS FOR REAL** *Virgin America VUSCD 91* [1]	28	3
3 Apr 99		**BABYLON** *Warner Esp. WESP 006CD1* [2]	65	1

[1] Paula Abdul featuring Ofra Haza [2] Black Dog featuring Ofra Haza

HAZIZA *Sweden, male production duo (1 WEEK)* pos/wks

Date		Title / Label	pos	wks
28 Apr 01		**ONE MORE** *Tidy Trax TIDY 152T*	75	1

Lee HAZLEWOOD – *See Nancy SINATRA*

Murray HEAD *UK, male vocalist (15 WEEKS)* pos/wks

Date		Title / Label	pos	wks
29 Jan 72		**SUPERSTAR** *MCA MMKS 5077*	47	1
10 Nov 84		**ONE NIGHT IN BANGKOK** *RCA CHESS 1*	12	13
16 Feb 85		**ONE NIGHT IN BANGKOK (re-entry)** *RCA CHESS 1*	74	1

'Superstar' was one of four tracks on a maxi single, two of which were credited during the disc's one week on the chart. The other track credited was 'I Don't Know How to Love Him' by Yvonne Elliman

Roy HEAD *US, male vocalist (5 WEEKS)* pos/wks

Date		Title / Label	pos	wks
4 Nov 65		**TREAT HER RIGHT** *Vocalion V-P 9248*	30	5

HEADBANGERS *UK, male vocal / instrumental group (3 WEEKS)* pos/wks

Date		Title / Label	pos	wks
10 Oct 81		**STATUS ROCK** *Magnet MAG 206*	60	3

HEADBOYS *UK, male vocal / instrumental group (8 WEEKS)* pos/wks

Date		Title / Label	pos	wks
22 Sep 79		**THE SHAPE OF THINGS TO COME** *RSO 40*	45	8

HEADGIRL – *See MOTÖRHEAD; GIRLSCHOOL*

Max HEADROOM – *See ART OF NOISE*

HEADS *UK, male instrumental group (4 WEEKS)* pos/wks

Date		Title / Label	pos	wks
21 Jun 86		**AZTEC LIGHTNING (THEME FROM BBC WORLD CUP GRANDSTAND)** *BBC RESL 184*	45	4

HEADS with Shaun RYDER *US / UK, male / female vocal / instrumental group (1 WEEK)* pos/wks

Date		Title / Label	pos	wks
9 Nov 96		**DON'T TAKE MY KINDNESS FOR WEAKNESS** *Radioactive MCSTD 48024*	60	1

Heads are Talking Heads minus lead singer David Byrne

See also TALKING HEADS

HEADSWIM *UK, male vocal / instrumental group (5 WEEKS)* pos/wks

Date		Title / Label	pos	wks
25 Feb 95		**CRAWL** *Epic 6612252*	64	1
14 Feb 98		**TOURNIQUET** *Epic 6650442*	30	3
16 May 98		**BETTER MADE** *Epic 6658402*	42	1

Jeremy HEALY and AMOS *UK, male production / vocal duo – Jeremy Healy and Amos Pizzey (7 WEEKS)* pos/wks

Date		Title / Label	pos	wks
12 Oct 96		**STAMP!** *Positiva CDTIV 65*	11	5
31 May 97		**ARGENTINA** *Positiva CDTIV 74*	30	2

Imogen HEAP – *See URBAN SPECIES*

HEAR 'N' AID *International, male / female vocal / instrumental charity assembly (6 WEEKS)* pos/wks

Date		Title / Label	pos	wks
19 Apr 86		**STARS** *Vertigo HEAR 1*	26	6

HEAR'SAY *UK, male / female vocal group from Popstars TV programme (45 WEEKS)* pos/wks

Date		Title / Label	pos	wks
24 Mar 01	★	**PURE AND SIMPLE** *Polydor 5870069* ◆ ■	1	25
7 Jul 01	★	**THE WAY TO YOUR LOVE** *Polydor 5871482* ■	1	13
13 Oct 01		**THE WAY TO YOUR LOVE (re-entry)** *Polydor 5871482*	60	4
8 Dec 01	●	**EVERYBODY** *Polydor 5705122*	4	3+

HEART (456 Top 500) *Giants of Stateside AOR, who first tasted success in Canada and are regarded as key players on the Seattle music scene. Fronted by Californian-born Wilson sisters Ann (v/g/f) b. 19 Jun 1951 and Nancy (g/v) b. 16 Mar 1954. UK chart career began a full decade after US debut (76 WEEKS)* pos/wks

Date		Title / Label	pos	wks
29 Mar 86		**THESE DREAMS** *Capitol CL 394* ▲	62	4
13 Jun 87	●	**ALONE** *Capitol CL 448* ▲	3	16
19 Sep 87		**WHO WILL YOU RUN TO** *Capitol CL 457*	30	7
12 Dec 87		**THERE'S THE GIRL** *Capitol CL 473*	34	7
5 Mar 88	●	**NEVER / THESE DREAMS (re-issue)** *Capitol CL 482*	8	9
14 May 88		**WHAT ABOUT LOVE** *Capitol CL 487*	14	6
22 Oct 88		**NOTHIN' AT ALL** *Capitol CL 507*	38	3
24 Mar 90	●	**ALL I WANNA DO IS MAKE LOVE TO YOU** *Capitol CL 569*	8	13
28 Jul 90		**I DIDN'T WANT TO NEED YOU** *Capitol CL 580*	47	3
17 Nov 90		**STRANDED** *Capitol CL 595*	60	2
14 Sep 91		**YOU'RE THE VOICE** *Capitol CLS 624*	56	2
20 Nov 93		**WILL YOU BE THERE (IN THE MORNING)** *Capitol CDCLS 700*	19	4

HEARTBEAT *UK, male / female vocal / instrumental group (5 WEEKS)* pos/wks

Date		Title / Label	pos	wks
24 Oct 87		**TEARS FROM HEAVEN** *Priority P 17*	32	4
23 Apr 88		**THE WINNER** *Priority P 19*	70	1

HEARTBEAT COUNTRY *UK, male vocalist – Bill Maynard (1 WEEK)* pos/wks

31 Dec 94	**HEARTBEAT** *MMM MMM 01CD*	**75**	1

HEARTBREAKER – *See DEMON vs HEARTBREAKER*

HEARTBREAKERS – *See Tom PETTY and the HEARTBREAKERS; Stevie NICKS*

HEARTISTS *Italy, male DJ / production trio (5 WEEKS)* pos/wks

9 Aug 97	**BELO HORIZONTI** *VC VCRD 23*	**42**	3
31 Jan 98	**BELO HORIZONTI (re-mix)** *VC VCRD 28*	**40**	2

Ted HEATH and his Music *UK, orchestra (56 WEEKS)* pos/wks

16 Jan 53	**VANESSA** *Decca F 9983*	**11**	1
3 Jul 53 ●	**HOT TODDY** *Decca F 10093*	**6**	11
23 Oct 53	**DRAGNET** *Decca F 10176*	**12**	1
27 Nov 53 ●	**DRAGNET (re-entry)** *Decca F 10176*	**9**	1
11 Dec 53	**DRAGNET (2nd re-entry)** *Decca F 10176*	**11**	1
15 Jan 54	**DRAGNET (3rd re-entry)** *Decca F 10176*	**11**	1
5 Feb 54	**DRAGNET (4th re-entry)** *Decca F 10176*	**12**	1
12 Feb 54 ●	**SKIN DEEP** *Decca F 10246*	**9**	3
6 Jul 56	**THE FAITHFUL HUSSAR** *Decca F 10746*	**18**	9
14 Mar 58 ●	**SWINGIN' SHEPHERD BLUES** *Decca F 11000*	**3**	14
11 Apr 58	**TEQUILA** *Decca F 11003*	**21**	6
4 Jul 58	**TOM HARK** *Decca F 11025*	**24**	2
5 Oct 61	**SUCU SUCU** *Decca F 11392*	**36**	4
9 Nov 61	**SUCU SUCU (re-entry)** *Decca F 11392*	**47**	1

HEATWAVE (417 Top 500) *Internationally successful UK-based soul / disco band formed Germany 1973 by brothers Johnnie and Keith Wilder (Ohio, US). Group's keyboard player and main songwriter, UK-born Rod Temperton, later penned many hits including several for Michael Jackson (80 WEEKS)* pos/wks

22 Jan 77 ●	**BOOGIE NIGHTS** *GTO GT 77*	**2**	14
7 May 77	**TOO HOT TO HANDLE / SLIP YOUR DISC TO THIS** *GTO GT 91*	**15**	11
14 Jan 78	**THE GROOVE LINE** *GTO GT 115*	**12**	8
3 Jun 78	**MIND BLOWING DECISIONS** *GTO GT 226*	**12**	11
4 Nov 78 ●	**ALWAYS AND FOREVER / MIND BLOWING DECISIONS (re-mix)** *GTO GT 236*	**9**	14
26 May 79	**RAZZLE DAZZLE** *GTO GT 248*	**43**	5
17 Jan 81	**GANGSTERS OF THE GROOVE** *GTO GT 285*	**19**	8
21 Mar 81	**JITTERBUGGIN'** *GTO GT 290*	**34**	7
1 Sep 90	**MIND BLOWING DECISIONS (re-recording)** *Brothers Organisation HW 1*	**65**	2

HEAVEN 17 (370 Top 500) *Politically astute electronic pop trio from Sheffield, UK; Martyn Ware (k), Ian Craig Marsh (k) (both previously in Human League) and Glenn Gregory (v). Act, named after a fictional band in cult film A Clockwork Orange, reunited and played first ever gigs in 1997 (87 WEEKS)* pos/wks

21 Mar 81	**(WE DON'T NEED THIS) FASCIST GROOVE THANG** *Virgin VS 400*	**45**	5
5 Sep 81	**PLAY TO WIN** *Virgin VS 433*	**46**	7
14 Nov 81	**PENTHOUSE AND PAVEMENT** *Virgin VS 455*	**57**	3
30 Oct 82	**LET ME GO** *Virgin VS 532*	**41**	6
16 Apr 83 ●	**TEMPTATION** *Virgin VS 570*	**2**	13
25 Jun 83 ●	**COME LIVE WITH ME** *Virgin VS 607*	**5**	11
10 Sep 83	**CRUSHED BY THE WHEELS OF INDUSTRY** *Virgin VS 628*	**17**	7
1 Sep 84	**SUNSET NOW** *Virgin VS 708*	**24**	6
27 Oct 84	**THIS IS MINE** *Virgin VS 722*	**23**	7
19 Jan 85	**. . . (AND THAT'S NO LIE)** *Virgin VS 740*	**52**	5
17 Jan 87	**TROUBLE** *Virgin VS 920*	**51**	3
21 Nov 92 ●	**TEMPTATION (re-mix)** *Virgin VS 1446*	**4**	11
27 Feb 93	**(WE DON'T NEED THIS) FASCIST GROOVE THANG (re-mix)** *Virgin VSCDT 1451*	**40**	2
10 Apr 93	**PENTHOUSE AND PAVEMENT (re-mix)** *Virgin VSCDT 1457*	**54**	1

Carol Kenyon is the uncredited vocalist on 'Temptation'. 'Fascist Groove Thang' in 1993 is a re-recording

HEAVENS CRY *Holland, male production duo (1 WEEK)* pos/wks

6 Oct 01	**TILL TEARS DO US PART** *Tidy Trax 158 CD*	**68**	1

HEAVY D and the BOYZ *Jamaica / US, male rap / vocal duo (28 WEEKS)* pos/wks

6 Dec 86	**MR BIG STUFF** *MCA MCA 1106*	**61**	8
15 Jul 89	**WE GOT OUR OWN THANG** *MCA MCA 23942*	**69**	2
6 Jul 91 ●	**NOW THAT WE FOUND LOVE** *MCA MCS 1550*	**2**	12
28 Sep 91	**IS IT GOOD TO YOU** *MCA MCS 1564*	**46**	3
8 Oct 94	**THIS IS YOUR NIGHT** *MCA MCSTD 2010*	**30**	3

HEAVY PETTIN' *UK, male vocal / instrumental group (2 WEEKS)* pos/wks

17 Mar 84	**LOVE TIMES LOVE** *Polydor HEP 3*	**69**	2

HEAVY STEREO *UK, male vocal / instrumental group (4 WEEKS)* pos/wks

22 Jul 95	**SLEEP FREAK** *Creation CRESCD 203*	**46**	1
28 Oct 95	**SMILER** *Creation CRESCD 213*	**46**	1
10 Feb 96	**CHINESE BURN** *Creation CRESCD 218*	**45**	1
24 Aug 96	**MOUSE IN A HOLE** *Creation CRESCD 230*	**53**	1

HEAVY WEATHER *US, male vocalist – Peter Lee (1 WEEK)* pos/wks

29 Jun 96	**LOVE CAN'T TURN AROUND** *Pukka CDPUKKA 6*	**56**	1

Bobby HEBB *US, male vocalist (15 WEEKS)* pos/wks

8 Sep 66	**SUNNY** *Philips BF 1503*	**12**	9
19 Aug 72	**LOVE LOVE LOVE** *Philips 6051 023*	**32**	6

HED BOYS *UK, male instrumental / production duo (6 WEEKS)* pos/wks

6 Aug 94	**GIRLS + BOYS** *Deconstruction 74321223322*	**21**	4
4 Nov 95	**GIRLS + BOYS (re-mix)** *Deconstruction 74321322032*	**36**	2

See also Joey NEGRO; JAKATTA; Li KWAN; RAVEN MAIZE; AKABU featuring Linda CLIFFORD

HEDGEHOPPERS ANONYMOUS *UK, male vocal / instrumental group (12 WEEKS)* pos/wks

30 Sep 65 ●	**IT'S GOOD NEWS WEEK** *Decca F 12241*	**5**	12

HEFNER *UK, male vocal / instrumental group (3 WEEKS)* pos/wks

26 Aug 00	**GOOD FRUIT** *Too Pure PURE 108CDS*	**50**	1
14 Oct 00	**THE GREEDY UGLY PEOPLE** *Too Pure PURE 111CDS*	**64**	1
8 Sep 01	**ALAN BEAN** *Too Pure PURE 118CDS*	**58**	1

Neal HEFTI *US, male orchestra (4 WEEKS)* pos/wks

9 Apr 88	**BATMAN THEME** *RCA PB 49571*	**55**	4

Den HEGARTY *UK, male vocalist (2 WEEKS)* pos/wks

31 Mar 79	**VOODOO VOODOO** *Magnet MAG 143*	**73**	2

See also DARTS

Anita HEGERLAND – *See Mike OLDFIELD*

HEINZ *UK, male vocalist – Heinz Burt (35 WEEKS)* pos/wks

8 Aug 63 ●	**JUST LIKE EDDIE** *Decca F 11693*	**5**	15
28 Nov 63	**COUNTRY BOY** *Decca F 11768*	**26**	9
27 Feb 64	**YOU WERE THERE** *Decca F 11831*	**26**	8
15 Oct 64	**QUESTIONS I CAN'T ANSWER** *Columbia DB 7374*	**39**	2
18 Mar 65	**DIGGIN' MY POTATOES** *Columbia DB 7482* [1]	**49**	1

[1] Heinz and the Wild Boys

HELICOPTER *UK, male instrumental / production duo – Dylan Barnes and Rob Davy (4 WEEKS)* pos/wks

27 Aug 94	**ON YA WAY** *Helicopter TIG 007CD*	**32**	2
22 Jun 96	**ON YA WAY (re-mix)** *Systematic SYSCD 27*	**37**	2

See also MUTINY UK

HELIOCENTRIC WORLD *UK, male / female vocal / instrumental group (2 WEEKS)* pos/wks

14 Jan 95	**WHERE'S YOUR LOVE BEEN** *Talkin Loud TLKCD 51*	**71**	2

HELIOTROPIC featuring Verna V *UK, male production duo (2 WEEKS)*

Date	Title / Label	pos	wks
16 Oct 99	**ALIVE** *Multiply CDMULTY 52*	33	2

Pete HELLER *UK, male DJ / producer (7 WEEKS)*

Date	Title / Label	pos	wks
15 May 99	**BIG LOVE** *Essential Recordings ESCD 4*	12	7

HELLER & FARLEY PROJECT *UK, male instrumental / production duo – Pete Heller and Terry Farley (7 WEEKS)*

Date	Title / Label	pos	wks
24 Feb 96	**ULTRA FLAVA** *AM:PM 5814372*	22	3
28 Dec 96	**ULTRA FLAVA (re-mix)** *AM:PM 5820552*	32	4

See also FIRE ISLAND; Pete HELLER; STYLUS TROUBLE

HELLO *UK, male vocal / instrumental group (21 WEEKS)*

Date	Title / Label	pos	wks
9 Nov 74 ●	**TELL HIM** *Bell 1377*	6	12
18 Oct 75 ●	**NEW YORK GROOVE** *Bell 1438*	9	9

HELLOWEEN *US, male vocal / instrumental group (7 WEEKS)*

Date	Title / Label	pos	wks
27 Aug 88	**DR STEIN** *Noise International 7HELLO 1*	57	3
12 Nov 88	**I WANT OUT** *Noise International 7HELLO 2*	69	2
2 Mar 91	**KIDS OF THE CENTURY** *EMI EM 178*	56	2

Bobby HELMS *US, male vocalist (7 WEEKS)*

Date	Title / Label	pos	wks
29 Nov 57	**MY SPECIAL ANGEL** *Brunswick 05721* [1]	22	3
21 Feb 58	**NO OTHER BABY** *Brunswick 05730*	30	1
1 Aug 58	**JACQUELINE** *Brunswick 05748* [1]	20	3

[1] Bobby Helms with the Anita Kerr Singers

Jimmy HELMS *US, male vocalist (10 WEEKS)*

Date	Title / Label	pos	wks
24 Feb 73 ●	**GONNA MAKE YOU AN OFFER YOU CAN'T REFUSE** *Cube BUG 27*	8	10

HELTAH SKELTAH and ORIGINOO GUNN CLAPPAZ as the FABULOUS FIVE *US, male rap / vocal / production group (1 WEEK)*

Date	Title / Label	pos	wks
1 Jun 96	**BLAH** *Priority PTYCD 117*	60	1

Eddie HENDERSON *US, male instrumentalist – trumpet (6 WEEKS)*

Date	Title / Label	pos	wks
28 Oct 78	**PRANCE ON** *Capitol CL 16015*	44	6

Joe 'Mr Piano' HENDERSON *UK, male instrumentalist – piano (23 WEEKS)*

Date	Title / Label	pos	wks
3 Jun 55	**SING IT WITH JOE** *Polygon P 1167*	14	4
2 Sep 55	**SING IT AGAIN WITH JOE** *Polygon P 1184*	18	3
25 Jul 58	**TRUDIE** *Pye Nixa N 15147*	14	12
24 Oct 58	**TRUDIE (re-entry)** *Pye Nixa N 15147*	23	2
23 Oct 59	**TREBLE CHANCE** *Pye 7N 15224*	28	1
24 Mar 60	**OOH! LA! LA!** *Pye 7N 15257*	46	1

First two hits are medleys as follows: Sing It with Joe: Margie / I'm Nobody's Sweetheart / Somebody Stole My Gal / Moonlight Bay / By the Light of the Silvery Moon / Cuddle Up a Little Closer. Sing It Again With Joe: Put Your Arms Around Me Honey / Ain't She Sweet / When You're Smiling / Shine on Harvest Moon / My Blue Heaven / Show Me the Way to Go Home

Wayne HENDERSON – *See Roy AYERS*

Billy HENDRIX *Germany, male producer – Sharam Jey (2 WEEKS)*

Date	Title / Label	pos	wks
12 Sep 98	**THE BODY SHINE (EP)** *Hooj Choons HOOJ 65CD*	55	2

Tracks on The Body Shine (EP): The Body Shine / Funky Shine / Colour Systems Inc's Amber Dub / Timewriter re-mix

Jimi HENDRIX EXPERIENCE (361 Top 500) *Guitar ace and hugely influential 20th-century icon, b. Johnny Allen Hendrix, 27 Nov 1942, Seattle, US, renamed James Marshall Hendrix, d. 18 Sep 1970, London. After being 'discovered' and then managed by Animals' bassist Chas Chandler, the left-handed guitarist and vocalist formed The Jimi Hendrix Experience, featuring Mitch Mitchell (d) and Noel Redding (b). His timeless appeal consistently generates annual global album sales of around three million (88 WEEKS)*

Date	Title / Label	pos	wks
29 Dec 66 ●	**HEY JOE** *Polydor 56 139*	6	11
23 Mar 67 ●	**PURPLE HAZE** *Track 604 001*	3	14
11 May 67 ●	**THE WIND CRIES MARY** *Track 604 004*	6	11
30 Aug 67	**BURNING OF THE MIDNIGHT LAMP** *Track 604 007*	18	9
23 Oct 68 ●	**ALL ALONG THE WATCHTOWER** *Track 604 025*	5	11
16 Apr 69	**CROSSTOWN TRAFFIC** *Track 604 029*	37	3
7 Nov 70 ★	**VOODOO CHILE** *Track 2095 001*	1	13
30 Oct 71	**GYPSY EYES / REMEMBER** *Track 2094 010*	35	5
12 Feb 72	**JOHNNY B GOODE** *Polydor 2001 277* [1]	35	5
21 Apr 90	**CROSSTOWN TRAFFIC (re-issue)** *Polydor PO 71* [1]	61	3
20 Oct 90	**ALL ALONG THE WATCHTOWER (EP)** *Polydor PO 100* [1]	52	3

[1] Jimi Hendrix

Tracks on All Along the Watchtower (EP): All Along the Watchtower / Voodoo Chile / Hey Joe (re-issues)

Nona HENDRYX *US, female vocalist (2 WEEKS)*

Date	Title / Label	pos	wks
16 May 87	**WHY SHOULD I CRY** *EMI America EA 234*	60	2

Don HENLEY *US, male vocalist (30 WEEKS)*

Date	Title / Label	pos	wks
12 Feb 83	**DIRTY LAUNDRY** *Asylum E 9894*	59	3
9 Feb 85	**THE BOYS OF SUMMER** *Geffen A 4945*	12	10
29 Jul 89	**THE END OF THE INNOCENCE** *Geffen GEF 57*	48	5
3 Oct 92	**SOMETIMES LOVE JUST AIN'T ENOUGH** *MCA MCS 1692* [1]	22	6
18 Jul 98	**BOYS OF SUMMER (re-issue)** *Geffen GFSTD 22350*	12	6

[1] Patty Smyth with Don Henley

See also EAGLES

Clarence 'Frogman' HENRY *US, male vocalist (35 WEEKS)*

Date	Title / Label	pos	wks
4 May 61 ●	**BUT I DO** *Pye International 7N 25078*	3	19
13 Jul 61 ●	**YOU ALWAYS HURT THE ONE YOU LOVE** *Pye International 7N 25089*	6	12
21 Sep 61	**LONELY STREET / WHY CAN'T YOU** *Pye International 7N 25108*	42	2
17 Jul 93	**(I DON'T KNOW WHY) BUT I DO (re-issue)** *MCA MCSTD 1797*	65	2

Kevin HENRY – *See LA MIX*

Paul HENRY and the Mayson GLEN ORCHESTRA *UK, male vocalist / orchestra (2 WEEKS)*

Date	Title / Label	pos	wks
14 Jan 78	**BENNY'S THEME** *Pye 7N 46027*	39	2

Pauline HENRY *UK, female vocalist (21 WEEKS)*

Date	Title / Label	pos	wks
18 Sep 93	**TOO MANY PEOPLE** *Sony S2 6595942*	38	2
6 Nov 93	**FEEL LIKE MAKING LOVE** *Sony S2 6597972*	12	7
29 Jan 94	**CAN'T TAKE YOUR LOVE** *Sony S2 6599902*	30	3
21 May 94	**WATCH THE MIRACLE START** *Sony S2 6602772*	54	1
30 Sep 95	**SUGAR FREE** *Sony S2 6624362*	57	2
23 Dec 95	**LOVE HANGOVER** *Sony S2 6626132*	37	3
24 Feb 96	**NEVER KNEW LOVE LIKE THIS** *Sony S2 6629382* [1]	40	2
1 Jun 96	**HAPPY** *Sony S2 6630692*	46	1

[1] Pauline Henry featuring Wayne Marshall

Pierre HENRY *France, male instrumentalist (1 WEEK)*

Date	Title / Label	pos	wks
4 Oct 97	**PSYCHE ROCK** *Hi-Life 4620312*	58	1

HEPBURN *UK, female vocal / instrumental group (15 WEEKS)*

Date	Title / Label	pos	wks
29 May 99 ●	**I QUIT** *Columbia 6674012*	8	7
28 Aug 99	**BUGS** *Columbia 6677382*	14	5
19 Feb 00	**DEEP DEEP DOWN** *Columbia 6683382*	16	3

HERD *UK, male vocal / instrumental group (35 WEEKS)*

Date	Title / Label	pos	wks
13 Sep 67 ●	**FROM THE UNDERWORLD** *Fontana TF 856*	6	13
20 Dec 67	**PARADISE LOST** *Fontana TF 887*	15	9
10 Apr 68 ●	**I DON'T WANT OUR LOVING TO DIE** *Fontana TF 925*	5	13

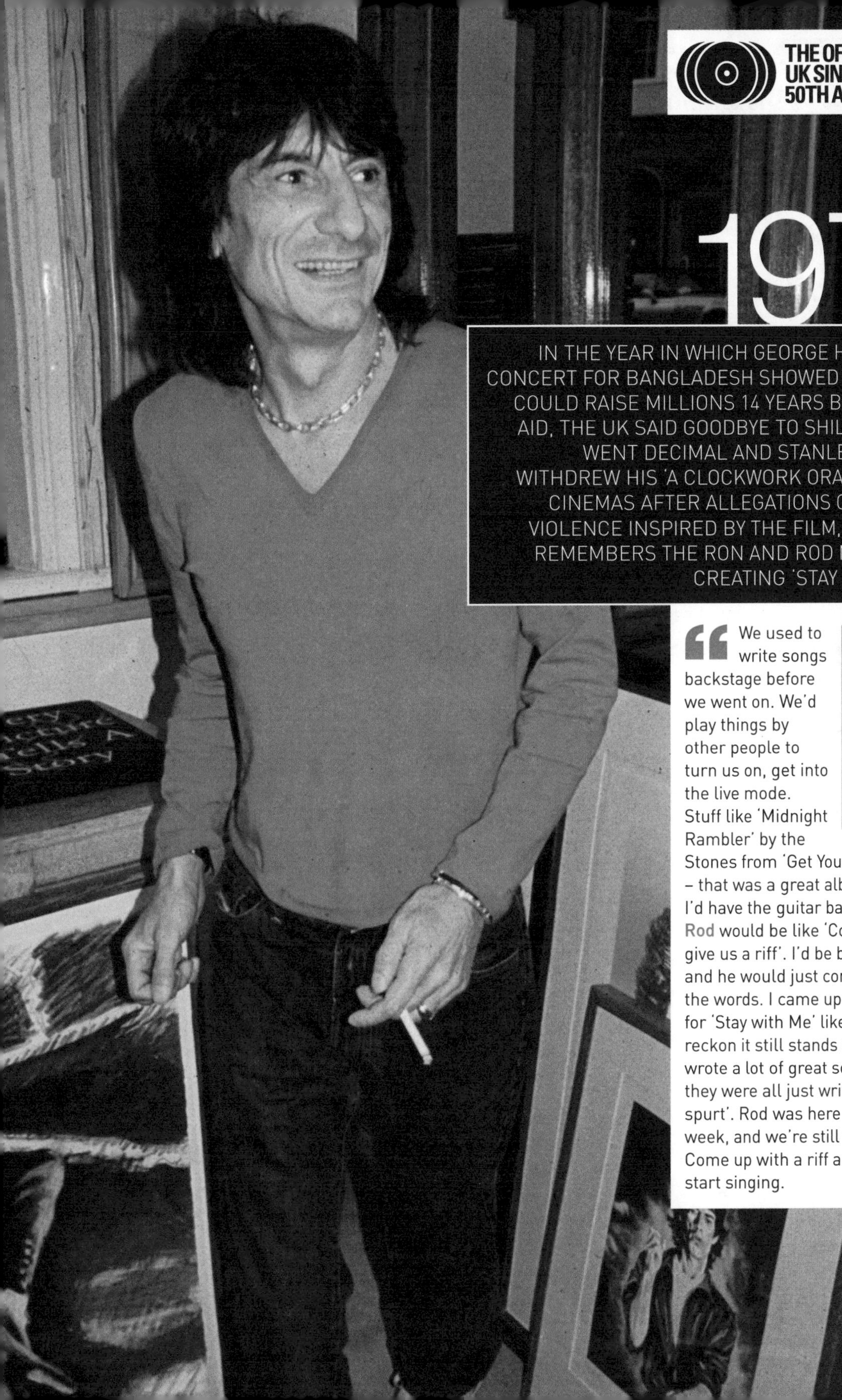

1971

IN THE YEAR IN WHICH GEORGE HARRISON'S CONCERT FOR BANGLADESH SHOWED THAT ROCK COULD RAISE MILLIONS 14 YEARS BEFORE LIVE AID, THE UK SAID GOODBYE TO SHILLINGS AND WENT DECIMAL AND STANLEY KUBRICK WITHDREW HIS 'A CLOCKWORK ORANGE' FROM CINEMAS AFTER ALLEGATIONS OF COPYCAT VIOLENCE INSPIRED BY THE FILM, **RON WOOD** REMEMBERS THE RON AND ROD METHOD OF CREATING 'STAY WITH ME' ...

"We used to write songs backstage before we went on. We'd play things by other people to turn us on, get into the live mode. Stuff like 'Midnight Rambler' by the Stones from 'Get Your Ya-Ya's Out!' – that was a great album! Anyway, I'd have the guitar back there and **Rod** would be like 'Come on, Ron, give us a riff'. I'd be banging away, and he would just come out with the words. I came up with the riff for 'Stay with Me' like that, and I reckon it still stands up today. We wrote a lot of great songs that way: they were all just written 'on the spurt'. Rod was here the other week, and we're still the same. Come up with a riff and he'll start singing."

SINGLE OF THE YEAR 'Hot Love' T. Rex
ALBUM OF THE YEAR 'Bridge Over Troubled Water' Simon and Garfunkel

HERMAN'S HERMITS (78 Top 500) *Manchester quintet fronted by teenage vocalist Peter Noone, b. 5 Nov 1947, whose US popularity in the mid-1960s rivalled The Beatles. This band sold more than 40 million records and at times had three singles simultaneously in the US Top 20 (211 WEEKS)*

			pos	wks
20 Aug 64	★	**I'M INTO SOMETHING GOOD** *Columbia DB 7338*	1	15
19 Nov 64		**SHOW ME GIRL** *Columbia DB 7408*	19	9
18 Feb 65	●	**SILHOUETTES** *Columbia DB 7475*	3	12
29 Apr 65	●	**WONDERFUL WORLD** *Columbia DB 7546*	7	9
2 Sep 65		**JUST A LITTLE BIT BETTER** *Columbia DB 7670*	15	9
23 Dec 65	●	**A MUST TO AVOID** *Columbia DB 7791*	6	11
24 Mar 66		**YOU WON'T BE LEAVING** *Columbia DB 7861*	20	7
23 Jun 66		**THIS DOOR SWINGS BOTH WAYS** *Columbia DB 7947*	18	7
6 Oct 66	●	**NO MILK TODAY** *Columbia DB 8012*	7	11
1 Dec 66		**EAST WEST** *Columbia DB 8076*	37	7
9 Feb 67	●	**THERE'S A KIND OF HUSH** *Columbia DB 8123*	7	11
17 Jan 68		**I CAN TAKE OR LEAVE YOUR LOVING** *Columbia DB 8327*	11	9
1 May 68		**SLEEPY JOE** *Columbia DB 8404*	12	10
17 Jul 68	●	**SUNSHINE GIRL** *Columbia DB 8446*	8	14
18 Dec 68	●	**SOMETHING'S HAPPENING** *Columbia DB 8504*	6	15
23 Apr 69	●	**MY SENTIMENTAL FRIEND** *Columbia DB 8563*	2	12
8 Nov 69		**HERE COMES THE STAR** *Columbia DB 8626*	33	9
7 Feb 70	●	**YEARS MAY COME, YEARS MAY GO** *Columbia DB 8656*	7	11
2 May 70		**YEARS MAY COME, YEARS MAY GO (re-entry)** *Columbia DB 8656*	45	1
23 May 70		**BET YER LIFE I DO** *RAK 102*	22	10
14 Nov 70		**LADY BARBARA** *RAK 106* [1]	13	12

[1] Peter Noone and Herman's Hermits

See also Peter NOONE

HERMES HOUSE BAND
Holland, male / female vocal / instrumental group (3 WEEKS)

			pos	wks
15 Dec 01	●	**COUNTRY ROADS** *EMI / Liberty CDHHB 001*	7	3+

HERNANDEZ *UK, male vocalist (3 WEEKS)*

			pos	wks
15 Apr 89		**ALL MY LOVE** *Epic HER 1*	58	3

Patrick HERNANDEZ *Guadeloupe, male vocalist (14 WEEKS)*

			pos	wks
16 Jun 79	●	**BORN TO BE ALIVE** *Gem GEM 4*	10	14

HERREYS *Sweden, male vocal group (3 WEEKS)*

			pos	wks
26 May 84		**DIGGI LOO-DIGGI LEY** *Panther PAN 5*	46	3

Kristin HERSH *US, female vocalist (3 WEEKS)*

			pos	wks
22 Jan 94		**YOUR GHOST** *4AD BAD 4001CD*	45	2
16 Apr 94		**STRINGS** *4AD BAD 4006CD*	60	1

Nick HEYWARD *UK, male vocalist (65 WEEKS)*

			pos	wks
19 Mar 83		**WHISTLE DOWN THE WIND** *Arista HEY 1*	13	8
4 Jun 83		**TAKE THAT SITUATION** *Arista HEY 2*	11	10
24 Sep 83		**BLUE HAT FOR A BLUE DAY** *Arista HEY 3*	14	8
3 Dec 83		**ON A SUNDAY** *Arista HEY 4*	52	5
2 Jun 84		**LOVE ALL DAY** *Arista HEY 5*	31	6
3 Nov 84		**WARNING SIGN** *Arista HEY 6*	25	8
5 Jan 85		**WARNING SIGN (re-entry)** *Arista HEY 6*	72	1
8 Jun 85		**LAURA** *Arista HEY 8*	45	4
10 May 86		**OVER THE WEEKEND** *Arista HEY 9*	43	5
10 Sep 88		**YOU'RE MY WORLD** *Warner Bros. W 7758*	67	2
21 Aug 93		**KITE** *Epic 6594882*	44	2
16 Oct 93		**HE DOESN'T LOVE YOU LIKE I DO** *Epic 6597282*	58	2
30 Sep 95		**THE WORLD** *Epic 6623845*	47	2
13 Jan 96		**ROLLERBLADE** *Epic 6627912*	37	2

See also HAIRCUT 100

HHC *UK, male DJ / production duo (1 WEEK)*

			pos	wks
19 Apr 97		**WE'RE NOT ALONE** *Perfecto PERF 138CD*	44	1

HI-FIVE *US, male vocal group (8 WEEKS)*

			pos	wks
1 Jun 91		**I LIKE THE WAY (THE KISSING GAME)** *Jive JIVE 271* ▲	43	6
24 Oct 92		**SHE'S PLAYING HARD TO GET** *Jive JIVE 316*	55	2

HI-GATE *UK, male production duo – Julius (Judge Jules) O'Riordan and Paul Masterson and female vocalist (14 WEEKS)*

			pos	wks
29 Jan 00	●	**PITCHIN' (IN EVERY DIRECTION)** *Incentice CENT 3CD*	6	6
26 Aug 00		**I CAN HEAR VOICES / CANED AND UNABLE** *Incentive CENT 9 CDS*	12	5
7 Apr 01		**GONNA WORK IT OUT** *Incentive CENT 20CDS*	25	3

See also YOMANDA; CANDY GIRLS; SLEAZESISTERS

HI GLOSS *US, disco aggregation (13 WEEKS)*

			pos	wks
8 Aug 81		**YOU'LL NEVER KNOW** *Epic EPC A 1387*	12	13

HI-LUX *UK, male instrumental / production duo (3 WEEKS)*

			pos	wks
18 Feb 95		**FEEL IT** *Cheeky CHEKCD 006*	41	2
2 Sep 95		**NEVER FELT THIS WAY / FEEL IT (re-issue)** *Champion CHAMPCD 319*	58	1

HI POWER *Germany, male rap group (1 WEEK)*

			pos	wks
1 Sep 90		**CULT OF SNAP / SIMBA GROOVE** *Rumour RUMAT 24*	73	1

HI-TEK featuring JONELL *US, male producer – Tony Cottrell (1 WEEK)*

			pos	wks
20 Oct 01		**ROUND & ROUND** *Rawkus RWK 3432*	73	1

HI-TEK 3 featuring YA KID K
Belgium, male / female vocal / instrumental group (10 WEEKS)

			pos	wks
3 Feb 90		**SPIN THAT WHEEL** *Brothers Organisation BORG 1*	69	3
29 Sep 90		**SPIN THAT WHEEL (TURTLES GET REAL) (re-issue)** *Brothers Organisation BORG 16*	15	7

See also TECHNOTRONIC

HI TENSION *UK, male vocal / instrumental group (23 WEEKS)*

			pos	wks
6 May 78		**HI TENSION** *Island WIP 6422*	13	12
12 Aug 78	●	**BRITISH HUSTLE / PEACE ON EARTH** *Island WIP 6446*	8	11

'Peace on Earth' credited with 'British Hustle' from 2 Sep 1978 to end of record's chart run

Al HIBBLER *US, male vocalist (17 WEEKS)*

			pos	wks
13 May 55	●	**UNCHAINED MELODY** *Brunswick 05420*	2	17

Hinda HICKS *UK, female vocalist (15 WEEKS)*

			pos	wks
7 Mar 98		**IF YOU WANT ME** *Island CID 689*	25	3
16 May 98		**YOU THINK YOU OWN ME** *Island CID 700*	19	4
15 Aug 98		**I WANNA BE YOUR LADY** *Island CID 709*	14	5
24 Oct 98		**TRULY** *Island CID 721*	31	2
14 Oct 00		**MY REMEDY** *Island CID 765*	61	1

Bertie HIGGINS *US, male vocalist (4 WEEKS)*

			pos	wks
5 Jun 82		**KEY LARGO** *Epic EPC A 2168*	60	4

HIGH *UK, male vocal group (11 WEEKS)*

			pos	wks
25 Aug 90		**UP AND DOWN** *London LON 272*	53	4
27 Oct 90		**TAKE YOUR TIME** *London LON 280*	56	2
12 Jan 91		**BOX SET GO** *London LONG 286*	28	3
6 Apr 91		**MORE . . .** *London LON 297*	67	2

HIGH FIDELITY *UK, male vocal / instrumental group (1 WEEK)*

			pos	wks
25 Jul 98		**LUV DUP** *Plastique FAKE 03CDS*	70	1

HIGH NUMBERS *UK, male vocal / instrumental group (4 WEEKS)*

			pos	wks
5 Apr 80		**I'M THE FACE** *Back Door DOOR 4*	49	4

The High Numbers were an early version of the Who

HIGH SOCIETY *UK, male vocal / instrumental group (4 WEEKS)* pos/wks

15 Nov 80 I NEVER GO OUT IN THE RAIN *Eagle ERS 002* 53 4

HIGHLY LIKELY *UK, male vocal / instrumental group (4 WEEKS)* pos/wks

21 Apr 73 WHATEVER HAPPENED TO YOU ('LIKELY LADS' THEME) *BBC RESL 10* 35 4

HIGHWAYMEN *US, male vocal group (18 WEEKS)* pos/wks

7 Sep 61 ★ MICHAEL *HMV POP 910* ▲ 1 14
7 Dec 61 THE GYPSY ROVER *HMV POP 948* 41 3
11 Jan 62 THE GYPSY ROVER (re-entry) *HMV POP 948* 43 1

HIJACK *UK, male rap group (3 WEEKS)* pos/wks

6 Jan 90 THE BADMAN IS ROBBIN' *Rhyme Syndicate 655517 7* 56 3

Benny HILL *UK, male comedian / vocalist (43 WEEKS)* pos/wks

16 Feb 61 GATHER IN THE MUSHROOMS *Pye 7N 15327* 12 8
1 Jun 61 TRANSISTOR RADIO *Pye 7N 15359* 24 6
16 May 63 HARVEST OF LOVE *Pye 7N 15520* 20 8
13 Nov 71 ★ ERNIE (THE FASTEST MILKMAN IN THE WEST) *Columbia DB 8833* 1 17
30 May 92 ERNIE (THE FASTEST MILKMAN IN THE WEST) (re-issue) *EMI ERN 1* 29 4

Chris HILL *UK, male vocalist / DJ / producer (14 WEEKS)* pos/wks

6 Dec 75 ● RENTA SANTA *Philips 6006 491* 10 7
4 Dec 76 ● BIONIC SANTA *Philips 6006 551* 10 7

Dan HILL *Canada, male vocalist (13 WEEKS)* pos/wks

18 Feb 78 SOMETIMES WHEN WE TOUCH *20th Century BTC 2355* 46 1
4 Mar 78 SOMETIMES WHEN WE TOUCH (re-entry) *20th Century BTC 2355* 13 12

Faith HILL *US, female vocalist (32 WEEKS)* pos/wks

14 Nov 98 THIS KISS *Warner Brothers W463CD* 13 11
17 Apr 99 LET ME LET GO *Warner Bros. W473CD* 72 1
20 May 00 BREATHE *WEA WEA 520CD* 33 2
21 Apr 01 THE WAY YOU LOVE ME *Warner Brothers W51CD* 15 5
30 Jun 01 ● THERE YOU'LL BE *Warner Brothers W 563CD* 3 11
13 Oct 01 BREATHE (re-mix) *Warner Brothers W 572CD* 36 2

Lauryn HILL *US, female vocalist (35 WEEKS)* pos/wks

6 Sep 97 THE SWEETEST THING *Columbia 6649785* [1] 18 4
27 Dec 97 ALL MY TIME *World Entertainment OWECD 2* 57 1
3 Oct 98 ● DOO WOP (THAT THING) *Ruffhouse 6665152* ▲ 3 7
27 Feb 99 ● EX-FACTOR *Columbia / Ruffhouse 6669452* 4 9
22 May 99 EX-FACTOR (re-entry) *Columbia / Ruffhouse 6669452* 67 1
10 Jul 99 EVERYTHING IS EVERYTHING *Columbia / Ruffhouse 6675742* 19 6
11 Dec 99 TURN YOUR LIGHTS DOWN LOW *Columbia 6684362* [2] 15 7

[1] Refugee Camp Allstars featuring Lauryn Hill [2] Bob Marley featuring Lauryn Hill

See also FUGEES

Lonnie HILL *US, male vocalist (4 WEEKS)* pos/wks

22 Mar 86 GALVESTON BAY *10 TEN 111* 51 4

Roni HILL *US, female vocalist (4 WEEKS)* pos/wks

7 May 77 YOU KEEP ME HANGIN' ON - STOP IN THE NAME OF LOVE *(MEDLEY) Creole CR 138* 36 4

Vince HILL (346 Top 500) *Easy listening balladeer, b. 16 Apr 1937, Coventry, UK. Member of critically acclaimed Raindrops (with Jackie Lee and composer Johnny Worth) and regularly heard on 'live' radio before starting 60s chart run (91 WEEKS)* pos/wks

7 Jun 62 THE RIVER'S RUN DRY *Piccadilly 7N 35043* 49 1
28 Jun 62 THE RIVER'S RUN DRY (re-entry) *Piccadilly 7N 35043* 41 1
6 Jan 66 TAKE ME TO YOUR HEART AGAIN *Columbia DB 7781* 13 11
17 Mar 66 HEARTACHES *Columbia DB 7852* 28 5
2 Jun 66 MERCI CHERI *Columbia DB 7924* 36 6
9 Feb 67 ● EDELWEISS *Columbia DB 8127* 2 17
11 May 67 ROSES OF PICARDY *Columbia DB 8185* 13 11
27 Sep 67 LOVE LETTERS IN THE SAND *Columbia DB 8268* 23 9
26 Jun 68 THE IMPORTANCE OF YOUR LOVE *Columbia DB 8414* 32 12
12 Feb 69 DOESN'T ANYBODY KNOW MY NAME? *Columbia DB 8515* 50 1
25 Oct 69 LITTLE BLUE BIRD *Columbia DB 8616* 42 1
25 Sep 71 LOOK AROUND (AND YOU'LL FIND ME THERE) *Columbia DB 8804* 12 16

HILLMAN MINX

UK / France, male / female vocal / instrumental group (1 WEEK) pos/wks

5 Sep 98 I'VE HAD ENOUGH *Mercury MERCD 509* 72 1

HILLTOPPERS *US, male vocal group (30 WEEKS)* pos/wks

27 Jan 56 ● ONLY YOU (AND YOU ALONE) *London HLD 8221* 3 22
10 Aug 56 ONLY YOU (AND YOU ALONE) (re-entry) *London HLD 8221* 24 1
14 Sep 56 TRYIN' *London HLD 8298* 30 1
5 Apr 57 MARIANNE *London HLD 8381* 20 2
26 Apr 57 MARIANNE (re-entry) *London HLD 8381* 23 4

Ronnie HILTON (183 Top 500) *Favourite 1950s balladeer, b. Adrian Hill, 26 Jan 1926, Hull, UK, d. 21 Feb 2001. Despite the rise of rock 'n' roll, he amassed a formidable selection of best-sellers, albeit mainly with cover versions (the customary UK practice in the 1950s) (136 WEEKS)* pos/wks

26 Nov 54 ● I STILL BELIEVE *HMV B 10785* 3 14
10 Dec 54 VENI VIDI VICI *HMV B 10785* 12 8
11 Mar 55 ● A BLOSSOM FELL *HMV B 10808* 10 5
26 Aug 55 STARS SHINE IN YOUR EYES *HMV B 10901* 13 7
11 Nov 55 THE YELLOW ROSE OF TEXAS *HMV B 10924* 15 2
10 Feb 56 YOUNG AND FOOLISH *HMV POP 154* 17 1
24 Feb 56 YOUNG AND FOOLISH (re-entry) *HMV POP 154* 20 1
9 Mar 56 YOUNG AND FOOLISH (2nd re-entry) *HMV POP 154* 19 1
20 Apr 56 ★ NO OTHER LOVE *HMV POP 198* 1 14
29 Jun 56 ● WHO ARE WE *HMV POP 221* 6 12
21 Sep 56 A WOMAN IN LOVE *HMV POP 248* 30 1
9 Nov 56 TWO DIFFERENT WORLDS *HMV POP 274* 13 13
24 May 57 ● AROUND THE WORLD *HMV POP 338* 4 18
2 Aug 57 WONDERFUL! WONDERFUL! *HMV POP 364* 27 2
21 Feb 58 MAGIC MOMENTS *HMV POP 446* 22 2
18 Apr 58 I MAY NEVER PASS THIS WAY AGAIN *HMV POP 468* [1] 30 1
2 May 58 I MAY NEVER PASS THIS WAY AGAIN (re-entry) *HMV POP 468* [1] 30 1
6 Jun 58 I MAY NEVER PASS THIS WAY AGAIN (2nd re-entry) *HMV POP 468* [1] 27 1
9 Jan 59 THE WORLD OUTSIDE *HMV POP 559* [1] 18 6
21 Aug 59 THE WONDER OF YOU *HMV POP 638* 22 3
21 May 64 DON'T LET THE RAIN COME DOWN *HMV POP 1291* 21 10
11 Feb 65 A WINDMILL IN OLD AMSTERDAM *HMV POP 1378* 23 13

[1] Ronnie Hilton with the Michael Sammes Singers

HINDSIGHT *UK, male vocal / instrumental group (3 WEEKS)* pos/wks

5 Sep 87 LOWDOWN *Circa YR 5* 62 3

Deni HINES *Australia, female vocalist (6 WEEKS)* pos/wks

14 Jun 97 IT'S ALRIGHT *Mushroom D 1593* 35 2
20 Sep 97 I LIKE THE WAY *Mushroom MUSH 7CDX* 37 2
28 Feb 98 DELICIOUS *Mushroom MUSH 20CD* [1] 52 1
23 May 98 JOY *Mushroom MUSH 30CDS* 47 1

[1] Deni Hines featuring Don-E

Gregory HINES – *See Luther VANDROSS*

HIPSWAY *UK, male vocal / instrumental group (21 WEEKS)* pos/wks

13 Jul 85 THE BROKEN YEARS *Mercury MER 193* 72 3
14 Sep 85 ASK THE LORD *Mercury MER 195* 72 1
22 Feb 86 THE HONEYTHIEF *Mercury MER 212* 17 9
10 May 86 ASK THE LORD (re-recording) *Mercury LORD 1* 50 5

			pos	wks
20 Sep 86		**LONG WHITE CAR** *Mercury MER 230*	55	2
1 Apr 89		**YOUR LOVE** *Mercury MER 279*	66	1

HISTORY featuring Q-TEE
UK, male production duo and female rapper (2 WEEKS)

			pos	wks
21 Apr 90		**AFRIKA** *SBK SBK 7008*	42	5

AFRIKA – *See Q.TEE*

Carol HITCHCOCK *Australia, female vocalist (5 WEEKS)*

			pos	wks
30 May 87		**GET READY** *A & M AM 391*	56	5

HITHOUSE *Holland, male producer – Peter Slaghuis (13 WEEKS)*

			pos	wks
5 Nov 88		**JACK TO THE SOUND OF THE UNDERGROUND** *Supreme SUPE 137*	14	12
19 Aug 89		**MOVE YOUR FEET TO THE RHYTHM OF THE BEAT** *Supreme SUPE 149*	69	1

HITMAN HOWIE TEE – *See REAL ROXANNE*

Helen HOBSON – *See Cliff RICHARD*

Edmund HOCKRIDGE *Canada, male vocalist (18 WEEKS)*

			pos	wks
17 Feb 56	●	**YOUNG AND FOOLISH** *Nixa N 15039*	10	7
13 Apr 56		**YOUNG AND FOOLISH (re-entry)** *Nixa N 15039*	28	1
4 May 56		**YOUNG AND FOOLISH (2nd re-entry)** *Nixa N 15039*	26	1
11 May 56		**NO OTHER LOVE** *Nixa N 15048*	24	2
1 Jun 56		**NO OTHER LOVE (re-entry)** *Nixa N 15048*	29	1
15 Jun 56		**NO OTHER LOVE (2nd re-entry)** *Nixa N 15048*	30	1
31 Aug 56		**BY THE FOUNTAINS OF ROME** *Pye Nixa N 15063*	17	5

Eddie HODGES *US, male vocalist (10 WEEKS)*

			pos	wks
28 Sep 61		**I'M GONNA KNOCK ON YOUR DOOR** *London HLA 9369*	37	6
9 Aug 62		**(GIRLS GIRLS GIRLS) MADE TO LOVE** *London HLA 9576*	37	4

Roger HODGSON – *See SUPERTRAMP*

Susanna HOFFS *US, female vocalist (8 WEEKS)*

			pos	wks
2 Mar 91		**MY SIDE OF THE BED** *Columbia 6565547*	44	4
11 May 91		**UNCONDITIONAL LOVE** *Columbia 6567827*	65	2
19 Oct 96		**ALL I WANT** *London LONCD 387*	32	2

See also BANGLES

Hulk HOGAN with GREEN JELLY *US, male wrestler / vocalist and US, male vocal / instrumental group (4 WEEKS)*

			pos	wks
25 Dec 93		**I'M THE LEADER OF THE GANG** *Arista 74321174892* [1]	25	4

HOLE *US, female / male vocal / instrumental group (15 WEEKS)*

			pos	wks
17 Apr 93		**BEAUTIFUL SON** *City Slang EFA 0491603*	54	1
9 Apr 94		**MISS WORLD** *City Slang EFA 049362*	64	1
15 Apr 95		**DOLL PARTS** *Geffen GFSTD 91*	16	3
29 Jul 95		**VIOLET** *Geffen GFSTD 94*	17	2
12 Sep 98		**CELEBRITY SKIN** *Geffen GFSTD 22345*	19	4
30 Jan 99		**MALIBU** *Geffen GFSTD 22369*	22	2
10 Jul 99		**AWFUL** *Geffen INTDE 97098*	42	2

HOLE IN ONE *Holland, male DJ / producer (2 WEEKS)*

			pos	wks
15 Feb 97		**LIFE'S TOO SHORT** *Manifesto FESCD 21*	36	2

Jools HOLLAND and JAMIROQUAI
UK, male instrumentalist – piano and UK, male vocalist (3 WEEKS)

			pos	wks
24 Feb 01		**I'M IN THE MOOD FOR LOVE** *Warner Esp. WSMS 001CD*	29	3

HOLLAND-DOZIER featuring Lamont DOZIER
US, male vocal duo (5 WEEKS)

			pos	wks
28 Oct 72		**WHY CAN'T WE BE LOVERS** *Invictus INV 525*	29	5

Jennifer HOLLIDAY *US, female vocalist (6 WEEKS)*

			pos	wks
4 Sep 82		**AND I'M TELLING YOU I'M NOT GOING** *Geffen GEF A 2644*	32	6

Michael HOLLIDAY *UK, male vocalist – Norman Milne (65 WEEKS)*

			pos	wks
30 Mar 56		**NOTHIN' TO DO** *Columbia DB 3746*	20	1
27 Apr 56		**NOTHIN' TO DO (re-entry)** *Columbia DB 3746*	23	2
15 Jun 56		**THE GAL WITH THE YALLER SHOES** *Columbia DB 3783*	13	3
22 Jun 56		**HOT DIGGITY (DOG ZIGGITY BOOM)** *Columbia DB 3783*	14	5
3 Aug 56		**HOT DIGGITY (DOG ZIGGITY BOOM) / THE GAL WITH THE YALLER SHOES** *Columbia DB 3783*	17	3
5 Oct 56		**TEN THOUSAND MILES** *Columbia DB 3813*	24	3
17 Jan 58	★	**THE STORY OF MY LIFE** *Columbia DB 4058*	1	15
14 Mar 58		**IN LOVE** *Columbia DB 4087*	26	3
16 May 58	●	**STAIRWAY OF LOVE** *Columbia DB 4121*	3	13
11 Jul 58		**I'LL ALWAYS BE IN LOVE WITH YOU** *Columbia DB 4155*	27	1
1 Jan 60	★	**STARRY EYED** *Columbia DB 4378* [1]	1	12
14 Apr 60		**SKYLARK** *Columbia DB 4437*	39	3
1 Sep 60		**LITTLE BOY LOST** *Columbia DB 4475*	50	1

[1] Michael Holliday with the Michael Sammes Singers

When 'Hot Diggity (Dog Ziggity Boom) / Gal With the Yaller Shoes' re-entered the chart on 3 Aug 1956, 'Hot Diggity (Dog Ziggity Boom)' was listed by itself on 3 Aug and 10 Aug. Both sides were listed on 17 Aug - 'Gal With the Yaller Shoes' peaking at No.25

HOLLIES (26 Top 500) *Distinctive, influential and well-respected Manchester group: Allan Clarke (v), Graham Nash (g), Tony Hicks (g), Eric Haydock (b), Bobby Elliott (d). They were among the most regular chart visitors of the 1960s, and their No.1s span 23 years (318 WEEKS)*

			pos	wks
30 May 63		**(AIN'T THAT) JUST LIKE ME** *Parlophone R 5030*	25	10
29 Aug 63		**SEARCHIN'** *Parlophone R 5052*	12	14
21 Nov 63	●	**STAY** *Parlophone R 5077*	8	16
27 Feb 64	●	**JUST ONE LOOK** *Parlophone R 5104*	2	13
21 May 64	●	**HERE I GO AGAIN** *Parlophone R 5137*	4	12
17 Sep 64	●	**WE'RE THROUGH** *Parlophone R 5178*	7	11
28 Jan 65	●	**YES I WILL** *Parlophone R 5232*	9	13
27 May 65	★	**I'M ALIVE** *Parlophone R 5287*	1	14
2 Sep 65	●	**LOOK THROUGH ANY WINDOW** *Parlophone R 5322*	4	11
9 Dec 65		**IF I NEEDED SOMEONE** *Parlophone R 5392*	20	9
24 Feb 66	●	**I CAN'T LET GO** *Parlophone R 5409*	2	10
23 Jun 66	●	**BUS STOP** *Parlophone R 5469*	5	9
13 Oct 66	●	**STOP STOP STOP** *Parlophone R 5508*	2	12
16 Feb 67	●	**ON A CAROUSEL** *Parlophone R 5562*	4	11
1 Jun 67	●	**CARRIE-ANNE** *Parlophone R 5602*	3	11
27 Sep 67		**KING MIDAS IN REVERSE** *Parlophone R 5637*	18	8
27 Mar 68	●	**JENNIFER ECCLES** *Parlophone R 5680*	7	11
2 Oct 68		**LISTEN TO ME** *Parlophone R 5733*	11	11
5 Mar 69	●	**SORRY SUZANNE** *Parlophone R 5765*	3	12
4 Oct 69	●	**HE AIN'T HEAVY, HE'S MY BROTHER** *Parlophone R 5806*	3	15
18 Apr 70	●	**I CAN'T TELL THE BOTTOM FROM THE TOP** *Parlophone R 5837*	7	10
3 Oct 70		**GASOLINE ALLEY BRED** *Parlophone R 5862*	14	7
22 May 71		**HEY WILLY** *Parlophone R 5905*	22	7
26 Feb 72		**THE BABY** *Polydor 2058 199*	26	6
2 Sep 72		**LONG COOL WOMAN IN A BLACK DRESS** *Parlophone R 5939*	32	8
13 Oct 73		**THE DAY THAT CURLY BILLY SHOT DOWN CRAZY SAM MCGHEE** *Polydor 2058 403*	24	6
9 Feb 74	●	**THE AIR THAT I BREATHE** *Polydor 2058 435*	2	13
14 Jun 80		**SOLDIER'S SONG** *Polydor 2059 246*	58	3
29 Aug 81		**HOLLIEDAZE (MEDLEY)** *EMI 5229*	28	7
3 Sep 88	★	**HE AIN'T HEAVY, HE'S MY BROTHER (re-issue)** *EMI EM 74*	1	11
3 Dec 88		**THE AIR THAT I BREATHE (re-issue)** *EMI EM 80*	60	5
20 Mar 93		**THE WOMAN I LOVE** *EMI CDEM 264*	42	2

Loleatta HOLLOWAY *US, female vocalist (21 WEEKS)*

			pos	wks
31 Aug 91		**GOOD VIBRATIONS** *Interscope A 8764* [1] ▲	14	7
18 Jan 92		**TAKE ME AWAY** *PWL Continental PWL 210* [2]	25	5
26 Mar 94		**STAND UP** *Six6 SIXCD 111*	68	1
1 Apr 95		**KEEP THE FIRE BURNIN'** *Columbia 6611552* [3]	49	1
11 Apr 98		**SHOUT TO THE TOP** *JBO JNR 5001573* [4]	23	2

UK No.1 ★ UK Top 10 ● Still on chart + UK million seller ◆ UK entry at No.1 ■ US No.1 ▲

		pos	wks
20 Feb 99	(YOU GOT ME) BURNING UP *Wonderboy WBOYD 013* [5]	14	4
25 Nov 00	DREAMIN' *Defected DFECT 22CDS*	59	1

[1] Marky Mark and the Funky Bunch featuring Loleatta Holloway [2] Cappella featuring Loleatta Holloway [3] Dan Hartman starring Loleatta Holloway [4] Fire Island featuring Loleatta Holloway [5] Cevin Fisher / Loleatta Holloway

HOLLOWAY & CO *UK, male producer – Nicky Holloway (1 WEEK)* pos/wks

		pos	wks
21 Aug 99	I'LL DO ANYTHING - TO MAKE YOU MINE *INCredible INCS 2CD*	58	1

Buddy HOLLY (99 Top 500) *Highly respected and exceptionally influential singer / songwriter, b. Charles Hardin Holley, 7 Sep 1936, Texas, US, d. 3 Feb 1959 (aka 'the day the music died'). Despite a relatively brief career, his records and songs are still frequently heard around the globe (190 WEEKS)* pos/wks

		pos	wks
6 Dec 57 ●	PEGGY SUE *Coral Q 72293*	6	17
14 Mar 58	LISTEN TO ME *Coral Q 72288*	16	2
20 Jun 58 ●	RAVE ON *Coral Q 72325*	5	14
29 Aug 58	EARLY IN THE MORNING *Coral Q 72333*	17	4
16 Jan 59	HEARTBEAT *Coral Q 72346*	30	1
27 Feb 59 ★	IT DOESN'T MATTER ANYMORE *Coral Q 72360*	1	21
31 Jul 59	MIDNIGHT SHIFT *Brunswick 05800*	26	3
11 Sep 59	PEGGY SUE GOT MARRIED *Coral Q 72376*	13	10
28 Apr 60	HEARTBEAT (re-issue) *Coral Q 72392*	30	3
26 May 60	TRUE LOVE WAYS *Coral Q 72397*	25	7
20 Oct 60	LEARNING THE GAME *Coral Q 72411*	36	3
26 Jan 61	WHAT TO DO *Coral Q 72419*	34	6
6 Jul 61	BABY I DON'T CARE / VALLEY OF TEARS *Coral Q 72432*	12	14
15 Mar 62	LISTEN TO ME (re-issue) *Coral Q 72449*	48	1
13 Sep 62	REMINISCING *Coral Q 72455*	17	11
14 Mar 63 ●	BROWN-EYED HANDSOME MAN *Coral Q 72459*	3	17
6 Jun 63 ●	BO DIDDLEY *Coral Q 72463*	4	12
5 Sep 63 ●	WISHING *Coral Q 72466*	10	11
19 Dec 63	WHAT TO DO (re-recording) *Coral Q 72469*	27	8
14 May 64	YOU'VE GOT LOVE *Coral Q 72472* [1]	40	6
10 Sep 64	LOVE'S MADE A FOOL OF YOU *Coral Q 72475*	39	6
3 Apr 68	PEGGY SUE / RAVE ON (re-issue) *MCA MU 1012*	32	9
10 Dec 88	TRUE LOVE WAYS (re-issue) *MCA MCA 1302*	65	4

[1] Buddy Holly and the Crickets

Buddy Holly's version of 'Love's Made a Fool of You' is not the same version as the Crickets' hit of 1959, on which Holly did not appear. 'Valley of Tears' was not listed together with 'Baby I Don't Care' until 13 Jul 1961

HOLLY and the IVYS *UK, male / female vocal / instrumental group (4 WEEKS)* pos/wks

		pos	wks
19 Dec 81	CHRISTMAS ON 45 *Decca SANTA 1*	40	4

HOLLYWOOD ARGYLES *US, male vocal group (10 WEEKS)* pos/wks

		pos	wks
21 Jul 60	ALLEY-OOP *London HLU 9146* ▲	24	10

HOLLYWOOD BEYOND *UK, male group (14 WEEKS)* pos/wks

		pos	wks
12 Jul 86 ●	WHAT'S THE COLOUR OF MONEY? *WEA YZ 76*	7	10
20 Sep 86	NO MORE TEARS *WEA YZ 81*	47	4

Eddie HOLMAN *US, male vocalist (13 WEEKS)* pos/wks

		pos	wks
19 Oct 74 ●	(HEY THERE) LONELY GIRL *ABC 4012*	4	13

David HOLMES *UK, male producer (9 WEEKS)* pos/wks

		pos	wks
6 Apr 96	GONE *Go! Discs GODCD 140*	75	1
23 Aug 97	GRITTY SHAKER *Go.Beat GOBCD 2*	53	1
10 Jan 98	DON'T DIE JUST YET *Go.Beat GOLCD 6*	33	3
4 Apr 98	MY MATE PAUL *Go.Beat GOBCD 8*	39	2
19 Aug 00	69 POLICE *Go.Beat / Polydor GOBCD 30*	53	1
26 May 01	DEVOTION *Tidy Trax TIDY 154CD*	66	1

Rupert HOLMES *US, male vocalist (14 WEEKS)* pos/wks

		pos	wks
12 Jan 80	ESCAPE (THE PINA COLADA SONG) *Infinity INF 120* ▲	23	7
22 Mar 80	HIM *MCA 565*	31	7

Adele HOLNESS – *See Ben SHAW featuring Adele HOLNESS*

John HOLT *Jamaica, male vocalist (14 WEEKS)* pos/wks

		pos	wks
14 Dec 74 ●	HELP ME MAKE IT THROUGH THE NIGHT *Trojan TR 7909*	6	14

Nichola HOLT *UK, female vocalist (1 WEEK)* pos/wks

		pos	wks
21 Oct 00	THE GAME *RCA 74321798992*	72	1

A HOMEBOY, a HIPPIE and a FUNKI DREDD *UK, male vocal / instrumental group (9 WEEKS)* pos/wks

		pos	wks
13 Oct 90	TOTAL CONFUSION *Tam Tam 7TTT 031*	56	3
29 Dec 90	FREEDOM *Tam Tam 7TTT 039*	68	4
8 Jan 94	HERE WE GO AGAIN *Polydor PZCD 302*	57	2

HONDY *Italy, female vocalist (2 WEEKS)* pos/wks

		pos	wks
12 Apr 97	HONDY (NO ACCESS) *Manifesto FESCD 20*	26	2

HONEYBUS *UK, male vocal / instrumental group (12 WEEKS)* pos/wks

		pos	wks
20 Mar 68 ●	I CAN'T LET MAGGIE GO *Deram DM 182*	8	12

HONEYCOMBS *UK, male / female vocal / instrumental group – lead vocal Dennis D'Ell (Dalziel) (39 WEEKS)* pos/wks

		pos	wks
23 Jul 64 ★	HAVE I THE RIGHT *Pye 7N 15664*	1	15
22 Oct 64	IS IT BECAUSE *Pye 7N 15705*	38	6
29 Apr 65	SOMETHING BETTER BEGINNING *Pye 7N 15827*	39	4
5 Aug 65	THAT'S THE WAY *Pye 7N 15890*	12	14

HONEYCRACK *UK, male vocal / instrumental group (9 WEEKS)* pos/wks

		pos	wks
4 Nov 95	SITTING AT HOME *Epic 6625382*	42	2
24 Feb 96	GO AWAY *Epic 6628642*	41	2
11 May 96	KING OF MISERY *Epic 6631472*	32	2
20 Jul 96	SITTING AT HOME (re-issue) *Epic 6635032*	32	2
16 Nov 96	ANYWAY *EG EGO 52A*	67	1

HONEYDRIPPERS *UK / US, male vocal / instrumental group (3 WEEKS)* pos/wks

		pos	wks
2 Feb 85	SEA OF LOVE *Es Paranza YZ 33*	56	3

See also Robert PLANT

HONEYZ *UK / France, female vocal trio (57 WEEKS)* pos/wks

		pos	wks
5 Sep 98 ●	FINALLY FOUND *1st Avenue / Mercury HNZCD 1*	4	12
19 Dec 98 ●	END OF THE LINE *1st Avenue / Mercury HNZCD 2*	5	12
24 Apr 99	END OF THE LINE (re-entry) *1st Avenue / Mercury HNZCD 2*	64	2
24 Apr 99 ●	LOVE OF A LIFETIME *1st Avenue / Mercury HNZCD 3*	9	9
23 Oct 99 ●	NEVER LET YOU DOWN *1st Avenue / Mercury HNZCD 4*	7	6
11 Mar 00 ●	WON'T TAKE IT LYING DOWN *1st Avenue / Mercury HNZCD 5*	7	7
13 May 00	WON'T TAKE IT LYING DOWN (re-entry) *1st Avenue / Mercury HNZCD 5*	72	1
28 Oct 00	NOT EVEN GONNA TRIP *1st Avenue / Mercury HNZCD 7*	24	3
25 Nov 00	NOT EVEN GONNA TRIP (re-entry) *1st Avenue / Mercury HNZCD 7*	68	1
13 Jan 01	NOT EVEN GONNA TRIP (2nd re-entry) *1st Avenue / Mercury HNZCD 7*	71	1
18 Aug 01	I DON'T KNOW *1st Avenue / Mercury HNZCD 8*	28	3

HONKY *UK, male vocal / instrumental group (5 WEEKS)* pos/wks

		pos	wks
28 May 77	JOIN THE PARTY *Creole CR 137*	28	5

HONKY *UK, male vocal / instrumental group (5 WEEKS)* pos/wks

		pos	wks
30 Oct 93	THE HONKY DOODLE DAY EP *ZTT ZANG 45CD*	61	1
19 Feb 94	THE WHISTLER *ZTT ZANG 48CD*	41	2
20 Apr 96	HIP HOP DON'T YA DROP *Higher Ground HIGHS 1CD*	70	1
10 Aug 96	WHAT'S GOIN DOWN *Higher Ground HIGHS 2CD*	49	1

Tracks on The Honky Doodle Day EP: KKK (Boom Boom Tra La La La) / Honky Doodle Dub / Chains

Frank HOOKER and POSITIVE PEOPLE *US, male / female vocal / instrumental group (4 WEEKS)* pos/wks

		pos	wks
5 Jul 80	THIS FEELIN' *DJM DJS 10947*	48	4

John Lee HOOKER *US, male vocalist (23 WEEKS)* pos/wks

Date		Title	pos	wks
11 Jun 64		DIMPLES *Stateside SS 297*	23	10
24 Oct 92		BOOM BOOM *Pointblank POB 3*	16	5
16 Jan 93		BOOGIE AT RUSSIAN HILL *Pointblank POBDX 4*	53	2
15 May 93		GLORIA *Exile VANCD 11* [1]	31	3
11 Feb 95		CHILL OUT (THINGS GONNA CHANGE) *Pointblank POBD 10*	45	2
20 Apr 96		BABY LEE *Silvertone ORECD 81* [2]	65	1

[1] Van Morrison and John Lee Hooker [2] John Lee Hooker with Robert Cray

HOOTERS *US, male vocal / instrumental group (9 WEEKS)* pos/wks

Date		Title	pos	wks
21 Nov 87		SATELLITE *CBS 651168 7*	22	9

HOOTIE & THE BLOWFISH
US, male vocal / instrumental group (6 WEEKS) pos/wks

Date		Title	pos	wks
25 Feb 95		HOLD MY HAND *Atlantic A 7230CD*	50	3
27 May 95		LET HER CRY *Atlantic A 7188CD*	75	1
4 May 96		OLD MAN AND ME (WHEN I GET TO HEAVEN) *Atlantic A 5513CD*	57	1
7 Nov 98		I WILL WAIT *Atlantic AT 0048CD*	57	1

HOPE A.D. *UK, male producer – David Hope (1 WEEK)* pos/wks

Date		Title	pos	wks
4 Jun 94		TREE FROG *Sun-Up SUN 003CD*	73	1

See also *MIND OF KANE*

Mary HOPKIN (470 Top 500) *Propelled to stardom from TV talent show 'Opportunity Knocks' witnessed by Twiggy who recommended the Welsh singer (b. 3 May 1950) to Paul McCartney. The Beatle produced 'Those Were the Days', originally a Russian folk song, which ironically knocked 'Hey Jude' from the No.1 spot (74 WEEKS)* pos/wks

Date		Title	pos	wks
4 Sep 68	★	THOSE WERE THE DAYS *Apple 2*	1	21
2 Apr 69	●	GOODBYE *Apple 10*	2	14
31 Jan 70	●	TEMMA HARBOUR *Apple 22*	6	11
28 Mar 70	●	KNOCK KNOCK WHO'S THERE *Apple 26*	2	14
31 Oct 70		THINK ABOUT YOUR CHILDREN *Apple 30*	19	7
2 Jan 71		THINK ABOUT YOUR CHILDREN (re-entry) *Apple 30*	46	2
31 Jul 71		LET MY NAME BE SORROW *Apple 34*	46	1
20 Mar 76		IF YOU LOVE ME *Good Earth GD 2*	32	4

Anthony HOPKINS *UK, male actor / vocalist (1 WEEK)* pos/wks

Date		Title	pos	wks
27 Dec 86		DISTANT STAR *Juice AA 5*	75	1

Nick HORNBY – See *PRETENDERS*

Bruce HORNSBY and the RANGE
US, male vocal / instrumental group (15 WEEKS) pos/wks

Date		Title	pos	wks
2 Aug 86		THE WAY IT IS *RCA PB 49805* ▲	15	10
25 Apr 87		MANDOLIN RAIN *RCA PB 49769*	70	1
28 May 88		THE VALLEY ROAD *RCA PB 49561*	44	4

HORNY UNITED – See *BONEY M*

HORSE *UK, female / male vocal / instrumental group (10 WEEKS)* pos/wks

Date		Title	pos	wks
24 Nov 90		CAREFUL *Capitol CL 587*	52	3
21 Aug 93		SHAKE THIS MOUNTAIN *Oxygen GASPD 7*	52	2
23 Oct 93		GOD'S HOME MOVIE *Oxygen GASXD 10*	56	1
15 Jan 94		CELEBRATE *Oxygen GASPD 11*	49	2
5 Apr 97		CAREFUL (re-mix) *Stress CDSTRX 79*	44	2

Johnny HORTON *US, male vocalist (15 WEEKS)* pos/wks

Date		Title	pos	wks
26 Jun 59		THE BATTLE OF NEW ORLEANS *Philips PB 932* ▲	16	4
19 Jan 61		NORTH TO ALASKA *Philips PB 1062*	23	11

HOT BLOOD *France, male instrumental group (5 WEEKS)* pos/wks

Date		Title	pos	wks
9 Oct 76		SOUL DRACULA *Creole CR 132*	32	5

HOT BUTTER *US, production duo - Bill and Steve Jerome featuring Stan Free (synth) (19 WEEKS)* pos/wks

Date		Title	pos	wks
22 Jul 72	●	POPCORN *Pye International 7N 25583*	5	16
23 Dec 72		POPCORN (re-entry) *Pye International 7N 25583*	50	3

HOT CHOCOLATE (34 Top 500) *London-based band who were chart regulars throughout the 1970s and 1980s. Group founders were West Indian-born Errol Brown (v) and Tony Wilson (b/v). The act had at least one hit every year between 1970 and 1984. 'You Sexy Thing' was the only song to make the Top 10 in the 70s, 80s and 90s (283 WEEKS)* pos/wks

Date		Title	pos	wks
15 Aug 70	●	LOVE IS LIFE *RAK 103*	6	12
6 Mar 71		YOU COULD HAVE BEEN A LADY *RAK 110*	22	9
28 Aug 71	●	I BELIEVE (IN LOVE) *RAK 118*	8	11
28 Oct 72		YOU'LL ALWAYS BE A FRIEND *RAK 139*	23	8
14 Apr 73	●	BROTHER LOUIE *RAK 149*	7	10
18 Aug 73		RUMOURS *RAK 157*	44	3
16 Mar 74	●	EMMA *RAK 168*	3	10
30 Nov 74		CHERI BABE *RAK 188*	31	9
24 May 75		DISCO QUEEN *RAK 202*	11	7
9 Aug 75	●	A CHILD'S PRAYER *RAK 212*	7	10
8 Nov 75	●	YOU SEXY THING *RAK 221*	2	12
20 Mar 76		DON'T STOP IT NOW *RAK 230*	11	8
26 Jun 76		MAN TO MAN *RAK 238*	14	8
21 Aug 76		HEAVEN IS IN THE BACK SEAT OF MY CADILLAC *RAK 240*	25	8
18 Jun 77	★	SO YOU WIN AGAIN *RAK 259*	1	11
26 Nov 77	●	PUT YOUR LOVE IN ME *RAK 266*	10	9
4 Mar 78		EVERY 1'S A WINNER *RAK 270*	12	11
2 Dec 78		I'LL PUT YOU TOGETHER AGAIN *RAK 286*	13	11
19 May 79		MINDLESS BOOGIE *RAK 292*	46	5
28 Jul 79		GOING THROUGH THE MOTIONS *RAK 296*	53	4
3 May 80	●	NO DOUBT ABOUT IT *RAK 310*	2	11
19 Jul 80		ARE YOU GETTING ENOUGH OF WHAT MAKES YOU HAPPY *RAK 318*	17	7
13 Dec 80		LOVE ME TO SLEEP *RAK 324*	50	5
30 May 81		YOU'LL NEVER BE SO WRONG *RAK 331*	52	4
17 Apr 82	●	GIRL CRAZY *RAK 341*	7	11
10 Jul 82	●	IT STARTED WITH A KISS *RAK 344*	5	12
25 Sep 82		CHANCES *RAK 350*	32	5
7 May 83	●	WHAT KINDA BOY YOU LOOKING FOR (GIRL) *RAK 357*	10	9
17 Sep 83		TEARS ON THE TELEPHONE *RAK 363*	37	5
4 Feb 84		I GAVE YOU MY HEART (DIDN'T I) *RAK 369*	13	10
17 Jan 87	●	YOU SEXY THING (re-mix) *EMI 5592*	10	10
4 Apr 87		EVERY 1'S A WINNER (re-mix) *EMI 5607*	69	2
6 Mar 93		IT STARTED WITH A KISS (re-issue) *EMI CDEMCTS 7*	31	5
22 Nov 97	●	YOU SEXY THING (re-issue) *EMI CDHOT 100*	6	8
14 Feb 98		IT STARTED WITH A KISS (2nd re-issue) *EMI CDHOT 101* [1]	18	3

[1] Hot Chocolate featuring Errol Brown

HOT GOSSIP – See *Sarah BRIGHTMAN*

HOT HOUSE *UK, male / female vocal / instrumental group (3 WEEKS)* pos/wks

Date		Title	pos	wks
14 Feb 87		DON'T COME TO STAY *Deconstruction CHEZ 1*	74	1
24 Sep 88		DON'T COME TO STAY (re-issue) *Deconstruction PB 42233*	70	2

HOT 'N' JUICY – See *MOUSSE T*

HOT RODS – See *EDDIE and the HOT RODS*

HOT STREAK *US, male vocal / instrumental group (8 WEEKS)* pos/wks

Date		Title	pos	wks
10 Sep 83		BODY WORK *Polydor POSP 642*	19	8

HOTHOUSE FLOWERS
Ireland, male vocal / instrumental group (36 WEEKS) pos/wks

Date		Title	pos	wks
14 May 88		DON'T GO *London LON 174*	11	8
23 Jul 88		I'M SORRY *London LON 187*	53	3
12 May 90		GIVE IT UP *London LON 258*	30	5
28 Jul 90		I CAN SEE CLEARLY NOW *London LON 269*	23	7
20 Oct 90		MOVIES *London LON 276*	68	2
13 Feb 93		EMOTIONAL TIME *London LONCD 335*	38	4
8 May 93		ONE TONGUE *London LOCDP 340*	45	3

19 Jun 93		**ISN'T IT AMAZING** *London LOCDP 343*	46	2
27 Nov 93		**THIS IS IT (YOUR SOUL)** *London LONCD 346*	67	1
16 May 98		**YOU CAN LOVE ME NOW** *London LONCD 410*	65	1

HOTLEGS *UK, male vocal / instrumental group (14 WEEKS)* pos/wks

4 Jul 70	●	**NEANDERTHAL MAN** *Fontana 6007 019*	2	14

HOTSHOTS *UK, male vocal group (15 WEEKS)* pos/wks

2 Jun 73	●	**SNOOPY VS THE RED BARON** *Mooncrest MOON 5*	4	15

Steven HOUGHTON *UK, male vocalist (22 WEEKS)* pos/wks

29 Nov 97	●	**WIND BENEATH MY WINGS** *RCA 74321529272*	3	15
7 Mar 98		**TRULY** *RCA 74321558552*	23	5
2 May 98		**TRULY (re-entry)** *RCA 74321558552*	72	2

A HOUSE *Ireland, male vocal / instrumental group (8 WEEKS)* pos/wks

13 Jun 92		**ENDLESS ART** *Setanta AHOU 1*	46	3
8 Aug 92		**TAKE IT EASY ON ME** *Setanta AHOU 2*	55	2
25 Jun 94		**WHY ME** *Setanta CDAHOU 4*	52	1
1 Oct 94		**HERE COME THE GOOD TIMES** *Setanta CDAHOUS 5*	37	2

HOUSE ENGINEERS *UK, male vocal / instrumental duo (2 WEEKS)* pos/wks

5 Dec 87		**GHOST HOUSE** *Syncopate SY 8*	69	2

HOUSE OF GLASS *Italy, male production duo – Bini & Martini (1 WEEK)* pos/wks

14 Apr 01		**DISCO DOWN** *Azuli AZNY 138*	72	1

See also ECLIPSE; BINI & MARTINI; GOODFELLAS featuring Lisa MILLETT

HOUSE OF LOVE *UK, male vocal / instrumental group (21 WEEKS)* pos/wks

22 Apr 89		**NEVER** *Fontana HOL 1*	41	2
18 Nov 89		**I DON'T KNOW WHY I LOVE YOU** *Fontana HOL 2*	41	3
3 Feb 90		**SHINE ON** *Fontana HOL 3*	20	4
7 Apr 90		**BEATLES AND THE STONES** *Fontana HOL 4*	36	4
26 Oct 91		**THE GIRL WITH THE LONELIEST EYES** *Fontana HOL 5*	58	1
2 May 92		**FEEL** *Fontana HOL 6*	45	3
27 Jun 92		**YOU DON'T UNDERSTAND** *Fontana HOL 7*	46	3
5 Dec 92		**CRUSH ME** *Fontana HOL 810*	67	1

HOUSE OF PAIN *US, male rap group (24 WEEKS)* pos/wks

10 Oct 92		**JUMP AROUND** *Ruffness XLS 32*	32	4
22 May 93	●	**JUMP AROUND / TOP O' THE MORNING TO YA (re-issue)** *Ruffness XL 43CD*	8	7
23 Oct 93		**SHAMROCKS AND SHENANIGANS / WHO'S THE MAN** *Ruffness XLS 46CD*	23	4
16 Jul 94		**ON POINT** *Ruffness XLS 52CD*	19	3
12 Nov 94		**IT AIN'T A CRIME** *Ruffness XLS 55CD1*	37	2
1 Jul 95		**OVER THERE (I DON'T CARE)** *Ruffness XLS 61CD1*	20	3
5 Oct 96		**FED UP** *Tommy Boy TBCD 7744*	68	1

HOUSE OF VIRGINISM
Sweden, male vocal / instrumental group (6 WEEKS) pos/wks

20 Nov 93		**I'LL BE THERE FOR YOU (DOYA DODODO DOYA)** *ffrr FCD 221*	29	3
30 Jul 94		**REACHIN** *ffrr FCD 238*	35	2
17 Feb 96		**EXCLUSIVE** *Logic 74321324102*	67	1

HOUSE OF ZEKKARIYAS – See WOMACK and WOMACK

HOUSE TRAFFIC
Italy / UK, male / female vocal / production duo (3 WEEKS) pos/wks

4 Oct 97		**EVERY DAY OF MY LIFE** *Logic 74321249442*	24	3

HOUSEMARTINS *UK, male vocal / instrumental group fronted by Norman Cook (b) and Paul Heaton (v) (59 WEEKS)* pos/wks

8 Mar 86		**SHEEP** *Go! Discs GOD 9*	54	3
5 Apr 86		**SHEEP (re-entry)** *Go! Discs GOD 9*	71	1
7 Jun 86	●	**HAPPY HOUR** *Go! Discs GOD 11*	3	13
4 Oct 86		**THINK FOR A MINUTE** *Go! Discs GOD 13*	18	8
6 Dec 86	★	**CARAVAN OF LOVE** *Go! Discs GOD 16*	1	11
23 May 87		**FIVE GET OVER EXCITED** *Go! Discs GOD 18*	11	6
5 Sep 87		**ME AND THE FARMER** *Go! Discs GOD 19*	15	5
21 Nov 87		**BUILD** *Go! Discs GOD 21*	15	8
23 Apr 88		**THERE IS ALWAYS SOMETHING THERE TO REMIND ME** *Go! Discs GOD 22*	35	4

HOUSEMASTER BOYZ and the RUDE BOY OF HOUSE
US, male vocal / instrumental group (14 WEEKS) pos/wks

9 May 87		**HOUSE NATION** *Magnetic Dance MAGD 1*	48	6
12 Sep 87	●	**HOUSE NATION (re-entry)** *Magnetic Dance MAGD 1*	8	8

HOUSETRAP – See DJ SANDY VS HOUSETRAP

Thelma HOUSTON *US, female vocalist (22 WEEKS)* pos/wks

5 Feb 77		**DON'T LEAVE ME THIS WAY** *Motown TMG 1060* ▲	13	8
27 Jun 81		**IF YOU FEEL IT** *RCA 77*	48	4
1 Dec 84		**YOU USED TO HOLD ME SO TIGHT** *MCA MCA 932*	49	8
21 Jan 95		**DON'T LEAVE ME THIS WAY (re-recording)** *Dynamo DYND 001*	35	2

Whitney HOUSTON (28 Top 500) *Multi-award-winning, record-shattering vocalist b. 9 Aug 1963, New Jersey, US. She recorded the second biggest selling UK single by a female, and scored a record seven successive No.1s in the US. In 2001, with sales exceeding 140 million behind her, she signed a record-breaking $100 million recording deal (312 WEEKS)* pos/wks

16 Nov 85	★	**SAVING ALL MY LOVE FOR YOU** *Arista ARIST 640* ▲	1	16
25 Jan 86		**HOLD ME** *Asylum EKR 32* [1]	44	5
25 Jan 86	●	**HOW WILL I KNOW** *Arista ARIST 656* ▲	5	12
12 Apr 86	●	**GREATEST LOVE OF ALL** *Arista ARIST 658* ▲	8	11
23 May 87	★	**I WANNA DANCE WITH SOMEBODY (WHO LOVES ME)** *Arista RIS 1* ▲	1	16
22 Aug 87		**DIDN'T WE ALMOST HAVE IT ALL** *Arista RIS 31* ▲	14	8
14 Nov 87	●	**SO EMOTIONAL** *Arista RIS 43* ▲	5	11
12 Mar 88		**WHERE DO BROKEN HEARTS GO** *Arista 109793* ▲	14	8
28 May 88	●	**LOVE WILL SAVE THE DAY** *Arista 111516*	10	7
24 Sep 88	★	**ONE MOMENT IN TIME** *Arista 111613*	1	12
9 Sep 89		**IT ISN'T, IT WASN'T, IT AIN'T NEVER GONNA BE** *Arista 112545* [2]	29	5
20 Oct 90	●	**I'M YOUR BABY TONIGHT** *Arista 113594* ▲	5	9
22 Dec 90		**ALL THE MAN THAT I NEED** *Arista 114000* ▲	13	10
29 Dec 90		**I'M YOUR BABY TONIGHT (re-entry)** *Arista 113594*	69	1
6 Jul 91		**MY NAME IS NOT SUSAN** *Arista 114510*	29	5
28 Sep 91		**I BELONG TO YOU** *Arista 114727*	54	2
14 Nov 92	★	**I WILL ALWAYS LOVE YOU** *Arista 74321120657* ◆ ▲	1	23
20 Feb 93	●	**I'M EVERY WOMAN** *Arista 74321131502*	4	11
24 Apr 93	●	**I HAVE NOTHING** *Arista 74321146142*	3	10
31 Jul 93		**RUN TO YOU** *Arista 74321153332*	15	6
6 Nov 93		**QUEEN OF THE NIGHT** *Arista 74321169302*	14	5
18 Dec 93		**I WILL ALWAYS LOVE YOU (re-entry)** *Arista 74321120657*	25	6
22 Jan 94		**SOMETHING IN COMMON** *MCA MCSTD 1957* [3]	16	5
18 Nov 95		**EXHALE (SHOOP SHOOP)** *Arista 74321332472* ▲	11	9
24 Feb 96		**COUNT ON ME** *Arista 74321345842* [4]	12	6
21 Dec 96		**STEP BY STEP** *Arista 74321449332*	13	13
29 Mar 97		**I BELIEVE IN YOU AND ME** *Arista 74321468602*	16	5
19 Dec 98	●	**WHEN YOU BELIEVE** *Columbia 6667522* [5]	4	11
6 Mar 99	●	**IT'S NOT RIGHT (BUT IT'S OK)** *Arista 74321652402*	3	15
27 Mar 99		**WHEN YOU BELIEVE (re-entry)** *Columbia 6667522* [5]	68	2
3 Jul 99	●	**MY LOVE IS YOUR LOVE** *Arista 74321672862*	2	12
11 Dec 99		**I LEARNED FROM THE BEST** *Arista 74321723992*	19	11
17 Jun 00	●	**IF I TOLD YOU THAT** *Arista 74321766282* [6]	9	9
26 Aug 00		**IF I TOLD YOU THAT (re-entry)** *Arista 74321766282* [6]	51	2
14 Oct 00	●	**COULD I HAVE THIS KISS FOREVER** *Arista 74321795992* [7]	7	8
30 Dec 00		**HEARTBREAK HOTEL** *Arista 74321820572* [8]	26	5

[1] Teddy Pendergrass with Whitney Houston [2] Aretha Franklin and Whitney Houston [3] Bobby Brown and Whitney Houston [4] Whitney Houston and CeCe Winans [5] Mariah Carey and Whitney Houston [6] Whitney Houston / George Michael [7] Whitney Houston and Enrique Iglesias [8] Whitney Houston featuring Faith Evans and Kelly Price

Adina HOWARD *US, female vocalist (16 WEEKS)* pos/wks

4 Mar 95		**FREAK LIKE ME** *East West A 4473CD*	67	1

6 May 95	**FREAK LIKE ME (re-entry)** *East West A 4473CD*	33	3
23 Nov 96 ●	**WHAT'S LOVE GOT TO DO WITH IT** *Interscope IND 97008* [1]	2	12

[1] Warren G featuring Adina Howard

Billy HOWARD *UK, male comedian / vocalist (12 WEEKS)* pos/wks

13 Dec 75 ●	**KING OF THE COPS** *Penny Farthing PEN 892*	6	12

Miki HOWARD *US, female vocalist (2 WEEKS)* pos/wks

26 May 90	**UNTIL YOU COME BACK (THAT'S WHAT I'M GONNA DO)** *East West 7935*	67	2

Nick HOWARD *Australia, male vocalist (1 WEEK)* pos/wks

21 Jan 95	**EVERYBODY NEEDS SOMEBODY** *Bell 74321220942*	64	1

Robert HOWARD – *See Kym MAZELLE*

HOWLIN' WOLF *US, male vocalist – Chester Burnette (5 WEEKS)* pos/wks

4 Jun 64	**SMOKESTACK LIGHTNIN'** *Pye International 7N 25244*	42	5

H 20 *UK, male vocal / instrumental group (16 WEEKS)* pos/wks

21 May 83	**DREAM TO SLEEP** *RCA 330*	17	10
13 Aug 83	**JUST OUTSIDE OF HEAVEN** *RCA 349*	38	6

H20 *US / Switzerland, male / female vocal / instrumental group (4 WEEKS)* pos/wks

14 Sep 96	**NOBODY'S BUSINESS** *AM:PM 5818832* [1]	19	3
30 Aug 97	**SATISFIED (TAKE ME HIGHER)** *AM:PM 5823252*	66	1

[1] H20 featuring Billie

Al HUDSON *US, male vocalist (22 WEEKS)* pos/wks

9 Sep 78	**DANCE, GET DOWN (FEEL THE GROOVE) / HOW DO YOU DO** *ABC 4229*	57	4
15 Sep 79	**YOU CAN DO IT** *MCA 511* [1]	15	10
8 Dec 79	**MUSIC** *MCA 542* [2]	56	6
29 Jun 85	**LET'S TALK** *MCA 972*	64	2

[1] Al Hudson and the Partners [2] One Way featuring Al Hudson

Lavine HUDSON *UK, female vocalist (3 WEEKS)* pos/wks

21 May 88	**INTERVENTION** *Virgin VS 1067*	57	3

HUDSON-FORD *UK, male vocal / instrumental duo – Richard Hudson and John Ford (20 WEEKS)* pos/wks

18 Aug 73 ●	**PICK UP THE PIECES** *A & M AMS 7078*	8	9
16 Feb 74	**BURN BABY BURN** *A & M AMS 7096*	15	9
29 Jun 74	**FLOATING IN THE WIND** *A & M AMS 7116*	35	2

See also MONKS

HUE AND CRY

UK, male vocal / instrumental duo – Pat and Greg Kane (59 WEEKS) pos/wks

13 Jun 87 ●	**LABOUR OF LOVE** *Circa YR 4*	6	16
19 Sep 87	**STRENGTH TO STRENGTH** *Circa YR 6*	46	5
30 Jan 88	**I REFUSE** *Circa YR 8*	47	3
22 Oct 88	**ORDINARY ANGEL** *Circa YR 18*	42	6
28 Jan 89	**LOOKING FOR LINDA** *Circa YR 24*	15	9
6 May 89	**VIOLENTLY (EP)** *Circa YR 29*	21	6
30 Sep 89	**SWEET INVISIBILITY** *Circa YR 37*	55	3
25 May 91	**MY SALT HEART** *Circa YR 64*	47	3
3 Aug 91	**LONG TERM LOVERS OF PAIN (EP)** *Circa YR 71*	48	3
11 Jul 92	**PROFOUNDLY YOURS** *Fidelity FIDEL 1*	74	1
13 Mar 93	**LABOUR OF LOVE (re-mix)** *Circa HUESCD 1*	25	4

Tracks on Violently (EP): Violently / The Man with the Child In His Eyes / Calamity John. Tracks on Long Term Lovers of Pain (EP): Long Term Lovers of Pain / Heart of Saturday Night / Remembrance and Gold / Stars Crash Down

HUES CORPORATION *US, male / female vocal group (16 WEEKS)* pos/wks

27 Jul 74 ●	**ROCK THE BOAT** *RCA APBO 0232* ▲	6	10
19 Oct 74	**ROCKIN' SOUL** *RCA PB 10066*	24	6

HUFF & HERB *UK, male DJ / production duo (4 WEEKS)* pos/wks

6 Dec 97	**FEELING GOOD** *Planet 3 GXY 2018CD*	31	3
7 Nov 98	**FEELING GOOD '98 (re-mix)** *Planet 3 GXY 2020CD*	69	1

HUFF AND PUFF *UK, male instrumental / production duo (4 WEEKS)* pos/wks

2 Nov 96	**HELP ME MAKE IT** *Skyway SKYWCD 4*	31	2
21 Jun 97	**HELP ME MAKE IT (re-mix)** *Skyway SKYWCD 8*	37	2

David HUGHES *UK, male vocalist (1 WEEK)* pos/wks

21 Sep 56	**BY THE FOUNTAINS OF ROME** *Philips PB 606*	27	1

HUGO and LUIGI *US, orchestra and chorus (2 WEEKS)* pos/wks

24 Jul 59	**LA PLUME DE MA TANTE** *RCA 1127*	29	2

HUMAN LEAGUE (135 Top 500)

Early-1980s UK pop sensation. Fronted by Phil Oakey (b. 2 Oct 1955, Sheffield) (v/syn) and joined in 1980 by vocalists Joanne Catherall and Susanne Sulley. The group, which also topped the US chart, won Best Newcomers at the 1982 Brit Awards (156 WEEKS) pos/wks

3 May 80	**HOLIDAY 80 (DOUBLE SINGLE)** *Virgin SV 105*	56	5
21 Jun 80	**EMPIRE STATE HUMAN** *Virgin VS 351*	62	2
28 Feb 81	**BOYS AND GIRLS** *Virgin VS 395*	48	4
2 May 81	**THE SOUND OF THE CROWD** *Virgin VS 416*	12	10
8 Aug 81 ●	**LOVE ACTION (I BELIEVE IN LOVE)** *Virgin VS 435*	3	13
10 Oct 81 ●	**OPEN YOUR HEART** *Virgin VS 453*	6	9
5 Dec 81 ★	**DON'T YOU WANT ME** *Virgin VS 466* ◆ ▲	1	13
9 Jan 82 ●	**BEING BOILED** *EMI FAST 4*	6	9
6 Feb 82	**HOLIDAY 80 (DOUBLE SINGLE) (re-entry)** *Virgin SV 105*	46	5
20 Nov 82 ●	**MIRROR MAN** *Virgin VS 522*	2	10
23 Apr 83 ●	**(KEEP FEELING) FASCINATION** *Virgin VS 569*	2	9
5 May 84	**THE LEBANON** *Virgin VS 672*	11	6
23 Jun 84	**THE LEBANON (re-entry)** *Virgin VS 672*	75	1
30 Jun 84	**LIFE ON YOUR OWN** *Virgin VS 688*	16	6
17 Nov 84	**LOUISE** *Virgin VS 723*	13	10
23 Aug 86 ●	**HUMAN** *Virgin VS 880* ▲	8	8
22 Nov 86	**I NEED YOUR LOVING** *Virgin VS 900*	72	1
15 Oct 88	**LOVE IS ALL THAT MATTERS** *Virgin VS 1025*	41	5
18 Aug 90	**HEART LIKE A WHEEL** *Virgin VS 1262*	29	5
7 Jan 95 ●	**TELL ME WHEN** *East West YZ 882CD1*	6	9
18 Mar 95	**ONE MAN IN MY HEART** *East West YZ 904CD1*	13	8
17 Jun 95	**FILLING UP WITH HEAVEN** *East West YZ 944CD1*	36	2
28 Oct 95	**DON'T YOU WANT ME (re-mix)** *Virgin VSCDT 1557*	16	3
20 Jan 96	**STAY WITH ME TONIGHT** *East West EW 020CD*	40	2
11 Aug 01	**ALL I EVER WANTED** *Papillon BTFLYS 0012*	47	1

Tracks on double single: Being Boiled / Marianne / Rock and Roll - Nightclubbing / Dancevision

HUMAN MOVEMENT featuring Sophie MOLETA

UK, male production duo and Australia, female vocalist (1 WEEK) pos/wks

3 Feb 01	**LOVE HAS COME AGAIN** *Renaissance Recordings RENCDS 005*	53	1

HUMAN NATURE *Australia, male vocal group (7 WEEKS)* pos/wks

10 May 97	**WISHES** *Epic 6644485*	44	1
30 Aug 97	**WHISPER YOUR NAME** *Epic 6649465*	53	1
10 Mar 01	**HE DON'T LOVE YOU** *Epic 6708922*	18	4
30 Jun 01	**WHEN WE WERE YOUNG** *Epic 6713792*	43	1

HUMAN RESOURCE

Holland, male instrumental / production group (14 WEEKS) pos/wks

14 Sep 91	**DOMINATOR** *R&S RSUK 4*	36	7
21 Dec 91	**THE COMPLETE DOMINATOR (re-mix)** *R&S RSUK 4X*	18	7

HUMANOID *UK, male producer – Brian Dougans (14 WEEKS)* pos/wks

26 Nov 88	**STAKKER HUMANOID** *Westside WSR 12*	17	8

		pos	wks
22 Apr 89	**SLAM** *Westside WSR 14*	54	2
8 Aug 92	**STAKKER HUMANOID (re-issue)** *Jumpin' + Pumpin' TOT 27*	40	3
3 Mar 01	**STAKKER HUMANOID (re-mix)** *Jumpin' + Pumpin' CDSTOT 43*	65	1

See also FUTURE SOUND OF LONDON

HUMATE *Germany, male production trio (4 WEEKS)*

		pos	wks
30 Jan 99	**LOVE STIMULATION** *Deviant DVNT 22CDS*	18	4

HUMBLE PIE *UK, male vocal / instrumental group (10 WEEKS)*

		pos	wks
23 Aug 69 ●	**NATURAL BORN BUGIE** *Immediate IM 082*	4	10

Engelbert HUMPERDINCK (54 Top 500)

Internationally popular cabaret entertainer and easy-on-the-ear vocalist, b. Arnold Dorsey, 2 May 1936, Madras, India. After a slow career start, an unlikely name change helped him to become one of the biggest-earning performers of the 1960s. This Vegas veteran was the UK's biggest-selling artist of 1967 and has reportedly amassed a personal fortune of £100m (239 WEEKS)

		pos	wks
26 Jan 67 ★	**RELEASE ME** *Decca F 12541* ◆	1	56
25 May 67 ●	**THERE GOES MY EVERYTHING** *Decca F 12610*	2	29
23 Aug 67 ★	**THE LAST WALTZ** *Decca F 12655* ◆	1	27
10 Jan 68 ●	**AM I THAT EASY TO FORGET** *Decca F 12722*	3	13
24 Apr 68 ●	**A MAN WITHOUT LOVE** *Decca F 12770*	2	15
25 Sep 68 ●	**LES BICYCLETTES DE BELSIZE** *Decca F 12834*	5	15
5 Feb 69 ●	**THE WAY IT USED TO BE** *Decca F 12879*	3	14
9 Aug 69	**I'M A BETTER MAN (FOR HAVING LOVED YOU)** *Decca F 12957*	15	13
15 Nov 69 ●	**WINTER WORLD OF LOVE** *Decca F 12980*	7	13
30 May 70	**MY MARIE** *Decca F 13032*	31	7
12 Sep 70	**SWEETHEART** *Decca F 13068*	22	6
31 Oct 70	**SWEETHEART (re-entry)** *Decca F 13068*	50	1
11 Sep 71	**ANOTHER TIME ANOTHER PLACE** *Decca F 13212*	13	12
4 Mar 72	**TOO BEAUTIFUL TO LAST** *Decca F 13281*	14	10
20 Oct 73	**LOVE IS ALL** *Decca F 13443*	44	3
17 Nov 73	**LOVE IS ALL (re-entry)** *Decca F 13443*	45	1
30 Jan 99	**QUANDO QUANDO QUANDO** *The Hit Label HLC 15*	40	3
6 May 00	**HOW TO WIN YOUR LOVE** *Universal TV 8822682*	59	1

HUNDRED REASONS *UK, male vocal / instrumental group (3 WEEKS)*

		pos	wks
18 Aug 01	**EP TWO** *Columbia 6713922*	47	1
15 Dec 01	**EP THREE** *Columbia 6720782*	37	2

Tracks on EP Two: Remmus / Soapbox / Shine. Tracks on EP Three: I'll Find You / Sunny / Slow Motion

Peter HUNNIGALE – *See ARSENAL FC*

Geraldine HUNT *Canada, female vocalist (5 WEEKS)*

		pos	wks
25 Oct 80	**CAN'T FAKE THE FEELING** *Champagne FIZZ 501*	44	5

Lisa HUNT – *See LOVESTATION*

Marsha HUNT *US, female vocalist (3 WEEKS)*

		pos	wks
21 May 69	**WALK ON GILDED SPLINTERS** *Track 604 030*	46	2
2 May 70	**KEEP THE CUSTOMER SATISFIED** *Track 604 037*	41	1

Tommy HUNT *US, male vocalist (17 WEEKS)*

		pos	wks
11 Oct 75	**CRACKIN' UP** *Spark SRL 1132*	39	5
21 Aug 76	**LOVING ON THE LOSING SIDE** *Spark SRL 1146*	28	9
4 Dec 76	**ONE FINE MORNING** *Spark SRL 1148*	44	3

Alfonzo HUNTER *US, male rap / instrumentalist (2 WEEKS)*

		pos	wks
22 Feb 97	**JUST THE WAY** *Cooltempo CDCOOL 326*	38	2

HUNTER featuring Ruby TURNER *UK, male gladiator / vocalist and UK, female vocalist (1 WEEK)*

		pos	wks
9 Dec 95	**SHAKABOOM!** *Telstar HUNTCD 1* [1]	64	1

Ian HUNTER *UK, male vocalist (10 WEEKS)*

		pos	wks
3 May 75	**ONCE BITTEN TWICE SHY** *CBS 3194*	14	10

See also MOTT THE HOOPLE

Tab HUNTER *US, male actor / vocalist – Andrew Arthur Kelm (30 WEEKS)*

		pos	wks
8 Feb 57 ★	**YOUNG LOVE** *London HLD 8380* ▲	1	18
12 Apr 57 ●	**NINETY-NINE WAYS** *London HLD 8410*	5	11
5 Jul 57	**NINETY-NINE WAYS (re-entry)** *London HLD 8410*	29	1

Terry HUNTER *US, male DJ / producer (1 WEEK)*

		pos	wks
26 Jul 97	**HARVEST FOR THE WORLD** *Delirious DELICD 4*	48	1

Steve 'Silk' HURLEY *US, male producer (9 WEEKS)*

		pos	wks
10 Jan 87 ★	**JACK YOUR BODY** *DJ International LON 117*	1	9

HURLEY & TODD *UK / South Africa, male production duo (2 WEEKS)*

		pos	wks
29 Apr 00	**SUNSTORM** *Multiply CDMULTY 58*	38	2

HURRICANE – *See PUFF DADDY*

HURRICANE #1 *UK, male vocal / instrumental group (17 WEEKS)*

		pos	wks
10 May 97	**STEP INTO MY WORLD** *Creation CRESCD 253*	29	2
5 Jul 97	**JUST ANOTHER ILLUSION** *Creation CRESCD 264*	35	2
6 Sep 97	**CHAIN REACTION** *Creation CRESCD 271*	30	2
1 Nov 97	**STEP INTO MY WORLD (re-mix)** *Creation CRESCD 276*	19	3
21 Feb 98	**ONLY THE STRONGEST WILL SURVIVE** *Creation CRERSCD 285*	19	6
24 Oct 98	**RISING SIGN** *Creation CRESCD 303*	47	1
3 Apr 99	**THE GREATEST HIGH** *Creation CRESCD 309*	43	1

HURRICANES – *See JOHNNY and the HURRICANES*

Phil HURTT *US, male vocalist (5 WEEKS)*

		pos	wks
11 Nov 78	**GIVING IT BACK** *Fantasy FTC 161*	36	5

HUSTLERS CONVENTION featuring Dave LAUDAT and Ondrea DUVERNEY *UK, male instrumental / production duo (1 WEEK)*

		pos	wks
20 May 95	**DANCE TO THE MUSIC** *Stress CDSTR 53*	71	1

See also SEX-O-SONIQUE; FULL INTENTION; DISCO TEX presents CLOUDBURST

Willie HUTCH *US, male vocalist (8 WEEKS)*

		pos	wks
4 Dec 82	**IN AND OUT** *Motown TMG 1285*	51	7
6 Jul 85	**KEEP ON JAMMIN'** *Motown ZB 40173*	73	1

June HUTTON *US, female vocalist (7 WEEKS)*

		pos	wks
7 Aug 53 ●	**SAY YOU'RE MINE AGAIN** *Capitol CL 13918* [1]	10	3
4 Sep 53 ●	**SAY YOU'RE MINE AGAIN (re-entry)** *Capitol CL 13918* [1]	6	4

[1] June Hutton and Axel Stordahl with the Boys Next Door

HWA featuring SONIC THE HEDGEHOG *UK, male producer – Jeremy Healy (6 WEEKS)*

		pos	wks
5 Dec 92	**SUPERSONIC** *Internal Affairs KGB 008*	33	6

HYBRID *UK, male production trio (4 WEEKS)*

		pos	wks
10 Jul 99	**FINISHED SYMPHONY** *Distinctive DISNCD 52*	58	1
11 Sep 99	**IF I SURVIVE** *Distinctive DISNCD 55* [1]	52	1
3 Jun 00	**KID 2000** *Virgin / EMI VTS CD2* [2]	32	2

[1] Hybrid featuring Julee Cruise [2] Hybrid featuring Chrissie Hynde

Brian HYLAND (492 Top 500)

Successful teen-targeted vocalist, b. 12 Nov 1943, New York, US. First hit the top in the US while still at high school, and teen separation saga 'Sealed with a Kiss' reached UK Top 10 twice. Both these songs were later UK No.1s by Bombalurina and Jason Donovan respectively (72 WEEKS) pos/wks

7 Jul 60 ●	**ITSY BITSY TEENIE WEENIE YELLOW POLKADOT BIKINI** *London HLR 9161* ▲	8	13
20 Oct 60	**FOUR LITTLE HEELS** *London HLR 9203*	29	6
10 May 62 ●	**GINNY COME LATELY** *HMV POP 1013*	5	15
2 Aug 62 ●	**SEALED WITH A KISS** *HMV POP 1051*	3	15
8 Nov 62	**WARMED OVER KISSES** *HMV POP 1079*	28	6
27 Mar 71	**GYPSY WOMAN** *Uni UN 530*	45	1
10 Apr 71	**GYPSY WOMAN (re-entry)** *Uni UN 530*	42	5
28 Jun 75 ●	**SEALED WITH A KISS (re-issue)** *ABC 4059*	7	11

Sheila HYLTON

Jamaica, female vocalist (12 WEEKS) pos/wks

15 Sep 79	**BREAKFAST IN BED** *United Artists BP 304*	57	5
17 Jan 81	**THE BED'S TOO BIG WITHOUT YOU** *Island WIP 6671*	35	7

Phyllis HYMAN

US, female vocalist (9 WEEKS) pos/wks

16 Feb 80	**YOU KNOW HOW TO LOVE ME** *Arista ARIST 323*	47	6
12 Sep 81	**YOU SURE LOOK GOOD TO ME** *Arista ARIST 424*	56	3

Dick HYMAN TRIO

US, male instrumentalist trio – Dick Hyman, keyboards (10 WEEKS) pos/wks

16 Mar 56 ●	**THEME FROM 'THE THREEPENNY OPERA'** *MGM 890*	9	10

Chrissie HYNDE

US, female vocalist / instrumentalist (38 WEEKS) pos/wks

3 Aug 85 ★	**I GOT YOU BABE** *DEP International DEP20* [1]	1	13
18 Jun 88 ●	**BREAKFAST IN BED** *DEP International DEP29* [1]	6	11
12 Oct 91	**SPIRITUAL HIGH (STATE OF INDEPENDENCE)** *Arista 114528* [2]	66	2
23 Jan 93	**SPIRITUAL HIGH (STATE OF INDEPENDENCE) (re-mix)** *Arista 74321 127712* [2]	47	2
18 Mar 95 ★	**LOVE CAN BUILD A BRIDGE** *London CO CD1* [3]	1	8
3 Jun 00	**KID 2000** *Virgin / EMI VTS CD2* [4]	32	2

[1] UB40 featuring Chrissie Hynde [2] Moodswings featuring Chrissie Hynde [3] Cher, Chrissie Hynde and Neneh Cherry with Eric Clapton [4] Hybrid featuring Chrissie Hynde

See also PRETENDERS

HYPER GO GO

UK, male instrumental / production duo (15 WEEKS) pos/wks

22 Aug 92	**HIGH** *Deconstruction 74321110497*	30	5
31 Jul 93	**NEVER LET GO** *Positiva CDTIV 3*	45	3
5 Feb 94	**RAISE** *Positiva CDTIV 9*	36	2
26 Nov 94	**IT'S ALRIGHT** *Positiva CDTIV 20*	49	1
6 Apr 96	**DO WATCHA DO** *Avex UK AVEXCD 24* [1]	54	1
12 Oct 96	**HIGH (re-mix)** *Distinctive DISNCD 24*	32	2
12 Apr 97	**DO WATCHA DO (re-mix)** *Distinctive DISNCD 28* [1]	60	1

[1] Hyper Go Go and Adeva

HYPERLOGIC

UK, male instrumental / production duo (3 WEEKS) pos/wks

29 Jul 95	**ONLY ME** *Systematic SYSCD 15*	35	2
9 May 98	**ONLY ME (re-mix)** *Tidy Trax TIDY 113CD1*	48	1

HYPERSTATE

UK, male / female vocal / instrumental duo (1 WEEK) pos/wks

6 Feb 93	**TIME AFTER TIME** *M & G MAGCD 34*	71	1

HYPNOTIST

UK, male producer – Caspar Pound (5 WEEKS) pos/wks

28 Sep 91	**THE HOUSE IS MINE** *Rising High RSN 4*	65	2
21 Dec 91	**THE HARDCORE EP** *Rising High RSN 13*	68	3

Tracks on The Hardcore EP: Hardcore U Know the Score / The Ride / Night of the Livin' E Heads / God of the Universe

HYSTERIC EGO

UK, male producer – Rob White (8 WEEKS) pos/wks

31 Aug 96	**WANT LOVE** *WEA WEA 070CD*	28	4
21 Jun 97	**MINISTRY OF LOVE** *WEA WEA 094CD*	39	2
28 Feb 98	**WANT LOVE - THE REMIXES** *WEA WEA 150CD*	46	1
13 Feb 99	**TIME TO GET BACK** *WEA WEA 198CD*	50	1

HYSTERICS

UK, male vocal / instrumental group (5 WEEKS) pos/wks

12 Dec 81	**JINGLE BELLS LAUGHING ALL THE WAY** *Record Delivery KA 5*	44	5

HYSTERIX

UK, male / female vocal / instrumental group (4 WEEKS) pos/wks

7 May 94	**MUST BE THE MUSIC** *Deconstruction 74321207362*	40	3
18 Feb 95	**EVERYTHING** *Deconstruction 74321236882*	65	1

I

I-LEVEL

UK, male vocal / instrumental group (9 WEEKS) pos/wks

16 Apr 83	**MINEFIELD** *Virgin VS 563*	52	6
18 Jun 83	**TEACHER** *Virgin VS 595*	56	3

I MONSTER

UK, male production / vocal duo – Dean Honer and Jarrod Gosling (6 WEEKS) pos/wks

16 Jun 01	**DAYDREAM IN BLUE** *Instant Karma KARMA 7 CD*	20	6

Janis IAN

US, female vocalist (10 WEEKS) pos/wks

17 Nov 79	**FLY TOO HIGH** *CBS 7936*	44	7
28 Jun 80	**THE OTHER SIDE OF THE SUN** *CBS 8611*	44	3

IAN VAN DAHL

Belgium, male / female production / vocal group (18 WEEKS) pos/wks

21 Jul 01 ●	**CASTLES IN THE SKY** *Nulife 74321867142*	5	16
22 Dec 01 ●	**WILL I** *Nulife 74321903402*	5	2

ICE CUBE

US, male rapper – O'Shea Jackson (23 WEEKS) pos/wks

27 Mar 93	**IT WAS A GOOD DAY** *Fourth & Broadway BRCD 270*	27	4
7 Aug 93	**CHECK YO SELF** *Fourth & Broadway BRCD 283* [1]	36	4
11 Sep 93	**WICKED** *Fourth & Broadway BRCD 282*	62	1
18 Dec 93	**REALLY DOE** *Fourth & Broadway BRCD 302*	66	1
26 Mar 94	**YOU KNOW HOW WE DO IT** *Fourth & Broadway BRCD 303*	41	3
27 Aug 94	**BOP GUN (ONE NATION)** *Fourth & Broadway BRCD 308* [2]	22	3
24 Dec 94	**YOU KNOW HOW WE DO IT (re-entry)** *Fourth & Broadway BRCD 303*	46	2
11 Mar 95	**HAND OF THE DEAD BODY** *Virgin America VUSCD 88* [3]	41	2
15 Apr 95	**NATURAL BORN KILLAZ** *Death Row A 8197CD* [4]	45	2
22 Mar 97	**THE WORLD IS MINE** *Jive JIVECD 419*	60	1

[1] Ice Cube featuring Das EFX [2] Ice Cube featuring George Clinton [3] Scarface featuring Ice Cube [4] Dr Dre and Ice Cube

ICE MC

UK, male rapper – Ian Campbell (5 WEEKS) pos/wks

6 Aug 94	**THINK ABOUT THE WAY (BOM DIGI DIGI BOM...)** *WEA YZ 829CD*	42	2
8 Apr 95	**IT'S A RAINY DAY** *Eternal YZ 902CD*	73	1
14 Sep 96	**BOM DIGI BOM (THINK ABOUT THE WAY) (re-issue)** *Eternal WEA 073CD*	38	2

ICE-T

US, male rapper – Tracy Morrow (29 WEEKS) pos/wks

18 Mar 89	**HIGH ROLLERS** *Sire W 7574*	63	2
17 Feb 90	**YOU PLAYED YOURSELF** *Sire W 9994*	64	2
29 Sep 90	**SUPERFLY 1990** *Capitol CL 586* [1]	48	3
8 May 93	**I AIN'T NEW TA THIS** *Rhyme Syndicate SYNDD 1*	62	2
18 Dec 93	**THAT'S HOW I'M LIVIN'** *Rhyme Syndicate SYNDD 2*	21	6
9 Apr 94	**GOTTA LOTTA LOVE** *Rhyme Syndicate SYNDD 3*	24	4
10 Dec 94	**BORN TO RAISE HELL** *Fox 74321230152* [2]	47	2

Date		Title	Pos	Wks
1 Jun 96		**I MUST STAND** *Rhyme Syndicate SYNDD 5*	23	3
7 Dec 96		**THE LANE** *Rhyme Syndicate SYNDD 6*	18	5

[1] Curtis Mayfield and Ice-T [2] Motörhead / Ice-T / Whitfield Crane

ICEBERG SLIMM *UK, male rapper (2 WEEKS)* pos/wks

Date		Title	Pos	Wks
7 Oct 00		**NURSERY RHYMES** *Polydor 5877632*	37	2

ICEHOUSE *New Zealand, male vocal / instrumental group (28 WEEKS)* pos/wks

Date		Title	Pos	Wks
5 Feb 83		**HEY LITTLE GIRL** *Chrysalis CHS 2670*	17	10
23 Apr 83		**STREET CAFE** *Chrysalis COOL 1*	62	4
3 May 86		**NO PROMISES** *Chrysalis CHS 2978*	72	1
29 Aug 87		**CRAZY** *Chrysalis CHS 3156*	74	1
13 Feb 88		**CRAZY (re-entry)** *Chrysalis CHS 3156*	38	8
14 May 88		**ELECTRIC BLUE** *Chrysalis CHS 3239*	53	4

ICICLE WORKS *UK, male vocal / instrumental group – lead vocal Ian McNabb (28 WEEKS)* pos/wks

Date		Title	Pos	Wks
24 Dec 83		**LOVE IS A WONDERFUL COLOUR** *Beggars Banquet BEG 99*	15	8
10 Mar 84		**BIRDS FLY (WHISPER TO A SCREAM) / IN THE CAULDRON OF LOVE** *Beggars Banquet BEG 108*	53	4
26 Jul 86		**UNDERSTANDING JANE** *Beggars Banquet BEG 160*	52	3
4 Oct 86		**WHO DO YOU WANT FOR YOUR LOVE?** *Beggars Banquet BEG 172*	54	4
14 Feb 87		**EVANGELINE** *Beggars Banquet BEG 181*	53	4
30 Apr 88		**LITTLE GIRL LOST** *Beggars Banquet BEG 215*	59	4
17 Mar 90		**MOTORCYCLE RIDER** *Epic WORKS 100*	73	1

ICON *UK, male / female vocal / instrumental duo (1 WEEK)* pos/wks

Date		Title	Pos	Wks
15 Jun 96		**TAINTED LOVE** *Eternal WEA 057CD*	51	1

IDEAL *UK, male producer – Jon Da Silva (2 WEEKS)* pos/wks

Date		Title	Pos	Wks
6 Aug 94		**HOT** *Cleveland City CLECD 13019*	49	2

IDEAL US featuring LIL' Mo

US, male vocal group featuring female vocalist (3 WEEKS) pos/wks

Date		Title	Pos	Wks
23 Sep 00		**WHATEVER** *Virgin VUSCD 172*	31	3

IDES OF MARCH *US, male vocal / instrumental group (9 WEEKS)* pos/wks

Date		Title	Pos	Wks
6 Jun 70		**VEHICLE** *Warner Bros. WB 7378*	31	9

Eric IDLE featuring Richard WILSON

UK, male actors / vocalists (3 WEEKS) pos/wks

Date		Title	Pos	Wks
17 Dec 94		**ONE FOOT IN THE GRAVE** *Victa CDVICTA 1*	50	3

IDLEWILD *UK, male vocal / instrumental group (15 WEEKS)* pos/wks

Date		Title	Pos	Wks
9 May 98		**A FILM FOR THE FUTURE** *Food CDFOOD 111*	53	1
25 Jul 98		**EVERYONE SAYS YOU'RE SO FRAGILE** *Food CDFOOD 113*	47	1
24 Oct 98		**I'M A MESSAGE** *Food CDFOOD 114*	41	1
13 Feb 99		**WHEN I ARGUE I SEE SHAPES** *Food CDFOOD 116*	19	2
2 Oct 99		**LITTLE DISCOURAGE** *Food CDFOOD 124*	24	2
8 Apr 00		**ACTUALLY IT'S DARKNESS** *Food CDFOOD127*	23	3
24 Jun 00		**THESE WOODEN IDEAS** *Food CDFOOD 132*	32	3
28 Oct 00		**ROSEABILITY** *Food CDFOODS 134*	38	2

Billy IDOL (282 Top 500) *Snarling rock 'n' roll rebel of the 1980s. Former vocalist of punk hitmakers Generation X, b. William Broad, 30 Nov 1955, Middlesex, UK. He had his greatest success in the US, where four singles reached the Top 10 and 'Mony Mony' reached No.1 (106 WEEKS)* pos/wks

Date		Title	Pos	Wks
11 Sep 82		**HOT IN THE CITY** *Chrysalis CHS 2625*	58	4
24 Mar 84		**REBEL YELL** *Chrysalis IDOL 2*	62	2
30 Jun 84		**EYES WITHOUT A FACE** *Chrysalis IDOL 3*	18	11
29 Sep 84		**FLESH FOR FANTASY** *Chrysalis IDOL 4*	54	3
13 Jul 85	●	**WHITE WEDDING** *Chrysalis IDOL 5*	6	15
14 Sep 85	●	**REBEL YELL (re-issue)** *Chrysalis IDOL 6*	6	12
4 Oct 86		**TO BE A LOVER** *Chrysalis IDOL 8*	22	8
7 Mar 87		**DON'T NEED A GUN** *Chrysalis IDOL 9*	26	5
13 Jun 87		**SWEET SIXTEEN** *Chrysalis IDOL 10*	17	9
3 Oct 87	●	**MONY MONY** *Chrysalis IDOL 11* ▲	7	10
16 Jan 88		**HOT IN THE CITY (re-mix)** *Chrysalis IDOL 12*	13	9
13 Aug 88		**CATCH MY FALL** *Chrysalis IDOL 13*	63	3
28 Apr 90		**CRADLE OF LOVE** *Chrysalis IDOL 14*	34	4
11 Aug 90		**L.A. WOMAN** *Chrysalis IDOL 15*	70	2
22 Dec 90		**PRODIGAL BLUES** *Chrysalis IDOL 16*	47	4
26 Jun 93		**SHOCK TO THE SYSTEM** *Chrysalis CDCHS 3994*	30	3
10 Sep 94		**SPEED** *Fox 74321223472*	47	2

Frank IFIELD (130 Top 500) *Early 60s superstar, b. 30 Nov 1937, Coventry, UK, and raised in Australia. This pop vocalist / yodeller had four No.1s in 12 months with revivals of US standards. Unlike many of his early 1960s UK contemporaries, his records also did well internationally (162 WEEKS)* pos/wks

Date		Title	Pos	Wks
19 Feb 60		**LUCKY DEVIL** *Columbia DB 4399*	22	5
7 Apr 60		**LUCKY DEVIL (re-entry)** *Columbia DB 4399*	33	2
29 Sep 60		**GOTTA GET A DATE** *Columbia DB 4496*	49	1
5 Jul 62	★	**I REMEMBER YOU** *Columbia DB 4856* ◆	1	28
25 Oct 62	★	**LOVESICK BLUES** *Columbia DB 4913*	1	17
24 Jan 63	★	**THE WAYWARD WIND** *Columbia DB 4960*	1	13
11 Apr 63	●	**NOBODY'S DARLIN' BUT MINE** *Columbia DB 7007*	4	16
27 Jun 63	★	**CONFESSIN' (THAT I LOVE YOU)** *Columbia DB 7062*	1	16
17 Oct 63		**MULE TRAIN** *Columbia DB 7131*	22	6
9 Jan 64	●	**DON'T BLAME ME** *Columbia DB 7184*	8	13
23 Apr 64		**ANGRY AT THE BIG OAK TREE** *Columbia DB 7263*	25	8
23 Jul 64		**I SHOULD CARE** *Columbia DB 7319*	33	3
1 Oct 64		**SUMMER IS OVER** *Columbia DB 7355*	25	6
19 Aug 65		**PARADISE** *Columbia DB 7655*	26	9
23 Jun 66		**NO ONE WILL EVER KNOW** *Columbia DB 7940*	25	4
8 Dec 66		**CALL HER YOUR SWEETHEART** *Columbia DB 8078*	24	11
7 Dec 91		**SHE TAUGHT ME HOW TO YODEL** *EMI 7YODEL 1* [1]	40	4

[1] Frank Ifield featuring the Backroom Boys

Enrique IGLESIAS *Spain, male vocalist (19 WEEKS)* pos/wks

Date		Title	Pos	Wks
11 Sep 99	●	**BAILAMOS** *Interscope IND 97131* ▲	4	9
18 Dec 99		**RHYTHM DIVINE** *Interscope 4972242*	45	2
14 Oct 00	●	**COULD I HAVE THIS KISS FOREVER** *Arista 74321795992* [1]	7	8

[1] Whitney Houston and Enrique Iglesias

Julio IGLESIAS (460 Top 500) *Spain's most successful vocalist of all time with reported world sales of more than 225 million albums; b. 23 Sep 1943, Madrid. Suave singer was still adding to his hits and awards in late 1990s, when son Enrique also became a leading Latin recording artist (75 WEEKS)* pos/wks

Date		Title	Pos	Wks
24 Oct 81	★	**BEGIN THE BEGUINE (VOLVER A EMPEZAR)** *CBS A 1612*	1	14
6 Mar 82	●	**QUIEREME MUCHO (YOURS)** *CBS A 1939*	3	9
9 Oct 82		**AMOR** *CBS A 2801*	32	7
9 Apr 83		**HEY!** *CBS JULIO 1*	31	7
7 Apr 84		**TO ALL THE GIRLS I'VE LOVED BEFORE** *CBS A 4252* [1]	17	10
7 Jul 84		**ALL OF YOU** *CBS A 4522* [2]	43	8
6 Aug 88	●	**MY LOVE** *CBS JULIO 2* [3]	5	11
4 Jun 94		**CRAZY** *Columbia 6603695*	43	3
27 Aug 94		**CRAZY (re-entry)** *Columbia 6603695*	50	2
26 Nov 94		**FRAGILE** *Columbia 6610192*	53	2
31 Dec 94		**FRAGILE (re-entry)** *Columbia 6610192*	66	2

[1] Julio Iglesias and Willie Nelson [2] Julio Iglesias and Diana Ross [3] Julio Iglesias featuring Stevie Wonder

IGNORANTS *UK, male vocal duo (3 WEEKS)* pos/wks

Date		Title	Pos	Wks
25 Dec 93		**PHAT GIRLS** *Spaghetti CIOCD 8*	59	3

IIO *US, male / female production duo – Marcus Moser and Nadia Li (8 WEEKS)* pos/wks

Date		Title	Pos	Wks
10 Nov 01	●	**RAPTURE** *Made / Data / MoS DATA 27CDS*	2	8+

ILLEGAL MOTION featuring Simone CHAPMAN

UK, male / female vocal / instrumental duo (1 WEEK) pos/wks

Date		Title	Pos	Wks
9 Oct 93		**SATURDAY LOVE** *Arista 74321163032*	67	1

ILLICIT featuring GRAM'MA FUNK *UK, male producer (1 WEEK)* pos/wks

2 Sep 00	**CHEEKY ARMADA** *Yola YOLACDX 01*	72	1

IMAANI
UK, female vocalist – Imaani Saleem (aka Melanie Crosdale) (7 WEEKS) pos/wks

9 May 98	**WHERE ARE YOU** *EMI CDEM 510*	15	7

IMAGINATION (284 Top 500) *Distinctive London-based trio, who created a unique blend of soul and dance music: Leee John (v), Ashley Ingram (v/k), Errol Kennedy (d). One of the most original British acts of the early 1980s, they were fronted by a charismatic and flamboyant lead singer (105 WEEKS)* pos/wks

16 May 81 ●	**BODY TALK** *R & B RBS 201*	4	18
5 Sep 81	**IN AND OUT OF LOVE** *R & B RBS 202*	16	9
14 Nov 81	**FLASHBACK** *R & B RBS 206*	16	13
6 Mar 82 ●	**JUST AN ILLUSION** *R & B RBS 208*	2	11
26 Jun 82 ●	**MUSIC AND LIGHTS** *R & B RBS 210*	5	9
25 Sep 82	**IN THE HEAT OF THE NIGHT** *R & B RBS 211*	22	8
11 Dec 82	**CHANGES** *R & B RBS 213*	31	8
4 Jun 83	**LOOKING AT MIDNIGHT** *R & B RBS 214*	29	7
5 Nov 83	**NEW DIMENSIONS** *R & B RBS 216*	56	3
26 May 84	**STATE OF LOVE** *R & B RBS 218*	67	2
24 Nov 84	**THANK YOU MY LOVE** *R & B RBS 219*	22	15
16 Jan 88	**INSTINCTUAL** *RCA PB 41697*	62	2

IMAJIN *US, male vocal group (7 WEEKS)* pos/wks

27 Jun 98	**SHORTY (YOU KEEP PLAYIN' WITH MY MIND)** *Jive 0521212* [1]	22	3
20 Feb 99	**NO DOUBT** *Jive 0521772*	42	2
24 Apr 99	**BOUNCE, ROCK, SKATE, ROLL** *Jive 0522142*	45	1
12 Feb 00	**FLAVA** *Jive 9250012*	64	1

[1] Imajin featuring Keith Murray

See also BABY DC

Natalie IMBRUGLIA *Australia, female vocalist (44 WEEKS)* pos/wks

8 Nov 97 ●	**TORN** *RCA 74321527982*	2	17
14 Mar 98 ●	**BIG MISTAKE** *RCA 74321566782*	2	10
6 Jun 98	**WISHING I WAS THERE** *RCA 74321585062*	19	5
17 Oct 98 ●	**SMOKE** *RCA 74321621942*	5	7
10 Nov 01	**THAT DAY** *RCA 74321896792*	11	4
29 Dec 01	**THAT DAY (re-entry)** *RCA 74321896792*	66	1

IMMACULATE FOOLS *UK, male vocal / instrumental group (4 WEEKS)* pos/wks

26 Jan 85	**IMMACULATE FOOLS** *A & M AM 227*	51	4

IMMATURE featuring SMOOTH
US, male vocal group and US, female vocalist (2 WEEKS) pos/wks

16 Mar 96	**WE GOT IT** *MCA MCSTD 48009* [1]	26	2

IMPALAS *US, male vocal group (1 WEEK)* pos/wks

21 Aug 59	**SORRY (I RAN ALL THE WAY HOME)** *MGM 1015*	28	1

IMPEDANCE *UK, male producer – Daniel Haydon (4 WEEKS)* pos/wks

11 Nov 89	**TAINTED LOVE** *Jumpin' & Pumpin' TOT 4*	54	4

IMPERIAL DRAG *UK, male vocal / instrumental group (1 WEEK)* pos/wks

12 Oct 96	**BOY OR A GIRL** *Columbia 6632992*	54	1

IMPERIAL TEEN
US, male / female vocal / instrumental group (1 WEEK) pos/wks

7 Sep 96	**YOU'RE ONE** *Slash LASCD 57*	69	1

See also FAITH NO MORE

IMPERIALS *US, male vocal group (9 WEEKS)* pos/wks

24 Dec 77	**WHO'S GONNA LOVE ME** *Power Exchange PX 266*	17	9

IMPOSTER – *See Elvis COSTELLO*

IMPRESSIONS *US, male vocal group (10 WEEKS)* pos/wks

22 Nov 75	**FIRST IMPRESSIONS** *Curtom K 16638*	16	10

IN CROWD *UK, male vocal / instrumental group (1 WEEK)* pos/wks

20 May 65	**THAT'S HOW STRONG MY LOVE IS** *Parlophone R 5276*	48	1

IN TUA NUA
Ireland, male / female vocal / instrumental group (2 WEEKS) pos/wks

14 May 88	**ALL I WANTED** *Virgin VS 1072*	69	2

INAURA *UK, male vocal / instrumental group (1 WEEK)* pos/wks

18 May 96	**COMA AROMA** *EMI CDEM 421*	57	1

INCANTATION *UK, male instrumental group (12 WEEKS)* pos/wks

4 Dec 82	**CACHARPAYA (ANDES PUMPSA DAESI)** *Beggars Banquet BEG 84*	12	12

INCOGNITO *UK, male / female vocal / instrumental group (38 WEEKS)* pos/wks

15 Nov 80	**PARISIENNE GIRL** *Ensign ENY 44*	73	2
29 Jun 91 ●	**ALWAYS THERE** *Talkin Loud TLK 10* [1]	6	9
14 Sep 91	**CRAZY FOR YOU** *Talkin Loud TLK 14* [2]	59	2
6 Jun 92	**DON'T YOU WORRY 'BOUT A THING** *Talkin Loud TLK 21*	19	6
15 Aug 92	**CHANGE** *Talkin Loud TLK 26*	52	2
21 Aug 93	**STILL A FRIEND OF MINE** *Talkin Loud TLKCD 42*	47	2
20 Nov 93	**GIVIN' IT UP** *Talkin Loud TLKCD 44*	43	2
12 Mar 94	**PIECES OF A DREAM** *Talkin Loud TLKCD 46*	35	2
27 May 95	**EVERYDAY** *Talkin Loud TLKCD 55*	23	3
5 Aug 95	**I HEAR YOUR NAME** *Talkin Loud TLKCD 56*	42	3
11 May 96	**JUMP TO MY LOVE / ALWAYS THERE (re-recording)** *Talkin Loud TLCD 7*	29	3
26 Oct 96	**OUT OF THE STORM** *Talkin Loud TLCD 14*	57	1
10 Apr 99	**NIGHTS OVER EGYPT** *Talkin Loud TLCD 40*	56	1

[1] Incognito featuring Jocelyn Brown [2] Incognito featuring Chyna

INCUBUS *US male vocal / instrumental group (3 WEEK)* pos/wks

20 May 00	**PARDON ME** *Epic 6693462*	61	1
23 Jun 01	**DRIVE** *Epic 6713782*	40	2

INDEEP *US, male / female vocal / rap group (11 WEEKS)* pos/wks

22 Jan 83	**LAST NIGHT A DJ SAVED MY LIFE** *Sound of New York SNY 1*	13	9
14 May 83	**WHEN BOYS TALK** *Sound of New York SNY 3*	67	2

INDIA *US, female vocalist (14 WEEKS)* pos/wks

26 Feb 94	**LOVE AND HAPPINESS (YEMAYA Y OCHUN)** *Cooltempo CDCOOL 287* [1]	50	2
5 Aug 95	**I CAN'T GET NO SLEEP** *A & M 5811412* [2]	44	2
16 Mar 96	**OYE COMO VA** *Media MCSTD 40013* [3]	36	2
8 Feb 97	**RUNAWAY** *Talkin Loud TLCD20* [4]	24	4
19 Jul 97	**OYE COMO VA (re-issue)** *Nukleuz MCSTD 40120* [3]	56	1
31 Jul 99	**TO BE IN LOVE** *Defected DEFECT 5CDS* [5]	23	3

[1] River Ocean featuring India [2] Masters At Work presents India [3] Tito Puente Jr and the Latin Rhythm featuring Tito Puente, India and Cali Aleman [4] Nuyorican Soul featuring India [5] MAW presents India

INDIAN VIBES *UK, male vocal / instrumental group (2 WEEKS)* pos/wks

24 Sep 94	**MATHAR** *Virgin International DINSD 136*	68	1
2 May 98	**MATHAR (re-mix)** *VC Recordings VCRD 32*	52	1

INDO *US, female vocal duo (3 WEEKS)* pos/wks

18 Apr 98	**R U SLEEPING** *Satellite 74321568212*	31	3

INDUSTRY STANDARD *UK, male DJ / production duo (3 WEEKS)* pos/wks

10 Jan 98	**VOLUME 1 (WHAT YOU WANT WHAT YOU NEED)** *Satellite 74321543742*	34	3

INFINITI – *See GRAND PUBA*

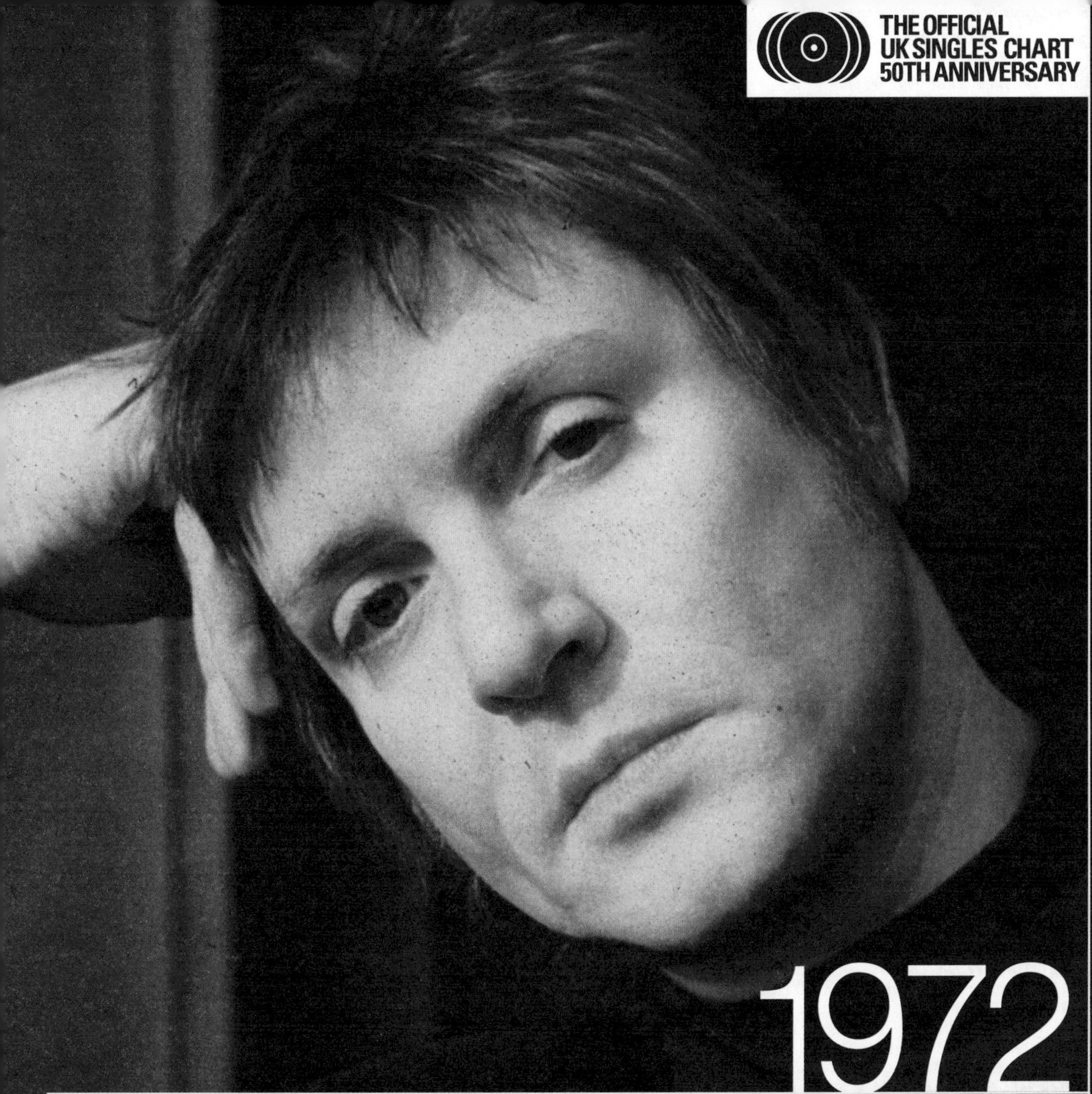

1972

IN THE YEAR IN WHICH BLOODY SUNDAY INFLAMED THE CONFLICT IN NORTHERN IRELAND, NIXON BECAME THE FIRST US PRESIDENT TO MAKE AN OFFICIAL VISIT TO CHINA, MARLON BRANDO'S MAFIA 'GODFATHER' PACKED THEM IN AT THE CINEMAS, AND TEENY BOP TRIUMPHED THANKS TO NEW ACTS THE OSMONDS AND DAVID CASSIDY, **SIMON LE BON** BUYS HIS FIRST POP SINGLE ...

“'A Horse With No Name' by **America** was the first record I ever bought at a little shop in Pinner [north-west London]. Such a good pop song. Good lyrics, which I think is one of the factors that makes a great pop song. I was always involved with literature at school. I did drama and studied poetry for years so I've always thought a song has got to say something.”

SINGLE OF THE YEAR 'Without You' Nilsson
ALBUM OF THE YEAR 'Electric Warrior' T. Rex

INGRAM *US, male vocal / instrumental group (2 WEEKS)* pos/wks

11 Jun 83	**SMOOTHIN' GROOVIN'** *Streetwave WAVE 3*	56	2

James INGRAM *US, male vocalist (42 WEEKS)* pos/wks

12 Feb 83	**BABY COME TO ME** *Qwest K 15005* [1] ▲	11	10
18 Feb 84	**YAH MO B THERE** *Qwest W 9394* [2]	44	5
7 Apr 84	**YAH MO B THERE (re-entry)** *Qwest W 9394* [2]	69	3
12 Jan 85	**YAH MO B THERE (2nd re-entry)** *Qwest W 9394* [2]	12	8
11 Jul 87 ●	**SOMEWHERE OUT THERE** *MCA MCA 1132* [3]	8	13
31 Mar 90	**SECRET GARDEN** *Qwest W 9992* [4]	67	1
16 Apr 94	**THE DAY I FALL IN LOVE** *Columbia 6600282* [5]	64	2

[1] Patti Austin and James Ingram [2] James Ingram with Michael McDonald [3] Linda Ronstadt and James Ingram [4] Quincy Jones featuring Al B Sure!, James Ingram, El DeBarge and Barry White [5] Dolly Parton and James Ingram

INK SPOTS *US, male vocal group (4 WEEKS)* pos/wks

29 Apr 55 ●	**MELODY OF LOVE** *Parlophone R 3977*	10	4

John INMAN *UK, male actor / vocalist (6 WEEKS)* pos/wks

25 Oct 75	**ARE YOU BEING SERVED SIR** *DJM DJS 602*	39	6

INMATES *UK, male vocal / instrumental group (9 WEEKS)* pos/wks

8 Dec 79	**THE WALK** *Radar ADA 47*	36	9

INNER CIRCLE *Jamaica, male vocal / instrumental group (35 WEEKS)* pos/wks

24 Feb 79	**EVERYTHING IS GREAT** *Island WIP 6472*	37	8
12 May 79	**STOP BREAKING MY HEART** *Island WIP 6488*	50	3
31 Oct 92	**SWEAT (A LA LA LA LA LONG)** *Magnet 9031776802*	43	5
1 May 93 ●	**SWEAT (A LA LA LA LA LONG) (re-entry)** *Magnet 9031776802*	3	14
31 Jul 93	**BAD BOYS** *Magnet MAG 1017CD*	52	3
10 Sep 94	**GAMES PEOPLE PLAY** *Magnet MAG 1026CD*	67	2

INNER CITY (410 Top 500) *House act from Detroit, US, formed by New York-born producer and club DJ Kevin Saunderson, b. 9 May 1964, which featured distinctive vocalist Paris Grey. Quickly became first house act to reach the UK Top 10 with initial three hits (81 WEEKS)* pos/wks

3 Sep 88 ●	**BIG FUN** *10 TEN 240* [1]	8	14
10 Dec 88 ●	**GOOD LIFE** *10 TEN 249*	4	12
22 Apr 89 ●	**AIN'T NOBODY BETTER** *10 TEN 252*	10	7
29 Jul 89	**DO YOU LOVE WHAT YOU FEEL** *10 TEN 273*	16	7
18 Nov 89	**WATCHA GONNA DO WITH MY LOVIN'** *10 TEN 290*	12	9
13 Oct 90	**THAT MAN (HE'S ALL MINE)** *10 TEN 334*	42	4
23 Feb 91	**TILL WE MEET AGAIN** *Ten TEN 337*	47	2
7 Dec 91	**LET IT REIGN** *Ten TEN 392*	51	2
4 Apr 92	**HALLELUJAH '92** *Ten TEN 398*	22	4
13 Jun 92	**PENNIES FROM HEAVEN** *Ten TEN 405*	24	4
12 Sep 92	**PRAISE** *Ten TENX 408*	59	2
27 Feb 93	**TILL WE MEET AGAIN (re-mix)** *Ten TENCD 414*	55	1
14 Aug 93	**BACK TOGETHER AGAIN** *Six6 SIXCD 104*	49	1
5 Feb 94	**DO YA** *Six6 SIXCD 107*	44	2
9 Jul 94	**SHARE MY LIFE** *Six6 SIXCD 114*	62	1
10 Feb 96	**YOUR LOVE** *Six6 SIXCD 127*	28	2
5 Oct 96	**DO ME RIGHT** *Six6 SIXXCD 2*	47	1
6 Feb 99 ●	**GOOD LIFE (BUENA VIDA) (re-recording)** *Pias Recordings PIASX 002CD*	10	6

[1] Inner City featuring Kevin Saunderson

INNER SANCTUM *Canada, male producer – Steve Bolton (1 WEEK)* pos/wks

23 May 98	**HOW SOON IS NOW** *Malarky MLKD 6*	75	1

INNERZONE ORCHESTRA *US, male producer – Carl Craig (1 WEEK)* pos/wks

28 Sep 96	**BUG IN THE BASSBIN** *Mo Wax MW 049CD*	68	1

INNOCENCE *UK, male / female vocal / instrumental group (33 WEEKS)* pos/wks

3 Mar 90	**NATURAL THING** *Cooltempo COOL 201*	16	7
21 Jul 90	**SILENT VOICE** *Cooltempo COOL 212*	37	5
13 Oct 90	**LET'S PUSH IT** *Cooltempo COOL 220*	25	6
8 Dec 90	**A MATTER OF FACT** *Cooltempo COOL 223*	37	7
30 Mar 91	**REMEMBER THE DAY** *Cooltempo COOL 226*	56	2
20 Jun 92	**I'LL BE THERE** *Cooltempo COOL 255*	26	3
3 Oct 92	**ONE LOVE IN MY LIFETIME** *Cooltempo COOL 263*	40	2
21 Nov 92	**BUILD** *Cooltempo COOL 267*	72	1

INSANE CLOWN POSSE *US, male rap duo (2 WEEKS)* pos/wks

17 Jan 98	**HALLS OF ILLUSION** *Island CID 685*	56	1
6 Jun 98	**HOKUS POKUS** *Island CIDX 705*	53	1

INSPIRAL CARPETS
UK, male vocal / instrumental group (50 WEEKS) pos/wks

18 Nov 89	**MOVE** *Cow DUNG 6*	49	2
17 Mar 90	**THIS IS HOW IT FEELS** *Cow DUNG 7*	14	8
30 Jun 90	**SHE COMES IN THE FALL** *Cow DUNG 10*	27	6
17 Nov 90	**ISLAND HEAD (EP)** *Cow DUNG 11*	21	4
30 Mar 91	**CARAVAN** *Cow DUNG 13*	30	5
22 Jun 91	**PLEASE BE CRUEL** *Cow DUNG 15*	50	2
29 Feb 92	**DRAGGING ME DOWN** *Cow DUNG 16*	12	5
30 May 92	**TWO WORLDS COLLIDE** *Cow DUNG 17*	32	2
19 Sep 92	**GENERATIONS** *Cow DUNG 18T*	28	3
14 Nov 92	**BITCHES BREW** *Cow DUNG 20T*	36	2
5 Jun 93	**HOW IT SHOULD BE** *Cow DUNG 22CD*	49	1
22 Jan 94	**SATURN 5** *Cow DUNG 23CD*	20	4
5 Mar 94	**I WANT YOU** *Cow DUNG 24CD* [1]	18	3
7 May 94	**UNIFORM** *Cow DUNG 26CD*	51	1
16 Sep 95	**JOE** *Cow DUNG 27CD*	37	2

[1] Inspiral Carpets featuring Mark E Smith

Tracks on Island Head (EP): Biggest Mountain / Gold Top / Weakness / I'll Keep It In Mind

INSPIRATIONAL CHOIR *US, male / female choir (11 WEEKS)* pos/wks

22 Dec 84	**ABIDE WITH ME** *Epic A 4997*	44	5
14 Dec 85	**ABIDE WITH ME (re-issue)** *Portrait A 4997*	36	6

Label credits the Royal Choral Society

INSTANT FUNK *US, male vocal / instrumental group (5 WEEKS)* pos/wks

20 Jan 79	**GOT MY MIND MADE UP** *Salsoul SSOL 114*	46	5

INTASTELLA
UK, male / female vocal / instrumental group (6 WEEKS) pos/wks

25 May 91	**DREAM SOME PARADISE** *MCA MCS 1520*	69	1
24 Aug 91	**PEOPLE** *MCA MCS 1559*	74	2
16 Nov 91	**CENTURY** *MCA MCS 1585*	70	2
23 Sep 95	**THE NIGHT** *Planet 3 GXY 2005CD*	60	1

INTELLIGENT HOODLUM *US, male rapper (3 WEEKS)* pos/wks

6 Oct 90	**BACK TO REALITY** *A & M AM 598*	55	3

INTERACTIVE
Germany, male instrumental / production group (4 WEEKS) pos/wks

13 Apr 96	**FOREVER YOUNG** *Ffrreedom TABCD 235*	28	4

INTRUDERS *US, male vocal group (21 WEEKS)* pos/wks

13 Apr 74	**I'LL ALWAYS LOVE MY MAMA** *Philadelphia International PIR 2159*	32	7
6 Jul 74	**WIN PLACE OR SHOW (SHE'S A WINNER)** *Philadelphia International PIR 2212*	14	9
22 Dec 84	**WHO DO YOU LOVE?** *Streetwave KHAN 34*	65	5

INVADERS OF THE HEART – *See Jah WOBBLE'S INVADERS of the HEART*

INVISIBLE GIRLS – *See Pauline MURRAY and the INVISIBLE GIRLS*

INVISIBLE MAN *UK, male producer – Graham Mew (1 WEEK)* pos/wks

17 Apr 99	**GIVE A LITTLE LOVE** *Serious SERR 006CD*	48	1

INXS (197 Top 500) *Stadium-packing rock sextet led by Australian Michael Hutchence (b. 22 Jan 1960, Sydney; d. 22 Nov 1997). Both Hutchence and group won Brit awards in 1991, and the video for their US chart-topper 'Need You Tonight' won five MTV awards in 1988 (132 WEEKS)*

Date		Title / Label	pos	wks
19 Apr 86		WHAT YOU NEED *Mercury INXS 5*	51	6
28 Jun 86		LISTEN LIKE THIEVES *Mercury INXS 6*	46	7
30 Aug 86		KISS THE DIRT (FALLING DOWN THE MOUNTAIN) *Mercury INXS 7*	54	3
24 Oct 87		NEED YOU TONIGHT *Mercury INXS 8* ▲	58	3
9 Jan 88		NEW SENSATION *Mercury INXS 9*	25	6
12 Mar 88		DEVIL INSIDE *Mercury INXS 10*	47	5
25 Jun 88		NEVER TEAR US APART *Mecury INXS 11*	24	7
12 Nov 88	●	NEED YOU TONIGHT (re-issue) *Mercury INXS 12*	2	11
8 Apr 89		MYSTIFY *Mercury INXS 13*	14	7
15 Sep 90		SUICIDE BLONDE *Mercury INXS 14*	11	6
8 Dec 90		DISAPPEAR *Mercury INXS 15*	21	8
26 Jan 91		GOOD TIMES *Atlantic A 7751* [1]	18	8
30 Mar 91		BY MY SIDE *Mercury INXS 16*	42	4
13 Jul 91		BITTER TEARS *Mercury INXS 17*	30	3
2 Nov 91		SHINING STAR (EP) *Mercury INXS 18*	27	3
18 Jul 92		HEAVEN SENT *Mercury INXS 19*	31	3
5 Sep 92		BABY DON'T CRY *Mercury INXS 20*	20	5
14 Nov 92		TASTE IT *Mercury INXS 23*	21	4
13 Feb 93		BEAUTIFUL GIRL *Mercury INXCD 24*	23	5
23 Oct 93		THE GIFT *Mercury INXCD 25*	11	4
11 Dec 93		PLEASE (YOU GOT THAT . . .) *Mercury INXCD 26*	50	3
22 Oct 94		THE STRANGEST PARTY (THESE ARE THE TIMES) *Mercury INXCD 27*	15	5
22 Mar 97		ELEGANTLY WASTED *Mercury INXCD 28*	20	4
7 Jun 97		EVERYTHING *Mercury INXDD 29*	71	1
18 Aug 01		PRECIOUS HEART *Duty Free / Decode DFTELCD 001* [2]	14	4
29 Sep 01		PRECIOUS HEART (re-entry) *Duty Free / Decode DFTELCD 001* [2]	57	1
3 Nov 01		I'M SO CRAZY *Credence CDCRED 016* [3]	19	5
15 Dec 01		I'M SO CRAZY (re-entry) *Credence CDCRED 016* [3]	71	1

[1] Jimmy Barnes and INXS [2] Tall Paul vs Inxs [3] Par-T-One vs Inxs

Tracks on Shining Star (EP): Shining Star / Send a Message (Live) / Faith in Each Other (Live) / Bitter Tears (Live). Although uncredited, 'Please (You Got That...)' is a duet with Ray Charles

Sweetie IRIE – *See ASWAD; SCRITTI POLITTI; Ed CASE*

Tippa IRIE *UK, male vocalist (14 WEEKS)*

Date		Title / Label	pos	wks
22 Mar 86		HELLO DARLING *Greensleeves / UK Bubblers TIPPA 4*	22	7
19 Jul 86		HEARTBEAT *Greensleeves / UK Bubblers TIPPA 5*	59	3
15 May 93		SHOUTING FOR THE GUNNERS *London LONCD 342* [1]	34	3
8 Jul 95		STAYING ALIVE 95 *Telstar CDSTAS 2776* [2]	48	1

[1] Arsenal FA Cup Squad featuring Tippa Irie and Peter Hunnigale [2] Fever featuring Tippa Irie

IRON MAIDEN (139 Top 500) *Legendary London-based group named after a medieval torture device. Lead vocalists have included Paul Di'Anno and Blaze Bayley, but it was with frontman Bruce Dickinson that they enjoyed a period as arguably the world's top metal band (154 WEEKS)*

Date		Title / Label	pos	wks
23 Feb 80		RUNNING FREE *EMI 5032*	34	5
7 Jun 80		SANCTUARY *EMI 5065*	29	5
8 Nov 80		WOMEN IN UNIFORM *EMI 5105*	35	4
14 Mar 81		TWILIGHT ZONE / WRATH CHILD *EMI 5145*	31	5
27 Jun 81		PURGATORY *EMI 5184*	52	3
26 Sep 81		MAIDEN JAPAN *EMI 5219*	43	4
20 Feb 82	●	RUN TO THE HILLS *EMI 5263*	7	10
15 May 82		THE NUMBER OF THE BEAST *EMI 5287*	18	8
23 Apr 83		FLIGHT OF ICARUS *EMI 5378*	11	6
2 Jul 83		THE TROOPER *EMI 5397*	12	7
18 Aug 84		2 MINUTES TO MIDNIGHT *EMI 5849*	11	6
3 Nov 84		ACES HIGH *EMI 5502*	20	5
5 Oct 85		RUNNING FREE (LIVE) *EMI 5532*	19	5
14 Dec 85		RUN TO THE HILLS (LIVE) *EMI 5542*	26	6
6 Sep 86		WASTED YEARS *EMI 5583*	18	4
22 Nov 86		STRANGER IN A STRANGE LAND *EMI 5589*	22	4
27 Dec 86		STRANGER IN A STRANGE LAND (re-entry) *EMI 5589*	71	2
26 Mar 88	●	CAN I PLAY WITH MADNESS *EMI EM 49*	3	6
13 Aug 88	●	THE EVIL THAT MEN DO *EMI EM 64*	5	6
19 Nov 88	●	THE CLAIRVOYANT *EMI EM 79*	6	8
18 Nov 89	●	INFINITE DREAMS *EMI EM 117*	6	5
30 Dec 89		INFINITE DREAMS (re-entry) *EMI EM 117*	74	1
22 Sep 90	●	HOLY SMOKE *EMI EM 153*	3	4
5 Jan 91	★	BRING YOUR DAUGHTER ... TO THE SLAUGHTER *EMI EMPD 171* ■	1	5
25 Apr 92	●	BE QUICK OR BE DEAD *EMI EM 229*	2	4
11 Jul 92		FROM HERE TO ETERNITY *EMI EMS 240*	21	4
13 Mar 93	●	FEAR OF THE DARK (LIVE) *EMI CDEMS 263*	8	3
16 Oct 93	●	HALLOWED BE THY NAME (LIVE) *EMI CDEM 288*	9	3
7 Oct 95	●	MAN ON THE EDGE *EMI CDEMS 398*	10	3
21 Sep 96		VIRUS *EMI CDEM 443*	16	3
21 Mar 98		THE ANGEL AND THE GAMBLER *EMI CDEM 507*	18	3
20 May 00	●	THE WICKER MAN *EMI CDEMS 568*	9	4
4 Nov 00		OUT OF THE SILENT PLANET *EMI CDEM 576*	20	3

IRONHORSE *Canada, male vocal / instrumental group (3 WEEKS)*

Date		Title / Label	pos	wks
5 May 79		SWEET LUI-LOUISE *Scotti Brothers K 11271*	60	3

Big Dee IRWIN *US, male vocalist – Difosco Erwin (17 WEEKS)*

Date		Title / Label	pos	wks
21 Nov 63	●	SWINGING ON A STAR *Colpix PX 11010*	7	17

Single was a vocal duet by Big Dee Irwin and Little Eva (uncredited)

Chris ISAAK *US, male vocalist (22 WEEKS)*

Date		Title / Label	pos	wks
24 Nov 90	●	WICKED GAME *London LON 279*	10	10
2 Feb 91		BLUE HOTEL *Reprise W 0005*	17	7
3 Apr 93		CAN'T DO A THING (TO STOP ME) *Reprise W 0161CD*	36	3
10 Jul 93		SAN FRANCISCO DAYS *Reprise W 0182CD*	62	1
2 Oct 99		BABY DID A BAD BAD THING *Reprise W 503CD*	44	1

ISHA-D *UK, male / female vocal / instrumental duo (4 WEEKS)*

Date		Title / Label	pos	wks
22 Jul 95		STAY (TONIGHT) *Cleveland City Blues CCBCD 15005*	28	3
5 Jul 97		STAY (re-issue) *Satellite 74321498212*	58	1

Ronald ISLEY – *See ISLEY BROTHERS; Rod STEWART; R KELLY; Warren G*

ISLEY BROTHERS (272 Top 500) *Cincinnati brothers who have had five decades of US hits: Ronald, O'Kelly (d. 1986) and Rudolph Isley. These influential singers / songwriters / producers and label-owners penned pop anthem 'Shout', and have US hits covering six decades. On 14 Jul 2001, the Isley Brothers became the first act in history to have six decades of US Hot 100 hits (108 WEEKS)*

Date		Title / Label	pos	wks
25 Jul 63		TWIST AND SHOUT *Stateside SS 112*	42	1
28 Apr 66		THIS OLD HEART OF MINE (IS WEAK FOR YOU) *Tamla Motown TMG 555*	47	1
1 Sep 66		I GUESS I'LL ALWAYS LOVE YOU *Tamla Motown TMG 572*	45	2
23 Oct 68	●	THIS OLD HEART OF MINE (IS WEAK FOR YOU) (re-entry) *Tamla Motown TMG 555*	3	16
15 Jan 69		I GUESS I'LL ALWAYS LOVE YOU (re-issue) *Tamla Motown TMG 683*	11	9
16 Apr 69	●	BEHIND A PAINTED SMILE *Tamla Motown TMG 693*	5	12
25 Jun 69		IT'S YOUR THING *Major Minor MM 621*	30	5
30 Aug 69		PUT YOURSELF IN MY PLACE *Tamla Motown TMG 708*	13	11
22 Sep 73		THAT LADY *Epic EPC 1704*	14	9
19 Jan 74		HIGHWAYS OF MY LIFE *Epic EPC 1980*	25	8
25 May 74		SUMMER BREEZE *Epic EPC 2244*	16	8
10 Jul 76	●	HARVEST FOR THE WORLD *Epic EPC 4369*	10	8
13 May 78		TAKE ME TO THE NEXT PHASE *Epic EPC 6292*	50	4
3 Nov 79		IT'S A DISCO NIGHT (ROCK DON'T STOP) *Epic EPC 7911*	14	11
16 Jul 83		BETWEEN THE SHEETS *Epic A 3513*	52	3

ISLEY JASPER ISLEY *US, male vocal / instrumental group (5 WEEKS)*

Date		Title / Label	pos	wks
23 Nov 85		CARAVAN OF LOVE *Epic A 6612*	52	5

ISOTONIK *UK, male producer – Chris Paul (9 WEEKS)*

Date		Title / Label	pos	wks
11 Jan 92		DIFFERENT STROKES *Ffrreedom TAB 101*	12	5
2 May 92		EVERYWHERE I GO / LET'S GET DOWN *Ffrreedom TAB 108*	25	4

'Let's Get Down' listed only from 9 May 1992

See also Chris PAUL

IT BITES *UK, male vocal / instrumental group (21 WEEKS)*

Date		Title / Label	pos	wks
12 Jul 86	●	CALLING ALL THE HEROES *Virgin VS 872*	6	12
18 Oct 86		WHOLE NEW WORLD *Virgin VS 896*	54	3
23 May 87		THE OLD MAN AND THE ANGEL *Virgin VS 941*	72	1
13 May 89		STILL TOO YOUNG TO REMEMBER *Virgin VS 1184*	66	3
24 Feb 90		STILL TOO YOUNG TO REMEMBER (re-issue) *Virgin VS 1238*	60	2

IT'S IMMATERIAL *UK, male vocal / instrumental group (10 WEEKS)*

Date		Title / Label	pos	wks
12 Apr 86		DRIVING AWAY FROM HOME (JIM'S TUNE) *Siren SIREN 15*	18	7
2 Aug 86		ED'S FUNKY DINER (FRIDAY NIGHT, SATURDAY MORNING) *Siren SIREN 24*	65	3

ITTY BITTY BOOZY WOOZY
Holland, male instrumental / production duo (2 WEEKS)

Date		Title / Label	pos	wks
25 Nov 95		TEMPO FIESTA (PARTY TIME) *Systematic SYSCD 23*	34	2

See also KLUBBHEADS

Burl IVES *US, male vocalist (25 WEEKS)*

Date		Title / Label	pos	wks
25 Jan 62	●	A LITTLE BITTY TEAR *Brunswick 05863*	9	15
17 May 62		FUNNY WAY OF LAUGHIN' *Brunswick 05868*	29	10

IVY LEAGUE *UK, male vocal group (31 WEEKS)*

Date		Title / Label	pos	wks
4 Feb 65	●	FUNNY HOW LOVE CAN BE *Piccadilly 7N 35222*	8	9
6 May 65		THAT'S WHY I'M CRYING *Piccadilly 7N 35228*	22	8
24 Jun 65	●	TOSSING AND TURNING *Piccadilly 7N 35251*	3	13
14 Jul 66		WILLOW TREE *Piccadilly 7N 35326*	50	1

IZIT *UK, male / female vocal / instrumental group (3 WEEKS)*

Date		Title / Label	pos	wks
2 Dec 89		STORIES *ffrr F 122*	52	3

J

Ray J *US, male vocalist (12 WEEKS)*

Date		Title / Label	pos	wks
17 Oct 98		THAT'S WHY I LIE *Atlantic AT 0049CD*	71	1
16 Jun 01	●	ANOTHER DAY IN PARADISE *WEA WEA 327CD1* [1]	5	10
11 Aug 01		WAIT A MINUTE *Atlantic AT 0106CD* [2]	54	1

[1] Brandy and Ray J [2] Ray J featuring Lil' Kim

J PAC *UK, male vocal / instrumental duo (2 WEEKS)*

Date		Title / Label	pos	wks
22 Jul 95		ROCK 'N' ROLL (DOLE) *East West YZ 953CD*	51	2

JA RULE *US, male rapper – Jeffrey Atkins (15 WEEKS)*

Date		Title / Label	pos	wks
3 Mar 01		BETWEEN YOU AND ME *Def Jam 5727402* [1]	26	3
10 Nov 01	●	I'M REAL *Epic 6720322* [2] ▲	4	8+
10 Nov 01		LIVIN' IT UP *Def Jam 5888142* [3]	27	4

[1] Ja Rule featuring Christina Milian [2] Jennifer Lopez featuring Ja Rule [3] Ja Rule featuring Case

See also JAY-Z

JACK 'N' CHILL *UK, male instrumental group (21 WEEKS)*

Date		Title / Label	pos	wks
6 Jun 87		THE JACK THAT HOUSE BUILT *Oval / 10 / Virgin TEN 174*	48	5
9 Jan 88	●	THE JACK THAT HOUSE BUILT (re-entry) *Oval / 10 / Virgin TEN 174*	6	11
9 Jul 88		BEATIN' THE HEAT *10 TEN 234*	42	5

Terry JACKS *Canada, male vocalist (21 WEEKS)*

Date		Title / Label	pos	wks
23 Mar 74	★	SEASONS IN THE SUN *Bell 1344* ▲	1	12
29 Jun 74	●	IF YOU GO AWAY *Bell 1362*	8	9

See also POPPY FAMILY

Chad JACKSON *UK, male DJ / producer – Mark Chadwick (10 WEEKS)*

Date		Title / Label	pos	wks
2 Jun 90	●	HEAR THE DRUMMER (GET WICKED) *Big Wave BWR 36*	3	10

Dee D JACKSON *UK, female vocalist – Deirdre Cozier (14 WEEKS)*

Date		Title / Label	pos	wks
22 Apr 78	●	AUTOMATIC LOVER *Mercury 6007 171*	4	9
2 Sep 78		METEOR MAN *Mercury 6007 182*	48	5

Freddie JACKSON *US, male vocalist (31 WEEKS)*

Date		Title / Label	pos	wks
23 Nov 85		YOU ARE MY LADY *Capitol CL 379*	49	4
22 Feb 86		ROCK ME TONIGHT (FOR OLD TIME'S SAKE) *Capitol CL 358*	18	9
11 Oct 86		TASTY LOVE *Capitol CL 428*	73	1
7 Feb 87		HAVE YOU EVER LOVED SOMEBODY *Capitol CL 437*	33	6
9 Jul 88		NICE 'N' SLOW *Capitol CL 502*	56	2
15 Oct 88		CRAZY (FOR ME) *Capitol CL 510*	41	3
5 Sep 92		ME AND MRS JONES *Capitol CL 668*	32	5
15 Jan 94		MAKE LOVE EASY *RCA 74321179162*	70	1

Gisele JACKSON *US, female vocalist (1 WEEK)*

Date		Title / Label	pos	wks
30 Aug 97		LOVE COMMANDMENTS *Manifesto FESCD 28*	54	1

Janet JACKSON (41 Top 500) *Multi-award-winning, record-breaking vocalist / performer, b. 16 May 1966, Indiana, US. Although not an overnight sensation, the youngest of the talented Jackson family became one of the world's biggest-selling recording artists and has amassed a staggering collection of gold albums and singles (274 WEEKS)*

Date		Title / Label	pos	wks
22 Mar 86	●	WHAT HAVE YOU DONE FOR ME LATELY *A & M AM 308*	3	14
31 May 86		NASTY *A & M AM 316*	19	9
9 Aug 86	●	WHEN I THINK OF YOU *A & M AM 337* ▲	10	10
1 Nov 86		CONTROL *A & M AM 359*	42	5
21 Mar 87	●	LET'S WAIT AWHILE *Breakout USA 601*	3	10
13 Jun 87		PLEASURE PRINCIPLE *Breakout USA 604*	24	5
14 Nov 87		FUNNY HOW TIME FLIES (WHEN YOU'RE HAVING FUN) *A&M Breakout USA 613*	59	2
2 Sep 89		MISS YOU MUCH *Breakout USA 663* ▲	22	7
4 Nov 89		RHYTHM NATION *Breakout USA 673*	23	5
27 Jan 90		COME BACK TO ME *Breakout USA 681*	20	7
31 Mar 90		ESCAPADE *Breakout USA 684* ▲	17	7
7 Jul 90		ALRIGHT *A & M USA 693*	20	5
8 Sep 90		BLACK CAT *A & M AM 587* ▲	15	6
27 Oct 90		LOVE WILL NEVER DO (WITHOUT YOU) *A & M AM 700* ▲	34	4
15 Aug 92	●	THE BEST THINGS IN LIFE ARE FREE *Perspective PERSS 7400* [1]	2	13
8 May 93	●	THAT'S THE WAY LOVE GOES *Virgin VSCDG 1460* ▲	2	10
31 Jul 93		IF *Virgin VSCDT 1474*	14	7
20 Nov 93	●	AGAIN *Virgin VSCDG 1481* ▲	6	11
12 Mar 94		BECAUSE OF LOVE *Virgin VSCDG 1488*	19	4
18 Jun 94		ANY TIME ANY PLACE *Virgin VSCDT 1501*	13	5
26 Nov 94		YOU WANT THIS *Virgin VSCDT 1519*	14	3
18 Mar 95	●	WHOOPS NOW / WHAT'LL I DO *Virgin VSCDT 1533*	9	8
10 Jun 95	●	SCREAM *Epic 6620222* [2]	3	12
24 Jun 95		SCREAM (re-mix) *Epic 6621277* [2]	43	2
23 Sep 95	●	RUNAWAY *A & M 5811972*	6	7
2 Dec 95		SCREAM (re-entry) *Epic 6620222* [2]	72	1
16 Dec 95	●	THE BEST THINGS IN LIFE ARE FREE (re-mix) *A & M 5813092* [3]	7	7
6 Apr 96		TWENTY FOREPLAY *A & M 5815112*	22	4
4 Oct 97	●	GOT 'TIL IT'S GONE *Virgin VSCDG 1666* [4]	6	9
13 Dec 97	●	TOGETHER AGAIN *Virgin VSCDG 1670*	4	19
4 Apr 98	●	I GET LONELY *Virgin VSCDT 1683* [5]	5	7
27 Jun 98		GO DEEP *Virgin VSCDT 1680*	13	5

			pos	wks
19 Dec 98		**EVERY TIME** *Virgin VSCDT 1720*	46	1
17 Apr 99		**GIRLFRIEND / BOYFRIEND** *Interscope IND 95640* [6]	11	7
1 May 99	●	**WHAT'S IT GONNA BE?!** *Elektra E3762CD1* [7]	6	7
19 Aug 00	●	**DOESN'T REALLY MATTER** *Def Soul 5629152* ▲	5	11
21 Apr 01	●	**ALL FOR YOU** *Virgin VSCDT 1801* ▲	3	11
11 Aug 01		**SOMEONE TO CALL MY LOVER** *Virgin VSCDT 1813*	11	5
22 Dec 01		**SON OF A GUN (I BETCHA THINK THIS SONG IS ABOUT YOU)** *Virgin VUSCD 232* [8]	13	2

[1] Luther Vandross and Janet Jackson with special guests BBD and Ralph Tresvant [2] Michael Jackson and Janet Jackson [3] Luther Vandross and Janet Jackson [4] Janet featuring Q-Tip and Joni Mitchell [5] Janet featuring BLACKstreet [6] BLACKstreet with Janet [7] Busta Rhymes featuring Janet [8] Janet with Carly Simon featuring Missy Elliott

See also Herb ALPERT

Jermaine JACKSON *US, male vocalist (43 WEEKS)*

			pos	wks
10 May 80	●	**LET'S GET SERIOUS** *Motown TMG 1183*	8	11
26 Jul 80		**BURNIN' HOT** *Motown TMG 1194*	32	6
30 May 81		**YOU LIKE ME DON'T YOU** *Motown TMG 1222*	41	5
12 May 84		**SWEETEST SWEETEST** *Arista JJK 1*	52	4
27 Oct 84		**WHEN THE RAIN BEGINS TO FALL** *Arista ARIST 584* [1]	68	2
16 Feb 85	●	**DO WHAT YOU DO** *Arista ARIST 609*	6	13
21 Oct 89		**DON'T TAKE IT PERSONAL** *Arista 112634*	69	2

[1] Jermaine Jackson and Pia Zadora

First hit features uncredited vocals of Stevie Wonder

See also JACKSONS

Joe JACKSON *UK, male vocalist (49 WEEKS)*

			pos	wks
4 Aug 79		**IS SHE REALLY GOING OUT WITH HIM?** *A & M AMS 7459*	13	9
12 Jan 80	●	**IT'S DIFFERENT FOR GIRLS** *A & M AMS 7493*	5	9
4 Jul 81		**JUMPIN' JIVE** *A & M AMS 8145* [1]	43	5
8 Jan 83	●	**STEPPIN' OUT** *A & M AMS 8262*	6	8
12 Mar 83		**BREAKING US IN TWO** *A & M AM 101*	59	4
28 Apr 84		**HAPPY ENDING** *A & M AM 186*	58	3
7 Jul 84		**BE MY NUMBER TWO** *A & M AM 200*	70	2
7 Jun 86		**LEFT OF CENTER** *A & M AM 320* [2]	32	9

[1] Joe Jackson's Jumpin' Jive [2] Suzanne Vega featuring Joe Jackson

Michael JACKSON (7 Top 500)

The self-proclaimed 'King of Pop' b. 29 Aug 1958, Indiana, US, is arguably the best known living musical entertainer. The youngest vocalist (age 11, fronting the Jackson Five) to top the US singles chart, he was also the first artist to enter that chart at No.1 (with 'You Are Not Alone'). In 1991 he became the first US act to enter the UK chart at No.1 since Elvis Presley in 1960 (whose daughter, Lisa Marie, he married in 1994). This outstanding, innovative singer / songwriter and performer has broken countless other records for his singles, albums, videos and tours. 'Thriller' is the world's biggest-selling record with global sales of more than 47 million, including 26 million in the US alone. It topped the US album chart for an unprecedented 37 weeks and had a record 12 Grammy nominations. Also on the album front, 'History' sold more copies in its first week than any previous double album. 'Dangerous' sold a staggering 10 million worldwide in its first month and 'Invincible' returned him to the top in 2001. Both 'Thriller' and 'Bad' have sold more than three million copies in the UK. Jackson, whose private life and physical appearance have attracted much media attention, was the first entertainer to earn more than $100 million in a year, and the first to receive an award for selling at least 100 million albums outside of the US (493 WEEKS)

			pos	wks
12 Feb 72	●	**GOT TO BE THERE** *Tamla Motown TMG 797*	5	11
20 May 72	●	**ROCKIN' ROBIN** *Tamla Motown TMG 816*	3	14
19 Aug 72	●	**AIN'T NO SUNSHINE** *Tamla Motown TMG 826*	8	11
25 Nov 72	●	**BEN** *Tamla Motown TMG 834* ▲	7	14
18 Nov 78		**EASE ON DOWN THE ROAD** *MCA 396* [1]	45	4
15 Sep 79	●	**DON'T STOP 'TIL YOU GET ENOUGH** *Epic EPC 7763* ▲	3	12
24 Nov 79	●	**OFF THE WALL** *Epic EPC 8045*	7	10
9 Feb 80	●	**ROCK WITH YOU** *Epic EPC 8206* ▲	7	9
3 May 80	●	**SHE'S OUT OF MY LIFE** *Epic EPC 8384*	3	9
26 Jul 80		**GIRLFRIEND** *Epic EPC 8782*	41	5
23 May 81	★	**ONE DAY IN YOUR LIFE** *Motown TMG 976*	1	14
1 Aug 81		**WE'RE ALMOST THERE** *Motown TMG 977*	46	4
6 Nov 82	●	**THE GIRL IS MINE** *Epic EPC A 2729* [2]	8	9
15 Jan 83		**THE GIRL IS MINE (re-entry)** *Epic EPC A 2729* [2]	75	1
29 Jan 83	★	**BILLIE JEAN** *Epic EPC A 3084* ▲	1	15
9 Apr 83	●	**BEAT IT** *Epic EPC A 3258* ▲	3	12
11 Jun 83	●	**WANNA BE STARTIN' SOMETHIN'** *Epic A 3427*	8	9
23 Jul 83		**HAPPY (LOVE THEME FROM 'LADY SINGS THE BLUES')** *Tamla Motown TMG 986*	52	3
15 Oct 83	●	**SAY SAY SAY** *Parlophone R 6062* [3] ▲	2	15
19 Nov 83	●	**THRILLER** *Epic A 3643*	10	18
31 Mar 84		**P.Y.T. (PRETTY YOUNG THING)** *Epic A 4136*	11	8
2 Jun 84	●	**FAREWELL MY SUMMER LOVE** *Motown TMG 1342*	7	12
11 Aug 84		**GIRL YOU'RE SO TOGETHER** *Motown TMG 1355*	33	8
8 Aug 87	★	**I JUST CAN'T STOP LOVING YOU** *Epic 650202 7* ▲	1	9
26 Sep 87	●	**BAD** *Epic 651155 7* ▲	3	11
5 Dec 87	●	**THE WAY YOU MAKE ME FEEL** *Epic 651275 7* ▲	3	10
20 Feb 88		**MAN IN THE MIRROR** *Epic 651388 7* ▲	21	5
28 May 88		**GET IT** *Motown ZB 41883* [4]	37	4
16 Jul 88	●	**DIRTY DIANA** *Epic 651546 7* ▲	4	8
10 Sep 88		**ANOTHER PART OF ME** *Epic 652844 7*	15	6
26 Nov 88	●	**SMOOTH CRIMINAL** *Epic 653026 7*	8	10
25 Feb 89	●	**LEAVE ME ALONE** *Epic 654672 7*	2	9
15 Jul 89		**LIBERIAN GIRL** *Epic 654947 0*	13	6
23 Nov 91	★	**BLACK OR WHITE** *Epic 6575987* ■ ▲	1	10
18 Jan 92		**BLACK OR WHITE (re-mix)** *Epic 6577316*	14	4
15 Feb 92	●	**REMEMBER THE TIME / COME TOGETHER** *Epic 6577747*	3	8
2 May 92	●	**IN THE CLOSET** *Epic 6580187*	8	6
25 Jul 92	●	**WHO IS IT** *Epic 6581797*	10	7
12 Sep 92		**JAM** *Epic 6583607*	13	5
5 Dec 92	●	**HEAL THE WORLD** *Epic 6584887*	2	15
27 Feb 93	●	**GIVE IN TO ME** *Epic 6590692*	2	9
10 Jul 93	●	**WILL YOU BE THERE** *Epic 6592222*	9	8
18 Dec 93		**GONE TOO SOON** *Epic 6599762*	33	5
10 Jun 95	●	**SCREAM** *Epic 6620222* [5]	3	12
24 Jun 95		**SCREAM (re-mix)** *Epic 6621277* [5]	43	2
2 Sep 95	★	**YOU ARE NOT ALONE** *Epic 6623102* ▲	1	15
2 Dec 95		**SCREAM (re-entry)** *Epic 6620222* [5]	72	1
9 Dec 95	★	**EARTH SONG** *Epic 6626955* ◆ ■	1	17
20 Apr 96	●	**THEY DON'T CARE ABOUT US** *Epic 6629502*	4	12
3 Aug 96		**THEY DON'T CARE ABOUT US (re-entry)** *Epic 6629502*	66	1
17 Aug 96		**THEY DON'T CARE ABOUT US (2nd re-entry)** *Epic 6629502*	66	1
24 Aug 96	●	**WHY** *Epic 6629502* [6]	2	9
16 Nov 96	●	**STRANGER IN MOSCOW** *Epic 6637872*	4	10
1 Mar 97		**STRANGER IN MOSCOW (re-entry)** *Epic 6637872*	69	1
3 May 97	★	**BLOOD ON THE DANCEFLOOR** *Epic 6644625* ■	1	9
19 Jul 97	●	**HISTORY / GHOSTS** *Epic 6647962*	5	8
20 Oct 01	●	**YOU ROCK MY WORLD** *Epic 6720292*	2	11+
22 Dec 01		**CRY** *Epic 6721822*	25	2+

[1] Diana Ross and Michael Jackson [2] Michael Jackson and Paul McCartney [3] Paul McCartney and Michael Jackson [4] Stevie Wonder and Michael Jackson [5] Michael Jackson and Janet Jackson [6] 3T featuring Michael Jackson

The sleeve of 'I Just Can't Stop Loving You' credits Siedah Garrett but the label does not. 'Come Together' was listed only from 7 Mar 1992. It peaked at No.10. Chart rules allow for a maximum of three formats; the additional three formats of 'Scream' - which each included re-mixed versions - were therefore listed separately (see 24 Jun 1995)

Mick JACKSON *UK, male vocalist (16 WEEKS)*

			pos	wks
30 Sep 78		**BLAME IT ON THE BOOGIE** *Atlantic K 11102*	15	8
3 Feb 79		**WEEKEND** *Atlantic K 11224*	38	8

Millie JACKSON *US, female vocalist (8 WEEKS)*

			pos	wks
18 Nov 72		**MY MAN, A SWEET MAN** *Mojo 2093 022*	50	1
10 Mar 84		**I FEEL LIKE WALKIN' IN THE RAIN** *Sire W 9348*	55	2
15 Jun 85		**ACT OF WAR** *Rocket EJS 8* [1]	32	5

[1] Elton John and Millie Jackson

Stonewall JACKSON *US, male vocalist (2 WEEKS)*

			pos	wks
17 Jul 59		**WATERLOO** *Philips PB 941*	24	2

Tony JACKSON – *See Q*

Tony JACKSON and the VIBRATIONS

UK, male vocal / instrumental group (3 WEEKS) pos/wks

Date		Title / Label	Pos	Wks
8 Oct 64		BYE BYE BABY *Pye 7N 15685*	38	3

See also SEARCHERS

Wanda JACKSON *US, female vocalist (11 WEEKS)* pos/wks

Date		Title / Label	Pos	Wks
1 Sep 60		LET'S HAVE A PARTY *Capitol CL 15147*	32	8
26 Jan 61		MEAN MEAN MAN *Capitol CL 15176*	46	1
9 Feb 61		MEAN MEAN MAN (re-entry) *Capitol CL 15176*	40	2

JACKSON SISTERS *US, female vocal group (2 WEEKS)* pos/wks

Date		Title / Label	Pos	Wks
20 Jun 87		I BELIEVE IN MIRACLES *Urban URB 4*	72	2

JACKSONS (57 Top 500)

One of the world's biggest-selling and most popular groups: brothers Jackie, Tito, Jermaine, Marlon and solo superstar Michael Jackson, with Randy joining in 1977. The Indiana quintet topped the US chart with their first four hits, and have reportedly sold more than 100 million records (235 WEEKS) pos/wks

Date		Title / Label	Pos	Wks
31 Jan 70	●	I WANT YOU BACK *Tamla Motown TMG 724* [1] ▲	2	13
16 May 70	●	ABC *Tamla Motown TMG 738* [1] ▲	8	11
1 Aug 70	●	THE LOVE YOU SAVE *Tamla Motown TMG 746* [1] ▲	7	9
21 Nov 70	●	I'LL BE THERE *Tamla Motown TMG 758* [1] ▲	4	16
10 Apr 71		MAMA'S PEARL *Tamla Motown TMG 769* [1]	25	7
17 Jul 71		NEVER CAN SAY GOODBYE *Tamla Motown TMG 778* [1]	33	7
11 Nov 72	●	LOOKIN' THROUGH THE WINDOWS *Tamla Motown TMG 833* [1]	9	11
23 Dec 72		SANTA CLAUS IS COMING TO TOWN *Tamla Motown TMG 837* [1]	43	3
17 Feb 73	●	DOCTOR MY EYES *Tamla Motown TMG 842* [1]	9	10
9 Jun 73		HALLELUJAH DAY *Tamla Motown TMG 856* [1]	20	9
8 Sep 73		SKYWRITER *Tamla Motown TMG 865* [1]	25	8
9 Apr 77		ENJOY YOURSELF *Epic EPC 5063*	42	4
4 Jun 77	★	SHOW YOU THE WAY TO GO *Epic EPC 5266*	1	10
13 Aug 77		DREAMER *Epic EPC 5458*	22	9
5 Nov 77		GOIN' PLACES *Epic EPC 5732*	26	7
11 Feb 78		EVEN THOUGH YOU'VE GONE *Epic EPC 5919*	31	4
23 Sep 78	●	BLAME IT ON THE BOOGIE *Epic EPC 6683*	8	12
3 Feb 79		DESTINY *Epic EPC 6983*	39	6
24 Mar 79	●	SHAKE YOUR BODY (DOWN TO THE GROUND) *Epic EPC 7181*	4	12
25 Oct 80		LOVELY ONE *Epic EPC 9302*	29	6
13 Dec 80		HEARTBREAK HOTEL *Epic EPC 9391*	44	6
28 Feb 81	●	CAN YOU FEEL IT *Epic EPC 9554*	6	15
4 Jul 81	●	WALK RIGHT NOW *Epic EPC A 1294*	7	11
7 Jul 84		STATE OF SHOCK *Epic A 4431* [2]	14	8
8 Sep 84		TORTURE *Epic A 4675*	26	6
16 Apr 88	●	I WANT YOU BACK (re-mix) *Motown ZB 41913*	8	9
13 May 89		NOTHIN' (THAT COMPARES 2 U) *Epic 654808 7*	33	6

[1] Jackson Five [2] Jacksons, lead vocals Mick Jagger and Michael Jackson

JACKY – *See Jackie LEE*

JACQUELINE – *See MACK VIBE featuring JACQUELINE*

JADA – *See SKIP RAIDERS featuring JADA*

JADE *US, female vocal group (28 WEEKS)* pos/wks

Date		Title / Label	Pos	Wks
20 Mar 93	●	DON'T WALK AWAY *Giant W 0160CD*	7	8
3 Jul 93		I WANNA LOVE YOU *Giant 74321151662*	13	7
18 Sep 93		ONE WOMAN *Giant 74321165122*	22	5
5 Feb 94		ALL THRU THE NITE *Giant 74321187552* [1]	32	3
11 Feb 95		EVERY DAY OF THE WEEK *Giant 74321260242*	19	5

[1] P.O.V. duet with Jade

JADE 4 U – *See Praga KHAN*

JAGGED EDGE *UK, male vocal / instrumental group (2 WEEKS)* pos/wks

Date		Title / Label	Pos	Wks
15 Sep 90		YOU DON'T LOVE ME *Polydor PO 97*	66	2

JAGGED EDGE featuring NELLY

US, male vocal group and male rapper (3 WEEKS) pos/wks

Date		Title / Label	Pos	Wks
27 Oct 01		WHERE THE PARTY AT? *Columbia 6719012*	25	3

Mick JAGGER *UK, male vocalist (42 WEEKS)* pos/wks

Date		Title / Label	Pos	Wks
14 Nov 70		MEMO FROM TURNER *Decca F 13067*	32	5
7 Jul 84		STATE OF SHOCK *Epic A 4431* [1]	14	8
16 Feb 85		JUST ANOTHER NIGHT *CBS A 4722*	32	6
7 Sep 85	★	DANCING IN THE STREET *EMI America EA 204* [2] ■	1	12
12 Sep 87		LET'S WORK *CBS 651028 7*	31	7
6 Feb 93		SWEET THING *Atlantic A 7410CD*	24	4

[1] Jacksons, lead vocals Mick Jagger and Michael Jackson [2] David Bowie and Mick Jagger

See also ROLLING STONES

JAGS *UK, male vocal / instrumental group (11 WEEKS)* pos/wks

Date		Title / Label	Pos	Wks
8 Sep 79		BACK OF MY HAND *Island WIP 6501*	17	10
2 Feb 80		WOMAN'S WORLD *Island WIP 6531*	75	1

JAHEIM *US, male vocalist (5 WEEKS)* pos/wks

Date		Title / Label	Pos	Wks
24 Mar 01		COULD IT BE *Warner Brothers W 551CD*	33	3
11 Aug 01		JUST IN CASE *Warner Brothers W 564CD*	34	2

JAKATTA *UK, male producer – Dave Lee (15 WEEKS)* pos/wks

Date		Title / Label	Pos	Wks
24 Feb 01	●	AMERICAN DREAM *Rulin RULIN 15CDS*	3	13
2 Jun 01		AMERICAN DREAM (re-entry) *Rulin RULIN 15CDS*	73	1
11 Aug 01		AMERICAN DREAM (re-mix) *Rulin RULIN 20CDS*	63	1

See also Li KWAN; HED BOYS; Joey NEGRO; RAVEN MAIZE; AKABU featuring Linda CLIFFORD

JALN BAND *UK / Jamaica, male vocal / instrumental group (17 WEEKS)* pos/wks

Date		Title / Label	Pos	Wks
11 Sep 76		DISCO MUSIC (I LIKE IT) *Magnet MAG 73*	21	9
27 Aug 77		I GOT TO SING *Magnet MAG 97*	40	4
1 Jul 78		GET UP *Magnet MAG 118*	53	4

JAM (84 Top 500)

Influential and extremely popular punk-based mod trio from Surrey: Paul Weller (v/g), Bruce Foxton (b), Rick Buckler (d). They hold the record for the most simultaneous Top 75 singles with 13 (all reactivated by their 1982 dissolution) (205 WEEKS) pos/wks

Date		Title / Label	Pos	Wks
7 May 77		IN THE CITY *Polydor 2058 866*	40	6
23 Jul 77		ALL AROUND THE WORLD *Polydor 2058 903*	13	8
5 Nov 77		THE MODERN WORLD *Polydor 2058 945*	36	4
11 Mar 78		NEWS OF THE WORLD *Polydor 2058 995*	27	5
26 Aug 78		DAVID WATTS / 'A' BOMB IN WARDOUR STREET *Polydor 2059 054*	25	8
21 Oct 78		DOWN IN THE TUBE STATION AT MIDNIGHT *Polydor POSP 8*	15	7
17 Mar 79		STRANGE TOWN *Polydor POSP 34*	15	9
25 Aug 79		WHEN YOU'RE YOUNG *Polydor POSP 69*	17	7
3 Nov 79	●	THE ETON RIFLES *Polydor POSP 83*	3	12
22 Mar 80	★	GOING UNDERGROUND / DREAMS OF CHILDREN *Polydor POSP 113* ■	1	9
26 Apr 80		ALL AROUND THE WORLD (re-entry) *Polydor 2058 903*	43	3
26 Apr 80		DAVID WATTS / 'A' BOMB IN WARDOUR STREET (re-entry) *Polydor 2059 054*	54	3
26 Apr 80		IN THE CITY (re-entry) *Polydor 2058 866*	40	4
26 Apr 80		NEWS OF THE WORLD (re-entry) *Polydor 2058 995*	53	3
26 Apr 80		STRANGE TOWN (re-entry) *Polydor POSP 34*	44	4
26 Apr 80		THE MODERN WORLD (re-entry) *Polydor 2058 945*	52	3
23 Aug 80	★	START! *Polydor 2059 266*	1	8
7 Feb 81		THAT'S ENTERTAINMENT (import) *Metronome 0030 364*	21	7
6 Jun 81	●	FUNERAL PYRE *Polydor POSP 257*	4	6
24 Oct 81	●	ABSOLUTE BEGINNERS *Polydor POSP 350*	4	6
13 Feb 82	★	TOWN CALLED MALICE / PRECIOUS *Polydor POSP 400* ■	1	8
3 Jul 82	●	JUST WHO IS THE FIVE O'CLOCK HERO *Polydor 2059 504*	8	5
18 Sep 82	●	THE BITTEREST PILL (I EVER HAD TO SWALLOW) *Polydor POSP 505*	2	7
4 Dec 82	★	BEAT SURRENDER *Polydor POSP 540* ■	1	9
22 Jan 83		ALL AROUND THE WORLD (2nd re-entry) *Polydor 2058 903*	38	4
22 Jan 83		DAVID WATTS / 'A' BOMB IN WARDOUR STREET (2nd re-entry) *Polydor 2059 054*	50	4

22 Jan 83	**DOWN IN THE TUBE STATION AT MIDNIGHT (re-entry)** *Polydor POSP 8*	30	6
22 Jan 83	**GOING UNDERGROUND / DREAMS OF CHILDREN (re-entry)** *Polydor POSP 113*	21	6
22 Jan 83	**IN THE CITY (2nd re-entry)** *Polydor 2058 866*	47	4
22 Jan 83	**NEWS OF THE WORLD (2nd re-entry)** *Polydor 2058 995*	39	4
22 Jan 83	**STRANGE TOWN (2nd re-entry)** *Polydor POSP 34*	42	5
22 Jan 83	**THE MODERN WORLD (2nd re-entry)** *Polydor 2058 945*	51	4
22 Jan 83	**WHEN YOU'RE YOUNG (re-entry)** *Polydor POSP 69*	53	4
29 Jan 83	**THAT'S ENTERTAINMENT** *Polydor POSP 482*	60	3
5 Feb 83	**START! (re-entry)** *Polydor 2059 266*	62	2
5 Feb 83	**THE ETON RIFLES (re-entry)** *Polydor POSP 83*	54	3
5 Feb 83	**TOWN CALLED MALICE / PRECIOUS (re-entry)** *Polydor POSP 400*	73	1
29 Jun 91	**THAT'S ENTERTAINMENT (re-issue)** *Polydor PO 155*	57	2
11 Oct 97	**THE BITTEREST PILL (I EVER HAD TO SWALLOW) (re-issue)** *Polydor 5715992*	30	2

See also Paul WELLER; Bruce FOXTON

JAM & SPOON featuring PLAVKA *Germany, male / female vocal / instrumental group – Jam El Mar and Mark Spoon (24 WEEKS)*

		pos	wks
2 May 92	**TALES FROM A DANCEOGRAPHIC OCEAN (EP)** *R&S RSUK 14* [1]	49	1
6 Jun 92	**THE COMPLETE STELLA (re-mix)** *R&S RSUK 14X* [1]	66	2
26 Feb 94	**RIGHT IN THE NIGHT (FALL IN LOVE WITH MUSIC)** *Epic 6600822*	31	4
24 Sep 94	**FIND ME (ODYSSEY TO ANYOONA)** *Epic 6608082*	37	3
10 Jun 95 ●	**RIGHT IN THE NIGHT (FALL IN LOVE WITH MUSIC) (re-issue)** *Epic 6620182*	10	8
16 Sep 95	**FIND ME (ODYSSEY TO ANYOONA) (re-issue)** *Epic 6623242*	22	3
25 Nov 95	**ANGEL (LADADI O-HEYO)** *Epic 6626382*	26	2
30 Aug 97	**KALEIDOSCOPE SKIES** *Epic 6647614*	48	1

[1] Jam and Spoon

Tracks on Tales From a Danceographic Ocean (EP): Stella / Keep on Movin' / My First Fantastic FF. 'The Complete Stella' is a re-mix of a track from the EP

See also TOKYO GHETTO PUSSY; STORM

JAM MACHINE *Italy / US, male vocal / instrumental group (1 WEEK)*

		pos	wks
23 Dec 89	**EVERYDAY** *Deconstruction PB 43299*	68	1

JAM ON THE MUTHA *UK, male vocal / instrumental group (2 WEEKS)*

		pos	wks
11 Aug 90	**HOTEL CALIFORNIA** *M & G MAGS 3*	62	2

JAM TRONIK
Germany, male / female vocal / instrumental group (7 WEEKS)

		pos	wks
24 Mar 90	**ANOTHER DAY IN PARADISE** *Debut DEBT 3093*	19	7

JAMAICA UNITED *Jamaica, male vocal ensemble (1 WEEK)*

		pos	wks
4 Jul 98	**RISE UP** *Columbia 6660522*	54	1

JAMELIA *UK, female vocalist – Jamelia Davis (18 WEEKS)*

		pos	wks
31 Jul 99	**I DO** *Parlophone Rhythm Series CDRHYTHM 21*	36	2
4 Mar 00 ●	**MONEY** *Parlophone Rhythm Series CDRYTHM 27* [1]	5	9
24 Jun 00	**CALL ME** *Parlophone Rhythm Series CDRHYTHM 28*	11	5
21 Oct 00	**BOY NEXT DOOR** *Parlophone Rhythm Series CDRHYTHM 29*	42	2

[1] Jamelia featuring Beenie Man

JAMES (357 Top 500) *Anthemic indie pop band formed 1982 in Manchester, UK, by mainstays Tim Booth (v) and Larry Gott (g). After several hitless years, critically acclaimed releases and record company changes, they became one of the most consistently successful acts of the 1990s (89 WEEKS)*

		pos	wks
12 May 90	**HOW WAS IT FOR YOU?** *Fontana JIM 5*	32	3
7 Jul 90	**COME HOME** *Fontana JIM 6*	32	4
8 Dec 90	**LOSE CONTROL** *Fontana JIM 7*	38	5
30 Mar 91 ●	**SIT DOWN** *Fontana JIM 8*	2	10
30 Nov 91 ●	**SOUND** *Fontana JIM 9*	9	7
1 Feb 92	**BORN OF FRUSTRATION** *Fontana JIM 10*	13	6
4 Apr 92	**RING THE BELLS** *Fontana JIM 11*	37	2
18 Jul 92	**SEVEN (EP)** *Fontana JIM 12*	46	2
11 Sep 93	**SOMETIMES** *Fontana JIMCD 13*	18	4
13 Nov 93	**LAID** *Fontana JIMCD 14*	25	4
2 Apr 94	**JAM J / SAY SOMETHING** *Fontana JIMCD 15*	24	4
22 Feb 97 ●	**SHE'S A STAR** *Fontana JIMCD 16*	9	5
3 May 97	**TOMORROW** *Fontana JIMCD 17*	12	3
5 Jul 97	**WALTZING ALONG** *Fontana JIMCD 18*	23	4
21 Mar 98	**DESTINY CALLING** *Fontana JIMCD 19*	17	4
6 Jun 98	**RUNAGROUND** *Fontana JIMCD 20*	29	2
21 Nov 98 ●	**SIT DOWN (re-mix)** *Fontana JIMCD 21*	7	7
31 Jul 99	**I KNOW WHAT I'M HERE FOR** *Mercury JIMCD22*	22	5
16 Oct 99	**JUST LIKE FRED ASTAIRE** *Mercury JIMCD 23*	17	3
25 Dec 99	**WE'RE GOING TO MISS YOU** *Mercury JIMCD 24*	48	2
7 Jul 01	**GETTING AWAY WITH IT (ALL MESSED UP)** *Mercury JIMCD 25*	22	3

Tracks on Seven (EP): Seven / Goalie's Ball / William Burroughs / Still Alive. 'Say Something' listed with 'Jam J' only for first two weeks of record's run

JAMES – *See CHRIS and JAMES*

David JAMES *UK, male DJ / producer (1 WEEK)*

		pos	wks
11 Aug 01	**ALWAYS A PERMANENT STATE** *Hooj Choons HOOJ 108CD*	60	1

Dick JAMES *UK, male vocalist – Isaac Vapnic (13 WEEKS)*

		pos	wks
20 Jan 56	**ROBIN HOOD** *Parlophone R 4117*	14	8
18 May 56	**ROBIN HOOD (re-entry) / THE BALLAD OF DAVY CROCKETT** *Parlophone R 4117*	29	1
11 Jan 57	**GARDEN OF EDEN** *Parlophone R 4255*	18	4

'Robin Hood' is with Stephen James and his Chums

Etta JAMES *US, female vocalist - Jamesetta Hawkins (7 WEEKS)*

		pos	wks
10 Feb 96 ●	**I JUST WANT TO MAKE LOVE TO YOU** *MCA MCSTD 48003*	5	7

Freddie JAMES *Canada, male vocalist (3 WEEKS)*

		pos	wks
24 Nov 79	**GET UP AND BOOGIE** *Warner Bros. K 17478*	54	3

Joni JAMES *US, female vocalist – Joan Babbo (2 WEEKS)*

		pos	wks
6 Mar 53	**WHY DON'T YOU BELIEVE ME?** *MGM 582* ▲	11	1
30 Jan 59	**THERE MUST BE A WAY** *MGM 1002*	24	1

Rick JAMES *US, male vocalist (30 WEEKS)*

		pos	wks
8 Jul 78	**YOU AND I** *Motown TMG 1110*	46	7
7 Jul 79	**I'M A SUCKER FOR YOUR LOVE** *Motown TMG 1146* [1]	43	8
6 Sep 80	**BIG TIME** *Motown TMG 1198*	41	6
4 Jul 81	**GIVE IT TO ME BABY** *Motown TMG 1229*	47	3
12 Jun 82	**STANDING ON THE TOP (PART 1)** *Motown TMG 1263* [2]	53	3
3 Jul 82	**DANCE WIT' ME** *Motown TMG 1266*	53	3

[1] Teena Marie, co-lead vocals Rick James [2] Temptations featuring Rick James

Sonny JAMES *US, male vocalist – James Loden (8 WEEKS)*

		pos	wks
30 Nov 56	**THE CAT CAME BACK** *Capitol CL 14635*	30	1
8 Feb 57	**YOUNG LOVE** *Capitol CL 14683*	11	7

Wendy JAMES *UK, female vocalist (4 WEEKS)*

		pos	wks
20 Feb 93	**THE NAMELESS ONE** *MCA MCSTD 1732*	34	3
17 Apr 93	**LONDON'S BRILLIANT** *MCA MCSTD 1763*	62	1

Jimmy JAMES and the VAGABONDS
UK, male vocal / instrumental group (25 WEEKS)

		pos	wks
11 Sep 68	**RED RED WINE** *Pye 7N 17579*	36	8
24 Apr 76	**I'LL GO WHERE YOUR MUSIC TAKES ME** *Pye 7N 45585*	23	8
17 Jul 76 ●	**NOW IS THE TIME** *Pye 7N 45606*	5	9

Tommy JAMES and the SHONDELLS
US, male vocal / instrumental group (25 WEEKS)

		pos	wks
21 Jul 66	**HANKY PANKY** *Roulette RK 7000* ▲	38	7
5 Jun 68 ★	**MONY MONY** *Major Minor MM 567*	1	18

JAMES BOYS *UK, male vocal duo (6 WEEKS)* pos/wks

19 May 73	**OVER AND OVER** *Penny Farthing PEN 806*	39	6

JAMESTOWN featuring JOCELYN BROWN *US, male instrumentalist / producer – Kent Brainerd and US, female vocalist (1 WEEK)* pos/wks

27 Mar 99	**I BELIEVE** *Playola 0091705 PLA*	62	1

JAMIROQUAI (205 Top 500) *One of world's biggest-selling acts of the late 1990s features headdress-wearing vocalist Jay Kay, b. 30 Dec 1969, Manchester, UK. Group, whose videos have also earned numerous accolades, sold seven million copies of 1996 album 'Travelling Without Moving' and 1999 album 'Synkronized' topped many European charts (128 WEEKS)* pos/wks

31 Oct 92	**WHEN YOU GONNA LEARN** *Acid Jazz JAZID 46*	52	2
20 Feb 93	**WHEN YOU GONNA LEARN (re-entry)** *Acid Jazz JAZID 46*	69	1
13 Mar 93 ●	**TOO YOUNG TO DIE** *Sony S2 6590112*	10	7
5 Jun 93	**BLOW YOUR MIND** *Sony S2 6592972*	12	6
14 Aug 93	**EMERGENCY ON PLANET EARTH** *Sony S2 6595782*	32	3
25 Sep 93	**WHEN YOU GONNA LEARN (re-issue)** *Sony S2 6596952*	28	3
8 Oct 94	**SPACE COWBOY** *Sony S2 6608512*	17	5
19 Nov 94	**HALF THE MAN** *Sony S2 6610032*	15	8
1 Jul 95 ●	**STILLNESS IN TIME** *Sony S2 6620255*	9	5
1 Jun 96	**DO U KNOW WHERE YOU'RE COMING FROM** *Renk CDRENK 63* [1]	12	5
31 Aug 96 ●	**VIRTUAL INSANITY** *Sony S2 6636132*	3	11
7 Dec 96 ●	**COSMIC GIRL** *Sony S2 6638292*	6	10
10 May 97 ●	**ALRIGHT** *Sony S2 6643252*	6	5
13 Dec 97	**HIGH TIMES** *Sony S2 6653702*	20	6
25 Jul 98 ★	**DEEPER UNDERGROUND** *Sony S2 6662182* ■	1	11
5 Jun 99 ●	**CANNED HEAT** *Sony S2 6673022*	4	10
25 Sep 99	**SUPERSONIC** *Sony S2 6678392*	22	4
11 Dec 99	**KING FOR A DAY** *Sony S2 6679732*	20	7
24 Feb 01	**I'M IN THE MOOD FOR LOVE** *Warner.Esp WSMS 001CD* [2]	29	3
25 Aug 01 ●	**LITTLE L** *Sony S2 6717182*	5	11
1 Dec 01	**YOU GIVE ME SOMETHING** *Sony S2 6720072*	16	5+

[1] M-Beat featuring Jamiroquai [2] Jools Holland and Jamiroquai

JAMMERS *US, male vocal / instrumental group (2 WEEKS)* pos/wks

29 Jan 83	**BE MINE TONIGHT** *Salsoul Sal 101*	65	2

JAN and DEAN *US, male vocal duo (18 WEEKS)* pos/wks

24 Aug 61	**HEART AND SOUL** *London HLH 9395*	24	8
15 Aug 63	**SURF CITY** *Liberty LIB 55580* ▲	26	10

JAN and KJELD *Denmark, male vocal duo (4 WEEKS)* pos/wks

21 Jul 60	**BANJO BOY** *Ember S 101*	36	4

JANE'S ADDICTION *US, male vocal / instrumental group (4 WEEKS)* pos/wks

23 Mar 91	**BEEN CAUGHT STEALING** *Warner Bros. W 0011*	34	3
1 Jun 91	**CLASSIC GIRL** *Warner Bros. W 0031*	60	1

Horst JANKOWSKI *Germany, male instrumentalist – piano (18 WEEKS)* pos/wks

29 Jul 65 ●	**A WALK IN THE BLACK FOREST** *Mercury MF 861*	3	18

Samantha JANUS *UK, female vocalist (3 WEEKS)* pos/wks

11 May 91	**A MESSAGE TO YOUR HEART** *Hollywood HWD 104*	30	3

Philip JAP *UK, male vocalist (8 WEEKS)* pos/wks

31 Jul 82	**SAVE US** *A & M AMS 8217*	53	4
25 Sep 82	**TOTAL ERASURE** *A & M JAP 1*	41	4

JAPAN (413 Top 500) *Rock quintet who subsequently became New Romantic figureheads fronted by David Sylvian (v), b. David Batt, 23 Feb 1958, London, UK, who later recorded critically acclaimed solo work. Group folded in 1982, but full line-up briefly reconvened as Rain Tree Crow in 1991 (81 WEEKS)* pos/wks

18 Oct 80	**GENTLEMEN TAKE POLAROIDS** *Virgin VS 379*	60	2
9 May 81	**THE ART OF PARTIES** *Virgin VS 409*	48	5
19 Sep 81	**QUIET LIFE** *Hansa HANSA 6*	19	9
7 Nov 81	**VISIONS OF CHINA** *Virgin VS 436*	32	12
23 Jan 82	**EUROPEAN SON** *Hansa HANSA 10*	31	6
20 Mar 82 ●	**GHOSTS** *Virgin VS 472*	5	8
22 May 82	**CANTONESE BOY** *Virgin VS 502*	24	6
3 Jul 82 ●	**I SECOND THAT EMOTION** *Hansa HANSA 12*	9	11
9 Oct 82	**LIFE IN TOKYO** *Hansa HANSA 17*	28	6
20 Nov 82	**NIGHT PORTER** *Virgin VS 554*	29	9
12 Mar 83	**ALL TOMORROW'S PARTIES** *Hansa HANSA 18*	38	4
21 May 83	**CANTON (LIVE)** *Virgin VS 581*	42	3

See also RAIN TREE CROW

JARK PRONGO *Holland, male production duo (1 WEEK)* pos/wks

3 Apr 99	**MOVIN' THRU YOUR SYSTEM** *Hooj Choons HOOJ 72CD*	58	1

See also GOODMEN; TOMBA VIRA; RIVA featuring Dannii MINOGUE; CHOCOLATE PUMA

Jean-Michel JARRE *France, male instrumentalist / producer (40 WEEKS)* pos/wks

27 Aug 77 ●	**OXYGENE PART IV** *Polydor 2001 721*	4	9
20 Jan 79	**EQUINOXE PART 5** *Polydor POSP 20*	45	5
23 Aug 86	**FOURTH RENDEZ-VOUS** *Polydor POSP 788*	65	4
5 Nov 88	**REVOLUTIONS** *Polydor PO 25*	52	2
7 Jan 89	**LONDON KID** *Polydor PO 32* [1]	52	3
7 Oct 89	**OXYGENE PART IV (re-mix)** *Polydor PO 55*	65	2
26 Jun 93	**CHRONOLOGIE PART 4** *Polydor POCS 274*	55	2
30 Oct 93	**CHRONOLOGIE PART 4 (re-mix)** *Polydor POCS 274*	56	1
22 Mar 97	**OXYGENE 8** *Epic 6643232*	17	3
5 Jul 97	**OXYGENE 10** *Epic 6647152*	21	2
11 Jul 98	**RENDEZ-VOUS '98** *Epic 6661102* [2]	12	6
26 Feb 00	**C'EST LA VIE** *Epic 6689302* [3]	40	1

[1] Jean-Michel Jarre featuring Hank Marvin [2] Jean-Michel Jarre and Apollo 440
[3] Jean-Michel Jarre featuring Natacha Atlas

Al JARREAU *US, male vocalist (30 WEEKS)* pos/wks

26 Sep 81	**WE'RE IN THIS LOVE TOGETHER** *Warner Bros. K 17849*	55	4
14 May 83	**MORNIN'** *WEA U9929*	28	6
16 Jul 83	**TROUBLE IN PARADISE** *WEA Int. U9871*	36	5
24 Sep 83	**BOOGIE DOWN** *WEA U9814*	63	3
16 Nov 85	**DAY BY DAY** *Polydor POSP 770* [1]	53	3
5 Apr 86	**THE MUSIC OF GOODBYE (LOVE THEME FROM 'OUT OF AFRICA')** *MCA MCA 1038* [2]	75	1
7 Mar 87 ●	**'MOONLIGHTING' THEME** *WEA U8407*	8	8

[1] Shakatak featuring Al Jarreau [2] Melissa Manchester and Al Jarreau

Kenny 'Jammin' JASON and 'Fast' Eddie SMITH *US, male DJ / production duo (4 WEEKS)* pos/wks

11 Apr 87	**CAN U DANCE** *Champion CHAMP 41* [1]	71	2
14 Nov 87	**CAN U DANCE (re-entry)** *Champion CHAMP 41* [1]	67	2

JAVELLS featuring Nosmo KING *UK, male / female vocal group (8 WEEKS)* pos/wks

9 Nov 74	**GOODBYE NOTHING TO SAY** *Pye Disco Demand DDS 2003*	26	8

Peter JAY and the JAYWALKERS *UK, male instrumental group – Peter Jay – drums (11 WEEKS)* pos/wks

8 Nov 62	**CAN CAN '62** *Decca F 11531*	31	11

Simone JAY – *See DJ DADO*

JAYDEE *Holland, male DJ / producer – Robin Albers (3 WEEKS)* pos/wks

20 Sep 97	**PLASTIC DREAMS** *R&S RS 97117CD*	18	3

Ollie JAYE – *See JON THE DENTIST vs Ollie JAYE*

JAYHAWKS *US, male / female vocal / instrumental group (1 WEEK)* pos/wks

15 Jul 95	**BAD TIME** *American 74321291632*	70	1

1973

IN THE YEAR IN WHICH BOTH PICASSO AND BRUCE LEE DIED, THE US PULLED OUT OF VIETNAM, THE MOVIE 'M*A*S*H' WAS A SURPRISE SMASH HIT FOR 20TH CENTURY FOX, THE MARRIAGE OF PRINCESS ANNE AND CAPTAIN MARK PHILLIPS WAS WATCHED BY 550 MILLION PEOPLE WORLDWIDE, AND GLAM ROCK RULED WITH NO.1S FROM SLADE, SWEET AND GARY GLITTER. TOTP, TOTP2 AND CD:UK PRODUCER **RIC BLAXILL** REMEMBERS THE GLAMOUR OF ROXY MUSIC ...

"I can remember seeing **Roxy Music** perform 'Street Life' on TOTP as a young boy and being amazed at the glamour of the band. The song was also catchy to my young ears, but what impressed me most was one of the band was playing an electric violin – and not just electric but it was transparent too. This impressed me so much that I did two things. I saved up my pocket money to buy my first ever single, and it also made me think that playing the violin was definitely the thing to do. So for some years after seeing Roxy Music on TOTP I began a career as a violinist. All the torturous practice got me as far as the school orchestra at secondary school. I never played anything as exciting as 'Street Life' (classical music and hymns just weren't my thing) and I soon realised that walking to school with a violin case in your early teens was asking for trouble! Plus punk came along and there was never much call for a fiddle solo in punk songs."

SINGLE OF THE YEAR 'Blockbuster' Sweet
ALBUM OF THE YEAR 'Don't Shoot Me I'm Only the Piano Player' Elton John

JAY-Z (429 Top 500) *Foremost East Coast rapper, b. Shawn Carter, 4 Dec 1969, New York, whose original rap name was "Jazzy". The owner of Roc-A-Fella Records has had UK hits with a dozen acts, six simultaneous US R&B chart entries (2001), and saw his last four albums top the US chart (78 WEEKS)*

Date	Title / Label	pos	wks
1 Mar 97	**CAN'T KNOCK THE HUSTLE** *Northwestside 74321447192* [1]	30	2
10 May 97	**AIN'T NO PLAYA** *Northwestside 74321474842* [2]	31	2
21 Jun 97 ●	**I'LL BE** *Def Jam 75710432* [3]	9	5
23 Aug 97	**WHO YOU WIT** *Qwest W 0411CD*	65	1
25 Oct 97	**SUNSHINE** *Northwestside 74321528702* [4]	25	2
14 Feb 98	**WISHING ON A STAR** *Northwestside 74321554632* [5]	13	4
27 Jun 98	**THE CITY IS MINE** *Northwestside 74321588012* [6]	38	2
12 Dec 98 ●	**HARD KNOCK LIFE (GHETTO ANTHEM)** *Northwestside 74321635332*	2	11
13 Mar 99	**CAN I GET A...** *Def Jam 5668472* [7]	24	3
10 Apr 99	**BE ALONE NO MORE** *Northwestside 74321658472* [8]	11	9
19 Jun 99	**LOBSTER & SCRIMP** *Virgin DINSD 186* [9]	48	1
6 Nov 99 ●	**HEARTBREAKER** *Columbia 6683012* ▲ [10]	5	13
4 Dec 99	**WHAT YOU THINK OF THAT** *Def Jam 8708292* [11]	58	1
26 Feb 00	**ANYTHING** *Def Jam 5626502*	18	4
24 Jun 00	**BIG PIMPIN'** *Def Jam 5627742*	29	3
16 Dec 00	**I JUST WANNA LOVE U (GIVE IT 2 ME)** *Def Jam 5727462*	17	8
23 Jun 01	**FIESTA** *Jive 9252142* [11]	23	3
27 Oct 01	**IZZO (H.O.V.A.)** *Roc-A-Fella / Def Jam 5888152*	21	4

[1] Jay-Z featuring Mary J Blige [2] Jay-Z featuring Foxy Brown [3] Foxy Brown featuring Jay-Z [4] Jay-Z featuring Babyface and Foxy Brown [5] Jay-Z featuring Gwen Dickey [6] Jay-Z featuring BLACKstreet [7] Jay-Z featuring Amil and Ja Rule [8] Another Level featuring Jay-Z [9] Timbaland featuring Jay-Z [10] Mariah Carey featuring Jay-Z [11] R Kelly featuring Jay-Z

JAZZ and the BROTHERS GRIMM
UK, male vocal / instrumental group (2 WEEKS)

Date	Title / Label	pos	wks
9 Jul 88	**(LET'S ALL GO BACK) DISCO NIGHTS** *Ensign ENY 616*	57	2

JAZZY JEFF & the FRESH PRINCE
US, male rap / DJ duo – Jeff Townes and Will Smith (49 WEEKS)

Date	Title / Label	pos	wks
4 Oct 86	**GIRLS AIN'T NOTHING BUT TROUBLE** *Champion Champ 18* [1]	21	8
3 Aug 91 ●	**SUMMERTIME** *Jive JIVECD 279* [1]	8	8
9 Nov 91	**RING MY BELL** *Jive JIVECD 288* [1]	53	2
11 Sep 93 ★	**BOOM! SHAKE THE ROOM** *Jive JIVECD 335*	1	13
20 Nov 93	**I'M LOOKING FOR THE ONE (TO BE WITH ME)** *Jive JIVECD 345*	24	4
19 Feb 94	**CAN'T WAIT TO BE WITH YOU** *Jive JIVECD 348*	29	4
4 Jun 94	**TWINKLE TWINKLE (I'M NOT A STAR)** *Jive JIVECD 354*	62	2
6 Aug 94	**SUMMERTIME (re-entry)** *Jive JIVECD 279* [1]	29	4
2 Dec 95	**BOOM! SHAKE THE ROOM (re-mix)** *Jive JIVECD 387*	40	2
11 Jul 98	**LOVELY DAZE** *Jive 0518902* [1]	37	2

[1] DJ Jazzy Jeff and the Fresh Prince

See also Will SMITH

JAZZY M *UK, male DJ / producer – Michael Connelly (2 WEEKS)*

Date	Title / Label	pos	wks
21 Oct 00	**JAZZIN' THE WAY YOU KNOW** *Perfecto PERF 08CDS*	47	2

JB's ALL STARS
UK, male / female vocal / instrumental group (4 WEEKS)

Date	Title / Label	pos	wks
11 Feb 84	**BACKFIELD IN MOTION** *RCA Victor RCA 384*	48	4

JC *UK, male producer (1 WEEK)*

Date	Title / Label	pos	wks
7 Feb 98	**SO HOT** *East West EW 146CD*	74	1

JC 001 *UK, male rapper (4 WEEKS)*

Date	Title / Label	pos	wks
24 Apr 93	**NEVER AGAIN** *Anxious ANX 1012CD*	67	2
26 Jun 93	**CUPID** *Anxious ANX 1014CD*	56	2

JD – *See SNOOP DOGGY DOGG*

JDS *Italy / UK, male DJ / production duo – Julian Napolitano and Darren Pearce (3 WEEKS)*

Date	Title / Label	pos	wks
27 Sep 97	**NINE WAYS** *ffrr FCD 310*	61	1
23 May 98	**LONDON TOWN** *Jive 0530042*	49	1
3 Mar 01	**NINE WAYS (re-mix)** *ffrr FCD 391*	47	1

Norma JEAN – *See Romina JOHNSON*

Wyclef JEAN *US, male vocalist / rapper / producer (67 WEEKS)*

Date	Title / Label	pos	wks
28 Jun 97	**WE TRYING TO STAY ALIVE** *Columbia 6646815* [1]	13	5
27 Sep 97	**GUANTANAMERA** *Columbia 6650852* [2]	25	2
28 Mar 98 ●	**NO, NO, NO** *Columbia 6656592* [3]	5	8
16 May 98 ●	**GONE TILL NOVEMBER** *Columbia 6658712*	3	9
14 Nov 98 ●	**ANOTHER ONE BITES THE DUST** *Dreamworks DRMCD 22364* [4]	5	6
23 Oct 99	**NEW DAY** *Columbia 6682122* [5]	23	2
16 Sep 00 ●	**IT DOESN'T MATTER** *Columbia 6697782* [6]	3	8
16 Dec 00 ●	**911** *Columbia 6706122* [7]	9	10
21 Jul 01 ●	**PERFECT GENTLEMEN** *Columbia 6710522*	4	14
8 Dec 01	**WISH YOU WERE HERE** *Columbia 6721562*	28	3

[1] Wyclef Jean & The Refugee Allstars [2] Wyclef Jean and The Refugee Allstars [3] Destiny's Child featuring Wyclef Jean [4] Queen with Wyclef Jean featuring Pras and Free [5] Wyclef Jean featuring Bono [6] Wyclef Jean featuring The Rock and Melky Sedeck [7] Wyclef Jean featuring Mary J Blige

See also FUGEES

JEFFERSON *UK, male vocalist (8 WEEKS)*

Date	Title / Label	pos	wks
9 Apr 69	**THE COLOUR OF MY LOVE** *Pye 7N 17706*	22	8

JEFFERSON STARSHIP – *See STARSHIP*

Garland JEFFREYS *US, male vocalist (1 WEEK)*

Date	Title / Label	pos	wks
8 Feb 92	**HAIL HAIL ROCK 'N' ROLL** *RCA PB 49171*	72	1

JELLYBEAN *US, male producer – John Benitez (47 WEEKS)*

Date	Title / Label	pos	wks
1 Feb 86	**SIDEWALK TALK** *EMI America EA 210* [1]	47	4
26 Sep 87	**THE REAL THING** *Chrysalis CHS 3167* [2]	13	10
28 Nov 87 ●	**WHO FOUND WHO** *Chrysalis CHS JEL 1* [3]	10	10
12 Dec 87	**JINGO** *Chrysalis JEL 2*	12	10
12 Mar 88	**JUST A MIRAGE** *Chrysalis JEL 3* [4]	13	10
20 Aug 88	**COMING BACK FOR MORE** *Chrysalis JEL 4* [5]	41	3

[1] Jellybean featuring Catherine Buchanan [2] Jellybean featuring Steven Dante [3] Jellybean featuring Elisa Fiorillo [4] Jellybean featuring Adele Bertei [5] Jellybean featuring Richard Darbyshire

JELLYFISH *US, male vocal / instrumental group (20 WEEKS)*

Date	Title / Label	pos	wks
26 Jan 91	**THE KING IS HALF UNDRESSED** *Charisma CUSS 1*	39	6
27 Apr 91	**BABY'S COMING BACK** *Charisma CUSS 2*	51	4
3 Aug 91	**THE SCARY-GO-ROUND EP** *Charisma CUSS 3*	49	3
26 Oct 91	**I WANNA STAY HOME** *Charisma CUSS 4*	59	2
1 May 93	**THE GHOST AT NUMBER ONE** *Charisma CUSDG 10*	43	3
17 Jul 93	**NEW MISTAKE** *Charisma CUSDG 11*	55	2

Tracks on The Scary-Go-Round EP: Now She Knows She's Wrong / Bedspring Kiss / She Still Loves Him (Live) / Baby's Coming Back (Live)

JERU THE DAMAJA *US, male rapper (1 WEEK)*

Date	Title / Label	pos	wks
7 Dec 96	**YA PLAYIN YASELF** *ffrr FCD 289*	67	1

JESSICA *Sweden, female vocalist (1 WEEK)*

Date	Title / Label	pos	wks
20 Mar 99	**HOW WILL I KNOW (WHO YOU ARE)** *Jive 0522412*	47	1

JESUS AND MARY CHAIN
UK, male vocal / instrumental group (59 WEEKS)

Date	Title / Label	pos	wks
2 Mar 85	**NEVER UNDERSTAND** *Blanco Y Negro NEG 8*	47	4
8 Jun 85	**YOU TRIP ME UP** *Blanco Y Negro NEG 13*	55	3
12 Oct 85	**JUST LIKE HONEY** *Blanco Y Negro NEG 17*	45	3
26 Jul 86	**SOME CANDY TALKING** *Blanco Y Negro NEG 19*	13	5
2 May 87 ●	**APRIL SKIES** *Blanco Y Negro NEG 24*	8	6
15 Aug 87	**HAPPY WHEN IT RAINS** *Blanco Y Negro NEG 25*	25	5
7 Nov 87	**DARKLANDS** *Blanco Y Negro NEG 29*	33	4

9 Apr 88		**SIDEWALKING** *Blanco Y Negro NEG 32*	**30**	3
23 Sep 89		**BLUES FROM A GUN** *Blanco Y Negro NEG 41*	**32**	2
18 Nov 89		**HEAD ON** *Blanco Y Negro NEG 42*	**57**	2
8 Sep 90		**ROLLERCOASTER (EP)** *Blanco Y Negro NEG 45*	**46**	2
15 Feb 92	●	**REVERENCE** *Blanco Y Negro NEG 55*	**10**	4
14 Mar 92		**FAR GONE AND OUT** *Blanco Y Negro NEG 56*	**23**	3
4 Jul 92		**ALMOST GOLD** *Blanco Y Negro NEG 57*	**41**	2
10 Jul 93		**SOUND OF SPEED (EP)** *Blanco Y Negro NEG 66CD*	**30**	2
30 Jul 94		**SOMETIMES ALWAYS** *Blanco Y Negro NEG 70CD*	**22**	3
22 Oct 94		**COME ON** *Blanco Y Negro NEG 73CD1*	**52**	2
17 Jun 95		**I HATE ROCK 'N' ROLL** *Blanco Y Negro NEG 81CD*	**61**	1
18 Apr 98		**CRACKING UP** *Creation CRESCD 292*	**35**	2
30 May 98		**ILOVEROCKNROLL** *Creation CRESCD 296*	**38**	1

Tracks on Rollercoaster (EP): Rollercoaster / Silverblade / Lowlife / Tower of Song. Tracks on Sound of Speed (EP): Snakedriver / Something I Can't Have / Write Record Release Blues / Little Red Rooster

JESUS JONES *UK, male vocal / instrumental group (52 WEEKS)* pos/wks

25 Feb 89		**INFO-FREAKO** *Food FOOD 18*	**42**	3
8 Jul 89		**NEVER ENOUGH** *Food FOOD 21*	**42**	3
23 Sep 89		**BRING IT ON DOWN** *Food FOOD 22*	**46**	3
7 Apr 90		**REAL REAL REAL** *Food FOOD 24*	**19**	8
6 Oct 90		**RIGHT HERE RIGHT NOW** *Food FOOD 25*	**31**	4
12 Jan 91	●	**INTERNATIONAL BRIGHT YOUNG THING** *Food FOOD 27*	**7**	7
2 Mar 91		**WHO? WHERE? WHY?** *Food FOOD 28*	**21**	7
20 Jul 91		**RIGHT HERE RIGHT NOW (re-issue)** *Food FOOD 30*	**31**	4
9 Jan 93	●	**THE DEVIL YOU KNOW** *Food CDPERV 1*	**10**	5
10 Apr 93		**THE RIGHT DECISION** *Food CDPERV 2*	**36**	3
10 Jul 93		**ZEROES & ONES** *Food CDFOODS 44*	**30**	3
14 Jun 97		**THE NEXT BIG THING** *Food CDFOOD 95*	**49**	1
16 Aug 97		**CHEMICAL #1** *Food CDFOOD 102*	**71**	1

JESUS LIZARD *US, male vocal / instrumental group (2 WEEKS)* pos/wks

6 Mar 93		**PUSS** *Touch And Go TG 83CD*	**12**	2

The listed flip side of 'Puss' was 'Oh, the Guilt' by Nirvana

JESUS LOVES YOU *UK, male vocalist – Boy George (18 WEEKS)* pos/wks

11 Nov 89		**AFTER THE LOVE** *More Protein PROT 2*	**68**	1
23 Feb 91		**BOW DOWN MISTER** *More Protein PROT 8*	**27**	8
8 Jun 91		**GENERATIONS OF LOVE** *More Protein PROT 10*	**35**	8
12 Dec 92		**SWEET TOXIC LOVE** *Virgin VS 1449*	**65**	1

JETHRO TULL *UK, male vocal / instrumental group (68 WEEKS)* pos/wks

1 Jan 69		**LOVE STORY** *Island WIP 6048*	**29**	8
14 May 69	●	**LIVING IN THE PAST** *Island WIP 6056*	**3**	14
1 Nov 69	●	**SWEET DREAM** *Chrysalis WIP 6070*	**7**	11
24 Jan 70	●	**TEACHER / THE WITCH'S PROMISE** *Chrysalis WIP 6077*	**4**	9
18 Sep 71		**LIFE IS A LONG SONG / UP THE POOL** *Chrysalis WIP 6106*	**11**	8
11 Dec 76		**RING OUT SOLSTICE BELLS (EP)** *Chrysalis CXP 2*	**28**	6
15 Sep 84		**LAP OF LUXURY** *Chrysalis TULL 1*	**70**	2
16 Jan 88		**SAID SHE WAS A DANCER** *Chrysalis TULL 4*	**55**	4
21 Mar 92		**ROCKS ON THE ROAD** *Chrysalis TULLX 7*	**47**	3
22 May 93		**LIVING IN THE (SLIGHTLY MORE RECENT) PAST** *Chrysalis CDCHSS 3970*	**32**	3

Tracks on Ring Out Solstice Bells (EP): Ring Out Solstice Bells / March the Mad Scientist / The Christmas Song / Pan Dance. 'Living in the (Slightly More Recent) Past' is a live version of the original

JETS *UK, male vocal / instrumental group (38 WEEKS)* pos/wks

22 Aug 81		**SUGAR DOLL** *EMI 5211*	**55**	3
31 Oct 81		**YES TONIGHT JOSEPHINE** *EMI 5247*	**25**	11
6 Feb 82		**LOVE MAKES THE WORLD GO ROUND** *EMI 5262*	**21**	9
24 Apr 82		**THE HONEYDRIPPER** *EMI 5289*	**58**	3
9 Oct 82		**SOMEBODY TO LOVE** *EMI 5342*	**56**	3
6 Aug 83		**BLUE SKIES** *EMI 5405*	**53**	3
17 Dec 83		**ROCKIN' AROUND THE CHRISTMAS TREE** *PRT 7P 297*	**62**	4
13 Oct 84		**PARTY DOLL** *PRT JETS 2*	**72**	2

JETS *US, male / female vocal / instrumental group (19 WEEKS)* pos/wks

31 Jan 87	●	**CRUSH ON YOU** *MCA MCA 1048*	**5**	13
25 Apr 87		**CURIOSITY** *MCA MCA 1119*	**41**	4
28 May 88		**ROCKET 2 U** *MCA MCA 1226*	**69**	2

Joan JETT and the BLACKHEARTS
US, female vocalist with male vocal / instrumental group (21 WEEKS) pos/wks

24 Apr 82	●	**I LOVE ROCK 'N' ROLL** *Epic EPC A 2152* ▲	**4**	10
10 Jul 82		**CRIMSON AND CLOVER** *Epic EPC A 2485*	**60**	3
20 Aug 88		**I HATE MYSELF FOR LOVING YOU** *London LON 195*	**46**	6
31 Mar 90		**DIRTY DEEDS** *Chrysalis CHS 3518* [1]	**69**	1
19 Feb 94		**I LOVE ROCK & ROLL (re-issue)** *Reprise W 0232CD*	**75**	1

[1] Joan Jett

JEWEL *US, female vocalist / instrumentalist – guitar (8 WEEKS)* pos/wks

14 Jun 97		**WHO WILL SAVE YOUR SOUL** *Atlantic A 8514CD*	**52**	1
9 Aug 97		**YOU WERE MEANT FOR ME** *Atlantic A 5463CD*	**53**	1
22 Nov 97		**YOU WERE MEANT FOR ME (re-entry)** *Atlantic A 5463CD*	**32**	2
21 Nov 98		**HANDS** *Atlantic AT 0055CD*	**41**	2
26 Jun 99		**DOWN SO LONG** *Atlantic AT 0069CD*	**38**	2

JEZ & CHOOPIE *UK / Israel, male DJ / production duo (2 WEEKS)* pos/wks

21 Mar 98		**YIM** *Multiply CDMULTY 31*	**36**	2

JFK *UK, male producer (1 WEEK)* pos/wks

15 Sep 01		**GOOD GOD** *Y2K Y2K 025CD*	**71**	1

JHELISA *US, female vocalist (1 WEEK)* pos/wks

1 Jul 95		**FRIENDLY PRESSURE** *Dorado DOR 040CD*	**75**	1

JIGSAW *UK, male vocal / instrumental group (16 WEEKS)* pos/wks

1 Nov 75	●	**SKY HIGH** *Splash CPI 1*	**9**	11
6 Aug 77		**IF I HAVE TO GO AWAY** *Splash CP 11*	**36**	5

JILTED JOHN *UK, male vocalist – Graham Fellows (12 WEEKS)* pos/wks

12 Aug 78	●	**JILTED JOHN** *EMI International INT 567*	**4**	12

JIMMY EAT WORLD *US, male vocal / instrumental group (1 WEEK)* pos/wks

17 Nov 01		**SALT SWEAT SUGAR** *Dreamworks 4508782*	**60**	1

JIMMY THE HOOVER
UK, male / female vocal / instrumental group (8 WEEKS) pos/wks

25 Jun 83		**TANTALISE (WO WO EE YEH YEH)** *Innervision A 3406*	**18**	8

JINGLE BELLES *US / UK, female vocal group (4 WEEKS)* pos/wks

17 Dec 83		**CHRISTMAS SPECTRE** *Passion PASH 14*	**37**	4

JINNY *Italy, female vocalist – Janine Brown (16 WEEKS)* pos/wks

29 Jun 91		**KEEP WARM** *Virgin VS 1356*	**68**	3
22 May 93		**FEEL THE RHYTHM** *Logic 401633001022*	**74**	1
15 Jul 95		**KEEP WARM (re-mix)** *Multiply CDMULTY 5*	**11**	8
16 Dec 95		**WANNA BE WITH YOU** *Multiply CDMULTY 8*	**30**	4

JIVE BUNNY and the MASTERMIXERS *UK, male DJ / production duo – Andy Pickles and Les Hemstock (68 WEEKS)* pos/wks

15 Jul 89	★	**SWING THE MOOD** *Music Factory Dance MFD 001*	**1**	19
14 Oct 89	★	**THAT'S WHAT I LIKE** *Music Factory Dance MFD 002*	**1**	12
16 Dec 89	★	**LET'S PARTY** *Music Factory Dance MFD 003* ■	**1**	6
17 Mar 90	●	**THAT SOUNDS GOOD TO ME** *Music Factory Dance MFD 004*	**4**	6
25 Aug 90	●	**CAN CAN YOU PARTY** *Music Factory Dance MFD 007*	**8**	6
17 Nov 90		**LET'S SWING AGAIN** *Music Factory Dance MFD 009*	**19**	5
22 Dec 90		**THE CRAZY PARTY MIXES** *Music Factory Dance MFD 010*	**13**	5
23 Mar 91		**OVER TO YOU JOHN (HERE WE GO AGAIN)** *Music Factory Dance MFD 012*	**28**	5

20 Jul 91		HOT SUMMER SALSA *Music Factory Dance MFD 013*	43	2
23 Nov 91		ROCK 'N' ROLL DANCE PARTY *Music Factory Dance MFD 015*	48	2

See also Liz KERSHAW and Bruno BROOKES

JJ *UK, male / female vocal / instumental duo (3 WEEKS)*

			pos	wks
9 Feb 91		IF THIS IS LOVE *Columbia 6566097*	55	3

See also DJ LUCK & MC NEAT

JJ72 *Ireland, male / female vocal / instrumental group (10 WEEKS)*

			pos	wks
3 Jun 00		LONG WAY SOUTH *Lakota LAK 0015CD*	68	1
26 Aug 00		OXYGEN *Lakota LAK 0016CD*	23	3
4 Nov 00		OCTOBER SWIMMER *Lakota LAK 0018CD*	29	3
10 Feb 01		SNOW *Lakota LAK 0019CD*	21	3

JKD BAND *UK, male vocal / instrumental group (4 WEEKS)*

			pos	wks
1 Jul 78		DRAGON POWER *Satril SAT 132*	58	4

JM SILK *US, male vocal / instrumental duo (6 WEEKS)*

			pos	wks
25 Oct 86		I CAN'T TURN AROUND *RCA PB 49793*	62	3
7 Mar 87		LET THE MUSIC TAKE CONTROL *RCA PB 49767*	47	3

JMD – *See TYREE*

JO JO GUNNE *US, male vocal / instrumental group (12 WEEKS)*

			pos	wks
25 Mar 72	●	RUN RUN RUN *Asylum AYM 501*	6	12

JOAN COLLINS FAN CLUB *UK, male vocalist – Julian Clary (3 WEEKS)*

			pos	wks
18 Jun 88		LEADER OF THE PACK *10 TEN 227*	60	3

John Paul JOANS *UK, male vocalist (7 WEEKS)*

			pos	wks
19 Dec 70		MAN FROM NAZARETH *RAK 107*	41	3
16 Jan 71		MAN FROM NAZARETH (re-entry) *RAK 107*	25	4

JOBOXERS *UK, male vocal / instrumental group (33 WEEKS)*

			pos	wks
19 Feb 83	●	BOXER BEAT *RCA BOXX 1*	3	15
21 May 83	●	JUST GOT LUCKY *RCA BOXX 2*	7	9
13 Aug 83		JOHNNY FRIENDLY *RCA BOXX 3*	31	8
12 Nov 83		JEALOUS LOVE *RCA BOXX 4*	72	1

JOCASTA *UK, male vocal / instrumental group (2 WEEKS)*

			pos	wks
15 Feb 97		GO *Epic 6641415*	50	1
3 May 97		CHANGE ME *Epic 6643902*	60	1

JOCKMASTER B.A. – *See MAD JOCKS featuring JOCKMASTER B.A.*

JOCKO *US, male rapper – DJ Jocko Henderson (3 WEEKS)*

			pos	wks
23 Feb 80		RHYTHM TALK *Philadelphia International PIR 8222*	56	3

JODE featuring YO-HANS *UK, male / female vocal duo (2 WEEKS)*

			pos	wks
19 Dec 98		WALK...(THE DOG) LIKE AN EGYPTIAN *Logic 74321640332* [1]	48	2

JODECI *US, male vocal group (19 WEEKS)*

			pos	wks
16 Jan 93		CHERISH *Uptown MCSTD 1726*	56	2
11 Dec 93		CRY FOR YOU *Uptown MCSTD 1951*	56	1
16 Jul 94		FEENIN' *Uptown MCSTD 1984*	18	3
28 Jan 95		CRY FOR YOU (re-issue) *Uptown MCSTD 2039*	20	3
24 Jun 95		FREEK 'N YOU *Uptown MCSTD 2072*	17	5
9 Dec 95		LOVE U 4 LIFE *Uptown MCSTD 2105*	23	3
25 May 96		GET ON UP *MCA MCSTD 48010*	20	2

JODIE *Australia, female vocalist (1 WEEK)*

			pos	wks
25 Feb 95		ANYTHING YOU WANT *Mercury MERCD 423*	47	1

JOE *US, male vocalist – Joseph Thomas (42 WEEKS)*

			pos	wks
22 Jan 94		I'M IN LUV *Mercury JOECD 1*	22	4
25 Jun 94		THE ONE FOR ME *Mercury JOECD 2*	34	2
22 Oct 94		ALL OR NOTHING *Mercury JOECD 3*	56	1
27 Apr 96		ALL THE THINGS (YOUR MAN WON'T DO) *Island CID 634*	34	3
14 Jun 97		DON'T WANNA BE A PLAYER *Jive JIVECD 410*	16	3
27 Sep 97		THE LOVE SCENE *Jive JIVECD 430*	22	2
10 Jan 98		GOOD GIRLS *Jive JIVECD 442*	29	3
22 Aug 98		NO ONE ELSE COMES CLOSE *Jive 0521682*	41	2
31 Oct 98		ALL THAT I AM *Jive 0518532*	52	1
11 Mar 00	●	THANK GOD I FOUND YOU *Columbia 6690582* [1] ▲	10	9
20 May 00		THANK GOD I FOUND YOU (re-entry) *Columbia 6690582* [1]	71	1
15 Jul 00		TREAT HER LIKE A LADY *Jive 9250772*	60	1
17 Feb 01	●	STUTTER *Jive 9251632* [2] ▲	7	8
5 May 01		I WANNA KNOW *Jive 9252102*	37	2

[1] Mariah Carey featuring Joe and 98 Degrees [2] Joe featuring Mystikal

JOE PUBLIC *US, male rap group (5 WEEKS)*

			pos	wks
11 Jul 92		LIVE AND LEARN *Columbia 6575267*	43	4
28 Nov 92		I'VE BEEN WATCHIN' *Columbia 6587657*	75	1

Billy JOEL (158 Top 500)

Platinum-plated singer / songwriter / pianist, b. 9 May 1949, Long Island, US. This relatively youthful Grammy Living Legend Award recipient was the first artist to have five albums pass the seven-million mark Stateside (146 WEEKS)

			pos	wks
11 Feb 78		JUST THE WAY YOU ARE *CBS 5872*	19	9
24 Jun 78		MOVIN' OUT (ANTHONY'S SONG) *CBS 6412*	35	6
2 Dec 78		MY LIFE *CBS 6821*	12	15
28 Apr 79		UNTIL THE NIGHT *CBS 7242*	50	3
12 Apr 80		ALL FOR LEYNA *CBS 8325*	40	4
9 Aug 80		IT'S STILL ROCK AND ROLL TO ME *CBS 8753* ▲	14	11
15 Oct 83	★	UPTOWN GIRL *CBS A 3775*	1	17
10 Dec 83	●	TELL HER ABOUT IT *CBS A 3655* ▲	4	10
18 Feb 84	●	AN INNOCENT MAN *CBS A 4142*	8	10
28 Apr 84		THE LONGEST TIME *CBS A 4280*	25	8
23 Jun 84		LEAVE A TENDER MOMENT ALONE / GOODNIGHT SAIGON *CBS A 4521*	29	7
22 Feb 86		SHE'S ALWAYS A WOMAN / JUST THE WAY YOU ARE (re-issue) *CBS A 6862*	53	1
20 Sep 86		A MATTER OF TRUST *CBS 650057 7*	52	4
30 Sep 89	●	WE DIDN'T START THE FIRE *CBS JOEL 1* ▲	7	10
16 Dec 89		LENINGRAD *CBS JOEL 3*	53	4
10 Mar 90		I GO TO EXTREMES *CBS JOEL 2*	70	2
29 Aug 92		ALL SHOOK UP *Columbia 6583437*	27	4
31 Jul 93	●	THE RIVER OF DREAMS *Columbia 6595432*	3	14
23 Oct 93		ALL ABOUT SOUL *Columbia 6597362*	32	4
26 Feb 94		NO MAN'S LAND *Columbia 6599202*	50	3

'Goodnight Saigon' listed only from 30 Jun 1984

JOHANN *Germany, male producer – Johann Bley (1 WEEK)*

			pos	wks
16 Mar 96		NEW KICKS *Perfecto PERF 118CD*	54	1

Angela JOHN – *See José PADILLA featuring Angela JOHN*

Elton JOHN (4 Top 500)

Flamboyant singer / songwriter / pianist, b. Reginald Dwight, 25 Mar 1947, Pinner, Middlesex, UK. Almost as famous for his outrageous wardrobe as his music, Elton was the biggest-selling pop act of the 1970s, and has sold more albums in the UK and US than any British male singer, with total worldwide sales exceeding 150 million. He is the only British act to enter the US singles chart at No.1 and also recorded the first two albums to enter the US chart at No.1. He holds the record for headlining appearances at New York's Madison Square Garden. Elton, twice chairman of Watford Football Club, is the only act to chart every year from 1971 to 1999 in the UK and US. His Greatest Hits album has sold more than 15 million in the US and he has topped the US Adult Contemporary chart a record 16 times. 'Candle In The Wind 1997' (which he performed at the funeral of Diana, Princess of Wales) topped the chart in almost every country. In the UK it sold more than five million in six weeks and in the US had record advance orders of 8.7 million (and total sales in excess of 11 million). It also spent a staggering three years in the Canadian Top 20, which included 45 weeks at No.1. It is the world's biggest-selling single, with sales of 33 million in three months. His lyric writing partners have included, most influentially, Bernie

Taupin and, more recently, Sir Tim Rice. He became Sir Elton John in 1998 (576 WEEKS) pos/wks

23 Jan 71 ● **YOUR SONG** *DJM DJS 233* 7 12
22 Apr 72 ● **ROCKET MAN (I THINK IT'S GOING TO BE A LONG LONG TIME)** *DJM DJX 501* 2 13
9 Sep 72 **HONKY CAT** *DJM DJS 269* 31 6
4 Nov 72 ● **CROCODILE ROCK** *DJM DJS 271* ▲ 5 14
20 Jan 73 ● **DANIEL** *DJM DJS 275* 4 10
7 Jul 73 ● **SATURDAY NIGHT'S ALRIGHT FOR FIGHTING** *DJM DJX 502* 7 9
29 Sep 73 ● **GOODBYE YELLOW BRICK ROAD** *DJM DJS 285* 6 16
8 Dec 73 **STEP INTO CHRISTMAS** *DJM DJS 290* 24 7
2 Mar 74 **CANDLE IN THE WIND** *DJM DJS 297* 11 9
1 Jun 74 **DON'T LET THE SUN GO DOWN ON ME** *DJM DJS 302* 16 8
14 Sep 74 **THE BITCH IS BACK** *DJM DJS 322* 15 7
23 Nov 74 ● **LUCY IN THE SKY WITH DIAMONDS** *DJM DJS 340* ▲ 10 10
8 Mar 75 **PHILADELPHIA FREEDOM** *DJM DJS 354* [1] ▲ 12 9
28 Jun 75 **SOMEONE SAVED MY LIFE TONIGHT** *DJM DJS 385* 22 5
4 Oct 75 **ISLAND GIRL** *DJM DJS 610* ▲ 14 8
20 Mar 76 ● **PINBALL WIZARD** *DJM DJS 652* 7 7
3 Jul 76 ★ **DON'T GO BREAKING MY HEART** *Rocket ROKN 512* [2] ▲ 1 14
25 Sep 76 **BENNIE AND THE JETS** *DJM DJS 10705* ▲ 37 5
13 Nov 76 **SORRY SEEMS TO BE THE HARDEST WORD** *Rocket ROKN 517* 11 10
26 Feb 77 **CRAZY WATER** *Rocket ROKN 521* 27 6
11 Jun 77 **BITE YOUR LIP (GET UP AND DANCE)** *Rocket ROKN 526* 28 4
15 Apr 78 **EGO** *Rocket ROKN 538* 34 6
21 Oct 78 **PART TIME LOVE** *Rocket XPRES 1* 15 13
16 Dec 78 ● **SONG FOR GUY** *Rocket XPRES 5* 4 10
12 May 79 **ARE YOU READY FOR LOVE** *Rocket XPRES 13* 42 6
24 May 80 **LITTLE JEANNIE** *Rocket XPRES 32* 33 7
23 Aug 80 **SARTORIAL ELOQUENCE** *Rocket XPRES 41* 44 5
21 Mar 81 **I SAW HER STANDING THERE** *DJM DJS 10965* [3] 40 4
23 May 81 **NOBODY WINS** *Rocket XPRES 54* 42 5
27 Mar 82 ● **BLUE EYES** *Rocket XPRES 71* 8 10
12 Jun 82 **EMPTY GARDEN** *Rocket XPRES 77* 51 4
30 Apr 83 ● **I GUESS THAT'S WHY THEY CALL IT THE BLUES** *Rocket XPRES 91* 5 15
30 Jul 83 ● **I'M STILL STANDING** *Rocket EJS 1* 4 11
15 Oct 83 **KISS THE BRIDE** *Rocket EJS 2* 20 7
10 Dec 83 **COLD AS CHRISTMAS** *Rocket EJS 3* 33 6
26 May 84 ● **SAD SONGS (SAY SO MUCH)** *Rocket PH 7* 7 12
11 Aug 84 ● **PASSENGERS** *Rocket EJS 5* 5 11
20 Oct 84 **WHO WEARS THESE SHOES** *Rocket EJS 6* 50 3
2 Mar 85 **BREAKING HEARTS (AIN'T WHAT IT USED TO BE)** *Rocket EJS 7* 59 3
15 Jun 85 **ACT OF WAR** *Rocket EJS 8* [4] 32 5
12 Oct 85 ● **NIKITA** *Rocket EJS 9* 3 13
9 Nov 85 **THAT'S WHAT FRIENDS ARE FOR** *Arista ARIST 638* [5] ▲ 16 9
7 Dec 85 **WRAP HER UP** *Rocket EJS 10* 12 10
1 Mar 86 **CRY TO HEAVEN** *Rocket EJS 11* 47 4
4 Oct 86 **HEARTACHE ALL OVER THE WORLD** *Rocket EJS 12* 45 4
29 Nov 86 **SLOW RIVERS** *Rocket EJS 13* [6] 44 8
20 Jun 87 **FLAMES OF PARADISE** *CBS 6508657* [7] 59 3
16 Jan 88 ● **CANDLE IN THE WIND** *Rocket EJS 15* 5 11
4 Jun 88 **I DON'T WANNA GO ON WITH YOU LIKE THAT** *Rocket EJS 16* 30 8
3 Sep 88 **TOWN OF PLENTY** *Rocket EJS 17* 74 1
6 May 89 **THROUGH THE STORM** *Arista 112185* [8] 41 3
26 Aug 89 **HEALING HANDS** *Rocket EJS 19* 45 5
4 Nov 89 **SACRIFICE** *Rocket EJS 20* 55 3
9 Jun 90 ★ **SACRIFICE / HEALING HANDS (re-issue)** *Rocket EJS 22* 1 15
18 Aug 90 **CLUB AT THE END OF THE STREET / WHISPERS** *Rocket EJS 23* 47 3
20 Oct 90 **YOU GOTTA LOVE SOMEONE** *Rocket EJS 24* 33 4
15 Dec 90 **EASIER TO WALK AWAY** *Rocket EJS 25* 67 1
29 Dec 90 **EASIER TO WALK AWAY (re-entry)** *Rocket EJS 25* 63 1
7 Dec 91 ★ **DON'T LET THE SUN GO DOWN ON ME** *Epic 6576467* [9] ■ ▲ 1 10
6 Jun 92 ● **THE ONE** *Rocket EJS 28* 10 8
1 Aug 92 **RUNAWAY TRAIN** *Rocket EJS 29* [10] 31 4
7 Nov 92 **THE LAST SONG** *Rocket EJS 30* 21 4
22 May 93 **SIMPLE LIFE** *Rocket EJSCD 31* 44 2
20 Nov 93 ● **TRUE LOVE** *Rocket EJSCX 32* [2] 2 10
26 Feb 94 ● **DON'T GO BREAKING MY HEART (re-recording)** *Rocket EJRCD 33* [11] 7 7
14 May 94 **AIN'T NOTHING LIKE THE REAL THING** *London LONCD 350* [12] 24 4
9 Jul 94 **CAN YOU FEEL THE LOVE TONIGHT** *Mercury EJCD 34* 14 9
8 Oct 94 **CIRCLE OF LIFE** *Rocket EJSCD 35* 11 12
4 Mar 95 **BELIEVE** *Rocket EJSCD 36* 15 7
20 May 95 **MADE IN ENGLAND** *Rocket EJSCD 37* 18 5
3 Feb 96 **PLEASE** *Rocket EJSCD 40* 33 3
14 Dec 96 ● **LIVE LIKE HORSES** *Rocket LLHDD 1* [13] 9 6
20 Sep 97 ★ **CANDLE IN THE WIND 1997 / SOMETHING ABOUT THE WAY YOU LOOK TONIGHT** *Rocket PTCD 1* ◆ ■ ▲ 1 24
14 Feb 98 **RECOVER YOUR SOUL** *Rocket EJSCD 42* 16 3
13 Jun 98 **IF THE RIVER CAN BEND** *Rocket EJSDD 43* 32 2
6 Mar 99 ● **WRITTEN IN THE STARS** *Mercury EJSCD 45* [14] 10 7
22 May 99 **WRITTEN IN THE STARS (re-entry)** *Mercury EJSCD 45* [14] 63 1
6 Oct 01 ● **I WANT LOVE** *Rocket / Mercury 5887062* 9 10

[1] Elton John Band [2] Elton John and Kiki Dee [3] Elton John Band featuring John Lennon and the Muscle Shoals Horns [4] Elton John and Millie Jackson [5] Dionne Warwick and Friends featuring Elton John, Stevie Wonder and Gladys Knight [6] Elton John and Cliff Richard [7] Jennifer Rush and Elton John [8] Aretha Franklin and Elton John [9] George Michael and Elton John [10] Elton John and Eric Clapton [11] Elton John with RuPaul [12] Marcella Detroit and Elton John [13] Elton John and Luciano Pavarotti [14] Elton John and LeAnn Rimes

'Bite Your Lip (Get Up and Dance)' was one side of a double-sided chart entry, the other being 'Chicago' by Kiki Dee. 'Wrap Her Up' features George Michael as uncredited co-vocalist. 'Candle in the Wind' 1988 was a live recording

Robert JOHN *US, male vocalist (13 WEEKS)* pos/wks

17 Jul 68 **IF YOU DON'T WANT MY LOVE** *CBS 3436* 42 5
20 Oct 79 **SAD EYES** *EMI American EA 101* ▲ 31 8

JOHNNA *US, female vocalist (3 WEEKS)* pos/wks

10 Feb 96 **DO WHAT YOU FEEL** *PWL International PWL 323CD* 43 2
11 May 96 **IN MY DREAMS** *PWL International PWL 325CD* 66 1

JOHNNY and CHARLEY *Spain, male vocal duo (1 WEEK)* pos/wks

14 Oct 65 **LA YENKA** *Pye International 7N 25326* 49 1

JOHNNY and the HURRICANES (363 Top 500) *Internationally successful instrumental quintet formed 1957, Ohio, US. Featured saxophonist Johnny Paris (born Pocisk) and organist Paul Tesluk. Specialised in rocking retreads of old standards. The Beatles supported them in Hamburg in Dec 1962 (88 WEEKS)* pos/wks

9 Oct 59 ● **RED RIVER ROCK** *London HL 8948* 3 16
25 Dec 59 **REVEILLE ROCK** *London HL 9017* 14 5
17 Mar 60 ● **BEATNIK FLY** *London HLI 9072* 8 19
16 Jun 60 ● **DOWN YONDER** *London HLX 9134* 8 11
29 Sep 60 ● **ROCKING GOOSE** *London HLX 9190* 3 20
2 Mar 61 **JA-DA** *London HLX 9289* 14 9
6 Jul 61 **OLD SMOKIE / HIGH VOLTAGE** *London HLX 9378* 24 8

JOHNNY CORPORATE *US, male production duo (2 WEEKS)* pos/wks

28 Oct 00 **SUNDAY SHOUTIN'** *Defected DFECT 21CDS* 45 2

JOHNNY HATES JAZZ
UK, male vocal / instrumental group (45 WEEKS) pos/wks

11 Apr 87 ● **SHATTERED DREAMS** *Virgin VS 948* 5 14
29 Aug 87 **I DON'T WANT TO BE A HERO** *Virgin VS 1000* 11 10
21 Nov 87 **TURN BACK THE CLOCK** *Virgin VS 1017* 12 11
27 Feb 88 **HEART OF GOLD** *Virgin VS 1045* 19 7
9 Jul 88 **DON'T SAY IT'S LOVE** *Virgin VS 1081* 48 3

JOHNSON *UK, male / female vocal / instrumental duo (1 WEEK)* pos/wks

27 Mar 99 **SAY YOU LOVE ME** *Higher Ground HIGHS 18CD* 56 1

Andreas JOHNSON *Sweden, male vocalist (12 WEEKS)* pos/wks

5 Feb 00 ● **GLORIOUS** *WEA WEA 254CD* 4 11
27 May 00 **THE GAMES WE PLAY** *WEA WEA 264* 41 1

Bryan JOHNSON *UK, male vocalist (11 WEEKS)* pos/wks

10 Mar 60 **LOOKING HIGH, HIGH, HIGH** *Decca F 11213* 20 11

Carey JOHNSON *Australia, male vocalist (8 WEEKS)*

			pos	wks
25 Apr 87		**REAL FASHION REGGAE STYLE** *Oval TEN 170*	19	8

Denise JOHNSON *UK, female vocalist (4 WEEKS)*

			pos	wks
24 Aug 91		**DON'T FIGHT IT FEEL IT** *Creation CRE 110* [1]	41	2
14 May 94		**RAYS OF THE RISING SUN** *Magnet MAG 1022CD*	45	2

[1] Primal Scream featuring Denise Johnson

Don JOHNSON *US, male vocalist (12 WEEKS)*

			pos	wks
18 Oct 86		**HEARTBEAT** *Epic 650064 7*	46	5
5 Nov 88		**TILL I LOVED YOU (LOVE THEME FROM 'GOYA')** *CBS BARB 2* [1]	16	7

[1] Barbra Streisand and Don Johnson

General JOHNSON – *See CHAIRMEN OF THE BOARD*

Holly JOHNSON *UK, male vocalist (38 WEEKS)*

			pos	wks
14 Jan 89	●	**LOVE TRAIN** *MCA MCA 1306*	4	11
1 Apr 89	●	**AMERICANOS** *MCA MCA 1323*	4	11
20 May 89	★	**FERRY 'CROSS THE MERSEY** *PWL PWL 41* [1] ■	1	7
24 Jun 89		**ATOMIC CITY** *MCA MCA 1342*	18	4
30 Sep 89		**HEAVEN'S HERE** *MCA MCA 1365*	62	2
1 Dec 90		**WHERE HAS LOVE GONE?** *MCA MCA 1460*	73	1
25 Dec 99		**THE POWER OF LOVE** *Pleasure Dome PLDCD 1005*	56	2

[1] Christians, Holly Johnson, Paul McCartney, Gerry Marsden and Stock Aitken Waterman

See also FRANKIE GOES TO HOLLYWOOD

Howard JOHNSON *US, male vocalist (6 WEEKS)*

			pos	wks
4 Sep 82		**KEEPIN' LOVE NEW / SO FINE** *A & M USA 1221*	45	6

'Keepin' Love New' listed 4 Sep 1982 only

Johnny JOHNSON and the BANDWAGON
US, male vocal group (50 WEEKS)

			pos	wks
16 Oct 68	●	**BREAKIN' DOWN THE WALLS OF HEARTACHE** *Direction 58-3670* [1]	4	15
5 Feb 69		**YOU** *Direction 58-3923* [1]	34	4
28 May 69		**LET'S HANG ON** *Direction 58-4180* [1]	36	6
25 Jul 70	●	**SWEET INSPIRATION** *Bell 1111*	10	12
24 Oct 70		**SWEET INSPIRATION (re-entry)** *Bell 1111*	46	1
28 Nov 70	●	**BLAME IT ON THE PONY EXPRESS** *Bell 1128*	7	12

[1] Bandwagon

Kevin JOHNSON *Australia, male vocalist (6 WEEKS)*

			pos	wks
11 Jan 75		**ROCK 'N ROLL (I GAVE YOU THE BEST YEARS OF MY LIFE)** *UK UKR 84*	23	6

Laurie JOHNSON *UK, orchestra (14 WEEKS)*

			pos	wks
28 Sep 61	●	**SUCU SUCU** *Pye 7N 15383*	9	12
17 May 97		**THEME FROM 'THE PROFESSIONALS'** *Virgin VSCDT 1643* [1]	36	2

[1] Laurie Johnson's London Big Band

LJ JOHNSON *US, male vocalist (6 WEEKS)*

			pos	wks
7 Feb 76		**YOUR MAGIC PUT A SPELL ON ME** *Philips 6006 492*	27	6

Lou JOHNSON *US, male vocalist (2 WEEKS)*

			pos	wks
26 Nov 64		**MESSAGE TO MARTHA (KENTUCKY BLUEBIRD)** *London HL 9929*	36	2

Marv JOHNSON *US, male vocalist (39 WEEKS)*

			pos	wks
12 Feb 60	●	**YOU GOT WHAT IT TAKES** *London HLT 9013*	7	16
5 May 60		**I LOVE THE WAY YOU LOVE** *London HLT 9109*	35	3
11 Aug 60		**AIN'T GONNA BE THAT WAY** *London HLT 9165*	50	1
22 Jan 69	●	**I'LL PICK A ROSE FOR MY ROSE** *Tamla Motown TMG 680*	10	11
25 Oct 69		**I MISS YOU BABY** *Tamla Motown TMG 713*	25	8

Orlando JOHNSON – *See SECCHI featuring Orlando JOHNSON*

Paul JOHNSON *UK, male vocalist (7 WEEKS)*

			pos	wks
21 Feb 87		**WHEN LOVE COMES CALLING** *CBS PJOHN 1*	52	5
25 Feb 89		**NO MORE TOMORROWS** *CBS PJOHN 7*	67	2

Paul JOHNSON *US, male producer / instrumentalist (8 WEEKS)*

			pos	wks
25 Sep 99	●	**GET GET DOWN** *Defected DEFECT 7CDS*	5	8

Puff JOHNSON *US, female vocalist (6 WEEKS)*

			pos	wks
18 Jan 97		**OVER AND OVER** *Columbia 6640345*	20	4
12 Apr 97		**FOREVER MORE** *Work 644075*	29	2

Romina JOHNSON *UK, female vocalist (13 WEEKS)*

			pos	wks
4 Mar 00	●	**MOVIN TOO FAST** *Locked On XL LOX 117CD* [1]	2	11
10 Jun 00		**MOVIN TOO FAST (re-entry)** *Locked On XL LOX 117CD* [1]	64	1
17 Jun 00		**MY FORBIDDEN LOVER** *51 Lexington CDLEX 1* [2]	59	1

[1] Artful Dodger and Romina Johnson [2] Romina Johnson featuring Luci Martin and Norma Jean

Teddy JOHNSON – *See Pearl CARR and Teddy JOHNSON*

JOHNSTON BROTHERS
UK, male vocal group – leader Johnny Johnston (33 WEEKS)

			pos	wks
3 Apr 53	●	**OH, HAPPY DAY** *Decca F 10071*	4	8
5 Nov 54		**WAIT FOR ME, DARLING** *Decca F 10362* [1]	18	1
21 Jan 55		**HAPPY DAYS AND LONELY NIGHTS** *Decca F 10389*	14	2
7 Oct 55	★	**HERNANDO'S HIDEAWAY** *Decca F 10608*	1	13
30 Dec 55	●	**JOIN IN AND SING AGAIN** *Decca F 10636* [2]	9	1
13 Apr 56		**NO OTHER LOVE** *Decca F 10721*	22	1
30 Nov 56		**IN THE MIDDLE OF THE HOUSE** *Decca F 10781*	27	1
7 Dec 56		**JOIN IN AND SING NO.3** *Decca F 10814*	30	1
28 Dec 56		**JOIN IN AND SING NO.3 (re-entry)** *Decca F 10814*	24	1
8 Feb 57		**GIVE HER MY LOVE** *Decca F 10828*	27	1
19 Apr 57		**HEART** *Decca F 10860*	23	3

[1] Joan Regan with the Johnston Brothers [2] Johnson Brothers and The George Chisholm Sour-Note Six

The following two hits were medleys: Join In and Sing Again: Sheik of Araby / Yes Sir That's My Baby / California Here I Come / Some of These Days / Charleston / Margie. Join In and Sing (No.3): Coal Black Morning / When You're Smiling / Alexander's Ragtime Band / Sweet Sue Just You / When You Wore a Tulip / If You Were the Only Girl in the World

Bruce JOHNSTON *US, male instrumentalist – keyboards (4 WEEKS)*

			pos	wks
27 Aug 77		**PIPELINE** *CBS 5514*	33	4

Jan JOHNSTON *UK, female vocalist (5 WEEKS)*

			pos	wks
8 Feb 97		**TAKE ME BY THE HAND** *AM:PM 5821012* [1]	28	2
12 Feb 00		**LOVE WILL COME** *Xtravaganza XTRAV6CDS* [2]	31	2
21 Apr 01		**FLESH** *Perfecto PERF 05CDS*	36	2
28 Jul 01		**SILENT WORDS** *Perfecto PERF 16CDS*	57	1
8 Sep 01		**SKYDIVE (I FEEL WONDERFUL) (2nd re-mix)** *Incentive CENT 22CDS* [1]	35	2

[1] Submerge featuring Jan Johnston [2] Tomski featuring Jan Johnston [1] Freefall featuring Jan Johnston

Sabrina JOHNSTON *US, female vocalist (19 WEEKS)*

			pos	wks
7 Sep 91	●	**PEACE** *East West YZ 616*	8	10
7 Dec 91		**FRIENDSHIP** *East West YZ 637*	58	4
11 Jul 92		**I WANNA SING** *East West YZ 661*	46	2
3 Oct 92		**PEACE (re-mix)** *Epic 6584377*	35	2
13 Aug 94		**SATISFY MY LOVE** *Champion CHAMPCD 311*	62	1

The listed flipside of 'Peace' (re-mix) was 'Gypsy Woman' (re-mix) by Crystal Waters

JOJO – *See 2PAC; K-CI & JOJO*

James JOLIS – *See Barry MANILOW*

UK No.1 ★ UK Top 10 ● Still on chart + UK million seller ◆ UK entry at No.1 ■ US No.1 ▲

JOLLY BROTHERS
Jamaica, male vocal / instrumental group (7 WEEKS) pos/wks

Date		Title / Label	Pos	Wks
28 Jul 79		**CONSCIOUS MAN** *United Artists UP 36415*	46	7

JOLLY ROGER *UK, male instrumentalist / producer (12 WEEKS)* pos/wks

Date		Title / Label	Pos	Wks
10 Sep 88		**ACID MAN** *10 TEN 236*	23	12

JOMALSKI – *See WILDCHILD*

JOMANDA *US, female vocal group (10 WEEKS)* pos/wks

Date		Title / Label	Pos	Wks
22 Apr 89		**MAKE MY BODY ROCK** *RCA PB 42749*	44	3
29 Jun 91		**GOT A LOVE FOR YOU** *Giant W 0040*	43	4
11 Sep 93		**I LIKE IT** *Big Beat A 8377CD*	67	1
13 Nov 93		**NEVER** *Big Beat A 8347CD*	40	2

JON and VANGELIS *UK, male vocalist and Greece, male multi-instrumentalist - Jon Anderson and Evangelos Papathanassiou (28 WEEKS)* pos/wks

Date		Title / Label	Pos	Wks
5 Jan 80	●	**I HEAR YOU NOW** *Polydor POSP 96*	8	11
12 Dec 81	●	**I'LL FIND MY WAY HOME** *Polydor JV 1*	6	13
30 Jul 83		**HE IS SAILING** *Polydor JV 4*	61	2
18 Aug 84		**STATE OF INDEPENDENCE** *Polydor JV 5*	67	2

See also VANGELIS

JON OF THE PLEASED WIMMIN *UK, male DJ / producer (5 WEEKS)* pos/wks

Date		Title / Label	Pos	Wks
18 Feb 95		**PASSION** *Perfecto YZ 884CD*	27	3
6 Apr 96		**GIVE ME STRENGTH** *Perfecto PERF 119CD*	30	2

JON THE DENTIST vs Ollie JAYE
UK, male DJs / producers (2 WEEKS) pos/wks

Date		Title / Label	Pos	Wks
24 Jul 99		**IMAGINATION** *Tidy Trax TIDY 126CD*	72	1
10 Jun 00		**FEEL SO GOOD** *Tidy Trax TIDY 135CD*	72	1

JONAH *Holland, male production group (4 WEEKS)* pos/wks

Date		Title / Label	Pos	Wks
22 Jul 00		**SSSST (LISTEN)** *VC Recordings VCRD 69*	25	4

JONELL – *See HI-TEK featuring JONELL*

Aled JONES *UK, male vocalist (24 WEEKS)* pos/wks

Date		Title / Label	Pos	Wks
20 Jul 85		**MEMORY: THEME FROM THE MUSICAL 'CATS'** *BBC RESL 175*	42	4
30 Nov 85	●	**WALKING IN THE AIR** *HMV ALED 1*	5	11
14 Dec 85		**PICTURES IN THE DARK** *Virgin VS 836* [1]	50	6
20 Dec 86		**A WINTER STORY** *HMV ALED 2*	51	3

[1] Mike Oldfield featuring Aled Jones, Anita Hegerland and Barry Palmer

Barbara JONES *Jamaica, female vocalist (7 WEEKS)* pos/wks

Date		Title / Label	Pos	Wks
31 Jan 81		**JUST WHEN I NEEDED YOU MOST** *Sonet SON 2221*	31	7

Catherine Zeta JONES *UK, female vocalist (9 WEEKS)* pos/wks

Date		Title / Label	Pos	Wks
19 Sep 92		**FOR ALL TIME** *Columbia 6583547*	36	5
26 Nov 94		**TRUE LOVE WAYS** *PolyGram TV TLWCD 2* [1]	38	3
1 Apr 95		**IN THE ARMS OF LOVE** *Wow! WOWCD 7101*	72	1

[1] David Essex and Catherine Zeta Jones

Donell JONES *US, male vocalist (18 WEEKS)* pos/wks

Date		Title / Label	Pos	Wks
15 Feb 97		**KNOCKS ME OFF MY FEET** *LaFace 74321458502*	58	1
22 Jan 00	●	**U KNOW WHAT'S UP** *LaFace 74321722752*	2	11
20 May 00		**SHORTY (GOT HER EYES ON ME)** *Laface 74321748902*	19	3
2 Dec 00		**TRUE STEP TONIGHT** *Nulife 74321811312* [1]	25	3

[1] True Steppers featuring Brian Harvey and Donell Jones

Georgia JONES – *See PLUX featuring Georgia JONES; DIVA SURPRISE featuring Georgia JONES*

Grace JONES *US, female vocalist (46 WEEKS)* pos/wks

Date		Title / Label	Pos	Wks
26 Jul 80		**PRIVATE LIFE** *Island WIP 6629*	17	8
20 Jun 81		**PULL UP TO THE BUMPER** *Island WIP 6696*	53	4
30 Oct 82		**THE APPLE STRETCHING / NIPPLE TO THE BOTTLE** *Island WIP 6779*	50	4
9 Apr 83		**MY JAMAICAN GUY** *Island IS 103*	56	3
12 Oct 85		**SLAVE TO THE RHYTHM** *ZTT IS 206*	12	8
18 Jan 86		**PULL UP TO THE BUMPER / LA VIE EN ROSE (re-issue)** *Island IS 240*	12	9
1 Mar 86		**LOVE IS THE DRUG** *Island IS 266*	35	4
15 Nov 86		**I'M NOT PERFECT (BUT I'M PERFECT FOR YOU)** *Manhattan MT 15*	56	3
7 May 94		**SLAVE TO THE RHYTHM (re-mix)** *Zance ZANG 50CD1*	28	2
25 Nov 00		**PULL UP TO THE BUMPER** *Club Tools 0120375 CLU* [1]	60	1

[1] Grace Jones vs Funkstar De Luxe

'La Vie En Rose' was listed only from 1 Feb 1986

Hannah JONES *US, female vocalist (9 WEEKS)* pos/wks

Date		Title / Label	Pos	Wks
14 Sep 91		**BRIDGE OVER TROUBLED WATER** *Dance Pool 6565467* [1]	21	8
30 Jan 93		**KEEP IT ON** *TMRC CDTMRC 7*	67	1

[1] PJB featuring Hannah and her Sisters

Howard JONES (294 Top 500) *Accomplished singer / songwriter, b. 23 Feb 1955, Southampton, UK, who was a regular chart visitor in the mid-1980s with his brand of synth-based pop. Jones, who was equally popular in the US, appeared at Live Aid (103 WEEKS)* pos/wks

Date		Title / Label	Pos	Wks
17 Sep 83	●	**NEW SONG** *WEA HOW 1*	3	12
26 Nov 83	●	**WHAT IS LOVE** *WEA HOW 2*	2	15
14 Jan 84		**NEW SONG (re-entry)** *WEA HOW 1*	60	3
18 Feb 84		**HIDE AND SEEK** *WEA HOW 3*	12	9
26 May 84	●	**PEARL IN THE SHELL** *WEA HOW 4*	7	10
11 Aug 84	●	**LIKE TO GET TO KNOW YOU WELL** *WEA HOW 5*	4	12
9 Feb 85	●	**THINGS CAN ONLY GET BETTER** *WEA HOW 6*	6	8
20 Apr 85	●	**LOOK MAMA** *WEA HOW 7*	10	6
29 Jun 85		**LIFE IN ONE DAY** *WEA HOW 8*	14	7
15 Mar 86		**NO ONE IS TO BLAME** *WEA HOW 9*	16	7
4 Oct 86		**ALL I WANT** *WEA HOW 10*	35	4
29 Nov 86		**YOU KNOW I LOVE YOU...DON'T YOU?** *WEA HOW 11*	43	3
21 Mar 87		**LITTLE BIT OF SNOW** *WEA HOW 12*	70	1
4 Mar 89		**EVERLASTING LOVE** *WEA HOW 13*	62	3
11 Apr 92		**LIFT ME UP** *East West HOW 15*	52	3

Janie JONES *UK, female vocalist (3 WEEKS)* pos/wks

Date		Title / Label	Pos	Wks
27 Jan 66		**WITCHES BREW** *HMV POP 1495*	46	3

Jimmy JONES *US, male vocalist (47 WEEKS)* pos/wks

Date		Title / Label	Pos	Wks
17 Mar 60	●	**HANDY MAN** *MGM 1051*	3	21
16 Jun 60	★	**GOOD TIMIN'** *MGM 1078*	1	15
18 Aug 60		**HANDY MAN (re-entry)** *MGM 1051*	32	3
8 Sep 60		**I JUST GO FOR YOU** *MGM 1091*	35	4
17 Nov 60		**READY FOR LOVE** *MGM 1103*	46	1
30 Mar 61		**I TOLD YOU SO** *MGM 1123*	33	3

Juggy JONES *US, male multi-instrumentalist (4 WEEKS)* pos/wks

Date		Title / Label	Pos	Wks
7 Feb 76		**INSIDE AMERICA** *Contempo CS 2080*	39	4

Kelly JONES – *See MANCHILD*

Lavinia JONES *South Africa, female vocalist (2 WEEKS)* pos/wks

Date		Title / Label	Pos	Wks
18 Feb 95		**SING IT TO YOU (DEE-DOOB-DEE-DOO)** *Virgin International DINDG 142*	45	2

Mick JONES – *See AZTEC CAMERA; CLASH*

Oran 'Juice' JONES *US, male vocalist (14 WEEKS)* pos/wks

Date		Title / Label	Pos	Wks
15 Nov 86	●	**THE RAIN** *Def Jam A 7303*	4	14

Paul JONES *UK, male vocalist – Paul Pond (34 WEEKS)* pos/wks

Date		Title / Label	Pos	Wks
6 Oct 66	●	**HIGH TIME** *HMV POP 1554*	4	15
19 Jan 67	●	**I'VE BEEN A BAD, BAD BOY** *HMV POP 1576*	5	9

23 Aug 67	**THINKIN' AIN'T FOR ME** *HMV POP 1602*	47	1
13 Sep 67	**THINKIN' AIN'T FOR ME (re-entry)** *HMV POP 1602*	32	7
5 Feb 69	**AQUARIUS** *Columbia DB 8514*	45	2

See also MANFRED MANN; BLUES BAND

Quincy JONES

US, male producer / instrumentalist – keyboards (42 WEEKS) pos/wks

29 Jul 78	**STUFF LIKE THAT** *A & M AMS 7367*	34	9
11 Apr 81	**AI NO CORRIDA (I-NO-KO-REE-DA)** *A & M AMS 8109* [1]	14	10
20 Jun 81	**RAZZAMATAZZ** *A & M AMS 8140*	11	9
5 Sep 81	**BETCHA' WOULDN'T HURT ME** *A & M AMS 8157*	52	3
13 Jan 90	**I'LL BE GOOD TO YOU** *Qwest W 2697* [2]	21	7
31 Mar 90	**SECRET GARDEN** *Qwest W 9992* [3]	67	1
14 Sep 96	**STOMP** *Qwest W 0372CD* [4]	28	2
1 Aug 98	**SOUL BOSSA NOVA** *Manifesto FESCD 48* [5]	47	1

[1] Quincy Jones featuring Dune [2] Quincy Jones featuring Ray Charles and Chaka Khan [3] Quincy Jones featuring Al B Sure!, James Ingram, El DeBarge and Barry White [4] Quincy Jones featuring Melle Mel, Coolio, Yo-Yo, Shaquille O'Neal, The Luniz [5] Cool, the Fab and the Groovy present Quincy Jones

Uncredited vocals on 'Stuff Like That' were by Ashford and Simpson and Chaka Khan, and on 'Razzamatazz' and 'Betcha' Wouldn't Hurt Me' by Patti Austin

Rickie Lee JONES *US, female vocalist (9 WEEKS)* pos/wks

23 Jun 79	**CHUCK E'S IN LOVE** *Warner Bros. K 17390*	18	9

Shirley JONES – *See PARTRIDGE FAMILY*

Sonny JONES featuring Tara CHASE

Germany, male vocalist and Canada, female rapper (2 WEEKS) pos/wks

7 Oct 00	**FOLLOW YOU FOLLOW ME** *Logic 74321772892*	42	2

Tammy JONES *UK, female vocalist (10 WEEKS)* pos/wks

26 Apr 75 ●	**LET ME TRY AGAIN** *Epic EPC 3211*	5	10

Tom JONES (16 Top 500)

Unmistakable entertainer who has been an international headliner for five decades, b Thomas Woodward, 7 Jun 1940, South Wales (re-named after the popular 1963 film). Despite failure of his first two Joe Meek-produced singles, the Welsh wonder became one of world's most popular singers, with hits in the pop, country, R&B and easy listening fields. The Vegas veteran, who hosted his own very successful late-1960s TV series, has had hits on 10 labels. This 60-something sex symbol, who was arguably the top British solo singer of the 1960s on both sides of Atlantic, had his biggest selling album in 1999 with 'Reload' (390 WEEKS) pos/wks

11 Feb 65 ★	**IT'S NOT UNUSUAL** *Decca F 12062*	1	14
6 May 65	**ONCE UPON A TIME** *Decca F 12121*	32	4
8 Jul 65	**WITH THESE HANDS** *Decca F 12191*	13	11
12 Aug 65	**WHAT'S NEW PUSSYCAT?** *Decca F 12203*	11	10
13 Jan 66	**THUNDERBALL** *Decca F 12292*	35	4
19 May 66	**ONCE THERE WAS A TIME / NOT RESPONSIBLE** *Decca F 12390*	18	9
18 Aug 66	**THIS AND THAT** *Decca F 12461*	44	3
10 Nov 66 ★	**GREEN, GREEN GRASS OF HOME** *Decca F 22511* ◆	1	22
16 Feb 67 ●	**DETROIT CITY** *Decca F 22555*	8	10
13 Apr 67 ●	**FUNNY FAMILIAR FORGOTTEN FEELINGS** *Decca F 12599*	7	15
26 Jul 67 ●	**I'LL NEVER FALL IN LOVE AGAIN** *Decca F 12639*	2	25
22 Nov 67 ●	**I'M COMING HOME** *Decca F 12693*	2	16
28 Feb 68 ●	**DELILAH** *Decca F 12747*	2	17
17 Jul 68 ●	**HELP YOURSELF** *Decca F 12812*	5	26
27 Nov 68	**A MINUTE OF YOUR TIME** *Decca F 12854*	14	15
14 May 69 ●	**LOVE ME TONIGHT** *Decca F 12924*	9	12
13 Dec 69 ●	**WITHOUT LOVE** *Decca F 12990*	10	11
14 Mar 70	**WITHOUT LOVE (re-entry)** *Decca F 12990*	49	1
18 Apr 70 ●	**DAUGHTER OF DARKNESS** *Decca F 13013*	5	15
15 Aug 70	**I (WHO HAVE NOTHING)** *Decca F 13061*	16	8
17 Oct 70	**I (WHO HAVE NOTHING) (re-entry)** *Decca F 13061*	47	3
16 Jan 71	**SHE'S A LADY** *Decca F 13113*	13	9
27 Mar 71	**SHE'S A LADY (re-entry)** *Decca F 13113*	47	1
5 Jun 71	**PUPPET MAN** *Decca F 13183*	49	1
19 Jun 71	**PUPPET MAN (re-entry)** *Decca F 13183*	50	1
23 Oct 71 ●	**TILL** *Decca F 13236*	2	15
1 Apr 72 ●	**THE YOUNG NEW MEXICAN PUPPETEER** *Decca F 13298*	6	12
14 Apr 73	**LETTER TO LUCILLE** *Decca F 13393*	31	8
7 Sep 74	**SOMETHING 'BOUT YOU BABY I LIKE** *Decca F 13550*	36	5
16 Apr 77	**SAY YOU'LL STAY UNTIL TOMORROW** *EMI 2583*	40	3
18 Apr 87 ●	**A BOY FROM NOWHERE** *Epic OLE 1*	2	12
30 May 87	**IT'S NOT UNUSUAL (re-issue)** *Decca F 103*	17	8
2 Jan 88	**I WAS BORN TO BE ME** *Epic OLE 4*	61	1
29 Oct 88 ●	**KISS** *China CHINA 11* [1]	5	7
29 Apr 89	**MOVE CLOSER** *Jive JIVE 203*	49	3
26 Jan 91	**COULDN'T SAY GOODBYE** *Dover ROJ 10*	51	2
16 Mar 91	**CARRYING A TORCH** *Dover ROJ 12*	57	2
4 Jul 92	**DELILAH (re-issue)** *The Hit Label TOM 10*	68	2
6 Feb 93	**ALL YOU NEED IS LOVE** *Childline CHILDCD 93*	19	4
5 Nov 94	**IF I ONLY KNEW** *ZTT ZANG 59CD*	11	9
25 Sep 99 ●	**BURNING DOWN THE HOUSE** *Gut CDGUT 26* [2]	7	7
18 Dec 99	**BABY, IT'S COLD OUTSIDE** *Gut CDGUT 29* [3]	17	7
18 Mar 00 ●	**MAMA TOLD ME NOT TO COME** *Gut CDGUT 031* [4]	4	7
20 May 00 ●	**SEX BOMB** *Gut CDGUT 33* [5]	3	10
18 Nov 00	**YOU NEED LOVE LIKE I DO** *GUT CDGUT 36* [6]	24	3

[1] Art of Noise featuring Tom Jones [2] Tom Jones and The Cardigans [3] Tom Jones and Cerys Matthews [4] Tom Jones and Stereophonics [5] Tom Jones and Mousse T [6] Tom Jones and Heather Small

Sue JONES-DAVIES – *See Julie COVINGTON, Rula LENSKA, Charlotte CORNWELL and Sue JONES-DAVIES*

JONESTOWN *US, male vocal duo (1 WEEK)* pos/wks

13 Jun 98	**SWEET THANG** *Universal UMD 70376*	49	1

Alison JORDAN *UK, female vocalist (4 WEEKS)* pos/wks

9 May 92	**BOY FROM NEW YORK CITY** *Arista 74321100427*	23	4

Dick JORDAN *UK, male vocalist (4 WEEKS)* pos/wks

17 Mar 60	**HALLELUJAH, I LOVE HER SO** *Oriole CB 1534*	47	1
9 Jun 60	**LITTLE CHRISTINE** *Oriole CB 1548*	39	3

Jack JORDAN – *See Frank CHACKSFIELD and his Orchestra*

Montell JORDAN *US, male vocalist (21 WEEKS)* pos/wks

13 May 95	**THIS IS HOW WE DO IT** *Def Jam DEFCD 07* ▲	11	8
2 Sep 95	**SOMETHIN' 4 DA HONEYZ** *Def Jam DEFCD 10*	15	4
19 Oct 96	**I LIKE** *Def Jam DEFCD 19* [1]	24	3
23 May 98	**LET'S RIDE** *Def Jam 5686912* [2]	25	2
8 Apr 00	**GET IT ON TONITE** *Def Soul 5627222*	15	4

[1] Montell Jordan featuring Slick Rick [2] Montell Jordan featuring Master P and Silkk the Shocker

Ronny JORDAN *UK, male instrumentalist – guitar (7 WEEKS)* pos/wks

1 Feb 92	**SO WHAT!** *Antilles ANN 14*	32	4
25 Sep 93	**UNDER YOUR SPELL** *Island CID 565*	72	1
15 Jan 94	**TINSEL TOWN** *Island CID 566*	64	1
28 May 94	**COME WITH ME** *Island CID 584*	63	1

JORIO *US, male producer – Fred Jorio (1 WEEK)* pos/wks

24 Feb 01	**REMEMBER ME** *Wonderboy WBOYD 021*	54	1

David JOSEPH *UK, male vocalist (21 WEEKS)* pos/wks

26 Feb 83	**YOU CAN'T HIDE (YOUR LOVE FROM ME)** *Island IS 101*	13	9
28 May 83	**LET'S LIVE IT UP (NITE PEOPLE)** *Island IS 116*	26	5
18 Feb 84	**JOYS OF LIFE** *Island IS 153*	61	2
31 May 86	**EXPANSIONS '86 (EXPAND YOUR MIND)** *Fourth & Broadway BRW 48* [1]	58	5

[1] Chris Paul featuring David Joseph

Dawn JOSEPH – *See LOGO featuring Dawn JOSEPH*

Martyn JOSEPH *UK, male vocalist (10 WEEKS)* pos/wks

20 Jun 92	**DOLPHINS MAKE ME CRY** *Epic 6581347*	34	4

UK No.1 ★ UK Top 10 ● Still on chart + UK million seller ◆ UK entry at No.1 ■ US No.1 ▲

1974

IN THE YEAR IN WHICH RICHARD NIXON BECAME THE FIRST AMERICAN PRESIDENT TO RESIGN, ISRAELI CUTLERY BOTHERER URI GELLER ENTERED THE PUBLIC EYE AND MUHAMMAD ALI BEAT GEORGE FOREMAN IN THE 'RUMBLE IN THE JUNGLE', PRODUCER **GUS DUDGEON** CASTS HIS MIND BACK TO A COLORADO COLLABORATION OF TWO POP HEAVYWEIGHTS ...

“The idea that we should record a version of 'Lucy In The Sky With Diamonds' came about because Bernie Taupin had been watching a rerun of 'Yellow Submarine' on TV, and had commented to **Elton** that it was bizarre that 'Lucy' had never been released as a single. Elton had been looking for a song that **Lennon** could record with him as a result of a bet that he had made with John, after Elton had played piano and sung the harmony vocals on John's 'Whatever Gets You Through the Night'. Elton was so convinced that John's single would be a huge hit that he had made a deal with John: that should it actually make it, then John, in turn, would have to record a song with Elton. Seeing that Elton's prediction had proven to be right, despite John's scepticism about the song's chances, he now had to live up to the deal at a time when his confidence was at an all-time low. However, Elton's enthusiasm and friendship had carried John along and he arrived at Caribou Ranch, in Colorado, for the session with May Pang, his new girlfriend, and a beat-up guitar. He was so nervous at the beginning of the session, as was I, that he asked me to get a decent sound on his amp. Seeing as I was recording my favourite Beatle, I inevitably had his guitar far too loud in the playback, and he kept leaning over and asking me to turn it down. Eventually, after having insisted that 'most of it's fookin' crap, Gus', he persuaded me to wipe 80 per cent of it, with the exception of his guitar on the reggae section (his arrangement idea, incidentally), which I was determined to keep. He then did the vocal harmonies in the chorus, and wound up telling all of us that he liked our version more than the original. What a bloke!!”

SINGLE OF THE YEAR 'She' Charles Aznavour
ALBUM OF THE YEAR 'The Singles 1969 - 1973' Carpenters

12 Sep 92	WORKING MOTHER *Epic 6582937*	65	1
9 Jan 93	PLEASE SIR *Epic 6588552*	45	3
3 Jun 95	TALK ABOUT IT IN THE MORNING *Epic 6613342*	43	2

JOURNEY *US, male vocal / instrumental group (9 WEEKS)* pos/wks

27 Feb 82	DON'T STOP BELIEVIN' *CBS A 1728*	62	4
11 Sep 82	WHO'S CRYING NOW *CBS A 2725*	46	5

Ruth JOY *UK, female vocalist (3 WEEKS)* pos/wks

26 Aug 89	DON'T PUSH IT *MCA RJOY 1*	66	2
22 Feb 92	FEEL *MCA MCS 1574*	67	1

JOY DIVISION *UK, male vocal / instrumental group (24 WEEKS)* pos/wks

28 Jun 80	LOVE WILL TEAR US APART *Factory FAC 23*	13	9
29 Oct 83	LOVE WILL TEAR US APART (re-entry) *Factory FAC 23*	19	7
18 Jun 88	ATMOSPHERE *Factory FAC 2137*	34	5
17 Jun 95	LOVE WILL TEAR US APART (re-mix) *London YOJCD 1*	19	3

JOY STRINGS *UK, male / female vocal / instrumental group (11 WEEKS)* pos/wks

27 Feb 64	IT'S AN OPEN SECRET *Regal-Zonophone RZ 501*	32	7
17 Dec 64	A STARRY NIGHT *Regal-Zonophone RZ 504*	34	4

JOYRIDER *UK, male vocal / instrumental group (4 WEEKS)* pos/wks

27 Jul 96	RUSH HOUR *Paradox PDOXD 012*	22	3
28 Sep 96	ALL GONE AWAY *A & M 5819552*	54	1

JT and the BIG FAMILY
Italy, male / female vocal / instrumental group (8 WEEKS) pos/wks

3 Mar 90 ●	MOMENTS IN SOUL *Champion CHAMP 237*	7	8

JT PLAYAZ *UK, male production team (4 WEEKS)* pos/wks

5 Apr 97	JUST PLAYIN' *Pukka CDJTP 1*	30	3
2 May 98	LET'S GET DOWN *MCA MCSTD 40161*	64	1

JTQ *UK, male instrumental group (6 WEEKS)* pos/wks

3 Apr 93	LOVE THE LIFE *Big Life BLRD 93* [1]	34	3
3 Jul 93	SEE A BRIGHTER DAY *Big Life BLRDA 97* [1]	49	2
25 Feb 95	LOVE WILL KEEP US TOGETHER *Acid Jazz JAZID 112CD* [2]	63	1

[1] JTQ with Noel McKoy [2] JTQ featuring Alison Limerick

JUDAS PRIEST *UK, male vocal / instrumental group (51 WEEKS)* pos/wks

20 Jan 79	TAKE ON THE WORLD *CBS 6915*	14	10
12 May 79	EVENING STAR *CBS 7312*	53	4
29 Mar 80	LIVING AFTER MIDNIGHT *CBS 8379*	12	7
7 Jun 80	BREAKING THE LAW *CBS 8644*	12	6
23 Aug 80	UNITED *CBS 8897*	26	8
21 Feb 81	DON'T GO *CBS 9520*	51	3
25 Apr 81	HOT ROCKIN' *CBS A 1153*	60	3
21 Aug 82	YOU'VE GOT ANOTHER THING COMIN' *CBS A 2611*	66	2
21 Jan 84	FREEWHEEL BURNIN' *CBS A 4054*	42	3
23 Apr 88	JOHNNY B GOODE *Atlantic A 9114*	64	2
15 Sep 90	PAINKILLER *CBS 656273 7*	74	1
23 Mar 91	A TOUCH OF EVIL *Columbia 6565897*	58	1
24 Apr 93	NIGHT CRAWLER *Columbia 6590972*	63	1

JUDGE DREAD (323 Top 500) *Humorous white 'rude' reggae performer named after a Prince Buster track, and whose first hits were inspired by Buster's single 'Big Five', b. Alex Hughes, 1944, d. (on stage at Canterbury) 13 Mar 1998. All his hits were judged unsuitable for radio play (95 WEEKS)* pos/wks

26 Aug 72	BIG SIX *Big Shot BI 608*	11	27
9 Dec 72 ●	BIG SEVEN *Big Shot BI 613*	8	18
21 Apr 73	BIG EIGHT *Big Shot BI 619*	14	10
5 Jul 75 ●	JE T'AIME (MOI NON PLUS) *Cactus CT 65*	9	9
27 Sep 75	BIG TEN *Cactus CT 77*	14	7
6 Dec 75	CHRISTMAS IN DREADLAND / COME OUTSIDE *Cactus CT 80*	14	7
8 May 76	THE WINKLE MAN *Cactus CT 90*	35	4
28 Aug 76	Y VIVA SUSPENDERS *Cactus CT 99*	27	4
2 Apr 77	5TH ANNIVERSARY (EP) *Cactus CT 98*	31	4
14 Jan 78	UP WITH THE COCK / BIG PUNK *Cactus CT 110*	49	1
16 Dec 78	HOKEY COKEY / JINGLE BELLS *EMI 2881*	59	4

Tracks on 5th Anniversary (EP): Jamaica Jerk (Off) / Bring Back the Skins / End of the World / Big Everything. 'Y Viva Suspenders' was listed, additionally, with 'Confessions Of A Bouncer' in its second week on the chart

JUICE *Denmark, female vocal trio (3 WEEKS)* pos/wks

18 Apr 98	BEST DAYS *Chrysalis CDCHS 5081*	28	2
22 Aug 98	I'LL COME RUNNIN' *Chrysalis CDCHS 5090*	48	1

JUICY *US, male / female vocal duo (5 WEEKS)* pos/wks

22 Feb 86	SUGAR FREE *Epic A 6917*	45	5

JUICY LUCY *UK, male vocal / instrumental group (17 WEEKS)* pos/wks

7 Mar 70	WHO DO YOU LOVE *Vertigo V 1*	14	12
10 Oct 70	PRETTY WOMAN *Vertigo 6059 015*	45	2
31 Oct 70	PRETTY WOMAN (re-entry) *Vertigo 6059 015*	44	3

Thomas JULES-STOCK *UK, male vocalist (1 WEEK)* pos/wks

15 Aug 98	DIDN'T I TELL YOU TRUE *Mercury MERCD 501*	59	1

JULIA and COMPANY *US, male / female vocal group (10 WEEKS)* pos/wks

3 Mar 84	BREAKIN' DOWN (SUGAR SAMBA) *London LON 46*	15	8
23 Feb 85	I'M SO HAPPY *Next Plateau LON 61*	56	2

JULUKA
UK / South Africa, male / female vocal / instrumental group (4 WEEKS) pos/wks

12 Feb 83	SCATTERLINGS OF AFRICA *Safari ZULU 1*	44	4

See also Johnny CLEGG featuring SAVUKA

JUMP *UK, male instrumental group (1 WEEK)* pos/wks

1 Mar 97	FUNKATARIUM *Heat Recordings HEATCD 005*	56	1

Wally JUMP Jr and the CRIMINAL ELEMENT
US, male producer – Arthur Baker (19 WEEKS) pos/wks

28 Feb 87	TURN ME LOOSE *London LON 126*	60	2
5 Sep 87	PUT THE NEEDLE TO THE RECORD *Cooltempo COOL 150* [1]	63	3
12 Dec 87	TIGHTEN UP / I JUST CAN'T STOP DANCIN' *Breakout USA 621*	24	7
19 Mar 88	PRIVATE PARTY *Breakout USA 624*	57	3
6 Oct 90	EVERYBODY (RAP) *Deconstruction PB 44701* [2]	30	4

[1] Criminal Element Orchestra [2] Criminal Element Orchestra and Wendell Williams

JUMPING JACKS – *See Danny PEPPERMINT and the JUMPING JACKS*

Rosemary JUNE *US, female vocalist (9 WEEKS)* pos/wks

23 Jan 59	(I'LL BE WITH YOU) IN APPLE BLOSSOM TIME *Pye International 7N 25005*	14	9

JUNGLE BOOK *US, male / female vocal group (8 WEEKS)* pos/wks

8 May 93	THE JUNGLE BOOK GROOVE *Hollywood HWCD 128*	14	8

JUNGLE BROTHERS
US, male rap duo – Nathaniel Hall and Michael Small (35 WEEKS) pos/wks

22 Oct 88	I'LL HOUSE YOU *Gee Street GEE 003* [1]	22	5
18 Mar 89	BLACK IS BLACK / STRAIGHT OUT OF THE JUNGLE *Gee Street GEE 15*	72	1
31 Mar 90	WHAT 'U' WAITIN' '4' *Eternal W 9865*	35	5
21 Jul 90	DOIN' OUR OWN DANG *Eternal W 9754*	33	6
19 Jul 97	BRAIN *Gee Street GEE 5000388*	52	1
29 Nov 97	JUNGLE BROTHER *Gee Street GEE 5000493*	56	1
9 May 98	JUNGLE BROTHER (re-entry) *Gee Street GEE 5000493*	18	4
11 Jul 98	I'LL HOUSE YOU '98 (re-mix) *Gee Street FCD 338*	26	5
28 Nov 98	BECAUSE I GOT IT LIKE THAT *Gee Street GEE 5003593*	32	2
10 Jul 99	V.I.P. *Gee Street / V2 GEE 5007953*	33	3

6 Nov 99	**GET DOWN** *Gee Street / V2 GEE 5010153*	52	1
25 Mar 00	**FREAKIN' YOU** *Gee Street GEE 5008808*	70	1

[1] Richie Rich meets the Jungle Brothers

'Doin' Our Own Dang' features the uncredited De La Soul and Monie Love

JUNGLE HIGH with BLUE PEARL

UK / Germany, male production / instrumental duo and UK / US, male / female vocal / instrumental group (1 WEEK)

		pos	wks
27 Nov 93	**FIRE OF LOVE** *Logic 74321170292* [1]	71	1

JUNIOR *UK, male vocalist – Norman Giscombe (57 WEEKS)*

		pos	wks
24 Apr 82 ●	**MAMA USED TO SAY** *Mercury MER 98*	7	13
10 Jul 82	**TOO LATE** *Mercury MER 112*	20	9
25 Sep 82	**LET ME KNOW / I CAN'T HELP IT** *Mercury MER 116*	53	3
23 Apr 83	**COMMUNICATION BREAKDOWN** *Mercury MER 134*	57	3
8 Sep 84	**SOMEBODY** *London LON 50*	64	2
9 Feb 85	**DO YOU REALLY (WANT MY LOVE)** *London LON 60*	47	4
30 Nov 85	**OH LOUISE** *London LON 75*	74	3
4 Apr 87 ●	**ANOTHER STEP (CLOSER TO YOU)** *MCA KIM 5* [1]	6	11
25 Aug 90	**STEP OFF** *MCA MCA 1432* [2]	63	3
15 Aug 92	**THEN CAME YOU** *MCA MCS 1676* [2]	32	5
31 Oct 92	**ALL OVER THE WORLD** *MCA MCS 1691* [2]	74	1

[1] Kim Wilde and Junior [2] Junior Giscombe

JUNIOR JACK *Italy, male producer – Vito Lucente (4 WEEKS)*

		pos	wks
16 Dec 00	**MY FEELING** *Defected DFECT 24CDS*	31	4

JUNIOR M.A.F.I.A. *US, male / female rap ensemble (2 WEEKS)*

		pos	wks
3 Feb 96	**I NEED YOU TONIGHT** *Big Beat A 8130CD* [1]	66	1
19 Oct 96	**GETTIN' MONEY** *Big Beat A 5674CD*	63	1

[1] Junior M.A.F.I.A. featuring Aaliyah

JUNIORS – *See DANNY and the JUNIORS*

JUNKIE XL *Holland, male producer / vocal duo – Tom Holkenborg and Patrick Tilon (1 WEEK)*

		pos	wks
22 Jul 00	**ZEROTONINE** *Manifesto FESCD71*	63	1

JUNO REACTOR *UK / Germany, male production duo (1 WEEK)*

		pos	wks
8 Feb 97	**JUNGLE HIGH** *Perfecto PERF 133CD*	45	1

JURASSIC 5 *US, male rap group (4 WEEKS)*

		pos	wks
25 Jul 98	**JAYOU** *Pan PAN 018CD*	56	1
24 Oct 98	**CONCRETE SCHOOLYARD** *Pan PAN 020CD*	35	3

Christopher JUST *Austria, male producer (2 WEEKS)*

		pos	wks
13 Dec 97	**I'M A DISCO DANCER** *Slut Trax SLUT 001CD*	72	1
6 Feb 99	**I'M A DISCO DANCER (re-mix)** *XL Recordings XLS 105CD*	69	1

JUST LUIS *Australia, male vocalist (3 WEEKS)*

		pos	wks
14 Oct 95	**AMERICAN PIE** *Pro-Activ CDPTV 1*	31	2
17 Feb 96	**AMERICAN PIE (re-entry)** *Pro-Activ CDPTV 1*	70	1

Jimmy JUSTICE *UK, male vocalist – James Little (35 WEEKS)*

		pos	wks
29 Mar 62 ●	**WHEN MY LITTLE GIRL IS SMILING** *Pye 7N 15421*	9	13
14 Jun 62 ●	**AIN'T THAT FUNNY** *Pye 7N 15443*	8	11
23 Aug 62	**SPANISH HARLEM** *Pye 7N 15457*	20	11

JUSTIFIED ANCIENTS OF MU MU

UK, male production duo (6 WEEKS)

		pos	wks
9 Nov 91 ●	**IT'S GRIM UP NORTH** *KLF Communications JAMS 028*	10	5
4 Jan 92	**IT'S GRIM UP NORTH (re-entry)** *KLF Communications JAMS 028*	67	1

See also KLF; 2K; TIMELORDS

JUSTIN *UK, male vocalist – Justin Osuji (13 WEEKS)*

		pos	wks
22 Aug 98	**THIS BOY** *Virgin STCDT 1*	34	2
16 Jan 99	**OVER YOU** *Virgin STCDT 2*	11	4
17 Jul 99	**IT'S ALL ABOUT YOU** *Innocent STCDT 3*	34	3
22 Jan 00	**LET IT BE ME** *Innocent STCDTX 4*	15	4

Bill JUSTIS *US, male instrumentalist – alto sax (8 WEEKS)*

		pos	wks
10 Jan 58	**RAUNCHY** *London HLS 8517*	24	2
31 Jan 58	**RAUNCHY (re-entry)** *London HLS 8517*	11	6

Patrick JUVET *Switzerland, male vocalist (19 WEEKS)*

		pos	wks
2 Sep 78	**GOT A FEELING** *Casablanca CAN 127*	34	7
4 Nov 78	**I LOVE AMERICA** *Casablanca CAN 132*	12	12

JX *UK, male producer – Jake Williams (33 WEEKS)*

		pos	wks
2 Apr 94	**SON OF A GUN** *Internal Dance IDC 5*	13	6
1 Apr 95	**YOU BELONG TO ME** *Ffrreedom TABCD 227*	17	5
19 Aug 95 ●	**SON OF A GUN (re-mix)** *Ffrreedom TABCD 233*	6	6
18 May 96 ●	**THERE'S NOTHING I WON'T DO** *Ffrreedom TABCD 241*	4	13
8 Mar 97	**CLOSE TO YOUR HEART** *Ffrreedom TABCD 245*	18	3

K

Frank K featuring Wiston OFFICE

Italy / US, male vocal / instrumental duo (1 WEEK)

		pos	wks
26 Jan 91	**EVERYBODY LET'S SOMEBODY LOVE** *Urban URB 66*	61	1

Leila K *Sweden, female rapper – Leila El Khalifi (22 WEEKS)*

		pos	wks
25 Nov 89 ●	**GOT TO GET** *Arista 112696* [1]	8	14
17 Mar 90	**ROK THE NATION** *Arista 112971* [1]	41	3
23 Jan 93	**OPEN SESAME** *Polydor PQCD 1*	23	4
3 Jul 93	**ÇA PLANE POUR MOI** *Polydor PQCD 3*	69	1

[1] Rob 'n' Raz featuring Leila K

K-CI & JOJO *US, male vocal duo – Cedric and Joel Hailey (29 WEEKS)*

		pos	wks
27 Jul 96	**HOW DO YOU WANT IT** *Death Row DRWCD 4* [1] ▲	17	4
23 Aug 97	**YOU BRING ME UP** *MCA MCSTD 48057*	21	2
18 Apr 98 ●	**ALL MY LIFE** *MCA MCSTD 48076* ▲	8	11
19 Sep 98	**DON'T RUSH (TAKE LOVE SLOWLY)** *MCA MCSTD 48090*	16	3
2 Oct 99	**TELL ME IT'S REAL** *MCA MCSTD 40211*	40	2
23 Sep 00	**TELL ME IT'S REAL (re-mix)** *AM:PM CDAMPM 135*	16	5
12 May 01	**CRAZY** *MCA MCSTD 40253*	35	2

[1] 2Pac featuring K-Ci and JoJo

K CREATIVE *UK, male vocal / instrumental group (2 WEEKS)*

		pos	wks
7 Mar 92	**THREE TIMES A MAYBE** *Talkin Loud TLK 17*	58	2

The listed flipside of 'Three Times a Maybe' was 'Feed the Feeling' by Perception

Ernie K-DOE *US, male vocalist (7 WEEKS)*

		pos	wks
11 May 61	**MOTHER-IN-LAW** *London HLU 9330* ▲	29	7

K-GEE *UK, male producer – Karl Gordon (3 WEEKS)*

		pos	wks
4 Nov 00	**I DON'T REALLY CARE** *Instant Karma KARMA 3CD*	22	3

K-KLASS *UK, male / female vocal / instrumental group (31 WEEKS)*

		pos	wks
4 May 91	**RHYTHM IS A MYSTERY** *Deconstruction CREED 11*	61	2
9 Nov 91 ●	**RHYTHM IS A MYSTERY (re-issue)** *Deconstruction R 6302*	3	10
25 Apr 92	**SO RIGHT** *Deconstruction R 6309*	20	5

7 Nov 92		**DON'T STOP** *Deconstruction R 6325*	32	3
27 Nov 93		**LET ME SHOW YOU** *Deconstruction CDR 6367*	13	7
28 May 94		**WHAT YOU'RE MISSING** *Deconstruction CDRS 6380*	24	3
1 Aug 98		**BURNIN'** *Parlophone CDK 2001*	45	1

K7 *US, male vocal / rap group (22 WEEKS)* pos/wks

11 Dec 93	●	**COME BABY COME** *Big Life BLRD 105*	3	16
2 Apr 94		**HI DE HO** *Big Life BLRD 108* [1]	17	5
25 Jun 94		**ZUNGA ZENG** *Big Life BLRD 111* [1]	63	1

[1] K7 and the Swing Kids

K3M *Italy, male / female vocal / instrumental duo (1 WEEK)* pos/wks

21 Mar 92		**LISTEN TO THE RHYTHM** *PWL Continental PWL 214*	71	1

K-WARREN featuring LEE-O
UK, male producer and UK, male vocalist (2 WEEKS) pos/wks

5 May 01		**COMING HOME** *Go! Beat GOBCD 41*	32	2

K2 FAMILY *UK, male production / rap / vocal group (3 WEEKS)* pos/wks

27 Oct 01		**BOUNCING FLOW** *Relentless RELENT 22CD*	27	3

KACI *US, female vocalist – Kaci Battaglia (12 WEEKS)* pos/wks

10 Mar 01		**PARADISE** *Curb / London CUBC 61*	11	9
28 Jul 01		**TU AMOR** *Curb / London CUBC 71*	24	3

Joshua KADISON *US, male vocalist (19 WEEKS)* pos/wks

26 Feb 94		**JESSIE** *SBK CDSBK 43*	69	2
1 Oct 94		**JESSIE** (re-entry) *SBK CDSBK 43*	48	3
12 Nov 94		**BEAUTIFUL IN MY EYES** *SBK CDSBK 50*	65	1
29 Apr 95		**JESSIE** (re-issue) *SBK CDSBK 53*	15	10
12 Aug 95		**BEAUTIFUL IN MY EYES** (re-issue) *SBK CDSBK 55*	37	3

KADOC *UK / Spain, male vocal / instrumental group (11 WEEKS)* pos/wks

6 Apr 96		**THE NIGHTTRAIN** *Positiva CDTIV 26*	14	8
17 Aug 96		**YOU GOT TO BE THERE** *Positiva CDTIV 58*	45	1
23 Aug 97		**ROCK THE BELLS** *Manifesto FESCD 30*	34	2

Bert KAEMPFERT *Germany, orchestra (10 WEEKS)* pos/wks

23 Dec 65		**BYE BYE BLUES** *Polydor BM 56 504*	24	10

KAJAGOOGOO
UK, male vocal / instrumental group – lead vocal Limahl (50 WEEKS) pos/wks

22 Jan 83	★	**TOO SHY** *EMI 5359*	1	13
2 Apr 83	●	**OOH TO BE AH** *EMI 5383*	7	8
4 Jun 83		**HANG ON NOW** *EMI 5394*	13	7
17 Sep 83	●	**BIG APPLE** *EMI 5423*	8	8
3 Mar 84		**THE LION'S MOUTH** *EMI 5449*	25	7
5 May 84		**TURN YOUR BACK ON ME** *EMI 5646*	47	4
21 Sep 85		**SHOULDN'T DO THAT** *Parlophone R 6106* [1]	63	3

[1] Kaja

KALEEF *UK, male rap / vocal group (12 WEEKS)* pos/wks

30 Mar 96		**WALK LIKE A CHAMPION** *Payday KACD 5* [1]	23	3
7 Dec 96		**GOLDEN BROWN** *Unity UNITY 010CD*	22	4
14 Jun 97		**TRIALS OF LIFE** *Unity UNITY 012CD*	75	1
11 Oct 97		**I LIKE THE WAY (THE KISSING GAME)** *Unity UNITY 015CD1*	58	1
24 Jan 98		**SANDS OF TIME** *Unity UNITY 016CD*	26	3

[1] Kaliphz featuring Prince Naseem

KALIN TWINS *US, male vocal duo – Herb and Hal Kalin (18 WEEKS)* pos/wks

18 Jul 58	★	**WHEN** *Brunswick 05751*	1	18

KALLAGHAN – *See N'n'G featuring KALLAGHAN*

Kitty KALLEN *US, female vocalist (23 WEEKS)* pos/wks

2 Jul 54	★	**LITTLE THINGS MEAN A LOT** *Brunswick 05287* ▲	1	23

Gunter KALLMAN CHOIR
Germany, male / female vocal group (3 WEEKS) pos/wks

24 Dec 64		**ELISABETH SERENADE** *Polydor NH 24678*	39	3

KAMASUTRA featuring Jocelyn BROWN
Italy, male DJ / production duo and US, female vocalist (1 WEEK) pos/wks

22 Nov 97		**HAPPINESS** *Sony S2 KAMCD 2*	45	1

Nick KAMEN *UK, male vocalist (33 WEEKS)* pos/wks

8 Nov 86	●	**EACH TIME YOU BREAK MY HEART** *WEA YZ 90*	5	12
28 Feb 87		**LOVING YOU IS SWEETER THAN EVER** *WEA YZ 106*	16	9
16 May 87		**NOBODY ELSE** *WEA YZ 122*	47	3
28 May 88		**TELL ME** *WEA YZ 184*	40	5
28 Apr 90		**I PROMISED MYSELF** *WEA YZ 454*	50	4

Ini KAMOZE *Jamaica, male vocalist (15 WEEKS)* pos/wks

7 Jan 95	●	**HERE COMES THE HOTSTEPPER** *Columbia 6610472* ▲	4	15

KANDI *US, female vocalist – Kandi Burruss (10 WEEKS)* pos/wks

11 Nov 00	●	**DON'T THINK I'M NOT** *Columbia 6705102*	9	10

KANDIDATE *UK, male vocal / instrumental group (28 WEEKS)* pos/wks

19 Aug 78		**DON'T WANNA SAY GOODNIGHT** *RAK 280*	47	6
17 Mar 79		**I DON'T WANNA LOSE YOU** *RAK 289*	11	12
4 Aug 79		**GIRLS GIRLS GIRLS** *RAK 295*	34	7
22 Mar 80		**LET ME ROCK YOU** *RAK 306*	58	3

Eden KANE (480 Top 500)
Last teen idol before The Beatles, b. Richard Sarstedt, 29 Mar 1942, Delhi, India. Stylish pop beat singer who, like Adam Faith, had many of his hits penned for him by Johnny Worth. Brothers Peter and Robin Sarstedt also had Top 3 entries (73 WEEKS) pos/wks

1 Jun 61	★	**WELL I ASK YOU** *Decca F 11353*	1	21
14 Sep 61	●	**GET LOST** *Decca F 11381*	10	11
18 Jan 62	●	**FORGET ME NOT** *Decca F 11418*	3	14
10 May 62	●	**I DON'T KNOW WHY** *Decca F 11460*	7	13
30 Jan 64	●	**BOYS CRY** *Fontana TF 438*	8	14

KANE GANG *UK, male vocal / instrumental group (37 WEEKS)* pos/wks

19 May 84		**SMALLTOWN CREED** *Kitchenware SK 11*	60	2
7 Jul 84		**CLOSEST THING TO HEAVEN** *Kitchenware SK 15*	12	11
10 Nov 84		**RESPECT YOURSELF** *Kitchenware SK 16*	21	10
26 Jan 85		**RESPECT YOURSELF** (re-entry) *Kitchenware SK 16*	75	1
9 Mar 85		**GUN LAW** *Kitchenware SK 20*	53	4
27 Jun 87		**MOTORTOWN** *Kitchenware SK 30*	45	5
16 Apr 88		**DON'T LOOK ANY FURTHER** *Kitchenware SK 33*	52	4

KANSAS *US, male vocal / instrumental group (7 WEEKS)* pos/wks

1 Jul 78		**CARRY ON WAYWARD SON** *Kirshner KIR 4932*	51	7

Mory KANTE *Guinea, male vocalist (14 WEEKS)* pos/wks

23 Jul 88		**YEKE YEKE** *London LON 171*	29	9
11 Mar 95		**YEKE YEKE** (re-issue) *Ffrreedom TABCD 226*	25	3
30 Nov 96		**YEKE YEKE** (re-mix) *ffrr FCD 288*	28	2

KAOMA *France, male / female vocal / instrumental group (20 WEEKS)* pos/wks

21 Oct 89	●	**LAMBADA** *CBS 655011 7*	4	18
27 Jan 90		**DANCANDO LAMBADA** *CBS 655235 7*	62	2

KAOTIC CHEMISTRY
UK, male instrumental / production group (1 WEEK) pos/wks

31 Oct 92		**LSD (EP)** *Moving Shadow SHADOW 20*	68	1

Tracks on LSD (EP): Space Cakes / LSD / Illegal Substances / Drumtrip II

KARIN – See UNIQUE 3

KARIYA *US, female vocalist (9 WEEKS)* pos/wks

8 Jul 89	LET ME LOVE YOU FOR TONIGHT *Sleeping Bag SBUK 4*	44 6
21 Oct 89	LET ME LOVE YOU FOR TONIGHT (re-entry) *Sleeping Bag SBUK 4*	57 3

Mick KARN *UK, male instrumentalist (6 WEEKS)* pos/wks

9 Jul 83	AFTER A FASHION *Musicfest FEST 1* [1]	39 4
17 Jan 87	BUOY *Virgin VS 910* [2]	63 2

[1] Midge Ure and Mick Karn [2] Mick Karn featuring David Sylvian

See also JAPAN

KARTOON KREW *US, rap / instrumental group (6 WEEKS)* pos/wks

7 Dec 85	INSPECTOR GADGET *Champion CHAMP 6*	58 6

KASENETZ-KATZ SINGING ORCHESTRAL CIRCUS *US, male vocal / instrumental group (15 WEEKS)* pos/wks

20 Nov 68	QUICK JOEY SMALL (RUN JOEY RUN) *Buddah 201 022*	19 15

KATCHA *UK, male DJ / producer (1 WEEK)* pos/wks

21 Aug 99	TOUCHED BY GOD *Hooj Choons HOOJ 77CD*	57 1

KATRINA and the WAVES *US / UK, female / male vocal / instrumental group (34 WEEKS)* pos/wks

4 May 85 ●	WALKING ON SUNSHINE *Capitol CL 354*	8 12
5 Jul 86	SUN STREET *Capitol CL 407*	22 9
8 Jun 96	WALKING ON SUNSHINE (re-issue) *EMI Premier PRESCD 2*	53 1
10 May 97 ●	LOVE SHINE A LIGHT *Eternal WEA 106CD1*	3 12

KAVANA *UK, male vocalist – Anthony Kavanagh (26 WEEKS)* pos/wks

11 May 96	CRAZY CHANCE *Nemesis NMSD 1*	35 3
24 Aug 96	WHERE ARE YOU *Nemesis NMSD 2*	26 2
11 Jan 97 ●	I CAN MAKE YOU FEEL GOOD *Nemesis NMSDX 3*	8 5
19 Apr 97 ●	MFEO *Nemesis NMSD 4*	8 4
13 Sep 97	CRAZY CHANCE 97 (re-recording) *Nemesis NMSD 5*	16 3
29 Aug 98	SPECIAL KIND OF SOMETHING *Virgin VSCDT 1704*	13 4
12 Dec 98	FUNKY LOVE *Virgin VSCDT 1711*	32 2
9 Jan 99	FUNKY LOVE (re-entry) *Virgin VSCDT 1711*	73 1
20 Mar 99	WILL YOU WAIT FOR ME *Virgin VSCDT 1726*	29 2

Niamh KAVANAGH *Ireland, female vocalist (5 WEEKS)* pos/wks

12 Jun 93	IN YOUR EYES *Arista 74321154152*	24 5

KAWALA *UK, male vocal / instrumental / production group (1 WEEK)* pos/wks

26 Feb 00	HUMANISTIC *Pepper 9230022*	68 1

Janet KAY *UK, female vocalist – Janet Bogle (24 WEEKS)* pos/wks

9 Jun 79 ●	SILLY GAMES *Scope SC 2*	2 14
11 Aug 90	SILLY GAMES *Arista 113452* [1]	22 7
11 Aug 90	SILLY GAMES (re-mix) *Music Factory Dance MFD 006*	62 3

[1] Lindy Layton featuring Janet Kay

Danny KAYE *US, male actor / vocalist – David Kaminsky (10 WEEKS)* pos/wks

27 Feb 53 ●	WONDERFUL COPENHAGEN *Brunswick 05023*	5 10

With Gordon Jenkins and his Orchestra and Chorus

KAYE SISTERS *UK, female vocal group (45 WEEKS)* pos/wks

25 May 56	IVORY TOWER *HMV POP 209* [1]	20 5
1 Nov 57 ●	GOT-TA HAVE SOMETHING IN THE BANK, FRANK *Philips PB 751* [2]	8 11
3 Jan 58	SHAKE ME I RATTLE / ALONE *Philips PB 752*	27 1
1 May 59 ●	COME SOFTLY TO ME *Philips PB 913* [2]	9 9
7 Jul 60 ●	PAPER ROSES *Philips PB 1024*	7 19

[1] Three Kayes [2] Frankie Vaughan and the Kaye Sisters

KAYESTONE *UK, male DJ / production duo (1 WEEK)* pos/wks

29 Jul 00	ATMOSPHERE *Distinctive DISNCD 62*	55 1

KC and the SUNSHINE BAND (289 Top 500)

Red-hot disco act from Florida, US, fronted by KC (b. Harry Wayne Casey, 31 Jan 1951, Florida) and including co-writer / producer Richard Finch (b). Internationally successful group whose wall-to-wall late 1970s hits included five US No.1s (104 WEEKS) pos/wks

17 Aug 74 ●	QUEEN OF CLUBS *Jayboy BOY 88*	7 12
23 Nov 74	SOUND YOUR FUNKY HORN *Jayboy BOY 83*	17 9
29 Mar 75	GET DOWN TONIGHT *Jayboy BOY 93* ▲	21 9
2 Aug 75 ●	THAT'S THE WAY (I LIKE IT) *Jayboy BOY 99* ▲	4 10
22 Nov 75	I'M SO CRAZY ('BOUT YOU) *Jayboy BOY 101*	34 3
17 Jul 76	(SHAKE SHAKE SHAKE) SHAKE YOUR BOOTY *Jayboy BOY 110* ▲	22 8
11 Dec 76	KEEP IT COMIN' LOVE *Jayboy BOY 112*	31 8
30 Apr 77	I'M YOUR BOOGIE MAN *TK XB 2167* ▲	41 4
6 May 78	BOOGIE SHOES *TK TKR 6025*	34 5
22 Jul 78	IT'S THE SAME OLD SONG *TK TKR 6037*	47 5
8 Dec 79 ●	PLEASE DON'T GO *TK TKR 7558* ▲	3 12
16 Jul 83 ★	GIVE IT UP *Epic EPC A 3017*	1 14
24 Sep 83	(YOU SAID) YOU'D GIMME SOME MORE *Epic A 2760*	41 3
11 May 91	THAT'S THE WAY I LIKE IT (re-mix) *Music Factory Dance M7FAC 2*	59 2

KÉ *US, male vocalist (1 WEEK)* pos/wks

13 Apr 96	STRANGE WORLD *Venture 74321349412*	73 1

Johnny KEATING *UK, orchestra (14 WEEKS)* pos/wks

1 Mar 62 ●	THEME FROM 'Z CARS' (JOHNNY TODD) *Piccadilly 7N 35032*	8 14

Ronan KEATING *Ireland, male vocalist (56 WEEKS)* pos/wks

7 Aug 99 ★	WHEN YOU SAY NOTHING AT ALL *Polydor 5612902* ■	1 15
27 Nov 99	WHEN YOU SAY NOTHING AT ALL (re-entry) *Polydor 5612902*	75 1
1 Jan 00	WHEN YOU SAY NOTHING AT ALL (2nd re-entry) *Polydor 5612902*	66 1
22 Jul 00 ★	LIFE IS A ROLLERCOASTER *Polydor 5619362* ■	1 14
2 Dec 00 ●	THE WAY YOU MAKE ME FEEL *Polydor 5878852*	6 11
28 Apr 01 ●	LOVIN' EACH DAY *Polydor 5876872*	2 14

See also BOYZONE

KEE – See BM DUBS

Kevin KEEGAN *UK, male footballer / vocalist (6 WEEKS)* pos/wks

9 Jun 79	HEAD OVER HEELS IN LOVE *EMI 2965*	31 6

Yvonne KEELEY – See Scott FITZGERALD

Nelson KEENE *UK, male vocalist (5 WEEKS)* pos/wks

25 Aug 60	IMAGE OF A GIRL *HMV POP 771*	37 4
29 Sep 60	IMAGE OF A GIRL (re-entry) *HMV POP 771*	45 1

KEITH *US, male vocalist (8 WEEKS)* pos/wks

26 Jan 67	98.6 *Mercury MF 955*	24 7
16 Mar 67	TELL ME TO MY FACE *Mercury MF 968*	50 1

KEITH 'N' SHANE *Ireland, male vocal duo (3 WEEKS)* pos/wks

23 Dec 00	GIRL YOU KNOW IT'S TRUE *Polydor 5879462*	36 3

See also BOYZONE

KELIS *US, female vocalist – Kelis Rogers (29 WEEKS)* pos/wks

26 Feb 00	CAUGHT OUT THERE *Virgin 8965102CD*	52 1
4 Mar 00 ●	CAUGHT OUT THERE *Virgin VUSCD 158*	4 10
20 May 00	CAUGHT OUT THERE (re-entry) *Virgin VUSCD 158*	64 2
17 Jun 00	GOOD STUFF *Virgin VUSCD 164*	19 5
8 Jul 00	GOT YOUR MONEY *Elektra E 7077CD* [1]	11 8

21 Oct 00	**GET ALONG WITH YOU** *Virgin VUSCD 174*	51	1
3 Nov 01	**YOUNG FRESH N' NEW** *Virgin VUSCD 212*	32	2

[1] Ol' Dirty Bastard featuring Kelis

Jerry KELLER *US, male vocalist (14 WEEKS)*

		pos	wks
28 Aug 59 ★	**HERE COMES SUMMER** *London HLR 8890*	1	14

Frank KELLY *Ireland, male vocalist (5 WEEKS)*

		pos	wks
24 Dec 83	**CHRISTMAS COUNTDOWN** *Ritz RITZ 062*	26	4
29 Dec 84	**CHRISTMAS COUNTDOWN (re-entry)** *Ritz RITZ 062*	54	1

Frankie KELLY *US, male vocalist / instrumentalist (2 WEEKS)*

		pos	wks
2 Nov 85	**AIN'T THAT THE TRUTH** *10 TEN 87*	65	2

Grace KELLY – *See Bing CROSBY*

Keith KELLY *UK, male vocalist (5 WEEKS)*

		pos	wks
5 May 60	**(MUST YOU ALWAYS) TEASE ME** *Parlophone R 4640*	46	1
19 May 60	**(MUST YOU ALWAYS) TEASE ME (re-entry)** *Parlophone R 4640*	27	3
18 Aug 60	**LISTEN LITTLE GIRL** *Parlophone R 4676*	47	1

R KELLY (142 Top 500) *Phenomenally successful R&B vocalist, b. 8 Jan 1971, Chicago, US, whose writing and production skills are constantly in demand by other top artists. Amazingly, 1998 album 'R' yielded seven Top 20 hits but never reached the Top 20 itself (153 WEEKS)*

		pos	wks
9 May 92	**SHE'S GOT THAT VIBE** *Jive JIVET 292* [1]	57	2
20 Nov 93	**SEX ME** *Jive JIVECD 346* [1]	75	1
14 May 94	**YOUR BODY'S CALLIN'** *Jive JIVECD 353*	19	4
3 Sep 94	**SUMMER BUNNIES** *Jive JIVECD 358*	23	3
22 Oct 94 ●	**SHE'S GOT THAT VIBE (re-issue)** *Jive JIVECD 364*	3	13
21 Jan 95 ●	**BUMP 'N' GRIND** *Jive JIVECD 368* ▲	8	9
6 May 95	**THE 4 PLAY EPS** *Jive JIVECD 376*	23	3
11 Nov 95	**YOU REMIND ME OF SOMETHING** *Jive JIVECD 388*	24	3
2 Mar 96	**DOWN LOW (NOBODY HAS TO KNOW)** *Jive JIVECD 392* [2]	23	3
22 Jun 96	**THANK GOD IT'S FRIDAY** *Jive JIVECD 395*	14	4
29 Mar 97 ★	**I BELIEVE I CAN FLY** *Jive JIVECD 415*	1	17
19 Jul 97 ●	**GOTHAM CITY** *Jive JIVECD 428*	9	8
18 Jul 98 ●	**BE CAREFUL** *Jive 0521452* [3]	7	6
5 Sep 98	**BE CAREFUL (re-entry)** *Jive 0521452* [3]	75	1
26 Sep 98	**HALF ON A BABY** *Jive 0521802*	16	4
14 Nov 98	**HOME ALONE** *Jive 0522392* [4]	17	5
28 Nov 98 ●	**I'M YOUR ANGEL** *Epic 6666282* [5] ▲	3	13
31 Jul 99	**DID YOU EVER THINK** *Jive 0523612*	20	5
16 Oct 99	**IF I COULD TURN BACK THE HANDS OF TIME (import)** *Jive 0523182*	57	2
30 Oct 99 ●	**IF I COULD TURN BACK THE HANDS OF TIME** *Jive 0523182*	2	19
19 Feb 00	**SATISFY YOU (import)** *Bad Boy / Arista 792832* [6]	73	1
4 Mar 00	**SATISFY YOU (IMPORT) (re-entry)** *Bad Boy / Arista 792832* [6]	73	1
11 Mar 00 ●	**SATISFY YOU** *Bad Boy / Arista 74321745592* [6]	8	8
22 Apr 00	**ONLY THE LOOT CAN MAKE ME HAPPY / WHEN A WOMAN'S FED UP / I CAN'T SLEEP BABY (IF I)** *Jive 9250282*	24	3
21 Oct 00	**I WISH** *Jive 9251262*	12	6
31 Mar 01	**THE STORM IS OVER NOW** *Jive 9251782*	18	6
23 Jun 01	**FIESTA** *Jive 9252142* [7]	23	3

[1] R Kelly and Public Announcement [2] R Kelly featuring Ronald Isley [3] Sparkle featuring R Kelly [4] R Kelly featuring Keith Murray [5] Celine Dion and R Kelly [6] Puff Daddy featuring R Kelly [7] R Kelly featuring Jay-Z

The 4 Play EP was available on two CDs, each featuring 'Your Body's Callin' and three further tracks

See also PUBLIC ANNOUNCEMENT

Ramona KELLY – *See Cevin FISHER*

Roberta KELLY *US, female vocalist (3 WEEKS)*

		pos	wks
21 Jan 78	**ZODIACS** *Oasis/Hansa 3*	48	1
4 Feb 78	**ZODIACS (re-entry)** *Oasis/Hansa 3*	44	2

KELLY FAMILY

Ireland, male / female vocal / instrumental group (1 WEEK)

		pos	wks
21 Oct 95	**AN ANGEL** *EMI CDEM 390*	69	1

Johnny KEMP *Barbados, male vocalist (1 WEEK)*

		pos	wks
27 Aug 88	**JUST GOT PAID** *CBS 651470 7*	68	1

Tara KEMP *US, female vocalist (2 WEEKS)*

		pos	wks
20 Apr 91	**HOLD YOU TIGHT** *Giant W 0020*	69	2

Graham KENDRICK *UK, male vocalist (4 WEEKS)*

		pos	wks
9 Sep 89	**LET THE FLAME BURN BRIGHTER** *Power P 30*	55	4

Eddie KENDRICKS *US, male vocalist (20 WEEKS)*

		pos	wks
3 Nov 73	**KEEP ON TRUCKIN'** *Tamla Motown TMG 873* ▲	18	14
16 Mar 74	**BOOGIE DOWN** *Tamla Motown TMG 888*	39	4
21 Sep 85	**A NIGHT AT THE APOLLO LIVE!** *RCA PB 49935* [1]	58	2

[1] Daryl Hall and John Oates featuring David Ruffin and Eddie Kendrick

A Night at the Apollo Live! is a medley of 'The Way You Do the Things You Do' and 'My Girl'. Kendricks dropped the 's' from his name for last hit

See also TEMPTATIONS

KENICKIE *UK, female / male vocal / instrumental group (13 WEEKS)*

		pos	wks
14 Sep 96	**PUNKA** *Emidisc CDDISC 001*	43	2
16 Nov 96	**MILLIONAIRE SWEEPER** *Emidisc CDDISC 002*	60	1
11 Jan 97	**IN YOUR CAR** *Emidisc CDDISC 005*	24	3
3 May 97	**NIGHTLIFE** *Emidisc CDDISC 006*	27	2
5 Jul 97	**PUNKA (re-issue)** *Emidisc CDDISC 007*	38	2
6 Jun 98	**I WOULD FIX YOU** *EMI CDEM 513*	36	2
22 Aug 98	**STAY IN THE SUN** *EMI CDEMS 520*	43	1

Jane KENNAWAY and STRANGE BEHAVIOUR

UK, female vocalist, male instrumental group (3 WEEKS)

		pos	wks
24 Jan 81	**I.O.U.** *Deram DM 436*	65	3

Brian KENNEDY *Ireland, male actor / vocalist (8 WEEKS)*

		pos	wks
22 Jun 96	**A BETTER MAN** *RCA 74321382642*	28	3
21 Sep 96	**LIFE, LOVE AND HAPPINESS** *RCA 74321409921*	27	3
5 Apr 97	**PUT THE MESSAGE IN THE BOX** *RCA 74321462272*	37	2

Kevin KENNEDY *UK, male vocalist (1 WEEK)*

		pos	wks
24 Jun 00	**BULLDOG NATION** *D2m 74321759742*	70	1

KENNY *Ireland, male vocalist – Tony Kenny (16 WEEKS)*

		pos	wks
3 Mar 73	**HEART OF STONE** *RAK 144*	11	13
30 Jun 73	**GIVE IT TO ME NOW** *RAK 153*	38	3

KENNY *UK, male vocal / instrumental group (39 WEEKS)*

		pos	wks
7 Dec 74 ●	**THE BUMP** *RAK 186*	3	15
8 Mar 75 ●	**FANCY PANTS** *RAK 196*	4	9
7 Jun 75	**BABY I LOVE YOU OK** *RAK 207*	12	7
16 Aug 75 ●	**JULIE ANN** *RAK 214*	10	8

Gerard KENNY *US, male vocalist (21 WEEKS)*

		pos	wks
9 Dec 78	**NEW YORK, NEW YORK** *RCA PB 5117*	43	8
21 Jun 80	**FANTASY** *RCA PB 5256*	65	1
5 Jul 80	**FANTASY (re-entry)** *RCA PB 5256*	34	5
18 Feb 84	**THE OTHER WOMAN, THE OTHER MAN** *Impression IMS 3*	69	4
4 May 85	**NO MAN'S LAND** *WEA YZ 38*	56	3

KENT *Sweden, male vocal / instrumental group (1 WEEK)*

		pos	wks
13 Mar 99	**747** *RCA 74321645912*	61	1

Klark KENT

US, male vocalist / multi-instrumentalist – Stewart Copeland (4 WEEKS) pos/wks

26 Aug 78		**DON'T CARE** *A & M AMS 7376*	48	4

See also POLICE

Carol KENYON – See Paul HARDCASTLE; HEAVEN 17; RAPINATION

KERBDOG *Ireland, male vocal / instrumental group (5 WEEKS)* pos/wks

12 Mar 94		**DRY RISER** *Vertigo VERCC 83*	60	1
6 Aug 94		**DUMMY CRUSHER** *Vertigo VERCD 86*	37	2
12 Oct 96		**SALLY** *Fontana KERCD 2*	69	1
29 Mar 97		**MEXICAN WAVE** *Fontana KERCD 3*	49	1

Dick KERR – See Slim DUSTY

ANITA KERR SINGERS – See Bobby HELMS

KERRI and MICK *Australia, female / male vocal duo (3 WEEKS)* pos/wks

28 Apr 84		**'SONS AND DAUGHTERS' THEME** *A1 A1 286*	68	3

KERRI-ANN *Ireland, female vocalist (1 WEEK)* pos/wks

8 Aug 98		**DO YOU LOVE ME BOY?** *Raglan Road 5671012*	58	1

Liz KERSHAW and Bruno BROOKES

UK, male / female vocal duo (3 WEEKS) pos/wks

2 Dec 89		**IT TAKES TWO BABY** *Spartan CIN 101* [1]	53	2
1 Dec 90		**LET'S DANCE** *Jive BRUNO 1* [2]	54	1

[1] Liz Kershaw, Bruno Brookes, Jive Bunny and Londonbeat [2] Bruno and Liz and the Radio 1 DJ Posse

Nik KERSHAW (356 Top 500)

One time jazz-funk guitarist whose melodic pop repertoire made him a mid-1980s teen idol, b. 1 Mar 1958, Bristol, UK. His 50 weeks on the singles chart in 1984 beat all other soloists. He appeared at Live Aid, and penned hits for Let Loose, The Hollies and a No.1 for Chesney Hawkes (89 WEEKS) pos/wks

19 Nov 83		**I WON'T LET THE SUN GO DOWN ON ME** *MCA MCA 816*	47	5
28 Jan 84	●	**WOULDN'T IT BE GOOD** *MCA NIK 2*	4	14
14 Apr 84		**DANCING GIRLS** *MCA NIK 3*	13	9
16 Jun 84	●	**I WON'T LET THE SUN GO DOWN ON ME (re-issue)** *MCA NIK 4*	2	13
15 Sep 84		**HUMAN RACING** *MCA NIK 5*	19	7
17 Nov 84	●	**THE RIDDLE** *MCA NIK 6*	3	11
16 Mar 85	●	**WIDE BOY** *MCA NIK 7*	9	8
3 Aug 85	●	**DON QUIXOTE** *MCA NIK 8*	10	7
30 Nov 85		**WHEN A HEART BEATS** *MCA NIK 9*	27	7
11 Oct 86		**NOBODY KNOWS** *MCA NIK 10*	44	3
13 Dec 86		**RADIO MUSICOLA** *MCA NIK 11*	43	2
4 Feb 89		**ONE STEP AHEAD** *MCA NIK 12*	55	1
27 Feb 99		**SOMEBODY LOVES YOU** *Eagle EAGXA 023*	70	1
7 Aug 99		**SOMETIMES** *Wall of Sound WALLD 054* [1]	56	1

[1] Les Rythmes Digitales featuring Nik Kershaw

KEVIN and PERRY – See PRECOCIOUS BRATS featuring KEVIN and PERRY

KEVIN THE GERBIL *UK, male gerbil vocalist (6 WEEKS)* pos/wks

4 Aug 84		**SUMMER HOLIDAY** *Magnet RAT 3*	50	6

KEY WEST – See ERIK

KEYNOTES – See Dave KING

Alicia KEYS *US, female vocalist (8 WEEKS)* pos/wks

10 Nov 01	●	**FALLIN'** *J 74321903692* ▲	3	8+

Chaka KHAN (318 Top 500)

Powerful and influential soul diva b. Yvette Stevens, 23 Mar 1953, Illinois, US. Fronted funk troupe Rufus for six years, went solo 1978. Prince-penned 'I Feel For You' was the first UK No.1 to feature rap elements (courtesy of Grandmaster Melle Mel) (97 WEEKS) pos/wks

2 Dec 78		**I'M EVERY WOMAN** *Warner Bros. K 17269*	11	13
31 Mar 84	●	**AIN'T NOBODY** *Warner Bros. RCK 1* [1]	8	12
20 Oct 84	★	**I FEEL FOR YOU** *Warner Bros. W 9209*	1	16
19 Jan 85		**THIS IS MY NIGHT** *Warner Bros. W 9097*	14	6
20 Apr 85		**EYE TO EYE** *Warner Bros. W 9009*	16	7
12 Jul 86		**LOVE OF A LIFETIME** *Warner Bros. W 8671*	52	4
21 Jan 89		**IT'S MY PARTY** *Warner Bros. W 7678*	71	2
6 May 89	●	**I'M EVERY WOMAN (re-mix)** *Warner Bros. W 2963*	8	8
8 Jul 89	●	**AIN'T NOBODY (re-mix)** *Warner Bros. W 2880* [1]	6	9
7 Oct 89		**I FEEL FOR YOU (re-mix)** *Warner Bros. W 2764*	45	2
13 Jan 90		**I'LL BE GOOD TO YOU** *Qwest W 2697* [2]	21	7
28 Mar 92		**LOVE YOU ALL MY LIFETIME** *Warner Bros. W 0087*	49	3
17 Jul 93		**DON'T LOOK AT ME THAT WAY** *Warner Bros. W 0192CD*	73	1
19 Aug 95		**WATCH WHAT YOU SAY** *Cooltempo CDCOOL 308* [3]	28	3
1 Mar 97		**NEVER MISS THE WATER** *Reprise W 1393CD* [4]	59	1
11 Nov 00		**ALL GOOD** *Tommy Boy TBCD 2154B* [5]	33	3

[1] Rufus and Chaka Khan [2] Quincy Jones featuring Ray Charles and Chaka Khan [3] Guru featuring Chaka Khan [4] Chaka Khan featuring Me'Shell Ndegeocello [5] De La Soul featuring Chaka Khan

See also Quincy JONES

Praga KHAN *Belgium, male producer – Maurice Engelen (9 WEEKS)* pos/wks

4 Apr 92		**FREE YOUR BODY / INJECTED WITH A POISON** *Profile PROFT 347* [1]	16	6
11 Jul 92		**RAVE ALERT** *Profile PROF 369*	39	2
24 Nov 01		**INJECTED WITH A POISON (re-mix)** *Nukleuz NUKC 0238*	52	1

[1] Praga Khan featuring Jade 4 U

Mary KIANI *UK, female vocalist (15 WEEKS)* pos/wks

12 Aug 95		**WHEN I CALL YOUR NAME** *Mercury MERCD 440*	18	4
23 Dec 95		**I GIVE IT ALL TO YOU / I IMAGINE** *Mercury MERCD 449*	35	4
27 Apr 96		**LET THE MUSIC PLAY** *Mercury MERCD 456*	19	3
18 Jan 97		**100%** *Mercury MERCD 469*	23	3
21 Jun 97		**WITH OR WITHOUT YOU** *Mercury MERCD 487*	46	1

KICK HORNS – See DODGY

KICK SQUAD

UK / Germany, male vocal / instrumental group (2 WEEKS) pos/wks

10 Nov 90		**SOUND CLASH (CHAMPION SOUND)** *Kickin KICK 2*	59	2

KICKING BACK with TAXMAN *UK, male / female vocal / instrumental duo with male rapper (8 WEEKS)* pos/wks

17 Mar 90		**DEVOTION** *10 TEN 297*	47	4
7 Jul 90		**EVERYTHING** *10 TEN 307*	54	4

KICKS LIKE A MULE *UK, male instrumental / production duo – Nick Halkes and Richard Russell (6 WEEKS)* pos/wks

1 Feb 92	●	**THE BOUNCER** *Tribal Bass TRIBE 3S*	7	6

K.I.D. *Antilles, male / female vocal / instrumental group (4 WEEKS)* pos/wks

28 Feb 81		**DON'T STOP** *EMI 5143*	49	4

KID 'N' PLAY *US, male rap duo (7 WEEKS)* pos/wks

18 Jul 87		**LAST NIGHT** *Cooltempo COOL 148*	71	1
26 Mar 88		**DO THIS MY WAY** *Cooltempo COOL 164*	48	3
17 Sep 88		**GITTIN' FUNKY** *Cooltempo COOL 168*	55	3

KID ROCK *US, male vocalist / rapper – Bob Ritchie (8 WEEKS)* pos/wks

23 Oct 99		**COWBOY** *Atlantic AT 0076CD*	36	2
9 Sep 00		**AMERICAN BAD ASS** *Atlantic AT 0085CD*	25	4
12 May 01		**BAWITDABA** *Atlantic AT 0098CD*	41	2

KID UNKNOWN *UK, male producer – Paul Fitzpatrick (1 WEEK)* pos/wks

2 May 92		NIGHTMARE *Warp WAP 20CD*	64	1

Carol KIDD featuring Terry WAITE
UK, female / male vocal duo (3 WEEKS) pos/wks

17 Oct 92		WHEN I DREAM *The Hit Label HLS 1*	58	3

Johnny KIDD and the PIRATES
UK, male vocal / instrumental group (62 WEEKS) pos/wks

12 Jun 59		PLEASE DON'T TOUCH *HMV POP 615* [1]	26	3
17 Jul 59		PLEASE DON'T TOUCH (re-entry) *HMV POP 615* [1]	25	2
12 Feb 60		YOU GOT WHAT IT TAKES *HMV POP 698*	25	3
16 Jun 60	★	SHAKIN' ALL OVER *HMV POP 753*	1	19
6 Oct 60		RESTLESS *HMV POP 790*	22	7
13 Apr 61		LINDA LU *HMV POP 853*	47	1
10 Jan 63		A SHOT OF RHYTHM AND BLUES *HMV POP 1088*	48	1
25 Jul 63	●	I'LL NEVER GET OVER YOU *HMV POP 1173*	4	15
28 Nov 63		HUNGRY FOR LOVE *HMV POP 1228*	20	10
30 Apr 64		ALWAYS AND EVER *HMV POP 1269*	46	1

[1] Johnny Kidd

Nicole KIDMAN *Australia, female vocalist (7 WEEKS)* pos/wks

6 Oct 01		COME WHAT MAY *Interscope / Polydor 4976302* [1]	27	5
22 Dec 01	★	SOMETHIN' STUPID *Chrysalis CDCHS 5132* [2] ■	1	2+

[1] Nicole Kidman and Ewan McGregor [2] Robbie Williams and Nicole Kidman

KIDS FROM 'FAME' *US, male / female vocal group (36 WEEKS)* pos/wks

14 Aug 82	●	HI-FIDELITY *RCA 254* [1]	5	10
2 Oct 82	●	STARMAKER *RCA 280*	3	10
11 Dec 82		MANNEQUIN *RCA 299* [2]	50	6
9 Apr 83		FRIDAY NIGHT (LIVE VERSION) *RCA 320*	13	10

[1] Kids from Fame featuring Valerie Landsberg [2] Kids from Fame featuring Gene Anthony Ray

Greg KIHN BAND *US, male vocal / instrumental group (2 WEEKS)* pos/wks

23 Apr 83		JEOPARDY *Beserkley E 9847*	63	2

KILLAH PRIEST *US, male rapper (1 WEEK)* pos/wks

7 Feb 98		ONE STEP *Geffen GFSTD 22318*	45	1

KILLING JOKE *UK, male vocal / instrumental group (48 WEEKS)* pos/wks

23 May 81		FOLLOW THE LEADERS *Malicious Damage EGMDS 101*	55	5
20 Mar 82		EMPIRE SONG *Malicious Damage EGO 4*	43	4
30 Oct 82		BIRDS OF A FEATHER *EG EGO 10*	64	2
25 Jun 83		LET'S ALL (GO TO THE FIRE DANCES) *EG EGO 11*	51	3
15 Oct 83		ME OR YOU? *EG EGO 14*	57	1
7 Apr 84		EIGHTIES *EG EGO 16*	60	5
21 Jul 84		A NEW DAY *EG EGO 17*	56	2
2 Feb 85		LOVE LIKE BLOOD *EG EGO 20*	16	9
30 Mar 85		KINGS AND QUEENS *EG EGO 21*	58	3
16 Aug 86		ADORATIONS *EG EGO 27*	42	6
18 Oct 86		SANITY *EG EGO 30*	70	1
7 May 94		MILLENNIUM *Butterfly BFLD 12*	34	2
16 Jul 94		PANDEMONIUM *Butterfly BFLD 17*	28	3
4 Feb 95		JANA *Butterfly BFLDA 21*	54	1
23 Mar 96		DEMOCRACY *Butterfly BFLDA 33*	39	1

Andy KIM *Canada, male vocalist (12 WEEKS)* pos/wks

24 Aug 74	●	ROCK ME GENTLY *Capitol CL 15787* ▲	2	12

KINANE *Ireland, female vocalist (4 WEEKS)* pos/wks

18 May 96		ALL THE LOVER I NEED *Coliseum TOGA 003CD* [1]	59	1
21 Sep 96		THE WOMAN IN ME *Coliseum TOGA 007CD* [1]	73	1
16 May 98		HEAVEN *Coalition COLA 047CD*	49	1
22 Aug 98		SO FINE *Coalition COLA 055CD1*	63	1

[1] Bianca Kinane

KING *UK / Ireland, male vocal / instrumental group (44 WEEKS)* pos/wks

12 Jan 85	●	LOVE AND PRIDE *CBS A 4988*	2	14
23 Mar 85		WON'T YOU HOLD MY HAND NOW *CBS A 6094*	24	8
17 Aug 85	●	ALONE WITHOUT YOU *CBS A 6308*	8	9
19 Oct 85		THE TASTE OF YOUR TEARS *CBS A 6618*	11	9
11 Jan 86		TORTURE *CBS A 6761*	23	4

See also Paul KING

Albert KING – *See Gary MOORE*

BB KING *US, male vocalist / instrumentalist – guitar (10 WEEKS)* pos/wks

15 Apr 89	●	WHEN LOVE COMES TO TOWN *Island IS 411* [1]	6	7
18 Jul 92		SINCE I MET YOU BABY *Virgin VS 1423* [2]	59	3

[1] U2 with BB King [2] Gary Moore and BB King

Ben E KING *US, male vocalist – Benjamin Nelson (35 WEEKS)* pos/wks

2 Feb 61		FIRST TASTE OF LOVE *London HLK 9258*	27	11
22 Jun 61		STAND BY ME *London HLK 9358*	50	1
6 Jul 61		STAND BY ME (re-entry) *London HLK 9358*	27	6
5 Oct 61		AMOR, AMOR *London HLK 9416*	38	4
14 Feb 87	★	STAND BY ME (re-issue) *Atlantic A 9361*	1	11
4 Jul 87		SAVE THE LAST DANCE FOR ME *Manhattan MT 25*	69	2

See also DRIFTERS

Carole KING *US, female vocalist – Carole Klein (29 WEEKS)* pos/wks

20 Sep 62	●	IT MIGHT AS WELL RAIN UNTIL SEPTEMBER *London HLU 9591*	3	13
7 Aug 71	●	IT'S TOO LATE *A & M AMS 849* ▲	6	12
28 Oct 72		IT MIGHT AS WELL RAIN UNTIL SEPTEMBER (re-issue) *London HL 10391*	43	4

Dave KING *UK, male vocalist (29 WEEKS)* pos/wks

17 Feb 56	●	MEMORIES ARE MADE OF THIS *Decca F 10684* [1]	5	15
13 Apr 56		YOU CAN'T BE TRUE TO TWO *Decca F 10720* [1]	11	9
21 Dec 56		CHRISTMAS AND YOU *Decca F 10791*	23	2
24 Jan 58		THE STORY OF MY LIFE *Decca F 10973*	20	3

[1] Dave King featuring The Keynotes

Denis KING – *See STUTZ BEARCATS and the Denis KING ORCHESTRA; KING BROTHERS*

Diana KING *Jamaica, female vocalist (22 WEEKS)* pos/wks

8 Jul 95	●	SHY GUY *Columbia 6621682*	2	13
28 Oct 95		AIN'T NOBODY *Columbia 6625495*	13	5
1 Nov 97		I SAY A LITTLE PRAYER *Columbia 6651472*	17	4

Evelyn 'Champagne' KING (458 Top 500) *Bubbly soul / disco vocalist*
b. 29 Jun 1960, New York, US. Ground-breaking debut hit 'Shame' was the biggest selling transatlantic 12-inch single at the time. It earned her a US gold record and a silver disc in the UK despite failing to reach the Top 30 (76 WEEKS) pos/wks

13 May 78		SHAME *RCA PC 1122*	39	23
3 Feb 79		I DON'T KNOW IF IT'S RIGHT *RCA PB 1386*	67	2
27 Jun 81		I'M IN LOVE *RCA 95* [1]	27	11
26 Sep 81		IF YOU WANT MY LOVIN' *RCA 131* [1]	43	6
28 Aug 82	●	LOVE COME DOWN *RCA 249* [1]	7	13
20 Nov 82		BACK TO LOVE *RCA 287* [1]	40	4
19 Feb 83		GET LOOSE *RCA 315* [1]	45	5
9 Nov 85		YOUR PERSONAL TOUCH *RCA PB 49915*	37	5
29 Mar 86		HIGH HORSE *RCA PB 49891*	55	3
23 Jul 88		HOLD ON TO WHAT YOU'VE GOT *Manhattan MT 49*	47	3
10 Oct 92		SHAME (re-mix) *Network NWKTEN 56* [2]	74	1

[1] Evelyn King [2] Altern 8 vs Evelyn King

1975

IN THE YEAR IN WHICH 'JAWS' TERRIFIED THE TRUNKS OFF SURFERS AND SWIMMERS EVERYWHERE, MAGGIE THATCHER WAS ELECTED PRIME MINISTER AND ROLLERMANIA MADE THE BAY CITY ROLLERS ARGUABLY THE HOTTEST ACT SINCE THE BEATLES, **BRIAN MAY** TALKS ABOUT 'BOHEMIAN RHAPSODY', THE SINGLE, YOU, THE READERS OF BRITISH HIT SINGLES VOTED THE BEST HIT SINGLE OF ALL TIME ...

" The song was conceived by Freddie Mercury as an extravagant album track for the LP 'A Night at the Opera' in 1975, and executed by Queen, just the four of us, on 24-track analogue tape at a time when the technology had to be pushed farther than ever before to capture the extreme multi-tracking this epic demanded. It seemed an adventurous choice for the first single from the album, but we were advised that radio would never play the track unless it was edited down to the normal three and a half minutes. With typical arrogance we insisted that the track could only go out in its original form, over seven minutes long. The single, accompanied by a hastily thrown-together video clip (since hailed as the beginning of the video age – forgive us!), was so arresting it immediately stormed every radio and sales chart in the known world, and in the UK it stayed at the No.1 slot for nine weeks. "

SINGLE OF THE YEAR 'Bohemian Rhapsody' Queen
ALBUM OF THE YEAR 'The Best of the Stylistics' Stylistics

Jonathan KING (208 Top 500) *King of the pseudonyms, b. 6 Dec 1944, London, UK. A multi-faceted pop maestro who masterminded numerous hits and helped to guide the early careers of Genesis, Bay City Rollers and 10cc. Was Jailed in 2001 (128 WEEKS)*

Date		Title / Label	pos	wks
29 Jul 65	●	**EVERYONE'S GONE TO THE MOON** *Decca F 12187*	4	11
10 Jan 70		**LET IT ALL HANG OUT** *Decca F 12988*	26	7
16 Jan 71		**IT'S THE SAME OLD SONG** *B & C CB 139* [1]	19	9
3 Apr 71		**SUGAR SUGAR** *RCA 2064* [2]	12	14
29 May 71		**LAZY BONES** *Decca F 13177*	23	8
20 Nov 71		**HOOKED ON A FEELING** *Decca F 13241*	23	10
5 Feb 72		**FLIRT** *Decca F 13276*	22	9
14 Oct 72	●	**LOOP DI LOVE** *UK 7* [3]	4	13
26 Jan 74		**(I CAN'T GET NO) SATISFACTION** *UK 53* [4]	29	5
6 Sep 75	●	**UNA PALOMA BLANCA** *UK 105*	5	11
20 Sep 75		**CHICK-A-BOOM (DON'T YA JES LOVE IT)** *UK 2012 002* [5]	36	4
7 Feb 76		**IN THE MOOD** *UK 121* [6]	46	3
26 Jun 76	●	**IT ONLY TAKES A MINUTE** *UK 135* [7]	9	9
7 Oct 78		**ONE FOR YOU ONE FOR ME** *GTO GT 237*	29	6
16 Dec 78		**LICK A SMURP FOR CHRISTMAS (ALL FALL DOWN)** *Petrol GAS 1 / Magnet MAG 139* [8]	58	4
16 Jun 79		**YOU'RE THE GREATEST LOVER** *UK International INT 586*	67	2
3 Nov 79		**GLORIA** *Ariola ARO 198*	65	3

[1] Weathermen [2] Sakkarin [3] Shag [4] Bubblerock [5] 53rd and 3rd featuring the Sound of Shag [6] Sound 9418 [7] One Hundred Ton and a Feather [8] Father Abraphart and the Smurps

Nosmo KING – *See JAVELLS featuring Nosmo KING*

Paul KING *UK, male vocalist (3 WEEKS)*

Date		Title / Label	pos	wks
2 May 87		**I KNOW** *CBS PKING 1*	59	3

See also KING

Solomon KING *US, male vocalist (28 WEEKS)*

Date		Title / Label	pos	wks
3 Jan 68	●	**SHE WEARS MY RING** *Columbia DB 8325*	3	18
1 May 68		**WHEN WE WERE YOUNG** *Columbia DB 8402*	21	10

KING ADORA *UK, male vocal / instrumental group (5 WEEKS)*

Date		Title / Label	pos	wks
4 Nov 00		**SMOULDER** *Superior Quality / A&M RQSD 010CD*	62	1
3 Mar 01		**SUFFOCATE** *Superior Quality / A&M RQS 11DD*	39	2
26 May 01		**BIONIC** *Superior Quality / A&M RQS 012CD*	30	2

KING BEE *UK, male rapper (6 WEEKS)*

Date		Title / Label	pos	wks
26 Jan 91		**MUST BEE THE MUSIC** *Columbia 6565827* [1]	44	4
23 Mar 91		**BACK BY DOPE DEMAND** *First Bass 7RUFF 6X*	61	2

[1] King Bee featuring Michele

KING BROTHERS (476 Top 500) *Britain's top male group before The Beatles; brothers Denis (v/p), Michael (v/g) and Tony (v/b) King from Essex, UK. Poll-winning MOR-slanted trio made first of many TV appearances in 1953 (when Denis was 14). Denis became one of UK's top TV theme writers (74 WEEKS)*

Date		Title / Label	pos	wks
31 May 57	●	**A WHITE SPORT COAT (AND A PINK CARNATION)** *Parlophone R 4310*	6	14
9 Aug 57		**IN THE MIDDLE OF AN ISLAND** *Parlophone R 4338*	19	13
6 Dec 57		**WAKE UP LITTLE SUSIE** *Parlophone R 4367*	22	3
31 Jan 58		**PUT A LIGHT IN THE WINDOW** *Parlophone R 4389*	29	1
14 Feb 58		**PUT A LIGHT IN THE WINDOW (re-entry)** *Parlophone R 4389*	28	1
28 Feb 58		**PUT A LIGHT IN THE WINDOW (2nd re-entry)** *Parlophone R 4389*	25	2
14 Apr 60	●	**STANDING ON THE CORNER** *Parlophone R 4639*	4	11
28 Jul 60		**MAIS OUI** *Parlophone R 4672*	16	10
12 Jan 61		**DOLL HOUSE** *Parlophone R 4715*	21	8
2 Mar 61		**SEVENTY SIX TROMBONES** *Parlophone R 4737*	19	11

KING KURT *UK, male vocal / instrumental group (16 WEEKS)*

Date		Title / Label	pos	wks
15 Oct 83		**DESTINATION ZULULAND** *Stiff BUY 189*	36	6
28 Apr 84		**MACK THE KNIFE** *Stiff BUY 199*	55	4
4 Aug 84		**BANANA BANANA** *Stiff BUY 206*	54	4
15 Nov 86		**AMERICA** *Polydor KURT 1*	73	1
2 May 87		**THE LAND OF RING DANG DO** *Polydor KURT 2*	67	1

KING SUN-D'MOET *US, male rap / DJ duo (3 WEEKS)*

Date		Title / Label	pos	wks
11 Jul 87		**HEY LOVE** *Flame MELT 5*	66	3

Tony KING – *See Kylie MINOGUE*

KING TRIGGER *UK, male / female vocal / instrumental group (4 WEEKS)*

Date		Title / Label	pos	wks
14 Aug 82		**THE RIVER** *Chrysalis CHS 2623*	57	4

KINGDOM COME *US, male vocal / instrumental group (2 WEEKS)*

Date		Title / Label	pos	wks
16 Apr 88		**GET IT ON** *Polydor KCS 1*	75	1
6 May 89		**DO YOU LIKE IT** *Polydor KCS 3*	73	1

KINGMAKER *UK, male vocal / instrumental group (22 WEEKS)*

Date		Title / Label	pos	wks
18 Jan 92		**IDIOTS AT THE WHEEL (EP)** *Scorch SCORCH 3*	30	3
23 May 92		**EAT YOURSELF WHOLE** *Scorch SCORCHG 5*	15	3
31 Oct 92		**ARMCHAIR ANARCHIST** *Scorch SCORCHG 6*	47	2
8 May 93		**10 YEARS ASLEEP** *Scorch CDSCORCHS 8*	15	4
19 Jun 93		**QUEEN JANE** *Scorch CDSCORS 9*	29	4
30 Oct 93		**SATURDAY'S NOT WHAT IT USED TO BE** *Scorch CDSCORCH 10*	63	1
15 Apr 95		**YOU AND I WILL NEVER SEE THINGS EYE TO EYE** *Scorch CDSCORCHS 11*	33	3
3 Jun 95		**IN THE BEST POSSIBLE TASTE (PART 2)** *Scorch CDSCORCHS 12*	41	2

Tracks on Idiots at the Wheel (EP): Really Scrape the Sky / Revelation / Every Teenage Suicide / Strip Away

KINGS OF CONVENIENCE *Norway, male vocal / instrumental duo (2 WEEKS)*

Date		Title / Label	pos	wks
21 Apr 01		**TOXIC GIRL** *Source SOURCDSE 1025*	44	1
14 Jul 01		**FAILURE** *Source SOURCD 036*	63	1

KINGS OF SWING ORCHESTRA *Australia, orchestra (5 WEEKS)*

Date		Title / Label	pos	wks
1 May 82		**SWITCHED ON SWING** *Philips Swing 1*	48	5

KINGS OF TOMORROW featuring Julie McKNIGHT *US, male production / instrumental duo and female vocalist (4 WEEKS)*

Date		Title / Label	pos	wks
14 Apr 01		**FINALLY** *Distance DI 2029*	54	1
29 Sep 01		**FINALLY (re-mix)** *Defected DFECT 37CDS*	24	3

KINGSMEN *US, male vocal / instrumental group (7 WEEKS)*

Date		Title / Label	pos	wks
30 Jan 64		**LOUIE LOUIE** *Pye International 7N 25231*	26	7

KINGSTON TRIO *US, male vocal / instrumental group (15 WEEKS)*

Date		Title / Label	pos	wks
21 Nov 58	●	**TOM DOOLEY** *Capitol CL 14951* ▲	5	14
4 Dec 59		**SAN MIGUEL** *Capitol CL 15073*	29	1

KINKS (71 Top 500) *Well-respected and innovative London band, who had few equals in the 1960s: Ray Davies (v/g), Dave Davies (g), Pete Quaife (b), Mick Avory (d). Ray Davies, regarded as one of rock's premier songwriters, remains active almost 40 years after the group's first hit (215 WEEKS)*

Date		Title / Label	pos	wks
13 Aug 64	★	**YOU REALLY GOT ME** *Pye 7N 15673*	1	12
29 Oct 64	●	**ALL DAY AND ALL OF THE NIGHT** *Pye 7N 15714*	2	14
21 Jan 65	★	**TIRED OF WAITING FOR YOU** *Pye 7N 15759*	1	10
25 Mar 65		**EVERYBODY'S GONNA BE HAPPY** *Pye 7N 15813*	17	8
27 May 65	●	**SET ME FREE** *Pye 7N 15854*	9	11
5 Aug 65	●	**SEE MY FRIEND** *Pye 7N 15919*	10	9
2 Dec 65	●	**TILL THE END OF THE DAY** *Pye 7N 15981*	8	12
3 Mar 66	●	**DEDICATED FOLLOWER OF FASHION** *Pye 7N 17064*	4	11
9 Jun 66	★	**SUNNY AFTERNOON** *Pye 7N 17125*	1	13
24 Nov 66	●	**DEAD END STREET** *Pye 7N 17222*	5	11
11 May 67	●	**WATERLOO SUNSET** *Pye 7N 17321*	2	11
18 Oct 67	●	**AUTUMN ALMANAC** *Pye 7N 17400*	3	11
17 Apr 68		**WONDERBOY** *Pye 7N 17468*	36	5
17 Jul 68		**DAYS** *Pye 7N 17573*	12	10

16 Apr 69	**PLASTIC MAN** *Pye 7N 17724*	31	4
10 Jan 70	**VICTORIA** *Pye 7N 17865*	33	4
4 Jul 70 ●	**LOLA** *Pye 7N 17961*	2	14
12 Dec 70 ●	**APEMAN** *Pye 7N 45016*	5	14
27 May 72	**SUPERSONIC ROCKET SHIP** *RCA 2211*	16	8
27 Jun 81	**BETTER THINGS** *Arista ARIST 415*	46	5
6 Aug 83	**COME DANCING** *Arista ARIST 502*	12	9
15 Oct 83	**DON'T FORGET TO DANCE** *Arista ARIST 524*	58	3
15 Oct 83	**YOU REALLY GOT ME (re-issue)** *PRT KD1*	47	4
18 Jan 97	**THE DAYS EP** *When! WENX 1016*	35	2

Tracks on The Days EP: Days / You Really Got Me / Dead End Street / Lola

KINKY *UK, female rapper (1 WEEK)* pos/wks

24 Aug 96	**EVERYBODY** *Feverpitch CDFVR 1009*	71	1

See also ERASURE

KINKY MACHINE *UK, male vocal / instrumental group (4 WEEKS)* pos/wks

6 Mar 93	**SUPERNATURAL GIVER** *Lemon LEMON 006CD*	70	1
29 May 93	**SHOCKAHOLIC** *Oxygen GASPD 5*	70	1
14 Aug 93	**GOING OUT WITH GOD** *Oxygen GASPD 9*	74	1
2 Jul 94	**10 SECOND BIONIC MAN** *Oxygen GASPD 14*	66	1

Fern KINNEY *US, female vocalist – Fern Kinney-Lewis (11 WEEKS)* pos/wks

16 Feb 80 ★	**TOGETHER WE ARE BEAUTIFUL** *WEA K 79111*	1	11

KINSHASA BAND – *See Johnny WAKELIN*

Kathy KIRBY *UK, female vocalist (54 WEEKS)* pos/wks

15 Aug 63	**DANCE ON** *Decca F 11682*	11	13
7 Nov 63 ●	**SECRET LOVE** *Decca F 11759*	4	18
20 Feb 64 ●	**LET ME GO LOVER!** *Decca F 11832*	10	11
7 May 64	**YOU'RE THE ONE** *Decca F 11892*	17	9
4 Mar 65	**I BELONG** *Decca F 12087*	36	3

Bo KIRKLAND and Ruth DAVIS
US, male / female vocal duo (9 WEEKS) pos/wks

4 Jun 77	**YOU'RE GONNA GET NEXT TO ME** *EMI International INT 532*	12	9

KISS *US, male vocal / instrumental group (57 WEEKS)* pos/wks

30 Jun 79	**I WAS MADE FOR LOVIN' YOU** *Casablanca CAN 152*	50	7
20 Feb 82	**A WORLD WITHOUT HEROES** *Casablanca KISS 002*	55	3
30 Apr 83	**CREATURES OF THE NIGHT** *Casablanca KISS 4*	34	4
29 Oct 83	**LICK IT UP** *Vertigo KISS 5*	31	5
8 Sep 84	**HEAVEN'S ON FIRE** *Vertigo VER 12*	43	3
9 Nov 85	**TEARS ARE FALLING** *Vertigo KISS 6*	57	2
3 Oct 87 ●	**CRAZY CRAZY NIGHTS** *Vertigo KISS 7*	4	9
5 Dec 87	**REASON TO LIVE** *Vertigo KISS 8*	33	7
10 Sep 88	**TURN ON THE NIGHT** *Vertigo KISS 9*	41	3
18 Nov 89	**HIDE YOUR HEART** *Vertigo KISS 10*	59	2
31 Mar 90	**FOREVER** *Vertigo KISS 11*	65	2
11 Jan 92 ●	**GOD GAVE ROCK AND ROLL TO YOU II** *Interscope A 8696*	4	8
9 May 92	**UNHOLY** *Mercury KISS 12*	26	2

KISS AMC *UK, female rap duo (5 WEEKS)* pos/wks

1 Jul 89	**A BIT OF . . .** *Syncopate SY 29*	58	2
19 Aug 89	**A BIT OF U2 (re-entry)** *Syncopate SY 29*	58	2
3 Feb 90	**MY DOCS** *Syncopate XAMC 1*	66	1

Before the re-entry of 'A Bit of U2', copyright problems meant that the disc was unable to be given its full title

KISSING THE PINK
UK, male / female vocal / instrumental group (14 WEEKS) pos/wks

5 Mar 83	**LAST FILM** *Magnet KTP 3*	19	14

Mac and Katie KISSOON
Trinidad / UK, male / female vocal duo (33 WEEKS) pos/wks

19 Jun 71	**CHIRPY CHIRPY CHEEP CHEEP** *Young Blood YB 1026*	41	1
18 Jan 75 ●	**SUGAR CANDY KISSES** *Polydor 2058 531*	3	10
3 May 75 ●	**DON'T DO IT BABY** *State STAT 4*	9	8
30 Aug 75	**LIKE A BUTTERFLY** *State STAT 9*	18	9
15 May 76	**THE TWO OF US** *State STAT 21*	46	5

Kevin KITCHEN *UK, male vocalist (3 WEEKS)* pos/wks

20 Apr 85	**PUT MY ARMS AROUND YOU** *China WOK 1*	64	3

Joy KITIKONTI *Italy, male producer – Massimo Chiticonti (2 WEEKS)* pos/wks

17 Nov 01	**JOYENERGIZER** *BXR BXRC 0347*	57	2

Eartha KITT *US, female vocalist (34 WEEKS)* pos/wks

1 Apr 55 ●	**UNDER THE BRIDGES OF PARIS** *HMV B 10647*	7	9
10 Jun 55	**UNDER THE BRIDGES OF PARIS (re-entry)** *HMV B 10647*	20	1
3 Dec 83	**WHERE IS MY MAN** *Record Shack SOHO 11*	36	11
7 Jul 84	**I LOVE MEN** *Record Shack SOHO 21*	50	3
12 Apr 86	**THIS IS MY LIFE** *Record Shack SOHO 61*	73	1
1 Jul 89	**CHA CHA HEELS** *Arista 112331* [1]	32	7
5 Mar 94	**IF I LOVE YA THEN I NEED YA IF I NEED YA THEN I WANT YOU AROUND** *RCA 74321190342*	43	2

[1] Eartha Kitt and Bronski Beat

KITTIE *Canada, female vocal / instrumental group (2 WEEKS)* pos/wks

25 Mar 00	**BRACKISH** *Epic 6691292*	46	1
22 Jul 00	**CHARLOTTE** *Epic 6696222*	60	1

KLAXONS *Belgium, male vocal / instrumental group (6 WEEKS)* pos/wks

10 Dec 83	**THE CLAP CLAP SOUND** *PRT 7P 290*	45	6

KLEEER *US, male / female vocal / instrumental group (10 WEEKS)* pos/wks

17 Mar 79	**KEEEP YOUR BODY WORKING** *Atlantic LV 21*	51	6
14 Mar 81	**GET TOUGH** *Atlantic 11560*	49	4

KLESHAY *UK, female vocal trio (5 WEEKS)* pos/wks

19 Sep 98	**REASONS** *Epic KLE 1CD*	33	2
20 Feb 99	**RUSH** *Epic KLE 2CD*	19	3

KLF *UK, male vocal / instrumental duo – Bill Drummond and Jimmy Cauty (51 WEEKS)* pos/wks

11 Aug 90 ●	**WHAT TIME IS LOVE? (LIVE AT TRANCENTRAL)** *KLF Communications KLF 004* [1]	5	12
19 Jan 91 ★	**3 AM ETERNAL** *KLF Communications KLF 005* [1]	1	11
4 May 91 ●	**LAST TRAIN TO TRANCENTRAL** *KLF Communications KLF 008*	2	9
7 Dec 91 ●	**JUSTIFIED AND ANCIENT** *KLF Communications KLF 099* [2]	2	12
7 Mar 92 ●	**AMERICA: WHAT TIME IS LOVE? (re-mix)** *KLF Communications KLFUSA 004*	4	7

[1] KLF featuring the Children of the Revolution [2] KLF guest vocals: Tammy Wynette

See also JUSTIFIED ANCIENTS OF MU MU; TIMELORDS; 2K

KLUBBHEADS
Holland, male instrumental / production group (10 WEEKS) pos/wks

11 May 96 ●	**KLUBBHOPPING** *AM:PM 5815572*	10	6
16 Aug 97	**DISCOHOPPING** *AM:PM 5823032*	35	2
15 Aug 98	**KICKIN' HARD** *Wonderboy WBOYD 011*	36	2

See also ITTY BITTY BOOZY WOOZY

KLUSTER featuring Ron CARROLL
France, male DJ / production duo (1 WEEK) pos/wks

28 Apr 01	**MY LOVE** *Scorpio Music 1928112*	73	1

KNACK *US, male vocal / instrumental group (12 WEEKS)* pos/wks

30 Jun 79 ●	**MY SHARONA** *Capitol CL 16087* ▲	6	10
13 Oct 79	**GOOD GIRLS DON'T** *Capitol CL 16097*	66	2

KNACK – *See MOUNT RUSHMORE presents THE KNACK*

Beverley KNIGHT *UK, female vocalist – Beverley Smith (27 WEEKS)* pos/wks

		pos	wks
8 Apr 95	FLAVOUR OF THE OLD SCHOOL *Dome CDDOME 101*	50	2
2 Sep 95	DOWN FOR THE ONE *Dome CDDOME 102*	55	1
21 Oct 95	FLAVOUR OF THE OLD SCHOOL (re-mix) *Dome CDDOME 105*	33	2
23 Mar 96	MOVING ON UP (ON THE RIGHT SIDE) *Dome CDDOME 107*	42	1
30 May 98	MADE IT BACK *Parlophone Rhythm CDRHYTHM 11* [1]	21	3
22 Aug 98	REWIND (FIND A WAY) *Parlophone Rhythm CDRHYTHS 13*	40	2
10 Apr 99	MADE IT BACK 99 (re-mix) *Parlophone Rhythm CDRHYTHM 18*	19	5
17 Jul 99	GREATEST DAY *Parlophone Rhythm CDRHYTHS 22*	14	5
4 Dec 99	SISTA SISTA *Parlophone Rhythm CDRHYTHM 26*	31	2
17 Nov 01	GET UP *Parlophone CDRS 6564*	17	4

[1] Beverley Knight featuring Redman

Frederick KNIGHT *US, male vocalist (10 WEEKS)* pos/wks

		pos	wks
10 Jun 72	I'VE BEEN LONELY SO LONG *Stax 2025 098*	22	10

Gladys KNIGHT and the PIPS (103 Top 500) *One of soul music's foremost female singers for almost 40 years; b. 28 May 1944, Georgia, US. The celebrated vocalist (who first appeared on US TV aged eight) and her family quartet The Pips (they split in 1989), were inducted into the Rock and Roll Hall of Fame in 1996 (187 WEEKS)* pos/wks

		pos	wks
8 Jun 67	TAKE ME IN YOUR ARMS AND LOVE ME *Tamla Motown TMG 604*	13	15
27 Dec 67	I HEARD IT THROUGH THE GRAPEVINE *Tamla Motown TMG 629*	47	1
17 Jun 72	JUST WALK IN MY SHOES *Tamla Motown TMG 813*	35	8
25 Nov 72	HELP ME MAKE IT THROUGH THE NIGHT *Tamla Motown TMG 830*	11	17
3 Mar 73	LOOK OF LOVE *Tamla Motown TMG 844*	21	9
26 May 73	NEITHER ONE OF US *Tamla Motown TMG 855*	31	7
5 Apr 75 ●	THE WAY WE WERE - TRY TO REMEMBER *Buddah BDS 428*	4	15
2 Aug 75 ●	BEST THING THAT EVER HAPPENED TO ME *Buddah BDS 432*	7	10
15 Nov 75	PART TIME LOVE *Buddah BDS 438*	30	5
8 May 76 ●	MIDNIGHT TRAIN TO GEORGIA *Buddah BDS 444* ▲	10	9
21 Aug 76	MAKE YOURS A HAPPY HOME *Buddah BDS 447*	35	4
6 Nov 76	SO SAD THE SONG *Buddah BDS 448*	20	9
15 Jan 77	NOBODY BUT YOU *Buddah BDS 451*	34	2
28 May 77 ●	BABY DON'T CHANGE YOUR MIND *Buddah BDS 458*	4	12
24 Sep 77	HOME IS WHERE THE HEART IS *Buddah BDS 460*	35	4
8 Apr 78	THE ONE AND ONLY *Buddah BDS 470*	32	4
13 May 78	THE ONE AND ONLY (re-entry) *Buddah BDS 470*	66	1
24 Jun 78	COME BACK AND FINISH WHAT YOU STARTED *Buddah BDS 473*	15	13
30 Sep 78	IT'S A BETTER THAN GOOD TIME *Buddah BDS 478*	59	4
30 Aug 80	TASTE OF BITTER LOVE *CBS 8890*	35	6
8 Nov 80	BOURGIE BOURGIE *CBS 9081*	32	6
26 Dec 81	WHEN A CHILD IS BORN *CBS S 1758* [1]	74	2
9 Nov 85	THAT'S WHAT FRIENDS ARE FOR *Arista ARIST 638* [2] ▲	16	9
16 Jan 88	LOVE OVERBOARD *MCA MCA 1223*	42	4
10 Jun 89 ●	LICENCE TO KILL *MCA MCA 1339* [3]	6	11

[1] Johnny Mathis and Gladys Knight [2] Dionne Warwick and Friends featuring Elton John, Stevie Wonder and Gladys Knight [3] Gladys Knight

Jordan KNIGHT *US, male vocalist (9 WEEKS)* pos/wks

		pos	wks
16 Oct 99 ●	GIVE IT TO YOU *Interscope 4971672*	5	8
15 Jan 00	GIVE IT TO YOU (re-entry) *Interscope 4971672*	61	1

See also NEW KIDS ON THE BLOCK

Robert KNIGHT *US, male vocalist (26 WEEKS)* pos/wks

		pos	wks
17 Jan 68	EVERLASTING LOVE *Monument MON 1008*	40	2
24 Nov 73 ●	LOVE ON A MOUNTAIN TOP *Monument MNT 1875*	10	16
9 Mar 74	EVERLASTING LOVE (re-issue) *Monument MNT 2106*	19	8

Mark KNOPFLER *UK, male vocalist / instrumentalist – guitar (7 WEEKS)* pos/wks

		pos	wks
12 Mar 83	GOING HOME (THEME OF 'LOCAL HERO') *Vertigo DSTR 4*	56	3
16 Mar 96	DARLING PRETTY *Vertigo VERCD 88*	33	2
25 May 96	CANNIBALS *Vertigo VERCD 89*	42	2

See also DIRE STRAITS

KNOWLEDGE *Italy, male production duo (1 WEEK)* pos/wks

		pos	wks
8 Nov 97	AS (UNTIL THE DAY) *ffrr FCD 312*	70	1

Buddy KNOX *US, male vocalist (5 WEEKS)* pos/wks

		pos	wks
10 May 57	PARTY DOLL *Columbia DB 3914* ▲	29	3
16 Aug 62	SHE'S GONE *Liberty LIB 55473*	45	2

Frankie KNUCKLES *US, male producer (19 WEEKS)* pos/wks

		pos	wks
17 Jun 89	TEARS *ffrr F 108* [1]	50	3
21 Oct 89	YOUR LOVE *Trax TRAXT 3*	59	4
27 Jul 91	THE WHISTLE SONG *Virgin America VUS 47*	17	5
23 Nov 91	IT'S HARD SOMETIMES *Virgin America VUS 52*	67	1
6 Jun 92	RAIN FALLS *Virgin America VUST 60* [2]	48	2
27 May 95	TOO MANY FISH *Virgin America VUSCD 89* [3]	34	2
18 Nov 95	WHADDA U WANT (FROM ME) *Virgin America VUSCD 98* [3]	36	2

[1] Frankie Knuckles presents Satoshi Tomiie [2] Frankie Knuckles featuring Lisa Michaelis [3] Frankie Knuckles featuring Adeva

Moe KOFFMAN QUARTETTE *Canada, male instrumental group, Moe Koffman – flute (2 WEEKS)* pos/wks

		pos	wks
28 Mar 58	SWINGIN' SHEPHERD BLUES *London HLJ 8549*	23	2

Mike KOGLIN *Germany, male producer (4 WEEKS)* pos/wks

		pos	wks
28 Nov 98	THE SILENCE *Multiply CDMULTY 44*	20	2
29 May 99	ON MY WAY *Multiply CDMULTY 51* [1]	28	2

[1] Mike Koglin featuring Beatrice

KOKOMO *US, male instrumentalist – piano (7 WEEKS)* pos/wks

		pos	wks
13 Apr 61	ASIA MINOR *London HLU 9305*	35	7

KOKOMO *UK, male / female vocal / instrumental group (3 WEEKS)* pos/wks

		pos	wks
29 May 82	A LITTLE BIT FURTHER AWAY *CBS A 2064*	45	3

KON KAN *Canada, male vocal / instrumental duo – Barry Harris and Kevin Wynne (13 WEEKS)* pos/wks

		pos	wks
4 Mar 89 ●	I BEG YOUR PARDON *Atlantic A 8969*	5	13

John KONGOS *South Africa, male vocalist / multi-instrumentalist (25 WEEKS)* pos/wks

		pos	wks
22 May 71 ●	HE'S GONNA STEP ON YOU AGAIN *Fly BUG 8*	4	14
20 Nov 71 ●	TOKOLOSHE MAN *Fly BUG 14*	4	11

KONKRETE *UK, female production duo (1 WEEK)* pos/wks

		pos	wks
22 Sep 01	LAW UNTO MYSELF *Perfecto PERF 23CDS*	60	1

KOOL and the GANG (83 Top 500) *One of the most consistently successful R&B acts, hailing from New Jersey and including Robert 'Kool' Bell (b) and James 'JT' Taylor (v). The band spent 10 years as top US R&B stars before starting their impressive run of international hits (207 WEEKS)* pos/wks

		pos	wks
27 Oct 79 ●	LADIES NIGHT *Mercury KOOL 7*	9	12
19 Jan 80	TOO HOT *Mercury KOOL 8*	23	8
12 Jul 80	HANGIN' OUT *De-Lite KOOL 9*	52	4
1 Nov 80 ●	CELEBRATION *De-Lite KOOL 10* ▲	7	13
21 Feb 81	JONES VS JONES / SUMMER MADNESS *De-Lite KOOL 11*	17	11
30 May 81	TAKE IT TO THE TOP *De-Lite DE 2*	15	9
31 Oct 81	STEPPIN' OUT *De-Lite DE 4*	12	13
19 Dec 81 ●	GET DOWN ON IT *De-Lite DE 5*	3	12
6 Mar 82	TAKE MY HEART (YOU CAN HAVE IT IF YOU WANT IT) *De-Lite DE 6*	29	7
7 Aug 82	BIG FUN *De-Lite DE 7*	14	8
16 Oct 82 ●	OOH LA LA LA (LET'S GO DANCIN') *De-Lite DE 9*	6	9
4 Dec 82	HI DE HI, HI DE HO *De-Lite DE 14*	29	8
10 Dec 83	STRAIGHT AHEAD *De-Lite DE 15*	15	10
11 Feb 84 ●	JOANNA / TONIGHT *De-Lite DE 16*	2	11
14 Apr 84 ●	(WHEN YOU SAY YOU LOVE SOMEBODY) IN THE HEART *De-Lite DE 17*	7	8

UK No.1 ★ UK Top 10 ● Still on chart + UK million seller ◆ UK entry at No.1 ■ US No.1 ▲

1976

IN THE YEAR IN WHICH NASA'S VIKING 1 PROBE TRANSMITTED THE FIRST PICTURES FROM THE SURFACE OF MARS, ROBERT DE NIRO ASKED THE WORLD "ARE YOU LOOKING AT ME?!" IN 'TAXI DRIVER', AND THE SEX PISTOLS, CLASH AND DAMNED LED THE PUNK REVOLUTION, **CHRIS THOMPSON** OF MANFRED MANN'S EARTH BAND REMEMBERS THE AGGRO ENCOUNTERED OVER A DECISION TO RECORD A SPRINGSTEEN SONG ...

"The previous Earth Band album with another singer hadn't done incredibly well and the next record was going to be make or break. It was a difficult record to make; in fact, the record company hated it, if I remember rightly. The label boss stormed out of the studio saying he wasn't going to give us any more of the advance because he thought the record was rubbish – that was after listening to 'Blinded By the Light', I think! Anyway it came out and did pretty well. I once asked **Bruce Springsteen** [who wrote the song] if he liked our version of 'Blinded' and he changed the subject. I don't think he liked it at all. I know he hated the Pointer Sisters' 'Fire'. I think he probably found it a complete and utter bastardisation of his work because he's pretty precious about his work – rightly so, I suppose!"

SINGLE OF THE YEAR 'Save Your Kisses For Me' Brotherhood of Man
ALBUM OF THE YEAR 'Greatest Hits' ABBA

1976

24 Nov 84	**FRESH** *De-Lite DE 18*	11	12
9 Feb 85	**MISLED** *De-Lite DE 19*	28	5
11 May 85 ●	**CHERISH** *De-Lite DE 20*	4	22
2 Nov 85	**EMERGENCY** *De-Lite DE 21*	50	3
22 Nov 86	**VICTORY** *Club JAB 44*	67	2
20 Dec 86	**VICTORY (re-entry)** *Club JAB 44*	30	10
21 Mar 87	**STONE LOVE** *Club JAB 47*	45	4
31 Dec 88	**CELEBRATION (re-mix)** *Club JAB 78*	56	5
6 Jul 91	**GET DOWN ON IT (re-mix)** *Mercury MER 346*	69	1

'Jones vs Jones' and 'Summer Madness' were labelled as A and B sides with 'Funky Stuff' and 'Hollywood Swinging' as the C and D sides of a two-disc release

KOOL ROCK STEADY – See *TYREE*

KOON + STEPHENSON – See *WESTBAM*

KORGIS *UK, male vocal / instrumental duo (27 WEEKS)* pos/wks

23 Jun 79	**IF I HAD YOU** *Rialto TREB 103*	13	12
24 May 80 ●	**EVERYBODY'S GOT TO LEARN SOMETIME** *Rialto TREB 115*	5	12
30 Aug 80	**IF IT'S ALRIGHT WITH YOU BABY** *Rialto TREB 118*	56	3

KORN *US, male vocal / instrumental group (14 WEEKS)* pos/wks

19 Oct 96	**NO PLACE TO HIDE** *Epic 6638452*	26	2
15 Feb 97	**A.D.I.D.A.S.** *Epic 6642042*	22	2
7 Jun 97	**GOOD GOD** *Epic 6646585*	25	2
22 Aug 98	**GOT THE LIFE** *Epic 6663912*	23	2
8 May 99	**FREAK ON A LEASH** *Epic 6672522*	24	2
12 Feb 00	**FALLING AWAY FROM ME** *Epic 6688692*	24	2
3 Jun 00	**MAKE ME BAD** *Epic 6694332*	25	2

KOSHEEN *UK, male production duo and female vocalist (12 WEEKS)* pos/wks

17 Jun 00	**EMPTY SKIES / HIDE U** *Moksha Recordings MOKSHA 05CD*	73	1
14 Apr 01	**(SLIP & SLIDE) SUICIDE** *Moksha Recordings MOKSHA 07CD*	50	2
1 Sep 01 ●	**HIDE U (re-mix)** *Arista 74321879412*	6	6
27 Oct 01	**HIDE U (re-entry of re-mix)** *Arista 74321879412*	55	1
22 Dec 01	**CATCH** *Moksha / Arista 74321913722*	15	2+

KP & ENVYI
US, female vocal / rap duo – Kia Philips and Susan Hedgepath (4 WEEKS) pos/wks

13 Jun 98	**SWING MY WAY** *East West E 3849 CD*	14	4

KRAFTWERK (486 Top 500) *Acclaimed German band who greatly influenced dance and rock music. Founder members were multi-instrumentalists / vocalists Ralf Hutter and Florian Schneider. 'The Model' was the first German record to top the UK chart. Hip hop's pioneers acknowledge their debt to this seminal electronic group (72 WEEKS)* pos/wks

10 May 75	**AUTOBAHN** *Vertigo 6147 012*	11	9
28 Oct 78	**NEON LIGHTS** *Capitol CL 15998*	53	3
9 May 81	**POCKET CALCULATOR** *EMI 5175*	39	6
11 Jul 81	**COMPUTER LOVE / THE MODEL** *EMI 5207*	36	8
26 Dec 81 ★	**COMPUTER LOVE / THE MODEL (re-entry)** *EMI 5207*	1	13
20 Feb 82	**SHOWROOM DUMMIES** *EMI 5272*	25	5
6 Aug 83	**TOUR DE FRANCE** *EMI 5413*	22	8
25 Aug 84	**TOUR DE FRANCE (re-entry)** *EMI 5413*	24	11
1 Jun 91	**THE ROBOTS** *EMI EM 192*	20	4
2 Nov 91	**RADIOACTIVITY (re-mix)** *EMI EM 201*	43	2
23 Oct 99	**TOUR DE FRANCE (re-issue)** *EMI 8874210*	61	1
18 Mar 00	**EXPO 2000** *EMI CDEM 562*	27	2

Billy J KRAMER and the DAKOTAS *Another successful Brian Epstein-managed and George Martin-produced group, led by well-groomed photogenic vocalist, b. William H. Ashton, 19 Aug 1943, Lancashire, UK. Winners of Melody Maker Best Newcomer of 1963 poll. Had most of their hits penned by Lennon and McCartney (71 WEEKS)* pos/wks

2 May 63 ●	**DO YOU WANT TO KNOW A SECRET?** *Parlophone R 5023*	2	15
1 Aug 63 ★	**BAD TO ME** *Parlophone R 5049*	1	14
7 Nov 63 ●	**I'LL KEEP YOU SATISFIED** *Parlophone R 5073*	4	13
27 Feb 64 ★	**LITTLE CHILDREN** *Parlophone R 5105*	1	13
23 Jul 64 ●	**FROM A WINDOW** *Parlophone R 5156*	10	8
20 May 65	**TRAINS AND BOATS AND PLANES** *Parlophone R 5285*	12	8

KRANKIES *UK, male / female vocal duo (6 WEEKS)* pos/wks

7 Feb 81	**FAN'DABI'DOZI** *Monarch MON 21*	71	1
7 Mar 81	**FAN'DABI'DOZI (re-entry)** *Monarch MON 21*	46	5

Lenny KRAVITZ *US, male vocalist (68 WEEKS)* pos/wks

2 Jun 90	**MR CABDRIVER** *Virgin America VUS 20*	58	2
4 Aug 90	**LET LOVE RULE** *Virgin America VUS 26*	39	4
30 Mar 91	**ALWAYS ON THE RUN** *Virgin America VUS 34*	41	3
15 Jun 91	**IT AIN'T OVER TIL IT'S OVER** *Virgin America VUS 43*	11	8
14 Sep 91	**STAND BY MY WOMAN** *Virgin America VUS 45*	55	3
20 Feb 93 ●	**ARE YOU GONNA GO MY WAY** *Virgin America VUSDG 65*	4	11
22 May 93	**BELIEVE** *Virgin America VUSCD 72*	30	5
28 Aug 93	**HEAVEN HELP** *Virgin America VUSDG 73*	20	7
4 Dec 93	**BUDDHA OF SUBURBIA** *Arista 74321177052* [1]	35	3
4 Dec 93	**IS THERE ANY LOVE IN YOUR HEART** *Virgin America VUSDG 76*	52	2
9 Sep 95	**ROCK AND ROLL IS DEAD** *Virgin America VUSCD 93*	22	3
23 Dec 95	**CIRCUS** *Virgin America VUSCD 96*	54	2
2 Mar 96	**CAN'T GET YOU OFF MY MIND** *Virgin America VUSCD 100*	54	2
16 May 98	**IF YOU CAN'T SAY NO** *Virgin VUSCD 130*	48	2
10 Oct 98	**I BELONG TO YOU** *Virgin VUSCD 138*	75	1
20 Feb 99 ★	**FLY AWAY** *Virgin VUSCD 141* ■	1	10

[1] David Bowie featuring Lenny Kravitz

KRAZE *US, male / female vocal / instrumental group (6 WEEKS)* pos/wks

22 Oct 88	**THE PARTY** *MCA MCA 1288*	29	5
17 Jun 89	**LET'S PLAY HOUSE** *MCA MCA 1337*	71	1

KREUZ *UK, male vocal group (1 WEEK)* pos/wks

8 Jul 95	**PARTY ALL NIGHT** *Diesel DES 004C*	75	1

Chantal KREVIAZUK *Canada, female vocalist (1 WEEK)* pos/wks

6 Mar 99	**LEAVING ON A JET PLANE** *Epic 6666272*	59	1

KREW-KATS *UK, male instrumental group (10 WEEKS)* pos/wks

9 Mar 61	**TRAMBONE** *HMV POP 840*	33	9
18 May 61	**TRAMBONE (re-entry)** *HMV POP 840*	49	1

KRIS KROSS
US, male rap duo – Chris Kelly and Chris Smith (22 WEEKS) pos/wks

30 May 92 ●	**JUMP** *Ruff House 6578547* ▲	2	8
25 Jul 92	**WARM IT UP** *Ruff House 6582187*	16	6
17 Oct 92	**I MISSED THE BUS** *Ruff House 6583927*	57	1
19 Dec 92	**IT'S A SHAME** *Ruff House 6588587*	31	5
11 Sep 93	**ALRIGHT** *Ruff House 6595652*	47	2

Marty KRISTIAN – See *NEW SEEKERS*

KROKUS *Switzerland / Malta, male vocal / instrumental group (2 WEEKS)* pos/wks

16 May 81	**INDUSTRIAL STRENGTH (EP)** *Ariola ARO 258*	62	2

Tracks on Industrial Strength (EP): Bedside Radio / Easy Rocker / Celebration / Bye Bye Baby

KRS ONE *US, male rapper – Lawrence Parker (8 WEEKS)* pos/wks

18 May 96	**RAPPAZ R N DAINJA** *Jive JIVECD 396*	47	1
8 Feb 97	**WORD PERFECT** *Jive JIVECD 418*	70	1
26 Apr 97	**STEP INTO A WORLD (RAPTURE'S DELIGHT)** *Jive JIVECD 411*	24	2
20 Sep 97	**HEARTBEAT / A FRIEND** *Jive JIVECD 431*	66	1
1 Nov 97	**DIGITAL** *ffrr FCD 316* [1]	13	3

[1] Goldie featuring KRS One

KRUSH *UK, male / female vocal / instrumental group (16 WEEKS)* pos/wks

5 Dec 87 ●	**HOUSE ARREST** *Club JAB 63*	3	15
14 Nov 92	**WALKING ON SUNSHINE** *Network NWK 55*	71	1

KRUSH PERSPECTIVE *US, female vocal group (2 WEEKS)* pos/wks

16 Jan 93	**LET'S GET TOGETHER (SO GROOVY NOW)** *Perspective PERD 7416*	61	2

UK No.1 ★ UK Top 10 ● Still on chart + UK million seller ◆ UK entry at No.1 ■ US No.1 ▲

KRUST featuring Saul WILLIAMS *UK, male producer / instrumentalist – Kirk Thompson and US, male poet / rapper (1 WEEK)* pos/wks

23 Oct 99	CODED LANGUAGE *Talkin Loud TLCD 51*	66	1

KULA SHAKER *UK, male vocal / instrumental group (48 WEEKS)* pos/wks

4 May 96	GRATEFUL WHEN YOU'RE DEAD - JERRY WAS THERE *Columbia KULACD 2*	35	3
6 Jul 96 ●	TATTVA *Columbia KULACD 3*	4	8
7 Sep 96 ●	HEY DUDE *Columbia KULACD 4*	2	7
23 Nov 96 ●	GOVINDA *Columbia KULACD 5*	7	8
8 Mar 97 ●	HUSH *Columbia KULACD 6*	2	8
9 Aug 97	HUSH (re-entry) *Columbia KULACD 6*	70	1
2 May 98 ●	SOUND OF DRUMS *Columbia KULA 21CD*	3	6
6 Mar 99	MYSTICAL MACHINE GUN *Columbia KULA 22CD*	14	3
15 May 99	SHOWER YOUR LOVE *Columbia KULA 23CD*	14	4

KULAY *Philippines, male / female vocal group (1 WEEK)* pos/wks

12 Sep 98	DELICIOUS *INCredible INCRL 4CD*	73	1

KUMARA *Holland, male production duo (1 WEEK)* pos/wks

7 Oct 00	SNAP YOUR FINGAZ *Y2K Y2K 018CD*	70	1

Charlie KUNZ *US, male instrumentalist – piano (4 WEEKS)* pos/wks

17 Dec 54	PIANO MEDLEY NO.114 *Decca F 10419*	20	3
14 Jan 55	PIANO MEDLEY NO.114 (re-entry) *Decca F 10419*	16	1

Medley titles: There Must Be a Reason / Hold My Hand / If I Give My Heart to You / Little Things Mean a Lot / Make Her Mine / My Son My Son

KURSAAL FLYERS *UK, male vocal / instrumental group (10 WEEKS)* pos/wks

20 Nov 76	LITTLE DOES SHE KNOW *CBS 4689*	14	10

KURUPT *US, male rapper (10 WEEKS)* pos/wks

13 Oct 01	IT'S OVER *Pias Recordings PIASB 024CD*	21	3
25 Aug 01	WHERE I WANNA BE *London LONCD461* [1]	14	6
13 Oct 01	WHERE I WANNA BE (re-entry) *London LONCD461* [1]	58	1

[1] Shade Sheist featuring Nate Dogg and Kurupt

KUT KLOSE *US, female vocal group (1 WEEK)* pos/wks

29 Apr 95	I LIKE *Elektra EKR 200CD*	72	1

Li KWAN *UK, male producer – Dave Lee (2 WEEKS)* pos/wks

17 Dec 94	I NEED A MAN *Deconstruction 74321252192*	51	2

See also Joey NEGRO; AKABU featuring Linda CLIFFORD; HED BOYS; RAVEN MAIZE; JAKATTA

KWS *UK, male vocal / instrumental group (36 WEEKS)* pos/wks

25 Apr 92 ★	PLEASE DON'T GO / GAME BOY *Network NWK 46*	1	16
22 Aug 92 ●	ROCK YOUR BABY *Network NWK 54*	8	7
12 Dec 92	HOLD BACK THE NIGHT *Network NWK 65* [1]	30	5
5 Jun 93	CAN'T GET ENOUGH OF YOUR LOVE *Network NWKCD 72*	71	1
9 Apr 94	IT SEEMS TO HANG ON *X-clusive XCLU 006CD*	58	1
2 Jul 94	AIN'T NOBODY (LOVES ME BETTER) *X-clusive XCLU 010CD* [2]	21	4
19 Nov 94	THE MORE I GET THE MORE I WANT *X-clusive XCLU 011CD* [3]	35	2

[1] KWS features guest vocal from the Trammps [2] KWS and Gwen Dickey [3] KWS featuring Teddy Pendergrass

'Game Boy' was listed only from 9 May 1992

KY-MANI – *See PM DAWN*

KYO – *See BEDROCK*

L

Jonny L *UK, male vocalist / instrumentalist / producer (2 WEEKS)* pos/wks

28 Aug 93	OOH I LIKE IT *XL Recordings XLS 44CD*	73	1
31 Oct 98	20 DEGREES *XL Recordings XLS 103CD* [1]	66	1

[1] Jonny L featuring Silvah Bullet

LA BELLE EPOQUE *France, female vocal duo (14 WEEKS)* pos/wks

27 Aug 77	BLACK IS BLACK *Harvest HAR 5133*	48	1
10 Sep 77 ●	BLACK IS BLACK (re-entry) *Harvest HAR 5133*	2	13

LA BOUCHE *US, male / female rap / vocal duo (12 WEEKS)* pos/wks

24 Sep 94	SWEET DREAMS *Bell 74321223912*	63	1
15 Jul 95	BE MY LOVER *Arista 74321265402*	27	4
30 Sep 95	FALLING IN LOVE *Arista 74321305102*	43	2
2 Mar 96	BE MY LOVER (re-mix) *Arista 74321339822*	25	4
7 Sep 96	SWEET DREAMS (re-issue) *Arista 74321398542*	44	1

LA GANZ *US, male vocal / instrumental group (1 WEEK)* pos/wks

9 Nov 96	LIKE A PLAYA *Jive JIVECD 405*	75	1

L.A. GUNS *US, male / female vocal / instrumental group (4 WEEKS)* pos/wks

30 Nov 91	SOME LIE 4 LOVE *Mercury MER 358*	61	1
21 Dec 91	THE BALLAD OF JAYNE *Mercury MER 361*	53	3

LA MIX *UK, male / female vocal / instrumental duo (25 WEEKS)* pos/wks

10 Oct 87	DON'T STOP (JAMMIN') *Breakout USA 615*	47	4
21 May 88 ●	CHECK THIS OUT *Breakout USA 629*	6	7
8 Jul 89	GET LOOSE *Breakout USA 659* [1]	25	6
16 Sep 89	LOVE TOGETHER *Breakout USA 662* [2]	66	2
15 Sep 90	COMING BACK FOR MORE *A & M AM 579*	50	3
19 Jan 91	MYSTERIES OF LOVE *A & M AM 707*	46	2
23 Mar 91	WE SHOULDN'T HOLD HANDS IN THE DARK *A & M AM 755*	69	1

[1] LA Mix featuring Jazzi P [2] LA Mix featuring Kevin Henry

LA NA NEE NEE NOO NOO – *See BANANARAMA*

Danny LA RUE *UK, male vocalist (9 WEEKS)* pos/wks

18 Dec 68	ON MOTHER KELLY'S DOORSTEP *Page One POF 108*	33	9

LA TREC – *See SASH!*

LaBELLE *US, female vocal group – lead vocal Patti LaBelle (9 WEEKS)* pos/wks

22 Mar 75	LADY MARMALADE (VOULEZ-VOUS COUCHER AVEC MOI CE SOIR?) *Epic EPC 2852* ▲	17	9

See also Patti LaBELLE

Patti LaBELLE *US, female vocalist – Patricia Holt (21 WEEKS)* pos/wks

3 May 86 ●	ON MY OWN *MCA MCA 1045* [1] ▲	2	13
2 Aug 86	OH, PEOPLE *MCA MCA 1075*	26	6
3 Sep 94	THE RIGHT KINDA LOVER *MCA MCSTD 1995*	50	2

[1] Patti LaBelle and Michael McDonald

See also LaBELLE

LADIES CHOICE *UK, male vocal / instrumental group (4 WEEKS)* pos/wks

25 Jan 86	FUNKY SENSATION *Sure Delight SD 01*	41	4

LADIES FIRST *UK, female vocal trio (2 WEEKS)* pos/wks

24 Nov 01		MESSIN' *Polydor 5873422*	30	2

LADY G – *See B15 PROJECT featuring Crissy D and Lady G*

LADY J – *See RAZE*

LADY OF RAGE *US, female rapper (1 WEEK)* pos/wks

8 Oct 94		AFRO PUFFS *Interscope A 8288CD*	72	1

LADY SAW *Jamaica, female vocalist (3 WEEKS)* pos/wks

16 Dec 00		BUMP N GRIND (I AM FEELING HOT TONIGHT) *Telstar CDSTAS 3129* [1]	59	1
20 Oct 01		SINCE I MET YOU LADY / SPARKLE OF MY EYES *DEP International DEPD 55* [2]	40	2

[1] M Dubs featuring Lady Saw [2] UB40 featuring Lady Saw

LADYSMITH BLACK MAMBAZO
South Africa, male vocal group (26 WEEKS) pos/wks

3 Jun 95		SWING LOW SWEET CHARIOT *PolyGram TV SWLOW 2* [1]	15	6
3 Jun 95		WORLD IN UNION '95 *PolyGram TV RUGBY 2* [2]	47	5
15 Nov 97		INKANYEZI NEZAZI (THE STAR AND THE WISEMAN) *A & M 5823892*	33	3
11 Jul 98		THE STAR AND THE WISEMAN (re-issue) *AM:PM 5825692*	63	1
16 Oct 99		AIN'T NO SUNSHINE *Universal Music TV 1564332* [3]	42	2
18 Dec 99		I SHALL BE THERE *Glow Worm / Epic 6683332* [4]	13	9

[1] Ladysmith Black Mambazo featuring China Black [2] Ladysmith Black Mambazo featuring PJ Powers [3] Ladysmith Black Mambazo featuring Des'ree [4] B*Witched featuring Ladysmith Black Mambazo

LAGUNA *Italy, male DJ / production duo (2 WEEKS)* pos/wks

1 Nov 97		SPILLER FROM RIO (DO IT EASY) *Positiva CDTIV 83*	40	2

LAID BACK *Denmark, male vocal / instrumental duo (4 WEEKS)* pos/wks

5 May 90		BAKERMAN *Arista 112356*	44	4

LAIN – *See WOOKIE*

Cleo LAINE *UK, female vocalist – Clementina Campbell (14 WEEKS)* pos/wks

29 Dec 60		LET'S SLIP AWAY *Fontana H 269*	42	1
14 Sep 61	●	YOU'LL ANSWER TO ME *Fontana H 326*	5	13

Frankie LAINE (35 Top 500) *Powerful-voiced No.1 hitmaker of the pre-rock years, b. Frank Lovecchio, 30 Mar 1913, Chicago, US. He spent an unequalled 27 weeks at the top of the UK chart in 1953, including a record 18 by 'I Believe'. At one time he had three singles in the Top 5 (281 WEEKS)* pos/wks

14 Nov 52	●	HIGH NOON (DO NOT FORSAKE ME) *Columbia DB 3113*	7	7
14 Nov 52	●	SUGARBUSH *Columbia DB 3123* [1]	8	2
5 Dec 52	●	SUGARBUSH (re-entry) *Columbia DB 3123* [1]	8	6
20 Mar 53		THE GIRL IN THE WOOD *Columbia DB 2907*	11	1
3 Apr 53	★	I BELIEVE *Philips PB 117*	1	36
8 May 53	●	TELL ME A STORY *Philips PB 126* [2]	5	15
4 Sep 53	●	WHERE THE WINDS BLOW *Philips PB 167*	2	12
11 Sep 53		TELL ME A STORY (re-entry) *Philips PB 126* [2]	12	1
16 Oct 53	★	HEY JOE! *Philips PB 172*	1	8
30 Oct 53	★	ANSWER ME *Philips PB 196*	1	17
8 Jan 54	●	BLOWING WILD *Philips PB 207*	2	12
26 Mar 54	●	GRANADA *Philips PB 242*	10	1
9 Apr 54	●	GRANADA (re-entry) *Philips PB 242*	9	1
16 Apr 54	●	THE KID'S LAST FIGHT *Philips PB 258*	3	10
13 Aug 54	●	MY FRIEND *Philips PB 316*	3	15
8 Oct 54	●	THERE MUST BE A REASON *Philips PB 306*	9	9
22 Oct 54	●	RAIN, RAIN, RAIN *Philips PB 311* [3]	8	16
11 Mar 55		IN THE BEGINNING *Philips PB 404*	20	1
24 Jun 55	●	COOL WATER *Philips PB 465* [4]	2	22
15 Jul 55	●	STRANGE LADY IN TOWN *Philips PB 478*	6	13
11 Nov 55		HUMMING BIRD *Philips PB 498*	16	1
25 Nov 55	●	HAWK-EYE *Philips PB 519*	7	8
20 Jan 56	●	SIXTEEN TONS *Philips PB 539* [4]	10	3
4 May 56		HELL HATH NO FURY *Philips PB 585*	28	1
7 Sep 56	★	A WOMAN IN LOVE *Philips PB 617*	1	21
28 Dec 56		MOONLIGHT GAMBLER *Philips PB 638*	13	12
29 Mar 57		MOONLIGHT GAMBLER (re-entry) *Philips PB 638*	28	1
26 Apr 57		LOVE IS A GOLDEN RING *Philips PB 676* [5]	19	5
4 Oct 57		GOOD EVENING FRIENDS / UP ABOVE MY HEAD, I HEAR MUSIC IN THE AIR *Philips PB 708* [6]	25	4
13 Nov 59	●	RAWHIDE *Philips PB 965*	6	17
31 Mar 60		RAWHIDE (re-entry) *Philips PB 965*	41	2
11 May 61		GUNSLINGER *Philips PB 1135*	50	1

[1] Doris Day and Frankie Laine [2] Jimmy Boyd - Frankie Laine [3] Frankie Laine and the Four Lads [4] Frankie Laine with the Mellomen [5] Frankie Laine and the Easy Riders [6] Frankie Laine and Johnnie Ray

Greg LAKE *UK, male vocalist (12 WEEKS)* pos/wks

6 Dec 75	●	I BELIEVE IN FATHER CHRISTMAS *Manticore K 13511*	2	7
25 Dec 82		I BELIEVE IN FATHER CHRISTMAS (re-entry) *Manticore K 13511*	72	3
24 Dec 83		I BELIEVE IN FATHER CHRISTMAS (2nd re-entry) *Manticore K 13511*	65	2

See also EMERSON, LAKE and PALMER

LAMB *UK, male / female vocal / production duo (4 WEEKS)* pos/wks

29 Mar 97		GORECKI *Fontana LAMCD 4*	30	2
3 Apr 99		B LINE *Fontana LAMCD 5*	52	1
22 May 99		ALL IN YOUR HANDS *Fontana LAMCD 6*	71	1

Annabel LAMB *UK, female vocalist (7 WEEKS)* pos/wks

27 Aug 83		RIDERS ON THE STORM *A & M AM 131*	27	7

LAMBCHOP *US, male / female vocal / instrumental group (1 WEEK)* pos/wks

20 May 00		UP WITH PEOPLE *City Slang 201592*	66	1

LAMBRETTAS *UK, male vocal / instrumental group (24 WEEKS)* pos/wks

1 Mar 80	●	POISON IVY *Rocket XPRESS 25*	7	12
24 May 80		D-A-A-ANCE *Rocket XPRESS 33*	12	8
23 Aug 80		ANOTHER DAY (ANOTHER GIRL) *Rocket XPRESS 36*	49	4

LAMPIES *US, male / female / canine cartoon vocal group (2 WEEKS)* pos/wks

22 Dec 01		LIGHT UP THE WORLD FOR CHRISTMAS *Bluecrest LAMPCD 001*	48	2+

LANCASTRIANS *UK, male vocal / instrumental group (2 WEEKS)* pos/wks

24 Dec 64		WE'LL SING IN THE SUNSHINE *Pye 7N 15732*	44	2

Major LANCE *US, male vocalist (2 WEEKS)* pos/wks

13 Feb 64		UM, UM, UM, UM, UM, UM *Columbia DB 7205*	40	2

LANCERS – *See Teresa BREWER*

Valerie LANDSBERG – *See KIDS FROM 'FAME'*

LANDSCAPE *UK, male vocal / instrumental group (20 WEEKS)* pos/wks

28 Feb 81	●	EINSTEIN A GO-GO *RCA 22*	5	13
23 May 81		NORMAN BATES *RCA 60*	40	7

Desmond LANE – *See Alma COGAN; Cyril STAPLETON and his Orchestra*

Ronnie LANE and SLIM CHANCE
UK, male vocalist and male instrumental group (12 WEEKS) pos/wks

12 Jan 74		HOW COME *GM GMS 011*	11	8
15 Jun 74		THE POACHER *GM GMS 024*	36	4

See also SMALL FACES

UK No.1 ★ UK Top 10 ● Still on chart + UK million seller ◆ UK entry at No.1 ■ US No.1 ▲

Don LANG *UK, male vocalist – Gordon Langhorn (18 WEEKS)* pos/wks

4 Nov 55		CLOUDBURST *HMV POP 115*	16	2
2 Dec 55		CLOUDBURST (re-entry) *HMV POP 115*	18	1
13 Jan 56		CLOUDBURST (2nd re-entry) *HMV POP 115*	20	1
5 Jul 57		SCHOOL DAY (RING! RING! GOES THE BELL) *HMV POP 350* [1]	26	2
23 May 58	●	WITCH DOCTOR *HMV POP 488* [1]	5	11
10 Mar 60		SINK THE BISMARCK *HMV POP 714*	43	1

[1] Don Lang and his Frantic Five

kd lang *Canada, female vocalist (25 WEEKS)* pos/wks

16 May 92		CONSTANT CRAVING *Sire W 0100*	52	4
22 Aug 92		CRYING *Virgin America VUS 63* [1]	13	6
27 Feb 93		CONSTANT CRAVING (re-issue) *Sire W 0157CD*	15	8
1 May 93		THE MIND OF LOVE *Sire W 0170CD1*	72	1
26 Jun 93		MISS CHATELAINE *Sire W 0181CDX*	68	2
11 Dec 93		JUST KEEP ME MOVING *Sire W 0227CD*	59	1
30 Sep 95		IF I WERE YOU *Sire W 0319CD*	53	1
18 May 96		YOU'RE OK *Warner Bros. W 0332CD*	44	2

[1] Roy Orbison (duet with kd lang)

Thomas LANG *UK, male vocalist (3 WEEKS)* pos/wks

30 Jan 88		THE HAPPY MAN *Epic VOW 4*	67	3

LANGE featuring Sarah DWYER
UK, male producer – Stuart Langelann and female vocalist (1 WEEK) pos/wks

19 Jun 99		I BELIEVE *Additive 12 AD039*	68	1

LANTERNS *UK, male / female vocal / instrumental trio (1 WEEK)* pos/wks

6 Feb 99		HIGHRISE TOWN *Columbia 6665712*	50	1

Mario LANZA *US, male vocalist – Alfredo Cocozza (32 WEEKS)* pos/wks

14 Nov 52	●	BECAUSE YOU'RE MINE *HMV DA 2017*	3	24
4 Feb 55		DRINKING SONG *HMV DA 2065*	13	1
18 Feb 55		I'LL WALK WITH GOD *HMV DA 2062*	18	1
22 Apr 55		SERENADE *HMV DA 2065*	19	1
6 May 55		I'LL WALK WITH GOD (re-entry) *HMV DA 2062*	20	1
6 May 55		SERENADE (re-entry) *HMV DA 2065*	15	2
14 Sep 56		SERENADE *HMV DA 2085*	25	1
12 Oct 56		SERENADE (re-entry) *HMV DA 2085*	29	1

DA 2065 and DA 2085 are two different songs

LAPTOP *US, male vocalist / instrumentalist – Jesse Hartman (1 WEEK)* pos/wks

12 Jun 99		NOTHING TO DECLARE *Island CID 744*	74	1

Julius LAROSA *US, male vocalist (9 WEEKS)* pos/wks

4 Jul 58		TORERO *RCA 1063*	15	9

LA's *UK, male vocal / instrumental group (20 WEEKS)* pos/wks

14 Jan 89		THERE SHE GOES *Go! Discs GOLASEP 2*	59	4
15 Sep 90		TIMELESS MELODY *Go! Discs GOLAS 4*	57	2
3 Nov 90		THERE SHE GOES (re-issue) *Go! Discs GOLAS 5*	13	9
16 Feb 91		FEELIN' *Go! Discs GOLAS 6*	43	3
10 May 97		FEVER PITCH THE EP *Blanco Y Negro NEG 104CD* [1]	65	1
2 Oct 99		THERE SHE GOES (2nd re-issue) *Polydor 5614032*	65	1

[1] Pretenders, La's, Orlando, Neil MacColl, Nick Hornby

Tracks on Fever Pitch the EP: Goin' Back - Pretenders / There She Goes - La's / How Can We Hang On To A Dream - Orlando / Football - Neil MacColl / Boo Hewerdine - Nick Hornby

Denise LASALLE *US, female vocalist – Denise Craig (13 WEEKS)* pos/wks

15 Jun 85	●	MY TOOT TOOT *Epic A 6334*	6	13

Lisa LASHES *UK, female DJ / producer (1 WEEK)* pos/wks

8 Jul 00		UNBELIEVABLE *Tidy Trax TIDY 138CD*	63	1

James LAST BAND *Germany, male orchestra (4 WEEKS)* pos/wks

3 May 80		THE SEDUCTION (LOVE THEME) *Polydor PD 2071*	48	4

LAST RHYTHM *Italy, male instrumental / production group (1 WEEK)* pos/wks

14 Sep 96		LAST RHYTHM *Stress CDSTR 76*	62	1

LATANZA WATERS – *See E-SMOOVE featuring Latanza WATERS*

LATE SHOW *UK, male vocal / instrumental group (6 WEEKS)* pos/wks

3 Mar 79		BRISTOL STOMP *Decca F 13822*	40	6

LATIN QUARTER
UK, male / female vocal / instrumental group (10 WEEKS) pos/wks

18 Jan 86		RADIO AFRICA *Rockin' Horse RH 102*	19	9
18 Apr 87		NOMZAMO (ONE PEOPLE ONE CAUSE) *Rockin' Horse RH 113*	73	1

LATIN RHYTHM – *See Tito PUENTE Jr and the LATIN RHYTHM featuring Tito PUENTE, INDIA and Cali ALEMAN*

LATIN THING
Canada / Spain, male / female vocal / instrumental group (1 WEEK) pos/wks

13 Jul 96		LATIN THING *Faze 2 CDFAZE 33*	41	1

Gino LATINO *Italy, male producer – Lorenzo Cherubini (7 WEEKS)* pos/wks

20 Jan 90		WELCOME *ffrr F 126*	17	7

LATINO RAVE – *See VARIOUS ARTISTS (MONTAGES)*

LATOUR *US, male vocalist / producer – William LaTour (7 WEEKS)* pos/wks

8 Jun 91		PEOPLE ARE STILL HAVING SEX *Polydor PO 147*	15	7

Stacy LATTISAW *US, female vocalist (14 WEEKS)* pos/wks

14 Jun 80	●	JUMP TO THE BEAT *Atlantic / Cotillion K 11496*	3	11
30 Aug 80		DYNAMITE *Atlantic K 11554*	51	3

Dave LAUDAT – *See HUSTLERS CONVENTION featuring Dave LAUDAT and Ondrea DUVERNEY*

LAUNCHERS – *See Ezz RECO and the LAUNCHERS with Boysie GRANT*

Cyndi LAUPER (293 Top 500) *Flamboyant and versatile singer / songwriter, b. 20 Jun 1953, New York, US. Her debut album, 'She's So Unusual' (1983), spawned four Top 5 US singles, and she won a Grammy for Best New Artist of 1984 (easily outpacing her major female rival, Madonna) (103 WEEKS)* pos/wks

14 Jan 84	●	GIRLS JUST WANT TO HAVE FUN *Portrait A 3943*	2	12
24 Mar 84		TIME AFTER TIME *Portrait A 4290* ▲	54	4
16 Jun 84	●	TIME AFTER TIME (re-entry) *Portrait A 4290*	3	13
1 Sep 84		SHE BOP *Portrait A 4620*	46	5
17 Nov 84		ALL THROUGH THE NIGHT *Portrait A 4849*	64	2
20 Sep 86		TRUE COLOURS *Portrait 650026 7* ▲	12	11
27 Dec 86		CHANGE OF HEART *Portrait CYNDI 1*	74	1
10 Jan 87		CHANGE OF HEART (re-entry) *Portrait CYNDI 1*	67	1
28 Mar 87		WHAT'S GOING ON *Portrait CYN 1*	57	3
20 May 89	●	I DROVE ALL NIGHT *Epic CYN 4*	7	12
5 Aug 89		MY FIRST NIGHT WITHOUT YOU *Epic CYN 5*	53	4
30 Dec 89		HEADING WEST *Epic CYN 6*	68	1
6 Jun 92		THE WORLD IS STONE *Epic 6579707*	15	7
13 Nov 93		THAT'S WHAT I THINK *Epic 6598782*	31	4
8 Jan 94		WHO LET IN THE RAIN *Epic 6590392*	32	4
17 Sep 94	●	HEY NOW (GIRLS JUST WANT TO HAVE FUN) *Epic 6608072*	4	13
11 Feb 95		I'M GONNA BE STRONG *Epic 6611962*	37	2
26 Aug 95		COME ON HOME *Epic 6614255*	39	2
1 Feb 97		YOU DON'T KNOW *Epic 6641845*	27	2

'Hey Now (Girls Just Want to Have Fun)' is a re-recording of her first hit

LAUREL and HARDY *UK, male vocal / instrumental duo (2 WEEKS)* pos/wks

2 Apr 83	**CLUNK CLINK** *CBS A 3213*	65	2

LAUREL and HARDY with the AVALON BOYS featuring Chill WILLS *UK / US, male vocal duo – Stan Laurel and Oliver Hardy with male vocal group (10 WEEKS)* pos/wks

22 Nov 75 ●	**THE TRAIL OF THE LONESOME PINE** *United Artists UP 36026*	2	10

LAURNEA *US, female vocalist (2 WEEKS)* pos/wks

12 Jul 97	**DAYS OF YOUTH** *Epic 6646932*	36	2

Lauren LAVERNE – *See KENICKIE; MINT ROYALE*

Joanna LAW *UK, female vocalist (8 WEEKS)* pos/wks

7 Jul 90	**FIRST TIME EVER** *Citybeat CBE 752*	67	3
14 Sep 96	**THE GIFT** *Deconstruction 74321401912* [1]	15	5

[1] Way Out West featuring Miss Joanna Law

Law's contribution to 'The Gift' is a sample from 'First Time Ever'

Steve LAWLER *UK, male DJ / producer (1 WEEK)* pos/wks

11 Nov 00	**RISE 'IN** *Bedrock BEDRCDS 008*	50	1

Billy LAWRENCE – *See RAMPAGE featuring Billy LAWRENCE*

Joey LAWRENCE *US, male vocalist (15 WEEKS)* pos/wks

26 Jun 93	**NOTHIN' MY LOVE CAN'T FIX** *EMI CDEM 271*	13	7
28 Aug 93	**I CAN'T HELP MYSELF** *EMI CDEM 277*	27	4
30 Oct 93	**STAY FOREVER** *EMI CDEM 289*	41	3
19 Sep 98	**NEVER GONNA CHANGE MY MIND** *Curb CUBC 34*	49	1

Lee LAWRENCE *UK, male vocalist – Leon Siroto (10 WEEKS)* pos/wks

20 Nov 53	**CRYING IN THE CHAPEL** *Decca F 10177*	11	1
11 Dec 53 ●	**CRYING IN THE CHAPEL (re-entry)** *Decca F 10177*	7	5
2 Dec 55	**SUDDENLY THERE'S A VALLEY** *Columbia DB 3681*	19	1
16 Dec 55	**SUDDENLY THERE'S A VALLEY (re-entry)** *Columbia DB 3681*	14	3

Both with Ray Martin and his Orchestra

Sophie LAWRENCE *UK, female vocalist (7 WEEKS)* pos/wks

3 Aug 91	**LOVE'S UNKIND** *IQ ZB 44821*	21	7

Steve LAWRENCE *US, male vocalist – Sidney Leibowitz (27 WEEKS)* pos/wks

21 Apr 60 ●	**FOOTSTEPS** *HMV POP 726*	4	13
18 Aug 60	**GIRLS, GIRLS, GIRLS** *London HLT 9166*	49	1
22 Aug 63 ●	**I WANT TO STAY HERE** *CBS AAG 163* [1]	3	13

[1] Steve and Eydie

Lindy LAYTON *UK, female vocalist (28 WEEKS)* pos/wks

10 Feb 90 ★	**DUB BE GOOD TO ME** *Go. Beat GOD 39* [1]	1	13
11 Aug 90	**SILLY GAMES** *Arista 113452* [2]	22	7
26 Jan 91	**ECHO MY HEART** *Arista 113845*	42	2
31 Aug 91	**WITHOUT YOU (ONE AND ONE)** *Arista 114636*	71	2
24 Apr 93	**WE GOT THE LOVE** *PWL International PWCD 250*	38	3
30 Oct 93	**SHOW ME** *PWL International PWCD 275*	47	1

[1] Beats International featuring Lindy Layton [2] Lindy Layton featuring Janet Kay

Peter LAZONBY *UK, male DJ / producer (1 WEEK)* pos/wks

10 Jun 00	**SACRED CYCLES** *Hooj Choons HOOJ 93CD*	49	1

Doug LAZY *US, male rapper (9 WEEKS)* pos/wks

15 Jul 89	**LET IT ROLL** *Atlantic A 8866* [1]	27	5
4 Nov 89	**LET THE RHYTHM PUMP** *Atlantic A 8784*	45	3
26 May 90	**LET THE RHYTHM PUMP (re-mix)** *East West A 7919*	63	1

[1] Raze presents Doug Lazy

LCD *UK, male production group (9 WEEKS)* pos/wks

27 Jun 98	**ZORBA'S DANCE** *Virgin VSCDT 1693*	20	5
9 Oct 99	**ZORBA'S DANCE (re-issue)** *Virgin VSCDT 1757*	22	4

Keith LE BLANC – *See Malcolm X*

LE CLICK *Sweden / US, male / female vocal duo (2 WEEKS)* pos/wks

30 Aug 97	**CALL ME** *Logic 74321509672*	38	2

Kele LE ROC *UK, female vocalist – Kelly Biggs (15 WEEKS)* pos/wks

31 Oct 98 ●	**LITTLE BIT OF LOVIN'** *1st Avenue / Wild Card / Polydor 5672812*	8	7
27 Mar 99 ●	**MY LOVE** *1st Avenue / Wild Card / Polydor 5636112*	8	7
30 Sep 00	**THINKING OF YOU** *Telstar CDSTAS 3136* [1]	70	1

[1] Curtis Lynch Jr featuring Kele Le Roc and Red Rat

Vicky LEANDROS *Greece, female vocalist (29 WEEKS)* pos/wks

8 Apr 72 ●	**COME WHAT MAY** *Philips 6000 049*	2	16
23 Dec 72	**THE LOVE IN YOUR EYES** *Philips 6000 081*	48	3
20 Jan 73	**THE LOVE IN YOUR EYES (re-entry)** *Philips 6000 081*	40	4
7 Apr 73	**THE LOVE IN YOUR EYES (2nd re-entry)** *Philips 6000 081*	46	1
7 Jul 73	**WHEN BOUZOUKIS PLAYED** *Philips 6000 111*	44	2
28 Jul 73	**WHEN BOUZOUKIS PLAYED (re-entry)** *Philips 6000 111*	45	3

Denis LEARY *US, male vocalist (2 WEEKS)* pos/wks

13 Jan 96	**ASSHOLE** *A & M 5813352*	58	2

LED ZEPPELIN *UK, male vocal / instrumental group (2 WEEKS)* pos/wks

13 Sep 97	**WHOLE LOTTA LOVE** *Atlantic AT700 13CD*	21	2

See also Robert PLANT

Angel LEE *UK, female vocalist (1 WEEK)* pos/wks

3 Jun 00	**WHAT'S YOUR NAME?** *WEA WEA 258CD*	39	1

Ann LEE *UK, female vocalist – Annerley Gordon (21 WEEKS)* pos/wks

11 Sep 99	**2 TIMES (import)** *ZYX ZYX 90188*	57	2
16 Oct 99 ●	**2 TIMES** *Systematic SYSCD 31*	2	16
4 Mar 00	**VOICES** *Systematic SYSCD 32*	27	3

Brenda LEE (79 Top 500) *Biggest-selling teenage female vocalist of the early rock years; b. Brenda Tarpley, 11 Dec 1944, Georgia, US. 'Little Miss Dynamite', who first recorded aged 11, had back-to-back UK / US hits in the early 1960s. She was inducted into the Country Music Hall of Fame in 1997 (210 WEEKS)* pos/wks

17 Mar 60	**SWEET NUTHIN'S** *Brunswick 05819*	45	1
7 Apr 60 ●	**SWEET NUTHIN'S (re-entry)** *Brunswick 05819*	4	18
30 Jun 60	**I'M SORRY** *Brunswick 05833* ▲	12	16
20 Oct 60	**I WANT TO BE WANTED** *Brunswick 05839* ▲	31	6
19 Jan 61	**LET'S JUMP THE BROOMSTICK** *Brunswick 05823*	12	15
6 Apr 61	**EMOTIONS** *Brunswick 05847*	45	1
20 Jul 61	**DUM DUM** *Brunswick 05854*	22	8
16 Nov 61	**FOOL NUMBER ONE** *Brunswick 05860*	38	3
8 Feb 62	**BREAK IT TO ME GENTLY** *Brunswick 05864*	46	2
5 Apr 62 ●	**SPEAK TO ME PRETTY** *Brunswick 05867*	3	12
21 Jun 62 ●	**HERE COMES THAT FEELING** *Brunswick 05871*	5	12
13 Sep 62	**IT STARTED ALL OVER AGAIN** *Brunswick 05876*	15	11
29 Nov 62 ●	**ROCKIN' AROUND THE CHRISTMAS TREE** *Brunswick 05880*	6	7
17 Jan 63 ●	**ALL ALONE AM I** *Brunswick 05882*	7	17
28 Mar 63 ●	**LOSING YOU** *Brunswick 05886*	10	16
18 Jul 63	**I WONDER** *Brunswick 05891*	14	9
31 Oct 63	**SWEET IMPOSSIBLE YOU** *Brunswick 05896*	28	6
9 Jan 64 ●	**AS USUAL** *Brunswick 05899*	5	15
9 Apr 64	**THINK** *Brunswick 05903*	26	8
10 Sep 64	**IS IT TRUE** *Brunswick 05915*	17	8
10 Dec 64	**CHRISTMAS WILL BE JUST ANOTHER LONELY DAY** *Brunswick 05921*	25	5

UK No.1 ★ UK Top 10 ● Still on chart + UK million seller ◆ UK entry at No.1 ■ US No.1 ▲

4 Feb 65	**THANKS A LOT** *Brunswick 05927*	41	2
29 Jul 65	**TOO MANY RIVERS** *Brunswick 05936*	22	12

Byron LEE – *See Boris GARDINER*

Curtis LEE *US, male vocalist (2 WEEKS)*

		pos	wks
31 Aug 61	**PRETTY LITTLE ANGEL EYES** *London HLX 9397*	47	1
14 Sep 61	**PRETTY LITTLE ANGEL EYES (re-entry)** *London HLX 9397*	48	1

Dave LEE – *See Joey NEGRO; JAKATTA; HED BOYS; AKABU featuring Linda CLIFFORD; Li KWAN; RAVEN MAIZE*

Dee C LEE *UK, female vocalist – Diane Sealey (20 WEEKS)*

		pos	wks
9 Nov 85 ●	**SEE THE DAY** *CBS A 6570*	3	12
8 Mar 86	**COME HELL OR WATERS HIGH** *CBS A 6869*	46	5
13 Nov 93	**NO TIME TO PLAY** *Cooltempo CDCOOL 282* [1]	25	3

[1] Guru featuring Dee C Lee

See also STYLE COUNCIL

Garry LEE and SHOWDOWN *Canada, male vocal / instrumental group (3 WEEKS)*

		pos	wks
31 Jul 93	**THE RODEO SONG** *Party Dish VCD 101*	44	3

Jackie LEE *UK, female vocalist – Jackie Hopkins (31 WEEKS)*

		pos	wks
10 Apr 68 ●	**WHITE HORSES** *Philips BF 1647* [1]	10	14
2 Jan 71	**RUPERT** *Pye 7N 45003*	14	17

[1] Jacky

Leapy LEE *UK, male vocalist – Lee Graham (28 WEEKS)*

		pos	wks
21 Aug 68 ●	**LITTLE ARROWS** *MCA MU 1028*	2	21
20 Dec 69	**GOOD MORNING** *MCA MK 5021*	47	1
10 Jan 70	**GOOD MORNING (re-entry)** *MCA MK 5021*	29	6

Peggy LEE *US, female vocalist – Norma Jean Egstrom (29 WEEKS)*

		pos	wks
24 May 57 ●	**MR. WONDERFUL** *Brunswick 05671*	5	13
15 Aug 58 ●	**FEVER** *Capitol CL 14902*	5	11
23 Mar 61	**TILL THERE WAS YOU** *Capitol CL 15184*	40	1
6 Apr 61	**TILL THERE WAS YOU (re-entry)** *Capitol CL 15184*	30	3
22 Aug 92	**FEVER (re-issue)** *Capitol PEG 1*	75	1

Toney LEE *US, male vocalist (4 WEEKS)*

		pos	wks
29 Jan 83	**REACH UP** *TMT TMT 2*	64	4

Tracey LEE *US, male vocalist (1 WEEK)*

		pos	wks
19 Jul 97	**THE THEME** *Universal UND 56133*	51	1

LEE-O – *See K-WARREN featuring LEE-O*

LEEDS UNITED FC *UK, male football team vocalists (13 WEEKS)*

		pos	wks
29 Apr 72 ●	**LEEDS UNITED** *Chapter One SCH 168*	10	10
25 Apr 92	**LEEDS LEEDS LEEDS** *Q Music LUFC 2*	61	1
9 May 92	**LEEDS LEEDS LEEDS (re-entry)** *Q Music LUFC 2*	54	2

Carol LEEMING – *See STAXX featuring Carol LEEMING*

Raymond LEFEVRE *France, orchestra (2 WEEKS)*

		pos	wks
15 May 68	**SOUL COAXING** *Major Minor MM 559*	46	2

LEFTFIELD *UK, male instrumental / production duo – Neil Barnes and Paul Daley (23 WEEKS)*

		pos	wks
12 Dec 92	**SONG OF LIFE** *Hard Hands HAND 002T*	59	1
13 Nov 93	**OPEN UP** *Hard Hands HAND 009CD* [1]	13	5
25 Mar 95	**ORIGINAL** *Hard Hands HAND 18CD* [2]	18	3
5 Aug 95	**THE AFRO-LEFT EP** *Hard Hands HAND 23CD* [3]	22	3
20 Jan 96	**RELEASE THE PRESSURE** *Hard Hands HAND 29CD*	13	3
18 Sep 99 ●	**AFRIKA SHOX** *Hard Hands HAND 057CD1* [4]	7	5
11 Dec 99	**DUSTED** *Hard Hands HAND 058CD1* [5]	28	2
22 Jan 00	**DUSTED (re-entry)** *Hard Hands HAND 058CD1* [5]	75	1

[1] Leftfield Lydon [2] Leftfield Halliday [3] Leftfield featuring Djum Djum [4] Leftfield / Bambaataa [5] Leftfield / Roots Manuva

Tracks on The Afro-Left EP: Afro-Left / Afro Ride / Afro Central / Afro Sol

LEGEND B *Germany, male production duo (1 WEEK)*

		pos	wks
22 Feb 97	**LOST IN LOVE** *Perfecto PERF 132CD*	45	1

LEILANI *UK, female vocalist – Leilani Sen (7 WEEKS)*

		pos	wks
6 Feb 99	**MADNESS THING** *ZTT ZTT 124CD*	19	4
12 Jun 99	**DO YOU WANT ME?** *ZTT ZTT 134CD*	40	2
3 Jun 00	**FLYING ELVIS** *ZTT ZTT 145CD*	73	1

Paul LEKAKIS *US, male vocalist (4 WEEKS)*

		pos	wks
30 May 87	**BOOM BOOM (LET'S GO BACK TO MY ROOM)** *Champion CHAMP 43*	60	4

LEMON PIPERS *US, male vocal / instrumental group (16 WEEKS)*

		pos	wks
7 Feb 68 ●	**GREEN TAMBOURINE** *Pye International 7N 25444* ▲	7	11
1 May 68	**RICE IS NICE** *Pye International 7N 25454*	41	5

LEMON TREES *UK, male vocal / instrumental group (9 WEEKS)*

		pos	wks
26 Sep 92	**LOVE IS IN YOUR EYES** *Oxygen GASP 1*	75	1
7 Nov 92	**THE WAY I FEEL** *Oxygen GASP 2*	62	2
13 Feb 93	**LET IT LOOSE** *Oxygen GASPD 3*	55	2
17 Apr 93	**CHILD OF LOVE** *Oxygen GASPD 4*	55	3
3 Jul 93	**I CAN'T FACE THE WORLD** *Oxygen GASPD 6*	52	1

LEMONHEADS *US / Australia, male vocal / instrumental group – lead vocal Evan Dando (26 WEEKS)*

		pos	wks
17 Oct 92	**IT'S A SHAME ABOUT RAY** *Atlantic A 7423*	70	1
5 Dec 92	**MRS ROBINSON / BEIN' AROUND** *Atlantic A 7401*	19	9
6 Feb 93	**CONFETTI / MY DRUG BUDDY** *Atlantic A 7430CD*	44	2
10 Apr 93	**IT'S A SHAME ABOUT RAY (re-issue)** *Atlantic A 5764CD*	31	3
16 Oct 93	**INTO YOUR ARMS** *Atlantic A 7302CD*	14	4
27 Nov 93	**IT'S ABOUT TIME** *Atlantic A 7296CD*	57	2
14 May 94	**BIG GAY HEART** *Atlantic A 7259CD*	55	2
28 Sep 96	**IF I COULD TALK I'D TELL YOU** *Atlantic A 5561CD*	39	2
14 Dec 96	**IT'S ALL TRUE** *Atlantic A 5635CD*	61	1

LEN *Canada, male / female DJ / vocal group (15 WEEKS)*

		pos	wks
18 Dec 99 ●	**STEAL MY SUNSHINE** *Columbia 6685062*	8	13
10 Jun 00	**CRYPTIK SOULS CREW** *Columbia 6693832*	28	2

LENA – *See Lena FIAGBE*

John LENNON (93 Top 500) *One of the century's greatest musical talents, b. 9 Oct 1940, Liverpool, d. 8 Dec 1980. World-famous singer / songwriter who, together with Paul McCartney, fronted The Beatles and penned their hits. Three of his singles topped the UK chart in the two months after his murder in New York (197 WEEKS)*

		pos	wks
9 Jul 69 ●	**GIVE PEACE A CHANCE** *Apple 13* [1]	2	13
1 Nov 69	**COLD TURKEY** *Apple APPLES 1001* [1]	14	8
21 Feb 70 ●	**INSTANT KARMA** *Apple APPLES 1003* [2]	5	9
20 Mar 71 ●	**POWER TO THE PEOPLE** *Apple R 5892* [3]	7	9
9 Dec 72 ●	**HAPPY XMAS (WAR IS OVER)** *Apple R 5970* [4]	4	8
24 Nov 73	**MIND GAMES** *Apple R 5994*	26	9
19 Oct 74	**WHATEVER GETS YOU THROUGH THE NIGHT** *Apple R 5998* [5] ▲	36	4
4 Jan 75	**HAPPY XMAS (WAR IS OVER) (re-entry)** *Apple R 5970* [4]	48	1
8 Feb 75	**#9 DREAM** *Apple R 6003*	23	8
3 May 75	**STAND BY ME** *Apple R 6005*	30	7
1 Nov 75 ●	**IMAGINE** *Apple R 6009*	6	11
8 Nov 80 ★	**(JUST LIKE) STARTING OVER** *Geffen K 79186* ▲	1	15
20 Dec 80 ●	**HAPPY XMAS (WAR IS OVER) (2nd re-entry)** *Apple R 5970* [4]	2	9
27 Dec 80 ★	**IMAGINE (re-entry)** *Apple R 6009* ◆	1	13
24 Jan 81	**GIVE PEACE A CHANCE (re-entry)** *Apple 13* [1]	33	5

			pos	wks
24 Jan 81	★	**WOMAN** *Geffen K 79195*	1	11
21 Mar 81		**I SAW HER STANDING THERE** *DJM DJS 10965* [6]	40	4
4 Apr 81		**WATCHING THE WHEELS** *Geffen K 79207*	30	6
19 Dec 81		**HAPPY XMAS (WAR IS OVER) (3rd re-entry)** *Apple R 5970* [4]	28	5
20 Nov 82		**LOVE** *Parlophone R 6059*	41	7
25 Dec 82		**HAPPY XMAS (WAR IS OVER) (4th re-entry)** *Apple R 5970* [4]	56	3
21 Jan 84	●	**NOBODY TOLD ME** *Ono Music / Polydor POSP 700*	6	6
17 Mar 84		**BORROWED TIME** *Polydor POSP 701*	32	6
30 Nov 85		**JEALOUS GUY** *Parlophone R 6117*	65	2
10 Dec 88		**IMAGINE / JEALOUS GUY / HAPPY XMAS (WAR IS OVER) (re-issue)** *Parlophone R 6199*	45	5
25 Dec 99	●	**IMAGINE (re-issue)** *Parlophone CDR 6534*	3	11
18 Mar 00		**IMAGINE (re-entry of re-issue)** *Parlophone CDR 6534*	42	2

[1] Plastic Ono Band [2] Lennon, Ono and the Plastic Ono Band [3] John Lennon / Plastic Ono Band [4] John and Yoko and the Plastic Ono Band with the Harlem Community Choir [5] John Lennon with the Plastic Ono Nuclear Band [6] Elton John Band featuring John Lennon and the Muscle Shoals Horns

See also BEATLES

Julian LENNON *UK, male vocalist (47 WEEKS)*

			pos	wks
6 Oct 84	●	**TOO LATE FOR GOODBYES** *Charisma JL 1*	6	11
15 Dec 84		**VALOTTE** *Charisma JL 2*	55	6
9 Mar 85		**SAY YOU'RE WRONG** *Charisma JL 3*	75	1
7 Dec 85		**BECAUSE** *EMI 5538*	40	7
11 Mar 89		**NOW YOU'RE IN HEAVEN** *Virgin VS 1154*	59	3
24 Aug 91	●	**SALTWATER** *Virgin VS 1361*	6	13
30 Nov 91		**HELP YOURSELF** *Virgin VS 1379*	53	2
25 Apr 92		**GET A LIFE** *Virgin VS 1398*	56	3
23 May 98		**DAY AFTER DAY** *Music From Another JULIAN 4CD*	66	1

Annie LENNOX *UK, female songwriter / vocalist (68 WEEKS)*

			pos	wks
3 Dec 88		**PUT A LITTLE LOVE IN YOUR HEART** *A & M AM 484* [1]	28	8
28 Mar 92	●	**WHY** *RCA PB 45317*	5	8
6 Jun 92		**PRECIOUS** *RCA 74321100257*	23	5
22 Aug 92	●	**WALKING ON BROKEN GLASS** *RCA 74321107227*	8	8
31 Oct 92		**COLD** *RCA 74321116902*	26	4
13 Feb 93	●	**LITTLE BIRD / LOVE SONG FOR A VAMPIRE** *RCA 74321133832*	3	12
18 Feb 95	●	**NO MORE 'I LOVE YOU'S** *RCA 74321257162*	2	12
10 Jun 95		**A WHITER SHADE OF PALE** *RCA 74321284822*	16	6
30 Sep 95		**WAITING IN VAIN** *RCA 74321316132*	31	3
9 Dec 95		**SOMETHING SO RIGHT** *RCA 74321332392* [2]	44	2

[1] Annie Lennox and Al Green [2] Annie Lennox featuring Paul Simon

See also EURYTHMICS

Rula LENSKA – *See Julie COVINGTON, Rula LENSKA, Charlotte CORNWELL and Sue JONES-DAVIES*

Phillip LEO *UK, male vocalist (3 WEEKS)*

			pos	wks
23 Jul 94		**SECOND CHANCE** *EMI CDEM 327*	57	2
25 Mar 95		**THINKING ABOUT YOUR LOVE** *EMI CDEM 358*	64	1

LES RYTHMES DIGITALES
UK, male DJ / producer – Jacques Lu Cont (Stuart Price) (3 WEEKS)

			pos	wks
25 Apr 98		**MUSIC MAKES YOU LOSE CONTROL** *Wall of Sound WALLD 037*	69	1
7 Aug 99		**SOMETIMES** *Wall of Sound WALLD 054* [1]	56	1
30 Oct 99		**JACQUES YOUR BODY (MAKE ME SWEAT)** *Wall of Sound WALLD 060*	60	1

[1] Les Rythmes Digitales featuring Nik Kershaw

LeSHAUN – *See LL COOL J*

LESS THAN JAKE *US, male vocal / instrumental group (2 WEEKS)*

			pos	wks
5 Aug 00		**ALL MY BEST FRIENDS ARE METALHEADS** *Golf CDSHOLE 027*	51	1
8 Sep 01		**GAINESVILLE ROCK CITY** *Golf CDSHOLE 48*	57	1

LESTER – *See Norman COOK*

Ketty LESTER *US, female vocalist – Revoyda Frierson (16 WEEKS)*

			pos	wks
19 Apr 62	●	**LOVE LETTERS** *London HLN 9527*	4	12
19 Jul 62		**BUT NOT FOR ME** *London HLN 9574*	45	4

LET LOOSE *UK, male vocal / instrumental group (62 WEEKS)*

			pos	wks
24 Apr 93		**CRAZY FOR YOU** *Vertigo VERCD 74*	44	3
9 Apr 94		**SEVENTEEN** *Mercury MERCD 400*	44	2
25 Jun 94	●	**CRAZY FOR YOU (re-issue)** *Mercury MERCD 402*	2	20
22 Oct 94		**SEVENTEEN (re-mix)** *Mercury MERCD 406*	11	6
24 Dec 94		**CRAZY FOR YOU (re-entry of re-issue)** *Mercury MERCD 402*	46	4
7 Jan 95		**SEVENTEEN (re-entry of re-mix)** *Mercury MERCD 406*	47	3
28 Jan 95		**ONE NIGHT STAND** *Mercury MERCD 419*	12	6
29 Apr 95	●	**BEST IN ME** *Mercury MERCD 428*	8	5
4 Nov 95		**EVERYBODY SAY EVERYBODY DO** *Mercury MERCD 446*	29	3
13 Jan 96		**EVERYBODY SAY EVERYBODY DO (re-entry)** *Mercury MERCD 446*	71	1
22 Jun 96	●	**MAKE IT WITH YOU** *Mercury MERCD 464*	7	6
7 Sep 96		**TAKE IT EASY** *Mercury MERCD 472*	25	2
16 Nov 96		**DARLING BE HOME SOON** *Mercury MERCD 475*	65	1

Gerald LETHAN – *See WALL OF SOUND featuring Gerald LETHAN*

LETTERMEN *US, male vocal group (3 WEEKS)*

			pos	wks
23 Nov 61		**THE WAY YOU LOOK TONIGHT** *Capitol CL 15222*	36	3

LEVEL 42 (112) Top 500 *Critically acclaimed Isle of Wight / Hong Kong / London band: Mark King (v/b), Boon Gould (g), Mike Lindup (k/v), Phil Gould (d). Boasting a world-class bass player in King, they went from Brit-funk cult heroes to international stardom (177 WEEKS)*

			pos	wks
30 Aug 80		**LOVE MEETING LOVE** *Polydor POSP 170*	61	4
18 Apr 81		**LOVE GAMES** *Polydor POSP 234*	38	6
8 Aug 81		**TURN IT ON** *Polydor POSP 286*	57	6
14 Nov 81		**STARCHILD** *Polydor POSP 343*	47	4
8 May 82		**ARE YOU HEARING (WHAT I HEAR)?** *Polydor POSP 396*	49	5
2 Oct 82		**WEAVE YOUR SPELL** *Polydor POSP 500*	43	4
15 Jan 83		**THE CHINESE WAY** *Polydor POSP 538*	24	8
16 Apr 83		**OUT OF SIGHT, OUT OF MIND** *Polydor POSP 570*	41	4
30 Jul 83	●	**THE SUN GOES DOWN (LIVING IT UP)** *Polydor POSP 622*	10	12
22 Oct 83		**MICRO KID** *Polydor POSP 643*	37	5
1 Sep 84		**HOT WATER** *Polydor POSP 697*	18	9
3 Nov 84		**THE CHANT HAS BEGUN** *Polydor POSP 710*	41	5
21 Sep 85	●	**SOMETHING ABOUT YOU** *Polydor POSP 759*	6	17
7 Dec 85		**LEAVING ME NOW** *Polydor POSP 776*	15	11
26 Apr 86	●	**LESSONS IN LOVE** *Polydor POSP 790*	3	13
14 Feb 87	●	**RUNNING IN THE FAMILY** *Polydor POSP 842*	6	10
25 Apr 87	●	**TO BE WITH YOU AGAIN** *Polydor POSP 855*	10	7
12 Sep 87	●	**IT'S OVER** *Polydor POSP 900*	10	8
12 Dec 87		**CHILDREN SAY** *Polydor POSP 911*	22	6
3 Sep 88		**HEAVEN IN MY HANDS** *Polydor PO 14*	12	5
29 Oct 88		**TAKE A LOOK** *Polydor PO 24*	32	4
21 Jan 89		**TRACIE** *Polydor PO 34*	25	5
28 Oct 89		**TAKE CARE OF YOURSELF** *Polydor PO 58*	39	3
17 Aug 91		**GUARANTEED** *RCA PB 44745*	17	4
19 Oct 91		**OVERTIME** *RCA PB 44997*	62	2
18 Apr 92		**MY FATHER'S SHOES** *RCA PB 45271*	55	1
26 Feb 94		**FOREVER NOW** *RCA 74321190272*	19	4
30 Apr 94		**ALL OVER YOU** *RCA 74321205662*	26	2
6 Aug 94		**LOVE IN A PEACEFUL WORLD** *RCA 74321220332*	31	3

LEVELLERS *UK, male vocal / instrumental group (56 WEEKS)*

			pos	wks
21 Sep 91		**ONE WAY** *China WOK 2008*	51	2
7 Dec 91		**FAR FROM HOME** *China WOK 2010*	71	1
23 May 92		**15 YEARS (EP)** *China WOKX 2020*	11	5
10 Jul 93		**BELARUSE** *China WOKCD 2034*	12	5
30 Oct 93		**THIS GARDEN** *China WOKCD 2039*	12	4
14 May 94		**JULIE (EP)** *China WOKCD 2042*	17	3
12 Aug 95		**HOPE ST** *China WOKCD 2059*	12	5
14 Oct 95		**FANTASY** *China WOKCD 2067*	16	3
23 Dec 95		**JUST THE ONE** *China WOKCD 2076* [1]	12	8
20 Jul 96		**EXODUS - LIVE** *China WOKCD 2082*	24	2
9 Aug 97		**WHAT A BEAUTIFUL DAY** *China WOKCD 2088*	13	5

1977

IN THE YEAR IN WHICH STEVE BIKO DIED IN POLICE CUSTODY, 'STAR WARS' TOOK MOVIE FANS TO A GALAXY FAR, FAR, AWAY, AND BOTH OF THE CENTURY'S TOP SELLING SINGERS – ELVIS PRESLEY AND BING CROSBY – DIED, **JONATHAN ROSS** RECALLS HEAD-BANGING THE BASEMENT CEILING AT THE HOPE AND ANCHOR ...

"I got almost all the Pistols stuff on Virgin, which was fantastic. Of course, that was the year of the Silver Jubilee; to coincide with this they released 'God Save the Queen', which I still think is one of the best rock 'n' roll singles ever made. After first seeing the **Sex Pistols** on Bill Grundy's *Tonight Show* and being, as scared as I was, delighted by the filth and the fury that occurred, by 1977 I was a full-blown punk, eager for a vinyl fix. It came my way via the very first punk album, by The Damned. I don't know when it came out but I bought it Easter 1977 and I was very, very proud of it and played it relentlessly. My second album purchase was The Clash. In fact, it was a great year because there were so many great singles coming out – all of the Stiff singles were terrific, so much fantastic punk stuff. Not only did you feel like part of a movement but the music itself was terrific. I remember getting some of the indie stuff like the 'Spiral Scratch' EP which actually came out in 76 but I didn't get till 77. The first gig I ever went to was also in 77, early 77: X-Ray Spex at the Hope and Anchor in Islington. I went downstairs to see the gig – which was fabulous – and I remember spending ages plucking up the courage to pogo, and thinking come on..., and then when I finally did pluck up the courage (it was in the basement of this pub) I leapt up and hit my head so hard on the low beam that I had to spend the rest of the gig sitting down at the back feeling sorry for myself."

SINGLE OF THE YEAR 'Mull Of Kintyre / Girls' School' Wings
ALBUM OF THE YEAR 'Arrival' ABBA

Date	Title	pos	wks
18 Oct 97	CELEBRATE *China WOKCD 2089*	28	2
20 Dec 97	DOG TRAIN *China WOKCD 2090*	24	5
14 Mar 98	TOO REAL *China WOKCD 2091*	46	1
24 Oct 98	BOZOS *China WOKCD 2096*	44	2
6 Feb 99	ONE WAY (re-recording) *China WOKCD 2102*	33	2
9 Sep 00	HAPPY BIRTHDAY REVOLUTION *China EW218CD*	57	1

[1] Levellers, special guest Joe Strummer

Tracks on 15 Years (EP): 15 Years / Dance Before the Storm / The River Flow (Live) / Plastic Jeezus. Tracks on Julie (EP): Julie / English Civil War / Lowlands of Holland / 100 Years of Solitude

LEVERT *US, male vocal group (10 WEEKS)*

Date	Title	pos	wks
22 Aug 87	● CASANOVA *Atlantic A 9217*	9	10

LEVERT SWEAT GILL *US, male vocal group (7 WEEKS)*

Date	Title	pos	wks
14 Mar 98	MY BODY *East West E 3857CD*	21	3
6 Jun 98	CURIOUS *East West E 3842CD*	23	2
12 Sep 98	DOOR #1 *East West E 3817CD*	45	2

Hank LEVINE *US, orchestra (4 WEEKS)*

Date	Title	pos	wks
21 Dec 61	IMAGE *HMV POP 947*	45	4

LEVITICUS *UK, male producer (1 WEEK)*

Date	Title	pos	wks
25 Mar 95	BURIAL *ffrr FCD 255*	66	1

Barrington LEVY *Jamaica, male vocalist (13 WEEKS)*

Date	Title	pos	wks
2 Feb 85	HERE I COME *London LON 62*	41	4
15 Jun 91	TRIBAL BASE *Desire WANT 44* [1]	20	6
24 Sep 94	WORK *MCA MCSTD 2003*	65	1
13 Oct 01	HERE I COME (SING DJ) *Nulife / Arista 74321895622* [2]	37	2

[1] Rebel MC featuring Tenor Fly and Barrington Levy [2] Talisman P Featuring Barrington Levy

Here I Come (Sing DJ) is a re-recording of Here I Come

Jona LEWIE *UK, male vocalist – John Lewis (20 WEEKS)*

Date	Title	pos	wks
10 May 80	YOU'LL ALWAYS FIND ME IN THE KITCHEN AT PARTIES *Stiff BUY 73*	16	9
29 Nov 80	● STOP THE CAVALRY *Stiff BUY 104*	3	11

On some copies first title was simply 'Kitchen at Parties'

See also Terry DACTYL and the DINOSAURS

CJ LEWIS *UK, male vocalist (32 WEEKS)*

Date	Title	pos	wks
23 Apr 94	● SWEETS FOR MY SWEET *Black Market BMITD 017*	3	13
23 Jul 94	● EVERYTHING IS ALRIGHT (UPTIGHT) *Black Market BMITD 019*	10	7
8 Oct 94	BEST OF MY LOVE *Black Market BMITD 021*	13	6
17 Dec 94	DOLLARS *Black Market BMITD 023*	34	4
9 Sep 95	R TO THE A *Black Market BMITD 030*	34	2

Danny J LEWIS *UK, male producer (2 WEEKS)*

Date	Title	pos	wks
20 Jun 98	SPEND THE NIGHT *Locked On LOX 98CD*	29	2

Darlene LEWIS *US, female vocalist (4 WEEKS)*

Date	Title	pos	wks
16 Apr 94	LET THE MUSIC (LIFT YOU UP) *KMS / Eastern Bloc KMSCD 10*	16	4

All formats of 'Let the Music Lift You Up' featured versions by Loveland featuring Rachel McFarlane and also by Darlene Lewis

Dee LEWIS *UK, female vocalist (5 WEEKS)*

Date	Title	pos	wks
18 Jun 88	BEST OF MY LOVE *Mercury DEE 3*	47	5

Donna LEWIS *UK, female vocalist (16 WEEKS)*

Date	Title	pos	wks
7 Sep 96	● I LOVE YOU ALWAYS FOREVER *Atlantic A 5495CD*	5	14
8 Feb 97	WITHOUT LOVE *Atlantic A 5468CD*	39	2

Gary LEWIS and the PLAYBOYS *US, male vocal / instrumental group (7 WEEKS)*

Date	Title	pos	wks
8 Feb 75	MY HEART'S SYMPHONY *United Artists UP 35780*	36	7

Huey LEWIS and the NEWS *US, male vocal / instrumental group (66 WEEKS)*

Date	Title	pos	wks
27 Oct 84	IF THIS IS IT *Chrysalis CHS 2803*	39	6
31 Aug 85	THE POWER OF LOVE *Chrysalis HUEY 1* ▲	11	10
23 Nov 85	HEART AND SOUL (EP) *Chrysalis HUEY 2*	61	4
8 Feb 86	● THE POWER OF LOVE / DO YOU BELIEVE IN LOVE (re-issue) *Chrysalis HUEY 3*	9	12
10 May 86	THE HEART OF ROCK AND ROLL *Chrysalis HUEY 4*	49	3
23 Aug 86	STUCK WITH YOU *Chrysalis HUEY 5* ▲	12	12
6 Dec 86	HIP TO BE SQUARE *Chrysalis HUEY 6*	41	8
21 Mar 87	SIMPLE AS THAT *Chrysalis HUEY 7*	47	5
16 Jul 88	PERFECT WORLD *Chrysalis HUEY 10*	48	6

Tracks on Heart and Soul (EP): Heart and Soul / Hope You Love Me Like You Say You Do / Heart of Rock and Roll / Buzz Buzz Buzz. 'Do You Believe in Love' listed only from 15 Feb 1986

Jerry LEWIS *US, male vocalist – Joseph Levitch (8 WEEKS)*

Date	Title	pos	wks
8 Feb 57	ROCK-A-BYE YOUR BABY WITH A DIXIE MELODY *Brunswick 05636*	12	7
5 Apr 57	ROCK-A-BYE YOUR BABY WITH A DIXIE MELODY (re-entry) *Brunswick 05636*	22	1

Jerry Lee LEWIS *Piano-pounding wild man of rock 'n' roll, b. 29 Sep 1935, Louisiana, US (68 WEEKS)*

Date	Title	pos	wks
27 Sep 57	● WHOLE LOTTA SHAKIN' GOIN' ON *London HLS 8457*	8	10
20 Dec 57	★ GREAT BALLS OF FIRE *London HLS 8529*	1	12
27 Dec 57	WHOLE LOTTA SHAKIN' GOIN' ON (re-entry) *London HLS 8457*	26	1
11 Apr 58	● BREATHLESS *London HLS 8592*	8	7
23 Jan 59	HIGH SCHOOL CONFIDENTIAL *London HLS 8780*	12	6
1 May 59	LOVIN' UP A STORM *London HLS 8840*	28	1
9 Jun 60	BABY, BABY, BYE BYE *London HLS 9131*	47	1
4 May 61	● WHAT'D I SAY *London HLS 9335*	10	12
3 Aug 61	WHAT'D I SAY (re-entry) *London HLS 9335*	49	2
6 Sep 62	SWEET LITTLE SIXTEEN *London HLS 9584*	38	5
14 Mar 63	GOOD GOLLY MISS MOLLY *London HLS 9688*	31	6
6 May 72	CHANTILLY LACE *Mercury 6052 141*	33	5

Linda LEWIS *UK, female vocalist (31 WEEKS)*

Date	Title	pos	wks
2 Jun 73	ROCK-A-DOODLE-DOO *Raft RA 18502*	15	11
12 Jul 75	● IT'S IN HIS KISS *Arista 17*	6	8
17 Apr 76	BABY I'M YOURS *Arista 43*	33	6
2 Jun 79	I'D BE SURPRISINGLY GOOD FOR YOU *Ariola ARO 166*	40	5
19 Aug 00	REACH OUT *Skint SKINT 54CD* [1]	61	1

[1] Midfield General featuring Linda Lewis

Ramsey LEWIS *US, male instrumentalist – piano (8 WEEKS)*

Date	Title	pos	wks
15 Apr 72	WADE IN THE WATER *Chess 6145 004*	31	8

Shirley LEWIS – *See Arthur BAKER*

John LEYTON *UK male vocalist / actor (70 WEEKS)*

Date	Title	pos	wks
3 Aug 61	★ JOHNNY REMEMBER ME *Top Rank JAR 577*	1	15
5 Oct 61	● WILD WIND *Top Rank JAR 585*	2	10
28 Dec 61	SON THIS IS SHE *HMV POP 956*	15	10
15 Mar 62	LONE RIDER *HMV POP 992*	40	5
3 May 62	LONELY CITY *HMV POP 1014*	14	11
23 Aug 62	DOWN THE RIVER NILE *HMV POP 1054*	42	3
21 Feb 63	CUPBOARD LOVE *HMV POP 1122*	22	12
18 Jul 63	I'LL CUT YOUR TAIL OFF *HMV POP 1175*	50	1
8 Aug 63	I'LL CUT YOUR TAIL OFF (re-entry) *HMV POP 1175*	36	2
20 Feb 64	MAKE LOVE TO ME *HMV POP 1264* [1]	49	1

[1] John Leyton and the LeRoys

LEYTON BUZZARDS *UK, male vocal / instrumental group (5 WEEKS)* pos/wks

			pos	wks
3 Mar 79		**SATURDAY NIGHT (BENEATH THE PLASTIC PALM TREES)** *Chrysalis CHS 2288*	53	5

LFO *UK, male instrumental group (15 WEEKS)* pos/wks

			pos	wks
14 Jul 90		**LFO** *Warp WAP 5*	12	10
6 Jul 91		**WE ARE BACK / NURTURE** *Warp 7WAP 14*	47	3
1 Feb 92		**WHAT IS HOUSE (EP)** *Warp WAP 17*	62	2

Tracks on What Is House (EP): Tan Ta Ra / Mashed Potato / What Is House / Syndrome

LIBERACE *US, male instrumentalist – piano (Wladziu Valentino Liberace) (2 WEEKS)* pos/wks

			pos	wks
17 Jun 55		**UNCHAINED MELODY** *Philips PB 430*	20	1
19 Oct 56		**I DON'T CARE (AS LONG AS YOU CARE FOR ME)** *Columbia DB 3834*	28	1

'I Don't Care' featured Liberace as vocalist too

LIBERATION *UK, male instrumental / production duo (3 WEEKS)* pos/wks

			pos	wks
24 Oct 92		**LIBERATION** *ZYX ZYX 68657*	28	3

LIBERTY *UK, male / female vocal group (11 WEEKS)* pos/wks

			pos	wks
6 Oct 01	●	**THINKING IT OVER** *V2 VVR 5017773*	5	8
15 Dec 01		**DOIN' IT** *V2 VVR 5017793*	14	3

LIBIDO *Norway, male vocal / instrumental group (1 WEEK)* pos/wks

			pos	wks
31 Jan 98		**OVERTHROWN** *Fire BLAZE 119CD*	53	1

LIBRA presents TAYLOR *US, male / female production / vocal trio (3 WEEKS)* pos/wks

			pos	wks
26 Oct 96		**ANOMALY - CALLING YOUR NAME** *Platipus PLATCD 24*	71	1
18 Mar 00		**ANOMALY - CALLING YOUR NAME (re-mix)** *Platipus PLATCD 56*	43	2

LICK THE TINS *UK, male / female vocal / instrumental group (8 WEEKS)* pos/wks

			pos	wks
29 Mar 86		**CAN'T HELP FALLING IN LOVE** *Sedition EDIT 3308*	42	8

Oliver LIEB presents SMOKED *Germany, male producer (1 WEEK)* pos/wks

			pos	wks
30 Sep 00		**METROPOLIS** *Duty Free DF 019CD*	72	1

See also LSG

Ben LIEBRAND *Holland, male DJ / producer (2 WEEKS)* pos/wks

			pos	wks
9 Jun 90		**PULS(T)AR** *Epic LIEB 1*	68	2

LIEUTENANT PIGEON *UK, male / female instrumental group (29 WEEKS)* pos/wks

			pos	wks
16 Sep 72	★	**MOULDY OLD DOUGH** *Decca F 13278*	1	19
16 Dec 72		**DESPERATE DAN** *Decca F 13365*	17	10

LIFEHOUSE *US, male vocal / instrumental group (4 WEEKS)* pos/wks

			pos	wks
8 Sep 01		**HANGING BY A MOMENT** *Dreamworks / Polydor 4975612*	25	4

LIFFORD – *See ARTFUL DODGER*

LIGHT OF THE WORLD *UK, male vocal / instrumental group (25 WEEKS)* pos/wks

			pos	wks
14 Apr 79		**SWINGIN'** *Ensign ENY 22*	45	5
14 Jul 79		**MIDNIGHT GROOVIN'** *Ensign ENY 29*	72	1
18 Oct 80		**LONDON TOWN** *Ensign ENY 43*	41	5
17 Jan 81		**I SHOT THE SHERIFF** *Ensign ENY 46*	40	5
28 Mar 81		**I'M SO HAPPY / TIME** *Ensign MER 64*	35	6
21 Nov 81		**RIDE THE LOVE TRAIN** *EMI 5242*	49	3

LIGHTER SHADE OF BROWN *US, male vocal duo (3 WEEKS)* pos/wks

			pos	wks
9 Jul 94		**HEY DJ** *Mercury MERCD 401*	33	3

Gordon LIGHTFOOT *Canada, male vocalist (26 WEEKS)* pos/wks

			pos	wks
19 Jun 71		**IF YOU COULD READ MY MIND** *Reprise RS 20974*	30	9
3 Aug 74		**SUNDOWN** *Reprise K 14327* ▲	33	7
15 Jan 77		**THE WRECK OF THE EDMUND FITZGERALD** *Reprise K 14451*	40	4
16 Sep 78		**DAYLIGHT KATY** *Warner Bros. K 17214*	41	6

Terry LIGHTFOOT'S NEW ORLEANS JAZZMEN *UK, vocalist / instrumentalist – clarinet – and male band (17 WEEKS)* pos/wks

			pos	wks
7 Sep 61		**TRUE LOVE** *Columbia DB 4696*	33	4
23 Nov 61		**KING KONG** *Columbia SCD 2165*	29	12
3 May 62		**TAVERN IN THE TOWN** *Columbia DB 4822*	49	1

LIGHTFORCE *Germany, male production duo (1 WEEK)* pos/wks

			pos	wks
28 Oct 00		**JOIN ME** *Slinky Music SLINKY 004CD*	53	1

LIGHTHOUSE FAMILY (401 Top 500) *Smooth, easy-on-the-ear pop / soul duo formed in Newcastle-upon-Tyne, UK; Nigerian-born Tunde Baiyewu (v) and Londoner Paul Tucker (k). After slow start, debut album 'Ocean Drive' (1995) sold more than 1.6 million in UK and made a name for them in Europe (82 WEEKS)* pos/wks

			pos	wks
27 May 95		**LIFTED** *Wild Card CARDW 17*	61	2
14 Oct 95		**OCEAN DRIVE** *Wild Card 5797072*	34	3
10 Feb 96	●	**LIFTED (re-issue)** *Wild Card 5779432*	4	10
1 Jun 96		**OCEAN DRIVE (re-issue)** *Wild Card 5766192*	11	8
21 Sep 96		**GOODBYE HEARTBREAK** *Wild Card 5753492*	14	6
21 Dec 96		**LOVING EVERY MINUTE** *Wild Card 5731012*	20	7
11 Oct 97	●	**RAINCLOUD** *Wild Card 5717932*	6	7
10 Jan 98	●	**HIGH** *Polydor 5691492*	4	14
27 Jun 98	●	**LOST IN SPACE** *Polydor 5670592*	6	8
10 Oct 98		**QUESTION OF FAITH** *Wild Card 5673932*	21	5
9 Jan 99		**POSTCARD FROM HEAVEN** *Wild Card 5633952*	24	6
24 Nov 01	●	**(I WISH I KNEW HOW IT WOULD FEEL TO BE) FREE / ONE** *Wild Card / Polydor 5873812*	6	6+

LIGHTNING SEEDS (310 Top 500) *Conceived as a 'perfect pop' studio project by producer and group veteran Ian Broudie (v/g) 4 Aug 1958, Liverpool, UK. England's most popular footballing anthem, 'Three Lions', became first song to top the charts twice with different lyrics (98 WEEKS)* pos/wks

			pos	wks
22 Jul 89		**PURE** *Ghetto GTG 4*	16	8
14 Mar 92		**THE LIFE OF RILEY** *Virgin VS 1402*	28	6
30 May 92		**SENSE** *Virgin VS 1414*	31	5
20 Aug 94		**LUCKY YOU** *Epic 6606282*	43	2
14 Jan 95		**CHANGE** *Epic 6609865*	13	6
15 Apr 95		**MARVELLOUS** *Epic 6614265*	24	5
22 Jul 95		**PERFECT** *Epic 6621792*	18	5
21 Oct 95		**LUCKY YOU (re-issue)** *Epic 6625182*	15	6
9 Mar 96		**READY OR NOT** *Epic 6629672*	20	4
1 Jun 96	★	**THREE LIONS (THE OFFICIAL SONG OF THE ENGLAND FOOTBALL TEAM)** *Epic 6632732* [1] ■	1	15
2 Nov 96		**WHAT IF...** *Epic 6638635*	14	3
11 Jan 97		**WHAT IF... (re-entry)** *Epic 6638635*	64	1
18 Jan 97		**SUGAR COATED ICEBERG** *Epic 6640432*	12	4
26 Apr 97	●	**YOU SHOWED ME** *Epic 6643282*	8	5
13 Dec 97		**WHAT YOU SAY** *Epic 6653572*	41	5
20 Jun 98	★	**3 LIONS '98** *Epic 6660982* [1] ■	1	13
27 Nov 99		**LIFE'S TOO SHORT** *Epic 6681502*	27	3
22 Jan 00		**LIFE'S TOO SHORT (re-entry)** *Epic 6681502*	73	1
18 Mar 00		**SWEETEST SOUL SENSATIONS** *Epic 6689422*	67	1

[1] Baddiel and Skinner and the Lightning Seeds

LIL BOW WOW *US, male rapper – Rashad Moss (9 WEEKS)* pos/wks

			pos	wks
14 Apr 01	●	**BOW WOW (THAT'S MY NAME)** *So So Def / Columbia 6709832*	6	9

LIL' DEVIOUS *UK, male production duo (1 WEEK)* pos/wks

			pos	wks
15 Sep 01		**COME HOME** *Rulin RULIN 16CDS*	55	1

LIL' KIM *US, female vocalist – Kimberly Jones (40 WEEKS)* pos/wks

			pos	wks
26 Apr 97		**NO TIME** *Atlantic A 5594CD* [1]	45	1

5 Jul 97		**CRUSH ON YOU** *Atlantic AT 0002CD*	36	2
16 Aug 97		**NOT TONIGHT** *Atlantic AT 0007CD*	11	5
25 Oct 97		**CRUSH ON YOU (re-entry)** *Atlantic AT 0002CD*	23	3
22 Aug 98		**HIT 'EM WIT DA HEE** *East West E3824 CD1* [2]	25	3
5 Feb 00		**NOTORIOUS B.I.G.** *Puff Daddy / Arista 74321737312* [3]	16	5
2 Sep 00		**NO MATTER WHAT THEY SAY** *Atlantic 7567846972*	35	2
30 Jun 01	★	**LADY MARMALADE** *Interscope / Polydor 4975612* [4] ■ ▲	1	16
11 Aug 01		**WAIT A MINUTE** *Atlantic AT 0106CD* [5]	54	1
22 Sep 01		**IN THE AIR TONITE** *WEA WEA 331CD* [6]	26	2

[1] Lil' Kim featuring Puff Daddy [2] Missy 'Misdemeanor' Elliott featuring Lil' Kim [3] Notorious B.I.G. featuring Puff Daddy and Lil' Kim [4] Christina Aguilera, Lil' Kim, Mya and Pink [5] Ray J featuring Lil' Kim [6] Lil' Kim featuring Phil Collins

LIL' LOUIS *US, male producer – Louis Burns (21 WEEKS)* pos/wks

29 Jul 89	●	**FRENCH KISS** *ffrr FX 115*	2	11
13 Jan 90		**I CALLED U** *ffrr F 123*	16	6
26 Sep 92		**SAVED MY LIFE** *ffrr FX 197* [1]	74	1
12 Aug 00		**HOW'S YOUR EVENING SO FAR** *ffrr FCD 384* [2]	23	3

[1] Lil' Louis and the World [2] Josh Wink and Lil' Louis

See also BLACK MAGIC

LIL' MISS MAX – *See BLUE ADONIS featuring LIL' MISS MAX*

LIL' MO *US, female vocalist (4 WEEKS)* pos/wks

21 Nov 98		**5 MINUTES** *Elektra E 3803CD* [1]	72	1
23 Sep 00		**WHATEVER** *Virgin VUSCD 172* [2]	31	3

[1] Lil' Mo featuring Missy 'Misdemeanor' Elliott [2] Ideal U.S. featuring Lil' Mo

LIL MO' YIN YANG *US, male instrumental / production duo – Erick 'More' Morillo and 'Lil' Louis Vega (2 WEEKS)* pos/wks

9 Mar 96		**REACH** *Multiply CDMULTY 9*	28	2

See also Erick 'More' MORILLO presents RAW; REEL 2 REAL

LIL' ROMEO *US, male rapper (1 WEEK)* pos/wks

22 Sep 01		**MY BABY** *Priority PTYCD 136*	67	1

LILY – *See MAXIMA featuring LILY*

LILYS *US, male vocal / instrumental group (4 WEEKS)* pos/wks

21 Feb 98		**A NANNY IN MANHATTAN** *Che CHE 77CD*	16	4

LIMA – *See Tom NOVY*

LIMAHL *UK, male vocalist – Chris Hamill (25 WEEKS)* pos/wks

5 Nov 83		**ONLY FOR LOVE** *EMI LML 1*	16	7
7 Jan 84		**ONLY FOR LOVE (re-entry)** *EMI LML 1*	75	1
2 Jun 84		**TOO MUCH TROUBLE** *EMI LML 2*	64	3
13 Oct 84	●	**NEVER ENDING STORY** *EMI LML 3*	4	14

See also KAJAGOOGOO

Alison LIMERICK *UK, female vocalist (39 WEEKS)* pos/wks

30 Mar 91		**WHERE LOVE LIVES** *Arista 144208*	27	8
12 Oct 91		**COME BACK (FOR REAL LOVE)** *Arista 114530*	53	2
21 Dec 91		**MAGIC'S BACK (THEME FROM 'THE GHOSTS OF OXFORD STREET')** *RCA PB 45223* [1]	42	4
29 Feb 92		**MAKE IT ON MY OWN** *Arista 114996*	16	6
18 Jul 92		**GETTIN' IT RIGHT** *Arista 74321102867*	57	2
28 Nov 92		**HEAR MY CALL** *Arista 115337*	73	1
8 Jan 94		**TIME OF OUR LIVES** *Arista 74321180332*	36	4
19 Mar 94		**LOVE COME DOWN** *Arista 74321191952*	36	2
25 Feb 95		**LOVE WILL KEEP US TOGETHER** *Acid Jazz JAZID 112CD* [2]	63	1
6 Jul 96	●	**WHERE LOVE LIVES (re-mix)** *Arista 74321381592*	9	6
14 Sep 96		**MAKE IT ON MY OWN (re-mix)** *Arista 74321407812*	30	2
23 Aug 97		**PUT YOUR FAITH IN ME** *MBA XES 9001*	42	1

[1] Malcolm McLaren featuring Alison Limerick [2] JTQ featuring Alison Limerick

LIMIT *Holland, male vocal / instrumental duo – Bernard Oates and Rob Van Schaik (8 WEEKS)* pos/wks

5 Jan 85		**SAY YEAH** *Portrait A 4808*	17	8

LIMMIE and the FAMILY COOKIN' *US, male / female vocal group (28 WEEKS)* pos/wks

21 Jul 73	●	**YOU CAN DO MAGIC** *Avco 6105 019*	3	13
20 Oct 73		**DREAMBOAT** *Avco 6105 025*	31	5
6 Apr 74	●	**A WALKIN' MIRACLE** *Avco 6105 027*	6	10

LIMP BIZKIT *US, male vocal / instrumental group (49 WEEKS)* pos/wks

15 Jul 00	●	**TAKE A LOOK AROUND (THEME FROM 'MI:2')** *Interscope 4973682*	3	13
11 Nov 00		**MY GENERATION** *Interscope IND 97448*	15	6
6 Jan 01		**MY GENERATION (re-entry)** *Interscope IND 97448*	65	2
27 Jan 01	★	**ROLLIN'** *Interscope IND 97474* ■	1	13
23 Jun 01	●	**MY WAY** *Interscope 4975732*	6	10
10 Nov 01		**BOILER** *Interscope 4976362*	18	5

LINA *US, female vocalist (1 WEEK)* pos/wks

3 Mar 01		**PLAYA NO MO'** *Atlantic AT 0094CD*	46	1

Bob LIND *US, male vocalist (10 WEEKS)* pos/wks

10 Mar 66	●	**ELUSIVE BUTTERFLY** *Fontana TF 670*	5	9
26 May 66		**REMEMBER THE RAIN** *Fontana TF 702*	46	1

LINDA and the FUNKY BOYS – *See Linda CARR*

LINDISFARNE *UK, male vocal / instrumental group (55 WEEKS)* pos/wks

26 Feb 72	●	**MEET ME ON THE CORNER** *Charisma CB 173*	5	11
13 May 72	●	**LADY ELEANOR** *Charisma CB 153*	3	11
23 Sep 72		**ALL FALL DOWN** *Charisma CB 191*	34	5
3 Jun 78	●	**RUN FOR HOME** *Mercury 6007 177*	10	15
7 Oct 78		**JUKE BOX GYPSY** *Mercury 6007 187*	56	4
10 Nov 90	●	**FOG ON THE TYNE (REVISITED)** *Best ZB 44083* [1]	2	9

[1] Gazza and Lindisfarne

LINDSAY *UK, female vocalist (4 WEEKS)* pos/wks

12 May 01		**NO DREAM IMPOSSIBLE** *Universal TV 1589562*	32	4

LINER *UK, male vocal / instrumental group (6 WEEKS)* pos/wks

10 Mar 79		**KEEP REACHING OUT FOR LOVE** *Atlantic K 11235*	49	3
26 May 79		**YOU AND ME** *Atlantic K 11285*	44	3

Andy LING *UK, male producer (1 WEEK)* pos/wks

13 May 00		**FIXATION** *Hooj Choons HOOJ 094CD*	55	1

Laurie LINGO and the DIPSTICKS *UK, male vocal duo – DJs Dave Lee Travis and Paul Burnett (7 WEEKS)* pos/wks

17 Apr 76	●	**CONVOY GB** *State STAT 23*	4	7

LINK *US, male rapper (1 WEEK)* pos/wks

7 Nov 98		**WHATCHA GONE DO?** *Relativity 6666055*	48	1

LINKIN PARK *US, male vocal / instrumental group (27 WEEKS)* pos/wks

27 Jan 01		**ONE STEP CLOSER** *Warner Brothers W 550CD*	24	4
21 Apr 01		**CRAWLING** *Warner Brothers W 556CD*	16	8
30 Jun 01		**PAPERCUT** *Warner Brothers W 562CD*	14	6
20 Oct 01	●	**IN THE END** *Warner Brothers W 569CD*	8	9

LINOLEUM *UK, male / female vocal / instrumental group (1 WEEK)* pos/wks

12 Jul 97		**MARQUIS** *Lino Vinyl LINO 004CD1*	73	1

LINX *UK, male vocal / instrumental duo – David Grant and Peter Martin (45 WEEKS)* pos/wks

20 Sep 80		**YOU'RE LYING** *Chrysalis CHS 2461*	15	10

7 Mar 81	●	**INTUITION** *Chrysalis CHS 2500*	7	11
13 Jun 81		**THROW AWAY THE KEY** *Chrysalis CHS 2519*	21	9
5 Sep 81		**SO THIS IS ROMANCE** *Chrysalis CHS 2546*	15	9
21 Nov 81		**CAN'T HELP MYSELF** *Chrysalis CHS 2565*	55	3
10 Jul 82		**PLAYTHING** *Chrysalis CHS 2621*	48	3

LIONROCK *UK, male producer – Justin Robertson (14 WEEKS)*

			pos	wks
5 Dec 92		**LIONROCK** *Deconstruction 74321124381*	63	1
8 May 93		**PACKET OF PEACE** *Deconstruction 74321144372*	32	3
23 Oct 93		**CARNIVAL** *Deconstruction 74321164862*	34	2
27 Aug 94		**TRIPWIRE** *Deconstruction 74321204702*	44	1
6 Apr 96		**STRAIGHT AT YER HEAD** *Deconstruction 74321342972*	33	2
27 Jul 96		**FIRE UP THE SHOESAW** *Deconstruction 74321382652*	43	1
14 Mar 98		**RUDE BOY ROCK** *Concrete HARD 31CD*	20	3
30 May 98		**SCATTER & SWING** *Concrete HARD 35CD*	54	1

LIPPS INC *US, male / female vocal / instrumental group (13 WEEKS)*

			pos	wks
17 May 80	●	**FUNKYTOWN** *Casablanca CAN 194* ▲	2	13

LIQUID *UK, male producer – Eamon Downes (20 WEEKS)*

			pos	wks
21 Mar 92		**SWEET HARMONY** *XL Recordings XLS 28*	15	6
5 Sep 92		**THE FUTURE MUSIC (EP)** *XL Recordings XLT 33*	59	2
20 Mar 93		**TIME TO GET UP** *XL Recordings XLS 40CD*	46	2
8 Jul 95		**SWEET HARMONY / ONE LOVE FAMILY (re-mix)** *XL Recordings XLS 65CD*	14	6
21 Oct 95		**CLOSER** *XL Recordings XLS 66CD*	47	2
25 Jul 98		**STRONG** *Higher Ground HIGHS 7CD*	59	1
21 Oct 00		**ORLANDO DAWN** *Xtravaganza XTRAV 16CDS*	53	1

Tracks on The Future Music (EP): Liquid Is Liquid / Music / House (Is a Feeling) / The Year 3000. On the first two hits act also included Shane Heneghan

LIQUID CHILD *Germany, male production duo (2 WEEKS)*

			pos	wks
23 Oct 99		**DIVING FACES** *Essential Recordings ESCD 9*	25	2

LIQUID GOLD

UK, male / female vocal / instrumental group (46 WEEKS)

			pos	wks
2 Dec 78		**ANYWAY YOU DO IT** *Creole CR 159*	41	7
23 Feb 80	●	**DANCE YOURSELF DIZZY** *Polo POLO 1*	2	14
31 May 80	●	**SUBSTITUTE** *Polo POLO 4*	8	9
1 Nov 80		**THE NIGHT THE WINE AND THE ROSES** *POLO 6*	32	7
28 Mar 81		**DON'T PANIC** *Polo POLO 8*	42	5
21 Aug 82		**WHERE DID WE GO WRONG** *Polo POLO 23*	56	4

LIQUID OXYGEN *US, male producer (2 WEEKS)*

			pos	wks
28 Apr 90		**THE PLANET DANCE (MOVE YA BODY)** *Champion CHAMP 242*	56	2

LISA LISA *US, female vocalist (32 WEEKS)*

			pos	wks
4 May 85		**I WONDER IF I TAKE YOU HOME** *CBS A 6057* [1]	53	6
3 Aug 85		**I WONDER IF I TAKE YOU HOME (re-entry)** *CBS A 6057* [1]	12	11
31 Oct 87		**LOST IN EMOTION** *CBS 651036 7* [2] ▲	58	4
13 Jul 91		**LET THE BEAT HIT 'EM** *Columbia 6572867* [2]	17	6
24 Aug 91		**LET THE BEAT HIT 'EM PART 2** *Columbia 6573747* [2]	49	2
26 Mar 94		**SKIP TO MY LU** *Chrysalis CDCHS 5006*	34	3

[1] Lisa Lisa and Cult Jam with Full Force [2] Lisa Lisa and Cult Jam

LISA MARIE – *See Malcolm McLAREN*

LISA MARIE EXPERIENCE *UK, male instrumental / production duo – Dean Marriot and Neil Hynde (15 WEEKS)*

			pos	wks
27 Apr 96	●	**KEEP ON JUMPIN'** *ffrr FCD 271*	7	10
20 Jul 96		**KEEP ON JUMPIN' (re-entry)** *ffrr FCD 271*	61	3
10 Aug 96		**DO THAT TO ME** *Positiva CDTIV 57*	33	2

LIT *US, male vocal / instrumental group (7 WEEKS)*

			pos	wks
26 Jun 99		**MY OWN WORST ENEMY** *RCA 74321669992*	16	4
25 Sep 99		**ZIP - LOCK** *RCA 74321701852*	60	1
19 Aug 00		**OVER MY HEAD** *Capitol 8889532*	37	2

LITHIAM and Sonya MADAN

US, male producer and UK, female vocalist (2 WEEKS)

			pos	wks
1 Mar 97		**RIDE A ROCKET** *ffrr FCD 293*	40	2

Sonya Madan is lead singer of Echobelly

See also ECHOBELLY

De Etta LITTLE and Nelson PIGFORD

US, female / male vocal duo (5 WEEKS)

			pos	wks
13 Aug 77		**YOU TAKE MY HEART AWAY** *United Artists UP 36257*	35	5

LITTLE ANGELS *UK, male vocal / instrumental group (41 WEEKS)*

			pos	wks
4 Mar 89		**BIG BAD EP** *Polydor LTLEP 2*	74	1
24 Feb 90		**KICKING UP DUST** *Polydor LTL 5*	46	4
12 May 90		**RADICAL YOUR LOVER** *Polydor LTL 6* [1]	34	4
4 Aug 90		**SHE'S A LITTLE ANGEL** *Polydor LTL 7*	21	3
2 Feb 91		**BONEYARD** *Polydor LTL 8*	33	4
30 Mar 91		**PRODUCT OF THE WORKING CLASS** *Polydor LTL 9*	40	2
1 Jun 91		**YOUNG GODS** *Polydor LTL 10*	34	2
20 Jul 91		**I AIN'T GONNA CRY** *Polydor LTL 11*	26	3
7 Nov 92		**TOO MUCH TOO YOUNG** *Polydor LTL 12*	22	3
9 Jan 93		**WOMANKIND** *Polydor LTLCD 13*	12	5
24 Apr 93		**SOAPBOX** *Polydor LTLCD 14*	33	4
25 Sep 93		**SAIL AWAY** *Polydor LTLCD 15*	45	3
9 Apr 94		**TEN MILES HIGH** *Polydor LTLCD 16*	18	3

[1] Little Angels featuring the Big Bad Horns

Tracks on Big Bad EP: She's a Little Angel / Don't Waste My Time / Better Than the Rest / Sex in Cars

LITTLE ANTHONY and the IMPERIALS

US, male vocal group (4 WEEKS)

			pos	wks
31 Jul 76		**BETTER USE YOUR HEAD** *United Artists UP 36141*	42	4

LITTLE BENNY and the MASTERS *US, male rapper / instrumentalist – trumpet – and male instrumental group (7 WEEKS)*

			pos	wks
2 Feb 85		**WHO COMES TO BOOGIE** *Bluebird 10 BR 13*	33	7

LITTLE CAESAR *UK, male vocalist (3 WEEKS)*

			pos	wks
9 Jun 90		**THE WHOLE OF THE MOON** *A1 EAU 1*	68	3

LITTLE EVA *US, female vocalist – Eva Boyd (45 WEEKS)*

			pos	wks
6 Sep 62	●	**THE LOCO-MOTION** *London HL 9581* ▲	2	17
3 Jan 63		**KEEP YOUR HANDS OFF MY BABY** *London HLU 9633*	30	5
7 Mar 63		**LET'S TURKEY TROT** *London HLU 9687*	13	12
29 Jul 72		**THE LOCO-MOTION (re-entry)** *London HL 9581*	11	11

See also Big Dee IRWIN

LITTLE LOUIE – *See Louie VEGA and Marc ANTHONY*

LITTLE MS MARCIE – *See MELT featuring LITTLE MS MARCIE*

LITTLE RICHARD (239 Top 500) *Frantic, no-holds-barred rock 'n' roll singer / songwriter and piano-pounder, b. Richard Penniman, 5 Dec 1935, Georgia, US. This legendary performer's wild vocals and unrestrained stage show influenced many later stars. Both The Beatles and The Rolling Stones supported him on tour (116 WEEKS)*

			pos	wks
14 Dec 56		**RIP IT UP** *London HLO 8336*	30	1
8 Feb 57	●	**LONG TALL SALLY** *London HLO 8366*	3	16
22 Feb 57		**TUTTI FRUTTI** *London HLO 8366*	29	1
8 Mar 57		**SHE'S GOT IT** *London HLO 8382*	15	7
15 Mar 57	●	**THE GIRL CAN'T HELP IT** *London HLO 8382*	9	11
24 May 57		**SHE'S GOT IT (re-entry)** *London HLO 8382*	28	2
28 Jun 57	●	**LUCILLE** *London HLO 8446*	10	9
13 Sep 57		**JENNY JENNY** *London HLO 8470*	11	5
29 Nov 57		**KEEP A KNOCKIN'** *London HLO 8509*	21	7
28 Feb 58	●	**GOOD GOLLY MISS MOLLY** *London HLU 8560*	8	9
11 Jul 58		**OOH! MY SOUL** *London HLO 8647*	30	1
25 Jul 58		**OOH! MY SOUL (re-entry)** *London HLO 8647*	22	3

			pos	wks
2 Jan 59	●	**BABY FACE** *London HLU 8770*	2	15
3 Apr 59		**BY THE LIGHT OF THE SILVERY MOON** *London HLU 8831*	17	5
5 Jun 59		**KANSAS CITY** *London HLU 8868*	26	5
11 Oct 62		**HE GOT WHAT HE WANTED (BUT HE LOST WHAT HE HAD)** *Mercury AMT 1189*	38	4
4 Jun 64		**BAMA LAMA BAMA LOO** *London HL 9896*	20	7
2 Jul 77		**GOOD GOLLY MISS MOLLY / RIP IT UP** *Creole CR 140*	37	4
14 Jun 86		**GREAT GOSH A'MIGHTY ! (IT'S A MATTER OF TIME)** *MCA MCA 1049*	62	2
25 Oct 86		**OPERATOR** *WEA YZ 89*	67	2

The 1977 versions of 'Good Golly Miss Molly' and 'Rip It Up' on Creole are re-recordings

LITTLE STEVEN *US, male vocalist / instrumentalist – guitar (3 WEEKS)* pos/wks

			pos	wks
23 May 87		**BITTER FRUIT** *Manhattan MT 21*	66	3

LITTLE T – *See REBEL MC*

LITTLE TONY and his BROTHERS

Italy, male vocalists – led by Anthony Ciacci (3 WEEKS) pos/wks

			pos	wks
15 Jan 60		**TOO GOOD** *Decca F 11190*	19	3

LITTLE TREES *Denmark, female vocal group (7 WEEKS)* pos/wks

			pos	wks
1 Sep 01		**HELP! I'M A FISH** *RCA 74321874652*	11	7

LIVE *US, male vocal / instrumental group (13 WEEKS)* pos/wks

			pos	wks
18 Feb 95		**I ALONE** *Radioactive RAXTD 13*	48	4
1 Jul 95		**SELLING THE DRAMA** *Radioactive RAXTD 17*	30	2
7 Oct 95		**ALL OVER YOU** *Radioactive RAXTD 20*	48	1
13 Jan 96		**LIGHTNING CRASHES** *Radioactive RAXTD 23*	33	2
15 Mar 97		**LAKINI'S JUICE** *Radioactive RAD 49023*	29	2
12 Jul 97		**FREAKS** *Radioactive RAXTD 29*	60	1
5 Feb 00		**THE DOLPHIN'S CRY** *Radioactive RAXTD 39*	62	1

LIVE REPORT *UK, male vocal / instrumental group (1 WEEK)* pos/wks

			pos	wks
20 May 89		**WHY DO I ALWAYS GET IT WRONG** *Brouhaha CUE 7*	73	1

LIVERPOOL EXPRESS

UK, male vocal / instrumental group (26 WEEKS) pos/wks

			pos	wks
26 Jun 76		**YOU ARE MY LOVE** *Warner Bros. K 16743*	11	9
16 Oct 76		**HOLD TIGHT** *Warner Bros. K 16799*	46	2
18 Dec 76		**EVERY MAN MUST HAVE A DREAM** *Warner Bros. K 16854*	17	11
4 Jun 77		**DREAMIN'** *Warner Bros. K 16933*	40	4

LIVERPOOL FC *UK, male football team vocalists (21 WEEKS)* pos/wks

			pos	wks
28 May 77		**WE CAN DO IT (EP)** *State STAT 50*	15	4
23 Apr 83		**LIVERPOOL (WE'RE NEVER GONNA...) / LIVERPOOL (ANTHEM)** *Mean MEAN 102*	54	4
17 May 86		**SITTING ON THE TOP OF THE WORLD** *Columbia DB 9116*	50	2
14 May 88	●	**ANFIELD RAP (RED MACHINE IN FULL EFFECT)** *Virgin LFC 1*	3	6
18 May 96	●	**PASS AND MOVE (IT'S THE LIVERPOOL GROOVE)** *Telstar LFCCD 96* [1]	4	5

[1] Liverpool FC and the Boot Room Boyz

Tracks on We Can Do It (EP): We Can Do It / Liverpool Lou / We Shall Not Be Moved / You'll Never Walk Alone

LIVIN' JOY *US / Italy, male / female vocal / instrumental group – leader Paolo Visnadi (44 WEEKS)* pos/wks

			pos	wks
3 Sep 94		**DREAMER** *Undiscovered MCSTD 1993*	18	6
13 May 95	★	**DREAMER (re-mix)** *Undiscovered MCSTD 2056* ■	1	11
15 Jun 96	●	**DON'T STOP MOVIN'** *Undiscovered MCSTD 40041*	5	14
2 Nov 96	●	**FOLLOW THE RULES** *Undiscovered MCSTD 40081*	9	5
5 Apr 97		**WHERE CAN I FIND LOVE** *Undiscovered MCSTD 40108*	12	4
23 Aug 97		**DEEP IN YOU** *Universal MCSTD 40136*	17	4

See also ALEX PARTY

LIVING COLOUR *US, male vocal / instrumental group (22 WEEKS)* pos/wks

			pos	wks
27 Oct 90		**TYPE** *Epic LCL 7*	75	1
2 Feb 91		**LOVE REARS ITS UGLY HEAD** *Epic 6565937*	12	11
1 Jun 91		**SOLACE OF YOU** *Epic 6569087*	33	5
26 Oct 91		**CULT OF PERSONALITY** *Epic 6575357*	67	2
20 Feb 93		**LEAVE IT ALONE** *Epic 6589762*	34	2
17 Apr 93		**AUSLANDER** *Epic 6591732*	53	1

LIVING IN A BOX *UK, male vocal / instrumental group (62 WEEKS)* pos/wks

			pos	wks
4 Apr 87	●	**LIVING IN A BOX** *Chrysalis LIB 1*	5	13
13 Jun 87		**SCALES OF JUSTICE** *Chrysalis LIB 2*	30	6
26 Sep 87		**SO THE STORY GOES** *Chrysalis LIB 3* [1]	34	8
30 Jan 88		**LOVE IS THE ART** *Chrysalis LIB 4*	45	4
18 Feb 89	●	**BLOW THE HOUSE DOWN** *Chrysalis LIB 5*	10	9
10 Jun 89		**GATECRASHING** *Chrysalis LIB 6*	36	6
23 Sep 89	●	**ROOM IN YOUR HEART** *Chrysalis LIB 7*	5	13
30 Dec 89		**DIFFERENT AIR** *Chrysalis LIB 8*	64	1
13 Jan 90		**DIFFERENT AIR (re-entry)** *Chrysalis LIB 8*	57	2

[1] Living in a Box featuring Bobby Womack

Dandy LIVINGSTONE

Jamaica, male vocalist – Robert Livingstone Thompson (19 WEEKS) pos/wks

			pos	wks
2 Sep 72		**SUZANNE BEWARE OF THE DEVIL** *Horse HOSS 16*	14	11
13 Jan 73		**BIG CITY / THINK ABOUT THAT** *Horse HOSS 25*	26	8

LL COOL J (454 Top 500) *With a moniker abbreviated from Ladies Love Cool James, this whizz kid was born James Todd Smith, 18 Jun 1968, New York, US. The first solo rap act to score a UK Top 10 hit with 'I Need Love', which was also the first successful rap 'ballad', he amassed a record eight US No.1 rap hits (76 WEEKS)* pos/wks

			pos	wks
4 Jul 87		**I'M BAD** *Def Jam 650856 7*	71	1
12 Sep 87	●	**I NEED LOVE** *Def Jam 651101 7*	8	10
21 Nov 87		**GO CUT CREATOR GO** *Def Jam LLCJ 1*	66	2
13 Feb 88		**GOING BACK TO CALI / JACK THE RIPPER** *Def Jam LLCJ 2*	37	4
10 Jun 89		**I'M THAT TYPE OF GUY** *Def Jam LLCJ 3*	43	5
1 Dec 90		**AROUND THE WAY GIRL / MAMA SAID KNOCK YOU OUT** *Def Jam 6564470*	41	4
9 Mar 91		**AROUND THE WAY GIRL (re-mix)** *Columbia 6564470*	36	4
10 Apr 93		**HOW I'M COMIN'** *Def Jam 6591692*	37	2
20 Jan 96		**HEY LOVER** *Def Jam DEFCD 14* [1]	17	4
1 Jun 96		**DOIN' IT** *Def Jam DEFCD 15* [2]	15	3
5 Oct 96	●	**LOUNGIN'** *Def Jam DEFCD 30*	7	8
8 Feb 97	★	**AIN'T NOBODY** *Geffen GFSTD 22195* ■	1	9
5 Apr 97	●	**HIT EM HIGH (THE MONSTARS' ANTHEM)** *Atlantic A 5449CD* [3]	8	6
1 Nov 97	●	**PHENOMENON** *Def Jam 5681172*	9	5
28 Mar 98	●	**FATHER** *Def Jam 5685292*	10	5
11 Jul 98		**ZOOM** *Interscope IND 95594* [4]	15	3
5 Dec 98		**INCREDIBLE** *Jive 0522102* [5]	52	1

[1] LL Cool J featuring Boyz II Men [2] LL Cool J, guest vocals by LeShaun [3] B Real / Busta Rhymes / Coolio / LL Cool J / Method Man [4] Dr Dre and LL Cool J [5] Keith Murray featuring LL Cool J

'Jack the Ripper' listed only from 20 Feb 1988

LLAMA FARMERS

UK, male / female vocal / instrumental group (2 WEEKS) pos/wks

			pos	wks
6 Feb 99		**BIG WHEELS** *Beggars Banquet BBQ 333CD*	67	1
15 May 99		**GET THE KEYS AND GO** *Beggars Banquet BBQ 335CD*	74	1

Kelly LLORENNA *UK, female vocalist (10 WEEKS)* pos/wks

			pos	wks
7 May 94		**SET YOU FREE** *All Around The World CDGLOBE 124* [1]	39	4
24 Feb 96		**BRIGHTER DAY** *Pukka CDPUKKA 5*	43	2
25 Jul 98		**HEART OF GOLD** *Diverse VERSE 2CD*	55	1
24 Mar 01		**TRUE LOVE NEVER DIES** *All Around The World CDGLOBE 240* [2]	34	3

[1] N-Trance featuring Kelly Llorenna [2] Flip and Fill featuring Kelly Llorenna

See also N-TRANCE

Don LLOYDIE – *See SOUNDMAN and Don LLOYDIE with Elisabeth TROY*

UK No.1 ★ UK Top 10 ● Still on chart + UK million seller ◆ UK entry at No.1 ■ US No.1 ▲

LNR *US, male vocal / instrumental duo (2 WEEKS)* pos/wks

3 Jun 89	**WORK IT TO THE BONE** *Kool Kat KOOL 501*	64	2

LO FIDELITY ALLSTARS
UK, male vocal / instrumental group (5 WEEKS) pos/wks

11 Oct 97	**DISCO MACHINE GUN** *Skint SKINT 30CD*	50	1
2 May 98	**VISION INCISION** *Skint SKINT 33CD*	30	2
28 Nov 98	**BATTLEFLAG** *Skint SKINT 38CD* [1]	36	2

[1] Lo Fidelity Allstars featuring Pigeonhed

LOBO *US, male vocalist – Kent LaVoie (25 WEEKS)* pos/wks

19 Jun 71 ●	**ME AND YOU AND A DOG NAMED BOO** *Philips 6073 801*	4	14
8 Jun 74 ●	**I'D LOVE YOU TO WANT ME** *UK 68*	5	11

LOBO *Holland, male vocalist – Imrich Lobo (11 WEEKS)* pos/wks

25 Jul 81 ●	**THE CARIBBEAN DISCO SHOW** *Polydor POSP 302*	8	11

LOCK 'N' LOAD *Holland, male DJ / production duo – Francis Rooijen and Nilz Pijpers (13 WEEKS)* pos/wks

15 Apr 00 ●	**BLOW YA MIND** *Pepper 9230162*	6	10
1 Jul 00	**BLOW YA MIND (re-entry)** *Pepper 9230162*	69	1
3 Mar 01	**HOUSE SOME MORE** *Pepper 9230422*	45	2

Hank LOCKLIN *US, male vocalist (41 WEEKS)* pos/wks

11 Aug 60 ●	**PLEASE HELP ME, I'M FALLING** *RCA 1188*	9	19
15 Feb 62	**FROM HERE TO THERE TO YOU** *RCA 1273*	44	3
15 Nov 62	**WE'RE GONNA GO FISHIN'** *RCA 1305*	18	11
5 May 66	**I FEEL A CRY COMING ON** *RCA 1510*	29	8

LOCKSMITH *US, male vocal / instrumental group (6 WEEKS)* pos/wks

23 Aug 80	**UNLOCK THE FUNK** *Arista ARIST 364*	42	6

LOCOMOTIVE *UK, male vocal / instrumental group (8 WEEKS)* pos/wks

16 Oct 68	**RUDI'S IN LOVE** *Parlophone R 5718*	25	8

John LODGE – *See Justin HAYWARD; MOODY BLUES*

LODGER *UK, male / female vocal / instrumental group (2 WEEKS)* pos/wks

2 May 98	**I'M LEAVING** *Island CID 693*	40	2

Lisa LOEB and NINE STORIES
US, female / male vocal / instrumental group (17 WEEKS) pos/wks

3 Sep 94 ●	**STAY (I MISSED YOU)** *RCA 74321212522* ▲	6	15
16 Sep 95	**DO YOU SLEEP?** *Geffen GFSTD 96*	45	2

Nils LOFGREN *US, male vocalist / instrumentalist – guitar (3 WEEKS)* pos/wks

8 Jun 85	**SECRETS IN THE STREET** *Towerbell TOW 68*	53	3

Johnny LOGAN *Ireland, male vocalist – Sean Sherrard (24 WEEKS)* pos/wks

3 May 80 ★	**WHAT'S ANOTHER YEAR** *Epic EPC 8572*	1	8
23 May 87 ●	**HOLD ME NOW** *Epic LOG 1*	2	11
22 Aug 87	**I'M NOT IN LOVE** *Epic LOG 2*	51	5

Kenny LOGGINS *US, male vocalist (21 WEEKS)* pos/wks

28 Apr 84 ●	**FOOTLOOSE** *CBS A 4101* ▲	6	10
1 Nov 86	**DANGER ZONE** *CBS A 7188*	45	11

LOGO featuring Dawn JOSEPH
UK, male production duo and female vocalist (1 WEEK) pos/wks

8 Dec 01	**DON'T PANIC** *Manifesto FESCD 89*	42	1

LOLA *US, female vocalist (1 WEEK)* pos/wks

28 Mar 87	**WAX THE VAN** *Syncopate SY 1*	65	1

LOLLY *UK, female vocalist – Anna Klumby (44 WEEKS)* pos/wks

10 Jul 99 ●	**VIVA LA RADIO** *Polydor 5639492*	6	9
18 Sep 99 ●	**MICKEY** *Polydor 5613682*	4	10
4 Dec 99 ●	**BIG BOYS DON'T CRY / ROCKIN' ROBIN** *Polydor 5615552*	10	9
6 May 00	**PER SEMPRE AMORE (FOREVER IN LOVE)** *Polydor 5617882*	11	8
8 Jul 00	**PER SEMPRE AMORE (FOREVER IN LOVE) (re-entry)** *Polydor 5617882*	63	2
9 Sep 00	**GIRLS JUST WANNA HAVE FUN** *Polydor 5619762*	14	6

Alain LOMBARD – *See Mady MESPLE and Danielle MILLET with the PARIS OPERA-COMIQUE ORCHESTRA conducted by Alain LOMBARD*

Julie LONDON *US, female vocalist (3 WEEKS)* pos/wks

5 Apr 57	**CRY ME A RIVER** *London HLU 8240*	22	3

Laurie LONDON *UK, male vocalist (12 WEEKS)* pos/wks

8 Nov 57	**HE'S GOT THE WHOLE WORLD IN HIS HANDS** *Parlophone R 4359* [1]	12	12

[1] Laurie London with Geoff Love his Orchestra and Chorus

LONDON BOYS *UK, male vocal duo (46 WEEKS)* pos/wks

10 Dec 88	**REQUIEM** *WEA YZ 345*	59	6
1 Apr 89 ●	**REQUIEM (re-entry)** *WEA YZ 345*	4	15
1 Jul 89 ●	**LONDON NIGHTS** *WEA YZ 393*	2	9
16 Sep 89	**HARLEM DESIRE** *WEA YZ 415*	17	7
2 Dec 89	**MY LOVE** *WEA YZ 433*	46	6
16 Jun 90	**CHAPEL OF LOVE** *East West YZ 458*	75	1
19 Jan 91	**FREEDOM** *East West YZ 554*	54	2

LONDON COMMUNITY GOSPEL CHOIR – *See Sal SOLO*

LONDON PHILHARMONIC ORCHESTRA – *See Cliff RICHARD*

LONDON STRING CHORALE *UK, orchestra / choir (13 WEEKS)* pos/wks

15 Dec 73	**GALLOPING HOME** *Polydor 2058 280*	49	3
19 Jan 74	**GALLOPING HOME (re-entry)** *Polydor 2058 280*	31	10

LONDON SYMPHONY ORCHESTRA *UK, orchestra (5 WEEKS)* pos/wks

6 Jan 79	**THEME FROM 'SUPERMAN' (MAIN TITLE)** *Warner Bros. K 17292*	32	5

Orchestra conducted by John Williams

LONDONBEAT *UK / US, male vocal group (45 WEEKS)* pos/wks

26 Nov 88	**9 AM (THE COMFORT ZONE)** *AnXious ANX 008*	19	10
18 Feb 89	**FAILING IN LOVE AGAIN** *AnXious ANX 007*	60	2
2 Dec 89	**IT TAKES TWO BABY** *Spartan CIN 101* [1]	53	2
1 Sep 90 ●	**I'VE BEEN THINKING ABOUT YOU** *AnXious ANX 14* ▲	2	13
24 Nov 90	**A BETTER LOVE** *AnXious ANX 21*	52	5
2 Mar 91	**NO WOMAN NO CRY** *AnXious ANX 25*	64	2
20 Jul 91	**A BETTER LOVE (re-issue)** *AnXious ANX 32*	23	6
27 Jun 92	**YOU BRING ON THE SUN** *AnXious ANX 37*	32	4
24 Oct 92	**THAT'S HOW I FEEL ABOUT YOU** *AnXious ANX 40*	69	1
8 Apr 95	**I'M JUST YOUR PUPPET ON A . . . (STRING)** *AnXious 74321270982*	55	1
20 May 95	**COME BACK** *AnXious 74321226682*	69	1

[1] Liz Kershaw, Bruno Brookes, Jive Bunny and Londonbeat

LONE JUSTICE
US, female / male vocal / instrumental group (4 WEEKS) pos/wks

7 Mar 87	**I FOUND LOVE** *Geffen GEF 18*	45	4

LONESTAR *US, male vocal / instrumental group (24 WEEKS)* pos/wks

15 Apr 00	**AMAZED** *BMG / Grapevine 74321742582* ▲	21	22
7 Oct 00	**SMILE** *BMG / Grapevine 74321786132*	55	2

Shorty LONG *US, male vocalist (7 WEEKS)* pos/wks

17 Jul 68	**HERE COMES THE JUDGE** *Tamla Motown TMG 663*	30	7

LONG AND THE SHORT *UK, male vocal / instrumental group (8 WEEKS)* pos/wks

10 Sep 64	THE LETTER *Decca F 11964*	35	5
24 Dec 64	CHOC ICE *Decca F 12043*	40	3

LONG RYDERS *US, male vocal / instrumental group (4 WEEKS)* pos/wks

5 Oct 85	LOOKING FOR LEWIS AND CLARKE *Island IS 237*	59	4

LONGPIGS *UK, male vocal / instrumental group (17 WEEKS)* pos/wks

22 Jul 95	SHE SAID *Mother MUMCD 66*	67	1
28 Oct 95	JESUS CHRIST *Mother MUMCD 68*	61	1
17 Feb 96	FAR *Mother MUMCD 71*	37	2
13 Apr 96	ON AND ON *Mother MUMCD 74*	16	3
22 Jun 96	SHE SAID (re-issue) *Mother MUMCD 77*	16	4
5 Oct 96	LOST MYSELF *Mother MUMCD 82*	22	3
9 Oct 99	BLUE SKIES *Mother MUMCD 113*	21	2
18 Dec 99	THE FRANK SONATA *Mother MUMCD 114*	57	1

Joe LONGTHORNE *UK, male vocalist (6 WEEKS)* pos/wks

30 Apr 94	YOUNG GIRL *EMI CDEM 310*	61	2
10 Dec 94	PASSING STRANGERS *EMI CDEM 362* [1]	34	4

[1] Joe Longthorne and Liz Dawn

LONYO *UK, male vocalist / producer – Lonyo Engele (9 WEEKS)* pos/wks

8 Jul 00 ●	SUMMER OF LOVE *Riverhorse RIVH CD3* [1]	8	7
7 Apr 01	GARAGE GIRLS *Riverhorse RIVHCD 12* [2]	39	2

[1] Lonyo – Comme Ci Comme Ça [2] Lonyo featuring MC Onyx Stone

LOOK *UK, male vocal / instrumental group (15 WEEKS)* pos/wks

20 Dec 80 ●	I AM THE BEAT *MCA 647*	6	12
29 Aug 81	FEEDING TIME *MCA 736*	50	3

LOOP DA LOOP *UK, male producer – Nick Dresti (4 WEEKS)* pos/wks

7 Jun 97	GO WITH THE FLOW *Manifesto FESCD 24*	47	1
20 Feb 99	HAZEL *Manifesto FESCD 53*	20	3

LOOSE ENDS 457 Top 500 *Soul / disco trio formed in London; Carl McIntosh (v/g), Jane Eugene (v) and Steve Nichol (k) - the latter two leaving in 1990. First UK group to top US R&B chart - achieved this feat with US-produced 'Hangin' on a String' and 'Slow Down' (76 WEEKS)* pos/wks

25 Feb 84	TELL ME WHAT YOU WANT *Virgin VS 658*	74	1
28 Apr 84	EMERGENCY (DIAL 999) *Virgin VS 677*	41	6
21 Jul 84	CHOOSE ME (RESCUE ME) *Virgin VS 697*	59	3
23 Feb 85	HANGIN' ON A STRING (CONTEMPLATING) *Virgin VS 748*	13	13
11 May 85	MAGIC TOUCH *Virgin VS 761*	16	7
27 Jul 85	GOLDEN YEARS *Virgin VS 795*	59	4
14 Jun 86	STAY A LITTLE WHILE, CHILD *Virgin VS 819*	52	5
20 Sep 86	SLOW DOWN *Virgin VS 884*	27	7
29 Nov 86	NIGHTS OF PLEASURE *Virgin VS 919*	42	7
4 Jun 88	MR BACHELOR *Virgin VS 1080*	50	4
25 Aug 90	DON'T BE A FOOL *10 TEN 312*	13	9
17 Nov 90	LOVE'S GOT ME *10 TEN 330*	40	4
20 Jun 92	HANGIN' ON A STRING (re-mix) *Ten TEN 406*	25	5
5 Sep 92	MAGIC TOUCH (re-mix) *Ten TEN 409*	75	1

Lisa 'Left Eye' LOPES *US, female vocalist (20 WEEKS)* pos/wks

1 Apr 00 ★	NEVER BE THE SAME AGAIN *Virgin VSCDT 1762* [1] ■	1	14
22 Jul 00	NEVER BE THE SAME AGAIN (re-entry) *Virgin VSCDT 1762* [1]	70	2
27 Oct 01	THE BLOCK PARTY *La Face / Arista 74321895912*	16	4

[1] Melanie C / Lisa 'Left Eye' Lopes

See also TLC

Jennifer LOPEZ *Globally successful, photogenic singer / actress. J. Lo, b. 24 Jul 1970, Bronx, New York, starred in such movies as 'The Wedding Planner', 'The Cell' and 'Selena' (life story of an earlier Latin superstar) and had much publicised romance with P Diddy (70 WEEKS)* pos/wks

3 Jul 99 ●	IF YOU HAD MY LOVE *Columbia 6675772* ▲	4	13
13 Nov 99 ●	WAITING FOR TONIGHT *Columbia 6683072*	5	12
1 Apr 00	FEELIN' SO GOOD *Columbia 6691972* [1]	15	6
20 Jan 01 ★	LOVE DON'T COST A THING *Epic 6707282* ■	1	10
21 Apr 01	LOVE DON'T COST A THING (re-entry) *Epic 6707282*	67	1
12 May 01 ●	PLAY *Epic 6712272*	3	10
28 Jul 01	PLAY (re-entry) *Epic 6712272*	75	1
18 Aug 01 ●	AIN'T IT FUNNY *Epic 6717592*	3	8
27 Oct 01	AIN'T IT FUNNY (re-entry) *Epic 6717592*	59	1
10 Nov 01 ●	I'M REAL *Epic 6720322* [2] ▲	4	8+

[1] Jennifer Lopez featuring Big Pun and Fat Joe [2] Jennifer Lopez featuring Ja Rule

Trini LOPEZ *US, male vocalist (37 WEEKS)* pos/wks

12 Sep 63 ●	IF I HAD A HAMMER *Reprise R 20198*	4	17
12 Dec 63	KANSAS CITY *Reprise R 20236*	35	5
12 May 66	I'M COMING HOME CINDY *Reprise R 20455*	28	5
6 Apr 67	GONNA GET ALONG WITHOUT YA NOW *Reprise R 20547*	41	5
19 Dec 81	TRINI TRAX *RCA 154*	59	5

LO-PRO – *See X-PRESS 2*

LORD ROCKINGHAM'S XI *UK, male / female instrumental group – leader Harry Robinson (21 WEEKS)* pos/wks

24 Oct 58 ★	HOOTS MON *Decca F 11059*	1	17
6 Feb 59	WEE TOM *Decca F 11104*	16	3
25 Sep 93	HOOTS MON (re-issue) *Decca 8820982*	60	1

LORD TANAMO *Trinidad and Tobago, male vocalist (2 WEEKS)* pos/wks

1 Dec 90	I'M IN THE MOOD FOR LOVE *Mooncrest MOON 1009*	58	2

LORD TARIQ and Peter GUNZ *US, male vocal / rap duo (3 WEEKS)* pos/wks

2 May 98	DEJA VU (UPTOWN BABY) *Columbia 6658722*	21	3

Jerry LORDAN *UK, male vocalist (15 WEEKS)* pos/wks

8 Jan 60	I'LL STAY SINGLE *Parlophone R 4588*	26	2
26 Feb 60	WHO COULD BE BLUER *Parlophone R 4627*	16	9
10 Mar 60	I'LL STAY SINGLE (re-entry) *Parlophone R 4588*	41	1
19 May 60	WHO COULD BE BLUER (re-entry) *Parlophone R 4627*	45	1
2 Jun 60	SING LIKE AN ANGEL *Parlophone R 4653*	36	2

Traci LORDS *US, female vocalist (1 WEEK)* pos/wks

7 Oct 95	FALLEN ANGEL *Radioactive RAXTD 18*	72	1

Sophia LOREN – *See Peter SELLERS*

Trey LORENZ *US, male vocalist (5 WEEKS)* pos/wks

21 Nov 92	SOMEONE TO HOLD *Epic 6587857*	65	2
30 Jan 93	PHOTOGRAPH OF MARY *Epic 6589542*	38	3

See also Mariah CAREY

LORI and the CHAMELEONS *UK, female / male vocal / instrumental group (1 WEEK)* pos/wks

8 Dec 79	TOUCH *Sire SIR 4025*	70	1

LORRAINE – *See BOMB THE BASS*

LOS BRAVOS *Spain / Germany, male vocal / instrumental group (24 WEEKS)* pos/wks

30 Jun 66 ●	BLACK IS BLACK *Decca F 22419*	2	13
8 Sep 66	I DON'T CARE *Decca F 22484*	16	11

LOS DEL CHIPMUNKS – *See CHIPMUNKS*

LOS DEL MAR featuring Wil VELOZ *Cuba / Canada, male vocal / instrumental group (7 WEEKS)* pos/wks

8 Jun 96	MACARENA *Pulse 8 CDLOSE 101*	66	2
6 Jul 96	MACARENA (re-entry) *Pulse 8 CDLOSE 101*	43	5

THE OFFICIAL UK SINGLES CHART 50TH ANNIVERSARY

1978

IN THE YEAR IN WHICH JIMMY CARTER MEDIATED THE CAMP DAVID ARAB-ISRAELI PEACE ACCORD, LOUISE BROWN BECAME THE FIRST TEST-TUBE BABY TO BE BORN, THE 'SON OF SAM' WAS CAPTURED IN NEW YORK CITY, AND FILM SOUNDTRACKS 'SATURDAY NIGHT FEVER' AND 'GREASE' BROKE RECORDS AND SPAWNED NUMEROUS HITS, AN IMPRESSIONABLE **JON BON JOVI** OWNS UP TO POSSESSING A CARDBOARD GUITAR NAMED ELTON ...

“As a kid my walls were literally wallpapered with with pictures from all the American rock magazines of my favourite bands. There were so many of them; it was never just any one person for me. I've liked different people for different things – Jimmy Page, Elton John, I even had a cardboard guitar I called Elton! – but someone I really liked for his singing was John Waite, singer with **The Babys**, who are one of my favourite bands. If I had to choose one song in particular it was 'Isn't It Time'.”

SINGLE OF THE YEAR 'You're the One That I Want' John Travolta and Olivia Newton-John
ALBUM OF THE YEAR 'Saturday Night Fever' soundtrack

LOS DEL RIO *Spain, male vocal / instrumental duo – Antonio Monge and Rafael Perdigones (19 WEEKS)* pos/wks

1 Jun 96		**MACARENA** *RCA 74321345372* ▲	64	1
13 Jul 96	●	**MACARENA (re-entry)** *RCA 74321345372*	2	18

LOS INDIOS TABAJARAS *Brazil, male instrumental guitar duo – Natalicio and Antenor Lima (17 WEEKS)* pos/wks

31 Oct 63	●	**MARIA ELENA** *RCA 1365*	5	17

LOS LOBOS *US, male vocal / instrumental group – lead vocal David Hildago (24 WEEKS)* pos/wks

6 Apr 85		**DON'T WORRY BABY / WILL THE WOLF SURVIVE** *London LASH 4*	57	4
18 Jul 87	★	**LA BAMBA** *Slash LASH 13* ▲	1	11
26 Sep 87		**COME ON LET'S GO** *Slash LASH 14*	18	9

LOS UMBRELLOS *Denmark, male / female vocal trio (2 WEEKS)* pos/wks

3 Oct 98		**NO TENGO DINERO** *Virgin VUSCD 139*	33	2

Joe LOSS *UK, orchestra (53 WEEKS)* pos/wks

29 Jun 61		**WHEELS CHA CHA** *HMV POP 880*	21	21
19 Oct 61		**SUCU SUCU** *HMV POP 937*	48	1
29 Mar 62		**THE MAIGRET THEME** *HMV POP 995*	20	10
1 Nov 62		**MUST BE MADISON** *HMV POP 1075*	20	13
5 Nov 64		**MARCH OF THE MODS** *HMV POP 1351*	35	4
24 Dec 64		**MARCH OF THE MODS (re-entry)** *HMV POP 1351*	31	4

LOST *UK, male / instrumental / production duo (1 WEEK)* pos/wks

22 Jun 91		**TECHNO FUNK** *Perfecto PT 44560*	75	1

LOST BOYZ *US, male rap group (2 WEEKS)* pos/wks

2 Nov 96		**MUSIC MAKES ME HIGH** *Universal MCSTD 48015*	42	1
12 Jul 97		**LOVE, PEACE & NAPPINESS** *Universal UND 56131*	57	1

LOST IT.COM *UK, male vocal / production duo (1 WEEK)* pos/wks

7 Apr 01		**ANIMAL** *Perfecto PERF 13CDS*	70	1

LOST TRIBE *UK, male production duo (3 WEEKS)* pos/wks

11 Sep 99		**GAMEMASTER** *Hooj Choons HOOJ 81CD*	24	3

LOST WITNESS
UK, male production duo and female vocalist (10 WEEKS) pos/wks

29 May 99		**HAPPINESS HAPPENING** *Ministry of Sound MOSCDS 129*	18	4
18 Sep 99		**RED SUN RISING** *Ministry of Sound MOSCDS 133*	22	3
16 Dec 00		**7 COLOURS** *Data DATA 15CDS*	28	3

LOSTPROPHETS *UK, male vocal / instrumental group (2 WEEKS)* pos/wks

8 Dec 01		**SHINOBI VS DRAGON NINJA** *Visible Noise TORMENT16*	41	2

LOTUS EATERS *UK, male vocal / instrumental duo – Peter Coyle and Jerry Kelley (16 WEEKS)* pos/wks

2 Jul 83		**FIRST PICTURE OF YOU** *Sylvan SYL 1*	15	12
8 Oct 83		**YOU DON'T NEED SOMEONE NEW** *Sylvan SYL 2*	53	4

Bonnie LOU *US, female vocalist – Bonnie Lou Kath (10 WEEKS)* pos/wks

5 Feb 54	●	**TENNESSEE WIG WALK** *Parlophone R 3730*	4	10

Lippy LOU *UK, female rapper (2 WEEKS)* pos/wks

22 Apr 95		**LIBERATION** *More Protein PROCD 105*	57	2

Louchie LOU and Michie ONE
UK, female rap duo – Louise Gold and Michelle Charles (36 WEEKS) pos/wks

29 May 93	●	**SHOUT** *ffrr FCD 211*	7	8
14 Aug 93		**SOMEBODY ELSE'S GUY** *ffrr FCD 216*	54	2
26 Aug 95		**GET DOWN ON IT** *China WOKCD 2054*	58	1
13 Apr 96	●	**CECILIA** *WEA WEA 042CD1* [1]	4	17
15 Jun 96		**GOOD SWEET LOVIN'** *Indochina ID 050CD*	34	2
24 Aug 96		**CECILIA (re-entry)** *WEA WEA 042CD1* [1]	65	1
7 Sep 96		**CECILIA (2nd re-entry)** *WEA WEA 042CD1* [1]	59	1
21 Sep 96		**NO MORE ALCOHOL** *WEA WEA 065CD1* [1]	24	4

[1] Suggs featuring Louchie Lou and Michie One

LOUD *UK, male vocal / instrumental group (2 WEEKS)* pos/wks

28 Mar 92		**EASY** *China WOK 2016*	67	2

John D LOUDERMILK *US, male vocalist (10 WEEKS)* pos/wks

4 Jan 62		**THE LANGUAGE OF LOVE** *RCA 1269*	13	10

Louie LOUIE *US, male vocalist (5 WEEKS)* pos/wks

19 Dec 92		**THE THOUGHT OF IT** *Hardback YZ 724*	34	5

LOUISE (431 Top 500) *First British female to have a string of Top 20s as both a group member (exited Eternal in July 1995) and solo singer, b. Louise Nurding, 4 Nov 1974, south London. Photogenic vocalist, who has sung on 17 Top 20 entries, is married to footballer Jamie Redknapp (78 WEEKS)* pos/wks

7 Oct 95	●	**LIGHT OF MY LIFE** *EMI CDEMS 397*	8	8
16 Mar 96		**IN WALKED LOVE** *EMI CDEMS 413*	17	6
8 Jun 96	●	**NAKED** *EMI CDEM 431*	5	8
31 Aug 96	●	**UNDIVIDED LOVE** *EMI CDEM 441*	5	6
30 Nov 96	●	**ONE KISS FROM HEAVEN** *EMI CDEM 454*	9	7
4 Oct 97	●	**ARMS AROUND THE WORLD** *EMI CDEM 490*	4	7
29 Nov 97	●	**LET'S GO ROUND AGAIN** *EMI CDEM 500*	10	9
4 Apr 98		**ALL THAT MATTERS** *1st Avenue CDEM 506*	11	5
20 Jun 98		**ALL THAT MATTERS (re-entry)** *1st Avenue CDEM 506*	73	1
29 Jul 00	●	**2 FACED** *1st Avenue / EMI CDEMS 570*	3	8
11 Nov 00		**BEAUTIFUL INSIDE** *1st Avenue / EMI CDEMS 575*	13	4
8 Sep 01	●	**STUCK IN THE MIDDLE WITH YOU** *1st Avenue / EMI CDEM 600*	4	9

See also ETERNAL

Darlene LOVE *US, female vocalist (5 WEEKS)* pos/wks

19 Dec 92		**ALL ALONE ON CHRISTMAS** *Arista 74321124767*	31	4
1 Jan 94		**ALL ALONE ON CHRISTMAS (re-entry)** *Arista 74321124767*	72	1

Geoff LOVE – *See MANUEL and his MUSIC OF THE MOUNTAINS; Laurie LONDON*

Helen LOVE *UK, male / female vocal / instrumental group (2 WEEKS)* pos/wks

20 Sep 97		**DOES YOUR HEART GO BOOM** *Che CHE 72CD*	71	1
19 Sep 98		**LONG LIVE THE UK MUSIC SCENE** *Che CHE 82CD*	65	1

Monie LOVE *UK, female rapper – Simone Johnson (51 WEEKS)* pos/wks

4 Feb 89		**I CAN DO THIS** *Cooltempo COOL 177*	37	4
24 Jun 89		**GRANDPA'S PARTY** *Cooltempo COOL 184*	16	9
14 Jul 90		**MONIE IN THE MIDDLE** *Cooltempo COOL 210*	46	3
22 Sep 90		**IT'S A SHAME (MY SISTER)** *Cooltempo COOL 219* [1]	12	8
1 Dec 90		**DOWN TO EARTH** *Cooltempo COOL 222*	31	6
6 Apr 91		**RING MY BELL** *Cooltempo COOL 224* [2]	20	5
25 Jul 92		**FULL TERM LOVE** *Cooltempo COOL 258*	34	4
13 Mar 93		**BORN 2 B.R.E.E.D.** *Cooltempo CDCOOL 269*	18	5
12 Jun 93		**IN A WORD OR 2 / THE POWER** *Cooltempo CDCOOL 273*	33	3
21 Aug 93		**NEVER GIVE UP** *Cooltempo CDCOOL 276*	41	2
22 Apr 00		**SLICE OF DA PIE** *Relentless RELENT 2CDS*	29	2

[1] Monie Love featuring True Image [2] Monie Love vs Adeva

Vikki LOVE – *See JUNGLE BROTHERS; NUANCE featuring Vikki LOVE*

LOVE AFFAIR
UK, male vocal / instrumental group – lead vocal Steve Ellis (56 WEEKS) pos/wks

3 Jan 68	★	**EVERLASTING LOVE** *CBS 3125*	1	12
17 Apr 68	●	**RAINBOW VALLEY** *CBS 3366*	5	13
11 Sep 68	●	**A DAY WITHOUT LOVE** *CBS 3674*	6	12
19 Feb 69		**ONE ROAD** *CBS 3994*	16	9
16 Jul 69	●	**BRINGING ON BACK THE GOOD TIMES** *CBS 4300*	9	10

LOVE AND MONEY *UK, male vocal / instrumental group (23 WEEKS)* pos/wks

24 May 86	**CANDYBAR EXPRESS** *Mercury MONEY 1*	56	4
25 Apr 87	**LOVE AND MONEY** *Mercury MONEY 4*	68	4
17 Sep 88	**HALLELUIAH MAN** *Fontana MONEY 5*	63	4
14 Jan 89	**STRANGE KIND OF LOVE** *Fontana MONEY 6*	45	5
25 Mar 89	**JOCELYN SQUARE** *Fontana MONEY 7*	51	4
16 Nov 91	**WINTER** *Fontana MONEY 9*	52	2

LOVE BITE *Italy, male / female production / vocal group (1 WEEK)* pos/wks

7 Oct 00	**TAKE YOUR TIME** *AM:PM CDAMPM134*	56	1

LOVE CITY GROOVE
UK, male / female vocal / rap / instrumental group (11 WEEKS) pos/wks

8 Apr 95 ●	**LOVE CITY GROOVE** *Planet 3 GXY 2003CD*	7	11

LOVE CONNECTION
Italy / Germany, male / female vocal / production group (1 WEEK) pos/wks

2 Dec 00	**THE BOMB** *Multiply CDMULTY 63*	53	1

LOVE DECADE *UK, male / female vocal / instrumental group (14 WEEKS)* pos/wks

6 Jul 91	**DREAM ON (IS THIS A DREAM)** *All Around the World GLOBE 100*	52	2
23 Nov 91	**SO REAL** *All Around the World GLOBE 106*	14	7
11 Apr 92	**I FEEL YOU** *All Around the World GLOBE 107*	34	3
6 Feb 93	**WHEN THE MORNING COMES** *All Around the World CDGLOBE 114*	69	1
17 Feb 96	**IS THIS A DREAM** *All Around the World CDGLOBE 132*	39	1

'Is This a Dream' in 1996 is a re-recording

LOVE DECREE *UK, male vocal / instrumental group (4 WEEKS)* pos/wks

16 Sep 89	**SOMETHING SO REAL (CHINHEADS THEME)** *Ariola 112642*	61	4

LOVE / HATE *US, male vocal / instrumental group (4 WEEKS)* pos/wks

30 Nov 91	**EVIL TWIN** *Columbia 6575967*	59	1
4 Apr 92	**WASTED IN AMERICA** *Columbia 6578897*	38	3

LOVE INCORPORATED featuring MC NOISE
UK, male vocal / production duo (3 WEEKS) pos/wks

9 Feb 91	**LOVE IS THE MESSAGE** *Love EVOL 1*	59	3

LOVE NELSON – *See FIRE ISLAND*

LOVE REACTION – *See ZODIAC MINDWARP and the LOVE REACTION*

LOVE SCULPTURE *UK, instrumental group (14 WEEKS)* pos/wks

27 Nov 68 ●	**SABRE DANCE** *Parlophone R 5744*	5	14

See also Dave EDMUNDS

LOVE SQUAD – *See Linda CARR*

A LOVE SUPREME *UK, male vocal / instrumental group (2 WEEKS)* pos/wks

17 Apr 99	**NIALL QUINN'S DISCO PANTS** *A Love Supreme / Cherry Red CDVINNIE 3*	59	2

[LOVE] TATTOO *Australia, male producer – Stephen Allkins (1 WEEK)* pos/wks

6 Oct 01	**DROP SOME DRUMS** *Positiva CDTIV 162*	58	1

LOVE TO INFINITY
UK, male / female vocal / instrumental group (4 WEEKS) pos/wks

24 Jun 95	**KEEP LOVE TOGETHER** *Mushroom D 00467*	38	2
18 Nov 95	**SOMEDAY** *Mushroom D 1143*	75	1
3 Aug 96	**PRAY FOR LOVE** *Mushroom D 1213*	69	1

LOVE TRIBE *US, male / female vocal / instrumental duo (3 WEEKS)* pos/wks

29 Jun 96	**STAND UP** *AM:PM 5816272*	23	3

LOVE UNLIMITED *US, female vocal group (19 WEEKS)* pos/wks

17 Jun 72	**WALKIN' IN THE RAIN WITH THE ONE I LOVE** *Uni UN 539*	14	10
25 Jan 75	**IT MAY BE WINTER OUTSIDE (BUT IN MY HEART IT'S SPRING)** *20th Century BTC 2149*	11	9

LOVE UNLIMITED ORCHESTRA *US, orchestra (10 WEEKS)* pos/wks

2 Feb 74 ●	**LOVE'S THEME** *Pye International 7N 25635* ▲	10	10

LOVEBUG STARSKI *US, male rapper – Kevin Smith (9 WEEKS)* pos/wks

31 May 86	**AMITYVILLE (THE HOUSE ON THE HILL)** *Epic A 7182*	12	9

LOVEDEEJAY AKEMI – *See YOSH presents LOVEDEEJAY AKEMI*

LOVEHAPPY
US / UK, male / female vocal / instrumental group (3 WEEKS) pos/wks

18 Feb 95	**MESSAGE OF LOVE** *MCA MCSTD 2040*	37	2
20 Jul 96	**MESSAGE OF LOVE (re-mix)** *MCA MCSTD 40052*	70	1

Bill LOVELADY *UK, male vocalist (10 WEEKS)* pos/wks

18 Aug 79	**REGGAE FOR IT NOW** *Charisma CB 337*	12	10

LOVELAND featuring the voice of Rachel McFARLANE *UK, male / female vocal / instrumental group (15 WEEKS)* pos/wks

16 Apr 94	**LET THE MUSIC (LIFT YOU UP)** *KMS / Eastern Bloc KMSCD 10*	16	4
5 Nov 94	**(KEEP ON) SHINING / HOPE (NEVER GIVE UP)** *Eastern Bloc BLOCCD 016*	37	2
14 Jan 95	**I NEED SOMEBODY** *Eastern Bloc BLOCCD 019*	21	3
10 Jun 95	**DON'T MAKE ME WAIT** *Eastern Bloc BLOC 20CD*	22	3
2 Sep 95	**THE WONDER OF LOVE** *Eastern Bloc BLOC 22CD*	53	1
11 Nov 95	**I NEED SOMEBODY (re-mix)** *Eastern Bloc BLOC 23CD*	38	2

All formats of 'Let the Music (Lift You Up)' featured versions by Loveland featuring Rachel McFarlane and also by Darlene Lewis

LOVER SPEAKS *UK, male vocal / instrumental duo (5 WEEKS)* pos/wks

16 Aug 86	**NO MORE 'I LOVE YOU'S'** *A & M AM 326*	58	5

Michael LOVESMITH *US, male vocalist (1 WEEK)* pos/wks

5 Oct 85	**AIN'T NOTHIN' LIKE IT** *Motown ZB 40369*	75	1

LOVESTATION
UK, male / female vocal / instrumental group (21 WEEKS) pos/wks

13 Mar 93	**SHINE ON ME** *RCA 743211337912* [1]	71	1
13 Nov 93	**BEST OF MY LOVE** *Fresh FRSHD 1*	73	1
18 Mar 95	**LOVE COME RESCUE ME** *Fresh FRSHD 22*	42	2
1 Aug 98	**TEARDROPS** *Fresh FRSHD 65*	14	6
5 Dec 98	**SENSUALITY** *Fresh FRSHD 71*	16	7
5 Feb 00	**TEARDROPS (re-mix)** *Fresh FRSHD 79*	24	4

[1] Lovestation featuring Lisa Hunt

Lene LOVICH *US, female vocalist – Lili Premilovich (38 WEEKS)* pos/wks

17 Feb 79 ●	**LUCKY NUMBER** *Stiff BUY 42*	3	11
12 May 79	**SAY WHEN** *Stiff BUY 46*	19	10
20 Oct 79	**BIRD SONG** *Stiff BUY 53*	39	7
29 Mar 80	**WHAT WILL I DO WITHOUT YOU** *Stiff BUY 69*	58	3
14 Mar 81	**NEW TOY** *Stiff BUY 97*	53	5
27 Nov 82	**IT'S YOU ONLY YOU (MEIN SCHMERZ)** *Stiff BUY 164*	68	2

LOVIN' SPOONFUL
US / Canada, male vocal / instrumental group (33 WEEKS) pos/wks

14 Apr 66 ●	**DAYDREAM** *Pye International 7N 25361*	2	13
14 Jul 66 ●	**SUMMER IN THE CITY** *Kama Sutra KAS 200* ▲	8	11
5 Jan 67	**NASHVILLE CATS** *Kama Sutra KAS 204*	26	7
9 Mar 67	**DARLING BE HOME SOON** *Kama Sutra KAS 207*	44	2

LOVINDEER *Jamaica, male vocalist (3 WEEKS)* pos/wks

27 Sep 86	**MAN SHORTAGE** *TSOJ TS 1*	69	3

Gary LOW *Italy, male vocalist (3 WEEKS)* pos/wks

8 Oct 83	I WANT YOU *Savoir Faire FAIS 004*	52	3

Patti LOW – *See BUG KANN and the PLASTIC JAM*

Jim LOWE *US, male vocalist (9 WEEKS)* pos/wks

26 Oct 56 ●	THE GREEN DOOR *London HLD 8317* [1]	8	9

[1] Jim Lowe and the High Fives

Nick LOWE *UK, male vocalist (27 WEEKS)* pos/wks

11 Mar 78 ●	I LOVE THE SOUND OF BREAKING GLASS *Radar ADA 1*	7	8
9 Jun 79	CRACKIN' UP *Radar ADA 34*	34	5
25 Aug 79	CRUEL TO BE KIND *Radar ADA 43*	12	11
26 May 84	HALF A BOY AND HALF A MAN *F. Beat XX 34*	53	3

LOWGOLD *UK, male vocal / instrumental group (4 WEEKS)* pos/wks

30 Sep 00	BEAUTY DIES YOUNG *Nude NUD 52CD*	67	1
10 Feb 01	MERCURY *Nude NUD 53CD*	48	1
12 May 01	COUNTERFEIT *Nude NUD 55CD*	52	1
8 Sep 01	BEAUTY DIES YOUNG (re-mix) *Nude NUD 59CD*	40	1

LOWRELL *US, male vocalist (9 WEEKS)* pos/wks

24 Nov 79	MELLOW MELLOW RIGHT ON *AVI AVIS 108*	37	9

LRS – *See D MOB*

L7 *US, female vocal / instrumental group (18 WEEKS)* pos/wks

4 Apr 92	PRETEND WE'RE DEAD *Slash LASH 34*	21	7
30 May 92	EVERGLADE *Slash LASH 36*	27	3
12 Sep 92	MONSTER *Slash LASH 38*	33	3
28 Nov 92	PRETEND WE'RE DEAD (re-issue) *Slash LASH 42*	50	3
9 Jul 94	ANDRES *Slash LASCD 48*	34	2

LSG *Germany, male DJ / producer – Oliver Lieb (1 WEEK)* pos/wks

10 May 97	NETHERWORLD *Hooj Choons HOOJCD 52*	63	1

L.T.D. *US, male vocal / instrumental group (3 WEEKS)* pos/wks

9 Sep 78	HOLDING ON (WHEN LOVE IS GONE) *A & M AMS 7378*	70	3

LUCAS *Denmark, male vocalist (4 WEEKS)* pos/wks

6 Aug 94	LUCAS WITH THE LID OFF *WEA YZ 832CD*	37	4

Carrie LUCAS *US, female vocalist (6 WEEKS)* pos/wks

16 Jun 79	DANCE WITH YOU *Solar FB 1482*	40	6

Tammy LUCAS – *See Teddy RILEY*

LUCIANA *UK, female vocalist (5 WEEKS)* pos/wks

23 Apr 94	GET IT UP FOR LOVE *Chrysalis CDCHS 5008*	55	2
6 Aug 94	IF YOU WANT *Chrysalis CDCHS 5009*	47	2
5 Nov 94	WHAT GOES AROUND / ONE MORE RIVER *Chrysalis CDCHS 5015*	67	1

LUCID *UK, male / female vocal / instrumental group (15 WEEKS)* pos/wks

8 Aug 98 ●	I CAN'T HELP MYSELF *ffrr FCD 339*	7	8
27 Feb 99	CRAZY *ffrr / Delirious / Indirect FCD 355*	14	5
16 Oct 99	STAY WITH ME TILL DAWN *ffrr FCD 368*	25	2

LUCKY MONKEYS *UK, male instrumental group (1 WEEK)* pos/wks

9 Nov 96	BJANGO *Hi-Life 5757132*	50	1

See also FLUKE

LUCY PEARL
US, male / female vocal / rap / instrumental / production trio (7 WEEKS) pos/wks

29 Jul 00	DANCE TONIGHT *Virgin VSCDT 1775*	36	2
25 Nov 00	DON'T MESS WITH MY MAN *Virgin VSCDT 1778*	20	4
28 Jul 01	WITHOUT YOU *Virgin VSCDT 1805*	51	1

LUDACRIS *US, male rapper – Christopher Bridges (16 WEEKS)* pos/wks

9 Jun 01	WHAT'S YOUR FANTASY *Def Jam 5729842*	19	5
18 Aug 01 ●	ONE MINUTE MAN *Elektra E 7245CD* [1]	10	8
29 Sep 01	AREA CODES *Def Jam 5887722* [2]	25	3

[1] Missy 'Misdemeanor' Elliott featuring Ludacris [2] Ludacris featuring Nate Dogg

Baz LUHRMANN *Australia, male producer (16 WEEKS)* pos/wks

12 Jun 99 ★	EVERYBODY'S FREE (TO WEAR SUNSCREEN) *EMI CDBAZ 001* ■	1	16

Uncredited vocals by actor Lee Perry

Robin LUKE *US, male vocalist (6 WEEKS)* pos/wks

17 Oct 58	SUSIE DARLIN' *London HLD 8676*	24	3
21 Nov 58	SUSIE DARLIN' (re-entry) *London HLD 8676*	23	1
5 Dec 58	SUSIE DARLIN' (2nd re-entry) *London HLD 8676*	23	2

LUKK featuring Felicia COLLINS
US, male / female vocal / instrumental group (1 WEEK) pos/wks

28 Sep 85	ON THE ONE *Important TAN 6*	72	1

LULU (114 Top 500) *One of Scotland's best-known female vocalists, b. Marie Lawrie, 3 Nov 1948, Strathclyde. She scored her first hit aged 15, had a US chart-topper ('To Sir With Love') aged 18, won the Eurovision Song Contest aged 20, and finally reached No.1 aged 44 (175 WEEKS)* pos/wks

14 May 64 ●	SHOUT *Decca F 11884* [1]	7	13
12 Nov 64	HERE COMES THE NIGHT *Decca F 12017*	50	1
17 Jun 65 ●	LEAVE A LITTLE LOVE *Decca F 12169*	8	11
2 Sep 65	TRY TO UNDERSTAND *Decca F 12214*	25	8
13 Apr 67 ●	THE BOAT THAT I ROW *Columbia DB 8169*	6	11
29 Jun 67	LET'S PRETEND *Columbia DB 8221*	11	11
8 Nov 67	LOVE LOVES TO LOVE LOVE *Columbia DB 8295*	32	6
28 Feb 68 ●	ME, THE PEACEFUL HEART *Columbia DB 8358*	9	9
5 Jun 68	BOY *Columbia DB 8425*	15	7
6 Nov 68 ●	I'M A TIGER *Columbia DB 8500*	9	13
12 Mar 69 ●	BOOM BANG-A-BANG *Columbia DB 8550*	2	13
22 Nov 69	OH ME OH MY (I'M A FOOL FOR YOU BABY) *Atco 226008*	47	2
26 Jan 74 ●	THE MAN WHO SOLD THE WORLD *Polydor 2001 490*	3	9
19 Apr 75	TAKE YOUR MAMA FOR A RIDE *Chelsea 2005 022*	37	4
12 Dec 81	I COULD NEVER MISS YOU (MORE THAN I DO) *Alfa ALFA 1700*	62	4
16 Jan 82	I COULD NEVER MISS YOU (MORE THAN I DO) (re-entry) *Alfa ALFA 1700*	63	1
19 Jul 86 ●	SHOUT *Jive LULU1 / Decca SHOUT 1*	8	11
30 Jan 93	INDEPENDENCE *Dome CDDOME 1001*	11	5
3 Apr 93	I'M BACK FOR MORE *Dome CDDOME 1002* [2]	27	5
4 Sep 93	LET ME WAKE UP IN YOUR ARMS *Dome CDDOME 1005*	51	2
9 Oct 93 ★	RELIGHT MY FIRE *RCA 74321167722* [3] ■	1	14
27 Nov 93	HOW 'BOUT US *Dome CDDOME 1007*	46	3
27 Aug 94	GOODBYE BABY AND AMEN *Dome CDDOME 1011*	40	2
26 Nov 94	EVERY WOMAN KNOWS *Dome CDDOME 1013*	44	2
29 May 99	HURT ME SO BAD *Rocket / Mercury 5726132*	42	2
8 Jan 00	BETTER GET READY *Mercury 5625852*	59	1
18 Mar 00	WHERE THE POOR BOYS DANCE *Mercury 1568452*	24	5

[1] Lulu and the Luvvers [2] Lulu and Bobby Womack [3] Take That featuring Lulu

The newly recorded 'Shout' entered the chart on 19 Jul 1986, and the next week the original Decca version by Lulu and the Luvvers also charted. For all subsequent weeks Gallup amalgamated both versions under one entry and we have added an extra week on chart for the 'double week' to take account of this

Bob LUMAN *US, male vocalist (21 WEEKS)* pos/wks

8 Sep 60 ●	LET'S THINK ABOUT LIVING *Warner Bros. WB 18*	6	18
15 Dec 60	WHY, WHY, BYE, BYE *Warner Bros. WB 28*	46	1
4 May 61	THE GREAT SNOWMAN *Warner Bros. WB 37*	49	2

LUMINAIRE – *See Jonathan PETERS presents LUMINAIRE*

LUNIZ *US, male rap duo – Jerrold 'Yukmouth' Ellis Jr and Garrick 'Knumbskull' Husbands (18 WEEKS)*

		pos	wks
17 Feb 96	● I GOT 5 ON IT *Virgin America VUSCD 101*	3	13
11 May 96	PLAYA HATA *Virgin America VUSCD 103*	20	3
31 Oct 98	I GOT 5 ON IT (re-mix) *Virgin VCRD 41*	28	2

LUPINE HOWL *UK, male vocal / instrumental group (1 WEEK)*

		pos	wks
22 Jan 00	VAPORIZER *Vinyl Hiss VHISSCD 001*	68	1

LURKERS *UK, male vocal / instrumental group (11 WEEKS)*

		pos	wks
3 Jun 78	AIN'T GOT A CLUE *Beggars Banquet BEG 6*	45	3
5 Aug 78	I DON'T NEED TO TELL HER *Beggars Banquet BEG 9*	49	4
3 Feb 79	JUST THIRTEEN *Beggars Banquet BEG 14*	66	2
9 Jun 79	OUT IN THE DARK / CYANIDE *Beggars Banquet BEG 19*	72	1
17 Nov 79	NEW GUITAR IN TOWN *Beggars Banquet BEG 28*	72	1

LUSCIOUS JACKSON *US, female vocal / instrumental group (5 WEEKS)*

		pos	wks
18 Mar 95	DEEP SHAG / CITYSONG *Capitol CDCL 739*	69	1
21 Oct 95	HERE *Capitol CDCL 758*	59	1
12 Apr 97	NAKED EYE *Capitol CDCL 786*	25	2
3 Jul 99	LADYFINGERS *Grand Royal / Parlophone CDCL 813*	43	1

LUSH *UK, female / male vocal / instrumental group (19 WEEKS)*

		pos	wks
10 Mar 90	MAD LOVE (EP) *4AD BAD 003*	55	1
27 Oct 90	SWEETNESS AND LIGHT *4AD BAD 0013*	47	2
19 Oct 91	NOTHING NATURAL *4AD AD 1016*	43	2
11 Jan 92	FOR LOVE (EP) *4AD BAD 2001*	35	2
11 Jun 94	DESIRE LINES *4AD BAD 4010CD*	60	1
11 Jun 94	HYPOCRITE *4AD BAD 4008CD*	52	2
20 Jan 96	SINGLE GIRL *4AD BAD 6001CD*	21	3
9 Mar 96	LADYKILLERS *4AD BAD 6002CD*	22	3
27 Jul 96	500 (SHAKE BABY SHAKE) *4AD BAD 6009CD*	21	3

Tracks on Mad Love (EP): De-Luxe / Leaves Me Cold / Downer / Thoughtforms. Tracks on For Love (EP): For Love / Starlust / Outdoor Miner / Astronaut

LUSTRAL *UK, male DJ / production duo – Ricky Simmons and Steve Jones (3 WEEKS)*

		pos	wks
18 Oct 97	EVERYTIME *Hooj Choons HOOJCD 55*	60	1
4 Dec 99	EVERYTIME (re-mix) *Hooj Choons HOOJ 83CD*	30	2

LUVVERS – *See LULU*

LUZON *US, male producer – Stacy Burket (1 WEEK)*

		pos	wks
14 Jul 01	THE BAGUIO TRACK *Renaissance RENCDS 006*	67	1

LV *US, male vocalist – Larry Sanders (25 WEEKS)*

		pos	wks
28 Oct 95	★ GANGSTA'S PARADISE *Tommy Boy MCSTD 2104* [1] ◆ ■ ▲	1	20
23 Dec 95	THROW YOUR HANDS UP / GANGSTA'S PARADISE *Tommy Boy TBCD 699*	24	4
4 May 96	I AM LV *Tommy Boy TBCD 7724*	64	1

[1] Coolio featuring LV

The version of 'Gangsta's Paradise' coupled with 'Throw Your Hands Up' is a re-recorded version without Coolio's vocals

Annabella LWIN *Burma, female vocalist (1 WEEK)*

		pos	wks
28 Jan 95	DO WHAT YOU DO *Sony S2 6611235*	61	1

LWS *Italy, male instrumental group (1 WEEK)*

		pos	wks
29 Oct 94	GOSP *Transworld TRANNY 4CD*	65	1

John LYDON *UK, male vocalist (6 WEEKS)*

		pos	wks
13 Nov 93	OPEN UP *Hard Hands HAND 009CD* [1]	13	5
2 Aug 97	SUN *Virgin VUSCD 122*	42	1

[1] Leftfield Lydon

See also PUBLIC IMAGE LTD; SEX PISTOLS

Frankie LYMON and the TEENAGERS *US, male vocal group (38 WEEKS)*

		pos	wks
29 Jun 56	★ WHY DO FOOLS FALL IN LOVE *Columbia DB 3772* [1]	1	16
29 Mar 57	I'M NOT A JUVENILE DELINQUENT *Columbia 33 DB 3878*	12	7
12 Apr 57	● BABY, BABY *Columbia DB 3878*	4	12
20 Sep 57	GOODY GOODY *Columbia DB 3983*	24	3

[1] Teenagers featuring Frankie Lymon

Des LYNAM featuring WIMBLEDON CHORAL SOCIETY *UK, male vocalist / TV presenter with choir (3 WEEKS)*

		pos	wks
12 Dec 98	IF - READ TO FAURE'S 'PAVANE' *BBC Worldwide WMSS 60062*	45	3

Curtis LYNCH Jr featuring Kele LE ROC and RED RAT *UK, male producer, UK, female vocalist and Jamaica, male vocalist (1 WEEK)*

		pos	wks
30 Sep 00	THINKING OF YOU *Telstar CDSTAS3136*	70	1

Kenny LYNCH *UK, male vocalist (59 WEEKS)*

		pos	wks
30 Jun 60	MOUNTAIN OF LOVE *HMV POP 751*	33	3
13 Sep 62	PUFF *HMV POP 1057*	33	5
25 Oct 62	PUFF (re-entry) *HMV POP 1057*	46	1
6 Dec 62	● UP ON THE ROOF *HMV POP 1090*	10	12
20 Jun 63	● YOU CAN NEVER STOP ME LOVING YOU *HMV POP 1165*	10	14
16 Apr 64	STAND BY ME *HMV POP 1280*	39	7
27 Aug 64	WHAT AM I TO YOU *HMV POP 1321*	37	4
1 Oct 64	WHAT AM I TO YOU (re-entry) *HMV POP 1321*	44	2
17 Jun 65	I'LL STAY BY YOU *HMV POP 1430*	29	7
20 Aug 83	HALF THE DAY'S GONE AND WE HAVEN'T EARNED A PENNY *Satril SAT 510*	50	4

Cheryl LYNN *US, female vocalist (2 WEEKS)*

		pos	wks
8 Sep 84	ENCORE *Streetwave KHAN 23*	68	2

Patti LYNN *UK, female vocalist (5 WEEKS)*

		pos	wks
10 May 62	JOHNNY ANGEL *Fontana H 391*	37	5

Tami LYNN *US, female vocalist (20 WEEKS)*

		pos	wks
22 May 71	● I'M GONNA RUN AWAY FROM YOU *Mojo 2092 001*	4	14
3 May 75	I'M GONNA RUN AWAY FROM YOU (re-issue) *Contempo Raries CS 9026*	36	6

Vera LYNN *UK, female vocalist – Vera Walsh (46 WEEKS)*

		pos	wks
14 Nov 52	● AUF WIEDERSEH'N SWEETHEART *Decca F 9927* ▲	10	1
14 Nov 52	● FORGET-ME-NOT *Decca F 9985*	7	1
14 Nov 52	● THE HOMING WALTZ *Decca F 9959*	9	3
28 Nov 52	● FORGET-ME-NOT (re-entry) *Decca F 9985*	5	5
5 Jun 53	THE WINDSOR WALTZ *Decca F 10092*	11	1
15 Oct 54	★ MY SON, MY SON *Decca F 10372* [1]	1	14
8 Jun 56	WHO ARE WE *Decca F 10715*	30	1
26 Oct 56	A HOUSE WITH LOVE IN IT *Decca F 10799*	17	13
15 Mar 57	THE FAITHFUL HUSSAR (DON'T CRY MY LOVE) *Decca F 10846*	29	2
21 Jun 57	TRAVELLIN' HOME *Decca F 10903*	20	5

[1] Vera Lynn with Frank Weir, his saxophone, his Orchestra and Chorus

Jeff LYNNE *UK, male vocalist (4 WEEKS)*

		pos	wks
30 Jun 90	EVERY LITTLE THING *Reprise W 9799*	59	4

See also ELECTRIC LIGHT ORCHESTRA

Shelby LYNNE *US, female vocalist (1 WEEK)*

		pos	wks
29 Apr 00	LEAVIN' *Mercury 5627372*	73	1

Philip LYNOTT *Ireland, male vocalist (36 WEEKS)*

		pos	wks
5 Apr 80	DEAR MISS LONELY HEARTS *Vertigo SOLO 1*	32	6
21 Jun 80	KING'S CALL *Vertigo SOLO 2*	35	6
21 Mar 81	YELLOW PEARL *Vertigo SOLO 3*	56	3
26 Dec 81	YELLOW PEARL (re-entry) *Vertigo SOLO 3*	14	9

18 May 85	● **OUT IN THE FIELDS** *10 TEN 49* [1]	5	10
24 Jan 87	**KING'S CALL (re-mix)** *Vertigo LYN 1*	68	2

[1] Gary Moore and Phil Lynott

See also THIN LIZZY

LYNYRD SKYNYRD *US, male vocal / instrumental group (21 WEEKS)*

		pos	wks
11 Sep 76	**SWEET HOME ALABAMA / DOUBLE TROUBLE** *MCA 251*	31	4
22 Dec 79	**SWEET HOME ALABAMA / DOUBLE TROUBLE (re-entry)** *MCA 251*	43	8
19 Jun 82	**SWEET HOME ALABAMA / DOUBLE TROUBLE (2nd re-entry)** *MCA 251*	21	9

Sweet Home Alabama / Double Trouble was the chart listing for what was also alternatively listed as the Freebird EP for the two re-entries

Barbara LYON *US, female vocalist (12 WEEKS)*

		pos	wks
24 Jun 55	**STOWAWAY** *Columbia DB 3619*	12	8
21 Dec 56	**LETTER TO A SOLDIER** *Columbia DB 3865*	27	4

LYTE FUNKIE ONES *US, male vocal / rap group (17 WEEKS)*

		pos	wks
22 May 99	**CAN'T HAVE YOU** *Logic 74321649152*	54	1
18 Sep 99	**SUMMER GIRLS** *Logic 74321701152*	16	7
5 Feb 00	● **GIRL ON TV** *Logic 74321717582*	6	9

Humphrey LYTTELTON BAND *UK, male jazz band – Humphrey Lyttelton – trumpet (6 WEEKS)*

		pos	wks
13 Jul 56	**BAD PENNY BLUES** *Parlophone R 4184*	19	6

M

M *UK, male vocalist / multi-instrumentalist - Robin Scott (39 WEEKS)*

		pos	wks
7 Apr 79	● **POP MUZIK** *MCA 413* ▲	2	14
8 Dec 79	**MOONLIGHT AND MUZAK** *MCA 541*	33	9
15 Mar 80	**THAT'S THE WAY THE MONEY GOES** *MCA 570*	45	5
22 Nov 80	**OFFICIAL SECRETS** *MCA 650*	64	2
10 Jun 89	**POP MUZIK (re-mix)** *Freestyle FRS 1*	15	9

Bobby M featuring Jean CARN *US, male / female vocal / instrumental duo (3 WEEKS)*

		pos	wks
29 Jan 83	**LET'S STAY TOGETHER** *Gordy TMG 1288*	53	3

M and O BAND *UK, male vocal / instrumental duo – Muff Murfin and Colin Owen (6 WEEKS)*

		pos	wks
28 Feb 76	**LET'S DO THE LATIN HUSTLE** *Creole CR 120*	16	6

M&S presents GIRL NEXT DOOR *UK, male production duo and female vocalist (13 WEEKS)*

		pos	wks
7 Apr 01	● **SALSOUL NUGGET (IF U WANNA)** *ffrr FCD 393*	6	13

M-BEAT *UK, male producer – Marlon Hart (24 WEEKS)*

		pos	wks
18 Jun 94	**INCREDIBLE** *Renk RENK 42CD* [1]	39	3
10 Sep 94	● **INCREDIBLE (re-mix)** *Renk CDRENK 44* [1]	8	9
17 Dec 94	**SWEET LOVE** *Renk CDRENK 49* [2]	18	7
1 Jun 96	**DO U KNOW WHERE YOU'RE COMING FROM** *Renk CDRENK 63* [3]	12	5

[1] M-Beat featuring General Levy [2] M-Beat featuring Nazlyn [3] M-Beat featuring Jamiroquai

M DUBS featuring LADY SAW *UK / Jamaica, male producer / female vocalist (1 WEEK)*

		pos	wks
16 Dec 00	**BUMP N GRIND (I AM FEELING HOT TONIGHT)** *Telstar CDSTAS 3129*	59	1

M PEOPLE (181 Top 500) *Clubland favourites turned pop soul sophisticates: Heather Small (v), backed by Paul Heard and Mike Pickering (both k / prog). In 1994 this Manchester act was voted Best British Dance Act at the Brits and won the 1993 Mercury Music Prize for their LP 'Elegant Slumming' (137 WEEKS)*

		pos	wks
26 Oct 91	**HOW CAN I LOVE YOU MORE?** *Deconstruction PB 44855*	29	9
7 Mar 92	**COLOUR MY LIFE** *Deconstruction PB 45241*	35	4
18 Apr 92	**SOMEDAY** *Deconstruction PB 45369* [1]	38	3
10 Oct 92	**EXCITED** *Deconstruction 74321116337*	29	5
6 Feb 93	● **HOW CAN I LOVE YOU MORE? (re-mix)** *Deconstruction 74321130232*	8	8
26 Jun 93	● **ONE NIGHT IN HEAVEN** *Deconstruction 74321151852*	6	11
25 Sep 93	● **MOVING ON UP** *Deconstruction 74321166162*	2	11
4 Dec 93	● **DON'T LOOK ANY FURTHER** *Deconstruction 74321177112*	9	10
12 Mar 94	● **RENAISSANCE** *Deconstruction 74321194132*	5	7
17 Sep 94	**ELEGANTLY AMERICAN: ONE NIGHT IN HEAVEN / MOVING ON UP (EP) (re-mix)** *Deconstruction 74321231882*	31	2
19 Nov 94	● **SIGHT FOR SORE EYES** *Deconstruction 74321245472*	6	9
4 Feb 95	● **OPEN YOUR HEART** *Deconstruction 74321261532*	9	7
24 Jun 95	● **SEARCH FOR THE HERO** *Deconstruction 74321287962*	9	7
14 Oct 95	**LOVE RENDEZVOUS** *Deconstruction 74321319282*	32	4
25 Nov 95	**ITCHYCOO PARK** *Deconstruction 74321330732*	11	8
4 Oct 97	● **JUST FOR YOU** *BMG 74321523002*	8	7
6 Dec 97	**FANTASY ISLAND** *BMG 74321542932*	33	8
28 Feb 98	**FANTASY ISLAND (re-entry)** *BMG 74321542932*	69	1
28 Mar 98	● **ANGEL STREET** *M People 74321564182*	8	6
7 Nov 98	**TESTIFY** *M People 74321621742*	12	6
13 Feb 99	**DREAMING** *M People 74321645352*	13	4

[1] M People with Heather Small

M + M *Canada, male / female vocal duo (4 WEEKS)*

		pos	wks
28 Jul 84	**BLACK STATIONS WHITE STATIONS** *RCA 426*	46	4

M + M are Martha and a Muffin

See also MARTHA and the MUFFINS

M3 *UK, male / female production / vocal trio (2 WEEKS)*

		pos	wks
30 Oct 99	**BAILAMOS** *Inferno CDFERN 21*	40	2

M2M *Norway, female vocal / instrumental duo – Marit Larson and Marion Raven (6 WEEKS)*

		pos	wks
1 Apr 00	**DON'T SAY YOU LOVE ME** *Atlantic AT 0081CD*	16	6

Timo MAAS *Germany, male DJ / producer (3 WEEKS)*

		pos	wks
1 Apr 00	**DER SCHIEBER** *48k / Perfecto SPECT 07CDS*	50	1
30 Sep 00	**UBIK** *Perfecto PERF 10CDS* [1]	33	2

[1] Timo Mass featuring Martin Bettinghaus

Scott MAC – See *SIGNUM*

Pete MAC Jr *US, male vocalist (4 WEEKS)*

		pos	wks
15 Oct 77	**THE WATER MARGIN** *BBC RESL 50*	37	4

This is the Japanese version of the song which shared chart credit with the English-language version by Godiego

See also GODIEGO

MAC BAND featuring the McCAMPBELL BROTHERS *US, male vocal group (17 WEEKS)*

		pos	wks
18 Jun 88	● **ROSES ARE RED** *MCA MCA 1264*	8	13
10 Sep 88	**STALEMATE** *MCA MCA 1271*	40	4

'Stalemate' credits the McCampbell Brothers on the sleeve only, not on the label

Keith MAC PROJECT *UK, male / female vocal / instrumental group (1 WEEK)*

Date		Title / Label	pos	wks
25 Jun 94		DE DAH DAH (SPICE OF LIFE) *Public Demand PPDCD 3*	66	1

David McALMONT *UK, male vocalist (17 WEEKS)*

Date		Title / Label	pos	wks
27 May 95	●	YES *Hut HUTCD 53* [1]	8	8
4 Nov 95		YOU DO *Hut HUTDG 57* [1]	17	4
27 Apr 96		HYMN *Blanco Y Negro NEG 87CD* [2]	65	1
9 Aug 97		LOOK AT YOURSELF *Hut HUTCD 87*	40	2
22 Nov 97		DIAMONDS ARE FOREVER *East West EW 141CD* [3]	39	2

[1] McAlmont and Butler [2] Ultramarine featuring David McAlmont [3] David McAlmont / David Arnold

Neil MacARTHUR *UK, male vocalist (5 WEEKS)*

Date		Title / Label	pos	wks
5 Feb 69		SHE'S NOT THERE *Deram DM 225*	34	5

Neil MacArthur is Colin Blunstone under a pseudonym

David MacBETH *UK, male vocalist (4 WEEKS)*

Date		Title / Label	pos	wks
30 Oct 59		MR BLUE *Pye 7N 15231*	18	4

Nicko McBRAIN *UK, male vocalist / instrumentalist – drums (1 WEEK)*

Date		Title / Label	pos	wks
13 Jul 91		RHYTHM OF THE BEAST *EMI NICK 01*	72	1

Frankie McBRIDE *Ireland, male vocalist (15 WEEKS)*

Date		Title / Label	pos	wks
9 Aug 67		FIVE LITTLE FINGERS *Emerald MD 1081*	19	15

Dan McCAFFERTY *UK, male vocalist (3 WEEKS)*

Date		Title / Label	pos	wks
13 Sep 75		OUT OF TIME *Mountain TOP 1*	41	3

CW McCALL *US, male vocalist – William Fries (10 WEEKS)*

Date		Title / Label	pos	wks
14 Feb 76	●	CONVOY *MGM 2006 560* ▲	2	10

David McCALLUM *UK, male actor / vocalist (4 WEEKS)*

Date		Title / Label	pos	wks
14 Apr 66		COMMUNICATION *Capitol CL 15439*	32	4

McCAMPBELL BROTHERS – *See MAC BAND featuring the McCAMPBELL BROTHERS*

Linda McCARTNEY *US, female vocalist (7 WEEKS)*

Date		Title / Label	pos	wks
28 Aug 71		BACK SEAT OF MY CAR *Apple R 5914* [1]	39	5
21 Nov 98		WIDE PRAIRIE *Parlophone CDR 6510*	74	1
6 Feb 99		THE LIGHT COMES FROM WITHIN *Parlophone CDR 6513*	56	1

[1] Paul and Linda McCartney

See also Paul McCARTNEY

Paul McCARTNEY (15 Top 500)

Pop's most successful singer / songwriter and the richest man in British music with, reportedly, a personal fortune of £500m, b. 18 Jun 1942, Liverpool. His composition 'Yesterday' is the world's most recorded song and has had more than seven million plays on US radio alone. 'Mull Of Kintyre' (with his group Wings) is one of the few two-million sellers in the UK. This entertainer, known for his charitable work, has broken indoor and outdoor attendance records around the world and a 1999 internet show attracted at least 50 million hits. Winner of a record number of Ivor Novello Awards, he was awarded the only Rhodium record (from Guinness) to honour outstanding sales and received. He also received a Lifetime Achievement Grammy (1990), and a knighthood in 1997. Sir Paul is the only artist to have No.1s as a solo artist, part of a duo, trio, quartet, quintet and charity group (410 WEEKS)

Date		Title / Label	pos	wks
22 Feb 71	●	ANOTHER DAY *Apple R 5889*	2	12
28 Aug 71		BACK SEAT OF MY CAR *Apple R 5914* [1]	39	5
26 Feb 72		GIVE IRELAND BACK TO THE IRISH *Apple R 5936* [2]	16	8
27 May 72	●	MARY HAD A LITTLE LAMB *Apple R 5949* [2]	9	11
9 Dec 72	●	HI HI HI / C MOON *Apple R 5973* [2]	5	13
7 Apr 73	●	MY LOVE *Apple R 5985* [3] ▲	9	11
9 Jun 73	●	LIVE AND LET DIE *Apple R 5987* [2]	9	13
15 Sep 73		LIVE AND LET DIE (re-entry) *Apple R 5987* [2]	49	1
3 Nov 73		HELEN WHEELS *Apple R 5993* [3]	12	12
2 Mar 74	●	JET *Apple R 5996* [3]	7	9
6 Jul 74	●	BAND ON THE RUN *Apple R 5997* [3] ▲	3	11
9 Nov 74		JUNIOR'S FARM *Apple R 5999* [3]	16	10
31 May 75	●	LISTEN TO WHAT THE MAN SAID *Capitol R 6006* [2] ▲	6	8
18 Oct 75		LETTING GO *Capitol R 6008* [2]	41	3
15 May 76	●	SILLY LOVE SONGS *Parlophone R 6014* [2] ▲	2	11
7 Aug 76	●	LET 'EM IN *Parlophone R 6015* [2]	2	10
19 Feb 77		MAYBE I'M AMAZED *Parlophone R 6017* [2]	28	5
19 Nov 77	★	MULL OF KINTYRE / GIRLS' SCHOOL *Capitol R 6018* [2] ◆	1	17
1 Apr 78	●	WITH A LITTLE LUCK *Parlophone R 6019* [2] ▲	5	9
1 Jul 78		I'VE HAD ENOUGH *Parlophone R 6020* [2]	42	7
9 Sep 78		LONDON TOWN *Parlophone R 6021* [2]	60	4
7 Apr 79	●	GOODNIGHT TONIGHT *Parlophone R 6023* [2]	5	10
16 Jun 79		OLD SIAM SIR *Parlophone R 6026* [2]	35	6
1 Sep 79		GETTING CLOSER / BABY'S REQUEST *Parlophone R 6027* [2]	60	3
1 Dec 79	●	WONDERFUL CHRISTMAS TIME *Parlophone R 6029*	6	8
19 Apr 80	●	COMING UP *Parlophone R 6035* ▲	2	9
21 Jun 80	●	WATERFALLS *Parlophone R 6037*	9	8
10 Apr 82	★	EBONY AND IVORY *Parlophone 6054* [4] ▲	1	10
3 Jul 82		TAKE IT AWAY *Parlophone R 6056*	15	10
9 Oct 82		TUG OF WAR *Parlophone R 6057*	53	3
6 Nov 82	●	THE GIRL IS MINE *Epic EPC A 2729* [5]	8	9
15 Jan 83		THE GIRL IS MINE (re-entry) *Epic EPC A 2729* [5]	75	1
15 Oct 83	●	SAY SAY SAY *Parlophone R 6062* [6] ▲	2	15
17 Dec 83	★	PIPES OF PEACE *Parlophone R 6064*	1	12
6 Oct 84	●	NO MORE LONELY NIGHTS (BALLAD) *Parlophone R 6080*	2	15
24 Nov 84	●	WE ALL STAND TOGETHER *Parlophone R 6086* [7]	3	13
30 Nov 85		SPIES LIKE US *Parlophone R 6118*	13	10
21 Dec 85		WE ALL STAND TOGETHER (re-entry) *Parlophone R 6086* [7]	32	5
26 Jul 86		PRESS *Parlophone R 6133*	25	8
13 Dec 86		ONLY LOVE REMAINS *Parlophone R 6148*	34	5
28 Nov 87	●	ONCE UPON A LONG AGO *Parlophone R 6170*	10	7
20 May 89	★	FERRY 'CROSS THE MERSEY *PWL PWL 41* [8] ■	1	7
20 May 89		MY BRAVE FACE *Parlophone R 6213*	18	5
29 Jul 89		THIS ONE *Parlophone R 6223*	18	6
25 Nov 89		FIGURE OF EIGHT *Parlophone R 6235*	42	3
17 Feb 90		PUT IT THERE *Parlophone R 6246*	32	2
20 Oct 90		BIRTHDAY *Parlophone R 6271*	29	3
8 Dec 90		ALL MY TRIALS *Parlophone CDR 6278*	35	5
9 Jan 93		HOPE OF DELIVERANCE *Parlophone CDR 6330*	18	6
6 Mar 93		C'MON PEOPLE *Parlophone CDRS 6338*	41	3
10 May 97		YOUNG BOY *Parlophone CDRS 6462*	19	3
19 Jul 97		THE WORLD TONIGHT *Parlophone CDR 6472*	23	2
27 Dec 97		BEAUTIFUL NIGHT *Parlophone CDR 6489*	25	4
6 Nov 99		NO OTHER BABY / BROWN EYED HANDSOME MAN *Parlophone CDR 6527*	42	2
10 Nov 01		FROM A LOVER TO A FRIEND *Parlophone CDR 6567*	45	2

[1] Paul and Linda McCartney [2] Wings [3] Paul McCartney and Wings [4] Paul McCartney with Stevie Wonder [5] Michael Jackson and Paul McCartney [6] Paul McCartney and Michael Jackson [7] Paul McCartney and the Frog Chorus [8] Christians, Holly Johnson, Paul McCartney, Gerry Marsden and Stock Aitken Waterman

R 6027 credits no label at all, although the number is a Parlophone one

See also BEATLES

Kirsty MacCOLL *UK, female vocalist (65 WEEKS)*

Date		Title / Label	pos	wks
13 Jun 81		THERE'S A GUY WORKS DOWN THE CHIPSHOP SWEARS HE'S ELVIS *Polydor POSP 250*	14	9
19 Jan 85	●	A NEW ENGLAND *Stiff BUY 216*	7	10
15 Nov 86		GREETINGS TO THE NEW BRUNETTE *Go! Discs GOD 15* [1]	58	2
5 Dec 87	●	FAIRYTALE OF NEW YORK *Pogue Mahone NY 7* [2]	2	9
8 Apr 89		FREE WORLD *Virgin KMA 1*	43	6
1 Jul 89		DAYS *Virgin KMA 2*	12	9
25 May 91		WALKING DOWN MADISON *Virgin VS 1348*	23	7
17 Aug 91		MY AFFAIR *Virgin VS 1354*	56	2
14 Dec 91		FAIRYTALE OF NEW YORK (re-issue) *PM YZ 628* [2]	36	5
4 Mar 95		CAROLINE *Virgin VSCDX 1517*	58	2
24 Jun 95		PERFECT DAY *Virgin VSCDT 1552* [3]	75	1
29 Jul 95		DAYS (re-issue) *Virgin VSCDT 1558*	42	3

[1] Billy Bragg with Johnny Marr and Kirsty MacColl [2] Pogues featuring Kirsty MacColl [3] Kirsty MacColl and Evan Dando

Neil MacCOLL – *See LA's; PRETENDERS*

Marilyn McCOO and Billy DAVIS Jr
US, female / male vocal duo (9 WEEKS) pos/wks

19 Mar 77 ●	**YOU DON'T HAVE TO BE A STAR (TO BE IN MY SHOW)** *ABC 4147* ▲	7	9

Van McCOY *US, orchestra (36 WEEKS)* pos/wks

31 May 75 ●	**THE HUSTLE** *Avco 6105 038* [1] ▲	3	12
1 Nov 75	**CHANGE WITH THE TIMES** *Avco 6105 042*	36	4
12 Feb 77	**SOUL CHA CHA** *H & L 6105 065*	34	6
9 Apr 77 ●	**THE SHUFFLE** *H & L 6105 076*	4	14

[1] Van McCoy with the Soul City Symphony

McCOYS *US, male vocal / instrumental group (18 WEEKS)* pos/wks

2 Sep 65 ●	**HANG ON SLOOPY** *Immediate IM 001* ▲	5	14
16 Dec 65	**FEVER** *Immediate IM 021*	44	4

George McCRAE *US, male vocalist (62 WEEKS)* pos/wks

29 Jun 74 ★	**ROCK YOUR BABY** *Jayboy BOY 85* ▲	1	14
5 Oct 74 ●	**I CAN'T LEAVE YOU ALONE** *Jayboy BOY 90*	9	9
14 Dec 74	**YOU CAN HAVE IT ALL** *Jayboy BOY 92*	23	9
22 Mar 75	**SING A HAPPY SONG** *Jayboy BOY 95*	38	4
19 Jul 75 ●	**IT'S BEEN SO LONG** *Jayboy BOY 100*	4	11
18 Oct 75	**I AIN'T LYIN'** *Jayboy BOY 105*	12	7
24 Jan 76	**HONEY I** *Jayboy BOY 107*	33	4
25 Feb 84	**ONE STEP CLOSER (TO LOVE)** *President PT 522*	57	4

Gwen McCRAE *US, female vocalist (5 WEEKS)* pos/wks

30 Apr 88	**ALL THIS LOVE THAT I'M GIVING** *Flame MELT 7*	63	2
13 Feb 93	**ALL THIS LOVE I'M GIVING (re-recording)** *KTDA CDKTDA 2* [1]	36	3

[1] Music and Mystery featuring Gwen McCrae

McCRARYS *US, male / female vocal group (4 WEEKS)* pos/wks

31 Jul 82	**LOVE ON A SUMMER NIGHT** *Capitol CL 251*	52	4

Mindy McCREADY *US, female vocalist (3 WEEKS)* pos/wks

1 Aug 98	**OH ROMEO** *BNA 74321597242*	41	3

Ian McCULLOCH *UK, male vocalist (14 WEEKS)* pos/wks

15 Dec 84	**SEPTEMBER SONG** *Korova KOW 40*	51	5
2 Sep 89	**PROUD TO FALL** *WEA YZ 417*	51	4
12 May 90	**CANDLELAND (THE SECOND COMING)** *East West YZ 452* [1]	75	1
22 Feb 92	**LOVER LOVER LOVER** *East West YZ 643*	47	4

[1] Ian McCulloch featuring Elizabeth Fraser

See also ECHO and the BUNNYMEN

Martine McCUTCHEON *UK, female vocalist (65 WEEKS)* pos/wks

18 Nov 95	**ARE YOU MAN ENOUGH** *Avex UK AVEX CD 14* [1]	62	1
17 Apr 99 ★	**PERFECT MOMENT** *Innocent SINCD 7* ■	1	15
14 Aug 99	**PERFECT MOMENT (re-entry)** *Innocent SINCD 7*	59	5
11 Sep 99 ●	**I'VE GOT YOU** *Innocent SINCD 12*	6	10
4 Dec 99 ●	**TALKING IN YOUR SLEEP / LOVE ME** *Innocent SINCD 14*	6	16
4 Nov 00 ●	**I'M OVER YOU** *Innocent SINCD 20*	2	10
3 Feb 01 ●	**ON THE RADIO** *Innocent SINCD 21*	7	8

[1] Uno Clio featuring Martine McCutcheon

Gene McDANIELS *US, male vocalist (2 WEEKS)* pos/wks

16 Nov 61	**TOWER OF STRENGTH** *London HLG 9448*	49	1
30 Nov 61	**TOWER OF STRENGTH (re-entry)** *London HLG 9448*	49	1

Julie McDERMOTT – *See THIRD DIMENSION featuring Julie McDERMOTT; AWESOME 3*

Charles McDEVITT SKIFFLE GROUP featuring Nancy WHISKEY
UK, male / female vocal / instrumental group (20 WEEKS) pos/wks

12 Apr 57 ●	**FREIGHT TRAIN** *Oriole CB 1352*	5	17
14 Jun 57	**GREENBACK DOLLAR** *Oriole CB 1371*	28	1
5 Jul 57	**GREENBACK DOLLAR (re-entry)** *Oriole CB 1371*	30	1
20 Sep 57	**FREIGHT TRAIN (re-entry)** *Oriole CB 1352*	27	1

Jane McDONALD *UK, female vocalist (7 WEEKS)* pos/wks

26 Dec 98 ●	**CRUISE INTO CHRISTMAS MEDLEY** *Focus Music Int CDFM 2*	10	7

Michael McDONALD *US, male vocalist / instrumentalist (48 WEEKS)* pos/wks

18 Feb 84	**YAH MO B THERE** *Qwest W 9394* [1]	44	5
7 Apr 84	**YAH MO B THERE (re-entry)** *Qwest W 9394* [1]	69	3
12 Jan 85	**YAH MO B THERE (2nd re-entry)** *Qwest W 9394* [1]	12	8
3 May 86 ●	**ON MY OWN** *MCA MCA 1045* [2] ▲	2	13
26 Jul 86	**I KEEP FORGETTIN'** *Warner Bros K 17992*	43	6
6 Sep 86	**SWEET FREEDOM** *MCA MCA 1073*	12	10
24 Jan 87	**WHAT A FOOL BELIEVES (re-issue)** *Warner Bros. W 8451* [3]	57	3

[1] James Ingram with Michael McDonald [2] Patti LaBelle and Michael McDonald [3] Doobie Brothers featuring Michael McDonald

The 1985 entry of 'Yah Mo B There' is a re-mix of the original hit with the same catalogue number

See also DOOBIE BROTHERS

Carrie McDOWELL *US, female vocalist (3 WEEKS)* pos/wks

26 Sep 87	**UH UH NO NO CASUAL SEX** *Motown ZV 41501*	68	3

John McENROE and Pat CASH with the FULL METAL RACKETS
US / Australia, male vocal / instrumental duo with UK backing group (1 WEEK) pos/wks

13 Jul 91	**ROCK 'N' ROLL** *Music for Nations KUT 141*	66	1

Reba McENTIRE *US, female vocalist (1 WEEK)* pos/wks

19 Jun 99	**DOES HE LOVE YOU** *MCA Nashville MCSTD 55569*	62	1

MACEO & THE MACKS *US male vocal / instrumental group (5 WEEKS)* pos/wks

16 May 87	**CROSS THE TRACK (WE BETTER GO BACK)** *Urban URBX1*	54	5

McFADDEN and WHITEHEAD
US, male vocal duo – Gene McFadden and John Whitehead (10 WEEKS) pos/wks

19 May 79 ●	**AIN'T NO STOPPIN' US NOW** *Philadelphia International PIR 7365*	5	10

Rachel McFARLANE *UK, female vocalist (2 WEEKS)* pos/wks

1 Aug 98	**LOVER** *Multiply CDMULTY 37*	38	2

See also LOVELAND featuring the voice of Rachel McFARLANE

Bobby McFERRIN *US, male vocalist (15 WEEKS)* pos/wks

24 Sep 88 ●	**DON'T WORRY BE HAPPY** *Manhattan MT 56* ▲	2	11
17 Dec 88	**THINKIN' ABOUT YOUR BODY** *Manhattan BLUE 6*	46	4

McGANNS *UK, male vocal trio (4 WEEKS)* pos/wks

14 Nov 98	**JUST MY IMAGINATION** *Coalition COLA 062CD*	59	1
6 Feb 99	**A HEARTBEAT AWAY** *Coalition COLA 069CD*	42	3

Mike McGEAR *UK, male vocalist (4 WEEKS)* pos/wks

5 Oct 74	**LEAVE IT** *Warner Bros. K 16446*	36	4

Maureen McGOVERN *US, female vocalist (8 WEEKS)* pos/wks

5 Jun 76	**THE CONTINENTAL** *20th Century BTC 2222*	16	8

Shane MacGOWAN *UK, male vocalist (9 WEEKS)* pos/wks

12 Dec 92	**WHAT A WONDERFUL WORLD** *Mute MUTE 151* [1]	72	1
3 Sep 94	**THE CHURCH OF THE HOLY SPOOK** *ZTT ZANG 57CD* [2]	74	1

15 Oct 94		**THAT WOMAN'S GOT ME DRINKING** *ZTT ZANG 56CD* [2]	34	3
29 Apr 95		**HAUNTED** *ZTT ZANG 65CD* [3]	30	2
20 Apr 96		**MY WAY** *ZTT ZANG 79CD*	29	2

[1] Nick Cave and Shane McGowan [2] Shane MacGowan and the Popes [3] Shane MacGowan and Sinead O'Connor

See also POGUES

Ewan McGREGOR – *See PF PROJECT featuring Ewan McGREGOR; Nicole KIDMAN and Ewan McGREGOR*

Freddie McGREGOR *Jamaica, male vocalist (16 WEEKS)*

			pos	wks
27 Jun 87	●	**JUST DON'T WANT TO BE LONELY** *Germain DG 24*	9	11
19 Sep 87		**THAT GIRL (GROOVY SITUATION)** *Polydor POSP 884*	47	5

Mary MacGREGOR *US, female vocalist (10 WEEKS)*

			pos	wks
19 Feb 77	●	**TORN BETWEEN TWO LOVERS** *Ariola America AA 111* ▲	4	10

McGUINNESS FLINT *UK, male vocal / instrumental group (26 WEEKS)*

			pos	wks
21 Nov 70	●	**WHEN I'M DEAD AND GONE** *Capitol CL 15662*	2	14
1 May 71	●	**MALT AND BARLEY BLUES** *Capitol CL 15682*	5	12

Barry McGUIRE *US, male vocalist (13 WEEKS)*

			pos	wks
9 Sep 65	●	**EVE OF DESTRUCTION** *RCA 1469* ▲	3	13

McGUIRE SISTERS *US, female vocal group (24 WEEKS)*

			pos	wks
1 Apr 55		**NO MORE** *Vogue Coral Q 72050*	20	1
15 Jul 55		**SINCERELY** *Vogue Coral Q 72050* ▲	14	4
1 Jun 56		**DELILAH JONES** *Vogue Coral Q 72161*	24	2
14 Feb 58		**SUGARTIME** *Coral Q 72305*	14	6
1 May 59		**MAY YOU ALWAYS** *Coral Q 72356*	15	10
17 Jul 59		**MAY YOU ALWAYS (re-entry)** *Coral Q 72356*	28	1

MACHEL *Trinidad, male vocalist (2 WEEKS)*

			pos	wks
14 Sep 96		**COME DIG IT** *London LONCD 386*	56	2

MACHINE HEAD *UK, male vocal / instrumental group (4 WEEKS)*

			pos	wks
27 May 95		**OLD** *Roadrunner RR 23403*	43	2
6 Dec 97		**TAKE MY SCARS** *Roadrunner RR 22573*	73	1
18 Dec 99		**FROM THIS DAY** *Roadrunner RR 21383*	74	1

Craig MACK *US, male rapper (5 WEEKS)*

			pos	wks
12 Nov 94		**FLAVA IN YA EAR** *Bad Boy 74321242582*	57	2
1 Apr 95		**GET DOWN** *Puff Daddy 74321263402*	54	1
7 Jun 97		**SPIRIT** *Perspective 5822312* [1]	35	2

[1] Sound of Blackness featuring Craig Mack

Lizzy MACK *UK, female vocalist (3 WEEKS)*

			pos	wks
5 Nov 94		**THE POWER OF LOVE** *Media MCSTD 2016* [1]	49	2
4 Nov 95		**DON'T GO** *Power Station MCSTD 40004*	52	1

[1] Fits of Gloom featuring Lizzy Mack

Lonnie MACK *US, male instrumentalist – guitar (3 WEEKS)*

			pos	wks
14 Apr 79		**MEMPHIS** *Lightning LIG 9011*	47	3

'Memphis' was coupled with 'Let's Dance' by Chris Montez as a double A-side

MACK VIBE featuring JACQUELINE
US, male / female vocal / instrumental duo (1 WEEK)

			pos	wks
4 Feb 95		**I CAN'T LET YOU GO** *MCA MCSTD 20020*	53	1

Maria McKEE *US, female vocalist (23 WEEKS)*

			pos	wks
15 Sep 90	★	**SHOW ME HEAVEN** *Epic 656303 7*	1	14
26 Jan 91		**BREATHE** *Geffen GFS 1*	59	1
1 Aug 92		**SWEETEST CHILD** *Geffen GFS 23*	45	4
22 May 93		**I'M GONNA SOOTHE YOU** *Geffen GFSTD 39*	35	3
18 Sep 93		**I CAN'T MAKE IT ALONE** *Geffen GFSTD 53*	74	1

Kenneth McKELLAR *UK, male vocalist (4 WEEKS)*

			pos	wks
10 Mar 66		**A MAN WITHOUT LOVE** *Decca F 12341*	30	4

Terence McKENNA – *See SHAMEN*

Gisele MacKENZIE *Canada, female vocalist – Gisele LeFleche (6 WEEKS)*

			pos	wks
17 Jul 53		**SEVEN LONELY DAYS** *Capitol CL 13920*	12	1
31 Jul 53		**SEVEN LONELY DAYS (re-entry)** *Capitol CL 13920*	11	1
21 Aug 53	●	**SEVEN LONELY DAYS (2nd re-entry)** *Capitol CL 13920*	6	4

Scott McKENZIE *US, male vocalist – Philip Blondheim (18 WEEKS)*

			pos	wks
12 Jul 67	★	**SAN FRANCISCO (BE SURE TO WEAR SOME FLOWERS IN YOUR HAIR)** *CBS 2816*	1	17
1 Nov 67		**LIKE AN OLD TIME MOVIE** *CBS 3009* [1]	50	1

[1] The Voice of Scott McKenzie

Ken MACKINTOSH his Saxophone and his Orchestra
UK, orchestra (9 WEEKS)

			pos	wks
15 Jan 54		**THE CREEP** *HMV BD 1295*	12	1
29 Jan 54	●	**THE CREEP (re-entry)** *HMV BD 1295*	10	1
7 Feb 58		**RAUNCHY** *HMV POP 426*	19	6
10 Mar 60		**NO HIDING PLACE** *HMV POP 713*	45	1

Brian McKNIGHT *US, male vocalist (4 WEEKS)*

			pos	wks
6 Jun 98		**ANYTIME** *Motown 8607752*	48	2
3 Oct 98		**YOU SHOULD BE MINE** *Motown 8608412*	36	2

Julie McKNIGHT – *See KINGS OF TOMORROW featuring Julie McKNIGHT*

Vivienne McKONE *UK, female vocalist (5 WEEKS)*

			pos	wks
25 Jul 92		**SING (OOH-EE-OOH)** *ffrr F 183*	47	4
31 Oct 92		**BEWARE** *ffrr F 202*	69	1

McKOY *UK, male / female vocal group (2 WEEKS)*

			pos	wks
6 Mar 93		**FIGHT** *Rightrack CDTUM 1*	54	2

Noel McKOY – *See JTQ; McKOY*

Craig McLACHLAN *Australia, male vocalist (40 WEEKS)*

			pos	wks
16 Jun 90	●	**MONA** *Epic 655784 7* [1]	2	11
4 Aug 90		**AMANDA** *Epic 656170 7* [1]	19	6
10 Nov 90		**I ALMOST FELT LIKE CRYING** *Epic 656310 7* [1]	50	3
23 May 92		**ONE REASON WHY** *Epic 6580677*	29	6
14 Nov 92		**ON MY OWN** *Epic 6584677*	59	2
24 Jul 93		**YOU'RE THE ONE THAT I WANT** *Epic 6595222* [2]	13	6
25 Dec 93		**GREASE** *Epic 6600242*	44	4
8 Jul 95		**EVERYDAY** *MDMC DEVCS 6* [3]	65	2

[1] Craig McLachlan and Check 1-2 [2] Craig McLachlan and Debbie Gibson [3] Craig McLachlan and the Culprits

Sarah McLACHLAN
Canada, female vocalist / instrumentalist (21 WEEKS)

			pos	wks
3 Oct 98		**ADIA** *Arista 74321613902*	18	5
14 Oct 00	●	**SILENCE (re-mix)** *Nettwerk 331072* [1]	3	16

[1] Delerium featuring Sarah McLachlan

Tommy McLAIN *US, male vocalist (1 WEEK)*

			pos	wks
8 Sep 66		**SWEET DREAMS** *London HL 10065*	49	1

Malcolm McLAREN *UK, male vocalist (65 WEEKS)*

			pos	wks
4 Dec 82	●	**BUFFALO GALS** *Charisma MALC 1* [1]	9	12
26 Feb 83		**SOWETO** *Charisma MALC 2* [2]	32	5

2 Jul 83 ●	**DOUBLE DUTCH** *Charisma MALC 3*	3	13
17 Dec 83	**DUCK FOR THE OYSTER** *Charisma MALC 4*	54	5
1 Sep 84	**MADAM BUTTERFLY (UN BEL DI VEDREMO)** *Charisma MALC 5*	13	9
27 May 89	**WALTZ DARLING** *Epic WALTZ 2* [3]	31	8
19 Aug 89	**SOMETHING'S JUMPIN' IN YOUR SHIRT** *Epic WALTZ 3* [4]	29	7
25 Nov 89	**HOUSE OF THE BLUE DANUBE** *Epic WALTZ 4* [3]	73	1
21 Dec 91	**MAGIC'S BACK (THEME FROM 'THE GHOSTS OF OXFORD STREET')** *RCA PB 45223* [5]	42	4
3 Oct 98	**BUFFALO GALS STAMPEDE (re-mix)** *Virgin VSCDT 1717* [6]	65	1

[1] Malcolm McLaren and the World's Famous Supreme Team [2] Malcolm McLaren and the McLarenettes [3] Malcolm McLaren and the Bootzilla Orchestra [4] Malcolm McLaren and the Bootzilla Orchestra featuring Lisa Marie [5] Malcolm McLaren featuring Alison Limerick [6] Malcolm McLaren and the World's Famous Supreme Team plus Rakim and Roger Sanchez

Bitty McLEAN *UK, male vocalist (50 WEEKS)* pos/wks

31 Jul 93 ●	**IT KEEP RAININ' (TEARS FROM MY EYES)** *Brilliant CDBRIL 1*	2	15
30 Oct 93	**PASS IT ON** *Brilliant CDBRIL 2*	35	3
15 Jan 94 ●	**HERE I STAND** *Brilliant CDBRIL 3*	10	6
9 Apr 94 ●	**DEDICATED TO THE ONE I LOVE** *Brilliant CDBRIL 4*	6	10
6 Aug 94	**WHAT GOES AROUND** *Brilliant CDBRIL 5*	36	3
8 Apr 95	**OVER THE RIVER** *Brilliant CDBRIL 9*	27	4
17 Jun 95	**WE'VE ONLY JUST BEGUN** *Brilliant CDBRIL 10*	23	5
30 Sep 95	**NOTHING CAN CHANGE THIS LOVE** *Brilliant CDBRIL 11*	55	2
27 Jan 96	**NATURAL HIGH** *Brilliant CDBRIL 12*	63	1
5 Oct 96	**SHE'S ALRIGHT** *Kuff KUFFD 9*	53	1

Don McLEAN *US, male vocalist / instrumentalist (68 WEEKS)* pos/wks

22 Jan 72 ●	**AMERICAN PIE** *United Artists UP 35325* ▲	2	16
13 May 72 ★	**VINCENT** *United Artists UP 35359*	1	15
14 Apr 73	**EVERYDAY** *United Artists UP 35519*	38	5
10 May 80 ★	**CRYING** *EMI 5051*	1	14
17 Apr 82	**CASTLES IN THE AIR** *EMI 5258*	47	8
5 Oct 91	**AMERICAN PIE (re-issue)** *Liberty EMCT 3*	12	10

Jackie McLEAN *US, male instrumentalist - alto sax (4 WEEKS)* pos/wks

7 Jul 79	**DR JACKYLL AND MISTER FUNK** *RCA PB 1575*	53	4

Phil McLEAN *US, male vocalist (4 WEEKS)* pos/wks

18 Jan 62	**SMALL SAD SAM** *Top Rank JAR 597*	34	4

Ian McNABB *UK, male vocalist (6 WEEKS)* pos/wks

23 Jan 93	**IF LOVE WAS LIKE GUITARS** *This Way Up WAY 233*	67	1
2 Jul 94	**YOU MUST BE PREPARED TO DREAM** *This Way Up WAY 3199* [1]	54	1
17 Sep 94	**GO INTO THE LIGHT** *This Way Up WAY 3699*	66	2
27 Apr 96	**DON'T PUT YOUR SPELL ON ME** *This Way Up WAY 5033*	72	1
6 Jul 96	**MERSEYBEAST** *This Way Up WAY 5266*	74	1

[1] Ian McNabb featuring Ralph Molina and Billy Talbot

See also ICICLE WORKS

Lutricia McNEAL *US, female vocalist (43 WEEKS)* pos/wks

29 Nov 97 ●	**AIN'T THAT JUST THE WAY** *Wildstar CXSTAS 2907*	6	18
23 May 98 ●	**STRANDED** *Wildstar CXSTAS 2973*	3	12
26 Sep 98 ●	**SOMEONE LOVES YOU HONEY** *Wildstar CDWILD 9*	9	7
19 Dec 98	**THE GREATEST LOVE YOU'LL NEVER KNOW** *Wildstar CDWILD 11*	17	6

Patrick MacNEE and Honor BLACKMAN
UK, male / female vocal duo (7 WEEKS) pos/wks

1 Dec 90 ●	**KINKY BOOTS** *Deram KINKY 1*	5	7

Rita MacNEIL *Canada, female vocalist (10 WEEKS)* pos/wks

6 Oct 90	**WORKING MAN** *Polydor PO 98*	11	10

Clyde McPHATTER *US, male vocalist (1 WEEK)* pos/wks

24 Aug 56	**TREASURE OF LOVE** *London HLE 8293*	27	1

Carmen McRAE – *See Sammy DAVIS Jr*

Ralph McTELL *UK, male vocalist – Ralph May (18 WEEKS)* pos/wks

7 Dec 74 ●	**STREETS OF LONDON** *Reprise K 14380*	2	12
20 Dec 75	**DREAMS OF YOU** *Warner Bros. K 16648*	36	6

MAD COBRA featuring Richie STEPHENS
Jamaica / UK, male vocal duo (2 WEEKS) pos/wks

15 May 93	**LEGACY** *Columbia 6592852*	64	2

MAD JOCKS featuring JOCKMASTER B.A.
UK, male vocal / instrumental group (9 WEEKS) pos/wks

19 Dec 87	**JOCK MIX 1** *Debut DEBT 3037*	46	5
18 Dec 93	**PARTY FOUR (EP)** *SMP CDSSKM 24*	57	4

Tracks on Party Four (EP): No Lager / Here We Go Again / Jock Party Mix / Jock Jak Mix

MAD MOSES *US, male DJ / producer - 'Mad' Mitch Moses (1 WEEK)* pos/wks

16 Aug 97	**PANTHER PARTY** *Hi-Life 5744932*	50	1

MAD STUNTMAN – *See REEL 2 REAL*

Sonya MADAN – *See LITHIAM and Sonya MADAN*

MADASUN *UK, female vocal group (13 WEEKS)* pos/wks

11 Mar 00	**DON'T YOU WORRY** *V2 VVR 5011523*	14	6
27 May 00	**WALKING ON WATER** *V2 VVR 5012418*	14	4
2 Sep 00	**FEEL GOOD** *V2 VVR 5012983*	29	3

Danny MADDEN *US, male vocalist (2 WEEKS)* pos/wks

14 Jul 90	**THE FACTS OF LIFE** *Eternal YZ 473*	72	2

MADDER ROSE *US, male / female vocal / instrumental group (2 WEEKS)* pos/wks

26 Mar 94	**PANIC ON** *Atlantic A 8301CD*	65	1
16 Jul 94	**CAR SONG** *Seed A 7256CD*	68	1

MADDOG – *See STRETCH 'N' VERN present MADDOG*

MADE IN LONDON *UK / Norway, female vocal group (6 WEEKS)* pos/wks

13 May 00	**DIRTY WATER** *RCA 74321746192*	15	5
9 Sep 00	**SHUT YOUR MOUTH** *RCA 74321772602*	74	1

MADEMOISELLE
France, male production / instrumental duo (1 WEEK) pos/wks

8 Sep 01	**DO YOU LOVE ME** *RCA 74321878952*	56	1

MADISON AVENUE *Australia, male producer – Andy Van Dorsselaer, and female vocalist – Cheyne Coates (25 WEEKS)* pos/wks

13 Nov 99	**DON'T CALL ME BABY** *VC Recordings VCRD 56*	30	4
29 Jan 00	**DON'T CALL ME BABY (re-entry)** *VC Recordings VCRD 56*	74	1
19 Feb 00	**DON'T CALL ME BABY (2nd re-entry)** *VC Recordings VCRD 56*	70	1
20 May 00 ★	**DON'T CALL ME BABY (re-issue)** *VC Recordings VCRD 64* ■	1	12
21 Oct 00 ●	**WHO THE HELL ARE YOU** *VC Recordings VCRD 70*	10	5
27 Jan 01	**EVERYTHING YOU NEED** *VC Recordings VCRD 82*	33	2

MADNESS (42 Top 500)
London-based band whose ska-rooted 'nutty' sound earned them a huge haul of hits. This good-time septet fronted by Graham 'Suggs' McPherson (b. 13 Jan 1961) spent more weeks on the chart in the 1980s than any other group (268 WEEKS) pos/wks

1 Sep 79	**THE PRINCE** *2 Tone TT 3*	16	11
10 Nov 79 ●	**ONE STEP BEYOND** *Stiff BUY 56*	7	14
5 Jan 80 ●	**MY GIRL** *Stiff BUY 62*	3	10
5 Apr 80 ●	**WORK REST AND PLAY (EP)** *Stiff BUY 71*	6	8
13 Sep 80 ●	**BAGGY TROUSERS** *Stiff BUY 84*	3	20
22 Nov 80 ●	**EMBARRASSMENT** *Stiff BUY 102*	4	12
24 Jan 81 ●	**THE RETURN OF THE LOS PALMAS SEVEN** *Stiff BUY 108*	7	11
25 Apr 81 ●	**GREY DAY** *Stiff BUY 112*	4	10
26 Sep 81 ●	**SHUT UP** *Stiff BUY 126*	7	9

5 Dec 81	●	**IT MUST BE LOVE** *Stiff BUY 134*	4	12
20 Feb 82		**CARDIAC ARREST** *Stiff BUY 140*	14	10
22 May 82	★	**HOUSE OF FUN** *Stiff BUY 146*	1	9
24 Jul 82	●	**DRIVING IN MY CAR** *Stiff BUY 153*	4	8
27 Nov 82	●	**OUR HOUSE** *Stiff BUY 163*	5	13
19 Feb 83	●	**TOMORROW'S (JUST ANOTHER DAY) / MADNESS (IS ALL IN THE MIND)** *Stiff BUY 169*	8	9
20 Aug 83	●	**WINGS OF A DOVE** *Stiff BUY 181*	2	10
5 Nov 83	●	**THE SUN AND THE RAIN** *Stiff BUY 192*	5	10
11 Feb 84		**MICHAEL CAINE** *Stiff BUY 196*	11	8
2 Jun 84		**ONE BETTER DAY** *Stiff BUY 201*	17	7
31 Aug 85		**YESTERDAY'S MEN** *Zarjazz JAZZ 5*	18	7
26 Oct 85		**UNCLE SAM** *Zarjazz JAZZ 7*	21	11
1 Feb 86		**SWEETEST GIRL** *Zarjazz JAZZ 8*	35	6
8 Nov 86		**(WAITING FOR) THE GHOST TRAIN** *Zarjazz JAZZ 9*	18	7
3 Jan 87		**(WAITING FOR) THE GHOST TRAIN (re-entry)** *Zarjazz JAZZ 9*	74	1
19 Mar 88		**I PRONOUNCE YOU** *Virgin VS 1054* [1]	44	4
15 Feb 92	●	**IT MUST BE LOVE (re-issue)** *Virgin VS 1405*	6	9
25 Apr 92		**HOUSE OF FUN (re-issue)** *Virgin VS 1413*	40	3
8 Aug 92		**MY GIRL (re-issue)** *Virgin VS 1425*	27	4
28 Nov 92		**THE HARDER THEY COME** *Go! Discs GOD 93*	44	3
27 Feb 93		**NIGHT BOAT TO CAIRO** *Virgin VSCDT 1447*	56	2
31 Jul 99	●	**LOVESTRUCK** *Virgin VSCDT 1737*	10	7
6 Nov 99		**JOHNNY THE HORSE** *Virgin VSCDT 1740*	44	2
11 Mar 00		**DRIP FED FRED** *Virgin VSCDT 1768* [2]	55	1

[1] The Madness [2] Madness featuring Ian Dury

Tracks on Work Rest and Play (EP): Night Boat to Cairo / Deceives the Eye / The Young and the Old / Don't Quote Me on That. 'Night Boat to Cairo' in 1993 is a re-issue of a track from the Work Rest and Play EP

MADONNA (5 Top 500)

The most successful female chart act of all time in the UK and US, with worldwide sales in excess of 140 million records, born Madonna Ciccone, 16 Aug 1958, Michigan. Continually ground-breaking and trend-setting, this often controversial artist has amassed an unequalled 35 consecutive UK Top 10 singles (includes two re-entries, a remix and a re-issue) and an unbeatable tally of Top 5 entries. She has also had more UK No.1 singles and albums than any other female soloist, and at one time held the top two slots on the singles chart (1985). Her accumulated UK Top 10 entries are more than The Beatles and Rolling Stones combined, and her album 'The Immaculate Collection' has sold more than 3.3 million copies in the UK alone. In the US, the multi-award-winning singer holds the female record for 27 consecutive Top 20 entries and 16 successive Top 5s plus a dozen No.1s - 10 of which she wrote. Madonna has produced more No.1s than any female, played to packed stadiums around the globe and starred in several successful films. Her 2000 album 'Music' topped the chart in 26 countries and shipped five million albums. She was again voted Best International Female Singer at the 2001 Brits and grossed £40 million for the 28 US dates of her Drowned World Tour - the highest figure for a female performer in that year. She is also the most performed artist on the TV show 'Stars In Their Eyes', with eight impressions in the first 14 series' up to 2002 (568 WEEKS)

			pos	wks
14 Jan 84	●	**HOLIDAY** *Sire W 9405*	6	11
17 Mar 84		**LUCKY STAR** *Sire W 9522*	14	9
2 Jun 84		**BORDERLINE** *Sire W 9260*	56	4
17 Nov 84	●	**LIKE A VIRGIN** *Sire W 9210* ▲	3	18
2 Mar 85	●	**MATERIAL GIRL** *Sire W 9083*	3	10
8 Jun 85	●	**CRAZY FOR YOU** *Geffen A 6323* ▲	2	15
27 Jul 85	★	**INTO THE GROOVE** *Sire W 8934*	1	14
3 Aug 85	●	**HOLIDAY (re-entry)** *Sire W 9405*	2	10
21 Sep 85	●	**ANGEL** *Sire W 8881*	5	9
12 Oct 85	●	**GAMBLER** *Geffen A 6585*	4	11
7 Dec 85	●	**DRESS YOU UP** *Sire W 8848*	5	11
4 Jan 86		**GAMBLER (re-entry)** *Geffen A 6585*	61	1
25 Jan 86	●	**BORDERLINE (re-entry)** *Sire W 9260*	2	9
26 Apr 86	●	**LIVE TO TELL** *Sire W 8717* ▲	2	12
28 Jun 86	★	**PAPA DON'T PREACH** *Sire W 8636* ▲	1	14
4 Oct 86	★	**TRUE BLUE** *Sire W 8550*	1	15
13 Dec 86	●	**OPEN YOUR HEART** *Sire W 8480* ▲	4	9
4 Apr 87	★	**LA ISLA BONITA** *Sire W 8378*	1	11
18 Jul 87	★	**WHO'S THAT GIRL** *Sire W 8341* ▲	1	10
19 Sep 87	●	**CAUSING A COMMOTION** *Sire W 8224*	4	9
12 Dec 87	●	**THE LOOK OF LOVE** *Sire W 8115*	9	7
18 Mar 89	★	**LIKE A PRAYER** *Sire W 7539* ▲	1	12
3 Jun 89	●	**EXPRESS YOURSELF** *Sire W 2948*	5	10
16 Sep 89	●	**CHERISH** *Sire W 2883*	3	8
16 Dec 89	●	**DEAR JESSIE** *Sire W 2668*	5	9
7 Apr 90	★	**VOGUE** *Sire W 9851* ▲	1	14
21 Jul 90	●	**HANKY PANKY** *Sire W 9789*	2	9
8 Dec 90	●	**JUSTIFY MY LOVE** *Sire W 9000* ▲	2	10
2 Mar 91	●	**CRAZY FOR YOU (re-mix)** *Sire W 0008*	2	8
13 Apr 91	●	**RESCUE ME** *Sire W 0024*	3	8
8 Jun 91	●	**HOLIDAY (re-issue)** *Sire W 0037*	5	7
25 Jul 92	●	**THIS USED TO BE MY PLAYGROUND** *Sire W 0122* ▲	3	9
17 Oct 92	●	**EROTICA** *Maverick W 0138*	3	8
12 Dec 92	●	**DEEPER AND DEEPER** *Maverick W 0146*	6	9
9 Jan 93		**EROTICA (re-entry)** *Maverick W 0138*	65	1
6 Mar 93	●	**BAD GIRL** *Maverick W 0145CD*	10	7
3 Apr 93	●	**FEVER** *Maverick W 0168CD*	6	6
31 Jul 93	●	**RAIN** *Maverick W 0190CD*	7	8
2 Apr 94	●	**I'LL REMEMBER** *Maverick W 0240CD*	7	8
8 Oct 94	●	**SECRET** *Maverick W 0268CD*	5	9
17 Dec 94		**TAKE A BOW** *Maverick W 0278CD* ▲	16	9
25 Feb 95	●	**BEDTIME STORY** *Maverick W 0285CD*	4	8
6 May 95		**BEDTIME STORY (re-entry)** *Maverick W 0285CD*	66	1
26 Aug 95	●	**HUMAN NATURE** *Maverick W 0300CD*	8	5
4 Nov 95	●	**YOU'LL SEE** *Maverick W 0324CD*	5	13
6 Jan 96		**OH FATHER** *Maverick W 0326CD*	16	6
23 Mar 96		**ONE MORE CHANCE** *Maverick W 0337CD*	11	4
2 Nov 96	●	**YOU MUST LOVE ME** *Warner Bros. W 0378CD*	10	4
28 Dec 96	●	**DON'T CRY FOR ME ARGENTINA** *Warner Bros. W 0384CD*	3	12
4 Jan 97		**YOU MUST LOVE ME (re-entry)** *Warner Bros. W 0378CD*	75	1
18 Jan 97		**YOU MUST LOVE ME (2nd re-entry)** *Warner Bros. W 0378CD*	71	1
29 Mar 97	●	**ANOTHER SUITCASE IN ANOTHER HALL** *Warner Bros. W 0388CD*	7	5
7 Mar 98	★	**FROZEN** *Maverick W 0433CD* ■	1	13
9 May 98	●	**RAY OF LIGHT** *Maverick W 0444CD*	2	9
18 Jul 98		**RAY OF LIGHT (re-entry)** *Maverick W 0444CD*	75	1
5 Sep 98	●	**DROWNED WORLD (SUBSTITUTE FOR LOVE)** *Maverick W 0453CD1*	10	5
5 Dec 98	●	**THE POWER OF GOODBYE / LITTLE STAR** *Maverick W 459CD*	6	9
13 Mar 99	●	**NOTHING REALLY MATTERS** *Maverick W 471CD*	7	8
5 Jun 99		**NOTHING REALLY MATTERS (re-entry)** *Maverick W 471CD*	75	1
19 Jun 99	●	**BEAUTIFUL STRANGER** *Maverick W 495CD*	2	16
11 Mar 00	★	**AMERICAN PIE** *Maverick W 519CD* ■	1	12
17 Jun 00		**AMERICAN PIE (re-entry)** *Maverick W 519CD*	68	2
2 Sep 00	★	**MUSIC** *Maverick W 537CD1* ■ ▲	1	23
9 Dec 00	●	**DON'T TELL ME** *Maverick W 547CD1*	4	10
28 Apr 01	●	**WHAT IT FEELS LIKE FOR A GIRL** *Maverick W 533CD*	7	9
14 Jul 01		**WHAT IT FEELS LIKE FOR A GIRL (re-entry)** *Maverick W 533CD*	66	2

MAGAZINE

UK, male vocal / instrumental group, lead vocal – Howard Devoto (7 WEEKS)

			pos	wks
11 Feb 78		**SHOT BY BOTH SIDES** *Virgin VS 200*	41	4
26 Jul 80		**SWEET HEART CONTRACT** *Virgin VS 368*	54	3

MAGIC AFFAIR

US / Germany, male / female vocal / instrumental group (8 WEEKS)

			pos	wks
4 Jun 94		**OMEN III** *EMI CDEM 317*	17	4
27 Aug 94		**GIVE ME ALL YOUR LOVE** *EMI CDEM 340*	30	2
5 Nov 94		**IN THE MIDDLE OF THE NIGHT** *EMI CDEM 349*	38	2

MAGIC LADY

US, female vocal duo (3 WEEKS)

			pos	wks
14 May 88		**BETCHA CAN'T LOSE (WITH MY LOVE)** *Motown ZB 42003*	58	3

MAGIC LANTERNS

UK, male vocal / instrumental group (3 WEEKS)

			pos	wks
7 Jul 66		**EXCUSE ME BABY** *CBS 202094*	46	1
28 Jul 66		**EXCUSE ME BABY (re-entry)** *CBS 202094*	44	1
11 Aug 66		**EXCUSE ME BABY (2nd re-entry)** *CBS 202094*	46	1

MAGNUM

UK, male vocal / instrumental group (26 WEEKS)

			pos	wks
22 Mar 80		**MAGNUM (DOUBLE SINGLE)** *Jet 175*	47	6
12 Jul 86		**LONELY NIGHT** *Polydor POSP 798*	70	2

19 Mar 88		DAYS OF NO TRUST *Polydor POSP 910*	32	4
7 May 88		START TALKING LOVE *Polydor POSP 920*	22	4
2 Jul 88		IT MUST HAVE BEEN LOVE *Polydor POSP 930*	33	4
23 Jun 90		ROCKIN' CHAIR *Polydor PO 88*	27	4
25 Aug 90		HEARTBROKE AND BUSTED *Polydor PO 94*	49	2

Tracks on double single: Invasion / Kingdom of Madness / All of My Life / Great Adventure

MAGOO *UK, male vocal / instrumental group (1 WEEK)* pos/wks

4 Apr 98		BLACK SABBATH / SWEET LEAF *Fierce Panda NING 47CD* [1]	60	1

[1] Magoo : Mogwai

MAGOO – *See TIMBALAND; Missy 'Misdemeanor' ELLIOTT*

Sean MAGUIRE *UK, male vocalist (34 WEEKS)* pos/wks

20 Aug 94		SOMEONE TO LOVE *Parlophone CDR 6390*	14	7
5 Nov 94		TAKE THIS TIME *Parlophone CDR 6395*	27	4
31 Dec 94		TAKE THIS TIME (re-entry) *Parlophone CDR 6395*	74	1
25 Mar 95		SUDDENLY *Parlophone CDR 6403*	18	5
24 Jun 95		NOW I'VE FOUND YOU *Parlophone CDLEEPYS 1*	22	3
18 Nov 95		YOU TO ME ARE EVERYTHING *Parlophone CDR 6420*	16	3
25 May 96		GOOD DAY *Parlophone CDR 6432*	12	4
3 Aug 96		DON'T PULL YOUR LOVE *Parlophone CDR 6440*	14	4
29 Mar 97		TODAY'S THE DAY *Parlophone CDR 6459*	27	3

Siobhan MAHER – *See OCEANIC*

MAHLATHINI and the MAHOTELLA QUEENS – *See ART OF NOISE*

MAI TAI *Guyana, female vocal group (30 WEEKS)* pos/wks

25 May 85	●	HISTORY *Virgin VS 773*	8	13
3 Aug 85	●	BODY AND SOUL *Virgin VS 801*	9	13
15 Feb 86		FEMALE INTUITION *Virgin VS 844*	54	4

MAIN INGREDIENT *US, male vocal group (7 WEEKS)* pos/wks

29 Jun 74		JUST DON'T WANT TO BE LONELY *RCA APBO 0205*	27	7

MAISONETTES *UK, male / female vocal group (12 WEEKS)* pos/wks

11 Dec 82	●	HEARTACHE AVENUE *Ready Steady Go! RSG 1*	7	12

Raven MAIZE *UK, male producer – Dave Lee (7 WEEKS)* pos/wks

5 Aug 89		FOREVER TOGETHER *Republic LIC 014*	67	1
18 Aug 01		THE REAL LIFE *Rulin / MoS / Credence RULIN 18CDS*	12	5
29 Sep 01		THE REAL LIFE (re-entry) *Rulin / MoS / Credence RULIN 18CDS*	60	1

See also Joey NEGRO; Li KWAN; AKABU featuring Linda CLIFFORD; JAKATTA; HED BOYS

J MAJIK featuring Kathy BROWN
UK, male producer and US, female vocalist (2 WEEKS) pos/wks

5 May 01		LOVE IS NOT A GAME *Defected DFECT 31CDS*	34	2

MAKADOPOULOS and his GREEK SERENADERS
Greece, male vocal / instrumental group (14 WEEKS) pos/wks

20 Oct 60		NEVER ON SUNDAY *Palette PG 9005*	36	14

MAKAVELI *US, male rapper – 2Pac (Tupac Shakur) (8 WEEKS)* pos/wks

12 Apr 97	●	TO LIVE & DIE IN LA *Interscope IND 95529*	10	4
9 Aug 97		TOSS IT UP *Interscope IND 95521*	15	3
14 Feb 98		HAIL MARY *Interscope IND 95575*	43	1

See also 2PAC

Jack E MAKOSSA *Kenya, male producer (5 WEEKS)* pos/wks

12 Sep 87		THE OPERA HOUSE *Champion CHAMP 50*	48	5

MALA – *See BOWA featuring MALA*

MALAIKA *US, female vocalist (1 WEEK)* pos/wks

31 Jul 93		GOTTA KNOW (YOUR NAME) *A & M 5802732*	68	1

Carl MALCOLM *Jamaica, male vocalist (8 WEEKS)* pos/wks

13 Sep 75	●	FATTIE BUM BUM *UK 108*	8	8

Valerie MALCOLM – *See CANDY GIRLS*

Stephen MALKMUS *US, male vocalist (1 WEEK)* pos/wks

28 Apr 01		DISCRETION GROVE *Domino RUG 123CD*	60	1

Timmy MALLETT – *See BOMBALURINA*

MAMA CASS *US, female vocalist – Ellen Cohen (27 WEEKS)* pos/wks

14 Aug 68		DREAM A LITTLE DREAM OF ME *RCA 1726*	11	12
16 Aug 69	●	IT'S GETTING BETTER *Stateside SS 8021*	8	15

See also MAMAS and the PAPAS

MAMAS and the PAPAS *Folk-rock harmony quartet who helped to make California the focal point of mid-60s music: singer / songwriter John Phillips (d. 2001) and wife Michelle, Canadian Dennis Doherty and (Mama) Cass Elliot (d. 1974). Quartet split in 1968 with Cass becoming solo hitmaker and Michelle an actress (71 WEEKS)* pos/wks

28 Apr 66		CALIFORNIA DREAMIN' *RCA 1503*	23	9
12 May 66	●	MONDAY MONDAY *RCA 1516* ▲	3	13
28 Jul 66		I SAW HER AGAIN *RCA 1533*	11	11
9 Feb 67		WORDS OF LOVE *RCA 1564*	47	3
6 Apr 67	●	DEDICATED TO THE ONE I LOVE *RCA 1576*	2	17
26 Jul 67	●	CREEQUE ALLEY *RCA 1613*	9	11
2 Aug 97	●	CALIFORNIA DREAMIN' (re-issue) *MCA MCSTD 48058*	9	7

See also MAMA CASS

MAMBAS – *See Marc ALMOND*

Cheb MAMI – *See STING*

A MAN CALLED ADAM
UK, male / female vocal / instrumental group (4 WEEKS) pos/wks

29 Sep 90		BAREFOOT IN THE HEAD *Big Life BLR 28*	70	2
20 Oct 90		BAREFOOT IN THE HEAD (re-entry) *Big Life BLR 28*	60	2

MAN TO MAN *US, male vocal / instrumental duo (19 WEEKS)* pos/wks

13 Sep 86		MALE STRIPPER *Bolts BOLTS 4* [1]	64	3
3 Jan 87		MALE STRIPPER (re-entry) *Bolts BOLTS 4* [1]	63	1
7 Feb 87	●	MALE STRIPPER (2nd re-entry) *Bolts BOLTS 4* [1]	4	12
4 Jul 87		I NEED A MAN / ENERGY'S EUROBEAT *Bolts BOLTS 5*	43	3

[1] Man 2 Man meet Man Parrish

MAN WITH NO NAME *UK, male producer – Martin Freeland (6 WEEKS)* pos/wks

30 Sep 95		FLOOR-ESSENCE *Perfecto PERF 108CD*	68	1
20 Jan 96		PAINT A PICTURE *Perfecto PERF 114CD* [1]	42	2
12 Oct 96		TELEPORT / SUGAR RUSH *Perfecto PERF 126CD*	55	1
2 May 98		VAVOOM! *Perfecto PERF 159CD1*	43	1
18 Jul 98		THE FIRST DAY (HORIZON) *Perfecto PERF 164CD*	72	1

[1] Man with No Name featuring Hannah

Melissa MANCHESTER – *See Al JARREAU*

MANCHESTER UNITED FOOTBALL CLUB
UK, male football team vocalists (56 WEEKS) pos/wks

8 May 76		MANCHESTER UNITED *Decca F 13633*	50	1
21 May 83		GLORY GLORY MAN UNITED *EMI 5390*	13	5
18 May 85	●	WE ALL FOLLOW MAN UNITED *Columbia DB 9107*	10	5
19 Jun 93		UNITED (WE LOVE YOU) *Living Beat LBECD 026* [1]	37	2
30 Apr 94	★	COME ON YOU REDS *PolyGram TV MANU 2*	1	15
13 May 95	●	WE'RE GONNA DO IT AGAIN *PolyGram TV MANU 952* [2]	6	6

UK No.1 ★ UK Top 10 ● Still on chart + UK million seller ◆ UK entry at No.1 ■ US No.1 ▲

1979

:AR IN WHICH MARGARET THATCHER ENTERED 10 DOWNING STREET AS THE UK'S
MALE PRIME MINISTER, LORD MOUNTBATTEN WAS KILLED BY AN IRA BOMB, NEW
NED ON THE CHARTS BY THE FIRST 2-TONE AND RAP HITS AND SONY LAUNCHED
.KMAN, **MEAT LOAF** REMEMBERS A MOTORCYCLE MOMENT AS 'BAT OUT OF HELL'
MADE ITS FIRST VISIT TO THE UK SINGLES CHART :..

"One of the most mind-blowing moments in my musical history was watching **Todd Rundgren** play the solo in 'Bat Out of Hell'. I don't think I have ever been so amazed at anything. He said, 'Do you want a solo on this?' Picked up a guitar and did it in one take and one take only. Jim [producer / songwriter Jim Steinman] said he wanted a motorcycle sound effect on the track. Todd goes, 'OK, you want a motorcycle, here's a motorcycle.' He plays through the first half of this song, and he gets to the motorcycle part. He goes over to this guitar rack with all the bells and whistles – the first one I'd ever seen – and twists and bends these knobs. 'Motorcycle it is,' he says. And using a whammy bar, without missing a beat, he goes rrrrraaaaaaabbbbbbrrrrrrrr."

SINGLE OF THE YEAR 'Bright Eyes' Art Garfunkel
ALBUM OF THE YEAR 'Parallel Lines' Blondie

4 May 96 ●	MOVE MOVE MOVE (THE RED TRIBE) *Music Collection MANUCD 1* [3]	6	11
3 Aug 96	MOVE MOVE MOVE (THE RED TRIBE) (re-entry) *Music Collection MANUCD 1* [3]	50	4
29 May 99	LIFT IT HIGH (ALL ABOUT BELIEF) *Music Collection MANUCD 4* [4]	11	6
21 Aug 99	LIFT IT HIGH (ALL ABOUT BELIEF) (re-entry) *Music Collection MANUCD 4* [4]	75	1

[1] Manchester United and the Champions [2] Manchester United Football Squad featuring Stryker [3] 1996 Manchester United FA Cup Squad [4] 1999 Manchester United Squad

MANCHILD *UK, male production duo (2 WEEKS)* pos/wks

16 Sep 00	THE CLICHES ARE TRUE *One Little Indian 176 TP7CD* [1]	60	1
25 Aug 01	NOTHING WITHOUT ME *One Little Indian 183 TP7CD*	40	1

[1] Manchild featuring Kelly Jones

See also STEREOPHONICS

Henry MANCINI *US, orchestra / chorus (23 WEEKS)* pos/wks

7 Dec 61	MOON RIVER *RCA 1256*	46	2
28 Dec 61	MOON RIVER (re-entry) *RCA 1256*	44	1
24 Sep 64 ●	HOW SOON *RCA 1414*	10	12
25 Mar 72	THEME FROM 'CADE'S COUNTY' *RCA 2182*	42	1
11 Feb 84	MAIN THEME FROM 'THE THORN BIRDS' *Warner Bros. 9677*	23	7

Steve MANDELL – *See 'DELIVERANCE' SOUNDTRACK*

MANFRED MANN (70 Top 500) *One of the most regular chart entrants of the 1960s: Manfred Mann (k), Mike Vickers (g), Tom McGuinness (b), Mike Hugg (d), Paul Jones (v) - Jones was replaced by Mike D'Abo in 1966. They were the first group from the south of England to top the US charts during 1964's so-called 'British Invasion' (217 WEEKS)* pos/wks

23 Jan 64 ●	5-4-3-2-1 *HMV POP 1252*	5	13
16 Apr 64	HUBBLE BUBBLE (TOIL AND TROUBLE) *HMV POP 1282*	11	8
16 Jul 64 ★	DO WAH DIDDY DIDDY *HMV POP 1320* ▲	1	14
15 Oct 64 ●	SHA LA LA *HMV POP 1346*	3	12
14 Jan 65 ●	COME TOMORROW *HMV POP 1381*	4	9
15 Apr 65	OH NO, NOT MY BABY *HMV POP 1413*	11	10
16 Sep 65 ●	IF YOU GOTTA GO, GO NOW *HMV POP 1466*	2	12
21 Apr 66 ★	PRETTY FLAMINGO *HMV POP 1523*	1	12
7 Jul 66	YOU GAVE ME SOMEBODY TO LOVE *HMV POP 1541*	36	4
4 Aug 66 ●	JUST LIKE A WOMAN *Fontana TF 730*	10	10
27 Oct 66 ●	SEMI-DETACHED SUBURBAN MR JAMES *Fontana TF 757*	2	12
30 Mar 67 ●	HA! HA! SAID THE CLOWN *Fontana TF 812*	4	11
25 May 67	SWEET PEA *Fontana TF 828*	36	4
24 Jan 68 ★	MIGHTY QUINN *Fontana TF 897*	1	11
12 Jun 68 ●	MY NAME IS JACK *Fontana TF 943*	8	11
18 Dec 68 ●	FOX ON THE RUN *Fontana TF 985*	5	12
30 Apr 69 ●	RAGAMUFFIN MAN *Fontana TF 1013*	8	11
8 Sep 73 ●	JOYBRINGER *Vertigo 6059 083* [1]	9	10
28 Aug 76 ●	BLINDED BY THE LIGHT *Bronze BRO 29* [1] ▲	6	10
20 May 78 ●	DAVY'S ON THE ROAD AGAIN *Bronze BRO 52* [1]	6	12
17 Mar 79	YOU ANGEL YOU *Bronze BRO 68* [1]	54	5
7 Jul 79	DON'T KILL IT CAROL *Bronze BRO 77* [1]	45	4

[1] Manfred Mann's Earth Band

MANHATTAN TRANSFER (487 Top 500) *Multi-faceted four-part harmony vocal group formed New York, US, 1969, whose recordings include songs from the 1930s to 80s. Their nostalgic sound earned them 10 Grammy awards, although, oddly, their No.1 hit did not chart in the US (72 WEEKS)* pos/wks

7 Feb 76	TUXEDO JUNCTION *Atlantic K 10670*	24	6
5 Feb 77 ★	CHANSON D'AMOUR *Atlantic K 10886*	1	13
28 May 77	DON'T LET GO *Atlantic K 10930*	32	6
18 Feb 78	WALK IN LOVE *Atlantic K 11075*	48	1
4 Mar 78	WALK IN LOVE (re-entry) *Atlantic K 11075*	12	11
20 May 78	ON A LITTLE STREET IN SINGAPORE *Atlantic K 11136*	20	9
16 Sep 78	WHERE DID OUR LOVE GO / JE VOULAIS TE DIRE (QUE JE T'ATTENDS) *Atlantic K 11182*	40	4
23 Dec 78	WHO, WHAT, WHEN, WHERE, WHY *Atlantic K 11233*	49	6
17 May 80	TWILIGHT ZONE - TWILIGHT TONE (MEDLEY) *Atlantic K 11476*	25	8
21 Jan 84	SPICE OF LIFE *Atlantic A 9728*	19	8

MANHATTANS *US, male vocal group (31 WEEKS)* pos/wks

19 Jun 76 ●	KISS AND SAY GOODBYE *CBS 4317* ▲	4	11
2 Oct 76 ●	HURT *CBS 4562*	4	11
23 Apr 77	IT'S YOU *CBS 5093*	43	3
26 Jul 80	SHINING STAR *CBS 8624*	45	4
6 Aug 83	CRAZY *CBS A 3578*	63	2

M.A.N.I.C. *UK, male vocal / production duo (1 WEEK)* pos/wks

18 Apr 92	I'M COMIN' HARDCORE *Union City UCRT 2*	60	1

MANIC MCs featuring Sara CARLSON

UK, male production duo and female vocalist (5 WEEKS) pos/wks

12 Aug 89	MENTAL *RCA PB 43037*	30	5

MANIC STREET PREACHERS (159 Top 500) *Best-selling Welsh act of the 1990s; James Dean Bradfield (v/g), Nicky Wire (b), Sean Moore (d) and Richey Edwards (v/g - missing and presumed dead since 1995). Won trophies for the Best British Group and Best Album at the 1997 and 1999 Brit Awards (145 WEEKS)* pos/wks

25 May 91	YOU LOVE US *Heavenly HVN 10*	62	2
10 Aug 91	STAY BEAUTIFUL *Columbia 6573377*	40	3
9 Nov 91	LOVE'S SWEET EXILE / REPEAT *Columbia 6575827*	26	3
1 Feb 92	YOU LOVE US (re-issue) *Columbia 6577247*	16	4
28 Mar 92	SLASH 'N' BURN *Columbia 6578737*	20	4
13 Jun 92	MOTORCYCLE EMPTINESS *Columbia 6580837*	17	6
19 Sep 92 ●	THEME FROM M.A.S.H. (SUICIDE IS PAINLESS) *Columbia 6583827*	7	6
21 Nov 92	LITTLE BABY NOTHING *Columbia 6587967*	29	3
12 Jun 93	FROM DESPAIR TO WHERE *Columbia 6593372*	25	4
31 Jul 93	LA TRISTESSE DURERA (SCREAM TO A SIGH) *Columbia 6594772*	22	5
2 Oct 93	ROSES IN THE HOSPITAL *Columbia 6597272*	15	3
12 Feb 94	LIFE BECOMING A LANDSLIDE *Columbia 6600702*	36	2
11 Jun 94	FASTER / PCP *Epic 6604472*	16	3
13 Aug 94	REVOL *Epic 6606862*	22	3
15 Oct 94	SHE IS SUFFERING *Epic 6608952*	25	3
27 Apr 96 ●	A DESIGN FOR LIFE *Epic 6630705*	2	10
27 Jul 96	A DESIGN FOR LIFE (re-entry) *Epic 6630705*	71	1
3 Aug 96 ●	EVERYTHING MUST GO *Epic 6634685*	5	6
12 Oct 96 ●	KEVIN CARTER *Epic 6637752*	9	4
14 Dec 96 ●	AUSTRALIA *Epic 6640442*	7	7
13 Sep 97	LITTLE BABY NOTHING (re-issue) *Epic MANIC 6CD*	50	1
13 Sep 97	LOVE'S SWEET EXILE (re-issue) *Epic MANIC 2CD*	55	1
13 Sep 97	MOTORCYCLE EMPTINESS (re-issue) *Epic MANIC 5CD*	41	2
13 Sep 97	SLASH 'N' BURN (re-issue) *Epic MANIC 4CD*	54	1
13 Sep 97	STAY BEAUTIFUL (re-issue) *Epic MANIC 1CD*	52	1
13 Sep 97	YOU LOVE US (2nd re-issue) *Epic MANIC 3CD*	49	1
5 Sep 98 ★	IF YOU TOLERATE THIS YOUR CHILDREN WILL BE NEXT *Epic 6663452* ■	1	10
5 Dec 98	IF YOU TOLERATE THIS YOUR CHILDREN WILL BE NEXT (re-entry) *Epic 6663452*	69	1
12 Dec 98	THE EVERLASTING *Epic 6666862*	11	8
20 Mar 99 ●	YOU STOLE THE SUN FROM MY HEART *Epic 6669532*	5	8
17 Jul 99	TSUNAMI *Epic 6674112*	11	5
22 Jan 00 ★	THE MASSES AGAINST THE CLASSES *Epic 6685302* ■	1	6
1 Apr 00	THE MASSES AGAINST THE CLASSES (re-entry) *Epic 6685302*	70	1
10 Mar 01 ●	FOUND THAT SOUL *Epic 6708332*	9	3
10 Mar 01 ●	SO WHY SO SAD *Epic 6708322*	8	7
21 Apr 01	FOUND THAT SOUL (re-entry) *Epic 6708332*	68	1
16 Jun 01	OCEAN SPRAY *Epic 6712532*	15	4
22 Sep 01	LET ROBESON SING *Epic 6717732*	19	2

The listed flipside of 'Theme From M.A.S.H. (Suicide Is Painless)' was '(Everything I Do) I Do It for You' by Fatima Mansions

Barry MANILOW (185 Top 500)

Middle-of-the-road superstar, b. Barry Pincus, 17 Jun 1946, Brooklyn, US. This crowd-pulling singer / songwriter / pianist with a vast and loyal following on both sides of the Atlantic has sold in excess of 50 million albums (136 WEEKS)

		pos	wks
22 Feb 75	MANDY *Arista 1* ▲	11	9
6 May 78	CAN'T SMILE WITHOUT YOU *Arista 176*	43	7
29 Jul 78	SOMEWHERE IN THE NIGHT / COPACABANA (AT THE COPA) *Arista 196*	42	10
23 Dec 78	COULD IT BE MAGIC *Arista ARIST 229*	25	10
8 Nov 80	LONELY TOGETHER *Arista ARIST 373*	21	13
7 Feb 81	I MADE IT THROUGH THE RAIN *Arista ARIST 384*	37	6
11 Apr 81	BERMUDA TRIANGLE *Arista ARIST 406*	15	9
26 Sep 81	LET'S HANG ON *Arista ARIST 429*	12	11
12 Dec 81	THE OLD SONGS *Arista ARIST 443*	48	8
20 Feb 82	IF I SHOULD LOVE AGAIN *Arista ARIST 453*	66	2
17 Apr 82	STAY *Arista ARIST 464* [1]	23	8
16 Oct 82 ●	I WANNA DO IT WITH YOU *Arista ARIST 495*	8	8
4 Dec 82	I'M GONNA SIT RIGHT DOWN AND WRITE MYSELF A LETTER *Arista ARIST 503*	36	7
25 Jun 83	SOME KIND OF FRIEND *Arista ARIST 516*	48	2
27 Aug 83	YOU'RE LOOKING HOT TONIGHT *Arista ARIST 542*	47	6
10 Dec 83	READ 'EM AND WEEP *Arista ARIST 551*	17	7
8 Apr 89	PLEASE DON'T BE SCARED *Arista 112186*	35	5
10 Apr 93	COPACABANA (AT THE COPA) (re-mix) *Arista 74321136912*	22	4
20 Nov 93	COULD IT BE MAGIC (re-recording) *Arista 74321174882*	36	3
6 Aug 94	LET ME BE YOUR WINGS *EMI CDEM 336* [2]	73	1

[1] Barry Manilow featuring Kevin Desimone and James Jolis [2] Barry Manilow and Debra Byrd

ARIST 464 was available as both a live and studio recording

MANIX

UK, male / female vocal / instrumental group (6 WEEKS)

		pos	wks
23 Nov 91	MANIC MINDS *Reinforced RIVET 1209*	63	2
7 Mar 92	OBLIVION (HEAD IN THE CLOUDS) (EP) *Reinforced RIVET 1212*	43	3
8 Aug 92	RAINBOW PEOPLE *Reinforced RIVET 1221*	57	1

Tracks on Oblivion (Head in the Clouds) (EP): Oblivion (Head in the Clouds) / Never Been to Belgium (Gotta Rush) / I Can't Stand It / You Held My Hand

MANKEY

UK, male producer – Andy Manston (1 WEEK)

		pos	wks
16 Nov 96	BELIEVE IN ME *Frisky DISKY 3*	74	1

MANKIND

UK, male instrumental group (12 WEEKS)

		pos	wks
25 Nov 78	DR WHO *Pinnacle PIN 71*	25	12

Aimee MANN

US, female vocalist (9 WEEKS)

		pos	wks
31 Oct 87	TIME STAND STILL *Vertigo RUSH 13* [1]	42	3
28 Aug 93	I SHOULD'VE KNOWN *Imago 72787250437*	55	2
20 Nov 93	STUPID THING *Imago 727872504527*	47	2
5 Mar 94	I SHOULD'VE KNOWN (re-issue) *Imago 72787250602*	45	2

[1] Rush with Aimee Mann

Johnny MANN SINGERS

US, male / female vocal group (13 WEEKS)

		pos	wks
12 Jul 67 ●	UP-UP AND AWAY *Liberty LIB 55972*	6	13

MANSUN

UK, male vocal / instrumental group (44 WEEKS)

		pos	wks
6 Apr 96	ONE (EP) *Parlophone CDR 6430*	37	2
15 Jun 96	TWO (EP) *Parlophone CDR 6437*	32	2
21 Sep 96	STRIPPER VICAR *Parlophone CDR 6447*	19	3
17 Dec 96	WIDE OPEN SPACE *Parlophone CDR 6453*	15	4
15 Feb 97 ●	SHE MAKES MY NOSE BLEED *Parlophone CDR 6453*	9	5
10 May 97	TAXLOSS *Parlophone CDRS 6465*	15	3
18 Oct 97 ●	CLOSED FOR BUSINESS *Parlophone CDRS6482*	10	3
11 Jul 98 ●	LEGACY (EP) *Parlophone CDRS 6497*	7	4
5 Sep 98	BEING A GIRL (PART ONE) (EP) *Parlophone CDR 6503*	13	3
7 Nov 98	NEGATIVE *Parlophone CDR 6508*	27	2
13 Feb 99	SIX *Parlophone CDR 6511*	16	3
12 Aug 00 ●	I CAN ONLY DISAPOINT U *Parlophone CDR 6544*	8	6
18 Nov 00	ELECTRIC MAN *Parlophone CDR 6550*	23	2
10 Feb 01	FOOL *Parlophone CDRS 6553*	28	2

Tracks on One (EP): Egg Shaped Fred / Ski Jump Nose / Lemonade Secret Drinker / Thief. Tracks on Two (EP): Take It Easy Chicken / Drastic Sturgeon / The Greatest Pain / Moronica. Tracks on Legacy (EP): CD#1 Legacy (Extended version) / Can't Afford To Die / Spasm of Identity / Check Under the Bed. CD#2 Legacy / Wide Open Space (The Perfecto Remix) / GSOH / Face In The Crowd. Tracks on Being a Girl (Part One) (EP): Being A Girl / I Care / Been Here Before / Hideout / Railings

MANTOVANI and his ORCHESTRA

UK, orchestra – leader Annunzio Paolo Mantovani (52 WEEKS)

		pos	wks
19 Dec 52 ●	WHITE CHRISTMAS *Decca F 10017*	6	3
29 May 53 ★	THE SONG FROM THE MOULIN ROUGE *Decca F 10094*	1	21
23 Oct 53 ●	SWEDISH RHAPSODY *Decca F 10168*	2	17
13 Nov 53 ●	THE SONG FROM THE MOULIN ROUGE (re-entry) *Decca F 10094*	10	1
4 Dec 53	THE SONG FROM THE MOULIN ROUGE (2nd re-entry) *Decca F 10094*	12	1
26 Feb 54	SWEDISH RHAPSODY (re-entry) *Decca F 10168*	12	1
11 Feb 55	LONELY BALLERINA *Decca F 10395*	16	3
18 Mar 55	LONELY BALLERINA (re-entry) *Decca F 10395*	18	1
31 May 57	AROUND THE WORLD *Decca F 10888*	20	4

See also David WHITFIELD

MANTRONIK vs EPMD

US, male vocalist / instrumentalist / producer – Curtis Mantronik, and US, male rap / DJ duo (1 WEEK)

		pos	wks
15 Aug 98	STRICTLY BUSINESS *Parlophone CDR 6502*	43	1

MANTRONIX

US / Jamaica, male vocal / instrumental duo (48 WEEKS)

		pos	wks
22 Feb 86	LADIES *10 TEN 116*	55	4
17 May 86	BASSLINE *10 TEN 118*	34	6
7 Feb 87	WHO IS IT? *10 TEN 137*	40	6
4 Jul 87	SCREAM (PRIMAL SCREAM) *10 TEN 169*	46	4
30 Jan 88	SING A SONG (BREAK IT DOWN) *10 TEN 206*	61	2
12 Mar 88	SIMPLE SIMON (YOU GOTTA REGARD) *10 TEN 217*	72	2
6 Jan 90 ●	GOT TO HAVE YOUR LOVE *Capitol CL 559* [1]	4	11
12 May 90 ●	TAKE YOUR TIME *Capitol CL 573* [1]	10	7
2 Mar 91	DON'T GO MESSIN' WITH MY HEART *Capitol CL 608*	22	5
22 Jun 91	STEP TO ME (DO ME) *Capitol CL 613*	59	1

[1] Mantronix featuring Wondress

MANUEL and The MUSIC OF THE MOUNTAINS

UK, orchestra – leader Geoff Love (31 WEEKS)

		pos	wks
28 Aug 59	THE HONEYMOON SONG *Columbia DB 4323*	29	2
25 Sep 59	THE HONEYMOON SONG (re-entry) *Columbia DB 4323*	22	5
6 Nov 59	THE HONEYMOON SONG (2nd re-entry) *Columbia DB 4323*	27	2
13 Oct 60	NEVER ON SUNDAY *Columbia DB 4515*	29	10
13 Oct 66	SOMEWHERE MY LOVE *Columbia DB 7969*	42	2
31 Jan 76 ●	RODRIGO'S GUITAR CONCERTO DE ARANJUEZ (THEME FROM 2ND MOVEMENT) *EMI 2383*	3	10

Roots MANUVA

UK, male rapper (6 WEEKS)

		pos	wks
11 Dec 99	DUSTED *Hard Hands HAND 058CD1* [1]	28	2
22 Jan 00	DUSTED (re-entry) *Hard Hands HAND 058CD1* [1]	75	1
4 Aug 01	WITNESS (1 HOPE) *Big Dada BDCDS 022*	45	2
20 Oct 01	DREAMY DAYS *Big Dada BDCDS 033*	53	1

[1] Leftfield / Roots Manuva

MARATHON

Germany / UK, male vocal / instrumental group (3 WEEKS)

		pos	wks
25 Jan 92	MOVIN' *Ten TEN 395*	36	3

MARAUDERS

UK, male vocal / instrumental group (4 WEEKS)

		pos	wks
8 Aug 63	THAT'S WHAT I WANT *Decca F 11695*	48	1
22 Aug 63	THAT'S WHAT I WANT (re-entry) *Decca F 11695*	43	3

MARBLES

UK, male vocal duo - Graham Bonnet and Trevor Garden (18 WEEKS) pos/wks

		pos	wks
25 Sep 68 ●	**ONLY ONE WOMAN** *Polydor 56 272*	5	12
26 Mar 69	**THE WALLS FELL DOWN** *Polydor 56 310*	28	6

MARC and the MAMBAS – *See Marc ALMOND*

MARC et CLAUDE *Germany, male DJ / production duo – Marc Romboy and Klaus Derichs (10 WEEKS)* pos/wks

		pos	wks
21 Nov 98	**LA** *Positiva CDTIV 104*	28	3
22 Jul 00	**I NEED YOUR LOVIN' (LIKE THE SUNSHINE)** *Positiva CDTIV 136*	12	7

MARCELS *US, male vocal group – lead vocal Cornelius Harp (17 WEEKS)* pos/wks

		pos	wks
13 Apr 61 ★	**BLUE MOON** *Pye International 7N 25073* ▲	1	13
8 Jun 61	**SUMMERTIME** *Pye International 7N 25083*	46	4

Little Peggy MARCH *US, female vocalist (7 WEEKS)* pos/wks

		pos	wks
12 Sep 63	**HELLO HEARTACHE, GOODBYE LOVE** *RCA 1362*	29	7

MARCO POLO *Italy, male instrumental / production duo (1 WEEK)* pos/wks

		pos	wks
8 Apr 95	**A PRAYER TO THE MUSIC** *Hi-Life HICD 7*	65	1

MARCY PLAYGROUND *US, male vocal / instrumental trio (3 WEEKS)* pos/wks

		pos	wks
18 Apr 98	**SEX AND CANDY** *EMI CDEM 508*	29	3

MARDI GRAS *UK, male vocal / instrumental group (9 WEEKS)* pos/wks

		pos	wks
5 Aug 72	**TOO BUSY THINKING 'BOUT MY BABY** *Bell 1226*	19	9

MARIA – *See Maria NAYLER*

Kelly MARIE *UK, female vocalist (36 WEEKS)* pos/wks

		pos	wks
2 Aug 80 ★	**FEELS LIKE I'M IN LOVE** *Calibre PLUS 1*	1	16
18 Oct 80	**LOVING JUST FOR FUN** *Calibre PLUS 4*	21	7
7 Feb 81	**HOT LOVE** *Calibre PLUS 5*	22	10
30 May 81	**LOVE TRIAL** *Calibre PLUS 7*	51	3

Rose MARIE *Ireland, female vocalist (5 WEEKS)* pos/wks

		pos	wks
19 Nov 83	**WHEN I LEAVE THE WORLD BEHIND** *A1 284*	75	1
3 Dec 83	**WHEN I LEAVE THE WORLD BEHIND (re-entry)** *A1 284*	63	2
24 Dec 83	**WHEN I LEAVE THE WORLD BEHIND (2nd re-entry)** *A1 284*	66	2

Teena MARIE *US, female vocalist – Mary Brockert (28 WEEKS)* pos/wks

		pos	wks
7 Jul 79	**I'M A SUCKER FOR YOUR LOVE** *Motown TMG 1146* [1]	43	8
31 May 80 ●	**BEHIND THE GROOVE** *Motown TMG 1185*	6	10
11 Oct 80	**I NEED YOUR LOVIN'** *Motown TMG 1203*	28	6
26 Mar 88	**OOO LA LA LA** *Epic 651423 7*	74	2
10 Nov 90	**SINCE DAY ONE** *Epic 656429 7*	69	2

[1] Teena Marie, co-lead vocals Rick James

MARILLION (293 Top 500) *Progressive rock group formed in Buckinghamshire and originally named after Tolkien's novel Silmarillion. They reached their peak of popularity in the 80s, when fronted by Scottish vocalist / songwriter Fish (b. Derek Dick, 25 Apr 1958). When Fish left in 1989 the band continued to make regular visits to the charts with Steve Hogarth in the role of vocalist / songwriter (103 WEEKS)* pos/wks

		pos	wks
20 Nov 82	**MARKET SQUARE HEROES** *EMI 5351*	60	2
12 Feb 83	**HE KNOWS YOU KNOW** *EMI 5362*	35	4
16 Apr 83	**MARKET SQUARE HEROES (re-entry)** *EMI 5351*	53	6
18 Jun 83	**GARDEN PARTY** *EMI 5393*	16	5
11 Feb 84	**PUNCH AND JUDY** *EMI MARIL 1*	29	4
12 May 84	**ASSASSING** *EMI MARIL 2*	22	5
18 May 85 ●	**KAYLEIGH** *EMI MARIL 3*	2	14
7 Sep 85 ●	**LAVENDER** *EMI MARIL 4*	5	9
30 Nov 85	**HEART OF LOTHIAN** *EMI MARIL 5*	29	6
23 May 87 ●	**INCOMMUNICADO** *EMI MARIL 6*	6	5
25 Jul 87	**SUGAR MICE** *EMI MARIL 7*	22	5
7 Nov 87	**WARM WET CIRCLES** *EMI MARIL 8*	22	4
26 Nov 88	**FREAKS (LIVE)** *EMI MARIL 9*	24	3
9 Sep 89	**HOOKS IN YOU** *Capitol MARIL 10*	30	3
9 Dec 89	**UNINVITED GUEST** *EMI MARIL 11*	53	2
14 Apr 90	**EASTER** *EMI MARIL 12*	34	2
8 Jun 91	**COVER MY EYES (PAIN AND HEAVEN)** *EMI MARIL 13*	34	4
3 Aug 91	**NO ONE CAN** *EMI MARIL 14*	33	4
5 Oct 91	**DRY LAND** *EMI MARIL 15*	34	2
23 May 92	**SYMPATHY** *EMI MARIL 16*	17	3
1 Aug 92	**NO ONE CAN (re-issue)** *EMI MARIL 17*	26	4
26 Mar 94	**THE HOLLOW MAN** *EMI CDEMS 307*	30	2
7 May 94	**ALONE AGAIN IN THE LAP OF LUXURY** *EMI CDEMS 318*	53	3
10 Jun 95	**BEAUTIFUL** *EMI CDMARILS 18*	29	2

See also FISH

MARILYN *UK, male vocalist – Peter Robinson (26 WEEKS)* pos/wks

		pos	wks
5 Nov 83 ●	**CALLING YOUR NAME** *Mercury MAZ 1*	4	12
11 Feb 84	**CRY AND BE FREE** *Mercury MAZ 2*	31	6
21 Apr 84	**YOU DON'T LOVE ME** *Mercury MAZ 3*	40	7
13 Apr 85	**BABY U LEFT ME (IN THE COLD)** *Mercury MAZ 4*	70	1

MARILYN MANSON *US, male vocal / instrumental group (18 WEEKS)* pos/wks

		pos	wks
7 Jun 97	**THE BEAUTIFUL PEOPLE** *Nothing 95541*	18	3
20 Sep 97	**TOURNIQUET** *Nothing 95552*	28	2
21 Nov 98	**THE DOPE SHOW** *Nothing 95610*	12	3
26 Jun 99	**ROCK IS DEAD** *Maverick W 486CD*	23	2
18 Nov 00	**DISPOSABLE TEENS** *Nothing 4974372*	12	3
3 Mar 01	**THE FIGHT SONG** *Nothing / Interscope 4974902*	24	3
15 Sep 01	**THE NOBODIES** *Nothing IND 97604*	34	2

Marino MARINI and his QUARTET

Italy, male vocalist and instrumental group (23 WEEKS) pos/wks

		pos	wks
3 Oct 58	**VOLARE (NEL BLU DIPINTO DI BLU)** *Durium DC 16632*	13	7
10 Oct 58 ●	**COME PRIMA** *Durium DC 16632*	2	14
20 Mar 59	**CIAO CIAO BAMBINA** *Durium DC 16636*	25	1
3 Apr 59	**CIAO CIAO BAMBINA (re-entry)** *Durium DC 16636*	24	1

MARION *UK, male vocal / instrumental group (9 WEEKS)* pos/wks

		pos	wks
25 Feb 95	**SLEEP** *London LONCD 360*	53	1
13 May 95	**TOYS FOR BOYS** *London LONCD 366*	57	1
21 Oct 95	**LET'S ALL GO TOGETHER** *London LONCD 371*	37	2
3 Feb 96	**TIME** *London LONCD 377*	29	2
30 Mar 96	**SLEEP (re-mix)** *London LONCD 381*	17	2
7 Mar 98	**MIYAKO HIDEAWAY** *London LONCD 403*	45	1

MARK 'OH *Germany, male producer – Marko Albrecht (3 WEEKS)* pos/wks

		pos	wks
6 May 95	**TEARS DON'T LIE** *Systematic SYSCD 9*	24	3

Pigmeat MARKHAM *US, male vocalist (8 WEEKS)* pos/wks

		pos	wks
17 Jul 68	**HERE COMES THE JUDGE** *Chess CRS 8077*	19	8

Biz MARKIE *US, male rapper (2 WEEKS)* pos/wks

		pos	wks
26 May 90	**JUST A FRIEND** *Cold Chillin' W 9823*	55	2

Yannis MARKOPOULOS *Greece, orchestra (8 WEEKS)* pos/wks

		pos	wks
17 Dec 77	**WHO PAYS THE FERRYMAN** *BBC RESL 51*	11	8

Guy MARKS *US, male vocalist (8 WEEKS)* pos/wks

		pos	wks
13 May 78	**LOVING YOU HAS MADE ME BANANAS** *ABC 4211*	25	8

MARKSMEN – *See HOUSTON WELLS*

MARKY MARK and the FUNKY BUNCH

US, male / female vocal / rap / instrumental group (14 WEEKS) pos/wks

		pos	wks
31 Aug 91	**GOOD VIBRATIONS** *Interscope A 8764* [1] ▲	14	7
2 Nov 91	**WILDSIDE** *Interscope A 8674*	42	3
12 Dec 92	**YOU GOTTA BELIEVE** *Interscope A 8480*	54	4

[1] Marky Mark and the Funky Bunch featuring Loleatta Holloway

UK No.1 ★ UK Top 10 ● Still on chart + UK million seller ◆ UK entry at No.1 ■ US No.1 ▲

Bob MARLEY and the WAILERS (124 Top 500) *Legendary, globally successful Jamaican group. Varying line-up included Bob Marley b. 6 Apr 1945, Jamaica, d. 11 May 1981, Miami, (v/g), Peter Tosh b. 19 Oct 1944, Jamaica, d. 11 Sep 1987, Jamaica (v/g), Bunny Wailer (v/prc). Their compilation 'Legend' is the biggest-selling reggae album in the UK and the US with combined sales of more than 12 million (167 WEEKS)* pos/wks

27 Sep 75 NO WOMAN NO CRY *Island WIP 6244* 22 7
25 Jun 77 EXODUS *Island WIP 6390* 14 9
10 Sep 77 WAITING IN VAIN *Island WIP 6402* 27 6
10 Dec 77 ● JAMMING / PUNKY REGGAE PARTY *Island WIP 6410* 9 12
25 Feb 78 ● IS THIS LOVE *Island WIP 6420* 9 9
10 Jun 78 SATISFY MY SOUL *Island WIP 6440* 21 10
20 Oct 79 SO MUCH TROUBLE IN THE WORLD *Island WIP 6510* 56 4
21 Jun 80 ● COULD YOU BE LOVED *Island WIP 6610* 5 12
13 Sep 80 THREE LITTLE BIRDS *Island WIP 6641* 17 9
13 Jun 81 ● NO WOMAN NO CRY (re-entry) *Island WIP 6244* 8 11
7 May 83 ● BUFFALO SOLDIER *Island/Tuff Gong 1S 108* 4 12
21 Apr 84 ● ONE LOVE - PEOPLE GET READY *Island IS 169* 5 11
23 Jun 84 WAITING IN VAIN (re-issue) *Island IS 180* 31 7
8 Dec 84 COULD YOU BE LOVED (re-issue) *Island IS 210* 71 2
18 May 91 ONE LOVE - PEOPLE GET READY (re-issue) *Tuff Gong TGX 1* 42 3
19 Sep 92 ● IRON LION ZION *Tuff Gong TGX 2* 5 9
28 Nov 92 WHY SHOULD I / EXODUS *Tuff Gong TGX 3* 42 3
2 Jan 93 WHY SHOULD I / EXODUS (re-entry) *Tuff Gong TGX 3* 75 1
20 May 95 KEEP ON MOVING *Tuff Gong TGXCD 4* 17 4
8 Jun 96 WHAT GOES AROUND COMES AROUND *Anansi ANACS 002* 42 1
25 Sep 99 ● SUN IS SHINING *Club Tools / Edel 0066895 CLU* [1] 3 10
11 Dec 99 TURN YOUR LIGHTS DOWN LOW *Columbia 6684362* [2] 15 7
22 Jan 00 RAINBOW COUNTRY *Club Tools 0067225CLU* [1] 11 6
24 Jun 00 JAMMIN' *Tuff Gong TGXCD 9* [3] 42 2

[1] Bob Marley vs Funkstar De Luxe [2] Bob Marley featuring Lauryn Hill [3] Bob Marley featuring MC Lyte

'Exodus' on Tuff Gong TGX 3 listed with 'Why Should I' only from 5 Dec 1992, and is a different version from the Island hit. It peaked at No.53

Ziggy MARLEY and the MELODY MAKERS
Jamaica, male / female vocal / instrumental group (11 WEEKS) pos/wks

11 Jun 88 TOMORROW PEOPLE *Virgin VS 1049* 22 10
23 Sep 89 LOOK WHO'S DANCING *Virgin America VUS 5* 65 1

Lene MARLIN
Norway, female vocalist – Lene Marlin Pederson (19 WEEKS) pos/wks

11 Mar 00 ● SITTING DOWN HERE *Virgin DINSD 183* 5 11
16 Sep 00 UNFORGIVABLE SINNER *Virgin DINSD 202* 13 6
13 Jan 01 WHERE I'M HEADED *Virgin DINSD 196* 31 2

MARLO *UK, male vocal / instrumental group (1 WEEK)* pos/wks

24 Jul 99 HOW DO I KNOW? *Polydor 5611362* 56 1

MARMALADE (201 Top 500) *The first Scottish group to top the chart: included Dean Ford (v), Junior Campbell (g/p/v), Alan Whitehead (d). This pop quintet, who first recorded as Dean Ford and The Gaylords, had a large late-1960s teen following (130 WEEKS)* pos/wks

22 May 68 ● LOVIN' THINGS *CBS 3412* 6 13
23 Oct 68 WAIT FOR ME MARIANNE *CBS 3708* 30 5
4 Dec 68 ★ OB-LA-DI, OB-LA-DA *CBS 3892* 1 20
11 Jun 69 ● BABY MAKE IT SOON *CBS 4287* 9 13
20 Dec 69 ● REFLECTIONS OF MY LIFE *Decca F 12982* 3 12
18 Jul 70 ● RAINBOW *Decca F 13035* 3 14
27 Mar 71 MY LITTLE ONE *Decca F 13135* 15 11
4 Sep 71 ● COUSIN NORMAN *Decca F 13214* 6 11
27 Nov 71 BACK ON THE ROAD *Decca F 13251* 35 7
22 Jan 72 BACK ON THE ROAD (re-entry) *Decca F 13251* 50 1
1 Apr 72 ● RADANCER *Decca F 13297* 6 12
21 Feb 76 ● FALLING APART AT THE SEAMS *Target TGT 105* 9 11

MARMION
Spain / Holland, male instrumental / production duo (2 WEEKS) pos/wks

18 May 96 SCHONEBERG *Hooj Choons HOOJCD 43* 53 1
14 Feb 98 SCHONEBERG (re-mix) *ffrr FCD 324* 56 1

Johnny MARR – *See Billy BRAGG; Kirsty MacCOLL; ELECTRONIC; SMITHS*

MARRADONA *UK, male DJ / production group (5 WEEKS)* pos/wks

26 Feb 94 OUT OF MY HEAD *Peach PWCD 282* 38 3
26 Jul 97 OUT OF MY HEAD 97 (re-mix) *Soopa SPCD 1* 39 2

M/A/R/R/S *UK, male instrumental / production group (14 WEEKS)* pos/wks

5 Sep 87 ★ PUMP UP THE VOLUME / ANITINA (THE FIRST TIME I SEE SHE DANCE) *4AD AD 70* 1 14

Gerry MARSDEN – *See CHRISTIANS; Holly JOHNSON; Paul McCARTNEY; STOCK AITKEN WATERMAN; GERRY and the PACEMAKERS*

Matthew MARSDEN *UK, male vocalist (10 WEEKS)* pos/wks

11 Jul 98 THE HEART'S LONE DESIRE *Columbia 6661152* 13 7
7 Nov 98 SHE'S GONE *Columbia 6664915* [1] 24 3

[1] Matthew Marsden featuring Destiny's Child

Stevie MARSH *UK, female vocalist (4 WEEKS)* pos/wks

4 Dec 59 IF YOU WERE THE ONLY BOY IN THE WORLD *Decca F 11181* 29 2
25 Dec 59 IF YOU WERE THE ONLY BOY IN THE WORLD (re-entry) *Decca F 11181* 24 2

MARSHA – *See SHAGGY*

Joy MARSHALL *UK, female vocalist (2 WEEKS)* pos/wks

23 Jun 66 THE MORE I SEE YOU *Decca F 12422* 34 2

Keith MARSHALL *UK, male vocalist (10 WEEKS)* pos/wks

4 Apr 81 ONLY CRYING *Arrival PIK 2* 12 10

Louise Claire MARSHALL – *See SILICONE SOUL*

Wayne MARSHALL *UK, male vocalist (7 WEEKS)* pos/wks

1 Oct 94 OOH AAH (G-SPOT) *Soultown SOULCDS 322* 29 3
3 Jun 95 SPIRIT *Soultown SOULCDS 00352* 58 1
24 Feb 96 NEVER KNEW LOVE LIKE THIS *Sony S2 6629382* [1] 40 2
7 Dec 96 G SPOT (re-mix) *MBA INTER 9006* 50 1

[1] Pauline Henry featuring Wayne Marshall

MARSHALL HAIN *UK, male / female vocal / instrumental duo – Julian Marshall and Kit Hain (19 WEEKS)* pos/wks

3 Jun 78 ● DANCING IN THE CITY *Harvest HAR 5157* 3 15
14 Oct 78 COMING HOME *Harvest HAR 5168* 39 4

MARTAY featuring ZZ TOP *UK, female rapper – Melone McKenzy and US, male vocal / instrumental trio (2 WEEKS)* pos/wks

16 Oct 99 GIMME ALL YOUR LOVIN' 2000 *Riverhorse RIVHCD 2* 28 2

Lena MARTELL *UK, female vocalist – Helen Thomson (18 WEEKS)* pos/wks

29 Sep 79 ★ ONE DAY AT A TIME *Pye 7N 46021* 1 18

MARTHA and the MUFFINS
Canada, female / male vocal / instrumental group (10 WEEKS) pos/wks

1 Mar 80 ● ECHO BEACH *Dindisc DIN 9* 10 10

See also M + M

MARTHA and the VANDELLAS – *See Martha REEVES and the VANDELLAS*

MARTIKA *US, female vocalist – Marta Marrera (57 WEEKS)* pos/wks

			pos	wks
29 Jul 89	●	TOY SOLDIERS *CBS 655049 7* ▲	5	11
14 Oct 89	●	I FEEL THE EARTH MOVE *CBS 655294 7*	7	14
13 Jan 90		MORE THAN YOU KNOW *CBS 655526 7*	15	7
17 Mar 90		WATER *CBS 655731 7*	59	3
17 Aug 91	●	LOVE . . . THY WILL BE DONE *Columbia 6573137*	9	9
30 Nov 91		MARTIKA'S KITCHEN *Columbia 6575687*	17	10
22 Feb 92		COLOURED KISSES *Columbia 6577097*	41	3

Billie Ray MARTIN

Germany, female vocalist – Birgit Dieckmann (20 WEEKS) pos/wks

			pos	wks
19 Nov 94		YOUR LOVING ARMS *Magnet MAG 1028CD*	38	3
20 May 95	●	YOUR LOVING ARMS (re-mix) *Magnet MAG 1031CD*	6	10
2 Sep 95		RUNNING AROUND TOWN *Magnet MAG 1035CD*	29	2
6 Jan 96		IMITATION OF LIFE *Magnet MAG 1040CD*	29	3
6 Apr 96		SPACE OASIS *Magnet MAG 1042CD*	66	1
21 Aug 99		HONEY *React CDREACT 129*	54	1

Dean MARTIN (129 Top 500) *Acclaimed vocalist / entertainer / film actor and cabaret performer, b. Dino Crocetti, 7 Jun 1917, Ohio, d. 25 Dec 1995. He first found fame partnering Jerry Lewis (1946-56), and had a long and successful solo career. He was a member of Frank Sinatra's 'Rat Pack' and had an impressive 46-year chart span (163 WEEKS)* pos/wks

			pos	wks
18 Sep 53	●	KISS *Capitol CL 13893*	9	1
2 Oct 53	●	KISS (re-entry) *Capitol CL 13893*	5	7
22 Jan 54	●	THAT'S AMORE *Capitol CL 14008*	2	11
1 Oct 54	●	SWAY *Capitol CL 14138*	6	7
22 Oct 54		HOW DO YOU SPEAK TO AN ANGEL *Capitol CL 14150*	15	2
19 Nov 54		HOW DO YOU SPEAK TO AN ANGEL (re-entry) *Capitol CL 14150*	17	4
28 Jan 55	●	THE NAUGHTY LADY OF SHADY LANE *Capitol CL 14226*	5	10
4 Feb 55		MAMBO ITALIANO *Capitol CL 14227*	14	2
25 Feb 55	●	LET ME GO, LOVER *Capitol CL 14226*	3	9
1 Apr 55	●	UNDER THE BRIDGES OF PARIS *Capitol CL 14255*	6	8
10 Feb 56	★	MEMORIES ARE MADE OF THIS *Capitol CL 14523* ▲	1	16
2 Mar 56		YOUNG AND FOOLISH *Capitol CL 14519*	20	1
27 Apr 56		INAMORATA *Capitol CL 14507*	21	3
22 Mar 57		THE MAN WHO PLAYS THE MANDOLINO *Capitol CL 14690*	21	2
13 Jun 58	●	RETURN TO ME *Capitol CL 14844*	2	22
29 Aug 58	●	VOLARE (NEL BLU DIPINTO DI BLU) *Capitol CL 14910*	2	14
27 Aug 64		EVERYBODY LOVES SOMEBODY *Reprise R 20281* ▲	11	13
12 Nov 64		THE DOOR IS STILL OPEN TO MY HEART *Reprise R 20307*	42	4
5 Feb 69	●	GENTLE ON MY MIND *Reprise RS 23343*	2	23
30 Aug 69		GENTLE ON MY MIND (re-entry) *Reprise RS 23343*	49	1
22 Jun 96		THAT'S AMORE (re-issue) *EMI Premier PRESCD 3*	43	2
21 Aug 99		SWAY (re-issue) *Capitol CDSWAY 001*	66	1

Juan MARTIN *Spain, male instrumentalist – guitar (7 WEEKS)* pos/wks

			pos	wks
28 Jan 84	●	LOVE THEME FROM 'THE THORN BIRDS' *WEA X 9518*	10	7

Linda MARTIN *Ireland, female vocalist (2 WEEKS)* pos/wks

			pos	wks
30 May 92		WHY ME *Columbia 6581317*	59	2

Luci MARTIN – *See Romina JOHNSON*

Marilyn MARTIN – *See Phil COLLINS*

Ray MARTIN and his Chorus and Orchestra

UK, orchestra (11 WEEKS) pos/wks

			pos	wks
14 Nov 52	●	BLUE TANGO *Columbia DB 3051*	8	1
28 Nov 52	●	BLUE TANGO (re-entry) *Columbia DB 3051*	10	3
4 Dec 53	●	SWEDISH RHAPSODY *Columbia DB 3346*	10	1
18 Dec 53	●	SWEDISH RHAPSODY (re-entry) *Columbia DB 3346*	4	3
15 Jun 56		THE CAROUSEL WALTZ *Columbia DB 3771*	28	1
3 Aug 56		THE CAROUSEL WALTZ (re-entry) *Columbia DB 3771*	24	2

See also Lee LAWRENCE

Ricky MARTIN (459 Top 500) *Bon-bon shaking, ex-boy band singer and soap star b. Enrique Martin Morales, 24 Dec 1971, Puerto Rico. The performer who put the Latin into platinum sold 15 million of his eponymous album, recorded the world's biggest-selling football single ('The Cup of Life') and has the world's biggest-selling Spanish language album ('Vuelve') (75 WEEKS)* pos/wks

			pos	wks
20 Sep 97	●	(UN, DOS, TRES) MARIA *Columbia 6649595*	6	6
11 Jul 98		THE CUP OF LIFE *Columbia 6661502*	29	3
17 Jul 99	★	LIVIN' LA VIDA LOCA *Columbia 6676402* ■ ▲	1	17
20 Nov 99		SHAKE YOUR BON-BON *Columbia 6683412*	12	9
29 Apr 00	●	PRIVATE EMOTION *Columbia 6692692* [1]	9	9
4 Nov 00	●	SHE BANGS *Columbia 6705422*	3	15
10 Mar 01	●	NOBODY WANTS TO BE LONELY *Columbia 6709462* [2]	4	12
28 Jul 01		LOADED *Columbia 6714642*	19	4

[1] Ricky Martin featuring Meja [2] Ricky Martin and Christina Aguilera

Tony MARTIN *US, male vocalist – Alvin Morris Jr (28 WEEKS)* pos/wks

			pos	wks
22 Apr 55	●	STRANGER IN PARADISE *HMV B 10849*	6	13
13 Jul 56	●	WALK HAND IN HAND *HMV POP 222*	2	15

Both with Hugo Winterhalter's Orchestra and Chorus

Vince MARTIN – *See TARRIERS*

Wink MARTINDALE *US, male vocalist (41 WEEKS)* pos/wks

			pos	wks
4 Dec 59		DECK OF CARDS *London HLD 8962*	18	5
15 Jan 60		DECK OF CARDS (re-entry) *London HLD 8962*	28	2
31 Mar 60		DECK OF CARDS (2nd re-entry) *London HLD 8962*	45	1
18 Apr 63	●	DECK OF CARDS (3rd re-entry) *London HLD 8962*	5	21
20 Oct 73		DECK OF CARDS (re-issue) *Dot DOT 109*	22	12

Al MARTINO (367 Top 500) *Big-voiced balladeer b. Alfred Cini, 7 Oct 1927, Philadelphia, US. First release topped the US chart and was the first ever UK No.1. After a few lean years, he returned to become one of the 1960s top-selling easy listening acts in the US (87 WEEKS)* pos/wks

			pos	wks
14 Nov 52	★	HERE IN MY HEART *Capitol CL 13779* ▲	1	18
21 Nov 52	●	TAKE MY HEART *Capitol CL 13769*	9	1
30 Jan 53	●	NOW *Capitol CL 13835*	3	12
10 Jul 53	●	RACHEL *Capitol CL 13879*	10	4
11 Sep 53		RACHEL (re-entry) *Capitol CL 13879*	12	1
4 Jun 54		WANTED *Capitol CL 14128*	12	1
18 Jun 54	●	WANTED (re-entry) *Capitol CL 14128*	4	14
1 Oct 54	●	THE STORY OF TINA *Capitol CL 14163*	10	8
1 Oct 54		WANTED (2nd re-entry) *Capitol CL 14128*	17	1
23 Sep 55		THE MAN FROM LARAMIE *Capitol CL 14343*	19	2
28 Oct 55		THE MAN FROM LARAMIE (re-entry) *Capitol CL 14343*	20	1
31 Mar 60		SUMMERTIME *Top Rank JAR 312*	49	1
29 Aug 63		I LOVE YOU BECAUSE *Capitol CL 15300*	48	1
22 Aug 70		SPANISH EYES *Capitol CL 15430*	49	1
14 Jul 73	●	SPANISH EYES (re-entry) *Capitol CL 15430*	5	21

John MARTYN – *See SISTER BLISS*

MARVELETTES *US, female vocal group (10 WEEKS)* pos/wks

			pos	wks
15 Jun 67		WHEN YOU'RE YOUNG AND IN LOVE *Tamla Motown TMG 609*	13	10

Hank MARVIN

UK, male vocalist / instrumentalist, guitar – Brian Rankin (36 WEEKS) pos/wks

			pos	wks
13 Sep 69	●	THROW DOWN A LINE *Columbia DB 8615* [1]	7	9
21 Feb 70		JOY OF LIVING *Columbia DB 8657* [1]	25	8
6 Mar 82		DON'T TALK *Polydor POSP 420*	49	4
22 Mar 86	★	LIVING DOLL *WEA YZ 65* [2]	1	11
7 Jan 89		LONDON KID *Polydor PO 32* [3]	52	3
17 Oct 92		WE ARE THE CHAMPIONS *PolyGram TV PO 229* [4]	66	1

[1] Cliff and Hank [2] Cliff Richard and the Young Ones featuring Hank B Marvin [3] Jean-Michel Jarre featuring Hank Marvin [4] Hank Marvin featuring Brian May

See also SHADOWS

Lee MARVIN *US, male actor / vocalist (23 WEEKS)* pos/wks

7 Feb 70	★	**WAND'RIN' STAR** *Paramount PARA 3004*	1	18
20 Jun 70		**WAND'RIN' STAR (re-entry)** *Paramount PARA 3004*	42	3
15 Aug 70		**WAND'RIN' STAR (2nd re-entry)** *Paramount PARA 3004*	47	2

'I Talk to the Trees' by Clint Eastwood, the flip side of 'Wand'rin' Star', was listed with 'Wand'rin' Star' for 7 Feb and 14 Feb 1970 only

MARVIN THE PARANOID ANDROID *UK, male robot (4 WEEKS)* pos/wks

16 May 81		**MARVIN** *Polydor POSP 261*	53	4

MARVIN and TAMARA *UK, male / female vocal duo – Marvin Simmonds and Tamara Nicole (9 WEEKS)* pos/wks

7 Aug 99		**GROOVE MACHINE** *Epic 6675582*	11	5
25 Dec 99		**NORTH, SOUTH, EAST, WEST** *Epic 6684902*	38	4

Richard MARX (462 Top 500) *Child jingle singer turned session singer turned singer / songwriter, b. 16 Sep 1962, Chicago, US. He scored 12 consecutive Top 20 entries in the US (first six hits in the Top 3) and sold more than 15 million albums. Married Cynthia Rhodes, lead singer of Animotion. Produced and wrote for *N Sync in 2000 (75 WEEKS)* pos/wks

27 Feb 88		**SHOULD'VE KNOWN BETTER** *Manhattan MT 32*	50	5
14 May 88		**ENDLESS SUMMER NIGHTS** *Manhattan MT 39*	50	3
17 Jun 89		**SATISFIED** *EMI-USA MT 64* ▲	52	4
2 Sep 89	●	**RIGHT HERE WAITING** *EMI-USA MT 72* ▲	2	10
11 Nov 89		**ANGELIA** *EMI-USA MT 74*	45	4
24 Mar 90		**TOO LATE TO SAY GOODBYE** *EMI-USA MT 80*	38	3
7 Jul 90		**CHILDREN OF THE NIGHT** *EMI-USA MT 84*	54	2
1 Sep 90		**ENDLESS SUMMER NIGHTS / HOLD ON TO THE NIGHTS (re-issue)** *EMI-USA MT 89* ▲	60	2
19 Oct 91		**KEEP COMING BACK** *Capitol CL 634*	55	2
9 May 92	●	**HAZARD** *Capitol CL 654*	3	15
29 Aug 92		**TAKE THIS HEART** *Capitol CL 667*	13	6
28 Nov 92		**CHAINS AROUND MY HEART** *Capitol CL 676*	29	6
29 Jan 94		**NOW AND FOREVER** *Capitol CDCLS 703*	13	6
30 Apr 94		**SILENT SCREAM** *Capitol CDCLS 714*	32	4
13 Aug 94		**THE WAY SHE LOVES ME** *Capitol CDCL 721*	38	3

MARXMAN *UK / Ireland, rap / instrumental group (5 WEEKS)* pos/wks

6 Mar 93		**ALL ABOUT EVE** *Talkin Loud TLKCD 35*	28	4
1 May 93		**SHIP AHOY** *Talkin Loud TLKCD 39*	64	1

Sinead O'Connor provides uncredited vocals on 'Ship Ahoy'

MARY JANE GIRLS *US, female vocal group (15 WEEKS)* pos/wks

21 May 83		**CANDY MAN** *Motown TMG 1301*	60	4
25 Jun 83		**ALL NIGHT LONG** *Gordy TMG 1309*	13	9
8 Oct 83		**BOYS** *Gordy TMG 1315*	74	1
18 Feb 95		**ALL NIGHT LONG (re-mix)** *Motown TMGCD 1436*	51	1

MARY MARY *US, female vocal duo – Erica and Tina Atkins (14 WEEKS)* pos/wks

10 Jun 00	●	**SHACKLES (PRAISE YOU)** *Columbia 6694202*	5	12
18 Nov 00		**I SINGS** *Columbia 6699742*	32	2

Carolyne MAS *US, female vocalist (2 WEEKS)* pos/wks

2 Feb 80		**QUOTE GOODBYE QUOTE** *Mercury 6167 873*	71	2

MASE *US, male rapper – Mason Betha (53 WEEKS)* pos/wks

29 Mar 97		**CAN'T NOBODY HOLD ME DOWN** *Arista 74321464552* [1] ▲	19	4
9 Aug 97	●	**MO MONEY MO PROBLEMS** *Puff Daddy 74321492492* [2]	6	10
27 Dec 97	●	**FEEL SO GOOD** *Puff Daddy 74321526442*	10	8
18 Apr 98		**WHAT YOU WANT** *Puff Daddy74321578772* [3]	15	5
19 Sep 98		**HORSE AND CARRIAGE** *Epic 6662612* [4]	12	4
10 Oct 98	●	**TOP OF THE WORLD** *Atlantic AT 0046CD* [5]	2	8
12 Dec 98	●	**TAKE ME THERE** *Interscope IND 95620* [6]	7	9
9 Jan 99		**TOP OF THE WORLD (re-entry)** *Atlantic AT 0046CD* [5]	61	1
10 Jul 99		**GET READY** *Puff Daddy / Arista 74321682602* [7]	32	4

[1] Puff Daddy featuring Mase [2] Notorious B.I.G. featuring Puff Daddy and Mase [3] Mase featuring Total [4] Cam'ron featuring Mase [5] Brandy featuring Mase [6] BLACKstreet and Mya featuring Mase & Blinky Blink [7] Mase featuring BLACKstreet

MASH *US, male vocal / instrumental group (12 WEEKS)* pos/wks

10 May 80	★	**THEME FROM M*A*S*H (SUICIDE IS PAINLESS)** *CBS 8536*	1	12

MASH! *UK / US, male / female vocal group (3 WEEKS)* pos/wks

21 May 94		**U DON'T HAVE TO SAY U LOVE ME** *React CDREACT 37*	37	2
4 Feb 95		**LET'S SPEND THE NIGHT TOGETHER** *Playa CDXPLAYA 2*	66	1

MASH UP – *See Matt DAREY*

MASON – *See CHICANE*

Barbara MASON *US, female vocalist (5 WEEKS)* pos/wks

21 Jan 84		**ANOTHER MAN** *Streetwave KHAN 3*	45	5

Glen MASON *UK, male vocalist (7 WEEKS)* pos/wks

28 Sep 56		**GLENDORA** *Parlophone R 4203*	28	2
16 Nov 56		**THE GREEN DOOR** *Parlophone R 4244*	24	5

Mary MASON *UK, female vocalist (6 WEEKS)* pos/wks

8 Oct 77		**ANGEL OF THE MORNING - ANY WAY THAT YOU WANT ME (MEDLEY)** *Epic EPC 5552*	27	6

MASQUERADE *UK, male / female vocal group (10 WEEKS)* pos/wks

11 Jan 86		**ONE NATION** *Streetwave KHAN 59*	54	6
5 Jul 86		**(SOLUTION TO) THE PROBLEM** *Streetwave KHAN 67*	65	2
26 Jul 86		**(SOLUTION TO) THE PROBLEM (re-entry)** *Streetwave KHAN 67*	64	2

MASS ORDER *US, male vocal / instrumental duo (5 WEEKS)* pos/wks

14 Mar 92		**LIFT EVERY VOICE (TAKE ME AWAY)** *Columbia 6577487*	35	3
23 May 92		**LET'S GET HAPPY** *Columbia 6580737*	45	2

MASS PRODUCTION *US, male vocal / instrumental group (7 WEEKS)* pos/wks

12 Mar 77		**WELCOME TO OUR WORLD (OF MERRY MUSIC)** *Atlantic K 10898*	44	3
17 May 80		**SHANTE** *Atlantic K 11475*	59	4

MASS SYNDICATE featuring Su Su BOBIEN *US, male producer and US, female vocalist (1 WEEK)* pos/wks

24 Oct 98		**YOU DON'T KNOW** *ffrr FCD 347*	71	1

Zeitia MASSIAH *UK, female vocalist (2 WEEKS)* pos/wks

12 Mar 94		**I SPECIALIZE IN LOVE** *Union City UCRCD 27*	74	1
24 Sep 94		**THIS IS THE PLACE** *Virgin VSCDT 1511*	62	1

MASSIEL *Spain, female vocalist (4 WEEKS)* pos/wks

24 Apr 68		**LA LA LA** *Philips BF 1667*	35	4

MASSIVE ATTACK *UK, male / female vocal / instrumental group (42 WEEKS)* pos/wks

23 Feb 91		**UNFINISHED SYMPATHY** *Wild Bunch WBRS 2* [1]	13	9
8 Jun 91		**SAFE FROM HARM** *Wild Bunch WBRS 3*	25	6
22 Feb 92		**MASSIVE ATTACK (EP)** *Wild Bunch WBRS 4*	27	4
29 Oct 94		**SLY** *Wild Bunch WBRDX 5*	24	4
21 Jan 95		**PROTECTION** *Wild Bunch WBRX 6* [2]	14	4
1 Apr 95		**KARMACOMA** *Wild Bunch WBRX 7*	28	4
19 Jul 97		**RISINGSON** *Circa WBRX 8*	11	3

9 May 98 ●	**TEARDROP** *Virgin WBRX 9*	10	6
25 Jul 98	**ANGEL** *Virgin WBRX 10*	30	2

[1] Massive [2] Massive Attack featuring Tracey Thorn

Tracks on Massive Attack (EP): Hymn of the Big Wheel / Home of the Whale / Be Thankful / Any Love. Teardrop features an uncredited vocal by Elizabeth Fraser from the Cocteau Twins

MASSIVO featuring TRACY *UK, male / female vocal / instrumental group (11 WEEKS)* pos/wks

26 May 90	**LOVING YOU** *Debut DEBT 3097*	25	11

MASTER P – *See Montell JORDAN*

MASTER SINGERS *UK, male vocal group (8 WEEKS)* pos/wks

14 Apr 66	**HIGHWAY CODE** *Parlophone R 5428*	25	6
17 Nov 66	**WEATHER FORECAST** *Parlophone R 5523*	50	1
29 Dec 66	**WEATHER FORECAST (re-entry)** *Parlophone R 5523*	45	1

MASTERMIXERS – *See JIVE BUNNY and the MASTERMIXERS*

Sammy MASTERS *US, male vocalist (5 WEEKS)* pos/wks

9 Jun 60	**ROCKIN' RED WING** *Warner Bros. WB 10*	36	5

MASTERS AT WORK present INDIA *US, male production / instrumental duo and female vocalist (5 WEEKS)* pos/wks

5 Aug 95	**I CAN'T GET NO SLEEP** *A & M 5811412*	44	2
31 Jul 99	**TO BE IN LOVE** *Defected DEFECT 5CDS* [1]	23	3

[1] MAW presents India

MASTERS OF CEREMONIES – *See DJ PIED PIPER and the MASTERS OF CEREMONIES*

MATCH *UK, male vocal / instrumental group (3 WEEKS)* pos/wks

16 Jun 79	**BOOGIE MAN** *Flamingo FM 2*	48	3

MATCHBOX *UK, male vocal / instrumental group (66 WEEKS)* pos/wks

3 Nov 79	**ROCKABILLY REBEL** *Magnet MAG 155*	18	12
19 Jan 80	**BUZZ BUZZ A DIDDLE IT** *Magnet MAG 157*	22	8
10 May 80	**MIDNITE DYNAMOS** *Magnet MAG 169*	14	12
27 Sep 80 ●	**WHEN YOU ASK ABOUT LOVE** *Magnet MAG 191*	4	12
29 Nov 80	**OVER THE RAINBOW – YOU BELONG TO ME** *(MEDLEY)*	15	11
4 Apr 81	**BABES IN THE WOOD** *Magnet MAG 193*	46	6
1 Aug 81	**LOVE'S MADE A FOOL OF YOU** *Magnet MAG 194*	63	3
29 May 82	**ONE MORE SATURDAY NIGHT** *Magnet MAG 223*	63	2

MATCHBOX 20 *US, male vocal / instrumental group (4 WEEKS)* pos/wks

11 Apr 98	**PUSH** *Atlantic AT 0021CD*	38	2
4 Jul 98	**3 AM** *Atlantic AT 0034CD*	64	1
17 Feb 01	**IF YOU'RE GONE** *Atlantic AT 0090CD*	50	1

MATCHROOM MOB – *See CHAS and DAVE*

Mireille MATHIEU *France, female vocalist (7 WEEKS)* pos/wks

13 Dec 67	**LA DERNIERE VALSE** *Columbia DB 8323*	26	7

Johnny MATHIS (180 Top 500) *Legendary MOR vocal superstar, b. 30 Sep 1935, San Francisco, US. Frank Sinatra and Elvis Presley are the only males with more hit albums in the US, where his greatest hits album charted for almost 10 years - a record for a solo performer (137 WEEKS)* pos/wks

23 May 58	**TEACHER, TEACHER** *Fontana H 130*	27	5
26 Sep 58 ●	**A CERTAIN SMILE** *Fontana H 142*	4	16
19 Dec 58	**WINTER WONDERLAND** *Fontana H 165*	17	3
7 Aug 59 ●	**SOMEONE** *Fontana H 199*	6	15
27 Nov 59	**THE BEST OF EVERYTHING** *Fontana H 218*	30	1
29 Jan 60	**MISTY** *Fontana H 219*	12	9
24 Mar 60	**YOU ARE BEAUTIFUL** *Fontana H 234*	38	8
14 Apr 60	**MISTY (re-entry)** *Fontana H 219*	46	2
26 May 60	**YOU ARE BEAUTIFUL (re-entry)** *Fontana H 234*	46	1
28 Jul 60	**STARBRIGHT** *Fontana H 254*	47	2
6 Oct 60 ●	**MY LOVE FOR YOU** *Fontana H 267*	9	18
4 Apr 63	**WHAT WILL MARY SAY** *CBS AAG 135*	49	1
25 Jan 75 ●	**I'M STONE IN LOVE WITH YOU** *CBS 2653*	10	12
13 Nov 76 ★	**WHEN A CHILD IS BORN (SOLEADO)** *CBS 4599*	1	12
25 Mar 78 ●	**TOO MUCH, TOO LITTLE, TOO LATE** *CBS 6164* [1] ▲	3	14
29 Jul 78	**YOU'RE ALL I NEED TO GET BY** *CBS 6483* [1]	45	6
11 Aug 79	**GONE GONE GONE** *CBS 7730*	15	10
26 Dec 81	**WHEN A CHILD IS BORN** *CBS S 1758* [2]	74	2

[1] Johnny Mathis and Deniece Williams [2] Johnny Mathis and Gladys Knight

Ivan MATIAS *US, male vocalist (1 WEEK)* pos/wks

6 Apr 96	**SO GOOD (TO COME HOME TO) / I'VE HAD ENOUGH** *Arista 74321345072*	69	1

MATT BIANCO *UK, male / female vocal / instrumental duo (65 WEEKS)* pos/wks

11 Feb 84	**GET OUT OF YOUR LAZY BED** *WEA BIANCO 1*	15	8
14 Apr 84	**SNEAKING OUT THE BACK DOOR / MATT'S MOOD** *WEA YZ 3*	44	7
10 Nov 84	**HALF A MINUTE** *WEA YZ 26*	23	10
2 Mar 85	**MORE THAN I CAN BEAR** *WEA YZ 34*	50	7
5 Oct 85	**YEH YEH** *WEA YZ 46*	13	10
1 Mar 86	**JUST CAN'T STAND IT** *WEA YZ 62*	66	2
14 Jun 86	**DANCING IN THE STREET** *WEA YZ 72*	64	3
4 Jun 88	**DON'T BLAME IT ON THAT GIRL / WAP-BAM-BOOGIE** *WEA YZ 188*	11	13
27 Aug 88	**GOOD TIMES** *WEA YZ 302*	55	3
4 Feb 89	**NERVOUS / WAP-BAM-BOOGIE (re-mix)** *WEA YZ 328*	59	2

'Matt's Mood' credited only from 5 May 1984. Act was a UK / Poland, male / female vocal / instrumental group on first five hits

Al MATTHEWS *US, male vocalist (8 WEEKS)* pos/wks

23 Aug 75	**FOOL** *CBS 3429*	16	8

Cerys MATTHEWS – *See Tom JONES; CATATONIA; SPACE*

Dave MATTHEWS BAND *US, male vocal / instrumental group (2 WEEKS)* pos/wks

1 Dec 01	**THE SPACE BETWEEN** *RCA 74321883192*	35	2

John MATTHEWS – *See UNDERCOVER*

MATTHEWS SOUTHERN COMFORT *UK, male vocal / instrumental group – lead vocalist Ian Matthews (18 WEEKS)* pos/wks

26 Sep 70 ★	**WOODSTOCK** *Uni UNS 526*	1	18

MATUMBI *UK, male vocal / instrumental group (7 WEEKS)* pos/wks

29 Sep 79	**POINT OF VIEW** *Matumbi RIC 101*	35	7

Susan MAUGHAN *UK, female vocalist (25 WEEKS)* pos/wks

11 Oct 62 ●	**BOBBY'S GIRL** *Philips 326544 BF*	3	19
14 Feb 63	**HAND A HANDKERCHIEF TO HELEN** *Philips 326562 BF*	41	3
9 May 63	**SHE'S NEW TO YOU** *Philips 326586 BF*	45	3

MAUREEN *UK, female vocalist – Maureen Walsh (22 WEEKS)* pos/wks

26 Nov 88 ●	**SAY A LITTLE PRAYER** *Rhythm King DOOD 3* [1]	10	10
16 Jun 90	**THINKING OF YOU** *Urban URB 55*	11	9
12 Jan 91	**WHERE HAS ALL THE LOVE GONE** *Urban URB 65*	51	3

[1] Bomb the Bass featuring Maureen

Some copies of 'Thinking of You' are credited to the fuller name of Maureen Walsh

Paul MAURIAT and his Orchestra *France, orchestra (14 WEEKS)* pos/wks

21 Feb 68	**LOVE IS BLUE (L'AMOUR EST BLEU)** *Philips BF 1637* ▲	12	14

1980

IN THE YEAR IN WHICH JOHN LENNON WAS MURDERED BY MARK CHAPMAN AND HAD THE FIRST OF THREE CONSECUTIVE POSTHUMOUS NO.1S, SADDAM HUSSEIN'S IRAQI FORCES INVADED IRAN, PHILIPS DEVELOPED THE COMPACT DISC, JOY DIVISION'S IAN CURTIS COMMITTED SUICIDE, AND ERNO RUBIK'S INGENIOUS CUBE BECAME THE TOY OF CHOICE FOR KIDS EVERYWHERE, ULTRAVOX'S **MIDGE URE** GETS BESTED BY THE JOE DOLCE MUSIC THEATRE ...

"**Joe Dolce** stole the No.1 spot from 'Vienna', but he only stole it for two weeks. Then John Lennon got shot and he stole it for three weeks. People tend to forget that. What he [Joe] did, I suppose, was give us the world's best-known No.2."

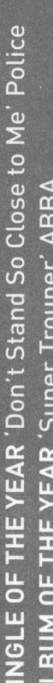

SINGLE OF THE YEAR 'Don't Stand So Close to Me' Police
ALBUM OF THE YEAR 'Super Trouper' ABBA

MAVERICKS *US, male vocal / instrumental group (23 WEEKS)* pos/wks

2 May 98 ●	**DANCE THE NIGHT AWAY** *MCA Nashville MCSTD 48081*	4	18
26 Sep 98	**I'VE GOT THIS FEELING** *MCA Nashville MCSTD 48095*	27	4
5 Jun 99	**SOMEONE SHOULD TELL HER** *MCA Nashville MCSTD 55567*	45	1

MAW – *See MASTERS AT WORK present INDIA*

MAX LINEN *UK, male production duo (1 WEEK)* pos/wks

17 Nov 01	**THE SOULSHAKER** *Global Cuts GC 73CD*	55	1

MAX Q *Australia, male vocal / instrumental duo (3 WEEKS)* pos/wks

17 Feb 90	**SOMETIMES** *Mercury MXQ 2*	53	3

MAX WEBSTER *Canada, male vocal / instrumental group (3 WEEKS)* pos/wks

19 May 79	**PARADISE SKIES** *Capitol CL 16079*	43	3

MAXEE *US, female vocalist (1 WEEK)* pos/wks

17 Mar 01	**WHEN I LOOK INTO YOUR EYES** *Mercury 5628702*	55	1

MAXIM *UK, male producer / vocalist – Keith Palmer (3 WEEKS)* pos/wks

10 Jun 00	**CARMEN QUEASY** *XL Recordings XLS 119CD*	33	2
23 Sep 00	**SCHEMING** *XL Recordings XLS 121CD*	53	1

See also PRODIGY

MAXIMA featuring LILY
UK / Spain, male / female vocal / instrumental duo (2 WEEKS) pos/wks

14 Aug 93	**IBIZA** *Yo! Yo! CDLILY 1*	55	2

MAXWELL *US, male vocalist (10 WEEKS)* pos/wks

11 May 96	**...TIL THE COPS COME KNOCKIN'** *Columbia 6631792*	63	1
24 Aug 96	**ASCENSION NO ONE'S GONNA LOVE YOU SO DON'T EVER WONDER** *Columbia 6636265*	39	3
1 Mar 97	**SUMTHIN' SUMTHIN' THE MANTRA** *Columbia 6638642*	27	3
24 May 97	**ASCENSION DON'T EVER WONDER (re-issue)** *Columbia 6645952*	28	3

MAXX *UK / Sweden / Germany, male / female vocal / instrumental group (24 WEEKS)* pos/wks

21 May 94 ●	**GET-A-WAY** *Pulse 8 CDLOSE 59*	4	12
6 Aug 94 ●	**NO MORE (I CAN'T STAND IT)** *Pulse 8 CDLOSE 66*	8	8
29 Oct 94	**YOU CAN GET IT** *Pulse 8 CDLOSE 75*	21	3
22 Jul 95	**I CAN MAKE YOU FEEL LIKE** *Pulse 8 CDLOSE 88*	56	1

Terry MAXX – *See FUNKSTAR DE LUXE*

Billy MAY and his Orchestra *US, orchestra (10 WEEKS)* pos/wks

27 Apr 56 ●	**MAIN TITLE THEME FROM 'MAN WITH THE GOLDEN ARM'** *Capitol CL 14551*	9	10

Brian MAY *UK, male vocalist / instrumentalist – guitar (33 WEEKS)* pos/wks

5 Nov 83	**STAR FLEET** *EMI 5436* [1]	65	3
7 Dec 91 ●	**DRIVEN BY YOU** *Parlophone R 6304*	6	9
5 Sep 92 ●	**TOO MUCH LOVE WILL KILL YOU** *Parlophone R 6320*	5	9
17 Oct 92	**WE ARE THE CHAMPIONS** *PolyGram TV PO 229* [2]	66	1
21 Nov 92	**BACK TO THE LIGHT** *Parlophone R 6329*	19	4
19 Jun 93	**RESURRECTION** *Parlophone CDRS 6351* [3]	23	3
18 Dec 93	**LAST HORIZON** *Parlophone CDR 6371*	51	2
6 Jun 98	**THE BUSINESS** *Parlophone CDR 6498*	51	1
12 Sep 98	**WHY DON'T WE TRY AGAIN** *Parlophone CDR 6504*	44	1

[1] Brian May and Friends [2] Hank Marvin featuring Brian May [3] Brian May with Cozy Powell

See also QUEEN

Lisa MAY *UK, female vocalist (2 WEEKS)* pos/wks

15 Jul 95	**WISHING ON A STAR** *Urban Gorilla UG 3CD* [1]	61	1
14 Sep 96	**THE CURSE OF VOODOO RAY** *Fontana VOOCD 1*	64	1

[1] 88.3 featuring Lisa MAY

Mary MAY *UK, female vocalist (1 WEEK)* pos/wks

27 Feb 64	**ANYONE WHO HAD A HEART** *Fontana TF 440*	49	1

Shernette MAY *UK, female vocalist (1 WEEK)* pos/wks

6 Jun 98	**ALL THE MAN THAT I NEED** *Virgin VSCDT 1691*	50	1

Simon MAY *UK, male vocalist (21 WEEKS)* pos/wks

9 Oct 76 ●	**SUMMER OF MY LIFE** *Pye 7N 45627*	7	8
21 May 77	**WE'LL GATHER LILACS – ALL MY LOVING (MEDLEY)** *Pye 7N 45688*	49	1
4 Jun 77	**WE'LL GATHER LILACS – ALL MY LOVING (MEDLEY) (re-entry)** *Pye 7N 45688*	50	1
26 Oct 85	**HOWARD'S WAY** *BBC RESL 174* [1]	21	11

[1] Simon May Orchestra

See also Anita DOBSON; Marti WEBB

MAYA – *See TAMPERER featuring MAYA*

Curtis MAYFIELD *US, male vocalist (20 WEEKS)* pos/wks

31 Jul 71	**MOVE ON UP** *Buddah 2011 080*	12	10
2 Dec 78	**NO GOODBYES** *Atlantic LV 1*	65	3
30 May 87	**(CELEBRATE) THE DAY AFTER YOU** *RCA MONK 6* [1]	52	2
29 Sep 90	**SUPERFLY 1990** *Capitol CL 586* [2]	48	3
16 Jun 01	**ASTOUNDED** *Virgin VUSCD 194* [3]	40	2

[1] Blow Monkeys with Curtis Mayfield [2] Curtis Mayfield and Ice-T [3] Bran Van 3000 featuring Curtis Mayfield

MAYTALS *Jamaica, male vocal / instrumental group (4 WEEKS)* pos/wks

25 Apr 70	**MONKEY MAN** *Trojan TR 7711*	50	1
9 May 70	**MONKEY MAN (re-entry)** *Trojan TR 7711*	47	3

MAYTE *US, female vocalist (1 WEEK)* pos/wks

18 Nov 95	**IF EYE LOVE U 2 NIGHT** *NPG 0061635*	67	1

MAZE featuring Frankie BEVERLY
US, male vocal / instrumental group (14 WEEKS) pos/wks

20 Jul 85	**TOO MANY GAMES** *Capitol CL 363*	36	7
23 Aug 86	**I WANNA BE WITH YOU** *Capitol CL 421*	55	3
27 May 89	**JOY AND PAIN** *Capitol CL 531* [1]	57	4

[1] Maze

Kym MAZELLE *US, female vocalist – Kimberley Grigsby (66 WEEKS)* pos/wks

12 Nov 88	**USELESS (I DON'T NEED YOU NOW)** *Syncopate SY 18*	53	3
14 Jan 89 ●	**WAIT** *RCA PB 42595* [1]	7	10
25 Mar 89	**GOT TO GET YOU BACK** *Syncopate SY 25*	29	4
7 Oct 89	**LOVE STRAIN** *Syncopate SY 30*	52	3
20 Jan 90	**WAS THAT ALL IT WAS** *Syncopate SY 32*	33	6
26 May 90	**USELESS (I DON'T NEED YOU NOW) (re-mix)** *Syncopate SY 36*	48	2
24 Nov 90	**MISSING YOU** *Ten TEN 345* [2]	22	7
25 May 91	**NO ONE CAN LOVE YOU MORE THAN ME** *Parlophone R 6287*	62	2
26 Dec 92	**LOVE ME THE RIGHT WAY** *Arista 74321128097* [3]	22	10
11 Jun 94	**NO MORE TEARS (ENOUGH IS ENOUGH)** *Bell 74321209032* [4]	13	7
8 Oct 94	**GIMME ALL YOUR LOVIN'** *Bell 74321231322* [5]	22	3
23 Dec 95	**SEARCHING FOR THE GOLDEN EYE** *Eternal WEA 027CD* [6]	40	3
28 Sep 96	**LOVE ME THE RIGHT WAY (re-mix)** *Logic 74321404442* [3]	55	1
16 Aug 97	**YOUNG HEARTS RUN FREE** *EMI CDEM 488*	20	4
19 Feb 00	**TRULY** *Island Blue PFACD 4* [7]	55	1

[1] Robert Howard and Kym Mazelle [2] Soul II Soul featuring Kym Mazelle [3] Rapination and Kym Mazelle [4] Kym Mazelle and Jocelyn Brown [5] Jocelyn Brown and Kym Mazelle [6] Motiv 8 and Kym Mazelle [7] Peshay featuring Kym Mazelle

MAZZY STAR *US, male / female vocal / instrumental duo (3 WEEKS)* pos/wks

27 Aug 94	**FADE INTO YOU** *Capitol CDCL 720*	48	1
2 Nov 96	**FLOWERS IN DECEMBER** *Capitol CDCL 781*	40	2

MC ALISTAIR – See *DREEM TEEM*

MC DUKE *UK, male rapper (1 WEEK)* pos/wks

11 Mar 89	**I'M RIFFIN (ENGLISH RASTA)** *Music of Life 7NOTE 25*	75	1

MC ERIC – See *TECHNOTRONIC*

MC FIXX IT – See *ANTICAPPELLA*

MC HAMMER – See *HAMMER*

MC KIE – See *TEEBONE featuring MC KIE and MC SPARKS*

MC LETHAL *UK, male producer (1 WEEK)* pos/wks

14 Nov 92	**THE RAVE DIGGER** *Network NWKT 60*	66	1

MC LYTE *US, female rapper – Lana Moorer (16 WEEKS)* pos/wks

15 Jan 94	**RUFFNECK** *Atlantic A 8336CD*	67	1
29 Jun 96	**KEEP ON KEEPIN' ON** *East West A 4287CD* [1]	39	2
18 Jan 97	**COLD ROCK A PARTY** *East West A 3975CD*	15	4
19 Apr 97	**KEEP ON KEEPIN' ON (re-issue)** *East West A 3950CD1* [1]	27	2
5 Sep 98	**I CAN'T MAKE A MISTAKE** *Elektra E 3813CD*	46	1
19 Dec 98	**IT'S ALL YOURS** *East West E 3789CD* [2]	36	4
24 Jun 00	**JAMMIN'** *Tuff Gong TGXCD 9* [3]	42	2

[1] MC Lyte featuring Xscape [2] MC Lyte featuring Gina Thompson [3] Bob Marley featuring MC Lyte

MC MARIO – See *AMBASSADORS OF FUNK featuring MC MARIO*

MC MIKEE FREEDOM – See *NOMAD*

MC MIKER 'G' and Deejay SVEN *Holland, male vocal / instrumental rap duo – Lucien Witteveen and Sven Van Veen (7 WEEKS)* pos/wks

6 Sep 86 ●	**HOLIDAY RAP** *Debut DEBT 3008*	6	7

MC NEAT – See *DJ LUCK & MC NEAT*

MC NOISE – See *LOVE INCORPORATED featuring MC NOISE*

MC NUMBER 6 – See *FAB*

MC ONYX STONE – See *LONYO*

MC PARKER – See *FAB*

MC RB – See *SUNSHIP featuring MCRB*

MC SAR – See *REAL McCOY*

MC SKAT KAT and the STRAY MOB *US, male cartoon feline rap / vocal group (2 WEEKS)* pos/wks

9 Nov 91	**SKAT STRUT** *Virgin America VUS 51*	64	2

MC SOLAAR – See *URBAN SPECIES; Missy 'Misdemeanor' ELLIOTT*

MC SPARKS – See *TEEBONE featuring MC KIE and MC SPARKS*

MC SPY-D + FRIENDS *UK, male / female vocal / instrumental group (2 WEEKS)* pos/wks

11 Mar 95	**THE AMAZING SPIDER-MAN** *Parlophone CDR 6404*	37	2

MC STYLES – See *Scott GARCIA featuring MC STYLES*

MC TUNES *UK, male rapper – Nicholas Lockett (19 WEEKS)* pos/wks

2 Jun 90 ●	**THE ONLY RHYME THAT BITES** *ZTT ZANG 3* [1]	10	10
15 Sep 90	**TUNES SPLITS THE ATOM** *ZTT ZANG 6* [1]	18	7
1 Dec 90	**PRIMARY RHYMING** *ZTT ZANG 10*	67	1
6 Mar 99	**THE ONLY RHYME THAT BITES 99** *ZTT ZTT 125CD* [1]	53	1

[1] MC Tunes versus 808 State

MC VIPER – See *REFLEX featuring MC VIPER*

MC WILDSKI *UK, male rapper (10 WEEKS)* pos/wks

8 Jul 89	**BLAME IT ON THE BASSLINE** *Go.Beat GOD 33* [1]	29	6
3 Mar 90	**WARRIOR** *Arista 112956*	49	4

[1] Norman Cook featuring MC Wildski

'Blame It on the Bassline' was listed with 'Won't Talk About It' by Norman Cook featuring Billy Bragg

M-D-EMM *UK, male producer – Mark Ryder (3 WEEKS)* pos/wks

22 Feb 92	**GET DOWN** *Strictly Underground 7STUR 13*	55	2
30 May 92	**MOVE YOUR FEET** *Strictly Underground STUR 15*	67	1

See also Mark *RYDER*

MDM *UK, male producer – Matt Darey (1 WEEK)* pos/wks

27 Oct 01	**MASH IT UP** *Nulife / Arista 74321870472*	66	1

See also Matt *DAREY; SUNBURST; MELT featuring LITTLE MS MARCIE*

ME AND YOU featuring WE THE PEOPLE BAND *Jamaica / UK, male / female vocal / instrumental group (9 WEEKS)* pos/wks

28 Jul 79	**YOU NEVER KNOW WHAT YOU'VE GOT** *Laser LAS 8*	31	9

ME ME ME *UK, male vocal / instrumental group (4 WEEKS)* pos/wks

17 Aug 96	**HANGING AROUND** *Indolent DUFF 005CD*	19	4

Abigail MEAD and Nigel GOULDING *UK / US, female / male producers – Vivian Kubrick and Nigel Goulding (10 WEEKS)* pos/wks

26 Sep 87 ●	**FULL METAL JACKET (I WANNA BE YOUR DRILL INSTRUCTOR)** *Warner Bros. W 8187*	2	10

MEAT BEAT MANIFESTO *UK, male production duo (1 WEEK)* pos/wks

20 Feb 93	**MINDSTREAM** *Play It Again Sam BIAS 232CD*	55	1

MEAT LOAF (157 Top 500) *Larger-than-life vocalist / actor; b. Marvin Lee Aday, 27 Sep 1948, Dallas, US. His collaborations with producer / songwriter Jim Steinman resulted in some of rock's finest recordings. His album 'Bat Out of Hell' sold more than 25 million copies and spent more than nine years in total in the UK chart (146 WEEKS)* pos/wks

20 May 78	**YOU TOOK THE WORDS RIGHT OUT OF MY MOUTH** *Epic EPC 5980*	33	8
19 Aug 78	**TWO OUT OF THREE AIN'T BAD** *Epic EPC 6281*	32	8
10 Feb 79	**BAT OUT OF HELL** *Epic EPC 7018*	15	7
26 Sep 81	**I'M GONNA LOVE HER FOR BOTH OF US** *Epic EPCA 1580*	62	3
28 Nov 81 ●	**DEAD RINGER FOR LOVE** *Epic EPCA 1697*	5	17
28 May 83	**IF YOU REALLY WANT TO** *Epic A 3357*	59	2
24 Sep 83	**MIDNIGHT AT THE LOST AND FOUND** *Epic A 3748*	17	8
14 Jan 84	**RAZOR'S EDGE** *Epic A 4080*	41	3
6 Oct 84	**MODERN GIRL** *Arista ARIST 585*	17	9
22 Dec 84	**NOWHERE FAST** *Arista ARIST 600*	67	4
23 Mar 85	**PIECE OF THE ACTION** *Arista ARIST 603*	47	5
30 Aug 86	**ROCK 'N' ROLL MERCENARIES** *Arista ARIST 666* [1]	31	6
22 Jun 91	**DEAD RINGER FOR LOVE (re-issue)** *Epic 6569827*	53	2
27 Jun 92	**TWO OUT OF THREE AIN'T BAD (re-issue)** *Epic 6574917*	69	1
9 Oct 93 ★	**I'D DO ANYTHING FOR LOVE (BUT I WON'T DO THAT)** *Virgin VSCDT 1443* ▲	1	19
18 Dec 93 ●	**BAT OUT OF HELL (re-issue)** *Epic 6600062*	8	9
19 Feb 94	**ROCK AND ROLL DREAMS COME THROUGH** *Virgin VSCDT 1479*	11	7
7 May 94	**OBJECTS IN THE REAR VIEW MIRROR MAY APPEAR CLOSER THAN THEY ARE** *Virgin VSCDT 1492*	26	4

		pos	wks
28 Oct 95 ●	**I'D LIE FOR YOU (AND THAT'S THE TRUTH)** *Virgin VSCDT 1563*	2	11
27 Jan 96 ●	**NOT A DRY EYE IN THE HOUSE** *Virgin VSCDT 1567*	7	6
27 Apr 96	**RUNNIN' FOR THE RED LIGHT (I GOTTA LIFE)** *Virgin VSCDX 1582*	21	3
17 Apr 99	**IS NOTHING SACRED** *Virgin VSCDT 1734* [2]	15	4

[1] Meat Loaf featuring John Parr [2] Meat Loaf featuring Patti Russo

'Dead Ringer for Love' features Cher as uncredited co-vocalist. 'I'd Do Anything For Love (But I Won't Do That) features uncredited vocals by Lorraine Crosby (aka Mrs Loud)

MECHANICS – *See MIKE and the MECHANICS*

MECO *US, orchestra – led by Meco Monardo (9 WEEKS)*

		pos	wks
1 Oct 77 ●	**STAR WARS THEME – CANTINA BAND** *RCA XB 1028* ▲	7	9

Glenn MEDEIROS *US, male vocalist (26 WEEKS)*

		pos	wks
18 Jun 88 ★	**NOTHING'S GONNA CHANGE MY LOVE FOR YOU** *London LON 184*	1	13
3 Sep 88	**LONG AND LASTING LOVE (ONCE IN A LIFETIME)** *London LON 202*	42	4
30 Jun 90	**SHE AIN'T WORTH IT** *London LON 265* [1] ▲	12	9

[1] Glenn Medeiros featuring Bobby Brown

Paul MEDFORD – *See Letitia DEAN and Paul MEDFORD*

MEDICINE HEAD *UK, male vocal / instrumental duo – John Fiddler and Peter Hope Evans (37 WEEKS)*

		pos	wks
26 Jun 71	**(AND THE) PICTURES IN THE SKY** *Dandelion DAN 7003*	22	8
5 May 73 ●	**ONE AND ONE IS ONE** *Polydor 2001 432*	3	13
4 Aug 73	**RISING SUN** *Polydor 2058 389*	11	9
9 Feb 74	**SLIP AND SLIDE** *Polydor 2058 436*	22	7

MEDICINE SHOW – *See DR HOOK*

Bill MEDLEY *US, male vocalist (29 WEEKS)*

		pos	wks
31 Oct 87 ●	**(I'VE HAD) THE TIME OF MY LIFE** *RCA PB 49625* [1] ▲	6	12
27 Aug 88	**HE AIN'T HEAVY, HE'S MY BROTHER** *Scotti Brothers PO 10*	25	6
15 Dec 90 ●	**(I'VE HAD) THE TIME OF MY LIFE (re-entry)** *RCA PB 49625* [1]	8	11

[1] Bill Medley and Jennifer Warnes

See also RIGHTEOUS BROTHERS

MEDWAY *US, male producer – Jesse Skeens (2 WEEKS)*

		pos	wks
29 Apr 00	**FAT BASTARDS (EP)** *Hooj Choons HOOJ 92CD*	69	1
10 Mar 01	**RELEASE** *Hooj Choons HOOJ 105*	67	1

Tracks on Fat Bastards (EP): Release / Flanker / Faith

Michael MEDWIN, Bernard BRESSLAW, Alfie BASS and Leslie FYSON *UK, male actors / vocalists (9 WEEKS)*

		pos	wks
30 May 58 ●	**THE SIGNATURE TUNE OF 'THE ARMY GAME'** *HMV POP 490*	5	9

See also Bernard BRESSLAW

MEECHIE *US, female vocalist (1 WEEK)*

		pos	wks
2 Sep 95	**YOU BRING ME JOY** *Vibe MCSTD 2069*	74	1

Tony MEEHAN *UK, male instrumental group, Tony Meehan – drums (4 WEEKS)*

		pos	wks
16 Jan 64	**SONG OF MEXICO** *Decca F 11801*	39	4

See also Jet HARRIS and Tony MEEHAN; SHADOWS

MEEKER *UK, female vocal / production duo (1 WEEK)*

		pos	wks
26 Feb 00	**SAVE ME** *Underwater H20 009 CD*	60	1

MEGA CITY FOUR *UK, male vocal / instrumental group (7 WEEKS)*

		pos	wks
19 Oct 91	**WORDS THAT SAY** *Big Life MEGA 2*	66	1
8 Feb 92	**STOP (EP)** *Big Life MEGA 3*	36	2
16 May 92	**SHIVERING SAND** *Big Life MEGA 4*	35	2
1 May 93	**IRON SKY** *Big Life MEGAD 5*	48	1
17 Jul 93	**WALLFLOWER** *Big Life MEGAD 6*	69	1

Tracks on Stop (EP): Stop / Desert Song / Back to Zero / Overlap

MEGABASS – *See VARIOUS ARTISTS (MONTAGES)*

MEGADETH *US, male vocal / instrumental group (32 WEEKS)*

		pos	wks
19 Dec 87	**WAKE UP DEAD** *Capitol CL 476*	65	2
27 Feb 88	**ANARCHY IN THE UK** *Capitol CL 480*	45	3
21 May 88	**MARY JANE** *Capitol CL 489*	46	2
13 Jan 90	**NO MORE MR NICE GUY** *SBK SBK 4*	13	6
29 Sep 90	**HOLY WARS . . . THE PUNISHMENT DUE** *Capitol CLP 588*	24	3
16 Mar 91	**HANGAR 18** *Capitol CLS 604*	26	4
27 Jun 92	**SYMPHONY OF DESTRUCTION** *Capitol CLS 662*	15	3
24 Oct 92	**SKIN O' MY TEETH** *Capitol CLP 669*	13	3
29 May 93	**SWEATING BULLETS** *Capitol CDCL 682*	26	3
7 Jan 95	**TRAIN OF CONSEQUENCES** *Capitol CDCL 730*	22	3

MEGAMAN – *See OXIDE & NEUTRINO*

MEHTA – *See José CARRERAS*

MEJA *Sweden, female vocalist – Meja Beckman (14 WEEKS)*

		pos	wks
24 Oct 98	**ALL 'BOUT THE MONEY** *Columbia 6665662*	12	5
29 Apr 00 ●	**PRIVATE EMOTION** *Columbia 6692692* [1]	9	9

[1] Ricky Martin featuring Meja

MEKKA *UK, male producer – Jake Williams (1 WEEK)*

		pos	wks
24 Mar 01	**DIAMOND BACK** *Perfecto PERF 12CDS*	67	1

MEKON featuring Roxanne SHANTE *UK, male producer – John Gosling and US, female rapper (1 WEEK)*

		pos	wks
23 Sep 00	**WHAT'S GOING ON** *Wall of Sound WALD 064*	43	1

Melle MEL – *See GRANDMASTER FLASH, Melle MEL and the FURIOUS FIVE*

MEL and KIM – *See Mel SMITH; Kim WILDE*

MEL and KIM *UK, female vocal duo – Mel and Kim Appleby (51 WEEKS)*

		pos	wks
20 Sep 86 ●	**SHOWING OUT (GET FRESH AT THE WEEKEND)** *Supreme SUPE 107*	3	19
7 Mar 87 ★	**RESPECTABLE** *Supreme SUPE 111*	1	15
11 Jul 87 ●	**F.L.M.** *Supreme SUPE 113*	7	10
27 Feb 88 ●	**THAT'S THE WAY IT IS** *Supreme SUPE 117*	10	7

See also Kim APPLEBY

George MELACHRINO ORCHESTRA *UK, orchestra (9 WEEKS)*

		pos	wks
12 Oct 56	**AUTUMN CONCERTO** *HMV B 10958*	18	9

MELANIE *US, female vocalist – Melanie Safka (35 WEEKS)*

		pos	wks
26 Sep 70 ●	**RUBY TUESDAY** *Buddah 2011 038*	9	14
9 Jan 71	**RUBY TUESDAY (re-entry)** *Buddah 2011 038*	43	1
16 Jan 71	**WHAT HAVE THEY DONE TO MY SONG MA** *Buddah 2011038*	39	1
1 Jan 72 ●	**BRAND NEW KEY** *Buddah 2011 105* ▲	4	12
16 Feb 74	**WILL YOU LOVE ME TOMORROW** *Neighbourhood NBH 9*	37	5
24 Sep 83	**EVERY BREATH OF THE WAY** *Neighbourhood HOOD NB1*	70	2

MELKY SEDECK *US, male / female vocal / instrumental duo (9 WEEKS)*

		pos	wks
8 May 99	**RAW** *MCA MCSTD 48107*	50	1
16 Sep 00 ●	**IT DOESN'T MATTER** *Columbia 6697782* [1]	3	8

[1] Wyclef Jean featuring The Rock and Melky Sedeck

John Cougar MELLENCAMP *US, male vocalist (18 WEEKS)*

		pos	wks
23 Oct 82	**JACK AND DIANE** *Riva RIVA 37* [1] ▲	25	8
1 Feb 86	**SMALL TOWN** *Riva JCM 5*	53	4

10 May 86	**R.O.C.K. IN THE USA** *Riva JCM 6*	67	3
3 Sep 94	**WILD NIGHT** *Mercury MERCD 409* [2]	34	3

[1] John Cougar [2] John Mellencamp featuring Me'Shell Ndegeocello

MELLOMEN – *See Rosemary CLOONEY; Frankie LAINE; Doris DAY*

Will MELLOR *UK, male actor / vocalist (9 WEEKS)*

		pos	wks
28 Feb 98 ●	**WHEN I NEED YOU** *Unity UNITY 017RCD*	5	6
27 Jun 98	**NO MATTER WHAT I DO** *Jive 0540012*	23	3

MELLOW TRAX

Germany, male producer – Christian Schwarnweber (2 WEEKS)

		pos	wks
14 Oct 00	**OUTTA SPACE** *Substance SUBS 3CDS*	41	2

MELODIANS *Jamaica, male vocal / instrumental group (1 WEEK)*

		pos	wks
10 Jan 70	**SWEET SENSATION** *Trojan TR 695*	41	1

MELODY MAKERS – *See Ziggy MARLEY and the MELODY MAKERS*

MELT featuring Little Ms MARCIE

UK, male producer – Matt Darey (1 WEEK)

		pos	wks
8 Apr 00	**HARD HOUSE MUSIC** *WEA WEA 257CD*	59	1

See also Matt DAREY; SUNBURST; MDM

MELTDOWN *UK / US, male instrumental / production duo (1 WEEK)*

		pos	wks
27 Apr 96	**MY LIFE IS IN YOUR HANDS** *Sony S3 DANU 7CD*	44	1

Harold MELVIN and the BLUENOTES

US, male vocal group (52 WEEKS)

		pos	wks
13 Jan 73 ●	**IF YOU DON'T KNOW ME BY NOW** *CBS 8496*	9	9
12 Jan 74	**THE LOVE I LOST (PART 1)** *Philadelphia International PIR 1879*	21	8
13 Apr 74	**SATISFACTION GUARANTEED (OR TAKE YOUR LOVE BACK)** *Philadelphia International PIR 2187*	32	6
31 May 75	**GET OUT (AND LET ME CRY)** *Route RT 06* [1]	35	5
28 Feb 76	**WAKE UP EVERYBODY (PART 1)** *Philadelphia International PIR 3866*	23	7
22 Jan 77 ●	**DON'T LEAVE ME THIS WAY** *Philadelphia International PIR 4909* [2]	5	10
2 Apr 77	**REACHING FOR THE WORLD** *ABC 4161* [1]	48	1
28 Apr 84	**DON'T GIVE ME UP** *London LON 47* [1]	59	4
4 Aug 84	**TODAY'S YOUR LUCKY DAY** *London LON 52* [3]	66	2

[1] Harold Melvin and the Blue Notes [2] Harold Melvin and the Bluenotes featuring Theodore Pendergrass [3] Harold Melvin and the Blue Notes featuring Nikko

MEMBERS *UK, male vocal / instrumental group (14 WEEKS)*

		pos	wks
3 Feb 79	**THE SOUND OF THE SUBURBS** *Virgin VS 242*	12	9
7 Apr 79	**OFFSHORE BANKING BUSINESS** *Virgin VS 248*	31	5

MEMBERS OF MAYDAY *Germany, male production duo (3 WEEKS)*

		pos	wks
23 Jun 01	**10 IN 01** *Deviant DVNT 42CDS*	31	3

MEMPHIS BLEEK featuring JAY-Z *US, male rappers (1 WEEK)*

		pos	wks
4 Dec 99	**WHAT YOU THINK OF THAT** *Def Jam 8708292*	58	1

MEN AT WORK *Australia, male vocal / instrumental group – lead vocal Colin James Hay (39 WEEKS)*

		pos	wks
30 Oct 82	**WHO CAN IT BE NOW?** *Epic EPC A 2392* ▲	45	5
8 Jan 83 ★	**DOWN UNDER** *Epic EPC A 1980* ▲	1	12
9 Apr 83	**OVERKILL** *Epic EPC A 3220*	21	10
2 Jul 83	**IT'S A MISTAKE** *Epic EPC A 3475*	33	6
10 Sep 83	**DR HECKYLL AND MR JIVE** *Epic EPC A 3668*	31	6

MEN OF VIZION *US, male vocal group (2 WEEKS)*

		pos	wks
27 Mar 99	**DO YOU FEEL ME? (...FREAK YOU)** *MJJ / Epic 6670912*	36	2

MEN THEY COULDN'T HANG

UK, male vocal / instrumental group (4 WEEKS)

		pos	wks
2 Apr 88	**THE COLOURS** *Magnet SELL 6*	61	4

MEN WITHOUT HATS

Canada, male vocal / instrumental group (11 WEEKS)

		pos	wks
8 Oct 83 ●	**THE SAFETY DANCE** *Statik TAK 1*	6	11

Sergio MENDES *Brazil, male conductor (5 WEEKS)*

		pos	wks
9 Jul 83	**NEVER GONNA LET YOU GO** *A & M AM 118*	45	5

Uncredited vocals by Joe Pizzulo and Leza Miller

Andrea MENDEZ *UK, female vocalist (1 WEEK)*

		pos	wks
3 Aug 96	**BRING ME LOVE** *AM:PM 5817872*	44	1

MENSWEAR *UK, male vocal / instrumental group (18 WEEKS)*

		pos	wks
15 Apr 95	**I'LL MANAGE SOMEHOW** *Laurel LAUCD 4*	49	1
1 Jul 95	**DAYDREAMER** *Laurel LAUCD 5*	14	4
30 Sep 95	**STARDUST** *Laurel LAUCD 6*	16	3
16 Dec 95	**SLEEPING IN** *Laurel LAUCD 7*	24	3
23 Mar 96 ●	**BEING BRAVE** *Laurel LAUCD 8*	10	4
7 Sep 96	**WE LOVE YOU** *Laurel LAUCD 11*	22	3

MENTAL AS ANYTHING

Australia, male vocal / instrumental group (13 WEEKS)

		pos	wks
7 Feb 87 ●	**LIVE IT UP** *Epic ANY 1*	3	13

Freddie MERCURY (422 Top 500)

Gregarious, versatile lead singer of Queen, b. Faroukh Bulsara, 5 Sep 1946, Zanzibar, Africa, d. 24 Nov 1991. UK-based performer was one of rock music's all-time great showmen, whose music has raised millions of pounds for Aids charities (79 WEEKS)

		pos	wks
22 Sep 84 ●	**LOVE KILLS** *CBS A 4735*	10	8
20 Apr 85	**I WAS BORN TO LOVE YOU** *CBS A 6019*	11	10
13 Jul 85	**MADE IN HEAVEN** *CBS A 6413*	57	4
21 Sep 85	**LIVING ON MY OWN** *CBS A 6555*	50	3
24 May 86	**TIME** *EMI EMI 5559*	32	5
7 Mar 87 ●	**THE GREAT PRETENDER** *Parlophone R 6151*	4	9
7 Nov 87 ●	**BARCELONA** *Polydor POSP 887* [1]	8	9
8 Aug 92 ●	**BARCELONA (re-issue)** *Polydor PO 221* [1]	2	8
12 Dec 92 ●	**IN MY DEFENCE** *Parlophone R 6331*	8	7
6 Feb 93	**THE GREAT PRETENDER (re-issue)** *Parlophone CDR 6336*	29	3
31 Jul 93 ★	**LIVING ON MY OWN (re-mix)** *Parlophone CDR 6355*	1	13

[1] Freddie Mercury and Montserrat Caballé

See also QUEEN

MERCURY REV *US, male vocal / instrumental group (8 WEEKS)*

		pos	wks
14 Nov 98	**GODDESS ON A HIWAY** *V2 VVR 5003323*	51	1
6 Feb 99	**DELTA SUN BOTTLENECK STOMP** *V2 VVR 5005413*	26	2
22 May 99	**OPUS 40** *V2 VVR 5006963*	31	2
28 Aug 99	**GODDESS ON A HIWAY (re-issue)** *V2 VVR 5008493*	26	2
6 Oct 01	**NITE AND FOG** *V2 VVR 5017723*	47	1

MERCY MERCY *UK, male vocal / instrumental group (2 WEEKS)*

		pos	wks
21 Sep 85	**WHAT ARE WE GONNA DO ABOUT IT?** *Ensign ENY 522*	59	2

MERLIN – *See BOMB THE BASS; BEATMASTERS*

MERO *UK, male vocal duo (2 WEEKS)*

		pos	wks
25 Mar 00	**IT MUST BE LOVE** *RCA 74321664772*	33	2

Tony MERRICK *UK, male vocalist (1 WEEK)*

		pos	wks
2 Jun 66	**LADY JANE** *Columbia DB 7913*	49	1

MERSEYBEATS *UK, male vocal / instrumental group (64 WEEKS)*

		pos	wks
12 Sep 63	**IT'S LOVE THAT REALLY COUNTS** *Fontana TF 412*	24	12

Date		Title / Label	pos	wks
16 Jan 64	●	**I THINK OF YOU** *Fontana TF 431*	5	17
16 Apr 64		**DON'T TURN AROUND** *Fontana TF 459*	13	11
9 Jul 64		**WISHIN' AND HOPIN'** *Fontana TF 482*	13	10
5 Nov 64		**LAST NIGHT** *Fontana TF 504*	40	3
14 Oct 65		**I LOVE YOU, YES I DO** *Fontana TF 607*	22	8
20 Jan 66		**I STAND ACCUSED** *Fontana TF 645*	38	3

MERSEYS *UK, male vocal duo (13 WEEKS)* pos/wks

Date		Title / Label	pos	wks
28 Apr 66	●	**SORROW** *Fontana TF 694*	4	13

MERTON PARKAS *UK, male vocal / instrumental group (6 WEEKS)* pos/wks

Date		Title / Label	pos	wks
4 Aug 79		**YOU NEED WHEELS** *Beggars Banquet BEG 22*	40	6

MERZ *UK, male vocalist / instrumentalist – Conrad Lambert (2 WEEKS)* pos/wks

Date		Title / Label	pos	wks
17 Jul 99		**MANY WEATHERS APART** *Epic 6674972*	48	1
16 Oct 99		**LOVELY DAUGHTER** *Epic 6679132*	60	1

Mady MESPLE and Danielle MILLET with the PARIS OPERA-COMIQUE ORCHESTRA conducted by Alain LOMBARD

France, female vocal duo and orchestra (4 WEEKS) pos/wks

Date		Title / Label	pos	wks
6 Apr 85		**FLOWER DUET (FROM 'LAKME')** *EMI 5481*	47	4

MESSIAH *UK, male instrumental / production group (13 WEEKS)* pos/wks

Date		Title / Label	pos	wks
20 Jun 92		**TEMPLE OF DREAMS** *Kickin KICK 12S*	20	5
26 Sep 92		**I FEEL LOVE** *Kickin KICK 22S* [1]	19	5
27 Nov 93		**THUNDERDOME** *WEA YZ 790CD1*	29	3

[1] Messiah featuring Precious Wilson

METAL GURUS *UK, male vocal / instrumental group (2 WEEKS)* pos/wks

Date		Title / Label	pos	wks
8 Dec 90		**MERRY XMAS EVERYBODY** *Mercury GURU 1*	55	2

METALHEADZ – *See GOLDIE*

METALLICA

US / Denmark, male vocal / instrumental group (59 WEEKS) pos/wks

Date		Title / Label	pos	wks
22 Aug 87		**THE $5.98 EP - GARAGE DAYS RE-REVISITED** *Vertigo METAL 112*	27	4
3 Sep 88		**HARVESTER OF SORROW** *Vertigo METAL 212*	20	3
22 Apr 89		**ONE** *Vertigo METAL 5*	13	7
10 Aug 91	●	**ENTER SANDMAN** *Vertigo METAL 7*	5	4
9 Nov 91		**THE UNFORGIVEN** *Vertigo METAL 8*	15	4
2 May 92	●	**NOTHING ELSE MATTERS** *Vertigo METAL 10*	6	6
31 Oct 92		**WHEREVER I MAY ROAM** *Vertigo METAL 9*	25	4
20 Feb 93		**SAD BUT TRUE** *Vertigo METCD 11*	20	3
1 Jun 96	●	**UNTIL IT SLEEPS** *Vertigo METCD 12*	5	4
28 Sep 96		**HERO OF THE DAY** *Vertigo METCD 13*	17	4
7 Dec 96		**MAMA SAID** *Vertigo METCD 14*	19	2
22 Nov 97		**THE MEMORY REMAINS** *Vertigo METCD 15*	13	3
7 Mar 98		**THE UNFORGIVEN II** *Vertigo METDD 17*	15	4
4 Jul 98		**FUEL** *Vertigo METCD 16*	31	2
27 Feb 99		**WHISKEY IN THE JAR** *Vertigo METCD 19*	29	2
12 Aug 00		**I DISAPPEAR** *Hollywood 0113875 HWR*	35	3

Tracks on The $5.98 EP: Garage Days Re-Revisited : Helpless / Crash Course in Brain Surgery / The Small Hours / Last Caress / Green Hell

METEORS *UK, male vocal / instrumental group (2 WEEKS)* pos/wks

Date		Title / Label	pos	wks
26 Feb 83		**JOHNNY REMEMBER ME** *ID EYE 1*	66	2

Pat METHENY GROUP – *See David BOWIE*

METHOD MAN *US, male rapper – Clifford Smith (14 WEEKS)* pos/wks

Date		Title / Label	pos	wks
29 Apr 95		**RELEASE YO' SELF** *Def Jam DEFCD 6*	46	1
29 Jul 95	●	**I'LL BE THERE FOR YOU - YOU'RE ALL I NEED TO GET BY** *Def Jam DEFCD 11* [1]	10	5
5 Apr 97	●	**HIT EM HIGH (THE MONSTARS' ANTHEM)** *Atlantic A 5449CD* [2]	8	6
22 May 99		**BREAK UPS 2 MAKE UPS** *Def Jam 8709272* [3]	33	2

[1] Method Man featuring Mary J Blige [2] B Real / Busta Rhymes / Coolio / LL Cool J / Method Man [3] Method Man featuring D'Angelo

MEZZOFORTE *Iceland, male instrumental group (10 WEEKS)* pos/wks

Date		Title / Label	pos	wks
5 Mar 83		**GARDEN PARTY** *Steinar STE 705*	17	9
11 Jun 83		**ROCKALL** *Steinar STE 710*	75	1

MFSB *US, orchestra (18 WEEKS)* pos/wks

Date		Title / Label	pos	wks
27 Apr 74		**TSOP (THE SOUND OF PHILADELPHIA)** *Philadelphia International PIR 2289* [1] ▲	22	9
26 Jul 75		**SEXY** *Philadelphia International PIR 3381*	37	5
31 Jan 81		**MYSTERIES OF THE WORLD** *Sound of Philadelphia PIR 9501*	41	4

[1] MFSB featuring the Three Degrees

MG's – *See BOOKER T and the MG's*

MIAMI SOUND MACHINE (495 Top 500)

Ground-breaking Latin combo formed by percussionist Emilio Estefan and fronted by wife Gloria, who achieved worldwide fame after they started recording in English. Miami honoured them by renaming a street Miami Sound Machine Boulevard. Gloria went on to become one of the world's top selling female artists (72 WEEKS) pos/wks

Date		Title / Label	pos	wks
11 Aug 84	●	**DR BEAT** *Epic A 4614*	6	14
17 May 86		**BAD BOY** *Epic A 6537*	16	11
16 Jul 88	●	**ANYTHING FOR YOU** *Epic 651673 7* [1] ▲	10	16
22 Oct 88	●	**1-2-3** *Epic 652958 7* [1]	9	9
17 Dec 88		**RHYTHM IS GONNA GET YOU** *Epic 654514 7* [1]	16	9
31 Dec 88		**1-2-3 (re-entry)** *Epic 652958 7* [1]	72	1
11 Feb 89	●	**CAN'T STAY AWAY FROM YOU** *Epic 651 444 7* [1]	7	12

[1] Gloria Estefan and Miami Sound Machine

See also Gloria ESTEFAN

George MICHAEL (48 Top 500)

Previously half of internationally celebrated duo Wham!, b. Georgios Panayiotou, 25 Jun 1963, London, UK. This multi-talented, award-winning singer / songwriter / producer / arranger and instrumentalist has successfully made the difficult transition from teeny-bopper hero to world-renowned solo star (249 WEEKS) pos/wks

Date		Title / Label	pos	wks
4 Aug 84	★	**CARELESS WHISPER** *Epic A 4603* ◆ ▲	1	17
5 Apr 86	★	**A DIFFERENT CORNER** *Epic A 7033*	1	10
31 Jan 87	★	**I KNEW YOU WERE WAITING (FOR ME)** *Epic DUET 2* [1] ▲	1	9
13 Jun 87	●	**I WANT YOUR SEX** *Epic LUST 1*	3	10
24 Oct 87	●	**FAITH** *Epic EMU 3* ▲	2	12
9 Jan 88		**FATHER FIGURE** *Epic EMU 4* ▲	11	6
23 Apr 88	●	**ONE MORE TRY** *Epic EMU 5* ▲	8	7
16 Jul 88		**MONKEY** *Epic EMU 6* ▲	13	6
3 Dec 88		**KISSING A FOOL** *Epic EMU 7*	18	6
25 Aug 90	●	**PRAYING FOR TIME** *Epic GEO 1* ▲	6	7
27 Oct 90		**WAITING FOR THAT DAY** *Epic GEO 2*	23	5
15 Dec 90		**FREEDOM!** *Epic GEO 3*	28	6
16 Feb 91		**HEAL THE PAIN** *Epic 6566477*	31	4
30 Mar 91		**COWBOYS AND ANGELS** *Epic 6567747*	45	3
7 Dec 91	★	**DON'T LET THE SUN GO DOWN ON ME** *Epic 6576467* [2] ■ ▲	1	10
13 Jun 92	●	**TOO FUNKY** *Epic 6580587*	4	9
1 May 93	★	**FIVE LIVE (EP)** *Parlophone CDRS 6340* [3] ■	1	11
24 Jul 93		**FIVE LIVE (EP) (re-entry)** *Parlophone CDRS 6340* [3]	74	1
20 Jan 96	★	**JESUS TO A CHILD** *Virgin VSCDG 1571* ■	1	10
20 Apr 96		**JESUS TO A CHILD (re-entry)** *Virgin VSCDG 1571*	68	1
4 May 96	★	**FASTLOVE** *Virgin VSCDG 1579* ■	1	14
4 May 96		**JESUS TO A CHILD (2nd re-entry)** *Virgin VSCDG 1571*	65	2
31 Aug 96	●	**SPINNING THE WHEEL** *Virgin VSCDG 1595*	2	12
1 Feb 97	●	**OLDER / I CAN'T MAKE YOU LOVE ME** *Virgin VSCDG 1626*	3	8
12 Apr 97		**OLDER / I CAN'T MAKE YOU LOVE ME (re-entry)** *Virgin VSCDG 1626*	70	1
10 May 97	●	**STAR PEOPLE '97** *Virgin VSCDG 1641*	2	9
7 Jun 97	●	**WALTZ AWAY DREAMING** *Aegean AECD 01*	10	4
19 Jul 97		**STAR PEOPLE '97 (re-entry)** *Virgin VSCDG 1641*	59	4
20 Sep 97	●	**YOU HAVE BEEN LOVED / THE STRANGEST THING '97** *Virgin VSCD 1663*	2	8
31 Oct 98	●	**OUTSIDE** *Epic 6665625*	2	14

13 Feb 99	**OUTSIDE (re-entry)** *Epic 6665625*	61	2
13 Mar 99 ●	**AS** *Epic 6670122* [4]	4	10
17 Jun 00 ●	**IF I TOLD YOU THAT** *Arista 74321766282* [5]	9	9
26 Aug 00	**IF I TOLD YOU THAT (re-entry)** *Arista 74321766282* [5]	51	2

[1] Aretha Franklin and George Michael [2] George Michael and Elton John [3] George Michael and Queen with Lisa Stansfield [4] George Michael and Mary J Blige [5] Whitney Houston / George Michael

Tracks on Five Live (EP): Somebody to Love / These Are the Days of Our Lives / Calling You / Papa Was a Rolling Stone - Killer (medley). The first track on the EP features Queen, the second Queen and Lisa Stansfield

See also Lisa MOORISH; Elton JOHN

MICHAEL SCHENKER GROUP – *See Michael SCHENKER GROUP*

MICHAELA *UK, female vocalist (6 WEEKS)* pos/wks

2 Sep 89	**H-A-P-P-Y RADIO** *London H 1*	62	4
28 Apr 90	**TAKE GOOD CARE OF MY HEART** *London WAC 90*	66	2

Lisa MICHAELIS – *See Frankie KNUCKLES*

Pras MICHEL
US, male rapper / producer – Prakazrel Michael (36 WEEKS) pos/wks

27 Jun 98 ●	**GHETTO SUPASTAR (THAT IS WHAT YOU ARE)** *Interscope IND 95593* [1]	2	17
7 Nov 98 ●	**BLUE ANGELS** *Ruffhouse 6666215* [2]	6	10
14 Nov 98 ●	**ANOTHER ONE BITES THE DUST** *Dreamworks DRMCD 22364* [3]	5	6
1 Sep 01	**MISS CALIFORNIA** *Elektra E 7192CD* [4]	25	3

[1] Pras Michel featuring Ol' Dirty Bastard introducing Mya [2] Pras [3] Queen with Wyclef Jean featuring Pras and Free [4] Dante Thomas featuring Pras

MICHELE – *See KING BEE*

Keith MICHELL *Australia, male vocalist (25 WEEKS)* pos/wks

27 Mar 71	**I'LL GIVE YOU THE EARTH (TOUS LES BATEAUX, TOUS LES OISEAUX)** *Spark SRL 1046*	43	1
17 Apr 71	**I'LL GIVE YOU THE EARTH (TOUS LES BATEAUX, TOUS LES OISEAUX) (re-entry)** *Spark SRL 1046*	30	10
26 Jan 80 ●	**CAPTAIN BEAKY / WILFRED THE WEASEL** *Polydor POSP 106*	5	10
29 Mar 80	**THE TRIAL OF HISSING SID** *Polydor HISS 1* [1]	53	4

[1] Keith Michell, Captain Beaky and his Band

MICHELLE *Trinidad, female vocalist (1 WEEK)* pos/wks

8 Jun 96	**STANDING HERE ALL ALONE** *Positiva CDTIV 54*	69	1

Yvette MICHELLE *US, female vocalist (3 WEEKS)* pos/wks

5 Apr 97	**I'M NOT FEELING YOU** *Loud 74321465222*	36	3

Lloyd MICHELS – *See MISTURA featuring Lloyd MICHELS*

MICK and PAT – *See PAT and MICK*

MICROBE *UK, male vocalist (7 WEEKS)* pos/wks

14 May 69	**GROOVY BABY** *CBS 4158*	29	7

MICRODISNEY *Ireland, male vocal / instrumental group (3 WEEKS)* pos/wks

21 Feb 87	**TOWN TO TOWN** *Virgin VS 927*	55	3

MIDDLE OF THE ROAD (452 Top 500) *Scottish vocal / instrumental pop quartet who re-located to Italy and were extremely successful across Europe. Fronted by sole female Sally Carr (Sarah Young) b. 28 Mar 1945, Glasgow. First hit reportedly sold close to 10 million copies worldwide (76 WEEKS)* pos/wks

5 Jun 71 ★	**CHIRPY CHIRPY CHEEP CHEEP** *RCA 2047*	1	34
4 Sep 71 ●	**TWEEDLE DEE TWEEDLE DUM** *RCA 2110*	2	17
11 Dec 71 ●	**SOLEY SOLEY** *RCA 2151*	5	12
25 Mar 72	**SACRAMENTO** *RCA 2184*	49	1
8 Apr 72	**SACRAMENTO (re-entry)** *RCA 2184*	23	6
29 Jul 72	**SAMSON AND DELILAH** *RCA 2237*	26	6

MIDDLESBROUGH FC featuring Bob MORTIMER and Chris REA
UK, male football team / vocal group (1 WEEK) pos/wks

24 May 97	**LET'S DANCE** *Magnet EW 112CD*	44	1

MIDFIELD GENERAL featuring LINDA LEWIS *UK, male producer – Damian Harris, and UK, female vocalist (1 WEEK)* pos/wks

19 Aug 00	**REACH OUT** *Skint / SKINT 54CD*	61	1

MIDGET *UK, male vocal / instrumental group (2 WEEKS)* pos/wks

31 Jan 98	**ALL FALL DOWN** *Radarscope TINYCDS 6X*	57	1
18 Apr 98	**INVISIBLE BALLOON** *Radarscope TINYCDS 7*	66	1

MIDI XPRESS *UK, male vocal / instrumental duo (1 WEEK)* pos/wks

11 May 96	**CHASE** *Labello Dance LAD 26CD*	73	1

Bette MIDLER *US, female vocalist (27 WEEKS)* pos/wks

17 Jun 89 ●	**WIND BENEATH MY WINGS** *Atlantic A 8972* ▲	5	12
13 Oct 90	**FROM A DISTANCE** *Atlantic A 7820*	45	5
15 Jun 91 ●	**FROM A DISTANCE (re-entry)** *Atlantic A 7820*	6	9
5 Dec 98	**MY ONE TRUE FRIEND** *Warner Brothers W 460CD*	58	1

MIDNIGHT COWBOY SOUNDTRACK *US, orchestra (4 WEEKS)* pos/wks

8 Nov 80	**MIDNIGHT COWBOY** *United Artists UP 634*	47	4

MIDNIGHT OIL *Australia, male vocal / instrumental group (32 WEEKS)* pos/wks

23 Apr 88	**BEDS ARE BURNING** *Sprint OIL 1*	48	5
2 Jul 88	**THE DEAD HEART** *Sprint OIL 2*	68	2
25 Mar 89 ●	**BEDS ARE BURNING (re-issue)** *Sprint OIL 3*	6	13
1 Jul 89	**THE DEAD HEART (re-issue)** *Sprint OIL 4*	62	4
10 Feb 90	**BLUE SKY MINE** *CBS OIL 5*	66	2
17 Apr 93	**TRUGANINI** *Columbia 6590492*	29	4
3 Jul 93	**MY COUNTRY** *Columbia 6593702*	66	1
6 Nov 93	**IN THE VALLEY** *Columbia 6598492*	60	1

MIDNIGHT STAR
US, male / female vocal / instrumental group (26 WEEKS) pos/wks

23 Feb 85	**OPERATOR** *Solar MCA 942*	66	2
28 Jun 86	**HEADLINES** *Solar MCA 1065*	16	8
4 Oct 86 ●	**MIDAS TOUCH** *Solar MCA 1096*	8	10
7 Feb 87	**ENGINE NO.9** *Solar MCA 1117*	64	3
2 May 87	**WET MY WHISTLE** *Solar MCA 1127*	60	3

MIDNITE BAND – *See Tony RALLO and the MIDNITE BAND*

MIGHTY AVENGERS
UK, male vocal / instrumental group (2 WEEKS) pos/wks

26 Nov 64	**SO MUCH IN LOVE** *Decca F 11962*	46	2

MIGHTY AVONS – *See LARRY CUNNINGHAM and the MIGHTY AVONS*

MIGHTY DUB KATZ *UK, male producer – Norman Cook (5 WEEKS)* pos/wks

7 Dec 96	**JUST ANOTHER GROOVE** *ffrr FCD 287*	43	1
2 Aug 97	**MAGIC CARPET RIDE** *ffrr FCD 306*	24	4

See also Norman COOK; BEATS INTERNATIONAL; HOUSEMARTINS; FATBOY SLIM; PIZZAMAN; FREAKPOWER

MIGHTY LEMON DROPS
UK, male vocal / instrumental group (6 WEEKS) pos/wks

13 Sep 86	**THE OTHER SIDE OF YOU** *Blue Guitar AZUR 1*	67	1
18 Apr 87	**OUT OF HAND** *Blue Guitar AZUR 4*	66	3
23 Jan 88	**INSIDE OUT** *Blue Guitar AZUR 6*	74	2

MIGHTY MIGHTY BOSSTONES
US, male vocal / instrumental group (6 WEEKS) pos/wks

25 Apr 98	**THE IMPRESSION THAT I GET** *Mercury 5748432*	12	5
27 Jun 98	**THE RASCAL KING** *Mercury 5661092*	63	1

MIGHTY MORPH'N POWER RANGERS
US, male / female vocal group (13 WEEKS) pos/wks

17 Dec 94 ●	**POWER RANGERS** *RCA 74321253022*	3	9
25 Feb 95	**POWER RANGERS (re-entry)** *RCA 74321253022*	57	2
25 Mar 95	**POWER RANGERS (2nd re-entry)** *RCA 74321253022*	65	1
8 Apr 95	**POWER RANGERS (3rd re-entry)** *RCA 74321253022*	74	1

MIGHTY WAH – *See WAH!*

MIGIL FIVE *UK, male vocal / instrumental group (20 WEEKS)* pos/wks

19 Mar 64 ●	**MOCKINGBIRD HILL** *Pye 7N 15597*	10	13
4 Jun 64	**NEAR YOU** *Pye 7N 15645*	31	7

MIG29 *Italy, male instrumental / production group (2 WEEKS)* pos/wks

22 Feb 92	**MIG29** *Champion CHAMP 292*	62	2

MIKAELA – *See SUPERCAR*

MIKE *UK, male producer – Mark Jolley (2 WEEKS)* pos/wks

19 Nov 94	**TWANGLING THREE FINGERS IN A BOX** *Pukka CDMIKE 100*	40	2

MIKE and the MECHANICS
UK, male vocal / instrumental group (67 WEEKS) pos/wks

15 Feb 86	**SILENT RUNNING (ON DANGEROUS GROUND)** *WEA U 8908*	21	9
31 May 86	**ALL I NEED IS A MIRACLE** *WEA U 8765*	53	4
14 Jan 89 ●	**THE LIVING YEARS** *WEA U 7717* ▲	2	11
16 Mar 91	**WORD OF MOUTH** *Virgin VS 1345*	13	10
15 Jun 91	**A TIME AND PLACE** *Virgin VS 1351*	58	3
8 Feb 92	**EVERYBODY GETS A SECOND CHANCE** *Virgin VS 1396*	56	4
25 Feb 95	**OVER MY SHOULDER** *Virgin VSCDT 1526*	12	9
17 Jun 95	**A BEGGAR ON A BEACH OF GOLD** *Virgin VSCDT 1535*	33	5
2 Sep 95	**ANOTHER CUP OF COFFEE** *Virgin VSCDT 1554*	51	4
17 Feb 96	**ALL I NEED IS A MIRACLE (re-mix)** *Virgin VSCDT 1576*	27	4
1 Jun 96	**SILENT RUNNING (re-issue)** *Virgin VSCDT 1585*	61	1
5 Jun 99	**NOW THAT YOU'VE GONE** *Virgin VSCDT 1732*	35	2
28 Aug 99	**WHENEVER I STOP** *Virgin VSCDT 1743*	73	1

See also GENESIS

MIKI and GRIFF
UK, female / male vocal duo – Miki and Griff Griffiths (25 WEEKS) pos/wks

2 Oct 59	**HOLD BACK TOMORROW** *Pye 7N 15213*	26	2
13 Oct 60	**ROCKIN' ALONE (IN AN OLD ROCKIN' CHAIR)** *Pye 7N 15296*	44	3
1 Feb 62	**A LITTLE BITTY TEAR** *Pye 7N 15412*	16	13
22 Aug 63	**I WANT TO STAY HERE** *Pye 7N 15555*	23	7

John MILES *UK, male vocalist / multi-instrumentalist (30 WEEKS)* pos/wks

18 Oct 75	**HIGH FLY** *Decca F 13595*	17	6
20 Mar 76 ●	**MUSIC** *Decca F 13627*	3	9
16 Oct 76	**REMEMBER YESTERDAY** *Decca F 13667*	32	5
18 Jun 77 ●	**SLOW DOWN** *Decca F 13709*	10	10

Robert MILES *Italy, male instrumentalist – keyboards – Roberto Concina (49 WEEKS)* pos/wks

24 Feb 96 ●	**CHILDREN** *Deconstruction 74321348322*	2	18
8 Jun 96 ●	**FABLE** *Deconstruction 74321382622*	7	7
3 Aug 96	**FABLE (re-entry)** *Deconstruction 74321382622*	71	1
31 Aug 96	**FABLE (2nd re-entry)** *Deconstruction 74321382622*	69	1
16 Nov 96 ●	**ONE & ONE** *Deconstruction 74321427692* [1]	3	17
29 Nov 97	**FREEDOM** *Deconstruction 74321536952* [2]	15	4
28 Jul 01	**PATHS** *Salt SALT 002CD* [3]	74	1

[1] Robert Miles featuring Maria Nayler [2] Robert Miles featuring Kathy Sledge [3] Robert Miles featuring Nina Miranda

June MILES-KINGSTON – *See Jimmy SOMERVILLE*

Paul MILES-KINGSTON – *See Sarah BRIGHTMAN*

Christina MILIAN – *See JA RULE*

MILK – *See Jason DOWNS featuring MILK*

MILK AND HONEY featuring Gali ATARI
Israel, male / female vocal / instrumental group (8 WEEKS) pos/wks

14 Apr 79 ●	**HALLELUJAH** *Polydor 2001 870*	5	8

MILK INCORPORATED
Belgium, male / female vocal / production group (3 WEEKS) pos/wks

28 Feb 98	**GOOD ENOUGH (LA VACHE)** *Malarky MLKD 5*	23	3

MILL GIRLS – *See Billy COTTON and his BAND*

MILLA *US, female vocalist (1 WEEK)* pos/wks

18 Jun 94	**GENTLEMAN WHO FELL** *SBK CDSBK 49*	65	1

Frankie MILLER *UK, male vocalist (32 WEEKS)* pos/wks

4 Jun 77	**BE GOOD TO YOURSELF** *Chrysalis CHS 2147*	27	6
14 Oct 78 ●	**DARLIN'** *Chrysalis CHS 2255*	6	15
20 Jan 79	**WHEN I'M AWAY FROM YOU** *Chrysalis CHS 2276*	42	5
21 Mar 92	**CALEDONIA** *MCS MCS 2001*	45	6

Gary MILLER *UK, male vocalist – Neville Williams (35 WEEKS)* pos/wks

21 Oct 55	**THE YELLOW ROSE OF TEXAS** *Nixa N 15004*	13	5
13 Jan 56 ●	**ROBIN HOOD** *Nixa N 15020*	10	6
11 Jan 57	**GARDEN OF EDEN** *Pye Nixa N 15070*	14	6
1 Mar 57	**GARDEN OF EDEN (re-entry)** *Pye Nixa N 15070*	27	1
19 Jul 57	**WONDERFUL, WONDERFUL** *Pye Nixa N 15094*	29	1
17 Jan 58	**THE STORY OF MY LIFE** *Pye Nixa N 15120*	14	6
21 Dec 61	**THERE GOES THAT SONG AGAIN / THE NIGHT IS YOUNG (AND YOU'RE SO BEAUTIFUL)** *Pye 7N 15404*	29	9
1 Mar 62	**THERE GOES THAT SONG AGAIN (re-entry)** *Pye 7N 15404*	48	1

'The Night Is Young' listed with 'There Goes That Song Again' only for weeks 21 and 28 Dec 1961 and 4 Jan 1962. It peaked at No.32

Glenn MILLER and his ORCHESTRA
US, orchestra, Glenn Miller – trombone (9 WEEKS) pos/wks

12 Mar 54	**MOONLIGHT SERENADE** *HMV BD 5942*	12	1
24 Jan 76	**MOONLIGHT SERENADE (re-issue) / LITTLE BROWN JUG / IN THE MOOD** *RCA 2644* ▲	13	8

US No.1 symbol refers only to 'In The Mood' which hit the top spot in 1939

Jody MILLER *US, female vocalist (1 WEEK)* pos/wks

21 Oct 65	**HOME OF THE BRAVE** *Capitol CL 15415*	49	1

Leza MILLER – *See Sergio MENDES*

Mitch MILLER his Orchestra and Chorus
US, orchestra and chorus (13 WEEKS) pos/wks

7 Oct 55 ●	**THE YELLOW ROSE OF TEXAS** *Philips PB 505* ▲	2	13

Ned MILLER *US, male vocalist (22 WEEKS)* pos/wks

14 Feb 63 ●	**FROM A JACK TO A KING** *London HL 9658*	2	21
18 Feb 65	**DO WHAT YOU DO DO WELL** *London HL 9937*	48	1

Roger MILLER *US, male vocalist (42 WEEKS)* pos/wks

18 Mar 65 ★	**KING OF THE ROAD** *Philips BF 1397*	1	15
3 Jun 65	**ENGINE ENGINE NO.9** *Philips BF 1416*	33	5
21 Oct 65	**KANSAS CITY STAR** *Philips BF 1437*	48	1
16 Dec 65	**ENGLAND SWINGS** *Philips BF 1456*	45	1
6 Jan 66	**ENGLAND SWINGS (re-entry)** *Philips BF 1456*	13	7
27 Mar 68	**LITTLE GREEN APPLES** *Mercury MF 1021*	19	10
2 Apr 69	**LITTLE GREEN APPLES (re-entry)** *Mercury MF 1021*	48	1
7 May 69	**LITTLE GREEN APPLES (2nd re-entry)** *Mercury MF 1021*	39	2

1981

IN THE YEAR IN WHICH THE POPE WAS SHOT BY A TURKISH JAILBREAKER IN ST PETER'S SQUARE, PAC MAN FEVER HIT THE ARCADES, THE LINESMAN COULD NOT BE SERIOUS BUT JOHN MCENROE WON WIMBLEDON, AND ADAM & THE ANTS WERE THE MOST CHARTED ACT OF THE YEAR, THE HUMAN LEAGUE'S **PHIL OAKEY** TELLS US ABOUT A NEAR-DEATH EXPERIENCE ...

“'Don't You Want Me' was the track I least wanted to release. We were a very avant-garde band at the time, and I took one day off from recording which was pretty unusual, leaving Jo Callis, the co-writer, and Martin Rushent to work on the track. When I went back I thought it was really middle of the road, and no matter how I tried to change it back I didn't manage it. I sort of thought it was the sell-out track on the album, and I never thought anyone would like it. The thing I'll never forget is that when it went to No.1 we were on tour in a very rickety bus. We were heading to Holyhead to do a show in Dublin, and on the way through Wales there was a massive snowstorm – the bus broke down after we'd driven into a ditch and suddenly there was no one else on the road to help us. So when we reached No.1 we were actually contemplating our deaths. The bus stopped and we couldn't restart it so we had no heat. We thought about getting into the luggage compartment and huddling together when a speculative tow truck came past and saved us, so I think we thought we might die.”

SINGLE OF THE YEAR 'Don't You Want Me' Human League
ALBUM OF THE YEAR 'King of the Wild Frontier' Adam and the Ants

Steve MILLER BAND *US, male vocal / instrumental group (36 WEEKS)* pos/wks

23 Oct 76		**ROCK 'N ME** *Mercury 6078 804* ▲	11	9
19 Jun 82	●	**ABRACADABRA** *Mercury STEVE 3* ▲	2	11
4 Sep 82		**KEEPS ME WONDERING WHY** *Mercury STEVE 4*	52	3
11 Aug 90	★	**THE JOKER** *Capitol CL 583* ▲	1	13

Suzi MILLER and the JOHNSTON BROTHERS
UK, female vocalist – Renee Lester and male vocal group (2 WEEKS) pos/wks

21 Jan 55		**HAPPY DAYS AND LONELY NIGHTS** *Decca F 10389*	14	2

Lisa MILLETT – *See SHEER BRONZE featuring Lisa MILLETT; GOODFELLAS featuring Lisa MILLETT; A.T.F.C. presents ONEPHATDEEVA; BABY BUMPS*

MILLI VANILLI *France / Germany, male duo – Rob Pilatus and Fabrice Morvan (50 WEEKS)* pos/wks

1 Oct 88	●	**GIRL YOU KNOW IT'S TRUE** *Cooltempo COOL 170*	3	13
17 Dec 88		**BABY DON'T FORGET MY NUMBER** *Cooltempo COOL 178* ▲	16	11
22 Jul 89		**BLAME IT ON THE RAIN** *Cooltempo COOL 180* ▲	53	5
30 Sep 89	●	**GIRL I'M GONNA MISS YOU** *Cooltempo COOL 191* ▲	2	15
2 Dec 89		**BLAME IT ON THE RAIN (re-entry)** *Cooltempo COOL 180*	52	5
10 Mar 90		**ALL OR NOTHING** *Cooltempo COOL 199*	74	1

MILLICAN and NESBITT
UK, male vocal duo – Alan Millican and Tim Nesbitt (14 WEEKS) pos/wks

1 Dec 73		**VAYA CON DIOS** *Pye 7N 45310*	20	11
18 May 74		**FOR OLD TIME'S SAKE** *Pye 7N 45357*	38	3

MILLIE *Jamaica, female vocalist – Millie Small (33 WEEKS)* pos/wks

12 Mar 64	●	**MY BOY LOLLIPOP** *Fontana TF 449*	2	18
25 Jun 64		**SWEET WILLIAM** *Fontana TF 479*	30	9
11 Nov 65		**BLOODSHOT EYES** *Fontana TF 617*	48	1
25 Jul 87		**MY BOY LOLLIPOP (re-issue)** *Island WIP 6574*	46	5

MILLIONAIRE HIPPIES
UK, male producer – Danny Rampling (4 WEEKS) pos/wks

18 Dec 93		**I AM THE MUSIC HEAR ME!** *Deconstruction 74321175432*	52	3
10 Sep 94		**C'MON** *Deconstruction 74321229372*	59	1

Garry MILLS *UK, male vocalist (31 WEEKS)* pos/wks

7 Jul 60	●	**LOOK FOR A STAR** *Top Rank JAR 336*	7	14
20 Oct 60		**TOP TEEN BABY** *Top Rank JAR 500*	24	12
22 Jun 61		**I'LL STEP DOWN** *Decca F 11358*	39	5

Hayley MILLS *UK, female vocalist (11 WEEKS)* pos/wks

19 Oct 61		**LET'S GET TOGETHER** *Decca F 21396*	17	11

Stephanie MILLS *US, female vocalist (33 WEEKS)* pos/wks

18 Oct 80	●	**NEVER KNEW LOVE LIKE THIS BEFORE** *20th Century TC 2460*	4	14
23 May 81		**TWO HEARTS** *20th Century TC 2492* [1]	49	5
15 Sep 84		**THE MEDICINE SONG** *Club JAB 8*	29	9
5 Sep 87		**(YOU'RE PUTTIN') A RUSH ON ME** *MCA MCA 1187*	62	2
1 May 93		**NEVER DO YOU WRONG** *MCA MCSTD 1767*	57	2
10 Jul 93		**ALL DAY ALL NIGHT** *MCA MCSTD 1778*	68	1

[1] Stephanie Mills featuring Teddy Pendergrass

Warren MILLS *Zambia, male vocalist (1 WEEK)* pos/wks

28 Sep 85		**SUNSHINE** *Jive JIVE 99*	74	1

MILLS BROTHERS *US, male vocal group (1 WEEK)* pos/wks

9 Jan 53	●	**THE GLOW WORM** *Brunswick 05007*	10	1

With Hal McIntyre and his Orchestra

MILLTOWN BROTHERS
UK, male vocal / instrumental group (16 WEEKS) pos/wks

2 Feb 91		**WHICH WAY SHOULD I JUMP?** *A & M AM 711*	38	5
13 Apr 91		**HERE I STAND** *A & M AM 758*	41	4
6 Jul 91		**APPLE GREEN** *A & M AM 787*	43	4
22 May 93		**TURN OFF** *A & M 5802692*	55	1
17 Jul 93		**IT'S ALL OVER NOW BABY BLUE** *A & M 5803332*	48	2

CB MILTON *Holland, male vocalist (5 WEEKS)* pos/wks

21 May 94		**IT'S A LOVING THING** *Logic 74321208062*	49	2
25 Mar 95		**IT'S A LOVING THING (re-mix)** *Logic 74321267212*	34	2
19 Aug 95		**HOLD ON** *Logic 74321292112*	62	1

Garnet MIMMS and TRUCKIN' CO
US, male vocalist and male instrumental group (1 WEEK) pos/wks

25 Jun 77		**WHAT IT IS** *Arista 109*	44	1

MIND OF KANE *UK, male producer – David Hope (1 WEEK)* pos/wks

27 Jul 91		**STABBED IN THE BACK** *Deja Vu DJV 007*	64	1

See also HOPE A.D.

MINDBENDERS (424 Top 500) *Manchester based vocal / instrumental group, named after the 1963 horror movie, who first found fame backing Wayne Fontana. Eric Stewart (g/v) later formed Hotlegs and 10 cc (79 WEEKS)* pos/wks

11 Jul 63		**HELLO JOSEPHINE** *Fontana TF 404* [1]	46	2
28 May 64		**STOP LOOK AND LISTEN** *Fontana TF 451* [1]	37	4
8 Oct 64	●	**UM UM UM UM UM UM** *Fontana TF 497* [1]	5	15
4 Feb 65	●	**GAME OF LOVE** *Fontana TF 535* [1] ▲	2	11
17 Jun 65		**JUST A LITTLE BIT TOO LATE** *Fontana TF 579* [1]	20	7
30 Sep 65		**SHE NEEDS LOVE** *Fontana TF 611* [1]	32	6
13 Jan 66	●	**A GROOVY KIND OF LOVE** *Fontana TF 644*	2	14
5 May 66		**CAN'T LIVE WITH YOU CAN'T LIVE WITHOUT YOU** *Fontana TF 697*	28	7
25 Aug 66		**ASHES TO ASHES** *Fontana TF 731*	14	9
20 Sep 67		**THE LETTER** *Fontana TF 869*	42	4

[1] Wayne Fontana and the Mindbenders

See also Wayne FONTANA

MINDS OF MEN
UK, male / female vocal / instrumental group (1 WEEK) pos/wks

22 Jun 96		**BRAND NEW DAY** *Perfecto PERF 121CD*	41	1

Sal MINEO *US, male vocalist (11 WEEKS)* pos/wks

12 Jul 57		**START MOVIN' (IN MY DIRECTION)** *Philips PB 707*	16	11

Marcello MINERBI *Italy, orchestra (16 WEEKS)* pos/wks

22 Jul 65	●	**ZORBA'S DANCE** *Durium DRS 54001*	6	16

MINI POPS *UK, male / female vocal group (2 WEEKS)* pos/wks

26 Dec 87		**SONGS FOR CHRISTMAS '87 (EP)** *Bright BULB 9*	39	2

Tracks on Songs for Christmas '87 (EP): Thanks for Giving Us Christmas / The Man in Red / Christmas Time Around the World / Shine On

MINIMAL FUNK 2 *Italy, male production duo (1 WEEK)* pos/wks

18 Jul 98		**THE GROOVY THANG** *Cleveland City CLECD 13046*	65	1

MINISTERS DE LA FUNK *US, male production trio (4 WEEKS)* pos/wks

11 Mar 00		**BELIEVE** *Defected DFECT 14CDS*	45	2
27 Jan 01		**BELIEVE (re-mix)** *Defected DFECT 26CDS* [1]	42	2

[1] Ministers De La Funk featuring Jocelyn Brown

MINISTRY *US, male vocal / instrumental group (3 WEEKS)* pos/wks

8 Aug 92		**NWO** *Sire W 0125TE*	49	1
6 Jan 96		**THE FALL** *Warner Bros. W 0328CD*	53	2

See also REVOLTING COCKS

MINK DE VILLE *US, male vocal / instrumental group (9 WEEKS)* pos/wks

6 Aug 77		**SPANISH STROLL** *Capitol CLX 103*	20	9

UK No.1 ★ UK Top 10 ● Still on chart + UK million seller ◆ UK entry at No.1 ■ US No.1 ▲

MINKY *UK, male producer – Gary Dedman (1 WEEK)* pos/wks

		pos	wks
30 Oct 99	THE WEEKEND HAS LANDED *Offbeat OFFCD 1001*	70	1

Liza MINNELLI *US, female vocalist (15 WEEKS)* pos/wks

		pos	wks
12 Aug 89 ●	LOSING MY MIND *Epic ZEE 1*	6	7
7 Oct 89	DON'T DROP BOMBS *Epic ZEE 2*	46	3
25 Nov 89	SO SORRY I SAID *Epic ZEE 3*	62	2
3 Mar 90	LOVE PAINS *Epic ZEE 4*	41	3

Dannii MINOGUE (490 Top 500) *Australian singer / actress, b. 20 Oct 1971, who like older sister Kylie had a chart comeback in 2001. The Minogues have had more singles success than any other sisters (72 WEEKS)* pos/wks

		pos	wks
30 Mar 91 ●	LOVE AND KISSES *MCA MCS 1529*	8	8
18 May 91	SUCCESS *MCA MCS 1538*	11	7
27 Jul 91 ●	JUMP TO THE BEAT *MCA MCS 1556*	8	6
19 Oct 91	BABY LOVE *MCA MCS 1580*	14	6
14 Dec 91	I DON'T WANNA TAKE THIS PAIN *MCA MCS 1600*	40	5
1 Aug 92	SHOW YOU THE WAY TO GO *MCA MCS 1671*	30	3
12 Dec 92	LOVE'S ON EVERY CORNER *MCA MCSR 1723*	44	4
17 Jul 93 ●	THIS IS IT *MCA MCSTD 1790*	10	8
2 Oct 93	THIS IS THE WAY *MCA MCSTD 1935*	27	3
11 Jun 94	GET INTO YOU *Mushroom D 11751*	36	2
23 Aug 97 ●	ALL I WANNA DO *Eternal WEA 119CD* [1]	4	8
1 Nov 97	EVERYTHING I WANTED *Eternal WEA 137CD* [1]	15	4
28 Mar 98	DISREMEMBRANCE *Eternal WEA 153CD* [1]	21	3
1 Dec 01 ●	WHO DO YOU LOVE NOW (STRINGER) *ffrr DFCD 002* [2]	3	5+

[1] Dannii [2] Riva featuring Dannii Minogue

Kylie MINOGUE (40 Top 500) *Biggest-selling female vocalist of the late 1980s, b. 28 May 1968, Melbourne. The Australian actress turned singer has had the best ever female chart career start with 13 successive Top 10 entries, and had the biggest selling single by a female soloist in 2001 (275 WEEKS)* pos/wks

		pos	wks
23 Jan 88 ★	I SHOULD BE SO LUCKY *PWL PWL 8*	1	16
14 May 88 ●	GOT TO BE CERTAIN *PWL PWL 12*	2	12
6 Aug 88 ●	THE LOCO-MOTION *PWL PWL 14*	2	11
22 Oct 88 ●	JE NE SAIS PAS POURQUOI *PWL PWL 21*	2	13
10 Dec 88 ★	ESPECIALLY FOR YOU *PWL PWL 24* [1]	1	14
6 May 89 ★	HAND ON YOUR HEART *PWL PWL 35*	1	11
5 Aug 89 ●	WOULDN'T CHANGE A THING *PWL PWL 42*	2	9
4 Nov 89 ●	NEVER TOO LATE *PWL PWL 45*	4	10
20 Jan 90 ★	TEARS ON MY PILLOW *PWL PWL 47*	1	8
12 May 90 ●	BETTER THE DEVIL YOU KNOW *PWL PWL 56*	2	10
3 Nov 90 ●	STEP BACK IN TIME *PWL PWL 64*	4	8
2 Feb 91 ●	WHAT DO I HAVE TO DO *PWL PWL 72*	6	8
1 Jun 91 ●	SHOCKED *PWL PWL 81*	6	7
7 Sep 91	WORD IS OUT *PWL PWL 204*	16	5
2 Nov 91 ●	IF YOU WERE WITH ME NOW *PWL PWL 208* [2]	4	7
30 Nov 91	KEEP ON PUMPIN' IT *PWL PWL 207* [3]	49	1
25 Jan 92 ●	GIVE ME JUST A LITTLE MORE TIME *PWL PWL 212*	2	8
25 Apr 92	FINER FEELINGS *PWL International PWL 227*	11	6
22 Aug 92	WHAT KIND OF FOOL (HEARD ALL THAT BEFORE) *PWL International PWL 241*	14	5
28 Nov 92	CELEBRATION *PWL International PWL 257*	20	7
10 Sep 94 ●	CONFIDE IN ME *Deconstruction 74321227482*	2	9
26 Nov 94	PUT YOURSELF IN MY PLACE *Deconstruction 74321246572*	11	9
22 Jul 95	WHERE IS THE FEELING *Deconstruction 74321293612*	16	3
14 Oct 95	WHERE THE WILD ROSES GROW *Mute CDMUTE 185* [4]	11	4
20 Sep 97	SOME KIND OF BLISS *Deconstruction 74321517252*	22	5
6 Dec 97	DID IT AGAIN *Deconstruction 74321535702*	14	6
21 Mar 98	BREATHE *Deconstruction 74321570132*	14	4
31 Oct 98	GBI *Arthrob ART 021CD* [5]	63	1
1 Jul 00 ★	SPINNING AROUND *Parlophone CDRS 6542* ■	1	11
23 Sep 00 ●	ON A NIGHT LIKE THIS *Parlophone CDRS 6546*	2	7
21 Oct 00 ●	KIDS *Chrysalis CDCHS 5119* [6]	2	17
23 Dec 00 ●	PLEASE STAY *Parlophone CDRS 6551*	10	7
13 Jan 01	ON A NIGHT LIKE THIS (re-entry) *Parlophone CDRS 6546*	71	1
10 Feb 01	KIDS (re-entry) *Chrysalis CDCHS 5119* [6]	73	1
29 Sep 01 ★	CAN'T GET YOU OUT OF MY HEAD *Parlophone CDRS 6562* ■	1	14+

[1] Kylie Minogue and Jason Donovan [2] Kylie Minogue and Keith Washington [3] Visionmasters with Tony King and Kylie Minogue [4] Nick Cave and Kylie Minogue [5] Towa Tei featuring Kylie Minogue [6] Robbie Williams / Kylie Minogue

Morris MINOR and the MAJORS *UK, male vocal / rap group (11 WEEKS)* pos/wks

		pos	wks
19 Dec 87 ●	STUTTER RAP (NO SLEEP 'TIL BEDTIME) *10 TEN 203*	4	11

Sugar MINOTT *Jamaica, male vocalist (16 WEEKS)* pos/wks

		pos	wks
28 Mar 81 ●	GOOD THING GOING (WE'VE GOT A GOOD THING GOING) *RCA 58*	4	12
17 Oct 81	NEVER MY LOVE *RCA 138*	52	4

MINT CONDITION *US, male vocal group (3 WEEKS)* pos/wks

		pos	wks
21 Jun 97	WHAT KIND OF MAN WOULD I BE *Wild Card 5710492*	38	2
4 Oct 97	LET ME BE THE ONE *Wild Card 5717132*	63	1

MINT JULEPS *UK, female vocal group (7 WEEKS)* pos/wks

		pos	wks
22 Mar 86	ONLY LOVE CAN BREAK YOUR HEART *Stiff BUY 241*	62	2
30 May 87	EVERY KINDA PEOPLE *Stiff BUY 257*	58	5

MINT ROYALE
UK, male production duo – Neil Claxton and Chris Baker (5 WEEKS) pos/wks

		pos	wks
5 Feb 00	DON'T FALTER *Faith & Hope FHCD 014* [1]	15	4
6 May 00	TAKE IT EASY *Faith & Hope FHCD 016*	66	1

[1] Mint Royale featuring Lauren Laverne

MINTY *Australia, female vocalist – Angela Kelly (1 WEEK)* pos/wks

		pos	wks
23 Jan 99	I WANNA BE FREE *Virgin VSCDT 1728*	67	1

MIRACLES (406 Top 500) *Motown's first US Top 10 act were fronted, between 1955 and 1972, by Smokey Robinson who wrote and produced hits for many Motown acts including this quartet (81 WEEKS)* pos/wks

		pos	wks
24 Feb 66	GOING TO A GO-GO *Tamla Motown TMG 547*	44	5
22 Dec 66	(COME 'ROUND HERE) I'M THE ONE YOU NEED *Tamla Motown TMG 584*	45	2
27 Dec 67	I SECOND THAT EMOTION *Tamla Motown TMG 631* [1]	27	11
3 Apr 68	IF YOU CAN WANT *Tamla Motown TMG 648* [1]	50	1
7 May 69 ●	TRACKS OF MY TEARS *Tamla Motown TMG 696* [1]	9	13
1 Aug 70 ★	THE TEARS OF A CLOWN *Tamla Motown TMG 745* [1] ▲	1	14
30 Jan 71	(COME 'ROUND HERE) I'M THE ONE YOU NEED (re-issue) *Tamla Motown TMG 761* [1]	13	9
5 Jun 71	I DON'T BLAME YOU AT ALL *Tamla Motown TMG 774* [1]	11	10
10 Jan 76 ●	LOVE MACHINE *Tamla Motown TMG 1015* ▲	3	10
2 Oct 76	THE TEARS OF A CLOWN (re-issue) *Tamla Motown TMG 1048* [1]	34	6

[1] Smokey Robinson and the Miracles

See also Smokey ROBINSON and the MIRACLES

MIRAGE *UK, male vocal / instrumental group (35 WEEKS)* pos/wks

		pos	wks
14 Jan 84	GIVE ME THE NIGHT (MEDLEY) *Passion PASH 15* [1]	49	4
9 May 87 ●	JACK MIX II / III *Debut DEBT 3022*	4	11
25 Jul 87	SERIOUS MIX *Debut DEBT 3028*	42	4
7 Nov 87 ●	JACK MIX IV *Debut DEBT 3035*	8	10
27 Feb 88	JACK MIX VII *Debut DEBT 3042*	50	3
2 Jul 88	PUSH THE BEAT *Debut DEBT 3050*	67	2
11 Nov 89	LATINO HOUSE *Debut DEBT 3085*	70	1

[1] Mirage featuring Roy Gayle

'Jack Mix III' listed with 'Jack Mix II' only from 6 Jun 1987

Nina MIRANDA – *See Robert MILES*

Danny MIRROR *Holland, male vocalist – Eddy Ouwens (9 WEEKS)* pos/wks

		pos	wks
17 Sep 77 ●	I REMEMBER ELVIS PRESLEY (THE KING IS DEAD) *Sonet SON 2121*	4	9

MIRRORBALL *UK, male production duo – Jamie White and Jamie Ford, and female vocalist (5 WEEKS)* pos/wks

		pos	wks
13 Feb 99	GIVEN UP *Multiply CDMULTY 46*	12	4
24 Jun 00	BURNIN' *Multiply CDMULTY 56*	47	1

See also TZANT; PF PROJECT featuring Ewan McGREGOR

MIRWAIS *France, male producer – Mirwais Ahmadzais (3 WEEKS)* pos/wks

20 May 00 **DISCO SCIENCE** *Epic 6693102* 68 1
23 Dec 00 **NAIVE SONG** *Epic 6706922* 50 2

MISHKA *Bermuda, male vocalist (2 WEEKS)* pos/wks

15 May 99 **GIVE YOU ALL THE LOVE** *Creation CRESCD 311* 34 2

MISS JANE *UK, female vocalist (1 WEEK)* pos/wks

30 Oct 99 **IT'S A FINE DAY** *G1 Recordings G 1001CD* 62 1

MISS SHIVA
Germany, female DJ / producer – Khadra Bungardt (2 WEEKS) pos/wks

10 Nov 01 **DREAMS** *VC Recordings VCRD 99* 30 3

MISS X *UK, female vocalist – Joyce Blair (6 WEEKS)* pos/wks

1 Aug 63 **CHRISTINE** *Ember S 175* 37 6

MISSION *UK, male vocal / instrumental group (58 WEEKS)* pos/wks

14 Jun 86 **SERPENTS KISS** *Chapter 22 CHAP 6* 70 3
26 Jul 86 **GARDEN OF DELIGHT / LIKE A HURRICANE** *Chapter 22 CHAP 7* ... 49 4
18 Oct 86 **STAY WITH ME** *Mercury MYTH 1* 30 4
17 Jan 87 **WASTELAND** *Mercury MYTH 2* 11 6
14 Mar 87 **SEVERINA** *Mercury MYTH 3* 25 5
13 Feb 88 **TOWER OF STRENGTH** *Mercury MYTH 4* 12 7
23 Apr 88 **BEYOND THE PALE** *Mercury MYTH 6* 32 4
13 Jan 90 **BUTTERFLY ON A WHEEL** *Mercury MYTH 8* 12 4
10 Mar 90 **DELIVERANCE** *Mercury MYTH 9* 27 4
2 Jun 90 **INTO THE BLUE** *Mercury MYTH 10* 32 3
17 Nov 90 **HANDS ACROSS THE OCEAN** *Mercury MYTH 11* 28 2
25 Apr 92 **NEVER AGAIN** *Mercury MYTH 12* 34 3
20 Jun 92 **LIKE A CHILD AGAIN** *Mercury MYTH 13* 30 2
17 Oct 92 **SHADES OF GREEN** *Vertigo MYTH 14* 49 2
8 Jan 94 **TOWER OF STRENGTH (re-mix)** *Vertigo MYTCD 15* 33 3
26 Mar 94 **AFTERGLOW** *Vertigo MYTCD 16* 53 1
4 Feb 95 **SWOON** *Neverland HOOKCD 002* 73 1

MISSJONES *US, female vocalist (1 WEEK)* pos/wks

10 Oct 98 **2 WAY STREET** *Motown 8608572* 49 1

MISTA E *UK, male producer – Damon Rochefort (5 WEEKS)* pos/wks

10 Dec 88 **DON'T BELIEVE THE HYPE** *Urban URB 28* 41 5

MIS-TEEQ *UK, female vocal group (28 WEEKS)* pos/wks

20 Jan 01 ● **WHY** *Inferno / Telstar CDFERN 35* 8 7
23 Jun 01 ● **ALL I WANT** *Inferno / Telstar CDSTAS 3184* 2 11
27 Oct 01 ● **ONE NIGHT STAND** *Inferno / Telstar CDSTAS 3208* ..... 5 10+

MISTURA featuring Lloyd MICHELS
US, male instrumental group, Lloyd Michels – trumpet (10 WEEKS) pos/wks

15 May 76 **THE FLASHER** *Route RT 30* 23 10

Des MITCHELL *UK / Belgium, male DJ / production trio (5 WEEKS)* pos/wks

29 Jan 00 ● **(WELCOME) TO THE DANCE** *Code Blue BLUE 0087CD1* 5 5

Guy MITCHELL (126 Top 500) *Extremely popular pre-rock vocalist, b. Al Cernik, 27 Feb 1927, Detroit, US, d. 1 Jul 1999. He appeared on the first and last charts of the 1950s, and was one of most consistently successful singers and performers of that decade (164 WEEKS)* pos/wks

14 Nov 52 ● **FEET UP!** *Columbia DB 3151* 2 10
13 Feb 53 ★ **SHE WEARS RED FEATHERS** *Columbia DB 3238* 1 15
24 Apr 53 ● **PRETTY LITTLE BLACK-EYED SUSIE** *Columbia DB 3255* 2 11
12 Jun 53 **SHE WEARS RED FEATHERS (re-entry)** *Columbia DB 3238* 12 1
28 Aug 53 ★ **LOOK AT THAT GIRL** *Philips PB 162* 1 14
6 Nov 53 ● **CHICKA BOOM** *Philips PB 178* 5 9
18 Dec 53 ● **CLOUD LUCKY SEVEN** *Philips BBL 7265* 2 16
15 Jan 54 ● **CHICKA BOOM (re-entry)** *Philips PB 178* 4 6
19 Feb 54 ● **THE CUFF OF MY SHIRT** *Philips PB 225* 9 1
26 Feb 54 **SIPPIN' SODA** *Philips PB 210* 11 1
19 Mar 54 **THE CUFF OF MY SHIRT (re-entry)** *Philips PB 225* 12 1
2 Apr 54 **THE CUFF OF MY SHIRT (2nd re-entry)** *Philips PB 225* 11 1
30 Apr 54 ● **A DIME AND A DOLLAR** *Philips PB 248* 8 1
14 May 54 ● **A DIME AND A DOLLAR (re-entry)** *Philips PB 248* 8 4
7 Dec 56 ★ **SINGING THE BLUES** *Philips PB 650* ▲ 1 22
15 Feb 57 ● **KNEE DEEP IN THE BLUES** *Philips PB 669* 3 12
26 Apr 57 ★ **ROCK-A-BILLY** *Philips PB 685* 1 14
26 Jul 57 **IN THE MIDDLE OF A DARK, DARK NIGHT / SWEET STUFF** *Philips PB 712* 27 2
23 Aug 57 **IN THE MIDDLE OF A DARK DARK NIGHT / SWEET STUFF (re-entry)** *Philips PB 712* 25 2
11 Oct 57 **CALL ROSIE ON THE PHONE** *Philips PB 743* 17 6
27 Nov 59 **HEARTACHES BY THE NUMBER** *Philips PB 964* ▲ 26 2
18 Dec 59 ● **HEARTACHES BY THE NUMBER (re-entry)** *Philips PB 964* 5 13

Joni MITCHELL
Canada, female vocalist – Roberta Anderson (24 WEEKS) pos/wks

13 Jun 70 **BIG YELLOW TAXI** *Reprise RS 20906* 11 15
4 Oct 97 ● **GOT 'TIL IT'S GONE** *Virgin VSCDG 1666* [1] 6 9

[1] Janet featuring Q-Tip and Joni Mitchell

VSCDG 1666 uses samples from RS 20906

Willie MITCHELL *US, male instrumentalist – guitar (3 WEEKS)* pos/wks

24 Apr 68 **SOUL SERENADE** *London HLU 10186* 43 1
11 Dec 76 **THE CHAMPION** *London HL 10545* 47 2

MIX FACTORY *UK, male / female vocal / instrumental group (2 WEEKS)* pos/wks

30 Jan 93 **TAKE ME AWAY (PARADISE)** *All Around The World CDGLOBE 120* 51 2

MIXMASTER *Italy, male producer – Daniele Davoli (10 WEEKS)* pos/wks

4 Nov 89 ● **GRAND PIANO** *BCM BCM 344* 9 10

MIXTURES *Australia, male vocal / instrumental group (21 WEEKS)* pos/wks

16 Jan 71 ● **THE PUSHBIKE SONG** *Polydor 2058 083* 2 21

Hank MIZELL *US, male vocalist (13 WEEKS)* pos/wks

20 Mar 76 ● **JUNGLE ROCK** *Charly CS 1005* 3 13

MK *US, male producer – Mark Kinchen (3 WEEKS)* pos/wks

4 Feb 95 **ALWAYS** *Activ CDTV 3* [1] 69 1
27 May 95 **BURNING '95** *Activ CDTVR 6* 44 2

[1] MK featuring Alana

Alana appears on both hits, although she is credited only on the first

MN8 *UK / Trinidad, male vocal group (38 WEEKS)* pos/wks

4 Feb 95 ● **I'VE GOT A LITTLE SOMETHING FOR YOU** *Columbia 6608802* 2 13
29 Apr 95 ● **IF YOU ONLY LET ME IN** *Columbia 6613252* 6 7
15 Jul 95 ● **HAPPY** *Columbia 6622192* 8 7
4 Nov 95 **BABY IT'S YOU** *Columbia 6624522* 22 2
6 Jan 96 **BABY IT'S YOU (re-entry)** *Columbia 6624522* 59 1
24 Feb 96 **PATHWAY TO THE MOON** *Columbia 6629212* 25 2
31 Aug 96 **TUFF ACT TO FOLLOW** *Columbia 6635345* 15 3
26 Oct 96 **DREAMING** *Columbia 6638302* 21 3

MNO *Belgium, male instrumental / production group (2 WEEKS)* pos/wks

28 Sep 91 **GOD OF ABRAHAM** *A & M AM 820* 66 2

MOBILES *UK, male / female vocal / instrumental group (14 WEEKS)* pos/wks

9 Jan 82 ● **DROWNING IN BERLIN** *Rialto RIA 3* 9 10
27 Mar 82 **AMOUR AMOUR** *Rialto RIA 5* 45 4

MOBO ALLSTARS

UK / US, male / female vocal / instrumental group (3 WEEKS) pos/wks

		pos	wks
26 Dec 98	AIN'T NO STOPPING US NOW *PolyGram TV 5632302*	47	3

Artists featured include: Another Level, Shola Ama, Kéllé Bryan, Celetia, Cleopatra, Damage, Des'ree, D'Influence, E17, Michelle Gayle, Glamma Kid, Lynden David Hall, Hinda Hicks, Honeyz, Kle'Shay, Kele Le Roc, Beverley Knight, Tony Momrelle, Nine Yards, Mica Paris, Karen Ramirez, Connor Reeves, Roachford, 7th Son, Byron Stingily, Truce, Soundproof, Ultimate Kaos

MOBY

US, male producer – Richard Hall (63 WEEKS) pos/wks

		pos	wks
27 Jul 91	GO *Outer Rhythm FOOT 15*	46	3
19 Oct 91 ●	GO (re-entry) *Outer Rhythm FOOT 15*	10	7
3 Jul 93	I FEEL IT *Equinox AXISCD 001*	38	3
11 Sep 93	MOVE *Mute CDMUTE 158*	21	5
28 May 94	HYMN *Mute CDMUTE 161*	31	2
29 Oct 94	FEELING SO REAL *Mute CDMUTE 173*	30	2
25 Feb 95	EVERY TIME YOU TOUCH ME *Mute CDMUTE 176*	28	3
1 Jul 95	INTO THE BLUE *Mute CDMUTE 179A*	34	2
7 Sep 96	THAT'S WHEN I REACH FOR MY REVOLVER *Mute CDMUTE 184*	50	1
15 Nov 97 ●	JAMES BOND THEME *Mute CDMUTE 210*	8	7
10 Jan 98	JAMES BOND THEME (re-entry) *Mute CDMUTE 210*	74	1
5 Sep 98	HONEY *Mute CDMUTE 218*	33	2
8 May 99	RUN ON *Mute CDMUTE 221*	33	2
24 Jul 99	BODYROCK *Mute CDMUTE 225*	38	2
23 Oct 99	WHY DOES MY HEART FEEL SO BAD *Mute CDMUTE 230*	16	4
18 Mar 00	NATURAL BLUES *Mute CDMUTE 251*	11	6
24 Jun 00 ●	PORCELAIN *Mute CDMUTE 252*	5	6
28 Oct 00	WHY DOES MY HEART FEEL SO BAD (re-issue) *Mute CDMUTE 255*	17	5

MOCA – *See David MORALES*

MOCHA – *See Missy 'Misdemeanor' ELLIOTT; Nicole RAY*

MOCK TURTLES

UK, male / female vocal / instrumental group (15 WEEKS) pos/wks

		pos	wks
9 Mar 91	CAN YOU DIG IT? *Siren SRN 136*	18	11
29 Jun 91	AND THEN SHE SMILES *Siren SRN 139*	44	4

MODERN LOVERS – *See Jonathan RICHMAN and the MODERN LOVERS*

MODERN ROMANCE (450 Top 500)

Latin-tinged London pop group which evolved out of new wave band The Leyton Buzzards. Lead singer Geoff Deane, who was replaced in 1982 by Michael J Mullins, later became a top TV scriptwriter (Birds of a Feather, Chef!, Babes in the Wood) (77 WEEKS) pos/wks

		pos	wks
15 Aug 81	EVERYBODY SALSA *WEA K 18815*	12	10
7 Nov 81 ●	AY AY AY AY MOOSEY *WEA K 18883*	10	12
30 Jan 82	QUEEN OF THE RAPPING SCENE (NOTHING EVER GOES THE WAY YOU PLAN) *WEA K 18928*	37	8
14 Aug 82	CHERRY PINK AND APPLE BLOSSOM WHITE *WEA K 19245* [1]	15	8
13 Nov 82 ●	BEST YEARS OF OUR LIVES *WEA ROM 1*	4	13
26 Feb 83 ●	HIGH LIFE *WEA ROM 2*	8	8
7 May 83	DON'T STOP THAT CRAZY RHYTHM *WEA ROM 3*	14	6
6 Aug 83 ●	WALKING IN THE RAIN *WEA X 9733*	7	12

[1] Modern Romance featuring John du Prez

MODERN TALKING

Germany, male vocal / instrumental duo – Thomas Anders and Dieter Bohlen (22 WEEKS) pos/wks

		pos	wks
15 Jun 85	YOU'RE MY HEART, YOU'RE MY SOUL *Magnet MAG 277*	69	2
17 Aug 85	YOU'RE MY HEART, YOU'RE MY SOUL (re-entry) *Magnet MAG 277*	56	5
12 Oct 85	YOU CAN WIN IF YOU WANT *Magnet MAG 282*	70	2
16 Aug 86 ●	BROTHER LOUIE *RCA PB 40875*	4	10
4 Oct 86	ATLANTIS IS CALLING (S.O.S. FOR LOVE) *RCA PB 40969*	55	3

MODETTES

UK, female vocal / instrumental group (6 WEEKS) pos/wks

		pos	wks
12 Jul 80	PAINT IT BLACK *Deram DET-R 1*	42	5
18 Jul 81	TONIGHT *Deram DET 3*	68	1

MODJO

France, male production / vocal duo – Yann Destagnol and Romain Tranchart (29 WEEKS) pos/wks

		pos	wks
16 Sep 00 ★	LADY (HEAR ME TONIGHT) *Polydor 5877582* ■	1	20
14 Apr 01	CHILLIN' *Polydor 5870092*	12	8
6 Oct 01	WHAT I MEAN *Polydor 5873462*	59	1

Domenico MODUGNO

Italy, male vocalist (13 WEEKS) pos/wks

		pos	wks
5 Sep 58 ●	VOLARE (NEL BLU DIPINTO DI BLU) *Oriole ICB 5000* ▲	10	12
27 Mar 59	CIAO CIAO BAMBINA (PIOVE) *Oriole CB 1489*	29	1

MOFFATTS

Canada, male vocal / instrumental group (6 WEEKS) pos/wks

		pos	wks
20 Feb 99	CRAZY *Chrysalis CDEM 533*	16	3
26 Jun 99	UNTIL YOU LOVED ME *Chrysalis CDEM 541*	36	2
23 Oct 99	MISERY *EMI CDEM 551*	47	1

MOGWAI

UK, male instrumental group (3 WEEKS) pos/wks

		pos	wks
4 Apr 98	SWEET LEAF / BLACK SABBATH *Fierce Panda NING 47CD* [1]	60	1
11 Apr 98	FEAR SATAN *Eye-Q EYEUK 032CD*	57	1
11 Jul 98	NO EDUCATION NO FUTURE (F**K THE CURFEW) *Chemikal CHEM 026CD*	68	1

[1] Mogwai: Magoo

MOHAWKS

Jamaica, male vocal / instrumental group (2 WEEKS) pos/wks

		pos	wks
24 Jan 87	THE CHAMP *Pama PM 1*	58	2

Frank'o MOIRAGHI featuring AMNESIA

Italy, male / female vocal / instrumental duo (4 WEEKS) pos/wks

		pos	wks
1 Jun 96	FEEL MY BODY *Multiply CDMULTY 10*	39	2
26 Oct 96	FEEL MY BODY (re-mix) *Multiply CDMULTY 15*	40	2

MOIST

Canada, male vocal / instrumental group (10 WEEKS) pos/wks

		pos	wks
12 Nov 94	PUSH *Chrysalis CDCHS 5016*	35	3
25 Feb 95	SILVER *Chrysalis CDCHS 5019*	50	2
29 Apr 95	FREAKY BE BEAUTIFUL *Chrysalis CDCHS 5022*	47	2
19 Aug 95	PUSH (re-issue) *Chrysalis CDCHS 5024*	20	3

MOJO

UK, male instrumental group (3 WEEKS) pos/wks

		pos	wks
22 Aug 81	DANCE ON *Creole CR 17*	70	3

MOJOLATORS featuring CAMILLA

US, male production duo and female vocalist (1 WEEK) pos/wks

		pos	wks
6 Oct 01	DRIFTING *Multiply CDMULTY 81*	52	1

MOJOS

UK, male vocal / instrumental group (26 WEEKS) pos/wks

		pos	wks
26 Mar 64 ●	EVERYTHING'S ALRIGHT *Decca F 11853*	9	11
11 Jun 64	WHY NOT TONIGHT *Decca F 11918*	25	10
10 Sep 64	SEVEN DAFFODILS *Decca F 11959*	30	5

MOKENSTEF

US, female vocal group (1 WEEK) pos/wks

		pos	wks
23 Sep 95	HE'S MINE *Def Jam DEFCD 13*	70	1

MOLELLA featuring the OUTHERE BROTHERS

Italy, male producer and US, male rap / vocal duo (10 WEEKS) pos/wks

		pos	wks
16 Dec 95 ●	IF YOU WANNA PARTY *Eternal WEA 030CD*	9	10

Sophie MOLETA – *See HUMAN MOVEMENT featuring Sophie MOLETA*

Ralph MOLINA – *See Ian McNABB*

Sam MOLLISON – *See SASHA*

MOLLY HALF HEAD

UK, male vocal / instrumental group (1 WEEK) pos/wks

		pos	wks
3 Jun 95	SHINE *Columbia 6620732*	73	1

MOLOKO *Ireland / UK, male / female vocal / instrumental duo – Roisin Murphy and Mark Brydon (31 WEEKS)*

		pos	wks
24 Feb 96	**DOMINOID** *Echo ECSCD 016*	65	1
25 May 96	**FUN FOR ME** *Echo ECSCD 20*	36	2
20 Jun 98	**THE FLIPSIDE** *Echo ECSCD 54*	53	1
27 Mar 99	**SING IT BACK** *Echo ECSCD 71*	45	2
4 Sep 99 ●	**SING IT BACK (re-mix)** *Echo ECSCD 82*	4	9
1 Apr 00 ●	**THE TIME IS NOW** *Echo ECSCD 88*	2	10
5 Aug 00	**PURE PLEASURE SEEKER** *Echo ECSCD 99*	21	5
25 Nov 00	**INDIGO** *Echo ECSCD 104*	51	1

MOMBASSA *UK, male production duo (1 WEEK)*

		pos	wks
8 Mar 97	**CRY FREEDOM** *Soundproof SPCD 021*	63	1

MOMENTS *US, male vocal group (32 WEEKS)*

		pos	wks
8 Mar 75 ●	**GIRLS** *All Platinum 6146 302* [1]	3	10
19 Jul 75 ●	**DOLLY MY LOVE** *All Platinum 6146 306*	10	9
25 Oct 75	**LOOK AT ME (I'M IN LOVE)** *All Platinum 6146 309*	42	4
22 Jan 77 ●	**JACK IN THE BOX** *All Platinum 6146 318*	7	9

[1] Moments and Whatnauts

Tony MOMRELLE *UK, male vocalist (1 WEEK)*

		pos	wks
15 Aug 98	**LET ME SHOW YOU** *Art & Soul ART 1CDS*	67	1

MONACO *UK, male vocal / instrumental duo – Peter Hook and David Potts (11 WEEKS)*

		pos	wks
15 Mar 97	**WHAT DO YOU WANT FROM ME?** *Polydor 5731912*	11	6
31 May 97	**SWEET LIPS** *Polydor 5710552*	18	4
20 Sep 97	**SHINE (SOMEONE WHO NEEDS ME)** *Polydor 5714182*	55	1

See also NEW ORDER

Pharoahe MONCH *US, male rapper (10 WEEKS)*

		pos	wks
19 Feb 00	**SIMON SAYS** *Rawkus RWK 205CD*	24	2
19 Aug 00	**LIGHT** *Rawkus RWK 259CD*	72	1
3 Feb 01	**OH NO** *Rawkus RWK 302* [1]	24	4
1 Dec 01	**GOT YOU** *Priority PTYCD 145*	27	3

[1] Mos Def and Nate Dogg featuring Pharoahe Monch

Jay MONDI and the LIVING BASS
US, male / female vocal / instrumental group (3 WEEKS)

		pos	wks
24 Mar 90	**ALL NIGHT LONG** *10 TEN 304*	63	3

MONDO KANE *UK, male vocal / instrumental group (3 WEEKS)*

		pos	wks
16 Aug 86	**NEW YORK AFTERNOON** *Lisson DOLE 2*	70	3

MONE *US, female vocalist (2 WEEKS)*

		pos	wks
12 Aug 95	**WE CAN MAKE IT** *A & M 5811592*	64	1
16 Mar 96	**MOVIN'** *AM:PM 5814392*	48	1

Zoot MONEY and the BIG ROLL BAND
UK, male vocal / instrumental group (8 WEEKS)

		pos	wks
18 Aug 66	**BIG TIME OPERATOR** *Columbia DB 7975*	25	8

MONEY MARK
US, male vocal / instrumentalist / producer (3 WEEKS)

		pos	wks
28 Feb 98	**HAND IN YOUR HEAD** *Mo Wax MW 066CD*	40	2
6 Jun 98	**MAYBE I'M DEAD** *Mo Wax MW 089CD1*	45	1

MONICA *US, female vocalist – Monica Arnold (37 WEEKS)*

		pos	wks
29 Jul 95	**DON'T TAKE IT PERSONAL (JUST ONE OF DEM DAYS)** *Arista 74321301452*	32	3
17 Feb 96	**LIKE THIS AND LIKE THAT** *Rowdy 74321344222*	33	2
8 Jun 96	**BEFORE YOU WALK OUT OF MY LIFE** *Rowdy 74321374042*	22	3
24 May 97	**FOR YOU I WILL** *Atlantic A 5437CD*	27	2
6 Jun 98 ●	**THE BOY IS MINE** *Atlantic AT 0036 CD* [1] ▲	2	20
17 Oct 98 ●	**THE FIRST NIGHT** *Rowdy 74321619342* ▲	6	6
4 Sep 99	**ANGEL OF MINE** *Arista 74321692892* ▲	55	1

[1] Brandy and Monica

MONIFAH *US, female vocalist (2 WEEKS)*

		pos	wks
30 Jan 99	**TOUCH IT** *Universal UND 56218*	29	2

TS MONK *US, male / female vocal / instrumental group (6 WEEKS)*

		pos	wks
7 Mar 81	**BON BON VIE** *Mirage K 11653*	63	2
25 Apr 81	**CANDIDATE FOR LOVE** *Mirage K 11648*	58	4

MONKEES (301 Top 500) *The world's top act of 1967: Davy Jones (v/g), Mike Nesmith (v/g), Peter Tork (v/k), Mickey Dolenz (v/d). This Anglo-American quartet was hand-picked for a Beatles-style TV series, which helped to rocket them, albeit briefly, to the very top (101 WEEKS)*

		pos	wks
5 Jan 67 ★	**I'M A BELIEVER** *RCA 1560* ▲	1	17
26 Jan 67	**LAST TRAIN TO CLARKSVILLE** *RCA 1547* ▲	23	7
6 Apr 67 ●	**A LITTLE BIT ME, A LITTLE BIT YOU** *RCA 1580*	3	12
22 Jun 67 ●	**ALTERNATE TITLE** *RCA 1604*	2	12
16 Aug 67	**PLEASANT VALLEY SUNDAY** *RC 1620*	11	8
15 Nov 67 ●	**DAYDREAM BELIEVER** *RCA 1645* ▲	5	17
27 Mar 68	**VALLERI** *RCA 1673*	12	8
26 Jun 68	**DW WASHBURN** *RCA 1706*	17	6
26 Mar 69	**TEAR DROP CITY** *RCA 1802*	46	1
25 Jun 69	**SOMEDAY MAN** *RCA 1824*	47	1
15 Mar 80	**THE MONKEES EP** *Arista ARIST 326*	33	9
18 Oct 86	**THAT WAS THEN, THIS IS NOW** *Arista ARIST 673*	68	1
1 Apr 89	**THE MONKEES EP** *Arista 112157*	62	2

Tracks on Arista 326 EP: I'm a Believer / Daydream Believer / Last Train to Clarksville / A Little Bit Me a Little Bit You. Tracks on Arista 112157 EP: Daydream Believer / Monkees Theme / Last Train to Clarksville

MONKEY MAFIA
UK, male vocal / instrumental / DJ / production group (3 WEEKS)

		pos	wks
10 Aug 96	**WORK MI BODY** *Heavenly HVN 53CD* [1]	75	1
7 Jun 97	**15 STEPS (EP)** *Heavenly HVN 67CD*	67	1
2 May 98	**LONG AS I CAN SEE THE LIGHT** *Heavenly HVN 84CD*	51	1

[1] Monkey Mafia featuring Patra

Tracks on 15 Steps (EP): Lion in the Hall / Krash the Decks: Slaughter the Vinyl / Metro Love / Beats in the Hall

MONKS *UK, male vocal / instrumental duo – Richard Hudson and John Ford (9 WEEKS)*

		pos	wks
21 Apr 79	**NICE LEGS SHAME ABOUT HER FACE** *Carrere CAR 104*	19	9

The Monks were Hudson-Ford under a different name

MONO *UK, male / female vocal / instrumental duo (1 WEEK)*

		pos	wks
2 May 98	**LIFE IN MONO** *Echo ECSCD 64*	60	1

MONOBOY featuring DELORES *Ireland, male producer – Ian Masterson and female vocalist (1 WEEK)*

		pos	wks
7 Jul 01	**THE MUSIC IN YOU** *Perfecto PERF 18CDS*	50	1

Matt MONRO (213 Top 500) *Superior British balladeer, b. Terence Parsons, 1 Dec 1932, London, d. 7 Feb 1985. This Sinatra-styled vocalist, who was renamed by hitmaker Winifred Atwell, had few MOR equals in the 1960s. In 1961, Billboard magazine named him Top International Act and Most Promising Male Singer (127 WEEKS)*

		pos	wks
15 Dec 60 ●	**PORTRAIT OF MY LOVE** *Parlophone R 4714*	3	16
9 Mar 61 ●	**MY KIND OF GIRL** *Parlophone R 4755*	5	12
18 May 61	**WHY NOT NOW / CAN THIS BE LOVE** *Parlophone R 4775*	24	9
28 Sep 61	**GONNA BUILD A MOUNTAIN** *Parlophone R 4819*	44	3
8 Feb 62 ●	**SOFTLY AS I LEAVE YOU** *Parlophone R 4868*	10	18
14 Jun 62	**WHEN LOVE COMES ALONG** *Parlophone R 4911*	46	3
8 Nov 62	**MY LOVE AND DEVOTION** *Parlophone R 4954*	29	5
14 Nov 63	**FROM RUSSIA WITH LOVE** *Parlophone R 5068*	20	13

			pos	wks
17 Sep 64	●	**WALK AWAY** *Parlophone R 5171*	4	20
24 Dec 64		**FOR MAMA** *Parlophone R 5215*	23	4
25 Mar 65		**WITHOUT YOU** *Parlophone R 5251*	37	4
21 Oct 65	●	**YESTERDAY** *Parlophone R 5348*	8	12
24 Nov 73		**AND YOU SMILED** *EMI 2091*	28	8

Gerry MONROE *UK, male vocalist (57 WEEKS)* pos/wks

			pos	wks
23 May 70	●	**SALLY** *Chapter One CH 122*	4	20
19 Sep 70		**CRY** *Chapter One CH 128*	38	5
14 Nov 70	●	**MY PRAYER** *Chapter One CH 132*	9	12
17 Apr 71		**IT'S A SIN TO TELL A LIE** *Chapter One CH 144*	13	12
21 Aug 71		**LITTLE DROPS OF SILVER** *Chapter One CH 152*	37	6
12 Feb 72		**GIRL OF MY DREAMS** *Chapter One CH 159*	43	2

Hollis P MONROE *Canada, male producer (1 WEEK)* pos/wks

			pos	wks
24 Apr 99		**I'M LONELY** *City Beat CBE 778CD*	51	1

MONSOON *UK, male / female vocal / instrumental group (12 WEEKS)* pos/wks

			pos	wks
3 Apr 82		**EVER SO LONELY** *Mobile Suit Corp CORP 2*	12	9
5 Jun 82		**SHAKTI (THE MEANING OF WITHIN)** *Mobile Suit Corp CORP 4*	41	3

MONSTA BOY featuring DENZIE
UK, male production / vocal instrumental duo (3 WEEKS) pos/wks

			pos	wks
7 Oct 00		**SORRY (I DIDN'T KNOW)** *Locked On LOX 125CD*	25	3

MONSTER MAGNET
US, male vocal / instrumental group (6 WEEKS) pos/wks

			pos	wks
29 May 93		**TWIN EARTH** *A & M 5802812*	67	1
18 Mar 95		**NEGASONIC TEENAGE WARHEAD** *A & M 5809812*	49	1
6 May 95		**DOPES TO INFINITY** *A & M 5810332*	58	1
23 Jan 99		**POWERTRIP** *A&M 5828232*	39	2
6 Mar 99		**SPACE LORD** *A&M 5632752*	45	1

MONTAGE *UK, female vocal trio (1 WEEK)* pos/wks

			pos	wks
15 Feb 97		**THERE AIN'T NOTHIN' LIKE THE LOVE** *Wildcard 5733172*	64	1

MONTANA SEXTET *US, male instrumental group (1 WEEK)* pos/wks

			pos	wks
15 Jan 83		**HEAVY VIBES** *Virgin VS 560*	59	1

MONTANO vs THE TRUMPET MAN
UK, male production / instrumental duo (1 WEEK) pos/wks

			pos	wks
18 Sep 99		**ITZA TRUMPET THING** *Serious SERR 010CD*	46	1

Hugo MONTENEGRO *US, orchestra (26 WEEKS)* pos/wks

			pos	wks
11 Sep 68	★	**THE GOOD THE BAD AND THE UGLY** *RCA 1727*	1	24
8 Jan 69		**HANG 'EM HIGH** *RCA 1771*	50	1
19 Mar 69		**THE GOOD, THE BAD AND THE UGLY (re-entry)** *RCA 1727*	48	1

Chris MONTEZ *US, male vocalist – Ezekiel Montanez (61 WEEKS)* pos/wks

			pos	wks
4 Oct 62	●	**LET'S DANCE** *London HLU 9596*	2	18
17 Jan 63	●	**SOME KINDA FUN** *London HLU 9650*	10	9
30 Jun 66	●	**THE MORE I SEE YOU** *Pye International 7N 25369*	3	13
22 Sep 66		**THERE WILL NEVER BE ANOTHER YOU** *Pye International 7N 25381*	37	4
14 Oct 72	●	**LET'S DANCE (re-issue)** *London HLU 10205*	9	14
14 Apr 79		**LET'S DANCE (2nd re-issue)** *Lightning LIG 9011*	47	3

The second re-issue of 'Let's Dance' on Lightning was coupled with 'Memphis' by Lonnie Mack as a double A-side

MONTROSE *US, male vocal / instrumental group (2 WEEKS)* pos/wks

			pos	wks
28 Jun 80		**SPACE STATION NO.5 / GOOD ROCKIN' TONIGHT** *Warner Brothers HM 9*	71	2

MONTROSE AVENUE *UK, male vocal / instrumental group (4 WEEKS)* pos/wks

			pos	wks
28 Mar 98		**WHERE DO I STAND?** *Columbia 6656072*	38	2
20 Jun 98		**SHINE** *Columbia 6660012*	58	1
17 Oct 98		**START AGAIN** *Columbia 6664255*	59	1

MONTY PYTHON *UK, male comedy group (9 WEEKS)* pos/wks

			pos	wks
5 Oct 91	●	**ALWAYS LOOK ON THE BRIGHT SIDE OF LIFE** *Virgin PYTH 1*	3	9

MONYAKA *US / Jamaica, male vocal / instrumental group (8 WEEKS)* pos/wks

			pos	wks
10 Sep 83		**GO DEH YAKA (GO TO THE TOP)** *Polydor POSP 641*	14	8

MOOD *UK, male vocal / instrumental group (10 WEEKS)* pos/wks

			pos	wks
6 Feb 82		**DON'T STOP** *RCA 171*	59	4
22 May 82		**PARIS IS ONE DAY AWAY** *RCA 211*	42	5
30 Oct 82		**PASSION IN DARK ROOMS** *RCA 276*	74	1

MOODSWINGS / CHRISSIE HYNDE *UK, male / instrumental group and US, female vocalist / instrumentalist (4 WEEKS)* pos/wks

			pos	wks
12 Oct 91		**SPIRITUAL HIGH (STATE OF INDEPENDENCE)** *Arista 114528*	66	2
23 Jan 93		**SPIRITUAL HIGH (STATE OF INDEPENDENCE) (re-mix)** *Arista 74321127712*	47	2

See also PRETENDERS

MOODY BLUES 246 Top 500 *Long-lived and internationally popular cosmic rock quintet from Birmingham, UK: line-up has included Denny Laine (v/g), Ray Thomas (fl/v), Mike Pinder, (k/v), Graeme Edge (d), Justin Hayward (v/g) and John Lodge (b/v). This album-orientated act has sold more than 50 million records worldwide (114 WEEKS)* pos/wks

			pos	wks
10 Dec 64	★	**GO NOW** *Decca F 12022*	1	14
4 Mar 65		**I DON'T WANT TO GO ON WITHOUT YOU** *Decca F 12095*	33	9
10 Jun 65		**FROM THE BOTTOM OF MY HEART** *Decca F 12166*	22	9
18 Nov 65		**EVERYDAY** *Decca F 12266*	44	2
27 Dec 67		**NIGHTS IN WHITE SATIN** *Deram DM 161*	19	11
7 Aug 68		**VOICES IN THE SKY** *Deram DM 196*	27	10
4 Dec 68		**RIDE MY SEE-SAW** *Deram DM 213*	42	1
2 May 70	●	**QUESTION** *Threshold TH 4*	2	12
6 May 72		**ISN'T LIFE STRANGE** *Threshold TH 9*	13	10
2 Dec 72	●	**NIGHTS IN WHITE SATIN (re-entry)** *Deram DM 161*	9	11
10 Feb 73		**I'M JUST A SINGER (IN A ROCK 'N' ROLL BAND)** *Threshold TH 13*	36	4
10 Nov 79		**NIGHTS IN WHITE SATIN (2nd re-entry)** *Deram DM 161*	14	12
20 Aug 83		**BLUE WORLD** *Threshold TH 30*	35	5
25 Jun 88		**I KNOW YOU'RE OUT THERE SOMEWHERE** *Polydor POSP 921*	52	4

Michael MOOG *US, male producer – Shivaun Gaines (3 WEEKS)* pos/wks

			pos	wks
11 Dec 99		**THAT SOUND** *ffrr FCD 374*	32	2
25 Aug 01		**YOU BELONG TO ME** *Strictly Rhythm SRUKECD 04*	62	1

MOOGWAI *Switzerland / Holland, production duo (2 WEEKS)* pos/wks

			pos	wks
6 May 00		**VIOLA** *Platipus PLATCD 71*	55	1
26 May 01		**THE LABYRINTH** *Platipus PLATCD 83*	68	1

MOONMAN *Holland, male DJ / producer – Ferry Corsten (4 WEEKS)* pos/wks

			pos	wks
9 Aug 97		**DON'T BE AFRAID** *Heat Recordings HEATCD 009*	60	1
27 Nov 99		**DON'T BE AFRAID '99 (re-mix)** *Heat Recordings HEATCD 022*	41	2
7 Oct 00		**GALAXIA** *Heat Recordings HEATCD 025* [1]	50	1

[1] Moonman featuring Chantal

See also Ferry CORSTEN; VERACOCHA; GOURYELLA; SYSTEM F

MOONTREKKERS *UK, male instrumental group (1 WEEK)* pos/wks

			pos	wks
2 Nov 61		**NIGHT OF THE VAMPIRE** *Parlophone R 4814*	50	1

Chanté MOORE *US, female vocalist (11 WEEKS)* pos/wks

			pos	wks
20 Mar 93		**LOVE'S TAKEN OVER** *MCA MCSTD 1744*	54	3
4 Mar 95		**FREE / SAIL ON** *MCA MCSTD 2042*	69	1
7 Apr 01		**STRAIGHT UP** *MCA MCSTD 40250*	11	6
2 Jun 01		**STRAIGHT UP (re-entry)** *MCA MCSTD 40250*	74	1

Dorothy MOORE *US, female vocalist (24 WEEKS)* pos/wks

19 Jun 76 ●	MISTY BLUE *Contempo CS 2087*	5	12
16 Oct 76	FUNNY HOW TIME SLIPS AWAY *Contempo CS 2092*	38	3
15 Oct 77	I BELIEVE YOU *Epic EPC 5573*	20	9

Dudley MOORE – *See Peter COOK*

Gary MOORE (297 Top 500) *Noted blues guitarist, b. 4 Apr 1952, Belfast. Played in early 1970s Irish band Skid Row (with Phil Lynott) as well as Thin Lizzy and Colosseum II, before successfully launching his solo career (103 WEEKS)* pos/wks

21 Apr 79 ●	PARISIENNE WALKWAYS *MCA 419*	8	11
21 Jan 84	HOLD ON TO LOVE *10 TEN 13*	65	3
11 Aug 84	EMPTY ROOMS *10 TEN 25*	51	5
18 May 85 ●	OUT IN THE FIELDS *10 TEN 49* [1]	5	10
27 Jul 85	EMPTY ROOMS (re-issue) *10 TEN 58*	23	8
20 Dec 86	OVER THE HILLS AND FAR AWAY *10 TEN 134*	20	8
28 Feb 87	WILD FRONTIER *10 TEN 159*	35	5
9 May 87	FRIDAY ON MY MIND *10 TEN 164*	26	6
29 Aug 87	THE LONER *10 TEN 178*	53	5
5 Dec 87	TAKE A LITTLE TIME (DOUBLE SINGLE) *10 TEN 190*	75	1
14 Jan 89	AFTER THE WAR *Virgin GMS 1*	37	4
18 Mar 89	READY FOR LOVE *Virgin GMS 2*	56	2
24 Mar 90	OH PRETTY WOMAN *Virgin VS 1233* [2]	48	3
12 May 90	STILL GOT THE BLUES (FOR YOU) *Virgin VS 1267*	31	7
18 Aug 90	WALKING BY MYSELF *Virgin VS 1281*	48	5
15 Dec 90	TOO TIRED *Virgin VS 1306*	71	1
22 Feb 92	COLD DAY IN HELL *Virgin VS 1393*	24	5
9 May 92	STORY OF THE BLUES *Virgin VS 1412*	40	4
18 Jul 92	SINCE I MET YOU BABY *Virgin VS 1423* [3]	59	3
24 Oct 92	SEPARATE WAYS *Virgin VS 1437*	59	1
8 May 93	PARISIENNE WALKWAYS (re-recording) *Virgin VSCDX 1456*	32	4
17 Jun 95	NEED YOUR LOVE SO BAD *Virgin VSCDG 1546*	48	2

[1] Gary Moore and Phil Lynott [2] Gary Moore featuring Albert King [3] Gary Moore and BB King

'Parisienne Walkways' features uncredited vocals by Phil Lynott. Tracks on double single: Take a Little Time / Out in the Fields / All Messed Up / Thunder Rising

Jackie MOORE *US, female vocalist (5 WEEKS)* pos/wks

15 Sep 79	THIS TIME BABY *CBS 7722*	49	5

Lynsey MOORE – *See RAMSEY and FEN featuring Lynsey MOORE*

Mandy MOORE *US, female vocalist (18 WEEKS)* pos/wks

6 May 00 ●	CANDY *Epic 6693452*	6	13
19 Aug 00	I WANNA BE WITH YOU *Epic 6695922*	21	5

Mark MOORE – *See S EXPRESS*

Melba MOORE *US, female vocalist – Melba Hill (29 WEEKS)* pos/wks

15 May 76 ●	THIS IS IT *Buddah BDS 443*	9	8
26 May 79	PICK ME UP I'LL DANCE *Epic EPC 7234*	48	5
9 Oct 82	LOVE'S COMIN' AT YA *EMI America EA 146*	15	8
15 Jan 83	MIND UP TONIGHT *Capitol CL 272*	22	6
5 Mar 83	UNDERLOVE *Capitol CL 281*	60	2

Ray MOORE *UK, male vocalist (9 WEEKS)* pos/wks

29 Nov 86	O' MY FATHER HAD A RABBIT *Play PLAY 213*	24	7
5 Dec 87	BOG EYED JOG *Play PLAY 224*	61	2

Sam MOORE and LOU REED *US, male vocalists (10 WEEKS)* pos/wks

17 Jan 87	SOUL MAN *A & M AM 364*	30	10

Tina MOORE *US, female vocalist (18 WEEKS)* pos/wks

30 Aug 97 ●	NEVER GONNA LET YOU GO *Delirious 74321511052*	7	15
25 Apr 98	NOBODY BETTER *RCA 74321571612*	20	3

Lisa MOORISH *UK, female vocalist (11 WEEKS)* pos/wks

7 Jan 95	JUST THE WAY IT IS *Go.Beat GODCD 123*	42	3
19 Aug 95	I'M YOUR MAN *Go.Beat GODCD 128*	24	3
3 Feb 96	MR FRIDAY NIGHT *Go.Beat GODCD 137*	24	3
18 May 96	LOVE FOR LIFE *Go.Beat GODCD 145*	37	2

'I'm Your Man' features the uncredited vocals of George Michael

M.O.P. *US, male rap group (19 WEEKS)* pos/wks

12 May 01 ●	COLD AS ICE *Epic 6711762*	4	10
18 Aug 01 ●	ANTE UP *Epic 6717882* [1]	7	7
13 Oct 01	ANTE UP (re-entry) *Epic 6717882* [1]	65	1
1 Dec 01	STAND CLEAR *Chrysalis CDEM 597* [2]	43	1

[1] M.O.P. featuring Busta Rhymes [2] Adam F featuring M.O.P.

Angel MORAES *US, male producer (2 WEEKS)* pos/wks

16 Nov 96	HEAVEN KNOWS – DEEP DEEP DOWN *ffrr FCD 282*	72	1
17 May 97	I LIKE IT *AM:PM 5871792*	70	1

David MORALES *US, male DJ / producer (21 WEEKS)* pos/wks

10 Jul 93	GIMME LUV (EENIE MEENIE MINY MO) *Mercury MERCD 390*	37	3
20 Nov 93	THE PROGRAM *Mercury MERCD 396*	66	1
24 Aug 96	IN DE GHETTO *Manifesto FESCD 12* [1]	35	2
15 Aug 98 ●	NEEDIN' U *Manifesto FESCD 46* [2]	8	8
24 Jun 00	HIGHER *Azuli AZNYCDX 120* [3]	41	2
20 Jan 01	NEEDIN' YOU II (re-mix) *Manifesto FESCD 78* [4]	11	5

[1] David Morales and the Bad Yard Club featuring Crystal Waters and Delta [2] David Morales presents The Face [3] David Morales and Albert Cabrera present Moca featuring Deanna [4] David Morales presents The Face featuring Juliet Roberts

See also BOSS; PULSE featuring Antoinette ROBERSON

Mike MORAN – *See Lynsey DE PAUL*

MORCHEEBA *UK, male / female vocal / instrumental group (13 WEEKS)* pos/wks

13 Jul 96	TAPE LOOP *Indochina ID 045CD*	42	1
5 Oct 96	TRIGGER HIPPIE *Indochina ID 052CD*	40	2
15 Feb 97	THE MUSIC THAT WE HEAR (MOOG ISLAND) *Indochina ID 054CD*	47	1
11 Oct 97	SHOULDER HOLSTER *Indochina ID 064CD*	53	1
11 Apr 98	BLINDFOLD *Indochina ID 070CD*	56	1
20 Jun 98	LET ME SEE *Indochina ID 076CD*	46	1
29 Aug 98	PART OF THE PROCESS *China WOKCD 2097*	38	2
5 Aug 00	ROME WASN'T BUILT IN A DAY *East West EW 214CD*	34	3
31 Mar 01	WORLD LOOKING IN *East West EW 225CD*	48	1

MORE *UK, male vocal / instrumental group (2 WEEKS)* pos/wks

14 Mar 81	WE ARE THE BAND *Atlantic K 11561*	59	2

MOREL *US, male vocalist / producer – Richard Morel (1 WEEK)* pos/wks

12 Aug 00	TRUE (THE FAGGOT IS YOU) *Hooj Choons HOOJ 097CD*	64	1

George MOREL featuring Heather WILDMAN *US, male / female vocal / instrumental duo (2 WEEKS)* pos/wks

26 Oct 96	LET'S GROOVE *Positiva CDTIV 62*	42	2

MORGAN *UK, male vocal / instrumental duo (1 WEEK)* pos/wks

27 Nov 99	MISS PARKER *Source CDSOUR 002*	74	1

Debelah MORGAN *US, female vocalist (9 WEEKS)* pos/wks

24 Feb 01 ●	DANCE WITH ME *Atlantic AT 0087CD*	10	9

Derrick MORGAN *Jamaica, male vocalist (1 WEEK)* pos/wks

17 Jan 70	MOON HOP *Crab 32*	49	1

Jamie J MORGAN *US, male vocalist (6 WEEKS)* pos/wks

10 Feb 90	WALK ON THE WILD SIDE *Tabu 655596 7*	27	6

Jane MORGAN *US, female vocalist – Jane Currier (22 WEEKS)* pos/wks

5 Dec 58 ★	THE DAY THE RAINS CAME *London HLR 8751*	1	16
22 May 59	IF ONLY I COULD LIVE MY LIFE AGAIN *London HLR 8810*	27	1
21 Jul 60	ROMANTICA *London HLR 9120*	39	5

Meli'sa MORGAN *US, female vocalist (7 WEEKS)* pos/wks

9 Aug 86	FOOL'S PARADISE *Capitol CL 415*	41	5
25 Jun 88	GOOD LOVE *Capitol CL 483*	59	2

Ray MORGAN *UK, male vocalist (6 WEEKS)* pos/wks

25 Jul 70	THE LONG AND WINDING ROAD *B & C CB 128*	32	6

Erick 'More' MORILLO presents RAW *US, male DJ / producer / instrumentalist and female vocalist (1 WEEK)* pos/wks

4 Feb 95	HIGHER (FEEL IT) *A & M 5809412*	74	1

See also LIL MO' YIN YANG

Alanis MORISSETTE *Canada, female vocalist (45 WEEKS)* pos/wks

5 Aug 95	YOU OUGHTA KNOW *Maverick W 0307CD*	22	7
28 Oct 95	HAND IN MY POCKET *Maverick W 0312CD*	26	3
24 Feb 96	YOU LEARN *Maverick W 0334CD*	24	4
20 Apr 96	IRONIC *Maverick W 0343CD*	11	9
3 Aug 96 ●	HEAD OVER FEET *Maverick W 0355CD*	7	7
7 Dec 96	ALL I REALLY WANT *Maverick W 0382CD*	59	1
31 Oct 98 ●	THANK U *Maverick W 0458CD*	5	10
13 Mar 99	JOINING YOU *Maverick W 472CD1*	28	2
31 Jul 99	SO PURE *Maverick W 492CD1*	38	2

Giorgio MORODER *Italy, male instrumentalist – synthesizer (36 WEEKS)* pos/wks

24 Sep 77	FROM HERE TO ETERNITY *Oasis 1* [1]	16	10
17 Mar 79	CHASE *Casablanca CAN 144*	48	6
22 Sep 84 ●	TOGETHER IN ELECTRIC DREAMS *Virgin VS 713* [2]	3	13
29 Jun 85	GOOD-BYE BAD TIMES *Virgin VS 772* [3]	44	5
11 Jul 98	CARRY ON *Almighty CDALMY 120* [4]	65	1
12 Feb 00	THE CHASE (re-recording) *Logic 74321732112* [5]	46	1

[1] Giorgio [2] Giorgio Moroder and Phil Oakey [3] Philip Oakey and Giorgio Moroder [4] Donna Summer and Giorgio Moroder [5] DJ Empire presents Giorgio Moroder

Ennio MORRICONE *Italy, orchestra (12 WEEKS)* pos/wks

11 Apr 81 ●	CHI MAI (THEME FROM THE TV SERIES 'THE LIFE AND TIMES OF DAVID LLOYD GEORGE') *BBC RESL 92*	2	12

Sarah Jane MORRIS – *See COMMUNARDS*

Diana MORRISON – *See Michael BALL*

Dorothy Combs MORRISON – *See Edwin HAWKINS SINGERS*

Mark MORRISON *Talented but notorious R&B singer / songwriter whose brushes with the law made him a regular subject of the tabloids. The singer, who changed his name to Abdul Rahman in 1998, b. 3 May 1972, Leicester, UK, spent several years living in the US. His first album included five Top 10 singles (68 WEEKS)* pos/wks

22 Apr 95	CRAZY *WEA YZ 907CD*	19	4
16 Sep 95	LET'S GET DOWN *WEA WEA 001CD*	39	2
16 Mar 96 ★	RETURN OF THE MACK *WEA WEA 040CD*	1	23
27 Jul 96 ●	CRAZY (re-mix) *WEA WEA 054CD1*	6	8
31 Aug 96	RETURN OF THE MACK (re-entry) *WEA WEA 040CD*	60	1
19 Oct 96	CRAZY (re-entry of re-mix) *WEA WEA 054CD1*	71	1
19 Oct 96 ●	TRIPPIN' *WEA WEA 079CD1*	8	6
21 Dec 96 ●	HORNY *WEA WEA 090CD1*	5	9
15 Mar 97 ●	MOAN & GROAN *WEA WEA 096CD1*	7	6
20 Sep 97	WHO'S THE MACK! *WEA WEA 128CD1*	13	5
4 Sep 99	BEST FRIEND *WEA WEA 221CD1* [1]	23	3

[1] Mark Morrison and Conner Reeves

Van MORRISON *UK, male vocalist – George Ivan (20 WEEKS)* pos/wks

20 Oct 79	BRIGHT SIDE OF THE ROAD *Mercury 6001 121*	63	3
1 Jul 89	HAVE I TOLD YOU LATELY *Polydor VANS 1*	74	1
9 Dec 89	WHENEVER GOD SHINES HIS LIGHT *Polydor VANS 2* [1]	20	6
15 May 93	GLORIA *Exile VANCD 11* [2]	31	3
18 Mar 95	HAVE I TOLD YOU LATELY THAT I LOVE YOU *RCA 74321271702* [3]	71	1
10 Jun 95	DAYS LIKE THIS *Exile VANCD 12*	65	1
2 Dec 95	NO RELIGION *Exile 5775792*	54	1
1 Mar 97	THE HEALING GAME *Exile 5733912*	46	1
6 Mar 99	PRECIOUS TIME *Pointblank / Virgin POBD 14*	36	2
22 May 99	BACK ON TOP *Exile / Pointblank / Virgin POBD 15*	69	1

[1] Van Morrison with Cliff Richard [2] Van Morrison and John Lee Hooker [3] Chieftains with Van Morrison

'Have I Told You Lately That I Love You' is a re-recording of his second hit

See also THEM

MORRISSEY (477 Top 500) *Witty, often provocative vocalist / lyricist and former frontman of The Smiths, born Stephen Morrissey, 22 May 1959, Manchester, UK. The first of 15 successive Top 40 singles entered at No.6, thereby immediately outdoing his previous band's chart peak (74 WEEKS)* pos/wks

27 Feb 88 ●	SUEDEHEAD *HMV POP 1618*	5	6
11 Jun 88 ●	EVERYDAY IS LIKE SUNDAY *HMV POP 1619*	9	6
11 Feb 89 ●	LAST OF THE FAMOUS INTERNATIONAL PLAYBOYS *HMV POP 1620*	6	5
29 Apr 89 ●	INTERESTING DRUG *HMV POP 1621*	9	4
25 Nov 89	OUIJA BOARD OUIJA BOARD *HMV POP 1622*	18	4
5 May 90	NOVEMBER SPAWNED A MONSTER *HMV POP 1623*	12	4
20 Oct 90	PICCADILLY PALARE *HMV POP 1624*	18	2
23 Feb 91	OUR FRANK *HMV POP 1625*	26	3
13 Apr 91	SING YOUR LIFE *HMV POP 1626*	33	2
27 Jul 91	PREGNANT FOR THE LAST TIME *HMV POP 1627*	25	4
12 Oct 91	MY LOVE LIFE *HMV POP 1628*	29	2
9 May 92	WE HATE IT WHEN OUR FRIENDS BECOME SUCCESSFUL *HMV POP 1629*	17	3
18 Jul 92	YOU'RE THE ONE FOR ME, FATTY *HMV POP 1630*	19	3
19 Dec 92	CERTAIN PEOPLE I KNOW *HMV POP 1631*	35	4
12 Mar 94 ●	THE MORE YOU IGNORE ME THE CLOSER I GET *Parlophone CDR 6372*	8	3
11 Jun 94	HOLD ON TO YOUR FRIENDS *Parlophone CDR 6383*	47	2
20 Aug 94	INTERLUDE *Parlophone CDR 6365* [1]	25	2
28 Jan 95	BOXERS *Parlophone CDR 6400*	23	3
2 Sep 95	DAGENHAM DAVE *RCA Victor 74321299802*	26	2
9 Dec 95	THE BOY RACER *RCA Victor 74321332952*	36	2
23 Dec 95	SUNNY *Parlophone CDR 6243*	42	2
2 Aug 97	ALMA MATTERS *Island CID 667*	16	3
18 Oct 97	ROY'S KEEN *Island CID 671*	42	1
10 Jan 98	SATAN REJECTED MY SOUL *Island CID 686*	39	2

[1] Morrissey and Siouxsie

See also SMITHS

MORRISTON ORPHEUS MALE VOICE CHOIR – *See ALARM*

Buddy MORROW *US, orchestra – Muni Zudecoff (1 WEEK)* pos/wks

20 Mar 53	NIGHT TRAIN *HMV B 10347*	12	1

Bob MORTIMER – *See EMF; MIDDLESBROUGH FC featuring Bob MORTIMER and Chris REA*

MOS DEF *US male rapper – Dante Smith (6 WEEKS)* pos/wks

24 Jun 00	UMI SAYS *Rawkus RWK 232CD*	60	1
4 Nov 00	MISS FAT BOOTY - PART II *Rawkus RWK 282CD* [1]	64	1
3 Feb 01	OH NO *Rawkus RWK 302* [2]	24	4

[1] Mos Def featuring Ghostface Killah [2] Mos Def and Nate Dogg featuring Pharoahe Monch

Mickie MOST *UK, male vocalist (1 WEEK)* pos/wks

25 Jul 63	MR. PORTER *Decca F 11664*	45	1

MOTELS
US / UK, male / female vocal / instrumental group (7 WEEKS) pos/wks

			pos	wks
11 Oct 80		**WHOSE PROBLEM?** *Capitol CL 16162*	42	4
10 Jan 81		**DAYS ARE O.K.** *Capitol CL 16149*	41	3

Wendy MOTEN *US, female vocalist (13 WEEKS)* pos/wks

			pos	wks
5 Feb 94	●	**COME IN OUT OF THE RAIN** *EMI-USA CDMT 105*	8	9
14 May 94		**SO CLOSE TO LOVE** *EMI-USA CDMTS 106*	35	4

MOTHER *UK, male instrumental / production duo (4 WEEKS)* pos/wks

			pos	wks
12 Jun 93		**ALL FUNKED UP** *Bosting BYSNCD 101*	34	2
1 Oct 94		**GET BACK** *Six6 SIXT 119*	73	1
31 Aug 96		**ALL FUNKED UP (re-mix)** *Six6 SIXXCD 1*	66	1

MOTHER'S PRIDE *UK, male DJ / production duo (2 WEEKS)* pos/wks

			pos	wks
21 Mar 98		**FLORIBUNDA** *Heat Recordings HEATCD 013*	42	1
6 Nov 99		**LEARNING TO FLY** *Devolution DEVR 001CDS*	54	1

MOTIV 8 *UK, male producer – Steve Rodway (10 WEEKS)* pos/wks

			pos	wks
17 Jul 93		**ROCKIN' FOR MYSELF** *Nuff Respect NUFF 002CD* [1]	67	1
7 May 94		**ROCKIN' FOR MYSELF (re-mix)** *WEA YZ 814CD*	18	4
21 Oct 95		**BREAK THE CHAIN** *Eternal WEA 010CD*	31	2
23 Dec 95		**SEARCHING FOR THE GOLDEN EYE** *Eternal WEA 027CD* [2]	40	3

[1] Motiv 8 featuring Angie Brown [2] Motiv 8 and Kym Mazelle

MOTIVATION *Holland, male producer – Francis Louwers (1 WEEK)* pos/wks

			pos	wks
17 Nov 01		**PARA MI** *Definitive CDDEF 1*	71	1

MÖTLEY CRÜE *US, male vocal / instrumental group (28 WEEKS)* pos/wks

			pos	wks
24 Aug 85		**SMOKIN' IN THE BOYS ROOM** *Elektra EKR 16*	71	2
8 Feb 86		**HOME SWEET HOME / SMOKIN' IN THE BOYS ROOM (re-issue)** *Elektra EKR 33*	51	3
1 Aug 87		**GIRLS, GIRLS, GIRLS** *Elektra EKR 59*	26	6
16 Jan 88		**YOU'RE ALL I NEED / WILD SIDE** *Elektra EKR 65*	23	4
4 Nov 89		**DR FEELGOOD** *Elektra EKR 97*	50	3
12 May 90		**WITHOUT YOU** *Elektra EKR 109*	39	3
7 Sep 91		**PRIMAL SCREAM** *Elektra EKR 133*	32	2
11 Jan 92		**HOME SWEET HOME (re-mix)** *Elektra EKR 136*	37	2
5 Mar 94		**HOOLIGAN'S HOLIDAY** *Elektra EKR 180CDX*	36	2
19 Jul 97		**AFRAID** *Elektra E 3936 CD1*	58	1

'Wild Side' listed with 'You're All I Need' only from 30 Jan 1988. It peaked at No.26

MOTÖRHEAD (411 Top 500)
Unashamedly loud mainstays of UK heavy rock formed in 1975 after Lemmy (v/b) (b. Ian Kilmister 24 Dec 1945, Stoke-on-Trent, UK) left Hawkwind. Much-touted in punk circles, they helped to show the way to 1980s heavy metal bands such as Metallica (81 WEEKS) pos/wks

			pos	wks
16 Sep 78		**LOUIE LOUIE** *Bronze BRO 60*	75	1
30 Sep 78		**LOUIE LOUIE (re-entry)** *Bronze BRO 60*	68	1
10 Mar 79		**OVERKILL** *Bronze BRO 67*	39	4
14 Apr 79		**OVERKILL (re-entry)** *Bronze BRO 67*	57	3
30 Jun 79		**NO CLASS** *Bronze BRO 78*	61	4
1 Dec 79		**BOMBER** *Bronze BRO 85*	34	7
3 May 80	●	**THE GOLDEN YEARS (EP)** *Bronze BRO 92*	8	7
1 Nov 80		**ACE OF SPADES** *Bronze BRO 106*	15	12
22 Nov 80		**BEER DRINKERS AND HELL RAISERS** *Big Beat SWT 61*	43	4
21 Feb 81	●	**ST VALENTINE'S DAY MASSACRE (EP)** *Bronze BRO 116* [1]	5	8
11 Jul 81	●	**MOTÖRHEAD (LIVE)** *Bronze BRO 124*	6	7
3 Apr 82		**IRON FIST** *Bronze BRO 146*	29	5
21 May 83		**I GOT MINE** *Bronze BRO 165*	46	2
30 Jul 83		**SHINE** *Bronze BRO 167*	59	2
1 Sep 84		**KILLED BY DEATH** *Bronze BRO 185*	51	2
5 Jul 86		**DEAF FOREVER** *GWR GWR 2*	67	1
5 Jan 91		**THE ONE TO SING THE BLUES** *Epic 6565787*	45	3
14 Nov 92		**'92 TOUR (EP)** *Epic 6588096*	63	1
11 Sep 93		**ACE OF SPADES (re-issue)** *WGAF CDWGAF 101*	23	5
10 Dec 94		**BORN TO RAISE HELL** *Fox 74321230152* [2]	47	2

[1] Motörhead and Girlschool (also known as Headgirl) [2] Motörhead / Ice-T / Whitfield Crane

Tracks on The Golden Years (EP): Dead Men Tell No Tales / Too Late Too Late / Leaving Here / Stone Dead Forever. Tracks on St Valentine's Day Massacre (EP): Please Don't Touch / Emergency / Bomber. Tracks on '92 Tour (EP): Hellraiser / You Better Run / Going to Brazil / Ramones

MOTORS *UK, male vocal / instrumental group (29 WEEKS)* pos/wks

			pos	wks
24 Sep 77		**DANCING THE NIGHT AWAY** *Virgin VS 186*	42	4
10 Jun 78	●	**AIRPORT** *Virgin VS 219*	4	13
19 Aug 78		**FORGET ABOUT YOU** *Virgin VS 222*	13	9
12 Apr 80		**LOVE AND LONELINESS** *Virgin VS 263*	58	3

MOTOWN SPINNERS – *See DETROIT SPINNERS*

MOTT THE HOOPLE *UK, male vocal / instrumental group (55 WEEKS)* pos/wks

			pos	wks
12 Aug 72	●	**ALL THE YOUNG DUDES** *CBS 8271*	3	11
16 Jun 73		**HONALOOCHIE BOOGIE** *CBS 1530*	12	9
8 Sep 73	●	**ALL THE WAY FROM MEMPHIS** *CBS 1764*	10	8
24 Nov 73	●	**ROLL AWAY THE STONE** *CBS 1895*	8	12
30 Mar 74		**GOLDEN AGE OF ROCK AND ROLL** *CBS 2177*	16	7
22 Jun 74		**FOXY FOXY** *CBS 2439*	33	5
2 Nov 74		**SATURDAY GIGS** *CBS 2754*	41	3

MOUNT RUSHMORE presents THE KNACK
UK, male production duo / female vocalist (1 WEEK) pos/wks

			pos	wks
3 Apr 99		**YOU BETTER** *Universal MCSTD 40192*	53	1

Nana MOUSKOURI *Greece, female vocalist (11 WEEKS)* pos/wks

			pos	wks
11 Jan 86	●	**ONLY LOVE** *Philips PH 38*	2	11

MOUSSE T
Germany, male producer – Mustafa Gundogdu (27 WEEKS) pos/wks

			pos	wks
6 Jun 98	●	**HORNY** *AM:PM 5826712* [1]	2	17
20 May 00	●	**SEX BOMB** *Gut CDGUT 33* [2]	3	10

[1] Mousse T vs Hot 'N' Juicy [2] Tom Jones and Mousse T

MOUTH and MACNEAL
Holland, male / female vocal duo (10 WEEKS) pos/wks

			pos	wks
4 May 74	●	**I SEE A STAR** *Decca F 13504*	8	10

MOVE (264 Top 500)
Innovative and influential Birmingham band, included Carl Wayne (v), Roy Wood (v/g). They were the first group heard on BBC Radio 1 ('Flowers in the Rain'), and had eight consecutive Top 20 entries. Wood later moved on to a successful solo career, helped to form ELO and went on to front Wizzard (110 WEEKS) pos/wks

			pos	wks
5 Jan 67	●	**NIGHT OF FEAR** *Deram DM 109*	2	10
6 Apr 67	●	**I CAN HEAR THE GRASS GROW** *Deram DM 117*	5	10
6 Sep 67	●	**FLOWERS IN THE RAIN** *Regal Zonophone RZ3001*	2	13
7 Feb 68	●	**FIRE BRIGADE** *Regal Zonophone RZ3005*	3	11
25 Dec 68	★	**BLACKBERRY WAY** *Regal Zonophone RZ3015*	1	12
23 Jul 69		**CURLY** *Regal Zonophone RZ3021*	12	12
25 Apr 70	●	**BRONTOSAURUS** *Regal Zonophone RZ3026*	7	10
3 Jul 71		**TONIGHT** *Harvest HAR 5038*	11	10
23 Oct 71		**CHINATOWN** *Harvest HAR 5043*	23	8
13 May 72	●	**CALIFORNIA MAN** *Harvest HAR 5050*	7	14

MOVEMENT *US, male vocal / instrumental group (2 WEEKS)* pos/wks

			pos	wks
24 Oct 92		**JUMP!** *Arista 74321116677*	57	2

MOVEMENT 98 featuring Carroll THOMPSON
UK, male / female vocal / instrumental group (8 WEEKS) pos/wks

			pos	wks
19 May 90		**JOY AND HEARTBREAK** *Circa YR 45*	27	5
15 Sep 90		**SUNRISE** *Circa YR 51*	58	3

MOVIN' MELODIES *Holland, male producer – Patrick Prinz (3 WEEKS)* pos/wks

22 Oct 94	**LA LUNA** *Effective EFFS 017CD* [1]	64	1
29 Jun 96	**INDICA** *Hooj Choons HOOJCD 44*	62	1
26 Jul 97	**ROLLERBLADE** *Movin' Melodies 5822352*	71	1

[1] Movin' Melodies Production

See also ARTEMESIA; ETHICS; SUBLIMINAL CUTS

Alison MOYET (276 Top 500) *After five Top 20 hits with Yazoo, the distinctive, bluesy-voiced vocalist (b. 18 Jun 1961, Essex, UK), nicknamed Alf, enjoyed a string of solo successes. Her biggest hits included revivals of songs made popular by Billie Holiday and Ketty Lester (107 WEEKS)* pos/wks

23 Jun 84 ●	**LOVE RESURRECTION** *CBS A 4497*	10	11
13 Oct 84 ●	**ALL CRIED OUT** *CBS A 4757*	8	11
1 Dec 84	**INVISIBLE** *CBS A 4930*	21	10
16 Mar 85 ●	**THAT OLE DEVIL CALLED LOVE** *CBS A 6044*	2	10
29 Nov 86 ●	**IS THIS LOVE?** *CBS MOYET 1*	3	16
7 Mar 87 ●	**WEAK IN THE PRESENCE OF BEAUTY** *CBS MOYET 2*	6	10
30 May 87	**ORDINARY GIRL** *CBS MOYET 3*	43	4
28 Nov 87 ●	**LOVE LETTERS** *CBS MOYET 5*	4	10
6 Apr 91	**IT WON'T BE LONG** *Columbia 6567577*	50	4
1 Jun 91	**WISHING YOU WERE HERE** *Columbia 6569397*	72	1
12 Oct 91	**THIS HOUSE** *Columbia 6575157*	40	5
16 Oct 93	**FALLING** *Columbia 6595962*	42	3
12 Mar 94	**WHISPERING YOUR NAME** *Columbia 6601622*	18	7
28 May 94	**GETTING INTO SOMETHING** *Columbia 6603565*	51	2
22 Oct 94	**ODE TO BOY** *Columbia 6607952*	59	1
26 Aug 95	**SOLID WOOD** *Columbia 6623265*	44	2

See also YAZOO

MOZAIC *UK, female vocal group (7 WEEKS)* pos/wks

5 Aug 95	**SING IT (THE HALLELUJAH SONG)** *Perfecto PERF 106CD*	14	4
10 Aug 96	**RAYS OF THE RISING SUN** *Perfecto PERF 123CD*	32	2
30 Nov 96	**MOVING UP MOVING ON** *Perfecto PERF 131CD*	62	1

MR and MRS SMITH
UK, male / female instrumental / production group (1 WEEK) pos/wks

12 Oct 96	**GOTTA GET LOOSE** *Hooj Choons HOOJCD 46*	70	1

MR BEAN and SMEAR CAMPAIGN featuring Bruce DICKINSON
UK, male comedian – Rowan Atkinson and male vocalist (5 WEEKS) pos/wks

4 Apr 92 ●	**(I WANT TO BE) ELECTED** *London LON 319*	9	5

MR BIG *UK, male vocal / instrumental group (14 WEEKS)* pos/wks

12 Feb 77 ●	**ROMEO** *EMI 2567*	4	10
21 May 77	**FEEL LIKE CALLING HOME** *EMI 2610*	35	4

MR BIG *US, male vocal / instrumental group (17 WEEKS)* pos/wks

7 Mar 92 ●	**TO BE WITH YOU** *Atlantic A 7514* ▲	3	11
23 May 92	**JUST TAKE MY HEART** *Atlantic A 7490*	26	4
8 Aug 92	**GREEN TINTED SIXTIES MIND** *Atlantic A 7468*	72	1
20 Nov 93	**WILD WORLD** *Atlantic A 7310CD*	59	1

MR BLOBBY *UK, male pink, yellow spotted blob vocalist (16 WEEKS)* pos/wks

4 Dec 93 ★	**MR BLOBBY** *Destiny Music CDDMUS 104*	1	12
16 Dec 95	**CHRISTMAS IN BLOBBYLAND** *Destiny DMUSCD 108*	36	4

MR BLOE *UK, male instrumental group (18 WEEKS)* pos/wks

9 May 70 ●	**GROOVIN' WITH MR BLOE** *DJM DJS 216*	2	18

MR FINGERS *US, male producer – Larry Heard (5 WEEKS)* pos/wks

17 Mar 90	**WHAT ABOUT THIS LOVE** *ffrr F 131*	74	1
7 Mar 92	**CLOSER** *MCA MCS 1601*	50	3
23 May 92	**ON MY WAY** *MCA MCS 1630*	71	1

MR FOOD *UK, male vocalist (3 WEEKS)* pos/wks

9 Jun 90	**. . . AND THAT'S BEFORE ME TEA!** *Tangible TGB 005*	62	3

MR HANKEY *US, male Xmas excrement vocalist (6 WEEKS)* pos/wks

25 Dec 99 ●	**MR HANKEY THE CHRISTMAS POO** *Columbia 6685582*	4	6

MR JACK *Belgium, male producer – Lucente Vito (2 WEEKS)* pos/wks

25 Jan 97	**WIGGLY WORLD** *Extravaganza 0090965*	32	2

MR LEE *US, male producer – Leroy Haggard (6 WEEKS)* pos/wks

6 Aug 88	**PUMP UP LONDON** *Breakout USA 639*	64	2
11 Nov 89	**GET BUSY** *Jive JIVE 231*	71	1
24 Feb 90	**GET BUSY (re-entry)** *Jive JIVE 231*	41	3

MR MISTER *US, male vocal / instrumental group (22 WEEKS)* pos/wks

21 Dec 85 ●	**BROKEN WINGS** *RCA PB 49945* ▲	4	13
1 Mar 86	**KYRIE** *RCA PB 49927* ▲	11	9

MR OIZO *France, male producer – Quentin Dupieux (15 WEEKS)* pos/wks

3 Apr 99 ★	**FLAT BEAT** *F Communications / Pias Recordings F 104CDUK* ■	1	13
7 Aug 99	**FLAT BEAT (re-entry)** *F Communications / Pias Recordings F 104CDUK*	60	2

MR PRESIDENT *Germany, male / female vocal group (13 WEEKS)* pos/wks

14 Jun 97 ●	**COCO JAMBOO** *WEA WEA 110CD*	8	11
20 Sep 97	**I GIVE YOU MY HEART** *WEA WEA 126CD*	52	1
25 Apr 98	**JOJO ACTION** *WEA WEA 156CD*	73	1

MR ROY *UK, male instrumental / production group (6 WEEKS)* pos/wks

7 May 94	**SOMETHING ABOUT YOU** *Fresh FRSHD 11*	74	1
21 Jan 95	**SAVED** *Fresh FRSHD 21*	24	4
16 Dec 95	**SOMETHING ABOUT U (CAN'T BE BEAT) (re-mix)** *Fresh FRSHCD 33*	49	1

MR RUMBLE – *See BM DUBS Present MR RUMBLE*

MR V *UK, male producer – Rob Villiers (2 WEEKS)* pos/wks

6 Aug 94	**GIVE ME LIFE** *Cheeky CHEKCD 005*	40	2

MR VEGAS *Jamaica, male vocalist – Clifford Smith (7 WEEKS)* pos/wks

22 Aug 98	**HEADS HIGH** *Greensleeves GRECD 650*	71	1
13 Nov 99	**HEADS HIGH (re-issue)** *Greensleeves GRECD 785*	16	6

MRS MILLS
UK, female instrumentalist – piano – Gladys Mills (6 WEEKS) pos/wks

14 Dec 61	**MRS MILLS MEDLEY** *Parlophone R 4856*	18	5
31 Dec 64	**MRS MILLS PARTY MEDLEY** *Parlophone R 5214*	50	1

Mrs Mills' Medley consisted of the following tunes: I Want to Be Happy / Sheik of Araby / Baby Face / Somebody Stole My Gal / Ma (He's Making Eyes At Me) / Swanee / Ain't She Sweet / California Here I Come

MRS WOOD *UK, female producer (6 WEEKS)* pos/wks

16 Sep 95	**JOANNA** *React CDREACT 066*	40	2
6 Jul 96	**HEARTBREAK** *React CDREACT 78* [1]	44	1
4 Oct 97	**JOANNA (re-mix)** *React CDREACT 107*	34	2
15 Aug 98	**1234** *React CDREACT 121*	54	1

[1] Mrs Wood featuring Eve Gallagher

MS DYNAMITE – *See STICKY featuring MS DYNAMITE*

MTUME *US, male / female vocal / instrumental group (12 WEEKS)* pos/wks

14 May 83	**JUICY FRUIT** *Epic A 3424*	34	9
22 Sep 84	**PRIME TIME** *Epic A 4720*	57	3

MUD (174 Top 500) *Rock 'n' roll-influenced Seventies stars: Les Gray (v), Rob Davis (g/v), Ray Stiles (b/v), Dave Mount (d/v). After joining RAK Records and teaming with writers / producers Nicky Chinn and Mike Chapman, this good-time British band had a noteworthy run of hits, including three No.1s. Davis (Rob D) is now a noted dance music producer and composer (139 WEEKS)*

Date		Title / Label	pos	wks
10 Mar 73		**CRAZY** *RAK 146*	12	12
23 Jun 73		**HYPNOSIS** *RAK 152*	16	13
27 Oct 73	●	**DYNA-MITE** *RAK 159*	4	12
19 Jan 74	★	**TIGER FEET** *RAK 166*	1	11
13 Apr 74	●	**THE CAT CREPT IN** *RAK 170*	2	9
27 Jul 74	●	**ROCKET** *RAK 178*	6	9
30 Nov 74	★	**LONELY THIS CHRISTMAS** *RAK 187*	1	10
15 Feb 75	●	**THE SECRETS THAT YOU KEEP** *RAK 194*	3	9
26 Apr 75	★	**OH BOY** *RAK 201*	1	9
21 Jun 75	●	**MOONSHINE SALLY** *RAK 208*	10	7
2 Aug 75		**ONE NIGHT** *RAK 213*	32	4
4 Oct 75	●	**L-L-LUCY** *Private Stock PVT 41*	10	6
29 Nov 75	●	**SHOW ME YOU'RE A WOMAN** *Private Stock PVT 45*	8	8
15 May 76		**SHAKE IT DOWN** *Private Stock PVT 65*	12	8
27 Nov 76	●	**LEAN ON ME** *Private Stock PVT 85*	7	9
21 Dec 85		**LONELY THIS CHRISTMAS (re-entry)** *RAK 187*	61	3

MUDHONEY *US, male vocal / instrumental group (2 WEEKS)*

Date		Title / Label	pos	wks
17 Aug 91		**LET IT SLIDE** *Subpop SP 15154*	60	1
24 Oct 92		**SUCK YOU DRY** *Reprise W 0137*	65	1

MUDLARKS *UK, male / female vocal group (19 WEEKS)*

Date		Title / Label	pos	wks
2 May 58	●	**LOLLIPOP** *Columbia DB 4099*	2	9
6 Jun 58	●	**BOOK OF LOVE** *Columbia DB 4133*	8	9
27 Feb 59		**THE LOVE GAME** *Columbia DB 4250*	30	1

MUFFINS – *See MARTHA and the MUFFINS*

Idris MUHAMMAD *US, male instrumentalist – drums (3 WEEKS)*

Date		Title / Label	pos	wks
17 Sep 77		**COULD HEAVEN EVER BE LIKE THIS** *Kudu 935*	42	3

Vocal by Frank Floyd

MUKKAA *UK, male instrumental / production duo (1 WEEK)*

Date		Title / Label	pos	wks
27 Feb 93		**BURUCHACCA** *Limbo LIMBO 008*	74	1

Maria MULDAUR *US, female vocalist (8 WEEKS)*

Date		Title / Label	pos	wks
29 Jun 74		**MIDNIGHT AT THE OASIS** *Reprise K 14331*	21	8

MULL HISTORICAL SOCIETY
UK, male vocal / instrumental group (1 WEEK)

Date		Title / Label	pos	wks
21 Jul 01		**ANIMAL CANNABUS** *Rough Trade RTRADESCD 021*	53	1

Arthur MULLARD – *See Hylda BAKER and Arthur MULLARD*

Larry MULLEN – *See Adam CLAYTON and Larry MULLEN*

Shawn MULLINS *US, male vocalist (11 WEEKS)*

Date		Title / Label	pos	wks
6 Mar 99	●	**LULLABY** *Columbia 6669592*	9	10
2 Oct 99		**WHAT IS LIFE** *Columbia 6678212*	62	1

MULU *UK, male / female vocal / instrumental duo (1 WEEK)*

Date		Title / Label	pos	wks
2 Aug 97		**PUSSYCAT** *Dedicated MULU 003CD1*	50	1

Samantha MUMBA *Ireland, female vocalist (51 WEEKS)*

Date		Title / Label	pos	wks
8 Jul 00	●	**GOTTA TELL YOU** *Wild Card / Polydor 5618832*	2	12
28 Oct 00	●	**BODY II BODY** *Wild Card / Polydor 5877742*	5	12
3 Mar 01	●	**ALWAYS COME BACK TO YOUR LOVE** *Wild Card / Polydor 5879252*	3	15
22 Sep 01	●	**BABY COME ON OVER** *Wild Card / Polydor 5872352*	5	10
22 Dec 01	●	**LATELY** *Wild Card / Polydor 5705232*	6	2+

Coati MUNDI – *See Kid CREOLE and the COCONUTS*

MUNDY *Ireland, male vocalist (2 WEEKS)*

Date		Title / Label	pos	wks
3 Aug 96		**TO YOU I BESTOW** *Epic MUNDY 1CD*	60	1
5 Oct 96		**LIFE'S A CINCH** *Epic MUNDY 2CD*	75	1

MUNGO JERRY (359 Top 500) *London-based good-time jug band, fronted by singer / songwriter Ray Dorset, b. 21 Mar 1946, Middlesex, UK. 'In the Summertime', the first three-track No.1, sold seven million worldwide, and their first two singles topped the chart. Dorset also penned Kelly Marie's No.1, 'Feels Like I'm In Love' (88 WEEKS)*

Date		Title / Label	pos	wks
6 Jun 70	★	**IN THE SUMMERTIME** *Dawn DNX 2502*	1	20
6 Feb 71		**BABY JUMP** *Dawn DNX 2505*	32	1
20 Feb 71	★	**BABY JUMP (re-entry)** *Dawn DNX 2505*	1	12
29 May 71	●	**LADY ROSE** *Dawn DNX 2510*	5	12
18 Sep 71		**YOU DON'T HAVE TO BE IN THE ARMY TO FIGHT IN THE WAR** *Dawn DNX 2513*	13	8
22 Apr 72		**OPEN UP** *Dawn DNX 2514*	21	8
7 Jul 73	●	**ALRIGHT ALRIGHT ALRIGHT** *Dawn DNS 1037*	3	12
10 Nov 73		**WILD LOVE** *Dawn DNS 1051*	32	5
6 Apr 74		**LONG LEGGED WOMAN DRESSED IN BLACK** *Dawn DNS 1061*	13	9
29 May 99		**SUPPORT THE TOON - IT'S YOUR DUTY (EP)** *Saraja TOONCD 001* [1]	57	1

[1] Mungo Jerry and Toon Travellers

Tracks on Support the Toon - It's Your Duty (EP): Blaydon Races / Going to Wembley / Bottle of Beer

MUNICH MACHINE *Germany, male instrumental group (8 WEEKS)*

Date		Title / Label	pos	wks
10 Dec 77		**GET ON THE FUNK TRAIN** *Oasis OASIS 2*	41	4
4 Nov 78		**A WHITER SHADE OF PALE** *Oasis OASIS 5* [1]	42	4

[1] Munich Machine introducing Chris Bennett

David MUNROW – *See EARLY MUSIC CONSORT directed by David MUNROW*

MUPPETS *US, frog-fronted puppet ensemble (15 WEEKS)*

Date		Title / Label	pos	wks
28 May 77	●	**HALFWAY DOWN THE STAIRS** *Pye 7N 45698*	7	8
17 Dec 77		**THE MUPPET SHOW MUSIC HALL EP** *Pye 7NX 8004*	19	7

'Halfway Down the Stairs' is sung by Jerry Nelson as Kermit the Frog's nephew, Robin. Tracks on The Muppet Show Music Hall EP: Don't Dilly Dally On the Way / Waiting at the Church / The Boy in the Gallery / Wotcher (Knocked 'Em in the Old Kent Road)

Lydia MURDOCK *US, female vocalist (9 WEEKS)*

Date		Title / Label	pos	wks
24 Sep 83		**SUPERSTAR** *Korova KOW 30*	14	9

Shirley MURDOCK *US, female vocalist (2 WEEKS)*

Date		Title / Label	pos	wks
12 Apr 86		**TRUTH OR DARE** *Elektra EKR 36*	60	2

Eddie MURPHY – *See Shabba RANKS*

Noel MURPHY *Ireland, male vocalist (4 WEEKS)*

Date		Title / Label	pos	wks
27 Jun 87		**MURPHY AND THE BRICKS** *Murphy's STACK 1*	57	4

Roisin MURPHY – *See Boris DLUGOSCH*

Walter MURPHY and the BIG APPLE BAND
US, orchestra (9 WEEKS)

Date		Title / Label	pos	wks
10 Jul 76		**A FIFTH OF BEETHOVEN** *Private Stock PVT 59* ▲	28	9

Anne MURRAY *Canada, female vocalist (40 WEEKS)*

Date		Title / Label	pos	wks
24 Oct 70		**SNOWBIRD** *Capitol CL 15654*	23	17
21 Oct 72		**DESTINY** *Capitol CL 15734*	41	4
9 Dec 78		**YOU NEEDED ME** *Capitol CL 16011* ▲	22	14
21 Apr 79		**I JUST FALL IN LOVE AGAIN** *Capitol CL 16069*	58	2
19 Apr 80		**DAYDREAM BELIEVER** *Capitol CL 16123*	61	3

Keith MURRAY *US, male rapper (10 WEEKS)*

Date		Title / Label	pos	wks
2 Nov 96		**THE RHYME** *Jive JIVECD 407*	59	1

1982

IN THE YEAR IN WHICH ARGENTINA SURRENDERED TO THE UK IN THE FALKLANDS WAR, BRITAIN RESUMED FULL DIPLOMATIC CONTACT WITH THE VATICAN AFTER A BREAK OF 400 YEARS, AND 'THRILLER' WOULD GO ON TO BECOME THE WORLD'S BEST SELLING ALBUM, **MARC ALMOND** DESCRIBES THE PERILS OF A 1982 VIDEO SHOOT ...

“We completed a hat-trick of hits when our third single, 'Say Hello, Wave Goodbye', got to No.3. It was accompanied by one of the campest videos so far – set in an imaginary pink Parisian jazz cellar, complete with existentialists and Apache dancers. In some ways it was a sterilised version of Soft Cell's world. I sat on a stool at the bar, clad in black like a Garlandesque torch singer. At one hilarious point in the video I attempt an Apache dance with an extremely busty young woman. This had to be filmed several times, owing to Eileen's large breasts getting in my face and knocking off my false eyelashes (which I flickered at the camera at every opportunity). When it was first shown on 'Top of the Pops' the switchboard was jammed with complaining callers. Exactly what they found offensive was never clear to me. Was it me? My unashamed campness that translated as a type of sexuality? Most likely because without an interpretation in sexual terms there would have literally been nothing to complain about. At the end of the video I threw my arms into the air and gave that famous last note all I've got. It could for me have been the last note in the world ever!”

SINGLE OF THE YEAR 'Come On Eileen' Dexy's Midnight Runners
ALBUM OF THE YEAR 'Kids from Fame' Kids from Fame

27 Jun 98	**SHORTY (YOU KEEP PLAYIN' WITH MY MIND)** *Jive 0521212* [1]	22	3
14 Nov 98	**HOME ALONE** *Jive 0522392* [2]	17	5
5 Dec 98	**INCREDIBLE** *Jive 0522102* [3]	52	1

[1] Imajin featuring Keith Murray [2] R Kelly featuring Keith Murray [3] Keith Murray featuring LL Cool J

Pauline MURRAY and the INVISIBLE GIRLS *UK, female vocalist with male (really) vocal / instrumental group (2 WEEKS)* pos/wks

2 Aug 80	**DREAM SEQUENCE (ONE)** *Illusive IVE 1*	67	2

Ruby MURRAY (247 Top 500) *Britain's singing sensation of 1955, b. 29 Mar 1935, Belfast, d. 17 Dec 1996. The name of this nasal-sounding 'girl next door', who became the first artist to have five simultaneous Top 20 hits, has now become a part of the English language (rhyming slang for a curry) (114 WEEKS)* pos/wks

3 Dec 54 ●	**HEARTBEAT** *Columbia DB 3542*	3	16
28 Jan 55 ★	**SOFTLY, SOFTLY** *Columbia DB 3558*	1	22
4 Feb 55 ●	**HAPPY DAYS AND LONELY NIGHTS** *Columbia DB3577*	6	8
4 Mar 55 ●	**LET ME GO LOVER** *Columbia DB 3577*	5	7
18 Mar 55 ●	**IF ANYONE FINDS THIS, I LOVE YOU** *Columbia DB 3580* [1]	4	11
1 Jul 55 ●	**EVERMORE** *Columbia DB 3617*	3	17
8 Jul 55	**SOFTLY, SOFTLY (re-entry)** *Columbia DB 3558*	20	1
14 Oct 55 ●	**I'LL COME WHEN YOU CALL** *Columbia DB 3643*	6	7
31 Aug 56	**YOU ARE MY FIRST LOVE** *Columbia DB 3770*	16	4
5 Oct 56	**YOU ARE MY FIRST LOVE (re-entry)** *Columbia DB 3770*	21	1
12 Dec 58	**REAL LOVE** *Columbia DB 4192*	18	6
5 Jun 59 ●	**GOODBYE JIMMY, GOODBYE** *Columbia DB 4305*	10	13
9 Oct 59	**GOODBYE JIMMY, GOODBYE (re-entry)** *Columbia DB 4305*	26	1

[1] Ruby Murray with Anne Warren

Junior MURVIN *Jamaica, male vocalist (9 WEEKS)* pos/wks

3 May 80	**POLICE AND THIEVES** *Island WIP 6539*	23	9

MUSE *UK, male vocal / instrumental group (27 WEEKS)* pos/wks

26 Jun 99	**UNO** *Mushroom / Taste Media MUSH 50CDS*	73	1
18 Sep 99	**CAVE** *Mushroom / Taste Media MUSH 58CDS*	52	1
4 Dec 99	**MUSCLE MUSEUM** *Mushroom / Taste Media MUSH 66CDS*	43	2
4 Mar 00	**SUNBURN** *Mushroom / Taste Media MUSH 68CDS*	22	2
17 Jun 00	**UNINTENDED** *Mushroom / Taste Media MUSH 72CDS*	20	4
21 Oct 00	**MUSCLE MUSEUM (re-issue)** *Mushroom / Taste Media MUSH 84CDS*	25	3
24 Mar 01	**PLUG IN BABY** *Mushroom / Taste Media MUSH 89CDS*	11	5
16 Jun 01	**NEW BORN** *Mushroom / Taste Media MUSH 92CDS*	12	4
1 Sep 01	**BLISS** *Mushroom / Taste Media MUSH 96CDS*	22	2
1 Dec 01	**HYPER MUSIC / FEELING GOOD** *Mushroom MUSH 97CDS*	24	3

MUSIC and MYSTERY featuring Gwen McCRAE *UK, male production group and US, female vocalist (3 WEEKS)* pos/wks

13 Feb 93	**ALL THIS LOVE I'M GIVING** *KTDA CDKTDA 2*	36	3

MUSIC RELIEF '94 *UK, male / female vocal / instrumental group (1 WEEK)* pos/wks

5 Nov 94	**WHAT'S GOING ON** *Jive RWANDACD 1*	70	1

MUSICAL YOUTH *UK, male vocal / instrumental group – lead vocal Dennis Seaton (55 WEEKS)* pos/wks

25 Sep 82 ★	**PASS THE DUTCHIE** *MCA YOU 1*	1	12
20 Nov 82	**YOUTH OF TODAY** *MCA YOU 2*	13	9
8 Jan 83	**PASS THE DUTCHIE (re-entry)** *MCA YOU 1*	65	1
12 Feb 83 ●	**NEVER GONNA GIVE YOU UP** *MCA YOU 3*	6	10
16 Apr 83	**HEARTBREAKER** *MCA YOU 4*	44	3
9 Jul 83	**TELL ME WHY** *MCA YOU 5*	33	6
22 Oct 83	**007** *MCA YOU 6*	26	6
14 Jan 84	**SIXTEEN** *MCA YOU 7*	23	8

See also Donna SUMMER

MUSIQUE *US, female vocal group – Nick Hanson and Moussa Clarke (12 WEEKS)* pos/wks

18 Nov 78	**IN THE BUSH** *CBS 6791*	16	12

MUSIQUE VS U2 *UK, male production duo Nick Hanson and Moussa Clarke and Ireland, male vocal / instrumental group (5 WEEKS)* pos/wks

2 Jun 01	**NEW YEAR'S DUB** *Serious SERR 030CD*	15	4
14 Jul 01	**NEW YEAR'S DUB (re-entry)** *Serious SERR 030CD*	75	1

See also PF PROJECT featuring Ewan McGREGOR

MUSTAFAS – *See STAIFFI and his MUSTAFAS*

MUTANT DISCO – *See PHATS AND SMALL*

MUTINY UK *UK, male production duo – Dylan Barnes and Rob Davy (3 WEEKS)* pos/wks

19 May 01	**SECRETS** *Sunflower VCRD 86* [1]	47	1
25 Aug 01	**VIRUS** *VC Recordings VCRD 91*	42	2

[1] Vocals by Lorraine Cato

See also HELICOPTER

MXM *Italy, male / female vocal / instrumental group (1 WEEK)* pos/wks

2 Jun 90	**NOTHING COMPARES 2 U** *London LON 267*	68	1

MY BLOODY VALENTINE *UK, male / female vocal / instrumental group (5 WEEKS)* pos/wks

5 May 90	**SOON** *Creation CRE 073*	41	3
16 Feb 91	**TO HERE KNOWS WHEN** *Creation CRE 085*	29	2

MY LIFE STORY *UK, male / female vocal / instrumental group (12 WEEKS)* pos/wks

17 Aug 96	**12 REASONS WHY I LOVE HER** *Parlophone CDR 6442*	32	2
9 Nov 96	**SPARKLE** *Parlophone CDR 6450*	34	2
1 Mar 97	**THE KING OF KISSINGDOM** *Parlophone CDRS 6457*	35	1
17 May 97	**STRUMPET** *Parlophone CDR 6464*	27	2
23 Aug 97	**DUCHESS** *Parlophone CDR 6474*	39	1
19 Jun 99	**IT'S A GIRL THING** *IT ITR 001*	37	2
30 Oct 99	**EMPIRE LINE** *IT ITR 003*	58	1
19 Feb 00	**WALK / DON'T WALK** *IT ITR 007*	48	1

MY VITRIOL *UK, male / female vocal / instrumental group (6 WEEKS)* pos/wks

22 Jul 00	**CEMENTED SHOES** *Infectious INFECT 89CDS*	65	1
11 Nov 00	**PIECES** *Infectious INFECT 94CDS*	56	1
24 Feb 01	**ALWAYS YOUR WAY** *Infectious INFECT 95CDS*	31	2
19 May 01	**GROUNDED** *Infectious INFECT 97CD*	29	2

MYA (499 Top 500) *Hip hop female vocalist b. 10 Oct 1979, Mya Harrison, Washington DC, US. 'Lady Marmalade', the 900th No.1, is the only song to top the UK and US chart twice (71 WEEKS)* pos/wks

27 Jun 98 ●	**GHETTO SUPASTAR (THIS IS WHAT YOU ARE)** *Interscope IND 95593* [1]	2	17
12 Dec 98 ●	**TAKE ME THERE** *Interscope IND 95620* [2]	7	9
17 Apr 99	**GIRLFRIEND/BOYFRIEND** *Interscope IND 95640* [3]	11	7
10 Feb 01 ●	**CASE OF THE EX** *Interscope 4974772*	3	11
24 Mar 01	**GIRLS DEM SUGAR** *Virgin VUSCD 173* [4]	13	5
9 Jun 01	**FREE** *Interscope 4975002*	11	6
30 Jun 01 ★	**LADY MARMALADE** *Interscope / Polydor 4975612* [5] ■ ▲	1	16

[1] Pras Michel featuring Ol' Dirty Bastard introducing Mya [2] BLACKstreet and Mya featuring Mase and Blinky Blink [3] BLACKstreet with Janet [4] Beenie Man featuring Mya [5] Christina Aguilera, Lil' Kim, Mya and Pink

Tim MYCROFT – *See SOUNDS NICE featuring Tim MYCROFT*

Alicia MYERS *US, female vocalist (3 WEEKS)* pos/wks

1 Sep 84	**YOU GET THE BEST FROM ME (SAY, SAY, SAY)** *MCA MCA 914*	58	3

Billie MYERS *UK, female vocalist (12 WEEKS)* pos/wks

11 Apr 98	●	**KISS THE RAIN** *Universal UND 56182*	4	9
25 Jul 98		**TELL ME** *Universal UND 56201*	28	3

Richard MYHILL *UK, male vocalist (9 WEEKS)* pos/wks

1 Apr 78		**IT TAKES TWO TO TANGO** *Mercury 6007 167*	17	9

Alannah MYLES *Canada, female vocalist (17 WEEKS)* pos/wks

17 Mar 90	●	**BLACK VELVET** *East West A 8742* ▲	2	15
16 Jun 90		**LOVE IS** *East West A 8918*	61	2

Marie MYRIAM *France, female vocalist (4 WEEKS)* pos/wks

28 May 77		**L'OISEAU ET L'ENFANT** *Polydor 2056 634*	42	4

MYRON *US male vocalist (1 WEEK)* pos/wks

22 Nov 97		**WE CAN GET DOWN** *Island Black Music CID 677*	74	1

MYSTERIANS – *See ? (QUESTION MARK) and the MYSTERIANS*

MYSTERY *Holland, male production duo (1 WEEK)* pos/wks

6 Oct 01		**MYSTERY** *Inferno CDFERN 42*	56	1

MYSTI – *See CAMOUFLAGE featuring MYSTI*

MYSTIC MERLIN *US, male vocal / instrumental group (9 WEEKS)* pos/wks

26 Apr 80		**JUST CAN'T GIVE YOU UP** *Capitol CL 16133*	20	9

MYSTIC 3 *UK / Italy, male production group (aka Blockster) (1 WEEK)* pos/wks

24 Jun 00		**SOMETHING'S GOIN' ON** *Rulin RULIN 2CDS*	63	1

MYSTICA *Israel, male production trio (2 WEEKS)* pos/wks

24 Jan 98		**EVER REST** *Perfecto PERF 152CD*	62	1
9 May 98		**AFRICAN HORIZON** *Perfecto PERF 161CD*	59	1

MYSTIKAL *US, male rapper – Michael Tyler (16 WEEKS)* pos/wks

9 Dec 00		**SHAKE YA ASS** *Jive 9251552*	30	5
17 Feb 01	●	**STUTTER** *Jive 9251632* [1] ▲	7	8
3 Mar 01		**DANGER (BEEN SO LONG)** *Jive 9251722* [2]	28	3

[1] Joe featuring Mystikal [2] Mystikal featuring Nivea

See also Mariah CAREY

MYTOWN *Ireland, male vocal group (2 WEEKS)* pos/wks

13 Mar 99		**PARTY ALL NIGHT** *Universal UND 56231*	22	2

MZ MAY – *See DREEM TEEM*

N

N-JOI *UK, male instrumental / production group (28 WEEKS)* pos/wks

27 Oct 90		**ANTHEM** *Deconstruction PB 44041*	45	5
2 Mar 91		**ADRENALIN (EP)** *Deconstruction PT 44344*	23	5
6 Apr 91	●	**ANTHEM (re-issue)** *Deconstruction PB 44445*	8	8
22 Feb 92		**LIVE IN MANCHESTER (PARTS 1 + 2)** *Deconstruction PT 45252*	12	5
24 Jul 93		**THE DRUMSTRUCK (EP)** *Deconstruction 74321154832*	33	3
17 Dec 94		**PAPILLON** *Deconstruction 74321252132*	70	1
8 Jul 95		**BAD THINGS** *Deconstruction 74321277292*	57	1

Tracks on Adrenalin (EP): Adrenalin / The Kraken / Rhythm Zone / Phoenix. Tracks on The Drumstruck (EP): The Void / Boom Bass / Drumstruck

N'n'G featuring KALLAGHAN
UK, male / female production / vocal group (6 WEEKS) pos/wks

1 Apr 00		**RIGHT BEFORE MY EYES** *Urban Heat UHTCD 003*	12	6

'N SYNC *US, male vocal group (66 WEEKS)* pos/wks

13 Sep 97		**TEARIN' UP MY HEART** *Arista 74321505152*	40	2
22 Nov 97		**I WANT YOU BACK** *Arista 74321541122*	62	1
27 Feb 99	●	**I WANT YOU BACK (re-issue)** *Transcontinental / Northwestside 74321646972*	5	8
8 May 99		**I WANT YOU BACK (re-entry of re-issue)** *Transcontinental / Northwestside 74321646972*	62	2
26 Jun 99	●	**TEARIN' UP MY HEART (re-issue)** *Northwestside / Arista 74321675832*	9	8
11 Sep 99		**TEARIN' UP MY HEART (re-entry of re-issue)** *Northwestside / Arista 74321675832*	73	2
8 Jan 00		**MUSIC OF MY HEART** *Epic 6685272* [1]	34	3
11 Mar 00	●	**BYE BYE BYE** *Jive 9250202*	3	8
22 Jul 00		**I'LL NEVER STOP** *Jive 9250762*	13	6
16 Sep 00	●	**IT'S GONNA BE ME** *Jive 9251082* ▲	9	8
2 Dec 00		**THIS I PROMISE YOU** *Jive 9251302*	21	7
21 Jul 01	●	**POP** *Jive 9252422*	9	8
8 Dec 01		**GONE** *Jive 9252772*	24	3

[1] 'N Sync / Gloria Estefan

N-TRANCE (481 Top 500) *Producers Dale Longworth and Kevin O'Toole are the nucleus of this multi-faceted Manchester act who emerged from the trance scene (73 WEEKS)* pos/wks

7 May 94		**SET YOU FREE** *All Around the World CDGLOBE 124* [1]	39	4
22 Oct 94		**TURN UP THE POWER** *All Around the World CDGLOBE 125*	23	3
14 Jan 95	●	**SET YOU FREE (re-mix)** *All Around the World CDGLOBE 126*	2	15
16 Sep 95	●	**STAYIN' ALIVE** *All Around the World CDGLOBE 131* [2]	2	11
24 Feb 96		**ELECTRONIC PLEASURE** *All Around the World CDGLOBE 135*	11	4
5 Apr 97		**D.I.S.C.O.** *All Around the World CDGLOBE 153*	11	6
23 Aug 97		**THE MIND OF THE MACHINE** *All Around the World CDGLOBE 159*	15	4
1 Nov 97	●	**DA YA THINK I'M SEXY** *All Around the World CDGLOBE 150* [3]	7	10
12 Sep 98		**PARADISE CITY** *All Around the World CDGLOBE 140*	28	3
19 Dec 98		**TEARS IN THE RAIN** *All Around the Globe CDGLOBE 185*	53	1
20 May 00		**SHAKE YA BODY** *All Around the World CDGLOBE 204*	37	1
22 Sep 01	●	**SET YOU FREE (2nd re-mix)** *All Around the World CDGLOBE 242*	4	11

[1] N-Trance featuring Kelly Llorenna [2] N-Trance featuring Ricardo Da Force [3] N-Trance featuring Rod Stewart

Although she is vocalist on all versions of 'Set You Free' Kelly Llorenna is given label credit only on the first entry. Similarly, Ricardo da Force appears on several tracks but receives label credit only for 'Stayin' Alive'

N-TYCE *UK, female vocal group (15 WEEKS)* pos/wks

5 Jul 97		**HEY DJ! (PLAY THAT SONG)** *Telstar CDSTAS 2885*	20	2
13 Sep 97		**WE COME TO PARTY** *Telstar CDSTAS 2915*	12	4
28 Feb 98		**TELEFUNKIN'** *Telstar CDSTAS 2944*	16	5
6 Jun 98		**BOOM BOOM** *Telstar CDSTAS 2971*	18	4

Jimmy NAIL (479 Top 500) *Singer / songwriter, b. James Michael Aloysius Bradford, 1954, Newcastle, UK, whose R&B mixed with a Geordie take on country provided a flip-side to his acting career which included key characters in both 'Auf Wiedersehen Pet' and 'Spender'. His longest stay on the charts was courtesy of another TV series, 'Crocodile Shoes', in which he combined acting and singing (73 WEEKS)* pos/wks

27 Apr 85	●	**LOVE DON'T LIVE HERE ANYMORE** *Virgin VS 764*	3	11
11 Jul 92	★	**AIN'T NO DOUBT** *East West YZ 686*	1	12
3 Oct 92		**LAURA** *East West YZ 702*	58	2
26 Nov 94	●	**CROCODILE SHOES** *East West YZ 867CD*	4	13
11 Feb 95		**COWBOY DREAMS** *East West YZ 878CD*	13	7

11 Mar 95		CROCODILE SHOES (re-entry) *East West YZ 867CD*	68	3
8 Apr 95		CROCODILE SHOES (2nd re-entry) *East West YZ 867CD*	56	4
6 May 95		CALLING OUT YOUR NAME *East West YZ 935CD*	65	1
28 Oct 95		BIG RIVER *East West EW 008CD*	18	5
23 Dec 95		LOVE *East West EW 018CD*	33	4
3 Feb 96		BIG RIVER (re-mix) *East West EW 024CD*	72	2
16 Nov 96		COUNTRY BOY *East West EW 070CD*	25	8
21 Nov 98		THE FLAME STILL BURNS *London LONCD 420* [1]	47	1

[1] Jimmy Nail with Strange Fruit

NAKATOMI *UK, male / female production group (2 WEEKS)* pos/wks

7 Feb 98		CHILDREN OF THE NIGHT *Peach PCHCD 006*	47	2

NAKED EYES *UK, male vocal / instrumental duo (3 WEEKS)* pos/wks

23 Jul 83		ALWAYS SOMETHING THERE TO REMIND ME *RCA 348*	59	3

NALIN I.N.C. *Germany, male production duo (1 WEEK)* pos/wks

28 Mar 98		PLANET VIOLET *Logic 74321565702*	51	1

See also NALIN & KANE

NALIN & KANE *Germany, male DJ / production duo – Andy Nalin and Harry Cane (6 WEEKS)* pos/wks

1 Nov 97		BEACHBALL *ffrr FCD 318*	48	1
3 Oct 98		BEACHBALL (re-mix) *LONDON FCD349*	17	5

See also NALIN I.N.C.

NANA – *See ARCHITECHS*

NAPOLEON XIV *US, male vocalist – Jerry Samuels (10 WEEKS)* pos/wks

4 Aug 66	●	THEY'RE COMING TO TAKE ME AWAY, HA-HAAA! *Warner Bros. WB 5831*	4	10

NARADA – *See Narada Michael WALDEN*

Michelle NARINE – *See BIG BASS vs Michelle NARINE*

NAS *US, male rapper – Nasir Jones (30 WEEKS)* pos/wks

28 May 94		IT AIN'T HARD TO TELL *Columbia 6604702*	64	1
17 Aug 96		IF I RULED THE WORLD *Columbia 6634022*	12	7
25 Jan 97		STREET DREAMS *Columbia 6641302*	12	4
14 Jun 97		HEAD OVER HEELS *Epic 6645942* [1]	18	3
29 May 99		HATE ME NOW *Columbia 6672562* [2]	14	6
15 Jan 00		NASTRADAMUS *Columbia 6685572*	24	3
22 Jan 00		HOT BOYZ *Elektra E 7002CD* [3]	18	3
21 Apr 01		OOCHIE WALLY *Columbia 67010852* [4]	30	3

[1] Allure featuring NAS [2] Nas featuring Puff Daddy [3] Missy 'Misdemeanor' Elliott featuring Nas, Eve and Q Tip [4] QB Finest featuring Nas and Bravehearts

Johnny NASH (277 Top 500) *US singer / songwriter / actor and label co-owner, b. 19 Aug 1940, Texas. This versatile vocalist first charted in his homeland in 1957. After recording in Jamaica in the late 1960s, he helped to popularise reggae on both sides of the Atlantic and introduced the public to Bob Marley's songs (106 WEEKS)* pos/wks

7 Aug 68	●	HOLD ME TIGHT *Regal Zonophone RZ 3010*	5	16
8 Jan 69	●	YOU GOT SOUL *Major Minor MM 586*	6	12
2 Apr 69	●	CUPID *Major Minor MM 603*	6	11
25 Jun 69		CUPID (re-entry) *Major Minor MM 603*	50	1
1 Apr 72		STIR IT UP *CBS 7800*	13	12
24 Jun 72	●	I CAN SEE CLEARLY NOW *CBS 8113* ▲	5	15
7 Oct 72	●	THERE ARE MORE QUESTIONS THAN ANSWERS *CBS 8351*	9	9
14 Jun 75	★	TEARS ON MY PILLOW *CBS 3220*	1	11
11 Oct 75		LET'S BE FRIENDS *CBS 3597*	42	3
12 Jun 76		(WHAT A) WONDERFUL WORLD *Epic EPC 4294*	25	7
9 Nov 85		ROCK ME BABY *2000 AD FED 19*	47	4
15 Apr 89		I CAN SEE CLEARLY NOW (re-mix) *Epic JN 1*	54	5

Leigh NASH – *See DELERIUM*

NASHVILLE TEENS *UK, male vocal / instrumental group (37 WEEKS)* pos/wks

9 Jul 64	●	TOBACCO ROAD *Decca F 11930*	6	13
22 Oct 64	●	GOOGLE EYE *Decca F 12000*	10	11
4 Mar 65		FIND MY WAY BACK HOME *Decca F 12089*	34	6
20 May 65		THIS LITTLE BIRD *Decca F 12143*	38	4
3 Feb 66		THE HARD WAY *Decca F 12316*	45	2
24 Feb 66		THE HARD WAY (re-entry) *Decca F 12316*	48	1

NATASHA *UK, female vocalist – Natasha England (16 WEEKS)* pos/wks

5 Jun 82	●	IKO IKO *Towerbell TOW 22*	10	11
4 Sep 82		THE BOOM BOOM ROOM *Towerbell TOW 25*	44	5

Ultra NATÉ *US, female vocalist – Ultra Naté Wyche (39 WEEKS)* pos/wks

9 Dec 89		IT'S OVER NOW *Eternal YZ 440*	62	3
23 Feb 91		IS IT LOVE? *Eternal YZ 509* [1]	71	1
29 Jan 94		SHOW ME *Warner Bros. W 0219CD*	62	1
14 Jun 97	●	FREE *AM:PM 5822432*	4	17
24 Jan 98		FREE (re-mix) *AM:PM 5825012*	33	2
18 Apr 98	●	FOUND A CURE *AM:PM 5826452*	6	7
25 Jul 98		NEW KIND OF MEDICINE *AM:PM 5827492*	14	5
22 Jul 00		DESIRE *AM:PM CDAMPM133*	40	2
9 Jun 01		GET IT UP (THE FEELING) *AM:PM CDAMPM 140*	51	1

[1] Basement Boys present Ultra Naté

NATIVE *UK, male production duo (2 WEEKS)* pos/wks

10 Feb 01		FEEL THE DRUMS *Slinky Music SLINKY 009CD*	46	2

NATURAL BORN CHILLERS *UK, male production duo (3 WEEKS)* pos/wks

1 Nov 97		ROCK THE FUNKY BEAT *East West EW 138CD1*	30	3

NATURAL BORN GROOVES *Belgium, male DJ / production duo – Burn Boon and Jaco van Rijsvijck (3 WEEKS)* pos/wks

2 Nov 96		FORERUNNER *XL XLS 76CD*	64	1
19 Apr 97		GROOVEBIRD *Positiva CDTIV 75*	21	2

NATURAL LIFE *UK, male / female vocal / instrumental group (3 WEEKS)* pos/wks

7 Mar 92		NATURAL LIFE *Tribe NLIFE 3*	47	3

NATURAL SELECTION *US, male vocal / instrumental duo (2 WEEKS)* pos/wks

9 Nov 91		DO ANYTHING *East West A 8724*	69	2

NATURALS *UK, male vocal / instrumental group (9 WEEKS)* pos/wks

20 Aug 64		I SHOULD HAVE KNOWN BETTER *Parlophone R 5165*	24	9

David NAUGHTON *US, male vocalist (6 WEEKS)* pos/wks

25 Aug 79		MAKIN' IT *RSO 32*	44	6

NAUGHTY BY NATURE *US, male rap group (17 WEEKS)* pos/wks

9 Nov 91		O.P.P. *Big Life BLR 62*	73	1
20 Jun 92		O.P.P. (re-issue) *Big Life BLR 74*	35	3
30 Jan 93		HIP HOP HOORAY *Big Life BLRD 89*	22	3
19 Jun 93		IT'S ON *Big Life BLRD 99*	48	2
27 Nov 93		HIP HOP HOORAY (re-mix) *Big Life BLRDA 104*	20	4
29 Apr 95		FEEL ME FLOW *Big Life BLRD 115*	23	3
11 Sep 99		JAMBOREE *Arista 74321692882* [1]	51	1

[1] Naughty By Nature featuring Zhané

NAVIGATOR – *See FREESTYLERS*

Maria NAYLER *UK, female vocalist (26 WEEKS)* pos/wks

9 Mar 96		BE AS ONE *Deconstruction 74321342962* [1]	17	4
16 Nov 96	●	ONE & ONE *Deconstruction 74321427692* [2]	3	17
7 Mar 98		NAKED AND SACRED *Deconstruction 74321534242*	32	3

		pos	wks
5 Sep 98	**WILL YOU BE WITH ME / LOVE IS THE GOD** *Deconstruction 74321591772*	65	1
27 May 00	**ANGRY SKIES** *Deconstruction 74321759492*	42	1

[1] Sasha and Maria [2] Robert Miles featuring Maria Nayler

NAZARETH (466 Top 500) *Earthy but versatile rock band formed 1969 in Dunfermline, Scotland, who throughout their 30-year career have been led by Dan McCafferty (v). Sole US Top 10 hit 'Love Hurts' also spent a record-shattering 60 weeks on the Norwegian chart (75 WEEKS)*

		pos	wks
5 May 73 ●	**BROKEN DOWN ANGEL** *Mooncrest MOON 1*	9	11
21 Jul 73 ●	**BAD BAD BOY** *Mooncrest MOON 9*	10	9
13 Oct 73	**THIS FLIGHT TONIGHT** *Mooncrest MOON 14*	11	13
23 Mar 74	**SHANGHAI'D IN SHANGHAI** *Mooncrest MOON 22*	41	4
14 Jun 75	**MY WHITE BICYCLE** *Mooncrest MOON 47*	14	8
15 Nov 75	**HOLY ROLLER** *Mountain TOP 3*	36	4
24 Sep 77	**HOT TRACKS (EP)** *Mountain NAZ 1*	15	11
18 Feb 78	**GONE DEAD TRAIN** *Mountain NAZ 002*	49	2
13 May 78	**PLACE IN YOUR HEART** *Mountain TOP 37*	70	1
27 May 78	**PLACE IN YOUR HEART (re-entry)** *Mountain TOP 37*	74	1
27 Jan 79	**MAY THE SUNSHINE** *Mountain NAZ 003*	22	8
28 Jul 79	**STAR** *Mountain TOP 45*	54	3

Tracks on Hot Tracks (EP): Love Hurts / This Flight Tonight / Broken Down Angel / Hair of the Dog

NAZLYN – *See M-BEAT*

Me'Shell NDEGEOCELLO *US, female vocalist / instrumentalist – bass (5 WEEKS)*

		pos	wks
12 Feb 94	**IF THAT'S YOUR BOYFRIEND (HE WASN'T LAST NIGHT)** *Maverick W 0223CD1*	74	1
3 Sep 94	**WILD NIGHT** *Mercury MERCD 409* [1]	34	3
1 Mar 97	**NEVER MISS THE WATER** *Reprise W 0393CD* [2]	59	1

[1] John Mellencamp featuring Me'Shell Ndegeocello [2] Chaka Khan featuring Me'Shell Ndegeocello

Youssou N'DOUR *Senegal, male vocalist (35 WEEKS)*

		pos	wks
3 Jun 89	**SHAKIN' THE TREE** *Virgin VS 1167* [1]	61	3
22 Dec 90	**SHAKIN' THE TREE (re-issue)** *Virgin VS 1322* [1]	57	4
25 Jun 94 ●	**7 SECONDS** *Columbia 6605082* [2]	3	21
24 Dec 94	**7 SECONDS (re-entry)** *Columbia 6605082* [2]	54	4
14 Jan 95	**UNDECIDED** *Columbia 6609712*	53	2
10 Oct 98	**HOW COME** *Interscope IND 95598* [3]	52	1

[1] Youssou N'Dour and Peter Gabriel [2] Youssou N'Dour (featuring Neneh Cherry) [3] Youssou N'Dour and Canibus

The re-issue of 'Shaking the Tree' was listed with its flip side, 'Solsbury Hill' by Peter Gabriel

NEARLY GOD *UK, male / female vocal / instrumental group (2 WEEKS)*

		pos	wks
20 Apr 96	**POEMS** *Durban Poison DPCD 3*	28	2

Terry NEASON *UK, female vocalist (1 WEEK)*

		pos	wks
25 Jun 94	**LIFEBOAT** *WEA YZ 830*	72	1

NEBULA II *UK, male instrumental / production group (3 WEEKS)*

		pos	wks
1 Feb 92	**SEANCE / ATHEAMA** *Reinforced RIVET 1211*	55	2
16 May 92	**FLATLINERS** *J4M 12NEBULA 2*	54	1

NED'S ATOMIC DUSTBIN *UK, male vocal / instrumental group (24 WEEKS)*

		pos	wks
14 Jul 90	**KILL YOUR TELEVISION** *Chapter 22 CHAP 48*	53	2
27 Oct 90	**UNTIL YOU FIND OUT** *Chapter 22 CHAP 52*	51	2
9 Mar 91	**HAPPY** *Columbia 6566807*	16	4
21 Sep 91	**TRUST** *Furtive 6574627*	21	4
10 Oct 92	**NOT SLEEPING AROUND** *Furtive 6583866*	19	3
5 Dec 92	**INTACT** *Furtive 6588166*	36	6
25 Mar 95	**ALL I ASK OF MYSELF IS THAT I HOLD TOGETHER** *Furtive 6613565*	33	2
15 Jul 95	**STUCK** *Furtive 6620562*	64	1

NEEDLE DAMAGE – *See DJ DAN presents NEEDLE DAMAGE*

Joey NEGRO *UK, male producer – Dave Lee (15 WEEKS)*

		pos	wks
16 Nov 91	**DO WHAT YOU FEEL** *Ten TEN 391*	36	3
21 Dec 91	**REACHIN' (re-mix)** *Republic LIC 160* [1]	70	1
18 Jul 92	**ENTER YOUR FANTASY (EP)** *Ten TEN 397*	35	3
25 Sep 93	**WHAT HAPPENED TO THE MUSIC** *Virgin VSCD 1466*	51	2
19 Feb 00 ●	**MUST BE THE MUSIC** *Incentive CENT 4CDS* [2]	8	5
16 Sep 00	**SATURDAY** *Yola YOLA CDX03* [2]	41	1

[1] Joey Negro presents Phase II [2] Joey Negro featuring Taka Boom

Tracks on Enter Your Fantasy (EP): Love Fantasy / Get Up / Enter Your Mind / Everybody

See also Li KWAN; RAVEN MAIZE; AKABU featuring Linda CLIFFORD; JAKATTA; HED BOYS

neil *UK, male actor/ vocalist – Nigel Planer (10 WEEKS)*

		pos	wks
14 Jul 84 ●	**HOLE IN MY SHOE** *WEA YZ 10*	2	10

Vince NEIL *US, male vocalist (1 WEEK)*

		pos	wks
3 Oct 92	**YOU'RE INVITED (BUT YOUR FRIEND CAN'T COME)** *Hollywood HWD 123*	63	1

NEJA *Italy, female vocalist (1 WEEK)*

		pos	wks
26 Sep 98	**RESTLESS (I KNOW YOU KNOW)** *Panorama CDPAN 1*	47	1

NEK *Italy, male vocalist (1 WEEK)*

		pos	wks
29 Aug 98	**LAURA** *Coalition COLA 054CD*	59	1

NELLY *US, male rapper – Cornell Haynes (31 WEEKS)*

		pos	wks
11 Nov 00 ●	**(HOT S**T) COUNTRY GRAMMAR** *Universal MCSTD 40242*	7	9
24 Feb 01	**EI** *Universal MCSTD 40249*	11	5
19 May 01 ●	**RIDE WIT ME** *Universal MCSTD 40252* [1]	3	12
15 Sep 01	**BATTER UP** *Universal MCSTD 40261* [2]	28	2
27 Oct 01	**WHERE THE PARTY AT?** *Columbia MCSTD 6719012* [3]	25	3

[1] Nelly featuring City Spud [2] Nelly and St Lunatics [3] Jagged Edge featuring Nelly

NELSON *US, male vocal duo (3 WEEKS)*

		pos	wks
27 Oct 90	**(CAN'T LIVE WITHOUT YOUR) LOVE AND AFFECTION** *DGC GEF 82* ▲	54	3

Bill NELSON *UK, male vocalist / instrumentalist – guitar and synthesizer (12 WEEKS)*

		pos	wks
24 Feb 79	**FURNITURE MUSIC** *Harvest HAR 5176* [1]	59	3
5 May 79	**REVOLT INTO STYLE** *Harvest HAR 5183* [1]	69	2
5 Jul 80	**DO YOU DREAM IN COLOUR?** *Cocteau COQ 1*	52	4
13 Jun 81	**YOUTH OF NATION ON FIRE** *Mercury WILL 2*	73	3

[1] Bill Nelson's Red Noise

See also BE BOP DELUXE

Phyllis NELSON *US, female vocalist (24 WEEKS)*

		pos	wks
23 Feb 85 ★	**MOVE CLOSER** *Carrere CAR 337*	1	21
21 May 94	**MOVE CLOSER (re-issue)** *EMI CDEMCT 9*	34	3

Ricky NELSON (149 Top 500) *TV star turned teen idol and later singer / songwriter, b. 8 May 1940, New Jersey, d. 31 Dec 1985. He was virtually raised on a US radio / TV family show. In the 1950s, he enjoyed sales on a par with Elvis Presley and Pat Boone. Both his father and his two sons also topped the US chart (1935 and 1990) (150 WEEKS)*

		pos	wks
21 Feb 58	**STOOD UP** *London HLP 8542*	27	1
7 Mar 58	**STOOD UP (re-entry)** *London HLP 8542*	29	1
22 Aug 58 ●	**POOR LITTLE FOOL** *London HLP 8670* ▲	4	13
7 Nov 58 ●	**SOMEDAY** *London HLP 8732*	9	13
21 Nov 58	**I GOT A FEELING** *London HLP 8732*	27	1

28 Nov 58	**POOR LITTLE FOOL (re-entry)** *London HLP 8670*	28	1
17 Apr 59 ●	**IT'S LATE** *London HLP 8817*	3	20
15 May 59	**NEVER BE ANYONE ELSE BUT YOU** *London HLP 8817*	19	1
5 Jun 59	**NEVER BE ANYONE ELSE BUT YOU (re-entry)** *London HLP 8817*	14	9
4 Sep 59	**SWEETER THAN YOU** *London HLP 8927*	19	3
11 Sep 59	**JUST A LITTLE TOO MUCH** *London HLP 8927*	11	8
15 Jan 60	**I WANNA BE LOVED** *London HLP 9021*	30	1
7 Jul 60	**YOUNG EMOTIONS** *London HLP 9121*	48	1
1 Jun 61 ●	**HELLO MARY LOU / TRAVELLIN' MAN** *London HLP 9347* ▲	2	18
16 Nov 61	**EVERLOVIN'** *London HLP 9440* [1]	23	5
29 Mar 62	**YOUNG WORLD** *London HLP 9524*	19	13
30 Aug 62	**TEENAGE IDOL** *London HLP 9583* [1]	39	4
17 Jan 63	**IT'S UP TO YOU** *London HLP 9648* [1]	22	9
17 Oct 63	**FOOLS RUSH IN** *Brunswick 05895* [1]	12	9
30 Jan 64	**FOR YOU** *Brunswick 05900* [1]	14	10
21 Oct 72	**GARDEN PARTY** *MCA MU 1165* [1]	41	4
24 Aug 91	**HELLO MARY LOU (GOODBYE HEART) (re-issue)** *Liberty EMCT 2*	45	5

[1] Rick Nelson

Sandy NELSON *US, male instrumentalist – drums (42 WEEKS)* pos/wks

		pos	wks
6 Nov 59 ●	**TEEN BEAT** *Top Rank JAR 197*	9	11
5 Feb 60	**TEEN BEAT (re-entry)** *Top Rank JAR 197*	25	1
14 Dec 61 ●	**LET THERE BE DRUMS** *London HLP 9466*	3	16
22 Mar 62	**DRUMS ARE MY BEAT** *London HLP 9521*	30	6
7 Jun 62	**DRUMMIN' UP A STORM** *London HLP 9558*	39	8

Shara NELSON *UK, female vocalist (23 WEEKS)* pos/wks

		pos	wks
24 Jul 93	**DOWN THAT ROAD** *Cooltempo CDCOOL 275*	19	6
18 Sep 93	**ONE GOODBYE IN TEN** *Cooltempo CDCOOL 279*	21	5
12 Feb 94	**UPTIGHT** *Cooltempo CDCOOL 286*	19	5
4 Jun 94	**NOBODY** *Cooltempo CDCOOL 290*	49	1
10 Sep 94	**INSIDE OUT / DOWN THAT ROAD (re-mix)** *Cooltempo CDCOOLX 295*	34	3
16 Sep 95	**ROUGH WITH THE SMOOTH** *Cooltempo CDCOOL 311*	30	2
5 Dec 98	**SENSE OF DANGER** *Pagan PAGAN 024CDS* [1]	61	1

[1] Presence featuring Shara Nelson

Shelley NELSON – *See TIN TIN OUT*

Willie NELSON *US, male vocalist (13 WEEKS)* pos/wks

		pos	wks
31 Jul 82	**ALWAYS ON MY MIND** *CBS A 2511*	49	3
7 Apr 84	**TO ALL THE GIRLS I'VE LOVED BEFORE** *CBS A 4252* [1]	17	10

[1] Julio Iglesias and Willie Nelson

NENA *Germany, female / male vocal / instrumental group – lead vocal Gabriele (Nena) Kerner (14 WEEKS)* pos/wks

		pos	wks
4 Feb 84 ★	**99 RED BALLOONS** *Epic A 4074*	1	12
5 May 84	**JUST A DREAM** *Epic H 3249*	70	2

N*E*R*D featuring Lee HARVEY and VITA *US, male vocal / production duo and US, male / female rappers (2 WEEKS)* pos/wks

		pos	wks
9 Jun 01	**LAPDANCE** *Virgin VUSCD 196*	33	2

NERIO'S DUBWORK – *See Darryl PANDY*

Frances NERO *US, female vocalist (9 WEEKS)* pos/wks

		pos	wks
13 Apr 91	**FOOTSTEPS FOLLOWING ME** *Debut DEBT 3109*	17	9

NERO and the GLADIATORS
UK, male instrumental group (6 WEEKS) pos/wks

		pos	wks
23 Mar 61	**ENTRY OF THE GLADIATORS** *Decca F 11329*	50	1
6 Apr 61	**ENTRY OF THE GLADIATORS (re-entry)** *Decca F 11329*	37	4
27 Jul 61	**IN THE HALL OF THE MOUNTAIN KING** *Decca F 11367*	48	1

Ann NESBY *US, female vocalist (3 WEEKS)* pos/wks

		pos	wks
21 Dec 96	**WITNESS (EP)** *AM:PM 5875612*	42	2
17 May 97	**HOLD ON (EP)** *AM:PM 5822332*	75	1

Tracks on Witness (EP): Can I Get a Witness / (mix) / In the Spirit / I'm Still Wearing Your Name. Tracks on Hold On (EP): Hold On (Mousse T's Uplifting Garage Edit) / Hold On (Mousse T's Hard Soul Remix) / Hold On (Klub Head Mix) / This Weekend (Laidback Mix)

Michael NESMITH *US, male vocalist (6 WEEKS)* pos/wks

		pos	wks
26 Mar 77	**RIO** *Island WIP 6373*	28	6

See also MONKEES

NETWORK *UK, male vocal / instrumental group (4 WEEKS)* pos/wks

		pos	wks
12 Dec 92	**BROKEN WINGS** *Chrysalis CHS 3923*	46	4

NEVADA *UK, male / female vocal / instrumental group (1 WEEK)* pos/wks

		pos	wks
8 Jan 83	**IN THE BLEAK MID WINTER** *Polydor POSP 203*	71	1

Robbie NEVIL *US, male vocalist (24 WEEKS)* pos/wks

		pos	wks
20 Dec 86 ●	**C'EST LA VIE** *Manhattan MT 14*	3	11
2 May 87	**DOMINOES** *Manhattan MT 19*	26	6
11 Jul 87	**WOT'S IT TO YA** *Manhattan MT 24*	43	7

Aaron NEVILLE – *See Linda RONSTADT; NEVILLE BROTHERS*

NEVILLE BROTHERS *US, male vocal / instrumental group (7 WEEKS)* pos/wks

		pos	wks
25 Nov 89	**WITH GOD ON OUR SIDE** *A & M AM 545*	47	6
7 Jul 90	**BIRD ON A WIRE** *A & M AM 568*	72	1

Jason NEVINS *US, male DJ / producer (24 WEEKS)* pos/wks

		pos	wks
21 Feb 98	**IT'S LIKE THAT (German import)** *Columbia 6652932* [1]	63	3
14 Mar 98	**IT'S LIKE THAT (US import)** *Columbia 6652932* [1]	65	1
21 Mar 98 ★	**IT'S LIKE THAT** *Sm:)e Communications SM 90652* [1] ◆ ■	1	16
18 Apr 98	**IT'S TRICKY (import)** *Epidrome EPD 6656982* [1]	74	1
26 Jun 99	**INSANE IN THE BRAIN** *INCredible INCRL 17CD* [2]	19	3

[1] Run-DMC vs Jason Nevins [2] Jason Nevins vs Cypress Hill

NEW ATLANTIC *UK, male instrumental / production duo - Richard Lloyd and Cameron Saunders (15 WEEKS)* pos/wks

		pos	wks
29 Feb 92	**I KNOW** *3 Beat 3BT 1*	12	7
3 Oct 92	**INTO THE FUTURE** *3 Beat 3BT 2* [1]	70	1
13 Feb 93	**TAKE OFF SOME TIME** *3 Beat 3BTCD 14*	64	1
26 Nov 94	**THE SUNSHINE AFTER THE RAIN** *Ffrreedom TABCD 223* [2]	26	6

[1] New Atlantic featuring Linda Wright [2] New Atlantic / U4EA featuring Berri

'The Sunshine After the Rain' was re-issued in 1995, credited simply to the vocalist Berri

NEW BOHEMIANS – *See Edie BRICKELL and the NEW BOHEMIANS*

NEW EDITION *US, male vocal group (36 WEEKS)* pos/wks

		pos	wks
16 Apr 83 ★	**CANDY GIRL** *London LON 21*	1	13
13 Aug 83	**POPCORN LOVE** *London LON 31*	43	5
23 Feb 85	**MR TELEPHONE MAN** *MCA MCA 938*	19	9
15 Apr 89	**CRUCIAL** *MCA MCA 23934*	70	1
10 Aug 96	**HIT ME OFF** *MCA MCSTD 48014*	20	4
7 Jun 97	**SOMETHING ABOUT YOU** *MCA MCSTD 48032*	16	4

See also BELL BIV DEVOE; Ralph TRESVANT; Bobby BROWN; Johnny GILL

NEW FOUND GLORY *US, male / female vocal group (1 WEEK)* pos/wks

		pos	wks
16 Jun 01	**HIT OR MISS (WAITED TOO LONG)** *MCA 1558232*	58	1

A NEW GENERATION
UK, male vocal / instrumental group (5 WEEKS) pos/wks

		pos	wks
26 Jun 68	**SMOKEY BLUE'S AWAY** *Spark SRL 1007*	38	5

NEW KIDS ON THE BLOCK (349 Top 500) *Highest earning boy band of all time: Jordan and Jon Knight, Donnie Wahlberg, Danny Wood, Joey McIntyre. Formed Boston, US, by producer / manager Maurice Starr as pop version of his act New Edition. In 1990, grossed reported $861 million and became the first group to score eight UK Top 10 entries in a year (90 WEEKS)*

Date		Title / Label	pos	wks
16 Sep 89		HANGIN' TOUGH *CBS BLOCK 1*	52	4
11 Nov 89	★	YOU GOT IT (THE RIGHT STUFF) *CBS BLOCK 2*	1	13
6 Jan 90	★	HANGIN' TOUGH (re-issue) *CBS BLOCK 3* ▲	1	9
17 Mar 90	●	I'LL BE LOVING YOU (FOREVER) *CBS BLOCK 4* ▲	5	8
12 May 90	●	COVER GIRL *CBS BLOCK 5*	4	8
16 Jun 90	●	STEP BY STEP *CBS BLOCK 6* ▲	2	7
4 Aug 90	●	TONIGHT *CBS BLOCK 7*	3	10
13 Oct 90	●	LET'S TRY AGAIN / DIDN'T I BLOW YOUR MIND *CBS BLOCK 8*	8	5
8 Dec 90	●	THIS ONE'S FOR THE CHILDREN *CBS BLOCK 9*	9	7
9 Feb 91		GAMES *CBS 6566267*	14	4
18 May 91		CALL IT WHAT YOU WANT *Columbia 6567857*	12	5
14 Dec 91	●	IF YOU GO AWAY *Columbia 6576667*	9	5
19 Feb 94		DIRTY DAWG *Columbia 6600362* [1]	27	3
26 Mar 94		NEVER LET YOU GO *Columbia 6602072* [1]	42	2

[1] NKOTB

NEW MODEL ARMY *UK, male vocal / instrumental group (33 WEEKS)*

Date		Title / Label	pos	wks
27 Apr 85		NO REST *EMI NMA 1*	28	5
3 Aug 85		BETTER THAN THEM / NO SENSE *EMI NMA 2*	49	2
30 Nov 85		BRAVE NEW WORLD *EMI NMA 3*	57	1
8 Nov 86		51ST STATE *EMI NMA 4*	71	2
28 Feb 87		POISON STREET *EMI NMA 5*	64	1
26 Sep 87		WHITE COATS (EP) *EMI NMA 6*	50	3
21 Jan 89		STUPID QUESTIONS *EMI NMA 7*	31	3
11 Mar 89		VAGABONDS *EMI NMA 8*	37	3
10 Jun 89		GREEN AND GREY *EMI NMA 9*	37	3
8 Sep 90		GET ME OUT *EMI NMA 10*	34	3
3 Nov 90		PURITY *EMI NMA 11*	61	2
8 Jun 91		SPACE *EMI NMA 12*	39	2
20 Feb 93		HERE COMES THE WAR *Epic 6589352*	25	2
24 Jul 93		LIVING IN THE ROSE (THE BALLADS EP) *Epic 6592492*	51	1

Better Than Them / No Sense are the lead tracks from The Acoustic EP which included the following tracks: Better Than Them / No Sense / Adrenalin / Trust. Tracks on White Coats (EP): White Coats / The Charge / Chinese Whispers / My Country. Tracks on Living in the Rose (The Ballads EP): Living in the Rose / Drummy B / Marry the Sea / Sleepwalking

NEW MUSIK *UK, male vocal / instrumental group (27 WEEKS)*

Date		Title / Label	pos	wks
6 Oct 79		STRAIGHT LINES *GTO GT 255*	53	5
19 Jan 80		LIVING BY NUMBERS *GTO GT 261*	13	8
26 Apr 80		THIS WORLD OF WATER *GTO GT 268*	31	7
12 Jul 80		SANCTUARY *GTO GT 275*	31	7

NEW ORDER (105 Top 500) *Innovative Mancunian group featuring three former members of critically acclaimed Joy Division: Bernard Sumner (v/g), Peter Hook (b), Stephen Morris (d), and augmented by Gillian Gilbert (k). 'Blue Monday' remains the UK's biggest-selling 12-inch single of all time (185 WEEKS)*

Date		Title / Label	pos	wks
14 Mar 81		CEREMONY *Factory FAC 33*	34	5
3 Oct 81		PROCESSION / EVERYTHING'S GONE GREEN *Factory FAC 53*	38	5
22 May 82		TEMPTATION *Factory FAC 63*	29	7
19 Mar 83		BLUE MONDAY *Factory FAC 73*	12	17
13 Aug 83	●	BLUE MONDAY (re-entry) *Factory FAC 73*	9	17
3 Sep 83		CONFUSION *Factory FAC 93*	12	7
7 Jan 84		BLUE MONDAY (2nd re-entry) *Factory FAC 73*	52	4
28 Apr 84		THIEVES LIKE US *Factory FAC 103*	18	5
25 May 85		THE PERFECT KISS *Factory FAC 123*	46	4
9 Nov 85		SUB-CULTURE *Factory FAC 133*	63	4
29 Mar 86		SHELLSHOCK *Factory FAC 143*	28	5
27 Sep 86		STATE OF THE NATION *Factory FAC 153*	30	3
27 Sep 86		THE PEEL SESSIONS (1ST JUNE 1982) *Strange Fruit SFPS 001*	54	1
15 Nov 86		BIZARRE LOVE TRIANGLE *Factory FAC 163*	56	2
1 Aug 87	●	TRUE FAITH *Factory FAC 183/7*	4	10
19 Dec 87		TOUCHED BY THE HAND OF GOD *Factory FAC 1937*	20	7
7 May 88	●	BLUE MONDAY (re-mix) *Factory FAC 737*	3	11
10 Dec 88		FINE TIME *Factory FAC 2237*	11	8
11 Mar 89		ROUND AND ROUND *Factory FAC 2637*	21	7
9 Sep 89		RUN 2 *Factory FAC 273*	49	2
2 Jun 90	★	WORLD IN MOTION . . . *Factory / MCA FAC 2937* [1]	1	12
17 Apr 93	●	REGRET *Centredate Co. NUOCD 1*	4	7
3 Jul 93		RUINED IN A DAY *Centredate Co. NUOCD 2*	22	4
4 Sep 93		WORLD (THE PRICE OF LOVE) *Centredate Co. NUOCD 3*	13	5
18 Dec 93		SPOOKY *Centredate Co. NUOCD 4*	22	4
19 Nov 94	●	TRUE FAITH (re-mix) *Centredate Co. NUOCD 5*	9	8
21 Jan 95		NINETEEN63 *London NUOCD 6*	21	4
5 Aug 95		BLUE MONDAY (2nd) (re-mix) *London NUOCD 7*	17	4
25 Aug 01	●	CRYSTAL *London NUOCD 8*	8	4
1 Dec 01		60 MILES AN HOUR *London NUOCD 9*	29	2

[1] Englandneworder

Group was male only on first hit. 'Blue Monday' in 1988 is a re-mixed version of the original 1983 hit which was made available on 7-inch for the first time, hence the slight difference in catalogue number. Sales for the re-mix and the original were combined from 7 May 1988 onwards when calculating its chart position. Tracks on The Peel Sessions (1st June 1982) EP: Turn the Heater On / We All Stand / Too Late / 5-8-6

See also JOY DIVISION; MONACO; ELECTRONIC; OTHER TWO

NEW ORLEANS JAZZMEN – *See Terry LIGHTFOOT and his NEW ORLEANS JAZZMEN*

NEW POWER GENERATION *US, male / female vocal / instrumental group (64 WEEKS)*

Date		Title / Label	pos	wks
31 Aug 91	●	GETT OFF *Paisley Park W 0056* [1]	4	8
21 Sep 91		CREAM *Paisley Park W 0061* [1] ▲	15	7
7 Dec 91		DIAMONDS AND PEARLS *Paisley Park W 0075* [1]	25	6
28 Mar 92		MONEY DON'T MATTER 2 NIGHT *Paisley Park W 0091* [1]	19	5
27 Jun 92		THUNDER *Paisley Park W 0113* [1]	28	3
18 Jul 92	●	SEXY MF / STROLLIN' *Paisley Park W 0123* [1]	4	7
10 Oct 92	●	MY NAME IS PRINCE *Paisley Park W 0132* [1]	7	5
14 Nov 92		MY NAME IS PRINCE (re-mix) *Paisley Park W 0142T* [1]	51	1
5 Dec 92		7 *Paisley Park W 0147* [1]	27	6
13 Mar 93		THE MORNING PAPERS *Paisley Park W 0162CD* [1]	52	3
1 Apr 95		GET WILD *NPG 0061045*	19	4
19 Aug 95		THE GOOD LIFE *NPG 0061515*	29	3
5 Jul 97		THE GOOD LIFE (re-entry) *NPG 0061515*	15	5
21 Nov 98		COME ON *RCA 74321634722*	65	1

[1] Prince and the New Power Generation

See also PRINCE

NEW RADICALS *US, male vocalist – Gregg Alexander (18 WEEKS)*

Date		Title / Label	pos	wks
3 Apr 99	●	YOU GET WHAT YOU GIVE *MCA MCSTD 48111*	5	17
25 Sep 99		SOMEDAY WE'LL KNOW *MCA MCSTD 40217*	48	1

NEW SEEKERS (165 Top 500) *Anglo-Australian vocal group formed by ex-Seeker Keith Potger with Eve Graham, Lyn Paul, Peter Doyle, Paul Layton and Marty Kristian. Hits included a Coca-Cola advertisement and a Eurovision entry. The group sold more than 25 million records worldwide and equalled the eight Top 20 entries by The Seekers (143 WEEKS)*

Date		Title / Label	pos	wks
17 Oct 70		WHAT HAVE THEY DONE TO MY SONG MA *Philips 6006 027*	48	1
31 Oct 70		WHAT HAVE THEY DONE TO MY SONG MA (re-entry) *Philips 6006 027*	44	1
10 Jul 71	●	NEVER ENDING SONG OF LOVE *Philips 6006 125*	2	19
18 Dec 71	★	I'D LIKE TO TEACH THE WORLD TO SING (IN PERFECT HARMONY) *Polydor 2058 184*	1	21
4 Mar 72	●	BEG STEAL OR BORROW *Polydor 2058 201*	2	13
10 Jun 72	●	CIRCLES *Polydor 2058 242*	4	16
2 Dec 72		COME SOFTLY TO ME *Polydor 2058 315* [1]	20	11
24 Feb 73		PINBALL WIZARD - SEE ME FEEL ME (MEDLEY) *Polydor 2058 338*	16	8
7 Apr 73		NEVERTHELESS *Polydor 2068 340* [2]	34	5
16 Jun 73		GOODBYE IS JUST ANOTHER WORD *Polydor 2058 368*	36	5
24 Nov 73	★	YOU WON'T FIND ANOTHER FOOL LIKE ME *Polydor 2058 421* [3]	1	16
9 Mar 74	●	I GET A LITTLE SENTIMENTAL OVER YOU *Polydor 2058 439* [3]	5	9
14 Aug 76		IT'S SO NICE (TO HAVE YOU HOME) *CBS 4391*	44	4

29 Jan 77		**I WANNA GO BACK** *CBS 4786*	25	4
15 Jul 78		**ANTHEM (ONE DAY IN EVERY WEEK)** *CBS 6413*	21	10

[1] New Seekers featuring Marty Kristian [2] Eve Graham and the New Seekers [3] New Seekers featuring Lyn Paul

NEW TONE AGE FAMILY – *See Dread FLIMSTONE and the MODERN TONE AGE FAMILY*

NEW VAUDEVILLE BAND
UK, male vocal / instrumental group (43 WEEKS) pos/wks

8 Sep 66	●	**WINCHESTER CATHEDRAL** *Fontana TF 741* ▲	4	19
26 Jan 67	●	**PEEK-A-BOO** *Fontana TF 784* [1]	7	11
11 May 67		**FINCHLEY CENTRAL** *Fontana TF 824*	11	9
2 Aug 67		**GREEN STREET GREEN** *Fontana TF 853*	37	4

[1] New Vaudeville Band featuring Tristram

NEW VISION *US, male vocal / instrumental duo (2 WEEKS)* pos/wks

29 Jan 00		**(JUST) YOU AND ME** *AM:PM CDAMPM 128*	23	2

NEW WORLD *Australia, male vocal / instrumental group (53 WEEKS)* pos/wks

27 Feb 71		**ROSE GARDEN** *RAK 111*	15	11
3 Jul 71	●	**TOM TOM TURNAROUND** *RAK 117*	6	15
4 Dec 71		**KARA KARA** *RAK 123*	17	13
13 May 72	●	**SISTER JANE** *RAK 130*	9	13
12 May 73		**ROOF TOP SINGING** *RAK 148*	50	1

NEW YORK CITY *US, male vocal group (11 WEEKS)* pos/wks

21 Jul 73		**I'M DOING FINE NOW** *RCA 2351*	20	11

NEW YORK SKYY
US, male / female vocal / instrumental group (2 WEEKS) pos/wks

16 Jan 82		**LET'S CELEBRATE** *Epic EPC A 1898*	71	1
30 Jan 82		**LET'S CELEBRATE (re-entry)** *Epic EPC A 1898*	67	1

NEWBEATS *US, male vocal group (22 WEEKS)* pos/wks

10 Sep 64		**BREAD AND BUTTER** *Hickory 1269*	15	9
23 Oct 71	●	**RUN, BABY, RUN (BACK INTO MY ARMS)** *London HL 10341*	10	13

Booker NEWBERRY III *US, male vocalist (11 WEEKS)* pos/wks

28 May 83	●	**LOVE TOWN** *Polydor POSP 613*	6	8
8 Oct 83		**TEDDY BEAR** *Polydor POSP 637*	44	3

Mickey NEWBURY *US, male vocalist (5 WEEKS)* pos/wks

1 Jul 72		**AMERICAN TRILOGY** *Elektra K 12047*	42	5

NEWCLEUS *US, male rap / instrumental group (6 WEEKS)* pos/wks

3 Sep 83		**JAM ON REVENGE (THE WIKKI WIKKI SONG)** *Beckett BKS 8*	44	6

Anthony NEWLEY (203 Top 500) *Acclaimed actor / singer and composer, b. 24 Sep 1931, London, UK, d. 14 Apr 1999. He appeared in more than 20 films before his singing career started. He was among the most innovative UK acts of the early rock years, before moving into musicals and cabaret (129 WEEKS)* pos/wks

1 May 59	●	**I'VE WAITED SO LONG** *Decca F 11127*	3	15
8 May 59		**IDLE ON PARADE (EP)** *Decca DFE 6566*	13	4
12 Jun 59	●	**PERSONALITY** *Decca F 11142*	6	12
15 Jan 60	★	**WHY** *Decca F 11194*	1	17
24 Mar 60	★	**DO YOU MIND** *Decca F 11220*	1	15
14 Jul 60	●	**IF SHE SHOULD COME TO YOU** *Decca F 11254*	4	15
24 Nov 60	●	**STRAWBERRY FAIR** *Decca F 11295*	3	11
16 Mar 61	●	**AND THE HEAVENS CRIED** *Decca F 11331*	6	12
15 Jun 61		**POP GOES THE WEASEL / BEE BOM** *Decca F 11362*	12	9
3 Aug 61		**WHAT KIND OF FOOL AM I?** *Decca F 11376*	36	8
25 Jan 62		**D-DARLING** *Decca F 11419*	25	6
26 Jul 62		**THAT NOISE** *Decca F 11486*	34	5

'Bee Bom' listed together with 'Pop Goes the Weasel' only for weeks of 15 and 22 Jun 1961. It peaked at No.15. Tracks on Idle on Parade (EP): I've Waited So Long / Idle Rock-a-Boogie / Idle on Parade / Saturday Night Rock-a-Boogie

Tara NEWLEY – *See E-ZEE POSSEE*

Brad NEWMAN *UK, male vocalist (1 WEEK)* pos/wks

22 Feb 62		**SOMEBODY TO LOVE** *Fontana H 357*	47	1

Dave NEWMAN *UK, male vocalist (6 WEEKS)* pos/wks

15 Apr 72		**THE LION SLEEPS TONIGHT** *Pye 7N 45134*	48	1
29 Apr 72		**THE LION SLEEPS TONIGHT (re-entry)** *Pye 7N 45134*	34	5

Paul NEWMAN – *See CAMISRA; ESCRIMA; PARTIZAN; TALL PAUL; GRIFTERS*

NEWS – *See Huey LEWIS and the NEWS*

NEWS *UK, male vocal / instrumental group (3 WEEKS)* pos/wks

29 Aug 81		**AUDIO VIDEO** *George GEORGE 1*	52	3

NEWTON *UK, male vocalist (6 WEEKS)* pos/wks

15 Jul 95		**SKY HIGH** *Bags Of Fun BAGSCD 6*	56	2
15 Feb 97		**SOMETIMES WHEN WE TOUCH** *Dominion CDDMIN 202*	32	3
16 Aug 97		**DON'T WORRY** *Dominion CDDMIN 206*	61	1

Juice NEWTON *US, female vocalist (6 WEEKS)* pos/wks

2 May 81		**ANGEL OF THE MORNING** *Capitol CL 16189*	43	6

Olivia NEWTON-JOHN (58 Top 500) *Top female vocalist in the US in the 1970s, b. 26 Sep 1948, Cambridge, UK. This photogenic Australian-raised singer / actress has won numerous pop and country awards and was the first female to score one dozen US Top 5 singles (234 WEEKS)* pos/wks

20 Mar 71	●	**IF NOT FOR YOU** *Pye International 7N 25543*	7	11
23 Oct 71	●	**BANKS OF THE OHIO** *Pye International 7N 25568*	6	17
11 Mar 72		**WHAT IS LIFE** *Pye International 7N 25575*	16	8
13 Jan 73		**TAKE ME HOME COUNTRY ROADS** *Pye International 7N 25599*	15	13
16 Mar 74		**LONG LIVE LOVE** *Pye International 7N 25638*	11	8
12 Oct 74		**I HONESTLY LOVE YOU** *EMI 2216* ▲	22	6
11 Jun 77	●	**SAM** *EMI 2616*	6	11
20 May 78	★	**YOU'RE THE ONE THAT I WANT** *RSO 006* [1] ◆ ▲	1	26
16 Sep 78	★	**SUMMER NIGHTS** *RSO 18* [1] ◆	1	19
4 Nov 78	●	**HOPELESSLY DEVOTED TO YOU** *RSO 17*	2	11
16 Dec 78	●	**A LITTLE MORE LOVE** *EMI 2879*	4	12
30 Jun 79		**DEEPER THAN THE NIGHT** *EMI 2954*	64	3
21 Jun 80	★	**XANADU** *Jet 185* [2]	1	11
23 Aug 80		**MAGIC** *Jet 196* ▲	32	7
25 Oct 80		**SUDDENLY** *Jet 7002* [3]	15	7
10 Oct 81	●	**PHYSICAL** *EMI 5234* ▲	7	16
16 Jan 82		**LANDSLIDE** *EMI 5257*	18	9
17 Apr 82		**MAKE A MOVE ON ME** *EMI 5291*	43	3
23 Oct 82		**HEART ATTACK** *EMI 5347*	46	4
15 Jan 83		**I HONESTLY LOVE YOU (re-issue)** *EMI 5360*	52	4
12 Nov 83		**TWIST OF FATE** *EMI 5438*	57	2
22 Dec 90	●	**THE GREASE MEGAMIX** *Polydor PO 114* [1]	3	10
23 Mar 91		**GREASE - THE DREAM MIX** *PWL / Polydor PO 136* [4]	47	2
4 Jul 92		**I NEED LOVE** *Mercury MER 370*	75	1
9 Dec 95		**HAD TO BE** *EMI CDEMS 410* [5]	22	4
25 Jul 98	●	**YOU'RE THE ONE THAT I WANT (re-issue)** *Polydor 0441332* [1]	4	9

[1] John Travolta and Olivia Newton-John [2] Olivia Newton-John and Electric Light Orchestra [3] Olivia Newton-John and Cliff Richard [4] Frankie Valli, John Travolta and Olivia Newton-John [5] Cliff Richard and Olivia Newton-John

NEXT *US, male vocal trio (8 WEEKS)* pos/wks

6 Jun 98		**TOO CLOSE** *Arista 74321580672* ▲	24	3
16 Sep 00		**WIFEY** *Arista 74321790912*	19	5

NEXT OF KIN *UK, male vocal / instrumental group (6 WEEKS)* pos/wks

20 Feb 99		**24 HOURS FROM YOU** *Universal MCSTD 40201*	13	4
19 Jun 99		**MORE LOVE** *Universal MCSTD 40207*	33	2

NIAGRA *UK, male / female vocal / DJ / production duo (1 WEEK)* pos/wks

27 Sep 97		**CLOUDBURST** *Freeflow FLOW CD2*	65	1

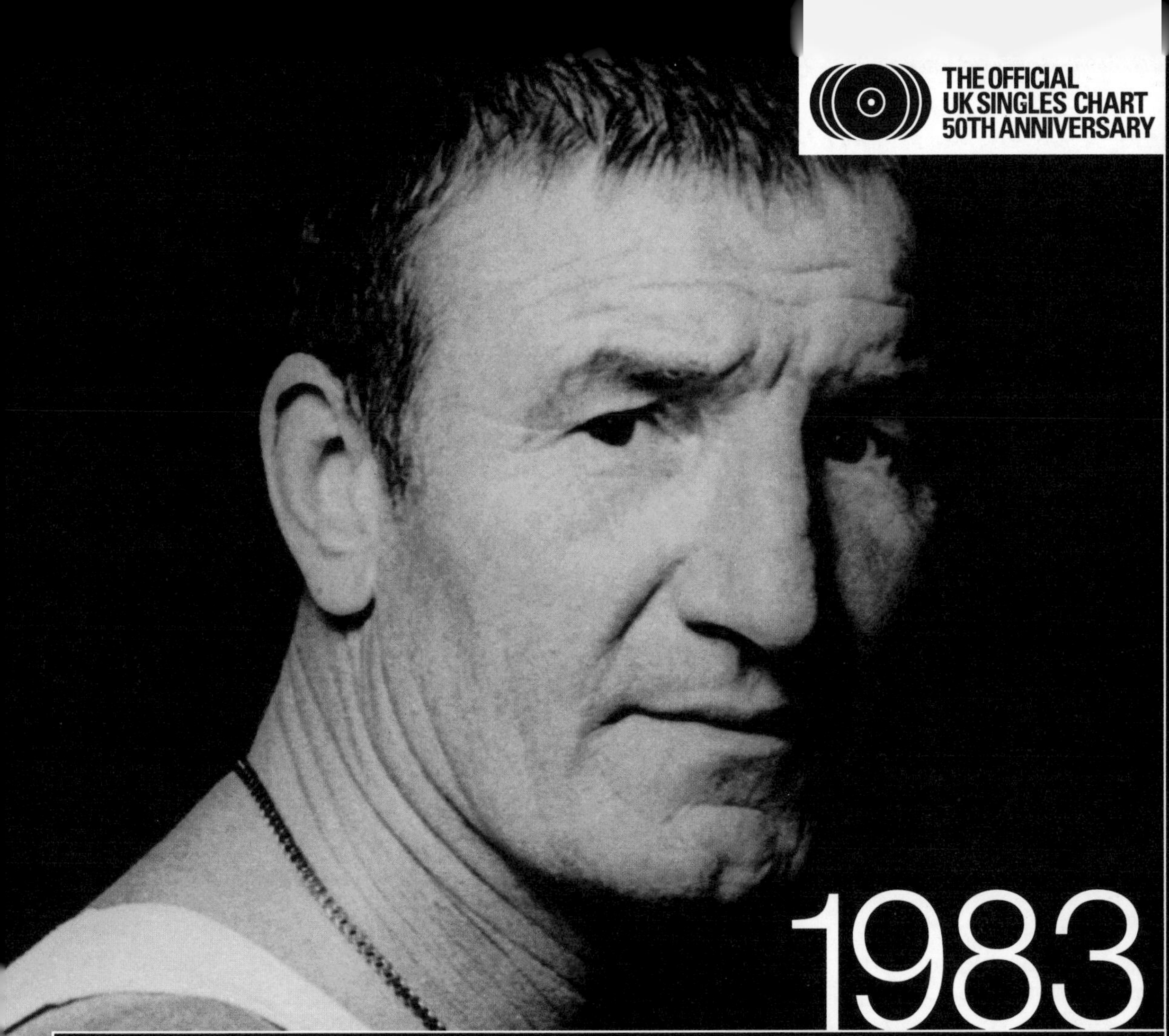

1983

IN THE YEAR IN WHICH HIV WAS DISCOVERED TO CAUSE AIDS, AMERICAN TROOPS INVADED GRENADA, SHERGAR WAS HORSE-NAPPED AND UK ACTS HAD THEIR BEST EVER SHOWING ON THE US TOP 100 TAKING HALF THE TOP 30 POSITIONS, ONE-TIME SALFORD JET AND CAPITAL GOLD DJ **MIKE SWEENEY** REMEMBERS HIS FIRST INTRODUCTION TO MORRISSEY ...

“I did an interview one afternoon on Piccadilly Radio. I'm told I've got this guy coming in, a local band [the Smiths] and the singer's called **Morrissey**. I remember saying, 'Morrissey what?' No, that's his name, just Morrissey. He doesn't have two names. I thought, OK, Ringo had only one name, wheel him in. So this guy came in – very weird, nice enough, by the way – very pleasant and very quiet. So I said to him, 'I've gotta tell you this – love your haircut.' I still had this mop-top Beatle cut at the time, but Morrissey had this quiff. Wow, I said, I used to have my hair like that when I was a kid. 'Cliff had his hair like you and Billy Fury.' And he said, 'I love Billy Fury.' So, of course, we got on. He was a regular bloke. So he gave me a vinyl copy of his record, 'This Charming Man' it was, and I put it on. When it had finished, I said to him, 'I'm gonna play the record again' because you could in those days. I literally put the needle back on the record again. I love riffs, so I said, listen, that's the best record I've heard since 'Pretty Vacant'. So I booked them for a TV show I was doing in the North West with Janice Long and by the time that happened it was a hit record, which was brilliant. It was a bit like booking The Beatles two months before 'Love Me Do'.”

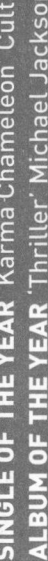

SINGLE OF THE YEAR 'Karma Chameleon' Culture Club
ALBUM OF THE YEAR 'Thriller' Michael Jackson

NICE *UK, male instrumental group (15 WEEKS)*

Date		Title / Label	pos	wks
10 Jul 68		**AMERICA** *Immediate IM 068*	21	15

Paul NICHOLAS *UK, male vocalist – Paul Beuselinck (31 WEEKS)*

Date		Title / Label	pos	wks
17 Apr 76		**REGGAE LIKE IT USED TO BE** *RSO 2090 185*	17	8
9 Oct 76	●	**DANCING WITH THE CAPTAIN** *RSO 2090 206*	8	9
4 Dec 76	●	**GRANDMA'S PARTY** *RSO 2090 216*	9	11
9 Jul 77		**HEAVEN ON THE 7TH FLOOR** *RSO 2090 249*	40	3

Sue NICHOLLS *UK, female vocalist (8 WEEKS)*

Date		Title / Label	pos	wks
3 Jul 68		**WHERE WILL YOU BE** *Pye 7N 17565*	17	8

Stevie NICKS *US, female vocalist (30 WEEKS)*

Date		Title / Label	pos	wks
15 Aug 81		**STOP DRAGGIN' MY HEART AROUND** *WEA K 79231* [1]	50	4
25 Jan 86		**I CAN'T WAIT** *Parlophone R 6110*	54	4
29 Mar 86		**TALK TO ME** *Parlophone R 6124*	68	2
6 May 89		**ROOMS ON FIRE** *EMI EM 90*	16	7
12 Aug 89		**LONG WAY TO GO** *EMI EM 97*	60	2
11 Nov 89		**WHOLE LOTTA TROUBLE** *EMI EM 114*	62	2
24 Aug 91		**SOMETIMES IT'S A BITCH** *EMI EM 203*	40	4
9 Nov 91		**I CAN'T WAIT (re-issue)** *EMI EM 214*	47	2
2 Jul 94		**MAYBE LOVE** *EMI CDEMS 328*	42	3

[1] Stevie Nicks with Tom Petty and the Heartbreakers

See also FLEETWOOD MAC

NICOLE *Germany, female vocalist – Nicole Hohloch (10 WEEKS)*

Date		Title / Label	pos	wks
8 May 82	★	**A LITTLE PEACE** *CBS A 2365*	1	9
21 Aug 82		**GIVE ME MORE TIME** *CBS A 2467*	75	1

NICOLE *US, female vocalist – Nicole McLeod (9 WEEKS)*

Date		Title / Label	pos	wks
28 Dec 85		**NEW YORK EYES** *Portrait A 6805* [1]	41	7
26 Dec 92		**ROCK THE HOUSE** *React 12REACT 12* [2]	63	1
6 Jul 96		**RUNNIN' AWAY** *Ore AG 18CD*	69	1

[1] Nicole with Timmy Thomas [2] Source featuring Nicole

NICOLE – *See Nicole RAY*

NICOLETTE *UK, female vocalist (1 WEEK)*

Date		Title / Label	pos	wks
23 Dec 95		**NO GOVERNMENT** *Talkin Loud TLCD 1*	67	1

NIGHTCRAWLERS featuring John REID
UK, male vocalist / multi-instrumentalist – John Reid (36 WEEKS)

Date		Title / Label	pos	wks
15 Oct 94		**PUSH THE FEELING ON** *ffrr FCD 245* [1]	22	5
4 Mar 95	●	**PUSH THE FEELING ON (re-mix)** *ffrr FCD 257*	3	11
27 May 95	●	**SURRENDER YOUR LOVE** *Final Vinyl 74321283982*	7	7
9 Sep 95		**DON'T LET THE FEELING GO** *Final Vinyl 7432129882*	13	4
20 Jan 96		**LET'S PUSH IT** *Final Vinyl 74321328142*	23	4
20 Apr 96		**SHOULD I EVER (FALL IN LOVE)** *Arista 74321358072*	34	2
27 Jul 96		**KEEP ON PUSHING OUR LOVE** *Arista 74321390422* [2]	30	2
3 Jul 99		**NEVER KNEW LOVE** *Riverhorse RIVHCD 1* [1]	59	1

[1] Nightcrawlers [2] Nightcrawlers featuring John Reid and Alysha Warren

Maxine NIGHTINGALE *UK, female vocalist (16 WEEKS)*

Date		Title / Label	pos	wks
1 Nov 75	●	**RIGHT BACK WHERE WE STARTED FROM** *United Artists UP 36015*	8	8
12 Mar 77		**LOVE HIT ME** *United Artists UP 36215*	11	8

NIGHTMARES ON WAX
UK, male production / instrumental group (6 WEEKS)

Date		Title / Label	pos	wks
27 Oct 90		**AFTERMATH / I'M FOR REAL** *Warp WAP 6*	38	5
26 Jun 99		**FINER** *Warp WAP 123CD*	63	1

NIGHTWRITERS *US, male vocal / instrumental duo (2 WEEKS)*

Date		Title / Label	pos	wks
23 May 92		**LET THE MUSIC USE YOU** *Ffrreedom TABX 112*	51	2

NIKKE? NICOLE! *US, female rapper (1 WEEK)*

Date		Title / Label	pos	wks
1 Jun 91		**NIKKE DOES IT BETTER** *Love EVOL 5*	73	1

Markus NIKOLAI *Germany, male producer (1 WEEK)*

Date		Title / Label	pos	wks
6 Oct 01		**BUSHES** *Southern Fried ECB 24CD*	74	1

NILSSON *US, male vocalist – Harry Nilsson (55 WEEKS)*

Date		Title / Label	pos	wks
27 Sep 69		**EVERYBODY'S TALKIN'** *RCA 1876*	50	1
11 Oct 69		**EVERYBODY'S TALKIN' (re-entry)** *RCA 1876*	23	9
14 Mar 70		**EVERYBODY'S TALKIN' (2nd re-entry)** *RCA 1876*	39	5
5 Feb 72	★	**WITHOUT YOU** *RCA 2165* ▲	1	20
3 Jun 72		**COCONUT** *RCA 2214*	42	5
16 Oct 76		**WITHOUT YOU (re-issue)** *RCA 2733*	22	8
20 Aug 77		**ALL I THINK ABOUT IS YOU** *RCA PB 9104*	43	3
19 Feb 94		**WITHOUT YOU (2nd re-issue)** *RCA 74321193092*	47	4

Charlotte NILSSON *Sweden, female vocalist (4 WEEKS)*

Date		Title / Label	pos	wks
3 Jul 99		**TAKE ME TO YOUR HEAVEN** *Arista 74321686952*	20	4

NINA and FREDERICK *Denmark, female / male vocal duo – Baron Frederick and Baroness Nina Van Pallandt (29 WEEKS)*

Date		Title / Label	pos	wks
18 Dec 59		**MARY'S BOY CHILD** *Columbia DB 4375*	26	1
10 Mar 60		**LISTEN TO THE OCEAN** *Columbia DB 4332*	47	1
7 Apr 60		**LISTEN TO THE OCEAN (re-entry)** *Columbia DB 4332*	46	1
17 Nov 60	●	**LITTLE DONKEY** *Columbia DB 4536*	3	10
28 Sep 61		**LONGTIME BOY** *Columbia DB 4703*	43	3
5 Oct 61		**SUCU-SUCU** *Columbia DB 4632*	23	13

NINE INCH NAILS *US, male vocal / instrumental group – leader Trent Reznor (15 WEEKS)*

Date		Title / Label	pos	wks
14 Sep 91		**HEAD LIKE A HOLE** *TVT IS 484*	45	4
16 Nov 91		**SIN** *TVT IS 508*	35	2
9 Apr 94		**MARCH OF THE PIGS** *TVT CID 592*	45	3
18 Jun 94		**CLOSER** *TVT CIDX 596*	25	3
13 Sep 97		**THE PERFECT DRUG** *Interscope IND 95542*	43	1
18 Dec 99		**WE'RE IN THIS TOGETHER** *Island 4971402*	39	2

999 *UK, male vocal / instrumental group (13 WEEKS)*

Date		Title / Label	pos	wks
25 Nov 78		**HOMICIDE** *United Artists UP 36467*	40	3
27 Oct 79		**FOUND OUT TOO LATE** *Radar ADA 46*	69	2
16 May 81		**OBSESSED** *Albion ION 1011*	71	1
18 Jul 81		**LIL RED RIDING HOOD** *Albion ION 1017*	59	3
14 Nov 81		**INDIAN RESERVATION** *Albion ION 1023*	51	4

911 *325* **Top 500** *Leading UK boy band: Lee Brennan, Jimmy Constable, Simon 'Spike' Dawbarn. Vocal trio formed in 1996, when they won GMTV 'Search for the Next Big Thing' contest. Tally of 10 consecutive Top 10s is among the best chart runs in history. Brennan is now recording solo (94 WEEKS)*

Date		Title / Label	pos	wks
11 May 96		**NIGHT TO REMEMBER** *Ginga CDGINGA 1*	38	2
10 Aug 96		**LOVE SENSATION** *Ginga CDGINGA 2*	21	4
9 Nov 96	●	**DON'T MAKE ME WAIT** *Ginga VSCDT 1618*	10	6
4 Jan 97		**DON'T MAKE ME WAIT (re-entry)** *Ginga VSCDT 1618*	63	2
22 Feb 97	●	**THE DAY WE FIND LOVE** *Virgin VSCDT 1619*	4	8
3 May 97	●	**BODYSHAKIN'** *Virgin VSCDT 1634*	3	7
12 Jul 97	●	**THE JOURNEY** *Virgin VSCDT 1645*	3	7
1 Nov 97	●	**PARTY PEOPLE...FRIDAY NIGHT** *Ginga / Virgin VSCDT 1658*	5	7
3 Jan 98		**PARTY PEOPLE...FRIDAY NIGHT (re-entry)** *Ginga / Virgin VSCDT 1658*	60	3
4 Apr 98	●	**ALL I WANT IS YOU** *Virgin VSCDT 1681*	4	6
20 Jun 98		**ALL I WANT IS YOU (re-entry)** *Virgin VSCDT 1681*	64	1
4 Jul 98	●	**HOW DO YOU WANT ME TO LOVE YOU?** *Ginga VSCDT 1686*	10	7
29 Aug 98		**HOW DO YOU WANT ME TO LOVE YOU? (re-entry)** *Ginga VSCDT 1686*	57	2
24 Oct 98	●	**MORE THAN A WOMAN** *Virgin VSCDT 1707*	2	9
2 Jan 99		**MORE THAN A WOMAN (re-entry)** *Virgin VSCDT 1707*	64	4
23 Jan 99	★	**A LITTLE BIT MORE** *Virgin VSCDT 1719* ■	1	9
15 May 99	●	**PRIVATE NUMBER** *Virgin VSCDT 1730*	3	7
23 Oct 99		**WONDERLAND** *Virgin VSCDT 1755*	13	3

9.9 *US, female vocal group (3 WEEKS)* pos/wks

		pos	wks
6 Jul 85	ALL OF ME FOR ALL OF YOU *RCA PB 49951*	53	3

NINE YARDS *UK, male vocal group (3 WEEKS)* pos/wks

		pos	wks
21 Nov 98	LONELINESS IS GONE *Virgin VSCDT 1696*	70	1
10 Apr 99	MATTER OF TIME *Virgin VSCDT 1723*	59	1
28 Aug 99	ALWAYS FIND A WAY *Virgin VSCDT 1746*	50	1

1910 FRUITGUM CO. *US, male vocal / instrumental group (16 WEEKS)* pos/wks

		pos	wks
20 Mar 68 ●	SIMON SAYS *Pye International 7N 25447*	2	16

1927 *Australia, male vocal / instrumental group (6 WEEKS)* pos/wks

		pos	wks
22 Apr 89	THAT'S WHEN I THINK OF YOU *WEA YZ 351*	46	6

98° *US, male vocal group (17 WEEKS)* pos/wks

		pos	wks
29 Nov 97	INVISIBLE MAN *Motown 8607092*	66	1
31 Oct 98	TRUE TO YOUR HEART *Motown 8608832* [1]	51	1
13 Mar 99	BECAUSE OF YOU *Motown 8609012*	36	2
11 Mar 00 ●	THANK GOD I FOUND YOU *Columbia 6690582* [2] ▲	10	9
11 Mar 00	THE HARDEST THING *Universal MCSTD 40228*	29	2
20 May 00	THANK GOD I FOUND YOU (re-entry) *Columbia 6690582* [2]	71	1
2 Dec 00	GIVE ME JUST ONE MORE NIGHT (UNA NOCHE) *Universal MCSTD 40243*	61	1

[1] 98 Degrees featuring Stevie Wonder [2] Mariah Carey featuring Joe and 98 Degrees

99TH FLOOR ELEVATORS *UK, male DJ / production duo (5 WEEKS)* pos/wks

		pos	wks
12 Aug 95	HOOKED *Labello Dance LAD 18CD* [1]	28	2
30 May 96	I'LL BE THERE *Labello Dance LAD 25CD1* [1]	37	2
8 Apr 00	HOOKED (re-mix) *Tripoli Trax TTRAX 061CD*	66	1

[1] 99th Floor Elevators featuring Tony De Vit

NIRVANA *UK / Ireland, male vocal / instrumental duo (6 WEEKS)* pos/wks

		pos	wks
15 May 68	RAINBOW CHASER *Island WIP 6029*	34	6

NIRVANA *US, male vocal / instrumental group (36 WEEKS)* pos/wks

		pos	wks
30 Nov 91 ●	SMELLS LIKE TEEN SPIRIT *DGC DGCS 5*	7	6
14 Mar 92 ●	COME AS YOU ARE *DGC DGCS 7*	9	5
25 Jul 92	LITHIUM *DGC DGCS 9*	11	6
12 Dec 92	IN BLOOM *Geffen GFS 34*	28	7
6 Mar 93	OH THE GUILT *Touch And Go TG 83CD*	12	2
11 Sep 93 ●	HEART-SHAPED BOX *Geffen GFSTD 54*	5	5
18 Dec 93	ALL APOLOGIES / RAPE ME *Geffen GFSTD 66*	32	5

The listed flip side of 'Oh the Guilt' was 'Puss' by Jesus Lizard

NITRO DELUXE
US, male multi-instrumentalist – Lee Junior (16 WEEKS) pos/wks

		pos	wks
14 Feb 87	THIS BRUTAL HOUSE *Cooltempo COOL 142*	47	7
13 Jun 87	THIS BRUTAL HOUSE (re-entry) *Cooltempo COOL 142*	62	4
6 Feb 88	LET'S GET BRUTAL (re-mix) *Cooltempo COOL*	24	5

'Let's Get Brutal' is a re-mixed version of 'This Brutal House'

NITZER EBB *UK, male vocal / instrumental group (3 WEEKS)* pos/wks

		pos	wks
11 Jan 92	GODHEAD *Mute 1MUTE 135T*	56	1
11 Apr 92	ASCEND *Mute 110MUTE 145*	52	1
4 Mar 95	KICK IT *Mute LCDMUTE 155*	75	1

NIVEA – *See MYSTIKAL*

NKOTB – *See NEW KIDS ON THE BLOCK*

NO AUTHORITY *US, male vocal group (1 WEEK)* pos/wks

		pos	wks
14 Mar 98	DON'T STOP *EPIC 6655592*	54	1

NO DICE *UK, male vocal / instrumental group (2 WEEKS)* pos/wks

		pos	wks
5 May 79	COME DANCING *EMI 2927*	65	2

NO DOUBT *US, male / female vocal / instrumental group – lead vocal Gwen Stefani (39 WEEKS)* pos/wks

		pos	wks
26 Oct 96	JUST A GIRL *Interscope IND 80034*	38	2
22 Feb 97 ★	DON'T SPEAK *Interscope IND 95515* ■	1	18
5 Jul 97 ●	JUST A GIRL (re-issue) *Interscope IND 95539*	3	7
4 Oct 97	SPIDERWEBS *Interscope IND 95551*	16	3
20 Dec 97	SUNDAY MORNING *Interscope IND 95566*	50	3
12 Jun 99	NEW *Higher Ground HIGHS 22CD*	30	2
25 Mar 00	EX-GIRLFRIEND *Interscope 4972992*	23	3
7 Oct 00	SIMPLE KIND OF LIFE *Interscope 4974162*	69	1

NO MERCY *US, male vocal / instrumental group (26 WEEKS)* pos/wks

		pos	wks
18 Jan 97 ●	WHERE DO YOU GO *Arista 74321401502*	2	15
24 May 97 ●	PLEASE DON'T GO *Arista 74321481372*	4	7
6 Sep 97	KISS YOU ALL OVER *Arista 7432151452*	16	4

NO SWEAT *Ireland, male vocal / instrumental group (5 WEEKS)* pos/wks

		pos	wks
13 Oct 90	HEART AND SOUL *London LON 274*	64	4
2 Feb 91	TEAR DOWN THE WALLS *London LON 257*	61	1

NO WAY JOSÉ *US, male instrumental group (6 WEEKS)* pos/wks

		pos	wks
3 Aug 85	TEQUILA *Fourth & Broadway BRW 28*	47	6

NO WAY SIS *UK, male vocal / instrumental group (4 WEEKS)* pos/wks

		pos	wks
21 Dec 96	I'D LIKE TO TEACH THE WORLD TO SING *EMI CDEM 461*	27	4

NOLANS (352 Top 500) *Dublin-born singing sisters with considerable MOR / pop appeal. Personnel on most hits: Anne, Maureen, Bernadette, Linda and Coleen Nolan. First European act to win the Grand Prize at the prestigious Tokyo Music Festival (1981) (90 WEEKS)* pos/wks

		pos	wks
6 Oct 79	SPIRIT BODY AND SOUL *Epic EPC 7796* [1]	34	6
22 Dec 79 ●	I'M IN THE MOOD FOR DANCING *Epic EPC 8068*	3	15
12 Apr 80	DON'T MAKE WAVES *Epic EPC 8349*	12	11
13 Sep 80 ●	GOTTA PULL MYSELF TOGETHER *Epic EPC 8878*	9	13
6 Dec 80	WHO'S GONNA ROCK YOU *Epic EPC 9325*	12	11
14 Mar 81 ●	ATTENTION TO ME *Epic EPC 9571*	9	13
15 Aug 81	CHEMISTRY *Epic EPC A 1485*	15	8
20 Feb 82	DON'T LOVE ME TOO HARD *Epic EPC A 1927*	14	12
1 Apr 95	I'M IN THE MOOD FOR DANCING (re-recording) *Living Beat LBECD 31*	51	1

[1] Nolan Sisters

NOMAD *UK, male / female vocal / instrumental duo – Damon Rochefort and Sharon Dee Clarke (22 WEEKS)* pos/wks

		pos	wks
2 Feb 91 ●	(I WANNA GIVE YOU) DEVOTION *Rumour RUMA 25* [1]	2	10
4 May 91	JUST A GROOVE *Rumour RUMA 33*	16	6
28 Sep 91	SOMETHING SPECIAL *Rumour RUMA 35*	73	1
25 Apr 92	YOUR LOVE IS LIFTING ME *Rumour RUMA 48*	60	2
7 Nov 92	24 HOURS A DAY *Rumour RUMA 60*	61	1
25 Nov 95	(I WANNA GIVE YOU) DEVOTION (re-mix) *Rumour RUMACD 75*	42	2

[1] Nomad featuring MC Mikee Freedom

NONCHALANT *US, female vocalist (1 WEEK)* pos/wks

		pos	wks
29 Jun 96	5 O'CLOCK *MCA MCSTD 48011*	44	1

Peter NOONE *UK, male vocalist (9 WEEKS)* pos/wks

		pos	wks
22 May 71	OH YOU PRETTY THING *RAK 114*	12	9

See also HERMAN'S HERMITS

NOOTROPIC *UK, male instrumental / production duo (1 WEEK)* pos/wks

		pos	wks
16 Mar 96	I SEE ONLY YOU *Hi-Life 5779832*	42	1

Ken NORDENE – *See Billy VAUGHN and his Orchestra*

Chris NORMAN – *See Suzi QUATRO; SMOKIE*

NORTH AND SOUTH *UK, male vocal / instrumental group (16 WEEKS)* pos/wks

17 May 97 ●	I'M A MAN NOT A BOY *RCA 74321461142*	7	5
9 Aug 97	TARANTINO'S NEW STAR *RCA 74321501242*	18	5
8 Nov 97	BREATHING *RCA 74321528422*	27	2
4 Apr 98	NO SWEAT '98 *RCA 74321562212*	29	4

NORTHERN LINE *UK / South Africa, male vocal group (12 WEEKS)* pos/wks

9 Oct 99	RUN FOR YOUR LIFE *Global Talent GTR 002CDS1*	18	4
11 Mar 00	LOVE ON THE NORTHERN LINE *Global Talent GTR 003CDS1*	15	5
17 Jun 00	ALL AROUND THE WORLD *Global Talent GTR 004CDS1*	27	3

NORTHERN UPROAR
UK, male vocal / instrumental group (11 WEEKS) pos/wks

21 Oct 95	ROLLERCOASTER / ROUGH BOYS *Heavenly HVN 047CD*	41	2
3 Feb 96	FROM A WINDOW / THIS MORNING *Heavenly HVN 051CD*	17	3
20 Apr 96	LIVIN' IT UP *Heavenly HVN 52CD*	24	2
22 Jun 96	TOWN *Heavenly HVN 54CD*	48	1
7 Jun 97	ANY WAY YOU LOOK *Heavenly HVN 70CD*	36	2
23 Aug 97	A GIRL I ONCE KNEW *Heavenly HVN 73CD*	63	1

NORTHSIDE *UK, male vocal / instrumental group (12 WEEKS)* pos/wks

9 Jun 90	SHALL WE TAKE A TRIP / MOODY PLACES *Factory FAC 268*	50	5
3 Nov 90	MY RISING STAR *Factory FAC 2987*	32	3
1 Jun 91	TAKE 5 *Factory FAC 3087*	40	4

Freddie NOTES and the RUDIES
Jamaica, male vocal / instrumental group (2 WEEKS) pos/wks

10 Oct 70	MONTEGO BAY *Trojan TR 7791*	45	2

NOTORIOUS B.I.G. *US, male rapper – Christopher Wallace (30 WEEKS)* pos/wks

29 Oct 94	JUICY *Bad Boy 74321240102*	72	1
1 Apr 95	BIG POPPA *Puff Daddy 74321263412*	63	1
15 Jul 95	CAN'T YOU SEE *Tommy Boy TBCD 700* [1]	43	2
19 Aug 95	ONE MORE CHANCE / STAY WITH ME *Puff Daddy 74321300782*	34	2
3 May 97 ●	HYPNOTIZE *Arista 74321466412* ▲	10	4
9 Aug 97 ●	MO MONEY MO PROBLEMS *Puff Daddy 74321492492* [2]	6	10
14 Feb 98	SKY'S THE LIMIT *Puff Daddy 74321561992* [3]	35	2
18 Jul 98	RUNNIN' *Black Jam BJAM 9005* [4]	15	3
5 Feb 00	NOTORIOUS B.I.G *Puff Daddy / Arista 74321737312* [5]	16	5

[1] Total featuring the Notorious B.I.G. [2] Notorious B.I.G. featuring Puff Daddy and Mase [3] Notorious B.I.G. featuring 112 [4] 2Pac and Notorious B.I.G. [5] Notorious B.I.G. featuring Puff Daddy and Lil' Kim

NOTTINGHAM FOREST FC with PAPER LACE
UK, football team with male vocal / instrumental group. (6 WEEKS) pos/wks

4 Mar 78	WE'VE GOT THE WHOLE WORLD IN OUR HANDS *Warner Bros. K 17110*	24	6

Heather NOVA *Bermuda, female vocalist (1 WEEK)* pos/wks

25 Feb 95	WALK THIS WORLD *Butterfly BFLD 19*	69	1

Nancy NOVA *UK, female vocalist (2 WEEKS)* pos/wks

4 Sep 82	NO, NO, NO *EMI 5328*	63	2

Tom NOVY *Germany, male producer (8 WEEKS)* pos/wks

2 May 98	SUPERSTAR *D:disco 74321569352* [1]	32	3
3 Jun 00	PUMPIN *Positiva CDTIV 132* [1]	19	3
2 Sep 00	I ROCK *Rulin RULIN 3CDS* [2]	55	1
4 Aug 01	NOW OR NEVER *Rulin RULIN 14CDS* [3]	64	1

[1] Novy vs Eniac [2] Tom Novy featuring Virginia [3] Tom Novy featuring Lima

NRG *UK, male DJ / production duo (2 WEEKS)* pos/wks

29 Mar 97	NEVER LOST HIS HARDCORE *Top Banana TOPCD 04*	71	1
12 Dec 98	NEVER LOST HIS HARDCORE '98 (re-mix) *Top Banana TOPCD 010*	61	1

NT GANG *Germany, male vocal / instrumental group (1 WEEK)* pos/wks

2 Apr 88	WAM BAM *Cooltempo COOL 163*	71	1

NU-BIRTH *UK, male production duo (2 WEEKS)* pos/wks

6 Sep 97	ANYTIME *XL XLS 85CD*	48	1
6 Jun 98	ANYTIME (re-issue) *Locked On LOX 97CD*	41	1

NU COLOURS *UK, male / female vocal / instrumental group (11 WEEKS)* pos/wks

6 Jun 92	TEARS *Wild Card CARD 1*	55	2
10 Oct 92	POWER *Wild Card CARD 3*	64	1
5 Jun 93	WHAT IN THE WORLD *Wild Card CARDD 4*	57	2
27 Nov 93	POWER (re-mix) *Wild Card CARDD 5*	40	2
25 May 96	DESIRE *Wild Card 5763652*	31	2
24 Aug 96	SPECIAL KIND OF LOVER *Wild Card 5752012*	38	2

NU GENERATION *UK, male producer – Aston Harvey (9 WEEKS)* pos/wks

29 Jan 00 ●	IN YOUR ARMS (RESCUE ME) *Concept CDCON 7*	8	8
21 Oct 00	NOWHERE TO RUN 2000 *Concept CDCON 16*	66	1

NU MATIC *UK, male instrumental / production duo (1 WEEK)* pos/wks

8 Aug 92	SPRING IN MY STEP *XL Recordings XLS 31*	58	1

NU SHOOZ *US, male / female vocal duo – John Smith and Valerie Day (17 WEEKS)* pos/wks

24 May 86 ●	I CAN'T WAIT *Atlantic A 9446*	2	14
26 Jul 86	POINT OF NO RETURN *Atlantic A 9392*	48	3

NU SOUL featuring Kelli RICH
US, male / female vocal / instrumental duo (2 WEEKS) pos/wks

13 Jan 96	HIDE-A-WAY *ffrr FCD 269*	27	2

NUANCE featuring Vikki LOVE
US, male / female vocal / instrumental group (3 WEEKS) pos/wks

19 Jan 85	LOVERIDE *Fourth & Broadway BRW 20*	59	3

NUBIAN PRINZ – *See POWERCUT featuring NUBIAN PRINZ*

NUFF JUICE – *See D MOB*

Gary NUMAN (127 Top 500)
The moody, synthesized sound of London-born Gary Webb (b. 8 Mar 1958) first hit the charts in 1979 under the group name Tubeway Army. Five-times chart hit 'Cars' was also the basis of Armand Van Helden's Top 20 hit 'Koochy' in 2000 (164 WEEKS) pos/wks

19 May 79 ★	ARE 'FRIENDS' ELECTRIC? *Beggars Banquet BEG 18* [1]	1	16
1 Sep 79 ★	CARS *Beggars Banquet BEG 23*	1	11
24 Nov 79 ●	COMPLEX *Beggars Banquet BEG 29*	6	9
24 May 80 ●	WE ARE GLASS *Beggars Banquet BEG 35*	5	7
30 Aug 80 ●	I DIE: YOU DIE *Beggars Banquet BEG 46*	6	7
20 Dec 80	THIS WRECKAGE *Beggars Banquet BEG 50*	20	7
29 Aug 81 ●	SHE'S GOT CLAWS *Beggars Banquet BEG 62*	6	6
5 Dec 81	LOVE NEEDS NO DISGUISE *Beggars Banquet BEG 68* [2]	33	7
6 Mar 82	MUSIC FOR CHAMELEONS *Beggars Banquet BEG 70*	19	7
19 Jun 82 ●	WE TAKE MYSTERY (TO BED) *Beggars Banquet BEG 77*	9	4
28 Aug 82	WHITE BOYS AND HEROES *Beggars Banquet BEG 81*	20	4
3 Sep 83	WARRIORS *Beggars Banquet BEG 95*	20	5
22 Oct 83	SISTER SURPRISE *Beggars Banquet BEG 101*	32	3
3 Nov 84	BERSERKER *Numa NU 4*	32	5
22 Dec 84	MY DYING MACHINE *Numa NU 6*	66	1
9 Feb 85	CHANGE YOUR MIND *Polydor POSP 722* [3]	17	8
25 May 85	THE LIVE EP *Numa NUM 7*	27	4
10 Aug 85	YOUR FASCINATION *Numa NU 9*	46	5
21 Sep 85	CALL OUT THE DOGS *Numa NU 11*	49	2
16 Nov 85	MIRACLES *Numa NU 13*	49	3
19 Apr 86	THIS IS LOVE *Numa NU 16*	28	3
28 Jun 86	I CAN'T STOP *Numa NU 17*	27	4
4 Oct 86	NEW THING FROM LONDON TOWN *Numa NU 19* [3]	52	3
6 Dec 86	I STILL REMEMBER *Numa NU 21*	74	1
28 Mar 87	RADIO HEART *GFM GFM 109* [4]	35	6

13 Jun 87		**LONDON TIMES** *GFM GFM 112* [4]	48	2
19 Sep 87		**CARS (E REG MODEL) / ARE 'FRIENDS' ELECTRIC? (re-mix)** *Beggars Banquet BEG 199*	16	7
30 Jan 88		**NO MORE LIES** *Polydor POSP 894* [3]	34	3
1 Oct 88		**NEW ANGER** *Illegal ILS 1003*	46	2
3 Dec 88		**AMERICA** *Illegal ILS 1004*	49	1
3 Jun 89		**I'M ON AUTOMATIC** *Polydor PO 43* [3]	44	2
16 Mar 91		**HEART** *IRS NUMAN 1*	43	2
21 Mar 92		**THE SKIN GAME** *Numa NU 23*	68	1
1 Aug 92		**MACHINE + SOUL** *Numa NUM 124*	72	1
4 Sep 93		**CARS (2nd re-mix)** *Beggars Banquet BEG 264CD*	53	1
16 Mar 96		**CARS (re-issue of re-mix)** *PolyGram TV PRMCD 1*	17	4

[1] Tubeway Army [2] Gary Numan and Dramatis [3] Sharpe and Numan [4] Radio Heart featuring Gary Numan

Tracks on The Live EP: Are 'Friends' Electric? / Berserker / Cars / We Are Glass. 'Cars' in 1996 is a re-issue of the 1987 remix

See also Paul GARDINER

NUMBER ONE CUP *US, male vocal / instrumental group (1 WEEK)* pos/wks

2 Mar 96		**DIVEBOMB** *Blue Rose BRRC 10032*	61	1

Jose NUNEZ featuring OCTAHVIA
US, male DJ / producer (2 WEEKS) pos/wks

5 Sep 98		**IN MY LIFE** *Ministry of Sound MOSCDS 126*	56	1
5 Jun 99		**HOLD ON** *Ministry of Sound MOSCDS 130*	44	1

Bobby NUNN *US, male vocalist / multi-instrumentalist (3 WEEKS)* pos/wks

4 Feb 84		**DON'T KNOCK IT (UNTIL YOU TRY IT)** *Motown TMG 1323*	65	3

NUSH *UK, male instrumental / production duo – Danny Matlock and Danny Harrison (7 WEEKS)* pos/wks

23 Jul 94		**U GIRLS** *Blunted Vinyl BLNCDX 006*	58	1
22 Apr 95		**MOVE THAT BODY** *Blunted Vinyl BLNCD 012*	46	2
16 Sep 95		**U GIRLS (LOOK SO SEXY) (re-mix)** *Blunted Vinyl BLNCD 13*	15	4

NUT *UK, female vocalist (4 WEEKS)* pos/wks

8 Jun 96		**BRAINS** *Epic NUTCD 2*	64	1
21 Sep 96		**CRAZY** *Epic NUTCD 5*	56	1
11 Jan 97		**SCREAM** *Epic NUTCD 6*	43	2

NUTTIN' NYCE *US, female vocal group (2 WEEKS)* pos/wks

10 Jun 95		**DOWN 4 WHATEVA** *Jive JIVECD 365*	62	1
12 Aug 95		**FROGGY STYLE** *Jive JIVECD 381*	68	1

NUYORICAN SOUL *US, male DJ / production group (8 WEEKS)* pos/wks

8 Feb 97		**RUNAWAY** *Talkin Loud TLCD20* [1]	24	4
10 May 97		**IT'S ALRIGHT, I FEEL IT!** *Talkin Loud TLCD 22* [2]	26	2
25 Oct 97		**I AM THE BLACK GOLD OF THE SUN** *Talkin Loud TLCD 26* [2]	31	2

[1] Nuyorican Soul featuring India [2] Nuyorican Soul featuring Jocelyn Brown

NWA *US, male rap group (15 WEEKS)* pos/wks

9 Sep 89		**EXPRESS YOURSELF** *Fourth & Broadway BRW 144*	50	4
26 May 90		**EXPRESS YOURSELF (re-entry)** *Fourth & Broadway BRW 144*	26	5
1 Sep 90		**GANGSTA, GANGSTA** *Fourth & Broadway BRW 191*	70	1
10 Nov 90		**100 MILES AND RUNNIN'** *Fourth & Broadway BRW 200*	38	3
23 Nov 91		**ALWAYZ INTO SOMETHIN'** *Fourth & Broadway BRW 238*	60	2

NYCC *Germany, male rap trio (6 WEEKS)* pos/wks

30 May 98		**FIGHT FOR YOUR RIGHT (TO PARTY)** *Control 0042645 CON*	14	5
19 Sep 98		**CAN YOU FEEL IT (ROCK DA HOUSE)** *Control 0042785 CON*	68	1

Joe NYE – *See DNA*

NYLON MOON *Italy, male instrumental duo (2 WEEKS)* pos/wks

13 Apr 96		**SKY PLUS** *Positiva CDTIV 50*	43	2

Michael NYMAN *UK, male instrumentalist – piano (2 WEEKS)* pos/wks

19 Mar 94		**THE HEART ASKS PLEASURE FIRST / THE PROMISE** *Virgin VEND 3*	60	2

O

O-TOWN *US, male vocal group (24 WEEKS)* pos/wks

28 Apr 01	●	**LIQUID DREAMS** *J 74321853202*	3	10
4 Aug 01	●	**ALL OR NOTHING** *J 74321875822*	4	10
3 Nov 01		**WE FIT TOGETHER** *J 74321893692*	20	3
22 Dec 01		**WE FIT TOGETHER (re-entry)** *J 74321893692*	74	1

Phil OAKEY – *See HUMAN LEAGUE; Giorgio MORODER*

Paul OAKENFOLD presents Afrika BAMBAATAA
UK, male producer and US, male rapper (1 WEEK) pos/wks

25 Aug 01		**PLANET ROCK** *Tommy Boy TBCD2266*	47	1

OASIS (29 Top 500) *Peerless Manchester-based, Beatles-influenced band: Liam (v) and Noel (g/v) Gallagher, Gem Archer (g), Andy Bell (b), Alan White (d). Tony McCarroll was replaced by Alan White in 1994. In 1999 Paul 'Bonehead' Arthurs was replaced by Gem Archer and Paul McGuigan was replaced by Andy Bell. The often controversial Britpop group smashed many records including most weeks on the chart in one year (134 in 1996) (309 WEEKS)* pos/wks

23 Apr 94		**SUPERSONIC** *Creation CRESCD 176*	31	3
2 Jul 94		**SHAKERMAKER** *Creation CRESCD 182*	11	5
20 Aug 94	●	**LIVE FOREVER** *Creation CRESCD 185*	10	5
22 Oct 94	●	**CIGARETTES AND ALCOHOL** *Creation CRESCD 190*	7	6
31 Dec 94		**CIGARETTES AND ALCOHOL (re-entry)** *Creation CRESCD 190*	69	1
31 Dec 94	●	**WHATEVER** *Creation CRESCD 195*	3	10
6 May 95	★	**SOME MIGHT SAY** *Creation CRESCD 204* ■	1	14
13 May 95		**SOME MIGHT SAY** *Creation CRE 204T*	71	1
24 Jun 95		**CIGARETTES AND ALCOHOL (2nd re-entry)** *Creation CRESCD 190*	53	3
24 Jun 95		**LIVE FOREVER (re-entry)** *Creation CRESCD 185*	50	3
24 Jun 95		**SHAKERMAKER (re-entry)** *Creation CRESCD 182*	52	3
24 Jun 95		**SUPERSONIC (re-entry)** *Creation CRESCD 176*	44	3
24 Jun 95		**WHATEVER (re-entry)** *Creation CRESCD 195*	48	3
26 Aug 95	●	**ROLL WITH IT** *Creation CRESCD 212*	2	11
26 Aug 95		**SOME MIGHT SAY (re-entry)** *Creation CRESCD 204*	73	1
11 Nov 95	●	**WONDERWALL** *Creation CRESCD 215*	2	20
25 Nov 95		**WIBBLING RIVALRY (INTERVIEWS WITH NOEL AND LIAM GALLAGHER)** *Fierce Panda NING 12CD* [1]	52	2
9 Dec 95		**WHATEVER (2nd re-entry)** *Creation CRESCD 195*	75	1
30 Dec 95		**CIGARETTES AND ALCOHOL (3rd re-entry)** *Creation CRESCD 190*	58	7
30 Dec 95		**SUPERSONIC (2nd re-entry)** *Creation CRESCD 176*	56	4
30 Dec 95		**WHATEVER (3rd re-entry)** *Creation CRESCD 195*	55	3
6 Jan 96		**LIVE FOREVER (2nd re-entry)** *Creation CRESCD 185*	64	1
6 Jan 96		**ROLL WITH IT (re-entry)** *Creation CRESCD 212*	65	3
6 Jan 96		**SHAKERMAKER (2nd re-entry)** *Creation CRESCD 182*	61	2
6 Jan 96		**SOME MIGHT SAY (2nd re-entry)** *Creation CRESCD 204*	59	3
20 Jan 96		**LIVE FOREVER (3rd re-entry)** *Creation CRESCD 185*	71	2
27 Jan 96		**WHATEVER (4th re-entry)** *Creation CRESCD 195*	61	3
24 Feb 96		**WHATEVER (5th re-entry)** *Creation CRESCD 195*	55	15
2 Mar 96		**CIGARETTES AND ALCOHOL (4th re-entry)** *Creation CRESCD 190*	62	4
2 Mar 96	★	**DON'T LOOK BACK IN ANGER** *Creation CRESCD 221* ■	1	16
2 Mar 96		**LIVE FOREVER (4th re-entry)** *Creation CRESCD 185*	74	2
2 Mar 96		**SHAKERMAKER (3rd re-entry)** *Creation CRESCD 182*	74	1
2 Mar 96		**SUPERSONIC (3rd re-entry)** *Creation CRESCD 176*	71	1
16 Mar 96		**SOME MIGHT SAY (3rd re-entry)** *Creation CRESCD 204*	75	1

13 Apr 96	**CIGARETTES AND ALCOHOL (5th re-entry)** *Creation CRESCD 190*	74	2
11 May 96	**CIGARETTES AND ALCOHOL (6th re-entry)** *Creation CRESCD 190*	72	3
17 Aug 96	**WHATEVER (6th re-entry)** *Creation CRESCD 195*	62	4
24 Aug 96	**CIGARETTES AND ALCOHOL (7th re-entry)** *Creation CRESCD 190*	72	1
24 Aug 96	**SOME MIGHT SAY (4th re-entry)** *Creation CRESCD 204*	70	1
24 Aug 96	**WONDERWALL (re-entry)** *Creation CRESCD 215*	60	5
21 Sep 96	**WHATEVER (7th re-entry)** *Creation CRESCD 195*	66	1
16 Nov 96	**CIGARETTES AND ALCOHOL (8th re-entry)** *Creation CRESCD 190*	38	5
16 Nov 96	**DON'T LOOK BACK IN ANGER (re-entry)** *Creation CRESCD 221*	53	5
16 Nov 96	**LIVE FOREVER (5th re-entry)** *Creation CRESCD 185*	42	2
16 Nov 96	**ROLL WITH IT (2nd re-entry)** *Creation CRESCD 212*	55	2
16 Nov 96	**SHAKERMAKER (4th re-entry)** *Creation CRESCD 182*	48	2
16 Nov 96	**SOME MIGHT SAY (5th re-entry)** *Creation CRESCD 204*	40	4
16 Nov 96	**SUPERSONIC (4th re-entry)** *Creation CRESCD 176*	47	2
16 Nov 96	**WHATEVER (8th re-entry)** *Creation CRESCD 195*	34	10
16 Nov 96	**WONDERWALL (2nd re-entry)** *Creation CRESCD 215*	36	9
28 Dec 96	**CIGARETTES AND ALCOHOL (9th re-entry)** *Creation CRESCD 190*	56	3
28 Dec 96	**DON'T LOOK BACK IN ANGER (2nd re-entry)** *Creation CRESCD 221*	53	3
28 Dec 96	**LIVE FOREVER (6th re-entry)** *Creation CRESCD 185*	59	3
28 Dec 96	**SOME MIGHT SAY (6th re-entry)** *Creation CRESCD 204*	58	3
4 Jan 97	**ROLL WITH IT (3rd re-entry)** *Creation CRESCD 212*	62	2
4 Jan 97	**SHAKERMAKER (5th re-entry)** *Creation CRESCD 182*	61	2
4 Jan 97	**SUPERSONIC (5th re-entry)** *Creation CRESCD 176*	63	1
19 Jul 97 ★	**D'YOU KNOW WHAT I MEAN?** *Creation CRESCD 256* ■	1	18
4 Oct 97 ●	**STAND BY ME** *Creation CRESCD 278*	2	18
24 Jan 98 ★	**ALL AROUND THE WORLD** *Creation CRESCD 282* ■	1	7
11 Apr 98	**ALL AROUND THE WORLD (re-entry)** *Creation CRESCD 282*	68	2
19 Feb 00 ★	**GO LET IT OUT** *Big Brother RKIDSCD 001* ■	1	10
29 Apr 00 ●	**WHO FEELS LOVE?** *Big Brother RKIDSCD 003*	4	7
6 May 00	**GO LET IT OUT (re-entry)** *Big Brother RKIDSCD 001*	52	2
1 Jul 00	**WHO FEELS LOVE? (re-entry)** *Big Brother RKIDSCD 003*	70	1
15 Jul 00 ●	**SUNDAY MORNING CALL** *Big Brother RKIDSCD004*	4	6

[1] Oas*s

Chart rules allow for a maximum of three formats; the 12-inch of 'Some Might Say' - already available on CD, 7-inch and cassette - was therefore listed separately

John OATES – *See Daryl HALL and John OATES*

OBERNKIRCHEN CHILDREN'S CHOIR

Germany, children's choir (26 WEEKS) pos/wks

22 Jan 54 ●	**THE HAPPY WANDERER** *Parlophone R 3799*	2	23
9 Jul 54 ●	**THE HAPPY WANDERER (re-entry)** *Parlophone R 3799*	8	3

OBI PROJECT featuring HARRY, ASHER D and DJ WHAT?

UK, male vocal / rap / production group (1 WEEK) pos/wks

4 Aug 01	**BABY, CAN I GET YOUR NUMBER** *East West EW 235CD*	75	1

Dermot O'BRIEN and his CLUBMEN

Ireland, male vocalist (2 WEEKS) pos/wks

20 Oct 66	**THE MERRY PLOUGHBOY** *Envoy ENV 016*	46	1
3 Nov 66	**THE MERRY PLOUGHBOY (re-entry)** *Envoy ENV 016*	50	1

Billy OCEAN

(141 Top 500) *Top British-based R&B singer / songwriter of the 1980s, b. Leslie Charles, 21 Jan 1950, Trinidad. He waited seven years after scoring his first four UK Top 20 hits before accumulating an impressive run of transatlantic successes, which included three US No.1s (153 WEEKS)* pos/wks

21 Feb 76 ●	**LOVE REALLY HURTS WITHOUT YOU** *GTO GT 52*	2	10
10 Jul 76	**L.O.D. (LOVE ON DELIVERY)** *GTO GT 62*	19	8
13 Nov 76	**STOP ME (IF YOU'VE HEARD IT ALL BEFORE)** *GTO GT 72*	12	11
19 Mar 77 ●	**RED LIGHT SPELLS DANGER** *GTO GT 85*	2	10
1 Sep 79	**AMERICAN HEARTS** *GTO GT 244*	54	5
19 Jan 80	**ARE YOU READY** *GTO GT 259*	42	7
13 Oct 84 ●	**CARIBBEAN QUEEN (NO MORE LOVE ON THE RUN)** *Jive JIVE 77* ▲	6	14
19 Jan 85	**LOVERBOY** *Jive JIVE 80*	15	10
11 May 85 ●	**SUDDENLY** *Jive JIVE 90*	4	14
17 Aug 85	**MYSTERY LADY** *Jive JIVE 98*	49	4
25 Jan 86 ★	**WHEN THE GOING GETS TOUGH, THE TOUGH GET GOING** *Jive JIVE 114*	1	13
12 Apr 86	**THERE'LL BE SAD SONGS (TO MAKE YOU CRY)** *Jive JIVE 117* ▲	12	13
9 Aug 86	**LOVE ZONE** *Jive JIVE 124*	49	3
11 Oct 86	**BITTERSWEET** *Jive JIVE 133*	44	4
10 Jan 87	**LOVE IS FOREVER** *Jive JIVE 134*	34	7
6 Feb 88 ●	**GET OUTTA MY DREAMS GET INTO MY CAR** *Jive BOS 1* ▲	3	11
7 May 88	**CALYPSO CRAZY** *Jive BOS 2*	35	4
6 Aug 88	**THE COLOUR OF LOVE** *Jive BOS 3*	65	3
6 Feb 93	**PRESSURE** *Jive BOSCD 6*	55	2

OCEAN COLOUR SCENE

UK, male vocal / instrumental group (62 WEEKS) pos/wks

23 Mar 91	**YESTERDAY TODAY** *!Phfft FIT 2*	49	1
17 Feb 96	**THE RIVERBOAT SONG** *MCA MCSTD 40021*	15	5
6 Apr 96 ●	**YOU'VE GOT IT BAD** *MCA MCSTD 40036*	7	4
15 Jun 96 ●	**THE DAY WE CAUGHT THE TRAIN** *MCA MCSTD 40046*	4	11
28 Sep 96 ●	**THE CIRCLE** *MCA MCSTD 40077*	6	6
28 Jun 97 ●	**HUNDRED MILE HIGH CITY** *MCA MCSTD 40133*	4	7
6 Sep 97 ●	**TRAVELLERS TUNE** *MCA MCSTD 40144*	5	5
22 Nov 97 ●	**BETTER DAY** *MCA MCSTD 40151*	9	5
28 Feb 98	**IT'S A BEAUTIFUL THING** *MCA MCSTD 40157*	12	4
4 Sep 99	**PROFIT IN PEACE** *Island CID 757*	13	5
27 Nov 99	**SO LOW** *Island CID 759*	34	2
8 Jul 00	**JULY / I AM THE NEWS** *Island CID 763*	31	2
7 Apr 01	**UP ON THE DOWN SIDE** *Island CID 774*	19	3
14 Jul 01	**MECHANICAL WONDER** *Island CID 779*	49	1
22 Dec 01	**CRAZY LOWDOWN WAYS** *Island CID 787*	64	1

OCEANIC

UK, male / female vocal / instrumental group (26 WEEKS) pos/wks

24 Aug 91 ●	**INSANITY** *Dead Dead Good GOOD 4*	3	15
30 Nov 91	**WICKED LOVE** *Dead Dead Good GOOD 5*	25	3
28 Dec 91	**WICKED LOVE (re-entry)** *Dead Dead Good GOOD 5*	65	2
13 Jun 92	**CONTROLLING ME** *Dead Dead Good GOOD 14*	14	5
14 Nov 92	**IGNORANCE** *Dead Dead Good GOOD 22* [1]	72	1

[1] Oceanic featuring Siobhan Maher

Des O'CONNOR

(235 Top 500) *Entertainer, comedian and MOR vocalist, b. 12 Jan 1932. This London-based all-rounder toured with Buddy Holly and Lonnie Donegan in the 1950s, had a series of hits in the 1960s and has been a top-rated TV star for the past six decades (117 WEEKS)* pos/wks

1 Nov 67 ●	**CARELESS HANDS** *Columbia DB 8275* [1]	6	17
8 May 68 ★	**I PRETEND** *Columbia DB 8397*	1	36
20 Nov 68 ●	**ONE, TWO, THREE O'LEARY** *Columbia DB 8492*	4	11
7 May 69	**DICK-A-DUM-DUM (KING'S ROAD)** *Columbia DB 8566*	14	10
29 Nov 69	**LONELINESS** *Columbia DB 8632*	18	11
14 Mar 70	**I'LL GO ON HOPING** *Columbia DB 8661*	30	7
26 Sep 70	**THE TIP OF MY FINGERS** *Columbia DB 8713*	15	15
8 Nov 86 ●	**THE SKYE BOAT SONG** *Tembo TML 119* [2]	10	10

[1] Des O'Connor with the Michael Sammes Singers [2] Roger Whittaker and Des O'Connor

Hazel O'CONNOR

UK, female vocalist (46 WEEKS) pos/wks

16 Aug 80 ●	**EIGHTH DAY** *A & M AMS 7553*	5	11
25 Oct 80	**GIVE ME AN INCH** *A & M AMS 7569*	41	4
21 Mar 81 ●	**D-DAYS** *Albion ION 1009*	10	9
23 May 81 ●	**WILL YOU** *A & M AMS 8131*	8	10
1 Aug 81	**(COVER PLUS) WE'RE ALL GROWN UP** *Albion ION 1018*	41	6
3 Oct 81	**HANGING AROUND** *Albion ION 1022*	45	3
23 Jan 82	**CALLS THE TUNE** *A & M AMS 8203*	60	3

Sinead O'CONNOR

Ireland, female vocalist (64 WEEKS) pos/wks

16 Jan 88	**MANDINKA** *Ensign ENY 611*	17	9
20 Jan 90 ★	**NOTHING COMPARES 2 U** *Ensign ENY 630* ▲	1	14
21 Jul 90	**THE EMPEROR'S NEW CLOTHES** *Ensign ENY 633*	31	5
20 Oct 90	**THREE BABIES** *Ensign ENY 635*	42	4
8 Jun 91	**MY SPECIAL CHILD** *Ensign ENY 646*	42	3

14 Dec 91	**SILENT NIGHT** *Ensign ENY 652*	60	4
12 Sep 92	**SUCCESS HAS MADE A FAILURE OF OUR HOME** *Ensign ENY 656*	18	4
12 Dec 92	**DON'T CRY FOR ME ARGENTINA** *Ensign ENY 657*	53	4
19 Feb 94	**YOU MADE ME THE THIEF OF YOUR HEART** *Island CID 588*	42	3
26 Nov 94	**THANK YOU FOR HEARING ME** *Ensign CDENYS 662*	13	7
29 Apr 95	**HAUNTED** *ZTT ZANG 65CD* [1]	30	2
26 Aug 95	**FAMINE** *Ensign CDENY 663*	51	1
17 May 97	**GOSPEL OAK (EP)** *Chrysalis CDCHS 5051*	28	3
6 Dec 97	**THIS IS A REBEL SONG** *Columbia 6652992*	60	1

[1] Shane MacGowan and Sinead O'Connor

Tracks on Gospel Oak (EP): This Is to Mother You / I Am Enough for Myself / Petit Poulet / 4 My Love

See also MARXMAN; Jah WOBBLE'S INVADERS of the HEART

OCTAHVIA – *See Jose NUNEZ featuring OCTAHVIA*

OCTOPUS *UK / France, male vocal / instrumental group (5 WEEKS)*

		pos	wks
22 Jun 96	**YOUR SMILE** *Food CDFOOD 78*	42	2
14 Sep 96	**SAVED** *Food CDFOODS 84*	40	2
23 Nov 96	**JEALOUSY** *Food CDFOODS 87*	59	1

Alan O'DAY *US, male vocalist (3 WEEKS)*

		pos	wks
2 Jul 77	**UNDERCOVER ANGEL** *Atlantic K 10926* ▲	43	3

ODETTA – *See Harry BELAFONTE*

Daniel O'DONNELL *Ireland, male vocalist (64 WEEKS)*

		pos	wks
12 Sep 92	**I JUST WANT TO DANCE WITH YOU** *Ritz RITZ 250P*	20	7
2 Jan 93	**THE THREE BELLS** *Ritz RITZCD 239*	71	1
8 May 93	**THE LOVE IN YOUR EYES** *Ritz RITZCD 257*	47	3
7 Aug 93	**WHAT EVER HAPPENED TO OLD FASHIONED LOVE** *Ritz RITZCD 262*	21	5
16 Apr 94	**SINGING THE BLUES** *Ritz RITZCD 270*	23	3
26 Nov 94	**THE GIFT** *Ritz RITZCD 275*	46	3
10 Jun 95	**SECRET LOVE** *Ritz RITZCD 285* [1]	28	3
9 Mar 96	**TIMELESS** *Ritz RITZCD 293* [1]	32	3
28 Sep 96	**FOOTSTEPS** *Ritz RITZCD 300*	25	5
7 Jun 97	**THE LOVE SONGS EP** *Ritz RITZCD 306*	27	4
11 Apr 98 ●	**GIVE A LITTLE LOVE** *Ritz RITZCD 315*	7	5
17 Oct 98	**THE MAGIC IS THERE** *Ritz RZCD 320*	16	4
20 Mar 99	**THE WAY DREAMS ARE** *Ritz RZCD 325*	18	3
24 Jul 99	**UNO MAS** *Ritz RZCD 326*	25	3
18 Dec 99	**A CHRISTMAS KISS** *Ritz RZCD 330*	20	4
15 Apr 00	**LIGHT A CANDLE** *Ritz RZCD 335*	23	4
16 Dec 00	**MORNING HAS BROKEN** *Ritz RZCD 341*	32	4

[1] Daniel O'Donnell and Mary Duff

Tracks on The Love Songs EP: Save the Last Dance for Me / I Can't Stop Loving You / You're the Only Good Thing / Limerick You're a Lady

ODYSSEY (399 Top 500) *Soul / disco vocal trio formed in New York, US, by non-natives Lillian and Louise Lopez (from Connecticut) and Manila-born Tony Reynolds (replaced 1978 by Bill McEachern). UK success not mirrored in US, where only their debut hit reached the Top 40 (82 WEEKS)*

		pos	wks
24 Dec 77 ●	**NATIVE NEW YORKER** *RCA PC 1129*	5	11
21 Jun 80 ★	**USE IT UP AND WEAR IT OUT** *RCA PB 1962*	1	12
13 Sep 80 ●	**IF YOU'RE LOOKIN' FOR A WAY OUT** *RCA 5*	6	15
17 Jan 81	**HANG TOGETHER** *RCA 23*	36	7
30 May 81 ●	**GOING BACK TO MY ROOTS** *RCA 85*	4	12
19 Sep 81	**IT WILL BE ALRIGHT** *RCA 128*	43	5
12 Jun 82 ●	**INSIDE OUT** *RCA 226*	3	11
11 Sep 82	**MAGIC TOUCH** *RCA 275*	41	5
17 Aug 85	**(JOY) I KNOW IT** *Mirror BUTCH 12*	51	4

Esther and Abi OFARIM *Israel, female / male vocal duo – Esther Zaled and Abraham Reichstadt (22 WEEKS)*

		pos	wks
14 Feb 68 ★	**CINDERELLA ROCKEFELLA** *Philips BF 1640*	1	13
19 Jun 68	**ONE MORE DANCE** *Philips BF 1678*	13	9

Wiston OFFICE – *See Frank K featuring Wiston OFFICE*

OFF-SHORE *Germany, male instrumental / production duo – Jens Lissat and Peter Harder (12 WEEKS)*

		pos	wks
22 Dec 90 ●	**I CAN'T TAKE THE POWER** *CBS 6565707*	7	11
17 Aug 91	**I GOT A LITTLE SONG** *Dance Pool 6568257*	64	1

OFFSPRING *US, male vocal / instrumental group – lead vocal Dexter Holland (56 WEEKS)*

		pos	wks
25 Feb 95	**SELF ESTEEM** *Golf CDSHOLE 001*	37	3
19 Aug 95	**GOTTA GET AWAY** *Out Of Step WOOS 2CDS*	43	2
1 Feb 97	**ALL I WANT** *Epitaph 64912*	31	2
26 Apr 97	**GONE AWAY** *Epitaph 64982*	42	1
30 Jan 99 ★	**PRETTY FLY (FOR A WHITE GUY)** *Columbia 666802* ■	1	11
8 May 99 ●	**WHY DON'T YOU GET A JOB?** *Columbia 6673542*	2	8
11 Sep 99	**THE KIDS AREN'T ALRIGHT** *Columbia 6677632*	11	6
4 Dec 99	**SHE'S GOT ISSUES** *Columbia 6683772*	41	2
18 Nov 00 ●	**ORIGINAL PRANKSTER** *Columbia 6699972*	6	8
31 Mar 01	**WANT YOU BAD** *Columbia 6709292*	15	5
19 May 01	**WANT YOU BAD (re-entry)** *Columbia 6709292*	34	4
7 Jul 01	**MILLION MILES AWAY** *Columbia 6714082*	21	4

OH WELL *Germany, male producer – Ackim Faulker (7 WEEKS)*

		pos	wks
14 Oct 89	**OH WELL** *Parlophone R 6236*	28	6
3 Mar 90	**RADAR LOVE** *Parlophone R 6244*	65	1

OHIO EXPRESS *US, male vocal / instrumental group (15 WEEKS)*

		pos	wks
5 Jun 68 ●	**YUMMY YUMMY YUMMY** *Pye International 7N 25459*	5	15

OHIO PLAYERS *US, male vocal / instrumental group (4 WEEKS)*

		pos	wks
10 Jul 76	**WHO'D SHE COO** *Mercury PLAY 001*	43	4

O'JAYS (494 Top 500) *One of the most consistently successful R&B vocal groups; members included Walter Williams and Eddie Levert (whose sons, Gerald and Sean, are in Levert). Formed in 1958 in Ohio, US, they have had five decades of US R&B hits, many produced and composed by Gamble and Huff (72 WEEKS)*

		pos	wks
23 Sep 72	**BACK STABBERS** *CBS 8270*	14	9
3 Mar 73 ●	**LOVE TRAIN** *CBS 1181* ▲	9	13
31 Jan 76	**I LOVE MUSIC** *Philadelphia International PIR 3879*	13	9
12 Feb 77	**DARLIN' DARLIN' BABY (SWEET, TENDER, LOVE)** *Philadelphia International PIR 4834*	24	6
8 Apr 78	**I LOVE MUSIC (re-issue)** *Philadelphia International PIR 6093*	36	3
17 Jun 78	**USED TA BE MY GIRL** *Philadelphia International PIR 6332*	12	12
30 Sep 78	**BRANDY** *Philadelphia International PIR 6658*	21	9
29 Sep 79	**SING A HAPPY SONG** *Philadelphia International PIR 7825*	39	6
30 Jul 83	**PUT OUR HEADS TOGETHER** *Philadelphia International A 3642*	45	5

John O'KANE *UK, male vocalist (4 WEEKS)*

		pos	wks
9 May 92	**STAY WITH ME** *Circa YR 88*	41	4

OL' DIRTY BASTARD *US, male rapper – Russell Jones (25 WEEKS)*

		pos	wks
27 Jun 98 ●	**GHETTO SUPERSTAR (THAT IS WHAT YOU ARE)** *Interscope IND 95593* [1]	2	17
8 Jul 00	**GOT YOUR MONEY** *Elektra E 7077CD* [2]	11	8

[1] Pras Michel featuring Ol' Dirty Bastard introducing Mya [2] Ol' Dirty Bastard featuring Kelis

See also WU-TANG CLAN

OLD SKOOL ORCHESTRA *UK, male DJ / production duo (1 WEEK)*

		pos	wks
23 Jan 99	**B-BOY HUMP** *East West EW 186CD1*	55	1

See also STRETCH 'N' VERN present MADDOG

Mike OLDFIELD 251 Top 500 *Composer / producer / multi-instrumentalist, b. 15 May 1953, Reading, UK. His chart-topping 1973 debut album, 'Tubular Bells', spent five years on the chart, and the belated 'Tubular Bells II' also reached UK No.1 (1992) (113 WEEKS)* pos/wks

13 Jul 74	**MIKE OLDFIELD'S SINGLE (THEME FROM TUBULAR BELLS)** *Virgin VS 101*	31	6
20 Dec 75 ●	**IN DULCE JUBILO / ON HORSEBACK** *Virgin VS 131*	4	10
27 Nov 76 ●	**PORTSMOUTH** *Virgin VS 163*	3	12
23 Dec 78	**TAKE 4 (EP)** *Virgin VS 238*	72	3
21 Apr 79	**GUILTY** *Virgin VS 245*	22	8
8 Dec 79	**BLUE PETER** *Virgin VS 317*	19	9
20 Mar 82	**FIVE MILES OUT** *Virgin VS 464* [1]	43	5
12 Jun 82	**FAMILY MAN** *Virgin VS 489* [1]	45	6
28 May 83 ●	**MOONLIGHT SHADOW** *Virgin VS 586* [2]	4	17
14 Jan 84	**CRIME OF PASSION** *Virgin VS 648* [1]	61	3
30 Jun 84	**TO FRANCE** *Virgin VS 686* [1]	48	7
14 Dec 85	**PICTURES IN THE DARK** *Virgin VS 836* [3]	50	6
3 Oct 92 ●	**SENTINEL** *WEA YZ 698*	10	6
19 Dec 92	**TATTOO** *WEA YZ 708*	33	5
17 Apr 93	**THE BELL** *WEA YZ 737CD*	50	2
9 Oct 93	**MOONLIGHT SHADOW (re-issue)** *Virgin VSCDT 1477*	52	2
17 Dec 94	**HIBERNACULUM** *WEA YZ 871CD*	47	3
2 Sep 95	**LET THERE BE LIGHT** *WEA YZ 880CD*	51	1
22 Nov 97	**WOMEN OF IRELAND** *WEA WEA 093CD*	70	1
24 Apr 99	**FAR ABOVE THE CLOUDS** *WEA WEA 206CD1*	53	1

[1] Mike Oldfield featuring Maggie Reilly [2] Mike Oldfield with vocals by Maggie Reilly [3] Mike Oldfield featuring Aled Jones, Anita Hegerland and Barry Palmer

Tracks on Take 4 (EP): Portsmouth / In Dulce Jubilo / Wrekorder Wrondo / Sailors Hornpipe. 'The Bell' credits Vivian Stanshall

Sally OLDFIELD *UK, female vocalist (13 WEEKS)* pos/wks

9 Dec 78	**MIRRORS** *Bronze BRO 66*	19	13

Misty OLDLAND *UK, female vocalist (7 WEEKS)* pos/wks

16 Oct 93	**GOT ME A FEELING** *Columbia 6597872*	59	2
12 Mar 94	**A FAIR AFFAIR (JE T'AIME)** *Columbia 6601612*	49	4
9 Jul 94	**I WROTE YOU A SONG** *Columbia 6603732*	73	1

OLGA *Italy, female vocalist (1 WEEK)* pos/wks

1 Oct 94	**I'M A BITCH** *UMM UMM 144UKCD*	68	1

OLIVE *UK, male / female vocal / instrumental group – vocal Ruth Ann Boyle (24 WEEKS)* pos/wks

7 Sep 96	**YOU'RE NOT ALONE** *RCA 74321406272*	42	4
15 Mar 97	**MIRACLE** *RCA 74321461242*	41	2
17 May 97 ★	**YOU'RE NOT ALONE (re-issue)** *RCA 74321473232* ■	1	13
16 Aug 97	**OUTLAW** *RCA 74321508372*	14	4
8 Nov 97	**MIRACLE (re-mix)** *RCA 74321530842*	41	1

OLIVER *US, male vocalist – William Swofford (18 WEEKS)* pos/wks

9 Aug 69 ●	**GOOD MORNING STARSHINE** *CBS 4435*	6	16
27 Dec 69	**GOOD MORNING STARSHINE (re-entry)** *CBS 4435*	39	2

Frankie OLIVER *UK, male vocalist (1 WEEK)* pos/wks

7 Jun 97	**GIVE HER WHAT SHE WANTS** *Island Jamaica IJCD 2011*	58	1

OLLIE and JERRY
US, male vocal duo – Ollie Brown and Jerry Knight (14 WEEKS) pos/wks

23 Jun 84 ●	**BREAKIN' ... THERE'S NO STOPPING US** *Polydor POSP 690*	5	11
9 Mar 85	**ELECTRIC BOOGALOO** *Polydor POSP 730*	57	3

OLYMPIC ORCHESTRA *UK, orchestra (15 WEEKS)* pos/wks

1 Oct 83	**REILLY** *Red Bus RBUS 82*	26	15

OLYMPIC RUNNERS *UK, male vocal / instrumental group (21 WEEKS)* pos/wks

13 May 78	**WHATEVER IT TAKES** *RCA PC 5078*	61	2
14 Oct 78	**GET IT WHILE YOU CAN** *Polydor RUN 7*	35	6
20 Jan 79	**SIR DANCEALOT** *Polydor POSP 17*	35	6
28 Jul 79	**THE BITCH** *Polydor POSP 63*	37	7

OLYMPICS *US, male vocal group (9 WEEKS)* pos/wks

3 Oct 58	**WESTERN MOVIES** *HMV POP 528*	12	8
19 Jan 61	**I WISH I COULD SHIMMY LIKE MY SISTER KATE** *Vogue V 9174*	40	1

OMAR *UK, male vocalist – Omar Hammer (18 WEEKS)* pos/wks

22 Jun 91	**THERE'S NOTHING LIKE THIS** *Talkin Loud TLK 9*	14	7
23 May 92	**YOUR LOSS MY GAIN** *Talkin Loud TLK 22*	47	2
26 Sep 92	**MUSIC** *Talkin Loud TLK 28*	53	2
23 Jul 94	**OUTSIDE / SATURDAY** *RCA 74321213982*	43	2
15 Oct 94	**KEEP STEPPIN'** *RCA 74321233682*	57	1
2 Aug 97	**SAY NOTHIN'** *RCA 74321502872*	29	2
18 Oct 97	**GOLDEN BROWN** *RCA 74321525422*	37	2

OMC *New Zealand, male vocalist – Paul Fuemana Lawrence (17 WEEKS)* pos/wks

20 Jul 96 ●	**HOW BIZARRE** *Polydor 5776202*	5	16
18 Jan 97	**ON THE RUN** *Polydor 5732452*	56	1

OMD – *See ORCHESTRAL MANOEUVRES IN THE DARK*

OMNI TRIO *UK, male producer –Rob Haigh (1 WEEK)* pos/wks

7 Jul 01	**THE ANGELS & SHADOWS PROJECT** *Moving Shadow SHADOW 150CD*	44	1

ONE *UK, male vocal group (2 WEEKS)* pos/wks

11 Jan 97	**ONE MORE CHANCE** *Mercury MERDD 478*	31	2

Michie ONE – *See Louchie LOU and Michie ONE*

ONE DOVE *UK, male / female vocal / instrumental group (9 WEEKS)* pos/wks

7 Aug 93	**WHITE LOVE** *Boy's Own BOICD 14*	43	3
16 Oct 93	**BREAKDOWN** *Boy's Own BOICD 15*	24	3
15 Jan 94	**WHY DON'T YOU TAKE ME** *Boy's Own BOICD 16*	30	3

187 LOCKDOWN *UK, male production duo – Danny Harrison and Julian Jonah (16 WEEKS)* pos/wks

15 Nov 97	**GUNMAN** *East West EW 140CD*	16	4
25 Apr 98 ●	**KUNG-FU** *East West EW 155CD*	9	5
25 Jul 98	**GUNMAN (re-mix)** *East West EW 176CD*	17	4
3 Oct 98	**THE DON** *East West EW 180CD*	29	2
13 Feb 99	**ALL 'N' ALL** *East West EW 194CD* [1]	43	1

[1] 187 Lockdown (featuring D'Empress)

See also REFLEX featuring MC VIPER

ONE HUNDRED TON AND A FEATHER – *See Jonathan KING*

ONE MINUTE SILENCE
UK, male vocal / rap / instrumental group (1 WEEK) pos/wks

20 Jan 01	**FISH OUT OF WATER** *V2 VVR 5013213*	56	1

112 *US, male vocalist (34 WEEKS)* pos/wks

28 Jun 97 ★	**I'LL BE MISSING YOU** *Puff Daddy 7421499102* [1] ◆■▲	1	21
10 Jan 98	**ALL CRIED OUT** *Epic 6652715* [2]	12	5
14 Feb 98	**SKY'S THE LIMIT** *Puff Daddy 7421561992* [3]	35	2
30 Jun 01	**IT'S OVER NOW** *Puff Daddy / Arista 74321849912*	22	3
8 Sep 01	**PEACHES & CREAM** *Arista 74321882632*	32	3

[1] Puff Daddy and faith Evans featuring 112 [2] Allure featuring 112 [3] Notorious B.I.G. featuring 112

ONE THE JUGGLER *UK, male vocal / instrumental group (1 WEEK)* pos/wks

19 Feb 83	**PASSION KILLER** *Regard RG 107*	71	1

1000 CLOWNS *US, male / female vocal / rap group (4 WEEKS)* pos/wks

22 May 99	**(NOT THE) GREATEST RAPPER** *Elektra E 3759CD*	23	4

THE OFFICIAL UK SINGLES CHART 50TH ANNIVERSARY

1984

IN THE YEAR IN WHICH THE MINERS' STRIKES HIT THE UK, THE CONSERVATIVE PARTY CONFERENCE IN BRIGHTON WAS BOMBED BY THE IRA, MARVIN GAYE DIED AND YUPPIE ENTERED THE DICTIONARY, AND THE UK'S FIRST THREE MILLION SELLER, 'DO THEY KNOW IT'S CHRISTMAS?' BY BAND AID, WAS RELEASED, **CLAIRE SWEENEY** REVEALS A POWERFUL INFLUENCE IN HER BID TO MAKE IT AS A SINGER ...

“In 1984 I saw the film 'Lady Sings the Blues' with **Diana Ross**. From there I became interested in Billie Holiday which developed into a love for jazz as my main musical influence. If it wasn't for that film, I wouldn't have developed my own singing style which has got me where I am today.”

SINGLE OF THE YEAR 'Two Tribes' Frankie Goes To Hollywood
ALBUM OF THE YEAR 'Legend' Bob Marley

1984

ONE TRIBE – *See OUR TRIBE / ONE TRIBE*

ONE 2 MANY

Norway, male / female vocal / instrumental group (11 WEEKS) pos/wks

12 Nov 88	**DOWNTOWN** *A & M AM 476*	65	4
3 Jun 89	**DOWNTOWN (re-issue)** *A & M AM 456*	43	7

ONE WAY *US, male vocal / instrumental group (8 WEEKS)* pos/wks

8 Dec 79	**MUSIC** *MCA 542* [1]	56	6
29 Jun 85	**LET'S TALK** *MCA 972*	64	2

[1] One Way featuring Al Hudson

Alexander O'NEAL (260 Top 500) *Soulful ex-vocalist with Minneapolis-based Flyte Time (line-up featured star producers Jimmy Jam and Terry Lewis, who worked on most of his hits), b. 15 Nov 1953, Mississippi, US. Co-wrote his biggest hit and clocked up impressive five Top 20 albums between 1985 and 1993 (112 WEEKS)* pos/wks

28 Dec 85 ●	**SATURDAY LOVE** *Tabu A 6829* [1]	6	11
15 Feb 86	**IF YOU WERE HERE TONIGHT** *Tabu A 6391*	13	10
5 Apr 86	**A BROKEN HEART CAN MEND** *Tabu A 6244*	53	4
6 Jun 87	**FAKE** *Tabu 650891 7*	33	6
31 Oct 87 ●	**CRITICIZE** *Tabu 651211 7*	4	14
6 Feb 88	**NEVER KNEW LOVE LIKE THIS** *Tabu 651382 7* [2]	26	7
25 Feb 88	**HEARSAY '88** *Tabu 654466 7*	56	2
28 May 88	**THE LOVERS** *Tabu 6515957*	28	4
23 Jul 88	**(WHAT CAN I SAY) TO MAKE YOU LOVE ME** *Tabu 652852 7*	27	5
24 Sep 88	**FAKE '88 (re-mix)** *Tabu 652949 7*	16	7
10 Dec 88	**CHRISTMAS SONG (CHESTNUTS ROASTING ON AN OPEN FIRE) / THANK YOU FOR A GOOD YEAR** *Tabu 653182 7*	30	5
25 Feb 89	**HEARSAY '89** *Tabu 654667 7*	56	2
2 Sep 89	**SUNSHINE** *Tabu 655191 7*	72	1
9 Dec 89	**HITMIX (OFFICIAL BOOTLEG MEGA-MIX)** *Tabu 655504 7*	19	7
24 Mar 90	**SATURDAY LOVE (re-mix)** *Tabu 655680 7* [1]	55	2
12 Jan 91	**ALL TRUE MAN** *Tabu 6565717*	18	6
23 Mar 91	**WHAT IS THIS THING CALLED LOVE?** *Tabu 6567317*	53	2
11 May 91	**SHAME ON ME** *Tabu 6568737*	71	1
9 May 92	**SENTIMENTAL** *Tabu 6580147*	53	2
30 Jan 93	**LOVE MAKES NO SENSE** *Tabu AMCD 7708*	28	6
3 Jul 93	**IN THE MIDDLE** *Tabu 5877152*	32	3
25 Sep 93	**ALL THAT MATTERS TO ME** *Tabu 6577232*	67	1
2 Nov 96	**LET'S GET TOGETHER** *EMI Premier PRESCD 11*	38	2
2 Aug 97	**BABY COME TO ME** *One World OWECD 1* [2]	56	1
12 Dec 98	**CRITICIZE '98 MIX (re-recording)** *One World OWECD 3*	51	1

[1] Cherrelle with Alexander O'Neal [2] Alexander O'Neal featuring Cherrelle

Shaquille O'NEAL *US, male rapper (4 WEEKS)* pos/wks

26 Mar 94	**I'M OUTSTANDING** *Jive JIVECD 349*	70	1
1 Feb 97	**YOU CAN'T STOP THE REIGN** *Interscope IND 95522*	40	2
17 Oct 98	**THE WAY IT'S GOIN' DOWN (T.W.I.S.M. FOR LIFE)** *A&M 5827932*	62	1+

ONEPHATDEEVA – *See A.T.F.C. presents ONEPHATDEEVA*

ONES *US, male production trio (10 WEEKS)* pos/wks

20 Oct 01 ●	**FLAWLESS** *Positiva CDTIV 164*	7	9
29 Dec 01	**FLAWLESS (re-entry)** *Positiva CDTIV 164*	74	1

ONLY ONES *UK, male vocal / instrumental group (2 WEEKS)* pos/wks

1 Feb 92	**ANOTHER GIRL – ANOTHER PLANET** *Columbia 6577507*	57	2

Yoko ONO *Japan, female vocalist (5 WEEKS)* pos/wks

28 Feb 81	**WALKING ON THIN ICE** *Geffen K 79202*	35	5

See also John LENNON

ONSLAUGHT *UK, male vocal / instrumental group (3 WEEKS)* pos/wks

6 May 89	**LET THERE BE ROCK** *London LON 224*	50	3

ONYX *US, male rap group (8 WEEKS)* pos/wks

28 Aug 93	**SLAM** *Columbia 6596302*	31	4
27 Nov 93	**THROW YA GUNZ** *Columbia 6598312*	34	3
20 Feb 99	**ROC-IN-IT** *Independiente ISOM 21MS* [1]	59	1

[1] Deejay Punk-Roc vs Onyx

OO LA LA *UK, male vocal / instrumental group (2 WEEKS)* pos/wks

5 Sep 92	**OO . . . AH . . . CANTONA** *North Speed OOAH 1*	64	2

OOBERMAN *UK, male / female vocal / instrumental group (5 WEEKS)* pos/wks

8 May 99	**BLOSSOMS FALLING** *Independiente ISOM 26MS*	39	2
17 Jul 99	**MILLION SUNS** *Independiente ISOM 30MS*	43	1
23 Oct 99	**TEARS FROM A WILLOW** *Independiente ISOM 37MS*	63	1
8 Apr 00	**SHORLEY WALL** *Independiente ISOM 41MS*	47	1

OOE – *See COLUMBO featuring OOE*

OPEN ARMS featuring ROWETTA

UK, male / female vocal / instrumental group (1 WEEK) pos/wks

15 Jun 96	**HEY MR DJ** *All Around the World CDGLOBE 136*	62	1

OPM *US, male vocal / instrumental group (14 WEEKS)* pos/wks

14 Jul 01 ●	**HEAVEN IS A HALFPIPE** *Atlantic AT 0107CD*	4	14

OPTIMYSTIC *UK, male / female vocal group (6 WEEKS)* pos/wks

17 Sep 94	**CAUGHT UP IN MY HEART** *WEA YZ 841CD*	49	3
10 Dec 94	**NOTHING BUT LOVE** *WEA 864CD1*	37	2
13 May 95	**BEST THING IN THE WORLD** *WEA YZ 920CD*	70	1

OPUS *Austria, male vocal / instrumental group (15 WEEKS)* pos/wks

15 Jun 85 ●	**LIVE IS LIFE** *Polydor POSP 743*	6	15

OPUS III *UK, male / female vocal / instrumental group (10 WEEKS)* pos/wks

22 Feb 92 ●	**IT'S A FINE DAY** *PWL International PWL 215*	5	8
27 Jun 92	**I TALK TO THE WIND** *PWL International PWL 235*	52	1
11 Jun 94	**WHEN YOU MADE THE MOUNTAIN** *PWL International PWCD 302*	71	1

ORANGE *UK, male vocal / instrumental group (1 WEEK)* pos/wks

8 Oct 94	**JUDY OVER THE RAINBOW** *Chrysalis CDCHS 5012*	73	1

ORANGE JUICE *UK, male vocal / instrumental group (34 WEEKS)* pos/wks

7 Nov 81	**L.O.V.E. . . . LOVE** *Polydor POSP 357*	65	2
30 Jan 82	**FELICITY** *Polydor POSP 386*	63	3
21 Aug 82	**TWO HEARTS TOGETHER / HOKOYO** *Polydor POSP 470*	60	2
23 Oct 82	**I CAN'T HELP MYSELF** *Polydor POSP 522*	42	3
19 Feb 83 ●	**RIP IT UP** *Polydor POSP 547*	8	11
4 Jun 83	**FLESH OF MY FLESH** *Polydor OJ 4*	41	6
25 Feb 84	**BRIDGE** *Polydor OJ 5*	67	2
12 May 84	**WHAT PRESENCE?** *Polydor OJ 6*	47	4
27 Oct 84	**LEAN PERIOD** *Polydor OJ 7*	74	1

See also Edwyn COLLINS

ORB *UK, male instrumental / production duo – Dr Alex Paterson and Kris Weston (32 WEEKS)* pos/wks

15 Jun 91	**PERPETUAL DAWN** *Big Life BLRD 46*	61	1
20 Jun 92 ●	**BLUE ROOM** *Big Life BLRT 75*	8	6
17 Oct 92	**ASSASSIN** *Big Life BLRT 81*	12	5
13 Nov 93 ●	**LITTLE FLUFFY CLOUDS** *Big Life BLRD 98*	10	5
5 Feb 94	**PERPETUAL DAWN (re-entry)** *Big Life BLRD 46*	18	5
27 May 95	**OXBOW LAKES** *Island CID 609*	38	2
8 Feb 97 ●	**TOXYGENE** *Island CID 652*	4	4
24 May 97	**ASYLUM** *Island CID 657*	20	2
24 Feb 01	**ONCE MORE** *Island CID 767*	38	2

Roy ORBISON (19 Top 500) *Unmistakable vocalist, b. 23 Apr 1936, Texas, d. 6 Dec 1988. The "Big O" recorded for legendary Sun label in the mid-1950s, and was the most popular US singer in Britain during the Beat Boom era (1963-65), when The Beatles supported him on tour. The performer, whose trademark was his dark glasses, had a hit span of 33 years, and was enjoying a successful comeback, both as a soloist and member of the Traveling Wilburys, when he died. This multi-award-winner is in the Grammy Hall of Fame as well as the Songwriters and Rock and Roll Halls of Fame (345 WEEKS)* pos/wks

28 Jul 60	**ONLY THE LONELY** *London HLU 9149*	36	1
11 Aug 60 ★	**ONLY THE LONELY (re-entry)** *London HLU 9149*	1	23
27 Oct 60	**BLUE ANGEL** *London HLU 9207*	11	16
25 May 61 ●	**RUNNING SCARED** *London HLU 9342* ▲	9	15
21 Sep 61	**CRYIN'** *London HLU 9405*	25	9
8 Mar 62 ●	**DREAM BABY** *London HLU 9511*	2	14
28 Jun 62	**THE CROWD** *London HLU 9561*	40	4
8 Nov 62	**WORKIN' FOR THE MAN** *London HLU 9607*	50	1
28 Feb 63 ●	**IN DREAMS** *London HLU 9676*	6	23
30 May 63 ●	**FALLING** *London HLU 9727*	9	11
19 Sep 63 ●	**BLUE BAYOU / MEAN WOMAN BLUES** *London HLU 9777*	3	19
20 Feb 64	**BORNE ON THE WIND** *London HLU 9845*	15	10
30 Apr 64 ★	**IT'S OVER** *London HLU 9882*	1	18
10 Sep 64 ★	**OH, PRETTY WOMAN** *London HLU 9919* ▲	1	18
19 Nov 64 ●	**PRETTY PAPER** *London HLU 9930*	6	11
11 Feb 65	**GOODNIGHT** *London HLU 9951*	14	9
22 Jul 65	**(SAY) YOU'RE MY GIRL** *London HLU 9978*	23	8
9 Sep 65	**RIDE AWAY** *London HLU 9986*	34	6
4 Nov 65	**CRAWLING BACK** *London HLU 10000*	19	9
27 Jan 66	**BREAKIN' UP IS BREAKIN' MY HEART** *London HLU 10015*	22	6
7 Apr 66	**TWINKLE TOES** *London HLU 10034*	29	5
16 Jun 66	**LANA** *London HLU 10051*	15	9
18 Aug 66 ●	**TOO SOON TO KNOW** *London HLU 10067*	3	17
1 Dec 66	**THERE WON'T BE MANY COMING HOME** *London HLU 10096*	12	9
23 Feb 67	**SO GOOD** *London HLU 10113*	32	6
24 Jul 68	**WALK ON** *London HLU 10206*	39	10
25 Sep 68	**HEARTACHE** *London HLU 10222*	44	4
30 Apr 69	**MY FRIEND** *London HLU 10261*	35	4
13 Sep 69	**PENNY ARCADE** *London HLU 10285*	40	3
11 Oct 69	**PENNY ARCADE (re-entry)** *London HLU 10285*	27	11
14 Jan 89 ●	**YOU GOT IT** *Virgin VS 1166*	3	10
1 Apr 89	**SHE'S A MYSTERY TO ME** *Virgin VS 1173*	27	5
4 Jul 92 ●	**I DROVE ALL NIGHT** *MCA MCS 1652*	7	10
22 Aug 92	**CRYING** *Virgin America VUS 63* [1]	13	6
7 Nov 92	**HEARTBREAK RADIO** *Virgin America VUS 68*	36	3
13 Nov 93	**I DROVE ALL NIGHT (re-issue)** *Virgin America VUSCD 79*	47	2

[1] Roy Orbison (duet with kd lang)

William ORBIT *UK, male producer – William Wainwright (18 WEEKS)* pos/wks

26 Jun 93	**WATER FROM A VINE LEAF** *Guerilla VSCDT 1465*	59	1
18 Dec 99 ●	**BARBER'S ADAGIO FOR STRINGS** *WEA WEA 247 CD*	4	13
25 Mar 00	**BARBER'S ADAGIO FOR STRINGS (re-entry)** *WEA WEA 247 CD*	69	2
6 May 00	**RAVEL'S PAVANE POUR UNE INFANTE DEFUNTE** *WEA WEA 269CD*	31	2

ORBITAL
UK, male instrumental duo – Paul and Phil Hartnoll (53 WEEKS) pos/wks

24 Mar 90	**CHIME** *ffrr F B5*	17	7
22 Sep 90	**OMEN** *ffrr F 145*	46	3
19 Jan 91	**SATAN** *ffrr FX 149*	31	4
15 Feb 92	**MUTATIONS (EP)** *ffrr FCD 181*	24	3
26 Sep 92	**RADICCIO (EP)** *Internal LIARX 1*	37	2
21 Aug 93	**LUSH** *Internal LIECD 7*	43	2
24 Sep 94	**ARE WE HERE** *Internal LIECD 15*	33	2
27 May 95	**BELFAST** *Volume VOLCD 1*	53	1
27 Apr 96	**THE BOX** *Internal LIECD 30*	11	4
11 Jan 97 ●	**SATAN (re-recording)** *Internal LIECD 37*	3	6
19 Apr 97 ●	**THE SAINT** *ffrr FCD 296*	3	7
20 Mar 99	**STYLE** *ffrr FCD 358*	13	4
17 Jul 99	**NOTHING LEFT** *ffrr FCD 365*	32	2
11 Mar 00	**BEACHED** *ffrr FCD 377* [1]	36	3
28 Apr 01	**FUNNY BREAK (ONE IS ENOUGH)** *ffrr FCD 395*	21	3

[1] Orbital and Angelo Badalamenti

Tracks on Mutations (EP): Chime Crime / Oolaa / Fahrenheit 3D 3 / Speed Freak. Tracks on Radiccio (EP): Halcyon / The Naked and the Dead / Sunday. The listed flip side of 'Belfast' was 'Innocent X' by Therapy?

ORCHESTRA ON THE HALF SHELL
US, male vocal / instrumental group (6 WEEKS) pos/wks

15 Dec 90	**TURTLE RHAPSODY** *SBK SBK 17*	36	6

ORCHESTRAL MANOEUVRES IN THE DARK (90 Top 500) *One of the most regular chart visitors of the 1980s had a nucleus of Andy McCluskey (v/syn/b) and Paul Humphries (syn), who left in 1989. This Liverpool-based synthesizer band had numerous international hits including 'Maid of Orleans', which was Germany's biggest seller in 1982 (201 WEEKS)* pos/wks

9 Feb 80	**RED FRAME WHITE LIGHT** *Dindisc DIN 6*	67	2
10 May 80	**MESSAGES** *Dindisc DIN 15*	13	11
4 Oct 80 ●	**ENOLA GAY** *Dindisc DIN 22*	8	15
29 Aug 81 ●	**SOUVENIR** *Dindisc DIN 24*	3	12
24 Oct 81 ●	**JOAN OF ARC** *Dindisc DIN 36*	5	14
23 Jan 82 ●	**MAID OF ORLEANS (THE WALTZ JOAN OF ARC)** *Dindisc DIN 40*	4	10
19 Feb 83	**GENETIC ENGINEERING** *Virgin VS 527*	20	8
9 Apr 83	**TELEGRAPH** *Virgin VS 580*	42	4
14 Apr 84 ●	**LOCOMOTION** *Virgin VS 660*	5	11
16 Jun 84	**TALKING LOUD AND CLEAR** *Virgin VS 685*	11	10
8 Sep 84	**TESLA GIRLS** *Virgin VS 705*	21	8
10 Nov 84	**NEVER TURN AWAY** *Virgin VS 727*	70	2
25 May 85	**SO IN LOVE** *Virgin VS 766*	27	7
20 Jul 85	**SECRET** *Virgin VS 796*	34	7
26 Oct 85	**LA FEMME ACCIDENT** *Virgin VS 811*	42	4
3 May 86	**IF YOU LEAVE** *Virgin VS 843*	48	4
6 Sep 86	**(FOREVER) LIVE AND DIE** *Virgin VS 888*	11	10
15 Nov 86	**WE LOVE YOU** *Virgin VS 911*	54	5
2 May 87	**SHAME** *Virgin VS 938*	52	3
6 Feb 88	**DREAMING** *Virgin VS 987*	50	3
2 Jul 88	**DREAMING (re-entry)** *Virgin VS 987*	60	3
30 Mar 91 ●	**SAILING ON THE SEVEN SEAS** *Virgin VS 1310*	3	13
6 Jul 91 ●	**PANDORA'S BOX** *Virgin VS 1331*	7	10
14 Sep 91	**THEN YOU TURN AWAY** *Virgin VS 1368*	50	4
7 Dec 91	**CALL MY NAME** *Virgin VS 1380*	50	2
15 May 93	**STAND ABOVE ME** *Virgin VSCDG 1444*	21	4
17 Jul 93	**DREAM OF ME (BASED ON LOVE'S THEME)** *Virgin VSCDT 1461*	24	5
18 Sep 93	**EVERYDAY** *Virgin VSCDT 1471*	59	2
17 Aug 96	**WALKING ON THE MILKY WAY** *Virgin VSCDT 1599*	17	5
2 Nov 96	**UNIVERSAL** *Virgin VSCDT 1606*	55	1
26 Sep 98	**THE OMD REMIXES (EP)** *Virgin VSCDT 1694*	35	2

Group often known as OMD. Tracks on the OMD Remixes (EP): Enola Gay / Souvenir / Electricity

Raul ORELLANA *Spain, male producer (8 WEEKS)* pos/wks

30 Sep 89	**THE REAL WILD HOUSE** *RCA BCM 322*	29	8

O.R.G.A.N. *Spain, male DJ / producer (2 WEEKS)* pos/wks

16 May 98	**TO THE WORLD** *Multiply CDMULTY 34*	33	2

ORIGIN *UK, male production duo (1 WEEK)* pos/wks

12 Aug 00	**WIDE EYED ANGEL** *Lost Language LOST 001CD*	73	1

ORIGIN UNKNOWN
UK, male instrumental / production duo (1 WEEK) pos/wks

13 Jul 96	**VALLEY OF THE SHADOWS** *Ram RAMM 16CD*	60	1

ORIGINAL *US, male vocal / instrumental duo – Everett Bradley and Walter Taieb (14 WEEKS)* pos/wks

14 Jan 95	**I LUV U BABY** *Ore AG 8CD*	31	3

			pos	wks
19 Aug 95	●	**I LUV U BABY (re-mix)** *Ore AGR 8CD*	2	9
11 Nov 95		**B 2 GETHER** *Ore AG 12CD*	29	2

ORIGINOO GUNN CLAPPAZ – *See HELTAH SKELTAH and ORIGINOO GUNN CLAPPAZ as the FABULOUS FIVE*

ORION
UK, male / female production / vocal / instrumental duo (2 WEEKS) pos/wks

			pos	wks
7 Oct 00		**ETERNITY** *Incentive CENT 11CDS*	38	2

ORLANDO – *See PRETENDERS; LA's*

Tony ORLANDO
US, male vocalist – Michael Anthony Orlando Cassavitis (11 WEEKS) pos/wks

			pos	wks
5 Oct 61	●	**BLESS YOU** *Fontana H 330*	5	11

See also DAWN

ORLONS *US, female / male vocal group (3 WEEKS)* pos/wks

			pos	wks
27 Dec 62		**DON'T HANG UP** *Cameo Parkway C 231*	50	1
10 Jan 63		**DON'T HANG UP (re-entry)** *Cameo Parkway C 231*	39	2

ORN *UK, male DJ / producer – Omio Nourizadeh (1 WEEK)* pos/wks

			pos	wks
1 Mar 97		**SNOW** *Deconstruction 74321447612*	61	1

Beth ORTON *UK, female vocalist (11 WEEKS)* pos/wks

			pos	wks
1 Feb 97		**TOUCH ME WITH YOUR LOVE** *Heavenly HVN 64CD*	60	1
5 Apr 97		**SOMEONE'S DAUGHTER** *Heavenly HVN 65CD*	49	1
14 Jun 97		**SHE CRIES YOUR NAME** *Heavenly HVN 68CD*	40	2
13 Dec 97		**BEST BIT (EP)** *Heavenly HVN 72CD* [1]	36	3
13 Mar 99		**STOLEN CAR** *Heavenly HVN 89CD*	34	2
25 Sep 99		**CENTRAL RESERVATION** *Heavenly HVN 92CD*	37	2

[1] Beth Orton featuring Terry Callier

Tracks on Best Bit (EP): Best Bit / Skimming Stone / Dolphins / Lean on Me

ORVILLE – *See Keith HARRIS and ORVILLE*

Jeffrey OSBORNE *US, male vocalist (38 WEEKS)* pos/wks

			pos	wks
17 Sep 83		**DON'T YOU GET SO MAD** *A & M AM 140*	54	2
14 Apr 84		**STAY WITH ME TONIGHT** *A & M AM 188*	18	11
23 Jun 84		**ON THE WINGS OF LOVE** *A & M AM 198*	11	14
20 Oct 84		**DON'T STOP** *A & M AM 222*	61	2
26 Jul 86		**SOWETO** *A & M AM 334*	44	5
6 Sep 86		**SOWETO (re-entry)** *A & M AM 334*	75	1
15 Aug 87		**LOVE POWER** *Arista RIS 27* [1]	63	3

[1] Dionne Warwick and Jeffrey Osborne

Joan OSBORNE *US, female vocalist (13 WEEKS)* pos/wks

			pos	wks
10 Feb 96	●	**ONE OF US** *Blue Gorilla JOACD 1*	6	10
8 Jun 96		**ST TERESA** *Blue Gorilla JOACD 3*	33	3

Tony OSBORNE SOUND *UK, orchestra (3 WEEKS)* pos/wks

			pos	wks
23 Feb 61		**THE MAN FROM MADRID** *HMV POP 827* [1]	50	1
3 Feb 73		**THE SHEPHERD'S SONG** *Philips 6006 266*	46	2

[1] Tony Osborne Sound featuring Joanne Brown

Ozzy OSBOURNE *UK, male vocalist (42 WEEKS)* pos/wks

			pos	wks
13 Sep 80		**CRAZY TRAIN** *Jet 197* [1]	49	4
15 Nov 80		**MR CROWLEY** *Jet 7003* [1]	46	3
26 Nov 83		**BARK AT THE MOON** *Epic A 3915*	21	8
2 Jun 84		**SO TIRED** *Epic A 4452*	20	9
1 Feb 86		**SHOT IN THE DARK** *Epic A 6859*	20	6
9 Aug 86		**THE ULTIMATE SIN / LIGHTNING STRIKES** *Epic A 7311*	72	1
20 May 89		**CLOSE MY EYES FOREVER** *Dreamland PB 49409* [2]	47	3
28 Sep 91		**NO MORE TEARS** *Epic 6574407*	32	3
30 Nov 91		**MAMA I'M COMING HOME** *Epic 6576177*	46	2
25 Nov 95		**PERRY MASON** *Epic 6626395*	23	2
31 Aug 96		**I JUST WANT YOU** *Epic 6635702*	43	1

[1] Ozzy Osbourne's Blizzard of Ozz [2] Lita Ford duet with Ozzy Osbourne

See also BLACK SABBATH

OSIBISA *Ghana / Nigeria, male vocal / instrumental group (12 WEEKS)* pos/wks

			pos	wks
17 Jan 76		**SUNSHINE DAY** *Bronze BRO 20*	17	6
5 Jun 76		**DANCE THE BODY MUSIC** *Bronze BRO 26*	31	6

Donny OSMOND (233 Top 500)
Teenage teen-idol vocalist, b. 9 Dec 1957, Utah, US. The main focal point of the hitmaking family act The Osmonds, he was one of the most popular pin-ups of the 1970s, and had three solo No.1s before his 16th birthday (118 WEEKS) pos/wks

			pos	wks
17 Jun 72	★	**PUPPY LOVE** *MGM 2006 104*	1	17
16 Sep 72	●	**TOO YOUNG** *MGM 2006 113*	5	12
21 Oct 72		**PUPPY LOVE (re-entry)** *MGM 2006 104*	45	2
11 Nov 72	●	**WHY** *MGM 2006 119*	3	20
23 Dec 72		**PUPPY LOVE (2nd re-entry)** *MGM 2006 104*	46	3
23 Dec 72		**TOO YOUNG (re-entry)** *MGM 2006 113*	47	3
27 Jan 73		**PUPPY LOVE (3rd re-entry)** *MGM 2006 104*	48	1
10 Mar 73	★	**THE TWELFTH OF NEVER** *MGM 2006 199*	1	14
18 Aug 73	★	**YOUNG LOVE** *MGM 2006 300*	1	10
10 Nov 73	●	**WHEN I FALL IN LOVE** *MGM 2006 365*	4	13
9 Nov 74		**WHERE DID ALL THE GOOD TIMES GO** *MGM 2006 468*	18	10
26 Sep 87		**I'M IN IT FOR LOVE** *Virgin VS 994*	70	1
6 Aug 88		**SOLDIER OF LOVE** *Virgin VS 1094*	29	8
12 Nov 88		**IF IT'S LOVE THAT YOU WANT** *Virgin VS 1140*	70	2
9 Feb 91		**MY LOVE IS A FIRE** *Capitol CL 600*	64	2

See also Donny and Marie OSMOND; OSMONDS

Donny and Marie OSMOND *US, male / female vocal duo (37 WEEKS)* pos/wks

			pos	wks
3 Aug 74	●	**I'M LEAVING IT (ALL) UP TO YOU** *MGM 2006 446*	2	12
14 Dec 74	●	**MORNING SIDE OF THE MOUNTAIN** *MGM 2006 474*	5	12
21 Jun 75		**MAKE THE WORLD GO AWAY** *MGM 2006 523*	18	6
17 Jan 76		**DEEP PURPLE** *MGM 2006 561*	25	7

See also Donny OSMOND; Marie OSMOND

Little Jimmy OSMOND *US, male vocalist (50 WEEKS)* pos/wks

			pos	wks
25 Nov 72	★	**LONG HAIRED LOVER FROM LIVERPOOL** *MGM 2006 109*	1	24
31 Mar 73	●	**TWEEDLE DEE** *MGM 2006 175*	4	13
19 May 73		**LONG HAIRED LOVER FROM LIVERPOOL (re-entry)** *MGM 2006 109*	41	3
23 Mar 74		**I'M GONNA KNOCK ON YOUR DOOR** *MGM 2006 389*	11	10

Marie OSMOND *US, female vocalist (15 WEEKS)* pos/wks

			pos	wks
17 Nov 73	●	**PAPER ROSES** *MGM 2006 315*	2	15

See also Donny and Marie OSMOND

OSMOND BOYS *US, male vocal group (6 WEEKS)* pos/wks

			pos	wks
9 Nov 91		**BOYS WILL BE BOYS** *Curb 6573847*	65	2
11 Jan 92		**SHOW ME THE WAY** *Curb 6577227*	60	4

OSMONDS (324 Top 500)
Top teeny-bop act, brothers Donny, Alan, Wayne, Merrill and Jay Osmond from Utah, US. Polished pop quintet created hysteria wherever they appeared. Osmond family (including Marie and Little Jimmy) had a record 13 UK hits in 1973 (94 WEEKS) pos/wks

			pos	wks
25 Mar 72		**DOWN BY THE LAZY RIVER** *MGM 2006 096*	40	5
11 Nov 72	●	**CRAZY HORSES** *MGM 2006 142*	2	18
14 Jul 73	●	**GOING HOME** *MGM 2006 288*	4	10
27 Oct 73	●	**LET ME IN** *MGM 2006 321*	2	14
20 Apr 74		**I CAN'T STOP** *MCA 129*	12	10
24 Aug 74	★	**LOVE ME FOR A REASON** *MGM 2006 458*	1	9
1 Mar 75		**HAVING A PARTY** *MGM 2006 492*	28	8
24 May 75	●	**THE PROUD ONE** *MGM 2006 520*	5	8
15 Nov 75		**I'M STILL GONNA NEED YOU** *MGM 2006 551*	32	4
30 Oct 76		**I CAN'T LIVE A DREAM** *Polydor 2066 726*	37	5

		pos	wks
23 Sep 95	**CRAZY HORSES (re-mix)** *Polydor 5793212*	50	1
12 Jun 99	**CRAZY HORSES (re-issue of re-mix)** *Polydor 5611372*	34	2

See also Donny OSMOND; Donny and Marie OSMOND

Gilbert O'SULLIVAN (160) Top 500

Distinctive Irish singer / songwriter / pianist, b. Raymond O'Sullivan, 1 Dec 1946, Waterford. His unusual image - short trousers, flat cap and pudding-basin haircut - helped to launch the successful international career of the performer voted No.1 UK Male Singer of 1972 (145 WEEKS)

		pos	wks
28 Nov 70 ●	**NOTHING RHYMED** *MAM 3*	8	11
3 Apr 71	**UNDERNEATH THE BLANKET GO** *MAM 13*	40	1
17 Apr 71	**UNDERNEATH THE BLANKET GO (re-entry)** *MAM 13*	42	3
24 Jul 71	**WE WILL** *MAM 30*	16	11
27 Nov 71 ●	**NO MATTER HOW I TRY** *MAM 53*	5	15
4 Mar 72 ●	**ALONE AGAIN (NATURALLY)** *MAM 66* ▲	3	12
17 Jun 72 ●	**OOH-WAKKA-DOO-WAKKA-DAY** *MAM 78*	8	11
21 Oct 72 ★	**CLAIR** *MAM 84*	1	14
17 Mar 73 ★	**GET DOWN** *MAM 96*	1	13
15 Sep 73	**OOH BABY** *MAM 107*	18	7
10 Nov 73 ●	**WHY OH WHY OH WHY** *MAM 111*	6	14
9 Feb 74	**HAPPINESS IS ME AND YOU** *MAM 114*	19	7
24 Aug 74	**A WOMAN'S PLACE** *MAM 122*	42	3
14 Dec 74	**CHRISTMAS SONG** *MAM 124*	12	6
14 Jun 75	**I DON'T LOVE YOU BUT I THINK I LIKE YOU** *MAM 130*	14	6
27 Sep 80	**WHAT'S IN A KISS?** *CBS 8929*	19	9
24 Feb 90	**SO WHAT** *Dover ROJ 3*	70	2

O.T. QUARTET – *See OUR TRIBE / ONE TRIBE*

OTHER TWO

UK, male / female vocal / instrumental duo (5 WEEKS)

		pos	wks
9 Nov 91	**TASTY FISH** *Factory FAC 3297*	41	3
6 Nov 93	**SELFISH** *London TWOCD 1*	46	2

Johnny OTIS SHOW

US, band – leader John Veliotes (22 WEEKS)

		pos	wks
22 Nov 57 ●	**MA (HE'S MAKING EYES AT ME)** *Capitol CL 14794* [1]	2	15
10 Jan 58	**BYE BYE BABY** *Capitol CL 14817* [2]	20	7

[1] Johnny Otis and his orchestra with Marie Adams and the Three Tons of Joy [2] Johnny Otis Show, vocals by Marie Adams and Johnny Otis

OTT

Ireland, male vocal group (18 WEEKS)

		pos	wks
15 Feb 97	**LET ME IN** *Epic 6642052*	12	5
17 May 97	**FOREVER GIRL** *Epic 6645082*	24	3
23 Aug 97	**ALL OUT OF LOVE** *Epic 6649152*	11	4
24 Jan 98	**THE STORY OF LOVE** *Epic OTT 1CD*	11	6

OTTAWAN

France, male / female vocal duo (45 WEEKS)

		pos	wks
13 Sep 80 ●	**D.I.S.C.O.** *Carrere CAR 161*	2	18
13 Dec 80	**YOU'RE OK** *Carrere CAR 168*	56	6
29 Aug 81 ●	**HANDS UP (GIVE ME YOUR HEART)** *Carrere CAR 183*	3	15
5 Dec 81	**HELP, GET ME SOME HELP!** *Carrere CAR 215*	49	6

John OTWAY and Wild Willy BARRETT

UK, male vocal / instrumental duo (12 WEEKS)

		pos	wks
3 Dec 77	**REALLY FREE** *Polydor 2058 951*	27	8
5 Jul 80	**DK 50-80** *Polydor 2059 250* [1]	45	4

[1] Otway and Barrett

OUI 3

UK / US / Switzerland, male / female rap / instrumental group (21 WEEKS)

		pos	wks
20 Feb 93	**FOR WHAT IT'S WORTH** *MCA MCSTD 1736*	28	6
24 Apr 93	**ARMS OF SOLITUDE** *MCA MCSTD 1759*	54	2
17 Jul 93	**BREAK FROM THE OLD ROUTINE** *MCA MCSTD 1793*	17	6
23 Oct 93	**FOR WHAT IT'S WORTH (re-mix)** *MCA MCSTD 1941*	26	3
29 Jan 94	**FACT OF LIFE** *MCA MCSTD 1939*	38	2
27 May 95	**JOY OF LIVING** *MCA MCSTD 2057*	55	2

OUR DAUGHTER'S WEDDING

US, male vocal / instrumental group (6 WEEKS)

		pos	wks
1 Aug 81	**LAWNCHAIRS** *EMI America EA 124*	49	6

OUR HOUSE

Australia, male instrumental production duo (1 WEEK)

		pos	wks
31 Aug 96	**FLOOR SPACE** *Perfecto PERF 125CD*	52	1

OUR KID

UK, male vocal group (11 WEEKS)

		pos	wks
29 May 76 ●	**YOU JUST MIGHT SEE ME CRY** *Polydor 2058 729*	2	11

OUR LADY PEACE

Canada, male vocal / instrumental group (1 WEEK)

		pos	wks
15 Jan 00	**ONE MAN ARMY** *Epic 6688662*	70	1

OUR TRIBE / ONE TRIBE

UK / US, male / female vocal / instrumental group (13 WEEKS)

		pos	wks
20 Jun 92	**WHAT HAVE YOU DONE (IS THIS ALL)** *Inner Rhythm HEART 03* [1]	52	2
27 Mar 93	**I BELIEVE IN YOU** *Ffrreedom TABCD 117* [2]	42	2
30 Apr 94	**HOLD THAT SUCKER DOWN** *Cheeky CHEKCD 004* [3]	24	3
21 May 94	**LOVE COME HOME** *Triangle BLUESCD 001* [4]	73	1
13 May 95	**HIGH AS A KITE** *ffrr FCD 259* [5]	55	1
30 Sep 95	**HOLD THAT SUCKER DOWN (re-mix)** *Cheeky CHEKCD 009* [3]	26	3
9 Dec 00	**HOLD THAT SUCKER DOWN (re-issue)** *Champion CHAMPCD 786* [3]	45	1

[1] One Tribe featuring Gem [2] Our Tribe [3] OT Quartet [4] Our Tribe with Franké Pharoah and Kristine W [5] One Tribe featuring Roger

OUT OF MY HAIR

UK, male vocal / instrumental group (1 WEEK)

		pos	wks
1 Jul 95	**MISTER JONES** *RCA 74321267812*	73	1

OUTHERE BROTHERS

US, male rap / vocal duo – Lamar Mahone and Craig Simpkins (50 WEEKS)

		pos	wks
18 Mar 95 ★	**DON'T STOP (WIGGLE WIGGLE)** *Eternal YZ 917CD*	1	15
17 Jun 95 ★	**BOOM BOOM BOOM** *Eternal YZ 938CD*	1	15
23 Sep 95 ●	**LA LA LA HEY HEY** *Eternal YZ 974CD*	7	7
16 Dec 95 ●	**IF YOU WANNA PARTY** *Eternal WEA 030CD* [1]	9	10
25 Jan 97	**LET ME HEAR YOU SAY 'OLE OLE'** *WEA 089CD*	18	3

[1] Molella featuring the Outhere Brothers

OUTKAST

US, male rap / vocal duo (23 WEEKS)

		pos	wks
23 Dec 00	**B.O.B (BOMBS OVER BAGHDAD)** *Laface / Arista 74321822942*	61	1
3 Feb 01	**MS JACKSON (import)** *Laface 73008245252*	48	4
3 Mar 01 ●	**MS JACKSON** *Laface / Arista 74321836822* ▲	2	10
9 Jun 01	**SO FRESH, SO CLEAN** *Laface / Arista 74321863402*	16	8

OUTLANDER

Belgium, male producer – Marcos Salon (3 WEEKS)

		pos	wks
31 Aug 91	**VAMP** *R&S RSUK 1*	51	2
7 Feb 98	**THE VAMP (REVAMPED)** *R&S RS 97113CDX*	62	1

OUTLAWS

UK, male instrumental group (4 WEEKS)

		pos	wks
13 Apr 61	**SWINGIN' LOW** *HMV POP 844*	46	2
8 Jun 61	**AMBUSH** *HMV POP 877*	43	2

See also Mike BERRY

OUTRAGE

US, male vocalist (2 WEEKS)

		pos	wks
11 Mar 95	**TALL 'N' HANDSOME** *Effective ECFL 001CD*	57	1
23 Nov 96	**TALL 'N' HANDSOME (re-mix)** *Positiva CDTIV 64*	51	1

OVERLANDERS

UK, male vocal / instrumental group – lead vocal Paul Arnold (10 WEEKS)

		pos	wks
13 Jan 66 ★	**MICHELLE** *Pye 7N 17034*	1	10

OVERWEIGHT POOCH featuring Ce Ce PENISTON

US, female rapper and female vocalist (2 WEEKS)

		pos	wks
18 Jan 92	**I LIKE IT** *A & M AM 847*	58	2

Mark OWEN *UK, male vocalist (24 WEEKS)*

			pos	wks
30 Nov 96	●	**CHILD** *RCA 74321424422*	3	11
15 Feb 97	●	**CLEMENTINE** *RCA 74321454982*	3	6
22 Feb 97		**CHILD (re-entry)** *RCA 74321424422*	45	4
23 Aug 97		**I AM WHAT I AM** *RCA 74321501222*	29	3

See also *TAKE THAT*

Reg OWEN and his Orchestra *UK, orchestra (10 WEEKS)*

			pos	wks
27 Feb 59		**MANHATTAN SPIRITUAL** *Pye International 7N 25009*	20	8
27 Oct 60		**OBSESSION** *Palette PG 9004*	43	2

Sid OWEN *UK, male vocalist (6 WEEKS)*

			pos	wks
16 Dec 95		**BETTER BELIEVE IT (CHILDREN IN NEED)** *Trinity TDM 001CD* [1]	60	1
8 Jul 00		**GOOD THING GOING** *Mushroom MUSH 74CDS*	14	5

[1] Sid Owen and Patsy Palmer

Robert OWENS *US, male vocalist (5 WEEKS)*

			pos	wks
7 Dec 91		**I'LL BE YOUR FRIEND** *Perfecto PB 45161*	75	2
26 Apr 97		**I'LL BE YOUR FRIEND (re-mix)** *Perfecto PERF 137CD1*	25	2
24 Feb 01		**MINE TO GIVE** *Science QEDCD 10* [1]	44	1

[1] Photek featuring Robert Owens

OXIDE & NEUTRINO *UK, male production / rap duo – Alex Rivers and Mark Oseitutu (35 WEEKS)*

			pos	wks
6 May 00	★	**BOUND 4 DA RELOAD (CASUALTY)** *East West OXIDE 01CD1* ■	1	11
30 Dec 00	●	**NO GOOD 4 ME** *East West OXIDE 02CD* [1]	6	8
26 May 01	●	**UP MIDDLE FINGER** *East West OXIDE 03CD*	7	7
28 Jul 01		**DEVIL'S NIGHTMARE** *East West OXIDE 07CD1*	16	5
8 Dec 01		**RAP DIS / ONLY WANNA KNOW U COS URE FAMOUS** *East West OXIDE 08CD*	12	4

[1] Oxide & Neutrino featuring Megaman, Romeo and Lisa Maffia

OZOMATLI *US, male vocal / instrumental group (2 WEEKS)*

			pos	wks
20 Mar 99		**CUT CHEMIST SUITE** *Almo Sounds CDALM 62*	58	1
22 May 99		**SUPER BOWL SUNDAE** *Almo Sounds CDALM 63*	68	1

P

Jazzi P *UK, female rapper (12 WEEKS)*

			pos	wks
8 Jul 89		**GET LOOSE** *Breakout USA 659* [1]	25	6
9 Jun 90		**FEEL THE RHYTHM** *A&M USA 691*	51	2
3 Aug 91		**REBEL WOMAN** *DNA 7DNA 001* [2]	42	4

[1] LA Mix featuring Jazzi P [2] DNA featuring Jazzi P

P J B featuring HANNAH and her SISTERS *Germany, male production group and US, female vocalists (8 WEEKS)*

			pos	wks
14 Sep 91		**BRIDGE OVER TROUBLED WATER** *Dance Pool 6565467*	21	8

See also *Hannah JONES*

Thom PACE *US, male vocalist (15 WEEKS)*

			pos	wks
19 May 79		**MAYBE** *RSO 34*	14	15

PACEMAKERS – See *GERRY and the PACEMAKERS*

PACIFICA *UK, male production duo (1 WEEK)*

			pos	wks
31 Jul 99		**LOST IN THE TRANSLATION** *Wildstar CDWILD 25*	54	1

PACK featuring Nigel BENN *UK, male vocal / instrumental group (2 WEEKS)*

			pos	wks
8 Dec 90		**STAND AND FIGHT** *IQ ZB 44237*	61	2

PACKABEATS *UK, male instrumental group (1 WEEK)*

			pos	wks
23 Feb 61		**GYPSY BEAT** *Parlophone R 4729*	49	1

José PADILLA featuring Angela JOHN *Spain, male DJ and UK, female vocalist (1 WEEK)*

			pos	wks
8 Aug 98		**WHO DO YOU LOVE** *Manifesto FESCD 45*	59	1

PAGANINI TRAXX *Italy, male DJ / producer (1 WEEK)*

			pos	wks
1 Feb 97		**ZOE** *Sony S3 DANUCD 18X*	47	1

Jimmy PAGE *UK, male guitarist (16 WEEKS)*

			pos	wks
17 Dec 94		**GALLOWS POLE** *Fontana PPCD 2* [1]	35	3
11 Apr 98		**MOST HIGH** *Mercury 5687512* [2]	26	2
1 Aug 98		**COME WITH ME (IMPORT)** *Epic 34K78954* [3]	75	1
8 Aug 98	●	**COME WITH ME** *Epic 6662842* [3]	2	10

[1] Jimmy Page and Robert Plant [2] Page and Plant [3] Puff Daddy featuring Jimmy Page

See also *LED ZEPPELIN*

Patti PAGE *US, female vocalist – Clara Ann Fowler (5 WEEKS)*

			pos	wks
27 Mar 53	●	**(HOW MUCH IS) THAT DOGGIE IN THE WINDOW** *Oriole CB 1156* ▲	9	5

Tommy PAGE *US, male vocalist (3 WEEKS)*

			pos	wks
26 May 90		**I'LL BE YOUR EVERYTHING** *Sire W 9959* ▲	53	3

Wendy PAGE – See *TIN TIN OUT*

PAGLIARO *Canada, male vocalist (6 WEEKS)*

			pos	wks
19 Feb 72		**LOVING YOU AIN'T EASY** *Pye 7N 45111*	31	6

PAID & LIVE featuring Lauryn HILL *US, male production duo and female rapper / vocalist (1 WEEK)*

			pos	wks
27 Dec 97		**ALL MY TIME** *World Entertainment OWECD 2*	57	1

Elaine PAIGE *UK, female vocalist – Elaine Bickerstaff (41 WEEKS)*

			pos	wks
21 Oct 78		**DON'T WALK AWAY TILL I TOUCH YOU** *EMI 2862*	46	5
6 Jun 81	●	**MEMORY** *Polydor POSP 279*	6	12
30 Jan 82		**MEMORY (re-entry)** *Polydor POSP 279*	67	3
14 Apr 84		**SOMETIMES (THEME FROM 'CHAMPIONS')** *Island IS 174*	72	1
5 Jan 85	★	**I KNOW HIM SO WELL** *RCA CHESS 3* [1]	1	16
21 Nov 87		**THE SECOND TIME (THEME FROM 'BILITIS')** *WEA YZ 163*	69	1
21 Jan 95		**HYMNE A L'AMOUR (IF YOU LOVE ME)** *WEA YZ 899CD*	68	1
24 Oct 98		**MEMORY (re-recording)** *WEA WEA 197CD*	36	2

[1] Elaine Paige and Barbara Dickson

Hal PAIGE and the WHALERS *US, male vocal / instrumental group (1 WEEK)*

			pos	wks
25 Aug 60		**GOING BACK TO MY HOME TOWN** *Melodisc MEL 1553*	50	1

Jennifer PAIGE *US, female vocalist (13 WEEKS)*

			pos	wks
12 Sep 98	●	**CRUSH** *EAR 0039425*	4	12
20 Mar 99		**SOBER** *EAR / Edel 0044185 ERE*	68	1

Orchestre de Chambre Jean-François PAILLARD *France, male conductor and orchestra (3 WEEKS)*

			pos	wks
20 Aug 88		**THEME FROM 'VIETNAM' (CANON IN D)** *Debut DEBT 3053*	61	3

PALE *Ireland, male vocal / instrumental group (2 WEEKS)*

			pos	wks
13 Jun 92		**DOGS WITH NO TAILS** *A & M AM 866*	51	2

PALE FOUNTAINS *UK, male vocal / instrumental group (6 WEEKS)* pos/wks

27 Nov 82	**THANK YOU** *Virgin VS 557*	48	6

PALE SAINTS *UK, male / female vocal / instrumental group (1 WEEK)* pos/wks

6 Jul 91	**KINKY LOVE** *4AD AD 1009*	72	1

PALE X *Holland, male producer (1 WEEK)* pos/wks

3 Feb 01	**NITRO** *Nukleuz NUKP 0280*	74	1

Nerina PALLOT *UK, female vocalist (1 WEEK)* pos/wks

18 Aug 01	**PATIENCE** *Polydor 5872122*	61	1

Barry PALMER – *See Mike OLDFIELD*

Patsy PALMER – *See Sid OWEN*

Robert PALMER (209 Top 500)

Grammy-winning UK rock-group veteran, b. 19 Jan 1949, Yorkshire. This vocalist's hottest run of transatlantic hits came after he fronted short-lived Anglo-American supergroup Power Station in 1985. He benefited from some striking award-winning videos featuring an all-female backing band (parodied in a 1999 Shania Twain video) (128 WEEKS) pos/wks

20 May 78	**EVERY KINDA PEOPLE** *Island WIP 6425*	53	4
7 Jul 79	**BAD CASE OF LOVIN' YOU (DOCTOR DOCTOR)** *Island WIP 6481*	61	2
6 Sep 80	**JOHNNY AND MARY** *Island WIP 6638*	44	8
22 Nov 80	**LOOKING FOR CLUES** *Island WIP 6651*	33	9
13 Feb 82	**SOME GUYS HAVE ALL THE LUCK** *Island WIP 6754*	16	8
2 Apr 83	**YOU ARE IN MY SYSTEM** *Island IS 104*	53	4
18 Jun 83	**YOU CAN HAVE IT (TAKE MY HEART)** *Island IS 121*	66	2
10 May 86 ●	**ADDICTED TO LOVE** *Island IS 270* ▲	5	15
19 Jul 86 ●	**I DIDN'T MEAN TO TURN YOU ON** *Island IS 283*	9	9
1 Nov 86	**DISCIPLINE OF LOVE** *Island IS 242*	68	1
26 Mar 88	**SWEET LIES** *Island IS 352*	58	3
11 Jun 88	**SIMPLY IRRESISTABLE** *EMI EM 61*	44	4
15 Oct 88 ●	**SHE MAKES MY DAY** *EMI EM 65*	6	12
13 May 89	**CHANGE HIS WAYS** *EMI EM 85*	28	7
26 Aug 89	**IT COULD HAPPEN TO YOU** *EMI EM 99*	71	1
3 Nov 90 ●	**I'LL BE YOUR BABY TONIGHT** *EMI EM 167* [1]	6	10
5 Jan 91 ●	**MERCY MERCY ME - I WANT YOU** *EMI EM 173*	9	9
15 Jun 91	**DREAMS TO REMEMBER** *EMI EM 193*	68	1
7 Mar 92	**EVERY KINDA PEOPLE (re-mix)** *Island IS 498*	43	3
17 Oct 92	**WITCHCRAFT** *EMI EM 251*	50	3
9 Jul 94	**GIRL U WANT** *EMI CDEMS 331*	57	2
3 Sep 94	**KNOW BY NOW** *EMI CDEMS 343*	25	5
24 Dec 94	**YOU BLOW ME AWAY** *EMI CDEMS 350*	38	4
14 Oct 95	**RESPECT YOURSELF** *EMI CDEMS 399*	45	2

[1] Robert Palmer and UB40

Suzanne PALMER – *See CLUB 69; ABSOLUTE*

Tyrone 'Visionary' PALMER – *See SLAM*

PAN POSITION

Italy / Venezuela, male instrumental / production group (1 WEEK) pos/wks

18 Jun 94	**ELEPHANT PAW (GET DOWN TO THE FUNK)** *Positiva CDTIV 13*	55	1

PANDORA'S BOX

US, male / female vocal / instrumental group (3 WEEKS) pos/wks

21 Oct 89	**IT'S ALL COMING BACK TO ME NOW** *Virgin VS 1216*	51	3

Darryl PANDY *US, male vocalist (5 WEEKS)* pos/wks

14 Dec 96	**LOVE CAN'T TURN AROUND** *4 Liberty LIBTCD 27* [1]	40	2
20 Feb 99	**RAISE YOUR HANDS** *VC Recordings VCRD 44* [2]	40	2
2 Oct 99	**SUNSHINE & HAPPINESS** *Azuli AZNYCD 103* [3]	68	1

[1] Farley 'Jackmaster' Funk with Darryl Pandy [2] Big Room Girl featuring Darryl Pandy [3] Darryl Pandy / Nerio's Dubwork

Johnny PANIC and the BIBLE OF DREAMS

UK, male / female vocal / instrumental group (2 WEEKS) pos/wks

2 Feb 91	**JOHNNY PANIC AND THE BIBLE OF DREAMS** *Fontana PANIC 1*	70	2

See also TEARS FOR FEARS

PANTERA *US, male vocal / instrumental group (8 WEEKS)* pos/wks

10 Oct 92	**MOUTH FOR WAR** *Atco A 5845T*	73	1
27 Feb 93	**WALK** *Atco B 6076CD*	35	2
19 Mar 94	**I'M BROKEN** *Atco B 5932CD1*	19	2
22 Oct 94	**PLANET CARAVAN** *East West A 5836CD1*	26	3

PAPA ROACH *US, male vocal / instrumental group (16 WEEKS)* pos/wks

17 Feb 01 ●	**LAST RESORT** *Dreamworks / Polydor 4509212*	3	10
5 May 01	**BETWEEN ANGELS & INSECTS** *Dreamworks / Polydor 4509082*	17	6

PAPER DOLLS *UK, female vocal group (13 WEEKS)* pos/wks

13 Mar 68	**SOMETHING HERE IN MY HEART (KEEPS A-TELLIN' ME NO)** *Pye 7N 17456*	11	13

PAPER LACE *UK, male vocal / instrumental group – lead vocal Phil Wright (41 WEEKS)* pos/wks

23 Feb 74 ★	**BILLY DON'T BE A HERO** *Bus Stop BUS 1014*	1	14
4 May 74 ●	**THE NIGHT CHICAGO DIED** *Bus Stop BUS 1016* ▲	3	11
24 Aug 74	**THE BLACK EYED BOYS** *Bus Stop BUS 1019*	11	10
4 Mar 78	**WE'VE GOT THE WHOLE WORLD IN OUR HANDS** *Warner Bros. K 17110* [1]	24	6

[1] Nottingham Forest FC with Paper Lace

PAPERDOLLS *UK, female vocal group (1 WEEK)* pos/wks

12 Sep 98	**GONNA MAKE YOU BLUSH** *MCA MCSTD 40175*	65	1

PAPPA BEAR featuring VAN DER TOORN

Germany, male rapper and Holland, male vocalist (1 WEEK) pos/wks

16 May 98	**CHERISH** *Universal UMD 70316*	47	1

PAR-T-ONE vs INXS *Italy, male production trio and Australia, male vocal / instrumental group (6 WEEKS)* pos/wks

3 Nov 01	**I'M SO CRAZY** *Credence CDCRED 016*	19	5
15 Dec 01	**I'M SO CRAZY (re-entry)** *Credence CDCRED 016*	71	1

Vanessa PARADIS *France, female vocalist (30 WEEKS)* pos/wks

13 Feb 88 ●	**JOE LE TAXI** *FA Productions POSP 902*	3	10
10 Oct 92 ●	**BE MY BABY** *Remark PO 235*	6	15
27 Feb 93	**SUNDAY MONDAYS** *Remark PZCD 251*	49	4
24 Jul 93	**JUST AS LONG AS YOU ARE THERE** *Remark PZCD 272*	57	1

PARADISE *UK, male vocal / instrumental group (4 WEEKS)* pos/wks

10 Sep 83	**ONE MIND, TWO HEARTS** *Priority P 1*	42	4

PARADISE LOST *UK, male vocal / instrumental group (3 WEEKS)* pos/wks

20 May 95	**THE LAST TIME** *Music For Nations CDKUT 165*	60	1
7 Oct 95	**FOREVER FAILURE** *Music For Nations CDKUT 169*	66	1
28 Jun 97	**SAY JUST WORDS** *Music For Nations CDKUT 174*	53	1

PARADISE ORGANISATION

UK, male instrumental / production group (1 WEEK) pos/wks

23 Jan 93	**PRAYER TOWER** *Cowboy RODEO 13*	70	1

PARADOX *UK, male instrumental duo (2 WEEKS)* pos/wks

24 Feb 90	**JAILBREAK** *Ronin 7R2*	66	2

Norrie PARAMOR *UK, orchestra (8 WEEKS)* pos/wks

17 Mar 60	**THEME FROM 'A SUMMER PLACE'** *Columbia DB 4419*	36	2
22 Mar 62	**THEME FROM 'Z CARS'** *Columbia DB 4789*	33	6

PARAMOUNT JAZZ BAND – *See Mr Acker BILK and his PARAMOUNT JAZZ BAND*

PARAMOUNTS *UK, male vocal / instrumental group (7 WEEKS)* pos/wks

16 Jan 64	**POISON IVY** *Parlophone R 5093*	35	7

PARCHMENT *UK, male / female vocal / instrumental group (5 WEEKS)* pos/wks

16 Sep 72	**LIGHT UP THE FIRE** *Pye 7N 45178*	31	5

PARIS *UK, male / female vocal group (4 WEEKS)* pos/wks

19 Jun 82	**NO GETTING OVER YOU** *RCA 222*	49	4

PARIS *US, male vocalist (2 WEEKS)* pos/wks

21 Jan 95	**GUERRILLA FUNK** *Priority PTYCD 100*	38	2

Mica PARIS *UK, female vocalist – Michelle Wallen (63 WEEKS)* pos/wks

7 May 88 ●	**MY ONE TEMPTATION** *Fourth & Broadway BRW 85*	7	11
30 Jul 88	**LIKE DREAMERS DO** *Fourth & Broadway BRW 108* [1]	26	5
22 Oct 88	**BREATHE LIFE INTO ME** *Fourth & Broadway BRW 115*	26	10
21 Jan 89	**WHERE IS THE LOVE** *Fourth & Broadway BRW 122* [2]	19	7
6 Oct 90	**CONTRIBUTION** *Fourth & Broadway BRW 188*	33	4
1 Dec 90	**SOUTH OF THE RIVER** *Fourth & Broadway BRW 199*	50	2
23 Feb 91	**IF I LOVE U 2 NITE** *Fourth & Broadway BRW 207*	43	3
31 Aug 91	**YOUNG SOUL REBELS** *Big Life BLR 57*	61	3
3 Apr 93	**I NEVER FELT LIKE THIS BEFORE** *Fourth & Broadway BRCD 263*	15	5
5 Jun 93	**I WANNA HOLD ON TO YOU** *Fourth & Broadway BRCD 275*	27	3
7 Aug 93	**TWO IN A MILLION** *Fourth & Broadway BRCD 285*	51	2
4 Dec 93	**WHISPER A PRAYER** *Fourth & Broadway BRCD 287*	65	1
8 Apr 95	**ONE** *Cooltempo CDCOOL 304*	29	4
16 May 98	**STAY** *Cooltempo CDCOOL 334*	40	2
14 Nov 98	**BLACK ANGEL** *Cooltempo CDCOOL 341*	72	1

[1] Mica Paris featuring Courtney Pine [2] Mica Paris and Will Downing

Ryan PARIS *France, male vocalist – Fabio Roscioli (10 WEEKS)* pos/wks

3 Sep 83 ●	**DOLCE VITA** *Carrere CAR 289*	5	10

PARIS & SHARP *UK, male production duo (1 WEEK)* pos/wks

1 Dec 01	**APHRODITE** *Cream / Parlophone CREAM 16CD*	61	1

PARIS ANGELS
UK, male / female vocal / instrumental group (5 WEEKS) pos/wks

3 Nov 90	**SCOPE** *Sheer Joy SHEER 0047*	75	1
20 Jul 91	**PERFUME** *Virgin VS 1360*	55	3
21 Sep 91	**FADE** *Virgin VS 1365*	70	1

PARIS RED
US / Germany, male / female vocal / instrumental duo (2 WEEKS) pos/wks

29 Feb 92	**GOOD FRIEND** *Columbia 6569417*	61	1
15 May 93	**PROMISES** *Columbia 6592342*	59	1

John PARISH and Polly Jean HARVEY *US, male producer / instrumentalist and UK, female vocalist (1 WEEK)* pos/wks

23 Nov 96	**THAT WAS MY VEIL** *Island CID 648*	75	1

See also PJ HARVEY

Simon PARK *UK, orchestra (24 WEEKS)* pos/wks

25 Nov 72	**EYE LEVEL** *Columbia DB 8946*	41	2
15 Sep 73 ★	**EYE LEVEL (re-entry)** *Columbia DB 8946* ◆	1	22

Graham PARKER and the RUMOUR
UK, male vocal / instrumental group (16 WEEKS) pos/wks

19 Mar 77	**THE PINK PARKER EP** *Vertigo PARK 001*	24	5
22 Apr 78	**HEY LORD, DON'T ASK ME QUESTIONS** *Vertigo PARK 002*	32	7
20 Mar 82	**TEMPORARY BEAUTY** *RCA PARK 100* [1]	50	4

[1] Graham Parker

Tracks on The Pink Parker EP: Hold Back the Night / (Let Me Get) Sweet on You / White Honey / Soul Shoes

Ray PARKER Jr *US, male vocalist (47 WEEKS)* pos/wks

25 Aug 84 ●	**GHOSTBUSTERS** *Arista ARIST 580* ▲	2	31
18 Jan 86	**GIRLS ARE MORE FUN** *Arista ARIST 641*	46	4
3 Oct 87	**I DON'T THINK THAT MAN SHOULD SLEEP ALONE** *Geffen GEF 27*	13	10
30 Jan 88	**OVER YOU** *Geffen GEF 33*	65	2

See also RAYDIO

Robert PARKER *US, male vocalist (8 WEEKS)* pos/wks

4 Aug 66	**BAREFOOTIN'** *Island WI 286*	24	8

Sara PARKER *US, female vocalist (2 WEEKS)* pos/wks

12 Apr 97	**MY LOVE IS DEEP** *Manifesto FESCD 22*	22	2

Jimmy PARKINSON *Australia, male vocalist (19 WEEKS)* pos/wks

2 Mar 56 ●	**THE GREAT PRETENDER** *Columbia DB 3729*	9	13
17 Aug 56	**WALK HAND IN HAND** *Columbia DB 3775*	30	1
5 Oct 56	**WALK HAND IN HAND (re-entry)** *Columbia DB 3775*	26	1
9 Nov 56	**IN THE MIDDLE OF THE HOUSE** *Columbia DB 3833*	26	2
30 Nov 56	**IN THE MIDDLE OF THE HOUSE (re-entry)** *Columbia DB 3833*	20	2

PARKS & WILSON *UK, male production duo – Michael Parks and Michael Wilson (1 WEEK)* pos/wks

9 Sep 00	**FEEL THE DRUM (EP)** *Hooj Choons HOOJ 099*	71	1

Tracks on Feel The Drum (EP): My Orbit / The Dragon / My Orbit (remix) / Drum Parade (No UFOs)

PARLIAMENT – *See Scott GROOVES*

John PARR *UK, male vocalist (22 WEEKS)* pos/wks

14 Sep 85 ●	**ST ELMO'S FIRE (MAN IN MOTION)** *London LON 73* ▲	6	13
18 Jan 86	**NAUGHTY NAUGHTY** *London LON 80*	58	3
30 Aug 86	**ROCK 'N' ROLL MERCENARIES** *Arista ARIST 666* [1]	31	6

[1] Meat Loaf featuring John Parr

Dean PARRISH *US, male vocalist (5 WEEKS)* pos/wks

8 Feb 75	**I'M ON MY WAY** *UK USA 2*	38	5

Man PARRISH *US, male DJ / producer (26 WEEKS)* pos/wks

26 Mar 83	**HIP HOP, BE BOP (DON'T STOP)** *Polydor POSP 575*	41	6
23 Mar 85	**BOOGIE DOWN (BRONX)** *Boiling Point POSP 731*	56	4
13 Sep 86	**MALE STRIPPER** *Bolts BOLTS 4* [1]	64	3
3 Jan 87	**MALE STRIPPER (re-entry)** *Bolts BOLTS 4* [1]	63	1
7 Feb 87 ●	**MALE STRIPPER (2nd re-entry)** *Bolts BOLTS 4* [1]	4	12

[1] Man 2 Man meet Man Parrish

Bill PARSONS *US, male vocalist (2 WEEKS)* pos/wks

10 Apr 59	**THE ALL AMERICAN BOY** *London HL 8798*	22	2

Record erroneously credited to Bill Parsons; actual vocalist is Bobby Bare

Alan PARSONS PROJECT
UK, male vocal / instrumental group (4 WEEKS) pos/wks

15 Jan 83	**OLD AND WISE** *Arista ARIST 494*	74	1
10 Mar 84	**DON'T ANSWER ME** *Arista ARIST 553*	58	3

UK No.1 ★ UK Top 10 ● Still on chart + UK million seller ◆ UK entry at No.1 ■ US No.1 ▲

PARTIZAN *UK, male DJ / production duo – 'Tall Paul' Newman and Craig Daniel-Yefet (3 WEEKS)* pos/wks

8 Feb 97		DRIVE ME CRAZY *Multiply CDMULTY 17*	36	2
6 Dec 97		KEEP YOUR LOVE *Multiply CDMULTY 29* [1]	53	1

[1] Partizan featuring Natalie Robb

See also TALL PAUL; ESCRIMA; CAMISRA; GRIFTERS

PARTNERS – *See Al HUDSON*

PARTNERS IN KRYME
US, male rap duo – James Alpem and Richard Usher (10 WEEKS) pos/wks

21 Jul 90	★	TURTLE POWER *SBK TURTLE 1*	1	10

David PARTON *UK, male vocalist (9 WEEKS)* pos/wks

15 Jan 77	●	ISN'T SHE LOVELY *Pye 7N 45663*	4	9

Dolly PARTON *US, female vocalist (33 WEEKS)* pos/wks

15 May 76	●	JOLENE *RCA 2675*	7	10
21 Feb 81		9 TO 5 *RCA 25* ▲	47	5
12 Nov 83	●	ISLANDS IN THE STREAM *RCA 378* [1] ▲	7	15
7 Apr 84		HERE YOU COME AGAIN *RCA 395*	75	1
16 Apr 94		THE DAY I FALL IN LOVE *Columbia 6600282* [2]	64	2

[1] Kenny Rogers and Dolly Parton [2] Dolly Parton and James Ingram

Stella PARTON *US, female vocalist (4 WEEKS)* pos/wks

22 Oct 77		THE DANGER OF A STRANGER *Elektra K 12272*	35	4

Don PARTRIDGE
UK, male vocalist / instrumentalist – one-man band (32 WEEKS) pos/wks

7 Feb 68	●	ROSIE *Columbia DB 8330*	4	12
29 May 68	●	BLUE EYES *Columbia DB 8416*	3	13
19 Feb 69		BREAKFAST ON PLUTO *Columbia DB 8538*	26	7

PARTRIDGE FAMILY *US, male / female vocal group (53 WEEKS)* pos/wks

13 Feb 71		I THINK I LOVE YOU *Bell 1130* [1] ▲	18	9
26 Feb 72		IT'S ONE OF THOSE NIGHTS (YES LOVE) *Bell 1203* [1]	11	11
8 Jul 72	●	BREAKING UP IS HARD TO DO *Bell MABEL 1* [1]	3	13
3 Feb 73	●	LOOKING THROUGH THE EYES OF LOVE *Bell 1278* [2]	9	9
19 May 73	●	WALKING IN THE RAIN *Bell 1293* [2]	10	11

[1] Partridge Family starring Shirley Jones featuring David Cassidy [2] Partridge Family starring David Cassidy

See also David CASSIDY

PARTY ANIMALS
Holland, male instrumental / production duo (3 WEEKS) pos/wks

1 Jun 96		HAVE YOU EVER BEEN MELLOW *Mokum DB 17553*	56	1
19 Oct 96		HAVE YOU EVER BEEN MELLOW (EP) *Mokum DB 17413*	43	2

Tracks on Have You Ever Been Mellow (EP): Have You Ever Been Mellow / Hava Naquilla / Aquarius

PARTY FAITHFUL
UK, male / female vocal / instrumental group (1 WEEK) pos/wks

22 Jul 95		BRASS: LET THERE BE HOUSE *Ore AG 10CD*	54	1

PASADENAS *UK, male vocal group (57 WEEKS)* pos/wks

28 May 88	●	TRIBUTE (RIGHT ON) *CBS PASA 1*	5	14
17 Sep 88		RIDING ON A TRAIN *CBS PASA 2*	13	9
26 Nov 88		ENCHANTED LADY *CBS PASA 3*	31	6
12 May 90		LOVE THING *CBS PASA 4*	22	5
14 Jul 90		REELING *CBS PASA 5*	75	1
1 Feb 92	●	I'M DOING FINE NOW *Columbia 6577187*	4	10
4 Apr 92		MAKE IT WITH YOU *Columbia 6579257*	20	4
6 Jun 92		I BELIEVE IN MIRACLES *Columbia 6580567*	34	3
29 Aug 92		MOVING IN THE RIGHT DIRECTION *Columbia 6583417*	49	2
21 Nov 92		LET'S STAY TOGETHER *Columbia 6587747*	22	3

PASSENGERS
Ireland / UK / Italy, male vocal / instrumental group (9 WEEKS) pos/wks

2 Dec 95	●	MISS SARAJEVO *Island CID 625*	6	9

PASSION *UK, male vocal / rap group (1 WEEK)* pos/wks

25 Jan 97		SHARE YOUR LOVE (NO DIGGITY) *Charm CRTCDS 269*	62	1

PASSIONS *UK, male / female vocal / instrumental group (8 WEEKS)* pos/wks

31 Jan 81		I'M IN LOVE WITH A GERMAN FILM STAR *Polydor POSP 222*	25	8

PAT and MICK
UK, male vocal duo – Pat Sharp and Mick Brown (27 WEEKS) pos/wks

9 Apr 88		LET'S ALL CHANT / ON THE NIGHT *PWL PWL 10* [1]	11	9
25 Mar 89	●	I HAVEN'T STOPPED DANCING YET *PWL PWL 33*	9	8
14 Apr 90		USE IT UP AND WEAR IT OUT *PWL PWL 55*	22	6
23 Mar 91		GIMME SOME *PWL PWL 75*	53	2
15 May 93		HOT HOT HOT *PWL International PARKCD 1*	47	2

[1] Mick and Pat

'On the Night' listed only from 4 Jun 1988. It peaked at No.70

PATIENCE and PRUDENCE *US, female vocal duo (8 WEEKS)* pos/wks

2 Nov 56		TONIGHT YOU BELONG TO ME *London HLU 8321*	28	3
1 Mar 57		GONNA GET ALONG WITHOUT YA NOW *London HLU 8369*	22	4
12 Apr 57		GONNA GET ALONG WITHOUT YA NOW (re-entry) *London HLU 8369*	24	1

PATRA *Jamaica, female vocalist (11 WEEKS)* pos/wks

25 Dec 93		FAMILY AFFAIR *Polydor PZCD 304* [1]	18	8
30 Sep 95		PULL UP TO THE BUMPER *Epic 6623942*	50	2
10 Aug 96		WORK MI BODY *Heavenly HVN 53CD* [2]	75	1

[1] Shabba Ranks featuring Patra and Terri & Monica [2] Monkey Mafia featuring Patra

PATRIC *UK, male vocalist (2 WEEKS)* pos/wks

9 Jul 94		LOVE ME *Bell 7432125352*	54	2

Dee PATTEN *UK, male DJ / producer (1 WEEK)* pos/wks

30 Jan 99		WHO'S THE BAD MAN? *Higher Ground HIGHS 15CD*	42	1

Kellee PATTERSON *US, female vocalist (7 WEEKS)* pos/wks

18 Feb 78		IF IT DON'T FIT DON'T FORCE IT *EMI International INT 544*	44	7

Rahsaan PATTERSON *US, male vocalist (2 WEEKS)* pos/wks

26 Jul 97		STOP BY *MCA MCSTD 48055*	50	1
21 Mar 98		WHERE YOU ARE *MCA MCSTD 48073*	55	1

Billy PAUL *US, male vocalist – Paul Williams (44 WEEKS)* pos/wks

13 Jan 73		ME AND MRS JONES *Epic EPC 1055* ▲	12	9
12 Jan 74		THANKS FOR SAVING MY LIFE *Philadelphia International PIR 1928*	33	6
22 May 76		LET'S MAKE A BABY *Philadelphia International PIR 4144*	30	5
30 Apr 77		LET 'EM IN *Philadelphia International PIR 5143*	26	5
16 Jul 77		YOUR SONG *Philadelphia International PIR 5391*	37	7
19 Nov 77		ONLY THE STRONG SURVIVE *Philadelphia International PIR 5699*	33	7
14 Jul 79		BRING THE FAMILY BACK *Philadelphia International PIR 7456*	51	5

Chris PAUL *UK, male producer / instrumentalist – guitar (8 WEEKS)* pos/wks

31 May 86		EXPANSIONS '86 (EXPAND YOUR MIND) *Fourth & Broadway BRW 48* [1]	58	5
21 Nov 87		BACK IN MY ARMS *Syncopate SY 5*	74	2
13 Aug 88		TURN THE MUSIC UP *Syncopate SY 13*	73	1

[1] Chris Paul featuring David Joseph

See also ISOTONIK

Frankie PAUL – *See APACHE INDIAN*

Les PAUL and Mary FORD
US, male instrumentalist – guitar, and female vocalist (4 WEEKS) pos/wks

			pos	wks
20 Nov 53	●	**VAYA CON DIOS (MAY GOD BE WITH YOU)** *Capitol CL 13943* ▲	7	4

Lyn PAUL *UK, female vocalist (6 WEEKS)* pos/wks

			pos	wks
28 Jun 75		**IT OUGHTA SELL A MILLION** *Polydor 2058 602*	37	6

See also NEW SEEKERS

Owen PAUL *UK, male vocalist – Owen McGee (14 WEEKS)* pos/wks

			pos	wks
31 May 86	●	**MY FAVOURITE WASTE OF TIME** *Epic A 7125*	3	14

PAUL and PAULA *US, male / female vocal duo – Ray Hildebrand and Jill Jackson (31 WEEKS)* pos/wks

			pos	wks
14 Feb 63	●	**HEY PAULA** *Philips 304012 BF* ▲	8	12
18 Apr 63	●	**YOUNG LOVERS** *Philips 304016 BF*	9	14
16 May 63		**HEY PAULA (re-entry)** *Philips 304012 BF*	37	5

Luciano PAVAROTTI *Italy, male vocalist (30 WEEKS)* pos/wks

			pos	wks
16 Jun 90	●	**NESSUN DORMA** *Decca PAV 03*	2	11
24 Oct 92		**MISERERE** *London LON 329* [1]	15	5
30 Jul 94		**LIBIAMO / LA DONNA E MOBILE** *Teldec YZ 843CD* [2]	21	4
14 Dec 96	●	**LIVE LIKE HORSES** *Rocket LLHDD 1* [3]	9	6
25 Jul 98		**YOU'LL NEVER WALK ALONE** *Decca 4607982* [4]	35	4

[1] Zucchero with Luciano Pavarotti [2] José Carreras featuring Placido Domingo and Luciano Pavarotti with Mehta [3] Elton John and Luciano Pavarotti [4] José Carreras, Placido Domingo and Luciano Pavarotti with Mehta

PAVEMENT *US, male vocal / instrumental group (6 WEEKS)* pos/wks

			pos	wks
28 Nov 92		**WATERY, DOMESTIC (EP)** *Big Cat ABB 38T*	58	1
12 Feb 94		**CUT YOUR HAIR** *Big Cat ABB 55SCD*	52	1
8 Feb 97		**STEREO** *Domino RUG 51CD*	48	1
3 May 97		**SHADY LANE** *Domino RUG 53CD*	40	1
22 May 99		**CARROT ROPE** *Domino RUG 90CD1*	27	2

Tracks on Watery, Domestic (EP): Texas Never Whispers / Frontwards / Feed 'Em / The Linden Lions / Shoot The Singer (1 Sick Verse)

Rita PAVONE *Italy, female vocalist (19 WEEKS)* pos/wks

			pos	wks
1 Dec 66		**HEART** *RCA 1553*	27	12
19 Jan 67		**YOU ONLY YOU** *RCA 1561*	21	7

Freda PAYNE *US, female vocalist (30 WEEKS)* pos/wks

			pos	wks
5 Sep 70	★	**BAND OF GOLD** *Invictus INV 502*	1	19
21 Nov 70		**DEEPER AND DEEPER** *Invictus INV 505*	33	9
27 Mar 71		**CHERISH WHAT IS DEAR TO YOU** *Invictus INV 509*	46	2

Tammy PAYNE *UK, female vocalist (2 WEEKS)* pos/wks

			pos	wks
20 Jul 91		**TAKE ME NOW** *Talkin Loud TLK 12*	55	2

Heather PEACE *UK, female vocalist (1 WEEK)* pos/wks

			pos	wks
13 May 00		**THE ROSE** *RCA 74321742892*	56	1

PEACE BY PIECE *UK, male vocal group (2 WEEKS)* pos/wks

			pos	wks
21 Sep 96		**SWEET SISTER** *Blanco Y Negro NEG 94CD*	46	1
25 Apr 98		**NOBODY'S BUSINESS** *Blanco Y Negro NEG 110CD1*	50	1

PEACH
UK / Belgium, female / male vocal / production group (1 WEEK) pos/wks

			pos	wks
17 Jan 98		**ON MY OWN** *Mute CDMUTE 215*	69	1

PEACHES and HERB *US, female / male vocal duo – Linda Green and Herbert Feemster (23 WEEKS)* pos/wks

			pos	wks
20 Jan 79		**SHAKE YOUR GROOVE THING** *Polydor 2066 992*	26	10
21 Apr 79	●	**REUNITED** *Polydor POSP 43* ▲	4	13

Mary PEARCE – *See UP YER RONSON featuring Mary PEARCE*

Natasha PEARL – *See TASTE XPERIENCE featuring NATASHA PEARL*

PEARL JAM *US, male vocal / instrumental group (41 WEEKS)* pos/wks

			pos	wks
15 Feb 92		**ALIVE** *Epic 6575727*	16	6
18 Apr 92		**EVEN FLOW** *Epic 6578577*	27	3
26 Sep 92		**JEREMY** *Epic 6582587*	15	4
1 Jan 94		**DAUGHTER** *Epic 6600202*	18	5
28 May 94		**DISSIDENT** *Epic 6604415*	14	4
26 Nov 94	●	**SPIN THE BLACK CIRCLE** *Epic 6610362*	10	3
25 Feb 95		**NOT FOR YOU** *Epic 6612032*	34	2
16 Dec 95		**I GOT ID** *Epic 6627162*	25	3
17 Aug 96		**WHO YOU ARE** *Epic 6635392*	18	2
31 Jan 98		**GIVEN TO FLY** *Epic 6653942*	12	3
23 May 98		**WISHLIST** *Epic 6657902*	30	2
14 Aug 99		**LAST KISS** *Epic 6674791*	42	1
13 May 00		**NOTHING AS IT SEEMS** *Epic 6693742*	22	2
22 Jul 00		**LIGHT YEARS** *Epic 6696282*	52	1

PEARLS *UK, female vocal duo (24 WEEKS)* pos/wks

			pos	wks
27 May 72		**THIRD FINGER, LEFT HAND** *Bell 1217*	31	6
23 Sep 72		**YOU CAME, YOU SAW, YOU CONQUERED** *Bell 1254*	32	5
24 Mar 73		**YOU ARE EVERYTHING** *Bell 1284*	41	3
1 Jun 74	●	**GUILTY** *Bell 1352*	10	10

Johnny PEARSON
UK, orchestra, Johnny Pearson – piano (15 WEEKS) pos/wks

			pos	wks
18 Dec 71	●	**SLEEPY SHORES** *Penny Farthing PEN 778*	8	15

PEBBLES *US, female vocalist – Perri McKissack (17 WEEKS)* pos/wks

			pos	wks
19 Mar 88	●	**GIRLFRIEND** *MCA MCA 1233*	8	11
28 May 88		**MERCEDES BOY** *MCA MCA 1248*	42	4
27 Oct 90		**GIVING YOU THE BENEFIT** *MCA MCA 1448*	73	2

PEDDLERS *UK, male vocal / instrumental group (14 WEEKS)* pos/wks

			pos	wks
7 Jan 65		**LET THE SUNSHINE IN** *Philips BF 1375*	50	1
23 Aug 69		**BIRTH** *CBS 4449*	17	9
31 Jan 70		**GIRLIE** *CBS 4720*	34	4

PEE BEE SQUAD *UK, male vocalist – Paul Burnett (3 WEEKS)* pos/wks

			pos	wks
5 Oct 85		**RUGGED AND MEAN, BUTCH AND ON SCREEN** *Project PRO 3*	52	3

Ann PEEBLES *US, female vocalist (3 WEEKS)* pos/wks

			pos	wks
20 Apr 74		**I CAN'T STAND THE RAIN** *London HL 10428*	50	1
4 May 74		**I CAN'T STAND THE RAIN (re-entry)** *London HL 10428*	41	2

PEECH BOYS *US, male vocal / instrumental group (3 WEEKS)* pos/wks

			pos	wks
30 Oct 82		**DON'T MAKE ME WAIT** *TMT TMT 7001*	49	3

Donald PEERS *UK, male vocalist (28 WEEKS)* pos/wks

			pos	wks
29 Dec 66		**GAMES THAT LOVERS PLAY** *Columbia DB 8079*	46	1
18 Dec 68	●	**PLEASE DON'T GO** *Columbia DB 8502*	3	18
30 Apr 69		**PLEASE DON'T GO (re-entry)** *Columbia DB 8502*	38	3
24 Jun 72		**GIVE ME ONE MORE CHANCE** *Decca F 13302*	36	6

PELE *UK, male / female vocal / instrumental group (3 WEEKS)* pos/wks

			pos	wks
15 Feb 92		**MEGALOMANIA** *M & G MAGS 20*	73	1
13 Jun 92		**FAIR BLOWS THE WIND FOR FRANCE** *M & G MAGS 24*	62	1
31 Jul 93		**FAT BLACK HEART** *M & G MAGCD 43*	75	1

Marti PELLOW *UK, male vocalist (8 WEEKS)* pos/wks

			pos	wks
16 Jun 01	●	**CLOSE TO YOU** *Mercury MERCD 532*	9	6
1 Dec 01		**I'VE BEEN AROUND THE WORLD** *Mercury 5887772*	28	2

See also WET WET WET

Debbie PENDER *US, female vocalist (1 WEEK)*

		pos	wks
30 May 98	**MOVIN' ON** *AM:PM 5826492*	41	1

Teddy PENDERGRASS *US, male vocalist (24 WEEKS)*

		pos	wks
21 May 77	**THE WHOLE TOWN'S LAUGHING AT ME** *Philadelphia International PIR 5116*	44	3
28 Oct 78	**ONLY YOU / CLOSE THE DOOR** *Philadelphia International PIR 6713*	41	6
23 May 81	**TWO HEARTS** *20th Century TC 2492* [1]	49	5
25 Jan 86	**HOLD ME** *Asylum EKR 32* [2]	44	5
28 May 88	**JOY** *Elektra EKR 75*	58	3
19 Nov 94	**THE MORE I GET THE MORE I WANT** *X-clusive XCLU 011CD* [3]	35	2

[1] Stephanie Mills featuring Teddy Pendergrass [2] Teddy Pendergrass with Whitney Houston [3] KWS featuring Teddy Pendergrass

Ce Ce PENISTON *US, female vocalist (53 WEEKS)*

		pos	wks
12 Oct 91	**FINALLY** *A & M AM 822*	29	7
11 Jan 92 ●	**WE GOT A LOVE THANG** *A & M AM 846*	6	8
18 Jan 92	**I LIKE IT** *A & M AM 847* [1]	58	2
21 Mar 92 ●	**FINALLY (re-issue)** *A & M AM 858*	2	8
23 May 92 ●	**KEEP ON WALKIN'** *A & M AM 878*	10	6
5 Sep 92	**CRAZY LOVE** *A & M AM 0060*	44	3
12 Dec 92	**INSIDE THAT I CRIED** *A & M AM 0121*	42	2
15 Jan 94	**I'M IN THE MOOD** *A & M 5804552*	16	4
2 Apr 94	**KEEP GIVIN' ME YOUR LOVE** *A & M 5805492*	36	2
6 Aug 94	**HIT BY LOVE** *A & M 5806932*	33	2
13 Sep 97	**FINALLY (re-mix)** *AM:PM 5823432*	26	5
7 Feb 98	**SOMEBODY ELSE'S GUY** *AM:PM 5825112*	13	4

[1] Overweight Pooch featuring Ce Ce Peniston

Dawn PENN
Jamaica, female vocalist – Dawn Pickering (12 WEEKS)

		pos	wks
11 Jun 94 ●	**YOU DON'T LOVE ME (NO, NO, NO)** *Big Beat A 8295CD*	3	12

Barbara PENNINGTON *US, female vocalist (8 WEEKS)*

		pos	wks
27 Apr 85	**FAN THE FLAME** *Record Shack SOHO 37*	62	3
27 Jul 85	**ON A CROWDED STREET** *Record Shack SOHO 49*	57	5

Tricia PENROSE *UK, female vocalist (2 WEEKS)*

		pos	wks
7 Dec 96	**WHERE DID OUR LOVE GO** *RCA 74321428152*	71	1
4 Mar 00	**DON'T WANNA BE ALONE** *Doop DP 2001CD*	44	1

PENTANGLE
UK, male / female vocal / instrumental group (4 WEEKS)

		pos	wks
28 May 69	**ONCE I HAD A SWEETHEART** *Big T BIG 124*	46	1
14 Feb 70	**LIGHT FLIGHT** *Big T BIG 128*	43	1
28 Feb 70	**LIGHT FLIGHT (re-entry)** *Big T BIG 128*	45	2

PENTHOUSE 4 *UK, male vocal / instrumental duo (3 WEEKS)*

		pos	wks
23 Apr 88	**BUST THIS HOUSE DOWN** *Syncopate SY 10*	56	3

PEOPLES CHOICE *US, male vocal / instrumental group (9 WEEKS)*

		pos	wks
20 Sep 75	**DO IT ANYWAY YOU WANNA** *Philadelphia International PIR 3500*	36	5
21 Jan 78	**JAM, JAM, JAM (ALL NIGHT LONG)** *Philadelphia International PIR 5891*	40	4

PEPE DELUXE *Finland, male DJ / production group (3 WEEKS)*

		pos	wks
26 May 01	**BEFORE YOU LEAVE** *Incredible 6712392*	20	3

Danny PEPPERMINT and the JUMPING JACKS
US, male vocal / instrumental group (8 WEEKS)

		pos	wks
18 Jan 62	**THE PEPPERMINT TWIST** *London HLL 9478*	26	8

PEPPERS *France, male instrumental group (12 WEEKS)*

		pos	wks
26 Oct 74 ●	**PEPPER BOX** *Spark SRL 1100*	6	12

PEPSI and SHIRLIE *UK, female vocal duo – Helen DeMacque and Shirley Holliman (24 WEEKS)*

		pos	wks
17 Jan 87 ●	**HEARTACHE** *Polydor POSP 837*	2	12
30 May 87 ●	**GOODBYE STRANGER** *Polydor POSP 865*	9	7
26 Sep 87	**CAN'T GIVE ME LOVE** *Polydor POSP 885*	58	3
12 Dec 87	**ALL RIGHT NOW** *Polydor POSP 896*	50	2

PERCEPTION *UK, male vocal group (2 WEEKS)*

		pos	wks
7 Mar 92	**FEED THE FEELING** *Talkin Loud TLK 17*	58	2

The listed flip side of 'Feed the Feeling' was 'Three Times a Maybe' by K-Creative

Lance PERCIVAL *UK, male vocalist (3 WEEKS)*

		pos	wks
28 Oct 65	**SHAME AND SCANDAL IN THE FAMILY** *Parlophone R 5335*	37	3

PERFECT CIRCLE – *See A PERFECT CIRCLE*

PERFECT DAY *UK, male vocal / instrumental group (4 WEEKS)*

		pos	wks
21 Jan 89	**LIBERTY TOWN** *London LON 214*	58	3
1 Apr 89	**JANE** *London LON 188*	68	1

PERFECT PHASE *Holland, male production duo (7 WEEKS)*

		pos	wks
25 Dec 99	**HORNY HORNS** *Positiva CDTIV 123*	21	7

PERFECTLY ORDINARY PEOPLE
UK, male vocal / instrumental group (3 WEEKS)

		pos	wks
22 Oct 88	**THEME FROM P.O.P.** *Urban URB 25*	61	3

PERFECTO ALLSTARZ *UK, male instrumental / production duo – Paul Oakenfold and Steve Osborne (11 WEEKS)*

		pos	wks
4 Feb 95 ●	**REACH UP (PAPA'S GOT A BRAND NEW PIG BAG)** *Perfecto YZ 892CD*	6	11

PERFUME *UK, male vocal / instrumental group (1 WEEK)*

		pos	wks
10 Feb 96	**HAVEN'T SEEN YOU** *Aromasound AROMA 005CDS*	71	1

Emilio PERICOLI *Italy, male vocalist (14 WEEKS)*

		pos	wks
28 Jun 62	**AL DI LA** *Warner Bros. WB 69*	30	14

Carl PERKINS *US, male vocalist (8 WEEKS)*

		pos	wks
18 May 56 ●	**BLUE SUEDE SHOES** *London HLU 8271*	10	8

PERPETUAL MOTION
UK, male instrumental / production group (5 WEEKS)

		pos	wks
2 May 98	**KEEP ON DANCIN' (LET'S GO)** *Positiva CDTIV 90*	12	5

Steve PERRY *UK, male vocalist (1 WEEK)*

		pos	wks
4 Aug 60	**STEP BY STEP** *HMV POP 745*	41	1

Nina PERSSON and David ARNOLD *Sweden, female vocalist and UK, male instrumentalist / producer (1 WEEK)*

		pos	wks
29 Apr 00	**THEME FROM 'RANDALL & HOPKIRK (DECEASED)'** *Island CID 762*	49	1

Jon PERTWEE *UK, male actor / vocalist (7 WEEKS)*

		pos	wks
1 Mar 80	**WORZEL'S SONG** *Decca F 13885*	33	7

PESHAY *UK, male DJ / producer – Paul Pesce (3 WEEKS)*

		pos	wks
9 May 98	**MILES FROM HOME** *Mo Wax MW 092*	75	1
17 Jul 99	**SWITCH** *Island Blue PFACD 1*	59	1
19 Feb 00	**TRULY** *Island Blue PFACD 4* [1]	55	1

[1] Peshay featuring Kym Mazelle

PET SHOP BOYS (64 Top 50) *Critically acclaimed and quintessentially English duo: former assistant editor of Smash Hits, Neil Tennant (v), and Chris Lowe (k). No duo has amassed more chart entries than this act, whose first hit was voted Best British Single at the 1987 Brit Awards (227 WEEKS)* pos/wks

Date		Title / Label	Pos	Wks
23 Nov 85	★	WEST END GIRLS *Parlophone R 6115* ▲	1	15
8 Mar 86		LOVE COMES QUICKLY *Parlophone R 6116*	19	9
31 May 86		OPPORTUNITIES (LET'S MAKE LOTS OF MONEY) *Parlophone R 6129*	11	8
4 Oct 86	●	SUBURBIA *Parlophone R 6140*	8	9
27 Jun 87	★	IT'S A SIN *Parlophone R 6158*	1	11
22 Aug 87	●	WHAT HAVE I DONE TO DESERVE THIS? *Parlophone R 6163* [1]	2	9
24 Oct 87	●	RENT *Parlophone R 6168*	8	7
12 Dec 87	★	ALWAYS ON MY MIND *Parlophone R 6171*	1	11
2 Apr 88	★	HEART *Parlophone R 6177*	1	10
24 Sep 88	●	DOMINO DANCING *Parlophone R 6190*	7	8
26 Nov 88	●	LEFT TO MY OWN DEVICES *Parlophone R 6198*	4	8
8 Jul 89	●	IT'S ALRIGHT *Parlophone R 6220*	5	8
6 Oct 90	●	SO HARD *Parlophone R 6269*	4	6
24 Nov 90		BEING BORING *Parlophone R 6275*	20	8
23 Mar 91	●	WHERE THE STREETS HAVE NO NAME - CAN'T TAKE MY EYES OFF YOU / HOW CAN YOU EXPECT TO BE TAKEN SERIOUSLY *Parlophone R 6285*	4	8
8 Jun 91		JEALOUSY *Parlophone R 6283*	12	5
26 Oct 91		DJ CULTURE *Parlophone R 6301*	13	3
23 Nov 91		DJ CULTURE (re-mix) *Parlophone 12RX 6301*	40	2
21 Dec 91		WAS IT WORTH IT? *Parlophone R 6306*	24	4
12 Jun 93	●	CAN YOU FORGIVE HER *Parlophone CDR 6348*	7	7
18 Sep 93	●	GO WEST *Parlophone CDR 6356*	2	9
11 Dec 93		I WOULDN'T NORMALLY DO THIS KIND OF THING *Parlophone CDR 6370*	13	7
16 Apr 94		LIBERATION *Parlophone CDR 6377*	14	5
11 Jun 94	●	ABSOLUTELY FABULOUS *Spaghetti CDR 6382* [2]	6	7
10 Sep 94		YESTERDAY WHEN I WAS MAD *Parlophone CDR 6386*	13	4
5 Aug 95		PANINARO *Parlophone CDR 6414*	15	4
4 May 96	●	BEFORE *Parlophone CDR 6431*	7	5
24 Aug 96	●	SE A VIDE E (THAT'S THE WAY LIFE IS) *Parlophone CDR 6443*	8	8
23 Nov 96		SINGLE *Parlophone CDR 6452*	14	3
29 Mar 97	●	A RED LETTER DAY *Parlophone CDR 6460*	9	3
5 Jul 97	●	SOMEWHERE *Parlophone CDR 6470*	9	5
31 Jul 99		I DON'T KNOW WHAT YOU WANT BUT I CAN'T GIVE IT ANYMORE *Parlophone CDR 6523*	15	3
9 Oct 99		NEW YORK CITY BOY *Parlophone CDR 6525*	14	4
15 Jan 00	●	YOU ONLY TELL ME YOU LOVE ME WHEN YOU'RE DRUNK *Parlophone CDR 6533*	8	4

[1] Pet Shop Boys and Dusty Springfield [2] Absolutely Fabulous

PETER and GORDON (437 Top 500) *UK duo, Peter Asher and Gordon Waller, who had transatlantic No.1 with debut single (penned, as were two other hits, by Asher's sister's boyfriend, Paul McCartney). Peter became a highly regarded Grammy-winning producer (77 WEEKS)* pos/wks

Date		Title / Label	Pos	Wks
12 Mar 64	★	A WORLD WITHOUT LOVE *Columbia DB 7225* ▲	1	14
4 Jun 64	●	NOBODY I KNOW *Columbia DB 7292*	10	11
8 Apr 65	●	TRUE LOVE WAYS *Columbia DB 7524*	2	15
24 Jun 65	●	TO KNOW YOU IS TO LOVE YOU *Columbia DB 7617*	5	10
21 Oct 65		BABY I'M YOURS *Columbia DB 7729*	19	9
24 Feb 66		WOMAN *Columbia DB 7834*	28	7
22 Sep 66		LADY GODIVA *Columbia DB 8003*	16	11

PETER, PAUL and MARY
US, male / female vocal / instrumental group (38 WEEKS) pos/wks

Date		Title / Label	Pos	Wks
10 Oct 63		BLOWING IN THE WIND *Warner Bros. WB 104*	13	16
16 Apr 64		TELL IT ON THE MOUNTAIN *Warner Bros. WB 127*	33	4
15 Oct 64		THE TIMES THEY ARE A-CHANGIN' *Warner Bros. WB 142*	44	2
17 Jan 70	●	LEAVING ON A JET PLANE *Warner Bros. WB 7340* ▲	2	16

PETERS and LEE *UK, male / female vocal duo – Lennie Peters and Dianne Lee (57 WEEKS)* pos/wks

Date		Title / Label	Pos	Wks
26 May 73	★	WELCOME HOME *Philips 6006 307*	1	24
3 Nov 73		BY YOUR SIDE *Philips 6006 339*	39	4
20 Apr 74	●	DON'T STAY AWAY TOO LONG *Philips 6006 388*	3	15
17 Aug 74		RAINBOW *Philips 6006 406*	17	7
6 Mar 76		HEY MR MUSIC MAN *Philips 6006 502*	16	7

Jonathan PETERS presents LUMINAIRE
US, male DJ / producer (1 WEEK) pos/wks

Date		Title / Label	Pos	Wks
24 Jul 99		FLOWER DUET *Pelican PELID 001*	75	1

Ray PETERSON *US, male vocalist (9 WEEKS)* pos/wks

Date		Title / Label	Pos	Wks
4 Sep 59		THE WONDER OF YOU *RCA 1131*	23	1
24 Mar 60		ANSWER ME *RCA 1175*	47	1
19 Jan 61		CORRINE, CORRINA *London HLX 9246*	48	1
2 Feb 61		CORRINE, CORRINA (re-entry) *London HLX 9246*	41	6

Tom PETTY and the HEARTBREAKERS
US, male vocal / instrumental group (43 WEEKS) pos/wks

Date		Title / Label	Pos	Wks
25 Jun 77		ANYTHING THAT'S ROCK 'N' ROLL *Shelter WIP 6396*	36	3
13 Aug 77		AMERICAN GIRL *Shelter WIP 6403*	40	5
15 Aug 81		STOP DRAGGIN' MY HEART AROUND *WEA K 79231* [1]	50	4
13 Apr 85		DON'T COME AROUND HERE NO MORE *MCA MCA 926*	50	4
13 May 89		I WON'T BACK DOWN *MCA MCA 1334* [2]	28	10
12 Aug 89		RUNNIN' DOWN A DREAM *MCA MCA 1359* [2]	55	4
25 Nov 89		FREE FALLIN' *MCA MCA 1381* [2]	64	2
29 Jun 91		LEARNING TO FLY *MCA MCS 1555*	46	4
4 Apr 92		TOO GOOD TO BE TRUE *MCA MCS 1616*	34	3
30 Oct 93		SOMETHING IN THE AIR *MCA MCSTD 1945* [2]	53	2
12 Mar 94		MARY JANE'S LAST DANCE *MCA MCSTD 1966*	52	2

[1] Stevie Nicks with Tom Petty and the Heartbreakers [2] Tom Petty

PF PROJECT featuring Ewan McGREGOR *UK, male production duo – Jamie White and Moussa Clarke and UK, male actor (11 WEEKS)* pos/wks

Date		Title / Label	Pos	Wks
15 Nov 97	●	CHOOSE LIFE *Positiva CDTIV 84*	6	11

See also TZANT and MUSIQUE vs U2

PHANTOMS – *See Johnny BRANDON*

PHARAO *Germany, male / female vocal / instrumental group (2 WEEKS)* pos/wks

Date		Title / Label	Pos	Wks
4 Mar 95		THERE IS A STAR *Epic 6611832*	43	2

PHARAOHS – *See SAM THE SHAM and the PHARAOHS*

PHARCYDE *US, male rap group (6 WEEKS)* pos/wks

Date		Title / Label	Pos	Wks
31 Jul 93		PASSIN' ME BY *Atlantic A 8360CD*	55	3
6 Apr 96		RUNNIN' *Go.Beat GODCD 142*	36	2
10 Aug 96		SHE SAID *Go.Beat GODCD 144*	51	1

Franke PHAROAH – *See FRANKE*

PHASE II *UK, male producer – Dave Lee (3 WEEKS)* pos/wks

Date		Title / Label	Pos	Wks
18 Mar 89		REACHIN' *Republic LICT 006*	70	1
21 Dec 91		REACHIN' (re-mix) *Republic LICT160* [1]	36	2

[1] Joey Negro presents Phase II

PHAT 'N' PHUNKY *UK, male production duo (1 WEEK)* pos/wks

Date		Title / Label	Pos	Wks
14 Jun 97		LET'S GROOVE *Chase CDCHASE 8*	61	1

PHATS & SMALL *UK, male DJ / production duo – Jason Hayward and Russell Small (36 WEEKS)* pos/wks

Date		Title / Label	Pos	Wks
10 Apr 99	●	TURN AROUND *Multiply CDMULTY 49*	2	16
14 Aug 99	●	FEEL GOOD *Multiply CDMULTY 54*	7	8
4 Dec 99		TONITE *Multiply CDMULTY 57*	11	6
30 Jun 01		THIS TIME AROUND *Multiply CDMULTY 75*	15	5
24 Nov 01		CHANGE *Multiply CDMULTY 80*	45	1

PHATT B *Holland, male DJ / producer – Bernsquil Verndoom (1 WEEK)* pos/wks

Date		Title / Label	Pos	Wks
11 Nov 00		AND DA DRUM MACHINE *Nulife / Arista 74321801902*	58	1

1985

IN A TRAGIC YEAR FOR FOOTBALL, BRADFORD CITY'S GROUND WAS ENGULFED IN FLAMES, KILLING 52 FANS, AND RIOTING AT THE HEYSEL STADIUM IN BRUSSELS CAUSED A WALL TO COLLAPSE CRUSHING 41. FAMINE STRUCK IN ETHIOPIA AND THE MUSIC WORLD STRUCK BACK WITH LIVE AID IN AN EFFORT TO RAISE FUNDS TO ALLEVIATE THE SUFFERING. LIVE AID PERFORMER **NIK KERSHAW** GIVES US THE LOW-DOWN ON HIS TWO TOP 10 HITS THAT YEAR ...

"I'd already sold a couple of million albums ['Human Racing'], played a sold-out UK and European tour and was still living in a two-up, one-down terraced house in Sible Hedingham. (They still haven't got the blue plaque on the wall.) In one of the bedrooms I'd fashioned what passed for a home studio in those days (Fostex four-track portastudio, drum machine, mike). In one corner languished my one and only keyboard, a Roland, which, if you held a key down and pressed the arpeggiator button, played the bass line to 'Don Quixote'. 'Wide Boy' was the only old song on the 'Riddle' album. It was written in 1980 when I was the guitarist in a jazz fusion band called – wait for it – Fusion! It was my party piece. They used to wheel me out from the back of the stage where me and my lager were hiding for my one vocal of the night. Can't imagine who I was thinking of when I wrote it. I was more into the neat, cyclic way the chords worked together than the lyric. Who was to know four years later it was to become autobiographical."

SINGLE OF THE YEAR 'The Power of Love' Jennifer Rush
ALBUM OF THE YEAR 'Born in the USA' Bruce Springsteen

PhD *UK, male vocal / instrumental duo – Jim Diamond and Tony Hymas (14 WEEKS)* pos/wks

			pos	wks
3 Apr 82	●	I WON'T LET YOU DOWN *WEA K 79209*	3	14

See also Jim DIAMOND

Barrington PHELOUNG *Australia, male conductor (2 WEEKS)* pos/wks

			pos	wks
13 Mar 93		'INSPECTOR MORSE' THEME *Virgin VSCDT 1458*	61	2

PHILADELPHIA INTERNATIONAL ALL-STARS
US, male / female vocal / instrumental group (8 WEEKS) pos/wks

			pos	wks
13 Aug 77		LET'S CLEAN UP THE GHETTO *Philadelphia International PIR 5451*	34	8

PHILHARMONIA ORCHESTRA, conductor Lorin MAAZEL
UK, orchestra and US, male conductor (7 WEEKS) pos/wks

			pos	wks
30 Jul 69		THUS SPAKE ZARATHUSTRA *Columbia DB 8607*	33	7

Chynna PHILLIPS *US, female vocalist (1 WEEK)* pos/wks

			pos	wks
3 Feb 96		NAKED AND SACRED *EMI CDEM 409*	62	1

Esther PHILLIPS *US, female vocalist – Esther Mae Jones (8 WEEKS)* pos/wks

			pos	wks
4 Oct 75	●	WHAT A DIFFERENCE A DAY MAKES *Kudu 925*	6	8

PHOEBE ONE *UK, female rapper (3 WEEKS)* pos/wks

			pos	wks
12 Dec 98		DOIN' OUR THING / ONE MAN'S BITCH *Mecca Recordings MECX 1020*	59	1
15 May 99		GET ON IT *Mecca Recordings MECX 1026*	38	2

PHOENIX *France, male vocal / instrumental group (1 WEEK)* pos/wks

			pos	wks
3 Feb 01		IF I EVER FEEL BETTER *Source DINSD 210*	65	1

Paul PHOENIX *UK, male vocalist (4 WEEKS)* pos/wks

			pos	wks
3 Nov 79		NUNC DIMITTIS *Different HAVE 20*	56	4

Full artist credit on hit as follows: Paul Phoenix (treble) with Instrumental Ensemble - James Watson (trumpet), John Scott (organ), conducted by Barry Rose

PHOTEK *UK, male producer – Rupert Parkes (4 WEEKS)* pos/wks

			pos	wks
22 Mar 97		NI-TEN-ICHI-RYU (TWO SWORDS TECHNIQUE) *Science QEDCD 2*	37	2
28 Feb 98		MODUS OPERANDI *Virgin QEDCD 6*	66	1
24 Feb 01		MINE TO GIVE *Science QEDCD 10* [1]	44	1

[1] Photek featuring Robert Owens

PHOTOS *UK, male / female vocal / instrumental group (4 WEEKS)* pos/wks

			pos	wks
17 May 80		IRENE *Epic EPC 8517*	56	4

PHUNKY PHANTOM *UK, male producer (3 WEEKS)* pos/wks

			pos	wks
16 May 98		GET UP STAND UP *Club for Life DISNCD 44*	27	3

PHUTURE ASSASSINS
UK, male instrumental / production group (1 WEEK) pos/wks

			pos	wks
6 Jun 92		FUTURE SOUND (EP) *Suburban Base SUBBASE 010*	64	1

Tracks on Future Sound (EP): Future Sound / African Sanctus / Rydim Come Foward / Freedom Sound

PIA – *See Pia ZADORA*

Edith PIAF *France, female vocalist (15 WEEKS)* pos/wks

			pos	wks
12 May 60		MILORD *Columbia DC 754*	41	4
3 Nov 60		MILORD (re-entry) *Columbia DC 754*	24	11

PIANOHEADZ *US, male DJ / production duo (2 WEEKS)* pos/wks

			pos	wks
11 Jul 98		IT'S OVER (DISTORTION) *Incredible Music INCRL 3CD*	39	2

PIANOMAN *UK, male producer – James Sammon (8 WEEKS)* pos/wks

			pos	wks
15 Jun 96	●	BLURRED *Ffrreedom TABCD 243*	6	7
26 Apr 97		PARTY PEOPLE (LIVE YOUR LIFE BE FREE) *3 Beat 3 BTCD1*	43	1

See also BASS BOYZ

Bobby 'Boris' PICKETT and the CRYPT-KICKERS
US, male vocal / instrumental group (13 WEEKS) pos/wks

			pos	wks
1 Sep 73	●	MONSTER MASH *London HLU 10320* ▲	3	13

Wilson PICKETT *US, male vocalist (61 WEEKS)* pos/wks

			pos	wks
23 Sep 65		IN THE MIDNIGHT HOUR *Atlantic AT 4036*	12	11
25 Nov 65		DON'T FIGHT IT *Atlantic AT 4052*	29	8
10 Mar 66		634-5789 *Atlantic AT 4072*	36	5
1 Sep 66		LAND OF 1000 DANCES *Atlantic 584 039*	22	9
15 Dec 66		MUSTANG SALLY *Atlantic 584 066*	28	7
27 Sep 67		FUNKY BROADWAY *Atlantic 584 130*	43	3
11 Sep 68		I'M A MIDNIGHT MOVER *Atlantic 584 203*	38	6
8 Jan 69		HEY JUDE *Atlantic 584 236*	16	9
21 Nov 87		IN THE MIDNIGHT HOUR (re-recording) *Motown ZB 41583*	62	3

PICKETTYWITCH
UK, male / female vocal / instrumental group (34 WEEKS) pos/wks

			pos	wks
28 Feb 70	●	THAT SAME OLD FEELING *Pye 7N 17887*	5	14
4 Jul 70		(IT'S LIKE A) SAD OLD KINDA MOVIE *Pye 7N 17951*	16	10
7 Nov 70		BABY I WON'T LET YOU DOWN *Pye 7N 45002*	27	10

Mauro PICOTTO *Italy, male producer (18 WEEKS)* pos/wks

			pos	wks
12 Jun 99		LIZARD (GONNA GET YOU) *VC Recordings VCRD 50*	27	3
20 Nov 99		LIZARD (GONNA GET YA) (re-mix) *VC Recordings VCRD 57*	33	2
15 Jul 00		IGUANA *VC Recordings VCRD 68*	33	3
13 Jan 01		KOMODO (SAVE A SOUL) *VC Recordings VCRD 85*	13	5
11 Aug 01		LIKE THIS LIKE THAT *VC Recordings VCRD 92*	21	4
25 Aug 01		VERDI *BXR BXRP 0318*	74	1

See also CRW; RAF

PIGBAG *UK, male instrumental group (20 WEEKS)* pos/wks

			pos	wks
7 Nov 81		SUNNY DAY *Y Records Y 12*	53	3
27 Feb 82		GETTING UP *Y Records Y 16*	61	3
3 Apr 82	●	PAPA'S GOT A BRAND NEW PIGBAG *Y Records Y 10*	3	11
10 Jul 82		THE BIG BEAN *Y Records Y 24*	40	3

PIGEON HED – *See LO FIDELITY ALLSTARS*

Nelson PIGFORD – *See De Etta LITTLE and Nelson PIGFORD*

PIGLETS *UK, female vocal group (12 WEEKS)* pos/wks

			pos	wks
6 Nov 71	●	JOHNNY REGGAE *Bell 1180*	3	12

Dick PIKE – *See Ruby WRIGHT*

P.I.L. – *See PUBLIC IMAGE LTD*

PILOT *UK, male vocal / instrumental group (29 WEEKS)* pos/wks

			pos	wks
2 Nov 74		MAGIC *EMI 2217*	11	11
18 Jan 75	★	JANUARY *EMI 2255*	1	10
19 Apr 75		CALL ME ROUND *EMI 2287*	34	4
27 Sep 75		JUST A SMILE *EMI 2338*	31	4

PILTDOWN MEN *US, male instrumental group (36 WEEKS)* pos/wks

			pos	wks
8 Sep 60		MCDONALD'S CAVE *Capitol CL 15149*	14	18
12 Jan 61		PILTDOWN RIDES AGAIN *Capitol CL 15175*	14	10
9 Mar 61		GOODNIGHT MRS. FLINTSTONE *Capitol CL 15186*	18	8

Courtney PINE *UK, male instrumentalist – saxophone (6 WEEKS)* pos/wks

			pos	wks
30 Jul 88		LIKE DREAMERS DO *Fourth & Broadway BRW 108* [1]	26	5
7 Jul 90		I'M STILL WAITING *Mango MNG 749* [2]	66	1

[1] Mica Paris featuring Courtney Pine [2] Courtney Pine featuring Carroll Thompson

PING PING and Al VERLAINE *Belgium, male vocal duo (4 WEEKS)* pos/wks

28 Sep 61	**SUCU SUCU** *Oriole CB 1589*	41	4

PINK *US, female vocalist – Alecia Moore (39 WEEKS)* pos/wks

10 Jun 00 ●	**THERE YOU GO** *LaFace / Arista 74321757602*	6	9
30 Sep 00 ●	**MOST GIRLS** *La Face / Arista 74321792012*	5	8
27 Jan 01 ●	**YOU MAKE ME SICK** *La Face / Arista 74321828702*	9	6
30 Jun 01 ★	**LADY MARMALADE** *Interscope / Polydor 4975612* [1] ■ ▲	1	16

[1] Christina Aguilera, Lil' Kim, Mya and Pink

PINK FLOYD *UK, male vocal / instrumental group (55 WEEKS)* pos/wks

30 Mar 67	**ARNOLD LAYNE** *Columbia DB 8156*	20	8
22 Jun 67 ●	**SEE EMILY PLAY** *Columbia DB 8214*	6	12
1 Dec 79 ★	**ANOTHER BRICK IN THE WALL (PART 2)** *Harvest HAR 5194* ◆ ▲	1	12
7 Aug 82	**WHEN THE TIGERS BROKE FREE** *Harvest HAR 5222*	39	5
7 May 83	**NOT NOW JOHN** *Harvest HAR 5224*	30	4
19 Dec 87	**ON THE TURNING AWAY** *EMI EM 34*	55	4
25 Jun 88	**ONE SLIP** *EMI EM 52*	50	3
4 Jun 94	**TAKE IT BACK** *EMI CDEMS 309*	23	4
29 Oct 94	**HIGH HOPES / KEEP TALKING** *EMI CDEMS 342*	26	3

PINKEES *UK, male vocal / instrumental group (9 WEEKS)* pos/wks

18 Sep 82 ●	**DANGER GAMES** *Creole CR 39*	8	9

PINKERTON'S ASSORTED COLOURS
UK, male vocal / instrumental group (12 WEEKS) pos/wks

13 Jan 66 ●	**MIRROR MIRROR** *Decca F 12307*	9	11
21 Apr 66	**DON'T STOP LOVING ME BABY** *Decca F 12377*	50	1

PINKY and PERKY *UK, pork puppet duo (3 WEEKS)* pos/wks

29 May 93	**REET PETITE** *Telstar CDPIGGY 1*	47	3

PIONEERS *Jamaica, male vocal / instrumental group (34 WEEKS)* pos/wks

18 Oct 69	**LONG SHOT KICK DE BUCKET** *Trojan TR 672*	21	10
10 Jan 70	**LONG SHOT KICK DE BUCKET (re-entry)** *Trojan TR 672*	40	1
31 Jul 71 ●	**LET YOUR YEAH BE YEAH** *Trojan TR 7825*	5	12
15 Jan 72	**GIVE AND TAKE** *Trojan TR 7846*	35	6
29 Mar 80	**LONG SHOT KICK DE BUCKET (re-issue)** *Trojan TRO 9063*	42	5

Re-issue of 'Long Shot Kick De Bucket' coupled with re-issue of Liquidator by Harry J All Stars

Billie PIPER (467 Top 500) *Youngest solo act to debut at No.1, b. 22 Sep 1982, Swindon, UK. One-time 'Smash Hits' model topped the chart at 15. Singer who is married to DJ / entrepreneur Chris Evans holds the record for being the only female to score three chart-toppers before her 18th birthday (74 WEEKS)* pos/wks

11 Jul 98 ★	**BECAUSE WE WANT TO** *Innocent SINCD 2* [1] ■	1	12
17 Oct 98 ★	**GIRLFRIEND** *Innocent SINCD 3* [1] ■	1	10
19 Dec 98 ●	**SHE WANTS YOU** *Innocent SINDXX 6* [1]	3	11
2 Jan 99	**GIRLFRIEND (re-entry)** *Innocent SINCD 3* [1]	71	2
13 Mar 99	**SHE WANTS YOU (re-entry)** *Innocent SINDXX 6* [1]	54	2
3 Apr 99 ●	**HONEY TO THE BEE** *Innocent SINCD 8* [1]	3	9
26 Jun 99	**HONEY TO THE BEE (re-entry)** *Innocent SINCD 8* [1]	70	2
27 May 00 ★	**DAY & NIGHT** *Innocent SINCD 11* ■	1	11
19 Aug 00	**DAY & NIGHT (re-entry)** *Innocent SINCD 11*	73	1
30 Sep 00 ●	**SOMETHING DEEP INSIDE** *Innocent SINCD 19*	4	8
23 Dec 00	**WALK OF LIFE** *Innocent SINCD 23*	25	5
13 Jan 01	**SOMETHING DEEP INSIDE (re-entry)** *Innocent SINCD 19*	67	1

[1] Billie

PIPKINS *UK, male vocal duo – Roger Greenaway and Tony Burrows (10 WEEKS)* pos/wks

28 Mar 70 ●	**GIMME DAT DING** *Columbia DB 8662*	6	10

See also BLUE MINK

PIPS – *See Gladys KNIGHT and the PIPS*

PIRANHAS *UK, male vocal / instrumental group (21 WEEKS)* pos/wks

2 Aug 80 ●	**TOM HARK** *Sire SIR 4044*	6	12
16 Oct 82	**ZAMBESI** *Dakota DAK 6* [1]	17	9

[1] Piranhas featuring Boring Bob Grover

PIRATES – *See Johnny KIDD and the PIRATES*

PITCH SHIFTER *UK, male vocal / instrumental group (3 WEEKS)* pos/wks

28 Feb 98	**GENIUS** *Geffen GFSTD 22324*	71	1
26 Sep 98	**MICROWAVED** *Geffen GFSTD 22348*	54	1
21 Oct 00	**DEAD BATTERY** *MCA MCSTD 40241*	71	1

Gene PITNEY (76 Top 500) *Leading US performer in the 1960s, b. 17 Feb 1941, Connecticut. This unmistakable vocalist and songwriter had a longer and more impressive track record in the UK than in his homeland. Nonetheless, it took him 28 years to reach No.1 (212 WEEKS)* pos/wks

23 Mar 61	**(I WANNA) LOVE MY LIFE AWAY** *London HL 9270*	26	11
8 Mar 62	**TOWN WITHOUT PITY** *HMV POP 952*	32	6
5 Dec 63 ●	**TWENTY FOUR HOURS FROM TULSA** *United Artists UP 1035*	5	19
5 Mar 64 ●	**THAT GIRL BELONGS TO YESTERDAY** *United Artists UP 1045*	7	12
15 Oct 64	**IT HURTS TO BE IN LOVE** *United Artists UP 1063*	36	4
12 Nov 64 ●	**I'M GONNA BE STRONG** *Stateside SS 358*	2	14
18 Feb 65 ●	**I MUST BE SEEING THINGS** *Stateside SS 390*	6	10
10 Jun 65 ●	**LOOKING THRU THE EYES OF LOVE** *Stateside SS 420*	3	12
4 Nov 65 ●	**PRINCESS IN RAGS** *Stateside SS 471*	9	12
17 Feb 66 ●	**BACKSTAGE** *Stateside SS 490*	4	10
9 Jun 66 ●	**NOBODY NEEDS YOUR LOVE** *Stateside SS 518*	2	13
10 Nov 66 ●	**JUST ONE SMILE** *Stateside SS 558*	8	12
23 Feb 67	**(IN THE) COLD LIGHT OF DAY** *Stateside SS 597*	38	6
15 Nov 67 ●	**SOMETHING'S GOTTEN HOLD OF MY HEART** *Stateside SS 2060*	5	13
3 Apr 68	**SOMEWHERE IN THE COUNTRY** *Stateside SS 2103*	19	9
27 Nov 68	**YOURS UNTIL TOMORROW** *Stateside SS 2131*	34	7
5 Mar 69	**MARIA ELENA** *Stateside SS 2142*	25	6
14 Mar 70	**A STREET CALLED HOPE** *Stateside SS 2164*	37	5
3 Oct 70	**SHADY LADY** *Stateside SS 2177*	29	8
28 Apr 73	**24 SYCAMORE** *Pye International 7N 25606*	34	7
2 Nov 74	**BLUE ANGEL** *Bronze BRO 11*	49	1
16 Nov 74	**BLUE ANGEL (re-entry)** *Bronze BRO 11*	39	3
14 Jan 89 ★	**SOMETHING'S GOTTEN HOLD OF MY HEART** *Parlophone R 6201* [1]	1	12

[1] Marc Almond featuring special guest star Gene Pitney

Mario PIU *Italy, male DJ / producer (14 WEEKS)* pos/wks

11 Dec 99 ●	**COMMUNICATION (SOMEBODY ANSWER THE PHONE)** *Incentive CENT 2CDS*	5	9
10 Mar 01	**THE VISION** *BXR BXRC 0253* [1]	16	4
21 Apr 01	**THE VISION (re-entry)** *BXR BXRC 0253* [1]	71	1

[1] Mario Piu presents DJ Arabesque

PIXIES *US, male / female vocal / instrumental group (13 WEEKS)* pos/wks

1 Apr 89	**MONKEY GONE TO HEAVEN** *4AD AD 904*	60	3
1 Jul 89	**HERE COMES YOUR MAN** *4AD AD 909*	54	1
28 Jul 90	**VELOURIA** *4AD AD 0009*	28	3
10 Nov 90	**DIG FOR FIRE** *4AD AD 0014*	62	1
8 Jun 91	**PLANET OF SOUND** *4AD AD 1008*	27	3
4 Oct 97	**DEBASER** *4AD BAD 7010CD*	23	2

PIZZAMAN *UK, male producer – Norman Cook (18 WEEKS)* pos/wks

27 Aug 94	**TRIPPIN' ON SUNSHINE** *Cowboy Records CDLOAD 16*	33	2
10 Jun 95	**SEX ON THE STREETS** *Cowboy Records CDLOAD 24*	24	4
18 Nov 95	**HAPPINESS** *Cowboy Records CDLOAD 29*	19	4
6 Jan 96	**SEX ON THE STREETS (re-entry)** *Cowboy Records CDLOAD 24*	23	4
1 Jun 96	**TRIPPIN' ON SUNSHINE (re-issue)** *Cowboy Records CDLOAD 32*	18	3
14 Sep 96	**HELLO HONKY TONKS (ROCK YOUR BODY)** *Cowboy Records CDLOAD 39*	41	1

See also MIGHTY DUB KATZ; FREAKPOWER; HOUSEMARTINS; Norman COOK; BEATS INTERNATIONAL; Norman COOK

PIZZICATO FIVE
Japan, male / female vocal / instrumental group (1 WEEK) pos/wks

1 Nov 97	**MON AMOUR TOKYO** *Matador OLE 2902*	72	1

Joe PIZZULO – *See Sergio MENDES*

PJ *Canada, male producer – Paul Jacobs (2 WEEKS)* pos/wks

20 Sep 97	**HAPPY DAYS** *Deconstruction 74321511822*	72	1
4 Sep 99	**HAPPY DAYS (re-mix)** *Defected DEFECT 6CDS*	57	1

PJ & DUNCAN – *See ANT & DEC*

PKA *UK, male producer – Phil Kelsey (2 WEEKS)* pos/wks

20 Apr 91	**TEMPERATURE RISING** *Stress SS 4*	68	1
7 Mar 92	**POWERGEN (ONLY YOUR LOVE)** *Stress PKA 1*	70	1

PLACEBO
US / Sweden / UK, male vocal / instrumental group (37 WEEKS) pos/wks

28 Sep 96	**TEENAGE ANGST** *Elevator Music FLOORCD 3*	30	3
1 Feb 97 ●	**NANCY BOY** *Elevator Music FLOORCD 4*	4	6
24 May 97	**BRUISE PRISTINE** *Elevator Music FLOORCD 5*	14	3
15 Aug 98 ●	**PURE MORNING** *Hut FLOORCD 6*	4	6
10 Oct 98 ●	**YOU DON'T CARE ABOUT US** *Hut FLOORCD 7*	5	5
6 Feb 99	**EVERY YOU EVERY ME** *Hut / Virgin FLOORCD 9*	11	5
29 Jul 00	**TASTE IN MEN** *Hut / Virgin FLOORCD 11*	16	6
7 Oct 00	**SLAVE TO THE WAGE** *Hut / Virgin FLOORCD 12*	19	3

PLANET FUNK
Italy / UK / Finland, male / female vocal / production group (11 WEEKS) pos/wks

10 Feb 01 ●	**CHASE THE SUN** *Virgin VSCDT 1794*	5	6
31 Mar 01	**CHASE THE SUN (re-entry)** *Virgin VSCDT 1794*	55	3

PLANET PATROL *US, male vocal / instrumental group (3 WEEKS)* pos/wks

17 Sep 83	**CHEAP THRILLS** *Polydor POSP 639*	64	3

PLANET PERFECTO *UK, male production group (15 WEEKS)* pos/wks

14 Aug 99	**NOT OVER YET 99** *Code Blue BLU 004CD1* [1]	16	4
13 Nov 99	**BULLET IN THE GUN** *Perfecto PERF 3CDS*	15	4
16 Sep 00 ●	**BULLET IN THE GUN 2000 (re-mix)** *Perfecto PERF 03CDSX*	7	6
29 Sep 01	**BITES DA DUST** *Perfecto PERF 19CDS*	52	1

[1] Planet Perfecto featuring Grace

PLANETS *UK, male vocal / instrumental group (8 WEEKS)* pos/wks

18 Aug 79	**LINES** *Rialto TREB 104*	36	6
25 Oct 80	**DON'T LOOK DOWN** *Rialto TREB 116*	66	2

Robert PLANT *UK, male vocalist (33 WEEKS)* pos/wks

9 Oct 82	**BURNING DOWN ONE SIDE** *Swansong SSK 19429*	73	1
16 Jul 83	**BIG LOG** *WEA B 9848*	11	10
30 Jan 88	**HEAVEN KNOWS** *Es Paranza A 9373*	33	5
28 Apr 90	**HURTING KIND (I'VE GOT MY EYES ON YOU)** *Es Paranza A 8985*	45	3
8 May 93	**29 PALMS** *Fontana FATEX 1*	21	5
3 Jul 93	**I BELIEVE** *Fontana FATEX 2*	64	2
25 Dec 93	**IF I WERE A CARPENTER** *Fontana FATEX 4*	63	2
17 Dec 94	**GALLOWS POLE** *Fontana PPCD 2* [1]	35	3
11 Apr 98	**MOST HIGH** *Mercury 5687512* [2]	26	2

[1] Jimmy Page and Robert Plant [2] Page and Plant

See also LED ZEPPELIN

PLASMATICS
US, female / male vocal / instrumental group (4 WEEKS) pos/wks

26 Jul 80	**BUTCHER BABY** *Stiff BUY 76*	55	4

PLASTIC BERTRAND
Belgium, male vocalist – Roger Jouret (17 WEEKS) pos/wks

13 May 78 ●	**ÇA PLANE POUR MOI** *Sire 6078 616*	8	12
5 Aug 78	**SHA LA LA LA LEE** *Vertigo 6059 209*	39	5

PLASTIC JAM – *See BUG KANN and the PLASTIC JAM*

PLASTIC ONO BAND – *See John LENNON*

PLASTIC PENNY *UK, male vocal / instrumental group (10 WEEKS)* pos/wks

3 Jan 68 ●	**EVERYTHING I AM** *Page One POF 051*	6	10

PLASTIC POPULATION – *See YAZZ*

PLATINUM HOOK *US, male vocal / instrumental group (1 WEEK)* pos/wks

2 Sep 78	**STANDING ON THE VERGE (OF GETTING IT ON)** *Motown TMG 1115*	72	1

PLATTERS (344 Top 500) *World's biggest selling vocal group in late 1950s, fronted by tenor Tony Williams b. 5 Apr 1928, New Jersey, US, d. 14 Aug 1992. Male / female doo-wop quintet appeared in more countries than any of their 1950s contemporaries (91 WEEKS)* pos/wks

7 Sep 56 ●	**THE GREAT PRETENDER / ONLY YOU (AND YOU ALONE)** *Mercury MT 117*	5	12
2 Nov 56 ●	**MY PRAYER** *Mercury MT 120* ▲	4	10
7 Dec 56	**THE GREAT PRETENDER / ONLY YOU (AND YOU ALONE) (re-entry)** *Mercury MT 117*	21	1
18 Jan 57	**MY PRAYER (re-entry)** *Mercury MT 120*	28	2
25 Jan 57	**YOU'LL NEVER, NEVER KNOW / IT ISN'T RIGHT** *Mercury MT 130*	23	1
8 Feb 57	**YOU'LL NEVER, NEVER KNOW / IT ISN'T RIGHT (re-entry)** *Mercury MT 130*	29	1
29 Mar 57	**MY PRAYER (2nd re-entry)** *Mercury MT 120*	22	1
29 Mar 57	**ONLY YOU (AND YOU ALONE) (2nd re-entry)** *Mercury MT 117*	18	3
12 Apr 57	**YOU'LL NEVER, NEVER KNOW / IT ISN'T RIGHT (2nd re-entry)** *Mercury MT 130*	29	1
17 May 57	**I'M SORRY** *Mercury MT 145*	18	6
5 Jul 57	**I'M SORRY (re-entry)** *Mercury MT 145*	23	1
19 Jul 57	**I'M SORRY (2nd re-entry)** *Mercury MT 145*	22	1
16 May 58 ●	**TWILIGHT TIME** *Mercury MT 214* ▲	3	18
16 Jan 59 ★	**SMOKE GETS IN YOUR EYES** *Mercury AMT 1016* ▲	1	20
28 Aug 59	**REMEMBER WHEN** *Mercury AMT 1053*	25	2
29 Jan 60	**HARBOUR LIGHTS** *Mercury AMT 1081*	11	11

PLAVKA – *See JAM & SPOON featuring PLAVKA*

PLAYBOY BAND – *See John FRED and the PLAYBOY BAND*

PLAYBOYS – *See Gary LEWIS and the PLAYBOYS*

PLAYER *US / UK, male vocal / instrumental group (7 WEEKS)* pos/wks

25 Feb 78	**BABY COME BACK** *RSO 2090 254* ▲	32	7

PLAYERS ASSOCIATION
US, male vocal / instrumental group (17 WEEKS) pos/wks

10 Mar 79 ●	**TURN THE MUSIC UP** *Vanguard VS 5011*	8	9
5 May 79	**RIDE THE GROOVE** *Vanguard VS 5012*	42	5
9 Feb 80	**WE GOT THE GROOVE** *Vanguard VS 5016*	61	3

PLAYGROUP *UK, male producer – Trevor Jackson (1 WEEK)* pos/wks

24 Nov 01	**NUMBER ONE** *Source SOURCD 026*	66	1

PLAYTHING *Italy, male production duo (1 WEEK)* pos/wks

5 May 01	**INTO SPACE** *Manifesto FESCD 81*	48	1

PLUS ONE featuring SIRRON

UK, male / female vocal / instrumental group (4 WEEKS) pos/wks

			pos	wks
19 May 90		IT'S HAPPENIN' *MCA MCA 1405*	40	4

PLUTO – *See Pluto SHERVINGTON*

PLUX featuring Georgia JONES

US, male / female vocal / instrumental group (2 WEEKS) pos/wks

			pos	wks
4 May 96		OVER AND OVER *ffrr FCD 277*	33	2

PM DAWN *US, male vocal / instrumental / rap duo – Attrell and Jarrett Cordes (39 WEEKS)* pos/wks

			pos	wks
8 Jun 91		A WATCHER'S POINT OF VIEW (DON'T CHA THINK) *Gee Street GEE 32*	36	5
17 Aug 91	●	SET ADRIFT ON MEMORY BLISS *Gee Street GEE 33* ▲	3	8
19 Oct 91		PAPER DOLL *Gee Street GEE 35*	49	3
22 Feb 92		REALITY USED TO BE A FRIEND OF MINE *Gee Street GEE 37*	29	4
7 Nov 92		I'D DIE WITHOUT YOU *Gee Street GEE 39*	30	5
13 Mar 93		LOOKING THROUGH PATIENT EYES *Gee Street GESCD 47*	11	7
12 Jun 93		MORE THAN LIKELY *Gee Street GESCD 49* [1]	40	3
30 Sep 95		DOWNTOWN VENUS *Gee Street GESCD 63*	58	2
6 Apr 96		SOMETIMES I MISS YOU SO MUCH *Gee Street GESCD 65*	58	1
31 Oct 98		GOTTA BE...MOVIN' ON UP *Gee Street GEE 5003933* [2]	68	1

[1] PM Dawn featuring Boy George [2] PM Dawn featuring Ky-Mani

POB featuring DJ Patrick REID

UK, male producer – Paul Brogden (1 WEEK) pos/wks

			pos	wks
11 Dec 99		BLUEBOTTLE / FLY *Platipus PLAT 63CD*	74	1

POETS *UK, male vocal / instrumental group (5 WEEKS)* pos/wks

			pos	wks
29 Oct 64		NOW WE'RE THRU *Decca F 11995*	31	5

POGUES *Ireland, male vocal / instrumental group (70 WEEKS)* pos/wks

			pos	wks
6 Apr 85		A PAIR OF BROWN EYES *Stiff BUY 220*	72	2
22 Jun 85		SALLY MACLENNANE *Stiff BUY 224*	51	4
14 Sep 85		DIRTY OLD TOWN *Stiff BUY 229*	62	3
8 Mar 86		POGUETRY IN MOTION (EP) *Stiff BUY 243*	29	6
30 Aug 86		HAUNTED *MCA MCA 1084*	42	4
28 Mar 87	●	THE IRISH ROVER *Stiff BUY 258* [1]	8	8
5 Dec 87	●	FAIRYTALE OF NEW YORK *Pogue Mahone NY 7* [2]	2	9
5 Mar 88		IF I SHOULD FALL FROM GRACE WITH GOD *Pogue Mahone PG 1*	58	3
16 Jul 88		FIESTA *Pogue Mahone PG 2*	24	5
17 Dec 88		YEAH, YEAH, YEAH, YEAH, YEAH *Pogue Mahone YZ 355*	43	4
8 Jul 89		MISTY MORNING, ALBERT BRIDGE *PM YZ 407*	41	3
16 Jun 90		JACK'S HEROES / WHISKEY IN THE JAR *PM YZ 500* [1]	63	2
15 Sep 90		SUMMER IN SIAM *PM YZ 519*	64	2
21 Sep 91		A RAINY NIGHT IN SOHO *PM YZ 603*	67	1
14 Dec 91		FAIRYTALE OF NEW YORK (re-issue) *PM YZ 628* [2]	36	5
30 May 92		HONKY TONK WOMEN *PM YZ 673*	56	2
21 Aug 93		TUESDAY MORNING *PM YZ 758 CD*	18	5
22 Jan 94		ONCE UPON A TIME *PM YZ 771CD*	66	2

[1] Pogues and the Dubliners [2] Pogues featuring Kirsty MacColl

Tracks on Poguetry in Motion (EP): London Girl / The Body of an American / A Rainy Night in Soho / Planxty Noel Hill

POINT BREAK *UK, male vocal group (21 WEEKS)* pos/wks

			pos	wks
9 Oct 99		DO WE ROCK *Eternal WEA 216CD1*	29	2
21 Jan 00	●	STAND TOUGH *Eternal WEA 248CD1*	7	5
22 Apr 00		FREAKYTIME *Eternal WEA 265CD1*	13	6
5 Aug 00		YOU *Eternal WEA 290CD1*	14	5
2 Dec 00		WHAT ABOUT US *Eternal WEA 314CD1*	24	3

POINTER SISTERS (372 Top 500) *Talented sibling vocal quartet formed 1971, Oakland, California, US, whose recordings touched many musical bases. Reduced to trio - June, Anita and Ruth - when Bonnie left in 1978. Soulful sisters surprisingly won a country music Grammy for 'Fairytale' in 1974 (87 WEEKS)* pos/wks

			pos	wks
3 Feb 79		EVERYBODY IS A STAR *Planet K 12324*	61	3
17 Mar 79		FIRE *Planet K 12339*	34	8
22 Aug 81	●	SLOWHAND *Planet K 12530*	10	11
5 Dec 81		SHOULD I DO IT? *Planet K 12578*	50	5
14 Apr 84	●	AUTOMATIC *Planet RPS 105*	2	15
23 Jun 84	●	JUMP (FOR MY LOVE) *Planet RPS 106*	6	10
11 Aug 84		I NEED YOU *Planet RPS 107*	25	9
27 Oct 84		I'M SO EXCITED *Planet RPS 108*	11	11
12 Jan 85		NEUTRON DANCE *Planet RPS 109*	31	7
20 Jul 85		DARE ME *RCA PB 49957*	17	8

POISON *US, male vocal / instrumental group (43 WEEKS)* pos/wks

			pos	wks
23 May 87		TALK DIRTY TO ME *Music For Nations KUT 125*	67	1
7 May 88		NOTHIN' BUT A GOOD TIME *Capitol CL 486*	35	3
5 Nov 88		FALLEN ANGEL *Capitol CL 500*	59	1
11 Feb 89		EVERY ROSE HAS ITS THORN *Capitol CL 520* ▲	13	9
29 Apr 89		YOUR MAMA DON'T DANCE *Capitol CL 523*	13	7
23 Sep 89		NOTHIN' BUT A GOOD TIME (re-issue) *Capitol CL 539*	48	3
30 Jun 90		UNSKINNY BOP *Capitol CL 582*	15	7
27 Oct 90		SOMETHING TO BELIEVE IN *Enigma CL 594*	35	4
23 Nov 91		SO TELL ME WHY *Capitol CL 640*	25	2
13 Feb 93		STAND *Capitol CDCL 679*	25	3
24 Apr 93		UNTIL YOU SUFFER SOME (FIRE AND ICE) *Capitol CDCL 685*	32	3

POKEMON ALLSTARS – *See 50 GRIND featuring POKEMON ALLSTARS*

POLECATS *UK, male vocal / instrumental group (18 WEEKS)* pos/wks

			pos	wks
7 Mar 81		JOHN I'M ONLY DANCING / BIG GREEN CAR *Mercury POLE 1*	35	8
16 May 81		ROCKABILLY GUY *Mercury POLE 2*	35	6
22 Aug 81		JEEPSTER / MARIE CELESTE *Mercury POLE 3*	53	4

POLICE (140 Top 500) *World-famous Anglo-American rock trio: Sting (b. Gordon Sumner) (v/b), Andy Summers (g/v), Stewart Copeland (d/v). These Brit and Grammy award winners were one of the 1980s' most popular acts. They had five successive albums entering the UK chart at No.1 (153 WEEKS)* pos/wks

			pos	wks
7 Oct 78		CAN'T STAND LOSING YOU *A & M AMS 7381*	42	5
28 Apr 79		ROXANNE *A & M AMS 7348*	12	9
7 Jul 79	●	CAN'T STAND LOSING YOU (re-entry) *A & M AMS 7381*	2	11
22 Sep 79	★	MESSAGE IN A BOTTLE *A & M AMS 7474*	1	11
17 Nov 79		FALL OUT *Illegal IL 001*	47	4
1 Dec 79	★	WALKING ON THE MOON *A & M AMS 7494*	1	10
16 Feb 80	●	SO LONELY *A & M AMS 7402*	6	10
14 Jun 80		SIX PACK *A & M AMPP 6001*	17	4
27 Sep 80	★	DON'T STAND SO CLOSE TO ME *A & M AMS 7564* ■	1	10
13 Dec 80	●	DE DO DO DO, DE DA DA DA *A & M AMS 7578*	5	8
26 Sep 81	●	INVISIBLE SUN *A & M AMS 8164*	2	8
24 Oct 81	★	EVERY LITTLE THING SHE DOES IS MAGIC *A & M AMS 8174*	1	13
12 Dec 81		SPIRITS IN THE MATERIAL WORLD *A & M AMS 8194*	12	8
28 May 83	★	EVERY BREATH YOU TAKE *A & M AM 117* ▲	1	11
23 Jul 83	●	WRAPPED AROUND YOUR FINGER *A & M AM 127*	7	7
5 Nov 83		SYNCHRONICITY II *A & M AM 153*	17	4
14 Jan 84		KING OF PAIN *A & M AM 176*	17	5
11 Oct 86		DON'T STAND SO CLOSE TO ME '86 (re-mix) *A & M AM 354*	24	4
13 May 95		CAN'T STAND LOSING YOU (LIVE) *A & M 5810372*	27	2
20 Dec 97		ROXANNE '97 (re-mix) *A & M 5824552* [1]	17	6
5 Aug 00		WHEN THE WORLD IS RUNNING DOWN *Pagan PAGAN 039CDS* [2]	28	3

[1] Sting and The Police [2] Different Gear vs The Police

Six Pack consists of six separate Police singles as follows: The Bed's Too Big Without You / Roxanne / Message in a Bottle / Walking on the Moon / So Lonely / Can't Stand Losing You. The last five titles were re-issues

See also STING; Klark KENT

Su POLLARD *UK, female vocalist (11 WEEKS)* pos/wks

			pos	wks
5 Oct 85		COME TO ME (I AM WOMAN) *Rainbow RBR 1*	71	1
1 Feb 86	●	STARTING TOGETHER *Rainbow RBR 4*	2	10

Jimi POLO *US, male vocalist (5 WEEKS)* pos/wks

			pos	wks
9 Nov 91		NEVER GOIN' DOWN *MCA MCS 1578* [1]	51	2

1 Aug 92		EXPRESS YOURSELF *Perfecto 74321101827*	59	2
9 Aug 97		EXPRESS YOURSELF (re-issue) *Perfecto PERF 146CD1*	62	1

[1] Adamski featuring Jimi Polo

The listed flip side of 'Never Goin' Down' was 'Born to Be Alive' by Adamski featuring Soho

POLTERGEIST *UK, male producer – Simon Berry (2 WEEKS)* pos/wks

6 Jul 96		VICIOUS CIRCLES *Manifesto FESCD 8*	32	2

See also VICIOUS CIRCLES

Peter POLYCARPOU *UK, male vocalist (4 WEEKS)* pos/wks

20 Feb 93		LOVE HURTS *Soundtrack Music CDEM 259*	26	4

POLYGON WINDOW *UK, male producer – Richard James (1 WEEK)* pos/wks

3 Apr 93		QUOTH *Warp WAP 33CD*	49	1

See also APHEX TWIN; AFX

PONI-TAILS *US, female vocal group (14 WEEKS)* pos/wks

19 Sep 58	●	BORN TOO LATE *HMV POP 516*	5	11
10 Apr 59		EARLY TO BED *HMV POP 596*	26	3

Brian POOLE and the TREMELOES 343 Top 500

Formed 1959 and signed by Decca in preference to The Beatles (auditioned same day). First south of England group to top the chart in Beat Boom era. Poole, b. 2 Nov 1941, Essex, UK, went solo in 1966, and group continued with even more success. Poole's daughters hit in the late 90s as Alisha's Attic (91 WEEKS) pos/wks

4 Jul 63	●	TWIST AND SHOUT *Decca F 11694*	4	14
12 Sep 63	★	DO YOU LOVE ME *Decca F 11739*	1	14
28 Nov 63		I CAN DANCE *Decca F 11771*	31	8
30 Jan 64	●	CANDY MAN *Decca F 11823*	6	13
7 May 64	●	SOMEONE, SOMEONE *Decca F 11893*	2	17
20 Aug 64		TWELVE STEPS TO LOVE *Decca F 11951*	32	7
31 Dec 64		THREE BELLS *Decca F 12037*	17	10
22 Jul 65		I WANT CANDY *Decca F 12197*	25	8

See also TREMELOES

Glyn POOLE *UK, male vocalist (8 WEEKS)* pos/wks

20 Oct 73		MILLY MOLLY MANDY *York SYK 565*	35	8

Ian POOLEY *Germany, male DJ / producer (2 WEEKS)* pos/wks

10 Mar 01		900 DEGREES *V2 VVR 5015143*	57	1
11 Aug 01		BALMES *V2 VVR 5016613* [1]	65	1

[1] Ian Pooley featuring Esthero

Iggy POP *US, male vocalist – James Jewel Osterburg (28 WEEKS)* pos/wks

13 Dec 86	●	REAL WILD CHILD (WILD ONE) *A & M AM 368*	10	11
10 Feb 90		LIVIN' ON THE EDGE OF THE NIGHT *Virgin America VUS 18*	51	4
13 Oct 90		CANDY *Virgin America VUS 29*	67	1
5 Jan 91		WELL DID YOU EVAH! *Chrysalis CHS 3646* [1]	42	4
4 Sep 93		THE WILD AMERICA (EP) *Virgin America VUSCD 74*	63	1
21 May 94		BESIDE YOU *Virgin America VUSCD 77*	47	2
23 Nov 96		LUST FOR LIFE *Virgin America VUSCD 116*	26	2
7 Mar 98		THE PASSENGER *Virgin VSCDT 1689*	22	3

[1] Deborah Harry and Iggy Pop

Tracks on The Wild America (EP): Wild America / Credit Card / Come Back Tomorrow / My Angel

LOS POP TOPS *Spain, male vocal group (6 WEEKS)* pos/wks

9 Oct 71		MAMY BLUE *A & M AMS 859*	35	6

POP WILL EAT ITSELF

UK, male vocal / instrumental group (43 WEEKS) pos/wks

30 Jan 88		THERE IS NO LOVE BETWEEN US ANYMORE *Chapter 22 CHAP 20*	66	1
23 Jul 88		DEF CON ONE *Chapter 22 PWEI 001*	63	4
11 Feb 89		CAN U DIG IT? *RCA PB 42621*	38	4
22 Apr 89		WISE UP! SUCKER *RCA PB 42761*	41	3
2 Sep 89		VERY METAL NOISE POLLUTION (EP) *RCA PB 42883*	45	3
9 Jun 90		TOUCHED BY THE HAND OF CICCIOLINA *RCA PB 43735*	28	4
13 Oct 90		DANCE OF THE MAD *RCA PB 44023*	32	2
12 Jan 91		X Y & ZEE *RCA PB 44243*	15	4
1 Jun 91		92° F *RCA PB 44555*	23	3
6 Jun 92		KARMADROME / EAT ME DRINK ME LOVE ME *RCA PB 45467*	17	2
29 Aug 92		BULLETPROOF! *RCA 74321110137*	24	3
16 Jan 93	●	GET THE GIRL! KILL THE BADDIES! *RCA 74321128802*	9	4
16 Oct 93		RSVP / FAMILIUS HORRIBILUS *Infectious INFECT 1CD*	27	2
12 Mar 94		ICH BIN EIN AUSLANDER *Infectious INFECT 4CD*	28	2
10 Sep 94		EVERYTHING'S COOL *Infectious INFECT 9CD*	23	2

Tracks on Very Metal Noise Pollution (EP): Def Con 1989 AD including the Twilight Zone / Preaching to the Perverted / PWEI-zation / 92° F

POPES – *See Shane MacGOWAN*

POPPERS presents AURA

UK, male production trio and UK, female vocalist (1 WEEK) pos/wks

25 Oct 97		EVERY LITTLE TIME *VC VCRD 26*	44	1

POPPY FAMILY *Canada, male / female vocal / instrumental group – Terry Jacks and Susan Peklevits (14 WEEKS)* pos/wks

15 Aug 70	●	WHICH WAY YOU GOIN' BILLY *Decca F 22976*	7	14

See also Terry JACKS

PORN KINGS *UK, male instrumental / production group (10 WEEKS)* pos/wks

28 Sep 96		UP TO NO GOOD *All Around the World CDGLOBE 145*	28	2
21 Jun 97		AMOUR (C'MON) *All Around the World CDGLOBE 152*	17	3
16 Jan 99	●	UP TO THE WILDSTYLE *All Around the World CDGLOBE 170* [1]	10	4
10 Feb 01		SLEDGER *All Around the World CDGLOBE 229*	71	1

[1] Porn Kings vs DJ Supreme

PORNO FOR PYROS *US, male vocal / instrumental group (2 WEEKS)* pos/wks

5 Jun 93		PETS *Warner Bros. W 0177 CD*	53	2

PORTISHEAD *UK, male / female vocal / instrumental group (20 WEEKS)* pos/wks

13 Aug 94		SOUR TIMES *Go.Beat GODCD 116*	57	1
14 Jan 95		GLORY BOX *Go.Beat GODCD 120*	13	7
22 Apr 95		SOUR TIMES (re-entry) *Go.Beat GODCD 116*	13	4
20 Sep 97	●	ALL MINE *Go.Beat 5715972*	8	4
22 Nov 97		OVER *Go.Beat 5719932*	25	2
14 Mar 98		ONLY YOU *Go.Beat 5694752*	35	2

Gary PORTNOY *US, male vocalist (3 WEEKS)* pos/wks

25 Feb 84		THEME FROM 'CHEERS' *Starblend CHEER 1*	58	3

PORTRAIT *US, male vocal group (6 WEEKS)* pos/wks

27 Mar 93		HERE WE GO AGAIN *Capitol CDCL 683*	37	3
8 Apr 95		I CAN CALL YOU *Capitol CDCL 740*	61	1
8 Jul 95		HOW DEEP IS YOUR LOVE *Capitol CDCL 751*	41	2

PORTSMOUTH SINFONIA *UK, orchestra (4 WEEKS)* pos/wks

12 Sep 81		CLASSICAL MUDDLY *Island WIP 6736*	38	4

Sandy POSEY *US, female vocalist (32 WEEKS)* pos/wks

15 Sep 66		BORN A WOMAN *MGM 1321*	24	11
5 Jan 67		SINGLE GIRL *MGM 1330*	15	13
13 Apr 67		WHAT A WOMAN IN LOVE WON'T DO *MGM 1335*	48	3
6 Sep 75		SINGLE GIRL (re-issue) *MGM 2006 533*	35	5

POSIES *US, male vocal / instrumental group (1 WEEK)* pos/wks

19 Mar 94		DEFINITE DOOR *Geffen GFSTD 68*	67	1

UK No.1 ★ UK Top 10 ● Still on chart + UK million seller ◆ UK entry at No.1 ■ US No.1 ▲

POSITIVE FORCE
US, female vocal duo – Brenda Reynolds and Vicki Drayton (9 WEEKS) pos/wks

22 Dec 79	**WE GOT THE FUNK** *Sugarhill SHL 102*	18	9

POSITIVE GANG
UK, male / female instrumental / vocal group (5 WEEKS) pos/wks

17 Apr 93	**SWEET FREEDOM** *PWL Continental PWCD 261*	34	4
31 Jul 93	**SWEET FREEDOM PART 2** *PWL Continental PWCD 264*	67	1

POSITIVE K *US, male rapper (2 WEEKS)* pos/wks

15 May 93	**I GOT A MAN** *Fourth & Broadway BRCD 280*	43	2

Mike POST *US, orchestra (18 WEEKS)* pos/wks

9 Aug 75	**AFTERNOON OF THE RHINO** *Warner Bros. K 16588* [1]	48	1
23 Aug 75	**AFTERNOON OF THE RHINO (re-entry)** *Warner Bros. K 16588* [1]	47	1
16 Jan 82	**THEME FROM 'HILL STREET BLUES'** *Elektra K 12576* [2]	25	11
29 Sep 84	**THE A TEAM** *RCA 443*	45	5

[1] Mike Post Coalition [2] Mike Post featuring Larry Carlton

POTTERS
UK, male Stoke City football supporters vocal group (2 WEEKS) pos/wks

1 Apr 72	**WE'LL BE WITH YOU** *Pye JT 100*	34	2

P.O.V. featuring JADE
US, male vocal group and female vocal group (3 WEEKS) pos/wks

5 Feb 94	**ALL THRU THE NITE** *Giant 74321187552*	32	3

POWDER *UK, male / female vocal / instrumental group (1 WEEK)* pos/wks

24 Jun 95	**AFRODISIAC** *Parkway PARK 002CD*	72	1

Bryan POWELL *UK, male vocalist (3 WEEKS)* pos/wks

13 Mar 93	**IT'S ALRIGHT** *Talkin' Loud TLKCD 34*	73	1
15 May 93	**I THINK OF YOU** *Talkin' Loud TLKCD 38*	61	1
7 Aug 93	**NATURAL** *Talkin' Loud TLKCD 41*	73	1

Cozy POWELL
UK, male instrumentalist, drums – Colin Flooks (38 WEEKS) pos/wks

8 Dec 73 ●	**DANCE WITH THE DEVIL** *RAK 164*	3	15
25 May 74	**THE MAN IN BLACK** *RAK 173*	18	8
10 Aug 74 ●	**NA NA NA** *RAK 180*	10	10
10 Nov 79	**THEME ONE** *Ariola ARO 189*	62	2
19 Jun 93	**RESURRECTION** *Parlophone CDRS 6351* [1]	23	3

[1] Brian May with Cozy Powell

Kobie POWELL – *See US3*

POWER CIRCLE – *See CHICANE*

P J POWERS – *See LADYSMITH BLACK MAMBAZO*

POWER OF DREAMS
Ireland, male vocal / instrumental group (2 WEEKS) pos/wks

19 Jan 91	**AMERICAN DREAM** *Polydor PO 117*	74	1
11 Apr 92	**THERE I GO AGAIN** *Polydor PO 200*	65	1

POWER STATION
UK / US, male vocal / instrumental group (17 WEEKS) pos/wks

16 Mar 85	**SOME LIKE IT HOT** *Parlophone R 6091*	14	8
11 May 85	**GET IT ON** *Parlophone R 6096*	22	7
9 Nov 85	**COMMUNICATION** *Parlophone R 6114*	75	1
12 Oct 96	**SHE CAN ROCK IT** *Chrysalis CDCHS 5039*	63	1

POWERCUT featuring NUBIAN PRINZ
US, male vocal / instrumental group (4 WEEKS) pos/wks

22 Jun 91	**GIRLS** *Eternal YZ 570*	50	4

POWERHOUSE *UK, male production duo (4 WEEKS)* pos/wks

20 Dec 97	**RHYTHM OF THE NIGHT** *Satellite 74321522592*	38	4

POWERHOUSE featuring Duane HARDEN
US, male producer – Lenny Fontana and male vocalist (5 WEEKS) pos/wks

22 May 99	**WHAT YOU NEED** *Defected DEFECT 3CDS*	13	5

POWERPILL *UK, male instrumental / production group (3 WEEKS)* pos/wks

6 Jun 92	**PAC-MAN** *Ffrreedom TABX 110*	43	3

Will POWERS *US, female vocalist – Lyn Goldsmith (9 WEEKS)* pos/wks

1 Oct 83	**KISSING WITH CONFIDENCE** *Island IS 134*	17	9

Hit features uncredited vocals by Carly Simon

PPK *Russia, male production / instrumental duo – Sergey Pimenov and Alexander Polyakov (4 WEEKS)* pos/wks

8 Dec 01 ●	**RESURECTION** *Perfecto PERF 32CDS*	3	4

PQM featuring CICA
US, male producer and female vocalist (1 WEEK) pos/wks

9 Dec 00	**THE FLYING SONG** *Renaissance / Yoshitoshi RENCDS 004*	68	1

Perez PRADO and his Orchestra *Cuba, orchestra (57 WEEKS)* pos/wks

25 Mar 55 ★	**CHERRY PINK AND APPLE BLOSSOM WHITE** *HMV B 10833* [1] ▲	1	17
25 Jul 58 ●	**PATRICIA** *RCA 1067*	8	16
10 Dec 94	**GUAGLIONE** *RCA 74321250192* [2]	41	6
8 Apr 95	**GUAGLIONE (re-entry)** *RCA 74321250192* [2]	58	2
6 May 95 ●	**GUAGLIONE (2nd re-entry)** *RCA 74321250192* [2]	2	16

[1] Perez 'Prez' Prado and his Orchestra, the King of the Mambo [2] Perez 'Prez' Prado and his Orchestra

PRAISE *UK, male / female vocal / instrumental group (7 WEEKS)* pos/wks

2 Feb 91 ●	**ONLY YOU** *Epic 6566117*	4	7

Uncredited vocals by Miriam Stockley

PRAS – *See Pras MICHEL*

PRATT and McCLAIN with BROTHERLOVE
US, male vocal duo with male instrumental group (6 WEEKS) pos/wks

1 Oct 77	**HAPPY DAYS** *Reprise K 14435*	31	6

PRAXIS *UK, male / female vocal / instrumental group (5 WEEKS)* pos/wks

25 Nov 95	**TURN ME OUT** *Stress CDSTR 40*	44	2
20 Sep 97	**TURN ME OUT (TURN TO SUGAR) (re-mix)** *ffrr FCD 314* [1]	35	3

[1] Praxis featuring Kathy Brown

PRAYING MANTIS *UK, male vocal / instrumental group (2 WEEKS)* pos/wks

31 Jan 81	**CHEATED** *Arista ARIST 378*	69	2

PRECIOUS *UK, female vocal group (20 WEEKS)* pos/wks

29 May 99 ●	**SAY IT AGAIN** *EMI CDEM 544*	6	9
28 Aug 99	**SAY IT AGAIN (re-entry)** *EMI CDEM 544*	53	2
1 Apr 00	**REWIND** *EMI CDEM 557*	11	5
15 Jul 00	**IT'S GONNA BE MY WAY** *EMI CDEM 569*	27	3
25 Nov 00	**NEW BEGINNING** *EMI CDEM 573*	50	1

PRECOCIOUS BRATS featuring KEVIN and PERRY *UK, male production duo – Julius O'Riordan (Judge Jules) and Matt Smith and UK, male / female vocal comedy duo – Harry Enfield and Kathy Burke (4 WEEKS)* pos/wks

6 May 00	**BIG GIRL** *Virgin / EMI VTSCD 1*	16	4

PREFAB SPROUT

UK, male / female vocal / instrumental group (60 WEEKS) pos/wks

			pos	wks
28 Jan 84		**DON'T SING** *Kitchenware SK 9*	62	2
20 Jul 85		**FARON YOUNG** *Kitchenware SK 22*	74	1
9 Nov 85		**WHEN LOVE BREAKS DOWN** *Kitchenware SK 21*	25	10
8 Feb 86		**JOHNNY JOHNNY** *Kitchenware SK 24*	64	2
13 Feb 88		**CARS AND GIRLS** *Kitchenware SK 35*	44	5
30 Apr 88	●	**THE KING OF ROCK 'N' ROLL** *Kitchenware SK 37*	7	10
23 Jul 88		**HEY MANHATTAN!** *Kitchenware SK 38*	72	2
18 Aug 90		**LOOKING FOR ATLANTIS** *Kitchenware SK 47*	51	3
20 Oct 90		**WE LET THE STARS GO** *Kitchenware SK 48*	50	3
5 Jan 91		**JORDAN: THE EP** *Kitchenware SK 49*	35	4
13 Jun 92		**THE SOUND OF CRYING** *Kitchenware SK 58*	23	5
8 Aug 92		**IF YOU DON'T LOVE ME** *Kitchenware SK 60*	33	4
3 Oct 92		**ALL THE WORLD LOVES LOVERS** *Kitchenware SK 62*	61	2
9 Jan 93		**LIFE OF SURPRISES** *Kitchenware SKCD 63*	24	4
10 May 97		**A PRISONER OF THE PAST** *Columbia SKZD 70*	30	2
2 Aug 97		**ELECTRIC GUITARS** *Columbia SKZD 71*	53	1

Tracks on Jordan: The EP: Carnival 2000 / The Ice Maiden / One of the Broken / Jordan: The Comeback

PRELUDE *UK, male / female vocal group (26 WEEKS)* pos/wks

			pos	wks
26 Jan 74		**AFTER THE GOLDRUSH** *Dawn DNS 1052*	21	9
26 Apr 80		**PLATINUM BLONDE** *EMI 5046*	45	7
22 May 82		**AFTER THE GOLDRUSH (re-recording)** *After Hours AFT 02*	28	7
31 Jul 82		**ONLY THE LONELY** *After Hours AFT 06*	55	3

PRESENCE *UK, male / female vocal / production group (2 WEEKS)* pos/wks

			pos	wks
5 Dec 98		**SENSE OF DANGER** *Pagan PAGAN 024CDS* [1]	61	1
19 Jun 99		**FUTURE LOVE** *Pagan PAGAN 028CDS*	66	1

[1] Presence featuring Shara Nelson

PRESIDENT BROWN – *See SABRE featuring PRESIDENT BROWN*

PRESIDENTS OF THE UNITED STATES OF AMERICA

US, male vocal / instrumental trio (21 WEEKS) pos/wks

			pos	wks
6 Jan 96		**LUMP** *Columbia 6624962*	15	7
20 Apr 96	●	**PEACHES** *Columbia 6631072*	8	7
20 Jul 96		**DUNE BUGGY** *Columbia 6634892*	15	4
2 Nov 96		**MACH 5** *Columbia 6638812*	29	2
1 Aug 98		**VIDEO KILLED THE RADIO STAR** *Maverick W 0450CD*	52	1

Elvis PRESLEY (1 Top 500)

The most important, most influential and most impersonated artist of the 20th century, b. 8 Jan 1935, Mississippi, US, d. 16 Aug 1977. The singer, whose first five US singles failed to reach the pop charts, went from rock 'n' roll rebel to Las Vegas veteran and on the way sold more records than any other performer in history. He holds, or has held, almost every chart-related record in the UK and US. No other solo artist of the rock era can match his number of best-selling singles and albums in the UK or US, nor his collection of platinum and gold records. The "King of Rock 'n' Roll" was the first artist to enter the UK chart at No.1, and the first to amass US advance orders in excess of one million copies for a single. He now has a 43-year span of UK Top 20 albums and also holds the record for most simultaneous UK album chart entries (27 in the Top 100) and held the record for the most entries on the UK single chart (nine). The best documented entertainer ever has won hundreds of awards, starred in dozens of successful films, broken numerous box office records in North America (the only continent he ever performed in), made Memphis a major tourist attraction and was the first artist credited with sales of one billion records (20 million of which were reportedly sold the day after his death) (1173 WEEKS) pos/wks

			pos	wks
11 May 56	●	**HEARTBREAK HOTEL** *HMV POP 182* ▲	2	21
25 May 56	●	**BLUE SUEDE SHOES** *HMV POP 213*	9	8
13 Jul 56		**I WANT YOU, I NEED YOU, I LOVE YOU** *HMV POP 235* ▲	25	2
3 Aug 56		**I WANT YOU, I NEED YOU, I LOVE YOU (re-entry)** *HMV POP 235*	14	9
17 Aug 56		**BLUE SUEDE SHOES (re-entry)** *HMV POP 213*	26	2
21 Sep 56	●	**HOUND DOG** *HMV POP 249* ▲	2	23
26 Oct 56		**HEARTBREAK HOTEL (re-entry)** *HMV POP 182*	23	1
16 Nov 56	●	**BLUE MOON** *HMV POP 272*	9	11
23 Nov 56		**I DON'T CARE IF THE SUN DON'T SHINE** *HMV POP 272*	29	1
7 Dec 56		**LOVE ME TENDER** *HMV POP 253* ▲	11	9
21 Dec 56		**I DON'T CARE IF THE SUN DON'T SHINE (re-entry)** *HMV POP 272*	23	3
15 Feb 57		**MYSTERY TRAIN** *HMV POP 295*	25	5
8 Mar 57		**RIP IT UP** *HMV POP 305*	27	1
10 May 57	●	**TOO MUCH** *HMV POP 330* ▲	6	8
14 Jun 57		**ALL SHOOK UP** *HMV POP 359*	24	1
28 Jun 57	★	**ALL SHOOK UP (re-entry)** *HMV POP 359* ▲	1	20
12 Jul 57	●	**(LET ME BE YOUR) TEDDY BEAR** *RCA1013* ▲	3	19
12 Jul 57		**TOO MUCH (re-entry)** *HMV POP 330*	26	1
30 Aug 57	●	**PARALYSED** *HMV POP 378*	8	10
4 Oct 57	●	**PARTY** *RCA 1020*	2	15
18 Oct 57		**GOT A LOT O' LIVIN' TO DO** *RCA 1020*	17	4
1 Nov 57		**LOVING YOU** *RCA 1013*	24	2
1 Nov 57		**TRYING TO GET TO YOU** *HMV POP 408*	16	4
8 Nov 57		**LAWDY MISS CLAWDY** *HMV POP 408*	15	5
15 Nov 57	●	**SANTA BRING MY BABY BACK (TO ME)** *RCA 1025*	7	8
17 Jan 58		**I'M LEFT, YOU'RE RIGHT, SHE'S GONE** *HMV POP 428*	21	2
24 Jan 58	★	**JAILHOUSE ROCK** *RCA 1028* ■ ▲	1	14
31 Jan 58		**JAILHOUSE ROCK (EP)** *RCA RCX 106*	18	5
7 Feb 58		**I'M LEFT, YOU'RE RIGHT, SHE'S GONE (re-entry)** *HMV POP 428*	29	1
28 Feb 58	●	**DON'T** *RCA 1043* ▲	2	11
2 May 58	●	**WEAR MY RING AROUND YOUR NECK** *RCA 1058*	3	10
25 Jul 58	●	**HARD HEADED WOMAN** *RCA 1070* ▲	2	11
3 Oct 58	●	**KING CREOLE** *RCA 1081*	2	15
23 Jan 59	★	**ONE NIGHT / I GOT STUNG** *RCA 1100*	1	12
24 Apr 59	★	**A FOOL SUCH AS I / I NEED YOUR LOVE TONIGHT** *RCA 1113*	1	15
24 Jul 59	●	**A BIG HUNK O' LOVE** *RCA 1136* ▲	4	9
12 Feb 60		**STRICTLY ELVIS (EP)** *RCA RCX 175*	26	1
7 Apr 60	●	**STUCK ON YOU** *RCA 1187* ▲	3	14
28 Jul 60	●	**A MESS OF BLUES** *RCA 1194*	2	18
3 Nov 60	★	**IT'S NOW OR NEVER** *RCA 1207* ◆ ■ ▲	1	19
19 Jan 61	★	**ARE YOU LONESOME TONIGHT?** *RCA 1216* ▲	1	15
9 Mar 61	★	**WOODEN HEART** *RCA 1226*	1	27
25 May 61	★	**SURRENDER** *RCA 1227* ▲	1	15
7 Sep 61	●	**WILD IN THE COUNTRY / I FEEL SO BAD** *RCA 1244*	4	12
2 Nov 61	★	**(MARIE'S THE NAME) HIS LATEST FLAME / LITTLE SISTER** *RCA 1258*	1	13
1 Feb 62	★	**ROCK-A-HULA BABY / CAN'T HELP FALLING IN LOVE** *RCA 1270*	1	20
10 May 62	★	**GOOD LUCK CHARM** *RCA 1280* ▲	1	17
21 Jun 62		**FOLLOW THAT DREAM (EP)** *RCA RCX 211*	34	2
30 Aug 62	★	**SHE'S NOT YOU** *RCA 1303*	1	14
29 Nov 62	★	**RETURN TO SENDER** *RCA 1320*	1	14
28 Feb 63		**ONE BROKEN HEART FOR SALE** *RCA 1337*	12	9
4 Jul 63	★	**(YOU'RE THE) DEVIL IN DISGUISE** *RCA 1355*	1	12
24 Oct 63		**BOSSA NOVA BABY** *RCA 1374*	13	8
19 Dec 63		**KISS ME QUICK** *RCA 1375*	14	10
12 Mar 64		**VIVA LAS VEGAS** *RCA 1390*	17	12
25 Jun 64	●	**KISSIN' COUSINS** *RCA 1404*	10	11
20 Aug 64		**SUCH A NIGHT** *RCA 1411*	13	10
29 Oct 64		**AIN'T THAT LOVING YOU BABY** *RCA 1422*	15	8
3 Dec 64		**BLUE CHRISTMAS** *RCA 1430*	11	7
11 Mar 65		**DO THE CLAM** *RCA 1443*	19	8
27 May 65	★	**CRYING IN THE CHAPEL** *RCA 1455*	1	15
11 Nov 65		**TELL ME WHY** *RCA 1489*	15	10
24 Feb 66		**BLUE RIVER** *RCA 1504*	22	7
7 Apr 66		**FRANKIE AND JOHNNY** *RCA 1509*	21	9
7 Jul 66	●	**LOVE LETTERS** *RCA 1526*	6	10
13 Oct 66		**ALL THAT I AM** *RCA 1545*	18	8
1 Dec 66	●	**IF EVERY DAY WAS LIKE CHRISTMAS** *RCA 1557*	9	7
9 Feb 67		**INDESCRIBABLY BLUE** *RCA 1565*	21	5
11 May 67		**YOU GOTTA STOP / THE LOVE MACHINE** *RCA 1593*	38	5
16 Aug 67		**LONG LEGGED GIRL (WITH THE SHORT DRESS ON)** *RCA RCA 1616*	49	2
21 Feb 68		**GUITAR MAN** *RCA 1663*	19	9
15 May 68		**U.S. MALE** *RCA 1688*	15	8
17 Jul 68		**YOUR TIME HASN'T COME YET BABY** *RCA 1714*	22	11
16 Oct 68		**YOU'LL NEVER WALK ALONE** *RCA 1747*	44	3
26 Feb 69		**IF I CAN DREAM** *RCA 1795*	11	10
11 Jun 69	●	**IN THE GHETTO** *RCA 1831*	2	16
6 Sep 69		**CLEAN UP YOUR OWN BACK YARD** *RCA 1869*	21	7

1986

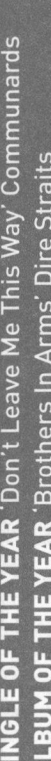

IN THE YEAR OF THE SPACE SHUTTLE CHALLENGER AND CHERNOBYL EXPLOSIONS, WHEN WHAM! SPLIT AND HOUSE ARRIVED, AND MARADONA'S "HAND OF GOD" HELPED ARGENTINA TO BEAT ENGLAND IN THE WORLD CUP QUARTER-FINALS, **SAM FOX** DESCRIBES THE EARLY DAYS OF A POP CAREER THAT MADE HER THE ONLY BRITISH FEMALE TO REGISTER THREE TOP 10S IN BOTH THE UK AND THE US IN THE 1980S ...

" I'd been approached by Stiff Records and a French label, because of my Page 3 fame, but I didn't like either of them. Then Jive rang and said they had a hit record for me – but I made certain I heard it before I signed. They played me 'Touch Me', and as soon as I heard the first four bars, even before I heard the words, I knew it was going to be a hit. Four months later, it got me a trip to the West Indies! 'Touch Me' had got to No.3 in the British charts and Bon Jovi was No.1 in America, so MTV ran a competition to win a holiday with Samantha Fox and Bon Jovi. They picked four girls and four boys to go to Jamaica for a weekend. I spent four days with Jon and the band and we got on really well. Then it was back to Britain to record the second single, which was harder than the first – no one wants to be a one-hit wonder. "

SINGLE OF THE YEAR 'Don't Leave Me This Way' Communards
ALBUM OF THE YEAR 'Brothers In Arms' Dire Straits

18 Oct 69		IN THE GHETTO (re-entry) *RCA 1831*	50	1
29 Nov 69	●	SUSPICIOUS MINDS *RCA 1900* ▲	2	14
28 Feb 70	●	DON'T CRY DADDY *RCA 1916*	8	11
16 May 70		KENTUCKY RAIN *RCA 1949*	21	11
11 Jul 70	★	THE WONDER OF YOU *RCA 1974*	1	20
8 Aug 70		KENTUCKY RAIN (re-entry) *RCA 1949*	46	1
14 Nov 70	●	I'VE LOST YOU *RCA 1999*	9	12
9 Jan 71	●	YOU DON'T HAVE TO SAY YOU LOVE ME *RCA 2046*	9	7
23 Jan 71		THE WONDER OF YOU (re-entry) *RCA 1974*	47	1
6 Mar 71		YOU DON'T HAVE TO SAY YOU LOVE ME (re-entry) *RCA 2046*	35	3
20 Mar 71	●	THERE GOES MY EVERYTHING *RCA 2060*	6	11
15 May 71	●	RAGS TO RICHES *RCA 2084*	9	11
17 Jul 71	●	HEARTBREAK HOTEL / HOUND DOG (re-issue) *RCA Maximillion 2104*	10	12
2 Oct 71		I'M LEAVIN' *RCA 2125*	23	9
4 Dec 71	●	I JUST CAN'T HELP BELIEVING *RCA 2158*	6	16
11 Dec 71		JAILHOUSE ROCK (re-issue) *RCA Maximillion 2153*	42	5
1 Apr 72	●	UNTIL IT'S TIME FOR YOU TO GO *RCA 2188*	5	9
17 Jun 72	●	AMERICAN TRILOGY *RCA 2229*	8	11
30 Sep 72	●	BURNING LOVE *RCA 2267*	7	9
16 Dec 72	●	ALWAYS ON MY MIND *RCA 2304*	9	13
26 May 73		POLK SALAD ANNIE *RCA 2359*	23	7
11 Aug 73		FOOL *RCA 2393*	15	10
24 Nov 73		RAISED ON ROCK *RCA 2435*	36	7
16 Mar 74		I'VE GOT A THING ABOUT YOU BABY *RCA APBO 0196*	33	5
13 Jul 74		IF YOU TALK IN YOUR SLEEP *RCA APBO 0280*	40	3
16 Nov 74	●	MY BOY *RCA 2458*	5	13
18 Jan 75	●	PROMISED LAND *RCA PB 10074*	9	8
24 May 75		T.R.O.U.B.L.E. *RCA 2562*	31	4
29 Nov 75		GREEN GREEN GRASS OF HOME *RCA 2635*	29	7
1 May 76		HURT *RCA 2674*	37	5
4 Sep 76	●	GIRL OF MY BEST FRIEND *RCA 2729*	9	12
25 Dec 76	●	SUSPICION *RCA 2768*	9	12
5 Mar 77	●	MOODY BLUE *RCA PB 0857*	6	9
13 Aug 77	★	WAY DOWN *RCA PB 0998*	1	13
3 Sep 77		ALL SHOOK UP (re-issue) *RCA PB 2694*	41	2
3 Sep 77		ARE YOU LONESOME TONIGHT (re-issue) *RCA PB 2699*	46	1
3 Sep 77		CRYING IN THE CHAPEL (re-issue) *RCA PB 2708*	43	2
3 Sep 77		IT'S NOW OR NEVER (re-issue) *RCA PB 2698*	39	2
3 Sep 77		JAILHOUSE ROCK (2nd re-issue) *RCA PB 2695*	44	2
3 Sep 77		RETURN TO SENDER (re-issue) *RCA PB 2706*	42	3
3 Sep 77		THE WONDER OF YOU (re-issue) *RCA PB 2709*	48	1
3 Sep 77		WOODEN HEART (re-issue) *RCA PB 2700*	49	1
10 Dec 77	●	MY WAY *RCA PB 1165*	9	8
24 Jun 78		DON'T BE CRUEL *RCA PB 9265*	24	12
15 Dec 79		IT WON'T SEEM LIKE CHRISTMAS (WITHOUT YOU) *RCA PB 9464*	13	6
30 Aug 80	●	IT'S ONLY LOVE / BEYOND THE REEF *RCA 4*	3	10
6 Dec 80		SANTA CLAUS IS BACK IN TOWN *RCA 16*	41	6
14 Feb 81		GUITAR MAN (re-master) *RCA 43*	43	4
18 Apr 81		LOVING ARMS *RCA 48*	47	6
13 Mar 82		ARE YOU LONESOME TONIGHT (LIVE) *RCA 196*	25	7
26 Jun 82		THE SOUND OF YOUR CRY *RCA 232*	59	2
5 Feb 83		JAILHOUSE ROCK (re-entry) *RCA 1028*	27	6
7 May 83		BABY I DON'T CARE *RCA 332*	61	3
3 Dec 83		I CAN HELP *RCA 369*	30	9
10 Nov 84		THE LAST FAREWELL *RCA 459*	48	6
19 Jan 85		THE ELVIS MEDLEY *RCA 476*	51	3
10 Aug 85		ALWAYS ON MY MIND (re-recording) *RCA PB 49944*	59	4
11 Apr 87		AIN'T THAT LOVIN' YOU BABY / BOSSA NOVA BABY (re-issues) *RCA ARON 1*	47	5
22 Aug 87		LOVE ME TENDER / IF I CAN DREAM (re-issues) *RCA ARON 2*	56	3
16 Jan 88		STUCK ON YOU (re-issue) *RCA PB 49595*	58	2
17 Aug 91		ARE YOU LONESOME TONIGHT (LIVE) (re-issue) *RCA PB 49177*	68	2
29 Aug 92		DON'T BE CRUEL (re-issue) *RCA 74321110777*	42	2
11 Nov 95		THE TWELFTH OF NEVER *RCA 74321320122*	21	3
18 May 96		HEARTBREAK HOTEL / I WAS THE ONE (2nd re-issue) *RCA 74321336862*	45	1
24 May 97		ALWAYS ON MY MIND (re-issue) *RCA 74321485412*	13	6
14 Apr 01		SUSPICIOUS MINDS (re-issue) *RCA 74321855822*	15	4
10 Nov 01		AMERICA THE BEAUTIFUL *RCA 74321904022*	69	1

Tracks on Jailhouse Rock (EP): Jailhouse Rock / Young and Beautiful / I Want to Be Free / Don't Leave Me Now / Baby I Don't Care. On Strictly Elvis (EP): Old Shep / Any Place Is Paradise / Paralysed / Is It So Strange. On Follow That Dream (EP): Follow That Dream / Angel / What a Wonderful Life / I'm Not the Marrying Kind. On 5 Jul 1962, a note on the Top 50 for that week stated: "Due to difficulties in assessing returns of Follow That Dream EP, it has been decided not to include it in Britain's Top 50. It is of course No.1 in the EP charts." Therefore this EP had only a two-week run on the chart when its sales would certainly have justified a much longer one. 'Beyond the Reef' listed only from 30 Aug to 13 Sep 1980. It peaked at No.7. RCA PB 49177 is a re-issue of RCA 196. 'Can't Help Falling in Love' credited from 1 Mar 1962. Tracks on The Elvis Medley: Jailhouse Rock / Teddy Bear / Hound Dog / Don't Be Cruel / Burning Love / Suspicious Minds. RCA PB 49944 is also an alternate version. 1997 Always On My Mind was re-issue of 1972 hit

Sharp-eyed readers will have counted 17 US No.1 hits listed for 'The King'. However, he actually scored 18 chart-toppers - with 'Don't Be Cruel' which gets an individual top placing in the US in addition to a joint listing with 'Hound Dog'

PRESSURE DROP *UK, male vocal / instrumental duo (2 WEEKS)* pos/wks

			pos	wks
21 Mar 98		SILENTLY BAD MINDED *Higher Ground HIGHS6 CD*	53	1
17 Mar 01		WARRIOR SOUND *Higher Ground 6697192*	72	1

Billy PRESTON

US, male vocalist / instrumentalist – keyboards (51 WEEKS) pos/wks

			pos	wks
23 Apr 69	★	GET BACK *Apple R 5777* [1] ■ ▲	1	17
2 Jul 69		THAT'S THE WAY GOD PLANNED IT *Apple 12*	11	10
16 Sep 72		OUTA SPACE *A & M AMS 7007*	44	3
3 Apr 76		GET BACK (re-entry) *Apple R 5777* [1]	28	5
15 Dec 79	●	WITH YOU I'M BORN AGAIN *Motown TMG 1159* [2]	2	11
8 Mar 80		IT WILL COME IN TIME *Motown TMG 1175* [2]	47	4
22 Apr 89		GET BACK (2nd re-entry) *Apple R 5777* [1]	74	1

[1] Beatles with Billy Preston [2] Billy Preston and Syreeta

Johnny PRESTON *US, male vocalist – Johnny Courville (45 WEEKS)* pos/wks

			pos	wks
12 Feb 60	★	RUNNING BEAR *Mercury AMT 1079* ▲	1	14
21 Apr 60	●	CRADLE OF LOVE *Mercury AMT 1092*	2	16
2 Jun 60		RUNNING BEAR (re-entry) *Mercury AMT 1079*	41	1
28 Jul 60		I'M STARTING TO GO STEADY *Mercury AMT 1104*	49	1
11 Aug 60		FEEL SO FINE *Mercury AMT 1104*	18	10
8 Dec 60		CHARMING BILLY *Mercury AMT 1114*	34	1
22 Dec 60		CHARMING BILLY (re-entry) *Mercury AMT 1114*	42	2

Mike PRESTON *UK, male vocalist – Jack Davis (33 WEEKS)* pos/wks

			pos	wks
30 Oct 59		MR BLUE *Decca F 11167*	12	8
25 Aug 60		I'D DO ANYTHING *Decca F 11255*	23	10
22 Dec 60		TOGETHERNESS *Decca F 11287*	41	5
9 Mar 61		MARRY ME *Decca F 11335*	14	10

PRETENDERS (196 Top 500) *Internationally successful, British-based post-punk group with an ever-changing line-up, but with ex-NME journalist Chrissie Hynde (b. 7 Sep 1951, Ohio, US) (v/g) as a common factor. Hynde was briefly married to the lead singer of Simple Minds, Jim Kerr, and had a child with Ray Davies of Kinks (132 WEEKS)* pos/wks

			pos	wks
10 Feb 79		STOP YOUR SOBBING *Real ARE 6*	34	9
14 Jul 79		KID *Real ARE 9*	33	7
17 Nov 79	★	BRASS IN POCKET *Real ARE 11*	1	17
5 Apr 80	●	TALK OF THE TOWN *Real ARE 12*	8	8
14 Feb 81		MESSAGE OF LOVE *Real ARE 15*	11	7
12 Sep 81		DAY AFTER DAY *Real ARE 17*	45	4
14 Nov 81	●	I GO TO SLEEP *Real ARE 18*	7	10
2 Oct 82		BACK ON THE CHAIN GANG *Real ARE 19*	17	9
26 Nov 83		2000 MILES *Real ARE 20*	15	9
9 Jun 84		THIN LINE BETWEEN LOVE AND HATE *Real ARE 22*	49	3
11 Oct 86	●	DON'T GET ME WRONG *Real YZ 85*	10	9
13 Dec 86	●	HYMN TO HER *Real YZ 93*	8	12
15 Aug 87		IF THERE WAS A MAN *Real YZ 149* [1]	49	6
23 Apr 94	●	I'LL STAND BY YOU *WEA YZ 815CD*	10	10
2 Jul 94		NIGHT IN MY VEINS *WEA YZ 825CD*	25	5
15 Oct 94		977 *WEA YZ 848CD1*	66	2
14 Oct 95		KID *WEA 014CD*	73	1

UK No.1 ★ UK Top 10 ● Still on chart + UK million seller ◆ UK entry at No.1 ■ US No.1 ▲

10 May 97	FEVER PITCH THE EP *Blanco Y Negro NEG 104CD* [2]	65	1
15 May 99	HUMAN *WEA WEA 207CD*	33	3

[1] Pretenders for 007 [2] Pretenders, La's, Orlando, Neil MacColl, Nick Hornby

Tracks on Fever Pitch the EP: Goin' Back - Pretenders; There She Goes - La's; How Can We Hang On To A Dream - Orlando; Football - Neil MacColl; Boo Hewerdine - Nick Hornby. 'Kid' in 1995 is a re-recording

See also Chrissie HYNDE

PRETTY BOY FLOYD *US, male vocal / instrumental group (1 WEEK)* pos/wks

10 Mar 90	ROCK AND ROLL (IS GONNA SET THE NIGHT ON FIRE) *MCA MCA 1393*	75	1

PRETTY THINGS *UK, male vocal / instrumental group (41 WEEKS)* pos/wks

18 Jun 64	ROSALYN *Fontana TF 469*	41	5
22 Oct 64 ●	DON'T BRING ME DOWN *Fontana TF 503*	10	11
25 Feb 65	HONEY I NEED *Fontana TF 537*	13	10
15 Jul 65	CRY TO ME *Fontana TF 585*	28	7
20 Jan 66	MIDNIGHT TO SIX MAN *Fontana TF 647*	46	1
5 May 66	COME SEE ME *Fontana TF 688*	43	5
21 Jul 66	A HOUSE IN THE COUNTRY *Fontana TF 722*	50	1
4 Aug 66	A HOUSE IN THE COUNTRY (re-entry) *Fontana TF 722*	50	1

Alan PRICE (374 Top 500) *One-time leader of The Animals (first called Alan Price Combo), who left in 1965, b. 19 Apr 1942, Durham, UK. Best known for keyboards and vocals but wrote the 1973 Bafta-winning film score for 'O Lucky Man!' and won Most Promising New Actor award in 1975 (87 WEEKS)* pos/wks

31 Mar 66 ●	I PUT A SPELL ON YOU *Decca F 12367* [1]	9	10
14 Jul 66	HI LILI, HI LO *Decca F 12442* [1]	11	12
2 Mar 67 ●	SIMON SMITH AND HIS AMAZING DANCING BEAR *Decca F 12570* [1]	4	12
2 Aug 67 ●	THE HOUSE THAT JACK BUILT *Decca F 12641* [1]	4	10
15 Nov 67	SHAME *Decca F 12691* [1]	45	2
31 Jan 68	DON'T STOP THE CARNIVAL *Decca F 12731* [1]	13	8
10 Apr 71	ROSETTA *CBS 7108* [2]	11	10
25 May 74 ●	JARROW SONG *Warner Bros. K 16372*	6	9
29 Apr 78	JUST FOR YOU *Jet UP 36358*	43	7
17 Feb 79	BABY OF MINE / JUST FOR YOU (re-issue) *Jet 135*	32	3
30 Apr 88	CHANGES *Ariola 109911*	54	4

[1] Alan Price Set [2] Fame and Price Together

Kelly PRICE *US, female vocalist (10 WEEKS)* pos/wks

7 Nov 98	FRIEND OF MINE *Island Black Music CID 723*	25	3
8 May 99	SECRET LOVE *Island Black Music CID 739*	26	2
30 Dec 00	HEARTBREAK HOTEL *Arista 74321820572* [1]	26	5

[1] Whitney Houston featuring Faith Evans and Kelly Price

Lloyd PRICE *US, male vocalist (36 WEEKS)* pos/wks

13 Feb 59 ●	STAGGER LEE *HMV POP 580* ▲	7	14
15 May 59	WHERE WERE YOU (ON OUR WEDDING DAY)? *HMV POP 598*	15	6
12 Jun 59 ●	PERSONALITY *HMV POP 626*	9	8
14 Aug 59	PERSONALITY (re-entry) *HMV POP 626*	25	2
11 Sep 59	I'M GONNA GET MARRIED *HMV POP 650*	23	5
21 Apr 60	LADY LUCK *HMV POP 712*	45	1

PRICKLY HEAT *UK, male producer (1 WEEK)* pos/wks

26 Dec 98	OOOIE, OOOIE, OOOIE *Virgin VSCDT 1727*	57	1

Dickie PRIDE *UK, male vocalist (1 WEEK)* pos/wks

30 Oct 59	PRIMROSE LANE *Columbia DB 4340*	28	1

Maxi PRIEST (281 Top 500) *Popular dancehall reggae star, b. Max Elliott, 10 Jun 1960, London, UK. This internationally acclaimed vocalist is the only UK reggae act to top the US chart ('Close to You', 1990). A duet with Roberta Flack, 'Set the Night to Music', also reached the US Top 10 in 1991 (106 WEEKS)* pos/wks

29 Mar 86	STROLLIN' ON *10 TEN 84*	32	9
12 Jul 86	IN THE SPRINGTIME *10 TEN 127*	54	3
8 Nov 86	CRAZY LOVE *10 TEN 135*	67	5
4 Apr 87	LET ME KNOW *10 TEN 156*	49	4
24 Oct 87	SOME GUYS HAVE ALL THE LUCK *10 TEN 198*	12	12
20 Feb 88	HOW CAN WE EASE THE PAIN *10 TEN 207*	41	6
4 Jun 88 ●	WILD WORLD *10 TEN 221*	5	9
27 Aug 88	GOODBYE TO LOVE AGAIN *10 TEN 238*	57	3
9 Jun 90 ●	CLOSE TO YOU *10 TEN 294* ▲	7	10
1 Sep 90	PEACE THROUGHOUT THE WORLD *10 TEN 317* [1]	41	4
1 Dec 90	HUMAN WORK OF ART *10 TEN 328*	75	1
15 Dec 90	HUMAN WORK OF ART (re-entry) *10 TEN 328*	71	3
24 Aug 91	HOUSECALL *Epic 6573477* [2]	31	7
5 Oct 91	JUST A LITTLE BIT LONGER (EP) *Ten TEN 343*	62	3
26 Sep 92	GROOVIN' IN THE MIDNIGHT *Ten TEN 412*	50	2
28 Nov 92	JUST WANNA KNOW / FE' REAL *Ten TEN 416* [3]	33	3
20 Mar 93	ONE MORE CHANCE *Ten TENCD 420*	40	3
8 May 93 ●	HOUSECALL (re-mix) *Epic 6592842* [2]	8	8
31 Jul 93	WAITING IN VAIN *GRP MCSTD 1921* [4]	65	2
22 Jun 96	THAT GIRL *Virgin America VUSCD 106* [5]	15	7
21 Sep 96	WATCHING THE WORLD GO BY *Virgin America VUSCD 108*	36	2

[1] Maxi Priest featuring Jazzie B [2] Shabba Ranks featuring Maxi Priest [3] Maxi Priest / Maxi Priest featuring Apache Indian [4] Lee Ritenour and Maxi Priest [5] Maxi Priest featuring Shaggy

Tracks on Just a Little Bit Longer (EP): Just a Little Bit Longer / Best of Me / Searching / Fever

PRIMA DONNA *UK, male / female vocal group (4 WEEKS)* pos/wks

26 Apr 80	LOVE ENOUGH FOR TWO *Ariola ARO 221*	48	4

Louis PRIMA *US, male vocalist (1 WEEK)* pos/wks

21 Feb 58	BUONA SERA *Capitol CL 14821*	25	1

PRIMAL SCREAM *UK, male vocal / instrumental group (49 WEEKS)* pos/wks

3 Mar 90	LOADED *Creation CRE 070*	16	9
18 Aug 90	COME TOGETHER *Creation CRE 078*	26	6
22 Jun 91	HIGHER THAN THE SUN *Creation CRE 096*	40	2
24 Aug 91	DON'T FIGHT IT FEEL IT *Creation CRE 110* [1]	41	2
8 Feb 92	DIXIE-NARCO (EP) *Creation CRE 117*	11	6
12 Mar 94 ●	ROCKS / FUNKY JAM *Creation CRESCD 129*	7	5
18 Jun 94	JAILBIRD *Creation CRESCD 145*	29	2
10 Dec 94	(I'M GONNA) CRY MYSELF BLIND *Creation CRESCD 183*	49	2
15 Jun 96	THE BIG MAN AND THE SCREAM TEAM MEET THE BARMY ARMY UPTOWN *Creation CRESCD 194* [2]	17	2
17 May 97 ●	KOWALSKI *Creation CRESCD 245*	8	3
28 Jun 97	STAR *Creation CRESCD 263*	16	3
25 Oct 97	BURNING WHEEL *Creation CRESCD 272*	17	2
20 Nov 99	SWASTIKA EYES *Creation CRESCD 326*	22	2
1 Apr 00	KILL ALL HIPPIES *Creation CRESCD 332*	24	2
23 Sep 00	ACCELERATOR *Creation CRESCD 333*	34	1

[1] Primal Scream featuring Denise Johnson [2] Primal Scream, Irvine Welsh and On-U Sound

Tracks on Dixie-Narco (EP): Movin' On Up / Stone My Soul / Carry Me Home / Screamadelica

See also Gary CLAIL ON-U SOUND SYSTEM

PRIME MOVERS *US, male vocal / instrumental group (1 WEEK)* pos/wks

8 Feb 86	ON THE TRAIL *Island IS 263*	74	1

PRIMITIVE RADIO GODS *US, male vocalist – Chris O'Connor (1 WEEK)* pos/wks

30 Mar 96	STANDING OUTSIDE A BROKEN PHONE BOOTH WITH MONEY IN MY HAND *Columbia 6627692*	74	1

PRIMITIVES *UK, male / female vocal / instrumental group (27 WEEKS)* pos/wks

27 Feb 88 ●	CRASH *Lazy PB 41761*	5	10
30 Apr 88	OUT OF REACH *Lazy PB 42011*	25	4
3 Sep 88	WAY BEHIND ME *Lazy PB 42209*	36	4
29 Jul 89	SICK OF IT *Lazy PB 42947*	24	4
30 Sep 89	SECRETS *Lazy PB 43173*	49	3
3 Aug 91	YOU ARE THE WAY *RCA PB 44481*	58	2

PRINCE 32 Top 500 *Prolific singer / songwriter / producer / multi-instrumentalist / actor / label and studio owner, b. Prince Rogers Nelson, 7 Jun 1958, Minneapolis, US. This often controversial entertainer has packed stadiums and collected awards worldwide. He has recorded under a variety of monikers including a symbol and 'The Artist Formerly Known As Prince' (305 WEEKS)*

Date		Title	pos	wks
19 Jan 80		I WANNA BE YOUR LOVER *Warner Bros. K 17537*	41	3
29 Jan 83		1999 *Warner Bros. W 9896*	25	7
30 Apr 83		LITTLE RED CORVETTE *Warner Bros. W 9688*	54	6
26 Nov 83		LITTLE RED CORVETTE (re-issue) *Warner Bros. W 9436*	66	2
30 Jun 84	●	WHEN DOVES CRY *Warner Bros. W 9286* ▲	4	15
22 Sep 84	●	PURPLE RAIN *Warner Bros. W 9174* [1]	8	9
8 Dec 84		I WOULD DIE 4 U *Warner Bros. W 9121* [1]	58	6
19 Jan 85	●	1999 / LITTLE RED CORVETTE (re-issue) *Warner Bros. W 1999*	2	10
23 Feb 85	●	LET'S GO CRAZY / TAKE ME WITH U *Warner Bros. W 2000* [1] ▲	7	9
25 May 85		PAISLEY PARK *WEA W 9052* [1]	18	10
27 Jul 85		RASPBERRY BERET *WEA W 8929* [1]	25	8
26 Oct 85		POP LIFE *Paisley Park W 8858* [1]	60	2
8 Mar 86	●	KISS *Paisley Park W 8751* [1] ▲	6	9
14 Jun 86		MOUNTAINS *Paisley Park W 8711* [1]	45	4
16 Aug 86		GIRLS AND BOYS *Paisley Park W 8586* [1]	11	8
1 Nov 86		ANOTHERLOVERHOLENYOHEAD *Paisley Park W 8521* [1]	36	3
14 Mar 87	●	SIGN 'O' THE TIMES *Paisley Park W 8399*	10	9
20 Jun 87		IF I WAS YOUR GIRLFRIEND *Paisley Park W 8334*	20	6
15 Aug 87		U GOT THE LOOK *Paisley Park W 8289*	11	9
28 Nov 87		I COULD NEVER TAKE THE PLACE OF YOUR MAN *Paisley Park W 8288*	29	6
7 May 88	●	ALPHABET STREET *Paisley Park W 7900*	9	6
23 Jul 88		GLAM SLAM *Paisley Park W 7806*	29	4
5 Nov 88		I WISH U HEAVEN *Paisley Park W 7745*	24	5
24 Jun 89	●	BATDANCE *Warner Bros. W 2924* ▲	2	12
9 Sep 89		PARTYMAN *Warner Bros. W 2814*	14	6
18 Nov 89		THE ARMS OF ORION *Warner Bros. W 2757* [2]	27	5
4 Aug 90	●	THIEVES IN THE TEMPLE *Paisley Park W 9751*	7	6
10 Nov 90		NEW POWER GENERATION *Paisley Park W 9525*	26	4
31 Aug 91	●	GETT OFF *Paisley Park W 0056* [3]	4	8
21 Sep 91		CREAM *Paisley Park W 0061* [3] ▲	15	7
7 Dec 91		DIAMONDS AND PEARLS *Paisley Park W 0075* [3]	25	6
28 Mar 92		MONEY DON'T MATTER 2 NIGHT *Paisley Park W 0091* [3]	19	5
27 Jun 92		THUNDER *Paisley Park W 0113* [3]	28	3
18 Jul 92	●	SEXY MF / STROLLIN' *Paisley Park W 0123* [3]	4	7
10 Oct 92	●	MY NAME IS PRINCE *Paisley Park W 0132* [3]	7	5
14 Nov 92		MY NAME IS PRINCE (re-mix) *Paisley Park W 0142T* [3]	51	1
5 Dec 92		7 *Paisley Park W 0147* [3]	27	6
13 Mar 93		THE MORNING PAPERS *Paisley Park W 0162CD* [3]	52	3
16 Oct 93		PEACH *Paisley Park W 0210CD*	14	5
11 Dec 93	●	CONTROVERSY *Paisley Park W 0215CD1*	5	5
9 Apr 94	★	THE MOST BEAUTIFUL GIRL IN THE WORLD *NPG NPG 60155*	1	12
4 Jun 94		THE BEAUTIFUL EXPERIENCE (re-mix) *NPG NPG 60212*	18	3
10 Sep 94		LETITGO *Warner Bros. W 0260CD*	30	4
18 Mar 95		PURPLE MEDLEY *Warner Bros. W 0289CD*	33	2
23 Sep 95		EYE HATE U *Warner Bros. W 0315CD*	20	3
9 Dec 95	●	GOLD *Warner Bros. W 0325CD*	10	9
3 Aug 96		DINNER WITH DELORES *Warner Bros. 9362437422*	36	2
14 Dec 96		BETCHA BY GOLLY WOW *NPG CDEM 463* [4]	11	7
8 Mar 97		THE HOLY RIVER *EMI CDEM 467* [4]	19	3
9 Jan 99	●	1999 (re-issue) *Warner Bros. W 467CD*	10	4
18 Dec 99		1999 (re-entry of re-issue) *Warner Bros. W 467CD*	40	5
26 Feb 00		THE GREATEST ROMANCE EVER SOLD *NPG / Arista 74321745002* [4]	65	1

[1] Prince and the Revolution [2] Prince with Sheena Easton [3] Prince and the New Power Generation [4] The Artist

Although uncredited, Sheena Easton also sings on 'U Got the Look'. 'The Beautiful Experience' was a seven-track CD featuring 'The Most Beautiful Girl in the World' and six further mixes of the track

PRINCE BUSTER
Jamaica, male vocalist – Buster Campbell (16 WEEKS)

Date		Title	pos	wks
23 Feb 67		AL CAPONE *Blue Beat BB 324*	18	13
4 Apr 98		WHINE AND GRINE *Island CID 691*	21	3

PRINCE CHARLES and the CITY BEAT BAND
US, male vocal / instrumental group (2 WEEKS)

Date		Title	pos	wks
22 Feb 86		WE CAN MAKE IT HAPPEN *PRT 7P 348*	56	2

PRINCE NASEEM – See *KALEEF*

PRINCESS *UK, female vocalist - Desiree Heslop (44 WEEKS)*

Date		Title	pos	wks
3 Aug 85	●	SAY I'M YOUR NUMBER ONE *Supreme SUPE 101*	7	12
9 Nov 85		AFTER THE LOVE HAS GONE *Supreme SUPE 103*	28	13
19 Apr 86		I'LL KEEP ON LOVING YOU *Supreme SUPE 105*	16	8
5 Jul 86		TELL ME TOMORROW *Supreme SUPE 106*	34	5
25 Oct 86		IN THE HEAT OF A PASSIONATE MOMENT *Supreme SUPE 109*	74	1
13 Jun 87		RED HOT *Polydor POSP 868*	58	5

PRINCESS IVORI *US, female rapper (2 WEEKS)*

Date		Title	pos	wks
17 Mar 90		WANTED *Supreme SUPE 163*	69	2

Patrick PRINZ – See *ARTEMESIA; ETHICS; MOVIN' MELODIES; SUBLIMINAL CUTS*

Maddy PRIOR – See *STATUS QUO; STEELEYE SPAN*

PRIVATE LIVES *UK, male vocal / instrumental duo (4 WEEKS)*

Date		Title	pos	wks
11 Feb 84		LIVING IN A WORLD (TURNED UPSIDE DOWN) *EMI PRIV 2*	53	4

PRIZNA featuring DEMOLITION MAN
UK, male vocal / instrumental group (2 WEEKS)

Date		Title	pos	wks
29 Apr 95		FIRE *Labello Blanco NLBCDX 18*	33	2

PJ PROBY 347 Top 500 *Controversial pony tail-wearing, trouser-splitting teen idol, b. James Marcus Smith, 6 Nov 1938, Texas, US. Mannered vocalist found success after relocating to UK, and adopting Tom Jones (the successful 60s film, not the singer) attire. Voted Brightest Hope of 1964 by Melody Maker readers (91 WEEKS)*

Date		Title	pos	wks
28 May 64	●	HOLD ME *Decca F 11904*	3	15
3 Sep 64	●	TOGETHER *Decca F 11967*	8	11
10 Dec 64	●	SOMEWHERE *Liberty LIB 10182*	6	12
25 Feb 65		I APOLOGISE *Liberty LIB 10188*	11	8
8 Jul 65		LET THE WATER RUN DOWN *Liberty LIB 10206*	19	8
30 Sep 65		THAT MEANS A LOT *Liberty LIB 10215*	30	6
25 Nov 65	●	MARIA *Liberty LIB 10218*	8	9
10 Feb 66		YOU'VE COME BACK *Liberty LIB 10223*	25	7
16 Jun 66		TO MAKE A BIG MAN CRY *Liberty LIB 10236*	34	3
27 Oct 66		I CAN'T MAKE IT ALONE *Liberty LIB 10250*	37	5
6 Mar 68		IT'S YOUR DAY TODAY *Liberty LBF 15046*	32	5
28 Dec 96		YESTERDAY HAS GONE *EMI Premier CDPRESX 13* [1]	58	1
11 Jan 97		YESTERDAY HAS GONE (re-entry) *EMI Premier CDPRESX 13* [1]	69	1

[1] PJ Proby and Marc Almond featuring the My Life Story Orchestra

PROCLAIMERS
UK, male vocal / instrumental duo – Charlie and Craig Reid (50 WEEKS)

Date		Title	pos	wks
14 Nov 87	●	LETTER FROM AMERICA *Chrysalis CHS 3178*	3	10
5 Mar 88		MAKE MY HEART FLY *Chrysalis CLAIM 1*	63	3
27 Aug 88		I'M GONNA BE (500 MILES) *Chrysalis CLAIM 2*	11	11
12 Nov 88		SUNSHINE ON LEITH *Chrysalis CLAIM 3*	41	5
11 Feb 89		I'M ON MY WAY *Chrysalis CLAIM 4*	43	4
24 Nov 90	●	KING OF THE ROAD (EP) *Chrysalis CLAIM 5*	9	8
19 Feb 94		LET'S GET MARRIED *Chrysalis CDCLAIMS 6*	21	4
16 Apr 94		WHAT MAKES YOU CRY *Chrysalis CDCLAIMS 7*	38	3
22 Oct 94		THESE ARMS OF MINE *Chrysalis CDCLAIM 8*	51	2

Tracks on King of the Road (EP): King of the Road / Long Black Veil / Lulu Selling Tea / Not Ever

PROCOL HARUM *UK, male vocal / instrumental group – lead vocal Gary Brooker (56 WEEKS)*

Date		Title	pos	wks
25 May 67	★	A WHITER SHADE OF PALE *Deram DM 126*	1	15
4 Oct 67	●	HOMBURG *Regal Zonophone RZ 3003*	6	10

24 Apr 68	**QUITE RIGHTLY SO** *Regal Zonophone RZ 3007*	50	1
18 Jun 69	**A SALTY DOG** *Regal Zonophone RZ 3019*	44	1
2 Jul 69	**A SALTY DOG (re-entry)** *Regal Zonophone RZ 3019*	44	1
16 Jul 69	**A SALTY DOG (2nd re-entry)** *Regal Zonophone RZ 3019*	44	1
22 Apr 72	**A WHITER SHADE OF PALE (re-issue)** *Fly Magnifly ECHO 101*	13	13
5 Aug 72	**CONQUISTADOR** *Chrysalis CHS 2003*	22	7
23 Aug 75	**PANDORA'S BOX** *Chrysalis CHS 2073*	16	7

Michael PROCTOR – *See URBAN BLUES PROJECT presents Michael PROCTER*

PRODIGY (175 Top 500)

Confrontational dance-rock collision masterminded by Liam Howlett (k/prog) and featuring charismatic Keith Flint (v). This act has achieved a run of 12 successive Top 20 singles, while their 1997 album 'Fat of the Land' debuted at No.1 in more than 20 countries, including the UK and the US. MC / dancer Maxim went solo in 2000 (139 WEEKS)

		pos	wks
24 Aug 91	● **CHARLY** *XL Recordings XLS 21CD*	3	10
4 Jan 92	● **EVERYBODY IN THE PLACE (EP)** *XL Recordings XLS 26CD1*	2	9
26 Sep 92	**FIRE / JERICHO** *XL Recordings XLS 30CD*	11	4
21 Nov 92	● **OUT OF SPACE / RUFF IN THE JUNGLE BIZNESS** *XL Recordings XLS 35CD*	5	12
17 Apr 93	**WIND IT UP (REWOUND)** *XL Recordings XLS 39CD*	11	7
16 Oct 93	● **ONE LOVE** *XL Recordings XLS 47CD*	8	6
28 May 94	● **NO GOOD (START THE DANCE)** *XL Recordings XLS 51CD*	4	12
24 Sep 94	**VOODOO PEOPLE** *XL Recordings XLS 54CD*	13	5
18 Mar 95	**POISON** *XL Recordings XLS 58CD*	15	6
30 Mar 96	★ **FIRESTARTER** *XL Recordings XLS 70CD* ■	1	19
20 Apr 96	**CHARLY (re-entry)** *XL Recordings XLS 21CD*	66	1
20 Apr 96	**FIRE / JERICHO (re-entry)** *XL Recordings XLS 30CD*	63	1
20 Apr 96	**NO GOOD (START THE DANCE) (re-entry)** *XL Recordings XLS 51CD*	57	2
20 Apr 96	**OUT OF SPACE / RUFF IN THE JUNGLE BIZNESS (re-entry)** *XL Recordings XLS 35CD*	52	2
20 Apr 96	**POISON (re-entry)** *XL Recordings XLS 58CD*	62	1
20 Apr 96	**VOODOO PEOPLE (re-entry)** *XL Recordings XLS 54CD*	75	1
20 Apr 96	**WIND IT UP (REWOUND) (re-entry)** *XL Recordings XLS 39CD*	71	1
27 Apr 96	**EVERYBODY IN THE PLACE (EP) (re-entry)** *XL Recordings XLS 26CD1*	69	1
23 Nov 96	★ **BREATHE** *XL Recordings XLS 80CD* ■	1	17
14 Dec 96	**FIRESTARTER (re-entry)** *XL Recordings XLS 70CD*	54	4
25 Jan 97	**FIRESTARTER (2nd re-entry)** *XL Recordings XLS 70CD*	53	7
5 Apr 97	**BREATHE (re-entry)** *XL Recordings XLS 80CD*	71	1
29 Nov 97	● **SMACK MY BITCH UP** *XL Recordings XLS 90CD*	8	10

Tracks on Everybody in the Place (EP): Everybody in the Place / Crazy Man / G-Force (Energy Flow) / Rip Up the Sound System

PRODUCT G&B – *See SANTANA*

PROFESSIONALS *UK, male vocal / instrumental group (4 WEEKS)*

		pos	wks
11 Oct 80	**1-2-3** *Virgin VS 376*	43	4

PROFESSOR – *See DJ PROFESSOR*

PROFESSOR T – *See SHUT UP AND DANCE*

PROGRAM 2 BELTRAM – *See BELTRAM*

PROGRESS FUNK *Italy, male production trio (1 WEEK)*

		pos	wks
11 Oct 97	**AROUND MY BRAIN** *Deconstruction 74321518182*	73	1

PROGRESS presents the BOY WUNDA

UK, male DJ / producer – Robert Webster (10 WEEKS)

		pos	wks
18 Dec 99	● **EVERYBODY** *Manifesto FESCD 65*	7	10

PROJECT featuring GERIDEAU

US, male vocal / instrumental duo (1 WEEK)

		pos	wks
27 Aug 94	**BRING IT BACK 2 LUV** *Fruittree FTREE 10CD*	65	1

PROJECT 1 *UK, male producer – Mark Williams (3 WEEKS)*

		pos	wks
16 May 92	**ROUGHNECK (EP)** *Rising High RSN 22*	49	2
29 Aug 92	**DON GARGON COMIN'** *Rising High RSN 35*	64	1

Tracks on Roughneck (EP): Come My Selector / Can't Take the Heartbreak / Live Vibe 4 (Summer Vibes)

PRONG *US, male vocal / instrumental group (1 WEEK)*

		pos	wks
25 Apr 92	**WHOSE FIST IS THIS ANYWAY (EP)** *Epic 6580026*	58	1

Tracks on Whose Fist Is This Anyway (EP): Prove You Wrong / Hell If I Could / (Get a) Grip (On Yourself) / Prove You Wrong (re-mix)

PROPAGANDA

Germany, male / female vocal / instrumental group (35 WEEKS)

		pos	wks
17 Mar 84	**DR MABUSE** *ZTT ZTAS 2*	27	9
4 May 85	**DUEL** *ZTT ZTAS 8*	21	12
10 Aug 85	**P MACHINERY** *ZTT ZTAS 12*	50	5
28 Apr 90	**HEAVEN GIVE ME WORDS** *Virgin VS 1245*	36	5
8 Sep 90	**ONLY ONE WORD** *Virgin VS 1271*	71	4

PROPELLERHEADS *UK, male instrumental / production duo – Alex Gifford and Will White (15 WEEKS)*

		pos	wks
7 Dec 96	**TAKE CALIFORNIA** *Wall of Sound WALLD 024*	69	1
17 May 97	**SPYBREAK!** *Wall of Sound WALLD 029X*	40	1
18 Oct 97	● **ON HER MAJESTY'S SECRET SERVICE** *East West EW 136CD* [1]	7	5
20 Dec 97	**HISTORY REPEATING** *Wall of Sound WALLD 036* [2]	19	7
27 Jun 98	**BANG ON!** *Wall of Sound WALLD 039*	53	1

[1] Propellerheads / David Arnold [2] Propellerheads featuring Miss Shirley Bassey

PROPHETS OF SOUND

UK, male instrumental / production duo (1 WEEK)

		pos	wks
14 Nov 98	**HIGH** *Distinctive DISNCD 47*	73	1

PROSPECT PARK / Carolyn HARDING

UK, male / female vocal / production duo (1 WEEK)

		pos	wks
8 Aug 98	**MOVIN' ON** *AM:PM 5827312*	55	1

Shaila PROSPERE – *See RIMES featuring Shaila PROSPERE*

Brian PROTHEROE *UK, male vocalist (6 WEEKS)*

		pos	wks
7 Sep 74	**PINBALL** *Chrysalis CHS 2043*	22	6

PROUD MARY *UK, male vocal / instrumental group (1 WEEK)*

		pos	wks
25 Aug 01	**VERY BEST FRIEND** *Sour Mash JDNCSCD 004*	75	1

Dorothy PROVINE *US, female vocalist (15 WEEKS)*

		pos	wks
7 Dec 61	**DON'T BRING LULU** *Warner Bros. WB 53*	17	12
28 Jun 62	**CRAZY WORDS, CRAZY TUNE** *Warner Bros. WB 70*	45	3

PSEUDO ECHO

Australia, male vocal / instrumental group (12 WEEKS)

		pos	wks
18 Jul 87	● **FUNKY TOWN** *RCA PB 49705*	8	12

PSG – *See COLOUR GIRL*

PSYCHEDELIC FURS

UK, male vocal / instrumental group (31 WEEKS)

		pos	wks
2 May 81	**DUMB WAITERS** *CBS A 1166*	59	2
27 Jun 81	**PRETTY IN PINK** *CBS A 1327*	43	5
31 Jul 82	**LOVE MY WAY** *CBS A 2549*	42	6
31 Mar 84	**HEAVEN** *CBS A 4300*	29	6
16 Jun 84	**GHOST IN YOU** *CBS A 4470*	68	2
23 Aug 86	**PRETTY IN PINK (re-recording)** *CBS A 7242*	18	9
9 Jul 88	**ALL THAT MONEY WANTS** *CBS FURS 4*	75	1

PSYCHIC TV

UK, male / female vocal / instrumental group (4 WEEKS) pos/wks

26 Apr 86	**GODSTAR** *Temple TOPY 009* [1]	67	2
20 Sep 86	**GOOD VIBRATIONS / ROMAN P** *Temple TOPY 23*	65	2

[1] Psychic TV and the Angels of Light

PSYCHOTROPIC – *See FREEFALL featuring PSYCHOTROPIC; SALT-N-PEPA*

PUBLIC ANNOUNCEMENT

US, male vocal / instrumental group (5 WEEKS) pos/wks

9 May 92	**SHE'S GOT THAT VIBE** *Jive JIVET 292* [1]	57	2
20 Nov 93	**SEX ME** *Jive JIVECD 346* [1]	75	1
4 Jul 98	**BODY BUMPIN' (YIPPEE-YI-YO)** *A & M 5826972*	38	2

[1] R Kelly and Public Announcement

See also R KELLY

PUBLIC DEMAND *UK, male vocal group (2 WEEKS)* pos/wks

15 Feb 97	**INVISIBLE** *ZTT ZANG 85CD*	41	2

PUBLIC DOMAIN *UK, male production / vocal group (16 WEEKS)* pos/wks

2 Dec 00 ●	**OPERATION BLADE (BASS IN THE PLACE)** *Xtrahard / Xtravaganza X2H1 CDS*	5	13
23 Jun 01	**ROCK DA FUNKY BEATS** *Xtrahard / Xtravaganza X2H3 CDS* [1]	19	3

[1] Public Domain featuring Chuck D

PUBLIC ENEMY *US, male rap group (53 WEEKS)* pos/wks

21 Nov 87	**REBEL WITHOUT A PAUSE** *Def Jam 651245 7*	37	5
2 Jan 88	**REBEL WITHOUT A PAUSE (re-entry)** *Def Jam 651245 7*	71	2
9 Jan 88	**BRING THE NOISE** *Def Jam 651335 7*	32	5
2 Jul 88	**DON'T BELIEVE THE HYPE** *Def Jam 652833 7*	18	5
15 Oct 88	**NIGHT OF THE LIVING BASEHEADS** *Def Jam 6530460*	63	2
24 Jun 89	**FIGHT THE POWER** *Motown ZB 42877*	29	5
20 Jan 90	**WELCOME TO THE TERRORDOME** *Def Jam 655476 0*	18	4
7 Apr 90	**911 IS A JOKE** *Def Jam 655830 7*	41	3
23 Jun 90	**BROTHERS GONNA WORK IT OUT** *Def Jam 656018 1*	46	2
3 Nov 90	**CAN'T DO NUTTIN' FOR YA MAN** *Def Jam 656385 7*	53	2
12 Oct 91	**CAN'T TRUSS IT** *Def Jam 6575307*	22	4
25 Jan 92	**SHUT 'EM DOWN** *Def Jam 6577617*	21	3
11 Apr 92	**NIGHTTRAIN** *Def Jam 6578647*	55	2
13 Aug 94	**GIVE IT UP** *Def Jam DEFCD 1*	18	3
29 Jul 95	**SO WATCHA GONNA DO NOW** *Def Jam DEFCD 5*	50	1
6 Jun 98	**HE GOT GAME** *Def Jam 5689852* [1]	16	4
25 Sep 99	**DO YOU WANNA GO OUR WAY???** *Pias Recordings PIASX 005CDX*	66	1

[1] Public Enemy featuring Stephen Stills

PUBLIC IMAGE LTD

UK, male vocal / instrumental group (61 WEEKS) pos/wks

21 Oct 78 ●	**PUBLIC IMAGE** *Virgin VS 228*	9	8
7 Jul 79	**DEATH DISCO** *Virgin VS 274*	20	7
20 Oct 79	**MEMORIES** *Virgin VS 299*	60	2
4 Apr 81	**FLOWERS OF ROMANCE** *Virgin VS 397*	24	7
17 Sep 83 ●	**THIS IS NOT A LOVE SONG** *Virgin VS 529*	5	10
19 May 84	**BAD LIFE** *Virgin VS 675*	71	2
1 Feb 86	**RISE** *Virgin VS 841*	11	8
3 May 86	**HOME** *Virgin VS 855*	75	1
22 Aug 87	**SEATTLE** *Virgin VS 988*	47	4
6 May 89	**DISAPPOINTED** *Virgin VS 1181*	38	5
20 Oct 90	**DON'T ASK ME** *Virgin VS 1231*	22	5
22 Feb 92	**CRUEL** *Virgin VS 1390*	49	2

Group often known as P.I.L.

See also John LYDON

Gary PUCKETT – *See UNION GAP featuring Gary PUCKETT*

Tito PUENTE Jr and the LATIN RHYTHM featuring Tito PUENTE, INDIA and Cali ALEMAN

US, male / female vocal / instrumental group (3 WEEKS) pos/wks

16 Mar 96	**OYE COMO VA** *Media MCSTD 40013*	36	2
19 Jul 97	**OYE COMA VA (re-mix)** *Nukleuz MCSTD 40120*	56	1

PUFF DADDY (320 Top 500) *World Music Award-winning rapper / songwriter / producer and record label owner now known as P Diddy, b. Sean Combs 1970, New York, US. Only producer to score three successive US No.1 singles in the 1990s. 'I'll Be Missing You', a tribute to (his discovery) Notorious B.I.G., is the most successful rap single of all time (96 WEEKS)* pos/wks

29 Mar 97	**CAN'T NOBODY HOLD ME DOWN** *Arista 74321464552* [1] ▲	19	4
26 Apr 97	**NO TIME** *Atlantic A 5594CD* [2]	45	1
28 Jun 97 ★	**I'LL BE MISSING YOU** *Puff Daddy 74321499102* [3] ◆ ■ ▲	1	21
9 Aug 97 ●	**MO MONEY MO PROBLEMS** *Puff Daddy 74321492492* [4]	6	10
13 Sep 97	**SOMEONE** *RCA 74321513942* [5]	34	2
1 Nov 97	**BEEN AROUND THE WORLD** *Puff Daddy 74321539442* [6]	20	4
3 Jan 98	**BEEN AROUND THE WORLD (re-entry)** *Puff Daddy 74321539442* [6]	56	2
7 Feb 98	**IT'S ALL ABOUT THE BENJAMINS** *Puff Daddy 74321561972* [6]	18	3
1 Aug 98	**COME WITH ME (import)** *Epic 34K78954* [7]	75	1
8 Aug 98 ●	**COME WITH ME** *Epic 6662842* [7]	2	10
1 May 99	**ALL NIGHT LONG** *Puff Daddy / Arista 74321665692* [8]	23	3
29 May 99	**HATE ME NOW** *Columbia 6672562* [9]	14	6
21 Aug 99	**P.E. 2000** *Puff Daddy / Arista 74321694972* [10]	13	4
20 Nov 99	**BEST FRIEND** *Puff Daddy / Arista 74321712312* [11]	24	4
5 Feb 00	**NOTORIOUS B.I.G.** *Puff Daddy / Arista 74321737312* [12]	16	5
19 Feb 00	**SATISFY YOU (import)** *Bad Boy / Arista 7928322* [13]	73	1
4 Mar 00	**SATISFY YOU (import) (re-entry)** *Bad Boy / Arista 7928322* [13]	73	1
11 Mar 00 ●	**SATISFY YOU** *Puff Daddy / Arista 74321745592* [13]	8	8
6 Oct 01	**BAD BOY FOR LIFE** *Bad Boy / Arista 74321889982* [14]	13	6

[1] Puff Daddy featuring Mase [2] Lil' Kim featuring Puff Daddy [3] Puff Daddy and Faith Evans featuring 112 [4] Notorious B.I.G. featuring Puff Daddy and Mase [5] SWV featuring Puff Daddy [6] Puff Daddy and the Family [7] Puff Daddy featuring Jimmy Page [8] Faith Evans featuring Puff Daddy [9] Nas featuring Puff Daddy [10] Puff Daddy featuring Hurricane G [11] Puff Daddy featuring Mario Winans [12] Notorious B.I.G. featuring Puff Daddy and Lil' Kim [13] Puff Daddy featuring R Kelly [14] P Diddy, Black Rob and Mark Curry

PULP (488 Top 500) *Jarvis Cocker b. 19 Sep 1963, Sheffield, UK, is frontman of Pulp, or Arabacus Pulp as his band was called in 1978. After countless line-up changes and modest commercial success, 17 years passed before No.1 album 'Different Class' and a string of Top 10 singles troubled the charts. Cocker's unique brand of wit and wisdom was then exposed to the wider world culminating in the legendary bottom-wiggling "protest" at Michael Jackson's 1996 Brit Awards performance (72 WEEKS)* pos/wks

27 Nov 93	**LIP GLOSS** *Island CID 567*	50	2
2 Apr 94	**DO YOU REMEMBER THE FIRST TIME** *Island CID 574*	33	4
4 Jun 94	**THE SISTERS (EP)** *Island CID 595*	19	4
3 Jun 95 ●	**COMMON PEOPLE** *Island CID 613*	2	13
7 Oct 95 ●	**MIS-SHAPES / SORTED FOR E'S AND WIZZ** *Island CID 620*	2	8
9 Dec 95 ●	**DISCO 2000** *Island CID 623*	7	11
30 Dec 95	**MIS-SHAPES / SORTED FOR E'S AND WIZZ (re-entry)** *Island CID 620*	62	3
6 Apr 96 ●	**SOMETHING CHANGED** *Island CID 632*	10	5
8 Jun 96	**SOMETHING CHANGED (re-entry)** *Island CID 632*	62	1
22 Jun 96	**SOMETHING CHANGED (2nd re-entry)** *Island CID 632*	61	1
7 Sep 96	**DO YOU REMEMBER THE FIRST TIME (re-entry)** *Island CID 574*	73	1
22 Nov 97 ●	**HELP THE AGED** *Island CID 679*	8	7
24 Jan 98	**HELP THE AGED (re-entry)** *Island CID 679*	68	2
28 Mar 98	**THIS IS HARDCORE** *Island CID 695*	12	4
20 Jun 98	**A LITTLE SOUL** *Island CID 708*	22	2
19 Sep 98	**PARTY HARD** *Island CID 719*	29	2
20 Oct 01	**SUNRISE / TREES** *Island CID 786*	23	2

Tracks on The Sisters (EP): Babies / Your Sister's Clothes / Seconds / His 'n' Hers

UK No.1 ★ UK Top 10 ● Still on chart + UK million seller ◆ UK entry at No.1 ■ US No.1 ▲

PULSE featuring Antoinette ROBERSON
US, male / female vocal / production duo (3 WEEKS) pos/wks

25 May 96	**THE LOVER THAT YOU ARE** *ffrr FCD 278*	22	3

Pulse is David Morales

PUNK CHIC *Sweden, male producer - Johan Strandkvist (1 WEEK)* pos/wks

6 Oct 01	**DJ SPINNIN'** *WEA WEA 333CD*	69	1

PURE SUGAR *UK, male / female vocal / instrumental trio (1 WEEK)* pos/wks

24 Oct 98	**DELICIOUS** *Geffen GFSTD 22355*	70	1

PURESSENCE *UK, male vocal / instrumental group (5 WEEKS)* pos/wks

23 May 98	**THIS FEELING** *Island CID 688*	33	2
8 Aug 98	**IT DOESN'T MATTER ANYMORE** *Island CID 703*	47	1
21 Nov 98	**ALL I WANT** *Island CID 722*	39	2

James and Bobby PURIFY
US, male vocal duo – James Purify and Robert Dickey (16 WEEKS) pos/wks

24 Apr 76	**I'M YOUR PUPPET** *Mercury 6167 324*	12	10
7 Aug 76	**MORNING GLORY** *Mercury 6167 380*	27	6

PURPLE HEARTS *UK, male vocal / instrumental group (5 WEEKS)* pos/wks

22 Sep 79	**MILLIONS LIKE US** *Fiction FICS 003*	57	3
8 Mar 80	**JIMMY** *Fiction FICS 9*	60	2

PURPLE KINGS *UK, male vocal / instrumental duo (3 WEEKS)* pos/wks

15 Oct 94	**THAT'S THE WAY YOU DO IT** *Positiva CDTIV 21*	26	3

PUSH *Belgium, male producer – Dirk Dierickx (15 WEEKS)* pos/wks

15 May 99	**UNIVERSAL NATION** *Bonzai / Inferno CDFERN 16*	36	2
9 Oct 99	**UNIVERSAL NATION '99 (re-mix)** *Inferno CDFERN 20*	35	2
23 Sep 00	**TILL WE MEET AGAIN** *Inferno CDFERN 29*	46	1
12 May 01	**STRANGE WORLD** *Inferno CDFERN 38*	21	4
20 Oct 01	**PLEASE SAVE ME** *Inferno / Five AM FAMFERN 1CD* [1]	36	2
3 Nov 01	**THE LEGACY** *Inferno CDFERN 43*	22	4

[1] Sunscreem vs Push

PUSSY 2000 *UK, male production duo (1 WEEK)* pos/wks

3 Nov 01	**IT'S GONNA BE ALRIGHT** *Ink NIBNE 9CD*	70	1

PUSSYCAT
Holland, male / female vocal / instrumental group (30 WEEKS) pos/wks

28 Aug 76 ★	**MISSISSIPPI** *Sonet SON 2077*	1	22
25 Dec 76	**SMILE** *Sonet SON 2096*	24	8

PYRAMIDS *Jamaica, male vocal / instrumental group (4 WEEKS)* pos/wks

22 Nov 67	**TRAIN TOUR TO RAINBOW CITY** *President PT 161*	35	4

PYTHON LEE JACKSON
Australia, male vocal / instrumental group (12 WEEKS) pos/wks

30 Sep 72 ●	**IN A BROKEN DREAM** *Youngblood YB 1002*	3	12

Uncredited lead vocals by Rod Stewart

Q

Q *UK, male instrumental / production duo (6 WEEKS)* pos/wks

5 Jun 93	**GET HERE** *Arista 74321145972* [1]	37	4
12 Mar 94	**(EVERYTHING I DO) I DO IT FOR YOU** *Bell 74321193062* [2]	47	2

[1] Q featuring Tracy Ackerman [2] Q featuring Tony Jackson

Q UNIQUE – *See C & C MUSIC FACTORY / CLIVILLES & COLE*

QATTARA
UK, male production duo – Andy Cato and Alex Whitcombe (2 WEEKS) pos/wks

15 Mar 97	**COME WITH ME** *Positiva CDTIV 71*	31	2

QB FINEST featuring NAS & BRAVEHEARTS
US, male rappers (3 WEEKS) pos/wks

21 Apr 01	**OOCHIE WALLY** *Columbia 6710852*	30	3

Q-BASS *UK, male production / instrumental group (1 WEEK)* pos/wks

8 Feb 92	**HARDCORE WILL NEVER DIE** *Suburban Base SUBBASE 007*	64	1

Q-CLUB *Italy, male / female vocal / instrumental group (3 WEEKS)* pos/wks

6 Jan 96	**TELL IT TO MY HEART** *Manifesto FESCD 5*	28	3

QFX *UK, male vocal / instrumental group (16 WEEKS)* pos/wks

6 May 95	**FREEDOM (EP)** *Epidemic EPICD 004*	41	3
3 Feb 96	**EVERYTIME YOU TOUCH ME** *Epidemic EPICD 006*	22	4
3 Aug 96	**YOU GOT THE POWER** *Epidemic EPICD 007*	33	3
18 Jan 97	**FREEDOM 2 (re-mix)** *Epidemic EPICD 008*	21	4
20 Mar 99	**SAY YOU'LL BE MINE** *Quality Recordings QUAL 005CD*	34	2

Tracks on Freedom (EP): Freedom / Metropolis / Sianora Baby / The Machine

Q-TEE *UK, female rapper (7 WEEKS)* pos/wks

21 Apr 90	**AFRIKA** *SBK SBK 7008* [1]	42	5
10 Feb 96	**GIMME THAT BODY** *Heavenly HVN 48CD*	40	2

[1] History featuring Q-Tee

Q-TEX *UK, male / female vocal / instrumental group (7 WEEKS)* pos/wks

9 Apr 94	**THE POWER OF LOVE** *Stoatin' STOAT 002CD*	65	1
26 Nov 94	**BELIEVE** *23rd Precinct THIRD 2CD*	41	2
15 Jun 96	**LET THE LOVE** *23rd Precinct THIRD 4CD*	30	2
30 Nov 96	**DO YOU WANT ME** *23rd Precinct THIRD 5CD*	48	1
28 Jun 97	**POWER OF LOVE '97 (re-mix)** *23rd Precinct THIRD 7CD*	49	1

Q-TIP *US, male rapper – John Davis (23 WEEKS)* pos/wks

4 Oct 97 ●	**GOT 'TIL IT'S GONE** *Virgin VSCDG 1666* [1]	6	9
19 Jun 99	**GET INVOLVED** *Hollywood 0101185 HWR* [2]	36	2
22 Jan 00	**HOT BOYZ** *Elektra E7002CD* [3]	18	3
12 Feb 00	**BREATHE AND STOP** *Arista 74321727062*	12	7
6 May 00	**VIVRANT THING** *Arista 74321751302*	39	2

[1] Janet featuring Q-Tip and Joni Mitchell [2] Raphael Saadiq and Q-Tip [3] Missy 'Misdemeanor' Elliott featuring Nas, Eve and Q-Tip

See also A TRIBE CALLED QUEST; DEEE-LITE

QUAD CITY DJs *US, male rap duo (1 WEEK)* pos/wks

15 Nov 97	**SPACE JAM** *Atlantic EW773*	57	1

See also TAG TEAM

QUADROPHONIA
Belgium, male instrumental / production group (15 WEEKS) pos/wks

13 Apr 91	**QUADROPHONIA** *ARS 6567687*	14	9
6 Jul 91	**THE WAVE OF THE FUTURE** *ARS 6569937*	40	3
21 Dec 91	**FIND THE TIME (PART ONE)** *ARS 6576260*	41	3

QUADS *UK, male vocal / instrumental group (2 WEEKS)* pos/wks

22 Sep 79	**THERE MUST BE THOUSANDS** *Big Bear BB 23*	66	2

QUAKE featuring Marcia RAE
UK, male producer and UK, female vocalist (1 WEEK) pos/wks

29 Aug 98 THE DAY WILL COME *ffrr FCD 344* 53 1

QUANTUM JUMP *UK, male vocal / instrumental group (10 WEEKS)* pos/wks

2 Jun 79 ● THE LONE RANGER *Electric WOT 33* 5 10

QUARTERFLASH
US, male / female vocal / instrumental group (5 WEEKS) pos/wks

27 Feb 82 HARDEN MY HEART *Geffen GEF A 1838* 49 5

QUARTZ *UK, male instrumental group (19 WEEKS)* pos/wks

17 Mar 90 WE'RE COMIN' AT YA *Mercury ITMR 2* [1] 65 2
2 Feb 91 ● IT'S TOO LATE *Mercury ITM 3* [2] 8 14
15 Jun 91 NAKED LOVE (JUST SAY YOU WANT ME) *Mercury ITM 4* [3] 39 3

[1] Quartz featuring Stepz [2] Quartz introducing Dina Carroll [3] Quartz and Dina Carroll

Jakie QUARTZ *France, female vocalist (3 WEEKS)* pos/wks

11 Mar 89 A LA VIE, A L'AMOUR *PWL PWL 30* 55 3

QUARTZ LOCK featuring Lonnie GORDON *UK, male production / instrumental duo and US, female vocalist (2 WEEKS)* pos/wks

7 Oct 95 LOVE EVICTION *X:Plode BANG 2CD* 32 2

Suzi QUATRO (223 Top 500) *Leather-clad US rock singer / guitarist, b. Suzi Quatrocchio, 3 Jun 1950, Detroit. Thanks partly to ultra-commercial songs and productions by Nicky Chinn and Mike Chapman, she was a regular hitmaker in Europe. In her homeland, however, only 'Stumblin' In' reached the Top 40 (122 WEEKS)* pos/wks

19 May 73 ★ CAN THE CAN *RAK 150* 1 14
28 Jul 73 ● 48 CRASH *RAK 158* 3 9
27 Oct 73 DAYTONA DEMON *RAK 161* 14 13
9 Feb 74 ★ DEVIL GATE DRIVE *RAK 167* 1 11
29 Jun 74 TOO BIG *RAK 175* 14 6
9 Nov 74 ● THE WILD ONE *RAK 185* 7 10
8 Feb 75 YOUR MAMA WON'T LIKE ME *RAK 191* 31 5
5 Mar 77 TEAR ME APART *RAK 248* 27 6
18 Mar 78 ● IF YOU CAN'T GIVE ME LOVE *RAK 271* 4 13
22 Jul 78 THE RACE IS ON *RAK 278* 43 5
11 Nov 78 STUMBLIN' IN *RAK 285* [1] 41 8
20 Oct 79 SHE'S IN LOVE WITH YOU *RAK 299* 11 9
19 Jan 80 MAMA'S BOY *RAK 303* 34 5
5 Apr 80 I'VE NEVER BEEN IN LOVE *RAK 307* 56 3
25 Oct 80 ROCK HARD *Dreamland DLSP 6* 68 2
13 Nov 82 HEART OF STONE *Polydor POSP 477* 60 3

[1] Suzi Quatro and Chris Norman

Finley QUAYE *UK, male vocal / instrumentalist (23 WEEKS)* pos/wks

21 Jun 97 SUNDAY SHINING *Epic 6644552* 16 6
13 Sep 97 ● EVEN AFTER ALL *Epic 6649712* 10 5
29 Nov 97 IT'S GREAT WHEN WE'RE TOGETHER *Epic 6653382* 29 3
7 Mar 98 YOUR LOVE GETS SWEETER *Epic 6656065* 16 5
15 Aug 98 ULTRA STIMULATION *Epic 6660792* 51 1
23 Sep 00 SPIRITUALIZED *Epic 6698032* 26 3

QUEEN (12 Top 500) *World-renowned British quartet: Freddie Mercury (v) (d. 1991), Brian May (g/v), John Deacon (b/v), Roger Taylor (d/v). 'Bohemian Rhapsody' is the only record to top the chart on two occasions selling more than a million each time and was No.1 in a record four calendar years. First act to have chart-topping singles in the 70s, 80s, 90s and 21st century, and sold more than 25 million Greatest Hits albums worldwide. They were given the Brits Outstanding Contribution to British Music Award (1992) and were inducted into Rock and Roll Hall of Fame (2000). 'Bohemian Rhapsody' is No.1 in the Top 100 of all time as voted by British Hit Singles readers (419 WEEKS)* pos/wks

9 Mar 74 ● SEVEN SEAS OF RHYE *EMI 2121* 10 10
26 Oct 74 ● KILLER QUEEN *EMI 2229* 2 12
25 Jan 75 NOW I'M HERE *EMI 2256* 11 7
8 Nov 75 ★ BOHEMIAN RHAPSODY *EMI 2375* ◆ 1 17
3 Jul 76 ● YOU'RE MY BEST FRIEND *EMI 2494* 7 8
27 Nov 76 ● SOMEBODY TO LOVE *EMI 2565* 2 9
19 Mar 77 TIE YOUR MOTHER DOWN *EMI 2593* 31 4
4 Jun 77 QUEEN'S FIRST EP *EMI 2623* 17 10
22 Oct 77 ● WE ARE THE CHAMPIONS *EMI 2708* 2 11
25 Feb 78 SPREAD YOUR WINGS *EMI 2757* 34 4
28 Oct 78 BICYCLE RACE / FAT BOTTOMED GIRLS *EMI 2870* 11 12
10 Feb 79 ● DON'T STOP ME NOW *EMI 2910* 9 12
14 Jul 79 LOVE OF MY LIFE *EMI 2959* 63 2
20 Oct 79 ● CRAZY LITTLE THING CALLED LOVE *EMI 5001* ▲ 2 14
2 Feb 80 SAVE ME *EMI 5022* 11 6
14 Jun 80 PLAY THE GAME *EMI 5076* 14 8
6 Sep 80 ● ANOTHER ONE BITES THE DUST *EMI 5102* ▲ 7 9
6 Dec 80 ● FLASH *EMI 5126* 10 13
14 Nov 81 ★ UNDER PRESSURE *EMI 5250* [1] 1 11
1 May 82 BODY LANGUAGE *EMI 5293* 25 6
12 Jun 82 LAS PALABRAS DE AMOR *EMI 5316* 17 8
21 Aug 82 BACKCHAT *EMI 5325* 40 4
4 Feb 84 ● RADIO GAGA *EMI QUEEN 1* 2 9
14 Apr 84 ● I WANT TO BREAK FREE *EMI QUEEN 2* 3 15
28 Jul 84 ● IT'S A HARD LIFE *EMI QUEEN 3* 6 9
22 Sep 84 HAMMER TO FALL *EMI QUEEN 4* 13 7
8 Dec 84 THANK GOD IT'S CHRISTMAS *EMI QUEEN 5* 21 6
16 Nov 85 ● ONE VISION *EMI QUEEN 6* 7 10
29 Mar 86 ● A KIND OF MAGIC *EMI QUEEN 7* 3 11
21 Jun 86 FRIENDS WILL BE FRIENDS *EMI QUEEN 8* 14 8
27 Sep 86 WHO WANTS TO LIVE FOREVER *EMI QUEEN 9* 24 5
13 May 89 ● I WANT IT ALL *Parlophone QUEEN 10* 3 7
1 Jul 89 ● BREAKTHRU' *Parlophone QUEEN 11* 7 7
19 Aug 89 THE INVISIBLE MAN *Parlophone QUEEN 12* 12 6
21 Oct 89 SCANDAL *Parlophone QUEEN 14* 25 4
9 Dec 89 THE MIRACLE *Parlophone QUEEN 15* 21 5
26 Jan 91 ★ INNUENDO *Parlophone QUEEN 16* ■ 1 6
25 May 91 HEADLONG *Parlophone QUEEN 18* 14 4
25 May 91 I'M GOING SLIGHTLY MAD *Parlophone QUEEN 17* 22 5
26 Oct 91 THE SHOW MUST GO ON *Parlophone QUEEN 19* 16 5
7 Dec 91 THE SHOW MUST GO ON (re-entry) *Parlophone QUEEN 19* 27 5
21 Dec 91 ★ BOHEMIAN RHAPSODY / THESE ARE THE DAYS OF OUR LIVES (re-issue) *Parlophone QUEEN 20* ◆ ■ 1 14
1 May 93 ★ FIVE LIVE (EP) *Parlophone CDRS 6340* [2] ■ 1 11
24 Jul 93 FIVE LIVE (EP) (re-entry) *Parlophone CDRS 6340* [2] 74 1
4 Nov 95 ● HEAVEN FOR EVERYONE *Parlophone CDQUEEN 21* 2 12
23 Dec 95 ● A WINTER'S TALE *Parlophone CDQUEEN 22* 6 6
9 Mar 96 TOO MUCH LOVE WILL KILL YOU *Parlophone CDQUEEN 23* 15 6
29 Jun 96 ● LET ME LIVE *Parlophone CDQUEEN 24* 9 4
30 Nov 96 YOU DON'T FOOL ME *Parlophone CDQUEEN 25* 17 4
17 Jan 98 NO ONE BUT YOU / TIE YOUR MOTHER DOWN *Parlophone CDQUEEN 27* 13 4
14 Nov 98 ● ANOTHER ONE BITES THE DUST *Dreamworks DRMCD 22364* [3] 5 6
18 Dec 99 UNDER PRESSURE (re-mix) *Parlophone CDQUEEN 28* [1] 14 7
29 Jul 00 ★ WE WILL ROCK YOU *RCA 74321774022* [4] ■ 1 12
4 Nov 00 WE WILL ROCK YOU (re-entry) *RCA 74321774022* [4] 72 1

[1] Queen and David Bowie [2] George Michael and Queen with Lisa Stansfield [3] Queen with Wyclef Jean featuring Pras and Free [4] Five and Queen

Tracks on Queen's First EP: Good Old Fashioned Lover Boy / Death on Two Legs (Dedicated to...) / Tenement Funster / White Queen (As it Began). Tracks on Five Live (EP): Somebody to Love / These Are the Days of Our Lives / Calling You / Papa Was a Rolling Stone - Killer (medley). Queen appear only on the first two tracks. The first credits George Michael and Queen and the second George Michael with Lisa Stansfield

QUEEN LATIFAH *US, female rapper – Dana Owens (17 WEEKS)* pos/wks

24 Mar 90 MAMA GAVE BIRTH TO THE SOUL CHILDREN *Gee Street GEE 26* [1] 14 7
26 May 90 FIND A WAY *Ahead of our Time CCUT 8* [2] 52 2
31 Aug 91 FLY GIRL *Gee Street GEE 34* 67 1
26 Jun 93 WHAT'CHA GONNA DO *Epic 6593072* [3] 21 4
26 Mar 94 U.N.I.T.Y. *Motown TMGCD 1422* 74 1
12 Apr 97 MR BIG STUFF *Motown 5736572* [4] 31 2

[1] Queen Latifah + De La Soul [2] Coldcut featuring Queen Latifah [3] Shabba Ranks featuring Queen Latifah [4] Queen Latifah, Shades and Free

UK No.1 ★ UK Top 10 ● Still on chart + UK million seller ◆ UK entry at No.1 ■ US No.1 ▲

THE OFFICIAL UK SINGLES CHART 50TH ANNIVERSARY

1987

IN THE YEAR OF THE ZEEBRUGGE FERRY DISASTER, THE NEW YORK STOCK EXCHANGE SUFFERED COLLAPSE ON BLACK MONDAY, MTV DEBUTED IN EUROPE, MIKHAIL GORBACHEV AND RONALD REAGAN SIGNED THE FIRST TREATY IN HISTORY TO CUT THEIR NUCLEAR ARSENALS AND 'FATAL ATTRACTION' SENT A SHIVER DOWN THE SPINES OF RABBIT-OWNING ADULTERERS, **GEORGE MICHAEL** REMEMBERS ONE OF HIS BREAKTHROUGH SOLO EFFORTS, 'FAITH'...

"The 'Faith' album had been extremely successful in America on the black charts. I think I was the first artist to have a No.1 single on the black charts who wasn't actually black. And after that I received two major awards at the American Music awards which were historically black awards. That created quite a lot of controversy, and I think quite rightly so."

SINGLE OF THE YEAR - 'Never Gunna Give You Up' Rick Astley
ALBUM OF THE YEAR - 'Whitney' Whitney Houston

1987

QUEEN PEN *US, female rapper – Lynise Walters (10 WEEKS)*

		pos	wks
7 Mar 98	**MAN BEHIND THE MUSIC** *Interscope IND 95562*	38	2
9 May 98	**ALL MY LOVE** *Interscope IND 95584* [1]	11	5
5 Sep 98	**IT'S TRUE** *Interscope IND 95597*	24	3

[1] Queen Pen featuring Eric Williams

QUEENS OF THE STONE AGE *US, male vocal / instrumental group (2 WEEKS)*

		pos	wks
26 Aug 00	**THE LOST ART OF KEEPING A SECRET** *Interscope 4973912*	31	2

QUEENSRYCHE *US, male vocal / instrumental group (21 WEEKS)*

		pos	wks
13 May 89	**EYES OF A STRANGER** *EMI USA MT 65*	59	1
10 Nov 90	**EMPIRE** *EMI USA MT 90*	61	1
20 Apr 91	**SILENT LUCIDITY** *EMI USA MT 94*	34	5
6 Jul 91	**BEST I CAN** *EMI USA MT 97*	36	3
7 Sep 91	**JET CITY WOMAN** *EMI USA MT 98*	39	2
8 Aug 92	**SILENT LUCIDITY (re-issue)** *EMI USA MT 104*	18	4
28 Jan 95	**I AM I** *EMI CDMT 109*	40	2
25 Mar 95	**BRIDGE** *EMI CDMT 111*	40	3

QUENCH *Australia, male instrumental / production duo (1 WEEK)*

		pos	wks
17 Feb 96	**DREAMS** *Infectious INFECT 3CD*	75	1

QUENTIN and ASH *UK, female vocal duo (3 WEEKS)*

		pos	wks
6 Jul 96	**TELL HIM** *East West EW 049CD*	25	3

? (QUESTION MARK) and the MYSTERIANS *US, male vocal / instrumental group (4 WEEKS)*

		pos	wks
17 Nov 66	**96 TEARS** *Cameo Parkway C428* ▲	37	4

QUESTIONS *UK, male vocal / instrumental group (8 WEEKS)*

		pos	wks
23 Apr 83	**PRICE YOU PAY** *Respond KOB 702*	56	3
17 Sep 83	**TEAR SOUP** *Respond KOB 705*	66	1
10 Mar 84	**TUESDAY SUNSHINE** *Respond KOB 707*	46	4

QUICK *UK, male vocal / instrumental group (7 WEEKS)*

		pos	wks
15 May 82	**RHYTHM OF THE JUNGLE** *Epic EPC A 2013*	41	7

Tommy QUICKLY and the REMO FOUR *UK, male vocal / instrumental group (8 WEEKS)*

		pos	wks
22 Oct 64	**WILD SIDE OF LIFE** *Pye 7N 15708*	33	8

QUIET FIVE *UK, male vocal / instrumental group (3 WEEKS)*

		pos	wks
13 May 65	**WHEN THE MORNING SUN DRIES THE DEW** *Parlophone R 5273*	45	1
21 Apr 66	**HOMEWARD BOUND** *Parlophone R 5421*	44	2

QUIET RIOT *US, male vocal / instrumental group (5 WEEKS)*

		pos	wks
3 Dec 83	**METAL HEALTH / CUM ON FEEL THE NOIZE** *Epic A 3968*	45	5

'Cum on Feel the Noize' credited only from 10 Dec 1983

Eimear QUINN *Ireland, female vocalist (2 WEEKS)*

		pos	wks
15 Jun 96	**THE VOICE** *Polydor 5768842*	40	2

Paul QUINN and EDWYN COLLINS *UK, male vocalists / instrumentalists (2 WEEKS)*

		pos	wks
11 Aug 84	**PALE BLUE EYES** *Swamplands SWP 1*	72	2

QUIREBOYS *UK, male vocal / instrumental group (27 WEEKS)*

		pos	wks
4 Nov 89	**7 O'CLOCK** *Parlophone R 6230*	36	4
6 Jan 90	**HEY YOU** *Parlophone R 6241*	14	7
7 Apr 90	**I DON'T LOVE YOU ANYMORE** *Parlophone R 6248*	24	6
8 Sep 90	**THERE SHE GOES AGAIN / MISLED** *Parlophone R 6267*	37	4
10 Oct 92	**TRAMPS AND THIEVES** *Parlophone RS 6323*	41	3
20 Feb 93	**BROTHER LOUIE** *Parlophone CDR 6335*	31	3

QUIVER – *See SUTHERLAND BROTHERS and QUIVER*

QUIVVER *UK, male instrumental / production duo (3 WEEKS)*

		pos	wks
5 Mar 94	**SAXY LADY** *A & M 5805152*	56	2
18 Nov 95	**BELIEVE IN ME** *Perfecto PERF 111CD*	56	1

QUO VADIS *UK, male production trio (1 WEEK)*

		pos	wks
16 Dec 00	**SONIC BOOM (LIFE'S TOO SHORT)** *Serious SERR 028CD*	49	1

QWILO & FELIX DA HOUSECAT *US, male / female vocal / DJ / production duo (1 WEEK)*

		pos	wks
6 Sep 97	**DIRTY MOTHA** *Manifesto FESCD 29*	66	1

R

Eddie RABBITT *US, male vocalist (14 WEEKS)*

		pos	wks
27 Jan 79	**EVERY WHICH WAY BUT LOOSE** *Elektra K 12331*	41	9
28 Feb 81	**I LOVE A RAINY NIGHT** *Elektra K 12498* ▲	53	5

Steve RACE *UK, male instrumentalist – piano (9 WEEKS)*

		pos	wks
28 Feb 63	**PIED PIPER (THE BEEJE)** *Parlophone R 4981*	29	9

RACEY *UK, male vocal / instrumental group (44 WEEKS)*

		pos	wks
25 Nov 78 ●	**LAY YOUR LOVE ON ME** *RAK 284*	3	14
31 Mar 79 ●	**SOME GIRLS** *RAK 291*	2	11
18 Aug 79	**BOY OH BOY** *RAK 297*	22	9
20 Dec 80	**RUNAROUND SUE** *RAK 325*	13	10

RACING CARS *UK, male vocal / instrumental group (7 WEEKS)*

		pos	wks
12 Feb 77	**THEY SHOOT HORSES DON'T THEY** *Chrysalis CHS 2129*	14	7

RACKETEERS – *See Elbow BONES and the RACKETEERS*

Jimmy RADCLIFFE *US, male vocalist (2 WEEKS)*

		pos	wks
4 Feb 65	**LONG AFTER TONIGHT IS ALL OVER** *Stateside SS 374*	40	2

RADHA KRISHNA TEMPLE *UK, male / female vocal / instrumental group (17 WEEKS)*

		pos	wks
13 Sep 69	**HARE KRISHNA MANTRA** *Apple 15*	12	9
28 Mar 70	**GOVINDA** *Apple 25*	23	8

RADICAL ROB *UK, male producer – Rob McLuan (1 WEEK)*

		pos	wks
11 Jan 92	**MONKEY WAH** *R&S RSUK 8*	67	1

Jack RADICS – *See Chaka DEMUS and PLIERS; SUPERCAT*

RADIO HEART featuring Gary NUMAN *UK, male instrumental group and male vocalist / instrumentalist (8 WEEKS)*

		pos	wks
28 Mar 87	**RADIO HEART** *GFM GFM 109*	35	6
13 Jun 87	**LONDON TIMES** *GFM GFM 112*	48	2

RADIO 1 DJ POSSE – *See Liz KERSHAW and Bruno BROOKES*

RADIO REVELLERS – *See Anthony STEEL and the RADIO REVELLERS*

RADIO STARS *UK, male vocal / instrumental group (3 WEEKS)*

		pos	wks
4 Feb 78	**NERVOUS WRECK** *Chiswick NS 23*	39	3

RADIOHEAD *UK, male vocal / instrumental group (52 WEEKS)* pos/wks

			pos	wks
13 Feb 93		**ANYONE CAN PLAY GUITAR** *Parlophone CDR 6333*	32	2
22 May 93		**POP IS DEAD** *Parlophone CDR 6345*	42	2
18 Sep 93	●	**CREEP** *Parlophone CDR 6359*	7	6
8 Oct 94		**MY IRON LUNG** *Parlophone CDR 6394*	24	2
11 Mar 95		**HIGH AND DRY / PLANET TELEX** *Parlophone CDR 6405*	17	4
27 May 95		**FAKE PLASTIC TREES** *Parlophone CDR 6411*	20	4
2 Sep 95		**JUST** *Parlophone CDR 6415*	19	3
3 Feb 96	●	**STREET SPIRIT (FADE OUT)** *Parlophone CDR 6419*	5	4
7 Jun 97	●	**PARANOID ANDROID** *Parlophone CDODATA S 01*	3	5
6 Sep 97	●	**KARMA POLICE** *Parlophone CDODATAS 03*	8	4
24 Jan 98	●	**NO SURPRISES** *Parlophone CDODATAS 04*	4	6
4 Apr 98		**NO SURPRISES (re-entry)** *Parlophone CDODATAS 04*	74	1
2 Jun 01	●	**PYRAMID SONG** *Parlophone CDSFHEIT 45102*	5	5
18 Aug 01		**KNIVES OUT** *Parlophone CDFHEIT 45103*	13	4

RADISH *US, male vocal / instrumental group (3 WEEKS)* pos/wks

			pos	wks
30 Aug 97		**LITTLE PINK STARS** *Mercury MERCD 494*	32	2
15 Nov 97		**SIMPLE SINCERITY** *Mercury MERCD 498*	50	1

Fonda RAE *US, female vocalist (4 WEEKS)* pos/wks

			pos	wks
6 Oct 84		**TUCH ME** *Streetwave KHAN 28*	49	4

Jesse RAE *UK, male vocalist (2 WEEKS)* pos/wks

			pos	wks
11 May 85		**OVER THE SEA** *Scotland-Video YZ 36*	65	2

Marcia RAE – *See QUAKE featuring Marcia RAE*

RAE & CHRISTIAN featuring VEBA
UK, male production duo and UK, female vocalist (1 WEEK) pos/wks

			pos	wks
6 Mar 99		**ALL I ASK** *Grand Central GCCD 120*	67	1

RAF *Italy, male producer – Mauro Picotto (6 WEEKS)* pos/wks

			pos	wks
14 Mar 92		**WE'VE GOT TO LIVE TOGETHER** *PWL Continental PWL 218*	34	3
5 Mar 94		**TAKE ME HIGHER** *Media MRLCD 0012*	71	1
23 Mar 96		**TAKE ME HIGHER (re-mix)** *Media MCSTD 40026*	59	1
27 Jul 96		**ANGEL'S SYMPHONY** *Media MCSTD 40051*	73	1

Gerry RAFFERTY *UK, male vocalist (47 WEEKS)* pos/wks

			pos	wks
18 Feb 78	●	**BAKER STREET** *United Artists UP 36346*	3	15
26 May 79	●	**NIGHT OWL** *United Artists UP 36512*	5	13
18 Aug 79		**GET IT RIGHT NEXT TIME** *United Artists BP 301*	30	9
22 Mar 80		**BRING IT ALL HOME** *United Artists BP 340*	54	4
21 Jun 80		**ROYAL MILE** *United Artists BP 354*	67	2
10 Mar 90		**BAKER STREET (re-mix)** *EMI EM 132*	53	4

RAGE *UK, male vocal / instrumental group (15 WEEKS)* pos/wks

			pos	wks
31 Oct 92	●	**RUN TO YOU** *Pulse 8 LOSE 33*	3	11
27 Feb 93		**WHY DON'T YOU** *Pulse 8 CDLOSE 39*	44	2
15 May 93		**HOUSE OF THE RISING SUN** *Pulse 8 CDLOSE 43*	41	2

RAGE AGAINST THE MACHINE
US, male vocal / instrumental group (19 WEEKS) pos/wks

			pos	wks
27 Feb 93		**KILLING IN THE NAME** *Epic 6584922*	25	4
8 May 93		**BULLET IN THE HEAD** *Epic 6592582*	16	4
4 Sep 93		**BOMBTRACK** *Epic 6594712*	37	2
13 Apr 96	●	**BULLS ON PARADE** *Epic 6631522*	8	3
7 Sep 96		**PEOPLE OF THE SUN** *Epic 6636282*	26	2
6 Nov 99		**GUERRILLA RADIO** *Epic 6683142*	32	2
15 Apr 00		**SLEEP NOW IN THE FIRE** *Epic 6691362*	43	2

RAGGA TWINS *UK, male vocal group (10 WEEKS)* pos/wks

			pos	wks
10 Nov 90		**ILLEGAL GUNSHOT / SPLIFFHEAD** *Shut Up and Dance SUAD 7*	51	2
6 Apr 91		**WIPE THE NEEDLE / JUGGLING** *Shut Up and Dance SUAD 12S*	71	2
6 Jul 91		**HOOLIGAN 69** *Shut Up and Dance SUAD 16S*	56	2
7 Mar 92		**MIXED TRUTH / BRING UP THE MIC SOME MORE** *Shut Up and Dance SUAD 27S*	65	2
11 Jul 92		**SHINE EYE** *Shut Up and Dance SUAD 32S* [1]	63	2

[1] Ragga Twins featuring Junior Reid

RAGING SPEEDHORN *UK, male vocal / instrumental group (1 WEEK)* pos/wks

			pos	wks
16 Jun 01		**THE GUSH** *ZTT GIR004CD*	47	1

RAGTIMERS *UK, male instrumental group (8 WEEKS)* pos/wks

			pos	wks
16 Mar 74		**THE STING** *Pye 7N 45323*	46	1
30 Mar 74		**THE STING (re-entry)** *Pye 7N 45323*	31	7

RAH BAND *UK, male / female vocal / instrumental group – Richard A and Liz Hewson (50 WEEKS)* pos/wks

			pos	wks
9 Jul 77	●	**THE CRUNCH** *Good Earth GD 7*	6	12
1 Nov 80		**FALCON** *DJM DJS 10954*	35	7
7 Feb 81		**SLIDE** *DJM DJS 10964*	50	7
1 May 82		**PERFUMED GARDEN** *KR KR 5*	45	7
9 Jul 83		**MESSAGES FROM THE STARS** *TMT TMT 5*	42	5
19 Jan 85		**ARE YOU SATISFIED? (FUNKA NOVA)** *RCA RCA 470*	70	2
30 Mar 85	●	**CLOUDS ACROSS THE MOON** *RCA PB 40025*	6	10

RAHSAAN – *See US3*

RAILWAY CHILDREN *UK, male vocal / instrumental group (13 WEEKS)* pos/wks

			pos	wks
24 Mar 90		**EVERY BEAT OF THE HEART** *Virgin VS 1237*	68	2
2 Jun 90		**MUSIC STOP** *Virgin VS 1255*	66	2
20 Oct 90		**SO RIGHT** *Virgin VS 1289*	68	1
2 Feb 91		**EVERY BEAT OF THE HEART (re-entry)** *Virgin VS 1237*	24	6
20 Apr 91		**SOMETHING SO GOOD** *Virgin VS 1318*	57	2

RAIN – *See Stephanie DE SYKES*

RAIN TREE CROW *UK, male vocal / instrumental group (1 WEEK)* pos/wks

			pos	wks
30 Mar 91		**BLACKWATER** *Virgin VS 1340*	62	1

Group is Japan under an assumed name

See also JAPAN

RAINBOW *UK, male vocal / instrumental group (62 WEEKS)* pos/wks

			pos	wks
17 Sep 77		**KILL THE KING** *Polydor 2066 845*	44	3
8 Apr 78		**LONG LIVE ROCK 'N' ROLL** *Polydor 2066 913*	33	3
30 Sep 78		**L.A. CONNECTION** *Polydor 2066 968*	40	4
15 Sep 79	●	**SINCE YOU'VE BEEN GONE** *Polydor POSP 70*	6	10
16 Feb 80	●	**ALL NIGHT LONG** *Polydor POSP 104*	5	11
31 Jan 81	●	**I SURRENDER** *Polydor POSP 221*	3	10
20 Jun 81		**CAN'T HAPPEN HERE** *Polydor POSP 251*	20	8
11 Jul 81		**KILL THE KING (re-issue)** *Polydor POSP 274*	41	4
3 Apr 82		**STONE COLD** *Polydor POSP 421*	34	4
27 Aug 83		**STREET OF DREAMS** *Polydor POSP 631*	52	3
5 Nov 83		**CAN'T LET YOU GO** *Polydor POSP 654*	43	2

RAINBOW COTTAGE *UK, male vocal / instrumental group (4 WEEKS)* pos/wks

			pos	wks
6 Mar 76		**SEAGULL** *Penny Farthing PEN 906*	33	4

RAINMAKERS *US, male vocal / instrumental group (11 WEEKS)* pos/wks

			pos	wks
7 Mar 87		**LET MY PEOPLE GO-GO** *Mercury MER 238*	18	11

Marvin RAINWATER *US, male vocalist – Marvin Percy (22 WEEKS)* pos/wks

			pos	wks
7 Mar 58	★	**WHOLE LOTTA WOMAN** *MGM 974*	1	15
6 Jun 58		**I DIG YOU BABY** *MGM 980*	19	7

RAISSA *UK, female vocalist – Raissa Khan-Panni (1 WEEK)* pos/wks

			pos	wks
12 Feb 00		**HOW LONG DO I GET** *Polydor 5616282*	47	1

Bonnie RAITT *US, female vocalist / instrumentalist (9 WEEKS)* pos/wks

			pos	wks
14 Dec 91		**I CAN'T MAKE YOU LOVE ME** *Capitol CL 639*	50	4

9 Apr 94	**LOVE SNEAKIN' UP ON YOU** *Capitol CDCL 713*	69	1
18 Jun 94	**YOU** *Capitol CDCLS 718*	31	2
11 Nov 95	**ROCK STEADY** *Capitol CDCL 763* [1]	50	2

[1] Bonnie Raitt and Bryan Adams

RAJA NEE *US, female vocalist (2 WEEKS)* pos/wks

4 Mar 95	**TURN IT UP** *Perspective 5874872*	42	2

Dionne RAKEEM *UK, female vocalist (2 WEEKS)* pos/wks

4 Aug 01	**SWEETER THAN WINE** *Virgin VSCDT 1809*	46	2

RAKIM *US, male rapper – William Griffin (5 WEEKS)* pos/wks

27 Dec 97	**GUESS WHO'S BACK** *Universal UND 56151*	32	3
22 Aug 98	**STAY A WHILE** *Universal UND 56203*	53	1
3 Oct 98	**BUFFALO GIRLS STAMPEDE (re-mix)** *Virgin VSCDT 1717* [1]	65	1

[1] Malcolm McLaren and the World's Famous Supreme Team plus Rakim and Roger Sanchez

See also Eric B and RAKIM

Tony RALLO and the MIDNITE BAND
France / US, male vocal / instrumental group (8 WEEKS) pos/wks

23 Feb 80	**HOLDIN' ON** *Calibre CAB 150*	34	8

Sheryl Lee RALPH *US, female vocalist (2 WEEKS)* pos/wks

26 Jan 85	**IN THE EVENING** *Arista ARIST 595*	64	2

RAM JAM *US, male vocal / instrumental group (20 WEEKS)* pos/wks

10 Sep 77 ●	**BLACK BETTY** *Epic EPC 5492*	7	12
17 Feb 90	**BLACK BETTY (re-mix)** *Epic 655430 7*	13	8

RAM JAM BAND – *See Geno WASHINGTON and the RAM JAM BAND*

RAMBLERS – *See Perry COMO*

RAMBLERS (from the Abbey Hey Junior School)
UK, children's choir (15 WEEKS) pos/wks

13 Oct 79	**THE SPARROW** *Decca F 13860*	11	15

Karen RAMIREZ *UK, female vocalist – Karen Ramelize (15 WEEKS)* pos/wks

28 Mar 98	**TROUBLED GIRL** *Manifesto FESCD 31*	50	1
27 Jun 98 ●	**LOOKING FOR LOVE** *Manifesto FESCD 44*	8	11
21 Nov 98	**IF WE TRY** *Manifesto FESCD 50*	23	3

RAMONES *US, male vocal / instrumental group (32 WEEKS)* pos/wks

21 May 77	**SHEENA IS A PUNK ROCKER** *Sire RAM 001*	22	7
6 Aug 77	**SWALLOW MY PRIDE** *Sire 6078 607*	36	3
30 Sep 78	**DON'T COME CLOSE** *Sire SRE 1031*	39	5
8 Sep 79	**ROCK 'N' ROLL HIGH SCHOOL** *Sire SIR 4021*	67	2
26 Jan 80 ●	**BABY I LOVE YOU** *Sire SIR 4031*	8	9
19 Apr 80	**DO YOU REMEMBER ROCK 'N' ROLL RADIO?** *Sire SIR 4037*	54	3
10 May 86	**SOMEBODY PUT SOMETHING IN MY DRINK / SOMETHING TO BELIEVE IN** *Beggars Banquet BEG 157*	69	1
19 Dec 92	**POISON HEART** *Chrysalis CHS 3917*	69	2

RAMP *UK, male instrumental / production duo (1 WEEK)* pos/wks

8 Jun 96	**ROCK THE DISCOTEK** *Loaded LOADCD 30*	49	1

RAMPAGE *UK, male DJ / production group (1 WEEK)* pos/wks

25 Nov 95	**THE MONKEES** *Almo Sounds CDALMOS 017*	51	1

RAMPAGE featuring Billy LAWRENCE
US, male rapper – Roger McNair and male vocalist (1 WEEK) pos/wks

18 Oct 97	**TAKE IT TO THE STREETS** *Elektra E 3914CD*	58	1

RAMRODS *US, male / female instrumental group (12 WEEKS)* pos/wks

23 Feb 61 ●	**RIDERS IN THE SKY** *London HLU 9282*	8	12

RAMSEY and FEN featuring Lynsey MOORE *UK, male production duo and female vocalist (1 WEEK)* pos/wks

10 Jun 00	**LOVE BUG** *Nebula VCNEBD 4*	75	1

RANCID *US, male vocal / instrumental group (1 WEEK)* pos/wks

7 Oct 95	**TIME BOMB** *Out Of Step WOOS 8CDS*	56	1

RANGE – *See Bruce HORNSBY and the RANGE*

RANI – *See DELERIUM featuring RANI*

RANGERS FC *UK, male football team vocalists (2 WEEKS)* pos/wks

4 Oct 97	**GLASGOW RANGERS (NINE IN A ROW)** *Gers GERSCD 1*	54	2

RANK 1 *Holland, male production duo – Piet Bervoets and Benno De Goeij (5 WEEKS)* pos/wks

15 Apr 00 ●	**AIRWAVE** *Manifesto FESCD 69*	10	5

RANKING ANN – *See SCRITTI POLITTI*

RANKING ROGER – *See Pato BANTON*

Shabba RANKS
Jamaica, male vocalist – Rawlston Fernando Gordon (67 WEEKS) pos/wks

16 Mar 91	**SHE'S A WOMAN** *Virgin VS 1333* [1]	20	7
18 May 91	**TRAILER LOAD A GIRLS** *Epic 6568747*	63	2
24 Aug 91	**HOUSECALL** *Epic 6573477* [2]	31	7
8 Aug 92	**MR LOVERMAN** *Epic 6582517*	23	7
28 Nov 92	**SLOW AND SEXY** *Epic 6587727* [3]	17	7
6 Mar 93	**I WAS A KING** *Motown TMGCD 1414* [4]	64	1
13 Mar 93 ●	**MR LOVERMAN (re-issue)** *Epic 6590782*	3	11
8 May 93 ●	**HOUSECALL (re-mix)** *Epic 6592842* [2]	8	8
26 Jun 93	**WHAT'CHA GONNA DO** *Epic 6593072* [5]	21	4
25 Dec 93	**FAMILY AFFAIR** *Polydor PZCD 304* [6]	18	8
29 Apr 95	**LET'S GET IT ON** *Epic 6614122*	22	3
5 Aug 95	**SHINE EYE GAL** *Epic 6622332* [7]	46	2

[1] Scritti Politti featuring Shabba Ranks [2] Shabba Ranks featuring Maxi Priest [3] Shabba Ranks featuring Johnny Gill [4] Eddie Murphy featuring Shabba Ranks [5] Shabba Ranks featuring Queen Latifah [6] Shabba Ranks featuring Patra and Terri & Monica [7] Shabba Ranks (featuring Mykal Rose)

Bubbler RANX – *See Peter ANDRE*

RAPINATION *Italy, male instrumental / production duo (12 WEEKS)* pos/wks

26 Dec 92	**LOVE ME THE RIGHT WAY** *Logic 74321128097* [1]	22	10
10 Jul 93	**HERE'S MY A** *Logic 74321153092* [2]	69	1
28 Sep 96	**LOVE ME THE RIGHT WAY (re-mix)** *Logic 7432140442* [1]	55	1

[1] Rapination featuring Kym Mazelle [2] Rapination featuring Carol Kenyon

RAPPIN' 4-TAY *US, male rapper (5 WEEKS)* pos/wks

24 Jun 95	**I'LL BE AROUND** *Cooltempo CDCOOL 306* [1]	30	4
30 Sep 95	**PLAYAZ CLUB** *Cooltempo CDCOOL 310*	63	1

[1] Rappin' 4-Tay featuring the Spinners

The Spinners on 'I'll Be Around' are the Detroit Spinners

RARE *UK, male / female vocal / instrumental group (1 WEEK)* pos/wks

17 Feb 96	**SOMETHING WILD** *Equator AXISCD 011*	57	1

RARE BIRD *UK, male vocal / instrumental group (8 WEEKS)* pos/wks

14 Feb 70	**SYMPATHY** *Charisma CB 120*	27	8

O RASBURY – *See Rahni HARRIS and F.L.O.*

RASHAAN – *See US3*

Roland RAT SUPERSTAR

UK, male rodent vocalist / rapper (20 WEEKS) pos/wks

		pos	wks
19 Nov 83	**RAT RAPPING** *Rodent RAT 1*	14	12
28 Apr 84	**LOVE ME TENDER** *Rodent RAT 2*	32	7
2 Mar 85	**NO.1 RAT FAN** *Rodent RAT 4*	72	1

RATPACK *UK, male instrumental / production duo (3 WEEKS)* pos/wks

		pos	wks
6 Jun 92	**SEARCHIN' FOR MY RIZLA** *Big Giant BIGT 02*	58	3

RATTLES *Germany, male vocal / instrumental group (15 WEEKS)* pos/wks

		pos	wks
3 Oct 70 ●	**THE WITCH** *Decca F 23058*	8	15

RATTY *Germany, male production group (1 WEEK)* pos/wks

		pos	wks
24 Mar 01	**SUNRISE (HERE I AM)** *Neo NEOCD 051*	51	1

RAVESIGNAL III

Belgium, male producer – Christian Bolland (2 WEEKS) pos/wks

		pos	wks
14 Dec 91	**HORSEPOWER** *R&S RSUK 6*	61	2

See also CJ BOLLAND

RAW – *See Erick 'More' MORILLO presents RAW*

RAW SILK *US, female vocal group (12 WEEKS)* pos/wks

		pos	wks
16 Oct 82	**DO IT TO THE MUSIC** *KR KR 14*	18	9
10 Sep 83	**JUST IN TIME** *West End WEND 2*	49	3

RAW STYLUS *UK, male / female vocal / instrumental duo (1 WEEK)* pos/wks

		pos	wks
26 Oct 96	**BELIEVE IN ME** *Wired WIRED 234*	66	1

Lou RAWLS *US, male vocalist (10 WEEKS)* pos/wks

		pos	wks
31 Jul 76 ●	**YOU'LL NEVER FIND ANOTHER LOVE LIKE MINE** *Philadelphia International PIR 4372*	10	10

Gene Anthony RAY – *See KIDS FROM 'FAME'*

Jimmy RAY *UK, male vocalist – James Edwards (6 WEEKS)* pos/wks

		pos	wks
25 Oct 97	**ARE YOU JIMMY RAY?** *Sony S2 6650125*	13	5
14 Feb 98	**GOIN' TO VEGAS** *Sony S2 6654652*	49	1

Johnnie RAY (122 Top 500)

A sensation in the 1950s, the heart-wrenching vocal delivery of the 'Cry Guy' (b. 10 Jan 1927, Oregon, US, d. 25 Feb 1990) influenced many acts, including Elvis, and Ray was the prime target for teen hysteria in pre-Presley days (168 WEEKS) pos/wks

		pos	wks
14 Nov 52	**WALKIN' MY BABY BACK HOME** *Columbia DB 3060*	12	1
19 Dec 52 ●	**FAITH CAN MOVE MOUNTAINS** *Columbia DB 3154* [1]	7	2
9 Jan 53 ●	**FAITH CAN MOVE MOUNTAINS (re-entry)** *Columbia DB 3154* [1]	9	1
3 Apr 53	**MA SAYS, PA SAYS** *Columbia DB3242* [2]	12	1
10 Apr 53 ●	**SOMEBODY STOLE MY GAL** *Philips PB 123*	6	1
17 Apr 53	**FULL TIME JOB** *Columbia DB 3242* [2]	11	1
24 Apr 53 ●	**SOMEBODY STOLE MY GAL (re-entry)** *Philips PB 123*	6	4
29 May 53	**SOMEBODY STOLE MY GAL (2nd re-entry)** *Philips PB 123*	12	1
24 Jul 53 ●	**LET'S WALK THAT-A-WAY** *Philips PB 157* [2]	4	14
7 Aug 53	**SOMEBODY STOLE MY GAL (3rd re-entry)** *Philips PB 123*	11	1
9 Apr 54 ★	**SUCH A NIGHT** *Philips PB 244*	1	18
8 Apr 55	**IF YOU BELIEVE** *Philips PB 379*	15	1
13 May 55 ●	**IF YOU BELIEVE (re-entry)** *Philips PB 379*	7	10
20 May 55	**PATHS OF PARADISE** *Philips PB 441*	20	1
7 Oct 55	**HERNANDO'S HIDEAWAY** *Philips PB 495*	11	5
14 Oct 55 ●	**HEY THERE** *Philips PB 495*	5	9
28 Oct 55 ●	**SONG OF THE DREAMER** *Philips PB 516*	10	5
17 Feb 56	**WHO'S SORRY NOW** *Philips PB 546*	17	2
20 Apr 56	**AIN'T MISBEHAVIN'** *Philips PB 580*	17	6
8 Jun 56	**AIN'T MISBEHAVIN' (re-entry)** *Philips PB 580*	24	1
12 Oct 56 ★	**JUST WALKING IN THE RAIN** *Philips PB 624*	1	19
18 Jan 57	**YOU DON'T OWE ME A THING** *Philips PB 655*	12	15
8 Feb 57 ●	**LOOK HOMEWARD, ANGEL** *Philips PB 655*	7	16
10 May 57 ★	**YES, TONIGHT JOSEPHINE** *Philips PB 686*	1	16
6 Sep 57	**BUILD YOUR LOVE (ON A STRONG FOUNDATION)** *Philips PB 721*	17	7
4 Oct 57	**GOOD EVENING FRIENDS / UP ABOVE MY HEAD I HEAR MUSIC IN THE AIR** *Philips PB 708* [3]	25	4
4 Dec 59	**I'LL NEVER FALL IN LOVE AGAIN** *Philips PB 952*	26	4
8 Jan 60	**I'LL NEVER FALL IN LOVE AGAIN (re-entry)** *Philips PB 952*	26	1
5 Feb 60	**I'LL NEVER FALL IN LOVE AGAIN (2nd re-entry)** *Philips PB 952*	28	1

[1] Johnnie Ray and the Four Lads [2] Doris Day and Johnnie Ray [3] Frankie Laine and Johnnie Ray

The chart history of 'You Don't Owe Me a Thing / Look Homeward Angel' is complicated and is as follows: 'You Don't Owe Me a Thing' entered the chart by itself on 18 Jan 1957. On 8 and 15 Feb 1957, 'Look Homeward Angel' was coupled with 'You Don't Owe Me a Thing', but from 22 Feb 1957 the two sides went their individual ways on the chart and were listed separately: 'You Don't Owe Me a Thing' for a further 10 weeks and 'Look Homeward Angel' for a further 14 weeks

Nicole RAY *US, female vocalist (5 WEEKS)* pos/wks

		pos	wks
22 Aug 98	**MAKE IT HOT** *East West E 3821CD* [1]	22	4
5 Dec 98	**I CAN'T SEE** *East West E 3801CD*	55	1

[1] Nicole featuring Missy 'Misdemeanor' Elliott and Mocha

RAYDIO *US, male vocal / instrumental group (21 WEEKS)* pos/wks

		pos	wks
8 Apr 78	**JACK AND JILL** *Arista 161*	11	12
8 Jul 78	**IS THIS A LOVE THING** *Arista 193*	27	9

See also Ray PARKER Jr

RAYVON – *See SHAGGY*

RAZE *US, male / female vocal / instrumental group (47 WEEKS)* pos/wks

		pos	wks
1 Nov 86	**JACK THE GROOVE** *Champion CHAMP 23*	57	7
3 Jan 87	**JACK THE GROOVE (re-entry)** *Champion CHAMP 23*	20	8
28 Feb 87	**LET THE MUSIC MOVE U** *Champion CHAMP 27*	57	3
31 Dec 88	**BREAK 4 LOVE** *Champion CHAMP 67*	28	11
15 Jul 89	**LET IT ROLL** *Atlantic A 8866* [1]	27	5
2 Sep 89	**BREAK 4 LOVE (re-entry)** *Champion CHAMP 67*	59	5
27 Jan 90	**ALL 4 LOVE (BREAK 4 LOVE 1990)** *Champion CHAMP 228* [2]	30	5
10 Feb 90	**CAN YOU FEEL IT / CAN YOU FEEL IT** *Champion CHAMP 227* [3]	62	1
24 Sep 94	**BREAK 4 LOVE (re-mix)** *Champion CHAMPCD 314*	44	2

[1] Raze presents Doug Lazy [2] Raze featuring Lady J and Secretary of Entertainment [3] Raze / Championship Legend

'Can You Feel It' by Championship Legend is a montage of six Raze tracks

RE-FLEX *UK, male vocal / instrumental group (9 WEEKS)* pos/wks

		pos	wks
28 Jan 84	**THE POLITICS OF DANCING** *EMI FLEX 2*	28	9

Chris REA (228 Top 500)

One of the most popular UK singer / songwriters of the late 1980s, b. 4 Mar 1951, Middlesbrough. He was already a major European star by the time he finally cracked the UK Top 10 with his 18th chart entry, 'The Road to Hell (Part 2)' (120 WEEKS) pos/wks

		pos	wks
7 Oct 78	**FOOL (IF YOU THINK IT'S OVER)** *Magnet MAG 111*	30	7
21 Apr 79	**DIAMONDS** *Magnet MAG 144*	44	3
27 Mar 82	**LOVING YOU** *Magnet MAG 215*	65	3
1 Oct 83	**I CAN HEAR YOUR HEARTBEAT** *Magnet MAG 244*	60	2
17 Mar 84	**I DON'T KNOW WHAT IT IS BUT I LOVE IT** *Magnet MAG 255*	65	2
30 Mar 85	**STAINSBY GIRLS** *Magnet MAG 276*	26	10
29 Jun 85	**JOSEPHINE** *Magnet MAG 280*	67	2
29 Mar 86	**IT'S ALL GONE** *Magnet MAG 283*	69	1
31 May 86	**ON THE BEACH** *Magnet MAG 294*	57	3
28 Jun 86	**ON THE BEACH (re-entry)** *Magnet MAG 294*	75	1
12 Jul 86	**ON THE BEACH (2nd re-entry)** *Magnet MAG 294*	66	4
6 Jun 87	**LET'S DANCE** *Magnet MAG 299*	12	10
29 Aug 87	**LOVING YOU AGAIN** *Magnet MAG 300*	47	4
5 Dec 87	**JOYS OF CHRISTMAS** *Magnet MAG 314*	67	1
13 Feb 88	**QUE SERA** *Magnet MAG 318*	73	2

13 Aug 88		**ON THE BEACH SUMMER '88** *WEA YZ 195*	12	6
22 Oct 88		**I CAN HEAR YOUR HEARTBEAT** *WEA YZ 320*	74	2
17 Dec 88		**THE CHRISTMAS EP** *WEA YZ 325*	53	3
18 Feb 89		**WORKING ON IT** *WEA YZ 350*	53	3
14 Oct 89	●	**THE ROAD TO HELL (PART 2)** *WEA YZ 431*	10	9
10 Feb 90		**TELL ME THERE'S A HEAVEN** *East West YZ 455*	24	6
5 May 90		**TEXAS** *East West YZ 468*	69	1
16 Feb 91		**AUBERGE** *East West YZ 555*	16	6
6 Apr 91		**HEAVEN** *East West YZ 566*	57	2
29 Jun 91		**LOOKING FOR THE SUMMER** *East West YZ 584*	49	3
9 Nov 91		**WINTER SONG** *East West YZ 629*	27	4
24 Oct 92		**NOTHING TO FEAR** *East West YZ 699*	16	4
28 Nov 92		**GOD'S GREAT BANANA SKIN** *East West YZ 706*	31	3
30 Jan 93		**SOFT TOP HARD SHOULDER** *East West YZ 710CD*	53	2
23 Oct 93		**JULIA** *East West YZ 772CD*	18	5
12 Nov 94		**YOU CAN GO YOUR OWN WAY** *East West YZ 835CD*	28	3
24 Dec 94		**TELL ME THERE'S A HEAVEN (re-issue)** *East West YZ 885CD*	70	1
16 Nov 96		**'DISCO' LA PASSIONE** *East West EW 072CD* [1]	41	1
24 May 97		**LET'S DANCE** *Magnet EW 112CD*	44	1

[1] Chris Rea and Shirley Bassey

Both 'On the Beach Summer '88' and 'I Can Hear Your Heartbeat' in 1988 are re-recordings. Tracks on Driving Home for Christmas (EP): Driving Home for Christmas / Footsteps in the Snow / Joys of Christmas / Smile

REACT 2 RHYTHM *UK, male production group (1 WEEK)* pos/wks

28 Jun 97		**INTOXICATION** *Jackpot WIN 014CD*	73	1

Eileen READ – *See CADETS with Eileen REID*

Eddi READER *UK, female vocalist (14 WEEKS)* pos/wks

4 Jun 94		**PATIENCE OF ANGELS** *Blanco Y Negro NEG 68CD*	33	5
13 Aug 94		**JOKE (I'M LAUGHING)** *Blanco Y Negro NEG 72CD*	42	3
5 Nov 94		**DEAR JOHN** *Blanco Y Negro NEG 75CD1*	48	2
22 Jun 96		**TOWN WITHOUT PITY** *Blanco Y Negro NEG 90CD1*	26	3
21 Aug 99		**FRAGILE THING** *Track TRACK 0004A* [1]	69	1

[1] Big Country featuring Eddi Reader

See also FAIRGROUND ATTRACTION

READY FOR THE WORLD
US, male vocal / instrumental group (8 WEEKS) pos/wks

26 Oct 85		**OH SHEILA** *MCA MCA 1005* ▲	50	5
14 Mar 87		**LOVE YOU DOWN** *MCA MCA 1110*	60	3

REAL EMOTION
UK, male / female vocal / instrumental group (1 WEEK) pos/wks

1 Jul 95		**BACK FOR GOOD** *Living Beat LBECD 34*	67	1

REAL McCOY
Germany / US, male / female vocal / instrumental duo (36 WEEKS) pos/wks

6 Nov 93		**ANOTHER NIGHT** *Logic 74321173732* [1]	61	1
5 Nov 94	●	**ANOTHER NIGHT (re-issue)** *Logic 74321236992* [1]	2	12
28 Jan 95	●	**RUN AWAY** *Logic 74321258822* [1]	6	10
22 Apr 95		**LOVE AND DEVOTION** *Logic 74321272702* [1]	11	8
26 Aug 95		**COME AND GET YOUR LOVE** *Logic 74321301272*	19	4
11 Nov 95		**AUTOMATIC LOVER (CALL FOR LOVE)** *Logic 74321325042*	58	1

[1] (MC Sar &) the Real McCoy

REAL PEOPLE *UK, male vocal / instrumental group (8 WEEKS)* pos/wks

16 Feb 91		**OPEN UP YOUR MIND (LET ME IN)** *CBS 6566127*	70	1
20 Apr 91		**THE TRUTH** *Columbia 6567877*	73	1
6 Jul 91		**WINDOW PANE (EP)** *Columbia 6569327*	60	1
11 Jan 92		**THE TRUTH (re-issue)** *Columbia 6576987*	41	3
23 May 92		**BELIEVER** *Columbia 6580067*	38	2

Tracks on Window Pane (EP): Window Pane / See Through You / Everything Must Change

REAL ROXANNE *US, female rapper – Joanne Martinez (10 WEEKS)* pos/wks

28 Jun 86		**BANG ZOOM (LET'S GO GO)** *Cooltempo COOL 124* [1]	11	9
12 Nov 88		**RESPECT** *Cooltempo COOL 176*	71	1

[1] Real Roxanne with Hitman Howie Tee

REAL THING (245 Top 500) *Liverpool vocal quartet comprising brothers Chris and Eddie Amoo, Ray Lake and Dave Smith. They were the UK's best-selling black group of the late 1970s, whose biggest hits returned to the Top 10 (when re-mixed) in the 1980s (114 WEEKS)* pos/wks

5 Jun 76	★	**YOU TO ME ARE EVERYTHING** *Pye International 7N 25709*	1	11
4 Sep 76	●	**CAN'T GET BY WITHOUT YOU** *Pye 7N 45618*	2	10
12 Feb 77		**YOU'LL NEVER KNOW WHAT YOU'RE MISSING** *Pye 7N 45662*	16	9
30 Jul 77		**LOVE'S SUCH A WONDERFUL THING** *Pye 7N 45701*	33	5
4 Mar 78		**WHENEVER YOU WANT MY LOVE** *Pye 7N 46045*	18	9
3 Jun 78		**LET'S GO DISCO** *Pye 7N 46078*	39	7
12 Aug 78		**RAININ' THROUGH MY SUNSHINE** *Pye 7N 46113*	40	8
17 Feb 79	●	**CAN YOU FEEL THE FORCE?** *Pye 7N 46147*	5	11
21 Jul 79		**BOOGIE DOWN (GET FUNKY NOW)** *Pye 7P 109*	33	6
22 Nov 80		**SHE'S A GROOVY FREAK** *Calibre CAB 105*	52	4
8 Mar 86	●	**YOU TO ME ARE EVERYTHING (THE DECADE RE-MIX 76-86)** *PRT 7P 349*	5	12
24 May 86	●	**CAN'T GET BY WITHOUT YOU (THE SECOND DECADE REMIX)** *PRT 7P 352*	6	13
7 Jun 86		**YOU TO ME ARE EVERYTHING (THE DECADE REMIX 76-86) (re-entry)** *PRT 7P 349*	72	1
2 Aug 86		**CAN YOU FEEL THE FORCE? ('86 REMIX)** *PRT 7P 358*	24	6
25 Oct 86		**STRAIGHT TO THE HEART** *Jive JIVE 129*	71	2

REAL TO REEL *US, male vocal / instrumental group (2 WEEKS)* pos/wks

21 Apr 84		**LOVE ME LIKE THIS** *Arista ARIST 565*	68	2

REBEL MC *UK, male rapper – Mike West (52 WEEKS)* pos/wks

27 May 89		**JUST KEEP ROCKIN'** *Desire WANT 9* [1]	11	12
7 Oct 89	●	**STREET TUFF** *Desire WANT 18* [2]	3	14
31 Mar 90		**BETTER WORLD** *Desire WANT 25*	20	6
2 Jun 90		**REBEL MUSIC** *Desire WANT 31*	53	2
6 Apr 91		**WICKEDEST SOUND** *Desire WANT 40* [3]	43	6
15 Jun 91		**TRIBAL BASE** *Desire WANT 44* [4]	20	6
31 Aug 91		**BLACK MEANING GOOD** *Desire WANT 47*	73	1
21 Mar 92		**RICH AH GETTING RICHER** *Big Life BLR 70* [5]	48	4
8 Aug 92		**HUMANITY** *Big Life BLR 78* [6]	62	1

[1] Double Trouble and the Rebel MC [2] Rebel MC and Double Trouble [3] Rebel MC featuring Tenor Fly [4] Rebel MC featuring Tenor Fly and Barrington Levy [5] Rebel MC introducing Little T [6] Rebel MC featuring Lincoln Thompson

REBEL ROUSERS – *See Cliff BENNETT and the REBEL ROUSERS*

REBELETTES – *See Duane EDDY and the REBELS*

REBELS – *See Duane EDDY and the REBELS*

Ezz RECO and the LAUNCHERS with Boysie GRANT
Jamaica, male vocal / instrumental group (4 WEEKS) pos/wks

5 Mar 64		**KING OF KINGS** *Columbia DB 7217*	44	4

RECOIL *UK, male vocal / instrumental group (1 WEEK)* pos/wks

21 Mar 92		**FAITH HEALER** *Mute MUTE 110*	60	1

RED *UK, male production duo – Ian Bland and Paul Fitzpatrick (1 WEEK)* pos/wks

20 Feb 01		**HEAVEN & EARTH** *Slinky Music SLINKY 008CD*	41	1

See also BEAT RENEGADES; DREAM FREQUENCY

RED BOX *UK, male vocal / instrumental duo – Julian Close and Simon Toulson (28 WEEKS)* pos/wks

24 Aug 85	●	**LEAN ON ME (AH-LI-AYO)** *Sire W 8926*	3	14
25 Oct 86	●	**FOR AMERICA** *Sire YZ 84*	10	12
31 Jan 87		**HEART OF THE SUN** *Sire YZ 100*	71	2

RED CAR AND THE BLUE CAR
UK, male vocal / instrumental group (4 WEEKS) pos/wks

14 Dec 91	**HOME FOR CHRISTMAS DAY** *Virgin VS 1394*	44 4

RED DRAGON with Brian and Tony GOLD
Jamaica, male vocal group (15 WEEKS) pos/wks

30 Jul 94 ●	**COMPLIMENTS ON YOUR KISS** *Mango CIDM 820*	2 13
31 Dec 94	**COMPLIMENTS ON YOUR KISS (re-entry)** *Mango CIDM 820*	49 2

RED EYE *UK, male instrumental / production duo (1 WEEK)* pos/wks

3 Dec 94	**KUT IT** *Champion CHAMPCD 315*	62 1

RED 5 *Germany, male producer – Thomas Kukula (10 WEEKS)* pos/wks

10 May 97	**I LOVE YOU … STOP!** *Multiply CDMULTY 20*	11 5
20 Dec 97	**LIFT ME UP** *Multiply CDMULTY 30*	26 5

RED HED – See *VINYLGROOVER and The RED HED*

RED HILL CHILDREN *UK, male / female children's choir (2 WEEKS)* pos/wks

30 Nov 96	**WHEN CHILDREN RULE THE WORLD** *Really Useful 5797262*	40 2

RED HOT CHILI PEPPERS
US, male vocal / instrumental group (58 WEEKS) pos/wks

10 Feb 90	**HIGHER GROUND** *EMI-USA MT 75*	55 3
23 Jun 90	**TASTE THE PAIN** *EMI-USA MT 85*	29 3
8 Sep 90	**HIGHER GROUND (re-issue)** *EMI-USA MT 88*	54 3
14 Mar 92	**UNDER THE BRIDGE** *Warner Bros. W 0084*	26 4
15 Aug 92	**BREAKING THE GIRL** *Warner Bros. W 0126*	41 3
5 Feb 94 ●	**GIVE IT AWAY** *Warner Bros. W 0225CD1*	9 4
30 Apr 94	**UNDER THE BRIDGE (re-issue)** *Warner Bros. W 0237CD*	13 6
2 Sep 95	**WARPED** *Warner Bros. W 0316CD*	31 2
21 Oct 95	**MY FRIENDS** *Warner Bros. W 0317CD*	29 2
17 Feb 96	**AEROPLANE** *Warner Bros. W 0331CD*	11 3
14 Jun 97 ●	**LOVE ROLLERCOASTER** *Geffen GFSTD 22188*	7 8
12 Jun 99	**SCAR TISSUE** *Warner Bros. W 490CD*	15 6
4 Sep 99	**AROUND THE WORLD** *Warner Bros. W 500CD1*	35 2
12 Feb 00	**OTHERSIDE** *Warner Bros. W 510CD1*	33 2
19 Aug 00	**CALIFORNICATION** *Warner Bros W 534CD*	16 5
13 Jan 01	**ROAD TRIPPIN'** *Warner Bros. W 546CD1*	30 2

RED JERRY – See *WESTBAM*

RED RAT – See *CARNIVAL featuring RIP vs RED RAT; Curtis LYNCH Jr featuring Kele LE ROC and RED RAT*

RED RAW featuring 007 *UK, male vocal / instrumental duo (1 WEEK)* pos/wks

28 Oct 95	**OOH LA LA LA** *Media MCSTD 2065*	59 1

RED SNAPPER
UK, male vocal / instrumental / production group (1 WEEK) pos/wks

21 Nov 98	**IMAGE OF YOU** *Warp WAP 111CD*	60 1

RED VENOM – See *BIG BOSS STYLUS presents RED VENOM*

REDBONE *US, male vocal / instrumental group (12 WEEKS)* pos/wks

25 Sep 71 ●	**WITCH QUEEN OF NEW ORLEANS** *Epic EPC 7351*	2 12

REDD KROSS *US, male vocal / instrumental group (4 WEEKS)* pos/wks

5 Feb 94	**VISIONARY** *This Way Up WAY 2733*	75 1
10 Sep 94	**YESTERDAY ONCE MORE** *A & M 5807932*	45 2
1 Feb 97	**GET OUT OF MYSELF** *This Way Up WAY 5466*	63 1

The listed flip side of 'Yesterday Once More' was 'Superstar' by Sonic Youth

Sharon REDD *US, female vocalist (32 WEEKS)* pos/wks

28 Feb 81	**CAN YOU HANDLE IT** *Epic EPC 9572*	31 8
2 Oct 82	**NEVER GIVE YOU UP** *Prelude PRL A2755*	20 9
15 Jan 83	**IN THE NAME OF LOVE** *Prelude PRL A2905*	31 5
22 Oct 83	**LOVE HOW YOU FEEL** *Prelude A3868*	39 5
1 Feb 92	**CAN YOU HANDLE IT (re-recording)** *EMI EM 219* [1]	17 5

[1] DNA featuring Sharon Redd

Otis REDDING (218 Top 500)
Peerless singer / songwriter, b. 9 Sep 1941, Georgia, US, d. 10 Dec 1967. He was one of the first and most influential Sixties soul stars. He replaced Elvis as the World's Top Male Singer in a Melody Maker poll shortly before his death in a plane crash (124 WEEKS) pos/wks

25 Nov 65	**MY GIRL** *Atlantic AT 4050*	11 16
7 Apr 66	**(I CAN'T GET NO) SATISFACTION** *Atlantic AT 4080*	33 4
14 Jul 66	**MY LOVER'S PRAYER** *Atlantic 584 019*	37 6
25 Aug 66	**I CAN'T TURN YOU LOOSE** *Atlantic 584 030*	29 8
24 Nov 66	**FA-FA-FA-FA-FA (SAD SONG)** *Atlantic 584 049*	23 9
26 Jan 67	**TRY A LITTLE TENDERNESS** *Atlantic 584 070*	46 4
23 Mar 67	**DAY TRIPPER** *Stax 601 005*	43 6
4 May 67	**LET ME COME ON HOME** *Stax 601 007*	48 1
15 Jun 67	**SHAKE** *Stax 601 011*	28 10
19 Jul 67	**TRAMP** *Stax 601 012* [1]	18 11
11 Oct 67	**KNOCK ON WOOD** *Stax 601 021* [1]	35 5
14 Feb 68	**MY GIRL (re-issue)** *Atlantic 584 092*	36 9
21 Feb 68 ●	**(SITTIN' ON) THE DOCK OF THE BAY** *Stax 601 031* ▲	3 15
29 May 68	**THE HAPPY SONG (DUM-DUM)** *Stax 601 040*	24 5
31 Jul 68	**HARD TO HANDLE** *Atlantic 584 199*	15 12
9 Jul 69	**LOVE MAN** *Atco 226 001*	43 3

[1] Otis Redding and Carla Thomas

Helen REDDY *Australia, female vocalist (18 WEEKS)* pos/wks

18 Jan 75 ●	**ANGIE BABY** *Capitol CL 15799* ▲	5 10
28 Nov 81	**I CAN'T SAY GOODBYE TO YOU** *MCA 744*	43 8

REDHEAD KINGPIN and the FBI
US, male rapper – David Guppy (11 WEEKS) pos/wks

22 Jul 89	**DO THE RIGHT THING** *10 TEN 271*	13 10
2 Dec 89	**SUPERBAD SUPERSLICK** *10 TEN 286*	68 1

REDMAN *US, male rapper – Reggie Noble (22 WEEKS)* pos/wks

25 Apr 98	**RAP SCHOLAR** *East West E 3853CD* [1]	42 1
30 May 98	**MADE IT BACK** *Parlophone Rhythm CDRHYTHM 11* [2]	21 3
24 Oct 98 ●	**HOW DEEP IS YOUR LOVE** *Island Black Music CID 725* [3]	9 7
16 Jan 99	**HOW DEEP IS YOUR LOVE (re-entry)** *Island Black Music CID 725* [3]	75 1
12 Jun 99	**DA GOODNESS** *Def Jam 8709232*	52 1
22 Jul 00	**OOOH** *Tommy Boy TBCD 2102* [4]	29 2
15 Sep 01	**SMASH SUMTHIN'** *Def Jam 5886932* [5]	11 7

[1] Das EFX featuring Redman [2] Beverley Knight featuring Redman [3] Dru Hill featuring Redman [4] De La Soul featuring Redman [5] Redman featuring Adam F

REDNEX *Sweden, male / female vocal / instrumental group (23 WEEKS)* pos/wks

17 Dec 94 ★	**COTTON EYE JOE** *Internal Affairs KGBCD 016*	1 16
25 Mar 95	**OLD POP IN AN OAK** *Internal Affairs KGBD 019*	12 6
21 Oct 95	**WILD 'N FREE** *Internal Affairs KGBD 024*	55 1

REDS UNITED
UK, male vocal group – 40 Manchester United FC fans (13 WEEKS) pos/wks

6 Dec 97	**SING UP FOR THE CHAMPIONS** *Music Collection MANUCDP 2*	12 9
9 May 98	**UNITED CALYPSO '98** *Music Collection MANUCDP 3*	33 4

REDSKINS *UK, male vocal / instrumental duo (12 WEEKS)* pos/wks

10 Nov 84	**KEEP ON KEEPIN' ON** *Decca F 1*	43 5
22 Jun 85	**BRING IT DOWN (THIS INSANE THING)** *Decca F 2*	33 5
22 Feb 86	**THE POWER IS YOURS** *Decca F 3*	59 2

Alex REECE *UK, male producer (7 WEEKS)* pos/wks

16 Dec 95	**FEEL THE SUNSHINE** *Blunted Vinyl BLNCD 016*	69 1
11 May 96	**FEEL THE SUNSHINE (re-mix)** *Fourth & Broadway BRCD 332*	26 3
27 Jul 96	**CANDLES** *Fourth & Broadway BRCD 333*	33 2
18 Nov 96	**ACID LAB** *Fourth & Broadway BRCD 344*	64 1

Jimmy REED *US, male vocalist (2 WEEKS)* pos/wks

10 Sep 64	**SHAME, SHAME, SHAME** *Stateside SS 330*	45	2

Lou REED *US, male vocalist – Lou Firbank (19 WEEKS)* pos/wks

12 May 73 ●	**WALK ON THE WILD SIDE** *RCA 2303*	10	9
17 Jan 87	**SOUL MAN** *A & M AM 364* [1]	30	10

[1] Sam Moore and Lou Reed

Dan REED NETWORK
US, male vocal / instrumental group (16 WEEKS) pos/wks

20 Jan 90	**COME BACK BABY** *Mercury DRN 2*	51	3
17 Mar 90	**RAINBOW CHILD** *Mercury DRN 3*	60	3
21 Jul 90	**STARDATE 1990 / RAINBOW CHILD (re-issue)** *Mercury DRN 4*	39	4
8 Sep 90	**LOVER / MONEY** *Mercury DRN 5*	45	3
13 Jul 91	**MIX IT UP** *Mercury MER 345*	49	2
21 Sep 91	**BABY NOW I** *Mercury MER 352*	65	1

Michael REED ORCHESTRA – *See Richard HARTLEY / Michael REED ORCHESTRA*

REEF *UK, male vocal / instrumental group (46 WEEKS)* pos/wks

15 Apr 95	**GOOD FEELING** *Sony S2 6613602*	24	4
3 Jun 95	**NAKED** *Sony S2 6620622*	11	5
5 Aug 95	**WEIRD** *Sony S2 6622772*	19	3
2 Nov 96 ●	**PLACE YOUR HANDS** *Sony S2 6635712*	6	7
25 Jan 97 ●	**COME BACK BRIGHTER** *Sony S2 6640972*	8	5
5 Apr 97	**CONSIDERATION** *Sony S2 6643125*	13	4
2 Aug 97	**YER OLD** *Sony S2 6647032*	21	3
10 Apr 99	**I'VE GOT SOMETHING TO SAY** *Sony S2 6669542*	15	6
5 Jun 99	**SWEETY** *Sony S2 6673732*	46	1
11 Sep 99	**NEW BIRD** *Sony S2 6678512*	73	1
12 Aug 00	**SET THE RECORD STRAIGHT** *Sony S2 6695952*	19	5
16 Dec 00	**SUPERHERO** *Sony S2 66999382*	55	1
19 May 01	**ALL I WANT** *Sony S2 6708222*	51	1

REEL *Ireland, male vocal group (1 WEEK)* pos/wks

24 Nov 01	**LIFT ME UP** *Universal TV 0154632*	39	1

REEL 2 REAL *US, male vocal / production duo – Erick Morillo and Mark 'The Mad Stuntman' Quashie (53 WEEKS)* pos/wks

12 Feb 94 ●	**I LIKE TO MOVE IT** *Positiva CDTIV 10* [1]	5	20
2 Jul 94 ●	**GO ON MOVE** *Positiva CDTIV 15* [1]	7	9
1 Oct 94	**CAN YOU FEEL IT** *Positiva CDTIV 22* [1]	13	5
3 Dec 94	**RAISE YOUR HANDS** *Positiva CDTIV 27* [1]	14	6
1 Apr 95	**CONWAY** *Positiva CDTIVS 30* [1]	27	4
6 Jul 96 ●	**JAZZ IT UP** *Positiva CDTIV 59*	7	7
5 Oct 96	**ARE YOU READY FOR SOME MORE** *Positiva CDTIV 56*	24	2

[1] Reel 2 Real featuring the Mad Stuntman

See also LIL MO' YIN YANG, ERICK 'MORE' MORILLO

Maureen REES *UK, female (TV learner driver) vocalist (4 WEEKS)* pos/wks

20 Dec 97	**DRIVING IN MY CAR** *Eagle EAGXS 014*	49	4

Tony REES and the COTTAGERS *UK, male vocal group (1 WEEK)* pos/wks

10 May 75	**VIVA EL FULHAM** *Sonet SON 2059*	46	1

REESE PROJECT *US, male producer – Kevin Saunderson (7 WEEKS)* pos/wks

8 Aug 92	**THE COLOUR OF LOVE** *Network NWK 51*	52	2
12 Dec 92	**I BELIEVE** *Network NWKT 63*	74	1
13 Mar 93	**SO DEEP** *Network NWKCD 68*	54	2
24 Sep 94	**THE COLOUR OF LOVE (re-mix)** *Network NWKCD 81*	55	1
6 May 95	**DIRECT-ME** *Network NWKCD 87*	44	1

Conner REEVES *UK, male vocalist (18 WEEKS)* pos/wks

30 Aug 97	**MY FATHER'S SON** *Wildstar CDWILD 1*	12	5
22 Nov 97	**EARTHBOUND** *Wildstar CDWILD 2*	14	4
11 Apr 98	**READ MY MIND** *Wildstar CXWILD 4*	19	4
3 Oct 98	**SEARCHING FOR A SOUL** *Wildstar CDWILD 6*	28	2
4 Sep 99	**BEST FRIEND** *WEA WEA 221CD1* [1]	23	3

[1] Mark Morrison and Conner Reeves

Jim REEVES (24 Top 500) *Internationally acclaimed velvet-voiced vocalist b. 20 Aug 1924, Texas, US, d. 31 Jul 1964. 'Gentleman Jim' had an impressive portfolio of posthumous hits, including a record-breaking eight albums simultaneously on the UK chart three months after his death (322 WEEKS)* pos/wks

24 Mar 60	**HE'LL HAVE TO GO** *RCA 1168*	36	1
7 Apr 60	**HE'LL HAVE TO GO (re-entry)** *RCA 1168*	12	30
16 Mar 61	**WHISPERING HOPE** *RCA 1223*	50	1
23 Nov 61	**YOU'RE THE ONLY GOOD THING (THAT HAPPENED TO ME)** *RCA 1261*	17	19
28 Jun 62	**ADIOS AMIGO** *RCA 1293*	23	21
22 Nov 62	**I'M GONNA CHANGE EVERYTHING** *RCA 1317*	42	2
13 Jun 63 ●	**WELCOME TO MY WORLD** *RCA 1342*	6	15
17 Oct 63	**GUILTY** *RCA 1364*	29	7
20 Feb 64 ●	**I LOVE YOU BECAUSE** *RCA 1385*	5	39
18 Jun 64 ●	**I WON'T FORGET YOU** *RCA 1400*	3	25
5 Nov 64 ●	**THERE'S A HEARTACHE FOLLOWING ME** *RCA 1423*	6	13
7 Jan 65	**I WON'T FORGET YOU (re-entry)** *RCA 1400*	47	1
4 Feb 65 ●	**IT HURTS SO MUCH (TO SEE YOU GO)** *RCA 1437*	8	10
15 Apr 65	**NOT UNTIL THE NEXT TIME** *RCA 1446*	13	12
6 May 65	**HOW LONG HAS IT BEEN** *RCA 1445*	45	5
15 Jul 65	**THIS WORLD IS NOT MY HOME** *RCA 1412*	22	9
11 Nov 65	**IS IT REALLY OVER** *RCA 1488*	17	9
18 Aug 66 ★	**DISTANT DRUMS** *RCA 1537*	1	25
2 Feb 67	**I WON'T COME IN WHILE HE'S THERE** *RCA 1563*	12	11
26 Jul 67	**TRYING TO FORGET** *RCA 1611*	33	5
22 Nov 67	**I HEARD A HEART BREAK LAST NIGHT** *RCA 1643*	38	6
27 Mar 68	**PRETTY BROWN EYES** *RCA 1672*	33	5
25 Jun 69	**WHEN TWO WORLDS COLLIDE** *RCA 1830*	17	17
6 Dec 69	**BUT YOU LOVE ME, DADDY** *RCA 1899*	15	16
21 Mar 70	**NOBODY'S FOOL** *RCA 1915*	32	5
12 Sep 70	**ANGELS DON'T LIE** *RCA 1997*	44	1
26 Sep 70	**ANGELS DON'T LIE (re-entry)** *RCA 1997*	32	2
26 Jun 71	**I LOVE YOU BECAUSE / HE'LL HAVE TO GO (re-issue) / MOONLIGHT & ROSES** *RCA Maximillion 2092*	34	8
19 Feb 72	**YOU'RE FREE TO GO** *RCA 2174*	48	2

Martha REEVES and the VANDELLAS (385 Top 500) *Fronted by Martha Reeves, b. 18 Jul 1941, Alabama, US, previously a secretary and backing vocalist for the Motown label. The female trio made their UK Top 20 debut six years after doing the same in the US and were inducted into the Rock and Roll Hall of Fame in 1995 (85 WEEKS)* pos/wks

29 Oct 64	**DANCING IN THE STREET** *Stateside SS 345* [1]	28	8
1 Apr 65	**NOWHERE TO RUN** *Tamla Motown TMG 502* [1]	26	8
1 Dec 66	**I'M READY FOR LOVE** *Tamla Motown TMG 582* [1]	22	8
30 Mar 67	**JIMMY MACK** *Tamla Motown TMG 599* [1]	21	9
17 Jan 68	**HONEY CHILE** *Tamla Motown TMG 636*	30	9
15 Jan 69 ●	**DANCING IN THE STREET (re-issue)** *Tamla Motown TMG 684*	4	12
16 Apr 69	**NOWHERE TO RUN (re-issue)** *Tamla Motown TMG 694*	42	3
29 Aug 70	**JIMMY MACK (re-entry)** *Tamla Motown TMG 599* [1]	21	12
13 Feb 71	**FORGET ME NOT** *Tamla Motown TMG 762*	11	8
8 Jan 72	**BLESS YOU** *Tamla Motown TMG 794*	33	5
23 Jul 88	**NOWHERE TO RUN (2nd re-issue)** *A&M AM 444*	52	3

[1] Martha and the Vandellas

The listed flip side of 'Nowhere to Run' in 1988 was 'I Got You (I Feel Good)' by James Brown

Vic REEVES *UK, male comedian / vocalist – Jim Moir (29 WEEKS)* pos/wks

27 Apr 91 ●	**BORN FREE** *Sense SIGH 710* [1]	6	6
26 Oct 91 ★	**DIZZY** *Sense SIGH 712* [2]	1	12
14 Dec 91	**ABIDE WITH ME** *Sense SIGH 713*	47	3
8 Jul 95 ●	**I'M A BELIEVER** *Parlophone CDR 6412* [3]	3	8

[1] Vic Reeves and the Roman Numerals [2] Vic Reeves and the Wonder Stuff
[3] EMF and Reeves and Mortimer

REFLEX featuring MC VIPER *UK, male production duo – Danny Harrison and Julian Jonah and male rapper (1 WEEK)* pos/wks

19 May 01	**PUT YOUR HANDS UP** *Gusto CDGUS 2*	72	1

See also 187 LOCKDOWN

REFUGEE ALLSTARS – *See* ...

REFUGEE CAMP ...

REFU ...

pos/wks

...	8	1
...	9	4
...	5	8
...	20	1
...	3	10
...	18	1
...	6	8
...	19	1
...	9	16
...	29	1
...	29	1
...	29	8
...	47	1
...	42	1

...n Brothers

...KS) pos/wks

...	11	12
...	55	2

...EEK) pos/wks

...	59	1

pos/wks

...	35	9
...	71	2

[1] Featuring Jazzy Joyce

REGGAE REVOLUTION – *See Pato BANTON*

REGGIE – *See TECHNOTRONIC*

REGINA *US, female vocalist (3 WEEKS)* pos/wks

1 Feb 86	**BABY LOVE** *Funkin' Marvellous MARV 01*	50	3

REID *UK, male vocal group (12 WEEKS)* pos/wks

8 Oct 88	**ONE WAY OUT** *Syncopate SY 16*	66	2
11 Feb 89	**REAL EMOTION** *Syncopate SY 24*	65	2
15 Apr 89	**GOOD TIMES** *Syncopate SY 27*	55	6
21 Oct 89	**LOVIN' ON THE SIDE** *Syncopate REID 1*	71	2

Ellen REID – *See CRASH TEST DUMMIES*

John REID – *See NIGHTCRAWLERS featuring John REID*

Junior REID – *See COLDCUT; RAGGA TWINS; SOUP DRAGONS*

Mike REID *UK, male actor / comedian (10 WEEKS)* pos/wks

22 Mar 75 ●	**THE UGLY DUCKLING** *Pye 7N 45434*	10	8
24 Apr 99	**THE MORE I SEE YOU** *Telstar TV CDSTAS 3049* [1]	46	2

[1] Barbara Windsor and Mike Reid

Neil REID *UK, male vocalist (26 WEEKS)* pos/wks

1 Jan 72 ●	**MOTHER OF MINE** *Decca F 13264*	2	20
8 Apr 72	**THAT'S WHAT I WANT TO BE** *Decca F 13300*	49	1
22 Apr 72	**THAT'S WHAT I WANT TO BE (re-entry)** *Decca F 13300*	45	5

Patrick REID – *See POB featuring DJ Patrick REID*

Maggie REILLY – *See Mike OLDFIELD*

Keith RELF *UK, male vocalist (1 WEEK)* pos/wks

26 May 66	**MR. ZERO** *Columbia DB 7920*	50	1

R.E.M. (128 Top 500) *"America's Best Rock Band", according to Rolling Stone: Michael Stipe (v), Peter Buck (g), Mike Mills (b), Bill Berry (d) (no longer in band). This Georgia group went from the US college circuit to packing stadiums worldwide. In 1996, the award-winning, platinum-album-earning quartet signed an $80 million record deal (164 WEEKS)* pos/wks

28 Nov 87	**THE ONE I LOVE** *IRS IRM 46*	51	8
30 Apr 88	**FINEST WORKSONG** *IRS IRM 161*	50	2
4 Feb 89	**STAND** *Warner Bros. W 7577*	51	3
3 Jun 89	**ORANGE CRUSH** *Warner Bros. W 2960*	28	5
12 Aug 89	**STAND (re-issue)** *Warner Bros. W 2833*	48	2
9 Mar 91	**LOSING MY RELIGION** *Warner Bros. W 0015*	19	9
18 May 91 ●	**SHINY HAPPY PEOPLE** *Warner Bros. W 0027*	6	11
17 Aug 91	**NEAR WILD HEAVEN** *Warner Bros. W 0055*	27	4
21 Sep 91	**THE ONE I LOVE (re-issue)** *IRS IRM 178*	16	6
16 Nov 91	**RADIO SONG** *Warner Bros. W 0072*	28	3
14 Dec 91	**IT'S THE END OF THE WORLD AS WE KNOW IT** *IRS IRM 180*	39	4
3 Oct 92	**DRIVE** *Warner Bros. W 0136*	11	5
28 Nov 92	**MAN ON THE MOON** *Warner Bros. W 0143*	18	8
20 Feb 93	**THE SIDEWINDER SLEEPS TONITE** *Warner Bros. W 0152CD1*	17	6
17 Apr 93 ●	**EVERYBODY HURTS** *Warner Bros W 0169CD1*	7	12
24 Jul 93	**NIGHTSWIMMING** *Warner Bros. W 0184CD*	27	5
11 Dec 93	**FIND THE RIVER** *Warner Bros. W 0211CD*	54	1
17 Sep 94 ●	**WHAT'S THE FREQUENCY, KENNETH** *Warner Bros. W 0265CD*	9	7
12 Nov 94	**BANG AND BLAME** *Warner Bros. W 0275CD*	15	4
4 Feb 95	**CRUSH WITH EYELINER** *Warner Bros. W 0281CD*	23	3
15 Apr 95 ●	**STRANGE CURRENCIES** *Warner Bros. W 0290CD*	9	4
29 Jul 95	**TONGUE** *Warner Bros. W 0308CD*	13	5
31 Aug 96 ●	**E-BOW THE LETTER** *Warner Bros. W 0369CD*	4	5
2 Nov 96	**BITTERSWEET ME** *Warner Bros. W 0377CD*	19	2
14 Dec 96	**ELECTROLITE** *Warner Bros. W 0383CD*	29	2
24 Oct 98 ●	**DAYSLEEPER** *Warner Bros. W 0455CD*	6	6
19 Dec 98	**LOTUS** *Warner Bros. W 466CD*	26	5
20 Mar 99 ●	**AT MY MOST BEAUTIFUL** *Warner Bros. W 477CD*	10	4
5 Feb 00 ●	**THE GREAT BEYOND** *Warner Bros. W 516CD*	3	10
12 May 01 ●	**IMITATION OF LIFE** *Warner Bros. W 559CD*	6	9
4 Aug 01	**ALL THE WAY TO RENO** *Warner Bros. W 568CD*	24	3
1 Dec 01	**I'LL TAKE THE RAIN** *Warner Bros. W 573CD*	44	1

REMBRANDTS *US, male vocal / instrumental group (28 WEEKS)* pos/wks

2 Sep 95 ●	**I'LL BE THERE FOR YOU (THEME FROM 'FRIENDS')** *East West A 4390CD*	3	12
20 Jan 96	**THIS HOUSE IS NOT A HOME** *East West A 4336CD*	58	1
24 May 97 ●	**I'LL BE THERE FOR YOU (THEME FROM 'FRIENDS') (re-entry)** *East West A 4390CD*	5	15

REMO FOUR – *See Tommy QUICKLY*

RENAISSANCE *UK, male / female vocal / instrumental group (11 WEEKS)* pos/wks

15 Jul 78 ●	**NORTHERN LIGHTS** *Warner Bros. K 17177*	10	11

RENÉ and ANGELA *US, male / female vocal duo (15 WEEKS)* pos/wks

15 Jun 85	**SAVE YOUR LOVE (FOR NUMBER 1)** *Club JAB 14* [1]	66	2
7 Sep 85	**I'LL BE GOOD** *Club JAB 18*	22	10
2 Nov 85	**SECRET RENDEZVOUS** *Champion CHAMP 5*	54	3

[1] René and Angela featuring Kurtis Blow

RENÉ and YVETTE *UK, male / female vocal duo (4 WEEKS)* pos/wks

22 Nov 86	**JE T'AIME (ALLO ALLO) / RENE DMC (DEVASTATING MACHO CHARISMA)** *Sedition EDIT 3319*	57	4

Nicole RENEE *US, female vocalist (1 WEEK)* pos/wks

12 Dec 98	**STRAWBERRY** *Atlantic AT 0050CD*	55	1

RENÉE and RENATO *UK / Italy, female / male vocal duo – Hilary Lester and Renato Pagliari (22 WEEKS)* pos/wks

30 Oct 82 ★	**SAVE YOUR LOVE** *Hollywood HWD 003*	1	16
12 Feb 83	**JUST ONE MORE KISS** *Hollywood HWD 006*	48	6

RENEGADE SOUNDWAVE
UK, male vocal / instrumental group (7 WEEKS) pos/wks

3 Feb 90	**PROBABLY A ROBBERY** *Mute MUTE 102*	38	6
5 Feb 94	**RENEGADE SOUNDWAVE** *Mute CDMUTE 146*	64	1

REO SPEEDWAGON
US, male vocal / instrumental group (38 WEEKS) pos/wks

11 Apr 81 ●	**KEEP ON LOVING YOU** *Epic EPC 9544* ▲	7	14
27 Jun 81	**TAKE IT ON THE RUN** *Epic EPC A 1207*	19	14
16 Mar 85	**CAN'T FIGHT THIS FEELING** *Epic A 4880* ▲	16	10

REPARATA and the DELRONS
US, female vocal group (12 WEEKS) pos/wks

20 Mar 68	**CAPTAIN OF YOUR SHIP** *Bell 1002*	13	10
18 Oct 75	**SHOES** *Dart 2066 562* [1]	43	2

[1] Reparata

REPUBLICA
UK, male / female vocal / instrumental group (18 WEEKS) pos/wks

27 Apr 96	**READY TO GO** *Deconstruction 74321326132*	43	2
1 Mar 97	**READY TO GO (re-issue)** *Deconstruction 74321421332*	13	6
3 May 97 ●	**DROP DEAD GORGEOUS** *Deconstruction 74321408442*	7	7
3 Oct 98	**FROM RUSH HOUR WITH LOVE** *Deconstruction 74321610472*	20	3

See also SAFFRON

RESONANCE featuring The BURRELLS
US, male producer and male vocal duo (1 WEEK) pos/wks

26 May 01	**DJ** *Strictly Rhythm SRUKCD 02*	67	1

REST ASSURED *UK, male production trio (7 WEEKS)* pos/wks

28 Feb 98	**TREAT INFAMY** *ffrr FCD 333*	14	7

REUNION *US, male vocal group (4 WEEKS)* pos/wks

21 Sep 74	**LIFE IS A ROCK (BUT THE RADIO ROLLED ME)** *RCA PB 10056*	33	4

REVILLOS – *See REZILLOS*

REVIVAL 3000 *UK, male DJ / production trio (1 WEEK)* pos/wks

1 Nov 97	**THE MIGHTY HIGH** *Hi-Life 5718092*	47	1

REVOLTING COCKS *US, male vocal / instrumental group (1 WEEK)* pos/wks

18 Sep 93	**DA YA THINK I'M SEXY** *Devotion CDDVN 111*	61	1

REVOLUTION – *See PRINCE*

Debbie REYNOLDS *US, female vocalist (17 WEEKS)* pos/wks

30 Aug 57 ●	**TAMMY** *Vogue-Coral Q 72274* ▲	2	17

Jody REYNOLDS *US, male vocalist (1 WEEK)* pos/wks

14 Apr 79	**ENDLESS SLEEP** *Lightning LIG 9015*	66	1

'Endless Sleep' was coupled with 'To Know Him Is to Love Him' by the Teddy Bears as a double A-side

LJ REYNOLDS *US, male vocalist (3 WEEKS)* pos/wks

30 Jun 84	**DON'T LET NOBODY HOLD YOU DOWN** *Club JAB 5*	53	3

REYNOLDS GIRLS
UK, female vocal duo – Linda and Aisling Reynolds (12 WEEKS) pos/wks

25 Feb 89 ●	**I'D RATHER JACK** *PWL PWL 25*	8	12

REZILLOS *UK, male / female vocal / instrumental group (21 WEEKS)* pos/wks

12 Aug 78	**TOP OF THE POPS** *Sire SIR 4001*	17	9
25 Nov 78	**DESTINATION VENUS** *Sire SIR 4008*	43	4
18 Aug 79	**I WANNA BE YOUR MAN / I CAN'T STAND MY BABY** *Sensible SAB 1*	71	1
1 Sep 79	**I WANNA BE YOUR MAN / I CAN'T STAND MY BABY (re-entry)** *Sensible SAB 1*	75	1
26 Jan 80	**MOTORBIKE BEAT** *Dindisc DIN 5* [1]	45	6

[1] Revillos

RHC *Belgium, male / female vocal / instrumental duo (1 WEEK)* pos/wks

11 Jan 92	**FEVER CALLED LOVE** *R&S RSUK 9*	65	1

RHODA with The SPECIAL AKA
UK, female vocalist and male vocal / instrumental group (5 WEEKS) pos/wks

23 Jan 82	**THE BOILER** *2 Tone CHSTT 18* [1]	35	5

See also SPECIALS

Busta RHYMES *US, male rapper – Trevor Smith (59 WEEKS)* pos/wks

11 May 96 ●	**WOO-HAH!! GOT YOU ALL IN CHECK** *Elektra EKR 220CD*	8	7
21 Sep 96	**IT'S A PARTY** *Elektra EKR 226CD* [1]	23	2
5 Apr 97 ●	**HIT EM HIGH (THE MONSTARS' ANTHEM)** *Atlantic A 5449CD* [2]	8	6
3 May 97	**DO MY THING** *Elektra EKR 235CD*	39	1
18 Oct 97	**PUT YOUR HANDS WHERE MY EYES COULD SEE** *Elektra E 3900CD*	16	3
20 Dec 97	**DANGEROUS** *Elektra E 3877CD*	32	4
18 Apr 98 ●	**TURN IT UP / FIRE IT UP** *Elektra E 3847CD*	2	10
11 Jul 98	**ONE** *Elektra E 3833CD1* [3]	23	3
30 Jan 99 ●	**GIMME SOME MORE** *Elektra E 3782CD*	5	6
1 May 99 ●	**WHAT'S IT GONNA BE?!** *Elektra E 3762CD1* [4]	6	7
22 Jul 00	**GET OUT** *Elektra E 7075CD*	57	1
16 Dec 00	**FIRE** *East West E 7136*	60	1
18 Aug 01 ●	**ANTE UP** *Epic 6717882* [5]	7	7
13 Oct 01	**ANTE UP (re-entry)** *Epic 6717882* [5]	65	1

[1] Busta Rhymes featuring Zhane [2] B Real / Busta Rhymes / Coolio / LL Cool J / Method Man [3] Busta Rhymes featuring Erykah Badu [4] Busta Rhymes featuring Janet [5] M.O.P. featuring Busta Rhymes

RHYTHIM IS RHYTHIM *US, male production group (1 WEEK)* pos/wks

11 Nov 89	**STRINGS OF LIFE** *Kool Kat KOOL 509*	74	1

RHYTHM BANGERS – *See Robbie RIVERA presents RHYTHM BANGERS*

RHYTHM ETERNITY
UK, male / female vocal / instrumental group (1 WEEK) pos/wks

23 May 92	**PINK CHAMPAGNE** *Dead Dead Good GOOD 15T*	72	1

RHYTHM FACTOR
US, male / female vocal / instrumental group (2 WEEKS) pos/wks

29 Apr 95	**YOU BRING ME JOY** *Multiply CDMULTY 4*	53	2

RHYTHM MASTERS *UK / Malta, male DJ / production duo (3 WEEKS)* pos/wks

16 Aug 97	**COME ON Y'ALL** *Faze 2 CDFAZE 37*	49	1
6 Dec 97	**ENTER THE SCENE** *Distinctive DISNCD 40* [1]	49	1
18 Aug 01	**UNDERGROUND** *Black & Blue NEOCD 056*	50	1

[1] DJ Supreme vs the Rhythm Masters

See also BIG ROOM GIRL featuring Darryl PANDY; RHYTHMATIC JUNKIES

RHYTHM-N-BASS *UK, male vocal group (4 WEEKS)*

			pos/wks
19 Sep 92		ROSES *Epic 6582907*	56 2
3 Jul 93		CAN'T STOP THIS FEELING *Epic 6592002*	59 2

RHYTHM OF LIFE
UK, male DJ / producer – Steve Burgess (2 WEEKS)

			pos/wks
13 May 00		YOU PUT ME IN HEAVEN WITH YOUR TOUCH *Xtravaganza XTRAV 4CDS*	24 2

RHYTHM ON THE LOOSE
UK, male producer – Geoff Hibbert (2 WEEKS)

			pos/wks
19 Aug 95		BREAK OF DAWN *Six6 SIXCD 126*	36 2

RHYTHM QUEST *UK, male producer – Mark Hadfield (2 WEEKS)*

			pos/wks
20 Jun 92		CLOSER TO ALL YOUR DREAMS *Network NWK 40*	45 2

RHYTHM SECTION *UK, male vocal / instrumental group (1 WEEK)*

			pos/wks
18 Jul 92		MIDSUMMER MADNESS (EP) *Rhythm Section RSEC 006*	66 1

Tracks on Midsummer Madness (EP): Dreamworld / Burnin' Up / Perfect Love 2am / Perfect Love 8am

RHYTHM SOURCE
UK, male / female vocal / instrumental group (1 WEEK)

			pos/wks
17 Jun 95		LOVE SHINE *A & M 5810672*	74 1

RHYTHMATIC *UK, male instrumental / production duo (3 WEEKS)*

			pos/wks
12 May 90		TAKE ME BACK *Network NWK 8*	74 1
26 May 90		TAKE ME BACK (re-entry) *Network NWK 8*	71 1
3 Nov 90		FREQUENCY *Network NWK 13*	62 1

RHYTHMATIC JUNKIES
UK, male vocal / production group (1 WEEK)

			pos/wks
15 May 99		THE FEELIN (CLAP YOUR HANDS) *Sound of Ministry RIDE 2CDS*	67 1

RHYTHMKILLAZ *Holland, male production duo (2 WEEKS)*

			pos/wks
31 Mar 01		WACK ASS MF *Incentive CENT 18 CDS*	32 2

RIALTO *UK, male vocal / instrumental group (8 WEEKS)*

			pos/wks
8 Nov 97		MONDAY MORNING 5:19 *East West EW 116CD*	37 2
17 Jan 98		UNTOUCHABLE *East West EW 107CD1*	20 3
28 Mar 98		DREAM ANOTHER DREAM *East West EW 156CD1*	39 2
17 Oct 98		SUMMER'S OVER *China WOKCDR 2099*	60 1

Reva RICE and Greg ELLIS *UK, male / female vocal duo (2 WEEKS)*

			pos/wks
27 Mar 93		NEXT TIME YOU FALL IN LOVE *Really Useful RURCD 12*	59 2

Charlie RICH *US, male vocalist (29 WEEKS)*

			pos/wks
16 Feb 74	●	THE MOST BEAUTIFUL GIRL *Epic EPC 1897* ▲	2 14
13 Apr 74		BEHIND CLOSED DOORS *Epic EPC 1539*	16 10
1 Feb 75		WE LOVE EACH OTHER *Epic EPC 2868*	37 5

Kelli RICH – *See NU SOUL featuring Kelli RICH*

Richie RICH *UK, DJ / producer (16 WEEKS)*

			pos/wks
16 Jul 88		TURN IT UP *Club JAB 68*	48 3
22 Oct 88		I'LL HOUSE YOU *Gee Street GEE 003* [1]	22 5
10 Dec 88		MY DJ (PUMP IT UP SOME) *Gee Street GEE 7*	74 1
2 Sep 89		SALSA HOUSE *ffrr F 113*	50 3
9 Mar 91		YOU USED TO SALSA *ffrr F 156* [2]	52 3
29 Mar 97		STAY WITH ME *Castle CATX 1001* [3]	58 1

[1] Richie Rich meets the Jungle Brothers [2] Richie Rich featuring Ralphi Rosario [3] Richie Rich and Esera Tuaolo

'You Used To Salsa' is a remix of 'Salsa House'

Tony RICH PROJECT
US, male vocalist – Antonio Jeffries (22 WEEKS)

			pos/wks
4 May 96	●	NOBODY KNOWS *LaFace 74321356422*	4 17
31 Aug 96		LIKE A WOMAN *LaFace 74321401612*	27 4
14 Dec 96		LEAVIN' *LaFace 74321438382*	52 1

Cliff RICHARD (2) (Top 500) *Britain's most successful solo vocalist, b. Harry Webb, 14 Oct 1940, Lucknow, India. Ex-member of Dick Teague Skiffle Group was instantly successful, and almost overnight became the UK's No.1 rock 'n' roll star despite bad press due to "too sexy" live performances. Many successes on film, stage, TV, radio and video. He has had hits in every major market around the globe and was named World's No.1 Artist by Billboard in 1963 (with Elvis second and Shadows third). Between 1959 and 2001, Cliff had a staggering 35 Top 10 albums including seven No.1s, and had more Top 10 albums in the 1980s than any other artist. He was seen on the first 'Top of the Pops' and has appeared on the TV show more often than any other artist. He is one of the few performers to top the chart with two different recordings of the same song (Living Doll). This seemingly ageless entertainer's record number of 64 Top 10 entries now spans 43 years, and at times he held the record for being the youngest (1959) and oldest (1999) British singer to top the singles chart. Cliff, who has sold more than 85 million records worldwide, was awarded the Outstanding Contribution to British Music trophy at the 1989 Brits, received an MBE in 1980 and a knighthood in 1995, and holds the unique achievement of a UK No.1 single in five different decades (1145 WEEKS)*

			pos/wks
12 Sep 58	●	MOVE IT! *Columbia DB 4178* [1]	2 17
21 Nov 58	●	HIGH CLASS BABY *Columbia DB 4203* [1]	7 10
30 Jan 59		LIVIN' LOVIN' DOLL *Columbia DB 4249* [1]	20 6
8 May 59	●	MEAN STREAK *Columbia DB 4290 A* [1]	10 9
15 May 59		NEVER MIND *Columbia DB 4290 B* [1]	21 2
10 Jul 59	★	LIVING DOLL *Columbia DB 4306* [1]	1 21
9 Oct 59		DYNAMITE *Columbia DB 4351 A* [1]	16 2
9 Oct 59	★	TRAVELLIN' LIGHT *Columbia DB 4351 B* [2]	1 17
30 Oct 59		DYNAMITE (re-entry) *Columbia DB 4351 A* [1]	21 2
11 Dec 59		LIVING DOLL (re-entry) *Columbia DB 4306* [1]	26 1
1 Jan 60		LIVING DOLL (2nd re-entry) *Columbia DB 4306* [1]	28 1
15 Jan 60		EXPRESSO BONGO (EP) *Columbia SEG 7971* [2]	14 7
22 Jan 60	●	A VOICE IN THE WILDERNESS *Columbia DB 4398* [2]	2 13
24 Mar 60	●	FALL IN LOVE WITH YOU *Columbia DB 4431* [2]	2 15
5 May 60		A VOICE IN THE WILDERNESS (re-entry) *Columbia DB 4398* [2]	36 2
30 Jun 60	★	PLEASE DON'T TEASE *Columbia DB 4479* [3]	1 18
22 Sep 60	●	NINE TIMES OUT OF TEN *Columbia DB 4506* [2]	3 12
1 Dec 60	★	I LOVE YOU *Columbia DB 4547* [2]	1 16
2 Mar 61	●	THEME FOR A DREAM *Columbia DB 4593* [2]	3 14
30 Mar 61	●	GEE WHIZ IT'S YOU *Columbia DC 756* [2]	4 14
22 Jun 61	●	A GIRL LIKE YOU *Columbia DB 4667* [2]	3 14
19 Oct 61	●	WHEN THE GIRL IN YOUR ARMS IS THE GIRL IN YOUR HEART *Columbia DB 4716*	3 15
11 Jan 62	★	THE YOUNG ONES *Columbia DB 4761* [2] ◆ ■	1 21
10 May 62	●	I'M LOOKING OUT THE WINDOW / DO YOU WANT TO DANCE *Columbia DB 4828* [4]	2 17
6 Sep 62	●	IT'LL BE ME *Columbia DB 4886* [2]	2 12
6 Dec 62	★	THE NEXT TIME / BACHELOR BOY *Columbia DB 4950* [2]	1 18
21 Feb 63	★	SUMMER HOLIDAY *Columbia DB 4977* [2]	1 18
9 May 63	●	LUCKY LIPS *Columbia DB 7034* [2]	4 15
22 Aug 63	●	IT'S ALL IN THE GAME *Columbia DB 7089*	2 13
7 Nov 63	●	DON'T TALK TO HIM *Columbia DB 7150* [2]	2 13
6 Feb 64	●	I'M THE LONELY ONE *Columbia DB 7203* [2]	8 10
13 Feb 64		DON'T TALK TO HIM (re-entry) *Columbia DB 7150* [2]	50 1
30 Apr 64	●	CONSTANTLY *Columbia DB 7272*	4 13
2 Jul 64	●	ON THE BEACH *Columbia DB 7305* [2]	7 13
8 Oct 64	●	THE TWELFTH OF NEVER *Columbia DB 7372*	8 11
10 Dec 64	●	I COULD EASILY FALL *Columbia DB 7420* [2]	6 11
11 Mar 65	★	THE MINUTE YOU'RE GONE *Columbia DB 7496*	1 14
10 Jun 65		ON MY WORD *Columbia DB 7596*	12 10
19 Aug 65		THE TIME IN BETWEEN *Columbia DB 7660* [2]	22 8
4 Nov 65	●	WIND ME UP (LET ME GO) *Columbia DB 7745*	2 16
24 Mar 66		BLUE TURNS TO GREY *Columbia DB 7866* [2]	15 9
21 Jul 66	●	VISIONS *Columbia DB 7968*	7 12
13 Oct 66	●	TIME DRAGS BY *Columbia DB 8017* [2]	10 12
15 Dec 66	●	IN THE COUNTRY *Columbia DB 8094* [2]	6 10
16 Mar 67	●	IT'S ALL OVER *Columbia DB 8150*	9 10

8 Jun 67		**I'LL COME RUNNIN'** *Columbia DB 8210*	**26**	8
16 Aug 67	●	**THE DAY I MET MARIE** *Columbia DB 8245*	**10**	14
15 Nov 67	●	**ALL MY LOVE** *Columbia DB 8293*	**6**	12
20 Mar 68	★	**CONGRATULATIONS** *Columbia DB 8376*	**1**	13
26 Jun 68		**I'LL LOVE YOU FOREVER TODAY** *Columbia DB 8437*	**27**	6
25 Sep 68		**MARIANNE** *Columbia DB 8476*	**22**	8
27 Nov 68		**DON'T FORGET TO CATCH ME** *Columbia DB 8503* [2]	**21**	10
26 Feb 69		**GOOD TIMES (BETTER TIMES)** *Columbia DB 8548*	**12**	11
28 May 69	●	**BIG SHIP** *Columbia DB 8581*	**8**	10
13 Sep 69	●	**THROW DOWN A LINE** *Columbia DB 8615* [5]	**7**	9
6 Dec 69		**WITH THE EYES OF A CHILD** *Columbia DB 8641*	**20**	11
21 Feb 70		**THE JOY OF LIVING** *Columbia DB 8657* [5]	**25**	8
6 Jun 70	●	**GOODBYE SAM, HELLO SAMANTHA** *Columbia DB 8685*	**6**	15
5 Sep 70		**I AIN'T GOT TIME ANYMORE** *Columbia DB 8708*	**21**	7
23 Jan 71		**SUNNY HONEY GIRL** *Columbia DB 8747*	**19**	8
10 Apr 71		**SILVERY RAIN** *Columbia DB 8774*	**27**	6
17 Jul 71		**FLYING MACHINE** *Columbia DB 8797*	**37**	7
13 Nov 71		**SING A SONG OF FREEDOM** *Columbia DB 8836*	**13**	12
11 Mar 72		**JESUS** *Columbia DB 8864*	**35**	3
26 Aug 72		**LIVING IN HARMONY** *Columbia DB 8917*	**12**	10
17 Mar 73	●	**POWER TO ALL OUR FRIENDS** *EMI 2012*	**4**	12
12 May 73		**HELP IT ALONG / TOMORROW RISING** *EMI 2022*	**29**	6
1 Dec 73		**TAKE ME HIGH** *EMI 2088*	**27**	12
18 May 74		**(YOU KEEP ME) HANGIN' ON** *EMI 2150*	**13**	8
7 Feb 76		**MISS YOU NIGHTS** *EMI 2376*	**15**	10
8 May 76	●	**DEVIL WOMAN** *EMI 2458*	**9**	8
21 Aug 76		**I CAN'T ASK FOR ANYTHING MORE THAN YOU** *EMI 2499*	**17**	8
4 Dec 76		**HEY MR DREAM MAKER** *EMI 2559*	**31**	5
5 Mar 77		**MY KINDA LIFE** *EMI 2584*	**15**	8
16 Jul 77		**WHEN TWO WORLDS DRIFT APART** *EMI 2633*	**46**	3
31 Mar 79		**GREEN LIGHT** *EMI 2920*	**57**	3
21 Jul 79	★	**WE DON'T TALK ANYMORE** *EMI 2975*	**1**	14
3 Nov 79		**HOT SHOT** *EMI 5003*	**46**	5
2 Feb 80	●	**CARRIE** *EMI 5006*	**4**	10
16 Aug 80	●	**DREAMIN'** *EMI 5095*	**8**	10
25 Oct 80		**SUDDENLY** *Jet 7002* [6]	**15**	7
24 Jan 81		**A LITTLE IN LOVE** *EMI 5123*	**15**	8
29 Aug 81	●	**WIRED FOR SOUND** *EMI 5221*	**4**	9
21 Nov 81	●	**DADDY'S HOME** *EMI 5251*	**2**	12
17 Jul 82	●	**THE ONLY WAY OUT** *EMI 5318*	**10**	9
25 Sep 82		**WHERE DO WE GO FROM HERE** *EMI 5341*	**60**	3
4 Dec 82		**LITTLE TOWN** *EMI 5348*	**11**	7
19 Feb 83	●	**SHE MEANS NOTHING TO ME** *Capitol CL 276* [7]	**9**	9
16 Apr 83	●	**TRUE LOVE WAYS** *EMI 5385* [8]	**8**	8
4 Jun 83		**DRIFTING** *DJM SHEIL 1* [9]	**64**	2
3 Sep 83		**NEVER SAY DIE (GIVE A LITTLE BIT MORE)** *EMI 5415*	**15**	7
26 Nov 83	●	**PLEASE DON'T FALL IN LOVE** *EMI 5437*	**7**	9
31 Mar 84		**BABY YOU'RE DYNAMITE / OCEAN DEEP** *EMI 5457*	**27**	6
19 May 84		**OCEAN DEEP (re-entry) / BABY YOU'RE DYNAMITE (re-entry)** *EMI 5457*	**72**	1
3 Nov 84		**SHOOTING FROM THE HEART** *EMI RICH 1*	**51**	4
9 Feb 85		**HEART USER** *EMI RICH 2*	**46**	3
14 Sep 85		**SHE'S SO BEAUTIFUL** *EMI 5531*	**17**	9
7 Dec 85		**IT'S IN EVERY ONE OF US** *EMI 5537*	**45**	6
22 Mar 86	★	**LIVING DOLL** *WEA YZ 65* [10]	**1**	11
4 Oct 86	●	**ALL I ASK OF YOU** *Polydor POSP 802* [11]	**3**	16
29 Nov 86		**SLOW RIVERS** *Rocket EJS 13* [12]	**44**	8
20 Jun 87	●	**MY PRETTY ONE** *EMI EM 4*	**6**	10
29 Aug 87	●	**SOME PEOPLE** *EMI EM 18*	**3**	10
31 Oct 87		**REMEMBER ME** *EMI EM 31*	**35**	4
13 Feb 88		**TWO HEARTS** *EMI EM 42*	**34**	3
3 Dec 88	★	**MISTLETOE AND WINE** *EMI EM 78*	**1**	8
10 Jun 89	●	**THE BEST OF ME** *EMI EM 92*	**2**	7
26 Aug 89	●	**I JUST DON'T HAVE THE HEART** *EMI EM 101*	**3**	8
14 Oct 89		**LEAN ON YOU** *EMI EM 105*	**17**	6
9 Dec 89		**WHENEVER GOD SHINES HIS LIGHT** *Polydor VANS 2* [13]	**20**	6
24 Feb 90		**STRONGER THAN THAT** *EMI EM 129*	**14**	5
25 Aug 90	●	**SILHOUETTES** *EMI EM 152*	**10**	7
13 Oct 90		**FROM A DISTANCE** *EMI EM 155*	**11**	6
8 Dec 90	★	**SAVIOUR'S DAY** *EMI XMAS 90*	**1**	7
14 Sep 91		**MORE TO LIFE** *EMI EM 205*	**23**	5
7 Dec 91	●	**WE SHOULD BE TOGETHER** *EMI XMAS 91*	**10**	6
11 Jan 92		**THIS NEW YEAR** *EMI EMS 218*	**30**	2
5 Dec 92	●	**I STILL BELIEVE IN YOU** *EMI EM 255*	**7**	6
27 Mar 93	●	**PEACE IN OUR TIME** *EMI CDEM 265*	**8**	5
12 Jun 93		**HUMAN WORK OF ART** *EMI CDEM 267*	**24**	4
2 Oct 93		**NEVER LET GO** *EMI CDEM 281*	**32**	3
18 Dec 93		**HEALING LOVE** *EMI CDEM 294*	**19**	5
10 Dec 94		**ALL I HAVE TO DO IS DREAM / MISS YOU NIGHTS (re-issue)** *EMI CDEM 359* [14]	**14**	6
25 Feb 95		**ALL I HAVE TO DO IS DREAM / MISS YOU NIGHTS (re-entry of re-issue)** *EMI CDEM 359* [14]	**58**	3
2 Oct 95		**MISUNDERSTOOD MAN** *EMI CDEM 394*	**19**	3
9 Dec 95		**HAD TO BE** *EMI CDEM 410* [15]	**22**	4
30 Mar 96		**THE WEDDING** *EMI CDEM 422* [16]	**40**	1
25 Jan 97		**BE WITH ME ALWAYS** *EMI CDEM 453*	**52**	1
24 Oct 98	●	**CAN'T KEEP THIS FEELING IN** *EMI CDEM 526*	**10**	4
7 Aug 99		**THE MIRACLE** *EMI / Blacknight CDEM 546*	**23**	2
27 Nov 99	★	**THE MILLENNIUM PRAYER** *Papillon PROMISECD 01*	**1**	16
15 Dec 01		**SOMEWHERE OVER THE RAINBOW / WHAT A WONDERFUL WORLD** *Papillon CLIFFCD 1*	**11**	3+

[1] Cliff Richard and the Drifters [2] Cliff Richard and the Shadows [3] Cliff Richard and The Shadows [4] Cliff Richard / The Shadows [5] Cliff and Hank [6] Olivia Newton-John and Cliff Richard [7] Phil Everly and Cliff Richard [8] Cliff Richard with the London Philharmonic Orchestra [9] Sheila Walsh and Cliff Richard [10] Cliff Richard and the Young Ones featuring Hank B Marvin [11] Cliff Richard and Sarah Brightman [12] Elton John and Cliff Richard [13] Van Morrison with Cliff Richard [14] Cliff Richard with Phil Everly / Cliff Richard [15] Cliff Richard and Olivia Newton-John [16] Cliff Richard featuring Helen Hobson

Tracks on Expresso Bongo (EP): Love / A Voice in the Wilderness / The Shrine on the Second Floor / Bongo Blues. 'Bongo Blues' features only The Shadows. 'Bachelor Boy' was listed with 'The Next Time' from 10 Jan 1963. 'Ocean Deep' listed from 28 Apr 1984 onwards. It peaked at No.41

Wendy RICHARD – *See Mike SARNE*

Lionel RICHIE (106 Top 500)

Singer / composer / producer, b. 20 Jun 1949, Alabama, US. Launched a solo career in 1982 after 12 years fronting The Commodores. Arguably the most successful US songwriter of the 1980s, who composed at least one US chart-topper per year for a record nine successive years (182 WEEKS)

			pos	wks
12 Sep 81	●	**ENDLESS LOVE** *Motown TMG 1240* [1] ▲	**7**	12
20 Nov 82	●	**TRULY** *Motown TMG 1284* ▲	**6**	11
29 Jan 83		**YOU ARE** *Motown TMG 1290*	**43**	7
7 May 83		**MY LOVE** *Motown TMG 1300*	**70**	3
1 Oct 83	●	**ALL NIGHT LONG (ALL NIGHT)** *Motown TMG 1319* ▲	**2**	16
3 Dec 83	●	**RUNNING WITH THE NIGHT** *Motown TMG 1324*	**9**	12
10 Mar 84	★	**HELLO** *Motown TMG 1330* ▲	**1**	15
23 Jun 84		**STUCK ON YOU** *Motown TMG 1341*	**12**	12
20 Oct 84		**PENNY LOVER** *Motown TMG 1356*	**18**	7
16 Nov 85	●	**SAY YOU, SAY ME** *Motown ZB 40421* ▲	**8**	11
26 Jul 86	●	**DANCING ON THE CEILING** *Motown LIO1*	**7**	11
11 Oct 86		**LOVE WILL CONQUER ALL** *Motown LIO 2*	**45**	5
20 Dec 86		**BALLERINA GIRL / DEEP RIVER WOMAN** *Motown LIO3*	**17**	8
28 Mar 87		**SELA** *Motown LIO4*	**43**	6
9 May 92		**DO IT TO ME** *Motown TMG 1407*	**33**	6
22 Aug 92	●	**MY DESTINY** *Motown TMG 1408*	**7**	13
28 Nov 92		**LOVE OH LOVE** *Motown TMG 1413*	**52**	3
26 Dec 92		**LOVE OH LOVE (re-entry)** *Motown TMG 1413*	**73**	1
6 Apr 96		**DON'T WANNA LOSE YOU** *Mercury MERCD 461*	**17**	5
23 Nov 96		**STILL IN LOVE** *Mercury MERCD 477*	**66**	1
27 Jun 98		**CLOSEST THING TO HEAVEN** *Mercury 5661312*	**26**	2
21 Oct 00		**ANGEL** *Mercury 5726702*	**18**	5
23 Dec 00		**DON'T STOP THE MUSIC** *Mercury 5688992*	**34**	5
17 Mar 01		**TENDER HEART** *Mercury 5728462*	**29**	3
23 Jun 01		**I FORGOT** *Mercury 5729922*	**34**	2

[1] Diana Ross and Lionel Richie

'Deep River Woman' was listed only from 17 Jan 1987. It has the following credit: background vocal 'Alabama'

RICH KIDS

UK, male vocal / instrumental group (5 WEEKS)

			pos	wks
28 Jan 78		**RICH KIDS** *EMI 2738*	**24**	5

1988

IN THE YEAR ACID HOUSE WAS ALL THE RAGE, LOCKERBIE IN SOUTHERN SCOTLAND WAS THE SCENE OF A PLANE CRASH WHICH KILLED 270, AND THE BISHOP OF TURIN ANNOUNCED THAT THE INFAMOUS SHROUD WAS A MEDIEVAL FAKE, **MARK NEVIN** (EX-FAIRGROUND ATTRACTION) TALKS US THROUGH THE CREATION OF A 'PERFECT' SONG ...

"The success of 'Perfect' changed my life – for better and worse! In 1988, I was completely broke and it was looking very grim. Then suddenly cheques were flying through my letterbox for amounts of money that were comical to me at the time. This, of course, brought all kinds of different problems and I have kept several lawyers busy for one reason or another since, but at the end of the day 'Perfect' has been great to me. It sounds like it should have been written in 20 minutes but it wasn't like that at all. It sort of evolved into its simplicity. I started writing a song called 'Perfect' while I was living in a bedsit in Cricklewood, but the song that it is now was written during a very unhappy time in Akron, Ohio – rubber-town USA, where Firestone and Goodyear tyres come from. I was working as a gardener for the chairman of Firestone. I recently re-recorded 'Perfect' as an extra track for a CD single as a kind of re-claiming thing. I usually do it on my solo gigs and people love to hear it and join in on the chorus."

Jonathan RICHMAN and the MODERN LOVERS
US, male vocal / instrumental group (27 WEEKS) pos/wks

16 Jul 77		**ROADRUNNER** *Beserkley BZZ 1*	11	9
29 Oct 77	●	**EGYPTIAN REGGAE** *Beserkley BZZ 2*	5	14
21 Jan 78		**MORNING OF OUR LIVES** *Beserkley BZZ 7* [1]	29	4

[1] Modern Lovers

Adam RICKITT *UK, male vocalist (19 WEEKS)* pos/wks

26 Jun 99	●	**I BREATHE AGAIN** *Polydor 5611862*	5	10
16 Oct 99		**EVERYTHING MY HEART DESIRES** *Polydor 5614392*	15	6
5 Feb 00		**BEST THING** *Polydor 5616132*	25	3

RICO – *See SPECIALS*

RIDE *UK, male vocal / instrumental group (22 WEEKS)* pos/wks

27 Jan 90		**RIDE (EP)** *Creation CRE 072T*	71	2
14 Apr 90		**PLAY (EP)** *Creation CRE 075T*	32	3
29 Sep 90		**FALL (EP)** *Creation CRE 087T*	34	3
16 Mar 91		**TODAY FOREVER (EP)** *Creation CRE 100T*	14	4
15 Feb 92	●	**LEAVE THEM ALL BEHIND** *Creation CRE 123T*	9	3
25 Apr 92		**TWISTERELLA** *Creation CRE 150T*	36	2
30 Apr 94		**BIRDMAN** *Creation CRESCD 155*	38	2
25 Jun 94		**HOW DOES IT FEEL TO FEEL** *Creation CRESCD 184*	58	1
8 Oct 94		**I DON'T KNOW WHERE IT COMES FROM** *Creation CRESCD 189R*	46	1
24 Feb 96		**BLACK NITE CRASH** *Creation CRESCD 199*	67	1

Tracks on Ride (EP): Chelsea Girl / Drive Blind / All I Can See / Close My Eyes. Tracks on Play (EP): Like a Daydream / Silver / Furthest Sense / Perfect Time. Tracks on Fall (EP): Dreams Burn Down / Taste / Hear and Now / Nowhere. Tracks on Today Forever (EP): Unfamiliar / Sennen / Beneath / Today

Andrew RIDGELEY *UK, male vocalist (3 WEEKS)* pos/wks

31 Mar 90		**SHAKE** *Epic AJR 1*	58	3

See also WHAM!

Stan RIDGWAY *US, male vocalist (12 WEEKS)* pos/wks

5 Jul 86	●	**CAMOUFLAGE** *IRS IRM 114*	4	12

RIGHEIRA *Italy, male vocal duo (3 WEEKS)* pos/wks

24 Sep 83		**VAMOS A LA PLAYA** *A & M AM 137*	53	3

RIGHT SAID FRED *UK, male vocal / instrumental group – lead vocal Richard Fairbrass (66 WEEKS)* pos/wks

27 Jul 91	●	**I'M TOO SEXY** *Tug SNOG 1* ▲	2	16
7 Dec 91	●	**DON'T TALK JUST KISS** *Tug SNOG 2* [1]	3	11
21 Mar 92	★	**DEEPLY DIPPY** *Tug SNOG 3*	1	14
1 Aug 92		**THOSE SIMPLE THINGS / DAYDREAM** *Tug SNOG 4*	29	5
27 Feb 93	●	**STICK IT OUT** *Tug CDCOMIC 1* [2]	4	7
23 Oct 93		**BUMPED** *Tug CDSNOG 7*	32	4
18 Dec 93		**HANDS UP (4 LOVERS)** *Tug CDSNOG 8*	60	3
19 Mar 94		**WONDERMAN** *Tug CDSNOG 9*	55	1
13 Oct 01		**YOU'RE MY MATE** *Kingsize 74321895632*	18	5

[1] Right Said Fred. Guest vocals: Jocelyn Brown [2] Right Said Fred and Friends

RIGHTEOUS BROTHERS (376 Top 500)
Pioneering, influential blue-eyed soul duo, Bill Medley b. 19 Sep 1940, California, US, and Bobby Hatfield b. 10 Aug 1940, Wisconsin, US. 'You've Lost That Lovin' Feelin'', has an unsurpassed seven million US radio plays and reached UK Top 10 three times (86 WEEKS) pos/wks

14 Jan 65	★	**YOU'VE LOST THAT LOVIN' FEELIN'** *London HLU 9943* ▲	1	10
12 Aug 65		**UNCHAINED MELODY** *London HL 9975*	14	12
13 Jan 66		**EBB TIDE** *London HL 10011*	48	2
14 Apr 66		**(YOU'RE MY) SOUL AND INSPIRATION** *Verve VS 535* ▲	15	10
10 Nov 66		**THE WHITE CLIFFS OF DOVER** *London HL 10086*	21	9
22 Dec 66		**ISLAND IN THE SUN** *Verve VS 547*	24	5
12 Feb 69	●	**YOU'VE LOST THAT LOVIN' FEELIN' (re-issue)** *London HL 10241*	10	11
19 Nov 77		**YOU'VE LOST THAT LOVIN' FEELIN' (2nd re-issue)** *Phil Spector International 2010 022*	42	4
27 Oct 90	★	**UNCHAINED MELODY (re-issue)** *Verve / Polydor PO 101*	1	14
15 Dec 90	●	**YOU'VE LOST THAT LOVIN' FEELIN' / EBB TIDE (3rd re-issue)** *Verve / Polydor PO 116*	3	9

Cheryl Pepsii RILEY *US, female vocalist (1 WEEK)* pos/wks

28 Jan 89		**THANKS FOR MY CHILD** *CBS 653153 7*	75	1

Jeannie C RILEY
US, female vocalist – Jeanne C Stephenson (15 WEEKS) pos/wks

16 Oct 68		**HARPER VALLEY P.T.A.** *Polydor 56748* ▲	12	15

Teddy RILEY *US, male producer (5 WEEKS)* pos/wks

21 Mar 92		**IS IT GOOD TO YOU** *MCA MCS 1611* [1]	53	2
19 Jun 93		**BABY BE MINE** *MCA MCSTD 1772* [2]	37	3

[1] Teddy Riley featuring Tammy Lucas [2] BLACKstreet featuring Teddy Riley

RIMES featuring Shaila PROSPERE
UK, male rapper – Julian Johnson (1 WEEK) pos/wks

22 May 99		**IT'S OVER** *Universal MCSTD 40199*	51	1

LeAnn RIMES (442 Top 500)
Teenage queen of country music, b. 28 Aug 1982, Mississippi. She first recorded at age 11; three years later she became both the youngest act to enter US album chart at No.1 and Best New Artist Grammy winner and, at 15, 'How Do I Live' broke several longevity records on the US chart (77 WEEKS) pos/wks

7 Mar 98	●	**HOW DO I LIVE** *Curb CUBCX 30*	7	33
12 Sep 98		**LOOKING THROUGH YOUR EYES / COMMITMENT** *Curb CUBC 32*	38	2
31 Oct 98		**HOW DO I LIVE (re-entry)** *Curb CUBCX 30*	72	1
12 Dec 98		**BLUE** *Curb CUBC 39*	23	6
6 Mar 99	●	**WRITTEN IN THE STARS** *Mercury EJSCD 45* [1]	10	7
22 May 99		**WRITTEN IN THE STARS (re-entry)** *Mercury EJSCD 45* [1]	63	1
18 Dec 99		**CRAZY** *Curb CUBC 52*	36	3
25 Nov 00	★	**CAN'T FIGHT THE MOONLIGHT** *Curb CUBC 58* ■	1	17
31 Mar 01		**I NEED YOU** *Curb CUBC 60*	13	6
19 May 01		**I NEED YOU (re-entry)** *Curb CUBC 60*	75	1

[1] Elton John and LeAnn Rimes

RIMSHOTS *US, male / female instrumental / vocal group (5 WEEKS)* pos/wks

19 Jul 75		**7-6-5-4-3-2-1 (BLOW YOUR WHISTLE)** *All Platinum 6146 304*	26	5

RIO and MARS
France / UK, male / female vocal / instrumental duo (3 WEEKS) pos/wks

28 Jan 95		**BOY I GOTTA HAVE YOU** *Dome CDDOME 1014*	43	2
13 Apr 96		**BOY I GOTTA HAVE YOU (re-issue)** *Feverpitch CDFVR 1007*	46	1

Miguel RIOS *Spain, male vocalist (12 WEEKS)* pos/wks

11 Jul 70		**SONG OF JOY** *A & M AMS 790*	16	12

Waldo de los RIOS
Argentina, orchestra, leader – Osvaldo Ferraro Guiterrez (16 WEEKS) pos/wks

10 Apr 71	●	**MOZART SYMPHONY NO.40 IN G MINOR K550 1ST MOVEMENT (ALLEGRO MOLTO)** *A & M AMS 836*	5	16

RIP PRODUCTIONS *UK, production duo (1 WEEK)* pos/wks

29 Nov 97		**THE CHANT (WE R) / RIP PRODUCTIONS** *Satellite 74321534022*	58	1

See also DOUBLE 99; CARNIVAL featuring RIP vs RED RAT

Minnie RIPERTON *US, female vocalist (10 WEEKS)* pos/wks

12 Apr 75	●	**LOVING YOU** *Epic EPC 3121* ▲	2	10

RISE
UK, male production duo – Paul Oakenfold and Steve Osborne (1 WEEK) pos/wks

3 Sep 94		**THE SINGLE** *East West YZ 839CD*	70	1

RITCHIE FAMILY *US, female vocal group (19 WEEKS)* pos/wks

23 Aug 75		**BRAZIL** *Polydor 2058 625*	41	4
18 Sep 76	●	**THE BEST DISCO IN TOWN** *Polydor 2058 777*	10	9
17 Feb 79		**AMERICAN GENERATION** *Mercury 6007 199*	49	6

Lee RITENOUR and Maxi PRIEST
US, male instrumentalist – guitar and UK, male vocalist (2 WEEKS) pos/wks

31 Jul 93		**WAITING IN VAIN** *GRP MCSTD 1921*	65	2

Tex RITTER *US, male vocalist (14 WEEKS)* pos/wks

22 Jun 56	●	**THE WAYWARD WIND** *Capitol CL 14581*	8	14

RIVA featuring Dannii MINOGUE
Holland, male production duo and Australia, female vocalist (5 WEEKS) pos/wks

1 Dec 01	●	**WHO DO YOU LOVE NOW (STRINGER)** *ffrr DFCD 002*	3	5+

See also JARK PRONGO; GOODMEN

Paco RIVAZ – *See GAMBAFREAKS*

RIVER CITY PEOPLE
UK, male / female vocal / instrumental group (27 WEEKS) pos/wks

12 Aug 89		**(WHAT'S WRONG WITH) DREAMING?** *EMI EM 95*	70	3
3 Mar 90		**WALKING ON ICE** *EMI EM 130*	62	2
30 Jun 90		**CARRY THE BLAME / CALIFORNIA DREAMIN'** *EMI EM 145*	13	10
22 Sep 90		**(WHAT'S WRONG WITH) DREAMING? (re-issue)** *EMI EM 156*	40	3
2 Mar 91		**WHEN I WAS YOUNG** *EMI EM 176*	62	2
28 Sep 91		**SPECIAL WAY** *EMI EM 207*	44	3
22 Feb 92		**STANDING IN THE NEED OF LOVE** *EMI EM 216*	36	4

RIVER DETECTIVES *UK, male vocal / instrumental duo (4 WEEKS)* pos/wks

29 Jul 89		**CHAINS** *WEA YZ 383*	51	4

RIVER OCEAN featuring INDIA
US, male producer – Louie Vega and female vocalist (2 WEEKS) pos/wks

26 Feb 94		**LOVE AND HAPPINESS (YEMAYA Y OCHUN)** *Cooltempo CDCOOL 287*	50	2

See also INDIA; Louie VEGA and Marc ANTHONY

Robbie RIVERA presents RHYTHM BANGERS
Puerto Rico, male producer (7 WEEKS) pos/wks

2 Sep 00		**BANG** *Multiply CDMULTY 64*	13	7

Danny RIVERS *UK, male vocalist (3 WEEKS)* pos/wks

12 Jan 61		**CAN'T YOU HEAR MY HEART** *Decca F 11294*	36	3

RM PROJECT *UK, production group (1 WEEK)* pos/wks

3 Jul 99		**GET IT UP** *Inferno CDFERN 15*	49	1

ROACH MOTEL *UK, male instrumental / production group (2 WEEKS)* pos/wks

21 Aug 93		**AFRO SLEEZE / TRANSATLANTIC** *Junior Boy's Own JBO 1412*	73	1
10 Dec 94		**HAPPY BIZZNESS / WILD LUV** *Junior Boy's Own JBO 24*	75	1

ROACHFORD *UK, male / female vocal / instrumental group – Andrew Roachford (61 WEEKS)* pos/wks

18 Jun 88		**CUDDLY TOY** *CBS ROA 2*	61	4
14 Jan 89	●	**CUDDLY TOY (re-issue)** *CBS ROA 4*	4	9
18 Mar 89		**FAMILY MAN** *CBS ROA 5*	25	6
1 Jul 89		**KATHLEEN** *CBS ROA 6*	43	5
13 Apr 91		**GET READY!** *Columbia 6567057*	22	8
19 Mar 94		**ONLY TO BE WITH YOU** *Columbia 6601562*	21	7
18 Jun 94		**LAY YOUR LOVE ON ME** *Columbia 6603722*	36	5
20 Aug 94		**THIS GENERATION** *Columbia 6607452*	38	4
3 Dec 94		**CRY FOR ME** *Columbia 6610742*	46	2
1 Apr 95		**I KNOW YOU DON'T LOVE ME** *Columbia 6612525*	42	2
11 Oct 97		**THE WAY I FEEL** *Columbia 6651042*	20	4
14 Feb 98		**HOW COULD I? (INSECURITY)** *Columbia 6653462*	34	3
11 Jul 98		**NAKED WITHOUT YOU** *Columbia 6659362*	53	2

ROB 'N' RAZ featuring Leila K
Sweden, male production duo and female rapper (17 WEEKS) pos/wks

25 Nov 89	●	**GOT TO GET** *Arista 112696*	8	14
17 Mar 90		**ROK THE NATION** *Arista 112971*	41	3

Kate ROBBINS and BEYOND
UK, female / male vocal / instrumental group (10 WEEKS) pos/wks

30 May 81	●	**MORE THAN IN LOVE** *RCA 69*	2	10

Marty ROBBINS *US, male vocalist – Marty Robinson (32 WEEKS)* pos/wks

29 Jan 60		**EL PASO** *Fontana H 233* ▲	19	7
7 Apr 60		**EL PASO (re-entry)** *Fontana H 233*	44	1
26 May 60		**BIG IRON** *Fontana H 229*	48	1
27 Sep 62	●	**DEVIL WOMAN** *CBS AAG 114*	5	17
17 Jan 63		**RUBY ANN** *CBS AAG 128*	24	6

Antoinette ROBERSON – *See PULSE featuring Antoinette ROBERSON*

Austin ROBERTS *US, male vocalist (7 WEEKS)* pos/wks

25 Oct 75		**ROCKY** *Private Stock PVT 33*	22	7

Joe ROBERTS *UK, male vocalist (17 WEEKS)* pos/wks

28 Aug 93		**BACK IN MY LIFE** *ffrr FCD 215*	59	1
29 Jan 94		**LOVER** *ffrr FCD 220*	22	5
14 May 94		**BACK IN MY LIFE (re-issue)** *ffrr FCD 230*	39	3
6 Aug 94		**ADORE** *ffrr FCD 240*	45	3
18 Feb 95		**YOU ARE EVERYTHING** *Columbia 6611755* [1]	28	4
24 Feb 96		**HAPPY DAYS** *Grass Green GRASS 10CD* [2]	63	1

[1] Melanie Williams and Joe Roberts [2] Sweet Mercy featuring Joe Roberts

Juliet ROBERTS *UK, female vocalist (34 WEEKS)* pos/wks

31 Jul 93		**CAUGHT IN THE MIDDLE** *Cooltempo CDCOOL 272*	24	6
6 Nov 93		**FREE LOVE** *Cooltempo CDCOOL 281*	25	3
19 Mar 94		**AGAIN / I WANT YOU** *Cooltempo CDCOOL 285*	33	3
2 Jul 94		**CAUGHT IN THE MIDDLE (re-mix)** *Cooltempo CDCOOL 291*	14	5
15 Oct 94		**I WANT YOU (re-issue)** *Cooltempo CDCOOL 297*	28	3
31 Jan 98		**SO GOOD / FREE LOVE 98 (re-mix)** *Delirious 74321554002*	15	4
23 Jan 99		**BAD GIRLS / I LIKE** *Delirious DELICD 11*	17	5
20 Jan 01		**NEEDIN' YOU II** *Manifesto FESCD 78* [1]	11	5

[1] David Morales presents The Face featuring Juliet Roberts

Malcolm ROBERTS *UK, male vocalist (29 WEEKS)* pos/wks

11 May 67		**TIME ALONE WILL TELL** *RCA 1578*	45	2
30 Oct 68	●	**MAY I HAVE THE NEXT DREAM WITH YOU** *Major Minor MM 581*	8	14
12 Feb 69		**MAY I HAVE THE NEXT DREAM WITH YOU (re-entry)** *Major Minor MM 581*	45	1
22 Nov 69		**LOVE IS ALL** *Major Minor MM 637*	12	12

B A ROBERTSON *UK, male vocalist (60 WEEKS)* pos/wks

28 Jul 79	●	**BANG BANG** *Asylum K 13152*	2	12
27 Oct 79	●	**KNOCKED IT OFF** *Asylum K 12396*	8	12
1 Mar 80		**KOOL IN THE KAFTAN** *Asylum K 12427*	17	12
31 May 80	●	**TO BE OR NOT TO BE** *Asylum K 12449*	9	11
17 Oct 81		**HOLD ME** *Swansong BAM 1* [1]	11	8
17 Dec 83		**TIME** *Epic A 3983* [2]	45	5

[1] B A Robertson and Maggie Bell [2] Frida and B A Robertson

Don ROBERTSON
US, male instrumentalist – piano and whistle (9 WEEKS) pos/wks

11 May 56	●	**THE HAPPY WHISTLER** *Capitol CL 14575*	8	9

Robbie ROBERTSON
Canada, male vocalist / instrumentalist (11 WEEKS) pos/wks

23 Jul 88	**SOMEWHERE DOWN THE CRAZY RIVER** *Geffen GEF 40*	15	10
11 Apr 98	**TAKE YOUR PARTNER BY THE HAND** *Polydor 5693272* [1]	74	1

[1] Howie B featuring Robbie Robertson

Ivo ROBIC *Croatia, male vocalist (1 WEEK)* pos/wks

6 Nov 59	**MORGEN** *Polydor 23923*	23	1

Dawn ROBINSON – *See FIRM*

Floyd ROBINSON *US, male vocalist (9 WEEKS)* pos/wks

16 Oct 59 ●	**MAKIN' LOVE** *RCA 1146*	9	9

Smokey ROBINSON *US, male vocalist (45 WEEKS)* pos/wks

23 Feb 74	**JUST MY SOUL RESPONDING** *Tamla Motown TMG 883*	35	6
24 Feb 79	**POPS WE LOVE YOU** *Motown TMG 1136* [1]	66	5
9 May 81 ★	**BEING WITH YOU** *Motown TMG 1223*	1	13
13 Mar 82	**TELL ME TOMORROW** *Motown TMG 1255*	51	4
28 Mar 87	**JUST TO SEE HER** *Motown ZB 41147*	52	6
17 Sep 88	**INDESTRUCTIBLE** *Arista 111717* [2]	55	4
25 Feb 89	**INDESTRUCTIBLE** *Arista 112074* [2]	30	7

[1] Diana Ross, Marvin Gaye, Smokey Robinson and Stevie Wonder [2] Four Tops featuring Smokey Robinson

The original US recording of 'Indestructible' was not issued until after the chart run of the UK-only mix

See also Smokey ROBINSON and the MIRACLES; MIRACLES

Smokey ROBINSON and the MIRACLES *Motown's first US Top 10 act was fronted, between 1955 and 1972, by William "Smokey" Robinson, b. 19 Feb 1940, Detroit. He wrote and produced hits for many Motown acts including this quartet. Smokey received coveted Grammy Living Legend Award in 1989 and has a US album chart span covering 36 years (64 WEEKS)* pos/wks

27 Dec 67	**I SECOND THAT EMOTION** *Tamla Motown TMG 631*	27	11
3 Apr 68	**IF YOU CAN WANT** *Tamla Motown TMG 648*	50	1
7 May 69 ●	**TRACKS OF MY TEARS** *Tamla Motown TMG 696*	9	13
1 Aug 70 ★	**THE TEARS OF A CLOWN** *Tamla Motown TMG 745* ▲	1	14
30 Jan 71	**(COME 'ROUND HERE) I'M THE ONE YOU NEED (re-issue)** *Tamla Motown TMG 761*	13	9
5 Jun 71	**I DON'T BLAME YOU AT ALL** *Tamla Motown TMG 774*	11	10
2 Oct 76	**THE TEARS OF A CLOWN (re-issue)** *Tamla Motown TMG 1048*	34	6

1976 re-issue of 'The Tears of a Clown' was a double A-side release with 'Tracks of My Tears'

See also MIRACLES; Smokey ROBINSON

Tom ROBINSON *UK, male vocalist / instrumentalist (41 WEEKS)* pos/wks

22 Oct 77 ●	**2-4-6-8 MOTORWAY** *EMI 2715* [1]	5	9
18 Feb 78	**DON'T TAKE NO FOR AN ANSWER** *EMI 2749* [1]	18	6
13 May 78	**UP AGAINST THE WALL** *EMI 2787* [1]	33	6
17 Mar 79	**BULLY FOR YOU** *EMI 2916* [1]	68	2
25 Jun 83 ●	**WAR BABY** *Panic NIC 2*	6	9
12 Nov 83	**LISTEN TO THE RADIO: ATMOSPHERICS** *Panic NIC 3*	39	6
15 Sep 84	**RIKKI DON'T LOSE THAT NUMBER** *Castaway TR 2*	58	3

[1] Tom Robinson Band

Vicki Sue ROBINSON *US, female vocalist (1 WEEK)* pos/wks

27 Sep 97	**HOUSE OF JOY** *Logic 74321511492*	48	1

ROBO BABE – *See SIR KILLALOT vs ROBO BABE*

ROBSON and JEROME
UK, male vocal duo – Robson Green and Jerome Flynn (45 WEEKS) pos/wks

20 May 95 ★	**UNCHAINED MELODY / (THERE'LL BE BLUEBIRDS OVER) THE WHITE CLIFFS OF DOVER** *RCA 74321284362* [1] ◆ ■	1	16
4 Nov 95	**UNCHAINED MELODY / (THERE'LL BE BLUEBIRDS OVER) THE WHITE CLIFFS OF DOVER (re-entry)** *RCA 74321284362* [1]	63	1
11 Nov 95 ★	**I BELIEVE / UP ON THE ROOF** *RCA 74321326882* ◆ ■	1	14
9 Nov 96 ★	**WHAT BECOMES OF THE BROKENHEARTED / SATURDAY NIGHT AT THE MOVIES / YOU'LL NEVER WALK ALONE** *RCA 74321424732* ■	1	14

[1] Robson Green and Jerome Flynn

ROBYN *Sweden, female vocalist – Robyn Carlsson (14 WEEKS)* pos/wks

20 Jul 96	**YOU'VE GOT THAT SOMETHIN'** *RCA 74321393462*	54	1
16 Aug 97	**DO YOU KNOW (WHAT IT TAKES)** *RCA 74321509932*	26	3
7 Mar 98 ●	**SHOW ME LOVE** *RCA 74321555032*	8	6
30 May 98	**DO YOU REALLY WANT ME** *RCA 74321582982*	20	4

John ROCCA – *See FREEEZ*

ROCHELLE *US, female vocalist (6 WEEKS)* pos/wks

1 Feb 86	**MY MAGIC MAN** *Warner Bros. W 8838*	27	6

THE ROCK – *See Wyclef JEAN*

Chubb ROCK *US, male rapper (1 WEEK)* pos/wks

19 Jan 91	**TREAT 'EM RIGHT** *Champion CHAMP 272*	67	1

Sir Monti ROCK III – *See DISCO TEX and the SEX-O-LETTES*

ROCK AID ARMENIA
UK, male vocal / instrumental charity ensemble (5 WEEKS) pos/wks

16 Dec 89	**SMOKE ON THE WATER** *Life Aid Armenia ARMEN 001*	39	5

ROCK CANDY *UK, male vocal / instrumental group (6 WEEKS)* pos/wks

11 Sep 71	**REMEMBER** *MCA MK 5069*	32	6

ROCK GODDESS *UK, female vocal / instrumental group (5 WEEKS)* pos/wks

5 Mar 83	**MY ANGEL** *A & M AMS 8311*	64	2
24 Mar 84	**I DIDN'T KNOW I LOVED YOU (TILL I SAW YOU ROCK 'N' ROLL)** *A & M AMS 185*	57	3

ROCKER'S REVENGE featuring Donnie CALVIN
US, male / female vocal / instrumental group (20 WEEKS) pos/wks

14 Aug 82 ●	**WALKING ON SUNSHINE** *London LON 11*	4	13
29 Jan 83	**THE HARDER THEY COME** *London LON 18*	30	7

ROCKET FROM THE CRYPT
US, male vocal / instrumental group (7 WEEKS) pos/wks

27 Jan 96	**BORN IN 69** *Elemental ELM 32CD*	68	1
13 Apr 96	**YOUNG LIVERS** *Elemental ELM 33CDS*	67	1
14 Sep 96	**ON A ROPE** *Elemental ELM 38CDS1*	12	4
29 Aug 98	**LIPSTICK** *Elemental ELM 48CDS1*	64	1

ROCKETS – *See Tony CROMBIE and his ROCKETS*

ROCKFORD FILES
UK, male instrumental / production duo (4 WEEKS) pos/wks

11 Mar 95	**YOU SEXY DANCER** *Escapade CDJAPE 7*	34	3
6 Apr 96	**YOU SEXY DANCER (re-issue)** *Escapade CDJAPE 14*	59	1

ROCKIN' BERRIES
UK, male vocal / instrumental group (41 WEEKS) pos/wks

1 Oct 64	**I DIDN'T MEAN TO HURT YOU** *Piccadilly 7N 35197*	43	1
15 Oct 64 ●	**HE'S IN TOWN** *Piccadilly 7N 35203*	3	13
21 Jan 65	**WHAT IN THE WORLD'S COME OVER YOU** *Piccadilly 7N 35217*	23	7
13 May 65 ●	**POOR MAN'S SON** *Piccadilly 7N 35236*	5	11
26 Aug 65	**YOU'RE MY GIRL** *Piccadilly 7N 35254*	40	7
6 Jan 66	**THE WATER IS OVER MY HEAD** *Piccadilly 7N 35270*	43	1
20 Jan 66	**THE WATER IS OVER MY HEAD (re-entry)** *Piccadilly 7N 35270*	50	1

ROCKNEY – *See CHAS and DAVE*

ROCKSTEADY CREW *US, male / female vocal group (16 WEEKS)* pos/wks

1 Oct 83	●	(HEY YOU) THE ROCKSTEADY CREW *Charisma / Virgin RSC 1*	6	12
5 May 84		UPROCK *Charisma / Virgin RSC 2*	64	4

ROCKWELL *US, male vocalist – Kennedy Gordy (11 WEEKS)* pos/wks

4 Feb 84	●	SOMEBODY'S WATCHING ME *Motown TMG 1331*	6	11

'Somebody's Watching Me' features uncredited vocal by Michael Jackson

ROCKY V – *See Joey B ELLIS*

ROCOCO
UK / Italy, male / female vocal / instrumental group (5 WEEKS) pos/wks

16 Dec 89		ITALO HOUSE MIX *Mercury MER 314*	54	5

RODEO JONES
UK / Grenada, male / female vocal / instrumental group (2 WEEKS) pos/wks

30 Jan 93		NATURAL WORLD *A & M AMCD 0165*	75	1
3 Apr 93		SHADES OF SUMMER *A & M AMCD 212*	59	1

Clodagh RODGERS *Ireland, female vocalist (59 WEEKS)* pos/wks

26 Mar 69	●	COME BACK AND SHAKE ME *RCA 1792*	3	14
9 Jul 69	●	GOODNIGHT MIDNIGHT *RCA 1852*	4	11
4 Oct 69		GOODNIGHT MIDNIGHT (re-entry) *RCA 1852*	48	1
8 Nov 69		BILJO *RCA 1891*	22	9
4 Apr 70		EVERYBODY GO HOME THE PARTY'S OVER *RCA 1930*	47	2
20 Mar 71	●	JACK IN THE BOX *RCA 2066*	4	10
9 Oct 71		LADY LOVE BUG *RCA 2117*	28	12

Jimmie RODGERS *US, male vocalist (37 WEEKS)* pos/wks

1 Nov 57		HONEYCOMB *Columbia DB 3986* ▲	30	1
20 Dec 57	●	KISSES SWEETER THAN WINE *Columbia DB 4052*	7	11
28 Mar 58		OH-OH, I'M FALLING IN LOVE AGAIN *Columbia DB 4078*	18	6
19 Dec 58		WOMAN FROM LIBERIA *Columbia DB 4206*	18	6
14 Jun 62	●	ENGLISH COUNTRY GARDEN *Columbia DB 4847*	5	13

Paul RODGERS *UK, male vocalist (2 WEEKS)* pos/wks

12 Feb 94		MUDDY WATER BLUES *Victory ROGCD 1*	45	2

See also FREE; BAD COMPANY

RODRIGUEZ – *See SASH!*

RODS – *See EDDIE and the HOT RODS*

Tommy ROE (471 Top 500) *One of the 1960s' most successful male solo pop singer / songwriters b. 9 May 1942, Georgia, US. Initially recorded Buddy Holly-influenced 'Sheila' with his group The Satins two years before solo version. Co-wrote twice-chart-topping song 'Dizzy' (74 WEEKS)* pos/wks

6 Sep 62	●	SHEILA *HMV POP 1060* ▲	3	14
6 Dec 62		SUSIE DARLIN' *HMV POP 1092*	37	5
21 Mar 63	●	THE FOLK SINGER *HMV POP 1138*	4	13
26 Sep 63	●	EVERYBODY *HMV POP 1207*	9	11
19 Dec 63		EVERYBODY (re-entry) *HMV POP 1207*	49	3
16 Apr 69	★	DIZZY *Stateside SS 2143* ▲	1	19
23 Jul 69		HEATHER HONEY *Stateside SS 2152*	24	9

ROFO *UK, male instrumental / production duo (3 WEEKS)* pos/wks

1 Aug 92		ROFO'S THEME *PWL Continental PWLT 236*	44	3

ROGER *US, male vocalist – Roger Troutman (8 WEEKS)* pos/wks

17 Oct 87		I WANT TO BE YOUR MAN *Reprise W 8229*	61	4
12 Nov 88		BOOM! THERE SHE WAS *Virgin VS 1143*	55	3
13 May 95		HIGH AS A KITE *ffrr FCD 259* [1]	55	1

[1] One Tribe featuring Roger

Julie ROGERS *UK, female vocalist – Julie Rolls (38 WEEKS)* pos/wks

13 Aug 64	●	THE WEDDING *Mercury MF 820* [1]	3	23
10 Dec 64		LIKE A CHILD *Mercury MF 838*	20	9
25 Mar 65		HAWAIIAN WEDDING SONG *Mercury MF 849*	31	6

[1] Julie Rogers with Johnny Arthey and his Orchestra and Chorus

Kenny ROGERS (269 Top 500) *Celebrated crossover country vocalist / actor, who was one of the US's top-selling artists of the past 30 years, b. 21 Aug 1938, Houston. This Grammy-winning ex-New Christy Minstrel has collected more than 20 US gold albums and is a household name in many countries (109 WEEKS)* pos/wks

18 Oct 69	●	RUBY, DON'T TAKE YOUR LOVE TO TOWN *Reprise RS 20829* [1]	2	23
7 Feb 70	●	SOMETHING'S BURNING *Reprise RS 20888* [1]	8	14
30 Apr 77	★	LUCILLE *United Artists UP 36242*	1	14
17 Sep 77		DAYTIME FRIENDS *United Artists UP 36289*	39	4
2 Jun 79		SHE BELIEVES IN ME *United Artists UP 36533*	42	7
26 Jan 80	★	COWARD OF THE COUNTY *United Artists UP 614*	1	12
15 Nov 80		LADY *United Artists UP 635* ▲	12	12
12 Feb 83		WE'VE GOT TONIGHT *Liberty UP 658* [2]	28	7
22 Oct 83		EYES THAT SEE IN THE DARK *RCA 358*	61	1
12 Nov 83	●	ISLANDS IN THE STREAM *RCA 378* [3] ▲	7	15

[1] Kenny Rogers and the First Edition [2] Kenny Rogers and Sheena Easton [3] Kenny Rogers and Dolly Parton

ROKOTTO *UK, male vocal / instrumental group (10 WEEKS)* pos/wks

22 Oct 77		BOOGIE ON UP *State STAT 62*	40	4
10 Jun 78		FUNK THEORY *State STAT 80*	49	6

ROLLERGIRL *Germany, female vocalist – Nicci Juice (3 WEEKS)* pos/wks

16 Sep 00		DEAR JESSIE *Neo NEOCD 038*	22	3

ROLLING STONES (17 Top 500) *"World's No. 1 rock group": Mick Jagger (v), Keith Richard (g), Brian Jones (g) (d. 1969), Bill Wyman (b) (left 1991), Charlie Watts (d) - Ron Wood (g) joined 1975. No group has accumulated more UK or US Top 10 albums (they have record 38 US gold albums) or grossed more income from touring than legendary British band who have broken box office records on every continent and are still world's highest earning live band. Ever controversial group were early members of Rock and Roll Hall of Fame; Jagger and Richard were inducted into Songwriters' Hall of Fame and group received a Grammy Lifetime Achievement award (1986) (366 WEEKS)* pos/wks

25 Jul 63		COME ON *Decca F 11675*	21	14
14 Nov 63		I WANNA BE YOUR MAN *Decca F 11764*	12	16
27 Feb 64	●	NOT FADE AWAY *Decca F 11845*	3	15
2 Jul 64	★	IT'S ALL OVER NOW *Decca F 11934*	1	15
19 Nov 64	★	LITTLE RED ROOSTER *Decca F 12014*	1	12
4 Mar 65	★	THE LAST TIME *Decca F 12104*	1	13
26 Aug 65	★	(I CAN'T GET NO) SATISFACTION *Decca F 12220* ▲	1	12
28 Oct 65	★	GET OFF OF MY CLOUD *Decca F 12263* ▲	1	12
10 Feb 66	●	19TH NERVOUS BREAKDOWN *Decca F 12331*	2	8
19 May 66	★	PAINT IT BLACK *Decca F 12395* ▲	1	10
29 Sep 66	●	HAVE YOU SEEN YOUR MOTHER BABY, STANDING IN THE SHADOW? *Decca F 12497*	5	8
19 Jan 67	●	LET'S SPEND THE NIGHT TOGETHER / RUBY TUESDAY *Decca F 12546* [1] ▲	3	10
23 Aug 67	●	WE LOVE YOU / DANDELION *Decca F 12654*	8	8
29 May 68	★	JUMPIN' JACK FLASH *Decca F 12782*	1	11
9 Jul 69	★	HONKY TONK WOMEN *Decca F 12952* ▲	1	17
24 Apr 71	●	BROWN SUGAR / BITCH / LET IT ROCK *Rolling Stones RS 19100* ▲	2	13
3 Jul 71		STREET FIGHTING MAN *Decca F 13195*	21	8
29 Apr 72	●	TUMBLING DICE *Rolling Stones RS 19103*	5	8
1 Sep 73	●	ANGIE *Rolling Stones RS 19105* ▲	5	10
3 Aug 74	●	IT'S ONLY ROCK AND ROLL *Rolling Stones RS 19114*	10	7
20 Sep 75		OUT OF TIME *Decca F 13597*	45	2
1 May 76	●	FOOL TO CRY *Rolling Stones RS 19121*	6	10
3 Jun 78	●	MISS YOU / FARAWAY EYES *Rolling Stones EMI 2802* ▲	3	13
30 Sep 78		RESPECTABLE *Rolling Stones EMI 2861*	23	9
5 Jul 80	●	EMOTIONAL RESCUE *Rolling Stones RSR 105*	9	8
4 Oct 80		SHE'S SO COLD *Rolling Stones RSR 106*	33	6
29 Aug 81	●	START ME UP *Rolling Stones RSR 108*	7	9
12 Dec 81		WAITING ON A FRIEND *Rolling Stones RSR 109*	50	6
12 Jun 82		GOING TO A GO GO *Rolling Stones RSR 110*	26	6

2 Oct 82	**TIME IS ON MY SIDE** *Rolling Stones RSR 111*	62	2
12 Nov 83	**UNDERCOVER OF THE NIGHT** *Rolling Stones RSR 113*	11	9
11 Feb 84	**SHE WAS HOT** *Rolling Stones RSR 114*	42	4
21 Jul 84	**BROWN SUGAR (re-issue)** *Rolling Stones SUGAR 1*	58	2
15 Mar 86	**HARLEM SHUFFLE** *Rolling Stones A 6864*	13	7
2 Sep 89	**MIXED EMOTIONS** *Rolling Stones 655193 7*	36	5
2 Dec 89	**ROCK AND A HARD PLACE** *Rolling Stones 655422 7*	63	1
23 Jun 90	**PAINT IT BLACK (re-issue)** *London LON 264*	61	3
30 Jun 90	**ALMOST HEAR YOU SIGH** *Rolling Stones 656065 7*	31	5
30 Mar 91	**HIGHWIRE** *Rolling Stones 6567567*	29	4
1 Jun 91	**RUBY TUESDAY (LIVE)** *Rolling Stones 6568927*	59	2
16 Jul 94	**LOVE IS STRONG** *Virgin VSCDT 1503*	14	5
8 Oct 94	**YOU GOT ME ROCKING** *Virgin VSCDG 1518*	23	3
10 Dec 94	**OUT OF TEARS** *Virgin VSCDT 1524*	36	4
15 Jul 95	**I GO WILD** *Virgin VSCDX 1539*	29	3
11 Nov 95	**LIKE A ROLLING STONE** *Virgin VSCDT 1562*	12	5
4 Oct 97	**ANYBODY SEEN MY BABY?** *Virgin VSCDT 1653*	22	3
7 Feb 98	**SAINT OF ME** *Virgin VSCDT 1667*	26	2
22 Aug 98	**OUT OF CONTROL** *Virgin VSCDT 1700*	51	1

US No.1 symbol referring to 'Let's Spend The Night Together / Ruby Tuesday' applies to Ruby Tuesday which hit the top spot in 1967

'Faraway Eyes' was listed from 15 July 1978, with a peak position of 10

ROLLINS BAND *US, male vocal / instrumental group (4 WEEKS)* pos/wks

12 Sep 92	**TEARING** *Imago 72787250187*	54	2
10 Sep 94	**LIAR / DISCONNECTED** *Imago 74321213052*	27	2

ROLLO *UK, male producer – Roland Armstrong (8 WEEKS)* pos/wks

29 Jan 94	**GET OFF YOUR HIGH HORSE** *Cheeky CHEKCD 003* [1]	43	2
1 Oct 94	**GET OFF YOUR HIGH HORSE (re-entry)** *Cheeky CHEKCD 003* [1]	47	2
10 Jun 95	**LOVE LOVE LOVE - HERE I COME** *Cheeky CHEKCD 007* [2]	32	2
8 Jun 96	**LET THIS BE A PRAYER** *Cheeky CHEKCD 013* [3]	26	2

[1] Rollo Goes Camping [2] Rollo Goes Mystic [3] Rollo Goes Spiritual with Pauline Taylor

ROMAN HOLLIDAY *UK, male vocal / instrumental group (19 WEEKS)* pos/wks

2 Apr 83	**STAND BY** *Jive JIVE 31*	61	3
2 Jul 83	**DON'T TRY TO STOP IT** *Jive JIVE 39*	14	9
24 Sep 83	**MOTORMANIA** *Jive JIVE 49*	40	7

ROMAN NUMERALS – *See Vic REEVES*

ROMANTICS – *See RUBY and the ROMANTICS*

Max ROMEO *Jamaica, male vocalist – Maxie Smith (25 WEEKS)* pos/wks

28 May 69 ●	**WET DREAM** *Unity UN 503*	10	24
29 Nov 69	**WET DREAM (re-entry)** *Unity UN 503*	50	1

Harry 'Choo-Choo' ROMERO
US, male producer and US, female vocalist (3 WEEKS) pos/wks

22 May 99	**JUST CAN'T GET ENOUGH** *AM:PM CDAMPM 121* [1]	39	2
1 Sep 01	**I WANT OUT (I CAN'T BELIEVE)** *Perfecto PERF 22CDS*	51	1

[1] Harry 'Choo Choo' Romero presents Inaya Day

See also CHOO CHOO PROJECT

RONALDO'S REVENGE *UK, male production duo (2 WEEKS)* pos/wks

1 Aug 98	**MAS QUE MANCADA** *AM:PM 5827532*	37	2

See also FULL INTENTION

RONDO VENEZIANO *Italy, orchestra (3 WEEKS)* pos/wks

22 Oct 83	**LA SERENISSIMA (THEME FROM 'VENICE IN PERIL')** *Ferroway 7 RON 1*	58	3

RONETTES *US, female vocal group (34 WEEKS)* pos/wks

17 Oct 63 ●	**BE MY BABY** *London HLU 9793*	4	13
9 Jan 64	**BABY, I LOVE YOU** *London HLU 9826*	11	14
27 Aug 64	**(THE BEST PART OF) BREAKIN' UP** *London HLU 9905*	43	3
8 Oct 64	**DO I LOVE YOU** *London HLU 9922*	35	4

RONNETTE – *See FIDELFATTI featuring RONNETTE*

Mick RONSON with Joe ELLIOTT
UK, male instrumental / vocal duo (1 WEEK) pos/wks

7 May 94	**DON'T LOOK DOWN** *Epic 6603582*	55	1

Linda RONSTADT *US, female vocalist (34 WEEKS)* pos/wks

8 May 76	**TRACKS OF MY TEARS** *Asylum K 13034*	42	3
28 Jan 78	**BLUE BAYOU** *Asylum K 13106*	35	4
26 May 79	**ALISON** *Asylum K 13149*	66	2
11 Jul 87 ●	**SOMEWHERE OUT THERE** *MCA MCA 1132* [1]	8	13
11 Nov 89 ●	**DON'T KNOW MUCH** *Elektra EKR 101* [2]	2	12

[1] Linda Ronstadt and James Ingram [2] Linda Ronstadt featuring Aaron Neville

ROOFTOP SINGERS *US, male / female vocal group (12 WEEKS)* pos/wks

31 Jan 63 ●	**WALK RIGHT IN** *Fontana 271700 TF* ▲	10	12

ROOTJOOSE *UK, male vocal / instrumental group (3 WEEKS)* pos/wks

17 May 97	**CAN'T KEEP LIVING THIS WAY** *Rage RAGECD 2*	73	1
2 Aug 97	**MR FIXIT** *Rage RAGECDX 3*	54	1
4 Oct 97	**LONG WAY** *Rage RAGECD 5*	68	1

ROOTS *US, male rap / production group (3 WEEKS)* pos/wks

3 May 97	**WHAT THEY DO** *Geffen GFSTD 22240*	49	1
6 Mar 99	**YOU GOT ME** *MCA MCSTD 48110* [1]	31	2

[1] Roots featuring Erykah Badu

Ralphi ROSARIO – *See Richie RICH*

Mykal ROSE – *See Shabba RANKS*

ROSE OF ROMANCE ORCHESTRA *UK, orchestra (1 WEEK)* pos/wks

9 Jan 82	**TARA'S THEME FROM 'GONE WITH THE WIND'** *BBC RESL 108*	71	1

ROSE ROYCE (250 Top 500) *The best-selling nine-piece soul / dance combo from Los Angeles, whose biggest hits featured vocalist Gwen Dickey, started as a backing band for Motown acts and topped the UK album chart with their Greatest Hits collection in 1980 (113 WEEKS)* pos/wks

25 Dec 76 ●	**CAR WASH** *MCA 267* ▲	9	12
22 Jan 77	**PUT YOUR MONEY WHERE YOUR MOUTH IS** *MCA 259*	44	5
2 Apr 77	**I WANNA GET NEXT TO YOU** *MCA 278*	14	8
24 Sep 77	**DO YOUR DANCE** *Whitfield K 17006*	30	6
14 Jan 78 ●	**WISHING ON A STAR** *Warner Bros. K 17060*	3	14
6 May 78	**IT MAKES YOU FEEL LIKE DANCIN'** *Warner Bros. K 17148*	16	10
16 Sep 78 ●	**LOVE DON'T LIVE HERE ANYMORE** *Whitfield K 17236*	2	10
3 Feb 79	**I'M IN LOVE (AND I LOVE THE FEELING)** *Whitfield K 17291*	51	4
17 Nov 79	**IS IT LOVE YOU'RE AFTER** *Whitfield K 17456*	13	13
8 Mar 80	**OOH BOY** *Whitfield K 17575*	46	7
21 Nov 81	**R.R. EXPRESS** *Warner Bros. K 17875*	52	3
1 Sep 84	**MAGIC TOUCH** *Streetwave KHAN 21*	43	8
6 Apr 85	**LOVE ME RIGHT NOW** *Streetwave KHAN 39*	60	3
11 Jun 88	**CAR WASH / IS IT LOVE YOU'RE AFTER (re-issue)** *MCA MCA 1253*	20	7
31 Oct 98	**CAR WASH (re-recording)** *MCA MCSTD 48096* [1]	18	3

[1] Rose Royce featuring Gwen Dickey

ROSE TATTOO *Australia, male vocal / instrumental group (4 WEEKS)* pos/wks

11 Jul 81	**ROCK 'N' ROLL OUTLAW** *Carrere CAR 200*	60	4

Jimmy ROSELLI *US, male vocalist (8 WEEKS)* pos/wks

5 Mar 83	**WHEN YOUR OLD WEDDING RING WAS NEW** *A1 282*	51	5
20 Jun 87	**WHEN YOUR OLD WEDDING RING WAS NEW (re-issue)** *First Night SCORE 9*	52	3

ROSIE – *See G NATION featuring ROSIE*

Diana ROSS (6) (Top 500)

Perennially popular ex-leader of the Supremes, the most successful girl group of all time, b. Diane Earle, 26 Mar 1944, Detroit, US. Ross continued to clock up worldwide hits after leaving trio in 1970 and sang lead on at least one hit every year for a record 33 years (1964-1996). The classy vocalist has also had more albums on the UK chart than any other American female artist. Diana, who starred in the movies 'Lady Sings the Blues' (1972), 'Mahogany' (76) and 'The Wiz' (78), moved from Motown to RCA in 1981 for a (female) record $20 million. In 1994, she was the star of the opening ceremony of football's World Cup, and in 1998 was sampled on chart-topping singles by Puff Daddy and Monica. In her homeland this supreme song stylist has clocked up a staggering 22 Top 5 entries during her career, even though she has not had a major hit there since 1984. She has been inducted into the Soul Train and Songwriters' Hall of Fame and was the recipient of a Lifetime Achievement trophy at the World Music Awards in 1996 (560 WEEKS)

			pos	wks
30 Aug 67	●	**REFLECTIONS** *Tamla Motown TMG 616* [1]	5	14
29 Nov 67		**IN AND OUT OF LOVE** *Tamla Motown TMG 632* [1]	13	13
10 Apr 68		**FOREVER CAME TODAY** *Tamla Motown TMG 650* [1]	28	8
3 Jul 68		**SOME THINGS YOU NEVER GET USED TO** *Tamla Motown TMG 662* [1]	34	6
20 Nov 68		**LOVE CHILD** *Tamla Motown TMG 677* [1] ▲	15	14
29 Jan 69	●	**I'M GONNA MAKE YOU LOVE ME** *Tamla Motown TMG 685* [2]	3	11
23 Apr 69		**I'M GONNA MAKE YOU LOVE ME (re-entry)** *Tamla Motown TMG 685* [2]	49	1
23 Apr 69		**I'M LIVING IN SHAME** *Tamla Motown TMG 695* [1]	14	9
2 Jul 69		**I'M LIVING IN SHAME (re-entry)** *Tamla Motown TMG 695* [1]	50	1
16 Jul 69		**NO MATTER WHAT SIGN YOU ARE** *Tamla Motown TMG 704* [1]	37	7
20 Sep 69		**I SECOND THAT EMOTION** *Tamla Motown TMG 709* [2]	18	8
13 Dec 69		**SOMEDAY WE'LL BE TOGETHER** *Tamla Motown TMG 721* [1] ▲	13	13
21 Mar 70		**WHY (MUST WE FALL IN LOVE)** *Tamla Motown TMG 730* [2]	31	7
18 Jul 70		**REACH OUT AND TOUCH** *Tamla Motown TMG 743*	33	5
12 Sep 70	●	**AIN'T NO MOUNTAIN HIGH ENOUGH** *Tamla Motown TMG 751* ▲	6	12
3 Apr 71	●	**REMEMBER ME** *Tamla Motown TMG 768*	7	12
31 Jul 71	★	**I'M STILL WAITING** *Tamla Motown TMG 781*	1	14
30 Oct 71	●	**SURRENDER** *Tamla Motown TMG 792*	10	11
13 May 72		**DOOBEDOOD'NDOOBE DOOBEDOOD'NDOOBE** *Tamla Motown TMG 812*	12	9
14 Jul 73	●	**TOUCH ME IN THE MORNING** *Tamla Motown TMG 861* ▲	9	12
13 Oct 73		**TOUCH ME IN THE MORNING (re-entry)** *Tamla Motown TMG 861*	50	1
5 Jan 74	●	**ALL OF MY LIFE** *Tamla Motown TMG 880*	9	13
23 Mar 74	●	**YOU ARE EVERYTHING** *Tamla Motown TMG 890* [3]	5	12
4 May 74		**LAST TIME I SAW HIM** *Tamla Motown TMG 893*	35	4
20 Jul 74		**STOP LOOK LISTEN (TO YOUR HEART)** *Tamla Motown TMG 906* [3]	25	8
24 Aug 74		**BABY LOVE (re-issue)** *Tamla Motown TMG 915* [1]	12	10
28 Sep 74		**LOVE ME** *Tamla Motown TMG 917*	38	5
29 Mar 75		**SORRY DOESN'T ALWAYS MAKE IT RIGHT** *Tamla Motown TMG 941*	23	9
3 Apr 76	●	**THEME FROM 'MAHOGANY' (DO YOU KNOW WHERE YOU'RE GOING TO)** *Tamla Motown TMG 1010* ▲	5	8
24 Apr 76	●	**LOVE HANGOVER** *Tamla Motown TMG 1024* ▲	10	10
10 Jul 76		**I THOUGHT IT TOOK A LITTLE TIME** *Tamla Motown TMG 1032*	32	5
16 Oct 76		**I'M STILL WAITING (re-issue)** *Tamla Motown TMG 1041*	41	4
19 Nov 77		**GETTIN' READY FOR LOVE** *Motown TMG 1090*	23	7
22 Jul 78		**LOVIN' LIVIN' AND GIVIN'** *Motown TMG 1112*	54	6
18 Nov 78		**EASE ON DOWN THE ROAD** *MCA 396* [4]	45	4
24 Feb 79		**POPS WE LOVE YOU** *Motown TMG 1136* [5]	66	5
21 Jul 79		**THE BOSS** *Motown TMG 1150*	40	7
6 Oct 79		**NO ONE GETS THE PRIZE** *Motown TMG 1160*	59	3
24 Nov 79		**IT'S MY HOUSE** *Motown TMG 1169*	32	10
19 Jul 80	●	**UPSIDE DOWN** *Motown TMG 1195* ▲	2	12
20 Sep 80	●	**MY OLD PIANO** *Motown TMG 1202*	5	9
15 Nov 80		**I'M COMING OUT** *Motown TMG 1210*	13	10
17 Jan 81		**IT'S MY TURN** *Motown TMG 1217*	16	8
28 Mar 81		**ONE MORE CHANCE** *Motown TMG 1227*	49	5
13 Jun 81		**CRYIN' MY HEART OUT FOR YOU** *Motown TMG 1233*	58	3
12 Sep 81	●	**ENDLESS LOVE** *Motown TMG 1240* [6] ▲	7	12
7 Nov 81	●	**WHY DO FOOLS FALL IN LOVE** *Capitol CL 226*	4	12
23 Jan 82		**TENDERNESS** *Motown TMG 1248*	73	1
30 Jan 82		**MIRROR MIRROR** *Capitol CL 234*	36	5
6 Feb 82		**TENDERNESS (re-entry)** *Motown TMG 1248*	75	1
29 May 82	●	**WORK THAT BODY** *Capitol CL 241*	7	11
7 Aug 82		**IT'S NEVER TOO LATE** *Capitol CL 256*	41	4
23 Oct 82		**MUSCLES** *Capitol CL 268*	15	9
15 Jan 83		**SO CLOSE** *Capitol CL 277*	43	4
23 Jul 83		**PIECES OF ICE** *Capitol CL 298*	46	3
7 Jul 84		**ALL OF YOU** *CBS A 4522* [7]	43	8
15 Sep 84		**TOUCH BY TOUCH** *Capitol CL 337*	47	6
28 Sep 85		**EATEN ALIVE** *Capitol CL 372*	71	1
25 Jan 86	★	**CHAIN REACTION** *Capitol CL 386*	1	17
3 May 86		**EXPERIENCE** *Capitol CL 400*	47	3
13 Jun 87		**DIRTY LOOKS** *EMI EM 2*	49	3
8 Oct 88		**MR LEE** *EMI EM 73*	58	2
26 Nov 88		**LOVE HANGOVER (re-mix)** *Motown ZB 42307*	75	1
18 Feb 89		**STOP! IN THE NAME OF LOVE (re-issue)** *Motown ZB 41963* [1]	62	1
6 May 89		**WORKIN' OVERTIME** *EMI EM 91*	32	5
29 Jul 89		**PARADISE** *EMI EM 94*	61	2
7 Jul 90		**I'M STILL WAITING (re-mix)** *Motown ZB 43781*	21	6
30 Nov 91	●	**WHEN YOU TELL ME THAT YOU LOVE ME** *EMI EM 217*	2	11
15 Feb 92		**THE FORCE BEHIND THE POWER** *EMI EM 221*	27	3
20 Jun 92	●	**ONE SHINING MOMENT** *EMI EM 239*	10	8
28 Nov 92		**IF WE HOLD ON TOGETHER** *EMI EM 257*	11	10
13 Mar 93		**HEART (DON'T CHANGE MY MIND)** *EMI CDEM 261*	31	3
9 Oct 93		**CHAIN REACTION (re-issue)** *EMI CDEM 290*	20	5
11 Dec 93		**YOUR LOVE** *EMI CDEM 299*	14	8
2 Apr 94		**THE BEST YEARS OF MY LIFE** *EMI CDEM 305*	28	4
9 Jul 94		**WHY DO FOOLS FALL IN LOVE (re-issue) / I'M COMING OUT (re-mix)** *EMI CDEM 332*	36	4
2 Sep 95		**TAKE ME HIGHER** *EMI CDEM 388*	32	4
25 Nov 95		**I'M GONE** *EMI CDEM 402*	36	3
17 Feb 96		**I WILL SURVIVE** *EMI CDEM 415* [8]	14	4
21 Dec 96		**IN THE ONES YOU LOVE** *EMI CDEM 457*	34	4
6 Nov 99	●	**NOT OVER YOU YET** *EMI CDEMS 553*	9	6
15 Jan 00		**NOT OVER YOU YET (re-entry)** *EMI CDEMS 553*	58	1

[1] Diana Ross and the Supremes [2] Diana Ross and the Supremes and the Temptations [3] Diana Ross and Marvin Gaye [4] Diana Ross and Michael Jackson [5] Diana Ross, Marvin Gaye, Smokey Robinson and Stevie Wonder [6] Diana Ross and Lionel Richie [7] Julio Iglesias and Diana Ross [8] Diana

See also SUPREMES

Ricky ROSS *UK, male vocalist (3 WEEKS)*

			pos	wks
18 May 96		**RADIO ON** *Epic 6631352*	35	2
10 Aug 96		**GOOD EVENING PHILADELPHIA** *Epic 6635335*	58	1

See also DEACON BLUE

Francis ROSSI *UK, male vocalist (6 WEEKS)*

			pos	wks
11 May 85		**MODERN ROMANCE (I WANT TO FALL IN LOVE AGAIN)** *Vertigo FROS 1* [1]	54	4
3 Aug 96		**GIVE MYSELF TO LOVE** *Virgin VSCDT 1594* [2]	42	2

[1] Francis Rossi and Bernard Frost [2] Francis Rossi of Status Quo

See also STATUS QUO

Nini ROSSO *Italy, male instrumentalist – trumpet (14 WEEKS)*

			pos	wks
26 Aug 65	●	**IL SILENZIO** *Durium DRS 54000*	8	14

David Lee ROTH *US, male vocalist (15 WEEKS)*

			pos	wks
23 Feb 85		**CALIFORNIA GIRLS** *Warner Bros. W 9102*	68	2
5 Mar 88		**JUST LIKE PARADISE** *Warner Bros. W 8119*	27	7
3 Sep 88		**DAMN GOOD / STAND UP** *Warner Bros. W 7753*	72	1
12 Jan 91		**A LIL' AIN'T ENOUGH** *Warner Bros. W 0002*	32	3
19 Feb 94		**SHE'S MY MACHINE** *Reprise W 0229CD*	64	1
28 May 94		**NIGHT LIFE** *Reprise W 0249CD*	72	1

See also VAN HALEN

ROTTERDAM TERMINATION SOURCE
Holland, male instrumental / production duo (6 WEEKS) pos/wks

7 Nov 92		**POING** *SEP EDGE 74*	27	4
25 Dec 93		**MERRY X-MESS** *React CDREACT 33*	73	2

ROULA – *See 20 FINGERS*

ROULETTES – *See Adam FAITH*

Demis ROUSSOS *Greece, male vocalist (44 WEEKS)* pos/wks

22 Nov 75	●	**HAPPY TO BE ON AN ISLAND IN THE SUN** *Philips 6042 033*	5	10
28 Feb 76		**CAN'T SAY HOW MUCH I LOVE YOU** *Philips 6042 114*	35	5
26 Jun 76	★	**THE ROUSSOS PHENOMENON (EP)** *Philips DEMIS 001*	1	12
2 Oct 76	●	**WHEN FOREVER HAS GONE** *Philips 6042 186*	2	10
19 Mar 77		**BECAUSE** *Philips 6042 245*	39	4
18 Jun 77		**KYRILA (EP)** *Philips Demis 002*	33	3

Tracks on The Roussos Phenomenon (EP): Forever and Ever / Sing an Ode to Love / So Dreamy / My Friend the Wind. Tracks on Kyrila (EP): Kyrila / I'm Gonna Fall in Love / I Dig You / Sister Emilyne

ROUTERS *US, male instrumental group (7 WEEKS)* pos/wks

27 Dec 62		**LET'S GO** *Warner Bros. WB 77*	32	7

Maria ROWE *UK, female vocalist (2 WEEKS)* pos/wks

20 May 95		**SEXUAL** *ffrr FCD 248*	67	2

ROWETTA – *See OPEN ARMS featuring ROWETTA*

Kevin ROWLAND – *See DEXY'S MIDNIGHT RUNNERS*

John ROWLES *New Zealand, male vocalist (28 WEEKS)* pos/wks

13 Mar 68	●	**IF I ONLY HAD TIME** *MCA MU 1000*	3	18
19 Jun 68		**HUSH… NOT A WORD TO MARY** *MCA MU 1023*	12	10

Lisa ROXANNE
UK, female vocalist – Lisa Roxanne Naraine (2 WEEKS) pos/wks

9 Jun 01		**NO FLOW** *Palm Pictures PPCD 70542*	18	2

ROXETTE (169 Top 500)
The most successful Scandinavian act in the US singles chart: Marie Fredriksson (v), Per Gessle (v/g). The duo, who have even appeared on postage stamps in their homeland, can claim total worldwide sales in excess of 40 million (143 WEEKS) pos/wks

22 Apr 89	●	**THE LOOK** *EMI EM 87* ▲	7	10
15 Jul 89		**DRESSED FOR SUCCESS** *EMI EM 96*	48	5
28 Oct 89		**LISTEN TO YOUR HEART** *EMI EM 108* ▲	62	3
2 Jun 90	●	**IT MUST HAVE BEEN LOVE** *EMI EM 141* ▲	3	14
11 Aug 90	●	**LISTEN TO YOUR HEART / DANGEROUS (re-issue)** *EMI EM 149*	6	9
27 Oct 90		**DRESSED FOR SUCCESS (re-issue)** *EMI EM 162*	18	7
9 Mar 91	●	**JOYRIDE** *EMI EM 177* ▲	4	10
11 May 91		**FADING LIKE A FLOWER (EVERY TIME YOU LEAVE)** *EMI EM 190*	12	6
7 Sep 91		**THE BIG L** *EMI EM 204*	21	6
23 Nov 91		**SPENDING MY TIME** *EMI EM 215*	22	4
28 Mar 92		**CHURCH OF YOUR HEART** *EMI EM 227*	21	4
1 Aug 92		**HOW DO YOU DO!** *EMI EM 241*	13	7
7 Nov 92		**QUEEN OF RAIN** *EMI EM 253*	28	4
24 Jul 93	●	**ALMOST UNREAL** *EMI CDEM 268*	7	9
18 Sep 93	●	**IT MUST HAVE BEEN LOVE (re-issue)** *EMI CDEM 285*	10	8
26 Mar 94		**SLEEPING IN MY CAR** *EMI CDEM 314*	14	6
4 Jun 94		**CRASH! BOOM! BANG!** *EMI CDEM 324*	26	5
17 Sep 94		**FIREWORKS** *EMI CDEM 345*	30	4
3 Dec 94		**RUN TO YOU** *EMI CDEM 360*	27	6
8 Apr 95		**VULNERABLE** *EMI CDEM 369*	44	2
25 Nov 95		**THE LOOK (re-mix)** *EMI CDEM 406*	28	3
30 Mar 96		**YOU DON'T UNDERSTAND ME** *EMI CDEM 418*	42	2
20 Jul 96		**JUNE AFTERNOON** *EMI CDEM 437*	52	1
20 Mar 99		**WISH I COULD FLY** *EMI CDEM 537*	11	7
9 Oct 99		**STARS** *EMI CDEM 550*	56	1

ROXY MUSIC (136 Top 500)
Stylish art-rock group regarded as highly influential pioneers. Nucleus of oft-changing group line-up: Bryan Ferry (v), Andy Mackay (sax), Phil Manzanera (g). A major act of its time, this group amassed eleven Top 11 albums (155 WEEKS) pos/wks

19 Aug 72	●	**VIRGINIA PLAIN** *Island WIP 6144*	4	12
10 Mar 73	●	**PYJAMARAMA** *Island WIP 6159*	10	12
17 Nov 73	●	**STREET LIFE** *Island WIP 6173*	9	12
12 Oct 74		**ALL I WANT IS YOU** *Island WIP 6208*	12	8
11 Oct 75	●	**LOVE IS THE DRUG** *Island WIP 6248*	2	10
27 Dec 75		**BOTH ENDS BURNING** *Island WIP 6262*	25	7
22 Oct 77		**VIRGINIA PLAIN (re-issue)** *Polydor 2001 739*	11	6
3 Mar 79		**TRASH** *Polydor POSP 32*	40	6
28 Apr 79	●	**DANCE AWAY** *Polydor POSP 44*	2	14
11 Aug 79	●	**ANGEL EYES** *Polydor POSP 67*	4	11
17 May 80	●	**OVER YOU** *Polydor POSP 93*	5	9
2 Aug 80	●	**OH YEAH (ON THE RADIO)** *Polydor 2001 972*	5	8
8 Nov 80		**THE SAME OLD SCENE** *Polydor ROXY 1*	12	7
21 Feb 81	★	**JEALOUS GUY** *EG ROXY 2*	1	11
3 Apr 82	●	**MORE THAN THIS** *EG ROXY 3*	6	8
19 Jun 82		**AVALON** *EG ROXY 4*	13	6
25 Sep 82		**TAKE A CHANCE WITH ME** *EG ROXY 5*	26	6
27 Apr 96		**LOVE IS THE DRUG (re-mix)** *EG VSCDT 1580*	33	2

See also Bryan FERRY

Billy Joe ROYAL *US, male vocalist (4 WEEKS)* pos/wks

7 Oct 65		**DOWN IN THE BOONDOCKS** *CBS 201802*	38	4

The Central Band of the ROYAL AIR FORCE, Conductor W/Cdr AE SIMS OBE *UK, military band (1 WEEK)* pos/wks

21 Oct 55		**THE DAM BUSTERS MARCH** *HMV B 10877*	18	1

ROYAL GUARDSMEN
US, male vocal / instrumental group (17 WEEKS) pos/wks

19 Jan 67	●	**SNOOPY VS THE RED BARON** *Stateside SS 574*	8	13
6 Apr 67		**RETURN OF THE RED BARON** *Stateside SS 2010*	37	4

ROYAL HOUSE *US, male DJ / producer – Todd Terry (18 WEEKS)* pos/wks

10 Sep 88		**CAN YOU PARTY** *Champion CHAMP 79*	14	14
7 Jan 89		**YEAH! BUDDY** *Champion CHAMP 91*	35	4

ROYAL PHILHARMONIC ORCHESTRA arranged and conducted by Louis CLARK *UK, orchestra and conductor (19 WEEKS)* pos/wks

25 Jul 81	●	**HOOKED ON CLASSICS** *RCA 109*	2	11
24 Oct 81		**HOOKED ON CAN-CAN** *RCA 151*	47	3
10 Jul 82		**BBC WORLD CUP GRANDSTAND** *BBC RESL 116*	61	3
7 Aug 82		**IF YOU KNEW SOUSA (AND FRIENDS)** *RCA 256*	71	2

Louis Clark did not conduct the third hit

See also Elvis COSTELLO

The Pipes and Drums and Military Band of the ROYAL SCOTS DRAGOON GUARDS *UK, military band (43 WEEKS)* pos/wks

1 Apr 72	★	**AMAZING GRACE** *RCA 2191*	1	24
19 Aug 72		**HEYKENS SERENADE / THE DAY IS ENDED** *RCA 2251*	30	7
2 Dec 72		**LITTLE DRUMMER BOY** *RCA 2301*	13	9
23 Dec 72		**AMAZING GRACE (re-entry)** *RCA 2191*	42	3

ROYALLE DELITE *US, female vocal group (6 WEEKS)* pos/wks

14 Sep 85		**(I'LL BE A) FREAK FOR YOU** *Streetwave KHAN 51*	45	6

ROYCE DA 5'9" – *See BAD MEETS EVIL*

RÖYKSOPP *Norway, male production duo (1 WEEK)* pos/wks

15 Dec 01		**POOR LENO** *Wall of Sound WALLD 073*	59	1

Lita ROZA *UK, female vocalist (18 WEEKS)* pos/wks

13 Mar 53	★	**(HOW MUCH IS) THAT DOGGIE IN THE WINDOW** *Decca F 10070*	1	11

1989

IN THE YEAR IN WHICH IRANIAN LEADER AYATOLLAH KHOMEINI IMPOSED A FATWA ON SALMAN RUSHDIE, PRO-DEMOCRACY PROTESTERS WERE MASSACRED BY THE CHINESE ARMY IN TIANANMEN SQUARE, THE BERLIN WALL FELL TO WORLDWIDE CELEBRATIONS, AND RECORD-BREAKING PRODUCERS/COMPOSERS STOCK AITKEN AND WATERMAN NOTCHED UP SEVEN NO.1s, **JON MOORE** FROM COLDCUT TELLS US ABOUT HIS 'TOP OF THE POPS' EXPERIENCE...

"We were doing 'People Hold On' on 'Top of the Pops' and **Barry Manilow** was on. I was really gobsmacked and everyone was keen to see what he looked like because he was quite a mythical character in some respects. To my great disappointment we were all cleared out of the building so Barry could perform in private, but I did ask for an autograph and one of his entourage kindly got it for me. 'TOTP' was a pretty scary experience because it was a combination of full-on TV stuff and the vaguely BBC back-to-school feel: quite utilitarian and small but it came across as quite exciting. I was lurking around throwing records around but I do remember meeting DLT – that seems like such a different era."

SINGLE OF THE YEAR 'Ride On Time' Black Box
ALBUM OF THE YEAR 'A New Flame' Simply Red

Date	Title	pos	wks
7 Oct 55	**HEY THERE** *Decca F 10611*	17	2
23 Mar 56	**JIMMY UNKNOWN** *Decca F 10679*	15	5

ROZALLA *Zimbabwe, female vocalist – Rozalla Miller (48 WEEKS)* pos/wks

Date	Title	pos	wks
27 Apr 91	**FAITH (IN THE POWER OF LOVE)** *Pulse 8 LOSE 7*	65	2
7 Sep 91 ●	**EVERYBODY'S FREE (TO FEEL GOOD)** *Pulse 8 LOSE 13*	6	11
16 Nov 91	**FAITH (IN THE POWER OF LOVE) (re-issue)** *Pulse 8 LOSE 15*	11	6
22 Feb 92	**ARE YOU READY TO FLY** *Pulse 8 LOSE 21*	14	6
9 May 92	**LOVE BREAKDOWN** *Pulse 8 LOSE 25*	65	2
15 Aug 92	**IN 4 CHOONS LATER** *Pulse 8 LOSE 29*	50	2
30 Oct 93	**DON'T PLAY WITH ME** *Pulse 8 CDLOSE 52*	50	1
5 Feb 94	**I LOVE MUSIC** *Epic 6598932*	18	5
6 Aug 94	**THIS TIME I FOUND LOVE** *Epic 6603742*	33	3
29 Oct 94	**YOU NEVER LOVE THE SAME WAY TWICE** *Epic 6609052*	16	5
4 Mar 95	**BABY** *Epic 6611955*	26	3
31 Aug 96	**EVERYBODY'S FREE (re-mix)** *Pulse 8 CDLOSE 110*	30	2

RTE CONCERT ORCHESTRA – *See Bill WHELAN featuring ANUNA and the RTE CONCERT ORCHESTRA*

RUBBADUBB *UK, male / female vocal / instrumental group (1 WEEK)* pos/wks

Date	Title	pos	wks
18 Jul 98	**TRIBUTE TO OUR ANCESTORS** *Perfecto PERF 165CD*	56	1

RUBETTES *Ex-Barry Blue backing band fronted by Alan Williams, b. 22 Dec 1950, Hertfordshire, UK, whose brand of 1970s good-time rock 'n' roll produced a string of European hits. Distinctive falsetto Paul Da Vinci left the group after singing on their three-million-selling debut hit (68 WEEKS)* pos/wks

Date	Title	pos	wks
4 May 74 ★	**SUGAR BABY LOVE** *Polydor 2058 442*	1	10
13 Jul 74	**TONIGHT** *Polydor 2058 499*	12	9
16 Nov 74 ●	**JUKE BOX JIVE** *Polydor 2058 529*	3	12
8 Mar 75 ●	**I CAN DO IT** *State STAT 1*	7	9
21 Jun 75	**FOE-DEE-O-DEE** *State STAT 7*	15	6
22 Nov 75	**LITTLE DARLING** *State STAT 13*	30	5
1 May 76	**YOU'RE THE REASON WHY** *State STAT 20*	28	4
25 Sep 76	**UNDER ONE ROOF** *State STAT 27*	40	3
12 Feb 77 ●	**BABY I KNOW** *State STAT 37*	10	10

Maria RUBIA – *See FRAGMA*

RUBY and the ROMANTICS *US, female / male vocal group (6 WEEKS)* pos/wks

Date	Title	pos	wks
28 Mar 63	**OUR DAY WILL COME** *London HLR 9679* ▲	38	6

RUDE BOY OF HOUSE – *See HOUSEMASTER BOYZ and the RUDE BOY OF HOUSE*

RUDIES – *See Freddie NOTES and the RUDIES*

RUFF DRIVERZ *UK, male / female vocal / production trio (21 WEEKS)* pos/wks

Date	Title	pos	wks
7 Feb 98	**DON'T STOP** *Inferno CDFERN 003*	30	2
23 May 98	**DEEPER LOVE** *Inferno CDFERN 006*	19	3
24 Oct 98	**SHAME** *Inferno CXFERN 9*	51	2
28 Nov 98 ●	**DREAMING** *Inferno CXFERN 11* [1]	10	8
24 Apr 99	**LA MUSICA** *Inferno CDFERN 14* [1]	14	4
2 Oct 99	**WAITING FOR THE SUN** *Inferno CDFERN 19*	37	2

[1] Ruff Driverz presents Arrola

RUFF ENDZ
US, male vocal duo – David Chance and Dante Jordan (5 WEEKS) pos/wks

Date	Title	pos	wks
19 Aug 00	**NO MORE** *Epic 6696202*	11	5

Frances RUFFELLE *UK, female vocalist (6 WEEKS)* pos/wks

Date	Title	pos	wks
16 Apr 94	**LONELY SYMPHONY** *Virgin VSCDT 1499*	25	6

Bruce RUFFIN *Jamaica, male vocalist – Bernard Downer (23 WEEKS)* pos/wks

Date	Title	pos	wks
1 May 71	**RAIN** *Trojan TR 7814*	19	11
24 Jun 72 ●	**MAD ABOUT YOU** *Rhino RNO 101*	9	12

David RUFFIN *US, male vocalist (10 WEEKS)* pos/wks

Date	Title	pos	wks
17 Jan 76 ●	**WALK AWAY FROM LOVE** *Tamla Motown TMG 1017*	10	8
21 Sep 85	**A NIGHT AT THE APOLLO LIVE!** *RCA PB 49935* [1]	58	2

[1] Daryl Hall and John Oates featuring David Ruffin and Eddie Kendrick

See also TEMPTATIONS

Jimmy RUFFIN (280 Top 500) *Major Motown hitmaker, b. 7 May 1939, Mississippi, US. After rejecting a job as the lead vocalist of The Temptations (taken by his brother David), he had a handful of UK / US hits (several charting twice). He relocated to the UK, and was in a one-off hit act, Council Collective, a Paul Weller project. Son Ray produces chart toppers Blue (106 WEEKS)* pos/wks

Date	Title	pos	wks
27 Oct 66 ●	**WHAT BECOMES OF THE BROKENHEARTED** *Tamla Motown TMG 577*	8	15
9 Feb 67	**I'VE PASSED THIS WAY BEFORE** *Tamla Motown TMG 593*	29	7
20 Apr 67	**GONNA GIVE HER ALL THE LOVE I'VE GOT** *Tamla Motown TMG 603*	26	6
9 Aug 69	**I'VE PASSED THIS WAY BEFORE (re-issue)** *Tamla Motown TMG 703*	33	6
28 Feb 70 ●	**FAREWELL IS A LONELY SOUND** *Tamla Motown TMG 726*	8	16
4 Jul 70 ●	**I'LL SAY FOREVER MY LOVE** *Tamla Motown TMG 740*	7	12
17 Oct 70 ●	**IT'S WONDERFUL (TO BE LOVED BY YOU)** *Tamla Motown TMG 753*	6	14
27 Jul 74 ●	**WHAT BECOMES OF THE BROKENHEARTED (re-issue)** *Tamla Motown TMG 911*	4	12
2 Nov 74	**FAREWELL IS A LONELY SOUND (re-issue)** *Tamla Motown TMG 922*	30	5
16 Nov 74	**TELL ME WHAT YOU WANT** *Polydor 2058 433*	39	4
3 May 80 ●	**HOLD ON TO MY LOVE** *RSO 57*	7	8
26 Jan 85	**THERE WILL NEVER BE ANOTHER YOU** *EMI 5541*	68	1

Kim RUFFIN – *See Chubby CHUNKS*

RUFFNECK featuring YAVAHN
US, male production group featuring US, female vocalist (6 WEEKS) pos/wks

Date	Title	pos	wks
11 Nov 95	**EVERYBODY BE SOMEBODY** *Positiva CDTIV 46*	13	4
7 Sep 96	**MOVE YOUR BODY** *Positiva CDTIV 61*	60	1
1 Dec 01	**EVERYBODY BE SOMEBODY (re-mix)** *Strictly Rhythm SRUKCD 08*	66	1

RUFUS – *See Chaka KHAN*

RUKMANI – *See SNAP*

RUMOUR – *See Graham PARKER and the RUMOUR*

RUMPLE-STILTS-SKIN
US, male / female vocal / instrumental group (4 WEEKS) pos/wks

Date	Title	pos	wks
24 Sep 83	**I THINK I WANT TO DANCE WITH YOU** *Polydor POSP 649*	51	4

RUN-DMC *US, male rap group (59 WEEKS)* pos/wks

Date	Title	pos	wks
19 Jul 86	**MY ADIDAS / PETER PIPER** *London LON 101*	62	2
6 Sep 86 ●	**WALK THIS WAY** *London LON 104*	8	10
7 Feb 87	**YOU BE ILLIN'** *Profile LON 118*	42	4
30 May 87	**IT'S TRICKY** *Profile LON 130*	16	7
12 Dec 87	**CHRISTMAS IN HOLLIS** *Profile LON 163*	56	4
21 May 88	**RUN'S HOUSE** *London LON 177*	37	4
2 Sep 89	**GHOSTBUSTERS** *MCA 1360*	65	2
1 Dec 90	**WHAT'S IT ALL ABOUT** *Profile PROF 315*	48	3
27 Mar 93	**DOWN WITH THE KING** *Profile PROFCD 39*	69	2
21 Feb 98	**IT'S LIKE THAT (German import)** *Columbia 6652932* [1]	63	3
14 Mar 98	**IT'S LIKE THAT (US import)** *Columbia 6652932* [1]	65	1
21 Mar 98 ★	**IT'S LIKE THAT** *Sm:)e Communications SM 90652* [1] ◆ ■	1	16
18 Apr 98	**IT'S TRICKY (import)** *Epidrome EPD 6656982* [1]	74	1

[1] Run-DMC vs Jason Nevins

Walk This Way featured Steve Tyler and Joe Perry of Aerosmith

RUN TINGS *UK, male instrumental / production duo (1 WEEK)* pos/wks

Date	Title	pos	wks
16 May 92	**FIRES BURNING** *Suburban Base SUBBASE 009*	58	1

Todd RUNDGREN *US, male vocalist (8 WEEKS)*

		pos	wks
30 Jun 73	**I SAW THE LIGHT** *Bearsville K 15506*	36	6
14 Dec 85	**LOVING YOU'S A DIRTY JOB BUT SOMEBODY'S GOTTA DO IT** *CBS A 6662* [1]	73	2

[1] Bonnie Tyler, guest vocals Todd Rundgren

RUNRIG *UK, male vocal / instrumental group (28 WEEKS)*

		pos	wks
29 Sep 90	**CAPTURE THE HEART (EP)** *Chrysalis CHS 3594*	49	2
7 Sep 91	**HEARTHAMMER (EP)** *Chrysalis CHS 3754*	25	4
9 Nov 91	**FLOWER OF THE WEST** *Chrysalis CHS 3805*	43	2
6 Mar 93	**WONDERFUL** *Chrysalis CDCHS 3952*	29	3
15 May 93	**THE GREATEST FLAME** *Chrysalis CDCHS 3975*	36	3
7 Jan 95	**THIS TIME OF YEAR** *Chrysalis CDCHS 5018*	38	2
6 May 95	**AN UBHAL AS AIRDE (THE HIGHEST APPLE)** *Chrysalis CDCHS 5021*	18	5
4 Nov 95	**THINGS THAT ARE** *Chrysalis CDCHS 5029*	40	2
12 Oct 96	**RHYTHM OF MY HEART** *Chrysalis CDCHS 5035*	24	2
11 Jan 97	**THE GREATEST FLAME (re-issue)** *Chrysalis CDCHSS 5045*	30	3

Tracks on Capture the Heart (EP): Stepping Down the Glory Road / Satellite Flood / Harvest Moon / The Apple Came Down. Tracks on Hearthammer (EP): Hearthammer / Pride of the Summer (Live) / Loch Lomond (Live) / Solus Na Madain

RuPAUL *US, male drag queen vocalist – Rupaul Charles (19 WEEKS)*

		pos	wks
26 Jun 93	**SUPERMODEL (YOU BETTER WORK)** *Union City UCRD 21*	39	4
18 Sep 93	**HOUSE OF LOVE / BACK TO MY ROOTS** *Union City UCRD 23*	40	2
22 Jan 94	**SUPERMODEL / LITTLE DRUMMER BOY (re-mix)** *Union City UCRD 25*	61	2
26 Feb 94 ●	**DON'T GO BREAKING MY HEART** *Rocket EJCD 33* [1]	7	7
21 May 94	**HOUSE OF LOVE** *Union City UCRDG 29*	68	1
28 Feb 98	**IT'S RAINING MEN…THE SEQUEL** *Logic 74321555412* [2]	21	3

[1] Elton John with RuPaul [2] Martha Wash featuring RuPaul

RUSH *Canada, male vocal / instrumental group (43 WEEKS)*

		pos	wks
11 Feb 78	**CLOSER TO THE HEART** *Mercury RUSH 7*	36	3
15 Mar 80	**SPIRIT OF RADIO** *Mercury RADIO 7*	13	7
28 Mar 81	**VITAL SIGNS / A PASSAGE TO BANGKOK** *Mercury VITAL7*	41	4
31 Oct 81	**TOM SAWYER** *Mercury EXIT 7*	25	6
4 Sep 82	**NEW WORLD MAN** *Mercury RUSH 8*	42	3
30 Oct 82	**SUBDIVISIONS** *Mercury RUSH 9*	53	2
7 May 83	**COUNTDOWN / NEW WORLD MAN (LIVE)** *Mercury RUSH 10*	36	5
26 May 84	**THE BODY ELECTRIC** *Vertigo RUSH 11*	56	3
12 Oct 85	**THE BIG MONEY** *Vertigo RUSH 12*	46	3
31 Oct 87	**TIME STAND STILL** *Vertigo RUSH 13* [1]	42	3
23 Apr 88	**PRIME MOVER** *Vertigo RUSH 14*	43	3
7 Mar 92	**ROLL THE BONES** *Atlantic A 7524*	49	1

[1] Rush with Aimee Mann

Donell RUSH *US, male vocalist (1 WEEK)*

		pos	wks
5 Dec 92	**SYMPHONY** *ID 6587977*	66	1

Jennifer RUSH *US, female vocalist (58 WEEKS)*

		pos	wks
29 Jun 85 ★	**THE POWER OF LOVE** *CBS A 5003* ◆	1	32
14 Dec 85	**RING OF ICE** *CBS A 4745*	14	10
20 Dec 86	**THE POWER OF LOVE (re-entry)** *CBS A 5003*	55	4
20 Jun 87	**FLAMES OF PARADISE** *CBS 650865 7* [1]	59	3
27 May 89	**TILL I LOVED YOU** *CBS 654843 7* [2]	24	9

[1] Jennifer Rush and Elton John [2] Placido Domingo and Jennifer Rush

Patrice RUSHEN *US, female vocalist (25 WEEKS)*

		pos	wks
1 Mar 80	**HAVEN'T YOU HEARD** *Elektra K 12414*	62	3
24 Jan 81	**NEVER GONNA GIVE YOU UP (WON'T LET YOU BE)** *Elektra K 12494*	66	3
24 Apr 82 ●	**FORGET ME NOTS** *Elektra K 13173*	8	11
10 Jul 82	**I WAS TIRED OF BEING ALONE** *Elektra K 13184*	39	5
9 Jun 84	**FEELS SO REAL (WON'T LET GO)** *Elektra E 9742*	51	3

RUSSELL *US, male vocalist – Russell Taylor (1 WEEK)*

		pos	wks
27 May 00	**FOOL FOR LOVE** *Rulin RULIN 1CDS*	52	1

Brenda RUSSELL *US, female vocalist (17 WEEKS)*

		pos	wks
19 Apr 80	**SO GOOD SO RIGHT / IN THE THICK OF IT** *A & M AM 7515*	51	5
12 Mar 88	**PIANO IN THE DARK** *Breakout USA 623*	23	12

Patti RUSSO – *See MEAT LOAF*

RUTH *UK, male vocal / instrumental group (1 WEEK)*

		pos	wks
12 Apr 97	**I DON'T KNOW** *Arc 5737812*	66	1

Paul RUTHERFORD *UK, male vocalist (6 WEEKS)*

		pos	wks
8 Oct 88	**GET REAL** *Fourth & Broadway BRW 113*	47	3
19 Aug 89	**OH WORLD** *Fourth & Broadway BRW 136*	61	3

See also FRANKIE GOES TO HOLLYWOOD

RUTHLESS RAP ASSASSINS *UK, male rappers (2 WEEKS)*

		pos	wks
9 Jun 90	**JUST MELLOW** *Syncopate SY 35*	75	1
1 Sep 90	**AND IT WASN'T A DREAM** *Syncopate SY 38* [1]	75	1

[1] featuring Tracey Carmen

RUTLES *UK, male vocal group (5 WEEKS)*

		pos	wks
15 Apr 78	**I MUST BE IN LOVE** *Warner Bros. K 17125*	39	3
13 May 78	**I MUST BE IN LOVE (re-entry)** *Warner Bros. K 17125*	64	1
16 Nov 96	**SHANGRI-LA** *Virgin America VUSCD 117*	68	1

RUTS *UK, male vocal / instrumental group (28 WEEKS)*

		pos	wks
16 Jun 79 ●	**BABYLON'S BURNING** *Virgin VS 271*	7	11
8 Sep 79	**SOMETHING THAT I SAID** *Virgin VS 285*	29	5
19 Apr 80	**STARING AT THE RUDE BOYS** *Virgin VS 327*	22	8
30 Aug 80	**WEST ONE (SHINE ON ME)** *Virgin VS 370*	43	4

Barry RYAN *UK, male vocalist – Barry Sapherson (33 WEEKS)*

		pos	wks
23 Oct 68 ●	**ELOISE** *MGM 1442*	2	12
19 Feb 69	**LOVE IS LOVE** *MGM 1464*	25	4
4 Oct 69	**THE HUNT** *Polydor 56 348*	34	5
21 Feb 70	**MAGICAL SPIEL** *Polydor 56 370*	49	1
16 May 70	**KITSCH** *Polydor 2001 035*	37	6
15 Jan 72	**CAN'T LET YOU GO** *Polydor 2001 256*	32	5

See also Paul and Barry RYAN

Joshua RYAN *US, male producer (3 WEEKS)*

		pos	wks
27 Jan 01	**PISTOL WHIP** *Nulife/Arista 74321825482*	29	3

Marion RYAN *UK, female vocalist – Marion Sapherson (11 WEEKS)*

		pos	wks
24 Jan 58 ●	**LOVE ME FOREVER** *Pye Nixa N 15121*	5	11

With the Peter Knight Orchestra and the Beryl Stott Chorus

Paul and Barry RYAN
UK, male vocal duo – Paul and Barry Sapherson (43 WEEKS)

		pos	wks
11 Nov 65	**DON'T BRING ME YOUR HEARTACHES** *Decca F 12260*	13	9
3 Feb 66	**HAVE PITY ON THE BOY** *Decca F 12319*	18	6
12 May 66	**I LOVE HER** *Decca F 12391*	17	8
14 Jul 66	**I LOVE HOW YOU LOVE ME** *Decca F 12445*	21	7
29 Sep 66	**HAVE YOU EVER LOVED SOMEBODY** *Decca F 12494*	49	1
8 Dec 66	**MISSY MISSY** *Decca F 12520*	43	4
2 Mar 67	**KEEP IT OUT OF SIGHT** *Decca F 12567*	30	6
29 Jun 67	**CLAIRE** *Decca F 12633*	47	2

See also Barry RYAN

Rebekah RYAN *UK, female vocalist (5 WEEKS)*

		pos	wks
18 May 96	**YOU LIFT ME UP** *MCA MCSTD 40022*	26	3
7 Sep 96	**JUST A LITTLE BIT OF LOVE** *MCA MCSTD 40063*	51	1
17 May 97	**WOMAN IN LOVE** *MCA MCSTD 40109*	64	1

Bobby RYDELL *US, male vocalist – Robert Ridarelli (60 WEEKS)* pos/wks

			pos	wks
10 Mar 60	●	WILD ONE *Columbia DB 4429*	7	14
23 Jun 60		WILD ONE (re-entry) *Columbia DB 4429*	47	1
30 Jun 60		SWINGIN' SCHOOL *Columbia DB 4471*	44	1
1 Sep 60		VOLARE *Columbia DB 4495*	46	1
15 Sep 60		VOLARE (re-entry) *Columbia DB 4495*	22	5
15 Dec 60		SWAY *Columbia DB 4545*	12	13
23 Mar 61		GOOD TIME BABY *Columbia DB 4600*	42	7
19 Apr 62		TEACH ME TO TWIST *Columbia DB 4802* [1]	45	1
20 Dec 62		JINGLE BELL ROCK *Cameo Parkway C 205* [1]	40	3
23 May 63		FORGET HIM *Cameo Parkway C 108*	13	14

[1] Chubby Checker and Bobby Rydell

Mitch RYDER and the DETROIT WHEELS
US, male vocal / instrumental group (5 WEEKS) pos/wks

			pos	wks
10 Feb 66		JENNY TAKE A RIDE *Stateside SS 481*	44	1
24 Feb 66		JENNY TAKE A RIDE (re-entry) *Stateside SS 481*	33	4

Mark RYDER *UK, male producer (2 WEEKS)* pos/wks

			pos	wks
31 Mar 01		JOY *Relentless / Public Demand RELENT 9CDS*	34	2

See also M-D-EMM

Shaun RYDER – *See BLACK GRAPE; HAPPY MONDAYS; HEADS with Shaun RYDER; Russell WATSON*

RYTHM SYNDICATE *US, male vocal / instrumental group (5 WEEKS)* pos/wks

			pos	wks
27 Jul 91		P.A.S.S.I.O.N. *Impact American EM 197*	58	5

S

Robin S *US, female vocalist – Robin Stone (37 WEEKS)* pos/wks

			pos	wks
16 Jan 93		SHOW ME LOVE *Champion CHAMPCD 300*	59	4
13 Mar 93	●	SHOW ME LOVE (re-entry) *Champion CHAMPCD 300*	6	13
31 Jul 93		LUV 4 LUV *Champion CHAMPCD 301*	11	7
4 Dec 93		WHAT I DO BEST *Champion CHAMPCD 307*	43	2
19 Mar 94		I WANT TO THANK YOU *Champion CHAMPCD 310*	48	1
5 Nov 94		BACK IT UP *Champion CHAMPCD 312*	43	2
8 Mar 97	●	SHOW ME LOVE (re-mix) *Champion CHAMPCD 326*	9	5
12 Jul 97		IT MUST BE LOVE *Atlantic A 5596CD*	37	2
4 Oct 97		YOU GOT THE LOVE *Champion CHAMPCD 330*	62	1

S CLUB 7 (240 Top 500) *Made-for-TV act (series seen in more than 100 countries) had the best start to its career of any mixed vocal group, with eight Top 3 hits from first eight releases including four No.1s. Award-winning septet is the largest vocal group ever to top the chart, comprising Jo O'Meara, Tina Barrett, Hannah Spearritt, Rachel Stevens, Paul Cattermole, Bradley McIntosh and Jon Lee (115 WEEKS)* pos/wks

			pos	wks
19 Jun 99	★	BRING IT ALL BACK *Polydor 5610852* ■	1	15
2 Oct 99	●	S CLUB PARTY *Polydor 5614172*	2	12
25 Dec 99	●	TWO IN A MILLION / YOU'RE MY NUMBER ONE *Polydor 5615962*	2	11
8 Jan 00		S CLUB PARTY (re-entry) *Polydor 5614172*	68	2
3 Jun 00	●	REACH *Polydor 5618302*	2	17
23 Sep 00	●	NATURAL *Polydor 5877602*	3	13
9 Dec 00	★	NEVER HAD A DREAM COME TRUE *Polydor 5879032* ■	1	16
6 Jan 01		NATURAL (re-entry) *Polydor 5877602*	56	3
5 May 01	★	DON'T STOP MOVIN' *Polydor 5870832* ■	1	19
5 May 01		NEVER HAD A DREAM COME TRUE (re-entry) *Polydor 5879032*	69	2
1 Dec 01	★	HAVE YOU EVER *Polydor 5705002* ■	1	5

S EXPRESS *UK, male / female vocal / instrumental group, fronted by Mark Moore (50 WEEKS)* pos/wks

			pos	wks
16 Apr 88	★	THEME FROM S-EXPRESS *Rhythm King LEFT 21*	1	13
23 Jul 88	●	SUPERFLY GUY *Rhythm King LEFT 28*	5	9
18 Feb 89	●	HEY MUSIC LOVER *Rhythm King LEFT 30*	6	10
16 Sep 89		MANTRA FOR A STATE OF MIND *Rhythm King LEFT 35*	21	8
15 Sep 90		NOTHING TO LOSE *Rhythm King SEXY 01*	32	4
30 May 92		FIND 'EM, FOOL 'EM, FORGET 'EM *Rhythm King 6580137*	43	2
11 May 96		THEME FROM S.EXPRESS (re-mix) *Rhythm King SEXY 9CD* [1]	14	4

[1] Mark Moore presents S Express

S-J *UK, female vocalist (4 WEEKS)* pos/wks

			pos	wks
11 Jan 97		FEVER *React CDREACT 93*	46	1
24 Jan 98		I FEEL DIVINE *React CDREACT 113*	30	2
7 Nov 98		SHIVER *React CDREACT 138*	59	1

Raphael SAADIQ *US, male vocalist (4 WEEKS)* pos/wks

			pos	wks
23 Nov 96		STRESSED OUT *Jive JIVECD 404* [1]	33	2
19 Jun 99		GET INVOLVED *Hollywood 0101185 HWR* [2]	36	2

[1] A Tribe Called Quest featuring Faith Evans and Raphael Saadiq [2] Raphael Saadiq and Q-Tip

SABRE featuring PRESIDENT BROWN
Jamaica, male vocal duo (1 WEEK) pos/wks

			pos	wks
19 Aug 95		WRONG OR RIGHT *Greensleeves GRECD 485*	71	1

SABRES – *See Denny SEYTON and the SABRES*

SABRES OF PARADISE *UK, male production group (8 WEEKS)* pos/wks

			pos	wks
2 Oct 93		SMOKEBELCH II *Sabres of Paradise PT 009CD*	55	3
9 Apr 94		THEME *Sabres of Paradise PT 014CD*	56	3
17 Sep 94		WILMOT *Warp WAP 50CD*	36	2

SABRINA *Italy, female vocalist – Sabrina Salerno (22 WEEKS)* pos/wks

			pos	wks
6 Feb 88		BOYS (SUMMERTIME LOVE) *IBIZA IBIZ 1*	60	3
11 Jun 88	●	BOYS (SUMMERTIME LOVE) (re-entry) *IBIZA IBIZ 1*	3	11
1 Oct 88		ALL OF ME *PWL PWL 19*	25	7
1 Jul 89		LIKE A YO-YO *Videogram DCUP 1*	72	1

SACRED SPIRIT *Germany, male production trio utilising Native American chants (5 WEEKS)* pos/wks

			pos	wks
15 Apr 95		YEHA-NOHA (WISHES OF HAPPINESS AND PROSPERITY) *Virgin VSCDT 1514*	71	1
18 Nov 95		WISHES OF HAPPINESS AND PROSPERITY (YEHA-NOHA) (re-issue) *Virgin VSC 1568*	37	2
16 Mar 96		WINTER CEREMONY (TOR-CHENEY-NAHANA) *Virgin VSCDT 1574*	45	2

SAD CAFE *UK, male vocal / instrumental group (44 WEEKS)* pos/wks

			pos	wks
22 Sep 79	●	EVERY DAY HURTS *RCA PB 5180*	3	12
19 Jan 80		STRANGE LITTLE GIRL *RCA PB 5202*	32	5
15 Mar 80		MY OH MY *RCA SAD 3*	14	11
21 Jun 80		NOTHING LEFT TOULOUSE *RCA SAD 4*	62	4
27 Sep 80		LA-DI-DA *RCA SAD 5*	41	6
20 Dec 80		I'M IN LOVE AGAIN *RCA SAD 6*	40	6

SADE *UK, female / male vocal / instrumental group, lead vocals – Helen Folasade Adu (69 WEEKS)* pos/wks

			pos	wks
25 Feb 84	●	YOUR LOVE IS KING *Epic A 4137*	6	11
19 May 84		YOUR LOVE IS KING (re-entry) *Epic A 4137*	75	1
26 May 84		WHEN AM I GONNA MAKE A LIVING *Epic A 4437*	36	5
15 Sep 84		SMOOTH OPERATOR *Epic A 4655*	19	10
12 Oct 85		THE SWEETEST TABOO *Epic A 6609*	31	5
11 Jan 86		IS IT A CRIME *Epic A 6742*	49	3
2 Apr 88		LOVE IS STRONGER THAN PRIDE *Epic SADE 1*	44	3
4 Jun 88		PARADISE *Epic SADE 2*	29	7
10 Oct 92		NO ORDINARY LOVE *Epic 6583562*	26	3
28 Nov 92		FEEL NO PAIN *Epic 6588297*	56	2

8 May 93		KISS OF LIFE *Epic 6591162*	44	3
5 Jun 93		NO ORDINARY LOVE (re-entry) *Epic 6583562*	14	8
31 Jul 93		CHERISH THE DAY *Epic 6594812*	53	2
18 Nov 00		BY YOUR SIDE *Epic 6699992*	17	5
24 Mar 01		KING OF SORROW *Epic 6708672*	59	1

Staff Sergeant Barry SADLER *US, male vocalist (8 WEEKS)* pos/wks

24 Mar 66		THE BALLAD OF THE GREEN BERETS *RCA 1506* ▲	24	8

SAFFRON *UK, female vocalist (2 WEEKS)* pos/wks

16 Jan 93		CIRCLES *WEA SAFF 9CD*	60	2

See also REPUBLICA

SAFFRONS – *See CINDY and the SAFFRONS*

SAFRI DUO *Denmark, male instrumental / production duo – Uffe Savery and Morten Friis (9 WEEKS)* pos/wks

3 Feb 01	●	PLAYED-A-LIVE (THE BONGO SONG) *AM:PM CDAMPM 141*	6	9

Mike SAGAR and The CRESTERS *UK, male vocalist (5 WEEKS)* pos/wks

8 Dec 60		DEEP FEELING *HMV POP 819*	44	5

SAGAT *US, male rapper (6 WEEKS)* pos/wks

4 Dec 93		FUNK DAT *ffrr FCD 224*	25	5
3 Dec 94		LUVSTUFF *ffrr FCD 250*	71	1

Carole Bayer SAGER *US, female vocalist (9 WEEKS)* pos/wks

28 May 77	●	YOU'RE MOVING OUT TODAY *Elektra K 12257*	6	9

Bally SAGOO *UK, male producer / instrumentalist (8 WEEKS)* pos/wks

3 Sep 94		CHURA LIYA *Columbia 6607092*	64	1
22 Apr 95		CHOLI KE PEECHE *Columbia 6613352*	45	1
19 Oct 96		DIL CHEEZ (MY HEART...) *Higher Ground 6634882*	12	3
1 Feb 97		TUM BIN JIYA *Higher Ground 6641372*	21	3

SAILOR *UK, male vocal / instrumental group (24 WEEKS)* pos/wks

6 Dec 75	●	GLASS OF CHAMPAGNE *Epic EPC 3770*	2	12
27 Mar 76	●	GIRLS GIRLS GIRLS *Epic EPC 3858*	7	8
19 Feb 77		ONE DRINK TOO MANY *Epic EPC 4804*	35	4

ST ANDREWS CHORALE *UK, church choir (5 WEEKS)* pos/wks

14 Feb 76		CLOUD 99 *Decca F 13617*	31	5

ST CECILIA *UK, male vocal / instrumental group (17 WEEKS)* pos/wks

19 Jun 71		LEAP UP AND DOWN (WAVE YOUR KNICKERS IN THE AIR) *Polydor 2058 104*	12	17

SAINT ETIENNE *UK, male / female vocal / instrumental group – lead vocal Sarah Cracknell (52 WEEKS)* pos/wks

18 May 91		NOTHING CAN STOP US / SPEEDWELL *Heavenly HVN 009*	54	3
7 Sep 91		ONLY LOVE CAN BREAK YOUR HEART / FILTHY *Heavenly HVN 12*	39	4
16 May 92		JOIN OUR CLUB / PEOPLE GET REAL *Heavenly HVN 15*	21	3
17 Oct 92		AVENUE *Heavenly HVN 2312*	40	2
13 Feb 93		YOU'RE IN A BAD WAY *Heavenly HVN 25CD*	12	5
22 May 93		HOBART PAVING / WHO DO YOU THINK YOU ARE *Heavenly HVN 29CD*	23	5
18 Dec 93		I WAS BORN ON CHRISTMAS DAY *Heavenly HVN 36CD* [1]	37	5
19 Feb 94		PALE MOVIE *Heavenly HVN 37CD*	28	3
28 May 94		LIKE A MOTORWAY *Heavenly HVN 40CD*	47	2
1 Oct 94		HUG MY SOUL *Heavenly HVN 42CD*	32	2
11 Nov 95		HE'S ON THE PHONE *Heavenly HVN 50CDR* [2]	11	5
7 Feb 98		SYLVIE *Creation CRESCD 279*	12	3
2 May 98		THE BAD PHOTOGRAPHER *Creation CRESCD 290*	27	2
20 May 00	●	TELL ME WHY (THE RIDDLE) *Deviant DVNT 36CDS* [3]	7	5
24 Jun 00		HEART FAILED (IN THE BACK OF A TAXI) *Mantra / Beggars Banquet MNT 54CD*	50	1
20 Jan 01		BOY IS CRYING *Mantra / Beggars Banquet MNT 60 CD*	34	2

[1] Saint Etienne co-starring Tim Burgess [2] Saint Etienne featuring Etienne Daho [3] Paul Van Dyk featuring Saint Etienne

See also Sarah CRACKNELL

ST GERMAIN *France, male producer (3 WEEKS)* pos/wks

31 Aug 96		ALABAMA BLUES (REVISITED) *F Communications F 050CD*	50	1
10 Mar 01		ROSE ROUGE *Blue Note CDROSE 001*	54	2

Barry ST JOHN *UK, female vocalist (1 WEEK)* pos/wks

9 Dec 65		COME AWAY MELINDA *Columbia DB 7783*	47	1

ST JOHN'S COLLEGE SCHOOL CHOIR and the Band of the GRENADIER GUARDS *UK, school choir and military band (3 WEEKS)* pos/wks

3 May 86		THE QUEEN'S BIRTHDAY SONG *Columbia Q1*	40	3

ST LOUIS UNION *UK, male vocal / instrumental group (10 WEEKS)* pos/wks

13 Jan 66		GIRL *Decca F 12318*	11	10

Crispian ST PETERS *UK, male vocalist – Peter Smith (31 WEEKS)* pos/wks

6 Jan 66	●	YOU WERE ON MY MIND *Decca F 12287*	2	14
31 Mar 66	●	THE PIED PIPER *Decca F 12359*	5	13
15 Sep 66		CHANGES *Decca F 12480*	49	1
29 Sep 66		CHANGES (re-entry) *Decca F 12480*	47	3

ST PHILIPS CHOIR *UK, choir (4 WEEKS)* pos/wks

12 Dec 87		SING FOR EVER *BBC RESL 222*	49	4

ST THOMAS MORE SCHOOL CHOIR – *See Scott FITZGERALD*

ST WINIFRED'S SCHOOL CHOIR *UK, school choir – lead vocal Dawn Ralph (11 WEEKS)* pos/wks

22 Nov 80	★	THERE'S NO ONE QUITE LIKE GRANDMA *MFP FP 900*	1	11

Buffy SAINTE-MARIE *Canada, female vocalist (29 WEEKS)* pos/wks

17 Jul 71	●	SOLDIER BLUE *RCA 2081*	7	18
18 Mar 72		I'M GONNA BE A COUNTRY GIRL AGAIN *Vanguard VRS 35143*	34	5
8 Feb 92		THE BIG ONES GET AWAY *Ensign ENY 650*	39	5
4 Jul 92		FALLEN ANGELS *Ensign ENY 655*	57	1

SAINTS *Australia, male vocal / instrumental group (4 WEEKS)* pos/wks

16 Jul 77		THIS PERFECT DAY *Harvest HAR 5130*	34	4

Kyu SAKAMOTO *Japan, male vocalist (13 WEEKS)* pos/wks

27 Jun 63	●	SUKIYAKI *HMV POP 1171* ▲	6	13

Ryuichi SAKAMOTO – *See David SYLVIAN*

SAKKARIN – *See Jonathan KING*

SALAD *UK / Holland, male / female vocal / instrumental group (5 WEEKS)* pos/wks

11 Mar 95		DRINK THE ELIXIR *Island Red CIRD 104*	66	1
13 May 95		MOTORBIKE TO HEAVEN *Island Red CIRD 106*	42	1
16 Sep 95		GRANITE STATUE *Island Red CIRD 108*	50	1
26 Oct 96		I WANT YOU *Island CID 646*	60	1
17 May 97		CARDBOY KING *Island CID 654*	65	1

SALFORD JETS *UK, male vocal / instrumental group (2 WEEKS)* pos/wks

31 May 80		WHO YOU LOOKING AT *RCA PB 5239*	72	2

SALSOUL ORCHESTRA – *See CHARO and the SALSOUL ORCHESTRA*

SALT TANK *UK, male production duo (4 WEEKS)*

			pos	wks
11 May 96		**EUGINA** *Internal LIECD 29*	40	2
3 Jul 99		**DIMENSION** *Hooj Choons HOOJ 74CD*	52	1
9 Dec 00		**EUGINA (re-mix)** *Lost Language LOST 004CD*	58	1

SALT-N-PEPA (220 Top 500) *Rappers Cheryl "Salt" James (b. 28 Mar 1969, Brooklyn, US) and Sandra "Pepa" Denton (b. 9 Nov 1969, Kingston, Jamaica), backed up by DJ Dee Dee "Spinderella" Roper, are the most commercially successful female rap troupe of all time (123 WEEKS)*

			pos	wks
26 Mar 88		**PUSH IT / I AM DOWN** *ffrr FFR 2*	41	6
25 Jun 88	●	**PUSH IT / TRAMP** *Champion CHAMP 51 & ffrr FFR 2*	2	13
3 Sep 88		**SHAKE YOUR THANG (IT'S YOUR THING)** *ffrr FFR 11* [1]	22	8
12 Nov 88	●	**TWIST AND SHOUT** *ffrr FFR 16*	4	9
14 Apr 90		**EXPRESSION** *ffrr F 127*	40	6
25 May 91	●	**DO YOU WANT ME** *ffrr F 151*	5	12
31 Aug 91	●	**LET'S TALK ABOUT SEX** *ffrr F 162*	2	13
30 Nov 91		**YOU SHOWED ME** *ffrr F 174*	15	9
28 Mar 92		**EXPRESSION (re-mix)** *ffrr F 182*	23	6
3 Oct 92		**START ME UP** *ffrr F 196*	39	3
9 Oct 93		**SHOOP** *ffrr FCD 219*	29	3
19 Mar 94	●	**WHATTA MAN** *ffrr FCD 222* [2]	7	10
28 May 94		**SHOOP (re-mix)** *ffrr FCD 234*	13	8
12 Nov 94		**NONE OF YOUR BUSINESS** *ffrr FCD 244*	19	4
7 Jan 95		**NONE OF YOUR BUSINESS (re-entry)** *ffrr FCD 244*	64	1
21 Dec 96		**CHAMPAGNE** *MCA MCSTD 48025*	23	6
29 Nov 97		**R U READY** *ffrr FCDP 322*	24	2
11 Dec 99		**THE BRICK TRACK VERSUS GITTY UP** *ffrr FCD 373* [3]	22	4

[1] Salt-N-Pepa featuring EU [2] Salt-N-Pepa with En Vogue [3] Saltnpepa

'I Am Down' listed only from 2 Apr 1988. The disc re-entered on 25 June when it was made available on Champion with a different flip side. Sales for both discs were amalgamated

SAM and DAVE
US, male vocal duo – Sam Moore and Dave Prater (39 WEEKS)

			pos	wks
16 Mar 67		**SOOTHE ME** *Stax 601 004*	48	2
13 Apr 67		**SOOTHE ME (re-entry)** *Stax 601 004*	35	6
1 Nov 67		**SOUL MAN** *Stax 601 023*	24	14
13 Mar 68		**I THANK YOU** *Stax 601 030*	34	9
29 Jan 69		**SOUL SISTER, BROWN SUGAR** *Atlantic 584 237*	15	8

See also Lou REED

SAM THE SHAM and the PHARAOHS
US, male vocal / instrumental group (18 WEEKS)

			pos	wks
24 Jun 65		**WOOLY BULLY** *MGM 1269*	11	15
4 Aug 66		**LIL' RED RIDING HOOD** *MGM 1315*	48	1
18 Aug 66		**LIL' RED RIDING HOOD (re-entry)** *MGM 1315*	46	2

Richie SAMBORA
US, male vocalist / instrumentalist – guitar (4 WEEKS)

			pos	wks
7 Sep 91		**BALLAD OF YOUTH** *Mercury MER 350*	59	1
7 Mar 98		**HARD TIMES COME EASY** *Mercury 5686972*	37	2
1 Aug 98		**IN IT FOR LOVE** *Mercury 5660632*	58	1

See also BON JOVI

Mike SAMMES SINGERS *UK, male / female vocal group (38 WEEKS)*

			pos	wks
15 Sep 66		**SOMEWHERE MY LOVE** *HMV POP 1546*	22	19
12 Jul 67		**SOMEWHERE MY LOVE (re-entry)** *HMV POP 1546*	14	19

See also Michael FLANDERS; Des O'CONNOR; Malcolm VAUGHAN; Michael HOLLIDAY; Andy STEWART; Jimmy YOUNG

Dave SAMPSON *UK, male vocalist (6 WEEKS)*

			pos	wks
19 May 60		**SWEET DREAMS** *Columbia DB 4449*	48	1
2 Jun 60		**SWEET DREAMS (re-entry)** *Columbia DB 4449*	29	5

SAMSON *UK, male vocal / instrumental group (6 WEEKS)*

			pos	wks
4 Jul 81		**RIDING WITH THE ANGELS** *RCA 67*	55	3
24 Jul 82		**LOSING MY GRIP** *Polydor POSP 471*	63	2
5 Mar 83		**RED SKIES** *Polydor POSP 554*	65	1

SAN JOSE featuring Rodriguez ARGENTINA
UK, male instrumental group (8 WEEKS)

			pos	wks
17 Jun 78		**ARGENTINE MELODY (CANCION DE ARGENTINA)** *MCA 369*	14	8

Rodriguez Argentina is Rod Argent

See also SILSOE; ARGENT

SAN REMO STRINGS *US, orchestra (8 WEEKS)*

			pos	wks
18 Dec 71		**FESTIVAL TIME** *Tamla Motown TMG 795*	39	8

Junior SANCHEZ featuring DAJAE
US, male DJ / producer and US, female vocalist (2 WEEKS)

			pos	wks
16 Oct 99		**B WITH U** *Manifesto FESCD 62*	31	2

Roger SANCHEZ *US, male producer (19 WEEKS)*

			pos	wks
3 Oct 98		**BUFFALO GALS STAMPEDE (re-mix)** *Virgin VSCDT 1717* [1]	65	1
20Feb 99		**I WANT YOUR LOVE** *Perpetual PERPCDS 001* [2]	31	2
29 Jan 00		**I NEVER KNEW** *INCredible INCS 4CDS* [3]	24	2
14 Jul 01	★	**ANOTHER CHANCE** *Defected DFECT 35CDS* ■	1	12
15 Dec 01		**YOU CAN'T CHANGE ME** *Defected DFECT 41CDS* [4]	25	3+

[1] Malcolm McLaren and the World's Famous Supreme Team plus Rakim and Roger Sanchez [2] Roger Sanchez presents Twilight [3] Roger Sanchez featuring Cooly's Hot Box [4] Roger Sanchez featuring Armand Van Helden and N'Dea Davenport

See also FUNK JUNKEEZ; EL MARIACHI; TRANSATLANTIC SOUL

Chris SANDFORD *UK, male vocalist (9 WEEKS)*

			pos	wks
12 Dec 63		**NOT TOO LITTLE - NOT TOO MUCH** *Decca F 11778*	17	9

SANDPIPERS *US, male vocal group (33 WEEKS)*

			pos	wks
15 Sep 66	●	**GUANTANAMERA** *Pye International 7N 25380*	7	17
5 Jun 68		**QUANDO M'INNAMORO (A MAN WITHOUT LOVE)** *A & M AMS 723*	33	6
26 Mar 69		**KUMBAYA** *A & M AMS 744*	38	1
9 Apr 69		**KUMBAYA (re-entry)** *A & M AMS 744*	49	1
27 Nov 76		**HANG ON SLOOPY** *Satril SAT 114*	32	8

SANDRA *Germany, female vocalist (8 WEEKS)*

			pos	wks
17 Dec 88		**EVERLASTING LOVE** *Siren SRN 85*	45	8

Jodie SANDS *US, female vocalist (10 WEEKS)*

			pos	wks
17 Oct 58		**SOMEDAY (YOU'LL WANT ME TO WANT YOU)** *HMV POP 533*	14	10

Tommy SANDS *US, male vocalist (7 WEEKS)*

			pos	wks
4 Aug 60		**THE OLD OAKEN BUCKET** *Capitol CL 15143*	25	7

SANDSTORM *US, male producer – Mark Picchiotti (1 WEEK)*

			pos	wks
13 May 00		**THE RETURN OF NOTHING** *Renaissance Recordings RENCDS 001*	54	1

Samantha SANG
Australia, female vocalist – Cheryl Gray (13 WEEKS)

			pos	wks
4 Feb 78		**EMOTION** *Private Stock PVT 128*	11	13

SANTA CLAUS and the CHRISTMAS TREES
UK, male vocal / instrumental group (10 WEEKS)

			pos	wks
11 Dec 82		**SINGALONG-A-SANTA** *Polydor IVY 1*	19	5
10 Dec 83		**SINGALONG-A-SANTA AGAIN** *Polydor IVY 2*	39	5

SANTA ESMERALDA and Leroy GOMEZ
US / France, male / female vocal / instrumental group (5 WEEKS)

			pos	wks
12 Nov 77		**DON'T LET ME BE MISUNDERSTOOD** *Philips 6042 325*	41	5

SANTANA *US, male vocal / instrumental group (45 WEEKS)*

			pos	wks
28 Sep 74		**SAMBA PA TI** *CBS 2561*	27	7

15 Oct 77	**SHE'S NOT THERE** *CBS 5671*	11	12
25 Nov 78	**WELL ALL RIGHT** *CBS 6755*	53	3
22 Mar 80	**ALL I EVER WANTED** *CBS 8160*	57	3
23 Oct 99	**SMOOTH** *Arista 74321709492* [1] ▲	75	1
1 Apr 00 ●	**SMOOTH (re-issue)** *Arista 74321748762* [1]	3	10
5 Aug 00 ●	**MARIA MARIA** *Arista 74321769372* [2] ▲	6	9

[1] Santana featuring Rob Thomas [2] Santana featuring the Product G&B

SANTO and JOHNNY

US, male instrumental duo – steel and electric guitars (5 WEEKS) pos/wks

16 Oct 59	**SLEEP WALK** *Pye International 7N 25037* ▲	22	4
31 Mar 60	**TEARDROP** *Parlophone R 4619*	50	1

SANTOS *Italy, male producer – Sante Pucello (6 WEEKS)* pos/wks

20 Jan 01 ●	**CAMELS** *Incentive CENT 15CDS*	9	6

Mike SARNE *UK, male vocalist – Mike Scheuer (43 WEEKS)* pos/wks

10 May 62 ★	**COME OUTSIDE** *Parlophone R 4902* [1]	1	19
30 Aug 62	**WILL I WHAT** *Parlophone R 4932* [2]	18	10
10 Jan 63	**JUST FOR KICKS** *Parlophone R 4974*	22	7
28 Mar 63	**CODE OF LOVE** *Parlophone R 5010*	29	7

[1] Mike Sarne with Wendy Richard [2] Mike Sarne with Billie Davis

Joy SARNEY *UK, female vocalist (6 WEEKS)* pos/wks

7 May 77	**NAUGHTY NAUGHTY NAUGHTY** *Alaska ALA 2005*	26	6

SARR BAND

Italy / UK / France, male / female vocal / instrumental group (1 WEEK) pos/wks

16 Sep 78	**MAGIC MANDRAKE** *Calendar DAY 111*	68	1

Peter SARSTEDT *UK, male vocalist (25 WEEKS)* pos/wks

5 Feb 69 ★	**WHERE DO YOU GO TO (MY LOVELY)** *United Artists UP 2262*	1	16
4 Jun 69 ●	**FROZEN ORANGE JUICE** *United Artists UP 35021*	10	9

Robin SARSTEDT *UK, male vocalist (9 WEEKS)* pos/wks

8 May 76 ●	**MY RESISTANCE IS LOW** *Decca F 13624*	3	9

SARTORELLO *Italy, male / female vocal / instrumental duo (1 WEEK)* pos/wks

10 Aug 96	**MOVE BABY MOVE** *Multiply CDMULTY 12*	56	1

SASH! (249 Top 500) *German pop / dance act named after instrumentalist / producer Sascha (aka Sasha) Lappessen, featuring programmers Thomas Alisson and Ralf Kappmeier. First four hits uniquely featured vocals in different languages (French, Spanish, English, Italian) (103 WEEKS)* pos/wks

1 Mar 97 ●	**ENCORE UNE FOIS** *Multiply CDMULTY 18*	2	15
5 Jul 97 ●	**ECUADOR** *Multiply CDMULTY 23* [1]	2	12
18 Oct 97 ●	**STAY** *Multiply CDMULTY 26* [2]	2	14
4 Apr 98 ●	**LA PRIMAVERA** *Multiply CXMULTY 32*	3	12
15 Aug 98 ●	**MYSTERIOUS TIMES** *Multiply CXMULTY 40* [3]	2	12
28 Nov 98 ●	**MOVE MANIA** *Multiply CDMULTY 45* [4]	8	10
3 Apr 99	**COLOUR THE WORLD** *Multiply CDMULTY 48*	15	6
12 Feb 00 ●	**ADELANTE** *Multiply CDMULTY 60*	2	10
22 Apr 00 ●	**JUST AROUND THE HILL** *Multiply CDMULTY 62* [3]	8	7
23 Sep 00 ●	**WITH MY OWN EYES** *Multiply CDMULTY 67*	10	5

[1] Sash! featuring Rodriguez [2] Sash! featuring La Trec [3] Sash! featuring Tina Cousins [4] Sash! featuring Shannon

SASHA *UK, male producer – Alexander Coe (15 WEEKS)* pos/wks

31 Jul 93	**TOGETHER** *ffrr FCD 212* [1]	57	1
19 Feb 94	**HIGHER GROUND** *Deconstruction 74321189002* [2]	19	3
27 Aug 94	**MAGIC** *Deconstruction 74321221862* [2]	32	4
9 Mar 96	**BE AS ONE** *Deconstruction 74321342962* [3]	17	4
23 Sep 00	**SCORCHIO** *Arista 74321788222* [4]	23	3

[1] Danny Campbell and Sasha [2] Sasha with Sam Mollison [3] Sasha and Maria [4] Sasha / Emerson

Joe SATRIANI *US, male instrumentalist – guitar (1 WEEK)* pos/wks

13 Feb 93	**THE SATCH EP** *Relativity 6589532*	53	1

Tracks on The Satch EP: The Extremist / Cryin / Banana Bongo / Crazy

SATURDAY NIGHT BAND

US, male vocal / instrumental group (9 WEEKS) pos/wks

1 Jul 78	**COME ON DANCE DANCE** *CBS 6367*	16	9

Deion SAUNDERS – *See HAMMER*

Kevin SAUNDERSON – *See INNER CITY*

Chantay SAVAGE *US, female vocalist (9 WEEKS)* pos/wks

4 May 96	**I WILL SURVIVE** *RCA 74321377682*	12	8
8 Nov 97	**REMINDING ME (OF SEF)** *Relativity 6560762* [1]	59	1

[1] Common featuring Chantay Savage

Edna SAVAGE *UK, female vocalist (1 WEEK)* pos/wks

13 Jan 56	**ARRIVEDERCI DARLING** *Parlophone R 4097*	19	1

SAVAGE GARDEN (303 Top 500) *Australian pop vocal / instrumental duo: Daniel Jones and Darren Hayes. Eponymous debut album sold more than 11 million copies worldwide and huge critical acclaim followed with a record-breaking 10 Arias at the 1997 Australian music industry awards. Duo went separate ways in 2001 (101 WEEKS)* pos/wks

21 Jun 97	**I WANT YOU** *Columbia 6645452*	11	7
27 Sep 97	**TO THE MOON AND BACK** *Columbia 6648932*	55	1
28 Feb 98 ●	**TRULY MADLY DEEPLY** *Columbia 6656022* ▲	4	23
22 Aug 98 ●	**TO THE MOON AND BACK (re-issue)** *Columbia 6662882*	3	16
12 Dec 98	**I WANT YOU '98 (re-mix)** *Columbia 6667332*	12	10
10 Jul 99	**THE ANIMAL SONG** *Columbia 6675882*	16	6
13 Nov 99 ●	**I KNEW I LOVED YOU** *Columbia 6683102* ▲	10	12
1 Apr 00	**CRASH AND BURN** *Columbia 6690442*	14	6
29 Jul 00 ●	**AFFIRMATION** *Columbia 6696882*	8	10
25 Nov 00	**HOLD ME** *Columbia 6706032*	16	5
20 Jan 01	**HOLD ME (re-entry)** *Columbia 6706032*	61	2
31 Mar 01	**THE BEST THING** *Columbia 6709852*	35	2
5 May 01	**THE BEST THING (re-entry)** *Columbia 6709852*	74	1

Telly SAVALAS *US, male actor (12 WEEKS)* pos/wks

22 Feb 75 ★	**IF** *MCA 174*	1	9
31 May 75	**YOU'VE LOST THAT LOVIN' FEELIN'** *MCA 189*	47	3

SAVANNA *UK, male vocal group (4 WEEKS)* pos/wks

10 Oct 81	**I CAN'T TURN AWAY** *R & B RBS 203*	61	4

SAVUKA – *See Johnny CLEGG and SAVUKA*

SAW DOCTORS *Ireland, male vocal / instrumental group (9 WEEKS)* pos/wks

12 Nov 94	**SMALL BIT OF LOVE** *Shamtown SAW 001CD*	24	3
27 Jan 96	**WORLD OF GOOD** *Shamtown SAW 002CD*	15	3
13 Jul 96	**TO WIN JUST ONCE** *Shamtown SAW 004CD*	14	2
6 Dec 97	**SIMPLE THINGS** *Shamtown SAW 006CD*	56	1

Nitin SAWHNEY featuring ESKA

UK, male instrumental / producer and UK, female vocalist (1 WEEK) pos/wks

28 Jul 01	**SUNSET** *V2 VVR 5016763*	65	1

See also COLOURS featuring EMMANUEL & ESKA; EN-CORE featuring Stephen EMMANUEL & ESKA

SAXON *UK, male vocal / instrumental group (61 WEEKS)* pos/wks

22 Mar 80	**WHEELS OF STEEL** *Carrere CAR 143*	20	11
21 Jun 80	**747 (STRANGERS IN THE NIGHT)** *Carrere CAR 151*	13	9
28 Jun 80	**BACKS TO THE WALL** *Carrere HM 6*	64	2
28 Jun 80	**BIG TEASER / RAINBOW THEME** *Carrere HM 5*	66	2
29 Nov 80	**STRONG ARM OF THE LAW** *Carrere CAR 170*	63	3

			pos	wks
11 Apr 81		**AND THE BANDS PLAYED ON** *Carrere CAR 180*	12	8
18 Jul 81		**NEVER SURRENDER** *Carrere CAR 204*	18	6
31 Oct 81		**PRINCESS OF THE NIGHT** *Carrere CAR 208*	57	3
23 Apr 83		**POWER AND THE GLORY** *Carrere SAXON 1*	32	5
30 Jul 83		**NIGHTMARE** *Carrere CAR 284*	50	3
31 Aug 85		**BACK ON THE STREETS** *Parlophone R 6103*	75	1
29 Mar 86		**ROCK 'N' ROLL GYPSY** *Parlophone R 6112*	71	1
30 Aug 86		**WAITING FOR THE NIGHT** *EMI EMI 5575*	66	2
5 Mar 88		**RIDE LIKE THE WIND** *EMI EM 43*	52	4
30 Apr 88		**I CAN'T WAIT ANYMORE** *EMI EM 54*	71	1

Al SAXON *UK, male vocalist – Allan Fowler (10 WEEKS)* pos/wks

			pos	wks
16 Jan 59		**YOU'RE THE TOP CHA** *Fontana H 164*	17	4
28 Aug 59		**ONLY SIXTEEN** *Fontana H 205*	24	3
22 Dec 60		**BLUE-EYED BOY** *Fontana H 278*	39	2
7 Sep 61		**THERE I'VE SAID IT AGAIN** *Piccadilly 7N 35011*	48	1

Leo SAYER (144 Top 500) *Distinctive singer / songwriter (b. 21 May 1948, Sussex, UK) who was a top singles and album act on both sides of the Atlantic in the late 1970s. His first seven hits all reached the Top 10 - a feat first achieved by his manager, Adam Faith (151 WEEKS)* pos/wks

			pos	wks
15 Dec 73	●	**THE SHOW MUST GO ON** *Chrysalis CHS 2023*	2	13
15 Jun 74	●	**ONE MAN BAND** *Chrysalis CHS 2045*	6	9
14 Sep 74	●	**LONG TALL GLASSES** *Chrysalis CHS 2052*	4	9
30 Aug 75	●	**MOONLIGHTING** *Chrysalis CHS 2076*	2	8
30 Oct 76	●	**YOU MAKE ME FEEL LIKE DANCING** *Chrysalis CHS 2119* ▲	2	12
29 Jan 77	★	**WHEN I NEED YOU** *Chrysalis CHS 2127* ▲	1	13
9 Apr 77	●	**HOW MUCH LOVE** *Chrysalis CHS 2140*	10	8
10 Sep 77		**THUNDER IN MY HEART** *Chrysalis CHS 2163*	22	8
16 Sep 78	●	**I CAN'T STOP LOVIN' YOU (THOUGH I TRY)** *Chrysalis CHS 2240*	6	11
25 Nov 78		**RAINING IN MY HEART** *Chrysalis CHS 2277*	21	10
5 Jul 80	●	**MORE THAN I CAN SAY** *Chrysalis CHS 2442*	2	11
13 Mar 82	●	**HAVE YOU EVER BEEN IN LOVE** *Chrysalis CHS 2596*	10	9
19 Jun 82		**HEART (STOP BEATING IN TIME)** *Chrysalis CHS 2616*	22	10
12 Mar 83		**ORCHARD ROAD** *Chrysalis CHS 2677*	16	8
15 Oct 83		**TILL YOU COME BACK TO ME** *Chrysalis LEO 01*	51	3
8 Feb 86		**UNCHAINED MELODY** *Chrysalis LEO 3*	54	4
13 Feb 93		**WHEN I NEED YOU (re-issue)** *Chrysalis CDCHS 3926*	65	2
8 Aug 98		**YOU MAKE ME FEEL LIKE DANCING** *Brothers Org. CDBRUV 8* [1]	32	3

[1] Groove Generation featuring Leo Sayer

Alexei SAYLE *UK, male comedian / vocalist (8 WEEKS)* pos/wks

			pos	wks
25 Feb 84		**'ULLO JOHN GOT A NEW MOTOR?** *Island IS 162*	15	8

SCAFFOLD *UK, male vocal group (62 WEEKS)* pos/wks

			pos	wks
22 Nov 67	●	**THANK U VERY MUCH** *Parlophone R 5643*	4	12
27 Mar 68		**DO YOU REMEMBER** *Parlophone R 5679*	34	5
6 Nov 68	★	**LILY THE PINK** *Parlophone R 5734*	1	24
1 Nov 69		**GIN GAN GOOLIE** *Parlophone R 5812*	38	11
24 Jan 70		**GIN GAN GOOLIE (re-entry)** *Parlophone R 5812*	50	1
1 Jun 74	●	**LIVERPOOL LOU** *Warner Bros. K 16400*	7	9

Boz SCAGGS *US, male vocalist (31 WEEKS)* pos/wks

			pos	wks
30 Oct 76		**LOWDOWN** *CBS 4563*	28	4
22 Jan 77	●	**WHAT CAN I SAY** *CBS 4869*	10	10
14 May 77		**LIDO SHUFFLE** *CBS 5136*	13	9
10 Dec 77		**HOLLYWOOD** *CBS 5836*	33	8

SCANTY SANDWICH
UK, male DJ / producer – Richard Marshall (8 WEEKS) pos/wks

			pos	wks
29 Jan 00	●	**BECAUSE OF YOU** *Southern Fried ECB 18CDS*	3	8

SCARFACE *US, male rapper – Brad Jordan (6 WEEKS)* pos/wks

			pos	wks
11 Mar 95		**HAND OF THE DEAD BODY** *Virgin America VUSCD 88* [1]	41	2
5 Aug 95		**I SEEN A MAN DIE** *Virgin America VUSCD 94*	55	2
5 Jul 97		**GAME OVER** *Virgin VUSCD 121*	34	2

[1] Scarface featuring Ice Cube

SCARFO *UK, male vocal / instrumental group (2 WEEKS)* pos/wks

			pos	wks
19 Jul 97		**ALKALINE** *Deceptive BLUFF 044CD*	61	1
18 Oct 97		**COSMONAUT NO.7** *Deceptive BLUFF 053CD*	67	1

SCARLET *UK, female vocal / instrumental duo – Cheryl Parker and Joe Youle (18 WEEKS)* pos/wks

			pos	wks
21 Jan 95		**INDEPENDENT LOVE SONG** *WEA YZ 820CD*	12	12
29 Apr 95		**I WANNA BE FREE (TO BE WITH HIM)** *WEA YZ 913CD*	21	4
5 Aug 95		**LOVE HANGOVER** *WEA YZ 969CD*	54	1
6 Jul 96		**BAD GIRL** *WEA WEA 046CD*	54	1

SCARLET FANTASTIC
UK, male / female vocal / instrumental group (12 WEEKS) pos/wks

			pos	wks
3 Oct 87		**NO MEMORY** *Arista RIS 36*	24	10
23 Jan 88		**PLUG ME IN (TO THE CENTRAL LOVE LINE)** *Arista 109693*	67	2

SCARLET PARTY *UK, male vocal / instrumental group (5 WEEKS)* pos/wks

			pos	wks
16 Oct 82		**101 DAM-NATIONS** *Parlophone R 6058*	44	5

SCATMAN JOHN *US, male vocalist – John Larkin (19 WEEKS)* pos/wks

			pos	wks
13 May 95	●	**SCATMAN (SKI-BA-BOP-BA-DOP-BOP)** *RCA 74321281712*	3	12
2 Sep 95	●	**SCATMAN'S WORLD** *RCA 74321289952*	10	7

Michael SCHENKER GROUP
Germany / UK, male vocal / instrumental group (9 WEEKS) pos/wks

			pos	wks
13 Sep 80		**ARMED AND READY** *Chrysalis CHS 2455*	53	3
8 Nov 80		**CRY FOR THE NATIONS** *Chrysalis CHS 2471*	56	3
11 Sep 82		**DANCER** *Chrysalis CHS 2636*	52	3

Lalo SCHIFRIN
Argentina, male conductor and US, orchestra (11 WEEKS) pos/wks

			pos	wks
9 Oct 76		**JAWS** *CTI CTSP 005*	14	9
25 Oct 97		**BULLITT** *Warner.esp WESP 002CD*	36	2

SCHILLER *Germany, male production duo – Christopher von Deylen and Mirko von Schlieffen (3 WEEKS)* pos/wks

			pos	wks
28 Apr 01		**DAS GLOCKENSPIEL** *Data DATA 22CDS*	17	3

Peter SCHILLING *Germany, male vocalist (6 WEEKS)* pos/wks

			pos	wks
5 May 84		**MAJOR TOM (COMING HOME)** *PSP/WEA X 9438*	42	5
16 Jun 84		**MAJOR TOM (COMING HOME) (re-entry)** *PSP/WEA X 9438*	73	1

Phillip SCHOFIELD *UK, male vocalist (6 WEEKS)* pos/wks

			pos	wks
5 Dec 92		**CLOSE EVERY DOOR** *Really Useful RUR 11*	27	6

SCIENCE DEPARTMENT featuring ERIRE
UK, male production duo and female vocalist (1 WEEK) pos/wks

			pos	wks
10 Nov 01		**BREATHE** *Renaissance Recordings RENCDS 010*	64	1

SCIENTIST *UK, male producer – Phil Sebastiane (13 WEEKS)* pos/wks

			pos	wks
6 Oct 90		**THE EXORCIST** *Kickin KICK 1*	62	3
1 Dec 90		**THE EXORCIST (re-mix)** *Kickin KICK 1TR*	46	3
15 Dec 90		**THE BEE** *Kickin KICK 3S*	52	3
26 Jan 91		**THE BEE (re-entry)** *Kickin KICK 3S*	47	3
11 May 91		**SPIRAL SYMPHONY** *Kickin KICK 5*	74	1

SCOOBIE *UK, male / female vocal / production / Celtic FC supporters group (2 WEEKS)* pos/wks

			pos	wks
22 Dec 01		**THE MAGNIFICENT 7** *Big Tongue BTR 001CDS*	58	2+

SCOOCH *UK, male / female vocal group (20 WEEKS)* pos/wks

			pos	wks
6 Nov 99		**WHEN MY BABY** *Accolade CDAC 002*	29	4
22 Jan 00	●	**MORE THAN I NEEDED TO KNOW** *Accolade CDAC 003*	5	5
6 May 00		**THE BEST IS YET TO COME** *Accolade CDAC 004*	12	4

1990

IN THE YEAR IN WHICH NINTENDO LAUNCHED THE GAME BOY AND EVERYONE STARTED SEEING TETRIS BLOCKS IN THEIR SLEEP, NELSON MANDELA WAS FREED AFTER BEING IMPRISONED FOR 26 YEARS AND THE GULF WAR BROKE OUT IN IRAQ AFTER SADDAM HUSSEIN'S INVASION OF KUWAIT, **PAUL OAKENFOLD** TAKES US BACK TO WHEN HE PRODUCED 'STEP ON' BY THE HAPPY MONDAYS...

“It was their biggest single to date, and an international hit. There were various mixes covering all genres from rock to dance, and it was a pioneering single in the sense of moving the whole alternative scene forward – a record that really put that band on the map. It's still being played today, so it's stood the test of time. When I was DJing on tour with U2 on the Zooropa tour in 1993, even the kids went mad for it. It's just one of those classic feel-good tunes.”

SINGLE OF THE YEAR 'The Power' Snap
ALBUM OF THE YEAR '...But Seriously' Phil Collins

8 Jul 00	THE BEST IS YET TO COME (re-entry) *Accolade CDAC 004*	64	1
5 Aug 00	FOR SURE *Accolade CDAS 005*	15	6

SCOOTER *UK / Germany, male vocal / instrumental group (14 WEEKS)* pos/wks

21 Oct 95	MOVE YOUR ASS *Club Tools 0061675 CLU*	23	4
17 Feb 96	BACK IN THE UK *Club Tools 0061955 CLU*	18	3
25 May 96	REBEL YELL *Club Tools 0062575 CLU*	30	2
19 Oct 96	I'M RAVING *Club Tools 0063015 CLU*	33	3
17 May 97	FIRE *Club Tools 006005 CLU*	45	2

SCORPIONS *Germany, male vocal / instrumental group (35 WEEKS)* pos/wks

26 May 79	IS THERE ANYBODY THERE / ANOTHER PIECE OF MEAT *Harvest HAR 5185*	39	4
25 Aug 79	LOVEDRIVE *Harvest HAR 5188*	69	2
31 May 80	MAKE IT REAL *Harvest HAR 5206*	72	2
20 Sep 80	THE ZOO *Harvest HAR 5212*	75	1
3 Apr 82	NO ONE LIKE YOU *Harvest HAR 5219*	65	3
1 May 82	NO ONE LIKE YOU (re-entry) *Harvest HAR 5219*	64	1
17 Jul 82	CAN'T LIVE WITHOUT YOU *Harvest HAR 5221*	63	2
4 Jun 88	RHYTHM OF LOVE *Harvest HAR 5240*	59	2
18 Feb 89	PASSION RULES THE GAME *Harvest 5242*	74	1
1 Jun 91	WIND OF CHANGE *Vertigo VER 54*	53	3
28 Sep 91 ●	WIND OF CHANGE (re-issue) *Vertigo VER 58*	2	9
30 Nov 91	SEND ME AN ANGEL *Vertigo VER 60*	27	3
28 Dec 91	SEND ME AN ANGEL (re-entry) *Vertigo VER 60*	68	2

SCOTLAND WORLD CUP SQUAD
UK, male football team vocalists (27 WEEKS) pos/wks

22 Jun 74	EASY EASY *Polydor 2058 452*	20	4
27 May 78 ●	OLE OLA (MULHER BRASILEIRA) *Riva 15* [1]	4	6
1 May 82 ●	WE HAVE A DREAM *WEA K 19145* [2]	5	9
9 Jun 90	SAY IT WITH PRIDE *RCA PB 43791* [2]	45	3
15 Jun 96	PURPLE HEATHER *Warner Bros. W 0354CD* [3]	16	5

[1] Rod Stewart featuring the Scottish World Cup Squad '78 [2] Scottish World Cup Squad [3] Rod Stewart with the Scottish Euro '96 Squad

Jack SCOTT *Canada, male vocalist – Jack Scafone Jr (28 WEEKS)* pos/wks

10 Oct 58 ●	MY TRUE LOVE *London HLU 8626*	9	10
25 Sep 59	THE WAY I WALK *London HLL 8912*	30	1
10 Mar 60	WHAT IN THE WORLD'S COME OVER YOU *Top Rank JAR 280*	11	15
2 Jun 60	BURNING BRIDGES *Top Rank JAR 375*	32	2

Jill SCOTT *US, female vocalist (4 WEEKS)* pos/wks

4 Nov 00	GETTIN' IN THE WAY *Epic 6705272*	30	3
7 Apr 01	A LONG WALK *Epic 6710382*	54	1

Linda SCOTT *US, female vocalist – Linda Sampson (14 WEEKS)* pos/wks

18 May 61 ●	I'VE TOLD EVERY LITTLE STAR *Columbia DB 4638*	7	13
14 Sep 61	DON'T BET MONEY HONEY *Columbia DB 4692*	50	1

Mike SCOTT *UK, male vocalist / instrumentalist (4 WEEKS)* pos/wks

16 Sep 95	BRING 'EM ALL IN *Chrysalis CDCHS 5025*	56	1
11 Nov 95	BUILDING THE CITY OF LIGHT *Chrysalis CDCHS 5026*	60	1
27 Sep 97	LOVE ANYWAY *Chrysalis CDCHS 5064*	50	1
14 Feb 98	RARE, PRECIOUS AND GONE *Chrysalis CDCHSS 5073*	74	1

Millie SCOTT *US, female vocalist (11 WEEKS)* pos/wks

12 Apr 86	PRISONER OF LOVE *Fourth & Broadway BRW 45*	52	4
23 Aug 86	AUTOMATIC *Fourth & Broadway BRW 51*	56	3
21 Feb 87	EV'RY LITTLE BIT *Fourth & Broadway BRW 58*	63	4

Simon SCOTT *UK, male vocalist (8 WEEKS)* pos/wks

13 Aug 64	MOVE IT BABY *Parlophone R 5164*	37	8

Tony SCOTT *Holland, male rapper (6 WEEKS)* pos/wks

15 Apr 89	THAT'S HOW I'M LIVING / THE CHIEF *Champion CHAMP 97* [1]	48	4
10 Feb 90	GET INTO IT / THAT'S HOW I'M LIVING (re-issue) *Champion CHAMP 232*	63	2

[1] Toni Scott

'The Chief' listed only from 22 Apr 1989

SCOTT & LEON *UK, male production duo – Scott Anderson and Leon McCormack (6 WEEKS)* pos/wks

30 Sep 00	YOU USED TO HOLD ME *AM:PM CDAMPM 137*	19	4
19 May 01	SHINE ON *AM:PM CDAMPM 143*	34	2

SCOTTISH RUGBY TEAM with Ronnie BROWNE
UK, male rugby team vocalists (1 WEEK) pos/wks

2 Jun 90	FLOWER OF SCOTLAND *Greentrax STRAX 1001*	73	1

SCREAMING BLUE MESSIAHS
US / UK, male vocal / instrumental group (6 WEEKS) pos/wks

16 Jan 88	I WANNA BE A FLINTSTONE *WEA YZ 166*	28	6

SCREAMING TREES *US, male vocal / instrumental group (2 WEEKS)* pos/wks

6 Mar 93	NEARLY LOST YOU *Epic 6582372*	50	1
1 May 93	DOLLAR BILL *Epic 6591792*	52	1

Tracks on 'Nearly Lost You': E.S.K. / Song of a Baker / Winter Song (acoustic)

SCRITTI POLITTI (434 Top 500) *Cerebral pop group increasingly influenced by dance and hip hop trends. Formed 1977 by Green Gartside (v/g/k) b. 22 Jun 1956, Cardiff, Wales. US-recorded minor hit, 'Perfect Way', was act's only US Top 20 entry. Legendary jazz trumpeter Miles Davis played on 'Oh Patti' (78 WEEKS)* pos/wks

21 Nov 81	THE SWEETEST GIRL *Rough Trade RT 091*	64	3
22 May 82	FAITHLESS *Rough Trade RT 101*	56	4
7 Aug 82	ASYLUMS IN JERUSALEM / JACQUES DERRIDA *Rough Trade RT 111*	43	5
10 Mar 84 ●	WOOD BEEZ (PRAY LIKE ARETHA FRANKLIN) *Virgin VS 657*	10	12
9 Jun 84	ABSOLUTE *Virgin VS 680*	17	9
17 Nov 84	HYPNOTIZE *Virgin VS 725*	68	2
11 May 85 ●	THE WORD GIRL *Virgin VS 747*	6	12
7 Sep 85	PERFECT WAY *Virgin VS 780*	48	5
7 May 88	OH PATTI (DON'T FEEL SORRY FOR LOVERBOY) *Virgin VS 1006*	13	9
27 Aug 88	FIRST BOY IN THIS TOWN (LOVE SICK) *Virgin VS 1082*	63	3
12 Nov 88	BOOM! THERE SHE WAS *Virgin VS 1143*	55	3
16 Mar 91	SHE'S A WOMAN *Virgin VS 1333* [1]	20	7
3 Aug 91	TAKE ME IN YOUR ARMS AND LOVE ME *Virgin VS 1346* [2]	47	3
31 Jul 99	TINSELTOWN TO THE BOOGIEDOWN *Virgin VSCDT 1731*	46	1

[1] Scritti Politti featuring Shabba Ranks [2] Scritti Politti and Sweetie Irie

Earl SCRUGGS – *See Lester FLATT and Earl SCRUGGS*

SEA FRUIT *UK, male vocal / instrumental group (1 WEEK)* pos/wks

24 Jul 99	HELLO WORLD *Electric Canyon ECCD 3055*	59	1

SEA LEVEL *US, male instrumental group (4 WEEKS)* pos/wks

17 Feb 79	FIFTY-FOUR *Capricorn POSP 28*	63	4

SEAFOOD *UK, male / female vocal / instrumental group (1 WEEK)* pos/wks

28 Jul 01	CLOAKING *Infectious INFEC 103CDS*	71	1

SEAHORSES *UK, male vocal / instrumental group (26 WEEKS)* pos/wks

10 May 97 ●	LOVE IS THE LAW *Geffen GFSTD 22243*	3	7
26 Jul 97 ●	BLINDED BY THE SUN *Geffen GFSTD 22266*	7	7
11 Oct 97	LOVE ME AND LEAVE ME *Geffen GFSTD 22282*	16	4
13 Dec 97	YOU CAN TALK TO ME *Geffen GFSTD 22297*	15	8

SEAL *UK, male vocalist (70 WEEKS)* pos/wks

8 Dec 90 ●	CRAZY *ZTT ZANG 8*	2	15
4 May 91	FUTURE LOVE (EP) *ZTT ZANG 11*	12	6

20 Jul 91	**THE BEGINNING** *ZTT ZANG 21*	24	6
16 Nov 91 ●	**KILLER (EP)** *ZTT ZANG 23*	8	8
29 Feb 92	**VIOLET** *ZTT ZANG 27*	39	2
21 May 94	**PRAYER FOR THE DYING** *ZTT ZANG 51CD*	14	5
30 Jul 94	**KISS FROM A ROSE** *ZTT ZANG 52CD1*	20	5
5 Nov 94	**NEWBORN FRIEND** *ZTT ZANG 58CD*	45	2
15 Jul 95 ●	**KISS FROM A ROSE / I'M ALIVE (re-issue)** *ZTT ZANG 70CD* ▲	4	13
9 Dec 95	**DON'T CRY / PRAYER FOR THE DYING (re-issue)** *ZTT ZANG 75CD*	51	2
29 Mar 97	**FLY LIKE AN EAGLE** *ZTT ZEAL 1CD*	13	5
14 Nov 98	**HUMAN BEINGS** *Warner Brothers W 464CD*	50	1

Tracks on Future Love (EP): Future Love Paradise / A Minor Groove / Violet. Tracks on Killer (EP): Killer / Hey Joe / Come See What Love Has Done

See also ADAMSKI

SEARCHERS (204 Top 500) *Merseybeat combo initially tipped to be as big as The Beatles, formed 1960: Mike Pender (v/g), John McNally (g/v), Tony Jackson (v/b) (left 1964 - replaced by Frank Allen), Chris Curtis (d). Unlike The Beatles, however, most of this influential act's early hits were cover versions of US originals (128 WEEKS)*

		pos	wks
27 Jun 63 ★	**SWEETS FOR MY SWEET** *Pye 7N 15533*	1	16
10 Oct 63	**SWEET NOTHINS** *Philips BF 1274*	48	2
24 Oct 63 ●	**SUGAR AND SPICE** *Pye 7N 15566*	2	13
16 Jan 64 ★	**NEEDLES AND PINS** *Pye 7N 15594*	1	15
16 Apr 64 ★	**DON'T THROW YOUR LOVE AWAY** *Pye 7N 15630*	1	11
16 Jul 64	**SOMEDAY WE'RE GONNA LOVE AGAIN** *Pye 7N 15670*	11	8
17 Sep 64 ●	**WHEN YOU WALK IN THE ROOM** *Pye 7N 15694*	3	12
3 Dec 64	**WHAT HAVE THEY DONE TO THE RAIN** *Pye 7N 15739*	13	11
4 Mar 65 ●	**GOODBYE MY LOVE** *Pye 7N 15794*	4	11
8 Jul 65	**HE'S GOT NO LOVE** *Pye 7N 15878*	12	10
14 Oct 65	**WHEN I GET HOME** *Pye 7N 15950*	35	3
16 Dec 65	**TAKE ME FOR WHAT I'M WORTH** *Pye 7N 15992*	20	8
21 Apr 66	**TAKE IT OR LEAVE IT** *Pye 7N 17094*	31	6
13 Oct 66	**HAVE YOU EVER LOVED SOMEBODY** *Pye 7N 17170*	48	2

SEASHELLS *UK, female vocal group (5 WEEKS)*

		pos	wks
9 Sep 72	**MAYBE I KNOW** *CBS 8218*	32	5

SEB *UK, male instrumentalist – keyboards (1 WEEK)*

		pos	wks
18 Feb 95	**SUGAR SHACK** *React CDREACT 50*	61	1

SEBADOH *US, male vocal / instrumental group (4 WEEKS)*

		pos	wks
27 Jul 96	**BEAUTY OF THE RIDE** *Domino RUG 47CD*	74	1
30 Jan 99	**FLAME** *Domino RUG 80CD1*	30	3

Jon SECADA *Cuba, male vocalist (42 WEEKS)*

		pos	wks
18 Jul 92 ●	**JUST ANOTHER DAY** *SBK SBK 35*	5	15
31 Oct 92	**DO YOU BELIEVE IN US** *SBK SBK 37*	30	4
6 Feb 93	**ANGEL** *SBK CDSBK 39*	23	5
17 Jul 93	**DO YOU REALLY WANT ME** *SBK CDSBK 41*	30	4
16 Oct 93	**I'M FREE** *SBK CDSBK 44*	50	2
14 May 94	**IF YOU GO** *SBK CDSBK 51*	39	4
2 Jul 94	**IF YOU GO (re-entry)** *SBK CDSBK 51*	71	1
4 Feb 95	**MENTAL PICTURE** *SBK CDSBK 54*	44	2
16 Dec 95	**IF I NEVER KNEW YOU (LOVE THEME FROM 'POCAHONTAS')** *Walt Disney WD 7023C* [1]	51	4
14 Jun 97	**TOO LATE, TOO SOON** *SBK CDSBK 57*	43	1

[1] Jon Secada and Shanice

SECCHI featuring Orlando JOHNSON *Italy / US, male vocal / instrumental duo (3 WEEKS)*

		pos	wks
4 May 91	**I SAY YEAH** *Epic 6568467*	46	3

Harry SECOMBE *UK, male vocalist (35 WEEKS)*

		pos	wks
9 Dec 55	**ON WITH THE MOTLEY (VESTA LA GIUBBA)** *Philips PB 523*	16	3
3 Oct 63	**IF I RULED THE WORLD** *Philips BF 1261*	44	2
21 Nov 63	**IF I RULED THE WORLD (re-entry)** *Philips BF 1261*	18	15
23 Feb 67 ●	**THIS IS MY SONG** *Philips BF 1539*	2	15

SECOND CITY SOUND *UK, male instrumental group (8 WEEKS)*

		pos	wks
20 Jan 66	**TCHAIKOVSKY ONE** *Decca F 12310*	22	7
2 Apr 69	**DREAM OF OLWEN** *Major Minor MM 600*	43	1

SECOND IMAGE *UK, male vocal / instrumental group (11 WEEKS)*

		pos	wks
24 Jul 82	**STAR** *Polydor POSP 457*	60	2
2 Apr 83	**BETTER TAKE TIME** *Polydor POSP 565*	67	2
26 Nov 83	**DON'T YOU** *MCA 848*	68	2
11 Aug 84	**SING AND SHOUT** *MCA 882*	53	3
2 Feb 85	**STARTING AGAIN** *MCA 936*	65	2

SECOND PHASE *US, male producer – Joey Beltram (2 WEEKS)*

		pos	wks
21 Sep 91	**MENTASM** *R&S RSUK 2*	48	2

SECOND PROTOCOL *UK, male production duo (2 WEEKS)*

		pos	wks
23 Sep 00	**BASSLICK** *East West EW 216CD*	58	2

SECRET AFFAIR *UK, male vocal / instrumental group (34 WEEKS)*

		pos	wks
1 Sep 79	**TIME FOR ACTION** *I-Spy SEE 1*	13	10
10 Nov 79	**LET YOUR HEART DANCE** *I-Spy SEE 3*	32	6
8 Mar 80	**MY WORLD** *I-Spy SEE 5*	16	9
23 Aug 80	**SOUND OF CONFUSION** *I-Spy SEE 8*	45	5
17 Oct 81	**DO YOU KNOW** *I-Spy SEE 10*	57	4

SECRET KNOWLEDGE *UK / US, male / female vocal / instrumental duo (2 WEEKS)*

		pos	wks
27 Apr 96	**LOVE ME NOW** *Deconstruction 74321342432*	66	1
24 Aug 96	**SUGAR DADDY** *Deconstruction 74321400242*	75	1

SECRET LIFE *UK, male vocal / production group (10 WEEKS)*

		pos	wks
12 Dec 92	**AS ALWAYS** *Cowboy 7RODEO 9*	45	4
7 Aug 93	**LOVE SO STRONG** *Cowboy RODEO 18CD*	38	2
7 May 94	**SHE HOLDS THE KEY** *Pulse 8 CDLOSE 58*	63	1
29 Oct 94	**I WANT YOU** *Pulse 8 CDLOSE 71*	70	1
28 Jan 95	**LOVE SO STRONG (re-mix)** *Pulse 8 CDLOSE 79*	37	2

SECRETARY OF ENTERTAINMENT – *See RAZE*

SECTION-X *France, male instrumental duo (1 WEEK)*

		pos	wks
8 Mar 97	**ATLANTIS** *Perfecto PERF 136*	42	1

Neil SEDAKA (100 Top 500) *The man who put the 'Tra-La-La' into 1960s pop, b. 13 Mar 1939, New York, US. Ultra-commercial singer / songwriter / pianist who enjoyed two separate chart runs as an artist and wrote many hits for numerous other acts (190 WEEKS)*

		pos	wks
24 Apr 59 ●	**I GO APE** *RCA 1115*	9	13
13 Nov 59 ●	**OH! CAROL** *RCA 1152*	3	17
14 Apr 60 ●	**STAIRWAY TO HEAVEN** *RCA 1178*	8	15
1 Sep 60	**YOU MEAN EVERYTHING TO ME** *RCA 1198*	45	3
2 Feb 61 ●	**CALENDAR GIRL** *RCA 1220*	8	14
18 May 61 ●	**LITTLE DEVIL** *RCA 1236*	9	12
21 Dec 61 ●	**HAPPY BIRTHDAY, SWEET SIXTEEN** *RCA 1266*	3	18
19 Apr 62	**KING OF CLOWNS** *RCA 1282*	23	11
19 Jul 62 ●	**BREAKING UP IS HARD TO DO** *RCA 1298* ▲	7	16
22 Nov 62	**NEXT DOOR TO AN ANGEL** *RCA 1319*	29	4
30 May 63	**LET'S GO STEADY AGAIN** *RCA 1343*	42	1
13 Jun 63	**LET'S GO STEADY AGAIN (re-entry)** *RCA 1343*	43	2
7 Oct 72	**OH CAROL / BREAKING UP IS HARD TO DO / LITTLE DEVIL (re-issue)** *RCA Maximillion 2259*	19	14
4 Nov 72	**BEAUTIFUL YOU** *RCA 2269*	43	3
24 Feb 73	**THAT'S WHEN THE MUSIC TAKES ME** *RCA 2310*	18	10
2 Jun 73	**STANDING ON THE INSIDE** *MGM 2006 267*	26	9
25 Aug 73	**OUR LAST SONG TOGETHER** *MGM 2006 307*	31	8
9 Feb 74	**A LITTLE LOVIN'** *Polydor 2058 434*	34	6
22 Jun 74	**LAUGHTER IN THE RAIN** *Polydor 2058 494* ▲	15	9
22 Mar 75	**THE QUEEN OF 1964** *Polydor 2058 546*	35	5

SEDUCTION *US, female vocal group (1 WEEK)* pos/wks

21 Apr 90	**HEARTBEAT** *Breakout USA 685*	75	1

SEEKERS (227 Top 500) *First Australian act to top UK single or album chart: Judith Durham (v), Keith Potger (g), Bruce Woodley (g), Athol Guy (b). Their unique harmony vocals were displayed on many of their hits, which were penned and produced by Tom Springfield. Durham went solo in 1967, and Potger later went on to form the New Seekers (120 WEEKS)* pos/wks

7 Jan 65 ★	**I'LL NEVER FIND ANOTHER YOU** *Columbia DB 7431*	1	23
15 Apr 65 ●	**A WORLD OF OUR OWN** *Columbia DB 7532*	3	18
28 Oct 65 ★	**THE CARNIVAL IS OVER** *Columbia DB 7711* ◆	1	17
24 Mar 66	**SOMEDAY ONE DAY** *Columbia DB 7867*	11	11
8 Sep 66 ●	**WALK WITH ME** *Columbia DB 8000*	10	12
24 Nov 66 ●	**MORNINGTOWN RIDE** *Columbia DB 8060*	2	15
23 Feb 67 ●	**GEORGY GIRL** *Columbia DB 8134*	3	11
20 Sep 67	**WHEN WILL THE GOOD APPLES FALL** *Columbia DB 8273*	11	12
13 Dec 67	**EMERALD CITY** *Columbia DB 8313*	50	1

Bob SEGER and the SILVER BULLET BAND
US, male vocal / instrumental group (30 WEEKS) pos/wks

30 Sep 78	**HOLLYWOOD NIGHTS** *Capitol CL 16004*	42	6
3 Feb 79	**WE'VE GOT TONITE** *Capitol CL 16028*	41	6
24 Oct 81	**HOLLYWOOD NIGHTS** *Capitol CL 223*	49	3
6 Feb 82	**WE'VE GOT TONITE** *Capitol CL 235*	60	4
9 Apr 83	**EVEN NOW** *Capitol CL 284*	73	2
28 Jan 95	**WE'VE GOT TONIGHT (re-issue)** *Capitol CDCL 734*	22	5
29 Apr 95	**NIGHT MOVES** *Capitol CDCL 741*	45	2
29 Jul 95	**HOLLYWOOD NIGHTS (re-issue)** *Capitol CDCL 749*	52	1
10 Feb 96	**LOCK AND LOAD** *Parlophone CDCL 765*	57	1

Capitol CL 223 and CL 235 were live versions of earlier studio hits

Shea SEGER *US, female vocalist (1 WEEK)* pos/wks

5 May 01	**CLUTCH** *RCA 74321828142*	47	1

SEIKO and Donnie WAHLBERG
Japan / US, female / male vocal duo (5 WEEKS) pos/wks

18 Aug 90	**THE RIGHT COMBINATION** *Epic 656203 7*	44	5

See also NEW KIDS ON THE BLOCK

SELECTER *UK, male / female vocal / instrumental group (28 WEEKS)* pos/wks

13 Oct 79 ●	**ON MY RADIO** *2 Tone CHSTT 4*	8	9
2 Feb 80	**THREE MINUTE HERO** *2 Tone CHSTT 8*	16	6
29 Mar 80	**MISSING WORDS** *2 Tone CHSTT 10*	23	8
23 Aug 80	**THE WHISPER** *Chrysalis CHSS 1*	36	5

SELENA vs X.MEN
UK, female vocalist and male production duo (1 WEEK) pos/wks

14 Jul 01	**GIVE IT UP** *Go.Beat GOBCD 40*	61	1

Peter SELLERS *UK, male actor (39 WEEKS)* pos/wks

2 Aug 57	**ANY OLD IRON** *Parlophone R 4337*	21	3
6 Sep 57	**ANY OLD IRON (re-entry)** *Parlophone R 4337*	17	8
10 Nov 60 ●	**GOODNESS GRACIOUS ME!** *Parlophone R 4702* [1]	4	14
12 Jan 61	**BANGERS AND MASH** *Parlophone R 4724* [1]	22	5
23 Dec 65	**A HARD DAY'S NIGHT** *Parlophone R 5393*	14	7
27 Nov 93	**A HARD DAY'S NIGHT (re-issue)** *EMI CDEMS 293*	52	2

[1] Peter Sellers and Sophia Loren

See also GOONS

Michael SEMBELLO *US, male vocalist (6 WEEKS)* pos/wks

20 Aug 83	**MANIAC** *Casablanca CAN 1017* ▲	43	6

SEMISONIC *US, male vocal / instrumental group (20 WEEKS)* pos/wks

10 Jul 99	**SECRET SMILE** *MCA MCSTD 40210*	13	11
6 Nov 99	**CLOSING TIME** *MCA MCSTD 40221*	25	5
1 Apr 00	**SINGING IN MY SLEEP** *MCA MCSTD 40227*	39	2
3 Mar 01	**CHEMISTRY** *MCA MCSTD 40248*	35	2

SEMPRINI *UK, male pianist and orchestra (8 WEEKS)* pos/wks

16 Mar 61	**MAIN THEME FROM 'EXODUS'** *HMV POP 842*	25	8

SENSATIONAL ALEX HARVEY BAND
UK, male vocal / instrumental group (25 WEEKS) pos/wks

26 Jul 75 ●	**DELILAH** *Vertigo ALEX 001*	7	7
22 Nov 75	**GAMBLIN' BAR ROOM BLUES** *Vertigo ALEX 002*	38	8
19 Jun 76	**THE BOSTON TEA PARTY** *Mountain TOP 12*	13	10

SENSELESS THINGS
UK, male vocal / instrumental group (19 WEEKS) pos/wks

22 Jun 91	**EVERYBODY'S GONE** *Epic 6569807*	73	1
28 Sep 91	**GOT IT AT THE DELMAR** *Epic 6574497*	50	3
11 Jan 92	**EASY TO SMILE** *Epic 6576957*	18	4
11 Apr 92	**HOLD IT DOWN** *Epic 6579267*	19	4
5 Dec 92	**HOMOPHOBIC ASSHOLE** *Epic 6588337*	52	2
13 Feb 93	**PRIMARY INSTINCT** *Epic 6589402*	41	2
12 Jun 93	**TOO MUCH KISSING** *Epic 6592502*	69	1
5 Nov 94	**CHRISTINE KEELER** *Epic 6609572*	56	1
28 Jan 95	**SOMETHING TO MISS** *Epic 6611162*	57	1

SENSER *UK, male / female vocal / instrumental group (5 WEEKS)* pos/wks

25 Sep 93	**THE KEY** *Ultimate TOPP 019CD*	47	1
19 Mar 94	**SWITCH** *Ultimate TOPP 022CD*	39	2
23 Jul 94	**AGE OF PANIC** *Ultimate TOPP 027CD*	52	1
17 Aug 96	**CHARMING DEMONS** *Ultimate TOPP 045CD*	42	1

Nick SENTIENCE – *See BK*

SEPULTURA *Brazil, male vocal / instrumental group (12 WEEKS)* pos/wks

2 Oct 93	**TERRITORY** *Roadrunner RR 23823*	66	2
26 Feb 94	**REFUSE-RESIST** *Roadrunner RR 23773*	51	2
4 Jun 94	**SLAVE NEW WORLD** *Roadrunner RR 23745*	46	2
24 Feb 96	**ROOTS BLOODY ROOTS** *Roadrunner RR 23205*	19	2
17 Aug 96	**RATAMAHATTA** *Roadrunner RR 23145*	23	2
14 Dec 96	**ATTITUDE** *Roadrunner RR 22995*	46	2

SERIAL DIVA *UK, male / female production group (3 WEEKS)* pos/wks

18 Jan 97	**KEEP HOPE ALIVE** *Sound Of Ministry SOMCD 26*	57	1
15 May 99	**PEARL RIVER** *Low Sense SENSECD 24* [1]	32	2

[1] Three 'N One presents Johnny Shaker featuring Serial Diva

SERIOUS DANGER *UK, male producer – Richard Phillips (4 WEEKS)* pos/wks

20 Dec 97	**DEEPER** *Fresh FRSHD 68*	40	3
2 May 98	**HIGH NOON** *Fresh FRSHD 69*	54	1

SERIOUS INTENTION *US, male vocal / instrumental group (6 WEEKS)* pos/wks

16 Nov 85	**YOU DON'T KNOW (OH-OH-OH)** *Important TAN 8*	75	1
5 Apr 86	**SERIOUS** *Pow Wow LON 93*	51	5

SERIOUS ROPE *UK, male / female vocal / production group (3 WEEKS)* pos/wks

22 May 93	**HAPPINESS** *Rumour RUMACD 64* [1]	54	2
1 Oct 94	**HAPPINESS - YOU MAKE ME HAPPY (re-mix)** *Mercury MERCD 407*	70	1

[1] Serious Rope presents Sharon Dee Clarke

Erick SERMON featuring Marvin GAYE
US, male rapper and US, male vocalist (2 WEEKS) pos/wks

6 Oct 01	**MUSIC** *Polydor 4976222*	36	2

SET THE TONE *UK, male vocal / instrumental group (4 WEEKS)* pos/wks

22 Jan 83	**DANCE SUCKER** *Island WIP 6836*	62	2
26 Mar 83	**RAP YOUR LOVE** *Island IS 110*	67	2

SETTLERS *UK, male / female vocal / instrumental group (5 WEEKS)* pos/wks

Date		Title / Label	pos	wks
16 Oct 71		THE LIGHTNING TREE *York SYK 505*	36	5

Brian SETZER ORCHESTRA
US, male vocal / instrumental group (3 WEEKS) pos/wks

Date		Title / Label	pos	wks
3 Apr 99		JUMP JIVE AN' WAIL *Interscope IND 95601*	34	3

Taja SEVELLE *US, female vocalist (13 WEEKS)* pos/wks

Date		Title / Label	pos	wks
20 Feb 88	●	LOVE IS CONTAGIOUS *Paisley Park W 8257*	7	9
14 May 88		WOULDN'T YOU LOVE TO LOVE ME? *Paisley Park W 8127*	59	4

702 *US, female vocal group (10 WEEKS)* pos/wks

Date		Title / Label	pos	wks
14 Dec 96		STEELO *Motown 8606072*	41	2
29 Nov 97		NO DOUBT *Motown 8607052*	59	1
7 Aug 99		WHERE MY GIRLS AT? *Motown TMGCD 1500*	22	4
27 Nov 99		YOU DON'T KNOW *Motown TMGCD 1502*	36	3

740 BOYZ *US, male vocal / instrumental duo (1 WEEK)* pos/wks

Date		Title / Label	pos	wks
4 Nov 95		SHIMMY SHAKE *MCA MCSTD 40002*	54	1

SEVEN GRAND HOUSING AUTHORITY
UK, male producer – Terence Parker (1 WEEK) pos/wks

Date		Title / Label	pos	wks
23 Oct 93		THE QUESTION *Olympic ELYCD 010*	70	1

7669 *US, female rap group (1 WEEK)* pos/wks

Date		Title / Label	pos	wks
18 Jun 94		JOY *Motown TMGCD 1429*	60	1

7TH HEAVEN *UK, male vocal group (5 WEEKS)* pos/wks

Date		Title / Label	pos	wks
14 Sep 85		HOT FUN *Mercury MER 199*	47	5

SEVERINE *France, female vocalist (11 WEEKS)* pos/wks

Date		Title / Label	pos	wks
24 Apr 71	●	UN BANC, UN ARBRE, UNE RUE *Philips 6009 135*	9	11

David SEVILLE *US, male vocalist – Ross Bagdasarian (6 WEEKS)* pos/wks

Date		Title / Label	pos	wks
23 May 58		WITCH DOCTOR *London HLU 8619* ▲	11	6

See also ALFI and HARRY; CHIPMUNKS

Janette SEWELL – *See DOUBLE TROUBLE*

SEX CLUB featuring BROWN SUGAR
US, male / female vocal / instrumental duo (1 WEEK) pos/wks

Date		Title / Label	pos	wks
28 Jan 95		BIG DICK MAN *Club Tools CLU 60775*	67	1

SEX-O-LETTES – *See DISCO TEX and the SEX-O-LETTES*

SEX-O-SONIQUE *UK, male production / instrumental duo – Mike Gray and Jon Pearn (3 WEEKS)* pos/wks

Date		Title / Label	pos	wks
6 Dec 97		I THOUGHT IT WAS YOU *ffrr FCD 321*	32	3

See also FULL INTENTION; HUSTLERS CONVENTION featuring Dave LAUDAT and Ondrea DUVERNEY

SEX PISTOLS (362 Top 500) *Provocative and influential quartet who popularised punk. Formed 1975 in London UK, split 1978: Johnny Rotten (v), Steve Jones (g), Paul Cook (d) and Glen Matlock (b) - replaced 1977 by Sid Vicious (d. 1979). Notorious group reunited for brief, and profitable, Filthy Lucre tour in 1996 (88 WEEKS)* pos/wks

Date		Title / Label	pos	wks
18 Dec 76		ANARCHY IN THE UK *EMI 2566*	38	4
4 Jun 77	●	GOD SAVE THE QUEEN *Virgin VS 181*	2	9
9 Jul 77	●	PRETTY VACANT *Virgin VS 184*	6	8
22 Oct 77	●	HOLIDAYS IN THE SUN *Virgin VS 191*	8	6
8 Jul 78	●	NO ONE IS INNOCENT / MY WAY *Virgin VS 220* [1]	7	10
3 Mar 79	●	SOMETHING ELSE / FRIGGIN' IN THE RIGGIN' *Virgin VS 240*	3	12
7 Apr 79	●	SILLY THING *Virgin VS 256*	6	8
30 Jun 79	●	C'MON EVERYBODY *Virgin VS 272*	3	9
13 Oct 79		THE GREAT ROCK 'N' ROLL SWINDLE *Virgin VS 290*	21	6
14 Jun 80		(I'M NOT YOUR) STEPPING STONE *Virgin VS 339*	21	8
3 Oct 92		ANARCHY IN THE UK (re-issue) *Virgin VS 1431*	33	3
5 Dec 92		PRETTY VACANT (re-issue) *Virgin VS 1448*	56	2
27 Jul 96		PRETTY VACANT (LIVE) *Virgin America VUSCD 113*	18	3

[1] Sex Pistols, punk prayer by Ronald Biggs

The listed flip side of 'Silly Thing' was 'Who Killed Bambi' by Ten Pole Tudor. The listed flip side of 'The Great Rock 'n' Roll Swindle' was 'Rock Around the Clock', also by Ten Pole Tudor

Denny SEYTON and the SABRES
UK, male vocal / instrumental group (1 WEEK) pos/wks

Date		Title / Label	pos	wks
17 Sep 64		THE WAY YOU LOOK TONIGHT *Mercury MF 824*	48	1

SFX *UK, male instrumental / production duo (3 WEEKS)* pos/wks

Date		Title / Label	pos	wks
15 May 93		LEMMINGS *Parlophone CDR 6343*	51	3

SHABOOM *UK, male instrumental / production group (1 WEEK)* pos/wks

Date		Title / Label	pos	wks
31 Jul 99		SWEET SENSATION *WEA WEA 218CD1*	64	1

SHACK *UK, male vocal / instrumental group (3 WEEKS)* pos/wks

Date		Title / Label	pos	wks
26 Jun 99		COMEDY *London LONCD 427*	44	1
14 Aug 99		NATALIE'S PARTY *London LONCD 436*	63	1
11 Mar 00		OSCAR *London LONCD 445*	67	1

SHADES *US, female vocal group (3 WEEKS)* pos/wks

Date		Title / Label	pos	wks
12 Apr 97		MR BIG STUFF *Motown 5736572* [1]	31	2
20 Sep 97		SERENADE *Motown 8606892*	75	1

[1] Queen Latifah, Shades and Free

SHADES OF LOVE *US, male instrumental / production duo (1 WEEK)* pos/wks

Date		Title / Label	pos	wks
22 Apr 95		KEEP IN TOUCH (BODY TO BODY) *Vicious Muzik MUZCD 102*	64	1

SHADES OF RHYTHM
UK, male instrumental / production group (25 WEEKS) pos/wks

Date		Title / Label	pos	wks
2 Feb 91		HOMICIDE / EXORCIST *ZTT ZANG 13*	53	3
13 Apr 91		SWEET SENSATION *ZTT ZANG 18*	54	4
20 Jul 91		THE SOUND OF EDEN *ZTT ZANG 22*	35	5
30 Nov 91		EXTACY *ZTT ZANG 24*	16	7
20 Feb 93		SWEET REVIVAL (KEEP IT COMIN') *ZTT ZANG 40CD*	61	1
11 Sep 93		SOUND OF EDEN (re-issue) *ZTT ZANG 44CD*	37	3
5 Nov 94		THE WANDERING DRAGON *Public Demand PPDCD 5*	55	1
21 Jun 97		PSYCHO BASE *Coalition CRUM 002CD*	57	1

SHADOWS (3 Top 500) *Headliners for five decades and Britain's most successful instrumental group: Hank Marvin (b. Brian Rankin, 28 Oct 1941, Newcastle-upon-Tyne) (g), Bruce Welch (b. Bruce Cripps, 2 Nov 1941, Bognor Regis) (g), 'Jet' Harris (b. Terence Hawkins, 6 Jul 1939, London) (b), Tony Meehan (b. Daniel Meehan, 2 Mar 1943, London) (d), Brian Bennett (b. 9 Feb 1940, London) (d). They began their chart life as The Drifters when backing Cliff Richard and went on to contribute significantly on 35 hits with Cliff. Their main claim to fame is as Britain's most influential and imitated act before The Beatles (770 WEEKS)* pos/wks

Date		Title / Label	pos	wks
12 Sep 58	●	MOVE IT *Columbia DB 4178* [1]	2	17
21 Nov 58	●	HIGH CLASS BABY *Columbia DB 4203* [1]	7	10
30 Jan 59		LIVIN' LOVIN' DOLL *Columbia DB 4249* [1]	20	6
8 May 59	●	MEAN STREAK *Columbia DB 4290 A* [1]	10	9
15 May 59		NEVER MIND *Columbia DB 4290 B* [1]	21	2
10 Jul 59	★	LIVING DOLL *Columbia DB 4306* [1]	1	21
9 Oct 59		DYNAMITE *Columbia DB 4351 A* [1]	16	2
9 Oct 59	★	TRAVELLIN' LIGHT *Columbia DB 4351 B* [2]	1	17
30 Oct 59		DYNAMITE (re-entry) *Columbia DB 4351 A* [1]	21	2
11 Dec 59		LIVING DOLL (re-entry) *Columbia DB 4306* [1]	26	1
1 Jan 60		LIVING DOLL (2nd re-entry) *Columbia DB 4306* [1]	28	1
15 Jan 60		EXPRESSO BONGO (EP) *Columbia SEG 7971* [2]	14	7
22 Jan 60	●	VOICE IN THE WILDERNESS *Columbia DB 4398* [2]	2	13
24 Mar 60	●	FALL IN LOVE WITH YOU *Columbia DB 4431* [2]	2	15

5 May 60 VOICE IN THE WILDERNESS (re-entry) *Columbia DB 4398* [2] ... 36 2
30 Jun 60 ★ PLEASE DON'T TEASE *Columbia 4479* [2] ... 1 18
21 Jul 60 ★ APACHE *Columbia DB 4484* ... 1 21
22 Sep 60 ● NINE TIMES OUT OF TEN *Columbia DB 4506* [2] ... 3 12
10 Nov 60 ● MAN OF MYSTERY / THE STRANGER *Columbia DB 4530* ... 5 15
1 Dec 60 ★ I LOVE YOU *Columbia DB 4547* [2] ... 1 16
9 Feb 61 ● F.B.I. *Columbia DB 4580* ... 6 19
2 Mar 61 ● THEME FOR A DREAM *Columbia DB 4593* [2] ... 3 14
30 Mar 61 ● GEE WHIZ IT'S YOU *Columbia DC 756* [2] ... 4 14
11 May 61 ● THE FRIGHTENED CITY *Columbia DB 4637* ... 3 20
22 Jun 61 ● A GIRL LIKE YOU *Columbia DB 4667* [2] ... 3 14
7 Sep 61 ★ KON-TIKI *Columbia DB 4698* ... 1 10
16 Nov 61 ● THE SAVAGE *Columbia DB 4726* ... 10 8
23 Nov 61 KON-TIKI (re-entry) *Columbia DB 4698* ... 37 2
11 Jan 62 ★ THE YOUNG ONES *Columbia DB 4761* [2] ◆ ■ ... 1 21
1 Mar 62 ★ WONDERFUL LAND *Columbia DB 4790* ... 1 19
10 May 62 ● I'M LOOKING OUT THE WINDOW / DO YOU WANT TO DANCE *Columbia DB 4828* [3] ... 2 17
2 Aug 62 ● GUITAR TANGO *Columbia DB 4870* ... 4 15
6 Sep 62 ● IT'LL BE ME *Columbia DB 4886* [2] ... 2 12
6 Dec 62 ★ THE NEXT TIME / BACHELOR BOY *Columbia DB 4950* [2] ... 1 18
13 Dec 62 ★ DANCE ON! *Columbia DB 4948* ... 1 15
21 Feb 63 ★ SUMMER HOLIDAY *Columbia DB 4977* [2] ... 1 18
7 Mar 63 ★ FOOT TAPPER *Columbia DB 4984* ... 1 16
9 May 63 ● LUCKY LIPS *Columbia DB 7034* [2] ... 4 15
6 Jun 63 ● ATLANTIS *Columbia DB 7047* ... 2 17
19 Sep 63 ● SHINDIG *Columbia DB 7106* ... 6 12
7 Nov 63 ● DON'T TALK TO HIM *Columbia DB 7150* [2] ... 2 13
5 Dec 63 GERONIMO *Columbia DB 7163* ... 11 12
6 Feb 64 ● I'M THE LONELY ONE *Columbia DB 7203* [2] ... 8 10
13 Feb 64 DON'T TALK TO HIM (re-entry) *Columbia DB 7150* [2] ... 50 1
5 Mar 64 THEME FOR YOUNG LOVERS *Columbia DB 7231* ... 12 10
7 May 64 ● THE RISE AND FALL OF FLINGEL BUNT *Columbia DB 7261* ... 5 14
2 Jul 64 ● ON THE BEACH *Columbia DB 7305* [2] ... 7 13
3 Sep 64 RHYTHM AND GREENS *Columbia DB 7342* ... 22 7
3 Dec 64 GENIE WITH THE LIGHT BROWN LAMP *Columbia DB 7416* ... 17 10
10 Dec 64 ● I COULD EASILY FALL *Columbia DB 7420* [2] ... 6 11
11 Feb 65 MARY ANNE *Columbia DB 7476* ... 17 10
10 Jun 65 STINGRAY *Columbia DB 7588* ... 19 7
5 Aug 65 ● DON'T MAKE MY BABY BLUE *Columbia DB 7650* ... 10 10
19 Aug 65 THE TIME IN BETWEEN *Columbia DB 7660* [2] ... 22 8
25 Nov 65 THE WAR LORD *Columbia DB 7769* ... 18 9
17 Mar 66 I MET A GIRL *Columbia DB 7853* ... 22 5
24 Mar 66 BLUE TURNS TO GREY *Columbia DB 7866* [2] ... 15 9
7 Jul 66 A PLACE IN THE SUN *Columbia DB 7952* ... 24 6
13 Oct 66 ● TIME DRAGS BY *Columbia DB 8017* [2] ... 10 12
3 Nov 66 THE DREAMS I DREAM *Columbia DB 8034* ... 42 6
15 Dec 66 ● IN THE COUNTRY *Columbia DB 8094* [2] ... 6 10
13 Apr 67 MAROC 7 *Columbia DB 8170* ... 24 8
27 Nov 68 DON'T FORGET TO CATCH ME *Columbia DB 8503* [2] ... 21 10
8 Mar 75 LET ME BE THE ONE *EMI 2269* ... 12 9
16 Dec 78 ● DON'T CRY FOR ME ARGENTINA *EMI 2890* ... 5 14
28 Apr 79 ● THEME FROM THE 'DEER HUNTER' (CAVATINA) *EMI 2939* ... 9 14
26 Jan 80 RIDERS IN THE SKY *EMI 5027* ... 12 12
23 Aug 80 EQUINOXE (PART V) *Polydor POSP 148* ... 50 3
2 May 81 THE THIRD MAN *Polydor POSP 255* ... 44 4

[1] Cliff Richard and the Drifters [2] Cliff Richard and the Shadows [3] Cliff Richard / The Shadows

All the Shadows hits without Cliff Richard were instrumentals except for 'Mary Anne', 'Don't Make My Baby Blue', 'I Met a Girl', 'The Dreams I Dream' and 'Let Me Be the One'. Tracks on Expresso Bongo (EP): Love / A Voice in the Wilderness / The Shrine on the Second Floor / Bongo Blues. Last track featured Shadows only

See also Cliff RICHARD; Hank MARVIN; Jet HARRIS and Tony MEEHAN

SHAFT *UK, male producer – Mark Pritchard (9 WEEKS)* pos/wks

21 Dec 91 ● ROOBARB AND CUSTARD *Ffrreedom TAB 100* ... 7 8
25 Jul 92 MONKEY *Ffrreedom TAB 114* ... 61 1

SHAFT
UK, male production duo – Elliot Ireland and Alex Rizzo (19 WEEKS) pos/wks

4 Sep 99 ● (MUCHO MAMBO) SWAY *Wonderboy WBOYD 015* ... 2 12
20 May 00 MAMBO ITALIANO *Wonderboy WBDD 017* ... 12 6
21 Jul 01 KIKI RIRI BOOM *Wonderboy WBOYD 026* ... 62 1

SHAG – *See Jonathan KING*

SHAGGY (226 Top 500) *Jamaican male vocalist – Orville Burrell, b. 22 Oct 1968, the biggest-selling act in 2001, with most chart weeks (120 WEEKS)* pos/wks

6 Feb 93 ★ OH CAROLINA *Greensleeves GRECD 361* ... 1 19
10 Jul 93 SOON BE DONE *Greensleeves GRECD 380* ... 46 3
8 Jul 95 ● IN THE SUMMERTIME *Virgin VSCDT 1542* [1] ... 5 9
23 Sep 95 ★ BOOMBASTIC *Virgin VSCDT 1536* ■ ... 1 12
13 Jan 96 WHY YOU TREAT ME SO BAD *Virgin VSCDT 1566* [2] ... 11 5
23 Mar 96 SOMETHING DIFFERENT / THE TRAIN IS COMING *Virgin VSCDT 1581* [3] ... 21 5
22 Jun 96 THAT GIRL *Virgin America VUSCDX 106* [4] ... 15 7
19 Jul 97 ● PIECE OF MY HEART *Virgin VSCDT 1647* [5] ... 7 6
17 Feb 01 IT WASN'T ME (import) *MCA 1558032* [6] ... 31 3
10 Mar 01 ★ IT WASN'T ME *MCA 1558022* [6] ◆ ■ ▲ ... 1 20
9 Jun 01 ★ ANGEL *MCA MCSTD 40257* [1] ■ ▲ ... 1 16
29 Sep 01 ● LUV ME LUV ME *MCA MCSTD 40263* ... 5 10
1 Dec 01 DANCE AND SHOUT / HOPE *MCA MCSTD 40272* ... 19 5+

[1] Shaggy featuring Rayvon [2] Shaggy featuring Grand Puba [3] Shaggy featuring Wayne Wonder / Shaggy [4] Maxi Priest featuring Shaggy [5] Shaggy featuring Marsha [6] Shaggy featuring Ricardo "Rikrok" Ducent

SHAH *UK, female vocalist (1 WEEK)* pos/wks

6 Jun 98 SECRET LOVE *Evocative EVOKE 5CDS* ... 69 1

SHAI *US, male vocal group (6 WEEKS)* pos/wks

19 Dec 92 IF I EVER FALL IN LOVE *MCA MCS 1727* ... 36 6

SHAKATAK (387 Top 500) *London-based pop / jazz / funk ensemble who were big in Japan. Sound was typified by tinkling piano of Bill Sharpe and Jill Saward's soothing vocals. Sharpe later hit with Gary Numan, while Nigel Wright (k) produced hits for Madonna, Take That, Robson and Jerome, Barbra Streisand, Cliff Richard and Boyzone (85 WEEKS)* pos/wks

8 Nov 80 FEELS LIKE THE RIGHT TIME *Polydor POSP 188* ... 41 5
7 Mar 81 LIVING IN THE UK *Polydor POSP 230* ... 52 4
25 Jul 81 BRAZILIAN DAWN *Polydor POSP 282* ... 48 3
21 Nov 81 EASIER SAID THAN DONE *Polydor POSP 375* ... 12 17
3 Apr 82 ● NIGHT BIRDS *Polydor POSP 407* ... 9 8
19 Jun 82 STREETWALKIN' *Polydor POSP 452* ... 38 6
4 Sep 82 INVITATIONS *Polydor POSP 502* ... 24 7
6 Nov 82 STRANGER *Polydor POSP 530* ... 43 3
4 Jun 83 DARK IS THE NIGHT *Polydor POSP 595* ... 15 8
27 Aug 83 IF YOU COULD SEE ME NOW *Polydor POSP 635* ... 49 4
7 Jul 84 ● DOWN ON THE STREET *Polydor POSP 688* ... 9 11
15 Sep 84 DON'T BLAME IT ON LOVE *Polydor POSP 699* ... 55 3
16 Nov 85 DAY BY DAY *Polydor POSP 770* [1] ... 53 3
24 Oct 87 MR MANIC AND SISTER COOL *Polydor MANIC 1* ... 56 3

[1] Shakatak featuring Al Jarreau

SHAKESPEAR'S SISTER *UK / US, female vocal / instrumental duo – Siobhan Fahey and Marcella (Detroit) Levy (52 WEEKS)* pos/wks

29 Jul 89 ● YOU'RE HISTORY *ffrr F 112* ... 7 9
14 Oct 89 RUN SILENT *ffrr F 119* ... 54 3
10 Mar 90 DIRTY MIND *ffrr F 128* ... 71 1
12 Oct 91 GOODBYE CRUEL WORLD *London LON 309* ... 59 2
25 Jan 92 ★ STAY *London LON 314* ... 1 16
16 May 92 ● I DON'T CARE *London LON 318* ... 7 7
18 Jul 92 GOODBYE CRUEL WORLD (re-issue) *London LON 322* ... 32 4
7 Nov 92 HELLO (TURN YOUR RADIO ON) *London LON 330* ... 14 6
27 Feb 93 MY 16TH APOLOGY (EP) *London LONCD 337* ... 61 1
22 Jun 96 I CAN DRIVE *London LONCD 383* ... 30 3

Tracks on My 16th Apology (EP): My 16th Apology / Catwoman / Dirty Mind (live re-recording) / Hot Love. From 1996 Shakespear's Sister was essentially just vocalist Siobhan Fahey

See also Marcella DETROIT; BANANARAMA

SHAKY and BONNIE – *See Shakin' STEVENS; Bonnie TYLER*

SHALAMAR

(191 Top 500) *Influential US dance-music vocal trio masterminded by 'Soul Train' TV producer Don Cornelius. Line-up 1979-1983: Jeffrey Daniel, Jody Watley, Howard Hewett. Regarded as fashion icons and trendsetters, they helped to introduce "body-popping" to Britain (134 WEEKS)*

Date		Title	pos	wks
14 May 77		**UPTOWN FESTIVAL** *Soul Train FB 0885*	30	5
9 Dec 78		**TAKE THAT TO THE BANK** *RCA FB 1379*	20	12
24 Nov 79		**THE SECOND TIME AROUND** *Solar FB 1709*	45	9
9 Feb 80		**RIGHT IN THE SOCKET** *Solar SO 2*	44	6
30 Aug 80		**I OWE YOU ONE** *Solar SO 11*	13	10
28 Mar 81		**MAKE THAT MOVE** *Solar SO 17*	30	10
27 Mar 82	●	**I CAN MAKE YOU FEEL GOOD** *Solar K 12599*	7	11
12 Jun 82	●	**A NIGHT TO REMEMBER** *Solar K 13162*	5	12
4 Sep 82	●	**THERE IT IS** *Solar K 13194*	5	10
27 Nov 82		**FRIENDS** *Solar CHUM 1*	12	10
11 Jun 83	●	**DEAD GIVEAWAY** *Solar E 9819*	8	10
13 Aug 83		**DISAPPEARING ACT** *Solar E 9807*	18	8
15 Oct 83		**OVER AND OVER** *Solar E 9792*	23	6
24 Mar 84		**DANCING IN THE SHEETS** *CBS A 4171*	41	3
31 Mar 84		**DEADLINE USA** *MCA MCA 866*	52	3
24 Nov 84		**AMNESIA** *Solar/MCA SHAL 1*	61	2
2 Feb 85		**MY GIRL LOVES ME** *MCA SHAL 2*	45	3
26 Apr 86		**A NIGHT TO REMEMBER (re-mix)** *MCA SHAL 3*	52	4

See also BABYFACE

SHAM ROCK

Ireland, male / female vocal / instrumental group (11 WEEKS)

Date		Title	pos	wks
7 Nov 98		**TELL ME MA** *Jive 0522352*	13	11

SHAM 69

UK, male vocal / instrumental group (53 WEEKS)

Date		Title	pos	wks
13 May 78		**ANGELS WITH DIRTY FACES** *Polydor 2059 023*	19	10
29 Jul 78	●	**IF THE KIDS ARE UNITED** *Polydor 2059 050*	9	9
14 Oct 78	●	**HURRY UP HARRY** *Polydor POSP 7*	10	8
24 Mar 79		**QUESTIONS AND ANSWERS** *Polydor POSP 27*	18	9
4 Aug 79	●	**HERSHAM BOYS** *Polydor POSP 64*	6	9
27 Oct 79		**YOU'RE A BETTER MAN THAN I** *Polydor POSP 82*	49	5
12 Apr 80		**TELL THE CHILDREN** *Polydor POSP 136*	45	3

SHAMEN

(439 Top 500) *Early and highly influential exponents of techno-rock fusion. The Shamen, named after South American Indian tribesmen, comprise duo Colin Angus and Richard West (Mr C) following the departure of founders Peter Stephenson and Keith McKenzie and the death by drowning of Will Sinnott in 1991 (77 WEEKS)*

Date		Title	pos	wks
7 Apr 90		**PRO-GEN** *One Little Indian 36 TP7*	55	4
22 Sep 90		**MAKE IT MINE** *One Little Indian 46 TP7*	42	5
6 Apr 91		**HYPERREAL** *One Little Indian 48 TP7*	29	5
27 Jul 91	●	**MOVE ANY MOUNTAIN (re-mix)** *One Little Indian 52 TP7*	4	10
18 Jul 92	●	**LSI** *One Little Indian 68 TP7*	6	8
5 Sep 92	★	**EBENEEZER GOODE** *One Little Indian 78 TP7*	1	10
7 Nov 92		**BOSS DRUM (re-mix)** *One Little Indian 88 TP12*	58	1
7 Nov 92	●	**BOSS DRUM** *One Little Indian 88 TP7*	4	7
19 Dec 92	●	**PHOREVER PEOPLE** *One Little Indian 98 TP7*	5	10
6 Mar 93		**RE: EVOLUTION** *One Little Indian 118 TP7CD* [1]	18	2
6 Nov 93		**THE SOS (EP)** *One Little Indian 108 TP7CD*	14	4
19 Aug 95		**DESTINATION ESCHATON** *One Little Indian 128 TP7CDL*	15	4
21 Oct 95		**TRANSAMAZONIA** *One Little Indian 138 TP7CD*	28	2
10 Feb 96		**HEAL (THE SEPARATION)** *One Little Indian 158 TP7CDL*	31	2
21 Dec 96		**MOVE ANY MOUNTAIN '96 (2nd re-mix)** *One Little Indian 169 TP7CD*	35	3

[1] Shamen with Terence McKenna

'Move Any Mountain' is a re-mix of 'Pro-Gen'. Tracks on The SOS (EP): Comin' On / Make It Mine / Possible Worlds (re-mix)

SHAMPOO

UK, female vocal duo – Jacqui Blake and Carrie Askew (28 WEEKS)

Date		Title	pos	wks
30 Jul 94		**TROUBLE** *Food CDFOOD 51*	11	12
15 Oct 94		**VIVA LA MEGABABES** *Food CDFOOD 54*	27	4
18 Feb 95		**DELICIOUS** *Food CDFOOD 58*	21	4
5 Aug 95		**TROUBLE (re-issue)** *Food CDFOOD 66*	36	3
13 Jul 96		**GIRL POWER** *Food CDFOOD 76*	25	4
21 Sep 96		**I KNOW WHAT BOYS LIKE** *Food CDFOOD 83*	42	1

Jimmy SHAND BAND

UK, male dance band (2 WEEKS)

Date		Title	pos	wks
23 Dec 55		**BLUEBELL POLKA** *Parlophone F 3436*	20	2

Paul SHANE and the YELLOWCOATS

UK, male vocalist with male / female vocal group (5 WEEKS)

Date		Title	pos	wks
16 May 81		**HI-DE-HI (HOLIDAY ROCK)** *EMI 5180*	36	5

SHANGRI-LAS

US, female vocal group (48 WEEKS)

Date		Title	pos	wks
8 Oct 64		**REMEMBER (WALKIN' IN THE SAND)** *Red Bird RB 10008*	14	13
14 Jan 65		**LEADER OF THE PACK** *Red Bird RB 10014* ▲	11	9
14 Oct 72	●	**LEADER OF THE PACK (re-issue)** *Kama Sutra 2013 024*	3	14
5 Jun 76	●	**LEADER OF THE PACK (2nd re-issue)** *Charly CS 1009*	7	12

From 19 Jun 1976 until 14 Aug 1976, the last week of the disc's chart run, the Charly and another Contempo release of 'Leader of the Pack' were bracketed together on the chart

SHANICE

US, female vocalist – Shanice Wilson (24 WEEKS)

Date		Title	pos	wks
23 Nov 91		**I LOVE YOUR SMILE** *Motown ZB 44907*	55	4
22 Feb 92	●	**I LOVE YOUR SMILE (re-mix)** *Motown TMG 1401*	2	10
14 Nov 92		**LOVIN' YOU** *Motown TMG 1409*	54	1
16 Jan 93		**SAVING FOREVER FOR YOU** *Giant W 0148CD*	42	3
13 Aug 94		**I LIKE** *Motown TMGCD 1427*	49	2
16 Dec 95		**IF I NEVER KNEW YOU (LOVE THEME FROM 'POCAHONTAS')** *Walt Disney WD 7023CD* [1]	51	4

[1] Jon Secada and Shanice

SHANKS & BIGFOOT

UK, male production duo aka Doolally – Stephen Meade and Daniel Langsman (24 WEEKS)

Date		Title	pos	wks
29 May 99	★	**SWEET LIKE CHOCOLATE** *Pepper / Jive / Chocolate Boy 0530352* ■	1	15
2 Oct 99		**SWEET LIKE CHOCOLATE (re-entry)** *Pepper / Jive / Chocolate Boy 0530352*	66	1
29 Jul 00		**SING-A-LONG** *Pepper 9230232*	12	7
23 Sep 00		**SING-A-LONG (re-entry)** *Pepper 9230232*	52	1

SHANNON

US, female vocalist – Brenda Shannon Greene (54 WEEKS)

Date		Title	pos	wks
19 Nov 83		**LET THE MUSIC PLAY** *Club LET 1*	51	3
28 Jan 84		**LET THE MUSIC PLAY (re-entry)** *Club LET 1*	14	12
7 Apr 84		**GIVE ME TONIGHT** *Club JAB 1*	24	7
30 Jun 84		**SWEET SOMEBODY** *Club JAB 3*	25	8
20 Jul 85		**STRONGER TOGETHER** *Club JAB 15*	46	6
6 Dec 97		**IT'S OVER LOVE** *Manifesto FESCD 37* [1]	16	8
28 Nov 98	●	**MOVE MANIA** *Multiply CDMULTY 45* [2]	8	10

[1] Todd Terry presents Shannon [2] Sash! featuring Shannon

Del SHANNON

(153 Top 500) *Early 1960s chart regular, b. Charles Westover, 30 Dec 1934, Michigan, US, d. 8 Feb 1990. This unmistakable singer / songwriter who used a falsetto vocal on most hits topped both the UK and US charts with the first of his many hits (147 WEEKS)*

Date		Title	pos	wks
27 Apr 61	★	**RUNAWAY** *London HLX 9317* ▲	1	22
14 Sep 61	●	**HATS OFF TO LARRY** *London HLX 9402*	6	12
7 Dec 61	●	**SO LONG BABY** *London HLX 9462*	10	11
15 Mar 62	●	**HEY! LITTLE GIRL** *London HLX 9515*	2	15
6 Sep 62		**CRY MYSELF TO SLEEP** *London HLX 9587*	29	6
11 Oct 62	●	**THE SWISS MAID** *London HLX 9609*	2	17
17 Jan 63	●	**LITTLE TOWN FLIRT** *London HLX 9653*	4	13
25 Apr 63	●	**TWO KINDS OF TEARDROPS** *London HLX 9710*	5	13
22 Aug 63		**TWO SILHOUETTES** *London HLX 9761*	23	8
24 Oct 63		**SUE'S GOTTA BE MINE** *London HLU 9800*	21	8
12 Mar 64		**MARY JANE** *Stateside SS 269*	35	5
30 Jul 64		**HANDY MAN** *Stateside SS 317*	36	4
14 Jan 65	●	**KEEP SEARCHIN' (WE'LL FOLLOW THE SUN)** *Stateside SS 368*	3	11
18 Mar 65		**STRANGER IN TOWN** *Stateside SS 395*	40	2

Roxanne SHANTE *US, female rapper (11 WEEKS)* pos/wks

1 Aug 87		HAVE A NICE DAY *Breakout USA 612*	58	3
4 Jun 88		GO ON GIRL *Breakout USA 633*	55	3
29 Oct 88		SHARP AS A KNIFE *Club JAB 73* [1]	45	3
14 Apr 90		GO ON GIRL (re-mix) *Breakout USA 689*	74	1
23 Sep 00		WHAT'S GOING ON *Wall of Sound WALLD 064* [2]	43	1

[1] Brandon Cooke featuring Roxanne Shante [2] Mekon featuring Roxanne Shante

Helen SHAPIRO (230 Top 500) *Youngest female chart-topper, b. 28 Sep 1946, London. Before she was 16 years old, she amassed four Top 5 hits (including two No.1s) and had been voted Britain's Top Female Singer. She headlined the first UK tour on which The Beatles appeared (as her support act) (119 WEEKS)* pos/wks

23 Mar 61	●	DON'T TREAT ME LIKE A CHILD *Columbia DB 4589*	3	20
29 Jun 61	★	YOU DON'T KNOW *Columbia DB 4670*	1	23
28 Sep 61	★	WALKIN' BACK TO HAPPINESS *Columbia DB 4715*	1	19
15 Feb 62	●	TELL ME WHAT HE SAID *Columbia DB 4782*	2	15
3 May 62		LET'S TALK ABOUT LOVE *Columbia DB 4824*	23	7
12 Jul 62	●	LITTLE MISS LONELY *Columbia DB 4869*	8	11
18 Oct 62		KEEP AWAY FROM OTHER GIRLS *Columbia DB 4908*	40	6
7 Feb 63		QUEEN FOR TONIGHT *Columbia DB 4966*	33	5
25 Apr 63		WOE IS ME *Columbia DB 7026*	35	6
24 Oct 63		LOOK WHO IT IS *Columbia DB 7130*	47	3
23 Jan 64		FEVER *Columbia DB 7190*	38	4

SHARADA HOUSE GANG
Italy, male / female vocal / instrumental group (4 WEEKS) pos/wks

12 Aug 95		KEEP IT UP *Media MCSTD 2071*	36	2
11 May 96		LET THE RHYTHM MOVE YOU *Media MCSTD 40035*	50	1
18 Oct 97		GYPSY BOY, GYPSY GIRL *Gut CXGUT 12*	52	1

SHARKEY
UK, male DJ / producer / instrumentalist – Jonathan Sharkey (1 WEEK) pos/wks

8 Mar 97		REVOLUTIONS (EP) *React CDREACT 95*	53	1

Tracks on Revolutions (EP): Revolution Part One / Revolution Part Two / Revolution Part Two (remix)

Feargal SHARKEY *Ireland, male vocalist (58 WEEKS)* pos/wks

13 Oct 84		LISTEN TO YOUR FATHER *Zarjazz JAZZ 1*	23	7
29 Jun 85		LOVING YOU *Virgin VS 770*	26	10
12 Oct 85	★	A GOOD HEART *Virgin VS 808*	1	16
4 Jan 86	●	YOU LITTLE THIEF *Virgin VS 840*	5	9
5 Apr 86		SOMEONE TO SOMEBODY *Virgin VS 828*	64	3
16 Jan 88		MORE LOVE *Virgin VS 992*	44	5
16 Mar 91		I'VE GOT NEWS FOR YOU *Virgin VS 1294*	12	8

See also UNDERTONES; ASSEMBLY

SHARONETTES *US, female vocal group (8 WEEKS)* pos/wks

26 Apr 75		PAPA OOM MOW MOW *Black Magic BM 102*	26	5
12 Jul 75		GOING TO A GO-GO *Black Magic BM 104*	46	3

Debbie SHARP – *See DREAM FREQUENCY*

Dee Dee SHARP *US, female vocalist (2 WEEKS)* pos/wks

25 Apr 63		DO THE BIRD *Cameo Parkway C 244*	46	2

Barrie K SHARPE – *See Diana BROWN and Barrie K SHARPE*

SHARPE and NUMAN – *See Gary NUMAN*

Rocky SHARPE and the REPLAYS
UK, male / female vocal group (41 WEEKS) pos/wks

16 Dec 78		RAMA LAMA DING DONG *Chiswick CHIS 104*	17	10
24 Mar 79		IMAGINATION *Chiswick CHIS 110*	39	6
25 Aug 79		LOVE WILL MAKE YOU FAIL IN SCHOOL *Chiswick CHIS 114* [1]	60	4
9 Feb 80		MARTIAN HOP *Chiswick CHIS 121* [1]	55	4
17 Apr 82		SHOUT SHOUT (KNOCK YOURSELF OUT) *Chiswick DICE 3*	19	9
7 Aug 82		CLAP YOUR HANDS *RAK 345*	54	3
26 Feb 83		IF YOU WANNA BE HAPPY *Polydor POSP 560*	46	5

[1] Rocky Sharpe and the Replays featuring the Top Liners

Ben SHAW featuring Adele HOLNESS
UK, male producer and female vocalist (1 WEEK) pos/wks

14 Jul 01		SO STRONG *Fire Recordings ERIF 009CDS*	72	1

Mark SHAW *UK, male vocalist (1 WEEK)* pos/wks

17 Nov 90		LOVE SO BRIGHT *EMI EM 161*	54	1

Sandie SHAW (125 Top 500) *Barefoot pop princess of the Sixties, b. Sandra Goodrich, 26 Feb 1947, Essex, UK. This distinctive vocalist, who has a 30-year chart span, was the first UK act to win the Eurovision Song Contest (with 'Puppet on a String' in 1967) (165 WEEKS)* pos/wks

8 Oct 64	★	(THERE'S) ALWAYS SOMETHING THERE TO REMIND ME *Pye 7N 15704*	1	11
10 Dec 64	●	GIRL DON'T COME *Pye 7N 15743*	3	12
18 Feb 65	●	I'LL STOP AT NOTHING *Pye 7N 15783*	4	11
13 May 65	★	LONG LIVE LOVE *Pye 7N 15841*	1	14
23 Sep 65	●	MESSAGE UNDERSTOOD *Pye 7N 15940*	6	10
18 Nov 65		HOW CAN YOU TELL *Pye 7N 15987*	21	9
27 Jan 66	●	TOMORROW *Pye 7N 17036*	9	9
19 May 66		NOTHING COMES EASY *Pye 7N 17086*	14	9
8 Sep 66		RUN *Pye 7N 17163*	32	5
24 Nov 66		THINK SOMETIMES ABOUT ME *Pye 7N 17212*	32	4
19 Jan 67		I DON'T NEED ANYTHING *Pye 7N 17239*	50	1
16 Mar 67	★	PUPPET ON A STRING *Pye 7N 17272*	1	18
12 Jul 67		TONIGHT IN TOKYO *Pye 7N 17346*	21	6
4 Oct 67		YOU'VE NOT CHANGED *Pye 7N 17378*	18	12
7 Feb 68		TODAY *Pye 7N 17441*	27	7
12 Feb 69	●	MONSIEUR DUPONT *Pye 7N 17675*	6	15
14 May 69		THINK IT ALL OVER *Pye 7N 17726*	42	4
21 Apr 84		HAND IN GLOVE *Rough Trade RT 130*	27	5
14 Jun 86		ARE YOU READY TO BE HEARTBROKEN? *Polydor POSP 793*	68	1
12 Nov 94		NOTHING LESS THAN BRILLIANT *Virgin VSCDT 1521*	66	2

Tracy SHAW *UK, female vocalist (1 WEEK)* pos/wks

4 Jul 98		HAPPENIN' ALL OVER AGAIN *Recognition CDREC 2*	46	1

Winifred SHAW *US, female vocalist (4 WEEKS)* pos/wks

14 Aug 76		LULLABY OF BROADWAY *United Artists UP 36131*	42	4

SHE – *See URBAN DISCHARGE featuring SHE*

SHE ROCKERS *UK, female rap duo (2 WEEKS)* pos/wks

13 Jan 90		JAM IT JAM *Jive JIVE 233*	58	2

George SHEARING QUINTET
UK, male instrumentalist – piano (15 WEEKS) pos/wks

19 Jul 62		LET THERE BE LOVE *Capitol CL 15257* [1]	11	14
4 Oct 62		BAUBLES, BANGLES AND BEADS *Capitol CL 15269*	49	1

[1] Nat 'King' Cole with George Shearing

Gary SHEARSTON *Australia, male vocalist (8 WEEKS)* pos/wks

5 Oct 74	●	I GET A KICK OUT OF YOU *Charisma CB 234*	7	8

SHED SEVEN *UK, male vocal / instrumental group (48 WEEKS)* pos/wks

25 Jun 94		DOLPHIN *Polydor YORCD 2*	28	4
27 Aug 94		SPEAKEASY *Polydor YORCD 3*	24	3
12 Nov 94		OCEAN PIE *Polydor YORCD 4*	33	2
13 May 95		WHERE HAVE YOU BEEN TONIGHT *Polydor YORCD 5*	23	2
27 Jan 96		GETTING BETTER *Polydor 5778912*	14	3
23 Mar 96	●	GOING FOR GOLD *Polydor 5762152*	8	5
18 May 96		BULLY BOY *Polydor 5765972*	22	3
31 Aug 96		ON STANDBY *Polydor 5752732*	12	4
23 Nov 96		CHASING RAINBOWS *Polydor 5759292*	17	5
14 Mar 98		SHE LEFT ME ON FRIDAY *Polydor 5695412*	11	4

Date		Title / Label	pos	wks
23 May 98		THE HEROES *Polydor 5699172*	18	3
22 Aug 98		DEVIL IN YOUR SHOES (WALKING ALL OVER) *Polydor 5672072*	37	2
5 Jun 99		DISCO DOWN *Polydor 5638752*	13	6
5 May 01		CRY FOR HELP *Artful CD 35ARTFUL*	30	2

SHEEP ON DRUGS *UK, male vocal / instrumental duo (5 WEEKS)* pos/wks

Date		Title / Label	pos	wks
27 Mar 93		15 MINUTES OF FAME *Transglobal CID 564*	44	2
30 Oct 93		FROM A TO H AND BACK AGAIN *Transglobal CID 575*	40	2
14 May 94		LET THE GOOD TIMES ROLL *Transglobal CID 576*	56	1

SHEER BRONZE featuring Lisa MILLETT
UK, male / female vocal / instrumental duo (1 WEEK) pos/wks

Date		Title / Label	pos	wks
3 Sep 94		WALKIN' ON *Go.Beat GODCD 115*	63	1

SHEER ELEGANCE *UK, male vocal group (23 WEEKS)* pos/wks

Date		Title / Label	pos	wks
20 Dec 75		MILKY WAY *Pye International 7N 25697*	18	10
3 Apr 76	●	LIFE IS TOO SHORT GIRL *Pye International 7N 25703*	9	9
24 Jul 76		IT'S TEMPTATION *Pye International 7N 25715*	41	4

Sheila B. DEVOTION
France, female vocalist – Anny Chancel – and male vocal trio (33 WEEKS) pos/wks

Date		Title / Label	pos	wks
11 Mar 78		SINGIN' IN THE RAIN PART 1 *Carrere EMI 2751*	11	13
22 Jul 78		YOU LIGHT MY FIRE *Carrere EMI 2828*	44	6
24 Nov 79		SPACER *Carrere CAR 128* [1]	18	14

[1] Sheila & B. Devotion

The label of some pressings of 'Spacer' simply credit Sheila B. Devotion

Shade SHEIST featuring Nate DOGG and KURUPT
US, male rappers – leader Tremayne Thompson (7 WEEKS) pos/wks

Date		Title / Label	pos	wks
25 Aug 01		WHERE I WANNA BE *London LONCD 461*	14	6
13 Oct 01		WHERE I WANNA BE (re-entry) *London LONCD 461*	58	1

Doug SHELDON *UK, male vocalist (15 WEEKS)* pos/wks

Date		Title / Label	pos	wks
9 Nov 61		RUNAROUND SUE *Decca F 11398*	36	3
4 Jan 62		YOUR MA SAID YOU CRIED IN YOUR SLEEP LAST NIGHT *Decca F 11416*	29	6
7 Feb 63		I SAW LINDA YESTERDAY *Decca F 11564*	36	6

Michelle SHELLERS – *See SOUL PROVIDERS featuring Michelle SHELLERS*

Pete SHELLEY *UK, male vocalist (1 WEEK)* pos/wks

Date		Title / Label	pos	wks
12 Mar 83		TELEPHONE OPERATOR *Genetic XX1*	66	1

See also BUZZCOCKS

Peter SHELLEY *UK, male vocalist (20 WEEKS)* pos/wks

Date		Title / Label	pos	wks
14 Sep 74	●	GEE BABY *Magnet MAG 12*	4	10
22 Mar 75	●	LOVE ME LOVE MY DOG *Magnet MAG 22*	3	10

Anne SHELTON *UK, female vocalist – Patricia Sibley (31 WEEKS)* pos/wks

Date		Title / Label	pos	wks
16 Dec 55		ARRIVEDERCI DARLING *HMV POP 146*	17	4
13 Apr 56		SEVEN DAYS *Philips PB 567*	20	4
24 Aug 56	★	LAY DOWN YOUR ARMS *Philips PB 616*	1	14
20 Nov 59		THE VILLAGE OF ST BERNADETTE *Philips PB 969*	27	1
26 Jan 61	●	SAILOR *Philips PB 1096*	10	8

SHENA *UK, female vocalist (3 WEEKS)* pos/wks

Date		Title / Label	pos	wks
2 Aug 97		LET THE BEAT HIT 'EM *VC VCRD 24*	28	2
1 Sep 01		I'LL BE WAITING *Rulin RULIN 17CDS* [1]	44	1

[1] Full Intention presents Shena

Vikki SHEPARD – *See SLEAZESISTERS*

Vonda SHEPARD *US, female vocalist (9 WEEKS)* pos/wks

Date		Title / Label	pos	wks
5 Dec 98	●	SEARCHIN' MY SOUL *Epic 6666332*	10	9

SHEPHERD SISTERS *US, female vocal group (6 WEEKS)* pos/wks

Date		Title / Label	pos	wks
15 Nov 57		ALONE (WHY MUST I BE) *HMV POP 411*	14	5
3 Jan 58		ALONE (WHY MUST I BE) (re-entry) *HMV POP 411*	22	1

SHERBET *Australia, male vocal / instrumental group (10 WEEKS)* pos/wks

Date		Title / Label	pos	wks
25 Sep 76	●	HOWZAT *Epic EPC 4574*	4	10

Tony SHERIDAN and the BEATLES
UK, male vocalist / instrumental group (1 WEEK) pos/wks

Date		Title / Label	pos	wks
6 Jun 63		MY BONNIE *Polydor NH 668833*	48	1

Allan SHERMAN *US, male vocalist – Allan Copelon (10 WEEKS)* pos/wks

Date		Title / Label	pos	wks
12 Sep 63		HELLO MUDDAH! HELLO FADDAH! *Warner Bros. WB 106*	14	10

Bobby SHERMAN *US, male vocalist (4 WEEKS)* pos/wks

Date		Title / Label	pos	wks
31 Oct 70		JULIE DO YA LOVE ME *CBS 5144*	28	4

SHERRICK *US, male vocalist (10 WEEKS)* pos/wks

Date		Title / Label	pos	wks
1 Aug 87		JUST CALL *Warner Bros. W 8380*	23	8
21 Nov 87		LET'S BE LOVERS TONIGHT *Warner Bros. W 8146*	63	2

Pluto SHERVINGTON *Jamaica, male vocalist (20 WEEKS)* pos/wks

Date		Title / Label	pos	wks
7 Feb 76	●	DAT *Opal Pal 5*	6	8
10 Apr 76		RAM GOAT LIVER *Trojan TR 7978*	43	4
6 Mar 82		YOUR HONOUR *KR KR 4* [1]	19	8

[1] Pluto

Holly SHERWOOD *US, female vocalist (7 WEEKS)* pos/wks

Date		Title / Label	pos	wks
5 Feb 72		DAY BY DAY *Bell 1182*	29	7

Tony SHEVETON *UK, male vocalist (1 WEEK)* pos/wks

Date		Title / Label	pos	wks
13 Feb 64		A MILLION DRUMS *Oriole CB 1895*	49	1

SHIMMON & WOOLFSON *UK, male DJ / production duo (1 WEEK)* pos/wks

Date		Title / Label	pos	wks
10 Jan 98		WELCOME TO THE FUTURE *React CDREACT 119*	69	1

SHIMON & Andy C *UK, male production duo (2 WEEKS)* pos/wks

Date		Title / Label	pos	wks
15 Sep 01		BODY ROCK *Ram RAMM 34CD*	58	2

SHINEHEAD *Jamaica, male vocalist (6 WEEKS)* pos/wks

Date		Title / Label	pos	wks
3 Apr 93		JAMAICAN IN NEW YORK *Elektra EKR 161CD*	30	5
26 Jun 93		LET 'EM IN *Elektra EKR 168CD*	70	1

SHIRELLES *US, female vocal group (29 WEEKS)* pos/wks

Date		Title / Label	pos	wks
9 Feb 61	●	WILL YOU LOVE ME TOMORROW *Top Rank JAR 540* ▲	4	15
31 May 62		SOLDIER BOY *HMV POP 1019* ▲	23	9
23 May 63		FOOLISH LITTLE GIRL *Stateside SS 181*	38	5

SHIRLEY and COMPANY *US, female vocalist and male vocal / instrumental backing group (9 WEEKS)* pos/wks

Date		Title / Label	pos	wks
8 Feb 75	●	SHAME SHAME SHAME *All Platinum 6146 301*	6	9

SHIVA *UK, male / female vocal / instrumental group (5 WEEKS)* pos/wks

Date		Title / Label	pos	wks
13 May 95		WORK IT OUT *ffrr FCD 261*	36	2
19 Aug 95		FREEDOM *ffrr FCD 263*	18	3

SHIVAREE *US, female /male vocal / instrumental group (1 WEEK)* pos/wks

Date		Title / Label	pos	wks
17 Feb 01		GOODNIGHT MOON *Capitol CDCL 825*	63	1

SHO NUFF *US, male vocal / instrumental group (4 WEEKS)* pos/wks

Date		Title / Label	pos	wks
24 May 80		IT'S ALRIGHT *Ensign ENY 37*	53	4

Michelle SHOCKED *US, female vocalist (10 WEEKS)* pos/wks

8 Oct 88	**ANCHORAGE** *Cooking Vinyl LON 193*	60	4
14 Jan 89	**IF LOVE WAS A TRAIN** *Cooking Vinyl LON 212*	63	3
11 Mar 89	**WHEN I GROW UP** *Cooking Vinyl LON 219*	67	3

SHOCKING BLUE
Holland, male / female vocal / instrumental group (14 WEEKS) pos/wks

17 Jan 70 ●	**VENUS** *Penny Farthing PEN 702* ▲	8	11
25 Apr 70	**MIGHTY JOE** *Penny Farthing PEN 713*	43	3

Troy SHONDELL *US, male vocalist (11 WEEKS)* pos/wks

2 Nov 61	**THIS TIME** *London HLG 9432*	22	11

SHONDELLS – *See Tommy JAMES and the SHONDELLS*

SHOOTING PARTY *UK, male vocal duo (2 WEEKS)* pos/wks

31 Mar 90	**LET'S HANG ON** *Lisson DOLE 15*	66	2

SHORTIE vs BLACK LEGEND
Italy, male production duo and male vocalist (2 WEEKS) pos/wks

4 Aug 01	**SOMEBODY** *WEA WEA 328 CD*	37	2

SHOWADDYWADDY (81 Top 500) *Rock 'n' roll revival octet from Leicester, UK, which included vocalists Dave Bartram and Buddy Gask. At the peak of their career, they had seven successive Top 5 entries with rousing revivals of old US rock 'n' roll songs (209 WEEKS)* pos/wks

18 May 74 ●	**HEY ROCK AND ROLL** *Bell 1357*	2	14
17 Aug 74	**ROCK 'N' ROLL LADY** *Bell 1374*	15	9
30 Nov 74	**HEY MR CHRISTMAS** *Bell 1387*	13	8
22 Feb 75	**SWEET MUSIC** *Bell 1403*	14	9
17 May 75 ●	**THREE STEPS TO HEAVEN** *Bell 1426*	2	11
6 Sep 75 ●	**HEARTBEAT** *Bell 1450*	7	7
15 Nov 75	**HEAVENLY** *Bell 1460*	34	6
29 May 76	**TROCADERO** *Bell 1476*	32	3
6 Nov 76 ★	**UNDER THE MOON OF LOVE** *Bell 1495*	1	15
5 Mar 77 ●	**WHEN** *Arista 91*	3	11
23 Jul 77 ●	**YOU GOT WHAT IT TAKES** *Arista 126*	2	10
5 Nov 77 ●	**DANCIN' PARTY** *Arista 149*	4	11
25 Mar 78 ●	**I WONDER WHY** *Arista 174*	2	11
24 Jun 78 ●	**A LITTLE BIT OF SOAP** *Arista 191*	5	12
4 Nov 78 ●	**PRETTY LITTLE ANGEL EYES** *Arista ARIST 222*	5	12
31 Mar 79	**REMEMBER THEN** *Arista 247*	17	8
28 Jul 79	**SWEET LITTLE ROCK 'N' ROLLER** *Arista 278*	15	9
10 Nov 79	**A NIGHT AT DADDY GEE'S** *Arista 314*	39	5
27 Sep 80	**WHY DO LOVERS BREAK EACH OTHER'S HEARTS** *Arista ARIST 359*	22	10
29 Nov 80	**BLUE MOON** *Arista ARIST 379*	32	9
13 Jun 81	**MULTIPLICATION** *Arista ARIST 416*	39	4
28 Nov 81	**FOOTSTEPS** *Bell BELL 1499*	31	9
28 Aug 82	**WHO PUT THE BOMP (IN THE BOMP-A-BOMP-A-BOMP)** *RCA 236*	37	6

SHOWDOWN – *See Garry LEE and SHOWDOWN*

SHOWDOWN *US, male vocal / instrumental group (3 WEEKS)* pos/wks

17 Dec 77	**KEEP DOIN' IT** *State STAT 63*	41	3

SHOWSTOPPERS *US, male vocal group (25 WEEKS)* pos/wks

13 Mar 68	**AIN'T NOTHING BUT A HOUSEPARTY** *Beacon 3-100*	11	15
13 Nov 68	**EENY MEENY** *MGM 1436*	33	7
30 Jan 71	**AIN'T NOTHING BUT A HOUSEPARTY (re-issue)** *Beacon BEA 100*	43	1
13 Feb 71	**AIN'T NOTHING BUT A HOUSEPARTY (re-entry of re-issue)** *Beacon BEA 100*	33	1
27 Feb 71	**AIN'T NOTHING BUT A HOUSEPARTY (2nd re-entry of re-issue)** *Beacon BEA 100*	36	1

SHRIEKBACK *UK, male vocal / instrumental group (4 WEEKS)* pos/wks

28 Jul 84	**HAND ON MY HEART** *Arista SHRK 1*	52	4

SHRINK *Holland, male DJ / production trio (4 WEEKS)* pos/wks

10 Oct 98	**NERVOUS BREAKDOWN** *VC Recordings VCRD42*	42	2
19 Aug 00	**ARE YOU READY TO PARTY** *Nulife 74321783772*	39	2

SHUT UP AND DANCE *UK, male vocal / production group (14 WEEKS)* pos/wks

21 Apr 90	**£20 TO GET IN** *Shut Up and Dance SUAD 3*	56	3
28 Jul 90	**LAMBORGHINI** *Shut Up and Dance SUAD 4*	55	2
8 Feb 92	**AUTOBIOGRAPHY OF A CRACKHEAD / THE GREEN MAN** *Shut Up and Dance SUAD 21*	43	2
30 May 92 ●	**RAVING I'M RAVING** *Shut Up and Dance SUAD 30S* [1]	2	2
15 Aug 92	**THE ART OF MOVING BUTTS** *Shut Up and Dance SUAD 34S* [2]	69	1
1 Apr 95	**SAVE IT 'TIL THE MOURNING AFTER** *Pulse 8 PULS 84CD*	25	3
8 Jul 95	**I LOVE U** *Pulse 8 PULS 90CD* [3]	68	1

[1] Shut Up and Dance featuring Peter Bouncer [2] Shut Up and Dance featuring Erin
[3] Shut Up and Dance featuring Richie Davis and Professor T

SHY *UK, male vocal / instrumental group (3 WEEKS)* pos/wks

19 Apr 80	**GIRL (IT'S ALL I HAVE)** *Gallery GA 1*	60	3

SHY FX
UK, male instrumentalist / producer – Andre Williams (4 WEEKS) pos/wks

1 Oct 94	**ORIGINAL NUTTAH** *Sound of Underground SOUR 008CD* [1]	39	3
20 Mar 99	**BAMBAATA 2012** *Ebony EBR 020CD*	60	1

[1] UK Apachi with Shy FX

SHYHEIM *US, male rapper (1 WEEK)* pos/wks

8 Jun 96	**THIS IZ REAL** *Noo Trybe VUSCD 105*	61	1

SIA *Australia, female vocalist – Sia Furler (8 WEEKS)* pos/wks

3 Jun 00 ●	**TAKEN FOR GRANTED** *Long Lost Brother S 002CD1*	10	5
18 Aug 01	**DESTINY** *Ultimate Dilemma UDRCDS 043* [1]	30	3

[1] Zero 7 featuring Sia and Sophie

Labi SIFFRE *UK, male vocalist (44 WEEKS)* pos/wks

27 Nov 71	**IT MUST BE LOVE** *Pye International 7N 25572*	14	12
25 Mar 72	**CRYING LAUGHING LOVING LYING** *Pye International 7N 25576*	11	9
29 Jul 72	**WATCH ME** *Pye International 7N 25586*	29	6
4 Apr 87 ●	**(SOMETHING INSIDE) SO STRONG** *China WOK 12*	4	13
21 Nov 87	**NOTHIN'S GONNA CHANGE** *China WOK 16*	52	4

SIGNUM *Holland, male production duo (2 WEEKS)* pos/wks

28 Nov 98	**WHAT YA GOT 4 ME** *Tidy Trax TIDY 118CD*	70	1
31 Jul 99	**COMING ON STRONG** *Tidy Trax TIDY 128T* [1]	66	1

[1] Signum featuring Scott Mac

SIGUE SIGUE SPUTNIK
UK, male vocal / instrumental group (20 WEEKS) pos/wks

1 Mar 86 ●	**LOVE MISSILE F1-11** *Parlophone SSS 1*	3	9
7 Jun 86	**21st CENTURY BOY** *Parlophone SSS 2*	20	5
19 Nov 88	**SUCCESS** *Parlophone SSS 3*	31	3
1 Apr 89	**DANCERAMA** *Parlophone SSS 5*	50	2
20 May 89	**ALBINONI VS STAR WARS** *Parlophone SSS 4*	75	1

SIL *Holland, male DJ / production duo (1 WEEK)* pos/wks

11 Apr 98	**WINDOWS '98** *Hooj Choons HOOJCD 60*	58	1

SILENCERS *UK, male vocal / instrumental group (7 WEEKS)* pos/wks

25 Jun 88	**PAINTED MOON** *RCA HUSH 1*	57	4
27 May 89	**SCOTTISH RAIN** *RCA PB 42701*	71	2
15 May 93	**I CAN FEEL IT** *RCA 74321147112*	62	1

SILENT UNDERDOG
UK, male instrumentalist – Paul Hardcastle (1 WEEK) pos/wks

		pos	wks
16 Feb 85	**PAPA'S GOT A BRAND NEW PIGBAG** *Kaz KAZ 50*	73	1

SILICONE SOUL featuring Louise Clare MARSHALL
UK, male production duo and UK, female vocalist (5 WEEKS) pos/wks

		pos	wks
6 Oct 01	**RIGHT ON!** *VC Recordings / Soma VCRD 96*	15	4
24 Nov 01	**RIGHT ON! (re-entry)** *VC Recordings / Soma VCRD 96*	68	1

SILJE *Norway, female vocalist (6 WEEKS)* pos/wks

		pos	wks
15 Dec 90	**TELL ME WHERE YOU'RE GOING** *EMI EM 159*	55	6

SILK *US, male vocal group (10 WEEKS)* pos/wks

		pos	wks
24 Apr 93	**FREAK ME** *Elektra EKR 165CD* ▲	46	5
5 Jun 93	**GIRL U FOR ME** *Elektra EKR 167CD*	67	2
9 Oct 93	**BABY IT'S YOU** *Elektra EKR 173CD*	44	2
26 Feb 94	**FREAK ME (re-entry)** *Elektra EKR 165CD*	72	1

SILKIE *UK, male / female vocal / instrumental group (6 WEEKS)* pos/wks

		pos	wks
23 Sep 65	**YOU'VE GOT TO HIDE YOUR LOVE AWAY** *Fontana TF 603*	28	6

SILKK THE SHOCKER – See Montell JORDAN

SILSOE *UK, male instrumentalist – Rod Argent (4 WEEKS)* pos/wks

		pos	wks
21 Jun 86	**AZTEC GOLD** *CBS A 7231*	48	4

'Aztec Gold' was the ITV theme to the 1986 World Cup

See also SAN JOSE featuring Rodriguez ARGENTINA; ARGENT

Luci SILVAS *UK, female vocalist (1 WEEK)* pos/wks

		pos	wks
17 Jun 00	**IT'S TOO LATE** *EMI CDEM 565*	62	1

SILVER BULLET *UK, male rapper – Richard Brown (20 WEEKS)* pos/wks

		pos	wks
2 Sep 89	**BRING FORTH THE GUILLOTINE** *Tam Tam TTT 013*	70	1
9 Dec 89	**20 SECONDS TO COMPLY** *Tam Tam 7TTT 019*	11	10
3 Mar 90	**BRING FORTH THE GUILLOTINE (re-entry)** *Tam Tam TTT 013*	45	5
13 Apr 91	**UNDERCOVER ANARCHIST** *Parlophone R 6284*	33	4

SILVER BULLET BAND – See Bob SEGER and the SILVER BULLET BAND

SILVER CITY *UK, male / female vocal / instrumental duo (1 WEEK)* pos/wks

		pos	wks
30 Oct 93	**LOVE INFINITY** *Silver City GFJMCD 1*	62	1

SILVER CONVENTION
Germany / US, female vocal group (35 WEEKS) pos/wks

		pos	wks
5 Apr 75	**SAVE ME** *Magnet MAG 26*	30	7
15 Nov 75	**FLY ROBIN FLY** *Magnet MAG 43* ▲	28	8
3 Apr 76 ●	**GET UP AND BOOGIE** *Magnet MAG 55*	7	11
19 Jun 76	**TIGER BABY / NO NO JOE** *Magnet MAG 69*	41	4
29 Jan 77	**EVERYBODY'S TALKIN' 'BOUT LOVE** *Magnet MAG 81*	25	5

SILVER SUN *UK, male vocal / instrumental group (13 WEEKS)* pos/wks

		pos	wks
2 Nov 96	**LAVA** *Polydor 5756872*	54	1
22 Feb 97	**LAST DAY** *Polydor 5732432*	48	1
3 May 97	**GOLDEN SKIN** *Polydor 5738272*	32	2
5 Jul 97	**JULIA** *Polydor 5711752*	51	1
18 Oct 97	**LAVA (re-issue)** *Polydor 5714242*	35	2
20 Jun 98	**TOO MUCH, TOO LITTLE, TOO LATE** *Polydor 5699152*	20	4
26 Sep 98	**I'LL SEE YOU AROUND** *Polydor 5674532*	26	2

SILVERCHAIR *Australia, male vocal / instrumental group (8 WEEKS)* pos/wks

		pos	wks
29 Jul 95	**PURE MASSACRE** *Murmur 6622642*	71	1
9 Sep 95	**TOMORROW** *Murmur 6623952*	59	2
5 Apr 97	**FREAK** *Murmur 6640765*	34	2
19 Jul 97	**ABUSE ME** *Murmur 6647907*	40	2
15 May 99	**ANA'S SONG** *Columbia 6673452*	45	1

Dooley SILVERSPOON *US, male vocalist (3 WEEKS)* pos/wks

		pos	wks
31 Jan 76	**LET ME BE THE NUMBER 1 (LOVE OF YOUR LIFE)** *Seville SEV 1020*	44	3

Harry SIMEONE CHORALE *US, choir (14 WEEKS)* pos/wks

		pos	wks
13 Feb 59	**LITTLE DRUMMER BOY** *Top Rank JAR 101*	13	7
22 Dec 60	**ONWARD CHRISTIAN SOLDIERS** *Ember EMBS 118*	35	1
5 Jan 61	**ONWARD CHRISTIAN SOLDIERS (re-entry)** *Ember EMBS 118*	38	1
21 Dec 61	**ONWARD CHRISTIAN SOLDIERS (2nd re-entry)** *Ember EMBS 118*	36	3
20 Dec 62	**ONWARD CHRISTIAN SOLDIERS (re-issue)** *Ember EMBS 144*	38	2

Gene SIMMONS *US, male vocalist (4 WEEKS)* pos/wks

		pos	wks
27 Jan 79	**RADIOACTIVE** *Casablanca CAN 134*	41	4

See also KISS

SIMON *UK, male producer – Simon Pearson (2 WEEKS)* pos/wks

		pos	wks
31 Mar 01	**FREE AT LAST** *Positiva CDTIV 152*	36	2

Carly SIMON (433 Top 500) *First charted in US in 1964 as half of folk duo Simon Sisters with sister Lucy, b. 25 Jun 1945, New York. Winner of 1971's Best New Artist Grammy was married to fellow singer / songwriter James Taylor (1972-1983). Elected to Songwriters Hall of Fame 1994 (78 WEEKS)* pos/wks

		pos	wks
16 Dec 72 ●	**YOU'RE SO VAIN** *Elektra K 12077* ▲	3	15
31 Mar 73	**THE RIGHT THING TO DO** *Elektra K 12095*	17	9
16 Mar 74	**MOCKINGBIRD** *Elektra K 12134* [1]	34	5
6 Aug 77 ●	**NOBODY DOES IT BETTER** *Elektra K 12261*	7	12
21 Aug 82 ●	**WHY** *WEA K 79300*	10	13
24 Jan 87 ●	**COMING AROUND AGAIN** *Arista ARIST 687*	10	12
10 Jun 89	**WHY (re-issue)** *WEA U 7501*	56	5
20 Apr 91	**YOU'RE SO VAIN (re-issue)** *Elektra EKR 123*	41	5
22 Dec 01	**SON OF A GUN (I BETCHA THINK THIS SONG IS ABOUT YOU)** *VIRGIN VUSCD 232* [2]	13	2+

[1] Carly Simon and James Taylor [2] Janet with Carly Simon featuring Missy Elliott

See also Will POWERS

Joe SIMON *US, male vocalist (10 WEEKS)* pos/wks

		pos	wks
16 Jun 73	**STEP BY STEP** *Mojo 2093 030*	14	10

Paul SIMON (384 Top 500) *Acclaimed award-winning singer / songwriter b. 13 Oct 1941, New Jersey, US. Recorded under various names in early 1960s before forming top duo Simon and Garfunkel. Married to actress Carrie Fisher (1983-85) and later Edie Brickell. He also helped to popularise world music (85 WEEKS)* pos/wks

		pos	wks
19 Feb 72 ●	**MOTHER AND CHILD REUNION** *CBS 7793*	5	12
29 Apr 72	**ME AND JULIO DOWN BY THE SCHOOLYARD** *CBS 7964*	15	9
16 Jun 73 ●	**TAKE ME TO THE MARDI GRAS** *CBS 1578*	7	11
22 Sep 73	**LOVES ME LIKE A ROCK** *CBS 1700*	39	5
10 Jan 76	**50 WAYS TO LEAVE YOUR LOVER** *CBS 3887* ▲	23	6
3 Dec 77	**SLIP SLIDIN' AWAY** *CBS 5770*	36	5
6 Sep 80	**LATE IN THE EVENING** *Warner Bros. K 17666*	58	4
13 Sep 86 ●	**YOU CAN CALL ME AL** *Warner Bros. W 8667*	4	13
13 Dec 86	**THE BOY IN THE BUBBLE** *Warner Bros. W 8509*	26	8
6 Oct 90	**THE OBVIOUS CHILD** *Warner Bros. W 9549*	15	10
9 Dec 95	**SOMETHING SO RIGHT** *RCA 74321332392* [1]	44	2

[1] Annie Lennox featuring Paul Simon

See also SIMON and GARFUNKEL

Ronni SIMON *UK, male vocalist (2 WEEKS)* pos/wks

		pos	wks
13 Aug 94	**B GOOD 2 ME** *Network NWKCD 80*	73	1
10 Jun 95	**TAKE YOU THERE** *Network NWKCD 85*	58	1

Tito SIMON *Jamaica, male vocalist (4 WEEKS)* pos/wks

		pos	wks
8 Feb 75	**THIS MONDAY MORNING FEELING** *Horse HOSS 57*	45	4

SIMON and GARFUNKEL (369 Top 500) *Ultra-successful, folk-rooted duo, Paul Simon and Art Garfunkel, who first charted in US as Tom and Jerry in 1957. Their 'Bridge Over Troubled Water' single and album (Top UK LP of both 1970 and 1971!) is regarded as among the all-time greatest recordings. In 1968 they had three of US Top 5 albums (87 WEEKS)*

Date	Title	pos	wks
24 Mar 66	● HOMEWARD BOUND *CBS 202045*	9	12
16 Jun 66	I AM A ROCK *CBS 202303*	17	10
10 Jul 68	● MRS. ROBINSON *CBS 3443* ▲	4	12
8 Jan 69	● MRS. ROBINSON (EP) *CBS EP 6400*	9	5
30 Apr 69	● THE BOXER *CBS 4162*	6	14
21 Feb 70	★ BRIDGE OVER TROUBLED WATER *CBS 4790* ▲	1	19
15 Aug 70	BRIDGE OVER TROUBLED WATER (re-entry) *CBS 4790*	45	1
7 Oct 72	AMERICA *CBS 8336*	25	7
7 Dec 91	A HAZY SHADE OF WINTER / SILENT NIGHT - SEVEN O'CLOCK NEWS *Columbia 6576537*	30	6
15 Feb 92	THE BOXER (re-issue) *Columbia 6578067*	75	1

Tracks on Mrs Robinson (EP): Mrs Robinson / Scarborough Fair - Canticle / Sounds of Silence / April Come She Will. This EP would have stayed more than five weeks on chart had a decision to exclude EPs from chart in Feb 1969 not been taken

See also Paul SIMON; Art GARFUNKEL

SIMONE *US, female vocalist (1 WEEK)*

Date	Title	pos	wks
23 Nov 91	MY FAMILY DEPENDS ON ME *Strictly Rhythm A 8678*	75	1

Nina SIMONE *US, female vocalist – Eunice Waymon (46 WEEKS)*

Date	Title	pos	wks
5 Aug 65	I PUT A SPELL ON YOU *Philips BF 1415*	49	1
16 Oct 68	● AIN'T GOT NO - I GOT LIFE / DO WHAT YOU GOTTA DO *RCA 1743*	2	18
15 Jan 69	I PUT A SPELL ON YOU (re-issue) *Philips BF 1736*	28	4
15 Jan 69	● TO LOVE SOMEBODY *RCA 1779*	5	9
31 Oct 87	● MY BABY JUST CARES FOR ME *Charly CYZ 7112*	5	11
9 Jul 94	FEELING GOOD *Mercury MERCD 403*	40	3

'Do What You Gotta Do' was listed only for the first eight weeks of the record's chart run. It peaked at No.7

Victor SIMONELLI presents SOLUTION
US, male producer (1 WEEK)

Date	Title	pos	wks
2 Nov 96	FEELS SO RIGHT *Soundproof MCSTD 40068*	63	1

SIMPLE MINDS (102 Top 500) *Most successful Scottish band of the 1980s, fronted by Jim Kerr (b. 9 Jul 1959, Glasgow), who married Chrissie Hynde, lead singer of Pretenders. Five of the quintet's albums entered UK chart at No.1, and world sales topped 30 million (187 WEEKS)*

Date	Title	pos	wks
12 May 79	LIFE IN A DAY *Zoom ZUM 10*	62	2
23 May 81	THE AMERICAN *Virgin VS 410*	59	3
15 Aug 81	LOVE SONG *Virgin VS 434*	47	4
7 Nov 81	SWEAT IN BULLET *Virgin VS 451*	52	3
10 Apr 82	PROMISED YOU A MIRACLE *Virgin VS 488*	13	11
28 Aug 82	GLITTERING PRIZE *Virgin VS 511*	16	11
13 Nov 82	SOMEONE SOMEWHERE (IN SUMMERTIME) *Virgin VS 538*	36	5
26 Nov 83	WATERFRONT *Virgin VS 636*	13	10
28 Jan 84	SPEED YOUR LOVE TO ME *Virgin VS 649*	20	4
24 Mar 84	UP ON THE CATWALK *Virgin VS 661*	27	5
20 Apr 85	● DON'T YOU (FORGET ABOUT ME) *Virgin VS 749* ▲	7	11
17 Aug 85	DON'T YOU (FORGET ABOUT ME) (re-entry) *Virgin VS 749*	61	8
12 Oct 85	● ALIVE AND KICKING *Virgin VS 817*	7	9
28 Dec 85	DON'T YOU (FORGET ABOUT ME) (2nd re-entry) *Virgin VS 749*	74	1
4 Jan 86	ALIVE AND KICKING (re-entry) *Virgin VS 817*	60	2
1 Feb 86	● SANCTIFY YOURSELF *Virgin SM 1*	10	7
15 Feb 86	DON'T YOU (FORGET ABOUT ME) (3rd re-entry) *Virgin VS 749*	62	3
15 Mar 86	DON'T YOU (FORGET ABOUT ME) (4th re-entry) *Virgin VS 749*	68	1
12 Apr 86	● ALL THE THINGS SHE SAID *Virgin VS 860*	9	8
14 Jun 86	ALL THE THINGS SHE SAID (re-entry) *Virgin VS 860*	73	1
15 Nov 86	GHOSTDANCING *Virgin VS 907*	13	6
3 Jan 87	GHOSTDANCING (re-entry) *Virgin VS 907*	68	2
20 Jun 87	PROMISED YOU A MIRACLE *Virgin SM 2*	19	7
18 Feb 89	★ BELFAST CHILD *Virgin SMX 3*	1	11
22 Apr 89	THIS IS YOUR LAND *Virgin SMX4*	13	4
29 Jul 89	KICK IT IN *Virgin SM 5*	15	5
9 Dec 89	THE AMSTERDAM EP *Virgin SMX 6*	18	6
23 Mar 91	● LET THERE BE LOVE *Virgin VS 1332*	6	7
25 May 91	SEE THE LIGHTS *Virgin VS 1343*	20	4
31 Aug 91	STAND BY LOVE *Virgin VS 1358*	13	4
26 Oct 91	REAL LIFE *Virgin VS 1382*	34	3
10 Oct 92	● LOVE SONG / ALIVE AND KICKING (re-issue) *Virgin VS 1440*	6	6
28 Jan 95	● SHE'S A RIVER *Virgin VSCDX 1509*	9	5
8 Apr 95	HYPNOTISED *Virgin VSCDX 1534*	18	5
14 Mar 98	GLITTERBALL *Chrysalis CDCHSS 5078*	18	2
30 May 98	WAR BABIES *Chrysalis CDCHS 5088*	43	1

The 1987 version of 'Promised You a Miracle' was a live recording. Tracks on The Amsterdam EP: Let It All Come Down / Jerusalem / Sign of the Times

SIMPLICIOUS *US, male vocal group (9 WEEKS)*

Date	Title	pos	wks
29 Sep 84	LET HER FEEL IT *Fourth & Broadway BRW 13*	65	3
2 Feb 85	LET HER FEEL IT (re-issue) *Fourth & Broadway BRW 18*	34	6

The re-issue of 'Let Her Feel It' was listed with 'Personality' by Eugene Wilde

SIMPLY RED (73 Top 500) *The unmistakable Mick Hucknall (b. 8 Jun 1960, Manchester, UK) quickly became the representative face and voice of this internationally popular outfit. Their 'Stars' album sold more than two million in the UK and was the biggest British seller in 1991 and 1992 (214 WEEKS)*

Date	Title	pos	wks
15 Jun 85	MONEY'S TOO TIGHT (TO MENTION) *Elektra EKR 9*	13	12
21 Sep 85	COME TO MY AID *Elektra EKR 19*	66	2
16 Nov 85	HOLDING BACK THE YEARS *Elektra EKR 29* ▲	51	4
8 Mar 86	JERICHO *WEA YZ 63*	53	3
17 May 86	● HOLDING BACK THE YEARS (re-issue) *WEA YZ 70*	2	13
9 Aug 86	OPEN UP THE RED BOX *WEA YZ 75*	61	4
14 Feb 87	THE RIGHT THING *WEA YZ 103*	11	10
23 May 87	INFIDELITY *Elektra YZ 114*	31	5
28 Nov 87	EV'RY TIME WE SAY GOODBYE *Elektra YZ 161*	11	9
12 Mar 88	I WON'T FEEL BAD *Elektra YZ 172*	68	3
28 Jan 89	IT'S ONLY LOVE *Elektra YZ 349*	13	8
8 Apr 89	● IF YOU DON'T KNOW ME BY NOW *Elektra YZ 377* ▲	2	10
8 Jul 89	A NEW FLAME *WEA YZ 404*	17	8
28 Oct 89	YOU'VE GOT IT *Elektra YZ 424*	46	3
21 Sep 91	SOMETHING GOT ME STARTED *East West YZ 614*	11	8
30 Nov 91	● STARS *East West YZ 626*	8	10
8 Feb 92	● FOR YOUR BABIES *East West YZ 642*	9	8
2 May 92	THRILL ME *East West YZ 671*	33	5
25 Jul 92	YOUR MIRROR *East West YZ 689*	17	4
21 Nov 92	MONTREUX (EP) *East West YZ 716*	11	10
30 Sep 95	★ FAIRGROUND *East West EW 001CD1* ■	1	14
16 Dec 95	REMEMBERING THE FIRST TIME *East West EW 015CD1*	22	6
24 Feb 96	NEVER NEVER LOVE *East West EW 029CD1*	18	4
22 Jun 96	WE'RE IN THIS TOGETHER *East West EW 046CD1*	11	6
9 Nov 96	● ANGEL *East West EW 074CD1*	4	13
20 Sep 97	NIGHT NURSE *East West EW 129CD1* [1]	13	8
16 May 98	● SAY YOU LOVE ME *East West EW 164CD*	7	7
22 Aug 98	● THE AIR THAT I BREATHE *East West EW 3821CD*	6	7
12 Dec 98	GHETTO GIRL *East West EW 191CD1*	34	2
30 Oct 99	AIN'T THAT A LOT OF LOVE *East West EW 208CD1*	14	6
19 Feb 00	YOUR EYES *East West EW 212CD1*	26	2

[1] Sly and Robbie featuring Simply Red

Tracks on Montreux (EP): Drowning In My Own Tears / Grandma's Hands / Lady Godiva's Room / Love for Sale

SIMPLY RED AND WHITE
UK, male Sunderland FC supporters vocal group (4 WEEKS)

Date	Title	pos	wks
6 Apr 96	DAYDREAM BELIEVER (CHEER UP PETER REID) *Ropery SHAYISGOD 1D*	41	3
4 May 96	DAYDREAM BELIEVER (CHEER UP PETER REID) (re-entry) *Ropery SHAYISGOD 1D*	74	1

SIMPLY SMOOTH *US, male / female vocal group (1 WEEK)*

Date	Title	pos	wks
17 Oct 98	LADY (YOU BRING ME UP) *Big Bang CDBANG 07*	70	1

Jessica SIMPSON *US, female vocalist (24 WEEKS)*

Date	Title	pos	wks
22 Apr 00	● I WANNA LOVE YOU FOREVER *Columbia 6691272*	7	9

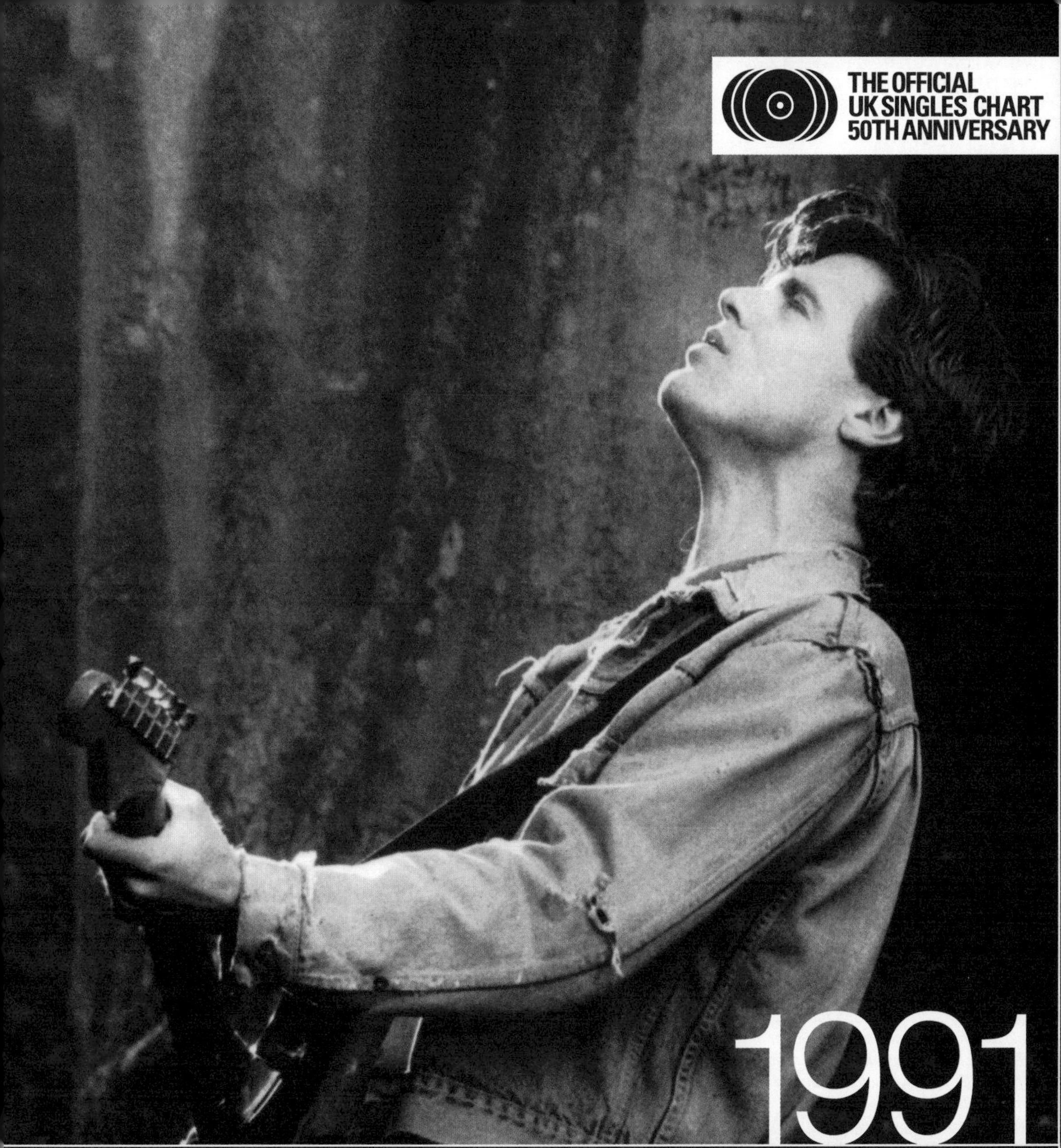

1991

IN THE YEAR IN WHICH JOHN MCCARTHY WAS FREED AFTER BEING HELD HOSTAGE BY ISLAMIC JIHAD TERRORISTS IN LEBANON, FREDDIE MERCURY DIED AND ANTHONY HOPKINS SPOOKED THE AUDIENCE IN 'SILENCE OF THE LAMBS', **BRYAN ADAMS** RECOUNTS HOW THE UK'S LONGEST-RUNNING NO.1 HIT STARTED LIFE AS A FOLK ARRANGEMENT ...

“This wasn't a brilliant plan. When we wrote the song it was just another record to me, and the fact that it was so successful was an incredible surprise to all of us. I can't believe it had been at No.1 for longer than my boyhood heroes, The Beatles, or The Rolling Stones. We had a great deal of trouble convincing the film company that our arrangement was going to work. They wanted to have period instruments used on the score so that it would blend in with the film, but I just couldn't imagine having lutes and mandolins on a rock record.”

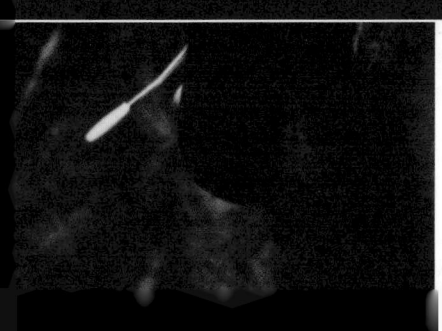

SINGLE OF THE YEAR '(Everything I Do) I Do It For You' Bryan Adams
ALBUM OF THE YEAR 'Greatest Hits' Eurythmics

8 Jul 00 I WANNA LOVE YOU FOREVER (re-entry) *Columbia 6691272* 68 2
15 Jul 00 I THINK I'M IN LOVE WITH YOU *Columbia 6695942*....................15 7
14 Jul 01 IRRESISTIBLE *Columbia 6714102*..11 6

Paul SIMPSON featuring ADEVA
US, producer / instrumentalist (8 WEEKS) pos/wks

25 Mar 89 MUSICAL FREEDOM (MOVING ON UP) *Cooltempo CDCOOL 182* 22 8

Vida SIMPSON *US, female vocalist (1 WEEK)* pos/wks

18 Feb 95 OOHHH BABY *Hi-Life HICD 6*..70 1

SIMPSONS *US, male / female cartoon group – lead vocals Bart Simpson (Nancy Cartwright) (19 WEEKS)* pos/wks

26 Jan 91 ★ DO THE BARTMAN *Geffen GEF 87*..1 12
6 Apr 91 ● DEEP DEEP TROUBLE *Geffen GEF 88* [1]....................................7 7

[1] Simpsons featuring Bart and Homer

W/Cdr AE SIMS – *See The Central Band of the ROYAL AIR FORCE*

Joyce SIMS *US, female vocalist (36 WEEKS)* pos/wks

19 Apr 86 ● ALL AND ALL *London LON 94*..16 10
13 Jun 87 LIFETIME LOVE *London LON 137*..34 6
9 Jan 88 ● COME INTO MY LIFE *London LON 161*....................................7 9
23 Apr 88 WALK AWAY *London LON 176*..24 6
17 Jun 89 LOOKING FOR A LOVE *ffrr F 109*...39 4
27 May 95 COME INTO MY LIFE (re-mix) *Club Tools 0060435 CLU*..............72 1

Kym SIMS *US, female vocalist (23 WEEKS)* pos/wks

7 Dec 91 ● TOO BLIND TO SEE IT *Atco B 8667*.......................................5 12
28 Mar 92 TAKE MY ADVICE *Atco B 8591*..13 7
27 Jun 92 A LITTLE BIT MORE *Atco B 8528*...30 3
8 Jun 96 WE GOTTA LOVE *Pulse 8 CDLOSE 104*......................................58 1

SIN WITH SEBASTIAN
Germany, male vocalist – Sebastian Roth (2 WEEKS) pos/wks

16 Sep 95 SHUT UP (AND SLEEP WITH ME) *Sing Sing 74321253592*........44 1
27 Jan 96 SHUT UP (AND SLEEP WITH ME) (re-mix) *Sing Sing 74321337972*..46 1

Frank SINATRA (11 Top 500) *Legendary entertainer regarded by many as the greatest song stylist of the 20th century, b. 12 Dec 1915, New Jersey, d. 14 May 1998. The vocalist (with Tommy Dorsey Orchestra) on first US No.1 'I'll Never Smile Again' (1940) was the first teen idol. 'Songs For Swingin' Lovers' is the only album to reach the UK Top 20 singles chart, and is one of 26 US gold albums amassed by the influential vocalist who has scored more US Top 10 LPs than any other solo artist. Sinatra, the first recipient of a Grammy Lifetime Achievement award (1965). He holds the UK chart longevity record with 'My Way' (440 WEEKS)* pos/wks

9 Jul 54 YOUNG-AT-HEART *Capitol CL 14064*......................................12 1
16 Jul 54 ★ THREE COINS IN THE FOUNTAIN *Capitol CL 14120*..................1 19
10 Jun 55 YOU MY LOVE *Capitol CL 14240*..13 3
22 Jul 55 YOU MY LOVE (re-entry) *Capitol CL 14240*..............................17 2
5 Aug 55 ● LEARNIN' THE BLUES *Capitol CL 14296*.................................2 13
12 Aug 55 YOU MY LOVE (2nd re-entry) *Capitol CL 14240*........................17 2
2 Sep 55 NOT AS A STRANGER *Capitol CL 14326*..................................18 1
13 Jan 56 ● LOVE AND MARRIAGE *Capitol CL 14503*..................................3 8
20 Jan 56 ● (LOVE IS) THE TENDER TRAP *Capitol CL 14511*.........................2 9
15 Jun 56 SONGS FOR SWINGIN' LOVERS (LP) *Capitol LCT 6106*..............12 8
22 Nov 57 ALL THE WAY *Capitol CL 14800*..29 1
29 Nov 57 CHICAGO *Capitol CL 14800*..25 1
6 Dec 57 ALL THE WAY / CHICAGO (re-entry) *Capitol CL 14800*..............21 1
13 Dec 57 ● ALL THE WAY (2nd re-entry) *Capitol CL 14800*.........................3 17
7 Feb 58 WITCHCRAFT *Capitol CL 14819*..12 8
14 Nov 58 MR. SUCCESS *Capitol CL 14956*..29 1
12 Dec 58 MR SUCCESS (re-entry) *Capitol CL 14956*..............................25 2
2 Jan 59 MR SUCCESS (2nd re-entry) *Capitol CL 14956*.........................26 1
10 Apr 59 FRENCH FOREIGN LEGION *Capitol CL 14997*............................18 5
15 May 59 COME DANCE WITH ME! (LP) *Capitol LCT 6179* [1]...................30 1
28 Aug 59 HIGH HOPES *Capitol CL 15052*..28 1
11 Sep 59 ● HIGH HOPES (re-entry) *Capitol CL 15052*..............................6 13
10 Mar 60 HIGH HOPES (2nd re-entry) *Capitol CL 15052*.........................42 1
7 Apr 60 IT'S NICE TO GO TRAV'LING *Capitol CL 15116*.........................48 2
16 Jun 60 RIVER STAY 'WAY FROM MY DOOR *Capitol CL 15135*..................18 9
8 Sep 60 NICE 'N' EASY *Capitol CL 15150*..15 12
24 Nov 60 OL' MACDONALD *Capitol CL 15168*.......................................11 8
20 Apr 61 MY BLUE HEAVEN *Capitol CL 15193*.......................................33 7
28 Sep 61 GRANADA *Reprise R 20010*..15 8
23 Nov 61 THE COFFEE SONG *Reprise R 20035*......................................39 3
5 Apr 62 EV'RYBODY'S TWISTIN' *Reprise R 20063*..............................22 12
13 Dec 62 ME AND MY SHADOW *Reprise R 20128* [2].............................20 7
7 Feb 63 ME AND MY SHADOW (re-entry) *Reprise R 20128* [2]...............47 2
7 Mar 63 MY KIND OF GIRL *Reprise R 20148* [3].................................35 6
24 Sep 64 HELLO DOLLY *Reprise R 20351* [3].......................................47 1
12 May 66 ★ STRANGERS IN THE NIGHT *Reprise R 23052* ▲..........................1 20
29 Sep 66 SUMMER WIND *Reprise RS 20509*...36 5
15 Dec 66 THAT'S LIFE *Reprise RS 20531*...44 5
23 Mar 67 ★ SOMETHIN' STUPID *Reprise RS 23166* [4] ▲............................1 18
23 Aug 67 THE WORLD WE KNEW (OVER AND OVER) *Reprise RS 20610*.....33 11
2 Apr 69 ● MY WAY *Reprise RS 20817*..5 42
4 Oct 69 ● LOVE'S BEEN GOOD TO ME *Reprise RS 20852*..........................8 18
31 Jan 70 MY WAY (re-entry) *Reprise RS 20817*..................................49 1
28 Feb 70 MY WAY (2nd re-entry) *Reprise RS 20817*............................30 5
11 Apr 70 MY WAY (3rd re-entry) *Reprise RS 20817*.............................33 9
27 Jun 70 MY WAY (4th re-entry) *Reprise RS 20817*.............................28 21
28 Nov 70 MY WAY (5th re-entry) *Reprise RS 20817*.............................18 16
6 Mar 71 I WILL DRINK THE WINE *Reprise RS 23487*............................16 12
27 Mar 71 MY WAY (6th re-entry) *Reprise RS 20817*.............................22 19
4 Sep 71 MY WAY (7th re-entry) *Reprise RS 20817*..............................39 8
1 Jan 72 MY WAY (8th re-entry) *Reprise RS 20817*..............................50 1
20 Dec 75 I BELIEVE I'M GONNA LOVE YOU *Reprise K 14400*....................34 7
9 Aug 80 THEME FROM 'NEW YORK, NEW YORK' *Reprise K 14502*........59 4
22 Feb 86 ● THEME FROM 'NEW YORK, NEW YORK' (re-entry) *Reprise K 14502*..4 10
4 Dec 93 ● I'VE GOT YOU UNDER MY SKIN *Island CID 578* [5].....................4 9
16 Apr 94 MY WAY (re-issue) *Reprise W 0163CD*.................................45 2
30 Jan 99 THEY ALL LAUGHED *Reprise W 469CD*..................................41 1

[1] Frank Sinatra with Billy May and His Orchestra [2] Frank Sinatra and Sammy Davis Jr [3] Frank Sinatra with Count Basie [4] Nancy Sinatra and Frank Sinatra [5] Frank Sinatra with Bono

Tracks on Songs for Swinging Lovers (LP): You Make Me Feel So Young / It Happened In Monterey / You're Getting to Be a Habit with Me / You Brought a New Kind of Love to Me / Too Marvellous for Words / Old Devil Moon / Pennies from Heaven / Love Is Here to Stay / I've Got You Under My Skin / I Thought About You / We'll Be Together Again / Makin' Whoopee / Swingin' Down the Lane / Anything Goes / How About You. Tracks on Come Dance With Me (LP): Come Dance With Me / Something's Gotta Give / Just in Time / Dancing in the Dark / Too Close for Comfort / I Could Have Danced All Night / Saturday Night Is the Loneliest Night of the Week / Day In Day Out / Cheek to Cheek / Baubles Bangles and Beads / The Song Is You / The Last Dance. 'All the Way' and 'Chicago', Capitol CL 14800, were at first billed separately, then together for one week, then 'All the Way' on its own. 'I've Got You Under My Skin' was the flip side of 'Stay (Faraway So Close)' by U2

Nancy SINATRA (307 Top 500) *Eldest child of legendary singer, b. 8 Jun 1940, New Jersey, US – days before father Frank's first US Top 10 entry. Was the subject of 1945 hit 'Nancy (with the Laughing Eyes'). 'Somethin' Stupid' is the only father-daughter chart topper (99 WEEKS)* pos/wks

27 Jan 66 ★ THESE BOOTS ARE MADE FOR WALKIN' *Reprise R 20432* ▲....1 14
28 Apr 66 HOW DOES THAT GRAB YOU, DARLIN'? *Reprise R 20461*..........19 8
19 Jan 67 ● SUGAR TOWN *Reprise RS 20527*..8 10
23 Mar 67 ★ SOMETHIN' STUPID *Reprise RS 23166* [1] ▲............................1 18
5 Jul 67 YOU ONLY LIVE TWICE / JACKSON *Reprise RS 20595* [2]........11 19
8 Nov 67 LADYBIRD *Reprise RS 20629* [3]..47 1
29 Nov 69 THE HIGHWAY SONG *Reprise RS 20869*................................21 10
21 Aug 71 ● DID YOU EVER *Reprise K 14093* [4]......................................2 19

[1] Nancy Sinatra and Frank Sinatra [2] Nancy Sinatra / Nancy Sinatra and Lee Hazlewood [3] Nancy Sinatra and Lee Hazlewood [4] Nancy and Lee

'Jackson' listed with 'You Only Live Twice' from 12 Jul 1967

SINCLAIR *UK, male vocalist (8 WEEKS)* pos/wks

21 Aug 93 AIN'T NO CASANOVA *Dome CDDOME 1004*...............................28 5

26 Feb 94	(I WANNA KNOW) WHY *Dome CDDOME 1009*	58	2
6 Aug 94	DON'T LIE *Dome CDDOME 1010*	70	1

Bob SINCLAR *France, male DJ / producer (7 WEEKS)* pos/wks

20 Mar 99	MY ONLY LOVE *East West EW 196CD* [1]	56	1
19 Aug 00 ●	I FEEL FOR YOU *Defected DEFECT 18CDS*	9	5
7 Apr 01	DARLIN' *Defected DFECT 30CDS* [2]	46	1

[1] Bob Sinclar featuring Lee A Genesis [2] Bob Sinclar featuring James Williams

SINDY *UK, female doll vocalist (1 WEEK)* pos/wks

5 Oct 96	SATURDAY NIGHT *Love This LUVTHISCD 13*	70	1

SINE *US, male / female vocal / instrumental group (9 WEEKS)* pos/wks

10 Jun 78	JUST LET ME DO MY THING *CBS 6351*	33	9

SINFONIA OF LONDON – *See Peter AUTY and the SINFONIA OF LONDON conducted by Howard BLAKE*

SINGING CORNER meets DONOVAN *UK, male vocalists (1 WEEK)* pos/wks

1 Dec 90	JENNIFER JUNIPER *Fontana SYP 1*	68	1

SINGING DOGS *Denmark, canine vocal group (4 WEEKS)* pos/wks

25 Nov 55	THE SINGING DOGS (MEDLEY) *Nixa N 15009* [1]	13	4

[1] Don Carlos presents The Singing Dogs

Medley songs: Pat-a-Cake / Three Blind Mice / Jingle Bells / Oh Susanna

SINGING NUN (Soeur Sourire) *Belgium, female vocalist – Jeanine Deckers (14 WEEKS)* pos/wks

5 Dec 63 ●	DOMINIQUE *Philips BF 1293* ▲	7	14

SINGING SHEEP *UK, computerised sheep noises (5 WEEKS)* pos/wks

18 Dec 82	BAA BAA BLACK SHEEP *Sheep BAA 1*	42	5

Maxine SINGLETON *US, female vocalist (3 WEEKS)* pos/wks

2 Apr 83	YOU CAN'T RUN FROM LOVE *Creole CR 50*	57	3

SINITTA (291 Top 500) *As well as a string of Hi-NRG dance hits, disco diva and Miquel Brown's daughter Sinitta Malone (b. 19 Oct 1966, Washington, DC) has starred in several London stage musicals including 'Mutiny' with David Essex and 'What a Feeling' with Luke Goss and Sonia (104 WEEKS)* pos/wks

8 Mar 86	SO MACHO / CRUISING *Fanfare FAN 7*	47	11
28 Jun 86 ●	SO MACHO / CRUISING (re-entry) *Fanfare FAN 7*	2	17
11 Oct 86	FEELS LIKE THE FIRST TIME *Fanfare FAN 8*	45	5
25 Jul 87 ●	TOY BOY *Fanfare FAN 12*	4	14
12 Dec 87	G.T.O. *Fanfare FAN 14*	15	9
19 Mar 88 ●	CROSS MY BROKEN HEART *Fanfare FAN 15*	6	9
24 Sep 88	I DON'T BELIEVE IN MIRACLES *Fanfare FAN 16*	22	8
3 Jun 89 ●	RIGHT BACK WHERE WE STARTED FROM *Fanfare FAN 18*	4	10
7 Oct 89	LOVE ON A MOUNTAIN TOP *Fanfare FAN 21*	20	6
21 Apr 90	HITCHIN' A RIDE *Fanfare FAN 24*	24	6
22 Sep 90	LOVE AND AFFECTION *Fanfare FAN 31*	62	3
4 Jul 92	SHAME SHAME SHAME *Arista 74321100327*	28	4
17 Apr 93	THE SUPREME EP *Arista 74321139592*	49	2

Tracks on The Supreme EP: Where Did Our Love Go / Stop! In the Name of Love / You Can't Hurry Love / Remember Me

SINNAMON *US, male vocal / instrumental group (1 WEEK)* pos/wks

28 Sep 96	I NEED YOU NOW *Worx WORXCD 003*	70	1

SIOUXSIE and the BANSHEES (150 Top 500) *Long-running commercially successful UK punk band included Susan 'Siouxsie' Dallion (v), Steve Severin (b) (also recorded as The Glove), Siouxsie's husband, Peter 'Budgie' Clark (d) (who recorded with Siouxsie as The Creatures) and, at times, Cure front man Robert Smith (g) (150 WEEKS)* pos/wks

26 Aug 78 ●	HONG KONG GARDEN *Polydor 2059 052*	7	10
31 Mar 79	THE STAIRCASE (MYSTERY) *Polydor POSP 9*	24	8
7 Jul 79	PLAYGROUND TWIST *Polydor POSP 59*	28	6
29 Sep 79	MITTAGEISEN (METAL POSTCARD) *Polydor 2059 151*	47	3
15 Mar 80	HAPPY HOUSE *Polydor POSP 117*	17	8
7 Jun 80	CHRISTINE *Polydor 2059 249*	22	8
6 Dec 80	ISRAEL *Polydor POSP 205*	41	8
30 May 81	SPELLBOUND *Polydor POSP 273*	22	8
1 Aug 81	ARABIAN KNIGHTS *Polydor POSP 309*	32	7
29 May 82	FIRE WORKS *Polydor POSPG 450*	22	6
9 Oct 82	SLOWDIVE *Polydor POSP 510*	41	4
4 Dec 82	MELT / IL EST NE LE DIVIN ENFANT *Polydor POSP 539*	49	5
1 Oct 83 ●	DEAR PRUDENCE *Wonderland SHE 4*	3	8
24 Mar 84	SWIMMING HORSES *Wonderland SHE 6*	28	4
2 Jun 84	DAZZLE *Wonderland SHE 7*	33	3
27 Oct 84	THE THORN EP *Wonderland SHEEP 8*	47	3
26 Oct 85	CITIES IN DUST *Wonderland SHE 9*	21	6
8 Mar 86	CANDYMAN *Wonderland SHE 10*	34	5
17 Jan 87	THIS WHEEL'S ON FIRE *Wonderland SHE 11*	14	6
28 Mar 87	THE PASSENGER *Wonderland SHE 12*	41	6
25 Jul 87	SONG FROM THE EDGE OF THE WORLD *Wonderland SHE 13*	59	3
30 Jul 88	PEEK-A-BOO *Wonderland SHE 14*	16	6
8 Oct 88	THE KILLING JAR *Wonderland SHE 15*	41	3
3 Dec 88	THE LAST BEAT OF MY HEART *Wonderland SHE 16*	44	1
25 May 91	KISS THEM FOR ME *Wonderland SHE 19*	32	4
13 Jul 91	SHADOWTIME *Wonderland SHE 20*	57	1
25 Jul 92	FACE TO FACE *Wonderland SHE 21*	21	4
20 Aug 94	INTERLUDE *Parlophone CDR 6365* [1]	25	2
7 Jan 95	O BABY *Wonderland SHECD 22*	34	3
18 Feb 95	STARGAZER *Wonderland SHECD 23*	64	1

[1] Morrissey and Siouxsie

Tracks on The Thorn (EP): Overground / Voices / Placebo Effect / Red Over White

See also GLOVE

SIR DOUGLAS QUINTET *US, male vocal / instrumental group (10 WEEKS)* pos/wks

17 Jun 65	SHE'S ABOUT A MOVER *London HLU 9964*	15	10

SIR KILLALOT vs ROBO BABE *UK, male robot rapper and female vocalist (3 WEEKS)* pos/wks

30 Dec 00	ROBOT WARS (ANDROID LOVE) *Polydor 5879362*	51	3

SIR MIX-A-LOT *US, male rapper (2 WEEKS)* pos/wks

8 Aug 92	BABY GOT BACK *Def American DEFA 20* ▲	56	2

SIRRON – *See PLUS ONE featuring SIRRON*

SISQO *US, male vocalist – Mark Andrews (43 WEEKS)* pos/wks

12 Feb 00	GOT TO GET IT *Def Soul 5626442*	14	4
22 Apr 00 ●	THONG SONG *Def Soul 5688902*	3	14
30 Sep 00 ●	UNLEASH THE DRAGON *Def Soul 5726422*	6	7
16 Dec 00	INCOMPLETE *Def Soul 5727542* ▲	13	8
28 Jul 01 ●	DANCE FOR ME *Def Soul 5887002*	6	10

SISSEL – *See Warren G*

SISTER BLISS *UK, female DJ / producer / instrumentalist – Ayalah Ben-Tovim (11 WEEKS)* pos/wks

15 Oct 94	CANTGETAMAN CANTGETAJOB (LIFE'S A BITCH) *Go.Beat GODCD 124* [1]	31	4
15 Jul 95	OH! WHAT A WORLD *Go.Beat GODCD 126* [1]	40	2
29 Jun 96	BADMAN *Junk Dog JDOGCD 1*	51	1

7 Oct 00		**SISTER SISTER** *Multiply CDMULTY 68*	34	2
24 Mar 01		**DELIVER ME** *Multiply CDMULTY 72* [2]	31	2

[1] Sister Bliss featuring Collette [2] Sister Bliss featuring John Martyn

SISTER SLEDGE (262 Top 500) *Successful US family group from Philadelphia: Kathy, Debra, Joni and Kim Sledge. They found more fame in the UK than in the US, and recorded some of the best-known disco records with noted producers / songwriters Nile Rodgers and Bernard Edwards (111 WEEKS)*

			pos	wks
21 Jun 75		**MAMA NEVER TOLD ME** *Atlantic K 10619*	20	6
17 Mar 79	●	**HE'S THE GREATEST DANCER** *Atlantic / Cotillion K 11257*	6	11
26 May 79	●	**WE ARE FAMILY** *Atlantic / Cotillion K 11293*	8	10
11 Aug 79		**LOST IN MUSIC** *Atlantic / Cotillion K 11337*	17	10
19 Jan 80		**GOT TO LOVE SOMEBODY** *Atlantic / Cotillion K 11404*	34	4
28 Feb 81		**ALL AMERICAN GIRLS** *Atlantic K 11656*	41	5
26 May 84		**THINKING OF YOU** *Cotillion / Atlantic B 9744*	11	13
8 Sep 84	●	**LOST IN MUSIC (re-mix)** *Cotillion / Atlantic B 9718*	4	12
17 Nov 84		**WE ARE FAMILY (re-mix)** *Cotillion / Atlantic B 9692*	33	4
1 Jun 85	★	**FRANKIE** *Atlantic A 9547*	1	16
31 Aug 85		**DANCING ON THE JAGGED EDGE** *Atlantic A 9520*	50	3
23 Jan 93	●	**WE ARE FAMILY (2nd re-mix)** *Atlantic A 4508CD*	5	8
13 Mar 93		**LOST IN MUSIC (2nd re-mix)** *Atlantic A 4509CD*	14	5
12 Jun 93		**THINKING OF YOU (re-mix)** *Atlantic A 4515CD*	17	4

SISTER 2 SISTER *Australia, female vocal duo – Christine and Sharon Muscat (5 WEEKS)*

			pos	wks
22 Apr 00		**SISTER** *Mushroom MUSH 70CDS*	18	4
28 Oct 00		**WHAT'S A GIRL TO DO** *Mushroom MUSH 76CDS*	61	1

SISTERS OF MERCY *UK, male / female vocal / instrumental group – leader Andrew Eldritch (40 WEEKS)*

			pos	wks
16 Jun 84		**BODY AND SOUL / TRAIN** *Merciful Release MR 029*	46	3
20 Oct 84		**WALK AWAY** *Merciful Release MR 033*	45	3
9 Mar 85		**NO TIME TO CRY** *Merciful Release MR 035*	63	2
3 Oct 87	●	**THIS CORROSION** *Merciful Release MR 39*	7	6
27 Feb 88		**DOMINION** *Merciful Release MR 43*	13	6
18 Jun 88		**LUCRETIA MY REFLECTION** *Merciful Release MR 45*	20	4
13 Oct 90		**MORE** *Merciful Release MR 47*	14	4
22 Dec 90		**DOCTOR JEEP** *Merciful Release MR 51*	37	4
2 May 92	●	**TEMPLE OF LOVE** *Merciful Release MR 53*	3	5
28 Aug 93		**UNDER THE GUN** *Merciful Release MR 59CDX*	19	3

SIVUCA *Brazil, male instrumentalist (3 WEEKS)*

			pos	wks
28 Jul 84		**AIN'T NO SUNSHINE** *London LON 51*	56	3

SIX BY SEVEN *UK, male vocal / instrumental group (1 WEEK)*

			pos	wks
9 May 98		**CANDLELIGHT** *Mantra MNT 34CD*	70	1

6 BY SIX *UK, male instrumental / production duo (1 WEEK)*

			pos	wks
4 May 96		**INTO YOUR HEART** *Six6 SIXCD 130*	51	1

SIX CHIX *UK, female vocal group (1 WEEK)*

			pos	wks
26 Feb 00		**ONLY THE WOMEN KNOW** *EMI CDCHIX 001*	72	1

666 *Germany, male / female vocal / instrumental group (1 WEEK)*

			pos	wks
3 Oct 98		**ALARMA** *Danceteria CDDAN 001*	58	1

666 *Holland, male production duo (4 WEEKS)*

			pos	wks
25 Nov 00		**DEVIL** *Echo ECSCD 102*	18	4

SIXPENCE NONE THE RICHER *US, male / female vocal / instrumental group (17 WEEKS)*

			pos	wks
29 May 99	●	**KISS ME** *Elektra E 3750CD*	4	12
18 Sep 99		**THERE SHE GOES** *Elektra E 3728CD*	14	5

60FT DOLLS *UK, male vocal / instrumental group (4 WEEKS)*

			pos	wks
3 Feb 96		**STAY** *Indolent DOLLS 002CD*	48	1
11 May 96		**TALK TO ME** *Indolent DOLLS 003CD*	37	1
20 Jul 96		**HAPPY SHOPPER** *Indolent DOLLS 005CD*	38	1
9 May 98		**ALISON'S ROOM** *Indolent DOLLS 007CD1*	61	1

SIZE 9 *US, male producer – Josh Wink (4 WEEKS)*

			pos	wks
17 Jun 95		**I'M READY** *Virgin America VUSCD 92*	52	1
11 Nov 95		**I'M READY (re-issue)** *VC VCRD 2* [1]	30	3

[1] Josh Wink's Size 9

See also Josh WINK

Roni SIZE / REPRAZENT *UK, male producer – Ryan Williams with male / female vocal / instrumental group (16 WEEKS)*

			pos	wks
14 Jun 97		**SHARE THE FALL** *Talkin Loud TLCD 21*	37	2
13 Sep 97		**HEROES** *Talkin Loud TLCD 25*	31	2
15 Nov 97		**BROWN PAPER BAG** *Talkin Loud TLCD 28*	20	3
14 Mar 98		**WATCHING WINDOWS** *Talkin Loud TLCD 31*	28	2
7 Oct 00		**WHO TOLD YOU** *Talkin Loud TLCD 61*	17	3
24 Mar 01		**DIRTY BEATS** *Talkin Loud TLCDD 63*	32	3
23 Jun 01		**LUCKY PRESSURE** *Talkin' Loud TLCD 64*	58	1

SIZZLA *Jamaica, male rapper – Miguel Collins (2 WEEKS)*

			pos	wks
17 Apr 99		**RAIN SHOWERS** *Xterminator EXTCDS 76*	51	2

SJ – *See S-J*

SKANDAL *UK, male vocal group (1 WEEK)*

			pos	wks
14 Oct 00		**CHAMPAGNE HIGHWAY** *Prestige Management CDGING 1*	53	1

SKATALITES *Jamaica, male instrumental group (6 WEEKS)*

			pos	wks
20 Apr 67		**GUNS OF NAVARONE** *Island WI 168*	36	6

SKEE-LO *US, male rapper – Antoine Roundtree (10 WEEKS)*

			pos	wks
9 Dec 95		**I WISH** *Wild Card 5777752*	15	8
27 Apr 96		**TOP OF THE STAIRS** *Wild Card 5763352*	38	2

Beverli SKEETE – *See DE-CODE featuring Beverli SKEETE*

Peter SKELLERN *UK, male vocalist (24 WEEKS)*

			pos	wks
23 Sep 72	●	**YOU'RE A LADY** *Decca F 13333*	3	11
29 Mar 75		**HOLD ON TO LOVE** *Decca F 13568*	14	9
28 Oct 78		**LOVE IS THE SWEETEST THING** *Mercury 6008 603* [1]	60	4

[1] Peter Skellern featuring Grimethorpe Colliery Band

SKID ROW *US, male vocal / instrumental group (27 WEEKS)*

			pos	wks
18 Nov 89		**YOUTH GONE WILD** *Atlantic A 8935*	42	3
3 Feb 90		**18 AND LIFE** *Atlantic A 8883*	12	6
31 Mar 90		**I REMEMBER YOU** *East West A 8886*	36	4
15 Jun 91		**MONKEY BUSINESS** *Atlantic A 7673*	19	3
14 Sep 91		**SLAVE TO THE GRIND** *Atlantic A 7603*	43	2
23 Nov 91		**WASTED TIME** *Atlantic A 7570*	20	3
29 Aug 92		**YOUTH GONE WILD / DELIVERING THE GOODS (re-issue)** *Atlantic A 7444*	22	4
18 Nov 95		**BREAKIN' DOWN** *Atlantic A 7135CD1*	48	2

SKIDS *UK, male vocal / instrumental group (60 WEEKS)*

			pos	wks
23 Sep 78		**SWEET SUBURBIA** *Virgin VS 227*	70	1
7 Oct 78		**SWEET SUBURBIA (re-entry)** *Virgin VS 227*	71	2
4 Nov 78		**THE SAINTS ARE COMING** *Virgin VS 232*	48	3
17 Feb 79	●	**INTO THE VALLEY** *Virgin VS 241*	10	11
26 May 79		**MASQUERADE** *Virgin VS 262*	14	9
29 Sep 79		**CHARADE** *Virgin VS 288*	31	6
24 Nov 79		**WORKING FOR THE YANKEE DOLLAR** *Virgin VS 306*	20	11
1 Mar 80		**ANIMATION** *Virgin VS 323*	56	3
16 Aug 80		**CIRCUS GAMES** *Virgin VS 359*	32	7
18 Oct 80		**GOODBYE CIVILIAN** *Virgin VS 373*	52	4
6 Dec 80		**WOMAN IN WINTER** *Virgin VSK 101*	49	3

UK No.1 ★ UK Top 10 ● Still on chart + UK million seller ◆ UK entry at No.1 ■ US No.1 ▲

SKIN *UK / Germany, male vocal / instrumental group (19 WEEKS)* pos/wks

			pos	wks
25 Dec 93		**THE SKIN UP (EP)** *Parlophone CDR 6363*	67	2
12 Mar 94		**HOUSE OF LOVE** *Parlophone CDR 6374*	45	2
30 Apr 94		**MONEY / UNBELIEVEABLE** *Parlophone CDR 6381*	18	3
23 Jul 94		**TOWER OF STRENGTH** *Parlophone CDR 6387*	19	3
15 Oct 94		**LOOK BUT DON'T TOUCH (EP) (re-issue)** *Parlophone CDRS 6391*	33	3
20 May 95		**TAKE ME DOWN TO THE RIVER** *Parlophone CDR 6409*	26	2
23 Mar 96		**HOW LUCKY YOU ARE** *Parlophone CDR 6426*	32	2
18 May 96		**PERFECT DAY** *Parlophone CDR 6433*	33	2

Tracks on The Skin Up (EP): Look But Don't Touch / Shine Your Light / Monkey (re-issue). Tracks on Look But Don't Touch (EP): Look But Don't Touch / Should I Stay or Should I Go / Pump It Up / Monkey

SKIN UP *UK, male producer (9 WEEKS)* pos/wks

			pos	wks
7 Sep 91		**IVORY** *Love EVOL 4*	48	3
14 Mar 92		**A JUICY RED APPLE** *Love EVOL 11*	32	4
18 Jul 92		**ACCELERATE** *Love EVOL 17*	45	2

SKINNER – See *LIGHTNING SEEDS*

SKINNY *UK, male vocal / instrumental / production duo (2 WEEKS)* pos/wks

			pos	wks
11 Apr 98		**FAILURE** *Cheeky CHEKCD 023*	31	2

SKIP RAIDERS featuring JADA
UK, male production duo and female vocalist (1 WEEK) pos/wks

			pos	wks
15 Jul 00		**ANOTHER DAY** *Perfecto PERF 4CDS*	46	1

SKIPWORTH and TURNER *US, male vocal duo (12 WEEKS)* pos/wks

			pos	wks
27 Apr 85		**THINKING ABOUT YOUR LOVE** *Fourth & Broadway BRW 23*	24	10
21 Jan 89		**MAKE IT LAST** *Fourth & Broadway BRW 118*	60	2

Nick SKITZ – See *FUNKY CHOAD featuring Nick SKITZ*

SKUNK ANANSIE
UK, male / female vocal / instrumental group (41 WEEKS) pos/wks

			pos	wks
25 Mar 95		**SELLING JESUS** *One Little Indian 101 TP7CD*	46	1
17 Jun 95		**I CAN DREAM** *One Little Indian 121 TP7CD*	41	2
2 Sep 95		**CHARITY** *One Little Indian 131 TP7CD*	40	2
27 Jan 96		**WEAK** *One Little Indian 141 TP7CD*	20	5
27 Apr 96		**CHARITY (re-issue)** *One Little Indian 151 TP7CD*	20	3
28 Sep 96		**ALL I WANT** *One Little Indian 161 TP7CD*	14	4
30 Nov 96		**TWISTED (EVERYDAY HURTS)** *One Little Indian 171 TP7CD*	26	4
1 Feb 97		**HEDONISM (JUST BECAUSE YOU FEEL GOOD)** *One Little Indian 181TP7CD*	13	6
14 Jun 97		**BRAZEN 'WEEP'** *One Little Indian 191TP7CD1*	11	5
13 Mar 99		**CHARLIE BIG POTATO** *Virgin VSCDT 1725*	17	3
22 May 99		**SECRETLY** *Virgin VSCDT 1733*	16	4
7 Aug 99		**LATELY** *Virgin VSCDT 1738*	33	2

SKY *UK / Australia, male instrumental group (11 WEEKS)* pos/wks

			pos	wks
5 Apr 80	●	**TOCCATA** *Ariola ARO 300*	5	11

SKYHOOKS *Australia, male vocal / instrumental group (1 WEEK)* pos/wks

			pos	wks
9 Jun 79		**WOMEN IN UNIFORM** *United Artists UP 36508*	73	1

SLACKER *UK, male production duo (4 WEEKS)* pos/wks

			pos	wks
26 Apr 97		**SCARED** *XL XLS 84CD*	36	2
30 Aug 97		**YOUR FACE** *XL XLS 87CD*	33	2

SLADE (38 Top 500) *Top group of the 1970s: Noddy Holder (v/g), Dave Hill (g), Jimmy Lea (b/p), Don Powell (d). They were the first act to have three singles enter at No.1. All six of the Wolverhampton band's chart-topping stompers were penned by Holder and Lea. Noddy, who is now a popular TV personality, was made an MBE in 2000 (279 WEEKS)* pos/wks

			pos	wks
19 Jun 71		**GET DOWN AND GET WITH IT** *Polydor 2058 112*	16	14
30 Oct 71	★	**COZ I LUV YOU** *Polydor 2058 155*	1	15
5 Feb 72	●	**LOOK WOT YOU DUN** *Polydor 2058 195*	4	10
3 Jun 72	★	**TAKE ME BAK 'OME** *Polydor 2058 231*	1	13
2 Sep 72	★	**MAMA WEER ALL CRAZEE NOW** *Polydor 2058 274*	1	10
25 Nov 72	●	**GUDBUY T'JANE** *Polydor 2058 312*	2	13
3 Mar 73	★	**CUM ON FEEL THE NOIZE** *Polydor 2058 339* ■	1	12
30 Jun 73	★	**SKWEEZE ME PLEEZE ME** *Polydor 2058 377* ■	1	10
6 Oct 73	●	**MY FRIEND STAN** *Polydor 2058 407*	2	8
15 Dec 73	★	**MERRY XMAS EVERYBODY** *Polydor 2058 422* ◆ ■	1	9
6 Apr 74	●	**EVERYDAY** *Polydor 2058 453*	3	7
6 Jul 74	●	**THE BANGIN' MAN** *Polydor 2058 492*	3	7
19 Oct 74	●	**FAR FAR AWAY** *Polydor 2058 522*	2	6
15 Feb 75		**HOW DOES IT FEEL** *Polydor 2058 547*	15	7
17 May 75	●	**THANKS FOR THE MEMORY (WHAM BAM THANK YOU MAM)** *Polydor 2058 585*	7	7
22 Nov 75		**IN FOR A PENNY** *Polydor 2058 663*	11	8
7 Feb 76		**LET'S CALL IT QUITS** *Polydor 2058 690*	11	7
5 Feb 77		**GYPSY ROAD HOG** *Barn 2014 105*	48	2
29 Oct 77		**MY BABY LEFT ME - THAT'S ALL RIGHT** *Barn 2014 114*	32	4
18 Oct 80		**SLADE ALIVE AT READING '80 (EP)** *Cheapskate CHEAP 5*	44	5
27 Dec 80		**MERRY XMAS EVERYBODY (re-recording)** *Cheapskate CHEAP 11* [1]	70	2
31 Jan 81	●	**WE'LL BRING THE HOUSE DOWN** *Cheapskate CHEAP 16*	10	9
4 Apr 81		**WHEELS AIN'T COMING DOWN** *Cheapskate CHEAP 21*	60	3
19 Sep 81		**LOCK UP YOUR DAUGHTERS** *RCA 124*	29	8
19 Dec 81		**MERRY XMAS EVERYBODY (re-entry)** *Polydor 2058 422*	32	4
27 Mar 82		**RUBY RED** *RCA 191*	51	3
27 Nov 82		**(AND NOW - THE WALTZ) C'EST LA VIE** *RCA 291*	50	6
25 Dec 82		**MERRY XMAS EVERYBODY (2nd re-entry)** *Polydor 2058 422*	67	3
19 Nov 83	●	**MY OH MY** *RCA 373*	2	11
10 Dec 83		**MERRY XMAS EVERYBODY (3rd re-entry)** *Polydor 2058 422*	20	5
4 Feb 84	●	**RUN RUNAWAY** *RCA 385*	7	10
17 Nov 84		**ALL JOIN HANDS** *RCA 455*	15	9
15 Dec 84		**MERRY XMAS EVERYBODY (4th re-entry)** *Polydor 2058 422*	47	4
26 Jan 85		**7 YEAR BITCH** *RCA 475*	60	3
23 Mar 85		**MYZSTERIOUS MIZSTER JONES** *RCA PB 40027*	50	5
30 Nov 85		**DO YOU BELIEVE IN MIRACLES** *RCA PB 40449*	54	6
21 Dec 85		**MERRY XMAS EVERYBODY (re-issue)** *Polydor POSP 780*	48	3
27 Dec 86		**MERRY XMAS EVERYBODY (re-entry of re-issue)** *Polydor POSP 780*	71	1
21 Feb 87		**STILL THE SAME** *RCA PB 41137*	73	2
19 Oct 91		**RADIO WALL OF SOUND** *Polydor PO 180*	21	5
26 Dec 98		**MERRY XMAS EVERYBODY '98 (re-mix)** *Polydor 5633532* [2]	30	3

[1] Slade and the Reading Choir [2] Slade vs Flush

Tracks on Slade Alive at Reading '80 (EP): When I'm Dancin' I Ain't Fightin' / Born to Be Wild / Somethin' Else / Pistol Packin' Mama / Keep a Rollin'

SLAM
UK, male production duo – Orde Meikle and Stuart McMillan (4 WEEKS) pos/wks

			pos	wks
17 Feb 01		**POSITIVE EDUCATION** *VC Recordings VCRD 84*	44	2
17 Mar 01		**NARCO TOURISTS** *Soma SOMA 100CD* [1]	66	1
7 Jul 01		**LIFETIMES** *Soma SOMA 107CDS* [2]	61	1

[1] Slam vs Unkle [2] Slam featuring Tyrone 'Visionary' Palmer

SLAMM *UK, male vocal / instrumental group (6 WEEKS)* pos/wks

			pos	wks
17 Jul 93		**ENERGIZE** *PWL International PWCD 266*	57	2
23 Oct 93		**VIRGINIA PLAIN** *PWL International PWCD 274*	60	1
22 Oct 94		**THAT'S WHERE MY MIND GOES** *PWL International PWCD 310*	68	1
4 Feb 95		**CAN'T GET BY** *PWL International PWCD 316*	47	2

SLARTA JOHN – See *HATIRAS featuring SLARTA JOHN*

Luke SLATER *UK, male producer (1 WEEK)* pos/wks

			pos	wks
16 Sep 00		**ALL EXHALE** *Novamute CDNOMU 79*	74	1

SLAUGHTER *US, male vocal / instrumental group (2 WEEKS)* pos/wks

			pos	wks
29 Sep 90		**UP ALL NIGHT** *Chrysalis CHS 3556*	62	1
2 Feb 91		**FLY TO THE ANGELS** *Chrysalis CHS 3634*	55	1

SLAVE *US, male vocal / instrumental group (3 WEEKS)* pos/wks

			pos	wks
8 Mar 80		**JUST A TOUCH OF LOVE** *Atlantic / Cotillion K 11442*	64	3

SLAYER *US, male vocal / instrumental group (3 WEEKS)*

		pos	wks
13 Jun 87	**CRIMINALLY INSANE** *Def Jam LON 133*	64	1
26 Oct 91	**SEASONS IN THE ABYSS** *Def American DEFA 9*	51	1
9 Sep 95	**SERENITY IN MURDER** *American 74321312482*	50	1

SLEAZESISTERS *UK, male producer – Paul Masterson (3 WEEKS)*

		pos	wks
29 Jul 95	**SEX** *Pulse 8 CDLOSE 92* [1]	53	1
30 Mar 96	**LET'S WHIP IT UP (YOU GO GIRL)** *Pulse 8 CDLOSE 102* [1]	46	1
26 Sep 98	**WORK IT UP** *Logic 74321616622* [2]	74	1

[1] Sleazesisters with Vikki Shepard [2] Sleaze Sisters

See also CANDY GIRLS; YOMANDA; HI-GATE

Kathy SLEDGE *US, female vocalist (7 WEEKS)*

		pos	wks
16 May 92	**TAKE ME BACK TO LOVE AGAIN** *Epic 6579837*	62	2
18 Feb 95	**ANOTHER STAR** *NRC DEACD 002*	54	1
29 Nov 97	**FREEDOM** *Deconstruction 74321536952* [1]	15	4

[1] Robert Miles featuring Kathy Sledge

See also SISTER SLEDGE

Percy SLEDGE *US, male vocalist (34 WEEKS)*

		pos	wks
12 May 66 ●	**WHEN A MAN LOVES A WOMAN** *Atlantic 584 001* ▲	4	17
4 Aug 66	**WARM AND TENDER LOVE** *Atlantic 584 034*	34	7
14 Feb 87 ●	**WHEN A MAN LOVES A WOMAN (re-issue)** *Atlantic YZ 96*	2	10

SLEEPER *UK, male / female vocal / instrumental group (29 WEEKS)*

		pos	wks
21 May 94	**DELICIOUS** *Indolent SLEEP 003CD*	75	1
21 Jan 95	**INBETWEENER** *Indolent SLEEP 006CD*	16	4
8 Apr 95	**VEGAS** *Indolent SLEEP 008CD*	33	3
7 Oct 95	**WHAT DO I DO NOW** *Indolent SLEEP 009CD1*	14	4
4 May 96 ●	**SALE OF THE CENTURY** *Indolent SLEEP 011CD*	10	5
13 Jul 96 ●	**NICE GUY EDDIE** *Indolent SLEEP 013CD*	10	5
5 Oct 96	**STATUESQUE** *Indolent SLEEP 014CD1*	17	3
4 Oct 97	**SHE'S A GOOD GIRL** *Indolent SLEEP 015CD*	28	2
6 Dec 97	**ROMEO ME** *Indolent SLEEP 17CD1*	39	2

SLICK *US, male / female vocal / instrumental group (15 WEEKS)*

		pos	wks
16 Jun 79	**SPACE BASS** *Fantasy FTC 176*	16	10
15 Sep 79	**SEXY CREAM** *Fantasy FTC 182*	47	5

Grace SLICK *US, female vocalist (4 WEEKS)*

		pos	wks
24 May 80	**DREAMS** *RCA PB 9534*	50	4

SLICK RICK – *See Montell JORDAN; Al B SURE!*

SLIK *UK, male vocal / instrumental group – lead vocal Midge Ure (18 WEEKS)*

		pos	wks
17 Jan 76 ★	**FOREVER AND EVER** *Bell 1464*	1	9
8 May 76	**REQUIEM** *Bell 1478*	24	9

SLIM CHANCE – *See Ronnie LANE and SLIM CHANCE*

SLIPKNOT *US, male vocal / instrumental group (9 WEEKS)*

		pos	wks
11 Mar 00	**WAIT AND BLEED** *Roadrunner RR 21125*	27	3
16 Sep 00	**SPIT IT OUT** *Roadrunner RR20903*	28	2
10 Nov 01	**LEFT BEHIND** *Roadrunner 23203355*	24	4

SLIPSTREEM *UK, male vocal group (7 WEEKS)*

		pos	wks
19 Dec 92	**WE ARE RAVING - THE ANTHEM** *Boogie Food 7BF 1*	18	7

SLITS *UK, female vocal / instrumental group (3 WEEKS)*

		pos	wks
13 Oct 79	**TYPICAL GIRLS / I HEARD IT THROUGH THE GRAPEVINE** *Island WIP 6505*	60	3

PF SLOAN *US, male vocalist (3 WEEKS)*

		pos	wks
4 Nov 65	**SINS OF THE FAMILY** *RCA 1482*	38	3

SLO-MOSHUN *UK, male instrumental / production duo (4 WEEKS)*

		pos	wks
5 Feb 94	**BELLS OF NY** *Six6 SIXCD 108*	29	3
30 Jul 94	**HELP MY FRIEND** *Six6 SIXCD 117*	52	1

SLOWDIVE *UK, male / female vocal / instrumental group (2 WEEKS)*

		pos	wks
15 Jun 91	**CATCH THE BREEZE / SHINE** *Creation CRE 112*	52	1
29 May 93	**OUTSIDE YOUR ROOM (EP)** *Creation CRESCD 119*	69	1

Tracks on Outside Your Room (EP): Outside Your Room / Alison / So Tired / Souvlaki Space Station

SL2 *UK, male DJ / production duo – Matt "Slipmatt" Nelson and John "Lime" Fernandez (25 WEEKS)*

		pos	wks
2 Nov 91	**DJS TAKE CONTROL / WAY IN MY BRAIN** *XL Recordings XLS 24*	11	5
4 Jan 92	**DJS TAKE CONTROL / WAY IN MY BRAIN (re-entry)** *XL Recordings XLS 24*	71	1
18 Apr 92 ●	**ON A RAGGA TIP** *XL Recordings XLS 29*	2	11
19 Dec 92	**WAY IN MY BRAIN (re-mix) / DRUMBEATS** *XL Recordings XLS 36*	26	6
15 Feb 97	**ON A RAGGA TIP '97 (re-mix)** *XL Recordings XLSR 29CD*	31	2

SLUSNIK LUNA *Finland, male producer – Niko Nyman (2 WEEKS)*

		pos	wks
1 Sep 01	**SUN** *Incentive CENT 29CDS*	40	2

SLY and the FAMILY STONE *US, male / female vocal / instrumental / production group (42 WEEKS)*

		pos	wks
10 Jul 68 ●	**DANCE TO THE MUSIC** *Direction 58 3568*	7	14
2 Oct 68	**M'LADY** *Direction 58 3707*	32	7
19 Mar 69	**EVERYDAY PEOPLE** *Direction 58 3938* ▲	36	1
9 Apr 69	**EVERYDAY PEOPLE (re-entry)** *Direction 58 3938*	37	4
8 Jan 72	**FAMILY AFFAIR** *Epic EPC 7632* ▲	15	8
15 Apr 72	**RUNNIN' AWAY** *Epic EPC 7810*	17	8

SLY FOX *US, male vocal / instrumental duo – Gary Cooper and Michael Camacho (16 WEEKS)*

		pos	wks
31 May 86 ●	**LET'S GO ALL THE WAY** *Capitol CL 403*	3	16

SLY and ROBBIE *Jamaica, male vocal / instrumental duo – Sly Dunbar and Robbie Shakespeare (23 WEEKS)*

		pos	wks
4 Apr 87	**BOOPS (HERE TO GO)** *Fourth & Broadway BRW 61*	12	11
25 Jul 87	**FIRE** *Fourth & Broadway BRW 71*	60	4
20 Sep 97	**NIGHT NURSE** *East West EW 129CD1* [1]	13	8

[1] Sly and Robbie featuring Simply Red

Heather SMALL *UK, female vocalist (9 WEEKS)*

		pos	wks
20 May 00	**PROUD** *Arista 74321748902*	16	5
19 Aug 00	**HOLDING ON** *Arista 74321781332*	58	1
18 Nov 00	**YOU NEED LOVE LIKE I DO** *GUT CDGUT 36* [1]	24	3

[1] Tom Jones and Heather Small

See also M PEOPLE

SMALL ADS *UK, male vocal / instrumental group (3 WEEKS)*

		pos	wks
18 Apr 81	**SMALL ADS** *Bronze BRO 115*	63	3

SMALL FACES (179 Top 500) *Revered London-based mod quartet: Steve Marriott (v/g) (d. 1991), Ronnie Lane (b) (d. 1997), Ian McLagan (k), Kenney Jones (d). Marriott and Lane penned most of the act's UK hits. Further international fame came when Marriott formed Humble Pie and the other members formed The Faces (137 WEEKS)*

		pos	wks
2 Sep 65	**WHATCHA GONNA DO ABOUT IT?** *Decca F 12208*	14	12
10 Feb 66 ●	**SHA-LA-LA-LA-LEE** *Decca F 12317*	3	11
12 May 66 ●	**HEY GIRL** *Decca F 12393*	10	9
11 Aug 66 ★	**ALL OR NOTHING** *Decca F 12470*	1	12
17 Nov 66 ●	**MY MIND'S EYE** *Decca F 12500*	4	11
9 Mar 67	**I CAN'T MAKE IT** *Decca F 12565*	26	7
8 Jun 67	**HERE COME THE NICE** *Immediate IM 050*	12	10

Date		Title / Label	pos	wks
9 Aug 67	●	ITCHYCOO PARK *Immediate IM 057*	3	14
6 Dec 67	●	TIN SOLDIER *Immediate IM 062*	9	12
17 Apr 68	●	LAZY SUNDAY *Immediate IM 064*	2	11
10 Jul 68		UNIVERSAL *Immediate IM 069*	16	11
19 Mar 69		AFTERGLOW OF YOUR LOVE *Immediate IM 077*	36	1
13 Dec 75	●	ITCHYCOO PARK (re-issue) *Immediate IMS 102*	9	11
20 Mar 76		LAZY SUNDAY (re-issue) *Immediate IMS 106*	39	5

SMALLER *UK, male vocal / instrumental group (2 WEEKS)* pos/wks

Date		Title / Label	pos	wks
28 Sep 96		WASTED *Better BETSCD 006*	72	1
29 Mar 97		IS *Better BETSCD 008*	55	1

SMART E'S *UK, male instrumental / production group (9 WEEKS)* pos/wks

Date		Title / Label	pos	wks
11 Jul 92	●	SESAME'S TREET *Suburban Base SUBBASE 12S*	2	9

S*M*A*S*H *UK, male vocal / instrumental group (1 WEEK)* pos/wks

Date		Title / Label	pos	wks
6 Aug 94		(I WANT TO) KILL SOMEBODY *Hi-Rise FLATSCD 5*	26	1

SMASH MOUTH *US, male vocal / instrumental group (9 WEEKS)* pos/wks

Date		Title / Label	pos	wks
25 Oct 97		WALKIN' ON THE SUN *Interscope IND 95555*	19	4
31 Jul 99		ALL STAR *Interscope 4971172*	24	5

SMASHING PUMPKINS
US, male / female vocal / instrumental group (36 WEEKS) pos/wks

Date		Title / Label	pos	wks
5 Sep 92		I AM ONE *Hut HUTT 18*	73	1
3 Jul 93		CHERUB ROCK *Hut HUTCD 31*	31	2
25 Sep 93		TODAY *Hut HUTCD 37*	44	2
5 Mar 94		DISARM *Hut HUTCD 43*	11	3
28 Oct 95		BULLET WITH BUTTERFLY WINGS *Hut HUTCD 63*	20	3
10 Feb 96		1979 *Hut HUTCD 67*	16	3
18 May 96	●	TONIGHT TONIGHT *Hut HUTDX 69*	7	6
23 Nov 96		THIRTY THREE *Hut HUTCD 78*	21	2
14 Jun 97	●	THE END IS THE BEGINNING IS THE END *Warner Bros. W 0404CD*	10	4
23 Aug 97		THE END IS THE BEGINNING IS THE END (re-mix) *Warner Bros. W 0410CD*	72	1
30 May 98		AVA ADORE *Hut HUTCD 101*	11	4
19 Sep 98		PERFECT *Hut HUTCD 106*	24	2
4 Mar 00		STAND INSIDE YOUR LOVE *Hut HUTCD 127*	23	2
23 Sep 00		TRY TRY TRY *Hut HUTCD 140*	73	1

SMEAR CAMPAIGN – *See MR BEAN and SMEAR CAMPAIGN featuring Bruce DICKINSON*

SMELLS LIKE HEAVEN *Italy, male producer – Fabio Paras (1 WEEK)* pos/wks

Date		Title / Label	pos	wks
10 Jul 93		LONDRES STRUTT *Deconstruction 74321154312*	57	1

Ann-Marie SMITH *UK, female vocalist (5 WEEKS)* pos/wks

Date		Title / Label	pos	wks
23 Jan 93		MUSIC *Synthetic CDR 6334* [1]	34	2
18 Mar 95		ROCKIN' MY BODY *Media MCSTD 2021* [2]	31	2
15 Jul 95		(YOU'RE MY ONE AND ONLY) TRUE LOVE *Media MCSTD 2060*	46	1

[1] Fargetta and Anne-Marie Smith [2] 49ers featuring Ann-Marie Smith

Elliott SMITH *US, male vocalist / instrumentalist (3 WEEKS)* pos/wks

Date		Title / Label	pos	wks
19 Dec 98		WALTZ #2 (XO) *DreamWorks DRMCD 22347*	52	1
1 May 99		BABY BRITAIN *DreamWorks DRMDM 50950*	55	1
8 Jul 00		SON OF SAM *DreamWorks DRMCD 4509492*	55	1

'Fast' Eddie SMITH – *See DJ 'FAST' EDDIE*

Hurricane SMITH *UK, male vocalist – Norman Smith (35 WEEKS)* pos/wks

Date		Title / Label	pos	wks
12 Jun 71	●	DON'T LET IT DIE *Columbia DB 8785*	2	12
29 Apr 72	●	OH BABE WHAT WOULD YOU SAY? *Columbia DB 8878*	4	16
2 Sep 72		WHO WAS IT *Columbia DB 8916*	23	7

Jimmy SMITH *US, male instrumentalist – organ (3 WEEKS)* pos/wks

Date		Title / Label	pos	wks
28 Apr 66		GOT MY MOJO WORKING *Verve VS 536*	48	2
19 May 66		GOT MY MOJO WORKING (re-entry) *Verve VS 536*	48	1

Keely SMITH *US, female vocalist (10 WEEKS)* pos/wks

Date		Title / Label	pos	wks
18 Mar 65		YOU'RE BREAKIN' MY HEART *Reprise R 20346*	14	10

Mandy SMITH *UK, female vocalist (2 WEEKS)* pos/wks

Date		Title / Label	pos	wks
20 May 89		DON'T YOU WANT ME BABY *PWL PWL 37*	59	2

Mark E SMITH – *See FALL; INSPIRAL CARPETS; DOSE*

Mel SMITH *UK, male vocalist (10 WEEKS)* pos/wks

Date		Title / Label	pos	wks
5 Dec 87	●	ROCKIN' AROUND THE CHRISTMAS TREE *10 TEN 2* [1]	3	7
21 Dec 91		ANOTHER BLOOMING CHRISTMAS *Epic 6576877*	59	3

[1] Mel and Kim (Kim was Kim Wilde)

Muriel SMITH with Wally STOTT and his Orchestra
US, female vocalist and male orchestra (17 WEEKS) pos/wks

Date		Title / Label	pos	wks
15 May 53	●	HOLD ME, THRILL ME, KISS ME *Philips PB 122*	3	17

O.C. SMITH *US, male vocalist (23 WEEKS)* pos/wks

Date		Title / Label	pos	wks
29 May 68	●	THE SON OF HICKORY HOLLER'S TRAMP *CBS 3343*	2	15
26 Mar 77		TOGETHER *Caribou CRB 4910*	25	8

Patti SMITH GROUP
US, female / male vocal / instrumental group (16 WEEKS) pos/wks

Date		Title / Label	pos	wks
29 Apr 78	●	BECAUSE THE NIGHT *Arista 181*	5	12
19 Aug 78		PRIVILEGE (SET ME FREE) *Arista 197*	72	1
2 Jun 79		FREDERICK *Arista 264*	63	3

Rex SMITH and Rachel SWEET
US, male / female vocalists (7 WEEKS) pos/wks

Date		Title / Label	pos	wks
22 Aug 81		EVERLASTING LOVE *CBS A 1405*	35	7

Richard Jon SMITH *South Africa, male vocalist (2 WEEKS)* pos/wks

Date		Title / Label	pos	wks
16 Jul 83		SHE'S THE MASTER OF THE GAME *Jive JIVE 38*	63	2

Rose SMITH – *See DELAKOTA*

Sheila SMITH – *See Cevin FISHER*

Whistling Jack SMITH *UK, male whistler (12 WEEKS)* pos/wks

Date		Title / Label	pos	wks
2 Mar 67	●	I WAS KAISER BILL'S BATMAN *Deram DM 112*	5	12

Will SMITH (304 Top 500)

Artist formerly known as the Fresh Prince is not only one of the 1990s' most successful rap stars, but also a top TV personality and movie actor, b. 25 Sep 1968, Philadelphia, US. The quadruple World Music Award winner (1999) helped to make rap respectable and accessible to all ages (100 WEEKS) pos/wks

Date		Title / Label	pos	wks
16 Aug 97	★	MEN IN BLACK *Columbia 6648682* ■	1	16
13 Dec 97		JUST CRUISIN' *Columbia 6653482*	23	6
7 Feb 98	●	GETTIN' JIGGY WIT IT *Columbia 6655605* ▲	3	10
1 Aug 98	●	JUST THE TWO OF US *Columbia 6662092*	2	10
5 Dec 98	●	MIAMI *Columbia 6666782*	3	14
13 Feb 99	●	BOY YOU KNOCK ME OUT *MJJ / Epic 6669372* [1]	3	8
15 May 99		BOY YOU KNOCK ME OUT (re-entry) *MJJ / Epic 6669372* [1]	69	1
10 Jul 99	●	WILD WILD WEST *Columbia 6675962* [2] ▲	2	16
20 Nov 99	●	WILL 2K *Columbia 6684452*	2	11
25 Mar 00		FREAKIN' IT *Columbia 6691052*	15	7
27 May 00		FREAKIN' IT (re-entry) *Columbia 6691052*	59	1

[1] Tatyana Ali featuring Will Smith [2] Will Smith featuring Dru Hill - additional vocals Kool Moe Dee

See also JAZZY JEFF & the FRESH PRINCE

SMITHS (286 Top 500) *Mancunian quartet with loyal fan base: Morrissey (b. Stephen Morrissey) (v), Johnny Marr (g), Andy Rourke (b), Mike Joyce (d). Their achievements include monopolising the Top 3 indie chart placings (Feb 1984) and having seven albums simultaneously in the UK chart (Mar 1995) (105 WEEKS)*

Date		Title / Label	pos	wks
12 Nov 83		THIS CHARMING MAN *Rough Trade RT 136*	25	12
28 Jan 84		WHAT DIFFERENCE DOES IT MAKE *Rough Trade RT 146*	12	9
2 Jun 84	●	HEAVEN KNOWS I'M MISERABLE NOW *Rough Trade RT 156*	10	8
1 Sep 84		WILLIAM, IT WAS REALLY NOTHING *Rough Trade RT 166*	17	6
9 Feb 85		HOW SOON IS NOW? *Rough Trade RT 176*	24	6
30 Mar 85		SHAKESPEARE'S SISTER *Rough Trade RT 181*	26	4
13 Jul 85		THAT JOKE ISN'T FUNNY ANYMORE *Rough Trade RT 186*	49	3
5 Oct 85		THE BOY WITH THE THORN IN HIS SIDE *Rough Trade RT 191*	23	5
31 May 86		BIG MOUTH STRIKES AGAIN *Rough Trade RT 192*	26	4
2 Aug 86		PANIC *Rough Trade RT 193*	11	8
1 Nov 86		ASK *Rough Trade RT 194*	14	5
7 Feb 87		SHOPLIFTERS OF THE WORLD UNITE *Rough Trade RT 195*	12	4
25 Apr 87	●	SHEILA TAKE A BOW *Rough Trade RT 196*	10	5
22 Aug 87		GIRLFRIEND IN A COMA *Rough Trade RT 197*	13	5
14 Nov 87		I STARTED SOMETHING I COULDN'T FINISH *Rough Trade RT 198*	23	4
19 Dec 87		LAST NIGHT I DREAMT THAT SOMEBODY LOVED ME *Rough Trade RT 200*	30	4
15 Aug 92	●	THIS CHARMING MAN (re-issue) *WEA YZ 0001*	8	5
12 Sep 92		HOW SOON IS NOW (re-issue) *WEA YZ 0002*	16	4
24 Oct 92		THERE IS A LIGHT THAT NEVER GOES OUT *WEA YZ 0003*	25	3
18 Feb 95		ASK (re-issue) *WEA YZ 0004CDX*	62	1

SMOKE *UK, male vocal / instrumental group (3 WEEKS)*

Date		Title / Label	pos	wks
9 Mar 67		MY FRIEND JACK *Columbia DB 8115*	45	3

SMOKE CITY
UK / Brazil, male / female vocal / instrumental group (5 WEEKS)

Date		Title / Label	pos	wks
12 Apr 97	●	UNDERWATER LOVE *Jive JIVECD 422*	4	5

SMOKED – *See Oliver LIEB presents SMOKED*

SMOKIE (216 Top 500) *British group who became European superstars, fronted by easily identifiable vocalist Chris Norman. Especially popular in Germany, many of their hits were penned by Mike Chapman and Nicky Chinn (125 WEEKS)*

Date		Title / Label	pos	wks
19 Jul 75	●	IF YOU THINK YOU KNOW HOW TO LOVE ME *RAK 206* [1]	3	9
4 Oct 75	●	DON'T PLAY YOUR ROCK 'N' ROLL TO ME *RAK 217* [1]	8	7
31 Jan 76		SOMETHING'S BEEN MAKING ME BLUE *RAK 227*	17	8
25 Sep 76		I'LL MEET YOU AT MIDNIGHT *RAK 241*	11	9
4 Dec 76	●	LIVING NEXT DOOR TO ALICE *RAK 244*	5	11
19 Mar 77		LAY BACK IN THE ARMS OF SOMEONE *RAK 251*	12	9
16 Jul 77	●	IT'S YOUR LIFE *RAK 260*	5	9
15 Oct 77	●	NEEDLES AND PINS *RAK 263*	10	9
28 Jan 78		FOR A FEW DOLLARS MORE *RAK 267*	17	6
20 May 78	●	OH CAROL *RAK 276*	5	13
23 Sep 78		MEXICAN GIRL *RAK 283*	19	9
19 Apr 80		TAKE GOOD CARE OF MY BABY *RAK 309*	34	7
13 May 95		LIVING NEXT DOOR TO ALICE (WHO THE F**K IS ALICE) *NOW CDWAG 245* [2]	64	2
12 Aug 95	●	LIVING NEXT DOOR TO ALICE (WHO THE F**K IS ALICE) (re-entry) *NOW CDWAG 245* [2]	3	17

[1] Smokey [2] Smokie featuring Roy 'Chubby' Brown

*'Living Next Door to Alice (Who The F**k Is Alice)' is a re-recorded version of 'Living Next Door to Alice'*

SMOKIN BEATS featuring Lyn EDEN
UK, male DJ / production duo and UK, female vocalist (3 WEEKS)

Date		Title / Label	pos	wks
17 Jan 98		DREAMS *AM:PM 5824711*	23	3

SMOKIN' MOJO FILTERS
UK / US, male / female vocal / instrumental charity group (5 WEEKS)

Date		Title / Label	pos	wks
23 Dec 95		COME TOGETHER (WAR CHILD) *Go! Discs GODCD 136*	19	5

SMOOTH *US, female vocalist (7 WEEKS)*

Date		Title / Label	pos	wks
22 Jul 95		MIND BLOWIN' *Jive JIVECD 379*	36	2
7 Oct 95		IT'S SUMMERTIME (LET IT GET INTO YOU) *Jive JIVECD 383*	46	1
16 Mar 96		LOVE GROOVE (GROOVE WITH YOU) *Jive JIVECD 390*	46	1
16 Mar 96		WE GOT IT *MCA MCSTD 48009* [1]	26	2
6 Jul 96		UNDERCOVER LOVER *Jive JIVECD 397*	41	1

[1] Immature featuring Smooth

Joe SMOOTH *US, male producer (4 WEEKS)*

Date		Title / Label	pos	wks
4 Feb 89		PROMISED LAND *DJ International DJIN 6*	56	4

SMOOTH TOUCH *US, male instrumental / production duo (1 WEEK)*

Date		Title / Label	pos	wks
2 Apr 94		HOUSE OF LOVE (IN MY HOUSE) *Six6 SIXCD 112*	58	1

Jean Jacques SMOOTHIE
UK, male DJ / producer – Steve Robson (7 WEEKS)

Date		Title / Label	pos	wks
13 Oct 01		2 PEOPLE *Echo ECSCD 112*	12	7

SMURFS *Holland, small blue creatures vocal group (52 WEEKS)*

Date		Title / Label	pos	wks
3 Jun 78	●	THE SMURF SONG *Decca F 13759* [1]	2	17
30 Sep 78		DIPPETY DAY *Decca F 13798* [1]	13	12
2 Dec 78		CHRISTMAS IN SMURFLAND *Decca F 13819*	19	7
7 Sep 96	●	I'VE GOT A LITTLE PUPPY *EMI TV CDSMURF 100*	4	10
21 Dec 96	●	YOUR CHRISTMAS WISH *EMI TV CDSMURF 102*	8	6

[1] Father Abraham and the Smurfs

Patty SMYTH – *See Don HENLEY*

SNAKEBITE *Italy, male production trio (2 WEEKS)*

Date		Title / Label	pos	wks
9 Aug 97		THE BIT GOES ON *Multiply CDMULTY 22*	25	2

SNAP (242 Top 500) *German-based producers Benito Benites (b. Michael Munzing) and John Garrett Virgo III (b. Luca Anzilotti) masterminded a string of worldwide dance hits for this act, which featured a host of mostly US vocalists and rappers including Turbo B, Jackie Harris, Penny Ford and Thea Austin (115 WEEKS)*

Date		Title / Label	pos	wks
24 Mar 90	★	THE POWER *Arista 113133*	1	15
16 Jun 90	●	OOOPS UP *Arista 113296*	5	12
22 Sep 90	●	CULT OF SNAP *Arista 113596*	8	7
8 Dec 90	●	MARY HAD A LITTLE BOY *Arista 113831*	8	10
30 Mar 91	●	SNAP MEGAMIX *Arista 114169*	10	6
21 Dec 91		THE COLOUR OF LOVE *Arista 114678*	54	3
4 Jul 92	★	RHYTHM IS A DANCER *Arista 115309*	1	19
9 Jan 93	●	EXTERMINATE! *Arista 74321106962* [1]	2	11
12 Jun 93	●	DO YOU SEE THE LIGHT (LOOKING FOR) *Arista 74321147622* [1]	10	8
17 Sep 94	●	WELCOME TO TOMORROW *Arista 74321223852* [2]	6	13
14 Jan 95		WELCOME TO TOMORROW (re-entry) *Arista 74321223852* [2]	75	1
1 Apr 95		THE FIRST THE LAST ETERNITY (TIL THE END) *Arista 74321254672* [2]	15	7
28 Oct 95		THE WORLD IN MY HANDS *Arista 74321314792* [2]	44	1
13 Apr 96		RAME *Arista 74321368902* [3]	50	1
24 Aug 96		THE POWER 96 *Arista 74321398672* [4]	42	1

[1] Snap featuring Niki Haris [2] Snap featuring Summer [3] Snap featuring Rukmani [4] Snap featuring Einstein

SNEAKER PIMPS
UK, male / female vocal / instrumental group (19 WEEKS)

Date		Title / Label	pos	wks
19 Oct 96		6 UNDERGROUND *Clean Up CUP 023CDS*	15	4
15 Mar 97		SPIN SPIN SUGAR *Clean Up CUP 033CDS*	21	3
7 Jun 97	●	6 UNDERGROUND (re-mix) *Clean Up CUP 036CDM*	9	4
30 Aug 97		POST MODERN SLEAZE *Clean Up CUP 038CDM*	22	3
7 Feb 98		SPIN SPIN SUGAR (re-mix) *Clean Up CUP 037X*	46	2
21 Aug 99		LOW FIVE *Clean Up CUP 052CDM*	39	2
30 Oct 99		TEN TO TWENTY *Clean Up CUP 054CDS*	56	1

THE OFFICIAL UK SINGLES CHART 50TH ANNIVERSARY

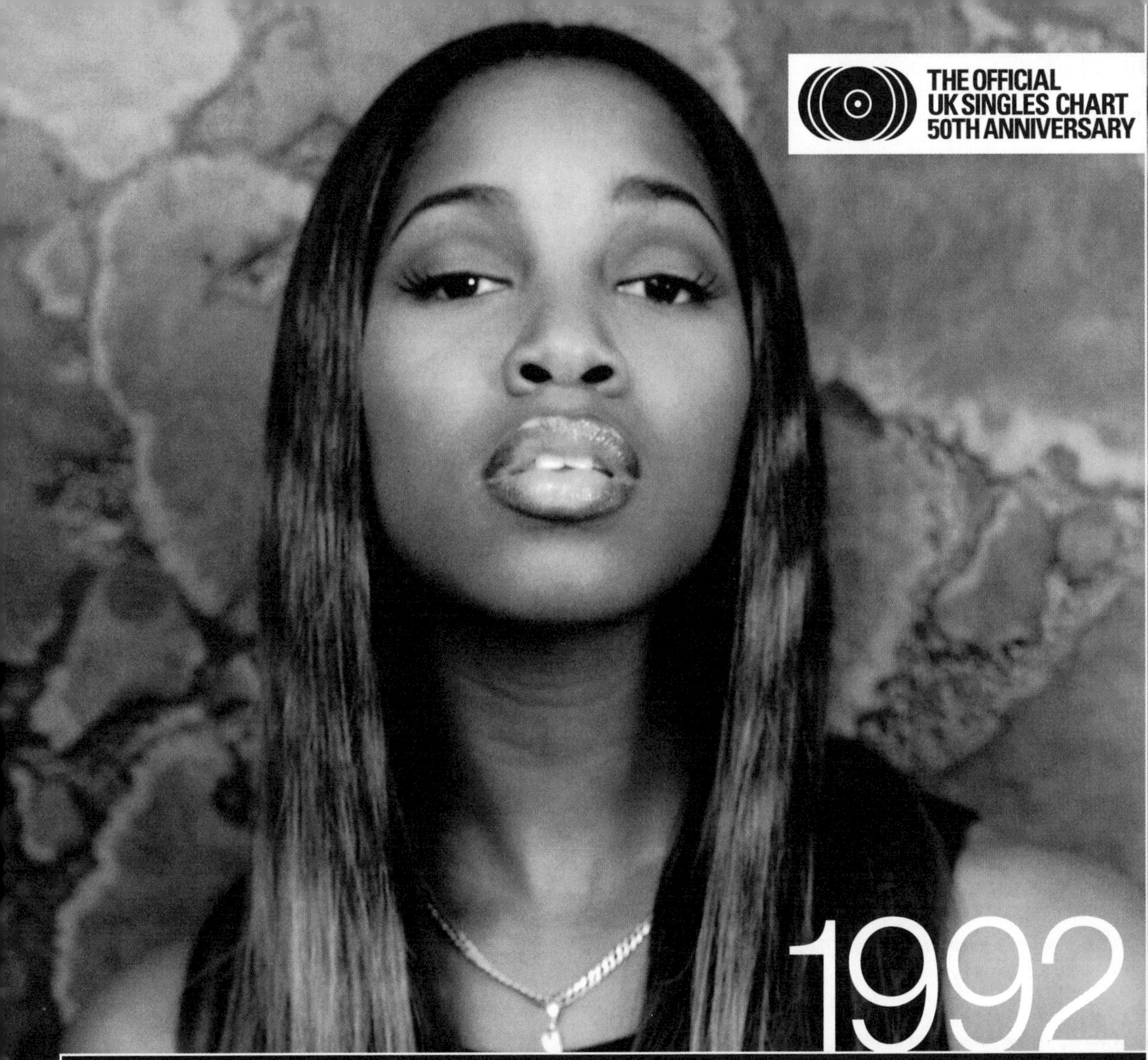

1992

IN THE YEAR IN WHICH QUEEN ELIZABETH HAD HER *ANNUS HORRIBILIS*, SOMALIA WAS RAVAGED BY FAMINE, BITTER FIGHTING BROKE OUT IN BOSNIA, SERBIAN FORCES CONTINUED THEIR SIEGE OF SARAJEVO, THE PREMIER LEAGUE WAS BORN AND THE WEDDING PRESENT EQUALLED ELVIS'S RECORD OF 12 HITS IN A YEAR, **JAMELIA** REMEMBERS HOW SHE HEARD HER HERO FOR THE FIRST TIME ON A TRIP TO THE HOSPITAL ...

“It was 1992. I was 12 years old and in hospital when I first heard **Mary J Blige**'s 'Real Love'. I would have it playing on my Walkman continuously. I sang along driving all the nurses and other patients mad! When I got out of hospital I saw the video for the first time. I wanted to get up and dance so much; unfortunately I couldn't because I was in a plaster cast which restricted my movement. Over the next couple of weeks I willed myself better just so I could pretend I was Mary! When the cast was removed that's just what I did. I had so much fun pretending I was a singer, so just imagine how much I'm loving being a real-life one!”

SINGLE OF THE YEAR 'I Will Always Love You' Whitney Houston
ALBUM OF THE YEAR 'Stars' Simply Red

SNIFF 'N' THE TEARS

UK, male vocal / instrumental group (5 WEEKS) pos/wks

23 Jun 79		**DRIVER'S SEAT** *Chiswick CHIS 105*	42	5

SNOOP DOGG

US, male rapper – Calvin Broadus (63 WEEKS) pos/wks

4 Dec 93		**WHAT'S MY NAME?** *Death Row A 8337CD* [1]	20	8
12 Feb 94		**GIN AND JUICE** *Death Row A 8316CD* [1]	39	3
20 Aug 94		**DOGGY DOGG WORLD** *Death Row A 8289CD* [1]	32	3
14 Dec 96		**SNOOP'S UPSIDE YA HEAD** *Interscope IND 95520* [2]	12	7
26 Apr 97		**WANTED DEAD OR ALIVE** *Def Jam 5744052* [3]	16	3
3 May 97		**VAPORS** *Interscope IND 95530* [1]	18	2
20 Sep 97		**WE JUST WANNA PARTY WITH YOU** *Columbia 6649902* [4]	21	2
24 Jan 98		**THA DOGGFATHER** *Interscope IND 95550* [1]	36	2
12 Dec 98		**COME AND GET WITH ME** *Elektra E 3787CD* [5]	58	1
25 Mar 00	●	**STILL D.R.E.** *Interscope 4972742* [6]	6	10
3 Feb 01	●	**THE NEXT EPISODE** *Interscope 4974762* [6]	3	10
17 Mar 01		**X** *Epic 6709072* [7]	14	7
28 Apr 01		**SNOOP DOGG** *Priority PTYCD 134*	13	5

[1] Snoop Doggy Dogg [2] Snoop Doggy Dogg featuring Charlie Wilson [3] 2Pac and Snoop Doggy Dogg [4] Snoop Doggy Dogg featuring JD [5] Keith Sweat featuring Snoop Dogg [6] Dr Dre featuring Snoop Dogg [7] Xzibit featuring Snoop Dogg

SNOW *Canada, male rapper – Darrin O'Brien (18 WEEKS)* pos/wks

13 Mar 93	●	**INFORMER** *East West America A 8436CD* ▲	2	15
5 Jun 93		**GIRL I'VE BEEN HURT** *East West America A 8417CD*	48	2
4 Sep 93		**UHH IN YOU** *Atlantic A 8378CD*	67	1

Mark SNOW *US, male instrumentalist – keyboards (15 WEEKS)* pos/wks

30 Mar 96	●	**THE X-FILES** *Warner Bros. W 0341CD*	2	15

Phoebe SNOW *US, female vocalist (7 WEEKS)* pos/wks

6 Jan 79		**EVERY NIGHT** *CBS 6842*	37	7

SNOWMAN – *See Peter AUTY and the SINFONIA OF LONDON conducted by Howard BLAKE*

SNOWMEN *UK, male vocal / instrumental group (12 WEEKS)* pos/wks

12 Dec 81		**HOKEY COKEY** *Stiff ODB 1*	18	8
18 Dec 82		**XMAS PARTY** *Solid STOP 006*	44	4

SNUG *UK, male vocal / instrumental group (1 WEEK)* pos/wks

18 Apr 98		**BEATNIK GIRL** *WEA WEA 151CDX*	55	1

SO *UK, male vocal / instrumental group (3 WEEKS)* pos/wks

13 Feb 88		**ARE YOU SURE** *Parlophone R 6173*	62	3

SO SOLID CREW

UK, male / female vocal / rap / production collective (22 WEEKS) pos/wks

18 Aug 01	★	**21 SECONDS** *Relentless RELENT 16CD* ■	1	13
17 Nov 01	●	**THEY DON'T KNOW** *Relentless RELENT 26CD*	3	7+
24 Nov 01		**21 SECONDS (re-entry)** *Relentless RELENT 16CD*	64	2

S.O.A.P. *Denmark, female vocal duo (2 WEEKS)* pos/wks

25 Jul 98		**THIS IS HOW WE PARTY** *Columbia 6661295*	36	2

SOAPY *UK, male instrumental / production duo (2 WEEKS)* pos/wks

14 Sep 96		**HORNY AS FUNK** *WEA WEA 074CD*	35	2

Gino SOCCIO *Canada, male instrumentalist – keyboards (5 WEEKS)* pos/wks

28 Apr 79		**DANCER** *Warner Bros. K 17357*	46	5

SOEUR SOURIRE – *See SINGING NUN (Soeur Sourire)*

SOFT CELL (273 Top 500)

Successful synth-driven duo from Leeds: Marc Almond (v), David Ball (k). The visually striking pair's revival of northern soul classic 'Tainted Love' was the Top UK single of 1981 and also broke the longevity record in the US Top 100 (107 WEEKS) pos/wks

1 Aug 81	★	**TAINTED LOVE** *Some Bizzare BZS 2*	1	16
14 Nov 81	●	**BEDSITTER** *Some Bizzare BZS 6*	4	12
9 Jan 82		**TAINTED LOVE (re-entry)** *Some Bizzare BZS 2*	43	10
6 Feb 82	●	**SAY HELLO WAVE GOODBYE** *Some Bizzare BZS 7*	3	9
29 May 82	●	**TORCH** *Some Bizzare BZS 9*	2	9
24 Jul 82		**TAINTED LOVE (2nd re-entry)** *Some Bizzare BZS 2*	50	4
21 Aug 82	●	**WHAT** *Some Bizzare BZS 11*	3	8
4 Dec 82		**WHERE THE HEART IS** *Some Bizzare BZS 16*	21	7
5 Mar 83		**NUMBERS / BARRIERS** *Some Bizzare BZS 17*	25	4
24 Sep 83		**SOUL INSIDE** *Some Bizzare BZS 20*	16	5
25 Feb 84		**DOWN IN THE SUBWAY** *Some Bizzare BZS 22*	24	6
9 Feb 85		**TAINTED LOVE (3rd re-entry)** *Some Bizzare BZS 2*	43	6
23 Mar 91		**SAY HELLO WAVE GOODBYE '91 (re-recording)** *Mercury SOFT 1* [1]	38	3
18 May 91	●	**TAINTED LOVE (re-issue)** *Mercury SOFT 2* [1]	5	8

[1] Soft Cell / Marc Almond

SOFT PARADE – *See ELECTRIC SOFT PARADE*

SOHO *UK, male / female vocal / instrumental group (11 WEEKS)* pos/wks

5 May 90		**HIPPY CHICK** *Savage 7SAV 106*	67	1
19 Jan 91	●	**HIPPY CHICK (re-entry)** *Savage 7SAV 106*	8	8
9 Nov 91		**BORN TO BE ALIVE** *MCA MCS 1578* [1]	51	2

[1] Adamski featuring Soho

The listed flip side of 'Born to Be Alive' was 'Never Goin' Down' by Adamski featuring Jimi Polo

SOLAR STONE *UK, male DJ / production trio (3 WEEKS)* pos/wks

21 Feb 98		**THE IMPRESSIONS EP** *Hooj Choons HOOJCD 57*	75	1
6 Nov 99		**SEVEN CITIES** *Hooj Choons HOOJ 85CD*	39	2

The Impressions EP: The Calling / Day By Day / The Calling / Day By Day / So Clear

SOLID GOLD CHARTBUSTERS

UK, male / female production / vocal group (1 WEEK) pos/wks

25 Dec 99		**I WANNA 1-2-1 WITH YOU** *Virgin VSCDT 1765*	62	1

SOLID HARMONIE *UK / US, female vocal group (11 WEEKS)* pos/wks

31 Jan 98		**I'LL BE THERE FOR YOU** *Jive JIVECD 437*	18	3
18 Apr 98		**I WANT YOU TO WANT ME** *Jive JIVECD 452*	16	3
15 Aug 98		**I WANNA LOVE YOU** *Jive 0521742*	20	4
21 Nov 98		**TO LOVE ONCE AGAIN** *Jive 0522472*	55	1

SOLO *UK, male producer – Stuart Crichton (4 WEEKS)* pos/wks

20 Jul 91		**RAINBOW (SAMPLE FREE)** *Reverb RVBT 003*	59	2
18 Jan 92		**COME ON!** *Reverb RVBT 008*	75	1
11 Sep 93		**COME ON! (re-mix)** *Stoatin' STOAT 003CD*	63	1

Sal SOLO *UK, male vocalist (13 WEEKS)* pos/wks

15 Dec 84		**SAN DAMIANO (HEART AND SOUL)** *MCA MCA 930*	15	10
6 Apr 85		**MUSIC AND YOU** *MCA MCA 946* [1]	52	3

[1] Sal Solo with the London Community Gospel Choir

SOLO U.S. *US, male vocal group (3 WEEKS)* pos/wks

3 Feb 96		**HEAVEN** *Perspective 5875212*	35	2
30 Mar 96		**WHERE DO U WANT ME TO PUT IT** *Perspective 5875312*	45	1

SOLUTION – *See Victor SIMONELLI presents SOLUTION*

Jimmy SOMERVILLE *UK, male vocalist (53 WEEKS)* pos/wks

11 Nov 89		**COMMENT TE DIRE ADIEU** *London LON 241* [1]	14	9
13 Jan 90	●	**YOU MAKE ME FEEL (MIGHTY REAL)** *London LON 249*	5	8
17 Mar 90		**READ MY LIPS (ENOUGH IS ENOUGH)** *London LON 254*	26	6

3 Nov 90 ●	TO LOVE SOMEBODY *London LON 281*	8	11
2 Feb 91	SMALLTOWN BOY (re-mix) *London LON 287* [2]	32	4
10 Aug 91	RUN FROM LOVE *London LON 301*	52	2
28 Jan 95	HEARTBEAT *London LONCD 358*	24	4
27 May 95	HURT SO GOOD *London LONCD 364*	15	6
28 Oct 95	BY YOUR SIDE *London LONCD 372*	41	2
13 Sep 97	DARK SKY *Gut CXGUT 11*	66	1

[1] Jimmy Somerville featuring June Miles-Kingston [2] Jimmy Somerville with Bronski Beat

See also BRONSKI BEAT; COMMUNARDS

SOMETHIN' FOR THE PEOPLE featuring TRINA and TAMARA

US, male vocal / instrumental group and female vocal duo (1 WEEK) pos/wks

7 Feb 98	MY LOVE IS THE SHHH! *Warner Bros W 0427CD*	64	1

SOMORE featuring Damon TRUEITT

US, male production group and male vocalist (2 WEEKS) pos/wks

24 Jan 98	I REFUSE (WHAT YOU WANT) *XL Recordings XLS 93CD*	21	2

SONGSTRESS

US, male production / vocal duo (1 WEEK) pos/wks

27 Feb 99	SEE LINE WOMAN '99 *Locked On LOX 106CD*	64	1

SONIA

(428 Top 500) *Bubbly teenage pop performer, b. Sonia Evans, 13 Feb 1971, Liverpool, UK. Singer / actress – the youngest UK female to reach No.1 since Mary Hopkin (1968) – was produced by the hit machine Stock Aitken and Waterman (78 WEEKS)* pos/wks

24 Jun 89 ★	YOU'LL NEVER STOP ME LOVING YOU *Chrysalis CHS 3385*	1	13
7 Oct 89	CAN'T FORGET YOU *Chrysalis CHS 3419*	17	6
9 Dec 89 ●	LISTEN TO YOUR HEART *Chrysalis CHS 3465*	10	10
7 Apr 90	COUNTING EVERY MINUTE *Chrysalis CHS 3492*	16	7
23 Jun 90	YOU'VE GOT A FRIEND *Jive CHILD 90* [1]	14	6
25 Aug 90	END OF THE WORLD *Chrysalis/PWL CHS 3557*	18	7
1 Jun 91 ●	ONLY FOOLS (NEVER FALL IN LOVE) *IQ ZB 44613*	10	8
31 Aug 91	BE YOUNG BE FOOLISH BE HAPPY *IQ ZB 44935*	22	5
16 Nov 91	YOU TO ME ARE EVERYTHING *IQ ZB 45121*	13	5
12 Sep 92	BOOGIE NIGHTS *Arista 74321113467*	30	3
1 May 93	BETTER THE DEVIL YOU KNOW *Arista 74321146872*	15	7
30 Jul 94	HOPELESSLY DEVOTED TO YOU *Cockney COCCD 2*	61	1

[1] Big Fun and Sonia featuring Gary Barnacle

SONIC SOLUTION

Belgium, male production duo – CJ Bolland and Steve Cop (1 WEEK) pos/wks

4 Apr 92	BEATSTIME *R&S RSUK 11*	59	1

SONIC SURFERS

Holland, male instrumental / production duo (2 WEEKS) pos/wks

20 Mar 93	TAKE ME UP *A & M AMCD 210* [1]	61	1
30 Jul 94	DON'T GIVE IT UP *Brilliant CDBRIL 6*	54	1

[1] Sonic Surfers featuring Jocelyn Brown

SONIC THE HEDGEHOG – *See HWA featuring SONIC THE HEDGEHOG*

SONIC YOUTH

US, male / female vocal / instrumental group (14 WEEKS) pos/wks

11 Jul 92	100% *DGC DGCS 11*	28	4
7 Nov 92	YOUTH AGAINST FASCISM *Geffen GFS 26*	52	2
3 Apr 93	SUGAR KANE *Geffen GFSTD 37*	26	3
7 May 94	BULL IN THE HEATHER *Geffen GFSTD 72*	24	2
10 Sep 94	SUPERSTAR *A & M 5807932*	45	2
11 Jul 98	SUNDAY *Geffen GFSTD 22332*	72	1

The listed flip side of 'Superstar' was 'Yesterday Once More' by Redd Kross

SONIQUE

UK, female vocalist / DJ – Sonia Clarke (42 WEEKS) pos/wks

13 Jun 98	I PUT A SPELL ON YOU *Serious SERR 001CD*	36	2
5 Dec 98	IT FEELS SO GOOD *Serious SERR 004CD*	24	3
3 Jun 00 ★	IT FEELS SO GOOD (re-mix) *Universal MCSTD 40233* ■	1	17
16 Sep 00 ●	SKY *Universal MCSTD 40240*	2	10
9 Dec 00 ●	I PUT A SPELL ON YOU (re-issue) *Universal MCSTD 40245*	8	10

SONNY

US, male vocalist – Salvatore Bono (11 WEEKS) pos/wks

19 Aug 65 ●	LAUGH AT ME *Atlantic AT 4038*	9	11

See also SONNY and CHER

SONNY and CHER

(426 Top 500) *Most successful US husband-and-wife recording team, Salvatore Bono, b 16 Feb 1935, Michigan, US, d. 5 Jan 1998, Cherilyn LaPierre, b. 20 May 1946, California, US. Married 1963-74 and was the major new act of 1965. Cher became a solo superstar and Sonny was elected mayor of Palm Springs (78 WEEKS)* pos/wks

12 Aug 65 ★	I GOT YOU BABE *Atlantic AT 4035* ▲	1	12
16 Sep 65	BABY DON'T GO *Reprise R 20309*	11	9
21 Oct 65	BUT YOU'RE MINE *Atlantic AT 4047*	17	8
17 Feb 66	WHAT NOW MY LOVE *Atlantic AT 4069*	13	11
30 Jun 66	HAVE I STAYED TOO LONG *Atlantic 584 018*	42	3
8 Sep 66 ●	LITTLE MAN *Atlantic 584 040*	4	10
17 Nov 66	LIVING FOR YOU *Atlantic 584 057*	44	4
2 Feb 67	THE BEAT GOES ON *Atlantic 584 078*	29	8
15 Jan 72 ●	ALL I EVER NEED IS YOU *MCA MU 1145*	8	12
22 May 93	I GOT YOU BABE (re-issue) *Epic 6592402*	66	1

See also SONNY; CHER

SONO

Germany, male production duo (1 WEEK) pos/wks

16 Jun 01	KEEP CONTROL *Code Blue BLU 020CD1*	66	1

SON'Z OF A LOOP DA LOOP ERA

UK, male producer – Danny Breaks (4 WEEKS) pos/wks

15 Feb 92	FAR OUT *Suburban Base SUBBASE 008*	36	3
17 Oct 92	PEACE + LOVEISM *Suburban Base SUBBASE 14*	60	1

SOOZY Q – *See BIG TIME CHARLIE*

SOPHIE – *See ZERO 7 featuring SIA and SOPHIE*

SORROWS

UK, male vocal / instrumental group (8 WEEKS) pos/wks

16 Sep 65	TAKE A HEART *Piccadilly 7N 35260*	21	8

S.O.S. BAND

US, male / female vocal / instrumental group (46 WEEKS) pos/wks

19 Jul 80	TAKE YOUR TIME (DO IT RIGHT) PART 1 *Tabu TBU 8564*	51	4
26 Feb 83	GROOVIN' (THAT'S WHAT WE'RE DOIN') *Tabu TBU A3120*	72	1
7 Apr 84	JUST BE GOOD TO ME *Tabu A 3626*	13	11
4 Aug 84	JUST THE WAY YOU LIKE IT *Tabu A 4621*	32	7
13 Oct 84	WEEKEND GIRL *Tabu A 4785*	51	5
29 Mar 86	THE FINEST *Tabu A 6997*	17	10
5 Jul 86	BORROWED LOVE *Tabu A 7241*	50	5
2 May 87	NO LIES *Tabu 650444 7*	64	3

Aaron SOUL

UK, male vocalist – Aaron Anyia (4 WEEKS) pos/wks

2 Jun 01	RING RING RING *Def Soul 5689042*	14	4

David SOUL

US, male actor / vocalist – David Solberg (56 WEEKS) pos/wks

18 Dec 76 ★	DON'T GIVE UP ON US *Private Stock PVT 84* ◆ ▲	1	16
26 Mar 77 ●	GOING IN WITH MY EYES OPEN *Private Stock PVT 99*	2	8
27 Aug 77 ★	SILVER LADY *Private Stock PVT 115*	1	14
17 Dec 77 ●	LET'S HAVE A QUIET NIGHT IN *Private Stock PVT 130*	8	9
27 May 78	IT SURE BRINGS OUT THE LOVE IN YOUR EYES *Private Stock PVT 137*	12	9

Jimmy SOUL

US, male vocalist (5 WEEKS) pos/wks

11 Jul 63	IF YOU WANNA BE HAPPY *Stateside SS 178* ▲	39	2
15 Jun 91	IF YOU WANNA BE HAPPY (re-issue) *Epic 6569647*	68	3

SOUL ASYLUM

US, male vocal / instrumental group (33 WEEKS) pos/wks

19 Jun 93	RUNAWAY TRAIN *Columbia 6593902*	37	8

		pos	wks
4 Sep 93	**SOMEBODY TO SHOVE** *Columbia 6596492*	34	3
13 Nov 93 ●	**RUNAWAY TRAIN (re-entry)** *Columbia 6593902*	7	11
22 Jan 94	**BLACK GOLD** *Columbia 6598442*	26	4
26 Mar 94	**SOMEBODY TO SHOVE (re-issue)** *Columbia 6602245*	32	3
15 Jul 95	**MISERY** *Columbia 6621092*	30	3
2 Dec 95	**JUST LIKE ANYONE** *Columbia 6624785*	52	1

SOUL BROTHERS *UK, male vocal / instrumental group (3 WEEKS)* pos/wks

		pos	wks
22 Apr 65	**I KEEP RINGING MY BABY** *Decca F 12116*	42	3

SOUL CITY ORCHESTRA

UK, male instrumental / production group (1 WEEK) pos/wks

		pos	wks
11 Dec 93	**IT'S JURASSIC** *London JURCD 1*	70	1

SOUL CITY SYMPHONY – *See Van McCOY*

SOUL FAMILY SENSATION

UK / US, male / female vocal / instrumental group (4 WEEKS) pos/wks

		pos	wks
11 May 91	**I DON'T EVEN KNOW IF I SHOULD CALL YOU BABY** *One Little Indian 47 TP7*	49	4

SOUL FOR REAL *US, male vocal group (4 WEEKS)* pos/wks

		pos	wks
8 Jul 95	**CANDY RAIN** *Uptown MCSTD 2052*	23	2
23 Mar 96	**EVERY LITTLE THING I DO** *Uptown MCSTD 48005*	31	2

SOUL II SOUL (354 Top 500) *Enormously influential dance music project led by entrepreneurial producer / DJ Jazzie B, b. Beresford Romeo, 16 Jan 1963, London. Act featured Nellee Hooper's innovative arrangements and was fronted by a succession of vocalists, most notably Caron Wheeler. Unlike UK contemporaries they were equally successful in US (89 WEEKS)* pos/wks

		pos	wks
21 May 88	**FAIRPLAY** *10 TEN 228* [1]	63	3
17 Sep 88	**FEEL FREE** *10 TEN 236* [2]	64	2
18 Mar 89 ●	**KEEP ON MOVING** *10 TEN 263* [3]	5	12
10 Jun 89 ★	**BACK TO LIFE (HOWEVER DO YOU WANT ME)** *10 TEN 265* [3]	1	14
9 Dec 89 ●	**GET A LIFE** *10 TEN 284*	3	13
5 May 90 ●	**A DREAM'S A DREAM** *10 TEN 300*	6	6
24 Nov 90	**MISSING YOU** *10 TEN 345* [4]	22	7
4 Apr 92 ●	**JOY** *Ten TEN 350*	4	7
13 Jun 92	**MOVE ME NO MOUNTAIN** *Ten TEN 400* [5]	31	4
26 Sep 92	**JUST RIGHT** *Ten TEN 410*	38	2
6 Nov 93	**WISH** *Virgin VSCDG 1480*	24	4
22 Jul 95	**LOVE ENUFF** *Virgin VSCDT 1527*	12	6
21 Oct 95	**I CARE (SOUL II SOUL)** *Virgin VSCDT 1560*	17	4
19 Oct 96	**KEEP ON MOVIN' (re-mix)** *Virgin VSCDT 1612*	31	2
30 Aug 97	**REPRESENT** *Island CID 668*	39	2
8 Nov 97	**PLEASURE DOME** *Island CID 669*	51	1

[1] Soul II Soul featuring Rose Windross [2] Soul II Soul featuring Do'reen [3] Soul II Soul featuring Caron Wheeler [4] Soul II Soul featuring Kym Mazelle [5] Soul II Soul, lead vocals Kofi

SOUL PROVIDERS featuring Michelle SHELLERS

UK, male production duo and US, female vocalist (1 WEEK) pos/wks

		pos	wks
14 Jul 01	**RISE** *AM:PM CDAMPM 147*	59	1

SOUL SONIC FORCE – *See Afrika BAMBAATAA, Paul OAKENFOLD*

S.O.U.L. S.Y.S.T.E.M. introducing Michelle VISAGE

US, male / female vocal / instrumental group (5 WEEKS) pos/wks

		pos	wks
16 Jan 93	**IT'S GONNA BE A LOVELY DAY** *Arista 74321125692*	17	5

See also C & C MUSIC FACTORY / CLIVILLES & COLE

SOUL U*NIQUE *UK, male / female vocal group (2 WEEKS)* pos/wks

		pos	wks
19 Feb 00	**BE MY FRIEND** *M&J MAJCD 2*	53	1
29 Jul 00	**3IL (THRILL)** *M&J MAJCD 3X*	66	1

SOUL VISION – *See EVERYTHING BUT THE GIRL*

SOULED OUT

Italy / US / UK, male / female vocal / instrumental group (1 WEEK) pos/wks

		pos	wks
9 May 92	**IN MY LIFE** *Columbia 6578367*	75	1

SOULSEARCHER

US, male / female production / vocal group (9 WEEKS) pos/wks

		pos	wks
13 Feb 99 ●	**CAN'T GET ENOUGH** *Defected DEFECT 1CDS*	8	7
8 Apr 00	**DO IT TO ME AGAIN** *Defected DFECT 15CDS*	32	2

SOULSONIC FORCE – *See Paul OAKENFOLD*

SOULWAX *Belgium, male vocal / instrumental duo (5 WEEKS)* pos/wks

		pos	wks
25 Mar 00	**CONVERSATION INTERCOM** *Pias Recordings PIASB 018CD*	65	1
24 Jun 00	**MUCH AGAINST EVERYONE'S ADVICE** *Pias Recordings PIASB 026CD*	56	1
30 Sep 00	**TOO MANY DJ'S** *Pias Recordings PIASB 036CD*	40	2
3 Mar 01	**CONVERSATION INTERCOM (re-mix)** *Pias Recordings PIASB 046CD*	50	1

SOUND 5 *UK, male vocal / instrumental group (1 WEEK)* pos/wks

		pos	wks
24 Apr 99	**ALA KABOO** *Gut CDGUT 23*	69	1

SOUND-DE-ZIGN *Holland, male DJ / production duo – Adri Blok and Arjen Rietvink (5 WEEKS)* pos/wks

		pos	wks
14 Apr 01	**HAPPINESS** *Nulife / Arista 74321844002*	19	5

SOUND FACTORY *Sweden, male vocal / instrumental duo (1 WEEK)* pos/wks

		pos	wks
5 Jun 93	**2 THE RHYTHM** *Logic 74321149422*	72	1

SOUND 9418 – *See Jonathan KING*

SOUND OF ONE featuring GLADEZZ

US, male / female vocal / instrumental duo (1 WEEK) pos/wks

		pos	wks
20 Nov 93	**AS I AM** *Cooltempo CDCOOL 280*	65	1

SOUNDGARDEN *US, male vocal / instrumental group (24 WEEKS)* pos/wks

		pos	wks
11 Apr 92	**JESUS CHRIST POSE** *A & M AM 862*	30	3
20 Jun 92	**RUSTY CAGE** *A & M AM 874*	41	1
21 Nov 92	**OUTSHINED** *A & M AM 0102*	50	1
26 Feb 94	**SPOONMAN** *A & M 5805392*	20	3
30 Apr 94	**THE DAY I TRIED TO LIVE** *A & M 5805952*	42	2
20 Aug 94	**BLACK HOLE SUN** *A & M 5807532*	12	5
28 Jan 95	**FELL ON BLACK DAYS** *A & M 5809472*	24	2
18 May 96	**PRETTY NOOSE** *A & M 5816202*	14	3
28 Sep 96	**BURDEN IN MY HAND** *A & M 5818552*	33	2
28 Dec 96	**BLOW UP THE OUTSIDE WORLD** *A & M 5819862*	40	2

SOUNDMAN and Don LLOYDIE with Elisabeth TROY

UK, male / female vocal / production group (2 WEEKS) pos/wks

		pos	wks
25 Feb 95	**GREATER LOVE** *Sound of Underground SOURCD 016*	49	2

SOUNDS INCORPORATED *UK, male instrumental group (11 WEEKS)* pos/wks

		pos	wks
23 Apr 64	**THE SPARTANS** *Columbia DB 7239*	30	6
30 Jul 64	**SPANISH HARLEM** *Columbia DB 7321*	35	5

SOUNDS NICE featuring Tim MYCROFT

UK, male instrumental group (11 WEEKS) pos/wks

		pos	wks
6 Sep 69	**LOVE AT FIRST SIGHT (JE T'AIME . . . MOI NON PLUS)** *Parlophone R 5797*	18	11

SOUNDS OF BLACKNESS

US, male / female gospel choir (32 WEEKS) pos/wks

		pos	wks
22 Jun 91	**OPTIMISTIC** *Perspective PERSS 786*	45	4
28 Sep 91	**THE PRESSURE PART 1** *Perspective PERSS 816*	71	1
15 Feb 92	**OPTIMISTIC (re-issue)** *Perspective PERSS 849*	28	4
25 Apr 92	**THE PRESSURE PART 1 (re-mix)** *Perspective PERSS 867*	49	2

8 May 93		**I'M GOING ALL THE WAY** *Perspective 5874252*	27	3
26 Mar 94		**I BELIEVE** *A & M 5874512*	17	4
2 Jul 94		**GLORYLAND** *Mercury MERCD 404* [1]	36	4
20 Aug 94		**EVERYTHING IS GONNA BE ALRIGHT** *A & M 5874672*	29	3
14 Jan 95		**I'M GOING ALL THE WAY (re-issue)** *A & M 5874832*	14	4
7 Jun 97		**SPIRIT** *A & M 5822292* [2]	35	2
14 Feb 98		**THE PRESSURE (2nd re-mix)** *AM:PM 5824872*	46	1

[1] Daryl Hall and the Sounds of Blackness [2] Sounds of Blackness / Craig Mack

SOUNDS ORCHESTRAL *UK, orchestra (18 WEEKS)* pos/wks

3 Dec 64	●	**CAST YOUR FATE TO THE WIND** *Piccadilly 7N 35206*	5	16
8 Jul 65		**MOONGLOW** *Piccadilly 7N 35248*	43	2

SOUNDSATION *UK, male producer (1 WEEK)* pos/wks

14 Jan 95		**PEACE AND JOY** *Ffrreedom TABCD 224*	48	1

SOUNDSCAPE *UK, male DJ / production group (1 WEEK)* pos/wks

14 Feb 98		**DUBPLATE CULTURE** *Satellite 74321552002*	61	1

SOUNDSOURCE
Sweden / UK, male instrumental / production group (1 WEEK) pos/wks

11 Jan 92		**TAKE ME UP** *ffrr FX 177*	62	1

SOUP DRAGONS *UK, male vocal / instrumental group (23 WEEKS)* pos/wks

20 Jun 87		**CAN'T TAKE NO MORE** *Raw TV RTV 3*	65	1
5 Sep 87		**SOFT AS YOUR FACE** *Raw TV RTV 4*	66	2
14 Jul 90	●	**I'M FREE** *Raw TV RTV 9* [1]	5	12
20 Oct 90		**MOTHER UNIVERSE** *Big Life BLR 30*	26	5
11 Apr 92		**DIVINE THING** *Big Life BLR 68*	53	3

[1] Soup Dragons featuring Junior Reid

SOURCE *UK, male producer – John Truelove (22 WEEKS)* pos/wks

2 Feb 91	●	**YOU GOT THE LOVE** *Truelove TLOVE 7001* [1]	4	11
26 Dec 92		**ROCK THE HOUSE** *React 12REACT 12* [2]	63	1
1 Mar 97	●	**YOU GOT THE LOVE (re-mix)** *React CDREACT 89* [1]	3	8
23 Aug 97		**CLOUDS** *XL Recordings XLS 83CD*	38	2

[1] Source featuring Candi Staton [2] Source featuring Nicole

SOURMASH *UK, male production trio (1 WEEK)* pos/wks

23 Dec 00		**PILGRIMAGE / MESCALITO** *Hooj Choons HOOJ 102*	73	1

SOUTH *UK, male vocal / instrumental group (1 WEEK)* pos/wks

17 Mar 01		**PAINT THE SILENCE** *Mo Wax MWR 134CD*	69	1

Joe SOUTH *US, male vocalist – Joe Souter (11 WEEKS)* pos/wks

5 Mar 69	●	**GAMES PEOPLE PLAY** *Capitol CL 15579*	6	11

SOUTH ST. PLAYER
US, male vocalist / producer – Roland Clark (1 WEEK) pos/wks

2 Sep 00		**WHO KEEPS CHANGING YOUR MIND** *Cream CREAM 4CD*	49	1

Jeri SOUTHERN *US, female vocalist (3 WEEKS)* pos/wks

21 Jun 57		**FIRE DOWN BELOW** *Brunswick 05665*	22	3

SOUTHLANDERS *Jamaica / UK, male vocal group (10 WEEKS)* pos/wks

22 Nov 57		**ALONE** *Decca F 10946*	17	10

SOUTHSIDE SPINNERS *Holland, male production duo – Marco Verkuylen and Benjamin Kuyten (7 WEEKS)* pos/wks

27 May 00	●	**LUVSTRUCK** *AM:PM CDAMPM 132*	9	7

SOUVLAKI *UK, male producer – Mark Summers (4 WEEKS)* pos/wks

15 Feb 97		**INFERNO** *Wonderboy WBOYD 003*	24	3
8 Aug 98		**MY TIME** *Wonderboy WBOYD 009*	63	1

SOVEREIGN COLLECTION *UK, orchestra (6 WEEKS)* pos/wks

3 Apr 71		**MOZART 40** *Capitol CL 15676*	27	6

Red SOVINE *US, male vocalist (8 WEEKS)* pos/wks

13 Jun 81	●	**TEDDY BEAR** *Starday SD 142*	4	8

SOX *UK, female vocal / instrumental group – lead vocal Samantha Fox (1 WEEK)* pos/wks

15 Apr 95		**GO FOR THE HEART** *Living Beat LBECD 33*	47	1

Bob B SOXX and the BLUE JEANS
US, male / female vocal group (2 WEEKS) pos/wks

31 Jan 63		**ZIP-A-DEE-DOO-DAH** *London HLU 9646*	45	2

SPACE *France, male instrumental group (12 WEEKS)* pos/wks

13 Aug 77	●	**MAGIC FLY** *Pye International 7N 25746*	2	12

SPACE *UK, male vocal / instrumental group (51 WEEKS)* pos/wks

6 Apr 96		**NEIGHBOURHOOD** *Gut CDGUT 1*	56	1
8 Jun 96		**FEMALE OF THE SPECIES** *Gut CDGUT 2*	14	10
7 Sep 96	●	**ME AND YOU VERSUS THE WORLD** *Gut CDGUT 4*	9	6
2 Nov 96		**NEIGHBOURHOOD (re-issue)** *Gut CDGUT 5*	11	6
22 Feb 97		**DARK CLOUDS** *Gut CDGUT 6*	14	4
10 Jan 98	●	**AVENGING ANGELS** *Gut CDGUT 16*	6	8
7 Mar 98	●	**THE BALLAD OF TOM JONES** *Gut CDGUT 018* [1]	4	8
4 Jul 98		**BEGIN AGAIN** *Gut CDGUT 19*	21	4
5 Dec 98		**THE BAD DAYS (EP)** *Gut CDGUT 22*	20	3
8 Jul 00		**DIARY OF A WIMP** *Gut CDGUT 34*	49	1

[1] Space with Cerys of Catatonia

Tracks on The Bad Days (EP): Bad Days / We Gotta Get Out of This Place / The Unluckiest Man in the World

SPACE BABY *UK, male producer – Matt Darey (1 WEEK)* pos/wks

8 Jul 95		**FREE YOUR MIND** *Hooj Choons HOOJ 34CD*	55	1

SPACE BROTHERS *UK, male production duo – Ricky Simmonds and Stephen Jones (19 WEEKS)* pos/wks

17 May 97		**SHINE** *Manifesto FESCD 23*	23	3
13 Dec 97		**FORGIVEN (I FEEL YOUR LOVE)** *Manifesto FESCD 36*	27	7
10 Jul 99		**LEGACY (SHOW ME LOVE)** *Manifesto FESCD 55*	31	3
9 Oct 99		**HEAVEN WILL COME** *Manifesto FESCD 61*	25	2
5 Feb 00		**SHINE 2000 (re-mix)** *Manifesto FESCD 67*	18	4

SPACE KITTENS *UK, male instrumental / production group (1 WEEK)* pos/wks

13 Apr 96		**STORM** *Hooj Choons HOOJCD 41*	58	1

SPACE MANOEVRES *UK, male producer – John Graham (2 WEEKS)* pos/wks

29 Jan 00		**STAGE ONE** *Hooj Choons HOOJ 79CD*	25	2

SPACE MONKEY *UK, male producer – Paul Goodchild (4 WEEKS)* pos/wks

8 Oct 83		**CAN'T STOP RUNNING** *Innervision A 3742*	53	4

SPACE RAIDERS *UK, male production trio (1 WEEK)* pos/wks

28 Mar 98		**GLAM RAID** *Skint SKINT 32CD*	68	1

SPACE 2000 *UK, male vocal / instrumental duo (1 WEEK)* pos/wks

12 Aug 95		**DO U WANNA FUNK** *Wired WIRED 218*	50	1

SPACECORN *Sweden, male DJ / producer – Daniel Ellenson (1 WEEK)* pos/wks

28 Apr 01		**AXEL F** *69 SN 069CD*	74	1

SPACEDUST *UK, male production duo – Paul Glancey and Duncan Glasson (12 WEEKS)* pos/wks

24 Oct 98	★	**GYM AND TONIC** *East West EW 188CD* ■	1	8

Date		Title / Label	pos	wks
9 Jan 99		**GYM AND TONIC (re-entry)** *East West EW 188CD*	55	2
27 Mar 99		**LET'S GET DOWN** *East West EW 195CD*	20	2

SPACEHOG *UK, male vocal / instrumental group (8 WEEKS)* pos/wks

Date		Title / Label	pos	wks
11 May 96		**IN THE MEANTIME** *Sire 7559643162*	70	1
28 Dec 96		**IN THE MEANTIME (re-entry)** *Sire 7559643162*	29	6
7 Feb 98		**CARRY ON** *Sire W 0428CD*	43	1

SPACEMAID *UK, male vocal / instrumental group (1 WEEK)* pos/wks

Date		Title / Label	pos	wks
5 Apr 97		**BABY COME ON** *Big Star STARC 105*	70	1

SPAGHETTI SURFERS
UK, male instrumental / production duo (1 WEEK) pos/wks

Date		Title / Label	pos	wks
22 Jul 95		**MISIRLOU (THE THEME TO THE MOTION PICTURE 'PULP FICTION')** *Tempo Toons CDTOON 4*	55	1

SPAGNA *Italy, female vocalist – Ivana Spagna (23 WEEKS)* pos/wks

Date		Title / Label	pos	wks
25 Jul 87	●	**CALL ME** *CBS 650279 7*	2	12
17 Oct 87		**EASY LADY** *CBS 651169 7*	62	3
20 Aug 88		**EVERY GIRL AND BOY** *CBS SPAG 1*	23	8

SPANDAU BALLET (133 Top 500) *Kilt-clad New Romantic revolutionaries. This London band went on to become smart-suited Top 10 regulars: Tony Hadley (v), Gary Kemp (g), Martin Kemp (b), Steve Norman (g/sax/prc), John Keeble (d). The Kemp brothers later went into the movies and TV, including lead roles in 'The Krays' (1990) and, for Martin, a part in 'EastEnders' (159 WEEKS)* pos/wks

Date		Title / Label	pos	wks
15 Nov 80	●	**TO CUT A LONG STORY SHORT** *Reformation CHS 2473*	5	11
24 Jan 81		**THE FREEZE** *Reformation CHS 2486*	17	8
4 Apr 81	●	**MUSCLEBOUND / GLOW** *Reformation CHS 2509*	10	10
18 Jul 81	●	**CHANT NO.1 (I DON'T NEED THIS PRESSURE ON)** *Reformation CHS 2528*	3	10
14 Nov 81		**PAINT ME DOWN** *Chrysalis CHS 2560*	30	5
30 Jan 82		**SHE LOVED LIKE DIAMOND** *Chrysalis CHS 2585*	49	4
10 Apr 82	●	**INSTINCTION** *Chrysalis CHS 2602*	10	11
2 Oct 82	●	**LIFELINE** *Chrysalis CHS 2642*	7	9
12 Feb 83		**COMMUNICATION** *Reformation CHS 2662*	12	10
23 Apr 83	★	**TRUE** *Reformation SPAN 1*	1	12
13 Aug 83	●	**GOLD** *Reformation SPAN 2*	2	9
9 Jun 84	●	**ONLY WHEN YOU LEAVE** *Reformation SPAN 3*	3	9
18 Aug 84		**ONLY WHEN YOU LEAVE (re-entry)** *Reformation SPAN 3*	74	1
25 Aug 84	●	**I'LL FLY FOR YOU** *Reformation SPAN 4*	9	9
20 Oct 84		**HIGHLY STRUNG** *Reformation SPAN 5*	15	5
8 Dec 84		**ROUND AND ROUND** *Reformation SPAN 6*	18	8
26 Jul 86		**FIGHT FOR OURSELVES** *Reformation A 7264*	15	7
8 Nov 86	●	**THROUGH THE BARRICADES** *Reformation SPANS 1*	6	10
14 Feb 87		**HOW MANY LIES** *Reformation SPANS 2*	34	4
3 Sep 88		**RAW** *CBS SPANS 3*	47	3
26 Aug 89		**BE FREE WITH YOUR LOVE** *CBS SPANS 4*	42	4

SPARKLE *US, female vocalist (10 WEEKS)* pos/wks

Date		Title / Label	pos	wks
18 Jul 98	●	**BE CAREFUL** *Jive 0521452* [1]	7	6
5 Sep 98		**BE CAREFUL (re-entry)** *Jive 0521452* [1]	75	1
7 Nov 98		**TIME TO MOVE ON** *Jive 0522032*	40	2
28 Aug 99		**LOVIN' YOU** *Jive 0523450*	65	1

[1] Sparkle featuring R Kelly

SPARKLEHORSE *US, male vocal / instrumental group (2 WEEKS)* pos/wks

Date		Title / Label	pos	wks
31 Aug 96		**RAINMAKER** *Capitol CDCL 777*	61	1
17 Oct 98		**SICK OF GOODBYES** *Parlophone CDCLS 808*	57	1

SPARKS (409 Top 500) *Eccentric pop / rock group, formed by Californian-born brothers Russell (v), 5 Oct 1953 and Ron Mael (k) 12 Aug 1948. Relocated to UK in 1973 and proved more successful in Europe than in their homeland. Voted Top Newcomers in the 1974 Record Mirror poll (81 WEEKS)* pos/wks

Date		Title / Label	pos	wks
4 May 74	●	**THIS TOWN AIN'T BIG ENOUGH FOR BOTH OF US** *Island WIP 6193*	2	10
20 Jul 74	●	**AMATEUR HOUR** *Island WIP 6203*	7	9
19 Oct 74		**NEVER TURN YOUR BACK ON MOTHER EARTH** *Island WIP 6211*	13	7
18 Jan 75		**SOMETHING FOR THE GIRL WITH EVERYTHING** *Island WIP 6221*	17	7
19 Jul 75		**GET IN THE SWING** *Island WIP 6236*	27	7
4 Oct 75		**LOOKS LOOKS LOOKS** *Island WIP 6249*	26	4
21 Apr 79		**THE NUMBER ONE SONG IN HEAVEN** *Virgin VS 244*	14	12
21 Jul 79	●	**BEAT THE CLOCK** *Virgin VS 270*	10	9
27 Oct 79		**TRYOUTS FOR THE HUMAN RACE** *Virgin VS 289*	45	5
29 Oct 94		**WHEN DO I GET TO SING 'MY WAY'** *Logic 74321234472*	38	3
11 Mar 95		**WHEN I KISS YOU (I HEAR CHARLIE PARKER PLAYING)** *Logic 74321264272*	36	2
20 May 95		**WHEN DO I GET TO SING 'MY WAY' (re-issue)** *Logic 74321274002*	32	2
9 Mar 96		**NOW THAT I OWN THE BBC** *Logic 74321348672*	60	1
25 Oct 97		**THE NUMBER ONE SONG IN HEAVEN (re-recording)** *Roadrunner RR 22692*	70	1
13 Dec 97		**THIS TOWN AIN'T BIG ENOUGH FOR BOTH OF US** *Roadrunner RR 22513* [1]	40	2

[1] Sparks vs Faith No More

Group was a UK / US group for first six hits

Bubba SPARXXX *US, male rapper – Warren Mathis (6 WEEKS)* pos/wks

Date		Title / Label	pos	wks
24 Nov 01	●	**UGLY** *Interscope / Polydor 4976542*	7	6+

SPEAR OF DESTINY *UK, male vocal / instrumental group (43 WEEKS)* pos/wks

Date		Title / Label	pos	wks
21 May 83		**THE WHEEL** *Epic A 3372*	59	5
21 Jan 84		**PRISONER OF LOVE** *Epic A 4068*	59	3
14 Apr 84		**LIBERATOR** *Epic A 4310*	67	2
15 Jun 85		**ALL MY LOVE (ASK NOTHING)** *Epic A 6333*	61	3
10 Aug 85		**COME BACK** *Epic A 6445*	55	3
7 Feb 87		**STRANGERS IN OUR TOWN** *10 TEN 148*	49	4
4 Apr 87		**NEVER TAKE ME ALIVE** *10 TEN 162*	14	11
25 Jul 87		**WAS THAT YOU?** *10 TEN 173*	55	4
3 Oct 87		**THE TRAVELLER** *10 TEN 189*	44	3
24 Sep 88		**SO IN LOVE WITH YOU** *Virgin VS 1123*	36	5

SPEARHEAD *US, male vocal / instrumental group (5 WEEKS)* pos/wks

Date		Title / Label	pos	wks
17 Dec 94		**OF COURSE YOU CAN** *Capitol CDCL 733*	74	1
22 Apr 95		**HOLE IN THE BUCKET** *Capitol CDCL 742*	55	1
15 Jul 95		**PEOPLE IN THA MIDDLE** *Capitol CDCLS 752*	49	2
15 Mar 97		**WHY OH WHY** *Capital CDCL 785*	45	1

Billie Jo SPEARS *US, female vocalist (40 WEEKS)* pos/wks

Date		Title / Label	pos	wks
12 Jul 75	●	**BLANKET ON THE GROUND** *United Artists UP 35805*	6	13
17 Jul 76	●	**WHAT I'VE GOT IN MIND** *United Artists UP 36118*	4	13
11 Dec 76		**SING ME AN OLD FASHIONED SONG** *United Artists UP 36179*	34	9
21 Jul 79		**I WILL SURVIVE** *United Artists UP 601*	47	5

Britney SPEARS (244 Top 500) *World's top selling teenager with album sales exceeding 37 million, b. 2 Dec 1981, Louisiana, US. Broke debut-act first-week UK sales record (464,000 for 'Baby One More Time') and is the youngest million-selling female in the history of the UK singles chart (114 WEEKS)* pos/wks

Date		Title / Label	pos	wks
27 Feb 99	★	**BABY ONE MORE TIME** *Jive 0522752* ◆ ■ ▲	1	22
26 Jun 99	●	**SOMETIMES** *Jive 0523202*	3	16
2 Oct 99	●	**(YOU DRIVE ME) CRAZY** *Jive 0550582*	5	11
29 Jan 00	★	**BORN TO MAKE YOU HAPPY** *Jive 9250022* ■	1	12
13 May 00	★	**OOPS!...I DID IT AGAIN** *Jive 9250542* ■	1	14
26 Aug 00	●	**LUCKY** *Jive 9251022*	5	11
16 Dec 00	●	**STRONGER** *Jive 9251502*	7	10
7 Apr 01		**DON'T LET ME BE THE LAST TO KNOW** *Jive 9251982*	12	8
27 Oct 01	●	**I'M A SLAVE 4 U** *Jive 9252892*	4	10+

SPECIALS (300 Top 500) *Midlands-based septet who led the early 1980s ska revival and, under Jerry Dammers (k), founded the trailblazing indie label 2 Tone. In 1981, Terry Hall (v), Neville Staples (v) and Lynval Golding (g) broke away to form Fun Boy Three (101 WEEKS)* pos/wks

Date		Title / Label	pos	wks
28 Jul 79	●	**GANGSTERS** *2 Tone CHSTT 1* [1]	6	12
27 Oct 79	●	**A MESSAGE TO YOU RUDY / NITE KLUB** *2 Tone CHSTT 5* [2]	10	14

UK No.1 ★ UK Top 10 ● Still on chart + UK million seller ◆ UK entry at No.1 ■ US No.1 ▲

Date	Title / Label	pos	wks
26 Jan 80 ★	**THE SPECIAL AKA LIVE EP** *2 Tone CHSTT 7* [1]	1	10
24 May 80 ●	**RAT RACE / RUDE BUOYS OUTA JAIL** *2 Tone CHSTT 11*	5	9
20 Sep 80 ●	**STEREOTYPE / INTERNATIONAL JET SET** *2 Tone CHSTT 13*	6	8
13 Dec 80 ●	**DO NOTHING / MAGGIE'S FARM** *2 Tone CHSTT 16*	4	11
20 Jun 81 ★	**GHOST TOWN** *2 Tone CHSTT 17*	1	14
23 Jan 82	**THE BOILER** *2 Tone CHSTT 18* [3]	35	5
3 Sep 83	**RACIST FRIEND / BRIGHT LIGHTS** *2 Tone CHSTT 25* [4]	60	3
17 Mar 84 ●	**NELSON MANDELA** *2 Tone CHSTT 26* [4]	9	10
8 Sep 84	**WHAT I LIKE MOST ABOUT YOU IS YOUR GIRLFRIEND** *2 Tone CHSTT 27* [4]	51	4
10 Feb 96	**HYPOCRITE** *Kuff KUFFD 3*	66	1

[1] Special AKA [2] Specials (featuring Rico+) [3] Rhoda with the Special AKA [4] Special A.K.A.

Tracks on The Special AKA Live EP: Too Much Too Young / Guns of Navarone / Long Shot Kick De Bucket / The Liquidator / Skinhead Moonstomp. 'Maggie's Farm' listed with 'Do Nothing' only from 10 Jan 1981. Group was male / female for last four hits

SPECTRUM *UK, male instrumental / production group (1 WEEK)* pos/wks

Date	Title / Label	pos	wks
26 Sep 92	**TRUE LOVE WILL FIND YOU IN THE END** *Silvertone ORE 44*	70	1

Chris SPEDDING
UK, male vocalist / instrumentalist – guitar (8 WEEKS) pos/wks

Date	Title / Label	pos	wks
23 Aug 75	**MOTOR BIKING** *RAK 210*	14	8

SPEECH *US, male vocalist (2 WEEKS)* pos/wks

Date	Title / Label	pos	wks
17 Feb 96	**LIKE MARVIN GAYE SAID (WHAT'S GOING ON)** *Cooltempo CDCOOL 314*	35	2

SPEEDY *UK, male / female vocal / instrumental group (1 WEEK)* pos/wks

Date	Title / Label	pos	wks
9 Nov 96	**BOY WONDER** *Boiler House! BOIL 2CD*	56	1

SPELLBOUND *India, female vocal duo (1 WEEK)* pos/wks

Date	Title / Label	pos	wks
31 May 97	**HEAVEN ON EARTH** *East West EW 098CD*	73	1

Johnnie SPENCE *UK, orchestra (15 WEEKS)* pos/wks

Date	Title / Label	pos	wks
1 Mar 62	**THE 'DR KILDARE' THEME** *Parlophone R 4872*	15	15

Don SPENCER *UK, male vocalist (12 WEEKS)* pos/wks

Date	Title / Label	pos	wks
21 Mar 63	**FIREBALL** *HMV POP 1087*	32	11
13 Jun 63	**FIREBALL (re-entry)** *HMV POP 1087*	49	1

Tracie SPENCER *US, female vocalist (3 WEEKS)* pos/wks

Date	Title / Label	pos	wks
4 May 91	**THIS HOUSE** *Capitol CL 612*	65	2
6 Nov 99	**IT'S ALL ABOUT YOU (NOT ABOUT ME)** *Parlophone Rhythm Series CDCL 815*	65	1

Jon SPENCER BLUES EXPLOSION
US, male vocal / instrumental group (1 WEEK) pos/wks

Date	Title / Label	pos	wks
10 May 97	**WAIL** *Mute CDMUTE 204*	66	1

SPHINX *UK / US, male vocal / instrumental group (2 WEEKS)* pos/wks

Date	Title / Label	pos	wks
25 Mar 95	**WHAT HOPE HAVE I** *Champion CHAMPCD 318*	43	2

SPICE GIRLS (109 Top 500) *Britain's most successful female vocal group: Geri Halliwell (Ginger Spice – left 1998), Melanie Chisholm (Mel C / Sporty Spice), Emma Bunton (Baby Spice), Victoria Adams – then Beckham (Posh Spice), Melanie Brown (Mel B / Mel G / Scary Spice). The girl-power group was the first act to put its first six singles at No.1 (179 WEEKS)* pos/wks

Date	Title / Label	pos	wks
20 Jul 96 ★	**WANNABE** *Virgin VSCDX 1588* ◆ ▲	1	26
26 Oct 96 ★	**SAY YOU'LL BE THERE** *Virgin VSCDT 1601* ■	1	17
28 Dec 96 ★	**2 BECOME 1** *Virgin VSCDT 1607* ◆ ■	1	19
15 Mar 97 ★	**MAMA / WHO DO YOU THINK YOU ARE** *Virgin VSCDT 1623* ■	1	15
17 May 97	**2 BECOME 1 (re-entry)** *Virgin VSCDT 1607*	54	4
25 Oct 97 ★	**SPICE UP YOUR LIFE** *Virgin VSCDT 1660* ■	1	15
27 Dec 97 ★	**TOO MUCH** *Virgin VSCDR 1669* ■	1	15
21 Mar 98 ●	**STOP** *Virgin VSCDT 1679*	2	15
11 Jul 98	**STOP (re-entry)** *Virgin VSCDT 1679*	52	2
1 Aug 98 ★	**VIVA FOREVER** *Virgin VSCDT 1692* ■	1	13
26 Dec 98 ★	**GOODBYE** *Virgin VSCDT 1721* ■	1	21
4 Nov 00 ★	**HOLLER / LET LOVE LEAD THE WAY** *Virgin VSCDT 1788* ■	1	17

See also Melanie B; Melanie C; Emma BUNTON; Victoria BECKHAM; Geri HALLIWELL

SPIDER *UK, male vocal / instrumental group (5 WEEKS)* pos/wks

Date	Title / Label	pos	wks
5 Mar 83	**WHY D'YA LIE TO ME** *RCA 313*	65	2
10 Mar 84	**HERE WE GO ROCK 'N' ROLL** *A & M AM 180*	57	3

SPIKEY TEE – *See BOMB THE BASS*

SPILLER *Italy / UK, male / female production / vocal duo – Cristiano Spiller and Sophie Ellis-Bextor (24 WEEKS)* pos/wks

Date	Title / Label	pos	wks
26 Aug 00 ★	**GROOVEJET (IF THIS AIN'T LOVE)** *Positiva CDTIV 137* ■	1	24

See also Sophie ELLIS-BEXTOR

SPIN CITY *UK / Ireland, male vocal group (3 WEEKS)* pos/wks

Date	Title / Label	pos	wks
26 Aug 00	**LANDSLIDE** *Epic 6696132*	30	3

SPIN DOCTORS *US, male vocal / instrumental group (28 WEEKS)* pos/wks

Date	Title / Label	pos	wks
15 May 93 ●	**TWO PRINCES** *Epic 6591452*	3	15
14 Aug 93	**LITTLE MISS CAN'T BE WRONG** *Epic 6584892*	23	5
9 Oct 93	**JIMMY OLSEN'S BLUES** *Epic 6597582*	40	2
4 Dec 93	**WHAT TIME IS IT** *Epic 6599552*	56	1
25 Jun 94	**CLEOPATRA'S CAT** *Epic 6604192*	29	2
30 Jul 94	**YOU LET YOUR HEART GO TOO FAST** *Epic 6606612*	66	1
29 Oct 94	**MARY JANE** *Epic 6609772*	55	1
8 Jun 96	**SHE USED TO BE MINE** *Epic 6632682*	55	1

SPINAL TAP *US / UK, male vocal / instrumental group (3 WEEKS)* pos/wks

Date	Title / Label	pos	wks
28 Mar 92	**BITCH SCHOOL** *MCA MCS 1624*	35	2
2 May 92	**THE MAJESTY OF ROCK** *MCA MCS 1629*	61	1

SPINNERS – *See DETROIT SPINNERS*

SPIRAL TRIBE *UK, male / female vocal / instrumental group (2 WEEKS)* pos/wks

Date	Title / Label	pos	wks
29 Aug 92	**BREACH THE PEACE (EP)** *Butterfly BLRT 79*	66	1
21 Nov 92	**FORWARD THE REVOLUTION** *Butterfly BLRT 85*	70	1

Tracks on Breach the Peace (EP): Breach the Peace / Do It / Seven / 25 Minute Warning

SPIRITS *UK, male / female vocal duo (5 WEEKS)* pos/wks

Date	Title / Label	pos	wks
19 Nov 94	**DON'T BRING ME DOWN** *MCA MCSTD 2018*	31	3
8 Apr 95	**SPIRIT INSIDE** *MCA MCSTD 2045*	39	2

SPIRITUAL COWBOYS – *See Dave STEWART*

SPIRITUALIZED
UK, male / female vocal / instrumental group (16 WEEKS) pos/wks

Date	Title / Label	pos	wks
30 Jun 90	**ANYWAY THAT YOU WANT ME / STEP INTO THE BREEZE** *Dedicated ZB 43783*	75	1
17 Aug 91	**RUN** *Dedicated SPIRT 002*	59	1
25 Jul 92	**MEDICATION** *Dedicated SPIRT 005T*	55	1
23 Oct 93	**ELECTRIC MAINLINE** *Dedicated SPIRT 007CD*	49	1
4 Feb 95	**LET IT FLOW** *Dedicated SPIRT 009CD* [1]	30	2
9 Aug 97	**ELECTRICITY** *Dedicated SPIRT 012CD1*	32	2
14 Feb 98	**I THINK I'M IN LOVE** *Dedicated SPIRT 014CD*	27	2
6 Jun 98	**THE ABBEY ROAD EP** *Dedicated SPIRT 015CD*	39	2
15 Sep 01	**STOP YOUR CRYING** *Spaceman / Arista OPM 002*	18	3
8 Dec 01	**OUT OF SIGHT** *Spaceman / Arista OPM 005*	65	1

[1] Spiritualized Electric Mainline

Tracks on The Abbey Road EP: Come Together / Broken Heart / Broken Heart (instrumental)

SPIRO and WIX *UK, male instrumental duo (2 WEEKS)* pos/wks

Date	Title / Label	pos	wks
10 Aug 96	**TARA'S THEME** *EMI Premier PRESCD 4*	29	2

SPITTING IMAGE *UK, male / female latex puppets (18 WEEKS)* pos/wks

10 May 86 ★	**THE CHICKEN SONG** *Virgin SPIT 1*		1	10
26 Jul 86	**THE CHICKEN SONG (re-entry)** *Virgin SPIT 1*		67	1
6 Dec 86	**SANTA CLAUS IS ON THE DOLE / FIRST ATHEIST TABERNACLE CHOIR** *Virgin VS 921*		22	7

SPLINTER *UK, male vocal / instrumental duo – Bill Elliott and Bob Purvis (10 WEEKS)* pos/wks

2 Nov 74	**COSTAFINE TOWN** *Dark Horse AMS 7135*	17	10

SPLIT ENZ
New Zealand / UK, male vocal / instrumental group (15 WEEKS) pos/wks

16 Aug 80	**I GOT YOU** *A & M AMS 7546*	12	11
23 May 81	**HISTORY NEVER REPEATS** *A & M AMS 8128*	63	4

A SPLIT SECOND
Belgium / Italy, male instrumental / production group (1 WEEK) pos/wks

14 Dec 91	**FLESH** *ffrr FX 178*	68	1

SPLODGENESSABOUNDS
UK, male vocal / instrumental group (17 WEEKS) pos/wks

14 Jun 80 ●	**SIMON TEMPLAR / TWO PINTS OF LAGER AND A PACKET OF CRISPS PLEASE** *Deram BUM 1*	7	8
6 Sep 80	**TWO LITTLE BOYS / HORSE** *Deram ROLF 1*	26	7
13 Jun 81	**COWPUNK MEDLUM** *Deram BUM 3*	69	2

SPOILED & ZIGO *Israel, male DJ / production duo (3 WEEKS)* pos/wks

12 Aug 00	**MORE & MORE** *Manifesto FESCD 72*	31	3

SPONGE *US, male vocal / instrumental group (1 WEEK)* pos/wks

19 Aug 95	**PLOWED** *Work 6623162*	74	1

SPOOKS *US, male / female vocal / rap group (17 WEEKS)* pos/wks

27 Jan 01 ●	**THINGS I'VE SEEN** *Epic 6706722*	6	10
5 May 01	**KARMA HOTEL** *Epic 6709012*	15	6
15 Sep 01	**SWEET REVENGE** *Epic 6718072*	67	1

SPOOKY *UK, male vocal / instrumental duo (1 WEEK)* pos/wks

13 Mar 93	**SCHMOO** *Guerilla GRRR 45CD*	72	1

SPORTY THIEVZ *US, male rap / vocal group (6 WEEKS)* pos/wks

10 Jul 99	**NO PIGEONS** *Columbia / Roc-A-Blok / Ruffhouse 6676022*	21	6

SPOTNICKS *Sweden, male instrumental group (37 WEEKS)* pos/wks

14 Jun 62	**ORANGE BLOSSOM SPECIAL** *Oriole CB 1724*	29	10
6 Sep 62	**ROCKET MAN** *Oriole CB 1755*	38	9
31 Jan 63	**HAVA NAGILA** *Oriole CB 1790*	13	12
25 Apr 63	**JUST LISTEN TO MY HEART** *Oriole CB 1818*	36	6

Dusty SPRINGFIELD (77 Top 500) *One of Britain's leading female vocalists of the 1960s, b. Mary O'Brien, 16 Apr 1939, London, d. 2 Mar 1999. After leaving The Springfields in 1963, she had numerous transatlantic solo hits, and during the Sixties was regularly voted UK's Top Female Singer (211 WEEKS)* pos/wks

21 Nov 63 ●	**I ONLY WANT TO BE WITH YOU** *Philips BF 1292*	4	18
20 Feb 64	**STAY AWHILE** *Philips BF 1313*	13	10
2 Jul 64 ●	**I JUST DON'T KNOW WHAT TO DO WITH MYSELF** *Philips BF 1348*	3	12
22 Oct 64 ●	**LOSING YOU** *Philips BF 1369*	9	13
18 Feb 65	**YOUR HURTIN' KINDA LOVE** *Philips BF 1396*	37	4
1 Jul 65 ●	**IN THE MIDDLE OF NOWHERE** *Philips BF 1418*	8	10
16 Sep 65 ●	**SOME OF YOUR LOVIN'** *Philips BF 1430*	8	12
27 Jan 66	**LITTLE BY LITTLE** *Philips BF 1466*	17	9
31 Mar 66 ★	**YOU DON'T HAVE TO SAY YOU LOVE ME** *Philips BF 1482*	1	13
7 Jul 66 ●	**GOIN' BACK** *Philips BF 1502*	10	10
15 Sep 66 ●	**ALL I SEE IS YOU** *Philips BF 1510*	9	12
23 Feb 67	**I'LL TRY ANYTHING** *Philips BF 1553*	13	9
25 May 67	**GIVE ME TIME** *Philips BF 1577*	24	6
10 Jul 68 ●	**I CLOSE MY EYES AND COUNT TO TEN** *Philips BF 1682*	4	12
4 Dec 68 ●	**SON-OF-A PREACHER MAN** *Philips BF 1730*	9	9
20 Sep 69	**AM I THE SAME GIRL** *Philips BF 1811*	43	3
18 Oct 69	**AM I THE SAME GIRL (re-entry)** *Philips BF 1811*	46	1
19 Sep 70	**HOW CAN I BE SURE** *Philips 6006 045*	36	4
20 Oct 79	**BABY BLUE** *Mercury DUSTY 4*	61	5
22 Aug 87 ●	**WHAT HAVE I DONE TO DESERVE THIS?** *Parlophone R 6163* [1]	2	9
25 Feb 89	**NOTHING HAS BEEN PROVED** *Parlophone R 6207*	16	7
2 Dec 89	**IN PRIVATE** *Parlophone R 6234*	14	10
26 May 90	**REPUTATION** *Parlophone R 6253*	38	6
24 Nov 90	**ARRESTED BY YOU** *Parlophone R 6266*	70	2
30 Oct 93	**HEART AND SOUL** *Columbia 6598562* [2]	75	1
10 Jun 95	**WHEREVER WOULD I BE** *Columbia 6620592* [3]	44	3
4 Nov 95	**ROLL AWAY** *Columbia 6623682*	68	1

[1] Pet Shop Boys and Dusty Springfield [2] Cilla Black with Dusty Springfield
[3] Dusty Springfield and Daryl Hall

See also SPRINGFIELDS

Rick SPRINGFIELD *Australia, male vocalist (13 WEEKS)* pos/wks

14 Jan 84	**HUMAN TOUCH / SOULS** *RCA RICK 1*	23	7
24 Mar 84	**JESSIE'S GIRL** *RCA RICK 2* ▲	43	6

'Souls' listed only from 11 Feb 1984. It peaked at No.24

SPRINGFIELDS
UK, male / female vocal / instrumental group (66 WEEKS) pos/wks

31 Aug 61	**BREAKAWAY** *Philips BF 1168*	31	8
16 Nov 61	**BAMBINO** *Philips BF 1178*	16	11
13 Dec 62 ●	**ISLAND OF DREAMS** *Philips 326557 BF*	5	26
28 Mar 63 ●	**SAY I WON'T BE THERE** *Philips 326577 BF*	5	15
25 Jul 63	**COME ON HOME** *Philips BF 1263*	31	6

See also Dusty SPRINGFIELD

Bruce SPRINGSTEEN (164 Top 500) *'The Boss', b. 23 Sep 1949, New Jersey, US. Singer / songwriter / guitarist / rock superstar, whose legendary stage performances have packed stadiums worldwide. He released the biggest-selling box set, and is one of world's best-selling album artists (144 WEEKS)* pos/wks

22 Nov 80	**HUNGRY HEART** *CBS 9309*	44	4
13 Jun 81	**THE RIVER** *CBS A 1179*	35	6
26 May 84	**DANCING IN THE DARK** *CBS A 4436*	28	7
6 Oct 84	**COVER ME** *CBS A 4662*	38	5
12 Jan 85 ●	**DANCING IN THE DARK (re-entry)** *CBS A 4436*	4	16
23 Mar 85	**COVER ME (re-entry)** *CBS A 4662*	16	8
15 Jun 85 ●	**I'M ON FIRE / BORN IN THE USA** *CBS A 6342*	5	12
3 Aug 85	**GLORY DAYS** *CBS A 6375*	17	6
14 Dec 85 ●	**SANTA CLAUS IS COMIN' TO TOWN / MY HOMETOWN** *CBS A 6773*	9	5
29 Nov 86	**WAR** *CBS 650193 7* [1]	18	7
7 Feb 87	**FIRE** *CBS 650381 7* [1]	54	2
23 May 87	**BORN TO RUN** *CBS BRUCE 2*	16	4
3 Oct 87	**BRILLIANT DISGUISE** *CBS 651141 7*	20	5
12 Dec 87	**TUNNEL OF LOVE** *CBS 651295 7*	45	4
18 Jun 88	**TOUGHER THAN THE REST** *CBS BRUCE 3*	13	8
24 Sep 88	**SPARE PARTS** *CBS BRUCE 4*	32	3
21 Mar 92	**HUMAN TOUCH** *Columbia 6578727*	11	5
23 May 92	**BETTER DAYS** *Columbia 6578907*	34	3
25 Jul 92	**57 CHANNELS (AND NOTHIN' ON)** *Columbia 6581387*	32	4
24 Oct 92	**LEAP OF FAITH** *Columbia 6583697*	46	3
10 Apr 93	**LUCKY TOWN (LIVE)** *Columbia 6592282*	48	3
19 Mar 94 ●	**STREETS OF PHILADELPHIA** *Columbia 6600652*	2	12
22 Apr 95	**SECRET GARDEN** *Columbia 6612955*	44	3
11 Nov 95	**HUNGRY HEART (re-issue)** *Columbia 6626252*	28	3
4 May 96	**THE GHOST OF TOM JOAD** *Columbia 6630315*	26	2
19 Apr 97	**SECRET GARDEN (re-issue)** *Columbia 6643245*	17	4

[1] Bruce Springsteen and The E-Street Band

SPRINGWATER *UK, male instrumentalist – Phil Cordell (12 WEEKS)* pos/wks

23 Oct 71 ●	**I WILL RETURN** *Polydor 2058 141*	5	12

1993

IN THE YEAR IN WHICH DAVID KORESH AND THE BRANCH DAVIDIAN CULT MET THEIR MAKER IN THE WACO SIEGE, YITZHAK RABIN AND YASSER ARAFAT SHOOK HANDS ON THE WHITE HOUSE LAWN IN A HISTORIC DEVELOPMENT IN THE ARAB-ISRAELI PEACE PROCESS, AND TAKE THAT BECAME THE FIRST ACT TO SCORE THREE SUCCESSIVE ENTRIES AT NO.1, THE EVER YOUTHFUL **LULU** TAKES US BACK EIGHT YEARS TO A DECISION THAT RE-LIT HER CHART CAREER...

“When the duet with **Take That** was talked about I wondered how it would work. When ‘Relight My Fire’ was suggested I thought, well, maybe it could work. When I heard the finished mix it did work and the rest is history. I found myself in my third decade in music making a number one record, having fun with one of the cutest boy bands ever!”

SINGLE OF THE YEAR ‘I’d Do Anything For Love (But I Won’t Do That)’ Meatloaf
ALBUM OF THE YEAR ‘Bat Out Of Hell II – Back Into Hell’ Meatloaf

1993

SPRINKLER *UK / US, male / female vocal / rap group (2 WEEKS)* pos/wks

			pos	wks
11 Jul 98		**LEAVE 'EM SOMETHING TO DESIRE** *Island CID 706*	45	2

SPYRO GYRA *US, male instrumental group (10 WEEKS)* pos/wks

			pos	wks
21 Jul 79		**MORNING DANCE** *Infinity INF 111*	17	10

SQUADRONAIRES – *See Joan REGAN*

SQUEEZE (221 Top 500) *Critically acclaimed London band, which had several UK / US best sellers. Featured noted singer / songwriters Glenn Tilbrook (g/v) and Chris Difford (v/g). Fluctuating line-up included Jools Holland (k) and Paul Carrack (v/k - also of Ace, and Mike and the Mechanics fame) (123 WEEKS)* pos/wks

			pos	wks
8 Apr 78		**TAKE ME I'M YOURS** *A & M AMS 7335*	19	9
10 Jun 78		**BANG BANG** *A & M AMS 7360*	49	5
18 Nov 78		**GOODBYE GIRL** *A & M AMS 7398*	63	2
24 Mar 79	●	**COOL FOR CATS** *A & M AMS 7426*	2	11
2 Jun 79	●	**UP THE JUNCTION** *A & M AMS 7444*	2	11
8 Sep 79		**SLAP AND TICKLE** *A & M AMS 7466*	24	8
1 Mar 80		**ANOTHER NAIL IN MY HEART** *A & M AMS 7507*	17	9
10 May 80		**PULLING MUSSELS (FROM THE SHELL)** *A & M AMS 7523*	44	6
16 May 81		**IS THAT LOVE** *A & M AMS 8129*	35	8
25 Jul 81		**TEMPTED** *A & M AMS 8147*	41	5
10 Oct 81	●	**LABELLED WITH LOVE** *A & M AMS 8166*	4	10
24 Apr 82		**BLACK COFFEE IN BED** *A & M AMS 8219*	51	4
23 Oct 82		**ANNIE GET YOUR GUN** *A & M AMS 8259*	43	4
15 Jun 85		**LAST TIME FOREVER** *A & M AM 255*	45	5
8 Aug 87		**HOURGLASS** *A & M AM 400*	16	10
17 Oct 87		**TRUST ME TO OPEN MY MOUTH** *A & M AM 412*	72	1
25 Apr 92		**COOL FOR CATS (re-issue)** *A & M AM 860*	62	2
24 Jul 93		**THIRD RAIL** *A & M 5803372*	39	3
11 Sep 93		**SOME FANTASTIC PLACE** *A & M 5803792*	73	1
9 Sep 95		**THIS SUMMER** *A & M 5811912*	36	3
18 Nov 95		**ELECTRIC TRAINS** *A & M 5812692*	44	2
15 Jun 96		**HEAVEN KNOWS** *A & M 5816052*	27	2
24 Aug 96		**THIS SUMMER (re-mix)** *A & M 5818372*	32	2

See also DIFFORD and TILBROOK

Billy SQUIER *US, male vocalist (3 WEEKS)* pos/wks

			pos	wks
3 Oct 81		**THE STROKE** *Capitol CL 214*	52	3

Dorothy SQUIRES *UK, female vocalist (56 WEEKS)* pos/wks

			pos	wks
5 Jun 53		**I'M WALKING BEHIND YOU** *Polygon P 1068*	12	1
24 Aug 61		**SAY IT WITH FLOWERS** *Columbia DB 4665* [1]	23	10
20 Sep 69		**FOR ONCE IN MY LIFE** *President PT 267*	24	10
20 Dec 69		**FOR ONCE IN MY LIFE (re-entry)** *President PT 267*	48	1
21 Feb 70		**TILL** *President PT 281*	25	10
9 May 70		**TILL (re-entry)** *President PT 281*	48	1
8 Aug 70		**MY WAY** *President PT 305*	40	5
19 Sep 70		**MY WAY (re-entry)** *President PT 305*	34	8
28 Nov 70		**MY WAY (2nd re-entry)** *President PT 305*	25	10

[1] Dorothy Squires and Russ Conway

ST LUNATICS – *See NELLY*

STABBS
Finland / US / Cameroon, male instrumental / production group (1 WEEK) pos/wks

			pos	wks
24 Dec 94		**JOY AND HAPPINESS** *Hi-Life HICD 3*	65	1

STACCATO
UK / Holland, male / female vocal / instrumental duo (1 WEEK) pos/wks

			pos	wks
20 Jul 96		**I WANNA KNOW** *Multiply CDMULTY 11*	65	1

Jim STAFFORD *US, male vocalist (16 WEEKS)* pos/wks

			pos	wks
27 Apr 74		**SPIDERS AND SNAKES** *MGM 2006 374*	14	8
6 Jul 74		**MY GIRL BILL** *MGM 2006 423*	20	8

Jo STAFFORD *US, female vocalist (28 WEEKS)* pos/wks

			pos	wks
14 Nov 52	★	**YOU BELONG TO ME** *Columbia DB 3152* ▲	1	19
19 Dec 52		**JAMBALAYA** *Columbia DB 3169*	11	2
7 May 54	●	**MAKE LOVE TO ME!** *Philips PB 233* ▲	8	1
9 Dec 55		**SUDDENLY THERE'S A VALLEY** *Philips PB 509*	12	5
3 Feb 56		**SUDDENLY THERE'S A VALLEY (re-entry)** *Philips PB 509*	19	1

Terry STAFFORD *US, male vocalist (9 WEEKS)* pos/wks

			pos	wks
7 May 64		**SUSPICION** *London HLU 9871*	31	9

STAIFFI and his MUSTAFAS
France, male vocal / instrumental group (1 WEEK) pos/wks

			pos	wks
28 Jul 60		**MUSTAFA CHA CHA CHA** *Pye International 7N 25057*	43	1

STAIND *US, male vocal / instrumental group (8 WEEKS)* pos/wks

			pos	wks
15 Sep 01		**IT'S BEEN AWHILE** *Elektra E 7252CD*	15	6
1 Dec 01		**OUTSIDE** *Elektra E 7277CD*	33	2

STAKKA BO *Sweden, male rap / DJ duo – Johan Renck and Oscar Franzen (12 WEEKS)* pos/wks

			pos	wks
25 Sep 93		**HERE WE GO** *Polydor PZCD 280*	13	8
18 Dec 93		**DOWN THE DRAIN** *Polydor PZCD 301*	64	4

Frank STALLONE *US, male vocalist (2 WEEKS)* pos/wks

			pos	wks
22 Oct 83		**FAR FROM OVER** *RSO 95*	68	2

STAMFORD BRIDGE *UK, male Chelsea FC supporters vocal group (1 WEEK)* pos/wks

			pos	wks
16 May 70		**CHELSEA** *Penny Farthing PEN 715*	47	1

STAN *UK, male vocal / instrumental duo (3 WEEKS)* pos/wks

			pos	wks
31 Jul 93		**SUNTAN** *Hug CDBUM 1*	40	3

Lisa STANSFIELD (211 Top 500) *Only UK act to have three US R&B No.1 hits, b. 11 Apr 1966, Lancashire. Like Yazz, she was featured vocalist on a Coldcut single before achieving a No.1 in her own right. This multi-Brit award winner has sold millions of records all around the world (127 WEEKS)* pos/wks

			pos	wks
25 Mar 89		**PEOPLE HOLD ON** *Ahead of Our Time CCUT 5* [1]	11	9
12 Aug 89		**THIS IS THE RIGHT TIME** *Arista 112512*	13	8
28 Oct 89	★	**ALL AROUND THE WORLD** *Arista 112693*	1	14
10 Feb 90	●	**LIVE TOGETHER** *Arista 112914*	10	6
12 May 90		**WHAT DID I DO TO YOU (EP)** *Arista 113168*	25	4
19 Oct 91	●	**CHANGE** *Arista 114820*	10	7
21 Dec 91		**ALL WOMAN** *Arista 115000*	20	8
14 Mar 92		**TIME TO MAKE YOU MINE** *Arista 115113*	14	8
6 Jun 92		**SET YOUR LOVING FREE** *Arista 74321100587*	28	4
19 Dec 92	●	**SOMEDAY (I'M COMING BACK)** *Arista 74321123567*	10	9
1 May 93	★	**FIVE LIVE (EP)** *Parlophone CDRS 6340* [2] ■	1	11
5 Jun 93	●	**IN ALL THE RIGHT PLACES** *MCA MCSTD 1780*	8	11
24 Jul 93		**FIVE LIVE (EP) (re-entry)** *Parlophone CDRS 6340* [2]	74	1
23 Oct 93		**SO NATURAL** *Arista 74321169132*	15	5
11 Dec 93		**LITTLE BIT OF HEAVEN** *Arista 74321178202*	32	4
18 Jan 97	●	**PEOPLE HOLD ON (THE BOOTLEG MIXES)** *Arista 74321452012* [3]	4	6
22 Mar 97	●	**THE REAL THING** *Arista 74321463222*	9	7
21 Jun 97		**NEVER, NEVER GONNA GIVE YOU UP** *Arista 74321490392*	25	3
4 Oct 97		**THE LINE** *RCA 74321511372*	64	1
23 Jun 01		**LET'S JUST CALL IT LOVE** *Arista 74321863422*	48	1

[1] Coldcut featuring Lisa Stansfield [2] George Michael and Queen with Lisa Stansfield [3] Lisa Stansfield vs The Dirty Rotten Scoundrels

Tracks on What Did I Do to You (EP): What Did I Do to You / My Apple Heart / Lay Me Down / Something's Happenin'. Tracks on Five Live (EP): Somebody to Love / These Are the Days of Our Lives / Calling You / Papa Was a Rolling Stone - Killer (medley). Lisa Stansfield appears only on the second track

Vivian STANSHALL – *See Mike OLDFIELD*

STANTON WARRIORS *UK, male production duo (1 WEEK)* pos/wks

22 Sep 01	DA ANTIDOTE *Mob MOBCD 006*	69	1

STAPLE SINGERS *US, male / female vocal group (14 WEEKS)* pos/wks

10 Jun 72	I'LL TAKE YOU THERE *Stax 2025 110* ▲	30	8
8 Jun 74	IF YOU'RE READY (COME GO WITH ME) *Stax 2025 224*	34	6

Cyril STAPLETON and his Orchestra *UK, orchestra (27 WEEKS)* pos/wks

27 May 55	ELEPHANT TANGO *Decca F 10488*	20	2
1 Jul 55	ELEPHANT TANGO (re-entry) *Decca F 10488*	20	1
22 Jul 55	ELEPHANT TANGO (2nd re-entry) *Decca F 10488*	19	1
23 Sep 55 ●	BLUE STAR (THE MEDIC THEME) *Decca F 10559* [1]	2	12
6 Apr 56	THE ITALIAN THEME *Decca F 10703*	18	2
1 Jun 56	THE HAPPY WHISTLER *Decca F 10735* [2]	22	4
19 Jul 57	FORGOTTEN DREAMS *Decca F 10912*	27	5

[1] Cyril Stapleton Orchestra featuring Julie Dawn [2] Cyril Stapleton Orchestra featuring Desmond Lane, penny whistle

STAR TURN ON 45 (PINTS)
UK, male vocalist – Steve O'Donnell (9 WEEKS) pos/wks

24 Oct 81	STARTURN ON 45 (PINTS) *V Tone V TONE 003*	45	4
30 Apr 88	PUMP UP THE BITTER *Pacific DRINK 1*	12	5

STARDUST
France, male / female vocal / instrumental group (3 WEEKS) pos/wks

8 Oct 77	ARIANA *Satril SAT 120*	42	3

STARDUST *France, male vocal / production group (26 WEEKS)* pos/wks

1 Aug 98	MUSIC SOUNDS BETTER WITH YOU (import) *Roule ROULE 305*	55	3
22 Aug 98 ●	MUSIC SOUNDS BETTER WITH YOU *Virgin DINSD 175*	2	23

Alvin STARDUST (231 Top 500) *Sixties hitmaker who became bill-topping Seventies vocalist, b. Bernard Jewry, 27 Sep 1942, London. After several minor hits as Shane Fenton, he collected a string of smashes as OTT rocker Stardust, and extended his chart span to almost 25 years. Father of current hitmaker Adam F (119 WEEKS)* pos/wks

3 Nov 73 ●	MY COO-CA-CHOO *Magnet MAG 1*	2	21
16 Feb 74 ★	JEALOUS MIND *Magnet MAG 5*	1	11
4 May 74 ●	RED DRESS *Magnet MAG 8*	7	8
31 Aug 74 ●	YOU YOU YOU *Magnet MAG 13*	6	10
30 Nov 74	TELL ME WHY *Magnet MAG 19*	16	8
1 Feb 75	GOOD LOVE CAN NEVER DIE *Magnet MAG 21*	11	9
12 Jul 75	SWEET CHEATIN' RITA *Magnet MAG 32*	37	4
5 Sep 81 ●	PRETEND *Stiff BUY 124*	4	10
21 Nov 81	A WONDERFUL TIME UP THERE *Stiff BUY 132*	56	8
5 May 84 ●	I FEEL LIKE BUDDY HOLLY *Chrysalis CHS 2784*	7	11
27 Oct 84 ●	I WON'T RUN AWAY *Chrysalis CHS 2829*	7	13
15 Dec 84	SO NEAR TO CHRISTMAS *Chrysalis CHS 2835*	29	4
23 Mar 85	GOT A LITTLE HEARTACHE *Chrysalis CHS 2856*	55	2

See also Shane FENTON and the FENTONES

STARFIGHTER *Belgium, male producer (3 WEEKS)* pos/wks

5 Feb 00	APACHE *Sound of Ministry MOSCDS 136*	31	3

STARGARD *US, female vocal group (14 WEEKS)* pos/wks

28 Jan 78	THEME FROM 'WHICH WAY IS UP' *MCA 346*	19	7
15 Apr 78	LOVE IS SO EASY *MCA 354*	45	1
9 Sep 78	WHAT YOU WAITIN' FOR *MCA 382*	39	6

STARGAZERS *UK / Australia, male / female vocal group (68 WEEKS)* pos/wks

13 Feb 53	BROKEN WINGS *Decca F 10047*	11	1
27 Feb 53 ★	BROKEN WINGS (re-entry) *Decca F 10047*	1	11
19 Feb 54 ★	I SEE THE MOON *Decca F 10213*	1	15
9 Apr 54	THE HAPPY WANDERER *Decca F 10259*	12	1
17 Dec 54 ★	THE FINGER OF SUSPICION *Decca F 10394* [1]	1	15
4 Mar 55	SOMEBODY *Decca F 10437*	20	1
3 Jun 55	THE CRAZY OTTO RAG *Decca F 10523*	18	3
9 Sep 55 ●	CLOSE THE DOOR *Decca F 10594*	6	9
11 Nov 55 ●	TWENTY TINY FINGERS *Decca F 10626*	4	11
22 Jun 56	HOT DIGGITY (DOG ZIGGITY BOOM) *Decca F 10731*	28	1

[1] Dickie Valentine with the Stargazers

STARGAZERS *UK, male vocal / instrumental group (3 WEEKS)* pos/wks

6 Feb 82	GROOVE BABY GROOVE (EP) *Epic EPC A 1924*	56	3

Tracks on Groove Baby Groove (EP): Groove Baby Groove / Jump Around / La Rock 'n' Roll (Quelques Uns à la Lune) / Red Light Green Light

STARJETS *UK, male vocal / instrumental group (5 WEEKS)* pos/wks

8 Sep 79	WAR STORIES *Epic EPC 7770*	51	5

STARLAND VOCAL BAND
US, male / female vocal group (10 WEEKS) pos/wks

7 Aug 76	AFTERNOON DELIGHT *RCA 2716* ▲	18	10

STARLIGHT *Italy, male instrumental / production group (11 WEEKS)* pos/wks

19 Aug 89 ●	NUMERO UNO *Citybeat CBE 742*	9	11

STARLITERS – *See Joey DEE and the STARLITERS*

STARPARTY
Holland, male production duo – Ferry Corsten and Robert Smit (2 WEEKS) pos/wks

26 Feb 00	I'M IN LOVE *Incentive CENT 5CDS*	26	2

See also Ferry CORSTEN; MOONMAN; SYSTEM F; GOURYELLA; VERACOCHA

Edwin STARR *US, male vocalist (70 WEEKS)* pos/wks

12 May 66	STOP HER ON SIGHT (SOS) *Polydor BM 56 702*	35	8
18 Aug 66	HEADLINE NEWS *Polydor 56 717*	39	3
11 Dec 68	STOP HER ON SIGHT (SOS) / HEADLINE NEWS (re-issue) *Polydor 56 753*	11	11
13 Sep 69	25 MILES *Tamla Motown TMG 672*	36	6
24 Oct 70 ●	WAR *Tamla Motown TMG 754* ▲	3	12
20 Feb 71	STOP THE WAR NOW *Tamla Motown TMG 764*	33	1
27 Jan 79 ●	CONTACT *20th Century BTC 2396*	6	12
26 May 79 ●	H.A.P.P.Y. RADIO *RCA TC 2408*	9	11
1 Jun 85	IT AIN'T FAIR *Hippodrome HIP 101*	56	4
30 Oct 93	WAR *Weekend CDWEEK 103* [1]	69	2

[1] Edwin Starr and Shadow

'Headline News' not listed with 'SOS' from 22 Jan 1969 to 19 Feb 1969. It therefore peaked at No.16. 'War' in 1993 was a re-recording and was listed with the flip side 'Wild Thing' by the Troggs and Wolf

See also UTAH SAINTS

Freddie STARR *UK, male vocalist – Fred Smith (14 WEEKS)* pos/wks

23 Feb 74 ●	IT'S YOU *Tiffany 6121 501*	9	10
20 Dec 75	WHITE CHRISTMAS *Thunderbird THE 102*	41	4

Kay STARR *US, female vocalist – Katherine Starks (58 WEEKS)* pos/wks

5 Dec 52 ★	COMES A-LONG A-LOVE *Capitol CL 13808*	1	16
24 Apr 53 ●	SIDE BY SIDE *Capitol CL 13871*	7	4
19 Mar 54 ●	CHANGING PARTNERS *Capitol CL 14050*	4	14
15 Oct 54	AM I A TOY OR TREASURE *Capitol CL 14151*	17	3
12 Nov 54	AM I A TOY OR TREASURE (re-entry) *Capitol CL 14151*	20	1
17 Feb 56 ★	ROCK AND ROLL WALTZ *HMV POP 168* ▲	1	20

Ringo STARR *UK, male vocalist - Richard Starkey (56 WEEKS)* pos/wks

17 Apr 71 ●	IT DON'T COME EASY *Apple R 5898*	4	11
1 Apr 72 ●	BACK OFF BOOGALOO *Apple R 5944*	2	10
27 Oct 73 ●	PHOTOGRAPH *Apple R 5992* ▲	8	13
23 Feb 74 ●	YOU'RE SIXTEEN *Apple R 5995* ▲	4	10
30 Nov 74	ONLY YOU *Apple R 6000*	28	11
6 Jun 92	WEIGHT OF THE WORLD *Private Music 115392*	74	1

See also BEATLES

STARS ON 54 *US, female vocal trio (3 WEEKS)*

			pos	wks
28 Nov 98		**IF YOU COULD READ MY MIND** *Tommy Boy TBCD 7497*	23	3

STARSAILOR *UK, male vocal / instrumental group (17 WEEKS)*

			pos	wks
17 Feb 01		**FEVER** *Chrysalis CDCHSS 5123*	18	3
5 May 01		**GOOD SOULS** *Chrysalis CDCHS 5125*	12	6
29 Sep 01	●	**ALCOHOLIC** *Chrysalis CDCHSS 5130*	10	6
22 Dec 01		**LULLABY** *Chrysalis CDCHS 5131*	36	2+

STARSHIP *US, female / male vocal / instrumental group (41 WEEKS)*

			pos	wks
26 Jan 80		**JANE** *Grunt FB 1750* [1]	21	9
16 Nov 85		**WE BUILT THIS CITY** *RCA PB 49929* ▲	12	12
8 Feb 86		**SARA** *RCA FB 49893* ▲	66	3
11 Apr 87	★	**NOTHING'S GONNA STOP US NOW** *Grunt FB 49757* ▲	1	17

[1] Jefferson Starship

STARSOUND *Holland, producer – Jaap Eggermont with male / female session singers (37 WEEKS)*

			pos	wks
18 Apr 81	●	**STARS ON 45** *CBS A 1102* ▲	2	14
4 Jul 81	●	**STARS ON 45 VOL2** *CBS A 1407*	2	10
19 Sep 81		**STARS ON 45 VOL3** *CBS A 1521*	17	6
27 Feb 82		**STARS ON STEVIE** *CBS A 2041*	14	7

STARTRAX *UK, male / female vocal group (8 WEEKS)*

			pos	wks
1 Aug 81		**STARTRAX CLUB DISCO** *Picksy KSY 1001*	18	8

STARVATION *Multinational, male / female vocal / instrumental charity assembly (6 WEEKS)*

			pos	wks
9 Mar 85		**STARVATION / TAM-TAM POUR L'ETHIOPE** *Zarjazz JAZZ 3*	33	6

STARVING SOULS *UK, male vocal / instrumental group (1 Week)*

			pos	wks
21 Oct 95		**I BE THE PROPHET** *Durban Poison DPCD 1*	66	1

STATE OF MIND
UK, male / female vocal / production group (3 WEEKS)

			pos	wks
18 Apr 98		**THIS IS IT** *Ministry of Sound MOSCDS 123*	30	2
25 Jul 98		**TAKE CONTROL** *Ministry of Sound MOSCDS 124*	46	1

STATIC REVENGER *US, male producer – Dennis White (3 WEEKS)*

			pos	wks
7 Jul 01		**HAPPY PEOPLE** *Incentive / Rulin CENRUL 1CDS*	23	3

STATIC-X *US, male vocal / instrumental group (1 WEEK)*

			pos	wks
6 Oct 01		**BLACK AND WHITE** *Warner W 560CD*	65	1

STATLER BROTHERS *US, male vocal group (4 WEEKS)*

			pos	wks
24 Feb 66		**FLOWERS ON THE WALL** *CBS 201976*	38	4

Candi STATON *Child gospel performer turned southern soul star turned disco diva, b. 1943, Alabama, US. The Grammy-nominated ex-wife of Clarence Carter first found US R&B fame in the late 1960s and last hit in UK after she had returned to gospel music (71 WEEKS)*

			pos	wks
29 May 76	●	**YOUNG HEARTS RUN FREE** *Warner Bros. K 16730*	2	13
18 Sep 76		**DESTINY** *Warner Bros. K 16806*	41	3
23 Jul 77	●	**NIGHTS ON BROADWAY** *Warner Bros. K 16972*	6	12
3 Jun 78		**HONEST I DO LOVE YOU** *Warner Bros. K 17164*	48	5
24 Apr 82		**SUSPICIOUS MINDS** *Sugarhill SH 112*	31	9
31 May 86		**YOUNG HEARTS RUN FREE (re-mix)** *Warner Bros. W 8680*	47	5
2 Feb 91	●	**YOU GOT THE LOVE** *Truelove TLOVE 7001* [1]	4	11
1 Mar 97	●	**YOU GOT THE LOVE (re-mix)** *React CDREACT 89* [1]	3	8
17 Apr 99		**LOVE ON LOVE** *React CDREACT 143*	27	3
7 Aug 99		**YOUNG HEARTS RUN FREE (re-recording)** *React CDREACT 158*	29	2

[1] Source featuring Candi Staton

STATUS IV *US, male vocal group (3 WEEKS)*

			pos	wks
9 Jul 83		**YOU AIN'T REALLY DOWN** *TMT TMT 4*	56	3

STATUS QUO (14) (Top 500) *Ever popular London-based three-chord boogie band: Francis Rossi (g/v), Rick Parfitt (g/v), Alan Lancaster (b), John Coghlan (d). These long-time festival favourites recorded as The Spectres and Traffic Jam before their psychedelic-sounding debut hit introduced them to the UK and US Top 20 (their only major American hit). No group has accumulated more British hit singles, and only The Beatles and Rolling Stones can better their tally of Top 20 albums. These heroes of the head-banging set who were chosen to open Live Aid in 1985 have been rockin' all over the world for more than 35 years (413 WEEKS)*

			pos	wks
24 Jan 68	●	**PICTURES OF MATCHSTICK MEN** *Pye 7N 17449*	7	12
21 Aug 68	●	**ICE IN THE SUN** *Pye 7N 17581*	8	12
28 May 69		**ARE YOU GROWING TIRED OF MY LOVE** *Pye 7N 17728*	46	2
18 Jun 69		**ARE YOU GROWING TIRED OF MY LOVE (re-entry)** *Pye 7N 17728*	50	1
2 May 70		**DOWN THE DUSTPIPE** *Pye 7N 17907*	12	17
7 Nov 70		**IN MY CHAIR** *Pye 7N 17998*	21	14
13 Jan 73	●	**PAPER PLANE** *Vertigo 6059 071*	8	11
14 Apr 73		**MEAN GIRL** *Pye 7N 45229*	20	11
8 Sep 73	●	**CAROLINE** *Vertigo 6059 085*	5	13
4 May 74	●	**BREAK THE RULES** *Vertigo 6059 101*	8	8
7 Dec 74	★	**DOWN DOWN** *Vertigo 6059 114*	1	11
17 May 75	●	**ROLL OVER LAY DOWN** *Vertigo QUO 13*	9	8
14 Feb 76	●	**RAIN** *Vertigo 6059 133*	7	7
10 Jul 76		**MYSTERY SONG** *Vertigo 6059 146*	11	9
11 Dec 76	●	**WILD SIDE OF LIFE** *Vertigo 6059 153*	9	12
8 Oct 77	●	**ROCKIN' ALL OVER THE WORLD** *Vertigo 6059 184*	3	16
2 Sep 78		**AGAIN AND AGAIN** *Vertigo QUO 1*	13	9
25 Nov 78		**ACCIDENT PRONE** *Vertigo QUO 2*	36	8
22 Sep 79	●	**WHATEVER YOU WANT** *Vertigo 6059 242*	4	9
24 Nov 79		**LIVING ON AN ISLAND** *Vertigo 6059 248*	16	10
11 Oct 80	●	**WHAT YOU'RE PROPOSING** *Vertigo QUO 3*	2	11
6 Dec 80		**LIES / DON'T DRIVE MY CAR** *Vertigo QUO 4*	11	10
28 Feb 81	●	**SOMETHING 'BOUT YOU BABY I LIKE** *Vertigo QUO 5*	9	7
28 Nov 81	●	**ROCK 'N' ROLL** *Vertigo QUO 6*	8	11
27 Mar 82	●	**DEAR JOHN** *Vertigo QUO 7*	10	8
12 Jun 82		**SHE DON'T FOOL ME** *Vertigo QUO 8*	36	5
30 Oct 82		**CAROLINE (LIVE AT THE NEC)** *Vertigo QUO 10*	13	7
10 Sep 83	●	**OL' RAG BLUES** *Vertigo QUO 11*	9	8
5 Nov 83		**A MESS OF BLUES** *Vertigo QUO 12*	15	6
10 Dec 83	●	**MARGUERITA TIME** *Vertigo QUO 14*	3	11
19 May 84		**GOING DOWN TOWN TONIGHT** *Vertigo QUO 15*	20	6
27 Oct 84	●	**THE WANDERER** *Vertigo QUO 16*	7	11
17 May 86	●	**ROLLIN' HOME** *Vertigo QUO 18*	9	6
26 Jul 86		**RED SKY** *Vertigo QUO 19*	19	8
4 Oct 86	●	**IN THE ARMY NOW** *Vertigo QUO 20*	2	14
6 Dec 86		**DREAMIN'** *Vertigo QUO 21*	15	8
26 Mar 88		**AIN'T COMPLAINING** *Vertigo QUO 22*	19	6
21 May 88		**WHO GETS THE LOVE?** *Vertigo QUO 23*	34	4
20 Aug 88		**RUNNING ALL OVER THE WORLD** *Vertigo QUAID 1*	17	6
3 Dec 88	●	**BURNING BRIDGES (ON AND OFF AND ON AGAIN)** *Vertigo QUO 25*	5	10
28 Oct 89		**NOT AT ALL** *Vertigo QUO 26*	50	2
29 Sep 90	●	**THE ANNIVERSARY WALTZ - PART 1** *Vertigo QUO 28*	2	9
15 Dec 90		**THE ANNIVERSARY WALTZ - PART 2** *Vertigo QUO 29*	16	7
7 Sep 91		**CAN'T GIVE YOU MORE** *Vertigo QUO 30*	37	3
18 Jan 92		**ROCK 'TIL YOU DROP** *Vertigo QUO 32*	38	3
10 Oct 92		**ROADHOUSE MEDLEY (ANNIVERSARY WALTZ PART 25)** *Polydor QUO 33*	21	4
6 Aug 94		**I DIDN'T MEAN IT** *Polydor QUOCD 34*	21	4
22 Oct 94		**SHERRI DON'T FAIL ME NOW** *Polydor QUOCD 35*	38	2
3 Dec 94		**RESTLESS** *Polydor QUOCD 36*	39	2
4 Nov 95		**WHEN YOU WALK IN THE ROOM** *PolyGram TV 5775122*	34	2
2 Mar 96		**FUN FUN FUN** *PolyGram TV 5762632* [1]	24	4
13 Apr 96		**DON'T STOP** *PolyGram TV 5766352*	35	2
9 Nov 96		**ALL AROUND MY HAT** *PolyGram TV 5759452* [2]	47	1
20 Mar 99		**THE WAY IT GOES** *Eagle EAGXS 075*	39	2
12 Jun 99		**LITTLE WHITE LIES** *Eagle EAGXS 101*	47	1
2 Oct 99		**TWENTY WILD HORSES** *Eagle EAGXS 105*	53	1
13 May 00		**MONY MONY** *Universal TV 1580132*	48	1

[1] Status Quo with the Beach Boys [2] Status Quo with Maddy Prior from Steeleye Span

'Don't Drive My Car' listed from 20 Dec 1980 only. 'Running All Over the World' is a re-recorded version of 'Rockin' All Over the World', with a slightly changed lyric, released to promote the Race Against Time of 28 Aug 1988

STAXX featuring Carol LEEMING
UK, male / female vocal / instrumental group (11 WEEKS) pos/wks

2 Oct 93		JOY *Champion CHAMPCD 303*	25	6
20 May 95		YOU *Champion CHAMPCD 316*	50	1
13 Sep 97		JOY (re-mix) *Champion CHAMPCD 328*	14	4

STEALER'S WHEEL
UK, male vocal / instrumental group (22 WEEKS) pos/wks

26 May 73	●	STUCK IN THE MIDDLE WITH YOU *A & M AMS 7036*	8	10
1 Sep 73		EVERYTHING'LL TURN OUT FINE *A & M AMS 7079*	33	6
26 Jan 74		STAR *A & M AMS 7094*	25	6

STEAM *US, male vocal / instrumental group (14 WEEKS)* pos/wks

31 Jan 70	●	NA NA HEY HEY KISS HIM GOODBYE *Fontana TF 1058* ▲	9	14

STEEL – *See UNITONE ROCKERS featuring STEEL*

Anthony STEEL and the RADIO REVELLERS
UK, male vocalist / male instrumental group (6 WEEKS) pos/wks

10 Sep 54		WEST OF ZANZIBAR *Polygon P 1114*	11	6

With Jackie Brown and his Music

STEEL HORSES – *See TRUMAN & WOLFF featuring STEEL HORSES*

STEEL PULSE *UK, male vocal / instrumental group (12 WEEKS)* pos/wks

1 Apr 78		KU KLUX KLAN *Island WIP 6428*	41	4
8 Jul 78		PRODIGAL SON *Island WIP 6449*	35	6
23 Jun 79		SOUND SYSTEM *Island WIP 6490*	71	2

Tommy STEELE (155 Top 500)
Britain's first home-grown rock 'n' roll star, b. Thomas Hicks, 17 Dec 1936, London. Just four months after his chart debut he was filming his life story. The singer / songwriter / guitarist, who topped the chart before Elvis, starred in many other movies and musicals (147 WEEKS) pos/wks

26 Oct 56		ROCK WITH THE CAVEMAN *Decca F 10795* [1]	13	4
30 Nov 56		ROCK WITH THE CAVEMAN (re-entry) *Decca F 10795* [1]	23	1
14 Dec 56	★	SINGING THE BLUES *Decca F 10819* [1]	1	13
15 Feb 57		KNEE DEEP IN THE BLUES *Decca F 10849* [1]	15	9
19 Apr 57		SINGING THE BLUES (re-entry) *Decca F 10819* [1]	24	1
3 May 57		BUTTERFINGERS *Decca F 10877* [1]	25	1
17 May 57	●	BUTTERFINGERS (re-entry) *Decca F 10877* [1]	8	17
17 May 57		SINGING THE BLUES (2nd re-entry) *Decca F 10819* [1]	29	1
16 Aug 57	●	WATER WATER / A HANDFUL OF SONGS *Decca F 10923* [1]	5	16
30 Aug 57		SHIRALEE *Decca F 10896* [1]	11	4
22 Nov 57		HEY YOU! *Decca F 10941* [1]	28	1
13 Dec 57		WATER WATER / A HANDFUL OF SONGS (re-entry) *Decca F 10923* [1]	28	1
7 Mar 58	●	NAIROBI *Decca F 10991*	3	11
25 Apr 58		HAPPY GUITAR *Decca F 10976*	20	5
18 Jul 58		THE ONLY MAN ON THE ISLAND *Decca F 11041* [1]	16	8
14 Nov 58	●	COME ON, LET'S GO *Decca F 11072*	10	13
14 Aug 59		TALLAHASSEE LASSIE *Decca F 11152*	16	4
28 Aug 59		GIVE! GIVE! GIVE! *Decca F 11152*	28	2
25 Sep 59		TALLAHASSEE LASSIE (re-entry) *Decca F 11152*	25	1
4 Dec 59	●	LITTLE WHITE BULL *Decca F 11177*	6	12
10 Mar 60		LITTLE WHITE BULL (re-entry) *Decca F 11177*	30	5
23 Jun 60	●	WHAT A MOUTH (WHAT A NORTH AND SOUTH) *Decca F 11245*	5	11
29 Dec 60		MUST BE SANTA *Decca F 11299*	40	1
17 Aug 61		THE WRITING ON THE WALL *Decca F 11372*	30	5

[1] Tommy Steele and the Steelmen

'A Handful of Songs' listed together with 'Water Water' from week of 23 Aug 1957

STEELEYE SPAN
UK, male / female vocal / instrumental group (18 WEEKS) pos/wks

8 Dec 73		GAUDETE *Chrysalis CHS 2007*	14	9
15 Nov 75	●	ALL AROUND MY HAT *Chrysalis CHS 2078*	5	9

STEELY DAN *US, male vocal / instrumental group (21 WEEKS)* pos/wks

30 Aug 75		DO IT AGAIN *ABC 4075*	39	4
11 Dec 76		HAITIAN DIVORCE *ABC 4152*	17	9
29 Jul 78		FM (NO STATIC AT ALL) *MCA 374*	49	4
2 Sep 78		FM (NO STATIC AT ALL) (re-entry) *MCA 374*	75	1
10 Mar 79		RIKKI DON'T LOSE THAT NUMBER *ABC 4241*	58	3

STEFY – *See DJH featuring STEFY*

Gwen STEFANI – *See EVE; NO DOUBT*

Jim STEINMAN *US, male producer (9 WEEKS)* pos/wks

4 Jul 81		ROCK 'N' ROLL DREAMS COME THROUGH *Epic EPC A 1236* [1]	52	7
23 Jun 84		TONIGHT IS WHAT IT MEANS TO BE YOUNG *MCA MCA 889* [2]	67	2

[1] Jim Steinman, vocals by Rory Dodd [2] Jim Steinman and Fire Inc

STEINSKI and MASS MEDIA
US, male / female production group (2 WEEKS) pos/wks

31 Jan 87		WE'LL BE RIGHT BACK *Fourth & Broadway BRW 59*	63	2

Mike STEIPHENSON – *See BURUNDI STEIPHENSON BLACK*

STELLA BROWNE *UK, male production duo (1 WEEK)* pos/wks

20 May 00		EVERY WOMAN NEEDS LOVE *Perfecto PERF 06*	55	1

Doreen STEPHENS – *See Billy COTTON and his BAND*

Richie STEPHENS *Jamaica, male vocalist (3 WEEKS)* pos/wks

15 May 93		LEGACY *Columbia 6592852* [1]	64	2
9 Aug 97		COME GIVE ME YOUR LOVE *Delirious 74321450442* [2]	61	1

[1] Mad Cobra featuring Richie Stephens [2] Richie Stephens and General Degree

Martin STEPHENSON and the DAINTEES
UK, male vocal / instrumental group (7 WEEKS) pos/wks

8 Nov 86		BOAT TO BOLIVIA *Kitchenware SL 27*	70	2
17 Jan 87		TROUBLE TOWN *Kitchenware SK 13* [1]	58	3
27 Jun 92		BIG SKY NEW LIGHT *Kitchenware SK 57*	71	2

[1] Daintees

STEPPENWOLF
US / Canada, male vocal / instrumental group (14 WEEKS) pos/wks

11 Jun 69		BORN TO BE WILD *Stateside SS 8017*	30	7
9 Aug 69		BORN TO BE WILD (re-entry) *Stateside SS 8017*	50	2
27 Feb 99		BORN TO BE WILD (re-issue) *MCA MCSTD 48104*	18	5

STEPS (94 Top 500)
Steptacular pop vocal quintet: Lisa Scott-Lee, Claire Richards, Faye Tozer, Lee Latchford-Evans, Ian Watkins (aka H). Hard-working live act whose 1999 tour was reportedly the biggest pop arena tour ever in the UK. The first UK mixed quintet to top the chart twice, they bagged 13 consecutive Top 5 singles (a feat bettered only by The Beatles), sold more than 12 million records and announced their split on Boxing Day 2001 (196 WEEKS) pos/wks

22 Nov 97		5, 6, 7, 8 *Jive JIVECD 438*	14	17
2 May 98	●	LAST THING ON MY MIND *Jive 0518492*	6	14
5 Sep 98	●	ONE FOR SORROW *Jive 0519092*	2	11
21 Nov 98	★	HEARTBEAT / TRAGEDY *Jive 0519142* ◆	1	30
20 Mar 99	●	BETTER BEST FORGOTTEN *Ebul / Jive 0519242*	2	15
10 Jul 99		BETTER BEST FORGOTTEN (re-entry) *Ebul / Jive 0519242*	49	2
24 Jul 99	●	LOVE'S GOT A HOLD ON MY HEART *Ebul / Jive 0519372*	2	11
23 Oct 99	●	AFTER THE LOVE HAS GONE *Ebul / Jive 0519462*	5	9
23 Oct 99		LOVE'S GOT A HOLD ON MY HEART (re-entry) *Ebul / Jive 0519372*	73	1
25 Dec 99	●	SAY YOU'LL BE MINE / BETTER THE DEVIL YOU KNOW *Ebul / Jive 9201008*	4	17
1 Jan 00		AFTER THE LOVE HAS GONE (re-entry) *Ebul / Jive 0519462*	60	2
15 Apr 00	●	DEEPER SHADE OF BLUE *Ebul / Jive 9201022*	4	9
15 Jul 00	●	WHEN I SAID GOODBYE / SUMMER OF LOVE *Ebul / Jive 9201162*	5	11

28 Oct 00 ★	**STOMP** *Ebul / Jive 9201212* ■	1	11
6 Jan 01 ●	**IT'S THE WAY YOU MAKE ME FEEL / TOO BUSY THINKING 'BOUT MY BABY** *Ebul / Jive 9201232*	2	11
16 Jun 01 ●	**HERE AND NOW / YOU'LL BE SORRY** *Ebul / Jive 9201322*	4	10
6 Oct 01 ●	**CHAIN REACTION / ONE FOR SORROW (re-mix)** *Ebul / Jive 9201422*	2	12
15 Dec 01 ●	**WORDS ARE NOT ENOUGH / I KNOW HIM SO WELL** *Ebul / Jive 9201452*	5	3+

STEREO MC's *UK, male / female vocal / rap group (37 WEEKS)* pos/wks

29 Sep 90	**ELEVATE MY MIND** *Fourth & Broadway BRW 186*	74	1
9 Mar 91	**LOST IN MUSIC** *Fourth & Broadway BRW 198*	46	3
26 Sep 92	**CONNECTED** *Fourth & Broadway BRW 262*	18	6
5 Dec 92	**STEP IT UP** *Fourth & Broadway BRW 266*	12	12
20 Feb 93	**GROUND LEVEL** *Fourth & Broadway BRCD 268*	19	5
29 May 93	**CREATION** *Fourth & Broadway BRCD 276*	19	4
26 May 01	**DEEP DOWN & DIRTY** *Island CID 777*	17	4
30 Jun 01	**DEEP DOWN & DIRTY (re-entry)** *Island CID 777*	62	1
1 Sep 01	**WE BELONG IN THIS WORLD TOGETHER** *Island CID 782*	59	1

STEREO NATION *UK, male vocal duo (3 WEEKS)* pos/wks

17 Aug 96	**I'VE BEEN WAITING** *EMI Premier PRESCD 5*	53	1
27 Oct 01	**LAILA** *Wizard WIZ 015* [1]	44	2

[1] Taz and Stereo Nation

STEREOLAB
UK / France, male / female vocal / instrumental group (6 WEEKS) pos/wks

8 Jan 94	**JENNY ONDIOLINE / FRENCH DISCO** *Duophonic UHF DUHFCD 01*	75	1
30 Jul 94	**PING PONG** *Duophonic UHF DUHFCD 04*	45	2
12 Nov 94	**WOW AND FLUTTER** *Duophonic UHF DUHFCD 07*	70	1
2 Mar 96	**CYBELE'S REVERIE** *Duophonic UHF DUHFCD 10*	62	1
13 Sep 97	**MISS MODULAR** *Duophonic DUHFCD 16*	60	1

STEREOPHONICS (329 Top 500) *1998 Best Newcomer Brit Award-winning rock trio - Kelly Jones (v,g), Richard Thomas (b) and Stuart Cable (d) – from Cwmaman, Wales, UK. Their 14 hit singles and two chart-topping albums of new material in the past five years cannot be bettered by any other group (94 WEEKS)* pos/wks

29 Mar 97	**LOCAL BOY IN THE PHOTOGRAPH** *V2 SPHD 2*	51	1
31 May 97	**MORE LIFE IN A TRAMP'S VEST** *V2 SPHD 4*	33	2
23 Aug 97	**A THOUSAND TREES** *V2 VVR 5000443*	22	3
8 Nov 97	**TRAFFIC** *V2 VVR 5000948*	20	3
21 Feb 98	**LOCAL BOY IN THE PHOTOGRAPH (re-issue)** *V2 VVR 5001263*	14	4
21 Nov 98 ●	**THE BARTENDER AND THE THIEF** *V2 VVR 5004653*	3	12
6 Mar 99 ●	**JUST LOOKING** *V2 VVR 5005303*	4	8
15 May 99 ●	**PICK A PART THAT'S NEW** *V2 VVR 5006778*	4	9
29 May 99	**JUST LOOKING (re-entry)** *V2 VVR 5005303*	73	1
4 Sep 99	**I WOULDN'T BELIEVE YOUR RADIO** *V2 VVR 5008823*	11	6
30 Oct 99	**I WOULDN'T BELIEVE YOUR RADIO (re-entry)** *V2 VVR 5008823*	71	1
20 Nov 99	**HURRY UP AND WAIT** *V2 VVR 5009323*	11	5
1 Jan 00	**HURRY UP AND WAIT (re-entry)** *V2 VVR 5009323*	53	3
18 Mar 00 ●	**MAMA TOLD ME NOT TO COME** *Gut CDGUT 031* [1]	4	7
31 Mar 01 ●	**MR WRITER** *V2 VVR 5015933*	5	12
23 Jun 01 ●	**HAVE A NICE DAY** *V2 VVR 5016243*	5	9
6 Oct 01	**STEP ON MY OLD SIZE NINES** *V2 VVR 5016253*	16	5
15 Dec 01 ●	**HANDBAGS AND GLADRAGS** *V2 VVR 5017753*	4	3+

[1] Tom Jones and Stereophonics

STETSASONIC *US, male rap group (3 WEEKS)* pos/wks

24 Sep 88	**TALKIN' ALL THAT JAZZ** *Breakout USA 640*	73	2
7 Nov 98	**TALKIN' ALL THAT JAZZ (re-mix)** *Tommy Boy TBCD 7310A*	54	1

STEVE and EYDIE – *See Steve LAWRENCE; Eydie GORME*

STEVE GIBBONS BAND – *See Steve GIBBONS BAND*

April STEVENS – *See Nino TEMPO and April STEVENS*

Cat STEVENS (321 Top 500) *Critically acclaimed folk-pop singer / songwriter, b. Steven Georgiou, 21 Jul 1947, London, UK, whose songs have been recorded by many top acts. One of world's biggest album sellers in 1970s. Semi-retired 1979, converted to Islamic faith and changed name to Yusuf Islam. Gave royalties for Boyzone version of 'Father and Son' to charity (96 WEEKS)* pos/wks

20 Oct 66	**I LOVE MY DOG** *Deram DM 102*	28	7
12 Jan 67 ●	**MATTHEW AND SON** *Deram DM 110*	2	10
30 Mar 67 ●	**I'M GONNA GET ME A GUN** *Deram DM 118*	6	10
2 Aug 67	**A BAD NIGHT** *Deram DM 140*	20	8
20 Dec 67	**KITTY** *Deram DM 156*	47	1
27 Jun 70 ●	**LADY D'ARBANVILLE** *Island WIP 6086*	8	13
28 Aug 71	**MOON SHADOW** *Island WIP 6092*	22	11
1 Jan 72 ●	**MORNING HAS BROKEN** *Island WIP 6121*	9	13
9 Dec 72	**CAN'T KEEP IT IN** *Island WIP 6152*	13	12
24 Aug 74	**ANOTHER SATURDAY NIGHT** *Island WIP 6206*	19	8
2 Jul 77	**(REMEMBER THE DAYS OF THE) OLD SCHOOL YARD** *Island WIP 6387*	44	3

Connie STEVENS *US, female vocalist – Concetta Ingolia (20 WEEKS)* pos/wks

5 May 60	**KOOKIE KOOKIE (LEND ME YOUR COMB)** *Warner Bros. WB 5* [1]	27	8
5 May 60 ●	**SIXTEEN REASONS** *Warner Bros. WB 3*	9	11
4 Aug 60	**SIXTEEN REASONS (re-entry)** *Warner Bros. WB 3*	45	1

[1] Edward Byrnes and Connie Stevens

Ray STEVENS *US, male vocalist – Ray Ragsdale (64 WEEKS)* pos/wks

16 May 70 ●	**EVERYTHING IS BEAUTIFUL** *CBS 4953* ▲	6	16
13 Mar 71 ●	**BRIDGET THE MIDGET (THE QUEEN OF THE BLUES)** *CBS 7070*	2	14
25 Mar 72	**TURN YOUR RADIO ON** *CBS 7634*	33	4
25 May 74 ★	**THE STREAK** *Janus 6146 201* ▲	1	12
21 Jun 75 ●	**MISTY** *Janus 6146 204*	2	10
27 Sep 75	**INDIAN LOVE CALL** *Janus 6146 205*	34	4
5 Mar 77	**IN THE MOOD** *Warner Bros. K 16875*	31	4

'In the Mood' features Ray Stevens not as a conventional vocalist, but as a group of chickens

Ricky STEVENS *UK, male vocalist (7 WEEKS)* pos/wks

14 Dec 61	**I CRIED FOR YOU** *Columbia DB 4739*	34	7

Shakin' STEVENS (39 Top 500) *Performs and records under a broad umbrella of styles from rock and country blues to cajun, b. Michael Barratt, 4 Mar 1948, Glamorgan, Wales. Shares with The Beatles (60s) and Elton John (70s) the distinction of being the most successful UK singles chart performer of a decade (80s) (277 WEEKS)* pos/wks

16 Feb 80	**HOT DOG** *Epic EPC 8090*	24	9
16 Aug 80	**MARIE MARIE** *Epic EPC 8725*	19	10
28 Feb 81 ★	**THIS OLE HOUSE** *Epic EPC 9555*	1	17
2 May 81 ●	**YOU DRIVE ME CRAZY** *Epic A 1165*	2	12
25 Jul 81 ★	**GREEN DOOR** *Epic A 1354*	1	12
10 Oct 81 ●	**IT'S RAINING** *Epic A 1643*	10	9
16 Jan 82 ★	**OH JULIE** *Epic EPC A 1742*	1	10
24 Apr 82 ●	**SHIRLEY** *Epic EPC A 2087*	6	6
21 Aug 82	**GIVE ME YOUR HEART TONIGHT** *Epic EPC A 2656*	11	10
16 Oct 82 ●	**I'LL BE SATISFIED** *Epic EPC A 2846*	10	8
11 Dec 82 ●	**THE SHAKIN' STEVENS EP** *Epic SHAKY 1*	2	7
23 Jul 83	**IT'S LATE** *Epic A 3565*	11	7
5 Nov 83 ●	**CRY JUST A LITTLE BIT** *Epic A 3774*	3	12
7 Jan 84 ●	**A ROCKIN' GOOD WAY** *Epic A 4071* [1]	5	9
24 Mar 84 ●	**A LOVE WORTH WAITING FOR** *Epic A 4291*	2	10
15 Sep 84 ●	**A LETTER TO YOU** *Epic A 4677*	10	8
24 Nov 84 ●	**TEARDROPS** *Epic A 4882*	5	9
2 Mar 85	**BREAKING UP MY HEART** *Epic A 6072*	14	7
12 Oct 85	**LIPSTICK POWDER AND PAINT** *Epic A 6610*	11	9
7 Dec 85 ★	**MERRY CHRISTMAS EVERYONE** *Epic A 6769*	1	8
8 Feb 86	**TURNING AWAY** *Epic A 6819*	15	7
1 Nov 86	**BECAUSE I LOVE YOU** *Epic SHAKY 2*	14	10
20 Dec 86	**MERRY CHRISTMAS EVERYONE (re-entry)** *Epic A 6769*	58	3
27 Jun 87	**A LITTLE BOOGIE WOOGIE (IN THE BACK OF MY MIND)** *Epic SHAKY 3*	12	10
19 Sep 87	**COME SEE ABOUT ME** *Epic SHAKY 4*	24	6

		pos	wks
28 Nov 87 ●	WHAT DO YOU WANT TO MAKE THOSE EYES AT ME FOR *Epic SHAKY 5*	5	8
23 Jul 88	FEEL THE NEED IN ME *Epic SHAKY 6*	26	5
15 Oct 88	HOW MANY TEARS CAN YOU HIDE *Epic SHAKY 7*	47	4
10 Dec 88	TRUE LOVE *Epic SHAKY 8*	23	6
18 Feb 89	JEZEBEL *Epic SHAKY 9*	58	2
13 May 89	LOVE ATTACK *Epic SHAKY 10*	28	4
24 Feb 90	I MIGHT *Epic SHAKY 11*	18	6
12 May 90	YES I DO *Epic SHAKY 12*	60	2
18 Aug 90	PINK CHAMPAGNE *Epic SHAKY 13*	59	2
13 Oct 90	MY CUTIE CUTIE *Epic SHAKY 14*	75	1
15 Dec 90	THE BEST CHRISTMAS OF THEM ALL *Epic SHAKY 15*	19	4
7 Dec 91	I'LL BE HOME THIS CHRISTMAS *Epic 6576507*	34	5
10 Oct 92	RADIO *Epic 6584367* [2]	37	3

[1] Shaky and Bonnie (Bonnie Tyler) [2] Shaky featuring Roger Taylor

Tracks on The Shakin' Stevens EP: Blue Christmas / Que Sera Sera / Josephine / Lawdy Miss Clawdy

STEVENSON'S ROCKET

UK, male vocal / instrumental group (5 WEEKS)

		pos	wks
29 Nov 75	ALRIGHT BABY *Magnet MAG 47*	37	2
20 Dec 75	ALRIGHT BABY (re-entry) *Magnet MAG 47*	45	3

Al STEWART *UK, male vocalist (6 WEEKS)*

		pos	wks
29 Jan 77	YEAR OF THE CAT *RCA 2771*	31	6

Amii STEWART *US, female vocalist (61 WEEKS)*

		pos	wks
7 Apr 79 ●	KNOCK ON WOOD *Atlantic / Hansa K 11214* ▲	6	12
16 Jun 79 ●	LIGHT MY FIRE / 137 DISCO HEAVEN (MEDLEY) *Atlantic / Hansa K 11278*	5	11
3 Nov 79	JEALOUSY *Atlantic / Hansa K 11386*	58	3
19 Jan 80	THE LETTER / PARADISE BIRD *Atlantic / Hansa K 11424*	39	4
19 Jul 80	MY GUY - MY GIRL (MEDLEY) *Atlantic / Hansa K 11550* [1]	39	5
29 Dec 84	FRIENDS *RCA 471*	12	11
17 Aug 85 ●	KNOCK ON WOOD / LIGHT MY FIRE (re-mix) *Sedition EDIT 3303*	7	12
25 Jan 86	MY GUY - MY GIRL (MEDLEY) *Sedition EDIT 3310* [2]	63	3

[1] Amii Stewart and Johnny Bristol [2] Amii Stewart and Deon Estus

Andy STEWART *UK, male vocalist (67 WEEKS)*

		pos	wks
15 Dec 60	DONALD, WHERE'S YOUR TROOSERS *Top Rank JAR 427* [1]	37	1
12 Jan 61	A SCOTTISH SOLDIER *Top Rank JAR 512* [1]	19	38
1 Jun 61	THE BATTLE'S O'ER *Top Rank JAR 565* [1]	28	13
12 Oct 61	A SCOTTISH SOLDIER (re-entry) *Top Rank JAR 512* [1]	43	2
12 Aug 65	DR FINLAY *HMV POP 1454*	50	1
26 Aug 65	DR FINLAY (re-entry) *HMV POP 1454*	43	4
9 Dec 89 ●	DONALD, WHERE'S YOUR TROOSERS (re-issue) *Stone SON 2353* [1]	4	8

[1] Andy Stewart with the Michael Sammes Singers

Billy STEWART *US, male vocalist (2 WEEKS)*

		pos	wks
8 Sep 66	SUMMERTIME *Chess CRS 8040*	39	2

Dave STEWART *UK, male instrumentalist – keyboards (30 WEEKS)*

		pos	wks
14 Mar 81	WHAT BECOMES OF THE BROKEN HEARTED *Stiff BROKEN 1* [1]	13	10
19 Sep 81 ★	IT'S MY PARTY *Stiff BROKEN 2* [2]	1	13
13 Aug 83	BUSY DOING NOTHING *Broken BROKEN 5* [2]	49	4
14 Jun 86	THE LOCOMOTION *Broken BROKEN 8* [2]	70	3

[1] Dave Stewart. Guest vocals: Colin Blunstone [2] Dave Stewart with Barbara Gaskin

Dave STEWART *UK, male instrumentalist – guitar (19 WEEKS)*

		pos	wks
24 Feb 90 ●	LILY WAS HERE *RCA ZB 43045* [1]	6	12
18 Aug 90	JACK TALKING *RCA PB 43907* [2]	69	2
3 Sep 94	HEART OF STONE *East West YZ 845CD*	36	5

[1] David A Stewart featuring Candy Dulfer [2] Dave Stewart and the Spiritual Cowboys

See also EURYTHMICS

Jermaine STEWART *US, male vocalist (42 WEEKS)*

		pos	wks
9 Aug 86 ●	WE DON'T HAVE TO TAKE OUR CLOTHES OFF TO HAVE A GOOD TIME *10 TEN 96*	2	14
1 Nov 86	JODY *10 TEN 143*	50	4
16 Jan 88 ●	SAY IT AGAIN *10 TEN 188*	7	12
2 Apr 88	GET LUCKY *Siren SRN 82*	13	9
24 Sep 88	DON'T TALK DIRTY TO ME *Siren SRN 86*	61	3

John STEWART *US, male vocalist (6 WEEKS)*

		pos	wks
30 Jun 79	GOLD *RSO 35*	43	6

Rod STEWART (8 Top 500)

World-renowned rock superstar b. 10 Jan 1945, London, UK, of Scottish parents. In the 1960s "Rod the Mod" recorded solo singles for Decca, EMI and Immediate, but is best remembered in that period as a member of the Five Dimensions, Hoochie Coochie Men, Steampacket, Shotgun Express and The Jeff Beck Group. Between 1969 and 1975, the gravel-voiced vocalist fronted The Faces as well as having a successful solo career. Over the past 30 years, Stewart has played to packed stadiums worldwide and amassed a vast collection of platinum and gold albums. In the US, he is one of the top selling UK artists of all time with eight Top 10 albums and 16 Top 10 singles. In Britain, he has scored 21 Top 10 LPs including seven solo No.1s. His writing skills have earned him a Lifetime Ivor Novello Award in the UK, while in the US he has recently been nominated for the prestigious Songwriters Hall of Fame. Stewart, whose love life also attracts much media attention, earned a Grammy Living Legend Award in 1989, Lifetime Achievement trophies from the Brits and World Music Awards and was inducted into the Rock and Roll Hall of Fame in 1994 (477 WEEKS)

		pos	wks
4 Sep 71	REASON TO BELIEVE *Mercury 6052 097*	19	2
18 Sep 71 ★	MAGGIE MAY *Mercury 6052 097* ▲	1	19
12 Aug 72 ★	YOU WEAR IT WELL *Mercury 6052 171*	1	12
18 Nov 72 ●	ANGEL / WHAT MADE MILWAUKEE FAMOUS (HAS MADE A LOSER OUT OF ME) *Mercury 6052 198*	4	11
5 May 73	I'VE BEEN DRINKING *RAK RR 4* [1]	27	6
8 Sep 73 ●	OH NO NOT MY BABY *Mercury 6052 371*	6	9
5 Oct 74 ●	FAREWELL - BRING IT ON HOME TO ME / YOU SEND ME *Mercury 6167 033*	7	7
7 Dec 74	YOU CAN MAKE ME DANCE SING OR ANYTHING (EVEN TAKE THE DOG FOR A WALK, MEND A FUSE, FOLD AWAY THE IRONING BOARD, OR ANY OTHER DOMESTIC SHORT COMINGS) *Warner Bros. K 16494* [2]	12	9
16 Aug 75 ★	SAILING *Warner Bros. K 16600*	1	11
15 Nov 75 ●	THIS OLD HEART OF MINE *Riva 1*	4	9
5 Jun 76 ●	TONIGHT'S THE NIGHT *Riva 3* ▲	5	9
21 Aug 76 ●	THE KILLING OF GEORGIE *Riva 4*	2	10
4 Sep 76 ●	SAILING (re-entry) *Warner Bros. K 16600*	3	20
20 Nov 76	GET BACK *Riva 6*	11	9
4 Dec 76	MAGGIE MAY (re-issue) *Mercury 6160 006*	31	7
23 Apr 77 ★	I DON'T WANT TO TALK ABOUT IT / FIRST CUT IS THE DEEPEST *Riva 7*	1	13
15 Oct 77 ●	YOU'RE IN MY HEART *Riva 11*	3	10
28 Jan 78 ●	HOT LEGS / I WAS ONLY JOKING *Riva 10*	5	8
27 May 78 ●	OLE OLA (MULHER BRASILEIRA) *Riva 15* [3]	4	6
18 Nov 78 ★	DA YA THINK I'M SEXY? *Riva 17* ▲	1	13
3 Feb 79	AIN'T LOVE A BITCH *Riva 18*	11	8
5 May 79	BLONDES (HAVE MORE FUN) *Riva 19*	63	3
31 May 80	IF LOVING YOU IS WRONG (I DON'T WANT TO BE RIGHT) *Riva 23*	23	9
8 Nov 80	PASSION *Riva 26*	17	10
20 Dec 80	MY GIRL *Riva 28*	32	7
17 Oct 81 ●	TONIGHT I'M YOURS (DON'T HURT ME) *Riva 33*	8	13
12 Dec 81	YOUNG TURKS *Riva 34*	11	9
27 Feb 82	HOW LONG *Riva 35*	41	4
4 Jun 83 ★	BABY JANE *Warner Bros. W 9608*	1	14
27 Aug 83 ●	WHAT AM I GONNA DO (I'M SO IN LOVE WITH YOU) *Warner Bros. W 9564*	3	8
10 Dec 83	SWEET SURRENDER *Warner Bros. W 9440*	23	9
26 May 84	INFATUATION *Warner Bros. W 9256*	27	7
28 Jul 84	SOME GUYS HAVE ALL THE LUCK *Warner Bros. W 9204*	15	10
24 May 86	LOVE TOUCH *Warner Bros. W 8668*	27	5
5 Jul 86	LOVE TOUCH (re-entry) *Warner Bros. W 8668*	69	3
12 Jul 86 ●	EVERY BEAT OF MY HEART *Warner Bros. W 8625*	2	9

20 Sep 86 **ANOTHER HEARTACHE** *Warner Bros. W 8631* ... 54 2
28 Mar 87 **SAILING (2nd re-entry)** *Warner Bros. K 16600* ... 41 3
28 May 88 **LOST IN YOU** *Warner Bros. W 7927* ... 21 6
13 Aug 88 **FOREVER YOUNG** *Warner Bros. W 7796* ... 57 3
6 May 89 **MY HEART CAN'T TELL YOU NO** *Warner Bros. W 7729* ... 49 4
11 Nov 89 **THIS OLD HEART OF MINE** *Warner Bros. W 2686* [4] ... 51 3
13 Jan 90 ● **DOWNTOWN TRAIN** *Warner Bros. W 2647* ... 10 12
24 Nov 90 ● **IT TAKES TWO** *Warner Bros. ROD 1* [5] ... 5 8
16 Mar 91 ● **RHYTHM OF MY HEART** *Warner Bros. W 0017* ... 3 11
15 Jun 91 ● **THE MOTOWN SONG** *Warner Bros. W 0030* [6] ... 10 8
7 Sep 91 **BROKEN ARROW** *Warner Bros. W 0059* ... 54 3
7 Mar 92 **PEOPLE GET READY** *Epic 6577567* [1] ... 49 3
18 Apr 92 **YOUR SONG / BROKEN ARROW (re-issue)** *Warner Bros. W 0104* ... 41 4
5 Dec 92 ● **TOM TRAUBERT'S BLUES (WALTZING MATILDA)** *Warner Bros. W 0144* ... 6 9
20 Feb 93 **RUBY TUESDAY** *Warner Bros. W 0158CD* ... 11 6
17 Apr 93 **SHOTGUN WEDDING** *Warner Bros. W 0171CD* ... 21 4
26 Jun 93 ● **HAVE I TOLD YOU LATELY** *Warner Bros. W 0185CD* ... 5 9
21 Aug 93 **REASON TO BELIEVE** *Warner Bros. W 0198CD1* ... 51 3
18 Dec 93 **PEOPLE GET READY** *Warner Bros. W 0226CD1* ... 45 4
15 Jan 94 ● **ALL FOR LOVE** *A & M 5804772* [7] ▲ ... 2 13
20 May 95 **YOU'RE THE STAR** *Warner Bros. W 0296CD* ... 19 5
19 Aug 95 **LADY LUCK** *Warner Bros. W 0310CD1* ... 56 1
15 Jun 96 **PURPLE HEATHER** *Warner Bros. W 0354CD* [8] ... 16 5
14 Dec 96 **IF WE FALL IN LOVE TONIGHT** *Warner Bros. W 0380CD* ... 58 1
1 Nov 97 ● **DA YA THINK I'M SEXY?** *All Around the World CDGLOBE 150* [9] ... 7 10
30 May 98 **OOH LA LA** *Warner Brothers W 0446CD* ... 16 5
5 Sep 98 **ROCKS** *Warner Brothers W 0452CD1* ... 55 1
17 Apr 99 **FAITH OF THE HEART** *Universal UND 56235* ... 60 1
24 Mar 01 **I CAN'T DENY IT** *Atlantic AT 0096CD* ... 26 2

[1] Jeff Beck and Rod Stewart [2] Faces / Rod Stewart [3] Rod Stewart featuring the Scottish World Cup Football Squad [4] Rod Stewart featuring Ronald Isley [5] Rod Stewart and Tina Turner [6] Rod Stewart with backing vocals by The Temptations [7] Bryan Adams, Rod Stewart and Sting [8] Rod Stewart with the Scottish Euro '96 Squad [9] N-Trance featuring Rod Stewart

'Reason to Believe' and 'People Get Ready' in 1993 were re-recordings. 'Reason to Believe' additionally credits Ronnie Wood on the sleeve

See also FACES; GLASS TIGER; PYTHON LEE JACKSON

STEX *UK, male / female vocal / instrumental group (2 WEEKS)* pos/wks

19 Jan 91 **STILL FEEL THE RAIN** *Some Bizarre SBZ 7002* ... 63 2

STICKY featuring MS DYNAMITE *UK, male producer – Richard Forbes and UK, female rapper (6 WEEKS)* pos/wks

23 Jun 01 **BOOO!** *ffrr / Public Demand / Social Circles FCD 399* ... 12 6

STIFF LITTLE FINGERS *Ireland, male vocal / instrumental group (39 WEEKS)* pos/wks

29 Sep 79 **STRAW DOGS** *Chrysalis CHS 2368* ... 44 4
16 Feb 80 **AT THE EDGE** *Chrysalis CHS 2406* ... 15 9
24 May 80 **NOBODY'S HERO / TIN SOLDIERS** *Chrysalis CHS 2424* ... 36 5
2 Aug 80 **BACK TO FRONT** *Chrysalis CHS 2447* ... 49 4
28 Mar 81 **JUST FADE AWAY** *Chrysalis CHS 2510* ... 47 6
30 May 81 **SILVER LINING** *Chrysalis CHS 2517* ... 68 3
23 Jan 82 **LISTEN (EP)** *Chrysalis CHS 2580* ... 33 6
18 Sep 82 **BITS OF KIDS** *Chrysalis CHS 2637* ... 73 2

Tracks on Listen (EP): That's When Your Blood Bumps / Two Guitars Clash / Listen / Sad-Eyed People

Curtis STIGERS *US, male vocalist (34 WEEKS)* pos/wks

18 Jan 92 ● **I WONDER WHY** *Arista 114716* ... 5 10
28 Mar 92 ● **YOU'RE ALL THAT MATTERS TO ME** *Arista 115273* ... 6 12
11 Jul 92 **SLEEPING WITH THE LIGHTS ON** *Arista 74321102307* ... 53 4
17 Oct 92 **NEVER SAW A MIRACLE** *Arista 74321117257* ... 34 4
3 Jun 95 **THIS TIME** *Arista 74321286962* ... 28 3
2 Dec 95 **KEEP ME FROM THE COLD** *Arista 74321319162* ... 57 1

Stephen STILLS *US, male vocalist / instrumentalist (8 WEEKS)* pos/wks

13 Mar 71 **LOVE THE ONE YOU'RE WITH** *Atlantic 2091 046* ... 37 4
6 Jun 98 **HE GOT GAME** *Def Jam 5689852* [1] ... 16 4

[1] Public Enemy featuring Stephen Stills

See also CROSBY, STILLS, NASH and YOUNG

STILTSKIN *UK, male vocal / instrumental group – lead vocal Ray Wilson (15 WEEKS)* pos/wks

7 May 94 ★ **INSIDE** *White Water LEV 1CD* ... 1 13
24 Sep 94 **FOOTSTEPS** *White Water WWRD 2* ... 34 2

STING (143 Top 500) *World's best known ex-Police-man, b. Gordon Sumner, 2 Oct 1951, Newcastle, UK. This singer / songwriter / bass player has amassed more solo hits than as front man of that top-selling trio. As a soloist, he has won both Brit and Grammy awards (152 WEEKS)* pos/wks

14 Aug 82 **SPREAD A LITTLE HAPPINESS** *A & M AMS 8242* ... 16 8
8 Jun 85 **IF YOU LOVE SOMEBODY SET THEM FREE** *A & M AM 258* ... 26 7
24 Aug 85 **LOVE IS THE SEVENTH WAVE** *A & M AM 272* ... 41 5
19 Oct 85 **FORTRESS AROUND YOUR HEART** *A & M AM 286* ... 49 3
7 Dec 85 **RUSSIANS** *A & M AM 292* ... 12 11
15 Feb 86 **MOON OVER BOURBON STREET** *A & M AM 305* ... 44 4
1 Mar 86 **RUSSIANS (re-entry)** *A & M AM 292* ... 71 1
7 Nov 87 **WE'LL BE TOGETHER** *A & M AM 410* ... 41 4
20 Feb 88 **ENGLISHMAN IN NEW YORK** *A & M AM 431* ... 51 3
9 Apr 88 **FRAGILE** *A & M AM 439* ... 70 2
11 Aug 90 **ENGLISHMAN IN NEW YORK (re-mix)** *A & M AM 580* ... 15 7
12 Jan 91 **ALL THIS TIME** *A & M AM 713* ... 22 4
9 Mar 91 **MAD ABOUT YOU** *A & M AM 721* ... 56 2
4 May 91 **THE SOUL CAGES** *A & M AM 759* ... 57 1
29 Aug 92 **IT'S PROBABLY ME** *A & M AM 883* [1] ... 30 5
13 Feb 93 **IF I EVER LOSE MY FAITH IN YOU** *A & M AMCD 0172* ... 14 6
24 Apr 93 **SEVEN DAYS** *A & M 5802232* ... 25 4
19 Jun 93 **FIELDS OF GOLD** *A & M 5803012* ... 16 6
4 Sep 93 **SHAPE OF MY HEART** *A & M 5803532* ... 57 1
20 Nov 93 **DEMOLITION MAN** *A & M 5804512* ... 21 4
15 Jan 94 ● **ALL FOR LOVE** *A & M 5804772* [2] ▲ ... 2 13
26 Feb 94 **NOTHING 'BOUT ME** *A & M 5805292* ... 32 3
29 Oct 94 ● **WHEN WE DANCE** *A & M 5808612* ... 9 7
11 Feb 95 **THIS COWBOY SONG** *A & M 5809652* [3] ... 15 6
20 Jan 96 **SPIRITS IN THE MATERIAL WORLD** *MCA MCSTD 2113* [4] ... 36 2
2 Mar 96 **LET YOUR SOUL BE YOUR PILOT** *A & M 5813312* ... 15 4
11 May 96 **YOU STILL TOUCH ME** *A & M 5815472* ... 27 3
22 Jun 96 **LIVE AT TFI FRIDAY (EP)** *A & M 5817652* ... 53 2
14 Sep 96 **I WAS BROUGHT TO MY SENSES** *A & M 5818912* ... 31 2
30 Nov 96 **I'M SO HAPPY I CAN'T STOP CRYING** *A & M 5820312* ... 54 1
20 Dec 97 **ROXANNE '97 (re-mix)** *A & M 5824552* [5] ... 17 6
25 Sep 99 **BRAND NEW DAY** *A&M / Polydor 4971522* ... 13 5
29 Jan 00 **DESERT SONG** *A&M / Mercury 4972402* [6] ... 15 6
22 Apr 00 **AFTER THE RAIN HAS FALLEN** *A&M / Mercury 4973252* ... 31 4

[1] Sting with Eric Clapton [2] Bryan Adams, Rod Stewart and Sting [3] Sting featuring Pato Banton [4] Pato Banton with Sting [5] Sting and The Police [6] Sting featuring Cheb Mami

Tracks on Live at TFI Friday (EP): You Still Touch Me / Lithium Sunset / Message in a Bottle

STINGERS – *See B BUMBLE and the STINGERS*

Byron STINGILY *US, male vocalist (14 WEEKS)* pos/wks

25 Jan 97 **GET UP (EVERYBODY)** *Manifesto FESCD 19* ... 14 5
1 Nov 97 **SING A SONG** *Manifesto FESCD 35* ... 38 2
31 Jan 98 **YOU MAKE ME FEEL (MIGHTY REAL)** *Manifesto FESCD 38* ... 13 4
13 Jun 98 **TESTIFY** *Manifesto FESCD 42* ... 48 1
12 Feb 00 **THAT'S THE WAY LOVE IS** *Manifesto FESCD 66* ... 32 2

STINX *UK, female vocal duo (3 WEEKS)* pos/wks

24 Mar 01 **WHY DO YOU KEEP ON RUNNING** *HEBS HEBS 1* ... 49 3

STIX 'N' STONED *UK, male instrumental / production duo (2 WEEKS)* pos/wks

20 Jul 96 **OUTRAGEOUS** *Positiva CDTIV 52* ... 39 2

Catherine STOCK *UK, female vocalist (6 WEEKS)*

			pos	wks
18 Oct 86		**TO HAVE AND TO HOLD** *Sierra FED 29*	17	6

STOCK AITKEN WATERMAN *UK, male producers (36 WEEKS)*

			pos	wks
25 Jul 87		**ROADBLOCK** *Breakout USA 611*	13	9
24 Oct 87	●	**MR SLEAZE** *London NANA 14*	3	10
12 Dec 87		**PACKJAMMED (WITH THE PARTY POSSE)** *Breakout USA 620*	41	6
21 May 88		**ALL THE WAY** *MCA GOAL 1* [1]	64	2
3 Dec 88		**SS PAPARAZZI** *PWL PWL 22*	68	2
20 May 89	★	**FERRY 'CROSS THE MERSEY** *PWL PWL 41* [2] ■	1	7

[1] England Football Team and the 'sound' of Stock, Aitken and Waterman [2] Christians, Holly Johnson, Paul McCartney, Gerry Marsden and Stock Aitken Waterman

The listed flip side of 'Mr Sleaze' was 'Love in the First Degree' by Bananarama

Miriam STOCKLEY – *See PRAISE; ATLANTIS vs AVATAR*

Rhet STOLLER *UK, male instrumentalist – guitar (8 WEEKS)*

			pos	wks
12 Jan 61		**CHARIOT** *Decca F 11302*	26	8

Morris STOLOFF *US, orchestra (11 WEEKS)*

			pos	wks
1 Jun 56	●	**MOONGLOW AND THE THEME FROM 'PICNIC'** *Brunswick 05553*	7	11

Angie STONE *US, female vocalist (4 WEEKS)*

			pos	wks
15 Apr 00		**LIFE STORY** *Arista 74321748492*	22	3
16 Dec 00		**KEEP YOUR WORRIES** *Virgin VUSCD 177* [1]	57	1

[1] Guru's Jazzmatazz featuring Angie Stone

R & J STONE *UK / US, male / female vocal duo – Russell and Joanne Stone (9 WEEKS)*

			pos	wks
10 Jan 76	●	**WE DO IT** *RCA 2616*	5	9

STONE ROSES (443 Top 500) *'Madchester', 'Baggy' pioneers who successfully combined rock guitar and acid house attitude, inspiring a massive return to guitar-based bands in northern Britain in the 90s. Ian Brown (v), John Squire (g), Mani (aka Gary Mountfield) (b), Reni (aka Alan Wren) (d/v), all from Manchester. Their eponymous debut album, which peaked no higher than No.19 in 1989, continues to register in the top five of best all-time album surveys (77 WEEKS)*

			pos	wks
29 Jul 89		**SHE BANGS THE DRUMS** *Silvertone ORE 6*	36	3
25 Nov 89	●	**WHAT THE WORLD IS WAITING FOR / FOOL'S GOLD** *Silvertone ORE 13*	8	14
6 Jan 90		**SALLY CINNAMON** *Revolver REV 36*	75	1
20 Jan 90		**SALLY CINNAMON (re-entry)** *Revolver REV 36*	46	4
3 Mar 90	●	**ELEPHANT STONE** *Silvertone ORE 1*	8	6
17 Mar 90		**MADE OF STONE** *Silvertone ORE 2*	20	4
31 Mar 90		**SHE BANGS THE DRUMS (re-entry)** *Silvertone ORE 6*	34	3
14 Jul 90	●	**ONE LOVE** *Silvertone ORE 17*	4	7
15 Sep 90		**WHAT THE WORLD IS WAITING FOR / FOOL'S GOLD (re-entry)** *Silvertone ORE 13*	22	5
14 Sep 91		**I WANNA BE ADORED** *Silvertone ORE 31*	20	3
11 Jan 92		**WATERFALL** *Silvertone ORE 35*	27	4
11 Apr 92		**I AM THE RESURRECTION** *Silvertone ORE 40*	33	2
30 May 92		**FOOL'S GOLD (re-issue)** *Silvertone ORET 13*	73	1
3 Dec 94	●	**LOVE SPREADS** *Geffen GFSTD 84*	2	8
11 Mar 95		**TEN STOREY LOVE SONG** *Geffen GFSTD 87*	11	3
29 Apr 95		**FOOL'S GOLD (2nd re-issue)** *Silvertone ORECD 71*	25	3
11 Nov 95		**BEGGING YOU** *Geffen GFSTD 22060*	15	3
6 Mar 99		**FOOL'S GOLD (re-mix)** *Jive Electro 0523092*	25	3

See also Ian BROWN; SEAHORSES

STONE TEMPLE PILOTS *US, male vocal / instrumental group (11 WEEKS)*

			pos	wks
27 Mar 93		**SEX TYPE THING** *Atlantic A 5769CD*	60	2
4 Sep 93		**PLUSH** *Atlantic A 7349CD*	23	4
27 Nov 93		**SEX TYPE THING (re-issue)** *Atlantic A 7293CD*	55	2
20 Aug 94		**VASOLINE** *Atlantic A 5650CD*	48	2
10 Dec 94		**INTERSTATE LOVE SONG** *Atlantic A 7192CD*	53	1

STONEBRIDGE McGUINNESS *UK, male vocal / instrumental duo (2 WEEKS)*

			pos	wks
14 Jul 79		**OO-EEH BABY** *RCA PB 5163*	54	2

STONEFREE *UK, male vocalist (1 WEEK)*

			pos	wks
23 May 87		**CAN'T SAY 'BYE** *Ensign ENY 607*	73	1

STONEPROOF *UK, male producer – John Graham (1 WEEK)*

			pos	wks
15 May 99		**EVERYTHING'S NOT YOU** *VC Recordings VCRD 47*	68	1

STONKERS – *See HALE and PACE and the STONKERS*

STOP THE VIOLENCE MOVEMENT *US, male / female rap charity ensemble (1 WEEK)*

			pos	wks
18 Feb 89		**SELF DESTRUCTION** *Jive BDPST 1*	75	1

Axel STORDAHL – *See June HUTTON*

STORM *UK, male / female vocal / instrumental group (10 WEEKS)*

			pos	wks
17 Nov 79		**IT'S MY HOUSE** *Scope SC 10*	36	10

STORM *Germany, male production duo – Jam El Mar and Mark Spoon (19 WEEKS)*

			pos	wks
29 Aug 98		**STORM** *Positiva CDTIV 94*	32	2
12 Aug 00	●	**TIME TO BURN** *Data DATA 16CDS*	3	10
23 Dec 00		**STORM ANIMAL** *Data DATA 20CDS*	21	5
26 May 01		**STORM (re-mix)** *Positiva CDTIV 154*	32	2

See also TOKYO GHETTO PUSSY; JAM & SPOON featuring PLAVKA

Danny STORM *UK, male vocalist (4 WEEKS)*

			pos	wks
12 Apr 62		**HONEST I DO** *Piccadilly 7N 35025*	42	4

Rebecca STORM *UK, female vocalist (13 WEEKS)*

			pos	wks
13 Jul 85		**THE SHOW (THEME FROM 'CONNIE')** *Towerbell TVP 3*	22	13

STORYVILLE JAZZ BAND – *See Bob WALLIS and his STORYVILLE JAZZ BAND*

Izzy STRADLIN' *US, male vocalist / instrumentalist – guitar (2 WEEKS)*

			pos	wks
26 Sep 92		**PRESSURE DROP** *Geffen GFS 25*	45	2

See also GUNS N' ROSES

Nick STRAKER BAND *UK, male vocal / instrumental group (15 WEEKS)*

			pos	wks
2 Aug 80		**A WALK IN THE PARK** *CBS 8525*	20	12
15 Nov 80		**LEAVING ON THE MIDNIGHT TRAIN** *CBS 9088*	61	3

Peter STRAKER and the HANDS OF DR TELENY *UK, male vocalist and male vocal / instrumental group (4 WEEKS)*

			pos	wks
19 Feb 72		**THE SPIRIT IS WILLING** *RCA 2163*	40	4

STRANGE BEHAVIOUR – *See Jane KENNAWAY and STRANGE BEHAVIOUR*

STRANGE FRUIT – *See Jimmy NAIL*

STRANGELOVE *UK, male vocal / instrumental group (8 WEEKS)*

			pos	wks
20 Apr 96		**LIVING WITH THE HUMAN MACHINES** *Food CDFOOD 70*	53	1
15 Jun 96		**BEAUTIFUL ALONE** *Food CDFOOD 81*	35	2
19 Oct 96		**SWAY** *Food CDFOOD 82*	47	1
26 Jul 97		**THE GREATEST SHOW ON EARTH** *Food CDFOODS 97*	36	2
11 Oct 97		**FREAK** *Food CDFOOD 105*	43	1
21 Feb 98		**ANOTHER NIGHT IN** *Food CDFOOD 110*	46	1

STRANGLERS (97 Top 500)

Arguably most commercially successful and long-lasting group to emerge from the punk / new wave scene: Hugh Cornwell (v/g), Jean-Jacques Burnel (b/v), Dave Greenfield (k), Jet Black (d). This London-based band had at least one hit every year between 1977 and 1992 (194 WEEKS)

Date		Title	pos	wks
19 Feb 77		**(GET A) GRIP (ON YOURSELF)** *United Artists UP 36211*	44	4
21 May 77	●	**PEACHES / GO BUDDY GO** *United Artists UP 36248*	8	14
30 Jul 77	●	**SOMETHING BETTER CHANGE / STRAIGHTEN OUT** *United Artists UP 36277*	9	8
24 Sep 77	●	**NO MORE HEROES** *United Artists UP 36300*	8	9
4 Feb 78		**FIVE MINUTES** *United Artists UP 36350*	11	9
6 May 78		**NICE 'N SLEAZY** *United Artists UP 36379*	18	8
12 Aug 78		**WALK ON BY** *United Artists UP 36429*	21	8
18 Aug 79		**DUCHESS** *United Artists BP 308*	14	9
20 Oct 79		**NUCLEAR DEVICE (THE WIZARD OF AUS)** *United Artists BP 318*	36	4
1 Dec 79		**DON'T BRING HARRY (EP)** *United Artists STR 1*	41	3
22 Mar 80		**BEAR CAGE** *United Artists BP 344*	36	5
7 Jun 80		**WHO WANTS THE WORLD** *United Artists BP 355*	39	4
31 Jan 81		**THROWN AWAY** *Liberty BP 383*	42	4
14 Nov 81		**LET ME INTRODUCE YOU TO THE FAMILY** *Liberty BP 405*	42	3
9 Jan 82	●	**GOLDEN BROWN** *Liberty BP 407*	2	12
24 Apr 82		**LA FOLIE** *Liberty BP 410*	47	3
24 Jul 82	●	**STRANGE LITTLE GIRL** *Liberty BP 412*	7	9
8 Jan 83	●	**EUROPEAN FEMALE** *Epic EPC A 2893*	9	6
26 Feb 83		**MIDNIGHT SUMMER DREAM** *Epic EPC A 3167*	35	4
6 Aug 83		**PARADISE** *Epic A 3387*	48	3
6 Oct 84		**SKIN DEEP** *Epic A 4738*	15	7
1 Dec 84		**NO MERCY** *Epic A 4921*	37	7
16 Feb 85		**LET ME DOWN EASY** *Epic A 6045*	48	4
23 Aug 86		**NICE IN NICE** *Epic 6500557*	30	5
18 Oct 86		**ALWAYS THE SUN** *Epic SOLAR 1*	30	5
13 Dec 86		**BIG IN AMERICA** *Epic HUGE 1*	48	6
7 Mar 87		**SHAKIN' LIKE A LEAF** *Epic SHEIK 1*	58	4
9 Jan 88	●	**ALL DAY AND ALL OF THE NIGHT** *Epic VICE 1*	7	7
28 Jan 89		**GRIP '89 (GET A) GRIP (ON YOURSELF) (re-mix)** *EMI EM 84*	33	3
17 Feb 90		**96 TEARS** *Epic TEARS 1*	17	6
21 Apr 90		**SWEET SMELL OF SUCCESS** *Epic TEARS 2*	65	2
5 Jan 91		**ALWAYS THE SUN (re-mix)** *Epic 6564307*	29	5
30 Mar 91		**GOLDEN BROWN (re-mix)** *Epic 6567617*	68	2
22 Aug 92		**HEAVEN OR HELL** *Psycho WOK 2025*	46	2

'Go Buddy Go' credited with 'Peaches' from 11 Jun 1977. 'Straighten Out' credited with 'Something Better Change' from 13 Aug 1977. Tracks on Don't Bring Harry (EP): Don't Bring Harry / Wired / Crabs (Live) / In the Shadows (Live)

STRAW *UK, male vocal / instrumental group (4 WEEKS)*

Date		Title	pos	wks
6 Feb 99		**THE AEROPLANE SONG** *WEA WEA 196CD*	37	2
24 Apr 99		**MOVING TO CALIFORNIA** *WEA WEA 205CD1*	50	1
3 Mar 01		**SAILING OFF THE EDGE OF THE WORLD** *Columbia 6708452*	52	1

STRAWBERRY SWITCHBLADE

UK, female vocal duo – Rose McDowell and Jill Bryson (26 WEEKS)

Date		Title	pos	wks
17 Nov 84	●	**SINCE YESTERDAY** *Korova KOW 38*	5	17
23 Mar 85		**LET HER GO** *Korova KOW 39*	59	5
21 Sep 85		**JOLENE** *Korova KOW 42*	53	4

STRAWBS *UK, male vocal / instrumental group (27 WEEKS)*

Date		Title	pos	wks
28 Oct 72		**LAY DOWN** *A & M AMS 7035*	12	13
27 Jan 73	●	**PART OF THE UNION** *A & M AMS 7047*	2	11
6 Oct 73		**SHINE ON SILVER SUN** *A & M AMS 7082*	34	3

STRAY CATS *US, male vocal / instrumental group (49 WEEKS)*

Date		Title	pos	wks
29 Nov 80	●	**RUNAWAY BOYS** *Arista SCAT 1*	9	10
7 Feb 81	●	**ROCK THIS TOWN** *Arista SCAT 2*	9	8
25 Apr 81		**STRAY CAT STRUT** *Arista SCAT 3*	11	10
20 Jun 81		**THE RACE IS ON** *Swansong SSK 19425* [1]	34	6
7 Nov 81		**YOU DON'T BELIEVE ME** *Arista SCAT 4*	57	3
6 Aug 83		**(SHE'S) SEXY AND 17** *Arista SCAT 6*	29	9
4 Mar 89		**BRING IT BACK AGAIN** *EMI USA MT 62*	64	3

[1] Dave Edmunds and the Stray Cats

STRAY MOB – *See MC SKAT KAT and the STRAY MOB*

STREETBAND *UK, male vocal / instrumental group (6 WEEKS)*

Date		Title	pos	wks
4 Nov 78		**TOAST / HOLD ON** *Logo GO 325*	18	6

See also Paul YOUNG

STREETS *UK, male producer – Mick Skinner (5 WEEKS)*

Date		Title	pos	wks
20 Oct 01		**HAS IT COME TO THIS** *WEA / 679 L 001*	18	4
1 Dec 01		**HAS IT COME TO THIS (re-entry)** *WEA / 679 L 001*	55	1

Barbra STREISAND (137 Top 500)

Acclaimed song stylist who has more gold albums than any other female, b. 24 Apr 1942, Brooklyn, US. This world-renowned MOR vocalist / actress has collected countless awards for her recordings and her stage and film work, and is a recipient of both Grammy Living Legend and Lifetime Achievement awards (155 WEEKS)

Date		Title	pos	wks
20 Jan 66		**SECOND HAND ROSE** *CBS 202025*	14	13
30 Jan 71		**STONEY END** *CBS 5321*	46	1
13 Feb 71		**STONEY END (re-entry)** *CBS 5321*	27	10
30 Mar 74		**THE WAY WE WERE** *CBS 1915* ▲	31	6
9 Apr 77	●	**LOVE THEME FROM 'A STAR IS BORN' (EVERGREEN)** *CBS 4855* ▲	3	19
25 Nov 78	●	**YOU DON'T BRING ME FLOWERS** *CBS 6803* [1] ▲	5	12
3 Nov 79	●	**NO MORE TEARS (ENOUGH IS ENOUGH)** *Casablanca CAN 174/ CBS 8000* [2] ▲	3	13
4 Oct 80	★	**WOMAN IN LOVE** *CBS 8966* ▲	1	16
6 Dec 80		**GUILTY** *CBS 9315* [3]	34	10
30 Jan 82		**COMIN' IN AND OUT OF YOUR LIFE** *CBS A 1789*	66	3
20 Mar 82		**MEMORY** *CBS A 1903*	34	6
5 Nov 88		**TILL I LOVED YOU (LOVE THEME FROM 'GOYA')** *CBS BARB 2* [4]	16	7
7 Mar 92		**PLACES THAT BELONG TO YOU** *Columbia 6577947*	17	5
5 Jun 93		**WITH ONE LOOK** *Columbia 6593422*	30	3
15 Jan 94		**THE MUSIC OF THE NIGHT** *Columbia 6597382* [5]	54	3
30 Apr 94		**AS IF WE NEVER SAID GOODBYE** *Columbia 6603572*	20	3
8 Feb 97	●	**I FINALLY FOUND SOMEONE** *A&M 5820832* [6]	10	7
15 Nov 97	●	**TELL HIM** *Epic 6653052* [7]	3	15
30 Oct 99		**IF YOU EVER LEAVE ME** *Columbia 6681242* [8]	26	3

[1] Barbra and Neil [2] Donna Summer and Barbra Streisand [3] Barbra Streisand and Barry Gibb [4] Barbra Streisand and Don Johnson [5] Barbra Streisand (duet with Michael Crawford) [6] Barbra Streisand and Bryan Adams [7] Barbra Streisand and Celine Dion [8] Barbra Streisand / Vince Gill

Neil was Neil Diamond. 'No More Tears (Enough Is Enough)' was released simultaneously on two different labels, a 7-inch single on Casablanca and a 12-inch on CBS

STRESS *UK, male vocal / instrumental group (1 WEEK)*

Date		Title	pos	wks
13 Oct 90		**BEAUTIFUL PEOPLE** *Eternal YZ 495*	74	1

STRETCH *UK, male vocal / instrumental group (9 WEEKS)*

Date		Title	pos	wks
8 Nov 75		**WHY DID YOU DO IT** *Anchor ANC 1021*	16	9

STRETCH 'N' VERN present MADDOG *UK, male instrumental / production duo – Stuart Collins and Julian Peake (14 WEEKS)*

Date		Title	pos	wks
14 Sep 96	●	**I'M ALIVE** *ffrr FCD 284*	6	9
9 Aug 97		**GET UP! GO INSANE!** *ffrr FCD 304*	17	5

STRICT INSTRUCTOR *Russia, female vocalist (1 WEEK)*

Date		Title	pos	wks
24 Oct 98		**STEP-TWO-THREE-FOUR** *All Around the World CDGLOBE 155*	49	1

STRIKE

UK / Australia, male / female vocal / instrumental group (24 WEEKS)

Date		Title	pos	wks
24 Dec 94		**U SURE DO** *Fresh FRSHD 19*	31	5
1 Apr 95	●	**U SURE DO (re-entry)** *Fresh FRSHD 19*	4	9
23 Sep 95		**THE MORNING AFTER (FREE AT LAST)** *Fresh FRSHD 37*	38	1
29 Jun 96		**INSPIRATION** *Fresh FRSHD 45*	27	2
16 Nov 96		**MY LOVE IS FOR REAL** *Fresh FRSHD 46*	35	2

31 May 97	**I HAVE PEACE** *Fresh FRSHCD 58*	17	4
25 Sep 99	**U SURE DO (re-mix)** *Fresh FRSHD 78*	53	1

STRIKERS *US, male vocal / instrumental group (5 WEEKS)*

		pos	wks
6 Jun 81	**BODY MUSIC** *Epic EPC A 1290*	45	5

STRING-A-LONGS *US, male instrumental group (16 WEEKS)*

		pos	wks
23 Feb 61 ●	**WHEELS** *London HLU 9278*	8	16

STRINGS OF LOVE
Italy, male / female vocal / instrumental group (2 WEEKS)

		pos	wks
3 Mar 90	**NOTHING HAS BEEN PROVED** *Breakout USA 688*	59	2

STROKES *US, male vocal / instrumental group (13 WEEKS)*

		pos	wks
7 Jul 01	**HARD TO EXPLAIN / NEW YORK CITY COPS** *Rough Trade RTRADESCD 023*	16	5
7 Jul 01	**MODERN AGE** *Rough Trade RTRADESCD 010*	74	1
21 Jul 01	**MODERN AGE (re-entry)** *Rough Trade RTRADESCD 010*	68	1
11 Aug 01	**MODERN AGE (2nd re-entry)** *Rough Trade RTRADESCD 010*	71	1
17 Nov 01	**LAST NITE** *Rough Trade RTRADESCD 041*	14	5

Modern Age is a 3-track CD featuring 'Modern Age', 'Last Nite' and 'Barely Legal'

Joe STRUMMER *UK, male vocalist – John Mellor (13 WEEKS)*

		pos	wks
2 Aug 86	**LOVE KILLS** *CBS A 7244*	69	1
23 Dec 95	**JUST THE ONE** *China WOKCD 2076* [1]	12	8
29 Jun 96 ●	**ENGLAND'S IRIE** *Radioactive RAXTD 25* [2]	6	4

[1] Levellers, special guest Joe Strummer [2] Black Grape featuring Joe Strummer and Keith Allen

See also CLASH

STRYKER – *See MANCHESTER UNITED FOOTBALL CLUB*

Chad STUART and Jeremy CLYDE *UK, male vocal duo (7 WEEKS)*

		pos	wks
28 Nov 63	**YESTERDAY'S GONE** *Ember EMB S 180*	37	7

STUDIO 45 *Germany, male DJ / production duo (2 WEEKS)*

		pos	wks
20 Feb 99	**FREAK IT!** *Azuli AZNYCD 090*	36	2

STUDIO 2 *Jamaica, male vocalist – Errol Jones (1 WEEK)*

		pos	wks
27 Jun 98	**TRAVELLING MAN** *Multiply CDMULTY 35*	40	1

STUMP *UK, male vocal / instrumental group (1 WEEK)*

		pos	wks
13 Aug 88	**CHARLTON HESTON** *Ensign ENY 614*	72	1

STUNTMASTERZ
UK, male production duo – Steve Harris and Pete Cook (9 WEEKS)

		pos	wks
3 Mar 01 ●	**THE LADYBOY IS MINE** *East West EW 226CD*	10	9

STUTZ BEARCATS and the Denis KING ORCHESTRA *UK, male / female vocal group with orchestra (6 WEEKS)*

		pos	wks
24 Apr 82	**THE SONG THAT I SING (THEME FROM 'WE'LL MEET AGAIN')** *Multi-Media Tapes MMT 6*	36	6

STYLE COUNCIL (296 Top 500)
Eighties chart regulars: Paul Weller (v/g), Mick Talbot (k) and sometimes Dee C Lee (v – former Wham! backing vocalist and Weller's wife). As with Weller's previous band, The Jam, most of this London act's hits were in their homeland (103 WEEKS)

		pos	wks
19 Mar 83 ●	**SPEAK LIKE A CHILD** *Polydor TSC 1*	4	8
28 May 83	**MONEY GO ROUND (PART 1)** *Polydor TSC 2*	11	6
13 Aug 83 ●	**LONG HOT SUMMER** *Polydor TSC 3*	3	9
20 Aug 83	**MONEY GO ROUND (PART 1) (re-entry)** *Polydor TSC 2*	74	1
19 Nov 83	**SOLID BOND IN YOUR HEART** *Polydor TSC 4*	11	8
18 Feb 84 ●	**MY EVER CHANGING MOODS** *Polydor TSC 5*	5	7
26 May 84 ●	**GROOVIN' (YOU'RE THE BEST THING / THE BIG BOSS GROOVE)** *Polydor TSC 6*	5	8
13 Oct 84 ●	**SHOUT TO THE TOP** *Polydor TSC 7*	7	8
11 May 85 ●	**WALLS COME TUMBLING DOWN!** *Polydor TSC 8*	6	7
6 Jul 85	**COME TO MILTON KEYNES** *Polydor TSC 9*	23	5
28 Sep 85	**THE LODGERS** *Polydor TSC 10*	13	6
5 Apr 86	**HAVE YOU EVER HAD IT BLUE** *Polydor CINE 1*	14	6
17 Jan 87 ●	**IT DIDN'T MATTER** *Polydor TSC 12*	9	5
14 Mar 87	**WAITING** *Polydor TSC 13*	52	3
31 Oct 87	**WANTED** *Polydor TSC 14*	20	4
28 May 88	**LIFE AT A TOP PEOPLE'S HEALTH FARM** *Polydor TSC 15*	28	3
23 Jul 88	**HOW SHE THREW IT ALL AWAY (EP)** *Polydor TSC 16*	41	2
18 Feb 89	**PROMISED LAND** *Polydor TSC 17*	27	5
27 May 89	**LONG HOT SUMMER 89 (re-mix)** *Polydor LHS 1*	48	2

'Paris Match' was listed with 'Long Hot Summer' from 3 Sep 1983. It peaked at No.7. Tracks on How She Threw It All Away (EP): How She Threw It All Away / Love the First Time / Long Hot Summer / I Do Like to Be B-Side the A-Side. The version of 'Long Hot Summer' on the EP is a re-recording of their third hit

STYLISTICS (166 Top 500)
Stylish and smooth vocal group from Philadelphia, US, fronted by falsetto-voiced Russell Thompkins Jr (b. 21 Mar 1951), whose UK hits continued after success in their homeland diminished. The quintet's Greatest Hits album topped the UK album chart in 1975 (143 WEEKS)

		pos	wks
24 Jun 72	**BETCHA BY GOLLY WOW** *Avco 6105 011*	13	12
4 Nov 72 ●	**I'M STONE IN LOVE WITH YOU** *Avco 6105 015*	9	10
17 Mar 73	**BREAK UP TO MAKE UP** *Avco 6105 020*	34	5
30 Jun 73	**PEEK-A-BOO** *Avco 6105 023*	35	6
19 Jan 74 ●	**ROCKIN' ROLL BABY** *Avco 6105 026*	6	9
13 Jul 74 ●	**YOU MAKE ME FEEL BRAND NEW** *Avco 6105 028*	2	14
19 Oct 74 ●	**LET'S PUT IT ALL TOGETHER** *Avco 6105 032*	9	9
25 Jan 75	**STAR ON A TV SHOW** *Avco 6105 035*	12	8
10 May 75 ●	**SING BABY SING** *Avco 6105 036*	3	10
26 Jul 75 ★	**CAN'T GIVE YOU ANYTHING (BUT MY LOVE)** *Avco 6105 039*	1	11
15 Nov 75 ●	**NA NA IS THE SADDEST WORD** *Avco 6105 041*	5	10
14 Feb 76 ●	**FUNKY WEEKEND** *Avco 6105 044*	10	7
24 Apr 76 ●	**CAN'T HELP FALLING IN LOVE** *H & L 6105 050*	4	7
7 Aug 76 ●	**16 BARS** *H & L 6105 059*	7	9
27 Nov 76	**YOU'LL NEVER GET TO HEAVEN (EP)** *H & L STYL 001*	24	9
26 Mar 77	**7000 DOLLARS AND YOU** *H & L 6105 073*	24	7

Tracks on You'll Never Get to Heaven (EP): You'll Never Get to Heaven / Country Living / You Are Beautiful / The Miracle

STYLUS TROUBLE *UK, male producer – Pete Heller (1 WEEK)*

		pos	wks
23 Jun 01	**SPUTNIK** *Junior London BRG 014*	63	1

See also HELLER & FARLEY PROJECT; Pete HELLER; FIRE ISLAND

STYX *US, male vocal / instrumental group (18 WEEKS)*

		pos	wks
5 Jan 80 ●	**BABE** *A & M AMS 7489* ▲	6	10
24 Jan 81	**THE BEST OF TIMES** *A & M AMS 8102*	42	5
18 Jun 83	**DON'T LET IT END** *A & M AM 120*	56	3

SUB SUB *UK, male instrumental / production group (12 WEEKS)*

		pos	wks
10 Apr 93 ●	**AIN'T NO LOVE (AIN'T NO USE)** *Rob's CDROB 9* [1]	3	11
19 Feb 94	**RESPECT** *Rob's CDROB 19*	49	1

[1] Sub Sub featuring Melanie Williams

SUBCIRCUS
Denmark / UK, male vocal / instrumental group (2 WEEKS)

		pos	wks
26 Apr 97	**YOU LOVE YOU** *Echo ECSCD 34*	61	1
12 Jul 97	**86'D** *Echo ECSCX 43*	56	1

SUBLIME *US, male vocal / instrumental group (1 WEEK)*

		pos	wks
5 Jul 97	**WHAT I GOT** *Gasoline Alley MCSTD 48045*	71	1

SUBLIMINAL CUTS
Holland, male producer – Patrick Prinz (3 WEEKS)

		pos	wks
15 Oct 94	**LE VOIE LE SOLEIL** *XL XLS 53CD*	69	1
20 Jul 96	**LE VOIE LE SOLEIL (re-mix)** *XL XLSR 53CD*	23	2

See also ARTEMESIA; ETHICS; MOVIN' MELODIES

SUBMERGE featuring Jan JOHNSTON *US, male producer / instrumentalist and US, female vocalist (2 WEEKS)* pos/wks

8 Feb 97	TAKE ME BY THE HAND *AM:PM 5821012*	28	2

SUBSONIC 2 *UK, male rap duo (3 WEEKS)* pos/wks

13 Jul 91	THE UNSUNG HEROES OF HIP HOP *Unity 6577947*	63	3

SUBTERRANIA featuring Ann CONSUELO *Sweden, male / female vocal / instrumental duo (1 WEEK)* pos/wks

5 Jun 93	DO IT FOR LOVE *Champion CHAMPCD 297*	68	1

SUEDE *London-based Britpop pioneers include photogenic frontman Brett Anderson (v) and co-writer Bernard Butler (g) who left 1994. MM's "Best Band in Britain" won the Mercury Music Prize for their 1993 self-titled debut album which sold more than 100,000 in its first week (68 WEEKS)* pos/wks

23 May 92	THE DROWNERS / TO THE BIRDS *Nude NUD 1S*	49	2
26 Sep 92	METAL MICKEY *Nude NUD 3S*	17	3
6 Mar 93 ●	ANIMAL NITRATE *Nude NUD 4CD*	7	7
29 May 93	SO YOUNG *Nude NUD 5CD*	22	3
26 Feb 94 ●	STAY TOGETHER *Nude NUD 9CD*	3	6
24 Sep 94	WE ARE THE PIGS *Nude NUD 10CD*	18	3
19 Nov 94	THE WILD ONES *Nude NUD 11CD1*	18	4
11 Feb 95	NEW GENERATION *Nude NUD 12CD1*	21	3
11 Mar 95	NEW GENERATION (re-entry) *Nude NUD 12CD1*	75	1
10 Aug 96 ●	TRASH *Nude NUD 21CD1*	3	6
26 Oct 96 ●	BEAUTIFUL ONES *Nude NUD 23CD1*	8	5
25 Jan 97 ●	SATURDAY NIGHT *Nude NUD 24CD1*	6	4
19 Apr 97 ●	LAZY *Nude NUD 27CD1*	9	3
23 Aug 97 ●	FILMSTAR *Nude NUD 30CD1*	9	4
24 Apr 99 ●	ELECTRICITY *Nude NUD 43CD1*	5	5
3 Jul 99	SHE'S IN FASHION *Nude NUD 44CD1*	13	5
18 Sep 99	EVERYTHING WILL FLOW *Nude NUD 45CD1*	24	2
20 Nov 99	CAN'T GET ENOUGH *Nude NUD 47CD1*	23	2

SUENO LATINO *Italy, male production duo (6 WEEKS)* pos/wks

23 Sep 89	SUENO LATINO *BCM BCM 323* [1]	47	5
11 Nov 00	SUENO LATINO (re-mix) *Distinctive DISNCD 64*	68	1

[1] Sueno Latino featuring Carolina Damas

SUGABABES *UK, female vocal group (26 WEEKS)* pos/wks

23 Sep 00 ●	OVERLOAD *London LONCD 449*	6	8
30 Dec 00	NEW YEAR *London LONCD 455*	12	9
21 Apr 01	RUN FOR COVER *London LONCD 459*	13	7
28 Jul 01	SOUL SOUND *London LONCD 460*	30	2

SUGAR *US, male vocal / instrumental group (7 WEEKS)* pos/wks

31 Oct 92	A GOOD IDEA *Creation CRE 143*	65	1
30 Jan 93	IF I CAN'T CHANGE YOUR MIND *Creation CRESCD 149*	30	2
21 Aug 93	TILTED *Creation CRECD 156*	48	1
3 Sep 94	YOUR FAVORITE THING *Creation CRESCD 186*	40	2
29 Oct 94	BELIEVE WHAT YOU'RE SAYING *Creation CRESCD 193*	73	1

SUGAR CANE *US, male / female vocal group (5 WEEKS)* pos/wks

30 Sep 78	MONTEGO BAY *Ariola Hansa AHA 524*	54	5

SUGAR RAY *US, male vocal / instrumental group (12 WEEKS)* pos/wks

31 Jan 98	FLY *Atlantic AT 0008CD*	58	1
29 May 99 ●	EVERY MORNING *Lava / Atlantic AT 0065CD*	10	9
20 Oct 01	WHEN IT'S OVER *Atlantic AT 0114CD*	32	2

SUGARCUBES *Iceland, male / female vocal / instrumental group (22 WEEKS)* pos/wks

14 Nov 87	BIRTHDAY *One Little Indian 7TP 7*	65	3
30 Jan 88	COLD SWEAT *One Little Indian 7TP 9*	56	4
16 Apr 88	DEUS *One Little Indian 7TP 10*	51	3
3 Sep 88	BIRTHDAY (re-recording) *One Little Indian 7TP 11*	65	3
16 Sep 89	REGINA *One Little Indian 26TP7*	55	2
11 Jan 92	HIT *One Little Indian 62 TP7*	17	6
3 Oct 92	BIRTHDAY (re-mix) *One Little Indian 104 TP12*	64	1

See also BJÖRK

SUGARHILL GANG *US, male rap group (16 WEEKS)* pos/wks

1 Dec 79 ●	RAPPER'S DELIGHT *Sugarhill SHL 101*	3	11
11 Sep 82	THE LOVER IN YOU *Sugarhill SH 116*	54	3
25 Nov 89	RAPPER'S DELIGHT (re-mix) *Sugarhill SHRD 0007*	58	2

SUGGS *UK, male vocalist – Graham McPherson (46 WEEKS)* pos/wks

12 Aug 95 ●	I'M ONLY SLEEPING / OFF ON HOLIDAY *WEA YZ 975CD*	7	6
14 Oct 95	CAMDEN TOWN *WEA WEA 019CD*	14	6
16 Dec 95	THE TUNE *WEA WEA 031CD*	33	3
13 Apr 96 ●	CECILIA *WEA WEA 042CD1* [1]	4	17
24 Aug 96	CECILIA (re-entry) *WEA WEA 042CD1* [1]	65	1
7 Sep 96	CECILIA (2nd re-entry) *WEA WEA 042CD1* [1]	59	1
21 Sep 96	NO MORE ALCOHOL *WEA WEA 065CD1* [1]	24	4
17 May 97	BLUE DAY *WEA WEA 112CD* [2]	22	5
5 Sep 98	I AM *WEA WEA 174CD*	38	3

[1] Suggs featuring Louchie Lou and Michie One [2] Suggs & Co featuring Chelsea Team

See also MADNESS

SULTANA *Italy, male instrumental / production group (1 WEEK)* pos/wks

26 Mar 94	TE AMO *Union City UCRD 28*	57	1

SULTANS OF PING *Ireland, male vocal / instrumental group (12 WEEKS)* pos/wks

8 Feb 92	WHERE'S ME JUMPER? *Divine ATHY 01* [1]	67	2
9 May 92	STUPID KID *Divine ATHY 02* [1]	67	1
10 Oct 92	VERONICA *Divine ATHY 03* [1]	69	1
9 Jan 93	YOU TALK TOO MUCH *Rhythm King 6588872* [1]	26	3
11 Sep 93	TEENAGE PUNKS *Epic 6595792*	49	2
30 Oct 93	MICHIKO *Epic 6598222*	43	2
19 Feb 94	WAKE UP AND SCRATCH ME *Epic 6601122*	50	1

[1] Sultans of Ping FC

SUM 41 *Canada, male vocal / instrumental group (12 WEEKS)* pos/wks

13 Oct 01 ●	FAT LIP *Mercury 5888012*	8	9
15 Dec 01	IN TOO DEEP *Mercury 5888982*	13	3+

SUMMER – *See SNAP*

Donna SUMMER (33) Top 500 *"Queen of disco music", b. LaDonna Gaines, 31 Dec 1948, Massachusetts, US. Germany was the launching pad for this diva, who had eight successive US Top 5 singles in the late 1970s. She was also the first female to score three consecutive US No.1 albums (299 WEEKS)* pos/wks

17 Jan 76 ●	LOVE TO LOVE YOU BABY *GTO GT 17*	4	9
29 May 76	COULD IT BE MAGIC *GTO GT 60*	40	7
25 Dec 76	WINTER MELODY *GTO GT 76*	27	6
9 Jul 77 ★	I FEEL LOVE *GTO GT 100*	1	11
20 Aug 77 ●	DEEP DOWN INSIDE (THEME FROM 'THE DEEP') *Casablanca CAN 111*	5	10
24 Sep 77	I REMEMBER YESTERDAY *GTO GT 107*	14	7
3 Dec 77 ●	LOVE'S UNKIND *GTO GT 113*	3	13
10 Dec 77 ●	I LOVE YOU *Casablanca CAN 114*	10	9
25 Feb 78	RUMOUR HAS IT *Casablanca CAN 122*	19	8
22 Apr 78	BACK IN LOVE AGAIN *GTO GT 117*	29	7
10 Jun 78	LAST DANCE *Casablanca TGIF 2*	70	1
24 Jun 78	LAST DANCE (re-entry) *Casablanca TGIF 2*	51	8
14 Oct 78 ●	MACARTHUR PARK *Casablanca CAN 131* ▲	5	10
17 Feb 79	HEAVEN KNOWS *Casablanca CAN 141*	34	8
12 May 79	HOT STUFF *Casablanca CAN 151* ▲	11	10
7 Jul 79	BAD GIRLS *Casablanca CAN 155* ▲	14	10
1 Sep 79	DIM ALL THE LIGHTS *Casablanca CAN 162*	29	9
3 Nov 79 ●	NO MORE TEARS (ENOUGH IS ENOUGH) *Casablanca CAN 174 / CBS 8000* [1] ▲	3	13
16 Feb 80	ON THE RADIO *Casablanca NB 2236*	32	6
21 Jun 80	SUNSET PEOPLE *Casablanca CAN 198*	46	5

UK No.1 ★ UK Top 10 ● Still on chart + UK million seller ◆ UK entry at No.1 ■ US No.1 ▲

1994

IN THE YEAR IN WHICH THE IRA DECLARED A CEASEFIRE, NELSON MANDELA'S ANC WAS VOTED INTO POWER IN SOUTH AFRICA, O J SIMPSON FOUND A MASSIVE WORLDWIDE AUDIENCE WHILE ESCAPING FROM THE POLICE IN A CHEROKEE JEEP, AND WHIGFIELD BECAME THE FIRST ARTIST TO DEBUT AT NO.1, **BECK** TALKS ABOUT HIS REASONING BEHIND HIS BREAKTHROUGH HIT 'LOSER'...

"The people who took that song to heart were the jock people, the popular people, the attractive, stronger ones. But it was really coming from someone – myself – feeling displaced from the 80s, a time of materialism where everybody was cashing in and making money. If you went to school and you were wearing the same shoes you had a year ago, and you'd grown out of them, and your toe was coming out of a hole, it was not your time. You were not accepted. The people who embraced it represented the reason the song was written."

SINGLE OF THE YEAR 'Love Is All Around' Wet Wet Wet
ALBUM OF THE YEAR 'Music Box' Mariah Carey

		pos	wks
27 Sep 80	**THE WANDERER** *Geffen K 79180*	48	6
17 Jan 81	**COLD LOVE** *Geffen K 79193*	44	3
10 Jul 82	**LOVE IS IN CONTROL (FINGER ON THE TRIGGER)** *Warner Bros. K 79302*	18	11
6 Nov 82	**STATE OF INDEPENDENCE** *Warner Bros. K 79344*	14	11
4 Dec 82	**I FEEL LOVE (re-mix)** *Casablanca FEEL 7*	21	10
5 Mar 83	**THE WOMAN IN ME** *Warner Bros. U 9983*	62	2
18 Jun 83	**SHE WORKS HARD FOR THE MONEY** *Mercury DONNA 1*	25	8
24 Sep 83	**UNCONDITIONAL LOVE** *Mercury DONNA 2*	14	12
21 Jan 84	**STOP LOOK AND LISTEN** *Mercury DONNA 3*	57	2
24 Oct 87	**DINNER WITH GERSHWIN** *Warner Bros. U 8237*	13	11
23 Jan 88	**ALL SYSTEMS GO** *WEA U 8122*	54	3
25 Feb 89 ●	**THIS TIME I KNOW IT'S FOR REAL** *Warner Bros. U 7780*	3	14
27 May 89 ●	**I DON'T WANNA GET HURT** *Warner Bros. U 7567*	7	9
26 Aug 89	**LOVE'S ABOUT TO CHANGE MY HEART** *Warner Bros. U 7494*	20	6
25 Nov 89	**WHEN LOVE TAKES OVER YOU** *WEA U 7361*	72	1
17 Nov 90	**STATE OF INDEPENDENCE (re-issue)** *Warner Bros. U 2857*	45	3
12 Jan 91	**BREAKAWAY** *Warner Bros. U 3308*	49	4
30 Nov 91	**WORK THAT MAGIC** *Warner Bros. U 5937*	74	1
12 Nov 94	**MELODY OF LOVE (WANNA BE LOVED)** *Mercury MERCD 418*	21	3
9 Sep 95 ●	**I FEEL LOVE** *Manifesto FESCD 1*	8	5
6 Apr 96	**STATE OF INDEPENDENCE (re-mix)** *Manifesto FESCD 7* [2]	13	5
11 Jul 98	**CARRY ON** *Almighty CDALMY 120* [3]	65	1
30 Oct 99	**I WILL GO WITH YOU (CON TE PARTIRO)** *Epic 6682092*	44	1

[1] Donna Summer and Barbra Streisand [2] Donna Summer featuring the All Star Choir [3] Donna Summer and Giorgio Moroder

'No More Tears (Enough Is Enough)' was released simultaneously on two different labels, a 7-inch single on Casablanca and a 12-inch on CBS. 'Unconditional Love' features the additional vocals of Musical Youth. 'I Feel Love' in 1995 is a re-recording

SUMMER DAZE *UK, male instrumental / production duo (1 WEEK)*

		pos	wks
26 Oct 96	**SAMBA MAGIC** *VC VCRD 14*	61	1

Mark SUMMERS *UK, male producer (6 WEEKS)*

		pos	wks
26 Jan 91	**SUMMER'S MAGIC** *Fourth & Broadway BRW 205*	27	6

SUNBURST *UK, male producer – Matt Darey (1 WEEK)*

		pos	wks
8 Jul 00	**EYEBALL (EYEBALL PAUL'S THEME)** *Virgin / EMI VTSCD 4*	48	1

See also MELT featuring LITTLE MS MARCIE; Matt DAREY; MDM

SUNDANCE – *See DJ 'FAST' EDDIE*

SUNDANCE *UK, male production duo (7 WEEKS)*

		pos	wks
8 Nov 97	**SUNDANCE** *React CDREACT 109*	33	2
3 Oct 98	**SUNDANCE '98 (re-mix)** *React CDREACTX 136*	37	2
27 Feb 99	**THE LIVING DREAM** *React CDREACT 134*	56	1
5 Feb 00	**WON'T LET THIS FEELING GO** *Inferno CDFERN 23*	40	2

SUNDAYS *UK, male / female vocal / instrumental group (12 WEEKS)*

		pos	wks
11 Feb 89	**CAN'T BE SURE** *Rough Trade RT 218*	45	5
3 Oct 92	**GOODBYE** *Parlophone R 6319*	27	2
20 Sep 97	**SUMMERTIME** *Parlophone CDRS 6475*	15	4
22 Nov 97	**CRY** *Parlophone CDR 6487*	43	1

SUNDRAGON *UK, male vocal / instrumental duo (1 WEEK)*

		pos	wks
21 Feb 68	**GREEN TAMBOURINE** *MGM 1380*	50	1

SUNFIRE *US, male vocal / instrumental group (11 WEEKS)*

		pos	wks
12 Mar 83	**YOUNG, FREE AND SINGLE** *Warner Bros. W 9897*	20	11

SUNKIDS featuring CHANCE
US, male production duo and US, female vocalist (2 WEEKS)

		pos	wks
13 Nov 99	**RESCUE ME** *AM:PM CDAMPM 126*	50	2

SUNNY *UK, female vocalist – Sunny Leslie (10 WEEKS)*

		pos	wks
30 Mar 74 ●	**DOCTOR'S ORDERS** *CBS 2068*	7	10

SUNSCREEM *UK, male / female vocal / instrumental group (35 WEEKS)*

		pos	wks
29 Feb 92	**PRESSURE** *Sony S2 6578017*	60	2
18 Jul 92	**LOVE U MORE** *Sony S2 6581727*	23	6
17 Oct 92	**PERFECT MOTION** *Sony S2 6584057*	18	5
9 Jan 93	**BROKEN ENGLISH** *Sony S2 6589032*	13	5
27 Mar 93	**PRESSURE US (re-mix)** *Sony S2 6591102*	19	5
2 Sep 95	**WHEN** *Sony S2 6623222*	47	2
18 Nov 95	**EXODUS** *Sony S2 6625342*	40	2
20 Jan 96	**WHITE SKIES** *Sony S2 6627425*	25	3
23 Mar 96	**SECRETS** *Sony S2 6629342*	36	2
6 Sep 97	**CATCH** *Pulse-8 CDLOSE 117*	55	1
20 Oct 01	**PLEASE SAVE ME** *Inferno / Five AM FAMFERN 1CD* [1]	36	2

[1] Sunscreem vs Push

Monty SUNSHINE – *See Chris BARBER'S JAZZ BAND*

SUNSHINE BAND – *See KC and the SUNSHINE BAND*

SUNSHIP featuring MCRB
UK, male producer and male vocalist (1 WEEK)

		pos	wks
1 Apr 00	**CHEQUE ONE-TWO** *Filter FILT 044*	75	1

SUPER FURRY ANIMALS
UK, male vocal / instrumental group (36 WEEKS)

		pos	wks
9 Mar 96	**HOMETOWN UNICORN** *Creation CRESCD 222*	47	1
11 May 96	**GOD! SHOW ME MAGIC** *Creation CRESCD 231*	33	2
13 Jul 96	**SOMETHING 4 THE WEEKEND** *Creation CRESCD 235*	18	3
12 Oct 96	**IF YOU DON'T WANT ME TO DESTROY YOU** *Creation CRESCD 243*	18	2
14 Dec 96	**THE MAN DON'T GIVE A FUCK** *Creation CRESCD 247*	22	2
24 May 97	**HERMANN LOVES PAULINE** *Creation CRESCD 252*	26	2
26 Jul 97	**THE INTERNATIONAL LANGUAGE OF SCREAMING** *Creation CRESCD 269*	24	2
4 Oct 97	**PLAY IT COOL** *Creation CRESCD 275*	27	2
6 Dec 97	**DEMONS** *Creation CRESCD 283*	27	2
6 Jun 98	**ICE HOCKEY HAIR** *Creation CRESCD 288*	12	3
22 May 99	**NORTHERN LITES** *Creation CRESCD 314*	11	4
21 Aug 99	**FIRE IN MY HEART** *Creation CRESCD 323*	25	3
29 Jan 00	**DO OR DIE** *Creation CRESCD 329*	20	2
21 Jul 01	**JUXTAPOZED WITH U** *Epic 6712242*	14	4
20 Oct 01	**(DRAWING) RINGS AROUND THE WORLD** *Epic 6719082*	28	2

SUPERCAR *Italy, male DJ production duo – Alberto Pizarelli and Ricki Pagano (6 WEEKS)*

		pos	wks
13 Feb 99	**TONITE** *Pepper 0530202*	15	5
21 Aug 99	**COMPUTER LOVE** *Pepper 0530392* [1]	67	1

[1] Supercar featuring Mikaela

SUPERCAT *Jamaica, male vocalist (5 WEEKS)*

		pos	wks
1 Aug 92	**IT FE DONE** *Columbia 6582737*	66	1
6 May 95	**MY GIRL JOSEPHINE** *Columbia 6614702* [1]	22	4

[1] Supercat featuring Jack Radics

SUPERFUNK *France, male production trio (2 WEEKS)*

		pos	wks
4 Mar 00	**LUCKY STAR** *Virgin DINSD 198* [1]	42	1
10 Jun 00	**THE YOUNG MC** *Virgin DINSD 206*	62	1

[1] Superfunk featuring Ron Carroll

SUPERGRASS *UK, male vocal / instrumental group (54 WEEKS)*

		pos	wks
29 Oct 94	**CAUGHT BY THE FUZZ** *Parlophone CDR 6396*	43	2
18 Feb 95	**MANSIZE ROOSTER** *Parlophone CDR 6402*	20	3
25 Mar 95	**LOSE IT** *Sub Pop SP 281*	75	1
13 May 95 ●	**LENNY** *Parlophone CDR 6410*	10	3
15 Jul 95 ●	**ALRIGHT / TIME** *Parlophone CDR 6413*	2	10
9 Mar 96 ●	**GOING OUT** *Parlophone CDR 6428*	5	6
12 Apr 97 ●	**RICHARD III** *Parlophone CDR 6461*	2	5
21 Jun 97 ●	**SUN HITS THE SKY** *Parlophone CDR 6469*	10	4
18 Oct 97	**LATE IN THE DAY** *Parlophone CDR 6484*	18	4

5 Jun 99	PUMPING ON YOUR STEREO *Parlophone CDR 6518*	11	6
21 Aug 99	PUMPING ON YOUR STEREO (re-entry) *Parlophone CDR 6518*	74	1
18 Sep 99 ●	MOVING *Parlophone CDR 6524*	9	5
4 Dec 99	MARY *Parlophone CDR 6531*	36	3
22 Jan 00	MARY (re-entry) *Parlophone CDR 6531*	72	1

SUPERMEN LOVERS *France, male production / vocal duo – Guillaume Atlan and Mani Hoffman (14 WEEKS)* pos/wks

15 Sep 01 ●	STARLIGHT *Independiente ISOM 53MS*	2	14

SUPERNATURALS *UK, male vocal / instrumental group (15 WEEKS)* pos/wks

26 Oct 96	LAZY LOVER *Food CDFOOD 85*	34	2
8 Feb 97	THE DAY BEFORE YESTERDAY'S MAN *Food CDFOODS 88*	25	3
26 Apr 97	SMILE *Food CDFOOD 92*	23	2
12 Jul 97	LOVE HAS PASSED AWAY *Food CDFOOD 99*	38	2
25 Oct 97	PREPARE TO LAND *Food CDFOODS 106*	48	1
1 Aug 98	I WASN'T BUILT TO GET UP *Food CDFOOD 112*	25	3
24 Oct 98	SHEFFIELD SONG *Food CDFOODS 115*	45	1
13 Mar 99	EVEREST *Food CDFOOD 119*	52	1

SUPERNOVA *UK, male / female vocal / instrumental duo (1 WEEK)* pos/wks

11 May 96	SOME MIGHT SAY *Sing Sing 74321369442*	55	1

SUPERSISTER *UK, female vocal group (8 WEEKS)* pos/wks

14 Oct 00	COFFEE *Gut CDGUT 35*	16	5
25 Aug 01	SHOPPING *Gut CDGUT 37*	36	2
17 Nov 01	SUMMER GONNA COME AGAIN *Gut CDGUT 38*	51	1

SUPERSTAR *UK, male vocal / instrumental group (2 WEEKS)* pos/wks

7 Feb 98	EVERY DAY I FALL APART *Camp Fabulous CFAB 003 CD*	66	1
25 Apr 98	SUPERSTAR *Camp Fabulous CFAB 007CD*	49	1

SUPERTRAMP *UK / US, male vocal / instrumental group (52 WEEKS)* pos/wks

15 Feb 75	DREAMER *A & M AMS 7132*	13	10
25 Jun 77	GIVE A LITTLE BIT *A & M AMS 7293*	29	7
31 Mar 79 ●	THE LOGICAL SONG *A & M AMS 7427*	7	11
30 Jun 79 ●	BREAKFAST IN AMERICA *A & M AMS 7451*	9	10
27 Oct 79	GOODBYE STRANGER *A & M AMS 7481*	57	3
30 Oct 82	IT'S RAINING AGAIN *A & M AMS 8255* [1]	26	11

[1] Supertramp featuring vocals by Roger Hodgson

SUPREMES (31 Top 500) *World's most successful female group: Diana Ross, Mary Wilson, Florence Ballard (d. 1976). Before Ross went solo in 1969, this Detroit-based trio had amassed a dozen US No.1s. They were inducted into the Rock and Roll Hall of Fame in 1988 (306 WEEKS)* pos/wks

3 Sep 64 ●	WHERE DID OUR LOVE GO *Stateside SS 327* ▲	3	14
22 Oct 64 ★	BABY LOVE *Stateside SS 350* ▲	1	15
21 Jan 65	COME SEE ABOUT ME *Stateside SS 376* ▲	27	6
25 Mar 65 ●	STOP! IN THE NAME OF LOVE *Tamla Motown TMG 501* ▲	7	12
10 Jun 65	BACK IN MY ARMS AGAIN *Tamla Motown TMG 516* ▲	40	5
9 Dec 65	I HEAR A SYMPHONY *Tamla Motown TMG 543* ▲	50	1
23 Dec 65	I HEAR A SYMPHONY (re-entry) *Tamla Motown TMG 543*	39	4
8 Sep 66 ●	YOU CAN'T HURRY LOVE *Tamla Motown TMG 575* ▲	3	12
1 Dec 66 ●	YOU KEEP ME HANGIN' ON *Tamla Motown TMG 585* ▲	8	10
2 Mar 67	LOVE IS HERE AND NOW YOU'RE GONE *Tamla Motown TMG 597* ▲	17	10
11 May 67 ●	THE HAPPENING *Tamla Motown TMG 607* ▲	6	12
30 Aug 67 ●	REFLECTIONS *Tamla Motown TMG 616* [1]	5	14
29 Nov 67	IN AND OUT OF LOVE *Tamla Motown TMG 632* [1]	13	13
10 Apr 68	FOREVER CAME TODAY *Tamla Motown TMG 650* [1]	28	8
3 Jul 68	SOME THINGS YOU NEVER GET USED TO *Tamla Motown TMG 662* [1]	34	6
20 Nov 68	LOVE CHILD *Tamla Motown TMG 677* [1] ▲	15	14
29 Jan 69 ●	I'M GONNA MAKE YOU LOVE ME *Tamla Motown TMG 685* [2]	3	11
23 Apr 69	I'M GONNA MAKE YOU LOVE ME (re-entry) *Tamla Motown TMG 685* [2]	49	1
23 Apr 69	I'M LIVIN' IN SHAME *Tamla Motown TMG 695* [1]	14	9
2 Jul 69	I'M LIVIN' IN SHAME (re-entry) *Tamla Motown TMG 695* [1]	50	1
16 Jul 69	NO MATTER WHAT SIGN YOU ARE *Tamla Motown TMG 704* [1]	37	7
20 Sep 69	I SECOND THAT EMOTION *Tamla Motown TMG 709* [2]	18	8
13 Dec 69	SOMEDAY WE'LL BE TOGETHER *Tamla Motown TMG 721* [1] ▲	13	13
21 Mar 70	WHY (MUST WE FALL IN LOVE) *Tamla Motown TMG 730* [2]	31	7
2 May 70 ●	UP THE LADDER TO THE ROOF *Tamla Motown TMG 735*	6	15
16 Jan 71 ●	STONED LOVE *Tamla Motown TMG 760*	3	13
26 Jun 71	RIVER DEEP MOUNTAIN HIGH *Tamla Motown TMG 777* [3]	11	10
21 Aug 71 ●	NATHAN JONES *Tamla Motown TMG 782*	5	11
20 Nov 71	YOU GOTTA HAVE LOVE IN YOUR HEART *Tamla Motown TMG 793* [3]	25	10
4 Mar 72 ●	FLOY JOY *Tamla Motown TMG 804*	9	10
15 Jul 72 ●	AUTOMATICALLY SUNSHINE *Tamla Motown TMG 821*	10	9
21 Apr 73	BAD WEATHER *Tamla Motown TMG 847*	37	4
24 Aug 74	BABY LOVE (re-issue) *Tamla Motown TMG 915* [1]	12	10
18 Feb 89	STOP! IN THE NAME OF LOVE (re-issue) *Motown ZB 41963* [1]	62	1

[1] Diana Ross and the Supremes [2] Diana Ross and the Supremes and the Temptations [3] Supremes and the Four Tops

AI B SURE! *US, male vocalist (13 WEEKS)* pos/wks

16 Apr 88	NITE AND DAY *Uptown W 8192*	44	5
30 Jul 88	OFF ON YOUR OWN (GIRL) *Uptown W 7870*	70	2
10 Jun 89	IF I'M NOT YOUR LOVER *Uptown W 2908* [1]	54	3
31 Mar 90	SECRET GARDEN *Qwest W 9992* [2]	67	1
12 Jun 93	BLACK TIE WHITE NOISE *Arista 74321148682* [3]	36	2

[1] Al B Sure featuring Slick Rick [2] Quincy Jones featuring Al B Sure!, James Ingram, El DeBarge and Barry White [3] David Bowie featuring Al B Sure!

SUREAL *UK, male / female production / vocal group (4 WEEKS)* pos/wks

7 Oct 00	YOU TAKE MY BREATH AWAY *Cream CREAM 7CD*	15	4

SURFACE *US, male vocal / instrumental duo (14 WEEKS)* pos/wks

23 Jul 83	FALLING IN LOVE *Salsoul SAL 104*	67	3
23 Jun 84	WHEN YOUR 'EX' WANTS YOU BACK *Salsoul SAL 106*	52	4
28 Feb 87	HAPPY *CBS 650393 7*	56	5
12 Jan 91	THE FIRST TIME *Columbia 6564767* ▲	60	2

SURFACE NOISE *UK, male instrumental group (11 WEEKS)* pos/wks

31 May 80	THE SCRATCH *WEA K 18291*	26	8
30 Aug 80	DANCIN' ON A WIRE *Groove Production GP102*	59	3

SURFARIS *US, male instrumental group (14 WEEKS)* pos/wks

25 Jul 63 ●	WIPE OUT *London HLD 9751*	5	14

SURPRISE SISTERS *UK, female vocal group (3 WEEKS)* pos/wks

13 Mar 76	LA BOOGA ROOGA *Good Earth GD 1*	38	3

SURVIVOR *US, male vocal / instrumental group – lead vocal Dave Bickler (26 WEEKS)* pos/wks

31 Jul 82 ★	EYE OF THE TIGER *Scotti Brothers SCT A 2411* ▲	1	15
1 Feb 86 ●	BURNING HEART *Scotti Brothers A 6708*	5	11

SUTHERLAND BROTHERS and QUIVER *UK, male vocal / instrumental group (20 WEEKS)* pos/wks

3 Apr 76 ●	ARMS OF MARY *CBS 4001*	5	12
20 Nov 76	SECRETS *CBS 4668*	35	4
2 Jun 79	EASY COME EASY GO *CBS 7121* [1]	50	4

[1] Sutherland Brothers

Pat SUZUKI *US, female vocalist (1 WEEK)* pos/wks

14 Apr 60	I ENJOY BEING A GIRL *RCA 1171*	49	1

SVENSON and GEILEN *Belgium, male producer and female vocalist (2 WEEKS)* pos/wks

22 Sep 01	THE BEAUTY OF SILENCE *Xtrahard / Xtravaganza X2H 5CDS*	41	2

See also – Johan GIELEN; AIRSCAPE; BLUE BAMBOO

Billy SWAN *US, male vocalist (13 WEEKS)* pos/wks

14 Dec 74	●	**I CAN HELP** *Monument MNT 2752* ▲	6	9
24 May 75		**DON'T BE CRUEL** *Monument MNT 3244*	42	4

SWAN LAKE *US, male producer – Todd Terry (4 WEEKS)* pos/wks

17 Sep 88		**IN THE NAME OF LOVE** *Champion CHAMP 86*	53	4

SWANS WAY
UK, male / female vocal / instrumental group (12 WEEKS) pos/wks

4 Feb 84		**SOUL TRAIN** *Exit EXT 3*	20	7
26 May 84		**ILLUMINATIONS** *Balgier PH 5*	57	5

Patrick SWAYZE featuring Wendy FRASER
US, male / female vocal duo (11 WEEKS) pos/wks

26 Mar 88		**SHE'S LIKE THE WIND** *RCA PB 49565*	17	11

Keith SWEAT *US, male vocalist (23 WEEKS)* pos/wks

20 Feb 88		**I WANT HER** *Vintertainment EKR 68*	26	10
14 May 88		**SOMETHING JUST AIN'T RIGHT** *Vintertainment EKR 72*	55	3
14 May 94		**HOW DO YOU LIKE IT** *Elektra EKR 185CD*	71	1
22 Jun 96		**TWISTED** *Elektra EKR 223CD*	39	2
23 Nov 96		**JUST A TOUCH** *Elektra EKR 227CD*	35	2
3 May 97		**NOBODY** *Elektra EKR 233CD* [1]	30	2
6 Dec 97		**I WANT HER (re-mix)** *Elektra E 3887CD*	44	1
12 Dec 98		**COME AND GET WITH ME** *Elektra E 3787CD* [2]	58	1
27 Mar 99		**I'M NOT READY** *Elektra E 3767CD*	53	1

[1] Keith Sweat featuring Athena Cage [2] Keith Sweat featuring Snoop Dogg

Michelle SWEENEY *US, female vocalist (1 WEEK)* pos/wks

29 Oct 94		**THIS TIME** *Big Beat A 8229CD*	57	1

SWEET (132 Top 500) *Glam-rock giants: Brian Connolly (v) (d. 1997), Andy Scott (g), Steve Priest (b), Mick Tucker (d) (d. 2002). The flamboyantly attired UK quartet was very popular in Europe and the US. Despite topping the chart only once, they achieved five No.2 hits (159 WEEKS)* pos/wks

13 Mar 71		**FUNNY FUNNY** *RCA 2051*	13	14
12 Jun 71	●	**CO-CO** *RCA 2087*	2	15
16 Oct 71		**ALEXANDER GRAHAM BELL** *RCA 2121*	33	5
5 Feb 72		**POPPA JOE** *RCA 2164*	11	12
10 Jun 72	●	**LITTLE WILLY** *RCA 2225*	4	14
9 Sep 72	●	**WIG-WAM BAM** *RCA 2260*	4	13
13 Jan 73	★	**BLOCKBUSTER** *RCA 2305*	1	15
5 May 73	●	**HELL RAISER** *RCA 2357*	2	11
22 Sep 73	●	**BALLROOM BLITZ** *RCA 2403*	2	9
19 Jan 74	●	**TEENAGE RAMPAGE** *RCA LPBO 5004*	2	8
13 Jul 74	●	**THE SIX TEENS** *RCA LPBO 5037*	9	7
9 Nov 74		**TURN IT DOWN** *RCA 2480*	41	2
15 Mar 75	●	**FOX ON THE RUN** *RCA 2524*	2	10
12 Jul 75		**ACTION** *RCA 2578*	15	6
24 Jan 76		**LIES IN YOUR EYES** *RCA 2641*	35	4
28 Jan 78	●	**LOVE IS LIKE OXYGEN** *Polydor POSP 1*	9	9
26 Jan 85		**IT'S... IT'S... THE SWEET MIX** *Anagram ANA 28*	45	5

It's... It's... the Sweet Mix is a medley of the following songs: Blockbuster / Fox on the Run / Teenage Rampage / Hell Raiser / Ballroom Blitz

Rachel SWEET *US, female vocalist (15 WEEKS)* pos/wks

9 Dec 78		**B-A-B-Y** *Stiff BUY 39*	35	8
22 Aug 81		**EVERLASTING LOVE** *CBS A 1405* [1]	35	7

[1] Rex Smith and Rachel Sweet

SWEET DREAMS *UK, male / female vocal duo – Polly Brown and Tony Jackson (12 WEEKS)* pos/wks

20 Jul 74	●	**HONEY HONEY** *Bradley's BRAD 7408*	10	12

SWEET DREAMS *UK, male / female vocal group (7 WEEKS)* pos/wks

9 Apr 83		**I'M NEVER GIVING UP** *Ariola ARO 333*	21	7

SWEET FEMALE ATTITUDE
UK, female vocal duo – Leanne Brown and Catherine Cassidy (14 WEEKS) pos/wks

15 Apr 00	●	**FLOWERS** *WEA WEA 267CD*	2	12
7 Oct 00		**8 DAYS A WEEK** *WEA WEA 296CD*	43	2

SWEET MERCY featuring Joe ROBERTS
UK, male production / instrumental duo and male vocalist (1 WEEK) pos/wks

24 Feb 96		**HAPPY DAYS** *Grass Green GRASS 10CD*	63	1

SWEET PEOPLE *France, male vocal / instrumental group (10 WEEKS)* pos/wks

4 Oct 80	●	**ET LES OISEAUX CHANTAIENT (AND THE BIRDS WERE SINGING)** *Polydor POSP 179*	4	8
29 Aug 87		**ET LES OISEAUX CHANTAIENT (AND THE BIRDS WERE SINGING) (re-entry)** *Polydor POSP 179*	73	2

SWEET PUSSY PAULINE – *See CANDY GIRLS*

SWEET SENSATION
UK, male vocal group – lead vocal Marcel King (17 WEEKS) pos/wks

14 Sep 74	★	**SAD SWEET DREAMER** *Pye 7N 45385*	1	10
18 Jan 75		**PURELY BY COINCIDENCE** *Pye 7N 45421*	11	7

SWEET TEE *US, female rapper – Toi Jackson (8 WEEKS)* pos/wks

16 Jan 88		**IT'S LIKE THAT Y'ALL / I GOT DA FEELIN'** *Cooltempo COOL 160*	31	6
13 Aug 94		**THE FEELING** *Deep Distraxion OILYCD 029* [1]	32	2

[1] Tin Tin Out featuring Sweet Tee

SWEETBACK *UK, male vocal / instrumental group (1 WEEK)* pos/wks

29 Mar 97		**YOU WILL RISE** *Epic 6643155*	64	1

SWEETBOX *Germany / US, male / female vocal / production duo – Rosan Roberto and Tina Harris (12 WEEKS)* pos/wks

22 Aug 98	●	**EVERYTHING'S GONNA BE ALRIGHT** *RCA 74321606842*	5	12

Sally SWEETLAND – *See Eddie FISHER*

SWERVEDRIVER *UK, male vocal / instrumental group (3 WEEKS)* pos/wks

10 Aug 91		**SANDBLASTED (EP)** *Creation CRE 102*	67	1
30 May 92		**NEVER LOSE THAT FEELING** *Creation CRE 120*	62	1
14 Aug 93		**DUEL** *Creation CRESCD 136*	60	1

Tracks on Sandblasted (EP): Sandblaster / Flawed / Out / Laze It Up

SWIMMING WITH SHARKS *Germany, female vocal duo (3 WEEKS)* pos/wks

7 May 88		**CARELESS LOVE** *WEA YZ 173*	63	3

SWING featuring DR ALBAN
US, male rapper and Nigeria, male vocalist (1 WEEK) pos/wks

29 Apr 95		**SWEET DREAMS** *Logic 74321251552*	59	1

SWING 52 *US, male vocal / instrumental group (1 WEEK)* pos/wks

25 Feb 95		**COLOR OF MY SKIN** *ffrr FCD 256*	60	1

SWING KIDS – *See K7*

SWING OUT SISTER
UK, male / female vocal / instrumental trio (55 WEEKS) pos/wks

25 Oct 86	●	**BREAKOUT** *Mercury SWING 2*	4	14
10 Jan 87	●	**SURRENDER** *Mercury SWING 3*	7	8
18 Apr 87		**TWILIGHT WORLD** *Mercury SWING 4*	32	6
11 Jul 87		**FOOLED BY A SMILE** *Mercury SWING 5*	43	4
8 Apr 89		**YOU ON MY MIND** *Fontana SWING 6*	28	9
8 Jul 89		**WHERE IN THE WORLD** *Fontana SWING 7*	47	4
11 Apr 92		**AM I THE SAME GIRL** *Fontana SWING 9*	21	6
20 Jun 92		**NOTGONNACHANGE** *Fontana SWING 10*	49	2
27 Aug 94		**LA LA (MEANS I LOVE YOU)** *Fontana SWIDD 11*	37	2

Act became male / female duo in 1989

SWINGING BLUE JEANS
UK, male vocal / instrumental group (57 WEEKS) pos/wks

Date		Title / Label	pos	wks
20 Jun 63		IT'S TOO LATE NOW *HMV POP 1170*	30	6
8 Aug 63		IT'S TOO LATE NOW (re-entry) *HMV POP 1170*	46	3
12 Dec 63	●	HIPPY HIPPY SHAKE *HMV POP 1242*	2	17
19 Mar 64		GOOD GOLLY MISS MOLLY *HMV POP 1273*	11	10
4 Jun 64	●	YOU'RE NO GOOD *HMV POP 1304*	3	13
20 Jan 66		DON'T MAKE ME OVER *HMV POP 1501*	31	8

SWIRL 360 *US, male vocal duo (1 WEEK)* pos/wks

Date		Title / Label	pos	wks
14 Nov 98		HEY NOW NOW *Mercury 5665352*	61	1

SWITCH *US, male vocal / instrumental group (3 WEEKS)* pos/wks

Date		Title / Label	pos	wks
10 Nov 84		KEEPING SECRETS *Total Experience RCA XE 502*	61	3

SWV *US, female vocal group (43 WEEKS)* pos/wks

Date		Title / Label	pos	wks
1 May 93		I'M SO INTO YOU *RCA 74321144972*	17	6
26 Jun 93		WEAK *RCA 74321153352* ▲	33	3
28 Aug 93	●	RIGHT HERE *RCA 74321160482*	3	12
26 Feb 94		DOWNTOWN *RCA 74321189012*	19	5
11 Jun 94		ANYTHING *RCA 74321212212*	24	3
25 May 96		YOU'RE THE ONE *RCA 74321383312*	13	3
21 Dec 96		IT'S ALL ABOUT U *RCA 74321442152*	36	5
12 Apr 97		CAN WE *Jive JIVECD 423*	18	4
13 Sep 97		SOMEONE *RCA 74321513942* [1]	34	2

[1] SWV featuring Puff Daddy

SYBIL *US, female vocalist – Sybil Lynch (69 WEEKS)* pos/wks

Date		Title / Label	pos	wks
1 Nov 86		FALLING IN LOVE *Champion CHAMP 22*	68	3
25 Apr 87		LET YOURSELF GO *Champion CHAMP 42*	32	6
29 Aug 87		MY LOVE IS GUARANTEED *Champion CHAMPX 55*	42	5
22 Jul 89		DON'T MAKE ME OVER *Champion CHAMP 213*	59	5
14 Oct 89		DON'T MAKE ME OVER (re-entry) *Champion CHAMP 213*	19	6
27 Jan 90	●	WALK ON BY *PWL PWL 48*	6	9
21 Apr 90		CRAZY FOR YOU *PWL PWL 53*	71	1
16 Jan 93	●	THE LOVE I LOST *PWL Sanctuary PWCD 253* [1]	3	13
20 Mar 93	●	WHEN I'M GOOD AND READY *PWL International PWCD 260*	5	13
26 Jun 93		BEYOND YOUR WILDEST DREAMS *PWL International PWCD 265*	41	2
11 Sep 93		STRONGER TOGETHER *PWL International PWCD 269*	41	2
11 Dec 93		MY LOVE IS GUARANTEED (re-mix) *PWL International PWCD 277*	48	1
9 Mar 96		SO TIRED OF BEING ALONE *PWL International PWL 324CD*	53	1
8 Mar 97		WHEN I'M GOOD AND READY (re-mix) *Next Plateau NP 14183*	66	1
26 Jul 97		STILL A THRILL *Coalition COLA 007CD*	55	1

[1] West End featuring Sybil

SYLK 130 *US, male production duo (2 WEEKS)* pos/wks

Date		Title / Label	pos	wks
25 Apr 98		LAST NIGHT A DJ SAVED MY LIFE *Sony S2 SYLK 1CD*	33	2

SYLVESTER *US, male vocalist – Sylvester James (45 WEEKS)* pos/wks

Date		Title / Label	pos	wks
19 Aug 78	●	YOU MAKE ME FEEL (MIGHTY REAL) *Fantasy FTC 160*	8	15
18 Nov 78		DANCE (DISCO HEAT) *Fantasy FTC 163*	29	12
31 Mar 79		I (WHO HAVE NOTHING) *Fantasy FTC 171*	46	5
7 Jul 79		STARS *Fantasy FTC 177*	47	3
11 Sep 82		DO YOU WANNA FUNK *London LON 13* [1]	32	8
3 Sep 83		BAND OF GOLD *London LON 33*	67	2

[1] Sylvester with Patrick Cowley

SYLVIA *US, female vocalist – Sylvia Robinson (11 WEEKS)* pos/wks

Date		Title / Label	pos	wks
23 Jun 73		PILLOW TALK *London HL 10415*	14	11

SYLVIA *Sweden, female vocalist – Sylvia Vrethammer (33 WEEKS)* pos/wks

Date		Title / Label	pos	wks
10 Aug 74	●	Y VIVA ESPANA *Sonet SON 2037*	4	19
4 Jan 75		Y VIVA ESPANA (re-entry) *Sonet SON 2037*	35	9
26 Apr 75		HASTA LA VISTA *Sonet SON 2055*	38	5

David SYLVIAN *UK, male vocalist – David Batt (36 WEEKS)* pos/wks

Date		Title / Label	pos	wks
7 Aug 82		BAMBOO HOUSES / BAMBOO MUSIC *Virgin VS 510* [1]	30	4
2 Jul 83		FORBIDDEN COLOURS *Virgin VS 601* [2]	16	8
2 Jun 84		RED GUITAR *Virgin VS 633*	17	5
18 Aug 84		THE INK IN THE WELL *Virgin VS 700*	36	3
3 Nov 84		PULLING PUNCHES *Virgin VS 717*	56	2
14 Dec 85		WORDS WITH THE SHAMAN *Virgin VS 835*	72	1
9 Aug 86		TAKING THE VEIL *Virgin VS 815*	53	3
17 Jan 87		BUOY *Virgin VS 910* [3]	63	2
10 Oct 87		LET THE HAPPINESS IN *Virgin VS 1001*	66	1
13 Jun 92		HEARTBEAT (TAINAI KAIKI II) RETURNING TO THE WOMB *Virgin America VUS 57* [4]	58	3
28 Aug 93		JEAN THE BIRDMAN *Virgin VSCDG 1462* [5]	68	2
27 Mar 99		I SURRENDER *Virgin VSCDT 1722*	40	2

[1] Sylvian Sakamoto [2] David Sylvian and Riuichi Sakamoto [3] Mick Karn featuring David Sylvian [4] David Sylvian / Riuichi Sakamoto featuring Ingrid Chavez [5] David Sylvian and Robert Fripp

SYMARIP *UK, male vocal / instrumental group (3 WEEKS)* pos/wks

Date		Title / Label	pos	wks
2 Feb 80		SKINHEAD MOONSTOMP *Trojan TRO 9062*	54	3

SYMBOLS *UK, male vocal / instrumental group (15 WEEKS)* pos/wks

Date		Title / Label	pos	wks
2 Aug 67		BYE BYE BABY *President PT 144*	44	3
3 Jan 68		(THE BEST PART OF) BREAKING UP *President PT 173*	25	12

Terri SYMON *UK, female vocalist (1 WEEK)* pos/wks

Date		Title / Label	pos	wks
10 Jun 95		I WANT TO KNOW WHAT LOVE IS *A & M 5810592*	54	1

SYMPOSIUM *UK, male vocal / instrumental group (10 WEEKS)* pos/wks

Date		Title / Label	pos	wks
22 Mar 97		FAREWELL TO TWILIGHT *Infectious INFECT 34CD*	25	2
31 May 97		THE ANSWER TO WHY I HATE YOU *Infectious INFECT 37CD*	32	2
30 Aug 97		FAIRWEATHER FRIEND *Infectious INFECT 44CD*	25	3
14 Mar 98		AVERAGE MAN *Infectious INFECT 52CD*	45	1
16 May 98		BURY YOU *Infectious INFECT 55CDS*	41	1
18 Jul 98		BLUE *Infectious INFECT 57CD*	48	1

SYREETA *US, female vocalist – Rita Wright (30 WEEKS)* pos/wks

Date		Title / Label	pos	wks
21 Sep 74		SPINNIN' AND SPINNIN' *Tamla Motown TMG 912*	49	3
1 Feb 75		YOUR KISS IS SWEET *Tamla Motown TMG 933*	12	8
12 Jul 75		HARMOUR LOVE *Tamla Motown TMG 954*	32	4
15 Dec 79	●	WITH YOU I'M BORN AGAIN *Motown TMG 1159* [1]	2	11
8 Mar 80		IT WILL COME IN TIME *Motown TMG 1175* [1]	47	4

[1] Billy Preston and Syreeta

SYSTEM *US, male vocal / instrumental duo (2 WEEKS)* pos/wks

Date		Title / Label	pos	wks
9 Jun 84		I WANNA MAKE YOU FEEL GOOD *Polydor POSP 685*	73	2

SYSTEM F *Holland, male producer – Ferry Corsten (10 WEEKS)* pos/wks

Date		Title / Label	pos	wks
3 Apr 99		OUT OF THE BLUE *Essential Recordings ESCD 1*	14	6
6 May 00		CRY *Essential Recordings ESCD 14*	19	4

See also Ferry CORSTEN; GOURYELLA; MOONMAN; VERACOCHA; STARPARTY

SYSTEM OF A DOWN *US, male vocal / instrumental group (4 WEEKS)* pos/wks

Date		Title / Label	pos	wks
3 Nov 01		CHOP SUEY *Columbia 6720342*	17	4

SYSTEM 7 *UK / France, male / female instrumental duo (2 WEEKS)* pos/wks

Date		Title / Label	pos	wks
13 Feb 93		7:7 EXPANSION *Butterfly BFLD 2*	39	1
17 Jul 93		SINBAD / QUEST *Butterfly BFLD 8*	74	1

T

T-BOZ *US, female vocalist (2 WEEKS)*

			pos	wks
23 Nov 96		**TOUCH MYSELF** *LaFace 74321422882*	48	1
14 Apr 01		**MY GETAWAY** *Maverick W 549CD* [1]	44	1

[1] Tionne "T-Boz" Watkins

See also TLC

T-CONNECTION *US, male vocal / instrumental group (27 WEEKS)*

			pos	wks
18 Jun 77		**DO WHAT YOU WANNA DO** *TK XC 9109*	11	8
14 Jan 78		**ON FIRE** *TK TKR 6006*	16	5
10 Jun 78		**LET YOURSELF GO** *TK TKR 6024*	52	3
24 Feb 79		**AT MIDNIGHT** *TK TKR 7517*	53	5
5 May 79		**SATURDAY NIGHT** *TK TKR 7536*	41	6

T-COY – *See VARIOUS ARTISTS (EPs and LPs)*

T-EMPO *UK, male / female vocal / instrumental group (4 WEEKS)*

			pos	wks
7 May 94		**SATURDAY NIGHT SUNDAY MORNING** *ffrr FCD 232*	19	3
9 Nov 96		**THE LOOK OF LOVE / THE BLUE ROOM** *ffrr FCD 281*	71	1

T-POWER *UK, male producer – Mark Royal (1 WEEK)*

			pos	wks
13 Apr 96		**POLICE STATE** *Sound of Underground TPOWCD 001*	63	1

T. REX (55 Top 500) *Influential acoustic act turned superstar glam rock boogie duo: singer / songwriter / guitarist Marc Bolan (b. Mark Feld, 30 Sep 1947, London, UK; d. 16 Sep 1977), and Steve Peregrin Took (percussion – replaced by Mickey Finn in 1969). (236 WEEKS)*

			pos	wks
8 May 68		**DEBORA** *Regal Zonophone RZ 3008* [1]	34	7
4 Sep 68		**ONE INCH ROCK** *Regal Zonophone RZ 3011* [1]	28	7
9 Aug 69		**KING OF THE RUMBLING SPIRES** *Regal Zonophone RZ 3022* [1]	44	1
24 Oct 70	●	**RIDE A WHITE SWAN** *Fly BUG 1*	2	20
27 Feb 71	★	**HOT LOVE** *Fly BUG 6*	1	17
10 Jul 71	★	**GET IT ON** *Fly BUG 10*	1	13
13 Nov 71	●	**JEEPSTER** *Fly BUG 16*	2	15
29 Jan 72	★	**TELEGRAM SAM** *T. Rex 101*	1	12
1 Apr 72	●	**DEBORA / ONE INCH ROCK (re-issue)** *Magnifly ECHO 102* [1]	7	10
13 May 72	★	**METAL GURU** *EMI MARC 1*	1	14
16 Sep 72	●	**CHILDREN OF THE REVOLUTION** *EMI MARC 2*	2	10
9 Dec 72	●	**SOLID GOLD EASY ACTION** *EMI MARC 3*	2	11
10 Mar 73	●	**20TH CENTURY BOY** *EMI MARC 4*	3	9
16 Jun 73	●	**THE GROOVER** *EMI MARC 5*	4	9
24 Nov 73		**TRUCK ON (TYKE)** *EMI MARC 6*	12	11
9 Feb 74		**TEENAGE DREAM** *EMI MARC 7* [2]	13	5
13 Jul 74		**LIGHT OF LOVE** *EMI MARC 8*	22	5
16 Nov 74		**ZIP GUN BOOGIE** *EMI MARC 9*	41	3
12 Jul 75		**NEW YORK CITY** *EMI MARC 10*	15	8
11 Oct 75		**DREAMY LADY** *EMI MARC 11* [3]	30	5
6 Mar 76		**LONDON BOYS** *EMI MARC 13*	40	3
19 Jun 76		**I LOVE TO BOOGIE** *EMI MARC 14*	13	9
2 Oct 76		**LASER LOVE** *EMI MARC 15*	41	4
2 Apr 77		**THE SOUL OF MY SUIT** *EMI MARC 16*	42	3
9 May 81		**RETURN OF THE ELECTRIC WARRIOR (EP)** *Rarn MBSF 001* [4]	50	4
19 Sep 81		**YOU SCARE ME TO DEATH** *Cherry Red CHERRY 29* [4]	51	4
27 Mar 82		**TELEGRAM SAM (re-entry)** *T. Rex 101*	69	2
18 May 85		**MEGAREX** *Marc on Wax TANX 1* [2]	72	2
9 May 87		**GET IT ON (re-mix)** *Marc on Wax MARC 10* [2]	54	4
24 Aug 91		**20TH CENTURY BOY (re-issue)** *Marc on Wax MARC 501* [2]	13	8
7 Oct 00		**GET IT ON** *All Around the World CDGLOBE 225* [5]	59	1

[1] Tyrannosaurus Rex [2] Marc Bolan and T. Rex [3] T. Rex Disco Party [4] Marc Bolan [5] Bus Stop featuring T. Rex

Tracks on Return of the Electric Warrior (EP): Sing Me a Song / Endless Sleep Extended / The Lilac Hand of Menthol Dan. Megarex is a medley of extracts from the following T. Rex hits: Truck On (Tyke) / The Groover / Telegram Sam / Shock Rock / Metal Guru / 20th Century Boy / Children of the Revolution / Hot Love

T-SHIRT *UK, female vocal duo (1 WEEK)*

			pos	wks
13 Sep 97		**YOU SEXY THING** *Eternal WEA 122CD*	63	1

T-SPOON *Holland, male / female vocal / instrumental group (15 WEEKS)*

			pos	wks
19 Sep 98	●	**SEX ON THE BEACH** *Control 0042395 CON*	2	13
23 Jan 99		**TOM'S PARTY** *Control 0043505 CON*	27	2

T2 featuring Robin S *US, male production duo (1 WEEK)*

			pos	wks
4 Oct 97		**YOU GOT THE LOVE** *Champion CHAMPCD 330*	62	1

TABERNACLE *UK, male instrumental / production group (2 WEEKS)*

			pos	wks
4 Mar 95		**I KNOW THE LORD** *Good Groove CDGG 1*	62	1
3 Feb 96		**I KNOW THE LORD (re-mix)** *Good Groove CDGGX 1*	55	1

TACK HEAD *US, male vocal / production / rap group (3 WEEKS)*

			pos	wks
30 Jun 90		**DANGEROUS SEX** *SBK SBK 7014*	48	3

TAFFY *UK, female vocalist – Catherine Quaye (14 WEEKS)*

			pos	wks
10 Jan 87	●	**I LOVE MY RADIO (MY DEE JAY'S RADIO)** *Transglobal TYPE 1*	6	10
18 Jul 87		**STEP BY STEP** *Transglobal TYPE 5*	59	4

TAG TEAM *US, male rap duo (8 WEEKS)*

			pos	wks
8 Jan 94		**WHOOMP! (THERE IT IS)** *Club Tools SHXCD 1*	34	5
29 Jan 94		**ADDAMS FAMILY (WHOOMP!)** *Atlas PZCD 305*	53	1
10 Sep 94		**WHOOMP! (THERE IT IS) (re-mix)** *Club Tools SHXR 1*	48	2

See also QUAD CITY DJs

TAK TIX *US, male / female vocal / production group (2 WEEKS)*

			pos	wks
20 Jan 96		**FEEL LIKE SINGING** *A & M 5813212*	33	2

TAKE 5 *US, male vocal group (4 WEEKS)*

			pos	wks
7 Nov 98		**I GIVE** *Edel 0039635 ERE*	70	1
27 Mar 99		**NEVER HAD IT SO GOOD** *Edel 0039355 ERE*	34	3

TAKE THAT (134 Top 500) *Record-breaking British boy band: Robbie Williams (v), Gary Barlow (v), Jason Orange (v), Howard Donald (v), Mark Owen (v). They were the first artists since The Beatles to score four consecutive chart-toppers, and the first act to release eight singles entering at No.1. Robbie Williams departed in July 1995 and Gary Barlow dissolved the band in Feb 1996 having sold nine million albums and 10 million singles (158 WEEKS)*

			pos	wks
23 Nov 91		**PROMISES** *RCA PB 45085*	38	2
8 Feb 92		**ONCE YOU'VE TASTED LOVE** *RCA PB 45257*	47	3
6 Jun 92	●	**IT ONLY TAKES A MINUTE** *RCA 74321101007*	7	8
15 Aug 92		**I FOUND HEAVEN** *RCA 74321108137*	15	6
10 Oct 92	●	**A MILLION LOVE SONGS** *RCA 74321116307*	7	9
12 Dec 92	●	**COULD IT BE MAGIC** *RCA 74321123137*	3	12
20 Feb 93	●	**WHY CAN'T I WAKE UP WITH YOU** *RCA 74321133102*	2	10
17 Jul 93	★	**PRAY** *RCA 74321154502* ■	1	11
9 Oct 93	★	**RELIGHT MY FIRE** *RCA 74321167722* [1] ■	1	14
18 Dec 93	★	**BABE** *RCA 74321182122* ■	1	10
9 Apr 94	★	**EVERYTHING CHANGES** *RCA 74321167732* ■	1	10
9 Jul 94	●	**LOVE AIN'T HERE ANYMORE** *RCA 74321214832*	3	10
15 Oct 94		**LOVE AIN'T HERE ANYMORE (re-entry)** *RCA 74321214832*	55	2
15 Oct 94	★	**SURE** *RCA 74321236622* ■	1	15
8 Apr 95	★	**BACK FOR GOOD** *RCA 74321271462* ■	1	13
5 Aug 95	★	**NEVER FORGET** *RCA 74321299572* ■	1	9

UK No.1 ★ UK Top 10 ● Still on chart + UK million seller ◆ UK entry at No.1 ■ US No.1 ▲

9 Mar 96	★	**HOW DEEP IS YOUR LOVE** *RCA 74321355592* ■	1	13
15 Jun 96		**HOW DEEP IS YOUR LOVE (re-entry)** *RCA 74321355592*	71	1

[1] Take That featuring Lulu

Billy TALBOT – *See Ian McNABB*

TALISMAN P featuring Barrington LEVY

UK, male producer and Jamaica, male vocalist (2 WEEKS) pos/wks

13 Oct 01		**HERE I COME (SING DJ)** *Nulife / Arista 74321895622*	37	2

TALK TALK

484 Top 500 *London-based synth-pop band who rapidly evolved into an organic, reflective rock group: Mark Hollis (v/g/k), Paul Webb (b) and Lee Harris (d). Act, who had several legal wrangles with label EMI, was also popular in Italy, where they scored four Top 20 singles (73 WEEKS)* pos/wks

24 Apr 82		**TALK TALK** *EMI 5284*	52	4
24 Jul 82		**TODAY** *EMI 5314*	14	13
13 Nov 82		**TALK TALK (re-mix)** *EMI 5352*	23	10
19 Mar 83		**MY FOOLISH FRIEND** *EMI 5373*	57	3
14 Jan 84		**IT'S MY LIFE** *EMI 5443*	46	5
7 Apr 84		**SUCH A SHAME** *EMI 5433*	49	6
11 Aug 84		**DUM DUM GIRL** *EMI 5480*	74	1
18 Jan 86		**LIFE'S WHAT YOU MAKE IT** *EMI EMI 5540*	16	9
15 Mar 86		**LIVING IN ANOTHER WORLD** *EMI EMI 5551*	48	4
17 May 86		**GIVE IT UP** *Parlophone R 6131*	59	3
19 May 90		**IT'S MY LIFE (re-issue)** *Parlophone R 6254*	13	9
1 Sep 90		**LIFE'S WHAT YOU MAKE IT (re-issue)** *Parlophone R 6264*	23	6

TALKING HEADS

US / UK, male / female vocal / instrumental group (54 WEEKS) pos/wks

7 Feb 81		**ONCE IN A LIFETIME** *Sire SIR 4048*	14	10
9 May 81		**HOUSES IN MOTION** *Sire SIR 4050*	50	3
21 Jan 84		**THIS MUST BE THE PLACE** *Sire W 9451*	51	3
3 Nov 84		**SLIPPERY PEOPLE** *EMI 5504*	68	2
12 Oct 85	●	**ROAD TO NOWHERE** *EMI EMI 5530*	6	16
8 Feb 86		**AND SHE WAS** *EMI EMI 5543*	17	8
6 Sep 86		**WILD WILD LIFE** *EMI EMI 5567*	43	4
16 May 87		**RADIO HEAD** *EMI EM 1*	52	2
13 Aug 88		**BLIND** *EMI EM 68*	59	3
10 Oct 92		**LIFETIME PILING UP** *EMI EM 250*	50	3

See also HEADS with Shaun RYDER

TALL PAUL *UK, male DJ / producer – Paul Newman (14 WEEKS)* pos/wks

29 Mar 97		**ROCK DA HOUSE** *VC Recordings VCRD 18*	12	4
29 May 99		**BE THERE** *Duty Free DF 009CD*	45	1
8 Apr 00		**FREEBASE** *Duty Free DF 015CD*	43	2
2 Jun 01		**ROCK DA HOUSE (re-mix)** *VC Recordings VCRD 89*	29	2
18 Aug 01		**PRECIOUS HEART** *Duty Free / Decode DFTELCD 001* [1]	14	4
29 Sep 01		**PRECIOUS HEART (re-entry)** *Duty Free / Decode DFTELCD 001* [1]	57	1

[1] Tall Paul vs Inxs

See also CAMISRA; ESCRIMA; PARTIZAN; GRIFTERS; Paul NEWMAN

TAMBA TRIO *Argentina, male vocal / instrumental group (2 WEEKS)* pos/wks

18 Jul 98		**MAS QUE NADA** *Talkin Loud TLCD 34*	34	2

TAMPERER featuring MAYA *Italy, male production duo – Alex Farolfi and Mario Fargetta and female vocalist (38 WEEKS)* pos/wks

25 Apr 98	★	**FEEL IT** *Pepper 0530032*	1	17
14 Nov 98	●	**IF YOU BUY THIS RECORD YOUR LIFE WILL BE BETTER** *Pepper 0530082*	3	14
12 Feb 00	●	**HAMMER TO THE HEART** *Pepper 9230032*	6	5
25 Mar 00		**HAMMER TO THE HEART (re-entry)** *Pepper 9230032*	68	2

TAMS *US, male vocal group – lead vocal Joseph Pope (31 WEEKS)* pos/wks

14 Feb 70		**BE YOUNG, BE FOOLISH, BE HAPPY** *Stateside SS 2123*	32	7
31 Jul 71	★	**HEY GIRL DON'T BOTHER ME** *Probe PRO 532*	1	17
21 Nov 87		**THERE AIN'T NOTHING LIKE SHAGGIN'** *Virgin VS 1029*	21	7

Norma TANEGA *US, female vocalist (8 WEEKS)* pos/wks

7 Apr 66		**WALKIN' MY CAT NAMED DOG** *Stateside SS 496*	22	8

The Children of TANSLEY SCHOOL *UK, children's choir (4 WEEKS)* pos/wks

28 Mar 81		**MY MUM IS ONE IN A MILLION** *EMI 5151*	27	4

Jimmy TARBUCK *UK, male vocalist (2 WEEKS)* pos/wks

16 Nov 85		**AGAIN** *Safari SAFE 68*	74	1
30 Nov 85		**AGAIN (re-entry)** *Safari SAFE 68*	68	1

Lord TARIQ and Peter GUNZ *US, male vocal / rap duo (3 WEEKS)* pos/wks

2 May 98		**DEJA VU (UPTOWN BABY)** *Columbia 6658722*	21	3

TARLISA – *See CO-RO featuring TARLISA*

Bill TARMEY *UK, male vocalist / actor (9 WEEKS)* pos/wks

3 Apr 93		**ONE VOICE** *Arista 74321140852*	16	4
19 Feb 94		**WIND BENEATH MY WINGS** *EMI CDEM 304*	40	3
19 Nov 94		**IOU** *EMI CDEM 361*	55	2

TARRIERS *US, male vocal / instrumental group (6 WEEKS)* pos/wks

14 Dec 56		**CINDY, OH CINDY** *London HLN 8340* [1]	26	1
1 Mar 57		**THE BANANA BOAT SONG** *Columbia DB 3891*	15	5

[1] Vince Martin and the Tarriers

TARTAN ARMY *UK, male vocal ensemble (4 WEEKS)* pos/wks

6 Jun 98		**SCOTLAND BE GOOD** *The Precious JWLCD 33*	54	4

A TASTE OF HONEY *US, female vocal duo – Janice Marie Johnson and Hazel Payne (19 WEEKS)* pos/wks

17 Jun 78	●	**BOOGIE OOGIE OOGIE** *Capitol CL 15988* ▲	3	16
18 May 85		**BOOGIE OOGIE OOGIE (re-mix)** *Capitol CL 357*	59	3

TASTE XPERIENCE featuring Natasha PEARL *UK, male instrumental / production group and UK, female vocalist (1 WEEK)* pos/wks

6 Nov 99		**SUMMERSAULT** *Manifesto FESCD 64*	66	1

TATA BOX INHIBITORS *Holland, male production duo (1 WEEK)* pos/wks

3 Feb 01		**FREET** *Hooj Choons HOOJ 103CD*	67	1

TATJANA *Croatia, female vocalist (2 WEEKS)* pos/wks

21 Sep 96		**SANTA MARIA** *Love This LUVTHISCDX 4*	40	2

TAVARES

448 Top 500 *Successful R&B and disco-era family group from Massachusetts, US, who started performing in 1963 (when aged 9-15) as Chubby and the Turnpikes; brothers Antone, 'Chubby', Ralph, Feliciano, Arthur Lee and Perry Lee Tavares (77 WEEKS)* pos/wks

10 Jul 76	●	**HEAVEN MUST BE MISSING AN ANGEL** *Capitol CL 15876*	4	11
9 Oct 76	●	**DON'T TAKE AWAY THE MUSIC** *Capitol CL 15886*	4	10
5 Feb 77		**MIGHTY POWER OF LOVE** *Capitol CL 15905*	25	6
9 Apr 77	●	**WHODUNIT** *Capitol CL 15914*	5	10
2 Jul 77		**ONE STEP AWAY** *Capitol CL 15930*	16	7
18 Mar 78		**THE GHOST OF LOVE** *Capitol CL 15968*	29	6
6 May 78	●	**MORE THAN A WOMAN** *Capitol CL 15977*	7	11
12 Aug 78		**SLOW TRAIN TO PARADISE** *Capitol CL 15996*	62	3
22 Feb 86		**HEAVEN MUST BE MISSING AN ANGEL (re-mix)** *Capitol TAV 1*	12	9
3 May 86		**IT ONLY TAKES A MINUTE** *Capitol TAV 2*	46	4

TAXMAN – *See KICKING BACK with TAXMAN*

TAYLOR – *See LIBRA presents TAYLOR*

Andy TAYLOR *UK, male vocalist (2 WEEKS)* pos/wks

20 Oct 90		**LOLA** *A & M AM 596*	60	2

See also DURAN DURAN

Becky TAYLOR *UK, female vocalist (1 WEEK)* pos/wks

16 Jun 01	SONG OF DREAMS *EMI Classics 8794880*	60 1

Dina TAYLOR – *See BBG*

Felice TAYLOR *US, female vocalist (13 WEEKS)* pos/wks

25 Oct 67	I FEEL LOVE COMIN' ON *President PT 155*	11 13

James TAYLOR *US, male vocalist (23 WEEKS)* pos/wks

21 Nov 70	FIRE AND RAIN *Warner Bros. WB 6104*	42 3
28 Aug 71 ●	YOU'VE GOT A FRIEND *Warner Bros. WB 16085* ▲	4 15
16 Mar 74	MOCKINGBIRD *Elektra K 12134* [1]	34 5

[1] Carly Simon and James Taylor

James TAYLOR QUARTET – *See JTQ*

John TAYLOR *UK, male vocalist (4 WEEKS)* pos/wks

15 Mar 86	I DO WHAT I DO . . . THEME FOR '9 1/2 WEEKS' *Parlophone R 6125*	42 4

See also DURAN DURAN

Johnnie TAYLOR *US, male vocalist (7 WEEKS)* pos/wks

24 Apr 76	DISCO LADY *CBS 4044* ▲	25 7

JT TAYLOR *US, male vocalist (5 WEEKS)* pos/wks

24 Aug 91	LONG HOT SUMMER NIGHT *MCA MCS 1567*	63 2
30 Nov 91	FEEL THE NEED *MCA MCS 1592*	57 1
18 Apr 92	FOLLOW ME *MCA MCS 1617*	59 2

Pauline TAYLOR *UK, female vocalist (3 WEEKS)* pos/wks

8 Jun 96	LET THIS BE A PRAYER *Cheeky CHEKCD 013* [1]	26 2
9 Nov 96	CONSTANTLY WAITING *Cheeky CHEKCD 015*	51 1

[1] Rollo Goes Spiritual with Pauline Taylor

R Dean TAYLOR *Canada, male vocalist (48 WEEKS)* pos/wks

19 Jun 68	GOTTA SEE JANE *Tamla Motown TMG 656*	17 12
3 Apr 71 ●	INDIANA WANTS ME *Tamla Motown TMG 763*	2 15
11 May 74 ●	THERE'S A GHOST IN MY HOUSE *Tamla Motown TMG 896*	3 12
31 Aug 74	WINDOW SHOPPING *Polydor 2058 502*	36 5
21 Sep 74	GOTTA SEE JANE (re-issue) *Tamla Motown TMG 918*	41 4

Roger TAYLOR *UK, male vocalist (18 WEEKS)* pos/wks

18 Apr 81	FUTURE MANAGEMENT *EMI 5157*	49 4
16 Jun 84	MAN ON FIRE *EMI 5478*	66 2
10 Oct 92	RADIO *Epic 6584367* [1]	37 3
14 May 94	NAZIS *Parlophone CDR 6379*	22 2
1 Oct 94	FOREIGN SAND *Parlophone CDR 6389* [2]	26 2
26 Nov 94	HAPPINESS *Parlophone CDR 6399*	32 2
10 Oct 98	PRESSURE ON *Parlophone CDR 6507*	45 1
10 Apr 99	SURRENDER *Parlophone CDR 6517*	38 2

[1] Shaky featuring Roger Taylor [2] Roger Taylor and Yoshiki

See also QUEEN

TAZ – *See STEREO NATION*

TC *Italy, male instrumental / production duo (5 WEEKS)* pos/wks

14 Mar 92	BERRY *Union City UCRT 1* [1]	73 1
21 Nov 92	FUNKY GUITAR *Union City UCRT 13* [2]	40 2
10 Jul 93	HARMONY *Union UCRD 20* [3]	51 2

[1] TC 1991 [2] TC 1992 [3] TC 1993

Kiri TE KANAWA *New Zealand, female vocalist (11 WEEKS)* pos/wks

28 Sep 91 ●	WORLD IN UNION *Columbia 6574817*	4 11

TEACH-IN

Holland, male / female vocal / instrumental group (7 WEEKS) pos/wks

12 Apr 75	DING-A-DONG *Polydor 2058 570*	13 7

TEAM *UK, male vocal / instrumental group (5 WEEKS)* pos/wks

1 Jun 85	WICKI WACKY HOUSE PARTY *EMI 5519*	55 5

TEAM DEEP *Belgium, male production duo (1 WEEK)* pos/wks

17 May 97	MORNINGLIGHT *Multiply CDMULTY 19*	42 1

TEARDROP EXPLODES

UK, male vocal / instrumental group (50 WEEKS) pos/wks

27 Sep 80	WHEN I DREAM *Mercury TEAR 1*	47 6
31 Jan 81 ●	REWARD *Vertigo TEAR 2*	6 13
2 May 81	TREASON (IT'S JUST A STORY) *Mercury TEAR 3*	18 8
29 Aug 81	PASSIONATE FRIEND *Zoo TEAR 5*	25 10
21 Nov 81	COLOURS FLY AWAY *Mercury TEAR 6*	54 3
19 Jun 82	TINY CHILDREN *Mercury TEAR 7*	44 7
19 Mar 83	YOU DISAPPEAR FROM VIEW *Mercury TEAR 8*	41 3

See also Julian COPE

TEARS FOR FEARS (168 Top 500)

Bath-based band at the forefront of the mid-1980s 'British Invasion' of the US: Roland Orzabal (v/g/k), Curt Smith (v/b; left in 1991). The first of their two US No.1s, 'Everybody Wants to Rule the World', also won the 1986 Brit award for Best Single (143 WEEKS) pos/wks

2 Oct 82 ●	MAD WORLD *Mercury IDEA 3*	3 16
5 Feb 83 ●	CHANGE *Mercury IDEA 4*	4 9
30 Apr 83 ●	PALE SHELTER *Mercury IDEA 5*	5 8
3 Dec 83	THE WAY YOU ARE *Mercury IDEA 6*	24 8
18 Aug 84	MOTHER'S TALK *Mercury IDEA 7*	14 8
1 Dec 84 ●	SHOUT *Mercury IDEA 8* ▲	4 16
30 Mar 85 ●	EVERYBODY WANTS TO RULE THE WORLD *Mercury IDEA 9* ▲	2 14
22 Jun 85	HEAD OVER HEELS *Mercury IDEA 10*	12 9
31 Aug 85	SUFFER THE CHILDREN *Mercury IDEA 1*	52 4
7 Sep 85	PALE SHELTER (re-issue) *Mercury IDEA 2*	73 2
12 Oct 85	I BELIEVE (A SOULFUL RE-RECORDING) *Mercury IDEA 11*	23 4
22 Feb 86	EVERYBODY WANTS TO RULE THE WORLD (re-entry) *Mercury IDEA 9*	73 1
31 May 86 ●	EVERYBODY WANTS TO RUN THE WORLD *Mercury RACE 1*	5 6
19 Jul 86	EVERYBODY WANTS TO RUN THE WORLD (re-entry) *Mercury RACE 1*	73 1
2 Sep 89 ●	SOWING THE SEEDS OF LOVE *Fontana IDEA 12*	5 9
18 Nov 89	WOMAN IN CHAINS *Fontana IDEA 13*	26 8
3 Mar 90	ADVICE FOR THE YOUNG AT HEART *Fontana IDEA 14*	36 4
22 Feb 92	LAID SO LOW (TEARS ROLL DOWN) *Fontana IDEA 17*	17 5
25 Apr 92	WOMAN IN CHAINS (re-issue) *Fontana IDEA 16* [1]	57 1
29 May 93	BREAK IT DOWN AGAIN *Mercury IDECD 18*	20 5
31 Jul 93	COLD *Mercury IDECD 19*	72 1
7 Oct 95	RAOUL AND THE KINGS OF SPAIN *Epic 6624765*	31 3
29 Jun 96	GOD'S MISTAKE *Epic 6634185*	61 1

[1] Tears For Fears featuring Oleta Adams

Mercury RACE 1 was a slightly changed version of Mercury IDEA 9, released to promote the Race Against Time of 15 May 1986. Oleta Adams is given no label credit on the original release of 'Woman In Chains'. From 1992 Tears For Fears was essentially a male vocalist / multi-instrumentalist - Roland Orzabal

TECHNATION *UK, male production duo (1 WEEK)* pos/wks

7 Apr 01	SEA OF BLUE *Slinky Music SLINKY 012CD*	56 1

TECHNICIAN 2 *UK, male instrumental / production group (1 WEEK)* pos/wks

14 Nov 92	PLAYING WITH THE BOY *MCA MCS 1710*	70 1

TECHNIQUE *UK, female vocal / instrumental duo (2 WEEKS)* pos/wks

10 Apr 99	SUN IS SHINING *Creation CRESCD 306*	64 1
28 Aug 99	YOU + ME *Creation CRESCD 315*	56 1

THE OFFICIAL UK SINGLES CHART 50TH ANNIVERSARY

1995

IN THE YEAR IN WHICH DAMIEN HIRST WAS ACCUSED OF FLOGGING A DEAD HORSE WITH HIS DEAD COWS AND SHEEP, TIMOTHY MCVEIGH WREAKED DESTRUCTION ON OKLAHOMA WITH A BOMB WHICH KILLED DOZENS AND INJURED HUNDREDS, ROGUE TRADER NICK LEESON WENT INTO HIDING AFTER BANKRUPTING BARINGS BANK AND BLUR WON A RECORD FOUR BRIT AWARDS, HERE'S HOW **NOEL GALLAGHER** SAW THE MUCH-HYPED BLUR VS OASIS HEAD TO HEAD ...

“You can manipulate the market, but at the end of the day it's like *Raging Bull* where Jake LaMotta says, "The jury's rigged in this town, but the people know who the champion is." But really I didn't enjoy the 'Country House' / 'Roll With It' thing. I didn't enjoy it being on *News at 10*. To me that demeans everything you stand for. That demeans everything about being in a rock 'n' roll band.”

SINGLE OF THE YEAR 'Unchained Melody / (There'll Be Bluebirds Over) The White Cliffs of Dover' Robson and Jerome

ALBUM OF THE YEAR 'The Colour of My Love' Celine Dion

TECHNO TWINS *UK, male / female vocal duo (2 WEEKS)* pos/wks

16 Jan 82	FALLING IN LOVE AGAIN *PRT 7P 224*	75	1
30 Jan 82	FALLING IN LOVE AGAIN (re-entry) *PRT 7P 224*	70	1

TECHNOCAT – *See Tom WILSON*

TECHNOHEAD *UK, male / female vocal / instrumental duo – Michael Wells and Lee Newman (20 WEEKS)* pos/wks

3 Feb 96 ●	I WANNA BE A HIPPY *Mokum DB 17703*	6	14
27 Apr 96	HAPPY BIRTHDAY *Mokum DB 17593*	18	5
12 Oct 96	BANANA-NA-NA (DUMB DI DUMB) *Mokum DB 17473*	64	1

See also GTO; TRICKY DISCO

TECHNOTRONIC *Belgium, male producer – Jo Bogaert (66 WEEKS)* pos/wks

2 Sep 89 ●	PUMP UP THE JAM *Swanyard SYR 4* [1]	2	15
3 Feb 90 ●	GET UP (BEFORE THE NIGHT IS OVER) *Swanyard SYR 8* [2]	2	10
7 Apr 90	THIS BEAT IS TECHNOTRONIC *Swanyard SYR 9* [3]	14	7
14 Jul 90 ●	ROCKIN' OVER THE BEAT *Swanyard SYR 14* [2]	9	9
6 Oct 90 ●	MEGAMIX *Swanyard SYR 19*	6	8
15 Dec 90	TURN IT UP *Swanyard SYD 9* [4]	42	4
25 May 91	MOVE THAT BODY *ARS 6568377* [5]	12	7
3 Aug 91	WORK *ARS 6573317* [5]	40	4
14 Dec 96	PUMP UP THE JAM (re-mix) *Worx WORXCD 004*	36	2

[1] Technotronic featuring Felly [2] Technotronic featuring Ya Kid K [3] Technotronic featuring MC Eric [4] Technotronic featuring Melissa and Einstein [5] Technotronic featuring Reggie

See also HI-TEK 3 featuring YA KID K

TEDDY BEARS *US, male / female vocal group (17 WEEKS)* pos/wks

19 Dec 58 ●	TO KNOW HIM IS TO LOVE HIM *London HLN 8733* ▲	2	16
14 Apr 79	TO KNOW HIM IS TO LOVE HIM (re-issue) *Lightning LIG 9015*	66	1

'To Know Him Is to Love Him' re-issue was coupled with 'Endless Sleep' by Jody Reynolds as a double A-side

TEEBONE featuring MC KIE and MC SPARKS *UK, male producer – Leon Thompson and UK, male rap duo (2 WEEKS)* pos/wks

5 Aug 00	FLY BI *East West EW 217CD*	43	2

TEENAGE FANCLUB
UK, male vocal / instrumental group (21 WEEKS) pos/wks

24 Aug 91	STAR SIGN *Creation CRE 105*	44	2
2 Nov 91	THE CONCEPT *Creation CRE 111*	51	1
8 Feb 92	WHAT YOU DO TO ME (EP) *Creation CRE 115*	31	2
26 Jun 93	RADIO *Creation CRESCD 130*	31	2
2 Oct 93	NORMAN 3 *Creation CRESCD 142*	50	1
2 Apr 94	FALLIN' *Epic 6602622* [1]	59	1
8 Apr 95	MELLOW DOUBT *Creation CRESCD 175*	34	2
27 May 95	SPARKY'S DREAM *Creation CRESCD 201*	40	2
2 Sep 95	NEIL JUNG *Creation CRESCD 210*	62	1
16 Dec 95	HAVE LOST IT (EP) *Creation CRESCD 216*	53	1
12 Jul 97	AIN'T THAT ENOUGH *Creation CRESCD 228*	17	3
30 Aug 97	I DON'T WANT CONTROL OF YOU *Creation CRESCD 238*	43	1
29 Nov 97	START AGAIN *Creation CRESCD 280*	54	1
28 Oct 00	I NEED DIRECTION *Columbia 6699512*	48	1

[1] Teenage Fanclub and De La Soul

Tracks on What You Do to Me (EP): What You Do to Me / B-Side / Life's a Gas / Filler. Tracks on Have Lost It (EP): 120 Mins / Don't Look Back / Everything Flows / Star Sign. This last track is a re-recorded version of their first hit

TEENAGERS – *See Frankie LYMON and the TEENAGERS*

Towa TEI featuring Kylie MINOGUE
Japan, male DJ / producer and Australia, female vocalist (1 WEEK) pos/wks

31 Oct 98	GBI *Athrob ART 021CD*	63	1

TEKNO TOO *UK, male instrumental / production duo (2 WEEKS)* pos/wks

13 Jul 91	JET-STAR *D-Zone DANCE 012*	56	2

TELETUBBIES *UK, male / female cuddly alien vocal group (32 WEEKS)* pos/wks

13 Dec 97 ★	TELETUBBIES SAY EH-OH! *BBC Worldwide WMXS 00092* ◆ ■	1	29
18 Jul 98	TELETUBBIES SAY EH-OH! (re-entry) *BBC Worldwide WMXS 00092*	66	2
15 Aug 98	TELETUBBIES SAY EH-OH! (2nd re-entry) *BBC Worldwide WMXS 00092*	72	1

TELEVISION *US, male vocal / instrumental group (10 WEEKS)* pos/wks

16 Apr 77	MARQUEE MOON *Elektra K 12252*	30	4
30 Jul 77	PROVE IT *Elektra K 12262*	25	4
22 Apr 78	FOXHOLE *Elektra K 12287*	36	2

TELEX *Belgium, male vocal / instrumental duo (7 WEEKS)* pos/wks

21 Jul 79	ROCK AROUND THE CLOCK *Sire SIR 4020*	34	7

Sylvia TELLA – *See BLOW MONKEYS*

TEMPERANCE SEVEN *UK, male vocal / instrumental band – lead vocal Paul MacDowell (45 WEEKS)* pos/wks

30 Mar 61 ★	YOU'RE DRIVING ME CRAZY *Parlophone R 4757*	1	16
15 Jun 61 ●	PASADENA *Parlophone R 4781*	4	17
28 Sep 61	HARD HEARTED HANNAH / CHILI BOM BOM *Parlophone R 4823*	28	4
7 Dec 61	THE CHARLESTON *Parlophone R 4851*	22	8

'Chili Bom Bom' listed with 'Hard Hearted Hannah' only for the weeks of 12 and 19 Oct 1961

TEMPLE OF THE DOG *US, male vocal / instrumental group (2 WEEKS)* pos/wks

24 Oct 92	HUNGER STRIKE *A & M AM 0091*	51	2

Nino TEMPO and April STEVENS *US, male / female vocal duo – Antonio and Carol Lo Tempio (19 WEEKS)* pos/wks

7 Nov 63	DEEP PURPLE *London HLK 9782* ▲	17	11
16 Jan 64	WHISPERING *London HLK 9829*	20	8

TEMPTATIONS (86 Top 500) *The world's most successful R&B vocal group: Eddie Kendricks (d. 1992), Otis Williams, Paul Williams (d. 1973), Melvin Franklin (d. 1995), David Ruffin (d. 1991). The Detroit quintet's biggest UK hit, 'My Girl', was a 27-year-old US No.1. The current line-up of the group is still doing well Stateside (203 WEEKS)* pos/wks

18 Mar 65	MY GIRL *Stateside SS 378* ▲	43	1
1 Apr 65	IT'S GROWING *Tamla Motown TMG 504*	49	1
15 Apr 65	IT'S GROWING (re-entry) *Tamla Motown TMG 504*	45	1
14 Jul 66	AIN'T TOO PROUD TO BEG *Tamla Motown TMG 565*	21	11
6 Oct 66	BEAUTY IS ONLY SKIN DEEP *Tamla Motown TMG 578*	18	10
15 Dec 66	(I KNOW) I'M LOSING YOU *Tamla Motown TMG 587*	19	9
6 Sep 67	YOU'RE MY EVERYTHING *Tamla Motown TMG 620*	26	15
6 Mar 68	I WISH IT WOULD RAIN *Tamla Motown TMG 641*	45	1
12 Jun 68	I COULD NEVER LOVE ANOTHER (AFTER LOVING YOU) *Tamla Motown TMG 658*	47	1
29 Jan 69 ●	I'M GONNA MAKE YOU LOVE ME *Tamla Motown TMG 685* [1]	3	11
5 Mar 69 ●	GET READY *Tamla Motown TMG 688*	10	9
23 Apr 69	I'M GONNA MAKE YOU LOVE ME (re-entry) *Tamla Motown TMG 685* [1]	49	1
23 Aug 69	CLOUD NINE *Tamla Motown TMG 707*	15	10
20 Sep 69	I SECOND THAT EMOTION *Tamla Motown TMG 709* [1]	18	8
17 Jan 70	I CAN'T GET NEXT TO YOU *Tamla Motown TMG 722* ▲	13	9
21 Mar 70	WHY (MUST WE FALL IN LOVE) *Tamla Motown TMG 730* [1]	31	7
13 Jun 70	PSYCHEDELIC SHACK *Tamla Motown TMG 741*	33	7
19 Sep 70 ●	BALL OF CONFUSION *Tamla Motown TMG 749*	7	12
19 Dec 70	BALL OF CONFUSION (re-entry) *Tamla Motown TMG 749*	48	3
22 May 71 ●	JUST MY IMAGINATION (RUNNING AWAY WITH ME) *Tamla Motown TMG 773* ▲	8	16
5 Feb 72	SUPERSTAR (REMEMBER HOW YOU GOT WHERE YOU ARE) *Tamla Motown TMG 800*	32	5
15 Apr 72	TAKE A LOOK AROUND *Tamla Motown TMG 808*	13	10
13 Jan 73	PAPA WAS A ROLLIN' STONE *Tamla Motown TMG 839* ▲	14	8
29 Sep 73	LAW OF THE LAND *Tamla Motown TMG 866*	41	4
12 Jun 82	STANDING ON THE TOP (PART 1) *Motown TMG 1263* [2]	53	3
17 Nov 84	TREAT HER LIKE A LADY *Motown TMG 1365*	12	10

			pos	wks
15 Aug 87		**PAPA WAS A ROLLIN' STONE (re-mix)** *Motown ZB 41431*	31	6
6 Feb 88		**LOOK WHAT YOU STARTED** *Motown ZB 41733*	63	2
21 Oct 89		**ALL I WANT FROM YOU** *Motown ZB 43233*	71	1
15 Feb 92	●	**MY GIRL (re-issue)** *Epic 6576767*	2	10
22 Feb 92		**THE JONES'** *Motown TMG 1403*	69	1

[1] Diana Ross and the Supremes and the Temptations [2] Temptations featuring Rick James

See also Rod STEWART

10 CC (192 Top 500) *Multi-talented Manchester supergroup: Graham Gouldman (previously penned hits for Hollies, Yardbirds and Herman's Hermits), Eric Stewart (ex-Mindbenders, Hotlegs), and Lol Creme and Kevin Godley (both ex-Hotlegs). Godley and Creme went on to have hits as a duo and produced award-winning videos (133 WEEKS)* pos/wks

			pos	wks
23 Sep 72	●	**DONNA** *UK 6*	2	13
19 May 73	★	**RUBBER BULLETS** *UK 36*	1	15
25 Aug 73	●	**THE DEAN AND I** *UK 48*	10	8
15 Jun 74	●	**WALL STREET SHUFFLE** *UK 69*	10	10
14 Sep 74		**SILLY LOVE** *UK 77*	24	7
5 Apr 75	●	**LIFE IS A MINESTRONE** *Mercury 6008 010*	7	8
31 May 75	★	**I'M NOT IN LOVE** *Mercury 6008 014*	1	11
29 Nov 75	●	**ART FOR ART'S SAKE** *Mercury 6008 017*	5	10
20 Mar 76	●	**I'M MANDY FLY ME** *Mercury 6008 019*	6	9
11 Dec 76	●	**THINGS WE DO FOR LOVE** *Mercury 6008 022*	6	11
16 Apr 77	●	**GOOD MORNING JUDGE** *Mercury 6008 025*	5	12
12 Aug 78	★	**DREADLOCK HOLIDAY** *Mercury 6008 035*	1	13
7 Aug 82		**RUN AWAY** *Mercury MER 113*	50	4
18 Mar 95		**I'M NOT IN LOVE (re-recording)** *Avex UK AVEXCD 2*	29	2

From 'Things We Do For Love' 10 CC were a male vocal / instrumental duo

See also WAX; Graham GOULDMAN

TEN CITY *US, male vocal / instrumental group (21 WEEKS)* pos/wks

			pos	wks
21 Jan 89	●	**THAT'S THE WAY LOVE IS** *Atlantic A 8963*	8	10
8 Apr 89		**DEVOTION** *Atlantic A 8916*	29	4
22 Jul 89		**WHERE DO WE GO?** *Atlantic A 8864*	60	1
27 Oct 90		**WHATEVER MAKES YOU HAPPY** *Atlantic A 7819*	60	2
15 Aug 92		**ONLY TIME WILL TELL / MY PEACE OF HEAVEN** *East West America A 8516*	63	2
11 Sep 93		**FANTASY** *Columbia 6595042*	45	2

TEN POLE TUDOR *UK, male vocal / instrumental group (40 WEEKS)* pos/wks

			pos	wks
7 Apr 79	●	**WHO KILLED BAMBI** *Virgin VS 256*	6	8
13 Oct 79		**ROCK AROUND THE CLOCK** *Virgin VS 290*	21	6
25 Apr 81	●	**SWORDS OF A THOUSAND MEN** *Stiff BUY 109*	6	12
1 Aug 81		**WUNDERBAR** *Stiff BUY 120*	16	9
14 Nov 81		**THROWING MY BABY OUT WITH THE BATHWATER** *Stiff BUY 129*	49	5

The listed flip side of 'Who Killed Bambi' was 'Silly Thing' by the Sex Pistols. The listed flip side of 'Rock Around the Clock' was 'The Great Rock 'n' Roll Swindle', also by the Sex Pistols

TEN SHARP *Holland, male vocal / instrumental duo (15 WEEKS)* pos/wks

			pos	wks
21 Mar 92	●	**YOU** *Columbia 6566647*	10	13
20 Jun 92		**AIN'T MY BEATING HEART** *Columbia 6580947*	63	2

10,000 MANIACS
US, female / male vocal / instrumental group (7 WEEKS) pos/wks

			pos	wks
12 Sep 92		**THESE ARE DAYS** *Elektra EKR 156*	58	3
10 Apr 93		**CANDY EVERYBODY WANTS** *Elektra EKR 160CD1*	47	3
23 Oct 93		**BECAUSE THE NIGHT** *Elektra EKR 175CD*	65	1

TEN YEARS AFTER *UK, male vocal / instrumental group (18 WEEKS)* pos/wks

			pos	wks
6 Jun 70	●	**LOVE LIKE A MAN** *Deram DM 299*	10	18

Danny TENAGLIA *US, male DJ / producer (5 WEEKS)* pos/wks

			pos	wks
5 Sep 98		**MUSIC IS THE ANSWER (DANCIN' AND PRANCIN')** *Twisted UK TWCD 10038* [1]	36	3
10 Apr 99		**TURN ME ON** *Twisted UK TWCD 10045* [2]	53	1
23 Oct 99		**MUSIC IS THE ANSWER (re-mix)** *Twisted UK TWCD 10052* [1]	50	1

[1] Danny Tenaglia and Celeda [2] Danny Tenaglia featuring Liz Torres

TENNESSEE THREE – *See Johnny CASH*

TENOR FLY *UK, male vocalist – Jonathan Sutter (17 WEEKS)* pos/wks

			pos	wks
6 Apr 91		**WICKEDEST SOUND** *Desire WANT 40* [1]	43	6
15 Jun 91		**TRIBAL BASE** *Desire WANT 44* [2]	20	6
7 Jan 95		**BRIGHT SIDE OF LIFE** *Mango CIDM 825*	51	2
7 Feb 98		**B-BOY STANCE** *Freskanova FND 7* [3]	23	3

[1] Rebel MC featuring Tenor Fly [2] Rebel MC featuring Tenor Fly and Barrington Levy [3] Freestylers featuring Tenor Fly

TENTH PLANET *UK, male / female vocal / production group (1 WEEK)* pos/wks

			pos	wks
14 Apr 01		**GHOSTS** *Nebula NEBCD 015*	59	1

Bryn TERFEL – *See Shirley BASSEY*

TERMINATERS – *See ARNEE and the TERMINATERS*

TERRA FIRMA *Italy, male producer – Claudio Giussani (1 WEEK)* pos/wks

			pos	wks
18 May 96		**FLOATING** *Platipus PLAT 21CD*	64	1

Tammi TERRELL – *See Marvin GAYE*

TERRIS *UK, male vocal / instrumental group (1 WEEK)* pos/wks

			pos	wks
17 Mar 01		**FABRICATED LUNACY** *Blanco Y Negro NEG 130CD*	62	1

TERRORIZE *UK, male producer – Shaun Imrei (6 WEEKS)* pos/wks

			pos	wks
2 May 92		**IT'S JUST A FEELING** *Hamster STER 1*	52	3
22 Aug 92		**FEEL THE RHYTHM** *Hamster 12STER 2*	69	1
14 Nov 92		**IT'S JUST A FEELING (re-issue)** *Hamster STER 8*	47	2

TERRORVISION *UK, male vocal / instrumental group (55 WEEKS)* pos/wks

			pos	wks
19 Jun 93		**AMERICAN TV** *Total Vegas CDVEGAS 3*	63	1
30 Oct 93		**NEW POLICY ONE** *Total Vegas CDVEGAS 4*	42	2
8 Jan 94		**MY HOUSE** *Total Vegas CDVEGAS 5*	29	4
9 Apr 94		**OBLIVION** *Total Vegas CDVEGAS 6*	21	5
25 Jun 94		**MIDDLEMAN** *Total Vegas CDVEGAS 7*	25	4
3 Sep 94		**PRETEND BEST FRIEND** *Total Vegas CDVEGAS 8*	25	3
29 Oct 94		**ALICE WHAT'S THE MATTER** *Total Vegas CDVEGAS 9*	24	4
18 Mar 95		**SOME PEOPLE SAY** *Total Vegas CDVEGAS 10*	22	3
2 Mar 96	●	**PERSEVERANCE** *Total Vegas CDVEGAS 11*	5	4
4 May 96		**CELEBRITY HIT LIST** *Total Vegas CDVEGAS 12*	20	3
20 Jul 96	●	**BAD ACTRESS** *Total Vegas CDVEGAS 13*	10	3
11 Jan 97		**EASY** *Total Vegas CDVEGASS 14*	12	4
3 Oct 98		**JOSEPHINE** *EMI CDVEGAS 15*	23	2
30 Jan 99	●	**TEQUILA** *Total Vegas CDVEGAS 16*	2	10
15 May 99		**III WISHES** *Total Vegas CDVEGAS 17*	42	1
27 Jan 01		**D'YA WANNA GO FASTER** *Papillion BTFLYS 0007*	28	2

Helen TERRY *UK, female vocalist (6 WEEKS)* pos/wks

			pos	wks
12 May 84		**LOVE LIES LOST** *Virgin VS 678*	34	6

Tony TERRY *US, male vocalist (6 WEEKS)* pos/wks

			pos	wks
27 Feb 88		**LOVEY DOVEY** *Epic TONY 2*	44	6

Todd TERRY PROJECT *US, male producer (33 WEEKS)* pos/wks

			pos	wks
12 Nov 88		**WEEKEND** *Sleeping Bag SBUK 1T*	56	3
14 Oct 95		**WEEKEND (re-mix)** *Ore AG 13CD*	28	3
13 Jul 96	●	**KEEP ON JUMPIN'** *Manifesto FESCD 11* [1]	8	6
12 Jul 97	●	**SOMETHING GOIN' ON** *Manifesto FESCD 25* [1]	5	10

6 Dec 97	IT'S OVER LOVE *Manfiesto FESCD 37* [2]	16	8
11 Apr 98	READY FOR A NEW DAY *Manifesto FESCD 40* [3]	20	2
3 Jul 99	LET IT RIDE *Innocent RESTCD 1*	58	1

[1] Todd Terry featuring Martha Wash and Jocelyn Brown [2] Todd Terry presents Shannon [3] Todd Terry featuring Martha Wash

See also GYPSYMEN; SWAN LAKE; BLACK RIOT; ROYAL HOUSE

TESLA *US, male vocal / instrumental group (1 WEEK)*

		pos	wks
27 Apr 91	SIGNS *Geffen GFS 3*	70	1

Joe TEX *US, male vocalist – Joe Arlington (11 WEEKS)*

		pos	wks
23 Apr 77 ●	AIN'T GONNA BUMP NO MORE (WITH NO BIG FAT WOMAN) *Epic EPC 5035*	2	11

TEXAS (212 Top 500) *Named after Wim Wenders' 'Paris, Texas' the Scots blues turned pop chart mainstays are: Sharleen Spiteri (v), Ally McErlaine (g), Johnny McElhone (b), Eddie Campbell (k), all from Glasgow. Stuart Kerr, Richard Hynde and Mykey Wilson have all contributed on drums with Tony McGovern (g) the most recent recruit to a band now well established among the multi-million-selling album elite (127 WEEKS)*

		pos	wks
4 Feb 89 ●	I DON'T WANT A LOVER *Mercury TEX 1*	8	11
6 May 89	THRILL HAS GONE *Mercury TEX 2*	60	3
5 Aug 89	EVERYDAY NOW *Mercury TEX 3*	44	5
2 Dec 89	PRAYER FOR YOU *Mercury TEX 4*	73	1
7 Sep 91	WHY BELIEVE IN YOU *Mercury TEX 5*	66	1
26 Oct 91	IN MY HEART *Mercury TEX 6*	74	1
8 Feb 92	ALONE WITH YOU *Mercury TEX 7*	32	4
25 Apr 92	TIRED OF BEING ALONE *Mercury TEX 8*	19	6
11 Sep 93	SO CALLED FRIEND *Vertigo TEXCD 9*	30	3
30 Oct 93	YOU OWE IT ALL TO ME *Vertigo TEXCD 10*	39	3
12 Feb 94	SO IN LOVE WITH YOU *Vertigo TEXCD 11*	28	2
18 Jan 97 ●	SAY WHAT YOU WANT *Mercury MERCD 480*	3	10
19 Apr 97 ●	HALO *Mercury MERCD 482*	10	7
9 Aug 97 ●	BLACK EYED BOY *Mercury MERCD 490*	5	6
15 Nov 97 ●	PUT YOUR ARMS AROUND ME *Mercury MERCD 497*	10	5
3 Jan 98	PUT YOUR ARMS AROUND ME (re-entry) *Mercury MERCD 497*	75	1
17 Jan 98	PUT YOUR ARMS AROUND ME (2nd re-entry) *Mercury MERCD 497*	64	2
21 Mar 98 ●	INSANE / SAY WHAT YOU WANT (ALL DAY EVERY DAY) (re-mix) *Mercury MERCD 499* [1]	4	7
1 May 99 ●	IN OUR LIFETIME *Mercury MERCD 517*	4	9
28 Aug 99 ●	SUMMER SON *Mercury MERCD 520*	5	9
27 Nov 99	WHEN WE ARE TOGETHER *Mercury MERCD 525*	12	9
14 Oct 00 ●	IN DEMAND *Mercury MERCD 528*	6	8
13 Jan 01	IN DEMAND (re-entry) *Mercury MERCD 528*	62	2
20 Jan 01 ●	INNER SMILE *Mercury MERCD 531*	6	8
21 Jul 01	I DON'T WANT A LOVER (re-mix) *Mercury MERCD 533*	16	4

[1] Texas featuring The Wu-Tang Clan

'Say What You Want (All Day Every Day)' is a new mix of the hit from 18 Jan 97 with rap by Method Man and The RZA

THAT KID CHRIS *US, male DJ / producer – Chris Staropoli (1 WEEK)*

		pos	wks
22 Feb 97	FEEL THA VIBE *Manifesto FESCD 16*	52	1

THAT PETROL EMOTION

UK, male vocal / instrumental group (24 WEEKS)

		pos	wks
11 Apr 87	BIG DECISION *Polydor TPE 1*	43	7
11 Jul 87	DANCE *Polydor TPE 2*	64	2
17 Oct 87	GENIUS MOVE *Virgin VS 1002*	65	2
31 Mar 90	ABANDON *Virgin VS 1242*	73	1
1 Sep 90	HEY VENUS *Virgin VS 1290*	49	4
9 Feb 91	TINGLE *Virgin VS 1312*	49	4
27 Apr 91	SENSITIZE *Virgin VS 1261*	55	4

THE AUDIENCE – *See THEAUDIENCE*

The THE *UK, male vocalist / multi-instrumentalist – Matt Johnson and backing musicians (52 WEEKS)*

		pos	wks
4 Dec 82	UNCERTAIN SMILE *Epic EPC A 2787*	68	3
17 Sep 83	THIS IS THE DAY *Epic A 3710*	71	3
9 Aug 86	HEARTLAND *Some Bizarre TRUTH 2*	29	10
25 Oct 86	INFECTED *Some Bizarre TRUTH 3*	48	5
24 Jan 87	SLOW TRAIN TO DAWN *Some Bizarre TENSE 1*	64	2
23 May 87	SWEET BIRD OF TRUTH *Epic TENSE 2*	55	2
1 Apr 89	THE BEAT(EN) GENERATION *Epic EMU 8*	18	5
22 Jul 89	GRAVITATE TO ME *Epic EMU 9*	63	3
7 Oct 89	ARMAGEDDON DAYS ARE HERE (AGAIN) *Epic EMU 10*	70	2
2 Mar 91	SHADES OF BLUE (EP) *Epic 6557968*	54	1
16 Jan 93	DOGS OF LUST *Epic 6584572*	25	4
17 Apr 93	SLOW EMOTION REPLAY *Epic 6590772*	35	3
19 Jun 93	LOVE IS STRONGER THAN DEATH *Epic 6593712*	39	3
15 Jan 94	DIS-INFECTED (EP) *Epic 6598112*	17	4
4 Feb 95	I SAW THE LIGHT *Epic 6610912*	31	2

Tracks on Shades of Blue (EP): Jealous of Youth / Another Boy Drowning (Live) / Solitude / Dolphins. Tracks on Dis-Infected (EP): This Was The Day / Dis-Infected / Helpline Operator (sickboy remix) / Dogs of Lust (germicide remix). 'That Was the Day' and 'Dis-Infected' on the EP are re-recordings of earlier hits. 'Dogs of Lust' is a re-mix

THEATRE OF HATE *UK, male vocal / instrumental group (9 WEEKS)*

		pos	wks
23 Jan 82	DO YOU BELIEVE IN THE WESTWORLD *Burning Rome BRR 2*	40	7
29 May 82	THE HOP *Burning Rome BRR 3*	70	2

THEAUDIENCE

UK, male / female, vocal / instrumental group (5 WEEKS)

		pos	wks
7 Mar 98	IF YOU CAN'T DO IT WHEN YOU'RE YOUNG, WHEN CAN YOU DO IT? *Mercury AUDCD 2*	48	1
23 May 98	A PESSIMIST IS NEVER DISAPPOINTED *Mercury AUDCD 3*	27	2
8 Aug 98	I KNOW ENOUGH (I DON'T GET ENOUGH) *Elleffe AUCD 4*	25	2

THEM *UK, male vocal / instrumental group (23 WEEKS)*

		pos	wks
7 Jan 65 ●	BABY PLEASE DON'T GO *Decca F 12018*	10	9
25 Mar 65 ●	HERE COMES THE NIGHT *Decca F 12094*	2	12
9 Feb 91	BABY PLEASE DON'T GO (re-issue) *London LON 292*	65	2

See also Van MORRISON

THEN JERICO *UK, male vocal / instrumental group (36 WEEKS)*

		pos	wks
31 Jan 87	LET HER FALL *London LON 97*	65	3
25 Jul 87	THE MOTIVE (LIVING WITHOUT YOU) *London LON 145*	18	12
24 Oct 87	MUSCLE DEEP *London LON 156*	48	4
28 Jan 89	BIG AREA *London LON 204*	13	7
8 Apr 89	WHAT DOES IT TAKE? *London LON 223*	33	4
12 Aug 89	SUGAR BOX *London LON 235*	22	6

THERAPY? *UK, male vocal / instrumental group (33 WEEKS)*

		pos	wks
31 Oct 92	TEETHGRINDER *A & M AM 0097*	30	2
20 Mar 93 ●	SHORTSHARPSHOCK (EP) *A & M AMCD 208*	9	4
12 Jun 93	FACE THE STRANGE (EP) *A & M 5803052*	18	3
28 Aug 93	OPAL MANTRA *A & M 5803612*	14	3
29 Jan 94	NOWHERE *A & M 5805052*	18	4
12 Mar 94	TRIGGER INSIDE *A & M 5805352*	22	3
11 Jun 94	DIE LAUGHING *A & M 5805892*	29	2
27 May 95	INNOCENT X *Volume VOLCD 1*	53	1
3 Jun 95	STORIES *A & M 5811052*	14	3
29 Jul 95	LOOSE *A & M 5811652*	25	3
18 Nov 95	DIANE *A & M 5812912*	26	2
14 Mar 98	CHURCH OF NOISE *A & M 5825392*	29	2
30 May 98	LONELY, CRYIN' ONLY *A & M 0441212*	32	1

Tracks on Shortsharpshock (EP): Screamager / Auto Surgery / Totally Random Man / Accelerator. Tracks on Face the Strange (EP): Turn / Speedball / Bloody Blue / Neckfreak. The listed flip side of 'Innocent X' was 'Belfast' by Orbital

THESE ANIMAL MEN

UK, male vocal / instrumental group (3 WEEKS)

		pos	wks
24 Sep 94	THIS IS THE SOUND OF YOUTH *Hi-Rise FLATSCD 7*	72	1

8 Feb 97		**LIFE SUPPORT MACHINE** *Hut HUTCD 76*	62	1
12 Apr 97		**LIGHT EMITTING ELECTRICAL WAVE** *Hut HUTCD 81*	72	1

THEY MIGHT BE GIANTS *US, male vocal / instrumental duo – John Flansburgh and John Linnell (18 WEEKS)*

			pos	wks
3 Mar 90	●	**BIRDHOUSE IN YOUR SOUL** *Elektra EKR 104*	6	11
2 Jun 90		**ISTANBUL (NOT CONSTANTINOPLE)** *Elektra EKR 110*	61	2
28 Jul 01		**BOSS OF ME** *Pias / Restless PIASREST 001 CD*	21	5

THIN LIZZY (210) Top 500

Accomplished Irish hard-rock group (which at times included noted guitarists Gary Moore, Snowy White and Midge Ure) was built around distinctive singer / bass guitarist Phil Lynott (d. 1986). After a slow start, they wrote their own chapter in British rock history (128 WEEKS)

			pos	wks
20 Jan 73	●	**WHISKEY IN THE JAR** *Decca F 13355*	6	12
29 May 76	●	**THE BOYS ARE BACK IN TOWN** *Vertigo 6059 139*	8	10
14 Aug 76		**JAILBREAK** *Vertigo 6059 150*	31	4
15 Jan 77		**DON'T BELIEVE A WORD** *Vertigo Lizzy 001*	12	7
13 Aug 77		**DANCIN' IN THE MOONLIGHT (IT'S CAUGHT ME IN ITS SPOTLIGHT)** *Vertigo 6059 177*	14	8
13 May 78		**ROSALIE - COWGIRLS' SONG (MEDLEY)** *Vertigo LIZZY 2*	20	13
3 Mar 79	●	**WAITING FOR AN ALIBI** *Vertigo LIZZY 003*	9	8
16 Jun 79		**DO ANYTHING YOU WANT TO** *Vertigo LIZZY 004*	14	9
20 Oct 79		**SARAH** *Vertigo LIZZY 5*	24	13
24 May 80		**CHINATOWN** *Vertigo LIZZY 6*	21	9
27 Sep 80	●	**KILLER ON THE LOOSE** *Vertigo LIZZY 7*	10	7
2 May 81		**KILLERS LIVE (EP)** *Vertigo LIZZY 8*	19	7
8 Aug 81		**TROUBLE BOYS** *Vertigo LIZZY 9*	53	4
6 Mar 82		**HOLLYWOOD (DOWN ON YOUR LUCK)** *Vertigo LIZZY 10*	53	3
12 Feb 83		**COLD SWEAT** *Vertigo LIZZY 11*	27	5
7 May 83		**THUNDER AND LIGHTNING** *Vertigo LIZZY 12*	39	2
6 Aug 83		**THE SUN GOES DOWN** *Vertigo LIZZY 13*	52	3
26 Jan 91		**DEDICATION** *Vertigo LIZZY 14*	35	3
23 Mar 91		**THE BOYS ARE BACK IN TOWN (re-issue)** *Vertigo LIZZY 15*	63	1

Tracks on Killers Live (EP): Bad Reputation / Are You Ready / Dear Miss Lonely Hearts

3RD BASS *US, male rap group (5 WEEKS)*

			pos	wks
10 Feb 90		**THE GAS FACE** *Def Jam 655627 0*	71	1
7 Apr 90		**BROOKLYN-QUEENS** *Def Jam 655830 7*	61	2
22 Jun 91		**POP GOES THE WEASEL** *Def Jam 6569547*	64	2

THIRD DIMENSION featuring Julie McDERMOTT *UK, male / female vocal / instrumental group (2 WEEKS)*

			pos	wks
12 Oct 96		**DON'T GO** *Soundproof MCSTD 40082*	34	2

THIRD EYE BLIND *US, male vocal / instrumental group (6 WEEKS)*

			pos	wks
27 Sep 97		**SEMI-CHARMED LIFE** *Elektra E 3907CD*	33	5
21 Mar 98		**HOW'S IT GOING TO BE** *Elektra E 3863CD*	51	1

3RD STOREE *US, male vocal group (1 WEEK)*

			pos	wks
5 Jun 99		**IF EVER** *Yab Yum / Elektra E 3752CD*	53	1

THIRD WORLD *Jamaica, male vocal / instrumental group (53 WEEKS)*

			pos	wks
23 Sep 78	●	**NOW THAT WE'VE FOUND LOVE** *Island WIP 6457*	10	9
6 Jan 79		**COOL MEDITATION** *Island WIP 6469*	17	10
16 Jun 79		**TALK TO ME** *Island WIP 6496*	56	5
6 Jun 81	●	**DANCING ON THE FLOOR (HOOKED ON LOVE)** *CBS A 1214*	10	15
17 Apr 82		**TRY JAH LOVE** *CBS A 2063*	47	6
9 Mar 85		**NOW THAT WE'VE FOUND LOVE (re-issue)** *Island IS 219*	22	8

THIRST *UK, male vocal / instrumental group (2 WEEKS)*

			pos	wks
6 Jul 91		**THE ENEMY WITHIN** *Ten TEN 379*	61	2

1300 DRUMS featuring the UNJUSTIFIED ANCIENTS OF M U *UK, male instrumental / production group (4 WEEKS)*

			pos	wks
18 May 96		**OOH! AAH! CANTONA** *Dynamo DYND 5*	11	4

THIS ISLAND EARTH *UK, male / female vocal / instrumental group (5 WEEKS)*

			pos	wks
5 Jan 85		**SEE THAT GLOW** *Magnet MAG 266*	47	5

THIS MORTAL COIL *UK, male / female vocal / instrumental group (3 WEEKS)*

			pos	wks
22 Oct 83		**SONG TO THE SIREN** *4AD AD 310*	66	2
12 Nov 83		**SONG TO THE SIREN (re-entry)** *4AD AD 310*	75	1

THIS WAY UP *UK, male vocal / instrumental duo (2 WEEKS)*

			pos	wks
22 Aug 87		**TELL ME WHY** *Virgin VS 954*	72	2

THIS YEAR'S BLONDE *UK, male / female vocal / instrumental group (8 WEEKS)*

			pos	wks
10 Oct 81		**PLATINUM POP** *Creole CR 19*	46	5
14 Nov 87		**WHO'S THAT MIX** *Debut DEBT 3034*	62	3

BJ THOMAS *US, male vocalist (4 WEEKS)*

			pos	wks
21 Feb 70		**RAINDROPS KEEP FALLING ON MY HEAD** *Wand WN1* ▲	38	3
2 May 70		**RAINDROPS KEEP FALLING ON MY HEAD (re-entry)** *Wand WN1*	49	1

Carla THOMAS – *See Otis REDDING*

Evelyn THOMAS *US, female vocalist (29 WEEKS)*

			pos	wks
24 Jan 76		**WEAK SPOT** *20th Century BTC 1014*	26	7
17 Apr 76		**DOOMSDAY** *20th Century BTC 1017*	41	1
1 May 76		**DOOMSDAY (re-entry)** *20th Century BTC 1017*	45	1
21 Apr 84	●	**HIGH ENERGY** *Record Shack SOHO 18*	5	17
25 Aug 84		**MASQUERADE** *Record Shack SOHO 25*	60	3

Jamo THOMAS and his PARTY BROTHERS ORCHESTRA *US, male vocalist (2 WEEKS)*

			pos	wks
26 Feb 69		**I SPY (FOR THE FBI)** *Polydor 56755*	48	1
12 Mar 69		**I SPY (FOR THE FBI) (re-entry)** *Polydor 56755*	44	1

Kenny THOMAS *UK, male vocalist (54 WEEKS)*

			pos	wks
26 Jan 91		**OUTSTANDING** *Cooltempo COOL 227*	12	10
1 Jun 91	●	**THINKING ABOUT YOUR LOVE** *Cooltempo COOL 235*	4	13
5 Oct 91		**BEST OF YOU** *Cooltempo COOL 243*	11	7
30 Nov 91		**TENDER LOVE** *Cooltempo COOL 247*	26	6
10 Jul 93		**STAY** *Cooltempo CDCOOL 271*	22	6
4 Sep 93		**TRIPPIN' ON YOUR LOVE** *Cooltempo CDCOOL 277*	17	5
6 Nov 93		**PIECE BY PIECE** *Cooltempo CDCOOL 283*	36	3
14 May 94		**DESTINY** *Cooltempo CDCOOL 289*	59	1
2 Sep 95		**WHEN I THINK OF YOU** *Cooltempo CDCOOL 309*	27	3

Lillo THOMAS *US, male vocalist (10 WEEKS)*

			pos	wks
27 Apr 85		**SETTLE DOWN** *Capitol CL 356*	66	2
21 Mar 87		**SEXY GIRL** *Capitol CL 445*	23	5
30 May 87		**I'M IN LOVE** *Capitol CL 450*	54	3

Mickey THOMAS – *See Elvin BISHOP*

Millard THOMAS – *See Harry BELAFONTE*

Nicky THOMAS *Jamaica, male vocalist (14 WEEKS)*

			pos	wks
13 Jun 70	●	**LOVE OF THE COMMON PEOPLE** *Trojan TR 7750*	9	14

Rob THOMAS – *See MATCHBOX 20; SANTANA*

Rufus THOMAS *US, male vocalist (12 WEEKS)*

			pos	wks
11 Apr 70		**DO THE FUNKY CHICKEN** *Stax 144*	18	12

Tasha THOMAS *US, female vocalist (3 WEEKS)*

			pos	wks
20 Jan 79		**SHOOT ME (WITH YOUR LOVE)** *Atlantic LV 4*	59	3

Timmy THOMAS *US, male vocalist (20 WEEKS)* pos/wks

Date		Title / Label	pos	wks
24 Feb 73		WHY CAN'T WE LIVE TOGETHER *Mojo 2027 012*	12	11
28 Dec 85		NEW YORK EYES *Portrait A 6805* [1]	41	7
14 Jul 90		WHY CAN'T WE LIVE TOGETHER (re-mix) *TK TKR 1*	54	2

[1] Nicole with Timmy Thomas

THOMAS and TAYLOR *US, male / female vocal duo (5 WEEKS)* pos/wks

Date		Title / Label	pos	wks
17 May 86		YOU CAN'T BLAME LOVE *Cooltempo COOL 123*	53	5

Amanda THOMPSON – *See Lesley GARRETT and Amanda THOMPSON*

Carroll THOMPSON – *See MOVEMENT 98 featuring Carroll THOMPSON; Courtney PINE*

Chris THOMPSON *UK, male vocalist (5 WEEKS)* pos/wks

Date		Title / Label	pos	wks
27 Oct 79		IF YOU REMEMBER ME *Planet K 12389*	42	5

Gina THOMPSON – *See MC LYTE*

Lincoln THOMPSON – *See REBEL MC*

Sue THOMPSON *US, female vocalist (9 WEEKS)* pos/wks

Date		Title / Label	pos	wks
2 Nov 61		SAD MOVIES (MAKE ME CRY) *Polydor NH 66967*	46	1
16 Nov 61		SAD MOVIES (MAKE ME CRY) (re-entry) *Polydor NH 66967*	48	1
21 Jan 65		PAPER TIGER *Hickory 1284*	50	1
11 Feb 65		PAPER TIGER (re-entry) *Hickory 1284*	30	6

THOMPSON TWINS (266 Top 500) *British-based synth-rock trio: Tom Bailey (v/syn), New Zealand-born Alannah Currie (v/prc/s), Joe Leeway (prc). Named after characters in a Tin Tin cartoon, they were joined on stage at Live Aid by Madonna and were at the forefront of second so-called 'British Invasion' (110 WEEKS)* pos/wks

Date		Title / Label	pos	wks
6 Nov 82		LIES *Arista ARIST 486*	67	3
29 Jan 83	●	LOVE ON YOUR SIDE *Arista ARIST 504*	9	12
16 Apr 83	●	WE ARE DETECTIVE *Arista ARIST 526*	7	9
16 Jul 83		WATCHING *Arista TWINS 1*	33	6
19 Nov 83	●	HOLD ME NOW *Arista TWINS 2*	4	15
4 Feb 84	●	DOCTOR DOCTOR *Arista TWINS 3*	3	10
31 Mar 84	●	YOU TAKE ME UP *Arista TWINS 4*	2	9
7 Jul 84		SISTER OF MERCY *Arista TWINS 5*	11	8
8 Sep 84		SISTER OF MERCY (re-entry) *Arista TWINS 5*	66	1
8 Dec 84		LAY YOUR HANDS ON ME *Arista TWINS 6*	13	9
31 Aug 85		DON'T MESS WITH DOCTOR DREAM *Arista TWINS 9*	15	6
19 Oct 85		KING FOR A DAY *Arista TWINS 7*	22	6
7 Dec 85		REVOLUTION *Arista TWINS 10*	56	3
4 Jan 86		REVOLUTION (re-entry) *Arista TWINS 10*	75	1
21 Mar 87		GET THAT LOVE *Arista TWINS 12*	68	2
11 Apr 87		GET THAT LOVE (re-entry) *Arista TWINS 12*	66	1
15 Oct 88		IN THE NAME OF LOVE '88 *Arista 111808*	46	3
28 Sep 91		COME INSIDE *Warner Bros. W 0058*	56	4
25 Jan 92		THE SAINT *Warner Bros. W 0080*	53	2

Tracey THORN – *See EVERYTHING BUT THE GIRL; MASSIVE ATTACK*

David THORNE *US, male vocalist (8 WEEKS)* pos/wks

Date		Title / Label	pos	wks
24 Jan 63		THE ALLEY CAT SONG *Stateside SS 141*	21	8

Ken THORNE *UK, orchestra (15 WEEKS)* pos/wks

Date		Title / Label	pos	wks
18 Jul 63	●	THEME FROM THE FILM 'THE LEGION'S LAST PATROL' *HMV POP 1176*	4	15

Trumpet solo by Ray Davies

THOSE 2 GIRLS *UK, female vocal duo (4 WEEKS)* pos/wks

Date		Title / Label	pos	wks
5 Nov 94		WANNA MAKE YOU GO . . . UUH! *Final Vinyl 74321233782*	74	1
4 Mar 95		ALL I WANT *Final Vinyl 74321254202*	36	3

THOUSAND YARD STARE
UK, male vocal / instrumental group (5 WEEKS) pos/wks

Date		Title / Label	pos	wks
26 Oct 91		SEASONSTREAM (EP) *Stifled Aardvark AARD 5T*	65	1
8 Feb 92		COMEUPPANCE *Stifled Aardvark AARD 007*	37	2
11 Jul 92		SPINDRIFT (EP) *Stifled Aardvark AARDT 010*	58	1
8 May 93		VERSION OF ME *Polydor AARDC 012*	57	1

Tracks on Seasonstream (EP): O-O AET / Village End / Keepsake / Worse for Wear
Tracks on Spindrift (EP): Wideshire Two / Hand, Son / Happenstance / Mocca Pune

THRASHING DOVES *UK, male vocal / instrumental group (3 WEEKS)* pos/wks

Date		Title / Label	pos	wks
24 Jan 87		BEAUTIFUL IMBALANCE *A & M TDOVE 1*	50	3

THREE AMIGOS *UK, male production trio (8 WEEKS)* pos/wks

Date		Title / Label	pos	wks
3 Jul 99		LOUIE LOUIE *Inferno CDFERN 17*	15	6
24 Mar 01		25 MILES 2001 *Wonderboy WBOYD 25*	30	2

3 COLOURS RED *UK, male vocal / instrumental group (17 WEEKS)* pos/wks

Date		Title / Label	pos	wks
18 Jan 97		NUCLEAR HOLIDAY *Creation CRESCD 250*	22	2
15 Mar 97		SIXTY MILE SMILE *Creation CRESCD 254*	20	3
10 May 97		PURE *Creation CRESCD 265*	28	1
12 Jul 97		COPPER GIRL *Creation CRESCD 270*	30	2
8 Nov 97		THIS IS MY HOLLYWOOD *Creation CRESCD 277*	48	1
23 Jan 99		BEAUTIFUL DAY *Creation CRESCD 308*	11	6
29 May 99		THIS IS MY TIME *Creation CRESCD 313*	36	2

THREE DEGREES (248 Top 500) *US R&B vocal group, who became top UK stars in the 1970s: Sheila Ferguson, Valerie Holiday, Fayette Pinkney. The trio, tagged by the media as "Prince Charles's favourites", was the first girl group to top the UK chart since The Supremes in 1964 (113 WEEKS)* pos/wks

Date		Title / Label	pos	wks
13 Apr 74		YEAR OF DECISION *Philadelphia International PIR 2073*	13	10
27 Apr 74		TSOP (THE SOUND OF PHILADELPHIA) *Philadelphia International PIR 2289* [1] ▲	22	9
13 Jul 74	★	WHEN WILL I SEE YOU AGAIN *Philadelphia International PIR 2155*	1	16
2 Nov 74		GET YOUR LOVE BACK *Philadelphia International PIR 2737*	34	4
12 Apr 75	●	TAKE GOOD CARE OF YOURSELF *Philadelphia International PIR 3177*	9	9
5 Jul 75		LONG LOST LOVER *Philadelphia International PIR 3352*	40	4
1 May 76		TOAST OF LOVE *Epic EPC 4215*	36	4
7 Oct 78		GIVING UP GIVING IN *Ariola ARO 130*	12	10
13 Jan 79	●	WOMAN IN LOVE *Ariola ARO 141*	3	11
24 Mar 79	●	THE RUNNER *Ariola ARO 154*	10	10
23 Jun 79		THE GOLDEN LADY *Ariola ARO 170*	56	3
29 Sep 79		JUMP THE GUN *Ariola ARO 183*	48	5
24 Nov 79	●	MY SIMPLE HEART *Ariola ARO 202*	9	11
5 Oct 85		THE HEAVEN I NEED *Supreme SUPE 102*	42	5
26 Dec 98		LAST CHRISTMAS *Wildstar CDWILD 15* [2]	54	2

[1] MFSB featuring the Three Degrees [2] Alien Voices featuring the Three Degrees

THREE DOG NIGHT *US, male vocal / instrumental group (23 WEEKS)* pos/wks

Date		Title / Label	pos	wks
8 Aug 70	●	MAMA TOLD ME NOT TO COME *Stateside SS 8052* ▲	3	14
29 May 71		JOY TO THE WORLD *Probe PRO 523* ▲	24	9

THREE DRIVES ON A VINYL
Holland, male vocal / instrumental group (7 WEEKS) pos/wks

Date		Title / Label	pos	wks
27 Jun 98		GREECE 2000 *Hooj Choons HOOJCD 63* [1]	44	1
30 Jan 99		GREECE 2000 (re-mix) *Hooj Choons HOOJ 70CD* [1]	12	4
17 Nov 01		SUNSET ON IBIZA *Xtravaganza XTRAV 27CDS*	44	2

[1] Three Drives

THREE GOOD REASONS
UK, male vocal / instrumental group (3 WEEKS) pos/wks

Date		Title / Label	pos	wks
10 Mar 66		NOWHERE MAN *Mercury MF 899*	47	3

3 JAYS *UK, male production / vocal trio (5 WEEKS)* pos/wks

Date		Title / Label	pos	wks
31 Jul 99		FEELING IT TOO *Multiply CDMULTY 53*	17	5

THREE KAYES – *See KAYE SISTERS*

UK No.1 ★ UK Top 10 ● Still on chart + UK million seller ◆ UK entry at No.1 ■ US No.1 ▲

3LW *US, female vocal group (12 WEEKS)* pos/wks

			pos	wks
2 Jun 01	●	**NO MORE (BABY I'MA DO RIGHT)** *Epic 6712722*	6	8
4 Aug 01		**NO MORE (BABY I'MA DO RIGHT) (re-entry)** *Epic 6712722*	74	1
8 Sep 01		**PLAYAS GON' PLAY** *Epic 6717932*	21	3

THREE 'N ONE *Germany, male production duo (3 WEEKS)* pos/wks

			pos	wks
7 Jun 97		**REFLECT** *ffrr FCD 301*	66	1
15 May 99		**PEARL RIVER** *Low Sense SENSECD 24* [1]	32	2

[1] Three 'N One presents Johnny Shaker featuring Serial Diva

3T *US, male vocal trio (45 WEEKS)* pos/wks

			pos	wks
27 Jan 96	●	**ANYTHING** *MJJ 6627152*	2	14
4 May 96		**24 / 7** *MJJ 6631995*	11	7
24 Aug 96	●	**WHY** *MJJ 6636482* [1]	2	9
7 Dec 96	●	**I NEED YOU** *Epic 6639912*	3	10
5 Apr 97	●	**GOTTA BE YOU** *Epic 6643645* [2]	10	5

[1] 3T featuring Michael Jackson [2] 3T: rap by Herbie

THREE TONS OF JOY – *See Johnny OTIS SHOW*

THRILLSEEKERS featuring Sheryl DEANE
UK, male producer / instrumentalist and female vocalist (2 WEEKS) pos/wks

			pos	wks
17 Feb 01		**SYNAESTHESIA (FLY AWAY)** *Neo NEOCD 050*	28	2

THROWING MUSES
US, male / female vocal / instrumental group (6 WEEKS) pos/wks

			pos	wks
9 Feb 91		**COUNTING BACKWARDS** *4AD AD 1001*	70	2
1 Aug 92		**FIREPILE (EP)** *4AD BAD 2012*	46	1
24 Dec 94		**BRIGHT YELLOW GUN** *4AD BAD 4018CD*	51	2
10 Aug 96		**SHARK** *4AD BAD 6016CD*	53	1

Tracks on Firepile (EP): Firepile / Manic Depression / Snailhead / City of the Dead

THS - THE HORN SECTION
US, male / female vocal / instrumental group (3 WEEKS) pos/wks

			pos	wks
18 Aug 84		**LADY SHINE (SHINE ON)** *Fourth & Broadway BRW 10*	54	3

Harry THUMANN
Germany, male instrumentalist – keyboards (6 WEEKS) pos/wks

			pos	wks
21 Feb 81		**UNDERWATER** *Decca F 13901*	41	6

See also WONDER DOG

THUNDER *UK, male vocal / instrumental group (52 WEEKS)* pos/wks

			pos	wks
17 Feb 90		**DIRTY LOVE** *EMI EM 126*	32	4
12 May 90		**BACKSTREET SYMPHONY** *EMI EM 137*	25	4
14 Jul 90		**GIMME SOME LOVIN'** *EMI EM 148*	36	3
29 Sep 90		**SHE'S SO FINE** *EMI EM 158*	34	3
23 Feb 91		**LOVE WALKED IN** *EMI EM 175*	21	4
15 Aug 92		**LOW LIFE IN HIGH PLACES** *EMI EM 242*	22	5
10 Oct 92		**EVERYBODY WANTS HER** *EMI EM 249*	36	4
13 Feb 93		**A BETTER MAN** *EMI CDBETTER 1*	18	4
19 Jun 93		**LIKE A SATELLITE (EP)** *EMI CDEM 272*	28	2
7 Jan 95		**STAND UP** *EMI CDEM 365*	23	4
25 Feb 95		**RIVER OF PAIN** *EMI CDEM 367*	31	2
6 May 95		**CASTLES IN THE SAND** *EMI CDEM 372*	30	3
23 Sep 95		**IN A BROKEN DREAM** *EMI CDEM 384*	26	2
25 Jan 97		**DON'T WAIT UP** *Raw Power RAWX 1020*	27	2
5 Apr 97		**LOVE WORTH DYING FOR** *Raw Power RAWX 1043*	60	1
7 Feb 98		**THE ONLY ONE** *Eagle EAGXA 016*	31	2
27 Jun 98		**PLAY THAT FUNKY MUSIC** *Eagle EAGXS 030*	39	2
20 Mar 99		**YOU WANNA KNOW** *Eagle EAGXA 037*	49	1

Tracks on Like a Satellite (EP): Like a Satellite / The Damage Is Done / Like a Satellite (Live) / Gimme Shelter

THUNDERBIRDS – *See Chris FARLOWE*

THUNDERBUGS
UK / France / Germany, female vocal / instrumental group (15 WEEKS) pos/wks

			pos	wks
18 Sep 99	●	**FRIENDS FOREVER** *First Avenue / Epic 6676932*	5	9
11 Dec 99		**FRIENDS FOREVER (re-entry)** *First Avenue / Epic 6676932*	71	1
18 Dec 99		**IT'S ABOUT TIME YOU WERE MINE** *First Avenue / Epic 6683972*	43	5

THUNDERCLAP NEWMAN *UK, male vocal / instrumental group – lead vocal John "Speedy" Keen (13 WEEKS)* pos/wks

			pos	wks
11 Jun 69	★	**SOMETHING IN THE AIR** *Track 604-031*	1	12
27 Jun 70		**ACCIDENTS** *Track 2094 001*	46	1

THUNDERTHIGHS *UK, female vocal group (5 WEEKS)* pos/wks

			pos	wks
22 Jun 74		**CENTRAL PARK ARREST** *Philips 6006 386*	30	5

Bobby THURSTON *US, male vocalist (10 WEEKS)* pos/wks

			pos	wks
29 Mar 80	●	**CHECK OUT THE GROOVE** *Epic EPC 8348*	10	10

TIFFANY *US, female vocalist – Tiffany Darwish (45 WEEKS)* pos/wks

			pos	wks
16 Jan 88	★	**I THINK WE'RE ALONE NOW** *MCA MCA 1211* ▲	1	13
19 Mar 88	●	**COULD'VE BEEN** *MCA TIFF 2* ▲	4	9
4 Jun 88	●	**I SAW HIM STANDING THERE** *MCA TIFF 3*	8	7
6 Aug 88		**FEELINGS OF FOREVER** *MCA TIFF 4*	52	2
12 Nov 88		**RADIO ROMANCE** *MCA TIFF 5*	13	11
11 Feb 89		**ALL THIS TIME** *MCA TIFF 6*	47	3

TIGER *UK / Ireland, male / female vocal / instrumental group (5 WEEKS)* pos/wks

			pos	wks
31 Aug 96		**RACE** *Trade 2 TRDCD 004*	37	2
16 Nov 96		**MY PUPPET PAL** *Trade 2 TRDCD 005*	62	1
22 Feb 97		**ON THE ROSE** *Trade 2 TRDCD 008*	57	1
22 Aug 98		**FRIENDS** *Trade 2 TRDCD 013*	72	1

TIGERTAILZ *US, male vocal / instrumental group (2 WEEKS)* pos/wks

			pos	wks
24 Jun 89		**LOVE BOMB BABY** *Music for Nations KUT 132*	75	1
16 Feb 91		**HEAVEN** *Music for Nations KUT 137*	71	1

TIGHT FIT *UK, male / female vocal group (49 WEEKS)* pos/wks

			pos	wks
18 Jul 81	●	**BACK TO THE SIXTIES** *Jive JIVE 002*	4	11
26 Sep 81		**BACK TO THE SIXTIES PART 2** *Jive JIVE 005*	33	5
23 Jan 82	★	**THE LION SLEEPS TONIGHT** *Jive JIVE 9*	1	15
1 May 82	●	**FANTASY ISLAND** *Jive JIVE 13*	5	12
31 Jul 82		**SECRET HEART** *Jive JIVE 20*	41	6

TIJUANA BRASS – *See Herb ALPERT*

TIK and TOK *UK, male vocal duo (2 WEEKS)* pos/wks

			pos	wks
8 Oct 83		**COOL RUNNING** *Survival SUR 016*	69	2

Tanita TIKARAM *UK, female vocalist (31 WEEKS)* pos/wks

			pos	wks
30 Jul 88	●	**GOOD TRADITION** *WEA YZ 196*	10	10
22 Oct 88		**TWIST IN MY SOBRIETY** *WEA YZ 321*	22	8
14 Jan 89		**CATHEDRAL SONG** *WEA YZ 331*	48	3
18 Mar 89		**WORLD OUTSIDE YOUR WINDOW** *WEA YZ 363*	58	2
13 Jan 90		**WE ALMOST GOT IT TOGETHER** *WEA YZ 443*	52	3
9 Feb 91		**ONLY THE ONES WE LOVE** *East West YZ 558*	69	1
4 Feb 95		**I MIGHT BE CRYING** *East West YZ 879CD*	64	2
6 Jun 98		**STOP LISTENING** *Mother MUMCD 102*	67	1
29 Aug 98		**I DON'T WANNA LOSE AT LOVE** *Mother MUMCD 105*	73	1

TILLMAN AND REIS *Germany, male production duo (1 WEEK)* pos/wks

			pos	wks
16 Sep 00		**BASSFLY** *Liquid Asset ASSET CD004*	70	1

Johnny TILLOTSON *US, male vocalist (50 WEEKS)* pos/wks

			pos	wks
1 Dec 60	★	**POETRY IN MOTION** *London HLA 9231*	1	15
2 Feb 61		**JIMMY'S GIRL** *London HLA 9275*	50	1
16 Feb 61		**JIMMY'S GIRL (re-entry)** *London HLA 9275*	43	1
12 Jul 62		**IT KEEPS RIGHT ON A-HURTIN'** *London HLA 9550*	31	10
4 Oct 62		**SEND ME THE PILLOW YOU DREAM ON** *London HLA 9598*	21	10

		pos	wks
27 Dec 62	**I CAN'T HELP IT** *London HLA 9642*	42	1
10 Jan 63	**I CAN'T HELP IT (re-entry)** *London HLA 9642*	47	1
24 Jan 63	**I CAN'T HELP IT (2nd re-entry)** *London HLA 9642*	41	4
9 May 63	**OUT OF MY MIND** *London HLA 9695*	34	5
14 Apr 79	**POETRY IN MOTION (re-issue)** *Lightning LIG 9016*	67	2

TILT *UK, male instrumental / production group (8 WEEKS)* pos/wks

		pos	wks
2 Dec 95	**I DREAM** *Perfecto PERF 112CD*	69	1
10 May 97	**MY SPIRIT** *Perfecto PERF 139CD*	61	1
13 Sep 97	**PLACES** *Perfecto PERF 149CD*	64	1
7 Feb 98	**BUTTERFLY** *Perfecto PERF 154CD1* [1]	41	1
27 Mar 99	**CHILDREN** *Deconstruction 74321648172*	51	1
8 May 99	**INVISIBLE** *Hooj Choons HOOJ 73CD*	20	2
12 Feb 00	**DARK SCIENCE (EP)** *Hooj Choons HOOJ 87*	55	1

[1] Tilt featuring Zee

Tracks on Dark Science (EP): 36 (two mixes) / Seduction Of Orpheus (two mixes)

TIMBALAND *US, male producer / rapper – Tim Mosley (13 WEEKS)* pos/wks

		pos	wks
23 Jan 99	**GET ON THE BUS** *East West E3780CD* [1]	15	5
13 Mar 99	**HERE WE COME** *Virgin DINSD 179* [2]	43	1
19 Jun 99	**LOBSTER & SCRIMP** *Virgin DINSD 186* [3]	48	1
21 Jul 01	**WE NEED A RESOLUTION** *Blackground VUSCD 206* [4]	20	4
1 Sep 01	**WE NEED A RESOLUTION (re-entry)** *Blackground VUSCD 206* [4]	65	2

[1] Destiny's Child featuring Timbaland [2] Timbaland / Missy Elliott and Magoo [3] Timbaland featuring Jay-Z [4] Aaliyah featuring Timbaland

TIMBUK 3 *US, male / female vocal / instrumental duo (7 WEEKS)* pos/wks

		pos	wks
31 Jan 87	**THE FUTURE'S SO BRIGHT I GOTTA WEAR SHADES** *IRS IRM 126*	21	7

TIME FREQUENCY
UK, male instrumental / production group (33 WEEKS) pos/wks

		pos	wks
6 Jun 92	**REAL LOVE** *Jive JIVET 307*	60	1
9 Jan 93	**NEW EMOTION** *Internal Affairs KGBCD 009*	36	6
12 Jun 93	**THE ULTIMATE HIGH / THE POWER ZONE** *Internal Affairs KGBD 010*	17	11
6 Nov 93 ●	**REAL LOVE (re-mix)** *Internal Affairs KGBCD 011*	8	6
1 Jan 94	**REAL LOVE (re-entry of re-mix)** *Internal Affairs KGBCD 011*	71	2
28 May 94	**SUCH A PHANTASY** *Internal Affairs KGBD 013*	25	4
8 Oct 94	**DREAMSCAPE '94** *Internal Affairs KGBD 015*	32	3

TIME OF THE MUMPH *UK, male producer – Mark Mumford (1 WEEK)* pos/wks

		pos	wks
11 Feb 95	**CONTROL** *Fresh FRSHD 24*	69	1

TIME UK *UK, male vocal / instrumental group (3 WEEKS)* pos/wks

		pos	wks
8 Oct 83	**THE CABARET** *Red Bus / Aroadia TIM 123*	63	3

TIME ZONE *UK / US, male vocal / instrumental duo (9 WEEKS)* pos/wks

		pos	wks
19 Jan 85	**WORLD DESTRUCTION** *Virgin VS 743*	44	9

TIMEBOX *UK, male vocal / instrumental group (4 WEEKS)* pos/wks

		pos	wks
24 Jul 68	**BEGGIN'** *Deram DM 194*	38	4

TIMELORDS *UK, male vocal / instrumental group (9 WEEKS)* pos/wks

		pos	wks
4 Jun 88 ★	**DOCTORIN' THE TARDIS** *KLF Communications KLF 003*	1	9

See also KLF; JUSTIFIED ANCIENTS OF MU MU; 2K

TIMEX SOCIAL CLUB
US, male vocal / instrumental group (9 WEEKS) pos/wks

		pos	wks
13 Sep 86	**RUMORS** *Cooltempo COOL 133*	13	9

TIN MACHINE *US / UK, male vocal / instrumental group (10 WEEKS)* pos/wks

		pos	wks
1 Jul 89	**UNDER THE GOD** *EMI-USA MT 68*	51	2
9 Sep 89	**TIN MACHINE / MAGGIE'S FARM (LIVE)** *EMI-USA MT 73*	48	2
24 Aug 91	**YOU BELONG IN ROCK 'N' ROLL** *London LON 305*	33	3
2 Nov 91	**BABY UNIVERSAL** *London LON 310*	48	3

See also David BOWIE

TIN TIN - *See Stephen 'Tin Tin' DUFFY*

TIN TIN OUT *UK, male instrumental / production duo – Lindsay Edwards and Darren Stokes (42 WEEKS)* pos/wks

		pos	wks
13 Aug 94	**THE FEELING** *Deep Distraxion OILYCD 029* [1]	32	2
25 Mar 95	**ALWAYS SOMETHING THERE TO REMIND ME** *WEA YZ 911CD* [2]	14	5
8 Feb 97	**ALL I WANNA DO** *VC VCRD 15*	31	2
10 May 97	**DANCE WITH ME** *VC VCRD 17* [3]	35	2
20 Sep 97	**STRINGS FOR YASMIN** *VC VCRD 20*	31	3
28 Mar 98 ●	**HERE'S WHERE THE STORY ENDS** *VC Recordings VCRD 30* [4]	7	10
12 Sep 98	**SOMETIMES** *VC Recordings VCRD 34* [4]	20	4
11 Sep 99	**ELEVEN TO FLY** *VC Recordings VCRDX 52* [5]	26	2
13 Nov 99 ●	**WHAT I AM** *VC Recordings VCRD 53* [6]	2	12

[1] Tin Tin Out featuring Sweet Tee [2] Tin Tin Out featuring Espiritu [3] Tin Tin Out featuring Tony Hadley [4] Tin Tin Out featuring Shelley Nelson [5] Tin Tin Out featuring Wendy Page [6] Tin Tin Out featuring Emma Bunton

TINA – *See Tina TURNER*

TINDERSTICKS *UK, male vocal / instrumental group (6 WEEKS)* pos/wks

		pos	wks
5 Feb 94	**KATHLEEN (EP)** *This Way Up WAY 2833CD*	61	1
18 Mar 95	**NO MORE AFFAIRS** *This Way Up WAY 3833*	58	1
12 Aug 95	**TRAVELLING LIGHT** *This Way Up WAY 4533*	51	1
7 Jun 97	**BATHTIME** *This Way Up WAY 6166*	38	1
1 Nov 97	**RENTED ROOMS** *This Way Up WAY 6566*	56	1
4 Sep 99	**CAN WE START AGAIN?** *Island CID 756*	54	1

Tracks on Kathleen (EP): Kathleen / Summat Moon / A Sweet Sweet Man / E-Type Joe

TINGO TANGO *UK, male instrumental group (2 WEEKS)* pos/wks

		pos	wks
21 Jul 90	**IT IS JAZZ** *Champion CHAMP 250*	68	2

TINMAN *UK, male producer – Paul Dakeyne (9 WEEKS)* pos/wks

		pos	wks
20 Aug 94 ●	**EIGHTEEN STRINGS** *ffrr FCD 242*	9	8
3 Jun 95	**GUDVIBE** *ffrr FCD 262*	49	1

TINY TIM *US, male vocalist (1 WEEK)* pos/wks

		pos	wks
5 Feb 69	**GREAT BALLS OF FIRE** *Reprise RS 20802*	45	1

TITANIC *Norway / UK, male instrumental group (12 WEEKS)* pos/wks

		pos	wks
25 Sep 71 ●	**SULTANA** *CBS 5365*	5	12

TITIYO *Sweden, female vocalist (6 WEEKS)* pos/wks

		pos	wks
3 Mar 90	**AFTER THE RAIN** *Arista 112722*	60	3
6 Oct 90	**FLOWERS** *Arista 113212*	71	1
5 Feb 94	**TELL ME I'M NOT DREAMING** *Arista 74321185622*	45	2

Cara TIVEY – *See Billy BRAGG*

TJR featuring XAVIER
UK, male instrumental / production group (2 WEEKS) pos/wks

		pos	wks
27 Sep 97	**JUST GETS BETTER** *Multiply CDMULTY 25*	28	2

TLC (395 Top 500) *Multi-award-winning 1990s female trio: Tionne "T-Boz" Watkins, Lisa "Left Eye" Lopes and Rozonda "Chilli" Thomas, formed and managed by fellow R&B hitmaker Pebbles. They have nine US gold singles, and The Supremes are only female group with more US No.1s (83 WEEKS)* pos/wks

		pos	wks
20 Jun 92	**AIN'T 2 PROUD 2 BEG** *Arista 115265*	13	5
22 Aug 92	**BABY-BABY-BABY** *LaFace 74321111297*	55	3
24 Oct 92	**WHAT ABOUT YOUR FRIENDS** *LaFace 74321118177*	59	2
21 Jan 95	**CREEP** *LaFace 74321254212* ▲	22	4
22 Apr 95	**RED LIGHT SPECIAL** *LaFace 74321273662*	18	4
5 Aug 95 ●	**WATERFALLS** *LaFace 74321298812* ▲	4	14

1996

IN THE YEAR IN WHICH THE TRAGIC EVENTS IN A SCHOOL IN DUNBLANE LED TO GREATER CONTROL OF FIREARMS IN THE UK, CJD WAS DISCOVERED TO BE LINKED TO EATING MEAT FROM CATTLE INFECTED WITH MAD COW DISEASE, TAKE THAT CALLED IT A DAY AND BOYZONE TOOK OVER THE BOY BAND CROWN JUST AS "GIRL POWER" STARTED TO EXPLODE, **SHIRLEY MANSON** FROM GARBAGE FONDLY REMEMBERS THE VIDEO FOR 'STUPID GIRL', THE BAND'S BIGGEST HIT TO DATE...

“This song really propelled our career into a different stratosphere. Suddenly we were all over the radio, not only in the UK but all over the world. The video too was a great success. A very simple performance shot by Sam Bayer who then took the film and scored and slashed it in his bathtub. Consequently he delivered a highly stylish and original video that became a staple on MTV. We were delighted by this turn of events. Still are!”

SINGLE OF THE YEAR 'Wannabe' Spice Girls
ALBUM OF THE YEAR 'Jagged Little Pill' Alanis Morissette

			pos	wks
4 Nov 95		**DIGGIN' ON YOU** *LaFace 74321319252*	18	5
13 Jan 96	●	**CREEP (re-issue)** *LaFace 74321340942*	6	7
3 Apr 99	●	**NO SCRUBS** *LaFace 74321660952* ▲	3	19
28 Aug 99	●	**UNPRETTY** *LaFace 74321695842* ▲	6	11
18 Dec 99		**DEAR LIE** *LaFace 74321724012*	31	9

See also T-BOZ; Lisa 'Left Eye' LOPES

T99 *Belgium, male instrumental / production group (10 WEEKS)*

		pos	wks
11 May 91	**ANASTHASIA** *XL XLS 19*	14	6
19 Oct 91	**NOCTURNE** *Emphasis 6574097*	33	4

TOADS – *See Stan FREBERG*

Art and Dotty TODD *US, male / female vocal duo (7 WEEKS)*

			pos	wks
13 Feb 53	●	**BROKEN WINGS** *HMV B 10399*	6	7

TOGETHER *UK, male vocal / instrumental group (8 WEEKS)*

		pos	wks
4 Aug 90	**HARDCORE UPROAR** *ffrr F 143*	12	8

TOKENS *US, male vocal group (12 WEEKS)*

		pos	wks
21 Dec 61	**THE LION SLEEPS TONIGHT (WIMOWEH)** *RCA 1263* ▲	11	12

TOKYO GHETTO PUSSY
Germany, male instrumental / production duo (4 WEEKS)

		pos	wks
16 Sep 95	**EVERYBODY ON THE FLOOR (PUMP IT)** *Epic 6611132*	26	2
16 Mar 96	**I KISS YOUR LIPS** *Epic 6623212*	55	2

See also JAM & SPOON featuring PLAVKA; STORM

TOL and TOL *Holland, male vocal / instrumental duo (2 WEEKS)*

		pos	wks
14 Apr 90	**ELENI** *Dover ROJ 5*	73	2

TOM TOM CLUB
US, female / male vocal / instrumental group (20 WEEKS)

			pos	wks
20 Jun 81	●	**WORDY RAPPINGHOOD** *Island WIP 6694*	7	9
10 Oct 81		**GENIUS OF LOVE** *Island WIP 6735*	65	2
7 Aug 82		**UNDER THE BOARDWALK** *Island WIP 6762*	22	9

TOMBA VIRA *Holland, male production duo (1 WEEK)*

		pos	wks
16 Jun 01	**THE SOUND OF: OH YEAH** *VC Recordings VCRD 88*	51	1

See also JARK PRONGO; GOODMEN; CHOCOLATE PUMA

TOMCAT *UK, male vocal / instrumental group (1 WEEK)*

		pos	wks
14 Oct 00	**CRAZY** *Virgin VSCDT 1785*	48	1

Satoshi TOMIIE – *See Frankie KNUCKLES*

Ricky TOMLINSON *UK, male actor / vocalist (3 WEEKS)*

		pos	wks
10 Nov 01	**ARE YOU LOOKIN' AT ME?** *All Around The World CDRICKY 1*	28	3

TOMSKI *UK, male producer – Tom Jankiewicz (3 WEEKS)*

		pos	wks
18 Apr 98	**14 HOURS TO SAVE THE EARTH** *Xtravaganza 0091515 EXT*	42	1
12 Feb 00	**LOVE WILL COME** *Xtravaganza XTRAV6CDS* [1]	31	2

[1] Tomski featuring Jan Johnston

TONE LOC *US, male rapper – Anthony Smith (19 WEEKS)*

		pos	wks
11 Feb 89	**WILD THING / LOC'ED AFTER DARK** *Fourth & Broadway BRW 121*	21	8
20 May 89	**FUNKY COLD MEDINA / ON FIRE** *Fourth & Broadway BRW 129*	13	9
5 Aug 89	**I GOT IT GOIN' ON** *Fourth & Broadway BRW 140*	55	2

TONGUE 'N' CHEEK
UK, male / female vocal / instrumental group (28 WEEKS)

		pos	wks
27 Feb 88	**NOBODY (CAN LOVE ME)** *Criminal BUS 6* [1]	59	6
25 Nov 89	**ENCORE** *Syncopate SY 33*	41	4
14 Apr 90	**TOMORROW** *Syncopate SY 34*	20	7
4 Aug 90	**NOBODY (re-recording)** *Syncopate SY 37*	37	5
19 Jan 91	**FORGET ME NOTS** *Syncopate SY 39*	26	6

[1] Tongue In Cheek

TONIGHT *UK, male vocal / instrumental group (10 WEEKS)*

		pos	wks
28 Jan 78	**DRUMMER MAN** *Target TDS 1*	14	8
20 May 78	**MONEY THAT'S YOUR PROBLEM** *Target TDS 2*	66	2

TONY TONI TONÉ *US, male vocal group (12 WEEKS)*

		pos	wks
30 Jun 90	**OAKLAND STROKE** *Wing WING 7*	50	5
9 Mar 91	**IT NEVER RAINS (IN SOUTHERN CALIFORNIA)** *Wing WING 10* [1]	69	2
4 Sep 93	**IF I HAD NO LOOT** *Polydor PZCD 292*	44	3
3 May 97	**LET'S GET DOWN** *Mercury MERCD 485* [2]	33	2

[1] Tony! Toni! Tone! [2] Tony Toni Tone featuring DJ Quick

TOO TOUGH TEE – *See DYNAMIX II featuring TOO TOUGH TEE*

TOON TRAVELLERS – *See MUNGO JERRY*

TOP *UK, male vocal / instrumental group (2 WEEKS)*

		pos	wks
20 Jul 91	**NUMBER ONE DOMINATOR** *Island IS 496*	67	2

TOP LINERS – *See Rocky SHARPE and the REPLAYS*

TOPLOADER *UK, male vocal / instrumental group (49 WEEKS)*

			pos	wks
22 May 99		**ACHILLES HEEL** *Sony S2 6671612*	64	1
7 Aug 99		**LET THE PEOPLE KNOW** *Sony S2 6677132*	52	1
4 Mar 00		**DANCING IN THE MOONLIGHT** *Sony S2 6689412*	19	7
13 May 00	●	**ACHILLES HEEL (re-issue)** *Sony S2 6691872*	8	7
2 Sep 00		**JUST HOLD ON** *Sony S2 6696242*	20	4
25 Nov 00	●	**DANCING IN THE MOONLIGHT (re-issue)** *Sony S2 6699852*	7	25
21 Apr 01		**ONLY FOR A WHILE** *Sony S2 S2 6708612*	19	4

TOPOL *Israel, male vocalist / actor – Chaim Topol (20 WEEKS)*

			pos	wks
20 Apr 67	●	**IF I WERE A RICH MAN** *CBS 202651*	9	20

Mel TORME *US, male vocalist (32 WEEKS)*

			pos	wks
27 Apr 56		**MOUNTAIN GREENERY** *Vogue / Coral Q 72150*	15	11
27 Jul 56	●	**MOUNTAIN GREENERY (re-entry)** *Vogue / Coral Q 72150*	4	13
3 Jan 63		**COMIN' HOME BABY** *London HLK 9643*	13	8

TORNADOS *UK, male instrumental group (59 WEEKS)*

			pos	wks
30 Aug 62	★	**TELSTAR** *Decca F 11494* ▲	1	25
10 Jan 63	●	**GLOBETROTTER** *Decca F 11562*	5	11
21 Mar 63		**ROBOT** *Decca F 11606*	17	12
6 Jun 63		**THE ICE CREAM MAN** *Decca F 11662*	18	9
10 Oct 63		**DRAGONFLY** *Decca F 11745*	41	2

Mitchell TOROK *US, male vocalist (19 WEEKS)*

			pos	wks
28 Sep 56	●	**WHEN MEXICO GAVE UP THE RHUMBA** *Brunswick 05586*	6	17
11 Jan 57		**RED LIGHT, GREEN LIGHT** *Brunswick 05626*	29	1
1 Feb 57		**WHEN MEXICO GAVE UP THE RHUMBA (re-entry)** *Brunswick 05586*	30	1

Liz TORRES – *See Danny TENAGLIA*

Emiliana TORRINI *Iceland, female vocalist (3 WEEKS)*

		pos	wks
10 Jun 00	**EASY** *One Little Indian 274 TP7CD*	63	1
9 Sep 00	**UNEMPLOYED IN SUMMERTIME** *One Little Indian 275 TP7CDL*	63	1
3 Feb 01	**TO BE FREE** *One Little Indian 276 TP7CD*	44	1

Peter TOSH *Jamaica, male vocalist (12 WEEKS)*

		pos	wks
21 Oct 78	**(YOU GOTTA WALK) DON'T LOOK BACK** *Rolling Stones 2859*	43	7

UK No.1 ★ UK Top 10 ● Still on chart + UK million seller ◆ UK entry at No.1 ■ US No.1 ▲

2 Apr 83	**JOHNNY B GOODE** *EMI RIC 115*	48	5

TOTAL *US, female vocal group (11 WEEKS)* pos/wks

15 Jul 95	**CAN'T YOU SEE** *Tommy Boy TBCD 700* [1]	43	2
14 Sep 96	**KISSIN' YOU** *Arista 74321404172*	29	2
15 Feb 97	**DO YOU THINK ABOUT US** *Puff Daddy 74321458492*	49	1
18 Apr 98	**WHAT YOU WANT** *Puff Daddy 74321578772* [2]	15	5
30 Sep 00	**I WONDER WHY HE'S THE GREATEST DJ** *Tommy Boy TBCD 2100* [3]	68	1

[1] Total featuring the Notorious B.I.G. [2] Mase featuring Total [3] Tony Touch featuring Total

TOTAL CONTRAST *UK, male vocal / instrumental duo – Robin Achampong and Delroy Murray (22 WEEKS)* pos/wks

3 Aug 85	**TAKES A LITTLE TIME** *London LON 71*	17	10
19 Oct 85	**HIT AND RUN** *London LON 76*	41	5
1 Mar 86	**THE RIVER** *London LON 83*	44	3
10 May 86	**WHAT YOU GONNA DO ABOUT IT** *London LON 95*	63	4

TOTO *US, male vocal / instrumental group (35 WEEKS)* pos/wks

10 Feb 79	**HOLD THE LINE** *CBS 6784*	14	11
5 Feb 83 ●	**AFRICA** *CBS A 2510* ▲	3	10
9 Apr 83	**ROSANNA** *CBS A 2079*	12	8
18 Jun 83	**I WON'T HOLD YOU BACK** *CBS A 3392*	37	5
18 Nov 95	**I WILL REMEMBER** *Columbia 6626552*	64	1

TOTO COELO *UK, female vocal group (14 WEEKS)* pos/wks

7 Aug 82 ●	**I EAT CANNIBALS PART 1** *Radialchoice TIC 10*	8	10
13 Nov 82	**DRACULA'S TANGO / MUCHO MACHO** *Radialchoice TIC 11*	54	4

TOTTENHAM HOTSPUR FA CUP FINAL SQUAD *UK, male football team vocalists (23 WEEKS)* pos/wks

9 May 81 ●	**OSSIE'S DREAM (SPURS ARE ON THEIR WAY TO WEMBLEY)** *Shelf SHELF 1*	5	8
1 May 82	**TOTTENHAM TOTTENHAM** *Shelf SHELF 2*	19	7
9 May 87	**HOT SHOT TOTTENHAM!** *Rainbow RBR 16*	18	5
11 May 91	**WHEN THE YEAR ENDS IN 1** *A1 A 1324*	44	3

All hits feature the vocal and instrumental talents of Chas and Dave

See also COCKEREL CHORUS

Tony TOUCH featuring TOTAL *US, male producer – Anthony Hernandez and US, female vocal group (1 WEEK)* pos/wks

30 Sep 00	**I WONDER WHY HE'S THE GREATEST DJ** *Tommy Boy TBCD 2100*	68	1

TOUCH & GO *UK, male / female vocal / production group (12 WEEKS)* pos/wks

7 Nov 98 ●	**WOULD YOU...?** *Oval VVR 5003083*	3	12

TOUCH OF SOUL *UK, male / female vocal / instrumental group (3 WEEKS)* pos/wks

19 May 90	**WE GOT THE LOVE** *Cooltempo COOL 204*	46	3

TOUR DE FORCE *UK, male production trio (1 WEEK)* pos/wks

16 May 98	**CATALAN** *East West EW 161CD*	71	1

TOURISTS *UK, male / female vocal / instrumental group (40 WEEKS)* pos/wks

9 Jun 79	**BLIND AMONG THE FLOWERS** *Logo GO 350*	52	5
8 Sep 79	**THE LONELIEST MAN IN THE WORLD** *Logo GO 360*	32	7
10 Nov 79 ●	**I ONLY WANT TO BE WITH YOU** *Logo GO 370*	4	14
9 Feb 80 ●	**SO GOOD TO BE BACK HOME AGAIN** *Logo TOUR 1*	8	9
18 Oct 80	**DON'T SAY I TOLD YOU SO** *RCA TOUR 2*	40	5

TOUTES LES FILLES *UK, female vocal group (1 WEEK)* pos/wks

4 Sep 99	**THAT'S WHAT LOVE CAN DO** *London LONCD 434*	44	1

Carol Lynn TOWNES *US, female vocalist (7 WEEKS)* pos/wks

4 Aug 84	**99 1/2** *Polydor POSP 693*	47	4
19 Jan 85	**BELIEVE IN THE BEAT** *Polydor POSP 720*	56	3

Fuzz TOWNSHEND *UK, male producer (1 WEEK)* pos/wks

6 Sep 97	**HELLO DARLIN** *Echo ECSCD 46*	51	1

Pete TOWNSHEND *UK, male vocalist (17 WEEKS)* pos/wks

5 Apr 80	**ROUGH BOYS** *Atco K 11460*	39	6
21 Jun 80	**LET MY LOVE OPEN YOUR DOOR** *Atco K 11486*	46	6
21 Aug 82	**UNIFORMS (CORPS D'ESPRIT)** *Atco K 11751*	48	5

See also WHO

TOXIC TWO *US, male instrumental / production duo – Ray Love and Damon Wild (6 WEEKS)* pos/wks

7 Mar 92	**RAVE GENERATOR** *PWL International PWL 223*	13	6

TOY - BOX *Denmark, male / female vocal duo (2 WEEKS)* pos/wks

18 Sep 99	**BEST FRIENDS** *Edel 0058245 ERE*	41	2

TOY DOLLS *UK, male vocal / instrumental group (12 WEEKS)* pos/wks

1 Dec 84 ●	**NELLIE THE ELEPHANT** *Volume VOL 11*	4	12

TOYAH (373 Top 500) *Visually striking punk / pop vocalist, b. Toyah Willcox 16 May 1958, Birmingham, UK. Came to prominence through acting – first major role in 1977 movie 'Jubilee'. Married King Crimson guitarist Robert Fripp in 1986. One of the first acts to chart regularly with EPs (87 WEEKS)* pos/wks

14 Feb 81 ●	**FOUR FROM TOYAH (EP)** *Safari TOY 1*	4	14
16 May 81 ●	**I WANT TO BE FREE** *Safari SAFE 34*	8	11
3 Oct 81 ●	**THUNDER IN THE MOUNTAINS** *Safari SAFE 38*	4	9
28 Nov 81	**FOUR MORE FROM TOYAH (EP)** *Safari TOY 2*	14	9
22 May 82	**BRAVE NEW WORLD** *Safari SAFE 45*	21	8
17 Jul 82	**IEYA** *Safari SAFE 28*	48	5
9 Oct 82	**BE LOUD BE PROUD (BE HEARD)** *Safari SAFE 52*	30	7
24 Sep 83	**REBEL RUN** *Safari SAFE 56*	24	5
19 Nov 83	**THE VOW** *Safari SAFE 58*	50	5
27 Apr 85	**DON'T FALL IN LOVE (I SAID)** *Portrait A 6160*	22	6
29 Jun 85	**SOUL PASSING THROUGH SOUL** *Portrait A 6359*	57	3
25 Apr 87	**ECHO BEACH** *EG EGO 31*	54	5

Tracks on Four From Toyah (EP): It's a Mystery / Revelations / War Boys / Angels and Demons. Tracks on Four More From Toyah (EP): Good Morning Universe / Urban Tribesman / In the Fairground / The Furious Futures

TOYS *US, female vocal group (17 WEEKS)* pos/wks

4 Nov 65 ●	**A LOVER'S CONCERTO** *Stateside SS 460*	5	13
27 Jan 66	**ATTACK** *Stateside SS 483*	36	4

T'PAU (440 Top 500) *Shropshire lads and a lass whose No.1 hit in 1987 had the distinction of being the 600th chart-topper. T'Pau (Mr Spock's Vulcan friend in 'Star Trek') comprised writers Carol Decker (v) and Ron Rogers (g), plus Michael Chetwood (k), Paul Jackson (b), Tim Burgess (d) and Taj Wyzgowski (g) (77 WEEKS)* pos/wks

8 Aug 87 ●	**HEART AND SOUL** *Siren SRN 41*	4	13
24 Oct 87 ★	**CHINA IN YOUR HAND** *Siren SRN 64*	1	15
30 Jan 88 ●	**VALENTINE** *Siren SRN 69*	9	8
2 Apr 88	**SEX TALK (LIVE)** *Siren SRN 80*	23	7
25 Jun 88	**I WILL BE WITH YOU** *Siren SRN 87*	14	6
1 Oct 88	**SECRET GARDEN** *Siren SRN 93*	18	7
3 Dec 88	**ROAD TO OUR DREAM** *Siren SRN 100*	42	6
25 Mar 89	**ONLY THE LONELY** *Siren SRN 107*	28	6
18 May 91	**WHENEVER YOU NEED ME** *Siren SRN 140*	16	6
27 Jul 91	**WALK ON AIR** *Siren SRN 142*	62	2
20 Feb 93	**VALENTINE (re-issue)** *Virgin VALEG 1*	53	1

TQ *US, male rapper – Terrance Quaites (35 WEEKS)* pos/wks

30 Jan 99 ●	**WESTSIDE** *Epic 6668102*	4	9
1 May 99 ●	**BYE BYE BABY** *Epic 6672372*	7	7

21 Aug 99	**BETTER DAYS** *Epic 6677532*	32	2
4 Sep 99 ●	**SUMMERTIME** *Northwestside 74321694672* [1]	7	7
29 Apr 00	**DAILY** *Epic 6692752*	14	5
13 Oct 01	**LET'S GET BACK TO BED ...BOY** *Epic 6718662* [2]	16	5

[1] Another Level featuring TQ [2] Sarah Connor featuring TQ

TRACIE *UK, female vocalist – Tracie Young (24 WEEKS)* pos/wks

26 Mar 83 ●	**THE HOUSE THAT JACK BUILT** *Respond KOB 701*	9	8
16 Jul 83	**GIVE IT SOME EMOTION** *Respond KOB 704*	24	9
14 Apr 84	**SOUL'S ON FIRE** *Respond KOB 708*	73	2
9 Jun 84	**(I LOVE YOU) WHEN YOU SLEEP** *Respond KOB 710*	59	3
17 Aug 85	**I CAN'T LEAVE YOU ALONE** *Respond SBS 1* [1]	60	2

[1] Tracie Young

Gordon TRACKS – *See AIR*

TRACY – *See MASSIVO featuring TRACY*

Jeanie TRACY *US, female vocalist (3 WEEKS)* pos/wks

11 Jun 94	**IF THIS IS LOVE** *Pulse 8 CDLOSE 63*	73	1
5 Nov 94	**DO YOU BELIEVE IN THE WONDER** *Pulse 8 CDLOSE 74*	57	1
13 May 95	**IT'S A MAN'S MAN'S MAN'S WORLD** *Pulse 8 CDLOSE 89* [1]	73	1

[1] Jeanie Tracy and Bobby Womack

TRAFFIC *UK, male vocal / instrumental group (40 WEEKS)* pos/wks

1 Jun 67 ●	**PAPER SUN** *Island WIP 6002*	5	10
6 Sep 67 ●	**HOLE IN MY SHOE** *Island WIP 6017*	2	14
29 Nov 67 ●	**HERE WE GO ROUND THE MULBERRY BUSH** *Island WIP 6025*	8	12
6 Mar 68	**NO FACE, NO NAME, NO NUMBER** *Island WIP 6030*	40	4

TRAIN *US, male vocal / instrumental group (8 WEEKS)* pos/wks

11 Aug 01 ●	**DROPS OF JUPITER (TELL ME)** *Columbia 6714472*	10	8

TRAMAINE *US, female vocalist (2 WEEKS)* pos/wks

5 Oct 85	**FALL DOWN (SPIRIT OF LOVE)** *A & M AM 281*	60	2

TRAMMPS *US, male vocal group (55 WEEKS)* pos/wks

23 Nov 74	**ZING WENT THE STRINGS OF MY HEART** *Buddah BDS 405*	29	10
1 Feb 75	**SIXTY MINUTE MAN** *Buddah BDS 415*	40	4
11 Oct 75 ●	**HOLD BACK THE NIGHT** *Buddah BDS 437*	5	8
13 Mar 76	**THAT'S WHERE THE HAPPY PEOPLE GO** *Atlantic K 10703*	35	8
24 Jul 76	**SOUL SEARCHIN' TIME** *Atlantic K 10797*	42	3
14 May 77	**DISCO INFERNO** *Atlantic K 10914*	16	7
24 Jun 78	**DISCO INFERNO (re-issue)** *Atlantic K 11135*	47	10
12 Dec 92	**HOLD BACK THE NIGHT** *Network NWK 65* [1]	30	5

[1] KWS features guest vocal from the Trammps

TRANCESETTERS *Holland, male production duo (2 WEEKS)* pos/wks

4 Mar 00	**ROACHES** *Hooj Choons HOOJ 89CD*	55	1
9 Jun 01	**SYNERGY** *Hooj Choons HOOJ 107*	72	1

TRANS-X
Canada, female / male vocal / instrumental group (9 WEEKS) pos/wks

13 Jul 85 ●	**LIVING ON VIDEO** *Boiling Point POSP 650*	9	9

TRANSA *UK, male DJ / production duo (2 WEEKS)* pos/wks

30 Aug 97	**PROPHASE** *Perfecto PERF 147CD*	65	1
21 Feb 98	**ENERVATE** *Perfecto PERF 155CD*	42	1

TRANSATLANTIC SOUL
US, male producer – Roger Sanchez (1 WEEK) pos/wks

22 Mar 97	**RELEASE YO SELF** *Deconstruction 74321459102*	43	1

TRANSFER *UK, male producer (1 WEEK)* pos/wks

3 Nov 01	**POSSESSION** *Mulitply CDMULTY 76*	54	1

TRANSFORMER 2
Belgium / Holland, male / female vocal / instrumental group (1 WEEK) pos/wks

24 Feb 96	**JUST CAN'T GET ENOUGH** *Positiva CDTIV 49*	45	1

See also CONVERT

TRANSISTER
UK / US, male / female vocal / instrumental group (1 WEEK) pos/wks

28 Mar 98	**LOOK WHO'S PERFECT NOW** *Virgin VSCDT 1678*	56	1

TRANSVISION VAMP
UK, female / male vocal / instrumental group (59 WEEKS) pos/wks

16 Apr 88	**TELL THAT GIRL TO SHUT UP** *MCA TVV 2*	45	3
25 Jun 88 ●	**I WANT YOUR LOVE** *MCA TVV 3*	5	13
17 Sep 88	**REVOLUTION BABY** *MCA TVV 4*	30	5
19 Nov 88	**SISTER MOON** *MCA TVV 5*	41	5
1 Apr 89 ●	**BABY I DON'T CARE** *MCA TVV 6*	3	11
10 Jun 89	**THE ONLY ONE** *MCA TVV 7*	15	6
5 Aug 89	**LANDSLIDE OF LOVE** *MCA TVV 8*	14	5
4 Nov 89	**BORN TO BE SOLD** *MCA TVV 9*	22	4
13 Apr 91	**(I JUST WANNA) B WITH U** *MCA TVV 10*	30	4
22 Jun 91	**IF LOOKS COULD KILL** *MCA TVV 11*	41	3

TRASH *UK, male vocal / instrumental group (3 WEEKS)* pos/wks

25 Oct 69	**GOLDEN SLUMBERS / CARRY THAT WEIGHT** *Apple 17*	35	3

TRASH CAN SINATRAS
UK, male vocal / instrumental group (1 WEEK) pos/wks

24 Apr 93	**HAYFEVER** *Go! Discs GODCD 98*	61	1

TRAVEL *France, male producer – Laurent Gutbier (2 WEEKS)* pos/wks

24 Apr 99	**BULGARIAN** *Tidy Trax TIDY 121CD*	67	2

TRAVELING WILBURYS
UK / US, male vocal / instrumental group (19 WEEKS) pos/wks

29 Oct 88	**HANDLE WITH CARE** *Wilbury W 7732*	21	13
11 Mar 89	**END OF THE LINE** *Wilbury W 7637*	52	4
30 Jun 90	**NOBODY'S CHILD** *Wilbury W 9773*	44	2

TRAVIS (491 Top 500)
Scottish melodic rock merchants named after a character from the 1984 movie 'Paris, Texas', consisting of English-born Fran Healy (v,g) and native Glaswegians Andy Dunlop (g), Dougie Payne (b) and Neil Primrose (d) whose Brit Award-winning 'The Man Who' was the best-selling album by a British act in the UK in 1999 (72 WEEKS) pos/wks

12 Apr 97	**U16 GIRLS** *Independiente ISOM 1MS*	40	2
28 Jun 97	**ALL I WANT TO DO IS ROCK** *Independiente ISOM 3MS*	39	2
23 Aug 97	**TIED TO THE 90'S** *Independiente ISOM 5MS*	30	2
25 Oct 97	**HAPPY** *Independiente ISOM 6MS*	38	2
11 Apr 98	**MORE THAN US (EP)** *Independiente ISOM 11MS*	16	3
20 Mar 99	**WRITING TO REACH YOU** *Independiente ISOM 22MS*	14	5
29 May 99	**DRIFTWOOD** *Independiente ISOM 27MS*	13	5
14 Aug 99 ●	**WHY DOES IT ALWAYS RAIN ON ME?** *Independiente ISOM 33MS*	10	8
20 Nov 99 ●	**TURN** *Independiente ISOM 39MS*	8	11
17 Jun 00 ●	**COMING AROUND** *Independiente ISOM 45MS*	5	7
12 Aug 00	**COMING AROUND (re-entry)** *Independiente ISOM 45MS*	55	2
2 Sep 00	**COMING AROUND (2nd re-entry)** *Independiente ISOM 45MS*	75	1
9 Jun 01 ●	**SING** *Independiente ISOM 49MS*	3	14
29 Sep 01	**SIDE** *Independiente ISOM 54MS*	14	8

Tracks on More Than Us (EP): More Than Us / Give Me Some Truth / All I Want to Do Is Rock / Funny Thing

Randy TRAVIS *US, male vocalist (6 WEEKS)* pos/wks

21 May 88	**FOREVER AND EVER, AMEN** *Warner Bros. W 8384*	55	6

John TRAVOLTA (350 Top 500)

Ever popular actor / singer, b. 18 Feb 1954, New Jersey, US. His influential music-based movies include 'Saturday Night Fever', 'Urban Cowboy' and 'Grease', whose retro 50s sound has timeless appeal. One of the few acts with two successive UK million sellers (90 WEEKS) pos/wks

20 May 78 ★	**YOU'RE THE ONE THAT I WANT** *RSO 006* [1] ◆ ▲	1	26
16 Sep 78 ★	**SUMMER NIGHTS** *RSO 18* [1] ◆	1	19
7 Oct 78 ●	**SANDY** *Polydor POSP 6*	2	15
2 Dec 78	**GREASED LIGHTNIN'** *Polydor POSP 14*	11	9
22 Dec 90 ●	**THE GREASE MEGAMIX** *Polydor PO 114* [1]	3	10
23 Mar 91	**GREASE - THE DREAM MIX** *PWL / Polydor PO 136* [2]	47	2
25 Jul 98 ●	**YOU'RE THE ONE THAT I WANT (re-issue)** *Polydor 0441332* [1]	4	9

[1] John Travolta and Olivia Newton-John [2] Frankie Valli, John Travolta and Olivia Newton-John

TREMELOES (69 Top 500)

Early-1960s backing band who become late-1960s stars: Len "Chip" Hawkes (v/b), Rick West (g), Alan Blakely (g), Dave Munden (d). After supporting Brian Poole on his many hits, this Essex group went on to score even more in their own right. Hawkes is the father of 1991 chart-topper Chesney Hawkes (222 WEEKS) pos/wks

4 Jul 63 ●	**TWIST AND SHOUT** *Decca F 11694*	4	14
12 Sep 63 ★	**DO YOU LOVE ME** *Decca F 11739*	1	14
28 Nov 63	**I CAN DANCE** *Decca F 11771*	31	8
30 Jan 64 ●	**CANDY MAN** *Decca F 11823*	6	13
7 May 64 ●	**SOMEONE SOMEONE** *Decca F 11893*	2	17
20 Aug 64	**TWELVE STEPS TO LOVE** *Decca F 11951*	32	7
31 Dec 64	**THREE BELLS** *Decca F 12037*	17	10
22 Jul 65	**I WANT CANDY** *Decca F 12197*	25	8
2 Feb 67 ●	**HERE COMES MY BABY** *CBS 202519*	4	11
27 Apr 67 ★	**SILENCE IS GOLDEN** *CBS 2723*	1	15
2 Aug 67 ●	**EVEN THE BAD TIMES ARE GOOD** *CBS 2930*	4	13
8 Nov 67	**BE MINE** *CBS 3043*	39	2
17 Jan 68 ●	**SUDDENLY YOU LOVE ME** *CBS 3234*	6	11
8 May 68	**HELULE HELULE** *CBS 2889*	14	9
18 Sep 68 ●	**MY LITTLE LADY** *CBS 3680*	6	12
11 Dec 68	**I SHALL BE RELEASED** *CBS 3873*	29	5
19 Mar 69	**HELLO WORLD** *CBS 4065*	14	8
1 Nov 69 ●	**(CALL ME) NUMBER ONE** *CBS 4582*	2	14
21 Mar 70	**BY THE WAY** *CBS 4815*	35	6
12 Sep 70 ●	**ME AND MY LIFE** *CBS 5139*	4	18
10 Jul 71	**HELLO BUDDY** *CBS 7294*	32	7

See also Brian POOLE and the TREMELOES

Jackie TRENT

UK, female vocalist – Yvonne Burgess (17 WEEKS) pos/wks

22 Apr 65 ★	**WHERE ARE YOU NOW (MY LOVE)** *Pye 7N 15776*	1	11
1 Jul 65	**WHEN THE SUMMERTIME IS OVER** *Pye 7N 15865*	39	2
2 Apr 69	**I'LL BE THERE** *Pye 7N 17693*	38	4

Ralph TRESVANT

US, male vocalist (21 WEEKS) pos/wks

12 Jan 91	**SENSITIVITY** *MCA MCS 1462*	18	8
15 Aug 92 ●	**THE BEST THINGS IN LIFE ARE FREE** *Perspective PERSS 7400* [1]	2	13

[1] Luther Vandross and Janet Jackson with special guests BBD and Ralph Tresvant

TREVOR & SIMON

UK, male production duo – Trevor Reilly and Simon Foy (5 WEEKS) pos/wks

10 Jun 00	**HANDS UP** *Substance SUBS 1CDS*	12	5

TRI

UK, male vocal / instrumental group (1 WEEK) pos/wks

2 Sep 95	**WE GOT THE LOVE** *Epic 6623642*	61	1

TRIBAL HOUSE

US, male vocal / instrumental group (2 WEEKS) pos/wks

3 Feb 90	**MOTHERLAND-A-FRI-CA** *Cooltempo COOL 198*	57	2

Tony TRIBE

Jamaica, male vocalist (2 WEEKS) pos/wks

16 Jul 69	**RED RED WINE** *Downtown DT 419*	50	1
9 Aug 69	**RED RED WINE (re-entry)** *Downtown DT 419*	46	1

A TRIBE CALLED QUEST

US, male rap group (18 WEEKS) pos/wks

18 Aug 90	**BONITA APPLEBUM** *Jive JIVE 256*	47	3
19 Jan 91	**CAN I KICK IT?** *Jive JIVE 265*	15	7
11 Jun 94	**OH MY GOD** *Jive JIVECD 355*	68	1
13 Jul 96	**1NCE AGAIN** *Jive JIVECD 399*	34	2
23 Nov 96	**STRESSED OUT** *Jive JIVECD 404* [1]	33	2
23 Aug 97	**THE JAM EP** *Jive JIVECD 427*	61	1
29 Aug 98	**FIND A WAY** *Jive 0518982*	41	2

[1] A Tribe Called Quest featuring Faith Evans and Raphael Saadiq

Tracks on The Jam EP: Jam / Get a Hold / Mardi Gras at Midnight / Same Ol' Thing

TRIBE OF TOFFS

UK, male vocal / instrumental group (5 WEEKS) pos/wks

24 Dec 88	**JOHN KETTLEY (IS A WEATHERMAN)** *Completely Different DAFT 1*	21	5

TRICKBABY

UK, female vocal / instrumental group (2 WEEKS) pos/wks

12 Oct 96	**INDIE-YARN** *Logic 74321423152*	47	2

TRICKSTER

UK, male producer – Liam Sullivan (3 WEEKS) pos/wks

4 Apr 98	**MOVE ON UP** *AM:PM 5825812*	19	3

TRICKY

UK, male vocalist / multi-instrumentalist – Adrian Thaws (29 WEEKS) pos/wks

5 Feb 94	**AFTERMATH** *Fourth & Broadway BRCD 288*	69	1
28 Jan 95	**OVERCOME** *Fourth & Broadway BRCD 304*	34	3
15 Apr 95	**BLACK STEEL** *Fourth & Broadway BRCD 320*	28	3
5 Aug 95	**THE HELL (EP)** *Fourth & Broadway BRCD 326* [1]	12	3
11 Nov 95	**PUMPKIN** *Fourth & Broadway BRCD 330*	26	2
9 Nov 96	**CHRISTIANSANDS** *Fourth & Broadway BRCD 340*	36	2
23 Nov 96 ●	**MILK** *Mushroom D 1494* [2]	10	7
11 Jan 97	**TRICKY KID** *Fourth & Broadway BRCD 341*	28	2
18 Jan 97	**MILK (re-entry)** *Mushroom D 1494* [2]	74	1
3 May 97	**MAKES ME WANNA DIE** *Fourth & Broadway BRCD 348*	29	2
30 May 98	**MONEY GREEDY / BROKEN HOMES** *Island CID 701*	25	2
21 Aug 99	**FOR REAL** *Island CID 753*	45	1

[1] Tricky vs the Gravediggaz [2] Garbage featuring Tricky

Tracks on The Hell (EP): Hell Is Round the Corner (original) / Hell Is Round the Corner (Hell and Water mix) / Psychosis / Tonite Is a Special Nite (Chaos mass confusion mix)

TRICKY DISCO

UK, male instrumental / production duo – Lee Newman and Michael Wells (10 WEEKS) pos/wks

28 Jul 90	**TRICKY DISCO** *Warp WAP 7*	14	8
20 Apr 91	**HOUSE FLY** *Warp 7WAP 11*	55	2

See also GTO; TECHNOHEAD

TRIFFIDS

Australia, male vocal / instrumental group (1 WEEK) pos/wks

6 Feb 88	**A TRICK OF THE LIGHT** *Island IS 350*	73	1

TRINA and TAMARA

US, female vocal duo (3 WEEKS) pos/wks

7 Feb 98	**MY LOVE IS THE SHHH!** *Warner Bros W 0427CD* [1]	64	1
12 Jun 99	**WHAT'D YOU COME HERE FOR?** *Columbia 6673382*	46	2

[1] Somethin' for the People featuring Trina and Tamara

TRINIDAD OIL COMPANY

Trinidad, male / female vocal / instrumental group (5 WEEKS) pos/wks

21 May 77	**THE CALENDAR SONG** *Harvest HAR 5122*	34	5

TRINITY – *See Julie DRISCOLL, Brian AUGER and the TRINITY*

TRIO

Germany, male vocal / instrumental group (10 WEEKS) pos/wks

3 Jul 82 ●	**DA DA DA** *Mobile Suit Corporation CORP 5*	2	10

TRIPLE X

Italy, male production duo (2 WEEKS) pos/wks

30 Oct 99	**FEEL THE SAME** *Sound of Ministry MOSCDS 135*	32	2

TRIPPING DAISY *US, male vocal / instrumental group (1 WEEK)* pos/wks

30 Mar 96	**PIRANHA** *Island CID 638*	72	1

TRISCO *UK, male production duo (2 WEEKS)* pos/wks

30 Jun 01	**MUSAK** *Positiva CDTIV 155*	28	2

TRIUMPH *Canada, male vocal / instrumental group (2 WEEKS)* pos/wks

22 Nov 80	**I LIVE FOR THE WEEKEND** *RCA 13*	59	2

TROGGS (365 Top 500) *Earthy Sixties pop quartet fronted by Reg Presley (Ball) b. 12 Jun 1943, Hampshire, UK. 'Wild Thing' topped the US chart and sold more than five million worldwide. The Presley-penned 'Love Is All Around' had a 15-week stay at No.1 in 1994 for Wet Wet Wet (87 WEEKS)* pos/wks

5 May 66 ●	**WILD THING** *Fontana TF 689* ▲	2	12
14 Jul 66 ★	**WITH A GIRL LIKE YOU** *Fontana TF 717*	1	12
29 Sep 66 ●	**I CAN'T CONTROL MYSELF** *Page One POF 001*	2	14
15 Dec 66 ●	**ANY WAY THAT YOU WANT ME** *Page One POF 010*	8	10
16 Feb 67	**GIVE IT TO ME** *Page One POF 015*	12	10
1 Jun 67	**NIGHT OF THE LONG GRASS** *Page One POF 022*	17	6
26 Jul 67	**HI HI HAZEL** *Page One POF 030*	42	3
18 Oct 67 ●	**LOVE IS ALL AROUND** *Page One POF 040*	5	14
28 Feb 68	**LITTLE GIRL** *Page One POF 056*	37	4
30 Oct 93	**WILD THING** *Weekend CDWEEK 103* [1]	69	2

[1] Troggs and Wolf

'Wild Thing' in 1993 is a re-recording and was listed with the flip side, 'War', by Edwin Starr and Shadow

TRONIKHOUSE *US, male producer – Kevin Saunderson (1 WEEK)* pos/wks

14 Mar 92	**UP TEMPO** *KMS UK KMSUK 1*	68	1

TROUBADOURS DU ROI BAUDOUIN *Zaire, male / female vocal group (11 WEEKS)* pos/wks

19 Mar 69	**SANCTUS (MISSA LUBA)** *Philips BF 1732*	28	6
7 May 69	**SANCTUS (MISSA LUBA) (re-entry)** *Philips BF 1732*	37	5

TROUBLE FUNK *US, male vocal / instrumental group (3 WEEKS)* pos/wks

27 Jun 87	**WOMAN OF PRINCIPLE** *Fourth & Broadway BRW 70*	65	3

Roger TROUTMAN – *See 2PAC*

Doris TROY *US, female vocalist (12 WEEKS)* pos/wks

19 Nov 64	**WHATCHA GONNA DO ABOUT IT** *Atlantic AT 4011*	37	7
21 Jan 65	**WHATCHA GONNA DO ABOUT IT (re-entry)** *Atlantic AT 4011*	38	5

Elisabeth TROY – *See SOUNDMAN and Don LLOYDIE with Elisabeth TROY; Y-TRIBE featuring Elisabeth TROY; MJ COLE*

TRU FAITH & DUB CONSPIRACY *UK, male production groups (5 WEEKS)* pos/wks

9 Sep 00	**FREAK LIKE ME** *Public Demand / Positiva CDTIV 138*	12	5

TRUBBLE *UK, female vocalist (5 WEEKS)* pos/wks

26 Dec 98	**DANCING BABY (OOGA-CHAKA)** *Island YYCD 1*	21	5

TRUCE *UK, female vocal group (6 WEEKS)* pos/wks

2 Sep 95	**THE FINEST** *Big Life BLRD 118*	54	1
30 Mar 96	**CELEBRATION OF LIFE** *Big Life BLRD 126*	51	1
29 Nov 97	**NOTHIN' BUT A PARTY** *Big Life BLRD 138*	71	1
5 Sep 98	**EYES DON'T LIE** *Big Life BLRD 146*	20	3

TRUCKIN' CO – *See Garnet MIMMS and TRUCKIN' CO*

Andrea TRUE CONNECTION *US, female vocalist, male instrumental backing group (16 WEEKS)* pos/wks

17 Apr 76 ●	**MORE MORE MORE** *Buddah BDS 442*	5	10
4 Mar 78	**WHAT'S YOUR NAME WHAT'S YOUR NUMBER** *Buddah BDS 467*	34	6

TRUE FAITH and Bridgette GRACE with FINAL CUT *US, male / female vocal / instrumental group (4 WEEKS)* pos/wks

2 Mar 91	**TAKE ME AWAY** *Network NWK 20*	51	4

TRUE IMAGE – *See Monie LOVE*

TRUE PARTY *UK, male production / vocal group (6 WEEKS)* pos/wks

2 Dec 00	**WHAZZUP** *Positiva CDBUD 001*	13	6

TRUE STEPPERS *UK, male production / instrumental duo – Jonny Linders and Andy Lysandrou (31 WEEKS)* pos/wks

29 Apr 00 ●	**BUGGIN** *Nulife 74321753342* [1]	6	8
26 Aug 00 ●	**OUT OF YOUR MIND** *Nulife 74321782942* [2]	2	16
2 Dec 00	**TRUE STEP TONIGHT** *Nulife 74321811312* [3]	25	3
6 Jan 01	**OUT OF YOUR MIND (re-entry)** *Nulife 74321782942* [2]	58	4

[1] True Steppers featuring Dane Bowers [2] True Steppers and Dane Bowers featuring Victoria Beckham [3] True Steppers featuring Brian Harvey and Donell Jones

Damon TRUEITT – *See SOMORE featuring DAMON TRUEITT*

TRUMAN & WOLFF featuring STEEL HORSES *UK, male production duo and UK, male rap group (1 WEEK)* pos/wks

22 Aug 98	**COME AGAIN** *Multiply CDMULTY 38*	57	1

TRUMPET MAN – *See MONTANO vs THE TRUMPET MAN*

TRUSSEL *US, male vocal / instrumental group (4 WEEKS)* pos/wks

8 Mar 80	**LOVE INJECTION** *Elektra K 12412*	43	4

TRUTH *UK, male vocal duo (6 WEEKS)* pos/wks

3 Feb 66	**GIRL** *Pye 7N 17035*	27	6

TRUTH *UK, male vocal / instrumental group (16 WEEKS)* pos/wks

11 Jun 83	**CONFUSION (HITS US EVERY TIME)** *Formation TRUTH 1*	22	7
27 Aug 83	**A STEP IN THE RIGHT DIRECTION** *Formation TRUTH 2*	32	7
4 Feb 84	**NO STONE UNTURNED** *Formation TRUTH 3*	66	2

TSD *UK, female vocal group (2 WEEKS)* pos/wks

17 Feb 96	**HEART AND SOUL** *Avex UK AVEXCD 21*	69	1
30 Mar 96	**BABY I LOVE YOU** *Avex UK AVEXCD 34*	64	1

Esera TUAOLO – *See Richie RICH*

TUBES *US, male vocal / instrumental group (18 WEEKS)* pos/wks

19 Nov 77	**WHITE PUNKS ON DOPE** *A & M AMS 7323*	28	4
28 Apr 79	**PRIME TIME** *A & M AMS 7423*	34	10
12 Sep 81	**DON'T WANT TO WAIT ANYMORE** *Capitol CL 208*	60	4

TUBEWAY ARMY – *See Gary NUMAN*

Barbara TUCKER *US, female vocalist (12 WEEKS)* pos/wks

5 Mar 94	**BEAUTIFUL PEOPLE** *Positiva CDTIV 11*	23	3
26 Nov 94	**I GET LIFTED** *Positiva CDTIV 23*	33	2
23 Sep 95	**STAY TOGETHER** *Positiva CDTIV 39*	46	1
8 Aug 98	**EVERYBODY DANCE (THE HORN SONG)** *Positiva CDTIV 96*	28	2
18 Mar 00	**STOP PLAYING WITH MY MIND** *Positiva CDTIV 127* [1]	17	4

[1] Barbara Tucker featuring Darryl D'Bonneau

Junior TUCKER *UK, male vocalist (2 WEEKS)* pos/wks

2 Jun 90	**DON'T TEST** *10 TEN 299*	54	2

Louise TUCKER *UK, female vocalist (5 WEEKS)* pos/wks

9 Apr 83	**MIDNIGHT BLUE** *Ariola ARO 289*	59	5

Tommy TUCKER *US, male vocalist (10 WEEKS)*

Date		Title / Label	pos	wks
26 Mar 64		HI-HEEL SNEAKERS *Pye International 7N 25238*	23	10

TUFF JAM *UK, male production duo (1 WEEK)*

Date		Title / Label	pos	wks
10 Oct 98		NEED GOOD LOVE *Locked On LOX 99CD*	44	1

TUKAN *Denmark, male production duo (3 WEEKS)*

Date		Title / Label	pos	wks
15 Dec 01		LIGHT A RAINBOW *Incentive CENT 33CDS*	38	3+

TURIN BRAKES *UK, male vocal / instrumental duo (8 WEEKS)*

Date		Title / Label	pos	wks
3 Mar 01		THE DOOR *Source SOURCDS 024*	67	1
12 May 01		UNDERDOG (SAVE ME) *Source SOURCDSE 101*	39	4
11 Aug 01		MIND OVER MONEY *Source SOURCD 038*	31	2
27 Oct 01		72 *Source SOURCD 041*	41	1

Ike and Tina TURNER

US, male / female vocal instrumental duo (44 WEEKS)

Date		Title / Label	pos	wks
9 Jun 66	●	RIVER DEEP - MOUNTAIN HIGH *London HL 10046*	3	13
28 Jul 66		TELL HER I'M NOT HOME *Warner Bros. WB 5753*	48	1
27 Oct 66		A LOVE LIKE YOURS *London HL 10083*	16	10
12 Feb 69		RIVER DEEP MOUNTAIN HIGH (re-issue) *London HLU 10242*	33	7
8 Sep 73	●	NUTBUSH CITY LIMITS *United Artists UP 35582*	4	13

See also Tina TURNER

Ruby TURNER *UK, female vocalist (31 WEEKS)*

Date		Title / Label	pos	wks
25 Jan 86		IF YOU'RE READY (COME GO WITH ME) *Jive JIVE 109* [1]	30	7
29 Mar 86		I'M IN LOVE *Jive JIVE 118*	61	4
13 Sep 86		BYE BABY *Jive JIVE 126*	52	3
14 Mar 87		I'D RATHER GO BLIND *Jive RTS 1*	24	8
16 May 87		I'M IN LOVE (re-issue) *Jive RTS 2*	57	2
13 Jan 90		IT'S GONNA BE ALRIGHT *Jive RTS 7*	57	3
5 Feb 94		STAY WITH ME BABY *M & G MAGCD 53*	39	3
9 Dec 95		SHAKABOOM! *Telstar HUNTCD 1* [2]	64	1

[1] Ruby Turner featuring Jonathan Butler [2] Hunter featuring Ruby Turner

Sammy TURNER *US, male vocalist (2 WEEKS)*

Date		Title / Label	pos	wks
13 Nov 59		ALWAYS *London HLX 8963*	26	2

Tina TURNER (66 Top 500)

Supreme soul singer-cum-rock legend, b. Anna Mae Bullock, 26 Nov 1939, Tennessee, US. After a successful, if stormy, partnership with husband Ike, she reached greater heights as a Grammy-winning soloist and is one of the world's most popular live acts (224 WEEKS)

Date		Title / Label	pos	wks
19 Nov 83	●	LET'S STAY TOGETHER *Capitol CL 316*	6	13
25 Feb 84		HELP *Capitol CL 325*	40	6
16 Jun 84	●	WHAT'S LOVE GOT TO DO WITH IT *Capitol CL 334* ▲	3	16
15 Sep 84		BETTER BE GOOD TO ME *Capitol CL 338*	45	5
17 Nov 84		PRIVATE DANCER *Capitol CL 343*	26	9
2 Mar 85		I CAN'T STAND THE RAIN *Capitol CL 352*	57	3
20 Jul 85	●	WE DON'T NEED ANOTHER HERO (THUNDERDOME) *Capitol CL 364*	3	12
12 Oct 85		ONE OF THE LIVING *Capitol CL 376*	55	2
2 Nov 85		IT'S ONLY LOVE *A & M AM 285* [1]	29	6
23 Aug 86		TYPICAL MALE *Capitol CL 419*	33	6
8 Nov 86		TWO PEOPLE *Capitol CL 430*	43	4
14 Mar 87		WHAT YOU GET IS WHAT YOU SEE *Capitol CL 439*	30	7
13 Jun 87		BREAK EVERY RULE *Capitol CL 452*	43	3
20 Jun 87		TEARING US APART *Duck W 8299* [2]	56	3
19 Mar 88		ADDICTED TO LOVE (LIVE) *Capitol CL 484*	71	2
2 Sep 89	●	THE BEST *Capitol CL 543*	5	12
18 Nov 89	●	I DON'T WANNA LOSE YOU *Capitol CL 553*	8	11
17 Feb 90		STEAMY WINDOWS *Capitol CL 560*	13	6
11 Aug 90		LOOK ME IN THE HEART *Capitol CL 584*	31	6
13 Oct 90		BE TENDER WITH ME BABY *Capitol CL 593*	28	4
24 Nov 90	●	IT TAKES TWO *Warner Bros. ROD 1* [3]	5	8
21 Sep 91		NUTBUSH CITY LIMITS (re-recording) *Capitol CL 630*	23	5
23 Nov 91		WAY OF THE WORLD *Capitol CL 637*	13	7
15 Feb 92		LOVE THING *Capitol CL 644*	29	4
6 Jun 92		I WANT YOU NEAR ME *Capitol CL 659*	22	4
22 May 93	●	I DON'T WANNA FIGHT *Parlophone CDRS 6346*	7	9
28 Aug 93		DISCO INFERNO *Parlophone CDR 6357*	12	6
30 Oct 93		WHY MUST WE WAIT UNTIL TONIGHT *Parlophone CDR 6366*	16	4
18 Nov 95	●	GOLDENEYE *Parlophone CDR 0071001*	10	9
23 Mar 96		WHATEVER YOU WANT *Parlophone CDR 6429*	23	6
8 Jun 96		ON SILENT WINGS *Parlophone CDR 6434*	13	6
27 Jul 96		MISSING YOU *Parlophone CDR 6441* [4]	12	5
19 Oct 96		SOMETHING BEAUTIFUL REMAINS *Parlophone CDR 6448*	27	2
21 Dec 96		IN YOUR WILDEST DREAMS *Parlophone CDR 6451* [5]	32	3
30 Oct 99	●	WHEN THE HEARTACHE IS OVER *Parlophone CDR 6529* [4]	10	7
12 Feb 00		WHATEVER YOU NEED *Parlophone CDR 6532*	27	3

[1] Bryan Adams and Tina Turner [2] Eric Clapton and Tina Turner [3] Rod Stewart and Tina Turner [4] Tina [5] Tina Turner featuring Barry White

See also Ike and Tina TURNER

TURNTABLE ORCHESTRA

US, male vocal / instrumental duo (4 WEEKS)

Date		Title / Label	pos	wks
21 Jan 89		YOU'RE GONNA MISS ME *Republic LIC 012*	52	4

TURTLES *US, male vocal / instrumental group (39 WEEKS)*

Date		Title / Label	pos	wks
23 Mar 67		HAPPY TOGETHER *London HL 10115* ▲	12	12
15 Jun 67	●	SHE'D RATHER BE WITH ME *London HLU 10135*	4	15
30 Oct 68	●	ELENORE *London HL 10223*	7	12

TUXEDOS – *See Bobby ANGELO and the TUXEDOS*

TWA *UK, male instrumental / production group (1 WEEK)*

Date		Title / Label	pos	wks
16 Sep 95		NASTY GIRLS *Mercury MERCD 441*	51	1

Shania TWAIN (489 Top 500)

Pop and country music queen, b. Eileen Regina Edwards 28 Aug 1965, Ontario, Canada. Self-penned 'Come On Over' album sold more than 30 million, including two million in the UK and record-breaking 18 million in the US. Tours in 1999 grossed $36.6 million (72 WEEKS)

Date		Title / Label	pos	wks
28 Feb 98	●	YOU'RE STILL THE ONE *Mercury 5684932*	10	10
13 Jun 98		WHEN *Mercury 5661192*	18	4
28 Nov 98	●	FROM THIS MOMENT ON *Mercury 5665632*	9	8
22 May 99	●	THAT DON'T IMPRESS ME MUCH *Mercury 8708032*	3	21
2 Oct 99	●	MAN! I FEEL LIKE A WOMAN! *Mercury 5623242*	3	18
26 Feb 00	●	DON'T BE STUPID (YOU KNOW I LOVE YOU) *Mercury 1721492*	5	9
13 May 00		DON'T BE STUPID (YOU KNOW I LOVE YOU) (re-entry) *Mercury 1721492*	60	2

TWEENIES *UK, male / female kiddie TV characters (43 WEEKS)*

Date		Title / Label	pos	wks
11 Nov 00	●	NUMBER 1 *BBC Music WMSS 60332*	5	18
31 Mar 01		BEST FRIENDS FOREVER *BBC Music WMSS 60382*	12	7
24 Apr 01		NUMBER 1 (re-entry) *BBC Music WMSS 60332*	72	4
26 May 01		BEST FRIENDS FOREVER (re-entry) *BBC Music WMSS 60382*	56	3
4 Aug 01		DO THE LOLLIPOP *BBC Music WMSS 60452*	17	8
15 Dec 01	●	I BELIEVE IN CHRISTMAS *BBC Music WMSS 60502*	9	3+

TWEETS *UK, male feathered vocal / instrumental group (34 WEEKS)*

Date		Title / Label	pos	wks
12 Sep 81	●	THE BIRDIE SONG (BIRDIE DANCE) *PRT 7P 219*	2	23
5 Dec 81		LET'S ALL SING LIKE THE BIRDIES SING *PRT 7P 226*	44	6
18 Dec 82		THE BIRDIE SONG (BIRDIE DANCE) (re-entry) *PRT 7P 219*	46	5

20 FINGERS *US, male instrumental / production duo – Charles Babie and Manfred Mohr (14 WEEKS)*

Date		Title / Label	pos	wks
26 Nov 94		SHORT DICK MAN *Multiply CDMULT 12* [1]	21	4
30 Sep 95		LICK IT *Zyx ZYX 75908* [2]	48	3
30 Sep 95		SHORT SHORT MAN (re-mix) *Multiply CXMULTY 7* [1]	11	7

[1] 20 Fingers featuring Gillette [2] 20 Fingers featuring Roula

21ST CENTURY GIRLS

UK, female vocal / instrumental group (4 WEEKS)

Date		Title / Label	pos	wks
12 Jun 99		21ST CENTURY GIRLS *EMI NTNCDS 001*	16	4

TWENTY 4 SEVEN featuring CAPTAIN HOLLYWOOD
US / Germany, male / female vocal / instrumental group (20 WEEKS) pos/wks

22 Sep 90 ● I CAN'T STAND IT *BCM BCMR 395* 7 10
24 Nov 90 ARE YOU DREAMING *BCM BCM 07504* 17 10

See also CAPTAIN HOLLYWOOD PROJECT

TWICE AS MUCH *UK, male vocal duo (9 WEEKS)* pos/wks

16 Jun 66 SITTIN' ON A FENCE *Immediate IM 033* 25 9

TWIGGY *UK, female vocalist – Lesley Hornby (10 WEEKS)* pos/wks

14 Aug 76 HERE I GO AGAIN *Mercury 6007 100* 17 10

TWILIGHT – *See Roger SANCHEZ*

TWIN HYPE *US, male rap duo (2 WEEKS)* pos/wks

15 Jul 89 DO IT TO THE CROWD *Profile PROF 255* 65 2

TWINKLE *UK, female vocalist – Lynn Ripley (20 WEEKS)* pos/wks

26 Nov 64 ● TERRY *Decca F 12013* 4 15
25 Feb 65 GOLDEN LIGHTS *Decca F 12076* 21 5

TWISTED SISTER *US, male vocal / instrumental group (28 WEEKS)* pos/wks

26 Mar 83 I AM (I'M ME) *Atlantic A 9854* 18 9
28 May 83 THE KIDS ARE BACK *Atlantic A 9827* 32 6
20 Aug 83 YOU CAN'T STOP ROCK 'N' ROLL *Atlantic A 9792* 43 4
2 Jun 84 WE'RE NOT GONNA TAKE IT *Atlantic A 9657* 58 6
18 Jan 86 LEADER OF THE PACK *Atlantic A 9478* 47 3

Conway TWITTY *US, male vocalist – Harold Jenkins (36 WEEKS)* pos/wks

14 Nov 58 ★ IT'S ONLY MAKE BELIEVE *MGM 992* ▲ 1 15
27 Mar 59 THE STORY OF MY LOVE *MGM 1003* 30 1
21 Aug 59 ● MONA LISA *MGM 1029* 5 14
21 Jul 60 IS A BLUE BIRD BLUE *MGM 1082* 43 3
23 Feb 61 C'EST SI BON *MGM 1118* 40 3

2 BAD MICE *UK, male instrumental / production group (4 WEEKS)* pos/wks

15 Feb 92 HOLD IT DOWN *Moving Shadow SHADOW 14* 70 1
8 Aug 92 HOLD IT DOWN (re-entry) *Moving Shadow SHADOW 14* 48 2
7 Sep 96 BOMBSCARE *Arista 74321397662* 46 1

TWO COWBOYS *Italy, male instrumental / production duo – Roberto Sagotto and Maurizio Braccagni (11 WEEKS)* pos/wks

9 Jul 94 ● EVERYBODY GONFI-GON *3 Beat TABCD 221* 7 11

2 EIVISSA *Germany, female vocal duo – Pascale Jean Louis and Ellen Helbig (6 WEEKS)* pos/wks

4 Oct 97 OH LA LA LA *Club Tools 0063475 CLU* 13 6

2 FOR JOY *UK, male instrumental / production duo (3 WEEKS)* pos/wks

1 Dec 90 IN A STATE *Mercury MER 333* 61 1
9 Nov 91 LET THE BASS KICK *All Around the World GLOBE 102* 67 2

2 FUNKY 2 starring Kathryn DION
UK, male / female vocal / instrumental group (4 WEEKS) pos/wks

6 Nov 93 BROTHERS AND SISTERS *Logic 74321170772* 56 2
30 Nov 96 BROTHERS AND SISTERS (re-mix) *All Around the World CDGLOBE 138* 36 2

2 HOUSE *US, male instrumental / production duo (1 WEEK)* pos/wks

21 Mar 92 GO TECHNO *Atlantic A 7519* 65 1

2 IN A ROOM
US, male vocal duo – Roger Pauletta and Rafael Vargas (15 WEEKS) pos/wks

18 Nov 89 SOMEBODY IN THE HOUSE SAY YEAH! *Big Life BLR 12* 66 1
26 Jan 91 ● WIGGLE IT *SBK SBK 19* 3 8
6 Apr 91 SHE'S GOT ME GOING CRAZY *SBK SBK 23* 54 2
22 Oct 94 EL TRAGO (THE DRINK) *Positiva CDTIV 18* 34 2
8 Apr 95 AHORA ES (NOW IS THE TIME) *Positiva CDTIV 32* 43 1
17 Aug 96 GIDDY-UP *Encore CDCOR 008* 74 1

2 IN A TENT *UK, male instrumental / production duo (7 WEEKS)* pos/wks

17 Dec 94 WHEN I'M CLEANING WINDOWS (TURNED OUT NICE AGAIN) *Love This SPONCD 1* 25 5
13 May 95 BOOGIE WOOGIE BUGLE BOY (DON'T STOP) *Bald Cat BALDCD 1* [1] 48 1
6 Jan 96 WHEN I'M CLEANING WINDOWS (TURNED OUT NICE AGAIN) (re-entry) *Love This SPONCD 1* 62 1

[1] 2 In a Tank

First hit features the vocals of George Formby

2K *UK, male production duo (2 WEEKS)* pos/wks

25 Oct 97 ***K THE MILLENNIUM *Blast First BFFP 146CDK* 28 2

See also KLF; TIMELORDS; JUSTIFIED ANCIENTS OF MU MU

2 MAD *UK, male vocal / instrumental duo (4 WEEKS)* pos/wks

9 Feb 91 THINKIN' ABOUT YOUR BODY *Big Life BLR 37* 43 4

TWO MAN SOUND
Belgium, male vocal / instrumental group (7 WEEKS) pos/wks

20 Jan 79 QUE TAL AMERICA *Miracle M 1* 46 7

TWO MEN, A DRUM MACHINE AND A TRUMPET
UK, male instrumental duo – Andy Cox and David Steele (17 WEEKS) pos/wks

9 Jan 88 TIRED OF GETTING PUSHED AROUND *London LON 141* 18 8
25 Jun 88 HEAT IT UP *Jive JIVE 174* [1] 21 9

[1] Wee Papa Girl Rappers featuring Two Men and a Drum Machine

See also FINE YOUNG CANNIBALS

TWO NATIONS *UK, male vocal / instrumental group (1 WEEK)* pos/wks

20 Jun 87 THAT'S THE WAY IT FEELS *10 TEN 168* 74 1

TWO PEOPLE *UK, male vocal / instrumental group (2 WEEKS)* pos/wks

31 Jan 87 HEAVEN *Polydor POSP 844* 63 2

2WO THIRD3 *UK, male vocal / instrumental group (15 WEEKS)* pos/wks

19 Feb 94 HEAR ME CALLING *Epic 6600642* 48 3
11 Jun 94 EASE THE PRESSURE *Epic 6604782* 45 2
8 Oct 94 I WANT THE WORLD *Epic 6608542* 20 5
17 Dec 94 I WANT TO BE ALONE *Epic 6610852* 29 5

2-4 FAMILY *UK / US / Korea, male / female rap / vocal group (1 WEEK)* pos/wks

29 May 99 LEAN ON ME (WITH THE FAMILY) *Epic 6670132* 69 1

2 UNLIMITED (253 Top 500) *The brainchild of Jean-Paul de Coster and Phil Wilde, fronted by the minimalist vocals / chants / raps of Dutch duo Ray Slijngaard and Anita Dels. Their youth-aimed, infectious dance tracks sold millions around Europe and gave them 11 successive UK Top 20 hits (112 WEEKS)* pos/wks

5 Oct 91 ● GET READY FOR THIS *PWL Continental PWL 206* 2 15
25 Jan 92 ● TWILIGHT ZONE *PWL Continental PWL 211* 2 10
2 May 92 ● WORKAHOLIC *PWL Continental PWL 228* 4 7
15 Aug 92 THE MAGIC FRIEND *PWL Continental PWL 240* 11 7
30 Jan 93 ★ NO LIMIT *PWL Continental PWCD 256* 1 16
8 May 93 ● TRIBAL DANCE *PWL Continental PWCD 262* 4 11
4 Sep 93 ● FACES *PWL Continental PWCD 268* 8 7
20 Nov 93 MAXIMUM OVERDRIVE *PWL Continental PWCD 276* 15 8
19 Feb 94 ● LET THE BEAT CONTROL YOUR BODY *PWL Continental PWCD 280* 6 9
21 May 94 ● THE REAL THING *PWL Continental PWCD 306* 6 7
1 Oct 94 NO ONE *PWL Continental PWCD 314* 17 6
25 Mar 95 HERE I GO *PWL Continental PWCD 317* 22 3

21 Oct 95		**DO WHAT'S GOOD FOR ME** *PWL Continental PWL 322CD1*	16	4
11 Jul 98		**WANNA GET UP** *Big Life BLRD 143*	38	2

In 1995 both Ray Slijngaard and Anita Dels left the act which was fronted by a Dutch female duo for 'Wanna Get Up'

2PAC *US, male rapper – Tupac Shakur (68 WEEKS)* pos/wks

13 Apr 96	●	**CALIFORNIA LOVE** *Death Row DRWCD 3* [1]	6	8
27 Jul 96		**HOW DO YOU WANT IT** *Death Row DRWCD 4* [2] ▲	17	4
30 Nov 96		**I AIN'T MAD AT CHA** *Death Row DRWCD 5*	13	9
26 Apr 97		**WANTED DEAD OR ALIVE** *Def Jam 5744052* [3]	16	3
10 Jan 98		**I WONDER IF HEAVEN GOT A GHETTO** *Jive JIVECD 446*	21	4
13 Jun 98		**DO FOR LOVE** *Jive 0518512* [4]	12	4
18 Jul 98		**RUNNIN'** *Black Jam BJAM 9005* [5]	15	3
28 Nov 98		**HAPPY HOME** *Eagle EAGXS 058*	17	2
20 Feb 99	●	**CHANGES** *Jive 0522832*	3	12
3 Jul 99		**DEAR MAMA** *Jive 0523702*	27	3
23 Jun 01	●	**UNTIL THE END OF TIME** *Interscope / Polydor 4975812*	4	11
10 Nov 01	●	**LETTER 2 MY UNBORN** *Interscope / Polydor 4976142*	21	5

[1] 2Pac featuring Dr Dre [2] 2Pac featuring K-Ci and JoJo [3] 2Pac and Snoop Doggy Dogg [4] 2Pac featuring Eric Williams [5] 2Pac and Notorious B.I.G.

See also MAKAVELI

TYGERS OF PAN TANG
UK, male vocal / instrumental group (15 WEEKS) pos/wks

14 Feb 81		**HELLBOUND** *MCA 672*	48	3
27 Mar 82		**LOVE POTION NO. 9** *MCA 769*	45	6
10 Jul 82		**RENDEZVOUS** *MCA 777*	49	4
11 Sep 82		**PARIS BY AIR** *MCA 790*	63	2

Bonnie TYLER (404 Top 500) *Raspy-voiced vocalist b. Gaynor Hopkins, 8 Jun 1953, Swansea, Wales. Made the US country Top 10 with 'It's A Heartache', and 'Total Eclipse of the Heart' was the first record by a Welsh artist to top the US pop chart (81 WEEKS)* pos/wks

30 Oct 76	●	**LOST IN FRANCE** *RCA 2734*	9	10
19 Mar 77		**MORE THAN A LOVER** *RCA PB 5008*	27	6
3 Dec 77	●	**IT'S A HEARTACHE** *RCA PB 5057*	4	12
30 Jun 79		**MARRIED MEN** *RCA PB 5164*	35	6
19 Feb 83	★	**TOTAL ECLIPSE OF THE HEART** *CBS TYLER 1* ▲	1	12
7 May 83		**FASTER THAN THE SPEED OF NIGHT** *CBS A 3338*	43	4
25 Jun 83		**HAVE YOU EVER SEEN THE RAIN** *CBS A 3517*	47	3
7 Jan 84	●	**A ROCKIN' GOOD WAY** *Epic A 4071* [1]	5	9
31 Aug 85	●	**HOLDING OUT FOR A HERO** *CBS A 4251*	2	13
14 Dec 85		**LOVING YOU'S A DIRTY JOB BUT SOMEBODY'S GOTTA DO IT** *CBS A 6662* [2]	73	2
28 Dec 91		**HOLDING OUT FOR A HERO (re-issue)** *Total TYLER 10*	69	2
27 Jan 96		**MAKING LOVE (OUT OF NOTHING AT ALL)** *East West EW 010CD*	45	2

[1] Shaky and Bonnie (Bonnie Tyler) [2] Bonnie Tyler, guest vocals Todd Rundgren

TYMES
US, male vocal group – lead vocal George Williams (41 WEEKS) pos/wks

25 Jul 63		**SO MUCH IN LOVE** *Cameo Parkway P 871* ▲	21	8
15 Jan 69		**PEOPLE** *Direction 58 3903*	16	10
21 Sep 74		**YOU LITTLE TRUSTMAKER** *RCA 2456*	18	9
21 Dec 74	★	**MS GRACE** *RCA 2493*	1	11
17 Jan 76		**GOD'S GONNA PUNISH YOU** *RCA 2626*	41	3

TYMES 4 *UK, female vocal group (5 WEEKS)* pos/wks

25 Aug 01		**BODYROCK** *Edel 0118635 ERE*	23	3
15 Dec 01		**SHE GOT GAME** *Blacklist 0133135 ERE*	40	2

TYPICALLY TROPICAL *UK, male vocal / instrumental duo – Jeff Calvert and Max West (11 WEEKS)* pos/wks

5 Jul 75	★	**BARBADOS** *Gull GULS 14*	1	11

TYREE *US, male producer – Tyree Cooper (10 WEEKS)* pos/wks

25 Feb 89		**TURN UP THE BASS** *ffrr FFR 24* [1]	12	7
6 May 89		**HARDCORE HIP HOUSE** *DJ International DJIN 11*	70	2
2 Dec 89		**MOVE YOUR BODY** *CBS 655470 7* [2]	72	1

[1] Tyree featuring Kool Rock Steady [2] Tyree featuring JMD

TYRESE *US, male vocalist (2 WEEKS)* pos/wks

31 Jul 99		**NOBODY ELSE** *RCA 74321688282*	59	1
25 Sep 99		**SWEET LADY** *RCA 74321700842*	55	1

TYRREL CORPORATION
UK, male vocal / instrumental duo (9 WEEKS) pos/wks

14 Mar 92		**THE BOTTLE** *Volante TYR 1*	71	1
15 Aug 92		**GOING HOME** *Volante TYR 2*	58	2
10 Oct 92		**WAKING WITH A STRANGER / ONE DAY** *Volante TYRS 3*	59	1
24 Sep 94		**YOU'RE NOT HERE** *Cooltempo CDCOOL 292*	42	2
14 Jan 95		**BETTER DAYS AHEAD** *Cooltempo CDCOOL 303*	29	3

TZANT *UK, male rap / instrumental duo – Jamie White and Marcus Thomas (aka ODC MC) (10 WEEKS)* pos/wks

7 Sep 96		**HOT AND WET (BELIEVE IT)** *Logic 74321376832*	36	2
25 Apr 98		**SOUNDS OF WICKEDNESS** *Logic 74321568842*	11	6
22 Aug 98		**BOUNCE WITH THE MASSIVE** *Logic 74321602102*	39	2

See also PF PROJECT

Judie TZUKE *UK, female vocalist (10 WEEKS)* pos/wks

14 Jul 79		**STAY WITH ME TILL DAWN** *Rocket XPRES 17*	16	10

U

UB40 (21 Top 500) *Reggae's most successful transatlantic group: includes brothers Ali (v/g) and Robin (v/g) Campbell, and Earl Falconer (b). Only three groups can claim more chart hits than this act, named after the number of the UK unemployment benefit form (330 WEEKS)* pos/wks

8 Mar 80	●	**KING / FOOD FOR THOUGHT** *Graduate GRAD 6*	4	13
14 Jun 80	●	**MY WAY OF THINKING / I THINK IT'S GOING TO RAIN** *Graduate GRAD 8*	6	10
1 Nov 80	●	**THE EARTH DIES SCREAMING / DREAM A LIE** *Graduate GRAD 10*	10	12
23 May 81		**DON'T LET IT PASS YOU BY / DON'T SLOW DOWN** *DEP International DEP 1*	16	9
8 Aug 81	●	**ONE IN TEN** *DEP International DEP 2*	7	10
13 Feb 82		**I WON'T CLOSE MY EYES** *DEP International DEP 3*	32	6
15 May 82		**LOVE IS ALL IS ALRIGHT** *DEP International DEP 4*	29	7
28 Aug 82		**SO HERE I AM** *DEP International DEP 5*	25	9
5 Feb 83		**I'VE GOT MINE** *DEP International 7 DEP 6*	45	4
20 Aug 83	★	**RED RED WINE** *DEP International 7 DEP 7* ▲	1	14
15 Oct 83	●	**PLEASE DON'T MAKE ME CRY** *DEP International 7 DEP 8*	10	8
10 Dec 83		**MANY RIVERS TO CROSS** *DEP International 7 DEP 9*	16	8
17 Mar 84		**CHERRY OH BABY** *DEP International DEP 10*	12	8
22 Sep 84	●	**IF IT HAPPENS AGAIN** *DEP International DEP 11*	9	8
1 Dec 84		**RIDDLE ME** *DEP International DEP 15*	59	2
3 Aug 85	★	**I GOT YOU BABE** *DEP International DEP 20* [1]	1	13
26 Oct 85	●	**DON'T BREAK MY HEART** *DEP International DEP 22*	3	13
12 Jul 86	●	**SING OUR OWN SONG** *DEP International DEP 23*	5	9
27 Sep 86		**ALL I WANT TO DO** *DEP International DEP 24*	41	4
17 Jan 87		**RAT IN MI KITCHEN** *DEP International DEP 25*	12	7
9 May 87		**WATCHDOGS** *DEP International DEP 26*	39	4
10 Oct 87		**MAYBE TOMORROW** *DEP International DEP 27*	14	8
27 Feb 88		**RECKLESS** *EMI EM 41* [2]	17	8
18 Jun 88	●	**BREAKFAST IN BED** *DEP International DEP 29* [1]	6	11
20 Aug 88		**WHERE DID I GO WRONG** *DEP International DEP 30*	26	6
17 Jun 89		**I WOULD DO FOR YOU** *DEP International DEP 32*	45	4
18 Nov 89	●	**HOMELY GIRL** *DEP International DEP 33*	6	10

27 Jan 90	**HERE I AM (COME AND TAKE ME)** *DEP International DEP 34*	46	3
31 Mar 90 ●	**KINGSTON TOWN** *DEP International DEP 35*	4	12
28 Jul 90	**WEAR YOU TO THE BALL** *DEP International DEP 36*	35	6
3 Nov 90 ●	**I'LL BE YOUR BABY TONIGHT** *EMI EM 167* [3]	6	10
1 Dec 90	**IMPOSSIBLE LOVE** *DEP International DEP 37*	47	2
2 Feb 91	**THE WAY YOU DO THE THINGS YOU DO** *DEP International DEP 38*	49	3
12 Dec 92	**ONE IN TEN (re-mix)** *ZTT ZANG 39* [4]	17	8
22 May 93 ★	**(I CAN'T HELP) FALLING IN LOVE WITH YOU** *DEP International DEPDG 40* ▲	1	16
21 Aug 93 ●	**HIGHER GROUND** *DEP International DEPD 41*	8	9
11 Dec 93	**BRING ME YOUR CUP** *DEP International DEPD 42*	24	6
2 Apr 94	**C'EST LA VIE** *DEP International DEPD 43*	37	3
27 Aug 94	**REGGAE MUSIC** *DEP International DEPDG 44*	28	2
4 Nov 95	**UNTIL MY DYING DAY** *DEP International DEPD 45*	15	6
30 Aug 97	**TELL ME IT IS TRUE** *DEP International DEP 48*	14	4
15 Nov 97	**ALWAYS THERE** *DEP International DEPD 49*	53	1
10 Oct 98 ●	**COME BACK DARLING** *DEP International DEPD 50*	10	6
19 Dec 98	**HOLLY HOLY** *DEP International DEPD 51*	31	3
1 May 99	**THE TRAIN IS COMING** *DEP International DEPD 52*	30	2
9 Dec 00	**LIGHT MY FIRE** *DEP International DEPD 53*	63	1
20 Oct 01	**SINCE I MET YOU LADY / SPARKLE OF MY EYES** *DEP International DEPD 55* [5]	40	2

[1] UB40 featuring Chrissie Hynde [2] Afrika Bambaataa and Family featuring UB40 [3] Robert Palmer and UB40 [4] 808 State vs UB40 [5] UB40 featuring Lady Saw

UBM *Germany, male / female vocal / instrumental group (1 WEEK)* pos/wks

23 May 98	**LOVIN' YOU** *Logic 74321571692*	46	1

UCC – *See URBAN COOKIE COLLECTIVE*

UFO *UK / Germany, male vocal / instrumental group (31 WEEKS)* pos/wks

5 Aug 78	**ONLY YOU CAN ROCK ME** *Chrysalis CHS 2241*	50	4
27 Jan 79	**DOCTOR DOCTOR** *Chrysalis CHS 2287*	35	6
31 Mar 79	**SHOOT SHOOT** *Chrysalis CHS 2318*	48	5
12 Jan 80	**YOUNG BLOOD** *Chrysalis CHS 2399*	36	5
17 Jan 81	**LONELY HEART** *Chrysalis CHS 2482*	41	5
30 Jan 82	**LET IT RAIN** *Chrysalis CHS 2576*	62	3
19 Mar 83	**WHEN IT'S TIME TO ROCK** *Chrysalis CHS 2672*	70	3

U4EA featuring BERRI – *See NEW ATLANTIC*

UGLY DUCKLING *US, male production / rap trio (1 WEEK)* pos/wks

13 Oct 01	**A LITTLE SAMBA** *XL Recordings XLS 135CD*	70	1

UGLY KID JOE *US, male vocal / instrumental group (28 WEEKS)* pos/wks

16 May 92 ●	**EVERYTHING ABOUT YOU** *Mercury MER 367*	3	9
22 Aug 92	**NEIGHBOR** *Mercury MER 374*	28	4
31 Oct 92	**SO DAMN COOL** *Mercury MER 383*	44	2
13 Mar 93 ●	**CATS IN THE CRADLE** *Mercury MERCD 385*	7	9
19 Jun 93	**BUSY BEE** *Mercury MERCD 389*	39	2
8 Jul 95	**MILKMAN'S SON** *Mercury MERCD 435*	39	2

UHF *US, male instrumental / production group (4 WEEKS)* pos/wks

14 Dec 91	**UHF / EVERYTHING** *XL Recordings XLS 25*	46	4

UK *UK, male vocal / instrumental group (2 WEEKS)* pos/wks

30 Jun 79	**NOTHING TO LOSE** *Polydor POSP 55*	67	2

UK *Canada / Spain, male vocal / instrumental group (1 WEEK)* pos/wks

3 Aug 96	**SMALL TOWN BOY** *Media MCSTD 400*	74	1

UK APACHI / APACHE
UK, male vocalist (3 WEEKS) pos/wks

1 Oct 94	**ORIGINAL NUTTAH** *Sound of Underground SOUR 008CD* [1]	39	3
28 Jul 01	**SIGNS** *Outcaste OUT 38CD1* [2]	63	1

[1] UK APACHI with SHY FX [2] DJ BADMARSH and SHRI featuring UK APACHE

UK MIXMASTERS *UK, male producer – Nigel Wright (15 WEEKS)* pos/wks

2 Feb 91	**THE NIGHT FEVER MEGAMIX** *IQ ZB 44339* [1]	23	5
27 Jul 91	**LUCKY 7 MEGAMIX** *IQ ZB 44731*	43	3
14 Dec 91	**BARE NECESSITIES MEGAMIX** *Connect ZB 35135*	14	7

[1] Mixmasters

UK PLAYERS *UK, male vocal / instrumental group (3 WEEKS)* pos/wks

14 May 83	**LOVE'S GONNA GET YOU** *RCA 326*	52	3

UK SUBS *UK, male vocal / instrumental group (39 WEEKS)* pos/wks

23 Jun 79	**STRANGLEHOLD** *Gem GEMS 5*	26	8
8 Sep 79	**TOMORROW'S GIRLS** *Gem GEMS 10*	28	6
1 Dec 79	**SHE'S NOT THERE / KICKS (EP)** *Gem GEMS 14*	36	7
8 Mar 80	**WARHEAD** *Gem GEMS 23*	30	4
17 May 80	**TEENAGE** *Gem GEMS 30*	32	5
25 Oct 80	**PARTY IN PARIS** *Gem GEMS 42*	37	4
18 Apr 81	**KEEP ON RUNNIN' (TILL YOU BURN)** *Gem GEMS 45*	41	5

Tracks on She's Not There / Kicks (EP): She's Not There / Kicks / Victim / The Same Thing

Tracey ULLMAN *UK, female vocalist (49 WEEKS)* pos/wks

19 Mar 83 ●	**BREAKAWAY** *Stiff BUY 168*	4	11
24 Sep 83 ●	**THEY DON'T KNOW** *Stiff BUY 180*	2	11
3 Dec 83 ●	**MOVE OVER DARLING** *Stiff BUY 195*	8	9
3 Mar 84	**MY GUY** *Stiff BUY 197*	23	6
28 Jul 84	**SUNGLASSES** *Stiff BUY 205*	18	9
27 Oct 84	**HELPLESS** *Stiff BUY 211*	61	3

ULTIMATE KAOS *UK, male vocal group (28 WEEKS)* pos/wks

22 Oct 94 ●	**SOME GIRLS** *Wild Card CARDD 12*	9	8
7 Jan 95	**SOME GIRLS (re-entry)** *Wild Card CARDD 12*	67	1
21 Jan 95	**HOOCHIE BOOTY** *Wild Card CARDW 14*	17	4
1 Apr 95	**SHOW A LITTLE LOVE** *Wild Card CARDW 18*	23	5
1 Jul 95	**RIGHT HERE** *Wild Card 5795832*	18	4
8 Mar 97	**CASANOVA** *Polydor 5759312*	24	3
18 Jul 98	**CASANOVA (re-issue)** *Mercury MERCD 505*	29	2
5 Jun 99	**ANYTHING YOU WANT (I'VE GOT IT)** *Mercury MERCD 510*	52	1

ULTRA *UK, male vocal / instrumental group (22 WEEKS)* pos/wks

18 Apr 98	**SAY YOU DO** *East West EW 124CD*	11	7
4 Jul 98	**SAY IT ONCE** *East West EW 171CD1*	16	6
10 Oct 98	**THE RIGHT TIME** *East West EW 182CD*	28	2
31 Oct 98	**THE RIGHT TIME (re-entry)** *East West EW 182CD*	74	1
16 Jan 99 ●	**RESCUE ME** *East West EW 193CD1*	8	6

ULTRA HIGH *UK, male vocalist – Michael McCloud (3 WEEKS)* pos/wks

2 Dec 95	**STAY WITH ME** *MCA MCSTD 40007*	36	2
20 Jul 96	**ARE YOU READY FOR LOVE** *MCA MCSTD 40039*	45	1

ULTRACYNIC
UK, male / female vocal / instrumental group (3 WEEKS) pos/wks

29 Aug 92	**NOTHING IS FOREVER** *380 PEW 2*	50	2
19 Apr 97	**NOTHING IS FOREVER (re-mix)** *All Around the World CDGLOBE 139*	47	1

ULTRAMARINE *UK, male instrumental duo (4 WEEKS)* pos/wks

24 Jul 93	**KINGDOM** *Blanco Y Negro NEG 65CD*	46	2
29 Jan 94	**BAREFOOT (EP)** *Blanco Y Negro NEG 67CD*	61	1
27 Apr 96	**HYMN** *Blanco Y Negro NEG 87CD* [1]	65	1

[1] Ultramarine featuring David McAlmont

Tracks on Barefoot (EP): Hooter / The Badger / Urf / Happy Land

ULTRA-SONIC *UK, male instrumental / production duo (2 WEEKS)* pos/wks

3 Sep 94	**OBSESSION** *Clubscene DCSRT 027*	75	1
21 Sep 96	**DO YOU BELIEVE IN LOVE** *Clubscene DCSRT 070*	47	1

ULTRASOUND
UK, male / female vocal / instrumental group (5 WEEKS) pos/wks

7 Mar 98		**BEST WISHES** *Nude NUD 33CD*	68	1
13 Jun 98		**STAY YOUNG** *Nude NUD 35CD1*	30	2
10 Apr 99		**FLOODLIT WORLD** *Nude NUD 41CD1*	39	2

ULTRAVOX (171 Top 500)
Ground-breaking British electro–rock quartet: Midge Ure (v/g) (replaced John Foxx in 1979), Billy Currie (k/syn), Chris Cross (b/syn), Warren Cann (d). Ex–Slik and Visage vocalist Ure was a driving force behind Band Aid hits, Live Aid and Nelson Mandela birthday concerts (142 WEEKS) pos/wks

5 Jul 80		**SLEEPWALK** *Chrysalis CHS 2441*	29	11
18 Oct 80		**PASSING STRANGERS** *Chrysalis CHS 2457*	57	4
17 Jan 81	●	**VIENNA** *Chrysalis CHS 2481*	2	14
28 Mar 81		**SLOW MOTION** *Island WIP 6691*	33	4
6 Jun 81	●	**ALL STOOD STILL** *Chrysalis CHS 2522*	8	10
22 Aug 81		**THE THIN WALL** *Chrysalis CHS 2540*	14	8
7 Nov 81		**THE VOICE** *Chrysalis CHS 2559*	16	12
25 Sep 82		**REAP THE WILD WIND** *Chrysalis CHS 2639*	12	9
27 Nov 82		**HYMN** *Chrysalis CHS 2657*	11	11
19 Mar 83		**VISIONS IN BLUE** *Chrysalis CHS 2676*	15	6
4 Jun 83		**WE CAME TO DANCE** *Chrysalis VOX 1*	18	7
11 Feb 84		**ONE SMALL DAY** *Chrysalis VOX 2*	27	6
19 May 84	●	**DANCING WITH TEARS IN MY EYES** *Chrysalis UV 1*	3	10
7 Jul 84		**LAMENT** *Chrysalis UV 2*	22	6
4 Aug 84		**DANCING WITH TEARS IN MY EYES (re–entry)** *Chrysalis UV 1*	74	1
25 Aug 84		**LAMENT (re–entry)** *Chrysalis UV 2*	73	1
20 Oct 84		**LOVE'S GREAT ADVENTURE** *Chrysalis UV 3*	12	9
27 Sep 86		**SAME OLD STORY** *Chrysalis UV 4*	31	4
22 Nov 86		**ALL FALL DOWN** *Chrysalis UV 5*	30	5
6 Feb 93		**VIENNA (re–issue)** *Chrysalis CDCHSS 3936*	13	4

UMBOZA
UK, male instrumental / production duo – Bryan Chamberlyn and Stuart Crichton (9 WEEKS) pos/wks

23 Sep 95		**CRY INDIA** *Positiva CDTIV 43*	19	4
20 Jul 96		**SUNSHINE** *Positiva CDTIV 47*	14	5

Piero UMILIANI
Italy, orchestra and chorus (8 WEEKS) pos/wks

30 Apr 77	●	**MAH NA MAH NA** *EMI International INT 530*	8	8

UNATION
UK, male / female vocal / instrumental group (3 WEEKS) pos/wks

5 Jun 93		**HIGHER AND HIGHER** *MCA MCSTD 1773*	42	2
7 Aug 93		**DO YOU BELIEVE IN LOVE** *MCA MCSTD 1796*	75	1

UNBELIEVABLE TRUTH
UK, male vocal / instrumental group (5 WEEKS) pos/wks

14 Feb 98		**HIGHER THAN REASON** *Virgin VSCDT 1676*	38	2
9 May 98		**SOLVED** *Virgin VSCDT 1684*	39	2
18 Jul 98		**SETTLE DOWN / DUNE SEA** *Virgin VSCDT 1697*	46	1

UNCANNY ALLIANCE
US, male / female vocal / instrumental duo (5 WEEKS) pos/wks

19 Dec 92		**I GOT MY EDUCATION** *A & M AM 0128*	39	5

UNCLE KRACKER
US, male vocalist – Matt Shafer (17 WEEKS) pos/wks

8 Sep 01	●	**FOLLOW ME** *Atlantic AT 0108CD*	3	17

UNCLE SAM
US, male vocalist (2 WEEKS) pos/wks

16 May 98		**I DON'T EVER WANT TO SEE YOU AGAIN** *Epic 6656382*	30	2

UNDERCOVER
UK, male vocal / instrumental group (29 WEEKS) pos/wks

15 Aug 92	●	**BAKER STREET** *PWL International PWL 239*	2	14
14 Nov 92	●	**NEVER LET HER SLIP AWAY** *PWL International PWL 255*	5	11
6 Feb 93		**I WANNA STAY WITH YOU** *PWL International PWCD 258*	28	3
14 Aug 93		**LOVESICK** *PWL International PWCD 271* [1]	62	1

[1] Undercover featuring John Matthews

UNDERTAKERS
UK, male vocal / instrumental group (1 WEEK) pos/wks

9 Apr 64		**JUST A LITTLE BIT** *Pye 7N 15607*	49	1

UNDERTONES
UK, male vocal / instrumental group (67 WEEKS) pos/wks

21 Oct 78		**TEENAGE KICKS** *Sire SIR 4007*	31	6
3 Feb 79		**GET OVER YOU** *Sire SIR 4010*	57	4
28 Apr 79		**JIMMY JIMMY** *Sire SIR 4015*	16	10
21 Jul 79		**HERE COMES THE SUMMER** *Sire SIR 4022*	34	6
20 Oct 79		**YOU'VE GOT MY NUMBER (WHY DON'T YOU USE IT?)** *Sire SIR 4024*	32	6
5 Apr 80	●	**MY PERFECT COUSIN** *Sire SIR 4038*	9	10
5 Jul 80		**WEDNESDAY WEEK** *Sire SIR 4042*	11	9
2 May 81		**IT'S GOING TO HAPPEN!** *Ardeck ARDS 8*	18	9
25 Jul 81		**JULIE OCEAN** *Ardeck ARDS 9*	41	5
9 Jul 83		**TEENAGE KICKS (re-issue)** *Ardeck ARDS 1*	60	2

UNDERWORLD
UK, male instrumental / vocal group (41 WEEKS) pos/wks

18 Dec 93		**SPIKEE / DOGMAN GO** *Junior Boy's Own JBO 17CD*	63	1
25 Jun 94		**DARK AND LONG** *Junior Boy's Own JBO 19CDS*	57	1
13 May 95		**BORN SLIPPY** *Junior Boy's Own JBO 29CDS*	52	2
18 May 96		**PEARL'S GIRL** *Junior Boy's Own JBO 38CDS1*	24	2
13 Jul 96	●	**BORN SLIPPY (re-mix)** *Junior Boy's Own JBO 44CDS*	2	16
9 Nov 96		**PEARL'S GIRL (re-issue)** *Junior Boy's Own JBO 45CDS1*	22	3
28 Dec 96		**BORN SLIPPY (re-entry of re-mix)** *Junior Boy's Own JBO 44CDS*	58	5
27 Mar 99		**PUSH UPSTAIRS** *Junior Boy's Own JBO 5005443*	12	4
5 Jun 99		**JUMBO** *Junior Boy's Own JBO 5007193*	21	2
28 Aug 99		**KING OF SNAKE** *Junior Boy's Own JBO 5008793*	17	3
2 Sep 00		**COWGIRL** *Junior Boy's Own JBO 5012513*	24	2

UNDISPUTED TRUTH
US, male / female vocal group (4 WEEKS) pos/wks

22 Jan 77		**YOU + ME = LOVE** *Warner Bros. K 16804*	43	4

U96
Germany, male producer – Alex Christiansen (7 WEEKS) pos/wks

29 Aug 92		**DAS BOOT** *M & G MAGS 28*	18	5
4 Jun 94		**INSIDE YOUR DREAMS** *Logic 74321209722*	44	1
29 Jun 96		**CLUB BIZARRE** *Urban 5750152*	70	1

UNION featuring the ENGLAND WORLD CUP SQUAD
UK / Holland, male instrumental group and UK, rugby team vocalists (7 WEEKS) pos/wks

12 Oct 91		**SWING LOW (RUN WITH THE BALL)** *Columbia 6575317*	16	7

UNION GAP featuring Gary PUCKETT
US, male vocal / instrumental group (47 WEEKS) pos/wks

17 Apr 68	★	**YOUNG GIRL** *CBS 3365*	1	17
7 Aug 68	●	**LADY WILLPOWER** *CBS 3551*	5	16
28 Aug 68		**WOMAN, WOMAN** *CBS 3110* [1]	48	1
15 Jun 74	●	**YOUNG GIRL (re-issue)** *CBS 8202* [1]	6	13

[1] Gary Puckett and the Union Gap

UNIQUE
US, male / female vocal / instrumental group (7 WEEKS) pos/wks

10 Sep 83		**WHAT I GOT IS WHAT YOU NEED** *Prelude A 3707*	27	7

UNIQUE 3
UK, male rap / DJ group (12 WEEKS) pos/wks

4 Nov 89		**THE THEME** *10 TEN 285*	61	3
14 Apr 90		**MUSICAL MELODY / WEIGHT FOR THE BASS** *10 TEN 298*	29	5
10 Nov 90		**RHYTHM TAKES CONTROL** *10 TEN 327* [1]	41	3
16 Nov 91		**NO MORE** *10 TEN 387*	74	1

[1] Unique 3 featuring Karin

UNIT FOUR PLUS TWO
UK, male vocal / instrumental group – lead vocal Peter Moules (29 WEEKS) pos/wks

13 Feb 64		**GREEN FIELDS** *Decca F 11821*	48	2
25 Feb 65	★	**CONCRETE AND CLAY** *Decca F 12071*	1	15
13 May 65		**(YOU'VE) NEVER BEEN IN LOVE LIKE THIS BEFORE** *Decca F 12144*	14	11
17 Mar 66		**BABY NEVER SAY GOODBYE** *Decca F 12333*	49	1

UNITED CITIZEN FEDERATION featuring Sarah BRIGHTMAN
UK, male production duo and UK, female vocalist (1 WEEK) pos/wks

14 Feb 98 **STARSHIP TROOPERS** *Coalition COLA 040CD*.......58 1

UNITED KINGDOM SYMPHONY *UK, orchestra (4 WEEKS)* pos/wks

27 Jul 85 **SHADES (THEME FROM THE CROWN PAINT TELEVISION COMMERCIAL)** *Food for Thought YUM 108*.......68 4

UNITONE – *See Laurel AITKEN and the UNITONE*

UNITONE ROCKERS featuring STEEL
UK, male vocal / instrumental group (1 WEEK) pos/wks

26 Jun 93 **CHILDREN OF THE REVOLUTION** *The Hit Label HLC 4*.......60 1

UNITY *UK, male / female vocal / instrumental group (2 WEEKS)* pos/wks

31 Aug 91 **UNITY** *Cardiac CNY 6*.......64 2

UNIVERSAL *Australia, male vocal group (6 WEEKS)* pos/wks

2 Aug 97 **ROCK ME GOOD** *London LONCD 397*.......19 4
18 Oct 97 **MAKE IT WITH YOU** *London LONCD 404*.......33 2

UNJUSTIFIED ANCIENTS OF M U – *See 1300 DRUMS featuring the UNJUSTIFIED ANCIENTS OF M U*

UNKLE *US / UK, male DJ / production duo – Josh Davis and James Lavelle (7 WEEKS)* pos/wks

20 Feb 99 ● **BE THERE** *Mo Wax MW 108CD1* [1].......8 6
17 Mar 01 **NARCO TOURISTS** *Soma SOMA 100CD* [2].......66 1

[1] Unkle featuring Ian Brown [2] Slam vs Unkle

UNO CLIO featuring Martine McCUTCHEON
UK, male instrumental group (1 WEEK) pos/wks

18 Nov 95 **ARE YOU MAN ENOUGH** *Avex UK AVEXCD 14*.......62 1

UNTOUCHABLES *US, male vocal / instrumental group (16 WEEKS)* pos/wks

6 Apr 85 **FREE YOURSELF** *Stiff BUY 221*.......26 11
27 Jul 85 **I SPY FOR THE FBI** *Stiff BUY 227*.......59 5

UP YER RONSON featuring Mary PEARCE
UK, male / female vocal / instrumental group (7 WEEKS) pos/wks

5 Aug 95 **LOST IN LOVE** *Hi-Life 5795572*.......27 3
30 Mar 96 **ARE YOU GONNA BE THERE** *Hi-Life 5763272*.......27 2
19 Apr 97 **I WILL BE RELEASED** *Hi-Life 5737352*.......32 2

Phil UPCHURCH COMBO
US, male instrumental group – Phil Upchurch – bass guitar (2 WEEKS) pos/wks

5 May 66 **YOU CAN'T SIT DOWN** *Sue WI 4005*.......39 2

UPSETTERS *Jamaica, male instrumental group (15 WEEKS)* pos/wks

4 Oct 69 ● **RETURN OF DJANGO / DOLLAR IN THE TEETH** *Upsetter US 301*.......5 15

UPSIDE DOWN *UK, male vocal group (16 WEEKS)* pos/wks

20 Jan 96 **CHANGE YOUR MIND** *World CDWORLD 1A*.......11 7
13 Apr 96 **EVERY TIME I FALL IN LOVE** *World CDWORLD 2A*.......18 3
8 Jun 96 **EVERY TIME I FALL IN LOVE (re-entry)** *World CDWORLD 2A*.......71 1
29 Jun 96 **NEVER FOUND A LOVE LIKE THIS BEFORE** *World CDWORLD 3A*.......19 3
23 Nov 96 **IF YOU LEAVE ME NOW** *World CDWORLD 4A*.......27 2

URBAN ALL STARS *UK, male producer – Norman Cook and US, male / female vocal / instrumental groups (2 WEEKS)* pos/wks

27 Aug 88 **IT BEGAN IN AFRICA** *Urban URB 23*.......64 2

URBAN BLUES PROJECT presents Michael PROCTER
US, male vocal / instrumental group (1 WEEK) pos/wks

10 Aug 96 **LOVE DON'T LIVE** *AM:PM 5817932*.......55 1

URBAN COOKIE COLLECTIVE
UK, male / female vocal / instrumental group (37 WEEKS) pos/wks

10 Jul 93 ● **THE KEY THE SECRET** *Pulse 8 CDLOSE 48*.......2 16
13 Nov 93 ● **FEELS LIKE HEAVEN** *Pulse 8 CDLOSE 55*.......5 9
19 Feb 94 **SAIL AWAY** *Pulse 8 CDLOSE 56*.......18 4
23 Apr 94 **HIGH ON A HAPPY VIBE** *Pulse 8 CDLOSE 60*.......31 3
15 Oct 94 **BRING IT ON HOME** *Pulse 8 CDLOSE 73*.......56 1
27 May 95 **SPEND THE DAY** *Pulse 8 CDLOSE 85*.......59 1
9 Sep 95 **REST OF MY LOVE** *Pulse 8 CDLOSE 93*.......67 1
16 Dec 95 **SO BEAUTIFUL** *Pulse 8 CDLOSE 100*.......68 1
24 Aug 96 **THE KEY THE SECRET (re-mix)** *Pulse 8 CDLOSE 109* [1].......52 1

[1] UCC

URBAN DISCHARGE featuring SHE
US, male / female vocal / instrumental group (1 WEEK) pos/wks

27 Jan 96 **WANNA DROP A HOUSE (ON THAT BITCH)** *MCA MCSTD 40020*.......51 1

URBAN HYPE *UK, male production / instrumental group – Robert Dibden and Mark Chitty (12 WEEKS)* pos/wks

11 Jul 92 ● **A TRIP TO TRUMPTON** *Faze 2 FAZE 5*.......6 8
17 Oct 92 **THE FEELING** *Faze 2 FAZE 10*.......67 1
9 Jan 93 **LIVING IN A FANTASY** *Faze 2 CDFAZE 13*.......57 3

URBAN SHAKEDOWN *UK / Italy, male DJ / production duo (8 WEEKS)* pos/wks

27 Jun 92 **SOME JUSTICE** *Urban Shakedown URBST 1*.......23 5
12 Sep 92 **BASS SHAKE** *Urban Shakedown URBST 2* [1].......59 2
10 Jun 95 **SOME JUSTICE (re-recording)** *Urban Shakedown URBCD 3* [2].......49 1

[1] Urban Shakedown featuring Mickey Finn [2] Urban Shakedown featuring DBO General

URBAN SOUL
UK / US, male / female vocal / production group (11 WEEKS) pos/wks

30 Mar 91 **ALRIGHT** *Cooltempo COOL 231*.......60 4
21 Sep 91 **ALRIGHT (re-mix)** *Cooltempo COOL 244*.......43 3
28 Mar 92 **ALWAYS** *Cooltempo COOL 251*.......41 3
13 Jun 98 **LOVE IS SO NICE** *VC Recordings VCRD 33*.......75 1

URBAN SPECIES *UK, male vocal / instrumental group (10 WEEKS)* pos/wks

12 Feb 94 **SPIRITUAL LOVE** *Talkin Loud TLKCD 45*.......35 4
16 Apr 94 **BROTHER** *Talkin Loud TLKCD 47*.......40 3
20 Aug 94 **LISTEN** *Talkin Loud TLKCD 50* [1].......47 2
6 Mar 99 **BLANKET** *Talkin Loud TLDD 39* [2].......56 1

[1] Urban Species featuring MC Solaar [2] Urban Species featuring Imogen Heap

Midge URE *UK, male vocalist (56 WEEKS)* pos/wks

12 Jun 82 ● **NO REGRETS** *Chrysalis CHS 2618*.......9 10
9 Jul 83 **AFTER A FASHION** *Musicfest FEST 1* [1].......39 4
14 Sep 85 ★ **IF I WAS** *Chrysalis URE 1*.......1 11
16 Nov 85 **THAT CERTAIN SMILE** *Chrysalis URE 2*.......28 4
8 Feb 86 **WASTELANDS** *Chrysalis URE 3*.......46 3
7 Jun 86 **CALL OF THE WILD** *Chrysalis URE 4*.......27 8
20 Aug 88 **ANSWERS TO NOTHING** *Chrysalis URE 5*.......49 4
19 Nov 88 **DEAR GOD** *Chrysalis URE 6*.......55 4
17 Aug 91 **COLD COLD HEART** *Arista 114555*.......17 7
25 May 96 **BREATHE** *Arista 74321371172*.......70 1

[1] Midge Ure and Mick Karn

See also SLIK; ULTRAVOX; RICH KIDS; VISAGE

URGE OVERKILL *US, male vocal / instrumental group (6 WEEKS)* pos/wks

21 Aug 93 **SISTER HAVANA** *Geffen GFSTD 51*.......67 1
16 Oct 93 **POSITIVE BLEEDING** *Geffen GFSTD 57*.......61 1
19 Nov 94 **GIRL YOU'LL BE A WOMAN SOON** *MCA MCSTD 2024*.......37 4

THE OFFICIAL UK SINGLES CHART 50TH ANNIVERSARY

1997

IN THE YEAR IN WHICH THE PRINCESS OF WALES DIED WHEN HER ARMOURED MERCEDES CRASHED IN A PARIS UNDERPASS, LABOUR WON THE BIGGEST ELECTION LANDSLIDE OF THE 20TH CENTURY, BRITISH RULE OF HONG KONG CAME TO AN END, AND THE PRINCESS DIANA TRIBUTE, 'CANDLE IN THE WIND 1997, BECAME THE WORLD'S BIGGEST SELLING SINGLE EVER, **ELTON JOHN** TELLS THE 'LOS ANGELES TIMES' ABOUT HOW THE SINGLE CAME ABOUT ...

"It all happened quickly. I got a call from Richard Branson, who said, 'You might have to get prepared to sing at the funeral,' but I really didn't know until Thursday of that week that I was definitely going to sing. I think it was a matter of protocol, whether everyone involved felt it was appropriate. When the coffin came into Westminster Abbey I cried and when it went out I cried, but the only time I came close to it during the song was at the beginning of the third verse. I just had to grit my teeth. I felt very much like a representative at that moment. It was an honour just to be invited to the funeral, but also to be able to sing that song. It's probably the biggest honour of my life. I don't think anything will ever match it for me. I was so touched by the way people reacted to Princess Diana's death... The way they waited 11 to 12 hours in the rain to sign the [memorial] books. Their dignity, their generosity, their genuine outpouring of grief. I've never seen anything like that. People say that's what it was like after the Second World War in England when people just got together and shared their emotions."

SINGLE OF THE YEAR 'I'll Be Missing You' Puff Daddy and Faith Evans (featuring 112)
ALBUM OF THE YEAR 'Spice' Spice Girls

URUSEI YATSURA
UK, male / female vocal / instrumental group (4 WEEKS) pos/wks

22 Feb 97 **STRATEGIC HAMLETS** *Che CHE 67CD* 64 1
28 Jun 97 **FAKE FUR** *Che CHE 70CD* 58 1
21 Feb 98 **HELLO TIGER** *Che CHE 75CD1* 40 1
6 Jun 98 **SLAIN BY ELF** *Che CHE 80CD1* 63 1

USA FOR AFRICA
US, male / female vocal charity ensemble, producer – Quincy Jones (9 WEEKS) pos/wks

13 Apr 85 ★ **WE ARE THE WORLD** *CBS USAID 1* ▲ 1 9

Soloists: Lionel Richie, Stevie Wonder, Paul Simon, Kenny Rogers, James Ingram, Tina Turner, Billy Joel, Michael Jackson, Diana Ross, Dionne Warwick, Willie Nelson, Al Jarreau, Bruce Springsteen, Kenny Loggins, Steve Perry, Daryl Hall, Huey Lewis, Cyndi Lauper, Kim Carnes, Bob Dylan, Ray Charles. Also credited: Dan Aykroyd, Harry Belafonte, Lindsey Buckingham, Sheila E, Bob Geldof, John Oates, Jackie Jackson, La Toya Jackson, Marlon Jackson, Randy Jackson, Tito Jackson, Waylon Jennings, The News, Bette Midler, Jeffrey Osborne, The Pointer Sisters, Smokey Robinson

USHER
US, male vocalist – Usher Raymond (45 WEEKS) pos/wks

18 Mar 95 **THINK OF YOU** *LaFace 74321269252* 70 1
31 Jan 98 ★ **YOU MAKE ME WANNA...** *LaFace 74321560652* ■ 1 12
2 May 98 **NICE & SLOW** *LaFace 74321579102* ▲ 24 5
2 May 98 **YOU MAKE ME WANNA... (re-entry)** *LaFace 74321560652* 72 1
3 Feb 01 ● **POP YA COLLAR** *LaFace 74321828692* 2 9
7 Jul 01 ● **U REMIND ME** *LaFace 74321863382* ▲ 3 9
20 Oct 01 ● **U GOT IT BAD** *Laface 74321898552* 5 8

US3
UK, male instrumental / production duo (15 WEEKS) pos/wks

10 Jul 93 **RIDDIM** *Blue Note CDCL 686* [1] 34 6
25 Sep 93 **CANTALOOP** *Blue Note CDCL 696* [2] 23 5
28 May 94 **I GOT IT GOIN' ON** *Blue Note CDCL 708* [3] 52 2
1 Mar 97 **COME ON EVERYBODY (GET DOWN)** *Blue Note CDCL 784* 38 2

[1] Us3 featuring Tukka Yoot [2] Us3 featuring Rahsaan [3] Us3 featuring Kobie Powell and Rahsaan

USURA
Italy, male / female vocal / instrumental group (15 WEEKS) pos/wks

23 Jan 93 ● **OPEN YOUR MIND** *Deconstruction 74321128042* 7 9
10 Jul 93 **SWEAT** *Deconstruction 74321154602* 29 3
6 Dec 97 **OPEN YOUR MIND 97 (re-mix)** *Malarky MLKD 4* [1] 21 3

[1] U.S.U.R.A.

UTAH SAINTS
UK, male instrumental / production duo – Jez Willis and Tim Garbutt (39 WEEKS) pos/wks

24 Aug 91 ● **WHAT CAN YOU DO FOR ME** *ffrr F 164* 10 11
6 Jun 92 ● **SOMETHING GOOD** *ffrr F 187* 4 9
8 May 93 ● **BELIEVE IN ME** *ffrr FCD 209* 8 6
17 Jul 93 **I WANT YOU** *ffrr FCD 213* 25 5
25 Jun 94 **I STILL THINK OF YOU** *ffrr FCD 225* 32 2
2 Sep 95 **OHIO** *ffrr FCD 264* 42 2
5 Feb 00 **LOVE SONG** *Echo ECSCD 83* 37 2
20 May 00 **FUNKY MUSIC (SHO NUFF TURNS ME ON)** *Echo ECSCD 96* 23 2

'Funky Music (Sho Nuff Turns Me On)' features uncredited vocal by Edwin Starr

U2
(44 Top 500) *Giants of contemporary rock: Bono (b. Paul Hewson) (v), The Edge (b. David Evans) (g), Adam Clayton (b), Larry Mullen Jr (d). Pollstar, which tracks revenues from US music tours, listed the band as the highest earners in 2001 with £78 million from 80 shows, a figure bettered only by The Rolling Stones in 1994 (254 WEEKS)* pos/wks

8 Aug 81 **FIRE** *Island WIP 6679* 35 6
17 Oct 81 **GLORIA** *Island WIP 6733* 55 4
3 Apr 82 **A CELEBRATION** *Island WIP 6770* 47 4
22 Jan 83 ● **NEW YEARS DAY** *Island WIP 6848* 10 8
2 Apr 83 **TWO HEARTS BEAT AS ONE** *Island IS 109* 18 5
15 Sep 84 ● **PRIDE (IN THE NAME OF LOVE)** *Island IS 202* 3 11
4 May 85 ● **THE UNFORGETTABLE FIRE** *Island IS 220* 6 6
28 Mar 87 ● **WITH OR WITHOUT YOU** *Island IS 319* ▲ 4 11
6 Jun 87 ● **I STILL HAVEN'T FOUND WHAT I'M LOOKING FOR** *Island IS 328* ▲ 6 11
12 Sep 87 ● **WHERE THE STREETS HAVE NO NAME** *Island IS 340* 4 6
26 Dec 87 **IN GOD'S COUNTRY (import)** *Island 7-99385* 48 4
1 Oct 88 ★ **DESIRE** *Island IS 400* 1 8
17 Dec 88 ● **ANGEL OF HARLEM** *Island IS 402* 9 6
15 Apr 89 ● **WHEN LOVE COMES TO TOWN** *Island IS 411* [1] 6 7
24 Jun 89 ● **ALL I WANT IS YOU** *Island IS 422* 4 6
2 Nov 91 ★ **THE FLY** *Island IS 500* ■ 1 5
14 Dec 91 **MYSTERIOUS WAYS** *Island IS 509* 13 7
14 Dec 91 **THE FLY (re-entry)** *Island IS 500* 62 1
7 Mar 92 ● **ONE** *Island IS 515* 7 6
20 Jun 92 **EVEN BETTER THAN THE REAL THING** *Island IS 525* 12 7
11 Jul 92 ● **EVEN BETTER THAN THE REAL THING (re-mix)** *Island REALU 2* 8 7
5 Dec 92 **WHO'S GONNA RIDE YOUR WILD HORSES** *Island IS 550* 14 8
4 Dec 93 ● **STAY (FARAWAY, SO CLOSE)** *Island CID 578* 4 9
17 Jun 95 ● **HOLD ME THRILL ME KISS ME KILL ME** *Atlantic A 7131CD* 2 14
15 Feb 97 ★ **DISCOTHEQUE** *Island CID 649* ■ 1 9
26 Apr 97 ● **STARING AT THE SUN** *Island CID 658* 3 6
17 May 97 **DISCOTHEQUE (re-entry)** *Island CID 649* 72 2
2 Aug 97 ● **LAST NIGHT ON EARTH** *Island CID 664* 10 4
6 Sep 97 **LAST NIGHT ON EARTH (re-entry)** *Island CID 664* 68 1
4 Oct 97 ● **PLEASE** *Island CID 673* 7 4
20 Dec 97 **IF GOD WILL SEND HIS ANGELS** *Island CID 684* 12 6
31 Oct 98 ● **SWEETEST THING** *Island CID 727* 3 13
21 Oct 00 ★ **BEAUTIFUL DAY** *Island CID 766* ■ 1 16
10 Feb 01 ● **STUCK IN A MOMENT YOU CAN'T GET OUT OF** *Island CID 770* 2 8
2 Jun 01 **NEW YEAR'S DUB** *Serious SERR 030CD* [2] 15 4
14 Jul 01 **NEW YEAR'S DUB (re-entry)** *Serious SERR 030CD* [2] 75 1
28 Jul 01 ● **ELEVATION** *Island CID 780* 3 8
1 Dec 01 ● **WALK ON** *Island CID 788* 5 5+

[1] U2 with BB King [2] Musique vs U2

'Stay (Faraway, So Close)' was listed with 'I've Got You Under My Skin' by Frank Sinatra with Bono, which was featured on many but not all formats

V

Verna V – *See HELIOTROPIC featuring Verna V*

VAGABONDS – *See Jimmy JAMES and the VAGABONDS*

Ricky VALANCE
UK, male vocalist – David Spencer (16 WEEKS) pos/wks

25 Aug 60 ★ **TELL LAURA I LOVE HER** *Columbia DB 4493* 1 16

Ritchie VALENS
US, male vocalist (5 WEEKS) pos/wks

6 Mar 59 **DONNA** *London HL 8803* 29 1
1 Aug 87 **LA BAMBA** *RCA PB 41435* 49 4

Caterina VALENTE with Werner Müller and the RIAS DANCE ORCHESTRA
France, female vocalist (14 WEEKS) pos/wks

19 Aug 55 ● **THE BREEZE AND I** *Polydor BM 6002* 5 14

Dickie VALENTINE
(337 Top 500) *UK's No.1 pre rock 'n' roll heart-throb in the mid 1950s, b. Richard Brice, 4 Nov 1929, London, d. 6 May 1971. Voted Top UK Male Vocalist while singing with the Ted Heath Orchestra and after going solo in 1954 (92 WEEKS)* pos/wks

20 Feb 53 **BROKEN WINGS** *Decca F 9954* 12 1
13 Mar 53 ● **ALL THE TIME AND EVERYWHERE** *Decca F 10038* 9 3
5 Jun 53 ● **IN A GOLDEN COACH (THERE'S A HEART OF GOLD)** *Decca F 10098* 7 1
5 Nov 54 **ENDLESS** *Decca F 10346* 19 1
17 Dec 54 ● **MISTER SANDMAN** *Decca F 10415* 5 12
17 Dec 54 ★ **THE FINGER OF SUSPICION** *Decca F 10394* [1] 1 15
18 Feb 55 ● **A BLOSSOM FELL** *Decca F 10430* 9 9

Date		Title	Pos	Wks
29 Apr 55		A BLOSSOM FELL (re-entry) *Decca F 10430*	18	1
3 Jun 55	●	I WONDER *Decca F 10493*	4	15
25 Nov 55	★	CHRISTMAS ALPHABET *Decca F 10628*	1	7
16 Dec 55		THE OLD PI-ANNA RAG *Decca F 10645*	15	5
7 Dec 56	●	CHRISTMAS ISLAND *Decca F 10798*	8	5
27 Dec 57		SNOWBOUND FOR CHRISTMAS *Decca F 10950*	28	1
13 Mar 59		VENUS *Pye Nixa 7N 15192*	28	1
3 Apr 59		VENUS (re-entry) *Pye Nixa 7N 15192*	25	1
17 Apr 59		VENUS (2nd re-entry) *Pye Nixa 7N 15192*	20	4
22 May 59		VENUS (3rd re-entry) *Pye Nixa 7N 15192*	25	1
19 Jun 59		VENUS (4th re-entry) *Pye Nixa 7N 15192*	28	1
23 Oct 59		ONE MORE SUNRISE (MORGEN) *Pye 7N 15221*	14	8

[1] Dickie Valentine with the Stargazers

VALENTINE BROTHERS *US, male vocal duo (1 WEEK)* pos/wks

23 Apr 83		MONEY'S TOO TIGHT (TO MENTION) *Energy NRG 1*	73	1

Joe VALINO *US, male vocalist (2 WEEKS)* pos/wks

18 Jan 57		THE GARDEN OF EDEN *HMV POP 283*	23	2

Frankie VALLI *US, male vocalist – Frankie Castellucio (52 WEEKS)* pos/wks

12 Dec 70		YOU'RE READY NOW *Philips 320226*	11	13
1 Feb 75	●	MY EYES ADORED YOU *Private Stock PVT 1* ▲	5	11
21 Jun 75		SWEARIN' TO GOD *Private Stock PVT 21*	31	5
17 Apr 76		FALLEN ANGEL *Private Stock PVT 51*	11	7
26 Aug 78	●	GREASE *RSO 012* ▲	3	14
23 Mar 91		GREASE - THE DREAM MIX *PWL / Polydor PO 136* [1]	47	2

[1] Frankie Valli, John Travolta and Olivia Newton-John

See also FOUR SEASONS

VAN DAHL – *See IAN VAN DAHL*

Mark VAN DALE with ENRICO
Belgium, male production duo (1 WEEK) pos/wks

3 Oct 98		WATER WAVE *Club Tools 0065815 CLU*	71	1

David VAN DAY *UK, male vocalist (3 WEEKS)* pos/wks

14 May 83		YOUNG AMERICANS TALKING *WEA DAY 1*	43	3

See also DOLLAR

VAN DER TOORN – *See PAPPA BEAR featuring VAN DER TOORN*

George VAN DUSEN *UK, male vocalist (4 WEEKS)* pos/wks

17 Dec 88		IT'S PARTY TIME AGAIN *Bri-Tone 7BT 001*	43	4

Paul VAN DYK *Germany, male DJ / producer (24 WEEKS)* pos/wks

17 May 97		FORBIDDEN FRUIT *Deviant DVNT 18CDR*	69	1
15 Nov 97		WORDS *Deviant DVNT 26CDS* [1]	54	1
5 Sep 98		FOR AN ANGEL *Deviant DVT 24CDS*	28	4
20 Nov 99		ANOTHER WAY / AVENUE *Deviant DVNT 35CDS*	13	5
8 Jan 00		ANOTHER WAY / AVENUE (re-entry) *Deviant DVNT 35CDS*	69	2
20 May 00	●	TELL ME WHY (THE RIDDLE) *Deviant DVNT 36CDS* [2]	7	5
2 Dec 00		WE ARE ALIVE *Deviant DVNT 38CDS*	15	6

[1] Paul Van Dyk featuring Toni Halliday [2] Paul Van Dyk featuring Saint Etienne

Leroy VAN DYKE *US, male vocalist (20 WEEKS)* pos/wks

4 Jan 62	●	WALK ON BY *Mercury AMT 1166*	5	17
26 Apr 62		BIG MAN IN A BIG HOUSE *Mercury AMT 1173*	34	3

Niels VAN GOGH *Germany, male producer (1 WEEK)* pos/wks

10 Apr 99		PULVERTURM *Logic 74321649192*	75	1

VAN HALEN *US / Holland, male vocal / instrumental group (51 WEEKS)* pos/wks

28 Jun 80		RUNNIN' WITH THE DEVIL *Warner Bros. HM 10*	52	3
4 Feb 84	●	JUMP *Warner Bros. W 9384* ▲	7	13
19 May 84		PANAMA *Warner Bros. W 9273*	61	2
5 Apr 86	●	WHY CAN'T THIS BE LOVE *Warner Bros. W 8740*	8	14
12 Jul 86		DREAMS *Warner Bros. W 8642*	62	2
6 Aug 88		WHEN IT'S LOVE *Warner Bros. W 7816*	28	7
1 Apr 89		FEELS SO GOOD *Warner Bros. W 7565*	63	1
22 Jun 91		POUNDCAKE *Warner Bros. W 0045*	74	1
19 Oct 91		TOP OF THE WORLD *Warner Bros. W 0066*	63	1
27 Mar 93		JUMP (LIVE) *Warner Bros. W 0155CD*	26	3
21 Jan 95		DON'T TELL ME *Warner Bros. W 0280CD*	27	2
1 Apr 95		CAN'T STOP LOVIN' YOU *Warner Bros. W 0288CD*	33	2

Armand VAN HELDEN *US, male DJ / producer (32 WEEKS)* pos/wks

8 Mar 97		THE FUNK PHENOMENA *ZYX ZYX 8523U8*	38	2
8 Nov 97		ULTRAFUNKULA *ffrr FCD 317*	46	1
6 Feb 99	★	YOU DON'T KNOW ME *ffrr FCD 357* [1] ■	1	11
1 May 99		FLOWERZ *ffrr FCD 361* [2]	18	5
15 May 99		YOU DON'T KNOW ME (re-entry) *ffrr FCD 357* [1]	72	1
20 May 00	●	KOOCHY *ffrr FCD 379*	4	7
3 Nov 01		WHY CAN'T YOU FREE SOME TIME *ffrr FCD 402*	34	2
15 Dec 01		YOU CAN'T CHANGE ME *Defected DFECT 41CDS* [3]	25	3+

[1] Armand Van Helden featuring Duane Harden [2] Armand Van Helden featuring Roland Clark [3] Roger Sanchez featuring Armand Van Helden and N'Dea Davenport

VAN TWIST
Zaire / Belgium, male / female vocal / instrumental group (2 WEEKS) pos/wks

16 Feb 85		SHAFT *Polydor POSP 729*	57	2

VANDELLAS – *See Martha REEVES and the VANDELLAS*

Luther VANDROSS (151 Top 500) *Superior soul singer / songwriter and producer, b. 20 Apr 1951, New York, US. Ex-David Bowie backing vocalist, who fronted chart group Change before embarking on a solo career that earned him 10 successive US platinum albums and a stack of awards (148 WEEKS)* pos/wks

19 Feb 83		NEVER TOO MUCH *Epic EPC A 3101*	44	6
26 Jul 86		GIVE ME THE REASON *Epic A 7288*	60	3
21 Feb 87		GIVE ME THE REASON (re-issue) *Epic 650216 7*	71	2
28 Mar 87		SEE ME *Epic LUTH 1*	60	4
11 Jul 87		I REALLY DIDN'T MEAN IT *Epic LUTH 3*	16	10
5 Sep 87		STOP TO LOVE *Epic LUTH 2*	24	7
7 Nov 87		SO AMAZING *Epic LUTH 4*	33	6
23 Jan 88		GIVE ME THE REASON (2nd re-issue) *Epic LUTH 5*	26	6
16 Apr 88		I GAVE IT UP (WHEN I FELL IN LOVE) *Epic LUTH 6*	28	5
9 Jul 88		THERE'S NOTHING BETTER THAN LOVE *Epic LUTH 7* [1]	72	1
8 Oct 88		ANY LOVE *Epic LUTH 8*	31	4
4 Feb 89		SHE WON'T TALK TO ME *Epic LUTH 9*	34	4
22 Apr 89		COME BACK *Epic LUTH 10*	53	3
28 Oct 89		NEVER TOO MUCH (re-mix) *Epic LUTH 12*	13	7
6 Jan 90		HERE AND NOW *Epic LUTH 13*	43	3
27 Apr 91		POWER OF LOVE - LOVE POWER *Epic 6568227*	46	5
18 Jan 92		THE RUSH *Epic 6577237*	53	3
15 Aug 92	●	THE BEST THINGS IN LIFE ARE FREE *Perspective PERSS 7400* [2]	2	13
22 May 93		LITTLE MIRACLES (HAPPEN EVERY DAY) *Epic 6590442*	28	3
18 Sep 93		HEAVEN KNOWS *Epic 6596522*	34	3
4 Dec 93		LOVE IS ON THE WAY *Epic 6599592*	38	2
17 Sep 94	●	ENDLESS LOVE *Epic 6608062* [3]	3	10
26 Nov 94		LOVE THE ONE YOU'RE WITH *Epic 6610612*	31	4
7 Jan 95		ENDLESS LOVE (re-entry) *Epic 6608062* [3]	70	2
4 Feb 95		ALWAYS AND FOREVER *Epic 6611942*	20	5
4 Feb 95		ENDLESS LOVE (2nd re-entry) *Epic 6608062* [3]	55	4
15 Apr 95		AIN'T NO STOPPING US NOW *Epic 6614242*	22	3
11 Nov 95		POWER OF LOVE - LOVE POWER (re-mix) *Epic 6625902*	31	3
16 Dec 95	●	THE BEST THINGS IN LIFE ARE FREE (re-mix) *A & M 5813092* [4]	7	7
23 Dec 95		EVERY YEAR EVERY CHRISTMAS *Epic 6627762*	43	2
12 Oct 96		YOUR SECRET LOVE *Epic 6638385*	14	5
28 Dec 96		I CAN MAKE IT BETTER *Epic 6640632*	44	2
20 Oct 01		TAKE YOU OUT *J 74321899442*	59	1

[1] Luther Vandross, duet with Gregory Hines [2] Luther Vandross and Janet Jackson with special guests BBD and Ralph Tresvant [3] Luther Vandross and Mariah Carey [4] Luther Vandross and Janet Jackson

VANESSA-MAE *Singapore, female instrumentalist – violin – Vanessa-Mae Vanakorn Nicholson (21 WEEKS)*

		pos	wks
28 Jan 95	TOCCATA AND FUGUE *EMI Classics MAE 8816812*	16	10
20 May 95	RED HOT *EMI CDMAE 2*	37	2
18 Nov 95	CLASSICAL GAS *EMI CDEM 404*	41	2
26 Oct 96	I'M A DOUN FOR LACK O' JOHNNIE (A LITTLE SCOTTISH FANTASY) *EMI CDMAE 3*	28	2
25 Oct 97	STORM *EMI CDEM 497*	54	1
20 Dec 97	I FEEL LOVE *EMI CDEM 553*	41	2
5 Dec 98	DEVIL'S TRILL / REFLECTION *EMI CDEM 530*	53	1
28 Jul 01	WHITE BIRD *EMI CDVAN 002*	66	1

VANGELIS *Greece, male instrumentalist – keyboards; Evangelos Papathanassiou (25 WEEKS)*

		pos	wks
9 May 81	CHARIOTS OF FIRE - TITLES *Polydor POSP 246* ▲	12	10
11 Jul 81	HEAVEN AND HELL, THIRD MOVEMENT (THEME FROM THE BBC-TV SERIES 'THE COSMOS') *BBC 1*	48	6
24 Apr 82	CHARIOTS OF FIRE - TITLES (re-entry) *Polydor POSP 246*	41	7
31 Oct 92	CONQUEST OF PARADISE *East West YZ 704*	60	2

See also JON and VANGELIS

VANILLA *UK, female vocal group (10 WEEKS)*

		pos	wks
22 Nov 97	NO WAY NO WAY *EMI CDEM 487*	75	1
27 Dec 97	NO WAY NO WAY (re-entry) *EMI CDEM 487*	14	7
23 May 98	TRUE TO US *EMI CDEM 509*	36	2

VANILLA FUDGE *US, male vocal / instrumental group (11 WEEKS)*

		pos	wks
9 Aug 67	YOU KEEP ME HANGIN' ON *Atlantic 584 123*	18	11

VANILLA ICE *US, male rapper – Robert Van Winkle (32 WEEKS)*

		pos	wks
24 Nov 90 ★	ICE ICE BABY *SBK SBK 18* ▲	1	13
2 Feb 91 ●	PLAY THAT FUNKY MUSIC *SBK SBK 20*	10	6
30 Mar 91	I LOVE YOU *SBK SBK 22*	45	5
29 Jun 91	ROLLIN' IN MY 5.0 *SBK SBK 27*	27	4
10 Aug 91	SATISFACTION *SBK SBK 29*	22	4

VANITY FARE *UK, male vocal / instrumental group (34 WEEKS)*

		pos	wks
28 Aug 68	I LIVE FOR THE SUN *Page One POF 075*	20	9
23 Jul 69 ●	EARLY IN THE MORNING *Page One POF 142*	8	12
27 Dec 69	HITCHIN' A RIDE *Page One POF 158*	16	13

Joe T VANNELLI PROJECT *Italy, male producer (2 WEEKS)*

		pos	wks
17 Jun 95	SWEETEST DAY OF MAY *Positiva CDTIV 36*	45	2

Randy VANWARMER
US, male vocalist – Randall Van Wormer (11 WEEKS)

		pos	wks
4 Aug 79 ●	JUST WHEN I NEEDED YOU MOST *Bearsville WIP 6516*	8	11

VAPORS *UK, male vocal / instrumental group (23 WEEKS)*

		pos	wks
9 Feb 80 ●	TURNING JAPANESE *United Artists BP 334*	3	13
5 Jul 80	NEWS AT TEN *United Artists BP 345*	44	4
11 Jul 81	JIMMIE JONES *Liberty BP 401*	44	6

VARDIS *UK, male vocal / instrumental group (4 WEEKS)*

		pos	wks
27 Sep 80	LET'S GO *Logo VAR 1*	59	4

Halo VARGA *US, male producer (1 WEEK)*

		pos	wks
9 Dec 00	FUTURE *Hooj Choons HOOJ 101CD*	67	1

VARIOUS ARTISTS (EPs and LPs) *(87 WEEKS)*

		pos	wks
15 Jun 56	CAROUSEL - ORIGINAL SOUNDTRACK (LP) *Capitol LCT 6105*	27	1
29 Jun 56 ●	ALL STAR HIT PARADE *Decca F 10752*	2	9
6 Jul 56	CAROUSEL - ORIGINAL SOUNDTRACK (LP) (re-entry) *Capitol LCT 6105*	26	1
26 Jul 57	ALL STAR HIT PARADE NO.2 *Decca F 10915*	15	7
9 Dec 89	THE FOOD CHRISTMAS EP *Food FOOD 23*	63	1
20 Jan 90	THE FURTHER ADVENTURES OF NORTH (EP) *Deconstruction PT 43372*	64	2
2 Nov 91	THE APPLE EP *Apple APP 1*	60	1
11 Jul 92	FOURPLAY (EP) *XL Recordings XLFP 1*	45	2
7 Nov 92	THE FRED EP *Heavenly HVN 19*	26	3
24 Apr 93	GIMME SHELTER (EP) *Food CDORDERA 1*	23	4
5 Jun 93	SUBPLATES VOLUME 1 (EP) *Suburban Base SUBBASE 24CD*	69	1
9 Oct 93	THE TWO TONE EP *2 Tone CHSTT 31*	30	3
4 Nov 95	HELP (EP) *Go! Discs GODCD 135*	51	2
16 Mar 96	NEW YORK UNDERCOVER (EP) *Uptown MCSTD 48002*	39	1
30 Mar 96	DANGEROUS MINDS (EP) *MCA MCSTD 48007*	35	1
29 Nov 97 ★	PERFECT DAY *Chrysalis CDNEED 01* ◆ ■	1	19
18 Apr 98	PERFECT DAY (re-entry) *Chrysalis CDNEED 01*	68	2
12 Sep 98	THE FULL MONTY-MONSTER MIX *RCA Victor 74321602582*	62	1
26 Sep 98	TRADE (EP) (DISC 2) *Tidy Trax TREP2*	75	1
10 Apr 99 ●	THANK ABBA FOR THE MUSIC *Epic ABCD 1*	4	13
25 Dec 99	IT'S ONLY ROCK 'N' ROLL *Universal TV 1566012*	19	8
26 Feb 00	IT'S ONLY ROCK 'N' ROLL (re-entry) *Universal TV 1566012*	67	2
17 Jun 00	PERFECT DAY (re-recording) *Chrysalis 8887840*	69	1
10 Nov 01	HARD BEAT EP 19 *Nukleuz NUKP 0369*	71	1

Tracks and artists on Carousel are as follows: Carousel Waltz - Orchestra conducted by Alfred Newman; You're a Queer One Julie Jordan - Barbara Ruick and Shirley Jones; Mister Snow - Barbara Ruick; If I Loved You - Shirley Jones and Gordon MacRae; June Is Busting Out All Over - Claramae Turner; Soliloquy - Gordon MacRae; Blow High Blow Low - Cameron Mitchell; When the Children Are Asleep - Robert Rounseville and Barbara Ruick; This Was a Real Nice Clambake - Barbara Ruick, Claramae Turner, Robert Rounseville and Cameron Mitchell; Stonecutters Cut It on Stone (There's Nothing So Bad for a Woman) - Cameron Mitchell; What's the Use of Wonderin' - Shirley Jones; You'll Never Walk Alone - Claramae Turner; If I Loved You - Gordon MacRae; You'll Never Walk Alone - Shirley Jones

*Tracks on All Star Hit Parade: Theme from The Threepenny Opera - Winifred Atwell; No Other Love - Dave King; My September Love - Joan Regan; A Tear Fell - Lita Roza; Out of Town - Dickie Valentine; It's Almost Tomorrow - David Whitfield. Tracks on All Star Hit Parade No.2: Around the World - Johnston Brothers; Puttin' On the Style - Billy Cotton; When I Fall In Love - Jimmy Young; A White Sport Coat - Max Bygraves; Freight Train - Beverley Sisters; Butterfly - Tommy Steele. Tracks on The Food Christmas EP: Like Princes Do - Crazyhead; I Don't Want That Kind of Love - Jesus Jones; Info Freako - Diesel Park West. Tracks on The Further Adventures of North (EP): Dream 17 - Annette; Carino 90 - T-Coy; The Way I Feel - Frequency 9; Stop This Thing - Dynasty of Two featuring Rowetta. Tracks on The Apple EP: Those Were the Days - Mary Hopkin; That's the Way God Planned It - Billy Preston; Sour Milk Sea - Jackie Lomax; Come and Get It - Badfinger. Tracks on Fourplay (EP): DJs Unite; Alright - Glide; Be Free - Noisy Factory; True Devotion - EQ. Tracks on The Fred EP: Deeply Dippy - Rockingbirds; Don't Talk Just Kiss - Flowered Up; I'm Too Sexy - Saint Etienne. Gimme Shelter EP was available on all four formats, each featuring an interview with the featured artist plus the following artists performing versions of Gimme Shelter: (cassette) Jimmy Somerville and Voice of the Beehive; Heaven 17; (12") Blue Pearl, 808 State and Robert Owens; Pop Will Eat Itself vs Gary Clail; Ranking Roger and the Mighty Diamonds; (CD) Thunder; Little Angels; Hawkwind and Sam Fox; (2nd CD) Cud with Sandie Shaw; Kingmaker; New Model Army and Tom Jones. Tracks on Subplates Volume 1 (EP): Style Warz - Son'z of a Loop Da Loop Era; Funky Dope Track - Q-Bass; The Chopper - DJ Hype; Look No Further - Run Tings. Tracks on The Two Tone EP: Gangsters - Special AKA; The Prince - Madness; On My Radio - Selecter; Tears of a Clown - Beat. Tracks on Help (EP): Lucky - Radiohead; 50ft Queenie (Live) PJ Harvey; Momentum - Guru featuring Big Shug; an untitled piece of incidental music. Tracks on New York Undercover (EP): Tell Me What You Like - Guy; Dom Perignon - Little Shawn; I Miss You - Monifah; Jeeps, Lex Coups, Bimax & Menz - Lost Boys. Tracks on Dangerous Minds (EP): Curiosity - Aaron Hall; Gin & Dance - De Vante; It's Alright - Sista featuring Craig Mack. Artists on Perfect Day are as follows: BBC Symphony Orchestra and Andrew Davis, Bono (U2), Boyzone, Brett Anderson (Suede), Brodsky Quartet, Burning Spear, Courtney Pine, David Bowie, Dr John, Elton John, Emmylou Harris, Evan Dando (Lemonheads), Gabrielle, Heather Small (M People), Huey (Fun Lovin' Criminals), Ian Broudie (Lightning Seeds), Joan Armatrading, Laurie Anderson, Lesley Garrett, Lou Reed, Robert Cray, Shane McGowan, Sheona White, Skye (Morcheeba), Suzanne Vega, Tammy Wynette, Thomas Allen, Tom Jones, Visual Ministry Orchestra. Tracks on The Full-Monty Monster Mix (medley): You Sexy Thing - Hot Chocolate; Hot Stuff - Donna Summer; You Can Leave Your Hat On - Tom Jones. CD also has a full version of 'You Can Leave Your Hat On' by Tom Jones and 'The Stripper' by David Rose. Tracks on Trade (EP) (disc 2): Put Your House in Order - Steve Thomas; The Dawn - Tony De Vit. Tracks on 'Thank ABBA For The Music' EP: 'Take A Chance On Me', 'Dancing Queen', 'Mamma Mia' and 'Thank You For The Music'- artists - Steps, Tina Cousins, Cleopatra, B*Witched and Billie. Artists on 'It's Only Rock 'n' Roll': Keith Richards, Kid Rock, Mary J Blige, Kelly Jones of Stereophonics, Jon Bon Jovi, Kéllé Bryan, Jay Kay of Jamiroquai, Ozzy Osbourne, Womack and Womack, Lionel Richie, Bonnie Raitt, Dolores O'Riordan of the Cranberries,*

James Brown, Spice Girls (minus Geri), Mick Jagger, Robin Williams, Jackson Browne, Iggy Pop, Chrissie Hynde, Skin of Skunk Anansie, Annie Lennox, Mark Owen, Natalie Imbruglia, Huey of Fun Lovin' Criminals, Dina Carroll, Gavin Rossdale of Bush, BB King, Joe Cocker, The Corrs, Steve Cradock and Simon Fowler of Ocean Colour Scene, Ronan Keating, Ray Barretto, Herbie Hancock, Francis Rossi and Rick Parfitt of Status Quo, S Club 7 and Eric Idle

VARIOUS ARTISTS (MONTAGES) *(31 WEEKS)*

			pos	wks
17 May 80		**CALIBRE CUTS** *Calibre CAB 502*	75	2
25 Nov 89		**DEEP HEAT '89** *Deep Heat DEEP 10*	12	11
3 Mar 90	●	**THE BRITS 1990** *RCA PB 43565*	2	7
28 Apr 90		**THE SIXTH SENSE** *Deep Heat DEEP 12*	49	2
10 Nov 90		**TIME TO MAKE THE FLOOR BURN** *Megabass MEGAX 1*	16	9

The following tracks are sampled: Calibre Cuts: Big Apples Rock - Black Ivory; Don't Hold Back - Chanson; The River Drive - Jupiter Beyond; Dancing in the Disco - LAX; Mellow Mellow Right On - Lowrell; Pata Pata - Osibisa; I Like It - Players Association; We Got the Funk - Positive Force; Holdin' On - Tony Rallo and the Midnight Band; Can You Feel the Force - Real Thing; Miami Heatwave - Seventh Avenue; Rappers Delight - Sugarhill Gang; Que Tal America - Two Man Sound; Remakes by session musicians: Ain't No Stoppin' Us Now, Bad Girls, We Are Family. Deep Heat '89 (credited to Latino Rave): Pump Up the Jam - Technotronic; Stakker Humanoid - Humanoid; A Day in the Life - Black Riot; Work it to the Bone - LNR; I Can Make U Dance - DJ 'Fast' Eddie; Voodoo Ray - A Guy Called Gerald; Numero Uno - Starlight; Bango (To the Batmobile) - Todd Terry; Break 4 Love - Raze; Don't Scandalize Mine - Sugar Bear. The Brits 1990: Street Tuff - Double Trouble and the Rebel MC; Voodoo Ray - A Guy Called Gerald; Theme From S-Express - S-Express; Hey DJ I Can't Dance to That Music You're Playing - Beatmasters; Eve of the War - Jeff Wayne; Pacific State - 808 State; We Call It Acieed - D Mob; Got to Keep On - Cookie Crew. The Sixth Sense (credited to Latino Rave): Get Up - Technotronic; The Magic Number - De La Soul; G'Ding G'Ding (Do Wanna Wanna) - Anna G; Show 'M the Bass - MC Miker G; Turn It Out (Go Base) - Rob Base; Eve of the War (War of the Worlds) - Project D; Moments In Love - 2 to the Power.Time to Make the Floor Burn (credited to Megabass): Do This My Way - Kid 'N' Play; Street Tuff - Double Trouble and the Rebel MC; Sex 4 Daze - Lake Eerie; Ride On Time - Black Box; Make My Body Rock - Jomanda; Don't Miss the Partyline - Bizz Nizz; Pump Pump It Up - Hypnotek; Big Fun - Inner City; Pump That Body - Mr Lee; Pump Up the Jam - Technotronic; This Beat Is Technotronic - Technotronic; Get Busy - Mr Lee; Touch Me - 49ers; Thunderbirds Are Go - FAB

Junior VASQUEZ *US, male DJ / producer (5 WEEKS)*

			pos	wks
15 Jul 95		**GET YOUR HANDS OFF MY MAN!** *Positiva CDTIV 37*	22	3
31 Aug 96		**IF MADONNA CALLS** *Multiply CDMULTY 13*	24	2

Elaine VASSELL – See *BEATMASTERS*

VAST *Australia, male vocal / instrumental group (1 WEEK)*

			pos	wks
16 Sep 00		**FREE** *Mushroom MUSH 79CDS*	55	1

Sven VATH *Germany, male DJ / producer (5 WEEKS)*

			pos	wks
24 Jul 93		**L'ESPERANZA** *Eye Q YZ 757*	63	2
6 Nov 93		**AN ACCIDENT IN PARADISE** *Eye Q YZ 778CD*	57	2
22 Oct 94		**HARLEQUIN - THE BEAUTY AND THE BEAST** *Eye Q YZ 857*	72	1

Frankie VAUGHAN (61 Top 500) *High-kicking 50s heart-throb vocalist, b. Frank Abelson, 3 Feb 1928, Liverpool, UK, d. 17 Sep 1999. This variety-show veteran, who received an OBE in 1965 for his charity work, was one of the most popular performers of the 1950s (232 WEEKS)*

			pos	wks
29 Jan 54		**ISTANBUL (NOT CONSTANTINOPLE)** *HMV B 10599* [1]	11	1
28 Jan 55		**HAPPY DAYS AND LONELY NIGHTS** *HMV B 10783*	12	3
22 Apr 55		**TWEEDLE DEE** *Philips PB 423*	17	1
2 Dec 55		**SEVENTEEN** *Philips PB 511*	18	3
3 Feb 56		**MY BOY FLAT TOP** *Philips PB 544*	20	2
9 Nov 56	●	**THE GREEN DOOR** *Philips PB 640*	2	15
11 Jan 57	★	**THE GARDEN OF EDEN** *Philips PB 660*	1	13
4 Oct 57	●	**MAN ON FIRE / WANDERIN' EYES** *Philips PB 729*	6	12
1 Nov 57	●	**GOT-TA HAVE SOMETHING IN THE BANK, FRANK** *Philips PB 751* [2]	8	11
20 Dec 57	●	**KISSES SWEETER THAN WINE** *Philips PB 775*	8	11
7 Mar 58		**CAN'T GET ALONG WITHOUT YOU / WE ARE NOT ALONE** *Philips PB 793*	11	6
9 May 58	●	**KEWPIE DOLL** *Philips PB 825*	10	12
1 Aug 58		**WONDERFUL THINGS** *Philips PB 834*	22	3
12 Sep 58		**WONDERFUL THINGS (re-entry)** *Philips PB 834*	27	3
10 Oct 58		**AM I WASTING MY TIME ON YOU** *Philips PB 865*	25	2
9 Jan 59		**AM I WASTING MY TIME ON YOU (re-entry)** *Philips PB 865*	27	2
30 Jan 59		**THAT'S MY DOLL** *Philips PB 895*	28	2
1 May 59	●	**COME SOFTLY TO ME** *Philips PB 913* [2]	9	9
24 Jul 59	●	**THE HEART OF A MAN** *Philips PB 930*	5	14
18 Sep 59		**WALKIN' TALL** *Philips PB 931*	28	1
2 Oct 59		**WALKIN' TALL (re-entry)** *Philips PB 931*	29	1
29 Jan 60		**WHAT MORE DO YOU WANT** *Philips PB 985*	25	2
22 Sep 60		**KOOKIE LITTLE PARADISE** *Philips PB 1054*	31	5
27 Oct 60		**MILORD** *Philips PB 1066*	34	6
9 Nov 61	★	**TOWER OF STRENGTH** *Philips PB 1195*	1	13
1 Feb 62		**DON'T STOP - TWIST!** *Philips 1219*	22	7
27 Sep 62		**HERCULES** *Philips 326542 BF*	42	4
24 Jan 63	●	**LOOP DE LOOP** *Philips 326566 BF*	5	12
20 Jun 63		**HEY MAMA** *Philips BF 1254*	21	9
4 Jun 64		**HELLO, DOLLY!** *Philips BF 1339*	18	11
11 Mar 65		**SOMEONE MUST HAVE HURT YOU A LOT** *Philips BF 1394*	46	1
23 Aug 67	●	**THERE MUST BE A WAY** *Columbia DB 8248*	7	21
15 Nov 67		**SO TIRED** *Columbia DB 8298*	21	9
28 Feb 68		**NEVERTHELESS** *Columbia DB 8354*	29	5

[1] Frankie Vaughan with the Peter Knight Singers [2] Frankie Vaughan and the Kaye Sisters

Malcolm VAUGHAN (278 Top 500) *Arguably the last of the hitmaking big-voiced tenors, b. Malcolm Thomas, 1930, Glamorgan, Wales. He was the straight man in a comedy duo with Kenny Earle, while enjoying his enviable run of UK ballad hits (at the height of the rock 'n' roll explosion) (106 WEEKS)*

			pos	wks
1 Jul 55	●	**EV'RY DAY OF MY LIFE** *HMV B 10874*	5	16
27 Jan 56		**WITH YOUR LOVE** *HMV POP 130* [1]	20	1
10 Feb 56		**WITH YOUR LOVE (re-entry)** *HMV POP 130* [1]	18	1
2 Mar 56		**WITH YOUR LOVE (2nd re-entry)** *HMV POP 130* [1]	20	1
26 Oct 56		**ST. THERESE OF THE ROSES** *HMV POP 250*	27	1
16 Nov 56	●	**ST. THERESE OF THE ROSES (re-entry)** *HMV POP 250*	3	19
12 Apr 57		**THE WORLD IS MINE** *HMV POP 303*	30	1
3 May 57		**THE WORLD IS MINE (re-entry)** *HMV POP 303*	29	2
10 May 57		**CHAPEL OF THE ROSES** *HMV POP 325*	13	8
31 May 57		**THE WORLD IS MINE (2nd re-entry)** *HMV POP 303*	26	1
29 Nov 57	●	**MY SPECIAL ANGEL** *HMV POP 419*	3	14
21 Mar 58		**TO BE LOVED** *HMV POP 459* [2]	14	12
17 Oct 58	●	**MORE THAN EVER (COME PRIMA)** *HMV POP 538* [2]	5	14
27 Feb 59		**WAIT FOR ME / WILLINGLY** *HMV POP 590*	28	1
13 Mar 59		**WAIT FOR ME (re-entry)** *HMV POP 590*	13	14

[1] Malcolm Vaughan with the Peter Knight Singers [2] Malcolm Vaughan with the Michael Sammes Singers

Norman VAUGHAN *UK, male vocalist (5 WEEKS)*

			pos	wks
17 May 62		**SWINGING IN THE RAIN** *Pye 7N 15438*	34	5

Sarah VAUGHAN *US, female vocalist (34 WEEKS)*

			pos	wks
27 Sep 57		**PASSING STRANGERS** *Mercury MT 164* [1]	22	2
11 Sep 59	●	**BROKEN HEARTED MELODY** *Mercury AMT 1057*	7	13
29 Dec 60		**LET'S / SERENATA** *Columbia DB 4542*	37	3
2 Feb 61		**LET'S / SERENATA (re-entry)** *Columbia DB 4542*	47	1
12 Mar 69		**PASSING STRANGERS (re-issue)** *Mercury MF 1082* [1]	20	15

[1] Billy Eckstine and Sarah Vaughan

Billy VAUGHN and his Orchestra *US, orchestra and chorus (8 WEEKS)*

			pos	wks
27 Jan 56		**THE SHIFTING WHISPERING SANDS PART 1** *London HLD 8205* [1]	20	1
23 Mar 56		**THEME FROM 'THE THREEPENNY OPERA'** *London HLD 8238*	12	7

[1] Billy Vaughn Orchestra and Chorus, narration by Ken Nordene

VDC – See *BLAST featuring VDC*

VEBA – See *RAE & CHRISTIAN featuring VEBA*

Bobby VEE (190 Top 500)

Early 1960s teen idol, b. Robert Velline, 30 Apr 1943, North Dakota, US. This photogenic, Buddy Holly-influenced teenaged vocalist (whose backing band once included Bob Dylan) was rarely away from the UK or US charts in the pre-Beat Boom years (134 WEEKS) pos/wks

Date		Title / Label	pos	wks
19 Jan 61	●	**RUBBER BALL** *London HLG 9255*	4	11
13 Apr 61	●	**MORE THAN I CAN SAY / STAYIN' IN** *London HLG 9316*	4	16
3 Aug 61	●	**HOW MANY TEARS** *London HLG 9389*	10	13
26 Oct 61	●	**TAKE GOOD CARE OF MY BABY** *London HLG 9438* ▲	3	16
21 Dec 61	●	**RUN TO HIM** *London HLG 9470*	6	15
8 Mar 62		**PLEASE DON'T ASK ABOUT BARBARA** *Liberty LIB 55419*	29	9
7 Jun 62	●	**SHARING YOU** *Liberty LIB 55451*	10	13
27 Sep 62		**A FOREVER KIND OF LOVE** *Liberty LIB 10046*	13	19
7 Feb 63	●	**THE NIGHT HAS A THOUSAND EYES** *Liberty LIB 10069*	3	12
20 Jun 63		**BOBBY TOMORROW** *Liberty LIB 55530*	21	10

'Staying In' listed with 'More Than I Can Say' from 13 Apr to 4 May 1961. It peaked at No.13

Louie VEGA and Marc ANTHONY

US, male vocal / instrumental duo (4 WEEKS) pos/wks

Date		Title / Label	pos	wks
5 Oct 91		**RIDE ON THE RHYTHM** *Atlantic A 7602* [1]	71	1
23 May 92		**RIDE ON THE RHYTHM (re-issue)** *Atlantic A 7486*	70	1
31 Jan 98		**RIDE ON THE RHYTHM (re-mix)** *Perfecto PERF 151CD1* [2]	36	2

[1] Little Louie Vega and Marc Anthony [2] Little Louie and Mark Anthony

See also LIL MO' YIN YANG

Suzanne VEGA

US, female vocalist (52 WEEKS) pos/wks

Date		Title / Label	pos	wks
18 Jan 86		**SMALL BLUE THING** *A & M AM 294*	65	3
22 Mar 86		**MARLENE ON THE WALL** *A & M AM 309*	21	9
7 Jun 86		**LEFT OF CENTER** *A & M AM 320* [1]	32	9
23 May 87		**LUKA** *A & M VEGA 1*	23	8
18 Jul 87		**TOM'S DINER** *A & M VEGA 2*	58	3
19 May 90		**BOOK OF DREAMS** *A & M AM 559*	66	1
28 Jul 90	●	**TOM'S DINER (re-mix)** *A & M AM 592* [2]	2	10
22 Aug 92		**IN LIVERPOOL** *A & M AM 0029*	52	2
24 Oct 92		**99.9 ºF** *A & M AM 0085*	46	2
19 Dec 92		**BLOOD MAKES NOISE** *A & M AM 0112*	60	3
6 Mar 93		**WHEN HEROES GO DOWN** *A & M AMCD 0158*	58	1
22 Feb 97		**NO CHEAP THRILL** *A & M 5818692*	40	1

[1] Suzanne Vega featuring Joe Jackson [2] DNA featuring Suzanne Vega

Tata VEGA

US, female vocalist (4 WEEKS) pos/wks

Date		Title / Label	pos	wks
26 May 79		**GET IT UP FOR LOVE / I JUST KEEP THINKING ABOUT YOU BABY** *Motown TMG 1140*	52	4

VEGAS

UK, male vocal / instrumental duo (10 WEEKS) pos/wks

Date		Title / Label	pos	wks
19 Sep 92		**POSSESSED** *RCA 74321110437*	32	4
28 Nov 92		**SHE** *RCA 74321124657*	43	4
3 Apr 93		**WALK INTO THE WIND** *RCA 74321122462*	65	2

Rosie VELA

US, female vocalist (7 WEEKS) pos/wks

Date		Title / Label	pos	wks
17 Jan 87		**MAGIC SMILE** *A & M AM 369*	27	7

Wil VELOZ – *See LOS DEL MAR featuring Wil VELOZ*

VELVELETTES

US, female vocal group (7 WEEKS) pos/wks

Date		Title / Label	pos	wks
31 Jul 71		**THESE THINGS WILL KEEP ME LOVING YOU** *Tamla Motown TMG 780*	34	7

VELVET UNDERGROUND

UK / US, male / female vocal / instrumental group (1 WEEK) pos/wks

Date		Title / Label	pos	wks
12 Mar 94		**VENUS IN FURS** *Sire W 0224CD*	71	1

VELVETS

US, male vocal group (2 WEEKS) pos/wks

Date		Title / Label	pos	wks
11 May 61		**THAT LUCKY OLD SUN** *London HLU 9328*	46	1
17 Aug 61		**TONIGHT (COULD BE THE NIGHT)** *London HLU 9372*	50	1

VENGABOYS (308 Top 500)

Hungary / Trinidad / Brazil / Holland, male / female vocal / production dance-pop troupe formed in 1992 by Spanish DJs Danski and Delmundo. In 1996 they added singers / dancers Kim, Robin (replaced by Yorick in 1999), Roy and Denice to front group. First Netherlands-based act to score six successive Top 5 singles, selling more than two million in the UK in 12 months (99 WEEKS) pos/wks

Date		Title / Label	pos	wks
28 Nov 98	●	**UP AND DOWN** *Positiva CDTIV 105*	4	15
13 Mar 99	●	**WE LIKE TO PARTY! (THE VENGABUS)** *Positiva CDTIV 108*	3	14
26 Jun 99	★	**BOOM, BOOM, BOOM, BOOM!!** *Positiva CDTIV 114* ■	1	15
11 Sep 99		**WE'RE GOING TO IBIZA (import)** *Jive 550422*	69	1
18 Sep 99	★	**WE'RE GOING TO IBIZA!** *Positiva CDTIV 119* ■	1	12
18 Dec 99	●	**KISS (WHEN THE SUN DON'T SHINE)** *Positiva CDTIV 122*	3	18
11 Mar 00	●	**SHALALA LALA** *Positiva CDTIV 126*	5	10
8 Jul 00	●	**UNCLE JOHN FROM JAMAICA** *Positiva CDTIV 135*	6	7
14 Oct 00		**CHEEKAH BOW BOW (THAT COMPUTER SONG)** *Positiva CDTIV 142*	19	5
24 Feb 01		**FOREVER AS ONE** *Positiva CDTIV 148*	28	2

VENT 414

UK, male vocal / instrumental group (1 WEEK) pos/wks

Date		Title / Label	pos	wks
28 Sep 96		**FIXER** *Polydor 5753292*	71	1

VENTURES

US, male instrumental group (31 WEEKS) pos/wks

Date		Title / Label	pos	wks
8 Sep 60	●	**WALK DON'T RUN** *Top Rank JAR 417*	8	13
1 Dec 60	●	**PERFIDIA** *London HLG 9232*	4	13
9 Mar 61		**RAM-BUNK-SHUSH** *London HLG 9292*	45	1
11 May 61		**LULLABY OF THE LEAVES** *London HLG 9344*	43	4

VERACOCHA

Holland, male production duo (4 WEEKS) pos/wks

Date		Title / Label	pos	wks
15 May 99		**CARTE BLANCHE** *Positiva CDTIV 110*	22	4

See also Ferry CORSTEN; GOURYELLA; MOONMAN; SYSTEM F

Al VERLAINE – *See PING PING and Al VERLAINE*

VERNONS GIRLS

UK, female vocal group (31 WEEKS) pos/wks

Date		Title / Label	pos	wks
17 May 62		**LOVER PLEASE** *Decca F 11450*	16	9
23 Aug 62		**LOVER PLEASE (re-entry) / YOU KNOW WHAT I MEAN** *Decca F 11450*	39	7
6 Sep 62		**LOCO-MOTION** *Decca F 11495*	47	1
18 Oct 62		**YOU KNOW WHAT I MEAN (re-entry)** *Decca F 11450*	37	3
15 Nov 62		**YOU KNOW WHAT I MEAN (2nd re-entry)** *Decca F 11450*	50	1
3 Jan 63		**FUNNY ALL OVER** *Decca F 11549*	31	8
18 Apr 63		**DO THE BIRD** *Decca F 11629*	50	1
2 May 63		**DO THE BIRD (re-entry)** *Decca F 11629*	44	1

'You Know What I Mean' was not coupled with 'Lover Please' on the chart of 23 Aug 1962, but both sides of this record were listed for the following six weeks

VERNON'S WONDERLAND

Germany, male producer – Matthias Hoffmann (1 WEEK) pos/wks

Date		Title / Label	pos	wks
25 May 96		**VERNON'S WONDERLAND** *Eye-Q Classics EYECL 004CD*	59	1

VERTICAL HORIZON

US, male vocal / instrumental group (2 WEEKS) pos/wks

Date		Title / Label	pos	wks
26 Aug 00		**EVERYTHING YOU WANT** *RCA 74321748692* ▲	42	2

VERUCA SALT

US, male / female vocal / instrumental group (5 WEEKS) pos/wks

Date		Title / Label	pos	wks
2 Jul 94		**SEETHER** *Scared Hitless FRET 003CD*	61	1
3 Dec 94		**SEETHER (re-issue)** *Hi-Rise FLATSDG 12*	73	1
4 Feb 95		**NUMBER ONE BLIND** *Hi-Rise FLATSCD 16*	68	1
22 Feb 97		**VOLCANO GIRLS** *Outpost OPRCD 22197*	56	1
30 Aug 97		**BENJAMIN** *Outpost OPRCD 22261*	75	1

VERVE

UK, male vocal / instrumental group (50 WEEKS) pos/wks

Date		Title / Label	pos	wks
4 Jul 92		**SHE'S A SUPERSTAR** *Hut HUT 16*	66	1
22 May 93		**BLUE** *Hut HUTCD 29*	69	1
13 May 95		**THIS IS MUSIC** *Hut HUTCD 54*	35	3
24 Jun 95		**ON YOUR OWN** *Hut HUTCD 55*	28	2
30 Sep 95		**HISTORY** *Hut HUTCD 59*	24	3
28 Jun 97	●	**BITTER SWEET SYMPHONY** *Hut HUTDG 82*	2	11

13 Sep 97 ★ THE DRUGS DON'T WORK *Hut HUTDG 88* ■ 1 12
6 Dec 97 ● LUCKY MAN *Hut HUTDG 92* 7 13
3 Jan 98 BITTER SWEET SYMPHONY (re-entry) *Hut HUTDG 82* 70 2
3 Jan 98 THE DRUGS DON'T WORK (re-entry) *Hut HUTDG 88* 66 1
30 May 98 SONNET (import) *Hut 8950752* 74 1

A VERY GOOD FRIEND OF MINE *Italy, male / female vocal / production / instrumental group (1 WEEK)* pos/wks

3 Jul 99 JUST ROUND *Positiva CDTIV 109* 55 1

VIBRATIONS – *See Tony JACKSON and the VIBRATIONS*

VIBRATORS *UK, male vocal / instrumental group (8 WEEKS)* pos/wks

18 Mar 78 AUTOMATIC LOVER *Epic EPC 6137* 35 5
17 Jun 78 JUDY SAYS (KNOCK YOU IN THE HEAD) *Epic EPC 6393* 70 3

VICE SQUAD *UK, male / female vocal / instrumental group (1 WEEK)* pos/wks

13 Feb 82 OUT OF REACH *Zonophone Z 26* 68 1

VICIOUS CIRCLES *UK, male producer – Simon Berry (1 WEEK)* pos/wks

16 Dec 00 VICIOUS CIRCLES *Platipus PLATCD 82* 68 1

See also POLTERGEIST

VICIOUS PINK *UK, male / female vocal / instrumental duo (4 WEEKS)* pos/wks

15 Sep 84 CCCAN'T YOU SEE *Parlophone R 6074* 67 4

Mike VICKERS – *See Kenny EVERETT*

Maria VIDAL *US, female vocalist (13 WEEKS)* pos/wks

24 Aug 85 BODY ROCK *EMI America EA 189* 11 13

VIDEO KIDS *Holland, male / female vocal duo (1 WEEK)* pos/wks

5 Oct 85 WOODPECKERS FROM SPACE *Epic A 6504* 72 1

VIDEO SYMPHONIC *UK, orchestra (3 WEEKS)* pos/wks

24 Oct 81 THE FLAME TREES OF THIKA *EMI EMI 5222* 42 3

VIENNA PHILHARMONIC ORCHESTRA *Austria, orchestra - conducted by Aram Khachturian (14 WEEKS)* pos/wks

18 Dec 71 THEME FROM 'THE ONEDIN LINE' *Decca F 13259* 15 14

VIEW FROM THE HILL *UK, male / female vocal / instrumental group (6 WEEKS)* pos/wks

19 Jul 86 NO CONVERSATION *EMI EMI 5565* 58 3
21 Feb 87 I'M NO REBEL *EMI EM 5580* 59 3

VIKKI *UK, female vocalist (3 WEEKS)* pos/wks

4 May 85 LOVE IS . . . *PRT 7P 326* 49 3

VILLAGE PEOPLE *US, male vocal group (66 WEEKS)* pos/wks

3 Dec 77 SAN FRANCISCO (YOU'VE GOT ME) *DJM DJS 10817* 45 5
25 Nov 78 ★ YMCA *Mercury 6007 192* ◆ 1 16
17 Mar 79 ● IN THE NAVY *Mercury 6007 209* 2 9
16 Jun 79 GO WEST *Mercury 6007 221* 15 8
9 Aug 80 CAN'T STOP THE MUSIC *Mercury MER 16* 11 11
9 Feb 85 SEX OVER THE PHONE *Record Shack SOHO 34* 59 5
4 Dec 93 YMCA (re-mix) *Bell 74321177182* 12 7
28 May 94 IN THE NAVY (re-mix) *Bell 74321198192* 36 2
27 Nov 99 YMCA (2nd re-mix) *Wrasse WRASX 002* 35 3

V.I.M. *UK, male instrumental / production group (1 WEEK)* pos/wks

26 Jan 91 MAGGIE'S LAST PARTY *F2 BOZ 1* 68 1

Gene VINCENT *US, male vocalist – Eugene Craddock (51 WEEKS)* pos/wks

13 Jul 56 BE-BOP-A-LULA *Capitol CL 14599* 30 2
24 Aug 56 BE-BOP-A-LULA (re-entry) *Capitol CL 14599* 16 3
28 Sep 56 BE-BOP-A-LULA (2nd re-entry) *Capitol CL 14599* 23 2
12 Oct 56 RACE WITH THE DEVIL *Capitol CL 14628* 28 1
19 Oct 56 BLUE JEAN BOP *Capitol CL 14637* 16 5
8 Jan 60 WILD CAT *Capitol CL 15099* 21 3
10 Mar 60 MY HEART *Capitol CL 15115* 16 6
10 Mar 60 WILD CAT (re-entry) *Capitol CL 15099* 39 3
28 Apr 60 MY HEART (re-entry) *Capitol CL 15115* 47 1
19 May 60 MY HEART (2nd re-entry) *Capitol CL 15115* 36 1
16 Jun 60 PISTOL PACKIN' MAMA *Capitol CL 15136* 15 9
1 Jun 61 SHE SHE LITTLE SHEILA *Capitol CL 15202* 22 10
17 Aug 61 SHE SHE LITTLE SHEILA (re-entry) *Capitol CL 15202* 44 1
31 Aug 61 I'M GOING HOME (TO SEE MY BABY) *Capitol CL 15215* 36 4

VINDALOO SUMMER SPECIAL *UK, male / female vocal / instrumental group (3 WEEKS)* pos/wks

19 Jul 86 ROCKIN' WITH RITA (HEAD TO TOE) *Vindaloo UGH 13* 56 3

Bobby VINTON *US, male vocalist (29 WEEKS)* pos/wks

2 Aug 62 ROSES ARE RED (MY LOVE) *Columbia DB 4878* ▲ 15 8
19 Dec 63 THERE! I'VE SAID IT AGAIN *Columbia DB 7179* ▲ 34 10
29 Sep 90 ● BLUE VELVET *Epic 6505240* ▲ 2 10
17 Nov 90 ROSES ARE RED (MY LOVE) (re-issue) *Epic 6564677* 71 1

VINYLGROOVER and The RED HED *UK, male production duo (1 WEEK)* pos/wks

27 Jan 01 ROK DA HOUSE *Nukleuz NUKP 0285* 72 1

VIOLINSKI *UK, male instrumental group (9 WEEKS)* pos/wks

17 Feb 79 CLOG DANCE *Jet 136* 17 9

VIPER *Belgium, male production group (1 WEEK)* pos/wks

7 Feb 98 THE TWISTER *Hooj Choons HOOJCD 59* 55 1

VIPERS SKIFFLE GROUP *UK, male vocal / instrumental group (18 WEEKS)* pos/wks

25 Jan 57 ● DON'T YOU ROCK ME DADDY-O *Parlophone R 4261* 10 9
22 Mar 57 ● THE CUMBERLAND GAP *Parlophone R 4289* 10 6
31 May 57 STREAMLINE TRAIN *Parlophone R 4308* 23 3

VIPs *UK, male vocal / instrumental group (4 WEEKS)* pos/wks

6 Sep 80 THE QUARTER MOON *Gem GEMS 39* 55 4

VIRGINIA – *See Tom NOVY*

VIRUS *UK, male instrumental / production duo (3 WEEKS)* pos/wks

26 Aug 95 SUN *Perfecto PERF 107CD* 62 1
25 Jan 97 MOON *Perfecto PERF 134CD* 36 2

VISAGE *UK, male vocal / instrumental group (56 WEEKS)* pos/wks

20 Dec 80 ● FADE TO GREY *Polydor POSP 194* 8 15
14 Mar 81 MIND OF A TOY *Polydor POSP 236* 13 8
11 Jul 81 VISAGE *Polydor POSP 293* 21 7
13 Mar 82 DAMNED DON'T CRY *Polydor POSP 390* 11 8
26 Jun 82 NIGHT TRAIN *Polydor POSP 441* 12 10
13 Nov 82 PLEASURE BOYS *Polydor POSP 523* 44 3
1 Sep 84 LOVE GLOVE *Polydor POSP 691* 54 3
28 Aug 93 FADE TO GREY (re-mix) *Polydor PZCD 282* 39 2

Michelle VISAGE – *See S.O.U.L. S.Y.S.T.E.M. introducing Michelle VISAGE*

VISCOUNTS *UK, male vocal group (18 WEEKS)* pos/wks

13 Oct 60 SHORT'NIN' BREAD *Pye 7N 15287* 16 8
14 Sep 61 WHO PUT THE BOMP (IN THE BOMP, BOMP, BOMP) *Pye 7N 15379* 21 10

VISION *UK, male vocal / instrumental group (1 WEEK)* pos/wks

9 Jul 83	**LOVE DANCE** *MVM MVM 2886*	74	1

VISIONMASTERS with Tony KING and Kylie MINOGUE
UK, male DJ / production duo, UK, male DJ / producer and Australia, female vocalist (1 WEEK) pos/wks

30 Nov 91	**KEEP ON PUMPIN' IT** *PWL PWL 207*	49	1

VITA – *See N*E*R*D featuring Lee HARVEY and VITA*

VIXEN *US, female vocal / instrumental group (21 WEEKS)* pos/wks

3 Sep 88	**EDGE OF A BROKEN HEART** *Manhattan MT 48*	51	4
4 Mar 89	**CRYIN'** *EMI Manhattan MT 60*	27	4
3 Jun 89	**LOVE MADE ME** *EMI-USA MT 66*	36	4
2 Sep 89	**EDGE OF A BROKEN HEART (re-issue)** *EMI-USA MT 48*	59	2
28 Jul 90	**HOW MUCH LOVE** *EMI-USA MT 87*	35	3
20 Oct 90	**LOVE IS A KILLER** *EMI-USA MT 91*	41	2
16 Mar 91	**NOT A MINUTE TOO SOON** *EMI-USA MT 93*	37	2

VOGGUE *Canada, female vocal duo (6 WEEKS)* pos/wks

18 Jul 81	**DANCIN' THE NIGHT AWAY** *Mercury MER 76*	39	6

VOICE OF THE BEEHIVE
US / UK, male / female vocal / instrumental group (51 WEEKS) pos/wks

14 Nov 87	**I SAY NOTHING** *London LON 151*	45	5
5 Mar 88	**I WALK THE EARTH** *London LON 169*	42	4
14 May 88	**DON'T CALL ME BABY** *London LON 175*	15	10
23 Jul 88	**I SAY NOTHING (re-issue)** *London LON 190*	22	6
22 Oct 88	**I WALK THE EARTH (re-issue)** *London LON 206*	46	4
13 Jul 91	**MONSTERS AND ANGELS** *London LON 302*	17	10
28 Sep 91	**I THINK I LOVE YOU** *London LON 308*	25	6
11 Jan 92	**PERFECT PLACE** *London LON 312*	37	6

VOICES OF LIFE *US, male / female vocal / production duo (2 WEEKS)* pos/wks

21 Mar 98	**THE WORD IS LOVE (SAY THE WORD)** *AM:PM 5825272*	26	2

Sterling VOID *UK, male instrumentalist / vocalist (3 WEEKS)* pos/wks

4 Feb 89	**RUNAWAY GIRL / IT'S ALL RIGHT** *ffrr FFR 21*	53	3

VOLATILE AGENTS featuring Simone BENN
UK, male production duo and UK, female vocalist (3 WEEKS) pos/wks

15 Dec 01	**HOOKED ON YOU** *Melting Pot MPRCD 10*	54	3+

VOLCANO
Norway / UK, male / female vocal / instrumental group (4 WEEKS) pos/wks

23 Jul 94	**MORE TO LOVE** *Deconstruction 74321221832*	32	3
18 Nov 95	**THAT'S THE WAY LOVE IS** *EXP EXPCD 002* [1]	72	1

[1] Volcano with Sam Cartwright

VOODOO & SERANO *Germany, male production duo – Reinhard Raith and Tommy Serano (4 WEEKS)* pos/wks

3 Feb 01	**BLOOD IS PUMPIN'** *Xtrahard / Xtravaganza X2H2 CDS*	19	4

VOYAGE *UK / France, disco aggregation (27 WEEKS)* pos/wks

17 Jun 78	**FROM EAST TO WEST / SCOTS MACHINE** *GTO GT 224*	13	13
25 Nov 78	**SOUVENIRS** *GTO GT 241*	56	7
24 Mar 79	**LET'S FLY AWAY** *GTO GT 245*	38	7

'Scots Machine' credited from 24 Jun 1978 until end of record's chart run

VOYAGER *UK, male vocal / instrumental group (8 WEEKS)* pos/wks

26 May 79	**HALFWAY HOTEL** *Mountain VOY 001*	33	8

VYBE *US, female vocal group (1 WEEK)* pos/wks

7 Oct 95	**WARM SUMMER DAZE** *Fourth & Broadway BRCD 315*	60	1

W

Kristine W *US, female vocalist – Kristine Weitz (8 WEEKS)* pos/wks

21 May 94	**LOVE COME HOME** *Triangle BLUESCD 001* [1]	73	1
25 Jun 94	**FEEL WHAT YOU WANT** *Champion CHAMPCD 304*	33	3
25 May 96	**ONE MORE TRY** *Champion CHAMPCD 317*	41	1
21 Dec 96	**LAND OF THE LIVING** *Champion CHAMPCD 324*	57	1
5 Jul 97	**FEEL WHAT YOU WANT (re-issue)** *Champion CHAMPCD 329*	40	2

[1] Our Tribe with Franké Pharoah and Kristine W

Bill WADDINGTON – *See CORONATION STREET CAST featuring Bill WADDINGTON*

Adam WADE with The George PAXTON Orchestra and Chorus
US, male vocalist (6 WEEKS) pos/wks

8 Jun 61	**TAKE GOOD CARE OF HER** *HMV POP 843*	38	1
22 Jun 61	**TAKE GOOD CARE OF HER (re-entry)** *HMV POP 843*	38	5

WAG YA TAIL *UK, male vocal / instrumental group (1 WEEK)* pos/wks

3 Oct 92	**XPAND YA MIND (EXPANSIONS)** *PWL International PWL 238*	49	1

WAH!
UK, male vocal / instrumental group – leader Pete Wylie (26 WEEKS) pos/wks

25 Dec 82 ●	**THE STORY OF THE BLUES** *Eternal JF 1*	3	12
19 Mar 83	**HOPE (I WISH YOU'D BELIEVE ME)** *WEA X 9880*	37	5
30 Jun 84	**COME BACK** *Beggars Banquet BEG 111* [1]	20	9

[1] Mighty Wah

See also Pete WYLIE

Donnie WAHLBERG – *See SEIKO and Donnie WAHLBERG; NEW KIDS ON THE BLOCK*

WAIKIKIS *Belgium, male instrumental group (2 WEEKS)* pos/wks

11 Mar 65	**HAWAII TATTOO** *Pye International 7N 25286*	41	2

WAILERS – *See Bob MARLEY and the WAILERS*

John WAITE *UK, male vocalist (13 WEEKS)* pos/wks

29 Sep 84 ●	**MISSING YOU** *EMI America EA 182* ▲	9	11
13 Feb 93	**MISSING YOU (re-issue)** *Chrysalis CDCHS 3938*	56	2

WAITRESSES *US, female vocal group (4 WEEKS)* pos/wks

18 Dec 82	**CHRISTMAS WRAPPING** *Ze / Island WIP 6821*	45	4

Johnny WAKELIN *UK, male vocalist (20 WEEKS)* pos/wks

18 Jan 75 ●	**BLACK SUPERMAN (MUHAMMAD ALI)** *Pye 7N 45420* [1]	7	10
24 Jul 76 ●	**IN ZAIRE** *Pye 7N 45595*	4	10

[1] Johnny Wakelin and the Kinshasa Band

Narada Michael WALDEN
US, male vocalist / producer (28 WEEKS) pos/wks

23 Feb 80	**TONIGHT I'M ALRIGHT** *Atlantic K 11437*	34	9
26 Apr 80 ●	**I SHOULDA LOVED YA** *Atlantic K 11413*	8	9
23 Apr 88 ●	**DIVINE EMOTIONS** *Reprise W 7967* [1]	8	10

[1] Narada

Gary WALKER *US, male vocalist – Gary Leeds (12 WEEKS)* pos/wks

24 Feb 66	**YOU DON'T LOVE ME** *CBS 202036*	26	6
26 May 66	**TWINKIE-LEE** *CBS 202081*	26	6

See also WALKER BROTHERS

UK No.1 ★ UK Top 10 ● Still on chart + UK million seller ◆ UK entry at No.1 ■ US No.1 ▲

1998

IN THE YEAR IN WHICH THE US GOVERNMENT APPROVED SALES OF VIAGRA, BILL CLINTON'S IMPEACHMENT OVER THE MONICA LEWINSKY AFFAIR GAVE A BOOST TO CIGAR SALES WORLDWIDE, AND ALL SAINTS AND B*WITCHED JOINED GIRL GROUP CHAMPS THE SPICE GIRLS WITH TWO CHART-TOPPERS APIECE, **FAYE TOZER** FROM STEPS TALKS ABOUT A TOP POP MOMENT ...

"I remember being in a taxi and the driver had the radio on and was playing 'Tragedy'. After it had finished, the DJ said, 'That's Britain's No.1 by Steps' and I felt all special for the rest of the day."

SINGLE OF THE YEAR 'Believe' Cher
ALBUM OF THE YEAR 'Urban Hymns' Verve

John WALKER *US, male vocalist – John Maus (6 WEEKS)* pos/wks

5 Jul 67		**ANNABELLA** *Philips BF 1593*	**48** 1
19 Jul 67		**ANNABELLA (re-entry)** *Philips BF 1593*	**24** 5

See also WALKER BROTHERS

Scott WALKER *US, male vocalist – Scott Engel (30 WEEKS)* pos/wks

6 Dec 67		**JACKIE** *Philips BF 1628*	**22** 9
1 May 68	●	**JOANNA** *Philips BF 1662*	**7** 11
11 Jun 69		**LIGHTS OF CINCINNATI** *Philips BF 1793*	**13** 10

See also WALKER BROTHERS

Junior WALKER and the ALL-STARS
US, male instrumental / vocal group (59 WEEKS) pos/wks

18 Aug 66		**HOW SWEET IT IS (TO BE LOVED BY YOU)** *Tamla Motown TMG 571*	**22** 10
2 Apr 69		**ROAD RUNNER** *Tamla Motown TMG 691*	**12** 12
18 Oct 69		**WHAT DOES IT TAKE (TO WIN YOUR LOVE)** *Tamla Motown TMG 712*	**13** 12
26 Aug 72		**WALK IN THE NIGHT** *Tamla Motown TMG 824*	**16** 11
27 Jan 73		**TAKE ME GIRL, I'M READY** *Tamla Motown TMG 840*	**16** 9
30 Jun 73		**WAY BACK HOME** *Tamla Motown TMG 857*	**35** 5

WALKER BROTHERS (331 Top 500) *Unrelated US trio, who were top UK teen idols in the mid-60s. Members Scott Walker (Engel) (v/b/k), John Walker (Maus) (v/g), Gary Walker (Leeds) (d) all had solo hits after trio split in 1967, with Scott (who first recorded solo in 1957) creating a large cult following (93 WEEKS)* pos/wks

29 Apr 65		**LOVE HER** *Philips BF 1409*	**20** 13
19 Aug 65	★	**MAKE IT EASY ON YOURSELF** *Philips BF 1428*	**1** 14
2 Dec 65	●	**MY SHIP IS COMING IN** *Philips BF 1454*	**3** 12
3 Mar 66	★	**THE SUN AIN'T GONNA SHINE ANYMORE** *Philips BF 1473*	**1** 11
14 Jul 66		**(BABY) YOU DON'T HAVE TO TELL ME** *Philips BF 1497*	**13** 8
22 Sep 66		**ANOTHER TEAR FALLS** *Philips BF 1514*	**12** 8
15 Dec 66		**DEADLIER THAN THE MALE** *Philips BF 1537*	**34** 6
9 Feb 67		**STAY WITH ME BABY** *Philips BF 1548*	**26** 6
18 May 67		**WALKING IN THE RAIN** *Philips BF 1576*	**26** 6
17 Jan 76	●	**NO REGRETS** *GTO GT 42*	**7** 9

See also Gary WALKER; John WALKER; Scott WALKER

WALL OF SOUND featuring Gerald LETHAN
US, male vocal / instrumental group (1 WEEK) pos/wks

31 Jul 93		**CRITICAL (IF YOU ONLY KNEW)** *Positiva CDTIV 4*	**73** 1

WALL OF VOODOO *US, male vocal / instrumental group (3 WEEKS)* pos/wks

19 Mar 83		**MEXICAN RADIO** *Illegal ILS 36*	**64** 3

Jerry WALLACE *US, male vocalist (1 WEEK)* pos/wks

23 Jun 60		**YOU'RE SINGING OUR LOVE SONG TO SOMEBODY ELSE** *London HLH 9110*	**46** 1

WALLFLOWERS *US, male vocal / instrumental group (1 WEEK)* pos/wks

12 Jul 97		**ONE HEADLIGHT** *Interscope IND 95532*	**54** 1

Bob WALLIS and his STORYVILLE JAZZ BAND *UK, male jazz band, Bob Wallis vocalist / instrumentalist – trumpet (7 WEEKS)* pos/wks

6 Jul 61		**I'M SHY MARY ELLEN, I'M SHY** *Pye Jazz 7NJ 2043*	**44** 2
4 Jan 62		**COME ALONG PLEASE** *Pye Jazz 7NJ 2048*	**33** 5

Joe WALSH *US, male vocalist (15 WEEKS)* pos/wks

16 Jul 77		**ROCKY MOUNTAIN WAY (EP)** *ABC ABE 12002*	**39** 4
8 Jul 78		**LIFE'S BEEN GOOD** *Asylum K 13129*	**14** 11

Tracks on Rocky Mountain Way (EP): Rocky Mountain Way / Turn to Stone / Meadows / Walk Away

Maureen WALSH – *See MAUREEN*

Sheila WALSH and Cliff RICHARD
UK, female / male vocal duo (2 WEEKS) pos/wks

4 Jun 83		**DRIFTING** *DJM SHEIL 1* [1]	**64** 2

Steve WALSH *UK, male DJ / vocalist (18 WEEKS)* pos/wks

18 Jul 87		**I FOUND LOVIN'** *A1 A1 299*	**74** 1
29 Aug 87	●	**I FOUND LOVIN' (re-entry)** *A1 A1 299*	**9** 12
12 Dec 87		**LET'S GET TOGETHER TONITE** *A1 A1 303*	**74** 1
30 Jul 88		**AIN'T NO STOPPING US NOW (PARTY FOR THE WORLD)** *A1 A1 304*	**44** 4

Trevor WALTERS *UK, male vocalist (22 WEEKS)* pos/wks

24 Oct 81		**LOVE ME TONIGHT** *Magnet MAG 198*	**27** 8
21 Jul 84	●	**STUCK ON YOU** *Sanity IS 002*	**9** 12
1 Dec 84		**NEVER LET HER SLIP AWAY** *Polydor POSP 716*	**73** 2

WAMDUE PROJECT *US, male producer – Chris Brann (19 WEEKS)* pos/wks

20 Nov 99		**KING OF MY CASTLE (import)** *Orange ORCDM 53584CD*	**61** 1
27 Nov 99	★	**KING OF MY CASTLE** *AM:PM CDAMPM 127* ■	**1** 15
25 Mar 00		**KING OF MY CASTLE (re-entry)** *AM:PM CDAMPM 127*	**74** 1
15 Apr 00		**YOU'RE THE REASON** *AM:PM CDAMPM 130*	**39** 2

WANG CHUNG *UK, male vocal / instrumental group (12 WEEKS)* pos/wks

28 Jan 84		**DANCE HALL DAYS** *Geffen A 3837*	**21** 12

WANNADIES
Sweden, male / female vocal / instrumental group (12 WEEKS) pos/wks

18 Nov 95		**MIGHT BE STARS** *Indolent DIE 003CD1*	**51** 2
24 Feb 96		**HOW DOES IT FEEL** *Indolent DIE 004CD1*	**53** 1
20 Apr 96		**YOU AND ME SONG** *Indolent DIE 005CD*	**18** 3
7 Sep 96		**SOMEONE SOMEWHERE** *Indolent DIE 006CD*	**38** 1
26 Apr 97		**HIT** *Indolent DIE 009CD1*	**20** 2
5 Jul 97		**SHORTY** *Indolent DIE 010CD1*	**41** 2
4 Mar 00		**YEAH** *RCA 74321745552*	**56** 1

Dexter WANSELL *US, male instrumentalist – keyboards (3 WEEKS)* pos/wks

20 May 78		**ALL NIGHT LONG** *Philadelphia International PIR 6255*	**59** 3

WAR
US / Canada / Denmark, male vocal / instrumental group (32 WEEKS) pos/wks

24 Jan 76		**LOW RIDER** *Island WIP 6267*	**12** 7
26 Jun 76		**ME AND BABY BROTHER** *Island WIP 6303*	**21** 7
14 Jan 78		**GALAXY** *MCA 339*	**14** 7
15 Apr 78		**HEY SENORITA** *MCA 359*	**40** 2
10 Apr 82		**YOU GOT THE POWER** *RCA 201*	**58** 4
6 Apr 85		**GROOVIN'** *Bluebird BR 16*	**43** 5

Anita WARD *US, female vocalist (11 WEEKS)* pos/wks

2 Jun 79	★	**RING MY BELL** *TK TKR 7543* ▲	**1** 11

Chrissy WARD *US, female vocalist (2 WEEKS)* pos/wks

24 Jun 95		**RIGHT AND EXACT** *Ore AG 6CD*	**62** 1
8 Feb 97		**RIGHT AND EXACT (re-mix)** *Ore AG 21CD*	**59** 1

Clifford T WARD *UK, male vocalist (16 WEEKS)* pos/wks

30 Jun 73	●	**GAYE** *Charisma CB 205*	**8** 11
26 Jan 74		**SCULLERY** *Charisma CB 221*	**37** 5

Michael WARD *UK, male vocalist (13 WEEKS)* pos/wks

29 Sep 73		**LET THERE BE PEACE ON EARTH (LET IT BEGIN WITH ME)** *Philips 6006 340*	**15** 10
15 Dec 73		**LET THERE BE PEACE ON EARTH (LET IT BEGIN WITH ME) (re-entry)** *Philips 6006 340*	**50** 3

Billy WARD and HIS DOMINOES *US, male vocal group (13 WEEKS)* pos/wks

13 Sep 57		**STARDUST** *London HLU 8465*	13	11
29 Nov 57		**DEEP PURPLE** *London HLU 8502*	30	1
3 Jan 58		**STARDUST (re-entry)** *London HLU 8465*	26	1

WARD BROTHERS *UK, male vocal / instrumental group (8 WEEKS)* pos/wks

10 Jan 87		**CROSS THAT BRIDGE** *Siren SIREN 37*	32	8

Justin WARFIELD – *See BOMB THE BASS*

WARM JETS
UK / Canada, male vocal / instrumental group (4 WEEKS) pos/wks

14 Feb 98		**NEVER NEVER** *Island WAY 6766*	37	2
25 Apr 98		**HURRICANE** *Island CID 697*	34	2

WARM SOUNDS *UK, male vocal duo (6 WEEKS)* pos/wks

4 May 67		**BIRDS AND BEES** *Deram DM 120*	27	6

Toni WARNE *UK, female vocalist (4 WEEKS)* pos/wks

25 Apr 87		**BEN** *Mint CHEW 110*	50	4

Jennifer WARNES *US, female vocalist (37 WEEKS)* pos/wks

15 Jan 83	●	**UP WHERE WE BELONG** *Island WIP 6830* [1] ▲	7	13
25 Jul 87		**FIRST WE TAKE MANHATTAN** *Cypress PB 49709*	74	1
31 Oct 87	●	**(I'VE HAD) THE TIME OF MY LIFE** *RCA PB 49625* [2] ▲	6	12
15 Dec 90	●	**(I'VE HAD) THE TIME OF MY LIFE (re-entry)** *RCA PB 49625* [2]	8	11

[1] Joe Cocker and Jennifer Warnes [2] Bill Medley and Jennifer Warnes

WARP BROTHERS *Germany, male DJ / production group (16 WEEKS)* pos/wks

11 Nov 00		**PHATT BASS (import)** *Dos or Die BMSCDM 40009*	58	3
9 Dec 00	●	**PHATT BASS** *Nulife / Arista 74321817102* [1]	9	8
17 Feb 01		**WE WILL SURVIVE** *Nulife / Arista 74321832722*	19	4
29 Dec 01		**BLAST THE SPEAKERS** *Nulife 74321899162*	40	1+

[1] Warp Brothers vs Aquagen

WARRANT *US, male vocal / instrumental group (7 WEEKS)* pos/wks

17 Nov 90		**CHERRY PIE** *CBS 6562587*	59	2
9 Mar 91		**CHERRY PIE (re-issue)** *Columbia 6566867*	35	5

Alysha WARREN *UK, female vocalist (4 WEEKS)* pos/wks

24 Sep 94		**I'M SO IN LOVE** *Wild Card CARDD 10*	61	1
25 Mar 95		**I THOUGHT I MEANT THE WORLD TO YOU** *Wild Card CARDD 16*	40	1
27 Jul 96		**KEEP ON PUSHING OUR LOVE** *Arista 74321390422* [1]	30	2

[1] Nightcrawlers featuring John Reid and Alysha Warren

Ann WARREN – *See Ruby MURRAY*

Nikita WARREN *Italy, female vocalist (1 WEEK)* pos/wks

13 Jul 96		**I NEED YOU** *VC VCRD 12*	48	1

WARRIOR *UK, male vocal / production / instrumental duo – Stacey Charles and Michael Woods (6 WEEKS)* pos/wks

21 Oct 00		**WARRIOR** *Incentive CENT 12CDS*	19	4
30 Jun 01		**VOODOO** *Incentive CENT 26CDS*	37	2

Dionne WARWICK (302 Top 500) *Super-stylish soul diva, b. 12 Dec 1940, New Jersey, US, whose classy and unmistakable vocals on songs written by Burt Bacharach and Hal David produced more than 30 US hits for her between 1962 and 1972. She is a cousin of Whitney Houston (101 WEEKS)* pos/wks

13 Feb 64		**ANYONE WHO HAD A HEART** *Pye International 7N 25234*	42	3
16 Apr 64	●	**WALK ON BY** *Pye International 7N 25241*	9	14
30 Jul 64		**YOU'LL NEVER GET TO HEAVEN (IF YOU BREAK MY HEART)** *Pye International 7N 25256*	20	8
8 Oct 64		**REACH OUT FOR ME** *Pye International 7N 25265*	23	7
1 Apr 65		**YOU CAN HAVE HIM** *Pye International 7N 25290*	37	5
13 Mar 68		**(THEME FROM) VALLEY OF THE DOLLS** *Pye International 7N 25445*	28	8
15 May 68	●	**DO YOU KNOW THE WAY TO SAN JOSE** *Pye International 7N 25457*	8	10
19 Oct 74		**THEN CAME YOU** *Atlantic K 10495* [1] ▲	29	6
23 Oct 82	●	**HEARTBREAKER** *Arista ARIST 496*	2	13
11 Dec 82	●	**ALL THE LOVE IN THE WORLD** *Arista ARIST 507*	10	10
26 Feb 83		**YOURS** *Arista ARIST 518*	66	2
28 May 83		**I'LL NEVER LOVE THIS WAY AGAIN** *Arista ARIST 530*	62	3
9 Nov 85		**THAT'S WHAT FRIENDS ARE FOR** *Arista ARIST 638* [2] ▲	16	9
15 Aug 87		**LOVE POWER** *Arista RIS 27* [3]	63	3

[1] Dionne Warwicke & the Detroit Spinners [2] Dionne Warwick and Friends featuring Elton John, Stevie Wonder and Gladys Knight [3] Dionne Warwick and Jeffrey Osborne

WAS (NOT WAS) *US, male vocal / instrumental duo – Don Fagenson and David Weiss (58 WEEKS)* pos/wks

3 Mar 84		**OUT COME THE FREAKS** *Ze / Geffen A 4178*	41	5
18 Jul 87		**SPY IN THE HOUSE OF LOVE** *Fontana WAS 2*	51	7
3 Oct 87	●	**WALK THE DINOSAUR** *Fontana WAS 3*	10	10
6 Feb 88		**SPY IN THE HOUSE OF LOVE (re-entry)** *Fontana WAS 2*	21	8
7 May 88		**OUT COME THE FREAKS (AGAIN)** *Fontana WAS 4*	44	3
16 Jul 88		**ANYTHING CAN HAPPEN** *Fontana WAS 5*	67	3
26 May 90		**PAPA WAS A ROLLING STONE** *Fontana WAS 7*	12	7
11 Aug 90		**HOW THE HEART BEHAVES** *Fontana WAS 8*	53	3
23 May 92		**LISTEN LIKE THIEVES** *Fontana WAS 10*	58	2
11 Jul 92	●	**SHAKE YOUR HEAD** *Fontana WAS 11*	4	9
26 Sep 92		**SOMEWHERE IN AMERICA (THERE'S A STREET NAMED AFTER MY DAD)** *Fontana WAS 12*	57	1

Fontana WAS 4 was a re-recorded version of their first hit. 'Shake Your Head' features uncredited vocals by Ozzy Osbourne and Kim Basinger. The group dropped the brackets from their name during the chart run of 'Papa Was A Rolling Stone'

Martha WASH *US, female vocalist (34 WEEKS)* pos/wks

28 Nov 92		**CARRY ON** *RCA 74321125457*	74	1
6 Mar 93		**GIVE IT TO YOU** *RCA 74321136562*	37	4
10 Jul 93		**RUNAROUND / CARRY ON (re-mix)** *RCA 74321153702*	49	2
18 Feb 95		**I FOUND LOVE** *Columbia 6612112* [1]	26	2
13 Jul 96	●	**KEEP ON JUMPIN'** *Manifesto FESCD 11* [2]	8	6
12 Jul 97	●	**SOMETHING GOIN' ON** *Manifesto FESCD 25* [2]	5	10
25 Oct 97		**CARRY ON (2nd re-mix)** *Delirious DELICD 6*	49	1
28 Feb 98		**IT'S RAINING MEN…THE SEQUEL** *Logic 74321555412* [3]	21	3
11 Apr 98		**READY FOR A NEW DAY** *Manifesto FESCD 40* [4]	20	2
15 Aug 98		**CATCH THE LIGHT** *Logic 74321587912*	45	1
3 Jul 99		**COME** *Logic 74321653942*	64	1
5 Feb 00		**IT'S RAINING MEN (re-recording)** *Logic 74321726282*	56	1

[1] C & C Music Factory featuring Martha Wash [2] Todd Terry featuring Martha Wash and Jocelyn Brown [3] Martha Wash featuring RuPaul [4] Todd Terry featuring Martha Wash

The listed flip side of 'I Found Love' was 'Take a Toke' by C & C Music Factory

See also WEATHER GIRLS

Dinah WASHINGTON *US, female vocalist (8 WEEKS)* pos/wks

30 Nov 61		**SEPTEMBER IN THE RAIN** *Mercury AMT 1162*	35	3
18 Jan 62		**SEPTEMBER IN THE RAIN (re-entry)** *Mercury AMT 1162*	49	1
4 Apr 92		**MAD ABOUT THE BOY** *Mercury DINAH 1*	41	4

Grover WASHINGTON Jr
US, male instrumentalist – saxophone (7 WEEKS) pos/wks

16 May 81		**JUST THE TWO OF US** *Elektra K 12514*	34	7

Although uncredited, Bill Withers sings on 'Just the Two of Us'

Keith WASHINGTON – *See Kylie MINOGUE*

Sarah WASHINGTON *UK, female vocalist (13 WEEKS)* pos/wks

14 Aug 93		**I WILL ALWAYS LOVE YOU** *Almighty CDALMY 33*	12	7
27 Nov 93		**CARELESS WHISPER** *Almighty CDALMY 43*	45	2

Date		Title	Pos	Wks
25 May 96		**HEAVEN** *AM:PM 5815352*	28	2
12 Oct 96		**EVERYTHING** *AM:PM 5818872*	30	2

Geno WASHINGTON and the RAM JAM BAND

US, male vocalist and UK, male instrumental backing group (20 WEEKS) pos/wks

Date		Title	Pos	Wks
19 May 66		**WATER** *Piccadilly 7N 35312*	39	8
21 Jul 66		**HI HI HAZEL** *Piccadilly 7N 35329*	45	3
25 Aug 66		**HI HI HAZEL (re-entry)** *Piccadilly 7N 35329*	48	1
6 Oct 66		**QUE SERA SERA** *Piccadilly 7N 35346*	43	3
2 Feb 67		**MICHAEL (HE'S A LOVER)** *Piccadilly 7N 35359*	39	5

W.A.S.P. *US, male vocal / instrumental group (38 WEEKS)* pos/wks

Date		Title	Pos	Wks
31 May 86		**WILD CHILD** *Capitol CL 388*	71	2
11 Oct 86		**95 - NASTY** *Capitol CL 432*	70	1
29 Aug 87		**SCREAM UNTIL YOU LIKE IT** *Capitol CL 458*	32	5
31 Oct 87		**I DON'T NEED NO DOCTOR (LIVE)** *Capitol CL 469*	31	5
20 Feb 88		**ANIMAL (F**K LIKE A BEAST)** *Music For Nations KUT 109*	61	3
4 Mar 89		**MEAN MAN** *Capitol CL 521*	21	5
27 May 89		**THE REAL ME** *Capitol CL 534*	23	5
9 Sep 89		**FOREVER FREE** *Capitol CL 546*	25	5
4 Apr 92		**CHAINSAW CHARLIE (MURDERS IN THE NEW MORGUE)** *Parlophone RS 6308*	17	2
6 Jun 92		**THE IDOL** *Parlophone RPD 6314*	41	2
31 Oct 92		**I AM ONE** *Parlophone 10RG 6324*	56	1
23 Oct 93		**SUNSET AND BABYLON** *Capitol CDCL 698*	38	2

WATERBOYS *UK / Ireland, male vocal / instrumental group (33 WEEKS)* pos/wks

Date		Title	Pos	Wks
2 Nov 85		**THE WHOLE OF THE MOON** *Ensign ENY 520*	26	7
14 Jan 89		**FISHERMAN'S BLUES** *Ensign ENY 621*	32	6
1 Jul 89		**AND A BANG ON THE EAR** *Ensign ENY 624*	51	4
6 Apr 91	●	**THE WHOLE OF THE MOON (re-issue)** *Ensign ENY 642*	3	9
8 Jun 91		**FISHERMAN'S BLUES (re-issue)** *Ensign ENY 645*	75	1
15 May 93		**THE RETURN OF PAN** *Geffen GFSTD 42*	24	3
24 Jul 93		**GLASTONBURY SONG** *Geffen GFSTD 49*	29	3

WATERFRONT *UK, male vocal / instrumental duo – Phil Cilia and Chris Duffy (19 WEEKS)* pos/wks

Date		Title	Pos	Wks
15 Apr 89		**BROKEN ARROW** *Polydor WON 3*	63	2
27 May 89		**CRY** *Polydor WON 1*	17	13
9 Sep 89		**NATURE OF LOVE** *Polydor WON 2*	63	4

WATERGATE *Turkey, male DJ / producer – Orhan Terzi (10 WEEKS)* pos/wks

Date		Title	Pos	Wks
13 May 00	●	**HEART OF ASIA** *Positiva CDTIV 129*	3	10

See also DJ QUICKSILVER

Dennis WATERMAN *UK, male vocalist (17 WEEKS)* pos/wks

Date		Title	Pos	Wks
25 Oct 80	●	**I COULD BE SO GOOD FOR YOU** *EMI 5009* [1]	3	12
17 Dec 83		**WHAT ARE WE GONNA GET 'ER INDOORS** *EMI MIN 101* [2]	21	5

[1] Dennis Waterman with the Dennis Waterman Band [2] Dennis Waterman and George Cole

Crystal WATERS *US, female vocalist (35 WEEKS)* pos/wks

Date		Title	Pos	Wks
18 May 91	●	**GYPSY WOMAN (LA DA DEE)** *A & M AM 772*	2	10
7 Sep 91		**MAKIN' HAPPY** *A & M AM 790*	18	6
11 Jan 92		**MEGAMIX** *A & M AM 843*	39	3
3 Oct 92		**GYPSY WOMAN (re-mix)** *Epic 6584377*	35	2
23 Apr 94		**100% PURE LOVE** *A & M 8586692*	15	7
2 Jul 94		**GHETTO DAY** *A & M 8589592*	40	2
25 Nov 95		**RELAX** *Manifesto FESCD 4*	37	2
24 Aug 96		**IN DE GHETTO** *Manifesto FESCD 12* [1]	35	2
19 Apr 97		**SAY ...IF YOU FEEL ALRIGHT** *Mercury 5742912*	45	1

[1] David Morales and the Bad Yard Club featuring Crystal Waters and Delta

The listed flip side of 'Gypsy Woman' (re-mix) was 'Peace' (re-mix) by Sabrina Johnston

Muddy WATERS

US, male vocalist / instrumentalist – guitar (6 WEEKS) pos/wks

Date		Title	Pos	Wks
16 Jul 88		**MANNISH BOY** *Epic MUD 1*	51	6

Roger WATERS *UK, male vocalist / instrumentalist (8 WEEKS)* pos/wks

Date		Title	Pos	Wks
30 May 87		**RADIO WAVES** *Harvest EM 6*	74	1
26 Dec 87		**THE TIDE IS TURNING (AFTER LIVE AID)** *Harvest EM 37*	54	4
5 Sep 92		**WHAT GOD WANTS PART 1** *Columbia 6581390*	35	3

Michael WATFORD *US, male vocalist (2 WEEKS)* pos/wks

Date		Title	Pos	Wks
26 Feb 94		**SO INTO YOU** *East West A 8309CD*	53	2

Tionne "T-Boz" WATKINS – *See T-BOZ, TLC TIONNE*

Jody WATLEY *US, female vocalist (35 WEEKS)* pos/wks

Date		Title	Pos	Wks
9 May 87		**LOOKING FOR A NEW LOVE** *MCA MCA 1107*	13	11
17 Oct 87		**DON'T YOU WANT ME** *MCA MCA 1198*	55	3
8 Apr 89		**REAL LOVE** *MCA MCA 1324*	31	7
12 Aug 89		**FRIENDS** *MCA MCA 1352* [1]	21	6
10 Feb 90		**EVERYTHING** *MCA MCA 1395*	74	2
11 Apr 92		**I'M THE ONE YOU NEED** *MCA MCS 1608*	50	3
21 May 94		**WHEN A MAN LOVES A WOMAN** *MCA MCSTD 1964*	33	2
25 Apr 98		**OFF THE HOOK** *Atlantic AT 0024CD1*	51	1

[1] Jody Watley with Eric B and Rakim

See also SHALAMAR

Johnny 'Guitar' WATSON

US, male vocalist / instrumentalist – guitar (8 WEEKS) pos/wks

Date		Title	Pos	Wks
28 Aug 76		**I NEED IT** *DJM DJS 10694*	35	5
23 Apr 77		**A REAL MOTHER FOR YA** *DJM DJS 10762*	44	3

Russell WATSON *UK, male vocalist (3 WEEKS)* pos/wks

Date		Title	Pos	Wks
30 Oct 99		**SWING LOW '99** *Decca / Universal TV 4669502*	38	2
22 Jul 00		**BARCELONA (FRIENDS UNTIL THE END)** *Decca 4672772* [1]	68	1

[1] Russell Watson and Shaun Ryder

WAVELENGTH *UK, male vocal group (12 WEEKS)* pos/wks

Date		Title	Pos	Wks
10 Jul 82		**HURRY HOME** *Ariola ARO 281*	17	12

WAX *US / UK, male vocal / instrumental duo – Andrew Gold and Graham Gouldman (16 WEEKS)* pos/wks

Date		Title	Pos	Wks
12 Apr 86		**RIGHT BETWEEN THE EYES** *RCA PB 40509*	60	5
1 Aug 87		**BRIDGE TO YOUR HEART** *RCA PB 41405*	12	11

See also Andrew GOLD; 10 CC; Graham GOULDMAN

Anthony WAY *UK, choirboy (2 WEEKS)* pos/wks

Date		Title	Pos	Wks
15 Apr 95		**PANIS ANGELICUS** *Decca 4481642*	55	2

A WAY OF LIFE

US, male / female vocal / instrumental group (3 WEEKS) pos/wks

Date		Title	Pos	Wks
21 Apr 90		**TRIPPIN' ON YOUR LOVE** *Eternal YZ 464*	55	3

WAY OF THE WEST *UK, male vocal / instrumental group (5 WEEKS)* pos/wks

Date		Title	Pos	Wks
25 Apr 81		**DON'T SAY THAT'S JUST FOR WHITE BOYS** *Mercury MER 66*	54	5

WAY OUT WEST *UK, male instrumental / production duo – Nick Warren and Jody Wisternoff (14 WEEKS)* pos/wks

Date		Title	Pos	Wks
3 Dec 94		**AJARE** *Deconstruction 74321243802*	52	1
2 Mar 96		**DOMINATION** *Deconstruction 74321342822*	38	2
14 Sep 96		**THE GIFT** *Deconstruction 74321401912* [1]	15	5
30 Aug 97		**BLUE** *Deconstruction 74321477512*	41	2
29 Nov 97		**AJARE (re-mix)** *Deconstruction 74321521352*	36	2
9 Dec 00		**THE FALL** *Wow WOW 005CD*	61	1
18 Aug 01		**INTENSIFY** *Distinctive Breaks DISNCD 74*	46	1

[1] Way Out West featuring Miss Joanna Law

Bruce WAYNE *Germany, male DJ / producer (2 WEEKS)* pos/wks

Date		Title	Pos	Wks
13 Dec 97		**READY** *Logic 74321527012*	44	1
4 Jul 98		**NO GOOD FOR ME** *Logic 74321587052*	70	1

Jeff WAYNE *US, orchestra (21 WEEKS)* pos/wks

9 Sep 78	EVE OF THE WAR *CBS 6496* [1]	36	8
10 Jul 82	MATADOR *CBS A 2493*	57	3
25 Nov 89 ●	EVE OF THE WAR (re-mix) *CBS 6551267* [1]	3	10

[1] Jeff Wayne's War Of The Worlds

WEATHER GIRLS
US, female vocal duo – Martha Wash and Izora Redman (14 WEEKS) pos/wks

27 Aug 83	IT'S RAINING MEN *CBS A 2924*	73	3
3 Mar 84 ●	IT'S RAINING MEN (re-entry) *CBS A 2924*	2	11

See also Martha WASH

WEATHER PROPHETS
UK, male vocal / instrumental group (2 WEEKS) pos/wks

28 Mar 87	SHE COMES FROM THE RAIN *Elevation ACID 1*	62	2

WEATHERMEN – *See Jonathan KING*

Marti WEBB *UK, female vocalist (42 WEEKS)* pos/wks

9 Feb 80 ●	TAKE THAT LOOK OFF YOUR FACE *Polydor POSP 100*	3	12
19 Apr 80	TELL ME ON A SUNDAY *Polydor POSP 111*	67	2
20 Sep 80	YOUR EARS SHOULD BE BURNING NOW *Polydor POSP 166*	61	4
8 Jun 85 ●	BEN *Starblend STAR 6*	5	11
20 Sep 86	ALWAYS THERE *BBC RESL 190* [1]	13	12
6 Jun 87	I CAN'T LET GO *Rainbow RBR 12*	65	1

[1] Marti Webb and the Simon May Orchestra

WEBB BROTHERS *US, male vocal duo (1 WEEK)* pos/wks

17 Feb 01	I CAN'T BELIEVE YOU'RE GONE *WEA WEA 320CD*	69	1

Joan WEBER *US, female vocalist (1 WEEK)* pos/wks

18 Feb 55	LET ME GO LOVER *Philips PB 389* ▲	16	1

WEDDING PRESENT
UK, male vocal / instrumental group (38 WEEKS) pos/wks

5 Mar 88	NOBODY'S TWISTING YOUR ARM *Reception REC 009*	46	2
1 Oct 88	WHY ARE YOU BEING SO REASONABLE NOW? *Reception REC 011*	42	2
7 Oct 89	KENNEDY *RCA PB 43117*	33	3
17 Feb 90	BRASSNECK *RCA PB 43403*	24	3
29 Sep 90	3 SONGS (EP) *RCA PB 44021*	25	4
11 May 91	DALLIANCE *RCA PB 44495*	29	3
27 Jul 91	LOVENEST *RCA PT 44750*	58	1
18 Jan 92	BLUE EYES *RCA PB 45185*	26	2
15 Feb 92	GO-GO DANCER *RCA PB 45183*	20	1
14 Mar 92	THREE *RCA PB 45181*	14	2
18 Apr 92	SILVER SHORTS *RCA PB 45311*	14	1
16 May 92 ●	COME PLAY WITH ME *RCA PB 45313*	10	2
13 Jun 92	CALIFORNIA *RCA PB 45315*	16	1
18 Jul 92	FLYING SAUCER *RCA 74321101157*	22	1
15 Aug 92	BOING! *RCA 74321101177*	19	1
19 Sep 92	LOVE SLAVE *RCA 743211101167*	17	1
17 Oct 92	STICKY *RCA 74321116917*	17	1
14 Nov 92	THE QUEEN OF OUTER SPACE *RCA 74321116927*	23	1
19 Dec 92	NO CHRISTMAS *RCA 74321116937*	25	1
10 Sep 94	YEAH YEAH YEAH YEAH *Island CID 585*	51	2
26 Nov 94	IT'S A GAS *Island CID 591*	71	1
31 Aug 96	2, 3, GO *Cooking Vinyl FRYCD 048*	67	1
25 Jan 97	MONTREAL *Cooking Vinyl FRYCD 053*	40	1

Tracks on 3 Songs (EP): Corduroy / Crawl / Make Me Smile (Come Up and See Me)

Fred WEDLOCK *UK, male vocalist (10 WEEKS)* pos/wks

31 Jan 81 ●	OLDEST SWINGER IN TOWN *Rocket XPRES 46*	6	10

WEE PAPA GIRL RAPPERS *UK, female rap / vocal duo – Samantha and Sandra Lawrence (27 WEEKS)* pos/wks

12 Mar 88	FAITH *Jive JIVE 164*	60	4
25 Jun 88	HEAT IT UP *Jive JIVE 174* [1]	21	9
1 Oct 88 ●	WEE RULE *Jive JIVE 185*	6	9
24 Dec 88	SOULMATE *Jive JIVE 193*	45	4
25 Mar 89	BLOW THE HOUSE DOWN *Jive JIVE 197*	65	1

[1] Wee Papa Girl Rappers featuring Two Men and a Drum Machine

Bert WEEDON *UK, male instrumentalist – guitar (38 WEEKS)* pos/wks

15 May 59 ●	GUITAR BOOGIE SHUFFLE *Top Rank JAR 117*	10	9
20 Nov 59	NASHVILLE BOOGIE *Top Rank JAR 221*	29	2
10 Mar 60	BIG BEAT BOOGIE *Top Rank JAR 300*	37	3
7 Apr 60	BIG BEAT BOOGIE (re-entry) *Top Rank JAR 300*	49	1
9 Jun 60	TWELFTH STREET RAG *Top Rank JAR 360*	47	2
28 Jul 60	APACHE *Top Rank JAR 415*	44	1
11 Aug 60	APACHE (re-entry) *Top Rank JAR 415*	24	3
27 Oct 60	SORRY ROBBIE *Top Rank JAR 517*	28	11
2 Feb 61	GINCHY *Top Rank JAR 537*	35	5
4 May 61	MR GUITAR *Top Rank JAR 559*	47	1

WEEKEND
International, male / female vocal / instrumental group (5 WEEKS) pos/wks

14 Dec 85	CHRISTMAS MEDLEY / AULD LANG SYNE *Lifestyle XY 1*	47	3

WEEKEND PLAYERS
UK, male / female production / vocal duo (3 WEEKS) pos/wks

8 Sep 01	21ST CENTURY *Multiply CDMULTY 78*	22	4

Michelle WEEKS *US, female vocalist (6 WEEKS)* pos/wks

2 Aug 97	MOMENT OF MY LIFE *Ministry of Sound MOSCDS 1* [1]	23	3
8 Nov 97	DON'T GIVE UP *Ministry of Sound MOSCDS 2*	28	2
11 Jul 98	GIVE ME LOVE *VC Recordings VCRD 37* [2]	59	1

[1] Bobby D'Ambrosio featuring Michelle Weeks [2] DJ Dado vs Michelle Weeks

WEEN – *See FOO FIGHTERS*

WEEZER *US, male vocal / instrumental group (17 WEEKS)* pos/wks

11 Feb 95	UNDONE - THE SWEATER SONG *Geffen GFSTD 85*	35	2
6 May 95	BUDDY HOLLY *Geffen GFSTD 88*	12	7
22 Jul 95	SAY IT AIN'T SO *Geffen GFSTD 95*	37	2
5 Oct 96	EL SCORCHO *Geffen GFSTD 22167*	50	1
14 Jul 01	HASH PIPE *Geffen 4975642*	21	3
3 Nov 01	ISLAND IN THE SUN *Geffen 4976102*	31	2

Frank WEIR *UK, orchestra (4 WEEKS)* pos/wks

15 Sep 60	CARIBBEAN HONEYMOON *Oriole CB 1559*	42	4

See also Vera LYNN

WEIRD SCIENCE *UK, male DJ / production duo (1 WEEK)* pos/wks

1 Jul 00	FEEL THE NEED *Nulife 74321751982*	62	1

Eric WEISSBERG – *See 'DELIVERANCE' SOUNDTRACK*

Denise WELCH *UK, female vocalist (3 WEEKS)* pos/wks

4 Nov 95	YOU DON'T HAVE TO SAY YOU LOVE ME / CRY ME A RIVER *Virgin VSCDT 1569*	23	3

Paul WELLER *UK, male vocalist (62 WEEKS)* pos/wks

18 May 91	INTO TOMORROW *Freedom High FHP 1* [1]	36	3
15 Aug 92	UH HUH OH YEH *Go! Discs GOD 86*	18	5
10 Oct 92	ABOVE THE CLOUDS *Go! Discs GOD 91*	47	2
17 Jul 93	SUNFLOWER *Go! Discs GODCD 102*	16	5
4 Sep 93	WILD WOOD *Go! Discs GODCD 104*	14	3
13 Nov 93	THE WEAVER (EP) *Go! Discs GODCD 107*	18	3
9 Apr 94	HUNG UP *Go! Discs GODCD 111*	11	3
5 Nov 94	OUT OF THE SINKING *Go! Discs GODCD 121*	20	3
6 May 95 ●	THE CHANGINGMAN *Go! Discs GODCD 127*	7	4
22 Jul 95 ●	YOU DO SOMETHING TO ME *Go! Discs GODCD 130*	9	6
30 Sep 95	BROKEN STONES *Go! Discs GODCD 132*	20	4
9 Mar 96	OUT OF THE SINKING *Go! Discs GODCD 143*	16	2

17 Aug 96	●	**PEACOCK SUIT** *Go! Discs GODCD 149*	5	5
9 Aug 97		**BRUSHED** *Island CID 666*	14	3
11 Oct 97		**FRIDAY STREET** *Island CID 676*	21	2
6 Dec 97		**MERMAIDS** *Island CID 683*	30	2
14 Nov 98		**BRAND NEW START** *Island CID 711*	16	3
9 Jan 99		**WILDWOOD (re-issue)** *Island CID 734*	22	3
2 Sep 00		**SWEET PEA, MY SWEET PEA** *Island CID 764*	44	1

[1] Paul Weller Movement

Tracks on The Weaver (EP): The Weaver / This Is No Time / Another New Day / Ohio (live). 'Out of the Sinking' in 1996 is a re-recording

See also COUNCIL COLLECTIVE; STYLE COUNCIL; JAM

Brandi WELLS *US, female vocalist (1 WEEK)* pos/wks

20 Feb 82		**WATCH OUT** *Virgin VS 479*	74	1

Houston WELLS and The MARKSMEN
UK, male vocal group (10 WEEKS) pos/wks

1 Aug 63		**ONLY THE HEARTACHES** *Parlophone R 5031*	22	10

Mary WELLS *US, female vocalist (25 WEEKS)* pos/wks

21 May 64	●	**MY GUY** *Stateside SS 288* ▲	5	14
30 Jul 64		**ONCE UPON A TIME** *Stateside SS 316* [1]	50	1
8 Jul 72		**MY GUY (re-issue)** *Tamla Motown TMG 820*	14	10

[1] Marvin Gaye and Mary Wells

Terri WELLS *US, female vocalist (9 WEEKS)* pos/wks

2 Jul 83		**YOU MAKE IT HEAVEN** *Phillyworld PWS 111*	53	2
5 May 84		**I'LL BE AROUND** *Phillyworld LON 48*	17	7

Alex WELSH BAND
UK, male instrumentalist – trumpet and band (4 WEEKS) pos/wks

10 Aug 61		**TANSY** *Columbia DB 4686*	45	4

Irvine WELSH – *See PRIMAL SCREAM*

WENDY and LISA *US, female vocal duo (31 WEEKS)* pos/wks

5 Sep 87		**WATERFALL** *Virgin VS 999*	66	4
16 Jan 88		**SIDESHOW** *Virgin VS 1012*	49	5
18 Feb 89		**ARE YOU MY BABY** *Virgin VS 1156*	70	3
29 Apr 89		**LOLLY LOLLY** *Virgin VS 1175*	64	3
8 Jul 89		**SATISFACTION** *Virgin VS 1194*	27	8
18 Nov 89		**WATERFALL (re-mix)** *Virgin VS 1223*	69	2
30 Jun 90		**STRUNG OUT** *Virgin VS 1272*	44	5
10 Nov 90		**RAINBOW LAKE** *Virgin VS 1280*	70	1

WES *France, male vocalist – Wes Madiko (7 WEEKS)* pos/wks

14 Feb 98		**ALANE** *Epic 6654682*	11	6
27 Jun 98		**I LOVE FOOTBALL** *Epic 6660772*	75	1

Dodie WEST *UK, female vocalist (4 WEEKS)* pos/wks

14 Jan 65		**GOIN' OUT OF MY HEAD** *Decca F 12046*	39	4

Keith WEST *UK, male vocalist (18 WEEKS)* pos/wks

9 Aug 67	●	**EXCERPT FROM 'A TEENAGE OPERA'** *Parlophone R 5623*	2	15
22 Nov 67		**SAM** *Parlophone R 5651*	38	3

Kit WEST – *See DEGREES OF MOTION featuring BITI*

WEST END *UK, female vocal group (2 WEEKS)* pos/wks

19 Aug 95		**LOVE RULES** *RCA 74321292702*	44	2

WEST END featuring SYBIL
UK, male production duo and female vocalist (13 WEEKS) pos/wks

16 Jan 93	●	**THE LOVE I LOST** *PWL Sanctuary PWCD253*	3	13

WEST HAM UNITED CUP SQUAD
UK, male football team vocalists (2 WEEKS) pos/wks

10 May 75		**I'M FOREVER BLOWING BUBBLES** *Pye 7N 45470*	31	2

WEST STREET MOB *US, male DJs / producers (3 WEEKS)* pos/wks

8 Oct 83		**BREAK DANCIN' - ELECTRIC BOOGIE** *Sugarhill SH 128*	71	1
22 Oct 83		**BREAK DANCIN' - ELECTRIC BOOGIE (re-entry)** *Sugarhill SH 128*	64	2

WESTBAM *Germany, male producer (9 WEEKS)* pos/wks

9 Jul 94		**CELEBRATION GENERATION** *Low Spirit PQCD 5*	48	2
19 Nov 94		**BAM BAM BAM** *Low Spirit PZCD 329*	57	1
3 Jun 95		**WIZARDS OF THE SONIC** *Urban PZCD 344*	32	2
23 Mar 96		**ALWAYS MUSIC** *Low Spirit 5779152* [1]	51	1
13 Jun 98		**WIZARDS OF THE SONIC (re-mix)** *Wonderboy WBOYD 010* [2]	43	2
28 Nov 98		**ROOF IS ON FIRE** *Logic 74321633162*	58	1

[1] Westbam / Koon + Stephenson [2] Westbam vs Red Jerry

WESTLIFE (217 Top 500) *Record-shattering Irish boy band: Bryan McFadden, Kian Egan, Mark Freehily, Nicky Byrne and Shane Filan. Only act to reach No.1 with their first seven releases – all entered at the top. They are also the first UK-based act to amass four No.1s in a year (124 WEEKS)* pos/wks

1 May 99	★	**SWEAR IT AGAIN** *RCA 74321662062* ■	1	12
14 Aug 99		**SWEAR IT AGAIN (re-entry)** *RCA 74321662062*	71	1
21 Aug 99	★	**IF I LET YOU GO** *RCA74321692352* ■	1	11
30 Oct 99	★	**FLYING WITHOUT WINGS** *RCA 74321709162* ■	1	13
25 Dec 99	★	**I HAVE A DREAM / SEASONS IN THE SUN** *RCA 74321726012* ■	1	17
8 Apr 00	★	**FOOL AGAIN** *RCA 74321751562* ■	1	10
1 Jul 00		**FOOL AGAIN (re-entry)** *RCA 74321751562*	60	2
30 Sep 00	★	**AGAINST ALL ODDS** *Columbia 6698872* [1] ■	1	11
11 Nov 00	★	**MY LOVE** *RCA 74321802792* ■	1	10
30 Dec 00	●	**WHAT MAKES A MAN** *RCA 74321826252*	2	13
13 Jan 01		**AGAINST ALL ODDS (re-entry)** *Columbia 6698872* [1]	68	1
17 Mar 01	★	**UPTOWN GIRL** *RCA 74321841682* ■	1	16
17 Nov 01	★	**QUEEN OF MY HEART** *RCA 74321899132* ■	1	7+

[1] Mariah Carey and Westlife

Kim WESTON – *See Marvin GAYE*

WESTWORLD
UK / US, male / female vocal / instrumental group (23 WEEKS) pos/wks

21 Feb 87		**SONIC BOOM BOY** *RCA BOOM 1*	11	7
2 May 87		**BA-NA-NA-BAM-BOO** *RCA BOOM 2*	37	5
25 Jul 87		**WHERE THE ACTION IS** *RCA BOOM 3*	54	4
17 Oct 87		**SILVERMAC** *RCA BOOM 4*	42	5
15 Oct 88		**EVERYTHING GOOD IS BAD** *RCA PB 42243*	72	2

WET WET WET (80 Top 500) *Perennially popular Glasgow quartet fronted by vocalist Marti Pellow (b. Mark McLoughlin, 23 Mar 1966). They were voted Best British Newcomers at the 1988 Brit Awards. 'Love Is All Around' holds the record for most weeks at No.1 by a UK act - 15 consecutive weeks (209 WEEKS)* pos/wks

11 Apr 87	●	**WISHING I WAS LUCKY** *Precious JEWEL 3*	6	14
25 Jul 87	●	**SWEET LITTLE MYSTERY** *Precious JEWEL 4*	5	12
5 Dec 87	●	**ANGEL EYES (HOME AND AWAY)** *Precious JEWEL 6*	5	12
19 Mar 88		**TEMPTATION** *Precious JEWEL 7*	12	8
14 May 88	★	**WITH A LITTLE HELP FROM MY FRIENDS** *Childline CHILD 1*	1	11
30 Sep 89	●	**SWEET SURRENDER** *Precious JEWEL 9*	6	8
9 Dec 89		**BROKE AWAY** *Precious JEWEL 10*	19	7
10 Mar 90		**HOLD BACK THE RIVER** *Precious JEWEL 11*	31	4
11 Aug 90		**STAY WITH ME HEARTACHE / I FEEL FINE** *Precious JEWEL 13*	30	4
14 Sep 91		**MAKE IT TONIGHT** *Precious JEWEL 15*	37	3
2 Nov 91		**PUT THE LIGHT ON** *Precious JEWEL 16*	56	2
4 Jan 92	★	**GOODNIGHT GIRL** *Precious JEWEL 17*	1	11
21 Mar 92		**MORE THAN LOVE** *Precious JEWEL 18*	19	5
11 Jul 92		**LIP SERVICE (EP)** *Precious JEWEL 19*	15	5
8 May 93		**BLUE FOR YOU / THIS TIME (LIVE)** *Precious JWLCD 20*	38	2
6 Nov 93		**SHED A TEAR** *Precious JWLCD 21*	22	5

8 Jan 94 COLD COLD HEART *Precious JWLCD 22* 23 4
21 May 94 ★ LOVE IS ALL AROUND *Precious JWLCD 23* ◆ 1 37
25 Mar 95 ● JULIA SAYS *Precious JWLDD 24* 3 9
17 Jun 95 ● DON'T WANT TO FORGIVE ME NOW *Precious JWLDD 25* 7 8
30 Sep 95 ● SOMEWHERE SOMEHOW *Precious JWLDD 26* 7 7
2 Dec 95 SHE'S ALL ON MY MIND *Precious JWLDD 27* 17 7
30 Mar 96 MORNING *Precious JWLDD 28* 16 4
22 Mar 97 ● IF I NEVER SEE YOU AGAIN *Precious JWLCD 29* 3 8
14 Jun 97 STRANGE *Precious JWLCD 30* 13 4
21 Jun 97 IF I NEVER SEE YOU AGAIN (re-entry) *Precious JWLCD 29* 72 1
19 Jul 97 STRANGE (re-entry) *Precious JWLCD 30* 74 1
16 Aug 97 ● YESTERDAY *Precious JWLCD 31* 4 6

The listed A-side with 'With a Little Help From My Friends' was 'She's Leaving Home' by Billy Bragg with Cara Tivey. Tracks on Lip Service (EP): Lip Service / High On the Happy Side / Lip Service (Live) / More Than Love (Live)

WE'VE GOT A FUZZBOX AND WE'RE GONNA USE IT
UK, female vocal / instrumental group (39 WEEKS) pos/wks

26 Apr 86 XX SEX / RULES AND REGULATIONS *Vindaloo UGH 11* 41 7
15 Nov 86 LOVE IS THE SLUG *Vindaloo UGH 14* 31 4
7 Feb 87 WHAT'S THE POINT *Vindaloo YZ 101* [1] 51 2
25 Feb 89 INTERNATIONAL RESCUE *WEA YZ 347* 11 10
20 May 89 PINK SUNSHINE *WEA YZ 401* [1] 14 10
5 Aug 89 SELF! *WEA YZ 408* [1] 24 6

[1] Fuzzbox

WHALE *Sweden, male / female vocal / instrumental group (8 WEEKS)* pos/wks

19 Mar 94 HOBO HUMPIN' SLOBO BABE *East West YZ 798CD* 46 2
15 Jul 95 I'LL DO YA *Hut HUTDG 51* 53 1
25 Nov 95 HOBO HUMPIN' SLOBO BABE (re-issue) *Hut HUTCD 64* 15 4
4 Jul 98 FOUR BIG SPEAKERS *Hut HUTCD 96* [1] 69 1

[1] Whale featuring Bus 75

WHALERS – *See Hal PAIGE and the WHALERS*

WHAM! (177 Top 500) *Teen-dream duo with a feel-good, pure pop sound: George Michael (v), Andrew Ridgeley (g). They were the only British group to have three chart-toppers in the UK and the US during the 1980s, a feat George later equalled as a solo artist (137 WEEKS)* pos/wks

16 Oct 82 ● YOUNG GUNS (GO FOR IT) *Innervision IVL A2766* 3 17
15 Jan 83 ● WHAM RAP! *Innervision IVL A2442* 8 11
14 May 83 ● BAD BOYS *Innervision A 3143* 2 14
30 Jul 83 ● CLUB TROPICANA *Innervision A 3613* 4 11
3 Dec 83 CLUB FANTASTIC MEGAMIX *Innervision A 3586* 15 8
26 May 84 ★ WAKE ME UP BEFORE YOU GO GO *Epic A 4440* ▲ 1 16
13 Oct 84 ★ FREEDOM *Epic A 4743* 1 14
15 Dec 84 ● LAST CHRISTMAS / EVERYTHING SHE WANTS *Epic A 4949* ◆ ▲ 2 13
23 Nov 85 ★ I'M YOUR MAN *Epic A 6716* 1 12
14 Dec 85 ● LAST CHRISTMAS (re-issue) *Epic WHAM 1* 6 7
21 Jun 86 ★ THE EDGE OF HEAVEN / WHERE DID YOUR HEART GO *Epic FIN 1* 1 10
20 Dec 86 LAST CHRISTMAS (2nd re-issue) *Epic 650269 7* 45 4

'Where Did Your Heart Go' listed only from 2 Aug 1986, peaking at No.28

WHATNAUTS – *See MOMENTS*

Rebecca WHEATLEY *UK, female vocalist (8 WEEKS)* pos/wks

26 Feb 00 ● STAY WITH ME (BABY) *BBC Music WMSS 60222* 10 7
13 May 00 STAY WITH ME (BABY) (re-entry) *BBC Music WMSS 60222* 71 1

WHEATUS *US, male vocal / instrumental group (32 WEEKS)* pos/wks

17 Feb 01 ● TEENAGE DIRTBAG *Columbia 6707962* 2 20
14 Jul 01 ● A LITTLE RESPECT *Columbia 6714282* 3 12

Caron WHEELER *UK, female vocalist (42 WEEKS)* pos/wks

18 Mar 89 ● KEEP ON MOVING *10 TEN 263* [1] 5 12
10 Jun 89 ★ BACK TO LIFE (HOWEVER DO YOU WANT ME) *10 TEN 265* [1] 1 14
8 Sep 90 LIVIN' IN THE LIGHT *RCA PB 43939* 14 6
10 Nov 90 UK BLAK *RCA PB 43719* 40 4
9 Feb 91 DON'T QUIT *RCA PB 44259* 53 3
7 Nov 92 I ADORE YOU *Perspective PERSS 7407* 59 2
11 Sep 93 BEACH OF THE WAR GODDESS *EMI CDEM 282* 75 1

[1] Soul II Soul featuring Caron Wheeler

Bill WHELAN featuring ANUNA and the RTE CONCERT ORCHESTRA *Ireland, male composer, male / female choir and orchestra (16 WEEKS)* pos/wks

17 Dec 94 ● RIVERDANCE *Son RTEBUACD 1* 9 16

WHEN IN ROME *UK, male vocal / instrumental group (3 WEEKS)* pos/wks

28 Jan 89 THE PROMISE *10 TEN 244* 58 3

WHIGFIELD *Denmark, female vocalist – Sannia Carlson (52 WEEKS)* pos/wks

17 Sep 94 ★ SATURDAY NIGHT *Systematic SYSCD 3* ◆ ■ 1 18
10 Dec 94 ● ANOTHER DAY *Systematic SYSCD 4* 7 10
10 Jun 95 ● THINK OF YOU *Systematic SYSCDP 10* 7 11
9 Sep 95 CLOSE TO YOU *Systematic SYCDP 18* 13 7
16 Dec 95 LAST CHRISTMAS / BIG TIME *Systematic SYSCD 24* 21 5
10 Oct 98 SEXY EYES - REMIXES *ZYX ZYX 8085R8* 68 1

WHIPPING BOY *Ireland, male vocal / instrumental group (4 WEEKS)* pos/wks

14 Oct 95 WE DON'T NEED NOBODY ELSE *Columbia 6622205* 51 1
3 Feb 96 WHEN WE WERE YOUNG *Columbia 6628062* 46 2
25 May 96 TWINKLE *Columbia 6632272* 55 1

Nancy WHISKEY – *See Charles McDEVITT SKIFFLE GROUP featuring Nancy WHISKEY*

WHISPERS *US, male vocal group (52 WEEKS)* pos/wks

2 Feb 80 ● AND THE BEAT GOES ON *Solar SO 1* 2 12
10 May 80 LADY *Solar SO 4* 55 3
12 Jul 80 MY GIRL *Solar SO 8* 26 6
14 Mar 81 ● IT'S A LOVE THING *Solar SO 16* 9 11
13 Jun 81 I CAN MAKE IT BETTER *Solar SO 19* 44 5
19 Jan 85 CONTAGIOUS *MCA MCA 937* 56 3
28 Mar 87 AND THE BEAT GOES ON (re-issue) *Solar MCA 1126* 45 4
23 May 87 ROCK STEADY *Solar MCA 1152* 38 6
15 Aug 87 SPECIAL F / X *Solar MCA 1178* 69 2

WHISTLE *US, male rap group (8 WEEKS)* pos/wks

1 Mar 86 ● (NOTHIN' SERIOUS) JUST BUGGIN' *Champion CHAMP 12* 7 8

Alex WHITCOMBE & BIG C
UK, male DJ and UK, male vocalist (1 WEEK) pos/wks

23 May 98 ICE RAIN *Xtravaganza 0091075 EXT* 44 1

Barry WHITE (176 Top 500) *Seventies soul and disco icon, b. 12 Sep 1944, Texas, US. This singer / songwriter / pianist / producer / arranger was behind best sellers by Love Unlimited and Love Unlimited Orchestra. Lovingly named the "Walrus of Love", his unmistakable deep voice has been in the charts for four decades (138 WEEKS)* pos/wks

9 Jun 73 I'M GONNA LOVE YOU JUST A LITTLE BIT MORE BABY *Pye International 7N 25610* 23 7
26 Jan 74 NEVER NEVER GONNA GIVE YA UP *Pye International 7N 25633* 14 11
17 Aug 74 ● CAN'T GET ENOUGH OF YOUR LOVE BABE *Pye International 7N 25661* ▲ 8 12
2 Nov 74 ★ YOU'RE THE FIRST, THE LAST, MY EVERYTHING *20th Century BTC 2133* 1 14
8 Mar 75 ● WHAT AM I GONNA DO WITH YOU *20th Century BTC 2177* 5 8
24 May 75 (FOR YOU) I'LL DO ANYTHING YOU WANT ME TO *20th Century BTC 2208* 20 6
27 Dec 75 ● LET THE MUSIC PLAY *20th Century BTC 2265* 9 8
6 Mar 76 ● YOU SEE THE TROUBLE WITH ME *20th Century BTC 2277* 2 10
21 Aug 76 BABY, WE BETTER TRY TO GET IT TOGETHER *20th Century BTC 2298* 15 7
13 Nov 76 DON'T MAKE ME WAIT TOO LONG *20th Century BTC 2309* 17 8

5 Mar 77		I'M QUALIFIED TO SATISFY *20th Century BTC 2328*	37	5
15 Oct 77		IT'S ECSTASY WHEN YOU LAY DOWN NEXT TO ME *20th Century BTC 2350*	40	3
16 Dec 78		JUST THE WAY YOU ARE *20th Century BTC 2380*	12	12
24 Mar 79		SHA LA LA MEANS I LOVE YOU *20th Century BTC 1041*	55	6
7 Nov 87		SHO' YOU RIGHT *Breakout USA 614*	14	7
16 Jan 88		NEVER NEVER GONNA GIVE YOU UP (re-mix) *Club JAB 59*	63	2
31 Mar 90		SECRET GARDEN *Qwest W 9992* [1]	67	1
21 Jan 95		PRACTICE WHAT YOU PREACH / LOVE IS THE ICON *A & M 5808992*	20	4
8 Apr 95		I ONLY WANT TO BE WITH YOU *A & M 5810252*	36	2
21 Dec 96		IN YOUR WILDEST DREAMS *Parlophone CDR 6451* [2]	32	3
4 Nov 00		LET THE MUSIC PLAY (re-mix) *Wonderboy WBOYD 020*	45	2

[1] Quincy Jones featuring Al B Sure!, James Ingram, El DeBarge and Barry White
[2] Tina Turner featuring Barry White

Chris WHITE *UK, male vocalist (4 WEEKS)* pos/wks

20 Mar 76		SPANISH WINE *Charisma CB 272*	37	4

Karyn WHITE *US, female vocalist (38 WEEKS)* pos/wks

5 Nov 88		THE WAY YOU LOVE ME *Warner Bros. W 7773*	42	5
18 Feb 89		SECRET RENDEZVOUS *Warner Bros. W 7562*	52	3
10 Jun 89		SUPERWOMAN *Warner Bros. W 2920*	11	13
9 Sep 89		SECRET RENDEZVOUS (re-issue) *Warner Bros. W 2855*	22	9
17 Aug 91		ROMANTIC *Warner Bros. W 0028* ▲	23	5
18 Jan 92		THE WAY I FEEL ABOUT YOU *Warner Bros. W 0073*	65	2
24 Sep 94		HUNGAH *Warner Bros. W 0264CD*	69	1

Snowy WHITE
UK, male vocalist / instrumentalist – guitar (12 WEEKS) pos/wks

24 Dec 83	●	BIRD OF PARADISE *Towerbell TOW 42*	6	10
28 Dec 85		FOR YOU *R4 FOR 3*	65	1
18 Jan 86		FOR YOU (re-entry) *R4 FOR 3*	72	1

Tam WHITE *UK, male vocalist (4 WEEKS)* pos/wks

15 Mar 75		WHAT IN THE WORLD'S COME OVER YOU *RAK 193*	36	4

Tony Joe WHITE *US, male vocalist (10 WEEKS)* pos/wks

6 Jun 70		GROUPIE GIRL *Monument MON 1043*	22	10

WHITE and TORCH *UK, male vocal / instrumental duo (4 WEEKS)* pos/wks

2 Oct 82		PARADE *Chrysalis CHS 2641*	54	4

WHITE PLAINS
UK, male group. Lead vocalist – Tony Burrows (56 WEEKS) pos/wks

7 Feb 70	●	MY BABY LOVES LOVIN' *Deram DM 280*	9	11
18 Apr 70		I'VE GOT YOU ON MY MIND *Deram DM 291*	17	11
24 Oct 70	●	JULIE DO YA LOVE ME *Deram DM 315*	8	14
12 Jun 71		WHEN YOU ARE A KING *Deram DM 333*	13	11
17 Feb 73		STEP INTO A DREAM *Deram DM 371*	21	9

WHITE STRIPES
US, male / female vocal / instrumental duo (2 WEEKS) pos/wks

24 Nov 01		HOTEL YORBA *XL Recordings XLS 139CD*	26	2

WHITE TOWN
UK, male vocalist / instrumentalist / producer – Jyoti Mishra (10 WEEKS) pos/wks

25 Jan 97	★	YOUR WOMAN *Chrysalis CDCHS 5052* ■	1	9
24 May 97		UNDRESSED *Chrysalis CDCHS 5058*	57	1

WHITE ZOMBIE *US, male vocal / instrumental group (4 WEEKS)* pos/wks

20 May 95		MORE HUMAN THAN HUMAN *Geffen GFSTD 92*	51	2
18 May 96		ELECTRIC HEAD PART 2 (THE ECSTASY) *Geffen GFSXD 22140*	31	2

WHITEHEAD BROS *US, male vocal duo (5 WEEKS)* pos/wks

14 Jan 95		YOUR LOVE IS A 187 *Motown TMGCD 1434*	32	3
13 May 95		FORGET I WAS A G *Motown TMGCD 1441*	40	2

WHITEHOUSE
US / UK, male vocal / instrumental / production duo (1 WEEK) pos/wks

15 Aug 98		AIN'T NO MOUNTAIN HIGH ENOUGH *Beautiful Noise BNOISE 2CD*	60	1

WHITEOUT *UK, male vocal / instrumental group (2 WEEKS)* pos/wks

24 Sep 94		DETROIT *Silvertone ORECD 66*	73	1
18 Feb 95		JACKIE'S RACING *Silvertone ORECD 68*	72	1

WHITESNAKE (261 Top 500)
Leading 1980s British rock group founded by ex-Deep Purple vocalist David Coverdale (b. 22 Sep 1949, North Yorkshire, UK), but with an ever-changing line-up. 'Whitesnake' (1987), their most successful album, shifted more than 10 million copies worldwide (112 WEEKS) pos/wks

24 Jun 78		SNAKE BITE (EP) *EMI International INEP 751* [1]	61	3
10 Nov 79		LONG WAY FROM HOME *United Artists BP 324*	55	2
26 Apr 80		FOOL FOR YOUR LOVING *United Artists BP 352*	13	9
12 Jul 80		READY AN' WILLING (SWEET SATISFACTION) *United Artists BP 363*	43	4
22 Nov 80		AIN'T NO LOVE IN THE HEART OF THE CITY *Sunburst/Liberty BP 381*	51	4
11 Apr 81		DON'T BREAK MY HEART AGAIN *Liberty BP 395*	17	9
6 Jun 81		WOULD I LIE TO YOU *Liberty BP 399*	37	6
6 Nov 82		HERE I GO AGAIN / BLOODY LUXURY *Liberty BP 416* ▲	34	10
13 Aug 83		GUILTY OF LOVE *Liberty BP 420*	31	5
14 Jan 84		GIVE ME MORE TIME *Liberty BP 422*	29	4
28 Apr 84		STANDING IN THE SHADOW *Liberty BP 423*	62	2
9 Feb 85		LOVE AIN'T NO STRANGER *Liberty BP 424*	44	4
28 Mar 87		STILL OF THE NIGHT *EMI EMI 5606*	16	8
6 Jun 87	●	IS THIS LOVE *EMI EM 3*	9	11
31 Oct 87	●	HERE I GO AGAIN (re-mix) *EMI EM 35*	9	11
6 Feb 88		GIVE ME ALL YOUR LOVE *EMI EM 23*	18	6
2 Dec 89		FOOL FOR YOUR LOVING *EMI EM 123*	43	2
10 Mar 90		THE DEEPER THE LOVE *EMI EM 128*	35	3
25 Aug 90		NOW YOU'RE GONE *EMI EM 150*	31	4
6 Aug 94		IS THIS LOVE / SWEET LADY LUCK (re-issue) *EMI CDEM 329*	25	4
7 Jun 97		TOO MANY TEARS *EMI CDEM 471* [2]	46	1

[1] David Coverdale's Whitesnake [2] David Coverdale and Whitesnake

Tracks on Snake Bite (EP): Bloody Mary / Steal Away / Ain't No Love In the Heart of the City / Come On. EM 123 is a re-recording of their third hit

David WHITFIELD (98 Top 500)
Most successful UK male singer in the US during the pre-rock years, b. 2 Feb 1925, Yorkshire, d. 16 Jan 1980. This operatic-style tenor had a formidable and predominantly female fan following in the 1950s (190 WEEKS) pos/wks

2 Oct 53	●	THE BRIDGE OF SIGHS *Decca F 10129*	9	1
16 Oct 53	★	ANSWER ME *Decca F 10192*	1	13
11 Dec 53		RAGS TO RICHES *Decca F 10207* [1]	12	1
8 Jan 54	●	RAGS TO RICHES (re-entry) *Decca F 10207* [1]	3	10
29 Jan 54		ANSWER ME (re-entry) *Decca F 10192*	12	1
19 Feb 54	●	THE BOOK *Decca F 10242*	5	12
28 May 54	●	THE BOOK (re-entry) *Decca F 10242*	10	3
18 Jun 54	★	CARA MIA *Decca F 10327*	1	25
12 Nov 54	●	SANTO NATALE (MERRY CHRISTMAS) *Decca F 10399*	2	10
11 Feb 55	●	BEYOND THE STARS *Decca F 10458*	8	9
27 May 55		MAMA *Decca F 10515*	20	1
24 Jun 55		MAMA (re-entry) *Decca F 10515*	19	2
8 Jul 55	●	EV'RYWHERE *Decca F 10515* [2]	3	20
29 Jul 55		MAMA (2nd re-entry) *Decca F 10515*	12	8
25 Nov 55	●	WHEN YOU LOSE THE ONE YOU LOVE *Decca F 10627* [3]	7	11
2 Mar 56		MY SEPTEMBER LOVE *Decca F 10690*	19	2
23 Mar 56		MY SEPTEMBER LOVE (re-entry) *Decca F 10690*	18	1
6 Apr 56	●	MY SEPTEMBER LOVE (2nd re-entry) *Decca F 10690*	3	20
24 Aug 56		MY SON JOHN *Decca F 10769*	22	4
31 Aug 56		MY UNFINISHED SYMPHONY *Decca F 10769*	29	1
7 Sep 56		MY SEPTEMBER LOVE (3rd re-entry) *Decca F 10690*	25	1

UK No.1 ★ UK Top 10 ● Still on chart + UK million seller ◆ UK entry at No.1 ■ US No.1 ▲

1999

IN THE YEAR IN WHICH THE MILLENNIUM STARTED BUGGING US, THE BRITISH GOVERNMENT TRANSFERRED POWER TO THE NORTHERN IRISH ASSEMBLY AS A RESULT OF THE GOOD FRIDAY AGREEMENT BEING IMPLEMENTED, 'THE BLAIR WITCH PROJECT' HAD CINEMA-GOERS HIDING BEHIND THEIR POPCORN, WESTLIFE BECAME THE FIRST ACT SINCE ELVIS TO SCORE FOUR NO.1S IN A YEAR, AND UK GARAGE DEBUTED ON THE CHARTS, **MARC (LARD) RILEY** RECOGNISES THE GENIUS OF EMINEM ...

“'Think about it before you walk in the door first – look at the store clerk – she's older than George Burns'. George Burns – not a reference point you'd exactly expect to find on one of the most important street tracks of the past 10 years, but 'Guilty Conscience' is exactly that. **Eminem**'s caustic, sometimes dark, sometimes childlike wit layered over **Dr Dre**'s beats were, to me, a revelation. The first time I heard 'My Name Is ...', I thought "novelty record". The second time I thought "very funny novelty record". The third hearing led me to discover 'The Slim Shady LP' – a work of brilliance bettered in the following years only by the same two men with 'The Marshall Mathers LP' and Dre's own '2001'. Phil Spector meets John Lydon for the millennium – genius!”

SINGLE OF THE YEAR 'The Millennium Prayer' Cliff Richard
ALBUM OF THE YEAR 'Come On Over' Shania Twain

Date		Title / Label	Pos	Wks
25 Jan 57	●	**THE ADORATION WALTZ** *Decca F 10833* [2]	9	11
5 Apr 57		**I'LL FIND YOU** *Decca F 10864*	28	2
7 Jun 57		**I'LL FIND YOU (re-entry)** *Decca F 10864*	27	2
14 Feb 58		**CRY MY HEART** *Decca F 10978* [3]	22	3
16 May 58		**ON THE STREET WHERE YOU LIVE** *Decca F 11018* [4]	16	14
8 Aug 58		**THE RIGHT TO LOVE** *Decca F 11039*	30	1
24 Nov 60		**I BELIEVE** *Decca F 11289*	49	1

[1] David Whitfield with Stanley Black and his Orchestra [2] David Whitfield with the Roland Shaw Orchestra [3] David Whitfield with chorus and Mantovani and his Orchestra [4] David Whitfield with Cyril Stapleton and his Orchestra

Slim WHITMAN (441 Top 500) *Distinctive country vocalist whose yodelling style made him a major 1950s pop star in UK, b. 20 Jan 1924, Florida, US. For 36 years, 'Rose Marie' held the record for most consecutive weeks at the top. At 53 (1977) he was the oldest act to top the chart with a new album. It was Whitman's singing that vanquished the aliens in the movie 'Mars Attacks!' (77 WEEKS)* pos/wks

Date		Title / Label	Pos	Wks
15 Jul 55	★	**ROSE MARIE** *London HL 8061*	1	19
29 Jul 55	●	**INDIAN LOVE CALL** *London L 1149*	7	12
23 Sep 55		**CHINA DOLL** *London L 1149*	15	2
9 Mar 56		**TUMBLING TUMBLEWEEDS** *London HLU 8230*	19	2
13 Apr 56		**I'M A FOOL** *London HLU 8252*	16	3
11 May 56		**I'M A FOOL (re-entry)** *London HLU 8252*	29	1
22 Jun 56		**SERENADE** *London HLU 8287*	24	3
27 Jul 56	●	**SERENADE (re-entry)** *London HLU 8287*	8	12
12 Apr 57	●	**I'LL TAKE YOU HOME AGAIN KATHLEEN** *London HLP 8403*	7	13
5 Oct 74		**HAPPY ANNIVERSARY** *United Artists UP 35728*	14	10

Roger WHITTAKER (383 Top 500) *World-renowned vocalist and whistler, b. 22 Mar 1936, Nairobi, Kenya. Easy-listening legend and popular live performer with more than 10 million albums sold in his home base, Germany (85 WEEKS)* pos/wks

Date		Title / Label	Pos	Wks
8 Nov 69		**DURHAM TOWN (THE LEAVIN')** *Columbia DB 8613*	12	18
11 Apr 70	●	**I DON'T BELIEVE IN IF ANYMORE** *Columbia DB 8664*	8	18
10 Oct 70		**NEW WORLD IN THE MORNING** *Columbia DB 8718*	17	14
3 Apr 71		**WHY** *Columbia DB 8752*	47	1
2 Oct 71		**MAMMY BLUE** *Columbia DB 8822*	31	10
26 Jul 75	●	**THE LAST FAREWELL** *EMI 2294*	2	14
8 Nov 86	●	**THE SKYE BOAT SONG** *Tembo TML 119* [1]	10	10

[1] Roger Whittaker and Des O'Connor

WHO (51 Top 500) *Legendary live band from London, whose 'Tommy' album (1969) popularised rock opera: Roger Daltrey (v), Pete Townshend (g), John Entwistle (b), Keith Moon (d) (d. 1978). These gold-record collectors have spent five decades breaking both guitars and box-office records (247 WEEKS)* pos/wks

Date		Title / Label	Pos	Wks
18 Feb 65	●	**I CAN'T EXPLAIN** *Brunswick 05926*	8	13
27 May 65	●	**ANYWAY ANYHOW ANYWHERE** *Brunswick 05935*	10	12
4 Nov 65	●	**MY GENERATION** *Brunswick 05944*	2	13
10 Mar 66	●	**SUBSTITUTE** *Reaction 591 001*	5	13
24 Mar 66		**A LEGAL MATTER** *Brunswick 05956*	32	6
1 Sep 66	●	**I'M A BOY** *Reaction 591 004*	2	13
1 Sep 66		**THE KIDS ARE ALRIGHT** *Brunswick 05965*	41	2
22 Sep 66		**THE KIDS ARE ALRIGHT (re-entry)** *Brunswick 05965*	48	1
15 Dec 66	●	**HAPPY JACK** *Reaction 591 010*	3	11
27 Apr 67	●	**PICTURES OF LILY** *Track 604 002*	4	10
26 Jul 67		**THE LAST TIME / UNDER MY THUMB** *Track 604 006*	44	3
18 Oct 67	●	**I CAN SEE FOR MILES** *Track 604 011*	10	12
19 Jun 68		**DOGS** *Track 604 023*	25	5
23 Oct 68		**MAGIC BUS** *Track 604 024*	26	6
19 Mar 69	●	**PINBALL WIZARD** *Track 604 027*	4	13
4 Apr 70		**THE SEEKER** *Track 604 036*	19	11
8 Aug 70		**SUMMERTIME BLUES** *Track 2094 002*	38	4
10 Jul 71	●	**WON'T GET FOOLED AGAIN** *Track 2094 009*	9	12
23 Oct 71		**LET'S SEE ACTION** *Track 2094 012*	16	12
24 Jun 72	●	**JOIN TOGETHER** *Track 2094 102*	9	9
13 Jan 73		**RELAY** *Track 2094 106*	21	5
13 Oct 73		**5.15** *Track 2094 115*	20	6
24 Jan 76	●	**SQUEEZE BOX** *Polydor 2121 275*	10	9
30 Oct 76	●	**SUBSTITUTE (re-issue)** *Polydor 2058 803*	7	7
22 Jul 78		**WHO ARE YOU** *Polydor WHO 1*	18	12
28 Apr 79		**LONG LIVE ROCK** *Polydor WHO 2*	48	5
7 Mar 81	●	**YOU BETTER YOU BET** *Polydor WHO 004*	9	8
9 May 81		**DON'T LET GO THE COAT** *Polydor WHO 005*	47	4
2 Oct 82		**ATHENA** *Polydor WHO 6*	40	4
26 Nov 83		**READY STEADY WHO (EP)** *Polydor WHO 7*	58	2
20 Feb 88		**MY GENERATION (re-issue)** *Polydor POSP 907*	68	2
27 Jul 96		**MY GENERATION (2nd re-issue)** *Polydor 8546372*	31	2

Tracks on Ready Steady Who (EP): Disguises / Circles / Batman / Bucket 'T' / Barbara Ann

See also HIGH NUMBERS

WHODINI *US, male rap / DJ duo (10 WEEKS)* pos/wks

Date		Title / Label	Pos	Wks
25 Dec 82		**MAGIC'S WAND** *Jive JIVE 28*	47	6
17 Mar 84		**MAGIC'S WAND (THE WHODINI ELECTRIC EP)** *Jive JIVE 61*	63	4

Tracks on The Whodini Electric EP: Jive Magic Wand / Nasty Lady / Rap Machine / The Haunted House of Rock

WHOOLIGANZ *US, male rap duo (2 WEEKS)* pos/wks

Date		Title / Label	Pos	Wks
13 Aug 94		**PUT YOUR HANDZ UP** *Positiva CDTIV 17*	53	2

WHOOSH *UK, male production trio (1 WEEK)* pos/wks

Date		Title / Label	Pos	Wks
13 Sep 97		**WHOOSH** *Wonderboy WBOYD 006*	72	1

WHYCLIFFE *UK, male vocalist (2 WEEKS)* pos/wks

Date		Title / Label	Pos	Wks
20 Nov 93		**HEAVEN** *MCA MCSTD 1944*	56	1
2 Apr 94		**ONE MORE TIME** *MCA MCSTD 1955*	72	1

WIDEBOYS featuring Dennis G
UK, male production duo and UK, male vocalist (6 WEEKS) pos/wks

Date		Title / Label	Pos	Wks
27 Oct 01		**SAMBUCA** *Locked On / 679 Recordings 679L 002CD*	15	6

Jane WIEDLIN *US, female vocalist (14 WEEKS)* pos/wks

Date		Title / Label	Pos	Wks
6 Aug 88		**RUSH HOUR** *Manhattan MT 36*	12	11
29 Oct 88		**INSIDE A DREAM** *Manhattan MT 55*	64	3

WIGAN'S CHOSEN FEW *Canada, male vocal / instrumental group and UK, crowd chants (11 WEEKS)* pos/wks

Date		Title / Label	Pos	Wks
18 Jan 75	●	**FOOTSEE** *Pye Disco Demand DDS 111*	9	11

WIGAN'S OVATION *UK, male vocal / instrumental group (19 WEEKS)* pos/wks

Date		Title / Label	Pos	Wks
15 Mar 75		**SKIING IN THE SNOW** *Spark SRL 1122*	12	10
28 Jun 75		**PER-SO-NAL-LY** *Spark SRL 1129*	38	6
29 Nov 75		**SUPER LOVE** *Spark SRL 1133*	41	3

WILCO *US, male vocal / instrumental group (1 WEEK)* pos/wks

Date		Title / Label	Pos	Wks
17 Apr 99		**CAN'T STAND IT** *Reprise W 475CD1*	67	1

Jack WILD *UK, male vocalist (2 WEEKS)* pos/wks

Date		Title / Label	Pos	Wks
2 May 70		**SOME BEAUTIFUL** *Capitol CL 15635*	46	2

WILD BOYS – See HEINZ

WILD CHERRY *US, male vocal / instrumental group (11 WEEKS)* pos/wks

Date		Title / Label	Pos	Wks
9 Oct 76	●	**PLAY THAT FUNKY MUSIC** *Epic EPC 4593* ▲	7	11

WILD COLOUR
UK, male / female vocal / instrumental group (2 WEEKS) pos/wks

Date		Title / Label	Pos	Wks
14 Oct 95		**DREAMS** *Perfecto PERF 105CD*	25	2

WILD PAIR – See Paula ABDUL

WILD WEEKEND *UK, male vocal / instrumental group (2 WEEKS)* pos/wks

Date		Title / Label	Pos	Wks
29 Apr 89		**BREAKIN' UP** *Parlophone R 6204*	74	1
5 May 90		**WHO'S AFRAID OF THE BIG BAD LOVE?** *Parlophone R 6249*	70	1

WILDCHILD *UK, male producer – Roger McKenzie (20 WEEKS)* pos/wks

22 Apr 95		**LEGENDS OF THE DARK BLACK PART 2** *Hi-Life HICD 9*	34	3
21 Oct 95		**RENEGADE MASTER (re-issue)** *Hi-Life 5771312*	11	4
23 Nov 96		**JUMP TO MY BEAT** *Hi-Life 5757372*	30	2
17 Jan 98	●	**RENEGADE MASTER '98** *Hi-Life 5692792*	3	10
25 Apr 98		**BAD BOY** *Polydor 5716072* [1]	38	1

[1] Wildchild featuring Jomalski

Although titled differently, first two hits are identical

Eugene WILDE *US, male vocalist – Ron Broomfield (15 WEEKS)* pos/wks

13 Oct 84		**GOTTA GET YOU HOME TONIGHT** *Fourth & Broadway BRW 15*	18	9
2 Feb 85		**PERSONALITY** *Fourth & Broadway BRW 18*	34	6

'Personality' was coupled with 'Let Her Feel It' by Simplicious

Kim WILDE (96 Top 500) *Most charted British female vocalist in the 1980s, b. Kim Smith, 18 Nov 1960, London. Neither Kim nor her father, rock 'n' roll star Marty Wilde, managed a UK No.1, but Kim did top the US chart (194 WEEKS)* pos/wks

21 Feb 81	●	**KIDS IN AMERICA** *RAK 327*	2	13
9 May 81	●	**CHEQUERED LOVE** *RAK 330*	4	9
1 Aug 81		**WATER ON GLASS / BOYS** *RAK 334*	11	8
14 Nov 81		**CAMBODIA** *RAK 336*	12	12
17 Apr 82		**VIEW FROM A BRIDGE** *RAK 342*	16	7
16 Oct 82		**CHILD COME AWAY** *RAK 352*	43	4
30 Jul 83		**LOVE BLONDE** *RAK 360*	23	8
12 Nov 83		**DANCING IN THE DARK** *RAK 365*	67	2
13 Oct 84		**THE SECOND TIME** *MCA KIM 1*	29	6
8 Dec 84		**THE TOUCH** *MCA KIM 2*	56	3
27 Apr 85		**RAGE TO LOVE** *MCA KIM 3*	19	8
25 Oct 86	●	**YOU KEEP ME HANGIN' ON** *MCA KIM 4* ▲	2	14
4 Apr 87	●	**ANOTHER STEP (CLOSER TO YOU)** *MCA KIM 5* [1]	6	11
8 Aug 87		**SAY YOU REALLY WANT ME** *MCA KIM 6*	29	5
5 Dec 87	●	**ROCKIN' AROUND THE CHRISTMAS TREE** *10 TEN 2* [2]	3	7
14 May 88		**HEY MISTER HEARTACHE** *MCA KIM 7*	31	5
16 Jul 88	●	**YOU CAME** *MCA KIM 8*	3	11
1 Oct 88	●	**NEVER TRUST A STRANGER** *MCA KIM 9*	7	9
3 Dec 88	●	**FOUR LETTER WORD** *MCA KIM 10*	6	12
4 Mar 89		**LOVE IN THE NATURAL WAY** *MCA KIM 11*	32	6
14 Apr 90		**IT'S HERE** *MCA KIM 12*	42	4
16 Jun 90		**TIME** *MCA KIM 13*	71	3
15 Dec 90		**I CAN'T SAY GOODBYE** *MCA KIM 14*	51	3
2 May 92		**LOVE IS HOLY** *MCA KIM 15*	16	6
27 Jun 92		**HEART OVER MIND** *MCA KIM 16*	34	3
12 Sep 92		**WHO DO YOU THINK YOU ARE** *MCA KIM 17*	49	3
10 Jul 93		**IF I CAN'T HAVE YOU** *MCA KIMTD 18*	12	8
13 Nov 93		**IN MY LIFE** *MCA KIMTD 19*	54	1
14 Oct 95		**BREAKIN' AWAY** *MCA KIMTD 21*	43	2
10 Feb 96		**THIS I SWEAR** *MCA KIMTD 22*	46	1

[1] Kim Wilde and Junior [2] Mel and Kim (Kim was Kim Wilde)

Marty WILDE (237 Top 500) *Early British rock 'n' roll singing idol, b. Reginald Smith, 15 Apr 1939, London. Although most of his best-sellers were cover versions (the normal practice at the time), he later penned hits for Lulu, Casuals, Status Quo and many for his daughter, Kim Wilde (117 WEEKS)* pos/wks

11 Jul 58	●	**ENDLESS SLEEP** *Philips PB 835*	4	14
6 Mar 59	●	**DONNA** *Philips PB 902*	3	16
5 Jun 59	●	**A TEENAGER IN LOVE** *Philips PB 926*	2	17
3 Jul 59		**DONNA (re-entry)** *Philips PB 902*	25	2
25 Sep 59	●	**SEA OF LOVE** *Philips PB 959*	3	12
11 Dec 59	●	**BAD BOY** *Philips PB 972*	7	8
10 Mar 60		**JOHNNY ROCCO** *Philips PB 1002*	30	4
19 May 60		**THE FIGHT** *Philips PB 1022*	47	1
22 Dec 60		**LITTLE GIRL** *Philips PB 1078*	16	9
26 Jan 61	●	**RUBBER BALL** *Philips PB 1101*	9	9
27 Jul 61		**HIDE AND SEEK** *Philips PB 1161*	47	2
9 Nov 61		**TOMORROW'S CLOWN** *Philips PB 1191*	33	5
24 May 62		**JEZEBEL** *Philips PB 1240*	19	11
25 Oct 62		**EVER SINCE YOU SAID GOODBYE** *Philips 326546 BF*	31	7

Matthew WILDER *US, male vocalist (11 WEEKS)* pos/wks

21 Jan 84	●	**BREAK MY STRIDE** *Epic A 3908*	4	11

WILDHEARTS *UK, male vocal / instrumental group (24 WEEKS)* pos/wks

20 Nov 93		**TV TAN** *Bronze YZ 784CD*	53	2
19 Feb 94		**CAFFEINE BOMB** *Bronze YZ 794CD*	31	3
9 Jul 94		**SUCKERPUNCH** *Bronze YZ 828CD*	38	2
28 Jan 95		**IF LIFE IS LIKE A LOVE BANK I WANT AN OVERDRAFT / GEORDIE IN WONDERLAND** *East West YZ 874CD*	31	3
6 May 95		**I WANNA GO WHERE THE PEOPLE GO** *East West YZ 923CD*	16	3
29 Jul 95		**JUST IN LUST** *East West YZ 967CD*	28	2
20 Apr 96		**SICK OF DRUGS** *Round WILD 1CD*	14	3
29 Jun 96		**RED LIGHT - GREEN LIGHT (EP)** *Round WILD 2CD*	30	2
16 Aug 97		**ANTHEM** *Mushroom MUSH 6CD*	21	2
18 Oct 97		**URGE** *Mushroom MUSH 14CD*	26	2

Tracks on Red Light - Green Light (EP): Red Light - Green Light / Got It On Tuesday / Do Anything / The British All-American Homeboy Crowd

Jonathan WILKES *UK, male vocalist (2 WEEKS)* pos/wks

17 Mar 01		**JUST ANOTHER DAY** *Innocent SINCD 25*	24	2

Sue WILKINSON *UK, female vocalist (8 WEEKS)* pos/wks

2 Aug 80		**YOU GOTTA BE A HUSTLER IF YOU WANNA GET ON** *Cheapskate CHEAP 2*	25	8

WILL TO POWER *US, male / female vocal / instrumental duo – Bob Rosenberg and Suzi Carr (18 WEEKS)* pos/wks

7 Jan 89	●	**BABY I LOVE YOUR WAY - FREEBIRD** *Epic 6530947* ▲	6	9
22 Dec 90		**I'M NOT IN LOVE** *Epic 6565377*	29	9

Alyson WILLIAMS *US, female vocalist (28 WEEKS)* pos/wks

4 Mar 89		**SLEEP TALK** *Def Jam 654656 7*	17	9
6 May 89		**MY LOVE IS SO RAW** *Def Jam 654898 7* [1]	34	5
19 Aug 89	●	**I NEED YOUR LOVIN'** *Def Jam 655143 7*	8	11
18 Nov 89		**I SECOND THAT EMOTION** *Def Jam 655456 7* [2]	44	3

[1] Alyson Williams featuring Nikki D [2] Alyson Williams with Chuck Stanley

Andy WILLIAMS (59 Top 500) *Leading MOR vocalist, who hosted a top-rated 1960s TV series, b. 3 Dec 1928, Iowa, US. He left the noted family act The Williams Brothers in 1951 and had an enviable portfolio of smooth UK and US hit singles and albums in the 1950s and 1960s. Had a surprise 1999 re-entry for 'Music to Watch Girls By' following its use in a TV car commercial (234 WEEKS)* pos/wks

19 Apr 57	★	**BUTTERFLY** *London HLA 8399*	1	15
21 Jun 57		**I LIKE YOUR KIND OF LOVE** *London HLA 8437*	16	10
30 Aug 57		**BUTTERFLY (re-entry)** *London HLA 8399*	29	1
14 Jun 62		**STRANGER ON THE SHORE** *CBS AAG 103*	30	10
21 Mar 63	●	**CAN'T GET USED TO LOSING YOU** *CBS AAG 138*	2	18
27 Feb 64		**A FOOL NEVER LEARNS** *CBS AAG 182*	40	4
16 Sep 65	●	**ALMOST THERE** *CBS 201813*	2	17
24 Feb 66		**MAY EACH DAY** *CBS 202042*	19	8
22 Sep 66		**IN THE ARMS OF LOVE** *CBS 202300*	33	7
4 May 67		**MUSIC TO WATCH GIRLS BY** *CBS 2675*	33	6
2 Aug 67		**MORE AND MORE** *CBS 2886*	45	1
13 Mar 68	●	**CAN'T TAKE MY EYES OFF YOU** *CBS 3298*	5	18
7 May 69		**HAPPY HEART** *CBS 4062*	47	1
21 May 69		**HAPPY HEART (re-entry)** *CBS 4062*	19	9
14 Mar 70	●	**CAN'T HELP FALLING IN LOVE** *CBS 4818*	3	17
1 Aug 70		**IT'S SO EASY** *CBS 5113*	13	13
7 Nov 70		**IT'S SO EASY (re-entry)** *CBS 5113*	49	1
21 Nov 70	●	**HOME LOVIN' MAN** *CBS 5267*	7	12
20 Mar 71	●	**(WHERE DO I BEGIN) LOVE STORY** *CBS 7020*	4	17
24 Jul 71		**(WHERE DO I BEGIN) LOVE STORY (re-entry)** *CBS 7020*	49	1
5 Aug 72		**LOVE THEME FROM 'THE GODFATHER'** *CBS 8166*	50	1
2 Sep 72		**LOVE THEME FROM 'THE GODFATHER' (re-entry)** *CBS 8166*	44	3
30 Sep 72		**LOVE THEME FROM 'THE GODFATHER' (2nd re-entry)** *CBS 8166*	42	5
8 Dec 73	●	**SOLITAIRE** *CBS 1824*	4	18
18 May 74		**GETTING OVER YOU** *CBS 2181*	35	5

Date		Title / Label	pos	wks
31 May 75		YOU LAY SO EASY ON MY MIND *CBS 3167*	32	7
6 Mar 76		THE OTHER SIDE OF ME *CBS 3903*	42	3
27 Mar 99	●	MUSIC TO WATCH GIRLS BY (re-issue) *Columbia 6671322*	9	6

Andy and David WILLIAMS *US, male vocal duo (5 WEEKS)* pos/wks

Date		Title / Label	pos	wks
24 Mar 73		I DON'T KNOW WHY *MCA MUS 1183*	37	5

Do not see Andy Williams. This Andy is the nephew of the other Andy

Billy WILLIAMS *US, male vocalist (9 WEEKS)* pos/wks

Date		Title / Label	pos	wks
2 Aug 57		I'M GONNA SIT RIGHT DOWN AND WRITE MYSELF A LETTER *Vogue Coral Q 72266*	22	8
18 Oct 57		I'M GONNA SIT RIGHT DOWN AND WRITE MYSELF A LETTER (re-entry) *Vogue Coral Q 72266*	28	1

Danny WILLIAMS (474 Top 500) *Velvet-voiced, British-based easy-listening vocalist; b. 7 Jan 1942, South Africa. Johnny Mathis-styled singer who won the UK 'Moon River' battle was first seen on rock 'n' roll TV show 'Drumbeat'. Had US Top 10 hit with 1964 UK flop 'White On White' (74 WEEKS)* pos/wks

Date		Title / Label	pos	wks
25 May 61		WE WILL NEVER BE AS YOUNG AS THIS AGAIN *HMV POP 839*	44	3
6 Jul 61		THE MIRACLE OF YOU *HMV POP 885*	41	8
2 Nov 61	★	MOON RIVER *HMV POP 932*	1	19
18 Jan 62		JEANNIE *HMV POP 968*	14	14
12 Apr 62	●	THE WONDERFUL WORLD OF THE YOUNG *HMV POP 1002*	8	13
5 Jul 62		TEARS *HMV POP 1035*	22	7
28 Feb 63		MY OWN TRUE LOVE *HMV POP 1112*	45	3
30 Jul 77		DANCIN' EASY *Ensign ENY 3*	30	7

Deniece WILLIAMS *US, female vocalist - Deniece Chandler (59 WEEKS)* pos/wks

Date		Title / Label	pos	wks
2 Apr 77	★	FREE *CBS 4978*	1	10
30 Jul 77	●	THAT'S WHAT FRIENDS ARE FOR *CBS 5432*	8	11
12 Nov 77		BABY BABY MY LOVE'S ALL FOR YOU *CBS 5779*	32	5
25 Mar 78	●	TOO MUCH, TOO LITTLE, TOO LATE *CBS 6164* [1] ▲	3	14
29 Jul 78		YOU'RE ALL I NEED TO GET BY *CBS 6483* [1]	45	6
5 May 84	●	LET'S HEAR IT FOR THE BOY *CBS A 4319* ▲	2	12
4 Aug 84		LET'S HEAR IT FOR THE BOY (re-entry) *CBS A 4319*	75	1

[1] Johnny Mathis and Deniece Williams

Diana WILLIAMS *US, female vocalist (3 WEEKS)* pos/wks

Date		Title / Label	pos	wks
25 Jul 81		TEDDY BEAR'S LAST RIDE *Capitol CL 207*	54	3

Don WILLIAMS *US, male vocalist (16 WEEKS)* pos/wks

Date		Title / Label	pos	wks
19 Jun 76		I RECALL A GYPSY WOMAN *ABC 4098*	13	10
23 Oct 76		YOU'RE MY BEST FRIEND *ABC 4144*	35	6

Eric WILLIAMS – *See QUEEN PEN; 2PAC*

Freedom WILLIAMS *US, male rapper (31 WEEKS)* pos/wks

Date		Title / Label	pos	wks
15 Dec 90	●	GONNA MAKE YOU SWEAT (EVERYBODY DANCE NOW) *CBS 6564540* [1] ▲	3	12
30 Mar 91		HERE WE GO *Columbia 6567537* [1]	20	7
6 Jul 91	●	THINGS THAT MAKE YOU GO HMMM... *Columbia 6566907* [1]	4	11
5 Jun 93		VOICE OF FREEDOM *Columbia 6593342*	62	1

[1] C & C Music Factory (featuring Freedom Williams)

Geoffrey WILLIAMS *UK, male vocalist (8 WEEKS)* pos/wks

Date		Title / Label	pos	wks
11 Apr 92		IT'S NOT A LOVE THING *EMI EM 228*	63	2
22 Aug 92		SUMMER BREEZE *EMI EM 245*	56	3
18 Jan 97		DRIVE *Hands On CDHOR 11*	52	2
19 Apr 97		SEX LIFE *Hands On CDHOR 12*	71	1

Iris WILLIAMS *UK, female vocalist (8 WEEKS)* pos/wks

Date		Title / Label	pos	wks
27 Oct 79		HE WAS BEAUTIFUL (CAVATINA) (THE THEME FROM 'THE DEER HUNTER') *Columbia DB 9070*	18	8

James WILLIAMS – *See Bob SINCLAIR; D TRAIN*

John WILLIAMS *UK, male instrumentalist - guitar (11 WEEKS)* pos/wks

Date		Title / Label	pos	wks
19 May 79		CAVATINA *Cube BUG 80*	13	11

John WILLIAMS *US, orchestra leader with US, orchestra (12 WEEKS)* pos/wks

Date		Title / Label	pos	wks
18 Dec 82		THEME FROM 'E.T.' (THE EXTRA-TERRESTRIAL) *MCA 800*	17	10
14 Aug 93		THEME FROM 'JURASSIC PARK' *MCA MCSTD 1927*	45	2

Kenny WILLIAMS *US, male vocalist (7 WEEKS)* pos/wks

Date		Title / Label	pos	wks
19 Nov 77		(YOU'RE) FABULOUS BABE *Decca FR 13731*	35	7

Larry WILLIAMS *US, male vocalist (18 WEEKS)* pos/wks

Date		Title / Label	pos	wks
20 Sep 57		SHORT FAT FANNIE *London HLN 8472*	21	8
17 Jan 58		BONY MORONIE *London HLU 8532*	11	10

Lenny WILLIAMS *US, male vocalist (7 WEEKS)* pos/wks

Date		Title / Label	pos	wks
5 Nov 77		SHOO DOO FU FU OOH *ABC 4194*	38	4
16 Sep 78		YOU GOT ME BURNING *ABC 4228*	67	3

Mark WILLIAMS – *See Karen BODDINGTON and Mark WILLIAMS*

Mason WILLIAMS *US, male instrumentalist – guitar (13 WEEKS)* pos/wks

Date		Title / Label	pos	wks
28 Aug 68	●	CLASSICAL GAS *Warner Bros. WB 7190*	9	13

Maurice WILLIAMS and the ZODIACS *US, male vocal group (9 WEEKS)* pos/wks

Date		Title / Label	pos	wks
5 Jan 61		STAY *Top Rank JAR 526* ▲	14	9

Melanie WILLIAMS *UK, female vocalist (21 WEEKS)* pos/wks

Date		Title / Label	pos	wks
10 Apr 93	●	AIN'T NO LOVE (AIN'T NO USE) *Rob's CDROB 9* [1]	3	11
9 Apr 94		ALL CRIED OUT *Columbia 6601872*	60	2
11 Jun 94		EVERYDAY THANG *Columbia 6604712*	38	3
17 Sep 94		NOT ENOUGH *Columbia 6607752*	65	1
18 Feb 95		YOU ARE EVERYTHING *Columbia 6611755* [2]	28	4

[1] Sub Sub featuring Melanie Williams [2] Melanie Williams and Joe Roberts

Robbie WILLIAMS (75 Top 500) *Former Take That teen idol who became a multi-award-winning vocalist and songwriter, b. 13 Feb 1974, Stoke-on-Trent, UK. This energetic and humorous showman has sold more than 10 million solo records in the UK and won more Brits than any other act (213 WEEKS)* pos/wks

Date		Title / Label	pos	wks
10 Aug 96	●	FREEDOM *Chrysalis CDFREE 1*	2	10
26 Oct 96		FREEDOM (re-entry) *Chrysalis CDFREE 1*	56	4
26 Apr 97	●	OLD BEFORE I DIE *Chrysalis CDCHS 5055*	2	9
5 Jul 97		OLD BEFORE I DIE (re-entry) *Chrysalis CDCHS 5055*	72	1
19 Jul 97		OLD BEFORE I DIE (2nd re-entry) *Chrysalis CDCHS 5055*	69	1
26 Jul 97	●	LAZY DAYS *Chrysalis CDCHS 5063*	8	5
27 Sep 97		SOUTH OF THE BORDER *Chrysalis CDCHS 5068*	14	4
13 Dec 97	●	ANGELS *Chrysalis CDCHS 5072* ◆	4	20
28 Mar 98	●	LET ME ENTERTAIN YOU *Chrysalis CDCHS 5080*	3	12
19 Sep 98	★	MILLENNIUM *Chrysalis CDCHS 5099* ■	1	20
12 Dec 98	●	NO REGRETS *Chrysalis CDCHS 5100*	4	13
2 Jan 99		ANGELS (re-entry) *Chrysalis CDCHS 5072*	57	4
27 Feb 99		ANGELS (2nd re-entry) *Chrysalis CDCHS 5072*	75	1
20 Mar 99		ANGELS (3rd re-entry) *Chrysalis CDCHS 5072*	75	1
27 Mar 99	●	STRONG *Chrysalis CDCHS 5107*	4	9
20 Nov 99	★	SHE'S THE ONE / IT'S ONLY US *Chrysalis CDCHS 5112* ■	1	16
1 Jan 00		ANGELS (4th re-entry) *Chrysalis CDCHS 5072*	71	1
8 Jan 00		MILLENNIUM (re-entry) *Chrysalis CDCHS 5099*	74	1
18 Mar 00		SHE'S THE ONE / IT'S ONLY US (re-entry) *Chrysalis CDCHS 5112*	57	4
12 Aug 00	★	ROCK DJ *Chrysalis CDCHS 5118* ■	1	17
21 Oct 00	●	KIDS *Chrysalis CHCHS 5119* [1]	2	17
16 Dec 00		ROCK DJ (re-entry) *Chrysalis CDCHS 5118*	60	3
23 Dec 00	●	SUPREME *Chrysalis CDCHS 5120*	4	10
10 Feb 01		KIDS (re-entry) *Chrysalis CHCHS 5119* [1]	73	1

21 Mar 01	● LET LOVE BE YOUR ENERGY *Chrysalis CDCHS 5124*	10	9
21 Jul 01	★ ETERNITY / THE ROAD TO MANDALAY *Chrysalis CDCHS 5126* ■	1	16
21 Jul 01	LET LOVE BE YOUR ENERGY (re-entry) *Chrysalis CDCHS 5124*	73	2
22 Dec 01	★ SOMETHIN' STUPID *Chrysalis CDCHS 5132* [2] ■	1	2+

[1] Robbie Williams / Kylie Minogue [2] Robbie Williams and Nicole Kidman

Saul WILLIAMS – *See KRUST featuring Saul WILLIAMS*

Vanessa WILLIAMS *US, female vocalist (24 WEEKS)* pos/wks

20 Aug 88	THE RIGHT STUFF *Wing WING 3*	71	1
25 Mar 89	DREAMIN' *Wing WING 4*	74	2
19 Aug 89	THE RIGHT STUFF (re-mix) *Wing WINR 3*	62	2
21 Mar 92	● SAVE THE BEST FOR LAST *Polydor PO 192* ▲	3	11
8 Apr 95	THE SWEETEST DAYS *Mercury MERCD 422*	41	2
8 Jul 95	THE WAY THAT YOU LOVE *Mercury MERCD 439*	52	1
18 Sep 95	COLOURS OF THE WIND *Walt Disney WD 7677CD*	21	5

Vesta WILLIAMS *US, female vocalist (13 WEEKS)* pos/wks

20 Dec 86	ONCE BITTEN TWICE SHY *A & M AM 362*	14	13

Wendell WILLIAMS *US, male rapper (6 WEEKS)* pos/wks

6 Oct 90	EVERYBODY (RAP) *Deconstruction PB 44701* [1]	30	4
18 May 91	SO GROOVY *Deconstruction PB 44567*	74	2

[1] Criminal Element Orchestra and Wendell Williams

WILLING SINNERS – *See Marc ALMOND*

Bruce WILLIS *US, male vocalist (30 WEEKS)* pos/wks

7 Mar 87	● RESPECT YOURSELF *Motown ZB 41117*	7	10
30 May 87	● UNDER THE BOARDWALK *Motown ZB 41349*	2	15
12 Sep 87	SECRET AGENT MAN - JAMES BOND IS BACK *Motown ZB 41437*	43	4
23 Jan 88	COMIN' RIGHT UP *Motown ZB 41453*	73	1

Chill WILLS – *See LAUREL and HARDY with the AVALON BOYS featuring Chill WILLS*

Viola WILLS *US, female vocalist (16 WEEKS)* pos/wks

6 Oct 79	● GONNA GET ALONG WITHOUT YOU NOW *Ariola / Hansa AHA 546*	8	10
15 Mar 86	BOTH SIDES NOW / DARE TO DREAM *Streetwave KHAN 66*	35	6

Al WILSON *US, male vocalist (5 WEEKS)* pos/wks

23 Aug 75	THE SNAKE *Bell 1436*	41	5

Charlie WILSON – *See SNOOP DOGGY DOGG; GAP BAND*

Dooley WILSON *US, male vocalist (9 WEEKS)* pos/wks

3 Dec 77	AS TIME GOES BY *United Artists UP 36331*	15	9

Disc has credit: 'With the voices of Humphrey Bogart and Ingrid Bergman'

Jackie WILSON (317 Top 500) *One of R&B music's greatest stage performers and most distinctive vocalists, b. 9 Jun 1934, Detroit, US, d. 21 Jan 1984 (after eight years in a semi-comatose state). He influenced Elvis Presley, Michael Jackson and Prince. 'Reet Petite' took a record 29 years, 42 days to reach the top (97 WEEKS)* pos/wks

15 Nov 57	● REET PETITE (THE SWEETEST GIRL IN TOWN) *Coral Q 72290*	6	14
14 Mar 58	TO BE LOVED *Coral Q 72306*	27	1
28 Mar 58	TO BE LOVED (re-entry) *Coral Q 72306*	23	6
16 May 58	TO BE LOVED (2nd re-entry) *Coral Q 72306*	23	1
15 Sep 60	(YOU WERE MADE FOR) ALL MY LOVE *Coral Q 72407*	33	6
3 Nov 60	(YOU WERE MADE FOR) ALL MY LOVE (re-entry) *Coral Q 72407*	47	1
22 Dec 60	ALONE AT LAST *Coral Q 72412*	50	1
14 May 69	(YOUR LOVE KEEPS LIFTING ME) HIGHER AND HIGHER *MCA BAG 2*	11	11
29 Jul 72	● I GET THE SWEETEST FEELING *MCA MU 1160*	9	13
3 May 75	I GET THE SWEETEST FEELING / (YOUR LOVE KEEPS LIFTING ME) HIGHER AND HIGHER (re-issue) *Brunswick BR 18*	25	8
29 Nov 86	★ REET PETITE (THE SWEETEST GIRL IN TOWN) (re-issue) *SMP SKM 3*	1	17
28 Feb 87	● I GET THE SWEETEST FEELING (2nd re-issue) *SMP SKM 1*	3	11
4 Jul 87	(YOUR LOVE KEEPS LIFTING ME) HIGHER AND HIGHER (2nd re-issue) *SMP SKM 10*	15	7

'Higher and Higher' was not listed together with 'I Get the Sweetest Feeling' on Brunswick until 17 May 1975

Mari WILSON *UK, female vocalist (34 WEEKS)* pos/wks

6 Mar 82	BEAT THE BEAT *Compact PINK 2*	59	3
8 May 82	BABY IT'S TRUE *Compact PINK 3*	42	6
11 Sep 82	● JUST WHAT I ALWAYS WANTED *Compact PINK 4*	8	10
13 Nov 82	(BEWARE) BOYFRIEND *Compact PINK 5*	51	4
19 Mar 83	CRY ME A RIVER *Compact PINK 6*	27	7
11 Jun 83	WONDERFUL *Compact PINK 7*	47	4

Meri WILSON *US, female vocalist (10 WEEKS)* pos/wks

27 Aug 77	● TELEPHONE MAN *Pye International 7N 25747*	6	10

Mike 'Hitman' WILSON *US, male producer (1 WEEK)* pos/wks

22 Sep 90	ANOTHER SLEEPLESS NIGHT *Arista 113506*	74	1

Precious WILSON – *See ERUPTION; MESSIAH*

Tom WILSON *UK, male producer (4 WEEKS)* pos/wks

2 Dec 95	TECHNOCAT *Pukka CDPUKKA 4* [1]	33	3
16 Mar 96	LET YOUR BODY GO *Clubscene DCSRT 050*	60	1

[1] Technocat featuring Tom Wilson

Victoria WILSON JAMES *US, female vocalist (1 WEEK)* pos/wks

9 Aug 97	REACH 4 THE MELODY *Sony S3 VWJCD1*	72	1

WILSON PHILLIPS *US, female vocal group (33 WEEKS)* pos/wks

26 May 90	● HOLD ON *SBK SBK 6* ▲	6	12
18 Aug 90	RELEASE ME *SBK SBK 11* ▲	36	5
10 Nov 90	IMPULSIVE *SBK SBK 16*	42	3
11 May 91	YOU'RE IN LOVE *SBK SBK 25* ▲	29	5
23 May 92	YOU WON'T SEE ME CRY *SBK SBK 34*	18	5
22 Aug 92	GIVE IT UP *SBK SBK 36*	36	3

WILT *Ireland, male vocal / instrumental group (2 WEEKS)* pos/wks

8 Apr 00	RADIO DISCO *Mushroom MUSH 71CDS*	56	1
8 Jul 00	OPEN ARMS *Mushroom MUSH 75CDS*	59	1

Chris WILTSHIRE – *See CLASS ACTION featuring Chris WILTSHIRE*

WIMBLEDON CHORAL SOCIETY *UK, choral group (8 WEEKS)* pos/wks

4 Jul 98	WORLD CUP '98 - PAVANE *Telstar CDSTAS 2979*	20	5
12 Dec 98	IF - READ TO FAURE'S 'PAVANE' *BBC Worldwide WMSS60062* [1]	45	3

[1] Des Lynam featuring Wimbledon Choral Society

WIN *UK, male vocal / instrumental group (3 WEEKS)* pos/wks

4 Apr 87	SUPER POPOID GROOVE *Swamplands LON 128*	63	3

WINANS *US, male vocal group (1 WEEK)* pos/wks

30 Nov 85	LET MY PEOPLE GO (PART 1) *Qwest W 8874*	71	1

BeBe WINANS – *See ETERNAL*

CeCe WINANS – *See Whitney HOUSTON*

Mario WINANS – *See PUFF DADDY*

WINDJAMMER *US, male vocal / instrumental group (12 WEEKS)* pos/wks

30 Jun 84	TOSSING AND TURNING *MCA MCA 897*	18	12

Rose WINDROSS – *See SOUL II SOUL*

Barbara WINDSOR and Mike REID
UK, female / male vocal duo (2 WEEKS) pos/wks

24 Apr 99	THE MORE I SEE YOU *Telstar CDSTAS 3049*	46	2

WING AND A PRAYER FIFE AND DRUM CORPS
US, male / female vocal / instrumental group (7 WEEKS) pos/wks

24 Jan 76	BABY FACE *Atlantic K 10705*	12	7

WINGER *US, male vocal / instrumental group (3 WEEKS)* pos/wks

19 Jan 91	MILES AWAY *Atlantic A 7802*	56	3

Pete WINGFIELD
UK, male vocalist / instrumentalist – piano (7 WEEKS) pos/wks

28 Jun 75 ●	EIGHTEEN WITH A BULLET *Island WIP 6231*	7	7

WINGS – *See Paul McCARTNEY*

Josh WINK *US, male producer – Joshua Winkelman (29 WEEKS)* pos/wks

6 May 95	DON'T LAUGH *XL XLS 62CD* [1]	38	2
21 Oct 95 ●	HIGHER STATE OF CONSCIOUSNESS *Manifesto FESCD 3*	8	8
30 Dec 95	HIGHER STATE OF CONSCIOUSNESS (re-entry) *Manifesto FESCD 3*	60	4
2 Mar 96	HYPNOTIZIN' *XL XLS 71CD* [1]	35	2
27 Jul 96 ●	HIGHER STATE OF CONSCIOUSNESS (re-mix) *Manifesto FESCD 9* [1]	7	10
12 Aug 00	HOW'S YOUR EVENING SO FAR *ffrr FCD 384* [2]	23	3

[1] Winx [2] Josh Wink and Lil' Louis

See also SIZE 9

Kate WINSLET *UK, female vocalist (4 WEEKS)* pos/wks

8 Dec 01 ●	WHAT IF *EMI / Liberty CDKATE 001*	6	4+

Edgar WINTER GROUP *US, male instrumental group (9 WEEKS)* pos/wks

26 May 73	FRANKENSTEIN *Epic EPC 1440* ▲	18	9

Ruby WINTERS *US, female vocalist (35 WEEKS)* pos/wks

5 Nov 77 ●	I WILL *Creole CR 141*	4	13
29 Apr 78	COME TO ME *Creole CR 153*	11	12
26 Aug 78	I WON'T MENTION IT AGAIN *Creole CR 160*	45	5
16 Jun 79	BABY LAY DOWN *Creole CR 171*	43	5

Steve WINWOOD *UK, male vocalist (33 WEEKS)* pos/wks

17 Jan 81	WHILE YOU SEE A CHANCE *Island WIP 6655*	45	5
9 Oct 82	VALERIE *Island WIP 6818*	51	4
28 Jun 86	HIGHER LOVE *Island IS 288* ▲	13	9
13 Sep 86	FREEDOM OVERSPILL *Island IS 294*	69	1
24 Jan 87	BACK IN THE HIGH LIFE AGAIN *Island IS 303*	53	2
19 Sep 87	VALERIE (re-mix) *Island IS 336*	19	8
11 Jun 88	ROLL WITH IT *Virgin VS 1085* ▲	53	4

See also Spencer DAVIS GROUP

WINX – *See Josh WINK*

WIRE *UK, male vocal / instrumental group (4 WEEKS)* pos/wks

27 Jan 79	OUTDOOR MINER *Harvest HAR 5172*	51	3
13 May 89	EARDRUM BUZZ *Mute MUTE 87*	68	1

WIRED
Holland / Finland, male production / instrumental duo (1 WEEK) pos/wks

20 Feb 99	TRANSONIC *Future Groove CDFGR 001*	73	1

WIRELESS *UK, male vocal / instrumental group (2 WEEKS)* pos/wks

28 Jun 97	I NEED YOU *Chrysalis CDCHS 5059*	68	1
7 Feb 98	IN LOVE WITH THE FAMILIAR *Chrysalis CDCHS 5075*	69	1

Norman WISDOM *UK, male comic actor / vocalist (20 WEEKS)* pos/wks

19 Feb 54 ●	DON'T LAUGH AT ME ('CAUSE I'M A FOOL) *Columbia DB 3133*	3	15
15 Mar 57	THE WISDOM OF A FOOL *Columbia DB 3903*	13	5

WISDOME *Italy, male / female production / vocal group (2 WEEKS)* pos/wks

11 Mar 00	OFF THE WALL *Positiva CDTIV 125*	33	2

WISEGUYS *UK, male DJ / producer – Theo Keating (13 WEEKS)* pos/wks

6 Jun 98	OOH LA LA *Wall of Sound WALLD 038*	55	1
12 Sep 98	START THE COMMOTION *Wall of Sound WALLD 044*	66	1
5 Jun 99 ●	OOH LA LA (re-issue) *Wall of Sound WALLD 038X*	2	10
11 Sep 99	START THE COMMOTION (re-issue) *Wall of Sound WALLD 059*	47	1

Bill WITHERS *US, male vocalist (29 WEEKS)* pos/wks

12 Aug 72	LEAN ON ME *A & M AMS 7004* ▲	18	9
14 Jan 78 ●	LOVELY DAY *CBS 5773*	7	8
25 May 85	OH YEAH! *CBS A 6154*	60	3
10 Sep 88 ●	LOVELY DAY (re-mix) *CBS 6530017*	4	9

See also Grover WASHINGTON Jr

WITNESS *UK, male vocal / instrumental group (2 WEEKS)* pos/wks

13 Mar 99	SCARS *Island CID 740*	71	1
19 Jun 99	AUDITION *Island CID 749*	71	1

WIX – *See SPIRO and WIX*

WIZZARD (436 Top 500) *Early 1970s chart champs led by extrovert Move and ELO frontman Roy Wood, b. 8 Nov 1946, Birmingham, UK. Big-budget Phil Spector-styled recordings are classics of their era. Wood also had several simultaneous solo successes (77 WEEKS)* pos/wks

9 Dec 72 ●	BALL PARK INCIDENT *Harvest HAR 5062*	6	12
21 Apr 73 ★	SEE MY BABY JIVE *Harvest HAR 5070*	1	17
1 Sep 73 ★	ANGEL FINGERS *Harvest HAR 5076*	1	10
8 Dec 73 ●	I WISH IT COULD BE CHRISTMAS EVERYDAY *Harvest HAR 5079* [1]	4	9
27 Apr 74 ●	ROCK 'N' ROLL WINTER *Warner Bros. K16497*	6	7
10 Aug 74	THIS IS THE STORY OF MY LOVE (BABY) *Warner Bros. K 16434*	34	4
21 Dec 74 ●	ARE YOU READY TO ROCK *Warner Bros. K 16497*	8	10
19 Dec 81	I WISH IT COULD BE CHRISTMAS EVERYDAY (re-issue) *Harvest HAR 5173* [1]	41	4
15 Dec 84	I WISH IT COULD BE CHRISTMAS EVERYDAY (re-entry of re-issue) *Harvest HAR 5173* [1]	23	4

[1] Wizzard featuring vocal backing by the Suedettes plus the Stockland Green Bilateral School First Year Choir with additional noises by Miss Snob and Class 3C

Jah WOBBLE'S INVADERS of the HEART
UK, male vocalist / multi-instrumentalist (10 WEEKS) pos/wks

1 Feb 92	VISIONS OF YOU *Oval OVAL 103*	35	5
30 Apr 94	BECOMING MORE LIKE GOD *Island CID 571*	36	2
25 Jun 94	THE SUN DOES RISE *Island CIDX 587*	41	3

First hit features the uncredited vocals of Sinead O'Connor

Terry WOGAN *Ireland, male vocalist (5 WEEKS)* pos/wks

7 Jan 78	FLORAL DANCE *Philips 6006 592*	21	5

WOLF – *See TROGGS*

WOLFSBANE *UK, male vocal / instrumental group (1 WEEK)* pos/wks

5 Oct 91	EZY *Def American DEFA 11*	68	1

UK No.1 ★ UK Top 10 ● Still on chart + UK million seller ◆ UK entry at No.1 ■ US No.1 ▲

Bobby WOMACK *US, male vocalist (21 WEEKS)*

		pos	wks
16 Jun 84	**TELL ME WHY** *Motown TMG 1339*	60	3
5 Oct 85	**I WISH HE DIDN'T TRUST ME SO MUCH** *MCA MCA 994*	64	2
26 Sep 87	**SO THE STORY GOES** *Chrysalis LIB 3* [1]	34	8
7 Nov 87	**LIVING IN A BOX** *MCA MCA 1210*	70	2
3 Apr 93	**I'M BACK FOR MORE** *Dome CDDOME 1002* [2]	27	5
13 May 95	**IT'S A MAN'S MAN'S MAN'S WORLD** *Pulse 8 CDLOSE 89* [3]	73	1

[1] Living in a Box featuring Bobby Womack [2] Lulu and Bobby Womack [3] Jeanie Tracy and Bobby Womack

See also Wilton FELDER

Lee Ann WOMACK *US, female vocalist (2 WEEKS)*

		pos	wks
9 Jun 01	**I HOPE YOU DANCE** *MCA Nashville MCSTD 40254*	40	2

WOMACK and WOMACK

US, male / female vocal duo – Linda and Cecil Womack (51 WEEKS)

		pos	wks
28 Apr 84	**LOVE WARS** *Elektra E 9799*	14	10
30 Jun 84	**BABY I'M SCARED OF YOU** *Elektra E 9733*	72	2
6 Dec 86	**SOUL LOVE - SOUL MAN** *Manhattan MT 16*	58	6
6 Aug 88 ●	**TEARDROPS** *Fourth & Broadway BRW 101*	3	17
12 Nov 88	**LIFE'S JUST A BALLGAME** *Fourth & Broadway BRW 116*	32	5
25 Feb 89	**CELEBRATE THE WORLD** *Fourth & Broadway BRW 125*	19	8
5 Feb 94	**SECRET STAR** *Warner Bros. W 0222CD* [1]	46	3

[1] House of Zekkariyas aka Womack and Womack

WOMBLES (313 Top 500)

Furriest (and possibly the tidiest) act in the Top 500 are natives of Wimbledon Common, London, and come under the musical guidance of songwriter and producer Mike Batt, b. 6 Feb 1950, Southampton, UK (98 WEEKS)

		pos	wks
26 Jan 74 ●	**THE WOMBLING SONG** *CBS 1794*	4	23
6 Apr 74 ●	**REMEMBER YOU'RE A WOMBLE** *CBS 2241*	3	16
22 Jun 74 ●	**BANANA ROCK** *CBS 2465*	9	13
12 Oct 74	**MINUETTO ALLEGRETTO** *CBS 2710*	16	9
7 Dec 74 ●	**WOMBLING MERRY CHRISTMAS** *CBS 2842*	2	8
10 May 75	**WOMBLING WHITE TIE AND TAILS** *CBS 3266*	22	7
9 Aug 75	**SUPER WOMBLE** *CBS 3480*	20	6
13 Dec 75	**LET'S WOMBLE TO THE PARTY TONIGHT** *CBS 3794*	34	5
21 Mar 98	**REMEMBER YOU'RE A WOMBLE (re-issue)** *Columbia 6656202*	13	5
13 Jun 98	**THE WOMBLING SONG (UNDERGROUND OVERGROUND) (re-issue)** *Columbia 6660412*	27	3
30 Dec 00	**I WISH IT COULD BE A WOMBLING MERRY CHRISTMAS EVERYDAY** *Dramatico DRAMCDS 0001* [1]	22	3

[1] Wombles with Roy Wood

Stevie WONDER (13 Top 500)

Multi-award-winner born Steveland Judkins, 13 May 1950, Michigan, is one of the most successful singer / songwriters of all time. The youngest artist to top the US singles and album chart (aged 13) also recorded Motown's biggest UK seller, 'I Just Called To Say I Love You'. Has recorded with many of the biggest names in music, and has had his songs sung and sampled by countless acts. No solo pop performer has amassed more Grammys and No.1 US R&B hits than the blind entertainer who helped to turn Martin Luther King's birthday into a US holiday, and whose charitable work is legendary (415 WEEKS)

		pos	wks
3 Feb 66	**UPTIGHT (EVERYTHING'S ALRIGHT)** *Tamla Motown TMG 545*	14	10
18 Aug 66	**BLOWIN' IN THE WIND** *Tamla Motown TMG 570*	36	5
5 Jan 67	**A PLACE IN THE SUN** *Tamla Motown TMG 588*	20	5
26 Jul 67 ●	**I WAS MADE TO LOVE HER** *Tamla Motown TMG 613*	5	15
25 Oct 67	**I'M WONDERING** *Tamla Motown TMG 626*	22	8
8 May 68	**SHOO BE DOO BE DOO DA DAY** *Tamla Motown TMG 653*	46	4
18 Dec 68 ●	**FOR ONCE IN MY LIFE** *Tamla Motown TMG 679*	3	13
19 Mar 69	**I DON'T KNOW WHY (I LOVE YOU)** *Tamla Motown TMG 690*	14	10
9 Jul 69	**I DON'T KNOW WHY (I LOVE YOU) (re-entry)** *Tamla Motown TMG 690*	43	1
16 Jul 69 ●	**MY CHERIE AMOUR** *Tamla Motown TMG 690*	4	15
15 Nov 69 ●	**YESTER-ME, YESTER-YOU, YESTERDAY** *Tamla Motown TMG 717*	2	13
28 Mar 70 ●	**NEVER HAD A DREAM COME TRUE** *Tamla Motown TMG 731*	6	12
18 Jul 70	**SIGNED SEALED DELIVERED I'M YOURS** *Tamla Motown TMG 744*	15	9
26 Sep 70	**SIGNED SEALED DELIVERED I'M YOURS (re-entry)** *Tamla Motown TMG 744*	49	1
21 Nov 70	**HEAVEN HELP US ALL** *Tamla Motown TMG 757*	29	11
15 May 71	**WE CAN WORK IT OUT** *Tamla Motown TMG 772*	27	7
22 Jan 72	**IF YOU REALLY LOVE ME** *Tamla Motown TMG 798*	20	7
3 Feb 73	**SUPERSTITION** *Tamla Motown TMG 841* ▲	11	9
19 May 73 ●	**YOU ARE THE SUNSHINE OF MY LIFE** *Tamla Motown TMG 852* ▲	7	11
13 Oct 73	**HIGHER GROUND** *Tamla Motown TMG 869*	29	5
12 Jan 74	**LIVING FOR THE CITY** *Tamla Motown TMG 881*	15	9
13 Apr 74 ●	**HE'S MISSTRA KNOW IT ALL** *Tamla Motown TMG 892*	10	9
19 Oct 74	**YOU HAVEN'T DONE NOTHIN'** *Tamla Motown TMG 921* ▲	30	5
11 Jan 75	**BOOGIE ON REGGAE WOMAN** *Tamla Motown TMG 928*	12	8
18 Dec 76 ●	**I WISH** *Motown TMG 1054* ▲	5	10
9 Apr 77 ●	**SIR DUKE** *Motown TMG 1068* ▲	2	9
10 Sep 77	**ANOTHER STAR** *Motown TMG 1083*	29	5
24 Feb 79	**POPS WE LOVE YOU** *Motown TMG 1136* [1]	66	5
24 Nov 79	**SEND ONE YOUR LOVE** *Motown TMG 1149*	52	3
26 Jan 80	**BLACK ORCHID** *Motown TMG 1173*	63	3
29 Mar 80	**OUTSIDE MY WINDOW** *Motown TMG 1179*	52	4
13 Sep 80 ●	**MASTERBLASTER (JAMMIN')** *Motown TMG 1204*	2	10
27 Dec 80 ●	**I AIN'T GONNA STAND FOR IT** *Motown TMG 1215*	10	10
7 Mar 81 ●	**LATELY** *Motown TMG 1226*	3	13
25 Jul 81 ●	**HAPPY BIRTHDAY** *Motown TMG 1235*	2	11
23 Jan 82	**THAT GIRL** *Motown TMG 1254*	39	6
10 Apr 82 ★	**EBONY AND IVORY** *Parlophone R 6054* [2] ▲	1	10
5 Jun 82 ●	**DO I DO** *Motown TMG 1269*	10	7
25 Sep 82	**RIBBON IN THE SKY** *Motown TMG 1280*	45	4
25 Aug 84 ★	**I JUST CALLED TO SAY I LOVE YOU** *Motown TMG 1349* ◆ ▲	1	24
1 Dec 84	**LOVE LIGHT IN FLIGHT** *Motown TMG 1364*	44	5
29 Dec 84	**DON'T DRIVE DRUNK** *Motown TMG 1372*	71	1
12 Jan 85	**DON'T DRIVE DRUNK (re-entry)** *Motown TMG 1372*	62	2
7 Sep 85 ●	**PART-TIME LOVER** *Motown ZB 40351* ▲	3	12
9 Nov 85	**THAT'S WHAT FRIENDS ARE FOR** *Arista ARIST 638* [3] ▲	16	9
23 Nov 85	**GO HOME** *Motown ZB 40501*	67	2
28 Dec 85	**I JUST CALLED TO SAY I LOVE YOU (re-entry)** *Motown TMG 1349*	64	2
8 Mar 86	**OVERJOYED** *Motown ZB 40567*	17	8
17 Jan 87	**STRANGER ON THE SHORE OF LOVE** *Motown WOND 2*	55	3
31 Oct 87	**SKELETONS** *Motown ZB 41439*	59	3
28 May 88	**GET IT** *Motown ZB 41883* [4]	37	4
6 Aug 88 ●	**MY LOVE** *CBS JULIO 2* [5]	5	11
20 May 89	**FREE** *Motown ZB 42855*	49	5
12 Oct 91	**FUN DAY** *Motown ZB 44957*	63	1
25 Feb 95	**FOR YOUR LOVE** *Motown TMGCD 1437*	23	4
22 Jul 95	**TOMORROW ROBINS WILL SING** *Motown 8603732*	71	1
19 Jul 97 ●	**HOW COME, HOW LONG** *Epic 6646202* [6]	10	5
31 Oct 98	**TRUE TO YOUR HEART** *Motown 8608832* [7]	51	1

[1] Diana Ross, Marvin Gaye, Smokey Robinson and Stevie Wonder [2] Paul McCartney with Stevie Wonder [3] Dionne Warwick and Friends featuring Elton John, Stevie Wonder and Gladys Knight [4] Stevie Wonder and Michael Jackson [5] Julio Iglesias featuring Stevie Wonder [6] Babyface featuring Stevie Wonder [7] 98 Degrees featuring Stevie Wonder

Wayne WONDER – *See SHAGGY*

WONDER DOG

Germany, canine vocalist – Harry Thumann (7 WEEKS)

		pos	wks
21 Aug 82	**RUFF MIX** *Flip FLIP 001*	31	7

WONDER STUFF *UK, male vocal / instrumental group (66 WEEKS)*

		pos	wks
30 Apr 88	**GIVE GIVE GIVE ME MORE MORE MORE** *Polydor GONE 3*	72	2
16 Jul 88	**A WISH AWAY** *Polydor GONE 4*	43	5
24 Sep 88	**IT'S YER MONEY I'M AFTER BABY** *Polydor GONE 5*	40	3
11 Mar 89	**WHO WANTS TO BE THE DISCO KING?** *Polydor GONE 6*	28	3
23 Sep 89	**DON'T LET ME DOWN GENTLY** *Polydor GONE 7*	19	4
11 Nov 89	**GOLDEN GREEN / GET TOGETHER** *Polydor GONE 8*	33	3
12 May 90	**CIRCLESQUARE** *Polydor GONE 10*	20	4
13 Apr 91 ●	**THE SIZE OF A COW** *Polydor GONE 11*	5	7
25 May 91	**CAUGHT IN MY SHADOW** *Polydor GONE 12*	18	3

		pos	wks
7 Sep 91	**SLEEP ALONE** *Polydor GONE 13*	43	2
26 Oct 91 ★	**DIZZY** *Sense SIGH 712* [1]	1	12
25 Jan 92 ●	**WELCOME TO THE CHEAP SEATS (EP)** *Polydor GONE 14*	8	5
25 Sep 93 ●	**ON THE ROPES (EP)** *Polydor GONCD 15*	10	4
27 Nov 93	**FULL OF LIFE (HAPPY NOW)** *Polydor GONCD 16*	28	3
26 Mar 94	**HOT LOVE NOW** *Polydor GONCD 17*	19	3
10 Sep 94	**UNBEARABLE** *Polydor GONCD 18*	16	3

[1] Vic Reeves and the Wonder Stuff

Tracks on Welcome to the Cheap Seats (EP): Welcome to the Cheap Seats / Me, My Mom, My Dad and My Brother / Will the Circle Be Unbroken / That's Entertainment. Tracks on On the Ropes (EP): On the Ropes / Professional Disturber of the Peace / Hank and John / Whites

WONDERS *US, male vocal / instrumental group (3 WEEKS)*

		pos	wks
22 Feb 97	**THAT THING YOU DO!** *Play-Tone 6640552*	22	3

WONDRESS – *See MANTRONIX*

Brenton WOOD *US, male vocalist – Alfred Smith (14 WEEKS)*

		pos	wks
27 Dec 67 ●	**GIMME LITTLE SIGN** *Liberty LBF 15021*	8	14

Roy WOOD *UK, male vocalist / multi-instrumentalist (44 WEEKS)*

		pos	wks
11 Aug 73	**DEAR ELAINE** *Harvest HAR 5074*	18	8
1 Dec 73 ●	**FOREVER** *Harvest HAR 5078*	8	13
15 Jun 74	**GOIN' DOWN THE ROAD** *Harvest HAR 5083*	13	7
31 May 75	**OH WHAT A SHAME** *Jet 754*	13	7
22 Nov 86	**WATERLOO** *IRS IRM 125* [1]	45	4
23 Dec 95	**I WISH IT COULD BE CHRISTMAS EVERYDAY** *Woody WOODY 001CD* [2]	59	2
30 Dec 00	**I WISH IT COULD BE A WOMBLING MERRY CHRISTMAS EVERYDAY** *Dramatico DRAMCDS 0001* [3]	22	3

[1] Doctor and the Medics featuring Roy Wood [2] Roy Wood Big Band [3] Wombles with Roy Wood

See also WIZZARD; ELECTRIC LIGHT ORCHESTRA; MOVE; WOMBLES

WOODENTOPS *UK, male vocal / instrumental group (1 WEEK)*

		pos	wks
11 Oct 86	**EVERYDAY LIVING** *Rough Trade RT 178*	72	1

Marcella WOODS – *See Matt DAREY*

Edward WOODWARD *UK, male vocalist (2 WEEKS)*

		pos	wks
16 Jan 71	**THE WAY YOU LOOK TONIGHT** *DJM DJS 232*	50	1
30 Jan 71	**THE WAY YOU LOOK TONIGHT (re-entry)** *DJM DJS 232*	42	1

WOOKIE *UK, male producer / vocalist - Jason Chue (11 WEEKS)*

		pos	wks
3 Jun 00	**WHAT'S GOING ON** *Soul II Soul S2SCD 001*	45	1
12 Aug 00 ●	**BATTLE** *Soul II Soul / Pias S2SPCD001* [1]	10	7
12 May 01	**BACK UP (TO ME)** *Soul II Soul S2SPCD 003* [1]	38	3

[1] Wookie featuring Lain

Sheb WOOLEY *US, male vocalist (8 WEEKS)*

		pos	wks
20 Jun 58	**THE PURPLE PEOPLE EATER** *MGM 981* ▲	12	8

WOOLPACKERS *UK, male vocal group (24 WEEKS)*

		pos	wks
16 Nov 96 ●	**HILLBILLY ROCK HILLBILLY ROLL** *RCA 74321425412*	5	14
29 Nov 97	**LINE DANCE PARTY** *RCA 74321512262*	25	10

WORKING WEEK
UK, male / female vocal / instrumental group (2 WEEKS)

		pos	wks
9 Jun 84	**VENCEREMOS - WE WILL WIN** *Virgin VS 684*	64	2

WORLD – *See LIL' LOUIS*

WORLD OF TWIST
UK, male / female vocal / instrumental group (12 WEEKS)

		pos	wks
24 Nov 90	**THE STORM** *Circa YR 55*	42	3
5 Jan 91	**THE STORM (re-entry)** *Circa YR 55*	74	2
23 Mar 91	**SONS OF THE STAGE** *Circa YR 62*	47	3
12 Oct 91	**SWEETS** *Circa YR 72*	58	2
22 Feb 92	**SHE'S A RAINBOW** *Circa YR 82*	62	2

WORLD PARTY
Ireland / UK, male vocal / instrumental group (29 WEEKS)

		pos	wks
14 Feb 87	**SHIP OF FOOLS** *Ensign ENY 606*	42	6
16 Jun 90	**MESSAGE IN THE BOX** *Ensign ENY 631*	39	6
15 Sep 90	**WAY DOWN NOW** *Ensign ENY 634*	66	2
18 May 91	**THANK YOU WORLD** *Ensign ENY 643*	68	1
10 Apr 93	**IS IT LIKE TODAY** *Ensign CDENY 658*	19	6
10 Jul 93	**GIVE IT ALL AWAY** *Ensign CDENY 659*	43	3
2 Oct 93	**ALL I GAVE** *Ensign CDENYS 660*	37	3
7 Jun 97	**BEAUTIFUL DREAM** *Chrysalis CDCHS 5053*	31	2

WORLD PREMIERE *US, male vocal / instrumental group (4 WEEKS)*

		pos	wks
28 Jan 84	**SHARE THE NIGHT** *Epic A 4133*	64	4

WORLD WARRIOR *UK, male producer – Simon Harris (1 WEEK)*

		pos	wks
16 Apr 94	**STREET FIGHTER II** *Living Beat LBECD 27*	70	1

See also Simon HARRIS

WORLDS APART *UK, male vocal group (17 WEEKS)*

		pos	wks
27 Mar 93	**HEAVEN MUST BE MISSING AN ANGEL** *Arista 74321139362*	29	3
3 Jul 93	**WONDERFUL WORLD** *Arista 74321153402*	51	1
25 Sep 93	**EVERLASTING LOVE** *Bell 74321164802*	20	4
26 Mar 94	**COULD IT BE I'M FALLING IN LOVE** *Bell 74321189952*	15	6
4 Jun 94	**BEGGIN' TO BE WRITTEN** *Bell 74321211982*	29	3

WORLD'S FAMOUS SUPREME TEAM
US, male vocal / scratch group (19 WEEKS)

		pos	wks
4 Dec 82 ●	**BUFFALO GALS** *Charisma MALC 1* [1]	9	12
25 Feb 84	**HEY DJ** *Charisma TEAM 1*	52	5
8 Dec 90	**OPERAA HOUSE** *Virgin VS 1273* [2]	75	1
3 Oct 98	**BUFFALO GALS STAMPEDE (Re-mix of first hit)** *Virgin VSCDT 1717* [3]	65	1

[1] Malcolm McLaren and the World's Famous Supreme Team [2] World Famous Supreme Team Show [3] Malcolm McLaren and the World's Famous Supreme Team plus Rakim and Roger Sanchez

W.O.S.P. *UK, male / female production / vocal duo (1 WEEK)*

		pos	wks
17 Nov 01	**GETTIN' INTO U** *Data DATA 26CDS*	48	1

WRECKX-N-EFFECT *US, male vocal group (18 WEEKS)*

		pos	wks
13 Jan 90	**JUICY** *Motown ZB 43295* [1]	29	7
5 Dec 92	**RUMP SHAKER** *MCA MCS 1725*	24	7
7 May 94	**WRECKX SHOP** *MCA MCSTD 1969* [2]	26	2
13 Aug 94	**RUMP SHAKER (re-issue)** *MCA MCSTD 1989*	40	2

[1] Wrecks-N-Effect [2] Wreckx-N-Effect featuring Apache Indian

Betty WRIGHT *US, female vocalist (23 WEEKS)*

		pos	wks
25 Jan 75	**SHOORAH SHOORAH** *RCA 2491*	27	7
19 Apr 75	**WHERE IS THE LOVE** *RCA 2548*	25	7
8 Feb 86	**PAIN** *Cooltempo COOL 117*	42	6
9 Sep 89	**KEEP LOVE NEW** *Sure Delight SD 11*	71	3

Ian WRIGHT *UK, male vocalist (2 WEEKS)*

		pos	wks
28 Aug 93	**DO THE RIGHT THING** *M & G MAGCD 45*	43	2

Linda WRIGHT – *See NEW ATLANTIC*

Ruby WRIGHT *US, female vocalist (15 WEEKS)*

		pos	wks
16 Apr 54 ●	**BIMBO** *Parlophone R 3816*	7	4

UK No.1 ★ UK Top 10 ● Still on chart + UK million seller ◆ UK entry at No.1 ■ US No.1 ▲

2000

IN THE YEAR IN WHICH CONCORDE CRASHED, AUSTRIA BECAME THE TARGET OF PROTESTS ACROSS EUROPE AFTER THE ELECTION OF JORG HAIDER'S FAR RIGHT FREEDOM PARTY IN A COALITION GOVERNMENT, GEORGE 'DUBYA' BUSH WON THE US PRESIDENCY IN A CONTROVERSIAL ELECTION BATTLE, AND A RECORD 43 SONGS TOPPED THE CHARTS. 'CAN WE FIX IT' SONGWRITER **PAUL K JOYCE** TALKS ABOUT HIS ASSOCIATION WITH **BOB THE BUILDER** ...

"My involvement with Bob the Builder began in May 1998 when, along with several other composers, I was asked to submit a theme song for a new animated children's series. I sat down with my guitar and wrote a very direct song, trying to make sure it would appeal to children and adults alike. Bob was an instant hit with kids and its punchy scripts and bold animation also began to attract an older audience. Soon 'Can We Fix It? – Yes We Can!' was being chanted on football terraces! The theme song was released in December 1999 and went on to topple Eminem's 'Stan' from the No.1 slot. Not content with this, Bob stopped Westlife from reaching the top of the charts (much to the delight of the music press) and went on to sell more than a million copies resulting in my receiving an Ivor Novello award for the best-selling single of 2000. This astonishing success has been the stuff that dreams are made of. Bob has definitely fixed it for me!"

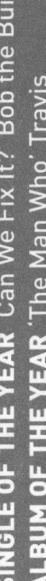

SINGLE OF THE YEAR 'Can We Fix It?' Bob the Builder
ALBUM OF THE YEAR 'The Man Who' Travis

21 May 54		BIMBO (re-entry) *Parlophone R 3816*	12	1
22 May 59		THREE STARS *Parlophone R 4556*	19	10

'Three Stars' is narrated by Dick Pike

Steve WRIGHT *UK, male vocalist (10 WEEKS)*

			pos	wks
27 Nov 82		I'M ALRIGHT *RCA 296* [1]	40	6
15 Oct 83		GET SOME THERAPY *RCA 362* [2]	75	1
1 Dec 84		THE GAY CAVALIEROS (THE STORY SO FAR) *MCA 925*	61	3

[1] Young Steve and the Afternoon Boys [2] Steve Wright and the Sisters of Soul

WU-TANG CLAN *US, male rap / instrumental group (21 WEEKS)*

			pos	wks
16 Aug 97		TRIUMPH *Loud 74321510212* [1]	46	1
21 Mar 98	●	SAY WHAT YOU WANT / INSANE *Mercury MERC 499* [2]	4	7
25 Nov 00	●	GRAVEL PIT *Loud / Epic 67015182*	6	13

[1] Wu-Tang Clan featuring Cappadonna [2] Texas featuring Wu-Tang Clan (rap by Method Man and RZA)

WUBBLE-U *UK, male production group (1 WEEK)*

			pos	wks
7 Mar 98		PETAL *Indolent DGOL 003CD1*	55	1

WURZELS *UK, male vocal / instrumental group (30 WEEKS)*

			pos	wks
2 Feb 67		DRINK UP THY ZIDER *Columbia DB 8081* [1]	45	1
15 May 76	★	THE COMBINE HARVESTER (BRAND NEW KEY) *EMI 2450*	1	13
11 Sep 76	●	I AM A CIDER DRINKER (PALOMA BLANCA) *EMI 2520*	3	9
25 Jun 77		FARMER BILL'S COWMAN (I WAS KAISER BILL'S BATMAN) *EMI 2637*	32	5
11 Aug 01		COMBINE HARVESTER 2001 (re-mix) *EMI Gold CDWURZ 001*	39	2

[1] Adge Cutler and the Wurzels

WWF SUPERSTARS *US / UK, male wrestling vocalists (15 WEEKS)*

			pos	wks
12 Dec 92	●	SLAM JAM *Arista 74321124887*	4	8
13 Feb 93		SLAM JAM (re-entry) *Arista 74321124887*	75	1
3 Apr 93		WRESTLEMANIA *Arista 74321136832*	14	5
10 Jul 93		USA *Arista 74321153092* [1]	71	1

[1] WWF Superstars featuring Hacksaw Jim Duggan

Robert WYATT *UK, male vocalist (11 WEEKS)*

			pos	wks
28 Sep 74		I'M A BELIEVER *Virgin VS 114*	29	5
7 May 83		SHIPBUILDING *Rough Trade RT 115*	35	6

Michael WYCOFF *US, male vocalist (2 WEEKS)*

			pos	wks
23 Jul 83		(DO YOU REALLY LOVE ME) TELL ME LOVE *RCA 348*	60	2

Pete WYLIE *UK, male vocalist (18 WEEKS)*

			pos	wks
3 May 86		SINFUL *Eternal MDM 7*	13	10
13 Sep 86		DIAMOND GIRL *Eternal MDM 12*	57	3
13 Apr 91		SINFUL! (SCARY JIGGIN' WITH DR LOVE) *Siren SRN 138* [1]	28	5

[1] Pete Wylie with the Farm

See also WAH!

Bill WYMAN *UK, male vocalist – William Perks (13 WEEKS)*

			pos	wks
25 Jul 81		(SI SI) JE SUIS UN ROCK STAR *A & M AMS 8144*	14	9
20 Mar 82		A NEW FASHION *A & M AMS 8209*	37	4

See also ROLLING STONES

Jane WYMAN – *See Bing CROSBY*

Tammy WYNETTE *US, female vocalist – Virginia Wynette Pugh (35 WEEKS)*

			pos	wks
26 Apr 75	★	STAND BY YOUR MAN *Epic EPC 7137*	1	12
28 Jun 75		D. I. V. O. R. C. E. *Epic EPC 3361*	12	7
12 Jun 76		I DON'T WANNA PLAY HOUSE *Epic EPC 4091*	37	4
7 Dec 91	●	JUSTIFIED AND ANCIENT *KLF Communications KLF 099* [1]	2	12

[1] KLF guest vocals: Tammy Wynette

Mark WYNTER (418 Top 500) *Teen-targeted pop singer turned actor, b. Terence Lewis, 29 Jan 1943, Surrey, UK. Boy-next-door type performer, whose hit portfolio contains a mix of revivals and cover versions. Moved into acting and TV presentation work (80 WEEKS)*

			pos	wks
25 Aug 60		IMAGE OF A GIRL *Decca F 11263*	11	10
10 Nov 60		KICKIN' UP THE LEAVES *Decca F 11279*	24	10
9 Mar 61		DREAM GIRL *Decca F 11323*	27	5
8 Jun 61		EXCLUSIVELY YOURS *Decca F 11354*	32	7
4 Oct 62	●	VENUS IN BLUE JEANS *Pye 7N 15466*	4	15
13 Dec 62	●	GO AWAY LITTLE GIRL *Pye 7N 15492*	6	11
6 Jun 63		SHY GIRL *Pye 7N 15525*	28	6
14 Nov 63		IT'S ALMOST TOMORROW *Pye 7N 15577*	12	12
9 Apr 64		ONLY YOU (AND YOU ALONE) *Pye 7N 15626*	38	4

X

Malcolm X *US, male orator (4 WEEKS)*

			pos	wks
7 Apr 84		NO SELL OUT *Tommy Boy IS 165*	60	4

Hit features credit: 'Music by Keith Le Blanc'

X MEN – *See SELENA VS X MEN*

XAVIER – *See TJR featuring XAVIER*

XAVIER *US, male / female vocal / instrumental group (3 WEEKS)*

			pos	wks
20 Mar 82		WORK THAT SUCKER TO DEATH / LOVE IS ON THE ONE *Liberty UP 651*	53	3

XPANSIONS *UK, male producer – Richie Malone (20 WEEKS)*

			pos	wks
6 Oct 90		ELEVATION *Optimism 113683*	49	5
23 Feb 91	●	MOVE YOUR BODY (ELEVATION) *Arista 113 683*	7	9
15 Jun 91		WHAT YOU WANT *Arista 114 246* [1]	55	2
26 Aug 95		MOVE YOUR BODY (re-mix) *Arista 74321294982* [2]	14	4

[1] Xpansions featuring Dale Joyner [2] Xpansions 95

'Move Your Body' is a re-mix of 'Elevation'

X-PRESS 2 *UK, male instrumental / production group (10 WEEKS)*

			pos	wks
5 Jun 93		LONDON X-PRESS *Junior Boy's Own JBO 12*	59	1
16 Oct 93		SAY WHAT! *Junior Boy's Own JBO 16CD*	32	2
30 Jul 94		ROCK 2 HOUSE / HIP HOUSIN' *Junior Boy's Own JBO 21CD* [1]	55	2
9 Mar 96		THE SOUND *Junior Boy's Own JBO 36*	38	1
12 Oct 96		TRANZ EURO XPRESS *Junior Boy's Own JBO 42CD*	45	1
30 Sep 00		AC / DC *Skint SKINT 57*	60	1
28 Apr 01		MUZIKIZUM *Skint SKINT 65*	52	1
20 Oct 01		SMOKE MACHINE *Skint SKINT 69*	43	1

[1] X-Press 2 featuring Lo-Pro

X-RAY SPEX *UK, male / female vocal / instrumental group (33 WEEKS)*

			pos	wks
29 Apr 78		THE DAY THE WORLD TURNED DAY-GLO *EMI International INT 553*	23	8
22 Jul 78		IDENTITY *EMI International INT 563*	24	10
4 Nov 78		GERM FREE ADOLESCENCE *EMI International INT 573*	19	11
21 Apr 79		HIGHLY INFLAMMABLE *EMI International INT 583*	45	4

XSCAPE *US, female vocal group (15 WEEKS)*

			pos	wks
20 Nov 93		JUST KICKIN' IT *Columbia 6598622*	49	2
5 Nov 94		JUST KICKIN' IT (re-issue) *Columbia 6608642*	54	2
7 Oct 95		FEELS SO GOOD *Columbia 6625022*	34	2

27 Jan 96 **WHO CAN I RUN TO** *Columbia 6628112* 31 3
29 Jun 96 **KEEP ON KEEPIN' ON** *East West A 4287CD* [1] 39 2
19 Apr 97 **KEEP ON KEEPIN' ON (re-issue)** *East West A 3950CD1* [1] 27 2
22 Aug 98 **THE ARMS OF THE ONE WHO LOVES YOU** *Columbia 6662522* 46 2

[1] MC Lyte featuring Xscape

XSTASIA *UK, male / female vocal / production duo (1 WEEK)* pos/wks

17 Mar 01 **SWEETNESS** *Liquid Asset ASSETCD 005* 65 1

X-STATIC *Italy, male / female vocal / instrumental group (2 WEEKS)* pos/wks

4 Feb 95 **I'M STANDING (HIGHER)** *Positiva CDTIV 25* 41 2

XTC *UK, male vocal / instrumental group (70 WEEKS)* pos/wks

12 May 79 **LIFE BEGINS AT THE HOP** *Virgin VS 259* 54 4
22 Sep 79 **MAKING PLANS FOR NIGEL** *Virgin VS 282* 17 11
6 Sep 80 **GENERALS AND MAJORS / DON'T LOSE YOUR TEMPER** *Virgin VS 365* 32 8
18 Oct 80 **TOWERS OF LONDON** *Virgin VS 372* 31 5
24 Jan 81 **SGT ROCK (IS GOING TO HELP ME)** *Virgin VS 384* 16 9
23 Jan 82 ● **SENSES WORKING OVERTIME** *Virgin VS 462* 10 9
27 Mar 82 **BALL AND CHAIN** *Virgin VS 482* 58 4
15 Oct 83 **LOVE ON A FARMBOY'S WAGES** *Virgin VS 613* 50 4
29 Sep 84 **ALL YOU PRETTY GIRLS** *Virgin VS 709* 55 5
28 Jan 89 **MAYOR OF SIMPLETON** *Virgin VS 1158* 46 5
4 Apr 92 **THE DISAPPOINTED** *Virgin VS 1404* 33 5
13 Jun 92 **THE BALLAD OF PETER PUMPKINHEAD** *Virgin VS 1415* 71 1

XZIBIT featuring SNOOP DOGG *US, male rappers (7 WEEKS)* pos/wks

17 Mar 01 **X** *Epic 6709072* 14 7

Y

Y?N-VEE *US, female vocal group (1 WEEK)* pos/wks

17 Dec 94 **CHOCOLATE** *RAL RALCD 2* 65 1

Y & T *US, male vocal / instrumental group (4 WEEKS)* pos/wks

13 Aug 83 **MEAN STREAK** *A & M AM 135* 41 4

Y-TRAXX *Belgium, male producer – Frédérique De Backer (1 WEEK)* pos/wks

24 May 97 **MYSTERY LAND (EP)** *ffrr FCD 292* 63 1

Tracks on Mystery Land (EP): Mystery Land (radio edit) / Trance Piano / Kiss the Sound / Mystery Land

Y-TRIBE featuring Elisabeth TROY *UK, male instrumental / production duo with female vocalist (3 WEEKS)* pos/wks

18 Dec 99 **ENOUGH IS ENOUGH** *Northwest 10 NORTHCD 002* 49 2
8 Jan 00 **ENOUGH IS ENOUGH (re-entry)** *Northwest 10 NORTHCD 002* 75 1

YA KID K – *See HI-TEK 3 featuring YA KID K; TECHNOTRONIC*

Weird Al YANKOVIC *US, male vocalist (8 WEEKS)* pos/wks

7 Apr 84 **EAT IT** *Scotti Bros. / Epic A 4257* 36 7
4 Jul 92 **SMELLS LIKE NIRVANA** *Scotti Bros PO 219* 58 1

YARBROUGH and PEOPLES *US, male / female vocal / instrumental duo – Calvin Yarbrough and Alisa Peoples (20 WEEKS)* pos/wks

27 Dec 80 ● **DON'T STOP THE MUSIC** *Mercury MER 53* 7 12
5 May 84 **DON'T WASTE YOUR TIME** *Total Experience XE 501* 60 3
11 Jan 86 **GUILTY** *Total Experience FB 49905* 53 3
5 Jul 86 **I WOULDN'T LIE** *Total Experience FB 49841* 61 2

YARDBIRDS *UK, male vocal / instrumental group (62 WEEKS)* pos/wks

12 Nov 64 **GOOD MORNING LITTLE SCHOOLGIRL** *Columbia DB 7391* 44 4
18 Mar 65 ● **FOR YOUR LOVE** *Columbia DB 7499* 3 12
17 Jun 65 ● **HEART FULL OF SOUL** *Columbia DB 7594* 2 13
14 Oct 65 ● **EVIL HEARTED YOU / STILL I'M SAD** *Columbia DB 7706* 3 10
3 Mar 66 ● **SHAPES OF THINGS** *Columbia DB 7848* 3 9
2 Jun 66 ● **OVER UNDER SIDEWAYS DOWN** *Columbia DB 7928* 10 9
27 Oct 66 **HAPPENINGS TEN YEARS TIME AGO** *Columbia DB 8024* 43 5

See also Eric CLAPTON; CREAM

YAVAHN – *See RUFFNECK featuring YAVAHN*

YAZOO *UK, female / male vocal / instrumental duo – Alison Moyet and Vince Clarke (55 WEEKS)* pos/wks

17 Apr 82 ● **ONLY YOU** *Mute MUTE 020* 2 14
17 Jul 82 ● **DON'T GO** *Mute YAZ 001* 3 11
20 Nov 82 **THE OTHER SIDE OF LOVE** *Mute YAZ 002* 13 9
21 May 83 ● **NOBODY'S DIARY** *Mute YAZ 003* 3 11
8 Dec 90 **SITUATION** *Mute YAZ 4* 14 8
4 Sep 99 **ONLY YOU (re-mix)** *Mute CDYAZ 5* 38 2

See also ASSEMBLY; Alison MOYET; ERASURE

YAZZ *UK, female vocalist (69 WEEKS)* pos/wks

20 Feb 88 ● **DOCTORIN' THE HOUSE** *Ahead of Our Time CCUT 27* [1] 6 9
23 Jul 88 ★ **THE ONLY WAY IS UP** *Big Life BLR 4* [2] 1 15
29 Oct 88 ● **STAND UP FOR YOUR LOVE RIGHTS** *Big Life BLR 5* 2 12
4 Feb 89 ● **FINE TIME** *Big Life BLR 6* 9 8
29 Apr 89 **WHERE HAS ALL THE LOVE GONE** *Big Life BLR 8* 16 6
23 Jun 90 **TREAT ME GOOD** *Big Life BLR 24* 20 5
28 Mar 92 **ONE TRUE WOMAN** *Polydor PO 198* 60 2
31 Jul 93 **HOW LONG** *Polydor PZCD 252* [3] 31 5
2 Apr 94 **HAVE MERCY** *Polydor PZCD 309* 42 3
9 Jul 94 **EVERYBODY'S GOT TO LEARN SOMETIME** *Polydor PZCD 316* 56 2
28 Sep 96 **GOOD THING GOING** *East West EW 062CD* 53 1
22 Mar 97 **NEVER CAN SAY GOODBYE** *East West EW 081CD* 61 1

[1] Coldcut featuring Yazz and the Plastic Population [2] Yazz and the Plastic Population [3] Yazz and Aswad

Trisha YEARWOOD *US, female vocalist (1 WEEK)* pos/wks

9 Aug 97 **HOW DO I LIVE** *MCA MCSTD 48064* 66 1

YELL! *UK, male vocal duo – Paul Varney and Daniel James (8 WEEKS)* pos/wks

20 Jan 90 ● **INSTANT REPLAY** *Fanfare FAN 22* 10 8

YELLO *Switzerland, male vocal / instrumental duo – Dieter Meier and Boris Blank (42 WEEKS)* pos/wks

25 Jun 83 **I LOVE YOU** *Stiff BUY 176* 41 4
26 Nov 83 **LOST AGAIN** *Stiff BUY 191* 73 1
9 Aug 86 **GOLDRUSH** *Mercury MER 218* 54 3
22 Aug 87 **THE RHYTHM DIVINE** *Mercury MER 253* [1] 54 2
27 Aug 88 ● **THE RACE** *Mercury YELLO 1* 7 11
17 Dec 88 **TIED UP** *Mercury YELLO 2* 60 5
25 Mar 89 **OF COURSE I'M LYING** *Mercury YELLO 3* 23 8
22 Jul 89 **BLAZING SADDLES** *Mercury YELLO 4* 47 2
8 Jun 91 **RUBBERBANDMAN** *Mercury YELLO 5* 58 2
5 Sep 92 **JUNGLE BILL** *Mercury MER 376* 61 2
7 Nov 92 **THE RACE / BOSTICH (re-issue)** *Mercury MER 382* 55 1
15 Oct 94 **HOW HOW** *Mercury MERCD 414* 59 1

[1] Yello featuring Shirley Bassey

YELLOW DOG *US / UK, male vocal / instrumental group (13 WEEKS)* pos/wks

4 Feb 78 ● **JUST ONE MORE NIGHT** *Virgin VS 195* 8 9
22 Jul 78 **WAIT UNTIL MIDNIGHT** *Virgin VS 217* 54 4

YELLOW MAGIC ORCHESTRA
Japan, male instrumental group (11 WEEKS) pos/wks

14 Jun 80	COMPUTER GAME (THEME FROM 'THE INVADERS') *A & M AMS 7502*	17	11

YELLOWCOATS – *See Paul SHANE and the YELLOWCOATS*

YES *UK / South Africa, male vocal / instrumental group (31 WEEKS)* pos/wks

17 Sep 77 ●	WONDROUS STORIES *Atlantic K 10999*	7	9
26 Nov 77	GOING FOR THE ONE *Atlantic K 11047*	24	4
9 Sep 78	DON'T KILL THE WHALE *Atlantic K 11184*	36	4
12 Nov 83	OWNER OF A LONELY HEART *Acto B 9817* ▲	28	9
31 Mar 84	LEAVE IT *Acto B 9787*	56	4
3 Oct 87	LOVE WILL FIND A WAY *Atco A 9449*	73	1

Group were UK only for first three hits

See also ANDERSON BRUFORD WAKEMAN HOWE

Melissa YIANNAKOU – *See DESIYA featuring Melissa YIANNAKOU*

YIN and YAN *UK, male vocal duo (5 WEEKS)* pos/wks

29 Mar 75	IF *EMI 2282*	25	5

Dwight YOAKAM *US, male vocalist (2 WEEKS)* pos/wks

10 Jul 99	CRAZY LITTLE THING CALLED LOVE *Reprise W 497CD*	43	2

YO-HANS – *See JODE*

YOMANDA *UK, male DJ / producer – Paul Masterson (18 WEEKS)* pos/wks

24 Jul 99 ●	SYNTH & STRINGS *Manifesto FESCD 59*	8	10
11 Mar 00	SUNSHINE *Manifesto FESCD 68*	16	6
2 Sep 00	ON THE LEVEL *Manifesto FESCD 73*	28	2

See also SLEAZESISTERS; CANDY GIRLS; HI-GATE

Tukka YOOT – *See US3*

YORK *Germany, male production / instrumental duo – Torsten and Jorg Stenzel (21 WEEKS)* pos/wks

9 Oct 99	THE AWAKENING *Manifesto FESCD 60*	11	5
10 Jun 00 ●	ON THE BEACH *Manifesto FESCD 70*	4	10
18 Nov 00	FAREWELL TO THE MOON *Manifesto FESCD 76*	37	2
27 Jan 01	THE FIELDS OF LOVE *Club Tools / Edel 0124095 CLU* [1]	16	4

[1] ATB featuring York

YOSH presents LOVEDEEJAY AKEMI
Holland, male producer (5 WEEKS) pos/wks

29 Jul 95	IT'S WHAT'S UPFRONT THAT COUNTS *Limbo LIMB 46CD*	69	1
2 Dec 95	IT'S WHAT'S UPFRONT THAT COUNTS (re-mix) *Limbo LIMB 50CD*	31	2
20 Apr 96	THE SCREAMER *Limbo LIMB 54CD*	38	2

YOSHIKI – *See Roger TAYLOR*

YOTHU YINDI *Australia, male vocal / instrumental group (1 WEEK)* pos/wks

15 Feb 92	TREATY *Hollywood HWD 116*	72	1

Faron YOUNG *US, male vocalist (23 WEEKS)* pos/wks

15 Jul 72 ●	IT'S FOUR IN THE MORNING *Mercury 6052 140*	3	23

Jimmy YOUNG (360 Top 500) *Distincitve balladeer who became a top radio DJ, b. 21 Sep, 1923, Gloucestershire, UK. Converted from record maker to record spinner and remained a star for five decades. First UK artist to reach No.1 with two successive singles (88 WEEKS)* pos/wks

9 Jan 53	FAITH CAN MOVE MOUNTAINS *Decca F 9986*	11	1
21 Aug 53 ●	ETERNALLY *Decca F 10130*	8	9
6 May 55 ★	UNCHAINED MELODY *Decca F 10502*	1	19
16 Sep 55 ★	THE MAN FROM LARAMIE *Decca F 10597*	1	12
23 Dec 55	SOMEONE ON YOUR MIND *Decca F 10640*	13	5
16 Mar 56 ●	CHAIN GANG *Decca F 10694*	9	6
8 Jun 56	THE WAYWARD WIND *Decca F 10736*	27	1
22 Jun 56	RICH MAN, POOR MAN *Decca F 10736*	25	1
28 Sep 56 ●	MORE *Decca F 10774*	4	17
3 May 57	ROUND AND ROUND *Decca F 10875*	30	1
10 Oct 63	MISS YOU *Columbia DB 7119*	15	13
26 Mar 64	UNCHAINED MELODY (re-recording) *Columbia DB 7234*	43	3

'Unchained Melody' on Columbia and 'Round and Round' are with the Michael Sammes Singers

John Paul YOUNG *Australia, male vocalist (16 WEEKS)* pos/wks

29 Apr 78 ●	LOVE IS IN THE AIR *Ariola ARO 117*	5	13
14 Nov 92	LOVE IS IN THE AIR (re-mix) *Columbia 6587697*	49	3

Karen YOUNG *UK, female vocalist (21 WEEKS)* pos/wks

6 Sep 69 ●	NOBODY'S CHILD *Major Minor MM 625*	6	21

Karen YOUNG *US, female vocalist (9 WEEKS)* pos/wks

19 Aug 78	HOT SHOT *Atlantic K 11180*	34	7
24 Feb 79	HOT SHOT (re-issue) *Atlantic LV 8*	75	1
15 Nov 97	HOT SHOT '97 (re-recording) *Distinctive DISNCD 37*	68	1

Neil YOUNG *Canada, male vocalist / instrumentalist (22 WEEKS)* pos/wks

11 Mar 72 ●	HEART OF GOLD *Reprise K 14140* ▲	10	11
6 Jan 79	FOUR STRONG WINDS *Reprise K 14493*	57	4
27 Feb 93	HARVEST MOON *Reprise W 0139CD*	36	3
17 Jul 93	THE NEEDLE AND THE DAMAGE DONE *Reprise W 0191CD*	75	1
30 Oct 93	LONG MAY YOU RUN (LIVE) *Reprise W 0207CD*	71	1
9 Apr 94	PHILADELPHIA *Reprise W 0242CD*	62	2

See also CROSBY, STILLS, NASH and YOUNG

Paul YOUNG (187 Top 500) *Soulful-sounding pop singer / songwriter (b. 17 Jan 1956, Bedfordshire, UK) who earlier fronted The Q-Tips and chart act Streetband. This multi-Brit Award winner sold seven million copies of his 'No Parlez' album (including more than one million in the UK) (134 WEEKS)* pos/wks

18 Jun 83 ★	WHEREVER I LAY MY HAT (THAT'S MY HOME) *CBS A 3371*	1	15
10 Sep 83 ●	COME BACK AND STAY *CBS A 3636*	4	9
19 Nov 83 ●	LOVE OF THE COMMON PEOPLE *CBS A 3585*	2	13
13 Oct 84 ●	I'M GONNA TEAR YOUR PLAYHOUSE DOWN *CBS A 4786*	9	7
8 Dec 84 ●	EVERYTHING MUST CHANGE *CBS A 4972*	9	11
9 Mar 85 ●	EVERYTIME YOU GO AWAY *CBS A 6300* ▲	4	11
22 Jun 85	TOMB OF MEMORIES *CBS A 6321*	16	7
17 Aug 85	TOMB OF MEMORIES (re-entry) *CBS A 6321*	74	1
4 Oct 86	WONDERLAND *CBS YOUNG 1*	24	5
29 Nov 86	SOME PEOPLE *CBS YOUNG 2*	56	3
7 Feb 87	WHY DOES A MAN HAVE TO BE STRONG? *CBS YOUNG 3*	63	2
12 May 90	SOFTLY WHISPERING I LOVE YOU *CBS YOUNG 4*	21	6
7 Jul 90	OH GIRL *CBS YOUNG 5*	25	6
6 Oct 90	HEAVEN CAN WAIT *CBS YOUNG 6*	71	2
12 Jan 91	CALLING YOU *CBS YOUNG 7*	57	2
30 Mar 91 ●	SENZA UNA DONNA (WITHOUT A WOMAN) *London LON 294* [1]	4	12
10 Aug 91	BOTH SIDES NOW *MCA MCS 1546* [2]	74	1
26 Oct 91	DON'T DREAM IT'S OVER *Columbia 6574117*	20	5
25 Sep 93	NOW I KNOW WHAT MADE OTIS BLUE *Columbia 6596412*	14	7
27 Nov 93	HOPE IN A HOPELESS WORLD *Columbia 6598652*	42	3
23 Apr 94	IT WILL BE YOU *Columbia 6602812*	34	4
17 May 97	I WISH YOU LOVE *East West EW 100CD1*	33	2

[1] Zucchero and Paul Young [2] Clannad and Paul Young

Retta YOUNG *US, female vocalist (7 WEEKS)* pos/wks

24 May 75	SENDING OUT AN S.O.S. *All Platinum 6146 305*	28	7

Tracie YOUNG – *See TRACIE*

UK No.1 ★ UK Top 10 ● Still on chart + UK million seller ◆ UK entry at No.1 ■ US No.1 ▲

2001

IN THE YEAR IN WHICH THE WORLD WAS OVERCOME BY THE TRAGIC EVENTS OF 11 SEPTEMBER AND THE RESULTING WAR IN AFGHANISTAN, AND GEORGE HARRISON LOST HIS BATTLE WITH CANCER, A BRIGHTER NOTE WAS STRUCK BY **HEAR'SAY** WHO SOLD 549,823 COPIES OF 'PURE AND SIMPLE' IN ITS FIRST WEEK: A RECORD FOR A DEBUT ACT WHICH EARNED THEM A GUINNESS WORLD RECORDS BRITISH HIT SINGLES NO.1 AWARD. THIS IS WHAT THE FIVE WINNERS OF THE 'POPSTARS' TV SERIES HAD TO SAY ABOUT THE BIGGEST DAY OF THEIR LIVES ...

“ **Danny Foster:** This is the biggest adventure of my life and getting to No.1 fulfils my ultimate ambition and proves people like our music. **Myleene Klass:** We've been in denial this week. We've made everbody touch wood who said it would get to No.1. The lid has been lifted on the music business. It gives everyone hope that they can be part of it. We were unknowns six months ago. And everyone who doesn't deserve to be part of it: we're coming to get you! **Suzanne Shaw:** "I'm having the most amazing time, but I'm also taking the music side of things really seriously. We're here to make hit singles and do well with our music. We don't want to be the same as everything else that's out there. **Noel Sullivan:** We would have been happy with any chart position, but this puts the icing on the cake. **Kym Marsh:** I'm speechless. This is amazing start. I never thought it would happen. ”

SINGLE OF THE YEAR 'Whole Again' Atomic Kitten
ALBUM OF THE YEAR 'No Angel' Dido

YOUNG and COMPANY
US, male / female vocal / instrumental group (12 WEEKS) pos/wks

			pos	wks
1 Nov 80		**I LIKE (WHAT YOU'RE DOING TO ME)** *Excalibur EXC 501*	20	12

YOUNG AND MOODY BAND
UK, male vocal / instrumental group (4 WEEKS) pos/wks

			pos	wks
10 Oct 81		**DON'T DO THAT** *Bronze BRO 130*	63	4

YOUNG BLACK TEENAGERS *US, male rap group (3 WEEKS)* pos/wks

			pos	wks
9 Apr 94		**TAP THE BOTTLE** *MCA MCSTD 1967*	39	3

YOUNG DISCIPLES
UK / US, male / female vocal / instrumental group (17 WEEKS) pos/wks

			pos	wks
13 Oct 90		**GET YOURSELF TOGETHER** *Talkin Loud TLK 2*	68	1
23 Feb 91		**APPARENTLY NOTHIN'** *Talkin Loud TLK 5*	46	4
3 Aug 91		**APPARENTLY NOTHIN' (re-entry)** *Talkin Loud TLK 5*	13	7
5 Oct 91		**GET YOURSELF TOGETHER (re-issue)** *Talkin Loud TLK 15*	65	2
5 Sep 92		**YOUNG DISCIPLES (EP)** *Talkin Loud TLKX 18*	48	3

Tracks on Young Disciples (EP): Move On / Freedom / All I Have In Me / Move On (re-mix)

YOUNG IDEA
UK, male vocal duo – Tony Cox and Douglas MacCrae-Brown (6 WEEKS) pos/wks

			pos	wks
29 Jun 67	●	**WITH A LITTLE HELP FROM MY FRIENDS** *Columbia DB 8205*	10	6

YOUNG MC *US, male rapper – Marvin Young (7 WEEKS)* pos/wks

			pos	wks
15 Jul 89		**BUST A MOVE** *Delicious Vinyl BRW 137*	73	2
17 Feb 90		**PRINCIPAL'S OFFICE** *Delicious Vinyl BRW 161*	54	3
17 Aug 91		**THAT'S THE WAY LOVE GOES** *Capitol CL 623*	65	2

YOUNG OFFENDERS
Ireland, male vocal / instrumental group (1 WEEK) pos/wks

			pos	wks
7 Mar 98		**THAT'S WHY WE LOSE CONTROL** *Columbia 6651942*	60	1

YOUNG ONES – *See Cliff RICHARD*

YOUNG RASCALS *US, male vocal / instrumental group (17 WEEKS)* pos/wks

			pos	wks
25 May 67	●	**GROOVIN'** *Atlantic 584 111* ▲	8	13
16 Aug 67		**A GIRL LIKE YOU** *Atlantic 584 128*	37	4

Leon YOUNG STRING CHORALE – *See Mr Acker BILK and his PARAMOUNT JAZZ BAND*

Sydney YOUNGBLOOD *US, male vocalist – Sydney Ford (31 WEEKS)* pos/wks

			pos	wks
26 Aug 89	●	**IF ONLY I COULD** *Circa YR 34*	3	14
9 Dec 89		**SIT AND WAIT** *Circa YR 40*	16	8
31 Mar 90		**I'D RATHER GO BLIND** *Circa YR 43*	44	5
29 Jun 91		**HOOKED ON YOU** *Circa YR 65*	72	2
20 Mar 93		**ANYTHING** *RCA 74321138672*	48	2

YOUNGER YOUNGER 28'S
UK, male / female vocal / instrumental group (1 WEEK) pos/wks

			pos	wks
5 Jun 99		**WE'RE GOING OUT** *V2 VVR 5006943*	61	1

Z

Z FACTOR *UK, male DJ / producer – Dave Lee (2 WEEKS)* pos/wks

			pos	wks
21 Feb 98		**GOTTA KEEP PUSHIN'** *ffrr FCD 329*	47	1
17 Nov 01		**RIDE THE RHYTHM** *Direction 6718482*	52	1

See also Joey NEGRO; Li KWAN; RAVEN MAIZE; AKUBU featuring Linda CLIFFORD; JAKATTA; HED BOYS

Z2 *UK, male production duo (1 WEEK)* pos/wks

			pos	wks
26 Feb 00		**I WANT YOU** *Platipus PLATCD 67* [1]	61	1

[1] Vocal by Alison Rivers

Helmut ZACHARIAS *Germany, orchestra (11 WEEKS)* pos/wks

			pos	wks
29 Oct 64	●	**TOKYO MELODY** *Polydor NH 52341*	9	11

Pia ZADORA *US, female vocalist (6 WEEKS)* pos/wks

			pos	wks
27 Oct 84		**WHEN THE RAIN BEGINS TO FALL** *Arista ARIST 584* [1]	68	2
12 Nov 88		**DANCE OUT OF MY HEAD** *Epic 6528867* [2]	65	4

[1] Jermaine Jackson and Pia Zadora [2] Pia

ZAGER and EVANS
US, male vocal duo – Denny Zager and Rick Evans (13 WEEKS) pos/wks

			pos	wks
9 Aug 69	★	**IN THE YEAR 2525 (EXORDIUM AND TERMINUS)** *RCA 1860* ▲	1	13

Michael ZAGER BAND
US, male / female vocal / instrumental group (12 WEEKS) pos/wks

			pos	wks
1 Apr 78	●	**LET'S ALL CHANT** *Private Stock PVT 143*	8	12

Gheorghe ZAMFIR
Romania, male instrumentalist – pipes (9 WEEKS) pos/wks

			pos	wks
21 Aug 76	●	**(LIGHT OF EXPERIENCE) DOINA DE JALE** *Epic EPC 4310*	4	9

Tommy ZANG *US, male vocalist (1 WEEK)* pos/wks

			pos	wks
16 Feb 61		**HEY GOOD LOOKING** *Polydor NH 66957*	45	1

ZAPP *US, male vocal / instrumental group (6 WEEKS)* pos/wks

			pos	wks
25 Jan 86		**IT DOESN'T REALLY MATTER** *Warner Bros. W 8879*	57	3
24 May 86		**COMPUTER LOVE (PART 1)** *Warner Bros. W 8805*	64	3

Francesco ZAPPALA *Italy, male producer (3 WEEKS)* pos/wks

			pos	wks
10 Aug 91		**WE GOTTA DO IT** *Fourth & Broadway BRW 225* [1]	57	2
2 May 92		**NO WAY OUT** *PWL Continental PWL 230*	69	1

[1] DJ Professor featuring Francesco Zappala

Lena ZAVARONI *UK, female vocalist (14 WEEKS)* pos/wks

			pos	wks
9 Feb 74	●	**MA HE'S MAKING EYES AT ME** *Philips 6006 367*	10	11
1 Jun 74		**PERSONALITY** *Philips 6006 391*	33	3

ZED BIAS *UK, male vocal / production group (4 WEEKS)* pos/wks

			pos	wks
15 Jul 00		**NEIGHBOURHOOD** *Locked On / XL Recordings LOX 122CD*	25	4

ZEE *UK, female vocalist (4 WEEKS)* pos/wks

			pos	wks
6 Jul 96		**DREAMTIME** *Perfecto PERF 122CD*	31	2
22 Mar 97		**SAY MY NAME** *Perfecto PERF 135CD*	36	1
7 Feb 98		**BUTTERFLY** *Perfecto PERF 154CD1* [1]	41	1

[1] Tilt featuring Zee

ZEPHYRS *UK, male vocal / instrumental group (1 WEEK)* pos/wks

			pos	wks
18 Mar 65		**SHE'S LOST YOU** *Columbia DB 7481*	48	1

ZERO B *UK, male instrumentalist – keyboards (6 WEEKS)* pos/wks

			pos	wks
22 Feb 92		**THE EP** *Ffrreedom TAB 102*	32	4
24 Jul 93		**RECONNECTION (EP)** *Internal LIECD 6*	54	2

Tracks on The EP: Lock Up / Spinning Wheel / Module / Eclipse. Tracks on Reconnection (EP): Lock Up / Lock Up (re-mix) / Oü Est Le Spoon / Love to Be In Love. All three versions of 'Lock Up' are different mixes of the same track

ZERO 7 *UK, male production duo (4 WEEKS)*

Date	Title / Label	pos	wks
18 Aug 01	**DESTINY** *Ultimate Dilemma UDRCDS043* [1]	30	3
17 Nov 01	**IN THE WAITING LINE** *Ultimate Dilemma UDRCDS045*	47	1

[1] Zero 7 featuring Sia and Sophie

ZERO VU featuring Lorna B
UK, male / female vocal / production group (1 WEEK)

Date	Title / Label	pos	wks
15 Mar 97	**FEELS SO GOOD** *Avex UK AVEXCD 53*	69	1

ZERO ZERO *UK, male instrumental / production duo (1 WEEK)*

Date	Title / Label	pos	wks
10 Aug 91	**ZEROXED** *Kickin KICK 9*	71	1

ZHANÉ *US, female vocal duo (18 WEEKS)*

Date	Title / Label	pos	wks
11 Sep 93	**HEY MR DJ** *Epic 6596102*	26	3
4 Dec 93	**HEY MR DJ (re-entry)** *Epic 6596102*	50	2
19 Mar 94	**GROOVE THANG** *Motown TMGCD 1423*	34	3
20 Aug 94	**VIBE** *Motown TMGCD 1430*	67	1
25 Feb 95	**SHAME** *Jive JIVECD 372*	66	1
21 Sep 96	**IT'S A PARTY** *Elektra EKR 226CD* [1]	23	2
8 Mar 97	**4 MORE** *Tommy Boy TBCD 7779A* [2]	52	1
26 Apr 97	**REQUEST LINE** *Motown 8606452*	22	3
30 Aug 97	**CRUSH** *Motown 5716712*	44	1
11 Sep 99	**JAMBOREE** *Arista 74321692882* [3]	51	1

[1] Busta Rhymes featuring Zhané [2] De La Soul featuring Zhané [3] Naughty By Nature featuring Zhané

ZIG and ZAG *Zog / Ireland, male puppet duo (12 WEEKS)*

Date	Title / Label	pos	wks
24 Dec 94 ●	**THEM GIRLS THEM GIRLS** *RCA 74321251042*	5	9
1 Jul 95	**HANDS UP! HANDS UP!** *RCA 74321284392*	21	3

ZIGZAG JIVE FLUTES – *See ELIAS and his ZIGZAG JIVE FLUTES*

ZION TRAIN *UK, male / female vocal / instrumental group (1 WEEK)*

Date	Title / Label	pos	wks
27 Jul 96	**RISE** *China WOKCD 2085*	61	1

ZODIAC MINDWARP and the LOVE REACTION
UK, male / female vocal / instrumental group (11 WEEKS)

Date	Title / Label	pos	wks
9 May 87	**PRIME MOVER** *Mercury ZOD 1*	18	6
14 Nov 87	**BACKSEAT EDUCATION** *Mercury ZOD 2*	49	3
2 Apr 88	**PLANET GIRL** *Mercury ZOD 3*	63	2

ZODIACS – *See Maurice WILLIAMS and the ZODIACS*

ZOE *UK, female vocalist – Zoe Pollock (22 WEEKS)*

Date	Title / Label	pos	wks
10 Nov 90	**SUNSHINE ON A RAINY DAY** *M & G MAGS 6*	53	5
24 Aug 91 ●	**SUNSHINE ON A RAINY DAY (re-mix)** *M & G MAGS 14*	4	11
2 Nov 91	**LIGHTNING** *M & G MAGS 18*	37	4
29 Feb 92	**HOLY DAYS** *M & G MAGS 21*	72	2

Rob ZOMBIE *US, male vocalist (2 WEEKS)*

Date	Title / Label	pos	wks
26 Dec 98	**DRAGULA** *Geffen GFSTD 22367*	44	2

ZOMBIE NATION *Germany, male production duo – Florian "Splank" Senfter and Emanuel "Mooner" Günther (16 WEEKS)*

Date	Title / Label	pos	wks
2 Sep 00	**KERNKRAFT 400 (import)** *TRANSK TRANSK 002*	61	1
30 Sep 00 ●	**KERNKRAFT 400** *Data DATA 11CDS*	2	15

ZOMBIES *UK, male vocal / instrumental group (16 WEEKS)*

Date	Title / Label	pos	wks
13 Aug 64	**SHE'S NOT THERE** *Decca F 11940*	12	11
11 Feb 65	**TELL HER NO** *Decca F 12072*	42	5

ZOO EXPERIENCE featuring DESTRY
UK, male instrumental group and US, male vocalist (1 WEEK)

Date	Title / Label	pos	wks
22 Aug 92	**LOVE'S GOTTA HOLD ON ME** *Cooltempo COOL 261*	66	1

ZUCCHERO *Italy, male vocalist / instrumentalist – guitar – Adelmo Fornaciari (24 WEEKS)*

Date	Title / Label	pos	wks
30 Mar 91 ●	**SENZA UNA DONNA (WITHOUT A WOMAN)** *London LON 294* [1]	4	12
18 Jan 92	**DIAMANTE** *London LON 313* [2]	44	7
24 Oct 92	**MISERERE** *London LON 329* [3]	15	5

[1] Zucchero and Paul Young [2] Zucchero with Randy Crawford [3] Zucchero with Luciano Pavarotti

ZZ TOP (330 Top 500)
Low-slung, guitar-driven blues-rock trio formed 1969 in Houston, Texas, US; long-bearded duo Billy Gibbons (v/g) and Dusty Hill (v/b) plus clean-shaven Frank Beard (d). Hugely popular stadium-packing festival headliners in the 1980s. Named to ensure they would be the last act in record racks and hit books (94 WEEKS)

Date	Title / Label	pos	wks
3 Sep 83	**GIMME ALL YOUR LOVIN'** *Warner Bros. W 9693*	61	3
26 Nov 83	**SHARP DRESSED MAN** *Warner Bros. W 9576*	53	3
31 Mar 84	**TV DINNERS** *Warner Bros. W 9334*	67	3
6 Oct 84 ●	**GIMME ALL YOUR LOVIN' (re-entry)** *Warner Bros. W 9693*	10	15
15 Dec 84	**SHARP DRESSED MAN (re-entry)** *Warner Bros. W 9576*	22	10
23 Feb 85	**LEGS** *Warner Bros. W 9272*	16	7
13 Jul 85	**THE ZZ TOP SUMMER HOLIDAY (EP)** *Warner Bros. W 8946*	51	5
19 Oct 85	**SLEEPING BAG** *Warner Bros. W 2001*	27	5
15 Feb 86	**STAGES** *Warner Bros. W 2002*	43	3
19 Apr 86	**ROUGH BOY** *Warner Bros. W 2003*	23	9
4 Oct 86	**VELCRO FLY** *Warner Bros. W 8650*	54	3
21 Jul 90	**DOUBLEBACK** *Warner Bros. W 9812*	29	6
13 Apr 91	**MY HEAD'S IN MISSISSIPPI** *Warner Bros W 0009*	37	5
11 Apr 92 ●	**VIVA LAS VEGAS** *Warner Bros. W 0098*	10	7
20 Jun 92	**ROUGH BOY (re-issue)** *Warner Bros. W 0111*	49	3
29 Jan 94	**PINCUSHION** *RCA 74321184732*	15	3
7 May 94	**BREAKAWAY** *RCA 74321192282*	60	1
29 Jun 96	**WHAT'S UP WITH THAT** *RCA 74321394822*	58	1
16 Oct 99	**GIMME ALL YOUR LOVIN' 2000** *Riverhorse RIVHCD 2* [1]	28	2

[1] Martay featuring ZZ Top

Tracks on Summer Holiday (EP): Tush / Got Me Under Pressure / Beer Drinkers and Hell Raisers / I'm Bad, I'm Nationwide

A-Z BY SONG TITLE

▶ What follows is an alphabetical index of the 23,182 songs that make up the 26,691 hit singles. For a detailed guide on to how to use this section and an explanation of all the symbols, turn the page

Meat Loaf can claim the longest hit single title in our song index with 1994's catchily named 'Objects in the Rear View Mirror May Appear Closer Than They Are', which comes in at 52 letters. Rod Stewart registers a massive 63 letters more for a song title with brackets, on the 1974 hymn to household chores 'You Can Make Me Dance Sing or Anything (Even Take the Dog for a Walk, Mend a Fuse, Fold Away the Ironing Board, or Any Other Domestic Short Comings)'

HOW TO USE THIS SECTION

This section contains an alphabetical index of every hit since 1952 in order of title, act name, highest position the hit reached on the chart and the year(s) in which it charted

▶ **Covers:** Different songs with the same title are differentiated by a letter in brackets after the song title: [A], [B], etc. Cover versions of the same song share the same letter. For example, there are seven versions of 'Around the World'. Four of these titles share the letter [A], which indicates that they are all covers of the same song (recorded individually by Bing Crosby, Ronnie Hilton, Gracie Fields and Mantovani). However, the fifth version is followed by the letter [B], which indicates that it is a different song (recorded by East 17). If the original version of a cover was never a chart hit, it will not be listed here.

Non-singles: In most cases, individual titles of songs on EP, LP, medley or megamix singles that made the chart are not listed here, although full track listings are included in the artist entries in the A-Z by artist section.

Most duets list both artists involved (eg 'Don't Let the Sun Go Down on Me' by Elton John and George Michael), but some hits are credited only to the main artist. For example, 'Zing a Little Zong' is credited to Bing Crosby. But if you look up his entry in the A-Z by artist section, a footnote for the hit explains that it was, in fact, a duet with Jane Wyman.

Act names use bold capital letters to indicate where to look them up alphabetically in the A-Z by artist section. Groups, bands, orchestras and ensembles are alphabetised according to the whole act name, while individual artists are ordered according to their surnames. Therefore, DANNY WILSON is a group and appears under 'D', while Jennifer LOPEZ is an individual and appears under 'L'.

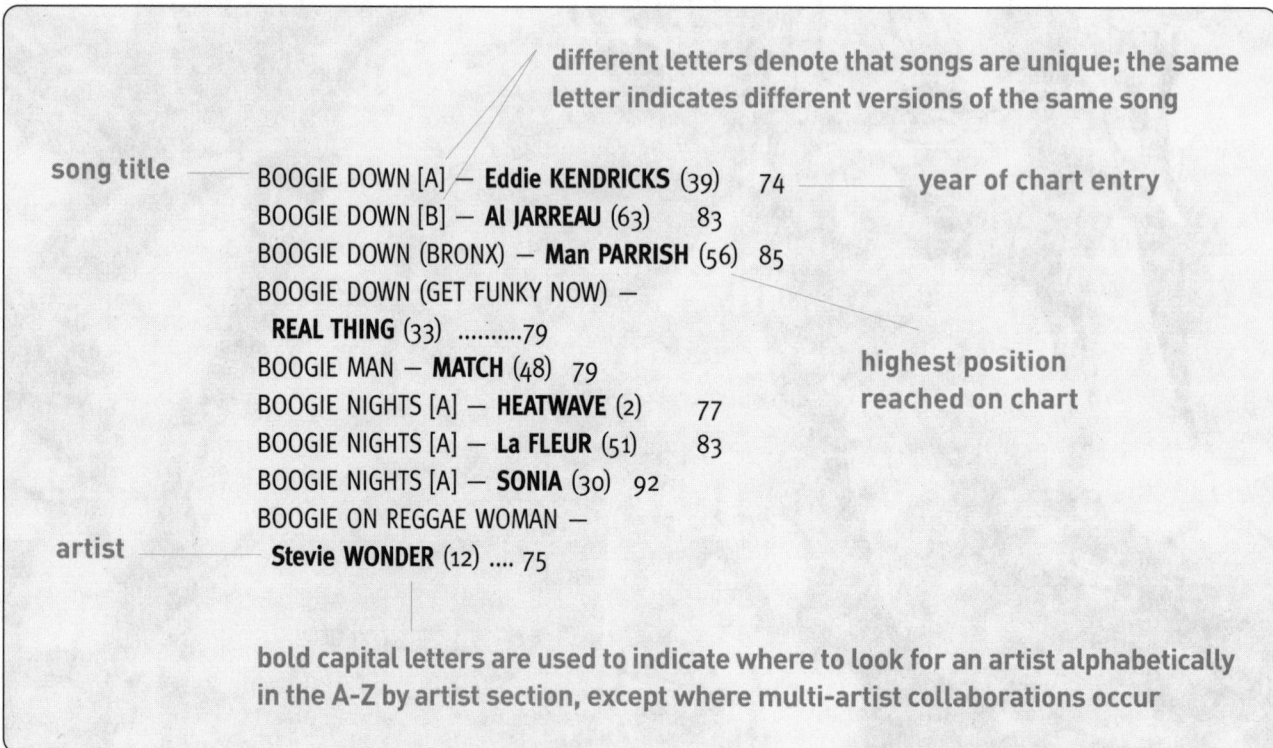

different letters denote that songs are unique; the same letter indicates different versions of the same song

song title — BOOGIE DOWN [A] – **Eddie KENDRICKS** (39) 74 — **year of chart entry**
BOOGIE DOWN [B] – **Al JARREAU** (63) 83
BOOGIE DOWN (BRONX) – **Man PARRISH** (56) 85
BOOGIE DOWN (GET FUNKY NOW) –
REAL THING (33) 79
BOOGIE MAN – **MATCH** (48) 79 — **highest position reached on chart**
BOOGIE NIGHTS [A] – **HEATWAVE** (2) 77
BOOGIE NIGHTS [A] – **La FLEUR** (51) 83
BOOGIE NIGHTS [A] – **SONIA** (30) 92
BOOGIE ON REGGAE WOMAN –
artist — **Stevie WONDER** (12) 75

bold capital letters are used to indicate where to look for an artist alphabetically in the A-Z by artist section, except where multi-artist collaborations occur

A BA NI BI – Izhar COHEN and the ALPHA-BETA (20) 78
'A' BOMB IN WARDOUR STREET – JAM (25) 78,80,83
A9 – ARIEL (28) 00
THE A TEAM – Mike POST (45) 84
AAAH D YAAA – GOATS (53) 93
AARON'S PARTY (COME GET IT) – Aaron CARTER (51) 00
ABACAB – GENESIS (9) 81
ABACUS (WHEN I FALL IN LOVE) – AXUS (62) 98
ABANDON [A] – DARE (71) 89
ABANDON [B] – THAT PETROL EMOTION (73) 90
ABANDON SHIP – BLAGGERS I.T.A. (48) 94
ABBA-ESQUE (EP) – ERASURE (1) 92
THE ABBEY ROAD EP – SPIRITUALIZED (39) 98
ABC – JACKSONS (8) 70
ABC AND D . . . – BLUE BAMBOO (23) 94
A.B.C. (FALLING IN LOVE'S NOT EASY) – DIRECT DRIVE (75) 85
ABIDE WITH ME [A] – INSPIRATIONAL CHOIR (36) 84,85
ABIDE WITH ME [A] – Vic REEVES (47) 91
ABOUT 3AM – DARK STAR (50) 99
ABOVE THE CLOUDS – Paul WELLER (47) 92
ABRACADABRA – Steve MILLER BAND (2) 82
ABRAHAM MARTIN AND JOHN – Marvin GAYE (9) 70
ABSOLUT(E) – Claudia BRUCKEN (71) 90
ABSOLUTE – SCRITTI POLITTI (17) 84
ABSOLUTE BEGINNERS [A] – JAM (4) 81
ABSOLUTE BEGINNERS [B] – David BOWIE (2) 86
ABSOLUTE E-SENSUAL – Jaki GRAHAM (69) 95
ABSOLUTE REALITY – ALARM (35) 85
ABSOLUTELY EVERYBODY – Vanessa AMOROSI (7) 00
ABSOLUTELY FABULOUS – PET SHOP BOYS (6) 94
ABSTAIN – FIVE THIRTY (75) 90
ABSURD – FLUKE (25) 97
ABUSE ME – SILVERCHAIR (40) 97
AC / DC – X-PRESS 2 (60) 00
ACAPULCO 1922 – Kenny BALL and his JAZZMEN (27) 63
ACCELERATE – SKIN UP (45) 92
ACCELERATOR – PRIMAL SCREAM (34) 00
ACCESS – DJ MISJAH and DJ TIM (16) 96,00
ACCIDENT OF BIRTH – Bruce DICKINSON (54) 97
ACCIDENT PRONE – STATUS QUO (36) 78
ACCIDENT WAITING TO HAPPEN (EP) – Billy BRAGG (33) 92
ACCIDENTS – THUNDERCLAP NEWMAN (46) 70
ACCIDENTS WILL HAPPEN – Elvis COSTELLO (28) 79
ACE OF SPADES – MOTÖRHEAD (15) 80,93
ACES HIGH – IRON MAIDEN (20) 84
ACHILLES HEEL – TOPLOADER (8) 99,00
ACHY BREAKY HEART [A] – Billy Ray CYRUS (3) 92
ACHY BREAKY HEART [A] – Alvin and the CHIPMUNKS featuring Billy Ray CYRUS (53) 92
ACID LAB – Alex REECE (64) 96
ACID MAN – JOLLY ROGER (23) 88
ACKEE 1-2-3 – BEAT (54) 83
THE ACOUSTICS (EP) – NEW MODEL ARMY (49) 85
ACPERIENCE – HARDFLOOR (60) 97
ACT OF WAR – Elton JOHN and Millie JACKSON (32) 85
ACTION [A] – SWEET (15) 75
ACTION [A] – DEF LEPPARD (14) 94
ACTION AND DRAMA – BIS (50) 99
ACTIV 8 (COME WITH ME) – ALTERN 8 (3) 91
ACTIVATED – Gerald ALSTON (73) 89
ACTUALLY IT'S DARKNESS – IDLEWILD (23) 00
ADDAMS FAMILY (WHOOMP!) – TAG TEAM (53) 94
ADDAMS GROOVE – HAMMER (4) 91
ADDICTED TO LOVE – Robert PALMER (5) 86
ADDICTED TO LOVE (LIVE) – Tina TURNER (71) 88
ADDICTION – ALMIGHTY (38) 93
ADELANTE – SASH! (2) 00
ADIA – Sarah McLACHLAN (18) 98
A.D.I.D.A.S. – KORN (22) 97
ADIDAS WORLD – Edwyn COLLINS (71) 97
ADIEMUS – ADIEMUS (48) 95
ADIOS AMIGO – Jim REEVES (23) 62
THE ADORATION WALTZ – David WHITFIELD (9) 57
ADORATIONS – KILLING JOKE (42) 86
ADORE – Joe ROBERTS (45) 94
ADORED AND EXPLORED – Marc ALMOND (25) 95
ADRENALIN (EP) – N-JOI (23) 91
ADRIFT (CAST YOUR MIND) – ANTARCTICA (72) 00
ADULT EDUCATION – Daryl HALL and John OATES (63) 84
THE ADVENTURES OF THE LOVE CRUSADER – Sarah BRIGHTMAN (53) 79
ADVICE FOR THE YOUNG AT HEART – TEARS FOR FEARS (36) 90
AEROPLANE – RED HOT CHILI PEPPERS (11) 96
THE AEROPLANE SONG – STRAW (37) 99
AFFAIR – CHERRELLE (67) 89
AFFIRMATION – SAVAGE GARDEN (8) 00
AFRAID – MOTLEY CRUE (58) 97
AFRICA – TOTO (3) 83
AFRICAN AND WHITE – CHINA CRISIS (45) 82
AFRICAN DREAM – Wasis DIOP featuring Lena FIAGBE (44) 96
AFRICAN HORIZON – MYSTICA (59) 98
AFRICAN REIGN – DEEP C (75) 91
AFRICAN WALTZ – Johnny DANKWORTH (9) 61
AFRIKA – Q-TEE (42) 90
AFRIKA SHOX – Afrika BAMBAATAA (7) 99
AFRO DIZZI ACT – CRY SISCO! (42) 89,90
AFRO KING – EMF (51) 95
AFRO PUFFS – LADY OF RAGE (72) 94
AFRO SLEEZE – ROACH MOTEL (73) 93
AFRODISIAC – POWDER (72) 95
THE AFRO-LEFT EP – LEFTFIELD (22) 95
AFTER A FASHION – Midge URE and Mick KARN (39) 83
AFTER ALL – FRANK AND WALTERS (11) 93
AFTER ALL THESE YEARS – FOSTER and ALLEN (43) 86
AFTER LOVE – BLANK & JONES (57) 00
AFTER THE FIRE – Roger DALTREY (50) 85
AFTER THE GOLDRUSH – PRELUDE (21) 74,82
AFTER THE LOVE – JESUS LOVES YOU (68) 89
AFTER THE LOVE HAS GONE [A] – EARTH WIND AND FIRE (4) 79
AFTER THE LOVE HAS GONE [A] – DAMAGE (42) 01
AFTER THE LOVE HAS GONE [B] – PRINCESS (28) 85
AFTER THE LOVE HAS GONE [C] – STEPS (5) 99,00
AFTER THE RAIN – TITIYO (60) 90
AFTER THE RAIN HAS FALLEN – STING (31) 00
AFTER THE WAR – Gary MOORE (37) 89
AFTER THE WATERSHED – CARTER – THE UNSTOPPABLE SEX MACHINE (11) 91
AFTER YOU'VE GONE – Alice BABS (43) 63
AFTERGLOW – MISSION (53) 94
AFTERGLOW OF YOUR LOVE – SMALL FACES (36) 69
AFTERMATH [A] – NIGHTMARES ON WAX (38) 90
AFTERMATH [B] – TRICKY (69) 94
AFTERNOON DELIGHT – STARLAND VOCAL BAND (18) 76
AFTERNOON OF THE RHINO – Mike POST (47) 75
(AFTERNOON) SOAPS – ARAB STRAP (74) 98
AFTERNOONS & COFFEESPOONS – CRASH TEST DUMMIES (23) 94
AGADOO – BLACK LACE (2) 84,98
AGAIN [A] – Jimmy TARBUCK (68) 85
AGAIN [B] – Janet JACKSON (6) 93
AGAIN [C] – Juliet ROBERTS (33) 94
AGAIN AND AGAIN – STATUS QUO (13) 78
AGAINST ALL ODDS [A] – Mariah CAREY and WESTLIFE (1) 00,01
AGAINST ALL ODDS (TAKE A LOOK AT ME NOW) [A] – Phil COLLINS (2) 84
AGAINST THE WIND – Maire BRENNAN (64) 92
AGE AIN'T NOTHING BUT A NUMBER – AALIYAH (32) 95
AGE OF LONELINESS – ENIGMA (21) 94
AGE OF LOVE – THE REMIXES – AGE OF LOVE (17) 97,98
AGE OF PANIC – SENSER (52) 94
AGENT DAN – AGENT PROVOCATEUR (49) 97
AHORA ES (NOW IS THE TIME) – 2 IN A ROOM (43) 95
AI NO CORRIDA (I-NO-KO-REE-DA) – Quincy JONES (14) 81
AIKEA-GUINEA – COCTEAU TWINS (41) 85
AIN'T COMPLAINING – STATUS QUO (19) 88
AIN'T DOIN' NOTHIN' – Jet BRONX and the FORBIDDEN (49) 77
AIN'T GOIN' TO GOA – ALABAMA 3 (40) 98
AIN'T GOING DOWN – Garth BROOKS (13) 94
AIN'T GONNA BE THAT WAY – Marv JOHNSON (50) 60
AIN'T GONNA BUMP NO MORE (WITH NO BIG FAT WOMAN) – Joe TEX (2) 77
AIN'T GONNA CRY AGAIN – Peter COX (37) 97
AIN'T GONNA WASH FOR A WEEK – BROOK BROTHERS (13) 61
AIN'T GOT A CLUE – LURKERS (45) 78
AIN'T GOT NO – I GOT LIFE – Nina SIMONE (2) 68
AIN'T IT FUN – GUNS N' ROSES (9) 93
AIN'T IT FUNNY – Jennifer LOPEZ (3) 01
AIN'T LOVE A BITCH – Rod STEWART (11) 79
AIN'T MISBEHAVIN' [A] – Johnnie RAY (17) 56
AIN'T MISBEHAVIN' [A] – Tommy BRUCE and the BRUISERS (3) 60
AIN'T MY BEATING HEART – TEN SHARP (63) 92
AIN'T NO CASANOVA – SINCLAIR (28) 93
AIN'T NO DOUBT – Jimmy NAIL (1) 92
AIN'T NO LOVE (AIN'T NO USE) – SUB SUB featuring Melanie WILLIAMS (3) 93
AIN'T NO LOVE IN THE HEART OF THE CITY – WHITESNAKE (51) 80
AIN'T NO MAN – Dina CARROLL (16) 92
AIN'T NO MOUNTAIN HIGH ENOUGH [A] – Diana ROSS (6) 70
AIN'T NO MOUNTAIN HIGH ENOUGH [A] – Jocelyn BROWN (35) 98
AIN'T NO MOUNTAIN HIGH ENOUGH [A] – WHITEHOUSE (60) 98
AIN'T NO MOUNTAIN HIGH ENOUGH – REMEMBER ME (MEDLEY) – BOYSTOWN GANG (46) 81
AIN'T NO NEED TO HIDE – Sandy B (60) 97
AIN'T NO PLAYA – JAY-Z featuring Foxy BROWN (31) 97
AIN'T NO PLEASING YOU – CHAS and DAVE (2) 82
AIN'T NO STOPPING – ENIGMA (11) 81
AIN'T NO STOPPIN' US – DJ LUCK & MC NEAT (8) 00
AIN'T NO STOPPIN' US NOW [A] – McFADDEN and WHITEHEAD (5) 79
AIN'T NO STOPPIN' US NOW [A] – BIG DADDY KANE (44) 90
AIN'T NO STOPPING US NOW [A] – Luther VANDROSS (22) 95
AIN'T NO STOPPING US NOW [A] – MOBO ALLSTARS (47) 98
AIN'T NO STOPPING US NOW (PARTY FOR THE WORLD) – Steve WALSH (44) 88
AIN'T NO SUNSHINE [A] – Michael JACKSON (8) 72
AIN'T NO SUNSHINE [A] – SIVUCA (56) 84
AIN'T NO SUNSHINE [A] – LADYSMITH BLACK MAMBAZO featuring DES'REE (42) 99
AIN'T NOBODY [A] – Chaka KHAN (6) 84,89
AIN'T NOBODY [A] – Jaki GRAHAM (44) 94
AIN'T NOBODY [A] – Diana KING (13) 95
AIN'T NOBODY [A] – COURSE (8) 97
AIN'T NOBODY [A] – LL COOL J (1) 97
AIN'T NOBODY BETTER – INNER CITY (10) 89
AIN'T NOBODY (LOVES ME BETTER) – KWS and Gwen DICKEY (21) 94
AIN'T NOTHIN' GOIN' ON BUT THE RENT – Gwen GUTHRIE (5) 86
AIN'T NOTHIN' GOIN' ON BUT THE RENT – Gwen GUTHRIE (42) 93
AIN'T NOTHIN' LIKE IT – Michael LOVESMITH (75) 85

AMERICA [B] – SIMON and GARFUNKEL (25) 72
AMERICA [C] – David ESSEX (32) 74
AMERICA [E] – Gary NUMAN (49) 88
AMERICA (I LOVE AMERICA) – FULL INTENTION (32) 96,97
AMERICA THE BEAUTIFUL – Elvis PRESLEY (69) 01
AMERICA: WHAT TIME IS LOVE – KLF (4) 92
AMERICA – WORLD CUP THEME 1994 – Leonard BERNSTEIN, ORCHESTRA and CHORUS (44) 94
THE AMERICAN – SIMPLE MINDS (59) 81
AMERICAN BAD ASS – KID ROCK (25) 00
AMERICAN DREAM [A] – CROSBY, STILLS, NASH and YOUNG (55) 89
AMERICAN DREAM [B] – POWER OF DREAMS (74) 91
AMERICAN DREAM [C] – JAKATTA (3) 01
AMERICAN GENERATION – RITCHIE FAMILY (49) 79
AMERICAN GIRL – Tom PETTY and the HEARTBREAKERS (40) 77
AMERICAN HEARTS – Billy OCEAN (54) 79
AMERICAN PIE [A] – Don McLEAN (2) 72,91
AMERICAN PIE [A] – CHUPITO (54) 95
AMERICAN PIE [A] – JUST LUIS (31) 95,96
AMERICAN PIE [A] – MADONNA (1) 00
AMERICAN TRILOGY [A] – Elvis PRESLEY (8) 72
AMERICAN TRILOGY [A] – Mickey NEWBURY (42) 72
AMERICAN TRILOGY [B] – DELGADOS (61) 00
AMERICAN TV – TERRORVISION (63) 93
AMERICAN WOMAN – GUESS WHO (19) 70
AMERICANOS – Holly JOHNSON (4) 89
AMIGO – BLACK SLATE (9) 80
AMIGOS PARA SIEMPRE (FRIENDS FOR LIFE) – José CARRERAS and Sarah BRIGHTMAN (11) 92
AMITYVILLE (THE HOUSE ON THE HILL) – LOVEBUG STARSKI (12) 86
AMNESIA [A] – SHALAMAR (61) 84
AMNESIA [B] – CHUMBAWAMBA (10) 98
AMONG MY SOUVENIRS – Connie FRANCIS (11) 59
AMOR – Julio IGLESIAS (32) 82
AMOR AMOR – Ben E KING (38) 61
AMOUR AMOUR – MOBILES (45) 82
AMOUR (C'MON) – PORN KINGS (17) 97
AMOUREUSE – Kiki DEE (13) 73,76
THE AMSTERDAM EP – SIMPLE MINDS (18) 89
AN ACCIDENT IN PARADISE – Sven VATH (57) 93
AN AFFAIR TO REMEMBER – Vic DAMONE (29) 57,58
AN ANGEL – KELLY FAMILY (69) 95
AN EVERLASTING LOVE – Andy GIBB (10) 78
AN INNOCENT MAN – Billy JOEL (8) 84
AN OLYMPIC RECORD – BARRON KNIGHTS (35) 68
AN UBHAL AS AIRDE (THE HIGHEST APPLE) – RUNRIG (18) 95
ANARCHY IN THE UK [A] – SEX PISTOLS (33) 76,92
ANARCHY IN THE UK [A] – MEGADETH (45) 88
ANARCHY IN THE UK [A] – GREEN JELLY (27) 93
ANA'S SONG – SILVERCHAIR (45) 99
ANASTHASIA – T99 (14) 91
ANCHORAGE – Michelle SHOCKED (60) 88
AND A BANG ON THE EAR – WATERBOYS (51) 89
AND DA DRUM MACHINE – PHATT B (58) 00
AND I LOVE YOU SO – Perry COMO (3) 73,74
AND I WISH – DOOLEYS (52) 81
AND I'M TELLING YOU I'M NOT GOING [A] – Jennifer HOLLIDAY (32) 82
AND I'M TELLING YOU I'M NOT GOING [A] – Donna GILES (27) 94,96
AND IT HURTS – DAYEENE (63) 99
AND IT WASN'T A DREAM – RUTHLESS RAP ASSASSINS (75) 90
(AND NOW – THE WALTZ) C'EST LA VIE – SLADE (50) 82
AND SHE WAS – TALKING HEADS (17) 86
AND SO I WILL WAIT FOR YOU – Dee FREDRIX (56) 93
AND SO IS LOVE – Kate BUSH (26) 94
... AND STONES – BLUE AEROPLANES (63) 90
... AND THAT'S BEFORE ME TEA! – MR FOOD (62) 90
... (AND THAT'S NO LIE) – HEAVEN 17 (52) 85
AND THE BAND PLAYED ON (DOWN AMONG THE DEAD MEN) – FLASH and the PAN (54) 78
AND THE BANDS PLAYED ON – SAXON (12) 81
AND THE BEAT GOES ON – WHISPERS (2) 80,87
AND THE HEAVENS CRIED – Anthony NEWLEY (6) 61
AND THE LEADER ROCKS ON – Gary GLITTER (58) 92
(AND THE) PICTURES IN THE SKY – MEDICINE HEAD (22) 71
AND THE SUN WILL SHINE – José FELICIANO (25) 69
AND THEN SHE KISSED ME – Gary GLITTER (39) 81
AND THEN SHE SMILES – MOCK TURTLES (44) 91
AND THEN THE RAIN FALLS – BLUE AMAZON (53) 97
AND YOU SMILED – Matt MONRO (28) 73
ANDRES – L7 (34) 94
ANDROGYNY – GARBAGE (24) 01
ANFIELD RAP (RED MACHINE IN FULL EFFECT) – LIVERPOOL FC (3) 88
ANGEL [A] – Rod STEWART (4) 72
ANGEL [B] – Aretha FRANKLIN (37) 73
ANGEL [B] – SIMPLY RED (4) 96
ANGEL [C] – MADONNA (5) 85
ANGEL [D] – AEROSMITH (69) 88
ANGEL [E] – EURYTHMICS (23) 90
ANGEL [F] – Jon SECADA (23) 93
ANGEL [G] – A-HA (41) 93
ANGEL [H] – GOLDIE (41) 95
ANGEL [I] – MASSIVE ATTACK (30) 98
ANGEL [J] – Tina COUSINS (46) 99
ANGEL [K] – Ralph FRIDGE (20) 00
ANGEL [L] – Lionel RICHIE (18) 00
ANGEL [M] – SHAGGY featuring RAYVON (1) 01
THE ANGEL AND THE GAMBLER – IRON MAIDEN (18) 98
ANGEL EYES – ROXY MUSIC (4) 79
ANGEL EYES (HOME AND AWAY) – WET WET WET (5) 87
ANGEL FACE – GLITTER BAND (4) 74
ANGEL FINGERS – WIZZARD (1) 73
ANGEL IN BLUE – J GEILS BAND (55) 82
ANGEL INTERCEPTOR – ASH (14) 95
ANGEL (LADADI O-HEYO) – JAM & SPOON featuring PLAVKA (26) 95
ANGEL OF HARLEM – U2 (9) 88
ANGEL OF MINE [A] – ETERNAL (4) 97
ANGEL OF MINE [A] – MONICA (55) 99
ANGEL OF THE MORNING [A] – PP ARNOLD (29) 68
ANGEL OF THE MORNING [A] – Juice NEWTON (43) 81
ANGEL OF THE MORNING – ANY WAY THAT YOU WANT ME (MEDLEY) – Mary MASON (27) 77
ANGEL STREET – M PEOPLE (8) 98
ANGELA JONES – Michael COX (7) 60
ANGELEYES – ABBA (3) 79
ANGELIA – Richard MARX (45) 89
ANGELO – BROTHERHOOD OF MAN (1) 77
ANGELS – Robbie WILLIAMS (4) 97,99,00
THE ANGELS AND SHADOWS PROJECT – OMNI TRIO (44) 01
ANGELS DON'T LIE – Jim REEVES (32) 70
ANGELS GO BALD: TOO – Howie B (36) 97
ANGEL'S HEAP – FINN (41) 95
ANGELS OF THE SILENCES – COUNTING CROWS (41) 96
ANGEL'S SYMPHONY – RAF (73) 96
ANGELS WITH DIRTY FACES – SHAM 69 (19) 78
ANGIE – ROLLING STONES (5) 73
ANGIE BABY – Helen REDDY (5) 75
ANGRY AT THE BIG OAK TREE – Frank IFIELD (25) 64
ANGRY CHAIR – ALICE IN CHAINS (33) 93
ANGRY SKIES – Maria NAYLER (42) 00
ANIMAL [A] – DEF LEPPARD (6) 87
ANIMAL [B] – LOST IT.COM (70) 01
ANIMAL ARMY – BABYLON ZOO (17) 96
ANIMAL CANNABUS – MULL HISTORICAL SOCIETY (53) 01
ANIMAL INSTINCT [A] – COMMODORES (74) 85
ANIMAL INSTINCT [B] – CRANBERRIES (54) 99
ANIMAL NITRATE – SUEDE (7) 93
THE ANIMAL SONG – SAVAGE GARDEN (16) 99
ANIMATION – SKIDS (56) 80
ANITINA (THE FIRST TIME I SEE SHE DANCE) – M/A/R/R/S (1) 87
ANNABELLA – John WALKER (24) 67
ANNIE GET YOUR GUN – SQUEEZE (43) 82
ANNIE I'M NOT YOUR DADDY – Kid CREOLE and the COCONUTS (2) 82
ANNIE'S SONG [A] – John DENVER (1) 74
ANNIE'S SONG [A] – James GALWAY (3) 78
ANNIVERSARY WALTZ – Anita HARRIS (21) 68
THE ANNIVERSARY WALTZ – PART 1 – STATUS QUO (2) 90
THE ANNIVERSARY WALTZ – PART 2 – STATUS QUO (16) 90
ANOMALY – CALLING YOUR NAME – LIBRA presents TAYLOR (43) 96,00
ANOTHER BLOOMING CHRISTMAS – Mel SMITH (59) 91
ANOTHER BODY MURDERED – FAITH NO MORE and BOO-YAA T.R.I.B.E. (26) 93
ANOTHER BRICK IN THE WALL (PART 2) – PINK FLOYD (1) 79
ANOTHER CHANCE – Roger SANCHEZ (1) 01
ANOTHER CUP OF COFFEE – MIKE and the MECHANICS (51) 95
ANOTHER DAY [A] – Paul McCARTNEY (2) 71
ANOTHER DAY [B] – WHIGFIELD (7) 94
ANOTHER DAY [C] – BUCKSHOT LEFONQUE (65) 97
ANOTHER DAY [D] – SKIP RAIDERS featuring JADA (46) 00
ANOTHER DAY (ANOTHER GIRL) – LAMBRETTAS (49) 80
ANOTHER DAY IN PARADISE [A] – Phil COLLINS (2) 89
ANOTHER DAY IN PARADISE [A] – JAM TRONIK (19) 90
ANOTHER DAY IN PARADISE [A] – Brandy and Ray J (5) 01
ANOTHER FUNNY HONEYMOON – David DUNDAS (29) 77
ANOTHER GIRL – ANOTHER PLANET – ONLY ONES (57) 92
ANOTHER HEARTACHE – Rod STEWART (54) 86
ANOTHER KIND OF LOVE – Hugh CORNWELL (71) 88
ANOTHER LONELY NIGHT IN NEW YORK – Robin GIBB (71) 84
ANOTHER LOVER – DANE (9) 01
ANOTHER MAN – Barbara MASON (45) 84
ANOTHER MONSTERJAM [A] – Simon HARRIS featuring EINSTEIN (65) 89
ANOTHER NAIL IN MY HEART – SQUEEZE (17) 80
ANOTHER NIGHT [A] – Aretha FRANKLIN (54) 86
ANOTHER NIGHT [B] – Jason DONOVAN (18) 90
ANOTHER NIGHT [C] – REAL McCOY (2) 93,94
ANOTHER NIGHT IN – STRANGELOVE (46) 98
ANOTHER ONE BITES THE DUST [A] – QUEEN (7) 80
ANOTHER ONE BITES THE DUST [A] – Pras MICHEL (5) 98
ANOTHER PART OF ME – Michael JACKSON (15) 88
ANOTHER PEARL – BADLY DRAWN BOY (41) 00
ANOTHER PIECE OF MEAT – SCORPIONS (39) 79
ANOTHER ROCK AND ROLL CHRISTMAS – Gary GLITTER (7) 84
ANOTHER SAD LOVE SONG – Toni BRAXTON (15) 93,94
ANOTHER SATURDAY NIGHT [A] – Sam COOKE (23) 63,86
ANOTHER SATURDAY NIGHT [A] – Cat STEVENS (19) 74

ANOTHER SILENT DAY – ADVENTURES (71) 84
ANOTHER SLEEPLESS NIGHT [A] – Jimmy CLANTON (50) 60
ANOTHER SLEEPLESS NIGHT [B] – Mike 'Hitman' WILSON (74) 90
ANOTHER SLEEPLESS NIGHT [B] – Shawn CHRISTOPHER (50) 91
ANOTHER STAR [A] – Stevie WONDER (29) 77
ANOTHER STAR [A] – Kathy SLEDGE (54) 95
ANOTHER STEP (CLOSER TO YOU) – Kim WILDE and JUNIOR (6) 87
ANOTHER SUITCASE IN ANOTHER HALL [A] – Barbara DICKSON (18) 77
ANOTHER SUITCASE IN ANOTHER HALL [A] – MADONNA (7) 97
ANOTHER TEAR FALLS – WALKER BROTHERS (12) 66
ANOTHER TIME ANOTHER PLACE – Engelbert HUMPERDINCK (13) 71
ANOTHER WAY – Paul VAN DYK (13) 99,00
ANOTHER WEEKEND – FIVE STAR (18) 88
ANOTHERLOVERHOLENYOHEAD – PRINCE (36) 86
ANSWER ME [A] – David WHITFIELD (1) 53,54
ANSWER ME [A] – Frankie LAINE (1) 53
ANSWER ME [A] – Ray PETERSON (47) 60
ANSWER ME [A] – Barbara DICKSON (9) 76
THE ANSWER TO WHY I HATE YOU – SYMPOSIUM (32) 97
ANSWERS TO NOTHING – Midge URE (49) 88
ANT RAP – ADAM and the ANTS (3) 81
ANTE UP – M.O.P. featuring Busta RHYMES (7) 01
ANTHEM [A] – N-JOI (8) 90,91
ANTHEM [B] – WILDHEARTS (21) 97
ANTHEM (ONE DAY IN EVERY WEEK) – NEW SEEKERS (21) 78
ANTI-SOCIAL – ANTHRAX (44) 89
ANTMUSIC – ADAM and the ANTS (2) 80
THE ANTMUSIC EP (THE B-SIDES) – ADAM and the ANTS (46) 82
ANY DREAM WILL DO – Jason DONOVAN (1) 91
ANY LOVE – Luther VANDROSS (31) 88
ANY OLD IRON – Peter SELLERS (17) 57
ANY OLD TIME – FOUNDATIONS (48) 68
ANY TIME ANY PLACE – Janet JACKSON (13) 94
ANY WAY THAT YOU WANT ME – TROGGS (8) 66
ANY WAY YOU LOOK – NORTHERN UPROAR (36) 97
ANYBODY SEEN MY BABY? – ROLLING STONES (22) 97
ANYMORE – Sarah CRACKNELL (39) 96
ANYONE CAN FALL IN LOVE – Anita DOBSON (4) 86
ANYONE CAN PLAY GUITAR – RADIOHEAD (32) 93
ANYONE FOR TENNIS (THE SAVAGE SEVEN THEME) – CREAM (40) 68
ANYONE WHO HAD A HEART [A] – Cilla BLACK (1) 64
ANYONE WHO HAD A HEART [A] – Dionne WARWICK (42) 64
ANYONE WHO HAD A HEART [A] – Mary MAY (49) 64
ANYTHING [A] – DIRECT DRIVE (67) 85
ANYTHING [B] – DAMNED (32) 86
ANYTHING [C] – Sydney YOUNGBLOOD (48) 93
ANYTHING [D] – CULTURE BEAT (5) 94
ANYTHING [E] – SWV (24) 94
ANYTHING [F] – 3T (2) 96
ANYTHING [G] – DAMAGE (68) 96
ANYTHING [H] – JAY-Z (18) 00
ANYTHING BUT DOWN – Sheryl CROW (19) 99
ANYTHING CAN HAPPEN – WAS (NOT WAS) (67) 88
ANYTHING FOR YOU – Gloria ESTEFAN and MIAMI SOUND MACHINE (10) 88
ANYTHING GOES – HARPERS BIZARRE (33) 67
ANYTHING IS POSSIBLE – Debbie GIBSON (51) 91
ANYTHING THAT'S ROCK 'N' ROLL – Tom PETTY and the HEARTBREAKERS (36) 77
ANYTHING YOU WANT – JODIE (47) 95
ANYTHING YOU WANT (I'VE GOT IT) – ULTIMATE KAOS (52) 99
ANYTIME [A] – NU-BIRTH (41) 97,98
ANYTIME [B] – Brian McKNIGHT (48) 98
ANYTIME YOU NEED A FRIEND – Mariah CAREY (8) 94
ANYWAY – HONEYCRACK (67) 96
ANYWAY ANYHOW ANYWHERE – WHO (10) 65
ANYWAY THAT YOU WANT ME – SPIRITUALIZED (75) 90
ANYWAY YOU DO IT – LIQUID GOLD (41) 78
ANYWAY YOU WANT IT – Dave CLARK FIVE (25) 64
ANYWHERE – DUBSTAR (37) 95
ANYWHERE FOR YOU – BACKSTREET BOYS (4) 97
ANYWHERE IS – ENYA (7) 95
APACHE [A] – Bert WEEDON (24) 60
APACHE [A] – SHADOWS (1) 60
APACHE [B] – STARFIGHTER (31) 00
APACHE DROPOUT – Edgar BROUGHTON BAND (33) 71
APEMAN – KINKS (5) 70
APHRODITE – PARIS & SHARP (61) 01
APOLLO 9 – Adam ANT (13) 84
APPARENTLY NOTHIN' [A] – YOUNG DISCIPLES (13) 91
APPARENTLY NOTHING [A] – BRAND NEW HEAVIES (32) 00
THE APPLE EP – VARIOUS ARTISTS (EPs and LPs) (60) 91
APPLE GREEN – MILLTOWN BROTHERS (43) 91
THE APPLE STRETCHING – Grace JONES (50) 82
APPLE TREE – Erykah BADU (47) 97
APPLEJACK – Jet HARRIS and Tony MEEHAN (4) 63
APRIL LOVE – Pat BOONE (7) 57
APRIL SKIES – JESUS AND MARY CHAIN (8) 87
AQUARIUS – LET THE SUNSHINE IN (MEDLEY) – FIFTH DIMENSION (11) 69
AQUARIUS – Paul JONES (45) 69
ARABIAN KNIGHTS – SIOUXSIE and the BANSHEES (32) 81
ARE EVERYTHING – BUZZCOCKS (61) 80
ARE 'FRIENDS' ELECTRIC? – Gary NUMAN (1) 79,87
ARE WE HERE – ORBITAL (33) 94
ARE YOU BEING SERVED – GRACE BROTHERS (51) 96
ARE YOU BEING SERVED SIR – John INMAN (39) 75
ARE YOU BLUE OR ARE YOU BLIND – BLUETONES (31) 95
ARE YOU DREAMING – CAPTAIN HOLLYWOOD PROJECT (17) 90
ARE YOU GETTING ENOUGH OF WHAT MAKES YOU HAPPY – HOT CHOCOLATE (17) 80
ARE YOU GONNA BE THERE – UP YER RONSON featuring Mary PEARCE (27) 96
ARE YOU GONNA GO MY WAY – Lenny KRAVITZ (4) 93
ARE YOU GROWING TIRED OF MY LOVE – STATUS QUO (46) 69
ARE YOU HEARING (WHAT I HEAR)? – LEVEL 42 (49) 82
ARE YOU JIMMY RAY? – Jimmy RAY (13) 97
ARE YOU LONESOME TONIGHT – Elvis PRESLEY (1) 61,77,82,91
ARE YOU LOOKIN' AT ME? – Ricky TOMLINSON (28) 01
ARE YOU MAN ENOUGH – UNO CLIO featuring Martine McCUTCHEON (62) 95
ARE YOU MINE – BROS (12) 91
ARE YOU MY BABY – WENDY and LISA (70) 89
ARE YOU OUT THERE – CRESCENDO (20) 95
ARE YOU READY [A] – Billy OCEAN (42) 80
ARE YOU READY? [B] – BREAK MACHINE (27) 84
ARE YOU READY [C] – AC/DC (34) 91
ARE YOU READY [D] – GYRES (71) 96
(ARE YOU READY) DO THE BUS STOP – FATBACK BAND (18) 75
ARE YOU READY FOR LOVE [A] – Elton JOHN (42) 79
ARE YOU READY FOR LOVE [B] – ULTRA HIGH (45) 96
ARE YOU READY FOR SOME MORE – REEL 2 REAL (24) 96
ARE YOU READY TO BE HEARTBROKEN – Sandie SHAW (68) 86
ARE YOU READY TO FLY – ROZALLA (14) 92
ARE YOU READY TO PARTY – SHRINK (39) 00
ARE YOU READY TO ROCK – WIZZARD (8) 74
ARE YOU SATISFIED? (FUNKA NOVA) – RAH BAND (70) 85
ARE YOU STILL HAVING FUN – Eagle-Eye CHERRY (21) 00
ARE YOU SURE [A] – ALLISONS (2) 61
ARE YOU SURE [B] – SO (62) 88
ARE YOU THAT SOMEBODY? – AALIYAH (11) 98
(ARE YOU) THE ONE THAT I'VE BEEN... – Nick CAVE and the BAD SEEDS (67) 97
AREA CODES – LUDACRIS featuring Nate DOGG (25) 01
ARGENTINA – AMOS (30) 97
ARGENTINE MELODY (CANCION DE ARGENTINA) – SAN JOSE featuring Rodriguez ARGENTINA (14) 78
ARIA – Mr Acker BILK and his PARAMOUNT JAZZ BAND (5) 76
ARIANA – STARDUST (42) 77
ARIENNE – Tasmin ARCHER (30) 93
ARIZONA SKY – CHINA CRISIS (47) 86
ARMAGEDDON DAYS ARE HERE (AGAIN) – The THE (70) 89
ARMAGEDDON IT – DEF LEPPARD (20) 88
ARMCHAIR ANARCHIST – KINGMAKER (47) 92
ARMED AND EXTREMELY DANGEROUS – FIRST CHOICE (16) 73
ARMED AND READY – Michael SCHENKER GROUP (53) 80
ARMS AROUND THE WORLD – LOUISE (4) 97
ARMS OF LOREN – E'VOKE (25) 96
ARMS OF MARY – SUTHERLAND BROTHERS and QUIVER (5) 76
THE ARMS OF ORION – PRINCE with Sheena EASTON (27) 89
ARMS OF SOLITUDE – OUI 3 (54) 93
THE ARMS OF THE ONE WHO LOVES YOU – XSCAPE (46) 98
ARMY – Ben FOLDS FIVE (28) 99
ARMY DREAMERS – Kate BUSH (16) 80
ARMY OF ME – BJÖRK (10) 95
ARMY OF TWO – DUM DUMS (27) 01
ARNOLD LAYNE – PINK FLOYD (20) 67
AROUND MY BRAIN – PROGRESS FUNK (73) 97
AROUND THE WAY GIRL – LL COOL J (36) 90,91
AROUND THE WORLD [A] – Bing CROSBY (5) 57
AROUND THE WORLD [A] – Gracie FIELDS (8) 57
AROUND THE WORLD [A] – MANTOVANI (20) 57
AROUND THE WORLD [A] – Ronnie HILTON (4) 57
AROUND THE WORLD [B] – EAST 17 (3) 94
AROUND THE WORLD [C] – DAFT PUNK (5) 97
AROUND THE WORLD [D] – RED HOT CHILI PEPPERS (35) 99
AROUND THE WORLD [E] – AQUA (26) 00
ARRANGED MARRIAGE – APACHE INDIAN (16) 93
ARRESTED BY YOU – Dusty SPRINGFIELD (70) 90
ARRIVEDERCI DARLING [A] – Anne SHELTON (17) 55
ARRIVEDERCI DARLING [A] – Edna SAVAGE (19) 56
ARSENAL NUMBER ONE – ARSENAL FC (46) 00
ART FOR ART'S SAKE – 10 CC (5) 75
THE ART OF DRIVING – BLACK BOX RECORDER (53) 00
ART OF LOVE – ART OF NOISE (67) 90

BABY IT'S YOU [A] — BEATLES (7) 95
BABY IT'S YOU [B] — SILK (44) 93
BABY IT'S YOU [C] — MN8 (22) 95,96
BABY JANE — Rod STEWART (1) 83
BABY JUMP — MUNGO JERRY (1) 71
BABY LAY DOWN — Ruby WINTERS (43) 79
BABY LEE — John Lee HOOKER (65) 96
BABY LET ME TAKE YOU HOME — ANIMALS (21) 64
BABY LOVE [A] — SUPREMES (1) 64,74
BABY LOVE [A] — Honey BANE (58) 81
BABY LOVE [B] — REGINA (50) 86
BABY LOVE [B] — Dannii MINOGUE (14) 91
BABY LOVER — Petula CLARK (12) 58
BABY MAKE IT SOON — MARMALADE (9) 69
BABY MY HEART — CRICKETS (33) 60
BABY NEVER SAY GOODBYE — UNIT FOUR PLUS TWO (49) 66
BABY NOW I — Dan REED NETWORK (65) 91
BABY NOW THAT I'VE FOUND YOU — FOUNDATIONS (1) 67
BABY OF MINE — Alan PRICE (32) 79
BABY ONE MORE TIME — Britney SPEARS (1) 99
BABY PLAYS AROUND (EP) — Elvis COSTELLO (65) 89
BABY PLEASE DON'T GO — THEM (10) 65,91
BABY ROO — Connie FRANCIS (5) 61
BABY SITTIN' — Bobby ANGELO and the TUXEDOS (30) 61
BABY SITTIN' BOOGIE — Buzz CLIFFORD (17) 61
BABY STOP CRYING — Bob DYLAN (13) 78
BABY TAKE A BOW — Adam FAITH (22) 62
BABY TALK — ALISHA (67) 86
BABY U LEFT ME (IN THE COLD) — MARILYN (70) 85
BABY UNIVERSAL — TIN MACHINE (48) 91
BABY WANTS TO RIDE — HANI (70) 00
BABY, WE BETTER TRY TO GET IT TOGETHER — Barry WHITE (15) 76
BABY WE CAN'T GO WRONG — Cilla BLACK (36) 74
BABY WHAT A BIG SURPRISE — CHICAGO (41) 77
BABY WHAT I MEAN — DRIFTERS (49) 67
(BABY) YOU DON'T HAVE TO TELL ME — WALKER BROTHERS (13) 66
BABY YOU'RE DYNAMITE — Cliff RICHARD (27) 84
BABYLON [B] — BLACK DOG featuring Ofra HAZA (65) 99
BABYLON [B] — Ofra HAZA (65) 99
BABYLON [A] — David GRAY (5) 00
BABYLON'S BURNING — RUTS (7) 79
BABY'S COMING BACK — JELLYFISH (51) 91
BABY'S FIRST CHRISTMAS — Connie FRANCIS (30) 61
BABY'S REQUEST — Paul McCARTNEY (60) 79
BACHELOR BOY — Cliff RICHARD and the SHADOWS (1) 62
BACHELORETTE — BJÖRK (21) 97
BACK AND FORTH [A] — CAMEO (11) 87
BACK AND FORTH [B] — AALIYAH (16) 94
BACK AROUND — ELEVATOR SUITE (71) 00
BACK BY DOPE DEMAND — KING BEE (61) 91
BACK FOR GOOD [A] — REAL EMOTION (67) 95
BACK FOR GOOD [A] — TAKE THAT (1) 95
BACK FROM THE EDGE — Bruce DICKINSON (68) 96
BACK HERE — BBMAK (37) 99,01
BACK HOME — ENGLAND WORLD CUP SQUAD (1) 70
BACK IN LOVE AGAIN — Donna SUMMER (29) 78
BACK IN MY ARMS — Chris PAUL (74) 87
BACK IN MY ARMS AGAIN — SUPREMES (40) 65
BACK IN MY ARMS (ONCE AGAIN) — Hazell DEAN (41) 84
BACK IN MY LIFE [A] — Joe ROBERTS (39) 93,94
BACK IN MY LIFE [B] — ALICE DEEJAY (4) 99
BACK IN THE DAY — AHMAD (64) 94
BACK IN THE HIGH LIFE AGAIN — Steve WINWOOD (53) 87
BACK IN THE UK — SCOOTER (18) 96
BACK IN THE USSR — BEATLES (19) 76
BACK IT UP — Robin S (43) 94
THE BACK OF LOVE — ECHO and the BUNNYMEN (19) 82
BACK OF MY HAND — JAGS (17) 79
BACK OFF BOOGALOO — Ringo STARR (2) 72
BACK ON MY FEET AGAIN — FOUNDATIONS (18) 68
BACK ON THE CHAIN GANG — PRETENDERS (17) 82
BACK ON THE ROAD [A] — MARMALADE (35) 71,72
BACK ON THE ROAD [B] — EARTH WIND AND FIRE (63) 80
BACK ON THE STREETS — SAXON (75) 85
BACK ON TOP — Van MORRISON (69) 99
BACK SEAT OF MY CAR — Linda McCARTNEY (39) 71
BACK STABBERS — O'JAYS (14) 72
BACK STREET LUV — CURVED AIR (4) 71
BACK TO EARTH — Yves DERUYTER (63) 01
BACK TO FRONT [A] — STIFF LITTLE FINGERS (49) 80
BACK TO FRONT [B] — ADAMSKI (63) 92
BACK TO LIFE (HOWEVER DO YOU WANT ME) — SOUL II SOUL featuring Caron WHEELER (1) 89
BACK TO LOVE [B] — Evelyn 'Champagne' KING (40) 82
BACK TO LOVE [A] — BRAND NEW HEAVIES (23) 94
BACK TO MY ROOTS — RuPAUL (40) 93
BACK TO REALITY — INTELLIGENT HOODLUM (55) 90
BACK TO SCHOOL AGAIN — FOUR TOPS (62) 82
BACK TO THE LIGHT — Brian MAY (19) 92
BACK TO THE OLD SCHOOL — BASSHEADS (12) 92
BACK TO THE SIXTIES — TIGHT FIT (4) 81
BACK TO THE SIXTIES PART 2 — TIGHT FIT (33) 81
BACK TO YOU — Bryan ADAMS (18) 97
BACK TOGETHER — BABYBIRD (22) 99
BACK TOGETHER AGAIN [A] — Roberta FLACK (3) 80
BACK TOGETHER AGAIN [A] — INNER CITY (49) 93
BACK UP (TO ME) — WOOKIE featuring LAIN (38) 01
BACK WITH THE BOYS AGAIN — Joe FAGIN (53) 86
BACK WITH THE KILLER AGAIN — AUTEURS (45) 96
BACKCHAT — QUEEN (40) 82
BACKFIELD IN MOTION — JB's ALL STARS (48) 84
BACKFIRED — Deborah HARRY (32) 81
BACKS TO THE WALL — SAXON (64) 80
BACKSEAT EDUCATION — ZODIAC MINDWARP and the LOVE REACTION (49) 87
BACKSTAGE — Gene PITNEY (4) 66
BACKSTREET SYMPHONY — THUNDER (25) 90
BACKSTROKIN' — FATBACK BAND (41) 80
BAD — Michael JACKSON (3) 87
BAD ACTRESS — TERRORVISION (10) 96
BAD AMBASSADOR — DIVINE COMEDY (34) 01
BAD BAD BOY — NAZARETH (10) 73
BAD BOY [A] — Marty WILDE (7) 59
BAD BOY [B] — ADICTS (75) 83
BAD BOY [C] — MIAMI SOUND MACHINE (16) ..86
BAD BOY [D] — WILDCHILD (38) 98
BAD BOY FOR LIFE — P DIDDY featuring Black Rob and Mark CURRY (13) 01
BAD BOYS [A] — WHAM! (2) 83
BAD BOYS [B] — INNER CIRCLE (52) 93
BAD CASE OF LOVIN' YOU (DOCTOR DOCTOR) — Robert PALMER (61) 79
BAD DAY — CARMEL (15) 83
THE BAD DAYS (EP) — SPACE (20) 98
BAD GIRL [A] — MADONNA (10) 93
BAD GIRL [B] — SCARLET (54) 96
BAD GIRL [C] — DJ RAP (32) 98
BAD GIRLS [A] — Donna SUMMER (14) 79
BAD GIRLS [A] — Juliet ROBERTS (17) 99
BAD HABIT — A.T.F.C. presents ONEPHATDEEVA (17) 00
BAD HABITS — Jenny BURTON (68) 85
BAD LIFE — PUBLIC IMAGE LTD (71) 84
BAD LOVE — Eric CLAPTON (25) 90
BAD LUCK — FM (54) 89
BAD MEDICINE — BON JOVI (17) 88
BAD MOON RISING — CREEDENCE CLEARWATER REVIVAL (1) 69,92
A BAD NIGHT — Cat STEVENS (20) 67
BAD OLD DAYS — CO-CO (13) 78
BAD OLD MAN — BABYBIRD (31) 98
BAD PENNY BLUES — Humphrey LYTTELTON BAND (19) 56
THE BAD PHOTOGRAPHER — SAINT ETIENNE (27) 98
BAD THING — CRY OF LOVE (60) 94
BAD THINGS — N-JOI (57) 95
BAD TIME — JAYHAWKS (70) 95
BAD TO ME — Billy J KRAMER and the DAKOTAS (1) 63
THE BAD TOUCH — BLOODHOUND GANG (4) 00
A BAD TOWN — BIG SOUND AUTHORITY (54) 85
BAD WEATHER — SUPREMES (37) 73
BAD YOUNG BROTHER — Derek B (16) 88
BADDER BADDER SCHWING — Freddy FRESH featuring FATBOY SLIM (34) 99
BADDEST RUFFEST — BACKYARD DOG (15) 01
BADGE — CREAM (18) 69,72
BADMAN [A] — COCKNEY REJECTS (65) 80
BADMAN [B] — SISTER BLISS (51) 96
THE BADMAN IS ROBBIN' — HIJACK (56) 90
BAG IT UP — Geri HALLIWELL (1) 00
BAGGY TROUSERS — MADNESS (3) 80
THE BAGUIO TRACK — LUZON (67) 01
BAILAMOS [A] — Enrique IGLESIAS (4) 99
BAILAMOS [B] — M3 (40) 99
BAILANDO CON LOBOS — CABANA (65) 95
BAKER STREET [A] — Gerry RAFFERTY (3) 78,90
BAKER STREET [A] — UNDERCOVER (2) 92
BAKERMAN — LAID BACK (44) 90
BALL AND CHAIN — XTC (58) 82
BALL OF CONFUSION — TEMPTATIONS (7) 70
BALL PARK INCIDENT — WIZZARD (6) 72
BALLAD OF A LANDLORD — Terry HALL (50) 97
BALLAD OF BONNIE AND CLYDE — Georgie FAME (1) 67
THE BALLAD OF CHASEY LAIN — BLOODHOUND GANG (15) 00
BALLAD OF DAVY CROCKETT [A] — Dick JAMES (14) 56
THE BALLAD OF DAVY CROCKETT [A] — Bill HAYES (2) 56
THE BALLAD OF DAVY CROCKETT [A] — Max BYGRAVES (20) 56
THE BALLAD OF DAVY CROCKETT [A] — Tennessee Ernie FORD (3) 56
THE BALLAD OF JAYNE — L.A. GUNS (53) 91
BALLAD OF JOHN AND YOKO — BEATLES (1) 69
THE BALLAD OF LUCY JORDAN — Marianne FAITHFULL (48) 79
BALLAD OF PALADIN — Duane EDDY and the REBELS (10) 62
THE BALLAD OF PETER PUMPKINHEAD [A] — CRASH TEST DUMMIES (30) 95
THE BALLAD OF PETER PUMPKINHEAD [A] — XTC (71) 92
THE BALLAD OF SPOTTY MULDOON — Peter COOK (34) 65
THE BALLAD OF THE GREEN BERETS — Staff Sergeant Barry SADLER (24) 66
THE BALLAD OF TOM JONES — SPACE with Cerys of CATATONIA (4) 98
BALLAD OF YOUTH — Richie SAMBORA (59) 91
BALLERINA GIRL — Lionel RICHIE (17) 86
BALLERINA (PRIMA DONNA) — Steve HARLEY and COCKNEY REBEL (51) 83
BALLOON — CATHERINE WHEEL (59) 92
BALLROOM BLITZ [A] — SWEET (2) 73
BALLROOM BLITZ [A] — Tia CARRERE (26) 92

BECAUSE THEY'RE YOUNG [A] – James DARREN (29)....60
BECAUSE WE WANT TO – Billie PIPER (1)....98
BECAUSE YOU LOVED ME (THEME FROM 'UP CLOSE AND PERSONAL') – Celine DION (5)....96
BECAUSE YOU'RE MINE [A] – Mario LANZA (3)....52
BECAUSE YOU'RE MINE [A] – Nat 'King' COLE (6)....52,53
BECAUSE YOU'RE YOUNG – CLASSIX NOUVEAUX (43)....82
BECOMING MORE LIKE ALFIE – DIVINE COMEDY (27)....96
BECOMING MORE LIKE GOD – Jah WOBBLE'S INVADERS OF THE HEART (36)....94
BED OF NAILS – Alice COOPER (38)....89
BED OF ROSES – BON JOVI (13)....93
BEDS ARE BURNING – MIDNIGHT OIL (6)....88,89
THE BED'S TOO BIG WITHOUT YOU – Sheila HYLTON (35)....81
BEDSITTER – SOFT CELL (4)....81
BEDTIME STORY – MADONNA (4)....95
THE BEE – SCIENTIST (47)....90,91
BEE BOM – Anthony NEWLEY (12)....61
BEE STING – CAMOUFLAGE featuring MYSTI (48)....77
BEEF – Gary CLAIL ON-U SOUND SYSTEM (64)....90
BEEN A LONG TIME – FOG (27)....94,98
BEEN AROUND THE WORLD – PUFF DADDY (20)....97,98
BEEN CAUGHT STEALING – JANE'S ADDICTION (34)....91
BEEN IT – CARDIGANS (56)....96
BEEN THINKING ABOUT YOU – Martine GIRAULT (63)....95
BEEP ME 911 – Missy 'Misdemeanor' ELLIOTT (14)....98
BEER DRINKERS AND HELL RAISERS – MOTÖRHEAD (43)....80
BEETHOVEN (I LOVE TO LISTEN TO) – EURYTHMICS (25)....87
BEETLEBUM – BLUR (1)....97
BEFORE – PET SHOP BOYS (7)....96
BEFORE TODAY – EVERYTHING BUT THE GIRL (25)....97
BEFORE YOU LEAVE – PEPE DELUXE (20)....01
BEFORE YOU LOVE ME – ALSOU (27)....01
BEFORE YOU WALK OUT OF MY LIFE – MONICA (22)....96
BEG STEAL OR BORROW – NEW SEEKERS (2)....72
A BEGGAR ON A BEACH OF GOLD – MIKE and the MECHANICS (33)....95
BEGGIN' – TIMEBOX (38)....68
BEGGIN' TO BE WRITTEN – WORLDS APART (29)....94
BEGGING YOU – STONE ROSES (15)....95
BEGIN AGAIN – SPACE (21)....98
BEGIN THE BEGUINE (VOLVER A EMPEZAR) – Julio IGLESIAS (1)....81
THE BEGINNING – SEAL (24)....91
BEHIND A PAINTED SMILE – ISLEY BROTHERS (5)....69
BEHIND CLOSED DOORS – Charlie RICH (16)....74
BEHIND THE COUNTER – FALL (75)....93
BEHIND THE GROOVE – Teena MARIE (6)....80
BEHIND THE MASK – Eric CLAPTON (15)....87
BEHIND THE WHEEL – DEPECHE MODE (21)....88
BEIN' AROUND – LEMONHEADS (19)....92
BEING A GIRL (PART ONE) (EP) – MANSUN (13)....98
BEING BOILED – HUMAN LEAGUE (6)....82
BEING BORING – PET SHOP BOYS (20)....90
BEING BRAVE – MENSWEAR (10)....96
BEING WITH YOU – Smokey ROBINSON (1)....81
BEL AMOUR – BEL AMOUR (23)....01
BELARUSE – LEVELLERS (12)....93
BELFAST [A] – BONEY M (8)....77
BELFAST [B] – BARNBRACK (45)....85
BELFAST [C] – ENERGY ORCHARD (52)....90
BELFAST [D] – ORBITAL (53)....95
BELFAST BOY – Don FARDON (32)....70
BELFAST CHILD – SIMPLE MINDS (1)....89
BELIEVE [A] – Lenny KRAVITZ (30)....93
BELIEVE [B] – Q-TEX (41)....94
BELIEVE [C] – Elton JOHN (15)....95
BELIEVE [D] – GOLDIE (36)....98
BELIEVE [E] – CHER (1)....98,99
BELIEVE [F] – MINISTERS DA LA FUNK featuring Jocelyn BROWN (42)....00,01
BELIEVE IN ME [A] – UTAH SAINTS (8)....93
BELIEVE IN ME [B] – QUIVVER (56)....95
BELIEVE IN ME [C] – MANKEY (74)....96
BELIEVE IN ME [D] – RAW STYLUS (66)....96
BELIEVE IN THE BEAT – Carol Lynn TOWNES (56)....85
BELIEVE WHAT YOU'RE SAYING – SUGAR (73)....94
BELIEVER – REAL PEOPLE (38)....92
BELIEVERS – BAZ (36)....01
THE BELL – Mike OLDFIELD (50)....93
BELL BOTTOM BLUES – Alma COGAN (4)....54
BELL BOTTOMED TEAR – BEAUTIFUL SOUTH (16)....92
THE BELLE OF ST MARK – Sheila E (18)....85
BELLISSIMA – DJ QUICKSILVER (4)....97
BELLS OF AVIGNON – Max BYGRAVES (36)....61
BELLS OF NY – SLO-MOSHUN (29)....94
BELO HORIZONTI – HEARTISTS (40)....97,98
BEN [A] – Marti WEBB (5)....85
BEN [A] – Michael JACKSON (7)....72
BEN [A] – Toni WARNE (50)....87
BEND IT – Dave DEE, DOZY, BEAKY, MICK and TICH (2)....66
BEND ME SHAPE ME [A] – AMEN CORNER (3)....68
BEND ME SHAPE ME [A] – AMERICAN BREED (24)....68
BENEDICTUS – BRAINBUG (24)....97
BENJAMIN – VERUCA SALT (75)....97
BENNIE AND THE JETS – Elton JOHN (37)....76
BENNY'S THEME – Paul HENRY and the Mayson GLEN ORCHESTRA (39)....78
BENTLEY'S GONNA SORT YOU OUT! – BENTLEY RHYTHM ACE (17)....97
BERMUDA TRIANGLE – Barry MANILOW (15)....81
BERNADETTE – FOUR TOPS (8)....67,72
BERRY – TC (73)....92
BERSERKER – Gary NUMAN (32)....84
BESAME MUCHO – Jet HARRIS (22)....62
BESIDE YOU – Iggy POP (47)....94
THE BEST – Tina TURNER (5)....89
BEST BIT (EP) – Beth ORTON featuring Terry CALLIER (36)....97
THE BEST CHRISTMAS OF THEM ALL – Shakin' STEVENS (19)....90
BEST DAYS – JUICE (28)....98
THE BEST DISCO IN TOWN – RITCHIE FAMILY (10)....76
BEST FRIEND [A] – BEAT (22)....80
BEST FRIEND [B] – Mark MORRISON and Conner REEVES (23)....99
BEST FRIEND [C] – PUFF DADDY (24)....99
BEST FRIENDS [A] – TOY - BOX (41)....99
BEST FRIENDS [B] – ALLSTARS (20)....01
BEST FRIENDS FOREVER – TWEENIES (12)....01
BEST FRIEND'S GIRL – ELECTRASY (41)....98
BEST I CAN – QUEENSRYCHE (36)....91
BEST IN ME – LET LOOSE (8)....95
THE BEST IS YET TO COME – SCOOCH (12)....00
BEST KEPT SECRET – CHINA CRISIS (36)....87
BEST LOVE – COURSE (51)....97
THE BEST OF EVERYTHING – Johnny MATHIS (30)....59
THE BEST OF LOVE – Michael BOLTON (14)....97
THE BEST OF ME [A] – Cliff RICHARD (2)....89
THE BEST OF ME [B] – Bryan ADAMS (47)....99, 00
BEST OF MY LOVE [A] – EMOTIONS (4)....77
BEST OF MY LOVE [A] – Dee LEWIS (47)....88
BEST OF MY LOVE [A] – LOVESTATION (73)....93
BEST OF MY LOVE [A] – CJ LEWIS (13)....94
THE BEST OF TIMES – STYX (42)....81
BEST OF YOU – Kenny THOMAS (11)....91
(THE BEST PART OF) BREAKING UP [A] – RONETTES (43)....64
(THE BEST PART OF) BREAKING UP [A] – SYMBOLS (25)....68
(THE BEST PART OF) BREAKING UP [A] – Roni GRIFFITH (63)....84
BEST REGRETS – GENEVA (38)....97
BEST THING – Adam RICKITT (25)....00
THE BEST THING – SAVAGE GARDEN (35)....01
BEST THING IN THE WORLD – OPTIMYSTIC (70)....95
BEST THING THAT EVER HAPPENED TO ME – Gladys KNIGHT and the PIPS (7)....75
THE BEST THINGS IN LIFE ARE FREE [A] – BELL BIV DEVOE (2)....92
THE BEST THINGS IN LIFE ARE FREE [A] – Luther VANDROSS and Janet JACKSON (7)....95
BEST WISHES – ULTRASOUND (68)....98
THE BEST YEARS OF MY LIFE – Diana ROSS (28)....94
BEST YEARS OF OUR LIVES – MODERN ROMANCE (4)....82
BET YER LIFE I DO – HERMAN'S HERMITS (22)....70
BETA – EMPIRION (75)....97
BETCHA BY GOLLY WOW [A] – STYLISTICS (13)....72
BETCHA BY GOLLY WOW [A] – PRINCE (11)....96
BETCHA CAN'T LOSE (WITH MY LOVE) – MAGIC LADY (58)....88
BETCHA CAN'T WAIT – EAST 17 (12)....99
BETCHA' WOULDN'T HURT ME – Quincy JONES (52)....81
BETTE DAVIS EYES – Kim CARNES (10)....81
BETTER BE GOOD TO ME – Tina TURNER (45)....84
BETTER BELIEVE IT (CHILDREN IN NEED) – Sid OWEN (60)....95
BETTER BEST FORGOTTEN – STEPS (2)....99
BETTER DAY – OCEAN COLOUR SCENE (9)....97
BETTER DAYS [A] – GUN (33)....89
BETTER DAYS [B] – Bruce SPRINGSTEEN (34)....92
BETTER DAYS [C] – TQ (32)....99
BETTER DAYS AHEAD – TYRREL CORPORATION (29)....95
BETTER DO IT SALSA – GIBSON BROTHERS (12)....80
BETTER GET READY – LULU (59)....00
A BETTER LOVE – LONDONBEAT (23)....90,91
BETTER LOVE NEXT TIME – DR HOOK (8)....80
BETTER MADE – HEADSWIM (42)....98
A BETTER MAN [A] – THUNDER (18)....93
A BETTER MAN [B] – Brian KENNEDY (28)....96
BETTER OFF ALONE – DJ JURGEN presents ALICE DEEJAY (2)....99
BETTER OFF WITHOUT YOU – Hazell DEAN (72)....91
BETTER TAKE TIME – SECOND IMAGE (67)....83
BETTER THE DEVIL YOU KNOW [A] – Kylie MINOGUE (2)....90
BETTER THE DEVIL YOU KNOW [A] – SONIA (15)....93
BETTER THE DEVIL YOU KNOW [B] – STEPS (4)....99
BETTER THINGS – KINKS (46)....81
BETTER USE YOUR HEAD – LITTLE ANTHONY and the IMPERIALS (42)....76
BETTER WATCH OUT – ANT & DEC (10)....96
BETTER WORLD – REBEL MC (20)....90
BETTY BETTY BETTY – Lonnie DONEGAN (11)....58
(BETWEEN A) ROCK AND A HARD PLACE – CUTTING CREW (66)....89
BETWEEN ANGELS & INSECTS – PAPA ROACH (17)....01
BETWEEN THE SHEETS – ISLEY BROTHERS (52)....83
BETWEEN THE WARS (EP) – Billy BRAGG (15)....85
BETWEEN YOU AND ME – JA RULE featuring Christina MILIAN (26)....01
BEWARE – Vivienne McKONE (69)....92
(BEWARE) BOYFRIEND – Mari WILSON (51)....82
BEYOND THE INVISIBLE – ENIGMA (26)....97

BRIDGE OVER TROUBLED WATER [A] —
SIMON and GARFUNKEL (1)........................70
BRIDGE TO YOUR HEART — WAX (12) 87
BRIDGET THE MIDGET (THE QUEEN OF
THE BLUES) — Ray STEVENS (2) 71
BRIGHT EYES [A] — Art GARFUNKEL (1) 79
BRIGHT EYES [A] — Stephen GATELY (3) 00
THE BRIGHT LIGHT — Tanya DONELLY (64)......97
BRIGHT LIGHTS — SPECIALS (60) 83
BRIGHT SIDE OF LIFE — TENOR FLY (51) 95
BRIGHT SIDE OF THE ROAD —
Van MORRISON (63)..79
BRIGHT YELLOW GUN —
THROWING MUSES (51) 94
BRIGHTER DAY — Kelly LLORENNA (43)............96
BRIGHTEST STAR — DRIZABONE (45)................94
BRILLIANT DISGUISE — Bruce SPRINGSTEEN (20)87
BRILLIANT FEELING — FULL MONTY
ALLSTARS featuring TJ DAVIS (72)..................96
BRILLIANT MIND — FURNITURE (21)..................86
BRIMFUL OF ASHA — CORNERSHOP (1) 97,98
BRING A LITTLE WATER SYLVIE —
Lonnie DONEGAN (7) 56,57
BRING 'EM ALL IN — Mike SCOTT (56) 95
BRING FORTH THE GUILLOTINE—
SILVER BULLET (45) 89,90
BRING IT ALL BACK — S CLUB 7 (1)..................99
BRING IT ALL HOME — Gerry RAFFERTY (54)....80
BRING IT BACK AGAIN — STRAY CATS (64) 89
BRING IT BACK 2 LUV —
PROJECT featuring GERIDEAU (65) 94
BRING IT DOWN (THIS INSANE THING) —
REDSKINS (33) 85
BRING IT ON [A] — N'dea DAVENPORT (52) 98
BRING IT ON [B] — GOMEZ (21) 99
BRING IT ON... BRING IT ON —
James BROWN (45) 83
BRING IT ON DOWN — JESUS JONES (46) 89
BRING IT ON HOME —
URBAN COOKIE COLLECTIVE (56) 94
BRING IT ON HOME TO ME — ANIMALS (7)......65
BRING ME CLOSER — ALTERED IMAGES (29)....83
BRING ME EDELWEISS — EDELWEISS (5)..........89
BRING ME LOVE — Andrea MENDEZ (44)..........96
BRING ME YOUR CUP — UB40 (24) 93
BRING MY FAMILY BACK — FAITHLESS (14) 99
BRING ON THE DANCING HORSES —
ECHO and the BUNNYMEN (21)......................85
BRING THE FAMILY BACK — Billy PAUL (51)......79
BRING THE NOISE [A] — PUBLIC ENEMY (32) ..88
BRING THE NOISE [A] —
ANTHRAX featuring Chuck D (14) 91
BRING UP THE MIC SOME MORE —
RAGGA TWINS (65) 92
BRING YOUR DAUGHTER . . .
TO THE SLAUGHTER — IRON MAIDEN (1) 91
BRINGING ON BACK THE GOOD TIMES —
LOVE AFFAIR (9) 69
BRISTOL STOMP — LATE SHOW (40)................79
BRITANNIA RAG — Winifred ATWELL (5) 52,53
BRITE SIDE — Deborah HARRY (59)..................89
BRITISH HUSTLE — HI TENSION (8)..................78
THE BRITISH WAY OF LIFE — CHORDS (54)......80
THE BRITS 1990 —
VARIOUS ARTISTS (MONTAGES) (2) 90
BROKE AWAY — WET WET WET (19) 89
BROKE / WON — BETA BAND (30) 01

BROKEN ARROW [A] — WATERFRONT (63)........89
BROKEN ARROW [B] —
Rod STEWART (41) 91,92
BROKEN DOLL —
Tommy BRUCE and the BRUISERS (36) 60
BROKEN DOWN ANGEL — NAZARETH (9).........73
BROKEN ENGLISH — SUNSCREEM (13).............93
A BROKEN HEART CAN MEND —
Alexander O'NEAL (53) 86
BROKEN HEART (THIRTEEN VALLEYS) —
BIG COUNTRY (47) 88
BROKEN HEARTED — Ken DODD (15) 70,71
BROKEN HEARTED MELODY —
Sarah VAUGHAN (7) 59
BROKEN HOMES — TRICKY (25)........................98
BROKEN LAND — ADVENTURES (20) 88
BROKEN NOSE — CATHERINE WHEEL (48)........98
BROKEN STONES — Paul WELLER (20) 95
BROKEN WINGS [A] — Art and Dotty TODD (6) 53
BROKEN WINGS [A] — Dickie VALENTINE (12) ..53
BROKEN WINGS [A] — STARGAZERS (1) 53
BROKEN WINGS [B] — MR MISTER (4) 85
BROKEN WINGS [B] — NETWORK (46) 92
THE BROKEN YEARS — HIPSWAY (72) 85
BRONTOSAURUS — MOVE (7) 70
BROOKLYN BEATS — Scotti DEEP (67).............97
BROOKLYN-QUEENS — 3RD BASS (61).............90
BROTHER [A] — CCS (25) 72
BROTHER [B] — URBAN SPECIES (40) 94
BROTHER BRIGHT — ÇA VA ÇA VA (65) 83
BROTHER LOUIE [A] — HOT CHOCOLATE (7) 73
BROTHER LOUIE [A] — QUIREBOYS (31)...........93
BROTHER LOUIE [B] — MODERN TALKING (4) ..86
BROTHER OF MINE —
ANDERSON BRUFORD WAKEMAN HOWE (63)89
BROTHERS AND SISTERS —
2 FUNKY 2 starring Kathryn DION (36) 93,96
BROTHERS GONNA WORK IT OUT —
PUBLIC ENEMY (46) 90
BROTHERS IN ARMS — DIRE STRAITS (16) 85
BROWN-EYED HANDSOME MAN [A] —
Buddy HOLLY (3)..63
BROWN EYED HANDSOME MAN [A] —
Paul McCARTNEY (42) 99
BROWN GIRL IN THE RING — BONEY M (1)..78,93
BROWN PAPER BAG —
Roni SIZE / REPRAZENT (20) 97
BROWN SKIN — india.arie (29)..........................01
BROWN SUGAR [A] — ROLLING STONES (2) 71,84
BROWN SUGAR [B] — D'ANGELO (24) 95
BRUISE PRISTINE — PLACEBO (14) 97
BRUSHED — Paul WELLER (14) 97
BRUTAL-8-E — ALTERN 8 (43) 92
BUBBLE — FLUKE (37) 94
BUBBLING HOT — Pato BANTON (15) 95
BUCK ROGERS — FEEDER (5) 01
THE BUCKET OF WATER SONG —
FOUR BUCKETEERS (26) 80
BUDDHA OF SUBURBIA —
David BOWIE featuring Lenny KRAVITZ (35)..93
BUDDY — DE LA SOUL (7) 89
BUDDY HOLLY — WEEZER (12) 95
BUDDY X [A] — Neneh CHERRY (35) 93
BUDDY X 99 [A] —
DREEM TEEM vs Neneh CHERRY (15) 99
BUFFALO BILL'S LAST SCRATCH —
BARRON KNIGHTS (49) 83

BUFFALO GALS [A] —
Malcolm McLAREN and the
WORLD'S FAMOUS SUPREME TEAM (9) 82
BUFFALO GALS STAMPEDE [A] —
Malcolm McLAREN (65)..................................98
BUFFALO SOLDIER —
Bob MARLEY and the WAILERS (4)................83
BUFFALO STANCE — Neneh CHERRY (3)...........88
THE BUG — DIRE STRAITS (67) 92
BUG A BOO — DESTINY'S CHILD (9) 99
BUG IN THE BASSBIN —
INNERZONE ORCHESTRA (68) 96
BUG POWDER DUST — BOMB THE BASS (24) ..94
BUGGIN — TRUE STEPPERS (6) 00
BUGS — HEPBURN (14) 99
BUILD [A] — HOUSEMARTINS (15) 87
BUILD [B] — INNOCENCE (72)...........................92
BUILD ME UP BUTTERCUP —
FOUNDATIONS (2) 68,98
BUILD YOUR LOVE — Johnnie RAY (17) 57
BUILDING THE CITY OF LIGHT —
Mike SCOTT (60) 95
BULGARIAN — TRAVEL (67) 99
BULL IN THE HEATHER — SONIC YOUTH (24) ..94
BULLDOG NATION — Kevin KENNEDY (70) 00
BULLET — FLUKE (23) 95
BULLET COMES — CHARLATANS (32)...............95
BULLET IN THE GUN —
PLANET PERFECTO (7)..............................99,00
BULLET IN THE HEAD —
RAGE AGAINST THE MACHINE (16) 93
BULLET WITH BUTTERFLY WINGS —
SMASHING PUMPKINS (20)..........................95
BULLETPROOF! — POP WILL EAT ITSELF (24) ..92
BULLFROG — GTO (72) 91
BULLITPROOF — BREAKBEAT ERA (65) 00
BULLITT — Lalo SCHIFRIN (36).........................97
BULLS ON PARADE —
RAGE AGAINST THE MACHINE (8) 96
BULLY BOY — SHED SEVEN (22) 96
BULLY FOR YOU — Tom ROBINSON (68) 79
THE BUMP — KENNY (3) 74
BUMP / RUN DADDY RUN — FUN LOVIN'
CRIMINALS (50) 01
BUMP 'N' GRIND — R KELLY (8).......................95
BUMP N GRIND (I AM FEELING HOT TONIGHT) —
M DUBS featuring LADY SAW (59) 00
BUMPED — RIGHT SAID FRED (32) 93
A BUNCH OF THYME — FOSTER and ALLEN (18)..82
BUONA SERA [A] — Louis PRIMA (25) 58
BUONA SERA [A] — Mr Acker BILK
and his PARAMOUNT JAZZ BAND (7) 60
BUONA SERA [A] — BAD MANNERS (34) 81
BUOY —
Mick KARN featuring David SYLVIAN (63) 87
BURDEN IN MY HAND — SOUNDGARDEN (33)..96
BURIAL — LEVITICUS (66) 95
BURLESQUE — FAMILY (13) 72
BURN [A] — DOCTOR and the MEDICS (29) 86
BURN [B] — Tina ARENA (47)...........................99
BURN BABY BURN [A] — HUDSON-FORD (15)....74
BURN BABY BURN [B] — ASH (13) 01

BURN IT UP —
BEATMASTERS with PP ARNOLD (14) 88
BURN RUBBER ON ME (WHY YOU
WANNA HURT ME) — GAP BAND (22) 80
BURNIN' [A] — DAFT PUNK (30) 97
BURNIN' [B] — K-KLASS (45) 98
BURNIN' [C] — MIRRORBALL (47).....................00
BURNIN' HOT — Jermaine JACKSON (32) 80
BURNIN' LOVE — CON FUNK SHUN (68) 86
BURNING '95 [A] — MK featuring ALANA (44) ..95
BURNING [B] — BABY BUMPS (17) 98
BURNING BRIDGES — Jack SCOTT (32) 60
BURNING BRIDGES (ON AND OFF AND
ON AGAIN) — STATUS QUO (5) 88
BURNING CAR — John FOXX (35) 80
BURNING DOWN ONE SIDE — Robert PLANT (73)82
BURNING DOWN THE HOUSE —
Tom JONES and the CARDIGANS (7).............99
BURNING HEART — SURVIVOR (5) 86
BURNING LOVE — Elvis PRESLEY (7) 72
BURNING OF THE MIDNIGHT LAMP —
Jimi HENDRIX EXPERIENCE (18) 67
BURNING THE GROUND — DURAN DURAN (31) 89
BURNING UP [A] — Tony DE VIT (25)................95
BURNING UP [B] — BINI & MARTINI (65) 01
BURNING WHEEL — PRIMAL SCREAM (17).........97
BURST — DARLING BUDS (50) 88
BURUCHACCA — MUKKAA (74)..........................93
BURUNDI BLACK —
BURUNDI STEIPHENSON BLACK (31) 71
BURUNDI BLUES — BEATS INTERNATIONAL (51)..90
BURY YOU — SYMPOSIUM (41) 98
BUS STOP — HOLLIES (5) 66
BUSHEL AND A PECK — Vivian BLAINE (12)......53
THE BUSINESS — Brian MAY (51).....................98
BUST A MOVE — YOUNG MC (73) 89
BUST THIS HOUSE DOWN — PENTHOUSE 4 (56) 88
BUSTED — Ray CHARLES (21) 63
BUSY BEE — UGLY KID JOE (39) 93
BUSY DOING NOTHING — Dave STEWART (49) 83
BUT I DO — Clarence 'Frogman' HENRY (3) 61
BUT NOT FOR ME [A] — Ella FITZGERALD (25)..59
BUT NOT FOR ME [A] — Ketty LESTER (45) 62
BUT YOU LOVE ME DADDY —
Jim REEVES (15) 69
BUT YOU'RE MINE — SONNY and CHER (17) 65
BUTCHER BABY — PLASMATICS (55) 80
BUTTERCUP — Carl ANDERSON (49) 85
BUTTERFINGERS — Tommy STEELE (8) 57
BUTTERFLY [A] — Andy WILLIAMS (1)...............57
BUTTERFLY [A] — Charlie GRACIE (12) 57
BUTTERFLY [B] — Danyel GERARD (11) 71
BUTTERFLY [C] — Mariah CAREY (22)................97
BUTTERFLY [D] — TILT featuring ZEE (41) 98
BUTTERFLY [E] — CRAZY TOWN (3)....................01
BUTTERFLY KISSES — Bob CARLISLE (56) 97
BUTTERFLY ON A WHEEL — MISSION (12)........90
BUZZ BUZZ A DIDDLE IT — MATCHBOX (22) 80
BUZZIN' — ASIAN DUB FOUNDATION (31) 98
BY MY SIDE — INXS (42) 91
BY THE DEVIL (I WAS TEMPTED) —
BLUE MINK (26) 73

BY THE FOUNTAINS OF ROME [A] – David HUGHES (27) 56
BY THE FOUNTAINS OF ROME [A] – Edmund HOCKRIDGE (17) 56
BY THE LIGHT OF THE SILVERY MOON – LITTLE RICHARD (17) 59
BY THE TIME THIS NIGHT IS OVER – Kenny G with Peabo BRYSON (56) 93
BY THE WAY [A] – BIG THREE (22) 63
BY THE WAY [B] – TREMELOES (35) 70
BY YOUR SIDE [A] – PETERS and LEE (39) 73
BY YOUR SIDE [B] – Jimmy SOMERVILLE (41) 95
BY YOUR SIDE [C] – SADE (17) 00
BYE BABY – Ruby TURNER (52) 86
BYE BYE BABY [A] – Johnny OTIS SHOW (20) 58
BYE BYE BABY [B] – SYMBOLS (44) 67
BYE BYE BABY [B] – BAY CITY ROLLERS (1) 75
BYE BYE BABY [C] – Tony JACKSON and the VIBRATIONS (38) 64
BYE BYE BABY [D] – TQ (7) 99
BYE BYE BLUES – Bert KAEMPFERT (24) 65
BYE BYE BYE – 'N SYNC (3) 00
BYE BYE LOVE – EVERLY BROTHERS (6) 57
B.Y.O.F. (BRING YOUR OWN FUNK) – FANTASTIC FOUR (62) 79
C MOON – Paul McCARTNEY (5) 72
C U WHEN U GET THERE – COOLIO (3) 97
C'MON PEOPLE (WE'RE MAKING IT NOW) – Richard ASHCROFT (21) 00
ÇA PLANE POUR MOI [A] – PLASTIC BERTRAND (8) 78
ÇA PLANE POUR MOI [A] – Leila K (69) 93
CABARET – Louis ARMSTRONG (1) 68
THE CABARET – TIME UK (63) 83
CACHARPAYA (ANDES PUMPSA DAESI) – INCANTATION (12) 82
CAFE DEL MAR – ENERGY 52 (12) 97,98
CAFFEINE BOMB – WILDHEARTS (31) 94
CALEDONIA – Frankie MILLER (45) 92
CALENDAR GIRL – Neil SEDAKA (8) 61
THE CALENDAR SONG – TRINIDAD OIL COMPANY (34) 77
CALIBRE CUTS – VARIOUS ARTISTS (MONTAGES) (75) 80
CALIFORNIA [A] – WEDDING PRESENT (16) 92
CALIFORNIA [B] – Belinda CARLISLE (31) 97
CALIFORNIA DREAMIN' [A] – MAMAS and the PAPAS (9) 66,97
CALIFORNIA DREAMIN' [A] – COLORADO (45) 78
CALIFORNIA DREAMIN' [A] – RIVER CITY PEOPLE (13) 90
CALIFORNIA GIRLS [A] – BEACH BOYS (26) 65
CALIFORNIA GIRLS [A] – David Lee ROTH (68) 85
CALIFORNIA HERE I COME [A] – Freddy CANNON (25) 60
CALIFORNIA HERE I COME [B] – Sophie B HAWKINS (53) 92
CALIFORNIA LOVE – 2PAC featuring Dr DRE (6) 96
CALIFORNIA MAN – MOVE (7) 72
CALIFORNIA SAGA – CALIFORNIA – BEACH BOYS (37) 73
CALIFORNIA SCREAMIN' – CARRIE (55) 98
CALIFORNICATION – RED HOT CHILI PEPPERS (16) 00
THE CALL – BACKSTREET BOYS (8) 01
CALL AND ANSWER – BARENAKED LADIES (52) 99
CALL HER YOUR SWEETHEART – Frank IFIELD (24) 66
CALL IT FATE – Richie DAN (34) 00
CALL IT LOVE – DEUCE (11) 95
CALL IT ROCK 'N' ROLL – GREAT WHITE (67) 91
CALL IT WHAT YOU WANT [A] – NEW KIDS ON THE BLOCK (12) 91
CALL IT WHAT YOU WANT [B] – CREDIT TO THE NATION (57) 93
CALL ME [A] – BLONDIE (1) 80,89
CALL ME [B] – GO WEST (12) 85
CALL ME [C] – SPAGNA (2) 87
CALL ME [D] – LE CLICK (38) 97
CALL ME [E] – JAMELIA (11) 00
(CALL ME) NUMBER ONE – TREMELOES (2) 69
CALL ME ROUND – PILOT (34) 75
CALL MY NAME – ORCHESTRAL MANOEUVRES IN THE DARK (50) 91
CALL OF THE WILD – Midge URE (27) 86
CALL OUT THE DOGS – Gary NUMAN (49) 85
CALL ROSIE ON THE PHONE – Guy MITCHELL (17) 57
CALL THE MAN – Celine DION (11) 97
THE CALL UP – CLASH (40) 80
CALL UP THE GROUPS – BARRON KNIGHTS (3) 64
CALLING – Geri HALLIWELL (7) 01
CALLING ALL THE HEROES – IT BITES (6) 86
CALLING AMERICA – ELECTRIC LIGHT ORCHESTRA (28) 86
CALLING ELVIS – DIRE STRAITS (21) 91
CALLING OCCUPANTS OF INTERPLANETARY CRAFT (THE RECOGNISED ANTHEM OF WORLD CONTACT DAY) – CARPENTERS (9) 77
CALLING OUT YOUR NAME – Jimmy NAIL (65) 95
CALLING YOU – Paul YOUNG (57) 91
CALLING YOUR NAME – MARILYN (4) 83
CALLS THE TUNE – Hazel O'CONNOR (60) 82
CALM DOWN (BASS KEEPS PUMPIN') – CHRIS and JAMES (74) 94
CALYPSO CRAZY – Billy OCEAN (35) 88
CAMBODIA – Kim WILDE (12) 81
CAMDEN TOWN – SUGGS (14) 95
CAMEL BOBSLED RACE – DJ SHADOW (62) 97
CAMELS – SANTOS (9) 01
CAMOUFLAGE – Stan RIDGWAY (4) 86
CAMPIONE 2000 – E-TYPE (58) 00
CAN CAN 62 [A] – Peter JAY and the JAYWALKERS (31) 62
CAN CAN [A] – BAD MANNERS (3) 81
CAN CAN YOU PARTY – JIVE BUNNY and the MASTERMIXERS (8) 90
CAN I – CASHMERE (29) 85
CAN I GET A... – JAY-Z (24) 99
CAN I GET A WITNESS – Sam BROWN (15) 89
CAN I GET OVER – DEFINITION OF SOUND (61) 92
CAN I KICK IT – A TRIBE CALLED QUEST (15) 91
CAN I PLAY WITH MADNESS – IRON MAIDEN (3) 88
CAN I TAKE YOU HOME LITTLE GIRL – DRIFTERS (10) 75
CAN I TOUCH YOU ... THERE – Michael BOLTON (6) 95
CAN I TRUST YOU – BACHELORS (26) 66
CAN THE CAN – Suzi QUATRO (1) 73
CAN THIS BE LOVE – Matt MONRO (24) 61
CAN U DANCE – DJ 'FAST' EDDIE (67) 87
CAN U DIG IT – POP WILL EAT ITSELF (38) 89
CAN U FEEL IT – DEEP CREED '94 (59) 94
CAN WE – SWV (18) 97
CAN WE FIX IT – BOB THE BUILDER (1) 00,01
CAN WE START AGAIN? – TINDERSTICKS (54) 99
CAN WE TALK ... – CODE RED (29) 97
CAN YOU DIG IT? – MOCK TURTLES (18) 91
CAN YOU DO IT – GEORDIE (13) 73
CAN YOU FEEL IT [A] – JACKSONS (6) 81
CAN YOU FEEL IT [B] – ELEVATION (62) 92
CAN YOU FEEL IT [C] – REEL 2 REAL (13) 94
CAN YOU FEEL IT [D] – CLS (46) 98
CAN YOU FEEL IT / CAN YOU FEEL IT – RAZE (62) 90
CAN YOU FEEL IT (ROCK DA HOUSE) – NYCC (68) 98
CAN YOU FEEL THE FORCE? – REAL THING (5) 79,86
CAN YOU FEEL THE LOVE TONIGHT – Elton JOHN (14) 94
(CAN YOU) FEEL THE PASSION – BLUE PEARL (14) 92
CAN YOU FORGIVE HER – PET SHOP BOYS (7) 93
CAN YOU FORGIVE ME – Karl DENVER (32) 63
CAN YOU HANDLE IT [A] – DNA featuring Sharon REDD (17) 92
CAN YOU HANDLE IT [A] – Sharon REDD (31) 81
CAN YOU KEEP A SECRET – BROTHER BEYOND (22) 88,89
CAN YOU PARTY – ROYAL HOUSE (14) 88
CAN YOU PLEASE CRAWL OUT YOUR WINDOW – Bob DYLAN (17) 66
CAN YOUR PUSSY DO THE DOG? – CRAMPS (68) 85
CANCER FOR THE CURE – EELS (60) 98
CANDIDA – DAWN (9) 71
CANDIDATE FOR LOVE – TS MONK (58) 81
CANDLE IN THE WIND – Elton JOHN (5) 74,88
CANDLE IN THE WIND 1997 – Elton JOHN (1) 97
CANDLEFIRE – DAWN OF THE REPLICANTS (52) 98
CANDLELAND (THE SECOND COMING) – Ian McCULLOCH (75) 90
CANDLELIGHT – SIX BY SEVEN (70) 98
CANDLES – Alex REECE (33) 96
CANDY [A] – CAMEO (27) 86
CANDY [B] – Iggy POP (67) 90
CANDY [C] – Mandy MOORE (6) 00
CANDY [D] – ASH (20) 01
CANDY EVERYBODY WANTS – 10,000 MANIACS (47) 93
CANDY GIRL [A] – NEW EDITION (1) 83
CANDY GIRL [B] – BABYBIRD (14) 97
CANDY MAN – Brian POOLE and the TREMELOES (6) 64
CANDY RAIN – SOUL FOR REAL (23) 95
CANDYBAR EXPRESS – LOVE AND MONEY (56) 86
CANDYMAN – SIOUXSIE and the BANSHEES (34) 86
CANED AND UNABLE – HI-GATE (12) 00
CANNED HEAT – JAMIROQUAI (4) 99
CANNIBALS – Mark KNOPFLER (42) 96
CANNONBALL – Duane EDDY and the REBELS (22) 59
CANNONBALL (EP) – BREEDERS (40) 93
CAN'T BE SURE – SUNDAYS (45) 89
CAN'T BE WITH YOU TONIGHT – Judy BOUCHER (2) 87
CAN'T BUY ME LOVE [A] – BEATLES (1) 64,84
CAN'T BUY ME LOVE [A] – Ella FITZGERALD (34) 64
CAN'T CHANGE ME – Chris CORNELL (62) 99
CAN'T CRY ANYMORE – Sheryl CROW (33) 95
CAN'T DO A THING (TO STOP ME) – Chris ISAAK (36) 93
CAN'T DO NUTTIN' FOR YA MAN – PUBLIC ENEMY (53) 90
CAN'T FAKE THE FEELING – Geraldine HUNT (44) 80
CAN'T FIGHT THE MOONLIGHT – LeAnn RIMES (1) 00
CAN'T FIGHT THIS FEELING – REO SPEEDWAGON (16) 85
CAN'T FORGET YOU – SONIA (17) 89
CAN'T GET ALONG WITHOUT YOU – Frankie VAUGHAN (11) 58
CAN'T GET ANY HARDER – James BROWN (59) 93
CAN'T GET BY – SLAMM (47) 95
CAN'T GET BY WITHOUT YOU – REAL THING (2) 76
CAN'T GET BY WITHOUT YOU (THE SECOND DECADE REMIX) – REAL THING (6) 86
CAN'T GET ENOUGH [A] – BAD COMPANY (15) 74
CAN'T GET ENOUGH [B] – SUEDE (23) 99
CAN'T GET ENOUGH [C] – SOULSEARCHER (8) 99
CAN'T GET ENOUGH OF YOU – Eddy GRANT (13) 81
CAN'T GET ENOUGH OF YOUR LOVE [A] – DARTS (43) 79
CAN'T GET ENOUGH OF YOUR LOVE [B] – KWS (71) 93
CAN'T GET ENOUGH OF YOUR LOVE [B] – Taylor DAYNE (14) 93
CAN'T GET ENOUGH OF YOUR LOVE BABE [B] – Barry WHITE (8) 74
CAN'T GET OUT OF BED – CHARLATANS (24) 94
CAN'T GET THE BEST OF ME – CYPRESS HILL (35) 00
CAN'T GET USED TO LOSING YOU [A] – Andy WILLIAMS (2) 63
CAN'T GET USED TO LOSING YOU [A] – BEAT (3) 83
CAN'T GET USED TO LOSING YOU [A] – COLOUR GIRL (31) 00
CAN'T GET YOU OFF MY MIND – Lenny KRAVITZ (54) 96
CAN'T GET YOU OUT OF MY HEAD – Kylie MINOGUE (1) 01
CAN'T GET YOU OUT OF MY THOUGHTS – DUM DUMS (18) 00
CAN'T GIVE ME LOVE – PEPSI and SHIRLIE (58) 87
CAN'T GIVE YOU ANYTHING (BUT MY LOVE) – STYLISTICS (1) 75
CAN'T GIVE YOU MORE – STATUS QUO (37) 91
CAN'T HAPPEN HERE – RAINBOW (20) 81
CAN'T HAVE YOU – LYTE FUNKIE ONES (54) 99
CAN'T HELP FALLING IN LOVE [A] – Elvis PRESLEY (1) 62
CAN'T HELP FALLING IN LOVE [A] – Andy WILLIAMS (3) 70
CAN'T HELP FALLING IN LOVE [A] – STYLISTICS (4) 76
CAN'T HELP FALLING IN LOVE [A] – LICK THE TINS (42) 86
CAN'T HELP IT – HAPPY CLAPPERS (18) 96
CAN'T HELP MYSELF – LINX (55) 81
CAN'T I – Nat 'King' COLE (6) 53
CAN'T KEEP IT IN – Cat STEVENS (13) 72
CAN'T KEEP LIVING THIS WAY – ROOTJOOSE (73) 97
CAN'T KEEP ME SILENT – ANGELIC (12) 01

CAN'T KEEP THIS FEELING IN – Cliff RICHARD (10) 98
CAN'T KNOCK THE HUSTLE – JAY-Z featuring Mary J BLIGE (30) 97
CAN'T LET GO [A] – EARTH WIND AND FIRE (46) 79
CAN'T LET GO [B] – Mariah CAREY (20) 92
CAN'T LET HER GO – BOYZ II MEN (23) 98
CAN'T LET YOU GO [A] – Barry RYAN (32) 72
CAN'T LET YOU GO [B] – RAINBOW (43) 83
CAN'T LIVE WITH YOU (CAN'T LIVE WITHOUT YOU) – MINDBENDERS (28) 66
CAN'T LIVE WITHOUT YOU – SCORPIONS (63) 82
(CAN'T LIVE WITHOUT YOUR) LOVE AND AFFECTION – NELSON (54) 90
CAN'T NOBODY HOLD ME DOWN – PUFF DADDY featuring MASE (19) 97
CAN'T SAY 'BYE – STONEFREE (73) 87
CAN'T SAY HOW MUCH I LOVE YOU – Demis ROUSSOS (35) 76
CAN'T SEE ME – Ian BROWN (21) 98
CANT SET RULES ABOUT LOVE – Adam ANT (47)90
CAN'T SHAKE LOOSE – Agnetha FALTSKOG (63) 83
CAN'T SHAKE THE FEELING – BIG FUN (8) 89
CAN'T SMILE WITHOUT YOU [A] – Barry MANILOW (43) 78
CAN'T SMILE WITHOUT YOU [A] – James BULLER (51) 99
CAN'T STAND IT – WILCO (67) 99
CAN'T STAND LOSING YOU – POLICE (2)78,79,95
CAN'T STAY AWAY FROM YOU – Gloria ESTEFAN and MIAMI SOUND MACHINE(7)89
CAN'T STOP – AFTER 7 (54) 90
CAN'T STOP LOSING YOU – FEEDER (12) 01
CAN'T STOP LOVIN' YOU – VAN HALEN (33) 95
CAN'T STOP RUNNING – SPACE MONKEY (53) 83
CAN'T STOP THE MUSIC – VILLAGE PEOPLE (11) 80
CAN'T STOP THESE THINGS – CHINA DRUM (65)96
CAN'T STOP THIS FEELING – RHYTHM-N-BASS (59) 93
CAN'T STOP THIS THING WE STARTED – Bryan ADAMS (12) 91
CAN'T TAKE MY EYES OFF YOU [A] – Andy WILLIAMS (5) 68
CAN'T TAKE MY EYES OFF YOU [A] – BOYSTOWN GANG (4) 82
CAN'T TAKE NO MORE – SOUP DRAGONS (65)87
CAN'T TAKE YOUR LOVE – Pauline HENRY (30) 94
CAN'T TRUSS IT – PUBLIC ENEMY (22) 91
CAN'T WAIT ANOTHER MINUTE – FIVE STAR (7)..86
CAN'T WAIT TO BE WITH YOU – JAZZY JEFF & the FRESH PRINCE (29) 94
CAN'T YOU HEAR MY HEART – Danny RIVERS (36) 61
CAN'T YOU HEAR MY HEART BEAT? – GOLDIE and the GINGERBREADS (25) 65
CAN'T YOU HEAR THE BEAT OF A BROKEN HEART – Iain GREGORY (39) 62
CAN'T YOU SEE – TOTAL featuring the NOTORIOUS B.I.G. (43) 95
CAN'T YOU SEE THAT SHE'S MINE – Dave CLARK FIVE (10) 64
(CAN'T YOU) TRIP LIKE I DO – FILTER and the CRYSTAL METHOD (39) 97
CANTALOOP – US3 (23) 93
CANTGETAMAN CANTGETAJOB (LIFE'S A BITCH) – SISTER BLISS (31) 94
CANTO DELLA TERRA – Andrea BOCELLI (24) 99,00
CANTON (LIVE) – JAPAN (42) 83
CANTONESE BOY – JAPAN (24) 82
CAPSTICK COMES HOME – Tony CAPSTICK and the CARLTON MAIN / FRICKLEY COLLIERY BAND (3) 81
CAPTAIN BEAKY – Keith MICHELL (5) 80
CAPTAIN DREAD – DREADZONE (49) 95
CAPTAIN KREMMEN (RETRIBUTION) – Kenny EVERETT (32) 77
THE CAPTAIN OF HER HEART – DOUBLE (8) 86
CAPTAIN OF YOUR SHIP – REPARATA and the DELRONS (13) 68
CAPTAIN SCARLET THEME – Barry GRAY ORCHESTRA (53) 86
CAPTURE THE HEART (EP) – RUNRIG (49) 90
CAR BOOT SALE – BILL (73) 93
CAR 67 – DRIVER 67 (7) 78
CAR SONG – MADDER ROSE (68) 94
CAR WASH [A] – ROSE ROYCE (9) 76,88
CAR WASH [A] – Gwen DICKEY (72) 90
CAR WASH [A] – ROSE ROYCE featuring Gwen DICKEY (18) 98
CARA MIA – David WHITFIELD (1) 54
CARAVAN [A] – Duane EDDY and the REBELS (42) 61
CARAVAN [B] – INSPIRAL CARPETS (30) 91
CARAVAN OF LOVE [A] – ISLEY JASPER ISLEY (52) 85
CARAVAN OF LOVE [A] – HOUSEMARTINS (1) ..86
CARAVAN SONG – Barbara DICKSON (41) 80
CARDBOY KING – SALAD (65) 97
CARDIAC ARREST – MADNESS (14) 82
CAREFUL – HORSE (44) 90,97
CARELESS HANDS – Des O'CONNOR (6) 67
CARELESS LOVE – SWIMMING WITH SHARKS (63) 88
CARELESS MEMORIES – DURAN DURAN (37) ..81
CARELESS WHISPER [A] – George MICHAEL (1)84
CARELESS WHISPER [A] – Sarah WASHINGTON (45) 93
CARIBBEAN BLUE – ENYA (13) 91
THE CARIBBEAN DISCO SHOW – LOBO (8) 81
CARIBBEAN HONEYMOON – Frank WEIR (42) ..60
CARIBBEAN QUEEN (NO MORE LOVE ON THE RUN) – Billy OCEAN (6) 84
CARMEN QUEASY – MAXIM (33) 00
CARNATION – Liam GALLAGHER and Steve CRADOCK (6) 99
CARNAVAL DE PARIS – Dario G (5) 98
CARNIVAL [A] – LIONROCK (34) 93
CARNIVAL [B] – CARDIGANS (35) 95
CARNIVAL IN HEAVEN – Malandra BURROWS (49) 97
THE CARNIVAL IS OVER – SEEKERS (1) 65
CAROLINA MOON – Connie FRANCIS (1) 58
CAROLINE [A] – STATUS QUO (5) 73,82
CAROLINE [B] – Kirsty MacCOLL (58) 95
CAROUSEL – ORIGINAL SOUNDTRACK (LP) – VARIOUS ARTISTS (EPs and LPs) (26) 56
THE CAROUSEL WALTZ – Ray MARTIN (24) 56
CARRIE [A] – Cliff RICHARD (4) 80
CARRIE [B] – EUROPE (22) 87
CARRIE-ANNE – HOLLIES (3) 67
CARROT ROPE – PAVEMENT (27) 99
CARRY ME HOME – GLOWORM (9) 94
CARRY ON [A] – Martha WASH (49) 92,93,97
CARRY ON [B] – SPACEHOG (43) 98
CARRY ON [C] – Donna SUMMER and Giorgio MORODER (65) 98
CARRY ON WAYWARD SON – KANSAS (51) 78
CARRY THAT WEIGHT – TRASH (35) 69
CARRY THE BLAME – RIVER CITY PEOPLE (13) 90
CARRYING A TORCH – Tom JONES (57) 91
CARS [A] – Gary NUMAN (1) 79,96
CARS [B] – FEAR FACTORY (57) 99
CARS (E REG MODEL) – Gary NUMAN (16) 87
CARS AND GIRLS – PREFAB SPROUT (44) 88
CARS (2ND RE-MIX) – Gary NUMAN (53) 93
CARTE BLANCHE – VERACOCHA (22) 99
CARTOON HEROES – AQUA (7) 00
CARTROUBLE – ADAM and the ANTS (33) 81
CASABLANCA – Kenny BALL and his JAZZMEN (21) 63
CASANOVA [A] – Petula CLARK (39) 63
CASANOVA [B] – COFFEE (13) 80
CASANOVA [B] – BABY D (67) 94
CASANOVA [C] – LEVERT (9) 87
CASANOVA [C] – ULTIMATE KAOS (24) 97,98
CASCADE – FUTURE SOUND OF LONDON (27) 93
CASE OF THE EX – MYA (3) 01
CASINO ROYALE – Herb ALPERT (27) 67
CASINO ROYALE / DEAD A'S – DJ Zinc / DJ Hype (58) 01
CASSIUS 1999 – CASSIUS (7) 99
CAST YOUR FATE TO THE WIND – SOUNDS ORCHESTRAL (5) 64
CASTLE ROCK – BLUETONES (7) 96
CASTLES IN SPAIN – ARMOURY SHOW (69) 84
CASTLES IN THE AIR [A] – Don McLEAN (47) ..82
CASTLES IN THE AIR [B] – COLOUR FIELD (51) 85
CASTLES IN THE SAND – THUNDER (30) 95
CASTLES IN THE SKY – IAN VAN DAHL (5) 01
CASUAL SUB (BURNING SPEAR) – ETA (28) 97,98
CAT AMONG THE PIGEONS – BROS (2) 88
THE CAT CAME BACK – Sonny JAMES (30) 56
THE CAT CREPT IN – MUD (2) 74
CAT PEOPLE (PUTTING OUT FIRE) – David BOWIE (26) 82
CATALAN – TOUR DE FORCE (71) 98
CATCH [A] – CURE (27) 87
CATCH [B] – SUNSCREEM (55) 97
CATCH [c] – KOSHEEN (15) 01
CATCH A FALLING STAR – Perry COMO (9) 58
CATCH A FIRE – HADDAWAY (39) 95
CATCH ME – ABSOLUTE (69) 98
CATCH MY FALL – Billy IDOL (63) 88
CATCH THE BREEZE – SLOWDIVE (52) 91
CATCH THE FIRE – DRIZABONE (54) 91
CATCH THE LIGHT – Martha WASH (45) 98
CATCH THE SUN – DOVES (32) 00
CATCH THE WIND – DONOVAN (4) 65
CATCH US IF YOU CAN – Dave CLARK FIVE (5) 65
CATERINA – Perry COMO (37) 62
THE CATERPILLAR – CURE (14) 84
CATH – BLUEBELLS (38) 83,84
CATHEDRAL PARK – DUBSTAR (41) 97
CATHEDRAL SONG – Tanita TIKARAM (48) 89
CATHY'S CLOWN – EVERLY BROTHERS (1) 60
CATS IN THE CRADLE [A] – UGLY KID JOE (7) ..93
CATS IN THE CRADLE [A] – Jason DOWNS featuring MILK (65) 01
CAUGHT A LITE SNEEZE – Tori AMOS (20) 96
CAUGHT BY THE FUZZ – SUPERGRASS (43) 94
CAUGHT IN MY SHADOW – WONDER STUFF (18) 91
CAUGHT IN THE MIDDLE – Juliet ROBERTS (14) 93,94
CAUGHT OUT THERE – KELIS (4) 00
CAUGHT UP IN MY HEART – OPTIMYSTIC (49) 94
CAUGHT UP IN THE RAPTURE – Anita BAKER (51) 87
CAUSING A COMMOTION – MADONNA (4) 87
CAVATINA – John WILLIAMS (13) 79
CAVE – MUSE (52) 99
CCCAN'T YOU SEE – VICIOUS PINK (67) 84
CECILIA – SUGGS featuring Louchie LOU and Michie ONE (4) 96
THE CEDAR ROOM – DOVES (33) 00
CELEBRATE [A] – AN EMOTIONAL FISH (46) 90
CELEBRATE [B] – HORSE (49) 94
CELEBRATE [C] – LEVELLERS (28) 97
CELEBRATE OUR LOVE – ALICE DEEJAY (17) 01
(CELEBRATE) THE DAY AFTER YOU – BLOW MONKEYS with Curtis MAYFIELD (52) 87
CELEBRATE THE WORLD – WOMACK and WOMACK (19) 89
CELEBRATION [A] – KOOL and the GANG (7) 80,88
CELEBRATION [A] – Kylie MINOGUE (20) 92
A CELEBRATION – U2 (47) 82
CELEBRATION GENERATION – WESTBAM (48) 94
CELEBRATION OF LIFE – TRUCE (51) 96
CELEBRITY HIT LIST – TERRORVISION (20) 96
CELEBRITY SKIN – HOLE (19) 98
CELL 151 – Steve HACKETT (66) 83
THE CELTIC SOUL BROTHERS – DEXY'S MIDNIGHT RUNNERS (20) 82,83
THE CELTS – ENYA (29) 92
CEMENT – FEEDER (53) 97
CEMENTED SHOES – MY VITRIOL (65) 00
CENTER CITY – FAT LARRY'S BAND (31) 77
CENTERFOLD [A] – J GEILS BAND (3) 82
CENTERFOLD [A] – Adam AUSTIN (41) 99
CENTRAL PARK ARREST – THUNDERTHIGHS (30) 74
CENTRAL RESERVATION – Beth ORTON (37) 99
CENTURY – INTASTELLA (70) 91
CEREMONY – NEW ORDER (34) 81
CERTAIN PEOPLE I KNOW – MORRISSEY (35) ..92
A CERTAIN SMILE – Johnny MATHIS (4) 58
THE CERTAINTY OF CHANCE – DIVINE COMEDY (49) 98
C'EST LA VIE [A] – Robbie NEVIL (3) 86
C'EST LA VIE [B] – UB40 (37) 94
C'EST LA VIE [C] – B*WITCHED (1) 98
C'EST LA VIE [D] – Jean-Michel JARRE (40) 00
C'EST SI BON – Conway TWITTY (40) 61
CHA CHA CHA – FLIPMODE SQUAD (54) 98

CHURA LIYA – **Bally SAGOO** (64) 94
CHURCH OF FREEDOM – **AMOS** (54) 95
CHURCH OF NOISE – **THERAPY?** (29) 98
THE CHURCH OF THE HOLY SPOOK – **Shane MacGOWAN** (74) 94
CHURCH OF THE POISON MIND – **CULTURE CLUB** (2) 83
CHURCH OF YOUR HEART – **ROXETTE** (21) 92
CIAO CIAO BAMBINA [A] – **Domenico MODUGNO** (29) 59
CIAO CIAO BAMBINA [A] – **Marino MARINI and his QUARTET** (24) 59
CIGARETTES AND ALCOHOL – **OASIS** (7)94,95,96
CINDERELLA ROCKEFELLA – **Esther and Abi OFARIM** (1) 68
CINDY INCIDENTALLY – **FACES** (2) 73
CINDY, OH CINDY [A] – **Eddie FISHER** (5) 56
CINDY, OH CINDY [A] – **Tony BRENT** (16) 56,57
CINDY, OH CINDY [A] – **TARRIERS** (26) 56
CINDY'S BIRTHDAY – **Shane FENTON and the FENTONES** (19) 62
CIRCLE – **Edie BRICKELL and the NEW BOHEMIANS** (74) 89
THE CIRCLE – **OCEAN COLOUR SCENE** (6) 96
CIRCLE IN THE SAND – **Belinda CARLISLE** (4) ..88
CIRCLE OF LIFE – **Elton JOHN** (11) 94
CIRCLE OF ONE – **Oleta ADAMS** (73) 91
CIRCLES [A] – **NEW SEEKERS** (4) 72
CIRCLES [B] – **SAFFRON** (60) 93
CIRCLES [C] – **Adam F** (20) 97
CIRCLESQUARE – **WONDER STUFF** (20) 90
CIRCUS [A] – **Lenny KRAVITZ** (54) 95
CIRCUS [B] – **Eric CLAPTON** (39) 98
THE CIRCUS [C] – **ERASURE** (6) 87
CIRCUS GAMES – **SKIDS** (32) 80
CITIES IN DUST – **SIOUXSIE and the BANSHEES** (21) 85
THE CITY IS MINE – **JAY-Z featuring BLACKSTREET** (38) 98
CITY LIGHTS – **David ESSEX** (24) 76
CITYSONG – **LUSCIOUS JACKSON** (69) 95
THE CIVIL WAR (EP) – **GUNS N' ROSES** (11) 93
CLAIR – **Gilbert O'SULLIVAN** (1) 72
CLAIRE – **Paul and Barry RYAN** (47) 67
THE CLAIRVOYANT – **IRON MAIDEN** (6) 88
THE CLAP CLAP SOUND – **KLAXONS** (45) 83
CLAP YOUR HANDS [A] – **Rocky SHARPE and the REPLAYS** (54) 82
CLAP YOUR HANDS [B] – **CAMISRA** (34) 99
THE CLAPPING SONG (EP) [A] – **Shirley ELLIS** (59)78
THE CLAPPING SONG [A] – **Shirley ELLIS** (6) ..65
THE CLAPPING SONG [A] – **BELLE STARS** (11)..82
CLARE – **FAIRGROUND ATTRACTION** (49) 89
CLASH CITY ROCKERS – **CLASH** (35) 78
CLASSIC – **Adrian GURVITZ** (8) 82
CLASSIC GIRL – **JANE'S ADDICTION** (60) 91
CLASSICAL GAS [A] – **Mason WILLIAMS** (9) 68
CLASSICAL GAS [A] – **VANESSA-MAE** (41) 95
CLASSICAL MUDDLY – **PORTSMOUTH SINFONIA** (38) 81
CLAUDETTE – **EVERLY BROTHERS** (1) 58
CLEAN CLEAN – **BUGGLES** (38) 80
CLEAN UP YOUR OWN BACK YARD – **Elvis PRESLEY** (21) 69
CLEMENTINE [A] – **Bobby DARIN** (8) 60
CLEMENTINE [B] – **Mark OWEN** (3) 97
CLEOPATRA'S CAT – **SPIN DOCTORS** (29) 94
CLEOPATRA'S THEME – **CLEOPATRA** (3) 98
THE CLICHES ARE TRUE – **MANCHILD featuring Kelly JONES** (60) 00
CLIMB EV'RY MOUNTAIN – **Shirley BASSEY** (1) 61
CLINT EASTWOOD – **GORILLAZ** (4) 01
CLIPPED – **CURVE** (36) 91
CLOAKING – **SEAFOOD** (71) 01
CLOG DANCE – **VIOLINSKI** (17) 79
CLOSE...BUT – **ECHOBELLY** (59) 94
CLOSE BUT NO CIGAR – **Thomas DOLBY** (22)..92
CLOSE EVERY DOOR – **Phillip SCHOFIELD** (27)92
CLOSE MY EYES FOREVER – **Lita FORD duet with Ozzy OSBOURE** (47) 89
CLOSE THE DOOR [A] – **STARGAZERS** (6) 55
CLOSE THE DOOR [B] – **Teddy PENDERGRASS** (41) 78
CLOSE TO ME – **CURE** (13) 85,90
CLOSE TO PERFECTION – **Miquel BROWN** (63) 85
CLOSE (TO THE EDIT) – **ART OF NOISE** (8) 84
CLOSE TO YOU [A] – **Maxi PRIEST** (7) 90
CLOSE TO YOU [B] – **BRAND NEW HEAVIES** (38) 95
CLOSE TO YOU [C] – **WHIGFIELD** (13) 95
CLOSE TO YOU [D] – **Marti PELLOW** (9) 01
CLOSE TO YOUR HEART – **JX** (18) 97
CLOSE YOUR EYES – **Tony BENNETT** (18) 55
CLOSED FOR BUSINESS – **MANSUN** (10) 97
CLOSER [A] – **MR FINGERS** (50) 92
CLOSER [B] – **NINE INCH NAILS** (25) 94
CLOSER [C] – **LIQUID** (47) 95
THE CLOSER I GET TO YOU – **Roberta FLACK** (42) 78
CLOSER THAN CLOSE – **Rosie GAINES** (4) 97
CLOSER THAN MOST – **BEAUTIFUL SOUTH** (22)..00
CLOSER TO ALL YOUR DREAMS – **RHYTHM QUEST** (45) 92
CLOSER TO ME – **FIVE** (4) 01
CLOSER TO THE HEART – **RUSH** (36) 78
CLOSEST THING TO HEAVEN [A] – **KANE GANG** (12) 84
CLOSEST THING TO HEAVEN [B] – **Lionel RICHIE** (26) 98
CLOSING TIME [A] – **DEACON BLUE** (42) 91
CLOSING TIME [B] – **SEMISONIC** (25) 99
CLOUD 8 – **FRAZIER CHORUS** (52) 90
CLOUD LUCKY SEVEN – **Guy MITCHELL** (2) 53
CLOUD NINE – **TEMPTATIONS** (15) 69
CLOUD 99 – **ST ANDREWS CHORALE** (31) 76
CLOUD NUMBER 9 – **Bryan ADAMS** (6) 99
CLOUDBURST [A] – **Don LANG** (16) 55,56
CLOUDBURST [B] – **NIAGRA** (65) 97
CLOUDBUSTING – **Kate BUSH** (20) 85
CLOUDS – **SOURCE** (38) 97
CLOUDS ACROSS THE MOON – **RAH BAND** (6) 85
THE CLOUDS WILL SOON ROLL BY – **Tony BRENT** (20) 58
CLOWN SHOES – **Johnny BURNETTE** (35) 62
CLUB AT THE END OF THE STREET – **Elton JOHN** (47) 90
CLUB BIZARRE – **U96** (70) 96
CLUB COUNTRY – **ASSOCIATES** (13) 82
CLUB FANTASTIC MEGAMIX – **WHAM!** (15) 83
CLUB FOR LIFE '98 – **CHRIS and JAMES** (66) ..98
CLUB LONELY – **GROOVE CONNEKTION 2** (54) 98
CLUB TROPICANA – **WHAM!** (4) 83
CLUBLAND – **Elvis COSTELLO** (60) 80
CLUNK CLINK – **LAUREL and HARDY** (65) 83
CLUTCH – **SHEA SEGER** (47) 01
C'MON – **MILLIONAIRE HIPPIES** (59) 94
C'MON AND GET MY LOVE – **D MOB with Cathy DENNIS** (15) 89
C'MON BILLY – **P J HARVEY** (29) 95
C'MON CINCINNATI – **DELAKOTA** (55) 98
C'MON EVERY BEATBOX – **BIG AUDIO DYNAMITE** (51) 86
C'MON EVERYBODY [A] – **Eddie COCHRAN** (6) 59,88
C'MON EVERYBODY [A] – **SEX PISTOLS** (3) 79
C'MON KIDS – **BOO RADLEYS** (18) 96
C'MON LET'S GO – **GIRLSCHOOL** (42) 81
C'MON MARIANNE – **GRAPEFRUIT** (31) 68
C'MON PEOPLE – **Paul McCARTNEY** (41) 93
COAST IS CLEAR – **CURVE** (34) 91
COCK A DOODLE DO IT – **EGGS ON LEGS** (42) 95
COCKNEY TRANSLATION – **Smiley CULTURE** (71) 85
CO-CO – **SWEET** (2) 71
COCO JAMBOO – **MR PRESIDENT** (8) 97
COCOMOTION – **EL COCO** (31) 78
COCONUT – **NILSSON** (42) 72
CODE OF LOVE – **Mike SARNE** (29) 63
CODE RED – **CONQUERING LION** (53) 94
CODED LANGUAGE – **KRUST featuring Saul WILLIAMS** (66) 99
COFFEE – **SUPERSISTER** (16) 00
COFFEE + TV – **BLUR** (11) 99
THE COFFEE SONG – **Frank SINATRA** (39) 61
COGNOSCENTI VS INTELLIGENTSIA – **CUBAN BOYS** (4) 99,00
COLD [A] – **Annie LENNOX** (26) 92
COLD [B] – **TEARS FOR FEARS** (72) 93
COLD AS CHRISTMAS – **Elton JOHN** (33) 83
COLD AS ICE [A] – **FOREIGNER** (24) 78,85
COLD AS ICE [A] – **M.O.P** (4) 01
COLD COLD HEART [A] – **Midge URE** (17) 91
COLD COLD HEART [B] – **WET WET WET** (23) ..94
COLD DAY IN HELL – **Gary MOORE** (24) 92
COLD HEARTED – **Paula ABDUL** (46) 90
COLD LOVE – **Donna SUMMER** (44) 81
COLD ROCK A PARTY – **MC LYTE** (15) 97
COLD SHOULDER – **CULTURE CLUB** (43) 99
COLD SWEAT [A] – **THIN LIZZY** (27) 83
COLD SWEAT [B] – **SUGARCUBES** (56) 88
COLD TURKEY – **John LENNON** (14) 69
COLD WORLD – **GENIUS / GZA featuring D'ANGELO** (40) 96
COLDCUT'S CHRISTMAS BREAK – **COLDCUT** (67) 89
COLETTE – **Billy FURY** (9) 60
COLOR OF MY SKIN – **SWING 52** (60) 95
THE COLOUR FIELD – **COLOUR FIELD** (43) 84
COLOUR MY LIFE – **M PEOPLE** (35) 92
THE COLOUR OF LOVE [A] – **Billy OCEAN** (65) 88
THE COLOUR OF LOVE [B] – **SNAP** (54) 91
THE COLOUR OF LOVE [C] – **REESE PROJECT** (52) 92,94
COLOUR OF MY LOVE – **JEFFERSON** (22) 69
COLOUR THE WORLD – **SASH!** (15) 99
COLOURED KISSES – **MARTIKA** (41) 92
COLOURS – **DONOVAN** (4) 65
THE COLOURS – **MEN THEY COULDN'T HANG** (61)88
COLOURS FLY AWAY – **TEARDROP EXPLODES** (54) 81
COLOURS OF THE WIND – **Vanessa WILLIAMS** (21) 95
COMA AROMA – **INAURA** (57) 96
THE COMANCHEROS – **Lonnie DONEGAN** (14)..62
COMBINE HARVESTER (BRAND NEW KEY) – **WURZELS** (1) 76,01
COME – **Martha WASH** (64) 99
COME AGAIN – **TRUMAN & WOLFF featuring STEEL HORSES** (57) 98
COME ALONG PLEASE – **Bob WALLIS and his STORYVILLE JAZZ BAND** (33) 62
COME AND GET IT – **BADFINGER** (4) 70
COME AND GET ME – **CLEOPATRA** (29) 00
COME AND GET WITH ME – **Keith SWEAT** (58) 98
COME AND GET YOUR LOVE – **REAL McCOY** (19) 95
COME AND STAY WITH ME – **Marianne FAITHFULL** (4) 65
COME AS YOU ARE – **NIRVANA** (9) 92
COME AWAY MELINDA – **Barry ST JOHN** (47) ..65
COME BABY COME – **K7** (3) 93
COME BACK [A] – **WAH!** (20) 84
COME BACK [B] – **SPEAR OF DESTINY** (55) 85
COME BACK [C] – **Luther VANDROSS** (53) 89
COME BACK [D] – **LONDONBEAT** (69) 95
COME BACK AND FINISH WHAT YOU STARTED – **Gladys KNIGHT and the PIPS** (15) 78
COME BACK AND SHAKE ME – **Clodagh RODGERS** (3) 69
COME BACK AND STAY – **Paul YOUNG** (4) 83
COME BACK BABY – **Dan REED NETWORK** (51)90
COME BACK BRIGHTER – **REEF** (8) 97
COME BACK DARLING – **UB40** (10) 98
COME BACK (FOR REAL LOVE) – **Alison LIMERICK** (53) 91
COME BACK JONEE – **DEVO** (60) 78
COME BACK MY LOVE – **DARTS** (2) 78
COME BACK TO ME [A] – **Janet JACKSON** (20)..90
COME BACK TO ME [B] – **ANGELHEART** (68) 96
COME BACK TO WHAT YOU KNOW – **EMBRACE** (6) 98
COME DANCE WITH ME (LP) – **Frank SINATRA** (30) 59
COME DANCING [A] – **NO DICE** (65) 79
COME DANCING [B] – **KINKS** (12) 83
COME DIG IT – **MACHEL** (56) 96
COME GET MY LOVIN' – **DIONNE** (69) 89
COME GIVE ME YOUR LOVE – **Richie STEPHENS** (61) 97
COME HELL OR WATERS HIGH – **DC LEE** (46)..86
COME HOME [A] – **Dave CLARK FIVE** (16) 65
COME HOME [B] – **JAMES** (32) 90
COME HOME [C] – **LIL' DEVIOUS** (55) 01
COME HOME WITH ME BABY – **DEAD OR ALIVE** (62) 89
COME IN OUT OF THE RAIN – **Wendy MOTEN** (8) 94
COME INSIDE – **THOMPSON TWINS** (56) 91
COME INTO MY LIFE [A] – **Joyce SIMS** (7) ..88,95
COME INTO MY LIFE [B] – **GALA** (38) 98
COME LIVE WITH ME – **HEAVEN 17** (5) 83
COME NEXT SPRING – **Tony BENNETT** (29) 56
COME ON [A] – **ROLLING STONES** (21) 63
COME ON [B] – **DJ SEDUCTION** (37) 92

COWBOY DREAMS — **Jimmy NAIL** (13) 95
COWBOY JIMMY JOE — **Alma COGAN** (37) 61
COWBOYS AND ANGELS — **George MICHAEL** (45) 91
COWBOYS AND INDIANS — **CROSS** (74)............87
COWBOYS & KISSES — **ANASTACIA** (28) 01
COWGIRL — **UNDERWORLD** (24).........................00
COWPUNCHER'S CANTATA — **Max BYGRAVES** (6) 52,53
COWPUNK MEDLUM — **SPLODGENESSABOUNDS** (69) 81
COZ I LUV YOU — **SLADE** (1).............................71
CRACKERS INTERNATIONAL (EP) — **ERASURE** (2) 88
CRACKIN' UP [A] — **Tommy HUNT** (39)..............75
CRACKIN' UP [B] — **Nick LOWE** (34)..................79
CRACKING UP — **JESUS AND MARY CHAIN** (35) 98
CRACKLIN' ROSIE — **Neil DIAMOND** (3) 70
CRADLE OF LOVE [A] — **Johnny PRESTON** (2) ..60
CRADLE OF LOVE [B] — **Billy IDOL** (34) 90
CRANK — **CATHERINE WHEEL** (66) 93
CRASH [A] — **PRIMITIVES** (5) 88
CRASH [B] — **FEEDER** (48) 97
CRASH AND BURN — **SAVAGE GARDEN** (14) 00
CRASH! BOOM! BANG! — **ROXETTE** (26) 94
CRASHIN' IN — **CHARLATANS** (31) 95
CRAWL — **HEADSWIM** (64) 95
CRAWLIN' BACK — **Roy ORBISON** (19) 65
CRAWLING — **LINKIN PARK** (16) 01
CRAWLING FROM THE WRECKAGE — **Dave EDMUNDS** (59).......................................79
CRAYZY MAN — **BLAST featuring VDC** (22) 94
CRAZY [A] — **MUD** (12) 73
CRAZY [B] — **MANHATTANS** (63) 83
CRAZY [C] — **ICEHOUSE** (38) 87,88
CRAZY [D] — **BOYS** (57) 90
CRAZY [E] — **Patsy CLINE** (14) 90
CRAZY [E] — **Julio IGLESIAS** (43) 94
CRAZY [E] — **LeAnn RIMES** (36) 99
CRAZY [F] — **SEAL** (2) 90
CRAZY [G] — **Bob GELDOF** (65) 94
CRAZY [H] — **AEROSMITH** (23) 94
CRAZY [I] — **ETERNAL** (15) 94
CRAZY [J] — **Mark MORRISON** (6) 95,96
CRAZY [K] — **NUT** (56) 96
CRAZY [L] — **AWESOME** (63) 98
CRAZY [M] — **MOFFATTS** (16) 99
CRAZY [N] — **LUCID** (14) 99
CRAZY [O] — **TOMCAT** (48)..................................00
CRAZY [P] — **K-CI & JOJO** (35)............................01
CRAZY CHANCE — **KAVANA** (16) 96,97
CRAZY CRAZY NIGHTS — **KISS** (4) 87
CRAZY CUTS — **GRANDMIXER DST** (71) 83,84
CRAZY DREAM — **Jim DALE** (24)..........................58
CRAZY (FOR ME) — **Freddie JACKSON** (41)........88
CRAZY FOR YOU [A] — **MADONNA** (2) 85,91
CRAZY FOR YOU [B] — **SYBIL** (71) 90
CRAZY FOR YOU [C] — **INCOGNITO** (59) 91
CRAZY FOR YOU [D] — **LET LOOSE** (2) 93,94
CRAZY HORSES — **OSMONDS** (2)............72,95,99
CRAZY LITTLE PARTY GIRL — **Aaron CARTER** (7) ..98
CRAZY LITTLE THING CALLED LOVE [A] — **QUEEN** (2) 79
CRAZY LITTLE THING CALLED LOVE [A] — **Dwight YOAKAM** (43) 99
CRAZY LOVE [A] — **Paul ANKA** (26) 58
CRAZY LOVE [B] — **Maxi PRIEST** (67) 86
CRAZY LOVE [C] — **Ce Ce PENISTON** (44)..........92
CRAZY LOVE [D] — **MJ COLE** (10) 00
CRAZY LOWDOWN WAYS — **OCEAN COLOUR SCENE** (64) 01
THE CRAZY OTTO RAG — **STARGAZERS** (18)......55
THE CRAZY PARTY MIXES — **JIVE BUNNY and the MASTERMIXERS** (13) 90
CRAZY TRAIN — **Ozzy OSBOURNE** (49) 80
CRAZY WATER — **Elton JOHN** (27) 77
CRAZY WORDS CRAZY TUNE — **Dorothy PROVINE** (45) 62
CRAZY YOU — **GUN** (21) 97
CREAM [A] — **PRINCE and the NEW POWER GENERATION** (15)........................91
CREAM [B] — **BLANK & JONES** (24) 99
CREAM (ALWAYS RISES TO THE TOP) — **Gregg DIAMOND BIONIC BOOGIE** (61)............79
CREATION — **STEREO MC's** (19) 93
CREATURES OF THE NIGHT — **KISS** (34) 83
CREDO — **FISH** (38) 92
THE CREEP [A] — **Ken MACKINTOSH** (10)..........54
CREEP [B] — **RADIOHEAD** (7) 93
CREEP [C] — **TLC** (6) 95,96
CREEQUE ALLEY — **MAMAS and the PAPAS** (9) 67
CREOLE JAZZ — **Mr Acker BILK and his PARAMOUNT JAZZ BAND** (22) 61
CRESCENT MOON — **Lynden David HALL** (45) ..98
CRIME OF PASSION — **Mike OLDFIELD** (61) 84
CRIMINALLY INSANE — **SLAYER** (64) 87
CRIMSON AND CLOVER — **Joan JETT and the BLACKHEARTS** (60) 82
CRISPY BACON — **Laurent GARNIER** (60)..........97
CRITICAL (IF YOU ONLY KNEW) — **WALL OF SOUND featuring Gerald LETHAN** (73) 93
CRITICIZE — **Alexander O'NEAL** (4) 87,98
CROCKETT'S THEME — **Jan HAMMER** (2)......87,91
CROCODILE ROCK — **Elton JOHN** (5) 72
CROCODILE SHOES — **Jimmy NAIL** (4)..........94,95
CROCODILES — **ECHO and the BUNNYMEN** (37)81
CROSS MY BROKEN HEART — **SINITTA** (6)........88
CROSS MY HEART — **EIGHTH WONDER** (13)......88
CROSS THAT BRIDGE — **WARD BROTHERS** (32)87
CROSS THE TRACK (WE BETTER GO BACK) — **MACEO & THE MACKS** (54)..........................87
CROSSROADS — **Tracy CHAPMAN** (61) 89
CROSSTOWN TRAFFIC — **Jimi HENDRIX EXPERIENCE** (37) 69,90
THE CROWD — **Roy ORBISON** (40)......................62
THE CROWN — **Gary BYRD and the GB EXPERIENCE** (6) 83
CRUCIAL — **NEW EDITION** (70) 89
CRUCIFIED — **ARMY OF LOVERS** (31)...........91,92
CRUCIFY — **Tori AMOS** (15) 92
CRUEL — **PUBLIC IMAGE LTD** (49) 92
THE CRUEL SEA — **DAKOTAS** (18) 63
CRUEL SUMMER [A] — **BANANARAMA** (8) 83,89
CRUEL SUMMER [A] — **ACE OF BASE** (8) 98
CRUEL TO BE KIND — **Nick LOWE** (12) 79
CRUISE INTO CHRISTMAS MEDLEY — **Jane McDONALD** (10) 98
CRUISIN' — **D'ANGELO** (31) 96
CRUISING — **SINITTA** (2)....................................86
THE CRUNCH — **RAH BAND** (6)..........................77
CRUSH [A] — **ZHANE** (44) 97
CRUSH [B] — **Jennifer PAIGE** (4) 98
CRUSH ME — **HOUSE OF LOVE** (67)...................92
CRUSH ON YOU [A] — **JETS** (5)..........................87
CRUSH ON YOU [A] — **Aaron CARTER** (9)..........97
CRUSH ON YOU [B] — **LIL' KIM** (23)...................97
CRUSH WITH EYELINER — **R.E.M.** (23) 95
CRUSHED BY THE WHEELS OF INDUSTRY — **HEAVEN 17** (17) 83
CRY [A] — **Gerry MONROE** (38)..........................70
CRY [B] — **GODLEY and CREME** (19) 85,86
CRY [C] — **WATERFRONT** (17) 89
CRY [D] — **SUNDAYS** (43) 97
CRY [E] — **SYSTEM F** (19) 00
CRY [F] — **Michael JACKSON** (25) 01
CRY AND BE FREE — **MARILYN** (31) 84
CRY BOY CRY — **BLUE ZOO** (13) 82
CRY DIGNITY — **DUB WAR** (59) 96
CRY FOR HELP [A] — **Rick ASTLEY** (7) 91
CRY FOR HELP [B] — **SHED SEVEN** (30) 01
CRY FOR ME — **ROACHFORD** (46) 94
CRY FOR THE NATIONS — **Michael SCHENKER GROUP** (56) 80
CRY FOR YOU — **JODECI** (20)........................93,95
CRY FREEDOM [A] — **George FENTON and Jonas GWANGWA** (75) ..88
CRY FREEDOM [B] — **MOMBASSA** (63).............97
CRY INDIA — **UMBOZA** (19) 95
CRY JUST A LITTLE BIT — **Shakin' STEVENS** (3)83
CRY LIKE A BABY — **BOX TOPS** (15)..................68
CRY ME A RIVER [A] — **Julie LONDON** (22)........57
CRY ME A RIVER [A] — **Mari WILSON** (27) 83
CRY ME A RIVER [A] — **Denise WELCH** (23) 95
CRY MY HEART — **David WHITFIELD** (22)..........58
CRY MYSELF TO SLEEP — **Del SHANNON** (29) ..62
CRY TO BE FOUND — **DEL AMITRI** (40) 98
CRY TO HEAVEN — **Elton JOHN** (47)..................86
CRY TO ME — **PRETTY THINGS** (28)...................65
CRY WOLF — **A-HA** (5) 86
CRYIN' [A] — **Roy ORBISON** (25).........................61
CRYING [A] — **Don McLEAN** (1) 80
CRYING [A] — **Roy ORBISON (duet with kd LANG)** (13) 92
CRYIN' [B] — **VIXEN** (27)......................................89
CRYIN' [C] — **AEROSMITH** (17) 93
CRYIN' IN THE RAIN — **EVERLY BROTHERS** (6) 62
CRYIN' MY HEART OUT FOR YOU — **Diana ROSS** (58) 81
CRYIN' TIME — **Ray CHARLES** (50)....................66
CRYING AT THE DISCOTHEQUE — **ALCAZAR** (13)01
THE CRYING GAME [A] — **Dave BERRY** (5) 64
THE CRYING GAME [A] — **BOY GEORGE** (22) 92
CRYING IN THE CHAPEL [A] — **Lee LAWRENCE** (7) 53
CRYING IN THE CHAPEL [A] — **Elvis PRESLEY** (1)...65,77
CRYING IN THE RAIN [A] — **A-HA** (13)................90
CRYING IN THE RAIN [B] — **CULTURE BEAT** (29)96
CRYING LAUGHING LOVING LYING — **Labi SIFFRE** (11)...72
CRYING OVER YOU — **Ken BOOTHE** (11)............74
THE CRYING SCENE — **AZTEC CAMERA** (70)......90
CRYPTIK SOULS CREW — **LEN** (28) 00
CRYSTAL — **NEW ORDER** (8) 01
CRYSTAL CLEAR — **GRID** (27) 93
C30, C60, C90, GO — **BOW WOW WOW** (34)....80
CUBA [A] — **GIBSON BROTHERS** (12)............79,80
CUBA [A] — **EL MARIACHI** (38) 96
CUBAN PETE — **Jim CARREY** (31) 95
CUBIK — **808 STATE** (10)..............................90,98
CUDDLY TOY — **ROACHFORD** (4) 88,89
THE CUFF OF MY SHIRT — **Guy MITCHELL** (9) ..54
CULT OF PERSONALITY — **LIVING COLOUR** (67) 91
CULT OF SNAP [A] — **HI POWER** (73) 90
CULT OF SNAP [A] — **SNAP** (8) 90
CUM ON FEEL THE NOIZE [A] — **SLADE** (1)........73
CUM ON FEEL THE NOIZE [A] — **QUIET RIOT** (45) 83
CUMBERLAND GAP [A] — **Lonnie DONEGAN** (1) 57
THE CUMBERLAND GAP [A] — **VIPERS SKIFFLE GROUP** (10) 57
THE CUP OF LIFE — **Ricky MARTIN** (29) 98
CUPBOARD LOVE — **John LEYTON** (22) 63
CUPID [A] — **Sam COOKE** (7) 61
CUPID [A] — **Johnny NASH** (6) 69
CUPID [B] — **JC 001** (56) 93
CUPID — I'VE LOVED YOU FOR A LONG TIME (MEDLEY) — **DETROIT SPINNERS** (4)....80
CURIOSITY — **JETS** (41)..87
CURIOUS — **LEVERT SWEAT GILL** (23) 98
CURLY — **MOVE** (12) 69
THE CURSE OF VOODOO RAY — **Lisa MAY** (64) 96
CUT CHEMIST SUITE — **OZOMATLI** (58) 99
CUT HERE — **CURE** (54) 01
CUT ME DOWN — **Lloyd COLE** (38) 86
CUT SOME RUG — **BLUETONES** (7) 96
CUT THE CAKE — **AVERAGE WHITE BAND** (31)..75
CUT YOUR HAIR — **PAVEMENT** (52) 94
A CUTE SWEET LOVE ADDICTION — **Johnny GILL** (46) 94
CUTS BOTH WAYS — **Gloria ESTEFAN** (49)........90
THE CUTTER — **ECHO and the BUNNYMEN** (8) 83
CUTTY SARK — **John BARRY ORCHESTRA** (35)..62
CYANIDE — **LURKERS** (72) 79
CYBELE'S REVERIE — **STEREOLAB** (62) 96
CYCLONE — **DUB PISTOLS** (63) 98
THE CYPHER: PART 3 — **Frankie CUTLASS** (59) 97
DA ANTIDOTE — **STANTON WARRIORS** (69) 01
DA DA DA — **TRIO** (2)..82
DA DOO RON RON — **CRYSTALS** (5) 63,74
DA-FORCE — **BEDLAM** (68)..................................99
DA FUNK — **DAFT PUNK** (7) 97
DA GOODNESS — **REDMAN** (52) 99
DA YA THINK I'M SEXY? [A] — **Rod STEWART** (1)...78,97
DA YA THINK I'M SEXY [A] — **REVOLTING COCKS** (61)...................................93
DA YA THINK I'M SEXY [A] — **N-TRANCE** (7)......97
D-A-A-ANCE — **LAMBRETTAS** (12).......................80
DADDY COOL [A] — **BONEY M** (6) 76,01
DADDY COOL — THE GIRL CAN'T HELP IT [B] — **DARTS** (6) 77
DADDY DON'T YOU WALK SO FAST — **Daniel BOONE** (17) 71
DADDY'S HOME — **Cliff RICHARD** (2) 81
DADDY'S LITTLE GIRL — **Nikki D** (75)................91
DAGENHAM DAVE — **MORRISSEY** (26)..............95
DAILY — **TQ** (14) 00
DALLIANCE — **WEDDING PRESENT** (29) 91
THE DAMBUSTERS MARCH — **The Central Band of the ROYAL AIR FORCE, Conductor W/Cdr AE SIMS OBE** (18) 55

DEADWEIGHT — BECK (23) ...97
DEAF FOREVER — MOTORHEAD (67) ...86
THE DEAL — Pat CAMPBELL (31) ...69
THE DEAN AND I — 10 CC (10) ...73
DEAR ADDY — Kid CREOLE and the COCONUTS (29) ...82
DEAR BOOPSIE — Pam HALL (54) ...86
DEAR DELILAH — GRAPEFRUIT (21) ...68
DEAR ELAINE — Roy WOOD (18) ...73
DEAR GOD — Midge URE (55) ...88
DEAR JESSIE [A] — MADONNA (5) ...89
DEAR JESSIE [A] — ROLLERGIRL (22) ...00
DEAR JOHN [A] — STATUS QUO (10) ...82
DEAR JOHN [B] — Eddi READER (48) ...94
DEAR LIE — TLC (32) ...99
DEAR LONELY HEARTS — Nat 'King' COLE (37) ...62
DEAR MAMA — 2PAC (27) ...99
DEAR MISS LONELY HEARTS — Philip LYNOTT (32) ...80
DEAR MRS APPLEBEE — David GARRICK (22) ...66
DEAR PRUDENCE — SIOUXSIE and the BANSHEES (3) ...83
DEATH DISCO — PUBLIC IMAGE LTD (20) ...79
DEATH OF A CLOWN — Dave DAVIES (3) ...67
DEBASER — PIXIES (23) ...97
DEBORA — T. REX (7) ...68,72
DECADENCE DANCE — EXTREME (36) ...91
THE DECEIVER — ALARM (51) ...84
DECEMBER — ALL ABOUT EVE (34) ...89
DECEMBER '63 (OH WHAT A NIGHT) — FOUR SEASONS (1) ...76,88
DECEMBER WILL BE MAGIC AGAIN — Kate BUSH (29) ...80
DECEPTION — FERGIE (47) ...00
DECK OF CARDS [A] — Max BYGRAVES (13) ...73
DECK OF CARDS [A] — Wink MARTINDALE (5) ...59,60,63,73
DEDICATED FOLLOWER OF FASHION — KINKS (4) ...66
DEDICATED TO THE ONE I LOVE [A] — MAMAS and the PAPAS (2) ...67
DEDICATED TO THE ONE I LOVE [A] — Bitty McLEAN (6) ...94
DEDICATION — THIN LIZZY (35) ...91
DEEE-LITE THEME — DEEE-LITE (25) ...90
DEEP — EAST 17 (5) ...93
THE DEEP — GLOBAL COMMUNICATION (51) ...97
DEEP AND WIDE AND TALL — AZTEC CAMERA (55) ...88
DEEP DOWN & DIRTY — STEREO MC's (17) ...01
DEEP DEEP DOWN — HEPBURN (16) ...00
DEEP DEEP TROUBLE — SIMPSONS (7) ...91
DEEP FEELING — Mike SAGAR (44) ...60
DEEP FOREST — DEEP FOREST (20) ...94
DEEP HEAT '89 — VARIOUS ARTISTS (MONTAGES) (12) ...89
DEEP (I'M FALLING DEEPER) — ARIEL (47) ...97
DEEP IN MY HEART — CLUBHOUSE (55) ...91
DEEP IN THE HEART OF TEXAS — Duane EDDY and the REBELS (19) ...62
DEEP IN YOU — LIVIN' JOY (17) ...97
DEEP INSIDE — Mary J BLIGE (42) ...99
DEEP MENACE (SPANK) — D'MENACE (20) ...98
DEEP PURPLE [A] — Billy WARD and HIS DOMINOES (30) ...57
DEEP PURPLE [A] — Nino TEMPO and April STEVENS (17) ...63
DEEP PURPLE [A] — Donny and Marie OSMOND (25) ...76
DEEP RIVER WOMAN — Lionel RICHIE (17) ...86
DEEP SHAG — LUSCIOUS JACKSON (69) ...95
DEEPER [A] — ESCRIMA (27) ...95
DEEPER [B] — DELIRIOUS? (20) ...97
DEEPER [C] — SERIOUS DANGER (40) ...97
DEEPER (EP) — DELIRIOUS? (36) ...97
DEEPER AND DEEPER [A] — Freda PAYNE (33) 70
DEEPER AND DEEPER [B] — MADONNA (6) ...92
DEEPER LOVE — RUFF DRIVERZ (19) ...98
A DEEPER LOVE [A] — Aretha FRANKLIN (5) ...94
A DEEPER LOVE [A] — C & C MUSIC FACTORY / CLIVILLES & COLE (15) ...92
DEEPER LOVE (SYMPHONIC PARADISE) — BBE (19) ...98
DEEPER SHADE OF BLUE — STEPS (4) ...00
DEEPER THAN THE NIGHT — Olivia NEWTON-JOHN (64) ...79
THE DEEPER THE LOVE — WHITESNAKE (35) ..90
DEEPER UNDERGROUND — JAMIROQUAI (1) ...98
DEEPLY DIPPY — RIGHT SAID FRED (1) ...92
DEF CON ONE — POP WILL EAT ITSELF (63) ...88
DEFINITE DOOR — POSIES (67) ...94
DEGREES — Ian POOLEY (57) ...01
DEJA VU — E-SMOOVE featuring Latanza WATERS (63) ..98
DEJA VU (UPTOWN BABY) — LORD TARIQ and Peter GUNZ (21) ...98
DELAWARE — Perry COMO (3) ...60
DELICATE — Terence Trent D'ARBY featuring DES'REE (14) ..93
DELICIOUS [A] — CATHERINE WHEEL (53) ...97
DELICIOUS [B] — KULAY (73) ...98
DELICIOUS [C] — Deni HINES featuring DON-E (52) ...98
DELICIOUS [D] — PURE SUGAR (70) ...98
DELICIOUS [E] — SLEEPER (75) ...94
DELICIOUS [F] — SHAMPOO (21) ...95
DELILAH [A] — Tom JONES (2) ...68,92
DELILAH [A] — SENSATIONAL Alex HARVEY BAND (7) ...75
DELILAH JONES — McGUIRE SISTERS (24) ...56
DELIVER ME — SISTER BLISS (31) ...01
DELIVERANCE — MISSION (27) ...90
DELIVERING THE GOODS — SKID ROW (22) ...92
DELLA AND THE DEALER — Hoyt AXTON (48) ..80
DELTA LADY — Joe COCKER (10) ...69
DELTA SUN BOTTLENECK STOMP — MERCURY REV (26) ...99
DEMOCRACY — KILLING JOKE (39) ...96
DEMOLITION MAN — STING (21) ...93
DEMONS [A] — SUPER FURRY ANIMALS (27) ...97
DEMONS [B] — FATBOY SLIM featuring Macy GRAY (16) ...01
DENIS — BLONDIE (2) ...78,88
DENISE — FOUNTAINS OF WAYNE (57) ...99
DER KOMMISSAR — AFTER THE FIRE (47) ...83
DER SCHIEBER — Timo MAAS (50) ...00
DESAFINADO [A] — Ella FITZGERALD (38) ...62
DESAFINADO [A] — Stan GETZ (11) ...62
DESERT DROUGHT — CAST (45) ...01
DESERT SONG — STING (15) ...00
DESIDERATA — Les CRANE (7) ...72
A DESIGN FOR LIFE — MANIC STREET PREACHERS (2) ...96
DESIRE [A] — U2 (1) ...88
DESIRE [B] — NU COLOURS (31) ...96
DESIRE [C] — BBE (19) ...98
DESIRE [D] — DJ ERIC (67) ...00
DESIRE [E] — Ultra NATE (40) ...00
DESIRE LINES — LUSH (60) ...94
DESIRE ME — DOLL (28) ...79
DESIREE — Neil DIAMOND (39) ...77
DESPERATE BUT NOT SERIOUS — Adam ANT (33) ...82
DESPERATE DAN — LIEUTENANT PIGEON (17) ..72
THE DESPERATE HOURS — Marc ALMOND (45) ...90
DESTINATION ESCHATON — SHAMEN (15) ...95
DESTINATION SUNSHINE — BALEARIC BILL (36) ..99
DESTINATION VENUS — REZILLOS (43) ...78
DESTINATION ZULULAND — KING KURT (36) ...83
DESTINY [A] — Anne MURRAY (41) ...72
DESTINY [B] — Candi STATON (41) ...76
DESTINY [C] — JACKSONS (39) ...79
DESTINY [D] — BABY D (69) ...93
DESTINY [E] — Kenny THOMAS (59) ...94
DESTINY [F] — DEM 2 (58) ...98
DESTINY [G] — ZERO 7 featuring SIA and SOPHIE (30) ...01
DESTINY CALLING — JAMES (17) ...98
DETROIT — WHITEOUT (73) ...94
DETROIT CITY — Tom JONES (8) ...67
DEUS — SUGARCUBES (51) ...88
DEUTSCHER GIRLS — ADAM and the ANTS (13)82
DEVIL — 666 (18) ...00
DEVIL GATE DRIVE — Suzi QUATRO (1) ...74
DEVIL IN YOUR SHOES (WALKING ALL OVER) — SHED SEVEN (37) ...98
DEVIL INSIDE — INXS (47) ...88
DEVIL OR ANGEL — Billy FURY (58) ...82
THE DEVIL WENT DOWN TO GEORGIA — Charlie DANIELS BAND (14) ...79
DEVIL WOMAN [A] — Marty ROBBINS (5) ...62
DEVIL WOMAN [B] — Cliff RICHARD (9) ...76
THE DEVIL YOU KNOW — JESUS JONES (10) ...93
THE DEVIL'S ANSWER — ATOMIC ROOSTER (4) 71
DEVIL'S BALL — DOUBLE (71) ...87
DEVIL'S GUN — CJ & CO (43) ...77
DEVIL'S HAIRCUT — BECK (22) ...96
DEVIL'S NIGHTMARE — OXIDE & NEUTRINO (16) ...01
DEVIL'S TOY — ALMIGHTY (36) ...91
DEVIL'S TRILL — VANESSA-MAE (53) ...98
DEVOTED TO YOU — CACIQUE (69) ...85
DEVOTION [A] — TEN CITY (29) ...89
DEVOTION [B] — KICKING BACK with TAXMAN (47) ...90
DEVOTION [C] — David HOLMES (66) ...01
DIABLO — GRID (32) ...95
DIAL MY HEART — BOYS (61) ...88
DIABLA — FUNK D'VOID (70) ...01
DIAMANTE — ZUCCHERO with Randy CRAWFORD (44) ...92
DIAMOND BACK — MEKKA (67) ...01
DIAMOND DEW — GORKY'S ZYGOTIC MYNCI (42) ...97
DIAMOND DOGS — David BOWIE (21) ...74
DIAMOND GIRL — Pete WYLIE (57) ...86
DIAMOND LIGHTS — GLENN and CHRIS (12) ...87
DIAMOND SMILES — BOOMTOWN RATS (13) ...79
DIAMONDS [A] — Jet HARRIS and Tony MEEHAN (1) ...63
DIAMONDS [B] — Chris REA (44) ...79
DIAMONDS [C] — Herb ALPERT (27) ...87
DIAMONDS AND PEARLS — PRINCE and the NEW POWER GENERATION (25) ...91
DIAMONDS ARE FOREVER [A] — David McALMONT (39) ...97
DIAMONDS ARE FOREVER [A] — Shirley BASSEY (38) ...72
DIANA — Paul ANKA (1) ...57
DIANE [A] — BACHELORS (1) ...64
DIANE [B] — THERAPY? (26) ...95
DIARY OF A WIMP — SPACE (49) ...00
THE DIARY OF HORACE WIMP — ELECTRIC LIGHT ORCHESTRA (8) ...79
DICK-A-DUM-DUM (KING'S ROAD) — Des O'CONNOR (14) ...69
DID IT AGAIN — Kylie MINOGUE (14) ...97
DID YOU EVER — Nancy SINATRA (2) ...71
DID YOU EVER REALLY LOVE ME — Nicki FRENCH (55) ...95
DID YOU EVER THINK — R KELLY (20) ...99
DID YOU HAVE TO LOVE ME LIKE YOU DID — COCONUTS (60) ...83
DIDN'T I (BLOW YOUR MIND THIS TIME) [A] — DELFONICS (22) ...71
DIDN'T I BLOW YOUR MIND [A] — NEW KIDS ON THE BLOCK (8) ...90
DIDN'T I TELL YOU TRUE — Thomas JULES-STOCK (59) ...98
DIDN'T WE ALMOST HAVE IT ALL — Whitney HOUSTON (14) ...87
DIE LAUGHING — THERAPY? (29) ...94
DIE YOUNG — BLACK SABBATH (41) ...80
DIFFERENT AIR — LIVING IN A BOX (57) ...89,90
A DIFFERENT BEAT — BOYZONE (1) ...96,97
A DIFFERENT CORNER — George MICHAEL (1) ..86
DIFFERENT STORY — BOWA featuring MALA (64) 91
DIFFERENT STROKES — ISOTONIK (12) ...92
DIFFERENT TIME DIFFERENT PLACE — Julia FORDHAM (41) ...94
DIG FOR FIRE — PIXIES (62) ...90
DIGERIDOO — APHEX TWIN (55) ...92
DIGGI LOO-DIGGI LEY — HERREYS (46) ...84
DIGGIN' MY POTATOES — HEINZ (49) ...65
DIGGIN' ON YOU — TLC (18) ...95
DIGGING IN THE DIRT — Peter GABRIEL (24) ...92
DIGGING THE GRAVE — FAITH NO MORE (16) ..95
DIGGING YOUR SCENE — BLOW MONKEYS (12)86
DIGITAL — GOLDIE featuring KRS ONE (13) ...97
DIGITAL LOVE, — DAFT PUNK (14) ...01
DIGNITY [A] — DEACON BLUE (20) ...88,94
DIGNITY [B] — Bob DYLAN (33) ...95
DIL CHEEZ (MY HEART...) — Bally SAGOO (12) ..96

DIM ALL THE LIGHTS — **Donna SUMMER** (29) ..79
A DIME AND A DOLLAR — **Guy MITCHELL** (8) ..54
DIMENSION — **SALT TANK** (52) ..99
DIMPLES — **John Lee HOOKER** (23) ..64
DIN DA DA — **Kevin AVIANCE** (65) ..98
DINAH — **BLACKNUSS** (56) ..97
DING DONG — **George HARRISON** (38) ..74
DING-A-DONG — **TEACH-IN** (13) ..75
DINNER WITH DELORES — **PRINCE** (36) ..96
DINNER WITH GERSHWIN — **Donna SUMMER** (13) 87
DIPPETY DAY — **SMURFS** (13) ..78
DIRECT-ME — **REESE PROJECT** (44) ..95
DIRGE — **DEATH IN VEGAS** (24) ..00
DIRT — **DEATH IN VEGAS** (61) ..97
DIRTY BEATS — **Roni SIZE / REPRAZENT** (32) ..01
DIRTY CASH — **ADVENTURES OF STEVIE V** (2) ..90,97
DIRTY DAWG — **NEW KIDS ON THE BLOCK** (27) 94
DIRTY DEEDS — **Joan JETT and the BLACKHEARTS** (69) ..90
DIRTY DEEDS DONE DIRT CHEAP — **AC/DC** (47) 80,93
DIRTY DIANA — **Michael JACKSON** (4) ..88
DIRTY LAUNDRY — **Don HENLEY** (59) ..83
DIRTY LOOKS — **Diana ROSS** (49) ..87
DIRTY LOVE — **THUNDER** (32) ..90
DIRTY MIND — **SHAKESPEAR'S SISTER** (71) ..90
DIRTY MONEY — **Dee FREDRIX** (74) ..93
DIRTY MOTHA — **QWILO and FELIX DA HOUSECAT** (66) ..97
DIRTY OLD TOWN — **POGUES** (62) ..85
DIRTY WATER — **MADE IN LONDON** (15) ..00
DISAPPEAR — **INXS** (21) ..90
DISAPPEARING ACT — **SHALAMAR** (18) ..83
DISAPPOINTED [A] — **PUBLIC IMAGE LTD** (38) ..89
DISAPPOINTED [B] — **ELECTRONIC** (6) ..92
THE DISAPPOINTED — **XTC** (33) ..92
DISARM — **SMASHING PUMPKINS** (11) ..94
DISCIPLINE OF LOVE — **Robert PALMER** (68) ..86
D.I.S.C.O. [A] — **OTTAWAN** (2) ..80
D.I.S.C.O. [A] — **N-TRANCE** (11) ..97
DISCO BABES FROM OUTER SPACE — **BABE INSTINCT** (21) ..99
DISCO BEATLEMANIA — **DBM** (45) ..77
DISCO CONNECTION — **Isaac HAYES** (10) ..76
DISCO COP — **BLUE ADONIS featuring LIL' MISS MAX** (27) ..98
DISCO DOWN [A] — **SHED SEVEN** (13) ..99
DISCO DOWN [B] — **HOUSE OF GLASS** (72) ..01
DISCO DUCK (PART ONE) — **Rick DEES and his CAST OF IDIOTS** (6) ..76
DISCO INFERNO [A] — **TRAMMPS** (16) ..77,78
DISCO INFERNO [A] — **Tina TURNER** (12) ..93
'DISCO' LA PASSIONE — **Chris REA and Shirley BASSEY** (41) ..96
DISCO LADY — **Johnnie TAYLOR** (25) ..76
DISCO MACHINE GUN — **LO FIDELITY ALLSTARS** (50) ..97
DISCO MUSIC (I LIKE IT) — **JALN BAND** (21) ..76
DISCO NIGHTS (ROCK FREAK) — **GQ** (42) ..79
DISCO QUEEN — **HOT CHOCOLATE** (11) ..75
DISCO SCIENCE — **MIRWAIS** (68) ..00
DISCO STOMP — **Hamilton BOHANNON** (6) ..75
DISCO 2000 — **PULP** (7) ..95
DISCOBUG '97 — **FREAKYMAN** (68) ..97
DISCOHOPPING — **KLUBBHEADS** (35) ..97
DISCONNECT — **ROLLINS BAND** (27) ..94
DISCO'S REVENGE — **GUSTO** (9) ..96
DISCOTHEQUE — **U2** (1) ..97
DISCRETION GLOVE — **Stephen MALKMUS** (60) 01
DISENCHANTED — **COMMUNARDS** (29) ..86
DISILLUSION — **BADLY DRAWN BOY** (26) ..00
DIS-INFECTED (EP) — **The THE** (17) ..94
DISPOSABLE TEENS — **MARILYN MANSON** (12) 00
DISREMEMBRANCE — **Dannii MINOGUE** (21) ..98
DISSIDENT — **PEARL JAM** (14) ..94
THE DISTANCE — **CAKE** (22) ..97
DISTANT DRUMS — **Jim REEVES** (1) ..66
DISTANT STAR — **Anthony HOPKINS** (75) ..86
DISTANT SUN — **CROWDED HOUSE** (19) ..93
DIVA — **DANA INTERNATIONAL** (11) ..98
DIVE! DIVE! DIVE! — **Bruce DICKINSON** (45) ..90
DIVE IN — **CATCH** (44) ..98
DIVE TO PARADISE — **EUROGROOVE** (31) ..95
DIVEBOMB — **NUMBER ONE CUP** (61) ..96
DIVINE EMOTIONS — **Narada Michael WALDEN** (8) 88
DIVINE HAMMER — **BREEDERS** (59) ..93
DIVINE THING — **SOUP DRAGONS** (53) ..92
DIVING FACES — **LIQUID CHILD** (25) ..99
D.I.V.O.R.C.E. [A] — **Tammy WYNETTE** (12) ..75
D.I.V.O.R.C.E. [A] — **Billy CONNOLLY** (1) ..75
DIXIE-NARCO (EP) — **PRIMAL SCREAM** (11) ..92
DIZZY [A] — **Tommy ROE** (1) ..69
DIZZY [A] — **Vic REEVES and the WONDER STUFF** (1) ..91
DJ [A] — **David BOWIE** (29) ..79
DJ [A] — **RESONANCE featuring The BURRELLS** (67) ..01
DJ CULTURE — **PET SHOP BOYS** (13) ..91
DJ SPINNIN' — **PUNK CHIC** (69) ..01
DJS TAKE CONTROL — **SL2** (11) ..91,92
DK 50-80 — **John OTWAY and Wild Willy BARRETT** (45) ..80
DO ANYTHING — **NATURAL SELECTION** (69) ..91
DO ANYTHING YOU WANNA DO — **EDDIE and the HOT RODS** (9) ..77
DO ANYTHING YOU WANT TO — **THIN LIZZY** (14) 79
DO FOR LOVE — **2PAC** (12) ..98
DO FRIES GO WITH THAT SHAKE — **George CLINTON** (57) ..86
DO I — **GIFTED** (60) ..97
DO I DO — **Stevie WONDER** (10) ..82
DO I HAVE TO SAY THE WORDS — **Bryan ADAMS** (30) ..92
DO I LOVE YOU — **RONETTES** (35) ..64
DO I QUALIFY? — **Lynden David HALL** (26) ..98
DO IT — **Tony DI BART** (21) ..94
DO IT AGAIN [A] — **BEACH BOYS** (1) ..68,91
DO IT AGAIN [B] — **STEELY DAN** (39) ..75
DO IT AGAIN - BILLIE JEAN (MEDLEY) — **CLUBHOUSE** (11) ..83
DO IT ANYWAY YOU WANNA — **PEOPLES CHOICE** (36) ..75
DO IT DO IT AGAIN — **Raffaella CARRA** (9) ..78
DO IT FOR LOVE [A] — **Danni'elle GAHA** (52) ..93
DO IT FOR LOVE [B] — **SUBTERRANIA featuring Ann CONSUELO** (68) 93
DO IT FOR LOVE [C] — **4MANDU** (45) ..96
DO IT NOW — **BRAIN BASHERS** (64) ..00
DO IT PROPERLY ('NO WAY BACK') / NO WAY BACK — **ADONIS featuring 2 PUERTO RICANS, A BLACK MAN AND A DOMINICAN** (47) ..87
DO IT TO ME — **Lionel RICHIE** (33) ..92
DO IT TO ME AGAIN — **SOULSEARCHER** (32) ..00
DO IT TO THE CROWD — **TWIN HYPE** (65) ..89
DO IT TO THE MUSIC — **RAW SILK** (18) ..82
DO ME — **BELL BIV DEVOE** (56) ..90
DO ME RIGHT — **INNER CITY** (47) ..96
DO MY THING — **Busta RHYMES** (39) ..97
DO NOT DISTURB — **BANANARAMA** (31) ..85
DO NOT PASS ME BY — **HAMMER** (14) ..92
DO NOTHING — **SPECIALS** (4) ..80
DO OR DIE — **SUPER FURRY ANIMALS** (20) ..00
DO RE ME SO FAR SO GOOD — **CARTER — THE UNSTOPPABLE SEX MACHINE** (22) ..92
DO SOMETHING — **Macy GRAY** (51) ..99
DO THAT TO ME — **LISA MARIE EXPERIENCE** (33) 96
DO THAT TO ME ONE MORE TIME — **CAPTAIN and TENNILLE** (7) ..80
DO THE BARTMAN — **SIMPSONS** (1) ..91
DO THE BIRD [A] — **Dee Dee SHARP** (46) ..63
DO THE BIRD [A] — **VERNONS GIRLS** (44) ..63
DO THE CLAM — **Elvis PRESLEY** (19) ..65
DO THE CONGA — **BLACK LACE** (10) ..84
DO THE FUNKY CHICKEN — **Rufus THOMAS** (18) ..70
(DO) THE HUCKLEBUCK — **COAST TO COAST** (5) ..81
DO THE LOLLIPOP — **TWEENIES** (17) ..01
DO THE RIGHT THING [A] — **REDHEAD KINGPIN and the FBI** (13) ..89
DO THE RIGHT THING [B] — **Ian WRIGHT** (43) ..93
(DO THE) SPANISH HUSTLE — **FATBACK BAND** (10) ..76
DO THEY KNOW IT'S CHRISTMAS? — **BAND AID** (1) ..84,85,89
DO THIS MY WAY — **KID 'N' PLAY** (48) ..88
DO U FEEL 4 ME — **EDEN** (51) ..93
DO U KNOW WHERE YOU'RE COMING FROM — **M-BEAT featuring JAMIROQUAI** (12) ..96
DO U STILL — **EAST 17** (7) ..96
DO U WANNA FUNK — **SPACE 2000** (50) ..95
DO WAH DIDDY DIDDY [A] — **MANFRED MANN** (1) 64
DO WAH DIDDY DIDDY [A] — **BLUE MELONS** (70) 96
DO WAH DIDDY [A] — **DJ OTZI** (9) ..01
DO WATCHA DO — **HYPER GO GO and ADEVA** (54) ..96,97
DO WE ROCK — **POINT BREAK** (29) ..99
DO WHAT YOU DO [A] — **Jermaine JACKSON** (6) 85
DO WHAT YOU DO [B] — **Annabella LWIN** (61) 95
DO WHAT YOU DO DO WELL — **Ned MILLER** (48) 65
DO WHAT YOU DO (EARWORM SONG) — **Clint BOON EXPERIENCE** (63) ..00
DO WHAT YOU FEEL [A] — **Joey NEGRO** (36) ..91
DO WHAT YOU FEEL [B] — **JOHNNA** (43) ..96
DO WHAT YOU GOTTA DO [A] — **FOUR TOPS** (11) 69
DO WHAT YOU GOTTA DO [A] — **Nina SIMONE** (2) ..68
DO WHAT YOU WANNA DO — **T-CONNECTION** (11) ..77
DO WHAT WE WOULD — **ACZESS** (65) ..01
DO WHAT'S GOOD FOR ME — **2 UNLIMITED** (16) 95
DO YA — **INNER CITY** (44) ..94
DO YA DO YA (WANNA PLEASE ME) — **Samantha FOX** (10) ..86
DO YA WANNA GET FUNKY WITH ME — **Peter BROWN** (43) ..78
DO YOU BELIEVE IN LOVE [A] — **Huey LEWIS and the NEWS** (9) ..86
DO YOU BELIEVE IN LOVE [B] — **UNATION** (75) 93
DO YOU BELIEVE IN LOVE [C] — **ULTRA-SONIC** (47) ..96
DO YOU BELIEVE IN MIRACLES — **SLADE** (54) ..85
DO YOU BELIEVE IN SHAME — **DURAN DURAN** (30) ..89
DO YOU BELIEVE IN THE WESTWORLD — **THEATRE OF HATE** (40) ..82
DO YOU BELIEVE IN THE WONDER — **Jeanie TRACY** (57) ..94
DO YOU BELIEVE IN US — **Jon SECADA** (30) ..92
DO YOU DREAM IN COLOUR? — **Bill NELSON** (52) 80
DO YOU FEEL LIKE I FEEL — **Belinda CARLISLE** (29) ..91
DO YOU FEEL LIKE WE DO — **Peter FRAMPTON** (39) ..76
DO YOU FEEL ME? (...FREAK YOU) — **MEN OF VIZION** (36) ..99
DO YOU FEEL MY LOVE [A] — **Eddy GRANT** (8) ..80,83
DO YOU KNOW [A] — **SECRET AFFAIR** (57) ..81
DO YOU KNOW [B] — **Michelle GAYLE** (6) ..97
DO YOU KNOW THE WAY TO SAN JOSE — **Dionne WARWICK** (8) ..68
DO YOU KNOW (WHAT IT TAKES) — **ROBYN** (26) 97
DO YOU LIKE IT — **KINGDOM COME** (73) ..89
DO YOU LOVE ME [A] — **Brian POOLE and the TREMELOES** (1) ..63
DO YOU LOVE ME [A] — **Dave CLARK FIVE** (30) 63
DO YOU LOVE ME [A] — **DEEP FEELING** (34) ..70
DO YOU LOVE ME [A] — **DUKE BAYSEE** (46) ..95
DO YOU LOVE ME [A] — **MADEMOISELLE** (56) ..01
DO YOU LOVE ME [B] — **Nick CAVE and the BAD SEEDS** (68) ..94
DO YOU LOVE ME BOY? — **KERRI-ANN** (58) ..98
DO YOU LOVE ME LIKE YOU SAY — **Terence Trent D'ARBY** (14) ..93
DO YOU LOVE WHAT YOU FEEL — **INNER CITY** (16) ..89
DO YOU MIND — **Anthony NEWLEY** (1) ..60
DO YOU REALLY LIKE IT — **DJ PIED PIPER and the MASTERS OF CEREMONIES** (1) ..01
(DO YOU REALLY LOVE ME) TELL ME LOVE — **Michael WYCOFF** (60) ..83
DO YOU REALLY LOVE ME TOO — **Billy FURY** (13) 64
DO YOU REALLY WANT ME [A] — **Jon SECADA** (30) ..93
DO YOU REALLY WANT ME [B] — **ROBYN** (20) ..98
DO YOU REALLY (WANT MY LOVE) — **JUNIOR** (47) 85
DO YOU REALLY WANT TO HURT ME — **CULTURE CLUB** (1) ..82
DO YOU REMEMBER — **SCAFFOLD** (34) ..68
DO YOU REMEMBER (LIVE) — **Phil COLLINS** (57) 90
DO YOU REMEMBER ROCK 'N' ROLL RADIO? — **RAMONES** (54) ..80
DO YOU REMEMBER THE FIRST TIME — **PULP** (33) ..94,96
DO YOU SEE — **Warren G** (29) ..95
DO YOU SEE THE LIGHT (LOOKING FOR) — **SNAP** (10) ..93
DO YOU SLEEP? — **Lisa LOEB and NINE STORIES** (45) ..95
DO YOU THINK ABOUT US — **TOTAL** (49) ..97
DO YOU UNDERSTAND — **ALMIGHTY** (38) ..96
DO YOU WANNA DANCE — **Barry BLUE** (7) ..73
DO YOU WANNA FUNK — **SYLVESTER** (32) ..82
DO YOU WANNA GET FUNKY — **C & C MUSIC FACTORY / CLIVILLES & COLE** (27) ..94
DO YOU WANNA GO OUR WAY??? — **PUBLIC ENEMY** (66) ..99

FAITH CAN MOVE MOUNTAINS [A] – **Johnnie RAY and the FOUR LADS** (7)........52,53
FAITH CAN MOVE MOUNTAINS [A] – **Jimmy YOUNG** (11)........53
FAITH CAN MOVE MOUNTAINS [A] – **Nat 'King' COLE** (10)........53
FAITH HEALER – **RECOIL** (60)........92
FAITH (IN THE POWER OF LOVE) – **ROZALLA** (11)........91
FAITH OF THE HEART – **Rod STEWART** (60)........99
FAITHFUL – **GO WEST** (13)........92
THE FAITHFUL HUSSAR (DON'T CRY MY LOVE) [A] – **Vera LYNN** (29)........57
THE FAITHFUL HUSSAR [A] – **Louis ARMSTRONG** (27)........56
THE FAITHFUL HUSSAR [A] – **Ted HEATH** (18)..56
FAITHLESS – **SCRITTI POLITTI** (56)........82
FAKE – **Alexander O'NEAL** (16)........87,88
FAKE FUR – **URUSEI YATSURA** (58)........97
FAKE PLASTIC TREES – **RADIOHEAD** (20)........95
FAKER – **AUDIOWEB** (70)........97
FALCON – **RAH BAND** (35)........80
FALL (EP) – **RIDE** (34)........90
THE FALL [A] – **MINISTRY** (53)........96
THE FALL [B] – **WAY OUT WEST** (61)........00
FALL AT YOUR FEET – **CROWDED HOUSE** (17)..91
FALL DOWN (SPIRIT OF LOVE) – **TRAMAINE** (60)85
FALL FROM GRACE – **ESKIMOS & EGYPT** (51)..93
FALL IN LOVE WITH ME [A] – **EARTH WIND AND FIRE** (47)........83
FALL IN LOVE WITH ME [B] – **BOOTH and the BAD ANGEL** (57)........98
FALL IN LOVE WITH YOU – **Cliff RICHARD and the SHADOWS** (2)........60
FALL OUT – **POLICE** (47)........79
FALL TO LOVE – **DIESEL PARK WEST** (48)........92
FALLEN ANGEL [A] – **Frankie VALLI** (11)........76
FALLEN ANGEL [B] – **POISON** (59)........88
FALLEN ANGEL [C] – **Traci LORDS** (72)........95
FALLEN ANGELS – **Buffy SAINTE-MARIE** (57)....92
FALLIN' [A] – **Connie FRANCIS** (20)........58
FALLIN' [B] – **TEENAGE FANCLUB and DE LA SOUL** (59)....94
FALLIN' [C] – **Alicia KEYS** (3)........01
FALLIN' IN LOVE – **HAMILTON, Joe FRANK and REYNOLDS** (33)..75
FALLING [A] – **Roy ORBISON** (9)........63
FALLING [B] – **Julee CRUISE** (7)........90
FALLING [C] – **Cathy DENNIS** (32)........93
FALLING [D] – **Alison MOYET** (42)........93
FALLING [E] – **ANT & DEC** (14)........97
FALLING [F] – **BOOM!** (11)........01
FALLING ANGELS RIDING – **David ESSEX** (29)..85
FALLING APART AT THE SEAMS – **MARMALADE** (9)........76
FALLING AWAY FROM ME – **KORN** (24)........00
FALLING IN AND OUT OF LOVE – **FEMME FATALE** (69)........89
FALLING IN LOVE [A] – **SURFACE** (67)........83
FALLING IN LOVE [B] – **SYBIL** (68)........86
FALLING IN LOVE [C] – **LA BOUCHE** (43)........95
FALLING IN LOVE AGAIN [A] – **TECHNO TWINS** (70)........82
FALLING IN LOVE AGAIN [B] – **Eagle-Eye CHERRY** (8)........98
FALLING IN LOVE (IS HARD ON THE KNEES) – **AEROSMITH** (22)........97
FALLING INTO YOU – **Celine DION** (10)........96
FALLING TO PIECES – **FAITH NO MORE** (41)....90
FAME [A] – **David BOWIE** (17)........75,90
FAME [B] – **Irene CARA** (1)........82
FAMILIUS HORRIBILUS – **POP WILL EAT ITSELF** (27)........93
FAMILY AFFAIR [A] – **SLY and the FAMILY STONE** (15)........72
FAMILY AFFAIR [A] – **BEF featuring Lalah HATHAWAY** (37)........91
FAMILY AFFAIR [A] – **Shabba RANKS featuring PATRA and TERRI & MONICA** (18)........93
FAMILY AFFAIR [B] – **Mary J BLIGE** (8)........01
FAMILY MAN [A] – **Mike OLDFIELD** (45)........82
FAMILY MAN [A] – **Daryl HALL and John OATES** (15)........83
FAMILY MAN [B] – **FLEETWOOD MAC** (54)........87
FAMILY MAN [C] – **ROACHFORD** (25)........89
FAMILY OF MAN – **FARM** (58)........90
FAMINE – **Sinead O'CONNOR** (51)........95
FAN MAIL – **DICKIES** (57)........80
FAN THE FLAME – **Barbara PENNINGTON** (62) 85
FANCY PANTS – **KENNY** (4)........75
FAN'DABI'DOZI – **KRANKIES** (46)........81
FANFARE FOR THE COMMON MAN – **EMERSON, LAKE and PALMER** (2)........77
FANLIGHT FANNY – **Clinton FORD** (22)........62
FANTASTIC DAY – **HAIRCUT 100** (9)........82
FANTASTIC VOYAGE – **COOLIO** (41)........94
FANTASY [A] – **EARTH WIND AND FIRE** (14)......78
FANTASY [A] – **BLACK BOX** (5)........90
FANTASY [B] – **Gerard KENNY** (34)........80
FANTASY [C] – **FANTASY UFO** (56)........90
FANTASY [D] – **TEN CITY** (45)........93
FANTASY [E] – **Mariah CAREY** (4)........95
FANTASY [F] – **LEVELLERS** (16)........95
FANTASY ISLAND [A] – **TIGHT FIT** (5)........82
FANTASY ISLAND [B] – **M PEOPLE** (33)......97,98
FANTASY REAL – **Phil FEARON** (41)........83
FAR – **LONGPIGS** (37)........96
FAR ABOVE THE CLOUDS – **Mike OLDFIELD** (53)99
FAR AND AWAY – **AIDA** (58)........00
FAR AWAY – **Shirley BASSEY** (24)........62
FAR FAR AWAY – **SLADE** (2)........74
FAR FROM HOME – **LEVELLERS** (71)........91
FAR FROM OVER – **Frank STALLONE** (68)........83
FAR GONE AND OUT – **JESUS AND MARY CHAIN** (23)........92
FAR OUT [A] – **SON'Z OF A LOOP DA LOOP ERA** (36)........92
FAR OUT [B] – **DEEJAY PUNK-ROC** (43)........98
FAR-OUT SON OF LUNG AND THE RAMBLINGS OF A MADMAN – **FUTURE SOUND OF LONDON** (22)95
FARAWAY EYES – **ROLLING STONES** (3)........78
FARAWAY PLACES – **BACHELORS** (36)........63
FAREWELL – **Rod STEWART** (7)........74
FAREWELL ANGELINA – **Joan BAEZ** (35)......65,66
FAREWELL IS A LONELY SOUND – **Jimmy RUFFIN** (8)........70,74
FAREWELL MR SORROW – **ALL ABOUT EVE** (36)..91
FAREWELL MY SUMMER LOVE [A] – **CHAOS** (55) 92
FAREWELL MY SUMMER LOVE [A] – **Michael JACKSON** (7)........84
FAREWELL TO THE MOON – **YORK** (37)........00
FAREWELL TO TWILIGHT – **SYMPOSIUM** (25)..97
FARMER BILL'S COWMAN (I WAS KAISER BILL'S BATMAN) – **WURZELS** (32)........77
FARON YOUNG – **PREFAB SPROUT** (74)........85
FASCINATED – **Lisa B** (35)........93
FASCINATING RHYTHM – **BASS-O-MATIC** (9)....90
FASHION – **David BOWIE** (5)........80
FASHION CRISIS HITS NEW YORK – **FRANK AND WALTERS** (42)........93
FASHION '98 – **GLAMMA KID** (49)........98
FAST AS YOU CAN – **Fiona APPLE** (33)........00
FAST CAR – **Tracy CHAPMAN** (5)........88
FASTER – **MANIC STREET PREACHERS** (16)......94
FASTER THAN THE SPEED OF NIGHT – **Bonnie TYLER** (43)........83
FASTLOVE – **George MICHAEL** (1)........96
FAT BASTARD – **MEDWAY** (69)........00
FAT BLACK HEART – **PELE** (75)........93
FAT BOTTOMED GIRLS – **QUEEN** (11)........78
FAT LIP – **SUM 41** (8)........01
FAT NECK – **BLACK GRAPE** (10)........96
FATAL HESITATION – **Chris DE BURGH** (44)......86
FATHER [A] – **CHRISTIANS** (55)........92
FATHER [B] – **LL COOL J** (10)........98
FATHER AND SON – **BOYZONE** (2)........95
FATHER CHRISTMAS DO NOT TOUCH ME – **GOODIES** (7)........74
FATHER FIGURE – **George MICHAEL** (11)........88
FATTIE BUM BUM [A] – **Carl MALCOLM** (8)......75
FATTIE BUM BUM [A] – **DIVERSIONS** (34)........75
FAVOURITE SHIRTS (BOY MEETS GIRL) – **HAIRCUT 100** (4)........81
FBI – **SHADOWS** (6)........61
FE' REAL – **Maxi PRIEST featuring APACHE INDIAN** (33) 92
F.E.A.R. – **Ian BROWN** (13)........01
FEAR LOVES THIS PLACE – **Julian COPE** (42) ..92
FEAR OF THE DARK [A] – **Gordon GILTRAP** (58)..79
FEAR OF THE DARK (LIVE) [B] – **IRON MAIDEN** (8)93
FEAR SATAN – **MOGWAI** (57)........98
FEAR: THE MINDKILLER – **EON** (63)........91
FED UP – **HOUSE OF PAIN** (68)........96
FEDORA (I'LL BE YOUR DAWG) – **CARAMBA** (56) 83
FEE FI FO FUM – **CANDY GIRLS** (23)........95
FEED MY FRANKENSTEIN – **Alice COOPER** (27)92
FEED THE FEELING – **PERCEPTION** (58)........92
FEED THE TREE – **BELLY** (32)........93
FEEDING TIME – **LOOK** (50)........81
FEEL [A] – **Ruth JOY** (67)........92
FEEL [B] – **HOUSE OF LOVE** (45)........92
FEEL EVERY BEAT – **ELECTRONIC** (39)........91
FEEL FREE – **SOUL II SOUL** (64)........88
FEEL GOOD [A] – **PHATS & SMALL** (7)........99
FEEL GOOD [B] – **MADASUN** (29)........00
FEEL IT [A] – **HI-LUX** (41)........95
FEEL IT [B] – **Carol BAILEY** (41)........95
FEEL IT [C] – **Neneh CHERRY** (68)........97
FEEL IT [D] – **TAMPERER featuring MAYA** (1) ..98
FEEL IT [E] – **Inaya DAY** (51)........00
FEEL LIKE CALLING HOME – **MR BIG** (35)........77
FEEL LIKE CHANGE – **BLACK** (56)........91
FEEL LIKE MAKIN' LOVE [A] – **George BENSON** (28)........83
FEEL LIKE MAKIN' LOVE [B] – **BAD COMPANY** (20)........75
FEEL LIKE MAKING LOVE [A] – **Roberta FLACK** (34)........74
FEEL LIKE MAKING LOVE [B] – **Pauline HENRY** (12)........93
FEEL LIKE SINGIN' [A] – **Sandy B** (60)........93
FEEL LIKE SINGING [B] – **TAK TIX** (33)........96
FEEL ME – **BLANCMANGE** (46)........82
FEEL ME FLOW – **NAUGHTY BY NATURE** (23) ..95
FEEL MY BODY – **Frank'o MOIRAGHI featuring AMNESIA** (39) ..96
FEEL NO PAIN – **SADE** (56)........92
FEEL SO FINE – **Johnny PRESTON** (18)........60
FEEL SO GOOD [A] – **MASE** (10)........97
FEEL SO GOOD [B] – **JON THE DENTIST vs Ollie JAYE** (72)........00
FEEL SO HIGH – **DES'REE** (13)........91,92
FEEL SO REAL [A] – **Steve ARRINGTON** (5)......85
FEEL SO REAL [B] – **DREAM FREQUENCY** (23)..92
FEEL SURREAL – **FREEFALL featuring PSYCHOTROPIC** (63)......91
FEEL THA VIBE – **THAT KID CHRIS** (52)........97
FEEL THE BEAT [A] – **CAMISRA** (32)........98
FEEL THE BEAT [B] – **DARUDE** (5)........00
FEEL THE DRUM (EP) – **PARKS & WILSON** (71)00
FEEL THE DRUMS – **NATIVE** (46)........01
FEEL THE MUSIC – **GURU** (34)........95
FEEL THE NEED [A] – **Leif GARRETT** (38)........79
FEEL THE NEED [A] – **G NATION featuring ROSIE** (58)........97
FEEL THE NEED [B] – **JT TAYLOR** (57)........91
FEEL THE NEED [C] – **WEIRD SCIENCE** (62)......00
FEEL THE NEED IN ME [A] – **DETROIT EMERALDS** (4)........73,77
FEEL THE NEED IN ME [A] – **FORREST** (17)......83
FEEL THE NEED IN ME [A] – **Shakin' STEVENS** (26)........88
FEEL THE PAIN – **DINOSAUR JR** (25)........94
FEEL THE RAINDROPS – **ADVENTURES** (58) 85
FEEL THE REAL – **David BENDETH** (44)........79
FEEL THE RHYTHM [A] – **Jazzi P** (51)........90
FEEL THE RHYTHM [B] – **TERRORIZE** (69)........92
FEEL THE RHYTHM [C] – **JINNY** (74)........93
FEEL THE SAME – **TRIPLE X** (32)........99
FEEL THE SUNSHINE – **Alex REECE** (26)......95,96
FEEL TOO BUSY THINKING 'BOUT MY BABY – **STEPS** (2)........01
FEEL WHAT YOU WANT – **Kristine W** (33) ..94,97
FEELIN' – **LA's** (43)........91
FEELIN' ALRIGHT – **EYC** (16)........93
THE FEELIN' (CLAP YOUR HANDS) – **RHYTHMATIC JUNKIES** (67)........99
FEELIN' INSIDE – **Bobby BROWN** (40)........97
FEELIN' SO GOOD – **Jennifer LOPEZ** (15)........00
FEELIN' YOU – **ALI** (63)........98
THE FEELING [A] – **URBAN HYPE** (67)........92
THE FEELING [B] – **TIN TIN OUT featuring SWEET TEE** (32)........94
FEELING FOR YOU – **CASSIUS** (16)........99
FEELING GOOD [A] – **Nina SIMONE** (40)........94
FEELING GOOD [A] – **HUFF & HERB** (31) 97,98
FEELING GOOD [A] – **MUSE** (24)........01
FEELING IT TOO – **3 JAYS** (17)........99

FEELING SO REAL – MOBY (30) 94
FEELING THIS WAY – CONDUCTOR & THE COWBOY (35) 00
FEELINGS – Morris ALBERT (4) 75
FEELINGS OF FOREVER – TIFFANY (52) 88
(FEELS LIKE) HEAVEN – FICTION FACTORY (6) 84
FEELS LIKE HEAVEN – URBAN COOKIE COLLECTIVE (5) 93
FEELS LIKE I'M IN LOVE – Kelly MARIE (1) 80
FEELS LIKE THE FIRST TIME [A] – FOREIGNER (39) 78
FEELS LIKE THE FIRST TIME [B] – SINITTA (45)86
FEELS LIKE THE RIGHT TIME – SHAKATAK (41)80
FEELS SO GOOD [A] – VAN HALEN (63) 89
FEELS SO GOOD [B] – XSCAPE (34) 95
FEELS SO GOOD [C] – Lorna B (69) 97
FEELS SO GOOD [D] – Melanie B (5)................01
FEELS SO REAL (WON'T LET GO) – Patrice RUSHEN (51) 84
FEELS SO RIGHT – Victor SIMONELLI presents SOLUTION (63) ..96
FEENIN' – JODECI (18) 94
FEET UP! – Guy MITCHELL (2)....................52
FELICITY – ORANGE JUICE (63) 82
FELL ON BLACK DAYS – SOUNDGARDEN (24)..95
FEMALE INTUITION – MAI TAI (54) 86
FEMALE OF THE SPECIES – SPACE (14) 96
FERGUS SINGS THE BLUES – DEACON BLUE (14)89
FERNANDO – ABBA (1) 76
FERRIS WHEEL – EVERLY BROTHERS (22) 64
FERRY ACROSS THE MERSEY [A] – GERRY and the PACEMAKERS (8) 64
FERRY 'CROSS THE MERSEY [A] – CHRISTIANS, Holly JOHNSON, Paul McCARTNEY, Gerry MARSDEN and STOCK AITKEN WATERMAN (1) 89
FESTIVAL TIME – SAN REMO STRINGS (39) 71
FEVER [A] – Peggy LEE (5) 58,92
FEVER [A] – Helen SHAPIRO (38) 64
FEVER [A] – McCOYS (44) 65
FEVER [A] – MADONNA (6) 93
FEVER [B] – S-J (46)....................97
FEVER [D] – STARSAILOR (18) 01
FEVER CALLED LOVE – RHC (65)....................92
FEVER PITCH THE EP – PRETENDERS, LA'S, ORLANDO, Nick HORNBY (65) 97
FICTION OF LIFE – CHINA DRUM (65) 97
FIELDS OF FIRE (400 MILES) – BIG COUNTRY (10)....................83
FIELDS OF GOLD – STING (16) 93
THE FIELDS OF LOVE – ATB featuring YORK (50) 01
FIESTA [A] – POGUES (24)....................88
FIESTA [A] – R Kelly featuring JAY-Z (23)..........01
!FIESTA FATAL! – B-TRIBE (64)....................93
FIFTEEN FEET OF PURE WHITE SNOW – Nick CAVE and the BAD SEEDS (52) 01
15 MINUTES OF FAME – SHEEP ON DRUGS (44) 93
15 STEPS (EP) – MONKEY MAFIA (67) 97
15 WAYS – FALL (65)....................94
15 YEARS (EP) – LEVELLERS (11)....................92
5TH ANNIVERSARY EP – JUDGE DREAD (31) 77
A FIFTH OF BEETHOVEN – Walter MURPHY and the BIG APPLE BAND (28) 76
50 FT QUEENIE – P J HARVEY (27) 93
50 WAYS TO LEAVE YOUR LOVER – Paul SIMON (23) 76
51ST STATE – NEW MODEL ARMY (71) 86
FIFTY-FOUR – SEA LEVEL (63) 79
54-46 (WAS MY NUMBER) – ASWAD (70)........84
57 CHANNELS (AND NOTHIN' ON) – Bruce SPRINGSTEEN (32) 92
59TH STREET BRIDGE SONG (FEELING GROOVY) – HARPERS BIZARRE (34)....................67
FIGARO – BROTHERHOOD OF MAN (1) 78
FIGHT – McKOY (54) 93
THE FIGHT – Marty WILDE (47) 60
FIGHT FOR OURSELVES – SPANDAU BALLET (15)86
FIGHT FOR YOUR RIGHT (TO PARTY) – NYCC (14)98
FIGHT MUSIC – D12 (11)....................01
THE FIGHT SONG – MARILYN MANSON (24) 01
FIGHT THE POWER – PUBLIC ENEMY (29)........89
FIGHT THE YOUTH – FISHBONE (60)................92
FIGHTING FIT – GENE (22)....................96
FIGURE OF EIGHT [A] – Paul McCARTNEY (42) 89
FIGURE OF 8 [A] – GRID (50)....................92
FIJI – ATLANTIS vs AVATAR (52) 00
FILL HER UP – GENE (36) 99
FILL ME IN – Craig DAVID (1) 00
FILLING UP WITH HEAVEN – HUMAN LEAGUE (36) 95
A FILM FOR THE FUTURE – IDLEWILD (53) 98
FILMSTAR – SUEDE (9) 97
FILTHY – SAINT ETIENNE (39) 91
THE FINAL COUNTDOWN – EUROPE (1) 86,00
FINALLY [A] – Ce Ce PENISTON (2) 91,92,97
FINALLY [B] – KINGS OF TOMORROW featuring Julie McKNIGHT (24) 01
FINALLY FOUND – HONEYZ (4) 98
FINCHLEY CENTRAL – NEW VAUDEVILLE BAND (11)....................67
FIND A WAY [A] – COLDCUT featuring QUEEN LATIFAH (52) 90
FIND A WAY [B] – A TRIBE CALLED QUEST (41)98
FIND 'EM, FOOL 'EM, FORGET 'EM – S EXPRESS (43)....................92
FIND ME (ODYSSEY TO ANYOONA) – JAM & SPOON featuring PLAVKA (22) 94,95
FIND MY LOVE – FAIRGROUND ATTRACTION (7)88
FIND MY WAY BACK HOME – NASHVILLE TEENS (34) 65
FIND THE ANSWER WITHIN – BOO RADLEYS (37) 95
FIND THE RIVER – R.E.M. (54)....................93
FIND THE TIME [A] – FIVE STAR (7) 86
FIND THE TIME (PART ONE) [B] – QUADROPHONIA (41)....................91
FINDERS KEEPERS – CHAIRMEN OF THE BOARD (21) 73
FINE DAY – Rolf HARRIS (24) 00
FINE TIME [A] – NEW ORDER (11) 88
FINE TIME [B] – YAZZ (9)....................89
FINER – NIGHTMARES ON WAX (63) 99
FINER FEELINGS – Kylie MINOGUE (11) 92
THE FINEST [A] – S.O.S. BAND (17)....................86
THE FINEST [A] – TRUCE (54) 95
FINEST WORKSONG – R.E.M. (50)....................88
FINETIME – CAST (17) 95
THE FINGER OF SUSPICION – Dickie VALENTINE with the STARGAZERS (1) 54
FINGERS AND THUMBS (COLD SUMMER'S DAY) – ERASURE (20) 95
FINGERS OF LOVE – CROWDED HOUSE (25)....94
FINGS AIN'T WOT THEY USED T'BE [A] – Max BYGRAVES (5) 60
FINGS AIN'T WOT THEY USED T'BE [A] – Russ CONWAY (47) 60
FINISHED SYMPHONY – HYBRID (58) 99
FIRE [A] – Crazy World of Arthur BROWN (1) ..68
FIRE [B] – POINTER SISTERS (34) 79
FIRE [B] – Bruce SPRINGSTEEN (54) 87
FIRE [C] – U2 (35) 81
FIRE [D] – SLY and ROBBIE (60) 87
FIRE [E] – PRODIGY (11) 92,96
FIRE [F] – PRIZNA featuring DEMOLITION MAN (33) 95
FIRE [G] – SCOOTER (45)....................97
FIRE [H] – Busta RHYMES (60) 00
FIRE AND RAIN – James TAYLOR (42) 70
FIRE BRIGADE – MOVE (3) 68
FIRE DOWN BELOW [A] – Jeri SOUTHERN (22) 57
FIRE DOWN BELOW [A] – Shirley BASSEY (30) 57
FIRE IN MY HEART – SUPER FURRY ANIMALS (25) 99
FIRE ISLAND – FIRE ISLAND (66) 92
FIRE OF LOVE – JUNGLE HIGH with BLUE PEARL (71) 93
FIRE UP THE SHOESAW – LIONROCK (43) 96
FIRE WIRE – COSMIC GATE (9) 01
FIRE WOMAN – CULT (15) 89
FIRE WORKS – SIOUXSIE and the BANSHEES (22) 82
FIREBALL [A] – Don SPENCER (32) 63
FIREBALL [B] – DEEP PURPLE (15)....................71
FIRED UP – ELEVATORMAN (44) 95
FIRED UP! – FUNKY GREEN DOGS (17) 97
FIREPILE (EP) – THROWING MUSES (46)..........92
FIRES BURNING – RUN TINGS (58) 92
FIRESTARTER – PRODIGY (1) 96,97
FIREWORKS – ROXETTE (30) 94
FIREWORKS (EP) – EMBRACE (34) 97
FIRM BIZ – FIRM featuring Dawn ROBINSON (18)97
FIRST ATHEIST TABERNACLE CHOIR – SPITTING IMAGE (22) 86
FIRST BOY IN THIS TOWN (LOVE SICK) – SCRITTI POLITTI (63)....................88
FIRST CUT IS THE DEEPEST [A] – PP ARNOLD (18) 67
FIRST CUT IS THE DEEPEST [A] – Rod STEWART (1) 77
FIRST DATE – BLINK 182 (31) 01
THE FIRST DAY (HORIZON) – MAN WITH NO NAME (72)....................98
FIRST IMPRESSIONS – IMPRESSIONS (16) 75
1ST MAN IN SPACE – THE ALL SEEING I (28) ..99
THE FIRST MAN YOU REMEMBER – Michael BALL (68) 89
THE FIRST NIGHT – MONICA (6) 98
FIRST OF MAY – BEE GEES (6) 69
1ST OF THA MONTH – BONE THUGS-N-HARMONY (15) 95,96
FIRST PICTURE OF YOU – LOTUS EATERS (15) 83
FIRST TASTE OF LOVE – Ben E KING (27) 61
THE FIRST THE LAST ETERNITY (TIL THE END) – SNAP (15) 95
FIRST THING IN THE MORNING – Kiki DEE (32)77
THE FIRST TIME [A] – Adam FAITH (5) 63
THE FIRST TIME [B] – Robin BECK (1)..............88
THE FIRST TIME [C] – SURFACE (60) 91
FIRST TIME EVER – Joanna LAW (67) 90
THE FIRST TIME EVER I SAW YOUR FACE [A] – Roberta FLACK (14) 72
THE FIRST TIME EVER I SAW YOUR FACE [A] – Celine DION (19) 00
FIRST WE TAKE MANHATTAN – Jennifer WARNES (74) 87
FISH OUT OF WATER – ONE MINUTE SILENCE (56) 01
FISHERMAN'S BLUES – WATERBOYS (32) 89,91
THE $5.98 EP – GARAGE DAYS RE-REVISITED – METALLICA (27)....................87
FIVE FATHOMS – EVERYTHING BUT THE GIRL (27) 99
5.15 – WHO (20) 73
555 – DELAKOTA (42) 99
5-4-3-2-1 – MANFRED MANN (5) 64
FIVE GET OVER EXCITED – HOUSEMARTINS (11) 87
FIVE LITTLE FINGERS – Frankie McBRIDE (19) 67
FIVE LIVE (EP) – George MICHAEL and QUEEN with Lisa STANSFIELD (1) 93
FIVE MILES OUT – Mike OLDFIELD (43) 82
5 MILES TO EMPTY – BROWNSTONE (12)........97
FIVE MINUTES [A] – STRANGLERS (11) 78
5 MINUTES [B] – LIL' MO featuring Missy 'Misdemeanor' ELLIOTT (72)....................98
5 O'CLOCK – NONCHALANT (44) 96
5 O'CLOCK WORLD – Julian COPE (42) 89
5-7-0-5 – CITY BOY (8) 78
5, 6, 7, 8 – STEPS (14) 97
5 STEPS – DRU HILL (22) 97
500 (SHAKE BABY SHAKE) – LUSH (21) 96
FIX – BLACKSTREET (7) 97
FIXATION – Andy LING (55)....................00
FIXER – VENT 414 (71)....................96
FLAGPOLE SITTA – HARVEY DANGER (57)........98
FLAME – SEBADOH (30) 99
THE FLAME [A] – ARCADIA (58)....................86
THE FLAME [B] – FINE YOUNG CANNIBALS (17) 96
THE FLAME STILL BURNS – Jimmy NAIL (47) ..98
THE FLAME TREES OF THIKA – VIDEO SYMPHONIC (42) 81
FLAMES OF PARADISE – Jennifer RUSH and Elton JOHN (59)..............87
FLAMING JUNE – BT (19) 97,98
FLAMING SWORD – CARE (48) 83
FLASH [A] – QUEEN (10) 80
FLASH [B] – BBE (5) 97
FLASH [B] – BK and Nick SENTIENCE (67)........01
FLASH [C] – GRIFTERS (63) 99
FLASHBACK – IMAGINATION (16)....................81
FLASHBACK JACK – ADAMSKI (46) 90
FLASHDANCE ... WHAT A FEELING [A] – Irene CARA (2)....................83
FLASHDANCE ... WHAT A FEELING [A] – BJORN AGAIN (65)....................93
THE FLASHER – MISTURA featuring Lloyd MICHELS (23) 76
FLAT BEAT – MR OIZO (1) 99
FLATLINERS – NEBULA II (54) 92
FLAVA [A] – Peter ANDRE (1)....................96
FLAVA [B] – IMAJIN (64)....................00
FLAVA IN YA EAR – Craig MACK (57)................94
FLAVOUR OF THE OLD SCHOOL – Beverley KNIGHT (33) 95
FLAVOR OF THE WEAK – AMERICAN HI-FI (31) 01

FLAWLESS – ONES (7) ...01
FLEE FLY FLO – FE-M@IL (46) ...00
FLESH [A] – A SPLIT SECOND (68) ...91
FLESH [A] – Jan JOHNSTON (36) ...01
FLESH FOR FANTASY – Billy IDOL (54) ...84
FLESH OF MY FLESH – ORANGE JUICE (41) ...83
FLETCH THEME – Harold FALTERMEYER (74) ...85
FLIGHT OF ICARUS – IRON MAIDEN (11) ...83
FLIGHT 643 – DJ TIESTO (56) ...01
FLIP – Jesse GREEN (26) ...76
THE FLIPSIDE – MOLOKO (53) ...98
FLIRT – Jonathan KING (22) ...72
FLIRTATION WALTZ – Winifred ATWELL (10) ...53
F.L.M. – MEL and KIM (7) ...87
FLOAT ON – FLOATERS (1) ...77
FLOATATION – GRID (60) ...90
FLOATING – TERRA FIRMA (64) ...96
FLOATING IN THE WIND – HUDSON-FORD (35) 74
FLOODLIT WORLD – ULTRASOUND (39) ...99
THE FLOOR – Johnny GILL (53) ...93
FLOOR-ESSENCE – MAN WITH NO NAME (68) 95
FLOOR SPACE – OUR HOUSE (52) ...96
THE FLORAL DANCE [A] – BRIGHOUSE and RASTRICK BRASS BAND (2) 77
FLORAL DANCE [A] – Terry WOGAN (21) ...78
FLORIBUNDA – MOTHER'S PRIDE (42) ...98
FLOWER DUET (FROM 'LAKME') [A] – Mady MESPLE and Danielle MILLET with the PARIS OPERA-COMIQUE ORCHESTRA conducted by Alain LOMBARD (47) ...85
FLOWER DUET [A] – Jonathan PETERS presents LUMINAIRE (75) ...99
FLOWER OF SCOTLAND – SCOTTISH RUGBY TEAM with Ronnie BROWNE (73) ...90
FLOWER OF THE WEST – RUNRIG (43) ...91
FLOWERS [A] – TITIYO (71) ...90
FLOWERS [B] – SWEET FEMALE ATTITUDE (2) 00
FLOWERS IN DECEMBER – MAZZY STAR (40) ...96
FLOWERS IN THE RAIN – MOVE (2) ...67
FLOWERS OF ROMANCE – PUBLIC IMAGE LTD (24) ...81
FLOWERS ON THE WALL – STATLER BROTHERS (38) ...66
FLOWERZ – Armand VAN HELDEN (18) ...99
FLOWTATION – Vincent DE MOOR (54) ...97
FLOY JOY – SUPREMES (9) ...72
FLY [A] – SUGAR RAY (58) ...98
FLY [B] – POB featuring DJ Patrick REID (74) ...99
THE FLY – U2 (1) ...91
FLY AWAY [A] – HADDAWAY (20) ...95
FLY AWAY [B] – Lenny KRAVITZ (1) ...99
FLY AWAY [C] – Vincent DE MOOR (30) ...01
FLY AWAY (BYE BYE) – EYES CREAM (53) ...99
FLY BI – TEEBONE featuring MC KIE and MC SPARKS (43) ...00
FLY GIRL – QUEEN LATIFAH (67) ...91
FLY LIFE – BASEMENT JAXX (19) ...97
FLY LIKE AN EAGLE – SEAL (13) ...97
FLY ROBIN FLY – SILVER CONVENTION (28) ...75
FLY TO THE ANGELS – SLAUGHTER (55) ...91
FLY TOO HIGH – Janis IAN (44) ...79
FLYING – CAST (4) ...96
FLYING ELVIS – LEILANI (73) ...00
FLYING HIGH [A] – COMMODORES (37) ...78
FLYING HIGH [B] – FREEEZ (35) ...81
FLYING HIGH [C] – CAPTAIN HOLLYWOOD PROJECT (58) ...95
FLYING MACHINE – Cliff RICHARD (37) ...71
FLYING SAUCER – WEDDING PRESENT (22) ...92
THE FLYING SONG – PQM featuring CICA (68) 00
FLYING WITHOUT WINGS – WESTLIFE (1) ...99
FLYSWATTER – EELS (55) ...00
FM (NO STATIC AT ALL) – STEELY DAN (49) ...78
FOE-DEE-O-DEE – RUBETTES (15) ...75
FOG ON THE TYNE (REVISITED) – GAZZA and LINDISFARNE (2) ...90
FOGGY MOUNTAIN BREAKDOWN – Lester FLATT and Earl SCRUGGS (39) ...67
FOGHORN – A (63) ...98
THE FOLK SINGER – Tommy ROE (4) ...63
FOLLOW ME [A] – JT TAYLOR (59) ...92
FOLLOW ME [B] – ALY-US (43) ...92
FOLLOW ME [C] – ATOMIC KITTEN (20) ...00
FOLLOW ME [D] – UNCLE KRACKER (3) ...01
FOLLOW THAT DREAM (EP) – Elvis PRESLEY (34) 62
FOLLOW THE LEADER – Eric B and RAKIM (21) 88
FOLLOW THE LEADERS – KILLING JOKE (55) ...81
FOLLOW THE RULES – LIVIN' JOY (9) ...96
FOLLOW YOU DOWN – GIN BLOSSOMS (30) ...96
FOLLOW YOU FOLLOW ME [A] – GENESIS (7) ...78
FOLLOW YOU FOLLOW ME [A] – Sonny JONES featuring Tara CHASE (42) ...00
FOLLOWING – BANGLES (55) ...87
THE FOOD CHRISTMAS EP – VARIOUS ARTISTS (EPs and LPs) (63) ...89
FOOD FOR THOUGHT [A] – BARRON KNIGHTS (46) ...79
FOOD FOR THOUGHT [B] – UB40 (4) ...80
FOOL [A] – Elvis PRESLEY (15) ...73
FOOL [B] – Al MATTHEWS (16) ...75
FOOL [C] – MANSUN (28) ...01
FOOL AGAIN – WESTLIFE (1) ...00
A FOOL AM I – Cilla BLACK (13) ...66
FOOL FOR LOVE – RUSSELL (52) ...00
FOOL FOR YOUR LOVING – WHITESNAKE (13) ...80,89
FOOL (IF YOU THINK IT'S OVER) [A] – Chris REA (30) ...78
FOOL IF YOU THINK IT'S OVER [A] – Elkie BROOKS (17) ...82
A FOOL NEVER LEARNS – Andy WILLIAMS (40) 64
FOOL NUMBER ONE – Brenda LEE (38) ...61
THE FOOL ON THE HILL – Shirley BASSEY (48) 71
FOOL TO CRY – ROLLING STONES (6) ...76
FOOLED AROUND AND FELL IN LOVE – Elvin BISHOP (34) ...76
FOOLED BY A SMILE – SWING OUT SISTER (43) 87
FOOLIN' YOURSELF – Paul HARDCASTLE (51) ...86
FOOLISH BEAT – Debbie GIBSON (9) ...88
FOOLISH LITTLE GIRL – SHIRELLES (38) ...63
FOOL'S GOLD – STONE ROSES (8) ...89,90,92,95,99
FOOL'S PARADISE – Meli'sa MORGAN (41) ...86
FOOLS RUSH IN [A] – Brook BENTON (50) ...61
FOOLS RUSH IN [A] – Ricky NELSON (12) ...63
FOOT STOMPIN' MUSIC – Hamilton BOHANNON (23) ...75
FOOT TAPPER – SHADOWS (1) ...63
FOOTLOOSE – Kenny LOGGINS (6) ...84
FOOTPRINT – DISCO CITIZENS (34) ...97
FOOTPRINTS IN THE SNOW – Johnny DUNCAN and the BLUE GRASS BOYS (27) ...57,58
FOOTSEE – WIGAN'S CHOSEN FEW (9) ...75
FOOTSTEPS [A] – Ronnie CARROLL (36) ...60
FOOTSTEPS [A] – Steve LAWRENCE (4) ...60
FOOTSTEPS [A] – SHOWADDYWADDY (31) ...81
FOOTSTEPS [B] – STILTSKIN (34) ...94
FOOTSTEPS [C] – Daniel O'DONNELL (25) ...96
FOOTSTEPS FOLLOWING ME – Frances NERO (17) ...91
FOR A FEW DOLLARS MORE – SMOKIE (17) ...78
FOR A FRIEND – COMMUNARDS (28) ...88
FOR A PENNY – Pat BOONE (19) ...59
FOR ALL THAT YOU WANT – Gary BARLOW (24) ...99
FOR ALL THE COWS – FOO FIGHTERS (28) ...95
FOR ALL TIME – Catherine Zeta JONES (36) ...92
FOR ALL WE KNOW [A] – Nicki FRENCH (42) ...95
FOR ALL WE KNOW [A] – Shirley BASSEY (6) ...71
FOR ALL WE KNOW [A] – CARPENTERS (18) ...71
FOR AMERICA – RED BOX (10) ...86
FOR AN ANGEL – Paul VAN DYK (28) ...98
FOR BRITAIN ONLY – Alice COOPER (66) ...82
(FOR GOD'S SAKE) GIVE MORE POWER TO THE PEOPLE – CHI-LITES (32) ...71
FOR HER LIGHT – FIELDS OF THE NEPHILIM (54) 90
FOR LOVE (EP) – LUSH (35) ...92
FOR MAMA – Matt MONRO (36) ...64
FOR OLD TIME'S SAKE – MILLICAN and NESBITT (38) ...74
FOR ONCE IN MY LIFE [A] – Stevie WONDER (3) 68
FOR ONCE IN MY LIFE [A] – Dorothy SQUIRES (24) ...69
FOR REAL – TRICKY (45) ...99
FOR SPACIOUS LIES – Norman COOK (48) ...89
FOR SURE – SCOOCH (15) ...00
FOR THE DEAD – GENE (14) ...96
FOR THE GOOD TIMES – Perry COMO (7) ...73
FOR THOSE ABOUT TO ROCK (WE SALUTE YOU) – AC/DC (15) ...82
FOR TOMORROW – BLUR (28) ...93
FOR WHAT IT'S WORTH – OUI 3 (26) ...93
FOR WHAT YOU DREAM OF – BEDROCK (25) ...96
FOR WHOM THE BELL TOLLS [A] – Simon DUPREE and the BIG SOUND (43) ...68
FOR WHOM THE BELL TOLLS [B] – BEE GEES (4) 93
FOR YOU [A] – Ricky NELSON (14) ...64
FOR YOU [B] – FARMERS BOYS (66) ...83
FOR YOU [C] – Snowy WHITE (65) ...85,86
FOR YOU [D] – ELECTRONIC (16) ...96
FOR YOU FOR LOVE – AVERAGE WHITE BAND (46) ...80
FOR YOU I WILL – MONICA (27) ...97
FOR YOU I'LL DO ANYTHING YOU WANT ME TO – Barry WHITE (20) ...75
FOR YOUR BABIES – SIMPLY RED (9) ...92
FOR YOUR BLUE EYES ONLY – Tony HADLEY (67) ...92
FOR YOUR EYES ONLY – Sheena EASTON (8) ...81
FOR YOUR LOVE [A] – YARDBIRDS (3) ...65
FOR YOUR LOVE [B] – Stevie WONDER (23) ...95
FORBIDDEN CITY – ELECTRONIC (14) ...96
FORBIDDEN COLOURS – David SYLVIAN (16) ...83
FORBIDDEN FRUIT – Paul VAN DYK (69) ...97
FORBIDDEN ZONE – BEDROCK (71) ...97
THE FORCE BEHIND THE POWER – Diana ROSS (27) ...92
FOREIGN SAND – Roger TAYLOR (26) ...94
FORERUNNER – NATURAL BORN GROOVES (64) 96
A FOREST – CURE (31) ...80
FOREST FIRE – Lloyd COLE (41) ...84
FOREVER [A] – Roy WOOD (8) ...73
FOREVER [B] – KISS (65) ...90
FOREVER [C] – DAMAGE (6) ...96
FOREVER [D] – CHARLATANS (12) ...99
FOREVER [E] – Tina COUSINS (45) ...99
FOREVER AND A DAY – BROTHERS IN RHYTHM (51) ...94
FOREVER AND EVER – SLIK (1) ...76
FOREVER AND EVER, AMEN – Randy TRAVIS (55) ...88
FOREVER AS ONE – VENGABOYS (28) ...01
FOREVER AUTUMN – Justin HAYWARD (5) ...78
FOREVER CAME TODAY – Diana ROSS and the SUPREMES (28) ...68
FOREVER FAILURE – PARADISE LOST (66) ...95
FOREVER FREE – W.A.S.P. (25) ...89
FOREVER GIRL – OTT (24) ...97
FOREVER IN BLUE JEANS – Neil DIAMOND (16) 79
FOREVER IN LOVE – Kenny G (47) ...93
FOREVER J – Terry HALL (67) ...94
A FOREVER KIND OF LOVE – Bobby VEE (13) ...62
(FOREVER) LIVE AND DIE – ORCHESTRAL MANOEUVRES IN THE DARK (11) ...86
FOREVER LOVE – Gary BARLOW (1) ...96
FOREVER MAN [A] – Eric CLAPTON (51) ...85
FOREVER MAN (HOW MANY TIMES) [A] – BEATCHUGGERS featuring Eric CLAPTON (26) 00
FOREVER MORE – Puff JOHNSON (29) ...97
FOREVER NOW – LEVEL 42 (19) ...94
FOREVER TOGETHER – Raven MAIZE (67) ...89
FOREVER YOUNG [A] – Rod STEWART (57) ...88
FOREVER YOUNG [B] – INTERACTIVE (28) ...96
FOREVER YOUR GIRL – Paula ABDUL (24) ...89
FOREVERGREEN – FINITRIBE (51) ...92
FORGET ABOUT THE WORLD – GABRIELLE (23) 96
FORGET ABOUT YOU – MOTORS (13) ...78
FORGET HIM [A] – Bobby RYDELL (13) ...63
FORGET HIM [A] – Billy FURY (59) ...83
FORGET I WAS A G – WHITEHEAD BROS (40) ...95
FORGET ME NOT [A] – Eden KANE (3) ...62
FORGET ME NOT [B] – Martha REEVES and the VANDELLAS (11) ...71
FORGET-ME-NOT – Vera LYNN (5) ...52
FORGET ME NOTS [A] – Patrice RUSHEN (8) ...82
FORGET ME NOTS [A] – TONGUE 'N' CHEEK (26) 91
FORGIVE ME – Lynden David HALL (30) ...00
FORGIVEN (I FEEL YOUR LOVE) – SPACE BROTHERS (27) ...97
FORGOT ABOUT DRE – DR DRE featuring EMINEM (7) ...00
FORGOTTEN DREAMS [A] – Cyril STAPLETON and his ORCHESTRA (27) ...57
FORGOTTEN DREAMS [A] – Leroy ANDERSON and his POPS CONCERT ORCHESTRA (24) ...57
FORGOTTEN TOWN – CHRISTIANS (22) ...87
FORT WORTH JAIL – Lonnie DONEGAN (14) ...59
FORTRESS AROUND YOUR HEART – STING (49) ...85
FORTUNES OF WAR – FISH (67) ...94

GIVE A LITTLE LOVE [D] — **INVISIBLE MAN** (48)99
GIVE A LITTLE LOVE BACK TO THE WORLD — **EMMA** (33) 90
GIVE AND TAKE [A] — **PIONEERS** (35) 72
GIVE AND TAKE [B] — **BRASS CONSTRUCTION** (62) 85
GIVE GIVE GIVE — **Tommy STEELE** (28)....59
GIVE GIVE GIVE ME MORE MORE MORE — **WONDER STUFF** (72)....88
GIVE HER MY LOVE — **JOHNSTON BROTHERS** (27) 57
GIVE HER WHAT SHE WANTS — **Frankie OLIVER** (58) 97
GIVE IN TO ME — **Michael JACKSON** (2)....93
GIVE IRELAND BACK TO THE IRISH — **Paul McCARTNEY** (16) 72
GIVE IT ALL AWAY — **WORLD PARTY** (43) 93
GIVE IT AWAY — **RED HOT CHILI PEPPERS** (9)..94
GIVE IT SOME EMOTION — **TRACIE** (24)....83
GIVE IT TO ME [A] — **TROGGS** (12)....67
GIVE IT TO ME [B] — **BAM BAM** (65) 88
GIVE IT TO ME BABY — **Rick JAMES** (47) 81
GIVE IT TO ME NOW — **KENNY** (38)....73
GIVE IT TO YOU [A] — **Martha WASH** (37) 93
GIVE IT TO YOU [B] — **Jordan KNIGHT** (5)....99,00
GIVE IT UP [A] — **KC and the SUNSHINE BAND** (1) 83
GIVE IT UP [A] — **CUT 'N' MOVE** (61) 93
GIVE IT UP [B] — **TALK TALK** (59) 86
GIVE IT UP [C] — **HOTHOUSE FLOWERS** (30) 90
GIVE IT UP [D] — **WILSON PHILLIPS** (36)....92
GIVE IT UP [E] — **GOODMEN** (5)....93
GIVE IT UP [F] — **PUBLIC ENEMY** (18)....94
GIVE IT UP [G] — **SELENA vs X.MEN** (61) 01
GIVE IT UP TURN IT LOOSE — **EN VOGUE** (22) 93
GIVE ME A LITTLE MORE TIME — **GABRIELLE** (5)....96
GIVE ME A REASON — **CORRS** (27) 01
GIVE ME ALL YOUR LOVE [A] — **WHITESNAKE** (18) 88
GIVE ME ALL YOUR LOVE [B] — **MAGIC AFFAIR** (30) 94
GIVE ME AN INCH — **Hazel O'CONNOR** (41)....80
GIVE ME BACK ME BRAIN — **DUFFO** (60)....79
GIVE ME BACK MY HEART — **DOLLAR** (4) 82
GIVE ME BACK MY MAN — **B-52's** (61)....80
GIVE ME FIRE — **GBH** (69) 82
GIVE ME JUST A LITTLE MORE TIME [A] — **CHAIRMEN OF THE BOARD** (3) 70
GIVE ME JUST A LITTLE MORE TIME [A] — **Kylie MINOGUE** (2) 92
GIVE ME JUST ONE MORE NIGHT (UNA NOCHE) — **98°** (61)....00
GIVE ME LIFE — **MR V** (40) 94
GIVE ME LOVE [A] — **DIDDY** (23)....94,97
GIVE ME LOVE [B] — **DJ DADO vs Michelle WEEKS** (59)....98
GIVE ME LOVE (GIVE ME PEACE ON EARTH) — **George HARRISON** (8)....73
GIVE ME MORE TIME [A] — **NICOLE** (75) 82
GIVE ME MORE TIME [B] — **WHITESNAKE** (29)..84
GIVE ME ONE MORE CHANCE [A] — **Donald PEERS** (36) 72
GIVE ME ONE MORE CHANCE [B] — **Luke GOSS and the BAND OF THIEVES** (68)..93
GIVE ME RHYTHM — **BLACK CONNECTION** (32) 98
GIVE ME SOME KINDA MAGIC — **DOLLAR** (34)..82
GIVE ME SOME MORE — **DJ GERT** (50)....01
GIVE ME STRENGTH — **JON OF THE PLEASED WIMMIN** (30) 96
GIVE ME THE NIGHT [A] — **George BENSON** (7) 80
GIVE ME THE NIGHT [A] — **MIRAGE** (49) 84
GIVE ME THE NIGHT [A] — **Randy CRAWFORD** (60) 97
GIVE ME THE REASON — **Luther VANDROSS** (26) 86,87,88
GIVE ME TIME — **Dusty SPRINGFIELD** (24)....67
GIVE ME TONIGHT — **SHANNON** (24)....84
GIVE ME YOU — **Mary J BLIGE** (19)....00
GIVE ME YOUR BODY — **CHIPPENDALES** (28) ..92
GIVE ME YOUR HEART TONIGHT — **Shakin' STEVENS** (11) 82
GIVE ME YOUR WORD [A] — **Tennessee Ernie FORD** (1)....55
GIVE ME YOUR WORD [A] — **Billy FURY** (27) 66
GIVE MYSELF TO LOVE — **Francis ROSSI** (42) ..96
GIVE PEACE A CHANCE — **John LENNON** (2) 69,81
GIVE UP THE FUNK (LET'S DANCE) — **BT EXPRESS** (52)....80
GIVE YOU — **DJAIMIN** (45) 92
GIVE YOU ALL THE LOVE — **MISHKA** (34) 99
GIVEN TO FLY — **PEARL JAM** (12) 98
GIVEN UP — **MIRRORBALL** (12) 99
GIVIN' IT UP — **INCOGNITO** (12)....93
GIVING HIM SOMETHING HE CAN FEEL — **ENVOGUE** (16) 92
GIVING IT ALL AWAY — **Roger DALTREY** (5)....73
GIVING IT BACK — **Phil HURTT** (36) 78
GIVING UP GIVING IN [A] — **THREE DEGREES** (12)78
GIVING UP GIVING IN [A] — **Sheena EASTON** (54)00
GIVING YOU THE BENEFIT — **PEBBLES** (73)....90
GIVING YOU THE BEST THAT I GOT — **Anita BAKER** (55) 88
G.L.A.D. — **Kim APPLEBY** (10)....91
GLAD ALL OVER [A] — **Dave CLARK FIVE** (1) 63,93
GLAD ALL OVER [A] — **CRYSTAL PALACE** (50) ..90
GLAD IT'S ALL OVER — **CAPTAIN SENSIBLE** (6) 84
GLAM — **Lisa B** (49) 93
GLAM RAID — **SPACE RAIDERS** (68)....98
GLAM ROCK COPS — **CARTER — THE UNSTOPPABLE SEX MACHINE** (24) 94
GLAM SLAM — **PRINCE** (29) 88
GLASGOW RANGERS (NINE IN A ROW) — **RANGERS FC** (54) 97
GLASS OF CHAMPAGNE — **SAILOR** (2) 75
GLASTONBURY SONG — **WATERBOYS** (29) 93
GLENDORA [A] — **Glen MASON** (28)....56
GLENDORA [A] — **Perry COMO** (18) 56
GLENN MILLER MEDLEY — **John ANDERSON BIG BAND** (61) 85,86
GLITTERBALL — **SIMPLE MINDS** (18) 98
GLITTERING PRIZE — **SIMPLE MINDS** (16) 82
GLOBETROTTER — **TORNADOS** (5) 63
GLORIA [A] — **Jonathan KING** (65) 79
GLORIA [A] — **Laura BRANIGAN** (6) 82
GLORIA [B] — **U2** (55) 81
GLORIA [C] — **Van MORRISON and John Lee HOOKER** (31)..93
GLORIOUS — **Andreas JOHNSON** (4) 00
GLORY BOX — **PORTISHEAD** (13) 95
GLORY DAYS — **Bruce SPRINGSTEEN** (17) 85
GLORY GLORY MAN UNITED — **MANCHESTER UNITED FOOTBALL CLUB** (13)..83
GLORY OF LOVE — **Peter CETERA** (3)....86
GLORY OF THE 80'S — **Tori AMOS** (46) 99
GLORYLAND — **Daryl HALL and the SOUNDS OF BLACKNESS** (36) 94
GLOW — **SPANDAU BALLET** (10) 81
GLOW OF LOVE — **CHANGE** (14) 80
THE GLOW WORM — **MILLS BROTHERS** (10) 53
GO [A] — **Scott FITZGERALD** (52) 88
GO [B] — **MOBY** (10) 91
GO [C] — **JOCASTA** (50) 97
GO AWAY [A] — **Gloria ESTEFAN** (13) 93
GO AWAY [B] — **HONEYCRACK** (41) 96
GO AWAY LITTLE GIRL — **Mark WYNTER** (6)....62
GO (BEFORE YOU BREAK MY HEART) — **Gigliola CINQUETTI** (8) 74
GO BUDDY GO — **STRANGLERS** (8) 77
GO CUT CREATOR GO — **LL COOL J** (66) 87
GO DEEP — **Janet JACKSON** (13)....98
GO DEH YAKA (GO TO THE TOP) — **MONYAKA** (14) 83
GO FOR IT! — **COVENTRY CITY CUP FINAL SQUAD** (61)....87
GO FOR IT (HEART AND FIRE) — **Joey B ELLIS** (20) 91
GO FOR THE HEART — **SOX** (47) 95
GO GO GO — **Chuck BERRY** (38) 63
GO HOME — **Stevie WONDER** (67)....85
GO INTO THE LIGHT — **Ian McNABB** (66)....94
GO LET IT OUT — **OASIS** (1) 00
GO NORTH — **Richard BARNES** (38)....70
GO NOW — **MOODY BLUES** (1) 64
GO ON BY — **Alma COGAN** (16) 55
GO ON GIRL — **Roxanne SHANTE** (55) 88,90
GO ON MOVE — **REEL 2 REAL** (7) 94
GO TECHNO — **2 HOUSE** (65)....92
GO THE DISTANCE — **Michael BOLTON** (14)....97
GO WEST [A] — **VILLAGE PEOPLE** (15) 79
GO WEST [A] — **PET SHOP BOYS** (2) 93
GO WILD IN THE COUNTRY — **BOW WOW WOW** (7) 82
GO WITH THE FLOW — **LOOP DA LOOP** (47) 97
GO YOUR OWN WAY — **FLEETWOOD MAC** (38) 77
GOD — **Tori AMOS** (44) 94
GOD GAVE ROCK AND ROLL TO YOU [A] — **ARGENT** (18) 73
GOD GAVE ROCK AND ROLL TO YOU II [A] — **KISS** (4)....92
GOD IS A DJ — **FAITHLESS** (6) 98
GOD OF ABRAHAM — **MNO** (66)....91
GOD ONLY KNOWS [A] — **BEACH BOYS** (2) 66
GOD ONLY KNOWS [A] — **DIESEL PARK WEST** (57)92
GOD SAVE THE QUEEN — **SEX PISTOLS** (2)....77
GOD! SHOW ME MAGIC — **SUPER FURRY ANIMALS** (33) 96
GOD THANK YOU WOMAN — **CULTURE CLUB** (31)86
GOD'S GONNA PUNISH YOU — **TYMES** (41) 76
GOD'S GREAT BANANA SKIN — **Chris REA** (31) 92
GOD'S HOME MOVIE — **HORSE** (56) 93
GOD'S KITCHEN — **BLANCMANGE** (65)....82
GOD'S MISTAKE — **TEARS FOR FEARS** (61) 96
GODDESS ON A HIWAY — **MERCURY REV** (26) 98,99
GODHEAD — **NITZER EBB** (56) 92
GODLESS — **DANDY WARHOLS** (66) 01
GODSPEED — **BT** (54) 98
GODSTAR — **PSYCHIC TV** (67) 86
GO-GO DANCER — **WEDDING PRESENT** (20) 92
GOIN' DOWN — **Melanie C** (4) 99
GOIN DOWN THE ROAD — **Roy WOOD** (13) 74
GOIN' OUT OF MY HEAD — **Dodie WEST** (39) 65
GOIN' PLACES — **JACKSONS** (26) 77
GOIN' TO THE BANK — **COMMODORES** (43) 86
GOIN' TO VEGAS — **Jimmy RAY** (49) 98
GOING BACK — **Dusty SPRINGFIELD** (10) 66
GOING BACK TO CALI — **LL COOL J** (37) 88
GOING BACK TO MY HOME TOWN — **Hal PAIGE and the WHALERS** (50) 60
GOING BACK TO MY ROOTS [A] — **ODYSSEY** (4)81
GOING BACK TO MY ROOTS [A] — **FPI PROJECT** (9) 89
GOING DOWN TO LIVERPOOL — **BANGLES** (56)86
GOING DOWN TOWN TONIGHT — **STATUS QUO** (20) 84
GOING FOR GOLD — **SHED SEVEN** (8) 96
GOING FOR THE ONE — **YES** (24)....77
GOING HOME [A] — **TYRREL CORPORATION** (58) 92
GOING HOME [B] — **OSMONDS** (4)....73
GOING HOME (THEME OF 'LOCAL HERO') — **Mark KNOPFLER** (56) 83
GOING IN WITH MY EYES OPEN — **David SOUL** (2)....77
GOING LEFT RIGHT — **DEPARTMENT S** (55) 81
GOING NOWHERE — **GABRIELLE** (9) 93
GOING OUT — **SUPERGRASS** (5) 96
GOING OUT OF MY HEAD — **FATBOY SLIM** (57) 97
GOING OUT WITH GOD — **KINKY MACHINE** (74)93
GOING ROUND — **D'BORA** (40)....95
GOING THROUGH THE MOTIONS — **HOT CHOCOLATE** (53) 79
GOING TO A GO-GO [A] — **MIRACLES** (44) 66
GOING TO A GO-GO [A] — **SHARONETTES** (46) 75
GOING TO A GO GO [A] — **ROLLING STONES** (26)....82
GOING UNDERGROUND [A] — **JAM** (1) 80,83
GOING UNDERGROUND [A] — **BUFFALO TOM** (6) 99
GOING UP THE COUNTRY — **CANNED HEAT** (19)69
GOLD [A] — **John STEWART** (43) 79
GOLD [B] — **SPANDAU BALLET** (2) 83
GOLD [C] — **EAST 17** (28) 92
GOLD [D] — **PRINCE** (10)....95
GOLDEN AGE OF ROCK AND ROLL — **MOTT THE HOOPLE** (16) 74
GOLDEN BROWN [A] — **STRANGLERS** (2)....82,91
GOLDEN BROWN [A] — **KALEEF** (22)....96
GOLDEN BROWN [A] — **OMAR** (37)....97
GOLDEN DAYS — **BUCKS FIZZ** (42)....84
GOLDEN GAZE — **Ian BROWN** (29)....00
GOLDEN GREEN — **WONDER STUFF** (33) 89
THE GOLDEN LADY — **THREE DEGREES** (56) 79
GOLDEN LIGHTS — **TWINKLE** (21)....65
GOLDEN SKIN — **SILVER SUN** (32)....97
GOLDEN SLUMBERS — CARRY THAT WEIGHT — **TRASH** (35) 69

GOTTA GET YOU HOME TONIGHT — Eugene WILDE (18) 84
GOTTA GO HOME — BONEY M (12) 79
GOTTA HAVE HOPE — BLACKOUT (46) 99
GOTTA HAVE RAIN — Max BYGRAVES (28) 58
GOT-TA HAVE SOMETHING IN THE BANK, FRANK — Frankie VAUGHAN and the KAYE SISTERS (8)....57
GOTTA KEEP PUSHIN' — Z FACTOR (47) 98
GOTTA KNOW (YOUR NAME) — MALAIKA (68) ..93
GOTTA LOTTA LOVE — ICE-T (24) 94
GOTTA PULL MYSELF TOGETHER — NOLANS (9) 80
GOTTA SEE BABY TONIGHT — Mr Acker BILK and his PARAMOUNT JAZZ BAND (24) 62
GOTTA SEE JANE — R Dean TAYLOR (17) 68,74
GOTTA TELL YOU — Samantha MUMBA (2) 00
GOURYELLA — GOURYELLA (15) 99
GOVINDA [A] — RADHA KRISHNA TEMPLE (23) 70
GOVINDA [B] — KULA SHAKER (7) 96
GRACE — BAND AKA (41) 82
GRACEADELICA — DARK STAR (25) 00
GRACELAND — BIBLE (51) 89
GRANADA [A] — Frankie LAINE (9) 54
GRANADA [A] — Frank SINATRA (15) 61
GRAND COOLIE DAM — Lonnie DONEGAN (6) ..58
GRAND PIANO — MIXMASTER (9) 89
GRANDAD — Clive DUNN (1) 70,71
GRANDMA'S PARTY — Paul NICHOLAS (9)....76
GRANDPA'S PARTY — Monie LOVE (16) 89
GRANITE STATUE — SALAD (50) 95
GRAPEVYNE — BROWNSTONE (16) 95
GRATEFUL WHEN YOU'RE DEAD — JERRY WAS THERE — KULA SHAKER (35) 96
THE GRAVE AND THE CONSTANT — FUN LOVIN' CRIMINALS (72) 96
GRAVEL PIT — WU-TANG CLAN (6) 00
GRAVITATE TO ME — The THE (63) 89
GRAVITY — James BROWN (65) 86
GREASE [A] — Frankie VALLI (3) 78
GREASE [A] — Craig McLACHLAN (44) 93
THE GREASE MEGAMIX [A] — John TRAVOLTA and Olivia NEWTON-JOHN (3) 90
GREASE – THE DREAM MIX [A] — Frankie VALLI, John TRAVOLTA and Olivia NEWTON-JOHN (47) 91
GREASED LIGHTNIN' — John TRAVOLTA (11) ...78
GREAT BALLS OF FIRE [A] — Jerry Lee LEWIS (1) ..57
GREAT BALLS OF FIRE [A] — TINY TIM (45) 69
THE GREAT BEYOND — R.E.M. (3) 00
THE GREAT ESCAPE — ENGLAND SUPPORTERS' BAND (46) 98
THE GREAT ESCAPE 2000 — ENGLAND SUPPORTERS' BAND (26) 00
GREAT GOSH A'MIGHTY ! (IT'S A MATTER OF TIME) — LITTLE RICHARD (62) 86
THE GREAT PRETENDER [A] — Jimmy PARKINSON (9)....56
THE GREAT PRETENDER [A] — Freddie MERCURY (4)....87,93
THE GREAT PRETENDER [A] — PLATTERS (5)....56
THE GREAT ROCK 'N' ROLL SWINDLE — SEX PISTOLS (21) 79
THE GREAT SNOWMAN — Bob LUMAN (49) 61
THE GREAT SONG OF INDIFFERENCE — Bob GELDOF (15)....90
GREAT THINGS — ECHOBELLY (13)....95
THE GREAT TRAIN ROBBERY — BLACK UHURU (62)....86
GREATER LOVE — SOUNDMAN and Don LLOYDIE with Elisabeth TROY (49) 95
THE GREATEST COCKNEY RIPOFF — COCKNEY REJECTS (21) 80
GREATEST DAY — Beverley KNIGHT (14) 99
THE GREATEST FLAME — RUNRIG (30) 93,97
THE GREATEST HIGH — HURRICANE #1 (43) 99
THE GREATEST LOVE OF ALL [A] — George BENSON (27) 77
GREATEST LOVE OF ALL [A] — Whitney HOUSTON (8) 86
THE GREATEST LOVE YOU'LL NEVER KNOW — Lutricia McNEAL (17) 98
THE GREATEST ROMANCE EVER SOLD — PRINCE (65)....00
THE GREATEST SHOW ON EARTH — STRANGELOVE (36) 97
THE GREATNESS AND PERFECTION OF LOVE — Julian COPE (52) 84
GREECE 2000 — THREE DRIVES (12)....98,99
GREED — Laurent GARNIER (36) 00
GREEDY FLY — BUSH (22) 97
THE GREEDY UGLY PEOPLE — HEFNER (64) 00
GREEN AND GREY — NEW MODEL ARMY (37) ..89
THE GREEN DOOR [A] — Frankie VAUGHAN (2) 56
THE GREEN DOOR [A] — Jim LOWE (8)....56
GREEN DOOR [A] — Glen MASON (24)....56
GREEN DOOR [A] — Shakin' STEVENS (1)....81
GREEN FIELDS [A] — BEVERLEY SISTERS (29) ..60
GREEN FIELDS [A] — UNIT FOUR PLUS TWO (48) 64
GREEN GREEN GRASS OF HOME [A] — Tom JONES (1)....66
GREEN GREEN GRASS OF HOME [A] — Elvis PRESLEY (29) 75
GREEN JEANS — FLEE-REKKERS (23) 60
THE GREEN LEAVES OF SUMMER — Kenny BALL and his JAZZMEN (7) 62
GREEN LIGHT — Cliff RICHARD (57) 79
THE GREEN MAN— SHUT UP AND DANCE (43) 92
THE GREEN MANALISHI (WITH THE TWO-PRONG CROWN) — FLEETWOOD MAC (10) 70
GREEN ONIONS — BOOKER T and the MG's (7)....79
GREEN RIVER — CREEDENCE CLEARWATER REVIVAL (19)....69
GREEN SHIRT — Elvis COSTELLO (68) 85
GREEN STREET GREEN — NEW VAUDEVILLE BAND (37) 67
GREEN TAMBOURINE [A] — LEMON PIPERS (7) 68
GREEN TAMBOURINE [A] — SUNDRAGON (50) ..68
GREEN TINTED SIXTIES MIND — MR BIG (72) ..92
GREENBACK DOLLAR — Charles McDEVITT SKIFFLE GROUP featuring Nancy WHISKEY (28) 57
GREENBANK DRIVE — CHRISTIANS (63)....90
GREENFIELDS — BROTHERS FOUR (40) 60
GREETINGS TO THE NEW BRUNETTE — Billy BRAGG with Johnny MARR and Kirsty MacCOLL (58) 86
GREY DAY — MADNESS (4)....81
GRIMLY FIENDISH — DAMNED (21)....85
GRIND — ALICE IN CHAINS (23) 95
GRIP '89 (GET A) GRIP (ON YOURSELF) — STRANGLERS (33) 89
GRITTY SHAKER — David HOLMES (53)....97
THE GROOVE — Rodney FRANKLIN (7)....80
GROOVE BABY GROOVE (EP) — STARGAZERS (56)82
GROOVE IS IN THE HEART — DEEE-LITE (2)....90,91
THE GROOVE LINE — HEATWAVE (12) 78
GROOVE MACHINE — MARVIN and TAMARA (11)..99
GROOVE OF LOVE — E.V.E. (30)....94
GROOVE THANG — ZHANE (34) 94
GROOVE TO MOVE — CHANNEL X (67)....91
GROOVEBIRD — NATURAL BORN GROOVES (21)..97
GROOVEJET (IF THIS AIN'T LOVE) — SPILLER (1) ..00
GROOVELINE — BLOCKSTER (18) 99
THE GROOVER — T. REX (4)....73
GROOVIN' [A] — YOUNG RASCALS (8) 67
GROOVIN' [A] — WAR (43) 85
GROOVIN' [A] — Pato BANTON (14) 96
GROOVIN' IN THE MIDNIGHT — Maxi PRIEST (50)92
GROOVIN' (THAT'S WHAT WE'RE DOIN') — S.O.S. BAND (72) 83
GROOVIN' WITH MR BLOE — MR BLOE (2) 70
GROOVY BABY — MICROBE (29) 69
GROOVY BEAT — D.O.P. (54) 96
GROOVY FEELING — FLUKE (45)....93
A GROOVY KIND OF LOVE [A] — MINDBENDERS (2) 66
A GROOVY KIND OF LOVE [A] — Les GRAY (32)77
A GROOVY KIND OF LOVE [A] — Phil COLLINS (1) 88
THE GROOVY THANG — MINIMAL FUNK 2 (65) 98
GROOVY TRAIN — FARM (6)....90
GROUND LEVEL — STEREO MC's (19)....93
GROUNDED — MY VITRIOL (29) 01
GROUPIE GIRL — Tony Joe WHITE (22) 70
G.T.O. — SINITTA (15)....87
GUAGLIONE — Perez PRADO (2) 94,95
GUANTANAMERA [A] — SANDPIPERS (7) 66
GUANTANAMERA [A] — FUGEES (25) 97
GUARANTEED — LEVEL 42 (17)....91
GUARDIAN ANGEL — Nino DE ANGELO (57)....84
GUARDIANS OF THE LAND — George BOWYER (33) 98
GUDBUY T'JANE — SLADE (2)....72
GUDVIBE — TINMAN (49) 95
GUERRILLA FUNK — PARIS (38) 95
GUERRILLA RADIO — RAGE AGAINST THE MACHINE (32) 99
GUESS I WAS A FOOL — ANOTHER LEVEL (5) ..98
GUESS WHO'S BACK — RAKIM (32)....97
GUIDING STAR — CAST (9) 97
GUILTY [A] — Jim REEVES (29) 63
GUILTY [B] — PEARLS (10) 74
GUILTY [C] — Mike OLDFIELD (22) 79
GUILTY [D] — Barbra STREISAND (34) 80
GUILTY [E] — CLASSIX NOUVEAUX (43) 81
GUILTY [F] — Paul HARDCASTLE (55)....84
GUILTY [G] — YARBROUGH and PEOPLES (53) 86
GUILTY CONSCIENCE — EMINEM featuring DR DRE (5) 99
GUILTY OF LOVE — WHITESNAKE (31) 83
GUITAR BOOGIE SHUFFLE — Bert WEEDON (10)59
GUITAR MAN [A] — Elvis PRESLEY (19) 68,81
THE GUITAR MAN [B] — BREAD (16)....72
GUITAR TANGO — SHADOWS (4) 62
GUITARRA G — BANDA SONARA (50) 01
GUN LAW — KANE GANG (53) 85
GUNMAN — 187 LOCKDOWN (16) 97,98
GUNS FOR HIRE — AC/DC (37)....83
GUNS OF NAVARONE — SKATALITES (36) 67
GUNSLINGER — Frankie LAINE (50) 61
GUNZ AND PIANOZ — BASS BOYZ (74) 96
GURNEY SLADE — Max HARRIS (11)....60
THE GUSH — RAGING SPEEDHORN (47)....01
GYM AND TONIC — SPACEDUST (1) 98,99
GYPSY — FLEETWOOD MAC (46) 82
GYPSY BEAT — PACKABEATS (49) 61
GYPSY BOY, GYPSY GIRL — SHARADA HOUSE GANG (52) 97
GYPSY EYES — Jimi HENDRIX EXPERIENCE (35)....71
GYPSY ROAD — CINDERELLA (54) 88
GYPSY ROAD HOG — SLADE (48)....77
GYPSY ROVER — HIGHWAYMEN (41)....61,62
GYPSY WOMAN [A] — Brian HYLAND (42) 71
GYPSY WOMAN [B] — Crystal WATERS (2) ..91,92
GYPSYS TRAMPS AND THIEVES — CHER (4) 71
HA CHA CHA (FUNKTION) — BRASS CONSTRUCTION (37) 77
HA HA SAID THE CLOWN — MANFRED MANN (4) 67
HAD TO BE — Cliff RICHARD and Olivia NEWTON-JOHN (22)95
HAIL CAESAR — AC/DC (56) 96
HAIL HAIL ROCK 'N' ROLL — Garland JEFFREYS (72) 92
HAIL MARY — MAKAVELI (43) 98
HAITIAN DIVORCE — STEELY DAN (17)....76
HALCYON — CHICANE (28) 00
HALE BOPP — DER DRITTE RAUM (75) 99
HALEY'S GOLDEN MEDLEY — Bill HALEY and his COMETS (50)....81
HALF A BOY AND HALF A MAN — Nick LOWE (53)....84
HALF A MINUTE — MATT BIANCO (23)....84
HALF AS MUCH — Rosemary CLOONEY (3) 52
HALF OF MY HEART — Emile FORD and the CHECKMATES (42) 61
HALF ON A BABY — R KELLY (16) 98
HALF THE DAY'S GONE AND WE HAVEN'T EARNT A PENNY — Kenny LYNCH (50)....83
HALF THE MAN — JAMIROQUAI (15)....94
HALF THE WORLD — Belinda CARLISLE (35) 92
HALFWAY AROUND THE WORLD — A*TEENS (30) 01
HALFWAY DOWN THE STAIRS — MUPPETS (7)..77
HALFWAY HOTEL — VOYAGER (33) 79
HALFWAY TO HEAVEN — EUROPE (42)....92
HALFWAY TO PARADISE — Billy FURY (3)....61
HALFWAY UP HALFWAY DOWN — Dennis BROWN (56) 82
HALLELUJAH — MILK AND HONEY featuring Gali ATARI (5)....79
HALLELUJAH DAY — JACKSONS (20)....73
HALLELUJAH FREEDOM — Junior CAMPBELL (10)72
HALLELUJAH I LOVE HER SO [A] — Dick JORDAN (47) 60
HALLELUJAH I LOVE HER SO [A] — Eddie COCHRAN (22)....60
HALLELUJAH MAN — LOVE AND MONEY (63)....88

HALLELUJAH '92 – INNER CITY (22) 92
HALLO SPACEBOY – David BOWIE (12) 96
HALLOWED BE THY NAME (LIVE) – IRON MAIDEN (9) 93
HALLS OF ILLUSION – INSANE CLOWN POSSE (56)................................98
HALO – TEXAS (10) 97
(HAMMER HAMMER) THEY PUT ME IN THE MIX – HAMMER (20)..91
HAMMER HORROR – Kate BUSH (44) 78
HAMMER TO FALL – QUEEN (13) 84
HAMMER TO THE HEART – TAMPERER featuring MAYA (6) 00
HAND A HANDKERCHIEF TO HELEN – Susan MAUGHAN (41) 63
HAND HELD IN BLACK AND WHITE – DOLLAR (19) 81
HAND IN GLOVE – Sandie SHAW (27)..............84
HAND IN HAND – GRACE (38) 97
HAND IN MY POCKET – Alanis MORISSETTE (26) 95
HAND IN YOUR HEAD – MONEY MARK (40) 98
HAND OF THE DEAD BODY – SCARFACE featuring ICE CUBE (41) 95
HAND ON MY HEART – SHRIEKBACK (52)........84
HAND ON YOUR HEART – Kylie MINOGUE (1) ..89
HANDBAGS AND GLADRAGS [A] – Chris FARLOWE (33)..67
HANDBAGS AND GLADRAGS [A] – STEREOPHONICS (4) 01
HANDFUL OF PROMISES – BIG FUN (21) 90
HANDFUL OF SONGS – Tommy STEELE (5)......57
HANDLE WITH CARE – TRAVELING WILBURYS (21) 88
HANDS – JEWEL (41) 98
HANDS ACROSS THE OCEAN – MISSION (28) ..90
HANDS OFF – SHE'S MINE – BEAT (9) 80
HANDS TO HEAVEN – BREATHE (4)..................88
HANDS UP [A] – CLUBZONE (50)......................94
HANDS UP [B] – TREVOR & SIMON (12) 00
HANDS UP (4 LOVERS) – RIGHT SAID FRED (60) 93
HANDS UP (GIVE ME YOUR HEART) – OTTAWAN (3)..81
HANDS UP! HANDS UP! – ZIG and ZAG (21) 95
HANDY MAN [A] – Jimmy JONES (3) 60
HANDY MAN [A] – Del SHANNON (36) 64
HANG 'EM HIGH – Hugo MONTENEGRO (50) ..69
HANG IN LONG ENOUGH – Phil COLLINS (34)..90
HANG MYSELF ON YOU – CANDYSKINS (65)....97
HANG ON IN THERE BABY [A] – Johnny BRISTOL (3)...74
HANG ON IN THERE BABY [A] – CURIOSITY (3)92
HANG ON NOW – KAJAGOOGOO (13) 83
HANG ON SLOOPY [A] – McCOYS (5) 65
HANG ON SLOOPY [A] – SANDPIPERS (32)......76
HANG ON TO A DREAM – Tim HARDIN (50) 67
HANG ON TO YOUR LOVE – Jason DONOVAN (8) 90
HANG TOGETHER – ODYSSEY (36) 81
HANG YOUR HEAD – DEACON BLUE (21)..........93
HANGAR 18 – MEGADETH (26)...........................91
HANGIN' – CHIC (64) 83
HANGIN' ON A STRING – LOOSE ENDS (13)85,92
HANGIN' OUT – KOOL and the GANG (52) 80
HANGIN' TOUGH – NEW KIDS ON THE BLOCK (1) 89,90
HANGING AROUND [A] – Hazel O'CONNOR (45) 81
HANGING AROUND [B] – ME ME ME (19) 96
HANGING AROUND [C] – CARDIGANS (17)........99
HANGING AROUND WITH THE BIG BOYS – BLOOMSBURY SET (56) 83
HANGING BY A MOMENT – LIFEHOUSE (25) 01
HANGING GARDEN – CURE (34) 82
HANGING ON THE TELEPHONE – BLONDIE (5) 78
HANGINAROUND – COUNTING CROWS (46) 99
HANGOVER – Betty BOO (50) 93
HANKY PANKY [A] – Tommy JAMES and the SHONDELLS (38) 66
HANKY PANKY [B] – MADONNA (2).................90
HANNA HANNA – CHINA CRISIS (44)................84
HAPPENIN' ALL OVER AGAIN [A] – Lonnie GORDON (4) 90
HAPPENIN' ALL OVER AGAIN [A] – Tracy SHAW (46)..98
THE HAPPENING – SUPREMES (6) 67
HAPPENINGS TEN YEARS TIME AGO – YARDBIRDS (43) 66
HAPPINESS [A] – Ken DODD (31) 64
HAPPINESS [B] – SERIOUS ROPE (54) 93
HAPPINESS [C] – Roger TAYLOR (32) 94
HAPPINESS [D] – PIZZAMAN (19) 95
HAPPINESS [E] – KAMASUTRA featuring Jocelyn BROWN (45)..97
HAPPINESS [F] – SOUND-DE-ZIGN (19) 01
HAPPINESS HAPPENING – LOST WITNESS (18)99
HAPPINESS IS JUST AROUND THE BEND – Cuba GOODING (72) 83
HAPPINESS IS ME AND YOU – Gilbert O'SULLIVAN (19) 74
HAPPINESS (MY VISION IS CLEAR) – BINI & MARTINI (53) 00
HAPPINESS – YOU MAKE ME HAPPY – SERIOUS ROPE (70) 94
HAPPY [A] – SURFACE (56) 87
HAPPY [A] – MN8 (8)..95
HAPPY [A] – Pauline HENRY (46) 96
HAPPY [B] – NED'S ATOMIC DUSTBIN (16) 91
HAPPY [C] – TRAVIS (38).................................97
HAPPY ANNIVERSARY [A] – Joan REGAN (29) ..60
HAPPY ANNIVERSARY [B] – Slim WHITMAN (14) 74
HAPPY BIRTHDAY [A] – Stevie WONDER (2) 81
HAPPY BIRTHDAY [B] – ALTERED IMAGES (2) ..81
HAPPY BIRTHDAY [C] – TECHNOHEAD (18) 96
HAPPY BIRTHDAY REVOLUTION – LEVELLERS (57)...00
HAPPY BIRTHDAY SWEET SIXTEEN – Neil SEDAKA (3)..61
HAPPY BIZZNESS – ROACH MOTEL (75) 94
HAPPY BUSMAN – FRANK AND WALTERS (49) 92
HAPPY DAY – BLINK (57) 94
HAPPY DAYS [A] – PRATT and McCLAIN with BROTHERLOVE (31)77
HAPPY DAYS [B] – SWEET MERCY featuring Joe ROBERTS (63)..96
HAPPY DAYS [C] – PJ (57) 97,99
HAPPY DAYS AND LONELY NIGHTS [A] – Frankie VAUGHAN (12) 55
HAPPY DAYS AND LONELY NIGHTS [A] – JOHNSTON BROTHERS (14) 55
HAPPY DAYS AND LONELY NIGHTS [A] – Ruby MURRAY (6) 55
HAPPY ENDING – Joe JACKSON (58) 84
HAPPY ENDINGS (GIVE YOURSELF A PINCH) – Lionel BART (68)...89
HAPPY EVER AFTER – Julia FORDHAM (27)......88
HAPPY FEELING – Hamilton BOHANNON (49)..75
HAPPY GO LUCKY ME – George FORMBY (40) 60
HAPPY GUITAR – Tommy STEELE (20) 58
HAPPY HEART – Andy WILLIAMS (19) 69
HAPPY HOME – 2PAC (17) 98
HAPPY HOUR – HOUSEMARTINS (3) 86
HAPPY HOUSE – SIOUXSIE and the BANSHEES (17) 80
HAPPY JACK – WHO (3)...................................66
HAPPY JUST TO BE WITH YOU – Michelle GAYLE (11).......................................95
HAPPY (LOVE THEME FROM 'LADY SINGS THE BLUES') – Michael JACKSON (52)..........83
THE HAPPY MAN – Thomas LANG (67)............88
HAPPY NATION – ACE OF BASE (40) 93,94
HAPPY PEOPLE – STATIC REVENGER (23)........01
H.A.P.P.Y. RADIO [A] – Edwin STARR (9) 79
H-A-P-P-Y RADIO [A] – MICHAELA (62) 89
HAPPY SHOPPER – 60FT DOLLS (38) 96
HAPPY SONG – Otis REDDING (24)..................68
HAPPY TALK – CAPTAIN SENSIBLE (1)..............82
HAPPY TO BE ON AN ISLAND IN THE SUN – Demis ROUSSOS (5) 75
HAPPY TO MAKE YOUR ACQUAINTANCE – Sammy DAVIS Jr (46) 60
HAPPY TOGETHER [A] – TURTLES (12) 67
HAPPY TOGETHER [A] – Jason DONOVAN (10)..91
THE HAPPY WANDERER [A] – OBERNKIRCHEN CHILDREN'S CHOIR (2) 54
THE HAPPY WANDERER [A] – STARGAZERS (12)..54
HAPPY WHEN IT RAINS – JESUS AND MARY CHAIN (25) 87
THE HAPPY WHISTLER [A] – Cyril STAPLETON and his ORCHESTRA (22) ..56
THE HAPPY WHISTLER [A] – Don ROBERTSON (8) 56
HAPPY XMAS (WAR IS OVER) – John LENNON (2) 72,75,80,81,82,88
HARBOUR LIGHTS – PLATTERS (11).................60
HARD AS A ROCK – AC/DC (33)........................95
HARD BEAT EP 19 – VARIOUS ARTISTS (EPs and LPs) (71)............01
A HARD DAY'S NIGHT [A] – BEATLES (1) 64,84
A HARD DAY'S NIGHT [A] – Peter SELLERS (14) 65,93
HARD HABIT TO BREAK – CHICAGO (8) 84
HARD HEADED WOMAN – Elvis PRESLEY (2) ..58
HARD HEARTED HANNAH – TEMPERANCE SEVEN (28) 61
HARD HOUSE MUSIC – MELT featuring LITTLE MS MARCIE (59) 00
HARD KNOCK LIFE (GHETTO ANTHEM) – JAY-Z (2) 98
A HARD RAIN'S A-GONNA FALL – Bryan FERRY (10) 73
HARD ROAD – BLACK SABBATH (33) 78
HARD TIMES COME EASY – Richie SAMBORA (37)..98
HARD TO EXPLAIN / NEW YORK CITY COPS – STROKES (16) 01
HARD TO HANDLE [A] – Otis REDDING (15)......68
HARD TO HANDLE [A] – BLACK CROWES (39) 90,91
HARD TO MAKE A STAND – Sheryl CROW (22) 97
HARD TO SAY I'M SORRY [A] – AZ YET featuring Peter CETERA (7)................97
HARD TO SAY I'M SORRY [A] – CHICAGO (4) ..82
HARD UP – AWESOME 3 (55) 90
THE HARD WAY – NASHVILLE TEENS (45) 66
THE HARDCORE EP – HYPNOTIST (68) 91
HARDCORE HEAVEN – DJ SEDUCTION (26) 92
HARDCORE HIP HOUSE – TYREE (70) 89
HARDCORE – THE FINAL CONFLICT – HARDCORE RHYTHM TEAM (69) 92
HARDCORE UPROAR – TOGETHER (12) 90
HARDCORE WILL NEVER DIE – Q-BASS (64) 92
HARDEN MY HEART – QUARTERFLASH (49) 82
HARDER BETTER FASTER STRONGER – DAFT PUNK (25) 01
THE HARDER I TRY – BROTHER BEYOND (2) ..88
THE HARDER THEY COME [A] – ROCKER'S REVENGE featuring Donnie CALVIN (30)........83
THE HARDER THEY COME [A] – MADNESS (44)92
THE HARDEST THING – 98 (29)........................00
HARDEST PART IS THE NIGHT – BON JOVI (68)85
HARDROCK – Herbie HANCOCK (65) 84
HARDTRANCE ACPERIENCE – HARDFLOOR (56)92
HARE KRISHNA MANTRA – RADHA KRISHNA TEMPLE (12) 69
HARLEM DESIRE – LONDON BOYS (17)............89
HARLEM SHUFFLE [A] – BOB and EARL (7).......69
HARLEM SHUFFLE [A] – ROLLING STONES (13) 86
HARLEQUIN – THE BEAUTY AND THE BEAST – Sven VATH (72)..94
HARMONICA MAN – BRAVADO (37) 94
HARMONY – TC (51) 93
HARMONY IN MY HEAD – BUZZCOCKS (32) 79
HARMOUR LOVE – SYREETA (32) 75
HARPER VALLEY P.T.A. – Jeannie C RILEY (12)..68
HARVEST FOR THE WORLD [A] – ISLEY BROTHERS (10) 76
HARVEST FOR THE WORLD [A] – CHRISTIANS (8)...88
HARVEST FOR THE WORLD [A] – Terry HUNTER (48) 97
HARVEST MOON – Neil YOUNG (36) 93
HARVEST OF LOVE – Benny HILL (20)..............63
HARVESTER OF SORROW – METALLICA (20)....88
HAS IT COME TO THIS – STREETS (18) 01
HASH PIPE – WEEZER (21)................................01
HASTA LA VISTA – SYLVIA (38) 75
HATE ME NOW – NAS featuring PUFF DADDY (14) 99
HATS OFF TO LARRY – Del SHANNON (6) 61
HAUNTED [A] – POGUES (42) 86
HAUNTED [A] – Shane MacGOWAN and Sinead O'CONNOR (30) 95
HAUNTED BY YOU – GENE (32)........................95
HAVA NAGILA – SPOTNICKS (13).......................63
HAVE A DRINK ON ME – Lonnie DONEGAN (8) 61
HAVE A GOOD FOREVER – COOLNOTES (73) ..85
HAVE A LITTLE FAITH – Joe COCKER (67) 95
HAVE A NICE DAY [A] – Roxanne SHANTE (58) 87
HAVE A NICE DAY [B] – STEREOPHONICS (5) ..01
HAVE FUN GO MAD – BLAIR (37) 95
HAVE I STAYED TOO LONG – SONNY and CHER (42) 66
HAVE I THE RIGHT [A] – HONEYCOMBS (1) 64
HAVE I THE RIGHT [A] – DEAD END KIDS (6) ..77
HAVE I TOLD YOU LATELY [A] – Van MORRISON (74) 89

HAVE I TOLD YOU LATELY [A] – Rod STEWART (5) 93
HAVE I TOLD YOU LATELY THAT I LOVE YOU [A] – CHIEFTANS with Van MORRISON (71) 95
HAVE LOST IT (EP) – TEENAGE FANCLUB (53) 95
HAVE LOVE, WILL TRAVEL (EP) – CRAZYHEAD (68) 89
HAVE MERCY – YAZZ (42) 94
HAVE PITY ON THE BOY – Paul and Barry RYAN (18) 66
HAVE YOU EVER? – BRANDY (13) 98
HAVE YOU EVER – S CLUB 7 (1) 01
HAVE YOU EVER BEEN IN LOVE – Leo SAYER (10)82
HAVE YOU EVER BEEN MELLOW – PARTY ANIMALS (56) 96
HAVE YOU EVER BEEN MELLOW (EP) – PARTY ANIMALS (43) 96
HAVE YOU EVER HAD IT BLUE – STYLE COUNCIL (14) 86
HAVE YOU EVER LOVED SOMEBODY [A] – Paul and Barry RYAN (49) 66
HAVE YOU EVER LOVED SOMEBODY [B] – SEARCHERS (48) 66
HAVE YOU EVER LOVED SOMEBODY [C] – Freddie JACKSON (33) 87
HAVE YOU EVER NEEDED SOMEONE SO BAD – DEF LEPPARD (16) 92
HAVE YOU EVER REALLY LOVED A WOMAN – Bryan ADAMS (4) 95
HAVE YOU EVER SEEN THE RAIN [A] – CREEDENCE CLEARWATER REVIVAL (36) 71
HAVE YOU EVER SEEN THE RAIN [A] – Bonnie TYLER (47) 83
HAVE YOU SEEN HER [A] – CHI-LITES (3) 72,75
HAVE YOU SEEN HER [A] – HAMMER (8) 90
HAVE YOU SEEN YOUR MOTHER BABY STANDING IN THE SHADOW – ROLLING STONES (5) 66
HAVEN'T SEEN YOU – PERFUME (71) 96
HAVEN'T STOPPED DANCING YET – GONZALEZ (15) 79
HAVEN'T YOU HEARD – Patrice RUSHEN (62)..80
HAVING A PARTY – OSMONDS (28) 75
HAWAII TATTOO – WAIKIKIS (41) 65
HAWAIIAN WEDDING SONG – Julie ROGERS (31) 65
HAWKEYE – Frankie LAINE (7) 55
HAYFEVER – TRASH CAN SINATRAS (61) 93
HAZARD – Richard MARX (3) 92
HAZEL – LOOP DA LOOP (20) 99
HAZELL – Maggie BELL (37) 78
HAZIN' & PHAZIN' – CHOO CHOO PROJECT (21)..00
HAZY SHADE OF WINTER [A] – BANGLES (11) ..88
A HAZY SHADE OF WINTER [B] – SIMON and GARFUNKEL (30) 91
HE AIN'T HEAVY, HE'S MY BROTHER [A] – HOLLIES (1) 69,88
HE AIN'T HEAVY, HE'S MY BROTHER [A] – Bill MEDLEY (25) 88
HE AIN'T NO COMPETITION – BROTHER BEYOND (6) 88
HE DOESN'T LOVE YOU LIKE I DO – Nick HEYWARD (58) 93
HE DON'T LOVE YOU – HUMAN NATURE (18) ..01
HE GOT GAME – PUBLIC ENEMY featuring Stephen STILLS (16) 98
HE GOT WHAT HE WANTED – LITTLE RICHARD (38) 62
HE IS SAILING – JON and VANGELIS (61) 83
HE KNOWS YOU KNOW – MARILLION (35) 83
HE REMINDS ME – Randy CRAWFORD (65) 83
HE THINKS HE'LL KEEP HER – Mary-Chapin CARPENTER (71) 93
HE WAS BEAUTIFUL (CAVATINA) (THE THEME FROM 'THE DEER HUNTER') – Iris WILLIAMS (18) 79
HE WASN'T MAN ENOUGH – Toni BRAXTON (5)..00
HEAD – Julian COPE (57) 91
HEAD ABOVE WATER – Clive GRIFFIN (60) 89
HEAD LIKE A HOLE – NINE INCH NAILS (45) 91
HEAD ON – JESUS AND MARY CHAIN (57) 89
HEAD OVER FEET – Alanis MORISSETTE (7) 96
HEAD OVER HEELS [A] – ABBA (25) 82
HEAD OVER HEELS [B] – TEARS FOR FEARS (12) 85
HEAD OVER HEELS [C] – Nic HAVERSON (48)..93
HEAD OVER HEELS [D] – ALLURE featuring NAS (18) 97
HEAD OVER HEELS IN LOVE – Kevin KEEGAN (31)79
HEAD TO TOE (EP) – BREEDERS (68) 94
HEADACHE – Frank BLACK (53) 94
HEADING WEST – Cyndi LAUPER (68) 89
HEADLESS CROSS – BLACK SABBATH (62) 89
HEADLIGHTS ON THE PARADE – BLUE NILE (72) 90
HEADLINE NEWS [A] – Edwin STARR (11) 66,68
HEADLINE NEWS [B] – William BELL (70) 86
HEADLINES – MIDNIGHT STAR (16) 86
HEADLONG – QUEEN (14) 91
HEADS DOWN NO NONSENSE MINDLESS BOOGIE – ALBERTO Y LOS TRIOS PARANOIAS (47) 78
HEADS HIGH – MR VEGAS (16) 98,99
HEAL THE PAIN – George MICHAEL (31) 91
HEAL (THE SEPARATION) – SHAMEN (31) 96
HEAL THE WORLD – Michael JACKSON (2) 92
THE HEALING GAME – Van MORRISON (46) 97
HEALING HANDS – Elton JOHN (1) 89,90
HEALING LOVE – Cliff RICHARD (19) 93
HEAR ME CALLING – 2WO THIRD3 (48) 94
HEAR MY CALL – Alison LIMERICK (73) 92
HEAR THE DRUMMER (GET WICKED) – Chad JACKSON (3) 90
HEAR YOU CALLING – AURORA (17) 99,00
HEARD IT ALL BEFORE – Sunshine ANDERSON (9) 01
HEARSAY '89 – Alexander O'NEAL (56) 89
HEART [A] – JOHNSTON BROTHERS (23) 57
HEART [A] – Max BYGRAVES (14) 57
HEART [B] – Rita PAVONE (27) 66
HEART [C] – PET SHOP BOYS (1) 88
HEART [D] – Gary NUMAN (43) 91
HEART AND SOUL [A] – JAN and DEAN (24) 61
HEART AND SOUL [B] – EXILE (54) 81
HEART AND SOUL [C] – T'PAU (4) 87
HEART AND SOUL [D] – NO SWEAT (64) 90
HEART AND SOUL [E] – Cilla BLACK with Dusty SPRINGFIELD (75) 93
HEART AND SOUL [F] – TSD (69) 96
HEART AND SOUL (EP) – Huey LEWIS and the NEWS (61) 85
THE HEART ASKS PLEASURE FIRST – Michael NYMAN (60) 94
HEART ATTACK – Olivia NEWTON-JOHN (46) 82
HEART ATTACK AND VINE – Screamin' Jay HAWKINS (42) 93
HEART (DON'T CHANGE MY MIND) – Diana ROSS (31) 93
HEART FAILED (IN THE BACK OF A TAXI) – SAINT ETIENNE (50) 00
HEART FULL OF SOUL – YARDBIRDS (2) 65
HEART GO BOOM – APOLLO FOUR FORTY (57)99
HEART LIKE A WHEEL – HUMAN LEAGUE (29) 90
THE HEART OF A MAN – Frankie VAUGHAN (5)59
HEART OF A TEENAGE GIRL [A] – George CHAKIRIS (49) 60
THE HEART OF A TEENAGE GIRL [A] – Craig DOUGLAS (10) 60
HEART OF ASIA – WATERGATE (3) 00
HEART OF GLASS [A] – BLONDIE (1) 79,95
HEART OF GLASS [A] – ASSOCIATES (56) 88
HEART OF GOLD [A] – Neil YOUNG (10) 72
HEART OF GOLD [B] – JOHNNY HATES JAZZ (19) 88
HEART OF GOLD [C] – FORCE & STYLES featuring Kelly LLORENNA (55) 98
HEART OF LOTHIAN – MARILLION (29) 85
THE HEART OF ROCK AND ROLL – Huey LEWIS and the NEWS (49) 86
HEART OF SOUL – CULT (51) 92
HEART OF STONE [A] – KENNY (11) 73
HEART OF STONE [B] – Suzi QUATRO (60) 82
HEART OF STONE [C] – BUCKS FIZZ (50) 88
HEART OF STONE [C] – CHER (43) 90
HEART OF STONE [D] – Dave STEWART (36) ..94
HEART OF THE SUN – RED BOX (71) 87
HEART OF THE WORLD – BIG COUNTRY (50) ..90
HEART ON MY SLEEVE – GALLAGHER and LYLE (6) 76
HEART OVER MIND – Kim WILDE (34) 92
HEART (STOP BEATING IN TIME) – Leo SAYER (22) 82
HEART USER – Cliff RICHARD (46) 85
HEARTACHE [A] – Roy ORBISON (44) 68
HEARTACHE [B] – GENE LOVES JEZEBEL (71) 86
HEARTACHE [C] – PEPSI and SHIRLIE (2) 87
HEARTACHE ALL OVER THE WORLD – Elton JOHN (45) 86
HEARTACHE AVENUE – MAISONETTES (7) 82
HEARTACHE TONIGHT – EAGLES (40) 79
HEARTACHES [A] – Patsy CLINE (31) 62
HEARTACHES [A] – Vince HILL (28) 66
HEARTACHES BY THE NUMBER – Guy MITCHELL (5) 59
HEARTBEAT [A] – Ruby MURRAY (3) 54
HEARTBEAT [B] – Buddy HOLLY (30) 59,60
HEARTBEAT [B] – ENGLAND SISTERS (33) 60
HEARTBEAT [B] – SHOWADDYWADDY (7) 75
HEARTBEAT [B] – Nick BERRY (2) 92
HEARTBEAT [B] – HEARTBEAT COUNTRY (75) 94
HEARTBEAT [C] – Sammy HAGAR (67) 80
HEARTBEAT [D] – Tippa IRIE (59) 86
HEARTBEAT [E] – Don JOHNSON (46) 86
HEARTBEAT [F] – SEDUCTION (75) 90
HEARTBEAT [G] – GRID (72) 92
HEARTBEAT [H] – Jimmy SOMERVILLE (24) 95
HEARTBEAT [I] – KRS ONE (66) 97
HEARTBEAT [J] – STEPS (1) 98
A HEARTBEAT AWAY – McGANNS (42) 99
HEARTBEAT (TAINAI KAIKI II) RETURNING TO THE WOMB – David SYLVIAN (58) 92
HEARTBREAK – MRS WOOD featuring Eve GALLAGHER (44) ..96
HEARTBREAK HOTEL [A] – Elvis PRESLEY (2) 56,71,96
HEARTBREAK HOTEL [A] – Stan FREBERG (24) 56
HEARTBREAK HOTEL [B] – JACKSONS (44) 80
HEARTBREAK HOTEL [C] – Whitney HOUSTON featuring Faith EVANS and Kelly PRICE (26) 00
HEARTBREAK RADIO – Roy ORBISON (36) 92
HEARTBREAK STATION – CINDERELLA (63) 91
HEARTBREAKER [A] – Dionne WARWICK (2) 82
HEARTBREAKER [B] – MUSICAL YOUTH (44) 83
HEARTBREAKER [C] – COLOR ME BADD (58) ..92
HEARTBREAKER [D] – Mariah CAREY featuring JAY-Z (5) 99
HEARTBROKE AND BUSTED – MAGNUM (49) ..90
HEARTHAMMER (EP) – RUNRIG (25) 91
HEARTLAND – The THE (29) 86
HEARTLIGHT – Neil DIAMOND (47) 82
HEARTLINE – Robin GEORGE (68) 85
THE HEART'S FILTHY LESSON – David BOWIE (35) 95
THE HEART'S LONE DESIRE – Matthew MARSDEN (13) 98
HEARTS ON FIRE [A] – Sam HARRIS (67) 85
HEARTS ON FIRE [B] – Bryan ADAMS (57) 87
HEART-SHAPED BOX – NIRVANA (5) 93
HEARTSONG – Gordon GILTRAP (21) 78
HEARTSPARK DOLLARSIGN – EVERCLEAR (48) 96
THE HEAT IS ON [A] – Agnetha FALTSKOG (35) ..83
THE HEAT IS ON [B] – Glenn FREY (12) 85
HEAT IT UP – TWO MEN, A DRUM MACHINE AND A TRUMPET (21) 88
HEAT OF THE BEAT – Roy AYERS (43) 79
HEAT OF THE MOMENT – ASIA (46) 82
HEAT OF THE NIGHT – Bryan ADAMS (50) 87
HEATHER HONEY – Tommy ROE (24) 69
HEATSEEKER – AC/DC (12) 88
HEAVEN [A] – Bryan ADAMS (38) 85
HEAVEN [B] – TWO PEOPLE (63) 87
HEAVEN [C] – CHIMES (24) 89,90
HEAVEN [D] – Chris REA (57) 91
HEAVEN [E] – TIGERTAILZ (71) 91
HEAVEN [F] – WHYCLIFFE (56) 93
HEAVEN [G] – FITS OF GLOOM (47) 94
HEAVEN [H] – Sarah WASHINGTON (28) 96
HEAVEN [I] – KINANE (49) 98
HEAVEN [J] – PSYCHEDELIC FURS (29) 84
HEAVEN [K] – SOLO U.S. (35) 96
HEAVEN & EARTH – RED (41) 01
HEAVEN AND HELL, THIRD MOVEMENT (THEME FROM THE BBC-TV SERIES 'THE COSMOS') – VANGELIS (48) 81
HEAVEN BESIDE YOU – ALICE IN CHAINS (35) 96
HEAVEN CAN WAIT – Paul YOUNG (71) 90
HEAVEN FOR EVERYONE – QUEEN (2) 95
HEAVEN GIVE ME WORDS – PROPAGANDA (36) 90
HEAVEN HELP – Lenny KRAVITZ (20) 93
HEAVEN HELP ME – Deon ESTUS (41) 89
HEAVEN HELP MY HEART – Tina ARENA (25) ..95

HEY DJ [A] – **LIGHTER SHADE OF BROWN** (33) 94
HEY DJ – I CAN'T DANCE (TO THAT MUSIC YOU'RE PLAYING) – **BEATMASTERS featuring BETTY BOO** (7) 89
HEY DJ! (PLAY THAT SONG) – **N-TYCE** (20) 97
HEY DUDE – **KULA SHAKER** (2) 96
HEY GIRL [A] – **SMALL FACES** (10)....................66
HEY GIRL [B] – **EXPRESSOS** (60) 80
HEY GIRL DON'T BOTHER ME – **TAMS** (1) 71
HEY GOD – **BON JOVI** (13)................................96
HEY GOOD LOOKIN' – **Bo DIDDLEY** (39) 65
HEY GOOD LOOKING – **Tommy ZANG** (45) 61
HEY JEALOUSY – **GIN BLOSSOMS** (24) 94
HEY JOE [A] – **Frankie LAINE** (1) 53
HEY JOE [B] – **Jimi HENDRIX EXPERIENCE** (6) ..67
HEY JUPITER – **Tori AMOS** (20) 96
HEY LITTLE GIRL [A] – **Del SHANNON** (2) 62
HEY LITTLE GIRL [B] – **ICEHOUSE** (17)..............83
HEY LORD, DON'T ASK ME QUESTIONS – **Graham PARKER and the RUMOUR** (32)........78
HEY LOVE – **KING SUN-D'MOET** (66)................87
HEY LOVER – **LL COOL J featuring BOYZ II MEN** (17) 96
HEY! LUCIANI – **FALL** (59) 86
HEY MAMA [A] – **Frankie VAUGHAN** (21).........63
HEY MAMA [B] – **Joe BROWN and the BRUVVERS** (33) 73
HEY MANHATTAN! – **PREFAB SPROUT** (72)......88
HEY MATTHEW – **Karel FIALKA** (9) 87
HEY MISS PAYNE – **CHEQUERS** (32) 76
HEY MR CHRISTMAS – **SHOWADDYWADDY** (13)..74
HEY MR DJ [A] – **ZHANE** (26)............................93
HEY MR DJ [B] – **OPEN ARMS featuring ROWETTA** (62)...........96
HEY MR DREAM MAKER – **Cliff RICHARD** (31) ..76
HEY MISTER HEARTACHE – **Kim WILDE** (31) 88
HEY MR MUSIC MAN – **PETERS and LEE** (16) 76
HEY MUSIC LOVER – **S EXPRESS** (6)................89
HEY NOW (GIRLS JUST WANT TO HAVE FUN) – **Cyndi LAUPER** (4) 94
HEY NOW NOW – **SWIRL 360** (61)....................98
HEY! PARADISE – **FLICKMAN** (69) 01
HEY PAULA – **PAUL and PAULA** (8)..................63
HEY ROCK AND ROLL – **SHOWADDYWADDY** (2) 74
HEY SENORITA – **WAR** (40) 78
HEY STOOPID – **Alice COOPER** (21) 91
HEY THERE [A] – **Johnnie RAY** (5) 55
HEY THERE [A] – **Lita ROZA** (17) 55
HEY THERE [A] – **Rosemary CLOONEY** (4)........55
HEY THERE [A] – **Sammy DAVIS Jr** (19) 55
(HEY THERE) LONELY GIRL [A] – **Eddie HOLMAN** (4) 74
HEY THERE LONELY GIRL [A] – **BIG FUN** (62) ..90
HEY VENUS – **THAT PETROL EMOTION** (49) 90
HEY! WHAT'S YOUR NAME – **BABY JUNE** (75)..92
HEY WILLY – **HOLLIES** (22) 71
HEY YOU [A] – **Tommy STEELE** (28) 57
HEY YOU [B] – **QUIREBOYS** (14) 90
(HEY YOU) THE ROCKSTEADY CREW – **ROCKSTEADY CREW** (6)..................................83
HEYKENS SERENADE – **The Pipes and Drums and Military Band of the ROYAL SCOTS DRAGOON GUARDS** (30) 72
HI DE HI, HI DE HO – **KOOL and the GANG** (29) 82
HI DE HI (HOLIDAY ROCK) – **Paul SHANE and the YELLOWCOATS** (36)......81
HI DE HO – **K7** (17) 94
HI HI HAZEL [A] – **Geno WASHINGTON and the RAM JAM BAND** (45) 66
HI HI HAZEL [A] – **TROGGS** (42) 67
HI HI HI – **Paul McCARTNEY** (5) 72
HI HO SILVER – **Jim DIAMOND** (5)....................86
HI! HOW YA DOIN'? – **Kenny G** (70) 84
HI LILI HI LO – **Alan PRICE** (11) 66
HI TENSION – **HI TENSION** (13) 78
HIBERNACULUM – **Mike OLDFIELD** (47)...........94
HIDDEN PLACE – **BJÖRK** (21) 01
HIDE AND SEEK [A] – **Marty WILDE** (47) 61
HIDE AND SEEK [B] – **Howard JONES** (12)........84
HIDE U – **KOSHEEN** (73) 00,01
HIDE YOUR HEART – **KISS** (59) 89
HIDEAWAY [A] – **Dave DEE, DOZY, BEAKY, MICK and TICH** (10) 66
HIDEAWAY [B] – **DE'LACY** (9) 95,98
HIDE-A-WAY – **NU SOUL featuring Kelli RICH** (27)...................96
HI-FIDELITY – **KIDS FROM 'FAME'** (5) 82
HIGH [A] – **CURE** (8) 92
HIGH [B] – **HYPER GO GO** (30)....................92,96
HIGH [C] – **FEEDER** (24).....................................97
HIGH [D] – **PROPHETS OF SOUND** (73)............98
HIGH [E] – **LIGHTHOUSE FAMILY** (4) 98
HIGH AND DRY – **RADIOHEAD** (17) 95
HIGH AS A KITE – **OUR TRIBE / ONE TRIBE** (55) ..95
HIGH CLASS BABY – **Cliff RICHARD** (7) 58
HIGH ENERGY – **Evelyn THOMAS** (5)................84
HIGH FIDELITY – **Elvis COSTELLO** (30) 80
HIGH FLY – **John MILES** (17) 75
HIGH HEAD BLUES – **BLACK CROWES** (25)......95
HIGH HOPES [A] – **Frank SINATRA** (6) 59,60
HIGH HOPES [B] – **PINK FLOYD** (26)................94
HIGH HORSE – **Evelyn 'Champagne' KING** (55)86
HIGH IN THE SKY – **AMEN CORNER** (6)...........68
HIGH LIFE – **MODERN ROMANCE** (8)................83
HIGH NOON [A] – **DJ SHADOW** (22)..................97
HIGH NOON [B] – **SERIOUS DANGER** (54) 98
HIGH NOON (DO NOT FORSAKE ME) – **Frankie LAINE** (7) 52
HIGH ON A HAPPY VIBE – **URBAN COOKIE COLLECTIVE** (31) 94
HIGH ON EMOTION – **Chris DE BURGH** (44) 84
HIGH ROLLERS – **ICE-T** (63)...............................89
HIGH SCHOOL CONFIDENTIAL – **Jerry Lee LEWIS** (12) 59
HIGH TIME – **Paul JONES** (4)............................66
HIGH TIMES – **JAMIROQUAI** (20) 97
HIGH VOLTAGE [A] – **JOHNNY and the HURRICANES** (24)................61
HIGH VOLTAGE (LIVE VERSION) [B] – **AC/DC** (48) 80
HIGHER [A] – **CREED** (47) 00,01
HIGHER [B] – **David MORALES** (41) 00
HIGHER AND HIGHER [A] – **Jackie WILSON** (15)87
HIGHER AND HIGHER [A] – **UNATION** (42)........93
HIGHER (FEEL IT) – **Erick 'More' MORILLO presents RAW** (74) 95
HIGHER GROUND [A] – **Stevie WONDER** (29) ..73
HIGHER GROUND [A] – **RED HOT CHILI PEPPERS** (54)........................90
HIGHER GROUND [B] – **GUN** (48).......................92
HIGHER GROUND [C] – **UB40** (8) 93
HIGHER GROUND [D] – **SASHA** (19) 94
HIGHER LOVE – **Steve WINWOOD** (13) 86
HIGHER STATE OF CONSCIOUSNESS – **Josh WINK** (7)...95,96
HIGHER THAN HEAVEN [A] – **AGE OF CHANCE** (53) 90
HIGHER THAN HEAVEN [B] – **Kéllé BRYAN** (14) 99
HIGHER THAN REASON – **UNBELIEVABLE TRUTH** (38)...........................98
HIGHER THAN THE SUN – **PRIMAL SCREAM** (40) 91
HIGHLIFE – **CYPRESS HILL** (35) 00
HIGHLY INFLAMMABLE – **X-RAY SPEX** (45) 79
HIGHLY STRUNG – **SPANDAU BALLET** (15) 84
HIGHRISE TOWN – **LANTERNS** (50) 99
HIGHWAY CODE – **MASTER SINGERS** (25)........66
HIGHWAY 5 – **BLESSING** (30) 91,92
HIGHWAY SONG – **Nancy SINATRA** (21)...........69
HIGHWAY TO HELL – **AC/DC** (14) 79,92
HIGHWAYS OF MY LIFE – **ISLEY BROTHERS** (25) 74
HIGHWIRE [A] – **Linda CARR** (15)......................75
HIGHWIRE [B] – **ROLLING STONES** (29) 91
HI-HEEL SNEAKERS – **Tommy TUCKER** (23) 64
HI-HO SILVER LINING – **Jeff BECK** (14) ..67,72,82
HI-LILI HI-LO – **Richard CHAMBERLAIN** (20) 63
HILLBILLY ROCK HILLBILLY ROLL – **WOOLPACKERS** (5) 96
HIM [A] – **Rupert HOLMES** (31) 80
HIM [B] – **Sarah BRIGHTMAN** (55)....................83
HIP HOP – **DEAD PREZ** (41)..............................00
HIP HOP, BE BOP (DON'T STOP) – **Man PARRISH** (41)..83
HIP HOP DON'T YA DROP – **HONKY** (70) 96
HIP HOP HOORAY – **NAUGHTY BY NATURE** (20)................................93
HIP HOUSE – **DJ 'FAST' EDDIE** (47).................89
HIP HOUSIN' – **X-PRESS 2** (55).........................94
HIP TO BE SQUARE – **Huey LEWIS and the NEWS** (41) 86
HIP TODAY – **EXTREME** (44) 95
HIPPY CHICK – **SOHO** (8) 90,91
HIPPY HIPPY SHAKE [A] – **SWINGING BLUE JEANS** (2) 63
HIPPY HIPPY SHAKE [A] – **GEORGIA SATELLITES** (63) 89
HIS GIRL – **GUESS WHO** (45) 67
HISTORY [A] – **MAI TAI** (8)................................85
HISTORY [B] – **VERVE** (24) 95
HISTORY [C] – **Michael JACKSON** (5) 97
HISTORY NEVER REPEATS – **SPLIT ENZ** (63) 81
HISTORY OF THE WORLD (PART 1) – **DAMNED** (51)...80
HISTORY REPEATING – **PROPELLERHEADS featuring Miss Shirley BASSEY** (19) 97
HIT [A] – **SUGARCUBES** (17) 92
HIT [B] – **WANNADIES** (20) 97
HIT AND MISS – **John BARRY ORCHESTRA** (10) 60
HIT AND RUN [A] – **GIRLSCHOOL** (32) 81
HIT AND RUN [B] – **TOTAL CONTRAST** (41) 85
HIT BY LOVE – **Ce Ce PENISTON** (33) 94
HIT 'EM HIGH (MONSTARS' ANTHEM) – **B REAL / BUSTA RHYMES / COOLIO / LL COOL J / METHOD MAN** (8) 97
HIT 'EM UP STYLE (OOPS!) – **BLU CANTRELL** (12) 01
HIT 'EM WIT DA HEE – **Missy 'Misdemeanor' ELLIOTT featuring LIL' KIM** (25) 98
HIT IT – **BEAT** (70)..81
HIT ME OFF – **NEW EDITION** (20) 96
HIT ME WITH YOUR RHYTHM STICK – **Ian DURY and the BLOCKHEADS** (1)....78,85,91
HIT OR MISS (WAITED TOO LONG) – **NEW FOUND GLORY** (58) 01
HIT THAT PERFECT BEAT – **BRONSKI BEAT** (3) 85
HIT THE GROUND – **DARLING BUDS** (27) 89
HIT THE GROUND RUNNING – **Tim FINN** (50) ..93
HIT THE NORTH – **FALL** (57) 87
HIT THE ROAD JACK – **Ray CHARLES** (6) 61
HITCHIN' A RIDE [A] – **VANITY FARE** (16) 69
HITCHIN' A RIDE [A] – **SINITTA** (24) 90
HITCHIN' A RIDE [B] – **GREEN DAY** (25) 97
HITMIX (OFFICIAL BOOTLEG MEGA-MIX) – **Alexander O'NEAL** (19) 89
HITS MEDLEY – **GIPSY KINGS** (53) 94
HITSVILLE UK – **CLASH** (56)..............................81
HOBART PAVING – **SAINT ETIENNE** (23) 93
HOBO HUMPIN' SLOBO BABE – **WHALE** (15) ..94,95
HOCUS POCUS – **FOCUS** (20) 73
HOGWASH FARM (THE DIESEL HANDS EP) – **DAWN OF THE REPLICANTS** (65)....................98
HOKEY COKEY [A] – **JUDGE DREAD** (59) 78
HOKEY COKEY [A] – **SNOWMEN** (18) 81
HOKEY COKEY [A] – **BLACK LACE** (31) 85
THE HOKEY COKEY [A] – **CAPTAIN SENSIBLE** (71) 94
HOKOYO – **ORANGE JUICE** (60) 82
HOKUS POKUS – **INSANE CLOWN POSSE** (53) 98
HOLD BACK THE NIGHT [A] – **TRAMMPS** (5) 75
HOLD BACK THE NIGHT [A] – **KWS features guest vocal from the TRAMMPS** (30) 92
HOLD BACK THE RIVER – **WET WET WET** (31)..90
HOLD BACK TOMORROW – **MIKI and GRIFF** (26) 59
HOLD IT – **Stephen 'Tin Tin' DUFFY** (55) 83
HOLD IT DOWN [A] – **SENSELESS THINGS** (19) 92
HOLD IT DOWN [B] – **2 BAD MICE** (48) 92
HOLD ME [A] – **Teddy PENDERGRASS with Whitney HOUSTON** (44) 86
HOLD ME [B] – **PJ PROBY** (3) 64
HOLD ME [B] – **B.A. ROBERTSON** (11) 81
HOLD ME [B] – **SAVAGE GARDEN** (16) 00,01
HOLD ME CLOSE – **David ESSEX** (1) 75
HOLD ME IN YOUR ARMS – **Rick ASTLEY** (10)..89
HOLD ME NOW [A] – **THOMPSON TWINS** (4) 83
HOLD ME NOW [B] – **Johnny LOGAN** (2) 87
HOLD ME THRILL ME KISS ME [A] – **Muriel SMITH** (3)..53
HOLD ME THRILL ME KISS ME [A] – **Gloria ESTEFAN** (11) 94,95
HOLD ME THRILL ME KISS ME KILL ME – **U2** (2) 95
HOLD ME TIGHT – **Johnny NASH** (5) 68

I DIDN'T MEAN IT – **STATUS QUO** (21) 94
I DIDN'T MEAN TO HURT YOU – **ROCKIN' BERRIES** (43) 64
I DIDN'T MEAN TO TURN YOU ON – **Robert PALMER** (9) 86
I DIDN'T WANT TO NEED YOU – **HEART** (47) ..90
I DIE: YOU DIE – **Gary NUMAN** (6) 80
I DIG YOU BABY – **Marvin RAINWATER** (19) 58
I DISAPPEAR – **METALLICA** (35) 00
I DO – **JAMELIA** (36) 99
I DO I DO I DO I DO I DO – **ABBA** (38)..........75
I DO WHAT I DO . . . THEME FOR '9 1/2 WEEKS' – **John TAYLOR** (42)..........86
I DON'T BELIEVE IN IF ANYMORE – **Roger WHITTAKER** (8) 70
I DON'T BELIEVE IN MIRACLES [A] – **Colin BLUNSTONE** (31) 72
I DON'T BELIEVE IN MIRACLES [B] – **SINITTA** (22) 88
I DON'T BLAME YOU AT ALL – **MIRACLES** (11)..71
I DON'T CARE [A] – **LIBERACE** (28) 56
I DON'T CARE [B] – **LOS BRAVOS** (16)..........66
I DON'T CARE [C] – **SHAKESPEAR'S SISTER** (7)92
I DON'T CARE IF THE SUN DON'T SHINE – **Elvis PRESLEY** (23) 56
I DON'T EVEN KNOW IF I SHOULD CALL YOU BABY – **SOUL FAMILY SENSATION** (49)..........91
I DON'T EVER WANT TO SEE YOU AGAIN – **UNCLE SAM** (30) 98
I DON'T KNOW [A] – **RUTH** (66)..........97
I DON'T KNOW [B] – **HONEYZ** (28)..........01
I DON'T KNOW ANYBODY ELSE – **BLACK BOX** (4)90
I DON'T KNOW HOW TO LOVE HIM [A] – **Petula CLARK** (47)..........72
I DON'T KNOW HOW TO LOVE HIM [A] – **Yvonne ELLIMAN** (47) 72
I DON'T KNOW IF IT'S RIGHT – **Evelyn 'Champagne' KING** (67)..........79
I DON'T KNOW WHAT IT IS BUT I LOVE IT – **Chris REA** (65)..........84
I DON'T KNOW WHAT YOU WANT BUT I CAN'T GIVE IT ANYMORE – **PET SHOP BOYS** (15) ..99
I DON'T KNOW WHERE IT COMES FROM – **RIDE** (46)..........94
I DON'T KNOW WHY [A] – **Eden KANE** (7)..........62
I DON'T KNOW WHY [B] – **Shawn COLVIN** (52) 93,95
I DON'T KNOW WHY [C] – **Andy and David WILLIAMS** (37) 73
(I DON'T KNOW WHY) BUT I DO – **Clarence 'Frogman' HENRY** (65) 93
I DON'T KNOW WHY I LOVE YOU – **HOUSE OF LOVE** (41) 89
I DON'T KNOW WHY (I LOVE YOU) – **Stevie WONDER** (14) 69
I DON'T LIKE MONDAYS – **BOOMTOWN RATS** (1) 79,94
I DON'T LOVE YOU ANYMORE – **QUIREBOYS** (24) 90
I DON'T LOVE YOU BUT I THINK I LIKE YOU – **Gilbert O'SULLIVAN** (14) 75
I DON'T MIND – **BUZZCOCKS** (55)..........78
I DON'T MIND AT ALL – **BOURGEOIS TAGG** (35)..88
I DON'T NEED ANYTHING – **Sandie SHAW** (50) ..67
I DON'T NEED NO DOCTOR (LIVE) – **W.A.S.P.** (31) 87
I DON'T NEED TO TELL HER – **LURKERS** (49) ..78
I DON'T REALLY CARE – **K-GEE** (22) 00
I DON'T REMEMBER – **Peter GABRIEL** (62) 83
I DON'T SMOKE – **DJ DEE KLINE** (11)..........00
I DON'T THINK SO – **DINOSAUR JR** (67) 95
I DON'T THINK THAT MAN SHOULD SLEEP ALONE – **Ray PARKER Jr** (13)..........87
I DON'T WANNA BE A STAR – **CORONA** (22)....95
I DON'T WANNA DANCE – **Eddy GRANT** (1) 82
I DON'T WANNA FIGHT – **Tina TURNER** (7) 93
I DON'T WANNA GET HURT – **Donna SUMMER** (7)..........89
I DON'T WANNA GO ON WITH YOU LIKE THAT – **Elton JOHN** (30)..........88
I DON'T WANNA LOSE AT LOVE – **Tanita TIKARAM** (73)..........98
I DON'T WANNA LOSE YOU [A] – **KANDIDATE** (11) 79
I DON'T WANNA LOSE YOU [B] – **Tina TURNER** (8) 89
I DON'T WANNA LOSE YOUR LOVE – **EMOTIONS** (40) 77
I DON'T WANNA PLAY HOUSE – **Tammy WYNETTE** (37) 76
I DON'T WANNA TAKE THIS PAIN – **Dannii MINOGUE** (40)..........91
I DON'T WANT A LOVER – **TEXAS** (8) 89,01
I DON'T WANT CONTROL OF YOU – **TEENAGE FANCLUB** (43) 97
I DON'T WANT NOBODY (TELLIN' ME WHAT TO DO) – **Cherie AMORE** (33)..........00
I DON'T WANT OUR LOVING TO DIE – **HERD** (5)..68
I DON'T WANT TO – **Toni BRAXTON** (9) 97
I DON'T WANT TO BE A FREAK (BUT I CAN'T HELP MYSELF) – **DYNASTY** (20) 79
I DON'T WANT TO BE A HERO – **JOHNNY HATES JAZZ** (11)..........87
I DON'T WANT TO GO ON WITHOUT YOU – **MOODY BLUES** (33) 65
(I DON'T WANT TO GO TO) CHELSEA – **Elvis COSTELLO** (16) 78
I DON'T WANT TO HURT YOU (EVERY SINGLE TIME) – **Frank BLACK** (63) 96
I DON'T WANT TO MISS A THING – **AEROSMITH** (4)..........98
I DON'T WANT TO PUT A HOLD ON YOU – **Berni FLINT** (3) 77
I DON'T WANT TO TALK ABOUT IT [A] – **Rod STEWART** (1) 77
I DON'T WANT TO TALK ABOUT IT [A] – **EVERYTHING BUT THE GIRL** (3)..........88
I DON'T WANT TO WAIT – **Paula COLE** (43) 98
I DON'T WANT YOUR LOVE – **DURAN DURAN** (14)..........88
I DREAM – **TILT** (69) 95
I DREAMED – **BEVERLEY SISTERS** (24) 57
I DROVE ALL NIGHT [A] – **Cyndi LAUPER** (7) 89
I DROVE ALL NIGHT [A] – **Roy ORBISON** (7)92,93
I EAT CANNIBALS PART 1 – **TOTO COELO** (8) ..82
I ENJOY BEING A GIRL – **Pat SUZUKI** (49) 60
I FEEL A CRY COMING ON – **Hank LOCKLIN** (29) 66
I FEEL DIVINE – **S-J** (30) 98
I FEEL FINE [A] – **BEATLES** (1) 64,84
I FEEL FINE [A] – **WET WET WET** (30) 90
I FEEL FOR YOU [A] – **Chaka KHAN** (1)........84,89
I FEEL FOR YOU [B] – **Bob SINCLAR** (9) 00
I FEEL FREE – **CREAM** (11) 66
I FEEL GOOD THINGS FOR YOU – **DADDY'S FAVOURITE** (44) 98,99
I FEEL IT – **MOBY** (38)..........93
I FEEL LIKE BUDDY HOLLY – **Alvin STARDUST** (7) 84
I FEEL LIKE WALKIN' IN THE RAIN – **Millie JACKSON** (55) 84
I FEEL LOVE [A] – **Donna SUMMER** (1) ..77,82,95
I FEEL LOVE (MEDLEY) [A] – **BRONSKI BEAT and Marc ALMOND** (3)..........85
I FEEL LOVE [A] – **MESSIAH** (19) 92
I FEEL LOVE [A] – **VANESSA-MAE** (41)..........97
I FEEL LOVE [B] – **CRW** (15)..........00
I FEEL LOVE COMIN' ON [A] – **Felice TAYLOR** (11)..........67
I FEEL LOVE COMIN' ON [A] – **DANA** (66) 82
I FEEL LOVED – **DEPECHE MODE** (12) 01
I FEEL SO BAD – **Elvis PRESLEY** (4)..........61
I FEEL SOMETHING IN THE AIR – **CHER** (43)....66
I FEEL THE EARTH MOVE – **MARTIKA** (7) 89
I FEEL YOU [A] – **LOVE DECADE** (34)..........92
I FEEL YOU [B] – **DEPECHE MODE** (8) 93
I FEEL YOU [C] – **Peter ANDRE** (1) 96,97
I FINALLY FOUND SOMEONE – **Barbra STREISAND and Bryan ADAMS** (10)....97
I FORGOT [A] – **COOLNOTES** (63)..........84
I FORGOT [B] – **Lionel RICHIE** (34)..........01
I FOUGHT THE LAW [A] – **Bobby FULLER FOUR** (33)..........66
I FOUGHT THE LAW [A] – **CLASH** (29) 88
I FOUND HEAVEN – **TAKE THAT** (15) 92
I FOUND LOVE [A] – **Darlene DAVIS** (55)..........87
I FOUND LOVE [B] – **LONE JUSTICE** (45) 87
I FOUND LOVE [C] – **C & C MUSIC FACTORY / CLIVILLES & COLE featuring Martha WASH**(26) 95
I FOUND LOVIN' [A] – **FATBACK BAND** (7) 84,86,87
I FOUND LOVIN' [A] – **Steve WALSH** (9) 87
I FOUND OUT – **CHRISTIANS** (56) 90
I FOUND OUT THE HARD WAY – **FOUR PENNIES** (14)..........64
I FOUND SOMEONE [A] – **CHER** (5) 87
I FOUND SOMEONE [B] – **Billy and Sarah GAINES** (48)..........97
I FOUND SUNSHINE – **CHI-LITES** (35) 74
I (FRIDAY NIGHT) – **DUBSTAR** (37) 00
I GAVE IT UP (WHEN I FELL IN LOVE) – **Luther VANDROSS** (28) 88
I GAVE YOU EVERYTHING – **CODE RED** (50) 96
I GAVE YOU MY HEART (DIDN'T I) – **HOT CHOCOLATE** (13) 84
I GET A KICK OUT OF YOU – **Gary SHEARSTON** (7) 74
I GET A LITTLE SENTIMENTAL OVER YOU – **NEW SEEKERS** (5) 74
I GET AROUND – **BEACH BOYS** (7) 64
I GET LIFTED – **Barbara TUCKER** (33) 94
I GET LONELY – **Janet JACKSON** (5)..........98
I GET SO EXCITED – **EQUALS** (44)..........68
I GET THE SWEETEST FEELING – **Jackie WILSON** (3)..........72,75,87
I GET WEAK – **Belinda CARLISLE** (10) 88
I GIVE – **TAKE 5** (70)..........98
I GIVE IT ALL TO YOU – **Mary KIANI** (35) 95
I GIVE YOU MY HEART – **MR PRESIDENT** (52) 97
I GO APE – **Neil SEDAKA** (9) 59
I GO TO EXTREMES – **Billy JOEL** (70) 90
I GO TO PIECES (EVERYTIME) – **Gerri GRANGER** (50) 78
I GO TO SLEEP – **PRETENDERS** (7) 81
I GO WILD – **ROLLING STONES** (29) 95
I GOT A FEELING – **Ricky NELSON** (27)..........58
I GOT A GIRL – **Lou BEGA** (55) 99
I GOT A LITTLE SONG – **OFF-SHORE** (64) 91
I GOT A MAN – **POSITIVE K** (43)..........93
I GOT DA FEELIN' – **SWEET TEE** (31)..........88
I GOT 5 ON IT – **LUNIZ** (3) 96,98
I GOT ID – **PEARL JAM** (25)..........95
I GOT IT GOIN' ON [A] – **Tone LOC** (55) 89
I GOT IT GOIN' ON [B] – **US3** (52)..........94
I GOT MINE – **MOTÖRHEAD** (46)..........83
I GOT MY EDUCATION – **UNCANNY ALLIANCE** (39) 92
I GOT RHYTHM – **HAPPENINGS** (28) 67
I GOT SOMEBODY ELSE – **CHANGING FACES** (42) 97
I GOT STUNG – **Elvis PRESLEY** (1)..........59
I GOT THE VIBRATION – **BLACK BOX** (21) 96
I GOT THIS FEELING – **BABY BUMPS** (22)........00
I GOT TO SING – **JALN BAND** (40) 77
I GOT YOU [A] – **James BROWN** (29)......66,88,92
I GOT YOU [B] – **SPLIT ENZ** (12) 80
I GOT YOU BABE [A] – **SONNY and CHER** (1)..65,93
I GOT YOU BABE [A] – **UB40 featuring Chrissie HYNDE** (1)..........85
I GOT YOU BABE [A] – **CHER** (35) 94
I GUESS I'LL ALWAYS LOVE YOU – **ISLEY BROTHERS** (11)..........66,69
I GUESS THAT'S WHY THEY CALL IT THE BLUES – **Elton JOHN** (5)..........83
I HAD TOO MUCH TO DREAM LAST NIGHT – **ELECTRIC PRUNES** (49) 67
I HATE MYSELF FOR LOVING YOU – **Joan JETT and the BLACKHEARTS** (46) 88
I HATE... PEOPLE – **ANTI-NOWHERE LEAGUE** (46) 82
I HATE ROCK 'N' ROLL – **JESUS AND MARY CHAIN** (61)..........95
I HAVE A DREAM [A] – **ABBA** (2)..........79
I HAVE A DREAM [A] – **WESTLIFE** (1)..........99
I HAVE NOTHING – **Whitney HOUSTON** (3) 93
I HAVE PEACE – **STRIKE** (17)..........97
I HAVEN'T STOPPED DANCING YET – **PAT and MICK** (9) 89
I HEAR A SYMPHONY – **SUPREMES** (39)..........65
I HEAR TALK – **BUCKS FIZZ** (34) 84
I HEAR YOU KNOCKING – **Dave EDMUNDS** (1) 70
I HEAR YOU NOW – **JON and VANGELIS** (8) 80
I HEAR YOUR NAME – **INCOGNITO** (42)..........95
I HEARD A HEART BREAK LAST NIGHT – **Jim REEVES** (38) 67
I HEARD A RUMOUR – **BANANARAMA** (14) 87
I HEARD IT THROUGH THE GRAPEVINE [A] – **Gladys KNIGHT and the PIPS** (47) 67
I HEARD IT THROUGH THE GRAPEVINE [A] – **Marvin GAYE** (1) 69,86

I RECALL A GYPSY WOMAN — Don WILLIAMS (13) 76
I REFUSE — HUE AND CRY (47) 88
I REFUSE (WHAT YOU WANT) — SOMORE featuring DAMON TRUEITT (21) 98
I REMEMBER — COOLIO (73) 94
I REMEMBER ELVIS PRESLEY (THE KING IS DEAD) — Danny MIRROR (4) 77
I REMEMBER YESTERDAY — Donna SUMMER (14) 77
I REMEMBER YOU [A] — Frank IFIELD (1) 62
I REMEMBER YOU [B] — SKID ROW (36) 90
I ROCK — Tom NOVY (55) 00
I SAVED THE WORLD TODAY — EURYTHMICS (11) 99
I SAW HER AGAIN — MAMAS and the PAPAS (11) 66
I SAW HER STANDING THERE [A] — Elton JOHN BAND featuring John LENNON and the MUSCLE SHOALS HORNS (40) 81
I SAW HIM STANDING THERE [A]— TIFFANY (8) 88
I SAW LINDA YESTERDAY — Doug SHELDON (36) 63
I SAW MOMMY KISSING SANTA CLAUS [A] — BEVERLEY SISTERS (6) 53
I SAW MOMMY KISSING SANTA CLAUS [A] — Billy COTTON and his BAND (11) 53
I SAW MOMMY KISSING SANTA CLAUS [A] — Jimmy BOYD (3) 53
I SAW THE LIGHT [A] — Todd RUNDGREN (36) 73
I SAW THE LIGHT [B] — The THE (31) 95
I SAY A LITTLE PRAYER [A] — Aretha FRANKLIN (4) 68
I SAY A LITTLE PRAYER [A] — Diana KING (17) 97
I SAY NOTHING — VOICE OF THE BEEHIVE (22) 87,88
I SAY YEAH — SECCHI featuring Orlando JOHNSON (46) 91
I SCARE MYSELF — Thomas DOLBY (46) 84
I SECOND THAT EMOTION [A] — MIRACLES (27) 67
I SECOND THAT EMOTION [A] — Diana ROSS and the SUPREMES and the TEMPTATIONS (18) 69
I SECOND THAT EMOTION [A] — JAPAN (9) 82
I SECOND THAT EMOTION [A] — Alyson WILLIAMS (44) 89
I SEE A STAR — MOUTH and MACNEAL (8) 74
I SEE ONLY YOU — NOOTROPIC (42) 96
I SEE THE MOON — STARGAZERS (1) 54
I SEE YOU BABY — GROOVE ARMADA (17) 99,00
I SEE YOUR SMILE — Gloria ESTEFAN (48) 93
I SEEN A MAN DIE — SCARFACE (55) 95
I SHALL BE RELEASED — TREMELOES (29) 68
I SHALL BE THERE — B*WITCHED featuring LADYSMITH BLACK MAMBAZO (13) 99
I SHOT THE SHERIFF [A] — Eric CLAPTON (9) 74,82
I SHOT THE SHERIFF [A] — LIGHT OF THE WORLD (40) 81
I SHOT THE SHERIFF [A] — Warren G (2) 97
I SHOULD BE SO LUCKY — Kylie MINOGUE (1) 88
I SHOULD CARE — Frank IFIELD (33) 64
I SHOULD HAVE KNOWN BETTER [A] — NATURALS (24) 64
I SHOULD HAVE KNOWN BETTER [B] — Jim DIAMOND (1) 84
I SHOULDA LOVED YA — Narada Michael WALDEN (8) 80
I SHOULD'VE KNOWN — Aimee MANN (45) 93,94
I SINGS — MARY MARY (32) 00
I SLEEP ALONE AT NIGHT — Jim DIAMOND (72) 85
I SPEAKA DA LINGO — BLACK LACE (49) 85
I SPECIALIZE IN LOVE [A] — Sharon BROWN (38) 82,94
I SPECIALIZE IN LOVE [A] — ARIZONA featuring ZEITIA (74) 94
I SPY FOR THE FBI [A] — Jamo THOMAS (44) 69
I SPY FOR THE FBI [A] — UNTOUCHABLES (59) 85
I STAND ACCUSED — MERSEYBEATS (38) 66
I STAND ALONE — E-MOTION (60) 96
I STARTED A JOKE — FAITH NO MORE (49) 98
I STARTED SOMETHING I COULDN'T FINISH — SMITHS (23) 87
I STILL BELIEVE [A] — Ronnie HILTON (3) 54
I STILL BELIEVE [B] — Mariah CAREY (16) 99
I STILL BELIEVE IN YOU — Cliff RICHARD (7) 92
I STILL HAVEN'T FOUND WHAT I'M LOOKING FOR [A] — U2 (6) 87
I STILL HAVEN'T FOUND WHAT I'M LOOKING FOR [A] — CHIMES (6) 90
I STILL LOVE YOU ALL — Kenny BALL and his JAZZMEN (24) 61
I STILL REMEMBER — Gary NUMAN (74) 86
I STILL THINK ABOUT YOU — DANGER DANGER (46) 92
I STILL THINK OF YOU — UTAH SAINTS (32) 94
I SURRENDER [A] — RAINBOW (3) 81
I SURRENDER [B] — Rosie GAINES (39) 97
I SURRENDER [C] — David SYLVIAN (40) 99
I SURRENDER (TO THE SPIRIT OF THE NIGHT) — Samantha FOX (25) 87
I SURRENDER TO YOUR LOVE — BY ALL MEANS (65) 88
I SWEAR — ALL-4-ONE (2) 94
I TALK TO THE TREES — Clint EASTWOOD (18) 70
I TALK TO THE WIND — OPUS III (52) 92
I THANK YOU [A] — SAM and DAVE (34) 68
I THANK YOU [B] — ADEVA (17) 89,96
I THINK I LOVE YOU [A] — PARTRIDGE FAMILY (18) 71
I THINK I LOVE YOU [A] — VOICE OF THE BEEHIVE (25) 91
I THINK I WANT TO DANCE WITH YOU — RUMPLE-STILTS-SKIN (51) 83
I THINK I'M IN LOVE — SPIRITUALIZED (27) 98
I THINK I'M IN LOVE WITH YOU — Jessica SIMPSON (15) 00
I THINK I'M PARANOID — GARBAGE (9) 98
I THINK IT'S GOING TO RAIN TODAY — UB40 (6) 80
I THINK OF YOU [A] — MERSEYBEATS (5) 64
I THINK OF YOU [B] — Perry COMO (14) 71
I THINK OF YOU [C] — DETROIT EMERALDS (27) 73
I THINK OF YOU [D] — Bryan POWELL (61) 93
I THINK WE'RE ALONE NOW — TIFFANY (1) 88
I THOUGHT I MEANT THE WORLD TO YOU — Alysha WARREN (40) 95
I THOUGHT IT TOOK A LITTLE TIME — Diana ROSS (32) 76
I THOUGHT IT WAS YOU [A] — Herbie HANCOCK (15) 78
I THOUGHT IT WAS YOU [A] — SEX-O-SONIQUE (32) 97
I THOUGHT IT WAS YOU [B] — Julia FORDHAM (45) 91,92
I THREW IT ALL AWAY — Bob DYLAN (30) 69
I TOLD YOU SO — Jimmy JONES (33) 61
I TOUCH MYSELF — DIVINYLS (10) 91
I TRY — Macy GRAY (6) 99
I TURN TO YOU [A] — Melanie C (1) 00
I TURN TO YOU [B] — Christina AGUILERA (19) 00
I UNDERSTAND [A] — G-CLEFS (17) 61
I UNDERSTAND [A] — FREDDIE and the DREAMERS (5) 64
I WALK THE EARTH — VOICE OF THE BEEHIVE (42) 88
I WANNA BE A FLINTSTONE — SCREAMING BLUE MESSIAHS (28) 88
I WANNA BE A HIPPY — TECHNOHEAD (6) 96
I WANNA BE A WINNER — BROWN SAUCE (15) 81
I WANNA BE ADORED — STONE ROSES (20) 91
I WANNA BE DOWN — BRANDY (36) 94,95
I WANNA BE FREE — MINTY (67) 99
I WANNA BE FREE (TO BE WITH HIM) — SCARLET (21) 95
I WANNA BE IN LOVE AGAIN — BEIJING SPRING (43) 93
I WANNA BE LOVED [A] — Ricky NELSON (30) 60
I WANNA BE LOVED [B] — Elvis COSTELLO (25) 84
I WANNA BE THE ONLY ONE — ETERNAL (1) 97
I WANNA BE WITH YOU [A] — COFFEE (57) 80
I WANNA BE WITH YOU [B] — MAZE featuring Frankie BEVERLY (55) 86
I WANNA BE WITH YOU [C] — Mandy MOORE (21) 00
I WANNA BE U — CHOCOLATE PUMA (6) 01
I WANNA BE YOUR LADY — Hinda HICKS (14) 98
I WANNA BE YOUR LOVER — PRINCE (41) 80
I WANNA BE YOUR MAN [A] — ROLLING STONES (12) 63
I WANNA BE YOUR MAN [A] — REZILLOS (71) 79
I WANNA BE YOUR MAN [B] — Chaka DEMUS and PLIERS (19) 94
I WANNA DANCE WIT CHOO — DISCO TEX and the SEX-O-LETTES (6) 75
I WANNA DANCE WITH SOMEBODY (WHO LOVES ME) — Whitney HOUSTON (1) 87
I WANNA DO IT WITH YOU — Barry MANILOW (8) 82
I WANNA GET NEXT TO YOU — ROSE ROYCE (14) 77
(I WANNA GIVE YOU) DEVOTION — NOMAD (2) 91,95
I WANNA GO BACK — NEW SEEKERS (25) 77
I WANNA GO HOME — Lonnie DONEGAN (5) 60
I WANNA GO WHERE THE PEOPLE GO — WILDHEARTS (16) 95
I WANNA HAVE SOME FUN — Samantha FOX (63) 89
I WANNA HOLD ON TO YOU — Mica PARIS (27) 93
I WANNA HOLD YOUR HAND — DOLLAR (9) 79
I WANNA KNOW [A] — STACCATO (65) 96
I WANNA KNOW [B] — JOE (37) 01
(I WANNA KNOW) WHY — SINCLAIR (58) 94
(I WANNA) LOVE MY LIFE AWAY — Gene PITNEY (26) 61
I WANNA LOVE YOU [A] — JADE (13) 93
I WANNA LOVE YOU [B] — SOLID HARMONIE (20) 98
I WANNA LOVE YOU FOREVER — Jessica SIMPSON (7) 00
I WANNA MAKE YOU FEEL GOOD — SYSTEM (73) 84
I WANNA 1-2-1 WITH YOU — SOLID GOLD CHARTBUSTERS (62) 99
I WANNA SEX YOU UP — COLOR ME BADD (1) 91
I WANNA SING — Sabrina JOHNSTON (46) 92
I WANNA STAY HOME — JELLYFISH (59) 91
I WANNA STAY WITH YOU [A] — GALLAGHER and LYLE (6) 76
I WANNA STAY WITH YOU [A] — UNDERCOVER (28) 93
I WANT AN ALIEN FOR CHRISTMAS — FOUNTAINS OF WAYNE (36) 97
I WANT CANDY [A] — Brian POOLE and the TREMELOES (25) 65
I WANT CANDY [A] — BOW WOW WOW (9) 82
I WANT CANDY [A] — CANDY GIRLS (30) 96
I WANT CANDY [A] — Aaron CARTER (31) 00
I WANT HER — Keith SWEAT (26) 88,97
I WANT IT ALL — QUEEN (3) 89
I WANT IT THAT WAY — BACKSTREET BOYS (1) 99
I WANT LOVE — Elton JOHN (9) 01
I WANT MORE — CAN (26) 76
I WANT OUT — HELLOWEEN (69) 88
I WANT OUT (I CAN'T BELIEVE) — Harry 'Choo-Choo' ROMERO (51) 01
I WANT THAT MAN — Deborah HARRY (13) 89
I WANT THE WORLD — 2WO THIRD3 (20) 94
I WANT TO BE ALONE — 2WO THIRD3 (29) 94
(I WANT TO BE) ELECTED — Bruce DICKINSON (9) 92
I WANT TO BE FREE — TOYAH (8) 81
I WANT TO BE STRAIGHT — Ian DURY and the BLOCKHEADS (22) 80
I WANT TO BE THERE WHEN YOU COME — ECHO and the BUNNYMEN (30) 97
I WANT TO BE WANTED — Brenda LEE (31) 60
I WANT TO BE YOUR MAN — ROGER (61) 87
I WANT TO BE YOUR PROPERTY — BLUE MERCEDES (23) 87
I WANT TO BREAK FREE — QUEEN (3) 84
I WANT TO GIVE — Perry COMO (31) 74
I WANT TO GO WITH YOU — Eddy ARNOLD (46) 66
I WANT TO HEAR IT FROM YOU — GO WEST (43) 87
I WANT TO HOLD YOUR HAND — BEATLES (1) 63,64,83
(I WANT TO) KILL SOMEBODY — S*M*A*S*H (26) 94
I WANT TO KNOW WHAT LOVE IS [A] — FOREIGNER (1) 84
I WANT TO KNOW WHAT LOVE IS [A] — Terri SYMON (54) 95
I WANT TO LIVE — GRACE (30) 95
I WANT TO STAY HERE [A] — Eydie GORME (3) 63
I WANT TO STAY HERE [A] — MIKI and GRIFF (23) 63
I WANT TO THANK YOU — Robin S (48) 94
I WANT TO TOUCH YOU — CATHERINE WHEEL (35) 92
I WANT TO WAKE UP WITH YOU — Boris GARDINER (1) 86

I'LL BE THERE FOR YOU — YOU'RE ALL I NEED TO GET BY — METHOD MAN featuring Mary J BLIGE (10) 95

I'LL BE WAITING [A] — Clive GRIFFIN (56) 91

I'LL BE WAITING [B] — FULL INTENTION presents SHENA (44) 01

(I'LL BE WITH YOU) IN APPLE BLOSSOM TIME — Rosemary JUNE (14) 59

I'LL BE YOUR BABY TONIGHT — Robert PALMER and UB40 (6) 90

I'LL BE YOUR EVERYTHING — Tommy PAGE (53) 90

I'LL BE YOUR FRIEND — Robert OWENS (25)91,97

I'LL BE YOUR SHELTER — Taylor DAYNE (43) ..90

I'LL COME RUNNIN' — JUICE (48) 98

I'LL COME RUNNING — Cliff RICHARD (26)....67

I'LL COME WHEN YOU CALL — Ruby MURRAY (6)55

I'LL CRY FOR YOU — EUROPE (28)....92

I'LL CUT YOUR TAIL OFF — John LEYTON (36) ..63

I'LL DO ANYTHING — TO MAKE YOU MINE — HOLLOWAY & CO. (58) 99

I'LL DO YA — WHALE (53) 95

I'LL FIND MY WAY HOME — JON and VANGELIS (6) 81

I'LL FIND YOU [A] — David WHITFIELD (27) 57

I'LL FIND YOU [B] — Michelle GAYLE (26) 94

I'LL FLY FOR YOU — SPANDAU BALLET (9) 84

I'LL GET BY [A] — Connie FRANCIS (19) 58

I'LL GET BY [A] — Shirley BASSEY (10)....61

I'LL GIVE YOU THE EARTH (TOUS LES BATEAUX, TOUS LES OISEAUX) — Keith MICHELL (30) ..71

I'LL GO ON HOPING — Des O'CONNOR (30) 70

I'LL GO WHERE YOUR MUSIC TAKES ME [A] — Jimmy JAMES and the VAGABONDS (23) 76

I'LL GO WHERE YOUR MUSIC TAKES ME [A] — Tina CHARLES (27) 78

I'LL HOUSE YOU — JUNGLE BROTHERS (26) 88,98

I'LL KEEP ON LOVING YOU — PRINCESS (16)....86

I'LL KEEP YOU SATISFIED — Billy J KRAMER and the DAKOTAS (4) 63

I'LL KEEP YOUR DREAMS ALIVE — George BENSON and Patti AUSTIN (68) 92

I'LL LOVE YOU FOREVER TODAY — Cliff RICHARD (27)....68

I'LL MAKE LOVE TO YOU — BOYZ II MEN (5)....94

I'LL MANAGE SOMEHOW — MENSWEAR (49)....95

I'LL MEET YOU AT MIDNIGHT — SMOKIE (11)....76

I'LL NEVER BREAK YOUR HEART — BACKSTREET BOYS (8)....95,96

I'LL NEVER FALL IN LOVE AGAIN [A] — Johnnie RAY (26) 59,60

I'LL NEVER FALL IN LOVE AGAIN [B] — Tom JONES (2) 67

I'LL NEVER FALL IN LOVE AGAIN [C] — Bobbie GENTRY (1) 69

I'LL NEVER FIND ANOTHER YOU — SEEKERS (1)65

I'LL NEVER GET OVER YOU [A] — Johnny KIDD and the PIRATES (4) 63

I'LL NEVER GET OVER YOU [B] — EVERLY BROTHERS (35) 65

I'LL NEVER GET OVER YOU (GETTING OVER ME) — EXPOS... (75) 93

I'LL NEVER LOVE THIS WAY AGAIN — Dionne WARWICK (62) 83

I'LL NEVER QUITE GET OVER YOU — Billy FURY (35) 66

I'LL NEVER STOP — 'N SYNC (13)....00

I'LL NEVER STOP LOVING YOU — Doris DAY (17) 55

I'LL PICK A ROSE FOR MY ROSE — Marv JOHNSON (10)....69

I'LL PUT YOU TOGETHER AGAIN — HOT CHOCOLATE (13) 78

I'LL REMEMBER — MADONNA (7) 94

I'LL REMEMBER TONIGHT — Pat BOONE (18) ..59

I'LL SAIL THIS SHIP ALONE — BEAUTIFUL SOUTH (31)....89

I'LL SAY FOREVER MY LOVE — Jimmy RUFFIN (7) 70

I'LL SEE YOU ALONG THE WAY — Rick CLARKE (63) 88

I'LL SEE YOU AROUND — SILVER SUN (26) 98

I'LL SEE YOU IN MY DREAMS — Pat BOONE (27) 62

I'LL SET YOU FREE — BANGLES (74) 89

I'LL SLEEP WHEN I'M DEAD — BON JOVI (17) ..93

I'LL STAND BY YOU — PRETENDERS (10)....94

I'LL STAY BY YOU — Kenny LYNCH (29)....65

I'LL STAY SINGLE — Jerry LORDAN (26) 60

I'LL STEP DOWN — Garry MILLS (39) 61

I'LL STICK AROUND — FOO FIGHTERS (18) 95

I'LL STOP AT NOTHING — Sandie SHAW (4) 65

I'LL TAKE THE RAIN — R.E.M. (44) 01

I'LL TAKE YOU HOME [A] — DRIFTERS (37) 63

I'LL TAKE YOU HOME [A] — Cliff BENNETT and the REBEL ROUSERS (42) 65

I'LL TAKE YOU HOME AGAIN KATHLEEN — Slim WHITMAN (7) 57

I'LL TAKE YOU THERE [A] — STAPLE SINGERS (30) 72

I'LL TAKE YOU THERE [A] — GENERAL PUBLIC (73) 94

I'LL TRY ANYTHING — Dusty SPRINGFIELD (13) 67

I'LL WAIT — Taylor DAYNE (29) 94

I'LL WALK WITH GOD — Mario LANZA (18) 55

ILLEGAL ALIEN — GENESIS (46) 84

ILLEGAL GUNSHOT — RAGGA TWINS (51) 90

ILLUMINATIONS — SWANS WAY (57)....84

ILLUSIONS — CYPRESS HILL (23)....96

ILOVEROCKNROLL — JESUS AND MARY CHAIN (38) 98

I'M A BELIEVER [A] — MONKEES (1)....67

I'M A BELIEVER [A] — Robert WYATT (29) 74

I'M A BELIEVER [A] — EMF (3) 95

I'M A BETTER MAN (FOR HAVING LOVED YOU) — Engelbert HUMPERDINCK (15)....69

I'M A BITCH — OLGA (68) 94

I'M A BOY — WHO (2) 66

I'M A DISCO DANCER — Christopher JUST (69) 97,99

I'M A DOUN FOR LACK O' JOHNNIE (A LITTLE SCOTTISH FANTASY) — VANESSA-MAE (28)..96

(I'M A) DREAMER — B B and Q BAND (35) 86

I'M A FOOL — Slim WHITMAN (16)....56

I'M A FOOL TO CARE — Joe BARRY (49)....61

I'M A LITTLE CHRISTMAS CRACKER — BOUNCING CZECKS (72) 84

I'M A MAN [A] — Spencer DAVIS GROUP (9) 67

I'M A MAN [A] — CHICAGO (8) 70

I'M A MAN NOT A BOY [A] — Chesney HAWKES (27) 91

I'M A MAN NOT A BOY [B] — NORTH AND SOUTH (7)....97

I'M A MAN — YE KE YE KE (MEDLEY) — CLUBHOUSE (69)....89

I'M A MESSAGE — IDLEWILD (41) 98

I'M A MIDNIGHT MOVER — Wilson PICKETT (38) 68

I'M A MOODY GUY — Shane FENTON and the FENTONES (22) 61

I'M A SLAVE 4 U — Britney SPEARS (4) 01

I'M A SUCKER FOR YOUR LOVE — Teena MARIE, co-lead vocals Rick JAMES (43)..79

I'M A TIGER — LULU (9) 68

I'M A WONDERFUL THING, BABY — Kid CREOLE and the COCONUTS (4) 82,93

I'M ALIVE [A] — HOLLIES (1)....65

I'M ALIVE [B] — ELECTRIC LIGHT ORCHESTRA (20)....80

I'M ALIVE [C] — CUT 'N' MOVE (49) 95

I'M ALIVE [D] — SEAL (4) 95

I'M ALIVE [E] — STRETCH 'N' VERN present MADDOG (6) 96

I'M ALL ABOUT YOU — DJ LUCK & MC NEAT featuimg Ari GOLD (18)....01

I'M ALL YOU NEED — Samantha FOX (41) 86

I'M ALRIGHT [A] — Steve WRIGHT (40) 82

I'M ALRIGHT [B] — Katherine E (41) 91

(I'M ALWAYS HEARING) WEDDING BELLS — Eddie FISHER (5)....55

(I'M ALWAYS TOUCHED BY YOUR) PRESENCE DEAR — BLONDIE (10) 78

I'M AN UPSTART — ANGELIC UPSTARTS (31)....79

I'M BACK FOR MORE — LULU and Bobby WOMACK (27) 93

I'M BAD — LL COOL J (71) 87

I'M BORN AGAIN — BONEY M (35) 79

I'M BROKEN — PANTERA (19)....94

I'M CHILLIN' — Kurtis BLOW (64)....86

I'M COMIN' HARDCORE — M.A.N.I.C. (60) 92

I'M COMING HOME — Tom JONES (2) 67

I'M COMING HOME CINDY — Trini LOPEZ (28)..66

I'M COMING OUT — Diana ROSS (13) 80,94

I'M COUNTING ON YOU — Petula CLARK (41) ..62

I'M CRYING — ANIMALS (8) 64

I'M DOIN' FINE — DAY ONE (68) 99

I'M DOING FINE — Jason DONOVAN (22)....90

I'M DOING FINE NOW [A] — NEW YORK CITY (20)....73

I'M DOING FINE NOW [B] — PASADENAS (4) 92

I'M EASY — FAITH NO MORE (3) 93

I'M EVERY WOMAN [A] — Chaka KHAN (8) ..78,89

I'M EVERY WOMAN [A] — Whitney HOUSTON (4)....93

I'M FALLING — BLUEBELLS (11) 84

I'M FOR REAL — NIGHTMARES ON WAX (38)....90

I'M FOREVER BLOWING BUBBLES [A] — WEST HAM UNITED CUP SQUAD (31) 75

I'M FOREVER BLOWING BUBBLES [A] — COCKNEY REJECTS (35)....80

I'M FREE [A] — Roger DALTREY (13)....73

I'M FREE [B] — SOUP DRAGONS (5)....90

I'M FREE [C] — Jon SECADA (50) 93

I'M GOIN' DOWN — Mary J BLIGE (12) 95

I'M GOING ALL THE WAY — SOUNDS OF BLACKNESS (14)....93,95

I'M GOING HOME — Gene VINCENT (36) 61

I'M GOING SLIGHTLY MAD — QUEEN (22) 91

I'M GONE — Diana ROSS (36) 95

I'M GONNA BE 500 MILES — PROCLAIMERS (11) 88

I'M GONNA BE A COUNTRY GIRL AGAIN — Buffy SAINTE-MARIE (34) 72

I'M GONNA BE STRONG [A] — Gene PITNEY (2)64

I'M GONNA BE STRONG [A] — Cyndi LAUPER (37) 95

I'M GONNA BE WARM THIS WINTER — Connie FRANCIS (48)....62

I'M GONNA CHANGE EVERYTHING — Jim REEVES (42) 62

(I'M GONNA) CRY MYSELF BLIND — PRIMAL SCREAM (49) 94

I'M GONNA GET MARRIED — Lloyd PRICE (23) 59

I'M GONNA GET ME A GUN — Cat STEVENS (6)67

I'M GONNA GET THERE SOMEHOW — Val DOONICAN (25)....65

I'M GONNA GET YA BABY — BLACK CONNECTION (62) 98

I'M GONNA GET YOU — BIZARRE INC (3) 92,93

I'M GONNA GIT YOU SUCKA — GAP BAND (63) 89

I'M GONNA KNOCK ON YOUR DOOR [A] — Eddie HODGES (37) 61

I'M GONNA KNOCK ON YOUR DOOR [A] — Little Jimmy OSMOND (11)....74

I'M GONNA LOVE HER FOR BOTH OF US — MEAT LOAF (62) 81

I'M GONNA LOVE YOU FOREVER — CROWN HEIGHTS AFFAIR (47)....78

I'M GONNA LOVE YOU JUST A LITTLE BIT MORE BABY — Barry WHITE (23)....73

I'M GONNA MAKE YOU LOVE ME — Diana ROSS and the SUPREMES and the TEMPTATIONS (3) 69

I'M GONNA MAKE YOU MINE [A] — Lou CHRISTIE (2)....69

I'M GONNA MAKE YOU MINE [B] — Tanya BLOUNT (69)....94

I'M GONNA MISS YOU FOREVER — Aaron CARTER (24) 98

I'M GONNA RUN AWAY FROM YOU — Tami LYNN (4) 71,75

I'M GONNA SIT RIGHT DOWN AND WRITE MYSELF A LETTER [A] — Billy WILLIAMS (22) 57

I'M GONNA SIT RIGHT DOWN AND WRITE MYSELF A LETTER [A] — Barry MANILOW (36)....82

I'M GONNA SOOTHE YOU — Maria McKEE (35) 93

I'M GONNA TEAR YOUR PLAYHOUSE DOWN — Paul YOUNG (9)....84

I'M IN A DIFFERENT WORLD — FOUR TOPS (27)..68

I'M IN A PHILLY MOOD — Daryl HALL (52) ..93,94

I'M IN FAVOUR OF FRIENDSHIP — FIVE SMITH BROTHERS (20) 55

I'M IN IT FOR LOVE — Donny OSMOND (70) 87

I'M IN LOVE [A] — FOURMOST (17) 63

I'M IN LOVE [B] — Evelyn 'Champagne' KING (27) 81

I'M IN LOVE [C] — Ruby TURNER (57)....86,87

I'M IN LOVE [D] — Lillo THOMAS (54) 87

I'M IN LOVE [E] — STARPARTY (26) 00

I'M IN LOVE AGAIN [A] — Fats DOMINO (12) 56

I'M IN LOVE AGAIN [B] — SAD CAFE (40)....80

I'M IN LOVE (AND I LOVE THE FEELING) — ROSE ROYCE (51) 79

I'M IN LOVE WITH A GERMAN FILM STAR — PASSIONS (25) 81

I'M IN LOVE WITH THE GIRL ON A CERTAIN MANCHESTER MEGASTORE CHECKOUT DESK — FRESHIES (54) 81

I'M IN LUV — JOE (22) 94

I'M IN THE MOOD — Ce Ce PENISTON (16) 94

I'M IN THE MOOD FOR DANCING — NOLANS (3) 79,95

I'M IN THE MOOD FOR LOVE [A] – LORD TANAMO (58) 90
I'M IN THE MOOD FOR LOVE [A] – Jools HOLLAND and JAMIROQUAI (29) 01
I'M IN YOU – Peter FRAMPTON (41) 77
I'M INTO SOMETHING GOOD – HERMAN'S HERMITS (1) 64
I'M JUST A BABY – Louise CORDET (13) 62
I'M JUST A SINGER (IN A ROCK 'N' ROLL BAND) – MOODY BLUES (36) 73
I'M JUST YOUR PUPPET ON A . . . (STRING) – LONDONBEAT (55) 95
I'M LEAVIN' – Elvis PRESLEY (23) 71
I'M LEAVING – LODGER (40) 98
I'M LEAVING IT UP TO YOU [A] – DALE and GRACE (42) 64
I'M LEAVING IT (ALL) UP TO YOU [A] – Donny and Marie OSMOND (2) 74
I'M LEFT, YOU'RE RIGHT, SHE'S GONE – Elvis PRESLEY (21) 58
I'M LIKE A BIRD – Nelly FURTADO (5) 01
I'M LIVING IN SHAME – Diana ROSS and the SUPREMES (14) 69
I'M LONELY – Hollis P MONROE (51) 99
I'M LOOKING FOR THE ONE (TO BE WITH ME) – JAZZY JEFF & the FRESH PRINCE (24) 93
I'M LOOKING OUT THE WINDOW – Cliff RICHARD (2) 62
I'M LOST WITHOUT YOU – Billy FURY (16) 65
I'M LUCKY – Joan ARMATRADING (46) 81
I'M MANDY FLY ME – 10 CC (6) 76
I'M NEVER GIVING UP – SWEET DREAMS (21) 83
IM NIN'ALU – Ofra HAZA (15) 88
I'M NO ANGEL – Marcella DETROIT (33) 94
I'M NO REBEL – VIEW FROM THE HILL (59) 87
I'M NOT A FOOL – COCKNEY REJECTS (65) 79
I'M NOT A JUVENILE DELINQUENT – Frankie LYMON and the TEENAGERS (12) 57
I'M NOT ASHAMED – BIG COUNTRY (69) 95
I'M NOT FEELING YOU – Yvette MICHELLE (36) 97
I'M NOT GIVING YOU UP – Gloria ESTEFAN (28) 96
I'M NOT GONNA LET YOU (GET THE BEST OF ME) – Colonel ABRAMS (24) 86
I'M NOT IN LOVE [A] – 10 CC (1) 75,95
I'M NOT IN LOVE [A] – Johnny LOGAN (51) 87
I'M NOT IN LOVE [A] – WILL TO POWER (29) ..90
I'M NOT IN LOVE [A] – FUN LOVIN' CRIMINALS (12) 97
I'M NOT PERFECT (BUT I'M PERFECT FOR YOU) – Grace JONES (56) 86
I'M NOT READY – Keith SWEAT (53) 99
I'M NOT SATISFIED – FINE YOUNG CANNIBALS (46) 90
I'M NOT SCARED – EIGHTH WONDER (7) 88
I'M NOT THE MAN I USED TO BE – FINE YOUNG CANNIBALS (20) 89
I'M NOT TO BLAME – ALIBI (51) 97
(I'M NOT YOUR) STEPPING STONE – SEX PISTOLS (21) 80
I'M ON AUTOMATIC – Gary NUMAN (44) 89
I'M ON FIRE [A] – 5000 VOLTS (4) 75
I'M ON FIRE [B] – Bruce SPRINGSTEEN (5) 85
I'M ON MY WAY [A] – Dean PARRISH (38) 75
I'M ON MY WAY [B] – PROCLAIMERS (43) 89
I'M ON MY WAY [C] – Betty BOO (44) 92
I'M ON MY WAY TO A BETTER PLACE – CHAIRMEN OF THE BOARD (30) 72,73
I'M ONLY SLEEPING – SUGGS (7) 95
I'M OUT OF YOUR LIFE – ARNIE'S LOVE (67) ..83
I'M OUTSTANDING – Shaquille O'NEAL (70) 94
I'M OUTTA LOVE – ANASTACIA (6) 00
I'M OVER YOU – Martine McCUTCHEON (2) 00
I'M QUALIFIED TO SATISFY – Barry WHITE (37)77
I'M RAVING – SCOOTER (33) 96
I'M READY [A] – CAVEMAN (65) 91
I'M READY [B] – SIZE 9 (30) 95
I'M READY [C] – Bryan ADAMS (20) 98
I'M READY FOR LOVE – Martha REEVES and the VANDELLAS (29) 66
I'M REAL [A] – James BROWN featuring FULL FORCE (31) 88
I'M REAL [B] – Jennifer LOPEZ featuring Ja RULE (4) 01
I'M RIFFIN (ENGLISH RASTA) – MC DUKE (75) 89
I'M RUSHING – BUMP (40) 92,95
I'M SHY MARY ELLEN I'M SHY – Bob WALLIS and his STORYVILLE JAZZ BAND (44) 61
I'M SICK OF YOU – GOODBYE MR MACKENZIE (49) 89
I'M SO BEAUTIFUL – DIVINE (52) 84
I'M SO CRAZY ('BOUT YOU) – KC and the SUNSHINE BAND (34) 75
I'M SO CRAZY – PAR-T-ONE vs INXS (19) 01
I'M SO EXCITED – POINTER SISTERS (11) 84
I'M SO GLAD I'M STANDING HERE TODAY – CRUSADERS, featured vocalist Joe COCKER (61)81
I'M SO HAPPY [A] – LIGHT OF THE WORLD (35)..81
I'M SO HAPPY [B] – JULIA and COMPANY (56) 85
I'M SO HAPPY [C] – Walter BEASLEY (70) 88
I'M SO HAPPY I CAN'T STOP CRYING – STING (54) 96
I'M SO IN LOVE – Alysha WARREN (61) 94
I'M SO INTO YOU – SWV (17) 93
I'M SO LONELY – CAST (14) 97
I'M SORRY [A] – PLATTERS (18) 57
I'M SORRY [B] – Brenda LEE (12) 60
I'M SORRY [C] – HOTHOUSE FLOWERS (53) 88
I'M SORRY I MADE YOU CRY – Connie FRANCIS (11) 58
I'M STANDING (HIGHER) – X-STATIC (41) 95
I'M STARTING TO GO STEADY – Johnny PRESTON (49) 60
I'M STILL GONNA NEED YOU – OSMONDS (32)75
I'M STILL IN LOVE WITH YOU – Al GREEN (35)72
I'M STILL STANDING – Elton JOHN (4) 83
I'M STILL WAITING [A] – Diana ROSS (1) 71,76,90
I'M STILL WAITING [A] – Courtney PINE (66) ..90
I'M STILL WAITING [B] – ANGELHEART (74) 97
I'M STONE IN LOVE WITH YOU [A] – STYLISTICS (9) 72
I'M STONE IN LOVE WITH YOU [A] – Johnny MATHIS (10) 75
I'M TELLIN YOU – Chubby CHUNKS (61) 99
I'M TELLING YOU NOW – FREDDIE and the DREAMERS (2) 63
I'M THAT TYPE OF GUY – LL COOL J (43) 89
I'M THE FACE – HIGH NUMBERS (49) 80
I'M THE LEADER OF THE GANG (I AM) [A] – Gary GLITTER (1) 73
I'M THE LEADER OF THE GANG [A] – Hulk HOGAN with GREEN JELLY (25) 93
I'M THE LONELY ONE – Cliff RICHARD and the SHADOWS (8) 64
I'M THE MAN – ANTHRAX (20) 87
I'M THE ONE – GERRY and the PACEMAKERS (2) 64
I'M THE ONE FOR YOU – ADEVA (51) 92
I'M THE ONE YOU NEED – Jody WATLEY (50)..92
I'M THE URBAN SPACEMAN – BONZO DOG DOO-DAH BAND (5) 68
I'M TIRED OF GETTING PUSHED AROUND – TWO MEN, A DRUM MACHINE AND A TRUMPET (18) 88
I'M TOO SCARED – Steven DANTE (34) 88
I'M TOO SEXY – RIGHT SAID FRED (2) 91
I'M WAKING UP TO US – BELLE & SEBASTIAN (39) 01
I'M WALKIN' – Fats DOMINO (19) 57
I'M WALKING BACKWARDS FOR CHRISTMAS – GOONS (4) 56
I'M WALKING BEHIND YOU [A] – Eddie FISHER (1) 53
I'M WALKING BEHIND YOU [A] – Dorothy SQUIRES (12) 53
I'M WONDERING – Stevie WONDER (22) 67
I'M YOUR ANGEL – Celine DION and R KELLY (3) 98
I'M YOUR BABY TONIGHT – Whitney HOUSTON (5) 90
I'M YOUR BOOGIE MAN – KC and the SUNSHINE BAND (41) 77
I'M YOUR MAN [A] – BLUE ZOO (55) 82
I'M YOUR MAN [B] – WHAM! (1) 85
I'M YOUR MAN [B] – Lisa MOORISH (24) 95
I'M YOUR PUPPET – James and Bobby PURIFY (12) 76
I'M YOUR TOY – Elvis COSTELLO (51) 82
IMAGE – Hank LEVINE (45) 61
IMAGE OF A GIRL [A] – Nelson KEENE (37) 60
IMAGE OF A GIRL [A] – Mark WYNTER (11) 60
IMAGE OF YOU – RED SNAPPER (60) 98
IMAGINATION [A] – Rocky SHARPE and the REPLAYS (39) 79
IMAGINATION [B] – BELOUIS SOME (17) 85,86
IMAGINATION [C] – JON THE DENTIST Vs Ollie JAYE (72) 99
IMAGINE [A] – John LENNON (1) ..75,80,88,99,00
IMAGINE [A] – Randy CRAWFORD (60) 82
IMAGINE [B] – Shola AMA (24) 00
IMAGINE ME IMAGINE YOU – FOX (15) 75
IMITATION OF LIFE [A] – Billie Ray MARTIN (29)..96
IMITATION OF LIFE [B] – R.E.M. (6) 01
IMMACULATE FOOLS – IMMACULATE FOOLS (51) 85
IMMORTALITY – Celine DION with BEE GEES (5) 98
IMPERIAL WIZARD – David ESSEX (32) 79
IMPORTANCE OF YOUR LOVE – Vince HILL (32) 68
IMPOSSIBLE [A] – CAPTAIN HOLLYWOOD PROJECT (29) 94
IMPOSSIBLE [B] – CHARLATANS (15) 00
THE IMPOSSIBLE DREAM – CARTER – THE UNSTOPPABLE SEX MACHINE (21) 92
IMPOSSIBLE LOVE – UB40 (47) 90
THE IMPRESSION THAT I GET – MIGHTY MIGHTY BOSSTONES (12) 98
THE IMPRESSIONS EP – SOLAR STONE (75) ..98
IMPULSIVE – WILSON PHILLIPS (42) 90
IN A BIG COUNTRY – BIG COUNTRY (17) 83
IN A BROKEN DREAM [A] – PYTHON LEE JACKSON (3) 72
IN A BROKEN DREAM [A] – THUNDER (26) 95
IN A GOLDEN COACH (THERE'S A HEART OF GOLD) [A] – Billy COTTON and his BAND (3) 53
IN A GOLDEN COACH (THERE'S A HEART OF GOLD) [A] – Dickie VALENTINE (7) 53
IN A LIFETIME – CLANNAD featuring BONO (17) 86,89
IN A LITTLE SPANISH TOWN – Bing CROSBY (22) 56
IN A PERSIAN MARKET – Sammy DAVIS Jr (28)56
IN A ROOM – DODGY (12) 96
IN A STATE – 2 FOR JOY (61) 90
IN A WORD OR 2 – Monie LOVE (33) 93
IN ALL THE RIGHT PLACES – Lisa STANSFIELD (8)93
IN AND OUT – Willie HUTCH (51) 82
IN AND OUT OF LOVE [A] – Diana ROSS and the SUPREMES (13) 67
IN AND OUT OF LOVE [B] – IMAGINATION (16) 81
IN AND OUT OF MY LIFE [A] – Tonja DANTZLER (66) 94
IN AND OUT OF MY LIFE [B] – A.T.F.C. presents ONEPHATDEEVA (11) 99
IN BETWEEN DAYS – CURE (15) 85
IN BLOOM – NIRVANA (28) 92
THE IN CROWD [A] – Dobie GRAY (25) 65
THE 'IN' CROWD [A] – Bryan FERRY (13) 74
IN DE GHETTO – David MORALES and the BAD YARD CLUB featuring Crystal WATERS and DELTA (35) 96
IN DEMAND – TEXAS (6) 00,01
IN DREAMS – Roy ORBISON (6) 63
IN DULCE DECORUM – DAMNED (72) 87
IN DULCE JUBILO – Mike OLDFIELD (4) 75
IN FOR A PENNY – SLADE (11) 75
IN 4 CHOONS LATER – ROZALLA (50) 92
IN GOD'S COUNTRY (IMPORT) – U2 (48) 87
IN IT FOR LOVE – Richie SAMBORA (58) 98
IN LIVERPOOL – Suzanne VEGA (52) 92
IN LOVE – Michael HOLLIDAY (26) 58
IN LOVE WITH LOVE – Deborah HARRY (45) 87
IN LOVE WITH THE FAMILIAR – WIRELESS (69)98
IN MY ARMS – ERASURE (13) 97
IN MY BED – DRU HILL (16) 97
IN MY CHAIR – STATUS QUO (21) 70
IN MY DEFENCE – Freddie MERCURY (8) 92
IN MY DREAMS [A] – Will DOWNING (34) 88
IN MY DREAMS [B] – JOHNNA (66) 96
IN MY HEART – TEXAS (74) 91
IN MY LIFE [A] – SOULED OUT (75) 92
IN MY LIFE [B] – Kim WILDE (54) 93
IN MY LIFE [C] – José NUNEZ featuring OCTAHVIA (56) 98
IN MY OWN TIME – FAMILY (4) 71
IN MY STREET – CHORDS (50) 80

I.O.I.O. – **BEE GEES** (49) 70
I.O.U. [A] – **Jane KENNAWAY and STRANGE BEHAVIOUR** (65) 81
I.O.U. [B] – **FREEEZ** (2) 83,87
IOU [C] – **Bill TARMEY** (55) 94
IRE FEELINGS (SKANGA) – **Rupie EDWARDS** (9) ..74
IRENE – **PHOTOS** (56) 80
IRIS – **GOO GOO DOLLS** (26) 98,99
THE IRISH ROVER – **POGUES and the DUBLINERS** (8) 87
IRON FIST – **MOTÖRHEAD** (29) 82
IRON HORSE – **CHRISTIE** (47) 72
IRON LION ZION – **Bob MARLEY and the WAILERS** (5) 92
IRON SKY – **MEGA CITY FOUR** (48) 93
IRONIC – **Alanis MORISSETTE** (11) 96
IRRESISTIBLE [A] – **Cathy DENNIS** (24) 92
IRRESISTIBLE [B] – **CORRS** (20) 00
IRRESISTIBLE [C] – **Jessica SIMPSON** (11) 01
IS – **SMALLER** (55) 97
IS A BLUE BIRD BLUE – **Conway TWITTY** (43) 60
IS IT A CRIME – **SADE** (49) 86
IS IT A DREAM [A] – **CLASSIX NOUVEAUX** (11) 82
IS IT A DREAM [B] – **DAMNED** (34) 85
IS IT BECAUSE – **HONEYCOMBS** (38) 64
IS IT GOOD TO YOU [A] – **HEAVY D and the BOYZ** (46) 91
IS IT GOOD TO YOU [A] – **Teddy RILEY** (53) 92
IS IT LIKE TODAY – **WORLD PARTY** (19) 93
IS IT LOVE? – **CHILI HI FLY** (37) 00
IS IT LOVE – **BASEMENT BOYS present Ultra NATÉ** (71) 91
IS IT LOVE YOU'RE AFTER – **ROSE ROYCE** (13) 79,88
IS IT REALLY OVER – **Jim REEVES** (17) 65
IS IT TRUE – **Brenda LEE** (17) 64
IS NOTHING SACRED – **MEAT LOAF** (15) 99
IS SHE REALLY GOING OUT WITH HIM? – **Joe JACKSON** (13) 79
IS THAT LOVE – **SQUEEZE** (35) 81
IS THAT YOUR FINAL ANSWER? (WHO WANTS TO BE A MILLIONAIRE – THE SINGLE) – **AMOURE** (33) 00
IS THERE ANY LOVE IN YOUR HEART – **Lenny KRAVITZ** (52) 93
IS THERE ANYBODY OUT THERE – **BASSHEADS** (5) 91,95
IS THERE ANYBODY THERE – **SCORPIONS** (39) 79
IS THERE SOMEONE OUT THERE? – **CODE RED** (34) 97
IS THERE SOMETHING I SHOULD KNOW [A] – **DURAN DURAN** (1) 83
IS THERE SOMETHING I SHOULD KNOW [A] – **ALLSTARS** (12) 01
IS THIS A DREAM – **LOVE DECADE** (39) 96
IS THIS A LOVE THING – **RAYDIO** (27) 78
IS THIS LOVE [A] – **Bob MARLEY and the WAILERS** (9) 78
IS THIS LOVE? [B] – **Alison MOYET** (3) 86
IS THIS LOVE [C] – **WHITESNAKE** (9) 87,94
IS THIS THE WAY TO AMARILLO – **Tony CHRISTIE** (18) 71
IS THIS WHAT I GET FOR LOVING YOU – **Marianne FAITHFULL** (43) 67
IS VIC THERE? – **DEPARTMENT S** (22) 81
IS YOUR LOVE IN VAIN – **Bob DYLAN** (56) 78
IS YOUR LOVE STRONG ENOUGH? – **Bryan FERRY** (22) 86
ISLAND GIRL – **Elton JOHN** (14) 75
ISLAND HEAD (EP) – **INSPIRAL CARPETS** (21) ..90
ISLAND IN THE SUN [A] – **Harry BELAFONTE** (3)57
ISLAND IN THE SUN [A] – **RIGHTEOUS BROTHERS** (36) 66
ISLAND IN THE SUN [B] – **WEEZER** (31) 01
ISLAND OF DREAMS – **SPRINGFIELDS** (5) 62
ISLAND OF LOST SOULS – **BLONDIE** (11) 82
ISLANDS IN THE STREAM – **Kenny ROGERS and Dolly PARTON** (7) 83
ISLE OF INNISFREE – **Bing CROSBY** (3) 52
ISMS – **DOG EAT DOG** (43) 96
ISN'T IT A WONDER – **BOYZONE** (2) 97
ISN'T IT AMAZING – **HOTHOUSE FLOWERS** (46) ..93
ISN'T IT MIDNIGHT – **FLEETWOOD MAC** (60) ..88
ISN'T IT TIME – **BABYS** (45) 78
ISN'T LIFE STRANGE – **MOODY BLUES** (13) 72
ISN'T SHE LOVELY – **David PARTON** (4) 77
ISOBEL – **BJÖRK** (23) 95
ISRAEL – **SIOUXSIE and the BANSHEES** (41) 80
ISRAELITES – **Desmond DEKKER and the ACES** (1) 69,75
ISTANBUL NOT CONSTANTINOPLE [A] – **Frankie VAUGHAN** (11) 54
ISTANBUL (NOT CONSTANTINOPLE) [B] – **THEY MIGHT BE GIANTS** (61) 90
IT AIN'T A CRIME – **HOUSE OF PAIN** (37) 94
IT AIN'T ENOUGH – **DREEM TEEM vs ARTFUL DODGER featuring MZ MAY and MC ALISTAIR** (20) 01
IT AIN'T FAIR – **Edwin STARR** (56) 85
IT AIN'T GONNA BE ME – **CJ BOLLAND** (35) 99
IT AIN'T HARD TO TELL – **NAS** (64) 94
IT AIN'T ME BABE – **Johnny CASH** (28) 65
IT AIN'T NECESSARILY SO – **BRONSKI BEAT** (16) 84
IT AIN'T OVER TIL IT'S OVER – **Lenny KRAVITZ** (11)91
IT AIN'T WHAT YOU DO IT'S THE WAY THAT YOU DO IT – **FUN BOY THREE and BANANARAMA** (4) 82
IT BEGAN IN AFRICA – **URBAN ALL STARS** (64)88
IT BEGAN IN AFRIKA – **CHEMICAL BROTHERS** (8) 01
IT COULD HAPPEN TO YOU – **Robert PALMER** (71)89
IT DIDN'T MATTER – **STYLE COUNCIL** (9) 87
IT DOESN'T HAVE TO BE – **ERASURE** (12) 87
IT DOESN'T HAVE TO BE THIS WAY – **BLOW MONKEYS** (5) 87
IT DOESN'T MATTER – **Wyclef JEAN featuring THE ROCK and MELKY SEDECK** (3) 00
IT DOESN'T MATTER ANYMORE [A] – **Buddy HOLLY** (1) 59
IT DOESN'T MATTER ANYMORE [B] – **PURESSENCE** (47) 98
IT DOESN'T REALLY MATTER – **ZAPP** (57) 86
IT DON'T COME EASY – **Ringo STARR** (4) 71
IT FE DONE – **SUPERCAT** (66) 92
IT FEELS SO GOOD – **SONIQUE** (1) 98,00
IT HAD TO BE YOU – **Harry CONNICK Jr** (32) 91
IT HURTS SO MUCH – **Jim REEVES** (8) 65
IT HURTS TO BE IN LOVE – **Gene PITNEY** (36) 64
IT IS JAZZ – **TINGO TANGO** (68) 90
IT IS TIME TO GET FUNKY – **D MOB** (9) 89
IT ISN'T RIGHT – **PLATTERS** (23) 57
IT ISN'T, IT WASN'T, IT AIN'T NEVER GONNA BE – **Aretha FRANKLIN and Whitney HOUSTON** (29) ..89
IT KEEPS RAININ' [A] – **Fats DOMINO** (49) 61
IT KEEP RAININ' (TEARS FROM MY EYES) [A] – **Bitty McLEAN** (2) 93
IT KEEPS RIGHT ON A HURTIN' – **Johnny TILLOTSON** (31) 62
IT MAKES ME WONDER – **Bruce FOXTON** (74) 84
IT MAKES YOU FEEL LIKE DANCIN' – **ROSE ROYCE** (16) 78
IT MAY BE WINTER OUTSIDE (BUT IN MY HEART IT'S SPRING) – **LOVE UNLIMITED** (11) 75
IT MIEK – **Desmond DEKKER and the ACES** (7) 69
IT MIGHT AS WELL RAIN UNTIL SEPTEMBER – **Carole KING** (3) 62,72
IT MUST BE HIM (SEUL SUR SON ETOILE) – **Vikki CARR** (2) 67
IT MUST BE LOVE [A] – **Labi SIFFRE** (14) 71
IT MUST BE LOVE [A] – **MADNESS** (4) 81,92
IT MUST BE LOVE [B] – **Robin S** (37) 97
IT MUST BE LOVE [C] – **MERO** (33) 00
IT MUST BE SANTA – **Joan REGAN** (42) 61
IT MUST HAVE BEEN LOVE [A] – **MAGNUM** (33) ..88
IT MUST HAVE BEEN LOVE [B] – **ROXETTE** (3)90,93
IT NEVER RAINS (IN SOUTHERN CALIFORNIA) – **TONY TONI TON...** (69) 91
IT ONLY TAKES A MINUTE [A] – **Jonathan KING** (9) 76
IT ONLY TAKES A MINUTE [A] – **TAVARES** (46) 86
IT ONLY TAKES A MINUTE [A] – **TAKE THAT** (7)92
IT ONLY TOOK A MINUTE – **Joe BROWN and the BRUVVERS** (6) 62,63
IT OUGHTA SELL A MILLION – **Lyn PAUL** (37) ..75
IT SEEMS TO HANG ON [A] – **ASHFORD and SIMPSON** (48) 78
IT SEEMS TO HANG ON [A] – **KWS** (58) 94
IT SHOULD HAVE BEEN ME [A] – **Yvonne FAIR** (5) 76
IT SHOULD'VE BEEN ME [A] – **ADEVA** (48) 91
IT STARTED ALL OVER AGAIN – **Brenda LEE** (15) 62
IT STARTED WITH A KISS – **HOT CHOCOLATE / Errol BROWN** (5) 82,93,98
IT SURE BRINGS OUT THE LOVE IN YOUR EYES – **David SOUL** (12) 78
IT TAKES ALL NIGHT LONG – **Gary GLITTER** (25) 77
IT TAKES TWO [A] – **Marvin GAYE** (16) 67
IT TAKES TWO BABY [A] – **Liz KERSHAW and Bruno BROOKES** (53) 89
IT TAKES TWO [A] – **Rod STEWART and Tina TURNER** (5) 90
IT TAKES TWO [B] – **Rob BASE and DJ E-Z ROCK** (24) 88,89
IT TAKES TWO TO TANGO – **Richard MYHILL** (17) 78
IT WAS A GOOD DAY – **ICE CUBE** (27) 93
IT WAS EASIER TO HURT HER – **Wayne FONTANA** (36) 65
IT WASN'T ME – **SHAGGY featuring Ricardo 'RIKROK' DUCENT** (1) 01
IT WILL BE ALRIGHT – **ODYSSEY** (43) 81
IT WILL BE YOU – **Paul YOUNG** (34) 94
IT WILL COME IN TIME – **Billy PRESTON and SYREETA** (47) 80
IT WILL MAKE ME CRAZY – **FELIX** (11) 92
IT WON'T BE LONG – **Alison MOYET** (50) 91
IT WON'T SEEM LIKE CHRISTMAS (WITHOUT YOU) – **Elvis PRESLEY** (13) 79
THE ITALIAN THEME – **Cyril STAPLETON and his ORCHESTRA** (18) ..56
ITALO HOUSE MIX – **ROCOCO** (54) 89
ITCHYCOO PARK [A] – **SMALL FACES** (3) 67,75
ITCHYCOO PARK [A] – **M PEOPLE** (11) 95
IT'LL BE ME – **Cliff RICHARD and the SHADOWS** (2) 62
IT'S A BEAUTIFUL THING – **OCEAN COLOUR SCENE** (12) 98
IT'S A BETTER THAN GOOD TIME – **Gladys KNIGHT and the PIPS** (59) 78
IT'S A DISCO NIGHT (ROCK DON'T STOP) – **ISLEY BROTHERS** (14) 1179
IT'S A FINE DAY [A] – **OPUS III** (5) 92
IT'S A FINE DAY [A] – **MISS JANE** (62) 99
IT'S A GAME – **BAY CITY ROLLERS** (16) 77
IT'S A GAS – **WEDDING PRESENT** (71) 94
IT'S A GIRL THING – **MY LIFE STORY** (37) 99
IT'S A GOOD LIFE – **Cevin FISHER featuring Romona KELLY** (54) 01
IT'S A HARD LIFE – **QUEEN** (6) 84
IT'S A HEARTACHE – **Bonnie TYLER** (4) 77
IT'S A LONG WAY TO THE TOP (IF YOU WANNA ROCK 'N' ROLL) – **AC/DC** (55) 80
IT'S A LOVE THING – **WHISPERS** (9) 81
IT'S A LOVING THING – **CB MILTON** (34) 94,95
IT'S A MAN'S MAN'S MAN'S WORLD [A] – **James BROWN** (13) 66
IT'S A MAN'S MAN'S MAN'S WORLD [A] – **BRILLIANT** (58) 85
IT'S A MAN'S MAN'S MAN'S WORLD [A] – **Jeanie TRACY and Bobby WOMACK** (73) 95
IT'S A MIRACLE – **CULTURE CLUB** (4) 84
IT'S A MISTAKE – **MEN AT WORK** (33) 83
IT'S A PARTY [A] – **Busta RHYMES featuring ZHANE** (23) 96
IT'S A PARTY [B] – **BOUNTY KILLER** (65) 99
IT'S A RAGGY WALTZ – **Dave BRUBECK QUARTET** (36) 62
IT'S A RAINY DAY – **ICE MC** (73) 95
IT'S A SHAME [A] – **DETROIT SPINNERS** (20) ..70
IT'S A SHAME [B] – **KRIS KROSS** (31) 92
IT'S A SHAME ABOUT RAY – **LEMONHEADS** (31) 92,93
IT'S A SHAME (MY SISTER) – **Monie LOVE** (12) 90
IT'S A SIN – **PET SHOP BOYS** (1) 87
IT'S A SIN TO TELL A LIE – **Gerry MONROE** (13) ..71
IT'S A TRIP (TUNE IN, TURN ON, DROP OUT) – **CHILDREN OF THE NIGHT** (52) 88
IT'S ABOUT TIME – **LEMONHEADS** (57) 93
IT'S ABOUT TIME YOU WERE MINE – **THUNDERBUGS** (43) 99
IT'S ALL ABOUT THE BENJAMINS – **PUFF DADDY** (18) 98
IT'S ALL ABOUT U – **SWV** (36) 96
IT'S ALL ABOUT YOU – **JUSTIN** (34) 99
IT'S ALL ABOUT YOU (NOT ABOUT ME) – **Tracie SPENCER** (65) 99

I'VE GOT NEWS FOR YOU — Feargal SHARKEY (12) 91
I'VE GOT SOMETHING TO SAY — REEF (15) 99
I'VE GOT THE MUSIC IN ME — Kiki DEE (19) 74
I'VE GOT THIS FEELING — MAVERICKS (27) 98
I'VE GOT TO LEARN TO SAY NO — Richard 'Dimples' FIELDS (56) 82
I'VE GOT YOU — Martine McCUTCHEON (6) 99
I'VE GOT YOU ON MY MIND [A] — Dorian GRAY (36) 68
I'VE GOT YOU ON MY MIND [A] — WHITE PLAINS (17) 70
I'VE GOT YOU UNDER MY SKIN [A] — FOUR SEASONS (12) 66
I'VE GOT YOU UNDER MY SKIN [A] — Neneh CHERRY (25) 90
I'VE GOT YOU UNDER MY SKIN [A] — Frank SINATRA with BONO (4) 93
(I'VE GOT YOUR) PLEASURE CONTROL — Simon HARRIS featuring Lonnie GORDON (60) 89
I'VE GOTTA GET A MESSAGE TO YOU — BEE GEES (1) 68
I'VE HAD ENOUGH [A] — Paul McCARTNEY (42)78
I'VE HAD ENOUGH [A] — Ivan MATIAS (69) 96
I'VE HAD ENOUGH [B] — EARTH WIND AND FIRE (29) 82
I'VE HAD ENOUGH [C] — HILLMAN MINX (72) ..98
(I'VE HAD) THE TIME OF MY LIFE — Bill MEDLEY and Jennifer WARNES (6)....87,90
I'VE JUST BEGUN TO LOVE YOU — DYNASTY (51) 80
I'VE LOST YOU — Elvis PRESLEY (9) 70
I'VE NEVER BEEN IN LOVE — Suzi QUATRO (56)..80
I'VE NEVER BEEN TO ME — CHARLENE (1)....82
I'VE PASSED THIS WAY BEFORE — Jimmy RUFFIN (29) 67,69
I'VE SEEN THE WORD — BLANCMANGE (65) 82
I'VE TOLD EVERY LITTLE STAR — Linda SCOTT (7) 61
I'VE WAITED SO LONG — Anthony NEWLEY (3) 59
IVORY — SKIN UP (48) 91
IVORY TOWER — KAYE SISTERS (20) 56
IZZO (H.O.V.A.) — JAY-Z (21) 01
JACK AND DIANE — John Cougar MELLENCAMP (25) 82
JACK AND JILL — RAYDIO (11) 78
JACK IN THE BOX [A] — Clodagh RODGERS (4) 71
JACK IN THE BOX [B] — MOMENTS (7) 77
JACK LE FREAK — CHIC (19) 87
JACK MIX II / III — MIRAGE (4) 87
JACK MIX IV — MIRAGE (8) 87
JACK MIX VII — MIRAGE (50) 88
JACK O' DIAMONDS — Lonnie DONEGAN (14) ..57
JACK TALKING — Dave STEWART (69) 90
THE JACK THAT HOUSE BUILT — JACK 'N' CHILL (6) 87,88
JACK THE GROOVE — RAZE (20) 86,87
JACK THE RIPPER [A] — LL COOL J (37) 88
JACK THE RIPPER [B] — Nick CAVE and the BAD SEEDS (68) 92
JACK TO THE SOUND OF THE UNDERGROUND — HITHOUSE (14) 88
JACK YOUR BODY — Steve 'Silk' HURLEY (1) 87
JACK'S HEROES — POGUES and the DUBLINERS (63) 90
JACKET HANGS — BLUE AEROPLANES (72) 90
JACKIE — Scott WALKER (22) 67
JACKIE WILSON SAID (I'M IN HEAVEN WHEN YOU SMILE) — DEXY'S MIDNIGHT RUNNERS (5) 82
JACKIE'S RACING — WHITEOUT (72) 95
JACKSON — Nancy SINATRA (11) 67
JACKY — Marc ALMOND (17) 91
JACQUELINE — Bobby HELMS (20) 58
JACQUES DERRIDA — SCRITTI POLITTI (43) 82
JACQUES YOUR BODY (MAKE ME SWEAT) — LES RYTHMES DIGITALES (60) 99
JA-DA — JOHNNY and the HURRICANES (14) 61
JADED [A] — GREEN DAY (28) 96
JADED [B] — AEROSMITH (13) 01
JAGUAR — DJ ROLANDO AKA AZTEC MYSTIC (43) 00
JAIL HOUSE RAP — FAT BOYS (63) 85
JAILBIRD — PRIMAL SCREAM (29) 94
JAILBREAK [A] — THIN LIZZY (31) 76
JAILBREAK [B] — PARADOX (66) 90
JAILHOUSE ROCK — Elvis PRESLEY (1) 58,71,77,83
JAILHOUSE ROCK (EP) — Elvis PRESLEY (18) 58
JAM — Michael JACKSON (13) 92
THE JAM EP — A TRIBE CALLED QUEST (61) 97
JAM IT JAM — SHE ROCKERS (58) 90
JAM J — JAMES (24) 94
JAM, JAM, JAM (ALL NIGHT LONG) — PEOPLES CHOICE (40) 78
JAM ON REVENGE (THE WIKKI WIKKI SONG) — NEWCLEUS (44) 83
JAMAICAN IN NEW YORK — SHINEHEAD (30) 93
JAMBALAYA [A] — Jo STAFFORD (11) 52
JAMBALAYA [A] — Fats DOMINO (41) 62
JAMBALAYA (ON THE BAYOU) [A] — CARPENTERS (12) 74
JAMBOREE — NAUGHTY BY NATURE featuring ZHANE. (51) 99
JAMES BOND THEME [A] — John BARRY ORCHESTRA (13) 62
JAMES BOND THEME [A] — MOBY (8) 97,98
JAMES HAS KITTENS — BLU PETER (70) 98
JAMMIN' IN AMERICA — GAP BAND (64) 84
JAMMING — Bob MARLEY and the WAILERS (9) 77,00
JANA — KILLING JOKE (54) 95
JANE [A] — STARSHIP (21) 80
JANE [B] — PERFECT DAY (68) 89
JANIE, DON'T TAKE YOUR LOVE TO TOWN — Jon BON JOVI (13) 97
JANUARY — PILOT (1) 75
JANUARY FEBRUARY — Barbara DICKSON (11) ..80
JAPANESE BOY — ANEKA (1) 81
JARROW SONG — Alan PRICE (6) 74
JAWS — Lalo SCHIFRIN (14) 76
JAYOU — JURASSIC 5 (56) 98
JAZZ CARNIVAL — AZYMUTH (19) 80
JAZZ IT UP — REEL 2 REAL (7) 96
JAZZ RAP — Kim CARNEGIE (73) 91
JAZZ THING — GANG STARR (66) 90
JAZZIN' THE WAY YOU KNOW — JAZZY M (47) ..00
JE NE SAIS PAS POURQUOI — Kylie MINOGUE (2) 88
JE SUIS MUSIC — CERRONE (39) 79
JE T'AIME... MOI NON PLUS [A] — Jane BIRKIN and Serge GAINSBOURG (1) 69,74
JE T'AIME (MOI NON PLUS) [A] — JUDGE DREAD (9) 75
JE T'AIME (ALLO ALLO) [A] — RENE and YVETTE (57) 86
JE VOULAIS TE DIRE (QUE JE T'ATTENDS) — MANHATTAN TRANSFER (40) 78
JEALOUS AGAIN — BLACK CROWES (70) 91
JEALOUS GUY [A] — ROXY MUSIC (1) 81
JEALOUS GUY [A] — John LENNON (45) 85,88
JEALOUS HEART [A] — CADETS with Eileen READ (42) 65
JEALOUS HEART [A] — Connie FRANCIS (44) 66
JEALOUS LOVE [A] — JOBOXERS (72) 83
JEALOUS LOVE [B] — Hazell DEAN (63) 84
JEALOUS MIND — Alvin STARDUST (1) 74
JEALOUSY [A] — Billy FURY (2) 61
JEALOUSY [B] — Amii STEWART (58) 79
JEALOUSY [C] — ADVENTURES OF STEVIE V (58) 91
JEALOUSY [D] — PET SHOP BOYS (12) 91
JEALOUSY [E] — OCTOPUS (59) 96
THE JEAN GENIE — David BOWIE (2) 72
JEAN THE BIRDMAN — David SYLVIAN (68) 93
JEANETTE — BEAT (45) 82
JEANNIE — Danny WILLIAMS (14) 62
JEANNIE, JEANNIE, JEANNIE — Eddie COCHRAN (31)61
JEANNY — FALCO (68) 86
JEANS ON — David DUNDAS (3) 76
JEDI WANNABE — BELLATRIX (65) 00
JEEPSTER [A] — T. REX (2) 71
JEEPSTER [A] — POLECATS (53) 81
JELLYHEAD — CRUSH (50) 96
JENNIFER ECCLES — HOLLIES (7) 68
JENNIFER JUNIPER [A] — DONOVAN (5) 68
JENNIFER JUNIPER [A] — SINGING CORNER meets DONOVAN (68) 90
JENNIFER SHE SAID — Lloyd COLE (31) 88
JENNY JENNY — LITTLE RICHARD (11) 57
JENNY ONDIOLINE — STEREOLAB (75) 94
JENNY TAKE A RIDE — Mitch RYDER and the DETROIT WHEELS (33)66
JEOPARDY — Greg KIHN BAND (63) 83
JEREMY — PEARL JAM (15) 92
JERICHO [A] — SIMPLY RED (53) 86
JERICHO [B] — PRODIGY (11) 92,96
JERUSALEM [A] — FALL (59) 88
JERUSALEM [A] — FAT LES (10) 00
JERUSALEM [B] — Herb ALPERT (42) 70,71
JESAMINE — CASUALS (2) 68
JESSE HOLD ON — B*WITCHED (4) 99,00
JESSIE — Joshua KADISON (15) 94,95
JESSIE'S GIRL — Rick SPRINGFIELD (43) 84
JESUS — Cliff RICHARD (35) 72
JESUS CHRIST — LONGPIGS (61) 95
JESUS CHRIST POSE — SOUNDGARDEN (30) 92
JESUS HAIRDO — CHARLATANS (48) 94
JESUS HE KNOWS ME — GENESIS (20) 92
JESUS SAYS — ASH (15) 98
JESUS TO A CHILD — George MICHAEL (1) 96
JET — Paul McCARTNEY (7) 74
JET CITY WOMAN — QUEENSRYCHE (39) 91
JET-STAR — TEKNO TOO (56) 91
JEWEL — CRANES (29) 93
JEZEBEL [A] — Marty WILDE (19) 62
JEZEBEL [A] — Shakin' STEVENS (58) 89
JIBARO — ELECTRA (54) 88
JIG A JIG — EAST OF EDEN (7) 71
JILTED JOHN — JILTED JOHN (4) 78
JIMMIE JONES — VAPORS (44) 81
JIMMY — PURPLE HEARTS (60) 80
JIMMY JIMMY — UNDERTONES (16) 79
JIMMY LEE — Aretha FRANKLIN (46) 87
JIMMY MACK — Martha REEVES and the VANDELLAS (21) 67,70
JIMMY OLSEN'S BLUES — SPIN DOCTORS (40) 93
JIMMY UNKNOWN — Lita ROZA (15) 56
JIMMY'S GIRL — Johnny TILLOTSON (43) 61
JINGLE BELL ROCK [A] — Max BYGRAVES (7) 59
JINGLE BELL ROCK [A] — Chubby CHECKER and Bobby RYDELL (40) 62
JINGLE BELLS — JUDGE DREAD (59) 78
JINGLE BELLS LAUGHING ALL THE WAY — HYSTERICS (44) 81
JINGO [A] — CANDIDO (55) 81
JINGO [A] — JELLYBEAN (12) 87
JINGO [A] — FKW (30) 94
JITTERBUGGIN' — HEATWAVE (34) 81
JIVE TALKIN' [A] — BEE GEES (5) 75
JIVE TALKIN' [A] — BOOGIE BOX HIGH (7) 87
JJ TRIBUTE — ASHA (38) 95
JOAN OF ARC — ORCHESTRAL MANOEUVRES IN THE DARK (5)81
JOANNA [A] — Scott WALKER (7) 68
JOANNA [B] — KOOL and the GANG (2) 84
JOANNA [C] — MRS WOOD (34) 95,97
JOCELYN SQUARE — LOVE AND MONEY (51) 89
JOCK MIX 1 — MAD JOCKS featuring JOCKMASTER B.A. (46)87
JOCKO HOMO — DEVO (62) 78
JODY — Jermaine STEWART (50) 86
JOE — INSPIRAL CARPETS (37) 95
JOE LE TAXI — Vanessa PARADIS (3) 88
JOE 90 (THEME) — Barry GRAY ORCHESTRA (53) 86
JOHN AND JULIE — Eddie CALVERT (6) 55
JOHN I'M ONLY DANCING [A] — David BOWIE (12) 72,79
JOHN I'M ONLY DANCING [A] — POLECATS (35) 81
JOHN KETTLEY (IS A WEATHERMAN) — TRIBE OF TOFFS (21) 88
JOHN WAYNE IS BIG LEGGY — HAYSI FANTAYZEE (11) 82
JOHNNY AND MARY — Robert PALMER (44) 80
JOHNNY ANGEL [A] — Shelley FABARES (41) 62
JOHNNY ANGEL [A] — Patti LYNN (37) 62
JOHNNY B GOODE [A] — Jimi HENDRIX EXPERIENCE (35) 72
JOHNNY B GOODE [A] — Peter TOSH (48) 83
JOHNNY B GOODE [A] — JUDAS PRIEST (64) 88
JOHNNY COME HOME — FINE YOUNG CANNIBALS (8) 85
JOHNNY COME LATELY — Steve EARLE (75) 88
JOHNNY DAY — Rolf HARRIS (44) 63
JOHNNY FRIENDLY — JOBOXERS (31) 83
JOHNNY GET ANGRY — Carol DEENE (32) 62
JOHNNY JOHNNY — PREFAB SPROUT (64) 86

LET'S LOVEDANCE TONIGHT – GARY'S GANG (49) ... 79
LET'S MAKE A BABY – Billy PAUL (30) ... 76
LET'S MAKE A NIGHT TO REMEMBER – Bryan ADAMS (10) ... 96
LET'S PARTY – JIVE BUNNY and the MASTERMIXERS (1) ... 89
LET'S PLAY HOUSE – KRAZE (71) ... 89
LET'S PRETEND – LULU (11) ... 67
LET'S PUSH IT [A] – INNOCENCE (25) ... 90
LET'S PUSH IT [B] – NIGHTCRAWLERS featuring John REID (23) ... 96
LET'S PUT IT ALL TOGETHER – STYLISTICS (9) 74
LET'S RIDE – Montell JORDAN (25) ... 98
LET'S ROCK – E-TRAX (60) ... 01
LET'S ROCK 'N' ROLL – Winifred ATWELL (24) 57
LET'S SEE ACTION – WHO (16) ... 71
LET'S SLIP AWAY – Cleo LAINE (42) ... 60
LET'S SPEND THE NIGHT TOGETHER [A] – ROLLING STONES (3) ... 67
LET'S SPEND THE NIGHT TOGETHER [A] – MASH! (66) ... 95
LET'S START OVER – Pamela FERNANDEZ (59) 95
LET'S START THE DANCE – Hamilton BOHANNON (56) ... 78
LET'S START TO DANCE AGAIN – Hamilton BOHANNON (49) ... 82
LET'S STAY TOGETHER [A] – Al GREEN (7) ... 72
LET'S STAY TOGETHER [A] – Bobby M featuring Jean CARN (53) ... 83
LET'S STAY TOGETHER [A] – Tina TURNER (6) 83
LET'S STAY TOGETHER [A] – PASADENAS (22) 92
LET'S STICK TOGETHER – Bryan FERRY (4) 76,88
LET'S SWING AGAIN – JIVE BUNNY and the MASTERMIXERS (19) ... 90
LET'S TALK – ONE WAY featuring Al HUDSON (64) ... 85
LET'S TALK ABOUT LOVE – Helen SHAPIRO (23) ... 62
LET'S TALK ABOUT SEX – SALT-N-PEPA (2) ... 91
LET'S THINK ABOUT LIVING – Bob LUMAN (6) 60
LET'S TRY AGAIN – NEW KIDS ON THE BLOCK (8) ... 90
LET'S TURKEY TROT – LITTLE EVA (13) ... 63
LET'S TWIST AGAIN [A] – Chubby CHECKER (2) ... 61,62,75
LET'S TWIST AGAIN [A] – John ASHER (14) ... 75
LET'S WAIT AWHILE – Janet JACKSON (3) ... 87
LET'S WALK THAT-A-WAY – Doris DAY and Johnnie RAY (4) ... 53
LET'S WHIP IT UP (YOU GO GIRL) – SLEAZESISTERS (46) ... 96
LET'S WOMBLE TO THE PARTY TONIGHT – WOMBLES (34) ... 75
LET'S WORK – Mick JAGGER (31) ... 87
LET'S WORK TOGETHER – CANNED HEAT (2) ... 70
THE LETTER [A] – LONG AND THE SHORT (35) 64
THE LETTER [B] – BOX TOPS (5) ... 67
THE LETTER [B] – MINDBENDERS (42) ... 67
THE LETTER [B] – Joe COCKER (39) ... 70
THE LETTER [B] – Amii STEWART (39) ... 80
LETTER FROM AMERICA – PROCLAIMERS (3) ... 87
LETTER FULL OF TEARS – Billy FURY (32) ... 62
LETTER TO A SOLDIER – Barbara LYON (27) ... 56
A LETTER TO ELISE – CURE (28) ... 92
LETTER TO LUCILLE – Tom JONES (31) ... 73
LETTER 2 MY UNBORN – 2PAC (4) ... 01
A LETTER TO YOU – Shakin' STEVENS (10) ... 84
LETTIN' YA MIND GO – DESERT (74) ... 01
LETTING GO – Paul McCARTNEY (41) ... 75
LETTING THE CABLES SLEEP – BUSH (51) ... 00
LEVI STUBBS' TEARS – Billy BRAGG (29) ... 86
LFO – LFO (12) ... 90
LIAR [A] – Graham BONNET (51) ... 81
LIAR [B] – ROLLINS BAND (27) ... 94
LIAR LIAR – CREDIT TO THE NATION (60) ... 95
LIARS' BAR – BEAUTIFUL SOUTH (43) ... 97
LIBERATION [A] – LIBERATION (28) ... 92
LIBERATION [B] – PET SHOP BOYS (14) ... 94
LIBERATION [C] – Lippy LOU (57) ... 95
LIBERATION (TEMPTATION – FLY LIKE AN EAGLE) – Matt DAREY (19) ... 99
LIBERATOR – SPEAR OF DESTINY (67) ... 84
LIBERIAN GIRL – Michael JACKSON (13) ... 89
LIBERTY TOWN – PERFECT DAY (58) ... 89
LIBIAMO – José CARRERAS featuring Placido DOMINGO and Luciano PAVAROTTI with MEHTA (21) ... 94
LICENCE TO KILL – Gladys KNIGHT and the PIPS (6) ... 89
LICK A SHOT – CYPRESS HILL (20) ... 94
LICK A SMURP FOR CHRISTMAS (ALL FALL DOWN) – Jonathan KING (58) ... 78
LICK IT – 20 FINGERS (48) ... 95
LICK IT UP – KISS (31) ... 83
LIDO SHUFFLE – Boz SCAGGS (13) ... 77
LIE TO ME – BON JOVI (10) ... 95
LIES [A] – STATUS QUO (11) ... 80
LIES [B] – THOMPSON TWINS (67) ... 82
LIES [C] – Jonathan BUTLER (18) ... 87
LIES [D] – EN VOGUE (44) ... 90
LIES [E] – EMF (28) ... 91
LIES IN YOUR EYES – SWEET (35) ... 76
LIFE [A] – HADDAWAY (6) ... 93
LIFE [B] – BLAIR (44) ... 96
LIFE [C] – DES'REE (8) ... 98
LIFE AIN'T EASY – CLEOPATRA (4) ... 98
LIFE AT A TOP PEOPLE'S HEALTH FARM – STYLE COUNCIL (28) ... 88
LIFE BECOMING A LANDSLIDE – MANIC STREET PREACHERS (36) ... 94
LIFE BEGINS AT THE HOP – XTC (54) ... 79
LIFE GOES ON – GEORGIE PORGIE (54) ... 00
LIFE IN A DAY – SIMPLE MINDS (62) ... 79
LIFE IN A NORTHERN TOWN – DREAM ACADEMY (15) ... 85
LIFE IN MONO – MONO (60) ... 98
LIFE IN ONE DAY – Howard JONES (14) ... 85
LIFE IN TOKYO – JAPAN (28) ... 82
LIFE IS A FLOWER – ACE OF BASE (5) ... 98
LIFE IS A HIGHWAY – Tom COCHRANE (62) ... 92
LIFE IS A LONG SONG – JETHRO TULL (11) ... 71
LIFE IS A MINESTRONE – 10 CC (7) ... 75
LIFE IS A ROCK (BUT THE RADIO ROLLED ME) – REUNION (33) ... 74
LIFE IS A ROLLERCOASTER – Ronan KEATING (1) 00
LIFE IS FOR LIVING – BARCLAY JAMES HARVEST (61) ... 80
LIFE IS SWEET – CHEMICAL BROTHERS (25) ... 95
LIFE IS TOO SHORT GIRL – SHEER ELEGANCE (9) 76
A LIFE LESS ORDINARY – ASH (10) ... 97
LIFE, LOVE AND HAPPINESS – Brian KENNEDY (27) ... 96
LIFE LOVE AND UNITY – DREADZONE (56) ... 96
THE LIFE OF RILEY – LIGHTNING SEEDS (28) ... 92
LIFE OF SURPRISES – PREFAB SPROUT (24) ... 93
LIFE ON MARS – David BOWIE (3) ... 73
LIFE ON YOUR OWN – HUMAN LEAGUE (16) ... 84
LIFE STORY – Angie STONE (22) ... 00
LIFE SUPPORT MACHINE – THESE ANIMAL MEN (62) ... 97
LIFE'S A CINCH – MUNDY (75) ... 96
LIFE'S BEEN GOOD – Joe WALSH (14) ... 78
LIFE'S JUST A BALLGAME – WOMACK and WOMACK (32) ... 88
LIFE'S TOO SHORT [A] – HOLE IN ONE (36) ... 97
LIFE'S TOO SHORT [B] – LIGHTNING SEEDS (27) ... 99,00
LIFE'S WHAT YOU MAKE IT – TALK TALK (16) 86,90
LIFEBOAT – Terry NEASON (72) ... 94
THE LIFEBOAT PARTY – Kid CREOLE and the COCONUTS (49) ... 83
LIFEFORMS – FUTURE SOUND OF LONDON (14) ... 94
LIFELINE – SPANDAU BALLET (7) ... 82
LIFESAVER – GURU (61) ... 96
LIFETIME LOVE – Joyce SIMS (34) ... 87
LIFETIME PILING UP – TALKING HEADS (50) ... 92
LIFETIMES – SLAM featuring Tyrone PALMER (61) ... 01
LIFT – 808 STATE (38) ... 91
LIFT EVERY VOICE (TAKE ME AWAY) – MASS ORDER (35) ... 92
LIFT IT HIGH (ALL ABOUT BELIEF) – MANCHESTER UNITED FOOTBALL CLUB (11) ... 99
LIFT ME UP [A] – Howard JONES (52) ... 92
LIFT ME UP [B] – RED 5 (26) ... 97
LIFT ME UP [C] – Geri HALLIWELL (1) ... 99,00
LIFTED – LIGHTHOUSE FAMILY (4) ... 95,96
LIFTING ME HIGHER – GEMS FOR JEM (28) ... 95
LIGHT – Pharoahe MONCH (72) ... 00
THE LIGHT – COMMON (56) ... 00
LIGHT A CANDLE – Daniel O'DONNELL (23) ... 00
LIGHT A RAINBOW – TUKAN (38) ... 01
LIGHT AIRCRAFT ON FIRE – AUTEURS (58) ... 96
THE LIGHT COMES FROM WITHIN – Linda McCARTNEY (56) ... 99
LIGHT EMITTING ELECTRICAL WAVE – THESE ANIMAL MEN (72) ... 97
LIGHT FLIGHT – PENTANGLE (43) ... 70
LIGHT MY FIRE [A] – DOORS (7) ... 67,91
LIGHT MY FIRE [A] – José FELICIANO (6) ... 68
LIGHT MY FIRE – 137 DISCO HEAVEN (MEDLEY) [A] – Amii STEWART (5) ... 79,85
LIGHT MY FIRE [A] – Mike FLOWERS POPS (39) ... 96
LIGHT MY FIRE [A] – UB40 (63) ... 00
LIGHT MY FIRE [B] – CLUBHOUSE (7) ... 93,94
(LIGHT OF EXPERIENCE) DOINA DE JALE – Gheorghe ZAMFIR (4) ... 76
LIGHT OF LOVE – T. REX (22) ... 74
LIGHT OF MY LIFE – LOUISE (8) ... 95
LIGHT OF THE WORLD – Kim APPLEBY (41) ... 93
LIGHT UP THE FIRE – PARCHMENT (31) ... 72
LIGHT UP THE NIGHT – BROTHERS JOHNSON (47) ... 80
LIGHT UP THE WORLD FOR CHRISTMAS – LAMPIES (48) ... 01
LIGHT YEARS – PEARL JAM (52) ... 00
LIGHTNIN' STRIKES – Lou CHRISTIE (11) ... 66
LIGHTNING – ZOE (37) ... 91
LIGHTNING CRASHES – LIVE (33) ... 96
LIGHTNING FLASH – BROTHERHOOD OF MAN (67) ... 82
LIGHTNING STRIKES – Ozzy OSBOURNE (72) ... 86
THE LIGHTNING TREE – SETTLERS (36) ... 71
LIGHTS OF CINCINNATI – Scott WALKER (13) ... 69
LIKE A BABY – Len BARRY (10) ... 66
LIKE A BUTTERFLY – Mac and Katie KISSOON (18) ... 75
LIKE A CHILD – Julie ROGERS (21) ... 64
LIKE A CHILD AGAIN – MISSION (30) ... 92
LIKE A FEATHER – Nikka COSTA (53) ... 01
LIKE A HURRICANE – MISSION (49) ... 86
LIKE A MOTORWAY – SAINT ETIENNE (47) ... 94
LIKE A PLAYA – LA GANZ (75) ... 96
LIKE A PRAYER – MADONNA (1) ... 89
LIKE A ROLLING STONE [A] – Bob DYLAN (4) ... 65
LIKE A ROLLING STONE [A] – ROLLING STONES (12) ... 95
LIKE A ROSE – A1 (6) ... 00
LIKE A SATELLITE (EP) – THUNDER (28) ... 93
LIKE A VIRGIN – MADONNA (3) ... 84
LIKE A WOMAN – Tony RICH PROJECT (27) ... 96
LIKE A YO-YO – SABRINA (72) ... 89
LIKE AN ANIMAL – GLOVE (52) ... 83
LIKE AN OLD TIME MOVIE – Scott McKENZIE (50) ... 67
LIKE CLOCKWORK – BOOMTOWN RATS (6) ... 78
LIKE DREAMERS DO [A] – APPLEJACKS (20) ... 64
LIKE DREAMERS DO [B] – Mica PARIS featuring Courtney PINE (26) ... 88
LIKE FLAMES – BERLIN (47) ... 87
LIKE I DO [A] – Maureen EVANS (3) ... 62
LIKE I DO [B] – FOR REAL (45) ... 97
LIKE I LIKE IT – AURRA (43) ... 85,86
LIKE I'VE NEVER BEEN GONE – Billy FURY (3) 63
LIKE LOVERS DO – Lloyd COLE (24) ... 95
LIKE MARVIN GAYE SAID (WHAT'S GOING ON) – SPEECH (35) ... 96
LIKE PRINCES DO – DIESEL PARK WEST (58) ... 89
LIKE SISTER AND BROTHER – DRIFTERS (7) ... 73
LIKE STRANGERS – EVERLY BROTHERS (11) ... 60
LIKE THIS AND LIKE THAT [A] – MONICA (33) ... 96
LIKE THIS AND LIKE THAT [B] – LaKiesha BERRI (54) ... 97
LIKE THIS LIKE THAT – Mauro PICOTTO (21) ... 01
LIKE TO GET TO KNOW YOU WELL – Howard JONES (4) ... 84
LIKE WE USED TO BE – Georgie FAME (33) ... 65
A LIL' AIN'T ENOUGH – David Lee ROTH (32) ... 91
LIL' DEVIL – CULT (11) ... 87
LIL' RED RIDING HOOD [A] – SAM THE SHAM and the PHARAOHS (46) ... 66
LIL RED RIDING HOOD [A] – 999 (59) ... 81
LILAC WINE – Elkie BROOKS (16) ... 78
LILY THE PINK – SCAFFOLD (1) ... 68
LILY WAS HERE – Candy DULFER (6) ... 90

LOC'ED AFTER DARK – **Tone LOC** (21)..............89
LOCAL BOY IN THE PHOTOGRAPH – **STEREOPHONICS** (14)................................97,98
LOCK AND LOAD – **Bob SEGER and the SILVER BULLET BAND** (57)96
LOCK UP YOUR DAUGHTERS – **SLADE** (29) 81
LOCKED OUT – **CROWDED HOUSE** (12) 94
LOCO – **FUN LOVIN' CRIMINALS** (5)..................01
LOCO IN ACAPULCO – **FOUR TOPS** (7) 88
LOCOMOTION – **ORCHESTRAL MANOEUVRES IN THE DARK** (5)..84
LOCO-MOTION [A] – **VERNONS GIRLS** (47) 62
THE LOCO-MOTION [A] – **LITTLE EVA** (2) 62,72
THE LOCOMOTION [A] – **Dave STEWART** (70) ..86
THE LOCO-MOTION [A] – **Kylie MINOGUE** (2) ..88
L.O.D. (LOVE ON DELIVERY) – **Billy OCEAN** (19) ..76
THE LODGERS – **STYLE COUNCIL** (13) 85
THE LOGICAL SONG – **SUPERTRAMP** (7)..........79
L'OISEAU ET L'ENFANT – **Marie MYRIAM** (42) ..77
LOLA [A] – **KINKS** (2)..70
LOLA [A] – **Andy TAYLOR** (60)...........................90
LOLLIPOP [A] – **CHORDETTES** (6) 58
LOLLIPOP [A] – **MUDLARKS** (2) 58
LOLLY LOLLY – **WENDY and LISA** (64)..............89
LONDINIUM – **CATATONIA** (20) 99
LONDON BOYS – **T. REX** (40) 76
LONDON CALLING – **CLASH** (11)..............79,88,91
LONDON GIRLS – **CHAS and DAVE** (63) 83
LONDON KID – **Jean-Michel JARRE featuring Hank MARVIN** (52)..........................89
LONDON NIGHTS – **LONDON BOYS** (2) 89
A LONDON THING – **Scott GARCIA featuring MC STYLES** (29) 97
LONDON TIMES – **RADIO HEART featuring Gary NUMAN**(48)......87
LONDON TONIGHT – **COLLAPSED LUNG** (31)....96
LONDON TOWN [A] – **Paul McCARTNEY** (60)....78
LONDON TOWN [B] – **LIGHT OF THE WORLD** (41)80
LONDON TOWN [C] – **BUCKS FIZZ** (34) 83
LONDON TOWN [D] – **JDS** (49)...........................98
LONDON X-PRESS – **X-PRESS 2** (59)................93
LONDON'S BRILLIANT – **Wendy JAMES** (62) 93
LONDON'S BRILLIANT PARADE – **Elvis COSTELLO** (48) 94
LONDRES STRUTT – **SMELLS LIKE HEAVEN** (57) 93
THE LONE RANGER – **QUANTUM JUMP** (5) 79
LONE RIDER – **John LEYTON** (40) 62
THE LONELIEST MAN IN THE WORLD – **TOURISTS** (32) 79
LONELINESS – **Des O'CONNOR** (18) 69
LONELINESS IS GONE – **NINE YARDS** (70) 98
LONELY [A] – **Eddie COCHRAN** (41) 60
LONELY [B] – **Mr Acker BILK and his PARAMOUNT JAZZ BAND** (14) 62
LONELY [C] – **Peter ANDRE** (6) 97,98
LONELY BALLERINA – **MANTOVANI** (16) 55
LONELY BOY [A] – **Paul ANKA** (3) 59
LONELY BOY [B] – **Andrew GOLD** (11) 77
LONELY BOY LONELY GUITAR – **Duane EDDY and the REBELS** (35) 63
THE LONELY BULL – **Herb ALPERT** (22)............63
LONELY CITY – **John LEYTON** (14) 62
LONELY, CRYIN' ONLY – **THERAPY?** (32) 98
LONELY DAYS – **BEE GEES** (33).......................70
LONELY DAYS, LONELY NIGHTS – **Don DOWNING** (32).......................................73
LONELY (HAVE WE LOST OUR LOVE) – **Lance ELLINGTON** (57) 93
LONELY HEART – **UFO** (41)...............................81
THE LONELY MAN THEME – **Cliff ADAMS ORCHESTRA** (39).........................60
LONELY NIGHT – **MAGNUM** (70) 86
THE LONELY ONE – **ALICE DEEJAY** (16) 00
LONELY PUP (IN A CHRISTMAS SHOP) – **Adam FAITH** (4)...60
LONELY STREET – **Clarence 'Frogman' HENRY** (42) 61
LONELY SYMPHONY – **Frances RUFFELLE** (25) 94
LONELY TEENAGER – **DION** (47) 61
LONELY THIS CHRISTMAS – **MUD** (1) 74,85
LONELY TOGETHER – **Barry MANILOW** (21) 80
THE LONER – **Gary MOORE** (53) 87
LONESOME – **Adam FAITH** (12) 62
LONESOME NUMBER ONE – **Don GIBSON** (47) 62
LONESOME (SI TU VOIS MA MERE) – **Chris BARBER'S JAZZ BAND** (27)....................59
LONESOME TRAVELLER – **Lonnie DONEGAN** (28)58
LONG AFTER TONIGHT IS ALL OVER – **Jimmy RADCLIFFE** (40)....................................65
LONG AND LASTING LOVE (ONCE IN A LIFETIME) – **Glenn MEDEIROS** (42) 88
THE LONG AND WINDING ROAD – **Ray MORGAN** (32) 70
LONG AS I CAN SEE THE LIGHT [A] – **CREEDENCE CLEARWATER REVIVAL** (20)........70
LONG AS I CAN SEE THE LIGHT [A] – **MONKEY MAFIA** (51) 98
LONG COOL WOMAN IN A BLACK DRESS – **HOLLIES** (32)...72
A LONG DECEMBER – **COUNTING CROWS** (62) 96,97
LONG HAIRED LOVER FROM LIVERPOOL – **Little Jimmy OSMOND** (1) 72,73
LONG HOT SUMMER – **STYLE COUNCIL** (3) 83,89
LONG HOT SUMMER NIGHT – **JT TAYLOR** (63)..91
LONG LEGGED GIRL (WITH THE SHORT DRESS ON) – **Elvis PRESLEY** (49) 67
LONG LEGGED WOMAN DRESSED IN BLACK – **MUNGO JERRY** (13) 74
LONG LIVE LOVE [A] – **Sandie SHAW** (1) 65
LONG LIVE LOVE [A] – **Nick BERRY** (47) 92
LONG LIVE LOVE [B] – **Olivia NEWTON-JOHN** (11) 74
LONG LIVE ROCK – **WHO** (48) 79
LONG LIVE ROCK 'N' ROLL – **RAINBOW** (33) 78
LONG LIVE THE UK MUSIC SCENE – **Helen LOVE** (65) 98
LONG LOST LOVER – **THREE DEGREES** (40) 75
LONG MAY YOU RUN (LIVE) – **Neil YOUNG** (71)93
THE LONG RUN – **EAGLES** (66) 79
LONG SHOT KICK DE BUCKET – **PIONEERS** (21).......................................69,70,80
LONG TALL GLASSES – **Leo SAYER** (4) 74
LONG TALL SALLY [A] – **Pat BOONE** (18) 56
LONG TALL SALLY [A] – **LITTLE RICHARD** (3)....57
LONG TERM LOVERS OF PAIN (EP) – **HUE AND CRY** (48)..91
LONG TIME – **ARROW** (30) 85
LONG TIME COMING – **BUMP & FLEX** (73) 98
LONG TIME GONE – **GALLIANO** (15)..................94
LONG TRAIN RUNNING [A] – **BANANARAMA** (30)91
LONG TRAIN RUNNIN' [A] – **DOOBIE BROTHERS** (7).......................................93
A LONG WALK – **Jill SCOTT** (54)........................01
LONG WAY – **ROOTJOOSE** (68) 97
LONG WAY AROUND – **Eagle-Eye CHERRY featuring Neneh CHERRY** (48)........................00
LONG WAY FROM HOME – **WHITESNAKE** (55)..79
LONG WAY SOUTH – **JJ72** (68)..........................00
LONG WAY TO GO – **Stevie NICKS** (60)...........89
LONG WHITE CAR – **HIPSWAY** (55) 86
LONGER – **Dan FOGELBERG** (59)......................80
THE LONGEST TIME – **Billy JOEL** (25) 84
LONGTIME BOY – **NINA and FREDERICK** (43) ..61
LONGVIEW – **GREEN DAY** (30)..........................95
LONNIE DONEGAN SHOWCASE (LP) – **Lonnie DONEGAN** (26) 56
LONNIE'S SKIFFLE PARTY – **Lonnie DONEGAN** (23) 58
LOO-BE-LOO – **CHUCKS** (22) 63
THE LOOK – **ROXETTE** (7) 89,95
LOOK AROUND – **Vince HILL** (12).......................71
LOOK AT ME – **Geri HALLIWELL** (2) 99
LOOK AT ME (I'M IN LOVE) – **MOMENTS** (42)..75
LOOK AT THAT GIRL – **Guy MITCHELL** (1) 53
LOOK AT YOURSELF – **David McALMONT** (40) 97
LOOK AWAY – **BIG COUNTRY** (7).....................86
LOOK BEFORE YOU LEAP – **Dave CLARK FIVE** (50) 66
LOOK BUT DON'T TOUCH (EP) – **SKIN** (33)......94
LOOK FOR A STAR – **Garry MILLS** (7) 60
LOOK HOMEWARD ANGEL – **Johnnie RAY** (7) ..57
LOOK INTO MY EYES – **BONE THUGS-N-HARMONY** (16).....................97
LOOK MAMA – **Howard JONES** (10) 85
LOOK ME IN THE HEART – **Tina TURNER** (31) ..90
LOOK OF LOVE [A] – **Gladys KNIGHT and the PIPS** (21)..................73
THE LOOK OF LOVE [A] – **T-EMPO** (71) 96
THE LOOK OF LOVE [B] – **ABC** (4) 82,83,90
THE LOOK OF LOVE [C] – **MADONNA** (9)..........87
LOOK THROUGH ANY WINDOW – **HOLLIES** (4) 65
LOOK UP TO THE LIGHT – **EVOLUTION** (55) 95
LOOK WHAT YOU DONE FOR ME – **Al GREEN** (44)72
LOOK WHAT YOU STARTED – **TEMPTATIONS** (63)88
LOOK WHO IT IS – **Helen SHAPIRO** (47)..........63
LOOK WHO'S DANCING – **Ziggy MARLEY and the MELODY MAKERS** (65)89
LOOK WHO'S PERFECT NOW – **TRANSISTER** (56)98
LOOK WHO'S TALKING – **DR ALBAN** (55) 94
LOOK WOT YOU DUN – **SLADE** (4) 72
LOOKIN' THROUGH THE WINDOWS – **JACKSONS** (9) 72
LOOKING AFTER NO.1 – **BOOMTOWN RATS** (11)..77
LOOKING AT MIDNIGHT – **IMAGINATION** (29) ..83
LOOKING FOR A LOVE – **Joyce SIMS** (39) 89
LOOKING FOR A NEW LOVE – **Jody WATLEY** (13)..87
LOOKING FOR A SONG – **BIG AUDIO DYNAMITE** (68) 94
LOOKING FOR ATLANTIS – **PREFAB SPROUT** (51)90
LOOKING FOR CLUES – **Robert PALMER** (33) ..80
LOOKING FOR LEWIS AND CLARK – **LONG RYDERS** (59) 85
LOOKING FOR LINDA – **HUE AND CRY** (15) 89
LOOKING FOR LOVE – **Karen RAMIREZ** (8) 98
LOOKING FOR LOVE TONIGHT – **FAT LARRY'S BAND** (46) 79
LOOKING FOR THE SUMMER – **Chris REA** (49) 91
LOOKING HIGH HIGH HIGH – **Bryan JOHNSON** (20) 60
LOOKING THROUGH PATIENT EYES – **PM DAWN** (11) 93
LOOKING THROUGH THE EYES OF LOVE [A] – **Gene PITNEY** (3) 65
LOOKING THROUGH THE EYES OF LOVE [A] – **PARTRIDGE FAMILY** (9) 73
LOOKING THROUGH YOUR EYES – **LeAnn RIMES** (38) 98
LOOKING UP – **Michelle GAYLE** (11) 93
LOOKS LIKE I'M IN LOVE AGAIN – **ERIK** (46) ..93
LOOKS LOOKS LOOKS – **SPARKS** (26) 75
LOOP-DE-LOOP – **Frankie VAUGHAN** (5) 63
LOOP DI LOVE – **Jonathan KING** (4) 72
LOOPS OF FURY (EP) – **CHEMICAL BROTHERS** (13) 96
LOOPS OF INFINITY – **COSMIC BABY** (70)........94
LOOPZILLA – **George CLINTON** (57) 82
LOOSE – **THERAPY?** (25) 95
LOOSE FIT – **HAPPY MONDAYS** (17) 91
LOPEZ – **808 STATE** (20)...................................97
LORDS OF THE NEW CHURCH – **Tasmin ARCHER** (26).......................................93
LORELEI – **Lonnie DONEGAN** (10) 60
LORRAINE – **BAD MANNERS** (21)......................80
LOS AMERICANOS – **ESPIRITU** (45)..................93
LOSE CONTROL – **JAMES** (38) 90
LOSE IT – **SUPERGRASS** (75) 95
LOSER – **BECK** (15) 94
LOSING MY GRIP – **SAMSON** (63) 82
LOSING MY MIND – **Liza MINNELLI** (6) 89
LOSING MY RELIGION – **R.E.M.** (19)..................91
LOSING YOU [A] – **Brenda LEE** (10) 63
LOSING YOU [B] – **Dusty SPRINGFIELD** (9) 64
LOST AGAIN – **YELLO** (73)................................83
LOST AND FOUND – **D*NOTE** (59)....................97
THE LOST ART OF KEEPING A SECRET – **QUEENS OF THE STONE AGE** (31) 00
LOST CAT – **CATATONIA** (41) 96
LOST IN AMERICA – **Alice COOPER** (22) 94
LOST IN EMOTION [A] – **LISA LISA** (58)............87
LOST IN EMOTION [B] – **John 'OO' FLEMING** (74)99
LOST IN FRANCE – **Bonnie TYLER** (9) 76
LOST IN LOVE [A] – **UP YER RONSON featuring Mary PEARCE** (27) 95
LOST IN LOVE [B] – **LEGEND B** (45) 97
LOST IN MUSIC [A] – **SISTER SLEDGE** (4) ..79,84,93
LOST IN MUSIC [B] – **STEREO MC's** (46) 91
LOST IN SPACE [A] – **APOLLO FOUR FORTY** (4)98
LOST IN SPACE [B] – **ELECTRASY** (60)..............98
LOST IN SPACE [C] – **LIGHTHOUSE FAMILY** (6) 98
LOST IN THE TRANSLATION – **PACIFICA** (54) ..99
LOST IN YOU [A] – **Rod STEWART** (21) 88
LOST IN YOU [B] – **Garth BROOKS** (70)............99
LOST IN YOUR EYES – **Debbie GIBSON** (34) 89
LOST IN YOUR LOVE – **Tony HADLEY** (42) 92
LOST JOHN – **Lonnie DONEGAN** (2)..................56
LOST MYSELF – **LONGPIGS** (22) 96

LOVE MAKES THE WORLD GO ROUND [A] – Perry COMO (6) 58
LOVE MAKES THE WORLD GO ROUND [A] – JETS (21) 82
LOVE MAKES THE WORLD GO ROUND [B] – DON-E (18) 92
LOVE MAN – Otis REDDING (43) 69
LOVE ME [A] – Yvonne ELLIMAN (6) 76
LOVE ME [A] – Martine McCUTCHEON (6) 99
LOVE ME [B] – Diana ROSS (38) 74
LOVE ME [C] – PATRIC (54) 94
LOVE ME AND LEAVE ME – SEAHORSES (16) ..97
LOVE ME AS THOUGH THERE WERE NO TOMORROW – Nat 'King' COLE (11) 56
LOVE ME BABY – Susan CADOGAN (22) 75
LOVE ME DO – BEATLES (4) 62,82,92
LOVE ME FOR A REASON [A] – OSMONDS (1)..74
LOVE ME FOR A REASON [A] – BOYZONE (2) ..94
LOVE ME FOREVER [A] – FOUR ESQUIRES (23)58
LOVE ME FOREVER [A] – Eydie GORME (21) 58
LOVE ME FOREVER [A] – Marion RYAN (5) 58
LOVE ME LIKE A LOVER – Tina CHARLES (31)..76
LOVE ME LIKE I LOVE YOU – BAY CITY ROLLERS (4) 76
LOVE ME LIKE THIS – REAL TO REEL (68) 84
LOVE ME LOVE MY DOG – Peter SHELLEY (3) 75
LOVE ME NOW [A] – Briana CORRIGAN (48) 96
LOVE ME NOW [B] – SECRET KNOWLEDGE (66) 96
LOVE ME OR LEAVE ME [A] – Sammy DAVIS Jr (8) 55
LOVE ME OR LEAVE ME [A] – Doris DAY (20) ..55
LOVE ME RIGHT NOW – ROSE ROYCE (60) 85
LOVE ME TENDER [A] – Elvis PRESLEY (11) 56,87
LOVE ME TENDER [A] – Richard CHAMBERLAIN (15) 62
LOVE ME TENDER [A] – Roland RAT SUPERSTAR (32) 84
LOVE ME THE RIGHT WAY – RAPINATION featuring Kym MAZELLE (22)92,96
LOVE ME TO SLEEP – HOT CHOCOLATE (50) ..80
LOVE ME TONIGHT [A] – Tom JONES (9) 69
LOVE ME TONIGHT [B] – Trevor WALTERS (27) 81
LOVE ME WARM AND TENDER – Paul ANKA (19) 62
LOVE ME WITH ALL YOUR HEART – Karl DENVER (37) 64
LOVE MEETING LOVE – LEVEL 42 (61) 80
LOVE MISSILE F1-11 – SIGUE SIGUE SPUTNIK (3) 86
LOVE MOVES (IN MYSTERIOUS WAYS) – Julia FORDHAM (19) 92
LOVE MY WAY – PSYCHEDELIC FURS (42) 82
LOVE NEEDS NO DISGUISE – Gary NUMAN and DRAMATIS (33) 81
LOVE NEVER DIES... – Belinda CARLISLE (54)..88
LOVE OF A LIFETIME [A] – Chaka KHAN (52) ..86
LOVE OF A LIFETIME [B] – HONEYZ (9) 99
LOVE OF MY LIFE [A] – DOOLEYS (9) 77
LOVE OF MY LIFE [B] – QUEEN (63) 79
LOVE OF THE COMMON PEOPLE [A] – Nicky THOMAS (9) 70
LOVE OF THE COMMON PEOPLE [A] – Paul YOUNG (2) 83
LOVE OF THE LOVED – Cilla BLACK (35) 63
LOVE OH LOVE – Lionel RICHIE (52) 92
LOVE ON A FARMBOY'S WAGES – XTC (50) 83
LOVE ON A MOUNTAIN TOP [A] – Robert KNIGHT (10) 73
LOVE ON A MOUNTAIN TOP [A] – SINITTA (20)89
LOVE ON A SUMMER NIGHT – McCRARYS (52)82
LOVE ON LOVE [A] – E-ZEE POSSEE (59) 90
LOVE ON LOVE [A] – Candi STATON (27) 99
LOVE ON THE LINE – BARCLAY JAMES HARVEST (63) 80
LOVE ON THE NORTHERN LINE – NORTHERN LINE (15) 00
LOVE ON THE ROCKS – Neil DIAMOND (17) 80
LOVE ON THE SIDE – BROKEN ENGLISH (69) ..87
LOVE ON YOUR SIDE – THOMPSON TWINS (9)83
LOVE OR MONEY [A] – BLACKWELLS (46) 61
LOVE OR MONEY [A] – Jimmy CRAWFORD (49) 61
LOVE OR MONEY [A] – Billy FURY (57) 82
LOVE OR MONEY [B] – Sammy HAGAR (67) 80
LOVE OR NOTHING – Diana BROWN and Barrie K SHARPE (71) 91
LOVE OVER GOLD (LIVE) – DIRE STRAITS (50) 84
LOVE OVERBOARD – Gladys KNIGHT and the PIPS (42) 88
LOVE PAINS [A] – Hazell DEAN (48) 89
LOVE PAINS [A] – Liza MINNELLI (41) 90
THE LOVE PARADE – DREAM ACADEMY (68) ..85
LOVE PATROL – DOOLEYS (29) 80
LOVE, PEACE & GREASE – BT (41) 97
LOVE PEACE AND HARMONY – DREAM FREQUENCY (71) 91
LOVE, PEACE & NAPPINESS – LOST BOYZ (57)97
LOVE PLUS ONE – HAIRCUT 100 (3) 82
LOVE POTION NO.9 – TYGERS OF PAN TANG (45)82
LOVE POWER – Dionne WARWICK and Jeffrey OSBORNE (63)87
LOVE REACTION – DIVINE (65) 83
LOVE REALLY HURTS WITHOUT YOU – Billy OCEAN (2) 76
LOVE REARS ITS UGLY HEAD – LIVING COLOUR (12) 91
LOVE REMOVAL MACHINE – CULT (18) 87
LOVE RENDEZVOUS – M PEOPLE (32) 95
LOVE RESURRECTION [A] – Alison MOYET (10) 84
LOVE RESURRECTION [A] – D'LUX (58) 96
LOVE ROLLERCOASTER – RED HOT CHILI PEPPERS (7) 97
LOVE RULES – WEST END (44) 95
THE LOVE SCENE – JOE (22) 97
LOVE SCENES – Beverley CRAVEN (34) 93
LOVE SEE NO COLOUR – FARM (35) 91,93
LOVE SENSATION – 911 (21) 96
LOVE SHACK – B-52's (2) 90,99
LOVE SHADOW – FASHION (51) 82
LOVE SHINE – RHYTHM SOURCE (74) 95
LOVE SHINE A LIGHT – KATRINA and the WAVES (3) 97
LOVE SHINES THROUGH – CHAKRA (67) 99
LOVE SHOULDA BROUGHT YOU HOME – Toni BRAXTON (33) 94
LOVE SHY – Kristine BLOND (22) 98,00
LOVE SICK – Bob DYLAN (64) 98
LOVE SITUATION – Mark FISHER featuring Dotty GREEN (59) 85
LOVE SLAVE – WEDDING PRESENT (17) 92
LOVE SNEAKIN' UP ON YOU – Bonnie RAITT (69) 94
A LOVE SO BEAUTIFUL – Michael BOLTON (27) ..95
LOVE SO BRIGHT – Mark SHAW (54) 90
LOVE SO RIGHT – BEE GEES (41) 76
LOVE SO STRONG – SECRET LIFE (37) 93,95
LOVE SONG [A] – DAMNED (20) 79
LOVE SONG [B] – SIMPLE MINDS (6) 81,92
LOVE SONG [C] – UTAH SAINTS (37) 00
LOVE SONG FOR A VAMPIRE – Annie LENNOX (3) 93
LOVE SONGS ARE BACK AGAIN (MEDLEY) – BAND OF GOLD (24) 84
THE LOVE SONGS EP – Daniel O'DONNELL (27) 97
LOVE SPREADS – STONE ROSES (2) 94
LOVE STIMULATION – HUMATE (18) 99
LOVE STORY – JETHRO TULL (29) 69
LOVE STRAIN – Kym MAZELLE (52) 89
A LOVE SUPREME – Will DOWNING (14) 88
LOVE TAKE OVER – FIVE STAR (25) 85
LOVE TAKES TIME – Mariah CAREY (37) 90
LOVE THE LIFE – JTQ (34) 93
LOVE THE ONE YOU'RE WITH [A] – Stephen STILLS (37) 71
LOVE THE ONE YOU'RE WITH [A] – BUCKS FIZZ (47) 86
LOVE THE ONE YOU'RE WITH [A] – Luther VANDROSS (31) 94
LOVE THEME FROM 'A STAR IS BORN' (EVERGREEN) – Barbra STREISAND (3) 77
LOVE THEME FROM SPARTACUS – Terry CALLIER (57) 98
LOVE THEME FROM THE GODFATHER – Andy WILLIAMS (42) 72
LOVE THEME FROM 'THE THORN BIRDS' – Juan MARTIN (10) 84
LOVE THING [A] – PASADENAS (22) 90
LOVE THING [B] – Tina TURNER (29) 92
LOVE THING [C] – EVOLUTION (32) 93
LOVE... THY WILL BE DONE – MARTIKA (9) 91
LOVE TIMES LOVE – HEAVY PETTIN' (69) 84
LOVE X LOVE – George BENSON (10) 80
LOVE TO HATE YOU – ERASURE (4) 91
LOVE II LOVE – DAMAGE (12) 96
LOVE TO LOVE YOU – CORRS (62) 97
LOVE TO LOVE YOU BABY – Donna SUMMER (4) 76
LOVE TO STAY – ALTERED IMAGES (46) 83
LOVE TOGETHER – LA MIX (66) 89
LOVE TOUCH – Rod STEWART (27) 86
LOVE TOWN – Booker NEWBERRY III (6) 83
LOVE TRAIN [A] – O'JAYS (9) 73
LOVE TRAIN [B] – Holly JOHNSON (4) 89
LOVE TRIAL – Kelly MARIE (51) 81
LOVE, TRUTH AND HONESTY – BANANARAMA (23) 88
LOVE U 4 LIFE – JODECI (23) 95
LOVE U MORE – SUNSCREEM (23) 92
LOVE UNLIMITED – FUN LOVIN' CRIMINALS (18) 98
LOVE WALKED IN – THUNDER (21) 91
LOVE WARS – WOMACK and WOMACK (14) 84
LOVE WHAT YOU DO – DIVINE COMEDY (26) ..01
LOVE WILL COME – TOMSKI (31) 00
LOVE WILL CONQUER ALL – Lionel RICHIE (45)86
LOVE WILL FIND A WAY [A] – David GRANT (24) 83
LOVE WILL FIND A WAY [B] – YES (73) 87
LOVE WILL KEEP US ALIVE – EAGLES (52) 96
LOVE WILL KEEP US TOGETHER [A] – CAPTAIN and TENNILLE (32) 75
LOVE WILL KEEP US TOGETHER [A] – JTQ featuring Alison LIMERICK (63) 95
LOVE WILL LEAD YOU BACK – Taylor DAYNE (69) 90
LOVE WILL MAKE YOU FAIL IN SCHOOL – Rocky SHARPE and the REPLAYS (60) 79
LOVE WILL NEVER DO (WITHOUT YOU) – Janet JACKSON (34) 90
LOVE WILL SAVE THE DAY – Whitney HOUSTON (10) 88
LOVE WILL TEAR US APART – JOY DIVISION (13) 80,83,95
LOVE WON'T LET ME WAIT – Major HARRIS (37) 75
LOVE WON'T WAIT – Gary BARLOW (1) 97
LOVE WORTH DYING FOR – THUNDER (60) 97
A LOVE WORTH WAITING FOR – Shakin' STEVENS (2) 84
LOVE YOU ALL MY LIFETIME – Chaka KHAN (49) 92
LOVE YOU ANYWAY – DE NADA (15) 01
LOVE YOU DOWN – READY FOR THE WORLD (60) 87
LOVE YOU INSIDE OUT – BEE GEES (13) 79
LOVE YOU MORE – BUZZCOCKS (34) 78
LOVE YOU SOME MORE – Cevin FISHER featuirng Sheila SMITH (60) 01
THE LOVE YOU SAVE – JACKSONS (7) 70
LOVE YOUR MONEY – DAISY CHAINSAW (26)..92
LOVE YOUR SEXY . . . !! – BYKER GROOOVE! (48) 94
LOVE ZONE – Billy OCEAN (49) 86
LOVEBIRDS – DODGY (65) 93
LOVEDRIVE – SCORPIONS (69) 79
LOVEFOOL – CARDIGANS (2) 96,97
LOVELIGHT (RIDE ON A LOVE TRAIN) – Jayn HANNA (42) 96
LOVELY DAUGHTER – MERZ (60) 99
LOVELY DAY – Bill WITHERS (4) 78,88
LOVELY DAZE – JAZZY JEFF & the FRESH PRINCE (37) 98
LOVELY MONEY – DAMNED (42) 82
LOVELY ONE – JACKSONS (29) 80
LOVELY THING – REGGAE PHILHARMONIC ORCHESTRA (71) 90
LOVENEST – WEDDING PRESENT (58) 91
LOVER [A] – Dan REED NETWORK (45) 90
LOVER [B] – Joe ROBERTS (22) 94
LOVER [C] – Rachel McFARLANE (38) 98
LOVER COME BACK TO ME – DEAD OR ALIVE (11) 85
THE LOVER IN ME – Sheena EASTON (15) 89
THE LOVER IN YOU – SUGARHILL GANG (54) ..82
LOVER LOVER LOVER – Ian McCULLOCH (47) 92
LOVER PLEASE – VERNONS GIRLS (16) 62
A LOVER SPURNED – Marc ALMOND (29) 90
THE LOVER THAT YOU ARE – PULSE featuring Antoinette ROBERSON (22) 96
LOVERBOY [A] – Billy OCEAN (15) 85
LOVERBOY [B] – CHAIRMEN OF THE BOARD (56)86
LOVERBOY [C] – Mariah featuring CAMEO (12) 01
LOVERIDE – NUANCE featuring Vikki LOVE (59)..85
A LOVER'S CONCERTO – TOYS (5) 65

MAIDS WHEN YOU'RE YOUNG NEVER WED AN OLD MAN – DUBLINERS (43) 67
THE MAIGRET THEME – Joe LOSS (20) 62
THE MAIN ATTRACTION – Pat BOONE (12) 62
MAIN THEME FROM 'EXODUS' – SEMPRINI (25) ..61
MAIN THEME FROM 'THE THORN BIRDS' – Henry MANCINI (23) 84
MAIN TITLE THEME FROM 'MAN WITH THE GOLDEN ARM' [A] – Billy MAY (9) 56
MAIN TITLE THEME FROM 'MAN WITH THE GOLDEN ARM' [A] – Jet HARRIS (12) 62
MAIS OUI – KING BROTHERS (16) 60
THE MAJESTY OF ROCK – SPINAL TAP (61) 92
MAJOR TOM (COMING HOME) – Peter SCHILLING (42) 84
MAJORCA – Petula CLARK (12) 55
MAKE A DAFT NOISE FOR CHRISTMAS – GOODIES (20) 75
MAKE A FAMILY – Gary CLARK (70) 93
MAKE A MOVE ON ME – Olivia NEWTON-JOHN (43) 82
MAKE BELIEVE IT'S YOUR FIRST TIME – CARPENTERS (60) 83
MAKE HER MINE – Nat 'King' COLE (11) 54
MAKE IT A PARTY – Winifred ATWELL (7) 56
MAKE IT EASY ON YOURSELF – WALKER BROTHERS (1) 65
MAKE IT HAPPEN – Mariah CAREY (17) 92
MAKE IT HOT – Nicole RAY featuring Missy 'Misdemeanor' ELLIOTT (22) 98
MAKE IT LAST [A] – SKIPWORTH and TURNER (60) 89
MAKE IT LAST [B] – EMBRACE (35) 01
MAKE IT MINE – SHAMEN (42) 90
MAKE IT ON MY OWN – Alison LIMERICK (16) 92,96
MAKE IT REAL – SCORPIONS (72) 80
MAKE IT RIGHT – Christian FALK featuring DEMETREUS (22) 00
MAKE IT SOON – Tony BRENT (9) 53
MAKE IT TONIGHT – WET WET WET (37) 91
MAKE IT WITH YOU [A] – BREAD (5) 70
MAKE IT WITH YOU [A] – PASADENAS (20) 92
MAKE IT WITH YOU [A] – LET LOOSE (7) 96
MAKE IT WITH YOU [B] – UNIVERSAL (33) 97
MAKE LOVE EASY – Freddie JACKSON (70) 94
MAKE LOVE LIKE A MAN – DEF LEPPARD (12) 92
MAKE LOVE TO ME! [A] – Jo STAFFORD (8) 54
MAKE LOVE TO ME [A] – John LEYTON (49) 64
MAKE LOVE TO ME [B] – Jill FRANCIS (70) 93
MAKE ME AN ISLAND – Joe DOLAN (3) 69
MAKE ME BAD – KORN (25) 00
MAKE ME LAUGH – ANTHRAX (26) 88
MAKE ME SMILE (COME UP AND SEE ME) – Steve HARLEY and COCKNEY REBEL (1) 75,92,95
MAKE MY BODY ROCK – JOMANDA (44) 89
MAKE MY DAY – Buju BANTON (72) 93
MAKE MY HEART FLY – PROCLAIMERS (63) 88
MAKE MY LOVE – Shawn CHRISTOPHER (57) ..94
MAKE SOMEONE HAPPY – Jimmy DURANTE (69) 96
MAKE THAT MOVE – SHALAMAR (30) 81
MAKE THE WORLD GO AWAY [A] – Eddy ARNOLD (8) 66
MAKE THE WORLD GO AWAY [A] – Donny and Marie OSMOND (18) 75
MAKE THE WORLD GO ROUND – Sandy B (20) 96,97,98
MAKE UP YOUR MIND – BASS JUMPERS (44) ..99
MAKE WAY FOR THE INDIAN – APACHE INDIAN and TIM DOG (29) 95
MAKE YOURS A HAPPY HOME – Gladys KNIGHT and the PIPS (35) 76
MAKES ME LOVE YOU – ECLIPSE (25) 99
MAKES ME WANNA DIE – TRICKY (29) 97
MAKIN' HAPPY – Crystal WATERS (18) 91
MAKIN' IT – David NAUGHTON (44) 79
MAKIN' LOVE – Floyd ROBINSON (9) 59
MAKIN' WHOOPEE – Ray CHARLES (42) 65
MAKING LOVE (OUT OF NOTHING AT ALL) – Bonnie TYLER (45) 96
MAKING PLANS FOR NIGEL – XTC (17) 79
MAKING THE MOST OF – DODGY (22) 95
MAKING TIME – CREATION (49) 66
MAKING UP AGAIN – GOLDIE (7) 78
MAKING YOUR MIND UP – BUCKS FIZZ (1) 81
MALE STRIPPER – Man PARRISH (4) 86,87
MALIBU – HOLE (22) 99
MALT AND BARLEY BLUES – McGUINNESS FLINT (5) 71
MAMA [A] – David WHITFIELD (12) 55
MAMA [A] – Connie FRANCIS (2) 60
MAMA [B] – Dave BERRY (5) 66
MAMA [C] – GENESIS (4) 83
MAMA [D] – Kim APPLEBY (19) 91
MAMA [E] – SPICE GIRLS (1) 97
MAMA I'M COMING HOME – Ozzy OSBOURNE (46) 91
MA-MA-MA-BELLE – ELECTRIC LIGHT ORCHESTRA (22) 74
MAMA NEVER TOLD ME – SISTER SLEDGE (20) 75
MAMA SAID [A] – Carleen ANDERSON (26) 94
MAMA SAID [B] – METALLICA (19) 96
MAMA SAID KNOCK YOU OUT – LL COOL J (41) ..90
MAMA TOLD ME NOT TO COME [A] – THREE DOG NIGHT (3) 70
MAMA TOLD ME NOT TO COME [A] – Tom JONES and STEREOPHONICS (4) 00
MAMA USED TO SAY [A] – JUNIOR (7) 82
MAMA USED TO SAY [A] – AZURE (56) 98
MAMA WEER ALL CRAZEE NOW – SLADE (1) 72
MAMA – WHO DA MAN? – Richard BLACKWOOD (3) 00
MAMA'S BOY – Suzi QUATRO (34) 80
MAMA'S PEARL – JACKSONS (25) 71
MAMBO ITALIANO [A] – Rosemary CLOONEY (1) 54
MAMBO ITALIANO [A] – Dean MARTIN (14) 55
MAMBO ITALIANO [A] – SHAFT (12) 00
MAMBO NO.5 (A LITTLE BIT OF...) [A] – Lou BEGA (1) 99
MAMBO NO.5 [A] – BOB THE BUILDER (1) 01
MAMBO ROCK – Bill HALEY and his COMETS (14) 55
MAMMA GAVE BIRTH TO THE SOUL CHILDREN – QUEEN LATIFAH + DE LA SOUL (14) 90
MAMMA MIA [A] – ABBA (1) 75
MAMMA MIA [A] – A TEENS (12) 99
MAMOUNA – Bryan FERRY (57) 95
MAMY BLUE [A] – LOS POP TOPS (35) 71
MAMY BLUE [A] – Roger WHITTAKER (31) 71
MAN – Rosemary CLOONEY (7) 54
MAN BEHIND THE MUSIC – QUEEN PEN (38) ..98
THE MAN DON'T GIVE A FUCK – SUPER FURRY ANIMALS (22) 96
THE MAN FROM LARAMIE [A] – Al MARTINO (19) 55
THE MAN FROM LARAMIE [A] – Jimmy YOUNG (1)55
MAN FROM MADRID – Tony OSBORNE SOUND (50) 61
MAN FROM NAZARETH – John Paul JOANS (25) 70,71
MAN! I FEEL LIKE A WOMAN! – Shania TWAIN (3) 99
THE MAN I LOVE – Kate BUSH (27) 94
THE MAN IN BLACK – Cozy POWELL (18) 74
MAN IN THE MIRROR – Michael JACKSON (21) 88
MAN IN THE MOON – CSILLA (69) 96
A MAN NEEDS TO BE TOLD – CHARLATANS (31) 01
MAN OF MYSTERY – SHADOWS (5) 60
MAN OF THE WORLD – FLEETWOOD MAC (2) ..69
MAN ON FIRE [A] – Frankie VAUGHAN (6) 57
MAN ON FIRE [B] – Roger TAYLOR (66) 84
MAN ON THE CORNER – GENESIS (41) 82
MAN ON THE EDGE – IRON MAIDEN (10) 95
MAN ON THE MOON – R.E.M. (18) 92
MAN OUT OF TIME – Elvis COSTELLO (58) 82
MAN SHORTAGE – LOVINDEER (69) 86
THE MAN THAT GOT AWAY – Judy GARLAND (18) 55
MAN TO MAN – HOT CHOCOLATE (14) 76
THE MAN WHO PLAYS THE MANDOLINO – Dean MARTIN (21) 57
THE MAN WHO SOLD THE WORLD [A] – LULU (3) 74
THE MAN WHO SOLD THE WORLD (LIVE) [A] – David BOWIE (39) 95
THE MAN WHO TOLD EVERYTHING – DOVES (32) 00
MAN WITH THE CHILD IN HIS EYES – Kate BUSH (6) 78
MAN WITH THE RED FACE – Laurent GARNIER (36) 00
A MAN WITHOUT LOVE [A] – Kenneth McKELLAR (30) 66
A MAN WITHOUT LOVE [A] – Engelbert HUMPERDINCK (2) 68
MANCHESTER UNITED – MANCHESTER UNITED FOOTBALL CLUB (50) 76
MANCHILD – Neneh CHERRY (5) 89
MANDINKA – Sinead O'CONNOR (17) 88
MANDOLIN RAIN – Bruce HORNSBY and the RANGE (70) 87
MANDOLINS IN THE MOONLIGHT – Perry COMO (13) 58
MANDY – Barry MANILOW (11) 75
MANDY (LA PANSE) – Eddie CALVERT (9) 58
MANEATER – Daryl HALL and John OATES (6) 82
MANGOS – Rosemary CLOONEY (17) 57
MANHATTAN SKYLINE – A-HA (13) 87
MANHATTAN SPIRITUAL – Reg OWEN (20) 59
MANIAC – Michael SEMBELLO (43) 83
MANIC MINDS – MANIX (63) 91
MANIC MONDAY – BANGLES (2) 86
MANNEQUIN – KIDS FROM 'FAME' (50) 82
MANNISH BOY – Muddy WATERS (51) 88
MAN-SIZE – P J HARVEY (42) 93
MANSIZE ROOSTER – SUPERGRASS (20) 95
MANTRA FOR A STATE OF MIND – S EXPRESS (21) 89
MANY RIVERS TO CROSS [A] – UB40 (16) 83
MANY RIVERS TO CROSS [A] – CHER (37) 93
MANY TEARS AGO – Connie FRANCIS (12) 61
MANY TOO MANY – GENESIS (43) 78
MANY WEATHERS APART – MERZ (48) 99
MARBLE BREAKS IRON BENDS – Peter FENTON (46) 66
MARBLEHEAD JOHNSON – BLUETONES (7) 96
MARBLES – BLACK GRAPE (46) 98
MARCH OF THE MODS – Joe LOSS (31) 64
MARCH OF THE PIGS – NINE INCH NAILS (45) 94
MARCH OF THE SIAMESE CHILDREN – Kenny BALL and his JAZZMEN (4) 62
MARCHETA – Karl DENVER (8) 61
MARGATE – CHAS and DAVE (46) 82
MARGIE – Fats DOMINO (18) 59
MARGO – Billy FURY (28) 59
MARGUERITA TIME – STATUS QUO (3) 83
MARIA [A] – PJ PROBY (8) 65
MARIA [B] – BLONDIE (1) 99
MARIA MARIA – SANTANA (6) 00
MARIA ELENA [A] – LOS INDIOS TABAJARAS (5)..63
MARIA ELENA [B] – Gene PITNEY (25) 69
MARIANA – GIBSON BROTHERS (11) 80
MARIANNE [A] – HILLTOPPERS (20) 57
MARIANNE [B] – Cliff RICHARD (22) 68
MARIE – BACHELORS (9) 65
MARIE CELESTE – POLECATS (53) 81
MARIE MARIE – Shakin' STEVENS (19) 80
(MARIE'S THE NAME) HIS LATEST FLAME – Elvis PRESLEY (1) 61
MARJORINE – Joe COCKER (48) 68
MARKET SQUARE HEROES – MARILLION (53) 82,83
MARLENE ON THE WALL – Suzanne VEGA (21) 86
MAROC 7 – SHADOWS (24) 67
MARQUEE MOON – TELEVISION (30) 77
MARQUIS – LINOLEUM (73) 97
MARRAKESH EXPRESS – CROSBY, STILLS, NASH and YOUNG (17) 69
MARRIED MEN – Bonnie TYLER (35) 79
MARRY ME – Mike PRESTON (14) 61
MARTA – BACHELORS (20) 67
MARTA'S SONG – DEEP FOREST (26) 95
MARTHA'S HARBOUR – ALL ABOUT EVE (10) ..88
MARTIAN HOP – Rocky SHARPE and the REPLAYS (55) 80
MARTIKA'S KITCHEN – MARTIKA (17) 91
MARVELLOUS – LIGHTNING SEEDS (24) 95
MARVIN – MARVIN THE PARANOID ANDROID (53) 81
MARY – SUPERGRASS (36) 99,00
MARY ANN – BLACK LACE (42) 79
MARY ANNE – SHADOWS (17) 65
MARY HAD A LITTLE BOY – SNAP (8) 90

MIDDLE OF THE NIGHT – BROTHERHOOD OF MAN (41) 78
MIDDLEMAN – TERRORVISION (25) 94
MIDLIFE CRISIS – FAITH NO MORE (10) 92
MIDNIGHT – Paul ANKA (26) 58
MIDNIGHT AT THE LOST AND FOUND – MEAT LOAF (17) 83
MIDNIGHT AT THE OASIS [A] – Maria MULDAUR (21) 74
MIDNIGHT AT THE OASIS [A] – BRAND NEW HEAVIES (13) 94
MIDNIGHT BLUE – Louise TUCKER (59) 83
MIDNIGHT COWBOY – MIDNIGHT COWBOY SOUNDTRACK (47) 80
MIDNIGHT FLYER – Nat 'King' COLE (23) 59
MIDNIGHT GROOVIN' – LIGHT OF THE WORLD (72) 79
MIDNIGHT IN A PERFECT WORLD – DJ SHADOW (54) 96
MIDNIGHT IN CHELSEA – Jon BON JOVI (4) 97
MIDNIGHT IN MOSCOW – Kenny BALL and his JAZZMEN (2) 61
MIDNIGHT RIDER – Paul DAVIDSON (10) 75
MIDNIGHT SHIFT – Buddy HOLLY (26) 59
MIDNIGHT SUMMER DREAM – STRANGLERS (35) 83
MIDNIGHT TO SIX MAN – PRETTY THINGS (46)66
MIDNIGHT TRAIN TO GEORGIA – Gladys KNIGHT and the PIPS (10) 76
MIDNITE – D'INFLUENCE (58) 95
MIDNITE DYNAMOS – MATCHBOX (14) 80
MIDNITE SPECIAL – Paul EVANS (41) 60
MIDSUMMER MADNESS (EP) – RHYTHM SECTION (66) 92
MIGHT BE STARS – WANNADIES (51) 95
THE MIGHTY HIGH – REVIVAL 3000 (47) 97
MIGHTY JOE – SHOCKING BLUE (43) 70
MIGHTY POWER OF LOVE – TAVARES (25) 77
MIGHTY QUINN – MANFRED MANN (1) 68
MIG29 – MIG29 (62) 92
MIKE OLDFIELD'S SINGLE (THEME FROM TUBULAR BELLS) – Mike OLDFIELD (31) 74
MILES AWAY [A] – John FOXX (51) 80
MILES AWAY [B] – WINGER (56) 91
MILES FROM HOME – PESHAY (75) 98
MILK – GARBAGE featuring TRICKY (10) 96,97
MILK AND ALCOHOL – DR FEELGOOD (9) 79
MILKMAN'S SON – UGLY KID JOE (39) 95
MILKY WAY – SHEER ELEGANCE (18) 75
THE MILL HILL SELF HATE CLUB – Edward BALL (57) 96
MILLENIUM [A] – KILLING JOKE (34) 94
MILLENNIUM [B] – Robbie WILLIAMS (1) 98,00
MILLENNIUM CHIMES – BIG BEN (53) 00
THE MILLENNIUM PRAYER – Cliff RICHARD (1) 99
MILLION DOLLAR LOVE – DUB WAR (73) 97
MILLION DRUMS – Tony SHEVETON (49) 64
A MILLION LOVE SONGS – TAKE THAT (7) 92
MILLION MILES AWAY – OFFSPRING (21) 01
MILLION SUNS – OOBERMAN (43) 99
MILLIONAIRE SWEEPER – KENICKIE (60) 96
MILLIONS LIKE US – PURPLE HEARTS (57) 79
MILLY MOLLY MANDY – Glyn POOLE (35) 73
MILORD [A] – Edith PIAF (24) 60
MILORD [A] – Frankie VAUGHAN (34) 60
MIND – FARM (31) 91
MIND ADVENTURES – DES'REE (43) 92
MIND BLOWIN' – SMOOTH (36) 95
MIND BLOWING DECISIONS – HEATWAVE (9) 78,90
MIND BODY SOUL – FANTASY UFO (50) 91
MIND GAMES – John LENNON (26) 73
MIND OF A TOY – VISAGE (13) 81
THE MIND OF LOVE – kd LANG (72) 93
THE MIND OF THE MACHINE – N-TRANCE (15) 97
MIND OVER MONEY – TURIN BRAKES (31) 01
MIND UP TONIGHT – Melba MOORE (22) 83
MINDLESS BOOGIE – HOT CHOCOLATE (46) 79
MINDSTREAM – MEAT BEAT MANIFESTO (55) 93
MINE – EVERYTHING BUT THE GIRL (58) 84
MINE ALL MINE – CA$HFLOW (15) 86
MINE TO GIVE – PHOTEK featuring Robert J OWENS (44) 01
MINEFIELD – I-LEVEL (52) 83
MINISTRY OF LOVE – HYSTERIC EGO (39) 97
MINNIE THE MOOCHER – REGGAE PHILHARMONIC ORCHESTRA (35) 88
MINORITY – GREEN DAY (18) 00
MINT CAR – CURE (31) 96
MINUETTO ALLEGRETTO – WOMBLES (16) 74
MINUTE BY MINUTE – DOOBIE BROTHERS (47) ..79
A MINUTE OF YOUR TIME – Tom JONES (14) ..68
THE MINUTE YOU'RE GONE – Cliff RICHARD (1) 65
MIRACLE [A] – Jon BON JOVI (29) 90
MIRACLE [B] – OLIVE (41) 97
THE MIRACLE [A]– QUEEN (21) 89
THE MIRACLE [B]– Cliff RICHARD (23) 99
MIRACLE GOODNIGHT – David BOWIE (40) 93
THE MIRACLE OF LOVE – EURYTHMICS (23) 86
THE MIRACLE OF YOU – Danny WILLIAMS (41) 61
MIRACLES – Gary NUMAN (49) 85
MIRROR IN THE BATHROOM – BEAT (4) 80,96
MIRROR MAN – HUMAN LEAGUE (2) 82
MIRROR MIRROR [A] – PINKERTON'S ASSORTED COLOURS (9) 66
MIRROR MIRROR [B] – Diana ROSS (36) 82
MIRROR MIRROR (MON AMOUR) – DOLLAR (4)81
MIRRORS – Sally OLDFIELD (19) 78
MIS-SHAPES – PULP (2) 95
MISERERE – ZUCCHERO with Luciano PAVAROTTI (15) 92
MISERY [A] – SOUL ASYLUM (30) 95
MISERY [B] – MOFFATTS (47) 99
MISFIT – CURIOSITY (7) 87
MISIRLOU (THE THEME TO THE MOTION PICTURE 'PULP FICTION') – SPAGHETTI SURFERS (55) 95
MISLED [A] – KOOL and the GANG (28) 85
MISLED [B] – QUIREBOYS (37) 90
MISLED [C] – Celine DION (15) 94,95
MISS AMERICA – BIG DISH (37) 91
MISS CALIFORNIA – Dante THOMAS featuring PRAS (25) 01
MISS CHATELAINE – kd LANG (68) 93
MISS FAT BOOTY – PART II – MOS DEF featuring GHOSTFACE KILLAH (64) 00
MISS HIT AND RUN – Barry BLUE (26) 74
MISS MODULAR – STEREOLAB (60) 97
MISS PARKER [A] – BENZ (35) 96
MISS PARKER [B] – MORGAN (74) 99
MISS SARAJEVO – PASSENGERS (6) 95
MISS THE GIRL – CREATURES (21) 83
MISS WORLD – HOLE (64) 94
MISS YOU [A] – Jimmy YOUNG (15) 63
MISS YOU [B] – ROLLING STONES (3) 78
MISS YOU LIKE CRAZY – Natalie COLE (2) 89
MISS YOU MUCH – Janet JACKSON (22) 89
MISS YOU NIGHTS – Cliff RICHARD (14) 76,94,95
MISSING [A] – Terry HALL (75) 89
MISSING [B] – EVERYTHING BUT THE GIRL (3) 94,95
MISSING WORDS – SELECTER (23) 80
MISSING YOU [A] – Chris DE BURGH (3) 88
MISSING YOU [B] – John WAITE (9) 84,93
MISSING YOU [B] – Tina TURNER (12) 96
MISSING YOU [C] – Mary J BLIGE (19) 97,98
MISSING YOU [C] – SOUL II SOUL featuring Kym MAZELLE (22) ..90
MISSING YOU NOW – Michael BOLTON featuring Kenny G (28) 92
MISSION OF LOVE – Jason DONOVAN (26) 92
MISSIONARY MAN – EURYTHMICS (31) 87
MISSISSIPPI – PUSSYCAT (1) 76
MISSY MISSY – Paul and Barry RYAN (43) 66
MISTAKES AND REGRETS – ... AND YOU WILL KNOW US BY THE TRAIL OF DEAD (69) 00
MISTER JONES – OUT OF MY HAIR (73) 95
MR. PORTER – Mickie MOST (45) 63
MISTER SANDMAN [A] – Max BYGRAVES (16) ..55
MISTER SANDMAN [A] – FOUR ACES (9) 55
MR BACHELOR – LOOSE ENDS (50) 88
MR BASS MAN – Johnny CYMBAL (24) 63
MR BIG STUFF [A] – HEAVY D and the BOYZ (61)86
MR BIG STUFF [A] – QUEEN LATIFAH, SHADES and FREE (31) 97
MR BLOBBY – MR BLOBBY (1) 93
MR BLUE [A] – David MacBETH (18) 59
MR BLUE [A] – Mike PRESTON (12) 59
MR BLUE SKY – ELECTRIC LIGHT ORCHESTRA (6) 78
MR CABDRIVER – Lenny KRAVITZ (58) 90
MR CROWLEY – Ozzy OSBOURNE (46) 80
MR CUSTER – Charlie DRAKE (12) 60
MR DEVIL – BIG TIME CHARLIE (39) 00
MR DJ [A] – CONCEPT (27) 85
MR DJ [B] – BLACKOUT (19) 01
MR E'S BEAUTIFUL BLUES – EELS (11) 00
MR FIXIT – ROOTJOOSE (54) 97
MR FRIDAY NIGHT – Lisa MOORISH (24) 96
MR GUDER – CARPENTERS (12) 74
MR GUITAR – Bert WEEDON (47) 61
MR HANKEY THE CHRISTMAS POO – MR HANKEY (4) 99
MR JONES – COUNTING CROWS (28) 94
MR KIRK'S NIGHTMARE – 4 HERO (73) 90
MR LEE – Diana ROSS (58) 88
MR LOVERMAN – Shabba RANKS (3) 92,93
MR MANIC AND SISTER COOL – SHAKATAK (56) 87
MR PHARMACIST – FALL (75) 86
MR PRESIDENT – D, B, M and T (33) 70
MR RAFFLES (MAN IT WAS MEAN) – Steve HARLEY and COCKNEY REBEL (13) 75
MR SANDMAN [A] – CHORDETTES (11) 54
MR SANDMAN [A] – Dickie VALENTINE (5) 54
MR SECOND CLASS – Spencer DAVIS GROUP (35) 68
MR SLEAZE – STOCK AITKEN WATERMAN (3) ..87
MR SOFT – Steve HARLEY and COCKNEY REBEL (8) 74
MR SOLITAIRE – ANIMAL NIGHTLIFE (25) 84
MR SUCCESS – Frank SINATRA (25) 58,59
MR TAMBOURINE MAN – BYRDS (1) 65
MR TELEPHONE MAN – NEW EDITION (19) 85
MR VAIN – CULTURE BEAT (1) 93
MR WENDAL – ARRESTED DEVELOPMENT (4) 93
MR WONDERFUL – Peggy LEE (5) 57
MR WRITER – STEREOPHONICS (5) 01
MR ZERO – Keith RELF (50) 66
MISTLETOE AND WINE – Cliff RICHARD (1) 88
MISTY [A] – Johnny MATHIS (12) 60
MISTY [A] – Ray STEVENS (2) 75
MISTY BLUE – Dorothy MOORE (5) 76
MISTY MORNING, ALBERT BRIDGE – POGUES (41) 89
MISUNDERSTANDING – GENESIS (42) 80
MISUNDERSTOOD MAN – Cliff RICHARD (19) ..95
MITCH – BISCUIT BOY (75) 01
MITTAGEISEN (METAL POSTCARD) – SIOUXSIE and the BANSHEES (47) 79
MIX IT UP – Dan REED NETWORK (49) 91
MIXED BIZNESS – BECK (34) 00
MIXED EMOTIONS – ROLLING STONES (36) 89
MIXED TRUTH – RAGGA TWINS (65) 92
MIYAKO HIDEAWAY – MARION (45) 98
M'LADY – SLY and the FAMILY STONE (32) 68
MMM MMM MMM MMM – CRASH TEST DUMMIES (2) 94
MMMBOP – HANSON (1) 97
MO MONEY MO PROBLEMS – NOTORIOUS B.I.G. featuring PUFF DADDY and MASE (6) 97
MOAN & GROAN – Mark MORRISON (7) 97
MOANIN' – Chris FARLOWE (46) 67
MOB RULES – BLACK SABBATH (46) 81
MOBILE – Ray BURNS (4) 55
MOCKINGBIRD [A] – Inez FOXX (33) 69
MOCKINGBIRD [A] – Carly SIMON and James TAYLOR (34) 74
MOCKINGBIRD [A] – BELLE STARS (51) 82
MOCKINGBIRD HILL – MIGIL FIVE (10) 64
THE MODEL – KRAFTWERK (1) 81
MODERN AGE – STROKES (68) 01
MODERN AGE (EP) – STROKES (71) 01
MODERN GIRL [A] – Sheena EASTON (8) 80
MODERN GIRL [B] – MEAT LOAF (17) 84
MODERN LOVE – David BOWIE (2) 83
MODERN ROMANCE (I WANT TO FALL IN LOVE AGAIN) – Francis ROSSI (54) 85
THE MODERN WORLD – JAM (36) 77,80,83
MODUS OPERANDI – PHOTEK (66) 98
MOIRA JANE'S CAFE – DEFINITION OF SOUND (34) 92
MOLLIE'S SONG – Beverley CRAVEN (61) 93
MOLLY – CARRIE (56) 98
MOMENT OF MY LIFE – Bobby D'AMBROSIO featuring Michelle WEEKS (23) 97
MOMENTS IN LOVE – ART OF NOISE (51) 85

MOVE THAT BODY [A] – **TECHNOTRONIC** (12) ..91
MOVE THAT BODY [B] – **NUSH** (46) 95
MOVE THE CROWD – **Eric B and RAKIM** (53) ..88
MOVE TO MEMPHIS – **A-HA** (47) 91
MOVE YOUR ASS – **SCOOTER** (23) 95
MOVE YOUR BODY [A] – **Gene FARROW and GF BAND** (33) 78
MOVE YOUR BODY [B] – **TYREE** (72) 89
MOVE YOUR BODY [C] – **XPANSIONS** (7) 91,95
MOVE YOUR BODY [D] – **ANTICAPPELLA** (21) 94,96
MOVE YOUR BODY [E] – **EUROGROOVE** (29) ..95,96
MOVE YOUR BODY [F] – **RUFFNECK featuring YAVAHN** (60) 96
MOVE YOUR BODY [G] – **EIFFEL 65** (3) 00
MOVE YOUR FEET – **M-D-EMM** (67)..................92
MOVE YOUR FEET TO THE RHYTHM OF THE BEAT – **HITHOUSE** (69)..89
MOVE YOUR LOVE – **DJH featuring STEFY** (73)................................91
MOVIE STAR – **HARPO** (24) 76
MOVIES [A] – **HOTHOUSE FLOWERS** (68) 90
MOVIES [B] – **ALIEN ANT FARM** (53) 01
MOVIN' [A] – **BRASS CONSTRUCTION** (23)..76,84
MOVIN' [A] – **400 BLOWS** (54) 85
MOVIN' [B] – **MARATHON** (36) 92
MOVIN' [C] – **MONE** (48) 96
MOVIN' ON [A] – **BANANARAMA** (24) 92
MOVIN' ON [B] – **APACHE INDIAN** (48) 93
MOVIN' ON [C] – **Debbie PENDER** (41) 98
MOVIN' ON [D] – **PROSPECT PARK / Carolyn HARDING** (55) 98
MOVIN' OUT (ANTHONY'S SONG) – **Billy JOEL** (35)...78
MOVIN' THRU YOUR SYSTEM – **JARK PRONGO** (58)...99
MOVIN TOO FAST – **ARTFUL DODGER and Romina JOHNSON** (2)..00
MOVING – **SUPERGRASS** (9) 99
MOVING IN THE RIGHT DIRECTION – **PASADENAS** (49)..92
MOVING ON – **DREADZONE** (58) 97
MOVING ON UP – **M PEOPLE** (2) 93,94
MOVING ON UP (ON THE RIGHT SIDE) – **Beverley KNIGHT** (42) 96
MOVING TO CALIFORNIA – **STRAW** (50) 99
MOVING UP MOVING ON – **MOZAIC** (62)..........96
MOZART 40 – **SOVEREIGN COLLECTION** (27) 71
MOZART SYMPHONY NO.40 IN G MINOR K550 1ST MOVEMENT (ALLEGRO MOLTO) – **Waldo de los RIOS** (5)...................................71
MRS HOOVER – **CANDYSKINS** (65) 96
MRS MILLS' MEDLEY – **MRS MILLS** (18) 61
MRS ROBINSON [A] – **SIMON and GARFUNKEL** (4) 68
MRS ROBINSON [A] – **LEMONHEADS** (19) 92
MRS ROBINSON (EP) – **SIMON and GARFUNKEL** (9) 69
MRS WASHINGTON – **GIGOLO AUNTS** (74) 94
MS GRACE – **TYMES** (1) 74
MS JACKSON – **OUTKAST** (2) 01
MUCH AGAINST EVERYONE'S ADVICE – **SOULWAX** (56) 00
MUCH LOVE – **Shola AMA** (17) 98
MUCHO MACHO – **TOTO COELO** (54) 82
MUCK IT OUT – **FARMERS BOYS** (48) 83
MUDDY WATER BLUES – **Paul RODGERS** (45)..94
MUHAMMAD ALI – **FAITHLESS** (29) 01
MULDER AND SCULLY – **CATATONIA** (3) 98
MULE (CHANT NO.2) – **BEGGAR and CO** (37) ..81
MULE SKINNER BLUES [A] – **Rusty DRAPER** (39) 60
MULE SKINNER BLUES [A] – **FENDERMEN** (32) 60
MULE TRAIN – **Frank IFIELD** (22)......................63
MULL OF KINTYRE – **Paul McCARTNEY** (1) 77
MULTIPLICATION [A] – **Bobby DARIN** (5) 61
MULTIPLICATION [A] – **SHOWADDYWADDY** (39)81
MUM'S GONE TO ICELAND – **BENNET** (34) 97
THE MUPPET SHOW MUSIC HALL EP – **MUPPETS** (19) 77
MURDER ON THE DANCEFLOOR – **Sophie ELLIS-BEXTOR** (2) 01
MURDER SHE WROTE [A] – **Tairrie B** (71) 90
MURDER SHE WROTE [B] – **Chaka DEMUS and PLIERS** (27) 94
MURPHY AND THE BRICKS – **Noel MURPHY** (57)87
MURPHY'S LAW – **CHERI** (13) 82
MUSAK – **TRISCO** (28) 01
MUSCLE DEEP – **THEN JERICO** (48)..................87
MUSCLE MUSEUM – **MUSE** (25) 99,00
MUSCLEBOUND – **SPANDAU BALLET** (10) 81
MUSCLES – **Diana ROSS** (15) 82
MUSIC [A] – **John MILES** (3) 76
MUSIC [A] – **Ann-Marie SMITH** (34)..................93
MUSIC [B] – **ONE WAY featuring Al HUDSON** (56)79
MUSIC [C] – **FR DAVID** (71) 83
MUSIC [D] – **D TRAIN** (23) 83,85
MUSIC [E] – **OMAR** (53)...................................92
MUSIC [F] – **MADONNA** (1)...............................00
MUSIC [G] – **Erick SERMON featuring Marvin GAYE** (36)............................01
MUSIC AND LIGHTS – **IMAGINATION** (5) 82
MUSIC AND YOU – **Sal SOLO** (52)......................85
MUSIC FOR CHAMELEONS – **Gary NUMAN** (19) 82
THE MUSIC I LIKE – **ALEXIA** (31) 98
MUSIC IN MY MIND – **Adam F** (27)...................98
THE MUSIC IN YOU – **MONOBOY featuring DELORES** (50).................................01
MUSIC IS A PASSION – **ATLANTIC OCEAN** (59) 94
THE MUSIC IS MOVING – **FARGETTA** (74) 96
MUSIC IS MY RADAR – **BLUR** (10)................00,01
MUSIC IS MOVING – **CORTINA** (42) 01
MUSIC IS THE ANSWER – **Danny TENAGLIA and CELEDA** (36) 98,99
MUSIC MAKES ME HIGH – **LOST BOYZ** (42) 96
MUSIC MAKES YOU FEEL LIKE DANCING – **BRASS CONSTRUCTION** (39) 80
MUSIC MAKES YOU LOSE CONTROL – **LES RYTHMES DIGITALES** (69) 98
THE MUSIC OF GOODBYE (LOVE THEME FROM 'OUT OF AFRICA') – **Al JARREAU** (75) 86
MUSIC OF MY HEART – **'N SYNC / Gloria ESTEFAN** (34) 00
THE MUSIC OF THE NIGHT [A] – **Michael CRAWFORD** (7)..................................87
THE MUSIC OF THE NIGHT [A] – **Barbra STREISAND (duet with Michael CRAWFORD)** (54) 94
THE MUSIC OF TORVILL AND DEAN (EP) – **Richard HARTLEY / Michael REED ORCHESTRA** (9) 84
MUSIC SAVED MY LIFE – **Cevin FISHER** (67)....99
MUSIC SOUNDS BETTER WITH YOU – **STARDUST** (2) 98
MUSIC STOP – **RAILWAY CHILDREN** (66)..........90
MUSIC TAKES YOU – **BLAME** (48) 92
THE MUSIC THAT WE HEAR (MOOG ISLAND) – **MORCHEEBA** (47) 97
MUSIC TO WATCH GIRLS BY – **Andy WILLIAMS** (9) 67,99
MUSICAL FREEDOM (MOVING ON UP) – **Paul SIMPSON featuring ADEVA** (22) 89
MUSICAL MELODY – **UNIQUE 3** (29) 90
THE MUSIC'S GOT ME [A] – **BASS BUMPERS** (25)94
THE MUSIC'S GOT ME [A] – **BROOKLYN BOUNCE** (67) 98
THE MUSIC'S NO GOOD WITHOUT YOU – **CHER** (8) 01
MUSIQUE – **DAFT PUNK** (7)..............................97
MUSKRAT – **EVERLY BROTHERS** (20)................61
MUSKRAT RAMBLE – **Freddy CANNON** (32)......61
MUST BE MADISON – **Joe LOSS** (20) 62
MUST BE SANTA – **Tommy STEELE** (40) 60
MUST BE THE MUSIC [A] – **HYSTERIX** (40) 94
MUST BE THE MUSIC [B] – **Joey NEGRO** (8) 00
MUST BEE THE MUSIC – **KING BEE** (44) 91
A MUST TO AVOID – **HERMAN'S HERMITS** (6) 65
MUSTAFA CHA CHA CHA – **STAIFFI and his MUSTAFAS** (43)....................60
MUSTANG SALLY [A] – **Wilson PICKETT** (28) 66
MUSTANG SALLY [A] – **COMMITMENTS** (63) 91
MUSTAPHA – **Bob AZZAM and His ORCHESTRA** (23)..............60
MUTANTS IN MEGA CITY ONE – **FINK BROTHERS** (50) 85
MUTATIONS (EP) – **ORBITAL** (24) 92
MUTUAL ATTRACTION – **CHANGE** (60)..............85
MUTUALLY ASSURED DESTRUCTION – **GILLAN** (32) 81
MUZIKIZUM – **X-PRESS 2** (52) 01
MY ADIDAS – **RUN-DMC** (62)...........................86
MY AFFAIR – **Kirsty MacCOLL** (56)....................91
MY ALL – **Mariah CAREY** (4) 98
MY ANGEL – **ROCK GODDESS** (64) 83
MY ARMS KEEP MISSING YOU – **Rick ASTLEY** (2)87
MY BABY – **LIL' ROMEO** (67) 01
MY BABY JUST CARES FOR ME – **Nina SIMONE** (5) 87
MY BABY LEFT ME [A] – **Dave BERRY** (37) 64
MY BABY LEFT ME - THAT'S ALL RIGHT (MEDLEY) [A] – **SLADE** (32) 77
MY BABY LOVES LOVIN' – **WHITE PLAINS** (9)..70
MY BAG – **Lloyd COLE** (46) 87
MY BEAT – **BLAZE featuring Palmer BROWN** (53)01
MY BEATBOX – **DEEJAY PUNK-ROC** (43) 98
MY BEAUTIFUL FRIEND – **CHARLATANS** (31) 99
MY BEST FRIEND'S GIRL – **CARS** (3)................78
MY BLUE HEAVEN – **Frank SINATRA** (33) 61
MY BODY – **LEVERT SWEAT GILL** (21) 98
MY BONNIE – **Tony SHERIDAN and the BEATLES** (48) 63
MY BOOK – **BEAUTIFUL SOUTH** (43)................90
MY BOOMERANG WON'T COME BACK – **Charlie DRAKE** (14) 61
MY BOY – **Elvis PRESLEY** (5)...........................74
MY BOY FLAT TOP – **Frankie VAUGHAN** (20) ..56
MY BOY LOLLIPOP – **MILLIE** (2) 64,87
MY BOYFRIEND'S BACK – **ANGELS** (50) 63
MY BRAVE FACE – **Paul McCARTNEY** (18) 89
MY BROTHER JAKE – **FREE** (4) 71
MY CAMERA NEVER LIES – **BUCKS FIZZ** (1)......82
MY CHERIE AMOUR – **Stevie WONDER** (4) 69
MY CHILD – **Connie FRANCIS** (26)....................65
MY COO-CA-CHOO – **Alvin STARDUST** (2) 73
MY COUNTRY – **MIDNIGHT OIL** (66) 93
MY CUTIE CUTIE – **Shakin' STEVENS** (75)........90
MY DEFINITION OF A BOOMBASTIC JAZZ STYLE – **DREAM WARRIORS** (13).......................................90
MY DESIRE – **AMIRA** (20)........................97,98,01
MY DESTINY – **Lionel RICHIE** (7)......................92
MY DING-A-LING – **Chuck BERRY** (1) 72
MY DIXIE DARLING – **Lonnie DONEGAN** (10)....57
MY DJ (PUMP IT UP SOME) – **Richie RICH** (74)88
MY DOCS – **KISS AMC** (66) 90
MY DRUG BUDDY – **LEMONHEADS** (44) 93
MY DYING MACHINE – **Gary NUMAN** (66) 84
MY EVER CHANGING MOODS – **STYLE COUNCIL** (5)...84
MY EYES ADORED YOU – **Frankie VALLI** (5) 75
MY FAMILY DEPENDS ON ME – **SIMONE** (75) ..91
MY FATHER'S EYES – **Eric CLAPTON** (33) 98
MY FATHER'S SHOES – **LEVEL 42** (55) 92
MY FATHER'S SON – **Conner REEVES** (12)........97
MY FAVORITE MISTAKE – **Sheryl CROW** (9)......98
MY FAVOURITE GAME – **CARDIGANS** (14) 98
MY FAVOURITE WASTE OF TIME – **Owen PAUL** (3) 86
MY FEELING – **JUNIOR JACK** (31) 00
MY FEET KEEP DANCING – **CHIC** (21) 79
MY FIRST NIGHT WITHOUT YOU – **Cyndi LAUPER** (53) 89
MY FOOLISH FRIEND – **TALK TALK** (57) 83
MY FORBIDDEN LOVER [A] – **CHIC** (15) 79
MY FORBIDDEN LOVER [A] – **Romina JOHNSON** (59) 00
MY FRIEND [A] – **Frankie LAINE** (3)..................54
MY FRIEND [B] – **Roy ORBISON** (35)................69
MY FRIEND [C] – **GROOVE ARMADA** (36)..........01
MY FRIEND JACK [A] – **SMOKE** (45)..................67
MY FRIEND JACK [A] – **BONEY M** (57) 80
MY FRIEND STAN – **SLADE** (2)..........................73
MY FRIEND THE SEA – **Petula CLARK** (7) 61
MY FRIENDS – **RED HOT CHILI PEPPERS** (29)..95
MY GENERATION [A] – **WHO** (2) 65,88,96
MY GENERATION [B] – **LIMP BIZKIT** (15)......00,01
MY GETAWAY – **T-BOZ** (44) 01
MY GIRL [A] – **Otis REDDING** (11) 65,68
MY GIRL [A] – **TEMPTATIONS** (2) 65,92
MY GIRL [A] – **WHISPERS** (26)..........................80
MY GIRL [B] – **MADNESS** (3) 80,92
MY GIRL [C] – **Rod STEWART** (32).....................80
MY GIRL BILL – **Jim STAFFORD** (20) 74
MY GIRL JOSEPHINE [A] – **Fats DOMINO** (32) ..61
MY GIRL JOSEPHINE [A] – **SUPERCAT** (22) 95
MY GIRL LOLLIPOP (MY BOY LOLLIPOP) – **BAD MANNERS** (9) 82
MY GIRL LOVES ME – **SHALAMAR** (45) 85
MY GUY [A] – **Mary WELLS** (5) 64,72
MY GUY [B] – **Tracey ULLMAN** (23) 84

MY GUY – MY GIRL (MEDLEY) [A] — **Amii STEWART and Johnny BRISTOL** (39)......80
MY GUY – MY GIRL (MEDLEY) [A] — **Amii STEWART and Deon ESTUS** (63)............86
MY HAND OVER MY HEART — **Marc ALMOND** (33) 92
MY HAPPINESS — **Connie FRANCIS** (4) 59
MY HEAD'S IN MISSISSIPPI — **ZZ TOP** (37) 91
MY HEART — **Gene VINCENT** (16).......................60
MY HEART CAN'T TELL YOU NO — **Rod STEWART** (49) 89
MY HEART GOES BANG (GET ME TO THE DOCTOR) — **DEAD OR ALIVE** (23).......................................85
MY HEART GOES BOOM — **FRENCH AFFAIR** (44)..00
MY HEART HAS A MIND OF ITS OWN — **Connie FRANCIS** (3)..60
MY HEART THE BEAT — **D-SHAKE** (42) 91
MY HEART WILL GO ON — **Celine DION** (1) 98
MY HEART'S BEATING WILD (TIC TAC TIC TAC) — **GIBSON BROTHERS** (56) 83
MY HEART'S SYMPHONY — **Gary LEWIS and the PLAYBOYS** (36) 75
MY HERO — **FOO FIGHTERS** (21) 98
MY HOMETOWN — **Bruce SPRINGSTEEN** (9) 85
MY HOUSE — **TERRORVISION** (29)....................94
MY IRON LUNG — **RADIOHEAD** (24) 94
MY JAMAICAN GUY — **Grace JONES** (56) 83
MY KIND OF GIRL [A] — **Matt MONRO** (5) 61
MY KIND OF GIRL [A] — **Frank SINATRA** (35).....63
MY KINDA LIFE — **Cliff RICHARD** (15) 77
MY KINGDOM — **FUTURE SOUND OF LONDON** (13) 96
MY LAST NIGHT WITH YOU — **ARROWS** (25) 75
MY LIFE — **Billy JOEL** (12)..................................78
MY LIFE IS IN YOUR HANDS — **MELTDOWN** (44)..96
MY LITTLE BABY — **Mike BERRY** (34) 63
MY LITTLE CORNER OF THE WORLD — **Anita BRYANT** (48) 60
MY LITTLE GIRL [A] — **CRICKETS** (17) 63
MY LITTLE GIRL [B] — **AUTUMN** (37) 71
MY LITTLE LADY — **TREMELOES** (6)...................68
MY LITTLE ONE — **MARMALADE** (15) 71
MY LOVE [A] — **Petula CLARK** (4).......................66
MY LOVE [B] — **Paul McCARTNEY** (9) 73
MY LOVE [C] — **Lionel RICHIE** (70) 83
MY LOVE [D] — **Julio IGLESIAS featuring Stevie WONDER** (5) 88
MY LOVE [E] — **LONDON BOYS** (46)..................89
MY LOVE [F] — **Mary J BLIGE** (29) 94
MY LOVE [G] — **Kele LE ROC** (8)........................99
MY LOVE [H] — **WESTLIFE** (1) 00
MY LOVE [I] — **KLUSTER featuring Ron CARROLL** (73) 01
MY LOVE AND DEVOTION [A] — **Doris DAY** (10) 52
MY LOVE AND DEVOTION [A] — **Matt MONRO** (29) 62
MY LOVE FOR YOU — **Johnny MATHIS** (9) 60
MY LOVE IS A FIRE — **Donny OSMOND** (64) 91
MY LOVE IS DEEP — **Sara PARKER** (22)............97
MY LOVE IS FOR REAL [A] — **Paula ABDUL featuring Ofra HAZA** (28) 95
MY LOVE IS FOR REAL [A] — **STRIKE** (35) 96
MY LOVE IS GUARANTEED — **SYBIL** (42)......87,93
MY LOVE IS MAGIC — **BAS NOIR** (73) 89
MY LOVE IS SO RAW — **Alyson WILLIAMS featuring Nikki D** (34) 89
MY LOVE IS THE SHHH! — **SOMETHIN' FOR THE PEOPLE featuring TRINA and TAMARA** (64) 98
MY LOVE IS WAITING — **Marvin GAYE** (34) 83
MY LOVE IS YOUR LOVE — **Whitney HOUSTON** (2)......................................99
MY LOVE LIFE — **MORRISSEY** (29) 91
MY LOVER'S PRAYER — **Otis REDDING** (37)......66
MY LOVIN' — **EN VOGUE** (4)..............................92
MY MAGIC MAN — **ROCHELLE** (27)....................86
MY MAMMY — **HAPPENINGS** (34) 67
MY MAN, A SWEET MAN — **Millie JACKSON** (50) 72
MY MAN AND ME — **Lynsey DE PAUL** (40) 75
MY MARIE — **Engelbert HUMPERDINCK** (31) 70
MY MATE PAUL — **David HOLMES** (39) 98
MY MELANCHOLY BABY [A] — **Tommy EDWARDS** (29) 59
MY MELANCHOLY BABY [A] — **CHAS and DAVE** (51)..83
MY MIND'S EYE — **SMALL FACES** (4) 66
MY MUM IS ONE IN A MILLION — **The Children of TANSLEY SCHOOL** (27) 81
MY NAME IS — **EMINEM** (2) 99
MY NAME IS JACK — **MANFRED MANN** (8) 68
MY NAME IS NOT SUSAN — **Whitney HOUSTON** (29) 91
MY NAME IS PRINCE — **PRINCE and the NEW POWER GENERATION** (7) 92
MY OH MY [A] — **SAD CAFE** (14) 80
MY OH MY [B] — **SLADE** (2) 83
MY OH MY [C] — **AQUA** (6)................................98
MY OLD MAN'S A DUSTMAN — **Lonnie DONEGAN** (1)......................................60
MY OLD PIANO — **Diana ROSS** (5)....................80
MY ONE SIN — **Nat 'King' COLE** (17) 55
MY ONE TEMPTATION — **Mica PARIS** (7) 88
MY ONE TRUE FRIEND — **Bette MIDLER** (58).....98
MY ONLY LOVE — **Bob SINCLAR** (56)................99
MY OWN SUMMER (SHOVE IT) — **DEFTONES** (29) 98
MY OWN TRUE LOVE — **Danny WILLIAMS** (45) 63
MY OWN WAY — **DURAN DURAN** (14) 81
MY OWN WORST ENEMY — **LIT** (16)..................99
MY PEACE OF HEAVEN — **TEN CITY** (63) 92
MY PERFECT COUSIN — **UNDERTONES** (9)........80
MY PERSONAL POSSESSION — **Nat 'King' COLE** (21) 57
MY PHILOSOPHY — **BOOGIE DOWN PRODUCTIONS** (69) 88
MY PRAYER [A] — **PLATTERS** (4) 56,57
MY PRAYER [A] — **Gerry MONROE** (9) 70
MY PREROGATIVE — **Bobby BROWN** (6) 88,95
MY PRETTY ONE — **Cliff RICHARD** (6) 87
MY PUPPET PAL — **TIGER** (62)..........................96
MY REMEDY — **Hinda HICKS** (61).......................00
MY RESISTANCE IS LOW — **Robin SARSTEDT** (3) 76
MY RISING STAR — **NORTHSIDE** (32) 90
MY SALT HEART — **HUE AND CRY** (47) 91
MY SENTIMENTAL FRIEND — **HERMAN'S HERMITS** (2) 69
MY SEPTEMBER LOVE — **David WHITFIELD** (3) 56
MY SHARONA — **KNACK** (6) 79
MY SHIP IS COMING IN — **WALKER BROTHERS** (3) 65
MY SIDE OF THE BED — **Susanna HOFFS** (44)..91
MY SIMPLE HEART — **THREE DEGREES** (9) 79
MY SISTER — **Juliana HATFIELD** (71) 93
MY 16TH APOLOGY (EP) — **SHAKESPEAR'S SISTER** (61) 93
MY SON JOHN — **David WHITFIELD** (22) 56
MY SON, MY SON — **Vera LYNN** (1) 54
MY SPECIAL ANGEL [A] — **Bobby HELMS** (22) ..57
MY SPECIAL ANGEL [A] — **Malcolm VAUGHAN** (3) 57
MY SPECIAL CHILD — **Sinead O'CONNOR** (42) ..91
MY SPECIAL DREAM — **Shirley BASSEY** (32) 64
MY SPIRIT — **TILT** (61) 97
MY STAR — **Ian BROWN** (5) 98
MY SUNDAY BABY — **DALE SISTERS** (36)..........61
MY SUPERSTAR — **DIMESTARS** (72) 01
MY SWEET JANE — **GUN** (51) 97
MY SWEET LORD — **George HARRISON** (1)........71
MY SWEET ROSALIE — **BROTHERHOOD OF MAN** (30) 76
MY TELEPHONE — **COLDCUT** (52) 89
MY TIME — **SOUVLAKI** (63) 98
MY TOOT TOOT — **Denise LA SALLE** (6)............85
MY TOWN — **GLASS TIGER** (33) 91
MY TRUE LOVE — **Jack SCOTT** (9) 58
MY UKELELE — **Max BYGRAVES** (19) 59
MY UNFINISHED SYMPHONY — **David WHITFIELD** (29)...................................56
MY UNKNOWN LOVE — **COUNT INDIGO** (59) 96
MY WAY [A] — **Eddie COCHRAN** (23) 63
MY WAY [B] — **Frank SINATRA** (5) 69,70,71,72,94
MY WAY [B] — **Dorothy SQUIRES** (25) 70
MY WAY [B] — **Elvis PRESLEY** (9).......................77
MY WAY [B] — **SEX PISTOLS** (7).........................78
MY WAY [B] — **Shane MacGOWAN** (29) 96
MY WAY [C] — **LIMP BIZKIT** (6)..........................01
MY WAY OF GIVING IN — **Chris FARLOWE** (48) 67
MY WAY OF THINKING — **UB40** (6) 80
MY WEAKNESS IS NONE OF YOUR BUSINESS — **EMBRACE** (9)..98
MY WHITE BICYCLE — **NAZARETH** (14)..............75
MY WOMAN'S MAN — **Dave DEE** (42) 70
MY WORLD [A] — **CUPID'S INSPIRATION** (33) ..68
MY WORLD [B] — **BEE GEES** (16) 72
MY WORLD [C] — **SECRET AFFAIR** (16) 80
MY WORLD OF BLUE — **Karl DENVER** (29)........64
MYFANWY — **David ESSEX** (41) 87
MYSTERIES OF LOVE — **LA MIX** (46)..................91
MYSTERIES OF THE WORLD — **MFSB** (41) 81
MYSTERIOUS GIRL — **Peter ANDRE** (2) 95,96
MYSTERIOUS TIMES — **SASH! featuring Tina COUSINS** (2) 98
MYSTERIOUS WAYS — **U2** (13)..........................92
MYSTERY [A] — **DIO** (34) 84
MYSTERY [B] — **MYSTERY** (56) 01
MYSTERY GIRL [A] — **Jess CONRAD** (18) 61
MYSTERY GIRL [B] — **DUKES** (47)........................81
MYSTERY LADY — **Billy OCEAN** (49)..................85
MYSTERY LAND (EP) — **Y-TRAXX** (63) 97
MYSTERY SONG — **STATUS QUO** (11)................76
MYSTERY TRAIN — **Elvis PRESLEY** (25) 57
MYSTICAL MACHINE GUN — **KULA SHAKER** (14)99
MYSTIFY — **INXS** (14) 89
MYZSTERIOUS MIZSTER JONES — **SLADE** (50)..85
NA NA HEY HEY KISS HIM GOODBYE [A] — **STEAM** (9) 70
NA NA HEY HEY KISS HIM GOODBYE [A] — **BANANARAMA** (5) 83
NA NA IS THE SADDEST WORD — **STYLISTICS** (5)75
NA NA NA — **Cozy POWELL** (10)........................74
NADINE (IS IT YOU) — **Chuck BERRY** (27) 64
NAGASAKI BADGER — **DISCO CITIZENS** (56) 98
NAGASAKI EP (I NEED A LOVER TONIGHT) — **Ken DOH** (7) 96
NAILS IN MY FEET — **CROWDED HOUSE** (22) ..93
NAIROBI — **Tommy STEELE** (3) 58
NAIVE SONG — **MIRWAIS** (50) 00
NAKED [A] — **REEF** (11).......................................95
NAKED [B] — **LOUISE** (5) 96
NAKED AND SACRED [A] — **Chynna PHILLIPS** (62) 96
NAKED AND SACRED [A] — **Maria NAYLER** (32) 98
NAKED EYE — **LUSCIOUS JACKSON** (25)............97
NAKED IN THE RAIN — **BLUE PEARL** (4) 90. 98
NAKED LOVE (JUST SAY YOU WANT ME) — **QUARTZ and Dina CARROLL** (39)....................91
NAKED WITHOUT YOU — **ROACHFORD** (53) 98
NAME AND NUMBER — **CURIOSITY** (14) 89
THE NAME OF THE GAME — **ABBA** (1) 77
THE NAMELESS ONE — **Wendy JAMES** (34) 93
NANCY BOY — **PLACEBO** (4)..............................97
A NANNY IN MANHATTAN — **LILYS** (16) 98
NAPPY LOVE — **GOODIES** (21) 75
NARCO TOURISTS — **SLAM vs UNKLE** (66) 01
NARCOTIC INFLUENCE — **EMPIRION** (64) 96
NASHVILLE BOOGIE — **Bert WEEDON** (29)........59
NASHVILLE CATS — **LOVIN' SPOONFUL** (26) 67
NASTRADAMUS — **NAS** (24)..............................00
NASTY — **Janet JACKSON** (19)...........................86
NASTY GIRLS — **TWA** (51) 95
NATALIE'S PARTY — **SHACK** (63) 99
NATHAN JONES [A] — **SUPREMES** (5) 71
NATHAN JONES [A] — **BANANARAMA** (15) 88
NATIONAL EXPRESS — **DIVINE COMEDY** (8)......99
NATIVE BOY (UPTOWN) — **ANIMAL NIGHTLIFE** (60) 83
NATIVE LAND — **EVERYTHING BUT THE GIRL** (73)84
NATIVE NEW YORKER [A] — **ODYSSEY** (5) 77
NATIVE NEW YORKER [A] — **BLACK BOX** (46) ..97
NATURAL [A] — **Bryan POWELL** (73)..................93
NATURAL [B] — **Peter ANDRE** (6) 97
NATURAL [C] — **S CLUB 7** (3)........................00,01
NATURAL BLUES — **MOBY** (11) 00
NATURAL BORN BUGIE — **HUMBLE PIE** (4) 69
NATURAL BORN KILLAZ — **DR DRE and ICE CUBE** (45)............................95
NATURAL HIGH [A] — **BLOODSTONE** (40)..........73
NATURAL HIGH [B] — **Bitty McLEAN** (63) 96
NATURAL LIFE — **NATURAL LIFE** (47) 92
NATURAL ONE — **FOLK IMPLOSION** (45) 96
NATURAL SINNER — **FAIR WEATHER** (6)............70
NATURAL THING — **INNOCENCE** (16) 90
NATURAL WORLD — **RODEO JONES** (75) 93
NATURE BOY [A] — **Bobby DARIN** (24) 61
NATURE BOY [A] — **George BENSON** (26) 77
NATURE BOY [A] — **CENTRAL LINE** (21) 83
NATURE OF LOVE — **WATERFRONT** (63)............89
NATURE'S TIME FOR LOVE — **Joe BROWN and the BRUVVERS** (26) 63
NAUGHTY CHRISTMAS (GOBLIN IN THE OFFICE) — **FAT LES** (21) 98
NAUGHTY GIRLS (NEED LOVE TOO) — **Samantha FOX featuring FULL FORCE** (31) 88
THE NAUGHTY LADY OF SHADY LANE [A] — **AMES BROTHERS** (6)..55
THE NAUGHTY LADY OF SHADY LANE [A] — **Dean MARTIN** (5) 55
NAUGHTY NAUGHTY — **John PARR** (58) 86

NAUGHTY NAUGHTY NAUGHTY – **Joy SARNEY** (26) ...77
THE NAUGHTY NORTH AND THE SEXY SOUTH – **E-MOTION** (17) ...96
NAZIS – **Roger TAYLOR** (22) ...94
NEANDERTHAL MAN – **HOTLEGS** (2) ...70
NEAR WILD HEAVEN – **R.E.M.** (27) ...91
NEAR YOU – **MIGIL FIVE** (31) ...64
NEARLY LOST YOU – **SCREAMING TREES** (50) 93
NECESSARY EVIL – **BODY COUNT** (45) ...94
NEED GOOD LOVE – **TUFF JAM** (44) ...98
NEED YOU TONIGHT – **INXS** (2) ...87,88
NEED YOUR LOVE SO BAD [A] – **FLEETWOOD MAC** (31) ...68,69
NEED YOUR LOVE SO BAD [A] – **Gary MOORE** (48) ...95
NEEDIN' U [A] – **David MORALES** (8) ...98
NEEDIN' YOU II [A] – **David MORALES presents THE FACE featuring Juliet ROBERTS** (11) ...01
THE NEEDLE AND THE DAMAGE DONE – **Neil YOUNG** (75) ...93
NEEDLES AND PINS [A] – **SEARCHERS** (1) ...64
NEEDLES AND PINS [A] – **SMOKIE** (10) ...77
NEGASONIC TEENAGE WARHEAD – **MONSTER MAGNET** (49) ...95
NEGATIVE – **MANSUN** (27) ...98
NEIGHBOR – **UGLY KID JOE** (28) ...92
NEIGHBOURHOOD [A] – **SPACE** (11) ...96
NEIGHBOURHOOD [B] – **ZED BIAS** (25) ...00
NEIL JUNG – **TEENAGE FANCLUB** (62) ...95
NEITHER ONE OF US – **Gladys KNIGHT and the PIPS** (31) ...73
NELLIE THE ELEPHANT – **TOY DOLLS** (4) ...84
NELSON MANDELA – **SPECIALS** (9) ...84
NE-NE NA-NA NA-NA NU-NU – **BAD MANNERS** (28) ...80
NEON KNIGHTS – **BLACK SABBATH** (22) ...80
NEON LIGHTS – **KRAFTWERK** (53) ...78
NERVOUS – **MATT BIANCO** (59) ...89
NERVOUS BREAKDOWN [A] – **Carleen ANDERSON** (27) ...94
NERVOUS BREAKDOWN [B] – **SHRINK** (42) ...98
NERVOUS SHAKEDOWN – **AC/DC** (35) ...84
NERVOUS WRECK – **RADIO STARS** (39) ...78
NESSUN DORMA [A] – **Luciano PAVAROTTI** (2) 90
NESSUN DORMA FROM 'TURANDOT' [A] – **Luis COBOS featuring Placido DOMINGO** (59) 90
NETHERWORLD – **LSG** (63) ...97
NEUROTICA – **CUD** (37) ...94
NEUTRON DANCE – **POINTER SISTERS** (31) ...85
NEVER [A] – **HEART** (8) ...88
NEVER [B] – **HOUSE OF LOVE** (41) ...89
NEVER [C] – **JOMANDA** (40) ...93
NEVER [D] – **ELECTRAFIXION** (58) ...95
NEVER 'AD NOTHIN' – **ANGELIC UPSTARTS** (52) 79
NEVER AGAIN [A] – **DISCHARGE** (64) ...81
NEVER AGAIN [B] – **MISSION** (34) ...92
NEVER AGAIN [C] – **JC 001** (67) ...93
NEVER AGAIN [D] – **HAPPY CLAPPERS** (49) ...96
NEVER AGAIN (THE DAYS TIME ERASED) – **CLASSIX NOUVEAUX** (44) ...81
NEVER BE ANYONE ELSE BUT YOU – **Ricky NELSON** (14) ...59
NEVER BE THE SAME AGAIN – **Melanie C and Lisa LOPES** (1) ...00
NEVER BEFORE – **DEEP PURPLE** (35) ...72
NEVER CAN SAY GOODBYE [A] – **JACKSONS** (33) 71
NEVER CAN SAY GOODBYE [A] – **Gloria GAYNOR** (2) ...74
NEVER CAN SAY GOODBYE [A] – **COMMUNARDS** (4) ...87
NEVER CAN SAY GOODBYE [A] – **YAZZ** (61) ...97
NEVER DO A TANGO WITH AN ESKIMO – **Alma COGAN** (6) ...55
NEVER DO YOU WRONG – **Stephanie MILLS** (57) ...93
NEVER ENDING SONG OF LOVE – **NEW SEEKERS** (2) ...71
NEVER ENDING STORY – **LIMAHL** (4) ...84
NEVER ENOUGH [A] – **JESUS JONES** (42) ...89
NEVER ENOUGH [B] – **CURE** (13) ...90
NEVER ENOUGH [C] – **Boris DLUGOSCH featuring Roisin MURPHY** (16) ...01
NEVER EVER – **ALL SAINTS** (1) ...97
NEVER FELT THIS WAY – **HI-LUX** (58) ...95
NEVER FORGET – **TAKE THAT** (1) ...95
NEVER FOUND A LOVE LIKE THIS BEFORE – **UPSIDE DOWN** (19) ...96
NEVER GIVE UP – **Monie LOVE** (41) ...93
NEVER GIVE UP ON A GOOD THING – **George BENSON** (14) ...82
NEVER GIVE YOU UP – **Sharon REDD** (20) ...82
NEVER GOIN' DOWN – **ADAMSKI and Jimi POLO** (51) ...91
NEVER GONNA BE THE SAME – **DANNY WILSON** (69) ...89
NEVER GONNA CHANGE MY MIND – **Joey LAWRENCE** (49) ...98
NEVER GONNA COME BACK DOWN – **BT** (51) ...01
NEVER GONNA CRY AGAIN – **EURYTHMICS** (63) 81
NEVER GONNA FALL IN LOVE AGAIN – **DANA** (31) 76
NEVER GONNA GIVE YOU UP [A] – **MUSICAL YOUTH** (6) ...83
NEVER GONNA GIVE YOU UP [B] – **Rick ASTLEY** (1) ...87
NEVER GONNA (GIVE YOU UP) [B] – **FKW** (48) 93
NEVER GONNA GIVE YOU UP (WON'T LET YOU BE) – **Patrice RUSHEN** (66) ...81
NEVER GONNA LET YOU GO [A] – **Sergio MENDES** (45) ...83
NEVER GONNA LET YOU GO [B] – **Tina MOORE** (7) ...97
NEVER GOODBYE – **Karl DENVER** (9) ...62
NEVER HAD A DREAM COME TRUE [A] – **Stevie WONDER** (6) ...70
NEVER HAD A DREAM COME TRUE [B] – **S CLUB 7** (1) ...00,01
NEVER HAD IT SO GOOD – **TAKE 5** (34) ...99
NEVER IN A MILLION YEARS – **BOOMTOWN RATS** (62) ...81
NEVER KNEW LOVE [A] – **Rick ASTLEY** (70) ...91
NEVER KNEW LOVE [B] – **Oleta ADAMS** (22) ...95
NEVER KNEW LOVE [C] – **NIGHTCRAWLERS featuring John REID** (59) ...99
NEVER KNEW LOVE LIKE THIS [A] – **Alexander O'NEAL and CHERRELLE** (26) ...88
NEVER KNEW LOVE LIKE THIS [B] – **Pauline HENRY featuring Wayne MARSHALL** (40) ...96
NEVER KNEW LOVE LIKE THIS BEFORE – **Stephanie MILLS** (4) ...80
NEVER LET GO [A] – **John BARRY ORCHESTRA** (49) ...60
NEVER LET GO [B] – **HYPER GO GO** (45) ...93
NEVER LET GO [C] – **Cliff RICHARD** (32) ...93
NEVER LET HER SLIP AWAY [A] – **Andrew GOLD** (5) ...78
NEVER LET HER SLIP AWAY [A] – **Trevor WALTERS** (73) ...84
NEVER LET HER SLIP AWAY [A] – **UNDERCOVER** (5) ...92
NEVER LET ME DOWN – **David BOWIE** (34) ...87
NEVER LET ME DOWN AGAIN – **DEPECHE MODE** (22) ...87
NEVER LET YOU DOWN – **HONEYZ** (7) ...99
NEVER LET YOU GO – **NEW KIDS ON THE BLOCK** (42) ...94
NEVER LOOK BACK – **DUMONDE** (36) ...01
NEVER LOSE THAT FEELING – **SWERVEDRIVER** (62) ...92
NEVER LOST HIS HARDCORE – **NRG** (61) ...97, 98
NEVER MIND – **Cliff RICHARD** (21) ...59
NEVER MIND THE PRESENTS – **BARRON KNIGHTS** (17) ...80
NEVER MISS THE WATER – **Chaka KHAN and Me'Shell NDEGEOCELLO** (59) ...97
NEVER MY LOVE – **Sugar MINOTT** (52) ...81
NEVER NEVER [A] – **ASSEMBLY** (4) ...83
NEVER NEVER [B] – **WARM JETS** (37) ...98
NEVER NEVER GONNA GIVE YA UP [A] – **Barry WHITE** (14) ...74, 88
NEVER, NEVER GONNA GIVE YOU UP [A] – **Lisa STANSFIELD** (25) ...97
NEVER NEVER LOVE – **SIMPLY RED** (18) ...96
NEVER NEVER NEVER – **Shirley BASSEY** (8) ...73
NEVER ON SUNDAY [A] – **CHAQUITO** (50) ...60
NEVER ON SUNDAY [A] – **Lynn CORNELL** (30) ...60
NEVER ON SUNDAY [A] – **Don COSTA** (27) ...60
NEVER ON SUNDAY [A] – **MAKADOPOULOS and his GREEK SERENADERS** (36) ...60
NEVER ON SUNDAY [A] – **MANUEL and his MUSIC OF THE MOUNTAINS** (29) ...60
NEVER SAW A MIRACLE – **Curtis STIGERS** (34) 92
NEVER SAY DIE – **BLACK SABBATH** (21) ...78
NEVER SAY DIE (GIVE A LITTLE BIT MORE) – **Cliff RICHARD** (15) ...83
NEVER SAY GOODBYE – **BON JOVI** (21) ...87
NEVER STOP [A] – **ECHO and the BUNNYMEN** (15) ...83
NEVER STOP [B] – **BRAND NEW HEAVIES** (43) 91
NEVER SURRENDER – **SAXON** (18) ...81
NEVER TAKE ME ALIVE – **SPEAR OF DESTINY** (14) ...87
NEVER TEAR US APART – **INXS** (24) ...88
NEVER THERE – **CAKE** (66) ...99
NEVER TOO FAR – **Mariah CAREY** (32) ...01
NEVER TOO LATE – **Kylie MINOGUE** (4) ...89
NEVER TOO MUCH – **Luther VANDROSS** (13) ...83,89
NEVER TRUST A STRANGER – **Kim WILDE** (7) ...88
NEVER TURN AWAY – **ORCHESTRAL MANOEUVRES IN THE DARK** (70) 84
NEVER TURN YOUR BACK ON MOTHER EARTH – **SPARKS** (13) ...74
NEVER UNDERSTAND – **JESUS AND MARY CHAIN** (47) ...85
NEVERTHELESS [A] – **Frankie VAUGHAN** (29) ...68
NEVERTHELESS [A] – **NEW SEEKERS** (34) ...73
NEW – **NO DOUBT** (30) ...99
NEW AMSTERDAM – **Elvis COSTELLO** (36) ...80
NEW ANGER – **Gary NUMAN** (46) ...88
NEW BEGINNING [A] – **Stephen GATELY** (3) ...00
NEW BEGINNING [B] – **PRECIOUS** (50) ...00
NEW BEGINNING (MAMBA SEYRA) – **BUCKS FIZZ** (8) ...86
NEW BIRD – **REEF** (73) ...99
NEW BORN – **MUSE** (12) ...01
A NEW DAY [B] – **KILLING JOKE** (56) ...84
NEW DAY [A] – **Wyclef JEAN featuring BONO** (23) 99
NEW DIMENSION – **IMAGINATION** (56) ...83
NEW DIRECTION – **FREAKPOWER** (60) ...96
NEW EMOTION – **TIME FREQUENCY** (36) ...93
A NEW ENGLAND – **Kirsty MacCOLL** (7) ...85
A NEW FASHION – **Bill WYMAN** (37) ...82
A NEW FLAME – **SIMPLY RED** (17) ...89
NEW GENERATION – **SUEDE** (21) ...95
NEW GRANGE – **CLANNAD** (65) ...83
NEW GUITAR IN TOWN – **LURKERS** (72) ...79
NEW KICKS – **JOHANN** (54) ...96
NEW KID IN TOWN – **EAGLES** (20) ...77
NEW KIND OF MEDICINE – **Ultra NATÉ** (14) ...98
NEW LIFE – **DEPECHE MODE** (11) ...81
NEW LIVE AND RARE (EP) – **DEEP PURPLE** (31) ...77
NEW LIVE AND RARE II (EP) – **DEEP PURPLE** (45) ...78
NEW LIVE AND RARE III (EP) – **DEEP PURPLE** (48) ...80
NEW MISTAKE – **JELLYFISH** (55) ...93
NEW MOON ON MONDAY – **DURAN DURAN** (9) 84
NEW ORLEANS [A] – **Gary 'US' BONDS** (16) ...61
NEW ORLEANS [A] – **Bern ELLIOTT and the FENMEN** (24) ...64
NEW ORLEANS [A] – **HARLEY QUINNE** (19) ...72
NEW ORLEANS [A] – **GILLAN** (17) ...81
NEW POLICY ONE – **TERRORVISION** (42) ...93
THE NEW POLLUTION – **BECK** (14) ...97
NEW POWER GENERATION – **PRINCE** (26) ...90
NEW SENSATION – **INXS** (25) ...88
NEW SONG – **Howard JONES** (3) ...83,84
A NEW SOUTH WALES – **ALARM** (31) ...89
NEW THING FROM LONDON TOWN – **Gary NUMAN** (52) ...86
NEW TOY – **Lene LOVICH** (53) ...81
NEW WAY, NEW LIFE – **ASIAN DUB FOUNDATION** (49) ...00
NEW WORLD IN THE MORNING – **Roger WHITTAKER** (17) ...70
NEW WORLD MAN – **RUSH** (42) ...82
NEW WORLD MAN (LIVE) – **RUSH** (36) ...83
NEW YEAR – **SUGABABES** (12) ...00
NEW YEARS DAY [A] – **U2** (10) ...83
NEW YEAR'S DUB [A] – **MUSIQUE vs U2** (15) ...01
NEW YORK AFTERNOON – **MONDO KANE** (70) 86
NEW YORK CITY – **T. REX** (15) ...75
NEW YORK CITY BOY – **PET SHOP BOYS** (14) ...99
NEW YORK EYES – **NICOLE with Timmy THOMAS** (41) ...85
NEW YORK GROOVE – **HELLO** (9) ...75

NO ONE IS TO BLAME — Howard JONES (16) ..86
NO ONE LIKE YOU — SCORPIONS (64) 82
NO ONE SPEAKS — GENEVA (32).......................96
NO ONE TO CRY TO — Ray CHARLES (38) 64
NO ONE WILL EVER KNOW — Frank IFIELD (25)66
NO ONE'S DRIVING — Dave CLARKE (37) 96
NO ORDINARY LOVE — SADE (14)................92,93
NO ORDINARY MORNING — CHICANE (28)........00
NO OTHER BABY [A] — Bobby HELMS (30) 58
NO OTHER BABY [A] — Paul McCARTNEY (42)..99
NO OTHER LOVE [A] — Ronnie HILTON (1)........56
NO OTHER LOVE [A] — Edmund HOCKRIDGE (24)56
NO OTHER LOVE [A] — JOHNSTON BROTHERS (22)56
NO PARTICULAR PLACE TO GO — Chuck BERRY (3)64
NO PIGEONS — SPORTY THIEVZ (21)................99
NO PLACE TO HIDE — KORN (26) 96
NO PROMISES — ICEHOUSE (72).......................86
NO RAIN — BLIND MELON (17) 93
NO REGRETS [A] — Shirley BASSEY (39) 65
NO REGRETS [B] — WALKER BROTHERS (7) 76
NO REGRETS [B] — Midge URE (9)....................82
NO REGRETS [C] — Robbie WILLIAMS (4) 98
NO RELIGION — Van MORRISON (54) 95
NO REST — NEW MODEL ARMY (28) 85
NO SCRUBS — TLC (3) 99
NO SELF CONTROL — Peter GABRIEL (33) 80
NO SELL OUT — Malcolm X (60) 84
NO SLEEP TILL BROOKLYN — BEASTIE BOYS (14)87
NO SON OF MINE — GENESIS (6) 91,92
NO STONE UNTURNED — TRUTH (66) 84
NO SURPRISES — RADIOHEAD (4) 98
NO SURRENDER — DEUCE (29) 96
NO SURVIVORS — GBH (63)...............................82
NO SWEAT '98 — NORTH AND SOUTH (29)......98
NO TENGO DINERO — LOS UMBRELLOS (33)....98
NO TIME — LIL' KIM featuring PUFF DADDY (45) 97
NO TIME TO BE 21 — ADVERTS (34) 78
NO TIME TO CRY — SISTERS OF MERCY (63) ..85
NO TIME TO PLAY — GURU featuring DC LEE (25) 93
NO WAY — FREAKPOWER (29)..........................98
NO WAY NO WAY — VANILLA (14) 97
NO WAY OUT — Francesco ZAPPALA (69) 92
NO WOMAN NO CRY [A] — Bob MARLEY and the WAILERS (8) 75,81
NO WOMAN NO CRY [A] — LONDONBEAT (64)...91
NO WOMAN, NO CRY [A] — FUGEES (2)............96
THE NOBODIES — MARILYN MANSON (34) 01
NOBODY [A] — Toni BASIL (52) 82
NOBODY [B] — TONGUE 'N' CHEEK (37) 88, 90
NOBODY [C] — Shara NELSON (49) 94
NOBODY [D] — Keith SWEAT (30) 97
NOBODY BETTER — Tina MOORE (20)..............98
NOBODY BUT YOU — Gladys KNIGHT and the PIPS (34) 77
NOBODY DOES IT BETTER — Carly SIMON (7)..77
NOBODY ELSE [A] — Nick KAMEN (47) 87
NOBODY ELSE [B] — TYRESE (59) 99
NOBODY I KNOW — PETER and GORDON (10)..64
NOBODY KNOWS [A] — Nik KERSHAW (44) 86
NOBODY KNOWS [B] — Tony RICH PROJECT (4)96
NOBODY MADE ME — Randy EDELMAN (60)....82
NOBODY NEEDS YOUR LOVE — Gene PITNEY (2) 66
NOBODY TOLD ME — John LENNON (6)............84
NOBODY WANTS TO BE LONELY — Ricky MARTIN and Christina AGUILERA (4) 01
NOBODY WINS — Elton JOHN (42) 81
NOBODY'S BUSINESS [A] — H2o (19) 96
NOBODY'S BUSINESS [B] — PEACE BY PIECE (50)98
NOBODY'S CHILD [A] — Karen YOUNG (6) 69
NOBODY'S CHILD [A] — TRAVELING WILBURYS (44) 90
NOBODY'S DARLIN' BUT MINE — Frank IFIELD (4)63
NOBODY'S DIARY — YAZOO (3) 83
NOBODY'S FOOL [A] — Jim REEVES (32) 70
NOBODY'S FOOL [B] — HAIRCUT 100 (9) 82
NOBODY'S HERO — STIFF LITTLE FINGERS (36)80
NOBODY'S SUPPOSED TO BE HERE — Deborah COX (55) 99
NOBODY'S TWISTING YOUR ARM — WEDDING PRESENT (46) 88
NOCTURNE — T99 (33) 91
NOMANSLAND (DAVID'S SONG) — DJ SAKIN & FRIENDS (14) 99
NOMZAMO (ONE PEOPLE ONE CAUSE) — LATIN QUARTER (73) 87
NON HO L'ETA PER AMARTI — Gigliola CINQUETTI (17)..................................64
NONE OF YOUR BUSINESS — SALT-N-PEPA (19) 94,95
(NONSTOPOPERATION) — DUST JUNKYS (47) ..97
NO ONE BUT YOU — QUEEN (13) 98
NORA MALONE — Teresa BREWER (26) 57
NORMAN — Carol DEENE (24) 62
NORMAN BATES — LANDSCAPE (40) 81
NORMAN 3 — TEENAGE FANCLUB (50) 93
NORTH COUNTRY BOY — CHARLATANS (4) 97
NORTH, SOUTH, EAST, WEST — MARVIN and TAMARA (44) 99
NORTH TO ALASKA — Johnny HORTON (23) 61
NORTHERN LIGHTS — RENAISSANCE (10) 78
NORTHERN LITES — SUPER FURRY ANIMALS (11) 99
NORTHERN STAR — Melanie C (4) 99
NOT A DRY EYE IN THE HOUSE — MEAT LOAF (7) 96
NOT A MINUTE TOO SOON — VIXEN (37)..........91
NOT ABOUT US — GENESIS (66) 98
NOT ALONE — Bernard BUTLER (27) 98
NOT ANYONE — BLACK BOX (31) 95
NOT AS A STRANGER — Frank SINATRA (18) 55
NOT AT ALL — STATUS QUO (50)......................89
NOT ENOUGH? — Melanie WILLIAMS (65) 94
NOT ENOUGH LOVE IN THE WORLD — CHER (31) 96
NOT EVEN GONNA TRIP — HONEYZ (24)......00,01
NOT FADE AWAY — ROLLING STONES (3) 64
NOT FOR YOU — PEARL JAM (34) 95
NOT GON' CRY — Mary J BLIGE (39) 96
NOT IF YOU WERE THE LAST JUNKIE ON EARTH — DANDY WARHOLS (13) 98
NOT NOW JOHN — PINK FLOYD (30) 83
NOT OVER YET [A] — GRACE (6).........................95
NOT OVER YET 99 [A] — Planet PERFECTO featuring GRACE (16) 99
NOT OVER YOU YET — Diana ROSS (9) 99,00
NOT RESPONSIBLE — Tom JONES (18)..............66
NOT SLEEPING AROUND — NED'S ATOMIC DUSTBIN (19) 92
NOT SO MANIC NOW — DUBSTAR (18) 96
NOT SUCH AN INNOCENT GIRL — Victoria BECKHAM (6) 01
NOT THAT KIND — ANASTACIA (11) 01
NOT THE GIRL YOU THINK YOU ARE — CROWDED HOUSE (20) 96
(NOT THE) GREATEST RAPPER — 1000 CLOWNS (23) 99
NOT TONIGHT — LIL' KIM (11) 97
NOT TOO LITTLE NOT TOO MUCH — Chris SANDFORD (17) 63
NOT UNTIL THE NEXT TIME — Jim REEVES (13) 65
NOT WHERE IT'S AT — DEL AMITRI (21) 97
NOTGONNACHANGE — SWING OUT SISTER (49) ..92
NOTHIN' AT ALL — HEART (38) 88
NOTHIN' BUT A GOOD TIME — POISON (35) 88,89
NOTHIN' BUT A PARTY — TRUCE (71)................97
NOTHIN' MY LOVE CAN'T FIX — Joey LAWRENCE (13) 93
NOTHIN' PERSONAL — DUST JUNKYS (62)........98
(NOTHIN' SERIOUS) JUST BUGGIN' — WHISTLE (7) 86
NOTHIN' (THAT COMPARES 2 U) — JACKSONS (33) 89
NOTHIN' TO DO — Michael HOLLIDAY (20) 56
NOTHING [A] — FRAZIER CHORUS (51) 90
NOTHING [B] — FLUFFY (52)..............................96
NOTHING AS IT SEEMS — PEARL JAM (22) 00
NOTHING 'BOUT ME — STING (32)....................94
NOTHING BUT LOVE — OPTIMYSTIC (37)..........94
NOTHING CAN CHANGE THIS LOVE — Bitty McLEAN (55)..95
NOTHING CAN DIVIDE US — Jason DONOVAN (5) 88
NOTHING CAN STOP ME — Gene CHANDLER (41) 68
NOTHING CAN STOP US — SAINT ETIENNE (54)91
NOTHING COMES EASY — Sandie SHAW (14) ..66
NOTHING COMPARES 2 U [A] — MXM (68)........90
NOTHING COMPARES 2 U [A] — Sinead O'CONNOR (1) 90
NOTHING ELSE MATTERS — METALLICA (6)......92
NOTHING EVER HAPPENS — DEL AMITRI (11) ..90
NOTHING HAS BEEN PROVED [A] — Dusty SPRINGFIELD (16) 89
NOTHING HAS BEEN PROVED [A] — STRINGS OF LOVE (59) 90
NOTHING IN PARTICULAR — BROTHERHOOD (55)96
NOTHING IS FOREVER — ULTRACYNIC (47) ..92,97
NOTHING IS REAL BUT THE GIRL — BLONDIE (26)...99
NOTHING LASTS FOREVER — ECHO and the BUNNYMEN (8) 97
NOTHING LEFT — ORBITAL (32) 99
NOTHING LEFT TOULOUSE — SAD CAFE (62)....80
NOTHING LESS THAN BRILLIANT — Sandie SHAW (66) 94
NOTHING NATURAL — LUSH (43) 91
NOTHING REALLY MATTERS — MADONNA (7) ..99
NOTHING RHYMED — Gilbert O'SULLIVAN (8) ..70
NOTHING TO DECLARE — LAPTOP (74) 99
NOTHING TO FEAR — Chris REA (16) 92
NOTHING TO LOSE [A] — UK (67).......................79
NOTHING TO LOSE [B] — S EXPRESS (32) 90
NOTHING WITHOUT ME — MANCHILD (40)........01
NOTHING'S GONNA CHANGE MY LOVE FOR YOU — Glenn MEDEIROS (1) 88
NOTHING'S GONNA STOP ME NOW — Samantha FOX (8)..87
NOTHING'S GONNA STOP US NOW — STARSHIP (1)...87
NOTHIN'S GONNA CHANGE — Labi SIFFRE (52) 87
NOTORIOUS — DURAN DURAN (7) 86,87
NOTORIOUS B.I.G. — NOTORIOUS B.I.G. (16)....00
NOVELTY WAVES — BIOSPHERE (51) 95
NOVEMBER RAIN — GUNS N' ROSES (4) 92
NOVEMBER SPAWNED A MONSTER — MORRISSEY (12) 90
NOVOCAINE FOR THE SOUL — EELS (10) 97
NOW [A] — Al MARTINO (3) 53
NOW [B] — Val DOONICAN (43) 68
NOW ALWAYS AND FOREVER — GAY DAD (41)..01
NOW AND FOREVER — Richard MARX (13)........94
(NOW AND THEN THERE'S) A FOOL SUCH AS I — Elvis PRESLEY (1) 59
NOW I KNOW WHAT MADE OTIS BLUE — Paul YOUNG (14)...93
NOW I'M HERE — QUEEN (11)............................75
NOW IS THE TIME — Jimmy JAMES and the VAGABONDS (5) 76
NOW IS TOMORROW — DEFINITION OF SOUND (46) 91
NOW IT'S GONE — CHORDS (63) 79
NOW I'VE FOUND YOU — Sean MAGUIRE (22)..95
NOW OR NEVER — Tom NOVY featuring LIMA (64) 01
NOW THAT I OWN THE BBC — SPARKS (60) 96
NOW THAT THE MAGIC HAS GONE — Joe COCKER (28) 92
NOW THAT WE'VE FOUND LOVE [A] — THIRD WORLD (10).....................................78,85
NOW THAT WE FOUND LOVE [A] — HEAVY D and the BOYZ (2) 91
NOW THAT YOU'VE GONE — MIKE and the MECHANICS (35).......................99
NOW THEY'LL SLEEP — BELLY (28) 95
NOW THOSE DAYS ARE GONE — BUCKS FIZZ (8) 82
NOW WE'RE THRU — POETS (31) 64
NOW YOU'RE GONE [A] — BLACK (66) 89
NOW YOU'RE GONE [B] — WHITESNAKE (31) 90
NOW YOU'RE IN HEAVEN — Julian LENNON (59)..89
NOWHERE — THERAPY? (18) 94
NOWHERE FAST — MEAT LOAF (67)...................84
NOWHERE GIRL — B-MOVIE (67) 82
NOWHERE LAND — CLUBHOUSE (56)................95
NOWHERE MAN — THREE GOOD REASONS (47)..66
NOWHERE TO RUN [A] — Martha REEVES and the VANDELLAS (26) 65,69,88
NOWHERE TO RUN 2000 [A] — NU GENERATION (66) 00
N-R-G — ADAMSKI (12).......................................90
NUCLEAR DEVICE (THE WIZARD OF AUS) — STRANGLERS (36) 79
NUCLEAR HOLIDAY — 3 COLOURS RED (22) 97
NUFF VIBES EP — APACHE INDIAN (5)..............93
#9 DREAM — John LENNON (23) 75
THE NUMBER OF THE BEAST — IRON MAIDEN (18) 82
NUMBER ONE [A] — EYC (27)............................94
NUMBER ONE [B] — A (47).................................98

PLEASE DON'T FALL IN LOVE – Cliff RICHARD (7) 83
PLEASE DON'T GO [A] – Donald PEERS (3) 68,69
PLEASE DON'T GO [B] – DOUBLE YOU? (41) 92
PLEASE DON'T GO [B] – KC and the SUNSHINE BAND (3) 79
PLEASE DON'T GO [B] – KWS (1)....92
PLEASE DON'T GO [C] – NO MERCY (4) 97
PLEASE DON'T MAKE ME CRY – UB40 (10)....83
PLEASE DON'T TEASE – Cliff RICHARD and the SHADOWS (1) 60
PLEASE DON'T TOUCH – Johnny KIDD and the PIRATES (25) 59
PLEASE DON'T TURN ME ON – ARTFUL DODGER (4) 00
PLEASE FORGIVE ME [A] – Bryan ADAMS (2) ..93
PLEASE FORGIVE ME [B] – David GRAY (18)99,00
PLEASE HELP ME, I'M FALLING – Hank LOCKLIN (9) 60
PLEASE MR POSTMAN [A] – BACKBEAT BAND (69)....94
PLEASE MR POSTMAN [A] – CARPENTERS (2) 75
PLEASE PLEASE ME [A] – BEATLES (2) 63,83
PLEASE PLEASE ME [A] – David CASSIDY (16) 74
PLEASE RELEASE ME – Mike FLOWERS POPS (39) 96
PLEASE SAVE ME – SUNSCREEM vs PUSH (36)01
PLEASE SIR – Martyn JOSEPH (45) 93
PLEASE STAY [A] – CRYIN' SHAMES (26) 66
PLEASE STAY [B] – Kylie MINOGUE (10) 00
PLEASE TELL HIM THAT I SAID HELLO – DANA (8) 75
PLEASE (YOU GOT THAT . . .) – INXS (50)....93
PLEASE YOURSELF – BIG SUPREME (64) 87
PLEASURE BOYS – VISAGE (44) 82
PLEASURE DOME – SOUL II SOUL (51) 97
PLEASURE LOVE – DE FUNK featuring F45 (49) ..99
PLEASURE PRINCIPLE – Janet JACKSON (24) ..87
PLENTY GOOD LOVIN' – Connie FRANCIS (18) 59
PLOWED – SPONGE (74) 95
PLUG ME IN (TO THE CENTRAL LOVE LINE) – SCARLET FANTASTIC (67) 88
PLUG IN BABY – MUSE (11) 01
PLUSH – STONE TEMPLE PILOTS (23) 93
THE POACHER – Ronnie LANE and SLIM CHANCE (36) 74
POCKET CALCULATOR – KRAFTWERK (39)....81
POEMS – NEARLY GOD (28) 96
POETRY IN MOTION – Johnny TILLOTSON (1)..60,79
POGUETRY IN MOTION (EP) – POGUES (29)....86
POING – ROTTERDAM TERMINATION SOURCE (27) 92
POINT OF NO RETURN [A] – NU SHOOZ (48) ..86
POINT OF NO RETURN [B] – CENTORY (67) 94
POINT OF VIEW – MATUMBI (35) 79
POISON [A] – Alice COOPER (2) 89
POISON [B] – BELL BIV DEVOE (19) 90
POISON [C] – PRODIGY (15) 95,96
POISON [D] – BARDOT (45) 01
POISON ARROW – ABC (6) 82
POISON HEART – RAMONES (69) 92
POISON IVY [A] – COASTERS (15) 59
POISON IVY [A] – PARAMOUNTS (35) 64
POISON IVY [A] – LAMBRETTAS (7)....80
POISON STREET – NEW MODEL ARMY (64) 87
POLICE AND THIEVES – Junior MURVIN (23)....80
POLICE OFFICER – Smiley CULTURE (12)....84
POLICE STATE – T-POWER (63) 96
POLICEMAN SKANK ... (THE STORY OF MY LIFE) – AUDIOWEB (21) 98
POLICY OF TRUTH – DEPECHE MODE (16) 90
THE POLITICS OF DANCING – RE-FLEX (28) 84
POLK SALAD ANNIE – Elvis PRESLEY (23) 73
POLYESTERDAY – GUS GUS (55) 98
PONY – GINUWINE (16) 97
PONY TIME – Chubby CHECKER (27)....61
POODLE ROCKIN' – GORKY'S ZYGOTIC MYNCI (52)....00
POOL HALL RICHARD – FACES (8)....73
POOR JENNY – EVERLY BROTHERS (14) 59
POOR LENO – RÖYKSOPP (59) 01
POOR LITTLE FOOL – Ricky NELSON (4) 58
POOR MAN'S SON – ROCKIN' BERRIES (5)....65
POOR ME – Adam FAITH (1) 60
POOR PEOPLE OF PARIS – Winifred ATWELL (1)56
POP – 'N SYNC (9)....01
POP COP – GYRES (71) 96
POP GO THE WORKERS – BARRON KNIGHTS (5) 65
POP GOES MY LOVE – FREEEZ (26) 83
POP GOES THE WEASEL [A] – Anthony NEWLEY (12) 61
POP GOES THE WEASEL [B] – 3RD BASS (64) 91
POP IS DEAD – RADIOHEAD (42) 93
POP LIFE – PRINCE (60) 85
POP MUZIK [A] – M (2)....79,89
POP MUZIK [A] – ALL SYSTEMS GO (63)....88
THE POP SINGER'S FEAR OF THE POLLEN COUNT – DIVINE COMEDY (17) 99
POP YA COLLAR – USHER (2) 01
POPCORN – HOT BUTTER (5) 72
POPCORN LOVE – NEW EDITION (43) 83
POPPA JOE – SWEET (11)....72
POPPA PICCOLINO – Diana DECKER (2)....53,54
POPPED!! – FOOL BOONA (52) 99
POPS WE LOVE YOU – Diana ROSS, Marvin GAYE, Smokey ROBINSON and Stevie WONDER (66) ..79
POPSCENE – BLUR (32)....92
PORCELAIN – MOBY (5)....00
PORT-AU-PRINCE – Winifred ATWELL and Frank CHACKSFIELD (18) 56
PORTRAIT OF MY LOVE – Matt MONRO (3) 60
PORTSMOUTH – Mike OLDFIELD (3) 76
PORTUGUESE WASHERWOMAN – Joe 'Fingers' CARR (20)....56
POSITIVE BLEEDING – URGE OVERKILL (61) 93
POSITIVE EDUCATION – SLAM (44) 01
A POSITIVE VIBRATION – BLACK BOX (21) 96
POSITIVELY FOURTH STREET – Bob DYLAN (8)65
POSSESSED – VEGAS (32) 92
POSSESSION – TRANSFER (54) 01
POSSIBLY MAYBE – BJÖRK (13)....96
POST MODERN SLEAZE – SNEAKER PIMPS (22)....97
POSTCARD FROM HEAVEN – LIGHTHOUSE FAMILY (24)....99
POSTMAN PAT – Ken BARRIE (44)....82,83
POUNDCAKE – VAN HALEN (74) 91
POUR SOME SUGAR ON ME – DEF LEPPARD (18) 87
POW POW POW – FONTANA featuring Darryl D'BONNEAU (62) 01
POWDER BLUE – ELBOW (41) 01
POWER – NU COLOURS (40) 92,93
POWER AND THE GLORY – SAXON (32) 83
THE POWER IS YOURS – REDSKINS (59) 86
POWER OF A WOMAN – ETERNAL (5) 95
THE POWER (OF ALL THE LOVE IN THE WORLD) – D:REAM (40)....95
P.OWER OF A.MERICAN N.ATIVES – DANCE 2 TRANCE (25) 93
THE POWER OF GOODBYE – MADONNA (6) 98
POWER OF LOVE [A] – DEEE-LITE (25) 90
POWER OF LOVE [B] – Q-TEX (49) 94,97
POWER OF LOVE - LOVE POWER – Luther VANDROSS (31) 91,95
THE POWER OF LOVE [A] – FRANKIE GOES TO HOLLYWOOD (1)00,84,85,93
THE POWER OF LOVE [A] – Holly JOHNSON (56) 99
THE POWER OF LOVE [B] – Celine DION (4) 94
THE POWER OF LOVE [B] – FITS OF GLOOM featuring Lizzy MACK (49) ..94
THE POWER OF LOVE [B] – Jennifer RUSH (1) 85,86
THE POWER OF LOVE [C] – Huey LEWIS and the NEWS (9) 85,86
POWER RANGERS – MIGHTY MORPH'N POWER RANGERS (3)..94,95
THE POWER [A] – SNAP featuring EINSTEIN (1)90,96
THE POWER [A] – Monie LOVE (33) 93
POWER TO ALL OUR FRIENDS – Cliff RICHARD (4) 73
POWER TO THE PEOPLE – John LENNON (7)....71
POWERGEN (ONLY YOUR LOVE) – PKA (70) 92
POWERTRIP – MONSTER MAGNET (39)....99
THE POWER ZONE – TIME FREQUENCY (17) 93
PRACTICE WHAT YOU PREACH – Barry WHITE (20) 95
PRAISE – INNER CITY (59)....92
PRAISE YOU – FATBOY SLIM (1) 99
PRANCE ON – Eddie HENDERSON (44)....78
PRAY [A] – HAMMER (8) 90
PRAY [B] – TAKE THAT (1) 93
PRAY [C] – Tina COUSINS (20) 98
PRAY FOR LOVE – LOVE TO INFINITY (69) 96
PRAYER FOR THE DYING – SEAL (14)....94,95
PRAYER FOR YOU – TEXAS (73) 89
A PRAYER TO THE MUSIC – MARCO POLO (65)95
PRAYER TOWER – PARADISE ORGANISATION (70)....93
PRAYING FOR TIME – George MICHAEL (6)....90
PREACHER MAN – BANANARAMA (20) 91
PREACHER, PREACHER – ANIMAL NIGHTLIFE (67) 85
PRECIOUS [A] – JAM (1) 82,83
PRECIOUS [B] – Annie LENNOX (23) 92
PRECIOUS HEART – TALL PAUL vs INXS (14)....01
PRECIOUS TIME – Van MORRISON (36) 99
PREGNANT FOR THE LAST TIME – MORRISSEY (25) 91
PREPARE TO LAND – SUPERNATURALS (48)....97
PRESENCE OF LOVE (LAUGHERNE) – ALARM (44) 88
PRESS – Paul McCARTNEY (25) 86
PRESSURE [A] – SUNSCREEM (60) 92
PRESSURE [B] – Billy OCEAN (55)....93
PRESSURE [C] – DRIZABONE (33) 94
THE PRESSURE – SOUNDS OF BLACKNESS (46) 91,92,98
PRESSURE DROP – Izzy STRADLIN' (45)....92
PRESSURE ON – Roger TAYLOR (45) 98
PRESSURE US – SUNSCREEM (19) 93
PRETEND [A] – Nat 'King' COLE (2)....53
PRETEND [A] – Alvin STARDUST (4) 81
PRETEND BEST FRIEND – TERRORVISION (25) 94
PRETEND WE'RE DEAD – L7 (21)....92
PRETENDER GOT MY HEART – ALISHA'S ATTIC (43) 01
PRETENDERS TO THE THRONE – BEAUTIFUL SOUTH (18)....95
PRETTIEST EYES – BEAUTIFUL SOUTH (37) 94
PRETTY BLUE EYES – Craig DOUGLAS (4)....60
PRETTY BROWN EYES – Jim REEVES (33) 68
PRETTY DEEP – Tanya DONELLY (55)....97
PRETTY FLAMINGO – MANFRED MANN (1) 66
PRETTY FLY (FOR A WHITE GUY) – OFFSPRING (1) 99
PRETTY GOOD YEAR – Tori AMOS (7)....94
PRETTY IN PINK – PSYCHEDELIC FURS (18)....81,86
PRETTY JENNY – Jess CONRAD (50) 62
PRETTY LITTLE ANGEL EYES [A] – Curtis LEE (47) 61
PRETTY LITTLE ANGEL EYES [A] – SHOWADDYWADDY (5) 78
PRETTY LITTLE BLACK-EYED SUSIE – Guy MITCHELL (2) 53
PRETTY NOOSE – SOUNDGARDEN (14)....96
PRETTY PAPER – Roy ORBISON (6) 64
PRETTY THING – Bo DIDDLEY (34) 63
PRETTY VACANT – SEX PISTOLS (6) 77,92,96
PRETTY WOMAN – JUICY LUCY (44) 70
THE PRICE OF LOVE [A] – EVERLY BROTHERS (2) 65
THE PRICE OF LOVE [A] – Bryan FERRY (49)....89
PRICE YOU PAY – QUESTIONS (56)....83
PRIDE (IN THE NAME OF LOVE) [A] – U2 (3)....84
PRIDE (IN THE NAME OF LOVE) [A] – C & C MUSIC FACTORY / CLIVILLES & COLE (15) 92
PRIMAL SCREAM – MÖTLEY CRÜE (32) 91
PRIMARY – CURE (43) 81
PRIMARY INSTINCT – SENSELESS THINGS (41)93
PRIMARY RHYMING – MC TUNES (67)....90
PRIME MOVER [A] – RUSH (43)....88
PRIME MOVER [B] – ZODIAC MINDWARP and the LOVE REACTION (18) 87
PRIME TIME [A] – TUBES (34) 79
PRIME TIME [B] – HAIRCUT 100 (46)....83
PRIME TIME [C] – MTUME (57) 84
PRIMROSE LANE – Dickie PRIDE (28) 59
THE PRINCE – MADNESS (16) 79
A PRINCE AMONG ISLANDS (EP) – CAPERCAILLIE (39) 92
PRINCE CHARMING – ADAM and the ANTS (1) 81
PRINCE IGOR – Warren G (15)....98
PRINCE OF DARKNESS – BOW WOW WOW (58)..81
PRINCE OF PEACE – GALLIANO (47) 92

R TO THE A — CJ LEWIS (34) ... 95
R U READY — SALT-N-PEPA (24) ... 97
R U SLEEPING — INDO (31) ... 98
RABBIT — CHAS and DAVE (8) ... 80
THE RACE [A] — YELLO (7) ... 88,92
RACE [B] — TIGER (37) ... 96
RACE FOR THE PRIZE — FLAMING LIPS (39) ... 99
THE RACE IS ON [A] — Suzi QUATRO (43) ... 78
THE RACE IS ON [B] — Dave EDMUNDS and the STRAY CATS (34) ... 81
RACE WITH THE DEVIL [A] — Gene VINCENT (28) 56
RACE WITH THE DEVIL [B] — GIRLSCHOOL (49) 80
RACE WITH THE DEVIL [B] — GUN (8) ... 68
RACHEL — Al MARTINO (10) ... 53
RACHMANINOFF'S 18TH VARIATION ON A THEME BY PAGANINI (THE STORY OF THREE LOVES) — Winifred ATWELL (9) ... 54
RACIST FRIEND — SPECIALS (60) ... 83
RADANCER — MARMALADE (6) ... 72
RADAR LOVE [A] — GOLDEN EARRING (7) ... 73,77
RADAR LOVE [A] — OH WELL (65) ... 90
RADIATION VIBE — FOUNTAINS OF WAYNE (32) .. 97
RADICAL YOUR LOVER — LITTLE ANGELS (34) .. 90
RADICCIO (EP) — ORBITAL (37) ... 92
RADIO [A] — Roger TAYLOR (37) ... 92
RADIO [B] — TEENAGE FANCLUB (31) ... 93
RADIO [C] — CORRS (18) ... 99
RADIO AFRICA — LATIN QUARTER (19) ... 86
RADIO DISCO — WILT (56) ... 00
RADIO GAGA — QUEEN (2) ... 84
RADIO HEAD — TALKING HEADS (52) ... 87
RADIO HEART — RADIO HEART featuring Gary NUMAN (35) ... 87
RADIO MUSICOLA — Nik KERSHAW (43) ... 86
RADIO #1 — AIR (31) ... 01
RADIO ON — Ricky ROSS (35) ... 96
RADIO RADIO — Elvis COSTELLO (29) ... 78
RADIO ROMANCE — TIFFANY (13) ... 88
RADIO SONG — R.E.M. (28) ... 91
RADIO WALL OF SOUND — SLADE (21) ... 91
RADIO WAVES — Roger WATERS (74) ... 87
RADIOACTIVE — Gene SIMMONS (41) ... 79
RADIOACTIVITY — KRAFTWERK (43) ... 91
RAG DOLL [A] — FOUR SEASONS (2) ... 64
RAG DOLL [B] — AEROSMITH (42) ... 90
RAG MAMA RAG — BAND (16) ... 70
RAGAMUFFIN MAN — MANFRED MANN (8) ... 69
RAGE HARD — FRANKIE GOES TO HOLLYWOOD (4) ... 86
RAGE TO LOVE — Kim WILDE (19) ... 85
RAGGA HOUSE (ALL NIGHT LONG) — Simon HARRIS (56) ... 90
RAGGAMUFFIN GIRL — APACHE INDIAN (31) ... 95
RAGING (EP) — BEYOND (68) ... 91
RAGS TO RICHES [A] — David WHITFIELD (3) .. 53,54
RAGS TO RICHES [A] — Elvis PRESLEY (9) ... 71
RAGTIME COWBOY JOE — CHIPMUNKS (11) ... 59
RAIN [A] — Bruce RUFFIN (19) ... 71
RAIN [B] — STATUS QUO (7) ... 76
RAIN [C] — CULT (17) ... 85
RAIN [D] — MADONNA (7) ... 93
RAIN [E] — GROOVE CORPORATION (71) ... 94
THE RAIN (SUPA DUPA FLY) — Missy 'Misdemeanor' ELLIOTT (16) ... 97
THE RAIN — Oran 'Juice' JONES (4) ... 86
RAIN AND TEARS — APHRODITE'S CHILD (29) .. 68
RAIN FALLS — Frankie KNUCKLES (48) ... 92
RAIN FOREST [A] — BIDDU (39) ... 76
RAIN FOREST [B] — Paul HARDCASTLE (41) 84,85
RAIN IN THE SUMMERTIME — ALARM (18) ... 87
RAIN KING — COUNTING CROWS (49) ... 94
RAIN OR SHINE — FIVE STAR (2) ... 86
RAIN RAIN RAIN — Frankie LAINE and the FOUR LADS (8) ... 54
RAIN SHOWERS — SIZZLA (51) ... 99
RAINBOW [A] — MARMALADE (3) ... 70
RAINBOW [B] — PETERS and LEE (17) ... 74
RAINBOW CHASER — NIRVANA (34) ... 68
RAINBOW CHILD — Dan REED NETWORK (39) .. 90
RAINBOW COUNTRY — Bob MARLEY and the WAILERS (11) ... 00
RAINBOW IN THE DARK — DIO (46) ... 83
RAINBOW LAKE — WENDY and LISA (70) ... 90
RAINBOW PEOPLE — MANIX (57) ... 92
RAINBOW (SAMPLE FREE) — SOLO (59) ... 91
RAINBOW THEME - FROZEN RAINBOW — SAXON (66) ... 80
RAINBOW VALLEY — LOVE AFFAIR (5) ... 68
RAINBOWS OF COLOUR — GROOVERIDER (40) 98
RAINCLOUD — LIGHTHOUSE FAMILY (6) ... 97
THE RAINDANCE — DARE (62) ... 89
RAINDROPS KEEP FALLIN' ON MY HEAD [A] — Bobbie GENTRY (40) ... 70
RAINDROPS KEEP FALLING ON MY HEAD [A] — BJ THOMAS (38) ... 70
RAINDROPS KEEP FALLING ON MY HEAD [A] — Sacha DISTEL (10) ... 70
RAININ' THROUGH MY SUNSHINE — REAL THING (40) ... 78
RAINING ALL OVER THE WORLD — ADVENTURES (68) ... 92
RAINING IN MY HEART — Leo SAYER (21) ... 78
RAINMAKER — SPARKLEHORSE (61) ... 96
RAINY DAY WOMEN NOS. 12 & 35 — Bob DYLAN (7) ... 66
RAINY DAYS AND MONDAYS — CARPENTERS (63) ... 93
RAINY NIGHT IN GEORGIA — Randy CRAWFORD (18) ... 81
A RAINY NIGHT IN SOHO — POGUES (67) ... 91
RAISE — HYPER GO GO (36) ... 94
RAISE YOUR HAND — Eddie FLOYD (42) ... 67
RAISE YOUR HANDS [A] — REEL 2 REAL (14) ... 94
RAISE YOUR HANDS [B] — BIG ROOM GIRL featuring Darryl PANDY (40) 99
RAISED ON ROCK — Elvis PRESLEY (36) ... 73
RAM GOAT LIVER — Pluto SHERVINGTON (43) ... 76
RAMA LAMA DING DONG — Rocky SHARPE and the REPLAYS (17) ... 78
RAMBLIN' ROSE — Nat 'King' COLE (5) ... 62
RAM-BUNK-SHUSH — VENTURES (45) ... 61
RAME — SNAP (50) ... 96
RAMONA — BACHELORS (4) ... 64
RANDY — BLUE MINK (9) ... 73
RANKING FULL STOP — BEAT (6) ... 79
RAOUL AND THE KINGS OF SPAIN — TEARS FOR FEARS (31) ... 95
RAP DIS / ONLY WANNA KNOW U COS URE FAMOUS — OXIDE & NEUTRINO (12) ... 01
RAP SCHOLAR — DAS EFX featuring REDMAN (42) ... 98
RAP SUMMARY — BIG DADDY KANE (52) ... 89
(RAP) SUPERSTAR / (ROCK) SUPERSTAR — CYPRESS HILL (13) ... 00
RAP YOUR LOVE — SET THE TONE (67) ... 83
RAPE ME — NIRVANA (32) ... 93
RAPP PAYBACK (WHERE IZ MOSES?) — James BROWN (39) ... 81
RAPPAZ R N DAINJA — KRS ONE (47) ... 96
RAPPER'S DELIGHT — SUGARHILL GANG (3) ... 79,89
RAPTURE [A] — BLONDIE (5) ... 81
RAPTURE [B] — IIO (2) ... 01
RARE, PRECIOUS AND GONE — Mike SCOTT (74) 98
THE RASCAL KING — MIGHTY MIGHTY BOSSTONES (63) ... 98
RASPBERRY BERET — PRINCE (25) ... 85
RASPUTIN — BONEY M (2) ... 78
RAT IN MI KITCHEN — UB40 (12) ... 87
RAT RACE — SPECIALS (5) ... 80
RAT RAPPING — Roland RAT SUPERSTAR (14) 83
RAT TRAP — BOOMTOWN RATS (1) ... 78
RATAMAHATTA — SEPULTURA (23) ... 96
THE RATTLER — GOODBYE MR MACKENZIE (37) .. 89
RATTLESNAKES — Lloyd COLE (65) ... 84
RAUNCHY [A] — Bill JUSTIS (11) ... 58
RAUNCHY [A] — Ken MACKINTOSH (19) ... 58
RAVE ALERT — Praga KHAN (39) ... 92
THE RAVE DIGGER — MC LETHAL (66) ... 92
RAVE GENERATOR — TOXIC TWO (13) ... 92
RAVE ON — Buddy HOLLY (5) ... 58,68
RAVEL'S PAVANE POUR UNE INFANTE DEFUNTE — William ORBIT (31) ... 00
RAVING I'M RAVING — SHUT UP AND DANCE (2) 92
RAW [A] — SPANDAU BALLET (47) ... 88
RAW [B] — ALARM (51) ... 91
RAW [C] — MELKY SEDECK (50) ... 99
RAW POWER — APOLLO FOUR FORTY (32) ... 97
RAWHIDE — Frankie LAINE (6) ... 59,60
RAY OF LIGHT — MADONNA (2) ... 98
RAYS OF THE RISING SUN [A] — Denise JOHNSON (45) ... 94
RAYS OF THE RISING SUN [A] — MOZAIC (32) .. 96
RAZOR'S EDGE — MEAT LOAF (41) ... 84
RAZZAMATAZZ — Quincy JONES (11) ... 81
RAZZLE DAZZLE [A] — Bill HALEY and his COMETS (13) ... 56
RAZZLE DAZZLE [B] — HEATWAVE (43) ... 79
RE: EVOLUTION — SHAMEN (18) ... 93
RE-REWIND THE CROWD SAY BO SELECTA — ARTFUL DODGER featuring Craig DAVID (2) .. 99
REACH [A] — Judy CHEEKS (17) ... 94,96
REACH [B] — LIL MO' YIN YANG (28) ... 96
REACH [C] — Gloria ESTEFAN (15) ... 96
REACH [D] — S CLUB 7 (2) ... 00
REACH FOR THE STARS — Shirley BASSEY (1) .. 61
REACH 4 THE MELODY — Victoria WILSON JAMES (72) ... 97
REACH OUT — MIDFIELD GENERAL featuring LINDA LEWIS (61) 00
REACH OUT AND TOUCH — Diana ROSS (33) .. 70
REACH OUT FOR ME — Dionne WARWICK (23) ... 64
REACH OUT I'LL BE THERE [A] — FOUR TOPS (1) ... 66,88
REACH OUT I'LL BE THERE [A] — Gloria GAYNOR (14) ... 75
REACH OUT I'LL BE THERE [A] — Michael BOLTON (37) ... 93
REACH UP — Toney LEE (64) ... 83
REACH UP (PAPA'S GOT A BRAND NEW PIG BAG) — PERFECTO ALLSTARZ (6) ... 95
REACHIN [A] — Joey NEGRO (70) ... 91
REACHIN [A] — HOUSE OF VIRGINISM (35) ... 94
REACHING FOR THE BEST — EXCITERS (31) ... 75
REACHING FOR THE WORLD — Harold MELVIN and the BLUENOTES (48) ... 77
READ 'EM AND WEEP — Barry MANILOW (17) .. 83
READ MY LIPS [A] — DSK (46) ... 91
READ MY LIPS [B] — ALEX PARTY (28) ... 96
READ MY LIPS (ENOUGH IS ENOUGH) — Jimmy SOMERVILLE (26) ... 90
READ MY MIND — Conner REEVES (19) ... 98
READY — Bruce WAYNE (44) ... 97
READY AN' WILLING (SWEET SATISFACTION) — WHITESNAKE (43) ... 80
READY FOR A NEW DAY — Martha WASH (20) ... 98
READY FOR LOVE [A] — Jimmy JONES (46) ... 60
READY FOR LOVE [B] — Gary MOORE (56) ... 89
READY OR NOT [A] — LIGHTNING SEEDS (20) .. 96
READY OR NOT [B] — DJ DADO (51) ... 99
READY OR NOT [C] — FUGEES (1) ... 96
READY OR NOT [C] — COURSE (5) ... 97
READY OR NOT [D] — A1 (3) ... 99
READY OR NOT HERE I COME — DELFONICS (41) 71
READY STEADY GO — GENERATION X (47) ... 78
READY STEADY WHO (EP) — WHO (58) ... 83
READY TO GO — REPUBLICA (13) ... 96,97
READY TO RECEIVE — ANIMALHOUSE (61) ... 00
READY TO RUN — DIXIE CHICKS (53) ... 99
READY, WILLING AND ABLE — Doris DAY (7) ... 55
REAL — Donna ALLEN (34) ... 95
REAL COOL WORLD — David BOWIE (53) ... 92
REAL EMOTION — REID (65) ... 89
REAL FASHION REGGAE STYLE — Carey JOHNSON (19) ... 87
REAL GONE KID — DEACON BLUE (8) ... 88
REAL GOOD — DOUBLE SIX (66) ... 98
REAL GOOD TIME — ALDA (7) ... 98
REAL GREAT BRITAIN — ASIAN DUB FOUNDATION (41) ... 00
REAL LIFE [A] — SIMPLE MINDS (34) ... 91
REAL LIFE [B] — BON JOVI (21) ... 99
THE REAL LIFE — RAVEN MAIZE (12) ... 01
REAL LOVE [A] — Ruby MURRAY (18) ... 58
REAL LOVE [B] — Jody WATLEY (31) ... 89
REAL LOVE [C] — DRIZABONE (16) ... 91,95
REAL LOVE [D] — DARE (67) ... 91
REAL LOVE [D] — TIME FREQUENCY (8) .. 92,93,94
REAL LOVE [E] — Mary J BLIGE (26) ... 92,93
REAL LOVE [F] — BEATLES (4) ... 96
THE REAL ME — W.A.S.P. (23) ... 89
A REAL MOTHER FOR YA — Johnny 'Guitar' WATSON (44) ... 77
REAL PEOPLE — APACHE INDIAN (66) ... 97
REAL REAL REAL — JESUS JONES (19) ... 90
THE REAL SLIM SHADY — EMINEM (1) ... 00

RHINESTONE COWBOY – Glen CAMPBELL (4)..75
THE RHYME – Keith MURRAY (59) 96
THE RHYTHM – CLOCK (28)..............................94
RHYTHM & BLUES ALIBI – GOMEZ (18)............99
RHYTHM AND GREENS – SHADOWS (22) 64
RHYTHM DIVINE – Enrique IGLESIAS (45)........99
THE RHYTHM DIVINE – YELLO featuring Shirley BASSEY (54)............87
RHYTHM IS A DANCER – SNAP (1) 92
RHYTHM IS A MYSTERY – K-KLASS (3) 91
RHYTHM IS GONNA GET YOU – Gloria ESTEFAN and MIAMI SOUND MACHINE (16) 88
RHYTHM NATION – Janet JACKSON (23) 89
RHYTHM OF LIFE – Oleta ADAMS (38) ..90,,91,95
RHYTHM OF LOVE – SCORPIONS (59).............88
RHYTHM OF MY HEART [A] – Rod STEWART (3)..91
RHYTHM OF MY HEART [A] – RUNRIG (24) 96
RHYTHM OF THE BEAST – Nicko McBRAIN (72)91
RHYTHM OF THE JUNGLE – QUICK (41) 82
RHYTHM OF THE NIGHT [A] – DeBARGE (4) 85
RHYTHM OF THE NIGHT [B] – POWERHOUSE (38)..97
THE RHYTHM OF THE NIGHT [C] – CORONA (2)94
RHYTHM OF THE RAIN [A] – CASCADES (5) 63
RHYTHM OF THE RAIN [A] – Jason DONOVAN (9)90
RHYTHM TAKES CONTROL – UNIQUE 3 (41) 90
RHYTHM TALK – JOCKO (56) 80
RIBBON IN THE SKY – Stevie WONDER (45)....82
RICE IS NICE – LEMON PIPERS (41) 68
RICH AH GETTING RICHER – REBEL MC (48)....92
RICH AND STRANGE – CUD (24) 92
RICH IN PARADISE – FPI PROJECT (9).............89
RICH KIDS – RICH KIDS (24) 78
RICH MAN POOR MAN – Jimmy YOUNG (25) ..56
RICHARD III – SUPERGRASS (2) 97
RICCOCHET – B B and Q BAND (71) 87
RICOCHET [A] – Joan REGAN (8)..................53,54
RICOCHET [B] – FAITH NO MORE (27).............95
RIDDIM – US3 (34) 93
RIDDLE – EN VOGUE (33) 00
THE RIDDLE – Nik KERSHAW (3)......................84
RIDDLE ME – UB40 (59) 84
RIDE (EP) – RIDE (71) 90
RIDE A ROCKET – LITHIAM and Sonya MADAN (40)........................97
RIDE A WHITE SWAN – T. REX (2)....................70
RIDE A WILD HORSE – Dee CLARK (16) 75
RIDE AWAY – Roy ORBISON (34) 65
RIDE LIKE THE WIND [A] – Christopher CROSS (69) 80
RIDE LIKE THE WIND [A] – EAST SIDE BEAT (3)91
RIDE LIKE THE WIND [A] – SAXON (52)............88
RIDE MY SEE-SAW – MOODY BLUES (42) 68
RIDE ON BABY – Chris FARLOWE (31).............66
RIDE ON THE RHYTHM – Louie VEGA and Marc ANTHONY (36) ..91,92,98
RIDE ON TIME – BLACK BOX (1) 89,91
RIDE THE BULLET – ARMY OF LOVERS (67) 92
RIDE THE GROOVE – PLAYERS ASSOCIATION (42) 79
RIDE THE LOVE TRAIN – LIGHT OF THE WORLD (49) 81
RIDE THE RHYTHM – Z FACTOR (52) 01
RIDE THE STORM – AKABU featuring Linda CLIFFORD (69) 01
RIDE THE TIGER – BOO RADLEYS (38) 97
RIDE-O-ROCKET – BROTHERS JOHNSON (50) ..78
RIDE WIT ME – NELLY featuring CITY SPUD (3) 01
RIDERS IN THE SKY [A] – RAMRODS (8) 61
RIDERS IN THE SKY [A] – SHADOWS (12) 80
RIDERS ON THE STORM [A] – DOORS (22) 71,76,91
RIDERS ON THE STORM [A] – Annabel LAMB (27)83
RIDICULOUS THOUGHTS – CRANBERRIES (20) 95
RIDING ON A TRAIN – PASADENAS (13) 88
RIDING ON THROUGH – DEEE-LITE (53)............91
RIDING WITH THE ANGELS – SAMSON (55)......81
RIGHT AND EXACT – Chrissy WARD (59) 95,97
RIGHT BACK WHERE WE STARTED FROM [A] – Maxine NIGHTINGALE (8) 75
RIGHT BACK WHERE WE STARTED FROM [A] – SINITTA (4) 89
RIGHT BEFORE MY EYES [A] – Patti DAY (69)..89
RIGHT BEFORE MY EYES [A] – N'N'G featuring KALLAGHAN (12) 00
RIGHT BESIDE YOU – Sophie B HAWKINS (13) 94
RIGHT BETWEEN THE EYES – WAX (60) 86
RIGHT BY YOUR SIDE – EURYTHMICS (10) 83
THE RIGHT COMBINATION – SEIKO and Donnie WAHLBERG (44) 90
THE RIGHT DECISION – JESUS JONES (36) 93
RIGHT HERE [A] – SWV (3) 93
RIGHT HERE [B] – ULTIMATE KAOS (18) 95
RIGHT HERE RIGHT NOW [A] – JESUS JONES (31) 90,91
RIGHT HERE RIGHT NOW [B] – DISCO CITIZENS (40)......................................95
RIGHT HERE RIGHT NOW [C] – FIERCE (25)......99
RIGHT HERE RIGHT NOW [D] – FATBOY SLIM (2) 99
RIGHT HERE WAITING – Richard MARX (2) 89
RIGHT IN THE NIGHT (FALL IN LOVE WITH MUSIC) – JAM & SPOON featuring PLAVKA (10) 94,95
RIGHT IN THE SOCKET – SHALAMAR (44)........80
THE RIGHT KINDA LOVER – Patti LaBELLE (50)94
RIGHT NEXT DOOR (BECAUSE OF ME) – Robert CRAY BAND (50) 87
RIGHT NOW [A] – CREATURES (14) 83
RIGHT NOW [B] – AIRHEAD (50) 92
RIGHT NOW [C] – ATOMIC KITTEN (10) 99
RIGHT ON! – SILICONE SOUL featuring Louise Clare MARSHALL (15) 01
RIGHT ON TRACK – BREAKFAST CLUB (54)......87
RIGHT SAID FRED – Bernard CRIBBINS (10) 62
THE RIGHT STUFF [A] – Bryan FERRY (37) 87
THE RIGHT STUFF [B] – Vanessa WILLIAMS (62).............................88,89
THE RIGHT THING – SIMPLY RED (11) 87
THE RIGHT THING TO DO – Carly SIMON (17)..73
THE RIGHT THING TO SAY – Nat 'King' COLE (42)..62
THE RIGHT TIME – ULTRA (28) 98
THE RIGHT TO LOVE – David WHITFIELD (30)..58
RIKKI DON'T LOSE THAT NUMBER [A] – STEELY DAN (58)..79
RIKKI DON'T LOSE THAT NUMBER [A] – Tom ROBINSON (58) 84
RING A DING GIRL – Ronnie CARROLL (46) 62
RING MY BELL [A] – Anita WARD (1) 79
RING MY BELL [A] – JAZZY JEFF & the FRESH PRINCE (53) 91
RING MY BELL [B] – Monie LOVE vs ADEVA (20) 91
RING OF BRIGHT WATER – Val DOONICAN (48)69
RING OF FIRE [A] – Duane EDDY and the REBELS (17) 61
RING OF FIRE [B] – ANIMALS (35)....................69
RING OF ICE – Jennifer RUSH (14)....................85
RING OUT SOLSTICE BELLS (EP) – JETHRO TULL (28) 76
RING RING [A] – ABBA (32) 74
RING RING [B] – DOLLAR (61) 82
RING RING RING – Aaron SOUL (14) 01
RING RING RING (HA HA HEY) – DE LA SOUL (10)91
RING THE BELLS – JAMES (37) 92
RINGO – Lorne GREENE (22)............................64
RIO [A] – Michael NESMITH (28) 77
RIO [B] – DURAN DURAN (9) 82
RIP IT UP [A] – LITTLE RICHARD (30)..........56,77
RIP IT UP [A] – Bill HALEY and his COMETS (4) ..56
RIP IT UP [A] – Elvis PRESLEY (27)..................57
RIP IT UP [B] – ORANGE JUICE (8)....................83
RIP PRODUCTIONS – RIP PRODUCTIONS (58) 97
RIPGROOVE – DOUBLE 99 (14) 97
RIPPED IN 2 MINUTES – A vs B (49) 98
RISE [A] – Herb ALPERT (13) 79
RISE [B] – PUBLIC IMAGE LTD (11) 86
RISE [C] – ZION TRAIN (61) 96
RISE [D] – Eddie AMADOR (19) 00
RISE [E] – GABRIELLE (1)..................................00
RISE [F] – SOUL PROVIDERS featuring Michelle SHELLERS (59)..................01
THE RISE AND FALL OF FLINGEL BUNT – SHADOWS (5) 64
RISE AND SHINE – CARDIGANS (29) 96
RISE 'IN – Steve LAWLER (50) 00
RISE TO THE OCCASION – CLIMIE FISHER (10) 87
RISE UP – JAMAICA UNITED (54)......................98
RISIN' TO THE TOP – Keni BURKE (70)............92
RISING SIGN – HURRICANE #1 (47)..................98
RISING SUN [A] – MEDICINE HEAD (11)............73
RISING SUN [B] – FARM (48)............................92
RISINGSON – MASSIVE ATTACK (11) 97
THE RIVER [A] – Bruce SPRINGSTEEN (35) 81
THE RIVER [B] – KING TRIGGER (57)................82
THE RIVER [C] – TOTAL CONTRAST (44) 86
THE RIVER [D] – BEAUTIFUL SOUTH (59) 00
RIVER DEEP MOUNTAIN HIGH [A] – Ike and Tina TURNER (3) 66,69
RIVER DEEP MOUNTAIN HIGH [A] – SUPREMES and the FOUR TOPS (11)..............71
THE RIVER (LE COLLINE SONO IN FIORE) – Ken DODD (3) 65
THE RIVER OF DREAMS – Billy JOEL (3) 93
RIVER OF PAIN – THUNDER (31) 95
RIVER STAY 'WAY FROM MY DOOR – Frank SINATRA (18)..60
THE RIVERBOAT SONG – OCEAN COLOUR SCENE (15) 96
RIVERDANCE – Bill WHELAN featuring ANUNA and the RTE CONCERT ORCHESTRA (9) 94
RIVERS OF BABYLON – BONEY M (1) 78
THE RIVERS OF BELIEF – ENIGMA (68) 92
THE RIVER'S RUN DRY – Vince HILL (41) 62
ROACHES – TRANCESETTERS (55)....................00
ROAD RAGE – CATATONIA (5) 98
ROAD RUNNER – Junior WALKER and the ALL-STARS (12) 69
THE ROAD TO HELL (PART 2) – Chris REA (10) 89
THE ROAD TO MANDALAY – Robbie WILLIAMS (1) 01
ROAD TO NOWHERE – TALKING HEADS (6)......85
ROAD TO OUR DREAM – T'PAU (42) 88
ROAD TO YOUR SOUL – ALL ABOUT EVE (37) 89
ROAD TRIPPIN' – RED HOT CHILI PEPPERS (30)..01
ROADBLOCK – STOCK AITKEN WATERMAN (13) 87
ROADHOUSE MEDLEY (ANNIVERSARY WALTZ PART 25) – STATUS QUO (21) 92
ROADRUNNER – Jonathan RICHMAN and the MODERN LOVERS (11) 77
ROAM – B-52's (17) 90
ROBERT DE NIRO'S WAITING – BANANARAMA (3) 84
ROBIN HOOD [A] – Dick JAMES (14) 56
ROBIN HOOD [A] – Gary MILLER (10) 56
ROBIN (THE HOODED MAN) – CLANNAD (42)..84
ROBIN'S RETURN – Neville DICKIE (33) 69
ROBOT – TORNADOS (17) 63
ROBOT MAN – Connie FRANCIS (2)..................60
ROBOT WARS (ANDROID LOVE) – SIR KILLALOT vs ROBO BABE (51) 00
THE ROBOTS – KRAFTWERK (20)......................91
ROCCO – DEATH IN VEGAS (51) 97
ROCHDALE COWBOY – Mike HARDING (22) 75
ROC-IN-IT – Deejay PUNK-ROC vs ONYX (59) ..99
THE ROCK [A] – DELAKOTA (60) 98
THE ROCK [B] – ALARM (31) 89
ROCK A HULA BABY – Elvis PRESLEY (1) 62
ROCK AND A HARD PLACE – ROLLING STONES (63) 89
ROCK AND ROLL DREAMS COME THROUGH – MEAT LOAF (11)..94
ROCK AND ROLL IS DEAD – Lenny KRAVITZ (22) 95
ROCK AND ROLL (IS GONNA SET THE NIGHT ON FIRE) – PRETTY BOY FLOYD (75) 90
ROCK AND ROLL MUSIC – BEACH BOYS (36) ..76
ROCK AND ROLL (PARTS 1 & 2) – Gary GLITTER (2)..72
ROCK AND ROLL WALTZ – Kay STARR (1) 56
ROCK AROUND THE CLOCK [A] – Bill HALEY and his COMETS (1) 55,56,57,68,74
ROCK AROUND THE CLOCK [A] – TELEX (34)....79
ROCK AROUND THE CLOCK [A] – TEN POLE TUDOR (21)....................................79
ROCK BOTTOM [A] – Lynsey DE PAUL (19) 77
ROCK BOTTOM [B] – BABYFACE (50)................94
ROCK DA FUNKY BEATS – PUBLIC DOMAIN featuring Chuck D (19)....................................01
ROCK DA HOUSE – TALL PAUL (12) 97,01
ROCK DJ – Robbie WILLIAMS (1) 00
ROCK HARD – Suzi QUATRO (68) 80
R.O.C.K. IN THE USA – John Cougar MELLENCAMP (67) 86
ROCK IS DEAD – MARILYN MANSON (23) 99
ROCK ISLAND LINE [A] – Lonnie DONEGAN (8) 56
ROCK ISLAND LINE [A] – Stan FREBERG (24) ..56
ROCK LOBSTER – B-52's (12) 79,86

SHINE EYE GAL – **Shabba RANKS** (46) 95
SHINE LIKE A STAR – **BERRI** (20) 95
SHINE ON [A] – **HOUSE OF LOVE** (20).............90
SHINE ON [B] – **DEGREES OF MOTION featuring BITI** (8) ..92,94
SHINE ON ME – **LOVESTATION** (71) 93
SHINE ON SILVER SUN – **STRAWBS** (34)..........73
SHINE (SOMEONE WHO NEEDS ME) – **MONACO** (55) 97
SHINEON – **SCOTT & LEON** (34) 01
SHINING LIGHT – **ASH** (8) 01
SHINING ROAD – **CRANES** (57) 94
SHINING STAR – **MANHATTANS** (45) 80
SHINING STAR (EP) – **INXS** (27).......................91
SHINOBI VS DRAGON NINJA – **LOSTPROPHETS** (41) 01
SHINY HAPPY PEOPLE – **R.E.M.** (6)..................91
SHINY SHINY – **HAYSI FANTAYZEE** (16)............83
SHIP AHOY – **MARXMAN** (64) 93
SHIP OF FOOLS [A] – **WORLD PARTY** (42) 87
SHIP OF FOOLS [B] – **ERASURE** (6).................88
SHIPBUILDING [A] – **Robert WYATT** (35) 83
SHIPBUILDING [A] – **Tasmin ARCHER** (40)........94
SHIPS IN THE NIGHT – **BE BOP DELUXE** (23) ..76
SHIPS (WHERE WERE YOU) – **BIG COUNTRY** (29) 93
SHIPWRECKED – **GENESIS** (54) 97
SHIRALEE – **Tommy STEELE** (11) 57
SHIRLEY – **Shakin' STEVENS** (6) 82
SHIVER [A] – **George BENSON** (19) 86
SHIVER [B] – **S-J** (59)...98
SHIVER [C] – **COLDPLAY** (35)............................00
SHIVERING SAND – **MEGA CITY FOUR** (35) 92
SHO' YOU RIGHT – **Barry WHITE** (14) 87
SHOCK THE MONKEY – **Peter GABRIEL** (58) 82
SHOCK TO THE SYSTEM – **Billy IDOL** (30) 93
SHOCK YOUR MAMA – **Debbie GIBSON** (74)....93
SHOCKAHOLIC – **KINKY MACHINE** (70) 93
SHOCKED – **Kylie MINOGUE** (6)........................91
SHOES – **REPARATA and the DELRONS** (43) ..75
SHOO BE DOO BE DOO DA DAY – **Stevie WONDER** (46)......................................68
SHOO DOO FU FU OOH – **Lenny WILLIAMS** (38) 77
SHOOP – **SALT-N-PEPA** (13)........................93,94
THE SHOOP SHOOP SONG (IT'S IN HIS KISS) – **CHER** (1)...91
SHOORAH SHOORAH – **Betty WRIGHT** (27) 75
SHOOT ALL THE CLOWNS – **Bruce DICKINSON** (37) 94
SHOOT ME (WITH YOUR LOVE) – **Tasha THOMAS** (59) 79
SHOOT ME WITH YOUR LOVE – **D:REAM** (7)....95
SHOOT SHOOT – **UFO** (48) 79
SHOOTING FROM MY HEART – **BIG BAM BOO** (61)89
SHOOTING FROM THE HEART – **Cliff RICHARD** (51)84
SHOOTING STAR [A] – **BOYZONE** (2) 97
SHOOTING STAR [B] – **DOLLAR** (14) 78
SHOPLIFTERS OF THE WORLD UNITE – **SMITHS** (12) 87
SHOPPING – **SUPERSISTER** (36) 01
SHORLEY WALL – **OOBERMAN** (47)..................00
SHORT CUT TO SOMEWHERE – **FISH** (75)........86
SHORT DICK MAN – **20 FINGERS** (21) 94
SHORT FAT FANNIE – **Larry WILLIAMS** (21) 57
SHORT SHORT MAN – **20 FINGERS** (11)............95
SHORT SKIRT LONG JACKET – **CAKE** (63)..........01
SHORT'NIN' BREAD – **VISCOUNTS** (16) 60
SHORT'NIN' BREAD ROCK – **Tony CROMBIE and his ROCKETS** (25) 56
SHORTSHARPSHOCK (EP) – **THERAPY?** (9) 93
SHORTY – **WANNADIES** (41) 97
SHORTY (GOT HER EYES ON ME) – **Donell JONES** (19) 00
SHORTY (YOU KEEP PLAYING WITH MY MIND) – **IMAJIN featuring Keith MURRAY** (22) 98
SHOT BY BOTH SIDES – **MAGAZINE** (41)..........78
SHOT DOWN IN THE NIGHT – **HAWKWIND** (59)80
SHOT IN THE DARK [A] – **Ozzy OSBOURNE** (20)..86
SHOT IN THE DARK [B] – **DJ HYPE** (63)...........93
SHOT OF POISON – **Lita FORD** (63) 92
SHOT OF RHYTHM AND BLUES – **Johnny KIDD and the PIRATES** (48) 63
SHOTGUN WEDDING [A] – **Roy C** (6) 66,72
SHOTGUN WEDDING [A] – **Rod STEWART** (21) 93
SHOULD I DO IT? – **POINTER SISTERS** (50)......81
SHOULD I EVER (FALL IN LOVE) – **NIGHTCRAWLERS featuring John REID** (34)....96
SHOULD I STAY – **GABRIELLE** (13)....................00
SHOULD I STAY OR SHOULD I GO – **CLASH** (1) 82,91
SHOULDER HOLSTER – **MORCHEEBA** (53)........97
SHOULDN'T DO THAT – **KAJAGOOGOO** (63) 85
SHOULD'VE KNOWN BETTER – **Richard MARX** (50)88
SHOUT [A] – **LULU** (7).................................64,86
SHOUT [A] – **Louchie LOU and Michie ONE** (7)93
SHOUT [B] – **TEARS FOR FEARS** (4) 84
SHOUT [C] – **ANT & DEC** (10) 97
SHOUT SHOUT (KNOCK YOURSELF OUT) – **Rocky SHARPE and the REPLAYS** (19) 82
SHOUT TO THE TOP [A] – **Fire ISLAND featuring Loleatta HOLLOWAY** (23)................98
SHOUT TO THE TOP [A] – **STYLE COUNCIL** (7) 84
SHOUTING FOR THE GUNNERS – **ARSENAL FC** (34) 93
THE SHOW – **Doug E FRESH and the GET FRESH CREW** (7)85
SHOW A LITTLE LOVE – **ULTIMATE KAOS** (23) 95
SHOW ME [A] – **DEXY'S MIDNIGHT RUNNERS** (16)81
SHOW ME [B] – **Lindy LAYTON** (47) 93
SHOW ME [C] – **Ultra NATÉ** (62) 94
SHOW ME [D] – **Dana DAWSON** (28)................96
SHOW ME GIRL – **HERMAN'S HERMITS** (19) 64
SHOW ME HEAVEN [A] – **Maria McKEE** (1)........90
SHOW ME HEAVEN [A] – **Tina ARENA** (29) 95
SHOW ME HEAVEN [A] – **CHIMIRA** (70) 97
SHOW ME LOVE [A] – **Robin S** (6) 93,97
SHOW ME LOVE [B] – **ROBYN** (8) 98
SHOW ME MARY – **CATHERINE WHEEL** (62) 93
SHOW ME THE MEANING OF BEING LONELY – **BACKSTREET BOYS** (3) 00
SHOW ME THE MONEY – **ARCHITECHS** (20) 01
SHOW ME THE WAY [A] – **Peter FRAMPTON** (10) 76
SHOW ME THE WAY [B] – **OSMOND BOYS** (60)..92
SHOW ME YOU'RE A WOMAN – **MUD** (8) 75
THE SHOW MUST GO ON [A] – **Leo SAYER** (2) 73
THE SHOW MUST GO ON [B] – **QUEEN** (16)......91
THE SHOW (THEME FROM 'CONNIE') – **Rebecca STORM** (22) 85
SHOW YOU THE WAY TO GO [A] – **Dannii MINOGUE** (30) 92
SHOW YOU THE WAY TO GO [A] – **JACKSONS** (1) 77
SHOWDOWN – **ELECTRIC LIGHT ORCHESTRA** (12) 73
SHOWER YOUR LOVE – **KULA SHAKER** (14)......99
SHOWING OUT (GET FRESH AT THE WEEKEND) – **MEL and KIM** (3) 86
SHOWROOM DUMMIES – **KRAFTWERK** (25) 82
THE SHUFFLE – **Van McCOY** (4) 77
SHUT 'EM DOWN – **PUBLIC ENEMY** (21) 92
SHUT UP – **MADNESS** (7) 81
SHUT UP AND DANCE – **AEROSMITH** (24)........94
SHUT UP AND FORGET ABOUT IT – **DANE** (9) ..01
SHUT UP AND KISS ME – **Mary-Chapin CARPENTER** (35) 95
SHUT UP (AND SLEEP WITH ME) – **SIN WITH SEBASTIAN** (44)........................95,96
SHUT YOUR MOUTH – **MADE IN LONDON** (74) 00
SHY BOY – **BANANARAMA** (4)..........................82
SHY GIRL – **Mark WYNTER** (28)........................63
SHY GUY – **Diana KING** (2) 95
(SI SI) JE SUIS UN ROCK STAR – **Bill WYMAN** (14) 81
SI TU DOIS PARTIR – **FAIRPORT CONVENTION** (21)............................69
SICK AND TIRED [A] – **Fats DOMINO** (26) 58
SICK AND TIRED [B] – **CARDIGANS** (34) 95
SICK MAN BLUES – **GOODIES** (4) 75
SICK OF DRUGS – **WILDHEARTS** (14)...............96
SICK OF GOODBYES – **SPARKLEHORSE** (57)....98
SICK OF IT – **PRIMITIVES** (24).........................89
SIDE BY SIDE – **Kay STARR** (7) 53
SIDE SADDLE – **Russ CONWAY** (1) 59
SIDE SHOW [A] – **CHANTER SISTERS** (43)........76
SIDE SHOW [B] – **WENDY and LISA** (49).........88
SIDE – **TRAVIS** (14) 01
THE SIDEBOARD SONG (GOT MY BEER IN THE SIDEBOARD HERE) – **CHAS and DAVE** (55)..79
SIDESHOW – **Barry BIGGS** (3) 76
SIDEWALK TALK – **JELLYBEAN** (47) 86
SIDEWALKING – **JESUS AND MARY CHAIN** (30) 88
THE SIDEWINDER SLEEPS TONITE – **R.E.M.** (17)..93
SIGHT FOR SORE EYES – **M PEOPLE** (6) 94
THE SIGN – **ACE OF BASE** (2) 94
SIGN 'O' THE TIMES – **PRINCE** (10)..................87
SIGN OF THE TIMES [A] – **Bryan FERRY** (37)....78
SIGN OF THE TIMES [B] – **BELLE STARS** (3) 83
SIGN OF THE TIMES [C] – **GRANDMASTER FLASH, Melle MEL and the FURIOUS FIVE** (72)..........85
A SIGN OF THE TIMES – **Petula CLARK** (49) 66
SIGN YOUR NAME – **Terence Trent D'ARBY** (2)88
THE SIGNATURE TUNE OF 'THE ARMY GAME' – **Michael MEDWIN, Bernard BRESSLAW, Alfie BASS and Leslie FYSON** (5) 58
SIGNED SEALED DELIVERED I'M YOURS [A] – **Stevie WONDER** (15) 70
SIGNED SEALED DELIVERED (I'M YOURS) [A] – **BOYSTOWN GANG** (50) 82
SIGNS... – **BLAMELESS** (49) 96
SIGNS [A] – **TESLA** (70) 91
SIGNS [B] – **DJ BADMARSH & SHRI featuring UK APACHE** (63).............................01
SILENCE – **DELERIUM** (73) 99,00
THE SILENCE – **Mike KOGLIN** (20)....................98
SILENCE IS GOLDEN – **TREMELOES** (1) 67
SILENT ALL THESE YEARS – **Tori AMOS** (26) ..91,92
SILENT LUCIDITY – **QUEENSRYCHE** (18) 91,92
SILENT NIGHT [A] – **Bing CROSBY** (8) 52
SILENT NIGHT [A] – **DICKIES** (47) 78
SILENT NIGHT [A] – **BROS** (2) 88
SILENT NIGHT [A] – **Sinead O'CONNOR** (60) 91
SILENT NIGHT – SEVEN O'CLOCK NEWS [A] – **SIMON and GARFUNKEL** (30)..........................91
SILENT RUNNING – **MIKE and the MECHANICS** (61) 96
SILENT RUNNING (ON DANGEROUS GROUND) – **MIKE and the MECHANICS** (21) 86
SILENT SCREAM – **Richard MARX** (32) 94
SILENT VOICE – **INNOCENCE** (37) 90
SILENT WORDS – **Jan JOHNSTON** (57) 01
SILENTLY BAD MINDED – **PRESSURE DROP** (53) 98
SILHOUETTES [A] – **HERMAN'S HERMITS** (3)....65
SILHOUETTES [A] – **Cliff RICHARD** (10) 90
SILK PYJAMAS – **Thomas DOLBY** (62).............92
SILLY GAMES [A] – **Janet KAY** (2)................79,90
SILLY GAMES [A] – **Lindy LAYTON featuring Janet KAY** (22) 90
SILLY LOVE – **10 CC** (24) 74
SILLY LOVE SONGS – **Paul McCARTNEY** (2) 76
SILLY THING – **SEX PISTOLS** (6) 79
SILVER [A] – **ECHO and the BUNNYMEN** (30) ..84
SILVER [B] – **MOIST** (50) 95
SILVER AND GOLD – **ASAP** (60)........................89
SILVER DREAM MACHINE (PART 1) – **David ESSEX** (4) 80
SILVER LADY – **David SOUL** (1) 77
SILVER LINING – **STIFF LITTLE FINGERS** (68)....81
SILVER MACHINE – **HAWKWIND** (3)........72,78,83
SILVER SCREEN SHOWER SCENE – **FELIX DA HOUSECAT** (55) 01
SILVER SHADOW – **ATLANTIC STARR** (41) 85
SILVER SHORTS – **WEDDING PRESENT** (14) 92
SILVER STAR – **FOUR SEASONS** (3)..................76
SILVER THUNDERBIRD – **Marc COHN** (54) 91
SILVERMAC – **WESTWORLD** (42) 87
SILVERY RAIN – **Cliff RICHARD** (27) 71
SIMBA GROOVE – **HI POWER** (73)....................90
SIMON SAYS [A] – **Pharoahe MONCH** (24) 00
SIMON SAYS [B] – **1910 FRUITGUM CO** (2) 68
SIMON SMITH AND HIS AMAZING DANCING BEAR – **Alan PRICE** (4) 67
SIMON TEMPLAR – **SPLODGENESSABOUNDS** (7)80
SIMPLE AS THAT – **Huey LEWIS and the NEWS** (47)....................87
SIMPLE GAME – **FOUR TOPS** (3) 71
SIMPLE KIND OF LIFE – **NO DOUBT** (69)..........00
SIMPLE LIFE – **Elton JOHN** (44).........................93
SIMPLE SIMON (YOU GOTTA REGARD) – **MANTRONIX** (72)..88
SIMPLE SINCERITY – **RADISH** (50) 97
SIMPLE THINGS – **SAW DOCTORS** (56)............97
THE SIMPLE THINGS – **Joe COCKER** (17) 94
THE SIMPLE TRUTH (A CHILD IS BORN) – **Chris DE BURGH** (36)............................87,88,91
SIMPLY IRRESISTABLE – **Robert PALMER** (44) 88
SIN – **NINE INCH NAILS** (35) 91
SINBAD QUEST – **SYSTEM 7** (74) 93
SINCE DAY ONE – **Teena MARIE** (69) 90

SINCE I DON'T HAVE YOU [A] – Art GARFUNKEL (38) 79
SINCE I DON'T HAVE YOU [A] – GUNS N' ROSES (10) 94
SINCE I LEFT YOU – AVALANCHES (16) 01
SINCE I MET YOU BABY [A] – Gary MOORE and BB KING (59) 92
SINCE I MET YOU BABY [A] – UB40 and LADY SAW (40) 01
SINCE YESTERDAY – STRAWBERRY SWITCHBLADE (5) 84
SINCE YOU'RE GONE – CARS (37) 82
SINCE YOU'VE BEEN GONE [A] – Aretha FRANKLIN (47) 68
SINCE YOU'VE BEEN GONE [B] – RAINBOW (6) 79
SINCERE – MJ COLE (13) 98,00
SINCERELY – McGUIRE SISTERS (14) 55
SINFUL – Pete WYLIE (13) 86,91
SING – TRAVIS (3) 01
SING A HAPPY SONG [A] – George McCRAE (38) 75
SING A HAPPY SONG [B] – O'JAYS (39) 79
SING A LITTLE SONG – Desmond DEKKER and the ACES (16) 75
SING-A-LONG [A] – A (57) 98
SING-A-LONG [B] – SHANKS & BIGFOOT (12) ..00
SING A SONG – Byron STINGILY (38) 97
SING A SONG (BREAK IT DOWN) – MANTRONIX (61) 88
SING A SONG OF FREEDOM – Cliff RICHARD (13) 71
SING AND SHOUT – SECOND IMAGE (53) 84
SING BABY SING – STYLISTICS (3) 75
SING DON'T SPEAK – BLACKFOOT SUE (36) 72
SING FOR EVER – ST PHILIPS CHOIR (49) 87
SING HALLELUJAH! – DR ALBAN (16) 93
SING IT AGAIN WITH JOE – Joe 'Mr Piano' HENDERSON (18) 55
SING IT BACK – MOLOKO (4) 99
SING IT (THE HALLELUJAH SONG) – MOZAIC (14) 95
SING IT TO YOU (DEE-DOOB-DEE-DOO) – Lavinia JONES (45) 95
SING IT WITH JOE – Joe 'Mr Piano' HENDERSON (14) 55
SING LIKE AN ANGEL – Jerry LORDAN (36) 60
SING LITTLE BIRDIE – Pearl CARR and Teddy JOHNSON (12) 59
SING ME – BROTHERS (8) 77
SING ME AN OLD FASHIONED SONG – Billie Jo SPEARS (34) 76
SING (OOH-EE-OOH) – Vivienne McKONE (47) 92
SING OUR OWN SONG – UB40 (5) 86
SING SING – GAZ (60) 79
SING UP FOR THE CHAMPIONS – REDS UNITED (12) 97
SING YOUR LIFE – MORRISSEY (33) 91
SINGALONG-A-SANTA – SANTA CLAUS and the CHRISTMAS TREES (19) 82
SINGALONG-A-SANTA AGAIN – SANTA CLAUS and the CHRISTMAS TREES (39) 83
THE SINGER SANG HIS SONG – BEE GEES (25) 68
SINGIN' IN THE RAIN PART 1 – Sheila B DEVOTION (11) 78
THE SINGING DOGS (MEDLEY) – SINGING DOGS (13) 55
SINGING IN MY SLEEP – SEMISONIC (39) 00
SINGING THE BLUES [A] – Guy MITCHELL (1) ..56
SINGING THE BLUES [A] – Tommy STEELE (1) 56,57
SINGING THE BLUES [A] – Dave EDMUNDS (28) 80
SINGING THE BLUES [A] – Daniel O'DONNELL (23) 94
SINGLE [A] – EVERYTHING BUT THE GIRL (20) 96
SINGLE [B] – PET SHOP BOYS (14) 96
THE SINGLE – RISE (70) 94
SINGLE GIRL [A] – Sandy POSEY (15) 67,75
SINGLE GIRL [B] – LUSH (21) 96
SINGLE LIFE – CAMEO (15) 85
THE SINGLES 1981-83 – BAUHAUS (52) 83
SINK THE BISMARCK – Don LANG (43) 60
SINK TO THE BOTTOM – FOUNTAINS OF WAYNE (42) 97
SINNER – Neil FINN (39) 98
SINS OF THE FAMILY – PF SLOAN (38) 65
SIPPIN' SODA – Guy MITCHELL (11) 54
SIR DANCEALOT – OLYMPIC RUNNERS (35) 79
SIR DUKE – Stevie WONDER (2) 77
SISSYNECK – BECK (30) 97
SISTA SISTA – Beverley KNIGHT (31) 99
SISTER [A] – BROS (10) 89
SISTER [B] – SISTER 2 SISTER (18) 00
SISTER DEW – dEUS (62) 99
SISTER FRICTION – HAYSI FANTAYZEE (62) 83
SISTER HAVANA – URGE OVERKILL (67) 93
SISTER JANE – NEW WORLD (9) 72
SISTER MOON – TRANSVISION VAMP (41) 88
SISTER OF MERCY – THOMPSON TWINS (11) ..84
SISTER PAIN – ELECTRAFIXION (27) 96
SISTER SISTER – SISTER BLISS (34) 00
SISTER SURPRISE – Gary NUMAN (32) 83
THE SISTERS (EP) – PULP (19) 94
SISTERS ARE DOIN' IT FOR THEMSELVES – EURYTHMICS and Aretha FRANKLIN (9) 85
SIT AND WAIT – Sydney YOUNGBLOOD (16) 89
SIT DOWN – JAMES (2) 91,98
SIT DOWN AND CRY – Erroll DUNKLEY (52) 80
THE SIT SONG – BARRON KNIGHTS (44) 80
SITTIN' ON A FENCE – TWICE AS MUCH (25) ..66
(SITTIN' ON) THE DOCK OF THE BAY – Otis REDDING (3) 68
SITTIN' UP IN MY ROOM – BRANDY (30) 96
SITTING AT HOME – HONEYCRACK (32) 95,96
SITTING DOWN HERE – Lene MARLIN (5) 00
SITTING IN THE PARK – Georgie FAME (12) 66
SITTING ON THE TOP OF THE WORLD – LIVERPOOL FC (50) 86
SITUATION – YAZOO (14) 90
SIX – MANSUN (16) 99
SIX FEET DEEP (EP) – GRAVEDIGGAZ (64) 95
SIX MILLION STEPS (WEST RUNS SOUTH) – Rahni HARRIS and F.L.O. (43) 78
SIX PACK – POLICE (17) 80
THE SIX TEENS – SWEET (9) 74
634-5789 – Wilson PICKETT (36) 66
6 UNDERGROUND – SNEAKER PIMPS (9) 96,97
SIXTEEN – MUSICAL YOUTH (23) 84
16 BARS – STYLISTICS (7) 76
SIXTEEN REASONS – Connie STEVENS (9) 60
SIXTEEN TONS [A] – Frankie LAINE (10) 56
SIXTEEN TONS [A] – Tennessee Ernie FORD (1) 56
THE 6TH SENSE – COMMON (56) 00
THE SIXTH SENSE – VARIOUS ARTISTS (MONTAGES) (49) 90
60 MILES AN HOUR – NEW ORDER (29) 01
68 GUNS – ALARM (17) 83
SIXTY MILE SMILE – 3 COLOURS RED (20) 97
SIXTY MINUTE MAN – TRAMMPS (40) 75
69 POLICE – David HOLMES (53) 00
THE SIZE OF A COW – WONDER STUFF (5) 91
SKA TRAIN – BEATMASTERS featuring Betty BOO (7) 89
SKAT STRUT – MC SKAT KAT and the STRAY MOB (64) 91
SKATEAWAY – DIRE STRAITS (37) 81
SKELETONS – Stevie WONDER (59) 87
SKIFFLE SESSION (EP) – Lonnie DONEGAN (20) 56
SKIING IN THE SNOW – WIGAN'S OVATION (12) 75
SKIN – CHARLOTTE (56) 99
SKIN DEEP [A] – Duke ELLINGTON (7) 54
SKIN DEEP [A] – Ted HEATH (9) 54
SKIN DEEP [B] – STRANGLERS (15) 84
THE SKIN GAME – Gary NUMAN (68) 92
SKIN O' MY TEETH – MEGADETH (13) 92
SKIN ON SKIN – GRACE (21) 96
SKIN TRADE – DURAN DURAN (22) 87
THE SKIN UP (EP) – SKIN (67) 93
SKINHEAD MOONSTOMP – SYMARIP (54) 80
SKIP TO MY LU – LISA LISA (34) 94
SKUNK FUNK – GALLIANO (41) 92
SKWEEZE ME PLEEZE ME – SLADE (1) 73
SKY – SONIQUE (2) 00
A SKY BLUE SHIRT AND A RAINBOW TIE – Norman BROOKS (17) 54
SKY HIGH [A] – JIGSAW (9) 75
SKY HIGH [A] – NEWTON (56) 95
SKY PILOT – ANIMALS (40) 68
SKY PLUS – NYLON MOON (43) 96
SKYDIVE – FREEFALL featuring Jan JOHNSTON (43) ..98,00,01
THE SKYE BOAT SONG – Roger WHITTAKER and Des O'CONNOR (10) ..86
SKYLARK – Michael HOLLIDAY (39) 60
SKY'S THE LIMIT – NOTORIOUS B.I.G. (35) 98
SKYWRITER – JACKSONS (25) 73
SLADE ALIVE AT READING '80 (EP) – SLADE (44) 80
SLAIN BY ELF – URUSEI YATSURA (63) 98
SLAM [A] – HUMANOID (54) 89
SLAM [B] – ONYX (31) 93
SLAM DUNK (DA FUNK) – FIVE (10) 97
SLAM JAM – WWF SUPERSTARS (4) 92,93
SLANG – DEF LEPPARD (17) 96
SLAP AND TICKLE – SQUEEZE (24) 79
SLASH 'N' BURN – MANIC STREET PREACHERS (20) 92,97
SLAVE NEW WORLD – SEPULTURA (46) 94
SLAVE TO LOVE – Bryan FERRY (10) 85
SLAVE TO THE GRIND – SKID ROW (43) 91
SLAVE TO THE RHYTHM – Grace JONES (12) ..85,94
SLAVE TO THE VIBE – AFTERSHOCK (11) 93
SLAVE TO THE WAGE – PLACEBO (19) 00
SLAVES NO MORE – BLOW MONKEYS (73) 89
SLEAZY BED TRACK – BLUETONES (35) 98
SLEDGEHAMMER – Peter GABRIEL (4) 86
SLEDGER – PORN KINGS (71) 01
SLEEP – MARION (17) 95,96
SLEEP ALONE – WONDER STUFF (43) 91
SLEEP FREAK – HEAVY STEREO (46) 95
SLEEP NOW IN THE FIRE – RAGE AGAINST THE MACHINE (43) 00
SLEEP ON THE LEFT SIDE – CORNERSHOP (23) ..98
SLEEP TALK – Alyson WILLIAMS (17) 89
SLEEP WALK – SANTO and JOHNNY (22) 59
SLEEP WELL TONIGHT – GENE (36) 94
SLEEP WITH ME – BIRDLAND (32) 90
SLEEPER – AUDIOWEB (50) 95,96
SLEEPIN' ON THE JOB – GILLAN (55) 80
SLEEPING BAG – ZZ TOP (27) 85
SLEEPING IN – MENSWEAR (24) 95
SLEEPING IN MY CAR – ROXETTE (14) 94
SLEEPING SATELLITE – Tasmin ARCHER (1) 92,93
SLEEPING WITH THE LIGHTS ON – Curtis STIGERS (53) 92
SLEEPING WITH VICTOR – Lynden David HALL (49) 00
SLEEPWALK – ULTRAVOX (29) 80
SLEEPY JOE – HERMAN'S HERMITS (12) 68
SLEEPY SHORES – Johnny PEARSON (8) 71
SLICE OF DA PIE – Monie LOVE (29) 00
SLID – FLUKE (59) 93
SLIDE [A] – RAH BAND (50) 81
SLIDE [B] – GOO GOO DOLLS (43) 99
SLIGHT RETURN – BLUETONES (2) 96
THE SLIGHTEST TOUCH – FIVE STAR (4) 87
SLIP AND DIP – COFFEE (57) 80
SLIP AND SLIDE – MEDICINE HEAD (22) 74
(SLIP & SLIDE) SUICIDE – KOSHEEN (50) 01
SLIP SLIDIN' AWAY – Paul SIMON (36) 77
SLIP YOUR DISC TO THIS – HEATWAVE (15) 77
SLIPPERY PEOPLE – TALKING HEADS (68) 84
SLIPPIN' – DMX (30) 99
SLIPPING AWAY – Dave EDMUNDS (60) 83
SLOOP JOHN B – BEACH BOYS (2) 66
SLOPPY HEART – FRAZIER CHORUS (73) 89
SLOW AND SEXY – Shabba RANKS featuring Johnny GILL (17) 92
SLOW DOWN [A] – John MILES (10) 77
SLOW DOWN [B] – LOOSE ENDS (27) 86
SLOW EMOTION REPLAY – The THE (35) 93
SLOW FLOW – BRAXTONS (26) 97
SLOW IT DOWN – EAST 17 (13) 93
SLOW MOTION – ULTRAVOX (33) 81
SLOW RIVERS – Elton JOHN and Cliff RICHARD (44) 86
SLOW TRAIN TO DAWN – The THE (64) 87
SLOW TRAIN TO PARADISE – TAVARES (62) 78
SLOW TWISTIN' – Chubby CHECKER (23) 62
SLOWDIVE – SIOUXSIE and the BANSHEES (41) ..82
SLOWHAND – POINTER SISTERS (10) 81
SLY – MASSIVE ATTACK (24) 94
SMACK MY BITCH UP – PRODIGY (8) 97
SMALL ADS – SMALL ADS (63) 81
SMALL BIT OF LOVE – SAW DOCTORS (24) 94
SMALL BLUE THING – Suzanne VEGA (65) 86
SMALL SAD SAM – Phil McLEAN (34) 62
SMALL TOWN – John Cougar MELLENCAMP (53) 86
SMALL TOWN BOY – UK (74) 96
A SMALL VICTORY – FAITH NO MORE (29) 92
SMALLTOWN BOY – BRONSKI BEAT (3) 84,91
SMALLTOWN CREED – KANE GANG (60) 84
SMARTY PANTS – FIRST CHOICE (9) 73
SMASH IT UP – DAMNED (35) 79
SMASH SUMTHIN' – REDMAN featuring Adam F (11) 01
S.M.D.U. – BROCK LANDARS (49) 98
SMELLS LIKE NIRVANA – Weird Al YANKOVIC (58) 92
SMELLS LIKE TEEN SPIRIT [A] – NIRVANA (7) ..91
SMELLS LIKE TEEN SPIRIT [A] – ABIGAIL (29) 94
SMILE [A] – Nat 'King' COLE (2) 54

SMILE [A] – Robert DOWNEY Jr (68) 93
SMILE [B] – PUSSYCAT (24) 76
SMILE [C] – Audrey HALL (14) 86
SMILE [D] – ASWAD (53) 90
SMILE [E] – SUPERNATURALS (23) 97
SMILE [F] – LONESTAR (55) 00
SMILE [G] – FUTURE BREEZE (67) 01
THE SMILE – David ESSEX (52) 83
A SMILE IN A WHISPER – FAIRGROUND ATTRACTION (75) 88
SMILER – HEAVY STEREO (46) 95
SMOKE – Natalie IMBRUGLIA (5) 98
SMOKE GETS IN YOUR EYES [A] – PLATTERS (1) 59
SMOKE GETS IN YOUR EYES [A] – BLUE HAZE (32) 72
SMOKE GETS IN YOUR EYES [A] – Bryan FERRY (17) 74
SMOKE GETS IN YOUR EYES [A] – John ALFORD (13) 96
SMOKE MACHINE – X-PRESS 2 (43) 01
SMOKE ON THE WATER [A] – DEEP PURPLE (21) 77
SMOKE ON THE WATER [A] – ROCK AID ARMENIA (39) 89
SMOKEBELCH II – SABRES OF PARADISE (55) 93
SMOKESTACK LIGHTNIN' – HOWLIN' WOLF (42) 64
SMOKEY BLUE'S AWAY – A NEW GENERATION (38) 68
SMOKIN' IN THE BOYS' ROOM [A] – BROWNSVILLE STATION (27) 74
SMOKIN' IN THE BOYS ROOM [A] – MÖTLEY CRÜE (51) 85,86
SMOKIN' ME OUT – Warren G (14) 97
SMOOTH – SANTANA (3) 99,00
SMOOTH CRIMINAL [A] – Michael JACKSON (8) 88
SMOOTH CRIMINAL [A] – ALIEN ANT FARM (3) 01
SMOOTH OPERATOR [A] – SADE (19) 84
SMOOTH OPERATOR [B] – BIG DADDY KANE (65) 89
SMOOTHIN' GROOVIN' – INGRAM (56) 83
SMOULDER – KING ADORA (62) 00
SMUGGLER'S BLUES – Glenn FREY (22) 85
THE SMURF – Tyrone BRUNSON (52) 82
THE SMURF SONG – SMURFS (2) 78
THE SNAKE – Al WILSON (41) 75
SNAKE BITE (EP) – WHITESNAKE (61) 78
SNAKE IN THE GRASS – Dave DEE, DOZY, BEAKY, MICK and TICH (23) 69
SNAP MEGAMIX – SNAP (10) 91
SNAP YOUR FINGAZ – KUMARA (70) 00
SNAPPINESS – BBG (28) 90,96
SNEAKIN' SUSPICION – DR FEELGOOD (47) 77
SNEAKING OUT THE BACK DOOR – MATT BIANCO (44) 84
SNOBBERY AND DECAY – ACT (60) 87
SNOOKER LOOPY – CHAS and DAVE (6) 86
SNOOP DOGG – SNOOP DOGGY DOGG (13) 01
SNOOP'S UPSIDE YA HEAD – SNOOP DOGGY DOGG (12) 96
SNOOPY VS THE RED BARON [A] – HOTSHOTS (4) 73
SNOOPY VS THE RED BARON [A] – ROYAL GUARDSMEN (8) 67
SNOT RAP – Kenny EVERETT (9) 83
SNOW [A] – ORN (61) 97
SNOW [B] – JJ72 (21) 01
SNOW COACH – Russ CONWAY (7) 59
SNOWBIRD – Anne MURRAY (23) 70
SNOWBOUND FOR CHRISTMAS – Dickie VALENTINE (28) 57
THE SNOWS OF NEW YORK – Chris DE BURGH (60) 95
SO AMAZING – Luther VANDROSS (33) 87
SO BEAUTIFUL [A] – URBAN COOKIE COLLECTIVE (68) 95
SO BEAUTIFUL [B] – Chris DE BURGH (29) 97
SO CALLED FRIEND – TEXAS (30) 93
SO CLOSE [A] – Diana ROSS (43) 83
SO CLOSE [B] – Daryl HALL and John OATES (69) 90
SO CLOSE [C] – Dina CARROLL (20) 92
SO CLOSE TO LOVE – Wendy MOTEN (35) 94
SO COLD THE NIGHT – COMMUNARDS (8) 86
SO DAMN COOL – UGLY KID JOE (44) 92
SO DEEP – REESE PROJECT (54) 93
SO DEEP IS THE NIGHT – Ken DODD (31) 64
SO DO I – Kenny BALL and his JAZZMEN (14) 62
SO EMOTIONAL – Whitney HOUSTON (5) 87
SO FAR AWAY – DIRE STRAITS (20) 85
SO FINE [A] – Howard JOHNSON (45) 82
SO FINE [B] – KINANE (63) 98
SO FRESH, SO CLEAN – OUTKAST (16) 01
SO GOOD [A] – Roy ORBISON (32) 67
SO GOOD [B] – ETERNAL (13) 94
SO GOOD [C] – BOYZONE (3) 95
SO GOOD [D] – Juliet ROBERTS (15) 98
SO GOOD SO RIGHT – Brenda RUSSELL (51) ..80
SO GOOD TO BE BACK HOME AGAIN – TOURISTS (8) 80
SO GOOD (TO COME HOME TO) – Ivan MATIAS (69) 96
SO GROOVY – Wendell WILLIAMS (74) 91
SO HARD – PET SHOP BOYS (4) 90
SO HELP ME GIRL – Gary BARLOW (11) 97
SO HERE I AM – UB40 (25) 82
SO HOT – JC (74) 98
SO IN LOVE – ORCHESTRAL MANOEUVRES IN THE DARK (27) 85
SO IN LOVE (THE REAL DEAL) – Judy CHEEKS (27) 93
SO IN LOVE WITH YOU [A] – Freddy BRECK (44) 74
SO IN LOVE WITH YOU [B] – SPEAR OF DESTINY (36) 88
SO IN LOVE WITH YOU [C] – TEXAS (28) 94
SO IN LOVE WITH YOU [D] – DUKE (22) 96,00
SO INTO YOU – Michael WATFORD (53) 94
SO IT WILL ALWAYS BE – EVERLY BROTHERS (23) 63
SO LET ME GO FAR – DODGY (30) 95
SO LITTLE TIME – ARKARNA (46) 97
SO LONELY – POLICE (6) 80
SO LONG [A] – FISCHER-Z (72) 80
SO LONG [B] – FIERCE (15) 99
SO LONG BABY – Del SHANNON (10) 61
SO LOW – OCEAN COLOUR SCENE (34) 99
SO MACHO – SINITTA (2) 86
SO MANY WAYS [A] – BRAXTONS (32) 97
SO MANY WAYS [B] – Ellie CAMPBELL (26) 99
SO MUCH IN LOVE [A] – TYMES (21) 63
SO MUCH IN LOVE [A] – ALL-4-ONE (49) 94
SO MUCH IN LOVE [B] – MIGHTY AVENGERS (46) 64
SO MUCH LOVE – Tony BLACKBURN (31) 68
SO MUCH TROUBLE IN THE WORLD – Bob MARLEY and the WAILERS (56) 79
SO NATURAL – Lisa STANSFIELD (15) 93
SO NEAR TO CHRISTMAS – Alvin STARDUST (29) 84
SO PURE [A] – BABY D (3) 96
SO PURE [B] – Alanis MORISSETTE (38) 99
SO REAL – LOVE DECADE (14) 91
SO RIGHT [A] – RAILWAY CHILDREN (68) 90
SO RIGHT [A] – K-KLASS (20) 92
SO SAD THE SONG – Gladys KNIGHT and the PIPS (20) 76
SO SAD (TO WATCH GOOD LOVE GO BAD) – EVERLY BROTHERS (4) 60
SO SORRY I SAID – Liza MINNELLI (62) 89
SO STRONG – Ben SHAW featuring Adele HOLNESS (72) 01
SO TELL ME WHY – POISON (25) 91
SO THE STORY GOES – LIVING IN A BOX featuring Bobby WOMACK (34) 87
SO THIS IS ROMANCE – LINX (15) 81
SO TIRED [A] – Frankie VAUGHAN (21) 67
SO TIRED [B] – Ozzy OSBOURNE (20) 84
SO TIRED OF BEING ALONE – SYBIL (53) 96
SO WHATCHA GONNA DO NOW – PUBLIC ENEMY (50) 95
SO WHAT – Gilbert O'SULLIVAN (70) 90
SO WHAT! – Ronny JORDAN (32) 92
SO WHAT IF I – DAMAGE (12) 01
SO WHY SO SAD – MANIC STREET PREACHERS (8) 01
SO YOU WIN AGAIN – HOT CHOCOLATE (1) 77
SO YOU'D LIKE TO SAVE THE WORLD – Lloyd COLE (72) 93
SO YOUNG [A] – SUEDE (22) 93
SO YOUNG [B] – CORRS (6) 98
SOAPBOX – LITTLE ANGELS (33) 93
SOBER [A] – DRUGSTORE (68) 98
SOBER [B] – Jennifer PAIGE (68) 99
SOCK IT 2 ME – Missy 'Misdemeanor' ELLIOTT (33) 97
SOFT AS YOUR FACE – SOUP DRAGONS (66) ..87
SOFT TOP HARD SHOULDER – Chris REA (53) 93
SOFTLY AS I LEAVE YOU – Matt MONRO (10) ..62
SOFTLY SOFTLY – EQUALS (48) 68
SOFTLY, SOFTLY – Ruby MURRAY (1) 55
SOFTLY WHISPERING I LOVE YOU [A] – CONGREGATION (4) 71
SOFTLY WHISPERING I LOVE YOU [A] – Paul YOUNG (21) 90
SOLACE OF YOU – LIVING COLOUR (33) 91
SOLD – BOY GEORGE (24) 87
SOLD ME DOWN THE RIVER – ALARM (43) 89
SOLD MY ROCK 'N' ROLL (GAVE IT FOR FUNKY SOUL) – Linda CARR (36) 76
SOLDIER BLUE – Buffy SAINTE-MARIE (7) 71
SOLDIER BOY [A] – SHIRELLES (23) 62
SOLDIER BOY [A] – CHEETAHS (39) 65
SOLDIER OF LOVE – Donny OSMOND (29) 88
SOLDIER'S SONG – HOLLIES (58) 80
SOLEY SOLEY – MIDDLE OF THE ROAD (5) 71
SOLID – ASHFORD and SIMPSON (3) 85
SOLID BOND IN YOUR HEART – STYLE COUNCIL (11) 83
SOLID GOLD EASY ACTION – T. REX (2) 72
SOLID ROCK (LIVE) – DIRE STRAITS (50) 84
SOLID WOOD – Alison MOYET (44) 95
SOLITAIRE [A] – Andy WILLIAMS (4) 73
SOLITAIRE [A] – CARPENTERS (32) 75
SOLOMON BITES THE WORM – BLUETONES (10) 98
SOLSBURY HILL – Peter GABRIEL (13) 77,90
(SOLUTION TO) THE PROBLEM – MASQUERADE (64) 86
SOLVED – UNBELIEVABLE TRUTH (39) 98
SOME BEAUTIFUL – Jack WILD (46) 70
SOME CANDY TALKING – JESUS AND MARY CHAIN (13) 86
SOME FANTASTIC PLACE – SQUEEZE (73) 93
SOME FINER DAY – ALL ABOUT EVE (57) 92
SOME GIRLS [A] – RACEY (2) 79
SOME GIRLS [B] – ULTIMATE KAOS (9) 94,95
SOME GUYS HAVE ALL THE LUCK [A] – Robert PALMER (16) 82
SOME GUYS HAVE ALL THE LUCK [A] – Rod STEWART (15) 84
SOME GUYS HAVE ALL THE LUCK [A] – Maxi PRIEST (12) 87
SOME JUSTICE – URBAN SHAKEDOWN (23) 92,95
SOME KIND OF A SUMMER – David CASSIDY (3) 73
SOME KIND OF BLISS – Kylie MINOGUE (22) ..97
SOME KIND OF FRIEND – Barry MANILOW (48) 83
SOME KIND OF HEAVEN – BBG (65) 90
SOME KIND OF WONDERFUL – BLOW MONKEYS (67) 87
SOME KINDA EARTHQUAKE – Duane EDDY and the REBELS (12) 59
SOME KINDA FUN – Chris MONTEZ (10) 63
SOME LIE 4 LOVE – L.A. GUNS (61) 91
SOME LIKE IT HOT – POWER STATION (14) 85
SOME MIGHT SAY [A] – DE-CODE featuring Beverli SKEETE (69) 96
SOME MIGHT SAY [A] – OASIS (1) 95,96
SOME MIGHT SAY [A] – SUPERNOVA (55) 96
SOME OF YOUR LOVIN' – Dusty SPRINGFIELD (8) 65
SOME OTHER GUY – BIG THREE (37) 63
SOME OTHER SUCKER'S PARADE – DEL AMITRI (46) 97
SOME PEOPLE [A] – Carol DEENE (25) 62
SOME PEOPLE [B] – BELOUIS SOME (33) 86
SOME PEOPLE [C] – Paul YOUNG (56) 86
SOME PEOPLE [D] – Cliff RICHARD (3) 87
SOME PEOPLE SAY – TERRORVISION (22) 95
SOME THINGS YOU NEVER GET USED TO – Diana ROSS and the SUPREMES (34) 68
SOMEBODY [A] – STARGAZERS (20) 55
SOMEBODY [B] – JUNIOR (64) 84
SOMEBODY [C] – DEPECHE MODE (16) 84
SOMEBODY [D] – Bryan ADAMS (35) 85
SOMEBODY [E] – BRILLIANT (67) 86
SOMEBODY [F] – SHORTIE vs BLACK LEGEND (37) 01
SOMEBODY ELSE'S GIRL – Billy FURY (18) 63
SOMEBODY ELSE'S GUY [A] – Ce Ce PENISTON (13) 98

STAY YOUNG – **ULTRASOUND** (30) 98
STAYIN' ALIVE [A] – **BEE GEES** (4) 78
STAYIN' ALIVE [A] – **Richard ACE** (66) 78
STAYIN' ALIVE [A] – **N-TRANCE featuring Ricardo DA FORCE** (2) 95
STAYING ALIVE 95 [A] – **FEVER featuring Tippa IRIE** (48) 95
STAYING IN – **Bobby VEE** (4) 61
STAYING OUT FOR THE SUMMER – **DODGY** (19) 94,95
STAYING TOGETHER – **Debbie GIBSON** (53) 88
STEAL MY SUNSHINE – **LEN** (8) 99
STEAL YOUR FIRE – **GUN** (24) 92
STEAL YOUR LOVE AWAY – **GEMINI** (37) 96
STEAM [A] – **Peter GABRIEL** (10) 93
STEAM [B] – **EAST 17** (7) 94
STEAMY WINDOWS – **Tina TURNER** (13) 90
STEEL BARS – **Michael BOLTON** (17) 92
A STEEL GUITAR AND A GLASS OF WINE – **Paul ANKA** (41) 62
STEELO – **702** (41) 96
STEM – **DJ SHADOW** (74) 96
STEP BACK IN TIME – **Kylie MINOGUE** (4) 90
STEP BY STEP [A] – **Steve PERRY** (41) 60
STEP BY STEP [B] – **Joe SIMON** (14) 73
STEP BY STEP [C] – **TAFFY** (59) 87
STEP BY STEP [D] – **NEW KIDS ON THE BLOCK** (2) 90
STEP BY STEP [E] – **Whitney HOUSTON** (13) 96
A STEP IN THE RIGHT DIRECTION – **TRUTH** (32) 83
STEP INSIDE LOVE – **Cilla BLACK** (8) 68
STEP INTO A DREAM – **WHITE PLAINS** (21) 73
STEP INTO A WORLD (RAPTURE'S DELIGHT) – **KRS ONE** (24) 97
STEP INTO CHRISTMAS – **Elton JOHN** (24) 73
STEP INTO MY WORLD – **HURRICANE #1** (19) 97
STEP INTO THE BREEZE – **SPIRITUALIZED** (75) 90
STEP IT UP – **STEREO MC's** (12) 92
STEP OFF – **JUNIOR** (63) 90
STEP OFF (PART 1) – **GRANDMASTER FLASH, Melle MEL and the FURIOUS FIVE** (8) 84
STEP ON – **HAPPY MONDAYS** (5) 90
STEP ON MY OLD SIZE NINES – **STEREOPHONICS** (16) 01
STEP RIGHT UP – **Jaki GRAHAM** (15) 86
STEP TO ME (DO ME) – **MANTRONIX** (59) 91
STEPPIN' OUT [A] – **KOOL and the GANG** (12) 81
STEPPIN' OUT [B] – **Joe JACKSON** (6) 83
STEPPING STONE [A] – **FARM** (58) 90
STEPPING STONE [A] – **ANT & DEC** (11) 96
STEPTOE AND SON AT BUCKINGHAM PALACE – **Wilfrid BRAMBELL and Harry H CORBETT** (25) 63
STEP-TWO-THREE-FOUR – **STRICT INSTRUCTOR** (49) 98
STEREO – **PAVEMENT** (48) 97
STEREOTYPE – **SPECIALS** (6) 80
STEREOTYPES – **BLUR** (7) 96
STEWBALL – **Lonnie DONEGAN** (2) 56
STICK IT OUT – **RIGHT SAID FRED** (4) 93
STICKS AND STONES – **CUD** (68) 94
STICKY – **WEDDING PRESENT** (17) 92
STIFF UPPER LIP – **AC/DC** (65) 00
STILL [A] – **Karl DENVER** (13) 63
STILL [A] – **Ken DODD** (35) 63
STILL [B] – **COMMODORES** (4) 79
STILL [C] – **Macy GRAY** (18) 00
STILL A FRIEND OF MINE – **INCOGNITO** (47) 93
STILL A THRILL – **SYBIL** (55) 97
STILL BE LOVIN' YOU – **DAMAGE** (11) 01
STILL BELIEVE – **Shola AMA** (26) 99
STILL D.R.E. – **DR DRE** (6) 00
STILL FEEL THE RAIN – **STEX** (63) 91
STILL GOT THE BLUES (FOR YOU) – **Gary MOORE** (31) 90
STILL I'M SAD – **YARDBIRDS** (3) 65
STILL IN LOVE [A] – **GO WEST** (43) 93
STILL IN LOVE [B] – **Lionel RICHIE** (66) 96
STILL OF THE NIGHT – **WHITESNAKE** (16) 87
STILL ON YOUR SIDE – **BBMAK** (8) 01
STILL THE SAME – **SLADE** (73) 87
STILL TOO YOUNG TO REMEMBER – **IT BITES** (60) 89,90
STILL WATER (LOVE) – **FOUR TOPS** (10) 70
STILL WATERS (RUN DEEP) – **BEE GEES** (18) 97
STILLNESS IN TIME – **JAMIROQUAI** (9) 95
THE STING – **RAGTIMERS** (31) 74
STING ME – **BLACK CROWES** (42) 92
STINGRAY – **SHADOWS** (19) 65
THE STINGRAY MEGAMIX – **FAB** (66) 90
STINKIN THINKIN – **HAPPY MONDAYS** (31) 92
STIR IT UP – **Johnny NASH** (13) 72
STOLEN CAR – **Beth ORTON** (34) 99
STOMP [A] – **BROTHERS JOHNSON** (6) 80
STOMP [A] – **Quincy JONES** (28) 96
STOMP [B] – **GOD'S PROPERTY** (60) 97
STOMP [C] – **STEPS** (1) 00
STONE BY STONE – **CATATONIA** (19) 01
STONE COLD – **RAINBOW** (34) 82
STONE LOVE – **KOOL and the GANG** (45) 87
STONED LOVE – **SUPREMES** (3) 71
STONEY END – **Barbra STREISAND** (27) 71
STONEY GROUND – **GUYS and DOLLS** (38) 76
THE STONK – **HALE and PACE and the STONKERS** (1) 91
STOOD ON GOLD – **GORKY'S ZYGOTIC MYNCI** (65) 01
STOOD UP – **Ricky NELSON** (27) 58
STOOL PIGEON – **Kid CREOLE and the COCONUTS** (7) 82
STOP [A] – **Sam BROWN** (4) 88,89
STOP [B] – **SPICE GIRLS** (2) 98
STOP (EP) – **MEGA CITY FOUR** (36) 92
STOP AND GO – **David GRANT** (19) 83
STOP BAJON... PRIMAVERA – **Tullio DE PISCOPO** (58) 87
STOP BREAKING MY HEART – **INNER CIRCLE** (50) 79
STOP BY – **Rahsaan PATTERSON** (50) 97
STOP DRAGGIN' MY HEART AROUND – **Stevie NICKS with Tom PETTY and the HEARTBREAKERS** (50) 81
STOP FEELING SORRY FOR YOURSELF – **Adam FAITH** (23) 65
STOP HER ON SIGHT (SOS) – **Edwin STARR** (11) 66,68
STOP! IN THE NAME OF LOVE – **Diana ROSS and the SUPREMES** (7) 65,89
STOP LISTENING – **Tanita TIKARAM** (67) 98
STOP LOOK AND LISTEN [A] – **Wayne FONTANA and The MINDBENDERS** (37) 64
STOP LOOK AND LISTEN [B] – **Donna SUMMER** (57) 84
STOP LOOK LISTEN (TO YOUR HEART) – **Diana ROSS and Marvin GAYE** (25) 74
STOP LOVING ME STOP LOVING YOU – **Daryl HALL** (30) 94
STOP ME (IF YOU'VE HEARD IT ALL BEFORE) – **Billy OCEAN** (12) 76
STOP PLAYING WITH MY MIND – **Barbara TUCKER** (17) 00
STOP STARTING TO START STOPPING (EP) – **D.O.P.** (58) 96
STOP STOP STOP – **HOLLIES** (2) 66
STOP THAT GIRL – **Chris ANDREWS** (36) 66
STOP THE CAVALRY – **Jona LEWIE** (3) 80
STOP THE ROCK – **APOLLO FOUR FORTY** (10) 99
STOP THE VIOLENCE – **BOOGIE DOWN PRODUCTIONS** (69) 88
STOP THE WAR NOW – **Edwin STARR** (33) 71
STOP THE WORLD – **EXTREME** (22) 92
STOP THIS CRAZY THING – **COLDCUT** (21) 88
STOP TO LOVE – **Luther VANDROSS** (24) 87
STOP YOUR CRYING – **SPIRITUALIZED** (18) 01
STOP YOUR SOBBING – **PRETENDERS** (34) 79
STORIES [A] – **IZIT** (52) 89
STORIES [B] – **THERAPY?** (14) 95
STORIES OF JOHNNY – **Marc ALMOND** (23) 85
STORM [A] – **SPACE KITTENS** (58) 96
STORM [B] – **VANESSA-MAE** (54) 97
STORM [C] – **STORM** (32) 98,01
THE STORM – **WORLD OF TWIST** (42) 90,91
STORM ANIMAL – **STORM** (21) 00
STORM IN A TEACUP – **FORTUNES** (7) 72
THE STORM IS OVER NOW – **R KELLY** (18) 01
STORMS IN AFRICA (PART II) – **ENYA** (41) 89
STORMTROOPER IN DRAG – **Paul GARDINER** (49) 81
THE STORY OF LOVE – **OTT** (11) 98
THE STORY OF MY LIFE [A] – **Alma COGAN** (25) 58
THE STORY OF MY LIFE [A] – **Dave KING** (20) 58
THE STORY OF MY LIFE [A] – **Gary MILLER** (14) 58
THE STORY OF MY LIFE [A] – **Michael HOLLIDAY** (1) 58
STORY OF MY LOVE – **Conway TWITTY** (30) 59
STORY OF THE BLUES – **Gary MOORE** (40) 92
THE STORY OF THE BLUES – **WAH!** (3) 82
THE STORY OF TINA [A] – **Al MARTINO** (10) 54
THE STORY OF TINA [A] – **Ronnie HARRIS** (12) 54
STOWAWAY – **Barbara LYON** (12) 55
STRAIGHT AHEAD – **KOOL and the GANG** (15) 83
STRAIGHT AT YER HEAD – **LIONROCK** (33) 96
STRAIGHT FROM THE HEART [A] – **Bryan ADAMS** (51) 86
STRAIGHT FROM THE HEART [B] – **DOOLALLY** (9) 98,99
STRAIGHT LINES – **NEW MUSIK** (53) 79
STRAIGHT OUT OF THE JUNGLE – **JUNGLE BROTHERS** (72) 89
STRAIGHT TO HELL – **CLASH** (17) 82
STRAIGHT TO MY FEET – **HAMMER** (57) 95
STRAIGHT TO THE HEART – **REAL THING** (71) 86
STRAIGHT TO YOU – **Nick CAVE and the BAD SEEDS** (68) 92
STRAIGHT UP [A] – **Paula ABDUL** (3) 89
STRAIGHT UP [B] – **Chanté MOORE** (11) 01
STRAIGHT UP NO BENDS – **Brian HARVEY** (26) 01
STRAIGHTEN OUT – **STRANGLERS** (9) 77
STRANDED [A] – **HEART** (60) 90
STRANDED [B] – **DEEP DISH** (60) 97
STRANDED [C] – **Lutricia McNEAL** (3) 98
STRANGE – **WET WET WET** (13) 97
STRANGE BAND – **FAMILY** (11) 70
STRANGE BREW – **CREAM** (17) 67
STRANGE CURRENCIES – **R.E.M.** (9) 95
STRANGE GLUE – **CATATONIA** (11) 98
STRANGE KIND OF LOVE – **LOVE AND MONEY** (45) 89
STRANGE KIND OF WOMAN – **DEEP PURPLE** (8) 71
STRANGE LADY IN TOWN – **Frankie LAINE** (6) 55
STRANGE LITTLE GIRL [A] – **SAD CAFE** (32) 80
STRANGE LITTLE GIRL [B] – **STRANGLERS** (7) 82
STRANGE MAGIC – **ELECTRIC LIGHT ORCHESTRA** (38) 76
STRANGE TOWN – **JAM** (15) 79,80,83
STRANGE WAY – **ALL ABOUT EVE** (50) 91
STRANGE WORLD [A] – **KÉ** (73) 96
STRANGE WORLD [B] – **PUSH** (21) 01
STRANGELOVE – **DEPECHE MODE** (16) 87
STRANGER – **SHAKATAK** (43) 82
THE STRANGER – **SHADOWS** (5) 60
STRANGER IN A STRANGE LAND – **IRON MAIDEN** (22) 86
STRANGER IN MOSCOW – **Michael JACKSON** (4) 96,97
STRANGER IN PARADISE [A] – **Bing CROSBY** (17) 55
STRANGER IN PARADISE [A] – **Don CORNELL** (19) 55
STRANGER IN PARADISE [A] – **Eddie CALVERT** (14) 55
STRANGER IN PARADISE [A] – **FOUR ACES** (6) 55
STRANGER IN PARADISE [A] – **Tony BENNETT** (1) 55
STRANGER IN PARADISE [A] – **Tony MARTIN** (6) 55
STRANGER IN TOWN – **Del SHANNON** (40) 65
A STRANGER ON HOME GROUND – **FAITH BROTHERS** (69) 85
STRANGER ON THE SHORE [A] – **Mr Acker BILK and his PARAMOUNT JAZZ BAND** (2) 61
STRANGER ON THE SHORE [A] – **Andy WILLIAMS** (30) 62
STRANGER ON THE SHORE OF LOVE – **Stevie WONDER** (55) 87
STRANGER THINGS – **ABC** (57) 97
STRANGERS IN OUR TOWN – **SPEAR OF DESTINY** (49) 87
STRANGERS IN THE NIGHT – **Frank SINATRA** (1) 66
STRANGERS WHEN WE MEET – **David BOWIE** (39) 95
THE STRANGEST PARTY (THESE ARE THE TIMES) – **INXS** (15) 94
THE STRANGEST THING '97 – **George MICHAEL** (2) 97
STRANGLEHOLD – **UK SUBS** (26) 79
STRATEGIC HAMLETS – **URUSEI YATSURA** (64) 97
STRAW DOGS – **STIFF LITTLE FINGERS** (44) 79
STRAWBERRY – **Nicole RENEE** (55) 98

THE SUN AIN'T GONNA SHINE ANYMORE [A] – **WALKER BROTHERS** (1) 66
THE SUN AIN'T GONNA SHINE ANYMORE [A] – **CHER** (26) 96
THE SUN ALWAYS SHINES ON TV [A] – **A-HA** (1) 85
THE SUN ALWAYS SHINES ON TV [A] – **DIVA** (53)95
THE SUN AND THE RAIN – **MADNESS** (5) 83
SUN ARISE – **Rolf HARRIS** (3) 62,97
SUN CITY – **ARTISTS UNITED AGAINST APARTHEID** (21) ..85
THE SUN DOES RISE – **Jah WOBBLE'S INVADERS of the HEART** (41)94
THE SUN DOESN'T SHINE – **BEATS INTERNATIONAL** (66) 91
THE SUN GOES DOWN – **THIN LIZZY** (52) 83
THE SUN GOES DOWN (LIVING IT UP) – **LEVEL 42** (10) 83
SUN HITS THE SKY – **SUPERGRASS** (10) 97
SUN IS SHINING [A] – **TECHNIQUE** (64) 99
SUN IS SHINING [B] – **Bob MARLEY vs FUNKSTAR DE LUXE** (3) 99
SUN KING – **CULT** (39) 89
THE SUN MACHINE – **E-ZEE POSSEE** (62) 90
SUN OF JAMAICA – **GOOMBAY DANCE BAND** (50) 82
THE SUN RISING – **BELOVED** (26) 89,97
SUN SHINING DOWN – **CIRCA featuring DESTRY** (70) 99
SUN STREET – **KATRINA and the WAVES** (22) 86
SUN WORSHIPPERS (POSITIVE THINKING) – **Diana BROWN and Barrie K SHARPE** (61) 90
SUNBURN [A] – **Graham GOULDMAN** (52) 79
SUNBURN [B] – **Michelle COLLINS** (28) 99
SUNBURN [C] – **MUSE** (22) 00
SUNCHYME – **Dario G** (2) 97
SUNDANCE – **SUNDANCE** (33) 97,98
SUNDAY [A] – **BUSTER** (49) 76
SUNDAY [B] – **SONIC YOUTH** (72) 98
SUNDAY GIRL – **BLONDIE** (1) 79
SUNDAY MONDAYS – **Vanessa PARADIS** (49) ..93
SUNDAY MORNING – **NO DOUBT** (50) 97
SUNDAY MORNING CALL – **OASIS** (4) 00
SUNDAY SHINING – **Finley QUAYE** (16) 97
SUNDAY SHOUTIN' – **JOHNNY CORPORATE** (45) 00
SUNDAY SUNDAY – **BLUR** (26) 93
SUNDOWN [A] – **Gordon LIGHTFOOT** (33) 74
SUNDOWN [A] – **ELWOOD** (72) 00
SUNFLOWER – **Paul WELLER** (16) 93
SUNGLASSES – **Tracey ULLMAN** (18) 84
SUNMACHINE – **Dario G** (17) 98
SUNNY [A] – **CHER** (32) 66
SUNNY [A] – **Georgie FAME** (13) 66
SUNNY [A] – **Bobby HEBB** (12) 66
SUNNY [A] – **BONEY M** (3) 77
SUNNY [B] – **MORRISSEY** (42) 95
SUNNY AFTERNOON – **KINKS** (1) 66
SUNNY CAME HOME – **Shawn COLVIN** (29) 98
SUNNY DAY – **PIGBAG** (53) 81
SUNNY HONEY GIRL – **Cliff RICHARD** (19) 71
SUNRISE [A] – **GOLDENSCAN** (52) 00
SUNRISE [B] – **MOVEMENT 98 featuring Carroll THOMPSON** (58) 90
SUNRISE [C] – **PULP** (23) 01
SUNSET – **Nitin SAWHNEY featuring ESKA** (65)01
SUNSET AND BABYLON – **W.A.S.P.** (38) 93
SUNSET (BIRD OF PREY) – **FATBOY SLIM** (9) ..00
SUNSET BOULEVARD – **Michael BALL** (72) 93
SUNRISE (HERE I AM) – **RATTY** (51) 01
SUNSET NOW – **HEAVEN 17** (24) 84
SUNSET ON IBIZA – **THREE DRIVES ON A VINYL** (44) 01
SUNSET PEOPLE – **Donna SUMMER** (46) 80
SUNSHINE [A] – **Warren MILLS** (74) 85
SUNSHINE [B] – **JAY-Z featuring BABYFACE and Foxy BROWN** (25) ..97
SUNSHINE [C] – **GABRIELLE** (9) 99
SUNSHINE [D] – **UMBOZA** (14) 96
SUNSHINE [E] – **Alexander O'NEAL** (72) 89
SUNSHINE [F] – **YOMANDA** (16) 00
SUNSHINE AFTER THE RAIN [A] – **Elkie BROOKS** (10) 77
THE SUNSHINE AFTER THE RAIN [A] – **BERRI** (4) 94,95
SUNSHINE & HAPPINESS – **Darryl PANDY** (68)99
SUNSHINE AND LOVE – **HAPPY MONDAYS** (62) ..92
SUNSHINE DAY [A] – **OSIBISA** (17) 76
SUNSHINE DAY [A] – **CLOCK** (58) 99
SUNSHINE GIRL – **HERMAN'S HERMITS** (8) 68
SUNSHINE OF LOVE – **Louis ARMSTRONG** (41) 68
SUNSHINE OF YOUR LOVE – **CREAM** (25) 68
THE SUNSHINE OF YOUR SMILE – **Mike BERRY** (9) 80
SUNSHINE ON A RAINY DAY – **ZOE** (4) 90,91
SUNSHINE ON LEITH – **PROCLAIMERS** (41) 88
SUNSHINE PLAYROOM – **Julian COPE** (64) 83
SUNSHINE SUPERMAN – **DONOVAN** (2) 66
SUNSTORM – **HURLEY & TODD** (38) 00
SUNSTROKE – **CHICANE** (21) 97
SUNTAN – **STAN** (40) 93
SUPER BOWL SUNDAE – **OZOMATLI** (68) 99
SUPER GRAN – **Billy CONNOLLY** (32) 85
SUPER LOVE – **WIGAN'S OVATION** (41) 75
SUPER POPOID GROOVE – **WIN** (63) 87
SUPER TROUPER [A] – **ABBA** (1) 80
SUPER TROUPER [A] – **A TEENS** (21) 99
SUPER WOMBLE – **WOMBLES** (20) 75
SUPERBAD SUPERSLICK – **REDHEAD KINGPIN and the FBI** (68) 89
SUPERFLY GUY – **S EXPRESS** (5) 88
SUPERFLY 1990 – **Curtis MAYFIELD and ICE-T** (48) 90
SUPERFREAKON – **Missy 'Misdemeanor' ELLIOTT** (72) 01
SUPERGIRL – **Graham BONNEY** (19) 66
SUPERHERO – **REEF** (55) 00
SUPERMAN (GIOCA JOUER) – **BLACK LACE** (9) 83
SUPERMARIOLAND – **AMBASSADORS OF FUNK featuring MC MARIO** (8) 92
SUPERMARKET SWEEP – **BAR CODES featuring Alison BROWN** (72) 94
SUPERMODEL – **RuPAUL** (39) 93,94
SUPERNATURAL – **Kim ENGLISH** (50) 97
SUPERNATURAL GIVER – **KINKY MACHINE** (70)93
SUPERNATURE – **CERRONE** (8) 78,96
SUPERNOVA – **FIVE THIRTY** (75) 91
SUPERSHIP – **George BENSON** (30) 75
SUPERSONIC [A] – **HWA featuring SONIC THE HEDGEHOG** (33) ..92
SUPERSONIC [B] – **OASIS** (31) 94,95,96,97
SUPERSONIC [C] – **JAMIROQUAI** (22) 99
SUPERSONIC ROCKET SHIP – **KINKS** (16) 72
SUPERSTAR [A] – **CARPENTERS** (18) 71
SUPERSTAR [A] – **SONIC YOUTH** (45) 94
SUPERSTAR [B] – **Murray HEAD** (47) 72
SUPERSTAR [C] – **Lydia MURDOCK** (14) 83
SUPERSTAR [D] – **Tom NOVY** (32) 98
SUPERSTAR [E] – **SUPERSTAR** (49) 98
SUPERSTAR (REMEMBER HOW YOU GOT WHERE YOU ARE) – **TEMPTATIONS** (32) 72
SUPERSTITION – **Stevie WONDER** (11) 73
SUPERSTITION – GOOD TIMES (MEDLEY) – **CLUBHOUSE** (59) 83
SUPERSTITIOUS – **EUROPE** (34) 88
SUPERSTRING – **CYGNUS X** (33) 01
SUPERSTYLIN' – **GROOVE ARMADA** (12) 01
SUPERWOMAN – **Karyn WHITE** (11) 89
SUPPORT THE TOON – IT'S YOUR DUTY (EP) – **MUNGO JERRY** (57) 99
SUPREME – **Robbie WILLIAMS** (4) 00
THE SUPREME EP – **SINITTA** (49) 93
SURE – **TAKE THAT** (1) 94
SURE SHOT – **BEASTIE BOYS** (27) 94
SURE THING – **DARLING BUDS** (71) 92
SURF CITY – **JAN and DEAN** (26) 63
SURFIN' USA [A] – **BEACH BOYS** (34) 63
SURFIN' USA [A] – **Aaron CARTER** (18) 98
SURPRISE – **BIZARRE INC** (21) 96
SURPRISE SURPRISE – **CENTRAL LINE** (48) 83
SURRENDER [A] – **Elvis PRESLEY** (1) 61
SURRENDER [B] – **Diana ROSS** (10) 71
SURRENDER [C] – **SWING OUT SISTER** (7) 87
SURRENDER [D] – **Roger TAYLOR** (38) 99
SURRENDER YOUR LOVE – **NIGHTCRAWLERS featuring John REID** (7) 95
SURROUND YOURSELF WITH SORROW – **Cilla BLACK** (3) 69
SURVIVAL CAR – **FOUNTAINS OF WAYNE** (53) 97
SURVIVE – **David BOWIE** (28) 00
SURVIVOR – **DESTINY'S CHILD** (1) 01
SUSANNA – **ART COMPANY** (12) 84
SUSANNAH'S STILL ALIVE – **Dave DAVIES** (20)67
SUSAN'S HOUSE – **EELS** (9) 97
SUSIE DARLIN' [A] – **Robin LUKE** (23) 58
SUSIE DARLIN' [A] – **Tommy ROE** (37) 62
SUSPICION [A] – **Terry STAFFORD** (31) 64
SUSPICION [A] – **Elvis PRESLEY** (9) 76
SUSPICIOUS MINDS [A] – **Elvis PRESLEY** (2)69,01
SUSPICIOUS MINDS [A] – **Candi STATON** (31) ..82
SUSPICIOUS MINDS [A] – **FINE YOUNG CANNIBALS** (8) 86
SUSSUDIO – **Phil COLLINS** (12) 85
SUZANNE BEWARE OF THE DEVIL – **Dandy LIVINGSTONE** (14) 72
SVEN SVEN SVEN – **BELL & SPURLING** (7) 01
SW LIVE (EP) – **Peter GABRIEL** (39) 94
SWALLOW MY PRIDE – **RAMONES** (36) 77
SWALLOWED – **BUSH** (7) 97
SWAMP THING – **GRID** (3) 94
SWAN LAKE – **CATS** (48) 69
SWASTIKA EYES – **PRIMAL SCREAM** (22) 99
SWAY [A] – **Dean MARTIN** (6) 54,99
SWAY [A] – **Bobby RYDELL** (12) 60
SWAY [B] – **STRANGELOVE** (47) 96
SWEAR IT AGAIN – **WESTLIFE** (1) 99
SWEARIN' TO GOD – **Frankie VALLI** (31) 75
SWEAT – **USURA** (29) 93
SWEAT (A LA LA LA LA LONG) – **INNER CIRCLE** (3) 92,93
SWEAT IN BULLET – **SIMPLE MINDS** (52) 81
SWEATING BULLETS – **MEGADETH** (26) 93
SWEDISH RHAPSODY [A] – **MANTOVANI** (2)53,54
SWEDISH RHAPSODY [A] – **Ray MARTIN** (4) 53
SWEET AND LOW – **Deborah HARRY** (57) 90
SWEET BABY – **Macy GRAY featuring Erykah BADU** (23) 01
SWEET BIRD OF TRUTH – **The THE** (55) 87
SWEET CAROLINE – **Neil DIAMOND** (8) 71
SWEET CATATONIA – **CATATONIA** (61) 96
SWEET CHEATIN' RITA – **Alvin STARDUST** (37) 75
SWEET CHILD O' MINE [A] – **GUNS N' ROSES** (6) 88,89
SWEET CHILD O' MINE [A] – **Sheryl CROW** (30)99
SWEET DANGER – **ANGELWITCH** (75) 80
SWEET DREAM – **JETHRO TULL** (7) 69
SWEET DREAMS [A] – **Dave SAMPSON** (29) 60
SWEET DREAMS (ARE MADE OF THIS) [B] – **EURYTHMICS** (2) 83,91
SWEET DREAMS [B] – **DJ SCOTT featuring Lorna B** (37) 95
SWEET DREAMS [B] – **SWING featuring Dr ALBAN**(59) 95
SWEET DREAMS [C] – **Tommy McLAIN** (49) 66
SWEET DREAMS [C] – **Roy BUCHANAN** (40) 73
SWEET DREAMS [C] – **Elvis COSTELLO** (42) 81
SWEET DREAMS [D] – **LA BOUCHE** (44) 94,96
SWEET EMOTION – **AEROSMITH** (74) 94
SWEET FREEDOM [A] – **Michael McDONALD** (12) 86
SWEET FREEDOM [B] – **POSITIVE GANG** (34) ..93
SWEET FREEDOM PART 2 – **POSITIVE GANG** (67)93
SWEET HARMONY [A] – **LIQUID** (14) 92,95
SWEET HARMONY [B] – **BELOVED** (8) 93
SWEET HEART CONTRACT – **MAGAZINE** (54) 80
SWEET HITCH-HIKER – **CREEDENCE CLEARWATER REVIVAL** (36) 71
SWEET HOME ALABAMA – **LYNYRD SKYNYRD** (21) 76,79,82
SWEET ILLUSION – **Junior CAMPBELL** (15) 73
SWEET IMPOSSIBLE YOU – **Brenda LEE** (28) ..63
SWEET INSPIRATION – **Johnny JOHNSON and the BANDWAGON** (10) 70
SWEET INVISIBILITY – **HUE AND CRY** (55) 89
SWEET JOHNNY – **GORKY'S ZYGOTIC MYNCI** (60)98
SWEET LADY – **TYRESE** (55) 99
SWEET LADY LUCK – **WHITESNAKE** (25) 94
SWEET LEAF – **MOGWAI** (60) 98
SWEET LIES [A] – **Robert PALMER** (58) 88
SWEET LIES [B] – **Ellie CAMPBELL** (42) 99
SWEET LIKE CHOCOLATE – **SHANKS & BIGFOOT** (1) 99
SWEET LIPS – **MONACO** (18) 97
SWEET LITTLE MYSTERY – **WET WET WET** (5) 87
SWEET LITTLE ROCK 'N' ROLLER – **SHOWADDYWADDY** (15) 79
SWEET LITTLE SIXTEEN [A] – **Chuck BERRY** (16) 58
SWEET LITTLE SIXTEEN [A] – **Jerry Lee LEWIS** (38) 62
SWEET LOVE [A] – **COMMODORES** (32) 77
SWEET LOVE [B] – **Anita BAKER** (13) 86

TAKE THIS TIME — Sean MAGUIRE (27) ... 94
TAKE TO THE MOUNTAINS — Richard BARNES (35) 70
TAKE YOU OUT — Luther VANDROSS (59) ... 01
TAKE YOU THERE — Ronni SIMON (58) ... 95
TAKE YOUR MAMA FOR A RIDE — LULU (37) ... 75
TAKE YOUR PARTNER BY THE HAND — Howie B featuring Robbie ROBERTSON (74) 98
TAKE YOUR TIME [A] — HIGH (56) ... 90
TAKE YOUR TIME [B] — MANTRONIX (10) ... 90
TAKE YOUR TIME [C] — LOVE BITE (56) ... 00
TAKE YOUR TIME (DO IT RIGHT) PART 1 — S.O.S. BAND (51) ... 80
TAKEN FOR GRANTED — SIA (10) ... 00
TAKES A LITTLE TIME — TOTAL CONTRAST (17) 85
TAKES TWO TO TANGO — Louis ARMSTRONG (6) 52
TAKIN' A CHANCE ON YOU — DOLLAR (62) ... 80
TAKING ON THE WORLD — GUN (50) ... 90
TAKING THE VEIL — David SYLVIAN (53) ... 86
TALES FROM A DANCEOGRAPHIC OCEAN EP — JAM & SPOON featuring PLAVKA (49) ... 92
TALES FROM THE HARD SIDE — BIOHAZARD (47) 94
TALK ABOUT IT IN THE MORNING — Martyn JOSEPH (43) ... 95
TALK BACK — DOUBLE TROUBLE (71) ... 90
TALK DIRTY TO ME — POISON (67) ... 87
TALK OF THE TOWN — PRETENDERS (8) ... 80
TALK TALK [A] — TALK TALK (23) ... 82
TALK TO ME [A] — THIRD WORLD (56) ... 79
TALK TO ME [B] — Stevie NICKS (68) ... 86
TALK TO ME [C] — Anita BAKER (68) ... 90
TALK TO ME [D] — 6oFT DOLLS (37) ... 96
TALKIN ALL THAT JAZZ — STETSASONIC (54) ... 88,98
TALKING IN YOUR SLEEP [A] — Crystal GAYLE (11) 78
TALKING IN YOUR SLEEP [A] — Martine McCUTCHEON (6) ... 99
TALKING IN YOUR SLEEP [B] — BUCKS FIZZ (15) ... 84
TALKING LOUD AND CLEAR — ORCHESTRAL MANOEUVRES IN THE DARK (11) ... 84
TALKING OF LOVE — Anita DOBSON (43) ... 87
TALKING WITH MYSELF — ELECTRIBE 101 (23) 90,98
TALL DARK STRANGER — Rose BRENNAN (31) ... 61
TALL 'N' HANDSOME — OUTRAGE (51) ... 95,96
TALLAHASSEE LASSIE [A] — Freddy CANNON (17) 59
TALLAHASSEE LASSIE [A] — Tommy STEELE (16) 59
TALLYMAN — Jeff BECK (30) ... 67
TALULA — Tori AMOS (22) ... 96
TAM-TAM POUR L'ETHIOPE — STARVATION (33) 85
TAMMY — Debbie REYNOLDS (2) ... 57
TANGERINE — FEEDER (60) ... 97
TANGO IN MONO — EXPRESSOS (70) ... 81
TANSY — Alex WELSH (45) ... 61
TANTALISE (WO WO EE YEH YEH) — JIMMY THE HOOVER (18) ... 83
TAP THE BOTTLE — YOUNG BLACK TEENAGERS (39) ... 94
TAP TURNS ON THE WATER — CCS (5) ... 71
TAPE LOOP — MORCHEEBA (42) ... 96
TARANTINO'S NEW STAR — NORTH AND SOUTH (18) ... 97
TARANTULA — FAITHLESS (29) ... 01
TARA'S THEME [A] — SPIRO and WIX (29) ... 96
TARA'S THEME FROM 'GONE WITH THE WIND' [A] — ROSE OF ROMANCE ORCHESTRA (71) ... 82
TARZAN BOY — BALTIMORA (3) ... 85
TASTE IN MEN — PLACEBO (16) ... 00
TASTE IT — INXS (21) ... 92
A TASTE OF AGGRO — BARRON KNIGHTS (3) ... 78
TASTE OF BITTER LOVE — Gladys KNIGHT and the PIPS (35) ... 80
A TASTE OF HONEY — Mr Acker BILK and his PARAMOUNT JAZZ BAND (16) ... 63
THE TASTE OF YOUR TEARS — KING (11) ... 85
TASTE THE PAIN — RED HOT CHILI PEPPERS (29) 90
TASTE YOUR LOVE — Horace BROWN (58) ... 95
TASTY FISH — OTHER TWO (41) ... 91
TASTY LOVE — Freddie JACKSON (73) ... 86
TATTOO — Mike OLDFIELD (33) ... 92
TATTOOED MILLIONAIRE — Bruce DICKINSON (18) ... 90
TATTVA — KULA SHAKER (4) ... 96
TAVERN IN THE TOWN — Terry LIGHTFOOT and his NEW ORLEANS JAZZMEN (49) ... 62
TAXI — J BLACKFOOT (48) ... 84
TAXLOSS — MANSUN (15) ... 97
TCHAIKOVSKY ONE — SECOND CITY SOUND (22) 66
TE AMO — SULTANA (57) ... 94
TEA FOR TWO CHA CHA — Tommy DORSEY ORCHESTRA starring Warren COVINGTON (3) ... 58
TEACH ME TO TWIST — Chubby CHECKER and Bobby RYDELL (45) ... 62
TEACH ME TONIGHT — DE CASTRO SISTERS (20) ... 55
TEACH YOU TO ROCK — Tony CROMBIE and his ROCKETS (25) ... 56
TEACHER [A] — JETHRO TULL (4) ... 70
TEACHER [B] — I-LEVEL (56) ... 83
THE TEACHER — BIG COUNTRY (28) ... 86
TEACHER, TEACHER — Johnny MATHIS (27) ... 58
TEAR DOWN THE WALLS — NO SWEAT (61) ... 91
A TEAR FELL — Teresa BREWER (2) ... 56
TEAR ME APART — Suzi QUATRO (27) ... 77
TEAR SOUP — QUESTIONS (66) ... 83
TEARDROP [A] — SANTO and JOHNNY (50) ... 60
TEARDROP [B] — MASSIVE ATTACK (10) ... 98
TEARDROP CITY — MONKEES (46) ... 69
TEARDROPS [A] — Shakin' STEVENS (5) ... 84
TEARDROPS [B] — WOMACK and WOMACK (3) 88
TEARDROPS [B] — LOVESTATION (14) ... 98,01
TEARIN' UP MY HEART — 'N SYNC (9) ... 97,99
TEARING — ROLLINS BAND (54) ... 92
TEARING US APART — Eric CLAPTON and Tina TURNER (56) ... 87
TEARS [A] — Danny WILLIAMS (22) ... 62
TEARS [B] — Ken DODD (1) ... 65
TEARS [C] — Frankie KNUCKLES (50) ... 89
TEARS [C] — NU COLOURS (55) ... 92
TEARS ARE FALLING — KISS (57) ... 85
TEARS ARE NOT ENOUGH — ABC (19) ... 81
TEARS DON'T LIE — MARK 'OH (24) ... 95
TEARS FROM A WILLOW — OOBERMAN (63) ... 99
TEARS FROM HEAVEN — HEARTBEAT (32) ... 87
THE TEARS I CRIED — GLITTER BAND (8) ... 75
TEARS IN HEAVEN — Eric CLAPTON (5) ... 92
TEARS IN THE RAIN — N-TRANCE (53) ... 98
TEARS IN THE WIND — CHICKEN SHACK (29) ... 69
THE TEARS OF A CLOWN [A] — MIRACLES (1) 70,76
TEARS OF A CLOWN [A] — BEAT (6) ... 79
TEARS OF THE DRAGON — Bruce DICKINSON (28) ... 94
TEARS ON MY PILLOW [A] — Johnny NASH (1) ... 75
TEARS ON MY PILLOW [B] — Kylie MINOGUE (1) ... 90
TEARS ON THE TELEPHONE [A] — Claude FRANCOIS (35) ... 76
TEARS ON THE TELEPHONE [B] — HOT CHOCOLATE (37) ... 83
TEARS RUN RINGS — Marc ALMOND (26) ... 88
TEARS WON'T WASH AWAY THESE HEARTACHES — Ken DODD (22) ... 69
TEASE ME — Chaka DEMUS and PLIERS (3) ... 93
(MUST YOU ALWAYS) TEASE ME — Keith KELLY (27) ... 60
TEASER — George BENSON (45) ... 87
TECHNARCHY — CYBERSONIK (73) ... 90
TECHNO FUNK — LOST (75) ... 91
TECHNO TRANCE — D-SHAKE (20) ... 90
TECHNOCAT — Tom WILSON (33) ... 95
TEDDY BEAR [A] — Red SOVINE (4) ... 81
TEDDY BEAR [B] — Booker NEWBURY III (44) ... 83
TEDDY BEAR'S LAST RIDE — Diana WILLIAMS (54) ... 81
TEEN ANGEL — Mark DINNING (37) ... 60
TEEN BEAT — Sandy NELSON (9) ... 59,60
TEENAGE — UK SUBS (32) ... 80
TEENAGE ANGST — PLACEBO (30) ... 96
TEENAGE DEPRESSION — EDDIE and the HOT RODS (35) ... 76
TEENAGE DIRTBAG — WHEATUS (2) ... 01
TEENAGE DREAM — T. REX (13) ... 74
TEENAGE IDOL — Ricky NELSON (39) ... 62
TEENAGE KICKS — UNDERTONES (31) ... 78,83
TEENAGE LAMENT 74 — Alice COOPER (12) ... 74
TEENAGE PUNKS — SULTANS OF PING (49) ... 93
TEENAGE RAMPAGE — SWEET (2) ... 74
TEENAGE SENSATION — CREDIT TO THE NATION (24) ... 94
TEENAGE TURTLES — BACK TO THE PLANET (52) 93
TEENAGE WARNING — ANGELIC UPSTARTS (29) ... 79
A TEENAGER IN LOVE [A] — Craig DOUGLAS (13) 59
A TEENAGER IN LOVE [A] — DION (28) ... 59
A TEENAGER IN LOVE [A] — Marty WILDE (2) ... 59
TEENSVILLE — Chet ATKINS (46) ... 60
TEETHGRINDER — THERAPY? (30) ... 92
TELEFUNKIN' — N-TYCE (16) ... 98
TELEGRAM SAM — T. REX (1) ... 72,82
TELEGRAPH — ORCHESTRAL MANOEUVRES IN THE DARK (42) ... 83
THE TELEPHONE ALWAYS RINGS — FUN BOY THREE (17) ... 82
TELEPHONE LINE — ELECTRIC LIGHT ORCHESTRA (8) ... 77
TELEPHONE MAN — Meri WILSON (6) ... 77
TELEPHONE OPERATOR — Pete SHELLEY (66) ... 83
TELEPHONE THING — FALL (58) ... 90
TELEPORT — MAN WITH NO NAME (55) ... 96
TELETUBBIES SAY EH-OH! — TELETUBBIES (1) 97,98
TELEVISION THE DRUG OF THE NATION — DISPOSABLE HEROES OF HIPHOPRISY (44) ... 92
TELL HER ABOUT IT — Billy JOEL (4) ... 83
TELL HER I'M NOT HOME — Ike and Tina TURNER (48) ... 66
TELL HER NO — ZOMBIES (42) ... 65
TELL HER THIS — DEL AMITRI (32) ... 95
TELL HIM [A] — Billie DAVIS (10) ... 63
TELL HIM [A] — EXCITERS (46) ... 63
TELL HIM [A] — HELLO (6) ... 74
TELL HIM [A] — QUENTIN and ASH (25) ... 96
TELL HIM [B] — Barbra STREISAND and Celine DION (3) ... 97
TELL IT LIKE IT T-I-IS — B-52's (61) ... 92
TELL IT ON THE MOUNTAIN — PETER, PAUL and MARY (33) ... 64
TELL IT TO MY HEART [A] — Taylor DAYNE (3) 88,96
TELL IT TO MY HEART [A] — Q-CLUB (28) ... 96
TELL IT TO THE RAIN — FOUR SEASONS (37) ... 67
TELL LAURA I LOVE HER — Ricky VALANCE (1) 60
TELL ME [A] — Melanie B (4) ... 00
TELL ME [B] — Nick KAMEN (40) ... 88
TELL ME [C] — GROOVE THEORY (31) ... 95
TELL ME [D] — DRU HILL (30) ... 97
TELL ME [E] — Billie MYERS (28) ... 98
TELL ME A STORY — Jimmy BOYD and Frankie LAINE (5) ... 53
TELL ME DO U WANNA — GINUWINE (16) ... 97
TELL ME (HOW IT FEELS) — 52ND STREET (54) 85
TELL ME I'M NOT DREAMING — TITIYO (45) ... 94
TELL ME IT IS TRUE — UB40 (14) ... 97
TELL ME IT'S REAL — K-CI & JOJO (16) ... 99,00
TELL ME MA — SHAM ROCK (13) ... 98
TELL ME ON A SUNDAY — Marti WEBB (67) ... 80
TELL ME THAT YOU LOVE ME — Paul ANKA (25) 57
TELL ME THE WAY — CAPPELLA (17) ... 95
TELL ME THERE'S A HEAVEN — Chris REA (24) ... 90,94
TELL ME TO MY FACE — KEITH (50) ... 67
TELL ME TOMORROW [A] — Smokey ROBINSON (51) ... 82
TELL ME TOMORROW [B] — PRINCESS (34) ... 86
TELL ME WHAT HE SAID — Helen SHAPIRO (2) 62
TELL ME WHAT YOU WANT [A] — Jimmy RUFFIN (39) ... 74
TELL ME WHAT YOU WANT [B] — LOOSE ENDS (74) ... 84
TELL ME WHAT YOU WANT [C] — BLU PETER (70) 98
TELL ME WHAT YOU WANT ME TO DO — Tevin CAMPBELL (63) ... 92
TELL ME WHEN [A] — APPLEJACKS (7) ... 64
TELL ME WHEN [B] — HUMAN LEAGUE (6) ... 95
TELL ME WHEN THE FEVER ENDED — ELECTRIBE 101 (32) ... 89
TELL ME WHERE YOU'RE GOING — SILJE (55) ... 90
TELL ME WHY [A] — Elvis PRESLEY (15) ... 65
TELL ME WHY [B] — Alvin STARDUST (16) ... 74
TELL ME WHY [C] — MUSICAL YOUTH (33) ... 83
TELL ME WHY [D] — Bobby WOMACK (60) ... 84
TELL ME WHY [E] — THIS WAY UP (72) ... 87
TELL ME WHY [F] — GENESIS (40) ... 93
TELL ME WHY (THE RIDDLE) — Paul VAN DYK featuring SAINT ETIENNE (7) ... 00
TELL THAT GIRL TO SHUT UP — TRANSVISION VAMP (45) ... 88
TELL THE CHILDREN — SHAM 69 (45) ... 80
TELLIN' STORIES — CHARLATANS (16) ... 97
TELSTAR — TORNADOS (1) ... 62
TEMMA HARBOUR — Mary HOPKIN (6) ... 70
TEMPERAMENTAL — EVERYTHING BUT THE GIRL (72) ... 00

THEME FROM P.O.P. – **PERFECTLY ORDINARY PEOPLE** (61) 88
THEME FROM 'RANDALL & HOPKIRK (DECEASED)' – **Nina PERSSON and David ARNOLD** (49) 00
THEME FROM S-EXPRESS – **S EXPRESS** (1) 88,96
THEME FROM 'SHAFT' [A] – **Isaac HAYES** (4) 71,00
THEME FROM 'SHAFT' [A] – **EDDY and the SOUL BAND** (13) 85
THEME FROM 'SUPERMAN' (MAIN TITLE) – **LONDON SYMPHONY ORCHESTRA** (32) 79
THEME FROM 'THE APARTMENT' – **FERRANTE and TEICHER** (44) 60
THEME FROM THE 'DEER HUNTER' (CAVATINA) – **SHADOWS** (9) 79
THEME FROM THE FILM 'THE LEGION'S LAST PATROL' – **Ken THORNE** (4) 63
THEME FROM 'THE HONG KONG BEAT' – **Richard DENTON and Martin COOK** (25) 78
THEME FROM 'THE ONEDIN LINE' – **VIENNA PHILHARMONIC ORCHESTRA** (15) 71
THEME FROM 'THE PERSUADERS' – **John BARRY ORCHESTRA** (13) 71
THEME FROM 'THE PROFESSIONALS' – **Laurie JOHNSON** (36) 97
THEME FROM THE THREEPENNY OPERA [A] – **Louis ARMSTRONG** (8) 56
THEME FROM 'THE THREEPENNY OPERA' [A] – **Dick HYMAN TRIO** (9) 56
THEME FROM "THE THREEPENNY OPERA" [A] – **Billy VAUGHN** (12) 56
THEME FROM 'THE TRAVELLING MAN' – **Duncan BROWNE** (68) 84
THEME FROM 'THE VALLEY OF THE DOLLS' [A] – **Dionne WARWICK** (28) 68
THEME FROM TURNPIKE (EP) – **dEUS** (68) 96
THEME FROM 'VIETNAM' (CANON IN D) – **Orchestre de Chambre Jean-François PAILLARD** (61) 88
THEME FROM 'WHICH WAY IS UP' – **STARGARD** (19) 78
THEME FROM 'Z CARS' [A] – **Norrie PARAMOR** (33) 62
THEME FROM 'Z CARS' JOHNNY TODD [A] – **Johnny KEATING** (8) 62
THEME ONE – **Cozy POWELL** (62) 79
THEN – **CHARLATANS** (12) 90
THEN CAME YOU [A] – **Dionne WARWICK and the DETRIOT SPINNERS** (29)......................74
THEN CAME YOU [A] – **JUNIOR** (32)..................92
THEN HE KISSED ME – **CRYSTALS** (2).............63
THEN I FEEL GOOD – **Katherine E** (56) 92
THEN I KISSED HER – **BEACH BOYS** (4) 67
THEN YOU CAN TELL ME GOODBYE – **CASINOS** (28) 67
THEN YOU TURN AWAY – **ORCHESTRAL MANOEUVRES IN THE DARK** (50) 91
THERE AIN'T NOTHIN' LIKE THE LOVE – **MONTAGE** (64) 97
THERE AIN'T NOTHING LIKE SHAGGIN' – **TAMS** (21) 87
THERE ARE MORE QUESTIONS THAN ANSWERS – **Johnny NASH** (9) 72
THERE ARE MORE SNAKES THAN LADDERS – **CAPTAIN SENSIBLE** (57) 84
THERE BUT FOR FORTUNE – **Joan BAEZ** (8) 65
THERE BUT FOR THE GRACE OF GOD – **FIRE ISLAND** (32) 94
THERE GOES MY EVERYTHING [A] – **Engelbert HUMPERDINCK** (2) 67
THERE GOES MY EVERYTHING [A] – **Elvis PRESLEY** (6) 71
THERE GOES MY FIRST LOVE – **DRIFTERS** (3)..75
THERE GOES THAT SONG AGAIN – **Gary MILLER** (29) 61,62
THERE GOES THE NEIGHBORHOOD – **Sheryl CROW** (19) 98
THERE I GO – **Vikki CARR** (50) 67
THERE I GO AGAIN – **POWER OF DREAMS** (65)92
THERE IS A LIGHT THAT NEVER GOES OUT – **SMITHS** (25) 92
THERE IS A MOUNTAIN – **DONOVAN** (8) 67
THERE IS A STAR – **PHARAO** (43) 95
THERE IS ALWAYS SOMETHING THERE TO REMIND ME – **HOUSEMARTINS** (35) 88
THERE IS NO LOVE BETWEEN US ANYMORE – **POP WILL EAT ITSELF** (66) 88
THERE IT IS – **SHALAMAR** (5) 82
THERE I'VE SAID IT AGAIN [A] – **Al SAXON** (48)61
THERE I'VE SAID IT AGAIN [A] – **Bobby VINTON** (34).......................................63
THERE MUST BE A REASON – **Frankie LAINE** (9)...54
THERE MUST BE A WAY [A] – **Joni JAMES** (24) 59
THERE MUST BE A WAY [A] – **Frankie VAUGHAN** (7) 67
THERE MUST BE AN ANGEL (PLAYING WITH MY HEART) – **EURYTHMICS** (1) 85
THERE MUST BE THOUSANDS – **QUADS** (66) ..79
THERE SHE GOES [A] – **LA's** (13)...........89,90,99
THERE SHE GOES [A] – **SIXPENCE NONE THE RICHER** (14).................99
THERE SHE GOES AGAIN – **QUIREBOYS** (37) ..90
THERE THERE MY DEAR – **DEXY'S MIDNIGHT RUNNERS** (7)....................80
THERE WILL NEVER BE ANOTHER TONIGHT – **Bryan ADAMS** (32)...91
THERE WILL NEVER BE ANOTHER YOU [A] – **Chris MONTEZ** (37) 66
THERE WILL NEVER BE ANOTHER YOU [B] – **Jimmy RUFFIN** (68) 85
THERE WON'T BE MANY COMING HOME – **Roy ORBISON** (12)..66
THERE YOU GO – **PINK** (6) 00
THERE YOU'LL BE – **Faith HILL** (3)....................01
(THERE'LL BE BLUEBIRDS OVER) THE WHITE CLIFFS OF DOVER – **ROBSON and JEROME** (1) 95
THERE'LL BE SAD SONGS (TO MAKE YOU CRY) – **Billy OCEAN** (12) 86
THERE'S A BRAND NEW WORLD – **FIVE STAR** (61) 88
THERE'S A GHOST IN MY HOUSE [A] – **R Dean TAYLOR** (3) 74
THERE'S A GHOST IN MY HOUSE [A] – **FALL** (30)87
THERE'S A GOLDMINE IN THE SKY – **Pat BOONE** (5) 57
THERE'S A GUY WORKS DOWN THE CHIPSHOP SWEARS HE'S ELVIS – **Kirsty MacCOLL** (14)..81
THERE'S A HEARTACHE FOLLOWING ME – **Jim REEVES** (6) 64
THERE'S A HOLE IN MY BUCKET – **Harry BELAFONTE** (32) 61
THERE'S A KIND OF HUSH [A] – **HERMAN'S HERMITS** (7) 67
THERE'S A KIND OF HUSH (ALL OVER THE WORLD) [A] – **CARPENTERS** (22) 76
THERE'S A SILENCE – **ELECTRIC SOFT PARADE** (52) 01
THERE'S A WHOLE LOT OF LOVING – **GUYS and DOLLS** (2)......................................75
(THERE'S) ALWAYS SOMETHING THERE TO REMIND ME – **Sandie SHAW** (1) 64
THERE'S GONNA BE A SHOWDOWN – **Archie BELL and the DRELLS** (36)..................73
THERE'S GOT TO BE A WAY – **Mariah CAREY** (54)91
THERE'S MORE TO LOVE – **COMMUNARDS** (20)..88
THERE'S NO LIVING WITHOUT YOU – **Will DOWNING** (67) 93
THERE'S NO ONE QUITE LIKE GRANDMA – **ST WINIFRED'S SCHOOL CHOIR** (1) 80
THERE'S NO OTHER WAY – **BLUR** (8)................91
THERE'S NOTHING BETTER THAN LOVE – **Luther VANDROSS** (72) 88
THERE'S NOTHING I WON'T DO – **JX** (4) 96
THERE'S NOTHING LIKE THIS – **OMAR** (14) 91
THERE'S SOMETHING WRONG IN PARADISE – **Kid CREOLE and the COCONUTS** (35) 83
THERE'S THE GIRL – **HEART** (34) 87
THERE'S YOUR TROUBLE – **DIXIE CHICKS** (26) 99
THESE ARE DAYS – **10,000 MANIACS** (58) 92
THESE ARE THE DAYS OF OUR LIVES – **QUEEN** (1) 91
THESE ARE THE TIMES – **DRU HILL** (4) 99
THESE ARMS OF MINE – **PROCLAIMERS** (51) 94
THESE BOOTS ARE MADE FOR WALKING [A] – **Nancy SINATRA** (1) 66
THESE BOOTS ARE MADE FOR WALKIN' [A] – **Billy Ray CYRUS** (63)...92
THESE DAYS – **BON JOVI** (7) 96
THESE DREAMS – **HEART** (8) 86,88
THESE EARLY DAYS – **EVERYTHING BUT THE GIRL** (75)....................88
THESE THINGS ARE WORTH FIGHTING FOR – **Gary CLAIL ON-U SOUND SYSTEM** (45)..........93
THESE THINGS WILL KEEP ME LOVING YOU – **VELVELETTES** (34) 71
THESE WOODEN IDEAS – **IDLEWILD** (32) 00
THEY ALL LAUGHED – **Frank SINATRA** (41) 99
(THEY CALL HER) LA BAMBA – **CRICKETS** (21) 64
THEY DON'T CARE ABOUT US – **Michael JACKSON** (4).......................................96
THEY DON'T KNOW [A] – **Tracey ULLMAN** (2) ..83
THEY DON'T KNOW [B] – **Jon B** (32) 98
THEY DON'T KNOW [C] – **SO SOLID CREW** (3)..01
(THEY LONG TO BE) CLOSE TO YOU [A] – **CARPENTERS** (6) 70
(THEY LONG TO BE) CLOSE TO YOU [A] – **Gwen GUTHRIE** (25) 86
THEY SAY IT'S GONNA RAIN – **Hazell DEAN** (58) 85
THEY SHOOT HORSES DON'T THEY – **RACING CARS** (14) 77
THEY'RE COMING TO TAKE ME AWAY HA-HAAA! – **NAPOLEON XIV** (4) 66
THEY'RE HERE – **EMF** (29) 92
THIEVES IN THE TEMPLE – **PRINCE** (7) 90
THIEVES LIKE US – **NEW ORDER** (18) 84
THIGHS HIGH (GRIP YOUR HIPS AND MOVE) – **Tom BROWNE** (45) 80
THIN LINE BETWEEN LOVE AND HATE – **PRETENDERS** (49) 84
THE THIN WALL – **ULTRAVOX** (14) 81
A THING CALLED LOVE – **Johnny CASH** (4) 72
THE THING I LIKE – **AALIYAH** (33)....................95
THINGS – **Bobby DARIN** (2)..............................62
THINGS CAN ONLY GET BETTER [A] – **Howard JONES** (6) 85
THINGS CAN ONLY GET BETTER [B] – **D:REAM** (1) 93,94,97
THINGS GET BETTER – **Eddie FLOYD** (31) 67
THINGS HAVE CHANGED – **Bob DYLAN** (58) 00
THINGS I'VE SEEN – **SPOOKS** (6) 01
THINGS THAT ARE – **RUNRIG** (40) 95
THINGS THAT MAKE YOU GO HMMM... – **C & C MUSIC FACTORY / CLIVILLES & COLE** (4) 91
THE THINGS THE LONELY DO – **AMAZULU** (43)86
THINGS THAT GO BUMP IN THE NIGHT – **ALLSTARS** (12) 01
THINGS WE DO FOR LOVE [A] – **10 CC** (6)........76
THINGS WE DO FOR LOVE [B] – **Horace BROWN** (27) 96
THINK [A] – **Brenda LEE** (26)............................64
THINK [B] – **Chris FARLOWE** (37)......................66
THINK [C] – **Aretha FRANKLIN** (26).............68,90
THINK ABOUT . . . – **DJH featuring STEFY** (22)...............................91
THINK ABOUT ME – **ARTFUL DODGER featuring Michelle ESCOFFERY** (11) 01
THINK ABOUT THAT – **Dandy LIVINGSTONE** (26) 73
THINK ABOUT THE WAY (BOM DIGI DIGI BOM...) – **ICE MC** (42) 94
THINK ABOUT YOUR CHILDREN – **Mary HOPKIN** (19).....................................70,71
THINK FOR A MINUTE – **HOUSEMARTINS** (18) 86
THINK I'M GONNA FALL IN LOVE WITH YOU – **DOOLEYS** (13) 77
THINK IT ALL OVER – **Sandie SHAW** (42) 69
THINK IT OVER – **CRICKETS** (11) 58
(THINK OF ME) WHEREVER YOU ARE – **Ken DODD** (21) 75
THINK OF YOU [A] – **USHER** (70).......................95
THINK OF YOU [B] – **WHIGFIELD** (7) 95
THINK SOMETIMES ABOUT ME – **Sandie SHAW** (32) 66
THINK TWICE – **Celine DION** (1)........................94
THINKIN' ABOUT YOUR BODY – **Bobby McFERRIN** (46) 88
THINKIN' AIN'T FOR ME – **Paul JONES** (32)......67
THINKING ABOUT YOUR BODY – **2 MAD** (43) ..91
THINKING ABOUT YOUR LOVE [A] – **SKIPWORTH and TURNER** (24) 85
THINKING ABOUT YOUR LOVE [A] – **Phillip LEO** (64)..95
THINKING ABOUT YOUR LOVE [B] – **Kenny THOMAS** (4) 91
THINKING IT OVER – **LIBERTY** (5) 01

TOMORROW TOMORROW – BEE GEES (23)......69
TOMORROW'S CLOWN – Marty WILDE (33)......61
TOMORROW'S GIRLS [A] – UK SUBS (28)........79
TOMORROW'S GIRLS [B] – Donald FAGEN (46)93
TOMORROW'S (JUST ANOTHER DAY) – MADNESS (8) 83
TOM'S DINER [A] – Suzanne VEGA (58) 87
TOM'S DINER [A] – DNA featuring Suzanne VEGA (2) 90
TOM'S PARTY – T-SPOON (27) 99
TONES OF HOME – BLIND MELON (62)............93
TONGUE – R.E.M. (13) 95
TONGUE TIED – CAT (17)..................................93
TONIGHT [A] – Shirley BASSEY (21) 62
TONIGHT [B] – MOVE (11) 71
TONIGHT [C] – RUBETTES (12)..........................74
TONIGHT [D] – Zaine GRIFF (54) 80
TONIGHT [E] – MODETTES (68) 81
TONIGHT [F] – Steve HARVEY (63) 83
TONIGHT [G] – KOOL and the GANG (2) 84
TONIGHT [H] – BOOMTOWN RATS (73)............84
TONIGHT [I] – David BOWIE (53).......................84
TONIGHT [J] – NEW KIDS ON THE BLOCK (3) ..90
TONIGHT [K] – DEF LEPPARD (34)....................93
TONIGHT (COULD BE THE NIGHT) – VELVETS (50)...61
TONIGHT I CELEBRATE MY LOVE – Peabo BRYSON and Roberta FLACK (2) 83
TONIGHT I'M ALRIGHT – Narada Michael WALDEN (34).........................80
TONIGHT I'M FREE – ANT & DEC (62)..............93
TONIGHT I'M GONNA LOVE YOU ALL OVER – FOUR TOPS (43) 82
TONIGHT I'M YOURS (DON'T HURT ME) – Rod STEWART (8) 81
TONIGHT IN TOKYO – Sandie SHAW (21) 67
TONIGHT IS WHAT IT MEANS TO BE YOUNG – Jim STEINMAN (67)...84
TONIGHT TONIGHT – SMASHING PUMPKINS (7) 96
TONIGHT TONIGHT TONIGHT – GENESIS (18) ..87
TONIGHT YOU BELONG TO ME – PATIENCE and PRUDENCE (28).......................56
TONIGHT'S THE NIGHT – Rod STEWART (5) 76
TONITE [A] – PHATS & SMALL (11) 99
TONITE [B] – SUPERCAR (15)............................99
TOO BEAUTIFUL TO LAST – Engelbert HUMPERDINCK (14).........................72
TOO BIG – Suzi QUATRO (14) 74
TOO BLIND TO SEE IT – Kym SIMS (5) 91
TOO BUSY THINKING 'BOUT MY BABY [A] – Marvin GAYE (5) 69
TOO BUSY THINKING 'BOUT MY BABY [A] – MARDI GRAS (19) 72
TOO BUSY THINKING 'BOUT MY BABY [A] – STEPS (2)..01
TOO CLOSE [A] – NEXT (24) 98
TOO CLOSE [A] – BLUE (1) 01
TOO DRUNK TO FUCK – DEAD KENNEDYS (36) 81
TOO FUNKY – George MICHAEL (4)..................92
TOO GONE, TOO LONG – EN VOGUE (20) 97
TOO GOOD – LITTLE TONY (19).........................60
TOO GOOD TO BE FORGOTTEN [A] – CHI-LITES (10) 74
TOO GOOD TO BE FORGOTTEN [A] – AMAZULU (5)..86
TOO GOOD TO BE TRUE – Tom PETTY and the HEARTBREAKERS (34) ..92
TOO HARD TO BE FREE – AMEN (72) 01
TOO HOT [A] – KOOL and the GANG (23) 80
TOO HOT [A] – COOLIO (9) 96
TOO HOT TO HANDLE – HEATWAVE (15)..........77
TOO HOT TO TROT – COMMODORES (38)........78
TOO LATE – JUNIOR (20) 82
TOO LATE FOR GOODBYES – Julian LENNON (6) 84
TOO LATE TO SAY GOODBYE – Richard MARX (38) 90
TOO LATE, TOO SOON – Jon SECADA (43) 97
TOO MANY BEAUTIFUL GIRLS – Clinton FORD (48) 61
TOO MANY BROKEN HEARTS – Jason DONOVAN (1) 89
TOO MANY DJ'S – SOULWAX (40) 00
TOO MANY FISH – Frankie KNUCKLES featuring ADEVA (34) 95
TOO MANY GAMES – MAZE featuring Frankie BEVERLY (36) 85
TOO MANY PEOPLE – Pauline HENRY (38) 93
TOO MANY RIVERS – Brenda LEE (22) 65
TOO MANY TEARS – David COVERDALE and WHITESNAKE (46) 97
TOO MANY WALLS – Cathy DENNIS (17) 91
TOO MUCH [A] – Elvis PRESLEY (6)..................57
TOO MUCH [B] – BROS (2) 89
TOO MUCH [C] – SPICE GIRLS (1) 97
TOO MUCH FOR ONE HEART – Michael BARRYMORE (25).............................95
TOO MUCH HEAVEN – BEE GEES (3)................78
TOO MUCH INFORMATION – DURAN DURAN (35)93
TOO MUCH KISSING – SENSELESS THINGS (69) 93
TOO MUCH LOVE WILL KILL YOU [A] – Brian MAY (5) 92
TOO MUCH LOVE WILL KILL YOU [A] – QUEEN (15) 96
TOO MUCH TEQUILA – CHAMPS (49) 60
TOO MUCH TOO LITTLE TOO LATE [A] – Johnny MATHIS and Deniece WILLIAMS (3) ..78
TOO MUCH, TOO LITTLE, TOO LATE [A] – SILVER SUN (20) 98
TOO MUCH TOO YOUNG – LITTLE ANGELS (22) 92
TOO MUCH TROUBLE – LIMAHL (64)................84
TOO NICE TO TALK TO – BEAT (7)....................80
TOO REAL – LEVELLERS (46)............................98
TOO RIGHT TO BE WRONG – CARTER TWINS (61)...97
TOO RISKY – Jim DAVIDSON (52) 80
TOO SHY – KAJAGOOGOO (1) 83
TOO SOON TO KNOW – Roy ORBISON (3) 66
TOO TIRED – Gary MOORE (71).........................90
TOO WICKED (EP) – ASWAD (61).......................91
TOO YOUNG [A] – Bill FORBES (29) 60
TOO YOUNG [A] – Donny OSMOND (5) 72
TOO YOUNG TO DIE – JAMIROQUAI (10) 93
TOO YOUNG TO GO STEADY – Nat 'King' COLE (8)...56
TOOK MY LOVE – BIZARRE INC (19) 93
TOOK THE LAST TRAIN – David GATES (50) 78
TOP O' THE MORNING TO YA – HOUSE OF PAIN (8)..93
TOP OF THE POPS – REZILLOS (17) 78
TOP OF THE STAIRS – SKEE-LO (38)................96
TOP OF THE WORLD [A] – CARPENTERS (5) 73
TOP OF THE WORLD [B] – VAN HALEN (63) 91
TOP OF THE WORLD [C] – BRANDY featuring MASE (2) 98,99
TOP OF THE WORLD (OLE, OLE, OLE) – CHUMBAWAMBA (21) 98
TOP TEEN BABY – Garry MILLS (24) 60
TOPSY (PARTS 1 AND 2) – Cozy COLE (29)......58
TORCH – SOFT CELL (2) 82
TORERO [A] – Julius LAROSA (15) 58
TORERO – CHA CHA CHA [A] – Renato CAROSONE and his SEXTET (25) 58
TORN – Natalie IMBRUGLIA (2) 97
TORN BETWEEN TWO LOVERS – Mary MacGREGOR (4) 77
TORTURE [A] – JACKSONS (26) 84
TORTURE [B] – KING (23) 86
TOSH – FLUKE (32) 95
TOSS IT UP – MAKAVELI (15) 97
TOSSING AND TURNING [A] – IVY LEAGUE (3) 65
TOSSING AND TURNING [B] – WINDJAMMER (18) 84
TOSSING AND TURNING [C] – CHAKKA BOOM BANG (57) 96
TOTAL CONFUSION – A HOMEBOY, a HIPPIE and a FUNKI DREDD (56) 90
TOTAL ECLIPSE OF THE HEART [A] – Bonnie TYLER (1)..83
TOTAL ECLIPSE OF THE HEART [A] – Nicki FRENCH (5) 94,95
TOTAL ERASURE – Philip JAP (41) 82
THE TOTAL MIX – BLACK BOX (12) 90
TOTTENHAM TOTTENHAM – TOTTENHAM HOTSPUR FA CUP FINAL SQUAD (19) 82
TOUCH – LORI and the CHAMELEONS (70)......79
THE TOUCH – Kim WILDE (56) 84
TOUCH BY TOUCH – Diana ROSS (47) 84
TOUCH IT – MONIFAH (29) 99
TOUCH ME [A] – 49ers (3)...............................89
TOUCH ME [B] – Rui DA SILVA featuring CASSANDRA (1) 01
TOUCH ME (ALL NIGHT LONG) – Cathy DENNIS (5) 91
TOUCH ME (I WANT YOUR BODY) – Samantha FOX (3)..86
TOUCH ME IN THE MORNING – Diana ROSS (9)..73
TOUCH ME TEASE ME – Foxy BROWN (26)......96
TOUCH ME TOUCH ME – Dave DEE, DOZY, BEAKY, MICK and TICH (13) 67
TOUCH ME WITH YOUR LOVE – Beth ORTON (60) 97
TOUCH MYSELF – T-BOZ (48) 96
A TOUCH OF EVIL – JUDAS PRIEST (58) 91
A TOUCH OF LOVE – CLEOPATRA (24) 99
A TOUCH OF VELVET A STING OF BRASS – Ron GRAINER ORCHESTRA (60) 78
TOUCH TOO MUCH – AC/DC (29)......................80
A TOUCH TOO MUCH – ARROWS (8)................74
TOUCHED BY GOD – KATCHA (57) 99
TOUCHED BY THE HAND OF CICCIOLINA – POP WILL EAT ITSELF (28) 90
TOUCHED BY THE HAND OF GOD – NEW ORDER (20)...87
TOUCHY! – A-HA (11) 88
TOUGHER THAN THE REST – Bruce SPRINGSTEEN (13) 88
TOUR DE FRANCE – KRAFTWERK (22) 83,84,99
TOURNIQUET [A] – MARILYN MANSON (28) 97
TOURNIQUET [B] – HEADSWIM (30) 98
TOUS LES GARÇONS ET LES FILLES – Françoise HARDY (36)....................................64
TOWER OF STRENGTH [A] – Frankie VAUGHAN (1).......................................61
TOWER OF STRENGTH [A] – Gene McDANIELS (49) 61
TOWER OF STRENGTH [B] – MISSION (12) ..88,94
TOWER OF STRENGTH [C] – SKIN (19)..............94
TOWERS OF LONDON – XTC (31)......................80
TOWN – NORTHERN UPROAR (48) 96
TOWN CALLED MALICE – JAM (1) 82,83
TOWN CLOWNS – BLAMELESS (56)..................95
TOWN CRIER – Craig DOUGLAS (36) 63
TOWN OF PLENTY – Elton JOHN (74) 88
TOWN TO TOWN – MICRODISNEY (55) 87
TOWN WITHOUT PITY [A] – Gene PITNEY (32) 62
TOWN WITHOUT PITY [A] – Eddi READER (26) 96
TOXIC GIRL – KINGS OF CONVENIENCE (44) 01
TOXYGENE – ORB (4)...97
TOY – CASUALS (30) 68
TOY BALLOONS – Russ CONWAY (7)................61
TOY BOY – SINITTA (4) 87
TOY SOLDIERS – MARTIKA (5) 89
TOYS FOR BOYS – MARION (57) 95
TRACEY IN MY ROOM – EBTG vs SOUL VISION (34) 01
TRACIE – LEVEL 42 (25) 89
TRACKS OF MY TEARS [A] – MIRACLES (9) 69
TRACKS OF MY TEARS [A] – Linda RONSTADT (42).......................................76
TRACKS OF MY TEARS [A] – Colin BLUNSTONE (60) 82
TRACKS OF MY TEARS [A] – GO WEST (16)......93
TRACY – CUFFLINKS (4)....................................69
TRADE (EP) (DISC 2) – VARIOUS ARTISTS (EPs and LPs) (75) 98
TRAFFIC – STEREOPHONICS (20) 97
TRAGEDY [A] – ARGENT (34) 72
TRAGEDY [B] – BEE GEES (1)............................79
TRAGEDY [B] – STEPS (1) 98
TRAGEDY AND MYSTERY – CHINA CRISIS (46)..83
TRAGIC COMIC – EXTREME (15)........................93
TRAIL OF TEARS – DOGS D'AMOUR (47) 89
THE TRAIL OF THE LONESOME PINE – LAUREL and HARDY with the AVALON BOYS featuring Chill WILLS (2) 75
TRAILER LOAD A GIRLS – Shabba RANKS (63) 91
TRAIN – SISTERS OF MERCY (46) 84
THE TRAIN IS COMING [A] – SHAGGY (21) 96
THE TRAIN IS COMING [A] – UB40 (30)............99
TRAIN OF CONSEQUENCES – MEGADETH (22) 95
TRAIN OF LOVE – Alma COGAN (27) 60
TRAIN OF THOUGHT [A] – A-HA (8) 86
TRAIN OF THOUGHT [B] – ESCRIMA (36)..........95
TRAIN TO SKAVILLE – ETHIOPIANS (40) 67
TRAIN TOUR TO RAINBOW CITY – PYRAMIDS (35) 67
TRAINS AND BOATS AND PLANES [A] – Billy J KRAMER and the DAKOTAS (12)..........65
TRAINS AND BOATS AND PLANES [A] – Burt BACHARACH (4)..65
TRAMBONE – KREW-KATS (33) 61
TRAMP [A] – Otis REDDING (18) 67
TRAMP [B] – SALT-N-PEPA (2).........................88
TRAMPOLENE – Julian COPE (31) 87
TRAMPS AND THIEVES – QUIREBOYS (41) 92

TRANCESCRIPT – HARDFLOOR (72) ... 93
TRANQUILLIZER – GENEVA (24) ... 97
TRANSAMAZONIA – SHAMEN (28) ... 95
TRANSATLANTIC – ROACH MOTEL (73) ... 93
TRANSFER AFFECTION – A FLOCK OF SEAGULLS (38) ... 83
TRANSISTOR RADIO – Benny HILL (24) ... 61
TRANSMISSION – GAY DAD (58) ... 01
TRANSONIC – WIRED (73) ... 99
TRANZ EURO XPRESS – X-PRESS 2 (45) ... 96
TRAPPED – Colonel ABRAMS (3) ... 85
TRASH [A] – ROXY MUSIC (40) ... 79
TRASH [B] – SUEDE (3) ... 96
THE TRAVELLER – SPEAR OF DESTINY (44) ... 87
TRAVELLERS TUNE – OCEAN COLOUR SCENE (5) 97
TRAVELIN' BAND – CREEDENCE CLEARWATER REVIVAL (8) ... 70
TRAVELIN' HOME – Vera LYNN (20) ... 57
TRAVELLIN' LIGHT – Cliff RICHARD and the SHADOWS (1) ... 59
TRAVELIN' MAN – Ricky NELSON (2) ... 61
TRAVELLING LIGHT – TINDERSTICKS (51) ... 95
TRAVELLING MAN – STUDIO 2 (40) ... 98
TREASON (IT'S JUST A STORY) – TEARDROP EXPLODES (18) ... 81
TREASURE OF LOVE – Clyde McPHATTER (27) ... 56
TREAT 'EM RIGHT – Chubb ROCK (67) ... 91
TREAT HER LIKE A LADY [A] – TEMPTATIONS (12) ... 84
TREAT HER LIKE A LADY [B] – Celine DION (29) ... 99
TREAT HER LIKE A LADY [C] – JOE (60) ... 00
TREAT HER RIGHT – Roy HEAD (30) ... 65
TREAT INFAMY – REST ASSURED (14) ... 98
TREAT ME GOOD – YAZZ (20) ... 90
TREAT ME LIKE A LADY – FIVE STAR (54) ... 90
TREAT ME RIGHT – ADEVA (62) ... 90
TREATY – YOTHU YINDI (72) ... 92
TREBLE CHANCE – Joe 'Mr Piano' HENDERSON (28) ... 59
TREE FROG – HOPE A.D. (73) ... 94
TREMELO SONG (EP) – CHARLATANS (44) ... 92
TREES – PULP (23) ... 01
THE TRIAL OF HISSING SID – Keith MICHELL (53) ... 80
TRIALS OF LIFE – KALEEF (75) ... 97
TRIBAL BASE – REBEL MC featuring TENOR FLY and Barrington LEVY (20) ... 91
TRIBAL DANCE – 2 UNLIMITED (4) ... 93
TRIBUTE (RIGHT ON) – PASADENAS (5) ... 88
TRIBUTE TO A KING – William BELL (31) ... 68
TRIBUTE TO BUDDY HOLLY – Mike BERRY (24) 61
TRIBUTE TO JIM REEVES – LARRY CUNNINGHAM and the MIGHTY AVONS (40) ... 64,65
TRIBUTE TO OUR ANCESTORS – RUBBADUBB (56) ... 98
A TRICK OF THE LIGHT – TRIFFIDS (73) ... 88
TRICK OF THE NIGHT – BANANARAMA (32) ... 87
TRICKY DISCO – TRICKY DISCO (14) ... 90
TRICKY KID – TRICKY (28) ... 97
TRIGGER HIPPIE – MORCHEEBA (40) ... 96
TRIGGER INSIDE – THERAPY? (22) ... 94
TRINI TRAX – Trini LOPEZ (59) ... 81
TRIP II THE MOON – ACEN (38) ... 92
A TRIP TO TRUMPTON – URBAN HYPE (6) ... 92
TRIPPIN' – Mark MORRISON (8) ... 96
TRIPPIN' ON SUNSHINE – PIZZAMAN (18) ... 94,96
TRIPPIN' ON YOUR LOVE [A] – A WAY OF LIFE (55) ... 90
TRIPPIN' ON YOUR LOVE [A] – Kenny THOMAS (17) ... 93
TRIPPY – ARAB STRAP (48) ... 98
TRIPWIRE – LIONROCK (44) ... 94
TRIUMPH – WU-TANG CLAN (46) ... 97
TROCADERO – SHOWADDYWADDY (32) ... 76
THE TROOPER – IRON MAIDEN (12) ... 83
TROPICALIA – BECK (39) ... 98
T.R.O.U.B.L.E. – Elvis PRESLEY (31) ... 75
TROUBLE [A] – GILLAN (14) ... 80
TROUBLE [B] – Lindsey BUCKINGHAM (31) ... 82
TROUBLE [C] – HEAVEN 17 (51) ... 87
TROUBLE [D] – SHAMPOO (11) ... 94,95
TROUBLE [E] – COLDPLAY (10) ... 00
TROUBLE [F] – CYPRESS HILL (33) ... 01
TROUBLE BOYS – THIN LIZZY (53) ... 81
TROUBLE IN PARADISE – Al JARREAU (36) ... 83
TROUBLE IS MY MIDDLE NAME [A] – BROOK BROTHERS (38) ... 63
TROUBLE IS MY MIDDLE NAME [A] – FOUR PENNIES (32) ... 66
TROUBLE TOWN – Martin STEPHENSON and the DAINTEES (58) 87
TROUBLE WITH HARRY – ALFI and HARRY (15) 56
TROUBLED GIRL – Karen RAMIREZ (50) ... 98
TRUCK ON (TYKE) – T. REX (12) ... 73
TRUDIE – Joe 'Mr Piano' HENDERSON (14) ... 58
TRUE – SPANDAU BALLET (1) ... 83
TRUE BLUE – MADONNA (1) ... 86
TRUE COLORS [A] – Cyndi LAUPER (12) ... 86
TRUE COLORS [A] – Phil COLLINS (26) ... 98
TRUE COLOURS [B] – GO WEST (48) ... 86
TRUE DEVOTION – Samantha FOX (62) ... 87
TRUE FAITH – NEW ORDER (4) ... 87,94
TRUE LOVE [A] – Bing CROSBY (4) ... 56,83
TRUE LOVE [A] – Terry LIGHTFOOT and his NEW ORLEANS JAZZMEN (33) ... 61
TRUE LOVE [A] – Richard CHAMBERLAIN (30) .. 63
TRUE LOVE [A] – Shakin' STEVENS (23) ... 88
TRUE LOVE [A] – Elton JOHN and Kiki DEE (2) 93
TRUE LOVE [B] – CHIMES (48) ... 90
TRUE LOVE FOR EVER MORE – BACHELORS (34) 65
TRUE LOVE NEVER DIES – FLIP & FILL featuring Kelly LLOREANNA (34) ... 01
TRUE LOVE WAYS [A] – Buddy HOLLY (25) 60,88
TRUE LOVE WAYS [A] – PETER and GORDON (2) 65
TRUE LOVE WAYS [A] – Cliff RICHARD (8) ... 83
TRUE LOVE WAYS [A] – David ESSEX and Catherine ZETA JONES (38) 94
TRUE LOVE WILL FIND YOU IN THE END – SPECTRUM (70) ... 92
TRUE SPIRIT – Carleen ANDERSON (24) ... 94
TRUE STEP TONIGHT – TRUE STEPPERS featuring Brian HARVEY and Donell JONES (25) ... 00
TRUE (THE FAGGOT IS YOU) – MOREL (64) ... 00
TRUE TO US – VANILLA (36) ... 98
TRUE TO YOUR HEART – 98° (51) ... 98
TRUGANINI – MIDNIGHT OIL (29) ... 93
TRULY [A] – Lionel RICHIE (6) ... 82
TRULY [A] – Steven HOUGHTON (23) ... 98
TRULY [B] – Hinda HICKS (31) ... 98
TRULY [C] – PESHAY featuring Kym MAZELLE (55) ... 00
TRULY MADLY DEEPLY – SAVAGE GARDEN (4) 98
TRUST [A] – BROTHER BEYOND (53) ... 90
TRUST [B] – NED'S ATOMIC DUSTBIN (21) ... 91
TRUST ME – GURU featuring N'Dea DAVENPORT (34) ... 93
TRUST ME TO OPEN MY MOUTH – SQUEEZE (72) ... 87
THE TRUTH [A] – Colonel ABRAMS (53) ... 85
THE TRUTH [B] – REAL PEOPLE (41) ... 91,92
TRUTH OR DARE – Shirley MURDOCK (60) ... 86
TRY – BROS (27) ... 91
TRY A LITTLE KINDNESS – Glen CAMPBELL (45) 70
TRY A LITTLE TENDERNESS – Otis REDDING (46) 67
TRY AGAIN – AALIYAH (5) ... 00
TRY JAH LOVE – THIRD WORLD (47) ... 82
TRY ME OUT – CORONA (6) ... 95
TRY MY WORLD – Georgie FAME (37) ... 67
TRY TO UNDERSTAND – LULU (25) ... 65
TRY TRY TRY [A] – Julian COPE (24) ... 95
TRY TRY TRY [B] – SMASHING PUMPKINS (73) 00
TRYIN' – HILLTOPPERS (30) ... 56
TRYIN' TO GET THE FEELING AGAIN – CARPENTERS (44) ... 94
TRYING TO FORGET – Jim REEVES (33) ... 67
TRYING TO GET TO YOU – Elvis PRESLEY (16) 57
TRYOUTS FOR THE HUMAN RACE – SPARKS (45) ... 79
TSOP THE SOUND OF PHILADELPHIA – MFSB featuring the THREE DEGREES (22) ... 74
TSUNAMI – MANIC STREET PREACHERS (11) ... 99
TU AMOR – KACI (24) ... 01
TU M'AIMES ENCORE (TO LOVE ME AGAIN) – Celine DION (7) ... 95
TUBTHUMPING – CHUMBAWAMBA (2) ... 97
TUBULAR BELLS – CHAMPS BOYS (41) ... 76
TUCH ME – Fonda RAE (49) ... 84
TUESDAY AFTERNOON – Jennifer BROWN (57) ... 99
TUESDAY MORNING – POGUES (18) ... 93
TUESDAY SUNSHINE – QUESTIONS (46) ... 84
TUFF ACT TO FOLLOW – MN8 (15) ... 96
TUG OF WAR – Paul McCARTNEY (53) ... 82
TULANE – Steve GIBBONS BAND (12) ... 77
TULIPS FROM AMSTERDAM – Max BYGRAVES (3) ... 58
TUM BIN JIYA – Bally SAGOO (21) ... 97
TUMBLING DICE – ROLLING STONES (5) ... 72
TUMBLING TUMBLEWEEDS – Slim WHITMAN (19) ... 56
THE TUNE – SUGGS (33) ... 95
TUNES SPLITS THE ATOM – MC TUNES versus 808 STATE (18) ... 90
TUNNEL OF LOVE [A] – DIRE STRAITS (54) ... 81
TUNNEL OF LOVE [B] – FUN BOY THREE (10) ... 83
TUNNEL OF LOVE [C] – Bruce SPRINGSTEEN (45) ... 87
TURN [A] – TRAVIS (8) ... 99
TURN [B] – FEEDER (27) ... 01
TURN OFF THE LIGHT – Nelly FURTADO (4) ... 01
TURN AROUND [A] – FAB! (59) ... 98
TURN AROUND [B] – PHATS & SMALL (2) ... 99
TURN AROUND AND COUNT 2 TEN – DEAD OR ALIVE (70) ... 88
TURN BACK THE CLOCK – JOHNNY HATES JAZZ (12) ... 87
TURN BACK TIME – AQUA (1) ... 98
TURN IT AROUND – ALENA (14) ... 99
TURN IT DOWN – SWEET (41) ... 74
TURN IT INTO LOVE – Hazell DEAN (21) ... 88
TURN IT ON – LEVEL 42 (57) ... 81
TURN IT ON AGAIN – GENESIS (8) ... 80
TURN IT UP [A] – CONWAY BROTHERS (11) ... 85
TURN IT UP [B] – Richie RICH (48) ... 88
TURN IT UP [C] – TECHNOTRONIC featuring MELISSA and EINSTEIN (42) ... 90
TURN IT UP [D] – Peter ANDRE (64) ... 95
TURN IT UP [E] – RAJA NEE (42) ... 95
TURN IT UP / FIRE IT UP – Busta RHYMES (2) 98
TURN IT UP (SAY YEAH) – DJ DUKE (31) ... 94
TURN ME LOOSE – Wally JUMP Jr and the CRIMINAL ELEMENT (60) 87
TURN ME ON – Danny TENAGLIA (53) ... 99
TURN ME ON TURN ME OFF – Honey BANE (37) 81
TURN ME OUT – PRAXIS (44) ... 95
TURN ME OUT (TURN TO SUGAR) – PRAXIS (35) 97
TURN OFF – MILLTOWN BROTHERS (55) ... 93
TURN ON THE NIGHT – KISS (41) ... 88
TURN ON TUNE IN COP OUT – FREAKPOWER (3) ... 93,95
TURN THE BEAT AROUND – Gloria ESTEFAN (21) 94
TURN THE MUSIC UP [A] – PLAYERS ASSOCIATION (8) ... 79
TURN THE MUSIC UP [A] – Chris PAUL (73) ... 88
TURN TO GOLD – David AUSTIN (68) ... 84
TURN TO STONE – ELECTRIC LIGHT ORCHESTRA (18) ... 77
TURN! TURN! TURN! – BYRDS (26) ... 65
TURN UP THE BASS – TYREE (12) ... 89
TURN UP THE NIGHT – BLACK SABBATH (37) .. 82
TURN UP THE POWER – N-TRANCE (23) ... 94
TURN YOUR BACK ON ME – KAJAGOOGOO (47) .. 84
TURN YOUR LIGHTS DOWN LOW – Bob MARLEY and the WAILERS (15) ... 99
TURN YOUR LOVE AROUND [A] – George BENSON (29) ... 81
TURN YOUR LOVE AROUND [A] – Tony DI BART (66) ... 96
TURN YOUR RADIO ON – Ray STEVENS (33) .. 72
TURNING AWAY – Shakin' STEVENS (15) ... 86
TURNING JAPANESE – VAPORS (3) ... 80
TURNING THE TOWN RED – Elvis COSTELLO (25) ... 84
TURQUOISE [A] – DONOVAN (30) ... 65
TURQUOISE [B] – CIRCULATION (64) ... 01
TURTLE POWER – PARTNERS IN KRYME (1) ... 90
TURTLE RHAPSODY – ORCHESTRA ON THE HALF SHELL (36) ... 90
TUSK – FLEETWOOD MAC (6) ... 79
TUTTI FRUTTI – LITTLE RICHARD (29) ... 57
TUXEDO JUNCTION – MANHATTAN TRANSFER (24) ... 76
TV – FLYING LIZARDS (43) ... 80
TV CRIMES – BLACK SABBATH (33) ... 92

UNDERGROUND [B] – **Ben FOLDS FIVE** (37) 96
UNDERGROUND [C] – **RHYTHM MASTERS** (50)..01
UNDERLOVE – **Melba MOORE** (60) 83
UNDERNEATH THE BLANKET GO – **Gilbert O'SULLIVAN** (40) 71
UNDERPASS – **John FOXX** (31)..........................80
UNDERSTAND THIS GROOVE – **FRANKE** (60)....92
UNDERSTANDING JANE – **ICICLE WORKS** (52)..86
UNDERWATER [A] – **Harry THUMANN** (41) 81
UNDERWATER [B] – **DELERIUM featuring RANI** (33) 01
UNDERWATER LOVE – **SMOKE CITY** (4)............97
UNDIVIDED LOVE – **LOUISE** (5) 96
UNDONE – THE SWEATER SONG – **WEEZER** (35) 95
UNDRESSED – **WHITE TOWN** (57) 97
UNEMPLOYED IN SUMMERTIME – **Emiliana TORRINI** (63) 00
UNEXPLAINED – **GRAVEDIGGAZ** (48)................98
UNEXPLAINED (EP) – **EMF** (18) 92
UNFINISHED SYMPATHY – **MASSIVE ATTACK** (13)91
UNFORGETTABLE – **Natalie COLE** (19) 91
THE UNFORGETTABLE FIRE – **U2** (6) 85
UNFORGIVABLE SINNER – **Lene MARLIN** (13) ..00
UNFORGIVEN – **D:REAM** (29)...........................93
THE UNFORGIVEN – **METALLICA** (15) 91
THE UNFORGIVEN II – **METALLICA** (15) 98
UNHOLY – **KISS** (26) 92
UNIFORM – **INSPIRAL CARPETS** (51) 94
UNIFORMS (CORPS D'ESPRIT) – **Pete TOWNSHEND** (48) 82
UNINTENDED – **MUSE** (20) 00
UNINVITED GUEST – **MARILLION** (53) 89
UNION CITY BLUE – **BLONDIE** (13) 79,95
UNION OF THE SNAKE – **DURAN DURAN** (3)....83
UNITED – **JUDAS PRIEST** (26) 80
UNITED CALYPSO '98 – **REDS UNITED** (33)......98
UNITED COLOURS – **BEST SHOT** (64) 94
UNITED (WE LOVE YOU) – **MANCHESTER UNITED FOOTBALL CLUB** (37) 93
UNITED WE STAND – **BROTHERHOOD OF MAN** (10) 70
UNITY – **UNITY** (64) 91
U.N.I.T.Y. – **QUEEN LATIFAH** (74).....................94
UNITY (PART 1 – THE THIRD COMING) – **Afrika BAMBAATAA and James BROWN** (49)..84
UNIVERSAL [A] – **SMALL FACES** (16) 68
UNIVERSAL [B] – **ORCHESTRAL MANOEUVRES IN THE DARK** (55)96
THE UNIVERSAL [C] – **BLUR** (5) 95
UNIVERSAL HEART-BEAT – **Juliana HATFIELD** (65) 95
UNIVERSAL NATION – **PUSH** (35) 99
THE UNKNOWN – **Mark B & BLADE** (49) 01
UNLEASH THE DRAGON – **SISQO** (6)................00
UNLOCK THE FUNK – **LOCKSMITH** (42) 80
UNO – **MUSE** (73) 99
UNO MAS – **Daniel O'DONNELL** (25)................99
UNPRETTY – **TLC** (6) 99
UNSAFE BUILDING 1990 – **ALARM** (54) 90
UNSKINNY BOP – **POISON** (15) 90
UNSQUARE DANCE – **Dave BRUBECK QUARTET** (14) 62
THE UNSUNG HEROES OF HIP HOP – **SUBSONIC 2** (63)..91
UNTIL IT SLEEPS – **METALLICA** (5) 96
UNTIL IT'S TIME FOR YOU TO GO [A] – **FOUR PENNIES** (19) 65
UNTIL IT'S TIME FOR YOU TO GO [A] – **Elvis PRESLEY** (5) 72
UNTIL MY DYING DAY – **UB40** (15) 95
UNTIL THE DAY – **FUNKY GREEN DOGS** (75)....98
UNTIL THE END OF TIME – **2PAC** (4) 01
UNTIL THE NIGHT – **Billy JOEL** (50)..................79
UNTIL THE TIME IS THROUGH – **FIVE** (2) 98
UNTIL YOU COME BACK TO ME – **ADEVA** (45) 92
UNTIL YOU COME BACK TO ME (THAT'S WHAT I'M GONNA DO) [A] – **Aretha FRANKLIN** (26) 74
UNTIL YOU COME BACK TO ME (THAT'S WHAT I'M GONNA DO) [A] – **Miki HOWARD** (67) 90
UNTIL YOU FIND OUT – **NED'S ATOMIC DUSTBIN** (51) 90
UNTIL YOU LOVED ME – **MOFFATTS** (36) 99
UNTIL YOU SUFFER SOME (FIRE AND ICE) – **POISON** (32) 93
UNTOUCHABLE – **RIALTO** (20)...........................98
UP ABOVE MY HEAD I HEAR MUSIC IN THE AIR – **Frankie LAINE and Johnnie RAY** (25) 57
UP AGAINST THE WALL – **Tom ROBINSON** (33)78
UP ALL NIGHT – **SLAUGHTER** (62)....................90
UP AND DOWN [A] – **HIGH** (53)........................90
UP AND DOWN [B] – **VENGABOYS** (4) 98
UP AROUND THE BEND [A] – **CREEDENCE CLEARWATER REVIVAL** (3)..........70
UP AROUND THE BEND [A] – **HANOI ROCKS** (61) 84
UP IN A PUFF OF SMOKE – **Polly BROWN** (43)74
UP MIDDLE FINGER – **OXIDE & NEUTRINO** (7) 01
UP ON THE CATWALK – **SIMPLE MINDS** (27) ..84
UP ON THE DOWN SIDE – **OCEAN COLOUR SCENE** (19) 01
UP ON THE ROOF [A] – **Kenny LYNCH** (10) 62
UP ON THE ROOF [A] – **Julie GRANT** (33) 63
UP ON THE ROOF [A] – **ROBSON and JEROME** (1) 95
UP ROCKING BEATS – **BOMFUNK MC'S** (11) 00
UP TEMPO – **TRONIKHOUSE** (68) 92
UP THE HILL BACKWARDS – **David BOWIE** (32)81
UP THE JUNCTION – **SQUEEZE** (2)....................79
UP THE LADDER TO THE ROOF – **SUPREMES** (6) 70
UP THE POOL – **JETHRO TULL** (11)....................71
UP TO NO GOOD – **PORN KINGS** (28).............96
UP TO THE WILDSTYLE – **PORN KINGS vs DJ SUPREME** (10) 99
UP, UP AND AWAY – **Johnny MANN SINGERS** (6) 67
UP WHERE WE BELONG – **Joe COCKER and Jennifer WARNES** (7) 83
UP WITH PEOPLE – **LAMBCHOP** (66) 00
UP WITH THE COCK – **JUDGE DREAD** (49)........78
UPFIELD – **Billy BRAGG** (46) 96
UPROCK – **ROCKSTEADY CREW** (64) 84
UPSIDE DOWN [A] – **Diana ROSS** (2) 80
UPSIDE DOWN [B] – **A TEENS** (10)....................01
UPTIGHT – **Shara NELSON** (19) 94
UPTIGHT (EVERYTHING'S ALRIGHT) – **Stevie WONDER** (14) 66
UPTOWN DOWNTOWN – **FULL INTENTION** (61) 96
UPTOWN FESTIVAL – **SHALAMAR** (30).............77
UPTOWN GIRL [A] – **Billy JOEL** (1) 83
UPTOWN GIRL [A] – **WESTLIFE** (1) 01
UPTOWN TOP RANKING [A] – **ALTHIA and DONNA** (1) 77
UPTOWN TOP RANKING [A] – **ALI and FRAZIER** (33) 93
UPTOWN UPTEMPO WOMAN – **Randy EDELMAN** (25) 76
URBAN CITY GIRL – **BENZ** (31) 96
URBAN GUERRILLA – **HAWKWIND** (39) 73
URBAN TRAIN – **DJ TIESTO featuring Kirsty HAWKSHAW** (22) 01
URGE – **WILDHEARTS** (26)................................97
THE URGE – **Freddy CANNON** (18)....................60
URGENT – **FOREIGNER** (45)..........................81,82
URGENTLY IN LOVE – **Billy CRAWFORD** (48) 98
USA – **WWF SUPERSTARS** (71) 93
USE IT UP AND WEAR IT OUT [A] – **ODYSSEY** (1) 80
USE IT UP AND WEAR IT OUT [A] – **PAT and MICK** (22) 90
USED TA BE MY GIRL – **O'JAYS** (12) 78
USELESS – **DEPECHE MODE** (28) 97
USELESS (I DON'T NEED YOU NOW) – **Kym MAZELLE** (48)...................................88,90
U16 GIRLS – **TRAVIS** (40) 97
UTOPIA – **GOLDFRAPP** (62) 01
V THIRTEEN – **BIG AUDIO DYNAMITE** (49) 87
VACATION – **Connie FRANCIS** (10)....................62
VADO VIA – **DRUPI** (17) 73
VAGABONDS – **NEW MODEL ARMY** (37) 89
VALENTINE – **T'PAU** (9) 88,93
VALENTINO – **Connie FRANCIS** (27)..................60
VALERIE – **Steve WINWOOD** (19) 82,87
VALLERI – **MONKEES** (12) 68
VALLEY OF TEARS [A] – **Fats DOMINO** (25)......57
VALLEY OF TEARS [B] – **Buddy HOLLY** (12) 61
VALLEY OF THE DOLLS – **GENERATION X** (23)....79
VALLEY OF THE SHADOWS – **ORIGIN UNKNOWN** (60)..................................96
THE VALLEY ROAD – **Bruce HORNSBY and the RANGE** (44)............88
VALOTTE – **Julian LENNON** (55).........................84
VAMOS A LA PLAYA – **RIGHEIRA** (53) 83
VAMP – **OUTLANDER** (51) 91,98
VANESSA – **Ted HEATH** (11)..............................53
VANITY KILLS – **ABC** (70) 85
VAPORIZER – **LUPINE HOWL** (68) 00
VAPORS – **SNOOP DOGG** (18) 97
VASOLINE – **STONE TEMPLE PILOTS** (48) 94
VAVOOM! – **MAN WITH NO NAME** (43) 98
VAYA CON DIOS (MAY GOD BE WITH YOU) [A] – **Les PAUL and Mary FORD** (7) 53
VAYA CON DIOS [A] – **MILLICAN and NESBITT** (20)73
VEGAS [A] – **SLEEPER** (33) 95
VEGAS [B] – **AGNELLI & NELSON** (48) 01
VEHICLE – **IDES OF MARCH** (31) 70
VELCRO FLY – **ZZ TOP** (54) 86
VELOURIA – **PIXIES** (28) 90
VELVET MOODS – **Johan GIELEN presents ABNEA** (74) 01
VENCEREMOS – WE WILL WIN – **WORKING WEEK** (64) 84
VENI VIDI VICI – **Ronnie HILTON** (12) 54
VENTOLIN – **APHEX TWIN** (49) 95
VENTURA HIGHWAY – **AMERICA** (43)................72
VENUS [A] – **Dickie VALENTINE** (20) 59
VENUS [A] – **Frankie AVALON** (16)....................59
VENUS [B] – **SHOCKING BLUE** (8) 70
VENUS [B] – **BANANARAMA** (8) 86
VENUS [B] – **DON PABLO'S ANIMALS** (4) 90
VENUS AND MARS – **Jo BREEZER** (27)..............01
VENUS AS A BOY – **BJÖRK** (29)........................93
VENUS IN BLUE JEANS – **Mark WYNTER** (4) 62
VENUS IN FURS – **VELVET UNDERGROUND** (71)..94
VERNON'S WONDERLAND – **VERNON'S WONDERLAND** (59) 96
VERONICA [A] – **Elvis COSTELLO** (31) 89
VERONICA [B] – **SULTANS OF PING** (69) 92
VERDI – **Mauro PICOTTO** (74) 01
VERSION OF ME – **THOUSAND YARD STARE** (57)93
VERY BEST FRIEND – **PROUD MARY** (75) 01
VERY METAL NOISE POLLUTION (EP) – **POP WILL EAT ITSELF** (45) 89
A VERY PRECIOUS LOVE – **Doris DAY** (16) 58
THE VERY THOUGHT OF YOU [A] – **Tony BENNETT** (21) 65
THE VERY THOUGHT OF YOU [A] – **Natalie COLE** (71) 92
VIBE – **ZHANE** (67) 94
VIBEOLOGY – **Paula ABDUL** (19) 92
VIBRATOR – **Terence Trent D'ARBY** (57) 95
VICIOUS CIRCLES [A] – **POLTERGEIST** (32) 96
VICIOUS CIRCLES [A] – **VICIOUS CIRCLES** (68) 00
VICTIM OF LOVE [A] – **ERASURE** (7) 87
VICTIM OF LOVE [B] – **Bryan ADAMS** (68)........87
VICTIMS – **CULTURE CLUB** (3) 83
VICTIMS OF SUCCESS – **DOGS D'AMOUR** (36) 90
VICTORIA [A] – **KINKS** (33) 70
VICTORIA [A] – **FALL** (35)..................................88
VICTORY – **KOOL and the GANG** (30) 86
VIDEO – **india.arie** (32) 01
VIDEO KILLED THE RADIO STAR [A] – **BUGGLES** (1) 79
VIDEO KILLED THE RADIO STAR [A] – **PRESIDENTS OF THE UNITED STATES OF AMERICA** (52) 98
VIDEOTHEQUE – **DOLLAR** (17) 82
VIENNA – **ULTRAVOX** (2)..............................81,93
VIENNA CALLING – **FALCO** (10) 86
VIETNAM – **Jimmy CLIFF** (46)............................70
VIEW FROM A BRIDGE – **Kim WILDE** (16) 82
A VIEW TO A KILL – **DURAN DURAN** (2) 85
VILLAGE OF ST BERNADETTE – **Anne SHELTON** (27) 59
VINCENT – **Don McLEAN** (1) 72
VINDALOO – **FAT LES** (2)..................................98
VIOLA – **MOOGWAI** (55) 00
VIOLAINE – **COCTEAU TWINS** (56)....................96
VIOLENCE OF SUMMER (LOVE'S TAKING OVER) – **DURAN DURAN** (20) 90
VIOLENTLY (EP) – **HUE AND CRY** (21) 89
VIOLENTLY HAPPY – **BJÖRK** (13) 94
VIOLET [A] – **SEAL** (39) 92
VIOLET [B] – **HOLE** (17) 95
V.I.P. – **JUNGLE BROTHERS** (33)........................99
VIRGIN MARY – **Lonnie DONEGAN** (27) 60
VIRGINIA PLAIN [A] – **ROXY MUSIC** (4)........72,77

VIRGINIA PLAIN [A] — SLAMM (60) 93
VIRTUAL INSANITY — JAMIROQUAI (3) 96
VIRUS [A] — IRON MAIDEN (16) 96
VIRUS [B] — MUTINY UK (42) 01
VISAGE — VISAGE (21) 81
THE VISION — Mario PIU presents DJ ARABESQUE (16) 01
VISION INCISION — LO FIDELITY ALLSTARS (30)98
VISION OF LOVE — Mariah CAREY (9) 90
VISION OF YOU — Belinda CARLISLE (41) 90,91
VISIONARY — REDD KROSS (75) 94
VISIONS [A] — Cliff RICHARD (7) 66
VISIONS [B] — Lena FIAGBE (48) 94
VISIONS IN BLUE — ULTRAVOX (15)..................83
VISIONS OF CHINA — JAPAN (32) 81
VISIONS OF YOU — Jah WOBBLE'S INVADERS of the HEART (35) 92
VITAL SIGNS — RUSH (41) 81
VITO SATAN — CAMPAG VELOCET (75) 00
VIVA BOBBY JOE — EQUALS (6) 69
VIVA EL FULHAM — Tony REES and the COTTAGERS (46) 75
VIVA FOREVER — SPICE GIRLS (1) 98
VIVA LA MEGABABES — SHAMPOO (27) 94
VIVA LA RADIO — LOLLY (6)..............................99
VIVA LAS VEGAS [A] — Elvis PRESLEY (17) 64
VIVA LAS VEGAS [A] — ZZ TOP (10) 92
VIVE LE ROCK — Adam ANT (50) 85
VIVID — ELECTRONIC (17) 99
VIVRANT THING — Q-TIP (39) 00
VOGUE — MADONNA (1).....................................90
THE VOICE [A] — ULTRAVOX (16) 81
THE VOICE [B] — Eimear QUINN (40) 96
VOICE IN THE WILDERNESS — Cliff RICHARD and the SHADOWS (2) 60
VOICE OF FREEDOM — Freedom WILLIAMS (62) 93
VOICES [A] — Dario G (37) 00
VOICES [B] — BEDROCK (44) 00
VOICES [C] — Ann LEE (27) 00
VOICES [D] — DISTURBED (52) 01
VOICES [E] — KC FLIGHTT vs FUNKY JUNCTION (59) 01
VOICES IN THE SKY — MOODY BLUES (27) 68
VOID — EXOTERIX (58).......................................93
VOLARE [A] — Charlie DRAKE (28) 58
VOLARE [A] — Dean MARTIN (2) 58
VOLARE [A] — Domenico MODUGNO (10) 58
VOLARE [A] — Marino MARINI and his QUARTET (13) 58
VOLARE [A] — Bobby RYDELL (22)....................60
VOLCANO GIRLS — VERUCA SALT (56) 97
VOLUME 1 (WHAT YOU WANT WHAT YOU NEED) — INDUSTRY STANDARD (34) 98
VOODOO — WARRIOR (37) 01
VOODOO CHILE — Jimi HENDRIX EXPERIENCE (1) 70
VOODOO PEOPLE — PRODIGY (13) 94,96
VOODOO RAY — A GUY CALLED GERALD (12) ..89
VOODOO VOODOO — Den HEGARTY (73) 79
VOULEZ-VOUS — ABBA (3) 79
THE VOW — TOYAH (50) 83
VOYAGE VOYAGE — DESIRELESS (5) 87,88
VOYEUR — Kim CARNES (68) 82
VULNERABLE — ROXETTE (44) 95
WACK ASS MF — RHYTHMKILLAZ (32) 01
WADE IN THE WATER — Ramsey LEWIS (31) 72
WAGES DAY — DEACON BLUE (18)....................89
THE WAGON — DINOSAUR JR (49) 91
WAIL — Jon SPENCER BLUES EXPLOSION (66) 97
WAIT — Kym MAZELLE (7) 89
WAIT A MINUTE — Ray J featuring LIL' KIM (54)01
WAIT AND BLEED — SLIPKNOT (27)..................00
WAIT FOR ME — Malcolm VAUGHAN (13).........59
WAIT FOR ME, DARLING — Joan REGAN with the JOHNSTON BROTHERS (18)..............54
WAIT FOR ME MARY-ANNE — MARMALADE (30)68
WAIT UNTIL MIDNIGHT — YELLOW DOG (54)....78
WAIT UNTIL TONIGHT (MY LOVE) — Phil FEARON (20) 83
WAITING [A] — STYLE COUNCIL (52) 87
WAITING [B] — GREEN DAY (34) 01
THE WAITING 18 — AMEN (61) 01
WAITING FOR A GIRL LIKE YOU — FOREIGNER (8) 81
WAITING FOR A STAR TO FALL — BOY MEETS GIRL (9) 88
WAITIN' FOR A SUPERMAN — FLAMING LIPS (73)99
WAITING FOR A TRAIN — FLASH and the PAN (7)83
WAITING FOR AN ALIBI — THIN LIZZY (9) 79
WAITING FOR SUMMER — DELIRIOUS? (26) 01
WAITING FOR THAT DAY — George MICHAEL (23)90
(WAITING FOR) THE GHOST TRAIN — MADNESS (18) 86,87
WAITING FOR THE GREAT LEAP FORWARDS — Billy BRAGG (52) 88
WAITING FOR THE LOVEBOAT — ASSOCIATES (53) 84
WAITING FOR THE NIGHT — SAXON (66) 86
WAITING FOR THE SUN — RUFF DRIVERZ (37)..99
WAITING FOR TONIGHT — Jennifer LOPEZ (5) ..99
WAITING HOPEFULLY — D*NOTE (46) 97
WAITING IN VAIN [A] — Bob MARLEY and the WAILERS (27) 77,84
WAITING IN VAIN [A] — Lee RITENOUR and Maxi PRIEST (65)............93
WAITING IN VAIN [A] — Annie LENNOX (31) 95
WAITING ON A FRIEND — ROLLING STONES (50) 81
WAKE ME UP BEFORE YOU GO GO — WHAM! (1) 84
WAKE UP — DANSE SOCIETY (61) 83
WAKE UP AND SCRATCH ME — SULTANS OF PING (50) 94
WAKE UP BOO! — BOO RADLEYS (9)................95
WAKE UP DEAD — MEGADETH (65) 87
WAKE UP EVERYBODY — Harold MELVIN and the BLUENOTES (23)......76
WAKE UP LITTLE SUSIE [A] — EVERLY BROTHERS (2) 57
WAKE UP LITTLE SUSIE [A] — KING BROTHERS (22)57
WAKE UP SUSAN — DETROIT SPINNERS (29) ..77
WAKING UP — ELASTICA (13)............................95
WAKING WITH A STRANGER — TYRREL CORPORATION (59) 92
WALHALLA — GOURYELLA (27) 99
WALK — PANTERA (35) 93
THE WALK [A] — INMATES (36) 79
THE WALK [B] — CURE (12) 83
WALK AWAY [A] — Shane FENTON and the FENTONES (38)........62
WALK AWAY [B] — Matt MONRO (4)..................64
WALK AWAY [C] — SISTERS OF MERCY (45)......84
WALK AWAY [D] — Joyce SIMS (24) 88
WALK AWAY FROM LOVE — David RUFFIN (10) 76
WALK AWAY RENEE — FOUR TOPS (3).............67
WALK DON'T RUN [A] — John BARRY ORCHESTRA (11) 60
WALK DON'T RUN [A] — VENTURES (8) 60
WALK / DON'T WALK — MY LIFE STORY (48)....00
WALK HAND IN HAND [A] — Jimmy PARKINSON (26) 56
WALK HAND IN HAND [A] — Ronnie CARROLL (13) 56
WALK HAND IN HAND [A] — Tony MARTIN (2)..56
WALK HAND IN HAND [A] — GERRY and the PACEMAKERS (29) 65
WALK IN LOVE — MANHATTAN TRANSFER (12) 78
A WALK IN THE BLACK FOREST — Horst JANKOWSKI (3) 65
WALK IN THE NIGHT [A] — Junior WALKER and the ALL-STARS (16) 72
WALK IN THE NIGHT [A] — Paul HARDCASTLE (54)88
A WALK IN THE PARK — Nick STRAKER BAND (20)80
WALK INTO THE WIND — VEGAS (65) 93
WALK LIKE A CHAMPION — KALEEF (23) 96
WALK LIKE A MAN [A] — FOUR SEASONS (12)..63
WALK LIKE A MAN [A] — DIVINE (23)................85
WALK LIKE A PANTHER '98 — The ALL SEEING I featuring Tony CHRISTIE (10) 99
WALK LIKE AN EGYPTIAN — BANGLES (3) ..86,90
WALK OF LIFE [A] — DIRE STRAITS (2)..............86
WALK OF LIFE [B] — Billie PIPER (25) 00
WALK ON [A] — Roy ORBISON (39) 68
WALK ON [B] — U2 (5) 01
WALK ON AIR — T'PAU (62) 91
WALK ON BY [A] — Leroy VAN DYKE (5) 62
WALK ON BY [B] — Dionne WARWICK (9) 64
WALK ON BY [B] — STRANGLERS (21) 78
WALK ON BY [B] — AVERAGE WHITE BAND (46) 79
WALK ON BY [B] — D TRAIN (44).......................82
WALK ON BY [B] — SYBIL (6)............................90
WALK ON BY [B] — GABRIELLE (7)....................97
WALK ON GILDED SPLINTERS — Marsha HUNT (46) 69
WALK ON THE WILD SIDE [A] — Lou REED (10) 73
WALK ON THE WILD SIDE [A] — BEAT SYSTEM (63) 90
WALK ON THE WILD SIDE [A] — Jamie J MORGAN (27) 90
WALK OUT TO WINTER — AZTEC CAMERA (64) 83
WALK RIGHT BACK [A] — EVERLY BROTHERS (1) ..61
WALK RIGHT BACK [A] — Perry COMO (33) 73
WALK RIGHT IN — ROOFTOP SINGERS (10) 63
WALK RIGHT NOW — JACKSONS (7) 81
WALK TALL — Val DOONICAN (3) 64
WALK THE DINOSAUR — WAS (NOT WAS) (10) 87
WALK...(THE DOG) LIKE AN EGYPTIAN — JODE (48)98
WALK THIS LAND — E-Z ROLLERS (18).............99
WALK THIS WAY — RUN-DMC (8)......................86
WALK THIS WORLD — Heather NOVA (69)........95
WALK THROUGH THE FIRE — Peter GABRIEL (69) 84
WALK THROUGH THE WORLD — Marc COHN (37)93
WALK WITH FAITH IN YOUR HEART — BACHELORS (22) 66
WALK WITH ME — SEEKERS (10) 66
WALK WITH ME MY ANGEL — Don CHARLES (39) 62
WALK WITH ME TALK WITH ME DARLING — FOUR TOPS (32) 72
WALKAWAY — CAST (9) 96
WALKIN' — CCS (7) 71
WALKIN' BACK TO HAPPINESS — Helen SHAPIRO (1)..61
WALKIN IN THE NAME — FUNKSTAR DE LUXE (42) 00
WALKIN' IN THE RAIN WITH THE ONE I LOVE — LOVE UNLIMITED (14) 72
A WALKIN' MIRACLE — LIMMIE and the FAMILY COOKIN' (6) 74
WALKIN' ON — SHEER BRONZE featuring Lisa MILLETT (63) 94
WALKIN' ON THE SUN — SMASH MOUTH (19)..97
WALKIN' ON UP — DJ PROFESSOR (64)............97
WALKIN' TALL [A] — Frankie VAUGHAN (28) 59
WALKIN' TALL [B] — Adam FAITH (23) 63
WALKIN' THE DOG — DENNISONS (36) 64
WALKIN' THE LINE — BRASS CONSTRUCTION (47) 83
WALKIN' TO MISSOURI — Tony BRENT (7) ..52,53
WALKING AFTER YOU: BEACON LIGHT — FOO FIGHTERS (20)...98
WALKING ALONE — Richard ANTHONY (37)......63
WALKING AWAY — Craig DAVID (3) 00
WALKING BY MYSELF — Gary MOORE (48) 90
WALKING DOWN MADISON — Kirsty MacCOLL (23)91
WALKING DOWN YOUR STREET — BANGLES (16) 87
WALKING IN MEMPHIS [A] — Marc COHN (22) ..91
WALKING IN MEMPHIS [A] — CHER (11) 95
WALKING IN MY SHOES — DEPECHE MODE (14) 93
WALKING IN MY SLEEP — Roger DALTREY (56)84
WALKING IN RHYTHM — BLACKBYRDS (23)......75
WALKING IN THE AIR [A] — Aled JONES (5) 85
WALKING IN THE AIR [A] — Peter AUTY and the SINFONIA OF LONDON conducted by Howard BLAKE (37) 85,87
WALKING IN THE AIR [A] — DIGITAL DREAM BABY (49) 91
WALKING IN THE RAIN [A] — WALKER BROTHERS (26)................................67
WALKING IN THE RAIN [A] — PARTRIDGE FAMILY (10) 73
WALKING IN THE RAIN [B] — MODERN ROMANCE (7)..................................83
WALKING IN THE SUNSHINE — BAD MANNERS (10)81
WALKING INTO SUNSHINE — CENTRAL LINE (42) 81
WALKING MY BABY BACK HOME — Johnnie RAY (12) 52
WALKING MY CAT NAMED DOG — Norma TANEGA (22) 66
WALKING ON AIR [A] — FRAZIER CHORUS (60) 91
WALKING ON AIR [B] — BAD BOYS INC (24) 93
WALKING ON BROKEN GLASS — Annie LENNOX (8)...92
WALKING ON ICE — RIVER CITY PEOPLE (62) ..90
WALKING ON SUNSHINE [A] — ROCKER'S REVENGE featuring Donnie CALVIN (4) 82
WALKING ON SUNSHINE [A] — Eddy GRANT (57) 89,01
WALKING ON SUNSHINE [A] — KRUSH (71) 92
WALKING ON SUNSHINE [B] — KATRINA and the WAVES (8) 85,96
WALKING ON THE CHINESE WALL — Philip BAILEY (34)..85
WALKING ON THE MILKY WAY — ORCHESTRAL MANOEUVRES IN THE DARK (17) 96
WALKING ON THE MOON — POLICE (1) 79
WALKING ON THIN ICE — Yoko ONO (35) 81
WALKING ON WATER — MADASUN (14) 00

WHAT BECOMES OF THE BROKEN HEARTED [A] – Dave STEWART guest vocals: Colin BLUNSTONE (13) 81
WHAT BECOMES OF THE BROKENHEARTED [A] – ROBSON and JEROME (1) 96
WHAT CAN I DO – CORRS (3) 98
WHAT CAN I SAY – Boz SCAGGS (10) 77
(WHAT CAN I SAY) TO MAKE YOU LOVE ME – Alexander O'NEAL (27) 88
WHAT CAN YOU DO FOR ME – UTAH SAINTS (10) 91
WHAT 'CHA GONNA DO – ETERNAL (16) 99
WHAT DID I DO TO YOU (EP) – Lisa STANSFIELD (25) 90
WHAT DIFFERENCE DOES IT MAKE – SMITHS (12) 84
WHAT DO I DO – Phil FEARON (5) 84
WHAT DO I DO NOW – SLEEPER (14) 95
WHAT DO I GET – BUZZCOCKS (37) 78
WHAT DO I HAVE TO DO – Kylie MINOGUE (6) 91
WHAT DO YA SAY – Chubby CHECKER (37) 63
WHAT DO YOU WANT – Adam FAITH (1) 59
WHAT DO YOU WANT FROM ME? – MONACO (11) 97
WHAT DO YOU WANT TO MAKE THOSE EYES AT ME FOR [A] – Emile FORD and the CHECKMATES (1) 59
WHAT DO YOU WANT TO MAKE THOSE EYES AT ME FOR [A] – Shakin' STEVENS (5) 87
WHAT DOES IT TAKE – THEN JERICO (33) 89
WHAT DOES IT TAKE (TO WIN YOUR LOVE) [A] – Junior WALKER and the ALL-STARS (13) 69
WHAT DOES IT TAKE (TO WIN YOUR LOVE) [A] – Kenny G (64) 86
WHAT DOES YOUR SOUL LOOK LIKE – DJ SHADOW (59) 95,98
WHAT EVER HAPPENED TO OLD FASHIONED LOVE – Daniel O'DONNELL (21) 93
WHAT GOD WANTS PART 1 – Roger WATERS (35) 92
WHAT GOES AROUND [A] – Bitty McLEAN (36) 94
WHAT GOES AROUND [B] – LUCIANA (67) 94
WHAT GOES AROUND COMES AROUND – Bob MARLEY and the WAILERS (42) 96
WHAT GOES ON – Bryan FERRY (67) 78
WHAT GOOD AM I – Cilla BLACK (24) 67
WHAT HAPPENED TO THE MUSIC – Joey NEGRO (51) 93
WHAT HAVE I DONE TO DESERVE THIS – PET SHOP BOYS and Dusty SPRINGFIELD (2) 87
WHAT HAVE THEY DONE TO MY SONG MA [A] – NEW SEEKERS (44) 70
WHAT HAVE THEY DONE TO MY SONG MA [A] – MELANIE (39) 71
WHAT HAVE THEY DONE TO THE RAIN – SEARCHERS (13) 64
WHAT HAVE YOU DONE FOR ME LATELY – Janet JACKSON (3) 86
WHAT HAVE YOU DONE (IS THIS ALL) – OUR TRIBE / ONE TRIBE (52) 92
WHAT HOPE HAVE I – SPHINX (43) 95
WHAT I AM [A] – Edie BRICKELL and the NEW BOHEMIANS (31) 89
WHAT I AM [A] – TIN TIN OUT featuring Emma BUNTON (2) 99
WHAT I CAN DO FOR YOU – Sheryl CROW (43) 95
WHAT I DO BEST – Robin S (43) 93
WHAT I GOT – SUBLIME (71) 97
WHAT I GOT IS WHAT YOU NEED – UNIQUE (27) 83
WHAT I LIKE MOST ABOUT YOU IS YOUR GIRLFRIEND – SPECIALS (51) 84
WHAT I MEAN – MODJO (59) 01
WHAT I MISS THE MOST – ALOOF (70) 98
WHAT IF... – LIGHTNING SEEDS (14) 96,97
WHAT IF – Kate WINSLET (6) 01
WHAT IN THE WORLD – NU COLOURS (57) 93
WHAT IN THE WORLD'S COME OVER YOU [A] – Jack SCOTT (11) 60
WHAT IN THE WORLD'S COME OVER YOU [A] – ROCKIN' BERRIES (23) 65
WHAT IN THE WORLD'S COME OVER YOU [A] – Tam WHITE (36) 75
WHAT IS A MAN – FOUR TOPS (16) 69
WHAT IS HOUSE (EP) – LFO (62) 92
WHAT IS LIFE [A] – Olivia NEWTON-JOHN (16) 72
WHAT IS LIFE [A] – Shawn MULLINS (62) 99
WHAT IS LIFE? [B] – BLACK UHURU (56) 84
WHAT IS LOVE [A] – Howard JONES (2) 83
WHAT IS LOVE [B] – DEEE-LITE (2) 90
WHAT IS LOVE [C] – HADDAWAY (2) 93
WHAT IS THIS THING CALLED LOVE – Alexander O'NEAL (53) 91
WHAT IS TRUTH – Johnny CASH (21) 70
WHAT IT FEELS LIKE FOR A GIRL – MADONNA (7) 01
WHAT IT IS [A] – Garnet MIMMS and TRUCKIN' CO (44) 77
WHAT IT IS [B] – Freddy FRESH (63) 99
WHAT IT'S LIKE – EVERLAST (34) 99
WHAT I'VE GOT IN MIND – Billie Jo SPEARS (4) 76
WHAT KIND OF FOOL – ALL ABOUT EVE (29) 88
WHAT KIND OF FOOL AM I? [A] – Anthony NEWLEY (36) 61
WHAT KIND OF FOOL AM I? [A] – Sammy DAVIS Jr (26) 62
WHAT KIND OF FOOL AM I? [A] – Shirley BASSEY (47) 63
WHAT KIND OF FOOL (HEARD IT ALL BEFORE) – Kylie MINOGUE (14) 92
WHAT KIND OF MAN WOULD I BE – MINT CONDITION (38) 97
WHAT KINDA BOY YOU LOOKING FOR (GIRL) – HOT CHOCOLATE (10) 83
WHAT MADE MILWAUKEE FAMOUS (HAS MADE A LOSER OUT OF ME) – Rod STEWART (4) 72
WHAT MAKES A MAN – WESTLIFE (2) 00
WHAT MAKES A MAN A MAN (LIVE) – Marc ALMOND (60) 93
WHAT MAKES YOU CRY – PROCLAIMERS (38) 94
WHAT MORE DO YOU WANT – Frankie VAUGHAN (25) 60
WHAT NOW – Adam FAITH (31) 63
WHAT NOW MY LOVE [A] – Shirley BASSEY (5) 62
WHAT NOW MY LOVE [A] – SONNY and CHER (13) 66
WHAT PRESENCE? – ORANGE JUICE (47) 84
WHAT THE WORLD IS WAITING FOR – STONE ROSES (8) 89,90
WHAT THEY DO – ROOTS (49) 97
WHAT TIME IS IT – SPIN DOCTORS (56) 93
WHAT TIME IS IT? – DUST JUNKYS (39) 98
WHAT TIME IS LOVE (LIVE AT TRANCENTRAL) – KLF (5) 90
WHAT TO DO – Buddy HOLLY (27) 61,63
WHAT TOOK YOU SO LONG – Emma BUNTON (1) 01
WHAT U DO – COLOURS featuring EMMANUEL & ESKA (51) 99
WHAT 'U' WAITIN' '4' – JUNGLE BROTHERS (35) 90
WHAT WILL I DO WITHOUT YOU – Lene LOVICH (58) 80
WHAT'LL I DO – Janet JACKSON (9) 95
WHAT WILL MARY SAY – Johnny MATHIS (49) 63
WHAT WOULD HAPPEN – Meredith BROOKS (49) 98
WHAT WOULD I BE – Val DOONICAN (2) 66
WHAT WOULD WE DO? – DSK (46) 91,97
WHAT WOULD YOU DO? – CITY HIGH (3) 01
WHAT WOULD YOU DO IF...? – CODE RED (55) 98
WHAT YA GOT 4 ME – SIGNUM (70) 98
WHAT YA LOOKIN' AT – CROW (60) 01
WHAT YOU DO – BIG BASS vs Michelle NARINE (67) 00
WHAT YOU DO TO ME (EP) – TEENAGE FANCLUB (31) 92
WHAT YOU GET IS WHAT YOU SEE – Tina TURNER (30) 87
WHAT YOU GONNA DO ABOUT IT – TOTAL CONTRAST (63) 86
WHAT YOU NEED [A] – INXS (51) 86
WHAT YOU NEED [B] – POWERHOUSE (13) 99
WHAT YOU SAY – LIGHTNING SEEDS (41) 97
WHAT YOU SEE IS WHAT YOU GET – Glen GOLDSMITH (33) 88
WHAT YOU THINK OF THAT – JAY-Z (58) 99
WHAT YOU WAITING FOR – STARGARD (39) 78
WHAT YOU WANT [A] – XPANSIONS (55) 91
WHAT YOU WANT [B] – FUTURE FORCE (47) 96
WHAT YOU WANT [C] – MASE / TOTAL (15) 98
WHAT YOU WON'T DO FOR LOVE – GO WEST (15) 93
WHAT YOU'RE MISSING – K-KLASS (24) 94
WHAT YOU'RE PROPOSING – STATUS QUO (2) 80
WHATCHA GONE DO? – LINK (48) 98
WHAT'CHA GONNA DO – Shabba RANKS featuring Queen LATIFAH (21) 93
WHATCHA GONNA DO WITH MY LOVIN' – INNER CITY (12) 89
WHATCHA GONNA DO ABOUT IT [A] – Doris TROY (37) 64,65
WHATCHA GONNA DO ABOUT IT? [A] – SMALL FACES (14) 65
WHATCHA GONNA DO NOW – Chris ANDREWS (40) 66
WHAT'D I SAY – Jerry Lee LEWIS (10) 61
WHAT'D YOU COME HERE FOR? – TRINA and TAMARA (46) 99
WHATEVER [A] – OASIS (3) 94,95,96
WHATEVER [A] – IDEAL US featuring LIL' MO (31) 99,00
WHATEVER [B] – EN VOGUE (14) 97
WHATEVER GETS YOU THROUGH THE NIGHT – John LENNON (36) 74
WHATEVER HAPPENED TO YOU ('LIKELY LADS' THEME) – HIGHLY LIKELY (35) 73
WHATEVER I DO (WHEREVER I GO) – Hazell DEAN (4) 84
WHATEVER IT TAKES – OLYMPIC RUNNERS (61) 78
WHATEVER LOLA WANTS – Alma COGAN (26) 57
WHATEVER MAKES YOU HAPPY – TEN CITY (60) 90
WHATEVER WILL BE WILL BE – Doris DAY (1) ..56
WHATEVER YOU NEED – Tina TURNER (27) 00
WHATEVER YOU WANT [A] – STATUS QUO (4) 79
WHATEVER YOU WANT [B] – Tina TURNER (23) 96
WHAT'S A GIRL TO DO – SISTER 2 SISTER (61) ..00
WHAT'S ANOTHER YEAR – Johnny LOGAN (1) ..80
WHAT'S GOIN DOWN – HONKY (49) 96
WHAT'S GOING ON [A] – MEKON featuring Roxanne SHANTE (43) 00
WHAT'S GOING ON [B] – Cyndi LAUPER (57) ..87
WHAT'S GOING ON [B] – MUSIC RELIEF '94 (70) 94
WHAT'S GOING ON [B] – ARTISTS AGAINST AIDS WORLDWIDE (6) 01
WHAT'S GOING ON [C] – WOOKIE (45) 00
WHAT'S IN A KISS? – Gilbert O'SULLIVAN (19) 80
WHAT'S IN A WORD – CHRISTIANS (33) 92
WHAT'S IN THE BOX (SEE WATCHA GOT) – BOO RADLEYS (25) 96
WHAT'S IT ALL ABOUT – RUN-DMC (48) 90
WHAT'S IT GONNA BE?! – Janet JACKSON / Busta RHYMES (6) 99
WHAT'S IT LIKE TO BE BEAUTIFUL – Lena FIAGBE (52) 94
WHAT'S LOVE GOT TO DO WITH IT [A] – Tina TURNER (3) 84
WHAT'S LOVE GOT TO DO WITH IT [A] – Warren G featuring Adina HOWARD (2) 96
WHAT'S MY AGE AGAIN? – BLINK 182 (17) 99,00
WHAT'S MY NAME? – SNOOP DOGG (20) 93
WHAT'S NEW PUSSYCAT – Tom JONES (11) 65
WHAT'S ON YOUR MIND – George BENSON (45) 81
WHAT'S SO DIFFERENT? – GINUWINE (10) 99
WHAT'S THAT TUNE (DOO DOO DOO DOO DOO-DOO-DOO-DOO-DOO-DOO) – DOROTHY (31) 95
WHAT'S THE COLOUR OF MONEY? – HOLLYWOOD BEYOND (7) 86
WHAT'S THE FREQUENCY, KENNETH – R.E.M. (9) 94
WHAT'S THE POINT – WE'VE GOT A FUZZBOX AND WE'RE GONNA USE IT (51) 87
WHAT'S UP [A] – 4 NON BLONDES (2) 93
WHAT'S UP [A] – DJ MIKO (6) 94
WHAT'S UP WITH THAT – ZZ TOP (58) 96
(WHAT'S WRONG WITH) DREAMING – RIVER CITY PEOPLE (40) 89,90
WHAT'S WRONG WITH THIS PICTURE – Chesney HAWKES (63) 93
WHAT'S YOUR FANTASY – LUDACRIS (19) 01
WHAT'S YOUR NAME – CHICORY TIP (13) 72
WHAT'S YOUR NAME? – Angel LEE (39) 00
WHAT'S YOUR NAME WHAT'S YOUR NUMBER – Andrea TRUE CONNECTION (34) 78
WHAT'S YOUR PROBLEM? – BLANCMANGE (40) ..85
WHAT'S YOUR SIGN? – DES'REE (19) 98
WHAT'S YOUR SIGN GIRL – Barry BIGGS (55) ..79
WHATTA MAN – SALT-N-PEPA with EN VOGUE (7) 94
WHAZZUP – TRUE PARTY (13) 00
THE WHEEL – SPEAR OF DESTINY (59) 83
WHEEL OF FORTUNE – ACE OF BASE (20) 93

WHEELS – STRING-A-LONGS (8) 61
WHEELS AIN'T COMING DOWN – SLADE (60) ..81
WHEELS CHA CHA – Joe LOSS (21) 61
WHEELS OF STEEL – SAXON (20) 80
WHEN [A] – KALIN TWINS (1) 58
WHEN [A] – SHOWADDYWADDY (3) 77
WHEN [B] – SUNSCREEM (47) 95
WHEN [C] – Shania TWAIN (18) 98
WHEN A CHILD IS BORN (SOLEADO) [A] – Johnny MATHIS (1) 76
WHEN A CHILD IS BORN [A] – Gladys KNIGHT and the PIPS (74) 81
WHEN A HEART BEATS – Nik KERSHAW (27) ..85
WHEN A MAN LOVES A WOMAN [A] – Percy SLEDGE (2) 66,87
WHEN A MAN LOVES A WOMAN [A] – Michael BOLTON (8) 91
WHEN A MAN LOVES A WOMAN [B] – Jody WATLEY (33) 94
WHEN A WOMAN – GABRIELLE (6) 00
WHEN AM I GONNA MAKE A LIVING – SADE (36) 84
WHEN BOUZOUKIS PLAYED – Vicky LEANDROS (44) 73
WHEN BOYS TALK – INDEEP (67) 83
WHEN CAN I SEE YOU – BABYFACE (35)..........94
WHEN CHILDREN RULE THE WORLD – RED HILL CHILDREN (40)....................96
WHEN DO I GET TO SING 'MY WAY' – SPARKS (32) 94,95
WHEN DOVES CRY [A] – PRINCE (4) 84
WHEN DOVES CRY [A] – GINUWINE (10) 97
WHEN DREAMS TURN TO DUST – Cathy DENNIS (43) 97
WHEN FOREVER HAS GONE – Demis ROUSSOS (2)....................76
WHEN HE SHINES – Sheena EASTON (12)........81
WHEN HEROES GO DOWN – Suzanne VEGA (58)93
WHEN I ARGUE I SEE SHAPES – IDLEWILD (19)99
WHEN I CALL YOUR NAME – Mary KIANI (18) ..95
WHEN I COME AROUND – GREEN DAY (27) 95
WHEN I COME HOME – Spencer DAVIS GROUP (12) 66
WHEN I DREAM [A] – TEARDROP EXPLODES (47) 80
WHEN I DREAM [B] – Carol KIDD featuring Terry WAITE (58) 92
WHEN I FALL IN LOVE [A] – Nat 'King' COLE (2)....................57,87
WHEN I FALL IN LOVE [A] – Donny OSMOND (4) 73
WHEN I FALL IN LOVE [A] – Rick ASTLEY (2)....87
WHEN I FALL IN LOVE [B] – ANT & DEC (12)....96
WHEN I GET HOME – SEARCHERS (35)............65
WHEN I GROW UP [A] – Michelle SHOCKED (67) 89
WHEN I GROW UP [B] – GARBAGE (9)..............99
WHEN I GROW UP (TO BE A MAN) – BEACH BOYS (27) 64
WHEN I KISS YOU (I HEAR CHARLIE PARKER PLAYING) – SPARKS (36)................95
WHEN I LEAVE THE WORLD BEHIND – Rose MARIE (63) 83
WHEN I LOOK INTO YOUR EYES [A] – FIREHOUSE (65) 92
WHEN I LOOK INTO YOUR EYES [B] – MAXEE (55) 01
WHEN I NEED YOU [A] – Leo SAYER (1)......77,93
WHEN I NEED YOU [A] – Will MELLOR (5)........98
WHEN I SAID GOODBYE – STEPS (5) 00
WHEN I SEE YOU SMILE – BAD ENGLISH (61)..89
WHEN I THINK OF YOU [A] – Janet JACKSON (10) 86
WHEN I THINK OF YOU [B] – Kenny THOMAS (27) 95
WHEN I THINK OF YOU [C] – Chris DE BURGH (59) 99
WHEN I WAS YOUNG [A] – ANIMALS (45) 67
WHEN I WAS YOUNG [B] – RIVER CITY PEOPLE (62) 91
WHEN I'M AWAY FROM YOU – Frankie MILLER (42) 79
WHEN I'M BACK ON MY FEET AGAIN – Michael BOLTON (44) 90
WHEN I'M CLEANING WINDOWS (TURNED OUT NICE AGAIN) – 2 IN A TENT (25) 94,96
WHEN I'M DEAD AND GONE – McGUINNESS FLINT (2) 70
WHEN I'M GOOD AND READY – SYBIL (5)......93,97
WHEN I'M SIXTY FOUR – Kenny BALL and his JAZZMEN (43) 67
WHEN IT'S LOVE – VAN HALEN (28) 88
WHEN IT'S OVER – SUGAR RAY (32) 01
WHEN IT'S TIME TO ROCK – UFO (70) 83
WHEN JOHNNY COMES MARCHING HOME – Adam FAITH (5)....................60
WHEN JULIE COMES AROUND – CUFFLINKS (10) 70
WHEN LOVE AND HATE COLLIDE – DEF LEPPARD (2) 95
WHEN LOVE BREAKS DOWN – PREFAB SPROUT (25) 85
WHEN LOVE COMES ALONG – Matt MONRO (46)62
WHEN LOVE COMES CALLING – Paul JOHNSON (52)....................87
WHEN LOVE COMES ROUND AGAIN (L'ARCA DI NOE) – Ken DODD (19) 71
WHEN LOVE COMES TO TOWN – U2 with BB KING (6) 89
WHEN LOVE TAKES OVER YOU – Donna SUMMER (72) 89
WHEN MEXICO GAVE UP THE RHUMBA – Mitchell TOROK (6) 56,57
WHEN MY BABY – SCOOCH (29)....................99
WHEN MY LITTLE GIRL IS SMILING [A] – Craig DOUGLAS (9) 62
WHEN MY LITTLE GIRL IS SMILING [A] – DRIFTERS (31) 62
WHEN MY LITTLE GIRL IS SMILING [A] – Jimmy JUSTICE (9) 62
WHEN MY LITTLE GIRL IS SMILING [B] – DRIFTERS (69)....................79
WHEN ONLY LOVE WILL DO – Richard DARBYSHIRE (54)....................94
WHEN ROCK 'N ROLL CAME TO TRINIDAD – Nat 'King' COLE (28) 57
WHEN SHE WAS MY GIRL – FOUR TOPS (3) 81
WHEN SMOKEY SINGS – ABC (11) 87
WHEN THE BOYS TALK ABOUT THE GIRLS – Valerie CARR (29) 58
WHEN THE FINGERS POINT – CHRISTIANS (34)87
WHEN THE GIRL IN YOUR ARMS IS THE GIRL IN YOUR HEART – Cliff RICHARD (3) 61
WHEN THE GOING GETS TOUGH, THE TOUGH GET GOING [A] – Billy OCEAN (1)................86
WHEN THE GOING GETS TOUGH [A] – BOYZONE (1) 99
WHEN THE HEARTACHE IS OVER – Tina TURNER (10) 99
WHEN THE HOODOO COMES – DIESEL PARK WEST (62) 89
WHEN THE LIGHTS GO OUT – FIVE (4) 98
WHEN THE MORNING COMES – LOVE DECADE (69) 93
WHEN THE MORNING SUN DRIES THE DEW – QUIET FIVE (45)....................65
WHEN THE NIGHT COMES – Joe COCKER (61)....................90,92
WHEN THE RAIN BEGINS TO FALL – Jermaine JACKSON and Pia ZADORA (68) 84
WHEN THE SH.. GOES DOWN – CYPRESS HILL (19) 93
WHEN THE SUMMERTIME IS OVER – Jackie TRENT (39) 65
WHEN THE SUN COMES SHININ' THRU – Long John BALDRY (29) 68
WHEN THE TIGERS BROKE FREE – PINK FLOYD (39)....................82
WHEN THE WIND BLOWS – David BOWIE (44) 86
WHEN THE WORLD IS RUNNING DOWN – DIFFERENT GEAR vs POLICE (28) 00
WHEN THE YEAR ENDS IN 1 – TOTTENHAM HOTSPUR FA CUP FINAL SQUAD (44) 91
WHEN TOMORROW COMES – EURYTHMICS (30) 86
WHEN TWO WORLDS COLLIDE – Jim REEVES (17) 69
WHEN TWO WORLDS DRIFT APART – Cliff RICHARD (46)....................77
WHEN WE ARE FAR FROM HOME – ENGLAND WORLD CUP SQUAD (66) 86
WHEN WE ARE TOGETHER – TEXAS (12)..........99
WHEN WE DANCE – STING (9) 94
WHEN WE WAS FAB – George HARRISON (25) 88
WHEN WE WERE YOUNG [A] – Solomon KING (21)....................68
WHEN WE WERE YOUNG [B] – BUCKS FIZZ (10) ..83
WHEN WE WERE YOUNG [C] – WHIPPING BOY (46) 96
WHEN WE WERE YOUNG [D] – HUMAN NATURE (43)....................01
WHEN WILL I BE FAMOUS – BROS (2) 87,88
WHEN WILL I BE LOVED – EVERLY BROTHERS (4)....................60
WHEN WILL I SEE YOU AGAIN [A] – THREE DEGREES (1)....................74
WHEN WILL I SEE YOU AGAIN [A] – BROTHER BEYOND (43) 89
WHEN WILL I SEE YOU AGAIN [A] – Sheila FERGUSON (60) 94
WHEN WILL THE GOOD APPLES FALL – SEEKERS (11)....................67
WHEN WILL YOU BE MINE – AVERAGE WHITE BAND (49) 79
WHEN WILL YOU MAKE MY TELEPHONE RING – DEACON BLUE (34) 88
WHEN WILL YOU SAY I LOVE YOU – Billy FURY (3) 63
WHEN YOU ARE A KING – WHITE PLAINS (13) 71
WHEN YOU ASK ABOUT LOVE [A] – CRICKETS (27)....................60
WHEN YOU ASK ABOUT LOVE [A] – MATCHBOX (4) 80
WHEN YOU BELIEVE – Mariah CAREY and Whitney HOUSTON (4) 98,99
WHEN YOU COME BACK TO ME – Jason DONOVAN (2) 89
WHEN YOU GET RIGHT DOWN TO IT – Ronnie DYSON (34)....................71
WHEN YOU GONNA LEARN – JAMIROQUAI (28) 92,93
WHEN YOU LOSE THE ONE YOU LOVE – David WHITFIELD (7)....................55
WHEN YOU MADE THE MOUNTAIN – OPUS III (71)....................94
WHEN YOU SAY NOTHING AT ALL – Ronan KEATING (1)....................99,00
(WHEN YOU SAY YOU LOVE SOMEBODY) IN THE HEART – KOOL and the GANG (7)....84
WHEN YOU TELL ME THAT YOU LOVE ME – Diana ROSS (2) 91
WHEN YOU WALK IN THE ROOM [A] – SEARCHERS (3) 64
WHEN YOU WALK IN THE ROOM [A] – CHILD (38) 78
WHEN YOU WALK IN THE ROOM [A] – Paul CARRACK (48) 87
WHEN YOU WALK IN THE ROOM [A] – STATUS QUO (34) 95
WHEN YOU WERE SWEET SIXTEEN – FUREYS (14)....................81
WHEN YOU WERE YOUNG – DEL AMITRI (20) 93
WHEN YOUR 'EX' WANTS YOU BACK – SURFACE (52) 84
WHEN YOUR OLD WEDDING RING WAS NEW – Jimmy ROSELLI (51) 83,87
WHEN YOU'RE GONE – Bryan ADAMS featuring Melanie C (3) 98
WHEN YOU'RE IN LOVE WITH A BEAUTIFUL WOMAN – DR HOOK (1)........79,92
WHEN YOU'RE NUMBER 1 – Gene CHANDLER (43)....................79
WHEN YOU'RE YOUNG – JAM (17) 79,83
WHEN YOU'RE YOUNG AND IN LOVE [A] – MARVELETTES (13) 67
WHEN YOU'RE YOUNG AND IN LOVE [A] – FLYING PICKETS (7)....................84
WHENEVER GOD SHINES HIS LIGHT – Van MORRISON with Cliff RICHARD (20)........89
WHENEVER YOU NEED ME – T'PAU (16) 91
WHENEVER YOU NEED SOMEBODY – Rick ASTLEY (3)....................87
WHENEVER YOU NEED SOMEONE – BAD BOYS INC (26)....................93
WHENEVER YOU WANT MY LOVE – REAL THING (18) 78
WHENEVER YOU'RE NEAR – CHER (72)...........93
WHENEVER YOU'RE READY – FIVE STAR (11)....................87
WHENEVER I STOP – MIKE and the MECHANICS (73)....................99
WHERE ARE THEY NOW? – GENE (22) 97
WHERE ARE YOU [A] – KAVANA (26)................96
WHERE ARE YOU [B] – IMAANI (15)..................98
WHERE ARE YOU BABY – Betty BOO (3)..........90
WHERE ARE YOU GOING TO MY LOVE – BROTHERHOOD OF MAN (22) 70
WHERE ARE YOU NOW? – GENERATOR (60) 99
WHERE ARE YOU NOW (MY LOVE) – Jackie TRENT (1) 65
WHERE CAN I FIND LOVE – LIVIN' JOY (12)......97

WHERE DID ALL THE GOOD TIMES GO – Donny OSMOND (18) 74
WHERE DID I GO WRONG – UB40 (26) 88
WHERE DID OUR LOVE GO [A] – SUPREMES (3) ..64
WHERE DID OUR LOVE GO [A] – MANHATTAN TRANSFER (40) 78
WHERE DID OUR LOVE GO [A] – Tricia PENROSE (71) 96
WHERE DID OUR LOVE GO? [B] – Donnie ELBERT (8) 72
WHERE DID WE GO WRONG – LIQUID GOLD (56) 82
WHERE DID YOUR HEART GO – WHAM! (1) 86
WHERE DO BROKEN HEARTS GO – Whitney HOUSTON (14) 88
(WHERE DO I BEGIN) LOVE STORY [A] – Andy WILLIAMS (4) 71
(WHERE DO I BEGIN) LOVE STORY [A] – Shirley BASSEY (34) 71
WHERE DO I STAND? – MONTROSE AVENUE (38) 98
WHERE DO U WANT ME TO PUT IT – SOLO U.S. (45) 96
WHERE DO WE GO – TEN CITY (60) 89
WHERE DO WE GO FROM HERE – Cliff RICHARD (60) 82
WHERE DO YOU GO – NO MERCY (2) 97
WHERE DO YOU GO TO MY LOVELY – Peter SARSTEDT (1) 69
WHERE DOES MY HEART BEAT NOW – Celine DION (72) 93
WHERE DOES THE TIME GO – Julia FORDHAM (41) 89
WHERE EAGLES FLY – CRYSTAL PALACE (50) ..90
WHERE HAS ALL THE LOVE GONE [A] – YAZZ (16) 89
WHERE HAS ALL THE LOVE GONE [A] – MAUREEN (51) 91
WHERE HAS LOVE GONE – Holly JOHNSON (73) 90
WHERE HAVE ALL THE COWBOYS GONE? – Paula COLE (15) 97
WHERE HAVE YOU BEEN TONIGHT – SHED SEVEN (23) 95
WHERE I FIND MY HEAVEN – GIGOLO AUNTS (29) 95
WHERE I WANNA BE – Shade SHEIST featuring Nate DOGG and KURUPT (14) 01
WHERE I'M HEADED – Lene MARLIN (31) 01
WHERE IN THE WORLD [A] – SWING OUT SISTER (47) 89
WHERE IN THE WORLD [B] – BBM (57) 94
WHERE IS MY MAN – Eartha KITT (36) 83
WHERE IS THE FEELING – Kylie MINOGUE (16) 95
WHERE IS THE LOVE [A] – Roberta FLACK (29) 72
WHERE IS THE LOVE [A] – Betty WRIGHT (25) 75
WHERE IS THE LOVE [A] – Mica PARIS and Will DOWNING (19) 89
WHERE IS THE LOVE? [B] – ADEVA (54) 97
WHERE IS THE LOVE (WE USED TO KNOW) – DELEGATION (22) 77
WHERE IS TOMORROW – Cilla BLACK (39) 68
WHERE IT'S AT – BECK (35) 96
WHERE LOVE LIVES – Alison LIMERICK (9) 91,96
WHERE MY GIRLS AT? – 702 (22) 99
WHERE THE ACTION IS – WESTWORLD (54) 87
WHERE THE BOYS ARE – Connie FRANCIS (5) ..61
WHERE THE HEART IS – SOFT CELL (21) 82
WHERE THE PARTY AT? – JAGGED EDGE featuring NELLY (25) 01
WHERE THE POOR BOYS DANCE – LULU (24) ..00
WHERE THE ROSE IS SOWN – BIG COUNTRY (29) 84
WHERE THE STREETS HAVE NO NAME – U2 (4) ..87
WHERE THE STREETS HAVE NO NAME – CAN'T TAKE MY EYES OFF YOU – PET SHOP BOYS (4) 91
WHERE THE WILD ROSES GROW – Nick CAVE and Kylie MINOGUE (11) 95
WHERE THE WINDS BLOW – Frankie LAINE (2) 53
WHERE WERE YOU – ADULT NET (66) 89
WHERE WERE YOU HIDING WHEN THE STORM BROKE – ALARM (22) 84
WHERE WERE YOU (ON OUR WEDDING DAY)?? – Lloyd PRICE (15) 59
WHERE WILL THE DIMPLE BE? – Rosemary CLOONEY (6) 55
WHERE WILL YOU BE – Sue NICHOLLS (17) 68
WHERE YOU ARE – Rahsaan PATTERSON (55) 98
WHERE YOU GONNA BE TONIGHT? – Willie COLLINS (46) 86
WHERE'S JACK THE RIPPER – GROOVERIDER (61) 99
WHERE'S ME JUMPER – SULTANS OF PING (67) 92
WHERE'S ROMEO – CA VA CA VA (49) 82
WHERE'S THE LOVE – HANSON (4) 97
WHERE'S YOUR HEAD AT? – BASEMENT JAXX (9) 01
WHERE'S YOUR LOVE BEEN – HELIOCENTRIC WORLD (71) 95
WHEREVER I LAY MY HAT (THAT'S MY HOME) – Paul YOUNG (1) 83
WHEREVER I MAY ROAM – METALLICA (25) 92
WHEREVER WOULD I BE – Dusty SPRINGFIELD and Daryl HALL (44) 95
WHEREVER YOU ARE – Neil FINN (32) 01
WHICH WAY SHOULD I JUMP – MILLTOWN BROTHERS (38) 91
WHICH WAY YOU GOIN' BILLY – POPPY FAMILY (7) 70
WHIGGLE IN LINE – BLACK DUCK (33) 94
WHILE I LIVE – Kenny DAMON (48) 66
WHILE YOU SEE A CHANCE – Steve WINWOOD (45) 81
WHINE AND GRINE – PRINCE BUSTER (21) 98
WHIP IT – DEVO (51) 80
WHIPPIN' PICCADILLY – GOMEZ (35) 98
WHISKEY IN THE JAR [A] – THIN LIZZY (6) 73
WHISKEY IN THE JAR [A] – DUBLINERS (63) 90
WHISKEY IN THE JAR [A] – POGUES (63) 90
WHISKEY IN THE JAR [A] – METALLICA (29) 99
THE WHISPER – SELECTER (36) 80
WHISPER A PRAYER – Mica PARIS (65) 93
WHISPER YOUR NAME – HUMAN NATURE (53) 97
WHISPERING [A] – BACHELORS (18) 63
WHISPERING [A] – Nino TEMPO and April STEVENS (20) 64
WHISPERING GRASS – Windsor DAVIES and Don ESTELLE (1) 75
WHISPERING HOPE – Jim REEVES (50) 61
WHISPERING YOUR NAME – Alison MOYET (18) ..94
WHISPERS – Elton JOHN (47) 90
WHISTLE DOWN THE WIND [A] – Nick HEYWARD (13) 83
WHISTLE DOWN THE WIND [B] – Tina ARENA (24) 98
THE WHISTLE SONG [A] – Frankie KNUCKLES (17) 91
THE WHISTLE SONG [A] – DJ ALIGATOR PROJECT (57) 00
THE WHISTLER – HONKY (41) 94
WHITE BIRD – VANESSA-MAE (66) 01
WHITE BOY WITH A FEATHER – Jason DOWNS featuring MILK (19) 01
WHITE BOYS AND HEROES – Gary NUMAN (20) ..82
WHITE CHRISTMAS [A] – MANTOVANI (6) 52
WHITE CHRISTMAS [A] – Pat BOONE (29) 57
WHITE CHRISTMAS [A] – Freddie STARR (41) ..75
WHITE CHRISTMAS [A] – Bing CROSBY (5) 77,85,98
WHITE CHRISTMAS [A] – DARTS (48) 80
WHITE CHRISTMAS [A] – Jim DAVIDSON (52) ..80
WHITE CHRISTMAS [A] – Keith HARRIS and ORVILLE (40) 85
WHITE CHRISTMAS [A] – Max BYGRAVES (71) 89
WHITE CLIFFS OF DOVER [A] – Mr Acker BILK and his PARAMOUNT JAZZ BAND (30) 60
WHITE CLIFFS OF DOVER [A] – RIGHTEOUS BROTHERS (21) 66
WHITE COATS (EP) – NEW MODEL ARMY (50) 87
WHITE HORSES – Jackie LEE (10) 68
WHITE LIE – FOREIGNER (58) 94
WHITE LIGHT, WHITE HEAT – David BOWIE (46) 83
WHITE LIGHTNING – FALL (56) 90
WHITE LINES (DON'T DON'T DO IT) [A] – GRANDMASTER FLASH, Melle MEL and the FURIOUS FIVE (7) 83,84,85
WHITE LINES (DON'T DO IT) [A] – GRANDMASTER FLASH, Melle MEL and the FURIOUS FIVE (59) 94
WHITE LINES (DON'T DO IT) [A] – DURAN DURAN (17) 95
WHITE LOVE – ONE DOVE (43) 93
(WHITE MAN) IN HAMMERSMITH PALAIS – CLASH (32) 78
WHITE NO SUGAR – Clint BOON EXPERIENCE (61) 99
WHITE PUNKS ON DOPE – TUBES (28) 77
WHITE RIBBON DAY – DELIRIOUS? (41) 97
WHITE RIOT – CLASH (38) 77
WHITE ROOM – CREAM (28) 69
WHITE SILVER SANDS – Bill BLACK'S COMBO (50) 60
WHITE SKIES – SUNSCREEM (25) 96
A WHITE SPORT COAT [A] – KING BROTHERS (6) 57
A WHITE SPORT COAT [A] – Terry DENE (18) ..57
WHITE WEDDING – Billy IDOL (6) 85
A WHITER SHADE OF PALE [A] – PROCOL HARUM (1) 67,72
A WHITER SHADE OF PALE [A] – MUNICH MACHINE (42) 78
A WHITER SHADE OF PALE [A] – Annie LENNOX (16) 95
WHO? – Ed CASE and SWEETIE IRIE (29) 01
WHO AM I [A] – Adam FAITH (5) 61
WHO AM I [B] – BEENIE MAN (10) 98
WHO ARE WE [A] – Ronnie HILTON (6) 56
WHO ARE WE [A] – Vera LYNN (30) 56
WHO ARE YOU – WHO (18) 78
WHO CAN I RUN TO – XSCAPE (31) 96
WHO CAN IT BE NOW? – MEN AT WORK (45) ..82
WHO CAN MAKE ME FEEL GOOD – BASSHEADS (38) 92
WHO COMES TO BOOGIE – LITTLE BENNY and the MASTERS (33) 85
WHO COULD BE BLUER – Jerry LORDAN (16) ..60
WHO DO U LOVE – Deborah COX (31) 96
WHO DO YOU LOVE [A] – JUICY LUCY (14) 70
WHO DO YOU LOVE? [B] – INTRUDERS (65) 84
WHO DO YOU LOVE [C] – José PADILLA featuring Angela JOHN (59) 98
WHO DO YOU LOVE NOW (STRINGER) – RIVA featuring Dannii MINOGUE (3) 01
WHO DO YOU THINK YOU ARE [A] – CANDLEWICK GREEN (21) 74
WHO DO YOU THINK YOU ARE [B] – Kim WILDE (49) 92
WHO DO YOU THINK YOU ARE [C] – SAINT ETIENNE (23) 93
WHO DO YOU THINK YOU ARE [D] – SPICE GIRLS (1) 97
WHO DO YOU WANT FOR YOUR LOVE – ICICLE WORKS (54) 86
WHO FEELS LOVE? – OASIS (4) 00
WHO FOUND WHO – JELLYBEAN featuring Elisa FIORILLO (10) 87
WHO GETS THE LOVE – STATUS QUO (34) 88
WHO IS IT [A] – MANTRONIX (40) 87
WHO IS IT [B] – Michael JACKSON (10) 92
WHO KEEPS CHANGING YOUR MIND – SOUTH ST PLAYER (49) 00
WHO KILLED BAMBI – TEN POLE TUDOR (6) ..79
WHO LET IN THE RAIN – Cyndi LAUPER (32) ..94
WHO LET THE DOGS OUT – BAHA MEN (2) 00
WHO LOVES YOU – FOUR SEASONS (6) 75
WHO MADE WHO – AC/DC (16) 86
WHO NEEDS LOVE (LIKE THAT) – ERASURE (10) 85,92
WHO PAYS THE FERRYMAN – Yannis MARKOPOULOS (11) 77
WHO PAYS THE PIPER – Gary CLAIL ON-U SOUND SYSTEM (31) 92
WHO PUT THE BOMP – VISCOUNTS (21) 61
WHO PUT THE BOMP (IN THE BOMP-A-BOMP-A-BOMP) – SHOWADDYWADDY (37) 82
WHO PUT THE LIGHTS OUT – DANA (14) 71
WHO THE HELL ARE YOU – MADISON AVENUE (10) 00
WHO TOLD YOU – Roni SIZE / REPRAZENT (17) 00
WHO WANTS THE WORLD – STRANGLERS (39) 80
WHO WANTS TO BE THE DISCO KING? – WONDER STUFF (28) 89
WHO WANTS TO LIVE FOREVER [A] – QUEEN (24) 86
WHO WANTS TO LIVE FOREVER [A] – Sarah BRIGHTMAN (45) 97
WHO WAS IT – Hurricane SMITH (23) 72
WHO WE BE – DMX (34) 01
WHO WEARS THESE SHOES – Elton JOHN (50) 84
WHO WERE YOU WITH IN THE MOONLIGHT – DOLLAR (14) 79
WHO, WHAT, WHEN, WHERE, WHY – MANHATTAN TRANSFER (49) 78
WHO WHERE WHY – JESUS JONES (21) 91
WHO WILL SAVE YOUR SOUL – JEWEL (52) 97

WHO WILL YOU RUN TO – HEART (30) 87
WHO YOU ARE – PEARL JAM (18) 96
WHO YOU LOOKING AT – SALFORD JETS (72) 80
WHO YOU WIT – JAY-Z (65).............................97
WHO'S THE BAD MAN? – Dee PATTEN (42) 99
WHO'S THE MAN – HOUSE OF PAIN (23) 93
WHOA – BLACK ROB (44) 00
WHO'D SHE COO – OHIO PLAYERS (43) 76
WHODUNIT – TAVARES (5) 77
WHOLE AGAIN – ATOMIC KITTEN (1) 01
WHOLE LOTTA LOVE [A] – CCS (13) 70
WHOLE LOTTA LOVE [A] – GOLDBUG (3) 96
WHOLE LOTTA LOVE [A] – LED ZEPPELIN (21)..97
WHOLE LOTTA ROSIE – AC/DC (36) 80
WHOLE LOTTA SHAKIN' GOIN' ON – Jerry Lee LEWIS (8) 57
WHOLE LOTTA TROUBLE – Stevie NICKS (62)..89
WHOLE LOTTA WOMAN – Marvin RAINWATER (1)58
WHOLE NEW WORLD – IT BITES (54) 86
A WHOLE NEW WORLD (ALADDIN'S THEME) – Regina BELLE and Peabo BRYSON (12) 93
THE WHOLE OF THE MOON [A] – WATERBOYS (3) 85,91
THE WHOLE OF THE MOON [A] – LITTLE CAESAR (68) 90
THE WHOLE TOWN'S LAUGHING AT ME – Teddy PENDERGRASS (44) 77
THE WHOLE WORLD LOST ITS HEAD – GO-GO's (29)...95
WHOOMP! (THERE IT IS) [A] – TAG TEAM (34) 94
WHOOMPH! (THERE IT IS) [A] – CLOCK (4)......95
WHOOMP THERE IT IS [A] – BM DUBS present MR RUMBLE (32) 01
WHOOPS NOW – Janet JACKSON (9)................95
WHOOSH – WHOOSH (72) 97
WHO'S AFRAID OF THE BIG BAD LOVE – WILD WEEKEND (70).......................................90
WHO'S AFRAID OF THE BIG BAD NOISE! – AGE OF CHANCE (65) 87
WHO'S COMING ROUND – 5050 (54)................01
WHO'S CRYING NOW – JOURNEY (46)..............82
WHO'S GONNA LOVE ME – IMPERIALS (17) 77
WHO'S GONNA RIDE YOUR WILD HORSES – U2 (14) 92
WHO'S GONNA ROCK YOU – NOLANS (12) 80
WHO'S IN THE HOUSE – BEATMASTERS (8) 89
WHO'S IN THE STRAWBERRY PATCH WITH SALLY – DAWN (37)....................74
WHO'S JOHNNY ('SHORT CIRCUIT' THEME) – El DeBARGE (60) 86
WHO'S LEAVING WHO – Hazell DEAN (4) 88
WHO'S LOVING MY BABY – Shola AMA (13)....97
WHO'S SORRY NOW [A] – Johnnie RAY (17) 56
WHO'S SORRY NOW [A] – Connie FRANCIS (1) 58
WHO'S THAT GIRL? [A] – EURYTHMICS (3) 83
WHO'S THAT GIRL [B] – FLYING PICKETS (71) 84
WHO'S THAT GIRL [C] – MADONNA (1) 87
WHO'S THAT GIRL [D] – EVE (6) 01
WHO'S THAT GIRL (SHE'S GOT IT) – A FLOCK OF SEAGULLS (66) 85
WHO'S THAT MIX – THIS YEAR'S BLONDE (62) 87
WHO'S THE DARKMAN – DARKMAN (46) 94
WHO'S THE MACK! – Mark MORRISON (13) 97
WHO'S ZOOMIN' WHO – Aretha FRANKLIN (11) 85
WHOSE FIST IS THIS ANYWAY (EP) – PRONG (58)..92
WHOSE LAW (IS IT ANYWAY) – GURU JOSH (26) 90
WHOSE PROBLEM? – MOTELS (42) 80
WHY [A] – Anthony NEWLEY (1) 60
WHY [A] – Frankie AVALON (20) 60
WHY [A] – Donny OSMOND (3) 72
WHY [B] – Roger WHITTAKER (47)....................71
WHY [C] – Carly SIMON (10)........................82,89
WHY [C] – GLAMMA KID (10) 99
WHY? [D] – BRONSKI BEAT (6) 84
WHY [E] – Annie LENNOX (5) 92
WHY [F] – D MOB with Cathy DENNIS (23)......94
WHY [G] – Ricardo DA FORCE (58) 96
WHY [H] – Michael JACKSON (2) 96
WHY [I] – 3T (2)...96
WHY [J] – MIS-TEEQ (8) 01
WHY ARE PEOPLE GRUDGEFUL – FALL (43) 93
WHY ARE YOU BEING SO REASONABLE NOW – WEDDING PRESENT (42) 88
WHY BABY WHY – Pat BOONE (17)..................57
WHY BELIEVE IN YOU – TEXAS (66) 91
WHY CAN'T YOU – Clarence 'Frogman' HENRY (42) 61
WHY CAN'T I BE YOU – CURE (21) 87
WHY CAN'T I WAKE UP WITH YOU – TAKE THAT (2)...93
WHY CAN'T THIS BE LOVE – VAN HALEN (8) 86
WHY CAN'T WE BE LOVERS – HOLLAND-DOZIER featuring Lamont DOZIER (29)...72
WHY CAN'T WE LIVE TOGETHER – Timmy THOMAS (12) 73,90
WHY CAN'T YOU FREE SOME TIME – Armand VAN HELDEN (34)...............................01
WHY DID YA – Tony DI BART (46)....................95
WHY DID YOU DO IT – STRETCH (16) 75
WHY DIDN'T YOU CALL ME – Macy GRAY (38) 00
WHY DO FOOLS FALL IN LOVE [A] – Alma COGAN (22) 56
WHY DO FOOLS FALL IN LOVE [A] – Frankie LYMON and the TEENAGERS (1)........56
WHY DO FOOLS FALL IN LOVE [A] – Diana ROSS (4)...81,94
WHY DO I ALWAYS GET IT WRONG – LIVE REPORT (73) 89
WHY DO LOVERS BREAK EACH OTHER'S HEARTS – SHOWADDYWADDY (22) 80
WHY DO YOU KEEP ON RUNNING – STINX (49) 01
WHY DOES A MAN HAVE TO BE STRONG – Paul YOUNG (63)..87
WHY DOES IT ALWAYS RAIN ON ME? – TRAVIS (10) 99
WHY DOES MY HEART FEEL SO BAD – MOBY (16) 99,00
WHY DON'T THEY UNDERSTAND – George HAMILTON IV (22) 58
WHY DON'T WE TRY AGAIN – Brian MAY (44) 98
WHY DON'T YOU – RAGE (44).........................93
WHY DON'T YOU BELIEVE ME – Joni JAMES (11)...53
WHY DON'T YOU DANCE WITH ME – FUTURE BREEZE (50).....................................97
WHY DON'T YOU GET A JOB? – OFFSPRING (2) 99
WHY DON'T YOU TAKE ME – ONE DOVE (30) ..94
WHY D'YA LIE TO ME – SPIDER (65)................83
WHY ME [A] – Linda MARTIN (59)....................92
WHY ME [B] – A HOUSE (52)...........................94
WHY ME [C] – ANT & DEC (27) 94
WHY (MUST WE FALL IN LOVE) – Diana ROSS and the SUPREMES and the TEMPTATIONS (31) 70
WHY MUST WE WAIT UNTIL TONIGHT – Tina TURNER (16) 93
WHY NOT NOW – Matt MONRO (24) 61
WHY NOT TONIGHT – MOJOS (25) 64
WHY OH WHY – SPEARHEAD (45)....................97
WHY OH WHY OH WHY – Gilbert O'SULLIVAN (6) 73
WHY SHE'S A GIRL FROM THE CHAINSTORE – BUZZCOCKS (61) 80
WHY SHOULD I – Bob MARLEY and the WAILERS (42) 92,93
WHY SHOULD I BE LONELY – Tony BRENT (24)..59
WHY SHOULD I CRY – Nona HENDRYX (60) 87
WHY SHOULD I LOVE YOU – DES'REE (44)......92
WHY WHY BYE BYE – Bob LUMAN (46) 60
WHY WHY WHY – DEJA VU (57) 94
WHY YOU FOLLOW ME – Eric BENET (48)........00
WHY YOU TREAT ME SO BAD – SHAGGY featuring GRAND PUBA (11) 96
WHY'S EVERYBODY ALWAYS PICKIN' ON ME? – BLOODHOUND GANG (56).............................97
WIBBLING RIVALRY (INTERVIEWS WITH NOEL AND LIAM GALLAGHER) – OASIS (52) 95
WICHITA LINEMAN – Glen CAMPBELL (7) 69
WICKED – ICE CUBE (62)................................93
WICKED GAME – Chris ISAAK (10)....................90
WICKED LOVE – OCEANIC (25).........................91
WICKED WAYS – BLOW MONKEYS (60)...........86
WICKEDEST SOUND – REBEL MC featuring TENOR FLY (43) 91
THE WICKER MAN – IRON MAIDEN (9) 00
WICKI WACKY HOUSE PARTY – TEAM (55) 85
WIDE AWAKE IN A DREAM – Barry BIGGS (44) 81
WIDE BOY – Nik KERSHAW (9) 85
WIDE EYED AND LEGLESS – Andy FAIRWEATHER-LOW (6) 75
WIDE EYED ANGEL – ORIGIN (73) 00
WIDE OPEN SPACE – MANSUN (15)..................96
WIDE PRAIRIE – Linda McCARTNEY (74) 98
WIFEY – NEXT (19)..00
WIG WAM BAM [A] – BLACK LACE (63) 86
WIG WAM BAM [A] – DAMIAN (49) 89
WIGGLE IT – 2 IN A ROOM (3)..........................91
WIGGLY WORLD – MR JACK (32) 97
WIG-WAM BAM – SWEET (4) 72
WIKKA WRAP – EVASIONS (20) 81
THE WILD AMERICA (EP) – Iggy POP (63) 93
WILD AND WONDERFUL – ALMIGHTY (50) 90
WILD BOYS – DURAN DURAN (2) 84
WILD CAT – Gene VINCENT (21) 60
WILD CHILD [A] – W.A.S.P. (71) 86
WILD CHILD [B] – ENYA (72) 01
WILD FLOWER – CULT (24) 87
WILD FRONTIER – Gary MOORE (35)................87
WILD HEARTED SON – CULT (40) 91
WILD HEARTED WOMAN – ALL ABOUT EVE (33) 88
WILD HONEY – BEACH BOYS (29)....................67
WILD IN THE COUNTRY – Elvis PRESLEY (4) 61
WILD IS THE WIND – David BOWIE (24) 81
WILD LOVE – MUNGO JERRY (32) 73
WILD LUV – ROACH MOTEL (75) 94
WILD 'N FREE – REDNEX (55) 95
WILD NIGHT – John Cougar MELLENCAMP (34)........................94
WILD ONE – Bobby RYDELL (7) 60
THE WILD ONE – Suzi QUATRO (7) 74
THE WILD ONES – SUEDE (18) 94
WILD SIDE – MOTLEY CRUE (23)......................88
WILD SIDE OF LIFE [A] – Tommy QUICKLY (33) 64
WILD SIDE OF LIFE [B] – STATUS QUO (9) 76
WILD SURF – ASH (31) 98
WILD THING [A] – TROGGS (2) 66,93
WILD THING [B] – GOODIES (21)......................75
WILD THING [C] – Tone LOC (21)......................89
WILD WEST HERO – ELECTRIC LIGHT ORCHESTRA (6)....................78
WILD WILD LIFE – TALKING HEADS (43) 86
WILD WILD WEST [A] – GET READY (65) 95
WILD WILD WEST [B] – Will SMITH featuring DRU HILL – additional vocals Kool Moe DEE (2) 99
WILD WIND – John LEYTON (2) 61
WILD WOMEN DO – Natalie COLE (16) 90
WILD WOOD – Paul WELLER (14) 93
WILD WORLD [A] – Jimmy CLIFF (8) 70
WILD WORLD [A] – Maxi PRIEST (5) 88
WILD WORLD [A] – MR BIG (59) 93
WILDLIFE (EP) – GIRLSCHOOL (58) 82
WILDSIDE – MARKY MARK and the FUNKY BUNCH (42)....91
WILDWOOD – Paul WELLER (22).......................99
WILFRED THE WEASEL – Keith MICHELL (5) 80
WILL I – IAN VAN DAHL (5) 01
WILL I EVER – ALICE DEEJAY (7) 00
WILL I WHAT – Mike SARNE with Billie DAVIS (18) 62
WILL THE WOLF SURVIVE – LOS LOBOS (57) 85
WILL 2K – Will SMITH (2) 99
WILL WE BE LOVERS – DEACON BLUE (31)......93
WILL YOU – Hazel O'CONNOR (8) 81
WILL YOU BE MY BABY – GRAND PUBA (53)..96
WILL YOU BE THERE – Michael JACKSON (9)......................................93
WILL YOU BE THERE (IN THE MORNING) – HEART (19) 93
WILL YOU BE WITH ME – Maria NAYLER (65) 98
WILL YOU LOVE ME TOMORROW [A] – SHIRELLES (4) 61
WILL YOU LOVE ME TOMORROW [A] – MELANIE (37) 74
WILL YOU LOVE ME TOMORROW [A] – Bryan FERRY (23) 93
WILL YOU MARRY ME – Paula ABDUL (73)......92
WILL YOU SATISFY? – CHERRELLE (57)............86
WILL YOU WAIT FOR ME – KAVANA (29) 99

YOU TO ME ARE EVERYTHING [A] – SONIA (13) 91
YOU TO ME ARE EVERYTHING [A] – Sean MAGUIRE (16) 95
YOU TO ME ARE EVERYTHING (THE DECADE REMIX 76-86) – REAL THING (5) 86
YOU TOOK THE WORDS RIGHT OUT OF MY MOUTH – MEAT LOAF (33) 78
YOU TRIP ME UP – JESUS AND MARY CHAIN (55) 85
YOU USED TO HOLD ME – SCOTT & LEON (19) 00
YOU USED TO HOLD ME SO TIGHT – Thelma HOUSTON (49) 84
YOU USED TO LOVE ME – Faith EVANS (42) 95
YOU USED TO SALSA – Richie RICH (52) 91
YOU WANNA KNOW – THUNDER (49) 99
YOU WANT IT YOU GOT IT – DETROIT EMERALDS (12) 73
YOU WANT THIS – Janet JACKSON (14) 94
YOU WEAR IT WELL [A] – Rod STEWART (1) 72
YOU WEAR IT WELL [B] – DeBARGE (54) 85
(YOU WERE MADE FOR) ALL MY LOVE – Jackie WILSON (33) 60
YOU WERE MADE FOR ME – FREDDIE and the DREAMERS (3) 63
YOU WERE MEANT FOR ME – JEWEL (32) 97
YOU WERE ON MY MIND – Crispian ST PETERS (2) 66
YOU WERE THERE – HEINZ (26) 64
YOU WEREN'T IN LOVE WITH ME – Billy FIELD (67) 82
YOU WILL RISE – SWEETBACK (64) 97
YOU WIN AGAIN – BEE GEES (1) 87
YOU WOKE UP MY NEIGHBOURHOOD – Billy BRAGG (54) 91
YOU WON'T BE LEAVING – HERMAN'S HERMITS (20) 66
YOU WON'T FIND ANOTHER FOOL LIKE ME – NEW SEEKERS (1) 73
YOU WON'T SEE ME CRY – WILSON PHILLIPS (18) 92
YOU WOULDN'T KNOW LOVE – CHER (55) 90
YOU YOU ROMEO – Shirley BASSEY (29) 57
YOU YOU YOU – Alvin STARDUST (6) 74
YOU'LL NEVER NEVER KNOW – PLATTERS (23) 57
YOU'RE ALL I NEED – MÖTLEY CRÜE (23) 88
YOU'RE THE STORY OF MY LIFE – Judy CHEEKS (30) 95
YOU'VE GOT TO GIVE ME ROOM – Oleta ADAMS (49) 91
YOU'LL ALWAYS BE A FRIEND – HOT CHOCOLATE (23) 72
YOU'LL ALWAYS FIND ME IN THE KITCHEN AT PARTIES – Jona LEWIE (16) 80
YOU'LL ANSWER TO ME – Cleo LAINE (5) 61
YOU'LL BE IN MY HEART – Phil COLLINS (17) 99
YOU'LL BE MINE (PARTY TIME) – Gloria ESTEFAN (18) 96
YOU'LL BE SORRY – STEPS (4) 01
YOU'LL NEVER BE SO WRONG – HOT CHOCOLATE (52) 81
YOU'LL NEVER FIND ANOTHER LOVE LIKE MINE – Lou RAWLS (10) 76
YOU'LL NEVER GET TO HEAVEN – Dionne WARWICK (20) 64
YOU'LL NEVER GET TO HEAVEN (EP) – STYLISTICS (24) 76
YOU'LL NEVER KNOW [A] – Shirley BASSEY (6) 61
YOU'LL NEVER KNOW [B] – HI GLOSS (12) 81
YOU'LL NEVER KNOW WHAT YOU'RE MISSING – REAL THING (16) 77
YOU'LL NEVER KNOW WHAT YOU'RE MISSING ('TIL YOU TRY) – Emile FORD and the CHECKMATES (12) 60
YOU'LL NEVER STOP ME LOVING YOU – SONIA (1) 89
YOU'LL NEVER WALK ALONE [A] – Gerry and the PACEMAKERS (1) 63
YOU'LL NEVER WALK ALONE [A] – Elvis PRESLEY (44) 68
YOU'LL NEVER WALK ALONE [A] – CROWD (1) 85
YOU'LL NEVER WALK ALONE [A] – José CARRERAS, Placido DOMINGO and Luciano PAVAROTTI with MEHTA (35) 98
YOU'LL SEE – MADONNA (5) 95
YOUNG AMERICANS – David BOWIE (18) 75
YOUNG AMERICANS TALKING – David VAN DAY (43) 83
YOUNG AND FOOLISH [A] – Ronnie HILTON (17) 56
YOUNG AND FOOLISH [A] – Edmund HOCKRIDGE (10) 56
YOUNG AND FOOLISH [A] – Dean MARTIN (20) 56
YOUNG AT HEART [A] – Frank SINATRA (12) 54
YOUNG AT HEART [B] – BLUEBELLS (1) 84,93
YOUNG BLOOD – UFO (36) 80
YOUNG BOY – Paul McCARTNEY (19) 97
YOUNG DISCIPLES (EP) – YOUNG DISCIPLES (48) 92
YOUNG EMOTIONS – Ricky NELSON (48) 60
YOUNG, FREE AND SINGLE – SUNFIRE (20) 83
YOUNG FRESH N' NEW – KELIS (32) 01
YOUNG GIFTED AND BLACK – BOB and MARCIA (5) 70
YOUNG GIRL [A] – UNION GAP featuring Gary PUCKETT (1) ..68,74
YOUNG GIRL [A] – Darren DAY (42) 94
YOUNG GIRL [A] – Joe LONGTHORNE (61) 94
YOUNG GIRLS & HAPPY ENDINGS – GORKY'S ZYGOTIC MYNCI (49) 97
YOUNG GODS – LITTLE ANGELS (34) 91
YOUNG GUNS (GO FOR IT) – WHAM! (3) 82
YOUNG HEARTS RUN FREE [A] – Candi STATON (2) 76,86,99
YOUNG HEARTS RUN FREE [A] – Kym MAZELLE (20) 97
YOUNG LIVERS – ROCKET FROM THE CRYPT (67) 96
YOUNG LOVE [A] – Tab HUNTER (1) 57
YOUNG LOVE [A] – Sonny JAMES (11) 57
YOUNG LOVE [A] – Donny OSMOND (1) 73
YOUNG LOVERS – PAUL and PAULA (9) 63
THE YOUNG MC – SUPERFUNK (62) 00
THE YOUNG NEW MEXICAN PUPPETEER – Tom JONES (6) 72
THE YOUNG OFFENDER'S MUM – CARTER – THE UNSTOPPABLE SEX MACHINE (34) 95
THE YOUNG ONES – Cliff RICHARD and the SHADOWS (1) 62
YOUNG PARISIANS – ADAM and the ANTS (9) 80
YOUNG SOUL REBELS – Mica PARIS (61) 91
YOUNG TURKS – Rod STEWART (11) 81
YOUNG WORLD – Ricky NELSON (19) 62
YOUNGER GIRL – CRITTERS (38) 66
YOUR BABY AIN'T YOUR BABY ANYMORE – Paul DA VINCI (20) 74
YOUR BABY'S GONE SURFIN' – Duane EDDY and the REBELS (49) 63
YOUR BODY'S CALLIN' – R KELLY (19) 94
YOUR CARESS (ALL I NEED) – DJ FLAVOURS (19) 97
YOUR CASSETTE PET – BOW WOW WOW (58) 80
YOUR CHEATING HEART – Ray CHARLES (13) 62
YOUR CHRISTMAS WISH – SMURFS (8) 96
YOUR DREAM – Adrian GURVITZ (61) 82
YOUR DRESS – John FOXX (61) 83
YOUR EARS SHOULD BE BURNING NOW – Marti WEBB (61) 80
YOUR EYES – SIMPLY RED (26) 00
YOUR FACE – SLACKER (33) 97
YOUR FASCINATION – Gary NUMAN (46) 85
YOUR FAVORITE THING – SUGAR (40) 94
YOUR GENERATION – GENERATION X (36) 77
YOUR GHOST – Kristin HERSH (45) 94
YOUR HONOUR – Pluto SHERVINGTON (19) 82
YOUR HURTIN' KIND OF LOVE – Dusty SPRINGFIELD (37) 65
YOUR KISS IS SWEET – SYREETA (12) 75
YOUR KISSES ARE CHARITY – CULTURE CLUB (25) 99
YOUR LATEST TRICK – DIRE STRAITS (26) 86
YOUR LOSS MY GAIN – OMAR (47) 92
YOUR LOVE [A] – HIPSWAY (66) 89
YOUR LOVE [B] – Frankie KNUCKLES (59) 89
YOUR LOVE [C] – Diana ROSS (14) 93
YOUR LOVE [D] – INNER CITY (28) 96
YOUR LOVE GETS SWEETER – Finley QUAYE (16) 98
(YOUR LOVE HAS LIFTED ME) HIGHER AND HIGHER – Rita COOLIDGE (48) 77
YOUR LOVE IS A 187 – WHITEHEAD BROS (32) 95
YOUR LOVE IS CALLING – EVOLUTION (60) 96
YOUR LOVE IS KING – SADE (6) 84
YOUR LOVE IS LIFTING ME – NOMAD (60) 92
(YOUR LOVE KEEPS LIFTING ME) HIGHER AND HIGHER – Jackie WILSON (11) 69,75
YOUR LOVE TAKES ME HIGHER – BELOVED (39) 90
YOUR LOVING ARMS – Billie Ray MARTIN (6) 94,95
YOUR LUCKY DAY IN HELL – EELS (35) 97
YOUR MA SAID YOU CRIED IN YOUR SLEEP LAST NIGHT – Doug SHELDON (29) 62
YOUR MAGIC PUT A SPELL ON ME – LJ JOHNSON (27) 76
YOUR MAMA DON'T DANCE – POISON (13) 89
YOUR MAMA WON'T LIKE ME – Suzi QUATRO (31) 75
YOUR MIRROR – SIMPLY RED (17) 92
YOUR NEW CUCKOO – CARDIGANS (35) 97
YOUR OWN SPECIAL WAY – GENESIS (43) 77
YOUR PAINTED SMILE – Bryan FERRY (52) 94
YOUR PERSONAL TOUCH – Evelyn 'Champagne' KING (37) 85
YOUR SECRET LOVE – Luther VANDROSS (14) 96
YOUR SMILE – OCTOPUS (42) 96
YOUR SONG [A] – Elton JOHN (7) 71
YOUR SONG [A] – Billy PAUL (37) 77
YOUR SONG [A] – Rod STEWART (41) 92
YOUR SWAYING ARMS – DEACON BLUE (23) 91
YOUR TENDER LOOK – Joe BROWN and the BRUVVERS (31) 62
YOUR TIME HASN'T COME YET BABY – Elvis PRESLEY (22) 68
YOUR TIME IS GONNA COME – DREAD ZEPPELIN (59) 90
YOUR TOWN – DEACON BLUE (14) 92
YOUR WOMAN – WHITE TOWN (1) 97
YOU'RE A BETTER MAN THAN I – SHAM 69 (49) 79
YOU'RE A LADY – Peter SKELLERN (3) 72
YOU'RE A STAR – AQUARIAN DREAM (67) 79
YOU'RE ALL I NEED TO GET BY [A] – Marvin GAYE (19) 68
YOU'RE ALL I NEED TO GET BY [A] – Johnny MATHIS and Deniece WILLIAMS (45) 78
YOU'RE ALL THAT MATTERS TO ME – Curtis STIGERS (6) 92
YOU'RE BREAKIN' MY HEART – Keely SMITH (14) 65
YOU'RE DRIVING ME CRAZY – TEMPERANCE SEVEN (1) 61
YOU'RE EVERYTHING TO ME – Boris GARDINER (11) 86
(YOU'RE) FABULOUS BABE – Kenny WILLIAMS (35) 77
YOU'RE FREE TO GO – Jim REEVES (48) 72
YOU'RE GONNA GET NEXT TO ME – Bo KIRKLAND and Ruth DAVIS (12) 77
YOU'RE GONNA MISS ME – TURNTABLE ORCHESTRA (52) 89
YOU'RE GORGEOUS – BABYBIRD (3) 96
(YOU'RE) HAVING MY BABY – Paul ANKA (6) ..74
YOU'RE HISTORY – SHAKESPEAR'S SISTER (7) 89
YOU'RE IN A BAD WAY – SAINT ETIENNE (12) 93
YOU'RE IN LOVE – WILSON PHILLIPS (29) 91
YOU'RE IN MY HEART [A] – Rod STEWART (3) 77
YOU'RE IN MY HEART [B] – David ESSEX (59) 83

PICTURE CREDITS

page 4 Pictorial Press
page 5 Rex Features
page 6 Courtesy of Musical Express
page 8 Courtesy of Derek Jackson
page 10 Pictorial Press
page 11 Paul Fenton Photography
page 14 Rex Features
page 15 Betty Halvagi
page 17 Hulton Archive
page 19 Rex Features
page 20 Rex Features
page 22 Rex Features (2)
page 24 Hulton Archive
page 25 Rex Features
page 26 Rex Features
page 27 Pictorial Press
page 28 Pictorial Press (2)
page 30 Pictorial Press (2)
page 32 Rex Features
page 33 Hulton Archive
page 34 Rex Features (2)
page 36 Rex Features
page 37 Pictorial Press
page 38 Rex Features (2)
page 40 Rex Features (2)
page 42 Rex Features
page 43 Tim Roney/IDOLS
page 44 Getty News
page 46 Rex Features
page 47 PA Photos
page 48 Popperfoto / Reuters
page 50 BMG
page 51 James Thackwell
page 52 Popperfoto/Reuters; The Mirror
page 53 Popperfoto/Reuters
page 54 Julian Burton/IDOLS
page 55 Pictorial Press
page 56 Popperfoto/Reuters
page 57 Independiente / Relentless
page 58 Parlophone
page 59 BMG
page 60 PA Photos
page 61 Daily Mail; David Redfern
page 62 Corinthians
page 63 Rex Features
page 64 Rex Features
page 65 Polygram
page 66 Rex Features
page 67 Hulton Archive
page 68 Parlophone
page 69 Hulton Archive
page 70 Mealey Photography / Liverpool City Council
page 71 PA Photos (2)
page 75 1952: Rex Features
page 79 1953: Hulton Archive
page 87 1954: Hulton Archive
page 99 1955: Rex Features (2)
page 107 1956: Rex Features; Hulton Archive
page 119 1957: Kathy Mclaren; Hulton Archive
page 127 1958: Getty News; Pictorial Press
page 135 1959: Rex Features (2)
page 147 1960: Steve Gillett
page 155 1961: Getty News; Rex Features
page 163 1962: Rex Features (2)
page 175 1963: Getty News; Hulton Archive
page 183 1964: Rex Features
page 191 1965: Rex Features; Pictorial Press
page 203 1966: Ron Cooper (Zabadak)
page 211 1967 Rex Features; Pictorial Press
page 219 1968 Rex Features (2)
page 231 1969: Rex Features; Hulton Archive
page 239 1970: Rex Features (2)
page 247 1971: Rex Features; Hulton Archive
page 259 1972: Rex Features; Redferns
page 267 1973: Pictorial Press
page 275 1974: Courtesy of Gus Dudgeon; Sam Emerson
page 283 1975: Rex Features
page 287 1976: CBS
page 295 1977: Rex Features (2)
page 303 1978: Rex Features; Pictorial Press
page 315 1979: Rex Features (2)
page 323 1980: Rex Features; Newspix
page 331 1981: IDOLS
page 343 1982: Rex Features
page 351 1983: Courtesy of Mike Sweeney; Rex Features
page 359 1984: Shalit Global Management; Rex Features
page 371 1985: Courtesy of Nik Kershaw
page 379 1986: Rex Features
page 387 1987: Rex Features
page 399 1988: Courtesy of Mark Nevin; Pictorial Press
page 407 1989: Corbis; Arista
page 415 1990: PA Photos; Pictorial Press
page 427 1991: A&M
page 435 1992: EMI Records; Rex Features
page 443 1993: Rex Features; IDOLS
page 455 1994: Rex Features
page 463 1995: Rex Features (2)
page 471 1996: Getty News; Mushroom Records
page 483 1997: Rex Features
page 491 1998: Jive Records
page 499 1999: Getty News
page 507 2000: Declan
page 511 2001: Rex Features
page 515 Pictorial Press (2)

BRITISH HIT SINGLES

CONTACT US

We thrive on your emails and letters so here are the contact details:

WRITE TO

The Editor, Guinness World Records Book of British Hit Singles, 338 Euston Road, London NW1 3BD

Email: editor@15th.britishhitsingles.com

Visit our website: www.britishhitsingles.com

VOTE FOR YOUR FAVOURITE No.1s

If you enjoyed voting in the British Hit Singles Top 100 Singles chart (results on page 16 of this book), you might like to pick your favourite No.1 hits by visiting www.theofficialcharts.com

SHOP A POP STAR

In next year's edition of British Hit Singles we will be publishing an illustrated "where are they now?" type of feature which will promote shockingly forgotten pop idols from way back when. Can you shop a pop star? Does your mum claim to have been the vocalist of a trend-setting 60s combo? Does your postman boast about his Top 40 chart entry from 1972? If you have an interesting story to tell and a good photo to go with it, drop us a line. Providing the subject can prove that they had at least one chart hit (no matter how minor) listed in our book, then we will consider exposing them in the pages of our 16th edition.

SHOP A POP STAR Three examples of just the sort of acts we are looking to hear from. Tony Jackson and The Vibrations (top), Lick The Tin (middle) and Hedgehoppers Anonymous (bottom). Apart from three great band names they all have one thing in common: a tiny chart career and a permanent place in our book. Where are they now and what are they doing?